NATIONAL CENTER FOR EDUCATION STATISTICS

Institute of Education Sciences

U.S. Department of Education
NCES 2009-020

Digest of Education Statistics 2008

March 2009

Thomas D. Snyder
National Center for
Education Statistics

Sally A. Dillow
Education Statistics
Services Institute—
American Institutes
for Research

Charlene M. Hoffman
Consultant

U.S. Department of Education
Arne Duncan
Secretary

Institute of Education Sciences
Sue Betka
Acting Director

National Center for Education Statistics
Stuart Kerachsky
Acting Commissioner

The National Center for Education Statistics (NCES) is the primary federal entity for collecting, analyzing, and reporting data related to education in the United States and other nations. It fulfills a congressional mandate to collect, collate, analyze, and report full and complete statistics on the condition of education in the United States; conduct and publish reports and specialized analyses of the meaning and significance of such statistics; assist state and local education agencies in improving their statistical systems; and review and report on education activities in foreign countries.

NCES activities are designed to address high-priority education data needs; provide consistent, reliable, complete, and accurate indicators of education status and trends; and report timely, useful, and high-quality data to the U.S. Department of Education, the Congress, the states, other education policymakers, practitioners, data users, and the general public. Unless specifically noted, all information contained herein is in the public domain.

We strive to make our products available in a variety of formats and in language that is appropriate to a variety of audiences. You, as our customer, are the best judge of our success in communicating information effectively. If you have any comments or suggestions about this or any other NCES product or report, we would like to hear from you. Please direct your comments to

National Center for Education Statistics
Institute of Education Sciences
U.S. Department of Education
1990 K Street NW
Washington, DC 20006-5651

March 2009

The NCES World Wide Web Home Page address is http://nces.ed.gov.
The NCES World Wide Web Electronic Catalog is http://nces.ed.gov/pubsearch.

Suggested Citation

Snyder, T.D., Dillow, S.A., and Hoffman, C.M. (2009). *Digest of Education Statistics 2008* (NCES 2009-020). National Center for Education Statistics, Institute of Education Sciences, U.S. Department of Education. Washington, DC.

Content Contact

Thomas D. Snyder
(202) 502-7452
tom.snyder@ed.gov

ISBN-13: 978-1-60175-787-6 (Paper)

FOREWORD

The 2008 edition of the *Digest of Education Statistics* is the 44th in a series of publications initiated in 1962. The *Digest* has been issued annually except for combined editions for the years 1977–78, 1983–84, and 1985–86. Its primary purpose is to provide a compilation of statistical information covering the broad field of American education from prekindergarten through graduate school. The *Digest* includes a selection of data from many sources, both government and private, and draws especially on the results of surveys and activities carried out by the National Center for Education Statistics (NCES). To qualify for inclusion in the *Digest*, material must be nationwide in scope and of current interest and value. The publication contains information on a variety of subjects in the field of education statistics, including the number of schools and colleges, teachers, enrollments, and graduates, in addition to educational attainment, finances, federal funds for education, libraries, and international comparisons. Supplemental information on population trends, attitudes on education, education characteristics of the labor force, government finances, and economic trends provides background for evaluating education data. Although the *Digest* contains important information on federal education funding, more detailed information on federal activities is available from federal education program offices.

The *Digest* contains seven chapters: All Levels of Education, Elementary and Secondary Education, Postsecondary Education, Federal Programs for Education and Related Activities, Outcomes of Education, International Comparisons of Education, and Libraries and Educational Technology. Preceding these chapters is an Introduction that provides a brief overview of current trends in American education, which supplements the tabular materials in chapters 1 through 7. The *Digest* concludes with three appendixes. The first appendix, Guide to Sources, provides a brief synopsis of the surveys used to generate the *Digest* tables; the second, Definitions, is included to help readers understand terms used in the *Digest*; and the third, Index of Table Numbers, allows readers to quickly locate tables on specific topics.

In addition to updating many of the statistics that have appeared in previous years, this edition contains new material, including

- number and percentage of public school students eligible for free or reduced-price lunch (table 42);
- percentage distribution of children at about 2 and 4 years of age, by type of child care arrangement and selected child and family characteristics (table 46);

- percentage distribution of quality ratings of child care arrangements of children at about 4 years of age, by type of arrangement and selected child and family characteristics (table 47);
- children's specific language, literacy, mathematics, color knowledge, and fine motor skills at about 4 years of age, by age of child and selected characteristics (table 114);
- average National Assessment of Educational Progress (NAEP) reading scale scores of 4th-, 8th-, and 12th-graders, by selected student and school characteristics (table 123);
- average NAEP writing scale score and percentage of students attaining NAEP writing achievement levels, by selected student characteristics and grade level (table 125);
- average NAEP mathematics scale scores of 4th-, 8th-, and 12th-graders, by selected student and school characteristics (table 136);
- average NAEP mathematics scale score of 8th-graders and percentage reporting various attitudes toward mathematics work, by frequency of attitude and selected student and school characteristics (table 137);
- average NAEP science scale score of 12th-graders and percentage reporting various attitudes toward science, by selected student and school characteristics (table 140);
- percentage of elementary and secondary school students who do homework outside of school, whose parents check that homework is done, and whose parents help with homework, by frequency and selected student and school characteristics (table 156);
- total full-year enrollment in degree-granting institutions, by control and type of institution and state or jurisdiction (table 222);
- degrees in Arabic, Chinese, Korean, and Russian conferred by degree-granting institutions, by level of degree (table 309);
- full-time, first-time degree/certificate seeking undergraduate students enrolled in degree-granting institutions, by participation and average amount awarded in financial aid programs, and type and control of institution (table 336); and
- percentage of 18- to 25-year-olds reporting substance abuse during the past 30 days and the past year, by drug used and selected characteristics (table 396).

Updates to tables from the next *Digest of Education Statistics* will appear on the NCES website prior to printing the full edition. The *Digest* can be accessed from http://nces.ed.gov/programs/digest.

Val Plisko
Associate Commissioner
Early Childhood, International, and Crosscutting Studies Division

Contents

	Page
Foreword	iii
List of Figures	vi
List of Tables	vii
Introduction	1
Guide to Tabular Presentation	7
Chapter 1. All Levels of Education	9
Chapter 2. Elementary and Secondary Education	53
Chapter 3. Postsecondary Education	269
Chapter 4. Federal Programs for Education and Related Activities	527
Chapter 5. Outcomes of Education	553
Chapter 6. International Comparisons of Education	577
Chapter 7. Libraries and Educational Technology	611

Appendixes

A. Guide to Sources	629
B. Definitions	669
C. Index of Table Numbers	683

List of Figures

Figure   **Page**

1. The structure of education in the United States   11

2. Enrollment, total expenditures in constant dollars, and expenditures as a percentage of the gross domestic product (GDP), by level of education: Selected years, 1965–66 through 2007–08   12

3. Percentage of persons 25 years old and over, by highest level of educational attainment: Selected years, 1940 through 2008   13

4. Percentage of persons 25 through 29 years old, by highest level of educational attainment: Selected years, 1940 through 2008   13

5. Highest level of education attained by persons 25 years old and over: March 2008   14

6. Enrollment, number of teachers, pupil/teacher ratio, and expenditures in public schools: 1960–61 through 2006–07   57

7. Total and full-day preprimary enrollment of 3- to 5-year-olds: October 1970 through October 2007 . .   58

8. Percentage change in public elementary and secondary enrollment, by state: Fall 2000 to fall 2006 .   58

9. Percentage of revenue for public elementary and secondary schools, by source of funds: 1970–71 through 2005–06   59

10. Current expenditure per pupil in fall enrollment in public elementary and secondary schools: 1970–71 through 2005–06   59

11. Enrollment, degrees conferred, and expenditures in degree-granting institutions: 1960–61 through 2006–07   272

12. Percentage change in total enrollment in degree-granting institutions, by state: Fall 2000 through fall 2006   273

13. Enrollment in degree-granting institutions, by age: Fall 1970 through fall 2017   273

14. Full-time-equivalent (FTE) students per staff member in public and private degree-granting institutions, by type of staff: 1976 and 2007   274

15. Trends in bachelor's degrees conferred by degree-granting institutions in selected fields of study: 1996–97, 2001–02, and 2006–07   274

16. Percentage distribution of total revenues of public degree-granting institutions, by source of funds: 2005–06   275

17. Percentage distribution of total revenues of private not-for-profit degree-granting institutions, by source of funds: 2005–06   275

18. Federal on-budget funds for education, by level or other educational purpose: Selected years, 1965 through 2008   535

19. Percentage of federal on-budget funds for education, by agency: Fiscal year 2007   536

20. Department of Education outlays, by type of recipient: Fiscal year 2008   536

21. Labor force participation rate of persons 20 to 64 years old, by age group and highest level of education: 2007   554

22. Unemployment rates of persons 25 years old and over, by highest level of education: 2007   555

23. Labor force status of 2006–07 high school dropouts and completers not enrolled in college: October 2007   555

24. Median annual earnings of persons 25 years old and over, by highest level of education and sex: 2007   556

25. Average salaries of bachelor's degree recipients 1 year after graduation, by field: 1991, 1994, and 2001   556

26. Percentage change in enrollment, by selected areas of the world and level of education: 1990 to 2005   579

27. Bachelor's degree recipients as a percentage of the population of the typical ages of graduation, by country: 2005   580

28. Public direct expenditures for education as a percentage of the gross domestic product (GDP), by country: 2005   580

29. Percentage of all public schools and instructional rooms with internet access: Various years, fall 1994 through fall 2005   612

List of Tables

Chapter 1. All Levels of Education

Enrollment, Teachers, and Schools

Table		Page
1.	Projected number of participants in educational institutions, by level and control of institution: Fall 2008	15
2.	Enrollment in educational institutions, by level and control of institution: Selected years, fall 1980 through fall 2008	15
3.	Enrollment in educational institutions, by level and control of institution: Selected years, 1869–70 through fall 2017	16
4.	Number of teachers in elementary and secondary schools, and instructional staff in postsecondary degree-granting institutions, by control of institution: Selected years, fall 1970 through fall 2017	18
5.	Number of educational institutions, by level and control of institution: Selected years, 1980–81 through 2006–07	19

Enrollment Rates

6.	Percentage of the population 3 to 34 years old enrolled in school, by sex, race/ethnicity, and age: Selected years, 1980 through 2007	20
7.	Percentage of the population 3 to 34 years old enrolled in school, by age group: Selected years, 1940 through 2007	22

Educational Attainment

8.	Percentage of persons age 25 and over and 25 to 29, by race/ethnicity, years of school completed, and sex: Selected years, 1910 through 2008	24
9.	Number of persons age 18 and over, by highest level of education attained, age, sex, and race/ethnicity: 2008	26
10.	Persons age 18 and over who hold at least a bachelor's degree in specific fields of study, by sex, race/ethnicity, and age: 2001	27
11.	Educational attainment of persons 18 years old and over, by state: 2000 and 2006	28
12.	Educational attainment of persons 25 years old and over, by race/ethnicity and state: 2006	29
13.	Educational attainment of persons 25 years old and over for the 25 largest states, by sex: 2006	31
14.	Educational attainment of persons 25 years old and over for the 15 largest metropolitan areas, by sex: 2008	31

Population

15.	Estimates of resident population, by age group: 1970 through 2008	32
16.	Estimates of resident population, by race/ethnicity and age group: Selected years, 1980 through 2008	33
17.	Estimated total and school-age resident populations, by state: Selected years, 1970 through 2007	34

Characteristics of Families With Children

18.	Number and percentage of family households, by family status and presence of own children under 18: Selected years, 1970 through 2007	35
19.	Characteristics of family households with own children under 18, by race/ethnicity and family structure: 2007	36

20. Household income, population poverty rates, and poverty status of 5- to 17-year-olds, by state: 1990, 2000, and 2005–07 37

21. Poverty status of all persons, persons in families, and related children under age 18, by race/ ethnicity: Selected years, 1959 through 2007 39

Opinions on and Parent Involvement in Education

22. Average grade that the public would give the public schools in their community and in the nation at large: 1974 through 2008. 42

23. Percentage of elementary and secondary school children whose parents were involved in school activities, by selected child, parent, and school characteristics: 1999, 2003, and 2007 43

24. Percentage of kindergartners through fifth-graders whose parents were involved in education-related activities, by selected child, parent, and school characteristics: 1999 and 2003 44

Finances

25. Expenditures of educational institutions related to the gross domestic product, by level of institution: Selected years, 1929–30 through 2007–08 45

26. Expenditures of educational institutions, by level and control of institution: Selected years, 1899–1900 through 2007–08. 46

27. Amount and percentage distribution of direct general expenditures of state and local governments, by function: Selected years, 1970–71 through 2005–06 47

28. Direct general expenditures of state and local governments for all functions and for education, by level of education and state: 2005–06 48

29. Direct general expenditures per capita of state and local governments for all functions and for education, by level of education and state: 2005–06. 49

30. Gross domestic product, state and local expenditures, personal income, disposable personal income, median family income, and population: Selected years, 1929 through 2007 50

31. Gross domestic product price index, Consumer Price Index, education price indexes, and federal budget composite deflator: Selected years, 1919 through 2007 51

Chapter 2. Elementary and Secondary Education

Enrollment

32. Historical summary of public elementary and secondary school statistics: Selected years, 1869–70 through 2005–06. 60

33. Enrollment in public elementary and secondary schools, by state or jurisdiction: Selected years, fall 1990 through fall 2008 62

34. Enrollment in public elementary and secondary schools, by level, grade, and state or jurisdiction: Fall 2006 64

35. Enrollment in public elementary and secondary schools, by level, grade, and state or jurisdiction: Fall 2005 66

36. Enrollment in public elementary and secondary schools, by level, grade, and state or jurisdiction: Fall 2004 68

37. Enrollment in public elementary and secondary schools, by grade: Selected years, fall 1980 through fall 2006 70

38. Number and percentage of homeschooled students ages 5 through 17 with a grade equivalent of kindergarten through 12th grade, by selected child, parent, and household characteristics: 1999 and 2003 71

39. Percentage distribution of students ages 5 through 17 attending kindergarten through 12th grade, by school type or participation in homeschooling and selected child, parent, and household characteristics: 1999 and 2003 72

40. Average daily attendance in public elementary and secondary schools, by state or jurisdiction: Selected years, 1969–70 through 2005–06.   73

41. Percentage distribution of enrollment in public elementary and secondary schools, by race/ethnicity and state or jurisdiction: Fall 1996 and fall 2006   74

42. Number and percentage of public school students eligible for free or reduced-price lunch, by state: 2000–01, 2004–05, 2005–06, and 2006–07   75

43. Enrollment of 3-, 4-, and 5-year-old children in preprimary programs, by level of program, control of program, and attendance status: Selected years, 1965 through 2007   76

44. Number of children under 6 years old and not yet enrolled in kindergarten, percentage in center-based programs, average weekly hours in nonparental care, and percentage in various types of primary care arrangements, by selected child and family characteristics: 2005   77

45. Child care arrangements of 3- to 5-year-old children who are not yet in kindergarten, by age and race/ethnicity: Various years, 1991 through 2005   78

46. Percentage distribution of children at about 2 and 4 years of age, by type of child care arrangement and selected child and family characteristics: 2003–04 and 2005–06.   79

47. Percentage distribution of quality rating of child care arrangements of children at about 4 years of age, by type of arrangement and selected child and family characteristics: 2005–06.   80

48. Children of prekindergarten through second-grade age, by enrollment status, selected maternal characteristics, and household income: 1995, 2001, and 2005.   81

49. Percentage of 3- to 5-year-olds not yet enrolled in kindergarten who have participated in home literacy activities with a family member, by type of activity and selected child and family characteristics: 1993, 2001, and 2005.   82

50. Children 3 to 21 years old served in federally supported programs for the disabled, by type of disability: Selected years, 1976–77 through 2006–07   83

51. Percentage distribution of students 6 to 21 years old served under Individuals with Disabilities Education Act, Part B, by educational environment and type of disability: Selected years, fall 1989 through fall 2006   84

52. Number and percentage of children served under Individuals with Disabilities Education Act, Part B, by age group and state or jurisdiction: Selected years, 1990–91 through 2006–07   85

53. Number of gifted and talented students in public elementary and secondary schools, by sex, race/ethnicity, and state: 2004 and 2006.   86

54. Percentage of gifted and talented students in public elementary and secondary schools, by sex, race/ethnicity, and state: 2004 and 2006.   87

55. Enrollment in grades 9 through 12 in public and private schools compared with population 14 to 17 years of age: Selected years, 1889–90 through fall 2008   88

56. Enrollment in foreign language courses compared with enrollment in grades 9 through 12 in public secondary schools: Selected years, fall 1948 through fall 2000   89

57. Number and percentage of schools with students enrolled in distance education courses and enrollment in distance education courses, by instructional level and district characteristics: 2002–03.   90

Private Elementary and Secondary Schools

58. Private elementary and secondary enrollment, teachers, and schools, by orientation of school and selected school characteristics: Fall 2005   91

59. Private elementary and secondary enrollment, number of schools, and average tuition, by school level, orientation, and tuition: 1999–2000 and 2003–04   92

60. Private elementary and secondary school full-time-equivalent staff and student to full-time-equivalent staff ratios, by orientation of school, school level, and type of staff: 2003–04   93

61. Enrollment and instructional staff in Catholic elementary and secondary schools, by level: Selected years, 1919–20 through 2007–08   95

62. Private elementary and secondary schools, enrollment, teachers, and high school graduates, by state: Selected years, 1997 through 2005   96

Teachers and Other Staff

63. Public elementary and secondary pupil/teacher ratios, by enrollment size, type, and level of school: Fall 1987 through fall 2006. 97

64. Public and private elementary and secondary teachers, enrollment, and pupil/teacher ratios: Selected years, fall 1955 through fall 2017 98

65. Public elementary and secondary teachers, by level and state or jurisdiction: Selected years, fall 2000 through fall 2006 99

66. Teachers, enrollment, and pupil/teacher ratios in public elementary and secondary schools, by state or jurisdiction: Selected years, fall 2000 through fall 2006 100

67. Highest degree earned, years of full-time teaching experience, and average class size for teachers in public elementary and secondary schools, by state: 2003–04. 101

68. Highest degree earned and years of full-time teaching experience for teachers in public and private elementary and secondary schools, by selected teacher characteristics: 1999–2000 and 2003–04. 102

69. Selected characteristics of public school teachers: Selected years, spring 1961 through spring 2001. 104

70. Percentage of public school teachers of grades 9 through 12, by field of main teaching assignment and selected demographic and educational characteristics: 2003–04. 105

71. Teachers' perceptions about serious problems in their schools, by control and level of school: Selected years, 1987–88 through 2003–04. 106

72. Teachers' perceptions about teaching and school conditions, by control and level of school: 1993–94, 1999–2000, and 2003–04 107

73. Mobility of public and private elementary and secondary teachers, by selected teacher and school characteristics: Selected years, 1987–88 through 2004–05 108

74. Average base salary for full-time teachers in public elementary and secondary schools, by highest degree earned and years of full-time teaching: Selected years, 1990–91 through 2003–04. 109

75. Average salaries for full-time teachers in public and private elementary and secondary schools, by selected characteristics: 2003–04 111

76. Average base salary for full-time public elementary and secondary school teachers with a bachelor's degree as their highest degree, by years of full-time teaching experience and state: 1993–94, 1999–2000, and 2003–04 113

77. Average base salary for full-time public elementary and secondary school teachers with a master's degree as their highest degree, by years of full-time teaching experience and state: 1993–94, 1999–2000, and 2003–04 114

78. Estimated average annual salary of teachers in public elementary and secondary schools: Selected years, 1959–60 through 2006–07. 115

79. Estimated average annual salary of teachers in public elementary and secondary schools, by state or jurisdiction: Selected years, 1969–70 through 2006–07 116

80. Staff employed in public elementary and secondary school systems, by functional area: Selected years, 1949–50 through fall 2006. 117

81. Staff employed in public elementary and secondary school systems, by type of assignment and state or jurisdiction: Fall 2006 118

82. Staff employed in public elementary and secondary school systems, by type of assignment and state or jurisdiction: Fall 2005 119

83. Staff employed in public elementary and secondary school systems, by type of assignment and state or jurisdiction: Fall 2004 120

84. Staff and teachers in public elementary and secondary school systems, by state or jurisdiction: Fall 2000 through fall 2006. 121

85. Staff, enrollment, and pupil/staff ratios in public elementary and secondary school systems, by state or jurisdiction: Fall 1999 through fall 2006 122

86. Principals in public and private elementary and secondary schools, by selected characteristics: 1993–94, 1999–2000, and 2003–04 123

Schools and School Districts

87. Number of public school districts and public and private elementary and secondary schools: Selected years, 1869–70 through 2006–07 124

88. Number and enrollment of regular public school districts, by enrollment size of district: Selected years, 1979–80 through 2006–07 125

89. Number of public elementary and secondary education agencies, by type of agency and state or jurisdiction: 2005–06 and 2006–07 126

90. Public elementary and secondary students, schools, pupil/teacher ratios, and finances, by type of locale: 2005–06 and 2006–07 127

91. Selected statistics on enrollment, teachers, dropouts, and graduates in public school districts enrolling more than 15,000 students: 1990, 2000, 2004–05, and 2006 129

92. Revenues, expenditures, poverty rate, and Title I allocations of public school districts enrolling more than 15,000 students: 2005–06 and fiscal year 2008 140

93. Enrollment, poverty, and federal funds for the 100 largest school districts, by enrollment size in 2006: Fall 2006, 2005–06, and fiscal year 2008 151

94. Public elementary and secondary schools, by type of school: Selected years, 1967–68 through 2006–07 154

95. Number and percentage distribution of public elementary and secondary schools and enrollment, by type and enrollment size of school: 2004–05, 2005–06, and 2006–07 155

96. Average enrollment and percentage distribution of public elementary and secondary schools, by type and size: Selected years, 1982–83 through 2006–07 156

97. Public elementary and secondary school students, by racial/ethnic enrollment concentration of school: Fall 1995, fall 2000, and fall 2006 157

98. Public elementary and secondary schools, by type and state or jurisdiction: 1990–91, 2000–01, and 2006–07 158

99. Public elementary schools, by grade span, average school size, and state or jurisdiction: 2006–07   159

100. Public secondary schools, by grade span, average school size, and state or jurisdiction: 2006–07   160

101. Number and enrollment of traditional public and public charter elementary and secondary schools and percentages of students, teachers, and schools, by selected characteristics: 2003–04   161

102. Percentage of public schools with permanent and portable (temporary) buildings and with environmental factors that interfere with instruction in classrooms, by selected school characteristics, type of factor, and extent of interference: 2005 163

103. Percentage of public schools with enrollment under, at, or over capacity, by selected school characteristics: 1999 and 2005 163

High School Completers and Dropouts

104. High school graduates, by sex and control of school: Selected years, 1869–70 through 2008–09 . 164

105. Public high school graduates, by state or jurisdiction: Selected years, 1980–81 through 2006–07 . 165

106. Averaged freshman graduation rates for public secondary schools, by state or jurisdiction: Selected years, 1990–91 through 2005–06 166

107. Public high school graduates and dropouts, by race/ethnicity and state or jurisdiction: 2005–06 . .   167

108. General Educational Development (GED) test takers and test passers, by age: 1971 through 2006   168

109. Percentage of high school dropouts among persons 16 through 24 years old (status dropout rate), by sex and race/ethnicity: Selected years, 1960 through 2007 169

110. Percentage of high school dropouts among persons 16 through 24 years old (status dropout rate), by income level, and percentage distribution of status dropouts, by labor force status and educational attainment: 1970 through 2007 170

111. Number of 14- through 21-year-old students served under Individuals with Disabilities Education Act, Part B, who exited school, by exit reason, age, and type of disability: United States and other jurisdictions, 2004–05 and 2005–06 171

Educational Achievement

112.   Percentage of children demonstrating specific cognitive and motor skills at about 9 months of age, by child's age and selected characteristics: 2001–02 172

113.   Percentage of children demonstrating specific mental skills, physical skills, and secure emotional attachment to parents at about 2 years of age, by selected characteristics: 2003–04 173

114.   Children's specific language, literacy, mathematics, color knowledge, and fine motor skills at about 4 years of age, by age of child and selected characteristics: 2005–06 174

115.   Mean reading scale scores and specific reading skills of fall 1998 first-time kindergartners, by time of assessment and selected characteristics: Selected years, fall 1998 through spring 2004 175

116.   Mean mathematics and science scale scores and specific mathematics skills of fall 1998 first-time kindergartners, by time of assessment and selected characteristics: Selected years, fall 1998 through spring 2004 176

117.   Average reading scale score, by age and selected student and school characteristics: Selected years, 1971 through 2004 177

118.   Average reading scale score, by sex, grade, race/ethnicity, and percentile: Selected years, 1992 through 2007 178

119.   Average reading scale score, by age and amount of time spent on reading and homework: Selected years, 1984 through 2004 179

120.   Percentage of students at or above selected reading score levels, by age, sex, and race/ethnicity: Selected years, 1971 through 2004 180

121.   Average reading scale score and percentage of 4th-graders in public schools attaining reading achievement levels, by race/ethnicity and state or jurisdiction: Selected years, 1992 through 2007   182

122.   Average reading scale score and percentage of 8th-graders in public schools attaining reading achievement levels, by locale and state or jurisdiction: Selected years, 1998 through 2007 184

123.   Average reading scale scores of 4th-, 8th-, and 12th-graders, by selected student and school characteristics: Selected years, 1992 through 2007 186

124.   Average reading scale scores of 4th- and 8th-graders, by selected student and parent characteristics and school type: Various years, 2000 through 2005 187

125.   Average writing scale score and percentage of students attaining writing achievement levels, by selected student characteristics and grade level: 2002 and 2007 188

126.   Percentage of students attaining U.S. history achievement levels, by grade level and selected student characteristics: 2001 and 2006 189

127.   Average U.S. history scale score, by grade level and selected student characteristics, and percentage distribution of 12th-graders, by selected student characteristics: 1994, 2001, and 2006 190

128.   Average civics scale score and percentage of students attaining civics achievement levels, by grade level and selected student characteristics: 1998 and 2006 191

129.   Average economics scale score of 12th-graders, percentage attaining economics achievement levels, and percentage with different levels of economics coursework, by selected student and school characteristics: 2006 192

130.   Percentage of students attaining geography achievement levels, by grade level and selected student characteristics: 2001 193

131.   Average mathematics scale score, by age and selected student and school characteristics: Selected years, 1973 through 2004 194

132.   Percentage of students at or above selected mathematics proficiency levels, by age, sex, and race/ethnicity: Selected years, 1978 through 2004 195

133.   Mathematics performance of 17-year-olds, by highest mathematics course taken, sex, and race/ethnicity: Selected years, 1978 through 2004 197

134.   Average mathematics scale score, percentage attaining mathematics achievement levels, and selected statistics on mathematics education of 4th-graders in public schools, by state or jurisdiction: Selected years, 1992 through 2007 198

135. Average mathematics scale score and percentage attaining mathematics achievement levels of 8th-graders in public schools, by level of parental education and state or jurisdiction: Selected years, 1990 through 2007 199

136. Average mathematics scale scores of 4th-, 8th-, and 12th-graders, by selected student and school characteristics: Selected years, 1990 through 2007 201

137. Average mathematics scale score of 8th-graders and percentage reporting various attitudes toward mathematics work, by frequency of attitude and selected student and school characteristics: 2007 202

138. Average science scale scores and percentage of 4th-, 8th-, and 12th-graders attaining science achievement levels, by selected student characteristics and percentile: 1996, 2000, and 2005 .. 203

139. Average science scale score for 8th-graders in public schools, by selected student characteristics and state or jurisdiction: 1996, 2000, and 2005... 204

140. Average science scale score of 12th-graders and percentage reporting various attitudes toward science, by selected student and school characteristics: 2005 206

141. SAT mean scores of college-bound seniors, by race/ethnicity: Selected years, 1986–87 through 2007–08... 207

142. SAT mean scores of college-bound seniors, by sex: 1966–67 through 2007–08.............. 208

143. SAT mean scores of college-bound seniors, by selected student characteristics: Selected years, 1995–96 through 2007–08... 209

144. SAT mean scores of college-bound seniors and percentage of graduates taking SAT, by state or jurisdiction: Selected years, 1987–88 through 2007–08 211

145. ACT score averages and standard deviations, by sex and race/ethnicity, and percentage of ACT test takers, by selected composite score ranges and planned fields of study: Selected years, 1995 through 2008 212

146. Percentage distribution of elementary and secondary school children, by average grades and selected child and school characteristics: 1996, 1999, and 2003 213

Coursetaking

147. Average number of Carnegie units earned by public high school graduates in various subject fields, by selected student characteristics: Selected years, 1982 through 2005 214

148. Average number of Carnegie units earned by public high school graduates in career/technical education courses, by selected student characteristics: Selected years, 1982 through 2005.... 217

149. Percentage of public and private high school graduates taking selected mathematics and science courses in high school, by sex and race/ethnicity: Selected years, 1982 through 2005 220

150. Percentage distribution of public and private high school graduates, by highest level of mathematics and science course completed and selected student characteristics: 2003–04.... 221

151. Percentage of public and private high school graduates earning minimum credits in selected combinations of academic courses, by sex and race/ethnicity: Selected years, 1982 through 2005   222

152. Public high schools that offered and students enrolled in dual credit, Advanced Placement, and International Baccalaureate courses, by school characteristics: 2003.................... 223

Student Activities and Behavior

153. Percentage of high school seniors who say they engage in various activities, by selected student and school characteristics: 1992 and 2004 224

154. Percentage of high school sophomores who participate in various school-sponsored extracurricular activities, by selected student characteristics: 1990 and 2002................ 225

155. Percentage distribution of 4th-graders, by time spent on homework and television viewing each day and selected student and school characteristics: Selected years, 1992 through 2000 226

156. Percentage of elementary and secondary school students who do homework outside of school, whose parents check that homework is done, and whose parents help with homework, by frequency and selected student and school characteristics: 2003 and 2007.................. 227

157. Tenth-graders' attendance patterns, by selected student and school characteristics: 1990 and 2002 229

158. Percentage of public schools reporting crime incidents, and number and rate of incidents, by school characteristics and type of incident: 1999–2000 and 2005–06 230

159. Percentage of schools with various security measures, by school control and selected characteristics: 2003–04 234

160. Number of students suspended and expelled from public elementary and secondary schools, by sex, race/ethnicity, and state: 2006 235

161. Percentage of students suspended and expelled from public elementary and secondary schools, by sex, race/ethnicity, and state: 2006 237

162. Percentage of students in grades 9 through 12 who reported experience with drugs and violence on school property, by race/ethnicity, grade, and sex: Selected years, 1997 through 2007 238

163. Percentage of 12- to 17-year-olds reporting substance abuse during the past 30 days and the past year, by drug used, sex, and race/ethnicity: Selected years, 1982 through 2006 239

164. Percentage of high school seniors reporting drug use, by type of drug and reporting period: Selected years, 1975 through 2007 240

State Regulations

165. Age range for compulsory school attendance and special education services, and policies on year-round schools and kindergarten programs, by state: Selected years, 1997 through 2008 241

166. Minimum length of school year and policy on textbook selection, by state: 2000, 2004, and 2006 . 242

167. State requirements for a standard high school diploma: 2006 243

168. States that use criterion-referenced tests (CRTs) aligned to state standards, by subject area and level: 2006–07 244

169. States using minimum-competency testing, by grade levels assessed, expected uses of standards, and state or jurisdiction: 2001–02 245

170. States requiring testing for initial certification of elementary and secondary teachers, by skills or knowledge assessment and state: 2007 and 2008 246

Revenues and Expenditures

171. Revenues for public elementary and secondary schools, by source of funds: Selected years, 1919–20 through 2005–06 247

172. Revenues for public elementary and secondary schools, by source and state or jurisdiction: 2005–06 248

173. Revenues for public elementary and secondary schools, by source and state or jurisdiction: 2004–05 249

174. Summary of expenditures for public elementary and secondary education, by purpose: Selected years, 1919–20 through 2005–06 250

175. Students transported at public expense and current expenditures for transportation: Selected years, 1929–30 through 2005–06 251

176. Current expenditures for public elementary and secondary education, by state or jurisdiction: Selected years, 1969–70 through 2005–06 252

177. Total expenditures for public elementary and secondary education, by function and state or jurisdiction: 2005–06 254

178. Total expenditures for public elementary and secondary education, by function and state or jurisdiction: 2004–05 256

179. Total expenditures for public elementary and secondary education, by function and subfunction: Selected years, 1990–91 through 2005–06 258

180. Expenditures for instruction in public elementary and secondary schools, by subfunction and state or jurisdiction: 2004–05 and 2005–06 260

181. Total and current expenditures per pupil in public elementary and secondary schools: Selected years, 1919–20 through 2005–06 261

182. Total and current expenditures per pupil in fall enrollment in public elementary and secondary education, by function and state or jurisdiction: 2005–06 262

183. Total and current expenditures per pupil in fall enrollment in public elementary and secondary education, by function and state or jurisdiction: 2004–05 263

184. Current expenditure per pupil in fall enrollment in public elementary and secondary schools, by state or jurisdiction: Selected years, 1969–70 through 2005–06 264

185. Current expenditure per pupil in average daily attendance in public elementary and secondary schools, by state or jurisdiction: Selected years, 1959–60 through 2005–06 266

Chapter 3. Postsecondary Education

Enrollment

186. Enrollment, staff, and degrees conferred in postsecondary institutions participating in Title IV programs, by type and control of institution, sex of student, type of staff, and type of degree: Fall 2005, fall 2006, and 2006–07 276

187. Historical summary of faculty, students, degrees, and finances in degree-granting institutions: Selected years, 1869–70 through 2006–07 277

188. Total fall enrollment in degree-granting institutions, by attendance status, sex of student, and control of institution: Selected years, 1947 through 2007 278

189. Total fall enrollment in degree-granting institutions, by control and type of institution: 1963 through 2007 279

190. Total fall enrollment in degree-granting institutions, by sex, age, and attendance status: Selected years, 1970 through 2017 280

191. Total fall enrollment in degree-granting institutions, by level of enrollment, sex, age, and attendance status of student: 2007 281

192. Total fall enrollment in degree-granting institutions, by control and type of institution, age, and attendance status of student: 2007 282

193. Total fall enrollment in degree-granting institutions, by level of enrollment, sex, attendance status, and type and control of institution: 2007 283

194. Total fall enrollment in degree-granting institutions, by level of enrollment, sex, attendance status, and type and control of institution: 2006 284

195. Total fall enrollment in degree-granting institutions, by level of enrollment, sex, attendance status, and type and control of institution: 2005 285

196. Total fall enrollment in degree-granting institutions, by attendance status, sex of student, and type and control of institution: Selected years, 1970 through 2006 286

197. Fall enrollment and number of degree-granting institutions, by control and affiliation of institution: Selected years, 1980 through 2006 287

198. Total first-time freshmen fall enrollment in degree-granting institutions, by attendance status, sex of student, and type and control of institution: 1955 through 2007 289

199. Total first-time freshmen fall enrollment in degree-granting institutions, by attendance status, sex, control of institution, and state or jurisdiction: Selected years, 2000 through 2006 290

200. Recent high school completers and their enrollment in college, by sex: 1960 through 2007 291

201. Recent high school completers and their enrollment in college, by race/ethnicity: 1960 through 2007 292

202. Graduation rates of previous year's 12th-graders and college attendance rates of those who graduated, by selected high school characteristics: 1999–2000 and 2003–04 294

203. Estimated rate of 2005–06 high school graduates attending degree-granting institutions, by state: 2006 295

204. Enrollment rates of 18- to 24-year-olds in degree-granting institutions, by type of institution and sex and race/ethnicity of student: 1967 through 2007 296

205.   Total undergraduate fall enrollment in degree-granting institutions, by attendance status, sex of
        student, and control of institution: 1967 through 2007 297

206.   Total graduate fall enrollment in degree-granting institutions, by attendance status, sex of student,
        and control of institution: 1969 through 2007 298

207.   Total first-professional fall enrollment in degree-granting institutions, by attendance status, sex of
        student, and control of institution: 1969 through 2007 299

208.   Total fall enrollment in degree-granting institutions, by state or jurisdiction: Selected years,
        1970 through 2006 300

209.   Total fall enrollment in public degree-granting institutions, by state or jurisdiction: Selected years,
        1970 through 2006 301

210.   Total fall enrollment in private degree-granting institutions, by state or jurisdiction: Selected years,
        1970 through 2006 302

211.   Total fall enrollment in all degree-granting institutions, by attendance status, sex, and state or
        jurisdiction: 2005 and 2006 303

212.   Total fall enrollment in public degree-granting institutions, by attendance status, sex, and state or
        jurisdiction: 2005 and 2006 304

213.   Total fall enrollment in private degree-granting institutions, by attendance status, sex, and state or
        jurisdiction: 2005 and 2006 305

214.   Total fall enrollment in private not-for-profit degree-granting institutions, by attendance status, sex,
        and state or jurisdiction: 2005 and 2006 306

215.   Total fall enrollment in degree-granting institutions, by control and type of institution and state or
        jurisdiction: 2005 and 2006 307

216.   Total fall enrollment in degree-granting institutions, by level of enrollment and state or jurisdiction:
        2004, 2005, and 2006 308

217.   Total fall enrollment in degree-granting institutions, by control, level of enrollment, type of
        institution, and state or jurisdiction: 2006 309

218.   Total fall enrollment in degree-granting institutions, by control, level of enrollment, type of
        institution, and state or jurisdiction: 2005 310

219.   Full-time-equivalent fall enrollment in degree-granting institutions, by control and type of institution:
        1967 through 2007 311

220.   Full-time-equivalent fall enrollment in degree-granting institutions, by control and type of institution
        and state or jurisdiction: 2000, 2005, and 2006 312

221.   Full-time-equivalent fall enrollment in degree-granting institutions, by control and state or
        jurisdiction: Selected years, 1980 through 2006 313

222.   Total full-year enrollment in degree-granting institutions, by control and type of institution and state
        or jurisdiction: 2005–06 and 2006–07 314

223.   Residence and migration of all freshmen students in degree-granting institutions, by state or
        jurisdiction: Fall 2006 315

224.   Residence and migration of all freshmen students in degree-granting institutions who graduated
        from high school in the previous 12 months, by state or jurisdiction: Fall 2006 316

225.   Residence and migration of all freshmen students in 4-year degree-granting institutions who
        graduated from high school in the previous 12 months, by state or jurisdiction: Fall 2006 317

226.   Total fall enrollment in degree-granting institutions, by race/ethnicity, sex, attendance status, and
        level of student: Selected years, 1976 through 2007 318

227.   Total fall enrollment in degree-granting institutions, by race/ethnicity of student and type and control
        of institution: Selected years, 1976 through 2007 321

228.   Fall enrollment in degree-granting institutions, by race/ethnicity of student and by state or
        jurisdiction: 2007 323

229.   Fall enrollment in degree-granting institutions, by race/ethnicity of student and by state or
        jurisdiction: 2006 325

230.   Total number of degree-granting institutions and fall enrollment in these institutions, by type and
        control of institution and percentage of minority enrollment: 2007 327

231. Number and percentage of students enrolled in postsecondary institutions, by level, disability status, and selected student characteristics: 2003–04 329

232. Enrollment in postsecondary education, by student level, type of institution, age, and major field of study: 2003–04 330

233. Graduate enrollment in science and engineering programs in degree-granting institutions, by discipline division: Fall 1994 through fall 2006 332

234. Number of degree-granting institutions and enrollment in these institutions, by size, type, and control of institution: Fall 2006 333

235. Selected statistics for degree-granting institutions enrolling more than 15,000 students in 2006: Selected years, 1990 through 2007 334

236. Enrollment of the 120 largest degree-granting college and university campuses, by selected characteristics and institution: Fall 2006 344

237. Enrollment and degrees conferred in degree-granting women's colleges, by selected characteristics and institution: Fall 2006 and 2006–07 345

238. Enrollment and degrees conferred in degree-granting institutions that serve large proportions of undergraduate Hispanic students, by selected characteristics and institution: Fall 2006 and 2006–07 346

239. Enrollment and degrees conferred in degree-granting tribally controlled institutions, by institution: Fall 2000 through fall 2006, and 2005–06 and 2006–07 353

240. Fall enrollment, degrees conferred, and expenditures in degree-granting historically Black colleges and universities, by institution: 2005, 2005–06, 2006, and 2006–07 354

241. Selected statistics on degree-granting historically Black colleges and universities, by control and type of institution: Selected years, 1990 through 2007 356

242. Fall enrollment in degree-granting historically Black colleges and universities, by type and control of institution: 1976 through 2006 357

Staff

243. Employees in degree-granting institutions, by sex, employment status, control and type of institution, and primary occupation: Selected years, fall 1987 through fall 2007 358

244. Total and full-time-equivalent staff in degree-granting institutions, by employment status, control of institution, and occupation: Fall 1976, fall 1997, and fall 2007 359

245. Employees in degree-granting institutions, by employment status, sex, control and type of institution, and primary occupation: Fall 2007 360

246. Employees in degree-granting institutions, by race/ethnicity, sex, employment status, control and type of institution, and primary occupation: Fall 2007 362

247. Number of full-time-equivalent (FTE) staff and faculty, and FTE staff and faculty/FTE student ratios in degree-granting institutions, by control and type of institution and state or jurisdiction: Fall 2005 363

248. Number of instructional faculty in degree-granting institutions, by employment status and control and type of institution: Selected years, fall 1970 through fall 2005 365

249. Full-time instructional faculty in degree-granting institutions, by race/ethnicity, sex, and academic rank: Fall 2003, fall 2005, and fall 2007 366

250. Percentage distribution of full-time faculty and instructional staff in degree-granting institutions, by type and control of institution, selected instruction activities, and number of classes taught for credit: Fall 2003 367

251. Percentage distribution of part-time faculty and instructional staff in degree-granting institutions, by type and control of institution, selected instruction activities, and number of classes taught for credit: Fall 2003 369

252. Full-time and part-time faculty and instructional staff in degree-granting institutions, by type and control of institution and selected characteristics: Fall 1992, fall 1998, and fall 2003 371

253. Full-time and part-time faculty and instructional staff in degree-granting institutions, by race/ethnicity, sex, and selected characteristics: Fall 2003 373

254. Full-time and part-time faculty and instructional staff in degree-granting institutions, by field and faculty characteristics: Fall 1992, fall 1998, and fall 2003 375

255. Full-time and part-time faculty and instructional staff in degree-granting institutions, by race/ethnicity, sex, and program area: Fall 1998 and fall 2003 377

256. Average base salary of full-time faculty and instructional staff in degree-granting institutions, by type and control of institution and field of instruction: Selected years, 1987–88 through 2003–04 379

257. Average salary of full-time instructional faculty on 9-month contracts in degree-granting institutions, by academic rank, control and type of institution, and sex: Selected years, 1970–71 through 2007–08 . 380

258. Average salary of full-time instructional faculty on 9-month contracts in degree-granting institutions, by sex, academic rank, and control and type of institution: Selected years, 1999–2000 through 2007–08 383

259. Average salary of full-time instructional faculty on 9-month contracts in degree-granting institutions, by control and type of institution and state or jurisdiction: 2006–07 384

260. Average salary of full-time instructional faculty on 9-month contracts in degree-granting institutions, by control and type of institution and state or jurisdiction: 2005–06 385

261. Average salary of full-time instructional faculty on 9-month contracts in 4-year degree-granting institutions, by type and control of institution, rank of faculty, and state or jurisdiction: 2006–07. . 386

262. Average salary of full-time instructional faculty on 9-month contracts in 4-year degree-granting institutions, by type and control of institution, rank of faculty, and state or jurisdiction: 2005–06. . 387

263. Average benefit expenditure for full-time instructional faculty on 9-month contracts in degree-granting institutions, by type of benefit and control of institution: Selected years, 1977–78 through 2006–07 388

264. Percentage of full-time instructional staff with tenure for degree-granting institutions with a tenure system, by academic rank, sex, and control and type of institution: Selected years, 1993–94 through 2005–06 390

Institutions

265. Degree-granting institutions, by control and type of institution: Selected years, 1949–50 through 2007–08 391

266. Degree-granting institutions and branches, by type and control of institution and state or jurisdiction: 2007–08 392

267. Degree-granting institutions that have closed their doors, by control and type of institution: 1969–70 through 2007–08 394

Degrees

268. Degrees conferred by degree-granting institutions, by level of degree and sex of student: Selected years, 1869–70 through 2017–18 395

269. Associate's degrees conferred by degree-granting institutions, by discipline division: 1995–96 through 2006–07 396

270. Associate's degrees and other subbaccalaureate awards conferred by degree-granting institutions, by length of curriculum, sex of student, and discipline division: 2006–07 397

271. Bachelor's degrees conferred by degree-granting institutions, by field of study: Selected years, 1970–71 through 2006–07 398

272. Master's degrees conferred by degree-granting institutions, by field of study: Selected years, 1970–71 through 2006–07 399

273. Doctor's degrees conferred by degree-granting institutions, by field of study: Selected years, 1970–71 through 2006–07 400

274. Bachelor's, master's, and doctor's degrees conferred by degree-granting institutions, by field of study and year: Selected years, 1970–71 through 2006–07 401

275. Bachelor's, master's, and doctor's degrees conferred by degree-granting institutions, by sex of student and discipline division: 2006–07 402

276. Degrees conferred by degree-granting institutions, by control of institution and level of degree: 1969–70 through 2006–07 417

277. Degrees conferred by degree-granting institutions, by control of institution, level of degree, and field of study: 2006–07 418

278. Number of degree-granting institutions conferring degrees, by control, level of degree, and field of study: 2006–07 419

279. Number of institutions and first-professional degrees conferred by degree-granting institutions in dentistry, medicine, and law, by sex of student: Selected years, 1949–50 through 2006–07 420

280. First-professional degrees conferred by degree-granting institutions, by sex of student, control of institution, and field of study: Selected years, 1985–86 through 2006–07 421

281. Associate's degrees conferred by degree-granting institutions, by race/ethnicity and sex of student: Selected years, 1976–77 through 2006–07 422

282. Associate's degrees conferred by degree-granting institutions, by sex, race/ethnicity, and field of study: 2006–07 423

283. Associate's degrees conferred by degree-granting institutions, by sex, race/ethnicity, and field of study: 2005–06 424

284. Bachelor's degrees conferred by degree-granting institutions, by race/ethnicity and sex of student: Selected years, 1976–77 through 2006–07 425

285. Bachelor's degrees conferred by degree-granting institutions, by sex, race/ethnicity, and field of study: 2006–07 426

286. Bachelor's degrees conferred by degree-granting institutions, by sex, race/ethnicity, and field of study: 2005–06 427

287. Master's degrees conferred by degree-granting institutions, by race/ethnicity and sex of student: Selected years, 1976–77 through 2006–07 428

288. Master's degrees conferred by degree-granting institutions, by sex, race/ethnicity, and field of study: 2006–07 429

289. Master's degrees conferred by degree-granting institutions, by sex, race/ethnicity, and field of study: 2005–06 430

290. Doctor's degrees conferred by degree-granting institutions, by race/ethnicity and sex of student: Selected years, 1976–77 through 2006–07 431

291. Doctor's degrees conferred by degree-granting institutions, by sex, race/ethnicity, and field of study: 2006–07 432

292. Doctor's degrees conferred by degree-granting institutions, by sex, race/ethnicity, and field of study: 2005–06 433

293. First-professional degrees conferred by degree-granting institutions, by race/ethnicity and sex of student: Selected years, 1976–77 through 2006–07 434

294. First-professional degrees conferred by degree-granting institutions, by sex, race/ethnicity, and field of study: 2006–07 435

295. First-professional degrees conferred by degree-granting institutions, by sex, race/ethnicity, and field of study: 2005–06 435

296. Degrees in agriculture and natural resources conferred by degree-granting institutions, by level of degree and sex of student: 1970–71 through 2006–07 436

297. Degrees in architecture and related services conferred by degree-granting institutions, by level of degree and sex of student: Selected years, 1949–50 through 2006–07 437

298. Degrees in the biological and biomedical sciences conferred by degree-granting institutions, by level of degree and sex of student: Selected years, 1951–52 through 2006–07 438

299. Degrees in biology, microbiology, and zoology conferred by degree-granting institutions, by level of degree: 1970–71 through 2006–07 439

300. Degrees in business conferred by degree-granting institutions, by level of degree and sex of student: Selected years, 1955–56 through 2006–07 440

301. Degrees in communication, journalism, and related programs and in communications technologies conferred by degree-granting institutions, by level of degree and sex of student: 1970–71 through 2006–07 441

302.   Degrees in computer and information sciences conferred by degree-granting institutions, by level of degree and sex of student: 1970–71 through 2006–07 442

303.   Degrees in education conferred by degree-granting institutions, by level of degree and sex of student: Selected years, 1949–50 through 2006–07 443

304.   Degrees in engineering and engineering technologies conferred by degree-granting institutions, by level of degree and sex of student: Selected years, 1949–50 through 2006–07 444

305.   Degrees in chemical, civil, electrical, and mechanical engineering conferred by degree-granting institutions, by level of degree: 1970–71 through 2006–07 445

306.   Degrees in English language and literature/letters conferred by degree-granting institutions, by level of degree and sex of student: Selected years, 1949–50 through 2006–07 446

307.   Degrees in modern foreign languages and literatures conferred by degree-granting institutions, by level of degree and sex of student: Selected years, 1949–50 through 2006–07 447

308.   Degrees in French, German, Italian, and Spanish conferred by degree-granting institutions, by level of degree: Selected years, 1949–50 through 2006–07 448

309.   Degrees in Arabic, Chinese, Korean, and Russian conferred by degree-granting institutions, by level of degree: 1969–70 through 2006–07 449

310.   Degrees in the health professions and related sciences conferred by degree-granting institutions, by level of degree and sex of student: 1970–71 through 2006–07 450

311.   Degrees in mathematics and statistics conferred by degree-granting institutions, by level of degree and sex of student: Selected years, 1949–50 through 2006–07 451

312.   Degrees in the physical sciences and science technologies conferred by degree-granting institutions, by level of degree and sex of student: Selected years, 1959–60 through 2006–07 .. 452

313.   Degrees in chemistry, geology and earth science, and physics conferred by degree-granting institutions, by level of degree: 1970–71 through 2006–07 453

314.   Degrees in psychology conferred by degree-granting institutions, by level of degree and sex of student: Selected years, 1949–50 through 2006–07 454

315.   Degrees in public administration and social services conferred by degree-granting institutions, by level of degree and sex of student: 1970–71 through 2006–07 455

316.   Degrees in the social sciences and history conferred by degree-granting institutions, by level of degree and sex of student: 1970–71 through 2006–07 456

317.   Degrees in economics, history, political science and government, and sociology conferred by degree-granting institutions, by level of degree: Selected years, 1949–50 through 2006–07 457

318.   Degrees in visual and performing arts conferred by degree-granting institutions, by level of degree and sex of student: 1970–71 through 2006–07 458

319.   Statistical profile of persons receiving doctor's degrees, by field of study and selected characteristics: 2004–05 and 2005–06 459

320.   Degrees conferred by degree-granting institutions, by control, level of degree, and state or jurisdiction: 2006–07 460

321.   Bachelor's and master's degrees conferred by degree-granting institutions, by field of study and state or jurisdiction: 2006–07 461

322.   Degrees conferred by degree-granting institutions, by level of degree and state or jurisdiction: 2005–06 and 2006–07 463

323.   Doctor's degrees conferred by the 60 institutions conferring the most doctor's degrees: 1997–98 through 2006–07 464

Outcomes

324.   Percentage distribution of 1990 high school sophomores, by highest level of education completed through 2000 and selected student characteristics: 2000 465

325.   Mean number of semester credits completed by bachelor's degree recipients, by course area and major: 1976, 1984, and 1992–93 466

326. Number and percentage of degree-granting institutions with first-year undergraduates using various selection criteria for admission, by type and control of institution: Selected years, 2000–01 through 2007–08 467

327. Number of applications, admissions, and enrollees; their distribution across institutions accepting various percentages of applications; and SAT and ACT scores of applicants, by type and control of institution: 2007–08 468

328. Percentage of degree-granting institutions offering remedial services, by type and control of institution: 1989–90 through 2007–08 469

329. Percentage distribution of enrollment and completion status of first-time postsecondary students starting during the 1995–96 academic year, by type of institution and other student characteristics: 2001 470

330. Average scores on Graduate Record Examination (GRE) general and subject tests: 1965 through 2007 472

Student Charges and Student Financial Assistance

331. Average undergraduate tuition and fees and room and board rates charged for full-time students in degree-granting institutions, by type and control of institution: 1964–65 through 2007–08 474

332. Average undergraduate tuition and fees and room and board rates charged for full-time students in degree-granting institutions, by type and control of institution and state or jurisdiction: 2006–07 and 2007–08 477

333. Undergraduate tuition and fees and room and board rates for full-time students in degree-granting institutions, by percentile of charges and control and type of institution: 2000–01 through 2007–08 478

334. Average graduate and first-professional tuition and required fees in degree-granting institutions, by first-professional field of study and control of institution: 1987–88 through 2007–08 479

335. Percentage of undergraduates receiving aid, by type and source of aid and selected student characteristics: 2003–04 480

336. Full-time, first-time degree/certificate seeking undergraduate students enrolled in degree-granting institutions, by participation and average amount awarded in financial aid programs, and type and control of institution: 2000–01 through 2005–06. 481

337. Average amount of financial aid awarded to full-time, full-year undergraduates, by type and source of aid and selected student characteristics: 2003–04 482

338. Average amount of financial aid awarded to part-time or part-year undergraduates, by type and source of aid and selected student characteristics: 2003–04 483

339. Amount borrowed, aid status, and sources of aid for full-time and part-time undergraduates, by control and type of institution: 2003–04 484

340. Percentage of full-time, full-year undergraduates receiving aid, by type and source of aid and control and type of institution: Selected years, 1992–93 through 2003–04 485

341. Average amount of financial aid awarded to full-time, full-year undergraduates, by type and source of aid and control and type of institution: Selected years, 1992–93 through 2003–04 486

342. Percentage of part-time or part-year undergraduates receiving aid, by type and source of aid and control and type of institution: Selected years, 1992–93 through 2003–04 488

343. Percentage of full-time and part-time undergraduates receiving federal aid, by aid program and control and type of institution: 2003–04 489

344. Amount borrowed, aid status, and sources of aid for full-time, full-year postbaccalaureate students, by level of study and control and type of institution: Selected years, 1992–93 through 2003–04 . 490

345. Amount borrowed, aid status, and sources of aid for part-time or part-year postbaccalaureate students, by level of study and control and type of institution: Selected years, 1992–93 through 2003–04 491

346. Percentage of full-time, full-year postbaccalaureate students receiving aid, by type of aid, level of study, and control and type of institution: Selected years, 1992–93 through 2003–04 492

347. Percentage of part-time or part-year postbaccalaureate students receiving aid, by type of aid, level of study, and control and type of institution: Selected years, 1992--93 through 2003–04 493

Revenue

348. Current-fund revenue of degree-granting institutions, by source of funds: Selected years, 1919–20 through 1995–96 494

349. Current-fund revenue of public degree-granting institutions, by source of funds: Selected years, 1980–81 through 2000–01 495

350. Revenues of public degree-granting institutions, by source of revenue and type of institution: 2003–04, 2004–05, and 2005–06 496

351. Revenues of public degree-granting institutions, by source of revenue and state or jurisdiction: 2005–06 498

352. Appropriations from state and local governments for public degree-granting institutions, by state or jurisdiction: Selected years, 1990–91 through 2005–06 499

353. Total revenue of private not-for-profit degree-granting institutions, by source of funds and type of institution: 1997–98 through 2005–06 500

354. Total revenue of private not-for-profit degree-granting institutions, by source of funds and type of institution: 2005–06 502

355. Total revenue of private for-profit degree-granting institutions, by source of funds and type of institution: 1999–2000 through 2005–06 503

356. Total revenue of private for-profit degree-granting institutions, by source of funds and type of institution: 2004–05 and 2005–06 504

357. Current-fund revenue received from the federal government by the 120 degree-granting institutions receiving the largest amounts, by control and rank order: 2005–06 505

358. Voluntary support for degree-granting institutions, by source and purpose of support: Selected years, 1959–60 through 2006–07 506

359. Endowment funds of the 120 colleges and universities with the largest endowments, by rank order: 2006 and 2007 507

Expenditures

360. Current-fund expenditures and current-fund expenditures per full-time-equivalent student in degree-granting institutions, by type and control of institution: Selected years, 1970–71 through 2000–01 508

361. Current-fund expenditures and educational and general expenditures of institutions of higher education, by purpose and per student: Selected years, 1929–30 through 1995–96 509

362. Expenditures of public degree-granting institutions, by purpose of expenditure and type of institution: 2003–04, 2004–05, and 2005–06 510

363. Expenditures of public degree-granting institutions, by type of institution, purpose of expenditure, and state or jurisdiction: 2003–04, 2004–05, and 2005–06 512

364. Total expenditures of private not-for-profit degree-granting institutions, by purpose and type of institution: 1996–97 through 2005–06 513

365. Total expenditures of private not-for-profit degree-granting institutions, by purpose and type of institution: 2005–06 515

366. Total expenditures of private for-profit degree-granting institutions, by purpose and type of institution: 1998–99 through 2005–06 516

367. Total expenditures of private for-profit degree-granting institutions, by purpose and type of institution: 2004–05 and 2005–06 518

368. Total expenditures of private not-for-profit and for-profit degree-granting institutions, by level and state or jurisdiction: 1998–99 through 2005–06 519

Adult Education

369. Participants in adult basic and secondary education programs, by type of program and state or jurisdiction: Selected fiscal years, 1990 through 2005 520

370. Participation of employed persons, 17 years old and over, in career-related adult education during the previous 12 months, by selected characteristics of participants: Various years, 1995 through 2005 521

371. Participation rate of persons, 17 years old and over, in adult education during the previous 12 months, by selected characteristics of participants: Selected years, 1991 through 2005 524

Vocational Education

372. Number of non-degree-granting Title IV institutions offering postsecondary education, by control and state or jurisdiction: Selected years, 2000–01 through 2007–08 526

Chapter 4. Federal Programs for Education and Related Activities

373. Federal support and estimated federal tax expenditures for education, by category: Selected fiscal years, 1965 through 2008 537

374. Federal on-budget funds for education, by agency: Selected fiscal years, 1970 through 2007 539

375. Federal on-budget funds for education, by level/educational purpose, agency, and program: Selected fiscal years, 1970 through 2008 540

376. Estimated federal support for education, by type of ultimate recipient and agency: Fiscal year 2007 547

377. U.S. Department of Education outlays, by type of recipient and level of education: Selected fiscal years, 1980 through 2008 548

378. U.S. Department of Education appropriations for major programs, by state or jurisdiction: Fiscal year 2007 549

379. Appropriations for Title I, No Child Left Behind Act of 2001, by program and state or jurisdiction: Fiscal years 2007 and 2008 550

380. Federal obligations for research, development, and R&D plant, by performers, fields of science, and category of obligation: Fiscal years 1999 through 2007 551

Chapter 5. Outcomes of Education

Educational Characteristics of the Workforce

381. Labor force participation rates and employment to population ratios of persons 16 to 64 years old, by highest level of education, age, sex, and race/ethnicity: 2007 557

382. Unemployment rate of persons 16 years old and over, by age, sex, race/ethnicity, and educational attainment: 2005, 2006, and 2007 558

383. Occupation of employed persons 25 years old and over, by educational attainment and sex: 2007 559

384. Median annual income of year-round, full-time workers 25 years old and over, by highest level of educational attainment and sex: 1990 through 2007 560

385. Distribution of earnings and median earnings of persons 25 years old and over, by highest level of educational attainment and sex: 2007 563

386. Literacy skills of adults, by type of literacy, proficiency levels, and selected characteristics: 1992 and 2003 565

387. Percentage of 12th-graders working different numbers of hours per week, by selected student characteristics and school locale type: 1992 and 2004 566

Recent High School and College Graduates

388. College enrollment and labor force status of 2005, 2006, and 2007 high school completers, by sex and race/ethnicity: 2005, 2006, and 2007 567

389. Labor force status of high school dropouts, by sex and race/ethnicity: Selected years, 1980 through 2007 569

390. Current postsecondary education and employment status, wages earned, and living arrangements of special education students out of secondary school up to 4 years, by type of disability: 2005 . 570

391. Full-time employment status of bachelor's degree recipients 1 year after graduation, by field of study: Selected years, 1976 through 2001.. 570

392. Percentage distribution of 1999–2000 bachelor's degree recipients 1 year after graduation, by field of study, time to completion, enrollment status, employment status, occupational area, job characteristics, and annual salaries: 2001.. 571

393. Enrollment in postbaccalaureate certificate or advanced degree programs and highest degree attained by 1992–93 bachelor's degree recipients, by education characteristics: 2003......... 572

394. Average annual salary of bachelor's degree recipients employed full time 1 year after graduation, by field of study: Selected years, 1976 through 2001 573

395. Percentage of 18- to 25-year-olds reporting substance abuse during the past 30 days and the past year, by drug used: Selected years, 1982 through 2006 574

396. Percentage of 18- to 25-year-olds reporting substance abuse during the past 30 days and the past year, by drug used and selected characteristics: 2000 and 2006 575

397. Percentage of 1972 high school seniors, 1992 high school seniors, and 2004 high school seniors who felt that certain life values were "very important," by sex: Selected years, 1972 through 2004 576

Chapter 6. International Comparisons of Education

Population, Enrollment, and Teachers

398. Selected population and finance statistics, school enrollment, and teachers, by major areas of the world: Selected years, 1980 through 2005 581

399. Selected population and enrollment statistics for countries with populations over 10 million, by continent: Selected years, 1990 through 2006.. 582

400. School-age populations as a percentage of total population, by age group and country: Selected years, 1985 through 2005 584

401. Percentage of population enrolled in secondary and postsecondary education, by age group and country: Selected years, 1985 through 2005 585

402. Pupils per teacher in public and private elementary and secondary schools, by level of education and country: Selected years, 1985 through 2006 586

Achievement, Instruction, and Student Activities

403. Average mathematics literacy, reading literacy, and science literacy scores of 15-year-olds, by sex and country: 2006 587

404. Mean scores and percentage distribution of 15-year-olds scoring at each mathematics literacy proficiency level, by country: 2006.. 588

405. Mean scores and percentage distribution of 15-year-olds scoring at each scientific literacy proficiency level, by country: 2006.. 589

406. Average fourth-grade mathematics scores, by content areas, index of time students spend doing mathematics homework in a normal school week, and country: 2003........................ 590

407. Average eighth-grade mathematics scores, by content areas, index of time students spend doing mathematics homework in a normal school week, and country: 2003........................ 591

408. Percentage of lesson time spent on various mathematics activities, yearly mathematics instructional time, and mathematics instructional time as a percentage of total instructional time in eighth grade, by country: 2003 593

409. Average size and scores of eighth-grade mathematics classes and Index of Teachers' Emphasis on Mathematics Homework (EMH), by country: 2003 595

410. Eighth-grade students' perceptions about mathematics and hours spent on leisure activities, by country: 2003 597

411. Average mathematics scores at the end of secondary school, by sex, average time spent studying mathematics out of school, and country: 1995 598

412. Average fourth-grade science scores in content areas and average time spent teaching science in school, by country: 2003 599

413. Average eighth-grade science scores in content areas and average time spent studying out of school, by country: 2003 600

414. Instructional practices and time spent teaching science in eighth grade, by country: 2003 602

Postsecondary Degrees

415. Number of bachelor's degree recipients per 100 persons of the typical age of graduation, by sex and country: 2002 through 2005 604

416. Percentage of bachelor's degrees awarded in mathematics and science, by field and country: Selected years, 1985 through 2005 605

417. Percentage of graduate degrees awarded in mathematics and science, by field and country: Selected years, 1985 through 2005 606

Finances

418. Public and private education expenditures per student, by level of education and country: Selected years, 2000 through 2005 607

419. Total public direct expenditures on education as a percentage of the gross domestic product, by level and country: Selected years, 1985 through 2005 608

Foreign Students in the United States

420. Foreign students enrolled in institutions of higher education in the United States and other jurisdictions, by continent, region, and selected countries of origin: Selected years, 1980–81 through 2006–07 609

Chapter 7. Libraries and Educational Technology

Libraries

421. Selected statistics on school libraries/media centers, by control and level of school: 1999–2000 and 2003–04 613

422. Selected statistics on public school libraries/media centers, by level and enrollment size of school: 2003–04 614

423. Selected statistics on public school libraries/media centers, by state: 2003–04 615

424. Collections, staff, and operating expenditures of degree-granting institution libraries: Selected years, 1976–77 through 2005–06 616

425. Collections, staff, and operating expenditures of the 60 largest college and university libraries: 2005–06 617

426. Public libraries, books and serial volumes, library visits, circulation, and reference transactions, by state: Fiscal year 2005 618

Computers and Technology

427. Public schools and instructional rooms with internet access, by selected school characteristics: Selected years, 1994 through 2005 619

428. Use of the Internet by persons 3 years old and over, by type of use and selected characteristics of students and other users: 2003 621

429. Number and percentage of home computer users, by type of application and selected characteristics: 1997 and 2003 623

430. Number and percentage of student home computer users, by type of application and selected characteristics: 2003 624

431. Student use of computers, by level of enrollment, age, and student and school characteristics: 1993, 1997, and 2003 625

432. Percentage of workers, 18 years old and over, using computers on the job, by type of computer application and selected characteristics: 1993, 1997, and 2003 627

Appendix A. Guide to Sources

A-1. Respondent counts for selected High School and Beyond surveys: 1982, 1984, and 1986 665

A-2. Design effects (DEFF) and root design effects (DEFT) for selected High School and Beyond surveys and subsamples: 1984 and 1986 666

A-3. Respondent counts of full-time workers from the Recent College Graduates survey: Selected years, 1976 to 1991 666

A-4. Sampling errors (95 percent confidence level) for percentages estimated from the Gallup Poll: 1992, 1993, and 1996 through 2008 667

A-5. Sampling errors (95 percent confidence level) for the difference in two percentages estimated from the Gallup Poll: 1992, 1993, and 1996 through 2008 667

A-6. Maximum differences required for significance (90 percent confidence level) between sample subgroups from the "Status of the American Public School Teacher" survey: 2000–01 667

INTRODUCTION

In fall 2008, about 74.1 million people were enrolled in American schools and colleges (table 1). About 4.6 million people were employed as elementary and secondary school teachers or as college faculty, in full-time equivalents (FTE). Other professional, administrative, and support staff at educational institutions totaled 5.2 million. All data for 2008 in this Introduction are projected. Some data for other years are projected or estimated as noted. In discussions of historical trends, different time periods and specific years are cited, depending on the timing of important changes as well as the availability of relevant data.

Elementary/Secondary Education

Enrollment

A pattern of annual increases in total public elementary and secondary school enrollment began in 1985 (table 3). Between 1985 and 2008, public school enrollment rose 26 percent, from 39.4 million to 49.8 million (table 2). Private school enrollment grew more slowly than public school enrollment during this period, rising 9 percent, from 5.6 million to 6.1 million. As a result, the percentage of elementary and secondary students enrolled in private schools declined from 12.4 percent in 1985 to 10.8 percent in 2008.

In public schools between 1985 and 2008, there was a 29 percent increase in elementary enrollment (prekindergarten through grade 8), compared with a 20 percent increase in secondary enrollment. Part of the relatively fast growth in public elementary school enrollment resulted from the expansion of prekindergarten programs (table 37). Between 1985 and 2006, enrollment in prekindergarten increased 611 percent, while enrollment in other elementary grades increased 23 percent. The number of children enrolled in prekindergarten increased from 0.2 million in 1985 to 1.1 million in 2006, and the number enrolled in kindergarten through grade 8 increased from 26.9 million to 33.1 million. Public secondary school enrollment declined 8 percent from 1985 to 1990, but then started increasing. For most of the period after 1992, secondary enrollment increased more rapidly than elementary enrollment, leading to relatively large secondary enrollment gains in recent years. For example, between 1998 and 2008, public secondary school enrollment rose 13 percent, compared with 5 percent for public elementary school enrollment. Overall, public school enrollment rose 7 percent between 1998 and 2008.

Since the enrollment rates of kindergarten, elementary, and secondary school-age children changed by less than 2 percentage points between 1985 and 2007 (table 7), increases in public and private elementary and secondary school enrollment have been driven primarily by increases in the number of children in these age groups. The enrollment rate of prekindergarten age children (ages 3 and 4) rose between 1985 and 2007, which was reflected by an increase in prekindergarten enrollment.

The National Center for Education Statistics (NCES) forecasts record levels of total elementary and secondary enrollment through at least 2017, reflecting expected increases in the school-age population. For public schools, the projected fall 2008 enrollment is expected to be a new record, and new records are expected every year through 2017, the last year for which NCES enrollment projections have been developed (table 3). Public elementary school enrollment (prekindergarten through grade 8) is projected to increase by 10 percent between 2008 and 2017. Public secondary school enrollment (grades 9 through 12) is expected to increase 5 percent between 2008 and 2017. Overall, total public school enrollment is expected to increase 9 percent between 2008 and 2017.

Teachers

A projected 3.7 million full-time-equivalent (FTE) elementary and secondary school teachers were engaged in classroom instruction in fall 2008 (table 4). This number has risen 15 percent since 1998. The 2008 projected number of FTE teachers includes 3.2 million public school teachers and 0.5 million private school teachers.

The number of public school teachers has risen faster than the number of public school students over the past 10 years, resulting in declines in the pupil/teacher ratio (table 64). In the fall of 2008, there were a projected 15.3 public school pupils per teacher, compared with 16.4 public school pupils per teacher 10 years earlier.

The average salary for public school teachers in 2006–07 was $50,816, about 3 percent higher than in 1996–97, after adjustment for inflation (table 78). The salaries of public school teachers have generally maintained pace with inflation since 1990–91.

Student Performance

Most of the student performance data in the *Digest* are drawn from the National Assessment of Educational Progress (NAEP). The NAEP assessments have been conducted using three basic designs: the national main NAEP, state NAEP, and long-term trend NAEP. The national main NAEP and state

NAEP provide current information about student performance in a variety of subjects, while long-term trend NAEP provides information on performance since the early 1970s in reading and mathematics only. Results from long-term trend NAEP are included in the discussion in chapter 2 of the *Digest*, while the information in this Introduction includes only results from the national main and state NAEP.

The main NAEP reports current information for the nation and specific geographic regions of the country. The assessment program includes students drawn from both public and nonpublic schools and reports results for student achievement at grades 4, 8, and 12. The main NAEP assessments follow the frameworks developed by the National Assessment Governing Board and use the latest advances in assessment methodology. The state NAEP is identical in content to the national main NAEP, but the state NAEP reports information only for public school students. Chapter 2 presents more information on the NAEP designs and methodology, and additional details appear in Appendix A: Guide to Sources.

Reading

Reported on a scale of 0 to 500, national average reading scores of 4th- and 8th-graders were higher in 2007 than in 1992, by 4 and 3 points, respectively (table 123). These 2007 scores were also higher than the 2005 scores. The reading score of 12th-graders was 6 points lower in 2005 (the most recent assessment year for grade 12) than in 1992. In the most recent assessment, females at each grade level outscored their male counterparts. For example, 12th-grade females scored 13 points higher than males in 2005. Average scores were higher in 2007 than in 1992 for White, Black, Hispanic, and Asian/Pacific Islander 4th-graders (ranging from 6 to 16 points) and for White, Black, and Hispanic 8th-graders (ranging from 5 to 7 points), while scores were lower in 2005 than in 1992 for White, Black, and Hispanic 12th-graders (ranging from 5 to 7 points).

The 2007 main NAEP reading assessment of states found that the average reading proficiency of public school 4th- and 8th-graders varied across participating jurisdictions (the 50 states, the Department of Defense overseas and domestic schools, and the District of Columbia). For 4th-graders in public schools, the U.S. average score was 220, with average scores in participating jurisdictions ranging from 197 in the District of Columbia to 236 in Massachusetts (table 121). For 8th-graders in public schools, the U.S. average score was 261, with average scores in participating jurisdictions ranging from 241 in the District of Columbia to 273 in the Department of Defense schools, Massachusetts, and Vermont (table 122).

Mathematics

From 1990 to 2007, average NAEP mathematics scores increased 27 points for 4th-graders and 19 points for 8th-graders (table 136). (NAEP mathematics scores are reported on a scale of 0 to 500.) Increases in scores were seen for both males and females and for most racial/ethnic groups. Both male and female 4th- and 8th-graders scored higher in 2007 than in any of the previous assessments. In 2007, at each grade, males outscored females by 2 points; these score gaps were not measurably different from the gaps in either 2005 or 1990. At grade 4, average scores in 2007 for White, Black, Hispanic, and Asian/Pacific Islander students were higher than the scores in any of the previous assessments. Although the score for American Indian/Alaska Native 4th-graders increased over time, there was no measurable difference between their 2005 and 2007 scores. At grade 8, average scores in 2007 for White, Black, and Hispanic students were higher than in any of the previous assessments. The average score for 8th-grade Asian/Pacific Islander students was higher in 2007 than in 1990, but not measurably different from their 2005 score. No measurable differences were detected in the scores for American Indian/Alaska Native 8th-graders over the assessment years.

The 2007 main NAEP assessment of states found that the average mathematics proficiency of public school 4th- and 8th-graders varied across participating jurisdictions (the 50 states, the Department of Defense overseas and domestic schools, and the District of Columbia). For 4th-graders in public schools, the U.S. average score was 239, with average scores in participating jurisdictions ranging from 214 in the District of Columbia to 252 in Massachusetts (table 134). For 8th-graders in public schools, the U.S. average score was 280, with average scores in participating jurisdictions ranging from 248 in the District of Columbia to 298 in Massachusetts (table 135).

Science

NAEP has assessed the science abilities of students in grades 4, 8, and 12 in both public and private schools since 1996, using a separate scale of 0 to 300 for each grade. The national average 4th-grade science score increased from 147 in 1996 to 151 in 2005; there was no measurable change in the 8th-grade score; and the 12th-grade score decreased from 150 in 1996 to 147 in 2005 (table 138). Certain subgroups outperformed others in science in 2005. For example, males outperformed females at all three grades. Male 4th-graders had a higher average score in 2005 than in 1996, and both male and female 12th-graders had lower scores in 2005 than in 1996. White students scored higher, on average, than Black and Hispanic students at all three grades in 2005. At grade 4, average scores were higher for White, Black, Hispanic, and Asian/Pacific Islander students in 2005 than in 1996. At grade 8, the average score for Black students was higher in 2005 than in 1996, but the scores did not measurably change for other racial/ethnic groups. At grade 12, there were no measurable changes in average scores for any racial/ethnic group when comparing results from 2005 with those from 1996.

International Comparisons

On the 2003 Trends in International Mathematics and Science Study (TIMSS), the average mathematics score of U.S. 4th-graders exceeded the international average for the 25 participating educational systems (table 406). (Most participating educational systems represent countries; however, some represent subnational entities with separate educational systems.)

U.S. 4th-graders outscored students in 13 educational systems, but were outperformed by students in 11 educational systems. Also on the 2003 TIMSS, U.S. 8th-graders exceeded the international average score for the 45 educational systems participating at the 8th-grade level (table 407). U.S. 8th-graders outscored students in 25 educational systems, and were outperformed by students in 9 educational systems.

On the 2006 Program for International Student Assessment (PISA), the average score of U.S. 15-year-olds in mathematics literacy was 474, which was lower than the Organization for Economic Cooperation and Development (OECD) average of 498 (table 403). (Possible scores on PISA assessments range from 0 to 1,000.) The average mathematics literacy score in the United States was lower than the average score in 23 of the other 29 OECD countries for which comparable PISA results were reported, higher than the average score in 4 of the other OECD countries, and not measurably different from the average score in 2 of the OECD countries. In science literacy, the average score of 15-year-olds in the United States was lower than the average score in 16 of the other 29 OECD countries, higher than the average score in 5 of the other OECD countries, and not measurably different from the average score in 8 of the OECD countries.

High School Graduates and Dropouts

About 3,328,000 high school students are expected to graduate during the 2008–09 school year (table 104), including 3,011,000 public school graduates and 317,000 private school graduates. High school graduates include only recipients of diplomas, not recipients of equivalency credentials. The number of high school graduates projected for 2008–09 is lower than the record-high projection of 3,346,000 graduates for 2007–08, but exceeds the high point during the baby boom era in 1976–77, when 3,152,000 students earned diplomas. In 2005–06, an estimated 73.4 percent of public high school students graduated on time—that is, received a diploma 4 years after beginning their freshman year (table 106).

The number of General Educational Development (GED) credentials issued rose from 330,000 in 1977 to 487,000 in 2000 (table 108). A record number of 648,000 GED credentials were issued in 2001. In that year, candidates who had already taken any of the five tests in the GED test battery had to complete the entire battery before the end of the year or else take all five tests over again. The reason is that a new GED test series was introduced in 2002. In the same year, data collection procedures changed, with data from the states on the number of credentials issued being replaced by test data from individual test-takers. In 2006, 464,000 passed the GED tests, up from 330,000 in 2002, the first year of the new test series.[1]

The percentage of dropouts among 16- to 24-year-olds has shown some decreases over the past 20 years. This percent-

age, known as the status dropout rate, includes all people in the 16- to 24-year-old age group who are not enrolled in school and who have not completed a high school program, regardless of when they left school. (People who left school but went on to receive a GED credential are not treated as dropouts.) Between 1987 and 2007, the status dropout rate declined from 12.6 percent to 8.7 percent (table 109). Although the status dropout rate declined for both Blacks and Hispanics during this period, their rates (8.4 and 21.4 percent, respectively) remained higher than the rate for Whites (5.3 percent) in 2007. This measure is based on the civilian noninstitutionalized population, which excludes people in prisons, people in the military, and other people not living in households.

Educational Technology

The number of computers in public schools has increased. In 2005, the average public school contained 154 instructional computers, compared with 90 in 1998 (table 427). One important technological advance that has come to classrooms following the introduction of computers has been connections to the Internet. The percentage of instructional rooms with access to the Internet increased from 51 percent in 1998 to 94 percent in 2005 (figure 29). Nearly all schools had access to the Internet in 2005 (table 427).

Postsecondary Education

College Enrollment

College enrollment was a projected 18.2 million in fall 2008, higher than in any previous year except 2007 (table 3). College enrollment is expected to continue setting new records throughout the fall 2009 through fall 2017 period. Between fall 2007 and fall 2017, enrollment is expected to increase by 10 percent. Despite decreases in the traditional college-age population during the late 1980s and early 1990s, total enrollment increased during this period (tables 7, 15, 188, and 204). The traditional college-age population (18 to 24 years old) rose 16 percent between 1997 and 2007, which was reflected by an increase of 26 percent in college enrollment. Between 1997 and 2007, the number of full-time students increased by 34 percent compared to a 15 percent increase in part-time students (table 188). During the same time period, the number of males enrolled increased 22 percent, while the number of females enrolled increased 29 percent.

Faculty

In fall 2007, degree-granting institutions—defined as postsecondary institutions that grant an associate's or higher degree and are eligible for Title IV federal financial aid programs—employed 1.4 million faculty members, including 0.7 million full-time and 0.7 million part-time faculty (table 245). In addition, degree-granting institutions employed 0.3 million graduate assistants.

---

[1] Information on changes in GED test series and reporting is based on the 2003 edition of *Who Passed the GED Tests?*, by the GED Testing Service of the American Council on Education, as well as communication with staff of the GED Testing Service.

Postsecondary Degrees

During the 2008–09 academic year, postsecondary degrees are projected to number 731,000 associate's degrees; 1,603,000 bachelor's degrees; 649,000 master's degrees; 93,300 first-professional degrees; and 61,700 doctor's degrees (table 268). Between 1996–97 and 2006–07, the number of degrees conferred rose at all levels. The number of associate's degrees was 27 percent higher in 2006–07 than in 1996–97, the number of bachelor's degrees was 30 percent higher, the number of master's degrees was 44 percent higher, the number of first-professional degrees was 14 percent higher, and the number of doctor's degrees was 32 percent higher.

Between 1996–97 and 2006–07, the number of bachelor's degrees awarded to males increased 25 percent, while the number awarded to females increased 34 percent. As a result, females earned 57 percent of all bachelor's degrees in 2006–07, compared with 56 percent in 1996–97. Between 1996–97 and 2006–07, the number of White students earning bachelor's degrees increased 22 percent, compared with larger increases of 55 percent for Black students, 84 percent for Hispanic students, 53 percent for Asian/Pacific Islander students, and 54 percent for American Indian/Alaska Native students (table 284). In 2006–07, White students earned 72 percent of all bachelor's degrees awarded (vs. 77 percent in 1996–97), Black students earned 10 percent (vs. 8 percent in 1996–97), Hispanic students earned 8 percent (vs. 5 percent in 1996–97), and Asian/Pacific Islander students earned 7 percent (vs. 6 percent in 1996–97). American Indian/Alaska Native students earned about 1 percent of the degrees in both years.

Undergraduate Prices

For the 2007–08 academic year, annual prices for undergraduate tuition, room, and board were estimated to be $11,578 at public institutions and $29,915 at private institutions (table 331). Between 1997–98 and 2007–08, prices for undergraduate tuition, room, and board at public institutions rose 30 percent, and prices at private institutions rose 23 percent, after adjustment for inflation.

Educational Attainment

The U.S. Census Bureau collects annual statistics on the educational attainment of the population. Between 1998 and 2008, the percentage of the adult population 25 years of age and over who had completed high school rose from 83 percent to 87 percent, and the percentage of adults with a bachelor's degree increased from 24 percent to 29 percent (table 8). High school completers include those people who graduated from high school with a diploma, as well as those who completed high school through equivalency programs. The percentage of young adults (25- to 29-year-olds) who had completed high school in 2008 was about the same as it was in 1998 (88 percent in both years). The percentage of young adults who had completed a bachelor's degree increased from 27 percent in 1998 to 31 percent in 2008.

Education Expenditures

Expenditures for public and private education, from pre-kindergarten through graduate school (excluding postsecondary schools not awarding associate's or higher degrees), are estimated at $1,017 billion for 2007–08 (table 25). Expenditures of elementary and secondary schools are expected to total $631 billion, while those of degree-granting postsecondary institutions are expected to total $386 billion. Total expenditures for education are expected to amount to 7.4 percent of the gross domestic product in 2007–08, about 0.5 percentage points higher than in 1997–98.

Interpreting Statistics

Readers should be aware of the limitations of statistics. These limitations vary with the exact nature of a particular survey. For example, estimates based on a sample of institutions will differ somewhat from the figures that would have been obtained if a complete census had been taken using the same survey procedures. Standard errors are available for sample survey data appearing in this report. In most cases, standard errors for all items appear in the printed table. In some cases, only standard errors for key items appear in the printed table. Standard errors that do not appear in the tables are available from NCES upon request. Although some of the surveys conducted by NCES are census or universe surveys (which attempt to collect information from all potential respondents), all surveys are subject to design, reporting, and processing errors and errors due to nonresponse. Differences in sampling, data collection procedures, coverage of target population, timing, phrasing of questions, scope of nonresponse, interviewer training, data processing, coding, and so forth mean that the results from the different sources may not be strictly comparable. More information on survey methodologies can be found in Appendix A: Guide to Sources.

Estimates presented in the text and figures are rounded from original estimates, not from a series of roundings. Percentages in the text are rounded to whole numbers, while ratios and percentage distributions are normally presented to one decimal place, where applicable.

Unless otherwise noted, all data in this report are for the 50 states and the District of Columbia. Unless otherwise noted, all financial data are in current dollars, meaning not adjusted for changes in the purchasing power of the dollar due to inflation. Price indexes for inflation adjustments can be found in table 31.

Common data elements are collected in different ways in different surveys. Since the *Digest* relies on a number of data sources, there are discrepancies in definitions and data across tables in the volume. For example, several different surveys collect data on public school enrollment, and while similar, the estimates are not identical. The definitions of racial/ethnic groups also differ across surveys, particularly with respect to whether Hispanic origin is considered an ethnic group regardless of race, or counted separately as a racial/ethnic group. Individual tables note the definitions used in the given studies.

All statements cited in the text about differences between two or more groups or changes over time were tested for statistical significance and are statistically significant at the .05 level. Various test procedures were used, depending on the nature of the statement tested. The most commonly used test procedures were t tests, equivalence tests, and linear trend tests. Equivalence tests were used to determine whether two statistics are substantively equivalent or substantively different. This was accomplished by using a hypothesis test to determine whether the confidence interval of the difference between sample estimates is substantively significant (i.e., greater or less than a preset substantively important difference). In most cases involving percentages, a difference of 3.0 was used to determine substantive equivalence or difference. In some comparisons involving only very small percentages, a lower difference was used. In cases involving only relatively large values, a larger difference was used, such as $1,000 in the case of annual salaries. Linear trend tests were conducted by evaluating the significance of the slope of a simple regression of the data over time, and a t test comparing the end points.

GUIDE TO TABULAR PRESENTATION

This section is intended to assist the reader in following the basic structure of the *Digest* tables and to provide a legend for some of the common symbols and indexes used throughout the book. Unless otherwise noted, all data are for the 50 states and the District of Columbia. Changes in survey instruments sometimes mean that data for specific categories are not available in a consistent manner over the entire reporting period. Because of these survey limitations, data for these specific categories may be noted as included with other categories where applicable.

Table Components

Title Describes the table content concisely. (Tables may not include data for all years implied in table titles. When this is the case, the title will include the term "Selected years.")

Unit indicator Informs the reader of the measurement unit in the table—"In thousands," "In millions of dollars," etc. Noted below the title unless several units are used, in which case the unit indicators are generally given in the spanner or individual column heads.

Spanner Describes a group of two or more columns.

Column head Describes a specific column.

Stub Describes a row or a group of rows. Each stub row is followed by a number of dots (leaders).

Field The area of the table which contains the data elements.

Example of Table Structure

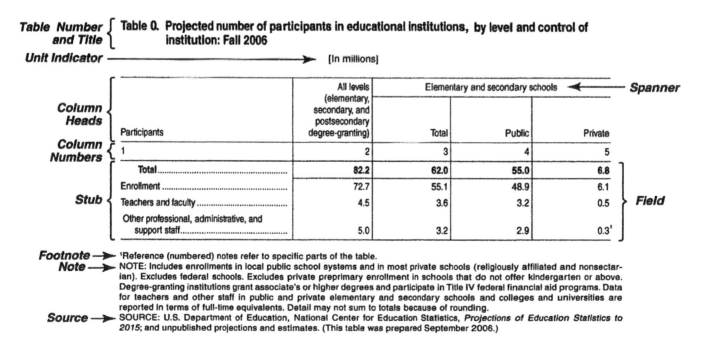

Table Number and Title: Table 0. Projected number of participants in educational institutions, by level and control of institution: Fall 2006

Unit Indicator: [In millions]

Participants	All levels (elementary, secondary, and postsecondary degree-granting)	Elementary and secondary schools		
		Total	Public	Private
1	2	3	4	5
Total	82.2	62.0	55.0	6.8
Enrollment	72.7	55.1	48.9	6.1
Teachers and faculty	4.5	3.6	3.2	0.5
Other professional, administrative, and support staff	5.0	3.2	2.9	0.3[1]

Footnote → [1]Reference (numbered) notes refer to specific parts of the table.
Note → NOTE: Includes enrollments in local public school systems and in most private schools (religiously affiliated and nonsectarian). Excludes federal schools. Excludes private preprimary enrollment in schools that do not offer kindergarten or above. Degree-granting institutions grant associate's or higher degrees and participate in Title IV federal financial aid programs. Data for teachers and other staff in public and private elementary and secondary schools and colleges and universities are reported in terms of full-time equivalents. Detail may not sum to totals because of rounding.
Source → SOURCE: U.S. Department of Education, National Center for Education Statistics, *Projections of Education Statistics to 2015*; and unpublished projections and estimates. (This table was prepared September 2006.)

Special notes   Symbols used to indicate why data do not appear in designated cell.

— Not available.

† Not applicable.

Rounds to zero.

! Interpret data with caution.

‡ Reporting standards not met.

Footnote   Describes a unique circumstance relating to a specific item within the table. Following are two typical examples:

Estimated   Based on available information from a subset of the population of interest.

Projected   Calculated from a forecasting model based on historical information.

Note   Furnishes general information that relates to the entire table.

Source   The document or reference from which the data are drawn. This note may also include the organizational unit responsible for preparing the data.

Descriptive Terms

Measures of central tendency   A number that is used to represent the "typical value" of a group of numbers. It is regarded as a measure of "location" or "central tendency" of a group of numbers.

Arithmetic mean (average)   is the most commonly used average. It is derived by summing the individual item values of a particular group and dividing that sum by the number of items. This value is often referred to simply as the "mean" or "average."

Median   is the measure of central tendency that occupies the middle position in a rank order of values. It generally has the same number of items above it as below it. If there is an even number of items in the group, the median is the average of the middle two items.

Average per capita,   or per person, figure represents an average computed for every person in a specified group, or population. It is derived by dividing the total for an item (such as income or expenditures) by the number of persons in the specified population.

Index number   A value that provides a means of measuring, summarizing, and communicating the nature of changes that occur from time to time or from place to place. An index is used to express changes in prices over periods of time, but may also be used to express differences between related subjects at a single point in time.

The *Digest* most often uses the Consumer Price Index to compare purchasing power over time.

To compute a price index, a base year or period is selected. The base-year price is then designated as the base or reference price to which the prices for other years or periods are related.

A method of expressing the price relationship is:

Index number =

$$\frac{\text{Price of a set of one or more items for related year}}{\text{Price of the same set of items for base year}} \times 100$$

When 100 is subtracted from the index number, the result equals the percent change in price from the base year.

Current and constant dollars   are used in a number of tables to express finance data. Unless otherwise noted, all figures are in current dollars, not adjusted for inflation. Constant dollars provide a measure of the impact of inflation on the current dollars.

Current dollar   figures reflect actual prices or costs prevailing during the specified year(s).

Constant dollar   figures attempt to remove the effects of price changes (inflation) from statistical series reported in dollar terms.

The constant dollar value for an item is derived by dividing the base-year price index (for example, the Consumer Price Index for 1999) by the price index for the year of data to be adjusted and multiplying by the price of item to be adjusted. The result is an adjusted dollar value as it would presumably exist if prices were the same as the base year—in other words, as if the dollar had constant purchasing power. Any changes in the constant dollar amounts would reflect only changes in the real values.

In the 2008 edition of the *Digest*, the following 26 tables include finance data that are adjusted to school year 2006–07 dollars: tables 26, 32, 74, 78, 79, 86, 171, 174, 175, 181, 184, 185, 256, 257, 263, 331, 334, 350, 353, 355, 360, 361, 362, 364, 366, and 424. Data adjusted to calendar year 2007 dollars appear in tables 20, 384, 394, and 418. Table 373 includes adjustments to fiscal year (FY) 2008 dollars.

CHAPTER 1
All Levels of Education

This chapter provides a broad overview of education in the United States. It brings together material from preprimary, elementary, secondary, and postsecondary education, as well as from the general population, to present a composite picture of the American educational system. Tables feature data on the total number of people enrolled in school, the number of teachers, the number of schools, and total expenditures for education at all levels. This chapter also includes statistics on education-related topics such as educational attainment, family characteristics, population, and opinions about schools. Economic indicators and price indexes have been added to facilitate analyses.

The U.S. system of education can be described as having three levels of formal education (elementary, secondary, and postsecondary) (figure 1). Students ordinarily spend from 6 to 8 years in the elementary grades, which may be preceded by 1 to 3 years in nursery school and kindergarten. The elementary school program is followed by a 4- to 6-year program in secondary school. Students normally complete the entire program through grade 12 by age 18.

High school graduates who decide to continue their education may enter a technical or vocational institution, a 2-year community or junior college, or a 4-year college or university. A 2-year college normally offers the first 2 years of a standard 4-year college curriculum and a selection of terminal vocational programs. Academic courses completed at a 2-year college are usually transferable for credit at a 4-year college or university. A technical or vocational institution offers postsecondary technical training leading to a specific career.

An associate's degree requires at least 2 years of college-level coursework, and a bachelor's degree normally requires 4 years of college-level coursework. At least 1 year of coursework beyond the bachelor's is necessary for a master's degree, while a doctor's degree usually requires a minimum of 3 or 4 years beyond the bachelor's.

Professional schools differ widely in admission requirements and program length. Medical students, for example, generally complete a bachelor's program of premedical studies at a college or university before they can enter the 4-year program at a medical school. Law programs normally require 3 years of coursework beyond the bachelor's degree level.

Many of the statistics in this chapter are derived from the statistical activities of the National Center for Education Statistics (NCES). In addition, substantial contributions have been drawn from the work of other groups, both governmental and nongovernmental, as shown in the source notes of the tables. Information on survey methodologies is contained in Appendix A: Guide to Sources and in the publications cited in the table source notes.

Enrollment and Attainment

Enrollment in elementary and secondary schools grew rapidly during the 1950s and 1960s, reaching a peak in 1971 (table 3 and figure 2). This enrollment rise was caused by what is known as the "baby boom," a dramatic increase in births following World War II. From 1971 to 1984, total elementary and secondary school enrollment decreased every year, reflecting the decline in the school-age population over that period. After these years of decline, enrollment in elementary and secondary schools started increasing in fall 1985, began hitting new record levels in the mid-1990s, and has continued to reach a new record level in each subsequent year.

School enrollment rates among 5- and 6-year-olds, 7- to 13-year-olds, and 14- to 17-year-olds remained relatively steady between 1985 and 2007 (table 7). Since the enrollment rates of elementary and secondary school-age children changed by less than 2 percentage points between 1985 and 2007, increases in public and private elementary and secondary school enrollment have been driven primarily by increases in the number of children in these age groups. Increases in the enrollment rate of prekindergarten age children (ages 3 and 4) between 1985 and 2007 have also contributed to overall enrollment increases.

Public school enrollment in prekindergarten through grade 8 rose from 29.9 million in fall 1990 to 34.2 million in 2003 (table 3). After a decrease of less than 1 percent between fall 2003 and fall 2004, elementary enrollment increased to a projected total of 34.9 million for fall 2008. Public elementary enrollment is projected to continue this pattern of annual increases through 2017 (the last year for which NCES has projected school enrollment). Public school enrollment in the upper grades rose from 11.3 million in 1990 to 15.1 million in 2006, with a projected enrollment of 14.9 million for 2008. Public secondary enrollment is projected to show a decrease of 3 percent between 2006 and 2011, and then increase again through 2017. Public secondary school enrollment in 2017 is expected to be about 5 percent higher than in 2008. Total public elementary and secondary enrollment is projected to set new records every year from 2008 to 2017.

College enrollment reached 14.5 million in fall 1992 and decreased to 14.3 million in fall 1995 (table 3). Total college enrollment increased 28 percent between 1995 and 2007, and a further increase of 10 percent is expected between fall 2007 and fall 2017. The percentage of 18- and 19-year-olds enrolled in school rose from 61 to 67 percent between 1996 and 2006. About 36 percent of 20- to 24-year-olds were enrolled in school in 2007.

Enrollment in Private Institutions

The percentage of students in private elementary and secondary schools declined from 11.7 percent in 1995 to 11.0 percent in 2005 (table 3). The percentage of college students who attended private colleges and universities rose from 22.2 to 25.5 percent between 1995 and 2005, and then continued to increase to 26.1 percent in 2007. In 2008, a projected 6.1 million students were enrolled in private schools at the elementary and secondary levels and 4.6 million students were in private (not-for-profit and for-profit) degree-granting institutions.

Educational Attainment of Adults

The percentages of adults 25 years old and over completing high school and higher education have been rising. In 2008, 87 percent of the population 25 years old and over had completed at least high school and 29 percent had completed a bachelor's or higher degree (table 8 and figure 3). These percentages are higher than in 1998, when 83 percent had completed at least high school and 24 percent had completed a bachelor's or higher degree. In 2008, about 8 percent of people 25 years old or over held a master's degree as their highest degree, 2 percent held a professional degree (e.g., medicine or law), and 1 percent held a doctor's degree (table 9 and figure 5).

Teachers and Faculty

An estimated 3.7 million elementary and secondary school full-time-equivalent (FTE) teachers were engaged in classroom instruction in the fall of 2008 (table 4). This number has risen about 15 percent since 1998. The number of FTE public school teachers in 2008 was about 3.2 million, and the number of FTE private school teachers was about 0.5 million. FTE faculty at postsecondary degree-granting institutions totaled an estimated 0.9 million in 2008, including 0.6 million at public institutions and 0.3 million at private institutions (table 1).

Expenditures

Expenditures of educational institutions rose to an estimated $1,017 billion for the 2007–08 school year (table 26). Elementary and secondary schools spent about 62 percent of this total, and colleges and universities accounted for the remaining 38 percent. After adjustment for inflation, total expenditures of all educational institutions rose by an estimated 36 percent between 1997–98 and 2007–08. Expenditures of elementary and secondary schools rose by an estimated 33 percent during this period, while total expenditures of colleges and universities rose by 41 percent. In 2007–08, expenditures of educational institutions were an estimated 7.4 percent of the gross domestic product (table 25).

Figure 1. The structure of education in the United States

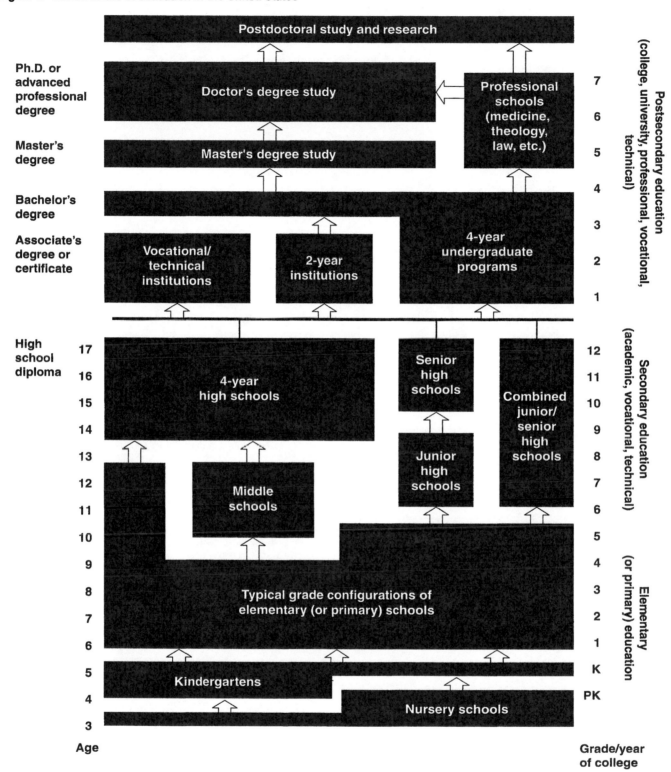

NOTE: Figure is not intended to show relative number of institutions nor relative size of enrollment for the different levels of education. Figure reflects typical patterns of progression rather than all possible variations. Adult education programs, while not separately delineated above, may provide instruction at the adult basic, adult secondary, or postsecondary education levels.
SOURCE: U.S. Department of Education, National Center for Education Statistics, Annual Reports Program.

Figure 2. Enrollment, total expenditures in constant dollars, and expenditures as a percentage of the gross domestic product (GDP), by level of education: Selected years, 1965–66 through 2007–08

Enrollment, in millions

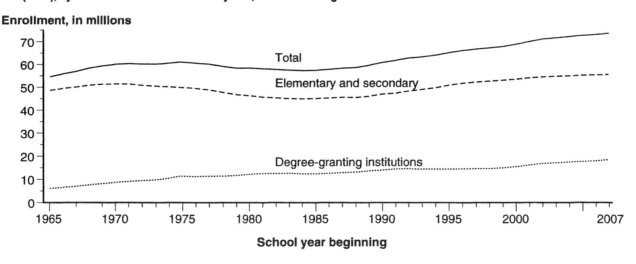

School year beginning

Expenditures, in billions of constant 2006–07 dollars

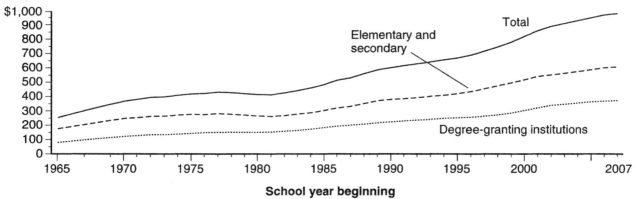

School year beginning

Percent of GDP

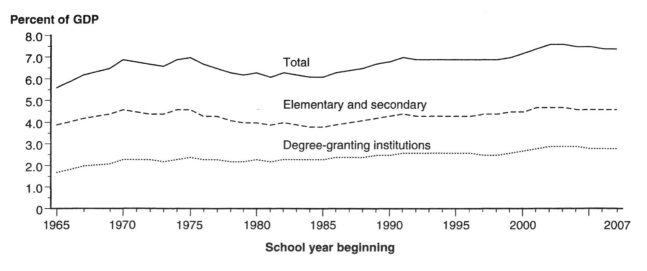

School year beginning

NOTE: Expenditure data for school years 2006 and 2007 (2006–07 and 2007–08) are estimated. Enrollment data for school year 2007–08 for elementary and secondary are projected.
SOURCE: U.S. Department of Education, National Center for Education Statistics, *Statistics of State School Systems*, 1965–66 through 1969–70; *Statistics of Public Elementary and Secondary School Systems*, 1970 through 1980; *Revenues and Expenditures for Public Elementary and Secondary Education*, 1970–71 through 1986–87; Common Core of Data (CCD), "State Nonfiscal Survey of Public Elementary and Secondary Education," 1985–86 through 2005–06; "National Public Education Financial Survey," 1987–88 through 2005–06; *Statistics of Nonpublic Elementary and Secondary Schools*, 1970–71 through 1979–80; Private School Universe Survey (PSS), 1989–90 through 2005–06; Higher Education General Information Survey (HEGIS), *Fall Enrollment in Institutions of Higher Education*, 1965–66 through 1985–86; *Financial Statistics of Institutions of Higher Education*, 1965–66 through 1985–86; 1986–87 through 2006–07 Integrated Postsecondary Education Data System (IPEDS), "Finance Survey," (IPEDS-FY87–89), and Spring 2001 through Spring 2007; and U.S. Department of Commerce, Bureau of Economic Analysis, retrieved August 12, 2008, from http://www.bea.gov/national/index.htm.

Figure 3.   Percentage of persons 25 years old and over, by highest level of educational attainment: Selected years, 1940 through 2008

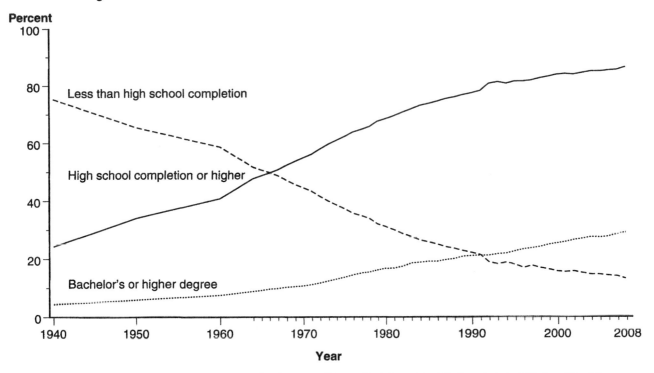

SOURCE: U.S. Department of Commerce, Census Bureau, *U.S. Census of Population, 1960, Volume 1, Part 1*; Current Population Reports, Series P-20; Current Population Survey (CPS), March 1961 through March 2008; and *1960 Census Monograph, Education of the American Population*, by John K. Folger and Charles B. Nam.

Figure 4.   Percentage of persons 25 through 29 years old, by highest level of educational attainment: Selected years, 1940 through 2008

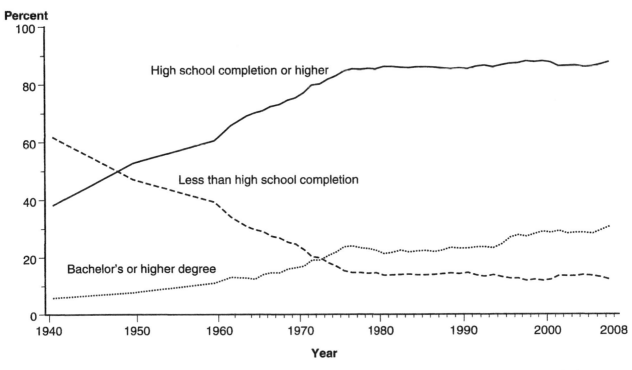

SOURCE: U.S. Department of Commerce, Census Bureau, *U.S. Census of Population, 1960, Volume 1, Part 1*; Current Population Reports, Series P-20; Current Population Survey (CPS), March 1961 through March 2008; and *1960 Census Monograph, Education of the American Population*, by John K. Folger and Charles B. Nam.

Figure 5.   Highest level of education attained by persons 25 years old and over: March 2008

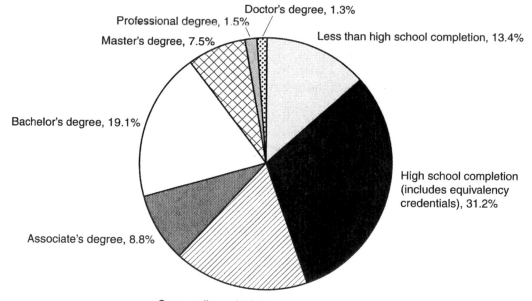

NOTE: Detail may not sum to totals because of rounding.
SOURCE: U.S. Department of Commerce, Census Bureau, Current Population Survey (CPS), March 2008.

Table 1. Projected number of participants in educational institutions, by level and control of institution: Fall 2008

[In millions]

Participants	All levels (elementary, secondary, and postsecondary degree-granting)	Elementary and secondary schools			Postsecondary degree-granting institutions		
		Total	Public	Private	Total	Public	Private
1	2	3	4	5	6	7	8
Total...........................	83.9	63.1	56.1	6.7	21.0	15.4	5.6
Enrollment	74.1	55.9	49.8	6.1	18.2	13.6	4.6
Teachers and faculty.......................	4.6	3.7	3.2	0.5	0.9	0.6	0.3
Other professional, administrative, and support staff.......................	5.2	3.4	3.0	0.3	1.8	1.2	0.6

NOTE: Includes enrollments in local public school systems and in most private schools (religiously affiliated and nonsectarian). Excludes federal schools. Excludes private preprimary enrollment in schools that do not offer kindergarten or above. Degree-granting institutions grant associate's or higher degrees and participate in Title IV federal financial aid programs. Data for teachers and other staff in public and private elementary and secondary schools and colleges and universities are reported in terms of full-time equivalents. Detail may not sum to totals because of rounding.

SOURCE: U.S. Department of Education, National Center for Education Statistics, *Projections of Education Statistics to 2017;* and unpublished projections and estimates. (This table was prepared October 2008.)

Table 2. Enrollment in educational institutions, by level and control of institution: Selected years, fall 1980 through fall 2008

[In thousands]

Level and control of institution	Fall 1980	Fall 1985	Fall 1990	Fall 1995	Fall 1998	Fall 1999	Fall 2000	Fall 2001	Fall 2002	Fall 2003	Fall 2004	Fall 2005	Fall 2006[1]	Projected fall 2007	Projected fall 2008
1	2	3	4	5	6	7	8	9	10	11	12	13	14	15	16
All levels...................	58,305	57,226	60,683	65,020	67,033	67,667	68,685	69,920	71,015	71,551	72,154	72,674	73,153	73,958	74,079
Public..............................	50,335	48,901	52,061	55,933	57,676	58,167	58,956	59,905	60,935	61,399	61,776	62,135	62,479	63,135	63,387
Private	7,971	8,325	8,622	9,087	9,357	9,500	9,729	10,014	10,080	10,152	10,379	10,539	10,674	10,823	10,692
Elementary and secondary schools[2]............	46,208	44,979	46,864	50,759	52,526	52,875	53,373	53,992	54,403	54,639	54,882	55,187	55,394	55,710	55,879
Public..............................	40,877	39,422	41,217	44,840	46,539	46,857	47,204	47,672	48,183	48,540	48,795	49,113	49,299	49,644	49,825
Private	5,331	5,557	5,648	5,918	5,988[3]	6,018	6,169[3]	6,320	6,220[3]	6,099	6,087[3]	6,073	6,095	6,066	6,054
Prekindergarten to grade 8....	31,639	31,229	34,392	37,096	38,121	38,277	38,594	38,961	39,031	38,990	38,934	38,929	38,932	39,271	39,585
Public..............................	27,647	27,034	29,878	32,341	33,346	33,488	33,688	33,938	34,116	34,202	34,179	34,205	34,221	34,589	34,903
Private.............................	3,992	4,195	4,514	4,756	4,776[3]	4,789	4,906[3]	5,023	4,915[3]	4,788	4,756[3]	4,723	4,711	4,681	4,681
Grades 9 to 12....................	14,570	13,750	12,472	13,662	14,405	14,598	14,779	15,031	15,373	15,649	15,948	16,258	16,462	16,439	16,294
Public..............................	13,231	12,388	11,338	12,500	13,193	13,369	13,515	13,734	14,067	14,338	14,617	14,908	15,078	15,055	14,922
Private.............................	1,339	1,362	1,134	1,163	1,212[3]	1,229	1,264[3]	1,296	1,306[3]	1,311	1,331[3]	1,350	1,384	1,385	1,372
Postsecondary degree-granting institutions..........	12,097	12,247	13,819	14,262	14,507	14,791	15,312	15,928	16,612	16,911	17,272	17,487	17,759	18,248[4]	18,200
Public..............................	9,457	9,479	10,845	11,092	11,138	11,309	11,753	12,233	12,752	12,859	12,980	13,022	13,180	13,491[4]	13,562
Undergraduate...............	8,442	8,477	9,710	9,904	9,950	10,110	10,539	10,986	11,433	11,523	11,651	11,698	11,847	12,138[4]	12,201
First-professional	114	112	112	115	121	123	124	128	132	134	136	138	140	143[4]	144
Graduate......................	901	890	1,023	1,074	1,067	1,077	1,089	1,119	1,187	1,201	1,194	1,186	1,193	1,211[4]	1,216
Private	2,640	2,768	2,974	3,169	3,369	3,482	3,560	3,695	3,860	4,053	4,292	4,466	4,579	4,757[4]	4,638
Undergraduate...............	2,033	2,120	2,250	2,328	2,487	2,571	2,616	2,730	2,824	2,957	3,130	3,266	3,337	3,466[4]	3,369
First-professional	163	162	162	183	182	180	183	181	187	195	199	199	204	208[4]	210
Graduate......................	443	486	563	659	701	730	761	784	849	901	963	1,001	1,038	1,083[4]	1,059

[1]Private elementary and secondary education data are projected.
[2]Includes enrollments in local public school systems and in most private schools (religiously affiliated and nonsectarian). Excludes homeschooled children who were not also enrolled in public and private schools. Based on the National Household Education Survey, the homeschooled children numbered approximately 1.5 million in 2007. Private elementary enrollment includes preprimary students in schools offering kindergarten or higher grades.
[3]Estimated.
[4]Data are actual.
NOTE: Degree-granting enrollment projections are based on the middle alternative projections published by the National Center for Education Statistics. Data through 1995 are for institutions of higher education, while later data are for degree-granting institutions. Degree-granting institutions grant associate's or higher degrees and participate in Title IV federal financial aid programs. The degree-granting classification is very similar to the earlier higher education classification, but it includes more 2-year colleges and excludes a few higher education institutions that did not grant degrees. (See Guide to Sources for details.) Detail may not sum to totals because of rounding. Some data have been revised from previously published figures. Private school enrollment data for fall 1999 are based on improved methodology for apportioning the grade-unclassified students.
SOURCE: U.S. Department of Education, National Center for Education Statistics, *Statistics of Public Elementary and Secondary School Systems, 1980;* Common Core of Data (CCD), "State Nonfiscal Survey of Public Elementary and Secondary Education," 1985–86 through 2006–07; Parent and Family Involvement in Education Survey of the National Household Education Surveys Program (PFI-NHES:2007); Private School Universe Survey (PSS), 1995–96 through 2005–06; *Projections of Education Statistics to 2017;* Higher Education General Information Survey (HEGIS), "Fall Enrollment in Institutions of Higher Education" surveys, 1980 and 1985; and 1990 through 2007 Integrated Postsecondary Education Data System (IPEDS), "Fall Enrollment Survey" (IPEDS-EF:90–99), and Spring 2001 through Spring 2008. (This table was prepared October 2008.)

Table 3. Enrollment in educational institutions, by level and control of institution: Selected years, 1869–70 through fall 2017

[In thousands]

Year	Total enrollment, all levels	Elementary and secondary, total	Public elementary and secondary schools			Private elementary and secondary schools[1]			Postsecondary degree-granting institutions[2]		
			Total	Prekindergarten through grade 8	Grades 9 through 12	Total	Prekindergarten through grade 8	Grades 9 through 12	Total	Public	Private
1	2	3	4	5	6	7	8	9	10	11	12
1869–70	—	—	6,872	6,792	80	—	—	—	52	—	—
1879–80	—	—	9,868	9,757	110	—	—	—	116	—	—
1889–90	14,491	14,334	12,723	12,520	203	1,611	1,516	95	157	—	—
1899–1900	17,092	16,855	15,503	14,984	519	1,352	1,241	111	238	—	—
1909–10	19,728	19,372	17,814	16,899	915	1,558	1,441	117	355	—	—
1919–20	23,876	23,278	21,578	19,378	2,200	1,699	1,486	214	598	—	—
1929–30	29,430	28,329	25,678	21,279	4,399	2,651	2,310	341	1,101	—	—
1939–40	29,539	28,045	25,434	18,832	6,601	2,611	2,153	458	1,494	797	698
1949–50	31,151	28,492	25,111	19,387	5,725	3,380	2,708	672	2,659	1,355	1,304
Fall 1959	44,497	40,857	35,182	26,911	8,271	5,675	4,640	1,035	3,640	2,181	1,459
Fall 1969	59,055	51,050	45,550	32,513	13,037	5,500 [3]	4,200 [3]	1,300 [3]	8,005	5,897	2,108
Fall 1970	59,838	51,257	45,894	32,558	13,336	5,363	4,052	1,311	8,581	6,428	2,153
Fall 1971	60,220	51,271	46,071	32,318	13,753	5,200 [3]	3,900 [3]	1,300 [3]	8,949	6,804	2,144
Fall 1972	59,941	50,726	45,726	31,879	13,848	5,000 [3]	3,700 [3]	1,300 [3]	9,215	7,071	2,144
Fall 1973	60,047	50,445	45,445	31,401	14,044	5,000 [3]	3,700 [3]	1,300 [3]	9,602	7,420	2,183
Fall 1974	60,297	50,073	45,073	30,971	14,103	5,000 [3]	3,700 [3]	1,300 [3]	10,224	7,989	2,235
Fall 1975	61,004	49,819	44,819	30,515	14,304	5,000 [3]	3,700 [3]	1,300 [3]	11,185	8,835	2,350
Fall 1976	60,490	49,478	44,311	29,997	14,314	5,167	3,825	1,342	11,012	8,653	2,359
Fall 1977	60,003	48,717	43,577	29,375	14,203	5,140	3,797	1,343	11,286	8,847	2,439
Fall 1978	58,897	47,637	42,551	28,463	14,088	5,086	3,732	1,353	11,260	8,786	2,474
Fall 1979	58,221	46,651	41,651	28,034	13,616	5,000 [3]	3,700 [3]	1,300 [3]	11,570	9,037	2,533
Fall 1980	58,305	46,208	40,877	27,647	13,231	5,331	3,992	1,339	12,097	9,457	2,640
Fall 1981	57,916	45,544	40,044	27,280	12,764	5,500 [3]	4,100 [3]	1,400 [3]	12,372	9,647	2,725
Fall 1982	57,591	45,166	39,566	27,161	12,405	5,600 [3]	4,200 [3]	1,400 [3]	12,426	9,696	2,730
Fall 1983	57,432	44,967	39,252	26,981	12,271	5,715	4,315	1,400	12,465	9,683	2,782
Fall 1984	57,150	44,908	39,208	26,905	12,304	5,700 [3]	4,300 [3]	1,400 [3]	12,242	9,477	2,765
Fall 1985	57,226	44,979	39,422	27,034	12,388	5,557	4,195	1,362	12,247	9,479	2,768
Fall 1986	57,709	45,205	39,753	27,420	12,333	5,452 [3]	4,116 [3]	1,336 [3]	12,504	9,714	2,790
Fall 1987	58,253	45,488	40,008	27,933	12,076	5,479	4,232	1,247	12,767	9,973	2,793
Fall 1988	58,485	45,430	40,189	28,501	11,687	5,242 [3]	4,036 [3]	1,206 [3]	13,055	10,161	2,894
Fall 1989	59,680	46,141	40,543	29,152	11,390	5,599	4,470	1,128	13,539	10,578	2,961
Fall 1990	60,683	46,864	41,217	29,878	11,338	5,648 [3]	4,514 [3]	1,134 [3]	13,819	10,845	2,974
Fall 1991	62,087	47,728	42,047	30,506	11,541	5,681	4,552	1,129	14,359	11,310	3,049
Fall 1992	62,987	48,500	42,823	31,088	11,735	5,677 [3]	4,560 [3]	1,117 [3]	14,487	11,385	3,103
Fall 1993	63,438	49,133	43,465	31,504	11,961	5,668	4,564	1,104	14,305	11,189	3,116
Fall 1994	64,177	49,898	44,111	31,898	12,213	5,787 [3]	4,656 [3]	1,131 [3]	14,279	11,134	3,145
Fall 1995	65,020	50,759	44,840	32,341	12,500	5,918	4,756	1,163	14,262	11,092	3,169
Fall 1996	65,911	51,544	45,611	32,764	12,847	5,933 [3]	4,755 [3]	1,178 [3]	14,368	11,120	3,247
Fall 1997	66,574	52,071	46,127	33,073	13,054	5,944	4,759	1,185	14,502	11,196	3,306
Fall 1998	67,033	52,526	46,539	33,346	13,193	5,988 [3]	4,776 [3]	1,212 [3]	14,507	11,138	3,369
Fall 1999	67,667	52,875	46,857	33,488	13,369	6,018	4,789	1,229	14,791	11,309	3,482
Fall 2000	68,685	53,373	47,204	33,688	13,515	6,169 [3]	4,906 [3]	1,264 [3]	15,312	11,753	3,560
Fall 2001	69,920	53,992	47,672	33,938	13,734	6,320	5,023	1,296	15,928	12,233	3,695
Fall 2002	71,015	54,403	48,183	34,116	14,067	6,220 [3]	4,915 [3]	1,306 [3]	16,612	12,752	3,860
Fall 2003	71,551	54,639	48,540	34,202	14,338	6,099	4,788	1,311	16,911	12,859	4,053
Fall 2004	72,154	54,882	48,795	34,179	14,617	6,087 [3]	4,756 [3]	1,331 [3]	17,272	12,980	4,292
Fall 2005	72,674	55,187	49,113	34,205	14,908	6,073	4,723	1,350	17,487	13,022	4,466
Fall 2006	73,153	55,394	49,299	34,221	15,078	6,095 [4]	4,711 [4]	1,384 [4]	17,759	13,180	4,579
Fall 2007[5]	73,958	55,710	49,644	34,589	15,055	6,066	4,681	1,385	18,248	13,491	4,757
Fall 2008[4]	74,079	55,879	49,825	34,903	14,922	6,054	4,681	1,372	18,200	13,562	4,638
Fall 2009[4]	74,532	56,116	50,067	35,240	14,826	6,049	4,695	1,355	18,416	13,748	4,668

See notes at end of table.

Table 3. Enrollment in educational institutions, by level and control of institution: Selected years, 1869–70 through fall 2017—Continued

[In thousands]

Year	Total enrollment, all levels	Elementary and secondary, total	Public elementary and secondary schools			Private elementary and secondary schools[1]			Postsecondary degree-granting institutions[2]		
			Total	Prekindergarten through grade 8	Grades 9 through 12	Total	Prekindergarten through grade 8	Grades 9 through 12	Total	Public	Private
1	2	3	4	5	6	7	8	9	10	11	12
Fall 2010[4]	75,013	56,400	50,353	35,653	14,700	6,047	4,721	1,326	18,613	13,890	4,722
Fall 2011[4]	75,603	56,781	50,722	36,096	14,626	6,059	4,760	1,300	18,822	14,041	4,781
Fall 2012[4]	76,323	57,275	51,194	36,527	14,667	6,081	4,813	1,267	19,048	14,201	4,847
Fall 2013[4]	77,116	57,817	51,701	36,972	14,729	6,116	4,879	1,237	19,299	14,380	4,919
Fall 2014[4]	77,979	58,446	52,284	37,403	14,881	6,162	4,933	1,228	19,533	14,547	4,986
Fall 2015[4]	78,843	59,127	52,910	37,711	15,199	6,217	4,976	1,241	19,716	14,677	5,039
Fall 2016[4]	79,679	59,786	53,503	38,052	15,451	6,283	5,021	1,262	19,893	14,804	5,089
Fall 2017[4]	80,523	60,443	54,087	38,399	15,689	6,356	5,066	1,290	20,080	14,942	5,138

—Not available.

[1]Beginning in fall 1980, data include estimates for an expanded universe of private schools. Therefore, direct comparisons with earlier years should be avoided.

[2]Data for 1869–70 through 1949–50 include resident degree-credit students enrolled at any time during the academic year. Beginning in 1959, data include all resident and extension students enrolled at the beginning of the fall term.

[3]Estimated.

[4]Projected.

[5]Data for elementary and secondary are projected; data for degree-granting institutions are actual.

NOTE: Elementary and secondary enrollment includes students in local public school systems and in most private schools (religiously affiliated and nonsectarian), but generally excludes homeschooled children and students in subcollegiate departments of colleges and in federal schools. Based on the National Household Education Survey, the home-schooled children numbered approximately 1.5 million in 2007. Excludes preprimary pupils in private schools that do not offer kindergarten or above. Postsecondary data through 1995 are for institutions of higher education, while later data are for degree-granting institutions. Degree-granting institutions grant associate's or higher degrees and participate in

Title IV federal financial aid programs. The degree-granting classification is very similar to the earlier higher education classification, but it includes more 2-year colleges and excludes a few higher education institutions that did not grant degrees. (See Guide to Sources for details.) Some data have been revised from previously published figures. Detail may not sum to totals because of rounding.

SOURCE: U.S. Department of Education, National Center for Education Statistics, *Annual Report of the Commissioner of Education, 1870* to *1910; Biennial Survey of Education in the United States, 1919–20* through *1949–50; Statistics of Public Elementary and Secondary School Systems, 1959* through *1980*; Common Core of Data (CCD), "State Nonfiscal Survey of Public Elementary and Secondary Education," 1981–82 through 2006–07; Parent and Family Involvement in Education Survey of the National Household Education Surveys Program (PFI-NHES:2007); Private School Universe Survey (PSS), 1989–90 through 2005–06; *Projections of Education Statistics to 2017*; Opening (Fall) Enrollment in Higher Education, 1959; Higher Education General Information Survey (HEGIS), "Fall Enrollment in Institutions of Higher Education" surveys, 1969 through 1985; and 1986 through 2007 Integrated Postsecondary Education Data System (IPEDS), "Fall Enrollment Survey" (IPEDS-EF:86–99), and Spring 2001 through Spring 2008. (This table was prepared October 2008.)

Table 4. Number of teachers in elementary and secondary schools, and instructional staff in postsecondary degree-granting institutions, by control of institution: Selected years, fall 1970 through fall 2017

[In thousands]

Year	All levels			Elementary and secondary teachers[1]			Degree-granting institutions instructional staff[2]		
	Total	Public	Private	Total	Public	Private	Total	Public	Private
1	2	3	4	5	6	7	8	9	10
1970	2,766	2,373	393	2,292	2,059	233	474	314	160
1975	3,081	2,641	440	2,453	2,198	255 [3]	628	443	185
1980	3,171	2,679	492	2,485	2,184	301	686 [3,4]	495 [3,4]	191 [3,4]
1981	3,145	2,636	509	2,440	2,127	313 [3]	705	509	196
1982	3,168	2,639	529	2,458	2,133	325 [3]	710 [3,4]	506 [3,4]	204 [3,4]
1983	3,200	2,651	549	2,476	2,139	337	724	512	212
1984	3,225	2,673	552	2,508	2,168	340 [3]	717 [3,4]	505 [3,4]	212 [3,4]
1985	3,264	2,709	555	2,549	2,206	343	715 [3,4]	503 [3,4]	212 [3,4]
1986	3,314	2,754	560	2,592	2,244	348 [3]	722 [3,4]	510 [3,4]	212 [3,4]
1987	3,424	2,831	592	2,631	2,279	352 [3]	793	553	240
1988	3,472	2,882	590	2,668	2,323	345 [3]	804 [3]	559 [3]	245 [3]
1989	3,537	2,934	603	2,713	2,357	356 [3]	824	577	247
1990	3,576	2,972	604	2,759	2,398	361 [3]	817 [3]	574 [3]	244 [3]
1991	3,623	3,013	610	2,797	2,432	365 [3]	826	581	245
1992	3,703	3,080	624	2,827	2,459	368 [3]	877 [3]	621 [3]	257 [3]
1993	3,790	3,154	636	2,874	2,504	370 [3]	915	650	265
1994	3,848	3,205	643	2,925	2,552	373 [3]	923 [3]	653 [3]	270 [3]
1995	3,906	3,255	651	2,974	2,598	376 [3]	932	657	275
1996	4,006	3,339	666	3,051	2,667	384 [3]	954 [3]	672 [3]	282 [3]
1997	4,127	3,441	687	3,138	2,746	391	990	695	295
1998	4,230	3,527	703	3,230	2,830	400 [3]	999 [3]	697 [3]	303 [3]
1999	4,347	3,624	723	3,319	2,911	408	1,028	713	315
2000	4,433	3,682	750	3,366	2,941	424 [3]	1,067 [3]	741 [3]	326 [3]
2001	4,554	3,771	783	3,440	3,000	441	1,113	771	342
2002	4,631	3,829	802	3,476	3,034	442 [3]	1,155 [3]	794 [3]	361 [3]
2003	4,663	3,840	823	3,490	3,049	441	1,174	792	382
2004	4,779	3,911	868	3,538	3,091	447 [3]	1,241 [3]	820 [3]	421 [3]
2005	4,883	3,984	899	3,593	3,143	450	1,290	841	449
2006	4,955	4,035	920	3,632	3,180	452 [5]	1,322 [3]	854 [3]	468 [3]
2007[6]	5,034	4,081	953	3,663	3,204	459	1,371	877	494
2008[5]	—	—	—	3,713	3,246	467	—	—	—
2009[5]	—	—	—	3,760	3,286	474	—	—	—
2010[5]	—	—	—	3,808	3,326	482	—	—	—
2011[5]	—	—	—	3,859	3,369	489	—	—	—
2012[5]	—	—	—	3,914	3,417	497	—	—	—
2013[5]	—	—	—	3,970	3,465	505	—	—	—
2014[5]	—	—	—	4,034	3,520	513	—	—	—
2015[5]	—	—	—	4,101	3,579	522	—	—	—
2016[5]	—	—	—	4,171	3,640	531	—	—	—
2017[5]	—	—	—	4,244	3,704	540	—	—	—

—Not available.

[1]Includes teachers in local public school systems and in most private schools (religiously affiliated and nonsectarian). Teachers are reported in terms of full-time equivalents.

[2]Data through 1995 are for institutions of higher education, while later data are for degree-granting institutions. Degree-granting institutions grant associate's or higher degrees and participate in Title IV federal financial aid programs. The degree-granting classification is very similar to the earlier higher education classification, but it includes more 2-year colleges and excludes a few higher education institutions that did not grant degrees. (See Guide to Sources for details.) Includes full-time and part-time faculty with the rank of instructor or above in colleges, universities, professional schools, and 2-year colleges. Excludes teaching assistants.

[3]Estimated.

[4]Inclusion of institutions is not consistent with surveys for 1987 and later years.

[5]Projected.

[6]Data for elementary and secondary are projected; data for degree-granting institutions are actual.

NOTE: Detail may not sum to totals because of rounding. Some data have been revised from previously published figures. Headcounts are used to report data for degree-granting institutions instructional staff.

SOURCE: U.S. Department of Education, National Center for Education Statistics, *Statistics of Public Elementary and Secondary Day Schools*, 1970 and 1975; Common Core of Data (CCD), "State Nonfiscal Survey of Public Elementary/Secondary Education," 1980 through 2006; Private School Universe Survey (PSS), 1989–90 through 2005–06; *Projections of Education Statistics to 2017*; Higher Education General Information Survey (HEGIS), "Fall Staff" survey, 1970 and 1975; 1987 through 2007 Integrated Postsecondary Education Data System (IPEDS), "Fall Staff Survey" (IPEDS-S:87–99), and Winter 2001–02 through Winter 2007–08; U.S. Equal Opportunity Commission, EEO-6, 1981 and 1983; and unpublished data. (This table was prepared October 2008.)

Table 5. Number of educational institutions, by level and control of institution: Selected years, 1980–81 through 2006–07

Level and control of institution	1980–81	1990–91	1995–96	1996–97	1997–98	1998–99	1999–2000	2000–01	2001–02	2002–03	2003–04	2004–05	2005–06	2006–07
1	2	3	4	5	6	7	8	9	10	11	12	13	14	15
All institutions	—	—	—	—	129,997	—	131,414	—	136,465	—	136,819	—	138,899	—
Elementary and secondary schools	106,746	109,228	122,059	—	123,403	—	125,007	—	130,007	—	130,407	—	132,436	—
Elementary	72,659	74,716	85,157	—	85,855	—	86,433	—	89,277	—	89,252	—	90,161	—
Secondary	24,856	23,602	23,530	—	24,169	—	24,903	—	24,884	—	25,476	—	26,727	—
Combined	5,202	8,847	11,205	—	11,412	—	12,197	—	14,430	—	13,931	—	14,964	—
Other[1]	4,029	2,063	2,167	—	1,967	—	1,474	—	1,416	—	1,749	—	584	—
Public schools	85,982	84,538	87,125	88,223	89,508	90,874	92,012	93,273	94,112	95,615	95,726	96,513	97,382	98,793
Elementary	59,326	59,015	61,165	61,805	62,739	63,462	64,131	64,601	65,228	65,718	65,758	65,984	67,291	68,990
Secondary	22,619	21,135	20,997	21,307	21,682	22,076	22,365	21,994	22,180	22,599	22,782	23,445	23,800	23,436
Combined	1,743	2,325	2,796	2,980	3,120	3,721	4,042	5,096	5,288	5,552	5,437	5,572	5,707	5,984
Other[1]	2,294	2,063	2,167	2,131	1,967	1,615	1,474	1,582	1,416	1,746	1,749	1,512	584	383
Private schools[2]	20,764	24,690	34,394	—	33,895	—	32,995	—	35,895	—	34,681	—	35,054	—
Elementary	13,333	15,701	23,992	—	23,116	—	22,302	—	24,049	—	23,494	—	22,870	—
Schools with highest grade of kindergarten	†	†	7,249	—	6,493	—	5,952	—	6,622	—	6,297	—	6,059	—
Secondary	2,237	2,467	2,533	—	2,487	—	2,538	—	2,704	—	2,694	—	2,927	—
Combined	3,459	6,522	8,409	—	8,292	—	8,155	—	9,142	—	8,494	—	9,257	—
Other[1]	1,735	(3)	(3)	—	(3)	—	(3)	—	(3)	—	(3)	—	(3)	—
Postsecondary Title IV institutions	—	—	—	6,669	6,594	6,431	6,407	6,479	6,458	6,354	6,412	6,383	6,463	6,536
Public	—	—	—	2,069	2,163	2,090	2,078	2,084	2,099	2,051	2,047	2,027	2,013	2,009
Private	—	—	—	4,600	4,431	4,341	4,329	4,395	4,359	4,303	4,365	4,356	4,450	4,527
Not-for-profit	—	—	—	2,027	2,007	1,986	1,936	1,950	1,941	1,921	1,913	1,875	1,866	1,848
For-profit	—	—	—	2,573	2,424	2,355	2,393	2,445	2,418	2,382	2,452	2,481	2,584	2,679
Title IV non-degree-granting institutions	—	—	—	2,660	2,530	2,383	2,323	2,297	2,261	2,186	2,176	2,167	2,187	2,222
Public	—	—	—	367	456	409	396	386	386	339	327	327	320	321
Private	—	—	—	2,293	2,074	1,974	1,927	1,911	1,875	1,847	1,849	1,840	1,867	1,901
Not-for-profit	—	—	—	334	300	291	255	255	265	256	249	238	219	208
For-profit	—	—	—	1,959	1,774	1,683	1,672	1,656	1,610	1,591	1,600	1,602	1,648	1,693
Title IV degree-granting institutions	3,231	3,559	3,706	4,009	4,064	4,048	4,084	4,182	4,197	4,168	4,236	4,216	4,276	4,314
2-year colleges	1,274	1,418	1,462	1,742	1,755	1,713	1,721	1,732	1,710	1,702	1,706	1,683	1,694	1,685
Public	945	972	1,047	1,088	1,092	1,069	1,068	1,076	1,085	1,081	1,086	1,061	1,053	1,045
Private	329	446	415	654	663	644	653	656	625	621	620	622	641	640
Not-for-profit	182	167	187	184	179	164	150	144	135	127	118	112	113	107
For-profit	147	279	228	470	484	480	503	512	490	494	502	510	528	533
4-year colleges	1,957	2,141	2,244	2,267	2,309	2,335	2,363	2,450	2,487	2,466	2,530	2,533	2,582	2,629
Public	552	595	608	614	615	612	614	622	628	631	634	639	640	643
Private	1,405	1,546	1,636	1,653	1,694	1,723	1,749	1,828	1,859	1,835	1,896	1,894	1,942	1,986
Not-for-profit	1,387	1,482	1,519	1,509	1,528	1,531	1,531	1,551	1,541	1,538	1,546	1,525	1,534	1,533
For-profit	18	64	117	144	166	192	218	277	318	297	350	369	408	453

—Not available.
†Not applicable.
[1]Includes special education, alternative, and other schools not classified by grade span. Because of changes in survey definitions, figures for "other" schools are not comparable from year to year.
[2]Data for 1980–81 and 1990–91 include schools with first or higher grades. Data for 1995–96 and later years include schools with kindergarten or higher grades.
[3]Included in other private school categories.
NOTE: Postsecondary data for 1980–81 and 1990–91 are for institutions of higher education, while later data are for Title IV degree-granting and non-degree-granting institutions. Degree-granting institutions grant associate's or higher degrees and participate in Title IV federal financial aid programs. The degree-granting classification is very similar to the earlier higher education classification, but it includes more 2-year colleges and excludes a few

higher education institutions that did not grant degrees. (See Guide to Sources for details.) Some data have been revised from previously published figures. Detail may not sum to totals because of rounding.
SOURCE: U.S. Department of Education, National Center for Education Statistics, Common Core of Data (CCD), "Public Elementary/Secondary School Universe Survey," 1989–90 through 2006–07; Private Schools in American Education; Statistics of Public Elementary and Secondary Day Schools, 1980–81; Schools and Staffing Survey (SASS), "Private School Data File," 1990–91; Private School Universe Survey (PSS), 1995–96 through 2005–06; Higher Education General Information Survey (HEGIS), "Institutional Characteristics of Colleges and Universities" survey, 1980–81; and 1990–91 through 2005–06 Integrated Postsecondary Education Data System (IPEDS), "Institutional Characteristics Survey" (IPEDS-IC:90–99), and Fall 2001 through Fall 2006. (This table was prepared September 2008.)

Table 6. Percentage of the population 3 to 34 years old enrolled in school, by sex, race/ethnicity, and age: Selected years, 1980 through 2007

Year and age	Total				Male				Female			
	Total	White	Black	Hispanic	Total	White	Black	Hispanic	Total	White	Black	Hispanic
1	2	3	4	5	6	7	8	9	10	11	12	13
1980												
Total, 3 to 34 years	**49.7** (0.21)	**48.8** (0.24)	**54.0** (0.68)	**49.8** (1.07)	**50.9** (0.30)	**50.0** (0.34)	**56.2** (0.98)	**49.9** (1.53)	**48.5** (0.30)	**47.7** (0.34)	**52.1** (0.94)	**49.8** (1.51)
3 and 4 years	36.7 (0.95)	37.4 (1.12)	38.2 (2.83)	28.5 (3.92)	37.8 (1.33)	39.2 (1.58)	36.4 (3.94)	30.1 (5.37)	35.5 (1.34)	35.5 (1.58)	40.0 (4.04)	26.6 (5.71)
5 and 6 years	95.7 (0.40)	95.9 (0.46)	95.5 (1.22)	94.5 (2.13)	95.0 (0.60)	95.4 (0.68)	94.1 (1.95)	94.0 (3.22)	96.4 (0.53)	96.5 (0.61)	97.0 (1.43)	94.9 (2.83)
7 to 9 years	99.1 (0.15)	99.1 (0.17)	99.4 (0.35)	98.4 (0.91)	99.0 (0.22)	99.0 (0.26)	99.5 (0.45)	97.7 (1.57)	99.2 (0.20)	99.2 (0.24)	99.3 (0.54)	99.0 (0.99)
10 to 13 years	99.4 (0.10)	99.4 (0.12)	99.4 (0.31)	99.7 (0.36)	99.4 (0.14)	99.4 (0.16)	99.4 (0.42)	99.4 (0.66)	99.4 (0.15)	99.3 (0.18)	99.3 (0.46)	99.9 (0.25)
14 and 15 years	98.2 (0.22)	98.7 (0.22)	97.9 (0.72)	94.3 (1.87)	98.7 (0.27)	98.9 (0.28)	98.4 (0.88)	96.7 (2.10)	97.7 (0.36)	98.5 (0.34)	97.3 (1.15)	92.1 (2.99)
16 and 17 years	89.0 (0.51)	89.2 (0.57)	90.7 (1.44)	81.8 (3.25)	89.1 (0.71)	89.4 (0.79)	90.7 (2.04)	81.5 (4.70)	88.8 (0.72)	89.0 (0.82)	90.6 (2.05)	82.2 (4.49)
18 and 19 years	46.4 (0.80)	47.0 (0.91)	45.8 (2.56)	37.8 (3.94)	47.0 (1.14)	48.5 (1.29)	42.9 (3.73)	36.9 (5.44)	45.8 (1.11)	45.7 (1.26)	48.3 (3.51)	38.8 (5.71)
20 and 21 years	31.0 (0.74)	33.0 (0.85)	23.3 (2.21)	19.5 (3.29)	32.6 (1.08)	34.8 (1.23)	22.8 (3.29)	21.4 (4.88)	29.5 (1.02)	31.3 (1.18)	23.7 (2.99)	17.6 (4.43)
22 to 24 years	16.3 (0.49)	16.8 (0.56)	13.6 (1.53)	11.7 (2.26)	17.8 (0.73)	18.7 (0.83)	13.4 (2.29)	10.7 (3.14)	14.9 (0.66)	15.0 (0.75)	13.7 (2.05)	12.6 (3.24)
25 to 29 years	9.3 (0.31)	9.4 (0.35)	8.8 (1.04)	6.9 (1.43)	9.8 (0.45)	9.8 (0.50)	10.6 (1.70)	6.8 (2.06)	8.8 (0.42)	9.1 (0.48)	7.5 (1.29)	6.9 (1.99)
30 to 34 years	6.4 (0.27)	6.4 (0.30)	6.9 (1.00)	5.1 (1.35)	5.9 (0.37)	5.6 (0.40)	7.2 (1.55)	6.2 (2.07)	7.0 (0.39)	7.2 (0.45)	6.6 (1.32)	4.1 (1.71)
1990												
Total, 3 to 34 years	**50.2** (0.23)	**49.8** (0.27)	**52.2** (0.71)	**47.2** (1.06)	**50.9** (0.32)	**50.4** (0.38)	**54.3** (1.02)	**46.8** (1.48)	**49.5** (0.32)	**49.2** (0.38)	**50.3** (0.99)	**47.7** (1.52)
3 and 4 years	44.4 (0.99)	47.2 (1.19)	41.8 (2.98)	30.7 (4.08)	43.9 (1.38)	47.9 (1.66)	38.1 (4.14)	28.0 (5.57)	44.9 (1.41)	46.6 (1.70)	45.5 (4.25)	33.6 (5.95)
5 and 6 years	96.5 (0.37)	96.7 (0.43)	96.5 (1.05)	94.9 (1.96)	96.5 (0.51)	96.8 (0.59)	96.2 (1.53)	95.8 (2.48)	96.4 (0.53)	96.7 (0.62)	96.9 (1.43)	93.9 (3.05)
7 to 9 years	99.7 (0.09)	99.7 (0.11)	99.8 (0.19)	99.5 (0.52)	99.7 (0.13)	99.7 (0.16)	99.9 (0.24)	99.5 (0.70)	99.6 (0.14)	99.7 (0.15)	99.8 (0.31)	99.4 (0.79)
10 to 13 years	99.6 (0.09)	99.7 (0.10)	99.9 (0.15)	99.1 (0.64)	99.6 (0.13)	99.6 (0.14)	99.9 (0.19)	99.0 (0.93)	99.7 (0.12)	99.7 (0.13)	99.8 (0.25)	99.1 (0.87)
14 and 15 years	99.0 (0.19)	99.0 (0.23)	99.4 (0.46)	99.0 (0.90)	99.1 (0.25)	99.2 (0.30)	99.7 (0.48)	99.1 (1.11)	98.9 (0.29)	98.9 (0.35)	99.1 (0.79)	98.8 (1.47)
16 and 17 years	92.5 (0.52)	93.5 (0.58)	91.7 (1.59)	85.4 (3.22)	92.6 (0.72)	93.4 (0.82)	93.0 (2.09)	85.5 (4.40)	92.4 (0.74)	93.7 (0.81)	90.5 (2.41)	85.3 (4.74)
18 and 19 years	57.2 (0.94)	59.1 (1.10)	55.0 (2.83)	44.0 (4.36)	58.2 (1.33)	59.7 (1.56)	60.4 (3.99)	40.7 (6.23)	56.3 (1.32)	58.5 (1.57)	49.8 (3.96)	47.2 (6.08)
20 and 21 years	39.7 (0.92)	43.1 (1.10)	28.3 (2.57)	27.2 (3.83)	40.3 (1.32)	44.2 (1.59)	31.0 (3.81)	21.7 (4.95)	39.2 (1.28)	42.0 (1.53)	25.8 (3.45)	33.1 (5.79)
22 to 24 years	21.0 (0.63)	21.9 (0.75)	19.7 (2.01)	9.9 (2.05)	22.3 (0.92)	23.7 (1.11)	19.3 (3.03)	11.2 (2.98)	19.9 (0.86)	20.3 (1.02)	20.0 (2.68)	8.4 (2.77)
25 to 29 years	9.7 (0.33)	10.4 (0.39)	6.1 (0.87)	6.3 (1.29)	9.2 (0.46)	10.0 (0.55)	4.7 (1.14)	4.6 (1.55)	10.2 (0.47)	10.7 (0.56)	7.3 (1.27)	8.1 (2.06)
30 to 34 years	5.8 (0.25)	6.2 (0.30)	4.5 (0.75)	3.6 (0.99)	4.8 (0.33)	5.0 (0.38)	2.3 (0.80)	4.0 (1.45)	6.9 (0.38)	7.4 (0.46)	6.3 (1.19)	3.1 (1.32)
1995												
Total, 3 to 34 years	**53.7** (0.21)	**53.8** (0.25)	**56.3** (0.58)	**49.7** (0.65)	**54.3** (0.29)	**54.2** (0.35)	**58.6** (0.83)	**49.1** (0.90)	**53.2** (0.30)	**53.4** (0.36)	**54.1** (0.80)	**50.3** (0.93)
3 and 4 years	48.7 (0.87)	52.2 (1.09)	47.8 (2.28)	36.9 (2.35)	49.4 (1.22)	51.1 (1.52)	52.4 (3.26)	40.8 (3.33)	48.1 (1.24)	53.5 (1.56)	43.4 (3.17)	32.7 (3.28)
5 and 6 years	96.0 (0.34)	96.6 (0.39)	95.4 (0.96)	93.9 (1.22)	95.3 (0.51)	95.9 (0.60)	94.6 (1.48)	93.6 (1.74)	96.8 (0.44)	97.4 (0.49)	96.3 (1.23)	94.3 (1.71)
7 to 9 years	98.7 (0.17)	98.9 (0.18)	97.7 (0.59)	98.5 (0.55)	98.9 (0.22)	99.0 (0.24)	98.1 (0.74)	98.8 (0.72)	98.5 (0.25)	98.9 (0.27)	97.2 (0.91)	98.2 (0.82)
10 to 13 years	99.1 (0.12)	99.0 (0.15)	99.2 (0.30)	99.2 (0.36)	99.1 (0.17)	99.0 (0.21)	99.5 (0.34)	98.8 (0.58)	99.0 (0.18)	98.9 (0.22)	98.9 (0.50)	99.5 (0.39)
14 and 15 years	98.9 (0.18)	98.8 (0.22)	99.0 (0.46)	98.9 (0.56)	99.0 (0.24)	98.9 (0.30)	99.6 (0.40)	98.4 (0.92)	98.8 (0.27)	98.7 (0.33)	98.3 (0.83)	99.4 (0.58)
16 and 17 years	93.6 (0.42)	94.4 (0.47)	93.0 (1.16)	88.2 (1.82)	94.5 (0.54)	95.0 (0.62)	95.6 (1.30)	88.4 (2.58)	92.6 (0.64)	93.8 (0.72)	90.3 (1.93)	88.0 (2.57)
18 and 19 years	59.4 (0.85)	61.8 (1.03)	57.5 (2.38)	46.1 (2.63)	59.5 (1.21)	61.9 (1.45)	59.2 (3.47)	47.4 (3.62)	59.2 (1.21)	61.8 (1.46)	56.1 (3.26)	44.8 (3.81)
20 and 21 years	44.9 (0.89)	49.7 (1.10)	37.8 (2.47)	27.1 (2.37)	44.7 (1.28)	50.0 (1.56)	36.7 (3.66)	24.8 (3.29)	45.1 (1.25)	49.3 (1.54)	38.7 (3.34)	29.2 (3.39)
22 to 24 years	23.2 (0.60)	24.4 (0.73)	20.0 (1.61)	15.6 (1.52)	22.8 (0.84)	24.1 (1.04)	20.6 (2.41)	14.8 (2.00)	23.6 (0.84)	24.8 (1.04)	19.5 (2.17)	16.6 (2.33)
25 to 29 years	11.6 (0.34)	12.3 (0.42)	10.0 (0.94)	7.1 (0.87)	11.0 (0.48)	12.2 (0.59)	6.3 (1.15)	5.6 (1.09)	12.2 (0.49)	12.3 (0.59)	13.0 (1.41)	8.7 (1.38)
30 to 34 years	5.9 (0.24)	5.7 (0.27)	7.7 (0.80)	4.7 (0.70)	5.4 (0.32)	5.0 (0.37)	6.9 (1.13)	4.5 (0.95)	6.5 (0.35)	6.3 (0.41)	8.3 (1.13)	4.9 (1.02)
2000												
Total, 3 to 34 years	**55.9** (0.22)	**56.0** (0.27)	**59.3** (0.60)	**51.3** (0.63)	**55.8** (0.31)	**55.8** (0.38)	**59.7** (0.85)	**50.5** (0.88)	**56.0** (0.31)	**56.1** (0.38)	**59.0** (0.83)	**52.2** (0.89)
3 and 4 years	52.1 (0.93)	54.6 (1.19)	59.8 (2.51)	35.9 (2.37)	50.8 (1.30)	54.1 (1.66)	58.0 (3.53)	31.9 (3.23)	53.4 (1.33)	55.2 (1.71)	61.8 (3.56)	40.0 (3.44)
5 and 6 years	95.6 (0.38)	95.5 (0.49)	96.7 (0.89)	94.3 (1.13)	95.1 (0.56)	94.5 (0.76)	96.0 (1.38)	95.4 (1.41)	96.1 (0.51)	96.4 (0.63)	97.5 (1.12)	93.1 (1.79)
7 to 9 years	98.1 (0.20)	98.4 (0.24)	97.5 (0.62)	97.5 (0.65)	98.0 (0.29)	98.1 (0.36)	98.2 (0.72)	96.6 (1.09)	98.2 (0.28)	98.6 (0.32)	96.7 (1.01)	98.4 (0.74)
10 to 13 years	98.3 (0.17)	98.5 (0.19)	98.5 (0.42)	97.4 (0.59)	98.3 (0.23)	98.1 (0.30)	98.8 (0.52)	98.4 (0.65)	98.3 (0.24)	98.8 (0.25)	98.1 (0.66)	96.4 (1.01)
14 and 15 years	98.7 (0.20)	98.9 (0.22)	99.6 (0.30)	96.2 (0.99)	98.7 (0.27)	98.8 (0.33)	99.6 (0.42)	96.9 (1.26)	98.6 (0.29)	99.0 (0.31)	99.6 (0.42)	95.4 (1.54)
16 and 17 years	92.8 (0.45)	94.0 (0.50)	91.7 (1.32)	87.0 (1.77)	92.7 (0.63)	94.7 (0.66)	88.9 (2.10)	85.7 (2.60)	92.9 (0.64)	93.3 (0.76)	94.6 (1.54)	88.3 (2.40)
18 and 19 years	61.2 (0.84)	63.9 (1.02)	57.2 (2.34)	49.5 (2.47)	58.3 (1.19)	61.2 (1.46)	51.5 (3.46)	48.0 (3.41)	64.2 (1.17)	66.7 (1.42)	62.2 (3.15)	51.1 (3.59)
20 and 21 years	44.1 (0.88)	49.2 (1.10)	37.4 (2.38)	26.1 (2.22)	41.0 (1.23)	45.8 (1.54)	31.3 (3.42)	24.2 (3.02)	47.3 (1.26)	52.7 (1.58)	42.3 (3.26)	28.1 (3.26)
22 to 24 years	24.6 (0.63)	24.9 (0.78)	24.0 (1.76)	18.2 (1.64)	23.9 (0.88)	25.0 (1.12)	22.0 (2.46)	15.2 (2.09)	25.3 (0.90)	24.8 (1.09)	25.8 (2.51)	21.6 (2.55)
25 to 29 years	11.4 (0.37)	11.1 (0.45)	14.5 (1.18)	7.4 (0.88)	10.0 (0.50)	10.5 (0.62)	11.6 (1.63)	5.1 (1.06)	12.7 (0.53)	11.8 (0.65)	16.7 (1.66)	9.5 (1.38)
30 to 34 years	6.7 (0.28)	6.1 (0.32)	9.9 (0.97)	5.6 (0.75)	5.6 (0.36)	4.7 (0.41)	8.5 (1.34)	5.7 (1.06)	7.7 (0.41)	7.4 (0.50)	11.2 (1.39)	5.5 (1.05)

See notes at end of table.

Table 6. Percentage of the population 3 to 34 years old enrolled in school, by sex, race/ethnicity, and age: Selected years, 1980 through 2007—Continued

Year and age	Total				Male				Female			
	Total	White	Black	Hispanic	Total	White	Black	Hispanic	Total	White	Black	Hispanic
1	2	3	4	5	6	7	8	9	10	11	12	13
2005												
Total, 3 to 34 years	56.5 (0.20)	57.6 (0.26)	58.5 (0.57)	50.9 (0.53)	55.8 (0.28)	57.1 (0.37)	58.8 (0.82)	48.4 (0.73)	57.2 (0.29)	58.0 (0.37)	58.1 (0.80)	53.7 (0.76)
3 and 4 years	53.6 (0.86)	58.5 (1.14)	52.4 (2.39)	43.0 (2.07)	52.8 (1.21)	54.8 (1.61)	54.8 (3.42)	43.0 (2.91)	54.4 (1.23)	60.3 (1.63)	50.1 (3.32)	43.0 (2.96)
5 and 6 years	95.4 (0.37)	95.9 (0.47)	95.9 (0.97)	93.8 (1.06)	94.8 (0.54)	95.4 (0.68)	94.8 (1.50)	92.4 (1.62)	96.1 (0.50)	96.3 (0.63)	97.1 (1.18)	95.3 (1.34)
7 to 9 years	98.6 (0.17)	99.0 (0.19)	98.7 (0.45)	97.4 (0.58)	98.2 (0.27)	98.9 (0.27)	98.0 (0.81)	96.0 (1.00)	99.0 (0.20)	99.0 (0.27)	99.5 (0.41)	98.8 (0.57)
10 to 13 years	98.6 (0.14)	99.0 (0.16)	98.5 (0.40)	97.9 (0.46)	98.4 (0.22)	99.1 (0.21)	97.6 (0.70)	97.2 (0.72)	98.9 (0.18)	98.8 (0.24)	99.5 (0.33)	98.6 (0.54)
14 and 15 years	98.0 (0.22)	98.6 (0.24)	96.1 (0.83)	97.3 (0.70)	97.5 (0.34)	98.4 (0.35)	93.3 (1.52)	97.8 (0.90)	98.4 (0.28)	98.7 (0.33)	98.8 (0.66)	96.7 (1.09)
16 and 17 years	95.1 (0.33)	96.1 (0.38)	93.6 (1.05)	92.6 (1.14)	95.1 (0.47)	95.9 (0.55)	93.6 (1.51)	92.5 (1.61)	95.1 (0.47)	96.3 (0.53)	93.6 (1.47)	92.6 (1.60)
18 and 19 years	67.6 (0.79)	71.6 (0.95)	62.0 (2.30)	54.3 (2.33)	66.5 (1.11)	69.8 (1.35)	66.9 (3.20)	51.8 (3.22)	68.8 (1.12)	73.5 (1.34)	57.4 (3.27)	57.2 (3.37)
20 and 21 years	48.7 (0.80)	54.4 (1.01)	37.9 (2.25)	30.0 (1.96)	45.3 (1.11)	50.5 (1.42)	35.5 (3.12)	25.2 (2.56)	52.3 (1.15)	58.5 (1.43)	40.4 (3.23)	35.3 (2.99)
22 to 24 years	27.3 (0.59)	27.8 (0.76)	28.6 (1.75)	19.5 (1.41)	25.2 (0.83)	26.4 (1.07)	24.0 (2.45)	17.5 (1.85)	29.2 (0.85)	29.1 (1.09)	32.5 (2.45)	21.8 (2.17)
25 to 29 years	11.9 (0.34)	12.5 (0.45)	11.9 (1.00)	7.8 (0.70)	9.6 (0.43)	10.2 (0.58)	9.1 (1.32)	5.6 (0.82)	14.2 (0.51)	14.7 (0.67)	14.2 (1.47)	10.4 (1.19)
30 to 34 years	6.9 (0.27)	6.9 (0.34)	9.8 (0.94)	4.2 (0.54)	5.9 (0.35)	6.5 (0.47)	6.3 (1.15)	2.6 (0.58)	7.9 (0.40)	7.4 (0.50)	12.7 (1.42)	6.1 (0.94)
2006												
Total, 3 to 34 years	56.0 (0.20)	56.8 (0.26)	58.3 (0.57)	51.3 (0.52)	55.5 (0.28)	56.4 (0.37)	58.9 (0.82)	49.0 (0.72)	56.6 (0.29)	57.1 (0.37)	57.7 (0.80)	53.9 (0.76)
3 and 4 years	55.7 (0.86)	58.2 (1.15)	59.6 (2.37)	48.8 (2.07)	56.0 (1.21)	58.3 (1.60)	58.0 (3.45)	49.1 (2.95)	55.4 (1.23)	58.1 (1.66)	61.0 (3.27)	48.5 (2.90)
5 and 6 years	94.6 (0.39)	95.6 (0.48)	92.4 (1.28)	93.4 (1.06)	94.4 (0.56)	95.9 (0.65)	93.3 (1.67)	91.7 (1.64)	94.8 (0.56)	95.3 (0.70)	91.4 (1.97)	95.3 (1.30)
7 to 9 years	98.2 (0.19)	98.5 (0.23)	97.1 (0.69)	98.1 (0.50)	98.1 (0.28)	98.5 (0.32)	97.4 (0.93)	97.7 (0.77)	98.3 (0.27)	98.6 (0.33)	96.8 (1.01)	98.5 (0.64)
10 to 13 years	98.3 (0.16)	98.6 (0.19)	97.1 (0.57)	98.2 (0.41)	98.2 (0.23)	98.6 (0.26)	96.7 (0.85)	97.9 (0.63)	98.4 (0.22)	98.5 (0.28)	97.5 (0.75)	98.6 (0.53)
14 and 15 years	98.3 (0.21)	98.4 (0.25)	97.4 (0.67)	98.4 (0.54)	98.2 (0.30)	97.9 (0.41)	97.6 (0.91)	99.0 (0.59)	98.4 (0.29)	99.0 (0.30)	97.2 (1.00)	97.7 (0.92)
16 and 17 years	94.6 (0.36)	95.9 (0.40)	93.6 (1.05)	91.1 (1.25)	94.1 (0.52)	95.5 (0.58)	91.6 (1.66)	91.7 (1.68)	95.0 (0.48)	96.2 (0.54)	95.7 (1.24)	90.4 (1.85)
18 and 19 years	65.5 (0.77)	67.9 (0.96)	65.4 (2.14)	53.4 (2.20)	63.6 (1.10)	65.4 (1.37)	65.4 (3.07)	51.5 (3.11)	67.4 (1.08)	70.5 (1.34)	65.3 (2.99)	55.4 (3.12)
20 and 21 years	47.5 (0.81)	52.9 (1.03)	39.0 (2.21)	30.6 (2.04)	44.0 (1.14)	49.2 (1.46)	38.4 (3.13)	24.1 (2.64)	51.1 (1.15)	56.5 (1.44)	39.6 (3.11)	37.5 (3.06)
22 to 24 years	26.7 (0.58)	27.4 (0.75)	28.1 (1.75)	17.9 (1.36)	25.0 (0.81)	26.2 (1.04)	24.9 (2.46)	16.0 (1.76)	28.5 (0.85)	28.7 (1.08)	31.0 (2.47)	20.1 (2.10)
25 to 29 years	11.7 (0.33)	12.5 (0.44)	11.7 (0.98)	7.3 (0.68)	10.4 (0.44)	11.9 (0.61)	9.4 (1.31)	5.4 (0.79)	13.0 (0.49)	13.2 (0.63)	13.7 (1.43)	9.7 (1.15)
30 to 34 years	7.2 (0.27)	7.4 (0.36)	8.1 (0.88)	5.3 (0.60)	5.9 (0.35)	6.3 (0.47)	6.5 (1.19)	3.5 (0.67)	8.5 (0.42)	8.5 (0.54)	9.4 (1.26)	7.3 (1.02)
2007												
Total, 3 to 34 years	56.1 (0.20)	56.6 (0.26)	58.6 (0.57)	51.7 (0.52)	55.4 (0.28)	56.0 (0.37)	59.7 (0.81)	49.4 (0.71)	56.8 (0.29)	57.3 (0.37)	57.7 (0.80)	54.3 (0.74)
3 and 4 years	54.5 (0.86)	56.3 (1.15)	59.1 (2.42)	48.2 (2.03)	54.4 (1.20)	53.8 (1.62)	60.2 (3.37)	50.7 (2.82)	54.7 (1.24)	58.9 (1.65)	58.0 (3.48)	45.6 (2.92)
5 and 6 years	94.7 (0.39)	95.0 (0.51)	93.9 (1.13)	94.3 (0.96)	94.0 (0.57)	94.0 (0.77)	93.7 (1.60)	94.1 (1.39)	95.3 (0.52)	96.0 (0.65)	94.1 (1.59)	94.5 (1.32)
7 to 9 years	98.1 (0.20)	98.6 (0.22)	98.2 (0.56)	96.3 (0.68)	98.1 (0.28)	98.3 (0.32)	98.3 (0.74)	96.4 (0.93)	98.1 (0.28)	98.8 (0.30)	98.6 (0.83)	96.2 (0.99)
10 to 13 years	98.6 (0.15)	98.6 (0.19)	99.0 (0.45)	99.0 (0.31)	98.4 (0.21)	98.5 (0.28)	97.1 (0.32)	99.0 (0.44)	98.7 (0.20)	98.7 (0.27)	98.8 (0.57)	99.0 (0.44)
14 and 15 years	98.7 (0.18)	98.8 (0.23)	98.0 (0.50)	98.4 (0.53)	98.4 (0.28)	98.3 (0.38)	99.1 (0.36)	97.8 (0.87)	99.0 (0.22)	99.2 (0.26)	98.8 (0.71)	99.1 (0.57)
16 and 17 years	94.3 (0.36)	95.6 (0.41)	93.7 (1.04)	90.6 (1.27)	94.4 (0.50)	95.2 (0.60)	95.6 (1.24)	91.1 (1.73)	94.1 (0.52)	96.0 (0.56)	91.8 (1.67)	90.0 (1.85)
18 and 19 years	66.8 (0.75)	69.7 (0.94)	61.8 (2.15)	57.2 (2.10)	66.3 (1.06)	69.3 (1.32)	61.6 (3.05)	55.2 (2.95)	67.2 (1.07)	70.1 (1.34)	62.0 (3.02)	59.2 (2.99)
20 and 21 years	48.4 (0.81)	54.5 (1.03)	38.1 (2.21)	32.3 (2.03)	43.7 (1.13)	49.9 (1.47)	37.7 (3.06)	24.6 (2.57)	53.3 (1.15)	59.2 (1.44)	38.5 (3.20)	41.0 (3.13)
22 to 24 years	27.3 (0.59)	28.4 (0.75)	27.8 (1.71)	18.8 (1.38)	25.4 (0.81)	26.9 (1.04)	28.6 (2.55)	14.4 (1.71)	29.2 (0.85)	29.9 (1.09)	27.1 (2.31)	23.7 (2.18)
25 to 29 years	12.4 (0.33)	12.5 (0.43)	15.3 (1.09)	8.3 (0.71)	10.2 (0.43)	10.6 (0.57)	10.7 (1.38)	6.7 (0.86)	14.7 (0.51)	14.4 (0.65)	19.2 (1.62)	10.3 (1.16)
30 to 34 years	7.2 (0.27)	7.4 (0.36)	9.6 (0.95)	4.5 (0.54)	6.4 (0.37)	6.7 (0.49)	9.1 (1.39)	3.1 (0.62)	7.9 (0.40)	8.0 (0.53)	9.9 (1.31)	6.1 (0.92)

NOTE: Includes enrollment in any type of graded public, parochial, or other private schools. Includes nursery schools, kindergartens, elementary schools, high schools, colleges, universities, and professional schools. Attendance may be on either a full-time or part-time basis and during the day or night. Enrollments in "special" schools, such as trade schools, business colleges, or correspondence schools, are not included. Beginning in 1994, preprimary enrollment was collected using new procedures and may not be comparable to figures for earlier years. Total includes persons from other racial/ethnic groups not shown separately. Race categories exclude persons of Hispanic ethnicity. Standard errors appear in parentheses.

SOURCE: U.S. Department of Commerce, Census Bureau, Current Population Survey (CPS), October, selected years, 1980 through 2007. (This table was prepared July 2008.)

Table 7. Percentage of the population 3 to 34 years old enrolled in school, by age group: Selected years, 1940 through 2007

Year	Total, 3 to 34 years	3 and 4 years	5 and 6 years	7 to 13 years	14 to 17 years	18 and 19 years old			20 to 24 years old			25 to 29 years	30 to 34 years
						Total	In elementary and secondary	In higher education	Total	20 and 21 years	22 to 24 years		
1	2	3	4	5	6	7	8	9	10	11	12	13	14
1940	— (†)	— (†)	— (†)	95.0 (†)	79.3 (†)	28.9 (—)	— (†)	— (†)	6.6 (†)	— (†)	— (†)	— (†)	— (†)
1945	— (†)	— (†)	— (†)	98.1 (†)	78.4 (†)	20.7 (—)	— (†)	— (†)	3.9 (†)	— (†)	— (†)	— (†)	— (†)
1947	— (†)	— (†)	73.8 (—)	98.5 (†)	79.3 (†)	24.3 (—)	— (†)	— (†)	10.2 (†)	— (†)	— (†)	3.0 (—)	— (†)
1948	— (†)	— (†)	74.7 (—)	98.1 (†)	81.8 (†)	26.9 (—)	— (†)	— (†)	9.7 (†)	— (†)	— (†)	2.6 (—)	— (†)
1949	— (†)	— (†)	76.2 (—)	98.6 (†)	81.6 (†)	25.3 (—)	— (†)	— (†)	9.2 (†)	— (†)	— (†)	3.8 (—)	— (†)
1950	— (†)	— (†)	74.4 (—)	98.7 (†)	83.7 (†)	29.4 (—)	— (†)	— (†)	9.0 (†)	— (†)	— (†)	3.0 (—)	0.9 (—)
1951	— (†)	— (†)	73.6 (—)	99.1 (†)	85.2 (†)	26.2 (—)	— (†)	— (†)	8.6 (†)	— (†)	— (†)	2.5 (—)	— (†)
1952	— (†)	— (†)	75.2 (—)	98.8 (†)	85.2 (†)	28.8 (—)	— (†)	— (†)	9.7 (†)	— (†)	— (†)	2.6 (—)	1.2 (—)
1953	— (†)	— (†)	78.6 (—)	99.4 (†)	85.9 (†)	31.2 (—)	— (†)	— (†)	11.1 (†)	— (†)	— (†)	2.9 (—)	1.7 (—)
1954	— (†)	— (†)	77.3 (—)	99.4 (†)	87.1 (†)	32.4 (—)	— (†)	— (†)	11.2 (†)	— (†)	— (†)	4.1 (—)	1.5 (—)
1955	— (†)	— (†)	78.1 (—)	99.2 (†)	86.9 (†)	31.5 (—)	— (†)	— (†)	11.1 (†)	— (†)	— (†)	4.2 (—)	1.6 (—)
1956	— (†)	— (†)	77.6 (—)	99.3 (†)	88.2 (†)	35.4 (—)	— (†)	— (†)	12.8 (†)	— (†)	— (†)	5.1 (—)	1.9 (—)
1957	— (†)	— (†)	78.6 (—)	99.5 (†)	89.5 (†)	34.9 (—)	— (†)	— (†)	14.0 (†)	— (†)	— (†)	— (†)	— (†)
1958	— (†)	— (†)	80.4 (—)	99.5 (†)	89.2 (†)	37.6 (—)	— (†)	— (†)	13.4 (†)	— (†)	— (†)	— (†)	— (†)
1959	— (†)	— (†)	80.0 (—)	99.4 (†)	90.2 (†)	36.8 (—)	— (†)	— (†)	12.7 (†)	— (†)	— (†)	— (†)	— (†)
1960	— (†)	— (†)	80.7 (—)	99.5 (†)	90.3 (†)	38.4 (—)	— (†)	— (†)	13.1 (†)	— (†)	— (†)	4.9 (—)	2.4 (—)
1961	— (†)	— (†)	81.7 (—)	99.3 (†)	91.4 (†)	38.0 (—)	— (†)	— (†)	13.7 (†)	— (†)	— (†)	— (†)	— (†)
1962	— (†)	— (†)	82.2 (—)	99.3 (†)	92.0 (†)	41.8 (—)	— (†)	— (†)	15.6 (†)	— (†)	— (†)	— (†)	— (†)
1963	— (†)	— (†)	82.7 (—)	99.3 (†)	92.9 (†)	40.9 (—)	— (†)	— (†)	17.3 (†)	— (†)	— (†)	— (†)	— (†)
1964	— (†)	— (†)	83.3 (—)	99.0 (†)	93.1 (†)	41.6 (—)	— (†)	— (†)	16.8 (†)	— (†)	— (†)	5.2 (—)	2.6 (—)
1965	55.5 (—)	10.6 (—)	84.9 (—)	99.4 (—)	93.2 (—)	46.3 (—)	— (†)	— (†)	19.0 (—)	27.6 (—)	13.2 (—)	6.1 (—)	3.2 (—)
1966	56.1 (—)	12.5 (—)	85.8 (—)	99.3 (—)	93.7 (—)	47.2 (—)	— (†)	— (†)	19.9 (—)	29.9 (—)	13.2 (—)	6.5 (—)	2.7 (—)
1967	56.6 (—)	14.2 (—)	87.4 (—)	99.3 (—)	93.7 (—)	47.6 (—)	— (†)	— (†)	22.0 (—)	33.3 (—)	13.6 (—)	6.6 (—)	4.0 (—)
1968	56.7 (—)	15.7 (—)	87.6 (—)	99.1 (—)	94.2 (—)	50.4 (—)	— (†)	— (†)	21.4 (—)	31.2 (—)	13.8 (—)	7.0 (—)	3.9 (—)
1969	57.0 (—)	16.1 (—)	88.4 (—)	99.2 (—)	94.0 (—)	50.2 (—)	— (†)	— (†)	23.0 (—)	34.1 (—)	15.4 (—)	7.9 (—)	4.8 (—)
1970	56.4 (0.22)	20.5 (0.73)	89.5 (0.53)	99.2 (0.08)	94.1 (0.27)	47.7 (0.85)	10.5 (0.52)	37.3 (0.83)	21.5 (0.47)	31.9 (0.85)	14.9 (0.52)	7.5 (0.33)	4.2 (0.27)
1971	56.2 (0.21)	21.2 (0.75)	91.6 (0.49)	99.1 (0.08)	94.5 (0.26)	49.2 (0.84)	11.5 (0.54)	37.7 (0.81)	21.9 (0.46)	32.2 (0.83)	15.4 (0.51)	8.0 (0.33)	4.9 (0.29)
1972	54.9 (0.21)	24.4 (0.80)	91.9 (0.50)	99.2 (0.08)	93.3 (0.28)	46.3 (0.82)	10.4 (0.50)	35.9 (0.79)	21.6 (0.45)	31.4 (0.79)	14.8 (0.50)	8.6 (0.33)	4.6 (0.27)
1973	53.5 (0.21)	24.2 (0.78)	92.5 (0.49)	99.2 (0.08)	92.9 (0.28)	42.9 (0.81)	10.0 (0.49)	32.9 (0.77)	20.8 (0.44)	30.1 (0.78)	14.5 (0.49)	8.5 (0.32)	4.5 (0.26)
1974	53.6 (0.21)	28.8 (0.83)	94.2 (0.43)	99.3 (0.08)	92.9 (0.28)	43.1 (0.80)	9.9 (0.48)	33.2 (0.76)	21.4 (0.44)	30.2 (0.76)	15.1 (0.50)	9.6 (0.33)	5.7 (0.29)
1975	53.7 (0.21)	31.5 (0.87)	94.7 (0.41)	99.3 (0.08)	93.6 (0.27)	46.9 (0.80)	10.2 (0.48)	36.7 (0.77)	22.4 (0.44)	31.2 (0.76)	16.2 (0.51)	10.1 (0.33)	6.6 (0.30)
1976	53.1 (0.21)	31.3 (0.90)	95.5 (0.38)	99.2 (0.09)	93.7 (0.27)	46.2 (0.79)	10.2 (0.48)	36.0 (0.76)	23.3 (0.44)	32.0 (0.75)	17.1 (0.51)	10.0 (0.33)	6.0 (0.28)
1977	52.5 (0.21)	32.0 (0.93)	95.8 (0.38)	99.4 (0.07)	93.7 (0.27)	46.2 (0.80)	10.4 (0.49)	35.7 (0.77)	22.9 (0.44)	31.8 (0.75)	16.5 (0.51)	10.8 (0.34)	6.9 (0.30)
1978	51.2 (0.21)	34.2 (0.94)	95.3 (0.41)	99.1 (0.09)	93.7 (0.27)	45.4 (0.80)	9.8 (0.48)	35.6 (0.77)	21.8 (0.43)	29.5 (0.73)	16.3 (0.50)	9.4 (0.31)	6.4 (0.28)
1979	50.3 (0.21)	35.1 (0.95)	95.8 (0.40)	99.2 (0.09)	93.6 (0.28)	45.0 (0.79)	10.3 (0.48)	34.6 (0.76)	21.7 (0.42)	30.2 (0.74)	15.8 (0.49)	9.6 (0.31)	6.4 (0.28)
1980	49.7 (0.21)	36.7 (0.95)	95.7 (0.40)	99.3 (0.09)	93.4 (0.29)	46.4 (0.80)	10.5 (0.49)	35.9 (0.77)	22.3 (0.43)	31.0 (0.74)	16.3 (0.49)	9.3 (0.30)	6.4 (0.30)
1981	48.9 (0.21)	36.0 (0.92)	94.0 (0.46)	99.2 (0.09)	94.1 (0.27)	49.0 (0.80)	11.5 (0.51)	37.5 (0.78)	22.5 (0.42)	31.6 (0.73)	16.5 (0.48)	9.0 (0.29)	6.9 (0.27)
1982	48.6 (0.22)	36.4 (0.96)	95.0 (0.44)	99.2 (0.10)	94.4 (0.29)	47.8 (0.85)	11.3 (0.54)	36.5 (0.81)	23.5 (0.45)	34.0 (0.79)	16.8 (0.50)	9.6 (0.31)	6.3 (0.27)
1983	48.4 (0.22)	37.5 (0.94)	95.4 (0.42)	99.2 (0.09)	95.0 (0.27)	50.4 (0.86)	12.8 (0.57)	37.6 (0.83)	22.7 (0.44)	32.5 (0.79)	16.6 (0.50)	9.6 (0.31)	6.4 (0.27)
1984	47.9 (0.22)	36.3 (0.92)	94.5 (0.45)	99.2 (0.09)	94.7 (0.28)	50.1 (0.88)	11.5 (0.56)	38.6 (0.86)	23.7 (0.45)	33.9 (0.80)	17.3 (0.51)	9.1 (0.30)	6.3 (0.27)

See notes at end of table.

Table 7. Percentage of the population 3 to 34 years old enrolled in school, by age group: Selected years, 1940 through 2007—Continued

Year	Total, 3 to 34 years	3 and 4 years	5 and 6 years	7 to 13 years	14 to 17 years	13 and 19 years old			20 to 24 years old			25 to 29 years	30 to 34 years
						Total	In elementary and secondary	In higher education	Total	20 and 21 years	22 to 24 years		
1	2	3	4	5	6	7	8	9	10	11	12	13	14
1985	48.3 (0.22)	38.9 (0.94)	96.1 (0.38)	99.2 (0.09)	94.9 (0.27)	51.6 (0.89)	11.2 (0.56)	40.4 (0.38)	24.0 (0.46)	35.3 (0.83)	16.9 (0.51)	9.2 (0.30)	6.1 (0.26)
1986	48.2 (0.22)	38.9 (0.93)	95.3 (0.40)	99.2 (0.10)	94.9 (0.28)	54.6 (0.90)	13.1 (0.61)	41.5 (0.89)	23.6 (0.46)	33.0 (0.83)	17.9 (0.53)	8.8 (0.29)	6.0 (0.25)
1987	48.6 (0.22)	38.3 (0.93)	95.1 (0.41)	99.5 (0.07)	95.0 (0.28)	55.6 (0.89)	13.1 (0.60)	42.5 (0.89)	25.5 (0.48)	38.7 (0.88)	17.5 (0.53)	9.0 (0.30)	5.8 (0.25)
1988	48.7 (0.24)	38.2 (1.01)	96.0 (0.41)	99.7 (0.07)	95.1 (0.30)	55.6 (0.96)	13.9 (0.67)	41.8 (0.95)	26.1 (0.53)	39.1 (0.96)	18.2 (0.60)	8.3 (0.31)	5.9 (0.27)
1989	49.0 (0.22)	39.1 (1.00)	95.2 (0.44)	99.3 (0.09)	95.7 (0.29)	56.0 (0.95)	14.4 (0.68)	41.6 (0.95)	27.0 (0.55)	38.5 (0.97)	19.9 (0.63)	9.3 (0.33)	5.7 (0.26)
1990	50.2 (0.23)	44.4 (0.99)	96.5 (0.37)	99.6 (0.06)	95.8 (0.28)	57.2 (0.94)	14.5 (0.67)	42.7 (0.94)	28.6 (0.54)	39.7 (0.92)	21.0 (0.63)	9.7 (0.33)	5.8 (0.25)
1991	50.7 (0.22)	40.5 (0.96)	95.4 (0.41)	99.6 (0.06)	96.0 (0.27)	59.6 (0.96)	15.6 (0.71)	44.0 (0.97)	30.2 (0.55)	42.0 (0.92)	22.2 (0.64)	10.2 (0.34)	6.2 (0.26)
1992	51.4 (0.22)	39.7 (0.95)	95.5 (0.41)	99.4 (0.08)	96.7 (0.25)	61.4 (0.96)	17.1 (0.74)	44.3 (0.98)	31.6 (0.56)	44.0 (0.95)	23.7 (0.65)	9.8 (0.34)	6.1 (0.26)
1993	51.8 (0.22)	40.4 (0.93)	95.4 (0.41)	99.5 (0.07)	96.5 (0.25)	61.6 (0.95)	17.2 (0.74)	44.4 (0.97)	30.8 (0.56)	42.7 (0.97)	23.6 (0.65)	10.2 (0.35)	5.9 (0.25)
1994	53.3 (0.21)	47.3[1] (0.87)	96.7 (0.32)	99.4 (0.08)	96.6 (0.22)	60.2 (0.87)	16.2 (0.65)	43.9 (0.88)	32.0 (0.51)	44.9 (0.88)	24.0 (0.59)	10.8 (0.33)	6.7 (0.25)
1995	53.7 (0.21)	48.7[1] (0.87)	96.0 (0.34)	98.9 (0.10)	96.3 (0.23)	59.4 (0.85)	16.3 (0.64)	43.1 (0.86)	31.5 (0.52)	44.9 (0.89)	23.2 (0.60)	11.6 (0.34)	5.9 (0.24)
1996	54.1 (0.22)	48.3[1] (0.91)	94.0 (0.43)	97.7 (0.15)	95.4 (0.26)	61.5 (0.87)	16.7 (0.67)	44.9 (0.89)	32.5 (0.55)	44.4 (0.93)	24.8 (0.65)	11.9 (0.36)	6.1 (0.25)
1997	55.6 (0.22)	52.6[1] (0.92)	96.5 (0.33)	99.1 (0.09)	96.6 (0.22)	61.5 (0.86)	16.7 (0.66)	44.7 (0.88)	34.3 (0.55)	45.9 (0.91)	26.4 (0.66)	11.8 (0.36)	5.7 (0.25)
1998	55.8 (0.22)	52.1[1] (0.92)	95.6 (0.37)	98.9 (0.10)	96.1 (0.24)	62.2 (0.84)	15.7 (0.63)	46.4 (0.86)	33.0 (0.55)	44.8 (0.91)	24.9 (0.65)	11.9 (0.37)	6.6 (0.27)
1999	56.0 (0.22)	54.2[1] (0.93)	96.0 (0.36)	98.7 (0.11)	95.8 (0.24)	60.6 (0.84)	16.5 (0.64)	44.1 (0.85)	32.8 (0.54)	45.3 (0.90)	24.5 (0.64)	11.1 (0.36)	6.2 (0.27)
2000	55.9 (0.22)	52.1[1] (0.93)	95.6 (0.38)	98.2 (0.13)	95.7 (0.25)	61.2 (0.84)	16.5 (0.64)	44.7 (0.85)	32.5 (0.53)	44.1 (0.88)	24.6 (0.63)	11.4 (0.37)	6.7 (0.28)
2001	56.4 (0.22)	52.4[1] (0.88)	95.3 (0.37)	98.3 (0.12)	95.8 (0.24)	61.1 (0.83)	17.1 (0.64)	44.0 (0.84)	34.1 (0.53)	46.1 (0.87)	25.5 (0.64)	11.8 (0.38)	6.9 (0.28)
2002	56.2 (0.21)	56.3[1] (0.89)	95.5 (0.37)	98.3 (0.12)	96.4 (0.22)	63.3 (0.83)	18.0 (0.67)	45.3 (0.86)	34.4 (0.52)	47.8 (0.87)	25.6 (0.62)	12.1 (0.37)	6.6 (0.27)
2003	56.2 (0.20)	55.1[1] (0.85)	94.5 (0.40)	98.3 (0.12)	96.2 (0.21)	64.5 (0.80)	17.9 (0.64)	46.6 (0.84)	35.6 (0.50)	48.3 (0.83)	27.8 (0.59)	11.8 (0.34)	6.8 (0.26)
2004	56.2 (0.20)	54.0[1] (0.85)	95.4 (0.37)	98.4 (0.12)	96.5 (0.21)	64.4 (0.80)	16.6 (0.62)	47.8 (0.83)	35.2 (0.49)	48.9 (0.82)	26.3 (0.58)	13.0 (0.35)	6.6 (0.26)
2005	56.5 (0.20)	53.6[1] (0.86)	95.4 (0.37)	98.6 (0.11)	96.5 (0.20)	67.6 (0.79)	18.3 (0.65)	49.3 (0.84)	36.1 (0.49)	48.7 (0.80)	27.3 (0.59)	11.9 (0.34)	6.9 (0.27)
2006	56.0 (0.20)	55.7[1] (0.86)	94.6 (0.39)	98.3 (0.12)	96.4 (0.21)	65.5 (0.77)	19.3 (0.64)	46.2 (0.81)	35.0 (0.49)	47.5 (0.81)	26.7 (0.58)	11.7 (0.33)	7.2 (0.27)
2007	56.1 (0.20)	54.5[1] (0.86)	94.7 (0.39)	98.4 (0.11)	96.4 (0.21)	66.8 (0.75)	17.9 (0.61)	46.9 (0.80)	35.7 (0.49)	48.4 (0.81)	27.3 (0.59)	12.4 (0.33)	7.2 (0.27)

—Not available.
†Not applicable.
[1]Preprimary enrollment collected using new procedures. Data may not be comparable to figures for earlier years.
NOTE: Data for 1940 are for April. Data for all other years are as of October. Includes enrollment in any type of graded public, parochial, or other private schools. Includes nursery schools, kindergartens, elementary schools, high schools, colleges, universities, and professional schools. Attendance may be on either a full-time or part-time basis and during the day or night.

Enrollments in "special" schools, such as trade schools, business colleges, or correspondence schools, are not included.
Standard errors appear in parentheses.
SOURCE: U.S. Department of Commerce, Census Bureau, *Historical Statistics of the United States, Colonial Times to 1970; Current Population Reports*, Series P-20, various years; and Current Population Survey, October, 1970 through 2007. (This table was prepared July 2008.)

Table 8. Percentage of persons age 25 and over and 25 to 29, by race/ethnicity, years of school completed, and sex: Selected years, 1910 through 2008

Age, year, and sex	Total — Less than 5 years of elementary school	Total — High school completion or higher[2]	Total — Bachelor's or higher degree[3]	White[1] — Less than 5 years of elementary school	White[1] — High school completion or higher[2]	White[1] — Bachelor's or higher degree[3]	Black[1] — Less than 5 years of elementary school	Black[1] — High school completion or higher[2]	Black[1] — Bachelor's or higher degree[3]	Hispanic — Less than 5 years of elementary school	Hispanic — High school completion or higher[2]	Hispanic — Bachelor's or higher degree[3]
1	2	3	4	5	6	7	8	9	10	11	12	13
Total, 25 and over												
1910[4]	23.8 (—)	13.5 (—)	2.7 (—)	— (†)	— (†)	— (†)	— (†)	— (†)	— (†)	— (†)	— (†)	— (†)
1920[4]	22.0 (—)	16.4 (—)	3.3 (—)	— (†)	— (†)	— (†)	— (†)	— (†)	— (†)	— (†)	— (†)	— (†)
1930[4]	17.5 (—)	19.1 (—)	3.9 (—)	— (†)	— (†)	— (†)	— (†)	— (†)	— (†)	— (†)	— (†)	— (†)
April 1940	13.7 (—)	24.5 (—)	4.6 (—)	10.9 (—)	26.1 (—)	4.9 (—)	41.8 (—)	7.7 (—)	1.3 (—)	— (†)	— (†)	— (†)
April 1950	11.1 (—)	34.3 (—)	6.2 (—)	8.9 (—)	36.4 (—)	6.6 (—)	32.6 (—)	13.7 (—)	2.2 (—)	— (†)	— (†)	— (†)
April 1960	8.3 (—)	41.1 (—)	7.7 (—)	6.7 (—)	43.2 (—)	8.1 (—)	23.5 (—)	21.7 (—)	3.5 (—)	— (†)	— (†)	— (†)
March 1970	5.3 (—)	55.2 (—)	11.0 (—)	4.2 (—)	57.4 (—)	11.6 (—)	14.7 (—)	36.1 (—)	6.1 (—)	— (†)	— (†)	— (†)
March 1975	4.2 (—)	62.5 (—)	13.9 (—)	2.6 (—)	65.8 (—)	14.9 (—)	12.3 (—)	42.6 (—)	6.4 (—)	18.2 (—)	38.5 (—)	6.6 (—)
March 1980	3.4 (0.08)	68.6 (0.20)	17.0 (0.16)	1.9 (0.07)	71.9 (0.21)	18.4 (0.18)	9.1 (0.47)	51.4 (0.81)	7.9 (0.44)	15.8 (0.87)	44.5 (1.18)	7.6 (0.63)
March 1985	2.7 (0.07)	73.9 (0.18)	19.4 (0.16)	1.4 (0.05)	77.5 (0.19)	20.8 (0.19)	6.1 (0.36)	59.9 (0.74)	11.1 (0.47)	13.5 (0.68)	47.9 (0.99)	8.5 (0.55)
March 1986	2.7 (0.07)	74.7 (0.18)	19.4 (0.16)	1.4 (0.05)	78.2 (0.19)	20.9 (0.19)	5.3 (0.33)	62.5 (0.72)	10.9 (0.47)	12.9 (0.64)	48.5 (0.96)	8.4 (0.53)
March 1987	2.4 (0.06)	75.6 (0.17)	19.9 (0.16)	1.3 (0.05)	79.0 (0.18)	21.4 (0.19)	4.9 (0.32)	63.6 (0.71)	10.8 (0.46)	11.9 (0.61)	50.9 (0.94)	8.6 (0.53)
March 1988	2.4 (0.06)	76.2 (0.17)	20.3 (0.16)	1.2 (0.05)	79.8 (0.18)	21.8 (0.19)	4.8 (0.31)	63.5 (0.70)	11.2 (0.46)	12.2 (0.60)	51.0 (0.92)	10.0 (0.55)
March 1989	2.5 (0.06)	76.9 (0.17)	21.1 (0.16)	1.2 (0.05)	80.7 (0.18)	22.8 (0.19)	5.2 (0.32)	64.7 (0.69)	11.7 (0.46)	12.2 (0.58)	50.9 (0.89)	9.9 (0.53)
March 1990	2.4 (0.06)	77.6 (0.17)	21.3 (0.16)	1.1 (0.05)	81.4 (0.17)	23.1 (0.19)	5.1 (0.31)	66.2 (0.67)	11.3 (0.45)	12.3 (0.58)	50.8 (0.88)	9.2 (0.51)
March 1991	2.4 (0.06)	78.4 (0.16)	21.4 (0.16)	1.1 (0.05)	82.4 (0.17)	23.3 (0.19)	4.7 (0.30)	66.8 (0.66)	11.5 (0.45)	12.5 (0.57)	51.3 (0.86)	9.7 (0.51)
March 1992	2.1 (0.06)	79.4 (0.16)	21.4 (0.16)	0.9 (0.04)	83.4 (0.16)	23.2 (0.19)	3.9 (0.27)	67.7 (0.65)	11.9 (0.45)	11.8 (0.55)	52.6 (0.85)	9.3 (0.49)
March 1993	2.1 (0.06)	80.2 (0.16)	21.9 (0.16)	0.8 (0.04)	84.1 (0.16)	23.8 (0.19)	3.7 (0.26)	70.5 (0.63)	12.2 (0.45)	11.8 (0.54)	53.1 (0.83)	9.0 (0.48)
March 1994	1.9 (0.05)	80.9 (0.15)	22.2 (0.16)	0.8 (0.04)	84.9 (0.16)	24.3 (0.19)	2.7 (0.22)	73.0 (0.61)	12.9 (0.46)	10.8 (0.48)	53.3 (0.78)	9.1 (0.45)
March 1995	1.8 (0.05)	81.7 (0.15)	23.0 (0.16)	0.7 (0.04)	85.9 (0.16)	25.4 (0.19)	2.5 (0.21)	73.8 (0.61)	13.3 (0.47)	10.6 (0.48)	53.4 (0.78)	9.3 (0.45)
March 1996	1.8 (0.05)	81.7 (0.16)	23.6 (0.17)	0.6 (0.04)	86.0 (0.16)	25.9 (0.20)	2.2 (0.18)	74.6 (0.53)	13.8 (0.42)	10.3 (0.42)	53.1 (0.68)	9.3 (0.40)
March 1997	1.7 (0.05)	82.1 (0.14)	23.9 (0.16)	0.6 (0.03)	86.3 (0.15)	26.2 (0.19)	2.0 (0.17)	75.3 (0.52)	13.3 (0.41)	9.4 (0.32)	54.7 (0.54)	10.3 (0.33)
March 1998	1.6 (0.05)	82.8 (0.14)	24.4 (0.16)	0.6 (0.03)	87.1 (0.14)	26.6 (0.19)	1.7 (0.15)	76.4 (0.50)	14.8 (0.42)	9.3 (0.31)	55.5 (0.53)	11.0 (0.33)
March 1999	1.6 (0.05)	83.4 (0.14)	25.2 (0.16)	0.6 (0.03)	87.7 (0.14)	27.7 (0.19)	1.7 (0.15)	77.4 (0.49)	15.5 (0.43)	9.0 (0.30)	56.1 (0.52)	10.9 (0.33)
March 2000	1.6 (0.05)	84.1 (0.13)	25.6 (0.16)	0.5 (0.03)	88.4 (0.14)	28.1 (0.19)	1.6 (0.15)	78.9 (0.48)	16.6 (0.44)	8.7 (0.29)	57.0 (0.51)	10.6 (0.32)
March 2001	1.6 (0.05)	84.3 (0.13)	26.1 (0.16)	0.5 (0.03)	88.7 (0.13)	28.6 (0.19)	1.3 (0.13)	79.5 (0.47)	16.1 (0.43)	9.3 (0.29)	56.5 (0.50)	11.2 (0.32)
March 2002	1.6 (0.03)	84.1 (0.09)	26.7 (0.11)	0.5 (0.02)	88.7 (0.10)	29.4 (0.14)	1.6 (0.11)	79.2 (0.34)	17.2 (0.31)	8.7 (0.19)	57.0 (0.34)	11.1 (0.21)
March 2003	1.6 (0.03)	84.6 (0.09)	27.2 (0.11)	0.5 (0.02)	89.4 (0.09)	30.0 (0.14)	1.5 (0.10)	80.3 (0.33)	17.4 (0.31)	8.2 (0.18)	57.0 (0.33)	11.4 (0.21)
March 2004	1.5 (0.03)	85.2 (0.09)	27.7 (0.11)	0.4 (0.02)	90.0 (0.09)	30.6 (0.14)	1.3 (0.09)	81.1 (0.32)	17.7 (0.31)	8.1 (0.18)	58.4 (0.32)	12.1 (0.21)
March 2005	1.6 (0.03)	85.2 (0.09)	27.6 (0.11)	0.5 (0.02)	90.1 (0.09)	30.5 (0.14)	1.5 (0.10)	81.5 (0.32)	17.7 (0.31)	7.9 (0.17)	58.5 (0.32)	12.0 (0.21)
March 2006	1.5 (0.03)	85.5 (0.09)	28.0 (0.11)	0.4 (0.02)	90.5 (0.09)	31.0 (0.14)	1.5 (0.10)	81.2 (0.32)	18.6 (0.31)	7.6 (0.17)	59.3 (0.31)	12.4 (0.21)
March 2007	1.5 (0.03)	85.7 (0.09)	28.7 (0.11)	0.4 (0.02)	90.6 (0.09)	31.8 (0.14)	1.2 (0.09)	82.8 (0.30)	18.7 (0.31)	6.9 (0.16)	60.3 (0.30)	12.7 (0.20)
March 2008	1.3 (0.03)	86.6 (0.08)	29.4 (0.11)	0.4 (0.02)	91.5 (0.08)	32.6 (0.14)	1.0 (0.08)	83.3 (0.30)	19.7 (0.32)	6.3 (0.15)	62.3 (0.29)	13.3 (0.21)
Total, 25 to 29												
1920[4]	— (†)	— (†)	— (†)	12.9 (—)	22.0 (—)	4.5 (—)	44.6 (—)	6.3 (—)	1.2 (—)	— (†)	— (†)	— (†)
April 1940	5.9 (—)	38.1 (—)	5.9 (—)	3.4 (—)	41.2 (—)	6.4 (—)	27.0 (—)	12.3 (—)	1.6 (—)	— (†)	— (†)	— (†)
April 1950	4.6 (—)	52.8 (—)	7.7 (—)	3.3 (—)	56.3 (—)	8.2 (—)	16.1 (—)	23.6 (—)	2.8 (—)	— (†)	— (†)	— (†)
April 1960	2.8 (—)	60.7 (—)	11.0 (—)	2.2 (—)	63.7 (—)	11.8 (—)	7.2 (—)	38.6 (—)	5.4 (—)	— (†)	— (†)	— (†)
March 1970	1.1 (—)	75.4 (—)	16.4 (—)	0.9 (—)	77.8 (—)	17.3 (—)	2.2 (—)	58.4 (—)	10.0 (—)	— (†)	— (†)	— (†)
March 1975	1.0 (—)	83.1 (—)	21.9 (—)	0.6 (—)	86.6 (—)	23.8 (—)	0.5 (—)	71.1 (—)	10.5 (—)	8.0 (—)	53.1 (—)	8.8 (—)
March 1980	0.8 (0.10)	85.4 (0.40)	22.5 (0.47)	0.3 (0.07)	89.2 (0.40)	25.0 (0.55)	0.6 (0.31)	76.7 (1.64)	11.6 (1.24)	6.7 (1.31)	58.0 (2.59)	7.7 (1.39)
March 1985	0.7 (0.09)	86.1 (0.37)	22.2 (0.45)	0.2 (0.06)	89.5 (0.38)	24.4 (0.53)	0.4 (0.23)	80.5 (1.42)	11.6 (1.15)	6.0 (1.05)	60.9 (2.17)	11.1 (1.39)
March 1986	0.9 (0.10)	86.1 (0.37)	22.4 (0.45)	0.4 (0.07)	89.6 (0.37)	25.2 (0.53)	0.5 (0.26)	83.5 (1.32)	11.8 (1.15)	5.6 (0.97)	59.1 (2.07)	9.0 (1.21)
March 1987	0.9 (0.10)	86.0 (0.37)	22.0 (0.44)	0.4 (0.08)	89.4 (0.38)	24.6 (0.53)	0.4 (0.23)	83.4 (1.32)	11.5 (1.13)	4.8 (0.88)	59.8 (2.04)	8.7 (1.17)
March 1988	1.0 (0.11)	85.9 (0.37)	22.7 (0.45)	0.3 (0.07)	89.7 (0.38)	25.1 (0.54)	0.3 (0.21)	80.9 (1.39)	12.0 (1.15)	6.0 (0.96)	62.3 (1.96)	11.3 (1.28)
March 1989	1.0 (0.11)	85.5 (0.38)	23.4 (0.45)	0.3 (0.07)	89.3 (0.38)	26.3 (0.55)	0.5 (0.25)	82.3 (1.35)	12.6 (1.17)	5.4 (0.89)	61.0 (1.92)	10.1 (1.19)
March 1990	1.2 (0.12)	85.7 (0.38)	23.2 (0.46)	0.3 (0.07)	90.1 (0.37)	26.4 (0.55)	1.0 (0.36)	81.7 (1.37)	13.4 (1.20)	7.3 (1.02)	58.2 (1.94)	8.1 (1.07)
March 1991	1.0 (0.11)	85.4 (0.39)	23.2 (0.46)	0.4 (0.08)	89.8 (0.39)	26.7 (0.56)	0.5 (0.26)	81.8 (1.36)	11.0 (1.10)	5.8 (0.93)	56.7 (1.96)	9.2 (1.15)
March 1992	0.9 (0.10)	86.3 (0.38)	23.6 (0.47)	0.3 (0.07)	90.7 (0.38)	27.2 (0.58)	0.8 (0.32)	80.9 (1.41)	11.0 (1.12)	5.2 (0.88)	60.9 (1.93)	9.5 (1.16)
March 1993	0.7 (0.09)	86.7 (0.38)	23.7 (0.48)	0.3 (0.07)	91.2 (0.37)	27.2 (0.59)	0.2 (0.18)	82.6 (1.36)	13.3 (1.22)	4.0 (0.76)	60.9 (1.90)	8.3 (1.08)
March 1994	0.8 (0.10)	86.1 (0.39)	23.3 (0.47)	0.2 (0.07)	91.1 (0.38)	27.1 (0.60)	0.6 (0.28)	84.1 (1.31)	13.6 (1.23)	3.6 (0.66)	60.3 (1.75)	8.0 (0.97)
March 1995	0.9 (0.11)	86.8 (0.39)	24.7 (0.49)	0.3 (0.08)	92.5 (0.36)	28.8 (0.62)	0.2 (0.17)	86.7 (1.23)	15.4 (1.31)	4.9 (0.79)	57.1 (1.80)	8.9 (1.04)

See notes at end of table.

Table 8. Percentage of persons age 25 and over and 25 to 29, by race/ethnicity, years of school completed, and sex: Selected years, 1910 through 2008—Continued

Age, year, and sex	Total			White[1]			Black[1]			Hispanic		
	Less than 5 years of elementary school	High school completion or higher[2]	Bachelor's or higher degree[3]	Less than 5 years of elementary school	High school completion or higher[2]	Bachelor's or higher degree[3]	Less than 5 years of elementary school	High school completion or higher[2]	Bachelor's or higher degree[3]	Less than 5 years of elementary school	High school completion or higher[2]	Bachelor's or higher degree[3]
1	2	3	4	5	6	7	8	9	10	11	12	13
March 1996.....	0.8 (0.11)	87.3 (0.40)	27.1 (0.53)	0.2 (0.07)	92.6 (0.38)	31.6 (0.67)	0.4 (0.20)	86.0 (1.14)	14.6 (1.16)	4.3 (0.65)	61.1 (1.58)	10.0 (0.97)
March 1997.....	0.8 (0.10)	87.4 (0.37)	27.8 (0.50)	0.1 (0.05)	92.9 (0.35)	32.6 (0.63)	0.6 (0.25)	86.9 (1.10)	14.2 (1.14)	4.2 (0.51)	61.8 (1.24)	11.0 (0.80)
March 1998.....	0.7 (0.09)	88.1 (0.36)	27.3 (0.50)	0.1 (0.05)	93.6 (0.34)	32.3 (0.64)	0.4 (0.21)	88.2 (1.04)	15.8 (1.18)	3.7 (0.48)	62.8 (1.23)	10.4 (0.78)
March 1999.....	0.6 (0.09)	87.8 (0.37)	28.2 (0.51)	0.1 (0.05)	93.0 (0.35)	33.6 (0.66)	0.2 (0.15)	88.7 (1.03)	15.0 (1.16)	3.2 (0.45)	61.6 (1.26)	8.9 (0.74)
March 2000.....	0.7 (0.09)	88.1 (0.37)	29.1 (0.52)	0.1 (0.04)	94.0 (0.33)	34.0 (0.67)	# (†)	86.8 (1.13)	17.8 (1.28)	3.8 (0.48)	62.8 (1.22)	9.7 (0.75)
March 2001.....	0.8 (0.11)	87.7 (0.38)	28.6 (0.52)	0.2 (0.06)	93.3 (0.36)	33.0 (0.68)	0.1 (0.10)	87.0 (1.11)	17.8 (1.27)	4.7 (0.54)	63.2 (1.23)	11.1 (0.80)
March 2002.....	1.1 (0.08)	86.4 (0.28)	29.3 (0.37)	0.1 (0.04)	93.0 (0.26)	35.9 (0.50)	0.6 (0.19)	87.6 (0.80)	18.0 (0.94)	4.7 (0.34)	62.4 (0.78)	8.9 (0.46)
March 2003.....	1.0 (0.08)	86.5 (0.27)	28.4 (0.36)	0.2 (0.04)	93.7 (0.25)	34.2 (0.49)	0.6 (0.19)	88.5 (0.78)	17.5 (0.93)	4.0 (0.30)	61.7 (0.75)	10.0 (0.47)
March 2004.....	1.1 (0.08)	86.6 (0.27)	28.7 (0.36)	0.3 (0.05)	93.3 (0.26)	34.5 (0.49)	0.3 (0.13)	88.7 (0.76)	17.1 (0.90)	4.1 (0.31)	62.4 (0.75)	10.9 (0.48)
March 2005.....	1.0 (0.08)	86.1 (0.27)	28.6 (0.36)	0.3 (0.05)	92.8 (0.26)	34.1 (0.48)	0.4 (0.15)	86.9 (0.79)	17.5 (0.89)	3.6 (0.28)	63.3 (0.74)	11.2 (0.48)
March 2006.....	0.9 (0.07)	86.4 (0.27)	28.4 (0.35)	0.2 (0.04)	93.4 (0.25)	34.3 (0.48)	0.4 (0.14)	86.3 (0.79)	18.7 (0.90)	3.5 (0.28)	63.2 (0.72)	9.5 (0.44)
March 2007.....	1.0 (0.08)	87.0 (0.26)	29.6 (0.35)	0.2 (0.04)	93.5 (0.25)	35.5 (0.47)	0.2 (0.11)	87.7 (0.75)	19.5 (0.90)	3.9 (0.29)	65.0 (0.71)	11.6 (0.47)
March 2008.....	0.6 (0.06)	87.8 (0.25)	30.8 (0.35)	0.1 (0.03)	93.7 (0.24)	37.1 (0.47)	0.3 (0.12)	87.5 (0.74)	20.4 (0.91)	2.5 (0.23)	68.3 (0.68)	12.4 (0.48)
Males, 25 and over												
April 1940	15.1 (—)	22.7 (—)	5.5 (—)	12.0 (—)	24.2 (—)	5.9 (—)	46.2 (—)	6.9 (—)	1.4 (—)	— (†)	— (†)	— (†)
April 1950	12.2 (—)	32.6 (—)	7.3 (—)	9.8 (—)	34.6 (—)	7.9 (—)	36.9 (—)	12.6 (—)	2.1 (—)	— (†)	— (†)	— (†)
April 1960	9.4 (—)	39.5 (—)	9.7 (—)	7.4 (—)	41.6 (—)	10.3 (—)	27.7 (—)	20.0 (—)	3.5 (—)	— (†)	— (†)	— (†)
March 1970	5.9 (—)	55.0 (—)	14.1 (—)	4.5 (—)	57.2 (—)	15.0 (—)	17.9 (—)	35.4 (—)	6.8 (—)	— (†)	— (†)	— (†)
March 1980	3.6 (0.12)	69.2 (0.30)	20.9 (0.26)	2.0 (0.10)	72.4 (0.31)	22.8 (0.29)	11.3 (0.78)	51.2 (1.23)	7.7 (0.66)	16.5 (1.30)	44.9 (1.74)	9.2 (1.01)
March 1990	2.7 (0.09)	77.7 (0.24)	24.4 (0.25)	1.3 (0.07)	81.6 (0.25)	26.7 (0.29)	6.4 (0.53)	65.8 (1.03)	11.9 (0.70)	12.9 (0.85)	50.3 (1.27)	9.8 (0.76)
March 1995	2.0 (0.08)	81.7 (0.22)	26.0 (0.25)	0.8 (0.06)	86.0 (0.22)	28.9 (0.29)	3.4 (0.37)	73.5 (0.91)	13.7 (0.71)	10.8 (0.69)	52.9 (1.11)	10.1 (0.67)
March 1996.....	1.9 (0.08)	81.9 (0.23)	26.0 (0.26)	0.7 (0.06)	86.1 (0.23)	28.8 (0.30)	2.9 (0.31)	74.6 (0.80)	12.5 (0.61)	10.1 (0.59)	53.0 (0.97)	10.3 (0.59)
March 1997.....	1.8 (0.07)	82.0 (0.21)	26.2 (0.24)	0.6 (0.05)	86.3 (0.21)	29.0 (0.28)	2.9 (0.30)	73.8 (0.79)	12.5 (0.60)	9.2 (0.44)	54.9 (0.76)	10.6 (0.47)
March 1998.....	1.7 (0.07)	82.8 (0.20)	26.5 (0.24)	0.7 (0.05)	87.1 (0.21)	29.3 (0.28)	2.3 (0.27)	75.4 (0.77)	14.0 (0.62)	9.3 (0.44)	55.7 (0.74)	11.1 (0.47)
March 1999.....	1.6 (0.07)	83.4 (0.20)	27.5 (0.24)	0.6 (0.05)	87.7 (0.20)	30.6 (0.28)	2.0 (0.25)	77.2 (0.74)	14.3 (0.62)	9.0 (0.43)	56.0 (0.75)	10.7 (0.46)
March 2000.....	1.6 (0.07)	84.2 (0.19)	27.8 (0.24)	0.6 (0.05)	88.5 (0.20)	30.8 (0.28)	2.1 (0.25)	79.1 (0.72)	16.4 (0.65)	8.2 (0.40)	56.6 (0.73)	10.7 (0.45)
March 2001.....	1.6 (0.07)	84.4 (0.19)	28.0 (0.24)	0.6 (0.05)	88.6 (0.19)	30.9 (0.28)	1.7 (0.22)	80.6 (0.69)	15.9 (0.64)	9.4 (0.42)	55.6 (0.72)	11.1 (0.45)
March 2002.....	1.7 (0.05)	83.8 (0.14)	28.5 (0.17)	0.5 (0.03)	88.5 (0.14)	31.7 (0.20)	1.9 (0.17)	79.0 (0.51)	16.5 (0.47)	9.0 (0.28)	56.1 (0.48)	11.0 (0.30)
March 2003.....	1.7 (0.05)	84.1 (0.13)	28.9 (0.17)	0.5 (0.03)	89.0 (0.14)	32.3 (0.20)	1.9 (0.17)	79.9 (0.50)	16.8 (0.47)	8.3 (0.26)	56.3 (0.46)	11.2 (0.29)
March 2004.....	1.7 (0.05)	84.8 (0.13)	29.4 (0.17)	0.5 (0.03)	89.9 (0.13)	32.9 (0.20)	1.5 (0.15)	80.8 (0.49)	16.6 (0.46)	8.4 (0.25)	57.3 (0.45)	11.8 (0.30)
March 2005.....	1.7 (0.05)	84.9 (0.13)	28.9 (0.17)	0.5 (0.03)	89.9 (0.13)	32.3 (0.20)	1.7 (0.16)	81.4 (0.48)	16.1 (0.45)	8.0 (0.24)	58.0 (0.44)	11.8 (0.29)
March 2006.....	1.6 (0.05)	85.0 (0.13)	29.2 (0.16)	0.4 (0.03)	90.2 (0.13)	32.8 (0.20)	1.7 (0.16)	80.7 (0.48)	17.5 (0.46)	7.8 (0.23)	58.5 (0.43)	11.9 (0.28)
March 2007.....	1.6 (0.04)	85.0 (0.13)	29.5 (0.16)	0.4 (0.03)	90.2 (0.13)	33.2 (0.20)	1.3 (0.14)	82.5 (0.46)	18.1 (0.47)	7.3 (0.22)	58.2 (0.42)	11.8 (0.28)
March 2008.....	1.4 (0.04)	85.9 (0.12)	30.1 (0.16)	0.4 (0.03)	91.1 (0.12)	33.8 (0.20)	1.1 (0.12)	82.1 (0.46)	18.7 (0.47)	6.5 (0.21)	60.9 (0.41)	12.6 (0.28)
Females, 25 and over												
April 1940	12.4 (—)	26.3 (—)	3.8 (—)	9.8 (—)	28.1 (—)	4.0 (—)	37.5 (—)	8.4 (—)	1.2 (—)	— (†)	— (†)	— (†)
April 1950	10.0 (—)	36.0 (—)	5.2 (—)	8.1 (—)	38.2 (—)	5.4 (—)	28.6 (—)	14.7 (—)	2.4 (—)	— (†)	— (†)	— (†)
April 1960	7.4 (—)	42.5 (—)	5.8 (—)	6.0 (—)	44.7 (—)	6.0 (—)	19.7 (—)	23.1 (—)	3.6 (—)	— (†)	— (†)	— (†)
March 1970	4.7 (—)	55.4 (—)	8.2 (—)	3.9 (—)	57.7 (—)	8.6 (—)	11.9 (—)	36.6 (—)	5.6 (—)	— (†)	— (†)	— (†)
March 1980	3.2 (0.11)	68.1 (0.28)	13.6 (0.21)	1.8 (0.09)	71.5 (0.30)	14.4 (0.23)	7.4 (0.58)	51.5 (1.10)	8.1 (0.60)	15.3 (1.20)	44.2 (1.66)	6.2 (0.80)
March 1990	2.2 (0.08)	77.5 (0.23)	18.4 (0.22)	1.0 (0.06)	81.3 (0.24)	19.8 (0.25)	4.0 (0.38)	66.5 (0.92)	10.8 (0.60)	11.7 (0.81)	51.3 (1.25)	8.7 (0.70)
March 1995	1.7 (0.07)	81.6 (0.21)	20.2 (0.22)	0.6 (0.05)	85.8 (0.22)	22.1 (0.26)	1.7 (0.24)	74.1 (0.81)	13.0 (0.62)	10.4 (0.67)	53.8 (1.09)	8.4 (0.61)
March 1996.....	1.7 (0.07)	81.6 (0.22)	21.4 (0.23)	0.5 (0.05)	85.9 (0.22)	23.2 (0.27)	1.6 (0.21)	74.6 (0.71)	14.8 (0.58)	10.5 (0.59)	53.3 (0.97)	8.3 (0.53)
March 1997.....	1.6 (0.06)	82.2 (0.20)	21.7 (0.21)	0.5 (0.04)	86.3 (0.20)	23.7 (0.25)	1.3 (0.18)	76.5 (0.68)	14.0 (0.56)	9.5 (0.45)	54.6 (0.76)	10.1 (0.46)
March 1998.....	1.6 (0.06)	82.9 (0.19)	22.4 (0.21)	0.6 (0.04)	87.1 (0.20)	24.1 (0.25)	1.2 (0.17)	77.1 (0.67)	15.4 (0.58)	9.2 (0.44)	55.3 (0.75)	10.9 (0.47)
March 1999.....	1.5 (0.06)	83.3 (0.19)	23.1 (0.22)	0.5 (0.04)	87.6 (0.19)	25.0 (0.26)	1.5 (0.19)	77.5 (0.66)	16.5 (0.59)	9.0 (0.42)	56.3 (0.73)	11.0 (0.46)
March 2000.....	1.5 (0.06)	84.0 (0.19)	23.6 (0.22)	0.4 (0.04)	88.4 (0.19)	25.5 (0.26)	1.1 (0.17)	78.7 (0.64)	16.8 (0.59)	9.3 (0.42)	57.5 (0.71)	10.6 (0.44)
March 2001.....	1.5 (0.06)	84.2 (0.18)	24.3 (0.22)	0.4 (0.04)	88.8 (0.19)	26.5 (0.26)	1.0 (0.16)	78.6 (0.64)	16.3 (0.58)	9.1 (0.41)	57.4 (0.70)	11.3 (0.45)
March 2002.....	1.5 (0.04)	84.4 (0.13)	25.1 (0.15)	0.5 (0.03)	88.9 (0.13)	27.3 (0.19)	1.4 (0.13)	79.4 (0.45)	17.7 (0.42)	8.3 (0.27)	57.9 (0.48)	11.2 (0.31)
March 2003.....	1.5 (0.04)	85.0 (0.13)	25.7 (0.15)	0.4 (0.03)	89.7 (0.13)	27.9 (0.19)	1.2 (0.12)	80.7 (0.44)	18.0 (0.43)	8.1 (0.26)	57.8 (0.46)	11.6 (0.30)
March 2004.....	1.4 (0.04)	85.4 (0.12)	26.1 (0.15)	0.4 (0.02)	90.1 (0.12)	28.4 (0.19)	1.1 (0.12)	81.2 (0.43)	18.5 (0.43)	7.8 (0.25)	59.5 (0.46)	12.3 (0.31)
March 2005.....	1.5 (0.04)	85.4 (0.12)	26.5 (0.15)	0.4 (0.03)	90.3 (0.12)	28.9 (0.19)	1.3 (0.12)	81.5 (0.42)	18.9 (0.43)	7.8 (0.25)	58.9 (0.45)	12.1 (0.30)
March 2006.....	1.5 (0.04)	85.9 (0.12)	26.9 (0.15)	0.4 (0.03)	90.8 (0.12)	29.3 (0.19)	1.3 (0.12)	81.5 (0.42)	19.5 (0.43)	7.4 (0.23)	60.1 (0.44)	12.9 (0.30)
March 2007.....	1.4 (0.04)	86.4 (0.12)	28.0 (0.16)	0.4 (0.03)	91.0 (0.12)	30.6 (0.19)	1.1 (0.11)	83.0 (0.40)	19.2 (0.42)	6.6 (0.22)	62.5 (0.43)	13.7 (0.30)
March 2008.....	1.3 (0.04)	87.2 (0.11)	28.8 (0.16)	0.4 (0.02)	91.8 (0.11)	31.5 (0.19)	1.0 (0.10)	84.2 (0.39)	20.5 (0.43)	6.1 (0.21)	63.7 (0.42)	14.1 (0.30)

—Not available.
†Not applicable.
#Rounds to zero.
[1]Includes persons of Hispanic ethnicity for years prior to 1980.
[2]Data for years prior to 1993 are for persons with 4 or more years of high school. Data for later years are for high school completers—i.e., those persons who graduated from high school with a diploma, as well as those who completed high school through equivalency programs, such as a GED program.
[3]Data for years prior to 1993 are for persons with 4 or more years of college.

[4]Estimates based on Census Bureau reverse projection of 1940 census data on education by age.
NOTE: Totals include other racial/ethnic groups not separately shown. Race categories exclude persons of Hispanic ethnicity except where otherwise noted. Standard errors appear in parentheses.
SOURCE: U.S. Department of Commerce, Census Bureau, U.S. Census of Population, 1960, Volume 1, part 1; *1960 Census Monograph, Education of the American Population*, by John K. Folger and Charles B. Nam; and Current Population Reports, Series P-20; various years; and Current Population Survey (CPS), March 1970 through March 2008. (This table was prepared September 2008.)

Table 9. Number of persons age 18 and over, by highest level of education attained, age, sex, and race/ethnicity: 2008

[In thousands]

Age, sex, and race/ethnicity	Total	Elementary: Less than 7 years	Elementary: 7 or 8 years	High school: 1 to 3 years	High school: 4 years	High school: Completion	College: Some college	College: Associate's degree	College: Bachelor's degree	College: Master's degree	College: Professional degree	College: Doctor's degree
1	2	3	4	5	6	7	8	9	10	11	12	13
Total, 18 and over	**224,703**	**6,503**	**4,927**	**17,334**	**3,245**	**69,480 (244.2)**	**44,168**	**18,589**	**40,070 (200.7)**	**14,893 (129.8)**	**3,009**	**2,485**
18 and 19 years old	7,869	45	78	2,607	509	2,161 (50.8)	2,429	31	5 (2.4)	5 (2.3)	‡	‡
20 to 24 years old	20,529	287	196	1,578	369	6,135 (84.9)	7,927	1,376	2,506 (54.7)	124 (12.2)	17	14
25 years old and over	196,305	6,171	4,653	13,149	2,366	61,183 (234.7)	33,812	17,182	37,559 (195.6)	14,765 (129.3)	2,991	2,472
25 to 29 years old	21,057	427	276	1,551	312	6,017 (84.1)	4,109	1,889	5,012 (76.9)	1,227 (38.4)	181	57
30 to 34 years old	19,089	499	269	1,189	244	5,280 (78.9)	3,287	1,829	4,409 (72.3)	1,565 (43.3)	309	210
35 to 39 years old	20,733	560	300	1,187	234	5,586 (81.1)	3,623	2,040	4,695 (74.5)	1,865 (47.2)	375	268
40 to 49 years old	44,100	1,221	669	2,619	504	13,750 (125.1)	7,598	4,397	8,889 (101.6)	3,233 (62.0)	668	553
50 to 59 years old	39,605	1,052	656	2,061	404	12,360 (118.9)	6,962	3,929	7,513 (93.7)	3,368 (63.3)	739	560
60 to 64 years old	14,931	437	335	898	131	4,632 (74.0)	2,710	1,222	2,634 (56.1)	1,377 (40.6)	268	289
65 years old and over	36,790	1,975	2,148	3,645	539	13,558 (124.2)	5,523	1,877	4,406 (72.2)	2,129 (50.4)	453	536
Males, 18 and over	**108,862**	**3,371**	**2,448**	**8,926**	**1,701**	**34,048 (187.8)**	**20,735**	**8,091**	**19,102 (145.6)**	**6,920 (90.0)**	**1,888**	**1,631**
18 and 19 years old	4,008	33	42	1,433	272	1,134 (36.9)	1,074	18	2 (1.6)	‡ (†)	‡	‡
20 to 24 years old	10,384	198	100	876	194	3,422 (63.8)	3,850	637	1,058 (35.6)	34 (6.4)	11	3
25 years old and over	94,470	3,140	2,306	6,617	1,236	29,491 (176.7)	15,810	7,436	18,042 (141.9)	6,886 (89.8)	1,877	1,628
25 to 29 years old	10,721	284	161	895	178	3,423 (63.8)	2,058	849	2,305 (52.5)	475 (23.9)	69	24
30 to 34 years old	9,489	295	146	664	137	2,933 (59.1)	1,539	830	2,060 (49.6)	623 (27.4)	150	110
35 to 39 years old	10,291	292	175	613	123	3,004 (59.8)	1,844	886	2,170 (50.9)	819 (31.4)	213	152
40 to 49 years old	21,754	700	366	1,499	273	7,183 (91.7)	3,422	1,849	4,116 (69.8)	1,579 (43.5)	399	368
50 to 59 years old	19,303	539	353	1,081	214	5,900 (83.3)	3,360	1,749	3,715 (66.4)	1,521 (42.7)	509	361
60 to 64 years old	7,150	197	158	409	61	2,002 (48.9)	1,261	576	1,398 (40.9)	703 (29.1)	186	199
65 years old and over	15,762	832	948	1,455	250	5,045 (77.2)	2,326	695	2,279 (52.2)	1,165 (37.4)	351	414
Females, 18 and over	**115,841**	**3,133**	**2,479**	**8,408**	**1,544**	**35,432 (190.9)**	**23,433**	**10,498**	**20,968 (152.0)**	**7,973 (96.4)**	**1,121**	**855**
18 and 19 years old	3,861	12	36	1,173	238	1,027 (35.1)	1,354	13	2 (1.7)	5 (2.3)	‡	‡
20 to 24 years old	10,145	88	96	702	176	2,713 (56.9)	4,076	738	1,448 (41.7)	89 (10.4)	7	11
25 years old and over	101,835	3,032	2,347	6,532	1,130	31,692 (182.2)	18,002	9,746	19,517 (147.1)	7,879 (95.9)	1,114	844
25 to 29 years old	10,337	143	115	656	133	2,594 (55.6)	2,051	1,039	2,708 (56.8)	752 (30.1)	112	33
30 to 34 years old	9,600	204	123	525	107	2,347 (52.9)	1,747	998	2,349 (53.0)	942 (33.6)	158	100
35 to 39 years old	10,442	269	126	574	111	2,582 (55.5)	1,779	1,153	2,526 (54.9)	1,046 (35.4)	163	116
40 to 49 years old	22,346	521	303	1,119	231	6,568 (87.8)	4,175	2,548	4,773 (75.1)	1,654 (44.5)	268	185
50 to 59 years old	20,302	512	303	980	190	6,460 (87.1)	3,602	2,180	3,798 (67.1)	1,848 (47.0)	229	200
60 to 64 years old	7,781	239	177	489	70	2,630 (56.0)	1,449	646	1,236 (38.5)	674 (28.5)	82	90
65 years old and over	21,028	1,143	1,200	2,190	290	8,513 (99.5)	3,197	1,181	2,127 (50.4)	964 (34.0)	102	121
White, 18 and over	**154,603**	**1,197**	**2,659**	**8,993**	**1,607**	**48,207 (215.7)**	**31,488**	**13,753**	**30,809 (180.0)**	**11,606 (115.4)**	**2,365**	**1,919**
18 and 19 years old	4,783	12	39	1,494	300	1,308 (39.6)	1,603	20	2 (1.7)	4 (2.1)	‡	‡
20 to 24 years old	12,742	35	57	655	145	3,564 (65.1)	5,349	923	1,916 (47.9)	83 (10.0)	8	5
25 years old and over	137,079	1,150	2,563	6,844	1,161	43,334 (207.1)	24,536	12,810	28,891 (175.1)	11,519 (115.0)	2,356	1,914
25 to 29 years old	12,544	32	87	562	113	3,330 (62.9)	2,447	1,314	3,636 (65.7)	853 (32.0)	137	33
30 to 34 years old	11,307	18	64	402	79	2,967 (59.5)	2,073	1,218	3,076 (60.5)	1,063 (35.7)	212	136
35 to 39 years old	12,951	36	92	397	65	3,379 (63.4)	2,384	1,423	3,424 (63.8)	1,297 (39.4)	288	167
40 to 49 years old	29,957	111	279	1,227	248	9,400 (104.4)	5,378	3,215	6,753 (89.0)	2,460 (54.2)	496	389
50 to 59 years old	29,246	167	298	1,075	224	9,218 (103.4)	5,229	3,101	6,051 (84.3)	2,811 (57.9)	598	474
60 to 64 years old	11,631	111	214	535	73	3,608 (65.5)	2,246	962	2,193 (51.2)	1,192 (37.8)	237	260
65 years old and over	29,442	673	1,528	2,646	358	11,432 (114.6)	4,779	1,577	3,760 (66.8)	1,844 (47.0)	389	456
Black, 18 and over	**25,478**	**486**	**480**	**3,037**	**552**	**8,903 (98.4)**	**5,491**	**2,081**	**3,113 (62.8)**	**1,055 (37.5)**	**143**	**136**
18 and 19 years old	1,144	6	12	478	80	305 (20.3)	257	6	‡ (†)	‡ (†)	‡	‡
20 to 24 years old	2,775	14	17	270	67	1,042 (37.3)	1,004	163	186 (15.9)	5 (2.6)	3	4
25 years old and over	21,559	466	450	2,289	405	7,556 (92.4)	4,230	1,912	2,927 (61.0)	1,050 (37.4)	140	132
25 to 29 years old	2,700	9	9	263	56	987 (36.3)	630	196	433 (24.2)	108 (12.1)	9	1
30 to 34 years old	2,329	3	12	157	38	833 (33.4)	517	232	392 (23.0)	116 (12.5)	18	13
35 to 39 years old	2,507	15	17	184	35	832 (33.4)	524	261	435 (24.2)	166 (15.0)	19	20
40 to 49 years old	5,255	51	49	455	105	1,919 (50.0)	1,120	558	710 (30.9)	223 (17.4)	31	35
50 to 59 years old	4,347	64	64	450	74	1,552 (45.2)	852	419	581 (28.0)	224 (17.4)	40	29
60 to 64 years old	1,345	37	25	184	22	455 (24.8)	236	120	172 (15.3)	76 (10.2)	6	13
65 years old and over	3,075	287	274	598	76	978 (36.1)	351	128	203 (16.6)	138 (13.7)	19	23
Hispanic, 18 and over	**30,285**	**4,328**	**1,533**	**4,451**	**879**	**9,130 (74.2)**	**4,684**	**1,730**	**2,539 (46.0)**	**750 (25.9)**	**189**	**73**
18 and 19 years old	1,394	26	22	463	103	424 (19.6)	351	5	1 (0.9)	‡ (†)	‡	‡
20 to 24 years old	3,617	233	114	552	141	1,235 (32.9)	968	191	170 (12.5)	11 (3.2)	#	1
25 years old and over	25,274	4,070	1,397	3,436	634	7,471 (70.2)	3,365	1,533	2,368 (44.6)	739 (25.7)	189	71
25 to 29 years old	4,275	379	170	672	133	1,388 (34.8)	734	271	445 (20.1)	64 (7.7)	15	5
30 to 34 years old	3,861	469	181	596	99	1,202 (32.5)	508	249	416 (19.4)	104 (9.8)	27	11
35 to 39 years old	3,650	488	170	560	109	1,080 (30.9)	483	244	355 (18.0)	128 (10.8)	26	8
40 to 49 years old	5,999	988	298	776	127	1,769 (39.0)	757	388	619 (23.6)	205 (13.7)	50	22
50 to 59 years old	3,754	716	241	422	90	1,033 (30.2)	537	228	293 (16.4)	145 (11.5)	41	7
60 to 64 years old	1,180	237	71	147	19	356 (18.0)	134	68	93 (9.3)	39 (6.0)	12	4
65 years old and over	2,555	792	266	265	58	643 (24.0)	213	86	146 (11.6)	53 (7.0)	17	14

†Not applicable.
#Rounds to zero.
‡Reporting standards not met.
NOTE: Total includes other racial/ethnic groups not shown separately. Although cells with fewer than 75,000 weighted persons are subject to relatively wide sampling variation, they are included in the table to permit various types of aggregations; see Guide to

Sources or http://www.census.gov/apsd/techdoc/cps/cps-main.html for information on calculating standard errors. Race categories exclude persons of Hispanic ethnicity. Detail may not sum to totals because of rounding. Standard errors appear in parentheses.
SOURCE: U.S. Department of Commerce, Census Bureau, Current Population Survey (CPS), March 2008. (This table was prepared August 2008.)

Table 10. Persons age 18 and over who hold at least a bachelor's degree in specific fields of study, by sex, race/ethnicity, and age: 2001

Field of study	Sex			Race/ethnicity					Age		
	Total	Males	Females	White	Black	Hispanic	Asian/Pacific Islander	American Indian/ Alaska Native	18 to 29 years old	30 to 49 years old	50 years old and over
1	2	3	4	5	6	7	8	9	10	11	12
	Number (in thousands)										
Total population, 18 and over (in thousands)	208,762 (680.6)	99,811 (484.3)	108,951 (477.6)	151,898 (779.3)	23,314 (234.3)	23,580 (273.6)	8,097 (252.9)	1,873 (135.5)	44,447 (572.0)	85,830 (721.6)	78,485 (703.0)
Degree holders											
Total	49,144 (595.5)	24,977 (422.6)	24,166 (419.3)	40,138 (548.5)	3,192 (142.5)	2,189 (145.7)	3,389 (177.9)	235 (49.2)	7,016 (245)	24,666 (444)	17,461 (378.5)
Agriculture/forestry	540 (68.7)	421 (60.6)	‡ (†)	473 (64.3)	‡ (†)	‡ (†)	‡ (†)	‡ (†)	‡ (†)	254 (47.1)	239 (45.7)
Art/architecture	1,450 (112.4)	649 (75.2)	801 (83.5)	1,156 (100.4)	‡ (†)	‡ (†)	‡ (†)	‡ (†)	259 (47.6)	748 (80.8)	443 (62.2)
Business/management	8,976 (275.8)	5,679 (218.3)	3,297 (167.9)	7,254 (248.7)	623 (65.4)	426 (66.1)	633 (80.2)	‡ (†)	1,202 (102.4)	5,102 (209.4)	2,672 (152.2)
Communications	1,164 (100.7)	577 (70.9)	586 (71.5)	945 (90.8)	‡ (†)	‡ (†)	‡ (†)	‡ (†)	301 (51.3)	706 (78.5)	157 (37.1)
Computer and information sciences	1,249 (104.3)	871 (87.0)	378 (57.4)	895 (88.4)	‡ (†)	‡ (†)	166 (41.4)	‡ (†)	268 (48.4)	828 (85.0)	152 (36.5)
Education	7,102 (246.1)	1,750 (123.0)	5,351 (212.3)	6,160 (229.6)	490 (58.1)	234 (49.1)	181 (43.2)	‡ (†)	663 (76.1)	2,891 (158.2)	3,548 (175.1)
Engineering	3,959 (184.8)	3,558 (174.2)	401 (59.2)	3,085 (163.4)	‡ (†)	173 (42.3)	559 (75.5)	‡ (†)	459 (63.3)	2,057 (133.7)	1,443 (112.1)
English/literature	1,527 (115.3)	597 (72.1)	930 (89.9)	1,316 (107.1)	‡ (†)	‡ (†)	‡ (†)	‡ (†)	241 (45.9)	633 (74.3)	654 (75.6)
Foreign languages	448 (62.6)	135 (34.4)	313 (52.3)	344 (54.9)	‡ (†)	‡ (†)	‡ (†)	‡ (†)	‡ (†)	219 (43.7)	189 (40.6)
Health sciences	2,298 (141.3)	482 (64.8)	1,817 (125.3)	1,811 (125.5)	173 (34.8)	‡ (†)	213 (46.9)	‡ (†)	382 (57.8)	1,247 (104.2)	670 (76.5)
Liberal arts/humanities	2,846 (157.0)	1,150 (99.9)	1,695 (121.1)	2,444 (145.6)	146 (31.9)	‡ (†)	142 (38.3)	‡ (†)	400 (59.1)	1,308 (106.7)	1,137 (99.6)
Mathematics/statistics	869 (87.1)	507 (66.5)	362 (56.2)	567 (70.4)	‡ (†)	‡ (†)	149 (39.2)	‡ (†)	‡ (†)	386 (58.1)	363 (56.3)
Natural sciences (biological and physical)	2,910 (158.8)	1,756 (123.2)	1,153 (100.1)	2,260 (140.1)	190 (36.4)	‡ (†)	345 (59.5)	‡ (†)	413 (60.1)	1,426 (111.4)	1,071 (96.6)
Philosophy/religion/theology	628 (74.1)	437 (61.8)	191 (40.9)	533 (68.3)	‡ (†)	‡ (†)	‡ (†)	‡ (†)	‡ (†)	268 (48.4)	255 (47.2)
Pre-professional	596 (72.1)	397 (58.9)	199 (41.7)	448 (62.6)	‡ (†)	‡ (†)	‡ (†)	‡ (†)	‡ (†)	306 (51.7)	216 (43.4)
Psychology	1,903 (128.6)	606 (72.7)	1,297 (106.1)	1,561 (116.6)	157 (33.0)	‡ (†)	‡ (†)	‡ (†)	428 (61.2)	940 (90.6)	535 (68.3)
Social sciences/history	2,436 (145.4)	1,026 (94.4)	1,410 (110.5)	1,981 (131.2)	260 (42.5)	‡ (†)	‡ (†)	‡ (†)	359 (56.0)	1,092 (97.6)	985 (92.7)
Other fields	8,243 (264.6)	4,377 (192.6)	3,866 (181.5)	6,907 (242.8)	417 (53.7)	337 (58.8)	559 (75.5)	‡ (†)	1,253 (104.5)	4,256 (191.5)	2,734 (153.9)
	Percentage distribution of degree holders, by field										
Total	100.0 (†)	100.0 (†)	100.0 (†)	100.0 (†)	100.0 (†)	100.0 (†)	100.0 (†)	100.0 (†)	100.0 (†)	100.0 (†)	100.0 (†)
Agriculture/forestry	1.1 (0.14)	1.7 (0.24)	0.5 (0.13)	1.2 (0.16)	0.7 (0.38)	1.1 (0.73)	0.5 (0.40)	‡ (†)	0.7 (0.29)	1.0 (0.19)	1.4 (0.26)
Art/architecture	3.0 (0.23)	2.6 (0.30)	3.3 (0.34)	2.9 (0.25)	3.3 (0.83)	4.8 (1.47)	2.2 (0.81)	4.4 (4.32)	3.7 (0.67)	3.0 (0.32)	2.5 (0.35)
Business/management	18.3 (0.52)	22.7 (0.78)	13.6 (0.65)	18.1 (0.57)	19.5 (1.86)	19.5 (2.72)	18.7 (2.16)	17.5 (7.98)	17.1 (1.33)	20.7 (0.76)	15.3 (0.81)
Communications	2.4 (0.20)	2.3 (0.28)	2.4 (0.29)	2.4 (0.22)	3.2 (0.82)	3.3 (1.23)	1.2 (0.60)	‡ (†)	4.3 (0.72)	2.9 (0.31)	0.9 (0.21)
Computer and information sciences	2.5 (0.21)	3.5 (0.34)	1.6 (0.24)	2.2 (0.22)	3.9 (0.91)	2.6 (1.10)	4.9 (1.19)	‡ (†)	3.8 (0.68)	3.4 (0.34)	0.9 (0.21)
Education	14.5 (0.47)	7.0 (0.48)	22.1 (0.79)	15.3 (0.53)	15.3 (1.69)	10.7 (2.13)	5.3 (1.24)	16.0 (7.69)	9.5 (1.03)	11.7 (0.61)	20.3 (0.90)
Engineering	8.1 (0.36)	14.2 (0.65)	1.7 (0.24)	7.7 (0.39)	3.6 (0.87)	7.9 (1.86)	16.5 (2.05)	11.4 (6.67)	6.5 (0.87)	8.3 (0.52)	8.3 (0.62)
English/literature	3.1 (0.23)	2.4 (0.29)	3.8 (0.37)	3.3 (0.26)	2.6 (0.75)	3.1 (1.19)	1.7 (0.71)	‡ (†)	3.4 (0.64)	2.6 (0.30)	3.7 (0.43)
Foreign languages	0.9 (0.13)	0.5 (0.14)	1.3 (0.22)	0.9 (0.14)	0.8 (0.42)	1.7 (0.90)	1.0 (0.56)	‡ (†)	0.6 (0.27)	0.9 (0.18)	1.1 (0.23)
Health sciences	4.7 (0.28)	1.9 (0.26)	7.5 (0.50)	4.5 (0.31)	5.4 (1.06)	4.4 (1.41)	6.3 (1.34)	2.1 (2.99)	5.4 (0.80)	5.1 (0.41)	3.8 (0.43)
Liberal arts/humanities	5.8 (0.31)	4.6 (0.39)	7.0 (0.49)	6.1 (0.35)	4.6 (0.98)	4.7 (1.45)	4.2 (1.11)	4.5 (4.37)	5.7 (0.82)	5.3 (0.42)	6.5 (0.55)
Mathematics/statistics	1.8 (0.18)	2.0 (0.26)	1.5 (0.23)	1.4 (0.17)	2.4 (0.72)	2.4 (1.05)	4.4 (1.13)	10.4 (6.41)	1.7 (0.46)	1.6 (0.23)	2.1 (0.32)
Natural sciences (biological and physical)	5.9 (0.31)	7.0 (0.48)	4.8 (0.41)	5.6 (0.34)	6.0 (1.11)	4.9 (1.49)	10.2 (1.67)	2.7 (3.41)	5.9 (0.83)	5.8 (0.44)	6.1 (0.54)
Philosophy/religion/theology	1.3 (0.15)	1.8 (0.25)	0.8 (0.17)	1.3 (0.17)	0.9 (0.45)	1.8 (0.90)	0.8 (0.49)	‡ (†)	1.5 (0.43)	1.1 (0.20)	1.5 (0.27)
Pre-professional	1.2 (0.15)	1.6 (0.23)	0.8 (0.17)	1.1 (0.16)	1.6 (0.59)	2.0 (0.97)	1.5 (0.67)	‡ (†)	1.1 (0.36)	1.2 (0.21)	1.2 (0.25)
Psychology	3.9 (0.26)	2.4 (0.29)	5.4 (0.45)	3.9 (0.29)	4.9 (1.01)	5.0 (1.50)	1.7 (0.72)	7.9 (5.65)	6.1 (0.85)	3.8 (0.36)	3.1 (0.39)
Social sciences/history	5.0 (0.29)	4.1 (0.37)	5.8 (0.45)	4.9 (0.32)	8.1 (1.28)	4.7 (1.45)	2.4 (0.85)	4.7 (4.45)	5.1 (0.78)	4.4 (0.39)	5.6 (0.52)
Other fields	16.8 (0.50)	17.5 (0.71)	16.0 (0.70)	17.2 (0.56)	13.1 (1.58)	15.4 (2.48)	16.5 (2.05)	9.9 (6.26)	17.9 (1.35)	17.3 (0.71)	15.7 (0.81)

†Not applicable.
‡Reporting standards not met.
NOTE: Race categories exclude persons of Hispanic ethnicity. Detail may not sum to totals because of rounding. Standard errors appear in parentheses.

SOURCE: U.S. Department of Commerce, Census Bureau, Survey of Income and Program Participation, 2001, unpublished tabulations. (This table was prepared September 2005.)

Table 11. Educational attainment of persons 18 years old and over, by state: 2000 and 2006

State	Percent of 18- to 24-year-olds who were high school completers[1] 2000	2006	Less than high school completion (2000)	High school completion or higher (2000)	Total (2000)	Bachelor's degree (2000)	Graduate or professional degree (2000)	Less than high school completion (2006)	High school completion or higher (2006)	Total (2006)	Bachelor's degree (2006)	Graduate or professional degree (2006)
1	2	3	4	5	6	7	8	9	10	11	12	13
United States	74.7 (0.02)	82.0 (0.11)	19.6 (0.01)	80.4 (0.01)	24.4 (0.01)	15.5 (0.01)	8.9 (#)	15.9 (0.04)	84.1 (0.04)	27.0 (0.05)	17.1 (0.04)	9.9 (0.03)
Alabama	72.2 (0.15)	79.7 (0.76)	24.7 (0.06)	75.3 (0.06)	19.0 (0.05)	12.1 (0.04)	6.9 (0.03)	20.0 (0.34)	80.0 (0.34)	21.0 (0.29)	13.5 (0.23)	7.5 (0.17)
Alaska......................	76.9 (0.40)	80.2 (2.23)	11.7 (0.12)	88.3 (0.12)	24.7 (0.16)	16.1 (0.13)	8.6 (0.10)	10.0 (0.62)	90.0 (0.62)	26.8 (1.01)	17.4 (0.85)	9.4 (0.60)
Arizona....................	69.2 (0.19)	77.7 (0.71)	19.0 (0.06)	81.0 (0.06)	23.5 (0.07)	15.1 (0.06)	8.4 (0.04)	16.4 (0.24)	83.6 (0.24)	25.5 (0.30)	16.3 (0.25)	9.3 (0.17)
Arkansas..................	75.4 (0.19)	83.7 (0.98)	24.7 (0.07)	75.3 (0.07)	16.7 (0.06)	11.0 (0.05)	5.7 (0.04)	19.4 (0.37)	80.6 (0.37)	18.6 (0.36)	12.2 (0.28)	6.4 (0.24)
California	70.7 (0.07)	81.2 (0.29)	23.2 (0.03)	76.8 (0.03)	26.6 (0.03)	17.1 (0.02)	9.5 (0.02)	19.9 (0.10)	80.1 (0.10)	29.1 (0.11)	18.6 (0.10)	10.4 (0.08)
Colorado	75.1 (0.15)	81.1 (0.80)	13.1 (0.05)	86.9 (0.05)	32.7 (0.06)	21.6 (0.06)	11.1 (0.04)	11.9 (0.21)	88.1 (0.21)	34.5 (0.28)	22.2 (0.24)	12.3 (0.22)
Connecticut..............	78.2 (0.21)	87.1 (0.74)	16.0 (0.06)	84.0 (0.06)	31.4 (0.08)	18.1 (0.07)	13.3 (0.06)	11.9 (0.25)	88.1 (0.25)	33.6 (0.42)	19.4 (0.32)	14.2 (0.27)
Delaware..................	77.6 (0.41)	80.2 (2.27)	17.4 (0.14)	82.6 (0.14)	25.0 (0.16)	15.6 (0.14)	9.4 (0.11)	14.2 (0.62)	85.8 (0.62)	28.1 (0.79)	17.1 (0.59)	11.1 (0.52)
District of Columbia	79.4 (0.40)	86.9 (1.45)	22.2 (0.18)	77.8 (0.18)	39.1 (0.21)	18.1 (0.17)	21.0 (0.18)	15.7 (0.73)	84.3 (0.73)	45.3 (0.87)	20.1 (0.82)	25.2 (0.79)
Florida.....................	71.7 (0.11)	80.2 (0.45)	20.1 (0.04)	79.9 (0.04)	22.3 (0.04)	14.2 (0.03)	8.1 (0.02)	15.3 (0.14)	84.7 (0.14)	25.3 (0.16)	16.4 (0.13)	8.9 (0.09)
Georgia....................	70.0 (0.15)	77.9 (0.53)	21.4 (0.05)	78.6 (0.05)	24.3 (0.05)	16.0 (0.05)	8.3 (0.04)	17.7 (0.18)	82.3 (0.18)	26.4 (0.20)	17.2 (0.16)	9.2 (0.14)
Hawaii.....................	85.8 (0.25)	90.5 (1.03)	15.4 (0.10)	84.6 (0.10)	26.2 (0.12)	17.8 (0.10)	8.4 (0.08)	11.0 (0.43)	89.0 (0.43)	29.5 (0.58)	19.7 (0.57)	9.7 (0.38)
Idaho.......................	77.3 (0.25)	82.5 (1.05)	15.3 (0.09)	84.7 (0.09)	21.7 (0.10)	14.9 (0.09)	6.8 (0.06)	12.5 (0.49)	87.5 (0.49)	23.6 (0.55)	16.5 (0.46)	7.1 (0.28)
Illinois.....................	76.0 (0.09)	83.3 (0.49)	18.6 (0.03)	81.4 (0.03)	26.1 (0.03)	16.6 (0.03)	9.5 (0.02)	15.0 (0.17)	85.0 (0.17)	28.8 (0.22)	18.1 (0.17)	10.7 (0.14)
Indiana....................	76.5 (0.15)	80.3 (0.66)	17.9 (0.05)	82.1 (0.05)	19.4 (0.05)	12.2 (0.04)	7.2 (0.04)	14.7 (0.20)	85.3 (0.20)	21.8 (0.24)	13.6 (0.19)	8.2 (0.16)
Iowa........................	81.4 (0.16)	86.1 (0.78)	13.9 (0.06)	86.1 (0.06)	21.2 (0.07)	14.7 (0.06)	6.5 (0.04)	11.2 (0.32)	88.8 (0.32)	24.3 (0.46)	16.7 (0.37)	7.6 (0.26)
Kansas....................	78.3 (0.18)	85.6 (0.89)	14.0 (0.06)	86.0 (0.06)	25.8 (0.08)	17.1 (0.06)	8.7 (0.05)	11.3 (0.29)	88.7 (0.29)	28.9 (0.43)	18.9 (0.33)	10.0 (0.30)
Kentucky	74.9 (0.15)	81.8 (0.74)	25.9 (0.06)	74.1 (0.06)	17.1 (0.05)	10.2 (0.04)	6.9 (0.03)	20.3 (0.30)	79.7 (0.30)	19.9 (0.29)	11.8 (0.22)	8.2 (0.18)
Louisiana	72.3 (0.15)	76.2 (0.89)	25.2 (0.06)	74.8 (0.06)	18.7 (0.05)	12.2 (0.04)	6.5 (0.03)	20.9 (0.33)	79.1 (0.33)	20.0 (0.27)	13.1 (0.24)	6.9 (0.17)
Maine.......................	78.9 (0.28)	83.8 (1.53)	14.6 (0.08)	85.4 (0.08)	22.9 (0.10)	15.0 (0.09)	7.9 (0.06)	11.1 (0.46)	88.9 (0.46)	25.9 (0.64)	16.9 (0.49)	9.0 (0.40)
Maryland..................	79.6 (0.16)	85.4 (0.67)	16.2 (0.05)	83.8 (0.05)	31.4 (0.07)	18.0 (0.06)	13.4 (0.05)	12.8 (0.18)	87.2 (0.18)	35.3 (0.28)	19.3 (0.27)	15.9 (0.22)
Massachusetts...........	82.2 (0.13)	86.8 (0.53)	15.2 (0.05)	84.8 (0.05)	33.2 (0.06)	19.5 (0.05)	13.7 (0.04)	12.0 (0.23)	88.0 (0.23)	36.7 (0.28)	21.2 (0.25)	15.5 (0.20)
Michigan..................	76.5 (0.10)	82.5 (0.46)	16.6 (0.03)	83.4 (0.03)	21.8 (0.04)	13.7 (0.03)	8.1 (0.02)	12.7 (0.17)	87.3 (0.17)	24.6 (0.24)	15.4 (0.19)	9.2 (0.15)
Minnesota................	79.3 (0.13)	86.0 (0.59)	12.1 (0.04)	87.9 (0.04)	27.4 (0.06)	19.1 (0.05)	8.3 (0.03)	9.3 (0.23)	90.7 (0.23)	30.2 (0.39)	20.8 (0.33)	9.4 (0.21)
Mississippi	71.3 (0.18)	77.1 (1.10)	27.1 (0.08)	72.9 (0.08)	16.9 (0.06)	11.1 (0.05)	5.8 (0.04)	22.3 (0.43)	77.7 (0.43)	18.7 (0.39)	12.4 (0.30)	6.3 (0.21)
Missouri	76.5 (0.13)	81.0 (0.63)	18.7 (0.05)	81.3 (0.05)	21.6 (0.05)	14.0 (0.04)	7.6 (0.03)	15.1 (0.22)	84.9 (0.22)	24.0 (0.27)	15.3 (0.23)	8.7 (0.19)
Montana...................	78.6 (0.31)	80.6 (1.88)	12.8 (0.10)	87.2 (0.10)	24.4 (0.13)	17.2 (0.11)	7.2 (0.08)	9.6 (0.49)	90.4 (0.49)	26.9 (0.66)	19.0 (0.70)	7.9 (0.48)
Nebraska	80.0 (0.21)	83.9 (1.00)	13.4 (0.07)	86.6 (0.07)	23.7 (0.09)	16.4 (0.08)	7.3 (0.06)	10.3 (0.38)	89.7 (0.38)	26.5 (0.54)	17.9 (0.48)	8.6 (0.33)
Nevada	66.7 (0.32)	78.0 (1.07)	19.3 (0.10)	80.7 (0.10)	18.2 (0.10)	12.1 (0.08)	6.1 (0.06)	15.9 (0.33)	84.1 (0.33)	20.9 (0.39)	13.7 (0.33)	7.1 (0.25)
New Hampshire	77.8 (0.29)	84.5 (1.55)	12.6 (0.08)	87.4 (0.08)	28.7 (0.11)	18.7 (0.10)	10.0 (0.07)	10.4 (0.38)	89.6 (0.38)	31.8 (0.58)	20.7 (0.43)	11.1 (0.42)
New Jersey...............	76.3 (0.14)	85.6 (0.51)	17.9 (0.04)	82.1 (0.04)	29.8 (0.05)	18.8 (0.04)	11.0 (0.04)	14.1 (0.18)	85.9 (0.18)	33.3 (0.23)	20.9 (0.21)	12.4 (0.14)
New Mexico..............	70.5 (0.24)	78.5 (1.46)	21.1 (0.09)	78.9 (0.09)	23.5 (0.09)	13.7 (0.07)	9.8 (0.06)	17.8 (0.47)	82.2 (0.47)	25.3 (0.46)	14.7 (0.35)	10.5 (0.31)
New York..................	76.1 (0.09)	83.6 (0.34)	20.9 (0.03)	79.1 (0.03)	27.4 (0.04)	15.6 (0.03)	11.8 (0.03)	15.9 (0.15)	84.1 (0.15)	31.1 (0.15)	17.8 (0.12)	13.3 (0.11)
North Carolina	74.2 (0.11)	81.2 (0.56)	21.9 (0.04)	78.1 (0.04)	22.5 (0.04)	15.3 (0.04)	7.2 (0.03)	17.9 (0.21)	82.1 (0.21)	24.8 (0.23)	16.5 (0.20)	8.3 (0.12)
North Dakota	84.4 (0.24)	91.6 (1.58)	16.1 (0.10)	83.9 (0.10)	22.0 (0.12)	16.5 (0.10)	5.5 (0.06)	12.2 (0.58)	87.8 (0.58)	26.4 (1.07)	19.4 (0.88)	6.9 (0.58)
Ohio........................	76.8 (0.09)	83.6 (0.44)	17.0 (0.03)	83.0 (0.03)	21.1 (0.03)	13.7 (0.03)	7.4 (0.02)	13.7 (0.14)	86.3 (0.14)	22.9 (0.17)	14.6 (0.15)	8.3 (0.12)
Oklahoma.................	74.8 (0.16)	80.8 (0.97)	19.4 (0.06)	80.6 (0.06)	20.3 (0.06)	13.5 (0.05)	6.8 (0.04)	15.9 (0.32)	84.1 (0.32)	22.0 (0.42)	14.7 (0.30)	7.3 (0.22)
Oregon....................	74.2 (0.17)	80.3 (0.93)	14.9 (0.05)	85.1 (0.05)	25.1 (0.06)	16.4 (0.06)	8.7 (0.04)	12.3 (0.30)	87.7 (0.30)	27.3 (0.38)	17.6 (0.28)	9.8 (0.23)
Pennsylvania.............	79.8 (0.09)	84.7 (0.48)	18.1 (0.03)	81.9 (0.03)	22.4 (0.03)	14.0 (0.03)	8.4 (0.02)	13.7 (0.17)	86.3 (0.17)	25.5 (0.19)	15.9 (0.14)	9.6 (0.12)
Rhode Island	81.3 (0.32)	88.2 (1.30)	22.0 (0.13)	78.0 (0.13)	25.6 (0.14)	15.9 (0.12)	9.7 (0.10)	12.2 (0.62)	82.8 (0.62)	29.1 (0.69)	18.0 (0.55)	11.1 (0.41)
South Carolina...........	74.3 (0.18)	80.9 (0.89)	23.7 (0.07)	76.3 (0.07)	20.4 (0.07)	13.5 (0.06)	6.9 (0.04)	18.5 (0.31)	81.5 (0.31)	22.9 (0.30)	15.0 (0.21)	7.8 (0.17)
South Dakota............	78.2 (0.33)	83.2 (1.61)	15.4 (0.12)	84.6 (0.12)	21.5 (0.13)	15.5 (0.12)	6.0 (0.08)	12.6 (0.67)	87.4 (0.67)	25.0 (0.85)	17.4 (0.73)	7.6 (0.50)
Tennessee	75.1 (0.16)	81.6 (0.68)	24.1 (0.06)	75.9 (0.06)	19.6 (0.06)	12.8 (0.05)	6.8 (0.03)	19.2 (0.24)	80.8 (0.24)	22.0 (0.26)	14.3 (0.20)	7.7 (0.15)
Texas	68.6 (0.08)	78.3 (0.39)	24.3 (0.03)	75.7 (0.03)	23.2 (0.03)	15.6 (0.03)	7.6 (0.02)	21.4 (0.15)	78.6 (0.15)	24.7 (0.15)	16.6 (0.13)	8.1 (0.08)
Utah........................	80.3 (0.16)	86.0 (0.84)	12.3 (0.07)	87.7 (0.07)	26.1 (0.09)	17.8 (0.08)	8.3 (0.06)	9.6 (0.38)	90.4 (0.38)	28.6 (0.41)	19.2 (0.36)	9.4 (0.31)
Vermont	83.0 (0.28)	89.6 (1.84)	13.6 (0.10)	86.4 (0.10)	29.4 (0.13)	18.3 (0.11)	11.1 (0.09)	9.0 (0.56)	91.0 (0.56)	32.9 (1.20)	20.1 (0.93)	12.8 (0.73)
Virginia....................	79.4 (0.13)	85.6 (0.58)	18.5 (0.05)	81.5 (0.05)	29.5 (0.06)	17.9 (0.05)	11.6 (0.04)	14.7 (0.22)	85.3 (0.22)	32.8 (0.25)	19.5 (0.19)	13.3 (0.18)
Washington...............	75.3 (0.16)	80.8 (0.64)	12.9 (0.05)	87.1 (0.05)	27.7 (0.06)	18.4 (0.05)	9.3 (0.04)	11.1 (0.20)	88.9 (0.20)	30.3 (0.29)	19.8 (0.20)	10.5 (0.17)
West Virginia.............	78.2 (0.22)	84.6 (1.03)	24.8 (0.09)	75.2 (0.09)	14.8 (0.07)	8.9 (0.06)	5.9 (0.05)	19.0 (0.49)	81.0 (0.49)	16.5 (0.45)	9.8 (0.36)	6.7 (0.26)
Wisconsin	78.9 (0.13)	84.5 (0.76)	14.9 (0.04)	85.1 (0.04)	22.4 (0.05)	15.2 (0.04)	7.2 (0.03)	11.6 (0.22)	88.4 (0.22)	25.5 (0.29)	17.1 (0.25)	8.4 (0.21)
Wyoming..................	79.0 (0.41)	86.9 (2.18)	12.1 (0.13)	87.9 (0.13)	21.9 (0.16)	14.9 (0.14)	7.0 (0.10)	10.0 (0.63)	90.0 (0.63)	21.8 (0.96)	14.6 (0.76)	7.3 (0.49)

#Rounds to zero.
[1] High school completers include diploma recipients and those completing through alternative credentials, such as a GED.
NOTE: Detail may not sum to totals because of rounding. Standard errors appear in parentheses.

SOURCE: U.S. Department of Commerce, Census Bureau, Census 2000 Summary File 3, retrieved October 11, 2006, from http://factfinder.census.gov/servlet/DatasetMainPage Servlet?_ds_name=DEC_2000_SF3_U&_program=DEC&_lang=en; Census Briefs, *Educational Attainment: 2000*; and American Community Survey, 2006. (This table was prepared June 2008.)

Table 12. Educational attainment of persons 25 years old and over, by race/ethnicity and state: 2006

State	Percent with high school completion or higher								Percent with bachelor's degree or higher							
	Total	White	Black	Hispanic	Asian	Hawaiian/ Pacific Islander	American Indian/Alaska Native	More than one race	Total	White	Black	Hispanic	Asian	Hawaiian/ Pacific Islander	American Indian/Alaska Native	More than one race
1	2	3	4	5	6	7	8	9	10	11	12	13	14	15	16	17
United States	84.1 (0.04)	88.9 (0.04)	79.5 (0.11)	60.3 (0.15)	85.7 (0.17)	84.9 (1.00)	79.2 (0.47)	86.3 (0.34)	27.0 (0.05)	29.9 (0.06)	16.9 (0.11)	12.3 (0.09)	49.6 (0.24)	13.9 (1.00)	13.1 (0.38)	24.6 (0.39)
Alabama	80.0 (0.34)	82.4 (0.34)	74.8 (0.61)	54.8 (3.41)	84.5 (3.22)	‡ (†)	77.3 (3.81)	70.2 (2.73)	21.0 (0.29)	23.0 (0.35)	14.3 (0.57)	13.2 (2.30)	54.1 (4.32)	‡ (†)	12.9 (3.46)	14.6 (3.05)
Alaska	90.0 (0.62)	94.0 (0.58)	91.4 (4.78)	72.6 (7.52)	76.6 (4.47)	‡ (†)	78.0 (1.99)	86.0 (3.95)	26.8 (1.01)	31.2 (1.24)	21.3 (6.63)	17.2 (4.14)	26.0 (3.49)	‡ (†)	8.3 (1.65)	16.6 (4.04)
Arizona	83.6 (0.24)	92.1 (0.21)	87.2 (1.54)	60.1 (0.91)	87.1 (1.46)	89.5 (8.38)	73.4 (1.53)	87.3 (1.87)	25.5 (0.30)	31.3 (0.37)	23.1 (1.54)	9.4 (0.42)	50.1 (2.55)	14.9 (5.44)	9.3 (0.89)	21.5 (1.88)
Arkansas	80.6 (0.37)	83.1 (0.44)	76.6 (1.07)	46.9 (2.78)	82.4 (3.68)	‡ (†)	74.6 (4.73)	77.0 (3.78)	18.6 (0.36)	19.9 (0.42)	13.1 (0.96)	7.5 (1.24)	39.2 (5.54)	‡ (†)	13.1 (2.92)	8.3 (1.83)
California	80.1 (0.10)	92.5 (0.09)	86.0 (0.41)	55.9 (0.27)	85.5 (0.30)	85.3 (1.63)	82.9 (1.35)	89.7 (0.67)	29.1 (0.11)	37.3 (0.17)	21.0 (0.42)	9.4 (0.17)	47.5 (0.38)	13.4 (1.67)	13.6 (0.98)	28.6 (0.88)
Colorado	88.1 (0.21)	93.7 (0.16)	86.5 (1.51)	62.9 (0.96)	87.7 (1.29)	‡ (†)	81.9 (3.31)	90.7 (1.99)	34.5 (0.28)	39.9 (0.38)	19.1 (1.78)	11.3 (0.51)	46.8 (2.09)	‡ (†)	22.6 (3.14)	28.9 (3.24)
Connecticut	88.1 (0.25)	91.0 (0.25)	82.2 (1.03)	68.2 (1.40)	88.9 (1.57)	‡ (†)	68.6 (6.81)	90.7 (2.84)	33.6 (0.42)	36.8 (0.46)	15.5 (1.16)	12.6 (0.98)	62.6 (2.88)	‡ (†)	17.9 (6.66)	31.4 (4.03)
Delaware	85.8 (0.62)	88.5 (0.74)	81.3 (2.25)	58.4 (4.17)	93.6 (2.41)	‡ (†)	‡ (†)	88.0 (5.55)	28.1 (0.79)	29.2 (0.83)	21.4 (2.09)	14.3 (3.18)	66.3 (4.66)	‡ (†)	‡ (†)	25.0 (7.50)
District of Columbia	84.3 (0.73)	98.3 (0.36)	78.6 (1.07)	56.6 (4.47)	90.6 (3.24)	‡ (†)	‡ (†)	88.9 (4.77)	45.3 (0.87)	85.0 (1.05)	19.8 (1.12)	31.1 (3.61)	68.1 (5.81)	‡ (†)	‡ (†)	55.0 (9.75)
Florida	84.7 (0.14)	89.2 (0.14)	77.1 (0.45)	73.5 (0.46)	85.7 (0.76)	87.4 (4.49)	84.0 (2.66)	86.1 (1.32)	25.3 (0.16)	27.5 (0.17)	15.6 (0.40)	21.7 (0.38)	46.0 (1.26)	14.2 (5.07)	13.7 (2.35)	22.9 (1.57)
Georgia	82.3 (0.18)	86.0 (0.21)	80.1 (0.39)	53.5 (1.57)	83.7 (1.21)	‡ (†)	80.0 (4.06)	86.3 (2.61)	26.4 (0.20)	30.4 (0.27)	18.2 (0.35)	11.4 (0.84)	48.5 (1.86)	‡ (†)	22.1 (4.21)	32.4 (3.10)
Hawaii	89.0 (0.43)	94.4 (0.52)	98.1 (1.35)	90.3 (1.42)	85.2 (0.81)	82.6 (1.87)	‡ (†)	92.1 (1.08)	29.5 (0.58)	41.8 (1.36)	27.6 (5.55)	15.7 (1.77)	30.3 (0.66)	10.6 (1.50)	‡ (†)	18.1 (1.49)
Idaho	87.5 (0.49)	90.9 (0.43)	‡ (†)	50.1 (2.73)	88.3 (3.82)	‡ (†)	77.0 (4.07)	81.7 (5.21)	23.6 (0.55)	24.8 (0.59)	‡ (†)	9.5 (1.52)	40.8 (6.39)	‡ (†)	12.1 (3.72)	18.9 (4.38)
Illinois	85.0 (0.17)	90.1 (0.17)	80.9 (0.49)	58.2 (0.83)	90.5 (0.77)	‡ (†)	76.1 (4.97)	83.6 (2.07)	28.8 (0.22)	32.1 (0.28)	17.5 (0.57)	10.8 (0.50)	60.7 (1.21)	‡ (†)	14.4 (3.75)	25.0 (2.28)
Indiana	85.3 (0.20)	86.7 (0.20)	81.6 (0.81)	58.2 (1.75)	91.8 (1.96)	‡ (†)	79.4 (5.87)	83.8 (2.41)	21.8 (0.24)	22.4 (0.26)	13.2 (0.91)	11.8 (1.19)	61.7 (3.34)	‡ (†)	22.3 (5.56)	20.1 (2.70)
Iowa	88.8 (0.32)	90.2 (0.29)	84.0 (0.40)	52.0 (3.25)	84.6 (3.24)	‡ (†)	82.1 (6.23)	93.9 (3.40)	24.3 (0.46)	24.4 (0.47)	15.9 (3.04)	7.8 (1.70)	56.9 (4.28)	‡ (†)	25.1 (7.37)	24.9 (7.45)
Kansas	88.7 (0.29)	91.6 (0.24)	84.1 (1.38)	57.3 (2.13)	85.8 (2.89)	‡ (†)	92.1 (2.25)	81.5 (2.98)	28.9 (0.43)	30.3 (0.46)	20.1 (2.00)	10.4 (1.19)	53.2 (3.83)	‡ (†)	23.8 (4.26)	22.5 (3.63)
Kentucky	79.7 (0.30)	79.9 (0.34)	80.2 (0.62)	61.0 (3.05)	89.2 (2.52)	‡ (†)	90.7 (5.09)	75.0 (4.56)	19.9 (0.29)	20.2 (0.34)	13.9 (0.94)	13.7 (1.82)	55.9 (3.59)	‡ (†)	7.7 (3.63)	15.1 (2.99)
Louisiana	79.1 (0.33)	83.5 (0.37)	69.6 (0.79)	69.4 (2.66)	83.4 (3.01)	‡ (†)	71.0 (5.15)	75.0 (3.84)	20.0 (0.27)	23.4 (0.38)	11.0 (0.44)	18.4 (1.93)	44.4 (3.37)	‡ (†)	10.1 (2.78)	17.0 (3.35)
Maine	88.9 (0.46)	89.1 (0.47)	91.5 (4.97)	79.7 (10.14)	87.5 (5.30)	‡ (†)	71.4 (8.68)	84.9 (4.50)	25.9 (0.64)	25.9 (0.63)	29.7 (9.59)	18.8 (6.02)	51.6 (9.82)	‡ (†)	9.5 (4.42)	15.1 (4.11)
Maryland	87.2 (0.18)	90.0 (0.24)	84.0 (0.40)	66.6 (1.73)	90.6 (0.75)	‡ (†)	84.7 (4.75)	90.6 (1.97)	35.3 (0.28)	39.1 (0.37)	24.2 (0.53)	21.4 (1.32)	61.8 (1.56)	‡ (†)	25.8 (6.50)	36.5 (3.25)
Massachusetts	88.0 (0.23)	90.4 (0.22)	82.1 (1.11)	66.4 (1.44)	82.0 (1.24)	‡ (†)	81.5 (5.21)	88.2 (2.19)	36.7 (0.28)	38.5 (0.37)	21.3 (1.17)	14.5 (0.91)	55.8 (1.87)	‡ (†)	21.5 (5.31)	36.9 (3.03)
Michigan	87.3 (0.17)	89.1 (0.18)	80.1 (0.62)	68.1 (1.84)	89.2 (1.46)	‡ (†)	84.6 (2.54)	84.2 (1.96)	24.6 (0.24)	25.5 (0.27)	15.2 (0.54)	15.4 (1.28)	60.1 (2.12)	‡ (†)	12.4 (1.91)	19.4 (2.19)
Minnesota	90.7 (0.23)	92.4 (0.19)	81.2 (1.86)	62.7 (3.05)	80.9 (2.33)	‡ (†)	82.2 (3.03)	87.0 (2.72)	30.2 (0.39)	30.9 (0.39)	20.9 (1.88)	15.8 (1.94)	40.7 (2.66)	‡ (†)	12.1 (2.26)	25.7 (3.68)
Mississippi	77.7 (0.43)	82.5 (0.49)	69.4 (0.73)	55.1 (3.60)	78.3 (5.59)	‡ (†)	64.0 (8.51)	79.4 (4.38)	18.7 (0.39)	22.3 (0.48)	11.3 (0.55)	13.9 (2.59)	48.3 (5.62)	‡ (†)	10.4 (4.14)	19.2 (4.96)
Missouri	84.9 (0.22)	86.0 (0.24)	80.3 (0.97)	67.1 (1.90)	83.3 (1.98)	‡ (†)	81.1 (3.09)	83.8 (2.03)	24.0 (0.27)	24.9 (0.29)	14.9 (0.78)	17.9 (1.96)	50.2 (3.14)	‡ (†)	24.4 (5.01)	19.7 (2.69)
Montana	90.4 (0.49)	91.1 (0.45)	‡ (†)	82.7 (6.45)	84.1 (7.17)	‡ (†)	77.5 (3.43)	93.6 (3.61)	26.9 (0.66)	27.7 (0.39)	‡ (†)	25.7 (6.90)	45.5 (10.30)	‡ (†)	10.4 (1.95)	15.8 (5.87)
Nebraska	89.7 (0.38)	92.5 (0.33)	88.3 (2.20)	51.8 (2.90)	81.2 (4.86)	‡ (†)	69.3 (6.10)	83.0 (6.10)	26.5 (0.54)	27.8 (0.60)	17.3 (2.59)	10.1 (1.60)	48.2 (5.72)	‡ (†)	12.7 (5.19)	13.3 (5.33)
Nevada	84.1 (0.33)	91.4 (0.38)	88.1 (1.19)	57.3 (1.09)	88.5 (1.18)	87.8 (3.73)	83.8 (2.63)	89.3 (2.35)	20.9 (0.39)	24.5 (0.54)	14.7 (1.40)	7.2 (0.58)	34.4 (1.62)	9.4 (4.08)	6.6 (2.38)	25.2 (3.68)
New Hampshire	89.6 (0.38)	89.7 (0.42)	81.6 (4.26)	85.7 (4.43)	93.7 (2.55)	‡ (†)	‡ (†)	85.4 (6.55)	31.8 (0.58)	31.1 (0.64)	32.9 (9.71)	28.2 (5.30)	62.7 (7.52)	‡ (†)	‡ (†)	38.7 (10.83)
New Jersey	85.9 (0.18)	90.1 (0.16)	81.4 (0.63)	67.3 (0.73)	91.8 (0.54)	‡ (†)	83.9 (5.91)	83.2 (2.39)	33.3 (0.23)	36.1 (0.26)	20.1 (0.64)	14.3 (0.54)	65.7 (0.84)	‡ (†)	15.7 (5.22)	32.3 (2.52)
New Mexico	82.2 (0.47)	93.3 (0.42)	81.5 (3.51)	70.0 (0.87)	83.5 (3.95)	‡ (†)	74.1 (1.99)	89.8 (2.82)	25.3 (0.46)	37.3 (0.69)	27.5 (4.23)	12.4 (0.58)	48.4 (5.48)	‡ (†)	9.8 (1.33)	35.1 (5.20)
New York	84.1 (0.15)	90.0 (0.13)	79.3 (0.38)	64.7 (0.60)	80.4 (0.65)	‡ (†)	34.0 (2.65)	84.6 (1.52)	31.1 (0.15)	36.0 (0.21)	19.4 (0.38)	14.7 (0.34)	44.7 (0.82)	‡ (†)	18.0 (2.71)	32.9 (2.01)
North Carolina	82.1 (0.21)	85.7 (0.22)	78.5 (0.45)	49.1 (1.60)	85.3 (1.66)	‡ (†)	66.9 (2.00)	79.4 (2.46)	24.8 (0.23)	27.9 (0.29)	15.3 (0.45)	10.6 (0.75)	52.8 (2.27)	‡ (†)	10.7 (1.44)	20.9 (2.31)
North Dakota	87.8 (0.58)	88.2 (0.56)	‡ (†)	‡ (†)	‡ (†)	‡ (†)	80.5 (5.68)	‡ (†)	26.4 (1.07)	26.8 (1.08)	‡ (†)	‡ (†)	‡ (†)	‡ (†)	13.3 (4.04)	‡ (†)

See notes at end of table.

Table 12.   Educational attainment of persons 25 years old and over, by race/ethnicity and state: 2006—Continued

State	Percent with high school completion or higher								Percent with bachelor's degree or higher							
	Total	White	Black	Hispanic	Asian	Hawaiian/ Pacific Islander	American Indian/Alaska Native	More than one race	Total	White	Black	Hispanic	Asian	Hawaiian/ Pacific Islander	American Indian/Alaska Native	More than one race
1	2	3	4	5	6	7	8	9	10	11	12	13	14	15	16	17
Ohio	86.3 (0.14)	87.4 (0.13)	79.3 (0.55)	71.5 (1.64)	89.0 (1.36)	‡	76.2 (2.96)	86.5 (1.94)	22.9 (0.17)	23.4 (0.18)	14.3 (0.50)	16.7 (1.26)	62.3 (2.33)	‡	10.9 (2.35)	17.4 (2.01)
Oklahoma	84.1 (0.32)	86.6 (0.32)	81.6 (1.37)	55.0 (2.31)	85.8 (2.85)	‡	80.6 (1.39)	81.6 (1.22)	22.0 (0.42)	24.0 (0.52)	14.8 (1.28)	10.5 (1.21)	43.3 (3.94)	‡	12.1 (0.99)	17.3 (1.41)
Oregon	87.7 (0.30)	91.0 (0.28)	84.3 (2.75)	54.3 (1.89)	83.9 (1.65)	90.0 (5.55)	85.9 (2.44)	87.5 (1.62)	27.3 (0.38)	28.7 (0.40)	15.6 (3.16)	10.1 (1.07)	42.3 (2.02)	14.8 (4.46)	15.1 (2.78)	22.5 (2.52)
Pennsylvania	86.3 (0.17)	87.9 (0.16)	79.7 (0.62)	63.5 (1.54)	84.9 (1.20)	‡	81.9 (5.10)	81.3 (2.67)	25.5 (0.19)	26.5 (0.18)	14.0 (0.64)	12.5 (0.92)	55.3 (1.83)	‡	21.4 (5.74)	19.5 (2.35)
Rhode Island	82.8 (0.62)	85.7 (0.66)	80.5 (3.10)	58.6 (3.00)	77.1 (4.19)	‡	71.5 (9.59)	87.2 (4.38)	29.1 (0.69)	31.1 (0.76)	18.8 (3.09)	13.5 (1.79)	48.5 (5.40)	‡	14.9 (9.15)	13.0 (4.23)
South Carolina	81.5 (0.31)	85.1 (0.33)	74.0 (0.76)	56.5 (2.41)	87.0 (2.31)	‡	74.4 (4.66)	88.1 (2.12)	22.9 (0.30)	27.3 (0.37)	11.0 (0.46)	10.8 (1.11)	48.0 (3.78)	‡	15.3 (4.45)	30.7 (3.48)
South Dakota	87.4 (0.67)	88.7 (0.64)	‡	51.5 (11.46)	‡	‡	78.8 (3.52)	‡	25.0 (0.85)	26.3 (0.93)	‡	5.4 (3.15)	‡	‡	9.0 (2.44)	‡
Tennessee	80.8 (0.24)	82.1 (0.25)	77.6 (0.76)	54.4 (2.31)	87.7 (2.33)	‡	77.0 (4.74)	80.1 (2.68)	22.0 (0.26)	23.2 (0.29)	14.5 (0.63)	11.5 (1.21)	54.7 (3.96)	‡	16.5 (3.32)	17.9 (3.00)
Texas	78.6 (0.15)	90.1 (0.13)	82.3 (0.45)	56.0 (0.37)	85.7 (0.67)	88.6 (6.20)	88.1 (1.70)	88.8 (1.10)	24.7 (0.15)	32.4 (0.20)	18.0 (0.41)	10.3 (0.22)	52.9 (1.00)	22.7 (8.59)	26.1 (2.27)	29.5 (1.51)
Utah	90.4 (0.38)	93.7 (0.29)	81.1 (7.96)	64.3 (2.17)	86.5 (2.59)	99.0 (1.01)	80.7 (4.34)	88.9 (3.56)	28.6 (0.41)	30.5 (0.47)	24.2 (5.81)	12.8 (1.61)	45.3 (4.97)	13.1 (3.88)	6.7 (2.66)	30.5 (6.50)
Vermont	91.0 (0.56)	91.2 (0.57)	‡	94.9 (4.20)	‡	‡	‡	88.2 (6.20)	32.9 (1.20)	32.7 (1.17)	‡	42.2 (10.56)	‡	‡	‡	24.7 (8.82)
Virginia	85.3 (0.22)	88.0 (0.21)	78.3 (0.56)	68.1 (1.42)	90.1 (0.81)	‡	80.8 (3.52)	89.9 (1.79)	32.8 (0.25)	35.6 (0.29)	17.7 (0.50)	23.9 (1.16)	57.1 (1.21)	‡	22.1 (4.07)	34.0 (2.59)
Washington	88.9 (0.20)	92.3 (0.17)	86.6 (1.34)	56.2 (1.44)	83.5 (1.15)	78.7 (4.00)	83.3 (1.64)	88.9 (1.52)	30.3 (0.29)	31.8 (0.33)	20.9 (1.50)	10.3 (0.86)	42.8 (1.17)	11.9 (3.71)	10.4 (1.55)	23.4 (2.00)
West Virginia	81.0 (0.49)	80.9 (0.50)	84.0 (2.00)	74.1 (5.39)	95.7 (2.88)	‡	‡	72.7 (7.43)	16.5 (0.45)	16.3 (0.43)	15.0 (2.19)	23.3 (6.51)	63.2 (7.62)	‡	‡	14.7 (6.04)
Wisconsin	88.4 (0.22)	90.2 (0.21)	76.9 (1.84)	63.9 (2.24)	79.7 (2.39)	‡	84.2 (3.56)	89.8 (2.59)	25.5 (0.29)	26.7 (0.29)	11.1 (1.10)	10.9 (1.35)	45.8 (3.82)	‡	11.3 (2.55)	25.2 (4.06)
Wyoming	90.0 (0.63)	91.5 (0.64)	‡	70.7 (3.73)	‡	‡	84.6 (5.98)	94.7 (3.89)	21.8 (0.96)	22.9 (1.07)	‡	8.1 (2.92)	‡	‡	7.1 (4.93)	19.4 (8.89)

†Not applicable.
‡Reporting standards not met.
NOTE: Race categories exclude persons of Hispanic ethnicity. Standard errors appear in parentheses.

SOURCE: U.S. Department of Commerce, Census Bureau, American Community Survey, 2006. (This table was prepared September 2008.)

Table 13. Educational attainment of persons 25 years old and over for the 25 largest states, by sex: 2006

State	Number of persons 25 years old and over (in thousands)						Percent with high school completion or higher						Percent with bachelor's or higher degree					
	Total		Males		Females		Total		Male		Female		Total		Male		Female	
1	2		3		4		5		6		7		8		9		10	
United States[1]	195,981	(90.7)	94,361	(56.0)	101,620	(52.6)	84.1	(0.04)	83.5	(0.05)	84.6	(0.05)	27.0	(0.05)	27.9	(0.06)	26.2	(0.07)
Alabama	3,024	(8.5)	1,425	(6.4)	1,599	(5.4)	80.0	(0.34)	79.1	(0.44)	80.8	(0.40)	21.0	(0.29)	21.7	(0.38)	20.3	(0.32)
Arizona	3,970	(7.9)	1,953	(4.9)	2,018	(5.7)	83.6	(0.24)	82.8	(0.32)	84.4	(0.29)	25.5	(0.30)	26.4	(0.42)	24.6	(0.35)
California	23,112	(24.2)	11,358	(17.1)	11,753	(12.5)	80.1	(0.10)	79.9	(0.14)	80.3	(0.11)	29.1	(0.11)	30.1	(0.13)	28.1	(0.15)
Colorado	3,120	(8.3)	1,548	(6.0)	1,571	(5.5)	88.1	(0.21)	87.5	(0.34)	88.8	(0.27)	34.5	(0.28)	35.6	(0.36)	33.5	(0.37)
Florida	12,464	(10.5)	5,983	(7.6)	6,481	(7.8)	84.7	(0.14)	83.9	(0.19)	85.4	(0.15)	25.3	(0.16)	26.9	(0.22)	23.8	(0.18)
Georgia	5,963	(10.5)	2,863	(7.5)	3,100	(6.2)	82.3	(0.18)	81.1	(0.30)	83.4	(0.20)	26.4	(0.20)	26.7	(0.24)	26.2	(0.27)
Illinois	8,341	(13.6)	4,009	(9.7)	4,332	(8.7)	85.0	(0.17)	84.7	(0.22)	85.3	(0.22)	28.8	(0.22)	29.8	(0.29)	27.9	(0.25)
Indiana	4,109	(8.9)	1,976	(6.6)	2,134	(5.9)	85.3	(0.20)	84.7	(0.27)	85.9	(0.28)	21.8	(0.24)	22.7	(0.30)	21.0	(0.30)
Louisiana	2,746	(8.3)	1,295	(6.1)	1,451	(5.6)	79.1	(0.33)	77.7	(0.41)	80.3	(0.41)	20.0	(0.27)	19.7	(0.39)	20.2	(0.35)
Maryland	3,719	(8.2)	1,746	(4.9)	1,973	(6.5)	87.2	(0.18)	86.4	(0.29)	87.9	(0.24)	35.3	(0.28)	36.2	(0.36)	34.4	(0.34)
Massachusetts	4,340	(8.3)	2,054	(5.4)	2,286	(5.3)	88.0	(0.23)	87.4	(0.30)	88.5	(0.28)	36.7	(0.28)	37.9	(0.35)	35.7	(0.33)
Michigan	6,648	(14.6)	3,207	(9.2)	3,440	(9.8)	87.3	(0.17)	86.4	(0.25)	88.0	(0.22)	24.6	(0.24)	25.5	(0.29)	23.9	(0.26)
Minnesota	3,397	(11.6)	1,663	(8.1)	1,734	(8.0)	90.7	(0.23)	89.8	(0.30)	91.4	(0.27)	30.2	(0.39)	30.8	(0.49)	29.7	(0.43)
Missouri	3,838	(11.8)	1,826	(6.0)	2,012	(8.4)	84.9	(0.22)	84.6	(0.30)	85.3	(0.27)	24.0	(0.27)	24.7	(0.34)	23.4	(0.35)
New Jersey	5,867	(9.8)	2,797	(7.4)	3,070	(6.9)	85.9	(0.18)	85.4	(0.26)	86.3	(0.22)	33.3	(0.23)	35.0	(0.27)	31.8	(0.29)
New York	12,846	(15.9)	6,052	(10.7)	6,794	(10.9)	84.1	(0.15)	83.9	(0.21)	84.2	(0.19)	31.1	(0.15)	31.8	(0.21)	30.5	(0.18)
North Carolina	5,838	(11.3)	2,777	(7.9)	3,061	(6.8)	82.1	(0.21)	80.6	(0.32)	83.5	(0.23)	24.8	(0.23)	25.0	(0.27)	24.5	(0.30)
Ohio	7,596	(13.6)	3,620	(7.6)	3,975	(8.9)	86.3	(0.14)	86.2	(0.18)	86.4	(0.17)	22.9	(0.17)	24.0	(0.22)	21.8	(0.21)
Pennsylvania	8,423	(14.6)	3,992	(10.9)	4,431	(9.9)	86.3	(0.17)	86.2	(0.22)	86.3	(0.20)	25.5	(0.19)	26.7	(0.25)	24.5	(0.21)
South Carolina	2,849	(6.2)	1,349	(5.3)	1,499	(3.9)	81.5	(0.31)	80.5	(0.44)	82.3	(0.35)	22.9	(0.30)	23.7	(0.39)	22.1	(0.37)
Tennessee	4,040	(9.1)	1,927	(6.4)	2,113	(5.6)	80.8	(0.24)	80.1	(0.34)	81.4	(0.31)	22.0	(0.26)	22.9	(0.30)	21.2	(0.35)
Texas	14,557	(16.6)	7,104	(12.6)	7,453	(11.7)	78.6	(0.15)	78.0	(0.19)	79.1	(0.17)	24.7	(0.15)	25.7	(0.20)	23.8	(0.17)
Virginia	5,078	(10.5)	2,425	(7.1)	2,653	(6.8)	85.3	(0.22)	84.7	(0.27)	85.9	(0.29)	32.8	(0.25)	33.5	(0.29)	32.0	(0.36)
Washington	4,246	(8.7)	2,079	(5.4)	2,167	(6.0)	88.9	(0.20)	88.8	(0.25)	89.0	(0.26)	30.3	(0.29)	31.8	(0.35)	28.9	(0.34)
Wisconsin	3,681	(13.5)	1,801	(9.4)	1,880	(6.8)	88.4	(0.22)	87.6	(0.33)	89.2	(0.24)	25.5	(0.29)	25.5	(0.39)	25.5	(0.36)

[1]Total includes all 50 states and the District of Columbia.
NOTE: Standard errors appear in parentheses. Detail may not sum to totals because of rounding.

SOURCE: U.S. Department of Commerce, Census Bureau, 2006 American Community Survey Public Use Microdata Sample (PUMS) data. (This table was prepared August 2008.)

Table 14. Educational attainment of persons 25 years old and over for the 15 largest metropolitan areas, by sex: 2008

Metropolitan area	Number of persons 25 years old and over (in thousands)						Percent with high school completion or higher						Percent with bachelor's or higher degree					
	Total		Males		Females		Total		Male		Female		Total		Male		Female	
1	2		3		4		5		6		7		8		9		10	
Atlanta-Sandy Springs-Gainesville, GA/AL, CSA	3,515	(64.6)	1,721	(45.4)	1,794	(46.3)	89.2	(0.57)	88.2	(0.85)	90.2	(0.77)	38.7	(0.90)	40.9	(1.30)	36.6	(1.25)
Boston-Worcester-Manchester, MA/NH, CSA	3,741	(66.6)	1,774	(46.1)	1,967	(48.5)	92.8	(0.46)	92.7	(0.68)	92.9	(0.64)	44.8	(0.89)	44.4	(1.30)	45.1	(1.23)
Chicago-Naperville-Michigan City, IL/IN/WI, CSA	6,117	(84.8)	2,918	(59.0)	3,199	(61.7)	87.7	(0.46)	86.8	(0.69)	88.6	(0.62)	35.1	(0.67)	36.3	(0.98)	34.0	(0.92)
Dallas-Fort Worth, TX, CSA	3,877	(67.8)	1,905	(47.7)	1,972	(48.6)	82.1	(0.68)	80.4	(1.00)	83.6	(0.92)	32.3	(0.83)	33.2	(1.19)	31.5	(1.15)
Detroit-Warren-Flint, MI, CSA	3,691	(66.2)	1,721	(45.4)	1,970	(48.5)	88.3	(0.58)	89.5	(0.81)	87.2	(0.83)	30.4	(0.83)	32.1	(1.24)	29.0	(1.12)
Houston-Baytown-Huntsville, TX, CSA	3,416	(63.7)	1,644	(44.4)	1,772	(46.1)	79.9	(0.75)	78.1	(1.12)	81.5	(1.01)	28.6	(0.85)	27.6	(1.21)	29.4	(1.19)
Los Angeles-Long Beach-Riverside, CA, CSA	11,273	(113.8)	5,514	(80.6)	5,758	(82.3)	79.2	(0.42)	78.8	(0.60)	79.6	(0.58)	29.4	(0.47)	30.5	(0.68)	28.3	(0.65)
Miami-Fort Lauderdale-Miami Beach, FL, MSA	3,665	(66.0)	1,740	(45.6)	1,926	(48.0)	86.6	(0.62)	86.1	(0.91)	87.1	(0.84)	31.5	(0.84)	31.8	(1.23)	31.2	(1.16)
Minneapolis-St. Paul-St. Cloud, MN/WI, CSA	2,132	(50.5)	1,036	(35.3)	1,096	(36.3)	93.3	(0.60)	93.9	(0.81)	92.6	(0.87)	39.4	(1.16)	41.3	(1.68)	37.5	(1.61)
New York-Newark-Bridgeport, NY/NJ/CT/PA, CSA	14,293	(127.3)	6,688	(88.6)	7,605	(94.2)	86.2	(0.32)	86.2	(0.46)	86.2	(0.43)	37.1	(0.44)	38.8	(0.65)	35.6	(0.60)
Philadelphia-Camden-Vineland, PA/NJ/DE/MD, CSA	3,815	(67.3)	1,789	(46.3)	2,026	(49.2)	89.1	(0.55)	88.1	(0.84)	90.0	(0.73)	31.3	(0.82)	31.7	(1.21)	31.0	(1.13)
Phoenix-Mesa-Scottsdale, AZ, MSA	2,903	(58.8)	1,457	(41.8)	1,447	(41.6)	85.9	(0.71)	85.9	(1.00)	85.9	(1.01)	27.3	(0.91)	29.3	(1.31)	25.4	(1.26)
San Jose-San Francisco-Oakland, CA, CSA	5,259	(78.8)	2,569	(55.4)	2,690	(56.6)	88.6	(0.48)	88.7	(0.69)	88.6	(0.67)	44.1	(0.75)	43.6	(1.07)	44.7	(1.05)
Seattle-Tacoma-Olympia, WA, CSA	2,587	(55.6)	1,259	(38.9)	1,328	(39.9)	94.1	(0.51)	93.7	(0.75)	94.5	(0.69)	36.4	(1.04)	36.7	(1.49)	36.2	(1.45)
Washington-Baltimore-Northern Virginia, DC/MD/VA/WV, CSA	5,317	(79.2)	2,543	(55.1)	2,774	(57.5)	90.8	(0.43)	90.2	(0.65)	91.4	(0.59)	45.3	(0.75)	47.3	(1.09)	43.5	(1.03)

NOTE: CSA = Combined Statistical Area, MSA = Metropolitan Statistical Area. Detail may not sum to totals because of rounding. Standard errors appear in parentheses.

SOURCE: U.S. Department of Commerce, Census Bureau, Current Population Survey (CPS), March 2008. (This table was prepared September 2008.)

Table 15. Estimates of resident population, by age group: 1970 through 2008

[In thousands]

Year	Total, all ages	Total, 3 to 34 years	3 and 4 years	5 and 6 years	7 to 13 years	14 to 17 years	18 and 19 years	20 and 21 years	22 to 24 years	25 to 29 years	30 to 34 years
1	2	3	4	5	6	7	8	9	10	11	12
1970	205,052	109,592	6,961	7,703	28,969	15,924	7,510	7,210	9,992	13,736	11,587
1971	207,661	111,202	6,805	7,344	28,892	16,328	7,715	7,350	10,809	14,041	11,917
1972	209,896	112,807	6,789	7,051	28,628	16,639	7,923	7,593	10,560	15,240	12,383
1973	211,909	114,426	6,938	6,888	28,158	16,867	8,114	7,796	10,725	15,786	13,153
1974	213,854	116,075	7,117	6,864	27,600	17,035	8,257	8,003	10,972	16,521	13,704
1975	215,973	117,435	6,912	7,013	26,905	17,128	8,478	8,196	11,331	17,280	14,191
1976	218,035	118,474	6,436	7,195	26,321	17,119	8,659	8,336	11,650	18,274	14,485
1977	220,239	119,261	6,190	6,978	25,877	17,045	8,675	8,550	11,949	18,277	15,721
1978	222,585	119,833	6,208	6,500	25,594	16,946	8,677	8,730	12,216	18,683	16,280
1979	225,055	120,544	6,252	6,256	25,175	16,611	8,751	8,754	12,542	19,178	17,025
1980	227,225	121,132	6,366	6,291	24,800	16,143	8,718	8,669	12,716	19,686	17,743
1981	229,466	121,999	6,535	6,315	24,396	15,609	8,582	8,759	12,903	20,169	18,731
1982	231,664	121,823	6,658	6,407	24,121	15,057	8,480	8,768	12,914	20,704	18,714
1983	233,792	122,302	6,877	6,572	23,709	14,740	8,290	8,652	12,981	21,414	19,067
1984	235,825	122,254	7,045	6,694	23,367	14,725	7,932	8,567	12,962	21,459	19,503
1985	237,924	122,512	7,134	6,916	22,976	14,888	7,637	8,370	12,895	21,671	20,025
1986	240,133	122,688	7,187	7,086	22,992	14,824	7,483	8,024	12,720	21,893	20,479
1987	242,289	122,672	7,132	7,178	23,325	14,502	7,502	7,742	12,450	21,857	20,984
1988	244,499	122,713	7,176	7,238	23,791	14,023	7,701	7,606	12,048	21,739	21,391
1989	246,819	122,655	7,315	7,184	24,228	13,536	7,898	7,651	11,607	21,560	21,676
1990	249,623	122,787	7,359	7,244	24,785	13,329	7,702	7,886	11,264	21,277	21,939
1991	252,981	123,210	7,444	7,393	25,216	13,491	7,208	8,029	11,205	20,923	22,301
1992	256,514	123,722	7,614	7,447	25,752	13,775	6,949	7,797	11,391	20,503	22,494
1993	259,919	124,371	7,887	7,549	26,212	14,096	6,985	7,333	11,657	20,069	22,584
1994	263,126	124,976	8,089	7,725	26,492	14,637	7,047	7,071	11,585	19,740	22,590
1995	266,278	125,478	8,107	8,000	26,825	15,013	7,182	7,103	11,197	19,680	22,372
1996	269,394	125,924	8,022	8,206	27,168	15,443	7,399	7,161	10,715	19,864	21,945
1997	272,647	126,422	7,915	8,232	27,683	15,769	7,569	7,309	10,601	19,899	21,446
1998	275,854	126,939	7,841	8,152	28,302	15,829	7,892	7,520	10,647	19,804	20,953
1999	279,040	127,446	7,772	8,041	28,763	16,007	8,094	7,683	10,908	19,575	20,603
2000[1]	282,194	128,062	7,729	7,979	29,073	16,122	8,185	7,996	11,132	19,306	20,541
2001[1]	285,112	128,553	7,654	7,912	29,167	16,184	8,169	8,281	11,516	18,938	20,732
2002[1]	287,888	129,094	7,651	7,797	29,174	16,353	8,121	8,310	11,989	18,896	20,802
2003[1]	290,448	129,490	7,715	7,717	29,035	16,497	8,165	8,264	12,372	19,051	20,673
2004[1]	293,192	130,094	7,940	7,707	28,638	16,813	8,261	8,226	12,644	19,458	20,408
2005[1]	295,896	130,357	8,065	7,768	28,295	17,068	8,259	8,282	12,665	19,945	20,010
2006[1]	298,755	130,780	8,068	7,995	28,014	17,207	8,319	8,383	12,611	20,575	19,607
2007	301,621	131,435	8,174	8,121	27,850	17,207	8,460	8,374	12,658	21,058	19,533
2008	304,483	132,289	8,244	8,124	27,925	16,959	8,717	8,430	12,714	21,463	19,712

[1]Revised from previously published figures.
NOTE: Detail may not sum to totals because of rounding. Estimates as of July 1.
SOURCE: U.S. Department of Commerce, Census Bureau, *Current Population Reports*, Series P-25, Nos. 1000, 1022, 1045, 1057, 1059, 1092, and 1095; and 2000 through 2008

Population Estimates, retrieved August 12, 2008, from http://www.census.gov/popest/national/asrh/2007-nat-res.html. (This table was prepared August 2008.)

Table 16. Estimates of resident population, by race/ethnicity and age group: Selected years, 1980 through 2008

Year and age group	Number (in thousands)								Percentage distribution							
	Total	White	Black	His-panic	Asian	Pacific Islander	American Indian/ Alaska Native	More than one race	Total	White	Black	His-panic	Asian	Pacific Islander	American Indian/ Alaska Native	More than one race
1	2	3	4	5	6	7	8	9	10	11	12	13	14	15	16	17
Total																
1980	227,225	181,140	26,215	14,869	3,665	(1)	1,336	—	100.0	79.7	11.5	6.5	1.6	(1)	0.6	—
1990	249,623	188,725	29,439	22,573	7,092	(1)	1,793	—	100.0	75.6	11.8	9.0	2.8	(1)	0.7	—
1995	266,278	194,389	32,500	28,158	9,188	(1)	2,044	—	100.0	73.0	12.2	10.6	3.5	(1)	0.8	—
2000[2]	282,194	195,770	34,413	35,649	10,458	369	2,104	3,431	100.0	69.4	12.2	12.6	3.7	0.1	0.7	1.2
2001[2]	285,112	196,321	34,814	37,069	10,866	376	2,130	3,536	100.0	68.9	12.2	13.0	3.8	0.1	0.7	1.2
2002[2]	287,888	196,775	35,185	38,488	11,264	383	2,155	3,639	100.0	68.4	12.2	13.4	3.9	0.1	0.7	1.3
2003[2]	290,448	197,148	35,511	39,844	11,635	389	2,178	3,742	100.0	67.9	12.2	13.7	4.0	0.1	0.7	1.3
2004[2]	293,192	197,657	35,889	41,202	11,988	396	2,205	3,854	100.0	67.4	12.2	14.1	4.1	0.1	0.8	1.3
2005[2]	295,896	198,092	36,253	42,603	12,347	403	2,231	3,967	100.0	66.9	12.3	14.4	4.2	0.1	0.8	1.3
2006[2]	298,755	198,589	36,646	44,054	12,712	410	2,259	4,084	100.0	66.5	12.3	14.7	4.3	0.1	0.8	1.4
2007[2]	301,621	199,092	37,037	45,504	13,080	417	2,287	4,205	100.0	66.0	12.3	15.1	4.3	0.1	0.8	1.4
2008[2]	304,483	199,559	37,430	46,976	13,446	424	2,315	4,333	100.0	65.5	12.3	15.4	4.4	0.1	0.8	1.4
Under 5																
1980	16,451	11,904	2,413	1,677	319	(1)	137	—	100.0	72.4	14.7	10.2	1.9	(1)	0.8	—
1990	18,856	12,757	2,825	2,497	593	(1)	184	—	100.0	67.7	15.0	13.2	3.1	(1)	1.0	—
1995	19,627	12,415	3,050	3,245	734	(1)	182	—	100.0	63.3	15.5	16.5	3.7	(1)	0.9	—
2000[2]	19,187	11,268	2,763	3,741	684	29	172	531	100.0	58.7	14.4	19.5	3.6	0.2	0.9	2.8
2001[2]	19,350	11,235	2,796	3,875	709	28	171	536	100.0	58.1	14.4	20.0	3.7	0.1	0.9	2.8
2002[2]	19,537	11,208	2,826	4,029	734	28	171	541	100.0	57.4	14.5	20.6	3.8	0.1	0.9	2.8
2003[2]	19,774	11,211	2,851	4,201	768	28	171	544	100.0	56.7	14.4	21.2	3.9	0.1	0.9	2.8
2004[2]	20,060	11,226	2,889	4,393	805	27	172	548	100.0	56.0	14.4	21.9	4.0	0.1	0.9	2.7
2005[2]	20,300	11,204	2,921	4,577	842	27	174	555	100.0	55.2	14.4	22.5	4.1	0.1	0.9	2.7
2006[2]	20,452	11,138	2,926	4,753	860	28	177	571	100.0	54.5	14.3	23.2	4.2	0.1	0.9	2.8
2007[2]	20,724	11,175	2,953	4,916	882	28	180	590	100.0	53.9	14.2	23.7	4.3	0.1	0.9	2.8
2008[2]	20,996	11,204	2,996	5,073	895	28	184	614	100.0	53.4	14.3	24.2	4.3	0.1	0.9	2.9
5 to 17																
1980	47,232	35,220	6,840	4,005	790	(1)	377	—	100.0	74.6	14.5	8.5	1.7	(1)	0.8	—
1990	45,359	—	—	—	—	—	—	—	—	—	—	—	—	—	—	—
1995	49,838	—	—	—	—	—	—	—	—	—	—	—	—	—	—	—
2000[2]	53,173	33,016	7,989	8,682	1,826	85	522	1,053	100.0	62.1	15.0	16.3	3.4	0.2	1.0	2.0
2001[2]	53,263	32,801	7,990	8,921	1,861	85	517	1,089	100.0	61.6	15.0	16.7	3.5	0.2	1.0	2.0
2002[2]	53,325	32,552	7,981	9,175	1,896	85	511	1,125	100.0	61.0	15.0	17.2	3.6	0.2	1.0	2.1
2003[2]	53,250	32,206	7,952	9,415	1,924	85	505	1,162	100.0	60.5	14.9	17.7	3.6	0.2	0.9	2.2
2004[2]	53,158	31,869	7,910	9,646	1,947	85	499	1,202	100.0	60.0	14.9	18.1	3.7	0.2	0.9	2.3
2005[2]	53,132	31,554	7,874	9,910	1,977	84	492	1,240	100.0	59.4	14.8	18.7	3.7	0.2	0.9	2.3
2006[2]	53,216	31,284	7,865	10,207	2,023	83	485	1,269	100.0	58.8	14.8	19.2	3.8	0.2	0.9	2.4
2007[2]	53,178	30,938	7,818	10,503	2,063	82	477	1,296	100.0	58.2	14.7	19.8	3.9	0.2	0.9	2.4
2008[2]	53,009	30,529	7,727	10,771	2,111	81	469	1,321	100.0	57.6	14.6	20.3	4.0	0.2	0.9	2.5
18 to 24																
1980	30,103	23,278	3,872	2,284	468	(1)	201	—	100.0	77.3	12.9	7.6	1.6	(1)	0.7	—
1990	26,853	—	—	—	—	—	—	—	—	—	—	—	—	—	—	—
1995	25,482	—	—	—	—	—	—	—	—	—	—	—	—	—	—	—
2000[2]	27,312	16,925	3,782	4,781	1,148	50	239	387	100.0	62.0	13.8	17.5	4.2	0.2	0.9	1.4
2001[2]	27,966	17,302	3,888	4,904	1,163	50	249	410	100.0	61.9	13.9	17.5	4.2	0.2	0.9	1.5
2002[2]	28,420	17,561	3,966	4,979	1,176	51	256	431	100.0	61.8	14.0	17.5	4.1	0.2	0.9	1.5
2003[2]	28,801	17,804	4,034	5,015	1,183	50	264	450	100.0	61.8	14.0	17.4	4.1	0.2	0.9	1.6
2004[2]	29,131	18,018	4,098	5,042	1,182	50	271	469	100.0	61.9	14.1	17.3	4.1	0.2	0.9	1.6
2005[2]	29,206	18,058	4,122	5,042	1,173	49	275	485	100.0	61.8	14.1	17.3	4.0	0.2	0.9	1.7
2006[2]	29,313	18,075	4,168	5,072	1,169	49	280	500	100.0	61.7	14.2	17.3	4.0	0.2	1.0	1.7
2007[2]	29,492	18,119	4,230	5,122	1,173	49	283	517	100.0	61.4	14.3	17.4	4.0	0.2	1.0	1.8
2008[2]	29,861	18,230	4,329	5,246	1,184	49	286	537	100.0	61.0	14.5	17.6	4.0	0.2	1.0	1.8
25 and over																
1980	133,438	110,737	13,091	6,903	2,088	(1)	620	—	100.0	83.0	9.8	5.2	1.6	(1)	0.5	—
1990	158,555	125,653	16,322	11,447	4,190	(1)	944	—	100.0	79.2	10.3	7.2	2.6	(1)	0.6	—
1995	171,332	131,839	18,250	14,519	5,628	(1)	1,096	—	100.0	76.9	10.7	8.5	3.3	(1)	0.6	—
2000[2]	182,521	134,560	19,879	18,445	6,800	205	1,171	1,460	100.0	73.7	10.9	10.1	3.7	0.1	0.6	0.8
2001[2]	184,533	134,983	20,140	19,370	7,134	212	1,193	1,501	100.0	73.1	10.9	10.5	3.9	0.1	0.6	0.8
2002[2]	186,606	135,454	20,412	20,304	7,459	220	1,216	1,543	100.0	72.6	10.9	10.9	4.0	0.1	0.7	0.8
2003[2]	188,624	135,926	20,674	21,212	7,760	227	1,239	1,586	100.0	72.1	11.0	11.2	4.1	0.1	0.7	0.8
2004[2]	190,843	136,544	20,991	22,121	8,054	235	1,263	1,634	100.0	71.5	11.0	11.6	4.2	0.1	0.7	0.9
2005[2]	193,259	137,276	21,335	23,074	8,355	242	1,290	1,687	100.0	71.0	11.0	11.9	4.3	0.1	0.7	0.9
2006[2]	195,774	138,091	21,688	24,023	8,661	250	1,317	1,743	100.0	70.5	11.1	12.3	4.4	0.1	0.7	0.9
2007[2]	198,227	138,860	22,037	24,963	8,962	258	1,345	1,802	100.0	70.1	11.1	12.6	4.5	0.1	0.7	0.9
2008[2]	200,617	139,596	22,379	25,885	9,256	265	1,375	1,861	100.0	69.6	11.2	12.9	4.6	0.1	0.7	0.9

—Not available.
[1]Included under Asian.
[2]Data on persons of more than one race group were collected beginning in 2000. Direct comparability of the data (other than Hispanic) prior to 2000 with the data for 2000 and later years is limited by the extent to which people reporting more than one race in later years had been reported in specific race groups in earlier years.

NOTE: Resident population includes civilian population and armed forces personnel residing within the United States; it excludes armed forces personnel residing overseas. Race categories exclude persons of Hispanic ethnicity. Detail may not sum to totals because of rounding. Some data have been revised from previously published figures. Estimates as of July 1. SOURCE: U.S. Department of Commerce, Census Bureau, Population Estimates, retrieved August 12, 2008, from http://www.census.gov/popest/national/asrh/2007-nat-res.html. (This table was prepared August 2008.)

Table 17. Estimated total and school-age resident populations, by state: Selected years, 1970 through 2007

[In thousands]

State	Total, all ages								5- to 17-year-olds							
	1970[1]	1980[1]	1990[1]	2000[2]	2004[2]	2005[2]	2006[2]	2007[2]	1970[1]	1980[1]	1990[1]	2000[2]	2004[2]	2005[2]	2006[2]	2007[2]
1	2	3	4	5	6	7	8	9	10	11	12	13	14	15	16	17
United States	203,302	226,546	248,765	282,194	293,192	295,896	298,755	301,621	52,540	47,407	45,178	53,173	53,158	53,132	53,216	53,178
Alabama	3,444	3,894	4,040	4,452	4,509	4,540	4,590	4,628	934	866	774	827	807	808	815	815
Alaska.............................	303	402	550	627	662	669	677	683	88	92	117	143	137	135	133	131
Arizona	1,775	2,718	3,665	5,167	5,744	5,952	6,166	6,339	486	578	686	990	1,074	1,106	1,143	1,170
Arkansas.........................	1,923	2,286	2,351	2,678	2,743	2,772	2,809	2,835	498	496	455	499	493	495	499	502
California	19,971	23,668	29,786	34,004	35,722	35,990	36,250	36,553	4,999	4,681	5,344	6,776	6,862	6,816	6,777	6,724
Colorado	2,210	2,890	3,294	4,328	4,609	4,674	4,766	4,862	589	592	607	807	817	821	832	843
Connecticut.....................	3,032	3,108	3,287	3,412	3,482	3,486	3,496	3,502	768	638	520	619	624	620	615	609
Delaware.........................	548	594	666	786	828	841	853	865	148	125	114	143	144	146	146	147
District of Columbia	757	638	607	572	580	582	585	588	164	109	80	82	81	79	79	78
Florida.............................	6,791	9,746	12,938	16,049	17,343	17,736	18,058	18,251	1,609	1,789	2,011	2,708	2,830	2,869	2,902	2,895
Georgia...........................	4,588	5,463	6,478	8,231	8,921	9,108	9,342	9,545	1,223	1,231	1,230	1,581	1,677	1,714	1,758	1,794
Hawaii.............................	770	965	1,108	1,212	1,254	1,268	1,279	1,283	204	198	196	217	211	207	202	199
Idaho...............................	713	944	1,007	1,300	1,392	1,426	1,464	1,499	200	213	228	272	273	278	284	289
Illinois.............................	11,110	11,427	11,431	12,439	12,680	12,720	12,777	12,853	2,859	2,401	2,095	2,369	2,334	2,323	2,317	2,308
Indiana............................	5,195	5,490	5,544	6,092	6,219	6,257	6,303	6,345	1,386	1,200	1,056	1,152	1,141	1,143	1,149	1,149
Iowa	2,825	2,914	2,777	2,928	2,946	2,956	2,973	2,988	743	604	525	545	522	519	518	515
Kansas............................	2,249	2,364	2,478	2,693	2,731	2,742	2,756	2,776	573	468	472	524	505	502	500	500
Kentucky	3,221	3,661	3,687	4,049	4,140	4,171	4,204	4,241	844	800	703	729	719	720	726	726
Louisiana	3,645	4,206	4,222	4,469	4,488	4,496	4,243	4,293	1,041	969	891	901	848	839	776	781
Maine..............................	994	1,125	1,228	1,277	1,309	1,312	1,315	1,317	260	243	223	231	220	216	212	209
Maryland..........................	3,924	4,217	4,781	5,311	5,538	5,573	5,602	5,618	1,038	895	803	1,004	1,009	1,003	994	982
Massachusetts.................	5,689	5,737	6,016	6,363	6,434	6,429	6,434	6,450	1,407	1,153	940	1,104	1,089	1,078	1,067	1,056
Michigan..........................	8,882	9,262	9,295	9,955	10,103	10,108	10,102	10,072	2,450	2,067	1,754	1,924	1,882	1,864	1,843	1,814
Minnesota	3,806	4,076	4,376	4,934	5,086	5,114	5,155	5,198	1,051	865	829	959	928	919	914	906
Mississippi	2,217	2,521	2,575	2,848	2,887	2,900	2,899	2,919	635	599	550	571	553	552	550	549
Missouri	4,678	4,917	5,117	5,606	5,745	5,788	5,838	5,878	1,183	1,008	944	1,058	1,037	1,035	1,036	1,032
Montana..........................	694	787	799	903	927	936	947	958	197	167	163	175	164	162	161	160
Nebraska	1,485	1,570	1,578	1,713	1,744	1,754	1,764	1,775	389	324	309	333	320	318	317	316
Nevada	489	800	1,202	2,018	2,330	2,409	2,492	2,565	127	160	204	369	425	438	453	465
New Hampshire	738	921	1,109	1,240	1,294	1,303	1,312	1,316	189	196	194	234	232	229	226	223
New Jersey	7,171	7,365	7,748	8,432	8,641	8,657	8,666	8,686	1,797	1,528	1,269	1,524	1,542	1,535	1,522	1,507
New Mexico	1,017	1,303	1,515	1,821	1,892	1,916	1,942	1,970	311	303	320	377	360	357	356	355
New York.........................	18,241	17,558	17,991	18,997	19,258	19,263	19,282	19,298	4,358	3,552	3,000	3,447	3,356	3,311	3,270	3,217
North Carolina	5,084	5,882	6,632	8,080	8,538	8,679	8,869	9,061	1,323	1,254	1,147	1,428	1,490	1,514	1,545	1,580
North Dakota	618	653	639	641	637	636	637	640	175	136	127	121	109	107	104	103
Ohio................................	10,657	10,798	10,847	11,364	11,453	11,460	11,464	11,467	2,820	2,307	2,012	2,132	2,069	2,051	2,037	2,015
Oklahoma	2,559	3,025	3,146	3,454	3,517	3,536	3,578	3,617	640	622	609	655	634	633	636	638
Oregon............................	2,092	2,633	2,842	3,431	3,583	3,630	3,691	3,747	534	525	521	624	621	621	626	627
Pennsylvania....................	11,801	11,864	11,883	12,286	12,349	12,367	12,403	12,433	2,925	2,376	1,996	2,191	2,117	2,095	2,079	2,057
Rhode Island	950	947	1,003	1,051	1,073	1,067	1,062	1,058	225	186	159	184	182	179	175	172
South Carolina.................	2,591	3,122	3,486	4,024	4,201	4,255	4,330	4,408	720	703	662	746	747	751	758	764
South Dakota	666	691	696	756	774	780	788	796	187	147	144	151	144	142	141	140
Tennessee	3,926	4,591	4,877	5,703	5,912	5,989	6,075	6,157	1,002	972	882	1,024	1,034	1,043	1,058	1,062
Texas	11,199	14,229	16,986	20,949	22,455	22,844	23,408	23,904	3,002	3,137	3,437	4,275	4,394	4,435	4,549	4,634
Utah................................	1,059	1,461	1,723	2,244	2,431	2,505	2,580	2,645	312	350	457	511	519	532	548	561
Vermont...........................	445	511	563	610	619	620	621	621	118	109	102	114	106	103	101	99
Virginia............................	4,651	5,347	6,189	7,105	7,464	7,558	7,640	7,712	1,197	1,114	1,060	1,279	1,301	1,304	1,308	1,308
Washington......................	3,413	4,132	4,867	5,912	6,190	6,271	6,375	6,468	881	826	893	1,121	1,114	1,112	1,114	1,113
West Virginia....................	1,744	1,950	1,793	1,807	1,805	1,806	1,809	1,812	442	414	337	300	285	283	283	283
Wisconsin	4,418	4,706	4,892	5,374	5,510	5,540	5,573	5,602	1,203	1,011	927	1,027	989	979	973	965
Wyoming..........................	332	470	454	494	503	507	513	523	92	101	101	98	90	89	89	89

[1]As of April 1.
[2]Estimates as of July 1.
NOTE: Resident population includes civilian population and armed forces personnel residing within the United States and within each state; it excludes armed forces personnel residing overseas. Some data have been revised from previously published figures. Detail may not sum to totals because of rounding.

SOURCE: U.S. Department of Commerce, Census Bureau, *Current Population Reports*, Series P-25, No. 1095; CPH-L-74 (1990 data); and 2000 through 2007 Population Estimates, retrieved August 12, 2008, from http://www.census.gov/popest/datasets.html. (This table was prepared August 2008.)

Table 18. Number and percentage of family households, by family status and presence of own children under 18: Selected years, 1970 through 2007

Family status	1970		1980		1990		2000		2005		2006		2007		Change, 1970 to 1990	Change, 1990 to 2007
1	2		3		4		5		6		7		8		9	10
	In thousands														Percent change	
All families	51,456	(257.3)	59,550	(271.4)	66,090	(307.8)	72,025	(311.6)	77,010	(226.6)	77,402	(226.9)	78,425	(227.5)	28.4	18.7
Married-couple family	44,728	(243.6)	49,112	(252.7)	52,317	(283.3)	55,311	(289.5)	58,109	(210.4)	58,179	(210.4)	58,945	(211.3)	17.0	12.7
Without own children under 18	19,196	(168.7)	24,151	(187.3)	27,780	(218.1)	30,062	(230.5)	31,929	(168.8)	32,197	(169.4)	32,787	(170.6)	44.7	18.0
With own children under 18	25,532	(192.0)	24,961	(190.1)	24,537	(206.4)	25,248	(214.1)	26,180	(155.3)	25,982	(154.8)	26,158	(155.2)	-3.9	6.6
One own child under 18	8,163	(112.5)	9,671	(122.0)	9,583	(133.0)	9,402	(136.2)	9,885	(99.6)	10,031	(100.2)	10,127	(100.7)	17.4	5.7
Two own children under 18	8,045	(111.7)	9,488	(120.9)	9,784	(134.3)	10,274	(142.1)	10,676	(103.3)	10,336	(101.7)	10,497	(102.4)	21.6	7.3
Three or more own children under 18	9,325	(119.9)	5,802	(95.3)	5,170	(98.5)	5,572	(105.9)	5,619	(75.9)	5,615	(75.8)	5,534	(75.3)	-44.6	7.0
Other family, male householder, no spouse present	1,228	(44.2)	1,733	(52.5)	2,884	(73.9)	4,028	(90.4)	4,893	(70.9)	5,130	(72.6)	5,063	(72.1)	134.9	75.6
Without own children under 18	887	(37.6)	1,117	(42.2)	1,731	(57.4)	2,242	(67.7)	2,859	(54.5)	3,035	(56.1)	3,049	(56.2)	95.2	76.1
With own children under 18	341	(23.3)	616	(31.3)	1,153	(46.9)	1,786	(60.5)	2,034	(46.0)	2,095	(46.7)	2,015	(45.8)	238.1	74.8
One own child under 18	179	(16.9)	374	(24.4)	723	(37.2)	1,131	(48.2)	1,227	(35.8)	1,313	(37.0)	1,243	(36.1)	303.9	71.9
Two own children under 18	87	(11.8)	165	(16.2)	307	(24.2)	483	(31.6)	563	(24.3)	588	(24.8)	553	(24.1)	252.9	80.1
Three or more own children under 18	75	(10.9)	77	(11.1)	123	(15.3)	171	(18.8)	244	(16.0)	194	(14.3)	218	(15.1)	64.0	77.2
Other family, female householder, no spouse present	5,500	(92.8)	8,705	(116.0)	10,890	(141.4)	12,687	(156.9)	14,009	(117.3)	14,093	(117.6)	14,416	(118.9)	98.0	32.4
Without own children under 18	2,642	(64.7)	3,261	(71.8)	4,290	(89.9)	5,116	(101.6)	5,703	(76.4)	5,703	(76.4)	5,832	(77.2)	62.4	35.9
With own children under 18	2,858	(67.2)	5,445	(92.3)	6,599	(111.0)	7,571	(122.8)	8,305	(91.6)	8,389	(92.1)	8,585	(93.1)	130.9	30.1
One own child under 18	1,008	(40.1)	2,398	(61.6)	3,225	(78.1)	3,777	(87.6)	4,081	(64.9)	4,184	(65.7)	4,280	(66.4)	219.9	32.7
Two own children under 18	810	(35.9)	1,817	(53.7)	2,173	(64.2)	2,458	(70.9)	2,626	(52.2)	2,739	(53.3)	2,765	(53.6)	168.3	27.2
Three or more own children under 18	1,040	(40.7)	1,230	(44.2)	1,202	(47.9)	1,336	(52.4)	1,597	(40.8)	1,466	(39.1)	1,540	(40.1)	15.6	28.1
	Percentage of all families														Change in percentage points	
All families	100.0	(†)	100.0	(†)	100.0	(†)	100.0	(†)	100.0	(†)	100.0	(†)	100.0	(†)	†	†
Married-couple family	86.9	(0.19)	82.5	(0.20)	79.2	(0.22)	76.8	(0.23)	75.5	(0.16)	75.2	(0.16)	75.2	(0.16)	-7.8	-4.0
Without own children under 18	37.3	(0.27)	40.6	(0.25)	42.0	(0.27)	41.7	(0.26)	41.5	(0.18)	41.6	(0.18)	41.8	(0.18)	4.7	-0.2
With own children under 18	49.6	(0.28)	41.9	(0.26)	37.1	(0.26)	35.1	(0.26)	34.0	(0.18)	33.6	(0.17)	33.4	(0.17)	-12.5	-3.8
One own child under 18	15.9	(0.20)	16.2	(0.19)	14.5	(0.19)	13.1	(0.18)	12.8	(0.12)	13.0	(0.12)	12.9	(0.12)	-1.4	-1.6
Two own children under 18	15.6	(0.20)	15.9	(0.19)	14.8	(0.19)	14.3	(0.19)	13.9	(0.13)	13.4	(0.13)	13.4	(0.13)	-0.8	-1.4
Three or more own children under 18	18.1	(0.21)	9.7	(0.15)	7.8	(0.14)	7.7	(0.14)	7.3	(0.10)	7.3	(0.10)	7.1	(0.09)	-10.3	-0.8
Other family, male householder, no spouse present	2.4	(0.09)	2.9	(0.09)	4.4	(0.11)	5.6	(0.12)	6.4	(0.09)	6.6	(0.09)	6.5	(0.09)	2.0	2.1
Without own children under 18	1.7	(0.07)	1.9	(0.07)	2.6	(0.09)	3.1	(0.09)	3.7	(0.07)	3.9	(0.07)	3.9	(0.07)	0.9	1.3
With own children under 18	0.7	(0.05)	1.0	(0.05)	1.7	(0.07)	2.5	(0.08)	2.6	(0.06)	2.7	(0.06)	2.6	(0.06)	1.1	0.8
One own child under 18	0.3	(0.03)	0.6	(0.04)	1.1	(0.06)	1.6	(0.07)	1.6	(0.05)	1.7	(0.05)	1.6	(0.05)	0.7	0.5
Two own children under 18	0.2	(0.02)	0.3	(0.03)	0.5	(0.04)	0.7	(0.04)	0.7	(0.03)	0.8	(0.03)	0.7	(0.03)	0.3	0.2
Three or more own children under 18	0.1	(0.02)	0.1	(0.02)	0.2	(0.02)	0.2	(0.03)	0.3	(0.02)	0.3	(0.02)	0.3	(0.02)	#	0.1
Other family, female householder, no spouse present	10.7	(0.17)	14.6	(0.18)	16.5	(0.20)	17.6	(0.20)	18.2	(0.14)	18.2	(0.14)	18.4	(0.14)	5.8	1.9
Without own children under 18	5.1	(0.12)	5.5	(0.12)	6.5	(0.13)	7.1	(0.14)	7.4	(0.10)	7.4	(0.10)	7.4	(0.10)	1.4	0.9
With own children under 18	5.6	(0.13)	9.1	(0.15)	10.0	(0.16)	10.5	(0.16)	10.8	(0.11)	10.8	(0.11)	10.9	(0.12)	4.4	1.0
One own child under 18	2.0	(0.08)	4.0	(0.10)	4.9	(0.12)	5.2	(0.12)	5.3	(0.08)	5.4	(0.08)	5.5	(0.08)	2.9	0.6
Two own children under 18	1.6	(0.07)	3.1	(0.09)	3.3	(0.10)	3.4	(0.10)	3.4	(0.07)	3.5	(0.07)	3.5	(0.07)	1.7	0.2
Three or more own children under 18	2.0	(0.08)	2.1	(0.07)	1.8	(0.07)	1.9	(0.07)	2.1	(0.05)	1.9	(0.05)	2.0	(0.05)	-0.2	0.1

†Not applicable.
#Rounds to zero.
NOTE: Own children are never-married sons and daughters, including stepchildren and adopted children, of the householder or married couple. Detail may not sum to totals because of rounding. Standard errors appear in parentheses.

SOURCE: U.S. Department of Commerce, Census Bureau, Current Population Reports, Series P20, *Household and Family Characteristics: 1995*; and *America's Families and Living Arrangements: 2000* and *2005–2007*, Current Population Survey (CPS), Annual Social and Economic Supplement, retrieved July 31, 2008, from http://www.census.gov/population/socdemo/hh-fam/cps2007/tabF2-all.xls. (This table was prepared August 2008.)

Table 19. Characteristics of family households with own children under 18, by race/ethnicity and family structure: 2007
[In thousands]

Race/ethnicity and family structure	Total families	Families with own children under 18 Total	Percent of all families	Percentage distribution	Families with 1 child under 18	2 children under 18	3 children under 18	4 or more under 18	Families with own children under 6 Total	Percent of all families	Families with own children under 3 Total	Percent of all families
1	2	3	4	5	6	7	8	9	10	11	12	13
All races[1]	78,425 (227.5)	36,757 (178.6)	46.9 (0.18)	100.0 (†)	15,651 (123.5)	13,815 (116.5)	5,188 (73.0)	2,104 (46.8)	16,306 (125.8)	20.8 (0.15)	9,469 (97.5)	12.1 (0.12)
Married-couple families	58,945 (211.3)	26,158 (155.2)	44.4 (0.21)	71.2 (0.24)	10,127 (100.7)	10,497 (102.4)	3,930 (63.7)	1,604 (40.9)	12,130 (109.7)	20.6 (0.17)	7,175 (85.4)	12.2 (0.14)
Families with male householder, no spouse present	5,063 (72.1)	2,015 (45.8)	39.8 (0.71)	5.5 (0.12)	1,243 (36.1)	553 (24.1)	171 (13.4)	47 (7.0)	803 (29.0)	15.9 (0.53)	503 (23.0)	9.9 (0.43)
Families with female householder, no spouse present	14,416 (118.9)	8,585 (93.1)	59.6 (0.42)	23.4 (0.23)	4,280 (66.4)	2,765 (53.6)	1,087 (33.7)	453 (21.8)	3,373 (59.1)	23.4 (0.36)	1,790 (43.2)	12.4 (0.28)
White, non-Hispanic	54,632 (206.3)	23,213 (147.4)	42.5 (0.22)	100.0 (†)	10,091 (100.5)	8,871 (94.5)	3,144 (57.1)	1,108 (34.1)	9,867 (99.5)	18.1 (0.17)	5,875 (77.5)	10.8 (0.14)
Married-couple families	44,327 (191.9)	17,849 (131.1)	40.3 (0.24)	76.9 (0.28)	7,076 (84.8)	7,188 (85.5)	2,630 (52.3)	954 (31.6)	7,996 (90.0)	18.0 (0.19)	4,821 (70.4)	10.9 (0.15)
Families with male householder, no spouse present	2,921 (55.0)	1,279 (36.6)	43.8 (0.94)	5.5 (0.15)	820 (29.3)	345 (19.0)	92 (9.8)	22 (4.8)	429 (21.2)	14.7 (0.67)	272 (16.9)	9.3 (0.55)
Families with female householder, no spouse present	7,384 (86.6)	4,085 (64.9)	55.3 (0.59)	17.6 (0.26)	2,195 (47.8)	1,337 (37.4)	422 (21.0)	131 (11.7)	1,442 (38.8)	19.5 (0.47)	782 (28.6)	10.6 (0.37)
Black[2]	9,272 (83.3)	5,057 (65.2)	54.5 (0.50)	100.0 (†)	2,282 (45.4)	1,686 (39.3)	697 (25.6)	392 (19.2)	2,182 (44.4)	23.5 (0.43)	1,176 (33.0)	12.7 (0.34)
Married-couple families	4,358 (61.1)	2,133 (43.9)	48.9 (0.74)	42.2 (0.68)	868 (28.5)	784 (27.1)	291 (16.6)	189 (13.4)	906 (29.1)	20.8 (0.60)	508 (21.9)	11.7 (0.47)
Families with male householder, no spouse present	864 (28.4)	329 (17.6)	38.1 (1.61)	6.5 (0.34)	200 (13.8)	89 (9.2)	28 (5.2)	12 (3.4)	146 (11.8)	16.9 (1.24)	90 (9.2)	10.4 (1.01)
Families with female householder, no spouse present	4,050 (59.1)	2,596 (48.2)	64.1 (0.74)	51.3 (0.69)	1,214 (33.5)	813 (27.6)	378 (18.9)	190 (13.4)	1,129 (32.4)	27.9 (0.69)	579 (23.3)	14.3 (0.54)
Hispanic	10,152 (82.3)	6,356 (70.1)	62.6 (0.47)	100.0 (†)	2,354 (45.7)	2,401 (46.1)	1,094 (31.7)	507 (21.8)	3,259 (53.0)	32.1 (0.45)	1,871 (41.0)	18.4 (0.38)
Married-couple families	6,762 (71.8)	4,392 (60.3)	65.0 (0.57)	69.1 (0.57)	1,451 (36.4)	1,768 (39.9)	797 (27.2)	376 (18.8)	2,352 (45.7)	34.8 (0.57)	1,364 (35.3)	20.2 (0.48)
Families with male householder, no spouse present	945 (29.6)	317 (17.3)	33.5 (1.50)	5.0 (0.27)	172 (12.8)	94 (9.4)	40 (6.2)	11 (3.2)	187 (13.3)	19.8 (1.26)	116 (10.5)	12.3 (1.04)
Families with female householder, no spouse present	2,445 (46.5)	1,647 (38.6)	67.4 (0.93)	25.9 (0.54)	731 (26.1)	539 (22.5)	258 (15.6)	119 (10.6)	720 (25.9)	29.4 (0.90)	390 (19.2)	16.0 (0.72)

†Not applicable.
[1]Race of family is defined as race of head of household. "All races" includes other race/ethnicity categories not separately shown.
[2]Includes Black persons of Hispanic ethnicity.
NOTE: Own children are never-married sons and daughters, including stepchildren and adopted children, of the householder or married couple. Detail may not sum to totals because of rounding. Standard errors appear in parentheses.

SOURCE: U.S. Department of Commerce, Census Bureau, *America's Families and Living Arrangements: 2007*, Current Population Survey (CPS), Annual Social and Economic Supplement, retrieved July 31, 2008, from http://www.census.gov/population/www/socdemo/hh-fam/cps2007.html. (This table was prepared August 2008.)

Table 20. Household income, population poverty rates, and poverty status of 5- to 17-year-olds, by state: 1990, 2000, and 2005–07

State	Median household income, in constant 2007 dollars[1]			Percent of persons in poverty			Poverty status of related children 5 through 17 years old[2]					
							1990[3]		2000[4]		2007	
	1990[3]	2000[4]	2005–07 (3-year average)	1990[3]	2000[4]	2005–07 (3-year average)	Number in poverty (in thousands)	Percent in poverty	Number in poverty (in thousands)	Percent in poverty	Number in poverty (in thousands)	Percent in poverty
1	2	3	4	5	6	7	8	9	10	11	12	13
United States	$48,526	$52,257	$49,668 (172.7)	13.1	12.4	12.5 (0.12)	7,545 (7.8)	17.0 (0.02)	7,974 (5.8)	15.4 (0.01)	8,727 (178)	16.5 (0.3)
Alabama	38,098	42,477	40,232 (865.9)	18.3	16.1	15.2 (0.91)	178 (1.2)	23.2 (0.16)	165 (1.2)	20.3 (0.11)	188 (28)	24.1 (3.2)
Alaska	66,854	64,174	60,124 (1,059.0)	9.0	9.4	8.8 (0.79)	11 (0.3)	9.6 (0.27)	14 (0.3)	10.3 (0.18)	10 (3)	7.3 (1.9)
Arizona	44,464	50,470	47,750 (971.1)	15.7	13.9	14.7 (0.85)	136 (1.0)	20.3 (0.15)	171 (1.3)	17.8 (0.11)	239 (34)	19.6 (2.5)
Arkansas	34,142	40,047	39,279 (808.6)	19.1	15.8	15.1 (0.97)	107 (0.9)	23.8 (0.20)	98 (0.6)	20.1 (0.13)	94 (16)	18.4 (2.9)
California	57,797	59,099	55,864 (432.7)	12.5	14.2	12.7 (0.30)	894 (3.3)	17.2 (0.06)	1,217 (4.6)	18.5 (0.04)	1,123 (74)	16.7 (1.0)
Colorado	48,662	58,739	57,333 (940.7)	11.7	9.3	10.3 (0.79)	82 (0.8)	13.7 (0.13)	79 (0.7)	10.0 (0.08)	98 (22)	11.4 (2.4)
Connecticut	67,360	67,116	62,893 (1,415.7)	6.8	7.9	8.7 (0.73)	50 (0.8)	9.8 (0.15)	58 (0.7)	9.6 (0.10)	75 (16)	12.3 (2.5)
Delaware	56,307	58,960	54,310 (1,213.1)	8.7	9.2	9.3 (0.79)	12 (0.3)	11.0 (0.27)	15 (0.4)	10.9 (0.22)	17 (4)	11.4 (2.5)
District of Columbia	49,610	49,933	49,474 (1,228.8)	16.9	20.2	19.2 (1.16)	18 (0.4)	24.1 (0.59)	24 (0.4)	30.4 (0.44)	22 (4)	‡ (†)
Florida	44,372	48,306	46,142 (486.6)	12.7	12.5	11.7 (0.43)	344 (2.0)	17.5 (0.10)	434 (2.0)	16.6 (0.07)	499 (47)	16.9 (1.5)
Georgia	46,855	52,803	49,387 (761.3)	14.7	13.0	13.5 (0.61)	228 (1.6)	18.9 (0.14)	248 (1.4)	16.1 (0.09)	327 (37)	18.2 (1.9)
Hawaii	62,691	61,995	63,164 (1,185.2)	8.3	10.7	8.4 (0.73)	20 (0.5)	10.5 (0.25)	27 (0.6)	12.9 (0.18)	22 (5)	10.8 (2.4)
Idaho	40,778	46,754	47,876 (927.2)	13.3	11.8	9.8 (0.79)	32 (0.5)	14.4 (0.23)	33 (0.6)	12.6 (0.14)	35 (7)	12.5 (2.4)
Illinois	52,072	57,976	51,320 (754.0)	11.9	10.7	10.7 (0.49)	328 (1.6)	15.9 (0.08)	309 (1.5)	13.4 (0.05)	294 (36)	13.4 (1.6)
Indiana	46,494	51,725	46,407 (863.6)	10.7	9.5	11.7 (0.73)	132 (1.1)	12.8 (0.10)	119 (1.4)	10.6 (0.08)	195 (29)	16.9 (2.3)
Iowa	42,347	49,114	49,262 (1,030.8)	11.5	9.1	10.2 (0.85)	65 (0.7)	12.6 (0.14)	50 (0.6)	9.5 (0.09)	52 (13)	10.5 (2.4)
Kansas	44,062	50,552	46,659 (976.4)	11.5	9.9	12.3 (0.91)	59 (0.7)	12.8 (0.15)	53 (0.6)	10.4 (0.10)	66 (14)	13.5 (2.7)
Kentucky	36,382	41,901	39,678 (758.8)	19.0	15.8	15.7 (0.97)	161 (1.1)	23.2 (0.16)	137 (1.0)	19.4 (0.10)	145 (25)	19.7 (3.0)
Louisiana	35,437	40,525	39,461 (900.4)	23.6	19.6	17.1 (1.03)	267 (1.6)	30.4 (0.19)	223 (1.1)	25.3 (0.11)	155 (25)	20.2 (3.0)
Maine	44,971	46,341	47,160 (1,128.6)	10.8	10.9	11.2 (0.91)	27 (0.4)	12.3 (0.20)	27 (0.5)	12.0 (0.15)	26 (6)	12.8 (2.9)
Maryland	63,590	65,788	65,124 (1,137.9)	8.3	8.5	9.0 (0.67)	82 (1.0)	10.5 (0.12)	96 (0.9)	9.8 (0.09)	103 (22)	10.3 (2.1)
Massachusetts	59,660	62,844	58,286 (1,458.5)	8.9	9.3	11.1 (0.67)	112 (1.1)	12.2 (0.12)	122 (1.3)	11.4 (0.08)	157 (26)	15.0 (2.3)
Michigan	50,083	55,583	49,394 (649.7)	13.1	10.5	12.0 (0.55)	288 (1.5)	16.7 (0.09)	238 (1.1)	12.7 (0.05)	270 (34)	15.1 (1.8)
Minnesota	49,903	58,624	57,815 (1,037.8)	10.2	7.9	8.5 (0.67)	93 (0.8)	11.4 (0.10)	81 (0.7)	8.7 (0.06)	99 (21)	11.6 (2.3)
Mississippi	32,510	38,986	35,971 (947.8)	25.2	19.9	21.1 (1.09)	177 (1.2)	32.6 (0.21)	146 (1.0)	26.0 (0.13)	172 (22)	32.6 (3.5)
Missouri	42,562	47,204	45,834 (854.7)	13.3	11.7	11.9 (0.73)	150 (1.1)	16.2 (0.12)	148 (1.1)	14.4 (0.08)	218 (31)	21.0 (2.7)
Montana	37,115	41,094	41,852 (842.7)	16.1	14.6	13.4 (0.91)	29 (0.5)	18.4 (0.30)	29 (0.5)	17.1 (0.20)	19 (4)	12.4 (2.6)
Nebraska	42,004	48,842	49,861 (1,040.2)	11.1	9.7	9.9 (0.79)	37 (0.6)	12.0 (0.18)	36 (0.6)	11.1 (0.12)	37 (8)	11.4 (2.4)
Nevada	50,068	55,476	53,008 (1,016.0)	10.2	10.5	10.0 (0.79)	23 (0.5)	11.7 (0.26)	44 (0.7)	12.3 (0.16)	50 (12)	11.2 (2.5)
New Hampshire	58,654	61,556	63,942 (1,274.0)	6.4	6.5	5.6 (0.61)	12 (0.3)	6.4 (0.16)	15 (0.3)	6.7 (0.12)	11 (4)	4.7 (1.6)
New Jersey	66,078	68,623	65,933 (1,394.7)	7.6	8.5	8.1 (0.55)	134 (1.2)	10.8 (0.10)	158 (1.3)	10.5 (0.07)	143 (25)	9.6 (1.6)
New Mexico	38,889	42,474	42,295 (1,057.8)	20.6	18.4	16.3 (1.09)	83 (0.8)	26.3 (0.25)	87 (0.7)	23.6 (0.17)	48 (11)	13.6 (2.8)
New York	53,223	53,997	49,546 (660.6)	13.0	14.6	14.4 (0.49)	531 (2.5)	18.1 (0.09)	640 (2.6)	19.1 (0.06)	624 (54)	19.3 (1.5)
North Carolina	43,022	48,760	43,035 (677.4)	13.0	12.3	14.1 (0.67)	180 (1.2)	16.0 (0.11)	207 (1.2)	14.9 (0.07)	327 (38)	20.5 (2.1)
North Dakota	37,478	43,061	44,743 (943.5)	14.4	11.9	10.6 (0.85)	20 (0.4)	15.9 (0.30)	15 (0.2)	12.2 (0.17)	10 (3)	9.5 (2.3)
Ohio	46,347	50,965	47,750 (652.3)	12.5	10.6	12.4 (0.55)	321 (1.6)	16.2 (0.08)	268 (1.5)	12.9 (0.05)	320 (37)	16.2 (1.7)
Oklahoma	38,066	41,562	41,046 (1,086.1)	16.7	14.7	14.7 (0.97)	119 (1.0)	19.9 (0.16)	113 (1.0)	17.7 (0.11)	114 (20)	16.9 (2.8)
Oregon	43,996	50,915	48,521 (996.3)	12.4	11.6	12.2 (0.91)	68 (0.8)	13.4 (0.15)	77 (0.7)	12.8 (0.11)	89 (19)	14.3 (2.8)
Pennsylvania	46,933	49,907	49,155 (612.0)	11.1	11.0	11.0 (0.49)	284 (1.5)	14.5 (0.08)	292 (1.5)	13.6 (0.05)	280 (35)	14.3 (1.7)
Rhode Island	51,957	52,376	54,009 (1,237.4)	9.6	11.9	10.7 (0.85)	19 (0.5)	12.3 (0.30)	28 (0.7)	15.6 (0.25)	20 (5)	12.1 (2.8)

See notes at end of table.

Table 20. Household income, population poverty rates, and poverty status of 5- to 17-year-olds, by state: 1990, 2000, and 2005-07—Continued

State	Median household income, in constant 2007 dollars[1]			Percent of persons in poverty			Poverty status of related children 5 through 17 years old[2]					
	1990[3]	2000[4]	2005-07 (3-year average)	1990[3]	2000[4]	2005-07 (3-year average)	1990[3] Number in poverty (in thousands)	1990[3] Percent in poverty	2000[4] Number in poverty (in thousands)	2000[4] Percent in poverty	2007 Number in poverty (in thousands)	2007 Percent in poverty
1	2	3	4	5	6	7	8	9	10	11	12	13
South Carolina	42,391	46,144	42,561 (983.8)	15.4	14.1	13.4 (0.91)	131 (1.2)	20.0 (0.19)	130 (1.2)	17.9 (0.12)	144 (25)	19.0 (3.0)
South Dakota	36,332	43,904	46,321 (974.8)	15.9	13.2	10.7 (0.79)	26 (0.5)	18.7 (0.33)	23 (0.3)	15.5 (0.21)	16 (3)	11.7 (2.3)
Tennessee	40,052	45,246	41,632 (725.9)	15.7	13.5	14.8 (0.79)	169 (1.2)	19.5 (0.13)	166 (1.2)	16.6 (0.10)	203 (29)	19.3 (2.5)
Texas	43,618	49,684	44,861 (482.7)	18.1	15.4	16.4 (0.49)	791 (3.1)	23.4 (0.09)	806 (2.6)	19.3 (0.06)	1,024 (71)	22.4 (1.4)
Utah	47,580	56,901	55,974 (1,026.4)	11.4	9.4	9.4 (0.73)	49 (0.7)	10.9 (0.16)	44 (0.6)	8.9 (0.09)	57 (11)	10.3 (1.9)
Vermont	48,100	50,840	51,566 (950.0)	9.9	9.4	8.4 (0.79)	11 (0.3)	10.7 (0.26)	11 (0.2)	9.9 (0.16)	9 (3)	10.1 (2.7)
Virginia	53,809	58,084	57,679 (1,007.4)	10.2	9.6	8.8 (0.55)	129 (1.2)	12.4 (0.12)	142 (1.3)	11.4 (0.08)	159 (26)	12.3 (1.9)
Washington	50,346	56,963	56,049 (967.9)	10.9	10.6	9.4 (0.67)	111 (0.9)	12.8 (0.10)	132 (1.4)	12.2 (0.09)	115 (23)	10.2 (2.0)
West Virginia	33,574	36,953	40,103 (796.2)	19.7	17.9	15.2 (0.91)	80 (0.8)	24.0 (0.23)	67 (0.6)	22.9 (0.17)	65 (10)	22.9 (3.1)
Wisconsin	47,535	54,493	50,619 (811.4)	10.7	8.7	10.4 (0.73)	121 (0.9)	13.3 (0.10)	100 (1.1)	10.0 (0.07)	132 (24)	14.0 (2.4)
Wyoming	43,747	47,152	48,205 (1,055.1)	11.9	11.4	10.5 (0.85)	12 (0.3)	12.6 (0.33)	12 (0.3)	12.5 (0.24)	9 (2)	9.9 (2.4)

†Not applicable.
‡Reporting standards not met.
[1]Adjusted by the Consumer Price Index research series using current methods (CPI-U-RS).
[2]Related children in a family include own children and all other children in the household who are related to the householder by birth, marriage, or adoption.
[3]Based on 1989 incomes collected in the 1990 census. Data may differ from figures derived from the Current Population Survey.
[4]Based on 1999 incomes collected in the 2000 census. Data may differ from figures derived from the Current Population Survey.
NOTE: Standard errors appear in parentheses. Standard errors in columns 12 and 13 cannot be shown with greater precision due to data source limitations.

SOURCE: U.S. Department of Commerce, Census Bureau, 1990 Summary Tape File 3 (STF 3), "Median Household Income in 1989" and "Poverty Status in 1989 by Family Type and Age," retrieved May 12, 2005, from http://factfinder.census.gov/servlet/DTGeoSearchByListServlet?ds_name=DEC_1990_STF3_&_lang=en&_ts=13404804959; Decennial Census, 1990, Minority Economic Profiles, unpublished data; Decennial Census, 2000, Summary Social, Economic, and Housing Characteristics, Census 2000 Summary File 4 (SF 4), "Poverty Status in 1999 of Related Children Under 18 Years by Family Type and Age," retrieved March 28, 2005, from http://factfinder.census.gov/servlet/DTGeoSearchByListServlet?ds_name=DEC_2000_SF4_U&_lang=en&_ts=13404942077; Current Population Reports, Series P-60, Income, Poverty, and Health Insurance Coverage in the United States: 2007, "Poverty Status by State: 2007" and "Poverty 2007," retrieved September 15, 2008, from http://www.census.gov/hhes/www/poverty/poverty07.html; and "Median Household Income by State," retrieved September 15, 2008, from http://www.census.gov/hhes/www/income/income07.html. (This table was prepared September 2008.)

Table 21. Poverty status of all persons, persons in families, and related children under age 18, by race/ethnicity: Selected years, 1959 through 2007

Year and race/ethnicity	Number below the poverty level (in thousands)						Percent below the poverty level					
	All persons	In families			In families with female householder, no husband present		All persons	In all families			In families with female householder, no husband present	
		Total	Householder[1]	Related children under 18	Total	Related children under 18		Total	Householder[1]	Related children under 18	Total	Related children under 18
1	2	3	4	5	6	7	8	9	10	11	12	13
Total												
1959	39,490 (641.5)	34,562 (489.5)	8,320 (178.3)	17,208 (289.6)	7,014 (160.3)	4,145 (117.4)	22.4 (0.34)	20.8 (0.17)	18.5 (0.31)	26.9 (0.30)	49.4 (0.71)	72.2 (1.00)
1960	39,851 (644.0)	34,925 (493.6)	8,243 (177.2)	17,288 (290.6)	7,247 (163.6)	4,095 (116.6)	22.2 (0.34)	20.7 (0.17)	18.1 (0.30)	26.5 (0.29)	48.9 (0.69)	68.4 (1.01)
1965	33,185 (595.4)	28,358 (419.2)	6,721 (156.2)	14,388 (255.6)	7,524 (167.4)	4,562 (124.1)	17.3 (0.30)	15.8 (0.14)	13.9 (0.26)	20.7 (0.26)	46.0 (0.66)	64.2 (0.96)
1970	25,420 (431.8)	20,330 (266.6)	5,260 (110.1)	10,235 (166.2)	7,503 (136.5)	4,689 (102.9)	12.6 (0.21)	10.9 (0.10)	10.1 (0.18)	14.9 (0.19)	38.1 (0.48)	53.0 (0.73)
1975	25,877 (435.2)	20,789 (271.0)	5,450 (112.4)	10,882 (173.0)	8,846 (151.3)	5,597 (114.2)	12.3 (0.20)	10.9 (0.10)	9.7 (0.17)	16.8 (0.20)	37.5 (0.43)	52.7 (0.67)
1980	29,272 (460.0)	22,601 (288.2)	6,217 (121.7)	11,114 (175.4)	10,120 (165.0)	5,866 (117.5)	13.0 (0.20)	11.5 (0.10)	10.3 (0.17)	17.9 (0.21)	36.7 (0.40)	50.8 (0.64)
1985	33,064 (513.3)	25,729 (336.0)	7,223 (141.0)	12,483 (200.4)	11,600 (190.8)	6,716 (134.8)	14.0 (0.21)	12.6 (0.11)	11.4 (0.18)	20.1 (0.23)	37.6 (0.40)	53.6 (0.65)
1986	32,370 (508.5)	24,754 (326.3)	7,023 (138.6)	12,257 (197.9)	11,944 (194.6)	6,943 (137.6)	13.6 (0.21)	12.0 (0.10)	10.9 (0.18)	19.8 (0.23)	38.3 (0.40)	54.4 (0.64)
1987	32,221 (507.5)	24,725 (326.0)	7,005 (138.3)	12,275 (198.1)	12,148 (196.8)	7,074 (139.2)	13.4 (0.21)	12.0 (0.10)	10.7 (0.18)	19.7 (0.23)	38.1 (0.40)	54.7 (0.64)
1988	31,745 (504.2)	24,048 (319.3)	6,876 (136.8)	11,935 (194.5)	11,972 (194.9)	6,742 (135.1)	13.0 (0.20)	11.6 (0.10)	10.4 (0.17)	19.0 (0.23)	37.2 (0.39)	50.6 (0.63)
1989	31,528 (548.0)	24,066 (348.2)	6,784 (147.9)	12,001 (212.7)	11,668 (208.8)	6,808 (148.2)	12.8 (0.22)	11.5 (0.11)	10.3 (0.19)	19.0 (0.25)	35.9 (0.42)	51.1 (0.69)
1990	33,585 (534.7)	25,232 (342.5)	7,098 (144.3)	12,715 (209.9)	12,578 (208.4)	7,363 (147.6)	13.5 (0.21)	12.0 (0.11)	10.7 (0.18)	19.9 (0.24)	37.2 (0.40)	53.4 (0.64)
1991	35,708 (549.1)	27,143 (362.1)	7,712 (151.9)	13,658 (220.3)	13,824 (222.2)	8,065 (156.2)	14.2 (0.22)	12.8 (0.11)	11.5 (0.19)	21.1 (0.24)	39.7 (0.39)	55.5 (0.62)
1992	38,014 (564.0)	28,961 (380.7)	7,960 (154.9)	14,521 (229.8)	14,205 (226.3)	8,032 (155.8)	14.8 (0.22)	13.3 (0.11)	11.7 (0.19)	21.6 (0.24)	39.0 (0.38)	54.3 (0.62)
1993	39,265 (571.8)	29,927 (390.5)	8,393 (160.2)	14,961 (234.6)	14,636 (231.0)	8,503 (161.5)	15.1 (0.22)	13.6 (0.11)	12.3 (0.19)	22.0 (0.24)	38.7 (0.38)	53.7 (0.60)
1994	38,059 (564.3)	28,985 (380.9)	8,053 (156.1)	14,610 (230.8)	14,380 (228.3)	8,427 (160.6)	14.5 (0.21)	13.1 (0.11)	11.6 (0.18)	21.2 (0.23)	38.6 (0.38)	52.9 (0.59)
1995	36,425 (553.8)	27,501 (365.8)	7,532 (149.7)	13,999 (224.1)	14,205 (226.3)	8,364 (159.8)	13.8 (0.21)	12.3 (0.10)	10.8 (0.18)	20.2 (0.23)	36.5 (0.37)	50.3 (0.58)
1996	36,529 (572.0)	27,376 (378.5)	7,708 (157.7)	13,764 (230.1)	13,796 (230.4)	7,990 (161.3)	13.7 (0.21)	12.2 (0.11)	11.0 (0.19)	19.8 (0.24)	35.8 (0.38)	49.3 (0.61)
1997	35,574 (565.6)	26,217 (366.2)	7,324 (152.8)	13,422 (226.2)	13,494 (227.0)	7,928 (160.5)	13.3 (0.21)	11.6 (0.11)	10.3 (0.18)	19.2 (0.23)	35.1 (0.38)	49.0 (0.61)
1998	34,476 (558.1)	25,370 (357.2)	7,186 (151.0)	12,845 (219.5)	12,907 (220.3)	7,627 (156.7)	12.7 (0.21)	11.2 (0.10)	10.0 (0.17)	18.3 (0.23)	33.1 (0.37)	46.1 (0.61)
1999	32,791 (547.3)	23,830 (340.8)	6,676 (144.4)	11,678 (206.0)	11,764 (207.0)	6,602 (143.4)	11.9 (0.20)	10.3 (0.10)	9.3 (0.17)	16.6 (0.22)	30.5 (0.37)	41.9 (0.61)
2000	31,581 (538.4)	22,347 (324.8)	6,222 (138.4)	11,005 (198.1)	10,926 (197.1)	6,116 (136.9)	11.3 (0.19)	9.6 (0.10)	8.6 (0.16)	15.6 (0.21)	28.5 (0.36)	39.8 (0.62)
2001	32,907 (548.1)	23,215 (334.2)	6,813 (146.2)	11,175 (200.1)	11,223 (200.6)	6,341 (139.9)	11.7 (0.20)	9.9 (0.10)	9.2 (0.17)	15.8 (0.21)	28.6 (0.36)	39.3 (0.60)
2002	34,570 (399.9)	24,534 (248.6)	7,229 (108.2)	11,646 (146.7)	11,657 (146.8)	6,564 (102.0)	12.1 (0.14)	10.4 (0.07)	9.6 (0.12)	16.3 (0.15)	28.8 (0.25)	39.6 (0.42)
2003	35,861 (407.8)	25,684 (257.3)	7,607 (111.6)	12,340 (152.5)	12,413 (153.1)	7,085 (106.8)	12.5 (0.14)	10.8 (0.07)	10.0 (0.12)	17.2 (0.16)	30.0 (0.25)	41.8 (0.42)
2004	37,040 (413.5)	26,544 (263.9)	7,854 (113.9)	12,473 (153.6)	12,823 (156.5)	7,132 (107.3)	12.7 (0.14)	11.0 (0.07)	10.2 (0.12)	17.3 (0.16)	30.5 (0.25)	41.9 (0.42)
2005	36,950 (413.0)	26,068 (260.3)	7,657 (112.1)	12,335 (152.5)	13,153 (159.2)	7,210 (108.0)	12.6 (0.14)	10.8 (0.07)	9.9 (0.12)	17.1 (0.16)	31.1 (0.25)	42.8 (0.43)
2006	36,460 (410.7)	25,915 (259.1)	7,668 (112.2)	12,299 (152.2)	13,199 (159.6)	7,341 (109.2)	12.3 (0.14)	10.6 (0.07)	9.8 (0.12)	16.9 (0.15)	30.5 (0.25)	42.1 (0.42)
2007	37,276 (414.6)	26,509 (263.6)	7,623 (111.8)	12,802 (156.3)	13,478 (161.9)	7,546 (111.1)	12.5 (0.14)	10.8 (0.07)	9.8 (0.12)	17.6 (0.16)	30.7 (0.25)	43.0 (0.42)
White												
1960[2]	28,309 (555.0)	24,262 (372.2)	6,115 (147.5)	11,229 (216.3)	4,296 (119.8)	2,357 (85.7)	17.8 (0.33)	16.2 (0.16)	14.9 (0.30)	20.0 (0.28)	39.0 (0.78)	59.9 (1.32)
1965[2]	22,496 (500.1)	18,508 (305.1)	4,824 (128.2)	8,595 (182.0)	4,092 (116.5)	2,321 (84.9)	13.3 (0.29)	11.7 (0.14)	11.1 (0.25)	14.4 (0.24)	35.4 (0.75)	52.9 (1.27)
1970[2]	17,484 (363.3)	13,323 (198.0)	3,708 (90.0)	6,138 (120.7)	3,761 (90.7)	2,247 (68.2)	9.9 (0.20)	8.1 (0.09)	8.0 (0.17)	10.5 (0.17)	28.4 (0.54)	43.1 (0.94)
1975[2]	17,770 (366.1)	13,799 (202.8)	3,838 (91.7)	6,748 (127.9)	4,577 (101.5)	2,813 (77.1)	9.7 (0.20)	8.3 (0.09)	7.7 (0.16)	12.5 (0.20)	29.4 (0.50)	44.2 (0.86)
1980[2]	19,699 (384.1)	14,587 (210.7)	4,195 (96.5)	6,817 (128.7)	4,940 (106.1)	2,813 (77.1)	10.2 (0.20)	8.6 (0.09)	8.0 (0.16)	13.4 (0.21)	28.0 (0.46)	41.6 (0.82)
1985[2]	22,860 (435.1)	17,125 (249.2)	4,983 (112.8)	7,838 (148.3)	5,990 (125.8)	3,372 (90.2)	11.4 (0.21)	9.9 (0.10)	9.1 (0.18)	15.6 (0.24)	29.8 (0.47)	45.2 (0.84)
1990[2]	22,326 (445.3)	15,916 (244.9)	4,622 (111.7)	7,696 (151.7)	5,210 (133.0)	3,597 (96.8)	10.7 (0.21)	9.0 (0.10)	8.1 (0.17)	15.1 (0.24)	29.8 (0.48)	45.9 (0.85)
1995[2]	24,423 (463.9)	17,593 (262.9)	4,994 (116.9)	8,474 (161.1)	7,047 (143.7)	4,051 (103.5)	11.2 (0.21)	9.6 (0.10)	8.5 (0.17)	15.5 (0.23)	29.7 (0.45)	42.5 (0.76)
1996[2]	24,650 (461.8)	17,621 (273.3)	5,059 (122.3)	8,488 (167.6)	7,073 (149.6)	4,029 (107.2)	11.2 (0.22)	9.6 (0.11)	8.6 (0.18)	15.5 (0.24)	29.8 (0.46)	43.1 (0.80)
1997[2]	24,396 (479.6)	17,258 (269.3)	4,990 (121.3)	8,441 (167.0)	7,296 (152.5)	4,186 (109.6)	11.0 (0.21)	9.3 (0.11)	8.4 (0.18)	15.4 (0.24)	30.7 (0.47)	44.3 (0.80)

See notes at end of table.

Table 21. Poverty status of all persons, persons in families, and related children under age 18, by race/ethnicity: Selected years, 1959 through 2007—Continued

		Number below the poverty level (in thousands)						Percent below the poverty level					
		In all families			In families with female householder, no husband present			In all families			In families with female householder, no husband present	
Year and race/ethnicity	All persons	Total	Householder[1]	Related children under 18	Total	Related children under 18	All persons	Total	Householder[1]	Related children under 18	Total	Related children under 18
1	2	3	4	5	6	7	8	9	10	11	12	13
1998	23,454 (471.2)	16,549 (261.4)	4,829 (119.0)	7,935 (160.6)	6,674 (144.4)	3,875 (104.9)	10.5 (0.21)	8.9 (0.10)	8.0 (0.17)	14.4 (0.23)	27.6 (0.45)	40.0 (0.78)
1999²	22,169 (459.8)	15,353 (248.1)	4,377 (112.4)	7,194 (151.2)	5,947 (134.6)	3,266 (95.2)	9.8 (0.20)	8.2 (0.10)	7.3 (0.17)	12.9 (0.22)	24.9 (0.44)	35.5 (0.78)
2000²	21,645 (454.8)	14,692 (240.6)	4,151 (109.1)	6,834 (146.5)	5,609 (130.0)	2,955 (90.0)	9.5 (0.20)	7.8 (0.10)	6.9 (0.16)	12.3 (0.22)	23.2 (0.42)	33.0 (0.78)
2001¹	22,739 (465.2)	15,369 (248.2)	4,579 (115.4)	7,086 (149.8)	5,972 (135.0)	3,291 (95.6)	9.9 (0.20)	9.9 (0.10)	7.4 (0.16)	12.8 (0.22)	24.3 (0.43)	34.7 (0.76)
2002³	15,567 (278.6)	9,389 (127.5)	3,208 (67.3)	3,848 (74.5)	3,733 (73.2)	1,949 (51.2)	8.0 (0.14)	8.0 (0.07)	6.0 (0.11)	8.9 (0.15)	20.0 (0.33)	29.2 (0.62)
2003³	15,902 (281.9)	9,658 (129.8)	3,270 (68.0)	3,957 (75.7)	3,959 (75.7)	2,033 (52.4)	8.2 (0.14)	6.1 (0.07)	6.1 (0.12)	9.3 (0.16)	21.1 (0.33)	30.7 (0.63)
2004³	16,908 (290.1)	10,323 (135.5)	3,505 (70.7)	4,190 (78.2)	4,116 (77.4)	2,114 (53.5)	8.7 (0.15)	6.5 (0.07)	6.5 (0.12)	9.9 (0.16)	21.7 (0.33)	31.5 (0.63)
2005³	16,227 (284.6)	9,604 (129.4)	3,285 (68.1)	3,973 (75.9)	4,278 (79.2)	2,158 (54.1)	8.3 (0.14)	6.0 (0.07)	6.1 (0.11)	9.5 (0.16)	22.6 (0.34)	33.1 (0.65)
2006³	16,013 (282.8)	9,676 (130.0)	3,372 (69.2)	3,930 (75.4)	4,353 (80.0)	2,206 (54.7)	8.2 (0.14)	6.1 (0.07)	6.2 (0.12)	9.5 (0.16)	22.5 (0.33)	32.9 (0.64)
2007³	16,032 (282.9)	9,553 (128.9)	3,184 (67.0)	3,996 (76.1)	4,099 (77.3)	2,101 (53.3)	8.2 (0.14)	6.0 (0.07)	5.9 (0.11)	9.7 (0.16)	21.4 (0.33)	32.4 (0.65)
Black²												
1959	9,927 (296.1)	9,112 (202.1)	1,860 (76.8)	5,022 (137.1)	2,416 (88.9)	1,475 (67.6)	55.1 (1.29)	54.9 (0.65)	48.1 (1.35)	65.5 (0.91)	70.6 (1.31)	81.6 (1.53)
1966	8,867 (285.2)	8,090 (186.5)	1,620 (71.2)	4,774 (132.9)	3,160 (103.7)	2,107 (82.3)	41.8 (1.18)	40.9 (0.59)	35.5 (1.19)	50.6 (0.87)	65.3 (1.15)	76.6 (1.36)
1970	7,548 (219.8)	6,683 (134.2)	1,481 (55.3)	3,922 (96.3)	3,656 (92.3)	2,383 (72.0)	33.5 (0.89)	32.2 (0.45)	29.5 (0.88)	41.5 (0.70)	58.7 (0.86)	67.7 (1.08)
1975	7,545 (219.8)	6,533 (132.3)	1,513 (56.0)	3,884 (95.7)	4,168 (99.9)	2,724 (77.7)	31.3 (0.85)	30.1 (0.43)	27.1 (0.82)	41.4 (0.70)	54.3 (0.78)	66.0 (1.01)
1980	8,579 (230.2)	7,190 (140.8)	1,826 (62.1)	3,906 (96.0)	4,984 (111.4)	2,944 (81.3)	32.5 (0.82)	31.1 (0.42)	28.9 (0.78)	42.1 (0.70)	53.4 (0.71)	64.8 (0.97)
1985	8,926 (246.7)	7,504 (153.2)	1,983 (68.7)	4,057 (103.9)	5,342 (123.1)	3,181 (89.9)	31.3 (0.82)	30.5 (0.43)	28.7 (0.79)	43.1 (0.74)	53.2 (0.72)	66.9 (0.99)
1990	9,837 (263.7)	8,160 (167.6)	2,193 (75.2)	4,412 (113.1)	6,005 (137.1)	3,543 (99.1)	31.9 (0.82)	31.0 (0.43)	29.3 (0.79)	44.2 (0.75)	50.6 (0.69)	64.7 (0.97)
1995	9,872 (264.0)	8,189 (168.0)	2,127 (73.9)	4,644 (116.7)	6,553 (145.0)	3,954 (105.9)	29.3 (0.77)	28.5 (0.40)	26.4 (0.74)	41.5 (0.70)	48.2 (0.64)	61.6 (0.91)
1996	9,694 (267.9)	7,993 (161.4)	2,206 (76.7)	4,411 (112.9)	6,123 (137.0)	3,619 (100.9)	28.4 (0.79)	27.6 (0.41)	26.1 (0.75)	39.5 (0.72)	46.4 (0.68)	58.2 (0.98)
1997	9,116 (262.9)	7,386 (153.6)	1,985 (72.5)	4,116 (108.5)	5,654 (130.6)	3,402 (97.4)	26.5 (0.77)	25.5 (0.40)	23.6 (0.72)	36.8 (0.71)	42.8 (0.67)	55.3 (0.99)
1998	9,091 (263.6)	7,259 (152.0)	1,981 (72.4)	4,073 (107.9)	5,629 (130.3)	3,366 (96.8)	26.1 (0.76)	24.7 (0.39)	23.4 (0.72)	36.4 (0.71)	42.8 (0.67)	54.7 (0.99)
1999	8,441 (257.8)	6,758 (145.5)	1,898 (70.7)	3,698 (102.1)	5,232 (124.8)	2,997 (90.7)	23.6 (0.72)	22.7 (0.38)	21.9 (0.69)	32.8 (0.69)	40.8 (0.68)	51.7 (1.03)
2000	7,982 (253.3)	6,221 (138.3)	1,685 (66.4)	3,495 (98.9)	4,774 (118.2)	2,830 (87.9)	22.5 (0.71)	21.2 (0.37)	19.1 (0.65)	30.9 (0.68)	38.6 (0.68)	49.4 (1.03)
2001	8,136 (255.5)	6,389 (140.6)	1,829 (69.3)	3,423 (97.7)	4,694 (117.1)	2,741 (86.4)	22.7 (0.71)	21.4 (0.37)	20.7 (0.67)	30.0 (0.67)	37.4 (0.67)	46.6 (1.02)
2002	8,602 (185.9)	6,761 (103.8)	1,923 (50.8)	3,570 (71.4)	4,980 (86.5)	2,855 (63.0)	24.1 (0.52)	22.8 (0.27)	21.5 (0.48)	32.1 (0.49)	38.2 (0.47)	47.5 (0.72)
2003	8,781 (197.6)	6,870 (104.9)	1,986 (51.7)	3,750 (73.4)	5,115 (87.9)	3,026 (65.1)	24.4 (0.52)	23.1 (0.27)	22.3 (0.49)	33.6 (0.50)	39.0 (0.47)	49.8 (0.72)
2004	9,014 (199.7)	7,153 (107.5)	2,035 (52.4)	3,702 (72.9)	5,247 (89.2)	2,963 (64.3)	24.7 (0.52)	23.8 (0.27)	22.8 (0.50)	33.4 (0.50)	39.6 (0.47)	49.2 (0.72)
2005	9,168 (201.5)	7,164 (107.6)	1,997 (51.9)	3,743 (73.4)	5,303 (89.7)	2,993 (64.7)	24.9 (0.52)	23.8 (0.27)	22.1 (0.49)	34.2 (0.51)	39.3 (0.47)	50.2 (0.72)
2006	9,048 (200.6)	7,072 (106.7)	2,007 (52.0)	3,690 (72.8)	5,180 (88.5)	2,971 (64.4)	24.3 (0.51)	23.1 (0.27)	21.6 (0.48)	33.0 (0.50)	39.1 (0.47)	49.7 (0.72)
2007	9,237 (203.0)	7,312 (108.9)	2,045 (52.5)	3,838 (74.4)	5,459 (91.3)	3,114 (66.1)	24.5 (0.51)	23.8 (0.27)	22.1 (0.48)	34.3 (0.50)	39.7 (0.47)	50.4 (0.71)
Hispanic												
1975	2,991 (176.8)	2,755 (90.2)	627 (41.3)	1,619 (67.7)	1,053 (54.0)	694 (43.5)	26.9 (1.41)	26.3 (0.70)	25.1 (1.41)	33.1 (1.09)	57.2 (1.88)	68.4 (2.37)
1980	3,491 (189.8)	3,143 (97.0)	751 (45.3)	1,718 (69.8)	1,319 (60.7)	809 (47.1)	25.7 (1.26)	25.1 (0.63)	23.2 (1.21)	33.0 (1.06)	54.5 (1.65)	65.0 (2.20)
1985	5,236 (202.8)	4,605 (107.7)	1,074 (48.7)	2,512 (76.6)	1,983 (67.4)	1,247 (52.7)	29.0 (1.01)	28.3 (0.51)	25.5 (0.98)	39.6 (0.89)	55.7 (1.21)	72.4 (1.57)
1990	6,006 (222.4)	5,091 (118.2)	1,244 (54.4)	2,750 (83.3)	2,115 (72.2)	1,314 (56.0)	28.1 (0.95)	26.9 (0.48)	25.0 (0.92)	37.7 (0.85)	53.0 (1.19)	68.4 (1.60)
1995	8,574 (256.1)	7,341 (147.3)	1,695 (64.1)	3,938 (101.9)	3,053 (88.3)	1,872 (67.6)	30.3 (0.85)	29.2 (0.43)	27.0 (0.84)	39.3 (0.73)	52.8 (0.99)	65.7 (1.34)
1996	8,697 (250.2)	7,515 (155.3)	1,748 (67.7)	4,090 (108.1)	3,020 (91.1)	1,779 (68.3)	29.4 (0.85)	28.5 (0.43)	26.4 (0.85)	39.9 (0.76)	53.5 (1.04)	67.4 (1.43)
1997	8,308 (246.9)	7,198 (151.2)	1,721 (67.1)	3,865 (104.7)	2,911 (89.3)	1,758 (67.9)	27.1 (0.82)	26.2 (0.41)	24.7 (0.81)	36.4 (0.73)	50.9 (1.03)	62.8 (1.43)
1998	8,070 (248.5)	6,814 (146.2)	1,648 (65.6)	3,670 (101.7)	2,837 (88.0)	1,739 (67.5)	25.6 (0.79)	24.3 (0.40)	22.7 (0.77)	33.6 (0.71)	46.7 (1.00)	59.6 (1.42)
1999	7,876 (247.8)	6,702 (144.7)	1,525 (62.9)	3,561 (99.9)	2,642 (84.6)	1,471 (61.7)	22.7 (0.72)	21.7 (0.37)	20.2 (0.72)	29.9 (0.66)	40.5 (0.95)	52.4 (1.47)
2000	7,747 (247.8)	6,430 (141.1)	1,431 (60.9)	3,342 (96.4)	2,444 (81.1)	1,303 (57.9)	21.5 (0.70)	20.3 (0.35)	18.5 (0.69)	27.6 (0.63)	37.8 (0.94)	48.3 (1.50)

See notes at end of table.

Table 21. Poverty status of all persons, persons in families, and related children under age 18, by race/ethnicity: Selected years, 1959 through 2007—Continued

Year and race/ethnicity	Number below the poverty level (in thousands)						Percent below the poverty level					
	All persons	In all families			In families with female householder, no husband present		All persons	In all families			In families with female householder, no husband present	
		Total	Householder[1]	Related children under 18	Total	Related children under 18		Total	Householder[1]	Related children under 18	Total	Related children under 18
1	2	3	4	5	6	7	8	9	10	11	12	13
2001	7,997 (251.7)	6,674 (144.4)	1,649 (65.6)	3,433 (97.9)	2,585 (83.6)	1,508 (62.6)	21.4 (0.68)	20.2 (0.35)	19.4 (0.67)	27.4 (0.62)	37.8 (0.92)	49.3 (1.41)
2002	8,555 (186.7)	7,184 (107.8)	1,792 (48.9)	3,653 (72.4)	2,554 (59.3)	1,501 (44.5)	21.8 (0.48)	20.8 (0.24)	19.7 (0.46)	28.2 (0.44)	36.4 (0.64)	47.9 (0.99)
2003	9,051 (192.6)	7,637 (111.9)	1,925 (50.8)	3,982 (76.0)	2,861 (63.1)	1,727 (48.0)	22.5 (0.48)	21.5 (0.24)	20.8 (0.47)	29.5 (0.44)	38.4 (0.63)	50.6 (0.95)
2004	9,122 (193.1)	7,705 (112.5)	1,958 (51.3)	3,985 (76.0)	3,072 (65.6)	1,837 (49.6)	21.9 (0.47)	21.1 (0.24)	20.5 (0.46)	28.6 (0.43)	39.3 (0.62)	51.9 (0.94)
2005	9,368 (196.0)	7,767 (113.1)	1,948 (51.2)	3,977 (75.9)	3,069 (65.6)	1,774 (48.7)	21.8 (0.46)	20.6 (0.23)	19.7 (0.45)	27.7 (0.42)	39.0 (0.61)	50.2 (0.94)
2006	9,243 (195.7)	7,650 (112.0)	1,922 (50.8)	3,959 (75.7)	3,189 (67.0)	1,848 (49.7)	20.6 (0.44)	19.5 (0.22)	18.9 (0.43)	26.6 (0.40)	36.9 (0.58)	47.2 (0.89)
2007	9,890 (202.5)	8,248 (117.4)	2,045 (52.5)	4,348 (79.9)	3,527 (70.9)	2,092 (53.2)	21.5 (0.44)	20.6 (0.23)	19.7 (0.44)	28.3 (0.41)	39.6 (0.58)	51.6 (0.88)
Asian/Pacific Islander[2]												
1990	858 (88.9)	712 (40.7)	— (†)	356 (28.6)	132 (17.3)	— (†)	12.2 (1.21)	11.3 (0.60)	— (†)	17.0 (1.23)	20.7 (2.41)	— (†)
1995	1,411 (112.3)	1,112 (51.3)	— (†)	532 (35.1)	266 (24.7)	— (†)	14.6 (1.11)	13.0 (0.55)	— (†)	18.6 (1.09)	28.9 (2.25)	— (†)
1996	1,454 (118.5)	1,172 (54.9)	— (†)	553 (37.2)	300 (27.3)	— (†)	14.5 (1.13)	13.2 (0.56)	— (†)	19.1 (1.14)	29.5 (2.24)	— (†)
1997	1,468 (119.0)	1,116 (53.5)	244 (24.6)	608 (39.1)	313 (27.9)	— (†)	14.0 (1.09)	12.0 (0.53)	10.2 (0.97)	19.9 (1.13)	33.6 (2.42)	— (†)
1998	1,360 (114.9)	1,087 (52.8)	270 (25.9)	542 (36.8)	373 (30.5)	— (†)	12.5 (1.02)	11.4 (0.51)	11.0 (0.99)	17.5 (1.07)	33.2 (2.20)	— (†)
1999	1,285 (111.9)	1,010 (50.8)	— (†)	367 (30.2)	275 (26.1)	— (†)	10.7 (0.91)	9.6 (0.45)	— (†)	11.5 (0.88)	22.9 (1.90)	— (†)
2000	1,258 (110.8)	895 (47.7)	235 (24.1)	407 (31.3)	289 (26.8)	128 (17.8)	9.9 (0.85)	8.1 (0.41)	8.8 (0.86)	12.5 (0.91)	23.4 (1.89)	32.3 (3.68)
2001	1,275 (111.5)	873 (47.1)	234 (24.1)	353 (29.6)	198 (22.1)	105 (16.1)	10.2 (0.87)	8.1 (0.41)	7.8 (0.77)	11.1 (0.87)	14.8 (1.52)	26.7 (3.49)
2002[4]	1,161 (76.0)	763 (31.3)	210 (16.2)	302 (19.5)	155 (13.9)	85 (10.3)	10.1 (0.65)	7.7 (0.30)	7.4 (0.55)	11.4 (0.69)	15.2 (1.25)	29.8 (3.02)
2003[4]	1,401 (82.9)	1,017 (36.3)	311 (19.8)	331 (20.4)	242 (17.4)	119 (12.2)	11.8 (0.68)	9.8 (0.33)	10.2 (0.61)	12.1 (0.70)	23.6 (1.48)	37.4 (3.02)
2004[4]	1,201 (77.2)	812 (32.3)	232 (17.1)	265 (18.2)	135 (13.0)	55 (8.3)	9.8 (0.62)	7.6 (0.29)	7.4 (0.52)	9.4 (0.61)	13.2 (1.18)	18.7 (2.53)
2005[4]	1,402 (83.0)	970 (35.4)	289 (19.1)	312 (19.8)	189 (15.4)	68 (9.2)	11.1 (0.64)	8.9 (0.30)	9.0 (0.56)	11.0 (0.66)	17.8 (1.31)	25.6 (2.99)
2006[4]	1,353 (81.7)	912 (34.3)	260 (18.1)	351 (21.0)	187 (15.3)	91 (10.7)	10.3 (0.61)	8.0 (0.28)	7.8 (0.52)	12.0 (0.67)	17.7 (1.31)	36.2 (3.38)
2007[4]	1,349 (81.8)	930 (34.7)	261 (18.1)	345 (20.9)	217 (16.5)	100 (11.2)	10.2 (0.60)	8.1 (0.28)	7.9 (0.52)	11.8 (0.67)	17.3 (1.19)	32.3 (2.96)

—Not available.
†Not applicable.
[1]Refers to the person who owns or rents (maintains) the housing unit.
[2]Includes persons of Hispanic ethnicity.
[3]Excludes persons of Hispanic ethnicity.
[4]Includes Asians only (i.e., does not include Pacific Islanders).

NOTE: Data are from the Current Population Survey and may differ from data shown in other tables obtained from the Decennial Census. Standard errors appear in parentheses.
SOURCE: U.S. Department of Commerce, Census Bureau, Current Population Reports, Series P-60, *Poverty in the United States*, selected years, 1959 through 2002; and *Income, Poverty, and Health Insurance Coverage in the United States*, 2003 through 2007. Current Population Survey (CPS), Annual Social and Economic Supplement, retrieved September 15, 2008, from http://pubdb3.census.gov/macro/032008/pov/toc.htm. (This table was prepared September 2008.)

Table 22. Average grade that the public would give the public schools in their community and in the nation at large: 1974 through 2008

Year	All adults		No children in school		Public school parents		Private school parents	
	Nation	Local community	Nation	Local community	Nation	Local community	Nation	Local community
1	2	3	4	5	6	7	8	9
1974	—	2.63	—	2.57	—	2.80	—	2.15
1975	—	2.38	—	2.31	—	2.49	—	1.81
1976	—	2.38	—	2.34	—	2.48	—	2.22
1977	—	2.33	—	2.25	—	2.59	—	2.05
1978	—	2.21	—	2.11	—	2.47	—	1.69
1979	—	2.21	—	2.15	—	2.38	—	1.88
1980	—	2.26	—	—	—	—	—	—
1981	1.94	2.20	—	2.12	—	2.36	—	1.88
1982	2.01	2.24	2.04	2.18	2.01	2.35	2.02	2.20
1983	1.91	2.12	1.92	2.10	1.92	2.31	1.82	1.89
1984	2.09	2.36	2.11	2.30	2.11	2.49	2.04	2.17
1985	2.14	2.39	2.16	2.36	2.20	2.44	1.93	2.00
1986	2.13	2.36	—	2.29	—	2.55	—	2.14
1987	2.18	2.44	2.20	2.38	2.22	2.61	2.03	2.01
1988	2.08	2.35	2.02	2.32	2.13	2.48	2.00	2.13
1989	2.01	2.35	1.99	2.27	2.06	2.56	1.93	2.12
1990	1.99	2.29	1.98	2.27	2.03	2.44	1.85	2.09
1991	2.00	2.36	—	—	—	—	—	—
1992	1.93	2.30	1.92	—	1.94	2.73	1.85	—
1993	1.95	2.41	1.97	2.40	1.97	2.48	1.80	2.11
1994	1.95	2.26	1.95	2.16	1.90	2.55	1.86	1.90
1995	1.97	2.28	1.98	2.25	1.93	2.41	1.81	1.85
1996	1.93	2.30	1.91	2.22	2.00	2.56	1.80	1.86
1997	1.97	2.35	1.99	2.27	2.01	2.56	1.99	1.87
1998	1.93	2.41	1.91	2.36	1.96	2.51	1.81	2.20
1999	2.02	2.44	2.03	2.42	1.97	2.56	—	—
2000	1.98	2.47	1.94	2.44	2.05	2.59	—	—
2001	2.01	2.47	2.00	2.42	2.04	2.66	—	—
2002	2.08	2.44	2.08	2.40	2.06	2.61	—	—
2003	2.11	2.41	2.09	2.32	2.16	2.57	—	—
2004	2.08	2.56	2.15	2.42	2.00	2.58	—	—
2005	2.06	2.45	2.07	2.43	2.11	2.60	—	—
2006	2.03	2.45	2.00	2.41	2.07	2.60	—	—
2007	1.90	2.31	1.89	2.27	1.96	2.54	—	—
2008	2.02	2.40	—	—	—	—	—	—

—Not available.
NOTE: Average based on a scale where A = 4, B = 3, C = 2, D = 1, and F = 0.

SOURCE: Phi Delta Kappa, *Phi Delta Kappan,* "The Annual Gallup Poll of the Public's Attitudes Toward the Public Schools," 1974 through 2008. (This table was prepared September 2008.)

Table 23. Percentage of elementary and secondary school children whose parents were involved in school activities, by selected child, parent, and school characteristics: 1999, 2003, and 2007

Percent of children whose parents report the following types of involvement in school activities

Child, parent, and school characteristic	1999				2003				2007			
	Attended a general school meeting	Attended parent-teacher conference	Attended a class event	Volunteered at school	Attended a general school meeting	Attended parent-teacher conference	Attended a class event	Volunteered at school	Attended a general school meeting	Attended parent-teacher conference	Attended a class event	Volunteered at school
1	2	3	4	5	6	7	8	9	10	11	12	13
Total	**78.3 (0.49)**	**72.8 (0.45)**	**65.4 (0.44)**	**36.8 (0.40)**	**87.7 (0.37)**	**77.1 (0.42)**	**69.9 (0.42)**	**41.8 (0.60)**	**89.4 (0.48)**	**78.1 (0.52)**	**74.5 (0.57)**	**46.4 (0.63)**
Sex of child												
Male	78.0 (0.62)	74.0 (0.60)	63.4 (0.62)	36.7 (0.65)	87.4 (0.49)	77.7 (0.63)	67.4 (0.75)	41.2 (0.87)	89.3 (0.70)	79.2 (0.65)	71.5 (0.90)	44.8 (0.95)
Female	78.6 (0.69)	71.5 (0.56)	67.4 (0.59)	37.0 (0.61)	87.9 (0.55)	76.5 (0.63)	72.6 (0.63)	42.4 (0.83)	89.6 (0.59)	76.8 (0.94)	77.7 (0.82)	48.1 (1.01)
Race/ethnicity of child												
White	80.5 (0.54)	73.6 (0.48)	71.6 (0.53)	42.7 (0.51)	88.7 (0.51)	76.4 (0.62)	74.1 (0.65)	48.4 (0.82)	90.9 (0.52)	77.8 (0.64)	80.1 (0.68)	54.2 (0.85)
Black	74.5 (1.12)	71.1 (1.23)	53.8 (1.29)	26.2 (1.21)	88.7 (0.85)	78.7 (1.35)	63.3 (1.54)	32.0 (1.65)	86.7 (1.77)	77.3 (1.98)	64.7 (2.31)	35.0 (1.89)
Hispanic	73.1 (1.18)	71.0 (1.05)	51.5 (1.02)	24.5 (0.90)	82.6 (1.05)	78.1 (1.10)	60.9 (1.36)	27.7 (1.23)	86.7 (1.14)	80.2 (1.05)	65.0 (1.46)	31.8 (1.34)
Asian[1]	— (†)	— (†)	— (†)	— (†)	— (†)	— (†)	— (†)	— (†)	91.0 (2.06)	79.9 (2.87)	71.4 (2.89)	45.8 (3.78)
Pacific Islander[1]	— (†)	— (†)	— (†)	— (†)	— (†)	— (†)	— (†)	— (†)	‡ (†)	‡ (7.16)	‡ (9.63)	‡ (12.64)
American Indian/Alaska Native[1]	— (†)	— (†)	— (†)	— (†)	— (†)	— (†)	— (†)	— (†)	94.2 (2.96)	79.7 (7.16)	80.8 (9.63)	58.4 (3.13)
Other[2]	76.7 (2.00)	73.2 (1.94)	62.4 (2.01)	30.7 (1.94)	87.5 (1.63)	77.6 (2.25)	68.5 (2.32)	37.2 (2.16)	89.2 (1.76)	73.6 (3.48)	75.7 (2.83)	44.8 (3.13)
Highest education level of parents												
Less than high school	57.4 (1.77)	60.0 (1.78)	37.8 (1.68)	12.9 (1.05)	69.8 (2.04)	67.8 (2.50)	42.4 (2.42)	15.6 (2.04)	75.2 (2.37)	69.7 (2.65)	48.1 (3.06)	19.5 (3.37)
High school/GED	72.7 (1.00)	69.7 (0.87)	58.7 (0.93)	26.0 (0.88)	83.6 (0.91)	75.4 (0.93)	62.1 (1.28)	30.3 (1.27)	84.5 (1.15)	74.3 (1.16)	65.1 (1.52)	33.0 (1.56)
Vocational/technical or some college	78.0 (1.04)	72.8 (0.97)	66.0 (1.05)	35.7 (1.07)	88.5 (0.67)	78.0 (1.02)	69.1 (0.93)	38.8 (1.26)	87.5 (1.56)	75.7 (1.48)	69.3 (1.60)	40.2 (1.66)
Associate's degree	81.7 (1.14)	75.8 (1.39)	68.7 (1.57)	41.5 (1.53)	88.6 (1.27)	76.6 (1.68)	73.0 (1.76)	39.7 (1.67)	91.9 (1.18)	80.2 (1.75)	76.9 (2.14)	45.3 (2.32)
Bachelor's degree	87.0 (0.73)	79.6 (0.84)	75.8 (0.93)	49.6 (1.10)	92.0 (0.75)	79.8 (0.89)	80.1 (0.95)	53.9 (1.29)	93.6 (0.75)	81.4 (1.00)	83.2 (0.95)	57.1 (1.44)
Graduate/professional degree	89.4 (0.70)	76.2 (1.09)	79.2 (0.98)	55.1 (1.21)	94.6 (0.74)	79.4 (0.99)	80.8 (1.09)	61.8 (1.57)	95.6 (0.64)	82.3 (1.13)	87.3 (0.95)	64.1 (1.33)
Family income												
$5,000 or less	67.0 (2.83)	66.7 (3.14)	47.4 (2.87)	17.6 (2.09)	77.7 (2.84)	72.4 (4.15)	55.6 (3.91)	27.3 (4.09)	76.3 (4.85)	66.1 (5.32)	44.7 (6.01)	27.8 (5.24)
$5,001 to 10,000	66.8 (2.13)	67.6 (2.25)	50.7 (2.23)	23.3 (1.91)	79.3 (3.26)	75.7 (3.28)	59.9 (3.60)	30.4 (3.35)	80.0 (3.45)	76.0 (3.81)	56.2 (4.56)	26.3 (4.53)
$10,001 to 15,000	67.1 (1.64)	70.0 (1.62)	49.9 (2.15)	20.4 (1.40)	80.0 (2.41)	75.6 (2.35)	53.4 (2.99)	22.5 (2.44)	76.7 (4.46)	73.0 (4.57)	56.8 (4.12)	28.8 (3.69)
$15,001 to 20,000	71.1 (1.76)	70.4 (1.52)	55.1 (1.89)	25.3 (1.70)	81.1 (2.60)	74.2 (2.23)	57.5 (2.28)	25.6 (2.44)	81.9 (3.07)	83.0 (2.54)	58.9 (4.17)	17.4 (2.12)
$20,001 to 25,000	70.6 (1.90)	67.0 (1.62)	53.4 (1.76)	26.2 (1.63)	83.5 (1.64)	79.1 (1.89)	62.4 (1.99)	27.0 (2.39)	84.8 (2.26)	78.9 (2.38)	64.7 (2.96)	29.9 (3.18)
$25,001 to 30,000	74.3 (1.35)	71.6 (1.31)	59.1 (1.71)	30.9 (1.69)	85.7 (1.46)	75.9 (2.41)	64.2 (2.23)	33.8 (2.86)	85.5 (3.09)	76.6 (3.20)	63.4 (3.20)	35.9 (3.53)
$30,001 to 35,000	79.0 (1.60)	73.8 (1.72)	67.6 (1.69)	37.9 (1.84)	84.5 (1.59)	76.3 (1.94)	64.7 (2.32)	33.5 (2.51)	85.6 (2.75)	72.4 (3.23)	67.6 (2.59)	31.5 (2.80)
$35,001 to 40,000	79.4 (1.38)	73.7 (1.38)	68.4 (1.64)	36.1 (1.84)	83.4 (2.50)	74.7 (2.10)	70.9 (2.41)	37.3 (3.50)	88.0 (1.65)	74.9 (2.85)	69.9 (2.57)	32.8 (2.52)
$40,001 to 50,000	81.6 (1.07)	75.1 (1.13)	72.8 (1.25)	40.1 (1.26)	87.5 (1.18)	79.3 (1.42)	68.5 (2.11)	40.0 (1.89)	88.8 (1.57)	79.4 (2.05)	74.3 (2.09)	40.8 (2.36)
$50,001 to 75,000	84.6 (0.78)	74.8 (0.91)	72.6 (0.90)	43.8 (1.05)	89.9 (0.79)	76.9 (0.96)	74.5 (1.04)	46.0 (1.27)	92.0 (0.73)	78.6 (0.96)	79.0 (1.15)	51.7 (1.18)
Over $75,000	88.5 (0.68)	77.3 (0.74)	79.3 (0.80)	54.9 (1.02)	93.9 (0.57)	78.6 (0.89)	79.3 (0.73)	56.8 (1.01)	95.0 (0.40)	79.9 (0.87)	85.4 (0.66)	62.0 (1.10)
Child attending public school	76.8 (0.54)	71.4 (0.50)	63.5 (0.48)	33.8 (0.41)	86.7 (0.40)	75.9 (0.45)	68.0 (0.47)	38.5 (0.64)	88.5 (0.53)	76.9 (0.59)	72.6 (0.66)	42.7 (0.69)
Elementary (kindergarten to grade 8)	81.7 (0.57)	80.9 (0.45)	66.9 (0.55)	38.1 (0.48)	90.9 (0.40)	85.1 (0.42)	71.7 (0.57)	42.8 (0.74)	91.7 (0.59)	85.1 (0.69)	76.1 (0.79)	48.5 (1.00)
Secondary (grades 9 to 12)	65.8 (0.99)	50.1 (1.10)	55.9 (0.97)	24.0 (0.77)	76.9 (1.06)	54.8 (1.02)	59.4 (1.06)	28.5 (0.98)	82.0 (1.12)	59.9 (1.14)	65.5 (1.27)	30.6 (1.05)
Child attending private school	91.4 (0.80)	85.0 (0.95)	81.7 (1.09)	63.8 (1.35)	95.7 (0.61)	86.6 (1.03)	85.6 (1.23)	68.7 (1.57)	96.3 (1.08)	86.5 (1.84)	88.1 (1.27)	74.1 (1.75)
Elementary (kindergarten to grade 8)	93.0 (0.73)	90.2 (0.81)	84.2 (1.11)	68.8 (1.37)	96.6 (0.69)	91.6 (0.92)	88.4 (1.22)	73.4 (1.90)	96.8 (1.46)	92.5 (1.61)	89.2 (1.65)	80.3 (1.87)
Secondary (grades 9 to 12)	85.9 (2.09)	66.9 (2.74)	73.0 (2.62)	46.3 (3.23)	93.0 (1.56)	72.2 (2.54)	77.6 (2.93)	55.2 (2.78)	95.2 (1.11)	71.2 (4.05)	85.2 (2.21)	58.6 (3.50)

—Not available.
†Not applicable.
‡Reporting standards not met.
[1]Included in "Other" in 1999 and 2003 data.
[2]Includes all other races or more than one race.
NOTE: Includes children enrolled in kindergarten through grade 12 and ungraded students. Excludes homeschooled children. The respondent was the parent most knowledgeable about the child's education. Responding parents reported on their own and their spouse's, or other household adults', activities. Race categories exclude persons of Hispanic ethnicity. Standard errors appear in parentheses.
SOURCE: U.S. Department of Education, National Center for Education Statistics, *Parent and Family Involvement in Education: 2002–03;* and Parent Survey (Parent:1999) and Parent and Family Involvement in Education Survey (PFI:2003 and 2007) of the National Household Education Surveys Program, unpublished tabulations. (This table was prepared August 2008.)

Table 24. Percentage of kindergartners through fifth-graders whose parents were involved in education-related activities, by selected child, parent, and school characteristics: 1999 and 2003

Child, parent, and school characteristic	Percent of children whose parents report that they did the following things with their children in the past month										Percent of children whose parents report that they involved their children in the following activities during the past week					
	1999					2003					1999			2003		
	Visited a library	Went to a play, concert, or other live show	Visited an art gallery, museum, or historical site	Visited a zoo or aquarium	Attended an event sponsored by a community, religious, or ethnic group[1]	Visited a library	Went to a play, concert, or other live show	Visited an art gallery, museum, or historical site	Visited a zoo or aquarium	Attended an event sponsored by a community, religious, or ethnic group[1]	Told a story	Worked on arts or crafts	Worked on household chores	Told a story	Worked on arts or crafts	Worked on household chores
1	2	3	4	5	6	7	8	9	10	11	12	13	14	15	16	17
Total	48.6 (0.64)	32.1 (0.55)	22.2 (0.67)	14.1 (0.47)	52.8 (0.63)	50.2 (0.80)	35.5 (0.87)	22.2 (0.83)	16.5 (0.69)	62.0 (0.80)	69.4 (0.60)	68.0 (0.60)	93.8 (0.33)	74.9 (0.66)	74.9 (0.70)	97.1 (0.21)
Sex of child																
Male	47.2 (0.91)	30.5 (0.84)	22.3 (0.93)	13.9 (0.70)	50.9 (0.89)	47.3 (1.08)	33.6 (1.09)	23.1 (1.12)	16.3 (0.88)	61.0 (1.08)	69.1 (0.76)	64.2 (0.81)	93.0 (0.41)	73.3 (0.86)	69.7 (0.98)	97.0 (0.33)
Female	50.1 (1.02)	33.7 (0.81)	22.1 (0.89)	14.3 (0.70)	54.8 (0.95)	53.1 (1.11)	37.5 (1.09)	21.2 (1.07)	16.7 (0.87)	63.0 (1.09)	69.7 (0.89)	71.9 (0.90)	94.6 (0.45)	76.6 (0.96)	80.2 (1.01)	97.3 (0.33)
Race/ethnicity of child																
White	48.9 (0.85)	33.9 (0.72)	22.3 (0.76)	12.0 (0.54)	54.6 (0.81)	49.1 (1.03)	37.2 (1.26)	21.2 (1.09)	13.6 (0.85)	64.6 (1.12)	70.9 (0.80)	72.4 (0.73)	96.2 (0.33)	76.0 (0.96)	75.4 (0.89)	98.4 (0.24)
Black	47.8 (1.76)	31.3 (1.60)	21.0 (1.52)	15.7 (1.24)	53.0 (1.40)	52.3 (2.50)	36.7 (2.23)	24.4 (1.97)	18.9 (1.55)	66.3 (2.35)	64.8 (1.73)	58.6 (1.82)	93.9 (0.79)	69.6 (2.00)	68.1 (2.14)	98.9 (0.43)
Hispanic	43.9 (1.65)	24.4 (1.10)	20.6 (1.26)	19.7 (1.02)	45.8 (1.32)	48.2 (1.77)	28.0 (1.53)	20.8 (1.38)	23.7 (1.32)	49.3 (1.75)	66.6 (1.49)	59.4 (1.33)	84.7 (1.19)	74.2 (1.55)	79.6 (1.45)	92.7 (0.86)
Other	61.6 (3.14)	34.9 (3.02)	29.8 (3.16)	18.1 (2.31)	51.7 (3.18)	61.0 (3.80)	37.4 (3.04)	29.9 (2.75)	18.3 (2.76)	62.3 (3.45)	74.0 (2.87)	69.1 (2.47)	92.0 (1.56)	79.9 (3.06)	73.6 (2.52)	93.3 (1.45)
Highest education level of parents																
Less than high school	34.5 (2.33)	17.5 (1.63)	12.1 (1.64)	15.2 (1.65)	36.7 (2.32)	36.1 (3.39)	20.0 (3.10)	9.3 (1.75)	15.3 (2.05)	34.3 (3.06)	61.9 (2.30)	54.4 (2.13)	81.8 (1.97)	67.2 (3.16)	74.8 (3.20)	94.9 (1.22)
High school/GED	40.3 (1.42)	25.9 (1.13)	16.0 (1.04)	12.8 (0.98)	42.6 (1.23)	44.5 (1.64)	28.6 (1.83)	17.8 (1.73)	16.5 (1.18)	50.5 (1.81)	66.5 (1.28)	64.3 (1.27)	92.8 (0.75)	71.3 (1.59)	75.5 (1.32)	97.1 (0.56)
Vocational/technical or some college	47.2 (1.41)	30.2 (1.30)	20.4 (1.21)	11.9 (0.90)	53.7 (1.43)	44.3 (2.04)	32.8 (1.89)	19.1 (1.32)	15.2 (1.29)	62.1 (1.64)	70.2 (1.23)	68.3 (1.18)	96.2 (0.58)	75.9 (1.54)	76.2 (1.51)	97.4 (0.56)
Associate's degree	50.4 (2.12)	35.5 (2.10)	22.0 (1.77)	14.3 (1.42)	53.6 (2.26)	47.4 (3.04)	41.1 (3.24)	22.0 (2.40)	15.4 (2.09)	67.0 (2.85)	70.0 (2.04)	71.9 (1.88)	95.4 (0.92)	76.0 (2.00)	73.6 (2.47)	96.9 (0.73)
Bachelor's degree	57.6 (1.52)	40.0 (1.24)	29.1 (1.37)	15.2 (1.03)	64.6 (1.22)	57.7 (1.74)	40.1 (1.61)	27.6 (1.70)	16.0 (1.32)	71.3 (1.63)	74.2 (1.39)	73.3 (1.10)	96.1 (0.66)	77.3 (1.60)	74.0 (1.48)	97.2 (0.46)
Graduate/professional degree	62.9 (1.53)	43.3 (1.77)	34.7 (1.73)	17.9 (1.33)	65.3 (1.68)	65.2 (2.04)	47.2 (2.53)	31.7 (2.02)	20.7 (1.82)	75.6 (1.55)	71.4 (1.73)	73.3 (1.53)	95.3 (0.79)	78.6 (1.64)	73.9 (1.72)	98.0 (0.46)
Family income																
$5,000 or less	42.7 (4.27)	24.9 (2.73)	16.5 (2.76)	16.6 (2.77)	37.3 (3.55)	38.2 (5.63)	25.7 (4.94)	13.2 (3.10)	18.7 (3.99)	52.9 (4.65)	67.5 (4.39)	55.9 (4.38)	90.9 (2.02)	79.5 (4.52)	78.9 (4.61)	94.3 (1.99)
$5,001 to 10,000	43.8 (2.86)	21.1 (2.34)	17.7 (2.07)	14.5 (1.65)	38.9 (2.62)	42.2 (4.99)	28.5 (4.74)	22.8 (4.05)	23.8 (4.05)	51.6 (4.74)	69.6 (2.30)	58.4 (2.93)	90.0 (1.69)	70.9 (3.88)	75.3 (3.30)	96.3 (1.62)
$10,001 to 15,000	44.8 (2.51)	24.5 (2.32)	18.2 (1.99)	15.3 (2.06)	45.5 (2.83)	49.1 (4.27)	27.3 (3.26)	20.7 (4.22)	20.9 (3.46)	49.1 (4.19)	66.7 (2.62)	61.2 (2.99)	91.9 (1.55)	70.0 (3.62)	74.6 (4.03)	93.8 (1.54)
$15,001 to 20,000	43.0 (3.07)	25.9 (2.37)	13.3 (1.74)	13.7 (1.61)	47.2 (2.78)	44.4 (3.95)	32.9 (3.75)	18.9 (2.83)	17.1 (2.61)	52.1 (4.19)	62.3 (2.29)	64.1 (2.70)	91.4 (1.35)	76.9 (3.45)	76.1 (3.74)	98.0 (0.60)
$20,001 to 25,000	38.9 (2.10)	26.3 (2.05)	18.7 (1.85)	14.7 (1.50)	47.7 (2.53)	48.4 (3.57)	26.0 (3.39)	16.3 (2.22)	16.4 (2.35)	57.8 (3.76)	68.1 (2.34)	63.9 (2.42)	90.5 (1.37)	71.6 (2.86)	80.6 (2.33)	96.0 (1.07)
$25,001 to 30,000	45.3 (2.27)	30.4 (2.35)	20.7 (1.97)	14.4 (1.70)	50.0 (2.30)	51.0 (3.71)	27.1 (3.35)	20.8 (3.12)	15.9 (2.50)	56.7 (3.96)	70.6 (2.32)	68.7 (2.42)	94.6 (0.87)	74.2 (2.86)	71.9 (3.47)	96.6 (1.06)
$30,001 to 35,000	49.2 (2.55)	31.3 (2.66)	21.4 (1.97)	11.9 (1.42)	53.7 (2.48)	44.9 (3.17)	33.2 (3.22)	18.3 (2.72)	17.1 (2.32)	59.7 (3.10)	69.3 (1.85)	66.1 (2.51)	93.2 (1.39)	73.3 (2.88)	78.1 (2.72)	97.9 (0.80)
$35,001 to 40,000	51.9 (2.30)	34.4 (2.60)	23.5 (2.18)	13.2 (1.48)	59.1 (2.45)	45.6 (4.30)	31.4 (3.79)	16.8 (2.99)	11.6 (2.92)	70.7 (3.70)	72.5 (1.94)	71.6 (1.96)	96.2 (0.89)	74.5 (3.68)	75.5 (2.97)	98.3 (0.99)
$40,001 to 50,000	52.1 (2.03)	32.5 (1.71)	23.1 (1.51)	13.1 (1.24)	58.5 (2.01)	52.2 (3.00)	35.8 (2.99)	20.9 (2.41)	14.8 (2.54)	63.1 (2.54)	69.0 (1.82)	72.2 (1.87)	95.7 (0.75)	75.7 (2.20)	71.9 (2.48)	97.0 (0.83)
$50,001 to 75,000	51.5 (1.67)	34.5 (1.47)	23.1 (1.37)	12.2 (0.86)	57.6 (1.72)	50.0 (1.65)	39.0 (1.59)	23.1 (1.42)	14.9 (1.27)	64.5 (1.42)	70.9 (1.43)	72.5 (1.41)	96.3 (0.64)	74.9 (1.53)	75.3 (1.55)	98.1 (0.37)
Over $75,000	55.5 (1.61)	44.5 (1.45)	31.6 (1.75)	15.8 (0.86)	61.9 (1.33)	55.8 (1.69)	42.6 (1.66)	27.3 (1.43)	16.9 (1.31)	67.9 (1.42)	71.4 (1.37)	74.4 (1.31)	95.4 (0.72)	76.8 (1.29)	73.3 (1.32)	97.4 (0.43)
Child attending public school	47.5 (0.68)	30.4 (0.58)	21.0 (0.70)	13.7 (0.49)	51.2 (0.68)	49.2 (0.87)	34.9 (0.88)	21.2 (0.92)	16.3 (0.71)	60.6 (0.85)	68.8 (0.65)	67.5 (0.66)	93.7 (0.38)	75.0 (0.68)	75.2 (0.72)	97.4 (0.21)
Child attending private school	56.4 (1.78)	44.3 (1.80)	31.0 (1.55)	17.1 (1.28)	64.8 (1.92)	57.0 (2.31)	40.0 (2.55)	29.0 (2.04)	17.9 (1.85)	72.2 (2.15)	73.7 (1.58)	71.6 (1.64)	94.7 (0.70)	74.2 (2.09)	72.1 (1.94)	95.1 (0.91)

[1] In 1999, one item was used to ask parents if they had attended an event sponsored by a community, ethnic, or religious group. In 2003, attendance at an event sponsored by a religious group was asked about separately from attendance at an event sponsored by a community or ethnic group.
NOTE: The respondent was the parent most knowledgeable about the child's education. The responding parent reported on their own and their spouse's, or other household adults', activities. Excludes homeschooled children. Race categories exclude persons of Hispanic ethnicity. Standard errors appear in parentheses.

SOURCE: U.S. Department of Education, National Center for Education Statistics, Parent Survey (Parent:1999) and Parent and Family Involvement in Education Survey (PFI:2003) of the National Household Education Surveys Program, unpublished tabulations. (This table was prepared June 2005.)

Table 25. Expenditures of educational institutions related to the gross domestic product, by level of institution: Selected years, 1929–30 through 2007–08

Year	Gross domestic product (GDP) (in billions of current dollars)	School year	Expenditures for education in current dollars					
			All educational institutions		All elementary and secondary schools		All postsecondary degree-granting institutions	
			Amount (in millions)	As a percent of GDP	Amount (in millions)	As a percent of GDP	Amount (in millions)	As a percent of GDP
1	2	3	4	5	6	7	8	9
1929	$103.6	1929–30	—	—	—	—	$632	0.6
1939	92.2	1939–40	—	—	—	—	758	0.8
1949	267.3	1949–50	$8,494	3.2	$6,249	2.3	2,246	0.8
1959	506.6	1959–60	22,314	4.4	16,713	3.3	5,601	1.1
1961	544.7	1961–62	26,828	4.9	19,673	3.6	7,155	1.3
1963	617.7	1963–64	32,003	5.2	22,825	3.7	9,178	1.5
1965	719.1	1965–66	40,558	5.6	28,048	3.9	12,509	1.7
1967	832.6	1967–68	51,558	6.2	35,077	4.2	16,481	2.0
1969	984.6	1969–70	64,227	6.5	43,183	4.4	21,043	2.1
1970	1,038.5	1970–71	71,575	6.9	48,200	4.6	23,375	2.3
1971	1,127.1	1971–72	76,510	6.8	50,950	4.5	25,560	2.3
1972	1,238.3	1972–73	82,908	6.7	54,952	4.4	27,956	2.3
1973	1,382.7	1973–74	91,084	6.6	60,370	4.4	30,714	2.2
1974	1,500.0	1974–75	103,903	6.9	68,846	4.6	35,058	2.3
1975	1,638.3	1975–76	114,004	7.0	75,101	4.6	38,903	2.4
1976	1,825.3	1976–77	121,793	6.7	79,194	4.3	42,600	2.3
1977	2,030.9	1977–78	132,515	6.5	86,544	4.3	45,971	2.3
1978	2,294.7	1978–79	143,733	6.3	93,012	4.1	50,721	2.2
1979	2,563.3	1979–80	160,075	6.2	103,162	4.0	56,914	2.2
1980	2,789.5	1980–81	176,378	6.3	112,325	4.0	64,053	2.3
1981	3,128.4	1981–82	190,825	6.1	120,486	3.9	70,339	2.2
1982	3,255.0	1982–83	204,661	6.3	128,725	4.0	75,936	2.3
1983	3,536.7	1983–84	220,993	6.2	139,000	3.9	81,993	2.3
1984	3,933.2	1984–85	239,351	6.1	149,400	3.8	89,951	2.3
1985	4,220.3	1985–86	259,336	6.1	161,800	3.8	97,536	2.3
1986	4,462.8	1986–87	280,964	6.3	175,200	3.9	105,764	2.4
1987	4,739.5	1987–88	301,786	6.4	187,999	4.0	113,787	2.4
1988	5,103.8	1988–89	333,246	6.5	209,377	4.1	123,868	2.4
1989	5,484.4	1989–90	365,825	6.7	231,170	4.2	134,656	2.5
1990	5,803.1	1990–91	395,318	6.8	249,230	4.3	146,088	2.5
1991	5,995.9	1991–92	417,944	7.0	261,755	4.4	156,189	2.6
1992	6,337.7	1992–93	439,876	6.9	274,635	4.3	165,241	2.6
1993	6,657.4	1993–94	461,157	6.9	287,807	4.3	173,351	2.6
1994	7,072.2	1994–95	485,369	6.9	302,400	4.3	182,969	2.6
1995	7,397.7	1995–96	508,523	6.9	318,046	4.3	190,476	2.6
1996	7,816.9	1996–97	538,854	6.9	338,951	4.3	199,903	2.6
1997	8,304.3	1997–98	570,471	6.9	361,615	4.4	208,856	2.5
1998	8,747.0	1998–99	603,847	6.9	384,638	4.4	219,209	2.5
1999	9,268.4	1999–2000	649,322	7.0	412,538	4.5	236,784	2.6
2000	9,817.0	2000–01	705,017	7.2	444,811	4.5	260,206	2.7
2001	10,128.0	2001–02	752,780	7.4	472,064	4.7	280,715	2.8
2002	10,469.6	2002–03	795,691	7.6	492,807	4.7	302,884	2.9
2003	10,960.8	2003–04	830,293	7.6	513,542	4.7	316,751	2.9
2004	11,685.9	2004–05	875,788	7.5	540,769	4.6	335,019	2.9
2005	12,421.9	2005–06	925,712	7.5	572,135	4.6	353,577	2.8
2006	13,178.4	2006–07 [1]	971,000	7.4	602,000	4.6	369,000	2.8
2007	13,807.5	2007–08 [1]	1,017,000	7.4	631,000	4.6	386,000	2.8

—Not available.

[1] Estimated.

NOTE: Total expenditures for public elementary and secondary schools include current expenditures, interest on school debt, and capital outlay. Data for private elementary and secondary schools are estimated. Expenditures for colleges and universities in 1929–30 and 1939–40 include current-fund expenditures and additions to plant value. Public and private degree-granting institutions data for 1949–50 through 1995–96 are for current-fund expenditures. Data for private degree-granting institutions for 1996–97 and later years are for total expenditures. Data for public degree-granting institutions for 1996–97 through 2000–01 are for current expenditures; data for later years are for total expenditures. Data through 1995–96 are for institutions of higher education, while later data are for degree-granting institutions. Degree-granting institutions grant associate's or higher degrees and participate in Title IV federal financial aid programs. The degree-granting classification is very similar to the earlier higher education classification, but it includes more 2-year colleges and excludes a few higher education institutions that did not grant degrees. (See Guide to Sources for details.) Some data have been revised from previously published figures. Detail may not sum to totals because of rounding.

SOURCE: U.S. Department of Education, National Center for Education Statistics, *Biennial Survey of Education in the United States*, 1929–30 through 1949–50; *Statistics of State School Systems*, 1951–52 through 1969–70; *Revenues and Expenditures for Public Elementary and Secondary Education*, 1970–71 through 1986–87; Common Core of Data (CCD), "National Public Education Financial Survey," 1987–88 through 2005–06; Higher Education General Information Survey (HEGIS), Financial Statistics of Institutions of Higher Education, 1965–66 through 1985–86; 1986–87 through 2005–06 Integrated Postsecondary Education Data System, "Finance Survey" (IPEDS-F:FY87–99), and Spring 2002 through Spring 2007. U.S. Department of Commerce, Bureau of Economic Analysis, retrieved August 12, 2008, from http://www.bea.gov/national/index.htm#gdpunpublished data. (This table was prepared August 2008.)

Table 26. Expenditures of educational institutions, by level and control of institution: Selected years, 1899–1900 through 2007–08

[In millions]

School year	Current dollars							Constant 2006-07 dollars[1]			
	Total	Elementary and secondary schools			Postsecondary degree-granting institutions			Total	Elementary and secondary schools		Postsecondary degree-granting institutions
		Total	Public	Private[2]	Total	Public	Private		Total	Public	
1	2	3	4	5	6	7	8	9	10	11	12
1899–1900	—	—	$215	—	—	—	—	—	—	—	—
1909–10	—	—	426	—	—	—	—	—	—	—	—
1919–20	—	—	1,036	—	—	—	—	—	—	$11,099	—
1929–30	—	—	2,317	—	$632 [3]	$292 [3]	$341 [3]	—	—	27,630	$7,540 [3]
1939–40	—	—	2,344	—	758 [3]	392 [3]	367 [3]	—	—	34,240	11,079 [3]
1949–50	$8,494	$6,249	5,838	$411	2,246	1,154	1,092	$73,218	$53,861	50,318	19,357
1959–60	22,314	16,713	15,613	1,100	5,601	3,131	2,470	155,026	116,115	108,473	38,911
1969–70	64,227	43,183	40,683	2,500	21,043	13,250	7,794	347,083	233,365	219,855	113,718
1970–71	71,575	48,200	45,500	2,700	23,375	14,996	8,379	367,808	247,688	233,814	120,120
1971–72	76,510	50,950	48,050	2,900	25,560	16,484	9,075	379,552	252,756	238,369	126,797
1972–73	82,908	54,952	51,852	3,100	27,956	18,204	9,752	395,362	262,050	247,267	133,312
1973–74	91,084	60,370	56,970	3,400	30,714	20,336	10,377	398,792	264,319	249,433	134,473
1974–75	103,903	68,846	64,846	4,000	35,058	23,490	11,568	409,535	271,356	255,590	138,179
1975–76	114,004	75,101	70,601	4,500	38,903	26,184	12,719	419,642	276,441	259,877	143,201
1976–77	121,793	79,194	74,194	5,000	42,600	28,635	13,965	423,613	275,445	258,055	148,167
1977–78	132,515	86,544	80,844	5,700	45,971	30,725	15,246	431,903	282,072	263,494	149,831
1978–79	143,733	93,012	86,712	6,300	50,721	33,733	16,988	428,340	277,185	258,411	151,154
1979–80	160,075	103,162	95,962	7,200	56,914	37,768	19,146	420,922	271,266	252,333	149,656
1980–81	176,378	112,325	104,125	8,200	64,053	42,280	21,773	415,647	264,702	245,378	150,945
1981–82	190,825	120,486	111,186	9,300	70,339	46,219	24,120	413,936	261,357	241,183	152,580
1982–83	204,661	128,725	118,425	10,300	75,936	49,573	26,363	425,665	267,730	246,307	157,936
1983–84	220,993	139,000	127,500	11,500	81,993	53,087	28,907	443,229	278,781	255,717	164,448
1984–85	239,351	149,400	137,000	12,400	89,951	58,315	31,637	461,965	288,353	264,420	173,612
1985–86	259,336	161,800	148,600	13,200	97,536	63,194	34,342	486,507	303,533	278,770	182,975
1986–87	280,964	175,200	160,900	14,300	105,764	67,654	38,110	515,632	321,532	295,288	194,100
1987–88	301,786	187,999	172,699	15,300	113,787	72,641	41,145	531,811	331,294	304,332	200,518
1988–89	333,246	209,377	192,977	16,400	123,868	78,946	44,922	561,325	352,679	325,055	208,646
1989–90	365,825	231,170	212,770	18,400	134,656	85,771	48,885	588,138	371,652	342,070	216,486
1990–91	395,318	249,230	229,430	19,800	146,088	92,961	53,127	602,607	379,916	349,734	222,691
1991–92	417,944	261,755	241,055	20,700	156,189	98,847	57,342	617,318	386,621	356,046	230,697
1992–93	439,876	274,635	252,935	21,700	165,241	104,570	60,671	630,033	393,358	362,278	236,674
1993–94	461,157	287,807	265,307	22,500	173,351	109,310	64,041	643,836	401,816	370,403	242,020
1994–95	485,369	302,400	279,000	23,400	182,969	115,465	67,504	658,756	410,426	378,667	248,330
1995–96	508,523	318,046	293,646	24,400	190,476	119,525	70,952	671,902	420,229	387,990	251,673
1996–97	538,854	338,951	313,151	25,800	199,903 [2]	125,978	73,925 [2]	692,228	435,427	402,283	256,801 [2]
1997–98	570,471	361,615	334,315	27,300	208,856 [2]	132,846	76,010 [2]	720,004	456,402	421,946	263,602 [2]
1998–99	603,847	384,638	355,838	28,800	219,209	140,539	78,670	749,159	477,198	441,468	271,960
1999–2000	649,322	412,538	381,838	30,700	236,784	152,325	84,459	782,975	497,452	460,433	285,522
2000–01	705,017	444,811	410,811	34,000	260,206	170,345	89,861	821,972	518,601	478,961	303,371
2001–02	752,780	472,064	435,364	36,700	280,715	183,436	97,280	862,390	540,800	498,757	321,589
2002–03	795,691	492,807	454,907	37,900	302,762	197,026	105,858	891,948	552,423	509,938	339,525
2003–04	830,293	513,542	474,242	39,300	316,751	205,069	111,682	910,809	563,341	520,230	347,467
2004–05	875,788	540,769	499,569	41,200	335,019	215,794	119,225	932,650	575,879	532,004	356,771
2005–06	925,712	572,135	528,735	43,400	353,577	226,550	127,027	949,651	586,930	542,408	362,721
2006–07[2]	971,000	602,000	556,000	46,000	369,000	237,000	131,000	971,000	602,000	556,000	369,000
2007–08[2]	1,017,000	631,000	583,000	48,000	386,000	250,000	136,000	981,000	608,000	562,000	372,000

—Not available.
[1]Constant dollars based on the Consumer Price Index, prepared by the Bureau of Labor Statistics, U.S. Department of Labor, adjusted to a school-year basis.
[2]Estimated.
[3]Data include current-fund expenditures and additions to plant value.
NOTE: Total expenditures for public elementary and secondary schools include current expenditures, interest on school debt, and capital outlay. Public and private degree-granting institutions data for 1929–30 through 1995–96 are for current-fund expenditures, except where noted. Data for private degree-granting institutions for 1996–97 and later years are for total expenditures. Data for public degree-granting institutions for 1996–97 through 2000–01 are for current expenditures; data for later years are for total expenditures. Data through 1995–96 are for institutions of higher education, while later data are for degree-granting institutions. Degree-granting institutions grant associate's or higher degrees and participate in Title IV federal financial aid programs. The degree-granting classification is very similar to the earlier higher education classification, but it includes more 2-year colleges and excludes a few higher education institutions that did not grant degrees. (See Guide to Sources for details.) Some data have been revised from previously published figures. Detail may not sum to totals because of rounding.
SOURCE: U.S. Department of Education, National Center for Education Statistics, *Annual Report of the Commissioner of Education*, 1899–1900 and 1909–10; *Biennial Survey of Education in the United States*, 1919–20 through 1949–50; *Statistics of State School Systems*, 1951–52 through 1969–70; *Revenues and Expenditures for Public Elementary and Secondary Education*, 1970–71 through 1986–87; Common Core of Data (CCD), "National Public Education Financial Survey," 1987–88 through 2005–06; Higher Education General Information Survey (HEGIS), Financial Statistics of Institutions of Higher Education, 1965–66 through 1985–86; 1986–87 through 2005–06 Integrated Postsecondary Education Data System, "Finance Survey," (IPEDS-F:FY87–99), and Spring 2001 through Spring 2007, and unpublished tabulations. (This table was prepared August 2008.)

Table 27. Amount and percentage distribution of direct general expenditures of state and local governments, by function: Selected years, 1970–71 through 2005–06

Function	1970–71	1980–81	1990–91	1994–95	1998–99	1999–2000	2000–01	2001–02	2002–03	2003–04	2004–05	2005–06
1	2	3	4	5	6	7	8	9	10	11	12	13
					Amount (in millions of current dollars)							
Total direct general expenditures	**$150,674**	**$407,449**	**$508,108**	**$1,146,188**	**$1,398,533**	**$1,502,768**	**$1,621,757**	**$1,732,478**	**$1,817,513**	**$1,903,194**	**$2,009,644**	**$2,121,946**
Education and libraries	60,174	147,649	313,744	383,557	490,100	528,767	571,374	602,954	630,246	664,561	699,247	738,464
Social services and income maintenance	30,376	92,555	214,919	303,208	338,964	365,226	396,086	433,685	467,625	501,116	537,983	557,496
Public welfare	18,226	54,121	130,402	193,110	215,190	233,350	257,380	281,176	306,463	335,257	362,007	370,325
Hospitals and health	11,205	36,101	81,110	105,946	119,361	127,342	134,010	147,065	154,878	159,676	170,244	181,565
Employment security administration[1]	945	2,276	3,250	3,946	4,130	4,178	4,359	5,082	5,267	4,679	4,383	4,614
Veterans' services	†	57	157	206	283	357	337	361	1,017	1,504	1,349	992
Transportation	19,819	39,231	75,410	88,938	110,163	118,974	130,422	136,824	142,255	141,959	147,629[2]	159,462[2]
Public safety	9,416	31,233	79,952	101,157	128,743	137,809	146,544	156,702	162,279	166,056	177,524	189,555
Police and fire protection	7,531	21,283	46,568	58,064	74,629	79,900	84,554	90,456	95,215	98,037	105,398	113,233
Correction	1,885	7,393	27,356	35,857	45,598	48,805	52,370	54,615	55,471	56,521	59,253	62,667
Protective inspection and regulation	†	2,557	6,008	7,236	8,516	9,104	9,620	11,631	11,593	11,498	12,873	13,655
Environment and housing	11,832	35,223	76,167	93,221	109,930	117,123	124,203	134,033	141,571	146,895	153,451	164,130
Natural resources, parks, and recreation	5,191	13,239	28,505	33,140	41,649	45,272	50,082	52,101	54,573	53,766	55,804	60,251
Housing and community development	2,554	7,086	16,643	21,509	25,254	26,590	27,402	31,623	35,275	37,221	39,995	41,980
Sewerage and sanitation	4,087	14,898	31,014	38,573	43,047	45,261	46,718	50,309	51,723	55,908	57,652	61,900
Governmental administration	6,703	20,001	48,461	60,018	76,699	81,659	85,910	92,779	98,658	100,741	106,601	111,335
Financial administration	2,271	7,230	16,995	22,380	27,593	29,300	30,007	32,660	34,911	36,163	36,549	37,441
General control[3]	4,432	12,771	31,466	37,638	49,106	52,360	55,903	60,119	63,747	64,579	70,052	73,894
Interest on general debt	5,089	17,131	52,234	56,970	67,294	69,814	73,836	75,287	77,277	81,723	80,980	85,660
Other direct general expenditures, not elsewhere classified	7,265	24,426	47,242	59,119	76,640	83,395	93,382	100,215	97,602	100,143	106,231	115,844
					Percentage distribution							
Total direct general expenditures	**100.0**	**100.0**	**100.0**	**100.0**	**100.0**	**100.0**	**100.0**	**100.0**	**100.0**	**100.0**	**100.0**	**100.0**
Education and libraries	39.9	36.2	34.5	33.5	35.0	35.2	35.2	34.8	34.7	34.9	34.8	34.8
Social services and income maintenance	20.2	22.7	23.7	26.5	24.2	24.3	24.4	25.0	25.7	26.3	26.8	26.3
Public welfare	12.1	13.3	14.4	16.8	15.4	15.5	15.9	16.2	16.9	17.6	18.0	17.5
Hospitals and health	7.4	8.9	8.9	9.2	8.5	8.5	8.3	8.5	8.5	8.4	8.5	8.6
Employment security administration[1]	0.6	0.6	0.4	0.3	0.3	0.3	0.3	0.3	0.3	0.2	0.2	0.2
Veterans' services	†	#	#	#	#	#	#	#	0.1	0.1	0.1	#
Transportation	13.2	9.6	8.3	7.8	7.9	7.9	8.0	7.9	7.8	7.5	7.3[2]	7.5[2]
Public safety	6.2	7.7	8.8	8.8	9.2	9.2	9.0	9.0	8.9	8.7	8.8	8.9
Police and fire protection	5.0	5.2	5.1	5.1	5.3	5.3	5.2	5.2	5.2	5.2	5.2	5.3
Correction	1.3	1.8	3.0	3.1	3.3	3.2	3.2	3.2	3.1	3.0	2.9	3.0
Protective inspection and regulation	†	0.6	0.7	0.6	0.6	0.6	0.6	0.7	0.6	0.6	0.6	0.6
Environment and housing	7.9	8.6	8.4	8.1	7.9	7.8	7.7	7.7	7.8	7.7	7.6	7.7
Natural resources, parks, and recreation	3.4	3.2	3.1	2.9	3.0	3.0	3.1	3.0	3.0	2.8	2.8	2.8
Housing and community development	1.7	1.7	1.8	1.9	1.8	1.8	1.7	1.8	1.9	2.0	2.0	2.0
Sewerage and sanitation	2.7	3.7	3.4	3.4	3.1	3.0	2.9	2.9	2.8	2.9	2.9	2.9
Governmental administration	4.4	4.9	5.3	5.2	5.5	5.4	5.3	5.4	5.4	5.3	5.3	5.2
Financial administration	1.5	1.8	1.9	2.0	2.0	1.9	1.9	1.9	1.9	1.9	1.8	1.8
General control[3]	2.9	3.1	3.5	3.3	3.5	3.5	3.4	3.5	3.5	3.4	3.5	3.5
Interest on general debt	3.4	4.2	5.8	5.0	4.8	4.6	4.6	4.3	4.3	4.3	4.0	4.0
Other direct general expenditures, not elsewhere classified	4.8	6.0	5.2	5.2	5.5	5.5	5.8	5.8	5.4	5.3	5.3	5.5

†Not applicable.
#Rounds to zero.
[1]Previously called social insurance administration.
[2]No longer includes transit subsidies.
[3]Includes judicial and legal expenditures and expenditures on general public buildings and other governmental administration.

NOTE: Excludes monies paid by states to the federal government. Some data have been revised from previously published figures. Detail may not sum to totals because of rounding.
SOURCE: U.S. Department of Commerce, Census Bureau, Governmental Finances. Retrieved July 8, 2008, from http://www.census.gov/govs/www/estimate06.html. (This table was prepared July 2008.)

Table 28. Direct general expenditures of state and local governments for all functions and for education, by level of education and state: 2005–06

[In millions of current dollars]

State	Total direct general expenditures[1]		Education expenditures									Other education[2]
			Total		Elementary and secondary education				Colleges and universities			
					Total		Current expenditure	Capital outlay	Total		Current expenditure	Capital outlay	
1	2		3		4		5	6	7		8	9	10
United States	$2,121,946	(1,909.8)	$727,967	(218.4)	$500,528	(200.2)	$441,271	$59,256	$191,758	(19.2)	$168,961	$22,798	$35,681
Alabama	30,721	(245.8)	10,910	(#)	6,552	(4.6)	5,809	744	3,743	(#)	3,103	640	615
Alaska	9,359	(35.6)	2,456	(39.3)	1,797	(39.4)	1,540	257	579	(#)	524	55	80
Arizona	35,747	(210.9)	11,800	(#)	7,738	(#)	6,594	1,144	3,575	(#)	3,161	414	488
Arkansas	16,585	(97.9)	6,383	(#)	4,131	(#)	3,681	450	1,906	(#)	1,659	247	347
California	293,473	(1,379.3)	92,371	(9.2)	64,121	(12.8)	54,081	10,040	24,336	(#)	20,892	3,444	3,914
Colorado	30,780	(215.5)	10,938	(#)	7,418	(#)	6,394	1,024	3,176	(#)	2,868	309	344
Connecticut	27,484	(52.2)	9,929	(19.9)	7,308	(19.7)	6,662	646	2,124	(#)	1,851	273	497
Delaware	7,459	(20.1)	2,646	(#)	1,616	(#)	1,388	228	862	(#)	733	129	167
District of Columbia	8,004	(#)	1,478	(#)	1,365	(#)	1,260	105	112	(#)	111	2	#
Florida	122,624	(539.5)	35,345	(#)	26,022	(#)	21,151	4,871	7,447	(#)	6,585	862	1,876
Georgia	54,210	(173.5)	21,292	(#)	15,405	(#)	13,474	1,931	4,531	(#)	4,026	505	1,356
Hawaii	9,846	(0.0)	2,913	(#)	1,937	(#)	1,776	161	936	(#)	852	84	40
Idaho	8,426	(33.7)	2,875	(#)	1,857	(#)	1,667	190	890	(#)	792	98	128
Illinois	84,195	(328.4)	29,445	(#)	20,689	(#)	18,669	2,020	7,420	(#)	6,928	491	1,337
Indiana	39,894	(283.2)	14,882	(89.3)	9,774	(89.9)	8,656	1,118	4,324	(#)	3,995	329	784
Iowa	20,605	(76.2)	7,779	(#)	4,662	(#)	4,069	593	2,765	(#)	2,460	304	353
Kansas	18,044	(113.7)	6,737	(0.7)	4,117	(0.4)	3,759	358	2,418	(#)	2,175	242	202
Kentucky	25,319	(48.1)	8,701	(#)	5,183	(#)	4,497	686	2,749	(#)	2,512	238	768
Louisiana	30,475	(94.5)	9,131	(#)	5,963	(#)	5,508	455	2,454	(#)	2,232	223	713
Maine	9,966	(32.9)	2,999	(18.3)	2,130	(18.1)	2,018	112	715	(#)	624	91	154
Maryland	39,382	(94.5)	14,392	(#)	9,723	(#)	8,700	1,023	4,051	(#)	3,684	367	619
Massachusetts	52,418	(104.8)	17,029	(51.1)	11,608	(51.1)	10,709	899	3,545	(#)	3,092	453	1,876
Michigan	66,534	(319.4)	26,336	(#)	17,233	(#)	15,501	1,732	8,298	(#)	7,135	1,163	805
Minnesota	38,762	(217.1)	13,055	(#)	8,899	(#)	7,835	1,063	3,402	(#)	3,157	245	754
Mississippi	19,250	(115.5)	6,430	(#)	3,997	(#)	3,583	413	2,131	(#)	1,863	269	302
Missouri	34,539	(252.1)	11,934	(#)	8,330	(#)	7,572	758	3,091	(#)	2,775	315	513
Montana	6,226	(19.3)	2,161	(#)	1,351	(0.0)	1,254	98	669	(#)	613	56	140
Nebraska	11,688	(87.7)	4,348	(#)	2,724	(#)	2,447	277	1,451	(#)	1,335	116	173
Nevada	16,099	(109.5)	5,129	(#)	3,809	(#)	3,049	760	1,172	(#)	1,008	164	149
New Hampshire	8,147	(28.5)	3,137	(#)	2,287	(#)	2,085	202	762	(#)	607	155	88
New Jersey	71,180	(227.8)	27,787	(16.7)	21,917	(17.5)	19,842	2,074	4,907	(#)	4,249	658	964
New Mexico	14,866	(50.5)	5,216	(#)	3,056	(#)	2,671	386	1,872	(#)	1,649	223	288
New York	194,728	(662.1)	57,190	(11.4)	45,451	(#)	41,506	3,944	9,770	(12.7)	8,706	1,064	1,969
North Carolina	55,905	(184.5)	19,964	(31.9)	11,502	(29.9)	10,443	1,059	7,866	(8.7)	6,772	1,093	597
North Dakota	4,515	(12.2)	1,665	(#)	949	(#)	856	93	662	(#)	617	45	55
Ohio	82,045	(336.4)	28,758	(#)	19,876	(#)	17,698	2,177	7,123	(#)	6,184	939	1,759
Oklahoma	20,832	(70.8)	8,029	(#)	5,018	(#)	4,581	437	2,630	(#)	2,300	330	380
Oregon	25,324	(141.8)	8,338	(#)	5,147	(#)	4,827	319	2,946	(#)	2,535	411	245
Pennsylvania	69,373	(286.0)	31,435	(#)	21,692	(#)	19,682	2,010	6,642	(#)	5,956	686	3,101
Rhode Island	8,247	(24.7)	2,710	(16.3)	1,957	(16.4)	1,892	64	596	(#)	519	77	157
South Carolina	29,057	(61.0)	10,565	(#)	6,939	(#)	5,810	1,129	2,805	(#)	2,442	363	821
South Dakota	4,665	(16.3)	1,539	(#)	1,011	(#)	929	82	434	(#)	380	54	94
Tennessee	34,386	(196.0)	10,900	(106.8)	7,393	(106.5)	6,690	703	2,847	(#)	2,635	212	660
Texas	138,254	(373.3)	56,039	(#)	38,567	(#)	32,395	6,171	15,635	(#)	13,805	1,829	1,838
Utah	15,611	(62.4)	5,937	(#)	3,291	(#)	2,786	505	2,385	(#)	2,212	173	262
Vermont	4,913	(10.8)	2,029	(0.8)	1,245	(#)	1,185	59	665	(#)	525	140	119
Virginia	50,390	(317.5)	19,243	(136.6)	13,152	(135.5)	11,791	1,361	5,327	(#)	4,473	854	764
Washington	45,175	(171.7)	15,350	(#)	9,545	(#)	8,122	1,423	4,746	(#)	4,151	595	1,060
West Virginia	11,435	(21.7)	4,280	(#)	2,604	(#)	2,416	187	1,259	(#)	1,057	202	418
Wisconsin	39,413	(157.7)	14,337	(2.9)	9,337	(2.8)	8,790	546	4,516	(#)	4,018	497	485
Wyoming	5,369	(40.3)	1,693	(#)	1,137	(#)	968	168	492	(#)	424	69	64

#Rounds to zero.

[1]Includes state and local government expenditures for education services, social services and income maintenance, transportation, public safety, environment and housing, governmental administration, interest on general debt, and other general expenditures.

[2]Includes assistance and subsidies to individuals, private elementary and secondary schools, and colleges and universities, as well as miscellaneous education expenditures.

NOTE: Current expenditure data in this table differ from figures appearing in other tables because of slightly varying definitions used in the Governmental Finances and Common Core of Data surveys. Detail may not sum to totals because of rounding. Standard errors appear in parentheses. Standard errors that are not shown are available upon request.
SOURCE: U.S. Department of Commerce, Census Bureau, Governmental Finances. Retrieved July 15, 2008, from http://www.census.gov/govs/www/estimate06.html. (This table was prepared August 2008.)

Table 29. Direct general expenditures per capita of state and local governments for all functions and for education, by level of education and state: 2005–06

State	Total, all direct general expenditures per capita[1]	Education expenditures							
		Total		Elementary and secondary education		Colleges and universities		Other education[2]	
		Amount per capita	As a percent of all functions	Amount per capita	As a percent of all functions	Amount per capita	As a percent of all functions	Amount per capita	As a percent of all functions
1	2	3	4	5	6	7	8	9	10
United States	$7,087	$2,431	34.3	$1,672	23.6	$640	9.0	$119	1.7
Alabama	6,680	2,372	35.5	1,425	21.3	814	12.2	134	2.0
Alaska	13,968	3,666	26.2	2,682	19.2	864	6.2	120	0.9
Arizona	5,797	1,914	33.0	1,255	21.6	580	10.0	79	1.4
Arkansas	5,900	2,271	38.5	1,470	24.9	678	11.5	123	2.1
California	8,050	2,534	31.5	1,759	21.8	668	8.3	107	1.3
Colorado	6,475	2,301	35.5	1,561	24.1	668	10.3	72	1.1
Connecticut	7,842	2,833	36.1	2,085	26.6	606	7.7	142	1.8
Delaware	8,740	3,100	35.5	1,894	21.7	1,011	11.6	196	2.2
District of Columbia	13,763	2,541	18.5	2,348	17.1	193	1.4	#	#
Florida	6,779	1,954	28.8	1,438	21.2	412	6.1	104	1.5
Georgia	5,789	2,274	39.3	1,645	28.4	484	8.4	145	2.5
Hawaii	7,659	2,266	29.6	1,507	19.7	728	9.5	31	0.4
Idaho	5,746	1,961	34.1	1,266	22.0	607	10.6	87	1.5
Illinois	6,561	2,295	35.0	1,612	24.6	578	8.8	104	1.6
Indiana	6,319	2,357	37.3	1,548	24.5	685	10.8	124	2.0
Iowa	6,910	2,609	37.8	1,563	22.6	927	13.4	118	1.7
Kansas	6,528	2,437	37.3	1,490	22.8	875	13.4	73	1.1
Kentucky	6,020	2,069	34.4	1,232	20.5	654	10.9	183	3.0
Louisiana	7,108	2,129	30.0	1,391	19.6	572	8.1	166	2.3
Maine	7,541	2,269	30.1	1,612	21.4	541	7.2	117	1.5
Maryland	7,013	2,563	36.5	1,731	24.7	721	10.3	110	1.6
Massachusetts	8,143	2,645	32.5	1,803	22.1	551	6.8	291	3.6
Michigan	6,590	2,609	39.6	1,707	25.9	822	12.5	80	1.2
Minnesota	7,502	2,527	33.7	1,722	23.0	658	8.8	146	1.9
Mississippi	6,614	2,209	33.4	1,373	20.8	732	11.1	104	1.6
Missouri	5,911	2,043	34.6	1,426	24.1	529	8.9	88	1.5
Montana	6,591	2,287	34.7	1,431	21.7	708	10.7	148	2.3
Nebraska	6,610	2,459	37.2	1,541	23.3	821	12.4	98	1.5
Nevada	6,451	2,055	31.9	1,526	23.7	470	7.3	60	0.9
New Hampshire	6,196	2,386	38.5	1,739	28.1	579	9.4	67	1.1
New Jersey	8,159	3,185	39.0	2,512	30.8	562	6.9	110	1.4
New Mexico	7,606	2,669	35.1	1,564	20.6	958	12.6	147	1.9
New York	10,086	2,962	29.4	2,354	23.3	506	5.0	102	1.0
North Carolina	6,312	2,254	35.7	1,299	20.6	888	14.1	67	1.1
North Dakota	7,100	2,619	36.9	1,492	21.0	1,041	14.7	86	1.2
Ohio	7,148	2,505	35.1	1,732	24.2	621	8.7	153	2.1
Oklahoma	5,820	2,243	38.5	1,402	24.1	735	12.6	106	1.8
Oregon	6,843	2,253	32.9	1,391	20.3	796	11.6	66	1.0
Pennsylvania	7,184	2,527	35.2	1,744	24.3	534	7.4	249	3.5
Rhode Island	7,725	2,538	32.9	1,833	23.7	559	7.2	147	1.9
South Carolina	6,724	2,445	36.4	1,606	23.9	649	9.7	190	2.8
South Dakota	5,967	1,968	33.0	1,293	21.7	555	9.3	120	2.0
Tennessee	5,694	1,805	31.7	1,224	21.5	472	8.3	109	1.9
Texas	5,881	2,384	40.5	1,641	27.9	665	11.3	78	1.3
Utah	6,122	2,328	38.0	1,290	21.1	935	15.3	103	1.7
Vermont	7,874	3,252	41.3	1,995	25.3	1,066	13.5	191	2.4
Virginia	6,593	2,518	38.2	1,721	26.1	697	10.6	100	1.5
Washington	7,063	2,400	34.0	1,492	21.1	742	10.5	166	2.3
West Virginia	6,288	2,354	37.4	1,432	22.8	692	11.0	230	3.7
Wisconsin	7,093	2,580	36.4	1,680	23.7	813	11.5	87	1.2
Wyoming	10,425	3,287	31.5	2,207	21.2	956	9.2	125	1.2

#Rounds to zero.
[1]Includes state and local government expenditures for education services, social services and income maintenance, transportation, public safety, environment and housing, governmental administration, interest on general debt, and other general expenditures.
[2]Includes assistance and subsidies to individuals, private elementary and secondary schools, and colleges and universities, as well as miscellaneous education expenditures.

NOTE: Per capita amounts are based on population figures as of July 2006. Detail may not sum to totals because of rounding.
SOURCE: U.S. Department of Commerce, Census Bureau, Governmental Finances, retrieved July 15, 2008, from http://www.census.gov/govs/www/estimate06.html; and GCT-T1 Population Estimates, retrieved July 15, 2008, from http://factfinder.census.gov/servlet/GCT Table? bm=y&-geo_id=01000US&-_box_head_nbr=GCT-T1&-ds_name=PEP_2006_EST&_lang=en&-_format=US-9&-_sse=on. (This table was prepared July 2008.)

Table 30. Gross domestic product, state and local expenditures, personal income, disposable personal income, median family income, and population: Selected years, 1929 through 2007

Year	Gross domestic product (in billions)		State and local direct general expenditures (in millions)[1]		Personal income (in billions)	Disposable personal income (in billions of chained 2000 dollars)[2]	Disposable personal income per capita		Median family income	Population (in thousands)	
	Current dollars	Chained 2000 dollars[2]	All direct general expenditures	Education expenditures			Current dollars	Chained 2000 dollars[2]		Midyear data[3]	Resident as of July 1[4]
1	2	3	4	5	6	7	8	9	10	11	12
1929	$103.6	$865.2	—	—	$85.1	$712.7	$684	$5,848	—	121,878	121,767
1939	92.2	950.7	—	—	72.9	774.9	545	5,914	—	131,028	130,880
1940	101.4	1,034.1	$9,229	$2,638	78.5	826.5	581	6,255	—	132,122	132,122
1950	293.8	1,777.3	22,787	7,177	229.0	1,260.0	1,385	8,306	3,319	151,684	152,271
1960	526.4	2,501.8	51,876	18,719	411.5	1,759.7	2,022	9,735	5,620	180,760	180,671
1970	1,038.5	3,771.9	131,332	52,718	838.8	2,781.7	3,587	13,563	9,867	205,089	205,052
1971	1,127.1	3,898.6	150,674	59,413	903.5	2,907.9	3,860	14,001	10,285	207,692	207,661
1972	1,238.3	4,105.0	168,550	65,814	992.7	3,046.5	4,140	14,512	11,116	209,924	209,896
1973	1,382.7	4,341.5	181,357	69,714	1,110.7	3,252.3	4,616	15,345	12,051	211,939	211,909
1974	1,500.0	4,319.6	198,959	75,833	1,222.6	3,228.5	5,010	15,094	12,902	213,898	213,854
1975	1,638.3	4,311.2	230,721	87,858	1,335.0	3,302.6	5,498	15,291	13,719	215,981	215,973
1976	1,825.3	4,540.9	256,731	97,216	1,474.8	3,432.2	5,972	15,738	14,958	218,086	218,035
1977	2,030.9	4,750.5	274,215	102,780	1,633.2	3,552.9	6,517	16,128	16,009	220,289	220,239
1978	2,294.7	5,015.0	296,984	110,758	1,837.7	3,718.8	7,224	16,704	17,640	222,629	222,585
1979	2,563.3	5,173.4	327,517	119,448	2,062.2	3,811.2	7,967	16,931	19,587	225,106	225,055
1980	2,789.5	5,161.7	369,086	133,211	2,307.9	3,857.7	8,822	16,940	21,023	227,726	227,225
1981	3,128.4	5,291.7	407,449	145,784	2,591.3	3,960.0	9,765	17,217	22,388	230,008	229,466
1982	3,255.0	5,189.3	436,733	154,282	2,775.3	4,044.9	10,426	17,418	23,433	232,218	231,664
1983	3,536.7	5,423.8	466,516	163,876	2,960.7	4,177.7	11,131	17,828	24,674	234,333	233,792
1984	3,933.2	5,813.6	505,008	176,108	3,289.5	4,494.1	12,319	19,011	26,433	236,394	235,825
1985	4,220.3	6,053.7	553,899	192,686	3,526.7	4,645.2	13,037	19,476	27,735	238,506	237,924
1986	4,462.8	6,263.6	605,623	210,819	3,722.4	4,791.0	13,649	19,906	29,458	240,683	240,133
1987	4,739.5	6,475.1	657,134	226,619	3,947.4	4,874.5	14,241	20,072	30,970	242,843	242,289
1988	5,103.8	6,742.7	704,921	242,683	4,253.7	5,082.6	15,297	20,740	32,191	245,061	244,499
1989	5,484.4	6,981.4	762,360	263,898	4,587.8	5,224.8	16,257	21,120	34,213	247,387	246,819
1990	5,803.1	7,112.5	834,818	288,148	4,878.6	5,324.2	17,131	21,281	35,353	250,181	249,623
1991	5,995.9	7,100.5	908,108	309,302	5,051.0	5,351.7	17,609	21,109	35,939	253,530	252,981
1992	6,337.7	7,336.6	981,253	324,652	5,362.0	5,536.3	18,494	21,548	36,573	256,922	256,514
1993	6,657.4	7,532.7	1,033,167	342,287	5,558.5	5,594.2	18,872	21,493	36,959	260,282	259,919
1994	7,072.2	7,835.5	1,077,665	353,287	5,842.5	5,746.4	19,555	21,812	38,782	263,455	263,126
1995	7,397.7	8,031.7	1,146,188	378,273	6,152.3	5,905.7	20,287	22,153	40,611	266,588	266,278
1996	7,816.9	8,328.9	1,189,356	398,859	6,520.6	6,080.9	21,091	22,546	42,300	269,714	269,394
1997	8,304.3	8,703.5	1,247,436	419,053	6,915.1	6,295.8	21,940	23,065	44,568	272,958	272,647
1998	8,747.0	9,066.9	1,314,496	450,365	7,423.0	6,663.9	23,161	24,131	46,737	276,154	275,854
1999	9,268.4	9,470.3	1,398,533	483,259	7,802.4	6,861.3	23,968	24,564	48,950	279,328	279,040
2000	9,817.0	9,817.0	1,502,768	521,612	8,429.7	7,194.0	25,472	25,472	50,732	282,433	282,194
2001	10,128.0	9,890.7	1,621,757	563,572	8,724.1	7,333.3	26,235	25,697	51,407	285,372	285,112
2002	10,469.6	10,048.8	1,732,478	594,694	8,881.9	7,562.2	27,167	26,238	51,680	288,215	287,888
2003	10,960.8	10,301.0	1,817,513	621,335	9,163.6	7,729.9	28,053	26,566	52,680	290,964	290,448
2004	11,685.9	10,675.8	1,903,194	655,361	9,727.2	8,008.9	29,563	27,274	54,061	293,644	293,192
2005	12,421.9	10,989.5	2,012,422	689,057	10,269.8	8,121.4	30,576	27,403	56,194	296,373	295,896
2006	13,178.4	11,294.8	2,121,946	727,967	10,993.9	8,407.0	32,222	28,098	58,407	299,199	298,755
2007	13,807.5	11,523.9	—	—	11,663.2	8,644.0	33,667	28,614	—	302,087	301,621

—Not available.

[1]Data for years prior to 1963 include expenditures for government fiscal years ending during that particular calendar year. Data for 1963 and later years are the aggregations of expenditures for government fiscal years that ended on June 30 of the stated year. General expenditures exclude expenditures of publicly owned utilities and liquor stores, and of insurance-trust activities. Intergovernmental payments between state and local governments are excluded. Payments to the federal government are included.

[2]Constant dollars based on a chain-price index, which uses the geometric mean of output weights of adjacent time periods compiled over a time series. Chain-price indexes reflect changes in prices, while implicit price deflators reflect both changes in prices and in the composition of output.

[3]Population of the United States including armed forces overseas. Includes Alaska and Hawaii beginning in 1960.

[4]Resident population of the United States. Includes Alaska and Hawaii beginning in 1958. Data for 1990 and later years include revisions based on the 2000 census.

NOTE: Gross domestic product (GDP) data are adjusted by the GDP chained weight price deflator. Personal income data are adjusted by the personal consumption deflator. Some data have been revised from previously published figures.

SOURCE: U.S. Department of Commerce, Census Bureau, Current Population Reports, *Money Income in the United States*, Series P-60, various years; Population Estimates, retrieved August 12, 2008, from http://www.census.gov/popest/datasets.html; and State and Local Government Finances, retrieved August 12, 2008, from http://www.census.gov/govs/www/estimate.html. U.S. Department of Commerce, Bureau of Economic Analysis, National Income and Product Accounts Tables, retrieved August 12, 2008, from http://www.bea.gov/national/index.htm. (This table was prepared August 2008.)

Table 31. Gross domestic product price index, Consumer Price Index, education price indexes, and federal budget composite deflator: Selected years, 1919 through 2007

Calendar year			School year					Federal fiscal year	
Year	Gross domestic product price index	Consumer Price Index[1]	Year	Consumer Price Index[2]	Higher Education Price Index	Research and Development Index	Academic Library Operations Index	Year	Federal budget composite deflator
1	2	3	4	5	6	7	8	9	10
1919	—	17.3	1919–20	19.1	—	—	—	1919	—
1929	11.9	17.1	1929–30	17.1	—	—	—	1929	—
1939	9.7	13.9	1939–40	14.0	—	—	—	1939	—
1949	16.4	23.8	1949–50	23.7	—	—	—	1949	0.1246
1950	16.5	24.1	1950–51	25.1	—	—	—	1950	0.1287
1956	19.4	27.2	1956–57	27.7	—	—	—	1956	0.1526
1957	20.0	28.1	1957–58	28.6	—	—	—	1957	0.1601
1958	20.5	28.9	1958–59	29.0	—	—	—	1958	0.1687
1959	20.8	29.1	1959–60	29.4	—	—	—	1959	0.1746
1960	21.0	29.6	1960–61	29.8	25.6	26.7	—	1960	0.1750
1961	21.3	29.9	1961–62	30.1	26.5	27.5	—	1961	0.1795
1962	21.6	30.2	1962–63	30.4	27.6	28.5	—	1962	0.1803
1963	21.8	30.6	1963–64	30.8	28.6	29.5	—	1963	0.1873
1964	22.1	31.0	1964–65	31.2	29.8	30.7	—	1964	0.1900
1965	22.5	31.5	1965–66	31.9	31.3	32.0	—	1965	0.1928
1966	23.2	32.4	1966–67	32.9	32.9	33.8	—	1966	0.1974
1967	23.9	33.4	1967–68	34.0	34.9	35.7	—	1967	0.2026
1968	24.9	34.8	1968–69	35.7	37.1	38.0	—	1968	0.2103
1969	26.2	36.7	1969–70	37.8	39.5	40.3	—	1969	0.2230
1970	27.5	38.8	1970–71	39.7	42.1	42.7	—	1970	0.2363
1971	28.9	40.5	1971–72	41.2	44.3	45.0	—	1971	0.2519
1972	30.2	41.8	1972–73	42.8	46.7	47.1	—	1972	0.2690
1973	31.9	44.4	1973–74	46.6	49.9	50.1	—	1973	0.2833
1974	34.7	49.3	1974–75	51.8	54.3	54.8	—	1974	0.3070
1975	38.0	53.8	1975–76	55.5	57.8	59.0	57.3	1975	0.3384
1976	40.2	56.9	1976–77	58.7	61.5	62.7	61.6	1976	0.3640
1977	42.8	60.6	1977–78	62.6	65.7	66.8	65.8	1977	0.3934
1978	45.8	65.2	1978–79	68.5	70.5	71.7	71.4	1978	0.4195
1979	49.6	72.6	1979–80	77.6	77.5	78.3	78.5	1979	0.4552
1980	54.1	82.4	1980–81	86.6	85.8	86.6	86.1	1980	0.5029
1981	59.1	90.9	1981–82	94.1	93.9	94.0	94.0	1981	0.5562
1982	62.7	96.5	1982–83	98.2	100.0	100.0	100.0	1982	0.5958
1983	65.2	99.6	1983–84	101.8	104.8	104.3	105.1	1983	0.6245
1984	67.7	103.9	1984–85	105.8	110.8	109.8	111.2	1984	0.6555
1985	69.7	107.6	1985–86	108.8	116.3	115.2	117.6	1985	0.6781
1986	71.3	109.6	1986–87	111.2	120.9	120.0	124.2	1986	0.6947
1987	73.2	113.6	1987–88	115.8	126.2	126.8	130.0	1987	0.7143
1988	75.7	118.3	1988–89	121.2	132.8	132.1	138.6	1988	0.7359
1989	78.6	124.0	1989–90	127.0	140.8	139.0	147.4	1989	0.7631
1990	81.6	130.7	1990–91	133.9	148.2	145.8	155.7	1990	0.7882
1991	84.5	136.2	1991–92	138.2	153.5	150.6	163.3	1991	0.8226
1992	86.4	140.3	1992–93	142.5	157.9	155.2	169.8	1992	0.8508
1993	88.4	144.5	1993–94	146.2	163.3	160.1	176.7	1993	0.8725
1994	90.3	148.2	1994–95	150.4	168.1	165.4	183.9	1994	0.8902
1995	92.1	152.4	1995–96	154.5	173.0	170.8	192.6	1995	0.9120
1996	93.9	156.9	1996–97	158.9	178.4	—	—	1996	0.9328
1997	95.4	160.5	1997–98	161.7	184.7	—	—	1997	0.9508
1998	96.5	163.0	1998–99	164.5	189.1	—	—	1998	0.9603
1999	97.9	166.6	1999–2000	169.3	196.9	—	—	1999	0.9748
2000	100.0	172.2	2000–01	175.1	206.5	—	—	2000	1.0000
2001	102.4	177.1	2001–02	178.2	215.0	—	—	2001	1.0234
2002	104.2	179.9	2002–03	182.1	221.2	—	—	2002	1.0425
2003	106.4	184.0	2003–04	186.1	231.5	—	—	2003	1.0703
2004	109.5	188.9	2004–05	191.7	239.8	—	—	2004	1.1014
2005	113.0	195.3	2005–06	199.0	251.8	—	—	2005	1.1419
2006	116.7	201.6	2006–07	204.1	260.3	—	—	2006	1.1806
2007	119.8	207.3	2007–08	211.7	—	—	—	2007	1.2064

—Not available.
[1]Index for urban wage earners and clerical workers through 1977; 1978 and later figures are for all urban consumers.
[2]Consumer Price Index adjusted to a school-year basis (July through June).
NOTE: Some data have been revised from previously published figures.

SOURCE: U.S. Department of Commerce, Bureau of Economic Analysis, National Income and Product Accounts, retrieved August 22, 2008, from http://www.bea.gov/national/nipaweb. U.S. Department of Labor, Bureau of Labor Statistics, Consumer Price Index, retrieved August 22, 2008, from http://data.bls.gov/cgi-bin/surveymost. Commonfund Institute, *Higher Education Price Index 2008 Update*. U.S. Office of Management and Budget, *Budget of the U.S. Government, Fiscal Year 2009, Historical Tables*. (This table was prepared August 2008.)

CHAPTER 2
Elementary and Secondary Education

This chapter contains a variety of statistics on public and private elementary and secondary education. Data are presented for enrollments, teachers and other school staff, schools, dropouts, achievement, school violence, and revenues and expenditures. These data are derived from surveys conducted by the National Center for Education Statistics (NCES) and other public and private organizations. The information ranges from counts of students and schools to state graduation requirements.

Enrollments

Public elementary and secondary school enrollment increased by 3 percent from 2001 to 2006, but enrollment at the elementary and secondary levels increased at different rates (table 37 and figure 6). Between 2001 and 2006, public elementary enrollment rose by 1 percent, while secondary enrollment increased by 10 percent. Enrollments in private elementary and secondary schools decreased by an estimated 4 percent between 2001 and 2006 (table 3).

In 2007, two-thirds of 3- to 5-year-olds were enrolled in preprimary education (nursery school and kindergarten), similar to the proportion in 2000 (table 43 and figure 7). However, the percentage of children in full-day programs increased from 2000 to 2007. In 2007, about 57 percent of the children enrolled in preprimary education attended preprimary school all day, compared with 53 percent in 2000.

A higher percentage of 4-year-old children (57 percent) were primarily cared for in center-based programs during the day in 2005–06 than were cared for in home-based settings by their parents (20 percent), in home-based settings by relatives (13 percent), or in home-based settings by nonrelatives (8 percent) (table 46). There were differences in the average quality of care children received in these settings. A higher percentage of children in Head Start and other center-based programs (35 percent) received high-quality care than those in home-based relative and nonrelative care (9 percent), according to the ratings of trained observers (table 47).

From 2001–02 to 2006–07, some increases occurred in the numbers and percentages of children being served in programs for those with disabilities. During the 2001–02 school year, 13 percent of students were served in these programs, compared with 14 percent in 2006–07 (table 50). Some of the change since 2001–02 may be attributed to the increasing percentage of children identified as having other

health impairments (limited strength, vitality, or alertness due to chronic or acute health problems such as a heart condition, tuberculosis, rheumatic fever, nephritis, asthma, sickle cell anemia, hemophilia, epilepsy, lead poisoning, leukemia, or diabetes), which rose from 0.7 to 1.2 percent of enrollment; autism, which rose from 0.2 to 0.5 percent of enrollment; and developmental delay, which rose from 0.5 to 0.7 percent of enrollment.

Teachers and Other School Staff

During the 1970s and early 1980s, public school enrollment decreased, while the number of teachers generally increased. As a result, the public school pupil/teacher ratio declined from 22.3 in 1970 to 17.9 in 1985 (table 64 and figure 6).[1] After 1985, the number of pupils per teacher continued to decline, reaching 17.2 in 1989. After a period of relative stability during the late 1980s through the mid-1990s, the ratio declined from 17.3 in 1995 to 16.0 in 2000. Some decreases have continued since then, and the public school pupil/teacher ratio was 15.5 in 2006. The projected pupil/teacher ratio for private schools for 2006 was 13.5.[1]

The average class size in 2003–04 was 20.4 pupils for public elementary schools and 24.7 for public secondary schools (table 67).

In 2003–04, some 75 percent of public school teachers were female, 41 percent were under 40, and 48 percent had a master's or higher degree (table 68). Compared to public school teachers, a lower percentage of private school teachers (35 percent) had a master's or higher degree. Seventy-six percent of private school teachers were female.

Public school principals tend to be older and have more advanced credentials than public school teachers. In 2003–04, some 15 percent of the public school principals were under age 40 and 98 percent of the public school principals had a master's or higher degree (table 86). A lower percentage of principals than of teachers were female. About 48 percent of public school principals were female, compared to 75 percent of teachers.

---

[1] The pupil/teacher ratio is based on all teachers—including teachers for students with disabilities and other special teachers—and all students enrolled in the fall of the school year. Unlike the pupil/teacher ratio, the average class size excludes students and teachers in classes that are exclusively for special education students. Class size averages are based on surveys of teachers reporting on the counts of students in their classes.

The numbers of both teaching and nonteaching staff employed by public schools grew during the 1970s, while the number of students declined (tables 80 and 3). Between 1970 and 1980, the percentage of staff who were teachers declined from 60 percent to 52 percent. From 1980 to 2006, the number of teachers and other staff grew at more similar rates (46 and 50 percent, respectively) than in the 1970s. As a result, the proportion of teachers among total staff was 1 percentage point lower in 2006 than in 1980, in contrast to the decrease of 8 percentage points during the 1970s. Two staff categories increased over 100 percent between 1980 and 2006—instructional aides, which rose 117 percent, and instructional coordinators, which rose 218 percent. Taken together, the percentage of staff with some instructional responsibilities (teachers and instructional aides) increased between 1980 and 2006, from 60 to 63 percent. In 2006, there were 8 pupils per staff member (total staff), compared with 10 pupils per staff member in 1980. In 2003, the number of pupils per staff member at private schools was 7 (table 60).

Schools

During most of the last century, the trend to consolidate small schools brought declines in the total number of public schools in the United States. In 1929–30, there were approximately 248,000 public schools, compared with about 99,000 in 2006–07 (table 87). But this number has been increasing in recent years; between 1996–97 and 2006–07, there was an increase of approximately 10,600 schools.

The shift in structure of public school systems toward middle schools (grade spans beginning with 4, 5, or 6 and ending with 6, 7, or 8) since the early 1970s has continued (table 94). The number of all elementary schools (beginning in grade 6 or below, with no grade higher than grade 8) rose by 12 percent to 68,990 between 1996–97 and 2006–07, and the subset of middle schools rose by 22 percent during the same time period. Meanwhile, the number of junior high schools (grades 7 and 8 or 7 to 9) declined by 16 percent. The average number of students in elementary schools declined from 478 students in 1996–97 to 473 in 2006–07 (table 96). The average enrollment size of secondary schools increased from 703 in 1995–96 to 722 in 2003–04, but then decreased to an average of 711 students in 2006–07. The average size of regular secondary schools, which exclude alternative, special education, and vocational education schools, rose from 777 to 811 between 1996–97 and 2006–07.

High School Graduates and Dropouts

About 3,328,000 high school students are expected to graduate during the 2008–09 school year (table 104), including 3,011,000 public school graduates and 317,000 private school graduates. High school graduates include only recipients of diplomas, not recipients of equivalency credentials. The 2008–09 projection of high school graduates is lower than the record-high projection of 3,346,000 graduates for 2007–08, but exceeds the high point during the baby boom era in 1976–77, when 3,152,000 students earned diplomas. In 2005–06, an estimated 73.4 percent of public high school students graduated on time—that is, received a diploma 4 years after beginning their freshman year (table 106).

The number of General Educational Development (GED) credentials issued rose from 330,000 in 1977 to 487,000 in 2000 (table 108). A record number of 648,000 GED credentials were issued in 2001. In that year, candidates who had already taken any of the five tests in the GED test battery had to complete the entire battery before the end of the year or else take all five tests over again. The reason is that a new GED test series was introduced in 2002. In the same year, data collection procedures changed, with data from the states on the number of credentials issued being replaced by test data from individual test-takers. In 2006, some 464,000 passed the GED tests, up from 330,000 in 2002, the first year of the new test series.[2]

The percentage of dropouts among 16- to 24-year-olds has shown some decreases over the past 20 years. This percentage, known as the status dropout rate, includes all people in the 16- to 24-year-old age group who are not enrolled in school and who have not completed a high school program, regardless of when they left school. (People who left school but went on to receive a GED credential are not treated as dropouts.) Between 1987 and 2007, the status dropout rate declined from 12.6 percent to 8.7 percent (table 109). Although the status dropout rate declined for both Blacks and Hispanics during this period, their rates (8.4 and 21.4 percent, respectively) remained higher than the rate for Whites (5.3 percent) in 2007. This measure is based on the civilian noninstitutionalized population, which excludes people in prisons, people in the military, and other people not living in households.

Achievement

Much of the student performance data in the *Digest* are drawn from the National Assessment of Educational Progress (NAEP). The NAEP assessments have been conducted using three basic designs: the national main NAEP, state NAEP, and long-term trend NAEP. The main NAEP reports current information for the nation and specific geographic regions of the country. The assessment program includes students drawn from both public and nonpublic schools and reports results for student achievement at grades 4, 8, and 12. The main NAEP assessments follow the frameworks developed by the National Assessment Governing Board and use the latest advances in assessment methodology. Because the assessment items reflect curricula associated with specific grade levels, the main NAEP uses samples of students at those grade levels.

---

[2] Information on changes in GED test series and reporting is based on the 2003 edition of *Who Passed the GED Tests?*, by the GED Testing Service of the American Council on Education, as well as communication with staff of the GED Testing Service.

Since 1990, NAEP assessments have also been conducted at the state level. Each participating state receives assessment results that report on the performance of students in that state. In its content, the state assessment is identical to the assessment conducted nationally. From 1990 through 2001, the national sample was a subset of the combined sample of students assessed in each participating state along with an additional sample from the states that did not participate in the state assessment. Since 2002, a combined sample of public schools has been selected for both state and national NAEP.

NAEP long-term trend assessments are designed to give information on the changes in the basic achievement level of America's youth since the early 1970s. They are administered nationally and report student performance at ages 9, 13, and 17 in reading and mathematics. Measuring long-term trends of student achievement requires the precise replication of past procedures. For example, students of specific ages are sampled in order to maintain consistency with the original sample design. Similarly, the long-term trend instrument does not evolve based on changes in curricula or in educational practices. The differences in procedures between the main NAEP and the long-term trend NAEP mean that their results cannot be compared directly.

Long-term trend data have shown improvements in achievement in a number of areas. The average reading score at age 9 was higher in 2004 than in any previous assessment year (table 117). The average score at age 13 was higher in 2004 than in 1971, but not measurably different from the average score in 1999. Between 1999 and 2004, average reading scores at age 17 showed no measurable changes. The average score for 17-year-olds in 2004 was similar to that in 1971.

Significant gaps in performance continue to exist between racial/ethnic subgroups. For Black 9-, 13-, and 17-year-olds, average reading scores in 2004 were higher than in 1971 (table 117). At age 9, Black students scored higher on average in 2004 than in any previous administration year. For White students, the average scores for 9- and 13-year-olds were also higher in 2004 than in 1971. Separate data for Hispanics were not gathered in 1971, but as with the other racial/ethnic groups, the average reading score for Hispanic students at age 9 was higher in 2004 than in any other assessment year. The average score for Hispanic students at age 13 increased between 1975 and 2004. The scores for 17-year-old Hispanic students also increased between 1975 and 2004, but no measurable changes were seen between 1999 and 2004.

Female students scored higher on average in reading assessments than their male counterparts in 2004. The gender score gap at age 9 decreased from 1971 to 2004. In contrast, there has been no measurable change in the gender score gap at age 13 between 2004 and any previous assessment year. For 17-year-olds, the gender score gap in 2004 was larger than the gaps in 1980 and 1988, but showed no measurable difference from the gaps in other assessment years.

On the main NAEP reading assessment, public school fourth-graders scored higher in 2007 than in all previous assessment years. The average reading score was up 2 points since 2005 (based on unrounded scores) and up 5 points compared to the first main NAEP reading assessment in 1992 (table 121).

The 2007 main NAEP reading assessment of states found that reading proficiency varied among public school fourth-graders in participating jurisdictions (the 50 states, the Department of Defense overseas and domestic schools, and the District of Columbia) (table 121). The U.S. average score was 220. The scores for the participating jurisdictions ranged from 197 in the District of Columbia to 236 in Massachusetts.

Mathematics achievement results from the long-term trend NAEP indicate a significant improvement for ages 9 and 13 between 1973 and 2004, but not for age 17 (table 131). The average score at age 9 in 2004 (241) was higher than in any previous year—up 9 points from 1999 and 22 points from 1973. The average score at age 13 in 2004 was higher than in any other assessment year. The 5-point increase between 1999 and 2004 resulted in an average score in 2004 that was 15 points higher than the average score in 1973. The average score at age 17 was not measurably different from the average score in 1973 or 1999. The apparent difference in average mathematics scores at age 9 between male and female students in 2004 was not statistically significant. Males had higher average scores than females at ages 13 and 17. The gender score gaps for 13- and 17-year-olds were measurably different between 1973 and 2004.

On the main NAEP mathematics assessment, the average score for public school eighth-graders in 2007 was 18 points higher than in 1990, the first assessment year. The average score in 2007 was higher than the score in any previous assessment (table 135).

The 2007 main NAEP assessment of states found that mathematics proficiency varied among public school eighth-graders in participating jurisdictions (the 50 states, the Department of Defense overseas and domestic schools, and the District of Columbia) (table 135). The main NAEP results are reported in the *Digest* in terms of both average scale scores and achievement levels. The achievement levels define what students who are performing at *Basic*, *Proficient*, and *Advanced* levels of achievement should know and be able to do. The *Basic* level denotes partial mastery of prerequisite knowledge and skills that are fundamental for proficient work at each grade. The *Proficient* level represents solid academic performance for each grade assessed; students reaching this level have demonstrated competency over challenging subject matter, including subject-matter knowledge, application of such knowledge to real-world situations, and analytical skills appropriate to the subject matter. The *Advanced* level signifies superior performance. Overall, 70 percent of these eighth-grade students performed at or above the Basic level in mathematics, and 31 percent performed at or above the Proficient level. The percentage of students performing at least at the Basic level in math ranged from 34 percent in the District of Columbia to 86 percent in North Dakota.

From 1996 to 2005, the national average 4th-grade science score increased from 147 to 151; there was no measurable change in the 8th-grade score; and the 12th-grade score decreased from 150 to 147 (table 138). Certain subgroups outperformed others in science in 2005. For example, males outperformed females at all three grades. White students scored higher, on average, than Black and Hispanic students at all three grades in 2005. At 4th grade, average scores increased for White, Black, Hispanic, and Asian/Pacific Islander students between 1996 and 2005. At 8th grade, the average score for Black students increased, but no measurable increases occurred for other racial/ethnic groups. At 12th grade, there were no measurable changes in average scores for any racial/ethnic group when comparing results from 2005 with those from 1996. Asian/Pacific Islander 4th-graders' 2000 results are not included because reporting standards were not met.

In addition to student performance data available through NAEP, the *Digest* presents data from other surveys to provide additional perspectives on student achievement. Differences among demographic groups in the acquisition of mental skills have been demonstrated at relatively early ages (table 113). In 2003–04, about 64 percent of 2-year-olds demonstrated skill in expressive vocabulary, which measured toddlers' skill in being able to communicate using gestures, words, and sentences. A higher percentage of females (69 percent) demonstrated expressive vocabulary than males (59 percent). Also, a higher percentage of White 2-year-olds (71 percent) demonstrated expressive vocabulary than Black, Hispanic, or American Indian/Alaska Native 2-year-olds (56, 54, and 50 percent, respectively). The percentage of 2-year-olds from families with high socioeconomic status (SES) who demonstrated expressive vocabulary (75 percent) was higher than the percentage of children from low-SES families (52 percent). Similar patterns of differences were observed among minority and economically disadvantaged children at about 4 years of age (table 114). There was little difference between the average literacy scores for female (13.7) and male (12.7) 48- to 57-month-olds. White (14.2) and Asian (17.5) 48- to 57-month-old children had higher literacy scores than Black (12.0), Hispanic (10.7), and American Indian/Alaska Native (9.6) children. Also, high-SES children (18.0) had higher average literacy scores than low-SES children (9.2). These same patterns were observed among 48- to 57-month-old children with respect to average mathematics scores.

The SAT (formerly known as the Scholastic Assessment Test and the Scholastic Aptitude Test) is not designed as an indicator of student achievement, but rather as an aid for predicting how well students will do in college. Between 1997–98 and 2004–05, the mathematics SAT average score increased by 8 points, but it declined by 5 points between 2004–05 and 2007–08 (table 142). The critical reading average score was 3 points lower in 2007–08 than in 1997–98.

The average number of science and mathematics courses completed by public high school graduates increased between 1982 and 2005. The average number of mathematics courses (Carnegie units) completed in high school rose from 2.6 in 1982 to 3.7 in 2005, and the number of science courses rose from 2.2 to 3.3 (table 147). The average number of courses in career/technical areas completed by all high school graduates was lower in 2005 (4.0 units) than in 1982 (4.6 units). As a result of the increased academic course load, the percentage of students completing the 1983 National Commission on Excellence recommendations for college-bound students (4 units of English, 3 units of social studies, 3 units of science, 3 units of mathematics, 2 units of foreign language, and .5 units of computer science) rose from 2 percent in 1982 to 36 percent in 2005 (table 151).

School Violence

In 2005–06, about 86 percent of public schools had a criminal incident, which is defined as a serious violent crime or a less serious crime such as a fight without weapons, theft, or vandalism (table 158). The percentage of schools having a criminal incident in 2005–06 was about the same as the percentage of schools having an incident in 1999–2000. In 2005–06, some 78 percent of schools reported a violent incident; 46 percent of schools reported a theft/larceny; and 68 percent reported other types of incidents. Overall, there were 5 crime incidents reported per 100 students.

Revenues and Expenditures

The state share of revenues for public elementary and secondary schools generally grew from the 1930s through the mid-1980s, while the local share declined during the same time period (table 171 and figure 9). However, this pattern changed in the late 1980s, when the local share began to increase at the same time the state share decreased. Between 1986–87 and 1993–94, the state share declined from 49.7 percent to 45.2 percent, while the local share rose from 43.9 percent to 47.8 percent. Between 1993–94 and 2000–01, the state share rose again to 49.7 percent, the highest share since 1986–87, but declined every school year afterward until 2005–06, when the state share was 46.5 percent. Between 1995–96 and 2005–06, the federal share of revenues rose to 9.1 percent. The local share declined from 45.9 percent in 1995–96 to 42.8 in 2002–03, and then increased to 44.4 percent in 2005–06.

After adjustment for inflation, current expenditures per student in fall enrollment in public schools rose during the 1980s, remained stable during the first part of the 1990s, and rose again after 1992–93 (table 181 and figure 10). There was an increase of 37 percent from 1980–81 to 1990–91; an increase of less than 1 percent from 1990–91 to 1994–95 (which resulted from small decreases at the beginning of this period, followed by small increases after 1992–93); and an increase of 25 percent from 1994–95 to 2005–06. In 2005–06, current expenditures per student in fall enrollment were $9,154 in unadjusted dollars. In 2005–06, some 55 percent of students in public schools were transported at public expense at a cost of $746 per pupil, also in unadjusted dollars (table 175).

Figure 6. Enrollment, number of teachers, pupil/teacher ratio, and expenditures in public schools: 1960–61 through 2006–07

Fall enrollment, in millions

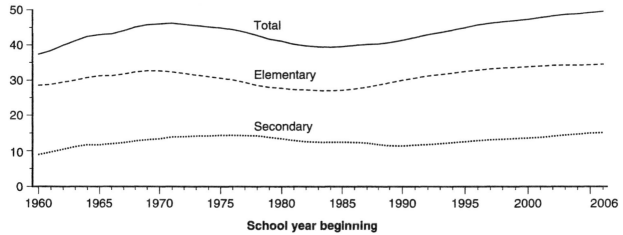

School year beginning

Teachers, in millions   **Pupil/teacher ratio**

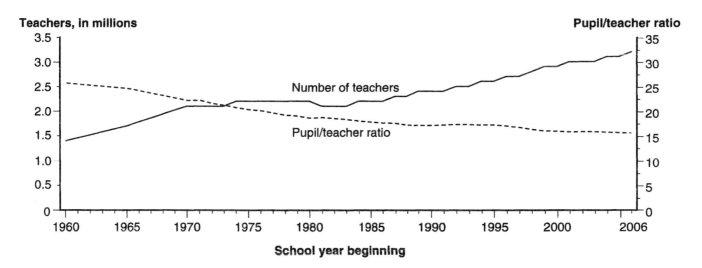

School year beginning

Current expenditures, in billions

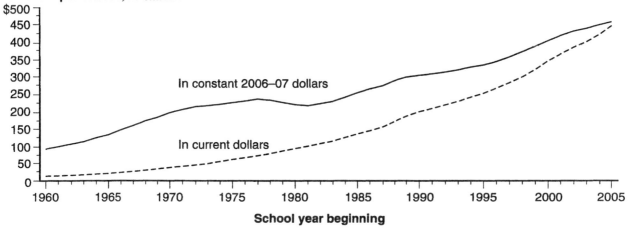

School year beginning

SOURCE: U.S. Department of Education, National Center for Education Statistics, *Statistics of State School Systems,* 1959–60 through 1969–70; *Statistics of Public Elementary and Secondary School Systems,* 1970 through 1980; *Revenues and Expenditures for Public Elementary and Secondary Education,* 1970–71 through 1980–81; and Common Core of Data (CCD), "State Nonfiscal Survey of Public Elementary/Secondary Education," 1981–82 through 2006–07, and "National Public Education Financial Survey," 1989–90 through 2005–06.

Figure 7. Total and full-day preprimary enrollment of 3- to 5-year-olds: October 1970 through October 2007

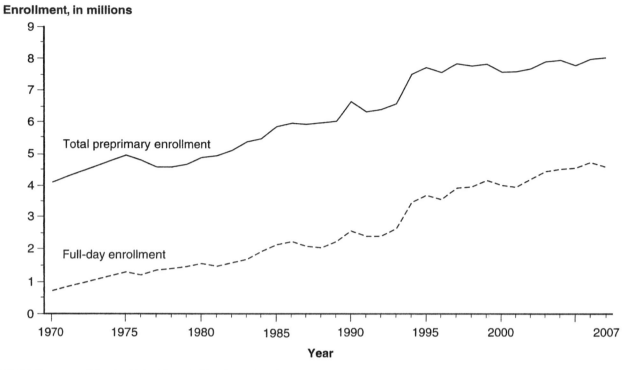

SOURCE: U.S. Department of Education, National Center for Education Statistics, *Preprimary Enrollment*, 1970 and 1975. U.S. Department of Commerce, Census Bureau, Current Population Survey (CPS), October 1976 through October 2007.

Figure 8. Percentage change in public elementary and secondary enrollment, by state: Fall 2000 to fall 2006

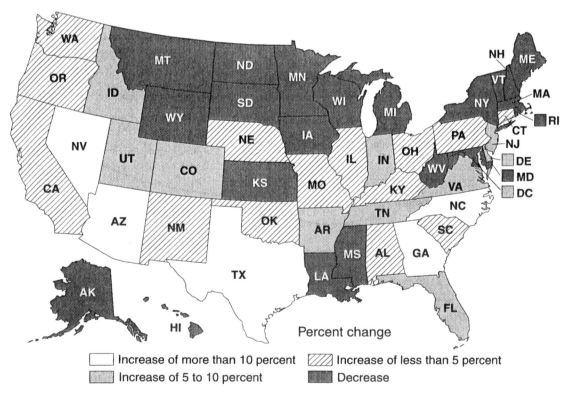

SOURCE: U.S. Department of Education, National Center for Education Statistics, Common Core of Data (CCD), "State Nonfiscal Survey of Public Elementary/Secondary Education," 2000–01 and 2006–07.

Figure 9. Percentage of revenue for public elementary and secondary schools, by source of funds: 1970–71 through 2005–06

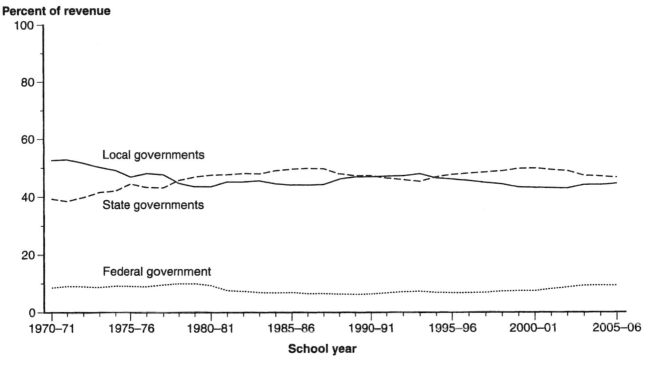

SOURCE: U.S. Department of Education, National Center for Education Statistics, *Revenues and Expenditures for Public Elementary and Secondary Education*, 1970–71 through 1986–87; and Common Core of Data (CCD), "National Public Education Financial Survey," 1987–88 through 2005–06.

Figure 10. Current expenditure per pupil in fall enrollment in public elementary and secondary schools: 1970–71 through 2005–06

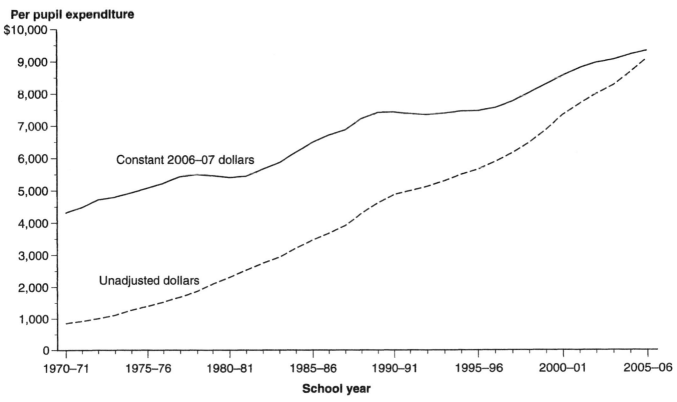

SOURCE: U.S. Department of Education, National Center for Education Statistics, *Revenues and Expenditures for Public Elementary and Secondary Education*, 1970–71 through 1986–87; and Common Core of Data (CCD), "National Public Education Financial Survey," 1987–88 through 2005–06.

Table 32. Historical summary of public elementary and secondary school statistics: Selected years, 1869–70 through 2005–06

Selected characteristic	1869–70	1879–80	1889–90	1899–1900	1909–10	1919–20	1929–30	1939–40	1949–50	1959–60	1969–70	1979–80	1989–90	1999–2000	2003–04	2004–05	2005–06
1	2	3	4	5	6	7	8	9	10	11	12	13	14	15	16	17	18
Population, pupils, and instructional staff																	
Total population (in thousands)[1]	38,558	50,156	62,622	75,995	90,490	104,514	121,878	131,028	149,188	177,830	201,385	225,055	246,819	279,040	290,448	293,192	295,896
5- to 17-year-olds (in thousands)[1]	11,683	15,066	18,473	21,573	24,011	27,571	31,414	30,151	30,223	43,881	52,386	48,043	44,947	52,811	53,250	53,158	53,132
5- to 17-year-olds as a percent of total population	30.3	30.0	29.5	28.4	26.5	26.4	25.8	23.0	20.3	24.7	26.0	21.3	18.2	18.9	18.3	18.1	18.0
Total enrollment in elementary and secondary schools (in thousands)[2]	7,562[3]	9,867	12,723	15,503	17,814	21,578	25,678	25,434	25,112	36,087	45,550	41,651	40,543	46,857	48,540	48,795	49,113
Prekindergarten and grades 1–8 (in thousands)	7,481[3]	9,757	12,520	14,984	16,899	19,378	21,279	18,833	19,387	27,602	32,513	28,034	29,152	33,488	34,202	34,179	34,205
Grades 9–12 (in thousands)	80[3]	110	203	519	915	2,200	4,399	6,601	5,725	8,485	13,037	13,616	11,390	13,369	14,338	14,617	14,908
Enrollment as a percent of total population	19.6[3]	19.7	20.3	20.4	19.7	20.6	21.1	19.4	16.8	20.3	22.6	18.5	16.4	16.8	16.7	16.6	16.6
Enrollment as a percent of 5- to 17-year-olds	64.7[3]	65.5	68.9	71.9	74.2	78.3	81.7	84.4	83.1	82.2	87.0	86.7	90.2	88.7	91.2	91.8	92.4
Percent of total enrollment in high schools (grades 9–12 and postgraduate)	1.1[3]	1.1	1.6	3.3	5.1	10.2	17.1	26.0	22.8	23.5	28.6	32.7	28.1	28.5	29.5	30.0	30.4
High school graduates (in thousands)	—	—	22	62	111	231	592	1,143	1,063	1,627	2,589	2,748	2,320	2,554	2,753	2,795	2,815
Average daily attendance (in thousands)	4,077	6,144	8,154	10,633	12,827	16,150	21,265	22,042	22,284	32,477	41,934	38,289	37,799	43,807	45,326	45,625	45,932
Total number of days attended by pupils enrolled (in millions)	539	801	1,098	1,535	2,011	2,615	3,673	3,858	3,964	5,782	7,501	6,835[4]	—	7,858	8,152	8,205	8,250
Percent of enrolled pupils attending daily	59.3	62.3	64.1	68.6	72.1	74.8	82.8	86.7	88.7	90.0	90.4	90.1[4]	—	94.3	92.8	—	—
Average length of school term, in days	132.2	130.3	134.7	144.3	157.5	161.9	172.7	175.0	177.9	178.0	178.9	178.5[4]	—	179.4	179.9	179.8	179.6
Average number of days attended per pupil	78.4	81.1	86.3	99.0	113.0	121.2	143.0	151.7	157.9	160.2	161.7	160.8[4]	—	—	—	—	—
Total instructional staff (in thousands)	—	—	—	—	—	678	880	912	963	1,457	2,286	2,406	2,986	3,819	4,053	4,120	4,151
Supervisors (in thousands)	—	—	—	—	—	7	7	5	—	—	—	—	—	—	—	—	—
Principals (in thousands)	—	—	—	—	—	14	31	32	43	64	91	106	126	137	165	166	156
Teachers, librarians, and other nonsupervisory instructional staff (in thousands)[5]	201	287	364	423	523	657	843	875	920	1,393	2,195	2,300	2,860	3,682	3,888	3,954	3,995
Males (in thousands)	78	123	126	127	110	93	140	195	196	404[4]	711[4]	782[4]	—	—	—	—	—
Females (in thousands)	123	164	238	296	413	585	703	681	724	989[4]	1,484[4]	1,518[4]	—	—	—	—	—
Percent male	38.7	42.8	34.5	29.9	21.1	14.1	16.6	22.2	21.3	29.0[4]	32.4[4]	34.0[4]	—	—	—	—	—
Total revenues and expenditures																	
Amounts in current dollars																	
Total revenue receipts (in millions)	—	—	$143	$220	$433	$970	$2,089	$2,261	$5,437	$14,747	$40,267	$96,881	$208,548	$372,944	$462,026	$487,754	$520,644
Federal government	—	—	—	—	—	2	7	40	156	652	3,220	9,504	12,701	27,098	41,923	44,810	47,554
State governments	—	—	—	—	—	160	354	684	2,166	5,768	16,063	45,349	98,239	184,613	217,384	228,554	242,151
Local sources, including intermediate	—	—	—	—	—	808	1,728	1,536	3,116	8,327	20,985	42,029	97,608	161,233	202,718	214,390	230,939
Percentage distribution of revenue receipts																	
Federal government	—	—	—	—	—	0.3	0.4	1.8	2.9	4.4	8.0	9.8	6.1	7.3	9.1	9.2	9.1
State governments	—	—	—	—	—	16.5	16.9	30.3	39.8	39.1	39.9	46.8	47.1	49.5	47.1	46.9	46.5
Local sources, including intermediate	—	—	—	—	—	83.2	82.7	68.0	57.3	56.5	52.1	43.4	46.8	43.2	43.9	44.0	44.4
Total expenditures for public schools (in millions)	$63	$78	$141	$215	$426	$1,036	$2,317	$2,344	$5,838	$15,613	$40,683	$95,962	$212,770	$381,838	$474,242	$499,569	$528,735
Current expenditures[6]	—	—	114	180	356	861	1,844	1,942	4,687	12,329[7]	34,218[7]	86,984[7]	188,229[7]	323,889[7]	403,390[7]	425,048[7]	449,595[7]
Capital outlay[8]	—	—	26	35	70	154	371	258	1,014	2,662	4,659	6,506	17,781	43,357	50,843	53,528	57,375
Interest on school debt	—	—	—	—	—	18	93	131	101	490	1,171	1,874	3,776	9,135	13,081	13,301	14,347
Other current expenditures[9]	—	—	—	—	—	3	10	13	36	133	636	598[10]	2,983	5,457	6,928	7,691	7,418
Percentage distribution of total expenditures																	
Current expenditures[6]	—	—	81.3	83.5	83.6	83.1	79.6	82.8	80.3	79.0[7]	84.1[7]	90.6[7]	88.5[7]	84.8[7]	85.1[7]	85.1[7]	85.0[7]
Capital outlay[8]	—	—	18.7	16.5	16.4	14.8	16.0	11.0	17.4	17.0	11.5	6.8	8.4	11.4	10.7	10.7	10.9
Interest on school debt	—	—	—	—	—	1.8	4.0	5.6	1.7	3.1	2.9	2.0	1.8	2.4	2.8	2.7	2.7
Other current expenditures[9]	—	—	—	—	—	0.3	0.4	0.6	0.6	0.8	1.6	0.6[10]	1.4	1.4	1.5	1.5	1.4

See notes at end of table.

Table 32. Historical summary of public elementary and secondary school statistics: Selected years, 1869–70 through 2005–06—Continued

Selected characteristic	1869–70	1879–80	1889–90	1899–1900	1909–10	1919–20	1929–30	1939–40	1949–50	1959–60	1969–70	1979–80	1989–90	1999–2000	2003–04	2004–05	2005–06
1	2	3	4	5	6	7	8	9	10	11	12	13	14	15	16	17	18
Teacher salaries; income and expenditures per pupil and per capita																	
Annual salary of classroom teachers[11]	$189	$195	$252	$325	$485	$871	$1,420	$1,441	$3,010	$4,995	$8,626	$15,970	$31,367	$41,807	$46,605	$47,659	$49,026
Personal income per member of labor force[1]	—	—	—	—	—	—	1,730	1,320	3,379	5,745	9,643	19,647	37,038	55,984	62,546	65,991	68,777
Total school expenditures per capita of total population	1.59	1.56	2.23	2.83	4.71	9.91	19.01	17.89	39	88	202	426	862	1,368	1,633	1,704	1,787
National income per capita[2]	—	—	—	—	—	—	772.90	627.35	1,595	2,563	4,418	9,994	19,555	29,518	33,164	35,154	37,087
Current expenditure per pupil in ADA[6,12,13]	—	—	13.99	16.67	27.85	53.32	86.70	88.09	210	375	816	2,272	4,980	7,394	8,900	9,316	9,788
Total expenditure per pupil in ADA[13,14]	15.55	12.71	17.23	20.21	33.23	64.16	108.49	105.74	260	471	955	2,491	5,550	8,592	10,310	10,781	11,350
National income per pupil in ADA[13]	—	—	—	—	—	—	4,430	3,729	10,680	14,035	21,217	58,740	127,690	188,024	212,513	225,900	238,920
Current expenditure per day per pupil in ADA[6,13,15]	—	—	0.10	0.12	0.18	0.33	0.50	0.50	1.17	2.11	4.56	12.73	—	—	—	—	—
Total expenditure per day per pupil in ADA[13]	0.12	0.10	0.13	0.14	0.21	0.40	0.63	0.60	1.46	2.65	5.34	13.95	—	—	—	—	—
Amounts in constant 2006–07 dollars[16]																	
Annual salary of classroom teachers[11]	$9,330	—	—	—	—	—	$16,935	$21,049	$25,945	$34,703	$46,615	$41,994	$50,429	$50,412	$51,124	$50,753	$50,294
Personal income per member of labor force[1]	—	—	—	—	—	—	20,637	19,281	29,128	39,915	52,110	51,663	59,545	67,508	68,611	70,276	70,556
Total school expenditures per capita of total population	—	—	—	—	—	106	227	261	337	610	1,092	1,121	1,386	1,650	1,791	1,815	1,833
National income per capita[2]	—	—	—	—	—	—	9,218	9,164	13,751	17,807	23,875	26,278	31,439	35,594	36,380	37,436	38,046
Current expenditure per pupil in ADA[6,12,13]	—	—	—	—	—	571	1,034	1,287	1,813	2,606	4,410	5,974	8,006	8,915	9,763	9,921	10,041
Total expenditure per pupil in ADA[13,14]	—	—	—	—	—	687	1,294	1,545	2,244	3,272	5,161	6,549	8,923	10,360	11,310	11,481	11,643
National income per pupil in ADA[13]	—	—	—	—	—	—	52,830	54,474	92,060	97,505	114,656	154,459	205,288	226,725	233,121	240,567	245,099
Current expenditure per day per pupil in ADA[6,13,15]	—	—	—	—	—	3.5	6.0	7.3	10.1	14.7	24.6	33.5	—	—	—	—	—
Total expenditure per day per pupil in ADA[13]	—	—	—	—	—	4.3	7.5	8.8	12.6	18.4	28.9	36.7	—	—	—	—	—

—Not available.

[1]Data on population and labor force are from the Census Bureau, and data on personal income and national income are from the Bureau of Economic Analysis, U.S. Department of Commerce. Population data through 1900 are based on total population. Population data from the decennial census. From 1909–10 to 1959–60, population data are total population, including armed forces overseas, as of July 1. Data for later years are for resident population that excludes armed forces overseas.

[2]Data for 1869–70 through 1959–60 are school year enrollment. Data for later years are fall enrollment.

[3]Data for 1870–71.

[4]Estimated by the National Center for Education Statistics.

[5]Prior to 1919–20, data are for the number of different persons employed rather than number of positions.

[6]Prior to 1919–20, includes interest on school debt.

[7]Because of the modification of the scope of "current expenditures for elementary and secondary schools," data for 1959–60 and later years are not entirely comparable with prior years.

[8]Beginning in 1969–70, includes capital outlay by state and local school building authorities.

[9]Includes summer schools, community colleges, and adult education. Beginning in 1959–60, also includes community services, formerly classified with "current expenditures for elementary and secondary schools."

[10]Excludes community colleges and adult education.

[11]Prior to 1959–60, average includes supervisors, principals, teachers, and other nonsupervisory instructional staff. Data for 1959–60 and later years are estimated by the National Education Association.

[12]Excludes current expenditures not allocable to pupil costs.

[13]"ADA" means average daily attendance in elementary and secondary schools.

[14]Expenditure figure is the sum of current expenditures allocable to pupil costs, capital outlay, and interest on school debt.

[15]Per-day rates derived by dividing annual rates by average length of term.

[16]Constant dollars based on the Consumer Price Index, prepared by the Bureau of Labor Statistics, U.S. Department of Labor, adjusted to a school-year basis.

NOTE: Some data have been revised from previously published figures. Beginning in 1959–60, data include Alaska and Hawaii. Detail may not sum to totals because of rounding.

SOURCE: U.S. Department of Education, National Center for Education Statistics, *Annual Report of the United States Commissioner of Education,* 1869–70 through 1909–10; *Biennial Survey of Education in the United States,* 1919–20 through 1949–50; *Statistics of State School Systems,* 1959–60 and 1969–70; *Statistics of Public Elementary and Secondary School Systems,* 1979–80; *Revenues and Expenditures for Public Elementary and Secondary Education, FY 1980;* Schools and Staffing Survey (SASS), "Public School Questionnaire," 1999–2000 and 2003–04; Common Core of Data (CCD), "State Nonfiscal Survey of Public Elementary/Secondary Education," 1989–90 through 2006–07, and "National Public Financial Survey," 1989–90 through 2005–06. Census Bureau, unpublished tabulations. Bureau of Economic Analysis, unpublished tabulations. Bureau of Labor Statistics, unpublished tabulations. (This table was prepared October 2008.)

Table 33. Enrollment in public elementary and secondary schools, by state or jurisdiction: Selected years, fall 1990 through fall 2008

State or jurisdiction	Total													Fall 2005			Fall 2006			Projected fall 2007 enrollment	Projected fall 2008 enrollment
	Fall 1990	Fall 1993	Fall 1994	Fall 1995	Fall 1996	Fall 1997	Fall 1998	Fall 1999	Fall 2000	Fall 2001	Fall 2002	Fall 2003	Fall 2004	Total	Prekindergarten to grade 8[1]	Grades 9 to 12[2]	Total	Prekindergarten to grade 8[1]	Grades 9 to 12[2]		
1	2	3	4	5	6	7	8	9	10	11	12	13	14	15	16	17	18	19	20	21	22
United States	41,216,683	43,464,916	44,111,482	44,840,481	45,611,046	46,126,897	46,538,585	46,857,149	47,203,539	47,671,870	48,183,086	48,540,215	48,795,465	49,113,298	34,205,172	14,908,126	49,298,945	34,221,430	15,077,515	49,644,000	49,825,000
Alabama	721,806	734,288	736,531	746,149	747,932	749,207	747,980	740,732	739,992	737,190	739,366	731,220	730,140	741,761	529,347	212,414	743,632	528,664	214,968	749,000	750,000
Alaska	113,903	125,948	127,057	127,618	129,919	132,123	135,373	134,391	133,356	134,349	134,364	133,933	132,970	133,288	91,225	42,063	132,608	90,167	42,441	134,000	132,000
Arizona	639,853	709,453	737,424	743,566	799,250	814,113	848,262	852,612	877,696	922,180	937,755	1,012,068	1,043,298	1,094,454	739,535	354,919	1,065,082	758,338	306,744	1,177,000	1,212,000
Arkansas	436,286	444,271	447,565	453,257	457,349	456,497	452,256	451,034	449,959	449,805	450,985	454,523	463,115	474,206	335,747	138,459	476,409	336,552	139,857	480,000	485,000
California	4,950,474	5,327,231	5,407,475	5,536,406	5,686,198	5,803,887	5,926,037	6,038,590	6,140,814	6,247,726	6,353,667	6,413,862	6,441,557	6,437,202	4,466,160	1,971,042	6,406,821	4,410,254	1,996,567	6,471,000	6,475,000
Colorado	574,213	625,062	640,521	656,279	673,438	687,167	699,135	708,109	724,508	742,145	751,862	757,693	765,976	779,826	549,875	229,951	794,026	559,041	234,985	803,000	812,000
Connecticut	469,123	496,298	506,824	517,935	527,129	535,164	544,698	553,993	562,179	570,228	570,023	577,203	577,390	575,059	399,705	175,354	575,100	398,063	177,037	566,000	561,000
Delaware	99,658	105,547	106,813	108,461	110,549	111,960	113,262	112,836	114,676	115,555	116,342	117,668	119,091	120,937	84,639	36,298	122,254	84,996	37,258	124,000	125,000
District of Columbia	80,694	80,678	80,450	79,802	78,648	77,111	71,889	77,194	68,925	75,392	76,166	78,057	76,714	76,876	55,637	21,239	72,850	52,383	20,467	76,000	75,000
Florida	1,861,592	2,040,763	2,111,188	2,176,222	2,242,212	2,294,077	2,337,633	2,381,396	2,434,821	2,500,478	2,539,929	2,587,628	2,639,336	2,675,024	1,873,395	801,629	2,671,513	1,866,562	804,951	2,771,000	2,812,000
Georgia	1,151,687	1,235,304	1,270,948	1,311,126	1,346,761	1,375,980	1,401,291	1,422,762	1,444,937	1,470,634	1,496,012	1,522,611	1,553,437	1,598,461	1,145,446	453,015	1,629,157	1,166,508	462,649	1,679,000	1,712,000
Hawaii	171,708	180,410	183,795	187,180	187,653	189,887	188,069	185,860	184,360	184,546	183,829	183,609	183,185	182,818	127,472	55,346	182,728	126,007	54,721	183,000	184,000
Idaho	220,840	236,774	240,448	243,097	245,252	244,403	244,722	245,136	245,117	246,521	248,604	252,120	256,084	261,982	182,829	79,153	267,380	187,005	80,375	272,000	276,000
Illinois	1,821,407	1,893,078	1,916,172	1,943,623	1,973,040	1,998,289	2,011,530	2,027,600	2,048,792	2,071,391	2,084,187	2,100,961	2,097,503	2,111,706	1,480,321	631,385	2,118,276	1,477,679	640,597	2,127,000	2,126,000
Indiana	954,525	965,633	969,022	977,263	982,876	986,836	989,001	988,702	989,267	996,133	1,003,875	1,011,130	1,021,348	1,035,074	724,467	310,607	1,045,940	730,108	315,832	1,043,000	1,044,000
Iowa	483,652	498,519	500,440	502,343	502,941	501,054	498,214	497,301	495,080	485,932	482,210	481,226	478,319	483,482	326,160	157,322	483,122	326,218	156,904	484,000	482,000
Kansas	437,034	457,614	460,838	463,008	466,293	468,687	472,353	472,188	470,610	470,205	470,957	470,490	469,136	467,525	320,601	146,924	469,506	326,225	143,281	462,000	461,000
Kentucky	636,401	655,265	657,642	659,821	656,089	669,322	655,687	648,180	665,850	654,363	660,782	663,885	674,796	679,878	487,435	192,443	683,173	487,192	195,981	683,000	686,000
Louisiana	784,757	800,560	797,933	797,366	793,296	776,813	768,734	756,579	743,089	731,328	730,464	727,709	724,281	654,526	482,082	172,444	675,851	492,116	183,735	614,000	602,000
Maine	215,149	216,995	212,601	213,569	213,593	212,579	211,051	209,253	207,037	205,586	204,337	202,084	198,820	195,498	133,491	62,007	193,986	132,338	61,648	189,000	186,000
Maryland	715,176	772,638	790,938	805,544	818,583	830,744	841,671	846,582	852,920	860,640	866,743	869,113	865,561	860,020	588,571	271,449	851,640	579,065	272,575	854,000	850,000
Massachusetts	834,314	877,726	893,727	915,007	933,898	949,006	962,317	971,425	975,150	973,139	982,989	980,459	975,574	971,909	675,398	296,511	968,661	670,628	298,033	960,000	952,000
Michigan	1,584,431	1,599,377	1,614,784	1,641,456	1,685,714	1,702,717	1,720,287	1,725,639	1,720,626	1,730,669	1,785,160	1,757,604	1,751,290	1,742,282	1,191,397	550,885	1,714,709	1,162,550	552,159	1,711,000	1,686,000
Minnesota	756,374	810,233	821,693	835,166	847,204	853,621	856,455	854,034	854,340	851,384	846,891	842,854	838,503	839,243	557,757	281,486	840,565	558,445	282,120	833,000	829,000
Mississippi	502,417	505,907	505,962	506,272	503,967	504,792	502,379	500,716	497,871	493,507	492,645	493,540	495,376	494,954	358,057	136,897	495,026	356,406	138,620	495,000	495,000
Missouri	816,558	866,378	878,541	889,881	900,517	910,613	913,494	914,110	912,744	909,792	906,499	905,941	905,449	917,705	635,142	282,563	920,353	634,275	286,078	917,000	917,000
Montana	152,974	163,009	164,341	165,547	164,627	162,335	159,988	157,556	154,875	151,947	149,995	148,356	146,705	145,416	97,770	47,646	144,418	97,021	47,397	143,000	142,000
Nebraska	274,081	285,097	287,100	289,744	291,967	292,681	291,140	288,261	286,199	285,095	285,402	285,542	285,761	286,646	195,055	91,591	287,580	195,769	91,811	288,000	288,000
Nevada	201,316	235,800	250,747	265,041	282,131	296,621	311,061	325,610	340,706	356,814	369,498	385,401	400,083	412,395	295,991	116,404	424,240	302,839	121,401	444,000	457,000
New Hampshire	172,785	185,360	189,319	194,171	198,308	201,629	204,713	206,783	208,461	206,847	207,671	207,417	206,852	205,767	138,586	67,181	203,551	136,188	67,363	200,000	198,000
New Jersey	1,089,646	1,151,307	1,174,206	1,197,381	1,227,832	1,250,276	1,268,996	1,289,256	1,313,405	1,341,656	1,367,438	1,380,753	1,393,347	1,395,602	970,725	424,877	1,388,850	963,548	425,302	1,393,000	1,393,000
New Mexico	301,881	322,292	327,248	329,640	332,632	331,673	328,753	324,495	320,306	320,260	320,234	323,066	326,102	326,758	229,552	97,206	328,220	230,091	98,129	329,300	330,000
New York	2,598,337	2,733,813	2,766,208	2,813,230	2,843,131	2,861,823	2,877,143	2,887,776	2,882,188	2,872,132	2,888,233	2,864,775	2,836,337	2,815,581	1,909,425	906,156	2,809,649	1,887,744	921,905	2,765,000	2,737,000
North Carolina	1,086,871	1,133,231	1,156,767	1,183,090	1,210,108	1,236,083	1,254,821	1,275,925	1,293,638	1,315,363	1,335,954	1,360,209	1,385,754	1,416,436	1,003,118	413,318	1,444,481	1,027,067	417,414	1,472,000	1,496,000
North Dakota	117,825	119,127	119,288	119,100	120,123	118,572	114,927	112,751	109,201	106,047	104,225	102,233	100,513	98,283	65,638	32,645	96,670	64,395	32,275	95,000	94,000

See notes at end of table.

Table 33. Enrollment in public elementary and secondary schools, by state or jurisdiction: Selected years, fall 1990 through fall 2008—Continued

State or jurisdiction	Fall 1990	Fall 1993	Fall 1994	Fall 1995	Fall 1996	Fall 1997	Fall 1998	Fall 1999	Fall 2000	Fall 2001	Fall 2002	Fall 2003	Fall 2004	Fall 2005 Total	Fall 2005 Prekindergarten to grade 8[1]	Fall 2005 Grades 9 to 12[2]	Fall 2006 Total	Fall 2006 Prekindergarten to grade 8[1]	Fall 2006 Grades 9 to 12[2]	Projected fall 2007 enrollment	Projected fall 2008 enrollment
1	2	3	4	5	6	7	8	9	10	11	12	13	14	15	16	17	18	19	20	21	22
Ohio	1,771,089	1,807,319	1,814,290	1,836,015	1,844,698	1,847,114	1,842,163	1,836,554	1,835,049	1,830,985	1,838,285	1,845,428	1,840,032	1,839,683	1,261,331	578,352	1,836,096	1,252,608	583,488	1,823,000	1,812,000
Oklahoma	579,087	604,076	609,718	616,393	620,695	623,681	628,492	627,032	623,110	622,139	624,548	626,160	629,476	634,739	456,963	177,776	639,391	459,953	179,438	639,000	643,000
Oregon	472,394	516,611	521,945	527,914	537,854	541,346	542,809	545,033	546,231	551,480	554,071	551,273	552,505	552,194	379,688	172,506	562,574	380,583	181,991	557,000	558,000
Pennsylvania	1,667,834	1,744,082	1,764,946	1,787,533	1,804,256	1,815,151	1,816,414	1,816,716	1,814,311	1,821,627	1,816,747	1,821,146	1,828,089	1,830,684	1,227,625	603,059	1,871,060	1,220,074	650,986	1,810,000	1,797,000
Rhode Island	138,813	145,676	147,487	149,799	151,324	153,321	154,785	156,454	157,347	158,046	159,205	159,375	156,498	153,422	103,870	49,552	151,612	101,996	49,616	148,000	145,000
South Carolina	622,112	643,696	648,725	645,586	652,816	659,273	664,600	666,780	677,411	676,198	694,389	699,198	703,736	701,544	498,030	203,514	703,119	497,102	206,017	704,000	706,000
South Dakota	129,164	142,825	143,482	144,685	143,331	142,443	132,495	131,037	128,603	127,542	130,048	125,537	122,798	122,012	83,530	38,482	121,158	83,137	38,021	121,000	120,000
Tennessee	824,595	866,557	881,425	893,770	904,818	893,044	905,454	916,202	909,161	924,899	927,608	936,681	941,091	953,928	676,576	277,352	978,368	691,971	286,397	968,000	974,000
Texas	3,382,887	3,608,262	3,677,171	3,748,167	3,828,975	3,891,877	3,945,367	3,991,783	4,059,619	4,163,447	4,259,823	4,331,751	4,405,215	4,525,394	3,268,339	1,257,055	4,599,509	3,319,782	1,279,727	4,759,000	4,872,000
Utah	446,652	471,365	474,675	477,121	481,812	482,957	481,176	450,255	481,485	484,684	489,262	495,981	503,607	508,430	357,644	150,786	523,586	371,326	152,260	542,000	554,000
Vermont	95,762	102,755	104,533	105,565	106,341	105,984	105,120	104,559	102,049	101,179	99,978	99,103	98,352	96,638	64,662	31,976	95,399	63,740	31,659	92,000	90,000
Virginia	998,601	1,045,471	1,060,809	1,079,854	1,096,093	1,110,815	1,124,022	1,133,994	1,144,915	1,163,091	1,177,229	1,192,092	1,204,739	1,213,616	841,299	372,317	1,220,440	841,685	378,755	1,234,000	1,242,000
Washington	839,709	915,952	938,314	956,572	974,504	991,235	998,053	1,003,714	1,004,770	1,009,200	1,014,798	1,021,349	1,020,005	1,031,985	699,482	332,503	1,026,774	694,858	331,916	1,033,000	1,032,000
West Virginia	322,389	314,383	310,511	307,112	304,052	301,419	297,530	291,811	286,367	282,885	282,455	281,215	280,129	280,866	197,189	83,677	281,939	197,573	84,366	279,000	278,000
Wisconsin	797,621	844,001	860,581	870,175	879,259	881,780	879,542	877,753	879,476	879,361	881,231	880,031	864,757	875,174	583,998	291,176	876,700	584,600	292,100	865,000	860,000
Wyoming	98,226	100,899	100,314	99,859	99,058	97,115	95,241	92,105	89,940	88,128	88,116	87,462	84,733	84,409	57,195	27,214	85,193	57,995	27,198	84,000	84,000
Bureau of Indian Education	—	—	—	—	—	—	50,125	49,076	46,938	46,476	46,126	45,828	45,828	50,938	36,133	14,805	—	—	—	—	—
DoD, overseas	—	—	—	—	80,715	78,254	78,170	108,035[3]	73,581	73,212	72,889	71,053	68,327	62,543	48,691	13,852	60,891	47,589	13,302	—	—
DoD, domestic	—	—	—	—	—	—	—	—	34,058	32,847	32,115	30,603	29,151	28,329	25,558	2,771	26,631	24,052	2,579	—	—
Other jurisdictions																					
American Samoa	12,463	14,484	14,445	14,576	14,766	15,214	15,372	15,477	15,702	15,897	15,984	15,893	16,126	16,438	11,766	4,672	16,427	11,755	4,672	—	—
Guam	26,391	30,920	32,185	32,960	33,393	32,444	32,222	32,951	32,473	31,992	—	31,572	30,605	30,986	21,946	9,040	—	—	—	—	—
Northern Marianas	6,449	8,188	8,429	8,809	9,041	9,246	9,498	9,732	10,004	10,479	11,251	11,244	11,601	11,718	8,427	3,291	11,695	8,504	3,191	—	—
Puerto Rico	644,734	631,460	621,121	627,620	618,861	617,157	613,862	613,019	612,725	604,177	596,502	584,916	575,648	563,490	399,384	164,106	544,138	382,600	161,538	—	—
U.S. Virgin Islands	21,750	22,752	23,126	22,737	22,385	22,136	20,976	20,866	19,459	18,780	18,333	17,716	16,429	16,750	11,728	5,022	16,284	11,237	5,047	—	—

—Not available.
[1]Includes elementary unclassified.
[2]Includes secondary unclassified.
[3]Includes both overseas and domestic schools.

NOTE: DoD = Department of Defense. Some data have been revised from previously published figures.
SOURCE: U.S. Department of Education, National Center for Education Statistics, Common Core of Data (CCD), "State Non-fiscal Survey of Public Elementary/Secondary Education," 1990–91 through 2006–07, and Projections of Education Statistics to 2017. (This table was prepared October 2008.)

Table 34. Enrollment in public elementary and secondary schools, by level, grade, and state or jurisdiction: Fall 2006

State or jurisdiction	Total, all grades	Prekindergarten through grade 8 and elementary ungraded													Grades 9 through 12 and secondary ungraded					
		Total	Prekinder-garten[1]	Kinder-garten	Grade 1	Grade 2	Grade 3	Grade 4	Grade 5	Grade 6	Grade 7	Grade 8	Elementary ungraded	Total	Grade 9	Grade 10	Grade 11	Grade 12	Secondary ungraded
1	2	3	4	5	6	7	8	9	10	11	12	13	14	15	16	17	18	19	20
United States	49,298,945 [2]	34,221,430	1,075,675 [2]	3,630,141	3,750,365	3,640,179	3,627,004	3,585,447	3,601,419	3,659,959	3,715,404	3,764,879	170,958	15,077,515	4,259,581	3,881,472	3,550,601	3,276,402	109,459
Alabama	743,632	528,664	3,872	58,209	60,977	58,289	57,413	56,720	56,326	57,483	59,802	59,573	0	214,968	64,943	55,864	49,690	44,471	0
Alaska	132,608	90,167	1,832	9,795	9,951	9,945	9,518	9,589	9,510	9,718	10,154	10,155	0	42,441	11,337	10,839	10,226	10,039	0
Arizona	1,065,082	758,338	14,403	85,429	85,431	83,819	82,026	81,292	81,966	81,115	82,015	80,641	201	306,744	84,121	79,483	72,572	70,551	17
Arkansas	476,409	336,552	10,895	38,058	37,689	36,298	35,753	35,581	35,058	34,793	36,009	36,026	392	139,857	38,937	37,233	33,902	29,617	168
California	6,406,821 [2]	4,410,254	119,895 [2]	454,605	477,226	465,948	467,831	470,542	478,821	485,405	493,306	491,871	4,804	1,996,567	545,466	517,813	487,440	443,253	2,595
Colorado	794,026	559,041	24,554	60,922	62,613	60,308	59,126	57,877	57,906	57,850	58,388	59,497	0	234,985	64,754	60,272	56,037	53,922	0
Connecticut	575,100	398,063	13,577	40,834	42,671	42,182	42,487	42,107	42,910	42,920	43,766	44,609	0	177,037	48,579	44,980	43,451	40,027	0
Delaware	122,254	84,996	662	8,604	9,717	9,351	9,176	8,982	9,039	9,306	9,897	10,262	0	37,258	11,785	9,770	8,221	7,482	0
District of Columbia	72,850	52,383	5,800	5,323	5,304	4,825	4,737	4,577	4,668	4,459	4,941	4,826	2,923	20,467	6,508	4,391	4,047	3,367	2,154
Florida	2,671,513	1,866,562	46,117	202,063	208,032	201,704	206,136	199,686	195,574	204,683	195,354	207,213	0	804,951	240,337	212,588	189,074	162,952	0
Georgia	1,629,157	1,166,508	39,318	130,453	129,876	125,241	126,293	121,155	122,020	121,879	123,370	126,903	0	462,649	145,883	121,715	104,649	90,402	0
Hawaii	180,728	126,007	1,486	13,953	14,366	13,887	13,839	13,687	13,988	13,667	13,534	13,512	88	54,721	16,419	14,240	13,302	10,675	85
Idaho	267,380	187,005	2,787	20,922	20,983	20,985	20,260	19,989	20,338	19,895	20,306	20,540	0	80,375	21,843	20,688	19,522	18,322	0
Illinois	2,118,276	1,477,679	75,275	147,440	155,861	153,266	155,356	153,480	154,719	160,650	162,594	159,038	0	640,597	180,641	166,115	150,475	143,366	0
Indiana	1,045,940	730,108	10,148	79,145	82,646	79,297	78,009	78,177	79,680	79,949	80,990	82,067	0	315,832	86,804	82,655	76,719	69,654	0
Iowa	483,122	326,218	8,255	37,592	34,981	34,698	34,540	34,245	34,329	34,576	35,971	37,031	3,019	156,904	40,126	39,556	38,774	38,448	0
Kansas	469,506	326,225	14,074	35,392	35,374	34,487	34,108	33,101	33,537	33,915	34,408	34,810	3,185	143,281	38,439	36,464	34,712	32,471	1,195
Kentucky	683,173 [2]	487,192	36,539 [2]	50,639	50,917	50,638	50,955	47,975	47,911	48,921	49,189	50,323	0	195,981	57,292	51,598	45,515	40,267	1,309
Louisiana	675,851	492,116	24,022	53,804	56,629	51,728	50,553	51,624	50,027	51,795	51,240	50,694	0	183,735	58,841	45,580	40,732	38,582	0
Maine	193,986	132,338	2,323	14,001	13,953	13,767	14,137	14,192	14,268	14,591	15,324	15,782	0	61,648	16,000	15,559	15,260	14,829	0
Maryland	851,640	579,065	25,674	56,133	59,586	58,630	60,287	61,045	62,293	63,627	65,458	66,332	0	272,575	78,874	68,921	64,124	60,656	0
Massachusetts	968,661	670,628	24,875	68,585	71,497	70,448	71,534	70,752	71,279	72,921	73,792	74,381	564	298,033	82,320	75,421	72,674	67,618	0
Michigan	1,714,709	1,162,550	18,251	129,669	123,220	120,312	120,128	120,169	121,040	125,072	128,283	130,582	25,824	552,159	151,742	142,842	128,161	116,774	12,640
Minnesota	840,565	558,445	12,319	60,712	60,338	59,468	59,017	59,257	59,172	60,664	62,879	64,619	0	282,120	68,807	69,631	70,409	73,273	0
Mississippi	495,026	356,406	2,685	39,617	41,527	38,636	37,289	36,873	36,945	38,318	39,581	38,819	6,116	138,620	42,005	35,506	30,232	26,732	4,145
Missouri	920,353	634,275	20,927	67,873	68,750	67,361	67,685	66,268	66,620	67,527	69,241	72,023	0	286,078	81,671	73,311	67,341	63,755	0
Montana	144,418	97,021	794	10,409	10,603	10,429	10,468	10,311	10,625	10,710	11,152	11,387	133	47,397	12,845	12,008	11,617	10,870	57
Nebraska	287,580	195,769	6,933	22,080	21,452	20,880	20,449	20,338	20,402	20,619	20,994	21,622	0	91,811	24,459	23,346	22,479	21,527	0
Nevada	424,240	302,839	2,937	31,746	33,938	33,946	33,278	32,711	32,969	33,595	33,137	33,557	1,025	121,401	41,149	33,777	25,182	21,262	31
New Hampshire	203,551	136,188	2,531	10,375	14,848	14,618	14,953	15,080	15,287	15,770	16,295	16,431	0	67,363	18,280	16,914	16,698	15,471	0
New Jersey	1,388,850	963,548	27,952	93,043	100,564	99,209	98,928	98,149	98,524	100,378	101,481	102,827	42,493	425,302	108,572	105,161	99,725	94,685	17,159
New Mexico	328,220	230,091	5,852	25,668	25,776	25,351	24,673	24,311	24,131	23,823	24,943	25,563	0	98,129	29,895	26,787	22,118	19,329	0
New York	2,809,649	1,887,744	44,649	186,373	200,298	194,190	194,135	192,095	197,006	199,867	208,458	210,851	59,822	921,905	250,358	233,088	195,277	179,030	64,152
North Carolina	1,444,481	1,027,067	16,601	118,443	119,653	113,975	112,003	108,731	106,929	108,435	111,332	110,965	0	417,414	128,905	108,148	95,805	84,556	0
North Dakota	96,670	64,395	977	6,650	6,704	6,747	6,910	6,931	7,005	7,130	7,467	7,874	0	32,275	8,283	8,199	7,975	7,818	0
Ohio	1,836,096	1,252,608	30,774	133,757	137,504	133,182	132,817	131,208	132,180	136,300	140,574	144,312	0	583,488	164,804	147,421	140,088	131,175	0
Oklahoma	639,391	459,953	34,378	49,362	51,739	47,605	46,759	45,369	44,658	45,179	46,022	46,050	2,832	179,438	51,070	46,155	42,614	38,453	1,146
Oregon	562,574	380,583	1,147	39,572	42,294	42,063	42,297	41,754	42,430	42,477	42,514	43,312	723	181,991	46,162	46,509	45,179	43,833	308
Pennsylvania	1,871,060	1,220,074	10,953	126,821	131,653	129,695	129,005	129,546	132,933	137,238	143,683	146,393	2,154	650,986	164,999	169,575	161,002	153,112	2,298
Rhode Island	151,612	101,996	1,764	10,231	10,429	9,871	11,173	11,135	11,324	11,594	12,281	12,194	0	49,616	13,935	12,964	11,885	10,332	0

See notes at end of table.

Table 34. Enrollment in public elementary and secondary schools, by level, grade, and state or jurisdiction: Fall 2006—Continued

		Prekindergarten through grade 8 and elementary ungraded												Grades 9 through 12 and secondary ungraded					
State or jurisdiction	Total, all grades	Total	Prekindergarten[1]	Kindergarten	Grade 1	Grade 2	Grade 3	Grade 4	Grade 5	Grade 6	Grade 7	Grade 8	Elementary ungraded	Total	Grade 9	Grade 10	Grade 11	Grade 12	Secondary ungraded
1	2	3	4	5	6	7	8	9	10	11	12	13	14	15	16	17	18	19	20
South Carolina	703,119	497,102	21,852	52,485	55,245	52,956	51,773	50,922	50,807	52,501	53,882	54,679	0	206,017	66,578	54,790	43,187	41,462	0
South Dakota	121,158	83,137	1,248	9,614	9,017	8,853	8,750	8,866	8,915	9,032	9,332	9,510	0	38,021	10,371	9,799	9,056	8,795	0
Tennessee	978,368	691,971	12,323	77,494	78,239	75,334	73,469	71,857	71,083	72,146	72,474	72,892	14,660	286,397	82,343	75,767	68,383	59,904	0
Texas	4,599,509	3,319,782	212,137	352,980	372,490	353,739	346,248	340,488	337,189	334,497	331,565	338,449	0	1,279,727	399,056	327,151	290,296	263,224	0
Utah	523,586	371,326	3,814	43,525	43,984	43,054	42,205	40,478	39,399	39,090	38,030	37,747	0	152,260	39,118	38,808	37,809	36,525	0
Vermont	95,399	63,740	4,308	6,198	6,206	6,394	6,477	6,521	6,559	6,826	7,065	7,186	0	31,659	8,168	7,944	7,948	7,599	0
Virginia	1,220,440	841,685	20,391	89,644	92,847	90,467	90,042	88,527	89,309	91,791	93,584	95,083	0	378,755	108,680	98,259	88,915	82,901	0
Washington	1,026,774	694,858	9,082	72,608	76,336	75,929	75,901	75,695	75,138	76,735	77,412	80,022	0	331,916	90,280	84,361	80,115	77,160	0
West Virginia	281,939	197,573	7,469	24,308	21,313	20,123	20,167	19,935	20,132	21,132	21,453	21,541	0	84,366	24,331	21,654	19,873	18,508	0
Wisconsin	876,700	584,600	33,821	60,408	60,696	59,703	59,554	59,356	60,261	61,257	63,938	65,606	0	292,100	75,282	72,425	73,694	70,699	0
Wyoming	85,193	57,995	423	6,575	6,422	6,348	6,377	6,191	6,280	6,138	6,544	6,697	0	27,198	7,184	7,427	6,420	6,167	0
Bureau of Indian Education	—	—	—	—	—	—	—	—	—	—	—	—	—	—	—	—	—	—	—
DoD, overseas	60,891	47,589	2,192	5,519	5,727	5,407	5,464	5,073	4,870	4,581	4,558	4,198	0	13,302	4,056	3,433	3,050	2,763	0
DoD, domestic	26,631	24,052	2,808	3,209	3,209	2,857	2,660	2,380	2,172	2,026	1,425	1,306	0	2,579	910	607	538	524	0
Other jurisdictions																			
American Samoa	16,427	11,755	1,560	1,014	1,125	1,101	1,157	1,109	1,074	1,162	1,221	1,232	0	4,672	1,311	1,151	1,097	1,064	49
Guam	—	—	—	—	—	—	—	—	—	—	—	—	—	—	—	—	—	—	—
Northern Marianas	11,695	8,504	579	725	940	910	904	892	865	826	839	939	85	3,191	980	849	644	718	0
Puerto Rico	544,138	382,600	207	35,468	42,270	40,659	41,342	41,624	41,704	42,003	44,785	42,914	9,624	161,538	41,511	41,545	38,733	34,829	4,920
U.S. Virgin Islands	16,284	11,237	(³)	1,018	1,070	1,127	1,125	1,315	1,214	1,255	1,775	1,338	0	5,047	1,834	1,256	1,005	952	0

[1]Data include imputations for nonrespondents.
[2]Includes imputations for underreporting.
[3]No prekindergarten pupils reported.

NOTE: DoD = Department of Defense.
SOURCE: U.S. Department of Education, National Center for Education Statistics, Common Core of Data (CCD), "State Non-fiscal Survey of Public Elementary/Secondary Education," 2006–07. (This table was prepared October 2008.)

Table 35. Enrollment in public elementary and secondary schools, by level, grade, and state or jurisdiction: Fall 2005

State or jurisdiction	Total, all grades	Prekindergarten through grade 8 and elementary ungraded													Grades 9 through 12 and secondary ungraded					
		Total	Prekinder-garten[1]	Kinder-garten	Grade 1	Grade 2	Grade 3	Grade 4	Grade 5	Grade 6	Grade 7	Grade 8	Elementary ungraded	Total	Grade 9	Grade 10	Grade 11	Grade 12	Secondary ungraded
1	2	3	4	5	6	7	8	9	10	11	12	13	14	15	16	17	18	19	20
United States	49,113,298[2]	34,205,172	1,036,466[2]	3,619,421	3,690,854	3,606,405	3,586,107	3,577,506	3,632,829	3,670,135	3,777,151	3,801,893	206,405	14,908,126	4,287,123	3,866,158	3,454,423	3,180,248	120,174
Alabama	741,761	529,347	2,623	58,692	59,756	57,545	56,618	55,919	57,115	58,438	61,130	59,643	1,868	212,414	65,192	55,492	48,278	43,452	0
Alaska	133,288	91,225	1,914	9,934	9,887	9,564	9,641	9,495	9,679	10,042	10,276	10,793	0	42,063	11,405	11,035	10,045	9,578	0
Arizona	1,094,454	739,535	9,979	83,529	83,426	80,750	80,091	80,458	79,659	80,391	80,393	80,683	176	354,919	99,040	92,746	83,935	79,180	18
Arkansas	474,206	335,747	10,372	38,070	37,271	35,714	35,564	34,951	34,623	35,281	36,098	37,279	524	138,459	38,952	37,331	32,603	29,351	222
California	6,437,202[2]	4,466,160	125,099[2]	458,440	473,239	469,553	471,246	477,828	485,857	489,656	491,516	489,560	34,166	1,971,042	546,914	515,681	467,241	423,241	17,965
Colorado	779,826	549,875	23,211	59,398	60,503	58,698	57,198	57,151	57,109	57,673	59,005	59,929	0	229,951	63,818	59,962	54,353	51,818	0
Connecticut	575,059	399,705	12,774	41,206	42,909	42,473	42,061	42,876	42,683	43,533	44,510	44,680	0	175,354	49,070	45,266	42,356	38,662	0
Delaware	120,937	84,639	680	8,511	9,566	9,011	9,034	8,896	9,059	9,532	9,858	10,492	0	36,298	11,638	9,279	7,826	7,555	0
District of Columbia	76,876	55,637	5,499	5,545	5,269	5,152	4,889	5,003	4,976	5,245	5,412	5,196	3,451	21,239	6,141	5,333	4,118	3,177	2,470
Florida	2,675,024	1,873,395	47,240	203,325	205,385	200,719	208,565	195,265	200,761	193,623	210,099	208,413	0	801,629	245,587	212,560	185,937	157,545	0
Georgia	1,598,461	1,145,446	38,633	128,397	125,153	122,084	121,345	119,028	120,287	121,969	124,872	123,678	0	453,015	145,243	120,058	99,914	87,800	0
Hawaii	182,818	127,472	1,412	14,236	14,023	13,965	13,821	14,127	14,169	14,209	13,721	13,696	93	55,346	17,167	14,278	12,914	10,899	88
Idaho	261,982	182,829	2,784	19,987	20,702	19,822	19,549	19,860	19,477	19,740	20,234	20,674	0	79,153	21,564	20,609	19,104	17,876	0
Illinois	2,111,706	1,480,321	72,131	147,726	154,061	153,558	155,155	154,372	158,822	162,949	160,362	160,911	274	631,385	179,703	165,477	147,500	138,518	187
Indiana	1,035,074	724,467	10,501	75,519	80,806	78,303	77,588	79,078	78,808	79,602	82,241	82,021	0	310,607	88,563	81,090	73,904	67,050	0
Iowa	483,482	326,160	6,826	37,435	34,499	34,341	34,064	34,160	34,270	35,380	37,040	38,145	0	157,322	41,059	40,151	38,501	37,611	0
Kansas	467,525	320,601	1,837	34,723	34,662	34,013	32,840	33,229	33,624	34,093	34,762	35,772	11,046	146,924	38,340	37,011	34,128	32,870	4,575
Kentucky	679,878	487,435	38,125	50,266	53,416	48,136	48,136	47,639	48,281	48,956	50,141	50,701	3,638	192,443	57,759	50,298	43,761	39,157	1,468
Louisiana	654,526	482,082	23,328	52,937	53,617	49,358	48,451	53,121	47,359	48,683	51,396	53,832	0	172,444	53,087	43,292	39,330	36,735	0
Maine	195,498	133,491	1,894	13,766	13,698	13,935	13,964	14,198	14,454	15,165	15,725	16,692	0	62,007	16,088	15,926	15,310	14,683	0
Maryland	860,020	588,571	24,219	56,858	58,661	60,342	61,064	62,347	63,983	65,661	67,036	68,400	0	271,449	79,788	70,031	62,864	58,766	0
Massachusetts	971,909	675,398	24,617	68,242	71,554	71,604	70,934	71,410	72,727	73,520	74,567	76,223	0	296,511	82,861	76,688	71,327	65,635	0
Michigan	1,742,282	1,191,397	25,009	131,886	123,620	121,806	121,190	121,830	124,713	128,451	133,086	134,113	25,693	550,885	157,709	143,122	124,460	113,351	12,243
Minnesota	839,243	557,757	11,633	59,666	59,400	58,602	58,728	58,563	59,913	61,379	64,193	65,416	264	281,486	69,317	71,029	68,967	72,173	0
Mississippi	494,954	358,057	2,488	40,346	40,443	37,598	36,830	36,787	37,972	38,744	40,868	38,907	7,074	136,897	41,191	35,019	29,599	26,383	4,705
Missouri	917,705	635,142	17,848	68,221	67,706	67,354	65,726	66,215	66,971	68,182	72,483	74,436	0	282,563	80,473	73,142	66,316	62,632	0
Montana	145,416	97,770	798	10,300	10,559	10,307	10,226	10,527	10,607	10,963	11,238	12,050	195	47,646	12,778	12,320	11,369	11,095	84
Nebraska	286,646	195,055	6,463	21,888	20,955	20,422	20,254	20,290	20,542	20,696	21,547	21,998	0	91,591	24,953	23,713	21,506	21,419	0
Nevada	412,395	295,991	2,812	29,978	33,338	32,560	31,971	32,222	32,947	32,743	32,938	33,502	980	116,404	39,421	32,585	23,868	20,501	29
New Hampshire	205,767	138,586	2,525	10,360	14,943	14,941	14,985	15,151	15,646	16,096	16,358	17,038	543	67,181	18,269	17,478	16,364	15,001	69
New Jersey	1,395,602	970,725	26,794	93,151	101,040	99,236	98,810	98,565	100,496	100,910	104,281	103,587	43,855	424,877	110,035	106,271	98,833	92,175	17,563
New Mexico	326,758	229,552	6,070	25,140	25,485	24,470	24,166	23,987	24,183	24,708	25,356	25,987	2,709	97,206	30,026	26,075	21,986	19,119	0
New York	2,815,581	1,909,425	40,519	189,924	199,641	196,759	195,922	196,074	202,331	205,818	213,746	216,226	52,260	906,156	257,444	233,911	186,182	173,867	54,752
North Carolina	1,416,436	1,003,118	9,847	116,829	114,554	110,707	107,336	105,392	106,210	110,275	110,074	111,894	0	413,318	128,333	108,210	94,508	82,267	0
North Dakota	98,283	65,638	1,052	6,579	6,907	6,918	6,915	7,016	7,077	7,300	7,881	7,993	0	32,645	8,484	8,261	8,011	7,889	0
Ohio	1,839,683	1,261,331	29,791	135,854	136,188	133,171	131,350	131,691	135,078	138,555	144,784	144,869	0	578,352	165,999	145,999	135,918	130,436	0
Oklahoma	634,739	456,963	33,418	48,667	51,206	46,889	45,263	44,194	44,786	45,611	46,408	47,812	2,709	177,776	50,065	46,551	42,054	38,013	1,093
Oregon	552,194	379,688	1,049	39,759	42,065	41,913	41,365	42,071	41,945	41,917	42,762	44,046	796	172,506	46,257	44,839	41,675	39,414	321
Pennsylvania	1,830,684	1,227,625	8,790	127,065	130,687	127,776	127,983	131,236	135,241	140,760	146,888	148,957	2,242	603,059	164,602	156,679	143,798	135,778	2,202
Rhode Island	153,422	103,870	1,688	9,580	10,029	11,281	11,229	11,484	11,555	12,212	12,342	12,470	0	49,552	14,193	13,007	11,765	10,587	0

See notes at end of table.

Table 35. Enrollment in public elementary and secondary schools, by level, grade, and state or jurisdiction: Fall 2005—Continued

State or jurisdiction	Total, all grades	Prekindergarten through grade 8 and elementary ungraded													Grades 9 through 12 and secondary ungraded					
		Total	Prekinder-garten[1]	Kinder-garten	Grade 1	Grade 2	Grade 3	Grade 4	Grade 5	Grade 6	Grade 7	Grade 8	Elementary ungraded	Total	Grade 9	Grade 10	Grade 11	Grade 12	Secondary ungraded
1	2	3	4	5	6	7	8	9	10	11	12	13	14	15	16	17	18	19	20
South Carolina	701,544	498,030	21,604	52,805	54,068	51,842	50,845	50,408	51,756	53,477	55,524	55,701	0	203,514	66,201	51,277	45,709	40,327	0
South Dakota	122,012	83,530	1,217	9,470	8,960	8,781	8,806	8,883	8,912	9,327	9,598	9,576	0	38,482	10,314	10,046	9,166	8,956	0
Tennessee	953,928	676,576	10,190	76,449	75,683	71,978	70,181	69,773	70,869	71,302	72,845	72,949	14,357	277,352	81,397	73,595	65,411	56,949	0
Texas	4,525,394	3,268,339	207,967	350,124	359,221	344,611	340,654	329,969	337,096	323,997	338,876	335,824	0	1,257,055	394,739	323,524	281,641	257,151	0
Utah	508,430	357,644	3,933	42,307	42,307	41,308	39,642	38,635	37,726	36,298	37,025	38,463	0	150,786	38,628	38,319	36,916	36,923	0
Vermont	96,638	64,662	4,061	6,069	6,441	6,429	6,486	6,549	6,827	7,075	7,166	7,559	0	31,976	8,327	8,142	7,888	7,499	120
Virginia	1,213,616	841,299	19,868	89,427	91,064	89,721	87,829	88,883	90,365	93,056	95,370	95,716	0	372,317	110,021	96,546	86,837	78,913	0
Washington	1,031,985	699,482	12,735	72,644	75,680	75,027	75,037	74,401	76,272	76,682	79,554	81,440	0	332,503	90,091	84,945	80,962	76,505	0
West Virginia	280,866	197,189	8,942	21,428	20,751	20,195	19,840	19,999	20,747	21,183	21,756	22,147	201	83,677	24,694	21,400	19,561	18,022	0
Wisconsin	875,174	583,998	31,218	60,382	59,593	58,978	58,664	59,984	60,304	62,737	65,153	66,985	0	291,176	76,674	73,409	71,428	69,665	0
Wyoming	84,409	57,195	439	6,381	6,257	6,185	6,056	6,111	5,960	6,340	6,647	6,819	0	27,214	7,509	7,150	6,476	6,079	0
Bureau of Indian Education	50,938	36,133	(³)	4,745	4,187	3,887	3,741	3,611	3,542	3,900	4,135	4,385	0	14,805	4,888	4,064	3,198	2,655	0
DoD, overseas	62,543	48,691	2,299	4,988	5,728	5,716	5,356	5,261	4,878	5,106	4,956	4,403	0	13,852	4,476	3,601	3,075	2,700	0
DoD, domestic	28,329	25,558	2,796	3,505	3,689	2,931	2,714	2,523	2,328	2,140	1,555	1,377	0	2,771	975	676	584	536	0
Other jurisdictions																			
American Samoa	16,438	11,766	1,560	1,022	1,125	1,101	1,157	1,109	1,074	1,162	1,224	1,232	0	4,672	1,311	1,151	1,097	1,064	49
Guam	30,986	21,946	446	2,311	2,478	2,485	2,372	2,480	2,534	2,085	2,412	2,343	0	9,040	3,164	2,423	1,994	1,459	0
Northern Marianas	11,718	8,427	580	727	883	899	906	870	867	872	937	810	76	3,291	1,038	821	750	682	0
Puerto Rico	563,490	399,384	212	37,695	43,944	42,566	42,261	43,432	43,286	43,570	46,370	42,804	13,244	164,106	41,804	43,878	38,830	33,016	6,578
U.S. Virgin Islands	16,750	11,728	(³)	993	1,124	1,121	1,219	1,277	1,331	1,444	1,845	1,371	3	5,022	1,911	1,113	998	1,000	0

[1]Data include imputations for nonrespondents.
[2]Includes imputations for underreporting.
[3]No prekindergarten pupils reported.

NOTE: DoD = Department of Defense.
SOURCE: U.S. Department of Education, National Center for Education Statistics, Common Core of Data (CCD), "State Non-fiscal Survey of Public Elementary/Secondary Education," 2004–05. (This table was prepared August 2008.)

Table 36. Enrollment in public elementary and secondary schools, by level, grade, and state or jurisdiction: Fall 2004

State or jurisdiction	Total, all grades	Prekindergarten through grade 8 and elementary ungraded												Grades 9 through 12 and secondary ungraded					
		Total	Prekindergarten[1]	Kindergarten	Grade 1	Grade 2	Grade 3	Grade 4	Grade 5	Grade 6	Grade 7	Grade 8	Elementary ungraded	Total	Grade 9	Grade 10	Grade 11	Grade 12	Secondary ungraded
1	2	3	4	5	6	7	8	9	10	11	12	13	14	15	16	17	18	19	20
United States	48,795,465[2]	34,178,784	990,421[2]	3,543,554	3,663,005	3,559,854	3,580,462	3,611,638	3,635,181	3,735,281	3,818,427	3,824,670	216,291	14,616,681	4,281,345	3,750,491	3,369,339	3,094,349	121,157
Alabama	730,140	521,757	1,994	56,964	58,567	55,661	54,954	56,182	57,293	59,406	61,450	59,286	0	208,383	64,569	53,604	47,538	42,672	0
Alaska	132,970	91,981	1,760	9,870	9,510	9,773	9,452	9,674	10,048	10,151	10,886	10,857	0	40,989	11,934	10,664	9,625	8,766	0
Arizona	1,043,298	722,208	9,730	80,614	79,773	78,239	78,495	77,110	77,929	77,592	79,811	78,595	4,320	321,090	91,860	82,536	75,259	71,035	400
Arkansas	463,115	328,188	7,688	36,967	36,286	34,795	34,444	33,884	34,457	34,740	36,881	37,369	677	134,927	38,279	35,794	31,928	28,640	286
California	6,441,557[2]	4,507,916	119,410[2]	455,155	477,554	474,856	481,280	488,045	492,895	491,264	492,879	498,806	35,772	1,933,641	549,463	497,197	459,125	409,576	18,280
Colorado	765,976	540,695	21,256	56,968	58,798	56,634	56,470	56,425	56,901	58,298	59,548	59,397	0	225,281	64,446	57,678	52,770	50,387	0
Connecticut	577,390	404,169	12,448	41,886	43,483	42,266	43,083	42,652	43,686	44,457	45,136	45,072	0	173,221	49,177	44,580	41,124	38,340	0
Delaware	119,091	83,599	670	8,279	9,111	8,861	8,783	8,872	9,172	9,491	9,866	10,494	0	35,492	11,249	9,081	7,772	7,390	0
District of Columbia	76,714	57,111	5,432	5,387	5,603	5,275	5,320	5,300	5,579	5,563	5,576	5,189	2,887	19,603	6,285	4,804	3,816	2,820	1,878
Florida	2,639,336	1,857,798	47,995	197,163	201,536	195,370	206,716	197,293	184,067	208,251	209,848	209,559	0	781,538	250,263	202,437	179,028	149,810	0
Georgia	1,553,437	1,118,379	37,791	122,495	120,880	117,310	117,092	116,129	118,762	122,861	122,627	122,432	0	435,058	142,079	113,044	96,063	83,872	0
Hawaii	183,185	128,788	1,288	13,576	14,207	13,899	14,298	14,289	14,548	14,299	13,849	14,422	113	54,397	16,971	13,682	12,845	10,794	105
Idaho	256,084	178,221	2,585	19,603	19,459	19,016	19,356	18,856	19,179	19,552	20,316	20,299	0	77,863	21,344	20,177	18,836	17,506	0
Illinois	2,097,503	1,483,645	68,764	145,797	154,861	152,864	156,370	158,622	160,365	161,487	162,047	162,192	276	613,858	178,240	159,950	142,828	132,658	182
Indiana	1,021,348	720,006	7,967	73,142	80,247	77,902	78,331	78,079	78,326	80,913	82,371	82,728	0	301,342	87,829	78,361	71,836	63,316	0
Iowa	478,319	324,169	6,108	36,713	33,916	33,626	33,588	33,743	34,716	36,141	37,521	38,097	0	154,150	41,196	39,580	36,940	36,434	0
Kansas	469,136	321,259	2,486	34,203	34,534	32,849	33,159	33,503	33,899	34,525	35,752	35,915	10,434	147,877	39,293	36,302	34,349	33,593	4,340
Kentucky	674,796	485,801	37,916	49,027	52,504	47,483	47,483	47,872	48,224	49,542	50,653	51,172	3,925	188,995	56,919	48,559	42,757	39,200	1,560
Louisiana	724,281	533,751	23,467	57,386	58,425	53,697	53,417	61,940	50,171	56,263	58,791	60,194	0	190,530	59,182	48,181	43,133	40,034	0
Maine	198,820	136,275	1,747	13,687	14,184	13,985	14,173	14,439	14,961	15,549	16,700	16,850	0	62,545	16,766	16,056	15,321	14,402	0
Maryland	865,561	597,417	23,380	54,838	60,854	61,152	62,144	63,776	65,688	66,799	69,219	69,567	0	268,144	81,270	68,249	61,193	57,432	0
Massachusetts	975,574	682,175	23,281	68,357	72,840	71,403	71,578	72,818	73,337	74,901	76,829	76,831	0	293,399	84,628	75,478	69,441	63,852	0
Michigan	1,751,290	1,211,698	20,360	131,141	124,663	122,038	122,480	125,319	127,648	132,348	136,430	137,898	31,373	539,592	158,797	135,116	120,228	111,055	14,396
Minnesota	838,503	558,447	11,173	58,657	58,523	58,093	58,048	59,338	60,554	62,870	65,175	66,016	0	280,056	70,751	69,691	67,978	71,636	0
Mississippi	495,376	361,087	2,623	39,547	39,967	37,520	37,004	38,311	38,525	39,603	41,076	39,115	7,796	134,289	40,195	34,245	29,012	25,801	5,036
Missouri	905,449	628,667	13,602	64,328	67,175	65,315	65,343	66,284	67,344	71,141	74,516	73,619	0	276,782	78,748	71,794	64,402	61,838	0
Montana	146,705	98,673	759	10,206	10,481	10,096	10,370	10,440	10,836	11,204	11,977	12,011	293	48,032	13,200	12,039	11,494	11,173	126
Nebraska	285,761	194,816	6,114	21,205	20,572	20,220	20,252	20,429	20,629	21,203	21,925	22,267	0	90,945	25,214	22,734	21,440	21,557	0
Nevada	400,083	288,754	2,894	29,877	32,258	31,338	31,333	31,950	31,439	32,304	32,364	32,472	525	111,329	36,056	30,706	23,167	21,385	15
New Hampshire	206,852	140,243	2,360	10,116	15,269	14,978	15,021	15,501	15,950	16,200	17,017	17,237	594	66,609	18,584	17,233	15,871	14,847	74
New Jersey	1,393,347	975,988	25,211	93,157	101,135	99,019	99,026	100,557	100,892	103,802	104,603	104,437	44,149	417,359	111,479	104,337	95,891	88,378	17,274
New Mexico	326,102	227,900	5,322	24,624	24,670	24,022	23,596	23,880	24,679	25,239	25,657	26,211	0	98,202	30,134	26,387	22,163	19,518	0
New York	2,836,337	1,942,961	39,801	188,633	203,159	198,215	202,014	202,267	208,162	211,816	219,122	218,176	51,596	893,376	262,635	227,717	183,622	166,975	52,427
North Carolina	1,385,754	985,740	12,468	111,753	111,489	105,683	104,054	104,337	106,846	108,064	111,067	109,979	0	400,014	126,414	103,929	90,414	79,257	0
North Dakota	100,513	67,122	1,089	6,643	7,116	6,958	7,044	7,069	7,321	7,726	8,029	8,127	0	33,391	8,547	8,515	8,186	8,143	0
Ohio	1,840,032	1,267,088	26,119	134,215	136,365	131,410	131,752	134,442	137,372	142,538	145,714	147,161	0	572,944	165,656	143,496	136,413	127,379	0
Oklahoma	629,476	452,952	31,803	47,152	50,685	45,295	43,924	44,372	45,177	46,058	47,939	47,270	3,277	176,524	50,035	45,741	41,485	37,938	1,325
Oregon	552,505	376,940	988	38,997	41,319	40,474	41,199	41,298	41,156	42,227	43,751	44,802	729	175,565	46,700	45,148	42,290	41,125	302
Pennsylvania	1,828,089	1,234,828	7,154	124,435	129,233	126,492	129,400	133,418	138,064	143,275	149,056	151,250	3,051	593,261	163,848	153,315	140,618	132,551	2,929
Rhode Island	156,498	107,040	1,633	8,824	11,661	11,408	11,580	11,731	12,273	12,365	12,782	12,783	0	49,458	14,591	12,763	11,571	10,533	0

See notes at end of table.

Table 36. Enrollment in public elementary and secondary schools, by level, grade, and state or jurisdiction: Fall 2004—Continued

State or jurisdiction	Total, all grades	Prekindergarten through grade 8 and elementary ungraded													Grades 9 through 12 and secondary ungraded					
		Total	Prekinder-garten[1]	Kinder-garten	Grade 1	Grade 2	Grade 3	Grade 4	Grade 5	Grade 6	Grade 7	Grade 8	Elementary ungraded	Total	Grade 9	Grade 10	Grade 11	Grade 12	Secondary ungraded
1	2	3	4	5	6	7	8	9	10	11	12	13	14	15	16	17	18	19	20
South Carolina	703,736	504,264	20,961	52,327	53,769	51,359	51,054	51,999	53,043	55,703	57,408	56,641	0	199,472	65,564	53,159	42,013	38,736	0
South Dakota	122,798	83,891	1,173	9,257	8,836	8,778	8,824	8,862	9,166	9,506	9,774	9,715	0	38,907	10,377	9,924	9,217	9,389	0
Tennessee	941,091[2]	670,880	8,132[2]	74,740	74,196	69,321	69,119	70,555	70,671	72,279	74,131	73,233	14,503	270,211	80,890	71,894	61,937	55,490	0
Texas	4,405,215	3,184,235	204,665	333,934	345,674	334,138	326,921	324,389	323,631	328,689	332,980	329,214	0	1,220,980	386,182	311,905	275,238	247,655	0
Utah	503,607	355,445	9,036	41,088	40,897	39,185	38,265	37,888	36,921	36,672	37,819	37,674	0	148,162	38,069	37,406	37,016	35,671	0
Vermont	98,352	65,935	3,714	6,249	6,452	6,521	6,550	6,807	7,068	7,254	7,474	7,846	0	32,417	8,533	8,237	7,873	7,552	222
Virginia	1,204,739	839,687	18,376	87,223	90,215	87,445	88,264	89,742	91,363	94,345	96,174	96,540	0	365,052	109,375	94,410	83,302	77,965	0
Washington	1,020,005	695,405	11,921	71,219	74,553	73,944	73,227	75,151	75,661	78,244	80,567	80,918	0	324,600	89,802	83,187	77,490	74,121	0
West Virginia	280,129	197,555	7,989	20,942	20,811	19,883	19,896	20,670	20,864	21,499	22,418	22,582	1	82,574	24,199	21,071	18,985	18,319	0
Wisconsin	864,757	577,950	27,444	58,724	58,521	57,807	58,874	59,267	61,493	62,557	66,095	67,168	0	286,807	76,173	71,196	69,928	69,510	0
Wyoming	84,733	57,285	374	6,264	6,209	5,983	6,042	5,862	6,230	6,505	6,831	6,985	0	27,448	7,355	7,202	6,568	6,323	0
Bureau of Indian Education	45,828	33,671	(³)	4,266	3,756	3,432	3,466	3,614	3,685	3,890	3,855	3,707	0	12,157	3,932	3,410	2,509	2,306	0
DoD, overseas	68,327	53,720	2,005	6,283	6,474	6,212	6,085	5,731	5,583	5,493	5,142	4,712	0	14,607	4,527	3,984	3,275	2,821	0
DoD, domestic	29,151	26,195	3,009	3,509	3,354	3,062	2,868	2,675	2,419	2,245	1,645	1,409	0	2,956	1,034	729	653	540	0
Other jurisdictions																			
American Samoa	16,126	11,873	1,547	1,016	1,129	1,109	1,080	1,185	1,218	1,258	1,216	1,115	0	4,253	1,140	1,122	1,051	878	62
Guam	30,605	21,686	430	2,203	2,463	2,362	2,463	2,509	2,110	2,439	2,335	2,372	0	8,919	2,815	2,587	1,860	1,657	0
Northern Marianas	11,601	8,416	580	686	921	886	872	851	877	951	880	834	78	3,185	979	857	681	668	0
Puerto Rico	575,648	408,607	199	38,375	45,988	43,084	43,612	44,497	45,012	45,002	46,246	43,212	13,380	167,041	45,140	44,949	37,422	32,917	6,613
U.S. Virgin Islands	16,429	11,650	(³)	989	1,088	1,112	1,094	1,315	1,386	1,460	1,747	1,288	171	4,779	1,676	1,145	1,029	929	0

[1]Data include imputations for nonrespondents.
[2]Includes imputations for underreporting.
[3]No prekindergarten pupils reported.
NOTE: DoD = Department of Defense. Some data have been revised from previously published figures.

SOURCE: U.S. Department of Education, National Center for Education Statistics, Common Core of Data (CCD), "State Non-fiscal Survey of Public Elementary/Secondary Education," 2004–05. (This table was prepared August 2008.)

Table 37. Enrollment in public elementary and secondary schools, by grade: Selected years, fall 1980 through fall 2006

Grade	Fall 1980	Fall 1985	Fall 1990	Fall 1992	Fall 1993	Fall 1994	Fall 1995	Fall 1996	Fall 1997	Fall 1998	Fall 1999	Fall 2000	Fall 2001	Fall 2002	Fall 2003	Fall 2004	Fall 2005	Fall 2006
1	2	3	4	5	6	7	8	9	10	11	12	13	14	15	16	17	18	19
									Number (in thousands)									
All grades	40,877	39,422	41,217	42,823	43,465	44,111	44,840	45,611	46,127	46,539	46,857	47,204	47,672	48,183	48,540	48,795	49,113	49,299
Elementary	27,647	27,034	29,878	31,088	31,504	31,898	32,341	32,764	33,073	33,346	33,488	33,688	33,938	34,116	34,202	34,179	34,205	34,221
Prekindergarten	96	151	303	505	545	603	637	670	695	729	751	776	865	915	950	990	1,036	1,076
Kindergarten	2,593	3,041	3,306	3,313	3,377	3,444	3,536	3,532	3,503	3,443	3,397	3,382	3,379	3,434	3,503	3,544	3,619	3,630
1st grade	2,894	3,239	3,499	3,542	3,529	3,593	3,671	3,770	3,755	3,727	3,684	3,636	3,614	3,594	3,613	3,663	3,691	3,750
2nd grade	2,800	2,941	3,327	3,431	3,429	3,440	3,507	3,600	3,689	3,681	3,656	3,634	3,593	3,565	3,544	3,580	3,606	3,640
3rd grade	2,893	2,895	3,297	3,361	3,437	3,439	3,445	3,524	3,597	3,696	3,691	3,676	3,653	3,623	3,611	3,580	3,586	3,627
4th grade	3,107	2,771	3,248	3,342	3,361	3,426	3,431	3,454	3,507	3,592	3,686	3,711	3,695	3,669	3,612	3,612	3,578	3,585
5th grade	3,130	2,776	3,197	3,325	3,350	3,372	3,438	3,453	3,458	3,520	3,604	3,707	3,727	3,711	3,685	3,635	3,633	3,601
6th grade	3,038	2,789	3,110	3,303	3,356	3,381	3,395	3,494	3,492	3,497	3,564	3,663	3,769	3,788	3,772	3,735	3,670	3,660
7th grade	3,085	2,938	3,067	3,299	3,355	3,404	3,422	3,464	3,520	3,530	3,541	3,629	3,720	3,821	3,841	3,818	3,777	3,715
8th grade	3,086	2,982	2,979	3,129	3,249	3,302	3,356	3,403	3,415	3,480	3,497	3,538	3,616	3,709	3,809	3,825	3,802	3,765
Elementary ungraded	924	511	543	539	515	494	502	401	442	451	417	336	306	287	256	216	206	171
Secondary	13,231	12,388	11,338	11,735	11,961	12,213	12,500	12,847	13,054	13,193	13,369	13,515	13,734	14,067	14,338	14,617	14,908	15,078
9th grade	3,377	3,439	3,169	3,352	3,487	3,604	3,704	3,801	3,819	3,856	3,935	3,963	4,012	4,105	4,190	4,281	4,287	4,260
10th grade	3,368	3,230	2,896	3,027	3,050	3,131	3,237	3,323	3,376	3,382	3,415	3,491	3,528	3,584	3,675	3,750	3,866	3,881
11th grade	3,195	2,866	2,612	2,656	2,751	2,748	2,826	2,930	2,972	3,021	3,034	3,083	3,174	3,229	3,277	3,369	3,454	3,551
12th grade	2,925	2,550	2,381	2,431	2,424	2,488	2,487	2,586	2,673	2,722	2,782	2,803	2,863	2,990	3,046	3,094	3,180	3,276
Secondary ungraded	366	303	282	269	248	242	245	206	214	212	203	175	157	160	149	121	120	109
									Percentage distribution									
All grades	100.0	100.0	100.0	100.0	100.0	100.0	100.0	100.0	100.0	100.0	100.0	100.0	100.0	100.0	100.0	100.0	100.0	100.0
Elementary	67.6	68.6	72.5	72.6	72.5	72.3	72.1	71.8	71.7	71.7	71.5	71.4	71.2	70.8	70.5	70.0	69.6	69.4
Prekindergarten	0.2	0.4	0.7	1.2	1.3	1.4	1.4	1.5	1.5	1.6	1.6	1.6	1.8	1.9	2.0	2.0	2.1	2.2
Kindergarten	6.3	7.7	8.0	7.7	7.8	7.8	7.9	7.7	7.6	7.4	7.3	7.2	7.1	7.1	7.2	7.3	7.4	7.4
1st grade	7.1	8.2	8.5	8.3	8.1	8.1	8.2	8.3	8.1	8.0	7.9	7.7	7.6	7.5	7.4	7.5	7.5	7.6
2nd grade	6.8	7.5	8.1	8.0	7.9	7.8	7.8	7.9	8.0	7.9	7.8	7.7	7.5	7.4	7.3	7.3	7.3	7.4
3rd grade	7.1	7.3	8.0	7.8	7.9	7.8	7.7	7.7	7.8	7.9	7.9	7.8	7.7	7.5	7.4	7.3	7.3	7.4
4th grade	7.6	7.0	7.9	7.8	7.7	7.8	7.7	7.6	7.6	7.7	7.9	7.9	7.8	7.6	7.5	7.4	7.3	7.3
5th grade	7.7	7.0	7.8	7.8	7.7	7.6	7.7	7.6	7.5	7.6	7.7	7.9	7.8	7.7	7.6	7.4	7.4	7.3
6th grade	7.4	7.1	7.5	7.7	7.7	7.7	7.6	7.6	7.6	7.5	7.6	7.8	7.9	7.9	7.8	7.7	7.5	7.4
7th grade	7.5	7.5	7.4	7.7	7.7	7.7	7.6	7.6	7.6	7.6	7.6	7.7	7.8	7.9	7.9	7.8	7.7	7.5
8th grade	7.5	7.6	7.2	7.3	7.5	7.5	7.5	7.5	7.4	7.5	7.5	7.5	7.6	7.7	7.8	7.8	7.7	7.6
Elementary ungraded	2.3	1.3	1.3	1.3	1.2	1.1	1.1	0.9	1.0	1.0	0.9	0.7	0.6	0.6	0.5	0.4	0.4	0.3
Secondary	32.4	31.4	27.5	27.4	27.5	27.7	27.9	28.2	28.3	28.3	28.5	28.6	28.8	29.2	29.5	30.0	30.4	30.6
9th grade	8.3	8.7	7.7	7.8	8.0	8.2	8.3	8.3	8.3	8.3	8.4	8.4	8.4	8.5	8.6	8.8	8.7	8.6
10th grade	8.2	8.2	7.0	7.1	7.0	7.1	7.2	7.3	7.3	7.3	7.3	7.4	7.4	7.4	7.6	7.7	7.9	7.9
11th grade	7.8	7.3	6.3	6.2	6.3	6.2	6.3	6.4	6.4	6.5	6.5	6.5	6.7	6.7	6.8	6.9	7.0	7.2
12th grade	7.2	6.5	5.8	5.7	5.6	5.6	5.5	5.7	5.8	5.8	5.9	5.9	6.0	6.2	6.3	6.3	6.5	6.6
Secondary ungraded	0.9	0.8	0.7	0.6	0.6	0.5	0.5	0.5	0.5	0.5	0.4	0.4	0.3	0.3	0.3	0.2	0.2	0.2

NOTE: Because of changes in reporting practices and imputation of data for nonrespondents since 1992, prekindergarten enrollment data for 1992 and later years are not comparable to prekindergarten enrollment data for prior years. Some data have been revised from previously published figures. Detail may not sum to totals because of rounding.

SOURCE: U.S. Department of Education, National Center for Education Statistics, *Statistics of Public Elementary and Secondary School Systems, 1980–81*; Common Core of Data (CCD), "State Nonfiscal Survey of Public Elementary/Secondary Education," 1985–86 through 2006–07. (This table was prepared October 2008.)

Table 38. Number and percentage of homeschooled students ages 5 through 17 with a grade equivalent of kindergarten through 12th grade, by selected child, parent, and household characteristics: 1999 and 2003

	1999						2003					
Selected characteristic	Number of students[1] (in thousands)		Number homeschooled (in thousands)		Percent homeschooled		Number of students[1] (in thousands)		Number homeschooled (in thousands)		Percent homeschooled	
1	2		3		4		5		6		7	
Total	50,188	(72.7)	850	(71.1)	1.7	(0.14)	50,707	(89.3)	1,096	(92.3)	2.2	(0.18)
Sex of child												
Male	25,515	(233.9)	417	(43.9)	1.6	(0.17)	25,819	(286.8)	569	(61.9)	2.2	(0.24)
Female	24,673	(238.7)	434	(46.1)	1.8	(0.19)	24,888	(277.7)	527	(58.2)	2.1	(0.23)
Race/ethnicity of child												
White	32,474	(168.2)	640	(62.3)	2.0	(0.19)	31,584	(187.2)	843	(77.5)	2.7	(0.25)
Black	8,047	(102.3)	84	(24.8)	1.0	(0.31)	7,985	(45.7)	103	(33.9)	1.3	(0.42)
Hispanic	7,043	(85.5)	77	(17.7)	1.1	(0.25)	8,075	(35.1)	59	(21.1)	0.7	(0.26)
Other	2,623	(114.2)	49	(17.2)	1.9	(0.65)	3,063	(161.1)	91	(31.5)	3.0	(1.02)
Grade equivalent[2]												
Kindergarten through 5th grade	24,428	(20.5)	428	(48.1)	1.8	(0.20)	24,269	(24.7)	472	(55.3)	1.9	(0.23)
Kindergarten	3,790	(20.0)	92	(19.7)	2.4	(0.52)	3,643	(24.7)	98	(23.5)	2.7	(0.64)
Grades 1 through 3	12,692	(6.2)	199	(36.7)	1.6	(0.29)	12,098	(#)	214	(33.3)	1.8	(0.28)
Grades 4 through 5	7,946	(1.3)	136	(22.5)	1.7	(0.28)	8,528	(#)	160	(30.1)	1.9	(0.35)
Grades 6 through 8	11,788	(3.4)	186	(28.0)	1.6	(0.24)	12,472	(6.5)	302	(44.9)	2.4	(0.36)
Grades 9 through 12	13,954	(70.5)	235	(33.2)	1.7	(0.24)	13,958	(81.8)	315	(47.0)	2.3	(0.33)
Number of children in the household												
One child	8,226	(153.8)	120	(20.3)	1.5	(0.24)	8,033	(218.1)	110	(22.3)	1.4	(0.28)
Two children	19,883	(211.4)	207	(27.1)	1.0	(0.14)	20,530	(319.4)	306	(45.1)	1.5	(0.22)
Three or more children	22,078	(241.2)	523	(65.2)	2.4	(0.30)	22,144	(362.8)	679	(80.2)	3.1	(0.36)
Number of parents in the household												
Two parents	33,007	(203.8)	683	(68.3)	2.1	(0.21)	35,936	(315.1)	886	(82.7)	2.5	(0.23)
One parent	15,454	(209.4)	142	(25.0)	0.9	(0.16)	13,260	(319.2)	196	(42.6)	1.5	(0.32)
Nonparental guardians	1,727	(86.0)	25	(14.4)	1.4	(0.82)	1,511	(100.1)	14	(11.1)	0.9	(0.74)
Parent participation in the labor force												
Two parents—both in labor force	22,880	(241.5)	237	(39.8)	1.0	(0.17)	25,108	(373.1)	274	(44.1)	1.1	(0.18)
Two parents—one in labor force	9,628	(194.4)	444	(53.8)	4.6	(0.55)	10,545	(297.2)	594	(73.7)	5.6	(0.67)
One parent in labor force	13,907	(220.0)	98	(21.8)	0.7	(0.16)	12,045	(267.9)	174	(39.8)	1.4	(0.33)
No parent participation in labor force	3,773	(162.3)	71	(18.8)	1.9	(0.48)	3,008	(171.4)	54	(23.7)	1.8	(0.78)
Highest education level of parents												
High school diploma or less	18,334	(217.3)	160	(26.5)	0.9	(0.15)	16,106	(272.3)	269	(51.6)	1.7	(0.32)
Vocational/technical or some college	15,177	(215.2)	287	(37.3)	1.9	(0.25)	16,068	(323.4)	338	(57.7)	2.1	(0.36)
Bachelor's degree	8,269	(182.5)	213	(36.2)	2.6	(0.42)	9,798	(277.3)	274	(47.2)	2.8	(0.48)
Graduate/professional degree	8,407	(207.1)	190	(39.8)	2.3	(0.46)	8,734	(238.1)	215	(44.2)	2.5	(0.51)
Household income												
$25,000 or less	16,776	(116.9)	262	(45.0)	1.6	(0.27)	12,375	(53.6)	283	(56.0)	2.3	(0.45)
$25,001 to $50,000	15,220	(232.7)	278	(36.7)	1.8	(0.24)	13,220	(270.2)	311	(49.9)	2.4	(0.37)
$50,001 to $75,000	8,576	(189.3)	162	(25.5)	1.9	(0.30)	10,961	(282.2)	264	(51.1)	2.4	(0.46)
Over $75,000	9,615	(211.2)	148	(26.5)	1.5	(0.28)	14,150	(261.7)	238	(45.8)	1.7	(0.33)
Urbanicity[3]												
Urban	37,415	(185.2)	575	(51.0)	1.5	(0.15)	40,180	(187.2)	794	(76.6)	2.0	(0.22)
Rural	12,773	(112.6)	275	(39.8)	2.2	(0.31)	10,527	(56.3)	302	(58.0)	2.9	(0.55)
Region												
Northeast	10,220	(103.7)	114	(30.1)	1.1	(0.30)	9,220	(42.6)	168	(53.3)	1.8	(0.58)
South	17,366	(122.5)	355	(48.4)	2.0	(0.28)	17,232	(55.0)	445	(66.7)	2.6	(0.39)
Midwest	12,040	(114.1)	166	(28.6)	1.4	(0.24)	11,949	(61.3)	238	(43.9)	2.0	(0.37)
West	10,560	(97.3)	215	(35.9)	2.0	(0.34)	12,305	(39.8)	245	(42.3)	2.0	(0.34)

#Rounds to zero.
[1]Refers to all students in public and private schools and homeschooled students.
[2]Students whose grade-equivalent was "ungraded" were excluded from the grade analysis. The percentage of students with an "ungraded" grade equivalent was 0.03 percent in 1999 and 0.02 percent in 2003.
[3]Urbanicity is based on a U.S. Census Bureau classification of places. Urban is a place with at least 50,000 people. Rural is a place not classified as urban.

NOTE: The number and percentage of homeschoolers exclude students who were enrolled in school for more than 25 hours a week and students who were only homeschooled due to a temporary illness. Race categories exclude persons of Hispanic ethnicity. Standard errors appear in parentheses.
SOURCE: U.S. Department of Education, National Center for Education Statistics, *Homeschooling in the United States: 2003*, Parent Survey (Parent:1999) and Parent and Family Involvement in Education Survey (PFI:2003) of the National Household Education Surveys Program. (This table was prepared September 2006.)

Table 39. Percentage distribution of students ages 5 through 17 attending kindergarten through 12th grade, by school type or participation in homeschooling and selected child, parent, and household characteristics: 1999 and 2003

Selected characteristic	1999								2003							
	Public school				Private school		Homeschooled[1]		Public school				Private school		Homeschooled[1]	
	Assigned		Chosen						Assigned		Chosen					
1	2		3		4		5		6		7		8		9	
Total..................................	76.1	(0.46)	12.3	(0.32)	10.0	(0.28)	1.7	(0.14)	72.1	(0.57)	15.0	(0.41)	10.8	(0.39)	2.2	(0.18)
Sex of child																
Male.......................	76.8	(0.62)	11.9	(0.43)	9.7	(0.34)	1.6	(0.17)	72.1	(0.70)	15.0	(0.56)	10.7	(0.48)	2.2	(0.24)
Female....................	75.3	(0.58)	12.6	(0.42)	10.3	(0.41)	1.8	(0.19)	72.1	(0.78)	14.9	(0.54)	10.8	(0.51)	2.1	(0.23)
Race/ethnicity of child																
White.......................	77.2	(0.56)	9.0	(0.33)	11.9	(0.39)	2.0	(0.19)	72.7	(0.67)	12.4	(0.47)	12.2	(0.48)	2.7	(0.25)
Black.......................	71.7	(1.17)	21.0	(1.14)	6.2	(0.47)	1.0	(0.31)	66.6	(1.49)	23.4	(1.45)	8.6	(0.85)	1.3	(0.42)
Hispanic..................	77.8	(1.02)	15.9	(0.90)	5.2	(0.40)	1.1	(0.25)	77.2	(1.17)	15.0	(0.99)	7.1	(0.66)	0.7	(0.26)
Other......................	71.0	(2.14)	16.1	(1.89)	11.0	(1.35)	1.9	(0.65)	67.1	(2.59)	18.7	(1.94)	11.3	(1.61)	3.0	(1.02)
Disability status of child as reported by parent																
Has a disability.........................	77.1	(0.90)	13.1	(0.74)	8.0	(0.49)	1.9	(0.27)	72.4	(1.12)	16.2	(0.75)	9.2	(0.70)	2.2	(0.35)
Does not have a disability..........................	75.8	(0.50)	12.0	(0.32)	10.5	(0.34)	1.7	(0.16)	72.0	(0.67)	14.5	(0.51)	11.3	(0.44)	2.1	(0.21)
Grade equivalent[2]																
Kindergarten through 5th grade..............	73.7	(0.67)	12.9	(0.46)	11.6	(0.41)	1.8	(0.20)	70.1	(0.70)	16.2	(0.56)	11.8	(0.53)	1.9	(0.23)
Kindergarten	68.1	(1.65)	13.6	(1.06)	15.9	(1.29)	2.4	(0.52)	69.0	(1.50)	15.5	(1.18)	12.8	(1.21)	2.7	(0.64)
Grades 1 through 3.................	74.5	(0.89)	13.1	(0.66)	10.9	(0.53)	1.6	(0.29)	70.0	(1.18)	16.2	(0.96)	12.1	(0.73)	1.8	(0.28)
Grades 4 through 5.................	75.3	(1.17)	12.3	(0.81)	10.7	(0.77)	1.7	(0.28)	70.7	(1.12)	16.5	(0.96)	10.9	(0.76)	1.9	(0.35)
Grades 6 through 8.................	79.1	(0.76)	9.8	(0.59)	9.5	(0.47)	1.6	(0.24)	73.3	(1.03)	14.1	(0.81)	10.2	(0.59)	2.4	(0.36)
Grades 9 through 12.................	77.5	(0.73)	13.2	(0.56)	7.5	(0.44)	1.7	(0.24)	74.6	(0.97)	13.6	(0.76)	9.5	(0.63)	2.3	(0.33)
Number of parents in the household																
Two parents........................	76.4	(0.56)	10.1	(0.34)	11.5	(0.37)	2.1	(0.21)	71.8	(0.67)	13.6	(0.51)	12.1	(0.47)	2.5	(0.23)
One parent..........................	75.6	(0.75)	16.1	(0.51)	7.3	(0.47)	0.9	(0.16)	72.9	(1.08)	18.1	(0.97)	7.6	(0.67)	1.5	(0.32)
Nonparental guardians	74.2	(2.48)	19.3	(2.44)	5.1	(0.84)	1.4	(0.82)	73.9	(2.88)	19.3	(2.42)	5.9	(1.27)	0.9	(0.74)
Highest education level of parents																
Less than a high school diploma	80.7	(1.33)	16.4	(1.39)	2.7	(0.51)	0.2	(0.10)	76.9	(2.06)	18.9	(1.76)	2.9	(1.18)	1.3	(0.73)
High school diploma or GED	80.6	(0.83)	12.7	(0.70)	5.6	(0.44)	1.1	(0.19)	77.8	(1.01)	15.5	(0.89)	4.9	(0.45)	1.8	(0.34)
Vocational/technical or some college..........	78.0	(0.70)	12.4	(0.58)	7.7	(0.40)	1.9	(0.25)	74.0	(0.97)	15.5	(0.74)	8.3	(0.58)	2.1	(0.36)
Bachelor's degree.......................	70.7	(1.12)	10.6	(0.69)	16.1	(0.76)	2.6	(0.42)	67.0	(1.12)	13.0	(0.89)	17.2	(0.94)	2.8	(0.48)
Graduate/professional degree	67.8	(1.09)	10.6	(0.72)	19.3	(0.82)	2.3	(0.46)	64.2	(1.43)	13.7	(1.05)	19.7	(1.16)	2.5	(0.51)
Poverty status of household																
Below poverty	77.0	(1.15)	16.9	(1.02)	4.3	(0.49)	1.9	(0.40)	76.2	(1.35)	17.6	(1.11)	3.6	(0.70)	2.7	(0.65)
Between poverty and 200 percent of poverty	78.0	(1.10)	13.8	(0.82)	5.7	(0.68)	2.4	(0.49)	75.7	(1.91)	16.3	(1.71)	4.7	(0.83)	3.3	(0.79)
At or above 200 percent of poverty.............	75.3	(0.49)	10.3	(0.29)	12.9	(0.40)	1.5	(0.13)	70.7	(0.65)	14.2	(0.50)	13.2	(0.50)	1.9	(0.19)
Urbanicity[3]																
Urban..................................	73.2	(0.53)	13.6	(0.36)	11.7	(0.33)	1.5	(0.15)	70.1	(0.61)	15.6	(0.46)	12.4	(0.42)	2.0	(0.22)
Rural...................................	84.6	(0.73)	8.3	(0.57)	5.0	(0.46)	2.2	(0.31)	79.9	(1.35)	12.6	(1.16)	4.6	(0.69)	2.9	(0.55)
Region																
Northeast..........................	75.1	(1.00)	11.1	(0.76)	12.6	(0.63)	1.1	(0.30)	71.6	(1.42)	11.9	(1.02)	14.6	(1.03)	1.8	(0.58)
South	77.1	(0.64)	11.6	(0.48)	9.3	(0.43)	2.0	(0.28)	74.2	(0.88)	14.9	(0.72)	8.3	(0.58)	2.6	(0.39)
Midwest............................	76.5	(0.80)	11.2	(0.66)	10.9	(0.61)	1.4	(0.24)	69.9	(1.27)	14.4	(0.92)	13.8	(1.04)	2.0	(0.37)
West.................................	74.8	(0.97)	15.7	(0.74)	7.5	(0.49)	2.0	(0.34)	71.9	(1.07)	17.9	(0.97)	8.3	(0.59)	2.0	(0.34)

[1]Excludes students who were enrolled in school for more than 25 hours a week and students who were only homeschooled due to a temporary illness.
[2]Students whose grade-equivalent was "ungraded" were excluded from the grade analysis. The percentage of students with an "ungraded" grade equivalent was 0.03 percent in 1999 and 0.02 percent in 2003.
[3]Urbanicity is based on a U.S. Census Bureau classification of places. Urban is a place with at least 50,000 people. Rural is a place not classified as urban.

NOTE: Race categories exclude persons of Hispanic ethnicity. Detail may not sum to totals because of rounding. Standard errors appear in parentheses.
SOURCE: U.S. Department of Education, National Center for Education Statistics, Parent Survey (Parent:1999) and Parent and Family Involvement in Education Survey (PFI:2003) of the National Household Education Surveys Program. (This table was prepared May 2007.)

Table 40. Average daily attendance in public elementary and secondary schools, by state or jurisdiction: Selected years, 1969–70 through 2005–06

State or jurisdiction	1969–70	1979–80	1989–90	1994–95	1999–2000	2000–01	2001–02	2002–03	2003–04	2004–05	2005–06
1	2	3	4	5	6	7	8	9	10	11	12
United States	41,934,376	38,288,911	37,799,296	40,720,763	43,806,726	44,075,930	44,604,592	45,017,360	45,325,731	45,625,458	45,931,617
Alabama	777,123	711,432	683,833	687,047	725,212	719,562	702,423	701,235	706,446	706,588	714,197
Alaska	72,489	79,945	98,213	113,874	122,412	122,932	123,316	123,145	122,341	121,699	122,010
Arizona	391,526	481,905	557,252	658,084	782,851	803,453	834,036	868,547	878,891	911,640	933,663
Arkansas	414,158	423,610	403,025	420,229	422,958	421,625	422,817	418,775	425,571	430,290	435,278
California[1]	4,418,423	4,044,736	4,893,341	5,198,308	5,957,216	6,075,001	6,219,160	6,312,362	6,384,882	6,373,959	6,349,270
Colorado	500,388	513,475	519,419	594,019	656,700	671,909	707,202	709,349	673,285	700,485	712,476
Connecticut	618,881	507,362	439,524	481,742	533,779	540,946	547,194	557,701	561,530	559,478	558,423
Delaware	120,819	94,058	89,838	98,793	106,444	105,681	107,730	109,945	108,751	110,393	113,986
District of Columbia	138,600	91,576	71,468	71,446	65,371	62,881	62,681	61,236	65,625	70,817	59,137
Florida	1,312,693	1,464,461	1,646,583	1,927,172	2,175,453	2,269,372	2,326,142	2,362,841	2,418,329	2,463,323	2,494,778
Georgia	1,019,427	989,433	1,054,097	1,181,724	1,326,713	1,347,218	1,379,176	1,400,007	1,424,004	1,460,767	1,499,317
Hawaii	168,140	151,563	157,360	169,254	171,180	171,117	170,268	169,797	167,739	169,825	168,009
Idaho	170,920	189,199	203,987	225,986	230,828	230,890	231,861	234,244	237,095	241,590	247,009
Illinois	2,084,844	1,770,435	1,587,733	1,734,175	1,789,089	1,805,582	1,837,863	1,855,417	1,862,274	1,862,046	1,871,619
Indiana	1,111,043	983,444	884,568	900,017	929,281	928,703	931,886	942,506	943,735	944,944	966,967
Iowa	624,403	510,081	450,224	478,285	471,384	467,404	462,276	459,761	457,771	456,559	477,491
Kansas	470,296	382,019	388,986	413,699	426,853	425,036	413,670	419,285	415,529	411,455	407,812
Kentucky	647,970	619,868	569,795	572,952	565,693	564,198	566,451	569,538	570,911	574,380	580,937
Louisiana	776,555	727,601	727,125	730,148	701,957	684,566	680,122	674,949	674,333	670,238	648,243
Maine	225,146	211,400	195,089	199,387	194,554	191,963	190,477	188,776	187,492	184,374	180,223
Maryland	785,989	686,336	620,617	701,594	791,133	797,522	807,331	809,398	808,557	804,696	800,553
Massachusetts	1,056,207	935,960	763,231	831,918	913,502	920,522	921,266	921,201	932,417	930,338	930,151
Michigan	1,991,235	1,758,427	1,446,996	1,492,653	1,574,894	1,577,260	1,588,300	1,591,900	1,590,555	1,583,496	1,574,023
Minnesota	864,595	748,606	699,001	770,549	818,819	820,457	818,160	813,660	792,896	788,354	787,521
Mississippi	524,623	454,401	476,048	470,974	468,746	465,505	461,951	461,269	463,470	463,816	461,112
Missouri	906,132	777,269	729,693	794,177	836,105	836,411	843,148	849,040	851,749	851,114	859,441
Montana	162,664	144,608	135,406	148,325	142,313	139,198	136,498	133,988	132,356	130,998	129,948
Nebraska	314,516	270,524	254,754	268,732	261,767	268,897	267,909	269,499	260,352	260,725	262,805
Nevada	113,421	134,995	173,149	229,862	305,067	321,679	334,853	346,512	364,409	378,186	383,403
New Hampshire	140,203	154,187	154,915	179,892	200,283	198,389	199,429	200,184	202,352	201,242	199,952
New Jersey	1,322,124	1,140,111	997,561	1,102,565	1,222,438	1,257,124	1,297,217	1,312,610	1,336,869	1,341,156	1,358,562
New Mexico	259,997	253,453	290,245	314,822	323,963	319,939	320,082	320,189	319,637	322,046	323,964
New York	3,099,192	2,530,289	2,244,110	2,388,973	2,595,070	2,598,176	2,610,320	2,614,977	2,599,902	2,581,772	2,556,705
North Carolina	1,104,295	1,072,150	1,012,274	1,071,640	1,185,737	1,203,143	1,225,681	1,242,234	1,264,266	1,289,444	1,319,335
North Dakota	141,961	118,986	109,659	111,502	105,123	103,420	100,028	97,879	96,231	94,823	92,843
Ohio	2,246,282	1,849,283	1,584,735	1,627,984	1,659,903	1,653,316	1,654,816	1,683,337	1,700,533	1,719,566	1,730,080
Oklahoma	560,993	548,065	543,170	570,381	586,266	580,754	580,894	581,767	583,932	587,188	591,486
Oregon	436,736	418,593	419,771	458,107	479,321	481,223	483,038	487,544	486,073	506,638	513,650
Pennsylvania	2,169,225	1,808,630	1,524,839	1,629,877	1,684,913	1,683,637	1,691,123	1,694,148	1,701,096	1,698,795	1,702,566
Rhode Island	163,205	139,195	125,934	136,229	144,422	144,895	145,330	144,813	143,792	143,939	139,001
South Carolina	600,292	569,612	569,029	608,699	624,456	623,008	628,510	629,997	635,750	639,950	647,703
South Dakota	158,543	124,934	119,823	128,335	122,252	120,966	118,919	118,383	116,651	115,148	114,673
Tennessee	836,010	806,696	761,766	806,895	844,878	846,551	849,413	850,322	859,522	868,129	881,414
Texas	2,432,420	2,608,817	3,075,333	3,364,830	3,706,550	3,771,568	3,860,613	3,940,776	4,016,791	4,084,792	4,186,812
Utah	287,405	312,813	408,917	442,617	448,096	447,450	448,557	451,063	456,183	464,645	478,233
Vermont	97,772	95,045	87,832	98,608	98,894	97,717	96,996	95,868	95,160	93,608	92,508
Virginia	995,580	955,105	989,197	1,079,496	1,195,123	1,087,591	1,099,677	1,109,459	1,118,446	1,133,882	1,141,790
Washington	764,735	710,929	755,141	870,163	925,696	927,530	931,533	933,702	937,656	941,238	946,824
West Virginia	372,278	353,264	301,947	287,937	273,277	264,798	262,581	260,365	266,078	271,197	271,780
Wisconsin	880,609	770,554	711,466	782,395	825,699	824,002	821,934	831,939	826,864	831,809	834,177
Wyoming	81,293	89,471	91,277	93,691	86,092	83,243	81,734	79,921	78,652	77,878	77,757
Other jurisdictions											
American Samoa	—	—	11,448	14,000	15,102	14,818	15,487	15,243	15,123	15,302	15,237
Guam	20,315	—	23,883	31,779	—	—	—	—	28,301	—	29,617
Northern Marianas	—	—	6,809	7,351	8,712	8,968	9,426	9,739	10,047	10,301	10,871
Puerto Rico	—	656,709	597,436	547,561	540,676	538,738	536,481	535,874	534,941	540,365	522,655
U.S. Virgin Islands	—	—	18,924	20,339	18,676	16,069	17,181	16,187	15,878	15,841	15,241

—Not available.
[1]Data for California for 1989–90 and earlier years are not strictly comparable with those for other states because California's attendance figures included excused absences.

SOURCE: U.S. Department of Education, National Center for Education Statistics, *Statistics of State School Systems, 1969–70*; *Revenues and Expenditures for Public Elementary and Secondary Education, 1979–80*; and Common Core of Data (CCD), "National Public Education Financial Survey," 1989–90 through 2005–06. (This table was prepared April 2008.)

Table 41. Percentage distribution of enrollment in public elementary and secondary schools, by race/ethnicity and state or jurisdiction: Fall 1996 and fall 2006

State or jurisdiction	Percentage distribution, fall 1996						Percentage distribution, fall 2006					
	Total	White	Black	Hispanic	Asian/Pacific Islander	American Indian/ Alaska Native	Total	White	Black	Hispanic	Asian/Pacific Islander	American Indian/ Alaska Native
1	2	3	4	5	6	7	8	9	10	11	12	13
United States	100.0	64.2	16.9	14.0	3.8	1.1	100.0	56.5	17.1	20.5	4.7	1.2
Alabama	100.0	61.5	36.4	0.7	0.6	0.7	100.0	59.1	35.9	3.2	1.1	0.8
Alaska.........................	100.0	63.1	4.7	2.9	4.5	24.8	100.0	57.4	4.6	4.4	7.0	26.6
Arizona	100.0	56.6	4.3	30.1	1.8	7.2	100.0	45.4	5.4	41.0	2.6	5.6
Arkansas.....................	100.0	73.5	23.5	1.8	0.7	0.4	100.0	67.6	22.7	7.5	1.5	0.7
California	100.0	39.5	8.7	39.7	11.2	0.9	100.0	30.2	7.8	49.5	11.7	0.8
Colorado	100.0	72.0	5.5	18.8	2.6	1.1	100.0	61.9	6.0	27.6	3.3	1.2
Connecticut..................	100.0	71.7	13.6	11.9	2.5	0.3	100.0	66.0	13.9	16.0	3.7	0.4
Delaware......................	100.0	63.9	29.9	4.3	1.8	0.2	100.0	53.9	33.0	9.8	3.0	0.4
District of Columbia	100.0	4.0	87.3	7.2	1.4	0.1	100.0	5.0	83.4	9.9	1.6	0.1
Florida.........................	100.0	56.7	25.4	15.9	1.8	0.2	100.0	48.4	23.9	25.0	2.4	0.3
Georgia.......................	100.0	57.9	37.6	2.6	1.7	0.1	100.0	48.2	39.2	9.5	2.9	0.1
Hawaii.........................	100.0	25.0	3.3	4.9	66.4	0.4	100.0	19.6	2.4	4.5	73.0	0.6
Idaho..........................	100.0	88.0	0.7	8.9	1.2	1.3	100.0	82.3	1.1	13.4	1.6	1.6
Illinois.........................	100.0	62.8	21.2	12.8	3.1	0.1	100.0	55.9	20.3	19.7	3.9	0.2
Indiana........................	100.0	85.4	11.2	2.4	0.8	0.2	100.0	79.5	12.6	6.3	1.3	0.3
Iowa...........................	100.0	92.2	3.4	2.4	1.6	0.5	100.0	85.9	5.3	6.2	2.0	0.6
Kansas........................	100.0	81.9	8.6	6.5	1.9	1.1	100.0	73.9	8.9	13.0	2.5	1.7
Kentucky	100.0	88.9	9.9	0.5	0.6	0.1	100.0	85.8	10.7	2.4	1.0	0.1
Louisiana	100.0	50.6	46.4	1.2	1.3	0.6	100.0	50.1	45.4	2.4	1.4	0.8
Maine..........................	100.0	97.2	0.9	0.4	0.9	0.6	100.0	94.6	2.3	1.0	1.4	0.7
Maryland......................	100.0	56.7	35.6	3.5	3.9	0.3	100.0	47.8	38.1	8.3	5.4	0.4
Massachusetts...............	100.0	77.9	8.4	9.6	4.0	0.2	100.0	72.9	8.4	13.6	4.9	0.3
Michigan	100.0	75.8	18.8	2.8	1.5	1.0	100.0	71.8	20.2	4.5	2.4	0.9
Minnesota	100.0	86.5	5.2	2.2	4.1	1.9	100.0	77.2	9.1	5.7	5.9	2.1
Mississippi	100.0	47.9	51.0	0.4	0.6	0.2	100.0	46.5	50.8	1.7	0.8	0.2
Missouri.......................	100.0	81.1	16.5	1.1	1.0	0.3	100.0	76.3	18.1	3.4	1.7	0.4
Montana.......................	100.0	87.2	0.6	1.5	0.8	9.9	100.0	83.9	1.0	2.5	1.2	11.4
Nebraska	100.0	86.4	6.0	4.9	1.3	1.4	100.0	76.5	7.7	12.2	1.9	1.7
Nevada	100.0	65.1	9.6	18.8	4.6	1.9	100.0	44.4	11.1	35.4	7.6	1.6
New Hampshire	100.0	96.4	1.0	1.3	1.1	0.2	100.0	92.9	1.8	2.9	2.0	0.3
New Jersey	100.0	62.5	18.5	13.5	5.4	0.2	100.0	55.7	17.4	18.8	7.9	0.2
New Mexico	100.0	38.8	2.4	47.7	1.0	10.2	100.0	30.6	2.6	54.6	1.3	10.9
New York......................	100.0	56.3	20.3	17.6	5.2	0.5	100.0	52.1	19.7	20.6	7.2	0.5
North Carolina	100.0	63.9	30.8	2.3	1.5	1.5	100.0	57.5	29.2	9.6	2.3	1.5
North Dakota	100.0	89.1	0.9	1.1	0.7	8.1	100.0	86.8	1.8	1.8	1.0	8.6
Ohio...........................	100.0	82.0	15.4	1.4	1.0	0.1	100.0	78.8	17.1	2.6	1.4	0.1
Oklahoma	100.0	68.8	10.5	4.3	1.3	15.1	100.0	58.6	10.8	9.5	1.8	19.3
Oregon........................	100.0	84.6	2.6	7.4	3.4	2.0	100.0	73.2	3.1	16.7	4.8	2.2
Pennsylvania.................	100.0	80.2	14.2	3.7	1.8	0.1	100.0	74.6	15.9	6.8	2.6	0.2
Rhode Island	100.0	78.3	7.3	10.7	3.3	0.5	100.0	69.5	8.8	18.0	3.1	0.7
South Carolina...............	100.0	56.0	42.2	0.8	0.8	0.2	100.0	53.9	39.8	4.6	1.4	0.3
South Dakota.................	100.0	83.7	1.0	0.8	0.8	13.8	100.0	84.5	1.7	2.1	1.0	10.6
Tennessee	100.0	74.6	23.4	0.9	1.0	0.1	100.0	69.1	24.8	4.4	1.5	0.2
Texas	100.0	45.6	14.3	37.4	2.4	0.3	100.0	35.7	14.4	46.3	3.3	0.3
Utah...........................	100.0	89.5	0.7	6.0	2.4	1.5	100.0	80.8	1.4	13.2	3.1	1.5
Vermont.......................	100.0	97.3	0.8	0.4	1.0	0.6	100.0	95.3	1.6	1.0	1.6	0.4
Virginia........................	100.0	67.7	25.5	3.3	3.4	0.2	100.0	59.3	26.7	8.3	5.4	0.3
Washington...................	100.0	77.5	4.8	8.3	6.7	2.7	100.0	68.9	5.7	14.3	8.4	2.6
West Virginia..................	100.0	95.2	4.0	0.5	0.3	0.1	100.0	93.3	5.1	0.8	0.7	0.1
Wisconsin.....................	100.0	82.6	9.6	3.5	2.9	1.3	100.0	77.3	10.5	7.2	3.6	1.5
Wyoming......................	100.0	89.0	1.2	6.2	0.8	2.8	100.0	84.5	1.5	9.4	1.1	3.5
Bureau of Indian Education	—	—	—	—	—	—	—	—	—	—	—	—
DoD, overseas	—	—	—	—	—	—	100.0	55.7	19.6	14.3	9.8	0.5
DoD, domestic	—	—	—	—	—	—	100.0	51.3	23.3	21.5	2.4	1.4
Other jurisdictions												
American Samoa	100.0	0.0	0.0	0.0	100.0	0.0	100.0	0.0	0.0	0.0	100.0	0.0
Guam......................	100.0	5.3	1.2	0.9	92.6	0.1	—	—	—	—	—	—
Northern Marianas.......	100.0	0.8	0.0	0.0	99.2	0.0	100.0	0.4	0.1	0.0	99.5	0.0
Puerto Rico.................	100.0	0.0	0.0	100.0	0.0	0.0	100.0	0.0	0.0	100.0	0.0	0.0
U.S. Virgin Islands........	100.0	1.1	84.6	14.0	0.2	#	100.0	1.1	83.3	15.3	0.2	0.2

—Not available.
#Rounds to zero.
NOTE: Percentage distribution based on students for whom race/ethnicity was reported, which may be less than the total number of students in the state. Race categories exclude persons of Hispanic ethnicity. DoD = Department of Defense. Detail may not sum to totals because of rounding.

SOURCE: U.S. Department of Education, National Center for Education Statistics, Common Core of Data (CCD), "State Nonfiscal Survey of Public Elementary/Secondary Education," 1996–97 and 2006–07. (This table was prepared October 2008.)

Table 42. Number and percentage of public school students eligible for free or reduced-price lunch, by state: 2000–01, 2004–05, 2005–06, and 2006–07

State or jurisdiction	Number of students				Number of students eligible for free/reduced-price lunch				Percent of students eligible for free/reduced-price lunch			
	2000–01	2004–05	2005–06	2006–07	2000–01	2004–05	2005–06	2006–07	2000–01	2004–05	2005–06	2006–07
1	2	3	4	5	6	7	8	9	10	11	12	13
United States	—	—	48,912,085	—	—	—	20,333,474	—	—	—	41.6	—
Alabama	728,351	721,205	741,547	743,469	335,143	376,494	383,219	379,537	46.0	52.2	51.7	51.0
Alaska	105,333	103,052	133,292	116,682	32,468	38,058	41,872	45,028	30.8	36.9	31.4	38.6
Arizona	—	933,789	1,094,454	1,014,149	—	500,442	492,450	434,432	—	53.6	45.0	42.8
Arkansas	449,959	463,121	474,206	476,132	205,058	240,352	250,641	279,400	45.6	51.9	52.9	58.7
California	6,050,753	6,322,433	6,312,103	6,210,343	2,820,611	3,100,883	3,063,627	3,119,120	46.6	49.0	48.5	50.2
Colorado	724,349	765,976	779,826	789,014	195,148	241,569	258,264	269,926	26.9	31.5	33.1	34.2
Connecticut	—	577,387	575,058	558,532	—	151,723	152,669	156,735	—	26.3	26.5	28.1
Delaware	114,676	119,091	120,937	121,886	37,766	42,411	43,682	45,163	32.9	35.6	36.1	37.1
District of Columbia	68,380	76,470	76,876	61,922	47,839	50,455	41,050	38,425	70.0	66.0	53.4	62.1
Florida	2,434,755	2,639,304	2,675,024	2,670,482	1,079,009	1,249,976	1,224,228	1,207,511	44.3	47.4	45.8	45.2
Georgia	1,444,937	1,553,435	1,598,461	1,628,309	624,511	743,797	795,394	819,824	43.2	47.9	49.8	50.3
Hawaii	184,357	184,096	184,925	179,730	80,657	76,597	74,926	73,650	43.8	41.6	40.5	41.0
Idaho	244,755	249,831	261,844	265,045	85,824	98,743	99,093	99,639	35.1	39.5	37.8	37.6
Illinois	—	1,989,386	2,111,706	1,944,728	—	785,978	785,715	794,322	—	39.5	37.2	40.8
Indiana	977,219	1,005,569	1,034,782	1,044,175	285,267	365,374	373,433	392,272	29.2	36.3	36.1	37.6
Iowa	492,021	477,007	481,099	481,181	131,553	148,429	154,416	155,065	26.7	31.1	32.1	32.2
Kansas	462,594	466,577	466,266	459,171	154,693	179,878	180,919	182,860	33.4	38.6	38.8	39.8
Kentucky	626,723	—	641,685	646,461	298,334	—	336,287	331,361	47.6	—	52.4	51.3
Louisiana	741,162	723,854	654,397	675,381	433,068	445,808	400,596	416,402	58.4	61.6	61.2	61.7
Maine	198,532	192,145	195,498	192,078	60,162	64,301	65,877	67,289	30.3	33.5	33.7	35.0
Maryland	852,911	865,553	860,020	850,026	255,872	277,669	272,069	274,539	30.0	32.1	31.6	32.3
Massachusetts	979,590	975,571	971,909	958,858	237,871	270,651	274,515	280,165	24.3	27.7	28.2	29.2
Michigan	1,703,260	1,625,345	1,711,544	1,713,777	504,044	584,773	609,754	619,879	29.6	36.0	35.6	36.2
Minnesota	854,154	838,433	839,084	838,453	218,867	247,520	253,938	259,532	25.6	29.5	30.3	31.0
Mississippi	497,421	493,682	494,954	494,686	319,670	318,743	344,107	334,359	64.3	64.6	69.5	67.6
Missouri	912,247	904,123	915,850	919,668	315,608	353,559	358,428	359,193	34.6	39.1	39.1	39.1
Montana	154,438	144,049	145,416	142,137	47,415	49,367	50,172	50,656	30.7	34.3	34.5	35.6
Nebraska	286,138	285,719	286,646	286,823	87,045	99,325	99,387	104,783	30.4	34.8	34.7	36.5
Nevada	282,621	397,502	412,407	—	92,978	114,155	170,039	—	32.9	28.7	41.2	—
New Hampshire	206,919	205,870	205,767	201,108	31,212	34,162	35,087	35,945	15.1	16.6	17.1	17.9
New Jersey	1,312,983	—	1,395,602	1,333,110	357,728	—	373,946	378,927	27.2	—	26.8	28.4
New Mexico	320,303	326,103	326,758	326,113	174,939	189,523	181,916	198,304	54.6	58.1	55.7	60.8
New York	2,859,927	2,836,334	2,838,209	2,753,057	1,236,945	515,130	1,260,933	1,229,063	43.3	18.2	44.4	44.6
North Carolina	1,194,371	1,351,576	1,416,436	1,422,787	470,316	624,500	603,316	624,349	39.4	46.2	42.6	43.9
North Dakota	109,201	100,508	98,284	96,587	31,840	29,204	29,064	29,246	29.2	29.1	29.6	30.3
Ohio	1,745,237	1,836,119	1,836,991	1,832,100	494,829	575,202	597,517	619,247	28.4	31.3	32.5	33.8
Oklahoma	623,110	628,837	634,739	638,736	300,179	339,012	346,070	352,841	48.2	53.9	54.5	55.2
Oregon	535,617	538,360	534,823	553,054	186,203	225,735	230,737	232,435	34.8	41.9	43.1	42.0
Pennsylvania	1,798,977	1,809,674	1,828,287	1,757,776	510,121	516,075	574,951	556,645	28.4	28.5	31.4	31.7
Rhode Island	157,347	154,863	151,690	149,441	52,209	50,172	53,521	49,558	33.2	32.4	35.3	33.2
South Carolina	677,411	701,700	701,544	702,851	320,254	367,133	361,567	360,907	47.3	52.3	51.5	51.3
South Dakota	128,598	122,791	122,008	115,450	37,857	36,845	39,059	34,996	29.4	30.0	32.0	30.3
Tennessee	—	—	953,798	958,352	—	—	448,431	466,781	—	—	47.0	48.7
Texas	4,059,353	4,403,057	4,523,873	4,566,432	1,823,029	2,098,348	2,181,697	2,172,930	44.9	47.7	48.2	47.6
Utah	470,265	494,533	508,430	520,331	135,428	160,051	164,255	160,559	28.8	32.4	32.3	30.9
Vermont	102,049	97,760	96,638	91,238	23,986	24,592	25,487	24,467	23.5	25.2	26.4	26.8
Virginia	1,067,710	1,147,470	1,214,229	1,172,057	320,233	374,532	377,725	383,298	30.0	32.6	31.1	32.7
Washington	—	1,019,982	1,031,985	1,021,710	—	368,022	376,198	375,159	—	36.1	36.5	36.7
West Virginia	286,285	280,124	280,703	281,070	143,446	141,053	137,878	139,804	50.1	50.4	49.1	49.7
Wisconsin	859,276	849,780	875,066	870,647	219,276	253,082	256,645	271,422	25.5	29.8	29.3	31.2
Wyoming	89,895	84,429	84,409	85,187	43,483	27,141	26,707	25,284	48.4	32.1	31.6	29.7

—Not available.
NOTE: Table reflects counts of students enrolled in schools for which both enrollment data and free/reduced price lunch eligibility data were reported.

SOURCE: U.S. Department of Education, National Center for Education Statistics, Common Core of Data (CCD), "Public Elementary/Secondary School Universe Survey," 2000–01, 2004–05, 2005–06 and 2006–07. (This table was prepared October 2008.)

Table 43. Enrollment of 3-, 4-, and 5-year-old children in preprimary programs, by level of program, control of program, and attendance status: Selected years, 1965 through 2007

[In thousands]

Year and age	Total population, 3 to 5 years old	Enrollment by level and control							Enrollment by attendance		
		Total	Percent enrolled	Nursery school		Kindergarten			Full-day	Part-day	Percent full-day
				Public	Private	Public	Private				
1	2	3	4	5	6	7	8		9	10	11
Total, 3 to 5 years old											
1965	12,549 (144.5)	3,407 (87.1)	27.1 (0.69)	127 (19.6)	393 (34.1)	2,291 (75.6)	596 (41.6)	— (†)	— (†)	— (†)
1970	10,949 (109.4)	4,104 (71.5)	37.5 (0.65)	332 (25.3)	762 (37.6)	2,498 (62.0)	511 (31.1)	698 (36.1)	3,405 (68.3)	17.0 (0.83)
1975	10,185 (105.8)	4,955 (71.2)	48.7 (0.70)	570 (32.7)	1,174 (45.5)	2,682 (62.7)	528 (31.6)	1,295 (47.4)	3,659 (68.3)	26.1 (0.88)
1980	9,284 (102.6)	4,878 (68.8)	52.5 (0.74)	628 (34.6)	1,353 (48.6)	2,438 (60.6)	459 (29.9)	1,551 (51.4)	3,327 (66.1)	31.8 (0.95)
1985	10,733 (115.6)	5,865 (77.6)	54.6 (0.72)	846 (42.0)	1,631 (56.0)	2,847 (68.8)	541 (34.1)	2,144 (62.3)	3,722 (74.2)	36.6 (0.95)
1990	11,207 (124.2)	6,659 (82.3)	59.4 (0.73)	1,199 (51.8)	2,180 (66.4)	2,772 (72.3)	509 (34.9)	2,577 (70.6)	4,082 (80.7)	38.7 (0.95)
1995[1]	12,518 (131.5)	7,739 (86.6)	61.8 (0.69)	1,950 (64.6)	2,381 (69.9)	2,800 (74.2)	608 (38.3)	3,689 (81.2)	4,051 (83.4)	47.7 (0.90)
2000[1]	11,858 (133.0)	7,592 (86.3)	64.0 (0.70)	2,146 (69.2)	2,180 (69.7)	2,701 (75.4)	565 (38.3)	4,008 (85.1)	3,584 (82.6)	52.8 (0.95)
2003[1]	12,204 (134.8)	7,921 (82.6)	64.9 (0.69)	2,512 (70.0)	2,347 (68.2)	2,539 (70.2)	523 (35.0)	4,429 (83.2)	3,492 (78.2)	55.9 (0.87)
2004[1]	12,362 (145.9)	7,969 (83.3)	64.5 (0.67)	2,428 (69.2)	2,243 (67.1)	2,812 (73.0)	484 (33.8)	4,507 (83.8)	3,461 (78.2)	56.6 (0.87)
2005[1]	12,134 (144.6)	7,801 (82.7)	64.3 (0.68)	2,409 (68.8)	2,120 (65.5)	2,804 (72.7)	468 (33.2)	4,548 (83.5)	3,253 (76.4)	58.3 (0.87)
2006[1]	12,186 (144.9)	8,010 (82.1)	65.7 (0.67)	2,481 (69.6)	2,156 (66.0)	2,960 (74.1)	413 (31.3)	4,723 (84.2)	3,286 (76.7)	59.0 (0.86)
2007[1]	12,326 (145.7)	8,056 (82.7)	65.4 (0.67)	2,532 (70.2)	2,037 (64.6)	3,088 (75.3)	400 (30.8)	4,578 (84.0)	3,478 (78.3)	56.8 (0.86)
3 years old											
1965	4,149 (84.9)	203 (24.3)	4.9 (0.59)	41 (11.1)	153 (21.2)	5 (3.9)	4 (3.5)	— (†)	— (†)	— (†)
1970	3,516 (63.2)	454 (28.1)	12.9 (0.80)	110 (14.6)	322 (24.1)	12 (4.9)	10 (4.5)	142 (16.5)	312 (23.8)	31.3 (3.07)
1975	3,177 (60.2)	683 (32.7)	21.5 (1.03)	179 (18.3)	474 (28.3)	11 (4.7)	18 (6.0)	259 (21.8)	423 (27.0)	37.9 (2.62)
1980	3,143 (60.7)	857 (35.7)	27.3 (1.14)	221 (20.5)	604 (31.6)	16 (5.7)	17 (5.9)	321 (24.3)	536 (30.2)	37.5 (2.36)
1985	3,594 (68.2)	1,035 (40.8)	28.8 (1.14)	278 (24.1)	679 (35.3)	52 (10.8)	26 (7.6)	350 (26.7)	685 (35.4)	33.8 (2.21)
1990	3,692 (72.7)	1,205 (45.1)	32.6 (1.22)	347 (28.1)	840 (40.3)	11 (5.4)	7 (4.2)	447 (31.4)	758 (38.9)	37.1 (2.20)
1995[1]	4,148 (77.4)	1,489 (49.2)	35.9 (1.19)	511 (33.7)	947 (43.0)	15 (6.1)	17 (6.5)	754 (39.6)	736 (39.2)	50.6 (2.06)
2000[1]	3,929 (78.2)	1,541 (50.5)	39.2 (1.29)	644 (38.3)	854 (42.7)	27 (8.5)	16 (6.7)	761 (40.9)	779 (41.3)	49.4 (2.10)
2003[1]	4,260 (81.3)	1,806 (50.5)	42.4 (1.19)	783 (39.6)	915 (42.0)	83 (14.1)	24 (7.7)	979 (43.0)	826 (40.4)	54.2 (1.84)
2004[1]	4,089 (85.7)	1,583 (48.8)	38.7 (1.19)	674 (37.2)	849 (40.6)	40 (9.9)	20 (7.0)	808 (39.9)	775 (39.3)	51.0 (1.97)
2005[1]	4,151 (86.3)	1,715 (49.7)	41.3 (1.20)	777 (39.4)	869 (41.1)	54 (11.4)	15 (6.0)	901 (41.6)	814 (40.1)	52.5 (1.89)
2006[1]	4,043 (85.2)	1,716 (49.2)	42.4 (1.22)	733 (38.4)	912 (41.6)	54 (11.5)	17 (6.4)	884 (41.2)	833 (40.3)	51.5 (1.89)
2007[1]	4,142 (86.2)	1,717 (49.7)	41.5 (1.20)	766 (39.1)	832 (40.4)	106 (15.9)	13 (5.7)	883 (41.3)	834 (40.4)	51.4 (1.89)
4 years old											
1965	4,238 (85.8)	683 (41.8)	16.1 (0.99)	68 (14.3)	213 (24.9)	284 (28.4)	118 (18.7)	— (†)	— (†)	— (†)
1970	3,620 (64.1)	1,007 (38.0)	27.8 (1.05)	176 (18.3)	395 (26.5)	318 (24.0)	117 (15.0)	230 (20.7)	776 (34.8)	22.8 (1.87)
1975	3,499 (63.1)	1,418 (41.0)	40.5 (1.17)	332 (24.5)	644 (32.3)	313 (23.8)	129 (15.7)	411 (26.9)	1,008 (37.8)	29.0 (1.70)
1980	3,072 (60.0)	1,423 (39.5)	46.3 (1.29)	363 (25.6)	701 (33.3)	239 (21.2)	120 (15.4)	467 (28.5)	956 (36.7)	32.8 (1.78)
1985	3,598 (68.2)	1,766 (45.1)	49.1 (1.25)	496 (31.1)	859 (38.5)	276 (24.0)	135 (17.1)	643 (34.6)	1,123 (41.8)	36.4 (1.72)
1990	3,723 (73.0)	2,087 (48.0)	56.1 (1.29)	695 (37.7)	1,144 (44.6)	157 (19.4)	91 (14.9)	716 (38.1)	1,371 (46.6)	34.3 (1.65)
1995[1]	4,145 (77.4)	2,553 (49.9)	61.6 (1.20)	1,054 (44.6)	1,208 (46.6)	207 (22.3)	84 (14.5)	1,104 (45.3)	1,449 (48.9)	43.3 (1.56)
2000[1]	3,940 (78.3)	2,556 (49.5)	64.9 (1.26)	1,144 (47.0)	1,121 (46.8)	227 (24.2)	65 (13.2)	1,182 (47.5)	1,374 (49.4)	46.2 (1.63)
2003[1]	4,076 (79.6)	2,785 (46.5)	68.3 (1.14)	1,324 (46.8)	1,176 (45.3)	184 (20.7)	101 (15.5)	1,400 (47.5)	1,384 (47.4)	50.3 (1.48)
2004[1]	4,339 (88.2)	2,969 (48.0)	68.4 (1.11)	1,462 (48.8)	1,213 (46.3)	208 (22.1)	85 (14.3)	1,484 (48.9)	1,485 (48.9)	50.0 (1.44)
2005[1]	4,028 (85.1)	2,668 (47.0)	66.2 (1.17)	1,295 (46.4)	1,083 (44.1)	215 (22.3)	75 (13.5)	1,332 (46.8)	1,336 (46.8)	49.9 (1.52)
2006[1]	4,095 (85.8)	2,817 (46.4)	68.8 (1.13)	1,401 (47.5)	1,067 (44.0)	306 (26.4)	43 (10.3)	1,418 (47.7)	1,399 (47.5)	50.3 (1.48)
2007[1]	4,092 (85.7)	2,774 (46.8)	67.8 (1.14)	1,417 (47.7)	993 (42.9)	295 (25.9)	69 (12.9)	1,297 (46.6)	1,476 (48.1)	46.8 (1.48)
5 years old[2]											
1965	4,162 (85.1)	2,521 (55.1)	60.6 (1.32)	18 (7.4)	27 (9.1)	2,002 (56.3)	474 (35.8)	— (†)	— (†)	— (†)
1970	3,814 (65.8)	2,643 (40.2)	69.3 (1.05)	45 (9.4)	45 (9.4)	2,168 (43.2)	384 (26.2)	326 (24.4)	2,317 (42.5)	12.3 (0.90)
1975	3,509 (63.2)	2,854 (32.6)	81.3 (0.93)	59 (10.7)	57 (10.6)	2,358 (39.2)	381 (26.0)	625 (32.0)	2,228 (40.2)	21.9 (1.09)
1980	3,069 (60.0)	2,598 (28.6)	84.7 (0.93)	44 (9.4)	48 (9.8)	2,183 (35.9)	322 (24.3)	763 (34.2)	1,835 (38.8)	29.4 (1.28)
1985	3,542 (67.7)	3,065 (30.6)	86.5 (0.86)	73 (12.7)	94 (14.4)	2,519 (40.6)	379 (27.7)	1,151 (41.9)	1,914 (44.6)	37.6 (1.32)
1990	3,792 (73.7)	3,367 (30.8)	88.8 (0.81)	157 (19.4)	196 (21.6)	2,604 (45.2)	411 (30.3)	1,414 (47.2)	1,953 (48.7)	42.0 (1.35)
1995[1]	4,224 (78.1)	3,697 (34.2)	87.5 (0.81)	385 (29.8)	226 (23.3)	2,578 (50.5)	507 (33.7)	1,830 (51.3)	1,867 (51.4)	49.5 (1.31)
2000[1]	3,989 (78.7)	3,495 (34.3)	87.6 (0.86)	359 (29.8)	206 (23.1)	2,447 (50.8)	484 (34.1)	2,065 (52.1)	1,431 (50.0)	59.1 (1.37)
2003[1]	3,867 (77.5)	3,331 (33.7)	86.1 (0.87)	404 (29.8)	256 (24.2)	2,272 (47.9)	398 (29.6)	2,050 (48.6)	1,281 (45.8)	61.5 (1.32)
2004[1]	3,934 (84.1)	3,417 (33.2)	86.9 (0.84)	293 (25.8)	181 (20.6)	2,564 (46.8)	380 (29.0)	2,215 (48.7)	1,201 (45.2)	64.8 (1.28)
2005[1]	3,955 (84.3)	3,418 (33.7)	86.4 (0.85)	337 (27.5)	168 (19.9)	2,535 (47.3)	378 (29.0)	2,316 (48.5)	1,102 (44.2)	67.7 (1.25)
2006[1]	4,049 (85.3)	3,476 (34.7)	85.9 (0.86)	346 (27.9)	178 (20.4)	2,599 (47.8)	353 (28.1)	2,422 (48.9)	1,054 (43.7)	69.7 (1.22)
2007[1]	4,091 (85.7)	3,565 (33.5)	87.1 (0.82)	349 (28.0)	212 (22.2)	2,687 (47.6)	317 (26.8)	2,397 (49.3)	1,168 (45.2)	67.2 (1.23)

—Not available.
†Not applicable.
[1]Data collected using new procedures. May not be comparable with figures prior to 1994.
[2]Enrollment data include only those students in preprimary programs.
NOTE: Data are based on sample surveys of the civilian noninstitutional population. Although cells with fewer than 75,000 children are subject to wide sampling variation, they are included in the table to permit various types of aggregations. Detail may not sum to totals because of rounding. Standard errors appear in parentheses.

SOURCE: U.S. Department of Education, National Center for Education Statistics, *Preprimary Enrollment*, 1965, 1970, and 1975. U.S. Department of Commerce, Census Bureau, Current Population Survey (CPS), October, 1980 through 2007. (This table was prepared August 2008.)

Table 44. Number of children under 6 years old and not yet enrolled in kindergarten, percentage in center-based programs, average weekly hours in nonparental care, and percentage in various types of primary care arrangements, by selected child and family characteristics: 2005

Selected child and family characteristic	Number of children, ages 0 to 5 (in thousands)	Percent in center-based programs	Average hours per week in nonparental care[1]	Percentage distribution, by type of primary care arrangement						
					Center-based care		Nonrelative care			
				Parental care only	Head Start	Other center-based	Family child care (in another home)	Sitter (in child's home)	Relative	Multiple arrangements[2]
1	2	3	4	5	6	7	8	9	10	11
Total preschool children..	20,665 (9.0)	36.1 (0.60)	29.3 (0.37)	39.8 (0.76)	5.1 (0.40)	27.3 (0.49)	8.3 (0.39)	2.3 (0.24)	15.4 (0.66)	1.7 (0.18)
Age										
Under 1 year	3,519 (#)	12.0 (1.13)	30.9 (0.95)	57.7 (1.81)	1.2 (0.57)	10.0 (1.07)	9.2 (0.90)	3.2 (0.60)	17.2 (1.42)	1.5 (0.47)
1 year old	3,988 (#)	16.9 (1.34)	31.2 (0.81)	48.5 (1.89)	0.7 (0.25)	15.0 (1.32)	11.1 (1.09)	3.4 (0.57)	19.1 (1.52)	2.2 (0.50)
2 years old	4,093 (#)	28.7 (1.84)	29.6 (0.75)	44.9 (1.97)	3.5 (0.98)	22.7 (1.66)	10.7 (1.13)	2.4 (0.49)	14.3 (1.17)	1.5 (0.38)
3 years old	4,070 (93.0)	42.5 (1.67)	28.9 (0.64)	34.0 (1.46)	5.3 (0.75)	33.2 (1.64)	7.6 (0.91)	1.7 (0.38)	16.7 (1.35)	1.5 (0.36)
4 years old	3,873 (92.0)	69.2 (1.36)	27.9 (0.67)	20.9 (1.44)	13.2 (1.12)	48.2 (1.29)	4.0 (0.73)	1.2 (0.50)	10.4 (1.29)	2.2 (0.44)
5 years old	1,123 (67.3)	68.7 (3.51)	26.9 (1.28)	21.1 (3.17)	10.4 (2.22)	48.4 (3.33)	4.6 (1.44)	0.8 (0.44)	13.6 (2.91)	1.1 (0.79)
Race/ethnicity										
White..............................	11,488 (99.2)	37.8 (0.87)	27.1 (0.48)	37.7 (0.97)	2.8 (0.35)	30.4 (0.82)	10.1 (0.59)	3.1 (0.35)	14.1 (0.82)	1.8 (0.26)
Black..............................	2,962 (5.2)	43.8 (2.44)	35.9 (0.85)	30.8 (2.67)	13.3 (2.10)	28.8 (2.32)	6.6 (1.05)	1.0 (0.54)	17.8 (2.76)	1.7 (0.57)
Hispanic	4,283 (4.1)	25.2 (1.28)	28.8 (0.76)	50.9 (1.43)	6.2 (0.76)	16.8 (1.01)	6.4 (0.80)	1.5 (0.32)	16.7 (0.96)	1.4 (0.35)
Other..............................	1,933 (100.2)	37.9 (2.72)	31.8 (0.91)	41.5 (2.80)	3.8 (0.94)	29.6 (2.43)	4.8 (0.76)	1.3 (0.35)	17.1 (2.03)	1.9 (0.68)
Number of parents in the household[3]										
Two parents.....................	16,275 (114.0)	34.4 (0.70)	27.0 (0.42)	43.3 (0.90)	3.4 (0.33)	27.7 (0.58)	8.6 (0.44)	2.4 (0.24)	12.9 (0.66)	1.7 (0.20)
One parent	4,055 (112.6)	42.2 (1.94)	35.1 (0.77)	26.1 (1.68)	11.1 (1.42)	26.3 (1.61)	7.8 (1.06)	1.6 (0.54)	25.3 (2.28)	1.8 (0.41)
Mother in household										
Yes	19,982 (65.8)	35.7 (0.59)	28.9 (0.38)	40.1 (0.78)	4.9 (0.42)	27.3 (0.47)	8.5 (0.40)	2.3 (0.23)	15.2 (0.67)	1.7 (0.18)
No	683 (63.8)	45.2 (4.17)	38.5 (1.87)	30.9 (3.95)	9.9 (2.44)	27.4 (3.62)	3.5 (1.26)	2.9 (1.76)	22.5 (3.75)	3.0 (1.38)
Mother's employment status[4]										
Currently employed...............	11,328 (197.3)	43.8 (0.81)	32.3 (0.40)	20.9 (0.97)	5.4 (0.64)	33.1 (0.81)	13.7 (0.68)	3.0 (0.32)	21.4 (0.92)	2.4 (0.29)
35 or more hours/week	7,038 (185.0)	47.5 (1.15)	37.1 (0.42)	14.9 (1.06)	5.7 (0.72)	36.3 (1.14)	16.6 (0.89)	2.4 (0.32)	22.0 (1.28)	2.1 (0.35)
Less than 35 hours/week ...	4,290 (156.5)	37.7 (1.52)	22.7 (0.64)	30.8 (2.00)	5.1 (0.99)	27.9 (1.43)	8.9 (0.99)	3.9 (0.64)	20.5 (1.38)	2.9 (0.49)
Looking for work................	1,416 (118.3)	22.6 (2.91)	26.0 (1.46)	55.0 (4.48)	4.9 (1.11)	17.1 (2.66)	3.7 (1.03)	1.8 (1.29)	16.7 (5.17)	0.9 (0.65)
Not in labor force..................	7,238 (173.7)	25.7 (1.03)	16.7 (0.69)	67.3 (1.13)	4.2 (0.50)	20.2 (0.91)	1.3 (0.26)	1.2 (0.22)	5.2 (0.61)	0.7 (0.19)
Mother's highest education[4]										
Less than high school	1,961 (99.4)	18.1 (1.58)	26.0 (1.58)	64.8 (2.31)	9.9 (1.33)	8.0 (1.03)	4.0 (0.89)	# (†)	12.2 (1.70)	1.0 (0.45)
High school/GED	5,590 (182.6)	30.3 (1.49)	29.2 (0.73)	45.4 (1.77)	8.0 (0.96)	20.0 (1.25)	6.3 (0.73)	1.2 (0.42)	17.3 (1.32)	1.8 (0.39)
Vocational/technical or some college	4,122 (145.7)	34.3 (1.80)	30.1 (1.02)	39.8 (2.17)	4.5 (0.68)	26.3 (1.59)	7.9 (0.94)	1.3 (0.42)	18.5 (1.76)	1.8 (0.47)
Associate's degree............	1,466 (78.9)	37.1 (2.76)	28.2 (1.04)	31.6 (2.90)	3.5 (1.22)	29.9 (2.48)	15.5 (1.96)	1.4 (0.56)	16.6 (2.27)	1.5 (0.62)
Bachelor's degree..............	4,593 (123.1)	45.2 (1.55)	27.9 (0.63)	33.2 (1.33)	1.9 (0.57)	38.2 (1.39)	9.9 (0.86)	3.6 (0.58)	11.5 (1.01)	1.8 (0.37)
Graduate/professional degree	2,250 (121.2)	47.1 (1.80)	30.0 (0.75)	25.7 (1.89)	1.2 (0.41)	40.3 (1.75)	11.6 (1.62)	6.5 (0.99)	13.0 (1.69)	1.7 (0.47)
Mother's home language[4]										
English	16,778 (117.0)	38.1 (0.63)	29.1 (0.41)	36.7 (0.86)	4.5 (0.49)	29.5 (0.53)	9.1 (0.44)	2.5 (0.26)	15.9 (0.77)	1.8 (0.21)
Non-English	3,205 (103.3)	23.5 (1.61)	26.9 (0.97)	57.9 (1.76)	7.1 (1.02)	15.9 (1.25)	5.5 (0.82)	1.0 (0.26)	11.5 (0.99)	1.0 (0.31)
Mother's age at first birth[4]										
Less than 18	1,744 (117.6)	27.7 (2.84)	32.8 (1.40)	50.3 (3.11)	10.4 (1.81)	15.4 (2.31)	4.8 (1.03)	2.0 (1.27)	15.9 (1.91)	1.1 (0.53)
18 or 19	2,529 (135.1)	28.4 (2.14)	30.6 (1.13)	46.6 (2.81)	7.6 (1.23)	17.6 (1.90)	7.1 (1.33)	0.9 (0.34)	19.4 (2.80)	0.8 (0.34)
20 or older.......................	15,709 (140.0)	37.8 (0.68)	28.3 (0.43)	37.9 (0.74)	3.9 (0.43)	30.2 (0.65)	9.1 (0.46)	2.5 (0.24)	14.4 (0.70)	1.9 (0.21)
Household income										
$15,000 or less	3,142 (79.3)	29.7 (2.19)	31.4 (1.11)	48.2 (2.35)	11.0 (1.61)	16.6 (1.80)	4.7 (0.90)	1.7 (0.67)	16.9 (2.31)	0.9 (0.35)
$15,001 to $25,000.............	2,770 (79.2)	29.0 (2.53)	31.0 (1.16)	48.9 (2.44)	8.5 (1.02)	19.2 (2.18)	4.5 (0.70)	1.5 (0.63)	15.9 (1.68)	1.5 (0.57)
$25,001 to $35,000.............	2,313 (94.5)	30.8 (2.06)	28.7 (1.01)	44.2 (2.22)	9.0 (1.52)	19.1 (1.89)	6.7 (1.39)	0.7 (0.31)	18.4 (1.99)	1.9 (0.52)
$35,001 to $50,000.............	2,943 (111.8)	28.3 (1.83)	29.5 (1.03)	48.5 (2.41)	4.2 (0.91)	21.2 (1.60)	6.7 (0.97)	0.8 (0.29)	16.7 (1.51)	2.0 (0.58)
More than $50,000..............	9,498 (112.8)	43.9 (0.95)	28.4 (0.42)	30.6 (1.03)	1.5 (0.27)	37.1 (0.88)	11.5 (0.71)	3.6 (0.38)	13.7 (0.84)	1.9 (0.26)
Poverty status[5]										
Above poverty threshold	15,900 (60.9)	38.4 (0.77)	29.0 (0.37)	36.6 (0.87)	3.5 (0.36)	30.6 (0.65)	9.6 (0.51)	2.5 (0.24)	15.3 (0.72)	1.9 (0.22)
At or below poverty threshold	4,766 (60.7)	28.3 (1.80)	30.2 (0.96)	50.5 (1.93)	10.4 (1.15)	16.4 (1.51)	3.9 (0.63)	1.7 (0.54)	15.9 (1.75)	1.1 (0.29)
Household size										
2 or 3 persons...................	5,469 (137.6)	38.2 (1.48)	32.5 (0.57)	30.6 (1.27)	5.9 (0.90)	28.9 (1.36)	11.6 (0.94)	2.2 (0.39)	18.5 (1.07)	2.2 (0.41)
4 persons........................	7,723 (172.4)	39.5 (1.17)	28.4 (0.56)	38.1 (1.26)	4.2 (0.56)	31.9 (0.95)	8.7 (0.65)	2.3 (0.35)	13.3 (1.14)	1.7 (0.33)
5 persons........................	4,279 (165.9)	34.0 (1.85)	26.8 (0.85)	44.3 (2.14)	5.6 (0.84)	24.2 (1.65)	7.2 (1.01)	3.1 (0.69)	14.4 (1.28)	1.2 (0.31)
6 or more persons................	3,194 (138.4)	26.8 (1.90)	27.6 (0.95)	53.7 (2.36)	5.4 (0.90)	17.7 (1.70)	3.3 (0.62)	1.4 (0.35)	16.7 (2.53)	1.8 (0.41)
Urbanicity										
Rural	4,328 (5.4)	32.5 (1.93)	29.7 (0.91)	37.5 (2.00)	5.8 (0.82)	22.5 (1.78)	10.6 (1.04)	1.4 (0.58)	20.0 (1.68)	2.2 (0.48)
Urban..............................	16,337 (7.5)	37.0 (0.58)	29.1 (0.37)	40.4 (0.88)	4.9 (0.43)	28.6 (0.54)	7.7 (0.44)	2.5 (0.27)	14.2 (0.70)	1.6 (0.18)

†Not applicable.
#Rounds to zero.
[1]Mean hours per week per child, among preschool children enrolled in any type of nonparental care arrangement. For children with more than one arrangement, the hours of each weekly arrangement were summed to calculate the total amount of time in child care per week.
[2]Children who spend equal hours per week in multiple nonparental care arrangements.
[3]Excludes children living apart from their parents.
[4]Excludes children living in households with no mother or female guardian present.

[5]Poverty status was determined by household income and number of persons in household.
NOTE: A child's "primary arrangement" was defined as the regular nonparental care arrangement or early childhood education program in which the child spent the most time per week. Race categories exclude persons of Hispanic ethnicity. Detail may not sum to totals because of rounding. Standard errors appear in parentheses.
SOURCE: U.S. Department of Education, National Center for Education Statistics, Early Childhood Program Participation Survey of the National Household Education Surveys Program (ECPP-NHES:2005). (This table was prepared October 2006.)

Table 45. Child care arrangements of 3- to 5-year-old children who are not yet in kindergarten, by age and race/ethnicity: Various years, 1991 through 2005

Child care arrangement	Total		Age						Race/ethnicity							
			3 years old		4 years old		5 years old		White		Black		Hispanic		Other	
1	2		3		4		5		6		7		8		9	
1991 children																
In thousands...................	8,402	(40.9)	3,733	(7.1)	3,627	(14.6)	1,042	(38.6)	5,850	(59.9)	1,236	(41.0)	999	(31.3)	317	(34.6)
Percent........................	100.0	(†)	44.4	(0.21)	43.2	(0.24)	12.4	(0.40)	69.6	(0.67)	14.7	(0.47)	11.9	(0.37)	3.8	(0.41)
Percent in nonparental arrangements																
Relative care.......................	16.9	(0.60)	16.2	(0.72)	18.0	(0.85)	15.6	(1.34)	14.8	(0.66)	24.1	(2.09)	19.6	(2.08)	19.4	(3.87)
Nonrelative care..................	14.8	(0.56)	14.8	(0.76)	14.7	(0.79)	14.9	(1.81)	17.3	(0.76)	7.9	(1.20)	9.4	(1.27)	12.1	(2.45)
Center-based programs[1]............	52.8	(0.89)	42.3	(1.44)	60.4	(1.04)	63.9	(2.12)	54.0	(0.95)	58.3	(2.49)	38.8	(2.20)	52.9	(3.45)
Percent with parental care only	31.0	(0.80)	37.8	(1.19)	26.0	(1.05)	24.3	(2.10)	30.6	(0.87)	24.8	(2.02)	40.7	(2.35)	32.8	(4.03)
1995 children																
In thousands...................	9,222	(52.9)	4,123	(8.3)	4,061	(12.5)	1,038	(48.3)	6,334	(94.0)	1,389	(56.1)	1,042	(38.8)	457	(39.1)
Percent........................	100.0	(†)	44.7	(0.25)	44.0	(0.24)	11.3	(0.46)	68.7	(0.94)	15.1	(0.60)	11.3	(0.42)	5.0	(0.42)
Percent in nonparental arrangements																
Relative care.......................	19.4	(0.64)	21.4	(1.23)	18.4	(0.95)	15.2	(2.14)	16.5	(0.84)	28.7	(2.78)	22.8	(2.01)	22.6	(3.75)
Nonrelative care..................	16.9	(0.84)	18.5	(1.35)	15.3	(1.03)	17.2	(2.19)	19.4	(1.04)	11.3	(1.65)	12.5	(1.64)	10.5	(2.74)
Center-based programs[1]............	55.1	(0.97)	40.7	(1.55)	64.8	(1.45)	74.5	(2.35)	56.9	(1.44)	59.8	(3.19)	37.4	(2.15)	56.7	(5.47)
Percent with parental care only	25.9	(1.01)	32.0	(1.95)	22.1	(1.24)	16.2	(1.78)	25.2	(1.39)	19.9	(2.50)	38.4	(2.33)	24.2	(3.59)
1999 children																
In thousands...................	8,518	(139.7)	3,809	(79.1)	3,703	(79.9)	1,006	(54.2)	5,384	(77.4)	1,214	(59.2)	1,376	(52.3)	545	(38.3)
Percent........................	100.0	(†)	44.7	(0.93)	43.5	(0.93)	11.8	(0.64)	63.2	(0.91)	14.2	(0.69)	16.2	(0.61)	6.4	(0.45)
Percent in nonparental arrangements																
Relative care.......................	22.8	(0.77)	24.3	(1.28)	22.0	(1.14)	20.2	(2.06)	18.7	(0.90)	33.4	(2.58)	26.5	(1.86)	30.0	(3.97)
Nonrelative care..................	16.1	(0.67)	16.3	(1.02)	15.9	(1.07)	16.1	(2.08)	19.4	(0.88)	7.4	(1.37)	12.7	(1.29)	10.4	(1.98)
Center-based programs[1]............	59.7	(0.63)	45.7	(1.28)	69.6	(1.19)	76.5	(2.40)	60.0	(0.81)	73.2	(2.40)	44.2	(2.19)	66.0	(4.10)
Percent with parental care only	23.1	(0.72)	30.8	(1.42)	17.7	(0.99)	13.5	(1.78)	23.2	(0.91)	13.7	(1.97)	33.4	(2.04)	16.6	(3.50)
2001 children																
In thousands...................	8,551	(11.0)	3,795	(91.4)	3,861	(89.0)	896	(47.0)	5,313	(68.0)	1,251	(55.1)	1,506	(43.5)	482	(38.3)
Percent........................	100.0	(†)	44.4	(1.06)	45.1	(1.04)	10.5	(0.55)	62.1	(0.79)	14.6	(0.64)	17.6	(0.51)	5.6	(0.45)
Percent in nonparental arrangements																
Relative care.......................	22.8	(0.89)	23.6	(1.39)	22.5	(1.33)	20.9	(2.66)	19.6	(1.01)	36.7	(3.42)	22.8	(1.89)	22.8	(3.54)
Nonrelative care..................	14.0	(0.65)	14.7	(1.17)	13.6	(0.95)	13.1	(2.13)	16.5	(0.98)	8.5	(1.65)	11.3	(1.43)	10.8	(2.72)
Center-based programs[1]............	56.4	(0.55)	42.8	(1.21)	65.9	(1.25)	73.0	(2.69)	59.1	(0.89)	63.1	(2.93)	39.9	(1.86)	61.8	(4.10)
Percent with parental care only	26.1	(0.67)	33.8	(1.29)	20.4	(1.11)	18.0	(2.49)	25.3	(0.99)	15.1	(2.22)	39.0	(2.03)	23.7	(3.90)
2005 children																
In thousands...................	9,066	(9.0)	4,070	(93.0)	3,873	(92.0)	1,123	(67.3)	5,177	(80.2)	1,233	(57.1)	1,822	(50.0)	834	(54.3)
Percent........................	100.0	(†)	44.9	(1.03)	42.7	(1.01)	12.4	(0.74)	57.1	(0.89)	13.6	(0.63)	20.1	(0.56)	9.2	(0.60)
Percent in nonparental arrangements																
Relative care.......................	22.6	(1.02)	24.0	(1.44)	20.8	(1.56)	23.8	(3.17)	21.4	(1.34)	25.0	(3.42)	22.6	(1.79)	26.4	(3.29)
Nonrelative care..................	11.6	(0.73)	14.4	(1.12)	9.2	(1.03)	9.9	(2.00)	15.0	(1.13)	5.2	(1.31)	8.1	(1.36)	8.1	(1.94)
Center-based programs[1]............	57.2	(0.83)	42.5	(1.67)	69.2	(1.36)	68.7	(3.51)	59.1	(1.32)	66.5	(3.41)	43.4	(2.10)	61.5	(3.31)
Percent with parental care only	26.3	(0.92)	33.4	(1.48)	20.6	(1.42)	20.4	(3.15)	24.1	(1.22)	19.5	(2.85)	38.0	(2.10)	24.7	(3.11)

†Not applicable.
[1]Center-based programs include day care centers, nursery schools, prekindergartens, preschools, and Head Start programs.
NOTE: Row percents for nonparental and parental care do not add to 100 percent because some children participated in more than one type of nonparental care arrangement. Race categories exclude persons of Hispanic ethnicity. Detail may not sum to totals because of rounding. Standard errors appear in parentheses.
SOURCE: U.S. Department of Education, National Center for Education Statistics, Early Childhood Education Survey, Parent Survey, and Early Childhood Program Participation Survey of the National Household Education Surveys Program (ECE-NHES:1991; Parent-NHES:1999; and ECPP-NHES:1995, 2001, and 2005). (This table was prepared July 2006.)

Table 46. Percentage distribution of children at about 2 and 4 years of age, by type of child care arrangement and selected child and family characteristics: 2003–04 and 2005–06

	Children at about 2 years of age in 2003–04						Children at about 4 years of age in 2005–06							
	Percentage distribution of children[1]	Percentage distribution by primary type of care arrangement[2]					Percentage distribution of children[7]	Percentage distribution by primary type of care arrangement[2]						
			Home-based care						Home-based care		Center-based care[5]			
Selected characteristic		No regular nonparental arrangement	Relative care[3]	Nonrelative care[4]	Center-based care[5]	Multiple arrangements[6]		No regular nonparental arrangement	Relative care[3]	Nonrelative care[4]	Total	Head Start	Other than Head Start	Multiple arrangements[6]
1	2	3	4	5	6	7	8	9	10	11	12	13	14	15
Total	100.0 (†)	50.6 (0.74)	18.6 (0.62)	14.6 (0.51)	15.8 (0.50)	0.5 (0.10)	100.0 (†)	20.0 (0.65)	13.1 (0.61)	7.6 (0.32)	57.5 (0.80)	12.7 (0.64)	44.8 (0.71)	1.9 (0.21)
Sex of child														
Male	51.2 (0.08)	50.0 (0.96)	19.1 (0.79)	14.3 (0.61)	16.3 (0.65)	0.3 (0.07)	51.2 (0.11)	19.3 (0.80)	13.1 (0.79)	7.5 (0.51)	58.0 (0.99)	12.9 (0.80)	45.1 (1.02)	2.1 (0.33)
Female	48.8 (0.08)	51.1 (1.01)	18.0 (0.78)	14.9 (0.71)	15.2 (0.63)	0.8 (0.19)	48.8 (0.11)	20.7 (0.90)	13.1 (0.86)	7.6 (0.52)	56.9 (1.00)	12.4 (0.74)	44.5 (0.91)	1.7 (0.20)
Race/ethnicity of child														
White	53.8 (0.53)	50.7 (1.07)	14.9 (0.88)	17.0 (0.75)	16.8 (0.73)	0.5 (0.13)	53.8 (0.59)	17.9 (0.98)	11.0 (0.74)	9.2 (0.49)	60.1 (1.04)	6.8 (0.61)	53.3 (1.00)	1.9 (0.28)
Black	13.7 (0.24)	37.1 (1.39)	26.0 (1.54)	12.0 (1.30)	24.1 (1.15)	0.8 (0.24)	13.8 (0.26)	16.0 (1.37)	13.9 (1.49)	4.3 (0.73)	62.4 (2.08)	25.4 (1.97)	37.1 (1.87)	3.3 (0.66)
Hispanic	25.3 (0.38)	57.4 (1.39)	21.4 (1.14)	11.6 (0.94)	9.2 (0.94)	0.4 (0.20)	25.1 (0.42)	27.2 (1.37)	15.9 (1.14)	6.2 (0.78)	49.4 (1.58)	18.6 (1.22)	30.9 (1.65)	1.2 (0.29)
Asian	2.7 (0.09)	55.5 (2.24)	23.8 (1.44)	10.9 (1.06)	9.4 (1.39)	0.5 (0.25)	2.6 (0.09)	17.5 (1.75)	16.0 (1.41)	3.4 (0.67)	60.7 (2.06)	5.5 (0.90)	55.3 (2.16)	2.3 (1.05)
Pacific Islander	0.2 (0.04)	73.5 (9.77)	23.5 (9.83)	‡ (†)	‡ (†)	‡ (†)	0.2 (0.05)	22.3 (6.82)	45.0 (14.27)	‡ (†)	19.9 (7.94)	5.0 (3.24)	14.9 (6.47)	‡ (†)
American Indian/Alaska Native	0.5 (0.06)	56.7 (3.20)	17.7 (3.16)	11.8 (3.90)	13.7 (2.77)	‡ (†)	0.5 (0.05)	20.0 (2.41)	14.0 (2.07)	5.3 (1.46)	59.6 (3.58)	31.1 (4.72)	28.5 (5.63)	1.1 (0.95)
More than one race	3.8 (0.28)	46.7 (3.01)	18.9 (1.89)	13.5 (2.25)	19.8 (2.23)	1.2 (0.64)	4.0 (0.28)	17.8 (2.13)	17.5 (2.44)	8.9 (2.06)	53.9 (3.41)	12.2 (2.33)	41.7 (3.27)	1.8 (0.85)
Age of child														
22 or fewer months	1.9 (0.29)	58.6 (4.73)	21.0 (4.62)	11.0 (3.41)	9.4 (2.77)	† (†)	† (†)	† (†)	† (†)	† (†)	† (†)	† (†)	† (†)	† (†)
23 months	38.3 (1.22)	54.1 (1.16)	17.0 (0.93)	13.6 (0.91)	14.5 (0.85)	0.7 (0.16)	† (†)	† (†)	† (†)	† (†)	† (†)	† (†)	† (†)	† (†)
24 months	38.0 (0.89)	49.1 (1.02)	18.5 (0.95)	15.6 (0.80)	16.6 (0.87)	0.2 (0.10)	† (†)	† (†)	† (†)	† (†)	† (†)	† (†)	† (†)	† (†)
25 months	12.4 (0.46)	44.8 (1.91)	23.1 (1.44)	14.7 (1.40)	16.8 (1.44)	0.5 (0.31)	† (†)	† (†)	† (†)	† (†)	† (†)	† (†)	† (†)	† (†)
26 or more months	9.4 (0.59)	47.6 (2.37)	18.6 (1.82)	14.8 (1.40)	17.9 (1.60)	1.1 (0.54)	† (†)	† (†)	† (†)	† (†)	† (†)	† (†)	† (†)	† (†)
Less than 48 months	†	†	†	†	†	†	16.4 (0.57)	27.3 (1.63)	13.9 (1.48)	8.7 (0.95)	48.0 (1.76)	10.6 (1.24)	37.4 (1.90)	2.2 (0.55)
48 to 52 months	†	†	†	†	†	†	38.1 (0.55)	19.9 (1.01)	13.0 (0.87)	8.3 (0.60)	56.8 (1.29)	12.0 (0.79)	44.8 (1.31)	2.0 (0.37)
53 to 57 months	†	†	†	†	†	†	36.5 (0.57)	16.5 (0.93)	13.1 (0.83)	6.7 (0.52)	62.2 (1.32)	14.4 (1.01)	47.8 (1.22)	1.5 (0.25)
58 or more months	†	†	†	†	†	†	9.0 (0.41)	20.9 (2.00)	12.0 (1.66)	6.3 (1.09)	58.1 (2.84)	12.0 (1.66)	46.1 (2.52)	2.7 (0.74)
Mother's employment status														
Full-time (35 hours or more)	34.6 (0.73)	15.6 (0.89)	30.4 (1.10)	26.0 (0.86)	27.1 (0.97)	0.8 (0.21)	39.4 (0.72)	8.5 (0.73)	18.5 (1.01)	13.4 (0.71)	57.4 (1.21)	11.4 (0.94)	46.1 (1.05)	2.1 (0.31)
Part-time (less than 35 hours)	20.2 (0.63)	35.4 (1.53)	26.4 (1.53)	20.5 (1.37)	16.7 (1.23)	1.1 (0.34)	19.7 (0.54)	13.4 (1.06)	15.9 (1.30)	8.5 (1.04)	59.3 (1.84)	10.1 (1.10)	49.2 (1.91)	2.9 (0.56)
Looking for work	6.3 (0.35)	71.1 (2.30)	11.5 (1.58)	3.8 (0.95)	13.4 (2.02)	0.1 (0.14)	5.4 (0.30)	28.5 (2.55)	12.6 (2.15)	2.1 (0.94)	54.7 (2.86)	24.3 (2.88)	30.4 (3.01)	2.0 (0.83)
Not in labor force	38.4 (0.78)	86.8 (0.75)	4.8 (0.48)	2.9 (0.35)	5.4 (0.46)	† (†)	34.3 (0.76)	35.6 (1.31)	4.6 (0.52)	1.5 (0.26)	57.3 (1.31)	13.7 (0.97)	43.7 (1.27)	1.0 (0.30)
No mother in household	0.4 (0.10)	21.3 (6.88)	30.9 (8.20)	17.7 (8.58)	30.1 (9.47)	‡ (†)	0.8 (0.12)	9.6 (4.50)	36.0 (7.05)	9.5 (4.19)	41.1 (7.47)	14.4 (5.29)	26.7 (6.56)	3.8 (2.78)
Parents' highest level of education														
Less than high school	12.8 (0.37)	67.6 (1.96)	17.5 (1.43)	6.8 (1.08)	7.6 (0.93)	0.4 (0.24)	10.4 (0.37)	34.0 (2.10)	16.5 (1.80)	4.0 (1.07)	43.4 (2.63)	22.2 (2.12)	21.2 (2.06)	2.1 (0.80)
High school completion	27.3 (0.45)	50.1 (1.32)	23.0 (1.17)	12.4 (0.91)	14.1 (0.84)	0.4 (0.16)	25.0 (0.58)	22.6 (1.23)	17.1 (1.14)	6.7 (0.64)	51.7 (1.69)	21.4 (1.37)	30.3 (1.35)	2.0 (0.31)
Some college/vocational	28.2 (0.49)	46.8 (1.53)	21.5 (1.21)	15.1 (0.93)	15.9 (0.94)	0.7 (0.20)	31.6 (0.63)	20.6 (1.18)	14.9 (0.99)	7.3 (0.57)	55.5 (1.47)	13.0 (1.05)	42.5 (1.28)	1.7 (0.33)
Bachelor's degree	16.9 (0.46)	48.6 (1.15)	14.3 (1.17)	17.7 (1.17)	18.7 (1.15)	0.7 (0.23)	16.8 (0.45)	16.0 (1.57)	8.4 (1.02)	8.1 (0.93)	65.7 (1.88)	3.3 (0.75)	62.4 (1.98)	1.8 (0.48)
Any graduate education	14.9 (0.35)	46.0 (1.92)	10.6 (1.05)	20.7 (1.57)	22.4 (1.49)	0.4 (0.16)	16.2 (0.36)	9.7 (0.83)	6.2 (0.90)	11.2 (1.16)	70.8 (1.57)	2.0 (0.52)	68.8 (1.67)	2.0 (0.51)
Poverty status[8]														
Below poverty threshold	23.9 (0.75)	61.8 (1.40)	18.0 (1.15)	7.8 (0.79)	11.7 (0.92)	0.7 (0.24)	24.8 (0.63)	27.6 (1.28)	15.0 (1.19)	4.4 (0.54)	51.0 (1.61)	26.3 (1.45)	24.7 (1.18)	2.0 (0.40)
At or above poverty threshold	76.1 (0.75)	47.0 (0.90)	18.7 (0.68)	16.7 (0.62)	17.1 (0.60)	0.5 (0.11)	75.2 (0.63)	17.4 (0.71)	12.5 (0.64)	8.6 (0.39)	59.6 (0.85)	8.2 (0.57)	51.4 (0.86)	1.9 (0.22)
Socioeconomic status[9]														
Lowest 20 percent	20.0 (0.51)	65.5 (1.51)	17.0 (1.25)	7.2 (0.82)	9.9 (0.76)	0.4 (0.18)	20.0 (0.52)	30.5 (1.27)	15.0 (1.34)	5.0 (0.68)	47.1 (1.80)	24.7 (1.56)	22.4 (1.46)	2.3 (0.57)
Middle 60 percent	60.0 (0.71)	47.2 (0.99)	21.8 (0.83)	14.9 (0.66)	15.4 (0.58)	0.6 (0.15)	60.0 (0.67)	19.6 (0.88)	15.0 (0.81)	7.4 (0.49)	56.2 (1.10)	12.5 (0.81)	43.7 (0.91)	1.8 (0.23)
Highest 20 percent	20.0 (0.48)	45.7 (1.68)	10.3 (0.84)	20.8 (1.50)	22.7 (1.44)	0.5 (0.21)	20.0 (0.47)	10.3 (0.93)	5.5 (0.73)	10.7 (0.90)	71.6 (1.39)	1.0 (0.23)	70.6 (1.42)	1.9 (0.42)

†Not applicable.
‡Reporting standards not met.
[1]Distribution of weighted Early Childhood Longitudinal Study, Birth Cohort survey population with data on primary care arrangements.
[2]Primary type of care arrangement is the type of nonparental care in which the child spent the most hours.
[3]Care provided in the child's home or in another private home by a relative (excluding parents).
[4]Care provided in the child's home or in another private home by a person unrelated to the child.
[5]Care provided in places such as early learning centers, nursery schools, and preschools, including Head Start.
[6]Children who spent an equal amount of time in each of two or more arrangements.
[7]Distribution of weighted Early Childhood Longitudinal Study, Birth Cohort survey population between 44 and 65 months of age with data on primary care arrangements.

[8]Poverty status based on Census Bureau guidelines from 2002, which identify a dollar amount determined to meet a household's needs, given its size and composition. In 2002, a family of four was considered to live below the poverty threshold if its income was less than or equal to $18,392.
[9]Socioeconomic status (SES) was measured by a composite score on parental education and occupations, and family income.
NOTE: Data are based on a representative sample of children born in 2001. Estimates for children at about 2 years of age weighted by W2R0. Estimates for children at about 4 years of age weighted by W3R0. Race categories exclude persons of Hispanic ethnicity. Detail may not sum to totals because of rounding and suppression of cells that do not meet standards. Standard errors appear in parentheses.
SOURCE: U.S. Department of Education, National Center for Education Statistics, Early Childhood Longitudinal Study, Birth Cohort, 9-month–Preschool Restricted-Use Data File and Electronic Codebook. (This table was prepared February 2008.)

Table 47. Percentage distribution of quality rating of child care arrangements of children at about 4 years of age, by type of arrangement and selected child and family characteristics: 2005–06

	Quality rating of primary type of child care arrangement[1]											
Selected characteristic	Home-based relative and nonrelative care[2,3]			Head Start and other center-based programs[4]			All center-based programs					
							Head Start[4]			Center-based care other than Head Start[4,5]		
	Low	Medium	High	Low	Medium	High	Low	Medium	High	Low	Medium	High
1	2	3	4	5	6	7	8	9	10	11	12	13
Total	42.6 (4.01)	47.9 (4.22)	9.5 (2.37)	9.5 (1.40)	55.8 (2.43)	34.7 (2.57)	3.2 (0.78)	56.7 (3.27)	40.1 (3.33)	11.6 (1.74)	55.5 (3.04)	32.9 (3.09)
Sex of child												
Male	45.5 (5.48)	44.1 (5.58)	10.4 (3.88)	6.4 (1.48)	53.3 (3.33)	40.3 (3.29)	2.2 (0.96)	56.5 (3.93)	41.3 (3.93)	7.9 (1.83)	52.2 (4.05)	39.9 (4.07)
Female	39.3 (5.23)	52.2 (5.83)	8.5 (2.45)	12.7 (2.32)	58.2 (3.32)	29.1 (3.23)	4.3 (1.14)	56.9 (4.83)	38.8 (4.88)	15.2 (2.83)	58.6 (3.98)	26.2 (3.70)
Race/ethnicity of child												
White	29.9 (4.72)	55.3 (5.34)	14.9 (4.09)	9.3 (1.79)	54.6 (3.76)	36.1 (3.68)	4.0 (1.92)	47.6 (8.27)	48.5 (8.28)	10.2 (1.94)	55.8 (3.99)	34.1 (3.82)
Black	52.8 (8.64)	47.2 (8.64)	‡	14.7 (3.72)	59.9 (4.52)	25.4 (3.89)	6.8 (1.57)	67.1 (4.41)	26.1 (4.61)	20.7 (6.22)	54.4 (6.72)	24.8 (4.23)
Hispanic	62.5 (8.53)	33.4 (8.03)	4.1 (2.31)	7.2 (2.79)	52.9 (4.25)	39.8 (4.77)	‡	56.2 (5.54)	43.4 (5.47)	11.7 (4.47)	50.8 (6.82)	37.6 (7.31)
Asian	‡	‡	‡	7.2 (3.52)	60.8 (8.13)	32.0 (7.99)	‡	‡	‡	7.8 (3.78)	63.7 (8.19)	23.6 (7.83)
Pacific Islander	‡	‡	‡	‡	73.5 (7.69)	23.5 (7.02)	‡	‡	‡	‡	‡	‡
American Indian/Alaska Native	‡	‡	‡	8.6 (4.86)	65.7 (7.78)	25.7 (6.77)	‡	‡	‡	‡	‡	‡
More than one race	‡	‡	‡	‡	‡	‡	‡	‡	‡	12.3 (6.65)	67.3 (9.09)	20.4 (7.10)
Age of child												
Less than 48 months	31.8 (7.35)	64.3 (7.24)	‡	10.2 (2.45)	56.8 (5.35)	33.0 (5.47)	‡	62.3 (8.56)	35.3 (8.44)	13.1 (3.62)	54.8 (7.33)	32.1 (7.16)
48 to 52 months	40.3 (6.19)	47.2 (6.86)	12.5 (4.19)	12.3 (2.58)	54.8 (4.11)	32.9 (3.71)	0.9 (0.49)	55.6 (6.30)	43.5 (6.33)	16.1 (3.22)	54.6 (4.99)	29.3 (4.36)
53 to 57 months	46.6 (6.49)	42.5 (6.69)	10.9 (3.14)	7.3 (1.66)	56.5 (3.22)	36.2 (3.36)	3.8 (1.34)	57.5 (4.02)	38.7 (4.06)	8.4 (2.07)	56.2 (4.22)	35.4 (4.29)
58 or more months	‡	‡	‡	7.2 (3.64)	55.0 (4.80)	37.8 (4.55)	14.8 (9.46)	46.1 (13.15)	39.1 (11.33)	5.0 (3.81)	57.5 (5.77)	37.5 (5.88)
Mother's employment status												
Full-time (35 hours or more)	36.6 (4.34)	56.6 (4.50)	6.9 (2.52)	14.9 (2.83)	55.3 (3.72)	29.8 (3.66)	4.9 (1.16)	47.7 (5.16)	47.4 (5.53)	17.7 (3.45)	57.4 (4.44)	25.0 (3.70)
Part-time (less than 35 hours)	48.9 (7.47)	35.1 (7.08)	16.0 (4.61)	5.7 (1.80)	60.9 (4.64)	33.4 (4.72)	3.2 (2.59)	59.8 (8.26)	37.0 (7.97)	6.5 (2.17)	61.2 (6.14)	32.3 (5.97)
Looking for work	‡	‡	‡	14.0 (5.16)	53.7 (6.25)	32.4 (6.61)	‡	73.4 (8.27)	24.2 (8.12)	22.4 (8.52)	39.2 (8.58)	38.4 (9.45)
Not in labor force	‡	‡	‡	3.5 (1.31)	53.3 (4.80)	43.2 (4.98)	1.7 (1.23)	58.9 (5.58)	39.4 (5.60)	4.2 (1.73)	51.2 (6.71)	44.7 (7.02)
No mother in household	‡	‡	‡	#	50.6 (39.00)	49.4 (39.00)	‡	‡	‡	‡	‡	‡
Parents' highest level of education												
Less than high school	63.0 (5.71)	31.8 (5.75)	5.1 (2.57)	12.5 (4.50)	59.1 (6.95)	28.3 (5.83)	‡	56.9 (7.43)	40.9 (7.36)	20.6 (7.95)	60.9 (10.59)	18.5 (7.52)
High school completion	40.1 (6.76)	52.3 (6.89)	7.6 (3.54)	6.0 (1.69)	49.9 (3.34)	44.1 (3.92)	4.9 (1.33)	54.9 (5.91)	40.3 (6.01)	6.7 (2.39)	47.2 (4.45)	46.1 (5.29)
Some college/vocational	29.9 (8.51)	62.1 (8.63)	8.0 (4.86)	16.1 (2.95)	58.8 (3.05)	25.1 (2.82)	2.8 (1.51)	60.4 (4.54)	36.8 (4.41)	22.4 (3.80)	58.1 (4.04)	19.5 (3.54)
Bachelor's degree	10.3 (5.73)	61.3 (8.63)	28.3 (7.99)	6.7 (2.43)	59.8 (6.64)	33.4 (6.78)	‡	‡	‡	7.3 (2.64)	60.2 (7.18)	32.6 (7.32)
Any graduate education	‡	‡	‡	5.0 (2.52)	53.6 (7.44)	41.4 (7.48)	‡	‡	‡	5.3 (2.66)	54.5 (7.47)	40.2 (7.47)
Poverty status[6]												
Below poverty threshold	68.1 (6.76)	28.3 (6.86)	3.6 (2.03)	9.2 (2.38)	59.1 (3.17)	31.7 (3.47)	2.6 (1.10)	57.9 (4.15)	39.6 (4.35)	15.4 (4.16)	60.2 (5.63)	24.4 (5.10)
At or above poverty threshold	35.8 (4.32)	53.2 (4.79)	11.1 (2.70)	9.6 (1.46)	54.7 (3.18)	35.7 (3.29)	3.8 (1.35)	55.5 (4.74)	40.6 (4.69)	10.8 (1.73)	54.5 (3.61)	34.7 (3.72)
Socioeconomic status[7]												
Lowest 20 percent	71.2 (7.12)	26.4 (7.02)	2.4 (1.80)	6.7 (2.19)	58.7 (4.31)	34.7 (4.41)	3.4 (1.25)	53.7 (5.22)	42.9 (5.54)	9.8 (3.99)	63.5 (7.31)	26.6 (6.57)
Middle 60 percent	43.3 (5.26)	49.7 (5.50)	7.0 (2.57)	11.3 (1.84)	56.3 (2.70)	32.4 (2.70)	3.2 (1.24)	59.3 (4.14)	37.5 (4.11)	14.1 (2.28)	55.2 (3.35)	30.7 (3.36)
Highest 20 percent	7.8 (4.79)	66.3 (7.41)	25.9 (6.85)	7.3 (2.54)	52.2 (6.28)	40.5 (6.20)	‡	‡	‡	7.5 (2.61)	52.7 (6.34)	39.8 (6.21)

†Not applicable.
#Rounds to zero.
‡Reporting standards not met.
[1]Primary type of care arrangement is the type of nonparental care in which the child spent the most hours.
[2]Care provided in the child's home or in another private home by a relative (excluding parents) or by a person unrelated to the child.
[3]Quality rating based on the Family Day Care Rating Scale (FDCRS). Low quality = score of 1 but less than 3. Medium quality = score of 3 but less than 5. High quality = score of 5 to 7.
[4]Quality rating based on the Early Childhood Environment Rating Scale (ECERS). Low quality = score of 1 but less than 3. Medium quality = score of 3 but less than 5. High quality = score of 5 to 7.
[5]Care provided in places such as early learning centers, nursery schools, and preschools, not classified as Head Start.
[6]Poverty status based on Census Bureau guidelines from 2002, which identify a dollar amount determined to meet a household's needs, given its size and composition. In 2002, a family of four was considered to live below the poverty threshold if its income was less than or equal to $18,392.
[7]Socioeconomic status (SES) was measured by a composite score on parental education and occupations, and family income.

NOTE: Estimates weighted by W33P0. Estimates pertain to children assessed between 44 months and 65 months of age. Rating is for child's primary type of care arrangement, which was the type of nonparental care in which the child spent the most hours. Children who were primarily cared for by parents or in multiple arrangements are not included in this table. Ratings of care arrangement quality using both the FDCRS and ECERS scales were based on interviewer observations of children's interactions with adults and peers, children's exposure to materials and activities, the extent to which and the manner in which routine care needs were met, and the furnishings and displays in the classroom. The FDCRS and ECERS metrics are designed to be equivalent. Race categories exclude persons of Hispanic ethnicity. Detail may not sum to totals because of rounding and suppression of cells that do not meet standards. Standard errors appear in parentheses.
SOURCE: U.S. Department of Education, National Center for Education Statistics, Early Childhood Longitudinal Study, Birth Cohort 9-month–Preschool Restricted-Use Data File and Electronic Codebook. (This table was prepared December 2008.)

Table 48. Children of prekindergarten through second-grade age, by enrollment status, selected maternal characteristics, and household income: 1995, 2001, and 2005

Maternal characteristic and household income	3- to 5-year-olds, not enrolled in school (includes homeschooled students)			Enrolled in nursery school or prekindergarten			Enrolled in kindergarten			Enrolled in first grade			Enrolled in second grade		
	1995	2001[1]	2005[1]	1995	2001[1]	2005[1]	1995	2001[1]	2005[1]	1995	2001[2]	2005[1]	1995	2001[2]	2005[1]
	2	3	4	5	6	7	8	9	10	11	12	13	14	15	16
Total children (in thousands)	4,586 (102.3)	3,990 (3.2)	4,156 (5.0)	4,642 (105.0)	4,586 (#)	4,926 (#)	4,149 (75.6)	3,831 (#)	3,717 (#)	4,025 (76.7)	4,333 (#)	4,118 (#)	3,777 (72.9)	3,934 (#)	3,900 (#)
Percentage distribution															
Mother's highest level of education[3]	100.0 (†)	100.0 (†)	100.0 (†)	100.0 (†)	100.0 (†)	100.0 (†)	100.0 (†)	100.0 (†)	100.0 (†)	100.0 (†)	100.0 (†)	100.0 (†)	100.0 (†)	100.0 (†)	100.0 (†)
Less than high school	16.3 (1.27)	16.4 (1.26)	13.8 (1.24)	6.8 (0.78)	8.0 (1.26)	6.8 (0.76)	13.4 (0.93)	10.7 (1.31)	9.5 (1.16)	12.3 (0.99)	11.7 (1.28)	10.0 (1.20)	15.0 (0.81)	13.5 (1.26)	10.3 (1.21)
High school/GED	41.1 (1.51)	39.7 (1.59)	37.2 (2.18)	30.7 (1.27)	26.1 (1.59)	24.6 (1.34)	36.4 (1.19)	30.3 (1.86)	27.5 (1.92)	34.9 (1.53)	30.3 (2.17)	31.1 (2.13)	35.6 (1.44)	32.8 (2.11)	29.5 (1.77)
Vocational/technical or some college	21.3 (1.34)	19.1 (1.30)	21.2 (1.43)	22.7 (1.01)	24.6 (1.30)	19.2 (1.32)	21.7 (1.00)	23.5 (1.84)	20.7 (1.70)	23.6 (1.29)	24.3 (1.87)	19.9 (1.94)	20.6 (0.94)	22.5 (2.18)	19.8 (1.64)
Associate's degree	7.0 (0.79)	5.9 (0.67)	6.8 (0.82)	8.6 (0.72)	7.7 (0.67)	8.4 (0.71)	7.0 (0.68)	7.6 (1.18)	7.7 (0.96)	7.3 (0.81)	7.5 (1.01)	10.3 (1.22)	7.6 (0.60)	7.5 (0.92)	8.0 (0.99)
Bachelor's degree	11.3 (0.86)	14.0 (1.16)	14.9 (1.20)	22.0 (1.10)	22.5 (1.16)	25.5 (1.13)	15.1 (0.98)	20.8 (1.58)	21.3 (1.42)	15.7 (1.02)	19.5 (1.68)	18.0 (1.23)	15.0 (0.94)	15.8 (1.70)	18.7 (1.46)
Graduate/professional degree	3.0 (0.48)	5.0 (0.63)	6.1 (0.73)	9.1 (0.70)	11.1 (0.63)	15.6 (0.94)	6.3 (0.69)	7.1 (1.02)	13.4 (1.43)	6.3 (0.49)	6.7 (1.04)	10.6 (1.22)	6.2 (0.67)	7.9 (1.28)	13.6 (1.62)
Mother's employment status[3]	100.0 (†)	100.0 (†)	100.0 (†)	100.0 (†)	100.0 (†)	100.0 (†)	100.0 (†)	100.0 (†)	100.0 (†)	100.0 (†)	100.0 (†)	100.0 (†)	100.0 (†)	100.0 (†)	100.0 (†)
Working 35 hours/week or more	33.4 (1.45)	36.7 (1.55)	33.5 (1.92)	38.5 (1.13)	43.7 (1.18)	39.4 (1.42)	35.9 (1.05)	38.9 (1.99)	36.9 (2.25)	38.5 (1.49)	46.1 (2.33)	40.7 (2.35)	40.5 (1.17)	42.3 (2.30)	41.2 (2.19)
Working less than 35 hours/week	17.8 (1.23)	19.2 (1.30)	21.1 (1.50)	23.7 (1.08)	22.8 (1.00)	24.4 (1.36)	20.8 (1.10)	22.6 (1.57)	21.5 (1.62)	20.8 (1.10)	19.7 (1.59)	20.7 (1.42)	21.4 (1.19)	20.1 (1.60)	22.7 (1.72)
Looking for work	6.8 (0.83)	5.7 (0.75)	8.7 (1.37)	5.8 (0.71)	3.9 (0.55)	4.0 (0.59)	5.6 (0.70)	3.9 (0.87)	7.3 (1.06)	5.0 (0.66)	4.1 (0.89)	5.7 (1.07)	5.4 (0.70)	5.1 (1.09)	4.9 (0.82)
Not in labor force	42.0 (1.68)	38.4 (1.48)	36.8 (1.79)	32.0 (1.28)	29.6 (1.27)	32.2 (1.35)	37.7 (1.18)	34.7 (2.16)	34.3 (1.99)	35.6 (1.57)	30.1 (2.05)	32.8 (1.97)	32.7 (1.30)	32.5 (2.22)	31.2 (1.99)
Household income	100.0 (†)	100.0 (†)	100.0 (†)	100.0 (†)	100.0 (†)	100.0 (†)	100.0 (†)	100.0 (†)	100.0 (†)	100.0 (†)	100.0 (†)	100.0 (†)	100.0 (†)	100.0 (†)	100.0 (†)
$10,000 or less	22.7 (1.21)	14.1 (1.07)	10.2 (1.06)	16.1 (1.06)	8.5 (0.81)	7.5 (0.90)	19.4 (1.24)	8.5 (1.22)	8.2 (0.95)	17.4 (1.19)	9.1 (1.18)	7.8 (1.05)	19.5 (1.34)	9.4 (1.07)	7.6 (1.08)
$10,001 to $20,000	15.7 (1.08)	14.5 (1.19)	12.0 (1.14)	10.4 (0.78)	12.7 (0.87)	9.7 (0.75)	12.6 (0.87)	14.1 (1.51)	11.1 (1.05)	13.2 (0.90)	14.0 (1.45)	10.4 (1.15)	11.6 (0.84)	12.4 (1.33)	12.5 (1.39)
$20,001 to $30,000	19.1 (1.12)	15.0 (0.94)	16.9 (1.38)	13.1 (0.81)	11.7 (0.74)	9.9 (1.18)	15.8 (0.76)	16.6 (1.41)	13.0 (1.32)	16.6 (0.91)	16.5 (1.71)	12.3 (1.32)	16.5 (1.05)	14.7 (1.54)	15.4 (1.71)
$30,001 to $40,000	16.2 (1.00)	13.6 (1.07)	15.3 (1.27)	12.4 (0.91)	9.7 (0.79)	9.9 (0.91)	15.1 (1.12)	12.2 (1.29)	11.1 (1.14)	14.1 (0.85)	10.7 (1.16)	10.7 (1.42)	16.1 (0.94)	12.4 (1.33)	10.6 (1.07)
$40,001 to $50,000	11.0 (0.74)	12.0 (1.05)	10.3 (1.12)	11.5 (0.96)	7.5 (0.58)	7.7 (0.64)	11.7 (0.88)	9.1 (1.16)	7.8 (1.07)	11.1 (0.77)	9.7 (1.34)	9.9 (1.14)	11.3 (0.92)	9.2 (1.08)	7.0 (0.87)
$50,001 to $75,000	10.5 (0.69)	18.8 (1.31)	20.0 (1.24)	19.3 (0.93)	21.2 (1.09)	20.8 (0.97)	14.4 (0.82)	20.9 (1.68)	18.4 (1.46)	15.6 (0.84)	18.3 (1.41)	20.4 (1.84)	15.0 (1.00)	19.6 (1.80)	20.3 (1.56)
More than $75,000	4.7 (0.70)	12.1 (0.99)	15.4 (1.30)	17.2 (1.06)	28.7 (1.09)	34.4 (1.13)	11.1 (0.62)	18.6 (1.30)	30.4 (1.54)	12.1 (0.73)	22.1 (1.86)	28.4 (1.56)	10.1 (0.79)	22.3 (1.78)	26.7 (1.83)

†Not applicable.
#Rounds to zero.
[1]Figures exclude children for whom no grade equivalent was available.
[2]Table includes a very small number of older children enrolled in first and second grade and excludes children for whom no grade equivalent was available.
[3]Excludes children living in households with no mother or female guardian present.
NOTE: Detail may not sum to totals because of rounding. Standard errors appear in parentheses.
SOURCE: U.S. Department of Education, National Center for Education Statistics, Early Childhood Program Participation Survey and Before- and After-School Programs and Activities Survey of the National Household Education Surveys Program (ECPP-NHES:1995, 2001, and 2005; and ASPA-NHES:2001 and 2005). (This table was prepared October 2006.)

Table 49. Percentage of 3- to 5-year-olds not yet enrolled in kindergarten who have participated in home literacy activities with a family member, by type of activity and selected child and family characteristics: 1993, 2001, and 2005

Selected child and family characteristic	Children (in thousands)			Percent participating three or more times in the past week												Visited a library[2]		
				Read to by family member[1]			Told a story by family member			Taught letters, words, or numbers			Did arts and crafts					
	1993	2001	2005	1993	2001	2005	1993	2001	2005	1993	2001	2005	1993	2001	2005	1993	2001	2005
1	2	3	4	5	6	7	8	9	10	11	12	13	14	15	16	17	18	19
Total	8,579 (42.0)	8,551 (11.0)	9,066 (9.0)	78 (0.7)	84 (0.8)	86 (0.7)	43 (0.9)	54 (0.9)	54 (1.0)	58 (0.8)	74 (1.0)	77 (0.9)	33 (0.8)	46 (1.0)	43 (1.2)	38 (1.0)	36 (1.1)	42 (1.2)
Age																		
3 years old	3,889 (8.2)	3,795 (91.4)	4,070 (93.0)	79 (1.0)	84 (1.1)	86 (1.2)	46 (1.3)	54 (1.4)	54 (1.9)	57 (1.3)	71 (1.7)	75 (1.2)	34 (1.3)	43 (1.7)	41 (1.8)	34 (1.9)	35 (1.9)	40 (1.7)
4 years old	3,713 (15.7)	3,861 (89.0)	3,873 (92.0)	78 (1.0)	85 (1.2)	85 (1.3)	41 (1.5)	55 (1.4)	53 (1.6)	58 (1.1)	77 (1.3)	77 (1.5)	33 (1.1)	48 (1.5)	44 (1.9)	41 (1.5)	37 (1.4)	44 (2.0)
5 years old	976 (39.4)	896 (47.0)	1,123 (67.3)	76 (2.1)	81 (2.7)	86 (2.2)	36 (2.7)	52 (3.0)	55 (3.4)	58 (2.8)	75 (2.5)	80 (2.3)	33 (2.3)	44 (2.7)	47 (3.5)	38 (2.7)	37 (3.4)	46 (4.0)
Sex																		
Male	4,453 (60.2)	4,292 (79.9)	4,707 (99.2)	77 (1.0)	82 (1.2)	85 (1.2)	43 (1.3)	53 (1.4)	53 (1.8)	58 (1.0)	73 (1.6)	75 (1.4)	31 (1.0)	41 (1.3)	39 (1.6)	38 (1.5)	35 (1.4)	44 (1.6)
Female	4,126 (65.0)	4,260 (79.6)	4,359 (99.6)	79 (1.0)	86 (1.0)	87 (0.9)	43 (1.2)	55 (1.3)	54 (1.6)	58 (1.4)	76 (1.3)	78 (1.2)	36 (1.2)	50 (1.5)	47 (1.6)	38 (1.1)	37 (1.6)	41 (1.7)
Race/ethnicity																		
White	5,902 (63.6)	5,313 (68.0)	5,177 (80.2)	85 (0.7)	89 (0.8)	92 (0.7)	44 (1.0)	58 (1.1)	53 (1.5)	58 (0.9)	75 (1.2)	76 (1.4)	36 (1.0)	49 (1.2)	47 (1.5)	42 (1.3)	39 (1.3)	45 (1.6)
Black	1,271 (44.9)	1,251 (55.1)	1,233 (57.1)	66 (2.4)	77 (2.6)	78 (3.1)	39 (2.7)	51 (2.9)	54 (3.6)	63 (2.7)	78 (3.4)	81 (3.1)	28 (2.4)	34 (3.3)	39 (4.0)	29 (2.6)	31 (2.6)	44 (3.8)
Hispanic	1,026 (34.1)	1,506 (43.5)	1,822 (50.0)	58 (2.4)	71 (1.9)	72 (2.0)	38 (2.2)	42 (2.1)	50 (2.4)	54 (1.9)	68 (2.0)	74 (2.2)	25 (2.1)	42 (2.2)	34 (2.5)	26 (1.6)	30 (2.0)	32 (2.1)
Other	381 (33.5)	482 (38.3)	834 (54.3)	73 (3.8)	87 (2.7)	88 (1.8)	50 (5.3)	60 (4.0)	64 (3.1)	59 (3.9)	78 (3.6)	82 (3.0)	32 (3.3)	46 (3.8)	47 (3.9)	43 (4.6)	38 (4.6)	48 (3.3)
Mother's highest level of education[3]																		
Less than high school	1,036 (50.1)	996 (54.5)	886 (59.4)	60 (2.7)	69 (2.8)	64 (3.3)	37 (3.2)	43 (3.7)	39 (3.5)	56 (2.7)	67 (3.0)	70 (3.0)	25 (2.2)	30 (2.9)	29 (3.2)	22 (2.7)	21 (2.4)	23 (3.2)
High school/GED	3,268 (79.6)	2,712 (89.0)	2,687 (117.9)	75 (1.3)	81 (1.6)	82 (1.6)	41 (1.3)	53 (1.7)	51 (2.4)	56 (1.3)	73 (1.5)	78 (1.9)	30 (1.2)	43 (1.7)	39 (2.3)	30 (1.8)	30 (1.9)	33 (2.5)
Vocational/technical or some college	2,291 (69.1)	1,833 (73.9)	1,782 (81.9)	83 (1.4)	85 (1.8)	88 (1.4)	45 (1.9)	53 (2.5)	56 (2.8)	60 (1.7)	76 (1.8)	78 (2.0)	37 (1.8)	47 (2.3)	45 (2.4)	44 (2.2)	38 (2.2)	47 (3.2)
Associate's degree	332 (25.7)	573 (40.9)	680 (44.1)	84 (3.1)	89 (2.5)	90 (2.3)	44 (4.3)	56 (3.2)	60 (3.6)	63 (3.9)	78 (3.5)	82 (2.8)	39 (4.1)	46 (3.8)	50 (3.5)	38 (4.1)	42 (4.3)	50 (4.1)
Bachelor's degree	912 (42.3)	1,553 (68.4)	1,949 (73.9)	90 (1.6)	93 (1.2)	93 (1.3)	48 (2.4)	58 (2.2)	57 (2.3)	57 (2.2)	76 (1.9)	75 (2.4)	37 (2.4)	53 (2.7)	47 (2.5)	55 (2.2)	46 (2.4)	53 (2.1)
Graduate/professional degree	569 (37.7)	685 (45.7)	879 (50.8)	90 (2.1)	96 (1.1)	94 (1.6)	50 (3.2)	67 (3.6)	63 (2.9)	60 (2.7)	80 (2.8)	75 (2.6)	42 (3.0)	55 (3.8)	48 (3.1)	59 (3.5)	55 (3.8)	58 (3.1)
Mother's employment status[3]																		
Employed	4,486 (77.3)	5,148 (84.2)	5,277 (111.1)	79 (1.0)	86 (1.0)	86 (1.0)	44 (1.0)	54 (1.3)	53 (1.5)	57 (1.2)	73 (1.3)	76 (1.3)	33 (1.1)	45 (1.5)	42 (1.7)	39 (1.2)	36 (1.2)	43 (1.6)
Unemployed	594 (45.0)	396 (36.9)	543 (63.7)	71 (3.4)	77 (5.0)	89 (2.6)	43 (2.9)	56 (5.6)	58 (6.8)	66 (3.7)	81 (5.0)	81 (3.6)	33 (3.9)	38 (5.2)	39 (5.1)	37 (3.7)	37 (4.8)	39 (4.5)
Not in labor force	3,328 (72.9)	2,809 (73.3)	3,043 (96.5)	79 (1.3)	83 (1.4)	85 (1.3)	43 (1.5)	54 (2.0)	55 (2.0)	58 (1.5)	76 (1.7)	76 (1.6)	34 (1.4)	48 (2.0)	45 (1.8)	37 (1.4)	38 (1.9)	43 (1.9)
Number of parents in the household																		
Two parents	6,226 (78.1)	6,416 (75.1)	7,000 (68.7)	81 (0.7)	87 (0.8)	87 (0.8)	44 (1.0)	55 (1.0)	53 (1.1)	57 (0.9)	74 (1.1)	76 (1.1)	35 (0.9)	48 (1.1)	44 (1.2)	41 (1.2)	38 (1.2)	43 (1.3)
None or one parent	2,353 (66.5)	2,135 (75.1)	2,066 (69.3)	71 (1.7)	76 (2.0)	83 (1.7)	41 (2.0)	51 (2.2)	55 (2.6)	59 (2.1)	73 (2.2)	78 (2.0)	30 (1.9)	39 (2.3)	41 (2.6)	30 (1.7)	30 (2.1)	40 (2.6)
Poverty status[4]																		
Above poverty threshold	6,323 (62.1)	6,620 (61.6)	7,095 (62.9)	82 (0.7)	87 (0.8)	88 (0.8)	44 (0.9)	55 (0.9)	55 (1.1)	57 (0.8)	75 (1.1)	77 (1.1)	36 (0.9)	47 (1.0)	45 (1.4)	41 (1.2)	39 (1.2)	44 (1.3)
At or below poverty threshold	2,256 (56.6)	1,931 (62.1)	1,971 (63.7)	67 (1.6)	74 (2.3)	78 (1.9)	39 (1.8)	51 (2.7)	51 (2.7)	60 (2.0)	72 (2.4)	76 (2.1)	27 (1.9)	40 (2.4)	38 (2.8)	28 (2.0)	27 (2.2)	36 (2.5)

[1]In 1993, respondents were asked about reading frequency in one of two versions. The percentages presented in the table are for all of the respondents who answered three or more times on either version of the questions.
[2]Refers to visiting a library at least once in the past month.
[3]Excludes children living in households with no mother or female guardian present.
[4]Poverty status was determined by household income and number of persons in household.

NOTE: Race categories exclude persons of Hispanic ethnicity. Detail may not sum to totals because of rounding. Standard errors appear in parentheses.
SOURCE: U.S. Department of Education, National Center for Education Statistics, School Readiness Survey and Early Childhood Program Participation Survey of the National Household Education Surveys Program (SR-NHES:1993 and ECPP-NHES:2001 and 2005). (This table was prepared October 2006.)

Table 50. Children 3 to 21 years old served in federally supported programs for the disabled, by type of disability: Selected years, 1976–77 through 2006–07

Type of disability	1976–77	1980–81	1990–91	1995–96	1996–97	1997–98	1998–99	1999–2000	2000–01	2001–02	2002–03	2003–04	2004–05	2005–06	2006–07
1	2	3	4	5	6	7	8	9	10	11	12	13	14	15	16
	Number served (in thousands)														
All disabilities	3,694	4,144	4,710	5,572	5,737	5,908	6,056	6,195	6,296	6,407	6,523	6,634	6,719	6,713	6,686
Specific learning disabilities	796	1,462	2,129	2,578	2,651	2,727	2,790	2,834	2,868	2,861	2,848	2,831	2,798	2,735	2,665
Speech or language impairments	1,302	1,168	985	1,022	1,045	1,060	1,068	1,080	1,409	1,391	1,412	1,441	1,463	1,468	1,475
Mental retardation	961	830	534	571	579	589	597	600	624	616	602	593	578	556	534
Emotional disturbance	283	347	389	437	446	454	462	469	481	483	485	489	489	477	464
Hearing impairments	88	79	58	67	68	69	70	71	78	78	78	79	79	79	80
Orthopedic impairments	87	58	49	63	66	67	69	71	83	83	83	77	73	71	69
Other health impairments[1]	141	98	55	133	160	190	220	253	303	350	403	464	521	570	611
Visual impairments	38	31	23	25	25	26	26	26	29	28	29	28	29	29	29
Multiple disabilities	—	68	96	93	98	106	106	111	133	136	138	140	140	141	142
Deaf-blindness	—	3	1	1	1	1	2	2	1	2	2	2	2	2	2
Autism	—	—	—	28	34	42	53	65	94	114	137	163	191	223	258
Traumatic brain injury	—	—	—	9	10	12	13	14	16	22	22	23	24	24	25
Developmental delay	—	—	—	—	—	2	12	19	178	242	283	305	332	339	333
Preschool disabled[2]	†	†	390	544	555	565	568	581	†	†	†	†	†	†	†
	Percentage distribution of children served														
All disabilities	100.0	100.0	100.0	100.0	100.0	100.0	100.0	100.0	100.0	100.0	100.0	100.0	100.0	100.0	100.0
Specific learning disabilities	21.5	35.3	45.2	46.3	46.2	46.2	46.1	45.7	45.5	44.7	43.7	42.7	41.6	40.7	39.9
Speech or language impairments	35.2	28.2	20.9	18.3	18.2	17.9	17.6	17.4	22.4	21.7	21.6	21.7	21.8	21.9	22.1
Mental retardation	26.0	20.0	11.3	10.2	10.1	10.0	9.9	9.7	9.9	9.6	9.2	8.9	8.6	8.3	8.0
Emotional disturbance	7.7	8.4	8.3	7.8	7.8	7.7	7.6	7.6	7.6	7.5	7.4	7.4	7.3	7.1	6.9
Hearing impairments	2.4	1.9	1.2	1.2	1.2	1.2	1.2	1.1	1.2	1.2	1.2	1.2	1.2	1.2	1.2
Orthopedic impairments	2.4	1.4	1.0	1.1	1.1	1.1	1.1	1.1	1.3	1.3	1.3	1.2	1.1	1.1	1.0
Other health impairments[1]	3.8	2.4	1.2	2.4	2.8	3.2	3.6	4.1	4.8	5.5	6.2	7.0	7.7	8.5	9.1
Visual impairments	1.0	0.7	0.5	0.4	0.4	0.4	0.4	0.4	0.5	0.4	0.4	0.4	0.4	0.4	0.4
Multiple disabilities	—	1.6	2.0	1.7	1.7	1.8	1.8	1.8	2.1	2.1	2.1	2.1	2.1	2.1	2.1
Deaf-blindness	—	0.1	#	#	#	#	#	#	#	#	#	#	#	#	#
Autism	—	—	—	0.5	0.6	0.7	0.9	1.0	1.5	1.8	2.1	2.5	2.8	3.3	3.9
Traumatic brain injury	—	—	—	0.2	0.2	0.2	0.2	0.2	0.2	0.3	0.3	0.4	0.4	0.4	0.4
Developmental delay	—	—	—	—	—	0.0	0.2	0.3	2.8	3.8	4.3	4.6	4.9	5.1	5.0
Preschool disabled[2]	†	†	8.3	9.8	9.7	9.6	9.4	9.4	†	†	†	†	†	†	†
	Number served as a percent of total enrollment[3]														
All disabilities	8.3	10.1	11.4	12.4	12.6	12.8	13.0	13.2	13.3	13.4	13.5	13.7	13.8	13.7	13.6
Specific learning disabilities	1.8	3.6	5.2	5.8	5.8	5.9	6.0	6.0	6.1	6.0	5.9	5.8	5.7	5.6	5.4
Speech or language impairments	2.9	2.9	2.4	2.3	2.3	2.3	2.3	2.3	3.0	2.9	2.9	3.0	3.0	3.0	3.0
Mental retardation	2.2	2.0	1.3	1.3	1.3	1.3	1.3	1.3	1.3	1.3	1.2	1.2	1.2	1.1	1.1
Emotional disturbance	0.6	0.8	0.9	1.0	1.0	1.0	1.0	1.0	1.0	1.0	1.0	1.0	1.0	1.0	0.9
Hearing impairments	0.2	0.2	0.1	0.1	0.1	0.1	0.2	0.2	0.2	0.2	0.2	0.2	0.2	0.2	0.2
Orthopedic impairments	0.2	0.1	0.1	0.1	0.1	0.1	0.1	0.2	0.2	0.2	0.2	0.2	0.2	0.1	0.1
Other health impairments[1]	0.3	0.2	0.1	0.3	0.4	0.4	0.5	0.5	0.6	0.7	0.8	1.0	1.1	1.2	1.2
Visual impairments	0.1	0.1	0.1	0.1	0.1	0.1	0.1	0.1	0.1	0.1	0.1	0.1	0.1	0.1	0.1
Multiple disabilities	—	0.2	0.2	0.2	0.2	0.2	0.2	0.2	0.3	0.3	0.3	0.3	0.3	0.3	0.3
Deaf-blindness	—	#	#	#	#	#	#	#	#	#	#	#	#	#	#
Autism	—	—	—	0.1	0.1	0.1	0.1	0.1	0.2	0.2	0.3	0.3	0.4	0.5	0.5
Traumatic brain injury	—	—	—	#	#	#	#	#	#	#	#	#	#	#	0.1
Developmental delay	—	—	—	—	—	#	#	#	0.4	0.5	0.6	0.6	0.7	0.7	0.7
Preschool disabled[2]	†	†	0.9	1.2	1.2	1.2	1.2	1.2	†	†	†	†	†	†	†

—Not available.
†Not applicable.
#Rounds to zero.
[1]Other health impairments include having limited strength, vitality, or alertness due to chronic or acute health problems such as a heart condition, tuberculosis, rheumatic fever, nephritis, asthma, sickle cell anemia, hemophilia, epilepsy, lead poisoning, leukemia, or diabetes.
[2]Includes preschool children ages 3–5 served under Chapter 1 and IDEA, Part B. Prior to 1987–88, these students were included in the counts by disability condition. Beginning in 1987–88, states were no longer required to report preschool children (ages 0–5) by disability condition. Beginning in 2000–01, preschool children were again identified by disability condition.
[3]Based on the total enrollment in public schools, prekindergarten through 12th grade.
NOTE: Includes students served under Chapter 1 of the Elementary and Secondary Education Act and under the Individuals with Disabilities Education Act (IDEA), formerly the Education of the Handicapped Act. Prior to October 1994, children and youth with disabilities were served under Chapter 1 as well as IDEA, Part B. In October 1994, funding for children and youth with

disabilities was consolidated under IDEA, Part B. Data reported in this table for years prior to 1994–95 include children ages 0–21 served under Chapter 1. Counts are based on reports from the 50 states and the District of Columbia only (i.e., table excludes data for other jurisdictions). Increases since 1987–88 are due in part to new legislation enacted in fall 1986, which added a mandate for public school special education services for 3- to 5-year-old disabled children. Some data have been revised from previously published figures. Detail may not sum to totals because of rounding.
SOURCE: U.S. Department of Education, Office of Special Education and Rehabilitative Services, Annual Report to Congress on the Implementation of the Individuals with Disabilities Education Act, selected years, 1977 through 2006; and Individuals with Disabilities Education Act (IDEA) database, retrieved August 1, 2008, from http://www.ideadata.org/PartBdata.asp. National Center for Education Statistics, Statistics of Public Elementary and Secondary School Systems, 1977; Common Core of Data (CCD), "State Nonfiscal Survey of Public Elementary/Secondary Education," 1981–82 through 2006–07. (This table was prepared October 2008.)

Table 51. Percentage distribution of students 6 to 21 years old served under Individuals with Disabilities Education Act, Part B, by educational environment and type of disability: Selected years, fall 1989 through fall 2006

Type of disability	All environments	Regular school, time outside regular class			Separate school for students with disabilities		Separate residential facility		Parentally placed in regular private schools	Homebound /hospital placement	Correctional facility
		Less than 21 percent	21–60 percent	More than 60 percent	Public	Private	Public	Private			
1	2	3	4	5	6	7	8	9	10	11	12
All students with disabilities											
1989	100.0	31.7	37.5	24.9	3.2	1.3	0.7	0.3	—	0.6	—
1990	100.0	33.1	36.4	25.0	2.9	1.3	0.6	0.3	—	0.5	—
1994	100.0	44.8	28.5	22.4	2.0	1.0	0.5	0.3	—	0.6	—
1995	100.0	45.7	28.5	21.5	2.1	1.0	0.4	0.3	—	0.5	—
1996	100.0	46.1	28.3	21.4	2.0	1.0	0.4	0.3	—	0.5	—
1997	100.0	46.8	28.8	20.4	1.8	1.0	0.4	0.3	—	0.5	—
1998	100.0	46.0	29.9	20.0	1.8	1.1	0.4	0.3	—	0.5	—
1999	100.0	45.9	29.8	20.3	1.9	1.0	0.4	0.3	—	0.5	—
2000	100.0	46.5	29.8	19.5	1.9	1.1	0.4	0.3	—	0.5	—
2001	100.0	48.2	28.5	19.2	1.7	1.2	0.4	0.4	—	0.4	—
2002	100.0	48.2	28.7	19.0	1.7	1.2	0.3	0.4	—	0.5	—
2003	100.0	49.9	27.7	18.5	1.7	1.1	0.3	0.4	—	0.5	—
2004											
All students with disabilities	**100.0**	**51.9**	**26.5**	**17.6**	**1.8**	**1.2**	**0.3**	**0.3**	**—**	**0.4**	**—**
Specific learning disabilities	100.0	51.2	35.8	12.0	0.3	0.4	0.1	0.1	—	0.2	—
Speech or language impairments	100.0	88.3	6.5	4.7	0.1	0.2	#	#	—	0.1	—
Mental retardation	100.0	13.1	29.7	50.8	4.4	1.0	0.3	0.3	—	0.4	—
Emotional disturbance	100.0	32.3	22.0	28.4	7.2	5.8	1.2	2.0	—	1.2	—
Multiple disabilities	100.0	12.8	16.9	45.2	12.7	8.1	0.9	1.3	—	2.2	—
Hearing impairments	100.0	46.9	18.8	20.9	4.3	2.6	5.9	0.4	—	0.2	—
Orthopedic impairments	100.0	48.2	19.5	25.8	4.0	0.8	0.1	0.1	—	1.5	—
Other health impairments[1]	100.0	53.7	29.3	13.6	0.8	0.8	0.1	0.2	—	1.4	—
Visual impairments	100.0	56.1	16.1	15.0	3.7	2.1	5.7	0.8	—	0.5	—
Autism	100.0	29.1	17.8	41.8	5.5	4.7	0.1	0.7	—	0.3	—
Deaf-blindness	100.0	19.4	15.6	35.1	8.5	6.9	7.6	2.9	—	3.9	—
Traumatic brain injury	100.0	37.5	28.4	25.9	2.7	3.1	0.2	0.6	—	1.5	—
Developmental delay	100.0	56.8	25.2	16.7	0.7	0.2	0.1	#	—	0.2	—
2005											
All students with disabilities	**100.0**	**54.2**	**25.1**	**16.7**	**1.8**	**1.2**	**0.3**	**0.3**	**—**	**0.5**	**—**
Specific learning disabilities	100.0	54.5	33.7	10.9	0.3	0.3	0.1	0.1	—	0.2	—
Speech or language impairments	100.0	88.7	6.2	4.6	0.1	0.3	#	#	—	0.1	—
Mental retardation	100.0	14.1	29.1	50.2	4.6	1.0	0.2	0.3	—	0.5	—
Emotional disturbance	100.0	34.7	21.6	26.8	6.9	5.7	1.2	1.8	—	1.3	—
Multiple disabilities	100.0	13.3	16.9	45.1	12.2	8.0	0.9	1.3	—	2.3	—
Hearing impairments	100.0	48.8	18.3	19.5	4.8	2.3	5.8	0.4	—	0.2	—
Orthopedic impairments	100.0	49.5	18.1	25.7	4.1	0.8	0.1	0.1	—	1.6	—
Other health impairments[1]	100.0	56.0	28.0	12.8	0.8	0.8	0.1	0.2	—	1.3	—
Visual impairments	100.0	58.2	15.2	14.2	4.1	1.6	5.4	0.7	—	0.6	—
Autism	100.0	31.4	18.2	39.8	5.1	4.4	0.1	0.6	—	0.4	—
Deaf-blindness	100.0	22.8	15.1	33.6	10.1	7.3	6.6	3.2	—	1.4	—
Traumatic brain injury	100.0	40.0	27.5	24.5	2.8	3.0	0.2	0.5	—	1.5	—
Developmental delay	100.0	59.5	23.4	15.8	0.7	0.3	0.1	#	—	0.2	—
2006											
All students with disabilities	**100.0**	**53.7**	**23.7**	**17.6**	**2.9** [2]	**(2)**	**0.4** [2]	**(2)**	**1.0** [3]	**0.4**	**0.4**
Specific learning disabilities	100.0	54.8	31.4	11.8	0.7 [2]	(2)	0.1 [2]	(2)	0.7 [3]	0.2	0.4
Speech or language impairments	100.0	84.2	6.1	6.8	0.3 [2]	(2)	# [2]	(2)	2.5 [3]	0.1	#
Mental retardation	100.0	16.0	28.7	48.4	5.6 [2]	(2)	0.4 [2]	(2)	0.2 [3]	0.5	0.3
Emotional disturbance	100.0	35.1	20.8	26.6	12.3 [2]	(2)	2.1 [2]	(2)	0.2 [3]	1.2	1.7
Multiple disabilities	100.0	13.4	16.7	44.4	20.5 [2]	(2)	2.0 [2]	(2)	0.4 [3]	2.3	0.3
Hearing impairments	100.0	48.8	17.8	19.8	8.2 [2]	(2)	4.2 [2]	(2)	1.0 [3]	0.2	0.1
Orthopedic impairments	100.0	47.0	19.0	26.3	5.3 [2]	(2)	0.2 [2]	(2)	0.7 [3]	1.4	#
Other health impairments[1]	100.0	54.8	26.5	14.9	1.6 [2]	(2)	0.2 [2]	(2)	0.8 [3]	1.0	0.2
Visual impairments	100.0	57.2	14.7	15.9	6.4 [2]	(2)	4.4 [2]	(2)	0.9 [3]	0.5	0.1
Autism	100.0	32.3	18.4	38.7	9.0 [2]	(2)	0.7 [2]	(2)	0.5 [3]	0.3	#
Deaf-blindness	100.0	21.0	13.5	34.8	20.7 [2]	(2)	7.6 [2]	(2)	0.6 [3]	1.8	#
Traumatic brain injury	100.0	41.7	26.1	23.7	5.7 [2]	(2)	0.6 [2]	(2)	0.6 [3]	1.4	0.2
Developmental delay	100.0	58.8	21.3	18.4	0.8 [2]	(2)	0.1 [2]	(2)	0.4 [3]	0.2	#

—Not available.
#Rounds to zero.
[1]Other health impairments include having limited strength, vitality, or alertness due to chronic or acute health problems such as a heart condition, tuberculosis, rheumatic fever, nephritis, asthma, sickle cell anemia, hemophilia, epilepsy, lead poisoning, leukemia, or diabetes.
[2]Data for 2006 combine public and private schools and combine public and private residential facilities.
[3]Students who are enrolled by their parents or guardians in regular private schools and have their basic education paid through private resources, but receive special education services at public expense. These students are not included under "Regular school, time outside general class" (columns 3 through 5).
NOTE: Data are for the 50 United States, the District of Columbia, and the Bureau of Indian Education schools taken on the Child Count date of the last Friday in October or December 1. Detail may not sum to totals because of rounding.
SOURCE: U.S. Department of Education, Office of Special Education Programs, Individuals with Disabilities Education Act (IDEA) database. Retrieved April 17, 2008, from https://www.ideadata.org/tables30th/ar_2-2.xls. (This table was prepared August 2008.)

Table 52. Number and percentage of children served under Individuals with Disabilities Education Act, Part B, by age group and state or jurisdiction: Selected years, 1990–91 through 2006–07

State or jurisdiction	3- to 21-year-olds served						As a percent of public school enrollment, 2006–07[1]	Percent change in number served, 2000–01 to 2006–07	3- to 5-year-olds served					
	1990–91	2000–01	2003–04	2004–05	2005–06	2006–07			1990–91	2000–01	2003–04	2004–05	2005–06	2006–07
1	2	3	4	5	6	7	8	9	10	11	12	13	14	15
United States	4,710,089	6,295,816	6,633,902	6,718,619	6,712,605	6,686,361	13.6	6.2	389,751	592,087	670,406	692,989	698,608	706,401
Alabama	94,601	99,828	93,056	93,402	92,635	89,013	12.0	-10.8	7,154	7,554	7,843	8,270	8,218	8,026
Alaska....................	14,390	17,691	17,959	18,134	17,997	17,760	13.4	0.4	1,458	1,637	1,968	2,002	2,082	1,987
Arizona..................	56,629	96,442	112,125	119,841	124,504	126,654	11.9	31.3	4,330	9,144	11,952	13,527	14,062	14,040
Arkansas................	47,187	62,222	66,793	68,088	67,314	68,133	14.3	9.5	4,626	9,376	10,670	11,638	10,286	11,689
California	468,420	645,287	675,763	675,417	676,318	672,737	10.5	4.3	39,627	57,651	61,950	63,240	66,653	67,052
Colorado................	56,336	78,715	82,447	83,249	83,498	83,559	10.5	6.2	4,128	8,202	9,673	10,307	10,540	10,939
Connecticut............	63,886	73,886	73,952	73,028	71,968	69,127	12.0	-6.4	5,466	7,172	8,135	7,978	7,881	6,833
Delaware................	14,208	16,760	18,417	18,698	18,857	19,366	15.8	15.5	1,493	1,652	2,031	1,975	2,073	2,213
District of Columbia	6,290	10,559	13,242	13,424	11,738	11,113	15.3	5.2	411	374	301	579	507	754
Florida...................	234,509	367,335	397,758	400,001	398,916	398,289	14.9	8.4	14,883	30,660	35,258	35,124	34,350	33,644
Georgia..................	101,762	171,292	190,948	195,928	197,596	196,810	12.1	14.9	7,098	16,560	20,260	20,801	20,728	20,410
Hawaii	12,705	23,951	23,266	22,711	21,963	21,099	11.7	-11.9	809	1,919	2,284	2,325	2,423	2,459
Idaho.....................	21,703	29,174	29,092	28,880	29,021	28,439	10.6	-2.5	2,815	3,591	3,807	3,910	4,043	3,889
Illinois...................	236,060	297,316	318,111	322,982	323,444	326,763	15.4	9.9	22,997	28,787	32,718	34,519	35,454	37,152
Indiana..................	112,949	156,320	171,896	175,205	177,826	179,043	17.1	14.5	7,243	15,101	18,439	19,008	19,228	19,364
Iowa......................	59,787	72,461	73,717	73,637	72,457	71,394	14.8	-1.5	5,421	5,580	5,985	6,059	6,118	6,199
Kansas...................	44,785	61,267	65,139	65,290	65,595	65,831	14.0	7.4	3,881	7,728	9,190	9,179	9,267	9,524
Kentucky................	78,853	94,572	103,783	106,916	108,798	109,354	16.0	15.6	10,440	16,372	20,219	20,777	21,317	21,007
Louisiana...............	72,825	97,938	101,933	102,498	90,453	89,422	13.2	-8.7	6,703	9,957	11,386	11,904	10,597	10,503
Maine....................	27,987	35,633	37,784	37,573	36,522	35,564	18.3	-0.2	2,895	3,978	4,647	4,806	4,348	4,145
Maryland................	88,017	112,077	113,865	112,404	110,959	106,739	12.5	-4.8	7,163	10,003	12,105	12,230	12,148	11,590
Massachusetts.........	149,743	162,216	159,042	161,992	162,654	165,959	17.1	2.3	12,141	14,328	14,822	14,821	15,195	15,813
Michigan................	166,511	221,456	238,292	242,083	243,607	241,941	14.1	9.3	14,547	19,937	23,465	24,058	24,290	24,268
Minnesota..............	79,013	109,880	114,193	115,491	116,511	117,924	14.0	7.3	8,646	11,522	12,987	12,783	13,402	13,989
Mississippi.............	60,872	62,281	66,848	68,883	68,099	67,590	13.7	8.5	5,642	6,944	7,994	8,361	8,319	8,430
Missouri.................	101,166	137,381	143,593	142,872	143,204	141,406	15.4	2.9	4,100	11,307	15,140	15,047	15,268	15,415
Montana.................	16,955	19,313	19,435	19,515	19,259	18,557	12.8	-3.9	1,751	1,635	1,798	1,878	1,925	1,941
Nebraska................	32,312	42,793	44,561	45,712	45,239	44,833	15.6	4.8	2,512	3,724	4,445	4,707	4,665	4,886
Nevada	18,099	38,160	45,201	47,015	47,794	48,230	11.4	26.4	1,401	3,676	4,933	5,185	5,492	5,669
New Hampshire	19,049	30,077	31,311	31,675	31,782	31,399	15.4	4.4	1,468	2,387	2,586	2,700	2,902	2,905
New Jersey.............	178,870	221,272	241,272	245,878	249,385	250,109	18.0	12.8	14,741	16,361	18,545	18,982	19,329	19,782
New Mexico	36,000	52,256	51,814	51,464	50,322	47,917	14.6	-8.3	2,210	4,970	5,656	6,207	6,441	6,300
New York................	307,366	441,333	442,665	452,312	447,422	451,929	16.1	2.4	26,266	51,665	55,588	60,692	58,297	60,156
North Carolina	122,942	173,067	193,956	193,377	192,820	192,451	13.3	11.2	10,516	17,361	21,018	20,210	20,543	20,433
North Dakota	12,294	13,652	14,044	14,681	13,883	13,825	14.3	1.3	1,164	1,247	1,501	1,531	1,520	1,567
Ohio......................	205,440	237,643	253,878	260,710	266,447	269,133	14.7	13.3	12,487	18,664	19,659	20,955	22,702	23,455
Oklahoma...............	65,457	85,577	93,045	95,022	96,601	95,860	15.0	12.0	5,163	6,393	7,769	8,080	8,149	7,625
Oregon...................	54,422	75,204	76,083	77,094	77,376	77,832	13.8	3.5	2,854	6,926	7,453	7,834	8,167	8,311
Pennsylvania...........	214,254	242,655	273,259	282,356	288,733	292,798	15.6	20.7	17,982	21,477	24,459	25,438	25,964	27,599
Rhode Island	20,646	30,727	32,223	31,532	30,681	30,243	19.9	-1.6	1,682	2,614	2,930	2,935	2,815	2,982
South Carolina.........	77,367	105,922	111,077	111,509	110,219	107,353	15.3	1.4	7,948	11,775	11,818	11,668	11,603	13,864
South Dakota	14,726	16,825	17,760	17,921	17,631	17,824	14.7	5.9	2,105	2,286	2,540	2,712	2,747	2,684
Tennessee..............	104,853	125,863	122,627	122,643	120,122	120,263	12.3	-4.4	7,487	10,699	11,121	11,713	12,008	11,967
Texas....................	344,529	491,642	506,771	514,236	507,405	494,302	10.7	0.5	24,848	36,442	40,607	41,564	40,236	39,351
Utah......................	46,606	53,921	57,745	59,840	60,526	61,166	11.7	13.4	3,424	5,785	6,733	7,221	7,462	7,597
Vermont	12,160	13,623	13,670	13,894	13,917	14,010	14.7	2.8	1,097	1,237	1,378	1,512	1,556	1,602
Virginia..................	112,072	162,212	172,788	174,417	174,640	170,794	14.0	5.3	9,892	14,444	16,422	16,996	17,480	16,968
Washington.............	83,545	118,851	123,673	124,067	124,498	122,979	12.0	3.5	9,558	11,760	13,010	13,086	13,429	13,174
West Virginia...........	42,428	50,333	50,772	50,377	49,677	49,054	17.4	-2.5	2,923	5,445	5,604	5,659	5,833	6,013
Wisconsin...............	85,651	125,358	127,828	129,179	130,076	128,526	14.7	2.5	10,934	14,383	15,393	15,955	16,077	15,591
Wyoming................	10,852	13,154	13,430	13,565	13,696	13,945	16.4	6.0	1,221	1,695	2,211	2,332	2,469	2,645
Bureau of Indian Education	6,997	8,448	8,343	8,051	7,795	6,918	—	-18.1	1,092	338	344	256	330	234
Other jurisdictions ...	38,986	70,670	83,948	93,716	93,256	102,995	—	45.7	3,892	8,168	9,392	8,704	5,149	7,749
American Samoa.............	363	697	1,135	1,239	1,211	1,146	7.0	64.4	48	48	138	98	80	78
Guam.....................	1,750	2,267	2,460	2,485	2,480	2,380	—	5.0	198	205	200	172	171	152
Northern Marianas	411	569	669	751	750	774	6.6	36.0	211	53	69	82	70	76
Palau.....................	—	131	—	—	—	—	—	—	—	10	—	—	—	—
Puerto Rico.............	35,129	65,504	77,932	87,485	87,125	97,129	17.9	48.3	3,345	7,746	8,806	8,185	4,677	7,314
U.S. Virgin Islands	1,333	1,502	1,752	1,756	1,690	1,566	9.6	4.3	90	106	179	167	151	129

—Not available.
[1]Percentage of students with disabilities is based on the total enrollment in public schools, pre-kindergarten through 12th grade.
NOTE: Prior to 1994, children and youth with disabilities were served under the Individuals with Disabilities Education Act (IDEA), Part B, and Chapter 1 of the Elementary and Secondary Education Act. In October 1994, funding for children and youth with disabilities was consolidated under IDEA, Part B. Data reported in this table for years prior to 1994 include children served under Chapter 1. Some data have been revised from previously published figures.

SOURCE: U.S. Department of Education, Office of Special Education and Rehabilitative Services, Annual Report to Congress on the Implementation of the Individuals with Disabilities Education Act, selected years, 1992 through 2006, and Individuals with Disabilities Education Act (IDEA) database, retrieved April 17, 2008, from http://www.ideadata.org/PartBdata.asp. National Center for Education Statistics, Common Core of Data (CCD), "State Nonfiscal Survey of Public Elementary/Secondary Education," 2006–07. (This table was prepared October 2008.)

Table 53. Number of gifted and talented students in public elementary and secondary schools, by sex, race/ethnicity, and state: 2004 and 2006

State	2004, total	2006							
		Total	Sex Male	Sex Female	Race/ethnicity White	Black	Hispanic	Asian/Pacific Islander	American Indian/Alaska Native
1	2	3	4	5	6	7	8	9	10
United States	3,202,760 (24,248)	3,236,990 (21,177)	1,579,000 (10,460)	1,657,990 (10,859)	2,191,210 (15,896)	296,150 (3,375)	414,060 (3,350)	304,220 (6,195)	31,360 (1,179)
Alabama	35,680 (798)	40,610 (361)	19,970 (184)	20,650 (184)	31,450 (338)	7,260 (109)	660 (14)	820 (6)	420 (6)
Alaska	5,390 (166)	5,620 (192)	2,810 (102)	2,810 (91)	4,390 (143)	160 (#)	160 (5)	490 (31)	420 (29)
Arizona	57,570 (1,275)	60,060 (711)	30,770 (412)	29,290 (306)	38,830 (544)	1,730 (20)	13,940 (178)	3,620 (29)	1,940 (394)
Arkansas	50,340 (3,219)	45,600 (1,870)	21,110 (924)	24,490 (967)	34,900 (1,253)	7,470 (677)	2,200 ! (860)	760 (26)	270 (41)
California	527,370 (10,256)	523,450 (13,209)	260,010 (6,688)	263,440 (6,567)	230,220 (7,405)	21,150 (559)	147,040 (2,827)	121,410 (5,930)	3,630 (276)
Colorado	50,350 (747)	54,000 (620)	27,770 (314)	26,240 (319)	40,420 (543)	2,280 (6)	8,190 (93)	2,730 (14)	400 (11)
Connecticut	15,980 (1,572)	20,170 (2,183)	9,660 (1,094)	10,510 (1,097)	15,470 (1,515)	1,710 (404)	1,350 (295)	1,560 (192)	90 (46)
Delaware	5,260 (†)	6,240 (†)	2,830 (†)	3,410 (†)	4,120 (†)	1,290 (†)	390 (†)	430 (†)	10 (†)
District of Columbia	— (—)	— (—)	— (—)	— (—)	— (—)	— (—)	— (—)	— (—)	— (—)
Florida	114,400 (1,095)	132,440 (893)	66,740 (462)	65,700 (438)	81,710 (761)	13,170 (92)	31,020 (106)	6,130 (23)	400 (6)
Georgia	136,620 (3,954)	150,680 (5,291)	71,110 (2,572)	79,560 (2,725)	110,350 (4,419)	26,370 (796)	4,470 (187)	9,250 (265)	240 (14)
Hawaii[2]	10,290 (993)	11,140 (†)	4,680 (†)	6,460 (†)	2,570 (†)	120 (†)	220 (†)	8,180 (†)	50 (†)
Idaho	9,920 (528)	10,650 (475)	5,570 (242)	5,070 (237)	9,850 (425)	50 (3)	450 (38)	240 (18)	40 (6)
Illinois	112,570 (4,554)	118,480 (5,016)	56,230 (2,375)	62,250 (2,674)	76,680 (3,996)	18,240 (1,697)	12,720 (225)	10,610 (667)	230 (24)
Indiana	74,780 (5,219)	82,830 (4,222)	37,930 (1,896)	44,900 (2,350)	72,400 (3,820)	5,320 (644)	2,560 (222)	2,450 (272)	110 (14)
Iowa	41,460 (1,657)	39,300 (1,030)	19,490 (516)	19,820 (533)	36,060 (970)	1,000 (17)	910 (86)	1,250 (71)	80 (6)
Kansas	15,150 (389)	14,430 (487)	7,810 (280)	6,610 (218)	12,760 (445)	390 (21)	500 (20)	650 (25)	120 (11)
Kentucky	85,660 (3,179)	96,600 (2,885)	45,310 (1,384)	51,290 (1,528)	89,170 (2,781)	5,150 (394)	890 (43)	1,310 (54)	70 (8)
Louisiana	28,020 (2,300)	22,010 (721)	10,710 (362)	11,300 (369)	15,740 (591)	4,590 (107)	510 (15)	1,010 (18)	160 (30)
Maine	5,640 (619)	6,030 (304)	2,960 (147)	3,060 (168)	5,750 (297)	50 (5)	40 (10)	160 (15)	20 ! (9)
Maryland[1]	117,010 (1,190)	137,410 (908)	65,760 (348)	71,650 (631)	86,470 (820)	22,510 (†)	10,480 (26)	17,520 (106)	430 (†)
Massachusetts	7,440 (6,408)	6,130 (4,750)	2,550 (2,312)	3,580 (2,467)	4,240 (3,918)	540 (1,255)	510 (117)	820 (507)	30 (21)
Michigan	65,970 (6,408)	54,950 (4,750)	26,470 (2,312)	28,480 (2,467)	44,610 (3,918)	5,510 (1,255)	1,050 (117)	3,600 (507)	190 (21)
Minnesota	73,940 (2,585)	72,280 (2,154)	35,550 (1,043)	36,740 (1,120)	56,970 (2,047)	4,590 (24)	2,460 (43)	7,560 (62)	710 (54)
Mississippi	30,510 (837)	31,070 (1,015)	15,110 (496)	15,970 (534)	22,580 (806)	7,520 (253)	410 (23)	530 (51)	40 (6)
Missouri	34,470 (898)	33,070 (831)	16,960 (424)	16,110 (422)	28,780 (767)	2,350 (93)	440 (18)	1,420 (47)	80 (6)
Montana	8,760 (401)	7,490 (251)	3,770 (133)	3,720 (125)	6,800 (235)	30 (3)	140 (10)	130 (9)	390 (31)
Nebraska	32,160 (824)	32,650 (604)	16,200 (307)	16,450 (305)	29,100 (581)	1,080 (11)	1,390 (57)	960 (12)	130 (7)
Nevada[2]	7,640 (23)	8,270 (†)	4,220 (†)	4,050 (†)	5,570 (†)	410 (†)	1,210 (†)	1,010 (†)	70 ! (7)
New Hampshire	4,450 (1,089)	4,700 (1,005)	2,350 (540)	2,350 (469)	4,380 (969)	40 (7)	50 (6)	220 (39)	10 ! (7)
New Jersey	88,960 (4,851)	97,260 (4,904)	43,920 (2,190)	53,350 (2,764)	64,810 (3,890)	8,620 (808)	9,360 (787)	14,390 (1,327)	90 (9)
New Mexico	36,410 (404)	12,950 (399)	6,890 (219)	6,050 (185)	7,180 (256)	240 (8)	4,280 (137)	510 (53)	740 (36)
New York	61,350 (5,223)	81,520 (3,741)	38,090 (1,799)	43,440 (1,955)	49,010 (3,322)	12,900 (358)	8,480 (177)	10,900 (342)	230 (24)
North Carolina	155,330 (10,613)	149,700 (4,678)	77,100 (2,261)	72,600 (2,429)	120,700 (3,981)	18,090 (639)	4,040 (168)	5,150 (155)	1,710 ! (777)
North Dakota	3,320 (305)	2,770 (162)	1,450 (87)	1,320 (76)	2,370 (100)	30 (1)	20 (#)	20 (2)	300 (123)
Ohio	133,690 (7,411)	127,610 (5,925)	64,720 (3,150)	62,900 (2,829)	108,200 (5,477)	13,890 (949)	1,540 (70)	3,860 (386)	130 (13)
Oklahoma	87,620 (2,447)	87,320 (2,151)	42,570 (990)	44,760 (1,192)	61,980 (1,581)	5,050 (93)	4,010 (94)	2,460 (46)	13,820 (692)
Oregon	39,440 (903)	38,570 (666)	17,970 (357)	20,600 (318)	32,590 (603)	640 (10)	1,750 (63)	3,110 (26)	480 (33)
Pennsylvania	85,070 (3,170)	75,930 (2,681)	37,090 (1,414)	37,000 (1,297)	63,480 (2,415)	6,680 (292)	1,370 (60)	4,350 (362)	50 (†)
Rhode Island	2,780 (531)	2,060 (300)	920 (134)	1,150 (168)	1,560 (252)	160 (41)	230 (30)	110 (13)	# (†)
South Carolina	88,070 (6,564)	77,520 (3,781)	36,580 (1,772)	40,940 (2,022)	59,580 (2,832)	14,660 (964)	1,510 (118)	1,620 (164)	160 (31)
South Dakota	2,940 (241)	3,070 (175)	1,680 (92)	1,390 (87)	2,790 (139)	20 (#)	20 (1)	50 (3)	190 (93)
Tennessee	32,630 (1,451)	17,100 (904)	8,810 (493)	8,290 (416)	14,540 (827)	1,650 (63)	260 (15)	620 (43)	30 (4)
Texas	344,500 (3,483)	344,640 (2,413)	167,640 (1,243)	177,000 (1,234)	175,730 (1,923)	28,260 (618)	115,950 (1,189)	23,630 (134)	1,070 (30)
Utah	23,510 (1,218)	25,660 (170)	12,090 (79)	13,570 (91)	20,380 (152)	320 (1)	2,880 (19)	1,890 (#)	190 (14)
Vermont	740 (151)	730 (129)	390 (70)	340 (61)	690 (121)	10 ! (3)	20 (5)	20 ! (6)	# (#)
Virginia	142,140 (3,772)	160,140 (3,319)	77,980 (1,608)	82,160 (1,732)	116,360 (2,709)	18,410 (1,070)	7,310 (117)	17,510 (165)	560 (107)
Washington	38,520 (843)	39,010 (1,289)	19,050 (573)	19,960 (726)	30,390 (1,170)	850 (12)	2,430 (89)	4,970 (90)	380 (17)
West Virginia	6,040 (493)	6,630 (559)	3,130 (305)	3,130 (262)	6,200 (504)	230 (35)	30 (4)	240 (40)	10 ! (#)
Wisconsin	62,000 (4,348)	56,450 (3,095)	27,340 (1,478)	29,100 (1,628)	48,560 (2,821)	3,370 (210)	2,180 (125)	1,900 (129)	440 (151)
Wyoming	2,910 ! (944)	2,030 (314)	990 (152)	1,040 (164)	1,830 (295)	30 (2)	80 (8)	70 (13)	30 (#)

—Not available.
†Not applicable.
#Rounds to zero.
! Interpret data with caution.
[1] Data are based on universe counts of schools and school districts; therefore, these figures do not have standard errors.

[2] Data for 2006 are based on universe counts of schools and school districts; therefore, these figures do not have standard errors.

NOTE: Race categories exclude persons of Hispanic ethnicity. Standard errors appear in parentheses. Detail may not sum to totals because of rounding.

SOURCE: U.S. Department of Education, Office for Civil Rights, Civil Rights Data Collection: 2004 and 2006. (This table was revised May 2008.)

Table 54. Percentage of gifted and talented students in public elementary and secondary schools, by sex, race/ethnicity, and state: 2004 and 2006

State	Total		Sex				Race/ethnicity									
			Male		Female		White		Black		Hispanic		Asian/Pacific Islander		American Indian/Alaska Native	
	2004	2006	2004	2006	2004	2006	2004	2006	2004	2006	2004	2006	2004	2006	2004	2006
1	2	3	4	5	6	7	8	9	10	11	12	13	14	15	16	17
United States	**6.7 (0.05)**	**6.7 (0.04)**	**6.3 (0.05)**	**6.3 (0.04)**	**7.0 (0.06)**	**7.0 (0.05)**	**7.9 (0.07)**	**8.0 (0.07)**	**3.5 (0.05)**	**3.6 (0.05)**	**4.3 (0.05)**	**4.2 (0.04)**	**11.9 (0.20)**	**13.1 (0.29)**	**5.2 (0.20)**	**5.2 (0.24)**
Alabama	4.8 (0.11)	5.5 (0.06)	4.6 (0.11)	5.2 (0.06)	4.9 (0.11)	5.7 (0.07)	6.3 (0.16)	7.1 (0.11)	2.4 (0.09)	2.8 (0.06)	2.3 (0.17)	2.9 (0.09)	9.4 (0.50)	10.2 (0.45)	4.9 (0.54)	6.1 (0.43)
Alaska	4.1 (0.19)	4.1 (0.19)	3.9 (0.19)	4.0 (0.19)	4.2 (0.19)	4.3 (0.19)	5.8 (0.22)	5.8 (0.22)	2.1 (0.03)	2.5 (0.02)	2.3 (0.11)	2.5 (0.13)	4.5 (0.45)	5.0 (0.52)	1.0 (0.08)	1.1 (0.12)
Arizona	5.9 (0.17)	6.3 (0.11)	5.9 (0.17)	6.3 (0.12)	5.9 (0.17)	6.3 (0.11)	8.4 (0.26)	9.1 (0.21)	3.5 (0.14)	3.4 (0.06)	3.3 (0.13)	3.5 (0.07)	13.9 (0.54)	14.2 (0.21)	4.0 (1.09)	3.7 (0.92)
Arkansas	9.9 (0.65)	9.5 (0.43)	8.8 (0.63)	8.6 (0.41)	11.0 (0.67)	10.5 (0.50)	11.2 (0.80)	10.7 (0.53)	7.1 (0.90)	7.3 (0.73)	5.8 ! (2.39)	5.8 ! (2.29)	10.6 (0.78)	10.3 (0.62)	4.7 (1.21)	8.2 (1.35)
California	8.4 (0.18)	8.3 (0.21)	8.0 (0.16)	8.0 (0.21)	8.8 (0.20)	8.6 (0.23)	12.0 (0.36)	11.9 (0.42)	4.6 (0.16)	4.3 (0.16)	5.1 (0.13)	4.8 (0.11)	14.6 (0.56)	16.1 (0.89)	6.5 (0.56)	5.8 (0.62)
Colorado	6.7 (0.11)	6.8 (0.11)	6.6 (0.11)	6.9 (0.11)	6.8 (0.12)	6.8 (0.11)	7.9 (0.14)	8.2 (0.16)	5.2 (0.03)	5.0 (0.02)	3.9 (0.14)	3.8 (0.07)	9.6 (0.11)	10.4 (0.09)	4.5 (0.39)	4.3 (0.29)
Connecticut	3.0 (0.32)	3.8 (0.41)	2.9 (0.31)	3.5 (0.40)	3.2 (0.34)	4.0 (0.44)	3.5 (0.38)	4.3 (0.44)	1.7 (0.44)	2.3 (0.59)	1.4 (0.33)	1.8 (0.42)	5.7 (0.68)	7.3 (0.95)	1.7 (0.44)	4.3 ! (2.37)
Delaware[1]	4.6 (†)	5.6 (†)	4.0 (†)	4.9 (†)	5.3 (†)	6.3 (†)	6.1 (†)	6.8 (†)	2.2 (†)	3.6 (†)	1.7 (†)	3.5 (†)	11.5 (†)	13.2 (†)	3.4 (†)	3.7 (†)
District of Columbia	— (†)	— (†)	— (†)	— (†)	— (†)	— (†)	— (†)	— (†)	— (†)	— (†)	— (†)	— (†)	— (†)	— (†)	— (†)	— (†)
Florida	4.5 (0.06)	4.7 (0.05)	4.5 (0.06)	4.7 (0.05)	4.5 (0.05)	4.8 (0.05)	5.7 (0.11)	6.1 (0.10)	2.0 (0.02)	2.0 (0.02)	4.0 (0.02)	4.4 (0.03)	8.8 (0.08)	9.3 (0.06)	4.6 (0.12)	5.0 (0.15)
Georgia	8.9 (0.30)	9.3 (0.35)	8.3 (0.29)	8.6 (0.33)	9.5 (0.31)	10.0 (0.39)	13.6 (0.59)	14.1 (0.69)	3.7 (0.15)	4.1 (0.15)	2.6 (0.25)	3.1 (0.17)	18.8 (0.41)	19.3 (0.71)	7.6 (0.49)	9.6 (0.65)
Hawaii[2]	5.7 (0.57)	6.2 (†)	4.4 (0.42)	5.1 (†)	7.0 (0.74)	7.5 (†)	7.7 (0.95)	9.7 (†)	2.9 (0.53)	2.9 (†)	2.6 (0.36)	3.9 (†)	5.5 (0.59)	5.8 (†)	4.3 (0.76)	4.8 (†)
Idaho	3.9 (0.23)	4.2 (0.20)	3.9 (0.21)	4.3 (0.20)	3.9 (0.24)	4.1 (0.21)	4.4 (0.26)	4.7 (0.23)	1.7 (0.20)	2.0 (0.14)	0.9 (0.13)	1.3 (0.12)	6.9 (0.38)	6.1 (0.46)	1.2 (0.28)	1.0 (0.23)
Illinois	5.4 (0.22)	5.8 (0.24)	5.0 (0.20)	5.4 (0.23)	5.8 (0.24)	6.3 (0.28)	6.7 (0.33)	7.0 (0.39)	2.5 (0.18)	4.2 (0.40)	2.8 (0.13)	3.1 (0.08)	13.1 (0.98)	13.3 (0.97)	5.4 (1.15)	5.1 (0.83)
Indiana	7.1 (0.49)	7.9 (0.40)	6.3 (0.44)	7.0 (0.36)	7.9 (0.55)	8.8 (0.49)	7.7 (0.52)	8.7 (0.50)	3.8 (0.78)	4.1 (0.54)	3.8 (0.66)	3.9 (0.39)	15.5 (2.71)	14.1 (2.08)	6.7 (1.64)	3.9 (0.56)
Iowa	8.5 (0.38)	8.2 (0.26)	8.2 (0.37)	7.9 (0.25)	8.9 (0.40)	8.5 (0.29)	9.0 (0.41)	8.8 (0.30)	4.6 (0.33)	3.9 (0.11)	3.7 (0.61)	3.1 (0.38)	13.5 (1.10)	12.2 (0.97)	3.6 (0.35)	2.9 (0.25)
Kansas	3.3 (0.11)	3.0 (0.12)	3.5 (0.11)	3.2 (0.13)	3.1 (0.11)	2.9 (0.12)	3.9 (0.15)	3.6 (0.16)	1.1 (0.05)	1.0 (0.04)	1.0 (0.08)	0.8 (0.04)	5.5 (0.17)	5.4 (0.25)	1.5 (0.19)	1.8 (0.20)
Kentucky	13.0 (0.54)	14.6 (0.50)	11.9 (0.51)	13.2 (0.47)	14.2 (0.57)	16.1 (0.60)	14.2 (0.62)	15.8 (0.64)	5.2 (0.54)	7.0 (0.60)	4.6 (0.46)	5.7 (0.38)	20.2 (1.48)	21.3 (1.14)	6.6 (1.24)	7.2 (0.96)
Louisiana	3.9 (0.32)	3.4 (0.13)	3.8 (0.31)	3.2 (0.13)	4.0 (0.34)	3.5 (0.14)	5.5 (0.60)	4.8 (0.26)	1.9 (0.07)	1.6 (0.04)	4.2 (0.34)	3.3 (0.12)	11.7 (0.91)	11.7 (0.34)	2.6 ! (1.04)	2.7 (0.78)
Maine	3.0 (0.36)	3.2 (0.19)	2.9 (0.33)	3.1 (0.18)	3.2 (0.39)	3.4 (0.22)	3.1 (0.37)	3.3 (0.20)	1.3 (0.22)	1.1 (0.12)	1.2 (0.27)	2.3 (0.54)	3.8 (0.80)	5.6 (0.60)	0.8 ! (0.35)	3.1 ! (1.29)
Maryland[1]	13.8 (†)	16.1 (†)	12.9 (†)	15.0 (†)	14.7 (†)	17.2 (†)	17.0 (†)	21.1 (†)	6.7 (†)	7.0 (†)	14.5 (†)	14.7 (†)	33.8 (†)	37.8 (†)	9.8 (†)	12.6 (†)
Massachusetts	0.8 (0.13)	0.7 (0.10)	0.7 (0.12)	0.6 (0.08)	0.9 (0.14)	0.8 (0.15)	0.8 (0.14)	0.6 (0.12)	0.7 (0.13)	0.7 (0.05)	0.8 ! (0.21)	0.5 (0.04)	1.9 (0.30)	1.7 (0.24)	0.9 ! (0.25)	0.5 (0.13)
Michigan	3.9 (0.37)	3.4 (0.29)	3.6 (0.35)	3.2 (0.28)	4.3 (0.40)	3.7 (0.32)	4.1 (0.41)	3.8 (0.34)	3.0 (0.62)	1.9 (0.44)	2.7 (0.54)	1.4 (0.18)	10.1 (1.56)	8.1 (1.30)	1.4 (0.25)	1.2 (0.19)
Minnesota	8.1 (0.37)	8.8 (0.28)	7.7 (0.36)	8.4 (0.26)	8.6 (0.38)	9.2 (0.32)	8.3 (0.44)	8.8 (0.36)	5.2 (0.34)	6.7 (0.11)	4.5 (0.20)	5.4 (0.18)	13.7 (0.33)	16.5 (0.25)	3.8 (0.57)	4.6 (0.54)
Mississippi	6.0 (0.19)	6.1 (0.20)	5.7 (0.18)	5.8 (0.19)	6.3 (0.22)	6.4 (0.22)	9.1 (0.38)	9.6 (0.41)	3.3 (0.21)	2.9 (0.11)	5.0 (0.43)	4.5 (0.37)	10.7 (0.48)	13.5 (1.47)	3.7 (0.93)	3.7 (0.64)
Missouri	3.8 (0.12)	3.6 (0.11)	3.8 (0.12)	3.5 (0.11)	3.8 (0.13)	3.6 (0.11)	4.3 (0.15)	4.0 (0.14)	1.7 (0.05)	1.5 (0.08)	1.4 (0.10)	1.3 (0.09)	9.0 (0.33)	9.1 (0.36)	2.0 (0.22)	2.4 (0.20)
Montana	5.6 (0.28)	5.2 (0.20)	5.4 (0.26)	5.0 (0.20)	5.9 (0.31)	5.3 (0.21)	6.0 (0.31)	5.7 (0.24)	2.8 (0.21)	2.2 (0.22)	3.3 (0.22)	3.9 (0.29)	9.9 (0.77)	8.2 (0.62)	2.9 (0.38)	2.1 (0.23)
Nebraska	11.4 (0.31)	11.4 (0.24)	10.9 (0.30)	11.0 (0.24)	11.9 (0.32)	11.8 (0.27)	12.8 (0.38)	13.3 (0.33)	6.4 (0.06)	4.8 (0.05)	4.5 (0.32)	3.9 (0.24)	17.0 (0.25)	18.2 (0.28)	4.6 (0.94)	3.1 (0.36)
Nevada[2]	1.9 (0.01)	1.9 (†)	2.1 (0.01)	1.9 (†)	1.8 (0.01)	1.9 (†)	2.8 (0.01)	3.0 (†)	0.8 (#)	0.9 (†)	0.8 (0.01)	0.8 (†)	2.8 (0.02)	3.1 (†)	1.0 (0.07)	1.1 (†)
New Hampshire	2.3 (0.55)	2.6 (0.54)	2.1 (0.49)	2.5 (0.56)	2.5 ! (0.62)	2.7 (0.54)	2.3 (0.56)	2.6 (0.58)	0.6 (0.11)	1.1 (0.19)	1.0 (0.20)	0.9 (0.10)	5.8 (1.25)	5.9 (1.07)	0.9 (0.09)	2.1 ! (1.20)
New Jersey	6.9 (0.38)	7.0 (0.35)	6.2 (0.34)	6.1 (0.31)	7.7 (0.42)	7.9 (0.43)	8.4 (0.53)	8.4 (0.55)	3.3 (0.35)	3.5 (0.36)	3.4 (0.39)	3.5 (0.33)	12.2 (1.13)	13.9 (1.50)	3.3 (0.59)	4.8 (0.61)
New Mexico	10.7 (0.26)	4.0 (0.14)	10.9 (0.27)	4.1 (0.15)	10.5 (0.26)	3.8 (0.14)	12.6 (0.42)	7.1 (0.31)	9.6 (0.18)	2.8 (0.11)	11.4 (0.37)	2.4 (0.11)	13.6 (1.09)	12.0 (1.34)	2.2 (0.17)	2.1 (0.15)
New York	2.2 (0.18)	2.9 (0.13)	2.0 (0.17)	2.6 (0.12)	2.3 (0.19)	3.2 (0.15)	3.4 (0.31)	3.3 (0.23)	0.8 (0.07)	2.4 (0.09)	0.4 (0.04)	1.5 (0.04)	1.7 (0.18)	5.5 (0.19)	1.4 (0.29)	1.5 (0.25)
North Carolina	10.9 (0.83)	10.8 (0.42)	10.3 (0.81)	10.2 (0.40)	11.6 (0.85)	11.3 (0.47)	15.7 (1.17)	15.4 (0.68)	3.9 (0.27)	4.3 (0.20)	3.0 (0.29)	3.1 (0.18)	16.5 (2.76)	17.3 (0.98)	6.3 (1.39)	6.2 ! (3.81)
North Dakota	3.1 (0.30)	2.8 (0.18)	3.0 (0.30)	2.9 (0.19)	3.2 (0.32)	2.8 (0.18)	2.8 (0.23)	2.8 (0.15)	2.3 (0.05)	1.7 (0.09)	1.5 (0.23)	1.4 (0.13)	8.1 (0.38)	5.4 (0.26)	7.0 ! (3.34)	3.3 ! (1.46)
Ohio	7.4 (0.40)	7.3 (0.33)	7.3 (0.40)	7.2 (0.34)	7.6 (0.40)	7.4 (0.35)	7.6 (0.48)	7.8 (0.42)	6.5 (0.37)	4.7 (0.37)	3.5 (0.26)	3.3 (0.28)	13.6 (1.44)	14.0 (1.64)	5.6 (0.62)	5.4 (0.60)
Oklahoma	14.0 (0.45)	13.7 (0.39)	13.1 (0.41)	13.0 (0.36)	15.0 (0.50)	14.4 (0.47)	16.6 (0.56)	16.2 (0.55)	7.7 (0.22)	7.4 (0.23)	7.0 (0.27)	6.8 (0.23)	23.6 (0.56)	21.5 (0.60)	11.3 (0.67)	11.8 (0.72)
Oregon	7.1 (0.20)	6.9 (0.16)	7.3 (0.20)	7.2 (0.17)	6.9 (0.21)	6.6 (0.16)	8.0 (0.24)	8.0 (0.22)	3.6 (0.05)	3.5 (0.09)	1.8 (0.10)	2.0 (0.09)	11.6 (0.14)	11.1 (0.21)	3.6 (0.42)	3.9 (0.31)
Pennsylvania	4.8 (0.19)	4.5 (0.17)	4.9 (0.20)	4.5 (0.17)	4.8 (0.19)	4.5 (0.18)	5.3 (0.23)	5.0 (0.22)	2.7 (0.16)	2.4 (0.15)	1.8 (0.38)	1.7 (0.12)	9.5 (0.87)	9.7 (0.96)	2.2 (0.35)	1.9 (0.36)
Rhode Island	1.8 (0.38)	1.4 (0.21)	1.6 (0.35)	1.2 (0.18)	2.1 (0.41)	1.6 (0.24)	2.0 (0.44)	1.5 (0.25)	1.5 (0.47)	1.2 ! (0.34)	1.2 (0.48)	1.0 (0.13)	2.2 (0.60)	2.3 (0.30)	0.9 ! (0.34)	0.3 ! (0.10)
South Carolina	12.7 (0.98)	11.0 (0.57)	11.7 (0.89)	10.1 (0.52)	13.9 (1.07)	11.9 (0.68)	17.8 (1.29)	15.9 (0.95)	5.9 (0.70)	5.1 (0.39)	5.1 (0.93)	4.6 (0.56)	21.6 (3.32)	19.3 (2.33)	8.3 (1.29)	8.2 (2.52)
South Dakota	2.2 (0.20)	2.7 (0.17)	2.3 (0.20)	2.8 (0.18)	2.1 (0.20)	2.5 (0.18)	2.4 (0.21)	2.9 (0.19)	1.2 (0.16)	0.9 (0.03)	0.6 (0.12)	0.7 (0.04)	3.3 (0.37)	4.2 (0.31)	1.3 ! (0.67)	1.4 ! (0.70)
Tennessee	3.3 (0.18)	1.7 (0.10)	3.1 (0.18)	1.7 (0.10)	3.5 (0.18)	1.7 (0.09)	2.9 (0.21)	2.0 (0.13)	4.5 (0.15)	0.7 (0.03)	1.6 (0.15)	0.6 (0.04)	7.9 (0.77)	4.2 (0.37)	2.9 (0.41)	1.4 (0.20)
Texas	8.0 (0.10)	7.6 (0.07)	7.5 (0.10)	7.2 (0.07)	8.5 (0.11)	8.0 (0.08)	11.2 (0.21)	10.8 (0.17)	4.9 (0.14)	4.4 (0.11)	5.6 (0.12)	5.5 (0.07)	16.4 (0.28)	16.0 (0.13)	7.1 (0.27)	7.1 (0.24)
Utah	4.6 (0.29)	5.0 (0.05)	4.3 (0.28)	4.6 (0.05)	5.0 (0.29)	5.5 (0.06)	4.5 (0.29)	4.9 (0.06)	5.1 (0.26)	4.6 (0.03)	4.4 (0.37)	4.1 (0.05)	11.7 (0.81)	12.0 (0.06)	2.6 (0.36)	2.7 (0.03)
Vermont	0.8 (0.17)	0.8 (0.15)	0.8 (0.17)	0.9 (0.16)	0.9 (0.17)	0.8 (0.15)	0.8 (0.17)	0.8 (0.15)	0.4 ! (0.16)	0.5 ! (0.16)	# (†)	1.3 ! (0.57)	0.2 ! (0.10)	1.4 ! (0.41)	# (†)	# (†)
Virginia	12.1 (0.38)	12.6 (0.32)	11.5 (0.36)	12.0 (0.30)	12.8 (0.40)	13.3 (0.37)	14.9 (0.55)	15.6 (0.50)	4.6 (0.21)	5.2 (0.35)	6.7 (0.65)	7.5 (0.23)	24.5 (0.83)	26.4 (0.46)	8.3 (2.41)	13.3 (2.61)
Washington	3.8 (0.10)	3.9 (0.13)	3.6 (0.10)	3.7 (0.12)	3.9 (0.10)	4.1 (0.16)	4.2 (0.14)	4.4 (0.19)	1.4 (0.02)	1.4 (0.02)	1.8 (0.12)	1.7 (0.09)	5.0 (0.09)	5.8 (0.12)	1.6 (0.28)	1.4 (0.10)
West Virginia	2.2 (0.19)	2.2 (0.21)	2.3 (0.20)	2.2 (0.22)	2.0 (0.18)	2.1 (0.21)	2.2 (0.19)	2.2 (0.21)	1.4 (0.17)	1.6 (0.32)	1.6 (0.37)	0.9 (0.23)	9.3 (1.90)	10.9 (2.21)	3.9 ! (1.25)	2.9 ! (0.82)
Wisconsin	6.8 (0.47)	6.4 (0.35)	6.4 (0.44)	6.1 (0.33)	7.3 (0.51)	6.8 (0.41)	7.8 (0.55)	7.1 (0.45)	2.0 (0.21)	3.7 (0.25)	2.4 (0.23)	3.5 (0.21)	6.7 (0.55)	6.1 (0.44)	4.6 ! (2.04)	3.2 ! (1.23)
Wyoming	3.2 ! (1.04)	2.2 (0.35)	2.8 ! (0.90)	2.0 (0.32)	3.7 ! (1.19)	2.3 (0.39)	3.5 ! (1.14)	2.3 (0.39)	1.5 ! (0.47)	2.0 (0.19)	1.2 (0.29)	0.9 (0.11)	3.6 (0.31)	6.7 (1.35)	0.7 ! (0.53)	1.0 (0.16)

—Not available.
†Not applicable.
#Rounds to zero.
!Interpret data with caution.
[1]Data are based on universe counts of schools and school districts; therefore, these figures do not have standard errors.
[2]Data for 2006 are based on universe counts of schools and school districts; therefore, these figures do not have standard errors.
NOTE: Race categories exclude persons of Hispanic ethnicity. Standard errors appear in parentheses.
SOURCE: U.S. Department of Education, Office for Civil Rights, Civil Rights Data Collection: 2004 and 2006. (This table was prepared May 2007.)

Table 55. Enrollment in grades 9 through 12 in public and private schools compared with population 14 to 17 years of age: Selected years, 1889–90 through fall 2008

[In thousands]

Year	Enrollment, grades 9 to 12[1]			Population 14 to 17 years of age[2]	Enrollment as a ratio of population 14 to 17 years of age[3]
	All schools	Public schools	Private schools		
1	2	3	4	5	6
1889–90	298	203	95	5,355	5.6
1899–1900	630	519	111	6,152	10.2
1909–10	1,032	915	117	7,220	14.3
1919–20	2,414	2,200	214	7,736	31.2
1929–30	4,741	4,399	341 [4]	9,341	50.7
1939–40	7,059	6,601	458 [5]	9,720	72.6
1949–50	6,397	5,725	672	8,405	76.1
Fall 1959	9,306	8,271	1,035	11,155	83.4
Fall 1963	12,170	10,883	1,287	13,492	90.2
Fall 1965	13,010	11,610	1,400	14,146	92.0
Fall 1966	13,294	11,894	1,400	14,398	92.3
Fall 1967	13,650	12,250	1,400	14,727	92.7
Fall 1968	14,118	12,718	1,400	15,170	93.1
Fall 1969	14,337	13,037	1,300 [6]	15,549	92.2
Fall 1970	14,647	13,336	1,311	15,924	92.0
Fall 1971	15,053	13,753	1,300 [6]	16,328	92.2
Fall 1972	15,148	13,848	1,300 [6]	16,639	91.0
Fall 1973	15,344	14,044	1,300 [6]	16,867	91.0
Fall 1974	15,403	14,103	1,300 [6]	17,035	90.4
Fall 1975	15,604	14,304	1,300 [6]	17,128	91.1
Fall 1976	15,656	14,314	1,342	17,119	91.5
Fall 1977	15,546	14,203	1,343	17,045	91.2
Fall 1978	15,441	14,088	1,353	16,946	91.1
Fall 1979	14,916	13,616	1,300 [6]	16,611	89.8
Fall 1980	14,570	13,231	1,339	16,143	90.3
Fall 1981	14,164	12,764	1,400 [6]	15,609	90.7
Fall 1982	13,805	12,405	1,400 [6]	15,057	91.7
Fall 1983	13,671	12,271	1,400	14,740	92.7
Fall 1984	13,704	12,304	1,400 [6]	14,725	93.1
Fall 1985	13,750	12,388	1,362	14,888	92.4
Fall 1986	13,669	12,333	1,336 [6]	14,824	92.2
Fall 1987	13,323	12,076	1,247	14,502	91.9
Fall 1988	12,893	11,687	1,206 [6]	14,023	91.9
Fall 1989	12,519	11,390	1,128 [6]	13,536	92.5
Fall 1990	12,472	11,338	1,134	13,329	93.6
Fall 1991	12,670	11,541	1,129	13,491	93.9
Fall 1992	12,852	11,735	1,117 [6]	13,775	93.3
Fall 1993	13,065	11,961	1,104	14,096	92.7
Fall 1994	13,344	12,213	1,131 [6]	14,637	91.2
Fall 1995	13,662	12,500	1,163	15,013	91.0
Fall 1996	14,025	12,847	1,178 [6]	15,443	90.8
Fall 1997	14,239	13,054	1,185	15,769	90.3
Fall 1998	14,405	13,193	1,212 [6]	15,829	91.0
Fall 1999	14,598	13,369	1,229	16,007	91.2
Fall 2000	14,779	13,515	1,264 [6]	16,122	91.7
Fall 2001	15,031	13,734	1,296	16,184	92.9
Fall 2002	15,373	14,067	1,306 [6]	16,353	94.0
Fall 2003	15,649	14,338	1,311	16,497	94.9
Fall 2004	15,948	14,617	1,331 [6]	16,813	94.9
Fall 2005	16,258	14,908	1,350	17,068	95.3
Fall 2006	16,462	15,078	1,384 [6]	17,207	95.7
Fall 2007[7]	16,439	15,055	1,385	17,207	95.5
Fall 2008[7]	16,294	14,922	1,372	16,959	96.1

[1]Includes a relatively small number of secondary ungraded students.
[2]Data for 1890 through 1950 are from the decennial censuses of population. Later data are Census Bureau estimates as of July 1 preceding the opening of the school year.
[3]Gross enrollment ratio based on school enrollment of all ages in grades 9 to 12 divided by the 14- to 17-year-old population. Differs from enrollment rates in other tables, which are based on the enrollment of persons in the given age group only.
[4]Data are for 1927–28.
[5]Data are for 1940–41.
[6]Estimated.
[7]Projected.
NOTE: Allocation of ungraded students to secondary levels based on proportions derived from prior years. Includes enrollment in public schools that are a part of state and local school systems and also in most private schools, both religiously affiliated and nonsectarian. Some data have been revised from previously published figures. Detail may not sum to totals because of rounding.

SOURCE: U.S. Department of Education, National Center for Education Statistics, *Annual Report of the Commissioner of Education*, 1890 through 1910; *Biennial Survey of Education in the United States*, 1919–20 through 1949–50; *Statistics of State School Systems*, 1951–52 through 1957–58; *Statistics of Public Elementary and Secondary School Systems*, 1959 through 1980; *Statistics of Nonpublic Elementary and Secondary Schools*, 1959 through 1980; Common Core of Data (CCD), "State Nonfiscal Survey of Public Elementary/Secondary Education," 1981–82 through 2006–07; Schools and Staffing Survey, Private School Data File, 1987–88; Private School Universe Survey (PSS), 1989–90 through 2005–06; *Projections of Education Statistics to 2017*; and unpublished data. U.S. Department of Commerce, Census Bureau, Current Population Reports, Series P-25, Nos. 1000, 1022, 1045, 1057, 1059, 1092, and 1095; and 2000 through 2007 Population Estimates, retrieved August 12, 2008, from http://www.census.gov/popest/national/asrh/2007-nat-res.html. (This table was prepared October 2008.)

Table 56. Enrollment in foreign language courses compared with enrollment in grades 9 through 12 in public secondary schools: Selected years, fall 1948 through fall 2000

[Number in thousands]

Language	Fall 1948	Fall 1960	Fall 1965	Fall 1968	Fall 1970	Fall 1974	Fall 1976	Fall 1982	Fall 1985	Fall 1990	Fall 1994	Fall 2000	Percent change in enrollment 1976 to 1990	Percent change in enrollment 1990 to 2000
1	2	3	4	5	6	7	8	9	10	11	12	13	14	15
Total enrollment, grades 9 to 12	5,602 [1]	8,589	11,610	12,718	13,336	14,103	14,314	12,405	12,388	11,338	12,213	13,514	-20.8	19.2
All foreign languages[2]														
Number enrolled	1,170	2,522	3,659	3,890	3,779	3,295	3,174	2,910	4,029	4,257	5,002	5,898	34.1	38.6
Percent of all students	20.9	29.4	31.5	30.6	28.3	23.3	22.2	23.3	32.2	37.5	41.0	43.6	†	†
Modern foreign languages														
Number enrolled	741	1,867	3,068	3,518	3,514	3,127	3,023	2,740	3,852	4,093	4,813	5,721	35.4	39.8
Percent of all students	13.2	21.7	26.4	27.7	26.4	22.1	21.1	21.9	31.1	36.1	39.4	42.3	†	†
Spanish														
Number enrolled	443	933	1,427	1,698	1,811	1,678	1,717	1,563	2,334	2,611	3,220	4,058	52.1	55.4
Percent of all students	7.9	10.9	12.3	13.4	13.6	11.9	12.0	12.5	18.8	23.0	26.4	30.0	†	†
French														
Number enrolled	254	744	1,251	1,328	1,231	978	888	858	1,134	1,089	1,106	1,075	22.6	-1.3
Percent of all students	4.5	8.7	10.8	10.4	9.2	6.9	6.2	6.9	9.2	9.6	9.1	8.0	†	†
German														
Number enrolled	43	151	328	423	411	393	353	267	312	295	326	283	-16.2	-4.1
Percent of all students	0.8	1.8	2.8	3.3	3.1	2.8	2.5	2.1	2.5	2.6	2.7	2.1	†	†
Russian														
Number enrolled	—	10	27	24	20	15	11	6	6	16	16	11	46.6	-35.6
Percent of all students	—	0.1	0.2	0.2	0.2	0.1	0.1	#	#	0.1	0.1	0.1	†	†
Italian														
Number enrolled	—	20	25	27	27	40	46	44	47	40	44	64	-11.4	58.7
Percent of all students	—	0.2	0.2	0.2	0.2	0.3	0.3	0.4	0.4	0.4	0.4	0.5	†	†
Japanese[3]														
Number enrolled	—	—	—	—	—	—	—	—	—	25	42	51	—	102.5
Percent of all students	—	—	—	—	—	—	—	—	—	0.2	0.3	0.4	†	†
Other modern foreign languages[4]														
Number enrolled	1	9	9	18	15	23	9	3	18	15	59	179	73.0	1,102.3
Percent of all students	#	0.1	0.1	0.1	0.1	0.2	0.1	#	0.1	0.1	0.5	1.3	†	†
Latin														
Number enrolled	429	655	591	372	265	167	150	170	177	164	189	177	8.9	8.3
Percent of all students	7.7	7.6	5.1	2.9	2.0	1.2	1.1	1.4	1.4	1.4	1.5	1.3	†	†

—Not available.
†Not applicable.
#Rounds to zero.
[1]Estimated.
[2]Includes enrollment in ancient Greek (not shown separately). Fewer than 1,000 students were enrolled in this language in each of the years shown.
[3]Until 1990, student enrollment in Japanese courses was included in the Other modern foreign languages category.

[4]Includes students enrolled in unspecified modern foreign languages. Since 1990, enrollment in Japanese courses is reported as a separate category.
NOTE: Percent change computed from unrounded numbers.
SOURCE: U.S. Department of Education, National Center for Education Statistics, Common Core of Data (CCD), "State Nonfiscal Survey of Public Elementary/Secondary Education," 1982 through 2000. American Council on the Teaching of Foreign Languages, *Foreign Language Enrollments in U.S. Public Secondary Schools, Fall 2000.* (This table was prepared April 2002.)

Table 57. Number and percentage of schools with students enrolled in distance education courses and enrollment in distance education courses, by instructional level and district characteristics: 2002–03

District characteristic	Number of schools with students enrolled in distance education courses					Percent of schools with students enrolled in distance education courses					Enrollment in distance education courses[1]				
	All instructional levels	Elementary schools	Middle or junior high schools	High schools	Combined or ungraded schools[2]	All instructional levels	Elementary schools	Middle or junior high schools	High schools	Combined or ungraded schools[2]	All instructional levels	Elementary schools	Middle or junior high schools	High schools	Combined or ungraded schools[2]
1	2	3	4	5	6	7	8	9	10	11	12	13	14	15	16
Total	8,210 (229)	130 (42)	580 (62)	6,250 (198)	1,250 (140)	9 (0.3)	# (†)	4 (0.4)	38 (1.2)	20 (1.8)	327,670 (36,233)	2,780! (1,564)	6,280 (1,247)	222,090 (26,660)	96,530 (26,828)
District enrollment size															
Less than 2,500	4,520 (175)	40! (30)	190 (45)	3,300 (161)	990 (123)	15 (0.6)	# (†)	4 (0.8)	44 (2.1)	29 (2.9)	117,730 (24,742)	80! (63)	1,260 (409)	74,160 (7,559)	42,240! (24,346)
2,500 to 9,999	1,670 (119)	20 (9)	160 (35)	1,360 (100)	130 (39)	6 (0.4)	# (†)	3 (0.8)	31 (2.0)	11 (3.0)	85,640 (7,597)	230! (125)	1,750 (639)	44,780 (6,148)	38,880 (3,490)
10,000 or more	2,020 (113)	60 (31)	240 (27)	1,590 (94)	120 (19)	6 (0.3)	# (†)	4 (0.5)	33 (1.9)	8 (1.6)	124,300 (25,922)	2,480! (1,563)	3,270 (1,030)	103,150 (24,010)	15,410! (11,373)
Metropolitan status															
Urban	960 (110)	50! (30)	90 (22)	760 (86)	60 (13)	5 (0.5)	# (†)	3 (0.6)	25 (2.7)	4 (1.3)	103,390 (25,612)	2,390! (1,565)	2,120 (996)	63,020 (25,477)	35,860 (1,650)
Suburban	2,980 (168)	30 (17)	280 (41)	2,400 (145)	270 (52)	7 (0.4)	# (†)	4 (0.6)	34 (1.7)	13 (2.4)	123,410 (27,446)	110! (64)	2,520 (683)	81,500 (8,967)	39,280 (25,200)
Rural	4,260 (162)	40! (28)	210 (47)	3,090 (115)	920 (124)	15 (0.6)	# (†)	4 (1.0)	47 (1.7)	32 (2.9)	100,870 (8,232)	270! (151)	1,640 (465)	77,570 (7,122)	21,390 (4,196)
Region															
Northeast	820 (88)	30! (16)	30! (17)	670 (76)	100 (30)	5 (0.5)	# (†)	1! (0.6)	25 (2.7)	12 (3.7)	42,070! (23,613)	100! (62)	190! (133)	17,420 (3,715)	24,350! (23,364)
Southeast	1,960 (128)	40! (26)	220 (34)	1,520 (108)	170 (35)	10 (0.5)	# (†)	6 (0.9)	45 (2.7)	14 (2.3)	59,010 (6,454)	1,390! (1,230)	2,530 (725)	50,410 (6,311)	4,680 (1,255)
Central	3,010 (174)	40! (28)	150 (34)	2,320 (123)	510 (90)	12 (0.6)	# (†)	3 (0.8)	47 (1.7)	28 (4.6)	108,140 (7,378)	940! (590)	1,050 (365)	60,560 (6,597)	45,590 (2,823)
West	2,410 (172)	20! (14)	180 (37)	1,750 (141)	460 (82)	8 (0.5)	# (†)	4 (0.7)	31 (2.0)	20 (2.6)	118,450 (27,630)	350! (224)	2,510 (996)	93,700 (25,509)	21,900! (11,645)
Poverty concentration															
Less than 10 percent	2,260 (144)	30! (16)	200 (33)	1,700 (113)	330 (78)	8 (0.5)	# (†)	4 (0.6)	36 (2.0)	29 (5.5)	77,380 (13,761)	570! (535)	2,030 (669)	57,320 (8,000)	17,470! (11,325)
10 to 19 percent	3,390 (154)	70! (39)	240 (34)	2,560 (141)	520 (84)	10 (0.4)	# (†)	4 (0.6)	40 (1.7)	23 (3.2)	97,300 (10,003)	1,450! (1,229)	1,710 (395)	77,810 (8,286)	16,330 (4,264)
20 percent or more	2,420 (134)	30 (9)	150 (42)	1,900 (115)	350 (72)	9 (0.5)	# (†)	4 (1.0)	40 (2.0)	16 (3.1)	93,280 (23,194)	760 (338)	2,540 (1,030)	83,100 (23,339)	6,880 (1,783)

†Not applicable.
#Rounds to zero.
!Interpret data with caution.
[1]Enrollment is based on students regularly enrolled in the districts. Enrollments include duplicated counts of students, since districts were instructed to count a student enrolled in each course in which he or she was enrolled.
[2]Combined or ungraded schools are those in which the grades offered in the school span both elementary and secondary grades or that are not divided into grade levels.

NOTE: Percentages are based on unrounded numbers. Percentages are based on the estimated 89,310 public schools in the nation in 2002–03. For the FRSS study sample, there were 3 cases for which district enrollment size was missing and 112 cases for which poverty concentration was missing. Detail may not sum to totals because of rounding or missing data.
SOURCE: U.S. Department of Education, National Center for Education Statistics, Fast Response Survey System (FRSS), "Distance Education Courses for Public Elementary and Secondary School Students: 2002–03," FRSS 84, 2003. (This table was prepared July 2005.)

Table 58. Private elementary and secondary enrollment, teachers, and schools, by orientation of school and selected school characteristics: Fall 2005

Selected school characteristic	Prekindergarten to grade 12 enrollment				Teachers[1]				Schools			
	Total	Catholic	Other religious	Nonsectarian	Total	Catholic	Other religious	Nonsectarian	Total	Catholic	Other religious	Nonsectarian
1	2	3	4	5	6	7	8	9	10	11	12	13
Total	6,073,240 (42,446)	2,402,800 (9,293)	2,303,330 (22,368)	1,367,120 (27,558)	449,810 (2,944)	149,760 (584)	178,720 (1,575)	121,330 (1,855)	35,050 (395)	7,740 (44)	16,160 (259)	11,150 (227)
Level of school												
Elementary	3,447,230 (28,118)	1,701,000 (9,970)	1,037,100 (14,831)	709,130 (12,793)	209,510 (1,406)	97,410 (613)	67,190 (643)	44,910 (779)	22,870 (333)	6,360 (40)	8,990 (211)	7,520 (193)
Secondary	859,800 (23,494)	597,680 (790)	135,790 (6,042)	126,330 (22,671)	70,680 (1,230)	42,680 (78)	13,590 (388)	14,410 (1,157)	2,930 (98)	1,080 (12)	840 (28)	1,010 (91)
Combined	1,766,220 (20,076)	104,120 (3,263)	1,130,450 (13,601)	531,660 (11,812)	169,630 (2,286)	9,680 (433)	97,940 (1,334)	62,010 (1,553)	9,260 (161)	300 (8)	6,340 (143)	2,610 (71)
Type of school												
Coed	5,665,240 (42,312)	2,162,040 (8,905)	2,188,480 (22,276)	1,314,730 (27,591)	412,860 (2,884)	130,900 (486)	167,830 (1,568)	114,130 (1,852)	33,700 (390)	7,290 (43)	15,660 (258)	10,750 (226)
All female	195,890 (1,860)	113,540 (1,860)	54,040 (†)	28,320 (†)	18,650 (295)	9,560 (295)	5,450 (†)	3,640 (†)	590 (3)	250 (3)	200 (†)	140 (†)
All male	212,110 (781)	127,220 (†)	60,820 (660)	24,070 (418)	18,300 (153)	9,310 (†)	5,440 (87)	3,560 (125)	760 (36)	210 (†)	300 (7)	260 (35)
School enrollment												
Less than 50	761,450 (18,785)	19,330 (1,432)	342,240 (11,519)	399,870 (10,507)	49,190 (1,057)	1,720 (184)	24,400 (722)	23,070 (637)	15,440 (355)	390 (34)	7,830 (244)	7,210 (205)
50 to 149	949,070 (9,737)	208,280 (1,257)	484,430 (7,108)	256,370 (4,872)	85,910 (1,078)	16,760 (150)	42,630 (834)	26,530 (601)	8,410 (104)	1,680 (8)	4,480 (84)	2,250 (52)
150 to 299	1,473,990 (9,832)	725,050 (4,774)	551,760 (8,343)	197,180 (1,046)	105,680 (737)	43,410 (241)	41,640 (684)	20,620 (63)	6,210 (50)	3,050 (21)	2,330 (44)	830 (5)
300 to 499	1,172,330 (13,161)	632,530 (4,879)	355,210 (9,134)	184,590 (8,446)	83,720 (999)	37,930 (333)	27,120 (635)	18,670 (698)	2,840 (33)	1,540 (12)	860 (22)	440 (21)
500 to 749	849,120 (21,313)	437,600 (6,097)	268,450 (2,725)	143,070 (19,955)	59,210 (964)	26,020 (510)	19,810 (458)	13,390 (597)	1,340 (41)	710 (9)	400 (4)	230 (39)
750 or more	867,280 (11,243)	380,010 (†)	301,230 (3,520)	186,040 (10,678)	66,100 (1,513)	23,930 (†)	23,110 (258)	19,050 (1,491)	810 (12)	370 (†)	260 (3)	180 (11)
Percent minority students												
None	394,080 (9,296)	43,320 (6,587)	287,720 (6,737)	63,040 (2,457)	30,890 (798)	3,300 (485)	23,830 (638)	3,760 (183)	5,320 (197)	360 (34)	3,720 (187)	1,240 (62)
1 to 9 percent	2,134,830 (14,724)	1,065,220 (7,602)	801,840 (7,532)	267,780 (6,255)	154,110 (1,387)	65,370 (553)	62,910 (754)	25,830 (666)	8,750 (96)	3,210 (20)	4,100 (86)	1,440 (29)
10 to 29 percent	1,662,220 (27,180)	636,360 (1,546)	636,700 (12,967)	589,160 (22,778)	147,200 (1,738)	42,000 (162)	49,040 (848)	56,160 (1,361)	9,210 (184)	1,850 (15)	3,610 (102)	3,760 (143)
30 to 49 percent	655,100 (12,339)	205,180 (759)	230,600 (7,677)	219,330 (6,733)	47,730 (818)	12,840 (36)	17,060 (629)	17,830 (432)	4,220 (133)	630 (10)	1,640 (95)	1,950 (72)
50 percent or more	1,027,020 (9,790)	452,730 (1,793)	346,480 (5,552)	227,810 (6,723)	69,380 (760)	26,250 (106)	25,890 (450)	17,740 (541)	7,550 (142)	1,690 (11)	3,100 (62)	2,760 (102)
Type of locale												
City	2,509,000 (19,613)	1,094,180 (6,460)	883,770 (11,944)	531,040 (10,606)	183,760 (1,378)	67,770 (467)	67,990 (838)	48,000 (685)	11,810 (149)	3,200 (31)	4,650 (72)	3,960 (88)
Suburban	2,430,620 (26,005)	983,870 (4,800)	875,210 (12,287)	571,540 (16,029)	173,110 (2,376)	59,800 (436)	64,850 (834)	48,460 (1,751)	12,800 (263)	2,860 (25)	5,030 (125)	4,910 (160)
Town	436,980 (7,068)	203,840 (†)	171,580 (6,060)	61,570 (3,596)	32,700 (595)	13,680 (†)	13,630 (571)	5,400 (155)	3,570 (152)	1,030 (†)	1,870 (123)	670 (82)
Rural	696,640 (25,237)	120,910 (7,006)	372,760 (10,218)	202,970 (22,589)	60,240 (1,442)	8,510 (474)	32,250 (830)	19,470 (1,153)	6,880 (206)	660 (25)	4,620 (184)	1,600 (98)

†Not applicable.
[1]Data reported in full-time equivalents (FTE). Excludes teachers who teach only prekindergarten students.
NOTE: Includes special education, vocational/technical education, and alternative schools. Tabulation includes schools that offer kindergarten or higher grade. Detail may not sum to totals because of rounding. Standard errors appear in parentheses.
SOURCE: U.S. Department of Education. National Center for Education Statistics, Private School Universe Survey (PSS), 2005–06. (This table was prepared June 2008.)

Table 59. Private elementary and secondary enrollment, number of schools, and average tuition, by school level, orientation, and tuition: 1999–2000 and 2003–04

School orientation and tuition	Kindergarten through 12th-grade enrollment[1]				Schools				Average tuition paid by students[2] (in current dollars)			
	Total	Elementary	Secondary	Combined	Total	Elementary	Secondary	Combined	Total	Elementary	Secondary	Combined
1	2	3	4	5	6	7	8	9	10	11	12	13
1999–2000												
Total	5,262,850 (131,001)	2,920,680 (55,056)	818,920 (34,102)	1,523,240 (88,816)	27,220 (239)	16,560 (278)	2,580 (126)	8,080 (276)	$4,689 (254.3)	$3,267 (128.3)	$6,053 (1,529.3)	$6,779 (798.1)
Catholic	2,548,710 (23,352)	1,810,330 (18,134)	616,190 (25,935)	122,190 (15,613)	7,930 (41)	6,530 (68)	1,100 (56)	300 (28)	3,236 (439.8)	2,451 (109.4)	4,845 (253.7)	6,780 (1,159.7)
Other religious	1,871,850 (86,781)	831,060 (41,035)	115,010 (10,980)	925,780 (66,926)	12,520 (271)	6,610 (231)	720 (76)	5,190 (243)	4,063 (936.7)	3,503 (609.1)	6,536 (787.7)	4,260 (1,240.4)
Nonsectarian	842,290 (61,373)	279,290 (28,987)	87,720 (11,774)	475,270 (43,377)	5,130 (156)	2,780 (153)	590 (90)	1,770 (151)	10,992 (928.4)	7,884 (1,727.8)	14,638 (1,279.2)	12,363 (3,043.5)
2003–04												
Total	5,059,450 (104,287)	2,675,960 (55,714)	832,320 (54,051)	1,551,170 (82,059)	28,380 (262)	17,330 (262)	2,660 (206)	8,400 (217)	$6,600 (144.5)	$5,049 (119.5)	$8,412 (433.4)	$8,302 (289.7)
Less than $2,499	825,410 (33,567)	614,780 (28,503)	‡ (†)	178,310 (14,033)	8,890 (318)	5,590 (235)	‡ (†)	2,910 (187)	1,755 (39.5)	1,856 (49.6)	‡ (†)	1,512 (84.4)
$2,500 to $3,499	1,056,200 (49,470)	779,200 (43,819)	‡ (†)	265,070 (25,565)	5,910 (281)	4,160 (218)	‡ (†)	1,700 (157)	3,313 (31.7)	3,358 (40.6)	‡ (†)	3,190 (42.3)
$3,500 to $5,999	1,561,900 (64,639)	856,260 (44,734)	319,590 (34,338)	386,050 (36,613)	6,890 (301)	4,660 (240)	710 (100)	1,520 (134)	4,992 (54.1)	5,098 (97.4)	4,901 (76.9)	4,831 (71.8)
$6,000 to $9,999	867,100 (70,159)	263,600 (30,526)	314,590 (37,104)	288,910 (43,797)	3,390 (208)	1,920 (165)	720 (105)	750 (94)	8,172 (140.5)	9,604 (270.0)	7,366 (120.3)	7,743 (213.1)
$10,000 or more	748,830 (65,828)	162,120 (18,476)	153,880 (27,201)	432,830 (52,538)	3,300 (196)	1,010 (143)	780 (90)	1,520 (138)	18,110 (407.5)	17,619 (823.9)	19,896 (1,089.0)	17,658 (558.0)
Catholic	2,320,040 (49,156)	1,645,680 (41,231)	584,250 (32,236)	90,110 (14,746)	7,920 (35)	6,530 (50)	1,060 (39)	320 (39)	4,254 (95.9)	3,533 (105.9)	6,046 (130.6)	5,801 (883.0)
Less than $2,499	508,950 (28,976)	478,010 (26,341)	‡ (†)	‡ (†)	2,520 (116)	2,370 (113)	‡ (†)	‡ (†)	1,803 (49.0)	1,838 (51.8)	‡ (†)	‡ (†)
$2,500 to $3,499	635,890 (37,479)	599,610 (36,557)	‡ (†)	‡ (†)	2,290 (113)	2,190 (110)	‡ (†)	‡ (†)	3,168 (27.7)	3,184 (29.8)	‡ (†)	‡ (†)
$3,500 to $5,999	825,850 (44,943)	522,410 (36,627)	284,710 (26,258)	‡ (†)	2,420 (135)	1,810 (123)	530 (49)	‡ (†)	4,727 (53.4)	4,615 (68.4)	4,897 (80.4)	‡ (†)
$6,000 to $9,999	307,270 (34,641)	‡ (†)	255,650 (31,681)	‡ (†)	550 (63)	‡ (†)	410 (46)	‡ (†)	7,428 (120.7)	‡ (†)	7,338 (127.4)	‡ (†)
$10,000 or more	‡ (†)	‡ (†)	‡ (†)	‡ (†)	‡ (†)	‡ (†)	‡ (†)	‡ (†)	‡ (†)	‡ (†)	‡ (†)	‡ (†)
Other religious	1,746,460 (63,090)	714,860 (28,935)	107,980 (33,776)	923,630 (48,379)	13,660 (203)	7,280 (200)	640 (175)	5,740 (182)	5,839 (143.9)	5,398 (161.4)	9,537 (962.6)	5,748 (230.3)
Less than $2,499	258,570 (16,268)	120,700 (10,263)	‡ (†)	137,010 (12,537)	5,390 (253)	2,830 (192)	‡ (†)	2,490 (183)	1,891 (66.3)	1,929 (122.6)	‡ (†)	1,864 (85.5)
$2,500 to $3,499	342,250 (25,879)	171,210 (16,475)	‡ (†)	169,300 (19,758)	3,180 (237)	1,820 (166)	‡ (†)	1,350 (139)	3,571 (82.6)	3,946 (133.6)	‡ (†)	3,194 (62.2)
$3,500 to $5,999	642,470 (45,686)	271,880 (24,925)	34,690 (18,788)	335,890 (35,041)	3,330 (210)	1,870 (139)	180 (82)	1,280 (130)	4,935 (57.4)	5,090 (98.1)	4,996 (244.4)	4,809 (82.3)
$6,000 to $9,999	319,250 (42,256)	101,120 (17,425)	‡ (†)	190,920 (34,055)	1,060 (116)	540 (73)	‡ (†)	410 (66)	7,872 (237.0)	8,771 (436.4)	‡ (†)	7,503 (273.3)
$10,000 or more	183,930 (21,087)	‡ (†)	‡ (†)	90,510 (17,086)	700 (76)	‡ (†)	‡ (†)	210 (40)	15,237 (566.0)	‡ (†)	‡ (†)	16,185 (1,179.3)
Nonsectarian	992,940 (71,519)	315,430 (30,820)	140,080 (27,556)	537,440 (59,332)	6,810 (136)	3,510 (141)	960 (108)	2,340 (144)	13,419 (379.1)	12,169 (468.5)	17,413 (1,987.6)	13,112 (480.4)
Less than $2,499	57,890 (8,890)	‡ (†)	‡ (†)	‡ (†)	990 (127)	‡ (†)	‡ (†)	‡ (†)	719 (309.9)	‡ (†)	‡ (†)	‡ (†)
$2,500 to $3,499	‡ (†)	‡ (†)	‡ (†)	‡ (†)	‡ (†)	‡ (†)	‡ (†)	‡ (†)	‡ (†)	‡ (†)	‡ (†)	‡ (†)
$3,500 to $5,999	93,530 (17,673)	61,960 (9,990)	‡ (†)	‡ (†)	1,140 (171)	970 (159)	‡ (†)	‡ (†)	7,718 (764.1)	9,209 (882.4)	‡ (†)	‡ (†)
$6,000 to $9,999	240,590 (30,450)	131,320 (22,258)	‡ (†)	‡ (†)	1,780 (175)	1,270 (148)	‡ (†)	‡ (†)	9,519 (293.3)	10,607 (379.7)	‡ (†)	‡ (†)
$10,000 or more	522,630 (55,040)	97,690 (16,359)	93,410 (22,905)	331,730 (47,865)	2,460 (172)	730 (129)	460 (77)	1,270 (128)	19,142 (571.0)	18,559 (855.5)	23,415 (1,493.6)	18,111 (618.0)

†Not applicable.
‡Reporting standards not met.
[1]Only includes kindergarten students who attend schools that offer first or higher grade.
[2]Tuition weighted by the number of students enrolled in schools.
NOTE: Excludes schools not offering first or higher grade. Elementary schools have grade 6 or lower and no grade higher than 8. Combined schools have no grade lower than 7. Combined schools have grades lower than 7 and higher than 8.

Excludes prekindergarten students. Includes schools reporting tuition of 0. Detail may not sum to totals because of rounding and cell suppression. Standard errors appear in parentheses.
SOURCE: U.S. Department of Education, National Center for Education Statistics, Schools and Staffing Survey (SASS), "Private School Questionnaire," 1999–2000 and 2003–04. (This table was prepared in August 2006.)

Table 60. Private elementary and secondary school full-time-equivalent staff and student to full-time-equivalent staff ratios, by orientation of school, school level, and type of staff: 2003–04

Type of staff	Total				Catholic			
	Total	Elementary[1]	Secondary[2]	Combined[3]	Total	Elementary[1]	Secondary[2]	Combined[3]
1	2	3	4	5	6	7	8	9
Number of schools	28,380 (262)	17,330 (252)	2,660 (206)	8,400 (217)	7,920 (35)	6,530 (50)	1,060 (39)	320 (39)
Enrollment (in thousands)	5,060 (104)	2,680 (56)	830 (54)	1,550 (82)	2,320 (49)	1,650 (41)	580 (32)	90 (15)
Total staff	**707,200 (15,342)**	**325,010 (6,805)**	**125,520 (8,244)**	**256,670 (13,136)**	**240,870 (4,555)**	**160,690 (3,518)**	**66,130 (3,172)**	**14,050 (2,166)**
Principals	27,090 (544)	14,490 (325)	2,740 (236)	9,860 (420)	7,750 (119)	6,090 (101)	1,230 (49)	430 (77)
Assistant principals	10,630 (444)	4,260 (196)	2,230 (183)	4,140 (354)	3,570 (163)	1,870 (124)	1,530 (109)	180 (49)
Other managers	19,670 (671)	7,290 (399)	4,740 (345)	7,640 (507)	5,760 (274)	2,430 (197)	2,830 (189)	500 (101)
Instruction coordinators	5,960 (393)	2,090 (182)	1,260 (218)	2,610 (269)	1,550 (211)	780 (138)	680 (146)	90 (30)
Teachers	416,930 (9,490)	197,090 (4,302)	69,200 (4,389)	150,540 (8,081)	149,280 (3,287)	100,360 (2,615)	40,720 (2,018)	8,200 (1,308)
Teacher aides	40,050 (1,667)	22,870 (948)	1,610 (425)	15,570 (1,391)	12,210 (610)	11,020 (507)	270 (57)	920 (405)
Other aides	8,220 (849)	3,930 (462)	‡ (†)	3,990 (737)	2,310 (435)	1,830 (246)	60 (27)	‡ (†)
Guidance counselors	10,200 (479)	2,400 (201)	3,860 (318)	3,950 (330)	4,490 (215)	1,530 (148)	2,650 (169)	320 (64)
Librarians/media specialists	11,060 (370)	5,280 (163)	1,820 (160)	3,970 (300)	4,400 (143)	3,080 (122)	1,080 (63)	240 (50)
Library/media center aides	3,360 (211)	1,590 (126)	700 (115)	1,070 (119)	1,410 (127)	920 (109)	400 (61)	90 (35)
Nurses	7,930 (962)	2,930 (145)	2,560 (899)	2,450 (202)	2,520 (114)	1,920 (105)	400 (60)	200 (49)
Student support staff[4]	19,100 (1,021)	7,600 (776)	3,380 (667)	8,110 (620)	3,940 (247)	2,700 (162)	800 (101)	440 (133)
Secretaries/clerical staff	43,840 (1,307)	18,360 (538)	8,920 (701)	16,570 (1,062)	14,810 (422)	8,790 (247)	5,240 (315)	780 (147)
Food service personnel	26,290 (1,189)	11,110 (444)	6,920 (922)	8,260 (733)	10,430 (417)	6,830 (314)	3,030 (296)	570 (115)
Custodial and maintenance	38,590 (1,263)	16,650 (443)	8,500 (796)	13,340 (1,001)	14,380 (342)	9,570 (298)	4,210 (257)	590 (101)
Other employees[5]	18,290 (2,842)	7,090 (1,831)	6,680 (2,228)	4,520 (598)	2,050 (259)	980 (152)	990 (198)	‡ (†)

Students per full-time-equivalent staff member

Type of staff	Total				Catholic			
	Total	Elementary[1]	Secondary[2]	Combined[3]	Total	Elementary[1]	Secondary[2]	Combined[3]
1	7	8	9	10	6	7	8	6
Total staff	7 (0.1)	8 (0.1)	7 (0.3)	6 (0.1)	10 (0.1)	10 (0.1)	9 (0.2)	6 (0.4)
Principals	187 (4.0)	185 (3.9)	304 (18.8)	157 (7.1)	299 (6.8)	270 (6.7)	474 (29.6)	210 (23.5)
Assistant principals	476 (16.5)	628 (29.0)	373 (18.1)	375 (25.0)	649 (24.6)	881 (54.1)	382 (16.9)	514 (128.9)
Other managers	257 (6.2)	367 (17.4)	175 (10.8)	203 (8.1)	403 (17.4)	677 (54.1)	207 (13.8)	180 (18.6)
Instruction coordinators	849 (57.3)	1,281 (115.3)	661 (124.6)	595 (63.4)	1,498 (224.6)	2,115 (480.8)	864 (213.6)	956 (339.4)
Teachers	12 (0.1)	14 (0.2)	12 (0.3)	10 (0.2)	16 (0.2)	16 (0.3)	14 (0.3)	11 (0.6)
Teacher aides	126 (4.9)	117 (4.5)	516 (139.6)	100 (8.6)	190 (9.8)	149 (7.1)	2,134 (416.0)	98 (67.5)
Other aides	616 (71.3)	680 (73.9)	‡ (†)	389 (89.2)	1,002 (203.9)	900 (125.5)	‡ (†)	‡ (†)
Guidance counselors	496 (20.5)	1,115 (92.7)	216 (13.6)	393 (29.9)	517 (23.9)	1,076 (105.9)	221 (7.9)	286 (50.7)
Librarians/media specialists	457 (9.9)	507 (12.7)	458 (28.0)	391 (16.6)	527 (14.5)	534 (16.1)	542 (33.1)	375 (69.7)
Library/media center aides	1,507 (91.8)	1,683 (132.8)	1,191 (238.1)	1,451 (142.2)	1,646 (156.8)	1,794 (226.3)	1,458 (260.7)	981 (392.9)
Nurses	638 (80.2)	913 (41.6)	‡ (†)	634 (52.8)	921 (41.0)	857 (42.6)	1,451 (174.0)	457 (119.8)
Student support staff[4]	265 (14.4)	352 (36.7)	246 (53.1)	191 (14.7)	589 (36.2)	610 (35.8)	733 (84.1)	203 (67.9)
Secretaries/clerical staff	115 (2.4)	146 (3.8)	93 (5.2)	94 (3.2)	157 (3.8)	187 (5.7)	111 (4.6)	116 (10.6)
Food service personnel	192 (8.6)	241 (10.1)	120 (17.6)	188 (13.9)	222 (8.9)	241 (11.7)	193 (15.0)	159 (26.7)
Custodial and maintenance	131 (3.3)	161 (3.7)	97 (7.3)	116 (5.3)	161 (4.3)	172 (4.6)	139 (6.4)	151 (15.2)
Other employees[5]	277 (40.8)	378 (91.0)	125 (58.5)	343 (40.1)	1,131 (151.6)	1,678 (286.2)	592 (150.8)	‡ (†)

See notes at end of table.

Table 60. Private elementary and secondary school full-time-equivalent staff and student to full-time-equivalent staff ratios, by orientation of school, school level, and type of staff: 2003–04—Continued

Type of staff	Other religious orientation				Nonsectarian			
	Total	Elementary[1]	Secondary[2]	Combined[3]	Total	Elementary[1]	Secondary[2]	Combined[3]
1	10	11	12	13	14	15	16	17
Number of schools	13,660 (203)	7,280 (200)	640 (175)	5,740 (182)	6,810 (136)	3,510 (141)	960 (108)	2,340 (144)
Enrollment (in thousands)	1,750 (63)	710 (29)	110 (34)	920 (48)	990 (72)	320 (31)	140 (28)	540 (59)
Total staff	246,390 (7,622)	99,660 (3,678)	17,540 (4,199)	129,190 (6,449)	219,940 (12,237)	64,660 (5,231)	41,850 (7,112)	113,430 (10,239)
Principals	12,720 (382)	5,360 (194)	650 (189)	6,710 (355)	6,620 (284)	3,030 (200)	860 (128)	2,730 (204)
Assistant principals	3,760 (289)	1,270 (125)	260 (84)	2,230 (254)	3,300 (239)	1,120 (129)	440 (97)	1,730 (207)
Other managers	6,750 (401)	2,530 (213)	610 (230)	3,610 (257)	7,170 (501)	2,330 (313)	1,300 (273)	3,530 (377)
Instruction coordinators	2,080 (232)	660 (90)	130 (56)	1,290 (204)	2,330 (262)	650 (101)	450 (171)	1,230 (162)
Teachers	154,340 (5,000)	62,300 (2,186)	10,550 (2,635)	81,490 (4,099)	113,300 (7,251)	34,430 (2,926)	17,930 (3,161)	60,950 (6,291)
Teacher aides	10,550 (688)	5,950 (461)	‡ (†)	4,480 (544)	17,290 (1,351)	5,890 (643)	1,230 (406)	10,160 (1,127)
Other aides	3,430 (605)	1,340 (276)	‡ (†)	2,070 (511)	2,470 (451)	770 (265)	‡ (†)	1,500 (372)
Guidance counselors	1,950 (181)	290 (45)	280 (107)	1,380 (122)	3,760 (392)	580 (113)	930 (256)	2,250 (305)
Librarians/media specialists	3,770 (204)	1,540 (114)	260 (101)	1,970 (144)	2,890 (252)	660 (96)	480 (115)	1,750 (218)
Library/media center aides	1,160 (111)	510 (69)	130 (54)	520 (75)	790 (130)	160 (32)	‡ (†)	460 (82)
Nurses	1,510 (115)	560 (58)	150 (47)	800 (84)	3,900 (939)	450 (76)	2,000 (901)	1,450 (185)
Student support staff[4]	3,810 (248)	1,910 (184)	260 (99)	1,640 (191)	11,350 (1,005)	2,990 (712)	2,320 (675)	6,030 (575)
Secretaries/clerical staff	15,960 (698)	6,090 (320)	1,200 (341)	8,670 (550)	13,070 (985)	3,480 (350)	2,470 (569)	7,120 (802)
Food service personnel	7,850 (505)	2,830 (209)	720 (205)	4,300 (502)	8,000 (1,015)	1,450 (230)	3,170 (866)	3,390 (505)
Custodial and maintenance	12,410 (513)	4,600 (251)	1,500 (351)	6,320 (446)	11,810 (1,038)	2,480 (247)	2,890 (701)	6,430 (832)
Other employees[5]	4,340 (711)	1,910 (435)	‡ (†)	1,720 (279)	11,890 (2,745)	4,190 (1,676)	4,980 (2,158)	2,720 (551)

Students per full-time-equivalent staff member

Type of staff	Other religious orientation				Nonsectarian			
	Total	Elementary[1]	Secondary[2]	Combined[3]	Total	Elementary[1]	Secondary[2]	Combined[3]
Total staff	7 (0.1)	7 (0.1)	6 (0.6)	7 (0.2)	5 (0.1)	5 (0.3)	3 (0.3)	5 (0.2)
Principals	137 (5.1)	133 (5.0)	166 (23.4)	138 (7.8)	150 (8.9)	104 (10.1)	163 (30.0)	197 (13.2)
Assistant principals	464 (31.2)	563 (62.8)	416 (77.5)	414 (40.5)	301 (16.5)	281 (31.2)	317 (69.4)	310 (28.3)
Other managers	259 (11.6)	283 (20.6)	176 (25.9)	256 (14.6)	139 (7.2)	135 (12.9)	108 (19.6)	152 (10.3)
Instruction coordinators	839 (96.9)	1,081 (138.7)	814 (489.3)	717 (136.7)	427 (46.2)	485 (75.6)	311 (144.5)	438 (66.9)
Teachers	11 (0.2)	11 (0.2)	10 (0.9)	11 (0.2)	9 (0.2)	9 (0.3)	8 (0.5)	9 (0.2)
Teacher aides	166 (12.4)	120 (8.6)	‡ (†)	206 (26.0)	57 (5.1)	54 (6.7)	114 (41.3)	53 (6.9)
Other aides	509 (104.6)	534 (109.4)	‡ (†)	446 (132.9)	401 (89.7)	412 (141.4)	‡ (†)	359 (128.7)
Guidance counselors	898 (61.4)	2,498 (420.6)	388 (50.6)	669 (50.0)	264 (30.8)	540 (136.6)	151 (48.9)	239 (37.1)
Librarians/media specialists	463 (19.1)	465 (26.4)	413 (47.9)	468 (30.9)	343 (15.3)	478 (41.3)	293 (47.9)	306 (16.5)
Library/media center aides	1,508 (143.3)	1,405 (168.3)	‡ (†)	1,791 (289.2)	1,257 (203.1)	1,919 (495.6)	‡ (†)	1,165 (155.1)
Nurses	1,156 (84.9)	1,269 (121.3)	731 (352.8)	1,155 (118.3)	254 (76.2)	703 (127.9)	‡ (†)	371 (53.8)
Student support staff[4]	458 (29.6)	374 (36.3)	411 (181.8)	565 (56.1)	87 (9.6)	105 (30.4)	60 (21.5)	89 (10.9)
Secretaries/clerical staff	109 (3.1)	117 (4.4)	90 (12.2)	107 (4.0)	76 (4.0)	91 (6.8)	57 (9.5)	75 (4.9)
Food service personnel	222 (14.9)	253 (18.9)	150 (55.0)	215 (24.9)	124 (16.2)	218 (40.6)	44 (11.8)	159 (17.8)
Custodial and maintenance	141 (4.6)	155 (8.1)	72 (15.7)	146 (7.8)	84 (5.4)	127 (11.0)	48 (9.0)	84 (6.3)
Other employees[5]	402 (65.4)	374 (81.4)	‡ (†)	537 (93.3)	83 (20.0)	‡ (†)	‡ (†)	198 (35.9)

†Not applicable.
‡Reporting standards not met.
[1]Includes schools beginning with grade 6 or below and with no grade higher than 8.
[2]Schools with no grade lower than 7.
[3]Schools with grades lower than 7 and higher than 8.
[4]Includes student support services professional staff, such as school psychologists, social workers, occupational therapists, and speech therapists.
[5]Includes health and other noninstructional aides, and other employees not identified by function.
NOTE: Data are based on a sample survey and may not be strictly comparable with data reported elsewhere. Excludes all prekindergarten students from calculations, but includes kindergarten students attending schools that offer first or higher grade. Includes only schools that offer first or higher grade. Standard errors appear in parentheses. Detail may not sum to totals because of rounding.
SOURCE: U.S. Department of Education, National Center for Education Statistics, Schools and Staffing Survey (SASS), "Private School Questionnaire," 2003–04. (This table was prepared August 2006.)

Table 61. Enrollment and instructional staff in Catholic elementary and secondary schools, by level: Selected years, 1919–20 through 2007–08

School year	Number of schools			Enrollment[1]			Instructional staff[2]		
	Total	Elementary[3]	Secondary	Total	Elementary	Secondary	Total	Elementary[3]	Secondary
1	2	3	4	5	6	7	8	9	10
1919–20	8,103	6,551	1,552	1,925,521	1,795,673	129,848	49,516	41,592	7,924
1929–30	10,046	7,923	2,123	2,464,467	2,222,598	241,869	72,552	58,245	14,307
1939–40	10,049	7,944	2,105	2,396,305	2,035,182	361,123	81,057	60,081	20,976
1949–50	10,778	8,589	2,189	3,066,387	2,560,815	505,572	94,295	66,525	27,770
Fall 1960	12,893	10,501	2,392	5,253,791	4,373,422	880,369	151,902	108,169	43,733
1969–70	11,352	9,366	1,986	4,367,000	3,359,000	1,008,000	195,400 [4]	133,200 [4]	62,200 [4]
1970–71	11,350	9,370	1,980	4,363,566	3,355,478	1,008,088	166,208	112,750	53,458
1974–75	10,127	8,437	1,690	3,504,000	2,602,000	902,000	150,179	100,011	50,168
1975–76	9,993	8,340	1,653	3,415,000	2,525,000	890,000	149,276	99,319	49,957
1979–80	9,640	8,100	1,540	3,139,000	2,293,000	846,000	147,294	97,724	49,570
1980–81	9,559	8,043	1,516	3,106,000	2,269,000	837,000	145,777	96,739	49,038
1981–82	9,494	7,996	1,498	3,094,000	2,266,000	828,000	146,172	96,847	49,325
1982–83	9,432	7,950	1,482	3,007,189	2,211,412	795,777	146,460	97,337	49,123
1983–84	9,401	7,937	1,464	2,969,000	2,179,000	790,000	146,913	98,591	48,322
1984–85	9,325	7,876	1,449	2,903,000	2,119,000	784,000	149,888	99,820	50,068
1985–86	9,220	7,790	1,430	2,821,000	2,061,000	760,000	146,594	96,741	49,853
1986–87	9,102	7,693	1,409	2,726,000	1,998,000	728,000	141,930	93,554	48,376
1987–88	8,992	7,601	1,391	2,623,031	1,942,148	680,883	139,887	93,199	46,688
1988–89	8,867	7,505	1,362	2,551,119	1,911,911	639,208	137,700	93,154	44,546
1989–90	8,719	7,395	1,324	2,589,000	1,983,000	606,000	136,900	94,197	42,703
1990–91	8,587	7,291	1,296	2,475,439	1,883,906	591,533	131,198	91,039	40,159
1991–92	8,508	7,239	1,269	2,442,924	1,856,302	586,622	153,334	109,084	44,250
1992–93	8,423	7,174	1,249	2,444,842	1,860,937	583,905	154,816	109,825	44,991
1993–94	8,345	7,114	1,231	2,444,609	1,859,947	584,662	157,201	112,199	45,002
1994–95	8,293	7,055	1,238	2,475,207	1,877,782	597,425	164,219	117,620	46,599
1995–96	8,250	7,022	1,228	2,491,111	1,884,461	606,650	166,759	118,753	48,006
1996–97	8,231	7,005	1,226	2,497,198	1,885,037	612,161	153,276	107,548	45,728
1997–98	8,223	7,004	1,219	2,497,894	1,879,737	618,157	152,260	105,717	46,542
1998–99	8,217	6,990	1,227	2,496,488	1,876,211	620,277	153,081	105,943	47,138
1999–2000	8,144	6,923	1,221	2,500,416	1,877,236	623,180	157,134	109,404	47,730
2000–01	8,146	6,920	1,226	2,491,559	1,863,682	627,877	160,731	111,937	48,794
2001–02	8,114	6,886	1,228	2,456,461	1,827,319	629,142	155,658	108,485	47,173
2002–03	8,000	6,785	1,215	2,396,027	1,765,893	630,134	163,004	112,884	50,120
2003–04	7,955	6,727	1,228	2,333,830	1,708,501	625,329	162,337	112,303	50,034
2004–05	7,799	6,574	1,225	2,269,685	1,642,868	626,817	160,153	107,764	52,389
2005–06	7,589	6,386	1,203	2,178,893	1,568,687	610,206	152,502 [5]	103,481 [5]	49,021 [5]
2006–07	7,498	6,288	1,210	2,168,222	1,544,695	623,527	159,135	107,682	51,453
2007–08	7,378	6,165	1,213	2,117,933	1,494,979	622,954	160,075	107,217	52,858

[1]Total enrollment is for kindergarten through grade 12, elementary enrollment is for kindergarten through grade 8, and secondary enrollment is for grades 9 through 12.
[2]From 1919–20 through fall 1960, includes part-time teachers. From 1969–70 through 1993–94, excludes part-time teachers. Beginning in 1994–95, reported in full-time equivalents (FTE).
[3]Includes middle schools.
[4]Includes estimates for the nonreporting schools.
[5]Excludes the Archdiocese of New Orleans.

NOTE: Data collected by the National Catholic Educational Association and data collected by the National Center for Education Statistics are not directly comparable because survey procedures and definitions differ. Some data have been revised from previously published figures.
SOURCE: National Catholic Educational Association, *A Statistical Report on Catholic Elementary and Secondary Schools for the Years 1967–68 to 1969–70; A Report on Catholic Schools,* 1970–71 through 1973–74; *A Statistical Report on U.S. Catholic Schools,* 1974–75 through 1980–81; and *United States Catholic Elementary and Secondary Schools,* 1981–82 through 2007–08. (This table was prepared May 2008.)

Table 62. Private elementary and secondary schools, enrollment, teachers, and high school graduates, by state: Selected years, 1997 through 2005

State	Schools, fall 2005		Enrollment in prekindergarten through grade 12										Teachers,[1] fall 2005		High school graduates, 2004–05	
			Fall 1997		Fall 1999		Fall 2001		Fall 2003		Fall 2005					
1	2		3		4		5		6		7		8		9	
United States	35,050	(395)	5,944,320	(18,543)	6,018,280	(30,179)	6,319,650	(40,272)	6,099,220	(41,219)	6,073,240	(42,446)	449,810	(2,944)	307,250	(9,318)
Alabama	500	(72)	82,060	(†)	81,040	(†)	92,380	(3,926)	99,580	(12,130)	92,280	(5,892)	6,740	(499)	5,190	(664)
Alaska	90	(23)	7,230	(†)	6,980	(†)	7,420	(†)	7,370	(424)	7,500	(1,028)	590	(46)	290	(†)
Arizona	400	(†)	59,730	(261)	58,740	(2,591)	78,660	(18,218)	75,360	(16,426)	66,840	(†)	4,130	(†)	2,630	(†)
Arkansas	230	(51)	30,410	(†)	29,400	(†)	32,570	(†)	31,300	(†)	35,390	(5,858)	2,440	(245)	3,920 !	(2,571)
California	4,180	(86)	721,210	(2,146)	724,010	(1,403)	757,750	(8,415)	740,460	(8,703)	737,490	(15,529)	49,960	(613)	33,540	(215)
Colorado	500	(29)	65,410	(†)	65,690	(†)	64,700	(†)	62,080	(476)	70,770	(1,160)	4,970	(29)	2,840	(†)
Connecticut	420	(11)	76,740	(785)	80,060	(391)	82,320	(†)	102,960	(25,024)	76,220	(1,619)	7,500	(114)	5,590	(†)
Delaware	140	(†)	36,730	(7,525)	26,940	(†)	31,690	(1,023)	33,020	(2,649)	29,830	(†)	2,270	(†)	1,660	(†)
District of Columbia	90	(†)	17,480	(†)	17,000	(†)	33,660	(14,373)	23,510	(6,121)	19,880	(†)	2,280	(†)	1,450	(†)
Florida	2,080	(105)	329,770	(2,120)	349,180	(4,957)	365,890	(8,301)	398,720	(14,590)	396,790	(7,429)	28,980	(420)	16,820	(130)
Georgia	790	(122)	126,520	(5,983)	137,420	(9,460)	137,060	(4,550)	144,850	(6,527)	152,600	(10,394)	12,400	(587)	7,300	(154)
Hawaii	120	(†)	35,530	(†)	35,550	(746)	42,980	(220)	39,940	(†)	32,810	(†)	2,540	(†)	1,670	(†)
Idaho	170 !	(53)	11,140	(†)	12,720	(†)	12,050	(†)	12,570	(†)	15,320	(2,518)	1,080	(207)	550	(†)
Illinois	1,810	(120)	345,250	(720)	347,750	(700)	357,390	(19,293)	316,430	(1,698)	317,940	(4,263)	19,990	(376)	14,350	(37)
Indiana	890	(110)	122,430	(1,222)	121,960	(†)	129,240	(326)	124,500	(455)	139,370	(17,870)	9,070	(1,051)	5,270	(389)
Iowa	290	(28)	64,320	(9,269)	54,640	(844)	51,540	(†)	53,850	(4,634)	60,960	(8,311)	4,330	(591)	3,270	(872)
Kansas	410	(112)	45,430	(1,964)	56,840	(12,716)	51,540	(8,341)	47,710	(2,151)	47,130	(1,654)	3,460	(249)	2,080	(†)
Kentucky	520	(129)	81,770	(1,078)	89,300	(6,657)	85,230	(3,227)	82,100	(1,525)	78,880	(1,228)	5,430	(129)	3,720	(†)
Louisiana	440	(32)	153,710	(1,198)	148,020	(†)	159,910	(11,381)	155,780	(3,515)	138,270	(525)	8,980	(79)	7,960	(†)
Maine	180	(17)	18,260	(†)	19,820	(261)	20,820	(174)	24,740	(3,629)	20,680	(337)	2,080	(49)	2,350	(†)
Maryland	830	(8)	154,920	(1,725)	166,570	(1,030)	175,740	(†)	172,360	(†)	170,350	(4,201)	14,200	(485)	8,520	(†)
Massachusetts	960	(53)	151,300	(†)	154,060	(147)	177,490	(9,836)	164,390	(6,636)	157,770	(3,273)	15,480	(330)	10,940	(73)
Michigan	990	(11)	211,950	(3,152)	208,470	(4,965)	198,380	(†)	180,080	(†)	166,950	(407)	10,930	(11)	8,050	(†)
Minnesota	610	(33)	97,470	(†)	101,360	(†)	112,310	(2,993)	106,010	(3,011)	104,730	(3,467)	7,020	(154)	4,270	(†)
Mississippi	330	(68)	57,150	(416)	67,200	(14,096)	67,380	(10,106)	57,110	(2,981)	57,930	(4,104)	4,440	(365)	3,150	(†)
Missouri	710	(57)	138,460	(6,478)	131,750	(†)	138,440	(4,321)	141,530	(9,966)	137,810	(10,580)	10,590	(1,106)	8,350	(1,026)
Montana	260 !	(118)	9,050	(†)	10,170	(487)	12,930	(1,895)	12,510	(2,091)	35,980 !	(22,655)	2,080 !	(1,085)	9,230 !	(8,769)
Nebraska	230	(†)	43,210	(†)	44,560	(†)	45,590	(618)	41,650	(†)	42,420	(†)	2,830	(†)	2,270	(†)
Nevada	170	(†)	15,360	(†)	17,350	(†)	20,370	(385)	23,930	(†)	29,120	(†)	1,520	(†)	660	(†)
New Hampshire	340	(†)	31,670	(1,565)	36,480	(†)	38,650	(†)	33,780	(†)	33,220	(†)	2,770	(†)	2,160	(†)
New Jersey	1,380	(55)	248,110	(8,025)	237,540	(2,316)	282,450	(4,182)	269,530	(7,577)	256,160	(8,439)	19,610	(713)	12,810	(226)
New Mexico	200	(18)	23,580	(84)	28,570	(220)	26,510	(†)	29,310	(3,928)	25,030	(141)	2,010	(18)	1,400	(†)
New York	2,220	(49)	531,510	(2,416)	542,520	(4,368)	559,670	(1,669)	515,620	(4,071)	510,750	(3,596)	41,180	(597)	28,510	(194)
North Carolina	660	(63)	105,450	(8,920)	104,370	(1,403)	116,500	(4,112)	126,230	(11,439)	117,280	(11,681)	9,760	(888)	5,330	(512)
North Dakota	50	(†)	7,970	(†)	7,730	(†)	7,180	(†)	6,840	(†)	7,290	(†)	540	(†)	420	(†)
Ohio	1,090	(54)	285,150	(3,088)	280,930	(1,730)	290,370	(7,180)	270,660	(7,094)	254,530	(9,821)	16,760	(839)	13,070	(359)
Oklahoma	250	(66)	39,580	(7,068)	45,660	(7,770)	46,570	(8,723)	34,300	(2,013)	35,350	(1,194)	3,050	(418)	1,780	(†)
Oregon	720 !	(234)	58,290	(4,441)	61,000	(5,195)	71,500	(15,519)	54,320	(†)	69,620	(14,139)	4,550	(557)	2,850	(159)
Pennsylvania	2,460	(52)	395,940	(5,960)	392,060	(6,679)	374,490	(†)	357,580	(3,364)	332,740	(3,918)	24,190	(258)	17,950	(†)
Rhode Island	180	(†)	30,310	(†)	29,570	(†)	30,970	(†)	31,960	(†)	30,600	(†)	2,660	(†)	1,810	(†)
South Carolina	440	(38)	82,390	(7,965)	86,810	(18,537)	70,950	(†)	73,800	(†)	70,240	(1,797)	5,300	(85)	2,950	(†)
South Dakota	90	(†)	10,350	(†)	10,120	(†)	11,740	(†)	11,980	(†)	12,700	(†)	920	(†)	510	(†)
Tennessee	640	(73)	91,880	(†)	104,150	(5,281)	98,790	(†)	93,390	(†)	105,240	(2,531)	9,000	(200)	5,860	(†)
Texas	1,740	(251)	283,120	(7,997)	277,770	(2,338)	314,210	(12,244)	271,380	(2,758)	304,170	(20,453)	22,770	(1,015)	11,500	(611)
Utah	130	(†)	18,250	(†)	15,900	(†)	20,040	(†)	19,990	(†)	21,220	(†)	1,620	(†)	1,090	(†)
Vermont	130	(†)	12,230	(398)	15,010	(1,829)	14,090	(†)	12,730	(†)	11,530	(†)	1,490	(†)	1,150	(†)
Virginia	990	(151)	115,560	(443)	116,110	(215)	129,470	(†)	131,160	(6,936)	155,220	(14,290)	13,610	(1,968)	7,100	(899)
Washington	790	(100)	88,160	(1,870)	88,080	(1,493)	91,150	(2,028)	101,130	(7,935)	119,640	(13,187)	7,950	(688)	4,600	(197)
West Virginia	150	(†)	15,260	(†)	16,370	(†)	16,560	(†)	15,300	(†)	16,120	(†)	1,380	(†)	800	(†)
Wisconsin	990	(11)	156,330	(†)	154,340	(1,581)	162,220	(9,080)	159,240	(11,743)	142,280	(137)	10,190	(17)	5,670	(†)
Wyoming	40	(†)	3,200	(†)	2,640	(†)	2,430	(†)	2,600	(†)	2,310	(†)	220	(†)	‡	(†)

†Not applicable.
!Interpret data with caution.
‡Reporting standards not met.
[1]Reported in full-time equivalents (FTE). Excludes teachers who teach only prekindergarten students.
NOTE: Includes special education, vocational/technical education, and alternative schools. Tabulation includes schools that offer kindergarten or higher grade. Includes enrollment of students in prekindergarten though grade 12 in schools that offer kindergarten or higher grade. Some data have been revised from previously published figures. Detail may not sum to totals because of rounding. Standard errors appear in parentheses.
SOURCE: U.S. Department of Education, National Center for Education Statistics, Private School Universe Survey (PSS), various years, 1997–98 through 2005–06. (This table was prepared June 2008.)

Table 63. Public elementary and secondary pupil/teacher ratios, by enrollment size, type, and level of school: Fall 1987 through fall 2006

Enrollment size, type, and level of school	1987	1988	1989	1990	1991	1992	1993	1994	1995	1996	1997	1998	1999	2000	2001	2002	2003	2004	2005	2006
1	2	3	4	5	6	7	8	9	10	11	12	13	14	15	16	17	18	19	20	21
All schools	**17.9**	**17.9**	**17.9**	**17.4**	**17.6**	**17.7**	**17.8**	**17.7**	**17.8**	**17.6**	**17.2**	**16.9**	**16.6**	**16.4**	**16.3**	**16.2**	**16.4**	**16.2**	**16.0**	**15.8**
Enrollment size of school																				
Under 300	14.6	14.8	14.6	14.0	14.1	14.1	14.3	14.1	14.1	14.0	13.7	13.6	13.3	13.1	12.9	12.8	13.0	12.8	12.7	12.7
300 to 499	17.6	17.7	17.6	17.0	17.1	17.0	17.3	17.2	17.1	16.9	16.5	16.2	15.8	15.5	15.4	15.3	15.5	15.2	15.0	14.9
500 to 999	18.5	18.4	18.5	18.0	18.1	18.1	18.2	18.1	18.2	17.9	17.5	17.1	16.8	16.7	16.5	16.5	16.6	16.4	16.2	15.9
1,000 to 1,499	18.5	18.3	18.5	17.9	18.2	18.6	18.5	18.6	18.7	18.5	18.1	17.7	17.6	17.4	17.4	17.4	17.6	17.3	16.9	16.7
1,500 or more	19.4	20.1	19.4	19.2	19.6	20.0	19.7	19.9	20.0	20.0	19.7	19.3	19.3	19.1	19.0	18.9	19.2	19.1	18.8	18.6
Type																				
Regular schools	18.1	18.0	18.1	17.6	17.7	17.8	17.9	17.8	17.9	17.7	17.3	17.0	16.7	16.5	16.4	16.3	16.5	16.3	16.1	15.9
Alternative	16.0	14.8	16.0	14.2	15.8	16.5	17.4	18.0	16.6	16.6	16.5	16.4	15.8	15.2	14.9	14.9	15.0	14.4	14.0	14.8
Special education	6.2	6.9	6.2	6.5	6.8	7.0	7.4	6.9	7.2	7.4	7.6	7.3	7.2	7.0	6.4	7.0	7.3	7.4	6.2	6.0
Vocational	13.0	—	13.0	13.0	12.3	13.0	13.1	12.9	12.7	12.9	12.9	13.1	13.0	12.7	12.7	9.9	10.3	11.5	12.0	13.4
Level and size																				
Elementary schools	18.6	18.6	18.6	18.1	18.2	18.1	18.2	18.0	18.1	17.8	17.4	17.0	16.7	16.5	16.3	16.2	16.3	16.0	15.8	15.6
Regular	18.7	18.7	18.7	18.2	18.2	18.1	18.3	18.0	18.1	17.9	17.4	17.0	16.7	16.5	16.3	16.2	16.3	16.0	15.8	15.6
Under 300	16.6	16.7	16.6	16.0	16.1	15.9	16.0	15.7	15.7	15.6	15.3	15.1	14.6	14.4	14.1	13.9	14.0	13.7	13.6	13.5
300 to 499	18.3	18.3	18.3	17.6	17.6	17.5	17.7	17.5	17.5	17.2	16.8	16.4	16.1	15.8	15.6	15.5	15.6	15.3	15.2	15.1
500 to 999	19.4	19.4	19.4	18.8	18.8	18.7	18.8	18.5	18.6	18.3	17.8	17.4	17.1	16.9	16.8	16.7	16.8	16.5	16.3	16.0
1,000 to 1,499	20.1	20.0	20.1	19.5	19.6	19.7	19.7	19.6	19.7	19.4	18.8	18.4	18.3	18.1	18.0	18.0	18.1	17.7	17.2	17.0
1,500 or more	19.5	18.9	19.5	19.9	20.9	20.3	21.2	20.4	20.9	21.2	20.7	19.9	20.0	20.5	20.2	20.3	20.8	20.5	19.6	19.4
Secondary schools	17.2	17.2	17.2	16.6	16.9	17.3	17.3	17.5	17.6	17.5	17.3	17.0	16.8	16.6	16.6	16.7	16.9	16.8	16.6	16.4
Regular	17.3	17.1	17.3	16.7	17.0	17.4	17.4	17.6	17.7	17.6	17.4	17.1	16.9	16.7	16.7	16.8	17.0	16.9	16.8	16.6
Under 300	12.4	12.7	12.4	12.3	12.3	12.3	12.6	12.7	12.8	12.7	12.5	12.5	12.0	12.0	11.9	12.0	12.3	12.0	12.2	12.0
300 to 499	15.5	15.4	15.5	14.9	15.1	15.3	15.5	15.7	15.7	15.5	15.3	15.1	14.6	14.5	14.4	14.4	14.7	14.7	14.6	14.3
500 to 999	16.8	16.6	16.8	16.1	16.4	16.7	16.7	16.8	16.9	16.7	16.4	16.2	16.0	15.8	15.7	15.8	16.0	15.9	15.8	15.6
1,000 to 1,499	17.9	17.7	17.9	17.2	17.5	17.9	17.8	17.9	18.0	17.9	17.5	17.2	17.1	16.8	16.8	16.9	17.2	17.0	16.8	16.5
1,500 or more	19.5	19.5	19.5	19.3	19.6	20.0	19.6	19.9	20.0	20.0	19.7	19.3	19.2	18.9	18.8	18.8	19.0	19.0	18.8	18.5
Combined schools	15.5	15.9	15.5	14.5	15.0	14.8	15.3	15.1	15.0	14.7	14.4	13.4	13.4	13.7	13.4	13.5	13.8	13.9	14.1	14.7
Under 300	9.5	9.8	9.5	8.9	9.3	9.3	9.6	9.3	9.0	8.7	8.6	8.9	9.1	9.2	9.1	9.1	9.5	9.2	9.5	10.1
300 to 499	14.4	15.3	14.4	14.2	14.3	14.4	14.8	14.4	14.7	14.3	14.0	13.6	13.8	13.5	13.1	13.1	14.4	13.4	13.9	14.3
500 to 999	17.6	17.1	17.6	16.3	16.7	15.6	16.5	16.6	16.6	16.6	16.2	15.5	14.9	15.8	15.6	16.0	15.4	15.8	15.9	16.0
1,000 to 1,499	19.0	18.5	19.0	17.8	17.9	18.6	18.6	18.3	18.2	18.4	18.0	16.9	16.9	17.5	18.1	17.7	17.5	17.4	16.4	17.3
1,500 or more	18.8	18.8	18.8	17.7	18.6	18.9	18.8	19.5	19.6	19.3	19.3	18.7	19.2	18.6	18.9	19.1	19.2	18.7	20.0	20.3
Ungraded	5.9	6.8	5.9	6.4	6.5	6.9	7.1	6.7	6.9	5.9	6.2	5.9	5.3	7.0	6.3	6.8	9.6	8.0	7.7	7.2

—Not available.
NOTE: Pupil/teacher ratios are based on data reported by types of schools rather than by instructional programs within schools. Only includes schools that reported both enrollment and teacher data. Ratios are based on data reported by schools and may differ from data reported in other tables that reflect aggregate totals reported by states.

SOURCE: U.S. Department of Education, National Center for Education Statistics, Common Core of Data (CCD), "Public Elementary/Secondary School Universe Survey," 1987–88 through 2006–07. (This table was prepared October 2008.)

Table 64. Public and private elementary and secondary teachers, enrollment, and pupil/teacher ratios: Selected years, fall 1955 through fall 2017

Year	Teachers (in thousands)			Enrollment (in thousands)			Pupil/teacher ratio		
	Total	Public	Private	Total	Public	Private	Total	Public	Private
1	2	3	4	5	6	7	8	9	10
1955	1,286	1,141	145 [1]	35,280	30,680	4,600 [1]	27.4	26.9	31.7 [1]
1960	1,600	1,408	192 [1]	42,181	36,281	5,900 [1]	26.4	25.8	30.7 [1]
1965	1,933	1,710	223	48,473	42,173	6,300	25.1	24.7	28.3
1970	2,292	2,059	233	51,257	45,894	5,363	22.4	22.3	23.0
1971	2,293	2,063	230 [1]	51,271	46,071	5,200 [1]	22.4	22.3	22.6 [1]
1972	2,337	2,106	231 [1]	50,726	45,726	5,000 [1]	21.7	21.7	21.6 [1]
1973	2,372	2,136	236 [1]	50,445	45,445	5,000 [1]	21.3	21.3	21.2 [1]
1974	2,410	2,165	245 [1]	50,073	45,073	5,000 [1]	20.8	20.8	20.4 [1]
1975	2,453	2,198	255 [1]	49,819	44,819	5,000 [1]	20.3	20.4	19.6 [1]
1976	2,457	2,189	268	49,478	44,311	5,167	20.1	20.2	19.3
1977	2,488	2,209	279	48,717	43,577	5,140	19.6	19.7	18.4
1978	2,479	2,207	272	47,637	42,551	5,086	19.2	19.3	18.7
1979	2,461	2,185	276 [1]	46,651	41,651	5,000 [1]	19.0	19.1	18.1 [1]
1980	2,485	2,184	301	46,208	40,877	5,331	18.6	18.7	17.7
1981	2,440	2,127	313 [1]	45,544	40,044	5,500 [1]	18.7	18.8	17.6 [1]
1982	2,458	2,133	325 [1]	45,166	39,566	5,600 [1]	18.4	18.6	17.2 [1]
1983	2,476	2,139	337	44,967	39,252	5,715	18.2	18.4	17.0
1984	2,508	2,168	340 [1]	44,908	39,208	5,700 [1]	17.9	18.1	16.8 [1]
1985	2,549	2,206	343	44,979	39,422	5,557	17.6	17.9	16.2
1986	2,592	2,244	348 [1]	45,205	39,753	5,452 [1]	17.4	17.7	15.7 [1]
1987	2,631	2,279	352	45,488	40,008	5,479	17.3	17.6	15.6
1988	2,668	2,323	345	45,430	40,189	5,242 [1]	17.0	17.3	15.2 [1]
1989	2,713	2,357	356	46,141	40,543	5,599	17.0	17.2	15.7
1990	2,759	2,398	361 [1]	46,864	41,217	5,648 [1]	17.0	17.2	15.6 [1]
1991	2,797	2,432	365	47,728	42,047	5,681	17.1	17.3	15.6
1992	2,827	2,459	368 [1]	48,500	42,823	5,677 [1]	17.2	17.4	15.4 [1]
1993	2,874	2,504	370	49,133	43,465	5,668	17.1	17.4	15.3
1994	2,925	2,552	373 [1]	49,898	44,111	5,787 [1]	17.1	17.3	15.5 [1]
1995	2,974	2,598	376	50,759	44,840	5,918	17.1	17.3	15.7
1996	3,051	2,667	384 [1]	51,544	45,611	5,933 [1]	16.9	17.1	15.5 [1]
1997	3,138	2,746	391	52,071	46,127	5,944	16.6	16.8	15.2
1998	3,230	2,830	400 [1]	52,526	46,539	5,988 [1]	16.3	16.4	15.0 [1]
1999	3,319	2,911	408	52,875	46,857	6,018	15.9	16.1	14.7
2000	3,366	2,941	424 [1]	53,373	47,204	6,169 [1]	15.9	16.0	14.5 [1]
2001	3,440	3,000	441	53,992	47,672	6,320	15.7	15.9	14.3
2002	3,476	3,034	442 [1]	54,403	48,183	6,220 [1]	15.7	15.9	14.1 [1]
2003	3,490	3,049	441	54,639	48,540	6,099	15.7	15.9	13.8
2004	3,538	3,091	447 [1]	54,882	48,795	6,087 [1]	15.5	15.8	13.6 [1]
2005	3,593	3,143	450	55,187	49,113	6,073	15.4	15.6	13.5
2006	3,632	3,180	452 [2]	55,394	49,299	6,095 [2]	15.2	15.5	13.5 [2]
2007[2]	3,663	3,204	459	55,710	49,644	6,066	15.2	15.5	13.2
2008[2]	3,713	3,246	467	55,879	49,825	6,054	15.0	15.3	13.0
2009[2]	3,760	3,286	474	56,116	50,067	6,049	14.9	15.2	12.8
2010[2]	3,808	3,326	482	56,400	50,353	6,047	14.8	15.1	12.5
2011[2]	3,859	3,369	489	56,781	50,722	6,059	14.7	15.1	12.4
2012[2]	3,914	3,417	497	57,275	51,194	6,081	14.6	15.0	12.2
2013[2]	3,970	3,465	505	57,817	51,701	6,116	14.6	14.9	12.1
2014[2]	4,034	3,520	513	58,446	52,284	6,162	14.5	14.9	12.0
2015[2]	4,101	3,579	522	59,127	52,910	6,217	14.4	14.8	11.9
2016[2]	4,171	3,640	531	59,786	53,503	6,283	14.3	14.7	11.8
2017[2]	4,244	3,704	540	60,443	54,087	6,356	14.2	14.6	11.8

[1]Estimated.
[2]Projected.
NOTE: Data for teachers are expressed in full-time equivalents (FTE). Counts of private school teachers and enrollment include prekindergarten through grade 12 in schools offering kindergarten or higher grades. Counts of public school teachers and enrollment include prekindergarten through grade 12. The pupil/teacher ratio includes teachers for students with disabilities and other special teachers, while these teachers are generally excluded from class size calculations. Ratios for public schools reflect totals reported by states and differ from totals reported for schools or school districts. Some data have been revised from previously published figures. Detail may not sum to totals because of rounding.
SOURCE: U.S. Department of Education, National Center for Education Statistics, *Statistics of Public Elementary and Secondary Day Schools*, 1955–56 through 1984–85; Common Core of Data (CCD), "State Nonfiscal Survey of Public Elementary/Secondary Education," 1985–86 through 2006–07; Private School Universe Survey (PSS), 1989–90 through 2005–06; *Projections of Education Statistics to 2017*; and unpublished data. (This table was prepared October 2008.)

Table 65. Public elementary and secondary teachers, by level and state or jurisdiction: Selected years, fall 2000 through fall 2006

State or jurisdiction	Fall 2000	Fall 2002	Fall 2003	Fall 2004	Fall 2005[1]				Fall 2006			
					Total	Elementary	Secondary	Ungraded	Total	Elementary	Secondary	Ungraded
1	2	3	4	5	6	7	8	9	10	11	12	13
United States...........	2,941,461 [2]	3,034,123 [2]	3,048,652 [2]	3,090,925 [2]	3,143,003 [2]	1,733,703 [2]	1,177,698 [2]	231,602 [2]	3,180,396 [2]	1,673,234 [2]	1,250,771	256,391
Alabama......................	48,194 [3]	47,115 [3]	58,070	51,594	57,757	43,348	14,409	0	56,134	34,385	21,749	0
Alaska........................	7,880	8,080	7,808	7,756	7,912	5,608	2,304	0	7,903	4,127	3,776	0
Arizona.......................	44,438	47,101	47,507	48,935	51,376	36,671	14,705	0	52,625	37,793	14,832	0
Arkansas....................	31,947	30,330	30,876	31,234	32,997	13,842	16,778	2,377	35,089	16,315	15,983	2,791
California....................	298,021 [3]	307,764 [3]	304,311 [3]	305,969 [3]	309,222 [3]	214,123 [3]	83,953	11,146	307,110 [3]	213,122 [3]	85,106	8,882
Colorado.....................	41,983	45,401 [2]	44,904	45,165	45,841	23,213	22,628	0	46,973	23,798	23,175	0
Connecticut.................	41,044	42,296	42,370	38,808	39,687	26,322	12,177	1,188	39,115	25,945	12,126	1,044
Delaware.....................	7,469	7,698	7,749	7,856	7,998	4,008	3,990	0	8,038	3,981	4,057	0
District of Columbia	4,949	5,005	5,676	5,387	5,481 [4]	2,885 [4]	2,316 [4]	280 [4]	5,394	2,837	2,273	284
Florida........................	132,030	138,226	144,955	154,864	158,962	70,501	62,190	26,271	162,851	72,116	64,334	26,401
Georgia.......................	91,043	96,044	97,150	104,987	108,535	65,470	43,065	0	113,597	68,690	44,907	0
Hawaii........................	10,927	10,973	11,129	11,146	11,226	5,868	5,321	37	11,271	5,943	5,289	39
Idaho..........................	13,714	13,896	14,049	14,269	14,521	7,515	7,006	0	14,770	7,690	7,080	0
Illinois........................	127,620	131,046	127,669	131,047	133,857	77,801	34,923	21,133	140,988	57,332	62,187	21,469
Indiana.......................	59,226	59,968	59,924	60,563	60,592	31,811	26,413	2,368	61,315	33,451	27,843	21
Iowa..........................	34,636	34,573	34,791	34,697	35,181	22,966	12,215	0	35,653	19,128	16,525	0
Kansas.......................	32,742	32,643	32,589	32,932	33,608	14,829	15,069	3,710	35,297	16,418	18,713	166
Kentucky.....................	39,589	40,662	41,246	41,463	42,413	24,407	9,811	8,195	43,371 [3]	21,615 [3]	10,101	11,655
Louisiana....................	49,915	50,062	50,495	49,192	44,660	31,392	13,268	0	45,951	32,186	13,765	0
Maine.........................	16,559	16,837	17,621	16,656	16,684	11,143	5,541	0	16,826	11,432	5,159	235
Maryland.....................	52,433	55,382	55,198	55,101	56,685	33,021	23,664	0	58,443	33,898	24,545	0
Massachusetts..............	67,432	74,214	72,062	73,399	73,596	40,862	20,253	12,481	73,157	41,984	20,793	10,380
Michigan.....................	97,031	89,595	97,014	100,638	98,069	41,545 [4]	43,751 [4]	12,773 [4]	98,037	38,666	39,265	20,106
Minnesota...................	53,457	52,808	51,611	52,152	51,107	25,398	24,312	1,397	51,880	25,905	24,387	1,588
Mississippi..................	31,006	31,598	32,591	31,321	31,433	14,987	12,035	4,411	32,351	15,669	12,408	4,274
Missouri......................	64,735	66,717	65,169	65,847	67,076	34,896	32,180	0	67,398	34,956	32,442	0
Montana......................	10,411	10,362	10,301	10,224	10,369	6,927	3,442	0	10,398	6,944	3,454	0
Nebraska.....................	20,983	21,043	20,921	21,236	21,359	13,799	7,560	0	21,459	13,588	7,755	116
Nevada	18,293	20,038	20,234	20,950	21,744	10,917	7,710	3,117	22,908	11,763	7,866	3,279
New Hampshire	14,341	14,977	15,112	15,298	15,536	10,665	4,871	0	15,515	10,582	4,933	0
New Jersey...................	99,061	107,004	109,077	114,875	112,673	43,891	68,782	0	112,301	45,494	48,157	18,650
New Mexico	21,042	21,172	21,569	21,730	22,021	15,212	6,809	0	22,016	15,628	6,388	0
New York......................	206,961	210,926	216,116	218,612 [4]	218,989	107,801	75,348	35,840	218,879	106,391	76,693	35,795
North Carolina	83,680	87,677	89,988	92,550	95,664	57,013	32,239	6,412	104,412	55,066	47,713	1,633
North Dakota	8,141	8,078	8,037	8,070	8,003	4,821	3,182	0	8,007	4,908	3,099	0
Ohio...........................	118,361	125,372	121,735	118,060	117,982	80,210	37,772	0	110,390	50,725	50,289	9,376
Oklahoma....................	41,318	40,638	39,253	40,416	41,833	20,286	16,931	4,616	42,206	20,668	17,059	4,479
Oregon.......................	28,094	27,126	26,732	27,431	28,346	13,364	9,573	5,409	26,443	17,697	7,856	890
Pennsylvania................	116,963	118,256	119,889	121,167	122,397	52,714	52,694	16,989	123,375	50,346	53,274	19,755
Rhode Island	10,645	11,196	11,918	11,781	14,180 [3]	7,307 [3]	6,873	0	11,381	5,407	5,974	0
South Carolina.................	45,380	46,528	45,830	46,914	48,212	33,512	13,848	852	49,733	33,316	13,995	2,422
South Dakota.................	9,397	9,257	9,245	9,064	9,129	5,638	2,547	944	9,070	5,721	2,547	802
Tennessee	57,164	58,652	59,584	60,022	59,596	41,831	16,822	943	62,176	43,484	18,210	482
Texas	274,826	288,655	289,481	294,547	302,425	149,960	116,750	35,715	311,649	155,549	119,809	36,291
Utah...........................	22,008	22,415	22,147	22,287 [3]	22,993	11,195	9,455	2,343	23,640	11,569	9,642	2,429
Vermont......................	8,414	8,542	8,749	8,720	8,851	3,365	3,542	1,944	8,859	3,413	3,614	1,832
Virginia.......................	86,977 [3]	99,919	90,573	93,732	103,944	39,018	64,926	0	105,039	39,639	65,400	0
Washington..................	51,098	52,953	52,824	53,125	53,508	26,234	22,224	5,050	53,743	26,319	22,181	5,243
West Virginia................	20,930	20,119	20,020	19,958	19,940	9,852	6,737	3,351	19,414	8,419	7,591	3,404
Wisconsin....................	60,165	60,385	58,216	60,521	60,127	40,522	19,391	214	59,089	27,921	31,003	165
Wyoming.....................	6,783	6,799	6,567	6,657	6,706	3,217	3,393	96	6,757	3,295	3,449	13
Bureau of Indian Education .	—	—	—	—	—	—	—	—	—	—	—	—
DoD, overseas	5,105	4,794	4,728	4,885	5,726	1,936	1,742	2,048	5,204	1,762	1,603	1,839
DoD, domestic	2,399	2,425	2,301	2,002	2,033	1,053	446	534	2,033	1,053	446	534
Other jurisdictions												
American Samoa	820	943	988	945	989	735	249	5	971	684	267	20
Guam........................	1,975	—	1,760	1,672	1,804	937	867	0	—	—	—	—
Northern Marianas........	526	545	550	579	614	333	276	5	579	322	253	4
Puerto Rico................	37,620	42,369	42,444	43,054	42,036	—	—	42,036	40,163	21,970	13,486	4,707
U.S. Virgin Islands.........	1,511	1,502	1,512	1,545	1,434	647	696	91	1,531	698	810	23

—Not available.
[1]Data have been revised from previously published figures.
[2]Includes imputed values for states.
[3]Includes imputations for underreporting of prekindergarten teachers.
[4]Imputed.

NOTE: Distribution of elementary and secondary teachers determined by reporting units. Teachers reported in full-time equivalents (FTE). DoD = Department of Defense.
SOURCE: U.S. Department of Education, National Center for Education Statistics, Common Core of Data (CCD), "State Nonfiscal Survey of Public Elementary/Secondary Education," 2000–01 through 2006–07. (This table was prepared August 2008.)

Table 66. Teachers, enrollment, and pupil/teacher ratios in public elementary and secondary schools, by state or jurisdiction: Selected years, fall 2000 through fall 2006

State or jurisdiction	Pupil/ teacher ratio, fall 2000	Pupil/ teacher ratio, fall 2002	Pupil/ teacher ratio, fall 2003	Fall 2004[1]			Fall 2005[1]			Fall 2006		
				Teachers	Enrollment	Pupil/ teacher ratio	Teachers	Enrollment	Pupil/ teacher ratio	Teachers	Enrollment	Pupil/ teacher ratio
1	2	3	4	5	6	7	8	9	10	11	12	13
United States	16.0 [2]	15.9 [2]	15.9 [2]	3,090,925 [2]	48,795,465 [2]	15.8 [2]	3,143,003 [2]	49,113,298 [2]	15.6 [2]	3,180,396 [2]	49,298,945 [2]	15.5 [2]
Alabama	15.4 [3]	15.7 [3]	12.6	51,594	730,140	14.2	57,757	741,761	12.8	56,134	743,632	13.2
Alaska	16.9	16.6	17.2	7,756	132,970	17.1	7,912	133,288	16.8	7,903	132,608	16.8
Arizona	19.8	19.9	21.3	48,935	1,043,298	21.3	51,376	1,094,454	21.3	52,625	1,065,082	20.2
Arkansas	14.1	14.9	14.7	31,234	463,115	14.8	32,997	474,206	14.4	35,089	476,409	13.6
California	20.6 [3]	20.6 [3]	21.1 [3]	305,969 [3]	6,441,557 [3]	21.1 [3]	309,222 [3]	6,437,202 [3]	20.8 [3]	307,110 [3]	6,406,821 [3]	20.9 [3]
Colorado	17.3	16.6	16.9	45,165	765,976	17.0	45,841	779,826	17.0	46,973	794,026	16.9
Connecticut	13.7	13.5	13.6	38,808	577,390	14.9	39,687	575,059	14.5	39,115	575,100	14.7
Delaware	15.4	15.1	15.2	7,856	119,091	15.2	7,998	120,937	15.1	8,038	122,254	15.2
District of Columbia	13.9	13.9	13.8	5,387	76,714	14.2	5,481 [4]	76,876	14.0 [4]	5,394	72,850	13.5
Florida	18.4	18.4	17.9	154,864	2,639,336	17.0	158,962	2,675,024	16.8	162,851	2,671,513	16.4
Georgia	15.9	15.6	15.7	104,987	1,553,437	14.8	108,535	1,598,461	14.7	113,597	1,629,157	14.3
Hawaii	16.9	16.8	16.5	11,146	183,185	16.4	11,226	182,818	16.3	11,271	180,728	16.0
Idaho	17.9	17.9	17.9	14,269	256,084	17.9	14,521	261,982	18.0	14,770	267,380	18.1
Illinois	16.1	15.9	16.5	131,047	2,097,503	16.0	133,857	2,111,706	15.8	140,988	2,118,276	15.0
Indiana	16.7	16.7	16.9	60,563	1,021,348	16.9	60,592	1,035,074	17.1	61,315	1,045,940	17.1
Iowa	14.3	13.9	13.8	34,697	478,319	13.8	35,181	483,482	13.7	35,653	483,122	13.6
Kansas	14.4	14.4	14.4	32,932	469,136	14.2	33,608	467,525	13.9	35,297	469,506	13.3
Kentucky	16.8	16.3	16.1	41,463	674,796	16.3	42,413	679,878	16.0	43,371 [3]	683,173 [3]	15.8 [3]
Louisiana	16.6	16.6	16.6	49,192	724,281	16.6	44,660	654,526	16.6	45,951	675,851	16.6
Maine	12.5	12.1	11.5	16,656	198,820	11.9	16,684	195,498	11.7	16,826	193,986	11.5
Maryland	16.3	15.7	15.7	55,101	865,561	15.7	56,685	860,020	15.2	58,443	851,640	14.6
Massachusetts	14.5	13.2	13.6	73,399	975,574	13.3	73,596	971,909	13.2	73,157	968,661	13.2
Michigan	17.7 [3]	19.9	18.1	100,638	1,751,290	17.4	98,069	1,742,282	17.8	98,037	1,714,709	17.5
Minnesota	16.0	16.0	16.3	52,152	838,503	16.1	51,107	839,243	16.4	51,880	840,565	16.2
Mississippi	16.1	15.6	15.1	31,321	495,376	15.8	31,433	494,954	15.7	32,351	495,026	15.3
Missouri	14.1	13.6	13.9	65,847	905,449	13.8	67,076	917,705	13.7	67,398	920,353	13.7
Montana	14.9	14.5	14.4	10,224	146,705	14.3	10,369	145,416	14.0	10,398	144,418	13.9
Nebraska	13.6	13.6	13.6	21,236	285,761	13.5	21,359	286,646	13.4	21,459	287,580	13.4
Nevada	18.6	18.4	19.0	20,950	400,083	19.1	21,744	412,395	19.0	22,908	424,240	18.5
New Hampshire	14.5	13.9	13.7	15,298	206,852	13.5	15,536	205,767	13.2	15,515	203,551	13.1
New Jersey	13.3	12.8	12.7	114,875	1,393,347	12.1	112,673	1,395,602	12.4	112,301	1,388,850	12.4
New Mexico	15.2	15.1	15.0	21,730	326,102	15.0	22,021	326,758	14.8	22,016	328,220	14.9
New York	13.9	13.7	13.3	218,612 [4]	2,836,337	13.0	218,989	2,815,581	12.9	218,879	2,809,649	12.8
North Carolina	15.5	15.2	15.1	92,550	1,385,754	15.0	95,664	1,416,436	14.8	104,412	1,444,481	13.8
North Dakota	13.4	12.9	12.7	8,070	100,513	12.5	8,003	98,283	12.3	8,007	96,670	12.1
Ohio	15.5	14.7	15.2	118,060	1,840,032	15.6	117,982	1,839,683	15.6	110,390	1,836,096	16.6
Oklahoma	15.1	15.4	16.0	40,416	629,476	15.6	41,833	634,739	15.2	42,206	639,391	15.1
Oregon	19.4	20.4	20.6	27,431	552,505	20.1	28,346	552,194	19.5	26,443	562,574	21.3
Pennsylvania	15.5	15.4	15.2	121,167	1,828,089	15.1	122,397	1,830,684	15.0	123,375	1,871,060	15.2
Rhode Island	14.8	14.2	13.4	11,781	156,498	13.3	14,180 [3]	153,422	10.8	11,381	151,612	13.3
South Carolina	14.9	14.9	15.3	46,914	703,736	15.0	48,212	701,544	14.6	49,733	703,119	14.1
South Dakota	13.7	14.0	13.6	9,064	122,798	13.5	9,129	122,012	13.4	9,070	121,158	13.4
Tennessee	15.9 [3]	15.8 [3]	15.7 [3]	60,022	941,091 [3]	15.7 [3]	59,596	953,928	16.0	62,176	978,368	15.7
Texas	14.8	14.8	15.0	294,547	4,405,215	15.0	302,425	4,525,394	15.0	311,649	4,599,509	14.8
Utah	21.9	21.8	22.4	22,287 [3]	503,607	22.6 [3]	22,993	508,430	22.1	23,640	523,586	22.1
Vermont	12.1	11.7	11.3	8,720	98,352	11.3	8,851	96,638	10.9	8,859	95,399	10.8
Virginia	13.2 [3]	11.8	13.2	93,732	1,204,739	12.9	103,944	1,213,616	11.7	105,039	1,220,440	11.6
Washington	19.7	19.2	19.3	53,125	1,020,005	19.2	53,508	1,031,985	19.3	53,743	1,026,774	19.1
West Virginia	13.7	14.0	14.0	19,958	280,129	14.0	19,940	280,866	14.1	19,414	281,939	14.5
Wisconsin	14.6	14.6	15.1	60,521	864,757	14.3	60,127	875,174	14.6	59,089	876,700	14.8
Wyoming	13.3	13.0 [3]	13.3	6,657	84,733	12.7	6,706	84,409	12.6	6,757	85,193	12.6
Bureau of Indian Education	—	—	—	—	45,828	—	—	50,938	—	—	—	—
DoD, overseas	14.4	15.2	15.0	4,885	68,327	14.0	5,726	62,543	10.9	5,204	60,891	11.7
DoD, domestic	14.2	13.2	13.3	2,002	29,151	14.6	2,033	28,329	13.9	2,033	26,631	13.1
Other jurisdictions												
American Samoa	19.1	17.0	16.1	945	16,126	17.1	989	16,438	16.6	971	16,427	16.9
Guam	16.4	—	17.9	1,672	30,605	18.3	1,804	30,986	17.2	—	—	—
Northern Marianas	19.0	20.6	20.4	579	11,601	20.0	614	11,718	19.1	579	11,695	20.2
Puerto Rico	16.3	14.1	13.8	43,054	575,648	13.4	42,036	563,490	13.4	40,163	544,138	13.5
U.S. Virgin Islands	12.9	12.2	11.7	1,545	16,429	10.6	1,434	16,750	11.7	1,531	16,284	10.6

—Not available.
[1]Data have been revised from previously published figures.
[2]Includes imputed values for states.
[3]Includes imputations for underreporting of prekindergarten teachers/enrollment.
[4]Imputed.

NOTE: Teachers reported in full-time equivalents (FTE). DoD = Department of Defense.
SOURCE: U.S. Department of Education, National Center for Education Statistics, Common Core of Data (CCD), "State Nonfiscal Survey of Public Elementary/Secondary Education," 2000–01 through 2006–07. (This table was prepared October 2008.)

Table 67. Highest degree earned, years of full-time teaching experience, and average class size for teachers in public elementary and secondary schools, by state: 2003–04

State	Total number of teachers (in thousands)	Percent of teachers, by highest degree earned[1] — Bachelor's	Master's	Education specialist[3]	Doctor's	Percent of teachers, by years of full-time teaching experience — Less than 3	3 to 9	10 to 20	Over 20	Average class size[2] — Elementary	Secondary
1	2	3	4	5	6	7	8	9	10	11	12
United States	3,250.6 (29.18)	50.8 (0.56)	40.9 (0.56)	6.0 (0.19)	1.2 (0.11)	12.2 (1.23)	32.9 (0.34)	28.4 (0.59)	26.5 (0.77)	20.4 (0.15)	24.7 (0.14)
Alabama	50.9 (2.34)	38.1 (2.08)	50.2 (2.39)	9.4 (1.37)	1.0 (0.35)	12.5 (1.94)	32.8 (2.76)	33.4 (1.88)	21.4 (1.66)	18.4 (0.38)	23.8 (0.66)
Alaska	8.6 (0.40)	58.4 (2.11)	34.3 (1.81)	5.6 (1.19)	1.4 (0.50)	13.0 (1.57)	36.8 (2.25)	31.2 (2.35)	18.9 (1.97)	20.5 (0.35)	23.3 (0.63)
Arizona	56.4 (2.27)	49.7 (2.21)	40.8 (2.07)	7.4 (1.30)	1.0 (0.37)	15.5 (1.73)	38.2 (2.08)	27.2 (1.72)	19.1 (1.84)	23.0 (0.39)	27.0 (0.55)
Arkansas	37.2 (1.80)	60.4 (2.56)	33.8 (2.45)	3.6 (0.62)	1.0 (0.35)	9.5 (2.15)	34.7 (2.58)	31.4 (2.37)	24.4 (1.90)	20.4 (0.64)	22.4 (0.62)
California	284.8 (16.87)	56.0 (1.76)	31.3 (1.65)	10.0 (0.95)	1.8 (0.52)	11.2 (1.45)	36.4 (1.48)	30.3 (1.66)	22.1 (1.79)	21.7 (0.26)	30.5 (0.53)
Colorado	49.1 (1.63)	44.5 (2.18)	47.7 (2.27)	5.4 (1.27)	0.9 (0.42)	12.0 (1.46)	37.4 (2.54)	30.2 (2.37)	20.5 (1.61)	22.1 (0.64)	24.5 (0.65)
Connecticut	45.0 (1.78)	24.5 (2.48)	55.9 (2.83)	16.1 (1.72)	2.2 (0.64)	9.8 (1.25)	29.7 (1.74)	31.0 (2.26)	29.4 (2.41)	19.5 (0.51)	22.3 (0.44)
Delaware	7.9 (0.60)	45.9 (3.20)	49.2 (3.29)	3.7 (1.09)	0.5 (0.36)	11.7 (1.74)	35.0 (3.39)	27.5 (3.15)	25.7 (3.17)	20.1 (0.75)	23.6 (0.82)
District of Columbia	5.4 (0.46)	48.2 (4.25)	41.8 (4.05)	6.2 (1.50)	3.3 (1.29)	15.5 (2.80)	29.8 (3.07)	28.7 (3.28)	26.0 (2.86)	19.0 (0.86)	22.8 (1.26)
Florida	156.8 (8.43)	61.8 (2.20)	32.7 (2.15)	2.4 (0.66)	1.5 (0.45)	14.3 (2.09)	27.9 (1.55)	32.0 (1.96)	25.8 (2.52)	21.2 (0.57)	27.6 (0.64)
Georgia	102.3 (3.08)	46.6 (2.71)	40.5 (2.00)	11.1 (1.81)	1.1 (0.53)	13.2 (2.18)	37.2 (2.01)	27.4 (2.61)	22.3 (1.96)	17.8 (0.59)	25.6 (0.76)
Hawaii	13.6 (0.54)	43.2 (2.43)	26.5 (2.29)	27.5 (2.19)	1.5 (0.59)	16.9 (1.80)	33.0 (2.45)	29.8 (2.27)	20.3 (1.86)	22.3 (0.71)	27.4 (1.93)
Idaho	15.4 (0.76)	71.9 (1.99)	24.9 (1.76)	1.9 (0.61)	0.2 (0.13)	12.3 (1.83)	28.4 (2.32)	36.0 (2.04)	23.3 (1.93)	22.9 (0.33)	24.1 (0.57)
Illinois	139.6 (6.23)	45.7 (2.40)	49.6 (2.89)	3.1 (0.90)	0.8 (0.71)	12.1 (1.67)	32.0 (2.57)	26.8 (2.51)	29.2 (2.87)	22.9 (0.72)	24.1 (0.66)
Indiana	63.0 (3.09)	37.3 (2.54)	56.3 (2.39)	4.3 (1.03)	1.3 (0.71)	11.2 (1.64)	27.1 (2.02)	35.9 (2.38)	25.8 (2.45)	21.3 (0.59)	25.3 (0.64)
Iowa	38.2 (1.03)	65.1 (2.01)	33.0 (1.95)	1.2 (0.50)	‡ (†)	8.4 (1.44)	27.9 (1.68)	27.1 (1.97)	36.7 (2.02)	20.9 (0.88)	23.9 (0.65)
Kansas	37.7 (1.31)	55.0 (2.32)	40.2 (2.28)	3.4 (0.62)	0.3 (0.41)	11.5 (2.00)	27.3 (1.87)	30.7 (1.62)	30.4 (2.10)	19.2 (0.68)	22.2 (0.76)
Kentucky	48.3 (1.80)	28.5 (2.05)	51.6 (2.33)	18.7 (1.90)	0.3 (0.18)	11.6 (1.59)	33.8 (2.03)	32.5 (1.79)	22.1 (1.99)	21.6 (0.57)	25.2 (0.49)
Louisiana	52.5 (1.69)	65.2 (2.43)	24.4 (1.96)	7.3 (1.16)	2.3 (0.65)	9.9 (1.40)	28.2 (2.06)	30.5 (1.99)	31.3 (2.72)	18.7 (0.59)	23.1 (0.58)
Maine	18.9 (0.79)	64.3 (2.34)	30.6 (2.22)	3.1 (0.86)	0.6 (0.27)	7.6 (1.29)	28.3 (1.99)	29.2 (2.20)	34.9 (2.10)	17.1 (0.49)	19.8 (0.54)
Maryland	59.3 (2.84)	42.7 (3.26)	46.6 (2.90)	8.3 (1.27)	1.4 (0.48)	16.0 (2.40)	33.7 (2.69)	22.2 (2.09)	28.1 (3.14)	20.7 (0.66)	25.9 (0.60)
Massachusetts	84.5 (3.81)	37.7 (2.79)	53.6 (2.85)	4.6 (0.97)	2.0 (0.36)	14.4 (1.68)	32.8 (2.29)	23.7 (2.34)	29.1 (2.38)	19.4 (0.48)	21.9 (0.50)
Michigan	100.1 (4.92)	43.3 (2.21)	50.5 (2.50)	4.0 (0.75)	1.0 (0.41)	11.2 (1.68)	35.4 (2.05)	27.3 (2.05)	26.1 (1.69)	21.9 (0.43)	26.5 (0.53)
Minnesota	61.0 (2.90)	49.0 (1.83)	43.6 (1.95)	5.7 (0.79)	0.9 (0.23)	10.4 (1.41)	33.5 (1.80)	28.5 (1.69)	27.6 (1.98)	22.3 (0.50)	26.0 (0.75)
Mississippi	34.4 (1.28)	62.3 (2.32)	30.6 (2.27)	3.9 (0.77)	1.0 (0.51)	16.3 (2.43)	28.0 (1.73)	25.5 (2.11)	30.3 (2.02)	20.4 (0.51)	22.4 (0.77)
Missouri	74.3 (5.34)	47.3 (2.45)	47.4 (2.50)	3.0 (0.77)	0.4 (0.16)	11.9 (1.53)	32.8 (1.90)	29.3 (1.92)	26.0 (2.44)	19.1 (0.51)	22.9 (0.65)
Montana	12.2 (0.76)	65.0 (1.94)	29.5 (1.83)	3.7 (0.75)	0.4 (0.24)	10.7 (1.33)	25.6 (1.86)	31.1 (1.98)	32.6 (2.09)	18.1 (0.44)	19.4 (0.62)
Nebraska	25.9 (1.03)	59.9 (2.49)	37.5 (2.32)	1.2 (0.47)	0.8 (0.38)	9.6 (1.40)	31.2 (1.96)	31.9 (2.07)	27.2 (1.79)	18.1 (0.57)	21.7 (0.68)
Nevada	19.9 (0.91)	43.4 (3.17)	48.9 (3.11)	6.2 (1.26)	0.8 (0.37)	13.7 (2.17)	38.7 (3.24)	25.2 (2.63)	22.4 (2.57)	22.6 (1.00)	29.9 (0.78)
New Hampshire	16.5 (0.64)	56.9 (2.59)	39.4 (2.46)	2.7 (1.04)	0.4 (0.28)	12.7 (2.04)	31.0 (2.29)	27.1 (2.74)	29.2 (2.18)	19.5 (0.53)	22.0 (1.01)
New Jersey	114.0 (4.11)	57.0 (2.59)	34.3 (2.48)	6.1 (1.09)	1.8 (0.48)	13.3 (1.74)	31.9 (1.74)	24.4 (2.07)	30.3 (2.52)	19.3 (0.72)	24.1 (0.94)
New Mexico	21.3 (0.88)	58.1 (2.20)	36.4 (2.28)	4.2 (1.04)	0.4 (0.26)	10.7 (1.96)	37.1 (2.35)	29.7 (1.74)	22.6 (2.19)	18.2 (0.40)	24.3 (0.67)
New York	234.1 (7.62)	21.4 (1.97)	67.2 (2.14)	8.8 (1.03)	2.0 (0.43)	13.1 (1.95)	36.5 (1.80)	27.8 (1.88)	22.6 (1.82)	19.8 (0.56)	23.6 (0.55)
North Carolina	95.6 (3.26)	67.0 (2.08)	27.6 (2.12)	3.1 (0.74)	1.0 (0.41)	13.8 (1.54)	34.9 (2.07)	29.4 (2.43)	21.9 (1.94)	20.3 (0.53)	24.3 (0.73)
North Dakota	9.7 (0.41)	71.7 (1.79)	24.6 (1.64)	2.4 (0.63)	0.4 (0.21)	10.5 (1.65)	21.8 (1.46)	31.4 (1.60)	36.3 (1.82)	17.2 (0.45)	19.5 (0.60)
Ohio	133.5 (4.62)	45.8 (2.12)	49.1 (2.17)	2.8 (0.53)	0.9 (0.36)	9.1 (1.92)	33.1 (1.80)	27.2 (1.90)	30.6 (1.82)	20.3 (0.40)	23.6 (0.42)
Oklahoma	46.0 (1.46)	66.3 (1.51)	30.2 (1.56)	2.7 (0.47)	0.4 (0.22)	8.8 (1.89)	31.1 (1.83)	31.8 (1.80)	28.3 (1.81)	19.9 (0.35)	23.2 (0.58)
Oregon	29.0 (1.48)	41.5 (2.26)	50.5 (2.33)	6.2 (1.17)	1.4 (0.63)	13.8 (2.22)	28.9 (1.99)	34.1 (2.55)	23.1 (2.17)	24.7 (0.54)	28.9 (0.71)
Pennsylvania	125.5 (4.65)	48.6 (1.96)	42.5 (1.93)	6.7 (0.90)	1.1 (0.45)	11.8 (1.55)	32.9 (1.68)	21.5 (1.87)	33.8 (2.32)	19.0 (0.54)	24.9 (0.47)
Rhode Island	13.8 (0.61)	48.0 (3.60)	45.8 (3.44)	4.7 (1.49)	0.66 (0.66)	10.8 (1.90)	35.3 (3.47)	28.2 (2.59)	25.6 (3.81)	19.6 (0.82)	22.4 (0.92)
South Carolina	47.5 (2.02)	47.0 (2.79)	42.9 (2.92)	7.5 (1.12)	0.6 (0.20)	8.5 (1.68)	29.5 (2.07)	31.2 (2.50)	30.8 (2.54)	18.5 (0.73)	23.8 (0.64)
South Dakota	10.8 (0.54)	72.9 (1.62)	24.0 (1.73)	1.7 (0.63)	0.6 (0.26)	9.3 (2.17)	29.1 (2.23)	29.3 (1.94)	32.4 (2.17)	17.8 (0.68)	23.2 (1.06)
Tennessee	64.6 (2.09)	46.1 (2.74)	43.2 (2.51)	8.5 (2.09)	0.6 (0.29)	10.7 (2.41)	29.9 (2.13)	27.5 (2.03)	31.8 (2.32)	19.0 (0.43)	24.5 (0.52)
Texas	291.0 (10.41)	71.9 (1.80)	22.4 (1.78)	3.8 (0.60)	1.0 (0.43)	13.4 (1.70)	33.9 (2.00)	30.7 (1.90)	22.0 (1.56)	18.7 (0.42)	22.3 (0.55)
Utah	23.4 (1.21)	65.2 (1.96)	24.2 (1.68)	7.8 (1.12)	0.7 (0.27)	17.9 (2.05)	30.1 (2.12)	29.5 (2.12)	22.6 (1.72)	24.3 (0.40)	29.0 (1.00)
Vermont	10.0 (0.45)	54.2 (3.21)	41.1 (3.37)	3.1 (1.09)	0.57 (0.57)	10.8 (1.71)	29.7 (2.67)	31.5 (2.80)	27.9 (2.57)	16.0 (0.46)	18.9 (0.89)
Virginia	92.2 (4.41)	58.6 (2.44)	34.1 (2.45)	4.3 (1.13)	0.53 (0.53)	12.7 (1.83)	33.8 (2.00)	24.9 (2.16)	28.6 (1.95)	19.1 (0.54)	22.7 (0.98)
Washington	63.5 (4.32)	42.6 (2.33)	50.7 (2.36)	4.6 (0.97)	0.36 (0.36)	11.7 (1.93)	34.5 (2.16)	27.2 (2.25)	26.7 (2.19)	21.9 (0.52)	26.5 (0.52)
West Virginia	22.9 (1.11)	36.9 (2.35)	53.5 (2.60)	7.2 (1.36)	0.15 (0.15)	7.4 (1.65)	18.6 (1.51)	23.9 (2.10)	50.1 (2.44)	18.8 (0.47)	22.1 (0.52)
Wisconsin	74.8 (3.62)	54.8 (2.72)	40.8 (2.62)	3.7 (0.87)	0.22 (0.22)	13.1 (2.40)	29.7 (1.81)	30.3 (1.93)	26.9 (1.66)	19.5 (0.48)	25.1 (0.74)
Wyoming	7.8 (0.42)	61.4 (3.46)	33.8 (3.11)	2.9 (0.87)	0.40 (0.40)	9.1 (2.88)	25.8 (2.90)	31.3 (3.08)	33.8 (3.34)	18.4 (0.67)	21.5 (0.80)

† Not applicable.
‡ Reporting standards not met.
[1] Teachers with less than a bachelor's degree are not shown separately.
[2] Elementary teachers are those who taught self-contained classes at the elementary level, and secondary teachers are those who taught departmentalized classes (e.g., science, art, social science, or other course subjects) at the secondary level. Teachers were classified as elementary or secondary on the basis of the grades they taught, rather than on the level of the school in which they taught.

[3] Includes certificate of advanced graduate studies.
NOTE: Data are based on a head count of all teachers rather than on the number of full-time-equivalent teachers appearing in other tables. Excludes prekindergarten teachers. Standard errors appear in parentheses. Detail may not sum to totals because of rounding, cell suppression, and omitted categories (less than bachelor's).
SOURCE: U.S. Department of Education, National Center for Education Statistics, Schools and Staffing Survey (SASS), "Public Teacher Questionnaire", 2003–04. (This table was prepared July 2006.)

Table 68. Highest degree earned and years of full-time teaching experience for teachers in public and private elementary and secondary schools, by selected teacher characteristics: 1999–2000 and 2003–04

Selected characteristic	Number of teachers, 1999–2000 (in thousands)	Number of teachers, 2003–04 (in thousands)	Percent of teachers, by highest degree earned, 2003–04					Percent of teachers, by years of full-time teaching experience, 2003–04			
			Less than bachelor's	Bachelor's	Master's	Education specialist[1]	Doctor's	Less than 3	3 to 9	10 to 20	Over 20
1	2	3	4	5	6	7	8	9	10	11	12
Public schools											
Total	3,002 (19.4)	3,251 (29.2)	1.1 (0.08)	50.8 (0.56)	40.9 (0.56)	6.0 (0.19)	1.2 (0.11)	12.2 (1.23)	32.9 (1.23)	28.4 (0.59)	26.5 (0.77)
Sex											
Males	754 (10.7)	813 (13.3)	2.6 (0.21)	50.2 (0.90)	40.5 (0.83)	5.1 (0.35)	1.7 (0.26)	12.0 (1.22)	33.9 (0.75)	25.4 (0.74)	28.8 (0.95)
Females	2,248 (16.0)	2,438 (23.5)	0.6 (0.07)	51.0 (0.61)	41.1 (0.61)	6.3 (0.23)	1.0 (0.10)	12.3 (1.26)	32.6 (0.43)	29.5 (0.69)	25.7 (0.84)
Race/ethnicity											
White	2,532 (17.2)[2]	2,702 (30.1)	1.0 (0.08)	49.8 (0.60)	42.3 (0.58)	5.9 (0.22)	1.1 (0.09)	11.5 (1.20)	32.0 (0.36)	29.1 (0.58)	27.4 (0.81)
Black	228 (6.0)[2]	257 (11.0)	1.8 (0.39)	52.3 (1.48)	38.3 (1.69)	5.6 (0.56)	2.0 (0.64)	14.9 (1.56)	35.5 (1.53)	22.1 (1.30)	27.6 (1.78)
Hispanic	169 (6.4)[2]	202 (11.3)	1.3 (0.36)	63.7 (2.14)	26.7 (2.03)	6.9 (1.17)	1.4 (0.51)	16.8 (1.87)	39.5 (1.89)	28.8 (2.26)	15.0 (1.58)
Asian	48 (2.7)[3]	42 (2.5)	0.5 (0.19)	45.5 (3.04)	40.6 (3.23)	10.4 (1.66)	3.1 (1.09)	15.9 (2.26)	41.6 (3.52)	26.0 (2.90)	16.5 (1.71)
Pacific Islander	—	6 (0.8)	‡ (†)	47.7 (6.35)	39.6 (6.85)	10.7 (3.21)	1.2 (0.84)	17.5 (4.14)	45.9 (6.35)	19.0 (6.33)	17.6 (4.24)
American Indian/Alaska Native	26 (1.9)[2]	17 (1.2)	1.8 (0.55)	52.9 (3.44)	40.8 (3.55)	3.7 (0.95)	0.8 (0.34)	14.4 (3.29)	31.2 (3.25)	30.1 (3.61)	24.3 (3.75)
More than one race	—	24 (2.2)	0.5 (0.32)	49.2 (5.18)	37.3 (4.96)	11.2 (2.70)	1.8 (0.75)	17.0 (3.72)	36.5 (4.77)	25.8 (4.97)	20.7 (3.70)
Age											
Less than 30	509 (9.2)	540 (27.4)	0.5 (0.08)	76.6 (1.22)	21.3 (1.25)	1.6 (0.26)	0.1 (0.04)	41.7 (2.58)	58.3 (2.58)	‡ (†)	‡ (†)
30 to 39	661 (9.8)	798 (14.5)	0.8 (0.12)	53.4 (0.89)	41.0 (0.88)	4.2 (0.31)	0.6 (0.13)	10.6 (1.16)	55.3 (1.16)	34.2 (1.00)	‡ (†)
40 to 49	953 (10.3)	840 (14.3)	1.5 (0.17)	46.2 (0.77)	44.5 (0.84)	6.2 (0.41)	1.5 (0.25)	6.8 (0.82)	23.5 (0.67)	44.5 (1.03)	25.2 (0.69)
50 to 59	786 (12.6)	942 (26.0)	1.2 (0.14)	40.0 (0.78)	47.8 (0.74)	9.3 (0.46)	1.7 (0.19)	2.8 (0.32)	11.3 (0.53)	26.1 (0.75)	59.8 (1.08)
60 or more	93 (4.0)	131 (4.8)	1.4 (0.27)	35.7 (1.83)	49.4 (2.08)	10.3 (1.18)	3.2 (0.72)	2.1 (0.43)	7.3 (0.95)	25.0 (1.59)	65.5 (1.78)
Level											
Elementary	1,602 (13.5)	1,716 (25.8)	0.4 (0.07)	52.0 (0.75)	40.6 (0.68)	6.2 (0.33)	0.8 (0.15)	11.5 (1.76)	33.5 (0.55)	29.4 (0.83)	25.7 (1.16)
General	1,019 (13.6)	1,130 (29.8)	0.4 (0.08)	55.0 (0.95)	38.1 (0.81)	5.7 (0.44)	0.8 (0.19)	11.1 (1.80)	34.2 (0.75)	29.0 (0.84)	25.8 (1.17)
Arts/music	33 (2.8)	101 (5.3)	0.3 (0.14)	52.8 (2.48)	42.8 (2.45)	3.5 (0.86)	0.7 (0.37)	12.5 (2.54)	28.4 (2.05)	32.7 (2.40)	26.4 (2.78)
English	[4] (†)	70 (5.1)	‡ (†)	40.6 (4.09)	48.7 (4.24)	9.4 (1.60)	1.3 (0.57)	8.5 (2.34)	28.8 (3.47)	34.4 (3.69)	28.3 (3.09)
ESL/bilingual	[4] (†)	25 (3.6)	‡ (†)	51.2 (6.39)	33.1 (5.69)	15.0 (5.02)	‡ (†)	11.5 (4.11)	44.7 (7.64)	31.3 (6.50)	12.5 (3.86)
Health/physical ed.	[4] (†)	73 (5.0)	‡ (†)	59.5 (3.48)	36.1 (3.32)	3.9 (1.02)	0.4 (0.26)	10.6 (2.49)	25.1 (2.52)	29.8 (2.62)	34.5 (3.46)
Mathematics	26 (2.5)	19 (2.3)	‡ (†)	50.1 (6.56)	44.7 (6.16)	4.2 (2.44)	‡ (†)	13.5 (4.00)	29.9 (5.31)	30.2 (5.32)	26.5 (5.31)
Science	[4] (†)	19 (3.0)	‡ (†)	50.4 (7.93)	40.8 (7.92)	7.9 (4.59)	‡ (†)	9.3 (3.30)	27.4 (5.91)	33.3 (8.23)	30.0 (6.65)
Special education	210 (5.8)	240 (20.6)	0.7 (0.31)	41.0 (1.66)	48.9 (1.77)	8.6 (0.86)	0.8 (0.48)	14.2 (1.92)	35.8 (1.49)	27.2 (1.53)	22.7 (1.74)
Other elementary	314 (8.4)	40 (3.5)	0.8 (0.28)	42.9 (4.07)	50.0 (4.27)	6.1 (1.68)	‡ (†)	9.8 (2.43)	34.2 (4.41)	32.1 (4.53)	24.0 (3.83)
Secondary	1,401 (17.7)	1,534 (26.0)	1.8 (0.13)	49.4 (0.64)	41.3 (0.66)	5.8 (0.22)	1.7 (0.12)	13.0 (0.71)	32.3 (0.51)	27.4 (0.58)	27.3 (0.54)
Arts/music	112 (4.1)	112 (4.1)	0.7 (0.13)	55.5 (2.01)	37.2 (1.91)	5.1 (0.61)	1.4 (0.39)	12.5 (1.16)	30.5 (1.70)	28.0 (1.62)	29.1 (1.59)
English	235 (5.0)	269 (9.0)	0.3 (0.09)	51.1 (1.40)	40.1 (1.28)	6.8 (0.60)	1.7 (0.34)	14.2 (0.99)	33.2 (1.18)	25.4 (1.15)	27.2 (1.10)
ESL/bilingual	[5] (†)	18 (2.5)	‡ (†)	43.6 (6.06)	49.4 (5.91)	5.4 (1.73)	1.6 (0.80)	18.9 (3.61)	33.6 (5.19)	28.9 (5.96)	18.6 (5.49)
Foreign language	[5] (†)	73 (3.3)	0.4 (0.16)	48.0 (2.13)	43.8 (2.29)	5.5 (0.86)	2.3 (0.64)	13.8 (1.41)	36.2 (1.90)	27.7 (1.70)	22.3 (2.09)
Health/physical ed.	[5] (†)	102 (4.3)	0.5 (0.18)	55.9 (1.83)	38.1 (1.91)	4.7 (0.89)	0.8 (0.20)	9.9 (1.56)	29.6 (1.89)	29.0 (2.20)	31.5 (1.79)
Mathematics	191 (4.3)	213 (5.5)	0.3 (0.11)	51.6 (1.36)	42.0 (1.30)	4.7 (0.58)	1.3 (0.27)	14.2 (1.53)	32.2 (1.31)	28.0 (1.29)	25.5 (1.17)
Science	159 (3.7)	189 (6.8)	0.2 (0.08)	48.4 (1.78)	44.2 (1.77)	4.4 (0.43)	2.8 (0.49)	12.5 (1.02)	34.0 (1.38)	28.3 (1.19)	25.2 (1.13)
Social studies	147 (4.3)	178 (5.7)	0.4 (0.22)	51.1 (1.56)	42.1 (1.40)	4.6 (0.52)	1.7 (0.39)	12.0 (0.92)	34.4 (1.26)	23.4 (1.26)	30.2 (1.28)
Special education	99 (2.3)	174 (7.5)	0.4 (0.13)	42.3 (3.22)	45.1 (1.92)	10.7 (0.94)	1.5 (0.38)	12.1 (1.50)	31.6 (1.25)	29.9 (1.46)	26.4 (1.72)
Vocational/technical	125 (3.2)	169 (5.7)	11.8 (1.09)	44.8 (6.72)	37.6 (4.08)	4.4 (0.52)	1.4 (0.41)	12.6 (1.22)	28.7 (1.34)	28.8 (1.15)	30.0 (1.59)
Other secondary	443 (8.5)	36 (2.1)	7.5 (7.76)	45.6 (3.30)	40.2 (2.71)	5.7 (1.20)	1.0 (0.40)	15.0 (2.41)	32.3 (2.81)	26.7 (2.50)	26.0 (2.61)
Private schools											
Total	449 (10.6)	467 (10.3)	9.2 (4.41)	55.5 (2.90)	29.5 (1.35)	3.6 (0.54)	2.2 (0.26)	24.8 (2.75)	33.0 (1.23)	23.9 (1.19)	18.3 (1.87)
Sex											
Males	107 (3.8)	110 (8.4)	6.5 (1.13)	49.1 (1.49)	36.5 (1.60)	3.8 (0.84)	4.0 (0.99)	25.6 (2.49)	32.3 (1.78)	21.4 (1.85)	20.6 (1.48)
Females	342 (7.7)	357 (14.3)	10.1 (5.69)	57.4 (3.92)	27.3 (1.53)	3.5 (0.54)	1.7 (0.30)	24.6 (3.07)	33.2 (1.54)	24.7 (1.43)	17.6 (2.11)
Race/ethnicity											
White	402 (9.6)[2]	411 (12.0)	8.5 (4.85)	55.5 (2.98)	30.4 (1.63)	3.5 (0.60)	2.1 (0.26)	23.7 (3.38)	33.0 (1.49)	24.2 (1.28)	19.0 (2.15)
Black	17 (1.4)[2]	19 (2.9)	17.9 (5.49)	60.2 (5.17)	16.9 (3.17)	2.9 (1.00)	2.1 (0.98)	29.8 (4.02)	31.2 (7.94)	20.9 (5.01)	18.2 (3.36)
Hispanic	21 (1.5)[2]	23 (3.1)	13.5 (2.34)	55.5 (3.71)	25.9 (3.05)	2.5 (1.59)	2.6 (1.52)	35.2 (3.46)	33.3 (3.63)	22.1 (3.09)	9.4 (2.53)
Age											
Less than 30	87 (3.1)	88 (3.7)	13.5 (1.65)	70.6 (1.87)	14.3 (1.40)	0.8 (0.42)	0.8 (0.37)	55.3 (2.87)	44.5 (2.81)	0.3 (0.14)	‡ (†)
30 to 39	101 (3.2)	103 (5.8)	9.3 (2.85)	57.5 (2.93)	28.1 (3.04)	3.3 (0.53)	1.8 (0.46)	26.3 (3.66)	52.3 (2.44)	21.4 (2.33)	‡ (†)
40 to 49	131 (4.2)	119 (7.1)	9.8 (4.12)	52.8 (3.22)	30.5 (1.92)	3.9 (0.88)	3.1 (0.64)	20.1 (2.16)	30.5 (3.43)	37.1 (1.75)	12.3 (1.59)
50 to 59	106 (3.2)	121 (11.1)	6.3 (11.09)	49.9 (6.72)	36.9 (4.08)	4.4 (0.86)	2.5 (0.50)	10.5 (8.31)	17.7 (2.13)	31.0 (3.77)	40.8 (6.01)
60 or more	25 (1.2)	37 (4.7)	7.0 (7.76)	40.6 (3.30)	41.5 (6.98)	7.5 (2.23)	3.4 (1.10)	9.9 (1.86)	9.8 (6.91)	21.7 (3.54)	58.6 (8.29)

See notes at end of table.

Table 68. Highest degree earned and years of full-time teaching experience for teachers in public and private elementary and secondary schools, by selected teacher characteristics: 1999–2000 and 2003–04—Continued

Selected characteristic	Number of teachers, 1999–2000 (in thousands)	Number of teachers, 2003–04 (in thousands)	Percent of teachers, by highest degree earned, 2003–04					Percent of teachers, by years of full-time teaching experience, 2003–04			
			Less than bachelor's	Bachelor's	Master's	Education specialist[1]	Doctor's	Less than 3	3 to 9	10 to 20	Over 20
1	2	3	4	5	6	7	8	9	10	11	12
Level											
Elementary	261 (5.8)	263 (17.5)	12.0 (6.69)	60.5 (5.01)	23.3 (1.53)	3.2 (0.67)	0.9 (0.22)	25.4 (3.89)	33.2 (1.77)	25.0 (1.80)	16.5 (2.56)
General	168 (4.0)	174 (17.1)	13.0 (9.87)	63.2 (6.93)	20.5 (2.69)	2.5 (0.55)	0.9 (0.26)	19.6 (6.79)	35.4 (3.85)	26.5 (2.76)	18.5 (3.30)
Arts/music	[4] (†)	21 (2.5)	14.7 (2.34)	52.3 (3.30)	27.4 (3.74)	5.5 (1.79)	‡ (†)	49.0 (3.59)	27.9 (3.68)	16.5 (2.58)	6.6 (1.55)
English	[4] (†)	8 (1.1)	3.7 (4.12)	53.4 (5.93)	36.1 (5.31)	3.7 (1.84)	3.2 (1.74)	23.8 (4.36)	27.9 (4.83)	26.9 (4.79)	21.3 (4.29)
Health/physical ed.	[4] (†)	14 (1.8)	11.3 (2.75)	67.6 (6.95)	18.1 (4.54)	1.9 (0.95)	‡ (†)	42.4 (6.88)	25.2 (7.73)	22.6 (6.65)	9.8 (2.36)
Mathematics	[4] (†)	6 (0.7)	4.8 (3.39)	60.3 (6.26)	33.4 (6.21)	‡ (†)	‡ (†)	24.2 (5.49)	31.5 (7.05)	21.9 (4.92)	22.4 (4.55)
Science	[4] (†)	5 (0.8)	‡ (†)	74.2 (7.13)	19.6 (6.90)	4.0 (1.98)	‡ (†)	26.1 (7.54)	28.1 (6.05)	24.0 (6.83)	21.8 (7.19)
Special education	16 (1.6)	12 (2.3)	5.6 (2.55)	52.2 (8.01)	33.3 (11.81)	8.9 (4.04)	‡ (†)	26.1 (8.02)	41.8 (7.02)	22.9 (4.46)	9.3 (3.39)
Other elementary	77 (2.2)	24 (3.5)	13.3 (2.96)	47.8 (6.61)	32.3 (9.54)	4.5 (1.43)	2.0 (1.03)	37.3 (6.33)	25.4 (12.04)	24.0 (4.85)	13.3 (3.14)
Secondary	188 (6.2)	204 (13.4)	5.7 (1.30)	49.0 (1.44)	37.4 (1.43)	4.1 (0.49)	3.9 (0.55)	24.1 (1.62)	32.7 (1.39)	22.5 (1.54)	20.7 (1.10)
Arts/music	[5] (†)	18 (1.9)	7.1 (2.15)	50.3 (4.71)	38.6 (4.67)	3.4 (1.80)	‡ (†)	28.6 (4.14)	33.6 (5.12)	23.7 (4.05)	14.1 (3.24)
English	33 (1.7)	38 (2.8)	4.3 (3.58)	48.6 (2.87)	38.6 (3.19)	5.1 (1.24)	3.3 (1.03)	19.5 (2.11)	30.5 (4.45)	25.0 (3.07)	24.9 (3.01)
Foreign language	[5] (†)	18 (2.1)	4.2 (5.86)	47.7 (5.46)	36.6 (6.02)	4.6 (2.24)	6.9 (2.32)	25.3 (4.07)	34.1 (5.96)	23.9 (4.10)	16.8 (3.43)
Health/physical ed.	[5] (†)	9 (1.0)	10.4 (3.83)	53.7 (5.46)	24.5 (4.98)	‡ (†)	‡ (†)	32.0 (5.74)	29.7 (5.25)	19.9 (5.64)	18.4 (4.54)
Mathematics	33 (1.6)	31 (3.2)	3.7 (1.51)	49.6 (3.23)	41.8 (2.84)	2.6 (1.44)	2.3 (1.39)	17.3 (2.82)	28.5 (3.01)	24.5 (2.88)	29.7 (3.55)
Science	23 (1.3)	27 (1.8)	1.9 (0.98)	47.4 (3.64)	41.0 (3.57)	3.8 (1.36)	5.9 (1.48)	25.3 (2.96)	35.1 (2.94)	19.0 (2.68)	20.6 (2.56)
Social studies	19 (1.1)	27 (2.4)	3.5 (1.15)	48.3 (3.65)	39.7 (3.69)	2.6 (0.82)	5.8 (1.48)	19.8 (4.74)	35.5 (3.03)	23.4 (3.79)	21.4 (2.79)
Special education	7 (1.0)	7 (1.5)	2.6 (1.30)	52.1 (6.47)	36.4 (7.21)	7.8 (2.79)	‡ (†)	20.7 (4.89)	47.0 (9.66)	20.3 (7.13)	12.0 (4.84)
Vocational/technical	4 (0.6)	5 (0.9)	24.9 (8.13)	45.2 (7.34)	20.9 (4.91)	4.7 (2.75)	4.3 (3.63)	39.5 (7.42)	23.1 (5.27)	22.1 (5.55)	15.4 (4.57)
Other secondary	69 (2.6)	24 (2.7)	11.8 (3.39)	45.7 (3.96)	31.5 (3.71)	6.2 (1.69)	4.7 (1.49)	33.7 (3.94)	32.9 (3.82)	18.8 (3.52)	14.6 (2.43)

—Not available.
†Not applicable.
‡Reporting standards not met.
[1]Includes certificate of advanced graduate studies.
[2]Data are only roughly comparable to 2003–04, because the new category of more than one race was introduced in 2003–04.
[3]Includes Pacific Islander.
[4]Included under other elementary.
[5]Included under other secondary.

NOTE: Excludes prekindergarten teachers. Data are based on a head count of full-time and part-time teachers rather than on the number of full-time-equivalent teachers reported in other tables. Detail may not sum to totals because of rounding and cell suppression. Race categories exclude persons of Hispanic ethnicity. Standard errors appear in parentheses.
SOURCE: U.S. Department of Education, National Center for Education Statistics, Schools and Staffing Survey (SASS), "Public Teacher Questionnaire," 1999–2000 and 2003–04; "Private Teacher Questionnaire," 1999–2000 and 2003–04; and "Charter Teacher Questionnaire," 1999–2000. (This table was prepared September 2006.)

Table 69. Selected characteristics of public school teachers: Selected years, spring 1961 through spring 2001

Selected characteristic	1961	1966	1971	1976	1981	1986	1991	1996	2001
1	2	3	4	5	6	7	8	9	10
Number of teachers (in thousands)	**1,408**	**1,710**	**2,055**	**2,196**	**2,185**	**2,206**	**2,398**	**2,164**	**2,979**
Sex (percent)									
Male	31.3	31.1	34.3	32.9	33.1	31.2	27.9	25.6	21.0
Female	68.7	68.9	65.7	67.1	66.9	68.8	72.1	74.4	79.0
Median age (years)									
All teachers	41	36	35	33	37	41	42	44	46
Males	34	33	33	33	38	42	43	46	47
Females	46	40	37	33	36	41	42	44	45
Marital status (percent)									
Single	22.3	22.0	19.5	20.1	18.5	12.9	11.7	12.4	15.2
Married	68.0	69.1	71.9	71.3	73.0	75.7	75.7	75.9	73.1
Widowed, divorced, or separated	9.7	9.0	8.6	8.6	8.5	11.4	12.6	11.8	11.7
Highest degree held (percent)									
Less than bachelor's	14.6	7.0	2.9	0.9	0.4	0.3	0.6	0.3	0.2
Bachelor's	61.9	69.6	69.6	61.6	50.1	48.3	46.3	43.6	43.1
Master's or specialist degree[1]	23.1	23.2	27.1	37.1	49.3	50.7	52.6	54.5	56.0
Doctor's	0.4	0.1	0.4	0.4	0.3	0.7	0.5	1.7	0.8
College credits earned in last 3 years									
Percent who earned credits	—	—	60.7	63.2	56.1	53.1	50.3	50.2	46.3
Mean number of credits earned[2]	—	—	14	—	9	4	4	—	—
Median years of teaching experience	11	8	8	8	12	15	15	15	14
Teaching for first year (percent)	8.0	9.1	9.1	5.5	2.4	3.1	3.0	2.1	3.1
Average number of pupils per class									
Elementary teachers, not departmentalized	29	28	27	25	25	24	23	24	21
Secondary and departmentalized elementary teachers	27	27	27	25	23	26	26	31	28
Mean number of students taught per day by secondary and departmentalized elementary teachers	—	132	135	127	118	97	93	97	86
Average number of hours in required school day	7.4	7.3	7.3	7.3	7.3	7.3	7.2	7.3	7.4
Average number of hours per week spent on all teaching duties									
All teachers	47	47	47	46	46	49	47	49	50
Elementary teachers	49	47	46	44	44	47	44	47	49
Secondary teachers	46	48	48	48	48	51	50	52	52
Average number of days of classroom teaching in school year	—	181	181	180	180	180	180	180	181
Average number of nonteaching days in school year	—	5	4	5	6	5	5	6	7
Average annual salary as classroom teacher (current dollars)	$5,264 [3]	$6,253	$9,261	$12,005	$17,209	$24,504	$31,790	$35,549	$43,262
Total income, including spouse's (if married) (current dollars)	—	—	15,021	19,957	29,831	43,413	55,491	63,171	77,739
Willingness to teach again (percent)									
Certainly would	49.9	52.6	44.9	37.5	21.8	22.7	28.6	32.1	31.7
Probably would	26.9	25.4	29.5	26.1	24.6	26.3	30.5	30.5	28.7
Chances about even	12.5	12.9	13.0	17.5	17.6	19.8	18.5	17.3	18.4
Probably would not	7.9	7.1	8.9	13.4	24.0	22.0	17.0	15.8	15.7
Certainly would not	2.8	2.0	3.7	5.6	12.0	9.3	5.4	4.3	5.6

—Not available.
[1]Figures for curriculum specialist or professional diploma based on 6 years of college study are not included.
[2]Measured in semester hours.
[3]Includes extra pay for extra duties.

NOTE: Data are based on sample surveys of public school teachers. See Guide to Sources for information on interpreting data from this survey. Data differ from figures appearing in other tables because of varying survey processing procedures and time period coverages. Detail may not sum to totals because of rounding.
SOURCE: National Education Association, *Status of the American Public School Teacher, 2000–01.* (This table was prepared August 2003.)

Table 70. Percentage of public school teachers of grades 9 through 12, by field of main teaching assignment and selected demographic and educational characteristics: 2003–04

Teacher characteristic	Total		Field of main teaching assignment									
			Arts and music	English or language arts	Foreign languages	Health and physical education	Mathematics	Natural sciences	Social sciences	Special education	Vocational/ technical	All other
1	2		3	4	5	6	7	8	9	10	11	12
Number of teachers (in thousands)	988.1	(19.27)	79.5 (2.92)	143.2 (5.13)	56.7 (2.11)	67.0 (2.85)	127.2 (3.53)	109.5 (4.38)	115.5 (3.42)	113.3 (5.03)	137.1 (4.49)	39.0 (1.92)
Total	100.0	(†)	100.0 (†)	100.0 (†)	100.0 (†)	100.0 (†)	100.0 (†)	100.0 (†)	100.0 (†)	100.0 (†)	100.0 (†)	100.0 (†)
Sex												
Male	44.1	(0.46)	45.5 (1.71)	26.1 (1.18)	21.9 (1.82)	63.1 (2.25)	45.1 (1.24)	51.3 (1.40)	65.1 (1.26)	27.9 (1.28)	50.1 (1.31)	47.6 (2.62)
Female	55.9	(0.46)	54.5 (1.71)	73.9 (1.18)	78.1 (1.82)	36.9 (2.25)	54.9 (1.24)	48.7 (1.40)	34.9 (1.26)	72.1 (1.28)	49.9 (1.31)	52.4 (2.62)
Race/ethnicity												
White	84.7	(0.89)	89.1 (1.26)	86.7 (1.10)	72.0 (2.88)	87.9 (1.30)	83.1 (1.48)	85.8 (1.22)	87.1 (1.23)	83.5 (1.69)	85.3 (1.10)	79.1 (1.90)
Black	7.1	(0.40)	5.5 (0.96)	6.9 (0.78)	4.5 (0.98)	6.1 (0.92)	6.8 (0.64)	6.5 (0.66)	5.9 (0.72)	9.4 (1.08)	8.9 (0.91)	9.6 (1.35)
Hispanic	5.4	(0.55)	3.6 (0.87)	3.8 (0.55)	20.8 (2.29)	3.8 (0.89)	6.3 (1.14)	4.0 (0.73)	3.6 (0.76)	4.8 (1.11)	3.9 (0.56)	7.7 (1.61)
Asian	1.3	(0.13)	0.7 (0.25)	1.1 (0.28)	1.5 (0.44)	0.5 (0.16)	2.5 (0.41)	2.0 (0.43)	1.3 (0.35)	0.8 (0.18)	0.4 (0.18)	2.1 (0.63)
Pacific Islander	0.2	(0.04)	‡ (†)	0.1 (0.07)	‡ (†)	0.2 (0.10)	0.1 (0.07)	0.3 (0.14)	0.3 (0.16)	0.3 (0.16)	0.1 (0.07)	‡ (†)
American Indian/Alaska Native	0.6	(0.06)	0.5 (0.12)	0.7 (0.15)	0.2 (0.08)	0.9 (0.34)	0.5 (0.13)	0.4 (0.13)	1.0 (0.35)	0.5 (0.17)	0.8 (0.25)	1.0 (0.30)
More than one race	0.7	(0.06)	0.5 (0.16)	0.7 (0.17)	1.0 (0.31)	0.6 (0.29)	0.7 (0.18)	1.0 (0.20)	0.9 (0.28)	0.7 (0.21)	0.5 (0.13)	0.4 (0.29)
Age												
Under 30 years	15.1	(0.45)	17.3 (1.41)	17.7 (0.93)	15.2 (1.39)	16.2 (1.84)	16.7 (1.00)	15.8 (1.02)	17.4 (1.01)	13.1 (1.15)	9.4 (0.77)	11.8 (1.91)
30 to 39 years	24.5	(0.49)	24.7 (1.56)	24.8 (1.16)	27.5 (1.89)	26.9 (1.60)	27.8 (1.15)	26.6 (1.29)	27.1 (1.37)	22.0 (1.21)	18.8 (0.86)	18.1 (1.95)
40 to 49 years	25.6	(0.41)	26.5 (1.66)	19.6 (1.12)	19.7 (1.70)	28.1 (2.02)	24.4 (1.18)	25.9 (1.45)	21.4 (1.27)	30.6 (1.48)	31.6 (1.17)	30.6 (2.55)
50 to 59 years	29.6	(0.50)	27.1 (1.67)	31.5 (1.18)	32.8 (1.90)	25.5 (1.69)	27.0 (1.24)	25.6 (1.25)	29.8 (1.30)	29.5 (1.48)	34.6 (1.10)	32.2 (2.45)
60 years and over	5.1	(0.19)	4.3 (0.79)	6.4 (0.59)	4.8 (0.72)	3.3 (0.58)	4.2 (0.41)	6.0 (0.74)	4.2 (0.54)	4.8 (0.77)	5.5 (0.54)	7.4 (1.23)
Age at which first began to teach full time or part time												
25 or under	56.0	(0.53)	64.6 (1.67)	56.5 (1.24)	56.2 (2.14)	70.1 (1.98)	61.1 (1.24)	51.4 (1.60)	56.3 (1.54)	53.3 (1.66)	47.5 (1.43)	43.9 (2.35)
26 to 35	28.1	(0.49)	24.2 (1.33)	30.0 (1.21)	26.8 (1.81)	25.2 (1.83)	23.3 (1.18)	32.3 (1.53)	30.9 (1.41)	29.9 (1.48)	28.8 (1.03)	24.6 (1.82)
36 to 45	11.4	(0.30)	9.2 (1.16)	9.8 (0.69)	13.2 (1.62)	3.5 (0.79)	10.6 (0.87)	11.1 (0.94)	9.3 (0.92)	12.1 (0.86)	16.9 (0.92)	20.5 (1.97)
46 to 55	4.1	(0.22)	1.8 (0.52)	3.4 (0.44)	3.4 (0.82)	1.0 (0.47)	4.2 (0.58)	4.6 (0.71)	3.3 (0.52)	4.4 (0.57)	6.2 (0.67)	10.7 (1.50)
56 or over	0.4	(0.06)	0.2 (0.11)	0.3 (0.11)	0.4 (0.22)	‡ (†)	0.9 (0.26)	0.6 (0.27)	0.3 (0.08)	0.3 (0.11)	0.7 (0.22)	0.2 (0.20)
Years of full-time teaching experience												
Less than 3 years	12.6	(0.67)	11.9 (1.18)	14.1 (0.98)	13.2 (1.41)	9.8 (1.47)	12.7 (1.30)	13.1 (0.86)	12.3 (0.79)	12.0 (1.58)	12.6 (1.15)	14.5 (1.67)
3 to 9 years	32.2	(0.43)	32.1 (1.86)	33.0 (1.28)	33.8 (1.68)	26.5 (1.56)	32.6 (1.40)	33.4 (1.29)	35.3 (1.30)	32.7 (1.32)	28.2 (1.05)	36.0 (2.50)
10 to 20 years	27.1	(0.41)	27.2 (1.69)	23.3 (0.98)	29.0 (1.91)	29.3 (1.96)	28.7 (1.44)	28.8 (1.14)	23.0 (1.26)	29.4 (1.64)	27.7 (1.09)	28.4 (1.95)
Over 20 years	28.0	(0.54)	28.8 (1.75)	29.6 (1.10)	24.1 (1.81)	34.3 (1.69)	26.0 (1.21)	24.7 (1.30)	29.5 (1.33)	25.9 (1.58)	31.5 (1.41)	21.2 (2.05)
Highest college degree												
Less than bachelor's degree	2.6	(0.20)	0.8 (0.28)	0.3 (0.09)	0.4 (0.15)	0.7 (0.27)	0.3 (0.08)	0.3 (0.14)	0.6 (0.29)	0.6 (0.21)	14.1 (1.17)	6.7 (1.44)
Bachelor's degree	47.9	(0.60)	55.5 (1.86)	49.3 (1.27)	46.3 (2.00)	54.8 (2.09)	50.8 (1.37)	43.5 (1.38)	50.1 (1.46)	43.0 (1.43)	44.0 (1.08)	41.4 (2.53)
Master's degree	42.0	(0.71)	37.4 (1.72)	41.2 (1.29)	46.0 (2.08)	39.4 (2.17)	43.7 (1.32)	46.8 (1.53)	43.1 (1.38)	43.9 (1.56)	36.4 (1.37)	44.8 (2.40)
Education specialist[1]	5.6	(0.23)	4.7 (0.76)	7.3 (0.77)	5.1 (0.80)	3.9 (0.73)	3.9 (0.48)	5.0 (0.56)	4.2 (0.48)	10.6 (0.97)	4.4 (0.51)	5.7 (1.15)
Doctorate or first professional	2.0	(0.15)	1.6 (0.48)	1.9 (0.35)	2.1 (0.73)	1.2 (0.31)	1.4 (0.27)	4.5 (0.76)	2.1 (0.40)	1.9 (0.42)	1.2 (0.32)	1.4 (0.47)
Undergraduate field of study[2]												
Arts and music	8.3	(0.21)	87.7 (0.96)	1.9 (0.26)	2.2 (0.79)	0.4 (0.15)	0.8 (0.18)	0.5 (0.19)	0.9 (0.26)	2.1 (0.37)	1.7 (0.38)	3.0 (0.73)
Education, instruction	8.4	(0.24)	2.5 (0.39)	9.8 (0.70)	6.1 (0.71)	1.9 (0.41)	10.0 (0.70)	6.8 (0.68)	10.7 (0.79)	17.6 (1.00)	3.0 (0.36)	13.0 (1.54)
Education, other	5.1	(0.23)	0.6 (0.32)	1.2 (0.23)	1.2 (0.60)	0.5 (0.25)	0.7 (0.18)	0.4 (0.16)	0.3 (0.09)	38.3 (1.55)	0.6 (0.19)	3.2 (0.66)
English and language arts	13.3	(0.35)	3.8 (0.64)	71.0 (1.15)	7.7 (0.91)	1.1 (0.48)	1.4 (0.35)	0.7 (0.28)	3.4 (0.58)	7.5 (0.77)	1.8 (0.33)	11.6 (1.80)
Foreign languages	4.5	(0.21)	0.1 (0.05)	1.2 (0.25)	65.3 (1.88)	0.2 (0.10)	0.3 (0.12)	0.1 (0.10)	1.3 (0.44)	0.9 (0.54)	0.3 (0.14)	5.4 (1.03)
Health and physical education	9.8	(0.30)	0.8 (0.25)	2.1 (0.37)	2.6 (0.85)	85.6 (1.20)	4.5 (0.55)	6.0 (0.72)	6.5 (0.70)	5.9 (0.71)	2.4 (0.37)	11.3 (1.78)
Mathematics and computer science	8.6	(0.21)	‡ (†)	0.6 (0.20)	1.0 (0.33)	0.3 (0.15)	61.3 (1.29)	1.4 (0.28)	0.5 (0.21)	0.6 (0.19)	0.8 (0.20)	4.0 (0.96)
Natural sciences	10.7	(0.37)	0.3 (0.12)	0.7 (0.26)	1.3 (0.51)	1.7 (0.52)	8.2 (0.66)	77.5 (1.22)	0.9 (0.25)	1.2 (0.21)	2.2 (0.33)	4.7 (1.00)
Social sciences	14.8	(0.31)	1.8 (0.31)	7.3 (0.65)	8.0 (1.18)	4.0 (0.69)	6.4 (0.65)	3.0 (0.42)	71.4 (1.23)	16.8 (1.09)	4.3 (0.51)	21.1 (1.89)
Vocational/technical education	12.7	(0.30)	1.2 (0.31)	2.3 (0.44)	2.4 (0.77)	3.6 (0.73)	5.3 (0.61)	2.5 (0.44)	2.5 (0.39)	6.4 (0.64)	67.7 (1.50)	11.7 (1.28)
Other	3.9	(0.21)	1.2 (0.37)	2.0 (0.41)	2.4 (0.86)	0.8 (0.27)	0.9 (0.24)	1.0 (0.28)	1.7 (0.47)	2.9 (0.62)	15.2 (1.18)	11.0 (1.74)

†Not applicable.
‡Reporting standards not met.
[1]Education specialist degrees or certificates are generally awarded for 1 year's work beyond the master's level.
[2]Data are for bachelor's degrees and major fields of study only.

NOTE: Race categories exclude persons of Hispanic ethnicity. Detail may not sum to totals because of rounding. Standard errors appear in parentheses.
SOURCE: U.S. Department of Education, National Center for Education Statistics, Schools and Staffing Survey (SASS), "Public Teacher Questionnaire," 2003–04. (This table was prepared July 2006.)

Table 71. Teachers' perceptions about serious problems in their schools, by control and level of school: Selected years, 1987–88 through 2003–04

Problem area	Public school teachers							Private school teachers						
	1987–88 total	1993–94 total	1999–2000 total	2003–04 Total	2003–04 Elementary schools	2003–04 Secondary schools	2003–04 Combined schools	1987–88 total	1993–94 total	1999–2000 total	2003–04 Total	2003–04 Elementary schools	2003–04 Secondary schools	2003–04 Combined schools
1	2	3	4	5	6	7	8	9	10	11	12	13	14	15
Percent of teachers indicating item is a serious problem														
Student tardiness	10.5 (0.18)	10.5 (0.28)	10.2 (0.22)	13.8 (0.30)	9.8 (0.39)	23.1 (0.58)	10.8 (0.96)	3.6 (0.38)	2.6 (0.23)	2.9 (0.21)	2.9 (0.40)	2.1 (0.45)	5.0 (0.83)	2.8 (0.65)
Student absenteeism	16.4 (0.23)	14.4 (0.29)	13.9 (0.26)	13.2 (0.31)	8.3 (0.37)	23.7 (0.59)	12.9 (1.04)	3.7 (0.39)	2.2 (0.19)	2.5 (0.22)	1.9 (0.23)	0.9 (0.17)	4.0 (0.75)	2.2 (0.48)
Teacher absenteeism	2.3 (0.09)	1.5 (0.09)	2.2 (0.10)	1.1 (0.08)	0.9 (0.12)	1.7 (0.15)	0.7 (0.16)	0.8 (0.13)	0.8 (0.10)	0.8 (0.11)	0.3 (0.09)	0.2 (0.07)	0.5 (0.24)	0.3 (0.15)
Students cutting class	5.9 (0.16)	5.1 (0.12)	4.7 (0.12)	5.6 (0.23)	1.5 (0.17)	14.5 (0.59)	4.4 (0.55)	0.9 (0.16)	0.7 (0.11)	0.8 (0.12)	0.5 (0.11)	0.2 (0.07)	0.9 (0.36)	0.7 (0.28)
Physical conflicts among students	5.8 (0.18)	8.2 (0.25)	4.8 (0.19)	— (†)	— (†)	— (†)	— (†)	1.3 (0.19)	1.5 (0.15)	1.0 (0.18)	— (†)	— (†)	— (†)	— (†)
Robbery or theft	3.7 (0.12)	4.1 (0.17)	2.4 (0.11)	— (†)	— (†)	— (†)	— (†)	1.3 (0.18)	0.8 (0.10)	0.9 (0.11)	— (†)	— (†)	— (†)	— (†)
Vandalism of school property	6.1 (0.15)	6.7 (0.23)	3.4 (0.15)	— (†)	— (†)	— (†)	— (†)	1.3 (0.19)	1.2 (0.11)	0.7 (0.11)	— (†)	— (†)	— (†)	— (†)
Student pregnancy	6.9 (0.17)	7.3 (0.24)	3.7 (0.12)	2.4 (0.12)	0.2 (0.06)	7.0 (0.34)	3.6 (0.49)	0.6 (0.12)	0.4 (0.06)	0.4 (0.09)	0.1 (0.05)	0.1 (0.04)	0.3 (0.19)	0.1 (0.05)
Student use of alcohol	11.4 (0.18)	9.3 (0.17)	7.4 (0.14)	— (†)	— (†)	— (†)	— (†)	3.6 (0.30)	3.1 (0.19)	3.1 (0.16)	— (†)	— (†)	— (†)	— (†)
Student drug abuse	8.0 (0.14)	5.7 (0.14)	6.0 (0.11)	— (†)	— (†)	— (†)	— (†)	1.8 (0.24)	1.3 (0.15)	1.8 (0.14)	— (†)	— (†)	— (†)	— (†)
Student possession of weapons	1.7 (0.06)	2.8 (0.12)	0.8 (0.06)	— (†)	— (†)	— (†)	— (†)	0.4 (0.11)	0.3 (0.06)	0.3 (0.06)	— (†)	— (†)	— (†)	— (†)
Verbal abuse of teachers	8.1 (0.21)	11.1 (0.26)	— (†)	— (†)	— (†)	— (†)	— (†)	2.0 (0.24)	2.3 (0.25)	— (†)	— (†)	— (†)	— (†)	— (†)
Student disrespect for teachers	— (†)	18.5 (0.35)	17.2 (0.34)	— (†)	— (†)	— (†)	— (†)	— (†)	3.4 (0.27)	3.8 (0.31)	— (†)	— (†)	— (†)	— (†)
Students dropping out	— (†)	5.8 (0.16)	4.6 (0.11)	3.3 (0.13)	0.3 (0.07)	9.6 (0.41)	4.3 (0.47)	— (†)	0.6 (0.09)	0.5 (0.10)	0.3 (0.09)	0.2 (0.08)	0.5 (0.26)	0.3 (0.12)
Student apathy	— (†)	23.6 (0.35)	20.6 (0.30)	16.6 (0.34)	9.9 (0.41)	30.4 (0.56)	19.5 (1.01)	— (†)	4.5 (0.28)	4.3 (0.29)	3.1 (0.39)	1.4 (0.24)	6.6 (0.95)	3.6 (0.70)
Lack of parental involvement	— (†)	27.6 (0.45)	23.7 (0.36)	21.6 (0.43)	19.3 (0.59)	26.3 (0.59)	22.7 (1.17)	— (†)	4.0 (0.26)	3.4 (0.30)	2.5 (0.37)	1.6 (0.27)	3.6 (0.77)	3.2 (0.69)
Poverty	— (†)	19.5 (0.52)	19.2 (0.43)	21.4 (0.46)	22.4 (0.65)	19.0 (0.57)	22.7 (1.31)	— (†)	2.7 (0.23)	2.1 (0.21)	2.2 (0.26)	1.8 (0.31)	3.4 (0.78)	2.2 (0.49)
Students come unprepared to learn	— (†)	28.8 (0.39)	29.5 (0.36)	26.8 (0.46)	23.7 (0.68)	33.5 (0.69)	26.1 (1.39)	— (†)	4.1 (0.28)	4.9 (0.36)	3.5 (0.30)	2.1 (0.55)	6.8 (0.99)	3.9 (0.70)
Percent of teachers indicating item happens daily														
Physical conflicts among students	— (†)	— (†)	— (†)	12.1 (0.29)	13.7 (0.43)	9.3 (0.38)	8.2 (0.95)	— (†)	— (†)	— (†)	2.3 (0.33)	2.6 (0.58)	1.0 (0.35)	2.6 (0.64)
Robbery or theft	— (†)	— (†)	— (†)	3.7 (0.17)	2.8 (0.22)	5.9 (0.24)	1.9 (0.40)	— (†)	— (†)	— (†)	0.4 (0.10)	# (†)	1.3 (0.40)	0.4 (0.22)
Vandalism of school property	— (†)	— (†)	— (†)	3.6 (0.16)	2.5 (0.21)	6.3 (0.33)	2.7 (0.52)	— (†)	— (†)	— (†)	0.5 (0.11)	0.1 (0.08)	0.8 (0.28)	0.8 (0.24)
Student use of alcohol	— (†)	— (†)	— (†)	3.1 (0.10)	0.3 (0.07)	9.0 (0.28)	3.5 (0.45)	— (†)	— (†)	(†)	0.7 (0.17)	# (†)	3.3 (0.86)	0.5 (0.21)
Student drug abuse	— (†)	— (†)	— (†)	4.5 (0.14)	0.5 (0.11)	13.0 (0.35)	4.4 (0.51)	— (†)	— (†)	— (†)	1.1 (0.26)	# (†)	5.2 (1.31)	0.8 (0.36)
Student possession of weapons	— (†)	— (†)	— (†)	0.5 (0.05)	0.1 (0.05)	1.2 (0.12)	0.3 (0.14)	— (†)	— (†)	— (†)	# (†)	# (†)	# (†)	0.1 (0.05)
Verbal abuse of teachers	— (†)	— (†)	— (†)	11.8 (0.31)	9.3 (0.39)	17.1 (0.50)	12.7 (1.10)	— (†)	— (†)	— (†)	2.4 (0.40)	1.2 (0.29)	4.0 (0.84)	3.3 (0.72)
Student disrespect for teachers	— (†)	— (†)	— (†)	21.6 (0.45)	18.5 (0.61)	28.3 (0.58)	20.9 (1.08)	— (†)	— (†)	— (†)	5.1 (0.37)	3.6 (0.56)	6.3 (1.05)	6.5 (1.12)
Racial tension	— (†)	— (†)	— (†)	2.4 (0.15)	1.8 (0.19)	3.9 (0.22)	1.5 (0.28)	— (†)	— (†)	— (†)	0.4 (0.08)	0.1 (0.06)	0.9 (0.36)	0.6 (0.20)

—Not available.
†Not applicable.
#Rounds to zero.
NOTE: Standard errors appear in parentheses.

SOURCE: U.S. Department of Education, National Center for Education Statistics, Schools and Staffing Survey (SASS), "Public Teacher Questionnaire," 1987–88, 1993–94, 1999–2000, and 2003–04; "Private Teacher Questionnaire," 1987–88, 1993–94, 1999–2000, and 2003–04; and "Charter Teacher Questionnaire," 1999–2000. (This table was prepared June 2008.)

Table 72. Teachers' perceptions about teaching and school conditions, by control and level of school: 1993–94, 1999–2000, and 2003–04

Percent of teachers somewhat agreeing or strongly agreeing with statement

Statement	Public total, 1993–94	Public total, 1999–2000	Public school teachers, 2003–04				Private total, 1993–94	Private total, 1999–2000	Private school teachers, 2003–04			
			Total	Elementary schools	Secondary schools	Combined schools			Total	Elementary schools	Secondary schools	Combined schools
1	2	3	4	5	6	7	8	9	10	11	12	13
The school administration's behavior toward the staff is supportive	79.2 (0.36)	78.8 (0.38)	85.2 (0.33)	85.8 (0.48)	84.1 (0.41)	84.3 (0.98)	88.2 (0.42)	87.3 (0.45)	91.1 (0.74)	91.4 (0.86)	89.6 (1.26)	91.4 (1.12)
My principal enforces school rules for student conduct and backs me up when I need it	80.8 (0.35)	82.2 (0.33)	87.2 (0.35)	87.8 (0.52)	85.8 (0.44)	87.7 (0.80)	88.4 (0.41)	88.3 (0.39)	92.2 (0.62)	92.0 (0.76)	91.0 (1.17)	92.9 (1.20)
The principal lets staff members know what is expected of them	85.6 (0.30)	87.7 (0.26)	91.8 (0.23)	92.4 (0.32)	91.0 (0.29)	90.1 (0.61)	88.2 (0.34)	89.8 (0.35)	93.8 (0.55)	93.6 (0.66)	93.4 (0.86)	94.1 (1.03)
Principal talks to me frequently about my instructional practices	44.3 (0.46)	45.6 (0.43)	— (†)	— (†)	— (†)	— (†)	54.0 (0.64)	50.4 (0.64)	— (†)	— (†)	— (†)	— (†)
In this school, staff members are recognized for a job well done	67.9 (0.39)	68.3 (0.42)	75.4 (0.38)	77.3 (0.55)	72.1 (0.40)	71.1 (1.28)	81.1 (0.40)	78.9 (0.50)	83.8 (1.09)	83.8 (1.25)	82.9 (1.58)	84.3 (1.91)
Principal knows what kind of school he/she wants and has communicated it to the staff	80.5 (0.36)	83.2 (0.28)	87.3 (0.30)	88.4 (0.40)	85.3 (0.43)	84.0 (1.07)	88.6 (0.38)	88.4 (0.43)	91.9 (0.68)	91.5 (0.81)	91.2 (0.90)	92.7 (1.21)
Most of my colleagues share my beliefs and values about what the central mission of the school should be	84.2 (0.22)	84.7 (0.26)	88.1 (0.26)	90.5 (0.38)	83.0 (0.41)	87.4 (0.86)	93.2 (0.37)	92.2 (0.31)	93.8 (0.50)	95.1 (0.55)	91.2 (1.02)	93.3 (1.08)
There is a great deal of cooperative effort among staff	77.5 (0.31)	78.4 (0.32)	83.2 (0.36)	85.1 (0.56)	79.0 (0.48)	82.8 (1.19)	90.5 (0.29)	89.0 (0.42)	91.1 (0.75)	91.5 (0.84)	88.6 (1.47)	91.8 (1.24)
I receive a great deal of support from parents for the work I do	52.5 (0.38)	57.9 (0.40)	61.1 (0.50)	63.2 (0.74)	56.7 (0.59)	61.1 (1.38)	84.6 (0.41)	84.0 (0.49)	86.0 (2.39)	88.3 (1.01)	81.5 (2.16)	85.1 (6.59)
I make a conscious effort to coordinate the content of my courses with that of other teachers	85.0 (0.25)	84.1 (0.24)	86.3 (0.31)	89.1 (0.45)	81.0 (0.40)	82.8 (0.96)	85.2 (0.44)	81.4 (0.55)	84.5 (1.20)	86.8 (1.10)	80.3 (1.54)	83.4 (2.03)
Routine duties and paperwork interfere with my job of teaching	70.8 (0.38)	71.1 (0.30)	70.8 (0.44)	71.2 (0.64)	70.7 (0.50)	65.9 (1.13)	40.1 (0.65)	44.5 (0.57)	40.8 (2.51)	42.2 (3.64)	44.1 (2.00)	37.5 (3.46)
Level of student misbehavior in this school interferes with my teaching	44.1 (0.40)	40.8 (0.42)	37.2 (0.53)	35.2 (0.83)	41.5 (0.59)	37.9 (1.48)	22.4 (0.43)	24.1 (0.61)	20.8 (2.55)	21.4 (1.47)	21.0 (1.92)	20.0 (6.60)
Amount of student tardiness and class cutting in this school interferes with my teaching	27.9 (0.32)	31.5 (0.35)	33.4 (0.45)	27.7 (0.62)	45.7 (0.64)	33.0 (1.32)	16.9 (0.75)	15.0 (0.43)	16.9 (1.01)	15.0 (1.14)	19.9 (1.59)	18.1 (1.93)
Rules for student behavior are consistently enforced by teachers in this school, even for students who are not in their classes	61.8 (0.42)	62.6 (0.39)	71.1 (0.46)	78.8 (0.60)	54.7 (0.55)	70.5 (1.08)	77.6 (0.50)	75.9 (0.51)	80.9 (1.51)	86.1 (1.12)	69.1 (2.45)	79.5 (2.42)
I am satisfied with my class sizes	64.9 (0.38)	67.7 (0.36)	69.1 (0.43)	69.7 (0.58)	65.2 (0.52)	83.7 (1.09)	84.4 (0.40)	85.7 (0.45)	87.6 (0.92)	85.4 (1.56)	85.4 (1.74)	91.5 (1.20)
I am satisfied with my teaching salary	44.9 (0.45)	39.4 (0.36)	45.9 (0.46)	44.2 (0.65)	49.4 (0.60)	46.2 (1.60)	41.6 (0.59)	42.6 (0.73)	50.6 (1.67)	43.7 (2.43)	54.1 (2.09)	57.9 (4.56)
I sometimes feel it is a waste of time to try to do my best as a teacher	26.8 (0.35)	20.3 (0.29)	16.7 (0.32)	14.6 (0.45)	20.8 (0.43)	18.4 (1.08)	10.2 (0.65)	10.5 (0.38)	8.7 (0.71)	8.5 (1.17)	7.8 (0.78)	9.3 (1.10)
I plan with the librarian/media specialist for the integration of services into my teaching	66.9 (0.42)	58.6 (0.38)	— (†)	— (†)	— (†)	— (†)	60.6 (0.71)	48.7 (0.74)	— (†)	— (†)	— (†)	— (†)
Necessary materials are available as needed by staff	73.1 (0.42)	75.0 (0.32)	79.0 (0.42)	79.7 (0.56)	76.9 (0.56)	83.2 (0.87)	85.7 (0.44)	89.0 (0.38)	91.8 (0.71)	91.0 (0.75)	91.5 (1.04)	93.0 (1.40)
I worry about the security of my job because of the performance of my students on state or local tests	— (†)	28.8 (0.37)	31.2 (0.43)	32.4 (0.55)	28.8 (0.57)	30.8 (1.15)	— (†)	6.7 (0.29)	7.8 (0.65)	9.0 (0.98)	7.9 (0.93)	6.2 (1.14)
I am given the support I need to teach students with special needs	— (†)	60.9 (0.33)	64.4 (0.46)	64.0 (0.63)	63.7 (0.65)	74.5 (1.37)	— (†)	67.1 (0.58)	71.8 (2.05)	68.6 (2.08)	70.8 (2.01)	76.5 (6.79)
I am generally satisfied with being a teacher at this school	— (†)	89.7 (0.24)	90.9 (0.28)	91.1 (0.40)	90.4 (0.31)	91.9 (0.75)	— (†)	93.3 (0.26)	95.2 (0.55)	94.8 (0.65)	95.7 (0.88)	95.4 (1.17)

—Not available.
†Not applicable.
NOTE: Standard errors appear in parentheses.

SOURCE: U.S. Department of Education, National Center for Education Statistics, Schools and Staffing Survey (SASS), "Public Teacher Questionnaire," 1993–94, 1999–2000, and 2003–04; "Private Teacher Questionnaire," 1993–94, 1999–2000, and 2003–04; and "Charter Teacher Questionnaire," 1999–2000. (This table was prepared August 2006.)

Table 73. Mobility of public and private elementary and secondary teachers, by selected teacher and school characteristics: Selected years, 1987–88 through 2004–05

Selected characteristic	Public — Left teaching 1987–88 to 1988–89	Public — Left teaching 1990–91 to 1991–92	Public — Left teaching 1993–94 to 1994–95	Public — Left teaching 1999–2000 to 2000–01	Public 2003–04 to 2004–05 Remained in same school	Public 2003–04 to 2004–05 Changed schools	Public 2003–04 to 2004–05 Left teaching	Private — Left teaching 1987–88 to 1988–89	Private — Left teaching 1990–91 to 1991–92	Private — Left teaching 1993–94 to 1994–95	Private — Left teaching 1999–2000 to 2000–01	Private 2003–04 to 2004–05 Remained in same school	Private 2003–04 to 2004–05 Changed schools	Private 2003–04 to 2004–05 Left teaching
1	2	3	4	5	6	7	8	9	10	11	12	13	14	15
Total	5.6 (0.30)	5.1 (0.36)	6.6 (0.34)	7.4 (0.37)	83.5 (0.59)	8.1 (0.49)	8.4 (0.44)	12.7 (0.85)	12.3 (0.80)	11.9 (0.70)	12.5 (0.69)	80.5 (2.00)	5.9 (0.55)	13.6 (2.18)
Sex														
Male	5.1 (0.52)	4.5 (0.60)	5.2 (0.32)	7.4 (0.67)	83.9 (1.00)	8.3 (0.84)	7.7 (0.68)	10.2 (1.72)	12.1 (1.91)	13.1 (1.20)	11.7 (1.48)	80.5 (2.04)	5.2 (0.79)	14.2 (2.06)
Female	5.8 (0.39)	5.3 (0.48)	7.1 (0.44)	7.4 (0.45)	83.4 (0.60)	8.1 (0.48)	8.6 (0.50)	13.4 (0.92)	12.3 (0.84)	11.6 (0.78)	12.8 (0.76)	80.5 (2.57)	6.1 (0.70)	13.4 (2.88)
Race/ethnicity														
White	5.7 (0.32)	5.1 (0.37)	6.5 (0.36)	7.5 (0.45)	83.9 (0.63)	7.9 (0.52)	8.2 (0.50)	12.1 (0.90)	12.0 (0.86)	11.7 (0.69)	12.3 (0.73)	81.3 (2.16)	5.7 (0.55)	13.0 (2.33)
Black	5.1 (1.84)	6.1 (1.45)	6.6 (1.48)	7.4 (1.60)	79.3 (2.64)	9.7 (1.11)	11.0 (2.31)	34.7 (8.35)	19.3 (6.76)	12.6 (4.52)	14.8 (5.09)	67.8 (11.35)	9.2 (2.97)	23.0 ! (13.00)
Hispanic	2.9 (0.84)	4.4 (0.99)	9.1 (2.14)	7.5 (1.67)	80.6 (3.14)	10.1 (2.22)	9.3 (1.89)	21.3 (6.46)	13.6 (4.32)	14.6 (4.31)	9.6 (2.85)	70.3 (6.25)	7.6 (2.90)	22.1 ! (5.72)
Asian/Pacific Islander	4.2 ! (2.77)	7.0 ! (5.37)	2.4 (0.71)	2.1 (0.87)	81.8 (6.71)	7.9 (2.47)	10.3 ! (5.52)	8.8 ! (10.39)	12.2 ! (6.51)	17.5 (8.67)	24.2 ! (12.23)	89.7 (3.65)	2.7 (1.11)	7.6 (2.84)
Asian	— (†)	— (†)	— (†)	— (†)	81.4 (7.39)	7.6 (2.43)	11.0 ! (6.34)	— (†)	— (†)	— (†)	— (†)	89.5 (3.85)	2.8 (1.20)	7.8 (3.01)
Native Hawaiian/Pacific Islander	— (†)	— (†)	— (†)	— (†)	‡ (†)	‡ (†)	‡ (†)	— (†)	— (†)	— (†)	— (†)	‡ (†)	‡ (†)	‡ (†)
American Indian/Alaska Native	3.1 ! (1.70)	— (†)	3.5 (1.06)	7.6 (3.68)	93.1 (2.54)	5.0 (2.08)	1.9 (0.77)	17.5 ! (15.61)	16.5 ! (18.44)	38.5 ! (20.33)	20.2 ! (12.71)	‡ (†)	‡ (†)	‡ (†)
More than one race	— (†)	— (†)	— (†)	— (†)	88.1 (5.10)	6.6 (3.19)	5.3 ! (3.19)	— (†)	— (†)	— (†)	— (†)	‡ (†)	‡ (†)	‡ (†)
Age														
Less than 25	4.3 (0.91)	9.1 (2.30)	3.8 (1.05)	9.3 (2.20)	79.5 (2.39)	15.7 (1.93)	4.8 (1.24)	19.0 (3.79)	23.8 (4.91)	20.0 (4.19)	29.9 (4.24)	67.1 (5.56)	14.9 (3.25)	18.0 (3.41)
25 to 29	9.0 (1.18)	9.0 (1.21)	10.0 (1.25)	9.7 (1.39)	75.1 (2.22)	14.3 (1.60)	10.6 (1.98)	17.6 (2.42)	17.8 (2.27)	13.1 (1.35)	18.6 (2.07)	68.6 (4.68)	10.2 (1.60)	21.2 (4.00)
30 to 39	5.8 (0.59)	4.2 (0.76)	6.7 (0.94)	6.5 (0.88)	84.2 (1.25)	9.0 (0.74)	6.8 (0.87)	12.4 (1.59)	13.7 (1.65)	14.9 (1.54)	13.7 (1.52)	80.6 (2.22)	5.2 (1.05)	14.2 (1.81)
40 to 49	2.4 (0.32)	2.0 (0.31)	3.9 (0.54)	4.6 (0.62)	87.6 (0.92)	7.1 (0.66)	5.3 (0.73)	10.5 (1.63)	7.7 (1.03)	8.7 (1.02)	8.5 (1.34)	84.3 (2.43)	5.0 (0.98)	10.7 (2.08)
50 to 59	5.7 (0.82)	6.7 (0.95)	6.3 (0.77)	8.1 (0.80)	85.5 (0.91)	4.8 (0.66)	9.8 (0.82)	11.3 (2.45)	9.6 (1.91)	8.2 (1.53)	5.9 (0.90)	87.5 (9.39)	3.9 (0.77)	8.6 ! (9.80)
60 to 64	23.4 (4.90)	26.8 (4.30)	30.5 (4.78)	25.7 (5.44)	69.4 (4.64)	2.5 (0.93)	28.0 (4.35)	16.9 (5.93)	17.8 (4.62)	13.1 (2.74)	18.1 (3.72)	77.2 (5.31)	2.0 (1.03)	20.7 (5.27)
65 and over	16.7 ! (8.48)	40.9 (13.80)	34.1 (7.79)	16.6 (5.44)	77.2 (6.23)	1.7 (0.83)	21.2 (5.95)	7.9 (3.16)	20.7 (5.83)	41.9 (8.67)	29.4 (7.60)	73.3 (7.94)	5.6 ! (6.36)	21.2 (7.31)
Full- and part-time teaching experience														
1 year or less	7.9 (0.96)	7.0 (1.31)	5.7 (0.82)	10.5 (1.93)	74.4 (2.62)	16.0 (1.81)	9.6 (1.66)	15.9 (2.73)	22.8 (2.85)	18.2 (2.12)	28.9 (3.95)	67.8 (6.72)	12.1 (2.82)	20.2 (4.36)
2 years	7.3 (1.81)	9.5 (1.89)	9.1 (1.51)	8.5 (1.94)	81.4 (1.81)	12.2 (1.37)	6.4 (1.43)	18.2 (3.32)	19.5 (3.19)	23.6 (2.72)	22.5 (3.24)	66.6 (14.18)	8.8 (2.83)	24.6 ! (16.24)
3 years	9.3 (1.50)	6.6 (1.24)	9.8 (1.42)	7.5 (1.60)	76.0 (3.37)	16.3 (3.03)	7.7 (1.55)	15.4 (3.80)	19.0 (3.35)	12.8 (2.15)	17.8 (2.49)	75.6 (2.80)	9.2 (2.07)	15.3 (2.47)
4 to 10 years	6.4 (0.89)	5.3 (0.89)	6.8 (0.94)	7.3 (0.72)	82.4 (1.04)	9.5 (0.55)	8.1 (0.98)	14.0 (1.91)	12.4 (1.73)	13.1 (1.51)	12.6 (1.37)	77.7 (2.31)	6.3 (0.73)	16.0 (2.54)
11 to 20 years	3.5 (0.42)	2.3 (0.30)	4.9 (0.64)	5.2 (0.74)	88.1 (0.96)	6.4 (0.63)	5.5 (0.70)	11.5 (1.73)	6.6 (1.00)	7.1 (0.93)	6.9 (1.13)	87.7 (2.31)	4.1 (0.75)	8.2 (1.75)
21 to 25 years	3.5 (0.87)	4.2 (0.87)	4.0 (0.81)	4.2 (0.68)	88.9 (1.33)	4.5 (0.83)	6.6 (1.23)	5.2 (2.36)	3.3 (1.40)	6.0 (1.64)	5.5 (1.32)	90.0 (4.28)	1.1 (0.47)	8.9 (4.25)
More than 25 years	11.3 (1.63)	11.0 (1.34)	12.0 (1.04)	11.4 (1.05)	82.1 (1.50)	3.6 (0.67)	14.3 (1.13)	8.4 (2.03)	15.0 (3.24)	12.7 (2.53)	10.0 (1.40)	87.0 (2.03)	4.5 (1.81)	8.5 (1.77)
Level taught														
Elementary	5.5 (0.39)	4.8 (0.45)	6.4 (0.53)	6.8 (0.45)	83.0 (0.90)	8.6 (0.70)	8.4 (0.68)	12.5 (0.99)	11.3 (1.02)	11.5 (0.96)	13.4 (0.84)	79.0 (3.21)	6.6 (1.04)	14.4 (3.64)
Secondary	5.6 (0.42)	5.5 (0.62)	6.7 (0.53)	8.6 (0.71)	84.0 (0.77)	7.6 (0.52)	8.4 (0.59)	12.9 (2.38)	13.3 (1.51)	12.6 (1.51)	8.5 (0.90)	82.5 (1.41)	5.0 (0.75)	12.5 (1.35)
School size														
Less than 150	7.3 (1.36)	4.4 (0.69)	6.4 (1.15)	9.5 (2.29)	76.1 (5.20)	11.8 (3.41)	12.1 (2.92)	16.6 (1.72)	16.3 (1.87)	14.8 (1.43)	14.6 (1.45)	69.4 (5.97)	7.8 (1.78)	22.7 (6.32)
150 to 349	4.8 (0.45)	3.9 (0.53)	7.8 (1.03)	6.7 (0.99)	80.5 (1.94)	9.2 (1.10)	10.3 (1.58)	10.9 (1.62)	13.3 (1.42)	12.6 (1.21)	13.1 (1.24)	81.0 (1.62)	6.6 (1.02)	12.4 (1.40)
350 to 499	6.1 (0.98)	6.4 (1.03)	5.8 (0.73)	7.4 (0.85)	83.9 (1.47)	7.5 (0.82)	8.6 (1.16)	10.7 (2.63)	6.3 (1.47)	12.1 (1.95)	10.3 (1.26)	85.1 (1.92)	5.2 (1.24)	9.8 (1.40)
500 to 749	5.6 (0.77)	4.7 (0.68)	7.6 (0.67)	7.1 (0.78)	84.8 (1.30)	8.2 (0.89)	7.0 (0.75)	9.6 (2.07)	9.8 (2.11)	7.1 (1.27)	11.1 (1.91)	86.3 (2.75)	4.0 (1.06)	9.8 (2.63)
750 or more	5.0 (0.48)	5.4 (0.54)	5.7 (0.57)	7.7 (0.74)	84.0 (0.98)	7.8 (0.66)	8.2 (0.79)	12.9 (3.14)	6.7 (2.58)	6.2 (1.18)	10.8 (1.64)	92.2 (1.43)	2.9 (1.05)	4.9 (0.90)
Percent minority enrollment														
Less than 5 percent	5.8 (0.60)	4.5 (0.51)	7.1 (0.68)	6.5 (0.78)	87.3 (1.33)	5.1 (0.70)	7.6 (1.13)	12.7 (1.27)	12.2 (1.35)	11.1 (0.99)	7.1 (0.96)	83.4 (7.63)	5.1 (0.99)	11.5 ! (8.06)
5 to 19 percent	5.8 (0.74)	5.5 (0.73)	6.0 (0.71)	6.9 (0.66)	85.9 (1.00)	6.6 (0.62)	7.5 (0.75)	10.3 (1.37)	12.2 (1.40)	11.1 (1.07)	7.6 (1.60)	82.8 (1.89)	4.7 (0.72)	12.5 (1.54)
20 to 49 percent	5.2 (0.64)	5.9 (0.73)	6.2 (0.82)	9.5 (1.09)	84.2 (1.03)	9.3 (0.88)	6.5 (0.60)	18.9 (4.18)	12.2 (2.01)	15.6 (2.28)	14.6 (1.45)	76.9 (2.26)	7.5 (1.14)	15.6 (2.00)
50 percent or more	5.3 (0.66)	4.9 (0.66)	6.9 (0.72)	7.3 (0.68)	79.7 (1.11)	9.9 (0.78)	10.3 (0.84)	13.6 (2.85)	13.1 (2.35)	13.2 (2.15)	13.1 (1.24)	72.7 (4.49)	8.8 (1.71)	18.5 (4.47)
Community type														
Central city	4.6 (0.59)	5.2 (0.65)	6.3 (0.64)	7.1 (0.65)	79.8 (1.22)	10.3 (0.83)	9.9 (1.05)	13.5 (1.67)	12.7 (1.40)	10.9 (0.75)	12.1 (0.96)	82.1 (1.60)	6.1 (0.68)	11.8 (1.58)
Urban fringe/large town	5.6 (0.59)	5.5 (0.75)	6.5 (0.70)	8.3 (0.77)	84.8 (0.87)	7.3 (0.54)	7.9 (0.63)	11.5 (1.51)	10.6 (1.21)	12.6 (1.32)	11.8 (1.23)	80.2 (2.22)	5.3 (0.62)	14.5 (1.93)
Rural/small town	5.7 (0.52)	4.8 (0.39)	6.8 (0.59)	6.3 (0.52)	85.0 (1.11)	7.3 (0.91)	7.7 (0.92)	15.0 (1.78)	13.9 (1.81)	13.6 (1.46)	15.5 (1.92)	80.0 (17.99)	8.5 (2.74)	15.5 ! (19.40)

—Not available.
†Not applicable.
!Interpret data with caution.
‡Reporting standards not met.
NOTE: Race categories exclude persons of Hispanic ethnicity. Detail may not sum to totals because of rounding. Standard errors appear in parentheses.

SOURCE: U.S. Department of Education, National Center for Education Statistics, Schools and Staffing Survey (SASS), *Characteristics of Stayers, Movers, and Leavers: Results From the Teacher Follow-up Survey 1994–95; Teacher Attrition and Mobility: Results From the Teacher Follow-up Survey: 2000–01*; "Public School Teacher Data File" and "Private School Teacher Data File," 2003–04; and Teacher Follow-up Survey (TFS), "Current and Former Teacher Data Files," 2004–05. (This table was prepared July 2007.)

Table 74. Average base salary for full-time teachers in public elementary and secondary schools, by highest degree earned and years of full-time teaching: Selected years, 1990–91 through 2003–04

Years of full-time teaching experience	Number of full-time teachers	Salary (current dollars)					Salary (constant 2006–07 dollars)[3]				
			Highest degree earned					Highest degree earned			
		All teachers[1]	Bachelor's degree	Master's degree	Education specialist[2]	Doctor's degree	All teachers[1]	Bachelor's degree	Master's degree	Education specialist[2]	Doctor's degree
1	2	3	4	5	6	7	8	9	10	11	12
1990–91											
Total	2,336,750 (20,958)	$31,300 (100)	$27,700 (100)	$35,000 (130)	$35,000 (390)	$40,100 (820)	$47,800 (150)	$42,300 (160)	$53,300 (190)	$56,800 (600)	$61,100 (1,240)
1 year or less	94,000 (3,014)	22,200 (200)	21,500 (210)	26,400 (860)	26,600 (980)	‡ (†)	33,900 (310)	32,800 (320)	40,300 (1,320)	40,600 (1,500)	‡ (†)
2 years	86,900 (2,963)	22,100 (160)	21,600 (150)	25,100 (510)	‡ (†)	‡ (†)	33,700 (250)	33,000 (220)	38,200 (770)	‡ (†)	‡ (†)
3 years	80,340 (2,542)	23,000 (180)	22,400 (170)	26,000 (690)	‡ (†)	‡ (†)	35,100 (270)	34,200 (270)	39,600 (1,060)	‡ (†)	‡ (†)
4 years	79,610 (3,271)	24,000 (240)	23,200 (250)	26,300 (530)	29,200 (1,490)	‡ (†)	36,500 (360)	35,300 (370)	40,200 (800)	44,500 (2,270)	‡ (†)
5 years	83,540 (3,238)	25,100 (200)	24,100 (240)	27,200 (440)	29,900 (2,190)	‡ (†)	38,200 (310)	36,700 (370)	41,500 (670)	45,500 (3,350)	‡ (†)
6 to 9 years	316,210 (6,805)	26,500 (110)	25,000 (140)	28,800 (240)	30,200 (760)	‡ (†)	40,400 (170)	38,100 (210)	43,900 (360)	46,000 (1,160)	‡ (†)
10 to 14 years	408,300 (7,843)	29,600 (160)	27,300 (170)	31,800 (300)	33,600 (590)	37,900 (1,940)	45,200 (250)	41,600 (260)	48,400 (460)	51,300 (900)	57,800 (2,960)
15 to 19 years	444,930 (7,580)	33,600 (210)	30,800 (250)	35,200 (250)	37,800 (840)	40,300 (1,550)	51,200 (320)	47,000 (390)	53,700 (380)	57,600 (1,280)	61,500 (2,360)
20 to 24 years	392,330 (8,038)	37,000 (200)	34,100 (270)	38,500 (240)	39,500 (840)	43,700 (1,390)	56,300 (310)	51,900 (420)	58,600 (370)	60,200 (1,280)	66,700 (2,120)
25 to 29 years	219,140 (6,214)	38,100 (310)	34,800 (410)	39,800 (370)	42,500 (1,260)	43,100 (2,180)	58,100 (470)	53,000 (620)	60,700 (560)	64,700 (1,920)	65,700 (3,320)
30 to 34 years	100,460 (4,766)	38,500 (380)	35,000 (450)	40,700 (490)	40,900 (1,600)	‡ (†)	58,700 (580)	53,400 (690)	62,000 (750)	62,400 (2,430)	‡ (†)
35 years or more	30,980 (2,515)	39,200 (890)	34,100 (1,260)	41,700 (1,120)	‡ (†)	‡ (†)	59,700 (1,350)	52,000 (1,920)	63,600 (1,700)	‡ (†)	‡ (†)
1993–94											
Total	2,329,730 (21,660)	$34,200 (90)	$30,200 (100)	$38,500 (150)	$40,700 (420)	$41,700 (1,330)	$47,700 (130)	$42,100 (140)	$53,700 (220)	$56,800 (590)	$58,100 (1,860)
1 year or less	105,540 (2,970)	23,600 (140)	23,000 (160)	27,000 (440)	28,500 (1,340)	‡ (†)	33,000 (200)	32,100 (230)	37,600 (620)	39,700 (1,870)	‡ (†)
2 years	95,880 (3,534)	24,400 (180)	23,700 (150)	27,200 (420)	25,200 (1,180)	‡ (†)	34,100 (250)	33,100 (210)	38,000 (590)	35,200 (1,640)	‡ (†)
3 years	87,840 (3,416)	25,300 (210)	24,300 (200)	30,000 (660)	28,700 (1,000)	‡ (†)	35,300 (290)	33,900 (280)	41,900 (920)	40,100 (1,400)	‡ (†)
4 years	98,760 (3,615)	26,300 (240)	25,200 (210)	30,200 (640)	‡ (†)	‡ (†)	36,700 (340)	35,100 (300)	42,200 (900)	‡ (†)	‡ (†)
5 years	90,470 (2,813)	27,100 (220)	25,800 (170)	30,100 (560)	30,600 (670)	‡ (†)	37,900 (300)	36,100 (240)	42,000 (780)	42,800 (940)	‡ (†)
6 to 9 years	306,960 (6,059)	29,200 (140)	27,100 (140)	32,200 (290)	34,300 (1,050)	32,200 (2,300)	40,700 (190)	37,900 (190)	45,000 (400)	47,900 (1,470)	44,900 (3,210)
10 to 14 years	362,360 (6,222)	32,300 (130)	29,800 (210)	34,700 (230)	37,300 (730)	39,600 (1,320)	45,100 (190)	41,500 (290)	48,500 (320)	52,100 (1,010)	55,300 (1,840)
15 to 19 years	372,480 (6,008)	36,100 (180)	33,300 (240)	38,400 (260)	38,600 (580)	40,300 (1,250)	50,400 (250)	46,400 (330)	53,500 (360)	54,000 (800)	56,300 (1,740)
20 to 24 years	407,660 (7,928)	39,600 (210)	36,500 (270)	41,400 (290)	43,600 (810)	46,100 (2,600)	55,300 (300)	51,000 (370)	57,700 (400)	60,800 (1,130)	64,400 (3,620)
25 to 29 years	264,520 (6,324)	42,800 (260)	38,800 (350)	45,000 (390)	46,000 (870)	53,700 (2,010)	59,800 (360)	54,200 (490)	62,800 (540)	64,200 (1,210)	74,900 (2,800)
30 to 34 years	105,460 (3,940)	43,600 (390)	39,500 (630)	45,400 (420)	49,500 (1,690)	‡ (†)	60,800 (540)	55,100 (880)	63,400 (580)	69,100 (2,360)	‡ (†)
35 years or more	31,790 (1,965)	42,800 (1,080)	37,400 (1,230)	46,000 (1,640)	45,000 (2,090)	‡ (†)	59,800 (1,510)	52,200 (1,720)	64,200 (2,290)	62,800 (2,910)	‡ (†)
1999–2000											
Total	2,742,210 (20,301)	$39,900 (120)	$35,300 (120)	$44,700 (170)	$48,000 (440)	$48,200 (1,420)	$48,100 (140)	$42,600 (140)	$53,900 (210)	$57,900 (530)	$58,092 (1,710)
1 year or less	172,710 (5,492)	29,300 (170)	28,100 (150)	34,000 (450)	33,400 (1,010)	‡ (†)	35,300 (200)	33,900 (180)	41,000 (540)	40,200 (1,220)	‡ (†)
2 years	161,220 (5,678)	29,700 (180)	28,800 (170)	33,000 (400)	‡ (†)	‡ (†)	35,800 (220)	34,700 (200)	39,800 (490)	‡ (†)	‡ (†)
3 years	145,290 (4,630)	30,700 (170)	29,700 (200)	34,400 (370)	34,500 (1,340)	‡ (†)	37,000 (200)	35,800 (240)	41,400 (450)	41,700 (1,620)	‡ (†)
4 years	133,840 (5,657)	32,400 (260)	30,800 (230)	35,900 (670)	37,100 (1,350)	‡ (†)	39,000 (310)	37,100 (280)	43,300 (800)	44,800 (1,630)	‡ (†)
5 years	120,490 (4,300)	32,400 (250)	31,000 (290)	34,900 (390)	35,800 (1,920)	‡ (†)	39,100 (310)	37,400 (350)	42,100 (470)	43,200 (2,310)	‡ (†)
6 to 9 years	385,840 (8,205)	35,000 (170)	32,600 (190)	37,800 (240)	40,200 (840)	41,300 (2,300)	42,200 (200)	39,400 (230)	45,600 (290)	48,400 (1,010)	49,700 (2,780)
10 to 14 years	382,730 (6,298)	39,300 (260)	36,200 (390)	42,100 (330)	44,800 (990)	36,500 (2,310)	47,400 (310)	43,600 (470)	50,700 (400)	54,100 (1,190)	44,000 (2,790)
15 to 19 years	321,740 (8,067)	43,400 (220)	40,300 (320)	45,900 (360)	47,300 (920)	34,900 (870)	52,300 (270)	48,600 (380)	55,400 (430)	57,000 (1,100)	42,100 (1,050)
20 to 24 years	351,730 (6,993)	45,700 (260)	41,300 (280)	48,500 (380)	49,000 (1,050)	33,400 (1,320)	55,000 (320)	49,800 (340)	58,500 (460)	59,100 (1,270)	40,300 (1,590)
25 to 29 years	329,170 (7,167)	48,500 (280)	44,800 (330)	50,200 (400)	54,200 (970)	38,200 (2,440)	58,500 (330)	54,000 (400)	60,500 (480)	65,400 (1,170)	46,000 (2,940)
30 to 34 years	185,470 (5,488)	52,200 (350)	47,300 (630)	54,200 (440)	56,000 (1,130)	‡ (†)	62,900 (420)	57,000 (760)	65,400 (530)	67,500 (1,360)	‡ (†)
35 years or more	51,990 (3,006)	50,600 (670)	46,700 (1,360)	52,300 (920)	56,200 (2,800)	‡ (†)	61,300 (810)	56,300 (1,640)	63,000 (1,110)	67,800 (3,370)	‡ (†)

See notes at end of table.

Table 74. Average base salary for full-time teachers in public elementary and secondary schools, by highest degree earned and years of full-time teaching: Selected years, 1990–91 through 2003–04—Continued

Years of full-time teaching experience	Number of full-time teachers	Salary (current dollars)					Salary (constant 2006–07 dollars)[3]				
		Highest degree earned					Highest degree earned				
		All teachers[1]	Bachelor's degree	Master's degree	Education specialist[2]	Doctor's degree	All teachers[1]	Bachelor's degree	Master's degree	Education specialist[2]	Doctor's degree
1	2	3	4	5	6	7	8	9	10	11	12
2003–04											
Total...............	2,948,230 (28,203)	$44,400 (240)	$39,200 (300)	$49,400 (200)	$52,900 (460)	$53,700 (1,290)	$48,700 (270)	$43,000 (330)	$54,200 (220)	$58,100 (500)	$59,000 (1,420)
1 year or less...............	177,920 (17,391)	33,200 (380)	31,800 (340)	38,600 (730)	44,300 (5,030)	37,300 (1,690)	36,400 (420)	34,900 (380)	42,300 (800)	48,600 (5,520)	40,900 (1,850)
2 years...............	153,950 (17,695)	34,100 (280)	32,700 (330)	37,900 (650)	34,000 (1,300)	‡ (†)	37,400 (310)	35,900 (370)	41,600 (710)	37,300 (1,430)	‡ (†)
3 years...............	168,140 (9,009)	35,200 (350)	33,400 (280)	40,200 (680)	40,300 (3,170)	‡ (†)	38,600 (380)	36,700 (310)	44,100 (750)	44,300 (3,480)	‡ (†)
4 years...............	159,490 (6,723)	36,300 (270)	34,600 (280)	40,300 (530)	38,500 (1,800)	‡ (†)	39,800 (290)	37,900 (310)	44,200 (580)	42,300 (1,970)	‡ (†)
5 years...............	153,180 (6,194)	37,400 (400)	34,900 (320)	40,800 (760)	42,800 (1,960)	‡ (†)	41,000 (440)	38,300 (360)	44,800 (840)	47,000 (2,150)	‡ (†)
6 to 9 years...............	498,590 (13,859)	40,300 (200)	37,100 (210)	43,700 (300)	45,800 (1,310)	44,300 (2,320)	44,300 (220)	40,700 (230)	47,900 (330)	50,300 (1,440)	48,600 (2,550)
10 to 14 years...............	433,530 (14,595)	44,300 (260)	39,700 (270)	47,900 (390)	50,000 (960)	55,000 (3,580)	48,600 (280)	43,600 (290)	52,500 (430)	54,900 (1,050)	60,400 (3,930)
15 to 19 years...............	343,970 (9,606)	49,200 (360)	44,300 (480)	52,300 (470)	56,300 (1,350)	58,400 (3,440)	54,000 (390)	48,600 (530)	57,400 (510)	61,700 (1,480)	64,000 (3,780)
20 to 24 years...............	285,980 (8,434)	50,800 (360)	46,400 (370)	54,000 (580)	54,900 (1,000)	53,600 (3,530)	55,700 (400)	50,900 (410)	59,200 (640)	60,200 (1,100)	58,800 (3,870)
25 to 29 years...............	283,460 (11,809)	52,800 (280)	48,600 (490)	55,000 (410)	55,900 (980)	65,200 (3,520)	57,900 (310)	53,400 (540)	60,300 (450)	61,300 (1,070)	71,500 (3,870)
30 to 34 years...............	223,710 (11,435)	56,300 (430)	51,300 (610)	58,100 (570)	62,400 (1,390)	60,800 (2,660)	61,700 (470)	56,300 (660)	63,700 (620)	68,500 (1,520)	66,700 (2,920)
35 years or more...............	66,310 (3,427)	58,200 (750)	55,400 (1,300)	59,100 (980)	61,300 (2,220)	‡ (†)	63,900 (830)	60,700 (1,420)	64,900 (1,070)	67,200 (2,440)	‡ (†)

†Not applicable.
‡Reporting standards not met.
[1]Includes teachers with levels of education below the bachelor's degree (not shown separately).
[2]Includes certificate of advanced graduate studies.
[3]Constant dollars based on the Consumer Price Index, prepared by the Bureau of Labor Statistics, U.S. Department of Labor, adjusted to a school-year basis.

NOTE: This table includes regular full-time teachers only; it excludes other staff even when they have full-time teaching duties (regular part-time teachers, itinerant teachers, long-term substitutes, administrators, library media specialists, other professional staff, and support staff). Some data have been revised from previously published figures. Detail may not sum to totals because of rounding. Standard errors appear in parentheses.
SOURCE: U.S. Department of Education, National Center for Education Statistics, Schools and Staffing Survey (SASS), "Public Teacher Questionnaire," 1990–91, 1993–94, 1999–2000, and 2003–04; and "Charter Teacher Questionnaire," 1999–2000. (This table was prepared July 2007.)

Table 75. Average salaries for full-time teachers in public and private elementary and secondary schools, by selected characteristics: 2003–04

Selected characteristic	Total earned income	Base salary	Number of full-time teachers (in thousands)	School year supplemental contract[1] — Number of teachers (in thousands)	School year supplemental contract[1] — Supplemental salary	Supplemental contract during summer — Number of teachers (in thousands)	Supplemental contract during summer — Supplemental salary	Number of teachers with nonschool employment (in thousands) — Teaching or tutor	Number of teachers with nonschool employment (in thousands) — Education related	Number of teachers with nonschool employment (in thousands) — Not education related
1	2	3	4	5	6	7	8	9	10	11
Public schools										
Total..........	$47,700 (240)	$44,400 (240)	2,948.2 (28.20)	1,185.9 (19.67)	$2,700 (60)	605.2 (14.05)	$2,500 (60)	120.8 (5.18)	83.7 (4.06)	263.9 (6.67)
Sex										
Males..........	51,000 (370)	45,000 (330)	750.5 (12.74)	426.6 (10.40)	3,700 (70)	183.0 (7.28)	3,000 (80)	37.1 (2.89)	36.0 (1.96)	120.1 (4.40)
Females..........	46,600 (240)	44,100 (250)	2,197.7 (22.90)	759.3 (14.53)	2,200 (80)	422.2 (11.16)	2,300 (60)	83.7 (3.86)	47.8 (3.36)	143.7 (4.95)
Race/ethnicity										
White..........	47,800 (270)	44,500 (280)	2,439.3 (29.86)	994.0 (17.73)	2,800 (70)	467.5 (11.87)	2,400 (60)	104.3 (4.72)	73.0 (3.77)	229.0 (5.70)
Black..........	46,600 (420)	43,300 (410)	241.2 (9.63)	85.7 (4.46)	2,400 (140)	68.4 (4.93)	3,000 (170)	9.5 (1.04)	5.7 (1.00)	17.0 (1.88)
Hispanic..........	47,400 (660)	44,000 (600)	187.7 (10.36)	78.5 (6.78)	2,400 (230)	51.2 (5.42)	2,500 (120)	4.1 (0.98)	3.4 (0.81)	11.5 (1.86)
Asian..........	49,000 (740)	46,800 (770)	38.0 (2.37)	11.3 (1.09)	2,600 (310)	8.5 (1.10)	2,500 (190)	1.3 (0.33)	0.5 (0.11)	2.0 (0.43)
American Indian/Alaska Native..........	42,600 (1,110)	39,300 (1,020)	15.0 (1.16)	6.5 (0.71)	2,900 (600)	3.8 (0.73)	1,900 (240)	0.4 (0.15)	0.5 (0.29)	1.7 (0.38)
Pacific Islander..........	46,600 (1,450)	42,800 (1,220)	5.1 (0.68)	2.2 (0.47)	3,000 (780)	1.6 (0.30)	2,400 (280)	0.4 (0.19)	0.2 (0.08)	0.4 (0.12)
More than one race..........	45,600 (1,570)	42,600 (1,390)	21.9 (2.09)	7.7 (1.16)	2,500 (220)	4.1 (0.95)	2,400 (290)	0.8 (0.31)	0.4 (0.18)	2.2 (0.53)
Age										
Less than 30..........	37,800 (300)	34,600 (280)	493.2 (21.85)	228.1 (9.75)	2,300 (80)	126.6 (8.42)	2,400 (110)	22.2 (2.44)	12.0 (1.81)	51.4 (4.28)
30 to 39..........	43,800 (220)	40,300 (220)	724.5 (13.52)	324.8 (9.14)	2,900 (120)	154.7 (6.97)	2,400 (80)	27.6 (2.52)	19.4 (1.57)	65.3 (4.38)
40 to 49..........	48,700 (250)	45,400 (200)	756.5 (14.12)	294.9 (8.76)	2,900 (170)	145.6 (5.15)	2,500 (80)	32.7 (2.48)	25.7 (1.88)	68.2 (3.44)
50 or more..........	54,700 (250)	51,500 (230)	973.9 (27.38)	338.1 (11.50)	2,800 (100)	178.3 (8.03)	2,700 (90)	38.3 (2.82)	26.6 (2.94)	78.9 (3.04)
Years of full-time and part-time teaching experience										
1 year or less..........	36,500 (500)	32,600 (410)	151.6 (15.47)	53.0 (4.81)	1,800 (100)	28.7 (4.42)	3,300 (400)	4.6 (1.02)	3.0 (0.61)	19.0 (2.82)
2 to 4 years..........	37,800 (240)	34,800 (200)	464.1 (26.82)	197.4 (11.10)	2,300 (90)	115.2 (9.08)	2,400 (80)	17.6 (2.36)	10.7 (1.49)	45.2 (4.03)
5 to 9 years..........	42,700 (190)	39,400 (160)	641.1 (16.17)	284.3 (10.62)	2,600 (120)	148.4 (7.22)	2,400 (80)	29.7 (3.01)	17.0 (1.55)	64.3 (3.48)
10 to 14 years..........	47,000 (300)	43,800 (260)	438.6 (14.16)	178.3 (7.17)	2,900 (140)	88.9 (6.03)	2,300 (100)	20.2 (2.58)	11.8 (1.46)	33.3 (2.29)
15 to 19 years..........	51,900 (410)	48,700 (360)	346.2 (10.03)	133.2 (5.40)	2,800 (210)	56.7 (3.15)	2,500 (140)	13.3 (1.76)	11.2 (1.40)	26.6 (2.01)
20 or more years..........	56,800 (230)	53,400 (200)	906.0 (26.90)	339.7 (10.80)	3,100 (130)	167.3 (6.99)	2,600 (90)	35.5 (2.31)	30.0 (2.41)	75.5 (3.67)
Level										
Elementary..........	46,700 (330)	44,400 (330)	1,522.7 (23.56)	461.2 (12.53)	2,100 (120)	304.7 (10.02)	2,200 (70)	52.9 (3.21)	32.7 (3.44)	106.2 (5.70)
Secondary..........	48,700 (260)	44,300 (250)	1,425.6 (24.05)	724.7 (15.05)	3,100 (70)	300.6 (8.62)	2,800 (70)	67.9 (3.86)	51.0 (2.26)	157.7 (4.79)

See notes at end of table.

Table 75. Average salaries for full-time teachers in public and private elementary and secondary schools, by selected characteristics: 2003–04—Continued

| Selected characteristic | Total earned income | | Base salary | | Number of full-time teachers (in thousands) | | School year supplemental contract[1] | | | | Supplemental contract during summer | | | | Number of teachers with nonschool employment (in thousands) | | | | | |
| | | | | | | | Number of teachers (in thousands) | | Supplemental salary | | Number of teachers (in thousands) | | Supplemental salary | | Teaching or tutor | | Education related | | Not education related | |
1	2		3		4		5		6		7		8		9		10		11	
Private schools																				
Total	$34,700	(1,910)	$31,700	(1,630)	366.5	(11.87)	84.6	(7.07)	$2,400	(130)	74.3	(3.97)	$3,100	(250)	24.5	(2.10)	12.7	(2.01)	37.1	(3.73)
Sex																				
Males	40,800	(650)	35,200	(580)	84.6	(6.15)	30.6	(2.45)	2,800	(200)	24.3	(2.25)	3,700	(320)	7.4	(0.92)	4.1	(0.68)	16.0	(1.80)
Females	32,800	(2,260)	30,600	(2,020)	281.9	(13.40)	53.9	(5.23)	2,200	(190)	50.0	(3.49)	2,800	(320)	17.1	(1.59)	8.6	(1.55)	21.2	(3.50)
Race/ethnicity																				
White	34,600	(2,140)	31,700	(1,880)	322.1	(11.91)	75.5	(6.49)	2,300	(140)	61.0	(3.77)	3,100	(310)	21.6	(1.95)	11.6	(1.99)	33.4	(3.71)
Black	31,500	(1,240)	27,900	(1,000)	15.7	(2.46)	2.3	(0.48)	2,200	(450)	5.0	(1.14)	3,000	(780)	0.7	(0.25)	0.5	(0.25)	1.3	(0.43)
Hispanic	35,700	(1,660)	32,000	(1,270)	16.6	(2.01)	4.0	(0.79)	3,600	(930)	4.7	(0.87)	3,600	(390)	1.5	(0.39)	0.3	(0.17)	1.5	(0.45)
Asian	37,300	(3,350)	34,500	(2,650)	6.8	(0.84)	1.1	(0.27)	1,900	(490)	2.1	(0.42)	3,200	(860)	0.4	(0.24)	0.2	(0.25)	0.5	(0.20)
American Indian/Alaska Native	35,800	(4,230)	31,900	(3,150)	1.7	(1.94)	0.5	(0.34)	†	(†)	0.5	(0.55)	†	(†)	0.1	(0.04)	‡	(†)	0.1	(0.07)
Pacific Islander	‡	(†)	‡	(†)	‡	(†)	‡	(†)	‡	(†)	‡	(†)	‡	(†)	‡	(†)	‡	(†)	‡	(†)
More than one race	38,600	(3,410)	36,900	(3,460)	2.7	(1.20)	1.0	(0.31)	‡	(†)	0.4	(0.20)	‡	(†)	0.1	(0.10)	‡	(†)	0.3	(0.14)
Age																				
Less than 30	29,100	(640)	25,900	(520)	74.6	(3.20)	20.2	(1.64)	2,300	(250)	19.6	(1.60)	2,700	(180)	6.6	(0.92)	2.7	(0.41)	10.0	(1.19)
30 to 39	33,200	(740)	30,100	(720)	80.3	(5.65)	19.7	(1.76)	2,500	(280)	17.6	(1.95)	3,100	(290)	5.3	(0.99)	2.9	(0.54)	8.7	(2.97)
40 to 49	34,600	(1,770)	31,900	(1,420)	88.4	(4.94)	21.5	(2.82)	2,400	(230)	17.8	(3.94)	3,000	(660)	4.9	(0.66)	2.7	(0.78)	8.4	(1.17)
50 or more	39,000	(4,480)	36,000	(3,990)	123.2	(12.45)	23.1	(2.91)	2,400	(240)	19.4	(2.19)	3,800	(380)	7.7	(1.22)	4.4	(0.87)	10.0	(1.42)
Years of full-time and part-time teaching experience																				
1 year or less	28,100	(1,100)	24,700	(1,040)	24.6	(3.43)	4.7	(0.68)	2,000	(320)	5.6	(0.81)	3,400	(540)	‡	(†)	‡	(†)	3.6	(2.36)
2 to 4 years	29,400	(2,930)	26,100	(2,430)	78.4	(14.11)	18.8	(1.67)	2,000	(310)	18.8	(1.67)	2,900	(220)	5.7	(0.83)	2.5	(0.42)	10.2	(1.19)
5 to 9 years	32,100	(880)	29,500	(780)	77.6	(3.94)	17.7	(2.10)	2,600	(340)	17.0	(1.91)	2,800	(200)	6.4	(1.02)	3.1	(0.70)	7.4	(1.70)
10 to 14 years	34,600	(3,070)	31,800	(2,680)	53.0	(5.17)	13.9	(2.34)	2,400	(280)	10.4	(1.46)	3,400	(450)	3.4	(0.76)	1.9	(0.50)	4.3	(0.84)
15 to 19 years	37,900	(4,030)	35,300	(3,690)	42.6	(3.78)	10.5	(1.61)	2,600	(340)	8.8	(3.73)	3,100	(1,110)	2.2	(0.47)	‡	(†)	3.5	(0.74)
20 or more years	41,700	(920)	38,500	(680)	90.3	(7.21)	19.0	(2.47)	2,700	(300)	13.7	(1.59)	3,600	(480)	6.0	(1.06)	3.2	(0.79)	8.2	(1.17)
Level																				
Elementary	31,400	(2,640)	29,200	(2,380)	209.9	(13.87)	30.1	(3.72)	2,200	(220)	37.0	(3.14)	2,900	(410)	12.3	(1.29)	6.2	(0.98)	17.5	(3.08)
Secondary	39,000	(730)	35,000	(570)	156.5	(9.42)	54.5	(4.01)	2,500	(180)	37.3	(3.37)	3,300	(250)	12.2	(1.35)	6.5	(1.22)	19.7	(1.87)

†Not applicable.
‡Reporting standards not met.
[1]Includes additional compensation for extracurricular instruction or other additional activities, and bonuses and state supplements.
NOTE: This table includes regular full-time teachers only; it excludes other staff even when they have full-time teaching duties (regular part-time teachers, itinerant teachers, long-term substitutes, administrators, library media specialists, other professional staff, and support staff). Race categories exclude persons of Hispanic ethnicity. Standard errors appear in parentheses. Detail may not sum to totals because of rounding, missing values in cells with too few cases to report, and survey item nonresponse.
SOURCE: U.S. Department of Education, National Center for Education Statistics, Schools and Staffing Survey (SASS), "Public Teacher Questionnaire" and "Private Teacher Questionnaire," 2003–04. (This table was prepared July 2006.)

Table 76. Average base salary for full-time public elementary and secondary school teachers with a bachelor's degree as their highest degree, by years of full-time teaching experience and state: 1993–94, 1999–2000, and 2003–04

State	1993–94			1999–2000			2003–04					
	Total	2 or fewer years	Over 20 years	Total	2 or fewer years	Over 20 years	Total	2 or fewer years	3 to 5 years	6 to 10 years	11 to 20 years	Over 20 years
1	2	3	4	5	6	7	8	9	10	11	12	13
United States	$30,150 (151)	$23,330 (98)	$38,090 (205)	$35,310 (116)	$28,450 (109)	$44,130 (230)	$39,200 (300)	$32,230 (290)	$34,240 (151)	$37,330 (204)	$42,540 (265)	$49,130 (327)
Alabama	24,450 (151)	22,220 (209)	26,110 (391)	31,300 (210)	28,280 (142)	33,840 (568)	32,750 (256)	29,640 (291)	30,930 (414)	32,590 (537)	36,180 (613)	37,610 (663)
Alaska	42,620 (308)	32,180 (251)	49,930 (569)	42,170 (269)	34,110 (290)	52,080 (480)	46,160 (720)	37,290 (1,113)	39,820 (638)	44,460 (968)	51,770 (1,019)	58,760 (943)
Arizona	28,050 (347)	22,590 (168)	35,180 (1,127)	30,110 (491)	25,020 (303)	39,120 (1,273)	33,370 (556)	29,510 (408)	30,920 (474)	32,180 (511)	36,150 (870)	44,060 (1,469)
Arkansas	24,970 (199)	20,680 (222)	28,350 (367)	29,810 (345)	25,780 (699)	34,110 (732)	32,710 (328)	26,590 (694)	29,350 (412)	32,110 (472)	35,440 (564)	38,080 (803)
California	37,330 (412)	27,710 (470)	44,920 (424)	41,930 (301)	32,820 (321)	53,250 (656)	51,210 (704)	38,920 (679)	42,830 (666)	49,460 (635)	57,860 (833)	63,110 (1,045)
Colorado	27,590 (391)	21,190 (318)	34,960 (958)	32,180 (428)	25,400 (252)	41,340 (776)	36,140 (699)	30,570 (534)	31,610 (488)	35,260 (875)	41,850 (1,215)	45,480 (2,188)
Connecticut	40,510 (645)	†	50,470 (814)	38,530 (883)	32,030 (344)	†	48,380 (1,997)	37,800 (820)	40,590 (1,951)	44,360 (3,208)	†	†
Delaware	31,400 (375)	‡	†	37,620 (893)	‡	†	41,210 (991)	‡	35,880 (887)	‡	48,350 (994)	†
District of Columbia	37,690 (645)	†	†	40,980 (593)	†	†	48,350 (1,290)	†	40,530 (1,228)	†	56,670 (1,684)	†
Florida	28,970 (229)	23,570 (308)	35,950 (514)	33,650 (407)	27,440 (314)	41,990 (570)	36,460 (624)	31,140 (612)	30,650 (367)	32,250 (345)	38,490 (650)	47,040 (843)
Georgia	25,650 (215)	22,100 (441)	29,940 (507)	33,610 (373)	29,410 (287)	38,730 (747)	37,160 (490)	32,220 (424)	34,590 (621)	37,540 (574)	40,840 (808)	45,020 (1,010)
Hawaii	34,060 (460)	24,940 (277)	43,990 (428)	36,710 (533)	27,370 (299)	49,690 (691)	39,250 (867)	32,620 (781)	35,430 (794)	37,430 (759)	42,240 (858)	52,650 (1,779)
Idaho	24,610 (252)	19,080 (281)	30,160 (573)	31,500 (208)	22,880 (245)	38,310 (294)	36,150 (627)	26,060 (579)	28,010 (730)	34,190 (843)	39,390 (757)	45,330 (794)
Illinois	29,480 (277)	23,430 (658)	36,520 (563)	35,250 (563)	28,230 (398)	43,610 (1,139)	38,730 (791)	33,180 (1,047)	34,470 (718)	36,190 (888)	42,290 (2,250)	49,120 (1,797)
Indiana	25,400 (329)	22,770 (194)	†	30,760 (296)	27,360 (186)	†	34,600 (640)	30,270 (337)	32,630 (599)	35,700 (643)	43,650 (1,343)	‡
Iowa	24,950 (319)	19,530 (242)	27,960 (664)	28,910 (279)	23,150 (253)	33,470 (430)	33,600 (696)	26,140 (457)	30,200 (3,349)	31,610 (827)	35,280 (813)	37,580 (840)
Kansas	25,930 (135)	22,850 (229)	29,330 (423)	29,430 (264)	26,110 (261)	33,250 (636)	32,290 (325)	28,500 (447)	29,940 (376)	30,810 (513)	33,770 (631)	36,990 (597)
Kentucky	24,910 (457)	21,620 (243)	†	27,720 (358)	24,650 (168)	†	31,610 (463)	28,490 (195)	30,030 (466)	33,360 (785)	‡	‡
Louisiana	22,520 (159)	18,470 (326)	27,590 (498)	28,020 (476)	24,620 (943)	32,330 (1,002)	32,590 (483)	28,380 (693)	28,450 (513)	31,340 (431)	34,540 (616)	39,200 (646)
Maine	28,550 (330)	20,080 (350)	33,670 (270)	34,690 (775)	27,390 (2,511)	37,570 (531)	36,650 (605)	27,300 (1,078)	28,310 (860)	32,670 (846)	38,590 (794)	43,490 (1,062)
Maryland	33,520 (476)	25,510 (239)	45,180 (456)	37,760 (683)	28,900 (337)	50,340 (597)	42,960 (1,313)	34,100 (381)	36,740 (502)	40,290 (764)	49,290 (3,755)	62,750 (2,717)
Massachusetts	34,340 (309)	24,690 (514)	37,410 (342)	40,410 (464)	29,950 (454)	46,600 (591)	43,930 (964)	35,830 (1,124)	38,620 (700)	44,450 (2,205)	48,570 (1,045)	54,780 (1,331)
Michigan	37,170 (670)	26,700 (947)	45,000 (1,000)	39,950 (838)	30,760 (457)	50,030 (608)	45,230 (682)	31,560 (693)	39,450 (911)	44,540 (1,078)	54,200 (1,107)	55,950 (1,245)
Minnesota	31,010 (419)	23,540 (629)	36,660 (652)	35,270 (685)	28,770 (783)	44,160 (962)	39,030 (566)	31,560 (761)	33,220 (541)	35,560 (469)	43,560 (660)	47,350 (783)
Mississippi	22,640 (106)	19,660 (138)	25,220 (170)	28,000 (186)	24,080 (218)	31,490 (300)	31,890 (425)	27,110 (306)	28,490 (316)	30,440 (669)	33,430 (557)	37,990 (555)
Missouri	23,510 (286)	20,340 (345)	28,110 (821)	28,020 (373)	24,940 (513)	30,550 (1,525)	31,340 (547)	27,220 (593)	29,540 (542)	31,440 (953)	34,190 (1,312)	36,040 (1,953)
Montana	24,070 (199)	18,720 (156)	29,940 (422)	27,920 (256)	21,080 (252)	34,110 (521)	31,870 (522)	23,190 (382)	25,240 (505)	28,110 (538)	34,620 (685)	38,530 (837)
Nebraska	22,580 (388)	18,760 (361)	25,440 (790)	26,000 (254)	21,940 (215)	28,950 (619)	30,300 (435)	26,720 (590)	27,970 (478)	28,970 (522)	32,590 (803)	33,690 (1,329)
Nevada	29,350 (285)	23,900 (291)	37,480 (755)	34,470 (434)	27,550 (293)	45,270 (895)	35,970 (700)	29,220 (632)	32,020 (420)	36,350 (529)	42,040 (1,042)	46,470 (1,091)
New Hampshire	31,280 (437)	‡	38,150 (519)	34,210 (542)	25,790 (974)	40,480 (609)	38,800 (644)	28,880 (649)	31,460 (509)	36,260 (878)	42,850 (1,070)	46,470 (1,091)
New Jersey	41,330 (744)	29,730 (479)	52,340 (770)	46,720 (653)	33,810 (290)	61,340 (698)	49,780 (1,049)	38,810 (616)	40,180 (878)	41,420 (614)	51,340 (1,569)	67,380 (1,456)
New Mexico	25,260 (280)	21,680 (280)	31,400 (383)	29,290 (363)	25,700 (321)	38,260 (1,106)	34,310 (470)	28,830 (752)	31,270 (426)	31,780 (439)	36,960 (559)	42,300 (930)
New York	39,650 (1,152)	27,790 (360)	52,140 (693)	41,600 (1,094)	33,250 (654)	55,630 (2,100)	42,630 (1,074)	37,410 (1,058)	37,860 (838)	‡	36,970 (561)	61,240 (1,827)
North Carolina	26,010 (220)	20,810 (182)	32,520 (273)	31,920 (331)	25,380 (510)	40,563 (500)	33,650 (479)	26,930 (566)	29,020 (633)	32,560 (465)	32,420 (553)	43,830 (730)
North Dakota	22,450 (193)	17,830 (282)	26,060 (512)	25,910 (279)	20,640 (297)	29,730 (461)	30,870 (490)	23,810 (613)	26,600 (669)	28,780 (617)	30,170 (381)	33,500 (660)
Ohio	30,370 (399)	22,010 (312)	35,420 (653)	35,120 (583)	25,730 (400)	43,640 (1,019)	41,600 (891)	30,430 (474)	33,460 (626)	39,340 (666)	47,660 (878)	52,220 (1,061)
Oklahoma	24,880 (108)	22,190 (198)	28,500 (325)	27,400 (224)	24,510 (179)	31,770 (566)	31,190 (211)	27,330 (456)	28,650 (276)	29,600 (158)	31,970 (236)	35,700 (260)
Oregon	31,310 (440)	22,440 (470)	36,960 (769)	38,370 (613)	27,350 (418)	44,180 (1,299)	42,430 (865)	33,030 (630)	34,170 (1,154)	38,200 (1,628)	45,670 (768)	51,340 (880)
Pennsylvania	37,260 (523)	26,690 (435)	44,790 (634)	42,620 (826)	28,940 (894)	54,710 (932)	44,250 (963)	‡	37,190 (683)	41,360 (1,062)	47,890 (1,351)	57,450 (993)
Rhode Island	38,000 (522)	‡	42,530 (268)	43,900 (357)	‡	52,310 (259)	49,360 (834)	‡	40,930 (885)	48,890 (1,514)	†	58,910 (741)
South Carolina	25,120 (286)	20,440 (151)	30,550 (526)	29,820 (300)	25,220 (175)	37,380 (538)	34,950 (483)	28,610 (1,161)	29,810 (284)	32,810 (423)	38,810 (552)	42,630 (682)
South Dakota	22,550 (186)	18,410 (303)	25,440 (386)	26,000 (230)	23,160 (826)	28,670 (307)	29,360 (301)	24,980 (437)	26,350 (289)	27,700 (536)	30,170 (381)	32,420 (493)
Tennessee	25,650 (291)	21,880 (297)	28,350 (557)	30,830 (378)	27,740 (386)	34,670 (1,188)	34,510 (432)	29,690 (624)	32,110 (922)	32,880 (591)	37,010 (794)	39,100 (756)
Texas	26,950 (295)	21,820 (295)	33,310 (476)	34,770 (386)	29,010 (322)	42,140 (458)	38,140 (278)	33,440 (564)	34,870 (362)	36,140 (315)	39,880 (333)	46,710 (455)
Utah	25,800 (195)	19,170 (223)	31,220 (356)	31,810 (375)	24,020 (271)	39,790 (691)	35,160 (525)	26,140 (259)	29,050 (511)	33,740 (327)	40,820 (753)	45,390 (679)
Vermont	29,750 (494)	‡	36,030 (873)	33,470 (733)	25,530 (671)	41,060 (1,235)	39,040 (840)	‡	31,850 (775)	36,680 (3,075)	39,490 (935)	46,720 (919)
Virginia	29,410 (378)	24,940 (310)	35,160 (584)	34,060 (424)	28,420 (311)	42,370 (1,270)	37,520 (583)	31,590 (556)	33,240 (570)	35,390 (734)	37,840 (767)	45,760 (1,585)
Washington	33,150 (490)	23,190 (273)	40,640 (390)	36,330 (359)	26,770 (233)	45,480 (368)	40,040 (916)	31,610 (610)	32,640 (801)	36,470 (563)	45,630 (1,170)	49,840 (1,000)
West Virginia	26,980 (183)	‡	29,090 (272)	30,040 (246)	‡	32,630 (284)	32,980 (344)	‡	29,320 (603)	31,240 (562)	34,030 (500)	35,910 (320)
Wisconsin	31,490 (351)	24,220 (249)	36,130 (773)	35,470 (331)	27,800 (194)	42,710 (696)	37,150 (634)	29,630 (479)	32,650 (658)	35,360 (697)	42,880 (829)	44,200 (1,291)
Wyoming	27,310 (247)	20,900 (137)	32,170 (448)	29,470 (248)	23,760 (266)	34,210 (487)	34,080 (576)	28,270 (1,408)	29,290 (685)	30,850 (724)	36,680 (1,120)	39,190 (1,900)

†Not applicable.
‡Reporting standards not met.
NOTE: This table includes regular full-time teachers only; it excludes other staff even when they have full-time teaching duties (regular part-time teachers, itinerant teachers, long-term substitutes, administrators, library media specialists, other professional staff, and support staff). Standard errors appear in parentheses.

SOURCE: U.S. Department of Education, National Center for Education Statistics, Schools and Staffing Survey (SASS), "Public School Teacher Questionnaire," 1993–94, 1999–2000, and 2003–04; and "Public Charter School Teacher Questionnaire," 1999–2000. (This table was prepared July 2006.)

Table 77. Average base salary for full-time public elementary and secondary school teachers with a master's degree as their highest degree, by years of full-time teaching experience and state: 1993–94, 1999–2000, and 2003–04

State	1993–94 Total	1993–94 6 to 10 years	1993–94 Over 20 years	1999–2000 Total	1999–2000 6 to 10 years	1999–2000 Over 20 years	2003–04 Total	2003–04 5 or fewer years	2003–04 6 to 10 years	2003–04 11 to 20 years	2003–04 Over 20 years
1	2	3	4	5	6	7	8	9	10	11	12
United States	$38,480 (154)	$32,600 (243)	$43,590 (242)	$44,700 (174)	$38,350 (237)	$50,760 (262)	$49,440 (202)	$39,790 (373)	$44,410 (281)	$50,770 (291)	$55,960 (303)
Alabama	28,920 (156)	28,160 (262)	29,930 (253)	36,930 (145)	35,790 (298)	38,870 (215)	39,730 (383)	34,140 (547)	38,370 (329)	40,980 (365)	42,870 (779)
Alaska	50,900 (373)	44,950 (826)	54,420 (526)	51,170 (662)	43,940 (576)	58,670 (860)	53,720 (1,005)	43,450 (1,112)	50,560 (1,420)	57,170 (1,064)	57,760 (1,387)
Arizona	35,280 (302)	29,840 (346)	40,670 (458)	38,150 (465)	33,130 (568)	45,050 (691)	41,310 (531)	34,210 (928)	37,850 (477)	43,230 (878)	46,850 (1,268)
Arkansas	29,070 (322)	25,360 (495)	30,890 (592)	34,830 (483)	‡ (†)	38,740 (666)	39,480 (639)	33,580 (907)	33,970 (1,210)	38,030 (737)	44,920 (912)
California	43,420 (636)	38,190 (617)	47,760 (439)	50,800 (537)	44,820 (766)	56,960 (572)	59,160 (761)	44,980 (909)	54,150 (819)	62,550 (1,089)	69,990 (999)
Colorado	36,580 (364)	30,050 (381)	41,650 (664)	41,200 (445)	37,350 (766)	47,410 (721)	47,960 (641)	38,020 (945)	42,330 (1,012)	49,560 (1,098)	55,610 (1,307)
Connecticut	49,310 (416)	43,420 (1,028)	54,360 (386)	50,620 (590)	43,240 (795)	59,920 (304)	57,340 (934)	43,290 (1,120)	50,720 (810)	61,590 (1,488)	66,970 (743)
Delaware	42,350 (535)	‡ (†)	46,460 (480)	48,120 (910)	‡ (†)	55,520 (1,366)	54,670 (913)	‡ (†)	46,820 (1,061)	57,730 (1,174)	63,070 (1,148)
District of Columbia	45,360 (828)	‡ (†)	50,710 (228)	51,040 (472)	‡ (†)	54,450 (451)	55,450 (1,568)	43,680 (1,813)	‡ (†)	60,080 (1,467)	63,570 (2,537)
Florida	33,150 (487)	28,830 (494)	38,010 (645)	39,330 (476)	32,340 (468)	44,940 (583)	42,120 (784)	33,570 (834)	35,420 (1,016)	41,340 (939)	49,860 (1,027)
Georgia	31,890 (227)	28,930 (453)	36,040 (329)	41,950 (524)	38,130 (581)	47,230 (475)	47,540 (752)	40,490 (1,121)	44,100 (418)	50,200 (1,090)	52,370 (1,322)
Hawaii	36,430 (731)	‡ (†)	43,230 (886)	41,280 (524)	‡ (†)	‡ (†)	42,910 (967)	37,550 (1,179)	‡ (†)	45,940 (1,377)	‡ (†)
Idaho	31,590 (440)	‡ (†)	34,140 (654)	42,380 (772)	‡ (†)	48,950 (1,559)	44,140 (857)	‡ (†)	38,380 (1,648)	45,930 (1,166)	48,580 (1,249)
Illinois	42,400 (588)	34,390 (692)	47,370 (886)	47,770 (953)	41,850 (1,166)	55,180 (1,087)	54,110 (1,253)	42,590 (2,237)	46,450 (1,114)	54,320 (2,228)	61,560 (1,612)
Indiana	38,040 (292)	31,170 (450)	41,560 (279)	45,480 (413)	36,090 (451)	49,420 (362)	49,760 (670)	‡ (†)	38,000 (1,355)	49,000 (1,004)	53,650 (576)
Iowa	32,220 (571)	27,710 (339)	34,820 (763)	38,010 (494)	33,960 (1,468)	39,340 (714)	41,880 (608)	‡ (†)	37,140 (1,001)	42,940 (1,159)	43,880 (900)
Kansas	32,560 (314)	27,180 (283)	35,800 (485)	36,140 (428)	31,990 (622)	38,480 (502)	40,400 (755)	35,310 (1,064)	34,940 (963)	40,120 (1,667)	43,700 (912)
Kentucky	31,390 (396)	22,800 (555)	35,140 (359)	36,380 (310)	32,810 (305)	41,260 (481)	40,570 (457)	‡ (†)	37,440 (1,813)	41,040 (555)	45,610 (913)
Louisiana	27,300 (262)	28,440 (653)	29,500 (361)	33,120 (806)	‡ (†)	35,150 (1,051)	38,000 (558)	‡ (†)	‡ (†)	36,750 (769)	40,860 (828)
Maine	33,060 (499)	‡ (†)	36,150 (255)	38,770 (458)	‡ (†)	42,340 (442)	42,460 (677)	29,830 (991)	36,100 (594)	43,780 (753)	47,860 (840)
Maryland	42,340 (406)	36,410 (689)	46,080 (575)	45,930 (1,055)	38,280 (736)	51,740 (900)	53,190 (1,307)	41,540 (1,215)	49,710 (4,001)	51,790 (1,561)	63,410 (1,462)
Massachusetts	39,710 (254)	34,790 (791)	42,330 (247)	47,630 (370)	41,960 (680)	52,390 (334)	53,500 (714)	42,360 (694)	48,280 (823)	56,090 (1,168)	61,270 (670)
Michigan	47,660 (488)	40,280 (1,312)	49,900 (482)	53,050 (651)	46,020 (968)	59,050 (1,034)	59,680 (906)	47,760 (2,452)	53,680 (1,813)	61,720 (1,073)	65,900 (1,194)
Minnesota	40,710 (552)	33,300 (1,049)	44,690 (475)	46,050 (674)	40,420 (1,136)	51,980 (1,175)	49,590 (731)	38,670 (953)	43,490 (621)	51,850 (1,136)	57,090 (1,137)
Mississippi	26,600 (200)	24,200 (382)	28,890 (301)	34,170 (326)	29,040 (271)	38,460 (348)	38,460 (479)	30,810 (1,013)	33,710 (594)	43,780 (629)	44,060 (571)
Missouri	33,180 (625)	27,370 (763)	38,290 (1,002)	37,400 (747)	31,650 (1,028)	44,150 (1,067)	40,880 (761)	34,170 (1,020)	37,090 (1,071)	40,160 (1,011)	46,110 (1,604)
Montana	32,270 (423)	26,250 (684)	35,390 (393)	35,960 (728)	28,230 (508)	41,050 (1,237)	39,650 (885)	29,930 (1,322)	‡ (†)	40,740 (796)	44,380 (1,218)
Nebraska	30,290 (538)	27,380 (1,109)	32,430 (903)	33,540 (536)	28,580 (667)	37,420 (936)	39,990 (784)	36,130 (904)	35,740 (1,248)	38,950 (1,233)	49,900 (1,023)
Nevada	38,570 (353)	‡ (†)	42,530 (571)	43,350 (429)	‡ (†)	49,500 (575)	45,770 (1,083)	35,580 (1,185)	44,120 (3,641)	48,050 (1,174)	49,900 (922)
New Hampshire	36,970 (505)	31,540 (889)	40,880 (595)	41,310 (689)	‡ (†)	46,210 (660)	45,140 (977)	‡ (†)	‡ (†)	49,800 (1,003)	52,340 (636)
New Jersey	50,950 (883)	39,430 (1,132)	58,160 (821)	57,410 (709)	‡ (†)	66,640 (670)	60,200 (1,571)	43,310 (799)	45,980 (962)	58,500 (2,452)	76,020 (1,723)
New Mexico	28,400 (281)	25,290 (476)	33,180 (477)	35,570 (539)	30,590 (835)	40,060 (742)	40,100 (810)	33,060 (1,387)	34,170 (572)	41,290 (759)	44,440 (1,013)
New York	47,440 (840)	37,930 (892)	58,710 (1,127)	53,130 (923)	42,590 (884)	66,450 (1,150)	56,650 (746)	45,710 (995)	50,450 (1,119)	61,290 (1,401)	67,470 (1,703)
North Carolina	29,180 (306)	25,350 (343)	33,390 (624)	36,810 (542)	33,780 (725)	41,890 (756)	42,720 (641)	33,670 (1,342)	36,440 (778)	43,620 (1,043)	48,390 (644)
North Dakota	28,520 (730)	‡ (†)	31,040 (1,162)	32,920 (559)	‡ (†)	35,380 (828)	39,710 (789)	‡ (†)	‡ (†)	39,620 (1,242)	43,130 (1,234)
Ohio	37,960 (550)	31,420 (1,307)	41,490 (766)	43,420 (585)	35,820 (1,054)	48,710 (836)	50,090 (689)	39,170 (1,098)	43,810 (692)	53,480 (1,108)	55,920 (852)
Oklahoma	28,510 (186)	25,430 (339)	30,460 (286)	31,990 (261)	28,260 (333)	34,280 (458)	34,580 (319)	29,280 (818)	31,370 (329)	33,700 (401)	38,060 (351)
Oregon	36,930 (471)	32,240 (522)	40,940 (714)	42,180 (588)	37,840 (764)	47,990 (1,031)	45,850 (647)	37,040 (770)	41,580 (1,019)	50,150 (1,019)	54,690 (808)
Pennsylvania	44,830 (816)	36,630 (1,649)	48,550 (875)	50,790 (1,027)	43,650 (1,633)	57,220 (1,154)	54,800 (925)	39,530 (1,277)	46,210 (1,322)	56,640 (2,337)	64,100 (910)
Rhode Island	41,630 (303)	‡ (†)	43,200 (261)	48,610 (204)	‡ (†)	52,300 (169)	55,110 (909)	‡ (†)	49,330 (2,504)	58,990 (1,214)	60,180 (1,080)
South Carolina	31,860 (208)	27,530 (286)	34,620 (234)	38,390 (528)	32,850 (657)	41,660 (960)	42,340 (625)	34,380 (1,594)	37,780 (814)	41,760 (997)	49,410 (679)
South Dakota	28,110 (449)	‡ (†)	29,320 (660)	32,800 (443)	‡ (†)	35,910 (727)	37,670 (801)	33,590 (747)	31,200 (971)	40,160 (1,346)	41,740 (1,162)
Tennessee	30,270 (350)	27,710 (409)	32,540 (455)	35,610 (414)	31,750 (533)	38,470 (648)	39,620 (543)	36,660 (1,126)	36,120 (835)	41,810 (1,182)	42,860 (892)
Texas	31,610 (277)	27,390 (692)	35,650 (529)	40,280 (453)	33,280 (548)	44,840 (764)	43,370 (723)	‡ (†)	37,590 (872)	43,480 (867)	49,650 (881)
Utah	32,590 (371)	‡ (†)	35,560 (281)	39,880 (586)	‡ (†)	44,960 (1,332)	43,370 (636)	‡ (†)	36,950 (1,534)	43,380 (922)	48,730 (598)
Vermont	36,770 (594)	‡ (†)	39,190 (730)	37,260 (668)	‡ (†)	42,340 (1,073)	44,740 (926)	‡ (†)	41,140 (1,342)	45,800 (871)	51,090 (1,076)
Virginia	33,740 (579)	‡ (†)	38,610 (760)	40,230 (668)	35,880 (668)	46,640 (1,263)	43,860 (948)	36,710 (808)	43,230 (829)	43,450 (1,725)	50,370 (1,581)
Washington	38,270 (398)	33,990 (713)	42,780 (525)	43,160 (364)	36,450 (533)	48,630 (566)	47,970 (500)	37,990 (737)	‡ (†)	51,300 (687)	55,050 (731)
West Virginia	32,130 (195)	28,230 (424)	33,970 (230)	36,590 (226)	‡ (†)	38,830 (240)	40,440 (716)	34,060 (1,895)	33,580 (668)	38,820 (611)	42,840 (1,081)
Wisconsin	40,920 (486)	35,470 (560)	42,670 (739)	46,420 (512)	39,570 (669)	49,520 (588)	47,750 (713)	35,510 (1,461)	40,870 (956)	48,330 (920)	53,980 (817)
Wyoming	32,490 (371)	‡ (†)	34,060 (663)	36,120 (497)	‡ (†)	38,480 (810)	41,610 (1,014)	‡ (†)	‡ (†)	40,480 (1,225)	44,440 (1,557)

†Not applicable.
‡Reporting standards not met.
NOTE: This table includes regular full-time teachers only; it excludes other staff even when they have full-time teaching duties (regular part-time teachers, itinerant teachers, long-term substitutes, administrators, library media specialists, other professional staff, and support staff). Standard errors appear in parentheses.

SOURCE: U.S. Department of Education, National Center for Education Statistics, Schools and Staffing Survey (SASS), "Public School Teacher Questionnaire," 1993–94, 1999–2000, and 2003–04; and "Public Charter School Teacher Questionnaire," 1999–2000. (This table was prepared July 2006.)

Table 78. Estimated average annual salary of teachers in public elementary and secondary schools: Selected years, 1959–60 through 2006–07

School year	Current dollars					Constant 2006–07 dollars[2]		
	All teachers	Elementary teachers	Secondary teachers	Wage and salary accruals per full-time-equivalent (FTE) employee[1]	Ratio of average teachers' salary to accruals per FTE employee	All teachers	Elementary teachers	Secondary teachers
1	2	3	4	5	6	7	8	9
1959–60	$4,995	$4,815	$5,276	$4,749	1.05	$34,703	$33,452	$36,655
1961–62	5,515	5,340	5,775	5,063	1.09	37,455	36,266	39,221
1963–64	5,995	5,805	6,266	5,478	1.09	39,680	38,422	41,474
1965–66	6,485	6,279	6,761	5,934	1.09	41,489	40,171	43,255
1967–68	7,423	7,208	7,692	6,533	1.14	44,558	43,267	46,172
1969–70	8,626	8,412	8,891	7,486	1.15	46,615	45,459	48,047
1970–71	9,268	9,021	9,568	7,998	1.16	47,626	46,357	49,168
1971–72	9,705	9,424	10,031	8,521	1.14	48,145	46,751	49,762
1972–73	10,174	9,893	10,507	9,056	1.12	48,517	47,177	50,105
1973–74	10,770	10,507	11,077	9,667	1.11	47,154	46,003	48,498
1974–75	11,641	11,334	12,000	10,411	1.12	45,883	44,673	47,298
1975–76	12,600	12,280	12,937	11,194	1.13	46,380	45,202	47,620
1976–77	13,354	12,989	13,776	11,971	1.12	46,447	45,177	47,915
1977–78	14,198	13,845	14,602	12,815	1.11	46,275	45,125	47,592
1978–79	15,032	14,681	15,450	13,825	1.09	44,797	43,751	46,043
1979–80	15,970	15,569	16,459	15,088	1.06	41,993	40,939	43,279
1980–81	17,644	17,230	18,142	16,520	1.07	41,579	40,604	42,753
1981–82	19,274	18,853	19,805	17,866	1.08	41,809	40,896	42,961
1982–83	20,695	20,227	21,291	18,950	1.09	43,043	42,069	44,282
1983–84	21,935	21,487	22,554	19,878	1.10	43,993	43,095	45,235
1984–85	23,600	23,200	24,187	20,819	1.13	45,550	44,778	46,683
1985–86	25,199	24,718	25,846	21,732	1.16	47,273	46,370	48,486
1986–87	26,569	26,057	27,244	22,650	1.17	48,760	47,821	49,999
1987–88	28,034	27,519	28,798	23,705	1.18	49,402	48,494	50,748
1988–89	29,564	29,022	30,218	24,655	1.20	49,798	48,885	50,900
1989–90	31,367	30,832	32,049	25,647	1.22	50,429	49,569	51,525
1990–91	33,084	32,490	33,896	26,794	1.23	50,432	49,526	51,670
1991–92	34,063	33,479	34,827	27,999	1.22	50,312	49,450	51,441
1992–93	35,029	34,350	35,880	29,058	1.21	50,172	49,199	51,391
1993–94	35,737	35,233	36,566	29,811	1.20	49,893	49,190	51,051
1994–95	36,675	36,088	37,523	30,606	1.20	49,776	48,980	50,927
1995–96	37,642	37,138	38,397	31,561	1.19	49,736	49,070	50,733
1996–97	38,443	38,039	39,184	32,789	1.17	49,385	48,866	50,337
1997–98	39,350	39,002	39,944	34,346	1.15	49,664	49,225	50,414
1998–99	40,544	40,165	41,203	35,978	1.13	50,301	49,830	51,118
1999–2000	41,807	41,306	42,546	37,800	1.11	50,412	49,808	51,303
2000–01	43,378	42,910	44,053	39,257	1.10	50,574	50,028	51,361
2001–02	44,655	44,177	45,310	40,031	1.12	51,157	50,609	51,907
2002–03	45,688	45,385	46,141	41,089	1.11	51,215	50,875	51,723
2003–04	46,605	46,275	46,682	42,617	1.09	51,124	50,762	51,209
2004–05	47,659	47,242	47,860	44,225	1.08	50,753	50,309	50,967
2005–06	49,026	48,641	49,261	45,991	1.07	50,294	49,899	50,535
2006–07	50,816	50,684	51,081	48,018	1.06	50,816	50,684	51,081

[1]Calendar-year data from the U.S. Department of Commerce, Bureau of Economic Analysis, have been converted to a school-year basis by averaging the two appropriate calendar years in each case.
[2]Constant dollars based on the Consumer Price Index, prepared by the Bureau of Labor Statistics, U.S. Department of Labor, adjusted to a school-year basis.

NOTE: Some data have been revised from previously published figures. Standard errors are not available for these estimates, which are based on state reports.
SOURCE: National Education Association, *Estimates of School Statistics*, 1959–60 through 2006–07; and unpublished tabulations. U.S. Department of Commerce, Bureau of Economic Analysis, National Income and Product Accounts, retrieved August 28, 2008, from http://www.bea.gov/national/nipaweb/SelectTable.asp. (This table was prepared September 2008.)

Table 79. Estimated average annual salary of teachers in public elementary and secondary schools, by state or jurisdiction: Selected years, 1969–70 through 2006–07

State	Current dollars							Constant 2006–07 dollars[1]							Percent change, 1999–2000 to 2006–07
	1969–70	1979–80	1989–90	1999–2000	2004–05	2005–06	2006–07	1969–70	1979–80	1989–90	1999–2000	2004–05	2005–06	2006–07	
1	2	3	4	5	6	7	8	9	10	11	12	13	14	15	16
United States...	$8,626	$15,970	$31,367	$41,807	$47,659	$49,026	$50,816	$46,615	$41,993	$50,429	$50,412	$50,753	$50,294	$50,816	0.8
Alabama	6,818	13,060	24,828	36,689	38,186	40,347	43,389	36,845	34,341	39,916	44,241	40,665	41,390	43,389	-1.9
Alaska	10,560	27,210	43,153	46,462	52,424	53,553	54,658	57,067	71,549	69,377	56,026	55,828	54,938	54,658	-2.4
Arizona	8,711	15,054	29,402	36,902	42,905	44,672	45,941	47,075	39,585	47,270	44,498	45,691	45,827	45,941	3.2
Arkansas	6,307	12,299	22,352	33,386	40,495	42,768	44,245	34,083	32,340	35,935	40,258	43,124	43,874	44,245	9.9
California	10,315	18,020	37,998	47,680	57,604	59,825	63,640	55,743	47,384	61,089	57,494	61,344	61,372	63,640	10.7
Colorado	7,761	16,205	30,758	38,163	43,949	44,439	45,833	41,941	42,611	49,450	46,018	46,803	45,588	45,833	-0.4
Connecticut	9,262	16,229	40,461	51,780	57,737	59,304	60,822	50,052	42,674	65,049	62,438	61,486	60,838	60,822	-2.6
Delaware	9,015	16,148	33,377	44,435	50,595	54,264	54,680	48,717	42,461	53,660	53,581	53,880	55,667	54,680	2.1
District of Columbia	10,285	22,190	38,402	47,076	58,456	59,000	59,000	55,581	58,349	61,739	56,766	62,251	60,526	59,000	3.9
Florida	8,412	14,149	28,803	36,722	41,590	43,302	45,308	45,459	37,205	46,307	44,281	44,290	44,422	45,308	2.3
Georgia	7,276	13,853	28,006	41,023	46,526	48,300	49,905	39,320	36,427	45,025	49,467	49,547	49,549	49,905	0.9
Hawaii	9,453	19,920	32,047	40,578	46,149	49,292	51,922	51,084	52,380	51,522	48,930	49,145	50,567	51,922	6.1
Idaho	6,890	13,611	23,861	35,547	40,864	41,150	42,798	37,234	35,790	38,361	42,864	43,517	42,214	42,798	-0.2
Illinois	9,569	17,601	32,794	46,486	57,539	58,686	58,246	51,711	46,282	52,723	56,054	61,275	60,204	58,246	3.9
Indiana	8,833	15,599	30,902	41,850	46,583	47,255	47,831	47,734	41,018	49,681	50,464	49,608	48,477	47,831	-5.2
Iowa	8,355	15,203	26,747	35,678	39,284	41,083	43,130	45,151	39,976	43,001	43,022	41,835	42,145	43,130	0.3
Kansas	7,612	13,690	28,744	34,981	39,345	41,467	43,334	41,136	35,998	46,212	42,181	41,900	42,539	43,334	2.7
Kentucky	6,953	14,520	26,292	36,380	40,959	42,592	43,646	37,574	38,181	42,270	43,868	43,618	43,693	43,646	-0.5
Louisiana	7,028	13,760	24,300	33,109	39,022	40,029	42,816	37,980	36,182	39,067	39,924	41,556	41,064	42,816	7.2
Maine	7,572	13,071	26,881	35,561	39,610	40,737	41,596	40,919	34,370	43,217	42,881	42,182	41,791	41,596	-3.0
Maryland	9,383	17,558	36,319	44,048	52,331	54,333	56,927	50,706	46,169	58,390	53,115	55,729	55,738	56,927	7.2
Massachusetts	8,764	17,253	34,712	46,580	54,701	56,369	58,624	47,361	45,367	55,807	56,168	58,253	57,827	58,624	4.4
Michigan	9,826	19,663	37,072	49,044	53,959	54,739	54,895	53,100	51,704	59,601	59,139	57,462	56,155	54,895	-7.2
Minnesota	8,658	15,912	32,190	39,802	46,906	48,489	49,634	46,788	41,841	51,752	47,995	49,952	49,743	49,634	3.4
Mississippi	5,798	11,850	24,292	31,857	38,212	40,576	40,182	31,333	31,160	39,054	38,414	40,693	41,625	40,182	4.6
Missouri	7,799	13,682	27,094	35,656	39,090	40,462	41,839	42,146	35,977	43,559	42,995	41,628	41,508	41,839	-2.7
Montana	7,606	14,537	25,081	32,121	38,485	39,832	41,225	41,103	38,225	40,323	38,733	40,984	40,862	41,225	6.4
Nebraska	7,375	13,516	25,522	33,237	39,456	40,382	42,044	39,855	35,540	41,032	40,078	42,018	41,426	42,044	4.9
Nevada	9,215	16,295	30,590	39,390	43,394	44,426	45,342	49,798	42,848	49,180	47,498	46,211	45,575	45,342	-4.5
New Hampshire	7,771	13,017	28,986	37,734	43,941	45,263	46,527	41,995	34,228	46,601	45,501	46,794	46,434	46,527	2.3
New Jersey	9,130	17,161	35,676	52,015	56,519	58,156	59,920	49,339	45,125	57,356	62,722	60,189	59,660	59,920	-4.5
New Mexico	7,796	14,887	24,756	32,554	39,391	41,637	42,780	42,130	39,146	39,800	39,255	41,949	42,714	42,780	9.0
New York	10,336	19,812	38,925	51,020	56,200	57,354	58,537	55,856	52,096	62,580	61,522	59,849	58,837	58,537	-4.9
North Carolina	7,494	14,117	27,883	39,404	43,348	43,922	46,410	40,498	37,121	44,828	47,515	46,163	45,058	46,410	-2.3
North Dakota	6,696	13,263	23,016	29,863	36,695	37,764	38,822	36,185	34,875	37,003	36,010	39,078	38,741	38,822	7.8
Ohio	8,300	15,269	31,218	41,436	48,692	50,314	51,937	44,854	40,150	50,189	49,965	51,853	51,615	51,937	3.9
Oklahoma	6,882	13,107	23,070	31,298	37,879	38,772	42,379	37,191	34,465	37,090	37,740	40,338	39,775	42,379	12.3
Oregon	8,818	16,266	30,840	42,336	48,320	50,044	50,911	47,653	42,772	49,581	51,050	51,457	51,338	50,911	-0.3
Pennsylvania	8,858	16,515	33,338	48,321	53,258	54,027	54,970	47,869	43,426	53,598	58,267	56,716	55,424	54,970	-5.7
Rhode Island	8,776	18,002	36,057	47,041	53,473	54,730	55,956	47,426	47,336	57,969	56,724	56,945	56,145	55,956	-1.4
South Carolina	6,927	13,063	27,217	36,081	42,189	43,011	44,133	37,434	34,349	43,757	43,508	44,928	44,123	44,133	1.4
South Dakota	6,403	12,348	21,300	29,071	34,040	34,709	35,378	34,602	32,469	34,244	35,055	36,250	35,607	35,378	0.9
Tennessee	7,050	13,972	27,052	36,328	42,076	42,537	43,816	38,099	36,740	43,492	43,806	44,808	43,637	43,816	#
Texas	7,255	14,132	27,496	37,567	41,011	41,744	44,897	39,206	37,160	44,205	45,300	43,674	42,824	44,897	-0.9
Utah	7,644	14,909	23,686	34,946	39,456	40,007	40,566	41,309	39,203	38,080	42,139	42,018	41,042	40,566	-3.7
Vermont	7,968	12,484	29,012	37,758	44,535	46,622	48,370	43,059	32,827	46,643	45,530	47,427	47,828	48,370	6.2
Virginia	8,070	14,060	30,938	38,744	42,768	43,823	44,727	43,611	36,971	49,739	46,719	45,545	44,956	44,727	-4.3
Washington	9,225	18,820	30,457	41,043	45,718	46,326	47,882	49,852	49,487	48,966	49,491	48,686	47,524	47,882	-3.3
West Virginia	7,650	13,710	22,842	35,009	38,360	38,284	40,531	41,341	36,051	36,723	42,215	40,851	39,274	40,531	-4.0
Wisconsin	8,963	16,006	31,921	41,153	44,299	46,390	47,901	48,436	42,088	51,319	49,624	47,175	47,590	47,901	-3.5
Wyoming	8,232	16,012	28,141	34,127	40,497	43,225	50,692	44,486	42,104	45,242	41,152	43,126	44,343	50,692	23.2

#Rounds to zero.
[1]Constant dollars based on the Consumer Price Index (CPI), prepared by the Bureau of Labor Statistics, U.S. Department of Labor, adjusted to a school-year basis. The CPI does not account for differences in inflation rates from state to state.

NOTE: Some data have been revised from previously published figures. Standard errors are not available for these estimates, which are based on state reports.
SOURCE: National Education Association, *Estimates of School Statistics*, 1969–70 through 2006–07. (This table was prepared July 2008.)

Table 80. Staff employed in public elementary and secondary school systems, by functional area: Selected years, 1949–50 through fall 2006

[In full-time equivalents]

School year	Total	School district administrative staff			Instructional staff						Support staff[1]
		Total	Officials and administrators	Instruction coordinators	Total	Principals and assistant principals	Teachers	Instructional aides	Librarians	Guidance counselors	
1	2	3	4	5	6	7	8	9	10	11	12
1949–50[2]	1,300,031	33,642	23,868	9,774	956,808	43,137	913,671	(3)	(3)	(3)	309,582
1959–60[2]	2,089,283	42,423	28,648	13,775	1,448,931	63,554	1,353,372	(3)	17,363	14,643	597,929
1969–70[2]	3,360,763	65,282	33,745	31,537	2,255,707	90,593	2,016,244	57,418	42,689	48,763	1,039,774
Fall 1980[2]	4,168,286	78,784	58,230	20,554	2,729,023	107,061	2,184,216	325,755	48,018	63,973	1,360,479
Fall 1990	4,494,076	75,868	—	—	3,051,404	127,417	2,398,169	395,959	49,909	79,950	1,366,804
Fall 1991	4,559,359	76,084	—	—	3,103,939	129,304	2,432,243	410,538	49,917	81,937	1,379,336
Fall 1992	4,708,286	78,414	45,712	32,702	3,139,544	121,936	2,458,956	427,279	50,324	81,049	1,490,328
Fall 1993	4,808,080	80,862	47,614	33,248	3,209,381	121,486	2,503,901	450,519	50,511	82,964	1,517,837
Fall 1994	4,904,757	81,867	48,827	33,040	3,280,752	120,017	2,551,875	473,348	50,668	84,844	1,542,138
Fall 1995	4,994,358	82,998	49,315	33,683	3,351,528	120,629	2,598,220	494,289	50,862	87,528	1,559,832
Fall 1996	5,091,205	81,975	48,480	33,495	3,447,580	123,734	2,667,419	516,356	51,464	88,607	1,561,650
Fall 1997	5,266,415	85,267	50,432	34,835	3,572,955	126,129	2,746,157	557,453	52,142	91,074	1,608,193
Fall 1998	5,419,181	88,939	52,975	35,964	3,693,630	129,317	2,830,286	588,108	52,805	93,114	1,636,612
Fall 1999	5,632,004	94,134	55,467	38,667	3,819,057	137,199	2,910,633	621,942	53,659	95,624	1,718,813
Fall 2000	5,709,753	97,270	57,837	39,433	3,876,628	141,792	2,941,461	641,392	54,246	97,737	1,735,855
Fall 2001	5,904,195	109,526	63,517	46,009	3,989,211	160,543	2,999,528	674,741	54,350	100,049	1,805,458
Fall 2002	5,954,661	110,777	62,781	47,996	4,016,963	164,171	3,034,123	663,552	54,205	100,912	1,826,921
Fall 2003	5,953,667	107,483	63,418	44,065	4,052,739	165,233	3,048,652	685,118	54,349	99,387	1,793,445
Fall 2004	6,058,174	111,832	64,101	47,731	4,120,063	165,657	3,090,925	707,514	54,145	101,822	1,826,279
Fall 2005	6,130,686	121,164	62,464	58,700	4,151,236	156,454	3,143,003	693,792	54,057	103,930	1,858,286
Fall 2006	6,163,962	125,063	59,737	65,326	4,198,932	154,630	3,180,396	705,638	54,445	103,823	1,839,967
					Percentage distribution						
1949–50[2]	100.0	2.6	1.8	0.8	73.6	3.3	70.3	(3)	(3)	(3)	23.8
1959–60[2]	100.0	2.0	1.4	0.7	69.4	3.0	64.8	(3)	0.8	0.7	28.6
1969–70[2]	100.0	1.9	1.0	0.9	67.1	2.7	60.0	1.7	1.3	1.5	30.9
Fall 1980[2]	100.0	1.9	1.4	0.5	65.5	2.6	52.4	7.8	1.2	1.5	32.6
Fall 1990	100.0	1.7	—	—	67.9	2.8	53.4	8.8	1.1	1.8	30.4
Fall 1991	100.0	1.7	—	—	68.1	2.8	53.3	9.0	1.1	1.8	30.3
Fall 1992	100.0	1.7	1.0	0.7	66.7	2.6	52.2	9.1	1.1	1.7	31.7
Fall 1993	100.0	1.7	1.0	0.7	66.7	2.5	52.1	9.4	1.1	1.7	31.6
Fall 1994	100.0	1.7	1.0	0.7	66.9	2.4	52.0	9.7	1.0	1.7	31.4
Fall 1995	100.0	1.7	1.0	0.7	67.1	2.4	52.0	9.9	1.0	1.8	31.2
Fall 1996	100.0	1.6	1.0	0.7	67.7	2.4	52.4	10.1	1.0	1.7	30.7
Fall 1997	100.0	1.6	1.0	0.7	67.8	2.4	52.1	10.6	1.0	1.7	30.5
Fall 1998	100.0	1.6	1.0	0.7	68.2	2.4	52.2	10.9	1.0	1.7	30.2
Fall 1999	100.0	1.7	1.0	0.7	67.8	2.4	51.7	11.0	1.0	1.7	30.5
Fall 2000	100.0	1.7	1.0	0.7	67.9	2.5	51.5	11.2	1.0	1.7	30.4
Fall 2001	100.0	1.9	1.1	0.8	67.6	2.7	50.8	11.4	0.9	1.7	30.6
Fall 2002	100.0	1.9	1.1	0.8	67.5	2.8	51.0	11.1	0.9	1.7	30.7
Fall 2003	100.0	1.8	1.1	0.7	68.1	2.8	51.2	11.5	0.9	1.7	30.1
Fall 2004	100.0	1.8	1.1	0.8	68.0	2.7	51.0	11.7	0.9	1.7	30.1
Fall 2005	100.0	2.0	1.0	1.0	67.7	2.6	51.3	11.3	0.9	1.7	30.3
Fall 2006	100.0	2.0	1.0	1.1	68.1	2.5	51.6	11.4	0.9	1.7	29.9
					Pupils per staff member						
1949–50[2]	19.3	746.4	1,052.1	2,569.2	26.2	582.1	27.5	(3)	(3)	(3)	81.1
1959–60[2]	16.8	829.3	1,228.1	2,554.1	24.3	553.6	26.0	(3)	2,026.3	2,402.7	58.8
1969–70[2]	13.6	697.7	1,349.8	1,444.3	20.2	502.8	22.6	793.3	1,067.0	934.1	43.8
Fall 1980[2]	9.8	518.9	702.0	1,988.8	15.0	381.8	18.7	125.5	851.3	639.0	30.0
Fall 1990	9.2	543.3	—	—	13.5	323.5	17.2	104.1	825.8	515.5	30.2
Fall 1991	9.2	552.6	—	—	13.5	325.2	17.3	102.4	842.3	513.2	30.5
Fall 1992	9.1	546.1	936.8	1,309.5	13.6	351.2	17.4	100.2	851.0	528.4	28.7
Fall 1993	9.0	537.5	912.9	1,307.3	13.5	357.8	17.4	96.5	860.5	523.9	28.6
Fall 1994	9.0	538.8	903.4	1,335.1	13.4	367.5	17.3	93.2	870.6	519.9	28.6
Fall 1995	9.0	540.3	909.3	1,331.2	13.4	371.7	17.3	90.7	881.6	512.3	28.7
Fall 1996	9.0	556.4	940.8	1,361.7	13.2	368.6	17.1	88.3	886.3	514.8	29.2
Fall 1997	8.8	541.0	914.6	1,324.2	12.9	365.7	16.8	82.7	884.6	506.5	28.7
Fall 1998	8.6	523.3	878.5	1,294.0	12.6	359.9	16.4	79.1	881.3	499.8	28.4
Fall 1999	8.3	497.8	844.8	1,211.8	12.3	341.5	16.1	75.3	873.2	490.0	27.3
Fall 2000	8.3	485.3	816.1	1,197.1	12.2	332.9	16.0	73.6	870.2	483.0	27.2
Fall 2001	8.1	435.3	750.5	1,036.1	12.0	296.9	15.9	70.7	877.1	476.5	26.4
Fall 2002	8.1	435.0	767.5	1,003.9	12.0	293.5	15.9	72.6	888.9	477.5	26.4
Fall 2003	8.2	451.6	765.4	1,101.6	12.0	293.8	15.9	70.8	893.1	488.4	27.1
Fall 2004	8.1	436.3	761.2	1,022.3	11.8	294.6	15.8	69.0	901.2	479.2	26.7
Fall 2005	8.0	405.3	786.3	836.7	11.8	313.9	15.6	70.8	908.5	472.6	26.4
Fall 2006	8.0	394.2	825.3	754.7	11.7	318.8	15.5	69.9	905.5	474.8	26.8

—Not available.

[1]Includes school district administrative support staff, school and library support staff, student support staff, and other support services staff.

[2]Because of classification revisions, categories other than teachers, principals, librarians, and guidance counselors are only roughly comparable to figures for years after 1980.

[3]Data included in column 8.

NOTE: Data for 1949–50 through 1969–70 are cumulative for the entire school year, rather than counts as of the fall of the year. Some data have been revised from previously published figures. Detail may not sum to totals because of rounding.

SOURCE: U.S. Department of Education, National Center for Education Statistics, *Statistics of State School Systems*, various years; *Statistics of Public Elementary and Secondary Schools*, various years; and Common Core of Data (CCD), "State Nonfiscal Survey of Public Elementary/Secondary Education," 1986–87 through 2006–07. (This table was prepared August 2008.)

Table 81. Staff employed in public elementary and secondary school systems, by type of assignment and state or jurisdiction: Fall 2006

[In full-time equivalents]

State or jurisdiction	Total	School district staff			School staff						Student support staff	Other support services staff
		Officials and administrators	Administrative support staff	Instruction coordinators	Principals and assistant principals	School and library support staff	Teachers	Instructional aides	Guidance counselors	Librarians		
1	2	3	4	5	6	7	8	9	10	11	12	13
United States[1]	6,163,962	59,737	177,232	65,326	154,630	295,641	3,180,396	705,638	103,823	54,445	254,647	1,112,447
Alabama[2,3,4]	109,816	281	1,185	970	3,043	8,065	56,134	6,648	1,842	1,424	2,805	27,419
Alaska[2]	16,853	493	716	189	743	1,199	7,903	2,274	285	167	479	2,405
Arizona	102,390	446	699	143	2,405	7,660	52,625	15,039	1,426	841	7,467	13,639
Arkansas	71,616	697	2,065	898	1,728	2,553	35,089	7,660	1,445	997	4,276	14,208
California[5,6]	579,825	2,991	22,961	6,854	14,328	37,065	307,110	68,071	6,500	1,255	15,340	97,350
Colorado	97,364	1,038	4,225	1,933	2,636	5,831	46,973	13,464	1,934	853	4,910	13,567
Connecticut	86,709	923	3,046	2,672	2,627	2,530	39,115	13,374	1,380	794	3,517	16,731
Delaware	15,403	313	347	308	403	417	8,038	1,536	279	131	788	2,843
District of Columbia[7]	12,194	131	692	107	393	411	5,394	1,349	100	41	600	2,976
Florida	321,600	2,021	15,094	709	7,731	16,706	162,851	29,642	6,043	2,798	12,688	65,317
Georgia	227,616	2,267	2,770	625	6,722	10,164	113,597	26,765	3,650	2,265	7,424	51,367
Hawaii	21,061	215	287	611	531	1,188	11,271	2,171	669	272	1,353	2,493
Idaho	26,312	132	556	254	730	1,139	14,770	2,838	593	164	544	4,592
Illinois[3,8,9]	221,553	42	2,302	845	3,838	11,442	140,988	30,173	1,807	2,208	7,094	20,814
Indiana	134,681	1,078	724	1,694	3,103	8,603	61,315	19,925	1,893	955	2,136	33,255
Iowa	69,690	988	708	441	2,236	4,337	35,653	10,115	1,192	525	1,908	11,587
Kansas	53,762	480	97	78	1,853	2,713	35,297	8,465	1,139	905	1,512	1,223
Kentucky	98,812	925	2,479	934	2,979	5,842	43,371	14,216	1,439	1,114	2,339	23,174
Louisiana	95,226	325	2,501	1,855	2,675	3,522	45,951	10,452	3,007	1,194	3,303	20,441
Maine	36,785	616	904	298	1,043	1,892	16,826	6,544	636	254	1,723	6,049
Maryland	113,474	3,091	2,206	1,793	3,634	6,525	58,443	10,175	2,365	1,203	4,146	19,893
Massachusetts[8]	136,563	1,721	4,899	952	3,908	5,534	73,157	21,276	2,181	927	7,618	14,390
Michigan	212,320	3,361	1,235	3,478	5,105	13,815	98,037	23,492	2,732	1,284	11,695	48,086
Minnesota	106,701	1,959	2,361	1,528	1,988	4,878	51,880	15,447	1,052	881	11,668	13,059
Mississippi	68,815	1,001	1,991	697	1,862	2,596	32,351	8,573	1,034	971	2,918	14,821
Missouri[9]	127,020	1,430	8,661	990	3,136	521	67,398	12,558	2,684	1,635	15,114	12,893
Montana[10,11]	19,023	171	487	174	534	191	10,398	2,014	449	378	713	3,514
Nebraska	42,938	588	826	791	1,030	1,776	21,459	5,378	790	563	1,284	8,453
Nevada[9,10]	33,949	197	974	75	1,036	1,686	22,908	4,159	856	355	661	1,042
New Hampshire	32,174	586	674	238	515	944	15,515	6,772	812	317	638	5,163
New Jersey[8,9,10,11]	205,372	1,438	6,212	2,808	1,341	8,859	112,301	25,974	2,651	1,819	13,964	28,005
New Mexico	46,551	723	1,776	248	1,134	2,210	22,016	5,261	720	288	3,820	8,355
New York	373,360	2,979	18,953	2,212	8,803	5,736	218,879	36,293	6,862	3,295	12,210	57,138
North Carolina	196,657	6,508	472	2,105	5,093	10,844	104,412	29,142	3,546	2,292	5,704	26,539
North Dakota	15,157	476	149	127	397	492	8,007	1,925	255	192	517	2,620
Ohio	242,574	2,135	14,625	1,773	5,216	14,876	110,390	18,025	3,814	1,449	19,000	51,271
Oklahoma	81,831	621	3,116	490	2,184	4,162	42,206	7,755	1,628	1,063	3,320	15,286
Oregon	51,067	236	3,470	338	1,641	4,956	26,443	4,396	1,029	403	865	7,290
Pennsylvania[3,8,9,10,11]	241,024	1,998	7,214	1,595	4,759	11,374	123,375	26,399	4,484	2,234	12,425	45,167
Rhode Island[3,6,8,9,10,11]	17,902	62	325	72	473	567	11,381	2,452	407	297	421	1,445
South Carolina	74,709	815	148	697	3,370	3,988	49,733	9,757	1,804	1,152	1,334	1,911
South Dakota	17,297	127	311	80	394	523	9,070	3,366	286	140	194	2,806
Tennessee	123,218	427	765	922	3,163	4,471	62,176	15,262	2,069	1,593	1,685	30,685
Texas	616,155	5,685	18,943	3,154	19,184	25,219	311,649	61,677	10,536	4,986	20,448	134,674
Utah	47,365	439	684	855	1,130	2,669	23,640	7,520	727	270	1,017	8,414
Vermont	19,232	145	431	315	446	947	8,859	4,330	437	258	924	2,140
Virginia	239,815	1,591	4,614	12,203	4,742	9,478	105,039	19,530	4,222	2,006	7,081	69,309
Washington	102,948	1,188	1,685	519	2,790	5,327	53,743	10,120	2,031	1,278	2,910	21,357
West Virginia[8,10]	39,217	170	1,667	166	1,096	1,632	19,414	3,416	1,706	365	1,713	7,872
Wisconsin	105,033	1,147	2,599	1,188	2,432	4,672	59,089	10,359	1,942	1,250	5,841	14,514
Wyoming	15,233	320	401	325	347	894	6,757	2,114	453	144	593	2,885
Bureau of Indian Education	—	—	—	—	—	—	—	—	—	—	—	—
DoD, overseas	8,338	65	72	91	235	789	5,204	486	237	138	247	774
DoD, domestic	3,574	58	10	31	102	291	2,033	179	97	68	89	616
Other jurisdictions												
American Samoa	1,869	54	63	69	67	157	971	107	42	20	218	101
Guam	—	—	—	—	—	—	—	—	—	—	—	—
Northern Marianas	1,160	5	77	8	33	63	579	229	19	1	40	106
Puerto Rico	71,962	570	63	431	1,395	5,425	40,163	230	932	1,109	4,628	17,016
U.S. Virgin Islands	3,020	59	161	43	83	72	1,531	362	89	33	170	417

—Not available.
[1]Includes imputations for undercounts in states as designated in footnotes 2 through 11.
[2]Includes imputations for instruction coordinators.
[3]Includes imputations for instructional aides.
[4]Includes imputations for guidance counselors.
[5]Includes imputations for prekindergarten teachers.
[6]Includes imputations for student support staff.
[7]Includes imputations for all staff, except guidance counselors and teachers.

[8]Includes imputations for library support staff.
[9]Includes imputations for school support staff.
[10]Includes imputations for administrative support staff.
[11]Includes imputations for other support services staff.
NOTE: DoD = Department of Defense.
SOURCE: U.S. Department of Education, National Center for Education Statistics, Common Core of Data (CCD), "State Nonfiscal Survey of Public Elementary/Secondary Education," 2006–07. (This table was prepared October 2008.)

Table 82. Staff employed in public elementary and secondary school systems, by type of assignment and state or jurisdiction: Fall 2005

[In full-time equivalents]

State or jurisdiction	Total	School district staff			School staff						Student support staff	Other support services staff
		Officials and administrators	Administrative support staff	Instruction coordinators	Principals and assistant principals	School and library support staff	Teachers	Instructional aides	Guidance counselors	Librarians		
1	2	3	4	5	6	7	8	9	10	11	12	13
United States[1]	6,130,686	62,464	182,005	58,700	156,454	289,682	3,143,003	693,792	103,930	54,057	230,549	1,156,050
Alabama	103,775	255	3,745	999	3,003	5,173	57,757	6,768	1,814	1,404	2,387	20,470
Alaska[2]	17,954	425	928	195	775	1,539	7,912	2,243	277	180	462	3,018
Arizona	100,162	453	555	158	2,311	7,866	51,376	14,520	1,373	824	7,403	13,323
Arkansas	70,673	670	1,766	672	1,677	1,699	32,997	7,381	1,441	1,014	4,908	16,448
California[3]	579,118	2,858	22,884	6,657	13,946	36,341	309,222	67,073	6,998	1,214	15,904	96,021
Colorado	93,148	1,100	2,561	1,550	2,477	5,090	45,841	10,527	1,424	841	4,009	17,728
Connecticut	84,669	1,363	1,679	412	2,318	3,684	39,687	12,488	1,399	815	4,736	16,088
Delaware	15,473	321	351	285	382	456	7,998	1,701	282	132	674	2,891
District of Columbia[4]	12,372	134	700	110	403	416	5,481	1,373	101	41	622	2,991
Florida	314,219	1,903	15,170	699	7,289	16,846	158,962	29,121	5,584	2,783	12,121	63,741
Georgia	218,965	2,217	2,739	551	6,374	9,907	108,535	25,512	3,536	2,216	7,004	50,374
Hawaii	21,059	212	284	573	493	1,252	11,226	2,158	672	292	1,363	2,534
Idaho	26,018	135	524	249	715	1,147	14,521	2,840	594	166	535	4,592
Illinois[5,6]	251,769	3,817	6,174	1,251	6,555	11,608	133,857	30,719	3,172	2,193	8,862	43,561
Indiana	133,096	1,029	760	1,681	3,026	8,492	60,592	19,830	1,804	963	2,016	32,903
Iowa	69,080	990	715	468	2,182	4,521	35,181	9,707	1,169	537	2,508	11,102
Kansas	65,537	1,265	870	132	1,738	2,672	33,608	7,500	1,135	925	3,197	12,495
Kentucky	97,937	857	2,445	911	2,276	5,941	42,413	14,096	1,456	1,111	3,098	23,333
Louisiana	92,612	311	2,340	1,772	2,553	3,359	44,660	10,319	2,955	1,150	3,028	20,165
Maine	35,249	662	695	348	952	1,753	16,684	6,046	633	261	1,430	5,785
Maryland	111,215	904	1,117	1,367	3,397	4,612	56,685	10,529	2,300	1,182	3,121	26,001
Massachusetts[7]	138,781	1,611	4,906	933	3,903	5,645	73,596	20,596	2,141	942	6,923	17,585
Michigan[3]	204,764	3,224	1,246	3,369	5,104	14,830	98,069	25,255	2,726	1,336	8,427	41,178
Minnesota	104,489	2,061	2,333	1,552	1,986	4,841	51,107	15,112	1,034	878	10,968	12,617
Mississippi	67,659	1,000	1,902	736	1,794	2,525	31,433	8,658	1,023	970	2,957	14,661
Missouri	128,794	1,360	8,465	961	3,093	516	67,076	12,332	2,635	1,632	4,591	26,133
Montana[6]	19,611	165	493	178	529	886	10,369	1,965	439	371	684	3,532
Nebraska	41,166	583	832	491	1,023	1,660	21,359	4,749	777	554	1,137	8,001
Nevada[8]	32,345	271	985	213	980	1,711	21,744	3,802	794	356	820	669
New Hampshire	32,022	552	645	220	513	927	15,536	6,712	826	305	649	5,137
New Jersey[9]	211,893	1,453	6,284	2,704	4,037	8,972	112,673	26,444	2,312	1,465	17,402	28,147
New Mexico	47,940	665	1,714	228	1,240	2,294	22,021	5,464	774	305	2,698	10,537
New York	373,504	2,981	18,954	2,220	8,806	5,739	218,989	36,293	6,865	3,296	12,219	57,142
North Carolina	182,107	1,725	3,612	1,005	4,950	6,810	95,664	28,725	3,646	2,340	5,703	27,927
North Dakota	15,128	481	161	121	393	499	8,003	1,876	275	200	525	2,594
Ohio	238,977	7,894	12,251	555	4,710	19,629	117,982	17,800	3,840	1,556	4,262	48,498
Oklahoma	81,857	628	3,185	494	2,186	4,229	41,833	7,868	1,586	1,047	3,258	15,543
Oregon	60,349	802	1,699	591	1,716	3,980	28,346	9,950	1,324	421	2,525	8,995
Pennsylvania	240,409	1,937	7,298	1,531	4,752	11,537	122,397	26,877	4,404	2,232	12,048	45,396
Rhode Island[2,3,5]	24,267	139	329	73	1,404	575	14,180	2,496	2,541	328	437	1,765
South Carolina[10]	67,992	301	2,677	718	3,371	3,792	48,212	3,614	1,775	1,144	1,764	624
South Dakota	19,018	447	315	376	404	531	9,129	3,427	319	143	1,107	2,820
Tennessee	114,171	319	2,310	492	3,509	4,742	59,596	13,621	2,023	1,569	1,632	24,358
Texas	598,513	5,216	18,013	3,007	18,407	24,192	302,425	61,268	10,251	4,907	19,858	130,969
Utah	45,821	390	708	795	1,083	2,602	22,993	7,292	686	268	978	8,026
Vermont	19,024	140	405	317	445	915	8,851	4,259	431	225	844	2,192
Virginia	233,898	1,610	5,004	11,571	4,621	10,705	103,944	18,965	3,331	2,001	6,803	65,343
Washington	113,845	927	1,766	429	2,826	3,956	53,508	10,191	2,011	1,253	2,883	34,095
West Virginia	38,152	451	1,686	372	1,046	454	19,940	3,280	693	381	1,634	8,215
Wisconsin	105,564	936	2,429	1,252	2,445	4,723	60,127	10,382	1,930	1,254	4,980	15,106
Wyoming	14,526	314	396	156	336	891	6,706	2,068	399	134	445	2,681
Bureau of Indian Education	—	—	—	—	—	—	—	—	—	—	—	—
DoD, overseas	9,099	66	76	89	253	822	5,726	537	300	151	287	792
DoD, domestic	3,671	58	10	31	102	359	2,033	179	97	97	89	616
Other jurisdictions												
American Samoa	1,446	62	14	23	67	51	989	41	33	20	82	64
Guam	3,455	16	164	105	59	308	1,804	662	44	13	65	215
Northern Marianas	1,234	7	76	10	34	69	614	249	18	1	57	99
Puerto Rico	75,023	1,687	70	423	1,489	4,685	42,036	247	1,016	1,118	3,742	18,510
U.S. Virgin Islands	2,664	77	121	8	85	80	1,434	284	79	23	174	299

—Not available.
[1]Includes imputations for undercounts in designated states.
[2]Includes imputations for instruction coordinators.
[3]Includes imputations for prekindergarten teachers.
[4]All staff data are imputed.
[5]Includes imputations for instructional aides.
[6]Includes imputations for administrative support staff, school and library support staff, and other support services staff.
[7]Includes imputations for library support staff.

[8]Includes imputations for officials and administrators, administrative support staff, and school and library support staff.
[9]Includes imputations for other support services staff.
[10]Includes imputations for administrative support staff and school support staff.
NOTE: DoD = Department of Defense. Some data have been revised from previously published figures.
SOURCE: U.S. Department of Education, National Center for Education Statistics, Common Core of Data (CCD), "State Nonfiscal Survey of Public Elementary/Secondary Education," 2005–06. (This table was prepared August 2008.)

Table 83. Staff employed in public elementary and secondary school systems, by type of assignment and state or jurisdiction: Fall 2004

[In full-time equivalents]

State or jurisdiction	Total	School district staff			School staff						Student support staff	Other support services staff
		Officials and administrators	Administrative support staff	Instruction coordinators	Principals and assistant principals	School and library support staff	Teachers	Instructional aides	Guidance counselors	Librarians		
1	2	3	4	5	6	7	8	9	10	11	12	13
United States[1]	6,058,174	64,101	170,296	47,731	165,657	300,554	3,090,925	707,514	101,822	54,145	203,181	1,152,248
Alabama	92,795	1,081	1,907	836	3,487	3,757	51,594	6,458	1,705	1,369	1,764	18,837
Alaska[2]	17,632	445	877	173	707	1,543	7,756	2,200	270	146	452	3,063
Arizona	97,953	418	516	192	2,223	9,269	48,935	13,713	1,351	827	7,202	13,307
Arkansas	66,127	659	1,851	623	1,569	1,573	31,234	7,196	1,264	954	3,760	15,444
California[3]	574,614	2,723	22,907	6,663	13,752	36,101	305,969	68,118	6,508	1,138	15,648	95,087
Colorado	91,337	1,010	2,518	1,425	2,442	5,071	45,165	10,269	1,409	842	3,802	17,384
Connecticut	83,879	1,383	1,727	369	2,258	3,877	38,808	12,689	1,352	789	4,633	15,994
Delaware	14,966	297	333	206	374	489	7,856	1,693	268	132	674	2,644
District of Columbia	12,162	130	686	105	398	414	5,387	1,339	99	41	608	2,955
Florida	311,853	1,892	15,599	677	7,242	16,220	154,864	31,517	5,942	2,800	11,920	63,180
Georgia	209,746	1,982	2,557	1,439	5,169	9,514	104,987	24,535	3,417	2,192	6,043	47,911
Hawaii	20,531	196	261	559	505	1,213	11,146	2,084	657	291	1,278	2,341
Idaho	25,533	115	535	264	716	1,085	14,269	2,736	590	171	523	4,529
Illinois[4,5]	261,194	3,942	6,949	1,059	6,457	13,320	131,047	34,411	3,117	2,176	8,599	50,117
Indiana	133,375	1,045	658	1,720	3,023	8,714	60,563	19,355	1,827	996	2,002	33,472
Iowa	68,450	945	716	482	2,195	4,533	34,697	9,475	1,157	561	2,507	11,182
Kansas	64,114	1,260	850	110	1,717	2,640	32,932	7,108	1,112	924	3,149	12,312
Kentucky	95,920	836	2,402	887	2,208	5,920	41,463	13,634	1,425	1,115	3,057	22,973
Louisiana	101,381	301	2,661	1,446	2,731	3,625	49,192	11,149	3,317	1,259	3,175	22,525
Maine	34,899	610	689	320	947	1,756	16,656	5,974	650	266	1,395	5,636
Maryland	108,296	834	1,070	1,285	3,226	4,640	55,101	9,747	2,230	1,140	3,088	25,935
Massachusetts[6]	137,613	1,603	4,610	908	3,892	6,312	73,399	19,652	2,117	949	6,712	17,459
Michigan	209,835	3,288	1,261	3,338	5,168	15,254	100,638	25,444	2,762	1,429	8,553	42,700
Minnesota	104,367	1,915	2,242	1,450	1,906	4,941	52,152	14,459	1,055	922	10,780	12,465
Mississippi	67,249	984	1,884	703	1,773	2,472	31,321	8,698	1,018	951	2,818	14,627
Missouri	126,792	1,325	8,585	1,024	3,066	516	65,847	12,061	2,582	1,622	4,521	25,643
Montana[5]	18,759	140	486	188	503	931	10,224	1,917	433	362	70	3,505
Nebraska	41,157	573	799	456	1,014	1,716	21,236	4,720	767	549	1,137	8,190
Nevada	31,260	263	965	546	924	1,705	20,950	3,683	713	343	438	730
New Hampshire	31,408	521	615	201	543	939	15,298	6,429	823	302	629	5,108
New Jersey	213,418	1,488	6,415	2,701	4,013	9,007	114,875	25,878	2,382	1,553	17,298	27,808
New Mexico	46,531	580	1,643	907	1,014	2,277	21,730	5,400	772	296	2,066	9,846
New York[7]	399,089	2,839	26,806	2,172	7,911	7,242	218,612	54,938	6,551	3,329	10,494	58,195
North Carolina	177,308	1,650	3,489	962	4,901	6,611	92,550	28,598	3,514	2,337	5,515	27,181
North Dakota	15,157	478	161	104	388	508	8,070	1,638	277	203	479	2,851
Ohio	239,988	7,991	12,682	601	4,792	19,771	118,060	17,321	3,828	1,642	3,960	49,340
Oklahoma	77,466	528	2,534	472	2,107	3,434	40,416	6,997	1,559	1,016	3,863	14,540
Oregon	56,637	639	1,540	495	1,592	3,778	27,431	9,585	1,221	431	1,934	7,991
Pennsylvania	237,122	1,709	6,772	1,457	4,686	11,425	121,167	26,510	4,409	2,225	11,573	45,189
Rhode Island [2,4,8,9]	22,838	155	343	204	1,955	653	11,781	2,567	2,574	215	549	1,842
South Carolina[10]	64,999	302	2,331	721	3,298	3,762	46,914	2,686	1,736	1,140	1,651	458
South Dakota	18,106	441	332	377	397	542	9,064	3,383	289	148	1,095	2,038
Tennessee	115,767	170	2,304	778	3,420	4,189	60,022	14,181	1,936	1,566	1,571	25,630
Texas	607,364	7,863	3,428	1,518	30,737	34,387	294,547	59,855	10,151	4,893	5,467	154,518
Utah	44,499	375	918	732	1,060	2,561	22,287	6,954	675	262	978	7,697
Vermont	18,899	148	395	296	432	961	8,720	4,339	426	220	819	2,143
Virginia	179,688	1,461	4,570	1,447	4,083	10,626	93,732	17,833	2,579	2,002	3,224	38,131
Washington	111,848	897	1,778	231	2,795	2,646	53,125	10,300	1,981	1,298	2,848	33,949
West Virginia	37,979	437	1,696	354	1,056	433	19,958	3,191	673	387	1,618	8,176
Wisconsin	104,018	926	65	1,395	2,473	4,788	60,521	10,951	1,963	1,292	4,784	14,860
Wyoming	14,256	308	378	153	332	893	6,657	1,946	389	132	458	2,610
Bureau of Indian Education	—	—	—	—	—	—	—	—	—	—	—	—
DoD, overseas	6,845	42	24	52	259	670	4,885	280	261	152	200	20
DoD, domestic	2,865	36	—	28	105	277	2,002	178	94	67	—	78
Other jurisdictions												
American Samoa	1,813	54	59	50	70	157	945	108	44	17	206	103
Guam	3,318	19	185	83	61	260	1,672	687	40	14	62	235
Northern Marianas	1,166	6	65	11	33	58	579	263	18	1	34	98
Puerto Rico	76,865	1,727	88	505	1,498	4,887	43,054	240	1,011	1,095	3,927	18,833
U.S. Virgin Islands	2,977	78	129	23	113	84	1,545	322	79	39	85	480

—Not available.
[1]Includes imputations for undercounts in designated states.
[2]Includes imputations for instruction coordinators.
[3]Includes imputations for prekindergarten teachers.
[4]Includes imputations for instructional aides.
[5]Includes imputations for administrative support staff, school and library support staff, and other support services staff.
[6]Includes imputations for library support staff.
[7]All staff data are imputed.

[8]Includes imputations for prekindergarten and kindergarten teachers.
[9]Includes imputations for librarians.
[10]Includes imputations for agency support staff and school support staff.
NOTE: Some data have been revised from previously published figures. DoD = Department of Defense.
SOURCE: U.S. Department of Education, National Center for Education Statistics, Common Core of Data (CCD), "State Nonfiscal Survey of Public Elementary/Secondary Education," 2004–05. (This table was prepared August 2008.)

Table 84. Staff and teachers in public elementary and secondary school systems, by state or jurisdiction: Fall 2000 through fall 2006

State or jurisdiction	Teachers as a percent of staff				Fall 2004[1]			Fall 2005[1]			Fall 2006		
	Fall 2000	Fall 2001	Fall 2002	Fall 2003	All staff	Teachers	Teachers as a percent of staff	All staff	Teachers	Teachers as a percent of staff	All staff	Teachers	Teachers as a percent of staff
1	2	3	4	5	6	7	8	9	10	11	12	13	14
United States[2]	51.5	50.8	51.0	51.2	6,058,174	3,090,925	51.0	6,130,686	3,143,003	51.3	6,163,962	3,180,396	51.6
Alabama	53.7 [3]	53.1 [3]	53.0 [3]	57.7	92,795	51,594	55.6	103,775	57,757	55.7	109,816 [3]	56,134	51.1 [3]
Alaska	49.3 [3]	48.1 [3]	47.2 [3]	47.2 [3]	17,632 [3]	7,756	44.0 [3]	17,954 [3]	7,912	44.1 [3]	16,853 [3]	7,903	46.9 [3]
Arizona	49.3	49.0	48.7	49.3	97,953	48,935	50.0	100,162	51,376	51.3	102,390	52,625	51.4
Arkansas	50.6	49.7	47.5	47.7	66,127	31,234	47.2	70,673	32,997	46.7	71,616	35,089	49.0
California	54.1 [3]	53.0 [3]	52.9 [3]	53.1 [3]	574,614 [3]	305,969 [3]	53.2 [3]	579,118 [3]	309,222 [3]	53.4 [3]	579,825 [3]	307,110 [3]	53.0 [3]
Colorado	50.7	50.4	50.2	50.2	91,337	45,165	49.4	93,148	45,841	49.2	97,364	46,973	48.2
Connecticut	50.0	49.2	49.0	49.6	83,879	38,808	46.3	84,669	39,687	46.9	86,709	39,115	45.1
Delaware	59.2	53.4	53.3	53.1	14,966	7,856	52.5	15,473	7,998	51.7	15,403	8,038	52.2
District of Columbia	46.2	43.5	43.3	53.5	12,162	5,387	44.3	12,372 [3]	5,481 [3]	44.3 [3]	12,194 [3]	5,394	44.2 [3]
Florida	47.8	47.6	48.1	49.0	311,853	154,864	49.7	314,219	158,962	50.6	321,600	162,851	50.6
Georgia	49.2	48.8	48.5	48.5	209,746	104,987	50.1	218,965	108,535	49.6	227,616	113,597	49.9
Hawaii	59.5	56.6	53.0	52.7	20,531	11,146	54.3	21,059	11,226	53.3	21,061	11,271	53.5
Idaho	56.2	55.9	55.8	55.9	25,533	14,269	55.9	26,018	14,521	55.8	26,312	14,770	56.1
Illinois	51.1 [3]	50.7 [3]	50.9 [3]	50.2 [3]	261,194 [3]	131,047	50.2 [3]	251,769 [3]	133,857	53.2 [3]	221,553 [3]	140,988	63.6 [3]
Indiana	46.7	46.3	47.2	45.9	133,375	60,563	45.4	133,096	60,592	45.5	134,681	61,315	45.5
Iowa	51.1	50.2	51.3	51.1	68,450	34,697	50.7	69,080	35,181	50.9	69,690	35,653	51.2
Kansas	50.9	50.8	51.1	51.1	64,114	32,932	51.4	65,537	33,608	51.3	53,762	35,297	65.7
Kentucky	44.1	42.6	42.4	43.0	95,920	41,463	43.2	97,937	42,413	43.3	98,812	43,371 [3]	43.9 [3]
Louisiana	49.3	49.2	48.9	49.0	101,381	49,192	48.5	92,612	44,660	48.2	95,226	45,951	48.3
Maine	49.7	49.1	48.7	49.1	34,899	16,656	47.7	35,249	16,684	47.3	36,785	16,826	45.7
Maryland	54.3	54.2	54.0	51.3	108,296	55,101	50.9	111,215	56,685	51.0	113,474	58,443	51.5
Massachusetts	55.1	54.9	51.6	53.6 [3]	137,613 [3]	73,399	53.3 [3]	138,781 [3]	73,596	53.0 [3]	136,563 [3]	73,157	53.6 [3]
Michigan	46.1	46.0	47.9	47.1 [3]	209,835	100,638	48.0	204,764 [3]	98,069	47.9 [3]	212,320	98,037	46.2
Minnesota	51.6 [3]	50.7	50.1 [3]	49.7	104,367	52,152	50.0	104,489	51,107	48.9	106,701	51,880	48.6
Mississippi	47.9	47.9	47.8	47.7	67,249	31,321	46.6	67,659	31,433	46.5	68,815	32,351	47.0
Missouri	53.2	52.3	52.1	51.8	126,792	65,847	51.9	128,794	67,076	52.1	127,020 [3]	67,398	53.1 [3]
Montana	53.5 [3]	53.4 [3]	55.4 [3]	55.2	18,759 [3]	10,224	54.5 [3]	19,611 [3]	10,369	52.9 [3]	19,023 [3]	10,398	54.7 [3]
Nebraska	52.6	52.0	51.6	51.6	41,157	21,236	51.6	41,166	21,359	51.9	42,938	21,459	50.0
Nevada	58.6	56.7	59.9	59.4	31,260	20,950	67.0	32,345 [3]	21,744	67.2 [3]	33,949 [3]	22,908	67.5 [3]
New Hampshire	51.1	50.4	49.8	49.0	31,408	15,298	48.7	32,022	15,536	48.5	32,174	15,515	48.2
New Jersey	53.4	53.6	53.7	53.5	213,418	114,875	53.8	211,893 [3]	112,673	53.2 [3]	205,372 [3]	112,301	54.7 [3]
New Mexico	46.8	48.6	48.3	48.1	46,531	21,730	46.7	47,940	22,021	45.9	46,551	22,016	47.3
New York	49.7	49.4	49.3	54.8	399,089 [3]	218,612 [3]	54.8 [3]	373,504	218,989	58.6	373,360	218,879	58.6
North Carolina	51.5	51.6	51.8	52.3	177,308	92,550	52.2	182,107	95,664	52.5	196,657	104,412	53.1
North Dakota	53.9	53.9	53.5	53.3	15,157	8,070	53.2	15,128	8,003	52.9	15,157	8,007	52.8
Ohio	53.1	53.1	51.7	50.2	239,988	118,060	49.2	238,977	117,982	49.4	242,574	110,390	45.5
Oklahoma	55.0	54.5	54.6	55.0	77,466	40,416	52.2	81,857	41,833	51.1	81,831	42,206	51.6
Oregon	50.0	49.3	49.3	49.3	56,637	27,431	48.4	60,349	28,346	47.0	51,067	26,443	51.8
Pennsylvania	52.2	51.7	51.1	51.4	237,122	121,167	51.1	240,409	122,397	50.9	241,024 [3]	123,375	51.2 [3]
Rhode Island	60.0	59.8	61.2	59.9 [3]	22,838 [3]	11,781 [3]	51.6 [3]	24,267 [3]	14,180 [3]	58.4 [3]	17,902 [3]	11,381	63.6 [3]
South Carolina	65.7 [3]	65.3 [3]	73.8 [3]	72.9 [3]	64,999 [3]	46,914	72.2 [3]	67,992 [3]	48,212	70.9 [3]	74,709 [3]	49,733	66.6 [3]
South Dakota	52.0	50.6	48.6	48.6	18,106	9,064	50.1	19,018	9,129	48.0	17,297 [3]	9,070	52.4 [3]
Tennessee	52.1	52.1	51.3	51.3	115,767	60,022	51.8	114,171	59,596	52.2	123,218	62,176	50.5
Texas	50.6	48.6	48.6	48.5	607,364	294,547	48.5	598,513	302,425	50.5	616,155	311,649	50.6
Utah	54.1	54.0	53.9	53.3	44,499	22,287	50.1	45,821	22,993	50.2	47,365	23,640	49.9
Vermont	47.3	47.4	46.5	46.8	18,899	8,720	46.1	19,024	8,851	46.5	19,232	8,859	46.1
Virginia	54.1 [3]	54.0	61.3	54.4	179,688	93,732	52.2	233,898	103,944	44.4	239,815	105,039	43.8
Washington	52.3	46.9	47.0	48.3	111,848	53,125	47.5	113,845	53,508	47.0	102,948	53,743	52.2
West Virginia	54.3	53.5	52.8	52.7	37,979	19,958	52.6	38,152	19,940	52.3	39,217 [3]	19,414	49.5 [3]
Wisconsin	56.3	54.6	53.3	55.7	104,018	60,521	58.2	105,564	60,127	57.0	105,033	59,089	56.3
Wyoming	48.6	48.7	49.1 [3]	46.5	14,256	6,657	46.7	14,526	6,706	46.2	15,233	6,757	44.4
Bureau of Indian Education	—	—	—	—	—	—	—	—	—	—	—	—	—
DoD, overseas	66.0	65.3	68.0	64.9	6,845	4,885	71.4	9,099	5,726	62.9	8,338	5,204	62.4
DoD, domestic	59.2	57.5	57.7	55.4	2,865	2,002	69.9	3,671	2,033	55.4	3,574	2,033	56.9
Other jurisdictions													
American Samoa	50.0	54.2	54.4	55.8	1,813	945	52.1	1,446	989	68.4	1,869	971	52.0
Guam	51.5	50.9	—	50.8	3,318	1,672	50.4	3,455	1,804	52.2	—	—	—
Northern Marianas	50.2	50.9	49.9	47.6	1,166	579	49.7	1,234	614	49.8	1,160	579	49.9
Puerto Rico	54.4	57.0	56.8	56.8	76,865	43,054	56.0	75,023	42,036	56.0	71,962	40,163	55.8
U.S. Virgin Islands	52.1	53.6	49.5	52.2	2,977	1,545	51.9	2,664	1,434	53.8	3,020	1,531	50.7

—Not available.
[1]Data revised from previously published figures.
[2]U.S. totals include imputations for underreporting and nonreporting states.
[3]Includes imputations for underreporting.

NOTE: DoD = Department of Defense.
SOURCE: U.S. Department of Education, National Center for Education Statistics, Common Core of Data (CCD), "State Nonfiscal Survey of Public Elementary/Secondary Education," 2000–01 through 2006–07. (This table was prepared October 2008.)

Table 85. Staff, enrollment, and pupil/staff ratios in public elementary and secondary school systems, by state or jurisdiction: Fall 1999 through fall 2006

State or jurisdiction	Pupil/staff ratio					Fall 2004[1]			Fall 2005[1]			Fall 2006		
	Fall 1999	Fall 2000	Fall 2001	Fall 2002	Fall 2003	Staff	Enrollment	Pupil/ staff ratio	Staff	Enrollment	Pupil/ staff ratio	Staff	Enrollment	Pupil/ staff ratio
1	2	3	4	5	6	7	8	9	10	11	12	13	14	15
United States[2]....	8.3	8.3	8.1	8.1	8.2	6,058,174	48,795,465	8.1	6,130,686	49,113,298	8.0	6,163,962	49,298,945	8.0
Alabama	8.4 [3]	8.2 [3]	8.4 [3]	8.3 [3]	7.3	92,795	730,140	7.9	103,775	741,761	7.1	109,816 [3]	743,632	6.8 [3]
Alaska	8.4 [3]	8.3 [3]	8.1 [3]	7.9 [3]	8.1 [3]	17,632 [3]	132,970	7.5 [3]	17,954 [3]	133,288	7.4 [3]	16,853 [3]	132,608	7.9 [3]
Arizona	9.7	9.7	9.8	9.7	10.5	97,953	1,043,298	10.7	100,162	1,094,454	10.9	102,390	1,065,082	10.4
Arkansas	7.5	7.1	6.8	7.1	7.0	66,127	463,115	7.0	70,673	474,206	6.7	71,616	476,409	6.7
California	11.3 [3]	11.1 [3]	10.9 [3]	10.9 [3]	11.2 [3]	574,614 [3]	6,441,557 [3]	11.2 [3]	579,118 [3]	6,437,202 [3]	11.1 [3]	579,825 [3]	6,406,821 [3]	11.0 [3]
Colorado	8.9	8.7	8.5	8.3	8.5	91,337	765,976	8.4	93,148	779,826	8.4	97,364	794,026	8.2
Connecticut	6.9	6.8	6.7	6.6	6.8	83,879	577,390	6.9	84,669	575,059	6.8	86,709	575,100	6.6
Delaware	8.4	9.1	8.2	8.1	8.1	14,966	119,091	8.0	15,473	120,937	7.8	15,403	122,254	7.9
District of Columbia	8.1	6.4	6.6	6.6	7.4	12,162	76,714	6.3	12,372 [3]	76,876	6.2 [3]	12,194 [3]	72,850	6.0 [3]
Florida	8.8	8.8	8.8	8.8	8.7	311,853	2,639,336	8.5	314,219	2,675,024	8.5	321,600	2,671,513	8.3
Georgia	7.7	7.8	7.7	7.6	7.6	209,746	1,553,437	7.4	218,965	1,598,461	7.3	227,616	1,629,157	7.2
Hawaii	10.4	10.0	9.5	8.9	8.7	20,531	183,185	8.9	21,059	182,818	8.7	21,061	180,728	8.6
Idaho	10.1	10.1	10.0	10.0	10.0	25,533	256,084	10.0	26,018	261,982	10.1	26,312	267,380	10.2
Illinois	8.3 [3]	8.2 [3]	8.1 [3]	8.1 [3]	8.3 [3]	261,194 [3]	2,097,503	8.0 [3]	251,769 [3]	2,111,706	8.4 [3]	221,553 [3]	2,118,276	9.6 [3]
Indiana	7.9	7.8	7.7	7.9	7.7	133,375	1,021,348	7.7	133,096	1,035,074	7.8	134,681	1,045,940	7.8
Iowa	7.5	7.3	7.0	7.2	7.1	68,450	478,319	7.0	69,080	483,482	7.0	69,690	483,122	6.9
Kansas	7.4	7.3	7.2	7.4	7.4	64,114	469,136	7.3	65,537	467,525	7.1	53,762	469,506	8.7
Kentucky	6.9	7.4	6.9	6.9	6.9	95,920	674,796	7.0	97,937	679,878	6.9	98,812	683,173 [3]	6.9 [3]
Louisiana	7.5	7.3	7.2	7.1	7.1	101,381	724,281	7.1	92,612	654,526	7.1	95,226	675,851	7.1
Maine	6.4	6.2	6.0	5.9	5.6	34,899	198,820	5.7	35,249	195,498	5.5	36,785	193,986	5.3
Maryland	9.0	8.8	8.7	8.4	8.1	108,296	865,561	8.0	111,215	860,020	7.7	113,474	851,640	7.5
Massachusetts	7.1	8.0	7.7	6.8	7.3 [3]	137,613 [3]	975,574	7.1 [3]	138,781 [3]	971,909	7.0 [3]	136,563 [3]	968,661	7.1 [3]
Michigan	8.2 [3]	8.2 [3]	8.1	9.5	8.5 [3]	209,835	1,751,290	8.3	204,764 [3]	1,742,282	8.5 [3]	212,320	1,714,709	8.1
Minnesota	8.2	8.2 [3]	8.1	8.0 [3]	8.1	104,367	838,503	8.0	104,489	839,243	8.0	106,701	840,565	7.9
Mississippi	7.8	7.7	7.6	7.4	7.2	67,249	495,376	7.4	67,659	494,954	7.3	68,815	495,026	7.2
Missouri	7.8	7.5	7.3	7.1	7.2	126,792	905,449	7.1	128,794	917,705	7.1	127,020 [3]	920,353	7.2 [3]
Montana	7.9 [3]	8.0 [3]	7.8 [3]	8.0 [3]	8.0	18,759 [3]	146,705	7.8 [3]	19,611 [3]	145,416	7.4 [3]	19,023 [3]	144,418	7.6 [3]
Nebraska	7.4	7.2	7.0	7.0	7.0	41,157	285,761	6.9	41,166	286,646	7.0	42,938	287,580	6.7
Nevada	10.8	10.9	10.5	11.0	11.3	31,260	400,083	12.8	32,345 [3]	412,395	12.7 [3]	33,949 [3]	424,240	12.5 [3]
New Hampshire	7.6	7.4	7.1	6.9	6.7	31,408	206,852	6.6	32,022	205,767	6.4	32,174	203,551	6.3
New Jersey	7.2	7.1	6.9	6.9	6.8	213,418	1,393,347	6.5	211,893 [3]	1,395,602	6.6 [3]	205,372 [3]	1,388,850	6.8 [3]
New Mexico	7.5	7.1	7.1	7.3	7.2	46,531	326,102	7.0	47,940	326,758	6.8	46,551	328,220	7.1
New York	7.1	6.9	6.8	6.7	7.3	399,089 [3]	2,836,337	7.1	373,504	2,815,581	7.5	373,360	2,809,649	7.5
North Carolina	8.0	8.0	7.9	7.9	7.9	177,308	1,385,754	7.8	182,107	1,416,436	7.8	196,657	1,444,481	7.3
North Dakota	7.5	7.2	7.1	6.9	6.8	15,157	100,513	6.6	15,128	98,283	6.5	15,157	96,670	6.4
Ohio	8.4	8.2	8.0	7.6	7.6	239,988	1,840,032	7.7	238,977	1,839,683	7.7	242,574	1,836,096	7.6
Oklahoma	8.5	8.3	8.1	8.4	8.8	77,466	629,476	8.1	81,857	634,739	7.8	81,831	639,391	7.8
Oregon	9.8	9.7	9.6	10.1	10.2	56,637	552,505	9.8	60,349	552,194	9.2	51,067	562,574	11.0
Pennsylvania	8.4	8.1	7.9	7.9	7.8	237,122	1,828,089	7.7	240,409	1,830,684	7.6	241,024 [3]	1,871,060	7.8 [3]
Rhode Island	8.7	8.9	8.5	8.7	8.0 [3]	22,838 [3]	156,498	6.9 [3]	24,267 [3]	153,422	6.3 [3]	17,902 [3]	151,612	8.5 [3]
South Carolina	7.8 [3]	9.8 [3]	9.5 [3]	11.0 [3]	11.1 [3]	64,999 [3]	703,736	10.8 [3]	67,992 [3]	701,544	10.3 [3]	74,709 [3]	703,119	9.4 [3]
South Dakota	7.5	7.1	6.9	6.8	6.6	18,106	122,798	6.8	19,018	122,012	6.4	17,297 [3]	121,158	7.0 [3]
Tennessee	8.2 [3]	8.3 [3]	8.3 [3]	8.1 [3]	8.1 [3]	115,767	941,091 [3]	8.1 [3]	114,171	953,928	8.4	123,218	978,368	7.9
Texas	7.6	7.5	7.1	7.2	7.3	607,364	4,405,215	7.3	598,513	4,525,394	7.6	616,155	4,599,509	7.5
Utah	11.9	11.8	11.8	11.8	11.9	44,499	503,607	11.3	45,821	508,430	11.1	47,365	523,586	11.1
Vermont	6.0	5.7	5.6	5.4	5.3	18,899	98,352	5.2	19,024	96,638	5.1	19,232	95,399	5.0
Virginia	7.2 [3]	7.1 [3]	7.0	7.2	7.2	179,688	1,204,739	6.7	233,898	1,213,616	5.2	239,815	1,220,440	5.1
Washington	10.5	10.3	9.0	9.0	9.3	111,848	1,020,005	9.1	113,845	1,031,985	9.1	102,948	1,026,774	10.0
West Virginia	7.5	7.4	7.5	7.4	7.4	37,979	280,129	7.4	38,152	280,866	7.4	39,217 [3]	281,939	7.2 [3]
Wisconsin	8.0	8.2	7.6	7.8	8.4	104,018	864,757	8.3	105,564	875,174	8.3	105,033	876,700	8.3
Wyoming	6.6	6.4	6.4	6.4 [3]	6.2	14,256	84,733	5.9	14,526	84,409	5.8	15,233	85,193	5.6
Bureau of Indian Education	—	—	—	—	—	—	45,828	—	—	50,938	—	—	—	—
DoD, overseas	9.3 [4]	9.5	9.3	10.3	9.8	6,845	68,327	10.0	9,099	62,543	6.9	8,338	60,891	7.3
DoD, domestic	—	8.4	7.6	7.6	7.4	2,865	29,151	10.2	3,671	28,329	7.7	3,574	26,631	7.5
Other jurisdictions														
American Samoa	9.6	9.6	9.4	9.2	9.0	1,813	16,126	8.9	1,446	16,438	11.4	1,869	16,427	8.8
Guam	8.9	8.5	8.5	—	9.1	3,318	30,605	9.2	3,455	30,986	9.0	—	—	—
Northern Marianas..	10.2	9.6	10.3	10.3	9.7	1,166	11,601	9.9	1,234	11,718	9.5	1,160	11,695	10.1
Puerto Rico	8.5	8.9	8.0	8.0	7.8	76,865	575,648	7.5	75,023	563,490	7.5	71,962	544,138	7.6
U.S. Virgin Islands...	7.0	6.7	6.7	6.0	6.1	2,977	16,429	5.5	2,664	16,750	6.3	3,020	16,284	5.4

—Not available.
[1]Data revised from previously published figures.
[2]U.S. totals include imputations for underreporting and nonreporting states.
[3]Includes imputations for underreporting.
[4]Includes both overseas and domestic schools.

NOTE: DoD = Department of Defense.
SOURCE: U.S. Department of Education, National Center for Education Statistics, Common Core of Data (CCD), "State Nonfiscal Survey of Public Elementary/Secondary Education," 1999–2000 through 2006–07. (This table was prepared October 2008.)

Table 86. Principals in public and private elementary and secondary schools, by selected characteristics: 1993–94, 1999–2000, and 2003–04

Characteristic	1993–94[1]	1999–2000[1]	2003–04[1]	Percentage distribution of principals, by highest degree earned, 2003–04				Average years of experience			Average annual salary of principals in current dollars		Average annual salary of principals in constant 2006–07 dollars[2]	
				Bachelor's or less	Master's	Education specialist[3]	Doctor's and first-professional	As a principal, 1993–94	As a principal, 2003–04	Teaching experience, 2003–04	1993–94	2003–04	1993–94	2003–04
1	2	3	4	5	6	7	8	9	10	11	12	13	14	15
Public schools														
Total	79,620 (235)	83,790 (327)	87,620 (307)	1.9 (0.24)	59.2 (0.71)	30.3 (0.69)	8.5 (0.43)	8.7 (0.10)	7.8 (0.10)	13.5 (0.11)	$54,900 (130)	$75,500 (190)	$76,600 (180)	$82,800 (200)
Sex														
Males	52,110 (613)	47,130 (604)	45,930 (707)	1.6 (0.25)	62.9 (1.04)	27.3 (0.93)	7.7 (0.51)	10.3 (0.16)	9.1 (0.16)	12.2 (0.13)	54,900 (160)	75,600 (290)	76,700 (220)	83,000 (320)
Females	27,500 (542)	36,660 (598)	41,690 (708)	2.2 (0.41)	55.1 (1.23)	33.1 (1.13)	9.7 (0.70)	5.6 (0.13)	6.3 (0.16)	14.9 (0.16)	54,700 (280)	75,400 (330)	76,400 (390)	82,700 (370)
Race/ethnicity														
White	67,080 (540)	68,930 (579)	72,200 (509)	1.8 (0.28)	58.8 (0.74)	30.8 (0.78)	8.6 (0.45)	9.0 (0.12)	8.0 (0.12)	13.5 (0.12)	54,500 (140)	75,100 (220)	76,000 (190)	82,400 (240)
Black	8,020 (351)	9,240 (321)	9,250 (377)	2.0 (0.53)	56.2 (2.32)	30.9 (1.94)	10.9 (1.68)	7.1 (0.21)	6.9 (0.33)	14.3 (0.40)	57,700 (450)	77,400 (670)	80,500 (630)	84,900 (730)
Hispanic	3,270 (258)	4,330 (300)	4,680 (355)	1.5 (0.61)	69.2 (3.85)	24.1 (3.68)	5.2 (1.35)	6.3 (0.43)	6.1 (0.43)	11.9 (0.55)	55,900 (800)	79,400 (1,370)	78,000 (1,110)	87,200 (1,500)
Asian	620[4] (109)	630[4] (124)	460 (87)	6.8 (2.16)	70.0 (10.11)	20.3 (10.38)	3.0 (1.23)	6.0[4] (0.60)	6.8 (1.17)	13.6 (1.29)	59,400[4] (1,430)	82,600 (1,670)	83,000[4] (1,990)	90,700 (1,830)
American Indian/Alaska Native	630 (67)	660 (60)	600 (80)	4.5 (2.07)	64.4 (5.17)	24.7 (4.67)	6.5 (2.26)	12.6 (0.67)	6.9 (0.63)	12.6 (0.94)	51,100 (1,730)	62,000 (2,130)	71,400 (2,420)	68,000 (2,330)
Pacific Islander	—	—	‡	‡	‡	‡	‡	‡	‡	‡	—	‡	—	‡
More than one race	—	—	350 (82)	3.2 (2.30)	48.5 (11.64)	35.6 (10.26)	12.7 (5.94)	—	5.6 (1.12)	13.2 (0.98)	—	75,800 (3,770)	—	83,200 (4,130)
Age														
Under 40	5,940 (273)	8,440 (302)	12,840 (477)	3.5 (0.84)	67.3 (1.98)	26.4 (1.81)	2.9 (0.40)	2.8 (0.13)	2.4 (0.10)	7.6 (0.14)	46,500 (470)	68,800 (540)	65,000 (660)	75,500 (600)
40 to 44	14,570 (496)	10,510 (317)	9,540 (449)	2.4 (0.68)	66.4 (1.85)	26.7 (1.73)	4.5 (0.62)	5.0 (0.12)	4.5 (0.18)	11.0 (0.21)	52,000 (390)	72,300 (660)	72,700 (540)	79,300 (730)
45 to 49	25,430 (429)	19,600 (535)	16,120 (526)	2.2 (0.72)	60.0 (1.81)	29.9 (1.59)	7.9 (0.85)	7.1 (0.13)	6.1 (0.16)	15.2 (0.20)	55,400 (260)	73,300 (530)	77,400 (360)	80,400 (580)
50 to 54	18,870 (539)	27,120 (606)	24,170 (669)	1.3 (0.29)	56.8 (1.47)	31.8 (1.16)	10.1 (1.06)	10.3 (0.18)	8.7 (0.19)	15.2 (0.21)	56,600 (360)	77,100 (440)	79,000 (510)	84,500 (480)
55 or over	14,820 (441)	18,130 (500)	24,960 (679)	1.3 (0.36)	53.9 (1.63)	32.5 (1.60)	12.3 (0.97)	15.1 (0.35)	11.9 (0.23)	15.9 (0.27)	57,800 (490)	80,100 (480)	80,700 (690)	87,900 (520)
Type of school														
Elementary	53,680 (294)	60,110 (253)	61,480 (361)	1.2 (0.22)	59.9 (0.96)	30.5 (0.99)	8.5 (0.57)	8.9 (0.14)	7.9 (0.13)	13.7 (0.13)	54,200 (170)	75,400 (220)	75,600 (240)	82,700 (250)
Secondary	18,260 (161)	20,450 (197)	19,700 (272)	2.9 (0.70)	56.4 (1.30)	30.7 (1.21)	10.0 (0.56)	8.0 (0.12)	7.5 (0.19)	13.1 (0.19)	56,600 (170)	79,400 (440)	79,000 (230)	87,100 (480)
Combined	2,750 (143)	3,230 (146)	6,450 (263)	5.6 (1.05)	60.9 (2.07)	27.9 (1.96)	5.6 (0.86)	7.5 (0.29)	7.4 (0.36)	12.7 (0.35)	52,800 (510)	64,700 (620)	73,800 (710)	70,900 (680)
Location of school														
City[5]	—	—	22,690 (425)	1.7 (0.36)	55.1 (1.70)	31.7 (1.39)	11.4 (1.11)	—	7.3 (0.17)	13.9 (0.23)	—	80,200 (380)	—	88,000 (410)
Suburban[6]	—	—	25,600 (506)	1.0 (0.27)	59.1 (1.30)	28.3 (1.35)	11.5 (0.96)	—	7.9 (0.23)	13.3 (0.23)	—	85,400 (470)	—	93,700 (520)
Town[7]	—	—	13,700 (424)	2.1 (0.77)	62.1 (1.86)	30.7 (1.69)	5.1 (0.64)	—	8.1 (0.28)	13.0 (0.27)	—	68,900 (500)	—	75,600 (550)
Rural[8]	—	—	25,640 (492)	2.8 (0.54)	61.2 (1.32)	30.9 (1.25)	5.1 (0.49)	—	7.9 (0.22)	13.6 (0.18)	—	65,000 (350)	—	71,300 (390)
Private schools														
Total	25,020 (198)	26,230 (259)	27,690 (677)	33.1 (1.27)	49.5 (1.20)	10.7 (0.61)	6.7 (0.53)	8.8 (0.20)	10.0 (0.24)	14.1 (0.25)	$32,100 (360)	$50,200 (610)	$44,800 (510)	$55,000 (670)
Sex														
Males	11,610 (301)	11,900 (308)	12,110 (552)	29.1 (1.74)	50.6 (1.72)	10.5 (0.95)	9.8 (1.13)	9.0 (0.26)	11.0 (0.35)	13.3 (0.35)	35,600 (560)	55,400 (1,000)	49,700 (790)	60,800 (1,100)
Females	13,410 (283)	14,330 (307)	15,580 (491)	36.2 (1.83)	48.8 (1.80)	10.8 (0.83)	4.3 (0.75)	8.6 (0.27)	9.2 (0.28)	14.7 (0.36)	29,200 (610)	46,300 (840)	40,700 (850)	50,700 (920)
Race/ethnicity														
White	23,130 (270)	23,320 (309)	24,850 (715)	32.3 (1.33)	50.2 (1.26)	11.1 (0.65)	6.4 (0.64)	8.7 (0.22)	10.3 (0.24)	14.4 (0.26)	32,000 (400)	50,600 (600)	44,600 (560)	55,500 (660)
Black	1,060 (124)	1,570 (164)	1,440 (155)	39.6 (6.00)	43.3 (6.40)	7.3 (3.50)	9.7 (4.10)	8.3 (1.04)	7.1 (1.08)	11.9 (1.35)	34,400 (2,480)	44,300 (3,460)	48,000 (3,460)	48,600 (3,800)
Hispanic	520 (91)	830 (135)	820 (116)	33.5 (6.35)	53.0 (6.98)	6.7 (3.27)	6.8 (4.10)	10.1 (1.43)	6.6 (1.29)	10.9 (1.50)	31,300 (1,960)	48,000 (3,940)	43,800 (2,730)	52,700 (4,320)
Age														
Under 40	4,790 (302)	3,750 (223)	4,420 (267)	54.2 (3.41)	39.7 (3.36)	4.9 (1.13)	1.2 (0.59)	3.5 (0.22)	2.9 (0.20)	6.3 (0.37)	26,300 (870)	40,900 (1,580)	36,700 (1,210)	44,900 (1,740)
40 to 44	4,400 (217)	3,450 (212)	3,040 (250)	45.3 (4.75)	43.9 (4.21)	7.2 (2.45)	3.7 (1.59)	5.3 (0.24)	5.4 (0.38)	10.6 (0.57)	30,500 (930)	43,600 (1,720)	42,600 (1,300)	47,900 (1,890)
45 to 49	5,140 (216)	5,210 (261)	4,020 (250)	32.7 (3.49)	50.4 (3.22)	8.7 (2.16)	8.3 (2.16)	8.3 (0.27)	7.6 (0.28)	12.9 (0.49)	34,600 (740)	51,700 (740)	48,400 (1,030)	56,700 (1,610)
50 to 54	4,120 (228)	5,840 (291)	5,820 (337)	27.1 (2.46)	53.0 (2.42)	12.3 (1.57)	7.6 (1.23)	9.6 (0.34)	10.1 (0.35)	14.7 (0.49)	37,700 (1,000)	52,400 (1,570)	52,700 (1,390)	57,500 (1,720)
55 or over	6,550 (244)	7,980 (276)	10,390 (425)	24.1 (1.64)	53.1 (1.81)	14.0 (1.11)	8.7 (1.21)	14.8 (0.40)	15.2 (0.40)	18.6 (0.44)	31,800 (760)	54,000 (1,110)	44,400 (1,060)	59,200 (1,220)
Type of school														
Elementary	13,350 (158)	15,810 (245)	16,750 (327)	33.4 (1.64)	50.0 (1.57)	12.0 (0.81)	4.6 (0.66)	9.4 (0.27)	9.9 (0.30)	14.3 (0.34)	28,800 (440)	47,200 (670)	40,200 (620)	51,800 (740)
Secondary	2,300 (244)	2,630 (133)	2,510 (364)	13.3 (3.27)	62.9 (4.33)	13.0 (2.76)	10.9 (2.56)	7.8 (0.36)	9.3 (0.77)	15.6 (0.68)	43,700 (780)	65,000 (2,590)	61,000 (1,090)	71,300 (2,840)
Combined	6,770 (115)	7,800 (265)	8,430 (281)	38.4 (2.36)	44.7 (2.35)	7.3 (0.93)	9.6 (1.10)	8.0 (0.34)	10.3 (0.39)	13.4 (0.39)	33,600 (1,110)	51,600 (1,520)	56,700 (1,550)	56,600 (1,660)

—Not available.
†Not applicable.
‡Reporting standards not met.
[1]Total differs from data appearing in other tables because of varying survey processing procedures and time period coverages.
[2]Constant dollars based on the Consumer Price Index, prepared by the Bureau of Labor Statistics, U.S. Department of Labor, adjusted to a school-year basis. Excludes principals reporting a salary of $0.
[3]Education specialist degrees or certificates are generally awarded for 1 year's work beyond the master's level. Includes certificate of advanced studies.
[4]Data include Pacific Islander.
[5]A city consists of a territory inside an urbanized area and inside a principal city.

[6]A suburb is a territory outside a principal city and inside an urbanized area. An urbanized area includes a central place and densely populated surrounding area with at least 50,000 people.
[7]A town is a territory within an urban cluster. An urban cluster is a central place with a densely populated adjacent territory including at least 2,500 people.
[8]A rural area is a Census-defined rural territory that is outside of an urbanized area and urban clusters.
NOTE: Race categories exclude persons of Hispanic ethnicity. Detail may not sum to totals because of rounding and survey item nonresponse. Standard errors appear in parentheses.
SOURCE: U.S. Department of Education, National Center for Education Statistics, Schools and Staffing Survey (SASS), "Public School Principal Questionnaire" and "Private School Principal Questionnaire", 1993–94, 1999–2000, and 2003–04. (This table was prepared July 2007.)

Table 87. Number of public school districts and public and private elementary and secondary schools: Selected years, 1869–70 through 2006–07

School year	Regular public school districts[1]	Public schools[2]					Private schools[2,3]		
		Total, all schools[4]	Total, schools with reported grade spans[5]	Schools with elementary grades		Schools with secondary grades	Total[4]	Schools with elementary grades	Schools with secondary grades
				Total	One-teacher				
1	2	3	4	5	6	7	8	9	10
1869–70	—	116,312	—	—	—	—	—	—	—
1879–80	—	178,122	—	—	—	—	—	—	—
1889–90	—	224,526	—	—	—	—	—	—	—
1899–1900	—	248,279	—	—	—	—	—	—	—
1909–10	—	265,474	—	—	212,448	—	—	—	—
1919–20	—	271,319	—	—	187,948	—	—	—	—
1929–30	—	248,117	—	238,306	148,712	23,930	—	9,275 [6]	3,258 [6]
1939–40	117,108 [7]	226,762	—	—	113,600	—	—	11,306 [6]	3,568 [6]
1949–50	83,718 [7]	—	—	128,225	59,652	24,542	—	10,375 [6]	3,331 [6]
1951–52	71,094 [7]	—	—	123,763	50,742	23,746	—	10,666 [6]	3,322 [6]
1959–60	40,520 [7]	—	—	91,853	20,213	25,784	—	13,574 [6]	4,061 [6]
1961–62	35,676 [7]	107,260	—	81,910	13,333	25,350	18,374	14,762 [6]	4,129 [6]
1963–64	31,705 [7]	104,015	—	77,584	9,895	26,431	—	—	4,451 [6]
1965–66	26,983 [7]	99,813	—	73,216	6,491	26,597	17,849 [6]	15,340 [6]	4,606 [6]
1967–68	22,010 [7]	—	94,197	70,879	4,146	27,011	—	—	—
1970–71	17,995 [7]	—	89,372	65,800	1,815	25,352	—	14,372 [6]	3,770 [6]
1973–74	16,730 [7]	—	88,655	65,070	1,365	25,906	—	—	—
1975–76	16,376 [7]	88,597	87,034	63,242	1,166	25,330	—	—	—
1976–77	16,271 [7]	—	86,501	62,644	1,111	25,378	19,910 [6]	16,385 [6]	5,904 [6]
1978–79	16,014 [7]	—	84,816	61,982	1,056	24,504	19,489 [6]	16,097 [6]	5,766 [6]
1979–80	15,944 [7]	87,004	—	—	—	—	—	—	—
1980–81	15,912 [7]	85,982	83,688	61,069	921	24,362	20,764 [6]	16,792 [6]	5,678 [6]
1982–83	15,824 [7]	84,740	82,039	59,656	798	23,988	—	—	—
1983–84	15,747 [7]	84,178	81,418	59,082	838	23,947	27,694	20,872	7,862
1984–85	—	84,007	81,147	58,827	825	23,916	—	—	—
1985–86	—	—	—	—	—	—	25,616	20,252	7,387
1986–87	15,713	83,455	82,190	60,784	763	23,389	—	—	—
1987–88	15,577	83,248	81,416	59,754	729	23,841	26,807	22,959	8,418
1988–89	15,376	83,165	81,579	60,176	583	23,638	—	—	—
1989–90	15,367	83,425	81,880	60,699	630	23,461	26,712	24,221	10,197
1990–91	15,358	84,538	82,475	61,340	617	23,460	24,690	22,223	8,989
1991–92	15,173	84,578	82,506	61,739	569	23,248	25,998	23,523	9,282
1992–93	15,025	84,497	82,896	62,225	430	23,220	—	—	—
1993–94	14,881	85,393	83,431	62,726	442	23,379	26,093	23,543	10,555
1994–95	14,772	86,221	84,476	63,572	458	23,668	—	—	—
1995–96	14,766	87,125	84,958	63,961	474	23,793	34,394	32,401	10,942
1996–97	14,841	88,223	86,092	64,785	487	24,287	—	—	—
1997–98	14,805	89,508	87,541	65,859	476	24,802	33,895	31,408	10,779
1998–99	14,891	90,874	89,259	67,183	463	25,797	—	—	—
1999–2000	14,928	92,012	90,538	68,173	423	26,407	32,995	30,457	10,693
2000–01	14,859	93,273	91,691	69,697	411	27,090	—	—	—
2001–02	14,559	94,112	92,696	70,516	408	27,468	35,895	33,191	11,846
2002–03	14,465	95,615	93,869	71,270	366	28,151	—	—	—
2003–04	14,383	95,726	93,977	71,195	376	28,219	34,681	31,988	11,188
2004–05	14,205	96,513	95,001	71,556	338	29,017	—	—	—
2005–06	14,166	97,382	96,798	72,998	335	29,507	35,054	32,127	12,184
2006–07	13,862	98,793	98,410	74,974	327	29,420	—	—	—

—Not available.
[1]Includes operating and nonoperating districts.
[2]Schools with both elementary and secondary programs are included under elementary schools and also under secondary schools.
[3]Data for most years prior to 1976–77 are partly estimated. Prior to 1995–96, excludes schools with highest grade of kindergarten.
[4]Includes regular schools and special schools not classified by grade span.
[5]Includes elementary, secondary, and combined elementary/secondary schools.
[6]These data cannot be compared directly with the data for years after 1980–81.
[7]Because of expanded survey coverage, data are not directly comparable with figures after 1983–84.

SOURCE: U.S. Department of Education, National Center for Education Statistics, *Annual Report of the Commissioner of Education*, 1870 through 1910; *Biennial Survey of Education in the United States*, 1919–20 through 1949–50; *Statistics of State School Systems*, 1959–60 through 1967–68; *Statistics of Public Elementary and Secondary School Systems*, 1970–71 through 1980–81; *Statistics of Public and Nonpublic Elementary and Secondary Day Schools*, 1968–69; *Statistics of Nonpublic Elementary and Secondary Schools*, 1970–71; *Private Schools in American Education*; Schools and Staffing Survey (SASS), "Private School Questionnaire," 1987–88 and 1990–91; Private School Universe Survey (PSS), 1989–90 through 2005–06; and Common Core of Data (CCD), "Local Education Agency Universe Survey" and "Public Elementary/Secondary School Universe Survey," 1982–83 through 2006–07. (This table was prepared September 2008.)

Table 88. Number and enrollment of regular public school districts, by enrollment size of district: Selected years, 1979–80 through 2006–07

Year	Total	25,000 or more	10,000 to 24,999	5,000 to 9,999	2,500 to 4,999	1,000 to 2,499	600 to 999	300 to 599	1 to 299	Size not reported
1	2	3	4	5	6	7	8	9	10	11
					Number of districts					
1979–80	15,944	181	478	1,106	2,039	3,475	1,841	2,298	4,223	303
1989–90	15,367	179	479	913	1,937	3,547	1,801	2,283	3,910	318
1994–95	14,772	207	542	996	2,013	3,579	1,777	2,113	3,173	372
1996–97	14,841	226	569	1,024	2,069	3,536	1,772	2,066	3,160	419
1997–98	14,805	230	572	1,038	2,079	3,524	1,775	2,044	3,165	378
1998–99	14,891	236	574	1,026	2,062	3,496	1,790	2,066	3,245	396
1999–2000	14,928	238	579	1,036	2,068	3,457	1,814	2,081	3,298	357
2000–01	14,859	240	581	1,036	2,060	3,448	1,776	2,107	3,265	346
2001–02	14,559	243	573	1,067	2,031	3,429	1,744	2,015	3,127	330
2002–03	14,465	248	587	1,062	2,033	3,411	1,745	1,987	3,117	275
2003–04	14,383	256	594	1,058	2,031	3,421	1,728	1,981	2,994	320
2004–05	14,205	264	589	1,056	2,018	3,391	1,739	1,931	2,881	336
2005–06	14,166	269	594	1,066	2,015	3,335	1,768	1,895	2,857	367
2006–07	13,862	275	598	1,066	2,006	3,334	1,730	1,898	2,691	264
					Percentage distribution of districts					
1979–80	100.0	1.1	3.0	6.9	12.8	21.8	11.5	14.4	26.5	1.9
1989–90	100.0	1.2	3.1	5.9	12.6	23.1	11.7	14.9	25.4	2.1
1994–95	100.0	1.4	3.7	6.7	13.6	24.2	12.0	14.3	21.5	2.5
1996–97	100.0	1.5	3.8	6.9	13.9	23.8	11.9	13.9	21.3	2.8
1997–98	100.0	1.6	3.9	7.0	14.0	23.8	12.0	13.8	21.4	2.6
1998–99	100.0	1.6	3.9	6.9	13.8	23.5	12.0	13.9	21.8	2.7
1999–2000	100.0	1.6	3.9	6.9	13.9	23.2	12.2	13.9	22.1	2.4
2000–01	100.0	1.6	3.9	7.0	13.9	23.2	12.0	14.2	22.0	2.3
2001–02	100.0	1.7	3.9	7.3	14.0	23.6	12.0	13.8	21.5	2.3
2002–03	100.0	1.7	4.1	7.3	14.1	23.6	12.1	13.7	21.5	1.9
2003–04	100.0	1.8	4.1	7.4	14.1	23.8	12.0	13.8	20.8	2.2
2004–05	100.0	1.9	4.1	7.4	14.2	23.9	12.2	13.6	20.3	2.4
2005–06	100.0	1.9	4.2	7.5	14.2	23.5	12.5	13.4	20.2	2.6
2006–07	100.0	2.0	4.3	7.7	14.5	24.1	12.5	13.7	19.4	1.9
					Number of students					
1979–80	41,882,000	11,415,000	7,004,000	7,713,000	7,076,000	5,698,000	1,450,000	1,005,000	521,000	†
1989–90	40,069,756	11,209,889	7,107,362	6,347,103	6,731,334	5,763,282	1,402,623	997,434	510,729	†
1994–95	43,669,683	13,063,753	8,113,872	6,868,964	7,032,980	5,835,233	1,393,734	927,198	433,949	†
1996–97	45,365,011	14,125,462	8,471,311	7,017,059	7,229,906	5,776,726	1,402,880	909,755	431,912	†
1997–98	45,872,785	14,445,720	8,540,624	7,123,005	7,272,764	5,753,977	1,402,274	899,840	434,581	†
1998–99	46,027,818	14,692,018	8,559,319	7,058,626	7,244,109	5,706,203	1,411,553	908,530	447,460	†
1999–2000	46,318,635	14,886,636	8,656,672	7,120,704	7,244,407	5,620,962	1,426,280	911,127	451,847	†
2000–01	46,588,307	15,083,671	8,750,743	7,144,242	7,235,089	5,597,023	1,400,732	927,146	449,661	†
2001–02	46,906,607	15,356,867	8,756,777	7,393,237	7,129,358	5,576,508	1,375,571	885,061	433,228	†
2002–03	47,379,395	15,690,805	8,957,891	7,348,643	7,150,205	5,547,189	1,375,070	874,163	435,429	†
2003–04	47,685,982	15,939,776	9,039,697	7,342,745	7,160,367	5,558,125	1,355,563	867,599	422,110	†
2004–05	47,800,967	16,182,672	8,980,096	7,346,960	7,134,861	5,533,156	1,368,546	851,455	403,221	†
2005–06	48,013,931	16,376,213	9,055,547	7,394,010	7,114,942	5,442,588	1,391,314	835,430	403,887	†
2006–07	48,105,937	16,496,573	9,083,944	7,395,889	7,092,532	5,433,770	1,363,287	840,032	399,910	†
					Percentage distribution of students					
1979–80	100.0	27.3	16.7	18.4	16.9	13.6	3.5	2.4	1.2	†
1989–90	100.0	28.0	17.7	15.8	16.8	14.4	3.5	2.5	1.3	†
1994–95	100.0	29.9	18.6	15.7	16.1	13.4	3.2	2.1	1.0	†
1996–97	100.0	31.1	18.7	15.5	15.9	12.7	3.1	2.0	1.0	†
1997–98	100.0	31.5	18.6	15.5	15.9	12.5	3.1	2.0	0.9	†
1998–99	100.0	31.9	18.6	15.3	15.7	12.4	3.1	2.0	1.0	†
1999–2000	100.0	32.1	18.7	15.4	15.6	12.1	3.1	2.0	1.0	†
2000–01	100.0	32.4	18.8	15.3	15.5	12.0	3.0	2.0	1.0	†
2001–02	100.0	32.7	18.7	15.8	15.2	11.9	2.9	1.9	0.9	†
2002–03	100.0	33.1	18.9	15.5	15.1	11.7	2.9	1.8	0.9	†
2003–04	100.0	33.4	19.0	15.4	15.0	11.7	2.8	1.8	0.9	†
2004–05	100.0	33.9	18.8	15.4	14.9	11.6	2.9	1.8	0.8	†
2005–06	100.0	34.1	18.9	15.4	14.8	11.3	2.9	1.7	0.8	†
2006–07	100.0	34.3	18.9	15.4	14.7	11.3	2.8	1.7	0.8	†

†Not applicable.
NOTE: Size not reported includes school districts reporting enrollment of zero. Regular districts exclude regional education service agencies and supervisory union administrative centers, state-operated agencies, federally operated agencies, and other types of local education agencies, such as independent charter schools. Enrollment totals differ from other tables because this table represents data reported by school districts rather than states or schools. Detail may not sum to totals because of rounding.
SOURCE: U.S. Department of Education, National Center for Education Statistics, Common Core of Data (CCD), "Local Education Agency Universe Survey," 1979–80 through 2006–07. (This table was prepared September 2008.)

Table 89. Number of public elementary and secondary education agencies, by type of agency and state or jurisdiction: 2005–06 and 2006–07

State or jurisdiction	Total agencies		Regular school districts, including supervisory union components[1]		Regional education service agencies and supervisory union administrative centers		State-operated agencies		Federally operated agencies		Independent charter schools and other agencies	
	2005–06	2006–07	2005–06	2006–07	2005–06	2006–07	2005–06	2006–07	2005–06	2006–07	2005–06	2006–07
1	2	3	4	5	6	7	8	9	10	11	12	13
United States	17,721	17,492	14,166	13,862	1,438	1,347	194	224	0	0	1,923	2,059
Alabama	165	163	165	133	0	1	0	29	0	0	0	0
Alaska.............................	54	54	54	53	0	0	0	1	0	0	0	0
Arizona	601	608	218	238	15	3	2	10	0	0	366	357
Arkansas.........................	291	292	253	254	15	15	3	3	0	0	20	20
California	1,128	1,130	987	989	132	131	9	10	0	0	0	0
Colorado	201	201	179	179	21	22	1	0	0	0	0	0
Connecticut.....................	196	198	166	169	6	6	7	7	0	0	17	16
Delaware	35	39	19	19	1	1	2	2	0	0	13	17
District of Columbia	53	56	1	1	0	0	0	0	0	0	52	55
Florida.............................	74	77	67	67	0	0	2	1	0	0	5	9
Georgia............................	204	204	180	182	16	16	5	5	0	0	3	1
Hawaii.............................	1	1	1	1	0	0	0	0	0	0	0	0
Idaho...............................	123	129	122	125	0	0	1	4	0	0	0	0
Illinois.............................	1,084	1,082	875	873	204	203	5	5	0	0	0	1
Indiana............................	364	367	294	294	29	29	4	4	0	0	37	40
Iowa	377	376	365	365	12	11	0	0	0	0	0	0
Kansas............................	312	332	300	323	0	0	12	9	0	0	0	0
Kentucky	196	195	176	175	18	18	2	2	0	0	0	0
Louisiana	88	99	68	68	0	0	7	6	0	0	13	25
Maine...............................	329	303	285	287	39	8	4	5	0	0	1	3
Maryland..........................	25	25	24	24	0	0	0	0	0	0	1	1
Massachusetts.................	495	392	350	250	86	78	1	0	0	0	58	64
Michigan	831	842	552	552	57	57	4	4	0	0	218	229
Minnesota	561	548	343	340	59	58	6	3	0	0	153	147
Mississippi	163	163	152	152	0	0	11	11	0	0	0	0
Missouri	532	550	524	524	0	0	4	5	0	0	4	21
Montana...........................	509	509	430	425	77	77	2	2	0	0	0	5
Nebraska	514	309	474	269	36	36	4	4	0	0	0	0
Nevada	18	19	17	17	0	0	0	1	0	0	1	1
New Hampshire	264	268	179	183	81	83	0	0	0	0	4	2
New Jersey	669	647	615	593	0	0	0	0	0	0	54	54
New Mexico	89	95	89	95	0	0	0	0	0	0	0	0
New York[2]	819	832	697	697	38	37	5	5	0	0	79	93
North Carolina	216	242	115	125	0	2	2	0	0	0	99	115
North Dakota	245	238	204	198	38	37	3	3	0	0	0	0
Ohio.................................	1,044	1,034	614	614	109	109	4	4	0	0	317	307
Oklahoma	600	600	540	540	0	0	3	0	0	0	57	60
Oregon.............................	221	223	200	199	20	20	1	3	0	0	0	1
Pennsylvania....................	730	737	501	501	101	104	11	11	0	0	117	121
Rhode Island	50	52	32	32	4	4	13	6	0	0	1	10
South Carolina.................	102	102	85	101	13	0	4	1	0	0	0	0
South Dakota...................	188	188	168	171	17	14	3	3	0	0	0	0
Tennessee	136	136	136	136	0	0	0	0	0	0	0	0
Texas	1,268	1,261	1,035	1,033	20	20	16	16	0	0	197	192
Utah	82	99	40	40	4	4	2	2	0	0	36	53
Vermont	363	358	302	292	60	60	1	0	0	0	0	6
Virginia............................	226	231	134	134	69	73	23	24	0	0	0	0
Washington......................	306	308	296	296	10	10	0	0	0	0	0	2
West Virginia....................	57	57	55	57	0	0	2	0	0	0	0	0
Wisconsin	460	459	440	425	17	0	3	3	0	0	0	31
Wyoming..........................	62	62	48	52	14	0	0	10	0	0	0	0
Bureau of Indian Education .	23	20	0	0	0	0	0	0	23	20	0	0
DoD, domestic	7	7	0	0	0	0	0	0	7	7	0	0
DoD, overseas	9	9	0	0	0	0	0	0	9	9	0	0
Other jurisdictions												
American Samoa	1	1	1	1	0	0	0	0	0	0	0	0
Guam	1	1	1	1	0	0	0	0	0	0	0	0
Northern Marianas.........	1	1	1	1	0	0	0	0	0	0	0	0
Puerto Rico..................	1	1	1	1	0	0	0	0	0	0	0	0
U.S. Virgin Islands..........	1	1	1	1	0	0	0	0	0	0	0	0

[1]Regular school districts include both independent districts and those that are a dependent segment of a local government. Includes nonoperating agencies. Components of supervisory unions operate schools, but share superintendent services with other districts.
[2]New York City counted as one school district.

NOTE: DoD = Department of Defense.
SOURCE: U.S. Department of Education, National Center for Education Statistics, Common Core of Data (CCD), "Local Education Agency Universe Survey," 2005–06 and 2006–07. (This table was prepared September 2008.)

Table 90. Public elementary and secondary students, schools, pupil/teacher ratios, and finances, by type of locale: 2005–06 and 2006–07

Selected characteristic	Total	City, large[1]	City, midsize[2]	City, small[3]	Suburban, large[4]	Suburban, midsize[5]	Suburban, small[6]	Town, fringe[7]	Town, distant[8]	Town, remote[9]	Rural, fringe[10]	Rural, distant[11]	Rural, remote[12]
1	2	3	4	5	6	7	8	9	10	11	12	13	14
Enrollment, schools, and pupil/ teacher ratios, fall 2006													
Enrollment (in thousands).............	49,066	7,710	3,601	3,774	15,957	1,665	1,075	1,784	2,364	1,881	4,492	3,332	1,430
Percentage distribution of enrollment, by race/ethnicity..........................	100.0	100.0	100.0	100.0	100.0	100.0	100.0	100.0	100.0	100.0	100.0	100.0	100.0
White..	56.5	22.7	40.3	54.4	56.7	71.2	69.3	75.6	70.5	67.8	75.1	80.8	77.8
Black..	17.1	30.4	28.2	17.9	15.8	9.8	8.8	7.7	12.0	11.1	11.2	10.1	7.2
Hispanic..	20.5	39.0	25.1	21.4	20.2	15.0	16.9	14.1	14.4	16.5	11.0	6.3	6.6
Asian/Pacific Islander..................	4.7	7.0	5.7	5.2	6.8	3.3	4.2	1.4	1.3	1.2	1.7	0.6	0.6
American Indian/Alaska Native......	1.2	0.9	0.7	1.1	0.5	0.7	0.9	1.1	1.8	3.4	0.9	2.2	7.8
Schools..	98,793	12,931	6,419	7,096	24,650	2,926	2,026	3,808	5,743	5,495	9,192	10,413	8,094
Average school size[13]......................	521	616	598	558	674	590	553	490	439	368	520	338	184
Pupil/teacher ratio[14]..........................	15.8	16.7	16.4	16.0	16.1	16.2	16.6	16.0	15.1	15.0	15.3	14.3	12.7
Enrollment (percentage distribution)...	100.0	15.7	7.3	7.7	32.5	3.4	2.2	3.6	4.8	3.8	9.2	6.8	2.9
Schools (percentage distribution).......	100.0	13.1	6.5	7.2	25.0	3.0	2.1	3.9	5.8	5.6	9.3	10.5	8.2
Revenues, 2005–06													
Total revenue (in millions of dollars)....	$529,720	$88,929	$37,353	$40,579	$181,208	$16,951	$10,776	$17,884	$23,473	$18,260	$45,264	$32,898	$16,145
Federal..	47,061	10,906	4,222	4,021	11,252	1,223	867	1,455	2,387	2,212	3,488	2,980	2,046
Title I..	11,371	3,798	1,045	941	2,202	246	167	303	559	522	556	572	461
Child Nutrition Act......................	8,910	1,967	794	750	2,093	243	155	285	491	414	734	648	335
Children with disabilities (IDEA)..	9,638	1,665	794	871	3,176	307	220	320	448	377	766	468	226
Impact aid..................................	1,236	85	90	59	218	22	7	42	40	143	75	122	332
Bilingual education.....................	320	93	30	33	81	5	5	9	14	10	11	15	14
Indian education.........................	100	9	4	5	6	1	1	3	7	12	5	12	36
Math, science, and professional development..........................	1,545	364	155	139	348	40	32	51	83	86	92	83	70
Safe and drug-free schools........	308	75	27	29	69	6	7	11	17	19	18	18	13
Title V, Part A............................	221	58	16	15	56	5	3	5	11	11	14	14	11
Vocational and technical education..............................	642	154	51	52	155	15	13	16	34	35	62	31	21
Other and unclassified...............	12,771	2,638	1,216	1,128	2,847	333	257	409	683	584	1,154	995	526
State (in millions of dollars)............	242,728	40,948	17,671	19,341	73,724	7,895	4,926	8,743	12,415	9,321	21,523	17,913	8,307
Special education programs........	15,218	2,880	1,214	1,075	5,810	454	317	428	588	413	1,006	690	343
Compensatory and basic skills ...	5,873	1,544	366	629	2,196	157	74	120	155	80	277	175	100
Bilingual education.....................	665	26	25	33	487	27	7	6	11	5	31	5	3
Gifted and talented	534	34	52	22	318	28	7	5	14	6	30	14	5
Vocational education	914	45	46	62	332	38	18	31	57	53	116	80	36
Other..	219,524	36,419	15,968	17,521	64,581	7,192	4,503	8,153	11,591	8,764	20,064	16,948	7,820
Local (in millions of dollars)[15].........	239,932	37,074	15,460	17,217	96,232	7,832	4,983	7,686	8,670	6,728	20,253	12,005	5,792
Property tax[16]...............................	147,248	19,062	9,066	10,315	63,209	4,185	3,224	5,039	5,770	4,599	11,656	7,293	3,831
Parent government contribution[16] .	39,189	11,260	2,722	2,475	14,555	1,708	526	492	528	202	2,091	1,391	338
Private (fees from individuals).....	13,176	1,088	756	938	5,018	482	312	507	642	509	1,483	1,001	439
Other[15]	40,319	5,665	2,915	3,489	13,449	1,457	921	1,648	1,731	1,417	4,122	2,321	1,184
Total revenue (percentage distribution)	100.0	100.0	100.0	100.0	100.0	100.0	100.0	100.0	100.0	100.0	100.0	100.0	100.0
Federal...	8.9	12.3	11.3	9.9	6.2	7.2	8.0	8.1	10.2	12.1	7.7	9.1	12.7
State...	45.8	46.0	47.3	47.7	40.7	46.6	45.7	48.9	52.9	51.0	47.6	54.4	51.4
Local...	45.3	41.7	41.4	42.4	53.1	46.2	46.2	43.0	36.9	36.8	44.7	36.5	35.9
Expenditures, 2005–06													
Total expenditures (in millions of dollars)..................	$536,511	$92,513	$37,757	$40,380	$184,135	$17,074	$10,859	$17,984	$23,535	$18,083	$45,623	$32,721	$15,847
Current expenditures for schools	441,978	75,372	31,275	33,914	149,763	13,995	8,861	15,009	19,787	15,553	37,022	27,787	13,640
Instruction..................................	271,753	47,611	18,952	20,823	92,101	8,581	5,374	9,208	12,067	9,441	22,484	16,922	8,188
Support services, students	22,677	3,193	1,706	1,901	8,463	711	469	767	994	811	1,925	1,205	531
Support services, instructional staff	21,228	4,053	1,791	1,727	7,021	642	412	632	919	706	1,693	1,118	513
Administration............................	32,337	4,761	2,223	2,351	10,788	1,029	665	1,151	1,566	1,298	2,862	2,367	1,277
Operation and maintenance........	43,280	7,422	2,997	3,318	14,779	1,422	881	1,440	1,918	1,546	3,521	2,649	1,387
Transportation	19,010	2,945	1,142	1,191	6,558	567	382	689	820	610	1,857	1,513	737
Food service	16,734	2,690	1,233	1,309	4,905	527	333	611	896	711	1,564	1,314	640
Other..	14,959	2,698	1,231	1,294	5,147	516	344	509	608	429	1,117	699	368
Other current expenditures	17,909	2,790	1,277	1,388	5,365	611	365	645	935	767	1,699	1,373	694
Interest on school debt	13,752	2,556	851	836	5,201	424	291	495	527	320	1,281	719	250
Capital outlay..................................	58,804	10,884	4,165	3,920	21,475	1,992	1,257	1,852	2,223	1,531	5,352	2,947	1,207
Current expenditures (percentage distribution)...............	100.0	100.0	100.0	100.0	100.0	100.0	100.0	100.0	100.0	100.0	100.0	100.0	100.0
Instruction..................................	61.5	63.2	60.6	61.4	61.5	61.3	60.6	61.4	61.0	60.7	60.7	60.9	60.0
Support services..........................	9.9	9.6	11.2	10.7	10.3	9.7	9.9	9.3	9.7	9.8	9.8	8.4	7.7
Administration............................	7.3	6.3	7.1	6.9	7.2	7.3	7.5	7.7	7.9	8.3	7.7	8.5	9.4
Operation and maintenance...........	9.8	9.8	9.6	9.8	9.9	10.2	9.9	9.6	9.7	9.9	9.5	9.5	10.2
Transportation	4.3	3.9	3.7	3.5	4.4	4.1	4.3	4.6	4.1	3.9	5.0	5.4	5.4
Food service and other..................	7.2	7.1	7.9	7.7	6.7	7.5	7.6	7.5	7.6	7.3	7.2	7.2	7.4

See notes at end of table.

Table 90. Public elementary and secondary students, schools, pupil/teacher ratios, and finances, by type of locale: 2005–06 and 2006–07—Continued

Selected characteristic	Total	City, large[1]	City, midsize[2]	City, small[3]	Suburban, large[4]	Suburban, midsize[5]	Suburban, small[6]	Town, fringe[7]	Town, distant[8]	Town, remote[9]	Rural, fringe[10]	Rural, distant[11]	Rural, remote[12]
1	2	3	4	5	6	7	8	9	10	11	12	13	14
Current expenditure per student (in dollars)	$9,151	$9,949	$8,852	$9,127	$9,529	$8,545	$8,451	$8,568	$8,400	$8,271	$8,561	$8,393	$9,406
Instruction expenditure per student (in dollars)	5,626	6,284	5,364	5,604	5,860	5,239	5,126	5,257	5,123	5,021	5,199	5,111	5,646

[1]Located inside an urbanized area and inside a principal city with a population of at least 250,000.

[2]Located inside an urbanized area and inside a principal city with a population of at least 100,000, but less than 250,000.

[3]Located inside an urbanized area and inside a principal city with a population less than 100,000.

[4]Located inside an urbanized area and outside a principal city with a population of 250,000 or more.

[5]Located inside an urbanized area and outside a principal city with a population of at least 100,000, but less than 250,000.

[6]Located inside an urbanized area and outside a principal city with a population less than 100,000.

[7]Located inside an urban cluster that is 10 miles or less from an urbanized area.

[8]Located inside an urban cluster that is more than 10 but less than or equal to 35 miles from an urbanized area.

[9]Located inside an urban cluster that is more than 35 miles from an urbanized area.

[10]Located outside any urbanized area or urban cluster, but 5 miles or less from an urbanized area or 2.5 miles or less from an urban cluster.

[11]Located outside any urbanized area or urban cluster and more than 5 miles but less than or equal to 25 miles from an urbanized area, or more than 2.5 miles but less than or equal to 10 miles from an urban cluster.

[12]Located outside any urbanized area or urban cluster, more than 25 miles from an urbanized area, and more than 10 miles from an urban cluster.

[13]Average for schools reporting enrollment. Enrollment data were available for 94,164 out of 98,793 institutions in 2006–07.

[14]Ratio for schools reporting both full-time-equivalent teachers and fall enrollment data.

[15]Includes tuition and fee revenues from other in-state school systems, which are excluded from state data reported through the "National Public Education Financial Survey."

[16]Property tax and parent government contributions are determined on the basis of independence or dependence of the local school system and are mutually exclusive.

NOTE: Detail may not sum to totals because of rounding. Race categories exclude persons of Hispanic ethnicity.

SOURCE: U.S. Department of Education, National Center for Education Statistics, Common Core of Data (CCD), "Public Elementary/Secondary School Universe Survey," 2006–07, and "Local Education Agency Universe Survey," 2005–06 and 2006–07; and "School District Finance Survey (Form F-33)," 2004–05. (This table was prepared September 2008.)

Table 91. Selected statistics on enrollment, teachers, dropouts, and graduates in public school districts enrolling more than 15,000 students: 1990, 2000, 2004–05, and 2006

Name of district	State	Enroll-ment, fall 1990	Enroll-ment, fall 2000	Enroll-ment, fall 2006	Percentage distribution of enrollment, by race, fall 2006						Number of classroom teachers, fall 2006	Pupil/teacher ratio, fall 2006	Total number of staff, fall 2006	Student/staff ratio, fall 2006	Percent dropouts from grades 9–12, 2004–05[1]					Number of high school graduates, 2004–05[2]	Number of schools, fall 2006
					White	Total	Black	Hispanic	Asian/Pacific Islander	American Indian/Alaska Native					Total	Grade 9	Grade 10	Grade 11	Grade 12		
1	2	3	4	5	6	7	8	9	10	11	12	13	14	15	16	17	18	19	20	21	22
Districts with more than 15,000 students	†	16,920,469	20,308,225	21,453,120	39.2	60.8	24.1	29.4	6.7	0.7	1,310,930	16.4	2,434,876	8.8	—	—	—	—	—	—	31,870
Baldwin County	AL	17,479	22,656	26,286	80.0	20.0	15.2	3.6	0.7	0.6	2,162	12.2	3,925	6.7	0.4	0.1	0.6	0.6	0.4	—	46
Birmingham City	AL	41,536	37,843	29,435	1.2	98.8	96.8	1.8	0.2	#	2,283	12.9	4,131	7.1	2.2	1.6	2.3	2.4	2.6	—	83
Huntsville City	AL	23,945	22,832	23,065	49.6	50.4	43.4	4.1	2.4	0.5	1,867	12.4	3,260	7.1	2.0	2.4	1.8	2.3	1.1	—	52
Jefferson County	AL	40,664	40,726	36,290	58.1	41.9	38.2	3.1	0.5	0.1	2,647	13.7	4,732	7.7	2.5	1.6	2.7	2.6	3.4	—	58
Madison County	AL	13,861	15,675	18,754	74.6	25.4	17.6	1.9	1.2	4.7	1,370	13.7	2,440	7.7	2.5	3.2	1.8	2.7	1.9	—	26
Mobile County	AL	67,203	64,976	65,097	44.9	55.1	50.8	1.1	2.1	1.0	4,789	13.6	9,279	7.0	1.7	1.6	1.8	1.7	1.6	—	114
Montgomery County	AL	35,956	33,267	31,867	17.5	82.5	78.2	1.9	2.2	0.2	2,372	13.4	4,456	7.2	4.8	1.6	5.9	6.7	6.0	—	61
Shelby County	AL	16,089	20,129	25,635	78.7	21.3	13.1	6.5	1.7	0.1	2,028	12.6	3,749	6.8	1.7	1.4	2.0	1.4	2.1	—	37
Tuscaloosa County	AL	14,426	15,666	16,712	72.5	27.5	25.1	1.7	0.5	0.1	1,261	13.3	2,303	7.3	3.5	3.0	4.3	4.0	2.8	—	30
Anchorage School	AK	42,300	49,526	49,230	57.2	42.8	8.4	6.9	12.3	15.1	2,853	17.3	5,752	8.6	8.3	5.0	5.9	8.6	14.4	2,549	95
Fairbanks North Star Borough	AK	14,961	15,659	15,017	68.8	31.2	7.8	5.0	3.4	15.0	813	18.5	1,831	8.2	11.0	10.9	13.2	11.9	7.4	830	34
Matanuska-Susitna Borough	AK	9,892	13,008	15,945	82.5	17.5	1.3	2.4	1.6	12.1	895	17.8	1,604	9.9	7.8	6.8	8.9	8.3	7.5	905	38
Alhambra Elementary	AZ	8,166	14,290	15,831	9.6	90.4	6.6	78.6	2.2	2.9	802	19.7	1,760	9.0	†	†	†	†	†	†	15
Amphitheater Unified	AZ	13,835	16,857	16,557	54.8	45.2	4.5	35.6	3.2	1.8	1,001	16.5	1,940	8.5	3.9	2.5	3.5	4.2	5.7	1,031	20
Cartwright Elementary	AZ	14,369	17,746	20,565	5.3	94.7	3.8	89.4	0.5	0.9	1,136	18.1	2,242	9.2	†	†	†	†	†	†	23
Chandler Unified	AZ	11,038	21,703	33,911	56.9	43.1	6.4	28.7	6.6	1.4	1,762	19.2	3,245	10.4	1.5	1.0	1.4	1.9	1.9	1,373	34
Deer Valley Unified	AZ	15,898	27,158	36,059	77.9	22.1	3.3	14.1	3.8	0.9	1,801	20.0	3,161	11.4	2.3	1.6	2.4	2.7	2.8	1,677	37
Dysart Unified	AZ	3,805	5,459	20,700	48.9	51.1	9.3	37.7	3.0	1.2	1,022	20.2	1,649	12.6	4.2	2.2	3.5	7.0	6.3	336	19
Gilbert Unified	AZ	10,863	29,188	37,797	74.0	26.0	4.4	16.3	4.5	0.9	2,140	17.7	4,015	9.4	1.2	0.3	0.9	2.0	2.0	2,300	39
Glendale Union High School	AZ	12,178	13,453	15,067	43.9	56.1	8.0	42.0	3.1	2.9	738	20.4	1,395	10.8	2.6	2.2	2.4	2.1	3.7	2,624	10
Kyrene Elementary	AZ	10,487	19,446	18,242	63.7	36.3	8.7	15.8	8.6	3.2	963	18.9	1,695	10.8	†	†	†	†	†	†	26
Mesa Unified	AZ	62,470	73,587	74,128	53.6	46.4	4.0	35.9	2.4	4.1	3,854	19.2	7,645	9.7	2.2	1.4	2.5	2.6	2.5	4,391	89
Paradise Valley Unified	AZ	26,698	34,882	34,648	70.7	29.3	3.4	21.5	3.2	1.2	1,931	17.9	3,135	11.1	2.0	0.9	1.5	2.6	3.2	2,237	46
Peoria Unified School	AZ	20,846	32,608	38,835	64.6	35.4	5.4	25.4	3.3	1.3	1,993	19.5	3,516	11.0	1.5	0.8	1.4	1.8	2.0	2,249	39
Phoenix Union High School	AZ	18,182	22,192	25,733	8.2	91.8	9.8	77.1	1.4	3.5	1,397	18.4	2,670	9.6	5.3	3.6	6.4	5.9	5.4	4,173	14
Scottsdale Unified	AZ	19,741	26,958	24,653	76.4	23.6	2.8	15.2	3.9	1.8	1,567	15.7	2,802	8.8	1.0	1.2	1.0	0.9	0.8	1,816	34
Sunnyside Unified	AZ	13,058	14,518	17,476	5.4	94.6	2.0	88.0	0.6	4.0	1,038	16.8	2,109	8.3	6.2	7.5	6.8	4.5	4.1	607	22
Tucson Unified	AZ	56,177	61,869	60,333	32.0	68.0	6.8	54.4	2.7	4.1	3,513	17.2	6,434	9.4	3.5	2.5	3.9	3.4	4.7	3,288	124
Washington Elementary	AZ	22,446	24,723	24,849	38.8	61.2	6.8	47.5	3.1	3.8	1,353	18.4	2,509	9.9	†	†	†	†	†	†	32
Little Rock	AR	25,813	25,502	26,879	23.6	76.4	68.2	6.1	1.7	0.3	1,858	14.5	3,667	7.3	6.8	6.1	6.9	7.0	7.5	1,242	49
Pulaski Co. Spec. School Dist.	AR	21,495	18,735	18,374	51.9	48.1	43.1	3.2	1.5	0.2	1,168	15.7	2,254	8.2	4.0	3.0	3.4	5.0	5.1	1,004	37
Springdale	AR	7,877	11,422	16,852	51.8	48.2	2.0	38.7	6.9	0.6	994	17.0	1,937	8.7	6.6	2.7	8.7	8.2	6.7	624	22
ABC Unified	CA	20,972	22,303	21,151	9.0	91.0	9.9	40.2	40.7	0.2	936	22.6	1,756	12.0	1.8	1.4	1.0	1.4	4.3	1,639	30
Alhambra Unified	CA	20,313	19,776	19,149	5.2	94.8	0.8	39.5	54.4	0.1	845	22.7	1,508	12.7	1.8	1.4	1.9	1.8	2.0	1,709	19
Alvord Unified	CA	14,853	17,664	19,847	16.8	83.2	5.0	72.4	5.4	0.4	861	23.0	1,612	12.3	0.4	0.2	0.3	0.3	1.0	899	21
Anaheim Elementary	CA	14,972	22,275	19,958	6.2	93.8	1.9	84.7	6.7	0.3	950	21.0	1,695	11.8	†	†	†	†	†	†	24
Anaheim Union High	CA	23,086	29,363	33,077	19.1	80.9	3.0	60.9	16.7	0.2	1,337	24.7	2,419	13.7	0.3	0.2	0.1	0.1	1.0	3,814	22
Antelope Valley Union High	CA	10,937	19,056	26,341	29.3	70.7	21.1	45.3	3.7	0.6	1,065	24.7	1,972	13.4	1.8	1.5	1.0	1.6	3.7	3,505	14
Antioch Unified	CA	13,045	20,018	20,476	30.4	69.6	21.0	35.1	12.5	1.0	973	21.0	1,454	14.1	3.0	0.3	0.7	1.5	9.8	1,152	26
Apple Valley Unified	CA	11,265	13,292	15,741	51.4	48.6	11.5	33.1	3.5	0.5	661	23.8	1,293	12.2	4.6	3.7	4.4	4.5	6.1	1,034	18
Bakersfield City Elementary	CA	24,911	27,674	27,403	13.2	86.8	11.5	72.6	1.5	1.1	1,362	20.1	2,522	10.9	†	†	†	†	†	†	43
Baldwin Park Unified	CA	15,878	17,473	19,784	4.9	95.1	3.1	85.8	6.0	0.1	847	23.4	1,485	13.3	6.6	4.0	3.9	6.4	14.1	1,027	23
Bellflower Unified	CA	9,917	14,935	15,009	18.9	81.1	15.9	54.2	10.7	0.3	674	22.3	1,210	12.4	1.7	0.5	0.4	0.9	5.3	882	15
Burbank Unified	CA	12,057	16,170	16,784	48.6	51.4	2.7	38.5	10.0	0.2	780	21.5	1,316	12.8	11.1	11.9	12.0	10.7	9.5	1,202	20
Cajon Valley Union Elementary	CA	17,328	19,059	16,613	53.0	47.0	7.2	36.6	3.5	0.7	784	21.2	1,378	12.1	0.6	0.6	0.5	0.6	0.7	†	30
Capistrano Unified	CA	26,852	45,074	51,512	71.5	28.5	1.5	19.2	7.4	0.3	2,237	23.0	3,933	13.1	0.6	0.6	0.5	0.6	0.7	3,027	61
Chaffey Joint Union High	CA	13,505	19,851	25,102	25.2	74.8	11.1	56.3	7.1	0.4	991	25.3	1,730	14.5	3.8	1.1	0.6	2.4	12.7	4,147	11

See notes at end of table.

Table 91. Selected statistics on enrollment, teachers, dropouts, and graduates in public school districts enrolling more than 15,000 students: 1990, 2000, 2004–05, and 2006—Continued

Name of district	State	Enroll-ment, fall 1990	Enroll-ment, fall 2000	Enroll-ment, fall 2006	Percentage distribution of enrollment, by race, fall 2006 — White	Minority — Total	Minority — Black	Minority — Hispanic	Minority — Asian/Pacific Islander	Minority — American Indian/Alaska Native	Number of classroom teachers, fall 2006	Pupil/teacher ratio, fall 2006	Total number of staff, fall 2006	Student/staff ratio, fall 2006	Percent dropouts from grades 9–12, 2004–05[1] — Total	Grade 9	Grade 10	Grade 11	Grade 12	Number of high school graduates, 2004–05[2]	Number of schools, fall 2006
1	2	3	4	5	6	7	8	9	10	11	12	13	14	15	16	17	18	19	20	21	22
Chino Valley Unified	CA	23,257	31,763	33,235	31.3	68.7	4.4	50.6	13.4	0.2	1,414	23.5	2,178	15.3	3.8	2.2	3.1	4.3	6.0	2,305	36
Chula Vista Elementary	CA	17,604	23,132	26,891	13.9	86.1	4.8	67.2	13.6	0.4	1,415	19.0	2,581	10.4	†	†	†	†	†	†	44
Clovis Unified	CA	23,224	32,717	37,101	55.2	44.8	3.7	24.1	15.8	1.1	1,729	21.5	2,996	12.4	1.1	0.4	0.6	0.6	2.7	2,203	47
Coachella Valley Unified	CA	9,091	12,636	17,499	1.4	98.6	0.5	97.5	0.3	0.3	826	21.2	1,574	11.1	5.5	7.2	4.8	5.5	2.6	736	23
Colton Joint Unified	CA	16,415	22,118	24,565	11.6	88.4	7.7	76.2	4.0	0.5	1,126	21.8	1,871	13.1	6.2	2.4	2.8	4.8	17.4	1,011	28
Compton Unified	CA	27,585	31,037	28,538	0.3	99.7	25.3	73.4	1.0	0.1	1,265	22.6	2,465	11.6	7.2	7.5	5.6	7.5	8.1	1,161	40
Conejo Valley Unified	CA	17,209	20,999	22,274	68.8	31.2	1.6	18.9	9.9	0.8	994	22.4	1,759	12.7	0.3	0.0	0.2	0.4	0.5	1,431	29
Corona-Norco Unified	CA	23,036	37,487	49,865	35.9	64.1	5.9	49.6	8.2	0.3	2,316	21.5	3,851	12.9	0.9	0.2	0.3	0.7	2.5	2,707	51
Covina-Valley Unified	CA	11,666	14,422	15,015	17.8	82.2	5.1	66.8	9.8	0.4	633	23.7	1,044	14.4	0.2	0.0	0.1	0.1	0.7	1,061	20
Cupertino Union School	CA	12,227	15,670	16,971	25.9	74.1	1.2	4.6	68.0	0.3	780	21.8	1,281	13.3	†	†	†	†	†	†	25
Desert Sands Unified	CA	16,058	23,500	28,277	28.4	71.6	2.1	67.0	2.2	0.4	1,238	22.8	2,011	14.1	2.8	0.7	3.1	2.7	5.6	1,544	32
Downey Unified	CA	15,418	21,474	22,456	11.0	89.0	3.9	80.0	4.7	0.4	985	22.8	1,652	13.6	1.8	1.3	0.4	0.9	4.6	1,332	20
East Side Union High	CA	21,973	24,282	25,998	11.8	88.2	4.3	46.1	37.3	0.4	1,191	21.8	2,017	12.9	7.5	8.0	3.7	3.0	15.2	4,949	20
Elk Grove Unified	CA	27,246	47,736	61,881	29.8	70.2	19.6	22.0	28.0	0.7	2,940	21.0	4,966	12.5	3.3	1.2	1.9	3.3	7.4	3,371	63
Escondido Union Elementary	CA	14,663	19,312	19,432	26.4	73.6	2.9	65.3	4.9	0.5	1,006	19.3	1,720	11.3	†	†	†	†	†	†	26
Fairfield-Suisun Unified	CA	20,227	22,263	23,074	28.1	71.9	22.6	31.5	16.8	0.9	1,135	20.3	1,962	11.8	4.1	1.4	1.2	2.6	12.3	1,292	32
Folsom-Cordova Unified	CA	12,656	16,277	18,793	62.9	37.1	8.3	15.3	12.4	1.0	856	22.0	1,482	12.7	2.1	1.7	1.5	2.6	2.8	1,035	35
Fontana Unified	CA	27,043	37,244	41,812	7.4	92.6	7.4	82.0	2.7	0.5	1,835	22.8	3,273	12.8	4.8	3.1	5.0	4.9	7.2	1,934	43
Fremont Unified	CA	27,172	31,078	32,087	25.5	74.5	5.7	16.0	52.2	0.4	1,511	21.2	2,314	13.9	1.0	0.7	0.7	1.1	1.6	1,958	41
Fresno Unified	CA	71,500	79,007	77,555	14.8	85.2	11.2	57.9	15.3	0.8	3,894	19.9	6,861	11.3	4.0	3.4	3.3	3.9	6.3	4,022	110
Fullerton Joint Union High	CA	12,729	15,165	16,499	26.9	73.1	2.4	49.0	21.6	0.2	586	28.2	1,076	15.3	0.4	0.2	0.4	0.6	1.0	2,961	8
Garden Grove Unified	CA	37,969	48,742	48,802	13.9	86.1	0.9	53.1	31.8	0.2	2,118	23.0	3,942	12.4	0.7	0.7	0.9	1.2	1.2	2,670	67
Glendale Unified	CA	25,459	30,329	27,420	56.8	43.2	1.2	22.4	19.4	0.2	1,157	23.7	2,147	12.8	1.5	0.5	0.6	0.9	3.3	2,133	32
Grossmont Union High	CA	18,647	23,639	23,870	56.2	43.8	8.9	27.3	5.7	2.0	1,115	21.4	1,524	15.7	1.0	0.3	0.6	8.6	2.7	4,508	19
Hacienda La Puente Unified	CA	23,267	24,646	22,355	5.6	94.4	1.6	76.2	16.3	0.3	1,096	20.4	1,751	12.8	12.4	13.8	14.8	3.1	11.9	1,556	39
Hayward Unified	CA	19,122	24,205	21,804	10.4	89.6	15.5	53.4	20.3	0.5	1,069	20.4	1,772	12.3	3.4	3.0	2.4	1.9	5.1	1,247	35
Hemet Unified	CA	12,811	17,451	23,541	44.7	55.3	7.1	43.6	3.4	1.3	1,051	22.4	1,807	13.0	1.2	1.9	0.3	5.6	2.8	991	29
Hesperia Unified	CA	13,113	15,360	21,890	35.1	64.9	7.3	54.4	2.4	0.8	944	23.2	1,766	12.4	5.8	4.8	5.5	1.0	7.7	1,038	29
Huntington Beach Union High	CA	14,039	14,359	15,913	48.2	51.8	1.4	20.6	24.4	5.5	635	25.1	1,195	13.3	1.0	0.1	0.0	0.1	2.6	3,045	9
Inglewood Unified	CA	16,355	17,295	15,945	0.5	99.5	41.1	57.5	0.9	0.1	961	16.6	1,283	12.4	0.1	0.0	0.0	4.8	0.4	684	20
Irvine Unified	CA	20,735	23,961	25,821	43.9	56.1	2.3	8.1	44.9	0.7	1,132	22.8	1,908	13.5	0.0	0.0	0.0	3.4	0.1	1,959	33
Jurupa Unified	CA	15,419	19,839	20,604	19.2	80.8	3.3	75.0	2.2	0.3	937	22.0	1,652	12.5	4.8	1.6	2.8	0.6	11.7	1,055	24
Kern Union High	CA	20,183	29,333	36,086	33.9	66.1	7.5	53.9	3.9	0.8	1,597	22.6	3,171	11.4	3.7	1.5	2.0	3.4	8.8	6,172	26
Lake Elsinore Unified	CA	11,000	17,178	21,525	41.3	58.7	4.9	48.9	4.1	0.5	965	22.3	1,729	12.4	0.4	0.1	0.5	0.6	0.7	1,119	24
Lancaster Elementary	CA	11,248	14,433	16,317	20.3	79.7	29.0	46.9	3.3	0.7	778	21.0	1,344	12.1	†	†	†	†	†	†	19
Lodi Unified	CA	23,954	27,339	31,266	30.5	69.5	8.9	36.7	23.2	0.7	1,586	19.7	2,734	11.4	5.4	2.8	3.2	3.4	12.6	1,738	54
Long Beach Unified	CA	71,342	93,694	90,663	17.6	82.4	19.0	53.8	9.3	0.3	4,213	21.5	8,083	11.2	3.2	1.4	1.6	3.0	7.3	4,956	91
Los Angeles Unified	CA	625,086	721,346	707,627	8.8	91.2	11.1	73.5	6.2	0.3	34,365	20.6	70,743	10.0	5.6	3.7	4.8	5.8	11.0	29,741	815
Lynwood Unified	CA	15,469	18,237	17,712	0.3	99.7	7.7	91.6	0.4	#	821	21.6	1,340	13.2	3.8	2.4	4.5	3.4	5.4	993	19
Madera Unified	CA	13,728	15,957	18,643	13.8	86.2	3.1	81.2	1.5	0.4	896	20.8	1,581	11.8	7.7	5.1	6.6	8.8	10.9	860	28
Manteca Unified	CA	13,356	15,746	23,643	30.8	69.2	10.2	44.5	13.2	1.3	1,088	21.7	1,778	13.3	0.9	0.7	0.4	0.5	2.4	1,221	27
Modesto City Elementary	CA	17,405	18,740	16,680	25.1	74.9	4.9	62.9	6.2	1.0	870	19.2	1,453	11.5	†	†	†	†	†	†	27
Modesto City High	CA	10,697	14,547	15,904	40.3	59.7	5.8	43.5	9.5	0.8	615	25.8	1,207	13.2	5.6	3.3	3.3	5.2	11.4	2,952	7
Montebello Unified	CA	32,938	34,794	33,819	2.1	97.9	0.3	93.9	3.6	0.1	1,460	23.2	2,704	12.5	0.4	4.1	4.4	6.0	0.5	1,800	29
Moreno Valley Unified	CA	29,064	32,730	37,351	14.6	85.4	19.9	60.0	5.1	0.5	1,639	22.8	2,890	12.9	6.5	1.7	1.8	2.8	13.6	1,837	38
Mt. Diablo Unified	CA	32,840	36,648	35,685	51.5	48.5	5.5	29.6	12.8	0.6	1,698	21.0	2,811	12.7	3.2	1.7	0.4	0.7	6.7	2,305	55
Murrieta Valley Unified	CA	3,990	12,065	21,246	56.7	43.3	6.7	25.6	10.5	1.3	912	23.3	1,649	12.9	1.4	0.2	0.4	0.7	5.2	1,003	18
Napa Valley Unified	CA	13,705	16,392	17,418	43.7	56.3	2.2	45.6	7.4	0.3	888	19.6	1,502	11.6	0.6	0.8	0.7	1.4	5.1	1,072	38
Newport-Mesa Unified	CA	16,434	21,658	21,421	51.9	48.1	1.3	40.4	6.1	0.4	1,016	21.1	2,004	10.7	1.4	3.0	3.2	3.9	1.5	1,402	32
Norwalk-La Mirada Unified	CA	19,179	23,610	22,551	13.7	86.3	3.5	74.4	7.9	0.4	914	24.7	1,814	12.4	1.4	0.8	0.7	1.4	3.1	1,293	29
Oakland Unified	CA	52,095	54,863	47,013	6.3	93.7	40.0	36.5	16.8	0.4	2,572	18.3	4,027	11.7	4.8	3.0	3.2	3.9	11.9	1,909	149
Oceanside Unified	CA	17,034	22,354	21,075	28.5	71.5	8.6	54.2	8.1	0.6	1,027	20.5	1,752	12.0	0.9	0.1	0.1	0.1	3.5	1,042	30

See notes at end of table.

Table 91. Selected statistics on enrollment, teachers, dropouts, and graduates in public school districts enrolling more than 15,000 students: 1990, 2000, 2004–05, and 2006—Continued

Name of district	State	Enroll-ment, fall 1990	Enroll-ment, fall 2000	Enroll-ment, fall 2006	White	Minority Total	Black	Hispanic	Asian/ Pacific Islander	American Indian/ Alaska Native	Number of classroom teachers, fall 2006	Pupil/ teacher ratio, fall 2006	Total number of staff, fall 2006	Student/ staff ratio, fall 2006	Percent dropouts Total	Grade 9	Grade 10	Grade 11	Grade 12	Number of high school graduates, 2004–05[1]	Number of schools, fall 2006
1	2	3	4	5	6	7	8	9	10	11	12	13	14	15	16	17	18	19	20	21	22
Ontario-Montclair Elementary	CA	21,033	26,407	24,177	6.6	93.4	3.6	86.3	3.2	0.3	1,178	20.5	1,955	12.4	†	†	†	†	†	†	34
Orange Unified	CA	25,224	31,097	30,327	39.2	60.8	1.7	46.0	12.6	0.6	1,373	22.1	2,658	11.4	1.4	1.6	0.8	0.9	2.2	1,887	42
Oxnard Elementary	CA	12,212	16,249	15,441	6.5	93.5	2.2	87.6	3.4	0.3	706	21.9	1,225	12.6	†	†	†	†	†	†	21
Oxnard Union High	CA	11,512	14,552	16,321	18.5	81.5	3.3	70.1	7.5	0.6	633	25.8	1,141	14.3	3.8	1.2	0.4	1.5	12.3	2,853	10
Pajaro Valley Unified School	CA	16,355	19,864	19,162	19.5	80.5	0.7	77.4	2.3	0.2	872	22.0	1,805	10.6	0.3	0.3	0.1	0.1	0.6	1,080	33
Palm Springs Unified	CA	14,427	20,847	24,263	20.5	79.5	5.2	70.0	3.7	0.7	1,095	22.2	1,802	13.5	6.5	3.2	3.6	6.0	14.3	1,049	24
Palmdale Elementary	CA	13,199	20,853	22,509	13.0	87.0	17.0	67.0	2.5	0.5	925	24.3	1,546	14.6	†	†	†	†	†	†	28
Panama Buena Vista Union Elementary	CA	10,066	12,843	15,792	35.6	64.4	11.5	44.6	7.6	0.7	783	20.2	1,326	11.9	†	†	†	†	†	†	22
Paramount Unified	CA	12,855	16,862	16,044	2.5	97.5	10.7	83.7	2.7	0.4	796	20.2	1,355	11.8	3.0	1.7	1.5	1.8	7.9	660	20
Pasadena Unified	CA	21,802	23,559	20,827	15.7	84.3	23.6	56.3	4.2	0.2	995	20.9	2,254	9.2	3.9	3.2	3.3	3.6	6.2	1,117	37
Placentia-Yorba Linda Unified	CA	21,438	26,046	26,419	55.1	44.9	2.1	31.8	10.8	0.2	1,105	23.9	2,022	13.1	0.3	0.3	0.2	0.3	0.4	1,656	32
Pomona Unified	CA	26,918	34,479	31,817	6.4	93.6	6.9	80.3	6.3	0.1	1,486	21.4	2,646	12.0	6.3	5.8	6.7	6.0	7.0	1,383	43
Poway Unified	CA	24,662	32,532	32,873	61.2	38.8	3.2	11.0	24.2	0.5	1,476	22.3	2,645	12.4	0.8	0.0	0.0	0.3	3.0	2,276	34
Redlands Unified	CA	16,002	19,411	21,438	41.8	58.2	8.0	37.9	11.6	0.7	945	22.7	1,547	13.9	1.4	0.5	0.7	0.9	3.7	1,486	23
Rialto Unified	CA	19,794	28,060	29,708	6.7	93.3	19.0	71.7	2.3	0.2	1,362	21.8	2,382	12.5	5.6	5.4	5.2	6.4	5.8	1,435	28
Riverside Unified	CA	31,326	38,124	43,464	33.0	67.0	9.2	52.3	5.0	0.5	1,798	24.2	3,323	13.1	0.9	0.9	0.7	0.9	1.1	2,636	48
Rowland Unified	CA	19,143	18,972	17,254	4.7	95.3	3.0	63.2	29.1	0.1	786	21.9	1,526	11.3	0.0	0.0	0.0	0.0	0.1	971	23
Sacramento City Unified	CA	49,557	52,734	49,355	21.4	78.6	21.6	32.2	23.7	1.2	2,479	19.9	4,265	11.6	4.0	5.7	3.1	3.7	3.3	2,451	93
Saddleback Valley Unified	CA	25,130	35,199	33,909	63.3	36.7	2.2	23.7	10.4	0.4	1,461	23.2	2,486	13.6	0.9	0.3	0.4	0.7	2.3	2,077	37
San Bernardino City Unified	CA	40,589	52,031	57,398	11.9	88.1	17.1	67.4	2.8	0.8	2,516	22.8	4,505	12.7	5.7	5.3	4.7	5.6	9.0	2,446	71
San Diego Unified	CA	121,152	141,804	130,983	25.5	74.5	13.5	44.2	16.3	0.6	7,135	18.4	13,304	9.8	2.9	3.0	2.3	2.6	3.8	6,653	223
San Francisco Unified	CA	61,688	59,979	56,183	10.2	89.8	13.4	23.5	52.3	0.6	3,103	18.1	4,561	12.3	1.9	2.9	1.5	2.1	1.7	3,789	118
San Jose Unified	CA	29,630	33,015	31,702	28.3	71.7	3.5	51.7	15.4	1.1	1,574	20.1	2,415	13.1	1.8	1.0	1.2	1.5	3.2	1,819	52
San Juan Unified	CA	47,690	50,266	47,862	68.3	31.7	7.5	15.7	6.6	2.0	2,262	21.2	4,384	10.9	5.7	3.4	4.6	5.2	9.4	3,848	81
San Marcos Unified	CA	9,108	12,804	16,844	40.1	59.9	3.2	47.8	8.2	0.7	733	23.0	1,331	12.7	2.4	0.0	0.6	0.7	10.0	645	19
San Ramon Valley Unified	CA	16,119	20,742	24,737	70.2	29.8	2.4	5.1	21.8	0.4	1,157	21.4	2,037	12.1	0.2	0.0	0.1	0.7	0.7	1,593	30
Santa Ana Unified	CA	45,964	60,643	57,286	3.4	96.6	0.7	92.5	3.3	0.1	2,453	23.4	5,228	11.0	2.7	1.8	1.9	3.2	4.6	2,735	60
Simi Valley Unified	CA	18,262	21,181	21,435	65.4	34.6	1.4	23.8	8.6	0.8	940	22.8	1,666	12.9	1.5	0.3	0.3	0.5	5.2	1,261	30
Stockton City Unified	CA	32,687	37,573	38,617	9.6	90.4	12.9	55.8	18.2	3.4	1,789	21.6	3,467	11.1	6.4	4.5	4.8	5.3	12.2	1,495	60
Sweetwater Union High	CA	27,894	35,330	42,085	11.2	88.8	4.7	71.8	11.8	0.5	1,911	22.0	3,680	11.4	1.8	0.3	0.8	1.4	5.2	5,313	29
Temecula Valley Unified	CA	7,596	18,980	28,680	59.1	40.9	5.2	23.3	11.0	1.3	1,349	21.3	2,274	12.6	1.0	0.3	0.7	0.9	2.5	1,416	31
Torrance Unified	CA	19,645	24,118	25,288	38.4	61.6	3.8	19.5	37.6	0.7	1,123	22.5	2,181	11.6	0.2	0.0	0.0	0.0	0.6	2,131	31
Tracy Joint Unified	CA	7,626	13,816	17,375	33.4	66.6	8.5	40.9	16.6	0.7	822	21.1	1,363	12.7	0.5	0.0	0.0	0.0	2.5	1,070	23
Tustin Unified	CA	10,831	16,963	20,515	36.3	63.7	2.7	43.5	17.1	0.3	870	23.6	1,527	13.4	0.4	0.1	0.4	0.2	1.0	994	28
Val Verde Unified	CA	—	11,242	18,922	8.8	91.2	17.4	69.6	4.0	0.2	821	23.0	1,461	12.9	7.9	4.8	9.0	12.1	8.8	685	21
Vallejo City Unified	CA	19,049	20,270	17,746	12.5	87.5	34.1	27.8	25.0	0.6	849	20.9	1,490	11.9	4.8	5.3	4.0	3.6	6.1	988	29
Ventura Unified	CA	15,383	17,527	17,285	50.9	49.1	2.2	42.0	3.7	1.1	823	21.0	1,435	12.0	2.7	0.3	0.5	2.0	8.8	1,090	31
Visalia Unified	CA	21,309	23,989	26,384	33.1	66.9	2.9	55.4	6.6	2.0	1,168	22.6	2,101	12.6	2.1	1.4	1.2	1.7	4.5	1,471	36
Vista Unified	CA	18,489	27,651	26,977	34.2	65.3	5.6	53.4	6.0	0.7	1,246	21.6	2,227	12.1	18.0	2.9	1.4	7.2	53.4	2,246	31
Walnut Valley Unified	CA	12,613	14,849	15,490	14.5	85.5	3.3	19.4	62.7	#	665	23.3	1,118	13.9	0.2	0.0	0.1	0.1	0.6	1,380	15
West Contra Costa Unified	CA	31,292	34,499	31,539	11.9	88.1	25.4	45.8	16.7	0.2	1,587	19.9	3,098	10.2	6.7	8.8	5.8	5.9	5.8	1,844	64
William S. Hart Union High	CA	10,278	17,001	24,318	57.0	43.0	4.7	27.2	10.6	0.5	984	24.7	1,636	14.9	1.9	1.2	1.7	1.9	3.1	3,062	19
Academy, School District No. 20	CO	10,986	17,628	21,204	82.3	17.7	4.2	7.6	5.0	0.8	1,284	16.5	2,568	8.3	1.8	0.3	0.9	1.6	4.4	1,432	29
Aurora, Joint District No. 28	CO	25,897	30,453	33,831	25.1	74.9	20.5	49.6	3.9	0.9	1,832	18.5	3,953	8.6	13.3	13.6	15.4	14.0	9.1	1,354	50
Boulder Valley	CO	21,502	27,508	28,171	77.2	22.8	1.6	14.2	6.4	0.6	1,710	16.5	3,652	7.7	2.7	1.2	2.0	3.2	4.6	1,945	54
Cherry Creek	CO	29,210	42,320	49,684	65.2	34.8	13.8	12.7	7.7	0.6	2,978	16.7	5,783	8.6	4.0	2.0	3.3	4.7	6.0	3,133	54
Colorado Springs	CO	30,009	32,699	30,029	63.7	36.3	10.4	21.6	2.7	1.6	1,879	16.0	3,932	7.6	8.7	6.9	5.7	8.0	13.9	1,920	62
Denver	CO	59,013	70,847	72,561	20.4	79.6	17.8	57.5	3.2	1.1	4,107	17.7	8,596	8.4	16.2	17.1	16.8	14.4	15.3	2,777	149
Douglas County	CO	13,125	34,918	50,370	85.9	14.1	2.0	7.1	4.3	0.7	2,813	17.9	5,909	8.5	2.0	0.9	1.4	3.0	0.6	2,404	68
Greeley	CO	11,657	15,998	18,069	45.3	54.7	1.2	51.8	1.0	0.7	1,073	16.8	2,152	8.4	12.8	4.4	12.0	16.0	20.5	911	31
Jefferson County	CO	76,275	87,703	86,154	75.6	24.4	1.9	17.7	3.6	1.2	4,809	17.9	10,424	8.3	7.6	1.6	5.2	8.4	16.1	5,616	160
Littleton	CO	15,524	16,516	15,989	82.8	17.2	2.0	11.3	3.2	0.6	904	17.7	1,912	8.4	2.3	1.2	1.6	3.2	3.4	1,286	25

See notes at end of table.

Table 91. Selected statistics on enrollment, teachers, dropouts, and graduates in public school districts enrolling more than 15,000 students: 1990, 2000, 2004–05, and 2006—Continued

Name of district	State	Enroll-ment, fall 1990	Enroll-ment, fall 2000	Enroll-ment, fall 2006	White	Minority Total	Black	Hispanic	Asian/ Pacific Islander	American Indian/ Alaska Native	Number of classroom teachers, fall 2006	Pupil/ teacher ratio, fall 2006	Total number of staff, fall 2006	Student/ staff ratio, fall 2006	Total	Grade 9	Grade 10	Grade 11	Grade 12	Number of high school graduates, 2004–05[2]	Number of schools, fall 2006
1	2	3	4	5	6	7	8	9	10	11	12	13	14	15	16	17	18	19	20	21	22
Mesa County Valley	CO	17,024	19,688	21,173	78.2	21.8	1.5	17.7	1.1	1.4	1,205	17.6	2,643	8.0	8.7	4.2	9.7	11.8	9.8	1,228	42
Northglenn-Thornton	CO	20,838	30,079	37,341	61.7	38.3	2.7	29.6	5.1	0.9	1,943	19.2	3,963	9.4	8.5	7.3	7.1	7.6	12.8	1,851	49
Poudre	CO	18,589	24,052	25,430	78.4	21.6	1.8	15.4	3.3	1.2	1,468	17.3	3,162	8.0	7.6	5.5	7.6	7.7	10.0	1,698	52
Pueblo	CO	18,364	17,636	17,915	34.2	65.8	2.7	61.1	0.7	1.3	1,111	16.1	2,226	8.0	10.8	12.3	12.0	11.2	6.0	1,021	38
Saint Vrain Valley	CO	15,070	19,620	24,011	68.1	31.9	1.2	26.4	3.5	0.9	1,247	19.3	2,313	10.4	6.1	3.0	4.0	6.8	11.1	1,345	44
Thompson	CO	12,019	14,766	15,310	82.0	18.0	1.2	14.4	1.5	0.9	822	18.6	1,797	8.5	3.5	1.6	2.9	6.4	3.2	1,087	30
Bridgeport	CT	19,687	22,432	21,248	9.4	90.6	42.1	45.4	3.0	0.2	1,255	16.9	2,702	7.9	6.7	5.5	7.3	9.0	5.1	939	39
Hartford	CT	25,418	22,543	22,329	6.0	94.0	40.8	52.0	1.0	0.3	1,592	14.0	3,613	6.2	5.7	6.4	5.4	6.0	3.8	766	42
New Haven	CT	17,881	19,549	19,981	11.2	88.8	52.4	34.8	1.4	0.2	1,392	14.4	3,218	6.2	5.7	4.6	6.5	7.2	5.0	860	48
Stamford	CT	11,574	14,791	15,045	41.8	58.2	22.1	29.7	6.3	0.0	1,114	13.5	2,037	7.4	2.0	1.8	2.4	2.1	1.6	884	21
Waterbury	CT	13,323	16,282	18,210	28.0	72.0	27.7	42.0	1.9	0.3	1,215	15.0	2,606	7.0	2.7	1.5	3.0	3.9	2.7	719	31
Christina	DE	17,872	19,882	18,495	40.8	59.2	42.4	12.0	4.4	0.3	1,190	15.5	2,548	7.3	7.7	9.9	8.0	6.5	5.0	907	29
Red Clay Consolidated	DE	14,551	15,827	15,594	49.1	50.9	26.7	20.2	3.8	0.2	933	16.7	1,821	8.6	6.1	8.1	7.1	4.2	3.4	730	28
District of Columbia[3]	DC	80,694	68,925	56,943	5.7	94.3	82.1	10.3	1.8	0.1	5,394	10.6	12,194	4.7	—	—	—	—	—	2,682	172
Alachua	FL	26,305	29,712	28,998	51.6	48.4	38.4	5.8	4.0	0.2	1,704	17.0	3,976	7.3	6.0	4.6	6.0	6.2	7.8	1,812	68
Bay	FL	21,827	25,755	27,005	77.7	22.3	15.8	3.9	2.1	0.5	1,739	15.5	3,513	7.7	1.5	1.4	1.8	1.1	1.5	1,412	46
Brevard	FL	56,503	70,597	74,785	74.6	25.4	15.0	8.0	2.0	0.2	4,723	15.8	9,170	8.2	1.4	1.8	1.4	1.3	0.6	4,364	127
Broward	FL	161,101	251,129	262,813	32.2	67.8	38.2	26.0	3.4	0.2	15,234	17.3	27,741	9.5	2.1	2.6	1.7	1.7	2.3	13,248	293
Charlotte	FL	13,030	17,170	17,888	81.6	18.4	8.8	7.6	1.7	0.4	1,027	17.4	2,349	7.6	2.6	1.3	2.9	3.3	3.1	1,248	23
Citrus	FL	11,697	15,199	16,087	89.1	10.9	4.5	4.6	1.4	0.4	1,034	15.6	2,268	7.1	5.1	4.3	4.6	5.7	6.3	929	24
Clay	FL	21,925	28,115	35,711	78.0	22.0	12.5	6.6	2.7	0.2	2,381	15.0	4,509	7.9	2.2	1.3	1.7	3.4	2.3	1,925	38
Collier	FL	20,850	34,203	43,144	44.9	55.1	11.4	42.2	1.1	0.3	2,743	15.7	5,615	7.7	2.8	2.8	2.9	2.6	2.6	2,170	63
Dade	FL	292,023	368,625	353,790	9.5	90.5	27.2	62.0	1.2	0.1	20,656	17.1	37,845	9.3	5.2	3.8	4.4	4.5	9.6	17,197	442
Duval	FL	111,142	125,846	125,176	44.0	56.0	45.4	6.6	3.8	0.2	7,776	16.1	12,986	9.6	7.0	7.4	6.6	6.7	7.4	5,873	176
Escambia	FL	42,950	45,012	42,708	55.8	44.2	37.6	3.2	2.7	0.8	2,844	15.0	5,697	7.5	4.6	4.9	4.4	3.4	5.6	2,072	81
Hernando	FL	12,831	17,215	22,450	80.0	20.0	7.1	11.5	1.2	0.3	1,539	14.6	3,011	7.5	3.4	3.2	3.1	4.8	2.8	1,012	28
Hillsborough	FL	124,337	164,311	193,517	45.2	54.8	23.2	28.4	2.9	0.2	10,210	19.0	21,538	9.0	2.5	2.4	2.3	3.1	2.0	9,252	280
Indian River	FL	11,683	14,979	17,611	66.9	33.1	15.3	16.4	1.2	0.2	1,082	16.7	2,180	8.1	1.5	1.1	1.1	2.0	2.1	1,010	28
Lake	FL	21,065	29,293	39,623	65.2	34.8	16.0	16.2	2.1	0.5	2,372	16.7	5,228	7.6	5.4	4.7	4.4	6.4	6.8	1,845	55
Lee	FL	43,240	58,401	78,981	54.9	45.1	14.2	28.9	1.6	0.3	4,648	17.0	9,038	8.7	3.6	3.5	3.5	4.0	3.8	3,461	105
Leon	FL	27,241	32,050	32,383	51.9	48.1	41.9	3.1	2.9	0.1	1,989	16.3	4,409	7.3	2.4	2.9	1.9	2.5	2.0	1,775	57
Manatee	FL	26,207	36,569	42,235	60.2	39.8	15.6	22.6	1.5	0.2	2,594	16.3	5,469	7.7	3.1	2.1	2.7	3.8	4.4	2,088	74
Marion	FL	29,577	38,562	42,572	63.5	36.5	20.3	14.2	1.4	0.6	2,614	16.3	5,999	7.1	4.4	2.9	4.3	4.5	7.4	2,141	63
Martin	FL	11,692	16,308	18,239	70.8	29.2	8.7	19.0	1.2	0.2	1,072	17.0	2,142	8.5	1.6	1.3	1.5	1.1	2.5	997	36
Okaloosa	FL	26,140	30,344	30,256	78.1	21.9	12.8	5.8	2.7	0.5	1,898	15.9	3,299	9.2	3.1	2.1	2.0	4.6	4.1	2,052	60
Orange	FL	102,672	150,681	175,245	35.7	64.3	28.3	31.3	4.3	0.4	10,975	16.0	22,848	7.7	2.0	2.2	1.9	1.9	2.1	8,789	230
Osceola	FL	19,514	34,566	52,012	34.1	65.9	10.9	52.2	2.6	0.3	2,858	18.2	6,441	8.1	5.1	4.7	4.7	5.9	5.8	2,330	61
Palm Beach	FL	105,712	153,871	171,431	42.8	57.2	29.7	24.2	2.7	0.6	10,633	16.1	19,127	9.0	3.2	3.3	2.9	3.3	3.1	8,572	263
Pasco	FL	33,891	49,704	64,689	79.5	20.5	5.2	13.0	2.0	0.3	4,123	15.7	8,491	7.6	5.0	4.4	5.2	5.2	5.4	2,890	95
Pinellas	FL	92,976	113,027	109,915	66.9	33.1	19.9	9.0	3.8	0.3	7,015	15.7	14,223	7.7	3.5	4.2	3.6	3.3	2.2	5,767	173
Polk	FL	64,579	79,477	92,801	54.6	45.4	22.1	21.7	1.4	0.6	6,478	14.3	12,623	7.4	6.0	5.4	6.5	6.0	6.6	4,034	152
Santa Rosa	FL	15,708	22,633	25,392	88.9	11.1	5.5	3.0	1.9	0.6	1,580	16.1	2,547	10.0	2.1	0.9	1.3	1.6	5.0	1,516	38
Sarasota	FL	26,881	35,533	42,190	76.1	23.9	9.7	12.1	1.8	0.2	2,715	15.5	5,617	7.5	3.3	2.6	3.8	3.5	3.7	2,436	61
Seminole	FL	48,831	60,869	66,351	63.2	36.8	14.2	18.5	3.8	0.3	4,185	15.9	7,599	8.7	1.5	1.7	1.1	1.5	1.7	3,697	79
St. Johns	FL	12,080	20,090	26,926	84.7	15.3	8.9	4.0	2.2	0.2	1,528	17.6	3,041	8.9	1.8	1.3	1.2	2.5	2.5	1,466	38
St. Lucie	FL	22,224	29,540	38,793	46.2	53.8	29.7	22.0	1.8	0.3	2,075	18.7	4,485	8.6	3.0	2.5	3.1	3.4	3.3	1,403	46
Volusia	FL	48,342	61,517	65,867	67.5	32.5	15.4	15.3	1.5	0.2	4,539	14.5	9,781	6.7	1.4	1.1	1.1	1.3	2.3	3,447	93
Atlanta City	GA	60,714	58,230	50,631	9.0	91.0	86.0	4.4	0.6	#	3,689	13.7	6,899	7.3	6.3	6.4	7.4	5.8	5.2	1,981	105
Bibb County	GA	24,378	24,739	25,223	22.7	77.3	74.1	1.8	1.3	0.1	1,685	15.0	3,750	6.7	8.6	10.5	8.2	7.5	6.3	873	47
Chatham County	GA	34,044	35,344	34,330	26.7	73.3	67.2	3.9	2.0	0.2	2,533	13.6	4,643	7.4	7.8	9.3	7.8	5.5	6.8	1,294	57

See notes at end of table.

Table 91. Selected statistics on enrollment, teachers, dropouts, and graduates in public school districts enrolling more than 15,000 students: 1990, 2000, 2004–05, and 2006—Continued

Name of district	State	Enroll-ment, fall 1990	Enroll-ment, fall 2000	Enroll-ment, fall 2006	White	Minority Total	Black	Hispanic	Asian/ Pacific Islander	American Indian/ Alaska Native	Number of classroom teachers, fall 2006	Pupil/ teacher ratio, fall 2006	Total number of staff, fall 2006	Student/ staff ratio, fall 2006	Total	Grade 9	Grade 10	Grade 11	Grade 12	Number of high school graduates, 2004–05[2]	Number of schools, fall 2006
1	2	3	4	5	6	7	8	9	10	11	12	13	14	15	16	17	18	19	20	21	22
Cherokee County	GA	16,086	26,043	35,068	81.1	18.9	6.4	10.7	1.5	0.2	2,425	14.5	4,444	7.9	6.1	5.1	6.3	6.7	6.7	1,432	35
Clayton County	GA	34,754	46,930	52,533	6.2	93.8	76.1	13.3	4.4	0.1	3,420	15.4	7,303	7.2	3.6	4.2	3.2	3.8	2.9	1,947	63
Cobb County	GA	69,441	95,781	107,274	50.4	49.6	30.6	14.5	4.3	0.2	7,739	13.9	13,945	7.7	4.3	3.4	4.0	4.9	5.4	5,998	114
Columbia County	GA	14,096	18,756	22,112	76.2	23.8	16.7	3.2	3.6	0.2	1,399	15.8	2,932	7.5	4.2	3.8	3.6	4.8	4.9	1,166	28
Coweta County	GA	10,430	16,766	21,352	71.7	28.3	22.1	5.1	0.9	0.2	1,463	14.6	3,072	7.0	4.0	3.9	5.2	4.6	1.9	980	30
DeKalb County	GA	74,108	95,958	101,396	10.4	89.6	77.6	8.7	3.3	0.1	7,134	14.2	14,578	7.0	4.8	5.0	4.4	5.4	4.1	4,332	150
Dougherty County	GA	18,482	16,799	16,528	11.6	88.4	86.8	1.1	0.4	0.1	1,075	15.4	2,513	6.6	10.0	11.7	10.4	9.2	6.7	646	28
Douglas County	GA	14,002	17,489	24,144	44.5	55.5	46.1	7.9	1.4	0.1	1,600	15.1	3,100	7.8	4.9	2.7	5.3	7.0	5.6	999	33
Fayette County	GA	13,105	19,590	22,494	67.7	32.3	22.5	5.7	3.9	0.2	1,583	14.2	3,011	7.5	1.3	1.5	1.2	0.9	1.6	1,587	29
Forsyth County	GA	7,742	17,131	28,171	85.8	14.2	1.7	8.8	3.5	0.1	1,893	14.9	3,513	8.0	4.0	2.5	4.3	4.8	5.0	1,014	27
Fulton County	GA	41,195	68,583	83,861	38.9	61.1	42.6	10.3	8.1	0.1	5,955	14.1	11,293	7.4	3.8	2.8	3.4	4.4	5.2	3,962	94
Gwinnett County	GA	63,930	110,075	152,043	40.6	59.4	27.3	21.4	10.6	0.1	10,341	14.7	18,929	8.0	4.8	4.7	5.2	4.6	4.8	6,582	108
Hall County	GA	13,738	20,330	24,877	59.6	40.4	5.4	33.3	1.5	0.1	1,707	14.6	3,094	8.0	8.3	6.8	8.7	9.7	8.9	1,033	34
Henry County	GA	10,929	23,601	37,368	51.1	48.9	40.8	5.3	2.6	0.2	2,482	15.1	4,594	8.1	6.2	6.1	7.5	5.4	5.6	1,478	40
Houston County	GA	16,249	21,529	25,193	58.0	42.0	35.3	4.4	2.1	0.2	1,781	14.1	3,624	7.0	3.6	4.1	3.8	4.2	2.1	1,309	35
Muscogee County	GA	30,038	32,916	33,115	32.0	68.0	62.0	4.1	1.7	0.2	2,313	14.3	5,144	6.4	6.4	7.8	6.1	6.3	4.8	1,448	65
Newton County	GA	8,054	11,734	18,498	45.5	54.5	48.4	4.9	1.0	0.3	1,225	15.1	2,461	7.5	3.3	2.8	3.9	3.5	3.0	605	21
Paulding County	GA	7,604	16,587	25,669	75.2	24.8	19.5	4.5	0.6	0.2	1,746	14.7	3,292	7.8	6.2	5.5	6.6	7.7	4.8	859	28
Richmond County	GA	33,660	35,424	33,391	22.2	77.8	74.3	2.3	1.1	0.1	2,283	14.6	4,754	7.0	5.8	6.9	5.8	5.7	3.8	1,478	61
Rockdale County	GA	10,942	13,519	15,350	36.4	63.6	52.2	9.6	1.6	0.2	1,001	15.3	2,046	7.5	4.7	4.3	6.0	3.1	4.5	817	20
Hawaii Department of Education	HI	171,309	184,360	180,728	19.6	80.4	2.4	4.5	73.0	0.6	11,270	16.0	21,059	8.6	4.7	2.8	4.7	5.4	6.7	10,813	286
Boise Independent District	ID	23,394	26,598	25,662	85.0	15.0	2.4	8.5	3.7	0.5	1,485	17.3	2,636	9.7	3.7	2.5	3.7	4.3	4.4	1,789	55
Meridian Joint District	ID	14,802	23,854	32,277	89.5	10.5	1.6	5.3	2.8	0.8	1,638	19.7	2,813	11.5	2.0	1.2	1.9	2.1	2.7	1,644	48
City of Chicago	IL	408,714	435,261	413,694	8.3	91.7	49.1	39.2	3.3	0.1	18,966	21.8	24,350	17.0	12.7	15.0	12.8	10.2	11.0	16,866	633
CUSD 300 (Carpentersville)	IL	11,196	16,711	19,161	62.4	37.6	5.0	27.5	4.9	0.3	973	19.7	1,337	14.3	2.8	1.4	2.9	3.8	3.5	1,088	24
Indian Prairie	IL	7,670	23,173	28,764	68.2	31.8	8.8	6.9	16.0	0.2	1,607	17.9	2,166	13.3	0.6	0.1	0.3	1.0	1.2	1,596	31
Naperville	IL	16,212	18,762	18,449	77.0	23.0	4.2	4.3	14.5	0.1	1,017	18.1	1,412	13.1	0.9	0.2	0.3	1.3	1.7	1,389	21
Plainfield	IL	3,324	11,986	26,770	66.8	33.2	8.5	20.0	4.6	0.2	1,398	19.1	1,923	13.9	—	—	—	—	—	935	25
Rockford	IL	27,255	27,399	29,515	42.2	57.8	32.4	22.2	3.1	0.1	1,539	19.2	1,945	15.2	10.2	12.3	8.7	8.0	9.8	1,272	52
SD U-46 (Elgin)	IL	27,726	36,767	40,380	43.2	56.8	7.0	41.9	7.7	0.2	2,002	20.2	2,644	15.3	5.3	3.9	4.9	6.0	7.0	2,192	57
Valley View	IL	11,781	13,558	17,963	34.8	65.2	25.0	33.8	6.3	0.1	917	19.6	1,278	14.1	1.3	0.1	0.3	1.4	5.0	843	20
Waukegan	IL	12,116	15,510	16,924	7.2	92.8	18.2	72.6	1.8	0.1	864	19.6	1,161	14.6	6.6	8.7	6.7	5.7	3.3	766	27
Evansville-Vanderburgh Sch. Corp.	IN	22,918	22,875	22,190	81.5	18.5	15.6	1.6	1.0	0.3	1,424	15.6	2,805	7.9	2.9	1.1	3.9	2.9	3.9	1,353	42
Fort Wayne	IN	31,611	31,843	31,884	58.7	41.3	26.5	11.6	2.7	0.6	1,874	17.0	3,717	8.6	4.0	2.8	4.4	3.8	5.7	1,622	54
Hamilton Southeastern Schools	IN	3,113	8,777	15,315	85.8	14.2	6.4	2.9	4.6	0.2	798	19.2	1,672	9.2	0.3	0.0	0.3	0.3	0.6	560	18
Indianapolis	IN	48,140	41,008	37,057	26.1	73.9	60.3	13.0	0.4	0.2	2,434	15.2	5,370	6.9	3.6	4.2	3.4	2.8	2.6	1,109	79
MSD Lawrence Township	IN	11,066	15,692	16,138	50.7	49.3	39.0	8.5	1.7	0.1	898	18.0	1,936	8.3	0.7	0.3	0.4	0.4	2.1	939	18
South Bend Community Sch. Corp.	IN	21,425	21,536	21,769	44.7	55.3	38.3	15.1	1.3	0.5	1,261	17.3	3,054	7.1	2.9	1.8	3.4	4.1	3.5	1,094	38
Vigo County School Corp.	IN	16,982	16,545	16,431	91.3	8.7	6.3	1.0	1.3	0.1	1,008	16.3	1,921	8.6	2.1	1.0	2.1	2.9	2.9	922	29
Cedar Rapids	IA	16,988	17,780	17,263	80.5	19.5	13.8	2.9	2.2	0.6	1,086	15.9	2,275	7.6	2.7	1.0	2.2	3.5	4.4	1,129	35
Davenport	IA	17,841	16,874	15,957	66.4	33.6	21.2	8.9	2.8	0.8	1,134	14.1	1,939	8.2	6.2	4.1	6.2	8.1	6.6	948	32
Des Moines Independent	IA	30,514	32,435	31,866	62.4	37.6	17.2	15.1	4.7	0.6	2,226	14.3	4,052	7.9	7.1	7.5	7.7	3.9	8.8	1,757	60
Blue Valley	KS	9,432	17,111	20,497	85.9	14.1	3.7	2.4	7.7	0.3	1,342	15.3	1,991	10.3	0.6	0.0	0.1	1.0	1.3	1,348	32
Kansas City	KS	21,948	21,173	19,992	17.6	82.4	44.8	34.0	3.2	0.5	1,371	14.6	1,988	10.1	4.1	3.9	5.4	3.9	3.2	1,034	45
Olathe	KS	14,868	20,703	25,492	80.9	19.1	6.0	8.8	4.0	0.3	1,925	13.2	2,949	8.6	1.2	0.0	0.4	1.6	3.0	1,501	46
Shawnee Mission	KS	30,563	30,765	28,518	78.0	22.0	8.4	9.7	3.1	0.8	1,888	15.1	2,731	10.4	1.6	0.9	1.3	1.9	2.3	2,213	50
Wichita	KS	46,847	48,228	46,938	45.0	55.0	22.4	23.8	5.5	3.3	2,824	16.6	4,456	10.5	4.2	2.4	4.0	5.5	5.5	2,315	90

See notes at end of table.

Table 91. Selected statistics on enrollment, teachers, dropouts, and graduates in public school districts enrolling more than 15,000 students: 1990, 2000, 2004–05, and 2006—Continued

Name of district	State	Enroll-ment, fall 1990	Enroll-ment, fall 2000	Enroll-ment, fall 2006	Percentage distribution of enrollment, by race, fall 2006						Number of classroom teachers, fall 2006	Pupil/ teacher ratio, fall 2006	Total number of staff, fall 2006	Student/ staff ratio, fall 2006	Percent dropouts from grades 9–12, 2004–05[1]					Number of high school graduates, 2004–05[2]	Number of schools, fall 2006
					White	Total	Minority Black	Hispanic	Asian/ Pacific Islander	American Indian/ Alaska Native					Total	Grade 9	Grade 10	Grade 11	Grade 12		
1	2	3	4	5	6	7	8	9	10	11	12	13	14	15	16	17	18	19	20	21	22
Boone Co.	KT	9,911	13,445	17,397	91.9	8.1	2.8	3.2	2.0	0.1	1,054	16.5	2,234	7.8	2.9	1.5	2.6	4.8	3.6	893	21
Fayette County	KT	32,083	33,130	34,335	64.4	35.6	24.4	7.7	3.4	0.2	2,601	13.2	5,167	6.6	4.3	5.0	4.3	3.5	3.9	1,901	65
Jefferson County	KT	91,450	96,860	92,659	56.6	43.4	37.0	4.0	2.3	0.1	5,971	15.5	12,954	7.2	6.8	3.8	7.7	7.9	9.3	5,165	171
Ascension Parish SB	LA	13,001	15,038	18,199	64.9	35.1	30.2	4.0	0.6	0.3	1,241	14.7	2,359	7.7	4.7	5.4	5.1	3.7	4.0	754	23
Bossier Parish SB	LA	17,804	18,797	19,393	62.9	37.1	31.0	4.1	1.6	0.3	1,245	15.6	2,560	7.6	4.2	4.8	3.8	3.0	5.2	1,055	35
Caddo Parish SB	LA	51,375	45,119	43,019	33.9	66.1	63.8	1.2	1.0	0.2	2,853	15.1	6,552	6.6	11.1	12.8	8.5	10.7	12.2	2,071	74
Calcasieu Parish SB	LA	32,917	32,261	32,247	63.1	36.9	34.6	1.2	0.9	0.2	2,280	14.1	4,695	6.9	4.4	4.4	4.0	5.0	4.3	1,694	60
East Baton Rouge Parish SB	LA	61,669	54,246	49,197	16.1	83.9	79.5	2.0	2.3	0.1	3,218	15.3	6,319	7.8	7.1	5.9	6.4	7.0	9.6	2,294	94
Jefferson Parish SB	LA	58,177	50,891	43,528	33.7	66.3	49.3	11.2	5.1	0.7	2,895	15.0	6,320	6.9	10.9	11.6	10.9	10.4	10.2	2,078	87
Lafayette Parish SB	LA	29,403	28,931	30,255	53.5	46.5	42.3	2.4	1.5	0.3	2,058	14.7	4,127	7.3	4.3	9.4	6.7	6.5	5.5	1,629	44
Livingston Parish SB	LA	16,310	19,723	23,155	92.1	7.9	6.1	1.3	0.3	0.2	1,413	16.4	2,886	8.0	4.3	3.2	5.1	5.0	3.9	1,062	40
Ouachita Parish SB	LA	17,667	17,479	18,937	67.2	32.8	31.0	1.0	0.7	0.1	1,246	15.2	2,804	6.8	5.5	6.2	6.8	3.8	4.7	964	35
Rapides Parish SB	LA	24,765	23,467	23,763	53.0	47.0	43.3	1.6	1.2	0.9	1,670	14.2	3,335	7.1	6.7	8.0	5.5	6.6	6.5	1,135	52
Saint Landry Parish SB	LA	17,213	15,457	15,457	42.0	58.0	56.9	0.5	0.4	0.1	1,036	14.9	2,150	7.2	5.4	8.8	5.6	3.8	2.1	815	39
Saint Tammany Parish SB	LA	27,522	32,392	34,857	78.2	21.8	17.4	2.5	1.5	0.4	2,562	13.6	5,069	6.9	4.3	3.5	3.7	5.2	5.1	1,960	52
Tangipahoa Parish SB	LA	16,724	18,197	19,487	51.3	48.7	46.1	1.8	0.5	0.2	1,134	17.2	2,473	7.9	8.1	7.2	7.6	7.4	10.4	1,043	37
Terrebonne Parish SB	LA	21,116	19,774	18,911	59.6	40.4	28.7	1.9	1.1	8.7	1,376	13.7	2,626	7.2	6.6	6.4	4.6	8.9	6.9	993	41
Anne Arundel County	MD	65,011	74,491	73,066	68.4	31.6	22.2	5.4	3.6	0.4	4,893	14.9	9,004	8.1	2.5	2.5	2.1	2.8	2.5	4,840	121
Baltimore City	MD	108,663	99,859	84,515	7.7	92.3	89.2	2.1	0.7	0.4	5,928	14.3	11,540	7.3	13.1	15.1	12.8	11.3	11.6	4,047	198
Baltimore County	MD	86,737	106,898	105,839	51.0	49.0	39.7	3.7	5.0	0.5	7,420	14.3	14,142	7.5	4.9	4.3	5.6	5.2	4.6	7,190	169
Calvert County	MD	10,398	16,170	17,474	79.7	20.3	16.7	1.9	1.5	0.3	1,071	16.3	2,146	8.1	2.2	1.3	2.9	2.8	1.7	1,246	27
Carroll County	MD	21,835	27,528	28,616	92.2	7.8	3.5	2.2	1.6	0.4	1,891	15.1	3,451	8.3	1.3	1.1	1.8	1.3	1.0	2,112	46
Cecil County	MD	12,868	15,905	16,421	86.2	13.8	9.5	2.8	1.2	0.3	1,140	14.4	2,107	7.8	4.4	3.6	2.6	6.1	5.9	1,015	29
Charles County	MD	18,708	23,468	26,623	43.7	56.3	49.0	3.3	3.2	0.8	1,635	16.3	3,065	8.7	3.8	3.1	3.2	3.8	5.4	1,743	35
Frederick County	MD	26,848	36,885	40,224	76.9	23.1	11.4	7.2	4.2	0.6	2,585	15.6	5,012	8.0	0.8	0.8	0.7	0.7	0.8	2,680	64
Harford County	MD	31,500	39,520	39,568	74.5	25.5	19.1	3.1	2.7	0.6	2,740	14.4	4,990	7.9	3.3	2.8	3.7	3.9	3.0	2,634	52
Howard County	MD	29,949	44,946	49,048	60.2	39.8	20.4	4.9	14.3	0.3	3,571	13.7	6,956	7.1	1.5	1.4	1.6	1.5	1.6	3,253	72
Montgomery County	MD	103,757	134,180	137,814	41.1	58.9	23.0	20.8	14.8	0.3	9,613	14.3	19,918	6.9	1.9	1.7	1.8	2.1	2.1	9,227	204
Prince George's County	MD	108,868	133,723	131,014	5.5	94.5	75.4	15.7	2.9	0.5	8,880	14.8	17,601	7.4	4.0	5.6	3.9	2.6	2.8	7,908	213
Saint Mary's County	MD	12,549	15,151	16,665	74.4	25.6	19.9	2.6	2.5	0.6	1,001	16.6	1,903	8.8	3.0	3.0	2.3	3.8	3.0	901	26
Washington County	MD	17,778	19,782	21,594	82.7	17.3	11.7	3.9	1.5	0.2	1,437	15.0	2,656	8.1	2.0	1.4	2.7	2.9	1.1	1,351	44
Boston	MA	60,543	63,024	56,388	13.7	86.3	41.5	35.7	8.7	0.5	4,275	13.2	7,033	8.0	7.6	6.1	8.0	7.7	9.2	3,196	139
Brockton	MA	14,529	16,791	15,612	33.5	66.5	48.9	14.1	2.6	0.9	1,089	14.3	1,921	8.1	6.4	4.9	8.8	6.9	5.2	838	25
Springfield	MA	24,194	26,526	25,791	19.1	80.9	26.6	52.0	2.2	0.1	2,215	11.6	3,446	7.5	12.4	9.9	15.0	10.4	16.7	946	44
Worcester	MA	21,066	25,828	23,603	43.4	56.6	13.1	35.0	8.0	0.5	1,764	13.4	3,378	7.0	5.4	4.7	5.6	6.2	5.6	1,235	44
Ann Arbor	MI	14,199	16,539	16,952	64.0	36.0	15.8	4.7	15.0	0.5	1,061	16.0	3,048	5.6	2.1	1.1	1.6	2.6	3.0	1,188	32
Chippewa Valley	MI	9,350	12,329	15,164	90.4	9.6	5.2	2.0	2.2	0.2	723	21.0	1,349	11.2	0.4	0.4	0.2	0.6	0.5	898	19
Dearborn City	MI	13,380	17,129	18,445	92.4	7.6	4.2	2.1	0.9	0.4	1,071	17.2	2,138	8.6	4.0	3.8	4.6	3.7	3.7	1,078	36
Detroit City	MI	168,116	162,194	117,609	2.4	97.6	90.0	6.4	0.8	0.3	7,127	16.5	16,272	7.2	9.6	11.2	9.1	8.6	6.7	5,673	233
Flint City	MI	27,601	22,532	17,565	15.7	84.3	81.1	2.4	0.3	0.4	1,064	16.5	2,520	7.0	2.9	3.5	3.1	2.7	1.0	672	47
Grand Rapids	MI	26,250	25,625	21,448	24.4	75.6	43.8	29.2	1.4	1.2	1,392	15.4	2,927	7.3	12.7	11.8	11.0	14.5	14.9	723	80
Lansing	MI	21,350	17,610	15,317	33.1	66.9	45.5	15.7	4.4	1.2	960	16.0	2,013	7.6	8.2	9.1	9.8	8.7	4.4	747	37
Livonia	MI	16,373	18,347	15,501	89.6	10.4	5.7	1.8	2.8	0.2	1,020	17.2	2,175	8.0	1.7	2.2	2.2	1.8	0.3	1,366	28
Plymouth-Canton	MI	14,955	16,518	18,888	78.6	21.4	7.1	2.0	12.0	0.4	976	19.4	1,896	10.0	1.2	1.1	1.0	0.8	2.0	1,085	27
Utica	MI	23,960	27,786	29,786	92.6	7.4	3.2	1.5	2.6	0.1	1,492	20.0	3,111	9.6	0.8	0.1	0.6	1.0	1.9	2,032	43
Walled Lake Consolidated Schools	MI	9,059	14,438	15,828	85.5	14.5	3.2	0.0	5.8	2.4	906	17.5	1,855	8.5	2.1	0.9	2.0	2.6	3.2	983	23
Warren Consolidated Schools	MI	14,336	14,602	15,476	84.7	15.3	8.4	0.8	5.6	0.5	811	19.1	1,574	9.8	0.7	0.1	0.4	0.7	1.5	1,049	26
Anoka-Hennepin	MN	34,524	41,314	41,310	81.8	18.2	7.8	3.0	6.2	1.2	2,518	16.4	4,814	8.6	2.4	0.3	0.6	1.7	6.8	2,809	59
Minneapolis	MN	36,763	48,834	37,033	28.5	71.5	41.3	16.3	9.6	4.3	2,216	16.7	5,274	7.0	11.6	6.8	6.6	8.7	24.4	1,748	115
Osseo	MN	19,483	22,017	22,071	58.5	41.5	21.9	5.5	13.4	0.7	1,293	17.1	2,645	8.3	1.9	0.2	1.4	2.1	4.3	1,314	32

See notes at end of table.

Table 91. Selected statistics on enrollment, teachers, dropouts, and graduates in public school districts enrolling more than 15,000 students: 1990, 2000, 2004–05, and 2006—Continued

Name of district	State	Enroll-ment, fall 1990	Enroll-ment, fall 2000	Enroll-ment, fall 2006	White	Minority Total	Black	Hispanic	Asian/Pacific Islander	American Indian/Alaska Native	Number of classroom teachers, fall 2006	Pupil/teacher ratio, fall 2006	Total number of staff, fall 2006	Student/staff ratio, fall 2006	Total	Grade 9	Grade 10	Grade 11	Grade 12	Number of high school graduates, 2004–05[1]	Number of schools, fall 2006[2]
1	2	3	4	5	6	7	8	9	10	11	12	13	14	15	16	17	18	19	20	21	22
Rochester	MN	13,887	15,929	16,237	73.5	26.5	11.0	6.3	8.8	0.4	962	16.9	1,922	8.5	2.5	0.8	0.8	3.3	5.3	1,206	41
Rosemount-Apple Valley-Eagan	MN	17,029	28,330	28,026	81.0	19.0	7.4	4.5	6.6	0.5	1,702	16.5	3,353	8.4	1.8	0.3	0.6	2.0	4.4	2,061	36
Saint Paul	MN	32,366	45,115	40,658	26.1	73.9	29.8	13.0	29.3	1.9	2,682	15.2	5,895	6.9	5.2	0.8	2.7	4.5	12.0	2,252	123
South Washington County School Dist.	MN	11,260	14,953	16,451	79.3	20.7	6.7	4.7	8.6	0.7	986	16.7	1,860	8.8	2.0	0.1	0.2	2.4	5.3	1,088	23
DeSoto County	MS	13,470	19,812	28,738	67.9	32.1	26.0	4.6	1.2	0.2	1,550	18.5	3,284	8.8	0.5	0.7	0.6	0.3	0.5	1,059	33
Jackson	MS	33,546	31,351	31,941	1.8	98.2	97.5	0.4	0.2	#	1,899	16.8	4,500	7.1	1.9	2.6	1.7	1.1	1.7	1,135	61
Rankin County	MS	12,824	15,013	17,398	75.9	24.1	21.5	1.3	1.1	0.1	1,191	14.6	2,131	8.2	1.2	0.8	1.0	1.4	2.2	812	25
Columbia	MO	12,786	16,178	17,090	68.2	31.8	22.5	3.9	5.0	0.3	1,287	13.3	2,437	7.0	4.6	0.7	3.4	5.9	8.8	1,098	31
Fort Zumwalt	MO	10,110	16,521	18,776	90.1	9.9	5.8	2.2	1.8	0.2	1,138	16.5	2,214	8.5	2.9	1.5	3.1	4.2	2.8	1,231	23
Francis Howell	MO	13,391	19,497	22,363	91.0	9.0	4.8	1.8	2.2	0.2	1,228	18.2	2,059	10.9	2.6	0.3	2.5	4.0	3.6	1,369	23
Hazelwood	MO	16,985	18,855	19,269	30.8	69.2	67.0	1.3	0.9	#	1,170	16.5	2,247	8.6	3.4	1.8	4.2	4.0	3.9	1,165	27
Kansas City	MO	34,486	37,298	26,980	13.7	86.3	64.5	19.6	2.0	0.2	2,039	13.2	3,888	6.9	4.4	4.9	5.2	3.6	3.1	1,498	71
Lee's Summit	MO	7,132	14,340	16,883	83.1	16.9	11.0	3.6	2.1	0.2	1,109	15.2	2,619	6.4	2.1	0.5	1.8	3.9	2.6	1,057	24
North Kansas City	MO	15,732	17,258	17,715	73.2	26.8	11.2	10.3	4.0	1.2	1,236	14.3	2,366	7.5	2.9	1.1	2.7	3.6	4.1	1,234	30
Parkway	MO	21,542	20,433	18,432	70.7	29.3	16.8	2.0	10.4	0.1	1,116	16.5	2,346	7.9	1.7	0.1	0.8	2.7	3.3	1,369	28
Rockwood	MO	15,608	21,203	22,544	83.1	16.9	10.9	1.6	4.2	0.2	1,403	16.1	3,015	7.5	1.3	0.6	1.5	1.6	1.5	1,508	31
Saint Louis City	MO	43,284	44,412	38,277	13.3	86.7	82.1	2.5	1.8	0.3	2,740	14.0	3,998	9.6	16.0	15.4	18.0	18.6	11.2	1,547	104
Springfield	MO	23,631	24,630	24,696	87.4	12.6	6.6	3.1	2.4	0.5	1,567	15.8	2,932	8.4	5.4	1.5	5.7	7.3	7.3	1,492	54
Lincoln	NE	27,986	31,354	32,934	78.8	21.2	8.9	6.7	3.9	1.6	2,382	13.8	4,476	7.4	5.0	0.6	2.3	5.7	11.1	2,066	64
Millard	NE	16,764	19,160	21,542	88.9	11.1	3.0	3.9	3.8	0.4	1,362	15.8	2,468	8.7	1.2	0.0	0.4	1.5	2.8	1,563	35
Omaha	NE	41,699	45,197	47,044	42.7	57.3	31.3	22.6	1.8	1.6	3,187	14.8	7,141	6.6	5.8	5.3	7.8	5.7	4.1	2,419	89
Clark County	NV	121,959	231,655	303,448	37.3	62.7	14.3	38.7	8.8	0.8	15,930	19.0	21,697	14.0	7.3	6.5	6.9	6.8	9.8	10,314	319
Washoe County	NV	38,466	56,268	64,954	55.9	44.1	3.8	31.6	6.3	2.4	3,600	18.0	5,022	12.9	2.0	1.3	2.0	1.9	3.6	2,651	101
Manchester	NH	14,604	17,407	17,154	78.6	21.4	7.1	11.3	2.5	0.5	1,212	14.2	2,028	8.5	5.3	1.5	4.5	5.7	11.5	1,285	22
Camden City	NJ	19,497	17,517	15,243	0.7	99.3	52.6	45.2	1.4	0.1	1,518	10.0	1,774	8.6	10.2	7.5	14.4	12.3	7.4	416	32
Elizabeth	NJ	15,266	19,674	21,214	9.5	90.5	24.4	64.4	1.7	0.0	2,038	10.4	2,401	8.8	4.4	2.0	7.6	4.2	2.8	968	30
Jersey City	NJ	28,585	31,347	28,910	9.2	90.8	36.4	38.5	14.6	1.3	2,700	10.7	3,345	8.6	7.2	9.0	7.1	7.1	5.0	1,469	38
Newark	NJ	48,433	42,150	41,266	7.5	92.5	59.0	32.6	0.8	0.1	3,181	13.0	4,652	8.9	2.9	2.4	4.0	2.5	2.6	2,057	73
Paterson	NJ	22,109	24,629	24,950	5.4	94.6	35.3	56.6	2.6	0.1	2,502	10.0	2,985	8.4	5.9	5.5	7.7	4.4	4.8	963	38
Toms River Regional	NJ	16,002	17,621	17,649	85.4	14.6	4.5	6.6	3.3	0.1	1,190	14.8	1,379	12.8	2.9	0.2	2.3	3.6	6.0	1,209	18
Albuquerque	NM	88,295	85,276	95,493	33.0	67.0	4.0	55.4	2.4	5.1	6,241	15.3	12,544	7.6	4.8	5.5	4.8	4.7	3.7	4,532	164
Las Cruces	NM	19,216	22,185	23,917	25.6	74.4	2.3	70.2	1.0	0.8	1,638	14.6	3,701	6.5	8.8	9.1	9.7	8.6	7.5	1,257	37
Brentwood Union	NY	11,749	15,565	16,587	11.7	88.3	18.7	67.5	1.9	0.1	1,155	14.4	2,388	6.9	15.5	17.8	19.5	14.5	6.3	887	17
Buffalo City	NY	47,235	45,721	36,540	25.3	74.7	57.6	14.1	1.5	1.6	2,861	12.8	5,067	7.2	8.9	5.2	9.2	11.6	12.0	1,667	60
New York City	NY	944,113	1,066,516	999,150	14.2	85.8	32.2	39.4	13.7	0.4	70,889	14.1	84,311	11.9	10.3	4.6	22.1	6.2	6.8	41,322	1,429
Rochester City	NY	32,705	36,294	33,337	12.0	88.0	65.3	20.8	1.6	0.3	2,861	11.7	5,562	6.0	10.4	9.7	12.3	9.5	9.6	1,121	61
Sachem Central	NY	15,187	14,948	15,387	88.0	12.0	1.4	6.2	4.3	0.1	1,146	13.4	2,042	7.5	1.3	0.2	0.2	2.4	2.8	1,020	18
Syracuse City	NY	22,432	23,015	21,178	31.2	68.8	53.9	10.6	2.9	1.4	1,856	11.4	3,859	5.5	11.0	12.2	11.6	13.1	5.9	812	34
Yonkers City	NY	18,621	26,237	24,708	17.8	82.2	27.5	48.5	6.1	0.2	1,729	14.3	3,528	7.0	7.5	5.6	5.4	13.1	8.1	1,049	39
Alamance-Burlington	NC	10,322	20,729	22,870	58.1	41.9	23.8	16.4	1.4	0.4	1,635	14.0	2,899	7.9	5.8	4.6	6.8	6.0	5.8	1,274	34
Buncombe County	NC	22,026	24,708	25,650	85.0	15.0	6.0	7.4	1.2	0.5	1,798	14.3	3,584	7.2	5.8	6.5	6.2	5.8	4.5	1,482	41
Cabarrus County	NC	12,853	19,115	26,015	69.9	30.1	17.0	11.0	1.7	0.4	1,800	14.5	3,287	7.9	5.5	5.5	6.8	5.8	4.8	1,250	31
Catawba County	NC	12,770	16,250	17,577	77.5	22.5	6.7	8.3	7.2	0.3	1,211	14.5	2,148	8.2	3.8	3.5	4.9	3.5	3.5	1,012	28
Charlotte-Mecklenburg	NC	77,069	103,336	128,789	37.2	62.8	43.7	14.1	4.4	0.5	9,408	13.7	17,670	7.3	3.7	4.3	3.7	2.9	3.7	5,661	158
Cleveland County	NC	8,131	9,663	17,395	67.7	32.3	28.6	2.8	0.9	0.1	1,305	13.3	2,471	7.0	5.4	7.0	5.3	4.3	4.3	945	28
Cumberland County	NC	44,612	50,850	53,621	39.3	60.7	49.9	7.1	1.8	2.0	3,993	13.4	7,599	7.1	3.5	3.9	3.9	4.3	2.0	3,154	90
Davidson County	NC	16,426	19,136	20,545	92.2	7.8	2.8	3.7	1.0	0.3	1,320	15.6	2,471	8.3	5.5	6.3	6.2	5.3	3.4	1,144	31

See notes at end of table.

Table 91. Selected statistics on enrollment, teachers, dropouts, and graduates in public school districts enrolling more than 15,000 students: 1990, 2000, 2004–05, and 2006—Continued

Name of district	State	Enroll-ment, fall 1990	Enroll-ment, fall 2000	Enroll-ment, fall 2006	Percentage distribution of enrollment, by race, fall 2006						Number of classroom teachers, fall 2006	Pupil/teacher ratio, fall 2006	Total number of staff, fall 2006	Student/staff ratio, fall 2006	Percent dropouts from grades 9–12, 2004–05[1]					Number of high school graduates, 2004–05[2]	Number of schools, fall 2006
					White	Total	Black	Hispanic	Asian/Pacific Islander	American Indian/Alaska Native					Total	Grade 9	Grade 10	Grade 11	Grade 12		
						Minority															
1	2	3	4	5	6	7	8	9	10	11	12	13	14	15	16	17	18	19	20	21	22
Durham Public	NC	18,517	29,728	31,260	25.2	74.8	55.7	16.2	2.6	0.2	2,423	12.9	5,456	5.7	6.0	7.0	6.8	5.1	3.8	1,648	46
Forsyth County	NC	37,625	44,769	51,325	48.2	51.8	34.2	15.6	1.8	0.2	4,058	12.6	6,933	7.4	6.4	5.4	6.1	6.7	8.1	2,638	77
Gaston County	NC	29,631	30,603	32,800	70.8	29.2	20.7	6.9	1.5	0.2	2,223	14.8	3,823	8.6	5.7	5.4	5.8	5.9	6.0	1,756	53
Guilford County	NC	24,575	63,417	71,722	43.4	56.6	42.7	8.2	5.1	0.6	5,405	13.3	9,551	7.5	3.2	3.7	3.6	2.8	2.4	3,968	117
Harnett County	NC	11,890	16,338	17,924	57.9	42.1	29.0	11.6	0.5	0.9	1,270	14.1	2,286	7.8	6.0	6.3	5.6	6.4	5.8	853	26
Iredell-Statesville	NC	10,610	17,235	21,023	73.8	26.2	14.9	8.3	2.8	0.2	1,488	14.1	2,801	7.5	5.3	4.8	5.7	6.6	4.1	1,085	34
Johnston County	NC	14,647	21,334	29,307	65.6	34.4	18.7	14.7	0.5	0.5	2,195	13.4	3,899	7.5	5.0	4.8	5.3	5.1	4.9	1,242	39
Nash-Rocky Mount	NC	11,653	18,342	18,429	37.9	62.1	54.0	6.4	1.2	0.4	1,331	13.8	2,542	7.2	6.8	6.9	7.8	7.3	4.9	1,016	28
New Hanover County	NC	19,090	21,605	24,001	66.5	33.5	26.3	5.3	1.5	0.4	1,763	13.6	3,620	6.6	6.9	4.5	7.0	7.4	10.2	1,332	37
Onslow County	NC	18,605	20,984	23,351	67.6	32.4	23.2	6.8	1.6	0.9	1,655	14.1	3,246	7.2	4.8	3.9	5.2	5.6	4.5	1,323	33
Pitt County	NC	17,629	20,040	22,763	41.2	58.8	51.0	6.3	1.3	0.2	1,734	13.1	3,134	7.3	7.2	8.2	6.7	5.7	7.7	1,114	35
Randolph County	NC	13,572	17,271	19,112	83.5	16.5	4.4	10.5	1.0	0.5	1,332	14.3	2,565	7.5	6.4	5.4	6.6	7.1	7.1	924	29
Robeson County	NC	23,251	23,911	21,190	18.6	81.4	28.9	7.8	0.5	44.1	1,712	14.2	3,446	7.0	8.1	8.0	10.5	8.5	3.7	1,103	42
Rowan-Salisbury	NC	16,403	20,472	21,190	69.3	30.7	20.8	8.3	1.3	0.3	1,555	13.6	2,932	7.2	6.0	4.8	5.8	6.6	7.2	1,198	33
Union County	NC	12,864	22,862	35,616	72.7	27.3	14.7	11.0	1.3	0.3	2,480	14.4	4,433	8.0	3.9	4.1	4.3	3.7	3.0	1,486	44
Wake County	NC	64,266	98,950	128,748	55.9	44.1	27.8	10.7	5.3	0.2	9,178	14.0	16,571	7.8	3.9	4.8	3.5	4.0	3.1	6,570	147
Wayne County	NC	13,653	19,279	19,608	47.5	52.5	40.5	10.7	1.1	0.2	1,428	13.7	2,662	7.4	5.8	6.2	5.3	6.6	5.0	1,024	33
Akron City	OH	33,213	31,464	26,424	45.2	54.8	51.6	1.4	1.8	0.1	2,015	13.1	5,832	4.5	4.8	4.9	3.6	5.9	5.2	1,582	60
Cincinnati City	OH	50,394	46,562	36,003	24.5	75.5	73.0	1.6	0.9	0.1	2,153	16.7	4,942	7.3	3.7	4.5	3.4	3.8	2.3	1,821	73
Cleveland Municipal City	OH	68,924	75,684	55,593	16.5	83.5	71.3	11.2	0.7	0.3	3,526	15.8	8,140	6.8	6.9	7.3	6.2	6.7	7.5	2,335	104
Columbus City	OH	63,956	64,511	56,003	29.3	70.7	63.2	5.3	2.0	0.3	3,129	17.9	7,546	7.4	5.4	5.6	5.5	4.8	5.9	2,582	136
Dayton City	OH	28,000	23,522	20,547	24.5	75.5	72.5	2.6	0.4	#	1,005	16.8	2,393	7.0	3.6	4.1	2.8	3.5	3.6	866	37
Hilliard City	OH	6,533	12,423	15,029	84.9	15.1	5.9	3.7	5.4	0.1	848	17.7	1,656	9.1	1.4	0.5	1.1	1.8	2.8	906	20
Lakota Local	OH	9,356	14,659	17,782	83.3	16.7	8.6	3.0	5.0	0.1	869	20.5	1,709	10.4	0.9	0.0	0.0	2.0	1.8	1,094	19
South-Western City	OH	16,605	19,216	21,476	77.9	22.1	12.0	8.2	1.7	0.3	1,085	19.8	2,415	8.9	2.4	2.7	1.7	2.3	3.0	1,109	36
Toledo City	OH	40,126	37,738	29,071	44.0	56.0	46.9	8.4	0.7	0.1	1,657	17.5	3,548	8.2	1.2	1.1	1.4	1.4	1.2	1,513	62
Broken Arrow	OK	13,872	14,990	15,588	76.6	23.4	5.3	5.7	2.5	9.9	964	16.2	1,908	8.2	3.8	2.0	2.5	4.7	6.3	926	22
Edmond	OK	13,041	17,084	19,712	76.6	23.4	10.8	4.7	4.0	3.9	996	19.8	2,242	8.8	0.7	0.6	0.6	0.8	0.9	1,311	22
Lawton	OK	17,727	17,338	17,062	47.6	52.4	32.5	10.6	2.5	6.8	1,131	15.1	2,263	7.5	3.3	0.9	5.2	3.6	3.8	919	35
Moore	OK	16,630	18,101	20,547	66.0	34.0	7.1	8.1	4.9	13.9	1,195	17.2	2,248	9.1	2.1	0.9	1.9	3.0	2.9	1,087	28
Oklahoma City	OK	36,038	39,750	40,778	23.4	76.6	31.9	36.6	2.8	5.3	2,440	16.7	4,671	8.7	6.2	6.9	7.0	5.7	4.1	1,475	96
Putnam City	OK	18,071	19,506	18,861	55.6	44.4	23.0	12.7	4.6	4.2	1,248	15.1	2,086	9.0	3.9	3.7	4.5	4.1	2.9	1,134	26
Tulsa	OK	40,732	42,812	41,438	34.7	65.3	35.2	18.6	1.5	10.0	2,714	15.3	6,116	6.8	8.1	7.7	8.7	8.1	7.9	1,779	86
Beaverton	OR	24,874	33,600	37,719	64.6	35.4	3.1	17.8	13.9	0.6	1,225	30.8	2,630	14.3	—	—	—	—	—	2,231	51
Bend-Lapine	OR	9,481	13,128	15,323	88.0	12.0	0.9	8.3	1.7	1.0	722	21.2	1,310	11.7	—	—	—	—	—	1,015	27
Eugene	OR	17,904	18,432	18,312	80.8	19.2	2.9	7.9	5.8	2.5	778	23.5	1,600	11.4	—	—	—	—	—	1,335	45
Hillsboro	OR	10,396	18,315	19,985	60.3	39.7	2.5	29.1	7.3	0.7	920	21.7	1,513	13.2	—	—	—	—	—	1,142	32
North Clackamas	OR	12,403	14,876	17,436	77.7	22.3	2.6	11.3	7.2	1.2	812	21.5	1,559	11.2	—	—	—	—	—	844	30
Portland	OR	53,042	53,141	46,348	56.6	43.4	16.3	14.2	11.0	1.9	2,498	18.6	4,255	10.9	—	—	—	—	—	2,429	97
Salem-Keizer	OR	27,756	35,108	39,585	61.8	38.2	1.2	30.9	4.2	1.8	2,077	19.1	4,004	9.9	—	—	—	—	—	2,084	67
Allentown City	PA	13,519	16,424	18,583	21.3	78.7	17.4	59.6	1.5	0.2	897	20.7	1,153	16.1	8.5	6.4	11.2	8.8	8.0	898	22
Bethlehem Area	PA	12,220	14,165	15,340	57.5	42.5	9.2	30.3	2.9	0.1	932	16.5	1,167	13.1	4.8	2.3	3.0	6.0	8.8	965	23
Central Bucks	PA	10,286	17,305	20,349	92.7	7.3	1.7	1.8	3.7	0.1	1,083	18.8	1,283	15.9	0.8	0.0	0.1	0.8	2.6	1,311	23
Philadelphia City	PA	190,978	201,190	178,201	13.2	86.8	64.4	16.4	5.7	0.2	9,917	18.0	12,599	14.1	10.0	7.1	11.7	11.4	10.7	10,819	274
Pittsburgh	PA	39,896	38,560	31,005	36.3	63.7	61.0	1.0	1.6	0.1	2,358	13.1	2,941	10.5	1.9	1.9	2.6	1.8	1.3	1,963	92
Reading	PA	11,965	15,487	17,958	13.0	87.0	13.6	72.6	0.8	#	918	19.6	1,214	14.8	10.7	3.7	15.3	13.4	10.1	654	19
Providence	RI	20,908	26,937	25,190	12.0	88.0	22.1	59.2	6.0	0.7	1,718	14.7	2,032	12.4	10.6	10.7	11.2	12.7	7.0	1,416	53
Aiken County	SC	23,964	25,147	25,028	58.8	41.2	35.7	4.6	0.7	0.3	1,660	15.1	2,447	10.2	3.9	4.1	4.4	4.2	2.8	1,153	41
Beaufort 01	SC	12,525	16,721	19,239	44.6	55.4	37.1	16.7	1.3	0.2	1,387	13.9	1,703	11.3	1.7	1.8	1.7	1.4	1.7	888	28

See notes at end of table.

Table 91. Selected statistics on enrollment, teachers, dropouts, and graduates in public school districts enrolling more than 15,000 students: 1990, 2000, 2004–05, and 2006—Continued

Name of district	State	Enroll-ment, fall 1990	Enroll-ment, fall 2000	Enroll-ment, fall 2006	Percentage distribution of enrollment, by race, fall 2006 — White	Minority Total	Black	Hispanic	Asian/ Pacific Islander	American Indian/ Alaska Native	Number of classroom teachers, fall 2006	Pupil/ teacher ratio, fall 2006	Total number of staff, fall 2006	Student/ staff ratio, fall 2006	Percent dropouts from grades 9–12, 2004–05[1] — Total	Grade 9	Grade 10	Grade 11	Grade 12	Number of high school graduates, 2004–05[1]	Number of schools, fall 2006[2]
1	2	3	4	5	6	7	8	9	10	11	12	13	14	15	16	17	18	19	20	21	22
Berkeley 01	SC	27,392	26,635	28,185	56.7	43.3	35.3	5.4	2.2	0.3	1,762	16.0	2,585	10.9	2.5	0.9	1.9	5.2	2.1	1,408	37
Charleston 01	SC	43,667	44,767	41,792	41.5	58.5	52.2	4.5	1.4	0.3	3,241	12.9	4,586	9.1	4.2	5.4	4.7	3.4	1.9	1,935	80
Dorchester 02	SC	13,737	16,678	20,206	63.7	56.3	29.8	3.4	2.5	0.5	1,285	15.7	1,532	13.2	3.2	3.3	3.2	3.4	2.8	915	16
Florence 01	SC	14,736	13,930	15,422	44.7	55.3	52.1	1.4	1.6	0.2	1,049	14.7	1,736	8.9	5.4	8.0	5.9	2.9	2.7	713	21
Greenville 01	SC	51,471	59,875	67,537	61.6	38.4	27.4	8.6	2.2	0.2	4,440	15.2	6,217	10.9	4.7	5.3	5.5	4.5	2.9	3,076	94
Horry 01	SC	24,085	29,894	36,124	67.8	32.2	24.2	6.0	1.5	0.5	2,399	15.1	3,764	9.6	3.2	2.4	3.6	4.2	2.5	1,676	49
Lexington 01	SC	11,204	17,285	20,247	85.0	15.0	8.9	3.6	2.0	0.5	1,474	13.7	1,924	10.5	1.5	1.6	1.4	1.1	1.8	1,067	22
Lexington 05	SC	11,688	15,064	16,732	66.5	33.5	29.0	2.0	2.3	0.2	1,243	13.5	1,603	10.4	1.2	1.2	0.5	1.6	1.5	970	19
Pickens 01	SC	14,298	15,938	16,530	86.1	13.9	9.5	2.9	1.2	0.4	1,088	15.2	1,497	11.0	3.2	3.0	3.1	2.9	3.9	769	25
Richland 01	SC	27,071	27,061	24,664	17.9	82.1	78.8	2.4	0.8	0.1	1,988	12.4	2,618	9.4	4.4	4.6	4.6	5.1	3.0	1,164	50
Richland 02	SC	12,792	17,409	22,320	33.6	66.4	58.8	4.7	2.8	0.1	1,624	13.7	1,967	11.3	2.3	1.7	2.3	2.5	2.9	1,040	25
York 03	SC	12,690	14,925	16,823	55.2	44.8	36.8	4.6	1.8	1.6	1,141	14.7	1,452	11.6	3.5	2.7	5.2	3.4	3.0	863	24
Sioux Falls	SD	16,120	19,097	19,771	83.4	16.6	6.0	4.9	2.1	3.6	1,308	15.1	1,467	13.5	6.6	2.3	4.9	5.2	13.7	1,265	48
Hamilton County	TN	22,874	39,915	40,922	60.2	39.8	34.0	3.9	1.7	0.2	2,964	13.8	6,325	6.5	4.9	4.0	5.0	6.2	4.8	1,926	77
Knox County	TN	50,429	51,944	59,663	79.5	20.5	15.5	2.9	1.8	0.3	3,639	16.4	6,816	8.8	2.4	0.1	0.2	3.0	6.8	3,088	86
Memphis City	TN	106,223	113,730	117,349	7.7	92.3	86.1	4.9	1.2	0.1	7,020	16.7	13,448	8.7	3.9	4.4	2.0	4.9	4.6	5,339	194
Montgomery County	TN	17,532	23,339	27,963	63.3	36.7	27.3	6.5	2.5	0.5	1,684	16.6	3,312	8.4	2.8	1.4	1.8	3.5	5.5	1,318	31
Nashville-Davidson County	TN	67,452	67,669	73,731	35.4	64.6	48.2	12.9	3.2	0.2	4,981	14.8	9,849	7.5	5.6	5.2	4.8	6.4	6.4	3,044	133
Rutherford County	TN	18,228	25,356	34,831	74.2	25.8	14.9	7.0	3.7	0.2	2,153	16.2	3,459	10.1	1.7	0.6	1.7	2.1	2.8	1,944	41
Shelby County	TN	37,605	46,972	47,126	57.8	42.2	34.1	3.6	4.0	0.4	2,817	16.7	5,013	9.4	0.5	0.5	0.6	0.7	0.2	2,413	49
Sumner County	TN	19,650	22,347	26,140	85.0	15.0	10.0	3.6	1.2	0.2	1,684	15.5	3,311	7.9	2.4	0.9	2.0	3.5	3.7	1,434	42
Williamson County	TN	11,502	19,545	27,797	89.2	10.8	4.4	2.8	3.5	0.1	1,720	16.2	3,146	8.8	1.3	0.0	0.2	1.3	4.0	1,609	36
Abilene ISD	TX	18,217	18,118	16,732	50.8	49.2	13.5	33.8	1.4	0.5	1,271	13.2	2,502	6.7	4.3	3.1	4.7	5.2	4.7	937	43
Aldine ISD	TX	41,372	52,520	58,831	4.2	95.8	31.4	62.4	1.9	0.1	3,923	15.0	8,003	7.4	4.2	3.5	4.5	3.5	5.7	2,231	69
Alief ISD	TX	29,774	42,151	45,696	4.4	95.6	37.2	45.9	12.4	0.1	3,238	14.1	6,147	7.4	4.5	2.8	5.7	4.6	6.0	2,159	44
Allen ISD	TX	4,859	10,604	16,463	67.7	32.3	10.4	10.4	9.2	0.6	1,068	15.4	1,837	9.0	1.0	0.3	0.5	1.1	2.2	950	20
Amarillo ISD	TX	27,374	28,908	30,394	45.5	54.5	11.3	40.1	2.7	0.3	2,129	14.3	3,936	7.7	3.4	1.9	3.3	3.8	5.0	1,557	54
Arlington ISD	TX	44,958	58,866	63,082	33.1	66.9	23.8	35.7	7.0	0.5	4,053	15.6	8,042	7.8	4.2	3.3	3.8	4.0	6.8	3,279	77
Austin ISD	TX	65,797	77,816	82,140	26.8	73.2	12.7	57.0	3.1	0.2	5,714	14.4	10,833	7.6	4.4	3.5	4.6	3.8	6.4	3,746	116
Beaumont ISD	TX	18,684	20,696	19,517	18.8	81.2	63.9	14.2	3.1	0.1	1,481	13.2	2,890	6.8	4.0	3.5	4.2	2.4	6.3	1,070	35
Birdville ISD	TX	18,466	21,246	22,541	57.7	42.3	7.1	28.9	5.7	0.7	1,405	16.0	1,981	11.4	2.0	1.4	2.2	2.1	2.6	1,263	34
Brownsville ISD	TX	34,906	40,898	48,334	1.6	98.4	0.2	97.9	0.4	#	3,166	15.3	7,030	6.9	4.2	2.2	6.2	3.8	5.8	1,697	54
Carrollton-Farmers Branch ISD	TX	16,234	24,134	26,252	25.8	74.2	14.2	48.9	10.8	0.4	1,813	14.5	3,260	8.1	1.6	1.0	1.8	1.4	2.5	1,404	45
Clear Creek ISD	TX	22,372	29,875	35,528	62.3	37.7	8.9	18.6	9.8	0.4	2,168	16.4	4,111	8.6	1.4	0.4	0.8	0.9	3.9	2,061	39
Conroe ISD	TX	23,288	34,928	44,460	65.0	35.0	6.6	24.9	3.0	0.5	2,775	16.0	5,244	8.5	2.3	2.2	2.1	2.5	2.4	2,482	51
Corpus Christi ISD	TX	41,881	39,138	38,930	17.0	83.0	5.4	75.6	1.7	0.2	2,396	16.3	4,996	7.8	4.3	3.0	4.5	4.7	5.6	2,102	62
Cypress-Fairbanks ISD	TX	41,196	63,497	92,135	41.4	58.6	14.6	35.2	8.5	0.3	5,838	15.8	11,282	8.2	0.9	0.6	0.8	0.7	1.7	4,622	75
Dallas ISD	TX	135,320	161,548	159,144	5.0	95.0	29.6	64.2	0.9	0.2	10,643	15.0	19,888	8.0	5.0	4.5	6.5	4.3	5.1	6,832	242
Denton ISD	TX	10,690	13,645	19,722	55.3	44.7	12.2	29.5	2.3	0.7	1,515	13.0	2,681	7.4	2.4	1.3	3.0	1.9	4.2	776	31
Ector County ISD	TX	26,993	26,831	26,472	31.8	68.2	5.4	61.3	0.8	0.7	1,662	15.9	3,283	8.1	7.8	3.1	6.8	10.0	13.9	1,297	39
Edinburg CISD	TX	13,685	22,005	28,772	2.1	97.9	0.3	96.9	0.6	0.1	1,836	15.7	3,945	7.3	4.2	3.1	4.9	5.1	4.3	1,227	37
El Paso ISD	TX	64,092	62,325	62,857	12.5	87.5	4.6	81.1	1.4	0.3	4,578	13.7	8,505	7.4	4.3	3.2	4.3	4.6	5.8	3,202	92
Fort Bend ISD	TX	36,270	53,999	67,014	25.5	74.5	32.2	22.4	19.7	0.2	4,119	16.3	8,141	8.2	2.0	1.0	1.3	1.4	4.5	4,423	66
Fort Worth ISD	TX	69,163	79,661	79,457	15.1	84.9	26.3	56.3	1.6	0.2	4,839	16.4	10,032	7.9	4.2	3.2	3.7	3.8	6.9	3,608	147
Frisco ISD	TX	1,310	7,234	23,777	64.5	35.5	11.1	13.3	10.0	0.6	1,687	14.1	2,943	8.2	1.3	0.6	0.5	0.7	2.8	613	35
Galena Park ISD	TX	15,593	18,885	21,275	7.7	92.3	20.8	70.1	1.3	0.1	1,532	13.9	2,943	7.2	2.8	1.9	2.4	3.9	3.6	1,115	23
Garland ISD	TX	37,978	50,312	56,955	32.6	67.4	18.7	40.6	7.6	0.5	3,774	15.1	7,111	8.0	2.2	1.4	1.6	2.1	4.1	3,088	73
Goose Creek CISD	TX	17,654	18,003	20,293	30.7	69.3	19.8	48.1	1.2	0.7	1,310	15.5	2,521	8.0	4.3	1.0	5.7	4.9	8.1	969	27
Grand Prairie ISD	TX	16,482	20,257	24,616	18.9	81.1	16.8	59.9	3.7	0.7	1,579	15.6	2,898	8.5	4.1	1.8	4.5	5.0	5.8	1,062	35
Harlingen CISD	TX	13,805	15,857	17,684	9.1	90.9	0.7	89.3	0.8	0.1	1,118	15.8	2,466	7.2	5.8	4.5	6.9	6.6	6.1	845	28
Houston ISD	TX	194,435	208,462	202,936	8.3	91.7	29.2	59.3	3.1	0.1	12,057	16.8	24,268	8.4	5.7	4.5	5.9	5.3	7.9	8,476	296

See notes at end of table.

Table 91. Selected statistics on enrollment, teachers, dropouts, and graduates in public school districts enrolling more than 15,000 students: 1990, 2000, 2004–05, and 2006—Continued

Name of district	State	Enrollment, fall 1990	Enrollment, fall 2000	Enrollment, fall 2006	Percentage distribution of enrollment, by race, fall 2006						Number of classroom teachers, fall 2006	Pupil/teacher ratio, fall 2006	Total number of staff, fall 2006	Student/staff ratio, fall 2006	Percent dropouts from grades 9–12, 2004–05[1]					Number of high school graduates, 2004–05[2]	Number of schools, fall 2006
					White	Total	Black	Hispanic	Asian/Pacific Islander	American Indian/Alaska Native					Total	Grade 9	Grade 10	Grade 11	Grade 12		
1	2	3	4	5	6	7	8	9	10	11	12	13	14	15	16	17	18	19	20	21	22
Humble ISD	TX	19,560	24,684	31,327	56.8	43.2	16.6	23.0	3.3	0.4	2,110	14.8	4,073	7.7	2.3	0.8	0.9	3.5	4.4	1,704	41
Hurst-Euless-Bedford ISD	TX	18,733	19,203	20,238	53.1	46.9	14.4	21.8	9.7	0.9	1,283	15.8	2,409	8.4	1.8	1.5	1.7	1.7	2.4	1,262	32
Irving ISD	TX	23,509	29,097	32,951	17.6	82.4	12.5	65.5	4.0	0.4	2,213	14.9	3,912	8.4	3.2	2.4	3.3	4.1	3.7	1,399	39
Judson ISD	TX	13,145	16,603	20,263	23.3	76.7	27.9	45.8	2.7	0.3	1,293	15.7	2,763	7.3	2.9	1.5	2.3	3.3	5.9	913	25
Katy ISD	TX	19,507	34,503	51,201	53.5	46.5	9.3	28.0	9.0	0.2	3,423	15.0	6,514	7.9	1.4	0.8	1.8	1.7	1.3	2,721	52
Keller ISD	TX	8,212	17,083	27,905	70.5	29.5	6.9	15.0	6.7	0.8	1,659	16.8	2,913	9.6	1.9	0.8	1.9	3.0	2.5	1,286	33
Killeen ISD	TX	22,131	29,887	36,651	36.6	63.4	38.6	20.1	4.0	0.7	2,554	14.4	5,287	6.9	3.8	3.5	4.1	3.5	4.5	1,545	53
Klein ISD	TX	26,220	32,376	41,612	46.4	53.6	15.7	29.1	8.4	0.4	2,623	15.9	5,050	8.2	2.4	1.7	2.5	2.5	3.1	2,286	39
La Joya ISD	TX	8,523	17,641	25,130	0.2	99.8	0.0	99.7	0.0	#	1,623	15.5	3,479	7.2	9.0	5.7	10.4	7.8	15.5	810	31
Lamar CISD	TX	12,335	15,159	20,708	32.5	67.5	17.4	45.8	4.1	0.2	1,292	16.0	2,589	8.0	2.9	2.4	3.0	3.0	3.8	994	30
Laredo ISD	TX	23,304	22,547	24,885	0.3	99.7	0.1	99.5	0.1	#	1,625	15.3	3,934	6.3	4.7	3.8	4.7	3.6	7.4	951	30
Leander ISD	TX	5,419	14,499	24,333	70.8	29.2	5.5	19.2	3.9	0.6	1,728	14.1	3,117	7.8	2.4	1.0	2.1	1.8	5.3	1,016	29
Lewisville ISD	TX	20,776	39,096	49,060	62.7	37.3	9.0	19.2	8.6	0.5	3,468	14.1	5,665	8.7	1.1	0.9	1.0	1.0	1.6	2,625	63
Lubbock ISD	TX	30,786	29,096	28,696	34.9	65.1	14.9	48.2	1.8	0.3	2,045	14.0	3,655	7.9	3.1	1.2	2.1	3.0	6.5	1,696	60
Mansfield ISD	TX	7,570	14,888	28,015	49.7	50.3	25.1	19.3	5.4	0.5	1,716	16.3	3,174	8.8	2.0	1.6	1.6	1.7	3.6	1,209	36
McAllen ISD	TX	18,432	21,747	24,570	6.4	93.6	0.5	91.1	1.9	0.1	1,724	14.3	3,457	7.1	4.9	4.6	5.8	4.5	4.5	1,247	31
McKinney ISD	TX	4,703	12,000	21,289	63.1	36.9	11.7	21.7	3.0	0.5	1,443	14.8	2,263	9.4	1.8	1.6	2.2	1.1	2.2	824	31
Mesquite ISD	TX	25,920	32,334	36,002	34.6	65.4	23.9	37.7	3.3	0.6	2,312	15.6	4,201	8.6	2.6	1.4	2.2	2.8	4.4	2,108	46
Midland ISD	TX	21,082	20,522	20,922	38.3	61.7	9.6	50.8	1.0	0.4	1,432	14.6	2,689	7.8	4.4	2.5	5.1	4.7	5.6	1,225	37
Mission CISD	TX	9,664	12,464	15,462	1.6	98.4	0.1	98.1	0.1	0.0	941	16.4	2,083	7.4	4.3	3.6	4.6	3.5	6.1	678	20
North East ISD	TX	39,909	50,875	61,255	41.1	58.9	9.5	45.5	3.6	0.3	4,081	15.0	7,849	7.8	1.4	1.0	1.3	1.4	2.2	3,514	72
Northside ISD	TX	50,229	63,739	82,587	26.2	73.8	8.0	62.3	3.2	0.3	5,226	15.8	10,863	7.6	2.6	1.7	3.0	2.6	3.6	4,238	95
Pasadena ISD	TX	37,643	42,577	49,851	14.2	85.8	7.7	74.6	3.2	0.2	3,305	15.1	6,541	7.6	4.7	3.3	5.0	4.3	7.9	1,923	65
Pearland ISD	TX	6,234	10,618	16,244	49.6	50.4	16.8	23.9	9.5	0.2	1,001	16.2	1,948	8.3	1.5	0.2	1.6	1.7	3.3	811	21
Pflugerville ISD	TX	6,482	14,545	19,811	33.8	66.2	22.8	34.5	8.7	0.3	1,256	15.8	2,101	9.4	2.6	1.3	3.0	2.4	4.4	942	27
Pharr-San Juan-Alamo ISD	TX	16,563	22,537	28,868	1.0	99.0	0.2	98.6	0.2	0.0	1,760	16.4	3,873	7.5	6.1	3.4	6.6	7.2	9.7	1,071	36
Plano ISD	TX	28,398	47,161	52,997	54.8	45.2	10.3	16.3	18.3	0.0	3,855	13.7	6,608	8.0	1.2	0.7	1.0	1.2	2.2	3,081	81
Richardson ISD	TX	32,555	35,138	34,042	34.6	65.4	25.9	31.2	7.9	0.4	2,289	14.9	4,578	7.4	2.0	1.0	1.7	1.8	3.7	1,981	58
Round Rock ISD	TX	19,636	31,536	39,211	54.7	45.3	10.3	24.4	10.1	0.4	2,655	14.8	4,814	8.1	2.4	1.1	2.5	2.7	3.6	2,204	47
San Antonio ISD	TX	60,161	57,273	55,406	3.0	97.0	8.1	88.5	0.2	0.1	3,494	15.9	7,759	7.1	6.5	4.6	6.8	6.8	9.0	2,520	107
Socorro ISD	TX	14,350	26,711	38,357	4.6	95.4	1.8	92.7	0.5	0.3	2,323	16.5	4,490	8.5	2.1	1.5	1.6	2.0	3.6	1,727	40
Spring Branch ISD	TX	23,661	31,659	32,160	33.2	66.8	7.6	53.1	5.9	0.2	2,320	13.9	4,548	7.1	2.8	2.0	3.2	2.7	3.7	1,823	51
Spring ISD	TX	18,537	23,034	32,255	20.6	79.4	38.5	35.9	4.8	0.2	2,084	15.5	3,913	8.2	2.8	1.9	3.2	2.6	4.0	1,448	32
Tyler ISD	TX	16,182	16,626	18,040	29.7	70.3	33.0	35.6	1.3	0.2	1,258	14.3	2,415	7.5	3.7	3.4	4.6	2.9	6.0	858	30
United ISD	TX	12,553	27,556	37,807	1.6	98.4	0.2	97.7	0.5	0.0	2,265	16.7	5,436	7.0	2.0	1.2	1.9	2.1	3.2	1,538	42
Waco ISD	TX	14,304	15,433	15,430	14.5	85.5	35.2	49.6	0.5	0.1	1,092	14.1	2,194	7.0	7.0	4.0	7.8	7.1	10.7	723	36
Weslaco ISD	TX	10,835	13,407	15,933	1.9	98.1	0.1	97.6	0.4	0.0	1,051	15.2	2,391	6.7	5.0	5.4	6.0	4.3	3.4	721	21
Ysleta ISD	TX	49,974	46,394	45,242	5.9	94.1	2.2	91.2	0.3	0.5	2,985	15.2	6,067	7.5	4.6	1.8	3.9	5.5	8.4	2,816	64
Alpine District	UT	38,852	47,117	56,460	88.7	11.3	0.7	8.1	2.1	0.5	2,267	24.9	4,410	12.8	4.7	0.4	0.7	2.3	16.3	3,295	71
Davis District	UT	55,558	59,578	62,193	88.0	12.0	1.5	7.1	2.4	0.9	2,802	22.2	5,604	11.1	1.6	0.0	0.6	1.1	4.5	3,690	99
Granite District	UT	78,554	71,328	67,502	64.6	35.4	2.1	25.2	6.9	1.3	3,199	21.1	6,502	10.4	6.0	1.1	2.3	4.8	16.5	3,916	124
Jordan District	UT	64,991	73,158	78,299	87.0	13.0	1.0	8.5	3.0	0.6	3,206	24.4	6,315	12.4	3.9	1.6	4.2	3.9	5.7	4,922	96
Nebo District	UT	16,393	21,094	25,602	89.2	10.8	0.6	8.2	1.3	0.8	1,073	23.9	1,338	19.1	1.2	0.0	0.2	0.5	4.3	1,364	44
Salt Lake District	UT	24,766	25,367	24,314	46.3	53.7	5.0	37.5	9.1	2.1	1,157	21.0	1,434	17.0	10.4	7.1	8.3	11.0	15.5	1,178	45
Washington District	UT	13,264	18,374	24,357	84.1	15.9	0.7	10.9	2.3	2.0	1,103	22.1	1,787	13.6	2.3	0.0	0.2	1.7	7.5	1,357	46
Weber District	UT	25,425	27,783	29,095	87.6	12.4	1.3	8.6	1.9	0.6	1,282	22.7	1,720	16.9	1.2	0.1	0.5	0.5	3.6	1,842	49
Arlington County	VA	14,825	18,870	18,456	46.8	53.2	14.1	28.2	10.9	0.1	1,951	9.5	4,265	4.3	4.0	2.9	4.8	2.9	5.6	1,102	33
Chesapeake City	VA	29,533	37,645	39,763	57.9	42.1	36.0	2.6	3.1	0.4	3,307	12.0	7,298	5.4	2.3	2.1	2.3	2.3	4.5	2,656	46
Chesterfield County	VA	44,480	51,212	58,455	62.6	37.4	27.2	6.4	3.1	0.7	4,547	12.9	8,904	6.6	3.6	2.8	3.2	3.5	5.2	3,730	61
Fairfax County	VA	128,766	156,412	163,952	52.4	47.6	11.3	17.1	18.9	0.3	13,384	12.2	36,318	4.5	3.0	4.2	3.0	0.4	4.3	11,384	207
Hampton City	VA	21,383	23,290	22,265	31.7	68.3	62.7	3.1	2.1	0.4	1,933	11.5	4,696	4.7	0.6	0.8	0.6	0.5	0.7	1,363	36

See notes at end of table.

Table 91. Selected statistics on enrollment, teachers, dropouts, and graduates in public school districts enrolling more than 15,000 students: 1990, 2000, 2004–05, and 2006—Continued

Name of district	State	Enroll-ment, fall 1990	Enroll-ment, fall 2000	Enroll-ment, fall 2006	Percentage distribution of enrollment, by race, fall 2006						Number of classroom teachers, fall 2006	Pupil/ teacher ratio, fall 2006	Total number of staff, fall 2006	Student/ staff ratio, fall 2006	Percent dropouts from grades 9-12, 2004-05[1]					Number of high school graduates, 2004-05[2]	Number of schools, fall 2006[3]
					White	Minority Total	Black	Hispanic	Asian/ Pacific Islander	American Indian/ Alaska Native					Total	Grade 9	Grade 10	Grade 11	Grade 12		
1	2	3	4	5	6	7	8	9	10	11	12	13	14	15	16	17	18	19	20	21	22
Hanover County	VA	11,328	16,611	19,201	86.3	13.7	10.0	1.6	1.7	0.4	1,752	11.0	4,221	4.5	1.5	0.5	0.8	1.8	3.2	1,325	23
Henrico County	VA	32,638	41,655	47,680	52.0	48.0	37.9	4.2	5.6	0.4	4,281	11.1	8,128	5.9	3.3	2.8	2.9	3.7	4.1	2,821	68
Loudoun County	VA	14,485	31,804	50,383	66.7	33.3	8.4	12.6	12.0	0.3	4,387	11.5	10,227	4.9	1.4	0.7	1.1	1.3	2.7	2,425	68
Newport News City	VA	28,925	33,008	32,373	32.3	67.7	58.4	6.0	2.6	0.6	2,584	12.5	6,765	4.8	0.4	0.1	0.4	0.6	0.8	1,732	49
Norfolk City	VA	36,541	37,349	35,610	25.5	74.5	68.0	3.9	2.4	0.2	3,186	11.2	6,309	5.6	1.3	1.8	1.3	0.4	0.8	1,384	57
Portsmouth City	VA	18,405	16,473	15,441	24.4	75.6	72.7	1.8	0.9	0.2	1,153	13.4	2,729	5.7	2.4	1.3	0.5	1.1	7.6	686	25
Prince William County	VA	41,888	54,646	70,948	43.6	56.4	23.3	25.3	7.5	0.3	5,334	13.3	10,397	6.8	2.4	2.3	2.0	2.0	3.3	3,792	83
Richmond City	VA	27,021	27,237	24,225	7.1	92.9	88.4	3.7	0.7	0.1	2,007	12.1	5,012	4.8	5.3	5.9	5.7	5.9	3.3	1,111	54
Spotsylvania County	VA	12,227	18,876	24,140	69.7	30.3	19.5	7.9	2.6	0.3	2,068	11.7	4,076	5.9	3.7	4.1	3.5	4.5	2.6	1,595	31
Stafford County	VA	12,555	21,124	26,508	67.0	33.0	20.8	8.9	2.9	0.4	2,013	13.2	4,434	6.0	2.6	2.3	2.3	2.3	3.5	1,637	29
Virginia Beach City	VA	70,266	76,586	72,538	59.1	40.9	28.4	5.5	6.5	0.4	5,967	12.2	12,730	5.7	1.9	1.5	1.4	2.7	2.4	4,640	88
Bellevue	WA	14,748	15,431	16,722	61.4	38.6	3.0	8.9	26.4	0.3	956	17.5	1,749	9.6	2.6	1.3	1.3	2.6	5.2	1,006	32
Bethel	WA	11,669	16,029	18,003	66.4	33.6	11.2	9.6	9.3	3.5	875	20.6	1,725	10.4	4.4	2.0	3.7	4.4	7.9	1,113	33
Edmonds	WA	18,868	22,067	21,030	68.5	31.5	6.3	9.1	14.6	1.5	1,083	19.4	2,094	10.0	4.9	0.9	2.1	4.0	12.7	1,096	43
Everett	WA	15,343	18,683	18,890	71.7	28.3	4.5	9.4	12.8	1.5	910	20.8	1,680	11.2	6.5	7.9	4.8	5.6	7.7	879	32
Evergreen (Clark)	WA	14,810	21,650	25,210	78.4	21.6	4.0	7.8	8.7	1.2	1,342	18.8	2,430	10.4	4.1	1.0	2.6	3.7	8.7	1,305	35
Federal Way	WA	18,168	22,623	22,759	49.9	50.1	13.9	16.7	18.0	1.4	1,175	19.4	2,164	10.5	4.2	4.5	4.1	4.4	3.5	1,234	44
Highline	WA	16,208	18,024	17,359	37.4	62.6	13.9	25.5	21.1	2.1	936	18.5	1,851	9.4	5.9	7.3	6.8	4.2	4.1	947	44
Issaquah	WA	8,888	14,259	16,298	73.9	26.1	2.3	4.5	18.6	0.7	800	20.4	1,495	10.9	1.4	0.7	1.0	1.1	2.9	1,041	26
Kent	WA	21,027	26,535	27,234	57.5	42.5	11.4	11.2	18.5	1.4	1,385	19.7	2,607	10.4	6.7	7.2	7.2	6.7	5.2	1,501	42
Lake Washington	WA	23,050	23,662	23,799	75.7	24.3	2.6	6.5	14.6	0.7	1,230	19.4	2,173	11.0	1.0	0.4	0.6	1.1	1.9	1,651	55
Northshore	WA	17,511	20,255	20,252	78.3	21.7	2.2	7.2	11.3	1.0	1,018	19.9	1,888	10.7	2.1	0.6	1.4	1.9	4.6	1,499	35
Puyallup	WA	15,100	19,757	21,018	79.8	20.2	4.4	6.9	7.2	1.8	1,050	20.0	1,940	10.8	4.1	2.0	2.7	5.9	6.1	1,254	33
Seattle	WA	43,593	47,575	46,113	42.4	57.6	21.8	11.4	22.3	2.2	2,494	18.5	4,819	9.6	6.1	5.6	6.1	7.4	5.4	2,697	112
Spokane	WA	29,186	31,725	30,181	84.0	16.0	4.6	4.0	3.3	4.1	1,765	17.1	3,236	9.3	9.3	7.9	7.6	12.1	10.0	1,884	66
Tacoma	WA	30,169	34,093	30,124	49.9	50.1	23.0	11.9	13.1	2.0	1,639	18.4	3,123	9.6	6.9	8.9	8.1	6.0	2.3	1,492	65
Vancouver	WA	16,423	21,892	22,421	75.3	24.7	5.4	11.6	5.8	1.8	1,141	19.7	2,307	9.7	3.4	0.8	1.6	5.3	6.0	1,211	41
Berkeley County	WV	10,415	13,076	16,322	83.7	16.3	10.3	4.9	0.9	0.2	896	18.2	1,984	8.2	4.7	5.1	3.9	5.9	3.5	811	29
Kanawha County	WV	34,284	29,250	28,104	85.8	14.2	12.4	0.5	1.2	0.1	1,611	17.4	3,407	8.2	5.2	5.9	5.3	5.0	4.5	1,617	72
Appleton Area	WI	12,876	14,793	15,243	79.7	20.3	3.4	5.5	10.7	0.8	971	15.7	1,595	9.6	0.7	0.0	0.2	0.7	1.8	1,182	36
Green Bay Area	WI	18,048	20,104	20,070	65.4	34.6	6.0	15.6	8.0	4.9	1,434	14.0	2,446	8.2	5.8	0.6	0.5	1.2	20.0	1,283	37
Kenosha	WI	16,219	20,099	22,482	64.4	35.6	15.9	17.6	1.7	0.4	1,361	16.5	2,480	9.1	3.1	2.8	1.6	4.6	3.1	1,479	40
Madison Metropolitan	WI	23,214	25,087	24,755	53.9	46.1	22.4	12.8	10.3	0.7	1,817	13.6	3,545	7.0	3.2	0.8	2.5	3.4	6.4	1,789	53
Milwaukee	WI	92,784	97,985	89,912	16.0	84.0	57.7	21.0	4.5	0.8	5,116	17.6	10,084	8.9	9.2	9.2	6.9	7.4	14.4	3,915	224
Racine	WI	21,904	21,102	21,696	51.9	48.1	26.7	19.6	1.5	0.3	1,327	16.3	2,488	8.7	4.9	0.9	0.9	2.9	14.5	1,243	35

—Not available.
†Not applicable.
#Rounds to zero.
[1]Alabama, Alaska, Arizona, Florida, Illinois, Maryland, New Jersey, New York, Tennessee, and Vermont reported data on an alternative July through June cycle, rather than the specified October through September cycle.
[2]Includes regular diplomas only.
[3]Data for total staff are imputed.

NOTE: Total enrollment, staff, and teacher data in this table reflect totals reported by school districts and may differ from data derived from summing school-level data to school district aggregates. SB = school board. ISD = independent school district. CISD = consolidated independent school district. Race categories exclude persons of Hispanic ethnicity. Detail may not sum to totals because of rounding.
SOURCE: U.S. Department of Education, National Center for Education Statistics, Common Core of Data (CCD), "Public Elementary/Secondary School Universe Survey," 2006–07; "Local Education Agency Universe Survey," 1990–91, 2000–01, 2005–06, and 2006–07; and "Local Education Agency-Level Public-Use Data File on Public School Dropouts: School Year 2004–05." (This table was prepared September 2008.)

Table 92. Revenues, expenditures, poverty rate, and Title I allocations of public school districts enrolling more than 15,000 students: 2005–06 and fiscal year 2008

Name of district	State	Revenues by source of funds, 2005–06 (in thousands of dollars)				Percentage distribution of revenues, 2005–06				Expenditures, 2005–06 (in thousands of dollars)					Poverty rate of 5- to 17-year-olds, 2005[1]	Current expenditure per pupil,[2] 2005–06	Title I allocations, fiscal year 2008, per poverty child[3]
											Current expenditures						
		Total	Federal	State	Local	Total	Federal	State	Local	Total[4]	Total	Instruction	Capital outlay	Interest on school debt			
1	2	3	4	5	6	7	8	9	10	11	12	13	14	15	16	17	18
Districts with more than 15,000 students	†	$222,926,950	$21,892,759	$104,716,790	$96,317,401	100.0	9.8	47.0	43.2	$230,003,266	$188,006,777	$116,347,149	$30,240,321	$6,483,163	17.9	$8,772	$1,591
Baldwin County	AL	234,316	20,180	105,214	108,922	100.0	8.6	44.9	46.5	244,873	213,235	125,561	22,751	4,639	15.6	8,215	1,231
Birmingham City	AL	332,468	47,478	144,294	140,696	100.0	14.3	43.4	42.3	351,163	273,887	143,983	67,752	1,355	33.3	8,847	1,357
Huntsville City	AL	204,401	20,299	98,684	85,418	100.0	9.9	48.3	41.8	207,829	197,336	117,941	7,566	613	15.1	8,528	1,337
Jefferson County	AL	306,247	25,131	169,148	111,968	100.0	8.2	55.2	36.6	304,511	258,433	155,861	32,796	7,058	16.0	7,212	1,340
Madison County	AL	143,093	9,592	87,302	46,199	100.0	6.7	61.0	32.3	162,128	127,421	75,829	27,588	4,612	9.7	7,020	1,056
Mobile County	AL	555,247	97,090	301,108	157,049	100.0	17.5	54.2	28.3	572,066	500,846	275,873	48,708	17,191	26.5	7,630	1,413
Montgomery County	AL	255,070	36,051	147,793	71,226	100.0	14.1	57.9	27.9	249,488	239,202	134,008	3,061	2,719	22.2	7,354	1,395
Shelby County	AL	224,127	13,420	109,820	100,887	100.0	6.0	49.0	45.0	232,518	196,494	116,724	22,794	8,258	7.6	7,951	1,110
Tuscaloosa County	AL	148,483	11,635	81,434	55,414	100.0	7.8	54.8	37.3	130,024	113,298	68,496	10,988	2,268	17.3	6,951	1,202
Anchorage School	AK	495,404	60,822	268,984	165,598	100.0	12.3	54.3	33.4	618,773	480,403	284,863	110,991	26,946	10.6	9,663	2,412
Fairbanks North Star Borough	AK	163,392	30,253	91,567	41,572	100.0	18.5	56.0	25.4	168,464	160,809	90,005	1,860	5,780	10.0	10,957	1,916
Matanuska-Susitna Borough	AK	161,802	15,430	104,617	41,755	100.0	9.5	64.7	25.8	188,987	156,911	88,893	26,514	5,562	11.5	10,119	1,933
Alhambra Elementary	AZ	117,273	19,593	62,420	35,260	100.0	16.7	53.2	30.1	114,469	96,250	58,603	4,427	5,065	28.6	6,191	1,448
Amphitheater Unified	AZ	137,184	12,327	50,991	73,866	100.0	9.0	37.2	53.8	122,133	113,335	62,565	4,588	3,854	15.2	6,759	1,303
Cartwright Elementary	AZ	137,873	21,800	85,288	30,785	100.0	15.8	61.9	22.3	130,379	124,647	76,720	5,474	9	23.0	6,137	1,438
Chandler Unified	AZ	254,432	13,376	128,104	112,952	100.0	5.3	50.3	44.4	268,147	195,104	116,659	63,095	8,214	10.2	6,120	1,068
Deer Valley Unified	AZ	260,082	13,844	111,783	134,455	100.0	5.3	43.0	51.7	250,946	206,535	125,698	31,345	13,066	9.1	5,935	1,072
Dysart Unified	AZ	168,186	9,012	101,490	57,684	100.0	5.4	60.3	34.3	185,298	186,257	59,046	75,081	2,768	13.7	5,985	1,256
Gilbert Unified	AZ	264,491	12,000	129,814	122,677	100.0	4.5	49.1	46.4	265,422	214,327	132,456	34,149	13,471	7.1	5,694	985
Glendale Union High School	AZ	134,170	10,216	55,031	68,923	100.0	7.6	41.0	51.4	159,787	104,729	61,028	50,203	4,437	21.1	7,004	1,190
Kyrene Elementary	AZ	154,216	8,627	55,108	90,481	100.0	5.6	35.7	58.7	144,480	117,456	74,546	5,694	17,329	4.7	6,408	620
Mesa Unified	AZ	570,482	40,514	273,960	256,008	100.0	7.1	48.0	44.9	530,985	484,868	299,633	33,377	9,052	14.5	6,497	1,393
Paradise Valley Unified	AZ	277,177	14,547	91,159	171,471	100.0	5.2	32.9	61.9	269,339	223,991	134,671	23,605	15,326	10.1	6,443	1,085
Peoria Unified School	AZ	296,335	16,023	155,358	124,954	100.0	5.4	52.4	42.2	298,409	239,729	142,446	49,944	8,433	10.1	6,347	1,074
Phoenix Union High School	AZ	268,860	25,124	53,682	190,054	100.0	9.3	20.0	70.7	282,697	221,839	123,017	47,655	12,141	28.1	8,870	1,364
Scottsdale Unified	AZ	229,966	12,070	38,063	179,833	100.0	5.2	16.6	78.2	254,003	183,062	108,954	55,762	13,966	7.7	6,796	1,016
Sunnyside Unified	AZ	136,194	25,829	74,833	35,532	100.0	19.0	54.9	26.1	130,636	122,737	65,752	7,832	0	33.2	7,351	1,537
Tucson Unified	AZ	507,545	70,587	230,316	206,642	100.0	13.9	45.4	40.7	500,668	448,735	241,303	36,086	15,743	18.8	7,410	1,591
Washington Elementary	AZ	211,565	27,831	94,251	89,483	100.0	13.2	44.5	42.3	206,058	162,659	100,279	31,380	6,165	16.2	6,550	1,292
Little Rock	AR	301,791	28,580	216,513	56,698	100.0	9.5	71.7	18.8	289,758	263,898	150,900	11,309	9,093	21.4	9,973	1,479
Pulaski Co. Spec. School Dist.	AR	180,206	15,212	134,574	30,420	100.0	8.4	74.7	16.9	172,244	152,923	92,862	8,152	3,475	15.8	8,227	1,401
Springdale	AR	135,972	11,691	100,881	23,400	100.0	8.6	74.2	17.2	147,573	123,843	81,261	18,596	5,122	15.3	7,770	1,275
ABC Unified	CA	187,281	15,699	143,818	27,764	100.0	8.4	76.8	14.8	185,266	162,318	100,814	5,564	1,673	15.4	7,494	1,216
Alhambra Unified	CA	183,999	20,070	123,404	40,525	100.0	10.9	67.1	22.0	206,243	159,411	93,709	33,383	2,761	26.1	8,199	1,264
Alvord Unified	CA	201,714	15,295	146,664	39,755	100.0	7.6	72.7	19.7	173,649	142,166	92,628	28,645	2,708	12.5	7,155	1,061
Anaheim Elementary	CA	182,089	20,901	97,105	64,083	100.0	11.5	53.3	35.2	199,294	163,526	106,152	28,190	1,606	17.2	7,904	1,567
Anaheim Union High	CA	353,590	43,009	227,961	82,620	100.0	12.2	64.5	23.4	363,464	265,698	166,378	59,981	6,562	13.6	8,024	1,317
Antelope Valley Union High	CA	214,283	13,941	148,691	51,651	100.0	6.5	69.4	24.1	229,012	180,479	111,979	41,912	4,187	18.3	7,130	1,217
Antioch Unified	CA	181,745	11,598	120,383	49,764	100.0	6.4	66.2	27.4	161,490	142,292	96,064	12,341	583	11.1	6,716	1,025
Apple Valley Unified	CA	125,251	11,078	84,477	29,696	100.0	8.8	67.4	23.7	142,826	104,712	67,041	35,536	1,325	19.6	6,663	1,310
Bakersfield City Elementary	CA	261,922	48,891	189,281	23,750	100.0	18.7	72.3	9.1	241,755	232,766	145,291	6,139	1,318	37.6	8,346	1,426
Baldwin Park Unified	CA	160,062	15,850	125,479	18,733	100.0	9.9	78.4	11.7	152,908	125,258	77,759	11,687	1,264	23.6	6,363	1,243
Bellflower Unified	CA	126,635	12,003	94,692	19,940	100.0	9.5	74.8	15.7	121,199	112,088	71,967	4,978	571	16.8	7,301	1,234
Burbank Unified	CA	141,799	8,367	88,333	45,099	100.0	5.9	62.3	31.8	134,189	122,523	82,239	6,994	2,089	14.1	7,360	1,121
Cajon Valley Union Elementary	CA	150,554	14,313	85,511	50,730	100.0	9.5	56.8	33.7	169,485	135,148	86,006	31,415	2,859	15.6	8,108	1,286
Capistrano Unified	CA	408,696	22,158	140,735	245,803	100.0	5.4	34.4	60.1	449,451	366,475	239,204	68,657	2,739	5.1	7,151	1,105
Chaffey Joint Union High	CA	216,860	11,474	147,013	58,373	100.0	5.3	67.8	26.9	233,091	180,586	114,339	37,467	5,492	15.6	7,229	1,214

See notes at end of table.

Table 92. Revenues, expenditures, poverty rate, and Title I allocations of public school districts enrolling more than 15,000 students: 2005–06 and fiscal year 2008—Continued

Name of district	State	Revenues by source of funds, 2005–06 (in thousands of dollars)				Percentage distribution of revenues, 2005–06				Expenditures, 2005–06 (in thousands of dollars)					Poverty rate of 5- to 17-year-olds, 2005[1]	Current expenditure per pupil,[2] 2005–06	Title I allocations, fiscal year 2008, per poverty child[3]
		Total	Federal	State	Local	Total	Federal	State	Local	Total[4]	Current expenditures						
											Total	Instruction	Capital outlay	Interest on school debt			
1	2	3	4	5	6	7	8	9	10	11	12	13	14	15	16	17	18
Chino Valley Unified	CA	263,136	14,456	177,004	71,676	100.0	5.5	67.3	27.2	268,914	219,164	144,617	37,109	5,562	10.0	6,505	1,083
Chula Vista Elementary	CA	249,739	21,237	108,497	120,005	100.0	8.5	43.4	48.1	251,398	212,984	137,366	22,335	10,562	14.3	8,046	1,076
Clovis Unified	CA	414,691	17,962	264,701	132,028	100.0	4.3	63.8	31.8	408,840	279,512	166,457	106,396	9,839	12.2	7,684	1,070
Coachella Valley Unified	CA	197,007	28,661	114,003	54,343	100.0	14.5	57.9	27.6	207,189	149,036	85,140	55,484	1,619	30.2	9,078	1,431
Colton Joint Unified	CA	221,755	20,338	165,692	35,725	100.0	9.2	74.7	16.1	225,837	175,035	102,398	44,940	2,933	18.7	7,082	1,366
Compton Unified	CA	278,948	42,906	195,351	40,691	100.0	15.4	70.0	14.6	280,569	236,981	138,924	27,334	4,220	31.9	7,838	1,528
Conejo Valley Unified	CA	193,356	7,195	79,352	106,809	100.0	3.7	41.0	55.2	190,964	159,425	105,360	20,377	1,951	7.5	7,099	963
Corona-Norco Unified	CA	475,912	26,873	288,824	160,215	100.0	5.6	60.7	33.7	549,080	341,520	219,895	162,689	17,023	9.2	7,188	1,098
Covina-Valley Unified	CA	127,673	9,316	95,928	22,429	100.0	7.3	75.1	17.6	142,605	114,503	68,592	19,472	894	14.4	7,484	988
Cupertino Union School	CA	129,567	5,001	34,173	90,393	100.0	3.9	26.4	69.8	127,996	116,753	77,482	7,726	3,216	5.4	7,045	982
Desert Sands Unified	CA	297,311	23,855	148,231	125,225	100.0	8.0	49.9	42.1	306,351	210,237	131,623	85,824	9,491	15.2	7,627	1,352
Downey Unified	CA	189,020	16,852	129,475	42,693	100.0	8.9	68.5	22.6	196,773	164,043	107,963	24,659	3,716	16.6	7,264	1,233
East Side Union High	CA	252,576	16,939	107,629	128,008	100.0	6.7	42.6	50.7	289,993	203,949	122,378	57,892	13,508	13.8	7,900	1,059
Elk Grove Unified	CA	653,443	41,007	430,227	182,209	100.0	6.3	65.8	27.9	669,174	465,030	293,317	156,912	5,262	14.5	7,657	1,361
Escondido Union Elementary	CA	162,236	17,848	87,373	57,015	100.0	11.0	53.9	35.1	168,559	145,304	92,709	19,174	3,457	14.5	7,393	1,223
Fairfield-Suisun Unified	CA	197,385	12,580	127,179	57,626	100.0	6.4	64.4	29.2	216,903	158,019	95,879	48,532	6,049	12.4	6,760	1,055
Folsom-Cordova Unified	CA	164,989	11,126	84,863	69,000	100.0	6.7	51.4	41.8	185,223	130,762	84,041	49,548	3,465	13.0	7,036	1,147
Fontana Unified	CA	381,615	36,925	295,898	48,792	100.0	9.7	77.5	12.8	393,527	332,892	199,986	44,552	3,519	20.1	7,939	1,352
Fremont Unified	CA	276,638	14,772	157,415	104,451	100.0	5.3	56.9	37.8	310,731	228,423	153,668	49,917	9,691	8.6	7,111	1,042
Fresno Unified	CA	719,209	113,778	505,426	100,005	100.0	15.8	70.3	13.9	694,101	637,514	382,434	20,129	15,070	34.7	8,065	1,571
Fullerton Joint Union High	CA	175,602	6,791	102,393	66,418	100.0	3.9	58.3	37.8	168,976	119,621	74,409	35,246	2,925	11.1	7,339	1,030
Garden Grove Unified	CA	419,282	45,741	265,465	108,076	100.0	10.9	63.3	25.8	407,076	395,798	252,750	2,963	122	15.7	7,984	1,558
Glendale Unified	CA	265,393	32,116	161,814	71,463	100.0	12.1	61.0	26.9	270,560	221,567	150,666	32,077	8,334	20.2	7,913	1,310
Grossmont Union High	CA	253,626	13,512	120,068	120,046	100.0	5.3	47.3	47.3	257,049	201,235	120,801	41,546	2,022	13.2	8,232	1,072
Hacienda La Puente Unified	CA	232,639	24,343	176,314	31,982	100.0	10.5	75.8	13.7	231,413	188,502	107,630	59,273	3,608	18.4	8,111	1,249
Hayward Unified	CA	203,287	20,864	123,316	59,107	100.0	10.3	60.7	29.1	194,207	176,152	112,401	5,818	1,293	16.1	7,922	1,248
Hemet Unified	CA	236,520	20,577	146,986	68,957	100.0	8.7	62.1	29.2	233,830	165,733	103,528	63,909	3,533	16.6	7,409	1,370
Hesperia Unified	CA	168,259	11,227	117,507	39,525	100.0	6.7	69.8	23.5	153,076	135,531	81,441	17,155	46	19.2	6,687	1,220
Huntington Beach Union High	CA	188,734	13,288	82,610	92,836	100.0	7.0	43.8	49.2	214,620	124,769	71,893	50,218	9,482	10.1	7,918	951
Inglewood Unified	CA	151,849	18,590	105,024	28,235	100.0	12.2	69.2	18.6	163,498	123,052	73,689	28,406	3,506	24.9	7,399	1,415
Irvine Unified	CA	220,480	11,758	65,511	143,211	100.0	5.3	29.7	65.0	295,826	188,591	121,172	89,835	10,473	5.7	7,397	973
Jurupa Unified	CA	186,026	19,632	123,855	42,539	100.0	10.6	66.6	22.9	186,142	161,975	102,343	19,135	4,163	17.1	7,697	1,346
Kern Union High	CA	338,816	31,355	191,444	116,017	100.0	9.3	56.5	34.2	356,477	295,627	160,122	81,140	9,457	27.3	8,352	1,305
Lake Elsinore Unified	CA	184,012	13,343	106,450	64,219	100.0	7.3	57.8	34.9	220,630	148,638	91,716	41,597	8,668	11.3	7,197	1,060
Lancaster Elementary	CA	150,646	16,149	107,840	26,657	100.0	10.7	71.6	17.7	154,288	118,549	75,714	12,650	1,391	21.2	7,383	1,270
Lodi Unified	CA	262,452	26,175	165,617	70,660	100.0	10.0	63.1	26.9	287,957	227,818	141,569	52,367	6,300	18.0	7,370	1,301
Long Beach Unified	CA	866,173	140,614	605,509	120,050	100.0	16.2	69.9	13.9	851,998	758,347	460,499	37,843	14,348	27.4	8,103	1,541
Los Angeles Unified	CA	8,297,754	1,174,255	5,671,268	1,452,231	100.0	14.2	68.3	17.5	9,136,581	7,001,506	4,250,025	1,691,347	250,996	26.5	9,626	1,868
Lynwood Unified	CA	192,829	19,011	154,577	19,241	100.0	9.9	80.2	10.0	200,519	147,716	90,845	47,680	822	27.0	8,111	1,257
Madera Unified	CA	165,720	20,293	105,707	39,720	100.0	12.2	63.8	24.0	205,917	138,663	84,342	61,330	2,232	30.1	7,707	1,368
Manteca Unified	CA	191,060	10,258	118,434	62,368	100.0	5.4	62.0	32.6	217,329	162,343	101,088	47,584	5,188	12.4	6,827	1,015
Modesto City Elementary	CA	310,246	30,650	184,133	95,463	100.0	9.9	59.4	30.8	327,360	264,048	164,596	50,882	1,765	25.5	7,927	1,348
Modesto City High	CA	(⁵)				(⁵)									17.3	(⁵)	1,162
Montebello Unified	CA	320,675	42,109	223,047	55,519	100.0	13.1	69.6	17.3	327,101	285,512	175,799	24,051	3,493	25.0	8,091	1,393
Moreno Valley Unified	CA	316,041	30,403	232,771	52,867	100.0	9.6	73.7	16.7	347,988	274,107	171,955	62,795	9,718	13.7	7,404	1,329
Mt. Diablo Unified	CA	349,944	33,557	183,731	142,656	100.0	6.7	52.5	40.8	373,979	277,932	180,125	78,977	11,927	9.5	7,746	1,120
Murrieta Valley Unified	CA	182,521	5,008	96,983	80,530	100.0	2.7	53.1	44.1	190,593	135,161	87,468	49,610	3,169	6.9	6,703	949
Napa Valley Unified	CA	148,000	10,654	41,304	96,042	100.0	7.2	27.9	64.9	159,270	135,118	89,414	17,590	3,048	9.5	7,762	1,034
Newport-Mesa Unified	CA	247,037	19,343	66,515	161,179	100.0	7.8	26.9	65.2	266,008	199,841	117,140	53,547	4,993	9.2	9,034	1,174
Norwalk-La Mirada Unified	CA	228,973	18,469	173,921	36,583	100.0	8.1	76.0	16.0	284,942	184,770	111,180	78,820	2,072	15.6	7,954	1,237
Oakland Unified	CA	544,354	78,128	303,382	162,844	100.0	14.4	55.7	29.9	574,697	417,440	236,879	90,512	20,696	22.1	8,672	1,764
Oceanside Unified	CA	195,771	21,943	107,910	65,918	100.0	11.2	55.1	33.7	211,392	166,920	106,303	39,673	4,406	17.5	7,812	1,253
Ontario-Montclair Elementary	CA	216,730	30,355	153,936	32,439	100.0	14.0	71.0	15.0	207,980	196,791	123,873	9,511	1,440	20.6	7,755	1,395
Orange Unified	CA	250,273	18,107	99,029	133,137	100.0	7.2	39.6	53.2	242,878	231,682	146,762	4,869	2,600	8.3	7,498	1,128

See notes at end of table.

Table 92. Revenues, expenditures, poverty rate, and Title I allocations of public school districts enrolling more than 15,000 students: 2005–06 and fiscal year 2008—Continued

Name of district	State	Revenues by source of funds, 2005–06 (in thousands of dollars)				Percentage distribution of revenues, 2005–06				Expenditures, 2005–06 (in thousands of dollars)						Poverty rate of 5- to 17-year-olds, 2005[1]	Current expenditure per pupil,[2] 2005–06	Title I allocations, fiscal year 2008, per poverty child[3]
		Total	Federal	State	Local	Total	Federal	State	Local	Total[4]	Current expenditures Total	Instruction	Capital outlay	Interest on school debt			
1	2	3	4	5	6	7	8	9	10	11	12	13	14	15	16	17	18
Oxnard Elementary	CA	151,870	19,665	91,162	41,043	100.0	12.9	60.0	27.0	158,482	128,641	85,198	23,062	4,265	18.4	8,038	1,238
Oxnard Union High	CA	142,352	12,465	69,422	60,465	100.0	8.8	48.8	42.5	144,902	127,950	76,788	10,104	3,114	17.4	7,928	1,163
Pajaro Valley Unified School	CA	202,733	37,096	99,401	66,236	100.0	18.3	49.0	32.7	213,775	186,020	106,740	22,778	1,687	18.4	9,624	1,242
Palm Springs Unified	CA	223,397	22,283	117,137	83,977	100.0	10.0	52.4	37.6	216,951	180,966	112,180	29,689	5,651	16.8	7,639	1,354
Palmdale Elementary	CA	222,944	40,909	159,657	22,378	100.0	18.3	71.6	10.0	219,147	170,142	103,843	7,595	3,484	20.5	7,454	1,301
Panama-Buena Vista Union Elementary	CA	140,684	8,178	105,452	27,054	100.0	5.8	75.0	19.2	139,997	112,333	72,547	21,604	391	14.2	7,387	978
Paramount Unified	CA	152,434	20,183	110,078	22,173	100.0	13.2	72.2	14.5	165,705	141,583	86,803	16,178	2,058	24.5	8,491	1,254
Pasadena Unified	CA	238,091	31,213	130,857	76,021	100.0	13.1	55.0	31.9	229,705	194,605	112,513	22,495	8,848	17.9	9,127	1,324
Placentia-Yorba Linda Unified	CA	215,989	14,014	107,736	94,239	100.0	6.5	49.9	43.6	229,692	200,568	125,599	24,685	1,074	6.6	7,496	1,087
Pomona Unified	CA	352,289	64,900	235,533	51,856	100.0	18.4	66.9	14.7	361,990	283,482	164,530	31,127	7,755	22.5	8,515	1,357
Poway Unified	CA	351,022	10,608	166,461	173,953	100.0	3.0	47.4	49.6	450,474	264,704	152,008	166,440	17,567	5.2	8,109	979
Redlands Unified	CA	175,293	11,876	113,343	50,074	100.0	6.8	64.7	28.6	184,485	150,167	96,516	25,480	3,680	12.3	7,041	1,247
Rialto Unified	CA	241,244	28,910	177,517	34,817	100.0	12.0	73.6	14.4	253,049	231,728	133,819	17,236	3,052	19.1	7,544	1,377
Riverside Unified	CA	391,043	36,540	251,745	102,758	100.0	9.3	64.4	26.3	383,404	314,206	199,222	57,242	3,385	14.3	7,298	1,344
Rowland Unified	CA	154,498	15,973	113,572	24,953	100.0	10.3	73.5	16.2	160,100	137,319	85,508	14,450	2,261	18.1	7,825	1,238
Sacramento City Unified	CA	573,623	80,420	360,147	133,056	100.0	14.0	62.8	23.2	569,519	452,973	266,185	87,020	19,507	22.2	8,986	1,587
Saddleback Valley Unified	CA	281,162	12,279	122,292	146,591	100.0	4.4	43.5	52.1	291,172	243,158	168,046	34,156	4,624	4.6	7,029	600
San Bernardino City Unified	CA	550,927	85,134	416,054	49,739	100.0	15.5	75.5	9.0	541,970	492,143	289,912	31,755	3,789	30.6	8,390	1,617
San Diego Unified	CA	1,404,140	159,576	566,739	677,825	100.0	11.4	40.4	48.3	1,532,235	1,234,922	719,740	223,475	71,248	18.4	9,321	1,570
San Francisco Unified	CA	593,468	65,909	217,610	309,949	100.0	11.1	36.7	52.2	586,939	469,937	254,337	75,260	6,886	15.3	8,357	1,508
San Jose Unified	CA	330,260	28,792	101,405	200,063	100.0	8.7	30.7	60.6	383,549	272,151	160,149	97,375	10,133	12.6	8,600	1,295
San Juan Unified	CA	452,930	41,671	273,659	137,600	100.0	9.2	60.4	30.4	436,542	384,421	240,430	30,982	13,178	13.5	7,955	1,379
San Marcos Unified	CA	157,868	9,659	85,146	63,063	100.0	6.1	53.9	39.9	157,746	113,268	71,262	38,659	3,116	13.0	7,005	977
San Ramon Valley Unified	CA	230,143	4,192	61,454	164,497	100.0	1.8	26.7	71.5	278,351	175,351	112,779	92,776	9,948	3.4	7,363	611
Santa Ana Unified	CA	548,889	78,647	322,882	147,360	100.0	14.3	58.8	26.8	560,924	482,642	295,198	68,630	6,287	17.3	8,138	1,717
Simi Valley Unified	CA	176,101	8,820	98,584	68,697	100.0	5.0	56.0	39.0	179,740	148,925	97,922	20,701	3,903	7.4	6,942	962
Stockton City Unified	CA	360,646	46,033	250,927	63,686	100.0	12.8	69.6	17.7	379,430	310,603	187,740	64,458	938	26.1	7,977	1,424
Sweetwater Union High	CA	527,183	29,210	369,292	128,681	100.0	5.5	70.1	24.4	538,603	338,387	203,927	169,486	15,341	18.4	8,083	1,308
Temecula Valley Unified	CA	234,800	7,926	124,780	102,094	100.0	3.4	53.1	43.5	229,360	175,697	119,360	45,891	5,470	6.2	6,436	997
Torrance Unified	CA	204,951	10,126	139,830	54,995	100.0	4.9	68.2	26.8	207,969	172,826	117,025	17,440	1,091	9.2	6,797	980
Tracy Joint Unified	CA	137,823	6,009	83,678	48,136	100.0	4.4	60.7	34.9	131,242	117,928	78,742	11,621	0	9.9	6,862	956
Tustin Unified	CA	171,550	8,881	65,984	96,675	100.0	5.2	38.5	56.4	165,193	140,334	91,507	11,900	7,499	8.3	6,949	1,079
Val Verde Unified	CA	234,210	10,304	189,974	33,932	100.0	4.4	81.1	14.5	219,185	129,501	74,462	86,872	2,799	14.5	7,489	1,224
Vallejo City Unified	CA	163,982	15,621	103,960	44,401	100.0	9.5	63.4	27.1	169,095	142,745	88,002	15,606	7,845	13.2	7,795	1,059
Ventura Unified	CA	184,226	14,282	73,522	96,422	100.0	7.8	39.9	52.3	150,650	133,666	77,622	7,775	3,397	11.7	7,618	993
Visalia Unified	CA	226,569	23,407	146,368	56,794	100.0	10.3	64.6	25.1	223,019	195,566	121,156	20,403	1,078	24.1	7,492	1,265
Vista Unified	CA	222,265	19,512	118,057	84,696	100.0	8.8	53.1	38.1	230,693	187,775	127,449	34,820	4,605	13.8	7,165	1,090
Walnut Valley Unified	CA	126,469	3,830	87,025	35,614	100.0	3.0	68.8	28.2	125,907	103,341	65,063	11,503	4,103	10.8	6,662	956
West Contra Costa Unified	CA	334,204	36,414	165,052	132,738	100.0	10.9	49.4	39.7	364,046	273,223	163,625	68,882	18,210	16.3	8,486	1,410
William S. Hart Union High	CA	189,592	5,939	129,622	54,031	100.0	3.1	68.4	28.5	234,552	168,711	94,976	48,160	7,444	8.2	7,198	953
Academy, School District No. 20...	CO	184,381	9,035	86,014	89,332	100.0	4.9	46.7	48.4	197,154	149,268	88,613	34,534	12,549	4.2	7,275	632
Aurora, Joint District No. 28...	CO	286,496	25,795	159,318	101,383	100.0	9.0	55.6	35.4	341,214	246,892	145,369	81,417	10,560	18.1	7,414	1,471
Boulder Valley	CO	267,139	12,522	60,115	194,502	100.0	4.7	22.5	72.8	252,798	227,323	143,546	10,810	6,736	7.4	8,138	1,090
Cherry Creek	CO	448,399	17,447	177,191	253,761	100.0	3.9	39.5	56.6	450,852	380,955	249,005	48,131	20,811	6.6	7,843	1,168
Colorado Springs	CO	282,426	21,958	120,843	139,625	100.0	7.8	42.8	49.4	301,739	276,326	147,687	13,066	8,949	14.2	8,926	1,392
Denver	CO	785,638	81,417	234,878	469,343	100.0	10.4	29.9	59.7	848,654	704,526	357,528	80,467	33,330	22.7	9,743	1,641
Douglas County	CO	432,175	10,599	169,336	252,240	100.0	2.5	39.2	58.4	451,344	374,475	216,323	46,422	30,078	2.8	7,795	801
Greeley	CO	146,247	15,349	79,534	51,364	100.0	10.5	54.4	35.1	145,439	126,400	76,105	11,276	6,607	14.6	6,955	1,363
Jefferson County	CO	807,076	37,259	328,874	440,943	100.0	4.6	40.7	54.6	867,642	717,691	385,478	94,601	41,757	7.7	8,313	1,467
Littleton	CO	148,138	5,151	64,888	78,099	100.0	3.5	43.8	52.7	161,068	125,441	77,263	28,125	5,930	5.8	7,776	1,044
Mesa County Valley	CO	161,770	14,095	85,203	62,472	100.0	8.7	52.7	38.6	238,880	153,147	89,940	78,103	6,618	16.1	7,445	1,361
Northglenn-Thornton	CO	336,914	15,301	175,753	145,860	100.0	4.5	52.2	43.3	369,511	271,378	168,316	71,212	20,407	9.4	7,219	1,168

See notes at end of table.

Table 92. Revenues, expenditures, poverty rate, and Title I allocations of public school districts enrolling more than 15,000 students: 2005–06 and fiscal year 2008—Continued

Name of district	State	Revenues by source of funds, 2005–06 (in thousands of dollars)				Percentage distribution of revenues, 2005–06				Expenditures, 2005–06 (in thousands of dollars)					Poverty rate of 5- to 17-year-olds, 2005[1]	Current expenditure per pupil[2] 2005–06	Title I allocations, fiscal year 2008, per poverty child[5]
		Total	Federal	State	Local	Total	Federal	State	Local	Total[4]	Current expenditures						
											Total	Instruction	Capital outlay	Interest on school debt			
1	2	3	4	5	6	7	8	9	10	11	12	13	14	15	16	17	18
Poudre	CO	229,291	14,166	82,132	132,993	100.0	6.2	35.8	58.0	257,178	216,023	112,868	24,722	14,132	10.6	8,567	1,137
Pueblo	CO	147,997	19,111	84,728	44,158	100.0	12.9	57.2	29.8	178,142	144,474	74,849	26,768	5,021	26.2	8,149	1,412
Saint Vrain Valley	CO	192,498	11,357	83,778	97,363	100.0	5.9	43.5	50.6	210,502	165,770	97,748	28,473	13,891	9.4	7,127	1,078
Thompson	CO	126,683	7,073	58,304	61,306	100.0	5.6	46.0	48.4	123,866	106,898	61,235	9,955	4,276	9.1	7,102	1,083
Bridgeport	CT	318,531	34,201	234,251	50,079	100.0	10.7	73.5	15.7	315,050	265,315	176,584	35,489	3,629	20.2	12,226	2,314
Hartford	CT	480,634	54,249	334,823	91,562	100.0	11.3	69.7	19.1	481,350	362,484	213,469	100,871	4,197	28.5	16,511	2,788
New Haven	CT	419,270	46,158	263,170	109,942	100.0	11.0	62.8	26.2	398,096	306,010	194,278	67,592	13,481	27.9	15,631	2,279
Stamford	CT	263,165	10,259	60,167	192,739	100.0	3.9	22.9	73.2	254,788	232,611	145,869	12,118	6,733	9.1	15,379	1,500
Waterbury	CT	228,506	25,586	133,488	69,432	100.0	11.2	58.4	30.4	233,106	224,500	132,231	4,749	345	26.8	12,420	2,018
Christina	DE	297,772	16,858	173,560	107,354	100.0	5.7	58.3	36.1	338,080	266,810	162,514	51,022	3,350	11.0	13,873	2,370
Red Clay Consolidated	DE	227,346	16,361	129,965	81,020	100.0	7.2	57.2	35.6	250,049	188,529	112,803	43,708	2,915	10.0	11,987	2,227
District of Columbia	DC	1,092,863	127,371	0	965,492	100.0	11.7	0.0	88.3	1,081,887	938,738	478,688	126,807	0	24.3	15,746	2,409
Alachua	FL	259,228	30,804	123,726	104,698	100.0	11.9	47.7	40.4	259,373	221,387	120,626	28,513	5,910	19.2	7,605	1,254
Bay	FL	254,874	23,114	102,761	128,999	100.0	9.1	40.3	50.6	234,969	201,849	123,233	24,255	4,335	18.5	7,309	1,249
Brevard	FL	649,861	51,463	290,653	307,745	100.0	7.9	44.7	47.4	678,153	548,972	344,913	110,531	16,917	12.5	7,297	1,312
Broward	FL	2,509,376	237,826	1,055,493	1,216,057	100.0	9.5	42.1	48.5	2,733,985	2,116,365	1,277,239	484,103	71,272	13.6	7,791	1,448
Charlotte	FL	183,053	14,432	36,626	131,995	100.0	7.9	20.0	72.1	174,198	140,598	78,063	29,106	575	14.1	7,852	992
Citrus	FL	147,728	12,568	51,355	83,805	100.0	8.5	34.8	56.7	147,470	120,303	67,209	23,552	257	20.6	7,608	1,205
Clay	FL	271,029	17,455	165,797	87,777	100.0	6.4	61.2	32.4	283,329	229,388	144,034	49,597	3,403	10.0	6,713	1,045
Collier	FL	519,821	41,384	79,896	398,541	100.0	8.0	15.4	76.7	502,659	413,284	222,535	73,304	11,087	13.8	9,546	1,088
Dade	FL	3,547,190	396,597	1,473,041	1,677,552	100.0	11.2	41.5	47.3	3,893,123	3,078,422	1,835,216	620,722	87,742	21.6	8,502	1,520
Duval	FL	1,091,677	115,047	515,553	461,077	100.0	10.5	47.2	42.2	1,101,192	966,794	564,700	122,492	10,640	14.8	7,633	1,410
Escambia	FL	382,583	50,840	200,029	131,714	100.0	13.3	52.3	34.4	379,208	344,434	185,017	27,550	3,238	21.8	7,925	1,315
Hernando	FL	203,323	15,895	89,374	98,054	100.0	7.8	44.0	48.2	187,720	150,521	87,102	28,561	7,638	17.8	6,934	1,208
Hillsborough	FL	1,767,683	246,951	886,776	633,956	100.0	14.0	50.2	35.9	1,807,826	1,369,437	823,943	293,853	52,364	16.5	7,068	1,451
Indian River	FL	171,157	12,200	30,255	128,702	100.0	7.1	17.7	75.2	195,313	130,246	73,358	58,506	5,028	16.0	7,555	1,167
Lake	FL	351,884	28,927	160,182	162,775	100.0	8.2	45.5	46.3	371,391	279,183	169,013	76,048	15,302	15.4	7,335	1,265
Lee	FL	796,722	65,221	148,090	583,411	100.0	8.2	18.6	73.2	827,023	559,642	314,798	228,017	24,867	13.7	7,399	1,318
Leon	FL	310,681	27,650	142,544	140,487	100.0	8.9	45.9	45.2	322,601	240,273	134,995	67,747	5,265	16.0	7,433	1,260
Manatee	FL	424,575	36,159	130,187	258,229	100.0	8.5	30.7	60.8	436,450	330,188	198,188	88,277	10,629	14.1	7,793	1,272
Marion	FL	369,910	40,094	187,606	142,210	100.0	10.8	50.7	38.4	364,551	296,655	160,724	55,394	5,737	20.8	7,057	1,291
Martin	FL	187,075	14,809	33,582	138,684	100.0	7.9	18.0	74.1	204,971	139,329	82,351	60,463	1,193	13.0	7,674	995
Okaloosa	FL	260,091	27,400	111,981	120,710	100.0	10.5	43.1	46.4	252,831	229,049	144,514	19,782	904	14.0	7,386	1,070
Orange	FL	1,738,157	146,724	699,562	891,871	100.0	8.4	40.2	51.3	1,763,715	1,297,445	753,494	388,204	58,782	16.6	7,388	1,407
Osceola	FL	477,114	41,629	227,590	207,895	100.0	8.7	47.7	43.6	457,890	351,831	200,072	88,260	14,204	18.8	7,065	1,272
Palm Beach	FL	1,928,698	142,941	443,563	1,342,194	100.0	7.4	23.0	69.6	2,096,947	1,459,819	901,464	519,326	81,236	14.6	8,345	1,403
Pasco	FL	568,273	51,721	282,171	234,381	100.0	9.1	49.7	41.2	630,965	456,101	265,367	159,737	12,057	14.3	7,266	1,296
Pinellas	FL	1,047,447	102,366	393,445	551,636	100.0	9.8	37.6	52.7	998,350	882,775	507,340	90,644	4,851	15.3	7,870	1,409
Polk	FL	837,268	83,205	425,406	328,657	100.0	9.9	50.8	39.3	882,982	705,767	445,073	149,786	18,111	18.5	7,891	1,377
Santa Rosa	FL	205,948	17,203	112,380	76,365	100.0	8.4	54.6	37.1	225,240	178,446	105,347	43,189	1,321	11.9	7,085	1,042
Sarasota	FL	518,465	26,664	86,780	405,021	100.0	5.1	16.7	78.1	515,485	394,289	232,461	108,115	4,526	12.3	9,412	1,089
Seminole	FL	553,790	40,497	272,416	240,877	100.0	7.3	49.2	43.5	579,373	476,667	299,563	87,031	13,770	9.6	7,059	1,263
St. Johns	FL	240,716	11,718	69,493	159,505	100.0	4.9	28.9	66.3	211,225	184,886	105,273	21,808	1,682	8.0	7,178	1,002
St. Lucie	FL	352,486	30,577	128,143	193,766	100.0	8.7	36.4	55.0	466,591	261,942	145,007	191,525	12,729	18.8	7,236	1,255
Volusia	FL	621,029	48,969	238,959	333,101	100.0	7.9	38.5	53.6	674,079	500,570	300,685	148,137	23,778	13.8	7,628	1,339
Atlanta City	GA	744,569	83,834	146,665	514,070	100.0	11.3	19.7	69.0	713,442	631,530	389,913	81,862	0	31.2	12,439	1,870
Bibb County	GA	231,172	32,011	109,301	89,860	100.0	13.8	47.3	38.9	231,599	205,958	118,657	23,837	1,796	31.7	8,156	1,578
Chatham County	GA	325,838	35,798	123,205	166,835	100.0	11.0	37.8	51.2	307,455	292,611	179,275	6,636	6,558	20.5	8,601	1,603
Cherokee County	GA	363,021	16,344	158,435	188,242	100.0	4.5	43.6	51.9	316,674	269,677	182,573	38,773	6,588	7.0	8,127	1,247
Clayton County	GA	508,169	54,562	251,142	202,465	100.0	10.7	49.4	39.8	485,764	446,883	282,410	38,143	0	18.5	8,487	1,555

See notes at end of table.

Table 92. Revenues, expenditures, poverty rate, and Title I allocations of public school districts enrolling more than 15,000 students: 2005–06 and fiscal year 2008—Continued

Name of district	State	Revenues by source of funds, 2005–06 (in thousands of dollars)				Percentage distribution of revenues, 2005–06				Expenditures, 2005–06 (in thousands of dollars)					Poverty rate of 5- to 17-year-olds, 2005[1]	Current expenditure per pupil,[2] 2005–06	Title I allocations, fiscal year 2008, per poverty child[3]
		Total	Federal	State	Local	Total	Federal	State	Local	Total[4]	Current expenditures						
											Total	Instruction	Capital outlay	Interest on school debt			
1	2	3	4	5	6	7	8	9	10	11	12	13	14	15	16	17	18
Cobb County	GA	1,123,467	68,185	400,985	654,297	100.0	6.1	35.7	58.2	1,023,920	860,886	572,392	151,039	7,231	8.4	8,066	1,574
Columbia County	GA	181,152	9,347	95,211	76,594	100.0	5.2	52.6	42.3	183,220	155,548	99,892	25,324	2,189	7.4	7,262	1,110
Coweta County	GA	190,199	11,818	81,663	96,718	100.0	6.2	42.9	50.9	183,111	153,352	99,233	25,316	2,784	10.7	7,474	1,177
DeKalb County	GA	1,102,028	85,470	444,185	572,373	100.0	7.8	40.3	51.9	1,134,249	1,019,680	621,322	114,569	0	18.2	9,967	1,699
Dougherty County	GA	173,271	26,011	88,507	58,753	100.0	15.0	51.1	33.9	191,661	146,709	88,154	43,732	623	28.3	8,802	1,428
Douglas County	GA	215,129	17,187	96,745	101,197	100.0	8.0	45.0	47.0	210,761	172,146	107,020	33,003	5,612	12.2	7,654	1,480
Fayette County	GA	206,975	7,184	85,996	113,795	100.0	3.5	41.5	55.0	207,228	180,931	118,390	18,291	4,662	4.5	8,098	789
Forsyth County	GA	264,006	8,521	91,798	163,687	100.0	3.2	34.8	62.0	324,531	200,111	133,236	107,852	16,201	5.2	7,819	1,205
Fulton County	GA	917,282	53,330	253,089	610,863	100.0	5.8	27.6	66.6	850,187	741,109	471,306	95,810	12,429	14.3	9,138	1,618
Gwinnett County	GA	1,424,897	81,934	552,630	790,333	100.0	5.8	38.8	55.5	1,493,189	1,206,315	750,668	260,382	24,806	8.7	8,343	1,745
Hall County	GA	214,335	17,351	100,962	96,022	100.0	8.1	47.1	44.8	200,428	184,445	117,233	13,150	2,722	11.4	7,659	1,223
Henry County	GA	355,858	15,623	159,971	180,264	100.0	4.4	45.0	50.7	391,880	285,976	199,054	89,830	12,824	8.0	8,086	1,216
Houston County	GA	240,225	19,614	128,702	91,909	100.0	8.2	53.6	38.3	249,049	208,770	133,425	36,379	2,880	16.7	8,484	1,403
Muscogee County	GA	355,347	37,628	189,513	128,206	100.0	10.6	53.3	36.1	316,566	277,469	167,616	37,327	0	23.9	8,282	1,501
Newton County	GA	163,511	12,422	87,463	63,626	100.0	7.6	53.5	38.9	156,568	129,829	82,713	24,435	2,245	15.6	7,599	1,349
Paulding County	GA	208,027	10,180	113,645	84,202	100.0	4.9	54.6	40.5	218,115	173,227	115,372	38,884	4,058	7.8	7,300	1,149
Richmond County	GA	334,078	45,608	167,007	121,463	100.0	13.7	50.0	36.4	337,825	285,050	174,719	49,251	3,349	32.8	8,406	1,598
Rockdale County	GA	149,138	9,078	67,309	72,751	100.0	6.1	45.1	48.8	146,137	122,093	76,969	23,793	251	13.1	8,178	1,316
Hawaii Department of Education	HI	2,705,532	225,393	2,431,735	48,404	100.0	8.3	89.9	1.8	1,939,968	1,805,522	1,077,351	74,988	0	11.2	9,876	1,868
Boise Independent District	ID	221,035	16,847	81,710	122,478	100.0	7.6	37.0	55.4	213,656	203,479	128,248	6,002	2,121	10.9	7,385	1,277
Meridian Joint District	ID	201,868	11,352	115,165	75,351	100.0	5.6	57.0	37.3	208,879	161,976	100,343	40,215	6,618	6.9	5,296	1,168
City of Chicago	IL	4,391,252	720,709	1,785,435	1,885,108	100.0	16.4	40.7	42.9	4,455,185	3,907,503	2,345,823	318,082	160,417	26.0	9,282	2,318
CUSD 300 (Carpentersville)	IL	171,405	8,588	42,746	120,071	100.0	5.0	24.9	70.1	167,191	145,931	89,840	14,976	6,284	7.5	7,747	1,236
Indian Prairie	IL	269,639	7,963	44,529	217,147	100.0	3.0	16.5	80.5	249,912	225,695	155,342	11,116	12,704	2.7	7,916	863
Naperville	IL	210,235	6,696	28,218	175,321	100.0	3.2	13.4	83.4	196,139	183,342	114,503	9,486	0	2.6	9,806	1,124
Plainfield	IL	218,837	3,738	83,230	131,869	100.0	1.7	38.0	60.3	266,315	178,094	112,654	71,056	12,741	3.1	7,308	754
Rockford	IL	292,674	37,462	116,065	139,147	100.0	12.8	39.7	47.5	272,279	252,154	146,276	6,879	8,117	19.3	8,652	1,791
SD U-46 (Elgin)	IL	381,407	23,046	121,504	236,857	100.0	6.0	31.9	62.1	383,613	328,976	190,553	31,127	10,569	11.2	8,296	1,332
Valley View	IL	179,025	7,800	53,480	117,745	100.0	4.4	29.9	65.8	194,044	147,316	90,002	44,296	1,622	7.6	8,413	1,195
Waukegan	IL	149,152	17,193	71,313	60,646	100.0	11.5	47.8	40.7	147,099	139,876	78,779	3,262	2,421	16.6	8,830	1,810
Evansville-Vanderburgh Sch. Corp.	IN	233,050	24,593	108,446	100,011	100.0	10.6	46.5	42.9	256,275	218,907	135,608	29,689	2,503	16.4	9,901	1,626
Fort Wayne	IN	363,184	30,267	167,892	165,025	100.0	8.3	46.2	45.4	348,296	310,665	191,673	23,236	2,684	17.8	9,832	1,736
Hamilton Southeastern Schools	IN	140,949	1,489	53,052	86,408	100.0	1.1	37.6	61.3	137,843	98,037	55,159	10,844	526	2.7	6,889	1,076
Indianapolis	IN	539,235	70,661	301,585	166,989	100.0	13.1	55.9	31.0	553,292	443,764	238,267	49,131	5,419	28.5	11,635	2,147
MSD Lawrence Township	IN	186,390	8,556	82,261	95,573	100.0	4.6	44.1	51.3	195,301	149,893	99,800	29,251	1,578	10.3	9,250	1,225
South Bend Community Sch. Corp.	IN	298,860	32,389	131,724	134,747	100.0	10.8	44.1	45.1	296,142	237,895	147,080	38,620	515	20.1	10,827	1,778
Vigo County School Corp.	IN	155,233	10,305	88,282	56,646	100.0	6.6	56.9	36.5	152,375	127,457	80,947	12,867	120	20.2	7,762	1,509
Cedar Rapids	IA	169,489	9,134	80,557	79,798	100.0	5.4	47.5	47.1	159,115	144,242	92,115	5,220	2,167	11.2	3,370	1,324
Davenport	IA	166,423	12,465	75,674	78,284	100.0	7.5	45.5	47.0	153,290	135,284	92,867	11,324	1,385	17.9	3,424	1,459
Des Moines Independent	IA	352,072	36,159	166,435	149,478	100.0	10.3	47.3	42.5	340,319	283,577	179,965	39,087	244	13.6	8,843	1,667
Blue Valley	KS	229,979	4,871	72,227	152,881	100.0	2.1	31.4	66.5	193,189	178,877	96,488	21,367	12,426	2.3	7,924	715
Kansas City	KS	204,694	21,194	121,472	62,028	100.0	10.4	59.3	30.3	196,303	180,274	103,761	10,309	5,708	26.7	9,004	1,855
Olathe	KS	258,084	11,279	124,997	121,808	100.0	4.4	48.4	47.2	237,506	205,753	129,439	18,032	11,653	5.4	8,347	1,386
Shawnee Mission	KS	283,766	11,787	101,554	170,425	100.0	4.2	35.8	60.1	267,934	224,663	144,279	33,561	9,674	4.8	7,877	768
Wichita	KS	484,596	58,489	278,891	147,216	100.0	12.1	57.6	30.4	463,263	417,538	225,575	33,293	11,132	16.6	8,601	2,131
Boone Co	KY	144,601	7,217	57,340	80,044	100.0	5.0	39.7	55.4	161,843	111,937	67,574	41,856	7,436	8.3	6,534	1,117
Fayette County	KY	375,213	31,145	127,154	216,914	100.0	8.3	33.9	57.8	340,729	288,726	172,767	40,192	9,700	16.0	8,174	1,473
Jefferson County	KY	986,526	114,949	409,390	462,187	100.0	11.7	41.5	46.8	942,280	861,271	459,443	52,096	20,620	15.3	8,741	1,770

See notes at end of table.

Table 92. Revenues, expenditures, poverty rate, and Title I allocations of public school districts enrolling more than 15,000 students: 2005–06 and fiscal year 2008—Continued

Name of district	State	Revenues by source of funds, 2005–06 (in thousands of dollars)				Percentage distribution of revenues, 2005–06				Expenditures, 2005–06 (in thousands of dollars)						Poverty rate of 5- to 17-year-olds, 2005[1]	Current expenditure per pupil,[2] 2005–06	Title I allocations, fiscal year 2008, per poverty child[3]
											Current expenditures							
		Total	Federal	State	Local	Total	Federal	State	Local	Total[4]	Total	Instruction	Capital outlay	Interest on school debt			
1	2	3	4	5	6	7	8	9	10	11	12	13	14	15	16	17	18
Ascension Parish SB	LA	158,389	20,610	67,465	70,314	100.0	13.0	42.6	44.4	145,007	134,721	85,750	7,912	2,096	13.5	7,508	1,222
Bossier Parish SB	LA	161,169	18,942	73,412	68,815	100.0	11.8	45.5	42.7	154,781	145,461	85,328	7,126	1,135	20.4	7,575	1,260
Caddo Parish SB	LA	405,585	52,901	187,599	165,085	100.0	13.0	46.3	40.7	404,267	361,057	211,422	38,577	3,331	30.6	8,218	1,401
Calcasieu Parish SB	LA	320,779	52,640	120,873	147,266	100.0	16.4	37.7	45.9	291,124	261,739	141,899	20,172	8,541	22.2	8,211	1,285
East Baton Rouge Parish SB	LA	531,036	103,663	160,215	267,158	100.0	19.5	30.2	50.3	467,808	424,169	246,793	42,252	0	28.0	8,493	1,439
Jefferson Parish SB	LA	576,105	144,780	149,445	281,880	100.0	25.1	25.9	48.9	431,497	401,020	235,919	14,812	12,081	20.3	9,634	1,487
Lafayette Parish SB	LA	279,208	45,160	101,911	132,137	100.0	16.2	36.5	47.3	253,821	241,612	154,590	6,626	4,545	19.2	7,862	1,358
Livingston Parish SB	LA	167,537	18,854	104,510	44,173	100.0	11.3	62.4	26.4	164,693	149,125	94,532	13,330	2,050	16.5	6,662	1,214
Ouachita Parish SB	LA	163,185	19,482	87,299	56,404	100.0	11.9	53.5	34.6	152,558	138,527	82,037	7,221	6,237	22.6	7,429	1,226
Rapides Parish SB	LA	199,395	35,918	98,742	64,735	100.0	18.0	49.5	32.5	198,277	180,927	109,287	12,948	3,804	27.1	7,546	1,282
Saint Landry Parish SB	LA	124,508	20,801	70,135	33,572	100.0	16.7	56.3	27.0	124,807	117,768	72,056	5,929	604	34.3	7,531	1,262
Saint Tammany Parish SB	LA	435,690	107,468	161,864	166,358	100.0	24.7	37.2	38.2	357,811	314,053	193,410	33,200	7,212	13.1	9,127	1,111
Tangipahoa Parish SB	LA	164,798	38,568	81,598	44,632	100.0	23.4	49.5	27.1	146,287	136,492	82,241	7,601	1,729	30.4	7,104	1,267
Terrebonne Parish SB	LA	168,558	27,313	80,423	60,822	100.0	16.2	47.7	36.1	145,928	142,131	88,860	3,173	60	26.6	7,457	1,263
Anne Arundel County	MD	843,819	45,111	250,654	548,054	100.0	5.3	29.7	64.9	852,787	740,389	447,170	83,837	10,100	6.1	10,064	1,844
Baltimore City	MD	1,111,963	130,664	736,766	244,533	100.0	11.8	66.3	22.0	1,073,880	956,167	557,526	60,305	3,159	28.4	10,910	2,236
Baltimore County	MD	1,210,105	85,998	458,372	665,735	100.0	7.1	37.9	55.0	1,231,603	1,105,429	678,947	83,174	12,211	7.4	10,327	2,125
Calvert County	MD	192,201	8,669	80,385	103,147	100.0	4.5	41.8	53.7	192,786	176,105	108,821	12,205	1,608	5.3	10,082	1,330
Carroll County	MD	312,834	14,003	131,276	167,555	100.0	4.5	42.0	53.6	306,452	275,179	161,509	21,454	2,322	4.0	9,509	997
Cecil County	MD	190,612	9,984	99,186	81,442	100.0	5.2	52.0	42.7	187,296	157,897	95,089	23,298	1,928	10.1	9,557	1,380
Charles County	MD	317,858	14,726	129,993	173,139	100.0	4.6	40.9	54.5	300,543	257,811	146,294	36,291	922	6.8	9,763	1,519
Frederick County	MD	440,159	17,200	177,088	245,871	100.0	3.9	40.2	55.9	446,983	379,418	229,402	53,972	7,668	5.0	9,564	1,536
Harford County	MD	470,593	23,029	188,703	258,861	100.0	4.9	40.1	55.0	482,901	378,923	231,702	71,653	3,615	6.2	9,423	1,498
Howard County	MD	626,100	18,334	181,901	425,865	100.0	2.9	29.1	68.0	690,536	568,709	361,929	104,845	11,274	3.7	11,703	1,056
Montgomery County	MD	2,157,876	91,123	418,717	1,648,036	100.0	4.2	19.4	76.4	2,099,080	1,792,567	1,140,692	237,838	33,078	5.4	12,859	2,276
Prince George's County	MD	1,656,012	107,664	794,996	753,352	100.0	6.5	48.0	45.5	1,575,692	1,362,659	763,809	133,901	18,972	9.4	10,221	1,980
Saint Mary's County	MD	187,564	13,322	83,564	90,678	100.0	7.1	44.6	48.3	183,097	157,723	90,781	20,532	2,417	9.4	9,473	1,364
Washington County	MD	221,545	15,880	105,756	99,909	100.0	7.2	47.7	45.1	221,505	201,370	122,378	14,137	1,646	10.6	9,525	1,528
Boston	MA	1,257,800	106,327	431,582	719,891	100.0	8.5	34.3	57.2	1,132,560	1,064,076	649,488	45,527	5,299	27.5	18,554	2,263
Brockton	MA	210,873	18,112	140,902	51,859	100.0	8.6	66.8	24.6	210,344	203,367	120,283	1,997	1,887	14.2	12,807	2,072
Springfield	MA	376,493	45,846	286,211	44,436	100.0	12.2	76.0	11.8	368,705	348,148	222,127	2,774	9,508	33.2	13,828	2,130
Worcester	MA	355,940	41,413	206,140	108,387	100.0	11.6	57.9	30.5	371,585	336,869	233,388	20,803	5,337	21.0	14,032	2,145
Ann Arbor	MI	222,052	4,928	90,587	126,537	100.0	2.2	40.8	57.0	248,064	198,828	112,197	37,786	6,766	9.4	11,593	1,331
Chippewa Valley	MI	148,299	1,691	91,424	55,184	100.0	1.1	61.6	37.2	199,396	115,024	74,062	59,796	22,767	6.4	7,749	1,224
Dearborn City	MI	210,324	14,180	112,805	83,339	100.0	6.7	53.6	39.6	222,292	194,462	113,527	17,842	7,744	35.6	10,709	1,695
Detroit City	MI	1,527,457	252,659	984,243	290,555	100.0	16.5	64.4	19.0	1,654,001	1,409,317	755,205	126,854	72,564	37.7	10,576	2,236
Flint City	MI	216,526	34,899	141,140	40,487	100.0	16.1	65.2	18.7	224,150	209,841	114,790	2,824	1,195	36.1	10,916	1,959
Grand Rapids	MI	264,192	27,736	152,292	84,164	100.0	10.5	57.6	31.9	279,992	232,142	139,289	40,493	4,874	24.9	10,902	1,828
Lansing	MI	180,164	21,418	109,545	49,201	100.0	11.9	60.8	27.3	215,089	175,861	96,225	33,367	3,312	29.7	10,998	1,693
Livonia	MI	194,822	1,732	117,897	75,193	100.0	0.9	60.5	38.6	195,457	179,341	102,515	5,602	5,219	6.5	9,904	1,257
Plymouth-Canton	MI	175,981	2,683	108,618	64,680	100.0	1.5	61.7	36.8	197,577	151,800	92,148	29,490	11,156	5.6	8,171	1,215
Utica	MI	285,676	9,549	186,241	89,886	100.0	3.3	65.2	31.5	313,388	257,798	161,282	37,821	10,495	6.9	8,661	1,294
Walled Lake Consolidated Schools	MI	183,526	2,651	103,613	77,262	100.0	1.4	56.5	42.1	192,826	160,072	93,553	18,375	10,807	5.7	10,137	1,202
Warren Consolidated Schools	MI	180,769	7,259	99,846	73,664	100.0	4.0	55.2	40.8	194,442	161,344	85,934	24,486	6,938	11.7	10,314	1,307
Anoka-Hennepin	MN	416,250	17,523	316,419	82,308	100.0	4.2	76.0	19.8	425,997	360,024	243,323	29,384	9,187	5.9	8,652	1,413
Minneapolis	MN	610,722	65,255	411,305	134,162	100.0	10.7	67.3	22.0	584,352	470,083	305,231	34,318	33,198	22.3	12,198	2,032
Osseo	MN	265,790	12,151	176,718	76,921	100.0	4.6	66.5	28.9	255,976	202,484	136,148	20,064	10,020	7.6	9,287	1,281
Rochester	MN	165,441	9,263	121,929	34,249	100.0	5.6	73.7	20.7	181,330	131,757	84,717	32,493	7,486	8.2	8,244	1,254
Rosemount-Apple Valley-Eagan	MN	283,643	9,098	212,167	62,378	100.0	3.2	74.8	22.0	307,212	244,943	173,816	45,945	5,414	3.9	8,664	704
Saint Paul	MN	568,094	61,883	420,146	86,065	100.0	10.9	74.0	15.1	573,945	487,303	333,998	35,106	14,720	21.6	11,807	1,830

See notes at end of table.

Table 92. Revenues, expenditures, poverty rate, and Title I allocations of public school districts enrolling more than 15,000 students: 2005–06 and fiscal year 2008—Continued

Name of district	State	Revenues by source of funds, 2005–06 (in thousands of dollars)				Percentage distribution of revenues, 2005–06				Expenditures, 2005–06 (in thousands of dollars)					Poverty rate of 5- to 17-year-olds, 2005	Current expenditure per pupil, 2005–06	Title I allocations, fiscal year 2008, per poverty child
		Total	Federal	State	Local	Total	Federal	State	Local	Total	Current expenditures						
											Total	Instruction	Capital outlay	Interest on school debt			
1	2	3	4	5	6	7	8	9	10	11	12	13	14	15	16	17	18
South Washington County School Dist	MN	168,612	4,805	120,324	43,483	100.0	2.8	71.4	25.8	163,930	125,564	82,330	13,893	7,994	3.0	7,733	732
DeSoto County	MS	183,666	14,174	101,071	68,421	100.0	7.7	55.0	37.3	269,348	153,013	91,375	109,625	6,504	10.9	5,633	1,003
Jackson	MS	266,798	53,709	122,080	91,009	100.0	20.1	45.8	34.1	268,618	248,739	141,031	12,311	4,586	33.1	7,676	1,439
Rankin County	MS	128,076	12,265	63,406	52,405	100.0	9.6	49.5	40.9	127,707	111,590	68,609	10,942	4,678	10.6	6,462	980
Columbia	MO	174,671	12,903	74,502	87,266	100.0	7.4	42.7	50.0	165,847	142,107	89,165	11,114	6,834	15.8	8,491	1,320
Fort Zumwalt	MO	164,572	5,841	63,557	95,174	100.0	3.5	38.6	57.8	142,496	129,822	76,627	5,204	5,210	4.3	6,941	632
Francis Howell	MO	178,700	6,637	65,857	106,206	100.0	3.7	36.9	59.4	166,302	145,325	91,450	5,104	8,228	3.2	7,104	741
Hazelwood	MO	189,401	7,282	73,609	108,510	100.0	3.8	38.9	57.3	191,718	144,823	89,357	36,656	7,827	11.3	7,406	1,206
Kansas City	MO	416,629	58,044	190,633	167,952	100.0	13.9	45.8	40.3	400,931	373,038	195,229	13,017	0	27.7	10,741	1,734
Lee's Summit	MO	175,227	4,784	68,399	102,044	100.0	2.7	39.0	58.2	164,897	134,412	83,403	15,732	10,142	6.2	8,067	1,010
North Kansas City	MO	183,966	10,074	55,157	118,735	100.0	5.5	30.0	64.5	184,210	138,189	86,033	33,146	7,858	9.5	7,911	1,073
Parkway	MO	197,316	5,183	42,938	149,195	100.0	2.6	21.8	75.6	205,719	172,253	95,982	24,795	4,982	3.9	9,169	625
Rockwood	MO	213,697	4,350	53,675	155,672	100.0	2.0	25.1	72.8	197,721	163,036	93,580	18,149	8,808	3.3	7,303	621
Saint Louis City	MO	484,076	67,979	223,278	192,819	100.0	14.0	46.1	39.8	479,064	439,864	233,502	23,391	124	34.6	10,770	1,652
Springfield	MO	197,757	20,009	66,723	111,025	100.0	10.1	33.7	56.1	197,069	173,161	101,660	13,911	7,952	16.2	7,138	1,479
Lincoln	NE	334,211	33,429	78,450	222,332	100.0	10.0	23.5	66.5	290,535	258,767	169,525	25,685	6,040	11.8	7,961	1,572
Millard	NE	203,368	7,716	62,112	133,540	100.0	3.8	30.5	65.7	189,687	155,184	96,781	28,400	5,248	4.3	7,424	1,836
Omaha	NE	481,362	66,310	173,465	241,587	100.0	13.8	36.0	50.2	447,072	385,862	217,602	43,869	12,720	18.7	8,265	2,018
Clark County	NV	2,608,292	178,590	1,456,009	973,693	100.0	6.8	55.8	37.3	2,898,553	2,085,834	1,252,700	620,518	178,985	14.1	7,092	1,448
Washoe County	NV	540,590	40,943	321,593	178,054	100.0	7.6	59.5	32.9	583,188	468,101	297,292	92,182	20,907	11.3	7,286	1,262
Manchester	NH	164,616	17,598	73,748	73,270	100.0	10.7	44.8	44.5	151,762	146,299	100,155	1,431	1,162	13.8	8,355	2,522
Camden City	NJ	401,941	32,944	351,301	17,696	100.0	8.2	87.4	4.4	358,928	318,217	182,659	28,380	214	36.9	20,077	2,501
Elizabeth	NJ	410,136	30,609	297,120	82,407	100.0	7.5	72.4	20.1	370,620	356,952	200,234	2,199	0	20.5	16,916	2,062
Jersey City	NJ	743,217	44,500	615,610	83,107	100.0	6.0	82.8	11.2	748,557	611,863	381,317	116,565	5,760	26.0	20,891	2,129
Newark	NJ	1,069,815	76,606	812,750	180,459	100.0	7.2	76.0	16.9	1,064,086	945,302	528,182	87,208	684	27.6	22,584	2,345
Paterson	NJ	527,248	37,149	447,759	42,340	100.0	7.0	84.9	8.0	525,042	477,368	273,752	14,355	1,139	28.1	18,862	2,057
Toms River Regional	NJ	222,770	8,095	92,031	122,644	100.0	3.6	41.3	55.1	222,379	198,126	116,719	19,030	4,340	7.0	11,059	1,546
Albuquerque	NM	805,387	82,042	603,903	119,442	100.0	10.2	75.0	14.8	831,890	703,818	419,582	113,270	5,627	16.6	7,486	1,555
Las Cruces	NM	211,345	23,661	153,254	34,430	100.0	11.2	72.5	16.3	208,328	182,518	106,278	20,575	2,647	27.4	7,661	1,349
Brentwood Union	NY	269,437	15,582	178,284	75,571	100.0	5.8	66.2	28.0	269,006	253,734	176,261	10,422	2,816	12.7	14,212	1,689
Buffalo City	NY	680,998	97,257	483,137	100,604	100.0	14.3	70.9	14.8	788,387	619,803	425,173	125,797	35,529	31.1	16,886	2,168
New York City	NY	17,451,165	1,936,055	7,472,905	8,042,205	100.0	11.1	42.8	46.1	18,584,181	15,757,417	12,149,252	1,900,914	506,675	26.6	15,539	2,332
Rochester City	NY	577,611	76,061	384,440	117,110	100.0	13.2	66.6	20.3	575,235	492,912	291,829	44,777	7,374	35.2	14,457	2,093
Sachem Central	NY	270,996	5,707	127,987	137,302	100.0	2.1	47.2	50.7	257,636	239,203	160,398	5,067	10,999	3.9	15,311	982
Syracuse City	NY	348,932	48,946	232,107	67,879	100.0	14.0	66.5	19.5	346,690	316,959	228,728	18,758	4,550	30.0	14,327	1,912
Yonkers City	NY	455,774	43,967	247,024	164,783	100.0	9.6	54.2	36.2	454,524	432,595	294,560	9,334	5,436	18.3	17,289	2,175
Alamance-Burlington	NC	159,357	16,643	101,815	40,899	100.0	10.4	63.9	25.7	163,576	149,311	95,787	11,702	2,349	15.6	6,798	1,213
Buncombe County	NC	229,770	19,644	125,709	84,417	100.0	8.5	54.7	36.7	208,396	186,988	116,864	15,148	6,008	15.9	7,323	1,274
Cabarrus County	NC	193,141	13,206	108,314	71,621	100.0	6.8	56.1	37.1	195,528	155,622	98,685	24,844	12,504	10.5	6,509	1,021
Catawba County	NC	143,672	10,933	83,444	49,295	100.0	7.6	58.1	34.3	147,414	117,112	78,174	24,666	5,636	12.8	6,843	997
Charlotte-Mecklenburg	NC	1,138,805	94,611	571,174	473,020	100.0	8.3	50.2	41.5	1,167,735	956,038	581,147	140,128	70,824	15.8	7,723	1,431
Cleveland County	NC	139,143	16,581	89,204	33,358	100.0	11.9	64.1	24.0	135,635	129,838	81,486	4,566	459	22.2	7,568	1,230
Cumberland County	NC	397,269	55,349	246,604	95,316	100.0	13.9	62.1	24.0	391,368	372,850	227,005	9,460	5,690	24.6	7,110	1,376
Davidson County	NC	136,602	10,142	91,098	35,362	100.0	7.4	66.7	25.9	133,249	124,582	74,234	6,660	1,875	11.9	6,205	1,010
Durham Public	NC	301,272	27,466	154,581	119,225	100.0	9.1	51.3	39.6	291,924	262,480	153,476	16,244	9,046	18.0	8,343	1,283
Forsyth County	NC	426,327	40,184	242,673	143,470	100.0	9.4	56.9	33.7	433,477	384,976	250,630	34,362	14,139	19.2	7,762	1,334

See notes at end of table.

Table 92. Revenues, expenditures, poverty rate, and Title I allocations of public school districts enrolling more than 15,000 students: 2005–06 and fiscal year 2008—Continued

Name of district	State	Revenues by source of funds, 2005–06 (in thousands of dollars) — Total	Federal	State	Local	% distribution of revenues 2005–06 — Total	Federal	State	Local	Expenditures 2005–06 (in thousands of dollars) — Total[4]	Current expenditures Total	Current expenditures Instruction	Capital outlay	Interest on school debt	Poverty rate of 5- to 17-year-olds, 2005[1]	Current expenditure per pupil,[2] 2005–06	Title I allocations, fiscal year 2008, per poverty child[3]
1	2	3	4	5	6	7	8	9	10	11	12	13	14	15	16	17	18
Gaston County	NC	234,492	23,923	148,788	61,781	100.0	10.2	63.5	26.3	233,062	213,334	134,446	14,669	5,059	16.0	6,607	1,294
Guilford County	NC	590,880	54,756	327,400	208,724	100.0	9.3	55.4	35.3	643,117	525,044	315,391	95,746	21,942	19.9	7,632	1,378
Harnett County	NC	127,884	14,235	84,600	29,049	100.0	11.1	66.2	22.7	122,394	114,690	74,094	4,254	3,397	19.5	6,531	1,217
Iredell-Statesville	NC	158,158	13,340	93,887	50,931	100.0	8.4	59.4	32.2	146,944	137,027	84,700	2,596	5,644	14.1	6,730	1,054
Johnston County	NC	227,627	17,418	135,148	75,061	100.0	7.7	59.4	33.0	239,081	195,286	127,734	30,992	12,789	15.0	7,070	1,221
Nash-Rocky Mount	NC	143,404	19,116	94,912	29,376	100.0	13.3	66.2	20.5	141,256	135,760	84,842	4,784	671	26.1	7,445	1,243
New Hanover County	NC	231,507	21,467	113,145	96,895	100.0	9.3	48.9	41.9	202,124	189,688	109,703	3,350	8,514	16.3	7,867	1,287
Onslow County	NC	181,937	23,096	108,728	50,113	100.0	12.7	59.8	27.5	166,211	156,368	96,942	7,308	2,216	21.5	6,815	1,244
Pitt County	NC	179,334	21,538	111,639	46,157	100.0	12.0	62.3	25.7	179,339	165,954	108,428	7,355	4,656	21.2	7,504	1,249
Randolph County	NC	133,450	11,518	86,807	35,125	100.0	8.6	65.0	26.3	125,079	118,029	76,210	2,397	4,583	15.4	6,332	1,195
Robeson County	NC	198,071	35,886	136,468	25,717	100.0	18.1	68.9	13.0	195,127	182,996	116,985	11,452	54	39.6	7,518	1,326
Rowan-Salisbury	NC	163,114	16,713	100,085	46,316	100.0	10.2	61.4	28.4	156,051	146,641	92,808	2,847	6,563	19.0	7,011	1,238
Union County	NC	222,678	17,264	138,042	67,372	100.0	7.8	62.0	30.3	284,484	209,458	134,571	56,134	16,491	11.3	6,676	1,056
Wake County	NC	1,052,989	67,553	552,264	433,172	100.0	6.4	52.4	41.1	1,173,179	883,716	539,611	219,641	62,745	11.3	7,333	1,385
Wayne County	NC	147,912	20,412	100,237	27,263	100.0	13.8	67.8	18.4	146,068	137,918	92,827	7,770	380	23.2	7,156	1,243
Akron City	OH	349,154	37,525	182,322	129,307	100.0	10.7	52.2	37.0	337,833	308,515	188,043	23,904	8	22.2	11,251	1,921
Cincinnati City	OH	542,108	66,585	191,167	284,356	100.0	12.3	35.3	52.5	599,178	467,683	282,875	113,274	738	26.7	12,684	1,991
Cleveland Municipal City	OH	897,692	122,333	514,940	260,419	100.0	13.6	57.4	29.0	863,053	726,839	462,833	96,290	9,003	39.2	12,364	2,005
Columbus City	OH	792,623	113,564	298,687	380,372	100.0	14.3	37.7	48.0	830,086	720,196	392,762	70,198	24,109	28.7	12,215	2,078
Dayton City	OH	310,624	32,755	163,221	114,648	100.0	10.5	52.5	36.9	293,390	220,789	104,659	57,372	120	32.8	12,946	1,799
Hilliard City	OH	163,142	4,978	49,804	108,360	100.0	3.1	30.5	66.4	147,924	137,378	87,957	4,832	4,439	6.8	9,250	1,193
Lakota Local	OH	161,258	5,018	56,527	99,713	100.0	3.1	35.1	61.8	150,784	134,462	72,643	8,825	6,728	5.2	9,703	1,186
South-Western City	OH	215,712	16,769	97,495	101,448	100.0	7.8	45.2	47.0	218,808	203,222	117,365	3,943	7,730	16.4	9,416	1,608
Toledo City	OH	487,272	42,060	299,044	146,168	100.0	8.6	61.4	30.0	479,748	378,667	226,578	83,684	7,184	31.0	12,447	1,877
Broken Arrow	OK	108,504	7,948	50,572	49,984	100.0	7.3	46.6	46.1	104,437	93,491	51,132	8,674	1,718	10.2	6,078	969
Edmond	OK	141,248	7,182	49,728	84,338	100.0	5.1	35.2	59.7	151,839	111,985	63,495	37,031	2,303	7.5	5,839	1,023
Lawton	OK	119,900	20,820	71,443	27,637	100.0	17.4	59.6	23.1	123,504	114,771	63,186	7,732	180	20.2	6,743	1,239
Moore	OK	125,299	9,376	70,058	45,865	100.0	7.5	55.9	36.6	127,799	114,626	68,108	12,160	960	8.1	5,723	1,014
Oklahoma City	OK	338,369	61,124	147,099	130,146	100.0	18.1	43.5	38.5	297,930	281,756	157,146	7,706	6,703	29.3	6,988	1,558
Putnam City	OK	137,185	12,999	62,454	61,732	100.0	9.5	45.5	45.0	140,844	122,918	69,552	16,865	874	16.7	6,400	1,257
Tulsa	OK	352,332	53,616	150,907	147,809	100.0	15.2	42.8	42.0	374,491	315,014	163,966	53,954	4,447	25.4	7,578	1,428
Beaverton	OR	321,555	19,158	146,469	155,928	100.0	6.0	45.6	48.5	358,718	275,025	165,885	57,716	25,042	9.9	7,506	1,346
Bend-Lapine	OR	129,135	10,517	46,750	71,868	100.0	8.1	36.2	55.7	122,716	108,168	64,030	6,026	7,754	14.5	7,366	1,337
Eugene	OR	175,141	15,531	60,728	98,882	100.0	8.9	34.7	56.5	191,891	155,561	94,030	26,593	8,853	13.3	8,416	1,272
Hillsboro	OR	168,777	13,691	83,969	71,117	100.0	8.1	49.8	42.1	165,117	146,977	86,621	5,678	12,013	10.6	7,463	1,268
North Clackamas	OR	132,335	8,485	71,412	52,438	100.0	6.4	54.0	39.6	132,498	117,087	67,357	4,805	8,438	9.7	6,920	1,272
Portland	OR	471,615	57,936	171,757	241,922	100.0	12.3	36.4	51.3	461,061	447,104	263,323	10,936	1,735	20.1	9,495	1,707
Salem-Keizer	OR	344,725	35,587	202,768	106,370	100.0	10.3	58.8	30.9	345,404	317,548	205,055	8,090	19,499	17.7	8,169	1,611
Allentown City	PA	171,539	18,921	70,162	82,456	100.0	11.0	40.9	48.1	171,281	143,545	94,838	6,933	2,277	29.1	7,923	1,812
Bethlehem Area	PA	184,128	8,952	37,981	137,195	100.0	4.9	20.6	74.5	202,606	133,987	83,865	42,134	9,038	13.2	8,796	1,467
Central Bucks	PA	238,275	4,345	35,329	198,601	100.0	1.8	14.8	83.3	223,575	186,957	116,925	17,832	12,764	2.9	9,341	1,174
Philadelphia City	PA	2,350,846	342,845	1,211,038	796,963	100.0	14.6	51.5	33.9	2,607,832	1,653,365	903,805	237,165	106,187	32.2	8,958	2,451
Pittsburgh	PA	628,050	68,186	206,350	353,514	100.0	10.9	32.9	56.3	612,430	485,878	288,012	58,221	21,424	22.6	14,947	2,267
Reading	PA	160,135	26,718	90,649	42,768	100.0	16.7	56.6	26.7	183,171	134,656	86,084	22,772	15,478	38.3	7,581	2,009
Providence	RI	396,311	54,343	224,713	117,255	100.0	13.7	56.7	29.6	383,202	360,369	196,498	8,332	8,411	36.6	14,069	2,200
Aiken County	SC	198,004	20,287	104,886	72,831	100.0	10.2	53.0	36.8	191,861	178,869	111,060	11,247	714	20.5	7,213	1,415
Beaufort 01	SC	205,630	17,950	44,954	142,726	100.0	8.7	21.9	69.4	194,479	167,102	96,128	13,814	11,649	16.9	8,800	1,350
Berkeley 01	SC	251,439	24,891	117,297	109,251	100.0	9.9	46.7	43.5	290,501	202,510	115,648	64,090	19,295	17.5	7,324	1,400
Charleston 01	SC	539,376	53,451	143,339	342,586	100.0	9.9	26.6	63.5	486,528	412,159	238,664	48,596	19,328	19.7	9,592	1,550

See notes at end of table.

Table 92. Revenues, expenditures, poverty rate, and Title I allocations of public school districts enrolling more than 15,000 students: 2005–06 and fiscal year 2008—Continued

| Name of district | State | Revenues by source of funds, 2005–06 (in thousands of dollars) | | | | Percentage distribution of revenues, 2005–06 | | | | Total[4] | Expenditures, 2005–06 (in thousands of dollars) | | | | Poverty rate of 5- to 17-year-olds, 2005[1] | Current expenditure per pupil,[2] 2005–06[1] | Title I allocations, fiscal year 2008, per poverty child[3] |
| | | | | | | | | | | | Current expenditures | | | | | | |
		Total	Federal	State	Local	Total	Federal	State	Local		Total	Instruction	Capital outlay	Interest on school debt			
1	2	3	4	5	6	7	8	9	10	11	12	13	14	15	16	17	18
Dorchester 02	SC	152,011	9,851	83,690	58,470	100.0	6.5	55.1	38.5	170,472	133,262	79,998	26,051	8,379	10.8	6,906	1,147
Florence 01	SC	135,585	16,143	64,999	54,443	100.0	11.9	47.9	40.2	129,090	119,147	72,073	5,776	505	22.3	7,902	1,341
Greenville 01	SC	594,646	49,035	272,239	273,372	100.0	8.2	45.8	46.0	783,897	472,202	278,553	248,364	55,914	15.7	6,990	1,598
Horry 01	SC	354,870	30,598	124,858	199,414	100.0	8.6	35.2	56.2	383,644	287,106	175,925	77,342	15,388	21.8	8,152	1,442
Lexington 01	SC	192,790	10,836	90,118	91,836	100.0	5.6	46.7	47.6	221,516	160,249	95,979	53,473	7,101	11.7	8,120	1,080
Lexington 05	SC	168,450	10,270	76,569	81,611	100.0	6.1	45.5	48.4	174,612	145,970	81,797	25,972	949	8.7	8,756	1,049
Pickens 01	SC	134,560	12,254	70,314	51,992	100.0	9.1	52.3	38.6	120,430	114,872	68,750	2,192	1,238	13.1	6,975	1,327
Richland 01	SC	319,836	29,935	119,862	170,039	100.0	9.4	37.5	53.2	423,210	266,786	155,493	135,734	18,166	21.9	10,703	1,606
Richland 02	SC	215,127	14,128	92,219	108,780	100.0	6.6	42.9	50.6	254,308	180,341	107,239	62,643	8,517	11.8	8,406	1,110
York 03	SC	152,721	11,167	73,559	67,995	100.0	7.3	48.2	44.5	157,385	130,629	77,229	20,014	5,510	15.4	7,807	1,314
Sioux Falls	SD	166,842	19,709	46,814	100,319	100.0	11.8	28.1	60.1	154,866	138,635	86,597	10,885	3,983	10.2	7,091	1,712
Hamilton County	TN	329,685	40,995	95,991	192,699	100.0	12.4	29.1	58.4	324,749	311,578	203,282	6,167	3,886	18.6	7,637	1,346
Knox County	TN	423,436	38,784	127,920	256,732	100.0	9.2	30.2	60.6	415,855	373,032	238,781	30,182	11,662	15.8	6,854	1,352
Memphis City	TN	1,032,125	140,491	368,104	523,530	100.0	13.6	35.7	50.7	1,021,710	928,391	581,315	81,554	682	27.4	7,719	1,488
Montgomery County	TN	175,482	21,677	87,019	66,786	100.0	12.4	49.6	38.1	221,066	167,411	101,000	47,556	5,708	14.8	6,199	1,214
Nashville-Davidson County	TN	681,050	68,208	173,087	439,755	100.0	10.0	25.4	64.6	701,092	603,700	373,810	71,912	21,996	20.6	8,303	1,434
Rutherford County	TN	211,109	15,651	101,319	94,139	100.0	7.4	48.0	44.6	272,151	196,558	134,869	58,878	11,706	8.8	5,904	1,017
Shelby County	TN	328,991	21,902	138,896	168,193	100.0	6.7	42.2	51.1	336,307	294,888	198,236	25,021	11,142	8.1	6,421	1,160
Sumner County	TN	172,811	13,810	85,124	73,877	100.0	8.0	49.3	42.8	169,590	165,017	109,038	3,098	0	11.4	6,458	1,028
Williamson County	TN	192,649	7,988	71,061	113,600	100.0	4.1	36.9	59.0	223,257	178,734	116,107	32,436	10,736	3.6	6,930	596
Abilene ISD	TX	142,504	22,714	62,735	57,055	100.0	15.9	44.0	40.0	156,498	131,925	83,332	20,034	2,897	23.3	7,921	1,233
Aldine ISD	TX	505,685	71,825	247,412	186,448	100.0	14.2	48.9	36.9	483,044	446,131	273,103	20,836	13,531	29.5	7,680	1,362
Alief ISD	TX	408,334	56,626	181,106	170,602	100.0	13.9	44.4	41.8	385,600	349,246	230,742	20,235	11,925	29.5	7,338	1,342
Allen ISD	TX	137,452	4,685	27,699	105,068	100.0	3.4	20.2	76.4	146,833	108,107	66,127	25,811	12,712	4.0	6,773	574
Amarillo ISD	TX	240,623	31,194	99,452	109,977	100.0	13.0	41.3	45.7	250,578	215,144	137,174	28,712	4,247	23.6	7,157	1,291
Arlington ISD	TX	503,710	50,029	117,254	336,427	100.0	9.9	23.3	66.8	473,875	433,202	278,122	8,191	29,953	16.0	6,833	1,312
Austin ISD	TX	861,984	84,971	83,088	693,925	100.0	9.9	9.6	80.5	952,590	660,697	388,313	126,928	21,419	20.5	8,141	1,455
Beaumont ISD	TX	206,906	53,357	32,142	121,407	100.0	25.8	15.5	58.7	192,327	176,623	104,092	11,193	1,910	26.8	9,025	1,257
Birdville ISD	TX	173,051	13,885	46,322	112,844	100.0	8.0	26.8	65.2	178,827	156,423	99,611	13,540	7,450	12.8	6,949	1,027
Brownsville ISD	TX	426,935	77,055	278,380	71,500	100.0	18.0	65.2	16.7	426,886	378,735	228,376	38,400	5,000	53.6	7,848	1,448
Carrollton-Farmers Branch ISD	TX	287,966	19,810	25,237	242,919	100.0	6.9	8.8	84.4	309,310	199,316	119,381	53,827	18,301	13.0	7,598	1,046
Clear Creek ISD	TX	296,302	17,404	49,619	229,279	100.0	5.9	16.7	77.4	373,669	235,128	149,881	112,006	25,682	8.7	6,674	1,016
Conroe ISD	TX	343,637	23,376	69,403	250,858	100.0	6.8	20.2	73.0	390,922	284,609	171,037	72,369	32,300	12.8	6,679	1,091
Corpus Christi ISD	TX	323,378	45,623	136,897	140,658	100.0	14.2	42.3	43.5	319,223	291,283	175,452	17,340	4,454	25.5	7,428	1,323
Cypress-Fairbanks ISD	TX	664,646	42,698	175,697	446,251	100.0	6.4	26.4	67.1	805,416	572,273	368,943	178,666	51,689	12.2	6,635	1,271
Dallas ISD	TX	1,556,872	210,079	226,097	1,120,696	100.0	13.5	14.5	72.0	1,828,174	1,261,081	767,180	472,624	62,872	26.7	7,821	1,644
Denton ISD	TX	175,101	13,258	25,666	136,093	100.0	7.6	14.7	77.8	225,743	143,909	88,535	65,346	15,705	12.3	7,840	1,354
Ector County ISD	TX	201,543	26,348	83,575	91,620	100.0	13.1	41.5	45.5	211,811	184,572	113,080	22,481	3,416	27.1	7,083	1,233
Edinburg CISD	TX	245,596	42,579	136,704	66,313	100.0	17.3	55.7	27.0	230,173	216,063	129,224	2,532	8,467	47.9	7,879	1,391
El Paso ISD	TX	539,616	87,228	263,772	188,616	100.0	16.2	48.9	35.0	566,646	483,798	293,721	65,652	14,328	35.2	7,582	1,445
Fort Bend ISD	TX	525,094	34,405	173,083	317,606	100.0	6.6	33.0	60.5	576,650	438,777	278,064	106,905	29,432	7.9	6,638	1,127
Fort Worth ISD	TX	712,933	119,688	246,250	346,995	100.0	16.8	34.5	48.7	651,893	616,864	360,309	3,891	19,605	26.3	7,679	1,462
Frisco ISD	TX	199,250	4,202	19,143	175,905	100.0	2.1	9.6	88.3	336,747	144,429	90,230	140,525	30,943	4.3	7,265	570
Galena Park ISD	TX	186,544	23,809	86,924	75,811	100.0	12.8	46.6	40.6	185,472	165,236	101,000	9,940	7,928	25.4	7,768	1,220
Garland ISD	TX	443,113	36,609	173,655	232,849	100.0	8.3	39.2	52.5	460,153	372,709	230,212	60,987	22,248	15.9	6,490	1,270
Goose Creek CISD	TX	189,400	21,454	23,283	144,663	100.0	11.3	12.3	76.4	194,006	154,542	89,867	26,031	10,955	21.7	7,645	1,215
Grand Prairie ISD	TX	197,243	20,500	101,022	75,721	100.0	10.4	51.2	38.4	186,774	164,037	102,325	6,063	14,088	19.6	6,856	1,235
Harlingen CISD	TX	139,063	20,465	74,266	44,332	100.0	14.7	53.4	31.9	146,932	126,429	77,943	14,734	3,563	38.2	7,169	1,274
Houston ISD	TX	1,900,199	295,857	275,291	1,329,051	100.0	15.6	14.5	69.9	2,001,122	1,571,231	932,412	320,095	89,293	30.8	7,472	1,564
Humble ISD	TX	244,577	15,382	74,528	154,667	100.0	6.3	30.5	63.2	307,724	193,687	120,339	99,337	13,356	9.5	6,520	995
Hurst-Euless-Bedford ISD	TX	172,112	12,406	18,677	141,029	100.0	7.2	10.9	81.9	163,262	141,738	89,296	4,006	14,594	12.6	7,095	1,010

See notes at end of table.

Table 92. Revenues, expenditures, poverty rate, and Title I allocations of public school districts enrolling more than 15,000 students: 2005–06 and fiscal year 2008—Continued

Name of district	State	Revenues by source of funds, 2005–06 (in thousands of dollars)				Percentage distribution of revenues, 2005–06				Expenditures, 2005–06 (in thousands of dollars)						Poverty rate of 5- to 17-year-olds, 2005[1]	Current expenditure per pupil,[2] 2005–06	Title I allocations, fiscal year 2008, per poverty child[3]
		Total	Federal	State	Local	Total	Federal	State	Local	Total[4]	Current expenditures						
											Total	Instruction	Capital outlay	Interest on school debt			
1	2	3	4	5	6	7	8	9	10	11	12	13	14	15	16	17	18
Irving ISD	TX	274,291	27,669	90,080	156,542	100.0	10.1	32.8	57.1	275,401	219,184	140,379	35,555	18,698	21.8	6,708	1,236
Judson ISD	TX	159,405	12,878	68,331	78,196	100.0	8.1	42.9	49.1	175,491	135,389	81,484	27,592	11,572	14.7	7,033	1,199
Katy ISD	TX	414,227	21,900	120,600	271,727	100.0	5.3	29.1	65.6	421,078	341,944	217,258	39,746	38,138	10.1	7,087	1,061
Keller ISD	TX	205,833	5,282	44,605	155,946	100.0	2.6	21.7	75.8	252,924	157,582	97,837	70,069	24,760	5.8	6,091	952
Killeen ISD	TX	316,647	71,390	170,109	75,148	100.0	22.5	53.7	23.7	302,805	262,215	162,347	30,001	7,602	16.6	7,582	1,326
Klein ISD	TX	313,553	19,372	115,270	178,911	100.0	6.2	36.8	57.1	351,966	261,899	158,113	74,756	13,830	13.1	6,642	1,081
La Joya ISD	TX	226,735	40,283	150,861	35,591	100.0	17.8	66.5	15.7	224,287	195,262	115,590	19,179	8,441	60.3	8,082	1,489
Lamar CISD	TX	171,657	13,798	47,771	110,088	100.0	8.0	27.8	64.1	226,145	142,940	88,040	71,921	10,321	17.3	7,270	1,238
Laredo ISD	TX	240,635	43,253	149,203	48,179	100.0	18.0	62.0	20.0	279,800	208,213	126,061	58,340	12,205	48.1	8,344	1,423
Leander ISD	TX	199,612	9,831	31,870	157,911	100.0	4.9	16.0	79.1	237,742	159,365	95,427	61,304	15,224	5.4	7,219	991
Lewisville ISD	TX	422,568	23,552	44,050	354,965	100.0	5.6	10.4	84.0	418,037	348,668	224,890	33,824	29,517	5.0	7,341	1,065
Lubbock ISD	TX	248,707	39,377	80,754	128,576	100.0	15.8	32.5	51.7	272,413	227,567	139,761	34,871	5,214	24.2	7,890	1,300
Mansfield ISD	TX	213,796	10,510	77,849	125,437	100.0	4.9	36.4	58.7	297,997	162,743	101,220	111,017	23,752	9.9	6,329	951
McAllen ISD	TX	210,011	32,070	91,135	86,806	100.0	15.3	43.4	41.3	211,247	194,817	120,152	8,099	5,813	34.9	7,973	1,256
McKinney ISD	TX	180,998	8,174	24,783	148,041	100.0	4.5	13.7	81.8	195,544	134,485	84,531	41,581	16,671	9.8	6,812	974
Mesquite ISD	TX	297,910	19,455	152,984	125,471	100.0	6.5	51.4	42.1	306,836	245,061	151,895	43,040	18,196	15.4	6,881	1,220
Midland ISD	TX	168,700	21,754	49,942	97,004	100.0	12.9	29.6	57.5	178,179	150,531	91,620	21,552	4,727	18.8	7,268	1,242
Mission CISD	TX	129,164	22,733	84,508	21,923	100.0	17.6	65.4	17.0	125,025	113,925	68,593	6,476	2,956	51.3	7,681	1,422
North East ISD	TX	518,662	35,735	91,958	390,969	100.0	6.9	17.7	75.4	653,692	439,072	275,986	173,380	38,546	14.2	7,340	1,293
Northside ISD	TX	672,158	52,375	236,073	383,710	100.0	7.8	35.1	57.1	761,692	537,869	324,192	171,554	45,236	15.1	6,833	1,355
Pasadena ISD	TX	397,550	43,518	196,018	158,014	100.0	10.9	49.3	39.7	443,404	350,710	214,601	70,252	20,017	26.0	7,124	1,328
Pearland ISD	TX	127,985	6,992	32,309	88,684	100.0	5.5	25.2	69.3	145,211	97,470	56,328	36,206	10,730	6.6	6,271	922
Pflugerville ISD	TX	153,906	9,341	38,471	106,094	100.0	6.1	25.0	68.9	175,987	125,044	76,668	35,514	13,830	11.8	6,665	961
Pharr-San Juan-Alamo ISD	TX	248,268	42,209	158,711	47,348	100.0	17.0	63.9	19.1	238,880	223,410	134,025	6,819	6,583	48.0	7,954	1,391
Plano ISD	TX	615,912	22,310	47,903	545,699	100.0	3.6	7.8	88.6	624,735	386,704	251,599	62,995	35,172	5.5	7,284	1,056
Richardson ISD	TX	371,470	31,864	36,115	303,491	100.0	8.6	9.7	81.7	352,993	256,846	165,716	40,473	16,791	16.3	7,308	1,236
Round Rock ISD	TX	347,064	17,959	34,711	294,394	100.0	5.2	10.0	84.8	296,020	272,161	163,208	6,989	13,873	5.6	7,191	1,053
San Antonio ISD	TX	522,507	96,815	261,726	163,966	100.0	18.5	50.1	31.4	546,526	466,716	271,489	43,414	25,998	31.4	8,272	1,576
Socorro ISD	TX	318,279	36,004	202,024	80,251	100.0	11.3	63.5	25.2	337,913	267,436	165,957	51,310	16,900	28.6	7,259	1,247
Spring Branch ISD	TX	319,770	37,384	33,121	249,265	100.0	11.7	10.4	78.0	326,830	257,046	160,131	28,323	20,425	20.6	7,860	1,263
Spring ISD	TX	284,322	26,718	111,764	145,840	100.0	9.4	39.3	51.3	365,387	217,545	131,134	118,103	28,011	21.0	6,931	1,227
Tyler ISD	TX	151,346	24,649	32,575	94,122	100.0	16.3	21.5	62.2	184,573	133,342	83,007	46,209	3,668	25.7	7,407	1,252
United ISD	TX	306,822	39,574	152,334	114,914	100.0	12.9	49.6	37.5	312,883	260,569	156,130	37,606	13,468	31.5	7,299	1,274
Waco ISD	TX	134,522	23,810	57,701	53,011	100.0	17.7	42.9	39.4	135,932	122,362	69,867	6,716	2,782	29.9	7,837	1,513
Weslaco ISD	TX	138,287	26,245	90,226	21,816	100.0	19.0	65.2	15.8	156,291	124,796	72,875	8,316	1,216	53.1	7,973	1,438
Ysleta ISD	TX	378,256	54,579	231,623	92,054	100.0	14.4	61.2	24.3	443,746	344,873	209,867	86,322	9,683	32.8	7,479	1,343
Alpine District	UT	338,381	30,990	201,345	106,046	100.0	9.2	59.5	31.3	342,743	272,383	182,557	51,762	13,592	6.6	4,918	1,182
Davis District	UT	387,460	33,373	232,883	121,204	100.0	8.6	60.1	31.3	391,760	325,083	202,322	43,749	12,045	5.7	5,266	1,182
Granite District	UT	438,162	49,884	238,873	149,405	100.0	11.4	54.5	34.1	415,275	350,329	220,419	52,578	0	10.7	5,202	1,353
Jordan District	UT	515,240	37,854	262,114	215,272	100.0	7.3	50.9	41.8	465,233	382,436	239,223	64,431	7,996	6.2	4,960	1,157
Nebo District	UT	162,194	16,090	97,358	48,746	100.0	9.9	60.0	30.1	187,589	122,919	77,680	54,975	6,714	7.3	5,101	1,072
Salt Lake District	UT	202,391	31,302	76,234	94,855	100.0	15.5	37.7	46.9	213,987	155,124	98,799	41,515	5,686	19.8	6,369	1,357
Washington District	UT	149,701	12,833	77,363	59,505	100.0	8.6	51.7	39.7	173,992	117,152	76,799	49,733	6,688	12.1	5,029	1,052
Weber District	UT	174,135	15,751	109,371	49,013	100.0	9.0	62.8	28.1	165,811	150,258	99,012	10,822	3,715	7.6	5,187	1,026
Arlington County	VA	367,657	13,644	43,029	310,984	100.0	3.7	11.7	84.6	367,268	301,661	181,565	35,106	10,514	9.9	16,339	1,249
Chesapeake City	VA	381,365	23,602	189,927	167,836	100.0	6.2	49.8	44.0	416,141	361,831	229,887	40,459	5,367	7.1	8,970	1,537
Chesterfield County	VA	510,235	24,816	237,277	248,142	100.0	4.9	46.5	48.6	505,444	439,195	274,529	50,520	12,657	6.8	7,673	1,368
Fairfax County	VA	2,067,838	83,028	392,286	1,592,524	100.0	4.0	19.0	77.0	2,199,898	1,950,204	1,182,107	182,516	52,793	5.4	11,909	1,741
Hampton City	VA	209,958	21,077	120,564	68,317	100.0	10.0	57.4	32.5	207,660	201,007	118,712	4,704	534	18.4	8,816	1,586
Hanover County	VA	167,008	6,500	70,044	90,464	100.0	3.9	41.9	54.2	178,631	145,464	98,230	26,454	5,369	4.8	7,802	719
Henrico County	VA	417,032	21,940	179,906	215,186	100.0	5.3	43.1	51.6	419,637	364,083	220,054	43,533	9,268	8.8	7,625	1,401
Loudoun County	VA	831,467	13,435	118,526	699,506	100.0	1.6	14.3	84.1	866,793	543,282	348,613	104,601	219,304	2.7	11,464	948

See notes at end of table.

Table 92. Revenues, expenditures, poverty rate, and Title I allocations of public school districts enrolling more than 15,000 students: 2005–06 and fiscal year 2008—Continued

Name of district	State	Revenues by source of funds, 2005–06 (in thousands of dollars)				Percentage distribution of revenues, 2005–06				Expenditures, 2005–06 (in thousands of dollars)						Poverty rate of 5- to 17-year-olds, 2005[1]	Current expenditure per pupil[2] 2005–06	Title I allocations, fiscal year 2008, per poverty child[3]
										Total[4]	Current expenditures							
		Total	Federal	State	Local	Total	Federal	State	Local		Total	Instruction	Capital outlay	Interest on school debt				
1	2	3	4	5	6	7	8	9	10	11	12	13	14	15	16	17	18
Newport News City	VA	318,316	34,509	168,627	115,180	100.0	10.8	53.0	36.2	317,087	280,388	169,871	22,781	5,282	19.8	8,461	1,647
Norfolk City	VA	354,784	45,103	190,218	119,463	100.0	12.7	53.6	33.7	353,089	325,651	210,937	19,579	84	26.1	9,042	1,750
Portsmouth City	VA	158,264	11,475	89,267	57,522	100.0	7.3	56.4	36.3	157,586	138,189	81,086	14,387	193	24.3	8,706	1,596
Prince William County	VA	768,833	31,853	306,983	429,997	100.0	4.1	39.9	55.9	779,722	633,677	365,858	104,101	20,508	6.4	9,256	1,386
Richmond City	VA	314,166	41,280	121,034	151,852	100.0	13.1	38.5	48.3	312,959	298,471	173,929	6,477	4,266	29.0	12,071	1,698
Spotsylvania County	VA	223,549	9,639	103,965	109,945	100.0	4.3	46.5	49.2	232,275	192,537	118,207	29,165	9,793	6.7	8,112	1,230
Stafford County	VA	238,131	11,603	112,576	113,952	100.0	4.9	47.3	47.9	279,035	216,294	135,412	62,144	49	4.3	8,262	786
Virginia Beach City	VA	729,334	58,432	336,273	334,629	100.0	8.0	46.1	45.9	735,916	656,756	390,198	47,793	16,468	9.5	8,839	1,672
Bellevue	WA	173,636	7,785	84,900	80,951	100.0	4.5	48.9	46.6	218,273	133,662	80,958	69,353	12,100	7.6	8,143	1,091
Bethel	WA	151,699	10,471	102,404	38,824	100.0	6.9	67.5	25.6	160,032	132,384	74,549	22,797	4,338	9.7	7,330	1,299
Edmonds	WA	198,349	14,513	111,421	72,415	100.0	7.3	56.2	36.5	197,008	165,098	98,823	20,380	10,176	9.1	7,700	1,183
Everett	WA	185,220	11,033	109,694	64,493	100.0	6.0	59.2	34.8	181,274	146,352	87,947	26,257	8,160	12.7	7,763	1,224
Evergreen (Clark)	WA	229,520	13,916	147,825	67,779	100.0	6.1	64.4	29.5	268,463	190,626	112,835	65,179	11,513	13.9	7,453	1,227
Federal Way	WA	186,941	13,987	119,701	53,253	100.0	7.5	64.0	28.5	183,532	170,378	104,274	6,552	5,878	11.4	7,415	1,214
Highline	WA	180,979	16,487	99,933	64,559	100.0	9.1	55.2	35.7	205,279	146,596	86,427	47,457	10,451	13.3	8,323	1,407
Issaquah	WA	155,860	4,612	81,131	70,117	100.0	3.0	52.1	45.0	166,632	118,359	70,518	35,732	10,054	3.8	7,381	647
Kent	WA	242,714	15,393	146,182	81,139	100.0	6.3	60.2	33.4	227,918	198,009	119,079	18,085	11,288	10.2	7,223	1,218
Lake Washington	WA	223,732	8,469	123,287	91,976	100.0	3.8	55.1	41.1	238,569	179,632	112,489	48,180	8,509	5.0	7,383	1,111
Northshore	WA	215,621	7,159	111,089	97,373	100.0	3.3	51.5	45.2	192,356	160,907	97,988	18,901	11,850	4.7	7,766	659
Puyallup	WA	191,738	7,785	116,702	67,251	100.0	4.1	60.9	35.1	218,274	153,946	92,708	51,713	12,029	6.5	7,432	1,151
Seattle	WA	557,532	50,277	260,714	246,541	100.0	9.0	46.8	44.2	552,617	421,203	241,388	128,210	1,900	13.4	9,140	1,631
Spokane	WA	299,299	32,607	181,570	85,122	100.0	10.9	60.7	28.4	322,247	255,909	155,577	52,868	7,263	19.0	8,255	1,523
Tacoma	WA	355,094	37,507	190,859	126,728	100.0	10.6	53.7	35.7	387,155	269,084	158,411	101,217	16,773	17.1	8,456	1,661
Vancouver	WA	201,351	17,712	125,608	58,031	100.0	8.8	62.4	28.8	205,117	178,709	105,459	16,773	8,255	17.7	7,937	1,497
Berkeley County	WV	158,724	14,264	93,045	51,415	100.0	9.0	58.6	32.4	157,998	141,045	83,164	13,343	1,248	13.3	9,028	1,461
Kanawha County	WV	286,640	34,850	147,461	104,329	100.0	12.2	51.4	36.4	284,693	265,399	161,364	8,097	799	20.8	9,479	1,659
Appleton Area	WI	159,040	8,716	88,076	62,248	100.0	5.5	55.4	39.1	168,924	143,331	91,997	18,115	2,926	7.3	9,422	1,533
Green Bay Area	WI	220,188	15,593	129,272	75,323	100.0	7.1	58.7	34.2	221,975	208,367	128,368	7,213	3,967	15.1	10,257	1,774
Kenosha	WI	231,925	15,018	141,633	75,274	100.0	6.5	61.1	32.5	225,340	214,416	136,001	5,651	3,940	12.7	9,688	1,800
Madison Metropolitan	WI	324,108	20,721	85,390	217,997	100.0	6.4	26.3	67.3	321,875	301,404	179,619	3,063	4,780	13.3	12,326	1,511
Milwaukee	WI	1,133,742	172,212	717,236	244,294	100.0	15.2	63.3	21.5	1,151,958	1,041,911	630,610	52,494	14,710	32.9	11,277	2,267
Racine	WI	220,786	15,829	144,035	60,922	100.0	7.2	65.2	27.6	223,124	212,912	136,388	4,821	3,145	15.1	10,055	1,891

†Not applicable.

[1]Poverty is defined based on the number of persons and related children in the family and their income. For information on poverty thresholds for 2005, see http://www.census.gov/hhes/www/poverty/threshld/thresh05.html.

[2]Current expenditure per pupil based on fall enrollment collected through the "School District Finance Survey (Form F-33)," 2005–06.

[3]Fiscal year 2008 Department of Education funds available for spending by school districts beginning with the 2008–09 school year divided by number of poverty children in 2005.

[4]Includes other expenditures not shown separately.

[5]Data included under Modesto City Elementary.

NOTE: Detail may not sum to totals because of rounding. SB = school board. ISD = independent school district. ISD = consolidated independent school district.

SOURCE: U.S. Department of Education, National Center for Education Statistics, Common Core of Data (CCD), "School District Finance Survey (Form F-33)," 2005–06, and "Local Education Agency Universe Survey," 2006–07; and unpublished Department of Education budget data. (This table was prepared September 2008.)

Table 93. Enrollment, poverty, and federal funds for the 100 largest school districts, by enrollment size in 2006: Fall 2006, 2005–06, and fiscal year 2008

							Revenues by source of funds, 2005–06				Revenue for selected federal programs (in thousands), 2005–06						Title I allocations (in thousands), fiscal year 2008[2]				
Name of district	State	Rank order	Enrollment, fall 2006	5- to 17-year-old population, 2005	5- to 17-year-olds in poverty, 2005	Poverty rate of 5- to 17-year-olds, 2005[1]	Total (in thousands)	Federal (in thousands)	Federal as a percent of total	Federal revenue per student[3]	Title I basic and concentration grants[3]	School lunch	Vocational education	Drug-free schools	Eisenhower math and science	Special education	Total	Basic grants	Concentration grants	Targeted grants	Education finance incentive grants
1	2	3	4	5	6	7	8	9	10	11	12	13	14	15	16	17	18	19	20	21	22
New York City	NY	1	999,150	1,371,739	365,056	26.6	$17,451,165	$1,936,055	11.1	$1,909	$906,128	$278,111	—	$19,386	$34,864	$278,903	$851,241	$346,102	$87,542	$227,974	$189,623
Los Angeles Unified	CA	2	707,627	874,982	231,576	26.5	8,297,754	1,174,255	14.2	1,614	556,289	142,181	$55,760	4,879	12,404	217,392	432,581	157,659	39,347	113,840	121,734
City of Chicago	IL	3	413,694	520,534	135,418	26.0	4,391,252	720,709	16.4	1,712	291,985	96,783	40,613	5,305	10,273	147,900	313,960	125,729	31,780	76,163	80,287
Dade	FL	4	353,790	410,366	88,751	21.6	3,547,190	396,597	11.2	1,095	125,907	71,776	26,675	2,654	7,511	86,108	134,859	51,836	13,373	38,394	31,256
Clark County	NV	5	303,448	311,645	43,949	14.1	2,608,292	178,590	6.8	607	55,697	39,570	3,971	1,216	3,327	43,420	63,625	25,448	6,565	17,190	14,421
Broward	FL	6	262,813	309,388	41,975	13.6	2,509,376	237,826	9.5	876	55,156	51,855	11,708	1,522	3,527	42,640	60,771	24,675	6,366	16,389	13,342
Houston ISD	TX	7	202,936	247,983	76,340	30.8	1,900,199	295,857	15.6	1,407	93,431	33,702	12,957	1,696	3,074	66,222	119,404	46,630	11,787	31,671	29,316
Hillsborough	FL	8	193,517	201,354	33,317	16.5	1,767,683	246,951	14.0	1,275	49,222	41,261	935	831	3,480	43,324	48,347	20,087	5,182	12,721	10,356
Hawaii Dept. of Education	HI	9	180,728	211,521	23,729	11.2	2,705,532	225,393	8.3	1,233	46,525	33,674	916	1,658	2,416	29,600	44,323	19,093	4,438	10,284	10,509
Philadelphia City	PA	10	178,241	266,016	85,700	32.2	2,350,846	342,345	14.6	1,858	149,970	—	26,351	2,103	7,189	62,564	210,050	72,619	18,734	53,742	64,954
Orange	FL	11	175,245	181,387	30,169	16.6	1,738,157	146,724	8.4	836	40,259	37,739	7,366	984	2,227	34,106	42,445	17,710	4,569	11,116	9,050
Palm Beach	FL	12	171,431	194,484	28,352	14.6	1,928,698	142,941	7.4	817	37,582	37,934	—	—	1,785	29,327	39,767	16,631	4,291	10,388	8,457
Fairfax County	VA	13	163,952	181,141	9,849	5.4	2,067,838	83,028	4.0	507	15,406	29,781	3,805	697	1,701	14,419	17,149	7,146	1,844	3,786	4,374
Dallas ISD	TX	14	159,144	186,895	49,967	26.7	1,556,872	210,079	13.5	1,303	64,382	25,670	10,653	1,193	2,136	54,474	82,128	35,681	9,019	19,437	17,991
Gwinnett County	GA	15	152,043	140,755	12,239	8.7	1,424,897	81,934	5.8	567	—	—	4,479	655	—	28,618	21,351	9,388	2,373	4,446	5,144
Montgomery County	MD	16	137,814	164,414	8,909	5.4	2,157,876	91,123	4.2	654	18,889	27,136	4,782	805	1,537	14,475	20,273	10,026	2,534	4,103	3,609
Prince George's County	MD	17	131,014	157,853	14,779	9.4	1,656,012	107,664	6.5	808	27,748	24,975	4,782	805	1,648	26,695	29,261	12,414	3,203	7,182	6,462
San Diego Unified	CA	18	130,983	159,576	29,285	18.4	1,404,140	159,576	11.4	1,205	56,846	24,474	8,848	1,371	1,235	28,813	45,987	19,225	4,859	11,288	10,616
Charlotte-Mecklenburg	NC	19	128,789	142,476	22,570	15.8	1,138,805	94,611	8.3	764	—	—	—	—	—	27,707	32,290	12,837	3,312	7,856	8,285
Wake County	NC	20	128,748	133,867	15,139	11.3	1,052,989	67,553	6.4	561	—	—	—	—	—	16,028	20,962	8,554	2,207	4,965	5,236
Duval	FL	21	125,176	153,059	22,609	14.8	1,091,677	115,047	10.5	908	32,582	32,616	7,223	853	1,364	23,895	31,885	13,456	3,472	8,245	6,712
Detroit City	MI	22	117,609	210,742	79,511	37.7	1,527,457	252,659	16.5	1,896	124,506	18,800	3,099	2,569	3,913	32,276	177,774	60,940	15,721	44,686	56,426
Memphis City	TN	23	117,349	135,941	37,238	27.4	1,032,125	140,491	13.6	1,168	42,915	23,681	—	—	3,760	37,954	55,409	20,583	5,310	13,249	16,266
Pinellas	FL	24	109,915	131,901	20,126	15.3	1,047,447	102,366	9.8	913	26,977	28,235	5,400	818	1,616	17,678	28,364	12,038	3,106	7,287	5,932
Cobb County	GA	25	107,274	112,603	9,418	8.4	1,123,467	68,185	6.1	539	—	—	—	—	—	13,551	14,823	6,269	1,611	3,290	3,653
Baltimore County	MD	26	105,839	131,322	9,727	7.4	1,210,105	85,998	7.1	813	20,889	21,746	6,507	549	1,265	14,243	20,673	9,606	2,428	4,654	3,985
DeKalb County	GA	27	101,396	116,065	21,112	18.2	1,102,028	85,470	7.8	835	—	—	—	—	—	28,764	35,864	13,760	3,550	8,363	10,192
Albuquerque	NM	28	95,493	107,133	17,735	16.6	805,387	82,042	10.2	873	25,376	15,953	3,296	316	953	16,946	27,583	10,863	2,766	6,388	7,567
Polk	FL	29	92,801	93,181	17,207	18.5	837,288	83,205	9.9	930	21,308	18,856	4,705	485	1,458	22,403	23,690	10,156	2,620	6,016	4,898
Jefferson County	KY	30	92,659	120,831	18,430	15.3	986,526	114,949	11.7	1,167	—	—	—	—	—	23,639	32,617	13,591	3,435	7,182	8,410
Cypress-Fairbanks ISD	TX	31	92,135	70,519	8,631	12.2	664,646	42,698	6.4	495	4,989	11,385	1,406	257	457	11,397	10,972	4,903	1,265	2,494	2,309
Long Beach Unified	CA	32	90,663	105,746	28,966	27.4	866,173	140,614	16.2	1,502	49,788	15,262	7,805	711	1,353	24,358	44,624	18,745	4,738	10,902	10,239
Milwaukee	WI	33	89,912	117,884	38,785	32.9	1,133,742	172,212	15.2	1,864	72,506	26,295	—	—	2,097	24,015	87,929	35,663	9,014	19,400	23,852
Jefferson County	CO	34	86,154	92,727	7,173	7.7	807,076	37,259	4.6	432	9,040	14,059	2,593	337	542	6,726	10,522	4,636	1,196	2,259	2,431
Baltimore City	MD	35	84,515	112,785	32,048	28.4	1,111,963	130,664	11.8	1,491	43,363	23,848	15,064	1,210	2,397	25,336	71,655	28,752	7,417	18,213	17,273
Fulton County	GA	36	83,861	94,612	13,560	14.3	917,282	53,330	5.8	658	—	—	—	—	—	14,407	21,946	8,795	2,269	5,011	5,871
Northside ISD	TX	37	82,587	74,508	11,250	15.1	672,158	52,375	7.8	665	11,515	11,621	2,540	324	696	15,129	15,247	6,575	1,696	3,623	3,354
Austin ISD	TX	38	82,140	93,158	19,087	20.5	861,984	84,971	9.9	1,047	21,115	14,071	4,135	460	965	20,770	27,772	12,099	3,058	6,551	6,064

See notes at end of table.

Table 93. Enrollment, poverty, and federal funds for the 100 largest school districts, by enrollment size in 2006: Fall 2006, 2005–06, and fiscal year 2008—Continued

Name of district	State	Rank order	Enrollment, fall 2006	5- to 17-year-old population, 2005	5- to 17-year-olds in poverty, 2005	Poverty rate of 5- to 17-year-olds, 2005[1]	Revenues by source of funds, 2005–06 Total (in thousands)	Federal (in thousands)	Federal as a percent of total	Federal revenue per student[3]	Revenue for selected federal programs (in thousands), 2005–06 Title I basic and concentration grants	School lunch	Vocational education	Drug-free schools	Eisenhower math and science	Special education	Title I allocations (in thousands), fiscal year 2008[2] Total	Basic grants	Concentration grants	Targeted grants	Education finance incentive grants
1	2	3	4	5	6	7	8	9	10	11	12	13	14	15	16	17	18	19	20	21	22
Fort Worth ISD	TX	39	79,457	94,953	24,953	26.3	712,933	119,688	16.8	1,490	39,402	16,574	—	584	1,270	21,636	36,471	15,632	3,951	8,770	8,118
Lee	FL	40	78,981	78,022	10,672	13.7	796,722	65,221	8.2	862	11,738	14,740	—	367	1,012	13,996	14,064	6,279	1,620	3,399	2,767
Jordan District	UT	41	78,299	82,813	5,175	6.2	515,240	37,854	7.3	491	4,349	12,212	1,571	243	710	8,167	5,989	2,960	0	1,380	1,649
Fresno Unified	CA	42	77,555	87,229	30,276	34.7	719,209	113,778	15.8	1,439	48,809	14,634	6,402	743	1,612	24,954	47,555	20,472	4,896	11,431	10,756
Brevard	FL	43	74,785	81,636	10,192	12.5	649,861	51,463	7.9	684	11,976	15,786	—	305	699	9,991	13,369	5,999	1,548	3,210	2,613
Mesa Unified	AZ	44	74,128	97,046	14,031	14.5	570,482	40,514	7.1	543	15,675	12,244	3,576	409	1,035	493	19,551	7,975	2,057	4,585	4,934
Nashville-Davidson County	TN	45	73,731	90,700	18,674	20.6	681,050	68,208	10.0	938	20,939	17,262	—	—	2,230	18,428	26,786	10,458	2,698	6,262	7,368
Anne Arundel County	MD	46	73,066	90,150	5,542	6.1	843,819	45,111	5.3	613	10,278	15,967	2,755	351	701	5,860	10,220	5,029	1,271	2,192	1,729
Denver	CO	47	72,561	82,789	18,832	22.7	785,638	81,417	10.4	1,126	27,637	15,821	4,518	610	1,430	15,344	30,908	11,875	3,064	7,121	8,848
Virginia Beach City	VA	48	72,538	84,521	8,025	9.5	729,334	58,432	8.0	786	11,879	13,755	3,751	337	1,087	8,202	13,420	5,831	1,504	2,898	3,188
Guilford County	NC	49	71,722	75,747	15,064	19.9	590,880	54,756	9.3	796	—	—	—	—	—	17,519	20,756	8,477	2,187	4,912	5,181
Prince William County	VA	50	70,948	69,838	4,451	6.4	768,833	31,853	4.1	465	5,811	11,125	1,466	354	674	7,936	6,168	3,195	0	1,442	1,532
Greenville 01	SC	51	67,537	73,811	11,616	15.7	594,646	49,035	8.2	726	15,571	13,401	2,466	403	1,154	11,900	18,565	7,447	1,882	4,029	5,207
Granite District	UT	52	67,502	75,014	8,056	10.7	438,162	49,884	11.4	741	9,933	12,181	2,747	322	716	11,671	10,898	4,585	1,183	2,296	2,833
Fort Bend ISD	TX	53	67,014	66,944	5,277	7.9	525,094	34,405	6.6	520	4,687	10,285	1,435	205	398	6,584	5,949	3,127	0	1,466	1,357
Seminole	FL	54	66,351	70,919	6,779	9.6	553,790	40,497	7.3	600	6,987	13,491	2,501	269	507	11,070	8,564	4,030	1,032	1,930	1,572
Volusia	FL	55	65,867	71,151	9,803	13.8	621,029	48,969	7.9	746	14,174	13,846	2,992	362	1,228	11,455	13,130	5,903	1,523	3,145	2,560
Mobile County	AL	56	65,097	77,632	20,566	26.5	555,247	97,090	17.5	1,479	30,276	20,374	5,790	774	2,396	18,966	29,067	11,449	2,954	6,931	7,733
Washoe County	NV	57	64,954	68,031	7,709	11.3	540,590	40,943	7.6	637	7,750	10,808	2,026	324	1,111	8,305	9,731	4,618	1,191	2,319	1,602
Pasco	FL	58	64,689	64,621	9,269	14.3	568,273	51,721	9.1	824	11,875	14,929	1,797	291	604	12,187	12,012	5,452	1,407	2,841	2,312
Arlington ISD	TX	59	63,082	69,512	11,139	16.0	503,710	50,029	9.9	789	10,996	10,011	1,851	289	634	14,137	14,613	6,327	1,632	3,456	3,199
El Paso ISD	TX	60	62,857	64,609	22,772	35.2	539,616	87,228	16.2	1,367	33,101	9,628	5,259	483	1,228	18,747	32,908	14,352	3,433	7,854	7,270
Davis District	UT	61	62,193	61,321	3,507	5.7	387,460	33,373	8.6	541	2,961	10,393	1,159	186	745	8,123	4,146	2,298	0	853	995
Elk Grove Unified	CA	62	61,881	53,130	7,682	14.5	653,443	41,007	6.3	675	11,799	8,626	1,821	220	511	8,997	10,455	4,848	1,251	2,412	1,944
North East ISD	TX	63	61,255	61,372	8,738	14.2	518,662	35,735	6.9	597	6,856	10,575	1,496	209	517	9,135	11,295	5,030	1,298	2,580	2,388
Tucson Unified	AZ	64	60,333	80,597	15,137	18.8	507,545	70,587	13.9	1,166	23,792	10,839	4,543	1,327	1,560	13,005	24,090	10,570	2,672	5,196	5,653
Knox County	TN	65	59,663	64,736	10,245	15.8	423,436	38,784	9.2	713	10,238	11,541	—	—	1,367	9,012	13,855	5,808	1,498	3,122	3,427
Aldine ISD	TX	66	58,831	55,372	16,337	29.5	505,685	71,825	14.2	1,236	16,893	10,085	2,106	360	694	22,482	22,247	9,311	2,402	5,470	5,064
Chesterfield County	VA	67	58,455	56,270	3,834	6.8	510,235	24,816	4.9	434	4,091	10,734	1,284	365	642	3,890	5,246	2,764	0	1,209	1,273
San Bernardino City Unified	CA	68	57,398	61,020	18,675	30.6	550,927	85,134	15.5	1,451	40,136	10,103	4,756	554	744	18,854	30,189	13,742	3,465	6,775	6,207
Santa Ana Unified	CA	69	57,286	65,573	11,375	17.3	548,889	78,647	14.3	1,326	28,258	11,096	2,021	458	699	16,502	19,527	9,529	2,409	4,033	3,556
Garland ISD	TX	70	56,955	55,908	8,902	15.9	443,113	36,609	8.3	638	5,497	9,098	1,455	232	450	10,309	11,309	5,035	1,299	2,584	2,391
District of Columbia	DC	71	56,943	80,807	19,634	24.3	1,092,863	127,371	11.7	2,137	64,248	10,035	—	1,189	5,960	15,446	47,308	20,218	4,978	11,828	10,284
Alpine District	UT	72	56,460	58,844	3,886	6.6	338,381	30,990	9.2	560	4,419	9,210	1,110	145	610	6,569	4,594	2,455	0	983	1,156
Boston	MA	73	56,388	80,050	21,995	27.5	1,257,800	106,327	8.5	1,854	43,428	18,955	—	—	1,476	11,549	49,776	18,592	4,796	11,353	15,034
San Francisco Unified	CA	74	56,183	68,353	10,454	15.3	593,468	65,909	11.1	1,172	18,259	—	4,061	498	404	11,118	15,769	7,454	1,829	3,490	2,997
Columbus City	OH	75	56,003	76,515	21,954	28.7	792,623	113,564	14.3	1,926	—	18,502	—	622	2,939	20,393	45,627	17,976	4,544	9,942	13,166
Cleveland Municipal City	OH	76	55,593	92,032	36,108	39.2	897,692	122,333	13.6	2,081	—	22,016	—	901	2,929	18,872	72,394	26,281	6,736	16,691	22,687

See notes at end of table.

Table 93. Enrollment, poverty, and federal funds for the 100 largest school districts, by enrollment size in 2006: Fall 2006, 2005–06, and fiscal year 2008—Continued

Name of district	State	Rank order	Enrollment, fall 2006	5- to 17-year-old population, 2005	5- to 17-year-olds in poverty, 2005	Poverty rate of 5- to 17-year-olds, 2005[1]	Total (in thousands)	Federal (in thousands)	Federal as a percent of total	Federal revenue per student[3]	Title I basic and concentration grants	School lunch	Vocational education	Drug-free schools	Eisenhower math and science	Special education	Total	Basic grants	Concentration grants	Targeted grants	Education finance incentive grants
1	2	3	4	5	6	7	8	9	10	11	12	13	14	15	16	17	18	19	20	21	22
San Antonio ISD	TX	77	55,406	66,817	20,984	31.4	522,507	96,815	18.5	1,716	32,858	11,483	5,174	618	1,185	25,230	33,067	15,026	3,797	7,397	6,847
Cumberland County	NC	78	53,621	56,592	13,945	24.6	397,266	55,349	13.9	1,055	—	—	—	—	—	14,226	19,189	7,884	2,034	4,512	4,759
Plano ISD	TX	79	52,997	71,487	3,912	5.5	615,912	22,310	3.6	419	2,562	6,730	1,128	161	425	4,374	4,132	2,236	0	985	911
Clayton County	GA	80	52,533	57,185	10,552	18.5	508,169	54,562	10.7	1,036	—	—	—	—	—	17,401	16,406	6,819	1,759	3,677	4,152
Osceola	FL	81	52,012	42,273	7,936	18.8	477,114	41,629	8.7	836	7,970	8,448	—	209	558	11,391	10,095	4,680	1,207	2,319	1,888
Capistrano Unified	CA	82	51,512	58,182	2,954	5.1	408,696	22,158	5.4	432	4,318	8,007	1,342	184	223	2,938	3,264	1,999	0	722	544
Forsyth County	NC	83	51,325	56,113	10,750	19.2	426,327	40,184	9.4	810	—	—	—	—	—	10,574	14,344	6,052	1,561	3,276	3,455
Katy ISD	TX	84	51,201	37,866	3,831	10.1	414,227	21,900	5.3	454	959	6,651	706	119	208	4,780	4,064	2,203	0	967	885
Atlanta City	GA	85	50,631	76,913	24,021	31.2	744,569	83,834	11.3	1,651	—	—	—	—	—	16,048	44,920	18,724	4,733	9,634	11,829
Loudoun County	VA	86	50,383	50,643	1,344	2.7	831,467	13,435	1.6	284	1,280	5,260	746	188	150	2,655	1,274	1,274	0	0	0
Douglas County	CO	87	50,370	51,555	1,457	2.8	432,175	10,599	2.5	221	813	6,230	668	104	121	1,023	1,167	1,167	0	0	0
Corona-Norco Unified	CA	88	49,865	45,087	4,167	9.2	475,912	26,873	5.6	566	4,743	7,212	1,258	161	201	7,752	4,576	2,549	0	1,142	886
Pasadena ISD	TX	89	49,851	48,256	12,560	26.0	397,550	43,518	10.9	884	10,432	6,898	1,786	242	532	14,056	16,682	7,136	1,841	4,002	3,704
Cherry Creek	CO	90	49,684	44,907	2,970	6.6	448,399	17,447	3.9	359	2,790	8,104	790	111	139	3,666	3,468	1,894	0	778	796
Sacramento City Unified	CA	91	49,355	65,611	14,540	22.2	573,623	80,420	14.0	1,595	28,148	9,705	4,872	492	839	13,768	23,078	10,509	2,656	5,223	4,690
Anchorage School	AK	92	49,230	53,869	5,707	10.6	495,404	60,822	12.3	1,223	13,426	11,794	4,471	626	1,014	8,084	13,764	6,128	0	3,794	3,841
East Baton Rouge Parish SB	LA	93	49,197	68,111	19,069	28.0	531,036	103,663	19.5	2,076	26,101	9,227	4,341	496	193	18,350	27,441	11,527	2,974	6,906	6,034
Lewisville ISD	TX	94	49,060	52,833	2,655	5.0	422,568	23,552	5.6	496	1,578	7,880	866	138	301	4,477	2,828	1,668	0	603	558
Howard County	MD	95	49,048	52,850	1,957	3.7	626,100	18,334	2.9	377	2,011	8,411	1,096	156	407	2,445	2,068	2,068	0	0	0
Garden Grove Unified	CA	96	48,802	56,164	8,805	15.7	419,282	45,741	10.9	923	14,697	8,302	3,065	357	407	12,623	13,722	6,297	2,491	2,704	2,229
Brownsville ISD	TX	97	48,334	41,942	22,493	53.6	426,935	77,055	18.0	1,597	24,520	9,858	4,726	438	561	22,019	32,577	12,662	3,266	8,646	8,003
San Juan Unified	CA	98	47,862	60,212	8,106	13.5	452,930	41,671	9.2	862	9,154	9,355	2,180	258	372	6,607	11,174	5,126	1,322	2,600	2,127
Henrico County	VA	99	47,680	49,578	4,376	8.8	417,032	21,940	5.3	460	4,525	8,558	1,410	161	607	4,406	6,129	3,176	0	1,432	1,521
Shelby County	TN	100	47,126	46,913	3,806	8.1	328,991	21,902	6.7	477	2,116	10,325	—	—	526	4,693	4,414	2,334	0	1,042	1,038

—Not available.

[1]Poverty is defined based on the number of persons and related children in the family and their income. For information on poverty thresholds for 2005, see http://www.census.gov/hhes/www/poverty/threshld/thresh05.html.

[2]Fiscal year 2008 Department of Education funds available for spending by school districts in the 2008–09 school year.

[3]Federal revenue per student is based on fall enrollment collected through the "School District Finance Survey (Form F-33)."

NOTE: Detail may not sum to totals because of rounding. SB = school board. ISD = independent school district.
SOURCE: U.S. Department of Education, National Center for Education Statistics, Common Core of Data (CCD), "School District Finance Survey (Form F-33)," 2005–06; and "Local Education Agency Universe Survey," 2006–07; and unpublished Department of Education budget data. (This table was prepared September 2008.)

Table 94. Public elementary and secondary schools, by type of school: Selected years, 1967–68 through 2006–07

		Schools with reported grade spans											
			Elementary schools				Secondary schools					Combined elementary/ secondary schools[6]	Other schools[1]
Year	Total, all public schools	Total	Total[2]	Middle schools[3]	One-teacher schools	Other elementary schools	Total[4]	Junior high[5]	3-year or 4-year high schools	5-year or 6-year high schools	Other secondary schools		
	1	2	3	4	5	6	7	8	9	10	11	12	13	14
1967–68	—	94,197	67,186	—	4,146	63,040	23,318	7,437	10,751	4,650	480	3,693	—
1970–71	—	89,372	64,020	2,080	1,815	60,125	23,572	7,750	11,265	3,887	670	1,780	—
1972–73	—	88,864	62,942	2,308	1,475	59,159	23,919	7,878	11,550	3,962	529	2,003	—
1974–75	—	87,456	61,759	3,224	1,247	57,288	23,837	7,690	11,480	4,122	545	1,860	—
1975–76	88,597	87,034	61,704	3,916	1,166	56,622	23,792	7,521	11,572	4,113	586	1,538	1,563
1976–77	—	86,501	61,123	4,180	1,111	55,832	23,857	7,434	11,658	4,130	635	1,521	—
1978–79	—	84,816	60,312	5,879	1,056	53,377	22,834	6,282	11,410	4,429	713	1,670	—
1980–81	85,982	83,688	59,326	6,003	921	52,402	22,619	5,890	10,758	4,193	1,778	1,743	2,294
1982–83	84,740	82,039	58,051	6,875	798	50,378	22,383	5,948	11,678	4,067	690	1,605	2,701
1983–84	84,178	81,418	57,471	6,885	838	49,748	22,336	5,936	11,670	4,046	684	1,611	2,760
1984–85	84,007	81,147	57,231	6,893	825	49,513	22,320	5,916	11,671	4,021	712	1,596	2,860
1986–87	83,455	82,190	58,801	7,452	763	50,586	21,406	5,142	11,453	4,197	614	1,983	1,265 [7]
1987–88	83,248	81,416	57,575	7,641	729	49,205	21,662	4,900	11,279	4,048	1,435	2,179	1,832 [7]
1988–89	83,165	81,579	57,941	7,957	583	49,401	21,403	4,687	11,350	3,994	1,372	2,235	1,586 [7]
1989–90	83,425	81,880	58,419	8,272	630	49,517	21,181	4,512	11,492	3,812	1,365	2,280	1,545 [7]
1990–91	84,538	82,475	59,015	8,545	617	49,853	21,135	4,561	11,537	3,723	1,314	2,325	2,063
1991–92	84,578	82,506	59,258	8,829	569	49,860	20,767	4,298	11,528	3,699	1,242	2,481	2,072
1992–93	84,497	82,896	59,676	9,152	430	50,094	20,671	4,115	11,651	3,613	1,292	2,549	1,601
1993–94	85,393	83,431	60,052	9,573	442	50,037	20,705	3,970	11,858	3,595	1,282	2,674	1,962
1994–95	86,221	84,476	60,808	9,954	458	50,396	20,904	3,859	12,058	3,628	1,359	2,764	1,745
1995–96	87,125	84,958	61,165	10,205	474	50,486	20,997	3,743	12,168	3,621	1,465	2,796	2,167
1996–97	88,223	86,092	61,805	10,499	487	50,819	21,307	3,707	12,424	3,614	1,562	2,980	2,131
1997–98	89,508	87,541	62,739	10,944	476	51,319	21,682	3,599	12,734	3,611	1,738	3,120	1,967
1998–99	90,874	89,259	63,462	11,202	463	51,797	22,076	3,607	13,457	3,707	1,305	3,721	1,615
1999–2000	92,012	90,538	64,131	11,521	423	52,187	22,365	3,566	13,914	3,686	1,199	4,042	1,474
2000–01	93,273	91,691	64,601	11,696	411	52,494	21,994	3,318	13,793	3,974	909	5,096	1,582
2001–02	94,112	92,696	65,228	11,983	408	52,837	22,180	3,285	14,070	3,917	908	5,288	1,416
2002–03	95,615	93,869	65,718	12,174	366	53,178	22,599	3,263	14,330	4,017	989	5,552	1,746
2003–04	95,726	93,977	65,758	12,341	376	53,041	22,782	3,251	14,595	3,840	1,096	5,437	1,749
2004–05	96,513	95,001	65,984	12,530	338	53,116	23,445	3,250	14,854	3,945	1,396	5,572	1,512
2005–06	97,382	96,798	67,291	12,545	335	54,411	23,800	3,249	15,103	3,910	1,538	5,707	584
2006–07	98,793	98,410	68,990	12,773	327	55,890	23,436	3,112	15,043	4,048	1,233	5,984	383

—Not available.
[1] Includes special education, alternative, and other schools not reported by grade span.
[2] Includes schools beginning with grade 6 or below and with no grade higher than 8.
[3] Includes schools with grade spans beginning with 4, 5, or 6 and ending with 6, 7, or 8.
[4] Includes schools with no grade lower than 7.
[5] Includes schools with grades 7 and 8 or grades 7 through 9.
[6] Includes schools beginning with grade 6 or lower and ending with grade 9 or above.

[7] Because of revision in data collection procedures, figures not comparable to data for other years.
SOURCE: U.S. Department of Education, National Center for Education Statistics, *Statistics of State School Systems*, 1967–68 and 1975–76; *Statistics of Public Elementary and Secondary Day Schools*, 1970–71, 1972–73, 1974–75, and 1976–77 through 1980–81; and Common Core of Data (CCD), "Public Elementary/Secondary School Universe Survey," 1982–83 through 2006–07. (This table was prepared September 2008.)

Table 95. Number and percentage distribution of public elementary and secondary schools and enrollment, by type and enrollment size of school: 2004–05, 2005–06, and 2006–07

Enrollment size of school	Number and percentage distribution of schools, by type						Enrollment totals and percentage distribution, by type of school[1]					
			Secondary[4]		Combined				Secondary[4]		Combined	
	Total[2]	Elementary[3]	All schools	Regular schools[6]	elementary/ secondary[5]	Other[2]	Total[2]	Elementary[3]	All schools	Regular schools[6]	elementary/ secondary[5]	Other[2]
1	2	3	4	5	6	7	8	9	10	11	12	13
2004–05[7]												
Total..................	96,513	65,984	23,445	19,028	5,572	1,512	48,583,506	31,161,899	15,877,599	15,411,760	1,502,102	41,906
Percent[8]..................	100.00	100.00	100.00	100.00	100.00	100.00	100.00	100.00	100.00	100.00	100.00	100.00
Under 100..................	11.03	6.21	17.81	9.09	41.68	51.19	0.96	0.65	1.08	0.63	5.88	16.18
100 to 199..................	9.69	8.59	11.11	10.35	16.97	24.91	2.78	2.75	2.27	1.86	8.29	24.28
200 to 299..................	11.56	12.85	8.20	8.56	9.80	8.53	5.61	6.87	2.86	2.61	8.07	15.27
300 to 399..................	13.53	15.96	7.82	8.55	7.35	9.56	9.09	11.78	3.82	3.65	8.57	23.33
400 to 499..................	13.20	16.23	6.06	6.80	5.78	3.75	11.37	15.35	3.81	3.74	8.62	11.65
500 to 599..................	10.80	13.06	5.76	6.53	4.23	1.37	11.35	15.05	4.44	4.40	7.72	5.15
600 to 699..................	8.14	9.49	5.36	6.11	3.38	0.00	10.11	12.93	4.87	4.85	7.33	0.00
700 to 799..................	5.56	6.24	4.36	4.99	2.23	0.34	7.96	9.82	4.57	4.58	5.57	1.78
800 to 999..................	6.60	6.68	7.24	8.37	3.08	0.34	11.25	12.47	9.08	9.17	9.17	2.34
1,000 to 1,499..................	5.96	4.08	12.25	14.21	2.96	0.00	13.66	10.02	21.00	21.31	11.91	0.00
1,500 to 1,999..................	2.16	0.49	7.23	8.44	1.57	0.00	7.12	1.74	17.51	17.87	9.06	0.00
2,000 to 2,999..................	1.43	0.10	5.53	6.48	0.64	0.00	6.46	0.51	18.29	18.75	5.08	0.00
3,000 or more..................	0.33	0.01	1.28	1.50	0.34	0.00	2.27	0.05	6.42	6.59	4.73	0.00
Average enrollment[8]..................	521	474	713	815	298	143	521	474	713	815	298	143
2005–06												
Total..................	97,382	67,291	23,800	19,252	5,707	584	48,912,085	31,104,018	16,219,309	15,685,032	1,526,186	62,572
Percent[8]..................	100.00	100.00	100.00	100.00	100.00	100.00	100.00	100.00	100.00	100.00	100.00	100.00
Under 100..................	11.03	6.22	18.42	9.27	37.01	57.49	0.96	0.65	1.11	0.63	5.04	18.57
100 to 199..................	9.63	8.57	10.98	10.16	16.33	23.00	2.75	2.74	2.25	1.82	7.53	25.47
200 to 299..................	11.47	12.63	8.45	8.69	10.30	8.62	5.55	6.76	2.96	2.64	7.98	16.67
300 to 399..................	13.58	16.03	7.79	8.66	8.32	5.75	9.11	11.86	3.82	3.68	9.09	15.48
400 to 499..................	13.16	16.15	6.11	6.88	6.86	2.26	11.31	15.28	3.87	3.77	9.63	7.58
500 to 599..................	11.00	13.36	5.66	6.44	5.25	1.23	11.55	15.44	4.37	4.31	9.01	5.22
600 to 699..................	8.14	9.46	5.28	6.06	4.42	0.41	10.10	12.91	4.83	4.79	9.04	2.15
700 to 799..................	5.63	6.31	4.40	5.07	2.77	0.41	8.07	9.95	4.64	4.63	6.53	2.50
800 to 999..................	6.58	6.76	6.82	8.00	3.54	0.41	11.20	12.63	8.59	8.73	9.93	2 77
1,000 to 1,499..................	5.89	4.00	11.96	14.05	3.40	0.41	13.49	9.82	20.64	21.00	12.77	3.58
1,500 to 1,999..................	2.08	0.42	7.11	8.43	1.00	0.00	6.86	1.48	17.33	17.79	5.37	0.00
2,000 to 2,999..................	1.47	0.09	5.67	6.72	0.46	0.00	6.66	0.45	18.90	19.40	3.44	0.00
3,000 or more..................	0.35	0.01	1.33	1.57	0.33	0.00	2.39	0.04	6.68	6.82	4.64	0.00
Average enrollment[8]..................	521	473	709	819	318	128	521	473	709	819	318	128
2006–07												
Total..................	98,793	68,990	23,436	19,379	5,984	383	49,065,594	31,273,476	16,068,448	15,577,348	1,672,583	51,087
Percent[8]..................	100.00	100.00	100.00	100.00	100.00	100.00	100.00	100.00	100.00	100.00	100.00	100.00
Under 100..................	10.71	5.92	18.00	9.79	36.67	60.16	0.94	0.63	1.10	0.66	4.88	16.36
100 to 199..................	9.60	8.40	11.10	10.25	17.81	17.89	2.75	2.68	2.27	1.86	7.97	18.99
200 to 299..................	11.53	12.59	8.62	8.84	11.05	6.78	5.58	6.73	3.02	2.72	8.41	12.25
300 to 399..................	13.75	16.22	8.07	8.83	7.40	7.59	9.24	12.01	3.96	3.80	7.91	19.24
400 to 499..................	13.44	16.53	6.07	6.79	6.86	3.52	11.57	15.66	3.83	3.75	9.45	11.30
500 to 599..................	10.98	13.30	5.78	6.47	4.62	1.63	11.53	15.37	4.45	4.37	7.79	6.29
600 to 699..................	8.20	9.63	5.21	5.98	3.52	0.27	10.17	13.14	4.75	4.78	7.03	1.22
700 to 799..................	5.60	6.40	4.04	4.63	2.45	0.81	8.01	10.08	4.24	4.27	5.63	4.23
800 to 999..................	6.62	6.74	7.09	8.16	3.46	0.27	11.27	12.59	8.94	9.02	9.42	1.72
1,000 to 1,499..................	5.67	3.80	11.68	13.47	3.61	1.08	13.01	9.32	20.16	20.41	13.45	8.39
1,500 to 1,999..................	2.10	0.38	7.32	8.55	1.34	0.00	6.93	1.35	17.78	18.22	7.14	0.00
2,000 to 2,999..................	1.48	0.08	5.74	6.71	0.84	0.00	6.71	0.38	19.11	19.58	6.08	0.00
3,000 or more..................	0.34	0.01	1.29	1.51	0.39	0.00	2.29	0.04	6.41	6.56	4.83	0.00
Average enrollment[8]..................	521	473	711	811	325	138	521	473	711	811	325	138

[1]Totals differ from those reported in other tables because this table represents data reported by schools rather than by states or school districts. Percentage distribution and average enrollment calculations exclude data for schools not reporting enrollment.
[2]Includes special education, alternative, and other schools not reported by grade span.
[3]Includes schools beginning with grade 6 or below and with no grade higher than 8.
[4]Includes schools with no grade lower than 7.
[5]Includes schools beginning with grade 6 or below and ending with grade 9 or above.
[6]Excludes special education schools, vocational schools, and alternative schools.

[7]Data have been revised from previously published figures.
[8]Data are for schools reporting their enrollment size. Enrollment data were available for 93,303 out of 96,513 schools in 2004–05, 93,845 out of 97,382 schools in 2005–06, and 94,164 out of 98,793 in 2006–07.
NOTE: Detail may not sum to totals because of rounding.
SOURCE: U.S. Department of Education, National Center for Education Statistics, Common Core of Data (CCD), "Public Elementary/Secondary School Universe Survey," 2004–05, 2005–06, and 2006–07. (This table was prepared September 2008.)

Table 96. Average enrollment and percentage distribution of public elementary and secondary schools, by type and size: Selected years, 1982–83 through 2006–07

Year	Average enrollment in schools, by type						Percentage distribution of schools, by enrollment size							
			Secondary[3]		Combined									
	Total[1]	Elementary[2]	All schools	Regular schools[6]	elementary/ secondary[4]	Other[5]	Under 200	200 to 299	300 to 399	400 to 499	500 to 599	600 to 699	700 to 999	1,000 or more
1	2	3	4	5	6	7	8	9	10	11	12	13	14	15
1982–83	478	399	719	—	478	142	21.9	13.8	15.5	13.1	10.2	7.1	10.2	8.3
1983–84	480	401	720	—	475	145	21.7	13.7	15.5	13.2	10.2	7.1	10.3	8.3
1984–85	482	403	721	—	476	146	21.5	13.6	15.5	13.2	10.3	7.1	10.4	8.4
1987–88	490	424	695	711	420	122	20.3	12.9	14.9	13.8	11.1	7.8	11.2	8.0
1988–89	494	433	689	697	412	142	20.0	12.5	14.7	13.8	11.4	8.0	11.6	8.0
1989–90	493	441	669	689	402	142	19.8	12.2	14.5	13.7	11.5	8.3	12.0	7.9
1990–91	497	449	663	684	398	150	19.7	11.9	14.2	13.6	11.7	8.5	12.3	8.1
1991–92	507	458	677	717	407	152	19.1	11.7	14.1	13.5	11.8	8.6	12.8	8.5
1992–93	513	464	688	733	423	135	18.6	11.6	13.9	13.5	11.9	8.7	13.1	8.7
1993–94	518	468	693	748	418	136	18.6	11.5	13.6	13.5	11.7	8.8	13.3	9.0
1994–95	520	471	696	759	412	131	18.6	11.4	13.6	13.4	11.8	8.7	13.3	9.2
1995–96	525	476	703	771	401	136	18.5	11.2	13.5	13.4	11.8	8.8	13.4	9.4
1996–97	527	478	703	777	387	135	18.7	11.3	13.2	13.2	11.8	8.8	13.6	9.5
1997–98	525	478	699	779	374	121	19.3	11.2	13.1	13.3	11.6	8.6	13.4	9.6
1998–99	524	478	707	786	290	135	19.6	11.2	13.1	13.2	11.5	8.5	13.3	9.6
1999–2000	521	477	706	785	282	123	20.0	11.3	13.3	13.2	11.2	8.4	13.1	9.5
2000–01	519	477	714	795	274	136	20.4	11.4	13.2	13.3	11.0	8.2	12.9	9.6
2001–02	520	477	718	807	270	138	20.5	11.5	13.3	13.1	10.9	8.1	12.7	9.7
2002–03	519	476	720	813	265	136	20.7	11.6	13.4	13.0	10.9	8.1	12.4	9.8
2003–04	521	476	722	816	269	142	20.7	11.6	13.5	13.2	10.8	8.0	12.3	9.9
2004–05	521	474	713	815	298	143	20.7	11.6	13.5	13.2	10.8	8.1	12.2	9.9
2005–06	521	473	709	819	318	128	20.7	11.5	13.6	13.2	11.0	8.1	12.2	9.8
2006–07	521	473	711	811	325	138	20.3	11.5	13.8	13.4	11.0	8.2	12.2	9.6

—Not available.
[1]Includes elementary, secondary, combined elementary/secondary, and other schools.
[2]Includes schools beginning with grade 6 or below and with no grade higher than 8.
[3]Includes schools with no grade lower than 7.
[4]Includes schools beginning with grade 6 or below and ending with grade 9 or above.
[5]Includes special education, alternative, and other schools not reported by grade span.
[6]Excludes special education schools, vocational schools, and alternative schools.

NOTE: Data reflect reports by schools rather than by states or school districts. Percentage distribution and average enrollment calculations exclude data for schools not reporting enrollment. Enrollment data were available for 94,164 out of 98,793 schools in 2006–07. Detail may not sum to totals because of rounding.
SOURCE: U.S. Department of Education, National Center for Education Statistics, Common Core of Data (CCD), "Public Elementary/Secondary School Universe Survey," 1982–83 through 2006–07. (This table was prepared September 2008.)

Table 97. Public elementary and secondary school students, by racial/ethnic enrollment concentration of school: Fall 1995, fall 2000, and fall 2006

Racial/ethnic group	Total	Distribution of students in racial/ethnic group, by percent minority in the school						Total	Distribution of students in each racial/ethnic group, by percent of that racial/ethnic group in the school					
		Less than 10 percent minority	10 to 24 percent minority	25 to 49 percent minority	50 to 74 percent minority	75 to 89 percent minority	90 percent or more minority		Less than 10 percent of group	10 to 24 percent of group	25 to 49 percent of group	50 to 74 percent of group	75 to 89 percent of group	90 percent or more of group
1	2	3	4	5	6	7	8	9	10	11	12	13	14	15
Total students enrolled, 1995	44,424,467	14,508,573	8,182,484	8,261,110	5,467,784	2,876,302	5,128,214	†	†	†	†	†	†	†
White	28,736,961	13,939,633	6,812,196	5,246,785	2,094,440	499,884	144,023	28,736,961	143,787	498,649	2,084,689	5,244,015	6,813,804	13,952,017
Minority	15,687,506	568,940	1,370,288	3,014,325	3,373,344	2,376,418	4,984,191	†	†	†	†	†	†	†
Black	7,510,678	198,386	598,716	1,588,850	1,622,448	941,335	2,560,943	7,510,678	657,403	1,119,556	1,873,303	1,386,802	811,898	1,661,716
Hispanic	6,016,293	174,140	415,761	932,949	1,289,184	1,099,109	2,105,150	6,016,293	646,364	847,792	1,359,649	1,360,020	874,878	927,590
Asian/Pacific Islander	1,656,787	142,886	259,335	367,888	379,110	297,680	209,888	1,656,787	703,101	435,495	301,984	135,001	67,558	13,648
American Indian/Alaska Native	503,748	53,528	96,476	124,638	82,602	38,294	108,210	503,748	223,244	75,019	63,070	39,200	15,084	88,131
Total students enrolled, 2000	46,120,425	12,761,478	8,736,252	8,760,300	6,013,131	3,472,083	6,377,181	†	†	†	†	†	†	†
White	28,146,613	12,218,862	7,271,285	5,566,681	2,303,106	596,478	190,201	28,146,613	189,779	595,137	2,294,232	5,556,108	7,279,301	12,232,056
Minority	17,973,812	542,616	1,464,967	3,193,619	3,710,025	2,875,605	6,186,980	†	†	†	†	†	†	†
Black	7,854,032	178,185	561,488	1,485,130	1,652,393	1,043,907	2,932,929	7,854,032	735,459	1,199,865	1,899,982	1,366,363	871,399	1,780,964
Hispanic	7,649,728	181,685	505,612	1,121,809	1,542,982	1,432,639	2,865,001	7,649,728	738,509	1,054,396	1,696,944	1,739,038	1,134,466	1,286,375
Asian/Pacific Islander	1,924,875	132,813	295,437	441,769	423,175	353,395	278,286	1,924,875	799,220	524,279	331,576	171,739	81,461	16,600
American Indian/Alaska Native	545,177	49,933	102,430	144,911	91,475	45,664	110,764	545,177	251,983	81,119	75,831	39,944	15,363	80,937
Total students enrolled, 2006	48,430,404	10,287,933	9,204,176	9,978,370	6,891,744	4,164,501	7,903,680	†	†	†	†	†	†	†
White	27,347,536	9,796,463	7,655,592	6,320,726	2,614,325	709,198	251,232	27,347,536	250,320	707,224	2,603,898	6,314,062	7,662,123	9,809,909
Minority	21,082,868	491,470	1,548,584	3,657,644	4,277,419	3,455,303	7,652,448	†	†	†	†	†	†	†
Black	8,275,666	155,744	540,244	1,499,391	1,725,076	1,167,149	3,188,062	8,275,666	860,667	1,395,172	1,996,139	1,419,113	871,982	1,732,593
Hispanic	9,938,381	183,775	587,440	1,433,226	1,928,013	1,830,633	3,975,294	9,938,381	854,191	1,343,881	2,124,521	2,326,375	1,595,158	1,694,255
Asian/Pacific Islander	2,279,868	110,441	321,727	562,243	510,165	405,255	370,037	2,279,868	938,203	624,914	372,685	222,123	99,394	22,549
American Indian/Alaska Native	588,953	41,510	99,173	162,784	114,165	52,266	119,055	588,953	276,079	86,056	86,725	42,682	20,038	77,373
Percent of students enrolled, 1995	100.0	32.7	18.4	18.6	12.3	6.5	11.5	†	†	†	†	†	†	†
White	100.0	48.5	23.7	18.3	7.3	1.7	0.5	100.0	0.5	1.7	7.3	18.2	23.7	48.6
Minority	100.0	3.6	8.7	19.2	21.5	15.1	31.8	†	†	†	†	†	†	†
Black	100.0	2.6	8.0	21.2	21.6	12.5	34.1	100.0	8.8	14.9	24.9	18.5	10.8	22.1
Hispanic	100.0	2.9	6.9	15.5	21.4	18.3	35.0	100.0	10.7	14.1	22.6	22.6	14.5	15.4
Asian/Pacific Islander	100.0	8.6	15.7	22.2	22.9	18.0	12.7	100.0	42.4	26.3	18.2	8.1	4.1	0.8
American Indian/Alaska Native	100.0	10.6	19.2	24.7	16.4	7.6	21.5	100.0	44.3	14.9	12.5	7.8	3.0	17.5
Percent of students enrolled, 2000	100.0	27.7	18.9	19.0	13.0	7.5	13.8	†	†	†	†	†	†	†
White	100.0	43.4	25.8	19.8	8.2	2.1	0.7	100.0	0.7	2.1	8.2	19.7	25.9	43.5
Minority	100.0	3.0	8.2	17.8	20.6	16.0	34.4	†	†	†	†	†	†	†
Black	100.0	2.3	7.1	18.9	21.0	13.3	37.3	100.0	9.4	15.3	24.2	17.4	11.1	22.7
Hispanic	100.0	2.4	6.6	14.7	20.2	18.7	37.5	100.0	9.7	13.8	22.2	22.7	14.8	16.8
Asian/Pacific Islander	100.0	6.9	15.3	23.0	22.0	18.4	14.5	100.0	41.5	27.2	17.2	8.9	4.2	0.9
American Indian/Alaska Native	100.0	9.2	18.8	26.6	16.8	8.4	20.3	100.0	46.2	14.9	13.9	7.3	2.8	14.8
Percent of students enrolled, 2006	100.0	21.2	19.0	20.6	14.2	8.6	16.3	†	†	†	†	†	†	†
White	100.0	35.8	28.0	23.1	9.6	2.6	0.9	100.0	0.9	2.6	9.5	23.1	28.0	35.9
Minority	100.0	2.3	7.3	17.3	20.3	16.4	36.3	†	†	†	†	†	†	†
Black	100.0	1.9	6.5	18.1	20.8	14.1	38.5	100.0	10.4	16.9	24.1	17.1	10.5	20.9
Hispanic	100.0	1.8	5.9	14.4	19.4	18.4	40.0	100.0	8.6	13.5	21.4	23.4	16.1	17.0
Asian/Pacific Islander	100.0	4.8	14.1	24.7	22.4	17.8	16.2	100.0	41.2	27.4	16.3	9.7	4.4	1.0
American Indian/Alaska Native	100.0	7.0	16.8	27.6	19.4	8.9	20.2	100.0	46.9	14.6	14.7	7.2	3.4	13.1

†Not applicable.
NOTE: Data reflect racial/ethnic data reported by schools. Because some schools do not report complete racial/ethnic data, totals may differ from figures in other tables. Excludes 1995 data for Idaho and 2000 data for Tennessee because racial/ethnic data were not reported. Race cate-gories exclude persons of Hispanic ethnicity. Detail may not sum to totals because of rounding.
SOURCE: U.S. Department of Education, National Center for Education Statistics, Common Core of Data (CCD), "Public Elementary/Secondary School Universe Survey," 1995–96, 2000–01, and 2006–07. (This table was prepared September 2008.)

Table 98. Public elementary and secondary schools, by type and state or jurisdiction: 1990–91, 2000–01, and 2006–07

| State or jurisdiction | Total, all schools, 1990–91 | Total, all schools, 2000–01 | Number of schools, 2006–07 | | | Combined elementary/secondary[3] | | | | Other[4] | Alternative[5] | Special education[5] | Charter[5] | One-teacher schools[5] |
			Total	Elementary[1]	Secondary[2]	Total	Prekindergarten, kindergarten, or 1st grade to grade 12	Other schools ending with grade 12	Other combined schools					
1	2	3	4	5	6	7	8	9	10	11	12	13	14	15
United States	84,538	93,273	98,793	68,990	23,436	5,984	3,320	1,819	845	383	6,638	1,956	4,132	327
Alabama	1,297	1,517	1,583	979	406	198	125	61	12	0	88	31	0	0
Alaska............................	498	515	503	185	84	234	215	12	7	0	49	1	23	5
Arizona	1,049	1,724	2,061	1,290	613	153	80	48	25	5	77	9	468	8
Arkansas........................	1,098	1,138	1,114	734	363	17	3	8	6	0	10	0	19	0
California	7,913	8,773	10,038	7,163	2,302	573	416	108	49	0	1,170	127	693	86
Colorado	1,344	1,632	1,736	1,239	411	86	38	39	9	0	84	8	135	3
Connecticut....................	985	1,248	1,114	835	256	23	11	9	3	0	38	37	16	1
Delaware........................	173	191	234	144	50	40	31	7	2	0	32	18	17	0
District of Columbia	181	198	235	164	45	16	7	4	5	10	11	14	59	0
Florida...........................	2,516	3,316	3,952	2,862	619	471	203	170	98	0	495	130	366	4
Georgia	1,734	1,946	2,463	2,017	387	59	19	24	16	0	210	90	55	0
Hawaii	235	261	286	208	52	26	22	3	1	0	1	3	28	0
Idaho..............................	582	673	726	439	231	56	35	14	7	0	91	10	30	13
Illinois............................	4,239	4,342	4,392	3,260	982	150	48	77	25	0	163	116	34	0
Indiana...........................	1,915	1,976	1,969	1,488	427	54	12	30	12	0	22	41	37	0
Iowa...............................	1,588	1,534	1,509	1,016	454	39	4	35	0	0	72	10	8	4
Kansas...........................	1,477	1,430	1,423	972	398	51	27	19	5	2	0	8	27	2
Kentucky	1,400	1,526	1,534	1,122	305	105	43	52	10	2	157	10	0	0
Louisiana	1,533	1,530	1,447	953	299	195	121	62	12	0	138	43	42	0
Maine	747	714	671	505	152	14	9	5	0	0	0	2	0	4
Maryland.........................	1,220	1,383	1,445	1,116	278	51	28	15	8	0	64	45	23	0
Massachusetts...............	1,842	1,905	1,879	1,474	360	41	20	14	7	4	0	4	59	3
Michigan	3,313	3,998	4,133	2,849	928	193	104	55	34	163	303	238	279	5
Minnesota.......................	1,590	2,362	2,665	1,544	823	298	102	133	63	0	712	300	155	1
Mississippi	972	1,030	1,062	764	234	58	45	10	3	6	64	0	1	0
Missouri	2,199	2,368	2,384	1,540	681	163	79	79	5	0	50	14	18	3
Montana..........................	900	879	831	479	352	0	0	0	0	0	4	2	0	66
Nebraska	1,506	1,326	1,166	777	331	58	57	1	0	0	0	31	0	36
Nevada...........................	354	511	590	433	115	42	15	22	5	0	41	0	22	11
New Hampshire	439	526	482	382	100	0	0	0	0	0	0	0	9	1
New Jersey	2,272	2,410	2,470	1,922	470	17	5	10	2	61	0	77	53	0
New Mexico	681	765	838	606	218	14	6	4	4	0	26	4	60	3
New York.........................	4,010	4,336	4,708	3,297	1,088	206	85	85	36	117	113	153	93	0
North Carolina	1,955	2,207	2,470	1,862	501	107	40	48	19	0	87	30	93	0
North Dakota	663	579	534	351	182	1	0	1	0	0	0	31	0	3
Ohio................................	3,731	3,916	3,972	2,721	1,019	232	56	65	111	0	8	40	305	1
Oklahoma	1,880	1,821	1,794	1,211	576	6	0	3	3	1	5	4	16	2
Oregon............................	1,199	1,273	1,284	926	295	63	37	20	6	0	40	2	70	11
Pennsylvania...................	3,260	3,252	3,286	2,357	816	105	45	34	26	8	0	2	119	0
Rhode Island	309	328	336	264	65	7	3	2	2	0	17	3	11	1
South Carolina...............	1,097	1,127	1,175	908	243	24	7	13	4	0	9	0	29	1
South Dakota.................	802	769	736	461	259	16	5	10	1	0	13	3	0	26
Tennessee	1,543	1,624	1,709	1,297	346	62	33	24	5	4	28	14	12	0
Texas	5,991	7,519	8,630	5,555	2,147	928	580	232	116	0	1,396	0	400	0
Utah................................	714	793	1,001	603	358	40	23	5	12	0	118	58	54	1
Vermont	397	393	330	255	56	19	12	7	0	0	1	0	0	1
Virginia...........................	1,811	1,969	2,202	1,782	358	62	54	8	0	0	226	58	3	0
Washington.....................	1,936	2,305	2,305	1,460	573	272	154	64	54	0	279	115	0	3
West Virginia...................	1,015	840	766	429	118	219	213	6	0	0	27	7	0	0
Wisconsin	2,018	2,182	2,237	1,539	602	96	31	55	10	0	76	8	188	7
Wyoming..........................	415	393	383	251	108	24	12	7	5	0	23	5	3	11
Bureau of Indian Education.................	—	189	186	109	25	52	46	3	3	0	0	0	0	—
DoD, domestic	—	71	68	56	6	6	1	2	3	0	0	0	0	0
DoD, overseas	—	156	140	94	34	12	10	2	0	0	0	0	0	0
Other jurisdictions														
American Samoa	30	31	31	24	6	0	0	0	0	1	0	1	0	0
Guam..........................	35	38	36	32	4	0	0	0	0	0	0	0	0	0
Northern Marianas......	26	29	30	22	6	0	0	0	0	2	1	0	0	0
Puerto Rico.................	1,619	1,543	1,515	901	393	196	19	5	172	25	8	25	0	0
U.S. Virgin Islands.......	33	36	34	23	10	1	0	0	1	0	1	0	0	0

—Not available.
[1]Includes schools beginning with grade 6 or below and with no grade higher than 8.
[2]Includes schools with no grade lower than 7.
[3]Includes schools beginning with grade 6 or below and ending with grade 9 or above.
[4]Includes schools not reported by grade span.

[5]Schools are also included under elementary, secondary, combined, or other as appropriate.
NOTE: DoD = Department of Defense.
SOURCE: U.S. Department of Education, National Center for Education Statistics, Common Core of Data (CCD), "Public Elementary/Secondary School Universe Survey," 1990–91, 2000–01, and 2006–07. (This table was prepared September 2008.)

Table 99. Public elementary schools, by grade span, average school size, and state or jurisdiction: 2006–07

State or jurisdiction	Total, all elementary schools	Total, all regular elementary schools[1]	Prekindergarten, kindergarten, or 1st grade to grades 3 or 4	Prekindergarten, kindergarten, or 1st grade to grade 5	Prekindergarten, kindergarten, or 1st grade to grade 6	Prekindergarten, kindergarten, or 1st grade to grade 8	Grade 4, 5, or 6 to grade 6, 7, or 8	Other grade spans	All elementary schools	Regular elementary schools[1]
1	2	3	4	5	6	7	8	9	10	11
United States	68,990	66,218	5,005	24,402	12,289	5,912	12,773	8,609	473	478
Alabama	979	954	86	296	181	66	208	142	485	487
Alaska	185	184	2	22	109	16	18	18	331	331
Arizona	1,290	1,250	58	246	341	390	173	82	537	542
Arkansas	734	710	121	141	196	6	144	126	413	413
California	7,163	6,910	170	2,404	2,150	815	1,042	582	572	584
Colorado	1,239	1,235	28	557	269	82	227	76	411	412
Connecticut	835	820	93	288	116	70	152	116	446	450
Delaware	144	141	26	55	13	7	35	8	548	551
District of Columbia	164	154	7	21	86	11	22	17	286	285
Florida	2,862	2,686	31	1,585	149	101	555	441	698	716
Georgia	2,017	1,746	33	1,032	34	14	435	469	670	671
Hawaii	208	208	0	73	100	5	26	4	540	540
Idaho	439	422	41	126	145	24	70	33	377	379
Illinois	3,260	3,155	315	805	354	723	554	509	441	445
Indiana	1,488	1,420	126	556	363	30	267	146	464	465
Iowa	1,016	1,011	115	334	196	18	224	129	295	296
Kansas	972	970	94	297	228	90	180	83	298	299
Kentucky	1,122	975	42	486	141	85	193	175	443	449
Louisiana	953	918	85	327	112	116	202	111	463	469
Maine	505	505	57	94	77	103	89	85	246	246
Maryland	1,116	1,088	17	634	137	42	225	61	505	512
Massachusetts	1,474	1,474	197	511	151	98	296	221	427	427
Michigan	2,849	2,658	250	975	341	184	515	584	403	407
Minnesota	1,544	1,126	110	331	407	128	219	349	399	436
Mississippi	764	611	75	120	122	40	138	269	505	505
Missouri	1,540	1,534	139	473	338	116	293	181	374	374
Montana	479	476	19	52	225	111	50	22	173	173
Nebraska	777	777	0	0	551	126	79	21	226	226
Nevada	433	422	7	214	94	20	73	25	683	684
New Hampshire	382	382	54	119	38	48	80	43	346	346
New Jersey	1,922	1,914	281	553	177	270	363	278	470	472
New Mexico	606	600	27	226	133	15	126	79	354	356
New York	3,297	3,263	275	1,257	439	166	743	417	537	538
North Carolina	1,862	1,840	82	1,031	55	123	440	131	552	554
North Dakota	351	314	10	50	161	50	24	56	183	183
Ohio	2,721	2,679	378	731	454	240	514	404	410	412
Oklahoma	1,211	1,207	73	352	133	312	224	117	359	360
Oregon	926	919	47	393	176	85	179	46	386	386
Pennsylvania	2,357	2,357	259	788	527	169	441	173	469	469
Rhode Island	264	248	28	101	41	4	42	48	379	382
South Carolina	908	886	40	444	58	25	225	116	549	549
South Dakota	461	445	14	120	94	98	82	53	186	186
Tennessee	1,297	1,289	172	478	99	179	280	89	514	515
Texas	5,555	5,410	589	2,321	633	121	1,249	642	553	563
Utah	603	580	10	121	370	21	41	40	522	533
Vermont	255	240	12	28	111	63	17	24	222	222
Virginia	1,782	1,511	50	835	154	9	309	425	537	538
Washington	1,460	1,382	45	574	392	78	231	140	427	441
West Virginia	429	429	62	162	35	29	111	30	351	351
Wisconsin	1,539	1,534	130	609	192	155	306	147	358	359
Wyoming	251	249	23	54	91	15	42	26	203	204
Bureau of Indian Education	109	109	6	5	26	64	4	4	—	—
DoD, domestic	56	56	16	13	6	1	9	11	381	381
DoD, overseas	94	94	6	20	39	8	18	3	447	447
Other jurisdictions										
American Samoa	24	24	1	0	0	21	1	1	490	490
Guam	32	32	0	23	0	0	7	2	—	—
Northern Marianas	22	22	0	2	10	0	2	8	324	324
Puerto Rico	901	900	64	4	785	4	27	17	275	276
U.S. Virgin Islands	23	23	0	0	22	0	1	0	376	376

—Not available.
[1]Excludes special education and alternative schools.
[2]Average for schools reporting enrollment data. Enrollment data were available for 66,052 out of 68,990 public elementary schools in 2006–07.

NOTE: Includes schools beginning with grade 6 or below and with no grade higher than 8. Excludes schools not reported by grade level, such as some special education schools for the disabled. DoD = Department of Defense.
SOURCE: U.S. Department of Education, National Center for Education Statistics, Common Core of Data (CCD), "Public Elementary/Secondary School Universe Survey," 2006–07. (This table was prepared September 2008.)

Table 100. Public secondary schools, by grade span, average school size, and state or jurisdiction: 2006–07

State or jurisdiction	Total, all secondary schools	Total, all regular secondary schools[1]	Schools, by grade span							Vocational schools[2]	Average number of students per school[3]	
			Grades 7 to 8 and 7 to 9	Grades 7 to 12	Grades 8 to 12	Grades 9 to 12	Grades 10 to 12	Other spans ending with grade 12	Other grade spans		All secondary schools	Regular secondary schools[1]
1	2	3	4	5	6	7	8	9	10	11	12	13
United States	**23,436**	**19,379**	**3,112**	**3,268**	**780**	**14,324**	**719**	**331**	**902**	**1,240**	**711**	**811**
Alabama	406	314	34	92	13	230	28	2	7	69	682	705
Alaska........................	84	66	16	22	2	42	2	0	0	1	501	602
Arizona	613	480	83	35	8	466	9	3	9	118	687	715
Arkansas.....................	363	358	58	140	6	98	40	1	20	24	487	491
California	2,302	1,566	331	315	55	1,576	0	0	25	0	939	1,321
Colorado	411	347	62	60	3	270	7	2	7	5	614	701
Connecticut..................	256	194	38	18	3	175	14	6	2	17	779	960
Delaware.....................	50	34	6	7	30	6	0	0	1	6	953	1,018
District of Columbia	45	39	9	4	0	29	0	0	3	5	424	475
Florida........................	619	415	18	69	24	405	16	25	62	46	1,100	1,598
Georgia	387	369	12	6	6	335	4	0	24	0	1,187	1,235
Hawaii	52	52	11	9	0	32	0	0	0	0	1,223	1,223
Idaho..........................	231	157	41	48	1	121	16	0	4	11	445	589
Illinois........................	982	837	148	68	25	621	20	59	41	50	733	810
Indiana........................	427	416	73	93	4	247	2	1	7	28	851	871
Iowa	454	383	49	84	0	303	9	4	5	0	385	445
Kansas........................	398	396	59	84	6	240	7	1	1	0	420	421
Kentucky	305	230	27	50	17	194	5	6	6	126	624	808
Louisiana	299	256	39	49	91	96	16	1	7	7	664	728
Maine.........................	152	123	15	11	1	124	1	0	0	27	536	544
Maryland......................	278	216	19	9	5	210	19	5	11	24	1,099	1,262
Massachusetts..................	360	330	36	37	5	277	1	1	3	30	872	869
Michigan	928	728	102	99	34	595	44	10	44	56	624	765
Minnesota	823	463	58	275	71	328	49	27	15	12	410	639
Mississippi	234	234	31	46	5	133	7	2	10	89	649	649
Missouri	681	594	77	205	1	349	22	10	17	61	558	563
Montana.......................	352	349	181	0	0	169	1	0	1	0	176	177
Nebraska	331	331	30	184	0	113	4	0	0	0	358	358
Nevada	115	103	18	6	5	79	2	5	0	1	1,119	1,204
New Hampshire	100	100	15	0	0	82	0	0	3	0	712	712
New Jersey	470	408	68	31	5	337	14	4	11	54	997	1,088
New Mexico	218	195	40	21	6	130	8	0	13	0	522	566
New York......................	1,088	965	89	165	14	684	23	4	109	30	857	897
North Carolina	501	466	26	15	9	409	5	5	32	9	888	944
North Dakota	182	182	12	115	3	48	2	1	1	6	219	219
Ohio..........................	1,019	953	140	141	50	628	17	13	30	75	661	671
Oklahoma.....................	576	572	95	0	0	413	50	3	15	0	352	353
Oregon........................	295	271	34	41	12	199	5	3	1	0	644	691
Pennsylvania..................	816	732	100	162	18	456	51	9	20	85	861	882
Rhode Island	65	53	8	1	1	52	0	0	3	12	806	931
South Carolina................	243	243	22	13	7	184	8	6	3	13	976	976
South Dakota.................	259	259	85	1	0	173	0	0	0	0	168	168
Tennessee	346	309	26	29	13	247	15	4	12	22	877	935
Texas	2,147	1,502	333	195	106	1,146	52	52	263	0	697	939
Utah	358	225	101	37	22	72	79	17	30	8	620	899
Vermont	56	55	9	18	0	29	0	0	0	15	591	602
Virginia........................	358	346	35	6	35	271	4	1	6	51	1,180	1,197
Washington....................	573	406	93	65	50	319	24	10	12	13	653	852
West Virginia..................	118	118	11	15	0	90	2	0	0	31	712	712
Wisconsin	602	549	62	62	6	427	11	28	6	3	521	558
Wyoming......................	108	90	27	10	2	65	4	0	0	0	302	346
Bureau of Indian Education...	25	25	1	6	0	18	0	0	0	0	—	—
DoD, domestic	6	6	1	0	1	4	0	0	0	0	429	429
DoD, overseas	34	34	2	17	0	15	0	0	0	0	446	446
Other jurisdictions												
American Samoa	6	5	0	0	0	5	1	0	0	1	771	887
Guam	4	4	0	0	0	4	0	0	0	0	—	—
Northern Marianas........	6	6	1	1	0	4	0	0	0	0	748	748
Puerto Rico..................	393	366	191	26	1	3	158	0	14	26	553	543
U.S. Virgin Islands..........	10	8	5	0	0	5	0	0	0	1	827	922

—Not available.
[1]Excludes vocational, special education, and alternative schools.
[2]Vocational schools are also included under appropriate grade span.
[3]Average for schools reporting enrollment data. Enrollment data were available for 22,594 out of 23,436 public secondary schools in 2006–07.

NOTE: Includes schools with no grade lower than 7. Excludes schools not reported by grade level, such as some special education schools for the disabled. DoD = Department of Defense.
SOURCE: U.S. Department of Education, National Center for Education Statistics, Common Core of Data (CCD), "Public Elementary/Secondary School Universe Survey," 2006–07. (This table was prepared September 2008.)

Table 101. Number and enrollment of traditional public and public charter elementary and secondary schools and percentages of students, teachers, and schools, by selected characteristics: 2003–04

Selected characteristic	Total elementary and secondary schools			Elementary schools			Secondary schools			Combined elementary/secondary schools		
	Total, all schools	Traditional (non-charter) schools	Public charter schools	Total, all schools	Traditional (non-charter) schools	Public charter schools	Total, all schools	Traditional (non-charter) schools	Public charter schools	Total, all schools	Traditional (non-charter) schools	Public charter schools
1	2	3	4	5	6	7	8	9	10	11	12	13
Number of schools	88,113 (282.8)	85,934 (284.7)	2,179 (41.9)	61,572 (387.9)	60,419 (375.6)	1,152 (88.2)	19,886 (305.4)	19,365 (297.0)	521 (71.1)	6,655 (292.3)	6,150 (275.5)	505 (70.6)
Enrollment (in thousands)	47,316 (497.8)	46,689 (507.2)	627 (42.1)	29,954 (307.7)	29,588 (304.4)	366 (32.6)	15,301 (443.3)	15,186 (443.9)	116 (20.4)	2,060 (124.5)	1,915 (124.1)	145 (22.8)
Percentage distribution of students												
Race/ethnicity	100.0 (†)	100.0 (†)	100.0 (†)	100.0 (†)	100.0 (†)	100.0 (†)	100.0 (†)	100.0 (†)	100.0 (†)	100.0 (†)	100.0 (†)	100.0 (†)
White	60.3 (0.48)	60.6 (0.49)	43.4 (3.24)	57.8 (0.63)	58.0 (.63)	42.9 (4.30)	63.4 (1.00)	63.6 (1.00)	34.5 (6.01)	74.2 (1.57)	75.9 (1.55)	51.8 (5.77)
Black	16.8 (0.35)	16.6 (0.35)	29.7 (3.06)	17.7 (0.46)	17.5 (0.47)	31.3 (3.96)	15.7 (0.52)	15.6 (0.52)	28.2 (7.72)	11.6 (1.12)	10.5 (0.97)	26.8 (6.60)
Hispanic	17.7 (0.49)	17.6 (0.49)	21.7 (2.29)	19.6 (0.69)	19.6 (0.70)	20.6 (3.55)	15.0 (0.81)	14.9 (0.82)	32.7 (4.85)	9.0 (1.10)	8.5 (1.18)	15.8 (3.27)
Asian/Pacific Islander	3.9 (0.19)	3.9 (0.19)	3.8 (0.81)	3.8 (0.14)	3.7 (0.14)	4.5 (1.12)	4.6 (0.43)	4.7 (0.43)	1.5 (0.35)	1.6 (0.30)	1.4 (0.31)	4.0 (1.90)
American Indian/Alaska Native	1.3 (0.04)	1.3 (0.04)	1.4 (0.24)	1.2 (0.05)	1.2 (0.05)	0.7 (0.12)	1.2 (0.06)	1.2 (0.06)	3.2 (1.13)	3.6 (0.29)	3.7 (0.32)	1.7 (0.54)
Percentage distribution of teachers												
Race/ethnicity[1]	100.0 (†)	100.0 (†)	100.0 (†)	100.0 (†)	100.0 (†)	100.0 (†)	100.0 (†)	100.0 (†)	100.0 (†)	100.0 (†)	100.0 (†)	100.0 (†)
White	84.4 (0.33)	84.5 (0.33)	71.1 (2.51)	83.4 (0.44)	83.5 (0.45)	72.4 (3.31)	85.4 (0.48)	85.5 (0.48)	62.4 (5.35)	90.1 (0.69)	91.3 (0.65)	73.2 (3.57)
Black	8.3 (0.22)	8.2 (0.22)	16.4 (2.14)	8.6 (0.28)	8.5 (0.29)	15.5 (2.98)	8.0 (0.37)	7.9 (0.36)	21.4 (4.72)	5.9 (0.57)	5.2 (0.53)	15.3 (3.55)
Hispanic	5.7 (0.28)	5.7 (0.28)	8.8 (1.34)	6.4 (0.42)	6.3 (0.43)	8.8 (2.05)	4.9 (0.30)	4.8 (0.30)	10.7 (2.87)	2.1 (0.27)	1.7 (0.26)	7.7 (1.83)
Asian/Pacific Islander	1.3 (0.05)	1.3 (0.05)	2.6 (0.46)	1.3 (0.06)	1.3 (0.06)	3.0 (0.72)	1.4 (0.10)	1.4 (0.10)	2.3 (0.93)	0.6 (0.12)	0.5 (0.12)	1.7 (0.66)
American Indian/Alaska Native	0.4 (0.02)	0.4 (0.02)	1.2 (0.39)	0.3 (0.02)	0.3 (0.02)	0.3 (0.13)	0.4 (0.03)	0.4 (0.03)	3.1 (1.81)	1.3 (0.18)	1.2 (0.18)	2.1 (0.99)
Years of full-time teaching experience	100.0 (†)	100.0 (†)	100.0 (†)	100.0 (†)	100.0 (†)	100.0 (†)	100.0 (†)	100.0 (†)	100.0 (†)	100.0 (†)	100.0 (†)	100.0 (†)
Less than 3	12.2 (1.23)	12.0 (1.30)	29.3 (1.67)	12.0 (1.63)	11.8 (1.64)	27.1 (2.27)	12.2 (0.66)	12.0 (0.67)	34.4 (2.90)	15.0 (1.35)	13.8 (1.36)	31.3 (3.80)
3 to 9	32.9 (0.34)	32.8 (0.38)	48.4 (1.89)	33.3 (0.52)	33.1 (0.53)	50.6 (2.97)	32.6 (0.52)	32.5 (0.52)	44.5 (3.22)	31.8 (1.26)	30.8 (1.20)	45.9 (3.77)
10 to 20	28.4 (0.59)	28.8 (0.62)	14.5 (1.58)	29.2 (0.88)	29.4 (0.89)	14.9 (2.43)	27.3 (0.45)	27.4 (0.45)	10.9 (2.96)	28.4 (1.27)	29.3 (1.35)	15.6 (2.53)
More than 20	26.5 (0.77)	26.4 (0.82)	7.7 (1.23)	25.5 (1.06)	25.7 (1.07)	7.4 (2.01)	28.0 (0.59)	28.1 (0.59)	10.2 (2.19)	24.8 (1.17)	26.1 (1.22)	7.3 (1.80)
Percentage distribution of schools												
Size of enrollment	100.0 (†)	100.0 (†)	100.0 (†)	100.0 (†)	100.0 (†)	100.0 (†)	100.0 (†)	100.0 (†)	100.0 (†)	100.0 (†)	100.0 (†)	100.0 (†)
Less than 300	29.2 (0.70)	28.2 (0.73)	67.9 (2.91)	25.6 (0.89)	25.0 (0.69)	60.3 (4.60)	29.0 (1.42)	27.6 (1.47)	81.4 (4.59)	62.5 (2.07)	61.8 (2.28)	71.4 (5.67)
300 to 599	38.9 (0.76)	39.4 (0.79)	19.2 (2.35)	46.1 (1.08)	46.5 (1.10)	23.7 (3.92)	22.2 (0.94)	22.5 (0.95)	12.0 (3.17)	22.8 (1.82)	23.4 (1.97)	16.4 (3.92)
600 to 999	21.6 (0.62)	21.9 (0.63)	9.9 (1.58)	23.6 (0.82)	23.3 (0.83)	13.4 (2.86)	19.4 (0.87)	19.8 (0.88)	4.4 (3.32)	9.7 (1.22)	9.9 (1.32)	7.3 (3.43)
1,000 or more	10.3 (0.38)	10.5 (0.38)	3.0 (0.75)	4.7 (0.35)	4.8 (0.35)	2.6 (1.04)	29.3 (1.20)	30.0 (1.26)	2.1 (1.35)	4.9 (0.73)	4.9 (0.78)	4.9 (2.05)
Percent minority enrollment	100.0 (†)	100.0 (†)	100.0 (†)	100.0 (†)	100.0 (†)	100.0 (†)	100.0 (†)	100.0 (†)	100.0 (†)	100.0 (†)	100.0 (†)	100.0 (†)
Less than 10.0	32.1 (0.58)	32.5 (0.59)	14.8 (3.96)	30.0 (0.69)	30.3 (0.71)	13.8 (4.54)	35.6 (1.31)	36.3 (1.31)	11.8 (11.16)	40.7 (2.04)	42.4 (2.12)	20.1 (7.08)
10.0 to 24.9	18.5 (0.65)	18.5 (0.65)	19.7 (3.64)	19.3 (0.85)	19.3 (0.85)	19.5 (4.68)	17.8 (1.22)	17.9 (1.26)	15.9 (4.19)	13.4 (1.86)	12.5 (1.80)	24.2 (7.19)
25.0 to 49.9	17.0 (0.49)	17.0 (0.49)	16.1 (2.69)	17.2 (0.64)	17.2 (0.64)	17.3 (4.10)	17.2 (0.81)	17.3 (0.84)	13.2 (4.30)	14.3 (1.48)	14.1 (1.60)	16.4 (5.54)
50.0 to 74.9	13.1 (0.59)	13.1 (0.60)	12.3 (2.45)	12.4 (0.68)	12.3 (0.69)	13.0 (3.60)	13.7 (1.21)	13.8 (1.22)	11.2 (3.72)	17.6 (2.23)	18.1 (2.35)	11.6 (5.40)
75.0 or more	19.4 (0.57)	18.9 (0.58)	37.1 (3.68)	21.2 (0.76)	20.9 (0.73)	36.4 (4.91)	15.6 (1.09)	14.7 (1.10)	47.9 (8.75)	14.0 (1.34)	12.9 (1.45)	27.7 (7.38)
Percent of students eligible for free or reduced-price lunch	100.0 (†)	100.0 (†)	100.0 (†)	100.0 (†)	100.0 (†)	100.0 (†)	100.0 (†)	100.0 (†)	100.0 (†)	100.0 (†)	100.0 (†)	100.0 (†)
Less than 15.0	22.0 (0.59)	21.6 (0.60)	38.9 (4.05)	19.4 (0.77)	19.1 (0.80)	33.5 (5.16)	30.7 (1.00)	30.1 (1.02)	55.6 (7.86)	19.9 (2.01)	18.7 (2.07)	33.9 (7.92)
15.0 to 29.9	16.8 (0.59)	17.0 (0.61)	9.7 (2.87)	16.0 (0.76)	16.2 (0.77)	10.1 (4.44)	21.0 (0.86)	21.4 (0.91)	6.7 (4.73)	11.1 (1.29)	11.0 (1.32)	11.7 (4.72)
30.0 to 49.9	22.3 (0.66)	22.4 (0.67)	16.4 (2.84)	22.3 (0.85)	22.4 (0.87)	18.0 (4.16)	21.3 (0.89)	21.5 (0.91)	13.0 (4.80)	25.0 (2.12)	25.7 (2.27)	16.2 (5.47)
50.0 to 74.9	21.0 (0.58)	21.3 (0.60)	12.5 (2.62)	22.3 (0.71)	22.5 (0.72)	13.7 (3.78)	15.4 (1.38)	15.4 (1.41)	12.8 (5.15)	25.9 (2.29)	27.2 (2.45)	9.6 (2.77)
75.0 or more	17.9 (0.65)	17.8 (0.66)	22.5 (3.35)	19.9 (0.68)	19.8 (0.69)	24.7 (4.63)	11.6 (1.50)	11.6 (1.53)	11.8 (5.37)	18.2 (1.79)	17.3 (1.77)	28.6 (8.45)

See notes at end of table.

Table 101. Number and enrollment of traditional public and public charter elementary and secondary schools and percentages of students, teachers, and schools, by selected characteristics: 2003–04—Continued

Selected characteristic	Total elementary and secondary schools			Elementary schools			Secondary schools			Combined elementary/secondary schools		
	Total, all schools	Traditional (non-charter) schools	Public charter schools	Total, all schools	Traditional (non-charter) schools	Public charter schools	Total, all schools	Traditional (non-charter) schools	Public charter schools	Total, all schools	Traditional (non-charter) schools	Public charter schools
1	2	3	4	5	6	7	8	9	10	11	12	13
Percent of schools with selected programs and services												
Programs with special instructional approaches	22.4 (0.65)	21.7 (0.67)	49.0 (3.90)	18.1 (0.74)	17.7 (0.76)	42.3 (5.04)	29.6 (1.62)	28.7 (1.73)	64.3 (7.05)	40.4 (2.69)	39.7 (2.89)	48.4 (8.68)
Talented/gifted program	68.9 (0.67)	69.6 (0.68)	38.9 (4.15)	70.3 (0.86)	71.0 (0.87)	38.4 (6.32)	71.7 (1.47)	72.4 (1.57)	42.8 (7.13)	47.0 (2.53)	47.9 (2.58)	35.9 (7.51)
Immersion in a foreign language program	4.0 (0.40)	4.1 (0.40)	2.5 (1.04)	4.7 (0.55)	4.7 (0.55)	4.2 (1.99)	3.0 (0.41)	3.0 (0.42)	‡ (†)	1.1 (0.29)	1.2 (0.31)	‡
A program for students with discipline or adjustment problems	31.9 (0.78)	32.3 (0.80)	17.8 (3.71)	26.7 (0.86)	27.0 (0.88)	11.9 (3.30)	46.9 (1.80)	47.5 (1.88)	24.4 (9.84)	35.7 (2.56)	36.6 (2.73)	24.4 (8.55)
Extended day program for students who need academic assistance	46.9 (0.72)	46.8 (0.76)	50.1 (3.98)	49.7 (0.83)	49.7 (0.86)	50.1 (6.11)	41.2 (1.33)	41.0 (1.36)	49.8 (7.22)	37.0 (2.30)	36.0 (2.42)	50.3 (8.26)
Before-school or after-school day care programs	33.1 (0.81)	32.9 (0.83)	40.4 (3.38)	44.1 (1.07)	43.8 (1.08)	61.4 (5.82)	5.4 (0.54)	5.3 (0.55)	8.4 (3.84)	13.8 (1.90)	12.8 (2.02)	25.4 (6.26)
Specialized career academy	6.4 (0.30)	6.4 (0.31)	6.5 (1.48)	0.8 (0.17)	0.8 (0.17)	‡ (†)	22.9 (1.08)	23.1 (1.14)	14.3 (4.10)	9.1 (1.18)	8.8 (1.08)	13.3 (5.95)
Advanced Placement (AP) courses	16.2 (0.40)	16.4 (0.41)	8.8 (1.78)	1.7 (0.32)	1.7 (0.33)	‡ (†)	56.0 (1.28)	57.1 (1.34)	14.5 (3.98)	31.9 (2.00)	32.6 (2.08)	22.8 (5.59)
International Baccalaureate	0.7 (0.11)	0.7 (0.11)	1.1 (0.67)	0.4 (0.13)	0.4 (0.13)	‡ (†)	2.0 (0.25)	2.0 (0.26)	‡ (†)	0.4 (0.21)	‡ (†)	4.4 (2.84)
Distance learning courses	12.2 (0.36)	12.2 (0.36)	8.4 (3.42)	2.6 (0.31)	2.7 (0.32)	‡ (†)	32.1 (1.15)	32.4 (1.12)	21.2 (9.75)	40.3 (2.25)	42.5 (2.52)	14.2 (5.58)
Entire school is for suspended students[2]	3.5 (0.35)	3.4 (0.35)	8.0 (3.12)	0.4 (0.17)	0.5 (0.18)	‡ (†)	7.5 (1.30)	7.0 (1.31)	25.5 (9.54)	20.4 (0.05)	21.4 (0.15)	8.0 (3.92)

†Not applicable.
‡Reporting standards not met.
[1]Based on data reported by schools.
[2]Entire school specifically for students who have been suspended or expelled, who have dropped out, or who have been referred for behavioral or adjustment problems.

NOTE: Race categories exclude persons of Hispanic ethnicity. Detail may not sum to totals because of rounding. Standard errors appear in parentheses.
SOURCE: U.S. Department of Education, National Center for Education Statistics, Schools and Staffing Survey (SASS), "Public School Questionnaire," 2003–04; and "Public Teacher Questionnaire," 2003–04. (This table was prepared June 2006.)

Table 102. Percentage of public schools with permanent and portable (temporary) buildings and with environmental factors that interfere with instruction in classrooms, by selected school characteristics, type of factor, and extent of interference: 2005

Type of environmental factor and extent of interference with ability to deliver classroom instruction	All public schools[1]		Instructional level				Size of school enrollment						Percent of students eligible for free or reduced-price lunch							
			Elementary		Secondary/ combined		Less than 350		350 to 699		700 or more		Less than 35 percent		35 to 49 percent		50 to 74 percent		75 percent or more	
1	2		3		4		5		6		7		8		9		10		11	
Estimated number of schools	80,910	(540)	61,590	(669)	19,320	(312)	27,300	(1,039)	32,710	(1,223)	20,900	(695)	32,880	(1,231)	13,400	(1,078)	18,620	(1,244)	16,010	(1,002)
Estimated enrollment (in thousands)	46,003	(457)	29,786	(457)	16,217	(195)	5,947	(331)	16,208	(605)	23,849	(699)	20,668	(721)	6,982	(531)	9,492	(721)	8,861	(670)
	Percent of schools																			
With permanent buildings	99	(0.4)	99	(0.5)	99	(0.5)	99	(0.5)	99	(0.6)	99	(0.5)	99	(0.5)	100	(†)	99	(0.7)	98	(1.2)
With portable (temporary) buildings	37	(1.9)	40	(2.5)	29	(1.9)	27	(3.1)	36	(2.9)	52	(2.8)	31	(2.9)	35	(4.6)	42	(3.3)	46	(3.9)
With portable classroom buildings	33	(1.7)	35	(2.1)	28	(1.9)	21	(2.6)	33	(2.7)	49	(2.9)	27	(2.7)	31	(4.4)	38	(3.0)	43	(3.9)
With environmental factors that interfere with instruction to a moderate or major extent																				
In permanent buildings[2]																				
Lighting, artificial	6	(0.9)	6	(1.1)	5	(1.0)	5	(2.0)	6	(1.4)	6	(1.4)	4	(1.2)	5	(2.7)	8	(2.0)	8	(2.0)
Lighting, natural	6	(0.8)	5	(1.0)	7	(1.1)	6	(1.6)	6	(1.5)	4	(0.8)	6	(1.3)	4	(1.8)	8	(2.3)	4	(1.4)
Heating	12	(1.3)	12	(1.5)	13	(1.8)	14	(2.4)	11	(1.9)	12	(2.0)	13	(2.1)	9	(2.4)	12	(2.7)	14	(2.2)
Air conditioning	16	(1.6)	16	(2.0)	17	(2.0)	16	(2.6)	16	(2.6)	17	(2.0)	19	(2.8)	11	(3.2)	15	(2.7)	16	(2.5)
Ventilation	12	(1.2)	11	(1.5)	12	(1.6)	11	(2.1)	12	(2.1)	12	(1.8)	12	(1.7)	10	(3.4)	12	(2.8)	13	(2.6)
Indoor air quality	9	(1.2)	9	(1.5)	9	(1.4)	8	(1.7)	11	(1.9)	9	(1.6)	10	(1.7)	6	(2.4)	10	(2.7)	10	(2.7)
Acoustics or noise control	12	(1.1)	12	(1.4)	12	(1.5)	12	(2.3)	13	(2.0)	12	(1.6)	8	(1.3)	10	(2.8)	20	(3.3)	14	(2.9)
Physical condition of buildings	10	(1.2)	10	(1.5)	12	(1.4)	10	(2.1)	11	(1.8)	10	(1.7)	9	(1.7)	7	(2.5)	14	(3.1)	13	(2.3)
Size or configuration of rooms	13	(1.1)	13	(1.4)	13	(1.2)	14	(2.3)	12	(2.0)	13	(1.7)	14	(1.9)	8	(2.5)	14	(2.9)	12	(2.2)
In portable buildings[3]																				
Lighting, artificial	8	(1.5)	8	(1.9)	5	(1.9)	11	(4.5)	3	(1.9)	10	(2.7)	5	(2.6)	#	(†)	12	(4.3)	11	(3.5)
Lighting, natural	9	(1.8)	9	(2.2)	9	(2.4)	11	(4.2)	5	(2.5)	12	(2.8)	7	(2.8)	2	(2.3)	14	(4.5)	11	(3.4)
Heating	9	(1.7)	9	(2.0)	9	(2.4)	11	(4.5)	6	(2.3)	12	(2.7)	9	(3.1)	7	(3.7)	10	(3.5)	10	(3.6)
Air conditioning	11	(2.0)	11	(2.3)	11	(2.6)	15	(5.3)	6	(2.3)	14	(3.1)	8	(3.0)	10	(4.5)	14	(4.6)	13	(3.8)
Ventilation	14	(1.8)	14	(2.1)	12	(2.7)	20	(5.8)	8	(2.4)	16	(3.3)	10	(3.2)	8	(3.7)	19	(5.0)	17	(3.9)
Indoor air quality	12	(1.9)	11	(2.3)	13	(2.8)	12	(4.2)	9	(2.9)	14	(3.2)	8	(2.8)	7	(3.5)	16	(4.6)	14	(3.4)
Acoustics or noise control	18	(2.1)	18	(2.5)	15	(2.8)	23	(4.8)	14	(3.4)	19	(3.4)	12	(3.8)	8	(3.8)	25	(5.1)	24	(4.3)
Physical condition of buildings	13	(1.9)	14	(2.3)	13	(2.7)	15	(5.1)	12	(3.1)	15	(2.9)	10	(3.2)	3	(2.0)	18	(4.5)	20	(3.9)
Size or configuration of rooms	16	(2.2)	16	(2.4)	16	(2.9)	15	(4.9)	16	(3.4)	18	(3.2)	9	(3.2)	15	(5.5)	16	(4.6)	26	(5.0)
	Percentage distribution of schools																			
By extent to which environmental factors interfere with instruction																				
In permanent buildings[2]	100	(†)	100	(†)	100	(†)	100	(†)	100	(†)	100	(†)	100	(†)	100	(†)	100	(†)	100	(†)
Not at all	56	(1.6)	56	(1.9)	58	(2.7)	55	(2.8)	56	(3.1)	59	(2.9)	57	(2.7)	62	(4.4)	51	(3.6)	57	(3.2)
Minor extent	33	(1.4)	34	(1.7)	30	(2.4)	34	(2.8)	33	(2.6)	32	(2.7)	32	(2.8)	32	(4.2)	38	(2.9)	32	(3.1)
Moderate extent	9	(1.0)	9	(1.3)	10	(1.4)	10	(2.0)	10	(1.8)	7	(1.2)	10	(1.9)	6	(2.3)	10	(2.5)	8	(2.0)
Major extent	1	(0.4)	1	(0.4)	2	(0.7)	1	(0.4)	1	(0.6)	2	(0.7)	1	(0.6)	#	(†)	1	(0.5)	3	(1.0)
In portable buildings[3]	100	(†)	100	(†)	100	(†)	100	(†)	100	(†)	100	(†)	100	(†)	100	(†)	100	(†)	100	(†)
Not at all	55	(3.3)	55	(3.7)	58	(4.3)	58	(6.8)	56	(5.7)	53	(4.3)	61	(6.1)	58	(9.3)	54	(6.4)	49	(5.6)
Minor extent	30	(3.1)	31	(3.6)	27	(3.5)	19	(5.4)	34	(5.8)	32	(3.8)	27	(4.7)	34	(8.5)	30	(6.5)	32	(5.5)
Moderate extent	13	(2.1)	12	(2.4)	14	(2.6)	21	(6.0)	10	(3.0)	10	(2.7)	13	(3.6)	7	(3.7)	13	(4.4)	16	(4.5)
Major extent	2	(0.8)	2	(1.0)	1	(0.8)	I	(1.4)	#	(†)	5	(1.9)	#	(†)	1	(0.9)	4	(2.4)	3	(1.9)

†Not applicable.
#Rounds to zero.
[1]Excludes special education, vocational, and alternative schools; schools without enrollment data; and schools offering only preprimary education.
[2]Data are based on the 99 percent of public schools with classrooms in permanent buildings.
[3]Data are based on the 33 percent of public schools with classrooms in portable (temporary) buildings.
NOTE: Detail may not sum to totals because of rounding. Standard errors appear in parentheses.
SOURCE: U.S. Department of Education, National Center for Education Statistics, Fast Response Survey System (FRSS), "Public School Principals' Perceptions of Their School Facilities: Fall 2005," FRSS 88, 2005, and unpublished tabulations. (This table was prepared June 2007.)

Table 103. Percentage of public schools with enrollment under, at, or over capacity, by selected school characteristics: 1999 and 2005

School enrollment versus design capacity	All public schools[1]		Instructional level				Size of school enrollment						Percent of students eligible for free or reduced-price lunch							
			Elementary		Secondary/ combined		Less than 350		350 to 699		700 or more		Less than 35 percent		35 to 49 percent		50 to 74 percent		75 percent or more	
1	2		3		4		5		6		7		8		9		10		11	
1999, total	100	(†)	100	(†)	100	(†)	100	(†)	100	(†)	100	(†)	100	(†)	100	(†)	100	(†)	100	(†)
Underenrolled by more than 25 percent	18	(1.5)	17	(1.7)	22	(2.5)	39	(4.0)	11	(2.0)	8	(1.7)	16	(2.0)	18	(3.1)	17	(4.1)	27	(4.4)
Underenrolled by 6 to 25 percent	33	(1.7)	31	(2.1)	39	(2.9)	32	(3.8)	36	(2.4)	31	(2.8)	38	(2.6)	32	(4.6)	29	(4.6)	25	(4.5)
Enrollment within 5 percent of capacity	26	(1.5)	28	(2.0)	20	(2.2)	16	(2.9)	34	(2.6)	25	(2.0)	25	(2.2)	26	(4.4)	32	(4.5)	23	(4.1)
Overenrolled by 6 to 25 percent	14	(1.2)	15	(1.5)	11	(1.8)	10	(2.4)	14	(2.0)	20	(1.8)	14	(2.1)	18	(3.6)	14	(3.3)	11	(3.0)
Overenrolled by more than 25 percent	8	(0.9)	8	(1.1)	8	(1.6)	3	(1.3)	6	(1.3)	16	(2.4)	6	(1.2)	6	(1.8)	7	(2.4)	14	(3.4)
2005, total	100	(†)	100	(†)	100	(†)	100	(†)	100	(†)	100	(†)	100	(†)	100	(†)	100	(†)	100	(†)
Underenrolled by more than 25 percent	21	(1.4)	20	(1.7)	24	(2.6)	41	(3.3)	14	(1.7)	6	(1.4)	19	(2.6)	25	(4.6)	24	(2.7)	19	(3.0)
Underenrolled by 6 to 25 percent	38	(1.8)	39	(2.1)	36	(2.6)	39	(3.4)	44	(2.9)	29	(2.4)	38	(2.7)	43	(4.0)	37	(2.8)	36	(4.1)
Enrollment within 5 percent of capacity	22	(1.5)	23	(1.9)	21	(1.9)	14	(2.3)	27	(2.5)	26	(2.4)	27	(2.5)	19	(3.3)	18	(3.1)	22	(2.9)
Overenrolled by 6 to 25 percent	10	(1.0)	10	(1.4)	11	(1.2)	4	(1.1)	9	(1.9)	20	(2.1)	11	(1.8)	6	(2.0)	12	(2.6)	9	(1.6)
Overenrolled by more than 25 percent	8	(1.0)	8	(1.3)	8	(1.0)	2	(0.9)	6	(1.4)	19	(2.5)	5	(1.0)	7	(2.3)	8	(2.2)	14	(2.9)

†Not applicable.
[1]Excludes special education, vocational, and alternative schools; schools without enrollment data; and schools offering only preprimary education.
NOTE: Detail may not sum to totals because of rounding. Standard errors appear in parentheses.
SOURCE: U.S. Department of Education, National Center for Education Statistics, Fast Response Survey System (FRSS), "Condition of America's Public School Facilities, 1999," FRSS 73, 1999, and "Public School Principals' Perceptions of Their School Facilities: Fall 2005," FRSS 88, 2005. (This table was prepared July 2007.)

Table 104. High school graduates, by sex and control of school: Selected years, 1869–70 through 2008–09

School year	High school graduates (in thousands)					Averaged freshman graduation rate for public schools[4]
	Total[1]	Sex		Control		
		Males	Females	Public[2]	Private[3]	
1	2	3	4	5	6	7
1869–70	16	7	9	—	—	—
1879–80	24	11	13	—	—	—
1889–90	44	19	25	22	22	—
1899–1900	95	38	57	62	33	—
1909–10	156	64	93	111	45	—
1919–20	311	124	188	231	80	—
1929–30	667	300	367	592	75	—
1939–40	1,221	579	643	1,143	78	—
1949–50	1,200	571	629	1,063	136	—
1959–60	1,858	895	963	1,627	231	—
1960–61	1,964	955	1,009	1,725	239	—
1961–62	1,918	938	980	1,678	240	—
1962–63	1,943	956	987	1,710	233	—
1963–64	2,283	1,120	1,163	2,008	275	—
1964–65	2,658	1,311	1,347	2,360	298	—
1965–66	2,665	1,323	1,342	2,367	298	—
1966–67	2,672	1,328	1,344	2,374	298	—
1967–68	2,695	1,338	1,357	2,395	300	—
1968–69	2,822	1,399	1,423	2,522	300	—
1969–70	2,889	1,430	1,459	2,589	300	78.7
1970–71	2,938	1,454	1,484	2,638	300	78.0
1971–72	3,002	1,487	1,515	2,700	302	77.4
1972–73	3,035	1,500	1,535	2,729	306	76.8
1973–74	3,073	1,512	1,561	2,763	310	75.4
1974–75	3,133	1,542	1,591	2,823	310	74.9
1975–76	3,148	1,552	1,596	2,837	311	74.9
1976–77	3,152	1,548	1,604	2,837	315	74.4
1977–78	3,127	1,531	1,596	2,825	302	73.2
1978–79	3,101	1,517	1,584	2,801	300	71.9
1979–80	3,043	1,491	1,552	2,748	295	71.5
1980–81	3,020	1,483	1,537	2,725	295	72.2
1981–82	2,995	1,471	1,524	2,705	290	72.9
1982–83	2,888	1,437	1,451	2,598	290	73.8
1983–84	2,767	—	—	2,495	272	74.5
1984–85	2,677	—	—	2,414	263	74.2
1985–86	2,643	—	—	2,383	260	74.3
1986–87	2,694	—	—	2,429	265	74.3
1987–88	2,773	—	—	2,500	273	74.2
1988–89	2,744	—	—	2,459	285	73.4
1989–90	2,589	—	—	2,320	269	73.6
1990–91	2,493	—	—	2,235	258	73.7
1991–92	2,478	—	—	2,226	252	74.2
1992–93	2,480	—	—	2,233	247	73.8
1993–94	2,464	—	—	2,221	243	73.1
1994–95	2,520	—	—	2,274	246	71.8
1995–96	2,518	—	—	2,273	245	71.0
1996–97	2,612	—	—	2,358	254	71.3
1997–98	2,704	—	—	2,439	265	71.3
1998–99	2,759	—	—	2,486	273	71.1
1999–2000	2,833	—	—	2,554	279	71.7
2000–01	2,848	—	—	2,569	279	71.7
2001–02	2,907	—	—	2,622	285	72.6
2002–03	3,016	—	—	2,720	296	73.9
2003–04[5,6]	3,054	—	—	2,753	301	74.3
2004–05	3,106	—	—	2,799	307	74.7
2005–06[6]	3,128	—	—	2,816	312	73.4
2006–07[7]	3,262	—	—	2,950	312	75.4
2007–08[7]	3,346	—	—	3,026	320	75.4
2008–09[7]	3,328	—	—	3,011	317	74.8

—Not available.

[1]Includes graduates of public and private schools.

[2]Data for 1929–30 and preceding years are from *Statistics of Public High Schools* and exclude graduates from high schools that failed to report to the Office of Education.

[3]For most years, private school data have been estimated based on periodic private school surveys.

[4]The averaged freshman graduation rate provides an estimate of the percentage of students who receive a regular diploma within 4 years of entering ninth grade. The rate uses aggregate student enrollment data to estimate the size of an incoming freshman class and aggregate counts of the number of diplomas awarded 4 years later.

[5]Includes estimates for New York and Wisconsin. Without estimates for these two states, the averaged freshman graduation rate for the remaining 48 states and the District of Columbia is 75.0 percent.

[6]Private school data are projected.

[7]Projected.

NOTE: Includes graduates of regular day school programs. Excludes graduates of other programs, when separately reported, and recipients of high school equivalency certificates. Some data have been revised from previously published figures. Detail may not sum to totals because of rounding.

SOURCE: U.S. Department of Education, National Center for Education Statistics, *Annual Report of the Commissioner of Education*, 1870 through 1910; *Biennial Survey of Education in the United States*, 1919–20 through 1949–50; *Statistics of State School Systems*, 1951–52 through 1957–58; *Statistics of Public Elementary and Secondary School Systems*, 1958–59 through 1980–81; *Statistics of Nonpublic Elementary and Secondary Schools*, 1959 through 1980; Common Core of Data (CCD), "State Nonfiscal Survey of Public Elementary/Secondary Education," 1981–82 through 2006–07; Private School Universe Survey (PSS), 1989 through 2005; and *Projections of Education Statistics to 2017*. (This table was prepared January 2009.)

Table 105. Public high school graduates, by state or jurisdiction: Selected years, 1980–81 through 2006–07

State or jurisdiction	1980–81	1990–91	1995–96	1999–2000	2000–01	2002–03	2003–04	2004–05	2005–06	Projected 2006–07 graduates	Percent change, 1999–2000 to 2006–07
1	2	3	4	5	6	7	8	9	10	11	12
United States	2,725,285	2,234,893	2,273,109	2,553,844	2,569,200	2,719,947	2,753,438[1]	2,799,250	2,815,544 [1]	2,950,450	15.5
Alabama	44,894	39,042	35,043	37,819	37,082	36,741	36,464	37,453	37,918	38,060	0.6
Alaska	5,343	5,458	5,945	6,615	6,812	7,297	7,236	6,909	7,361	7,930	19.9
Arizona	28,416	31,282	30,008	38,304	46,733	49,986	45,508	59,498	54,091	69,060	80.3
Arkansas	29,577	25,668	25,094	27,335	27,100	27,555	27,181	26,621	28,790	27,920	2.1
California	242,172	234,164	259,071	309,866	315,189	341,097	343,480	355,217	343,515	375,930	21.3
Colorado	35,897	31,293	32,608	38,924	39,241	42,379	44,777	44,532	44,424	46,890	20.5
Connecticut	38,369	27,290	26,319	31,562	30,388	33,667	34,573	35,515	36,222	37,450	18.7
Delaware	7,349	5,223	5,609	6,108	6,614	6,817	6,951	6,934	7,275	7,080	15.9
District of Columbia[2]	4,848	3,369	2,696	2,695	2,808	2,725	3,031	2,781	3,150 [3]	3,400	26.2
Florida	88,755	87,419	89,242	106,708	111,112	127,484	131,418	133,318	134,686	150,280	40.8
Georgia	62,963	60,088	56,271	62,563	62,499	66,890	68,550	70,834	73,498	76,550	22.4
Hawaii	11,472	8,974	9,387	10,437	10,102	10,013	10,324	10,813	10,922	10,680	2.3
Idaho	12,679	11,961	14,667	16,170	15,941	15,858	15,547	15,768	16,096	16,360	1.2
Illinois	136,795	103,329	104,626	111,835	110,624	117,507	124,763	123,615	126,817	130,080	16.3
Indiana	73,381	57,892	56,330	57,012	56,172	57,897	56,008	55,444	57,920	61,060	7.1
Iowa	42,635	28,593	31,689	33,926	33,774	34,860	34,339	33,547	33,693	35,480	4.6
Kansas	29,397	24,414	25,786	29,102	29,360	29,963	30,155	30,355	29,818	29,550	1.5
Kentucky	41,714	35,835	36,641	36,830	36,957	37,654	37,787	38,399	38,449	38,850	5.5
Louisiana	46,199	33,489	36,467	38,430	38,314	37,610	37,019	36,009	33,275	31,690	-17.5
Maine	15,554	13,151	11,795	12,211	12,654	12,947	13,278	13,077	12,950	13,390	9.7
Maryland	54,050	39,014	41,785	47,849	49,222	51,864	52,870	54,170	55,536	57,080	19.3
Massachusetts	74,831	50,216	47,993	52,950	54,393	55,987	58,326	59,665	61,272	62,460	18.0
Michigan	124,372	88,234	85,530	97,679	96,515	100,301	98,823	101,582	102,582	106,750	9.3
Minnesota	64,166	46,474	50,481	57,372	56,581	59,432	59,096	58,391	58,898	59,640	4.0
Mississippi	28,083	23,665	23,032	24,232	23,748	23,810	23,735	23,523	23,848	24,540	1.3
Missouri	60,359	46,928	49,011	52,848	54,138	56,925	57,983	57,841	58,417	59,680	12.9
Montana	11,634	9,013	10,139	10,903	10,628	10,657	10,500	10,335	10,283	10,130	-7.1
Nebraska	21,411	16,500	18,014	20,149	19,658	20,161	20,309	19,940	19,764	19,860	-1.4
Nevada	9,069	9,370	10,374	14,551	15,127	16,378	15,201	15,740	16,455	17,450	19.9
New Hampshire	11,552	10,059	10,094	11,829	12,294	13,210	13,309	13,775	13,988	14,240	20.4
New Jersey	93,168	67,003	67,704	74,420	76,130	81,391	83,826	86,502	90,049	95,590	28.4
New Mexico	17,915	15,157	15,402	18,031	18,199	16,923	17,892	17,353	17,822	17,430	-3.3
New York	198,465	133,562	134,401	141,731	141,884	143,818	142,526 [4]	153,203	161,817	158,850	12.1
North Carolina	69,395	62,792	57,014	62,140	63,288	69,696	72,126	75,010	76,710	81,080	30.5
North Dakota	9,924	7,573	8,027	8,606	8,445	8,169	7,888	7,555	7,192	7,220	-16.1
Ohio	143,503	107,484	102,098	111,668	111,281	115,762	119,029	116,702	117,356	119,710	7.2
Oklahoma	38,875	33,007	33,060	37,646	37,458	36,694	36,799	36,227	36,497	36,860	-2.1
Oregon	28,729	24,597	26,570	30,151	29,939	32,587	32,958	32,602	32,394	32,020	6.2
Pennsylvania	144,645	104,770	105,981	113,959	114,436	119,933	123,474	124,758	127,830 [3]	129,890	14.0
Rhode Island	10,719	7,744	7,689	8,477	8,603	9,318	9,258	9,881	10,108	10,180	20.1
South Carolina	38,347	32,999	30,182	31,617	30,026	32,482	33,235	33,439	34,970 [3]	38,080	20.4
South Dakota	10,385	7,127	8,532	9,278	8,881	8,999	9,001	8,585	8,589	8,240	-11.2
Tennessee	50,648	44,847	43,792	41,568	40,642	44,113	46,096	47,967	50,880	50,830	22.3
Texas	171,665	174,306	171,844	212,925	215,316	238,111	244,165	239,717	240,485	255,830	20.2
Utah	19,886	22,219	26,293	32,501	31,036	29,527	30,252	30,253	29,050	31,480	-3.1
Vermont	6,424	5,212	5,867	6,675	6,856	6,970	7,100	7,152	6,779	7,140	7.0
Virginia	67,126	58,441	58,166	65,596	66,067	72,943	72,042	73,667	69,597	78,710	20.0
Washington	50,046	42,514	49,862	57,597	55,081	60,435	61,274	61,094	60,213	65,050	12.9
West Virginia	23,580	21,064	20,335	19,437	18,440	17,287	17,339	17,137	16,763	17,260	-11.2
Wisconsin	67,743	49,340	52,651	58,545	59,341	63,272	62,784 [4]	63,229	63,003	64,120	9.5
Wyoming	6,161	5,728	5,892	6,462	6,071	5,845	5,833	5,616	5,527	5,380	-16.7
Bureau of Indian Education	—	—	—	—	—	—	—	—	—	—	—
DoD, overseas	—	—	2,674	2,642	2,621	2,641	2,766	—	—	—	—
DoD, domestic	—	—	—	560	568	590	584	—	—	—	—
Other jurisdictions											
American Samoa	—	597	719	698	722	832	852	905	879	—	—
Guam	—	1,014	987	1,406	1,371	1,502	1,346	1,179	—	—	—
Northern Marianas	—	273	325	360	361	422	575	614	670	—	—
Puerto Rico	—	29,329	29,499	30,856	30,154	31,408	30,083	29,071	31,896	—	—
U.S. Virgin Islands	—	981	937	1,060	966	886	816	940	—	—	—

—Not available.
[1]U.S. total includes estimates for nonreporting states.
[2]Beginning in 1985–86, graduates from adult programs are excluded.
[3]Projected data from NCES 2008-078, *Projections of Education Statistics to 2017*.
[4]Estimated high school graduates from NCES 2006-606rev, *The Averaged Freshman Graduation Rate for Public High Schools From the Common Core of Data: School Years 2002–03 and 2003–04.*

NOTE: Data include regular diploma recipients, but exclude students receiving a certificate of attendance and persons receiving high school equivalency certificates. DoD = Department of Defense. Detail may not sum to totals because of rounding.
SOURCE: U.S. Department of Education, National Center for Education Statistics; *Projections of Education Statistics to 2017;* Common Core of Data (CCD), "State Nonfiscal Survey of Public Elementary/Secondary Education," 1981–82 through 2006–07; and *The Averaged Freshman Graduation Rate for Public High Schools From the Common Core of Data: School Years 2002–03 and 2003–04.* (This table was prepared January 2009.)

Table 106. Averaged freshman graduation rates for public secondary schools, by state or jurisdiction: Selected years, 1990–91 through 2005–06

State or jurisdiction	1990–91	1993–94	1994–95	1995–96	1996–97	1997–98	1998–99	1999–2000	2000–01	2001–02	2002–03	2003–04	2004–05	2005–06
1	2	3	4	5	6	7	8	9	10	11	12	13	14	15
United States	**73.7**	**73.1**	**71.8**	**71.0**	**71.3**	**71.3**	**71.1**	**71.7**	**71.7**	**72.6**	**73.9**	**74.3** [1]	**74.7**	**73.4** [2]
Alabama	69.8	64.3	64.8	62.7	62.4	64.4	61.3	64.1	63.7	62.1	64.7	65.0	65.9	66.2
Alaska	74.6	73.8	71.2	68.3	67.9	68.9	70.0	66.7	68.0	65.9	68.0	67.2	64.1	66.5
Arizona	76.7	71.7	65.1	60.8	65.3	65.6	62.3	63.6	74.2	74.7	75.9	66.8	84.7	70.5
Arkansas	76.6	76.1	72.7	74.2	70.6	73.9	73.7	74.6	73.9	74.8	76.6	76.8	75.7	80.4
California	69.6	68.6	66.8	67.6	68.8	69.6	71.1	71.7	71.6	72.7	74.1	73.9	74.6	69.2
Colorado	76.3	77.3	76.0	74.8	74.7	73.9	73.4	74.1	73.2	74.7	76.4	78.7	76.7	75.5
Connecticut	80.2	79.9	77.2	76.1	76.7	76.9	76.0	81.9	77.5	79.7	80.9	80.7	80.9	80.9
Delaware	72.5	70.8	68.7	70.4	71.7	74.1	70.4	66.8	71.0	69.5	73.0	72.9	73.0	76.3
District of Columbia	54.5	58.7	54.6	49.7	54.6	53.9	52.0	54.5	60.2	68.4	59.6	68.2	66.3	65.4 [3]
Florida	65.6	64.2	63.5	62.3	62.7	62.1	61.4	61.0	61.2	63.4	66.7	66.4	64.6	63.6
Georgia	70.3	66.3	63.5	61.9	62.0	58.2	57.5	59.7	58.7	61.1	60.8	61.2	61.7	62.4
Hawaii	75.9	75.7	74.8	74.5	69.1	68.8	67.5	70.9	68.3	72.1	71.3	72.6	75.1	75.5
Idaho	79.6	79.9	80.2	80.5	80.1	79.7	79.5	79.4	79.6	79.3	81.4	81.5	81.0	80.5
Illinois	76.6	76.3	74.8	75.2	76.1	76.8	76.0	76.3	75.6	77.1	75.9	80.3	79.4	79.7
Indiana	76.9	74.7	73.8	73.6	74.0	73.8	74.3	71.8	72.1	73.1	75.5	73.5	73.2	73.3
Iowa	84.4	86.1	84.5	84.3	84.6	83.9	83.3	83.1	82.8	84.1	85.3	85.8	86.6	86.9
Kansas	80.8	80.2	78.8	77.1	76.9	76.0	76.7	77.1	76.5	77.1	76.9	77.9	79.2	77.5
Kentucky	72.9	79.2	73.8	71.3	71.1	70.2	70.0	69.7	69.8	69.8	71.7	73.0	75.9	77.2
Louisiana	57.5	61.5	62.4	61.7	59.3	61.3	61.1	62.2	63.7	64.4	64.1	69.4	63.9	59.5
Maine	80.7	74.0	73.6	73.7	75.2	78.5	74.7	75.9	76.4	75.6	76.3	77.6	78.6	76.3
Maryland	77.5	78.9	78.2	78.3	76.6	76.2	76.6	77.6	78.7	79.7	79.2	79.5	79.3	79.9
Massachusetts	79.1	79.7	78.1	78.0	78.4	78.3	77.9	78.0	78.9	77.6	75.7	79.3	78.7	79.5
Michigan	72.1	72.4	71.3	71.4	73.5	74.6	73.9	75.3	75.4	72.9	74.0	72.5	73.0	72.2
Minnesota	90.8	88.8	87.7	86.1	78.6	85.0	86.0	84.9	83.6	83.9	84.8	84.7	85.9	86.2
Mississippi	63.3	63.8	62.0	59.7	59.6	59.8	59.2	59.4	59.7	61.2	62.7	62.7	63.3	63.5
Missouri	76.0	76.8	76.0	75.0	74.7	75.2	75.8	76.3	75.5	76.8	78.3	80.4	80.6	81.0
Montana	84.4	85.5	86.5	83.9	83.2	82.2	81.3	80.8	80.0	79.8	81.0	80.4	81.5	81.9
Nebraska	86.7	87.2	86.9	86.6	84.8	85.6	87.3	85.7	83.8	83.9	85.2	87.6	87.8	87.0
Nevada	77.0	68.2	65.8	65.8	73.2	70.6	71.0	69.7	70.0	71.9	72.3	57.4	55.8	55.8
New Hampshire	78.6	80.5	78.4	77.5	77.3	76.7	75.3	76.1	77.8	77.8	78.2	78.7	80.1	81.1
New Jersey	81.4	83.4	82.1	82.8	83.9	76.3	77.5	83.6	85.4	85.8	87.0	86.3	85.1	84.8
New Mexico	70.1	66.9	64.4	63.7	62.5	61.6	63.3	64.7	65.9	67.4	63.1	67.0	65.4	67.3
New York	66.1	66.2	63.7	63.6	65.3	63.4	62.5	61.8	61.5	60.5	60.9	60.9 [4]	65.3	67.4
North Carolina	71.3	69.7	69.1	66.5	65.5	65.6	65.4	65.8	66.5	68.2	70.1	71.4	72.6	71.8
North Dakota	87.6	88.4	87.5	89.5	87.8	86.7	85.6	86.0	85.4	85.0	86.4	86.1	86.3	82.2
Ohio	77.5	81.1	79.9	74.5	76.4	77.0	75.0	75.2	76.5	77.5	79.0	81.3	80.2	79.2
Oklahoma	76.5	77.6	77.4	75.6	74.8	75.1	76.4	75.8	75.8	76.0	76.0	77.0	76.9	77.8
Oregon	72.7	72.9	71.2	68.3	69.1	69.0	68.2	69.6	68.3	71.0	73.7	74.2	74.2	73.0
Pennsylvania	79.7	81.0	80.1	80.0	79.8	79.4	79.1	78.7	79.0	80.2	81.7	82.2	82.5	83.5 [3]
Rhode Island	75.0	73.9	74.3	72.7	72.9	72.5	72.2	72.8	73.5	75.7	77.7	75.9	78.4	77.8
South Carolina	66.6	64.3	61.6	60.9	59.6	59.3	59.1	58.6	56.5	57.9	59.7	60.6	60.1	61.0 [3]
South Dakota	83.8	90.8	86.9	84.5	84.2	77.7	74.2	77.6	77.4	79.0	83.0	83.7	82.3	84.5
Tennessee	69.8	65.7	66.7	66.6	61.6	58.4	58.5	59.5	59.0	59.6	63.4	66.1	68.5	70.7
Texas	72.2	66.2	66.8	66.1	67.0	69.4	69.2	71.0	70.8	73.5	75.5	76.7	74.0	72.5
Utah	77.5	78.7	77.7	76.9	81.1	80.7	81.6	82.5	81.6	80.5	80.2	83.0	84.4	78.6
Vermont	79.5	83.5	88.9	85.3	83.6	83.9	81.9	81.0	80.2	82.0	83.6	85.4	86.5	82.3
Virginia	76.2	75.7	75.0	76.2	76.6	76.6	76.3	76.9	77.5	76.7	80.6	79.3	79.6	74.5
Washington	75.7	79.5	76.4	75.5	74.0	73.3	73.2	73.7	69.2	72.2	74.2	74.6	75.0	72.9
West Virginia	76.6	77.7	75.7	77.0	76.7	77.4	77.9	76.7	75.9	74.2	75.7	76.9	77.3	76.9
Wisconsin	85.2	84.7	84.0	83.6	83.7	83.1	82.6	82.7	83.3	84.8	85.8	85.8 [4]	86.7	87.5
Wyoming	81.1	84.0	78.8	77.7	78.4	77.1	76.6	76.3	73.4	74.4	73.9	76.0	76.7	76.1
Other jurisdictions														
American Samoa	85.3	83.7	78.7	79.7	79.7	76.6	80.4	71.9	77.0	82.9	81.0	80.2	81.1	81.0
Guam	48.2	45.4	45.2	44.6	45.4	39.5	54.7	52.9	51.7	—	56.3	48.4	—	—
Northern Marianas	—	78.9	62.9	62.9	68.4	63.4	63.5	61.1	62.7	65.2	65.2	75.3	75.4	80.3
Puerto Rico	60.9	57.1	60.4	60.8	61.5	61.9	63.6	64.7	65.7	66.2	67.8	64.8	61.7	68.6
U.S. Virgin Islands	53.2	59.2	59.7	54.2	62.0	58.6	58.6	53.8	57.3	48.7	53.5	—	—	—

—Not available.

[1]Includes estimates for New York and Wisconsin. Without estimates for these two states, the averaged freshman graduation rate for the remaining 48 states and the District of Columbia is 75.0 percent.

[2]U.S. total includes estimates for nonreporting states.

[3]Projected high school graduates from NCES 2008-078, *Projections of Education Statistics to 2017.*

[4]Estimated high school graduates from NCES 2006-606rev, *The Averaged Freshman Graduation Rate for Public High Schools From the Common Core of Data: School Years 2002–03 and 2003–04.*

NOTE: The averaged freshman graduation rate provides an estimate of the percentage of students who receive a regular diploma within 4 years of entering ninth grade. The rate uses aggregate student enrollment data to estimate the size of an incoming freshman class and aggregate counts of the number of diplomas awarded 4 years later. Some data have been revised from previously published figures.

SOURCE: U.S. Department of Education, National Center for Education Statistics, Common Core of Data (CCD), "State Nonfiscal Survey of Public Elementary/Secondary Education," 1986–87 through 2006–07; and *The Averaged Freshman Graduation Rate for Public High Schools From the Common Core of Data: School Years 2002–03 and 2003–04; and Projections of Education Statistics to 2017.* (This table was prepared January 2009.)

Table 107. Public high school graduates and dropouts, by race/ethnicity and state or jurisdiction: 2005–06

State or other jurisdiction	High school graduates, by race/ethnicity, 2005–06[1]						Event dropout rates (percent of 9th- to 12th-graders who dropped out) during 2005–06, by race/ethnicity					
	Total	White	Black	Hispanic	Asian/ Pacific Islander	American Indian/ Alaska Native	Total	White	Black	Hispanic	Asian/ Pacific Islander	American Indian/ Alaska Native
1	2	3	4	5	6	7	8	9	10	11	12	13
United States[2]	2,815,220	1,852,980	393,994	388,088	150,900	29,258	3.9	2.7	6.1	6.0	2.4	7.2
Alabama	37,918	24,680	12,026	478	391	343	2.5	2.3	2.9	2.9	1.2	1.3
Alaska	7,361	4,843	302	246	528	1,442	8.0	6.2	10.0	9.7	6.9	11.7
Arizona	54,091	30,551	2,703	16,369	1,689	2,779	6.4	4.9	7.0	8.2	3.7	10.3
Arkansas	28,790	21,017	5,951	1,183	467	172	3.1	2.7	4.2	3.8	2.4	2.5
California	343,515	138,584	25,355	124,409	52,334	2,833	3.7	2.3	6.5	4.8	1.8	4.3
Colorado	44,424	32,553	2,129	7,727	1,617	398	7.8	4.7	12.5	15.8	4.8	13.5
Connecticut	36,222	27,047	4,184	3,623	1,251	117	1.8	1.2	2.7	4.4	0.7	2.2
Delaware	7,275	4,646	2,002	361	246	20	5.5	4.2	7.3	9.8	2.9	6.8
District of Columbia[3]	3,150	—	—	—	—	—	‡	4.0	‡	‡	7.4	‡
Florida	134,686	76,980	26,759	26,495	4,018	434	4.1	2.9	5.8	5.0	1.7	3.7
Georgia	73,498	42,959	24,829	3,003	2,625	82	5.2	4.7	5.6	7.8	2.1	5.4
Hawaii	10,922	2,068	201	429	8,197	27	4.7	5.3	5.1	5.5	4.5	6.9
Idaho	16,096	14,192	91	1,359	251	203	2.7	2.1	4.8	6.4	1.2	5.6
Illinois	126,817	85,503	19,482	15,764	5,816	252	3.9	2.2	7.7	6.7	1.7	4.2
Indiana	57,920	49,885	5,140	1,953	804	138	2.9	2.5	5.0	4.8	1.7	3.4
Iowa	33,693	30,651	1,091	1,100	695	156	2.2	1.8	6.3	6.1	1.8	6.0
Kansas	29,818	24,517	2,152	2,058	772	319	2.4	1.9	4.4	4.5	2.4	3.7
Kentucky	38,449	—	—	—	—	—	3.3	—	—	—	—	—
Louisiana	33,275	19,483	12,396	533	626	237	8.4	5.7	12.0	9.8	5.6	8.6
Maine	12,950	12,359	219	107	196	69	5.4	5.3	5.5	8.1	5.7	10.1
Maryland	55,536	30,672	18,558	2,790	3,338	178	3.9	—	—	—	—	—
Massachusetts	61,272	48,093	4,765	5,358	2,905	151	3.4	2.3	6.6	7.9	2.7	6.5
Michigan	102,296	81,795	14,249	2,727	2,676	849	3.5	—	—	—	—	—
Minnesota	58,898	50,551	2,973	1,501	3,095	778	3.1	1.9	8.6	10.3	3.5	11.8
Mississippi	23,848	12,278	11,161	186	194	29	3.0	2.3	3.7	3.0	1.9	7.4
Missouri	58,417	47,534	8,401	1,257	1,028	197	4.1	3.3	7.9	6.3	2.0	6.5
Montana	10,283	9,071	44	201	153	814	3.7	3.1	6.2	5.4	1.2	8.5
Nebraska	19,764	16,931	1,032	1,236	352	213	2.8	1.9	8.0	6.4	2.7	7.3
Nevada	16,455	9,902	1,385	3,421	1,516	231	7.7	6.3	9.4	10.0	5.4	9.0
New Hampshire	13,988	—	—	—	—	—	3.2	3.1	3.6	6.6	1.7	4.9
New Jersey	90,049	56,056	13,916	12,775	7,088	214	1.6	1.0	2.5	2.9	0.6	2.8
New Mexico	17,822	6,901	425	8,197	270	2,029	5.5	4.5	5.2	5.9	3.3	6.6
New York	161,817	102,161	24,840	21,824	12,453	539	4.4	2.4	7.3	7.8	3.4	6.9
North Carolina	76,710	—	—	—	—	—	4.0	3.7	4.0	6.0	1.4	8.6
North Dakota	7,192	6,637	62	63	56	374	2.1	1.6	2.6	5.0	1.6	7.3
Ohio	117,356	98,744	14,919	1,922	1,641	130	4.0	2.7	9.8	8.3	1.8	7.9
Oklahoma	36,497	23,572	3,568	2,131	732	6,494	3.5	3.1	4.7	6.1	1.8	3.8
Oregon	32,394	26,248	746	3,139	1,664	597	4.6	—	—	—	—	—
Pennsylvania[3]	127,830	—	—	—	—	—	2.7	1.8	6.0	7.1	2.3	3.9
Rhode Island	10,108	7,666	819	1,292	277	54	4.1	3.1	5.7	7.6	4.8	7.6
South Carolina[3]	34,970	—	—	—	—	—	—	—	—	—	—	—
South Dakota	8,589	7,713	103	109	103	561	4.4	2.8	8.5	8.4	5.0	20.0
Tennessee	50,880	37,896	11,086	995	829	74	2.8	2.1	4.6	5.3	2.0	3.9
Texas	240,485	112,994	32,183	85,455	9,037	816	4.3	2.3	5.9	5.9	1.6	4.3
Utah	29,012	25,575	231	2,021	844	341	3.3	2.8	5.2	7.2	2.8	7.6
Vermont	6,779	6,451	87	72	118	51	‡	‡	‡	‡	‡	‡
Virginia	69,597	46,010	15,774	3,537	4,078	198	2.7	1.9	3.8	6.4	1.6	3.8
Washington	60,213	45,814	2,673	5,203	5,353	1,170	5.5	4.7	10.2	8.8	4.3	10.5
West Virginia	16,763	15,856	630	119	137	21	3.9	3.9	4.5	5.0	0.3	7.9
Wisconsin	63,003	53,607	4,040	2,430	2,150	776	2.2	1.3	7.7	4.9	2.2	5.9
Wyoming	5,527	4,897	64	341	65	160	5.7	4.7	8.9	10.4	3.8	21.2
Bureau of Indian Education	—	—	—	—	—	—	—	—	—	—	—	—
DoD, overseas	—	—	—	—	—	—	—	—	—	—	—	—
DoD, domestic	—	—	—	—	—	—	—	—	—	—	—	—
Other jurisdictions												
American Samoa	879	0	0	0	879	0	2.5	†	†	†	2.5	†
Guam	—	—	—	—	—	—	—	—	—	—	—	—
Northern Marianas	670	8	0	0	662	0	3.5	5.6	†	†	—	†
Puerto Rico	31,896	0	0	31,896	0	0	0.7	†	†	0.7	†	†
U.S. Virgin Islands	—	—	—	—	—	—	8.2	18.1	7.3	14.3	28.6	0.0

—Not available.
†Not applicable.
‡Reporting standards not met.
[1]Data differ slightly from figures reported in other tables due to varying reporting practices for racial/ethnic survey data.
[2]High school graduate counts include estimates for nonreporting states, based on 2005 12th-grade enrollment racial/ethnic distribution reported by state. Event dropout rate totals are totals for reporting states only.
[3]Projected high school graduates from NCES 2008-078, *Projections of Education Statistics to 2017.*

NOTE: Includes only graduates for whom race/ethnicity was reported. Race categories exclude persons of Hispanic ethnicity. Event dropout rates measure the percentage of public school students in grades 9 through 12 who dropped out of school between one October and the next. DoD = Department of Defense.
SOURCE: U.S. Department of Education, National Center for Education Statistics, Common Core of Data (CCD), "State Nonfiscal Survey of Public Elementary/Secondary Education," 2005–06 and 2006–07, and "State-Level Public School Dropouts," 2005–06; and unpublished tabulations. (This table was prepared January 2009.)

Table 108. General Educational Development (GED) test takers and test passers, by age: 1971 through 2006

| Year | Number of test takers (in thousands) | | | Percentage distribution of test passers, by age[1] | | | | |
	Total[2]	Completing test battery[3]	Passing tests[4]	19 years old or less	20 to 24 years old	25 to 29 years old	30 to 34 years old	35 years old or over
1	2	3	4	5	6	7	8	9
1971[5]	377	—	227	—	—	—	—	—
1972[5]	419	—	245	—	—	—	—	—
1973[5]	423	—	249	—	—	—	—	—
1974	—	—	294	35	27	13	9	17
1975	—	—	340	33	26	14	9	18
1976	—	—	333	31	28	14	10	17
1977	—	—	330	40	24	13	8	14
1978	—	—	381	31	27	13	10	18
1979	—	—	426	37	28	12	13	11
1980	—	—	479	37	27	13	8	15
1981	—	—	489	37	27	13	8	14
1982	—	—	486	37	28	13	8	15
1983	—	—	465	34	29	14	8	15
1984	—	—	427	32	28	15	9	16
1985	—	—	413	32	26	15	10	16
1986	—	—	428	32	26	15	10	17
1987	—	—	444	33	24	15	10	18
1988	—	—	410	35	22	14	10	18
1989	632	541	357	35	24	13	—	—
1990	714	615	410	36	25	13	10	15
1991	755	657	462	33	28	13	10	16
1992	739	639	457	33	28	13	9	17
1993	746	651	469	33	27	13	10	16
1994	774	668	491	36	25	13	9	15
1995	787	682	504	38	25	13	9	15
1996	824	716	488	39	25	13	9	14
1997	785	681	460	43	24	12	8	13
1998	776	673	481	44	24	11	7	13
1999	808	702	498	44	25	11	7	13
2000	811	699	487	45	25	11	7	13
2001	1,016	928	648	41	26	11	8	14
2002	557	467	330	49	25	10	6	11
2003	657	552	387	47	26	10	7	11
2004	666	570	406	46	26	11	6	10
2005	681	588	424	45	26	12	7	11
2006	676	580	464	46	25	12	6	11

—Not available.

[1]People who did not report their age were excluded from this calculation. Age data for 1988 and prior years are for all test takers and may not be comparable to data for later years.

[2]All people taking the GED tests (one or more subtests).

[3]People completing the entire GED battery of five tests.

[4]Data for 2002 and later years are for people passing the GED tests (i.e., earning both a passing total score on the test battery and a passing score on each individual test). Data for 2001 and prior years are for high school equivalency credentials issued by the states to GED test passers. In order to receive high school equivalency credentials in some states, GED test passers must meet additional state requirements (e.g., complete an approved course in civics or government).

[5]Includes other jurisdictions, such as Puerto Rico, Guam, and American Samoa.

NOTE: Data are for the United States only and exclude other jurisdictions, except where noted. Detail may not sum to totals because of rounding. Some data have been revised from previously published figures.

SOURCE: American Council on Education, General Educational Development Testing Service, the GED annual *Statistical Report*, 1971 through 1992; *Who Took the GED?* 1993 through 2001; *Who Passed the GED Tests?* 2002 through 2005; and *2006 GED Testing Program Statistical Report*. (This table was prepared July 2008.)

Table 109. Percentage of high school dropouts among persons 16 through 24 years old (status dropout rate), by sex and race/ethnicity: Selected years, 1960 through 2007

Year	Total status dropout rate				Male status dropout rate				Female status dropout rate			
	All races[1]	White	Black	Hispanic	All races[1]	White	Black	Hispanic	All races[1]	White	Black	Hispanic
1	2	3	4	5	6	7	8	9	10	11	12	13
1960[2]	27.2 (—)	— (†)	— (†)	— (†)	27.8 (—)	— (†)	— (†)	— (†)	26.7 (—)	— (†)	— (†)	— (†)
1967[3]	17.0 (—)	15.4 (—)	28.6 (—)	— (†)	16.5 (—)	14.7 (—)	30.6 (—)	— (†)	17.3 (—)	16.1 (—)	26.9 (—)	— (†)
1968[3]	16.2 (—)	14.7 (—)	27.4 (—)	— (†)	15.8 (—)	14.4 (—)	27.1 (—)	— (†)	16.5 (—)	15.0 (—)	27.6 (—)	— (†)
1969[3]	15.2 (—)	13.6 (—)	26.7 (—)	— (†)	14.3 (—)	12.6 (—)	26.9 (—)	— (†)	16.0 (—)	14.6 (—)	26.7 (—)	— (†)
1970[3]	15.0 (0.29)	13.2 (0.30)	27.9 (1.22)	— (†)	14.2 (0.42)	12.2 (0.42)	29.4 (1.82)	— (†)	15.7 (0.41)	14.1 (0.42)	26.6 (1.65)	— (†)
1971[3]	14.7 (0.28)	13.4 (0.29)	24.0 (1.14)	— (†)	14.2 (0.41)	12.6 (0.41)	25.5 (1.70)	— (†)	15.2 (0.40)	14.2 (0.42)	22.6 (1.54)	— (†)
1972	14.6 (0.28)	12.3 (0.29)	21.3 (1.07)	34.3 (2.22)	14.1 (0.40)	11.6 (0.40)	22.3 (1.59)	33.7 (3.23)	15.1 (0.39)	12.8 (0.41)	20.5 (1.44)	34.8 (3.05)
1973	14.1 (0.27)	11.6 (0.28)	22.2 (1.06)	33.5 (2.24)	13.7 (0.38)	11.5 (0.39)	21.5 (1.53)	30.4 (3.16)	14.5 (0.38)	11.8 (0.39)	22.8 (1.47)	36.4 (3.16)
1974	14.3 (0.27)	11.9 (0.28)	21.2 (1.05)	33.0 (2.08)	14.2 (0.39)	12.0 (0.40)	20.1 (1.51)	33.8 (2.99)	14.3 (0.38)	11.8 (0.39)	22.1 (1.45)	32.2 (2.90)
1975	13.9 (0.27)	11.4 (0.27)	22.9 (1.06)	29.2 (2.02)	13.3 (0.37)	11.0 (0.38)	23.0 (1.56)	26.7 (2.84)	14.5 (0.38)	11.8 (0.39)	22.9 (1.44)	31.6 (2.86)
1976	14.1 (0.27)	12.0 (0.28)	20.5 (1.00)	31.4 (2.01)	14.1 (0.38)	12.1 (0.39)	21.2 (1.49)	30.3 (2.94)	14.2 (0.37)	11.8 (0.39)	19.9 (1.35)	32.3 (2.76)
1977	14.1 (0.27)	11.9 (0.28)	19.8 (0.99)	33.0 (2.02)	14.5 (0.38)	12.6 (0.40)	19.5 (1.45)	31.6 (2.89)	13.8 (0.37)	11.2 (0.38)	20.0 (1.36)	34.3 (2.83)
1978	14.2 (0.27)	11.9 (0.28)	20.2 (1.00)	33.3 (2.00)	14.6 (0.38)	12.2 (0.40)	22.5 (1.52)	33.6 (2.88)	13.9 (0.37)	11.6 (0.39)	18.3 (1.31)	33.1 (2.78)
1979	14.6 (0.27)	12.0 (0.28)	21.1 (1.01)	33.8 (1.98)	15.0 (0.39)	12.6 (0.40)	22.4 (1.52)	33.0 (2.83)	14.2 (0.37)	11.5 (0.38)	20.0 (1.35)	34.5 (2.77)
1980	14.1 (0.26)	11.4 (0.27)	19.1 (0.97)	35.2 (1.89)	15.1 (0.39)	12.3 (0.40)	20.8 (1.47)	37.2 (2.72)	13.1 (0.36)	10.5 (0.37)	17.7 (1.28)	33.2 (2.61)
1981	13.9 (0.26)	11.3 (0.27)	18.4 (0.93)	33.2 (1.80)	15.1 (0.38)	12.5 (0.40)	19.9 (1.40)	36.0 (2.61)	12.8 (0.35)	10.2 (0.36)	17.1 (1.24)	30.4 (2.48)
1982	13.9 (0.27)	11.4 (0.29)	18.4 (0.97)	31.7 (1.93)	14.5 (0.40)	12.0 (0.42)	21.2 (1.50)	30.5 (2.73)	13.3 (0.38)	10.8 (0.40)	15.9 (1.26)	32.8 (2.71)
1983	13.7 (0.27)	11.1 (0.29)	18.0 (0.97)	31.6 (1.93)	14.9 (0.41)	12.2 (0.43)	19.9 (1.46)	34.3 (2.84)	12.5 (0.37)	10.1 (0.39)	16.2 (1.28)	29.1 (2.61)
1984	13.1 (0.27)	11.0 (0.29)	15.5 (0.91)	29.8 (1.91)	14.0 (0.40)	11.9 (0.43)	16.8 (1.37)	30.6 (2.78)	12.3 (0.37)	10.1 (0.39)	14.3 (1.22)	29.0 (2.63)
1985	12.6 (0.27)	10.4 (0.29)	15.2 (0.92)	27.6 (1.93)	13.4 (0.40)	11.1 (0.42)	16.1 (1.37)	29.9 (2.76)	11.8 (0.37)	9.8 (0.39)	14.3 (1.23)	25.2 (2.68)
1986	12.2 (0.27)	9.7 (0.28)	14.2 (0.90)	30.1 (1.88)	13.1 (0.40)	10.3 (0.42)	15.0 (1.33)	32.8 (2.66)	11.4 (0.37)	9.1 (0.39)	13.5 (1.21)	27.2 (2.63)
1987	12.6 (0.28)	10.4 (0.30)	14.1 (0.90)	28.6 (1.84)	13.2 (0.40)	10.8 (0.43)	15.0 (1.35)	29.1 (2.57)	12.1 (0.38)	10.0 (0.41)	13.3 (1.21)	28.1 (2.64)
1988	12.9 (0.30)	9.6 (0.31)	14.5 (1.00)	35.8 (2.30)	13.5 (0.44)	10.3 (0.46)	15.0 (1.48)	36.0 (3.19)	12.2 (0.42)	8.9 (0.43)	14.0 (1.36)	35.4 (3.31)
1989	12.6 (0.31)	9.4 (0.32)	13.9 (0.98)	33.0 (2.19)	13.6 (0.45)	10.3 (0.47)	14.9 (1.46)	34.4 (3.08)	11.7 (0.42)	8.5 (0.43)	13.0 (1.32)	31.6 (3.11)
1990	12.1 (0.29)	9.0 (0.30)	13.2 (0.94)	32.4 (1.91)	12.3 (0.42)	9.3 (0.44)	11.9 (1.30)	34.3 (2.71)	11.8 (0.41)	8.7 (0.42)	14.4 (1.34)	30.3 (2.70)
1991	12.5 (0.30)	8.9 (0.31)	13.6 (0.95)	35.3 (1.93)	13.0 (0.43)	8.9 (0.44)	13.5 (1.37)	39.2 (2.74)	11.9 (0.41)	8.9 (0.43)	13.7 (1.31)	31.1 (2.70)
1992[4]	11.0 (0.28)	7.7 (0.29)	13.7 (0.95)	29.4 (1.86)	11.3 (0.41)	8.0 (0.42)	12.5 (1.32)	32.1 (2.67)	10.7 (0.39)	7.4 (0.40)	14.8 (1.36)	26.6 (2.56)
1993[4]	11.0 (0.28)	7.9 (0.29)	13.6 (0.94)	27.5 (1.79)	11.2 (0.40)	8.2 (0.42)	12.6 (1.32)	28.1 (2.54)	10.9 (0.40)	7.6 (0.41)	14.4 (1.34)	26.9 (2.52)
1994[4]	11.4 (0.26)	7.7 (0.27)	12.6 (0.75)	30.0 (1.16)	12.3 (0.38)	8.0 (0.38)	14.1 (1.14)	31.6 (1.60)	10.6 (0.36)	7.5 (0.37)	11.3 (0.99)	28.1 (1.66)
1995[4]	12.0 (0.27)	8.6 (0.28)	12.1 (0.74)	30.0 (1.15)	12.2 (0.38)	9.0 (0.40)	11.1 (1.05)	30.0 (1.59)	11.7 (0.37)	8.2 (0.39)	12.9 (1.05)	30.0 (1.66)
1996[4]	11.1 (0.27)	7.3 (0.27)	13.0 (0.80)	29.4 (1.19)	11.4 (0.38)	7.3 (0.38)	13.5 (1.18)	30.3 (1.67)	10.9 (0.38)	7.3 (0.39)	12.5 (1.08)	28.3 (1.69)
1997[4]	11.0 (0.27)	7.6 (0.28)	13.4 (0.80)	25.3 (1.11)	11.9 (0.39)	8.5 (0.41)	13.3 (1.16)	27.0 (1.55)	10.1 (0.36)	6.7 (0.37)	13.5 (1.11)	23.4 (1.59)
1998[4]	11.8 (0.27)	7.7 (0.28)	13.8 (0.81)	29.5 (1.12)	13.3 (0.40)	8.6 (0.41)	15.5 (1.24)	33.5 (1.59)	10.3 (0.36)	6.9 (0.37)	12.2 (1.05)	25.0 (1.56)
1999[4]	11.2 (0.26)	7.3 (0.27)	12.6 (0.77)	28.6 (1.11)	11.9 (0.38)	7.7 (0.39)	12.1 (1.10)	31.0 (1.58)	10.5 (0.36)	6.9 (0.37)	13.0 (1.08)	26.0 (1.54)
2000[4]	10.9 (0.26)	6.9 (0.26)	13.1 (0.78)	27.8 (1.08)	12.0 (0.38)	7.0 (0.37)	15.3 (1.20)	31.8 (1.56)	9.9 (0.35)	6.9 (0.37)	11.1 (1.00)	23.5 (1.48)
2001[4]	10.7 (0.25)	7.3 (0.26)	10.9 (0.71)	27.0 (1.06)	12.2 (0.38)	7.9 (0.39)	13.0 (1.12)	31.6 (1.55)	9.3 (0.34)	6.7 (0.36)	9.0 (0.90)	22.1 (1.42)
2002[4]	10.5 (0.24)	6.5 (0.24)	11.3 (0.70)	25.7 (0.93)	11.8 (0.35)	6.7 (0.35)	12.8 (1.07)	29.6 (1.32)	9.2 (0.32)	6.3 (0.34)	9.9 (0.91)	21.2 (1.27)
2003[4,5]	9.9 (0.23)	6.3 (0.24)	10.9 (0.69)	23.5 (0.90)	11.3 (0.34)	7.1 (0.35)	12.5 (1.05)	26.7 (1.29)	8.4 (0.30)	5.6 (0.32)	9.5 (0.89)	20.1 (1.23)
2004[4,5]	10.3 (0.23)	6.8 (0.24)	11.8 (0.70)	23.8 (0.89)	11.6 (0.34)	7.1 (0.35)	13.5 (1.08)	28.5 (1.30)	9.0 (0.31)	6.4 (0.34)	10.2 (0.92)	18.5 (1.18)
2005[4,5]	9.4 (0.22)	6.0 (0.23)	10.4 (0.66)	22.4 (0.87)	10.8 (0.33)	6.6 (0.34)	12.0 (1.02)	26.4 (1.26)	8.0 (0.29)	5.3 (0.31)	9.0 (0.86)	18.1 (1.16)
2006[4,5]	9.3 (0.22)	5.8 (0.23)	10.7 (0.66)	22.1 (0.86)	10.3 (0.33)	6.4 (0.33)	9.7 (0.91)	25.7 (1.25)	8.3 (0.30)	5.3 (0.31)	11.7 (0.96)	18.1 (1.15)
2007[4,5]	8.7 (0.21)	5.3 (0.22)	8.4 (0.59)	21.4 (0.83)	9.8 (0.32)	6.0 (0.32)	8.0 (0.82)	24.7 (1.22)	7.7 (0.29)	4.5 (0.28)	8.8 (0.84)	18.0 (1.13)

—Not available.
†Not applicable.
[1]Includes other racial/ethnic categories not separately shown.
[2]Based on the April 1960 decennial census.
[3]White and Black include persons of Hispanic ethnicity.
[4]Because of changes in data collection procedures, data may not be comparable with figures for years prior to 1992.
[5]White and Black exclude persons identifying themselves as more than one race.

NOTE: "Status" dropouts are 16- to 24-year-olds who are not enrolled in school and who have not completed a high school program, regardless of when they left school. People who have received GED credentials are counted as high school completers. All data except for 1960 are based on October counts. Data are based on sample surveys of the civilian noninstitutionalized population, which excludes persons in prisons, persons in the military, and other persons not living in households. Race categories exclude persons of Hispanic ethnicity except where otherwise noted. Standard errors appear in parentheses.
SOURCE: U.S. Department of Commerce, Census Bureau, Current Population Survey (CPS), October 1967 through October 2007. (This table was prepared July 2008.)

Table 110. Percentage of high school dropouts among persons 16 through 24 years old (status dropout rate), by income level, and percentage distribution of status dropouts, by labor force status and educational attainment: 1970 through 2007

| Year | Status dropout rate | Status dropout rate, by family income quartile | | | | Percentage distribution of status dropouts, by labor force status | | | | Percentage distribution of status dropouts, by years of school completed | | | | |
| | | Lowest quartile | Middle low quartile | Middle high quartile | Highest quartile | Total | Employed[1] | Unemployed | Not in labor force | Total | Less than 9 years | 9 years | 10 years | 11 or 12 years |
1	2	3	4	5	6	7	8	9	10	11	12	13	14	15
1970	15.0 (0.29)	28.0 (0.92)	21.2 (0.65)	11.7 (0.50)	5.2 (0.34)	100.0 (†)	49.8 (1.06)	10.3 (0.65)	39.9 (1.04)	100.0 (†)	28.5 (0.96)	20.6 (0.86)	26.8 (0.94)	24.0 (0.91)
1971	14.7 (0.28)	28.8 (0.90)	20.7 (0.63)	10.9 (0.49)	5.1 (0.32)	100.0 (†)	49.5 (1.05)	10.9 (0.65)	39.6 (1.02)	100.0 (†)	27.9 (0.94)	21.7 (0.86)	27.8 (0.94)	22.7 (0.88)
1972	14.6 (0.28)	27.6 (0.85)	20.8 (0.62)	10.2 (0.46)	5.4 (0.33)	100.0 (†)	51.2 (1.03)	10.2 (0.63)	38.6 (1.01)	100.0 (†)	27.5 (0.92)	20.8 (0.84)	29.0 (0.94)	22.7 (0.87)
1973	14.1 (0.27)	28.0 (0.85)	19.6 (0.60)	9.9 (0.45)	4.9 (0.31)	100.0 (†)	53.2 (1.04)	9.2 (0.60)	37.5 (1.01)	100.0 (†)	26.5 (0.92)	20.9 (0.84)	27.4 (0.93)	25.3 (0.90)
1974	14.3 (0.27)	— (†)	— (†)	— (†)	— (†)	100.0 (†)	51.8 (1.02)	12.3 (0.67)	35.9 (0.98)	100.0 (†)	25.4 (0.89)	20.1 (0.82)	28.7 (0.93)	25.8 (0.90)
1975	13.9 (0.27)	28.8 (0.82)	18.0 (0.58)	10.2 (0.45)	5.0 (0.30)	100.0 (†)	46.0 (1.02)	15.6 (0.74)	38.4 (1.00)	100.0 (†)	23.5 (0.87)	21.1 (0.84)	27.5 (0.92)	27.9 (0.92)
1976	14.1 (0.27)	28.1 (0.79)	19.2 (0.60)	10.1 (0.45)	4.9 (0.29)	100.0 (†)	48.8 (1.01)	16.0 (0.74)	35.2 (0.97)	100.0 (†)	24.3 (0.87)	20.1 (0.81)	27.8 (0.91)	27.8 (0.91)
1977	14.1 (0.27)	28.5 (0.80)	19.0 (0.60)	10.4 (0.46)	4.5 (0.29)	100.0 (†)	52.9 (1.02)	13.6 (0.70)	33.6 (0.96)	100.0 (†)	24.3 (0.87)	21.7 (0.84)	27.3 (0.91)	26.6 (0.90)
1978	14.2 (0.27)	28.2 (0.80)	18.9 (0.60)	10.5 (0.46)	5.5 (0.31)	100.0 (†)	54.3 (1.01)	12.4 (0.67)	33.3 (0.95)	100.0 (†)	22.9 (0.85)	20.2 (0.81)	28.2 (0.91)	28.8 (0.91)
1979	14.6 (0.27)	28.1 (0.79)	18.5 (0.60)	11.5 (0.47)	5.6 (0.32)	100.0 (†)	54.0 (0.99)	12.7 (0.66)	33.3 (0.94)	100.0 (†)	22.6 (0.83)	21.0 (0.81)	28.6 (0.90)	27.8 (0.89)
1980	14.1 (0.26)	27.0 (0.77)	18.1 (0.60)	10.7 (0.46)	5.7 (0.32)	100.0 (†)	50.4 (1.01)	17.0 (0.76)	32.6 (0.95)	100.0 (†)	23.6 (0.86)	19.7 (0.80)	29.8 (0.93)	27.0 (0.90)
1981	13.9 (0.26)	26.4 (0.75)	17.8 (0.57)	11.1 (0.47)	5.2 (0.30)	100.0 (†)	49.8 (1.01)	18.3 (0.78)	31.9 (0.94)	100.0 (†)	24.3 (0.86)	18.6 (0.78)	30.2 (0.92)	26.9 (0.89)
1982	13.9 (0.27)	27.2 (0.78)	18.3 (0.63)	10.2 (0.48)	4.4 (0.29)	100.0 (†)	45.2 (1.06)	21.1 (0.37)	33.7 (1.01)	100.0 (†)	22.9 (0.90)	20.8 (0.87)	28.8 (0.96)	27.6 (0.95)
1983	13.7 (0.27)	26.5 (0.77)	17.8 (0.62)	10.5 (0.50)	4.1 (0.29)	100.0 (†)	48.4 (1.08)	18.2 (0.33)	33.4 (1.02)	100.0 (†)	23.6 (0.91)	19.3 (0.85)	28.8 (0.98)	28.8 (0.98)
1984	13.1 (0.27)	25.9 (0.76)	16.5 (0.61)	9.9 (0.48)	3.8 (0.29)	100.0 (†)	49.7 (1.11)	17.3 (0.84)	32.9 (1.05)	100.0 (†)	23.6 (0.95)	21.4 (0.91)	27.5 (1.00)	27.5 (0.99)
1985	12.6 (0.27)	27.1 (0.78)	14.7 (0.60)	8.3 (0.46)	4.0 (0.29)	100.0 (†)	50.1 (1.15)	17.5 (0.88)	32.4 (1.08)	100.0 (†)	23.9 (0.98)	21.0 (0.94)	27.9 (1.03)	27.2 (1.03)
1986	12.2 (0.27)	25.4 (0.75)	14.8 (0.60)	8.0 (0.45)	3.4 (0.28)	100.0 (†)	51.1 (1.18)	16.4 (0.87)	32.5 (1.10)	100.0 (†)	25.4 (1.03)	21.5 (0.97)	25.7 (1.03)	27.4 (1.05)
1987	12.6 (0.28)	25.5 (0.76)	16.6 (0.63)	8.0 (0.46)	3.6 (0.28)	100.0 (†)	52.4 (1.16)	13.6 (0.80)	34.0 (1.10)	100.0 (†)	25.9 (1.02)	20.7 (0.94)	26.0 (1.02)	27.5 (1.04)
1988	12.9 (0.30)	27.2 (0.85)	15.4 (0.68)	8.2 (0.51)	3.4 (0.30)	100.0 (†)	52.9 (1.27)	‡ (†)	‡ (†)	100.0 (†)	28.9 (1.15)	19.3 (1.00)	25.1 (1.10)	26.8 (1.12)
1989	12.6 (0.31)	25.0 (0.84)	16.2 (0.71)	8.7 (0.52)	3.3 (0.31)	100.0 (†)	53.2 (1.30)	13.8 (0.90)	33.0 (1.22)	100.0 (†)	29.4 (1.18)	20.8 (1.05)	24.9 (1.12)	25.0 (1.13)
1990	12.1 (0.27)	24.3 (0.82)	15.1 (0.65)	8.7 (0.51)	2.9 (0.28)	100.0 (†)	52.5 (1.29)	13.3 (0.88)	34.2 (1.23)	100.0 (†)	28.6 (1.17)	20.9 (1.05)	24.4 (1.11)	26.1 (1.14)
1991	12.5 (0.30)	25.9 (0.83)	15.5 (0.66)	7.7 (0.49)	3.0 (0.29)	100.0 (†)	47.5 (1.28)	15.8 (0.93)	36.7 (1.23)	100.0 (†)	28.6 (1.15)	20.5 (1.03)	26.1 (1.12)	24.9 (1.10)
1992[2]	11.0 (0.28)	23.4 (0.79)	12.9 (0.62)	7.3 (0.48)	2.4 (0.26)	100.0 (†)	47.6 (1.36)	15.0 (0.97)	37.4 (1.32)	100.0 (†)	21.6 (1.12)	17.5 (1.04)	24.4 (1.17)	36.5 (1.31)
1993[2]	11.0 (0.28)	22.9 (0.77)	12.7 (0.62)	6.6 (0.46)	2.9 (0.29)	100.0 (†)	48.7 (1.37)	12.8 (0.91)	38.5 (1.33)	100.0 (†)	20.5 (1.10)	16.6 (1.02)	24.1 (1.17)	38.8 (1.33)
1994[2]	11.4 (0.26)	20.7 (0.71)	13.7 (0.58)	8.7 (0.45)	4.9 (0.33)	100.0 (†)	49.5 (1.21)	13.0 (0.81)	37.5 (1.17)	100.0 (†)	23.9 (1.03)	16.2 (0.89)	20.3 (0.97)	39.6 (1.18)
1995[2]	12.0 (0.27)	23.2 (0.69)	13.8 (0.59)	8.3 (0.46)	3.6 (0.29)	100.0 (†)	48.9 (1.19)	14.2 (0.83)	37.0 (1.14)	100.0 (†)	22.2 (0.99)	17.0 (0.89)	22.5 (0.99)	38.3 (1.15)
1996[2]	11.1 (0.27)	22.0 (0.72)	13.6 (0.60)	7.0 (0.45)	3.2 (0.28)	100.0 (†)	47.3 (1.28)	15.0 (0.91)	37.7 (1.24)	100.0 (†)	20.3 (1.03)	17.7 (0.98)	22.6 (1.07)	39.4 (1.25)
1997[2]	11.0 (0.27)	21.8 (0.71)	13.5 (0.59)	6.2 (0.42)	3.4 (0.29)	100.0 (†)	53.3 (1.28)	13.2 (0.86)	33.5 (1.21)	100.0 (†)	19.9 (1.02)	15.7 (0.93)	22.3 (1.06)	42.1 (1.26)
1998[2]	11.8 (0.27)	22.3 (0.71)	14.9 (0.62)	7.7 (0.45)	3.5 (0.29)	100.0 (†)	55.1 (1.22)	10.3 (0.74)	34.6 (1.17)	100.0 (†)	21.0 (1.00)	14.9 (0.87)	21.4 (1.01)	42.6 (1.21)
1999[2]	11.2 (0.26)	21.0 (0.70)	14.3 (0.60)	7.4 (0.44)	3.9 (0.30)	100.0 (†)	55.6 (1.24)	10.0 (0.75)	34.4 (1.18)	100.0 (†)	22.2 (1.03)	16.3 (0.92)	22.5 (1.04)	39.0 (1.21)
2000[2]	10.9 (0.26)	20.7 (0.70)	12.8 (0.56)	8.3 (0.46)	3.5 (0.29)	100.0 (†)	56.9 (1.24)	12.3 (0.82)	30.8 (1.16)	100.0 (†)	21.5 (1.03)	15.3 (0.90)	23.1 (1.06)	40.0 (1.23)
2001[2]	10.7 (0.25)	19.3 (0.68)	13.4 (0.57)	9.0 (0.47)	3.2 (0.27)	100.0 (†)	58.3 (1.24)	14.8 (0.89)	26.9 (1.11)	100.0 (†)	18.4 (0.97)	16.8 (0.94)	23.8 (1.07)	40.9 (1.23)
2002[2]	10.5 (0.24)	18.8 (0.62)	12.3 (0.53)	8.4 (0.43)	3.8 (0.28)	100.0 (†)	57.4 (1.18)	13.3 (0.81)	29.2 (1.09)	100.0 (†)	22.8 (1.00)	17.1 (0.90)	21.3 (0.98)	38.9 (1.17)
2003[2]	9.9 (0.23)	19.5 (0.64)	10.8 (0.49)	7.3 (0.40)	3.4 (0.26)	100.0 (†)	53.5 (1.22)	13.7 (0.84)	32.9 (1.15)	100.0 (†)	21.2 (1.00)	18.2 (0.94)	20.7 (0.99)	40.0 (1.20)
2004[2]	10.3 (0.23)	18.0 (0.60)	12.7 (0.52)	8.2 (0.42)	3.7 (0.27)	100.0 (†)	53.0 (1.19)	14.3 (0.83)	32.7 (1.12)	100.0 (†)	21.4 (0.97)	15.9 (0.87)	22.5 (0.99)	40.3 (1.17)
2005[2]	9.4 (0.22)	17.9 (0.60)	11.5 (0.51)	7.1 (0.39)	2.7 (0.23)	100.0 (†)	56.9 (1.23)	11.9 (0.80)	31.2 (1.15)	100.0 (†)	18.9 (0.97)	16.8 (0.93)	21.4 (1.02)	42.9 (1.23)
2006[2]	9.3 (0.22)	16.5 (0.58)	12.1 (0.51)	6.3 (0.37)	3.8 (0.27)	100.0 (†)	56.4 (1.23)	11.7 (0.80)	32.0 (1.16)	100.0 (†)	22.1 (1.03)	13.4 (0.85)	20.7 (1.01)	43.9 (1.23)
2007[2]	8.7 (0.21)	16.7 (0.59)	10.5 (0.48)	6.4 (0.36)	3.2 (0.25)	100.0 (†)	55.5 (1.27)	11.2 (0.80)	33.3 (1.20)	100.0 (†)	21.2 (1.04)	16.9 (0.96)	22.9 (1.07)	39.0 (1.24)

—Not available.
†Not applicable.
‡Reporting standards not met.
[1]Includes persons employed, but not currently working.
[2]Because of changes in data collection procedures, data may not be comparable with figures for years prior to 1992.
NOTE: "Status" dropouts are 16- to 24-year-olds who are not enrolled in school and who have not completed a high school program, regardless of when they left school. People who have received GED credentials are counted as high school completers.

Data are based on sample surveys of the civilian noninstitutionalized population, which excludes persons in prisons, persons in the military, and other persons not living in households. Some data have been revised from previously published figures. Detail may not sum to totals because of rounding. Standard errors appear in parentheses.

SOURCE: U.S. Department of Commerce, Census Bureau, Current Population Survey (CPS), October 1970 through October 2007. (This table was prepared August 2008.)

Table 111. Number of 14- through 21-year-old students served under Individuals with Disabilities Education Act, Part B, who exited school, by exit reason, age, and type of disability: United States and other jurisdictions, 2004–05 and 2005–06

Age and type of disability	Total	Exiting school					Transferred to regular education[3]	Moved, known to be continuing
		Graduated with diploma	Received a certificate of attendance	Reached maximum age[1]	Dropped out[2]	Died		
1	2	3	4	5	6	7	8	9
2004–05[4]								
Total	393,579	214,986	60,123	5,214	111,343	1,913	67,707	207,797
Age								
14	7,101	128	41	†	6,669	263	18,794	43,814
15	11,767	51	44	†	11,338	334	15,781	47,947
16	24,833	1,718	632	†	22,088	395	14,320	47,521
17	125,619	79,091	16,079	†	30,056	393	11,149	38,731
18	145,129	93,411	24,970	703	25,783	262	5,686	20,629
19	51,530	29,707	10,621	412	10,647	143	1,452	6,285
20	16,604	7,572	4,259	1,169	3,529	75	373	2,102
21	10,996	3,308	3,477	2,930	1,233	48	152	768
Type of disability								
Specific learning disability	236,592	141,372	29,754	1,335	63,534	597	38,802	108,907
Mental retardation	47,025	16,684	16,573	1,915	11,505	348	2,342	20,731
Emotional disturbance	47,602	19,093	4,740	595	22,975	199	6,842	46,887
Speech or language impairment	8,769	5,714	789	37	2,203	26	9,973	5,060
Multiple disabilities	8,159	3,566	1,986	607	1,709	291	339	4,514
Other health impairment	28,883	17,939	3,353	146	7,189	256	7,418	15,803
Hearing impairment[5]	4,758	3,324	719	74	622	19	623	1,663
Orthopedic impairment	3,792	2,359	666	108	549	110	699	1,421
Visual impairment	1,813	1,312	243	36	208	14	183	488
Autism	3,909	2,196	978	291	423	21	267	1,499
Deaf-blindness	99	52	13	9	22	3	8	30
Traumatic brain injury	2,178	1,375	309	61	404	29	210	788
2005–06								
Total	396,857	224,343	60,864	5,424	104,101	2,125	71,397	210,984
Age								
14	5,935	93	23	†	5,490	329	19,591	45,635
15	11,067	75	54	†	10,567	371	17,111	49,035
16	27,713	4,810	623	†	21,885	395	15,526	48,667
17	142,510	94,529	17,466	†	30,103	412	11,478	39,079
18	141,364	91,785	25,028	749	23,517	285	5,576	19,859
19	42,605	23,694	9,857	372	8,509	173	1,489	5,923
20	15,397	6,585	4,272	1,471	2,969	100	422	1,971
21	10,266	2,772	3,541	2,832	1,061	60	204	815
Type of disability								
Specific learning disability	236,135	145,558	29,491	1,184	59,221	681	39,634	109,527
Mental retardation	46,588	17,111	16,562	2,125	10,409	381	2,301	21,050
Emotional disturbance	47,519	20,634	4,728	592	21,331	234	8,080	46,908
Speech or language impairment	8,923	6,005	825	43	2,028	22	10,512	5,139
Multiple disabilities	8,251	3,615	2,110	682	1,544	300	379	4,556
Other health impairment	32,274	20,464	3,781	178	7,545	306	8,251	17,389
Hearing impairment[5]	4,674	3,211	770	55	626	12	672	1,738
Orthopedic impairment	3,455	2,131	663	133	405	123	707	1,203
Visual impairment	1,766	1,273	245	28	201	19	217	581
Autism	4,876	2,783	1,297	326	446	24	409	2,038
Deaf-blindness	150	98	21	13	13	5	14	56
Traumatic brain injury	2,246	1,460	371	65	332	18	221	799

†Not applicable.

[1]Students may exit special education services due to maximum age beginning at age 18 depending on state law or practice or order of any court.

[2]"Dropped out" is defined as the total who were enrolled at some point in the reporting year, were not enrolled at the end of the reporting year, and did not exit through any of the other bases described. Beginning in 2004–05, includes students previously categorized as "moved, not known to continue."

[3]"Transferred to regular education" was previously labeled "no longer receives special education."

[4]Data have been revised from previously reported figures.

[5]Includes deaf and hard of hearing.

SOURCE: U.S. Department of Education, Office of Special Education Programs, Individuals with Disabilities Education Act (IDEA) database. Retrieved July 21, 2008, from https://www.ideadata.org/StateLevelFiles.asp. (This table was prepared July 2008.)

Table 112. Percentage of children demonstrating specific cognitive and motor skills at about 9 months of age, by child's age and selected characteristics: 2001–02

Age and selected characteristic	Number of children (in thousands)	Percentage distribution of children	Specific cognitive abilities							Specific motor abilities			
			Explores objects[1]	Explores purposefully[2]	Jabbers expressively[3]	Early problem solving[4]	Names objects[5]	Eye-hand coordination[6]	Sitting[7]	Prewalking[8]	Stands alone[9]	Skilful walking[10]	Balance[11]
1	2	3	4	5	6	7	8	9	10	11	12	13	14
8 through 10 months													
Total	2,880 (39.2)	100.0 (†)	98.6 (0.06)	83.2 (0.54)	29.6 (0.57)	3.7 (0.13)	0.6 (0.03)	89.1 (0.26)	86.8 (0.24)	64.7 (0.60)	18.6 (0.50)	8.4 (0.21)	1.7 (0.09)
Sex of child													
Male	1,459 (23.1)	50.6 (0.39)	98.6 (0.06)	82.7 (0.51)	28.8 (0.56)	3.5 (0.14)	0.6 (0.03)	89.3 (0.30)	87.0 (0.27)	65.1 (0.69)	18.5 (0.55)	8.3 (0.23)	1.7 (0.10)
Female	1,422 (22.0)	49.4 (0.39)	98.7 (0.09)	83.8 (0.68)	30.4 (0.71)	3.9 (0.18)	0.7 (0.05)	88.9 (0.36)	86.6 (0.33)	64.4 (0.78)	18.7 (0.67)	8.4 (0.29)	1.8 (0.14)
Race/ethnicity of child													
White	1,573 (28.6)	54.7 (0.61)	98.8 (0.07)	84.0 (0.68)	30.4 (0.72)	3.9 (0.17)	0.7 (0.04)	88.7 (0.37)	86.5 (0.34)	63.7 (0.82)	18.0 (0.66)	8.1 (0.27)	1.6 (0.10)
Black	381 (11.0)	13.3 (0.38)	98.1 (0.16)	80.8 (0.92)	27.9 (0.99)	3.4 (0.25)	0.6 (0.07)	91.1 (0.33)	88.6 (0.32)	69.8 (0.94)	22.9 (1.17)	10.4 (0.59)	2.6 (0.35)
Hispanic	716 (18.5)	24.9 (0.54)	98.5 (0.13)	82.3 (0.82)	29.0 (0.84)	3.1 (0.21)	0.6 (0.05)	88.4 (0.47)	86.1 (0.43)	63.4 (1.00)	17.0 (0.77)	7.8 (0.32)	1.6 (0.15)
Asian	77 (3.1)	2.7 (0.10)	98.8 (0.13)	83.3 (0.97)	28.2 (0.93)	3.1 (0.21)	0.5 (0.05)	89.4 (0.54)	87.1 (0.50)	65.0 (1.24)	18.1 (1.01)	8.1 (0.39)	1.6 (0.14)
Pacific Islander	6 (1.5)	0.2 (0.05)	98.9 (0.23)	81.8 (3.53)	23.7 (3.17)	2.0 (0.46)	0.3 (0.07)	95.4 (0.96)	93.0 (1.11)	79.9 (3.76)	34.6 (8.56)	15.0 (3.84)	3.9 (1.64)
American Indian/Alaska Native	10 (1.1)	0.4 (0.04)	98.4 (0.30)	80.3 (2.74)	27.3 (2.52)	3.4 (0.70)	0.6 (0.18)	90.2 (0.99)	86.7 (0.91)	66.7 (2.10)	19.6 (2.10)	8.5 (0.81)	3.5 (0.30)
More than one race	110 (9.2)	3.8 (0.31)	98.6 (0.15)	82.8 (1.30)	29.5 (1.56)	3.8 (0.57)	0.8 (0.22)	90.3 (0.91)	88.1 (0.85)	68.2 (2.13)	22.1 (2.03)	9.6 (0.79)	2.0 (0.31)
Months of age													
8 months	642 (32.8)	22.3 (0.99)	97.5 (0.14)	67.9 (1.04)	15.7 (0.53)	1.1 (0.09)	0.1 (0.02)	84.0 (0.52)	82.0 (0.46)	52.7 (1.08)	8.8 (0.63)	4.5 (0.22)	0.5 (0.05)
9 months	1,388 (28.3)	48.2 (0.76)	98.7 (0.06)	84.5 (0.43)	27.5 (0.44)	2.7 (0.09)	0.4 (0.02)	89.1 (0.32)	86.7 (0.30)	64.2 (0.74)	16.1 (0.55)	7.2 (0.21)	1.2 (0.07)
10 months	851 (24.2)	29.5 (0.90)	99.3 (0.07)	92.7 (0.33)	43.5 (0.74)	7.1 (0.27)	1.4 (0.08)	92.8 (0.26)	90.5 (0.25)	74.6 (0.63)	30.1 (0.85)	13.3 (0.42)	3.6 (0.25)
Primary type of care arrangement[12]													
No regular nonparental arrangement	1,458 (28.0)	50.6 (0.90)	98.5 (0.09)	82.4 (0.59)	28.7 (0.55)	3.4 (0.14)	0.6 (0.04)	88.2 (0.34)	86.0 (0.30)	63.1 (0.70)	17.7 (0.52)	8.0 (0.22)	1.6 (0.10)
Home-based care													
Relative care[13]	760 (27.1)	26.4 (0.81)	98.8 (0.08)	84.3 (0.67)	30.6 (0.79)	3.9 (0.22)	0.7 (0.06)	90.3 (0.35)	87.9 (0.33)	67.4 (0.84)	20.4 (0.81)	9.2 (0.38)	2.0 (0.19)
Nonrelative care[14]	431 (17.3)	15.0 (0.53)	98.8 (0.08)	84.7 (0.80)	31.3 (0.99)	4.2 (0.29)	0.8 (0.08)	89.9 (0.45)	87.5 (0.45)	66.0 (1.13)	19.2 (1.34)	8.6 (0.57)	1.8 (0.23)
Center-based care[15]	211 (14.0)	7.3 (0.48)	98.6 (0.19)	82.6 (1.43)	29.3 (1.54)	3.5 (0.39)	0.6 (0.08)	89.0 (0.71)	86.0 (0.71)	64.0 (1.72)	18.1 (1.51)	8.3 (0.66)	1.9 (0.32)
Multiple arrangements[16]	21 (4.4)	0.7 (0.15)	98.3 (0.36)	78.6 (3.50)	25.0 (2.87)	2.7 (0.60)	0.4 (0.11)	87.1 (2.77)	84.9 (2.35)	61.6 (4.67)	13.6 (2.60)	6.2 (0.89)	0.8 (0.18)
Parents' highest level of education													
Less than high school	383 (12.2)	13.3 (0.41)	98.4 (0.11)	80.1 (0.87)	26.0 (0.79)	2.8 (0.20)	0.5 (0.06)	88.9 (0.63)	86.5 (0.58)	64.4 (1.22)	17.4 (0.97)	8.1 (0.42)	1.7 (0.20)
High school completion	737 (21.5)	25.6 (0.65)	98.4 (0.13)	82.6 (0.85)	29.2 (0.78)	3.6 (0.20)	0.7 (0.06)	89.6 (0.46)	87.3 (0.42)	66.9 (0.94)	20.7 (0.87)	9.1 (0.39)	1.9 (0.20)
Some college/vocational	811 (23.6)	28.2 (0.66)	98.7 (0.08)	84.4 (0.62)	30.8 (0.72)	3.9 (0.21)	0.7 (0.05)	90.0 (0.33)	87.7 (0.31)	66.7 (0.79)	20.6 (0.79)	9.2 (0.34)	2.0 (0.15)
Bachelor's degree	496 (16.3)	17.3 (0.54)	98.8 (0.07)	83.9 (0.59)	30.2 (0.70)	3.8 (0.20)	0.7 (0.06)	88.2 (0.48)	86.0 (0.42)	62.4 (1.07)	16.2 (0.86)	7.4 (0.34)	1.4 (0.12)
Any graduate education	447 (15.7)	15.6 (0.52)	98.8 (0.11)	84.1 (0.95)	30.5 (0.92)	3.9 (0.22)	0.7 (0.06)	87.5 (0.58)	85.4 (0.52)	60.5 (1.22)	15.2 (0.91)	7.0 (0.40)	1.3 (0.18)
Poverty status[17]													
Below poverty threshold	682 (23.0)	23.7 (0.74)	98.3 (0.14)	80.9 (0.75)	27.1 (0.79)	3.1 (0.21)	0.5 (0.05)	89.1 (0.47)	86.8 (0.43)	65.5 (0.98)	19.2 (0.86)	8.7 (0.42)	1.9 (0.24)
At or above poverty threshold	2,198 (37.2)	76.3 (0.74)	98.7 (0.07)	84.0 (0.58)	30.4 (0.63)	3.8 (0.15)	0.7 (0.04)	89.1 (0.27)	86.8 (0.25)	64.5 (0.66)	18.4 (0.56)	8.3 (0.23)	1.7 (0.10)
Socioeconomic status[18]													
Lowest 20 percent	553 (17.5)	19.2 (0.59)	98.3 (0.13)	81.1 (0.72)	27.2 (0.74)	3.1 (0.18)	0.5 (0.04)	89.1 (0.45)	86.7 (0.43)	65.3 (0.92)	18.5 (0.91)	8.4 (0.38)	1.8 (0.19)
Middle 60 percent	1,724 (37.3)	59.9 (0.83)	98.6 (0.08)	83.4 (0.64)	30.0 (0.67)	3.8 (0.18)	0.7 (0.05)	89.4 (0.31)	87.2 (0.29)	65.6 (0.74)	19.7 (0.68)	8.8 (0.28)	1.9 (0.12)
Highest 20 percent	603 (18.1)	20.9 (0.61)	98.8 (0.09)	84.8 (0.73)	30.6 (0.78)	3.8 (0.18)	0.6 (0.04)	88.0 (0.45)	85.8 (0.40)	61.6 (0.96)	15.6 (0.65)	7.1 (0.28)	1.3 (0.13)
11 through 13 months													
Total	839 (32.1)	100.0 (†)	99.7 (0.05)	97.3 (0.15)	67.9 (0.54)	22.5 (0.55)	8.2 (0.37)	97.1 (0.17)	95.6 (0.19)	89.0 (0.54)	62.5 (1.29)	34.9 (0.95)	19.1 (0.84)
Months of age													
11 months	425 (19.6)	50.6 (1.54)	99.5 (0.10)	95.8 (0.28)	57.6 (0.77)	14.2 (0.59)	4.0 (0.33)	95.8 (0.28)	93.9 (0.29)	84.4 (0.86)	49.0 (1.74)	24.3 (1.05)	10.5 (0.77)
12 months	251 (14.9)	30.0 (1.29)	99.8 (0.03)	98.4 (0.13)	74.3 (0.83)	26.9 (0.94)	10.2 (0.65)	98.1 (0.21)	96.8 (0.26)	92.6 (0.71)	70.9 (2.09)	40.2 (1.65)	22.9 (1.50)
13 months	163 (12.1)	19.4 (1.16)	100.0 (0.01)	99.5 (0.08)	85.0 (0.62)	37.7 (1.04)	16.0 (0.87)	99.0 (0.27)	98.2 (0.30)	95.8 (0.85)	84.8 (2.24)	54.4 (1.81)	36.0 (1.83)
14 through 22 months	257 (19.7)	100.0 (†)	100.0 (0.01)	99.5 (0.14)	90.0 (0.60)	58.4 (1.44)	40.8 (1.71)	99.5 (0.12)	99.1 (0.13)	98.3 (0.28)	94.1 (0.91)	74.0 (1.35)	61.7 (1.82)

†Not applicable.
[1]Ability to explore objects, for example, reaching for and holding objects. The child may have no specific purpose except to play or discover.
[2]Ability to explore objects with a purpose, such as to explore a bell to understand the source of the sound.
[3]Measures proficiency in communication through diverse nonverbal sounds and gestures, such as vowel and vowel-consonant sounds.
[4]Measures proficiency in engaging in early problem solving, such as using a tool to reach an out-of-reach toy or locating a hidden toy.
[5]Measures proficiency in early communication skills, such as saying simple words like "mama" and "dada."
[6]Measures proficiency in being able to use visual tracking to guide hand movements to pick up a small object.
[7]Measures proficiency in ability to maintain control of the muscles used in sitting with and without support.
[8]Measures proficiency in ability to engage in various prewalking types of mobility, with and without support, such as shifting weight from one foot to the other.
[9]Measures proficiency in ability to walk with help and to stand independently.
[10]Measures proficiency in being able to walk independently.
[11]Measures proficiency in ability to maintain balance while shifting position.

[12]The type of nonparental care in which the child spent the most hours.
[13]Care provided in the child's home or in another private home by a relative (excluding parents).
[14]Care provided in the child's home or in another private home by a person unrelated to the child.
[15]Care provided in places such as early learning centers, nursery schools, and preschools, excluding Head Start.
[16]Children who spent an equal amount of time in each of two or more arrangements.
[17]Poverty status based on Census Bureau guidelines from 2002, which identify a dollar amount determined to meet a household's needs, given its size and composition. In 2002, a family of four was considered to live below the poverty threshold if its income was less than or equal to $18,392.
[18]Socioeconomic status (SES) was measured by a composite score on parental education and occupations, and family income.
NOTE: This table is based on a survey that sampled children born in 2001 and was designed to collect information about them for the first time when the children were older than 8 months of age (i.e., 8 to 10 months). As shown in the table, some children were older than this, although only 6.5 percent were over 13 months of age. Estimates weighted by W1C0. Race categories exclude persons of Hispanic ethnicity. Detail may not sum to totals because of rounding. Standard errors appear in parentheses.
SOURCE: U.S. Department of Education, National Center for Education Statistics, Early Childhood Longitudinal Study, Birth Cohort 9-month–Preschool Restricted-Use Data File and Electronic Codebook. (This table was prepared February 2008.)

Table 113. Percentage of children demonstrating specific mental skills, physical skills, and secure emotional attachment to parents at about 2 years of age, by selected characteristics: 2003–04

		Percent of children who demonstrate skills or secure emotional attachment											
Selected characteristic	Percentage distribution of children[1]	Specific mental skills[2]					Specific physical skills[2]						Secure emotional attachment to parents[3]
		Receptive vocabulary[4]	Expressive vocabulary[5]	Listening comprehension[6]	Matching/ discrimination[7]	Early counting[8]	Skillful walking[9]	Balance[10]	Fine motor control[11]	Uses stairs[12]	Alternating balance[13]	Motor planning[14]	
1	2	3	4	5	6	7	8	9	10	11	12	13	14
Total	100.0 (†)	84.5 (0.38)	63.9 (0.53)	36.6 (0.42)	31.9 (0.39)	3.9 (0.14)	92.6 (0.20)	89.4 (0.33)	55.5 (0.48)	48.1 (0.41)	30.0 (0.47)	10.2 (0.21)	61.6 (1.12)
Sex of child													
Male	51.1 (0.21)	81.4 (0.56)	59.2 (0.76)	32.9 (0.50)	28.4 (0.53)	3.8 (0.16)	92.0 (0.26)	88.4 (0.43)	54.2 (0.52)	46.9 (0.44)	28.7 (0.47)	9.6 (0.20)	55.0 (1.23)
Female	48.9 (0.21)	87.8 (0.38)	68.8 (0.59)	40.6 (0.50)	35.5 (0.48)	4.8 (0.20)	93.2 (0.20)	90.5 (0.32)	56.8 (0.53)	49.3 (0.47)	31.3 (0.55)	10.9 (0.26)	68.4 (1.27)
Race/ethnicity of child													
White	54.7 (0.60)	88.7 (0.40)	70.8 (0.63)	42.2 (0.52)	37.1 (0.49)	5.2 (0.21)	92.8 (0.23)	89.9 (0.38)	55.8 (0.58)	48.4 (0.50)	30.2 (0.59)	10.4 (0.26)	65.7 (1.41)
Black	13.4 (0.29)	79.4 (0.94)	53.7 (1.18)	34.4 (0.86)	25.5 (0.75)	2.2 (0.16)	93.3 (0.40)	87.9 (0.69)	53.5 (0.94)	50.2 (0.65)	28.2 (0.87)	9.4 (0.27)	57.4 (1.84)
Hispanic	24.5 (0.45)	78.3 (1.24)	55.0 (1.41)	31.7 (1.13)	30.7 (0.83)	3.7 (0.16)	91.6 (0.40)	90.0 (0.66)	53.5 (0.76)	47.5 (0.65)	28.2 (0.66)	9.9 (0.29)	60.9 (2.28)
Asian	2.5 (0.10)	83.2 (0.70)	67.7 (1.00)	39.8 (0.81)	36.7 (0.82)	4.5 (0.30)	95.3 (0.27)	89.6 (0.50)	56.9 (0.73)	49.5 (0.61)	31.8 (0.74)	11.2 (0.37)	62.4 (2.14)
Pacific Islander	0.2 (0.05)	78.9 (4.01)	59.4 (5.41)	36.3 (4.24)	21.7 (3.56)	1.4 (0.36)	95.2 (1.20)	90.0 (1.92)	55.0 (3.94)	47.2 (2.92)	28.9 (3.18)	9.7 (1.37)	‡ (5.19)
American Indian/Alaska Native	0.5 (0.06)	74.9 (4.10)	49.5 (5.70)	33.8 (5.41)	21.7 (3.24)	1.1 (0.46)	92.4 (0.53)	89.1 (0.92)	54.5 (1.30)	47.2 (1.07)	28.9 (1.19)	9.7 (0.53)	46.3 (3.12)
More than one race	3.9 (0.29)	85.0 (0.98)	64.5 (1.60)	37.0 (1.36)	32.2 (1.35)	3.7 (0.57)	92.4 (0.53)	89.1 (0.92)	54.5 (1.30)	47.2 (1.07)	28.9 (1.19)	9.7 (0.53)	61.6 (3.12)
Age of child													
22 months	2.0 (0.30)	78.1 (2.15)	53.1 (2.70)	28.4 (2.34)	24.5 (2.31)	2.9 (1.01)	90.9 (1.68)	86.5 (2.79)	53.4 (3.05)	46.5 (2.70)	29.2 (2.77)	10.6 (1.58)	65.1 (5.06)
23 months	45.3 (1.02)	86.5 (0.54)	60.1 (0.66)	33.4 (0.57)	25.8 (0.41)	2.8 (0.13)	95.9 (0.27)	88.0 (0.45)	54.3 (0.59)	47.0 (0.49)	30.4 (0.53)	9.7 (0.22)	62.7 (1.40)
24 months	38.9 (0.82)	86.9 (0.42)	56.6 (0.80)	34.9 (0.91)	34.3 (0.56)	4.6 (0.23)	95.0 (0.33)	90.2 (0.50)	57.5 (0.57)	48.6 (0.49)	30.4 (0.25)	10.7 (0.25)	60.8 (1.65)
25 months	13.7 (0.54)	87.4 (0.58)	68.3 (0.91)	40.3 (0.78)	35.4 (0.77)	5.0 (0.35)	95.0 (0.35)	90.2 (0.56)	57.5 (0.79)	50.0 (0.68)	32.4 (0.81)	11.4 (0.40)	59.8 (1.90)
Primary type of care arrangement[15]													
No regular nonparental arrangement	50.8 (0.75)	83.4 (0.50)	62.0 (0.70)	34.8 (0.56)	30.2 (0.52)	3.3 (0.17)	92.2 (0.26)	88.8 (0.43)	54.5 (0.55)	47.2 (0.47)	29.0 (0.52)	9.7 (0.22)	62.1 (1.35)
Home-based care	18.6 (0.63)	83.2 (0.70)	61.6 (1.04)	34.7 (0.84)	30.1 (0.78)	3.6 (0.29)	92.7 (0.30)	89.7 (0.46)	55.8 (0.79)	48.3 (0.67)	30.1 (0.77)	10.3 (0.35)	57.5 (1.93)
Relative care[16]	14.5 (0.51)	83.0 (0.72)	61.6 (1.00)	35.6 (0.82)	31.8 (0.82)	3.5 (0.30)	95.3 (0.27)	89.6 (0.50)	56.9 (0.73)	49.5 (0.61)	31.8 (0.74)	11.2 (0.37)	64.6 (2.23)
Nonrelative care[17]	4.1 (0.09)	81.7 (5.66)	63.1 (6.99)	38.0 (5.92)	33.8 (5.88)	6.2 (2.87)	91.3 (1.70)	87.1 (2.97)	52.4 (3.41)	45.8 (2.92)	27.9 (3.29)	9.8 (1.62)	72.2 (8.48)
Center-based care[18]	15.6 (0.57)	89.4 (0.60)	67.2 (0.74)	37.3 (0.74)	35.6 (0.74)	5.3 (0.47)	93.3 (0.31)	90.5 (0.52)	56.6 (0.73)	49.1 (0.61)	30.9 (0.74)	11.6 (0.35)	64.6 (1.87)
Multiple arrangements[19]	10.5 (0.09)	85.0 (1.00)	64.8 (1.60)	38.0 (1.36)	33.8 (1.35)	6.2 (0.57)	92.4 (0.53)	89.1 (0.92)	54.5 (1.30)	47.2 (1.07)	27.9 (1.19)	9.8 (0.53)	59.8 (8.48)
Mother's employment status													
Full-time (35 hours or more)	34.3 (0.77)	85.6 (0.57)	65.8 (0.83)	39.2 (0.64)	34.4 (0.62)	4.2 (0.24)	93.0 (0.24)	90.1 (0.42)	56.7 (0.65)	49.1 (0.56)	31.2 (0.66)	10.8 (0.31)	59.8 (1.58)
Part-time (less than 35 hours)	20.2 (0.66)	86.6 (0.64)	67.0 (0.98)	39.7 (0.80)	34.8 (0.80)	4.7 (0.37)	92.8 (0.34)	89.8 (0.47)	55.5 (1.04)	48.7 (0.85)	29.8 (0.60)	10.1 (0.30)	62.8 (1.54)
Looking for work	6.3 (0.30)	80.1 (1.28)	56.6 (1.77)	30.2 (1.33)	25.8 (1.20)	1.9 (0.04)	92.2 (0.48)	88.8 (0.81)	53.8 (1.04)	46.7 (0.85)	29.2 (0.54)	9.9 (0.37)	65.0 (3.07)
Not in labor force	38.8 (0.82)	83.1 (0.56)	56.1 (0.77)	34.7 (0.63)	30.1 (0.60)	3.4 (0.21)	92.2 (0.26)	88.8 (0.42)	54.7 (0.56)	47.3 (0.48)	30.5 (0.34)	9.9 (0.24)	56.9 (1.41)
No mother in household	0.4 (0.10)	79.3 (4.59)	54.8 (6.99)	30.5 (5.93)	26.8 (5.54)	5.1 (2.84)	95.8 (1.33)	91.2 (2.31)	57.5 (3.88)	49.9 (3.08)	31.7 (3.45)	10.7 (1.38)	56.9 (9.41)
Parents' highest level of education													
Less than high school	12.6 (0.38)	76.5 (0.97)	50.4 (1.28)	25.4 (0.66)	21.5 (0.78)	1.5 (0.13)	91.4 (0.43)	87.2 (0.71)	52.7 (0.84)	47.8 (0.69)	27.4 (0.71)	9.0 (0.28)	51.8 (2.87)
High school completion	26.6 (0.61)	81.6 (0.61)	58.8 (1.06)	36.7 (0.70)	27.4 (0.66)	2.5 (0.17)	92.4 (0.31)	89.4 (0.50)	52.6 (0.69)	47.9 (0.65)	29.7 (0.65)	10.0 (0.31)	54.8 (1.80)
Some college/vocational	28.3 (0.45)	84.5 (0.61)	64.1 (1.11)	42.5 (0.99)	31.8 (0.66)	4.2 (0.21)	92.6 (0.31)	89.0 (0.49)	55.6 (0.67)	49.1 (0.57)	30.9 (0.64)	10.4 (0.37)	62.6 (1.80)
Bachelor's degree	17.3 (0.39)	88.5 (0.60)	71.0 (1.13)	43.0 (0.97)	37.4 (0.98)	5.3 (0.27)	93.0 (0.36)	90.5 (0.52)	56.6 (0.80)	49.0 (0.68)	30.8 (0.77)	10.6 (0.35)	67.1 (2.12)
Any graduate education	15.4 (0.39)	90.4 (0.60)	74.7 (0.93)	46.5 (0.79)	41.4 (0.78)	7.1 (0.37)	93.0 (0.36)	90.2 (0.61)	56.5 (0.80)	48.9 (0.68)	30.8 (0.77)	10.6 (0.35)	72.8 (1.90)
Poverty status[20]													
Below poverty threshold	23.0 (0.80)	78.7 (0.85)	54.6 (1.11)	29.0 (0.81)	24.8 (0.72)	2.1 (0.18)	91.8 (0.32)	88.1 (0.53)	54.1 (0.70)	46.8 (0.60)	28.8 (0.67)	9.6 (0.28)	52.7 (1.73)
At or above poverty threshold	77.0 (0.80)	86.2 (0.37)	66.7 (0.53)	38.9 (0.44)	34.0 (0.42)	4.4 (0.18)	92.8 (0.21)	88.8 (0.35)	55.9 (0.53)	48.4 (0.45)	30.3 (0.51)	10.4 (0.23)	64.2 (1.22)
Socioeconomic status[21]													
Lowest 20 percent	19.0 (0.53)	77.3 (0.87)	51.6 (1.11)	26.4 (0.81)	22.5 (0.71)	1.6 (0.20)	91.7 (0.34)	88.0 (0.57)	53.6 (0.74)	46.4 (0.63)	28.2 (0.68)	9.4 (0.28)	51.5 (2.06)
Middle 60 percent	60.4 (0.55)	84.5 (0.46)	63.9 (0.68)	36.4 (0.55)	31.5 (0.51)	3.5 (0.17)	92.5 (0.24)	89.4 (0.40)	55.9 (0.59)	48.1 (0.51)	30.3 (0.58)	10.9 (0.29)	61.4 (1.43)
Highest 20 percent	20.5 (0.55)	91.1 (0.44)	75.4 (0.80)	46.7 (0.70)	41.5 (0.70)	7.0 (0.38)	93.4 (0.24)	90.8 (0.41)	57.2 (0.65)	49.5 (0.51)	31.5 (0.64)	10.9 (0.29)	71.5 (1.86)

†Not applicable.
[1] Distribution of weighted Early Childhood Longitudinal Study, Birth Cohort survey population between 22 and 25 months of age.
[2] Based on assessments collected using the Bayley Short Form Research Edition (BSF-R), a shortened field method of administering the Bayley Scales of Infant Development-II (BSID-II) (Bayley 1993). The scores are fully equaled with the BSID-II. The proficiency probabilities indicate mastery of a specific skill or ability within mental or physical domains.
[3] Secure attachment was measured by trained observers using Toddler Attachment Sort-45 Item (TAS-45) assessment. The formation of secure attachments in early childhood is an indicator that the child is able to use the parent as a secure base from which to explore novel stimuli in the environment freely and acquire a sense of self-confidence and adaptability to new and challenging situations. Other possible scale classifications in this metric were avoidant, ambivalent, and disorganized/disoriented.
[4] Ability to recognize and understand spoken words or to indicate a named object by pointing.
[5] Verbal expressiveness using gestures, words, and sentences.
[6] Ability to understand actions depicted by a story, in pictures, or by verbal instructions.
[7] Ability to match objects by their properties (e.g., color) or differentiate one object from another.
[8] Knowledge of counting words, knowledge of ordinality, and understanding of simple quantities.
[9] Ability to walk independently.
[10] Ability to maintain balance when changing position.
[11] Ability to use fine motor control with hands, such as grasping a pencil or holding a piece of paper while scribbling.
[12] Ability to walk up and down stairs, with and without alternating feet.
[13] Ability to maintain balance when changing position or when in motion, such as jumping.
[14] Ability to anticipate, regulate, and execute motor movements, such as being able to attempt to replicate the motions of others.
[15] The type of nonparental care in which the child spent the most hours.
[16] Care provided in the child's home or in another private home by a relative (excluding parents).
[17] Care provided in the child's home or in another private home by a person unrelated to the child.
[18] Care provided in places such as early learning centers, nursery schools, and preschools, including Head Start.
[19] Children who spent an equal amount of time in each of two or more arrangements.
[20] Poverty status based on Census Bureau guidelines from 2002, which identify a dollar amount determined to meet a household's needs, given its size and composition. In 2002, a family of four was considered to live below the poverty threshold if its income was less than or equal to $18,392.
[21] Socioeconomic status (SES) was measured by a composite score on parental education and occupations, and family income.
NOTE: Estimates weighted by W2R0. Estimates pertain to children assessed between 22 months and 25 months of age. Children younger than 22 months (less than 1 percent of the survey population) and children older than 25 months (approximately 9 percent of the survey population) are excluded from this table. Race categories exclude persons of Hispanic ethnicity. Detail may not sum to totals because of rounding. Standard errors appear in parentheses.
SOURCE: U.S. Department of Education, National Center for Education Statistics, Early Childhood Longitudinal Study, Birth Cohort 9-month–Preschool Restricted-Use Data File and Electronic Codebook. (This table was prepared February 2008.)

Table 114. Children's specific language, literacy, mathematics, color knowledge, and fine motor skills at about 4 years of age, by age of child and selected characteristics: 2005–06

Age and selected characteristic	Percentage distribution of children	Language		Literacy				Mathematics		Color knowledge—percent scoring 10 out of 10[9]	Fine motor score[10]
		Receptive vocabulary score[1]	Expressive vocabulary score[2]	Overall literacy score[3]	Percent proficient at letter recognition[4]	Phonological awareness score[5]	Conventions of print score[6]	Overall mathematics score[7]	Percent proficient in numbers and shapes[8]		
1	2	3	4	5	6	7	8	9	10	11	12
Less than 48 months											
Total	† (†)	7.8 (0.07)	2.1 (0.04)	10.7 (0.23)	22.9 (0.92)	3.0 (0.03)	2.0 (0.05)	18.7 (0.25)	44.8 (1.42)	49.0 (1.89)	2.5 (0.05)
48 through 57 months											
Total	100.0 (†)	8.6 (0.03)	2.4 (0.02)	13.2 (0.14)	32.7 (0.55)	3.3 (0.02)	2.5 (0.03)	22.8 (0.15)	65.4 (0.75)	63.6 (0.84)	3.4 (0.02)
Sex of child											
Male	51.6 (0.48)	8.4 (0.04)	2.3 (0.03)	12.7 (0.18)	30.8 (0.68)	3.3 (0.02)	2.4 (0.03)	22.3 (0.19)	62.3 (1.00)	61.3 (1.11)	3.1 (0.04)
Female	48.4 (0.48)	8.8 (0.05)	2.6 (0.02)	13.7 (0.20)	34.8 (0.76)	3.4 (0.03)	2.6 (0.04)	23.3 (0.18)	68.7 (0.93)	66.1 (1.29)	3.7 (0.04)
Race/ethnicity of child											
White	54.7 (0.69)	9.2 (0.05)	2.6 (0.03)	14.2 (0.21)	36.8 (0.79)	3.5 (0.03)	2.7 (0.04)	24.2 (0.21)	73.1 (0.99)	71.0 (1.11)	3.5 (0.03)
Black	13.3 (0.37)	8.0 (0.08)	2.4 (0.04)	12.0 (0.31)	28.3 (1.24)	3.2 (0.04)	2.3 (0.06)	20.6 (0.34)	54.7 (1.85)	55.3 (2.44)	3.2 (0.06)
Hispanic	24.9 (0.56)	7.4 (0.08)	2.1 (0.04)	12.0 (0.25)	23.0 (1.00)	3.0 (0.03)	2.0 (0.05)	20.1 (0.27)	51.4 (1.48)	50.2 (1.79)	3.3 (0.06)
Asian	2.5 (0.13)	7.9 (0.09)	2.1 (0.05)	17.5 (0.38)	49.4 (1.48)	3.9 (0.05)	3.3 (0.07)	26.3 (0.32)	81.2 (1.52)	70.7 (2.36)	4.5 (0.09)
Pacific Islander	0.1 (0.03)	‡ (†)	‡ (†)	‡ (†)	‡ (†)	‡ (†)	‡ (†)	‡ (†)	‡ (†)	‡ (†)	‡ (†)
American Indian/Alaska Native	0.5 (0.05)	7.9 (0.16)	2.1 (0.09)	9.6 (0.62)	18.8 (2.42)	2.9 (0.08)	1.8 (0.12)	17.6 (0.83)	39.9 (3.33)	43.9 (3.83)	3.0 (0.18)
More than one race	3.9 (0.31)	9.0 (0.12)	2.5 (0.05)	13.9 (0.51)	35.4 (1.88)	3.5 (0.08)	2.7 (0.10)	23.0 (0.56)	65.4 (2.71)	63.1 (2.97)	3.5 (0.11)
Primary type of care arrangement[11]											
No regular nonparental arrangement	18.2 (0.69)	8.1 (0.10)	2.3 (0.04)	11.4 (0.26)	25.6 (1.00)	3.1 (0.04)	2.2 (0.05)	20.6 (0.32)	53.4 (1.63)	51.6 (2.04)	3.1 (0.05)
Home-based care											
Relative care[12]	13.1 (0.65)	8.3 (0.09)	2.3 (0.05)	11.4 (0.31)	25.8 (1.23)	3.1 (0.04)	2.2 (0.06)	20.9 (0.31)	55.4 (1.69)	53.4 (2.58)	3.2 (0.07)
Nonrelative care[13]	7.5 (0.40)	8.6 (0.13)	2.5 (0.07)	12.8 (0.33)	31.5 (1.31)	3.3 (0.05)	2.4 (0.06)	23.2 (0.45)	67.6 (2.26)	63.8 (2.72)	3.3 (0.09)
Head Start	13.2 (0.73)	7.9 (0.08)	2.3 (0.05)	11.2 (0.23)	25.0 (0.91)	3.1 (0.03)	2.1 (0.05)	20.6 (0.30)	54.7 (1.79)	52.6 (2.55)	3.2 (0.07)
Other center-based care[14]	46.3 (0.83)	9.0 (0.04)	2.6 (0.03)	14.9 (0.22)	39.5 (0.84)	3.6 (0.03)	2.8 (0.04)	24.6 (0.21)	75.0 (0.91)	73.5 (1.19)	3.6 (0.04)
Multiple arrangements[15]	1.8 (0.23)	8.6 (0.22)	2.5 (0.10)	12.7 (0.64)	30.8 (2.49)	3.3 (0.08)	2.4 (0.12)	22.5 (0.71)	65.3 (4.67)	67.1 (5.44)	3.2 (0.23)
Mother's employment status											
Full-time (35 hours or more)	39.4 (0.85)	8.6 (0.05)	2.5 (0.03)	13.4 (0.21)	33.6 (0.82)	3.4 (0.03)	2.6 (0.04)	23.3 (0.18)	68.3 (0.90)	67.5 (1.09)	3.5 (0.05)
Part-time (less than 35 hours)	19.6 (0.60)	8.8 (0.07)	2.5 (0.04)	13.7 (0.24)	34.6 (0.94)	3.4 (0.03)	2.6 (0.05)	23.4 (0.26)	69.0 (1.24)	63.5 (2.06)	3.5 (0.05)
Looking for work	5.6 (0.34)	7.9 (0.14)	2.2 (0.07)	10.7 (0.39)	23.2 (1.55)	3.0 (0.05)	2.0 (0.08)	19.7 (0.58)	47.5 (3.00)	47.1 (3.83)	3.0 (0.11)
Not in labor force	34.6 (0.87)	8.6 (0.07)	2.4 (0.03)	13.1 (0.25)	32.5 (0.96)	3.3 (0.04)	2.5 (0.05)	22.4 (0.27)	63.2 (1.40)	62.1 (1.42)	3.3 (0.04)
No mother in household	0.8 (0.14)	8.2 (0.33)	2.2 (0.23)	10.7 (0.80)	23.4 (3.19)	3.0 (0.10)	2.0 (0.16)	20.6 (1.02)	53.8 (6.85)	58.7 (8.37)	3.0 (0.21)
Parents' highest level of education											
Less than high school	9.8 (0.42)	7.1 (0.12)	1.9 (0.06)	8.9 (0.27)	16.0 (1.07)	2.7 (0.04)	1.7 (0.06)	17.9 (0.38)	39.5 (2.07)	36.9 (2.75)	3.1 (0.09)
High school completion	25.1 (0.78)	7.9 (0.06)	2.3 (0.04)	10.6 (0.18)	22.8 (0.71)	3.0 (0.03)	2.0 (0.04)	19.9 (0.24)	50.5 (1.44)	51.3 (1.61)	3.1 (0.04)
Some college/vocational	32.0 (0.75)	8.6 (0.06)	2.5 (0.04)	12.4 (0.21)	29.8 (0.80)	3.2 (0.03)	2.4 (0.04)	22.4 (0.22)	64.5 (1.13)	64.5 (1.17)	3.4 (0.04)
Bachelor's degree	17.0 (0.57)	9.2 (0.07)	2.7 (0.04)	15.4 (0.28)	41.6 (1.12)	3.6 (0.04)	3.0 (0.05)	25.5 (0.21)	81.0 (1.04)	75.6 (1.68)	3.7 (0.08)
Any graduate education	16.2 (0.49)	9.7 (0.08)	2.7 (0.04)	18.1 (0.30)	51.9 (1.13)	4.0 (0.04)	3.5 (0.06)	27.4 (0.24)	86.0 (1.08)	81.0 (1.48)	3.9 (0.05)
Poverty status[16]											
Below poverty threshold	24.9 (0.71)	7.7 (0.06)	2.1 (0.03)	9.9 (0.17)	20.1 (0.68)	2.9 (0.02)	1.9 (0.04)	18.9 (0.22)	44.8 (1.39)	46.8 (1.76)	3.1 (0.05)
At or above poverty threshold	75.1 (0.71)	8.9 (0.03)	2.5 (0.02)	14.2 (0.16)	36.7 (0.60)	3.5 (0.02)	2.7 (0.03)	24.0 (0.16)	71.8 (0.76)	68.8 (0.91)	3.5 (0.03)
Socioeconomic status[17]											
Lowest 20 percent	19.6 (0.57)	7.3 (0.07)	2.0 (0.04)	9.2 (0.20)	17.2 (0.78)	2.8 (0.03)	1.7 (0.04)	18.0 (0.29)	40.1 (1.73)	42.8 (2.14)	3.0 (0.06)
Middle 60 percent	60.1 (0.79)	8.6 (0.04)	2.5 (0.03)	12.7 (0.14)	30.8 (0.55)	3.3 (0.02)	2.4 (0.03)	22.6 (0.17)	65.3 (0.94)	63.5 (1.06)	3.4 (0.03)
Highest 20 percent	20.3 (0.68)	9.8 (0.07)	2.8 (0.03)	18.0 (0.28)	51.2 (1.06)	4.0 (0.04)	3.4 (0.05)	27.5 (0.22)	87.1 (0.95)	81.7 (1.50)	3.9 (0.05)
58 or more months											
Total	† (†)	9.0 (0.11)	2.6 (0.04)	16.0 (0.35)	43.5 (1.31)	3.7 (0.05)	3.1 (0.07)	26.2 (0.31)	79.0 (1.20)	71.1 (2.09)	4.1 (0.07)

†Not applicable.
‡Reporting standards not met.
[1]Ability to recognize and understand spoken words or to indicate a named object by pointing. Potential score ranges from 0 to 15.
[2]Verbal expressiveness using gestures, words, and sentences. Potential score ranges from 0 to 5.
[3]Includes letter recognition, in both receptive and expressive modes; letter sounds; and early reading knowledge and skills. Potential score ranges from 0 to 37.
[4]Ability to identify a letter by either its name or the sounds it makes. Average score can be interpreted as the percentage of children who were proficient at recognizing the letters of the alphabet. Potential score ranges from 0 to 100.
[5]Measures understanding of the sounds and structure of spoken language, including rhyming, blending, segmenting, deleting, and substituting words, syllables, and sounds. Potential score ranges from 0 to 8.
[6]Understanding of what print represents and how it works. Potential score ranges from 0 to 44.
[7]Includes number sense, geometry, counting, operations, and patterns. Potential score ranges from 0 to 100.
[8]Ability to recognize single-digit numbers and basic geometric shapes. Average score can be interpreted as the percentage of children who were proficient. Potential score ranges from 0 to 100.
[9]Percentage of children who scored 10 on a test with a potential score range of 0 to 10. These children were able to name the colors of five pictured objects (2 points per correct answer).

[10]Measures the ability to use fine motor skills in drawing basic forms and shapes. Potential score ranges from 0 to 7.
[11]The type of nonparental care in which the child spent the most hours.
[12]Care provided in the child's home or in another private home by a relative (excluding parents).
[13]Care provided in the child's home or in another private home by a person unrelated to the child.
[14]Care provided in places such as early learning centers, nursery schools, and preschools, excluding Head Start.
[15]Children who spent an equal amount of time in each of two or more arrangements.
[16]Poverty status based on Census Bureau guidelines from 2002, which identify a dollar amount determined to meet a household's needs, given its size and composition. In 2002, a family of four was considered to live below the poverty threshold if its income was less than or equal to $18,392.
[17]Socioeconomic status (SES) was measured by a composite score on parental education and occupations, and family income.
NOTE: Estimates weighted by W3R0. Race categories exclude persons of Hispanic ethnicity. Detail may not sum to totals because of rounding. Standard errors appear in parentheses.
SOURCE: U.S. Department of Education, National Center for Education Statistics, Early Childhood Longitudinal Study, Birth Cohort 9-month–Preschool Restricted-Use Data File and Electronic Codebook. (This table was prepared April 2008.)

Table 115. Mean reading scale scores and specific reading skills of fall 1998 first-time kindergartners, by time of assessment and selected characteristics: Selected years, fall 1998 through spring 2004

Selected characteristic	Mean reading scale score						Score gain, fall 1998 to spring 2004	Percentage of children with specific reading skills, fifth grade, spring 2004		
	Kindergarten		First grade		Third grade, spring 2002	Fifth grade, spring 2004		Deriving meaning from text	Interpreting beyond text	Evaluating nonfiction
	Fall 1998	Spring 1999	Fall 1999	Spring 2000						
1	2	3	4	5	6	7	8	9	10	11
Total	30 (0.4)	41 (0.6)	48 (0.7)	72 (0.9)	120 (1.1)	141 (1.0)	111 (0.8)	75 (1.4)	47 (1.2)	8 (0.7)
Sex										
Male	29 (0.5)	41 (0.6)	48 (0.7)	73 (1.0)	119 (1.1)	141 (1.2)	112 (1.0)	76 (1.6)	48 (1.3)	7 (0.8)
Female	30 (0.5)	42 (0.8)	48 (0.9)	72 (1.2)	120 (1.5)	140 (1.3)	110 (1.1)	74 (1.9)	47 (1.5)	8 (0.9)
Race/ethnicity										
White	31 (0.4)	43 (0.7)	49 (0.7)	75 (1.0)	124 (0.9)	145 (0.9)	114 (0.8)	81 (1.2)	53 (1.1)	9 (0.8)
Black	26 (0.7)	38 (1.1)	43 (1.1)	64 (1.7)	107 (2.3)	129 (1.8)	102 (1.7)	58 (2.7)	33 (2.0)	2 (0.4)
Hispanic	29 (1.2)	41 (1.2)	47 (1.4)	69 (1.8)	117 (2.6)	137 (2.2)	108 (1.9)	72 (3.5)	43 (2.3)	4 (0.9)
Asian/Pacific Islander	32 (3.1)	44 (4.6)	52 (5.3)	75 (7.1)	117 (7.8)	143 (4.0)	111 (1.9)	79 (4.4)	49 (5.9)	11 (4.3)
Other	27 (2.2)	38 (2.5)	44 (3.6)	68 (5.4)	109 (9.6)	131 (8.4)	104 (6.2)	61 (12.1)	38 (8.8)	7 (5.3)
Parents' highest level of education[1]										
Less than high school	23 (0.7)	32 (0.9)	33 (1.4)	57 (2.9)	93 (3.1)	117 (3.0)	94 (2.9)	42 (4.7)	24 (2.5)	1 (0.2)
High school	26 (0.4)	38 (0.8)	42 (1.0)	65 (1.4)	112 (2.2)	134 (1.9)	108 (1.7)	67 (2.7)	39 (2.2)	3 (0.6)
Some college	29 (0.4)	41 (0.5)	47 (0.7)	71 (0.9)	120 (1.5)	140 (1.4)	111 (1.3)	75 (2.1)	46 (1.6)	6 (1.0)
Bachelor's or higher	34 (0.7)	47 (1.1)	54 (1.2)	82 (1.6)	130 (1.2)	151 (1.3)	117 (0.8)	88 (1.5)	60 (1.7)	13 (1.6)
Socioeconomic status[1]										
Lowest 20 percent	23 (0.4)	33 (0.7)	38 (0.9)	57 (1.7)	95 (2.4)	119 (1.9)	96 (1.8)	44 (3.1)	25 (1.7)	1 (0.3)
Middle 60 percent	29 (0.4)	41 (0.5)	47 (0.7)	72 (0.8)	120 (1.2)	140 (1.1)	112 (1.0)	76 (1.6)	46 (1.3)	6 (0.6)
Highest 20 percent	35 (0.9)	48 (1.3)	55 (1.5)	82 (2.0)	132 (1.2)	153 (1.6)	118 (1.0)	90 (1.7)	62 (2.2)	16 (2.3)
Number of family risk factors[1,2]										
No risks	32 (0.5)	44 (0.7)	51 (0.8)	77 (1.0)	127 (1.0)	147 (1.0)	115 (0.9)	84 (1.3)	55 (1.3)	10 (1.0)
One risk	27 (0.5)	39 (0.7)	44 (0.8)	68 (1.1)	114 (1.5)	135 (1.2)	109 (1.0)	70 (1.7)	40 (1.4)	4 (0.6)
Two or more risks	25 (0.6)	35 (1.3)	40 (1.0)	59 (1.5)	99 (2.3)	122 (2.2)	97 (1.9)	47 (3.6)	27 (2.0)	2 (0.5)
Kindergarten program type										
Half-day program	30 (0.6)	41 (0.8)	47 (0.8)	73 (1.2)	123 (1.3)	144 (1.1)	114 (1.0)	80 (1.6)	52 (1.2)	9 (0.9)
Full-day program	29 (0.5)	42 (0.8)	48 (1.0)	72 (1.3)	117 (1.7)	138 (1.6)	109 (1.2)	71 (2.2)	44 (1.8)	6 (0.9)
School type across all waves of the study										
Public school all years	29 (0.4)	40 (0.5)	46 (0.6)	71 (0.9)	118 (1.3)	139 (1.2)	110 (1.0)	73 (1.7)	46 (1.4)	7 (0.7)
Private school all years	35 (1.0)	47 (1.3)	56 (1.6)	85 (2.2)	131 (1.9)	153 (1.7)	118 (1.0)	91 (1.7)	62 (2.3)	13 (2.3)
Change in school type during study	32 (1.7)	45 (2.6)	52 (2.5)	77 (3.7)	123 (2.9)	143 (3.3)	111 (2.1)	78 (4.8)	49 (4.2)	9 (3.5)

[1]Status during kindergarten year.
[2]Family risk factors included living below the federal poverty level, primary home language was not English, mother's highest education was less than a high school diploma/GED, and living in a single-parent household. Values range from 0 to 4.
NOTE: Detail may not sum to totals because of rounding. Estimates reflect the sample of children assessed in English in all assessment years. ECLS-K was not administered in 2000–01, when most of the children in the sample were in second grade. Most of the children were in first grade in 1999–2000, but 5 percent were in kindergarten or other grades (e.g., second grade, ungraded classrooms); most were in third grade in 2001–02, but 11 percent were in second grade or other grades (e.g., fourth

grade, ungraded classrooms); most were in fifth grade in 2003–04, but 14 percent were in fourth grade or other grades (e.g., sixth grade). Reading scale ranges from 0 to 186. Data were calculated using C1_6FC0 weight and therefore differ from previously published figures. Race categories exclude persons of Hispanic ethnicity. Standard errors appear in parentheses.
SOURCE: U.S. Department of Education, National Center for Education Statistics, Early Childhood Longitudinal Study, Kindergarten Class of 1998–99 (ECLS-K), Longitudinal Kindergarten–Third Grade Public-Use Data File, fall 1998, spring 1999, fall 1999, spring 2000, and spring 2002, and Fifth-Grade Restricted-Use Data File. (This table was prepared September 2006.)

Table 116. Mean mathematics and science scale scores and specific mathematics skills of fall 1998 first-time kindergartners, by time of assessment and selected characteristics: Selected years, fall 1998 through spring 2004

Selected characteristic	Mathematics — Mean scale score							Percentage of children with specific skills, fifth grade, spring 2004			Science — Mean scale score		
	Kindergarten — Fall 1998	Kindergarten — Spring 1999	First grade — Fall 1999	First grade — Spring 2000	Third grade, spring 2002	Fifth grade, spring 2004	Score gain, fall 1998 to spring 2004	Place value	Rate and measurement	Fractions	Third grade, spring 2002	Fifth grade, spring 2004	Score gain, spring 2002 to spring 2004
1	2	3	4	5	6	7	8	9	10	11	12	13	14
Total	23 (0.3)	34 (0.4)	41 (0.6)	58 (0.6)	93 (1.0)	114 (1.0)	91 (0.8)	77 (1.7)	46 (1.7)	15 (1.1)	46 (0.6)	58 (0.7)	13 (0.4)
Sex													
Male	24 (0.4)	35 (0.5)	42 (0.8)	60 (0.9)	97 (1.1)	118 (1.1)	94 (1.0)	83 (1.9)	52 (2.0)	20 (1.6)	48 (0.6)	61 (0.7)	13 (0.4)
Female	23 (0.4)	33 (0.6)	40 (0.6)	57 (0.7)	89 (1.3)	110 (1.3)	88 (1.0)	72 (2.1)	40 (2.1)	11 (1.3)	43 (0.9)	55 (0.9)	12 (0.6)
Race/ethnicity													
White	25 (0.3)	36 (0.5)	43 (0.5)	62 (0.7)	98 (0.8)	119 (0.8)	94 (0.7)	84 (1.3)	54 (1.5)	19 (1.3)	49 (0.7)	62 (0.5)	13 (0.5)
Black	19 (0.5)	28 (0.7)	33 (0.8)	49 (1.0)	78 (1.8)	99 (2.2)	80 (1.9)	55 (4.0)	19 (2.0)	3 (0.8)	35 (1.1)	47 (1.3)	12 (0.5)
Hispanic	22 (0.7)	32 (0.9)	39 (0.9)	56 (1.1)	93 (1.7)	112 (2.0)	90 (1.6)	77 (3.0)	42 (3.8)	12 (2.5)	43 (1.2)	56 (1.2)	13 (0.7)
Asian/Pacific Islander	23 (2.2)	32 (3.7)	41 (3.4)	56 (5.4)	88 (8.6)	116 (5.8)	93 (3.8)	75 (11.2)	47 (11.7)	18 (5.8)	43 (5.5)	58 (4.9)	15 (1.4)
Other	21 (2.8)	31 (2.9)	38 (3.9)	54 (3.2)	87 (8.6)	106 (8.1)	86 (5.6)	65 (14.1)	38 (10.1)	13 (5.3)	41 (4.4)	52 (5.3)	12 (1.1)
Parents' highest level of education[1]													
Less than high school	16 (0.6)	24 (1.1)	29 (1.2)	44 (1.8)	71 (2.0)	90 (2.8)	74 (2.4)	40 (4.3)	13 (2.6)	2 (1.0)	34 (1.8)	43 (1.8)	9 (1.4)
High school	21 (0.6)	30 (0.7)	36 (0.9)	53 (1.2)	85 (1.6)	107 (1.7)	86 (1.2)	66 (3.0)	32 (2.4)	6 (1.2)	41 (1.2)	54 (1.2)	13 (0.4)
Some college	22 (0.4)	33 (0.6)	40 (0.7)	58 (0.8)	94 (1.3)	114 (1.2)	92 (1.0)	80 (2.1)	44 (2.3)	12 (1.6)	45 (0.7)	58 (0.8)	13 (0.5)
Bachelor's or higher	28 (0.8)	39 (0.8)	48 (1.0)	66 (1.1)	103 (1.3)	125 (1.3)	96 (1.1)	91 (1.5)	66 (2.6)	29 (2.8)	51 (1.0)	64 (0.8)	13 (0.5)
Socioeconomic status[1]													
Lowest 20 percent	17 (0.5)	25 (0.7)	30 (0.9)	45 (1.2)	73 (1.6)	93 (2.1)	76 (1.7)	44 (3.3)	15 (1.5)	2 (0.7)	33 (1.1)	45 (1.2)	11 (0.8)
Middle 60 percent	23 (0.4)	33 (0.5)	40 (0.6)	58 (0.8)	93 (1.2)	114 (1.1)	91 (0.9)	78 (1.9)	44 (2.2)	12 (1.3)	45 (0.7)	58 (0.7)	13 (0.4)
Highest 20 percent	29 (0.9)	40 (1.0)	47 (1.3)	67 (1.4)	106 (1.2)	127 (1.1)	98 (1.0)	94 (0.8)	70 (2.6)	32 (3.4)	53 (1.0)	66 (0.7)	13 (0.7)
Number of family risk factors[1][2]													
No risks	26 (0.4)	36 (0.5)	44 (0.7)	63 (0.8)	99 (0.9)	120 (0.9)	95 (0.8)	87 (1.4)	58 (1.8)	21 (1.5)	49 (0.7)	62 (0.6)	13 (0.4)
One risk	21 (0.4)	31 (0.7)	38 (0.8)	54 (0.9)	90 (1.4)	108 (1.2)	87 (0.9)	69 (2.2)	32 (2.3)	7 (1.0)	43 (0.8)	56 (0.9)	13 (0.7)
Two or more risks	18 (0.6)	26 (0.6)	31 (0.9)	47 (1.1)	75 (2.1)	96 (2.5)	78 (2.0)	49 (4.1)	19 (2.6)	4 (0.9)	34 (1.2)	45 (1.5)	11 (0.7)
Kindergarten program type													
Half-day program	24 (0.4)	34 (0.5)	41 (0.6)	60 (0.7)	96 (0.9)	118 (0.8)	94 (0.7)	84 (1.3)	52 (1.7)	18 (1.5)	48 (0.7)	61 (0.5)	13 (0.5)
Full-day program	23 (0.6)	34 (0.7)	40 (1.0)	58 (1.1)	91 (1.8)	111 (1.7)	88 (1.3)	72 (2.6)	41 (2.8)	13 (1.5)	44 (1.1)	56 (1.1)	13 (0.4)
School type across all waves of the study													
Public school all years	23 (0.4)	33 (0.5)	40 (0.6)	57 (0.7)	92 (1.3)	113 (1.2)	90 (0.9)	75 (1.9)	44 (1.9)	14 (1.2)	45 (0.8)	57 (0.8)	13 (0.4)
Private school all years	29 (0.9)	40 (1.1)	48 (1.3)	68 (1.6)	101 (1.8)	123 (1.6)	93 (1.0)	90 (2.3)	62 (3.6)	19 (3.1)	49 (1.1)	64 (1.0)	14 (0.5)
Change in school type during study	25 (1.3)	35 (1.7)	44 (2.2)	61 (2.3)	95 (2.9)	118 (2.9)	93 (2.1)	84 (4.0)	52 (5.2)	21 (4.2)	48 (2.1)	60 (1.9)	12 (1.2)

[1]Status during kindergarten year.
[2]Family risk factors included living below the federal poverty level, primary home language was not English, mother's highest education was less than a high school diploma/GED, and living in a single-parent household. Values range from 0 to 4.
NOTE: Detail may not sum to totals because of rounding. Estimates reflect sample of children assessed in English in all assessment years. ECLS-K was not administered in 2000–01, when most of the children in the sample were in second grade. Most of the children were in first grade in 1999–2000, but 5 percent were in kindergarten or other grades (e.g., second grade, ungraded classrooms); most were in third grade in 2001–02, but 11 percent were in second grade or other grades (e.g., fourth grade, ungraded classrooms); most were in fifth grade in 2003–04, but 14 percent were in fourth grade or other grades (e.g., sixth grade). Mathematics scale ranges from 0 to 153. Science scale ranges from 0 to 92. Data were calculated using C1_6FC0 weight and therefore differ from previously published figures. Race categories exclude persons of Hispanic ethnicity. Standard errors appear in parentheses.

SOURCE: U.S. Department of Education, National Center for Education Statistics, Early Childhood Longitudinal Study, Kindergarten Class of 1998–99 (ECLS-K), Longitudinal Kindergarten–Third Grade Public-Use Data File, fall 1998, spring 1999, fall 1999, spring 2000, and spring 2002, and Fifth-Grade Restricted-Use Data File. (This table was prepared September 2006.)

Table 117. Average reading scale score, by age and selected student and school characteristics: Selected years, 1971 through 2004

Selected student and school characteristic	1971		1975		1980		1984		1988		1990		1992		1994		1996		1999		2004	
1	2		3		4		5		6		7		8		9		10		11		12	
9-year-olds																						
All students	208	(1.0)	210	(0.7)	215	(1.0)	211	(0.8)	212	(1.1)	209	(1.2)	211	(0.9)	211	(1.2)	212	(1.0)	212	(1.3)	219	(1.1)
Sex																						
Male	201	(1.1)	204	(0.8)	210	(1.1)	207	(1.0)	207	(1.4)	204	(1.7)	206	(1.3)	207	(1.3)	207	(1.4)	209	(1.6)	216	(1.4)
Female	214	(1.0)	216	(0.8)	220	(1.1)	214	(0.9)	216	(1.3)	215	(1.2)	215	(0.9)	215	(1.4)	218	(1.1)	215	(1.5)	221	(1.0)
Race/ethnicity																						
White	214[1]	(0.9)	217	(0.7)	221	(0.8)	218	(0.9)	218	(1.4)	217	(1.3)	218	(1.0)	218	(1.3)	220	(1.2)	221	(1.6)	226	(1.1)
Black	170[1]	(1.7)	181	(1.2)	189	(1.8)	186	(1.3)	189	(2.4)	182	(2.9)	185	(2.2)	185	(2.3)	191	(2.6)	186	(2.3)	200	(2.2)
Hispanic	[2]	(†)	183	(2.2)	190	(2.3)	187	(3.0)	194	(3.5)	189	(2.3)	192	(3.1)	186	(3.9)	195	(3.4)	193	(2.7)	205	(1.7)
Region																						
Northeast	213	(1.7)	215	(1.3)	221	(2.1)	216	(2.2)	215	(2.6)	217	(2.2)	218	(2.6)	217	(2.9)	220	(1.8)	222	(3.5)	223	(2.5)
Southeast	194	(2.9)	201	(1.2)	210	(2.3)	204	(2.0)	207	(2.1)	197	(3.2)	199	(2.0)	208	(3.0)	206	(2.8)	205	(2.3)	218	(1.8)
Central	215	(1.2)	215	(1.2)	217	(1.4)	215	(1.9)	218	(2.2)	213	(2.0)	216	(1.6)	214	(2.3)	215	(2.6)	215	(3.9)	221	(2.3)
West	205	(2.0)	207	(2.0)	213	(1.8)	209	(2.0)	208	(2.6)	210	(2.8)	209	(2.3)	205	(2.8)	210	(1.9)	206	(1.8)	215	(1.5)
13-year-olds																						
All students	255	(0.9)	256	(0.8)	258	(0.9)	257	(0.6)	257	(1.0)	257	(0.8)	260	(1.2)	258	(0.9)	258	(1.0)	259	(1.0)	259	(1.0)
Sex																						
Male	250	(1.0)	250	(0.8)	254	(1.1)	253	(0.7)	252	(1.3)	251	(1.1)	254	(1.7)	251	(1.2)	251	(1.2)	254	(1.3)	254	(1.2)
Female	261	(0.9)	262	(0.9)	263	(0.9)	262	(0.7)	263	(1.0)	263	(1.1)	265	(1.2)	266	(1.2)	264	(1.2)	265	(1.2)	264	(1.3)
Race/ethnicity																						
White	261[1]	(0.7)	262	(0.7)	264	(0.7)	263	(0.6)	261	(1.1)	262	(0.9)	266	(1.2)	265	(1.1)	266	(1.0)	267	(1.2)	266	(1.0)
Black	222[1]	(1.2)	226	(1.2)	233	(1.5)	236	(1.2)	243	(2.4)	241	(2.2)	238	(2.3)	234	(2.4)	234	(2.6)	238	(2.4)	244	(2.0)
Hispanic	[2]	(†)	232	(3.0)	237	(2.0)	240	(2.0)	240	(3.5)	238	(2.3)	239	(3.5)	235	(1.9)	238	(2.9)	244	(2.9)	242	(1.6)
Parents' highest level of education																						
Not high school graduate	—	(†)	—	(†)	239	(1.1)	240	(1.2)	246	(2.1)	241	(1.8)	239	(2.6)	237	(2.4)	239	(2.8)	238	(3.4)	240	(2.7)
Graduated high school	—	(†)	—	(†)	253	(0.9)	253	(0.8)	253	(1.2)	251	(0.9)	252	(1.7)	251	(1.4)	251	(1.5)	251	(1.8)	251	(1.6)
Some education after high school	—	(†)	—	(†)	268	(1.0)	266	(1.1)	265	(1.7)	267	(1.7)	265	(2.7)	266	(1.9)	268	(2.3)	269	(2.4)	264	(2.0)
Graduated college	—	(†)	—	(†)	273	(0.9)	268	(0.9)	265	(1.6)	267	(1.1)	271	(1.5)	269	(1.2)	269	(1.4)	270	(1.2)	270	(1.0)
Region																						
Northeast	261	(2.0)	259	(1.8)	260	(1.8)	261	(0.8)	259	(2.4)	259	(1.8)	265	(3.2)	269	(2.0)	259	(2.6)	263	(2.9)	265	(1.9)
Southeast	245	(1.7)	249	(1.5)	253	(1.6)	256	(1.9)	258	(2.2)	256	(2.2)	254	(2.5)	253	(2.5)	251	(3.3)	254	(2.4)	257	(2.3)
Central	260	(1.8)	261	(1.4)	265	(1.4)	258	(1.3)	256	(2.0)	257	(1.5)	263	(3.0)	259	(3.3)	267	(1.8)	261	(1.9)	260	(2.1)
West	254	(1.3)	253	(1.7)	256	(2.0)	254	(1.1)	258	(2.1)	256	(1.6)	258	(1.6)	253	(2.1)	257	(1.7)	259	(2.2)	255	(1.6)
17-year-olds																						
All students	285	(1.2)	286	(0.8)	285	(1.2)	289	(0.8)	290	(1.0)	290	(1.1)	290	(1.1)	288	(1.3)	288	(1.1)	288	(1.3)	285	(1.2)
Sex																						
Male	279	(1.2)	280	(1.0)	282	(1.3)	284	(0.8)	286	(1.5)	284	(1.6)	284	(1.6)	282	(2.2)	281	(1.3)	281	(1.6)	278	(1.5)
Female	291	(1.3)	291	(1.0)	289	(1.2)	294	(0.9)	294	(1.5)	296	(1.2)	296	(1.1)	295	(1.5)	295	(1.2)	295	(1.4)	292	(1.3)
Race/ethnicity																						
White	291[1]	(1.0)	293	(0.6)	293	(0.9)	295	(0.9)	295	(1.2)	297	(1.2)	297	(1.4)	296	(1.5)	295	(1.2)	295	(1.4)	293	(1.1)
Black	239[1]	(1.7)	241	(2.0)	243	(1.8)	264	(1.2)	274	(2.4)	267	(2.3)	261	(2.1)	266	(3.9)	266	(2.7)	264	(1.7)	264	(2.7)
Hispanic	[2]	(†)	252	(3.6)	261	(2.7)	268	(2.9)	271	(4.3)	275	(3.6)	271	(3.7)	263	(4.9)	265	(4.1)	271	(3.9)	264	(2.9)
Parents' highest level of education																						
Not high school graduate	—	(†)	—	(†)	262	(1.5)	269	(1.4)	267	(2.0)	270	(2.8)	271	(3.9)	268	(2.7)	267	(3.2)	265	(3.6)	259	(3.4)
Graduated high school	—	(†)	—	(†)	277	(1.0)	281	(0.8)	282	(1.3)	283	(1.4)	280	(1.6)	276	(1.9)	273	(1.7)	274	(2.1)	274	(1.6)
Some education after high school	—	(†)	—	(†)	295	(1.2)	298	(0.9)	299	(2.2)	295	(1.9)	293	(1.9)	294	(1.6)	295	(2.2)	295	(1.8)	286	(1.9)
Graduated college	—	(†)	—	(†)	301	(1.0)	302	(0.9)	300	(1.4)	302	(1.5)	301	(1.7)	300	(1.7)	299	(1.5)	298	(1.3)	298	(1.3)
Region																						
Northeast	291	(2.8)	289	(1.7)	286	(2.4)	291	(2.5)	295	(2.9)	296	(1.8)	297	(3.2)	297	(4.2)	292	(2.8)	295	(4.0)	290	(2.5)
Southeast	271	(2.4)	277	(1.4)	280	(2.2)	284	(2.1)	286	(2.1)	285	(2.5)	278	(2.9)	283	(2.8)	279	(2.6)	279	(2.4)	281	(2.1)
Central	291	(2.1)	292	(1.4)	287	(2.2)	290	(1.8)	291	(1.9)	294	(2.4)	294	(2.1)	286	(3.7)	293	(2.1)	292	(1.5)	291	(2.2)
West	284	(1.8)	282	(1.9)	287	(2.1)	289	(1.6)	289	(1.8)	287	(2.6)	290	(2.3)	288	(2.8)	287	(2.4)	286	(3.0)	280	(2.5)

—Not available.
†Not applicable.
[1]Data for 1971 include persons of Hispanic ethnicity.
[2]Test scores of Hispanics were not tabulated separately.
NOTE: The NAEP reading scores have been evaluated at certain performance levels. Scale ranges from 0 to 500. Students scoring 150 (or higher) are able to follow brief written directions and carry out simple, discrete reading tasks. Students scoring 200 are able to understand, combine ideas, and make inferences based on short uncomplicated passages about specific or sequentially related information. Students scoring 250 are able to search for specific information, interrelate ideas, and make generalizations about literature, science, and social studies materials. Students scoring 300 are able to find, understand, summarize, and explain relatively complicated literary and informational material. Includes public and private schools. Excludes persons not enrolled in school and those who were unable to be tested due to limited proficiency in English or due to a disability. Race categories exclude persons of Hispanic ethnicity, except where noted. Some data have been revised from previously published figures. Standard errors appear in parentheses.
SOURCE: U.S. Department of Education, National Center for Education Statistics, National Assessment of Educational Progress (NAEP), *NAEP 2004 Trends in Academic Progress*; and NAEP Data Explorer (http://nces.ed.gov/nationsreportcard/nde/), retrieved January 2006. (This table was prepared February 2006.)

Table 118. Average reading scale score, by sex, grade, race/ethnicity, and percentile: Selected years, 1992 through 2007

Grade, race/ethnicity, and percentile	1992[1]	1994[1]	1998	2000	2002	2003	2005 Total	2005 Male	2005 Female	2007 Total	2007 Male	2007 Female
1	2	3	4	5	6	7	8	9	10	11	12	13
All students												
4th grade	217 (0.9)	214 (1.0)	215 (1.1)	213 (1.3)	219 (0.4)	218 (0.3)	219 (0.2)	216 (0.2)	222 (0.3)	221 (0.3)	218 (0.3)	224 (0.3)
8th grade	260 (0.9)	260 (0.8)	263 (0.8)	— (†)	264 (0.4)	263 (0.3)	262 (0.2)	257 (0.2)	267 (0.2)	263 (0.2)	258 (0.3)	268 (0.3)
12th grade	292 (0.6)	287 (0.7)	290 (0.6)	— (†)	287 (0.7)	— (†)	286 (0.6)	279 (0.8)	292 (0.7)	— (†)	— (†)	— (†)
Race/ethnicity												
4th grade												
White	224 (1.2)	224 (1.3)	225 (1.0)	224 (1.1)	229 (0.3)	229 (0.2)	229 (0.2)	226 (0.3)	232 (0.3)	231 (0.2)	228 (0.3)	234 (0.3)
Black	192 (1.7)	185 (1.8)	193 (1.9)	190 (1.8)	199 (0.5)	198 (0.4)	200 (0.3)	195 (0.4)	205 (0.5)	203 (0.4)	199 (0.5)	208 (0.5)
Hispanic	197 (2.6)	188 (3.4)	193 (3.2)	190 (2.9)	201 (1.3)	200 (0.6)	203 (0.5)	200 (0.5)	205 (0.6)	205 (0.5)	202 (0.6)	208 (0.5)
Asian/Pacific Islander	216 (2.9)	220 (3.8)	215 (5.6)	225 (5.2)	224 (1.6)	226 (1.2)	229 (0.7)	225 (1.0)	232 (0.8)	232 (1.0)	228 (1.1)	236 (1.1)
American Indian/Alaska Native	‡ (†)	211 (6.6)	‡ (†)	214 (6.0)	207 (2.0)	202 (1.4)	204 (1.3)	199 (1.4)	209 (1.6)	203 (1.2)	200 (1.5)	206 (1.5)
8th grade												
White	267 (1.1)	267 (1.0)	270 (0.9)	— (†)	272 (0.4)	272 (0.2)	271 (0.2)	266 (0.2)	277 (0.2)	272 (0.2)	267 (0.3)	277 (0.3)
Black	237 (1.7)	236 (1.8)	244 (1.2)	— (†)	245 (0.7)	244 (0.5)	243 (0.4)	237 (0.5)	249 (0.5)	245 (0.4)	238 (0.5)	251 (0.5)
Hispanic	241 (1.6)	243 (1.2)	243 (1.7)	— (†)	247 (0.8)	245 (0.7)	246 (0.4)	242 (0.5)	251 (0.5)	247 (0.4)	242 (0.6)	251 (0.6)
Asian/Pacific Islander	268 (3.9)	265 (3.0)	264 (7.1)	— (†)	267 (1.7)	270 (1.1)	271 (0.8)	266 (1.0)	275 (1.0)	271 (1.1)	266 (1.3)	275 (1.4)
American Indian/Alaska Native	‡ (†)	248 (4.7)	‡ (†)	— (†)	250 (3.5)	246 (3.0)	249 (1.4)	244 (1.9)	254 (1.7)	247 (1.2)	242 (1.5)	253 (1.5)
12th grade												
White	297 (0.6)	293 (0.7)	297 (0.7)	— (†)	292 (0.7)	— (†)	293 (0.7)	285 (1.0)	300 (0.7)	— (†)	— (†)	— (†)
Black	273 (1.4)	265 (1.6)	269 (1.4)	— (†)	267 (1.3)	— (†)	267 (1.2)	261 (1.7)	272 (1.6)	—	—	—
Hispanic	279 (2.7)	270 (1.7)	275 (1.5)	— (†)	273 (1.5)	— (†)	272 (1.2)	266 (1.7)	277 (1.7)	—	—	—
Asian/Pacific Islander	290 (3.2)	278 (2.4)	287 (2.7)	— (†)	286 (2.0)	— (†)	287 (1.9)	282 (2.8)	292 (2.3)	—	—	—
American Indian/Alaska Native	‡ (†)	274 (5.8)	‡ (†)	— (†)	‡ (†)	— (†)	279 (6.3)	‡	‡ (†)	—	—	—
Percentile[2]												
4th grade												
10th	170 (1.9)	159 (1.5)	163 (2.1)	159 (2.3)	170 (0.9)	169 (0.5)	171 (0.4)	167 (0.3)	175 (0.5)	174 (0.4)	170 (0.5)	179 (0.5)
25th	194 (1.1)	189 (1.1)	191 (1.7)	189 (1.4)	196 (0.5)	195 (0.4)	196 (0.3)	193 (0.3)	199 (0.3)	199 (0.3)	196 (0.4)	203 (0.4)
50th	219 (1.3)	219 (1.3)	217 (1.3)	218 (1.7)	221 (0.5)	221 (0.3)	221 (0.2)	219 (0.3)	224 (0.3)	224 (0.3)	221 (0.4)	227 (0.3)
75th	242 (1.1)	243 (1.3)	242 (0.9)	243 (0.8)	244 (0.5)	244 (0.3)	244 (0.3)	242 (0.4)	247 (0.4)	246 (0.3)	243 (0.3)	248 (0.4)
90th	261 (1.4)	263 (1.7)	262 (0.9)	262 (1.4)	263 (0.4)	264 (0.3)	263 (0.3)	260 (0.3)	266 (0.5)	264 (0.4)	261 (0.5)	267 (0.4)
8th grade												
10th	213 (1.2)	211 (1.9)	216 (1.7)	— (†)	220 (0.5)	217 (0.6)	216 (0.3)	210 (0.5)	223 (0.3)	217 (0.4)	211 (0.5)	225 (0.7)
25th	237 (1.1)	236 (1.1)	241 (0.7)	— (†)	244 (0.5)	242 (0.3)	240 (0.2)	235 (0.4)	246 (0.3)	242 (0.3)	237 (0.4)	247 (0.4)
50th	262 (1.1)	262 (0.7)	266 (0.7)	— (†)	267 (0.5)	266 (0.3)	265 (0.2)	260 (0.3)	269 (0.3)	265 (0.2)	261 (0.3)	270 (0.3)
75th	285 (0.8)	286 (1.1)	288 (1.0)	— (†)	288 (0.4)	288 (0.3)	286 (0.2)	282 (0.3)	291 (0.3)	287 (0.2)	282 (0.3)	291 (0.3)
90th	305 (1.3)	305 (1.2)	306 (0.8)	— (†)	305 (0.5)	305 (0.2)	305 (0.2)	300 (0.4)	309 (0.3)	305 (0.2)	300 (0.3)	309 (0.4)
12th grade												
10th	249 (0.8)	239 (0.9)	240 (0.6)	— (†)	237 (1.5)	— (†)	235 (1.1)	227 (2.3)	245 (1.2)	— (†)	— (†)	— (†)
25th	271 (0.8)	264 (0.9)	267 (0.8)	— (†)	263 (1.3)	— (†)	262 (0.8)	254 (0.9)	269 (1.3)	— (†)	— (†)	— (†)
50th	294 (0.8)	290 (0.6)	293 (0.6)	— (†)	289 (0.7)	— (†)	288 (0.8)	282 (0.9)	294 (0.8)	— (†)	— (†)	— (†)
75th	315 (0.5)	313 (0.8)	317 (0.7)	— (†)	312 (0.6)	— (†)	313 (1.1)	306 (1.1)	318 (0.7)	— (†)	— (†)	— (†)
90th	333 (0.7)	332 (1.2)	336 (0.8)	— (†)	332 (0.9)	— (†)	333 (1.1)	327 (1.3)	338 (1.0)	— (†)	— (†)	— (†)

—Not available. Data not collected.
†Not applicable.
‡Reporting standards not met.
[1]Accommodations were not permitted for this assessment.
[2]The percentile represents a specific point on the percentage distribution of all students ranked by their reading score from low to high. For example, 10 percent of students scored at or below the 10th percentile score, while 90 percent of students scored above it.

NOTE: Scale ranges from 0 to 500. Includes public and private schools. Excludes persons not enrolled in school and those who were unable to be tested due to limited proficiency in English or due to a disability. Race categories exclude persons of Hispanic ethnicity. Standard errors appear in parentheses.
SOURCE: U.S. Department of Education, National Center for Education Statistics, National Assessment of Educational Progress (NAEP), 1992, 1994, 1998, 2000, 2002, 2003, 2005, and 2007 Reading Assessments, retrieved May 28, 2008, from the NAEP Data Explorer (http://nces.ed.gov/nationsreportcard/nde). (This table was prepared June 2008.)

Table 119. Average reading scale score, by age and amount of time spent on reading and homework: Selected years, 1984 through 2004

Time spent on reading and homework	9-year-olds					13-year-olds					17-year-olds				
	1984	1994	1996	1999	2004	1984	1994	1996	1999	2004	1984	1994	1996	1999	2004
1	2	3	4	5	6	7	8	9	10	11	12	13	14	15	16
Average scale score															
Materials read a few times a year or more															
Poems	211 (1.9)	210 (2.9)	215 (2.8)	213 (2.7)	— (†)	260 (1.2)	261 (2.3)	262 (2.5)	263 (1.9)	— (†)	290 (1.5)	293 (2.1)	294 (2.8)	292 (2.6)	— (†)
Plays	211 (2.5)	207 (3.0)	214 (4.1)	211 (3.7)	— (†)	260 (1.3)	263 (2.1)	262 (2.4)	264 (2.3)	— (†)	290 (1.7)	294 (2.4)	293 (2.3)	294 (2.7)	— (†)
Biographies	213 (2.4)	210 (3.4)	220 (3.2)	215 (3.0)	— (†)	261 (1.3)	261 (2.1)	262 (2.2)	263 (2.1)	— (†)	292 (1.4)	293 (2.4)	293 (2.3)	291 (2.8)	— (†)
Science books	212 (1.6)	211 (2.6)	214 (2.0)	213 (2.1)	— (†)	259 (1.2)	260 (2.1)	261 (2.2)	261 (1.7)	— (†)	289 (1.4)	293 (2.3)	290 (2.2)	291 (2.3)	— (†)
Books about other times	211 (1.7)	211 (2.6)	213 (2.3)	213 (2.5)	— (†)	259 (1.1)	260 (2.2)	262 (2.2)	262 (2.1)	— (†)	289 (1.4)	293 (2.3)	292 (2.8)	292 (2.0)	— (†)
Frequency of reading for fun															
Daily	214 (1.1)	215 (2.3)	213 (2.0)	215 (2.4)	220 (1.5)	264 (1.4)	272 (3.2)	269 (3.3)	272 (3.2)	271 (2.8)	297 (1.5)	302 (4.2)	302 (5.2)	301 (4.9)	305 (3.7)
Weekly	212 (1.7)	214 (3.1)	212 (2.6)	215 (2.6)	224 (2.2)	255 (1.4)	255 (3.1)	258 (2.4)	263 (3.2)	261 (2.3)	290 (1.7)	286 (4.1)	290 (4.0)	289 (2.9)	287 (4.3)
Monthly	204 (3.3)	213 (5.8)	210 (5.0)	211 (4.2)	216 (4.6)	255 (2.1)	255 (5.7)	259 (4.6)	260 (3.7)	256 (3.9)	290 (1.8)	286 (4.5)	285 (5.6)	286 (4.8)	287 (4.7)
Yearly	197 (4.2)	— (†)	—	— (†)	209 (4.6)	252 (3.6)	252 (5.4)	— (†)	253 (4.4)	‡ (†)	279 (2.7)	281 (8.2)	285 (5.6)	283 (4.4)	272 (5.0)
Never	198 (2.7)	193 (3.9)	199 (4.3)	195 (3.3)	203 (4.4)	239 (2.5)	237 (5.1)	236 (4.8)	242 (5.3)	236 (3.9)	269 (2.4)	258 (5.2)	270 (5.0)	262 (5.0)	268 (5.8)
Reading of books, newspapers, and magazines															
Yearly/monthly	207 (1.6)	206 (3.8)	208 (3.1)	209 (2.9)	— (†)	244 (1.7)	245 (3.7)	249 (3.4)	252 (2.9)	— (†)	270 (2.0)	279 (4.0)	275 (4.5)	276 (3.8)	— (†)
Weekly	219 (2.5)	216 (3.7)	221 (4.7)	220 (3.5)	— (†)	261 (1.6)	262 (2.6)	262 (3.0)	251 (3.3)	— (†)	288 (1.5)	295 (2.8)	294 (3.2)	292 (2.2)	— (†)
Daily	211 (3.8)	—	— (†)	214 (6.3)	— (†)	269 (2.2)	275 (3.9)	270 (3.4)	271 (4.0)	— (†)	299 (1.9)	296 (4.0)	295 (4.8)	299 (6.5)	— (†)
Time spent on homework															
None	212 (0.9)	213 (2.0)	210 (1.9)	210 (1.9)	217 (2.0)	254 (1.0)	250 (1.7)	254 (1.3)	251 (2.0)	248 (1.7)	276 (0.8)	273 (2.3)	274 (1.9)	275 (2.3)	270 (2.0)
Didn't do assignment	199 (2.1)	200 (4.3)	196 (5.2)	204 (4.4)	204 (4.1)	247 (1.7)	243 (5.6)	249 (3.3)	249 (4.2)	245 (3.4)	287 (1.4)	285 (2.1)	281 (2.2)	282 (3.1)	279 (2.7)
Less than 1 hour	217 (0.8)	212 (1.4)	215 (1.0)	214 (1.5)	221 (1.0)	261 (0.6)	261 (1.3)	258 (1.6)	262 (1.5)	261 (1.2)	290 (0.9)	288 (1.6)	289 (1.5)	291 (2.3)	287 (1.6)
1 to 2 hours	216 (1.4)	214 (3.0)	219 (1.0)	215 (3.2)	221 (2.3)	267 (0.8)	268 (1.7)	266 (1.6)	268 (1.6)	268 (1.6)	296 (0.8)	297 (1.7)	296 (1.6)	296 (2.0)	295 (1.7)
More than 2 hours	201 (1.9)	193 (6.1)	199 (4.5)	197 (3.5)	207 (3.2)	265 (1.2)	270 (2.4)	268 (2.3)	269 (3.0)	272 (2.0)	303 (1.4)	306 (3.1)	307 (3.4)	300 (2.8)	304 (2.4)
Percent															
Materials read a few times a year or more															
Poems	70 (1.5)	62 (2.3)	60 (1.9)	64 (2.4)	— (†)	68 (1.3)	79 (1.4)	80 (1.9)	77 (1.6)	— (†)	76 (1.1)	85 (2.2)	80 (1.8)	85 (2.0)	— (†)
Plays	56 (1.4)	45 (2.2)	42 (2.4)	44 (2.2)	— (†)	59 (1.4)	63 (2.3)	67 (2.1)	61 (1.8)	— (†)	63 (1.0)	70 (2.1)	67 (1.6)	72 (1.9)	— (†)
Biographies	45 (1.5)	47 (2.1)	46 (2.4)	49 (3.0)	— (†)	62 (1.3)	68 (1.7)	65 (2.6)	72 (2.1)	— (†)	59 (1.2)	69 (1.8)	66 (1.7)	70 (1.9)	— (†)
Science books	84 (1.3)	87 (1.8)	83 (2.2)	80 (1.6)	— (†)	90 (1.1)	92 (1.4)	90 (1.9)	89 (1.2)	— (†)	70 (1.1)	84 (1.9)	82 (2.0)	84 (1.3)	— (†)
Books about other times	79 (1.2)	79 (2.0)	78 (1.6)	79 (1.9)	— (†)	83 (1.1)	83 (1.8)	84 (1.8)	84 (1.3)	— (†)	81 (0.9)	82 (2.0)	81 (1.9)	81 (2.0)	— (†)
Frequency of reading for fun															
Total	100 (†)	100 (†)	100 (†)	100 (†)	100 (†)	100 (†)	100 (†)	100 (†)	100 (†)	100 (†)	100 (†)	100 (†)	100 (†)	100 (†)	100 (†)
Daily	53 (0.8)	58 (1.6)	54 (1.8)	54 (1.6)	54 (1.6)	35 (1.0)	32 (1.8)	32 (2.1)	28 (1.7)	30 (1.9)	31 (1.1)	30 (2.6)	32 (2.7)	25 (1.7)	22 (2.9)
Weekly	28 (0.8)	25 (1.5)	27 (1.8)	26 (1.5)	26 (1.2)	35 (1.2)	32 (2.1)	31 (2.1)	36 (1.7)	31 (1.2)	33 (1.1)	31 (1.9)	32 (1.5)	28 (2.7)	30 (1.9)
Monthly	7 (0.6)	5 (0.6)	8 (1.0)	6 (0.6)	7 (0.5)	14 (0.8)	14 (1.7)	15 (1.4)	17 (1.6)	15 (1.2)	17 (0.5)	15 (1.5)	17 (1.6)	19 (1.7)	15 (1.6)
Yearly	3 (0.3)	3 (0.6)	3 (0.5)	4 (0.7)	5 (0.7)	7 (0.5)	10 (1.2)	9 (1.2)	10 (1.2)	9 (1.1)	10 (0.5)	12 (1.5)	12 (2.1)	12 (1.4)	14 (1.5)
Never	9 (0.5)	9 (0.8)	8 (0.8)	10 (0.8)	8 (0.8)	8 (0.6)	12 (1.7)	13 (1.5)	9 (1.4)	13 (1.3)	9 (0.6)	12 (1.4)	16 (2.1)	16 (2.4)	19 (1.8)
Reading of books, newspapers, and magazines															
Total	100 (†)	100 (†)	100 (†)	100 (†)	— (†)	100 (†)	100 (†)	100 (†)	100 (†)	— (†)	100 (†)	100 (†)	100 (†)	100 (†)	— (†)
Yearly/monthly	59 (1.5)	64 (1.8)	67 (2.3)	63 (2.6)	— (†)	30 (1.5)	34 (2.5)	32 (2.6)	32 (2.3)	— (†)	20 (1.0)	22 (1.7)	25 (2.1)	26 (2.1)	— (†)
Weekly	31 (1.5)	27 (1.8)	22 (1.9)	27 (2.4)	— (†)	49 (1.1)	47 (2.5)	47 (2.2)	49 (2.2)	— (†)	53 (1.2)	55 (2.3)	52 (2.6)	52 (2.2)	— (†)
Daily	11 (0.9)	9 (1.3)	10 (1.2)	11 (1.2)	— (†)	21 (1.1)	19 (1.7)	21 (1.7)	19 (1.9)	— (†)	27 (1.3)	23 (1.8)	23 (1.9)	21 (2.1)	— (†)
Time spent on homework															
Total	100 (†)	100 (†)	100 (†)	100 (†)	100 (†)	100 (†)	100 (†)	100 (†)	100 (†)	100 (†)	100 (†)	100 (†)	100 (†)	100 (†)	100 (†)
None	35 (1.3)	32 (2.1)	26 (1.6)	26 (1.6)	20 (1.5)	22 (0.7)	23 (1.4)	22 (1.8)	24 (1.7)	20 (1.3)	22 (0.9)	23 (1.4)	23 (1.4)	26 (1.0)	26 (1.0)
Didn't do assignment	4 (0.3)	4 (0.4)	4 (0.3)	4 (0.3)	6 (0.4)	4 (0.2)	6 (0.6)	5 (0.5)	5 (0.4)	6 (0.4)	11 (0.6)	11 (0.6)	13 (0.9)	13 (0.7)	13 (0.6)
Less than 1 hour	41 (1.0)	48 (1.7)	53 (1.5)	53 (1.4)	40 (1.4)	36 (0.6)	34 (1.0)	37 (1.2)	37 (1.4)	40 (1.2)	26 (0.9)	27 (1.5)	26 (2.6)	26 (2.2)	28 (1.0)
1 to 2 hours	13 (0.4)	11 (0.7)	13 (0.7)	13 (0.7)	26 (1.0)	29 (0.6)	28 (1.0)	27 (1.6)	27 (1.0)	26 (1.0)	27 (1.2)	26 (2.3)	25 (2.0)	23 (1.0)	22 (0.9)
More than 2 hours	6 (0.2)	4 (0.4)	4 (0.3)	5 (0.5)	8 (0.5)	9 (0.3)	9 (0.7)	8 (0.9)	8 (0.8)	8 (0.5)	13 (0.9)	13 (1.8)	11 (1.9)	12 (0.9)	11 (0.6)

—Not available.
†Not applicable.
‡Reporting standards not met.
NOTE: The NAEP reading scores have been evaluated at certain performance levels. Scale ranges from 0 to 500. Students scoring 150 (or higher) are able to follow brief written directions and carry out simple, discrete reading tasks. Students scoring 200 are able to understand, combine ideas, and make inferences based on short uncomplicated passages about specific or sequentially related information. Students scoring 250 are able to search for specific information, interrelate ideas, and make generalizations about litera-

ture, science, and social studies materials. Students scoring 300 are able to find, understand, summarize, and explain relatively complicated literary and informational material. Includes public and private schools. Excludes persons not enrolled in school and those who were unable to be tested due to limited proficiency in English or due to a disability. Detail may not sum to totals because of rounding. Standard errors appear in parentheses.

SOURCE: U.S. Department of Education, National Center for Education Statistics, National Assessment of Educational Progress (NAEP), NAEP Trends in Academic Progress, 1996 and 1999; and NAEP Data Explorer (http://nces.ed.gov/nationsreportcard/nde/), retrieved July 2005. (This table was prepared February 2006.)

Table 120. Percentage of students at or above selected reading score levels, by age, sex, and race/ethnicity: Selected years, 1971 through 2004

Selected characteristic	1971	1975	1980	1984	1988	1990	1992	1994	1996	1999	2004
1	2	3	4	5	6	7	8	9	10	11	12
9-year-olds											
Total											
Level 150	91 (0.5)	93 (0.4)	95 (0.4)	92 (0.4)	93 (0.7)	90 (0.9)	92 (0.4)	92 (0.7)	93 (0.6)	93 (0.7)	96 (0.3)
Level 200	59 (1.0)	62 (0.8)	68 (1.0)	62 (0.8)	63 (1.3)	59 (1.3)	62 (1.1)	63 (1.4)	64 (1.3)	64 (1.4)	70 (1.2)
Level 250	16 (0.6)	15 (0.6)	18 (0.8)	17 (0.7)	17 (1.1)	18 (1.0)	16 (0.8)	17 (1.2)	17 (0.8)	16 (1.0)	20 (1.0)
Male											
Level 150	88 (0.7)	91 (0.5)	93 (0.5)	90 (0.5)	90 (0.9)	88 (1.4)	90 (0.8)	90 (1.0)	92 (0.8)	91 (1.1)	95 (0.6)
Level 200	53 (1.2)	56 (1.0)	63 (1.1)	58 (1.0)	58 (1.8)	54 (1.9)	57 (1.6)	59 (1.5)	58 (2.0)	61 (1.8)	67 (1.7)
Level 250	12 (0.6)	12 (0.6)	15 (0.9)	16 (0.8)	16 (1.4)	16 (1.2)	14 (1.0)	15 (1.2)	14 (1.3)	15 (1.3)	19 (1.3)
Female											
Level 150	93 (0.5)	95 (0.3)	96 (0.4)	94 (0.5)	95 (1.0)	92 (1.1)	94 (0.6)	94 (0.8)	95 (0.6)	95 (0.8)	97 (0.5)
Level 200	65 (1.1)	68 (0.8)	73 (1.0)	65 (1.0)	67 (1.4)	64 (1.2)	67 (1.2)	67 (1.9)	70 (1.6)	67 (1.6)	74 (1.1)
Level 250	19 (0.8)	18 (0.8)	21 (1.0)	18 (0.8)	19 (1.2)	21 (1.2)	18 (1.1)	18 (1.5)	19 (1.3)	17 (1.3)	21 (1.3)
White											
Level 150	94[1] (0.4)	96 (0.3)	97 (0.2)	95 (0.3)	95 (0.7)	94 (0.9)	96 (0.5)	96 (0.5)	96 (0.6)	97 (0.4)	98 (0.4)
Level 200	65[1] (1.0)	69 (0.8)	74 (0.7)	69 (0.9)	68 (1.6)	66 (1.4)	69 (1.2)	70 (1.5)	71 (1.5)	73 (1.6)	78 (1.1)
Level 250	18[1] (0.7)	17 (0.7)	21 (0.9)	21 (0.8)	20 (1.5)	23 (1.2)	20 (1.0)	20 (1.5)	20 (1.1)	20 (1.4)	25 (1.2)
Black											
Level 150	70[1] (1.7)	81 (1.1)	85 (1.4)	81 (1.2)	83 (2.4)	77 (2.7)	80 (2.2)	79 (2.4)	84 (1.9)	82 (2.5)	91 (1.2)
Level 200	22[1] (1.5)	32 (1.5)	41 (1.9)	37 (1.5)	39 (2.9)	34 (3.4)	37 (2.2)	38 (2.8)	42 (3.2)	36 (3.0)	51 (3.0)
Level 250	2[1] (0.5)	2 (0.3)	4 (0.6)	5 (0.5)	6 (1.2)	5 (1.5)	5 (0.8)	4 (1.5)	6 (1.1)	4 (1.1)	8 (1.6)
Hispanic											
Level 150	[2] (†)	81 (2.5)	84 (1.8)	82 (3.0)	86 (3.5)	84 (1.8)	83 (2.6)	80 (4.6)	86 (2.4)	87 (3.3)	95 (1.4)
Level 200	[2] (†)	35 (3.0)	42 (2.6)	40 (2.7)	46 (3.3)	41 (2.7)	43 (3.5)	37 (4.6)	48 (3.8)	44 (3.4)	57 (2.8)
Level 250	[2] (†)	3 (0.5)	5 (1.4)	4 (0.6)	9 (2.3)	6 (2.0)	7 (2.3)	6 (1.6)	7 (3.2)	6 (1.7)	9 (1.8)
13-year-olds											
Total											
Level 150	100 (†)	100 (†)	100 (†)	100 (†)	100 (†)	100 (†)	100 (†)	99 (0.2)	100 (†)	100 (†)	— (†)
Level 200	93 (0.5)	93 (0.4)	95 (0.4)	94 (0.3)	95 (0.6)	94 (0.6)	93 (0.7)	92 (0.6)	92 (0.7)	93 (0.7)	94 (0.6)
Level 250	58 (1.1)	59 (1.0)	61 (1.1)	59 (0.8)	59 (1.3)	59 (1.0)	62 (1.4)	60 (1.2)	60 (1.3)	61 (1.5)	61 (1.3)
Level 300	10 (0.5)	10 (0.5)	11 (0.5)	11 (0.4)	11 (0.8)	11 (0.6)	15 (0.9)	14 (0.8)	14 (1.0)	15 (1.1)	13 (0.9)
Male											
Level 150	100 (†)	100 (†)	100 (†)	100 (†)	100 (†)	100 (†)	99 (0.4)	99 (0.3)	99 (0.4)	99 (0.3)	— (†)
Level 200	91 (0.7)	91 (0.5)	93 (0.6)	92 (0.4)	93 (1.0)	91 (0.9)	90 (1.1)	89 (1.1)	89 (1.2)	91 (0.9)	91 (0.8)
Level 250	52 (1.2)	52 (1.1)	56 (1.2)	54 (0.9)	52 (1.9)	52 (1.5)	55 (2.0)	53 (1.9)	53 (1.6)	55 (1.9)	55 (1.5)
Level 300	7 (0.5)	7 (0.4)	9 (0.7)	9 (0.5)	9 (0.9)	8 (0.8)	13 (1.1)	10 (0.7)	10 (1.0)	11 (1.1)	11 (0.9)
Female											
Level 150	100 (†)	100 (†)	100 (†)	100 (†)	100 (†)	100 (†)	100 (†)	100 (†)	100 (†)	100 (†)	— (†)
Level 200	95 (0.4)	96 (0.4)	96 (0.4)	96 (0.3)	97 (0.6)	96 (0.6)	95 (0.7)	95 (0.6)	95 (0.6)	96 (0.7)	96 (0.6)
Level 250	64 (1.1)	65 (1.2)	65 (1.1)	64 (0.8)	65 (1.4)	65 (1.5)	68 (1.4)	68 (1.7)	66 (1.6)	66 (1.9)	67 (1.8)
Level 300	12 (0.6)	13 (0.7)	13 (0.6)	13 (0.6)	13 (0.9)	14 (0.9)	18 (1.1)	18 (1.1)	17 (1.3)	18 (1.7)	15 (1.2)
White											
Level 150	100[1] (†)	100 (†)	100 (†)	100 (†)	100 (†)	100 (†)	100 (†)	100 (†)	100 (†)	100 (†)	— (†)
Level 200	96[1] (0.3)	96 (0.2)	97 (0.2)	96 (0.2)	96 (0.6)	96 (0.6)	96 (0.6)	95 (0.7)	95 (0.5)	96 (0.6)	96 (0.6)
Level 250	64[1] (0.9)	65 (0.9)	68 (0.8)	65 (0.8)	64 (1.5)	65 (1.2)	68 (1.4)	68 (1.3)	69 (1.4)	69 (1.7)	69 (1.3)
Level 300	11[1] (0.5)	12 (0.5)	14 (0.6)	13 (0.6)	12 (0.9)	13 (0.9)	18 (1.1)	17 (1.0)	17 (1.3)	18 (1.4)	17 (1.2)
Black											
Level 150	99[1] (0.3)	98 (0.3)	99 (0.3)	99 (0.2)	100 (†)	99 (‡)	99 (‡)	99 (‡)	99 (‡)	99 (‡)	— (†)
Level 200	74[1] (1.7)	77 (1.3)	84 (1.7)	85 (1.2)	91 (2.2)	88 (2.3)	82 (2.7)	81 (2.3)	82 (3.2)	85 (2.3)	89 (2.2)
Level 250	21[1] (1.2)	25 (1.6)	30 (2.0)	35 (1.3)	40 (2.3)	42 (3.5)	38 (2.7)	36 (3.5)	34 (3.9)	38 (2.7)	45 (2.8)
Level 300	1[1] (0.2)	2 (0.3)	2 (0.5)	3 (0.6)	5 (1.2)	5 (0.8)	6 (1.4)	4 (1.2)	3 (0.9)	5 (1.4)	5 (1.0)
Hispanic											
Level 150	[2] (†)	100 (†)	100 (†)	100 (†)	99 (‡)	99 (0.5)	98 (‡)	99 (‡)	99 (‡)	100 (†)	— (†)
Level 200	[2] (†)	81 (2.3)	87 (2.4)	86 (1.7)	87 (2.6)	86 (2.4)	83 (3.5)	82 (2.7)	85 (3.2)	89 (2.8)	88 (1.8)
Level 250	[2] (†)	32 (3.6)	35 (2.6)	39 (2.3)	38 (4.4)	37 (2.9)	41 (5.1)	34 (3.9)	38 (3.7)	43 (3.8)	43 (2.0)
Level 300	[2] (†)	2 (1.0)	2 (0.6)	4 (1.0)	4 (1.9)	4 (1.2)	6 (1.9)	4 (1.8)	5 (1.7)	6 (1.8)	4 (0.8)

See notes at end of table.

Table 120. Percentage of students at or above selected reading score levels, by age, sex, and race/ethnicity: Selected years, 1971 through 2004—Continued

Selected characteristic	1971		1975		1980		1984		1988		1990		1992		1994		1996		1999		2004	
1	2		3		4		5		6		7		8		9		10		11		12	
17-year-olds																						
Total																						
Level 150	100	(†)	100	(†)	100	(†)	100	(†)	100	(†)	100	(†)	100	(†)	100	(†)	100	(†)	100	(†)	—	(†)
Level 200	96	(0.3)	96	(0.3)	97	(0.3)	98	(0.1)	99	(0.3)	98	(0.3)	97	(0.4)	97	(0.5)	98	(0.5)	98	(0.4)	—	(†)
Level 250	79	(0.9)	80	(0.7)	81	(0.9)	83	(0.6)	86	(0.8)	84	(1.0)	83	(0.8)	81	(1.0)	82	(0.8)	82	(1.0)	80	(1.0)
Level 300	39	(1.0)	39	(0.8)	38	(1.1)	40	(1.0)	41	(1.5)	41	(1.0)	43	(1.1)	41	(1.2)	39	(1.4)	40	(1.4)	38	(1.2)
Male																						
Level 150	99	(0.1)	99	(0.2)	100	(†)	100	(†)	100	(†)	100	(†)	100	(†)	100	(†)	100	(†)	100	(†)	—	(†)
Level 200	95	(0.4)	95	(0.4)	96	(0.5)	98	(0.2)	99	(0.5)	97	(0.6)	96	(0.7)	96	(0.9)	96	(0.8)	97	(0.6)	—	(†)
Level 250	74	(1.0)	76	(0.8)	78	(1.0)	80	(0.7)	83	(1.4)	80	(1.4)	78	(1.2)	76	(1.5)	77	(1.2)	77	(1.5)	74	(1.4)
Level 300	34	(1.1)	34	(1.0)	35	(1.3)	36	(1.0)	37	(2.3)	36	(1.5)	38	(1.6)	36	(1.9)	34	(1.9)	34	(1.7)	33	(1.5)
Female																						
Level 150	100	(†)	100	(†)	100	(†)	100	(†)	100	(†)	100	(†)	100	(†)	100	(†)	100	(†)	100	(†)	—	(†)
Level 200	97	(0.3)	98	(0.4)	98	(0.3)	99	(0.1)	99	(0.3)	99	(0.3)	98	(0.4)	98	(0.5)	99	(0.5)	99	(0.4)	—	(†)
Level 250	83	(1.0)	84	(0.9)	84	(1.0)	87	(0.6)	88	(1.1)	89	(1.0)	87	(1.1)	86	(1.2)	87	(1.0)	87	(1.0)	86	(1.0)
Level 300	44	(1.2)	44	(0.9)	41	(1.2)	45	(1.1)	44	(2.0)	47	(1.3)	48	(1.5)	46	(1.5)	45	(1.7)	45	(1.8)	42	(1.5)
White																						
Level 150	100 [1]	(†)	100	(†)	100	(†)	100	(†)	100	(†)	100	(†)	100	(†)	100	(†)	100	(†)	100	(†)	—	(†)
Level 200	98 [1]	(0.2)	99	(0.1)	99	(0.1)	99	(0.1)	99	(0.3)	99	(0.2)	99	(0.3)	98	(0.4)	99	(0.4)	98	(0.4)	—	(†)
Level 250	84 [1]	(0.7)	86	(0.6)	87	(0.6)	88	(0.5)	89	(0.9)	88	(1.1)	88	(0.9)	86	(1.1)	87	(0.8)	87	(1.3)	86	(1.0)
Level 300	43 [1]	(0.9)	44	(0.8)	43	(1.1)	47	(1.1)	45	(1.6)	45	(1.6)	48	(1.2)	50	(1.4)	48	(1.4)	46	(1.5)	46	(1.5)	45	(1.4)
Black																						
Level 150	98 [1]	(0.4)	98	(0.8)	99	(0.3)	100	(†)	100	(†)	100	(†)	99	(‡)	99	(‡)	100	(†)	100	(†)	—	(†)
Level 200	82 [1]	(1.5)	82	(1.8)	86	(1.7)	96	(0.5)	98	(1.0)	96	(1.3)	92	(1.6)	93	(2.0)	95	(1.9)	95	(1.1)	—	(†)
Level 250	40 [1]	(1.6)	43	(1.6)	44	(2.0)	65	(1.5)	76	(2.4)	69	(2.8)	61	(2.3)	66	(4.1)	68	(4.0)	66	(2.5)	67	(3.0)
Level 300	8 [1]	(0.9)	8	(0.7)	7	(0.8)	16	(1.0)	25	(3.1)	20	(1.8)	17	(2.5)	22	(3.7)	18	(2.2)	17	(1.7)	17	(2.0)
Hispanic																						
Level 150	[2]	(†)	99	(0.4)	100	(†)	100	(†)	100	(†)	100	(†)	100	(†)	99	(‡)	100	(†)	100	(†)	—	(†)
Level 200	[2]	(†)	89	(2.4)	93	(1.8)	96	(0.7)	96	(2.4)	96	(2.1)	93	(2.3)	91	(3.4)	94	(1.9)	97	(‡)	—	(†)
Level 250	[2]	(†)	53	(4.1)	62	(3.1)	68	(2.4)	71	(4.8)	75	(4.7)	69	(4.0)	63	(4.4)	65	(4.2)	68	(4.3)	64	(3.7)
Level 300	[2]	(†)	13	(2.7)	17	(2.1)	21	(3.0)	23	(3.7)	27	(3.3)	27	(3.2)	20	(3.0)	20	(4.8)	24	(3.8)	20	(2.4)

—Not available.
†Not applicable.
‡Reporting standards not met.
[1] Data for 1971 include persons of Hispanic ethnicity.
[2] Test scores of Hispanics were not tabulated separately.
NOTE: The NAEP reading scores have been evaluated at certain performance levels. Scale ranges from 0 to 500. Students scoring 150 (or higher) are able to follow brief written directions and carry out simple, discrete reading tasks. Students scoring 200 are able to understand, combine ideas, and make inferences based on short uncomplicated passages about specific or sequentially related information. Students scoring 250 are able to search for specific information, interrelate ideas, and make generalizations about literature, sci-

ence, and social studies materials. Students scoring 300 are able to find, understand, summarize, and explain relatively complicated literary and informational material. Includes public and private schools. Excludes persons not enrolled in school and those who were unable to be tested due to limited proficiency in English or due to a disability. Race categories exclude persons of Hispanic ethnicity, except where noted. Standard errors appear in parentheses.
SOURCE: U.S. Department of Education, National Center for Education Statistics, National Assessment of Educational Progress (NAEP), *NAEP 1999 Trends in Academic Progress*; and NAEP Data Explorer (http://nces.ed.gov/nationsreportcard/nde/), retrieved July 2005. (This table was prepared February 2006.)

Table 121. Average reading scale score and percentage of 4th-graders in public schools attaining reading achievement levels, by race/ethnicity and state or jurisdiction: Selected years, 1992 through 2007

State or jurisdiction	Average scale score[1]							Average scale score[1] by race/ethnicity,[2] 2007					Percent attaining reading achievement levels, 2007		
	1992	1994	1998	2002	2003	2005	2007	White	Black	Hispanic	Asian/Pacific Islander	American Indian/ Alaska Native	At or above Basic[3]	At or above Proficient[4]	At Advanced[5]
1	2	3	4	5	6	7	8	9	10	11	12	13	14	15	16
United States	215 (1.0)	212 (1.1)	213 (1.2)	217 (0.5)	216 (0.3)	217 (0.2)	220 (0.3)	230 (0.2)	203 (0.4)	204 (0.5)	231 (1.0)	206 (1.2)	66 (0.3)	32 (0.3)	7 (0.1)
Alabama	207 (1.7)	208 (1.5)	211 (1.9)	207 (1.4)	207 (1.7)	208 (1.2)	216 (1.3)	227 (1.4)	201 (1.6)	197 (6.7)	‡ (†)	‡ (†)	62 (1.4)	29 (1.4)	7 (0.9)
Alaska	— (†)	— (†)	— (†)	— (†)	212 (1.6)	211 (1.4)	214 (1.0)	228 (1.2)	207 (3.2)	206 (4.4)	217 (3.1)	188 (1.9)	62 (1.2)	29 (1.0)	6 (0.8)
Arizona	209 (1.2)	206 (1.9)	206 (1.4)	205 (1.5)	209 (1.2)	207 (1.6)	210 (1.6)	224 (1.3)	206 (3.5)	197 (2.4)	229 (6.3)	187 (3.4)	56 (1.7)	24 (1.5)	5 (0.6)
Arkansas	211 (1.2)	209 (1.7)	209 (1.6)	213 (1.4)	214 (1.4)	217 (1.1)	217 (1.2)	226 (1.1)	195 (1.3)	202 (4.0)	‡ (†)	‡ (†)	64 (1.3)	29 (1.3)	5 (0.6)
California[6,7]	202 (2.0)	197 (1.8)	202 (2.5)	206 (2.5)	206 (1.2)	207 (0.7)	209 (1.0)	227 (1.2)	200 (2.4)	195 (0.9)	228 (2.6)	‡ (†)	53 (1.0)	23 (0.9)	5 (0.4)
Colorado	217 (1.1)	213 (1.3)	220 (1.4)	— (†)	224 (1.2)	224 (1.1)	224 (1.1)	234 (1.0)	210 (3.2)	204 (1.7)	233 (3.6)	‡ (†)	70 (1.3)	36 (1.4)	9 (1.0)
Connecticut	222 (1.3)	222 (1.6)	230 (1.6)	229 (1.1)	228 (1.1)	226 (1.0)	227 (1.3)	238 (1.3)	203 (3.0)	203 (2.7)	244 (3.6)	‡ (†)	73 (1.4)	41 (1.6)	12 (1.2)
Delaware	213 (0.6)	206 (1.1)	207 (1.7)	224 (0.6)	224 (0.7)	226 (0.8)	225 (0.7)	233 (0.9)	213 (1.0)	218 (2.3)	246 (3.6)	‡ (†)	73 (1.2)	34 (1.4)	7 (0.6)
District of Columbia	188 (0.8)	— (†)	179 (1.2)	191 (0.9)	188 (0.9)	191 (1.0)	197 (0.9)	258 (3.9)	192 (1.0)	206 (3.6)	‡ (†)	‡ (†)	39 (1.1)	14 (0.8)	4 (0.5)
Florida	208 (1.2)	205 (1.7)	206 (1.4)	214 (1.4)	218 (1.1)	220 (0.9)	224 (0.8)	232 (1.0)	208 (1.5)	218 (1.2)	241 (3.2)	‡ (†)	70 (1.0)	34 (1.0)	8 (0.6)
Georgia	212 (1.5)	207 (2.4)	209 (1.4)	215 (1.0)	214 (1.3)	214 (1.2)	219 (0.9)	230 (1.1)	205 (1.4)	212 (3.3)	232 (6.1)	‡ (†)	66 (1.3)	28 (1.5)	5 (0.7)
Hawaii	203 (1.7)	201 (1.7)	200 (1.5)	208 (0.9)	208 (1.4)	210 (1.0)	213 (1.1)	227 (2.2)	212 (4.6)	205 (4.1)	210 (1.2)	‡ (†)	59 (1.4)	26 (1.4)	5 (0.6)
Idaho	219 (0.9)	— (†)	— (†)	220 (1.1)	218 (1.0)	222 (0.9)	223 (0.8)	227 (0.7)	‡ (†)	204 (2.5)	‡ (†)	202 (10.9)	70 (1.0)	35 (1.2)	8 (0.6)
Illinois	— (†)	— (†)	— (†)	— (†)	216 (1.6)	217 (1.2)	219 (1.2)	230 (1.7)	201 (2.4)	205 (1.2)	240 (4.2)	‡ (†)	65 (1.6)	32 (1.3)	8 (0.9)
Indiana	221 (1.3)	220 (1.3)	225 (1.4)	222 (1.4)	220 (1.0)	218 (1.1)	222 (0.9)	226 (1.0)	201 (2.4)	207 (2.5)	241 (3.2)	‡ (†)	68 (1.2)	33 (1.3)	7 (0.7)
Iowa[6,7]	225 (1.1)	223 (1.3)	220 (1.6)	223 (1.1)	223 (1.1)	221 (0.9)	225 (1.1)	227 (1.1)	205 (4.0)	208 (3.1)	235 (6.9)	‡ (†)	74 (1.6)	36 (1.4)	7 (0.8)
Kansas[6,7]	— (†)	— (†)	221 (1.4)	222 (1.4)	220 (1.2)	221 (1.3)	225 (1.1)	229 (1.1)	208 (2.6)	209 (2.4)	229 (5.4)	‡ (†)	72 (1.2)	36 (1.5)	8 (0.9)
Kentucky	213 (1.3)	212 (1.6)	218 (1.5)	219 (1.1)	219 (1.2)	220 (1.1)	222 (1.1)	225 (1.1)	203 (2.2)	‡ (†)	233 (4.6)	‡ (†)	68 (1.4)	33 (1.4)	8 (0.7)
Louisiana	204 (1.2)	197 (1.3)	200 (1.6)	207 (1.7)	205 (1.4)	209 (1.3)	207 (1.6)	220 (1.8)	194 (1.7)	213 (5.5)	‡ (†)	‡ (†)	52 (2.0)	20 (1.4)	3 (0.6)
Maine	227 (1.1)	228 (1.3)	225 (1.4)	225 (1.1)	224 (0.9)	225 (0.9)	226 (0.9)	226 (0.9)	‡ (†)	‡ (†)	‡ (†)	‡ (†)	73 (1.1)	36 (1.4)	7 (0.8)
Maryland	211 (1.6)	210 (1.5)	212 (1.6)	217 (1.5)	219 (1.4)	220 (1.3)	225 (1.1)	236 (1.5)	208 (1.2)	213 (2.4)	243 (2.8)	‡ (†)	69 (1.3)	36 (1.5)	10 (0.7)
Massachusetts[6]	226 (0.9)	223 (1.3)	223 (1.4)	234 (1.8)	228 (1.2)	231 (0.9)	236 (1.1)	241 (1.1)	211 (2.1)	209 (2.0)	241 (3.5)	‡ (†)	81 (1.1)	49 (1.7)	16 (1.3)
Michigan	216 (1.5)	— (†)	216 (1.5)	219 (1.1)	219 (1.2)	218 (1.5)	220 (1.4)	227 (1.2)	197 (2.7)	210 (4.2)	233 (4.6)	‡ (†)	66 (1.7)	32 (1.6)	8 (0.7)
Minnesota[6,7]	221 (1.1)	218 (1.4)	219 (1.7)	225 (1.1)	223 (1.0)	225 (1.3)	225 (1.1)	231 (1.1)	198 (2.5)	200 (3.8)	218 (3.6)	205 (5.5)	73 (1.3)	37 (1.5)	9 (0.8)
Mississippi	199 (1.3)	202 (1.6)	203 (1.3)	203 (1.3)	205 (1.3)	204 (1.4)	208 (1.0)	222 (1.2)	195 (0.9)	209 (3.9)	235 (4.3)	‡ (†)	51 (1.4)	19 (1.0)	3 (0.4)
Missouri	220 (1.2)	217 (1.5)	216 (1.3)	220 (1.3)	222 (1.2)	221 (0.9)	221 (1.1)	226 (1.2)	200 (2.1)	213 (4.1)	245 (2.5)	‡ (†)	67 (1.3)	32 (1.3)	7 (0.6)
Montana[6,7]	— (†)	222 (1.4)	225 (1.5)	224 (1.8)	223 (1.2)	225 (1.1)	227 (1.0)	230 (0.9)	‡ (†)	220 (4.2)	‡ (†)	204 (3.1)	75 (1.0)	39 (1.8)	8 (0.9)
Nebraska[8]	221 (1.1)	220 (1.5)	— (†)	222 (1.5)	219 (1.0)	218 (1.2)	223 (1.3)	230 (0.9)	194 (3.7)	203 (2.8)	233 (4.6)	‡ (†)	71 (1.4)	35 (1.4)	8 (0.8)
Nevada	— (†)	—	206 (1.8)	209 (1.2)	207 (1.2)	207 (1.2)	211 (1.2)	224 (1.5)	202 (3.1)	196 (1.6)	220 (2.5)	‡ (†)	57 (1.3)	20 (1.3)	5 (0.5)
New Hampshire[6]	228 (1.2)	223 (1.5)	226 (1.7)	— (†)	228 (1.0)	227 (0.9)	229 (0.9)	230 (0.9)	215 (5.0)	209 (3.9)	235 (4.3)	‡ (†)	76 (0.9)	41 (1.5)	11 (0.9)
New Jersey	223 (1.4)	219 (1.2)	212 (1.6)	— (†)	225 (1.2)	223 (1.3)	231 (1.2)	238 (1.1)	212 (2.7)	214 (2.5)	245 (2.5)	‡ (†)	77 (1.3)	43 (1.5)	12 (0.9)
New Mexico	211 (1.5)	205 (1.7)	205 (1.4)	208 (1.6)	203 (1.5)	207 (1.3)	212 (1.3)	228 (1.9)	208 (4.0)	204 (1.4)	‡ (†)	197 (3.7)	58 (1.5)	24 (1.6)	5 (0.7)
New York[6,7]	215 (1.4)	212 (1.4)	215 (1.6)	222 (1.5)	222 (1.1)	223 (1.1)	224 (1.0)	234 (1.5)	208 (1.5)	206 (1.7)	236 (2.8)	‡ (†)	69 (1.2)	36 (1.3)	10 (0.9)
North Carolina	212 (1.1)	214 (1.5)	213 (1.6)	222 (1.0)	221 (1.0)	217 (1.0)	218 (0.9)	228 (1.1)	202 (1.1)	205 (2.2)	228 (5.0)	202 (4.3)	64 (1.2)	29 (1.1)	6 (0.5)
North Dakota[7]	226 (1.1)	225 (1.2)	— (†)	224 (1.0)	222 (0.9)	225 (0.7)	226 (0.9)	229 (0.7)	‡ (†)	‡ (†)	‡ (†)	204 (3.5)	75 (1.2)	35 (1.2)	6 (0.6)

See notes at end of table.

Table 121. Average reading scale score and percentage of 4th-graders in public schools attaining reading achievement levels, by race/ethnicity and state or jurisdiction: Selected years, 1992 through 2007—Continued

State or jurisdiction	Average scale score[1]							Average scale score[1] by race/ethnicity,[2] 2007					Percent attaining reading achievement levels, 2007		
	1992	1994	1998	2002	2003	2005	2007	White	Black	Hispanic	Asian/Pacific Islander	American Indian/ Alaska Native	At or above Basic[3]	At or above Proficient[4]	At Advanced[5]
	2	3	4	5	6	7	8	9	10	11	12	13	14	15	16
Ohio	217 (1.3)	— (†)	— (†)	222 (1.3)	222 (1.2)	223 (1.4)	226 (1.1)	231 (1.1)	204 (2.1)	214 (4.5)	‡ (†)	‡ (†)	73 (1.5)	36 (1.6)	8 (1.0)
Oklahoma	220 (0.9)	— (†)	219 (1.2)	213 (1.2)	214 (1.2)	214 (1.1)	217 (1.1)	223 (1.1)	204 (2.2)	198 (3.9)	221 (7.6)	213 (1.8)	65 (1.5)	27 (1.2)	4 (0.5)
Oregon	— (†)	— (†)	212 (1.8)	220 (1.4)	218 (1.3)	217 (1.4)	215 (1.4)	222 (1.3)	198 (3.8)	190 (2.3)	218 (6.3)	206 (7.2)	62 (1.5)	28 (1.5)	6 (0.7)
Pennsylvania[8]	221 (1.3)	215 (1.6)	— (†)	221 (1.2)	219 (1.3)	223 (1.3)	226 (1.0)	233 (0.8)	200 (2.9)	200 (5.0)	228 (3.7)	‡ (†)	73 (1.3)	40 (1.1)	11 (0.8)
Rhode Island[8]	217 (1.8)	220 (1.3)	218 (1.4)	220 (1.2)	216 (1.3)	216 (1.2)	219 (1.0)	227 (1.1)	198 (2.3)	198 (2.1)	219 (4.2)	‡ (†)	65 (1.2)	31 (1.2)	7 (0.7)
South Carolina	210 (1.3)	203 (1.4)	209 (1.4)	214 (1.3)	215 (1.3)	213 (1.3)	214 (1.2)	224 (1.2)	199 (1.5)	205 (3.5)	‡ (†)	‡ (†)	59 (1.5)	26 (1.3)	5 (0.5)
South Dakota	— (†)	— (†)	— (†)	— (†)	222 (1.2)	222 (0.5)	223 (1.0)	228 (0.9)	‡ (†)	209 (5.2)	‡ (†)	196 (2.6)	71 (1.2)	34 (1.6)	7 (0.8)
Tennessee[7,8]	212 (1.4)	213 (1.7)	212 (1.4)	214 (1.2)	212 (1.6)	214 (1.4)	216 (1.2)	224 (1.3)	192 (1.6)	208 (4.0)	‡ (†)	‡ (†)	61 (1.6)	27 (1.2)	6 (0.8)
Texas	213 (1.6)	212 (1.9)	214 (1.9)	217 (1.7)	215 (1.0)	219 (0.8)	220 (0.9)	232 (1.1)	207 (1.6)	212 (1.2)	236 (3.2)	‡ (†)	66 (1.1)	30 (1.1)	6 (0.5)
Utah	220 (1.1)	217 (1.3)	216 (1.2)	222 (1.0)	219 (1.0)	221 (1.1)	221 (1.2)	226 (1.0)	‡ (†)	201 (2.8)	217 (3.9)	‡ (†)	69 (1.4)	34 (1.4)	8 (0.5)
Vermont	— (†)	— (†)	— (†)	227 (1.1)	226 (0.9)	227 (0.9)	228 (0.8)	229 (0.9)	‡ (†)	216 (2.8)	‡ (†)	‡ (†)	74 (1.2)	41 (1.2)	11 (0.7)
Virginia	221 (1.4)	213 (1.5)	217 (1.2)	225 (1.3)	223 (1.5)	226 (0.8)	227 (1.1)	233 (1.3)	213 (1.4)	216 (2.8)	237 (2.7)	‡ (†)	74 (1.5)	38 (1.4)	9 (1.0)
Washington[7]	— (†)	— (†)	218 (1.4)	224 (1.2)	221 (1.1)	224 (1.1)	224 (1.4)	229 (1.4)	206 (3.5)	206 (2.3)	232 (3.6)	205 (5.0)	70 (1.5)	36 (1.7)	10 (1.1)
West Virginia	216 (1.3)	213 (1.1)	216 (1.7)	219 (1.2)	219 (1.0)	215 (0.8)	215 (1.1)	216 (1.1)	202 (2.9)	‡ (†)	‡ (†)	‡ (†)	63 (1.2)	28 (1.1)	5 (0.6)
Wisconsin[6,7,8]	224 (1.0)	224 (1.1)	222 (1.1)	— (†)	221 (0.8)	221 (1.0)	223 (1.2)	229 (1.2)	191 (4.2)	208 (2.8)	222 (4.4)	‡ (†)	70 (1.4)	36 (1.4)	8 (0.7)
Wyoming	223 (1.1)	221 (1.2)	218 (1.5)	221 (1.0)	222 (0.8)	223 (0.7)	225 (0.5)	228 (0.6)	‡ (†)	210 (2.4)	‡ (†)	200 (3.6)	73 (1.0)	36 (1.0)	8 (0.9)
Department of Defense dependents schools[9]	— (†)	— (†)	220 (0.7)	224 (0.4)	224 (0.5)	226 (0.6)	229 (0.5)	235 (0.8)	218 (1.6)	223 (1.4)	228 (2.1)	‡ (†)	78 (0.9)	40 (1.0)	8 (0.5)
Other jurisdictions															
Guam	182 (1.4)	181 (1.2)	— (†)	185 (1.3)	— (†)	— (†)	— (†)	— (†)	— (†)	— (†)	— (†)	— (†)	— (†)	— (†)	— (†)
U.S. Virgin Islands	171 (1.7)	— (†)	174 (2.2)	179 (1.9)	— (†)	— (†)	— (†)	— (†)	— (†)	— (†)	— (†)	— (†)	— (†)	— (†)	— (†)

—Not available.
†Not applicable.
‡Reporting standards not met.
[1]Scale ranges from 0 to 500.
[2]Race/ethnicity based on school records.
[3]Basic denotes partial mastery of the knowledge and skills that are fundamental for proficient work at the 4th-grade level.
[4]Proficient represents solid academic performance for 4th-graders. Students reaching this level have demonstrated competency over challenging subject matter.
[5]Advanced signifies superior performance.
[6]Did not satisfy one or more of the guidelines for school participation in 1998. Data are subject to appreciable nonresponse bias.

[7]Did not satisfy one or more of the guidelines for school participation in 2002. Data are subject to appreciable nonresponse bias.
[8]Did not satisfy one or more of the guidelines for school participation in 1994. Data are subject to appreciable nonresponse bias.
[9]Prior to 2005, NAEP divided the Department of Defense (DoD) schools into two jurisdictions, domestic and overseas. In 2005, NAEP began combining the DoD domestic and overseas schools into a single jurisdiction. Data shown in this table for years prior to 2005 were recalculated for comparability.
NOTE: The reading data include students for whom accommodations were permitted except for the 1992 and 1994 data. Race categories exclude persons of Hispanic ethnicity. Standard errors appear in parentheses.
SOURCE: U.S. Department of Education, National Center for Education Statistics, National Assessment of Educational Progress (NAEP), 1992, 1994, 1998, 2002, 2003, 2005, and 2007 Reading Assessments, retrieved May 16, 2008, from the NAEP Data Explorer (http://nces.ed.gov/nationsreportcard/nde/). (This table was prepared May 2008.)

Table 122. Average reading scale score and percentage of 8th-graders in public schools attaining reading achievement levels, by locale and state or jurisdiction: Selected years, 1998 through 2007

State or jurisdiction	Average scale score[1]					Percent attaining reading achievement levels, 2007				Average scale score by locale,[2] 2005		
	1998	2002	2003	2005	2007	Below Basic	At or above Basic[3]	At or above Proficient[4]	At Advanced[5]	Central city	Urban fringe/ large town	Rural/ small town
1	2	3	4	5	6	7	8	9	10	11	12	13
United States	261 (0.8)	263 (0.5)	261 (0.2)	260 (0.2)	261 (0.2)	27 (0.3)	73 (0.3)	29 (0.2)	2 (0.1)	254 (0.4)	264 (0.3)	262 (0.4)
Alabama	255 (1.4)	253 (1.3)	253 (1.5)	252 (1.4)	252 (1.0)	38 (1.2)	62 (1.2)	21 (1.3)	1 (0.4)	246 (2.8)	260 (3.1)	250 (1.6)
Alaska	— (†)	— (†)	256 (1.1)	259 (0.9)	259 (1.0)	29 (1.2)	71 (1.2)	27 (1.2)	2 (0.4)	‡ (†)	‡ (†)	‡ (†)
Arizona	260 (1.1)	257 (1.3)	255 (1.4)	255 (1.0)	255 (1.2)	35 (1.6)	65 (1.6)	24 (1.4)	2 (0.5)	253 (1.5)	258 (2.2)	253 (4.5)
Arkansas	256 (1.3)	260 (1.1)	258 (1.3)	258 (1.1)	258 (1.0)	30 (1.3)	70 (1.3)	25 (1.1)	1 (0.4)	257 (2.8)	261 (2.0)	257 (1.3)
California[6,7,8]	252 (1.6)	250 (1.8)	251 (1.3)	250 (0.6)	251 (0.8)	38 (0.8)	62 (0.8)	21 (0.8)	2 (0.3)	249 (0.9)	251 (0.9)	257 (3.6)
Colorado	264 (1.0)	— (†)	268 (1.2)	265 (1.1)	266 (1.0)	21 (1.2)	79 (1.2)	35 (1.5)	2 (0.5)	260 (2.1)	268 (1.5)	266 (2.0)
Connecticut	270 (1.0)	267 (1.2)	267 (1.1)	264 (1.3)	267 (1.6)	23 (1.7)	77 (1.7)	37 (1.7)	5 (0.4)	245 (3.0)	270 (1.5)	269 (1.8)
Delaware	254 (1.3)	267 (0.5)	265 (0.7)	266 (0.6)	265 (0.6)	23 (0.8)	77 (0.8)	31 (1.2)	2 (0.4)	266 (2.4)	265 (0.7)	269 (1.4)
District of Columbia	236 (2.1)	240 (0.9)	239 (0.8)	238 (0.9)	241 (0.7)	52 (1.1)	48 (1.1)	12 (1.0)	1 (0.3)	238 (0.9)	‡ (†)	‡ (†)
Florida	255 (1.4)	261 (1.6)	257 (1.3)	256 (1.2)	260 (1.2)	29 (1.3)	71 (1.3)	28 (1.3)	2 (0.4)	252 (2.4)	257 (1.5)	257 (2.6)
Georgia	257 (1.4)	258 (1.0)	258 (1.1)	257 (1.3)	259 (1.0)	30 (1.4)	70 (1.4)	26 (1.4)	2 (0.5)	245 (2.8)	261 (2.1)	257 (2.1)
Hawaii	249 (1.0)	252 (0.9)	251 (0.9)	249 (0.9)	251 (0.8)	38 (1.0)	62 (1.0)	20 (0.9)	1 (0.3)	255 (1.6)	249 (1.4)	243 (1.5)
Idaho	— (†)	266 (1.1)	264 (0.9)	264 (1.1)	265 (0.9)	22 (0.8)	78 (0.8)	32 (1.3)	2 (0.4)	266 (1.3)	264 (1.4)	263 (2.0)
Illinois	— (†)	— (†)	266 (1.0)	264 (1.0)	263 (1.0)	25 (1.1)	75 (1.1)	30 (1.5)	2 (0.4)	256 (1.9)	268 (1.5)	266 (2.1)
Indiana	— (†)	265 (1.3)	265 (1.0)	261 (1.1)	264 (1.1)	24 (1.1)	76 (1.1)	31 (1.5)	2 (0.5)	254 (2.1)	265 (2.0)	263 (1.6)
Iowa	— (†)	— (†)	268 (0.8)	267 (0.9)	267 (0.9)	20 (1.0)	80 (1.0)	36 (1.4)	2 (0.6)	262 (1.5)	272 (2.3)	268 (1.4)
Kansas[6,7,8]	268 (1.4)	269 (1.3)	266 (1.5)	267 (1.0)	267 (0.8)	19 (1.0)	81 (1.0)	35 (1.2)	2 (0.4)	262 (2.6)	270 (1.7)	267 (1.1)
Kentucky	262 (1.4)	265 (1.0)	266 (1.3)	264 (1.1)	262 (1.2)	27 (1.2)	73 (1.2)	28 (1.2)	3 (0.5)	271 (2.3)	262 (2.1)	263 (1.6)
Louisiana	252 (1.4)	256 (1.5)	253 (1.6)	253 (1.6)	253 (1.1)	36 (1.6)	64 (1.6)	19 (1.2)	1 (0.5)	247 (2.8)	255 (2.8)	255 (1.9)
Maine	271 (1.2)	270 (0.9)	268 (1.0)	270 (1.0)	270 (0.8)	17 (1.0)	83 (1.0)	37 (1.5)	3 (0.5)	269 (2.6)	265 (2.1)	269 (1.1)
Maryland[6,7]	261 (1.8)	263 (1.7)	262 (1.4)	261 (1.2)	265 (1.2)	24 (1.3)	76 (1.3)	33 (1.5)	3 (0.4)	251 (3.6)	262 (1.5)	266 (2.7)
Massachusetts	269 (1.4)	271 (1.3)	273 (1.0)	274 (1.0)	273 (1.0)	16 (0.9)	84 (0.9)	43 (1.5)	4 (0.7)	258 (1.4)	280 (1.3)	282 (3.1)
Michigan	— (†)	265 (1.6)	264 (1.8)	261 (1.2)	260 (1.2)	28 (1.5)	72 (1.5)	28 (1.3)	2 (0.4)	251 (2.9)	265 (1.4)	266 (2.2)
Minnesota[6,7]	265 (1.4)	— (†)	268 (1.1)	268 (1.2)	268 (0.9)	20 (1.2)	80 (1.2)	37 (1.2)	3 (0.5)	264 (3.2)	272 (1.6)	267 (1.6)
Mississippi	251 (1.2)	255 (0.9)	255 (1.4)	251 (1.3)	250 (1.1)	40 (1.4)	60 (1.4)	17 (1.4)	1 (0.3)	246 (2.9)	254 (2.1)	250 (1.8)
Missouri	262 (1.3)	268 (1.0)	267 (1.0)	265 (1.0)	263 (1.0)	25 (1.1)	75 (1.1)	31 (1.2)	3 (0.3)	258 (3.0)	267 (1.3)	266 (1.6)
Montana[6,7]	271 (1.3)	270 (1.0)	270 (1.0)	269 (0.7)	271 (0.8)	15 (1.0)	85 (1.0)	39 (1.4)	2 (0.4)	270 (1.6)	271 (1.8)	268 (0.9)
Nebraska	— (†)	270 (0.9)	266 (0.9)	267 (0.9)	267 (0.9)	21 (1.2)	79 (1.2)	35 (1.3)	3 (0.5)	266 (1.6)	268 (1.6)	268 (1.4)
Nevada	258 (1.0)	251 (0.8)	252 (0.8)	253 (0.9)	252 (0.8)	37 (0.9)	63 (0.9)	22 (1.0)	2 (0.4)	253 (1.4)	251 (1.4)	256 (1.5)
New Hampshire	— (†)	— (†)	271 (0.9)	270 (1.2)	270 (0.9)	18 (1.2)	82 (1.2)	37 (1.3)	3 (0.4)	264 (2.1)	270 (2.0)	272 (1.9)
New Jersey	— (†)	— (†)	268 (1.2)	269 (1.2)	270 (1.1)	19 (1.0)	81 (1.0)	39 (1.5)	4 (0.6)	‡ (†)	270 (1.3)	278 (3.0)
New Mexico	258 (1.2)	254 (1.0)	252 (0.9)	251 (1.0)	251 (0.8)	38 (1.3)	62 (1.3)	17 (0.9)	1 (0.3)	256 (1.9)	249 (1.9)	248 (1.7)
New York[6,7]	265 (1.5)	264 (1.5)	265 (1.3)	265 (1.0)	264 (1.1)	25 (1.3)	75 (1.3)	32 (1.4)	3 (0.3)	252 (1.5)	275 (1.4)	272 (1.4)
North Carolina	262 (1.1)	265 (1.1)	262 (1.0)	258 (0.9)	259 (1.1)	29 (1.3)	71 (1.3)	28 (1.1)	2 (0.4)	257 (1.6)	261 (1.9)	258 (1.5)
North Dakota[7]	— (†)	268 (0.8)	270 (0.8)	270 (0.6)	268 (0.7)	16 (1.0)	84 (1.0)	32 (1.3)	1 (0.5)	271 (1.5)	270 (1.8)	270 (0.8)

See notes at end of table.

Table 122. Average reading scale score and percentage of 8th-graders in public schools attaining reading achievement levels, by locale and state or jurisdiction: Selected years, 1998 through 2007—Continued

| State or jurisdiction | Average scale score[1] | | | | | Percent attaining reading achievement levels, 2007 | | | | Average scale score[1] by locale,[2] 2005 | | |
	1998	2002	2003	2005	2007	Below Basic	At or above Basic[3]	At or above Proficient[4]	At Advanced[5]	Central city	Urban fringe/large town	Rural/small town
	2	3	4	5	6	7	8	9	10	11	12	13
Ohio	— (†)	268 (1.6)	267 (1.3)	267 (1.3)	268 (1.2)	21 (1.2)	79 (1.2)	36 (1.6)	3 (0.6)	248 (3.1)	272 (1.6)	272 (2.2)
Oklahoma	265 (1.2)	262 (0.8)	262 (0.9)	260 (1.1)	260 (0.8)	28 (1.0)	72 (1.0)	26 (1.2)	1 (0.3)	252 (4.0)	264 (1.3)	259 (1.4)
Oregon[7]	266 (1.5)	268 (1.3)	264 (1.2)	263 (1.1)	266 (0.9)	23 (1.2)	77 (1.2)	34 (1.7)	3 (0.4)	264 (2.2)	264 (1.7)	261 (1.9)
Pennsylvania	— (†)	265 (1.0)	264 (1.2)	267 (1.3)	268 (1.2)	21 (1.4)	79 (1.4)	36 (1.5)	3 (0.6)	247 (3.9)	273 (1.9)	268 (1.4)
Rhode Island	264 (0.9)	262 (0.8)	261 (0.7)	261 (0.7)	258 (0.9)	31 (1.2)	69 (1.2)	27 (1.1)	2 (0.3)	245 (1.4)	267 (1.0)	275 (1.8)
South Carolina	255 (1.1)	258 (1.1)	258 (1.3)	257 (1.1)	257 (0.9)	31 (1.2)	69 (1.2)	25 (1.4)	2 (0.3)	259 (2.5)	262 (1.6)	253 (1.5)
South Dakota	— (†)	— (†)	270 (0.8)	269 (0.6)	270 (0.7)	17 (0.9)	83 (0.9)	37 (1.9)	2 (0.4)	267 (1.1)	271 (2.4)	269 (0.7)
Tennessee[7]	258 (1.2)	260 (1.4)	258 (1.2)	259 (0.9)	259 (1.0)	29 (1.3)	71 (1.3)	26 (1.1)	2 (0.4)	252 (1.7)	264 (2.3)	260 (1.6)
Texas	261 (1.4)	262 (1.4)	259 (1.1)	258 (0.6)	261 (0.9)	27 (1.0)	73 (1.0)	28 (1.2)	2 (0.3)	256 (1.1)	261 (1.1)	259 (1.6)
Utah	263 (1.0)	263 (1.1)	264 (0.8)	262 (0.8)	262 (1.0)	25 (1.1)	75 (1.1)	30 (1.2)	2 (0.4)	261 (1.4)	262 (1.0)	264 (3.0)
Vermont	— (†)	272 (0.9)	271 (0.8)	269 (0.7)	273 (0.8)	16 (1.1)	84 (1.1)	42 (1.3)	4 (0.6)	‡ (†)	‡	‡
Virginia	266 (1.1)	269 (1.0)	268 (1.1)	268 (1.0)	267 (1.1)	21 (1.2)	79 (1.2)	34 (1.6)	3 (0.4)	260 (1.7)	273 (1.6)	266 (2.1)
Washington[7]	264 (1.2)	268 (1.2)	264 (0.9)	265 (1.3)	265 (0.9)	23 (1.1)	77 (1.1)	34 (1.3)	3 (0.4)	264 (2.4)	265 (1.5)	265 (2.3)
West Virginia	262 (1.0)	264 (1.0)	260 (1.0)	255 (1.2)	255 (1.0)	32 (1.2)	68 (1.2)	23 (1.1)	1 (0.3)	261 (2.0)	259 (2.7)	252 (1.3)
Wisconsin[6,7]	265 (1.8)	— (†)	266 (1.3)	266 (1.1)	264 (1.0)	24 (1.3)	76 (1.3)	33 (1.7)	3 (0.4)	255 (2.6)	276 (1.6)	266 (1.6)
Wyoming	263 (1.3)	265 (0.7)	267 (0.5)	268 (0.7)	266 (0.7)	20 (1.1)	80 (1.1)	33 (1.0)	2 (0.5)	267 (1.6)	270 (3.7)	269 (0.8)
Department of Defense dependents schools[9]	269 (1.3)	273 (0.5)	272 (0.6)	271 (0.7)	273 (1.0)	13 (1.3)	87 (1.3)	39 (1.6)	2 (0.5)	‡ (†)	‡ (†)	‡ (†)
Other jurisdictions												
American Samoa	— (†)	198 (1.7)	— (†)	— (†)	— (†)	—	—	—	—	— (†)	— (†)	— (†)
Guam	— (†)	240 (1.2)	— (†)	— (†)	— (†)	—	—	—	—	— (†)	— (†)	— (†)
U.S. Virgin Islands	231 (2.1)	241 (1.3)	— (†)	— (†)	— (†)	—	—	—	—	— (†)	— (†)	— (†)

—Not available.
†Not applicable.
‡Reporting standards not met.
[1]Scale ranges from 0 to 500.
[2]Central city is a large or mid-size central city of a Metropolitan Statistical Area (MSA). Urban fringe/large town includes places that are within an MSA of a central city but not primarily within its central city, as well as towns that are incorporated places not within an MSA and have a population greater than or equal to 25,000. Rural/small town includes places that are defined as rural by the U.S. Census Bureau and have a population less than 2,500 and/or a population density of less than 1,000 per square mile, as well as towns that are incorporated places not within an MSA and have a population less than 25,000 but greater than or equal to 2,500.
[3]Basic denotes partial mastery of the knowledge and skills that are fundamental for proficient work at the 8th-grade level.
[4]Proficient represents solid academic performance for 8th-graders. Students reaching this level have demonstrated competency over challenging subject matter.

[5]Advanced signifies superior performance.
[6]Did not satisfy one or more of the guidelines for school participation in 1998. Data are subject to appreciable nonresponse bias.
[7]Did not satisfy one or more of the guidelines for school participation in 2002. Data are subject to appreciable nonresponse bias.
[8]Did not satisfy one or more of the guidelines for school participation in 2003. Data are subject to appreciable nonresponse bias.
[9]Prior to 2005, NAEP divided the Department of Defense (DoD) schools into two jurisdictions, domestic and overseas. In 2005, NAEP began combining the DoD domestic and overseas schools into a single jurisdiction. Data shown in this table for years prior to 2005 were recalculated for comparability.
NOTE: The reading data include students for whom accommodations were permitted. Standard errors appear in parentheses.
SOURCE: U.S. Department of Education, National Center for Education Statistics, National Assessment of Educational Progress (NAEP), 1998, 2000, 2002, 2003, 2005, and 2007 Reading Assessments, retrieved May 19, 2008, from the NAEP Data Explorer (http://nces.ed.gov/nationsreportcard/nde/). (This table was prepared May 2008.)

Table 123. Average reading scale scores of 4th-, 8th-, and 12th-graders, by selected student and school characteristics: Selected years, 1992 through 2007

Selected student or school characteristic	1992[1]		1994[1]		1998		2000		2002		2003		2005		2007	
1	2		3		4		5		6		7		8		9	
4th-graders, all students	**217**	**(0.9)**	**214**	**(1.0)**	**215**	**(1.1)**	**213**	**(1.3)**	**219**	**(0.4)**	**218**	**(0.3)**	**219**	**(0.2)**	**221**	**(0.3)**
Sex																
Male	213	(1.2)	209	(1.3)	212	(1.3)	208	(1.3)	215	(0.4)	215	(0.3)	216	(0.2)	218	(0.3)
Female	221	(1.0)	220	(1.1)	217	(1.3)	219	(1.4)	222	(0.5)	222	(0.3)	222	(0.3)	224	(0.3)
Race/ethnicity																
White	224	(1.2)	224	(1.3)	225	(1.0)	224	(1.1)	229	(0.3)	229	(0.2)	229	(0.2)	231	(0.2)
Black	192	(1.7)	185	(1.8)	193	(1.9)	190	(1.8)	199	(0.5)	198	(0.4)	200	(0.3)	203	(0.4)
Hispanic	197	(2.6)	188	(3.4)	193	(3.2)	190	(2.9)	201	(1.3)	200	(0.6)	203	(0.5)	205	(0.5)
Asian/Pacific Islander	216	(2.9)	220	(3.8)	215	(5.6)	225	(5.2)	224	(1.6)	226	(1.2)	229	(0.7)	232	(1.0)
American Indian/Alaska Native	‡	(†)	211	(6.6)	‡	(†)	214	(6.0)	207	(2.0)	202	(1.4)	204	(1.3)	203	(1.2)
Control of school																
Public	215	(1.0)	212	(1.1)	213	(1.2)	211	(1.4)	217	(0.5)	216	(0.3)	217	(0.2)	220	(0.3)
Private, total	232	(1.7)	231	(2.5)	232	(2.6)	231	(1.8)	234	(0.9)	235	(0.8)	‡	(†)	234	(1.1)
Catholic	229	(2.2)	229	(3.3)	232	(2.7)	229	(2.5)	234	(1.1)	235	(1.0)	234	(0.8)	232	(1.3)
Lutheran	—	(†)	—	(†)	—	(†)	—	(†)	236	(1.4)	232	(1.9)	231	(2.0)	—	(†)
Conservative Christian	—	(†)	—	(†)	—	(†)	—	(†)	229	(2.6)	‡	(†)	‡	(†)	—	(†)
8th-graders, all students	**260**	**(0.9)**	**260**	**(0.8)**	**263**	**(0.8)**	**—**	**(†)**	**264**	**(0.4)**	**263**	**(0.3)**	**262**	**(0.2)**	**263**	**(0.2)**
Sex																
Male	254	(1.1)	252	(1.0)	256	(1.0)	—	(†)	260	(0.5)	258	(0.3)	257	(0.2)	258	(0.3)
Female	267	(1.0)	267	(1.0)	270	(0.8)	—	(†)	269	(0.5)	269	(0.3)	267	(0.2)	268	(0.3)
Race/ethnicity																
White	267	(1.1)	267	(1.0)	270	(0.9)	—	(†)	272	(0.4)	272	(0.2)	271	(0.2)	272	(0.2)
Black	237	(1.7)	236	(1.8)	244	(1.2)	—	(†)	245	(0.7)	244	(0.5)	243	(0.4)	245	(0.4)
Hispanic	241	(1.6)	243	(1.2)	243	(1.7)	—	(†)	247	(0.8)	245	(0.7)	246	(0.4)	247	(0.4)
Asian/Pacific Islander	268	(3.9)	265	(3.0)	264	(7.1)	—	(†)	267	(1.7)	270	(1.1)	271	(0.8)	271	(1.1)
American Indian/Alaska Native	‡	(†)	248	(4.7)	‡	(†)	—	(†)	250	(3.5)	246	(3.0)	249	(1.4)	247	(1.2)
Parents' highest level of education																
Did not finish high school	243	(1.4)	238	(1.9)	242	(1.6)	—	(†)	248	(1.0)	245	(0.7)	244	(0.5)	245	(0.5)
Graduated high school	251	(1.4)	252	(1.2)	254	(1.3)	—	(†)	257	(0.5)	254	(0.4)	252	(0.4)	253	(0.4)
Some education after high school	265	(1.1)	266	(1.3)	268	(1.1)	—	(†)	268	(0.5)	267	(0.4)	265	(0.3)	266	(0.3)
Graduated college	271	(1.0)	270	(0.9)	273	(0.9)	—	(†)	274	(0.4)	273	(0.3)	272	(0.2)	273	(0.2)
Control of school																
Public	258	(1.0)	257	(0.8)	261	(0.8)	—	(†)	263	(0.5)	261	(0.2)	260	(0.2)	261	(0.2)
Private, total	278	(2.0)	279	(1.4)	281	(1.7)	—	(†)	281	(0.9)	282	(0.7)	‡	(†)	280	(0.9)
Catholic	275	(1.9)	279	(1.3)	282	(1.8)	—	(†)	281	(0.9)	281	(0.9)	280	(1.0)	282	(1.3)
Lutheran	—	(†)	—	(†)	—	(†)	—	(†)	281	(1.6)	281	(1.6)	280	(1.8)	—	(†)
Conservative Christian	—	(†)	—	(†)	—	(†)	—	(†)	‡	(†)	276	(1.5)	‡	(†)	—	(†)
12th-graders, all students	**292**	**(0.6)**	**287**	**(0.7)**	**290**	**(0.6)**	**—**	**(†)**	**287**	**(0.7)**	**—**	**(†)**	**286**	**(0.6)**	**—**	**(†)**
Sex																
Male	287	(0.7)	280	(0.8)	282	(0.8)	—	(†)	279	(0.9)	—	(†)	279	(0.8)	—	(†)
Female	297	(0.7)	294	(0.8)	298	(0.8)	—	(†)	295	(0.7)	—	(†)	292	(0.7)	—	(†)
Race/ethnicity																
White	297	(0.6)	293	(0.7)	297	(0.7)	—	(†)	292	(0.7)	—	(†)	293	(0.7)	—	(†)
Black	273	(1.4)	265	(1.6)	269	(1.4)	—	(†)	267	(1.3)	—	(†)	267	(1.2)	—	(†)
Hispanic	279	(2.7)	270	(1.7)	275	(1.5)	—	(†)	273	(1.5)	—	(†)	272	(1.2)	—	(†)
Asian/Pacific Islander	290	(3.2)	278	(2.4)	287	(2.7)	—	(†)	286	(2.0)	—	(†)	287	(1.9)	—	(†)
American Indian/Alaska Native	‡	(†)	274	(5.8)	‡	(†)	—	(†)	‡	(†)	—	(†)	279	(6.3)	—	(†)
Parents' highest level of education																
Did not finish high school	275	(1.4)	266	(1.5)	268	(1.8)	—	(†)	268	(1.5)	—	(†)	268	(1.7)	—	(†)
Graduated high school	283	(0.8)	277	(1.3)	279	(1.2)	—	(†)	278	(1.1)	—	(†)	274	(0.9)	—	(†)
Some education after high school	294	(0.8)	289	(1.0)	291	(1.0)	—	(†)	289	(1.0)	—	(†)	287	(0.8)	—	(†)
Graduated college	301	(0.8)	298	(1.0)	300	(0.7)	—	(†)	296	(0.8)	—	(†)	297	(0.7)	—	(†)
Control of school																
Public	290	(0.7)	286	(0.7)	289	(0.7)	—	(†)	—	(†)	—	(†)	285	(0.7)	—	(†)
Private, total	308	(1.3)	301	(1.9)	303	(1.6)	—	(†)	—	(†)	—	(†)	‡	(†)	—	(†)
Catholic	307	(1.5)	298	(2.4)	303	(2.2)	—	(†)	—	(†)	—	(†)	‡	(†)	—	(†)
Lutheran	—	(†)	—	(†)	—	(†)	—	(†)	—	(†)	—	(†)	—	(†)	—	(†)
Conservative Christian	—	(†)	—	(†)	—	(†)	—	(†)	—	(†)	—	(†)	—	(†)	—	(†)

—Not available.
†Not applicable.
‡Reporting standards not met.
[1]Accommodations were not permitted for this assessment.
NOTE: Scale ranges from 0 to 500. Includes public and private schools. Excludes persons not enrolled in school and those who were unable to be tested due to limited proficiency in English or due to a disability. Race categories exclude persons of Hispanic ethnicity. Some data have been revised from previously published figures. Standard errors appear in parentheses.
SOURCE: U.S. Department of Education, National Center for Education Statistics, National Assessment of Educational Progress (NAEP), 1992, 1994, 1998, 2000, 2002, 2003, 2005, and 2007 Reading Assessments, retrieved June 16, 2008, from the NAEP Data Explorer (http://nces.ed.gov/nationsreportcard/nde/). (This table was prepared June 2008.)

Table 124. Average reading scale scores of 4th- and 8th-graders, by selected student and parent characteristics and school type: Various years, 2000 through 2005

Year, grade, and school type	All students	Sex of child		Race/ethnicity of child					Highest education level of parents				
		Male	Female	White	Black	Hispanic	Asian/Pacific Islander	American Indian/Alaska Native	Less than high school	Graduated from high school	Some education after high school	Graduated from college	Unknown
1	2	3	4	5	6	7	8	9	10	11	12	13	14
2000													
4th-graders													
Public	211 (1.4)	206 (1.4)	217 (1.6)	223 (1.2)	189 (1.9)	188 (3.1)	223 (5.6)	‡ (†)	—	—	—	—	—
Private, total	231 (1.8)	225 (—)	238 (—)	236 (—)	213 ! (—)	215 (—)	236 ! (—)	‡ (†)	—	—	—	—	—
Catholic	229 (2.5)	224 (2.9)	233 (2.5)	236 (2.0)	209 ! (2.5)	211 ! (5.7)	‡ (†)	‡ (†)	—	—	—	—	—
Lutheran	‡ (†)	‡ (†)	‡ (†)	‡ (†)	‡ (†)	‡ (†)	‡ (†)	‡ (†)	—	—	—	—	—
Conservative Christian	‡ (†)	‡ (†)	‡ (†)	‡ (†)	‡ (†)	‡ (†)	‡ (†)	‡ (†)	—	—	—	—	—
2002													
4th-graders													
Public	217 (0.5)	214 (0.5)	220 (0.5)	227 (0.3)	198 (0.6)	199 (1.4)	223 (1.7)	207 (2.0)	—	—	—	—	—
Private, total	234 (0.9)	231 (—)	237 (—)	239 (—)	212 (—)	223 (—)	231 (—)	‡ (†)	—	—	—	—	—
Catholic	234 (1.1)	231 (1.3)	236 (1.2)	239 (0.8)	212 (3.1)	222 (3.1)	229 (4.3)	‡ (†)	—	—	—	—	—
Lutheran	236 (1.4)	234 (2.0)	238 (1.8)	238 (1.3)	‡ (†)	‡ (†)	‡ (†)	‡ (†)	—	—	—	—	—
Conservative Christian	229 (2.6)	226 (3.4)	233 (2.6)	234 (2.9)	216 ! (4.3)	‡ (†)	‡ (†)	‡ (†)	—	—	—	—	—
8th-graders													
Public	263 (0.5)	258 (0.5)	267 (0.5)	271 (0.5)	244 (0.8)	245 (0.9)	265 (1.8)	252 (2.5)	247 (1.0)	256 (0.5)	267 (0.6)	273 (0.5)	246 (0.8)
Private, total	281 (0.9)	276 (—)	285 (—)	285 (—)	263 (—)	266 (—)	285 (—)	‡ (†)	264 ! (—)	270 (—)	279 (—)	285 (—)	265 (—)
Catholic	281 (0.9)	276 (1.3)	285 (1.0)	285 (0.8)	261 (2.5)	271 (2.7)	282 (4.2)	‡ (†)	‡ (†)	272 (2.6)	278 (1.4)	285 (0.9)	266 (3.9)
Lutheran	281 (1.6)	278 (1.8)	284 (2.3)	283 (1.5)	216 ! (4.3)	‡ (†)	‡ (†)	‡ (†)	‡ (†)	271 (3.9)	284 (3.6)	284 (1.6)	‡ (†)
Conservative Christian	‡ (†)	‡ (†)	‡ (†)	‡ (†)	‡ (†)	‡ (†)	‡ (†)	‡ (†)	‡ (†)	‡ (†)	‡ (†)	‡ (†)	‡ (†)
2003													
4th-graders													
Public	216 (0.3)	213 (0.3)	220 (0.3)	227 (0.3)	197 (0.4)	199 (0.6)	225 (1.3)	202 (1.5)	—	—	—	—	—
Private, total	235 (0.8)	232 (—)	237 (—)	239 (—)	210 (—)	220 (—)	236 (—)	‡ (†)	—	—	—	—	—
Catholic	235 (1.0)	232 (1.2)	237 (1.2)	240 (0.9)	211 (2.4)	219 (1.9)	231 (3.6)	‡ (†)	—	—	—	—	—
Lutheran	232 (1.9)	229 (2.7)	234 (1.9)	236 (1.2)	206 ! (7.0)	‡ (†)	‡ (†)	‡ (†)	—	—	—	—	—
Conservative Christian	‡ (†)	‡ (†)	‡ (†)	‡ (†)	‡ (†)	‡ (†)	‡ (†)	‡ (†)	—	—	—	—	—
8th-graders													
Public	261 (0.2)	256 (0.3)	267 (0.3)	270 (0.2)	244 (0.5)	244 (0.7)	268 (1.2)	248 (1.7)	245 (0.6)	253 (0.4)	266 (0.4)	271 (0.3)	242 (0.6)
Private, total	282 (0.7)	278 (—)	287 (—)	286 (—)	261 (—)	269 (—)	286 (—)	‡ (†)	263 (—)	268 (—)	277 (—)	287 (—)	264 (—)
Catholic	281 (0.9)	277 (1.3)	286 (1.0)	286 (0.8)	260 (2.8)	270 (1.4)	280 (2.8)	‡ (†)	‡ (†)	269 (1.7)	277 (1.5)	285 (0.9)	265 (2.5)
Lutheran	281 (1.6)	275 (2.1)	288 (2.3)	284 (1.5)	260 ! (4.6)	‡ (†)	‡ (†)	‡ (†)	‡ (†)	271 (4.2)	276 (3.4)	286 (1.6)	‡ (†)
Conservative Christian	276 (1.5)	271 (2.0)	282 (1.9)	280 (1.6)	261 ! (6.4)	267 ! (7.1)	‡ (†)	‡ (†)	‡ (†)	263 (3.8)	275 (3.4)	282 (1.7)	258 (6.4)
2005													
4th-graders													
Public	217 (0.2)	214 (0.3)	221 (0.3)	228 (0.2)	199 (0.3)	201 (0.5)	227 (0.9)	205 (1.3)	—	—	—	—	—
Private, total	‡ (†)	‡ (†)	‡ (†)	‡ (†)	‡ (†)	‡ (†)	‡ (†)	‡ (†)	—	—	—	—	—
Catholic	234 (0.8)	232 (1.1)	236 (1.1)	239 (0.9)	214 (2.4)	222 (2.1)	232 (3.1)	‡ (†)	—	—	—	—	—
Lutheran	231 (2.0)	229 (2.9)	234 (2.3)	233 (2.1)	‡ (†)	‡ (†)	‡ (†)	‡ (†)	—	—	—	—	—
Conservative Christian	‡ (†)	‡ (†)	‡ (†)	‡ (†)	‡ (†)	‡ (†)	‡ (†)	‡ (†)	—	—	—	—	—
8th-graders													
Public	260 (0.2)	255 (0.2)	266 (0.2)	269 (0.2)	242 (0.4)	245 (0.4)	270 (0.8)	251 (1.2)	244 (0.5)	252 (0.3)	265 (0.2)	270 (0.2)	242 (0.4)
Private, total	‡ (†)	‡ (†)	‡ (†)	‡ (†)	‡ (†)	‡ (†)	‡ (†)	‡ (†)	‡ (†)	‡ (†)	‡ (†)	‡ (†)	‡ (†)
Catholic	280 (1.0)	275 (1.3)	284 (1.1)	285 (0.9)	259 (2.7)	268 (1.8)	280 (3.6)	‡ (†)	‡ (†)	269 (2.1)	276 (1.6)	284 (1.0)	258 (2.9)
Lutheran	280 (1.8)	274 (2.7)	285 (2.0)	284 (1.6)	252 ! (6.0)	‡ (†)	‡ (†)	‡ (†)	‡ (†)	270 (4.5)	275 (5.5)	286 (1.6)	‡ (†)
Conservative Christian	‡ (†)	‡ (†)	‡ (†)	‡ (†)	‡ (†)	‡ (†)	‡ (†)	‡ (†)	‡ (†)	‡ (†)	‡ (†)	‡ (†)	‡ (†)

—Not available.
†Not applicable.
!Interpret data with caution.
‡Reporting standards not met.
NOTE: The NAEP reading scale ranges from 0 to 500. Private totals include other private school categories not separately shown. Race categories exclude persons of Hispanic ethnicity. Standard errors appear in parentheses.

SOURCE: U.S. Department of Education, National Center for Education Statistics, National Assessment of Educational Progress (NAEP), *Student Achievement in Private Schools: Results From NAEP 2000–2005*; and the NAEP Data Explorer (http://nces.ed.gov/nationsreportcard/nde/), retrieved May 2006. (This table was prepared June 2006.)

Table 125. Average writing scale score and percentage of students attaining writing achievement levels, by selected student characteristics and grade level: 2002 and 2007

Grade, year, and achievement level	All students	Sex		Race/ethnicity					Parents' highest level of education				Free/reduced-price lunch eligibility		
		Male	Female	White	Black	Hispanic	Asian/ Pacific Islander	American Indian/ Alaska Native	Did not finish high school	Graduated high school	Some education after high school	Graduated college	Eligible	Not eligible	Information not available
1	2	3	4	5	6	7	8	9	10	11	12	13	14	15	16
Average scale score[1]															
4th-graders, 2002	154 (0.4)	146 (0.6)	163 (0.4)	161 (0.3)	140 (0.7)	141 (1.6)	167 (1.5)	139 (1.9)	— (†)	— (†)	— (†)	— (†)	141 (0.8)	163 (0.5)	161 (1.5)
8th-graders															
2002	153 (0.5)	143 (0.6)	164 (0.6)	161 (0.6)	135 (0.7)	137 (0.9)	161 (2.0)	137 (2.9)	136 (0.9)	144 (0.6)	156 (0.6)	165 (0.6)	136 (0.5)	162 (0.7)	161 (1.5)
2007	156 (0.2)	146 (0.3)	166 (0.3)	164 (0.2)	141 (0.4)	142 (0.6)	167 (1.2)	143 (1.3)	139 (0.6)	147 (0.5)	158 (0.4)	166 (0.3)	141 (0.3)	164 (0.3)	170 (1.2)
12th-graders															
2002	148 (0.8)	136 (0.8)	160 (0.9)	154 (0.8)	130 (1.3)	136 (1.5)	151 (2.4)	‡ (†)	129 (1.7)	139 (1.1)	149 (0.9)	158 (1.0)	132 (1.4)	152 (1.0)	156 (1.5)
2007	153 (0.6)	144 (0.6)	162 (0.7)	159 (0.6)	137 (1.0)	139 (1.0)	160 (1.7)	140 (3.9)	134 (1.0)	141 (0.8)	152 (0.7)	163 (0.6)	138 (0.7)	157 (0.6)	165 (1.5)
Percent attaining achievement levels															
4th-graders, 2002															
Below Basic	14 (0.4)	19 (0.5)	9 (0.3)	10 (0.2)	23 (0.8)	23 (1.6)	7 (1.1)	25 (2.6)	— (†)	— (†)	— (†)	— (†)	22 (0.8)	8 (0.3)	10 (1.1)
At or above Basic[2]	86 (0.4)	81 (0.5)	91 (0.3)	90 (0.2)	77 (0.8)	77 (1.6)	93 (1.1)	75 (2.6)	— (†)	— (†)	— (†)	— (†)	78 (0.8)	92 (0.3)	90 (1.1)
At or above Proficient[3]	28 (0.4)	20 (0.5)	36 (0.6)	34 (0.4)	14 (0.7)	17 (0.9)	41 (2.1)	15 (1.7)	— (†)	— (†)	— (†)	— (†)	15 (0.5)	36 (0.6)	34 (1.6)
At Advanced[4]	2 (0.1)	1 (0.1)	3 (0.2)	3 (0.2)	1 (0.2)	1 (0.2)	4 (0.6)	1 (0.5)	— (†)	— (†)	— (†)	— (†)	1 (0.1)	3 (0.2)	3 (0.3)
8th-graders															
2002															
Below Basic	15 (0.4)	21 (0.6)	9 (0.3)	10 (0.4)	26 (1.0)	27 (1.0)	12 (1.3)	27 (3.9)	26 (1.3)	19 (0.7)	11 (0.6)	9 (0.4)	26 (0.6)	9 (0.4)	11 (0.7)
At or above Basic[2]	85 (0.4)	79 (0.6)	91 (0.3)	90 (0.4)	74 (1.0)	73 (1.0)	88 (1.3)	73 (3.9)	74 (1.3)	81 (0.7)	89 (0.6)	91 (0.4)	74 (0.6)	91 (0.4)	89 (0.7)
At or above Proficient[3]	31 (0.6)	21 (0.6)	42 (0.8)	38 (0.6)	13 (0.6)	16 (1.1)	40 (2.6)	16 (2.5)	14 (1.0)	20 (0.6)	31 (0.8)	43 (0.8)	16 (0.6)	39 (0.8)	39 (1.7)
At Advanced[4]	2 (0.1)	1 (0.1)	3 (0.2)	3 (0.2)	# (†)	1 (0.2)	4 (0.8)	1 (#)	# (†)	1 (0.2)	1 (0.2)	4 (0.2)	1 (0.1)	3 (0.2)	4 (0.6)
2007															
Below Basic	12 (0.2)	17 (0.3)	7 (0.2)	7 (0.2)	19 (0.5)	20 (0.6)	8 (0.8)	21 (1.3)	21 (1.0)	16 (0.5)	9 (0.4)	7 (0.2)	20 (0.3)	7 (0.2)	5 (0.6)
At or above Basic[2]	88 (0.2)	83 (0.3)	93 (0.2)	93 (0.2)	81 (0.5)	80 (0.6)	92 (0.8)	79 (1.3)	79 (1.0)	84 (0.5)	91 (0.4)	93 (0.2)	80 (0.3)	93 (0.2)	95 (0.6)
At or above Proficient[3]	33 (0.3)	22 (0.3)	43 (0.4)	41 (0.3)	16 (0.6)	18 (0.5)	46 (1.4)	20 (1.6)	14 (0.6)	21 (0.6)	33 (0.5)	44 (0.4)	17 (0.3)	41 (0.4)	49 (1.8)
At Advanced[4]	2 (0.1)	1 (0.1)	3 (0.1)	3 (0.1)	# (†)	1 (0.1)	5 (0.5)	1 (0.4)	# (†)	# (†)	1 (0.1)	3 (0.1)	# (†)	3 (0.1)	4 (0.5)
12th-graders															
2002															
Below Basic	26 (0.7)	37 (1.0)	15 (0.7)	21 (0.7)	41 (1.7)	36 (1.8)	24 (2.3)	‡ (†)	43 (2.1)	32 (1.2)	23 (1.0)	18 (0.9)	40 (1.5)	23 (0.8)	19 (1.3)
At or above Basic[2]	74 (0.7)	63 (1.0)	85 (0.7)	79 (0.7)	59 (1.7)	64 (1.8)	76 (2.3)	‡ (†)	57 (2.1)	68 (1.2)	77 (1.0)	82 (0.9)	60 (1.5)	77 (0.8)	81 (1.3)
At or above Proficient[3]	24 (0.8)	14 (0.8)	33 (1.0)	28 (0.9)	9 (1.0)	13 (1.4)	25 (2.8)	‡ (†)	8 (1.4)	14 (1.1)	22 (1.3)	32 (1.0)	11 (1.0)	26 (1.0)	29 (1.6)
At Advanced[4]	2 (0.2)	1 (0.1)	3 (0.3)	2 (0.3)	# (†)	1 (0.2)	3 (1.1)	‡ (†)	# (†)	1 (0.2)	1 (0.2)	3 (0.4)	1 (0.2)	2 (0.3)	2 (0.4)
2007															
Below Basic	18 (0.5)	26 (0.6)	11 (0.5)	14 (0.5)	31 (1.2)	29 (1.1)	14 (1.5)	30 (5.3)	34 (1.5)	27 (1.1)	16 (0.7)	12 (0.4)	31 (1.0)	15 (0.5)	10 (1.0)
At or above Basic[2]	82 (0.5)	74 (0.6)	89 (0.5)	86 (0.5)	69 (1.2)	71 (1.1)	86 (1.5)	70 (5.3)	66 (1.5)	73 (1.1)	84 (0.7)	88 (0.4)	69 (1.0)	85 (0.5)	90 (1.0)
At or above Proficient[3]	24 (0.6)	16 (0.6)	32 (0.8)	30 (0.6)	9 (0.8)	11 (0.9)	30 (2.2)	12 (2.6)	8 (1.0)	13 (0.6)	20 (0.7)	34 (0.8)	11 (0.5)	27 (0.7)	36 (2.1)
At Advanced[4]	1 (0.1)	# (†)	1 (0.2)	1 (0.2)	# (†)	# (†)	1 (0.6)	# (†)	# (†)	# (†)	# (†)	2 (0.2)	# (†)	1 (0.5)	2 (0.4)

—Not available.
†Not applicable.
#Rounds to zero.
‡Reporting standards not met.
[1] Scale ranges from 1 to 300 for all three grades, but scores cannot be compared across grades. For example, a score of 156 at grade 8 does not denote higher performance than a score of 153 at grade 12.
[2] Basic denotes partial mastery of the knowledge and skills that are fundamental for proficient work at a given grade.
[3] Proficient represents solid academic performance. Students reaching this level have demonstrated competency over challenging subject matter.
[4] Advanced signifies superior performance for a given grade.

NOTE: Includes public and private schools. Excludes persons unable to be tested due to limited proficiency in English or due to a disability (if the accommodations provided were not sufficient to enable the test to properly reflect the students' writing proficiency). In 2002, the NAEP national samples of 4th- and 8th-graders were obtained by aggregating the samples from each state, rather than by independently selecting national samples for grades 4 and 8. As a consequence, the size of the national samples increased for these grade levels, and smaller differences were found to be statistically significant than would have been detected in previous assessments. Grade 4 was not included in the 2007 survey. Race categories exclude persons of Hispanic ethnicity. Some data have been revised from previously published figures. Detail may not sum to totals because of rounding. Standard errors appear in parentheses.
SOURCE: U.S. Department of Education, National Center for Education Statistics, National Assessment of Educational Progress (NAEP), 2002 and 2007 Writing Assessments, retrieved May 6, 2008, from the NAEP Data Explorer (http://nces.ed.gov/nationsreportcard/nde). (This table was prepared May 2008.)

Table 126. Percentage of students attaining U.S. history achievement levels, by grade level and selected student characteristics: 2001 and 2006

Selected student characteristic	Percent of 4th-graders						Percent of 8th-graders						Percent of 12th-graders					
	2001, At or above Basic[1]	2006					2001, At or above Basic[1]	2006					2001, At or above Basic[1]	2006				
		Below Basic	At or above Basic[1]	At or above Proficient[2]	At Advanced[3]			Below Basic	At or above Basic[1]	At or above Proficient[2]	At Advanced[3]			Below Basic	At or above Basic[1]	At or above Proficient[2]	At Advanced[3]	
1	2	3	4	5	6		7	8	9	10	11		12	13	14	15	16	
All students	66 (1.2)	30 (1.3)	70 (1.3)	18 (1.0)	2 (0.3)		62 (1.0)	35 (1.0)	65 (1.0)	17 (0.8)	1 (0.1)		43 (1.2)	53 (1.1)	47 (1.1)	13 (0.7)	1 (0.2)	
Sex																		
Male	65 (1.3)	31 (1.5)	69 (1.5)	20 (1.3)	2 (0.4)		62 (1.1)	33 (1.3)	67 (1.3)	19 (1.0)	2 (0.2)		45 (1.6)	50 (1.2)	50 (1.2)	15 (0.8)	1 (0.2)	
Female	67 (1.4)	30 (1.2)	70 (1.2)	16 (1.0)	1 (0.3)		61 (1.2)	36 (1.0)	64 (1.0)	14 (0.7)	1 (0.2)		40 (1.2)	56 (1.2)	44 (1.2)	11 (0.7)	1 (0.2)	
Race/ethnicity																		
White	76 (1.5)	16 (1.2)	84 (1.2)	26 (1.5)	2 (0.4)		71 (1.1)	21 (0.8)	79 (0.8)	23 (1.1)	2 (0.2)		49 (1.3)	44 (1.3)	56 (1.3)	16 (0.8)	1 (0.2)	
Black	41 (2.3)	54 (2.5)	46 (2.5)	5 (1.0)	# (†)		35 (2.1)	60 (1.7)	40 (1.7)	4 (0.5)	# (†)		19 (1.5)	80 (1.6)	20 (1.6)	2 (0.5)	# (†)	
Hispanic	40 (2.8)	51 (2.7)	49 (2.7)	6 (0.7)	1 (0.2)		36 (2.6)	54 (2.2)	46 (2.2)	6 (0.8)	# (0.1)		24 (2.3)	73 (1.4)	27 (1.4)	4 (0.6)	# (†)	
Asian/Pacific Islander	74 (4.5)	29 (4.8)	71 (4.8)	22 (4.3)	2 (—)		65 (3.0)	25 (4.4)	75 (4.4)	22 (3.0)	1 (0.6)		51 (6.7)	46 (3.5)	54 (3.5)	20 (3.1)	3 (0.7)	
American Indian/Alaska Native	‡ (†)	59 (7.7)	41 (7.7)	6 (3.2)	# (†)		57 (6.5)	57 (6.1)	43 (6.1)	5 (—)	# (†)		37 (7.8)	68 (7.3)	32 (7.3)	4 (2.9)	# (†)	
Parents' highest level of education																		
Not high school graduate	—	— (†)	— (†)	— (†)	— (†)		38 (4.1)	60 (2.2)	40 (2.2)	3 (0.9)	# (†)		19 (2.1)	82 (1.7)	18 (1.7)	3 (0.8)	# (†)	
Graduated high school	—	— (†)	— (†)	— (†)	— (†)		50 (1.8)	48 (2.2)	52 (2.2)	7 (0.7)	# (†)		25 (1.6)	69 (1.4)	31 (1.4)	5 (0.7)	# (†)	
Some college	—	— (†)	— (†)	— (†)	— (†)		69 (1.5)	30 (1.3)	70 (1.3)	14 (1.2)	1 (0.3)		39 (1.3)	55 (1.4)	45 (1.4)	9 (0.8)	# (†)	
Graduated college	—	— (†)	— (†)	— (†)	— (†)		77 (1.0)	21 (1.1)	79 (1.1)	27 (1.1)	2 (0.3)		58 (1.5)	40 (1.4)	60 (1.4)	20 (1.1)	2 (0.3)	
Free/reduced-price lunch eligibility																		
Eligible	45 (1.7)	49 (1.6)	51 (1.6)	6 (0.5)	# (†)		38 (1.7)	56 (1.6)	44 (1.6)	5 (0.5)	# (†)		22 (1.9)	76 (1.3)	24 (1.3)	3 (0.5)	# (†)	
Not eligible	79 (1.6)	16 (1.1)	84 (1.1)	27 (1.5)	3 (0.4)		71 (1.6)	22 (0.8)	78 (0.8)	23 (1.0)	2 (0.2)		44 (1.5)	48 (1.2)	52 (1.2)	15 (0.9)	1 (0.2)	
Not available	74 (2.8)	15 (4.0)	85 (4.0)	33 (4.7)	5 (1.7)		68 (2.2)	14 (3.2)	86 (3.2)	33 (3.8)	4 (1.1)		52 (2.9)	38 (3.7)	62 (3.7)	19 (2.6)	1 (0.5)	
Region																		
Northeast	—	25 (2.5)	75 (2.5)	19 (1.5)	2 (0.5)		— (†)	31 (2.4)	69 (2.4)	21 (2.1)	2 (0.4)		— (†)	44 (3.0)	56 (3.0)	19 (1.9)	2 (0.5)	
Midwest	—	20 (2.1)	80 (2.1)	25 (2.8)	2 (0.7)		— (†)	27 (1.8)	73 (1.8)	21 (1.7)	1 (0.3)		— (†)	50 (1.3)	50 (1.3)	14 (1.0)	1 (0.2)	
South	—	29 (2.1)	71 (2.1)	18 (2.0)	2 (0.5)		— (†)	36 (1.5)	64 (1.5)	15 (1.0)	1 (0.2)		— (†)	59 (2.0)	41 (2.0)	11 (1.0)	1 (0.2)	
West	—	45 (3.8)	55 (3.8)	11 (1.6)	1 (0.3)		— (†)	44 (2.6)	56 (2.6)	11 (1.3)	1 (0.2)		— (†)	‡ (†)	‡ (†)	‡ (†)	‡ (†)	

—Not available.
†Not applicable.
#Rounds to zero.
‡Reporting standards not met.
[1]Basic denotes partial mastery of the knowledge and skills that are fundamental for proficient work at a given grade.
[2]Proficient represents solid academic performance. Students reaching this level have demonstrated competency over challenging subject matter.
[3]Advanced signifies superior performance for a given grade.

NOTE: Includes public and private schools. Excludes students unable to be tested due to limited proficiency in English or due to a disability (if the accommodations provided were not sufficient to enable the test to properly reflect the students' U.S. history proficiency). Race categories exclude persons of Hispanic ethnicity. Totals include other racial/ethnic groups not shown separately. Standard errors appear in parentheses. Some data have been revised from previously published figures.
SOURCE: U.S. Department of Education, National Center for Education Statistics, National Assessment of Educational Progress (NAEP), 2001 and 2006 U.S. History Assessments, retrieved May 22, 2007, from the NAEP Data Explorer (http://nces.ed.gov/nationsreportcard/nde). (This table was prepared May 2007.)

Table 127. Average U.S. history scale score, by grade level and selected student characteristics, and percentage distribution of 12th-graders, by selected student characteristics: 1994, 2001, and 2006

Selected student characteristic	4th-graders 1994¹	4th-graders 2001	4th-graders 2006	8th-graders 1994¹	8th-graders 2001	8th-graders 2006	12th-graders 1994¹	12th-graders 2001	12th-graders 2006	Percentage distribution of 12th-graders 1994¹	Percentage distribution of 12th-graders 2001	Percentage distribution of 12th-graders 2006
1	2	3	4	5	6	7	8	9	10	11	12	13
All students	205 (1.0)	208 (0.9)	211 (1.1)	259 (0.6)	260 (0.8)	263 (0.8)	286 (0.8)	267 (0.9)	290 (0.7)	100 (†)	100 (†)	100 (†)
Sex												
Male	203 (1.5)	207 (1.1)	211 (1.2)	259 (0.8)	261 (0.9)	264 (0.9)	288 (0.8)	288 (1.1)	292 (0.9)	50 (0.8)	50 (0.7)	50 (0.4)
Female	206 (1.1)	209 (1.2)	211 (1.1)	259 (0.7)	260 (0.9)	261 (0.8)	285 (0.9)	286 (0.9)	288 (0.8)	50 (0.8)	50 (0.7)	50 (0.4)
Race/ethnicity												
White	214 (1.3)	217 (1.3)	223 (1.1)	266 (0.8)	268 (0.9)	273 (0.6)	292 (0.8)	292 (1.0)	297 (0.8)	75 (0.5)	72 (0.5)	66 (1.3)
Black	176 (1.6)	186 (2.0)	191 (1.9)	238 (1.6)	240 (1.9)	244 (1.2)	265 (1.5)	267 (1.4)	270 (1.3)	13 (0.3)	13 (0.2)	13 (0.9)
Hispanic	175 (2.6)	184 (2.6)	194 (1.9)	243 (1.4)	240 (2.0)	248 (1.2)	267 (1.7)	271 (1.9)	275 (1.0)	7 (0.5)	9 (0.4)	13 (1.2)
Asian/Pacific Islander	204 (3.6)	216 (3.7)	214 (5.1)	261 (5.0)	264 (2.8)	270 (3.0)	283 (3.5)	294 (6.0)	296 (2.6)	4 (0.3)	4 (0.3)	6 (0.6)
American Indian/Alaska Native	‡ (†)	‡ (†)	190 (5.9)	245 (3.4)	255 (4.4)	244 (6.3)	272 (3.0)	283 (4.2)	278 (4.1)	1 (0.3)	1 (0.2)	2 (0.7)
Parents' highest level of education												
Not high school graduate	— (†)	— (†)	— (†)	241 (1.3)	241 (2.8)	244 (1.2)	263 (1.4)	266 (1.6)	268 (1.2)	7 (0.4)	7 (0.4)	8 (0.4)
Graduated high school	— (†)	— (†)	— (†)	251 (0.8)	251 (1.0)	252 (1.3)	276 (1.1)	274 (1.1)	278 (1.0)	20 (0.7)	19 (0.6)	18 (0.6)
Some college	— (†)	— (†)	— (†)	264 (0.8)	264 (1.0)	265 (0.9)	287 (1.2)	286 (0.8)	290 (0.8)	25 (0.7)	24 (0.7)	23 (0.6)
Graduated college	— (†)	— (†)	— (†)	270 (0.8)	273 (0.9)	274 (0.8)	296 (0.9)	298 (1.2)	300 (0.8)	45 (1.0)	46 (1.1)	49 (1.0)
Free/reduced-price lunch eligibility												
Eligible	— (†)	188 (1.4)	195 (1.1)	— (†)	242 (1.3)	247 (1.1)	— (†)	269 (1.4)	273 (1.0)	— (†)	15 (0.9)	22 (1.0)
Not eligible	— (†)	219 (1.4)	224 (1.0)	— (†)	267 (1.1)	273 (0.7)	— (†)	289 (1.2)	295 (0.8)	— (†)	64 (2.2)	67 (1.4)
Not available	— (†)	217 (2.8)	227 (3.9)	— (†)	266 (2.0)	281 (2.7)	— (†)	294 (2.1)	300 (2.4)	— (†)	21 (2.5)	11 (1.3)
Region												
Northeast	— (†)	— (†)	215 (1.7)	— (†)	— (†)	267 (1.8)	— (†)	— (†)	297 (2.2)	— (†)	— (†)	20 (0.8)
Midwest	— (†)	— (†)	220 (2.2)	— (†)	— (†)	269 (1.4)	— (†)	— (†)	292 (1.1)	— (†)	— (†)	23 (0.7)
South	— (†)	— (†)	213 (2.0)	— (†)	— (†)	262 (1.2)	— (†)	— (†)	286 (1.4)	— (†)	— (†)	33 (0.8)
West	— (†)	— (†)	199 (2.9)	— (†)	— (†)	255 (1.9)	— (†)	— (†)	‡ (†)	— (†)	— (†)	‡ (†)

—Not available.
†Not applicable.
‡Reporting standards not met.
¹Accommodations were not permitted for this assessment.
NOTE: Scale ranges from 0 to 500. Includes public and private schools. Excludes students unable to be tested due to limited proficiency in English or due to a disability (if the accommodations provided were not sufficient to enable the test to properly reflect the students' proficiency in U.S. history). Race categories exclude persons of Hispanic ethnicity. Totals include other racial/ethnic groups not shown separately. Detail may not sum to totals because of rounding. Standard errors appear in parentheses. Some data have been modified from previously published figures.

SOURCE: U.S. Department of Education, National Center for Education Statistics, National Assessment of Educational Progress (NAEP), 1994, 2001, and 2006 U.S. History Assessments, retrieved June 6, 2007, from the NAEP Data Explorer (http://nces.ed.gov/nationsreportcard/nde/). (This table was prepared June 2007.)

Table 128. Average civics scale score and percentage of students attaining civics achievement levels, by grade level and selected student characteristics: 1998 and 2006

Selected student characteristic	Average scale score[1]				Percent of students attaining achievement levels							
					At or above Basic[2]				At or above Proficient[3]				At Advanced[4]			
	1998[5]		2006		1998[5]		2006		1998[5]		2006		1998[5]		2006	
1	2		3		4		5		6		7		8		9	
4th-graders	**150**	**(0.7)**	**154**	**(1.0)**	**69**	**(1.0)**	**73**	**(1.2)**	**23**	**(0.9)**	**24**	**(1.0)**	**2**	**(0.3)**	**1**	**(0.2)**
Sex																
Male	149	(1.0)	153	(1.1)	68	(1.2)	72	(1.3)	22	(1.2)	24	(1.2)	2	(0.4)	1	(0.3)
Female	151	(0.9)	155	(1.1)	70	(1.0)	75	(1.4)	23	(1.2)	24	(1.2)	1	(0.4)	1	(0.2)
Race/ethnicity																
White	158	(0.9)	164	(0.9)	78	(1.3)	85	(1.0)	29	(1.2)	34	(1.4)	2	(0.4)	2	(0.3)
Black	130	(1.1)	140	(1.5)	45	(1.7)	57	(2.3)	7	(1.1)	10	(1.2)	1	(0.3)	#	(†)
Hispanic	123	(2.2)	138	(1.3)	40	(2.8)	55	(2.0)	6	(1.1)	10	(1.1)	#	(†)	#	(0.1)
Asian/Pacific Islander	147	(4.0)	154	(3.8)	66	(5.5)	75	(4.5)	20	(3.5)	24	(4.0)	2	(0.9)	1	(0.6)
American Indian/Alaska Native	‡	(†)	124	(7.6)	‡	(†)	38	(11.3)	‡	(†)	7	(3.9)	‡	(†)	#	(†)
Free/reduced-price lunch eligibility																
Eligible	132	(0.9)	139	(1.1)	49	(1.3)	56	(1.6)	9	(0.9)	9	(0.8)	#	(†)	#	(†)
Not eligible	160	(1.1)	166	(0.8)	80	(1.4)	87	(0.9)	30	(1.3)	36	(1.4)	2	(0.5)	2	(0.3)
Not available	154	(2.2)	167	(2.1)	72	(3.1)	88	(2.2)	27	(2.5)	37	(4.0)	2	(0.9)	3	(1.4)
8th-graders	**150**	**(0.7)**	**150**	**(0.8)**	**70**	**(0.9)**	**70**	**(1.1)**	**22**	**(0.8)**	**22**	**(0.8)**	**2**	**(0.2)**	**2**	**(0.2)**
Sex																
Male	148	(0.9)	149	(1.0)	67	(1.1)	68	(1.3)	22	(1.0)	23	(0.9)	2	(0.3)	2	(0.3)
Female	152	(0.8)	151	(0.8)	73	(1.2)	72	(1.2)	22	(1.1)	21	(0.9)	1	(0.3)	1	(0.2)
Race/ethnicity																
White	158	(0.9)	161	(0.8)	78	(1.1)	82	(0.9)	28	(1.0)	30	(1.0)	2	(0.3)	2	(0.3)
Black	131	(1.2)	133	(1.5)	49	(1.7)	50	(2.0)	7	(1.0)	9	(1.1)	#	(†)	#	(0.2)
Hispanic	127	(1.3)	131	(1.1)	44	(2.3)	50	(2.2)	7	(1.0)	8	(1.0)	#	(0.2)	#	(†)
Asian/Pacific Islander	151	(8.9)	154	(3.2)	69	(9.5)	73	(4.0)	25	(5.8)	27	(3.2)	3	(1.3)	3	(0.9)
American Indian/Alaska Native	‡	(†)	127	(7.3)	‡	(†)	46	(9.5)	‡	(†)	7	(2.9)	‡	(†)	#	(†)
Parents' highest level of education																
Not high school graduate	—	(†)	129	(1.6)	—	(†)	47	(3.3)	—	(†)	6	(1.0)	—	(†)	#	(†)
Graduated high school	—	(†)	140	(1.3)	—	(†)	59	(1.8)	—	(†)	11	(1.0)	—	(†)	#	(0.2)
Some college	—	(†)	153	(1.0)	—	(†)	75	(1.7)	—	(†)	20	(1.3)	—	(†)	1	(0.3)
Graduated college	—	(†)	162	(0.9)	—	(†)	82	(0.9)	—	(†)	33	(1.2)	—	(†)	3	(0.4)
Free/reduced-price lunch eligibility																
Eligible	131	(1.1)	132	(1.0)	48	(1.6)	51	(1.5)	8	(0.8)	8	(0.5)	#	(0.2)	#	(0.1)
Not eligible	157	(1.0)	160	(0.8)	78	(1.2)	82	(1.0)	27	(1.2)	29	(0.9)	2	(0.3)	2	(0.3)
Not available	156	(2.2)	171	(2.4)	76	(2.7)	90	(2.2)	29	(2.1)	44	(4.1)	3	(0.6)	5	(1.8)
12th-graders	**150**	**(0.8)**	**151**	**(0.9)**	**65**	**(0.9)**	**66**	**(1.1)**	**26**	**(0.9)**	**27**	**(1.0)**	**4**	**(0.4)**	**5**	**(0.4)**
Sex																
Male	148	(1.1)	150	(1.1)	62	(1.2)	64	(1.5)	27	(1.2)	28	(1.2)	5	(0.6)	5	(0.5)
Female	152	(0.8)	152	(1.0)	68	(1.2)	67	(1.2)	26	(1.1)	26	(1.2)	3	(0.4)	4	(0.5)
Race/ethnicity																
White	157	(1.0)	158	(1.0)	73	(1.1)	74	(1.2)	32	(1.3)	34	(1.2)	5	(0.6)	6	(0.6)
Black	130	(1.6)	131	(1.4)	41	(2.0)	42	(1.9)	9	(1.3)	9	(1.1)	1	(0.3)	1	(0.3)
Hispanic	132	(1.1)	134	(1.1)	45	(1.9)	46	(1.7)	10	(1.2)	12	(1.2)	1	(0.3)	1	(0.3)
Asian/Pacific Islander	149	(5.2)	155	(3.1)	63	(4.8)	68	(3.7)	27	(6.6)	33	(3.9)	5	(2.3)	8	(1.6)
American Indian/Alaska Native	‡	(†)	131	(3.5)	‡	(†)	42	(8.0)	‡	(†)	9	(3.0)	‡	(†)	#	(†)
Parents' highest level of education																
Not high school graduate	—	(†)	126	(1.8)	—	(†)	35	(3.0)	—	(†)	8	(1.4)	—	(†)	1	(0.5)
Graduated high school	—	(†)	138	(1.0)	—	(†)	52	(1.6)	—	(†)	13	(1.2)	—	(†)	1	(0.3)
Some college	—	(†)	150	(0.9)	—	(†)	66	(1.4)	—	(†)	23	(1.2)	—	(†)	3	(0.5)
Graduated college	—	(†)	162	(1.1)	—	(†)	77	(1.2)	—	(†)	39	(1.4)	—	(†)	8	(0.7)
Free/reduced-price lunch eligibility																
Eligible	130	(1.4)	133	(1.0)	42	(2.1)	45	(1.5)	10	(1.7)	11	(1.1)	1	(0.4)	1	(0.4)
Not eligible	153	(1.0)	156	(1.0)	69	(1.1)	71	(1.2)	29	(1.3)	31	(1.2)	5	(0.5)	6	(0.5)
Not available	153	(1.3)	160	(2.4)	68	(1.6)	76	(3.1)	29	(1.5)	34	(2.8)	5	(0.7)	7	(1.3)

—Not available.
#Rounds to zero.
†Not applicable.
‡Reporting standards not met.
[1]Scale ranges from 0 to 300.
[2]Basic denotes partial mastery of the knowledge and skills that are fundamental for proficient work at a given grade.
[3]Proficient represents solid academic performance. Students reaching this level have demonstrated competency over challenging subject matter.
[4]Advanced signifies superior performance for a given grade.

[5]Accommodations were not permitted for this assessment.
NOTE: Includes public and private schools. Excludes students unable to be tested due to limited proficiency in English or due to a disability (if the accommodations provided were not sufficient to enable the test to properly reflect the students' proficiency in civics). Race categories exclude persons of Hispanic ethnicity. Totals include other racial/ethnic groups not shown separately. Standard errors appear in parentheses.
SOURCE: U.S. Department of Education, National Center for Education Statistics, National Assessment of Educational Progress (NAEP), 1998 and 2006 Civics Assessments, retrieved July 3, 2007, from the NAEP Data Explorer (http://nces.ed.gov/nationsreportcard/nde/). (This table was prepared July 2007.)

Table 129. Average economics scale score of 12th-graders, percentage attaining economics achievement levels, and percentage with different levels of economics coursework, by selected student and school characteristics: 2006

Selected student or school characteristic	Average scale score[1]	Percent of students attaining achievement levels				Percentage distribution of students by highest level of economics coursework taken				
		Below Basic	At or above Basic[2]	At or above Proficient[3]	At Advanced[4]	No economics courses	Combined course	Consumer economics/business	General economics	Advanced economics[5]
1	2	3	4	5	6	7	8	9	10	11
All students	150 (0.9)	21 (0.8)	79 (0.8)	42 (1.1)	3 (0.3)	13 (0.9)	12 (0.7)	11 (0.7)	49 (1.4)	16 (0.7)
Sex										
Male	152 (1.0)	21 (0.8)	79 (0.8)	45 (1.3)	4 (0.5)	13 (1.0)	10 (0.6)	10 (0.7)	50 (1.4)	16 (0.8)
Female	148 (0.9)	21 (0.9)	79 (0.9)	38 (1.3)	2 (0.3)	12 (0.9)	13 (0.9)	11 (0.8)	48 (1.6)	15 (0.8)
Race/ethnicity										
White	158 (0.8)	13 (0.7)	87 (0.7)	51 (1.2)	4 (0.4)	15 (1.1)	12 (0.8)	11 (0.8)	49 (1.6)	13 (0.9)
Black	127 (1.2)	43 (1.9)	57 (1.9)	16 (1.3)	# (†)	8 (0.8)	11 (0.9)	11 (1.2)	49 (1.7)	21 (1.1)
Hispanic	133 (1.2)	36 (1.6)	64 (1.6)	21 (1.2)	# (†)	8 (1.7)	13 (1.1)	7 (0.9)	55 (2.6)	18 (1.2)
Asian/Pacific Islander	153 (3.5)	20 (4.0)	80 (4.0)	44 (4.5)	4 (1.4)	13 (1.8)	10 (1.8)	10 (1.4)	45 (4.1)	22 (1.9)
American Indian/Alaska Native	137 (4.1)	28 (5.6)	72 (5.6)	26 (4.8)	2 (—)	11 (3.9)	18 (2.7)	17 (3.2)	41 (4.9)	13 (3.1)
Parents' highest level of education										
Not high school graduate	129 (1.4)	41 (2.1)	59 (2.1)	17 (1.7)	# (†)	10 (1.7)	13 (1.4)	10 (1.4)	53 (3.2)	14 (1.3)
Graduated high school	138 (1.2)	31 (1.5)	69 (1.5)	27 (1.4)	1 (0.3)	11 (1.2)	12 (1.0)	12 (1.0)	52 (1.7)	13 (0.9)
Some college	150 (0.8)	18 (1.1)	82 (1.1)	39 (1.4)	1 (0.4)	11 (1.0)	13 (0.9)	12 (1.0)	51 (1.9)	14 (1.0)
Graduated college	160 (0.9)	13 (0.8)	87 (0.8)	54 (1.3)	5 (0.6)	14 (1.0)	11 (0.8)	10 (0.7)	47 (1.5)	17 (1.0)
Free/reduced-price lunch eligibility										
Eligible	132 (0.9)	38 (1.1)	62 (1.1)	20 (1.1)	1 (0.2)	9 (0.7)	13 (1.1)	10 (0.9)	50 (1.6)	18 (0.8)
Not eligible	155 (0.9)	16 (0.8)	84 (0.8)	48 (1.2)	4 (0.4)	13 (1.1)	12 (0.8)	12 (0.9)	48 (1.6)	16 (0.9)
Not available	157 (1.9)	14 (1.7)	86 (1.7)	50 (2.8)	4 (1.1)	16 (3.0)	12 (1.6)	7 (1.1)	54 (3.1)	11 (1.4)
School location										
Central city	148 (1.4)	24 (1.3)	76 (1.3)	39 (1.8)	3 (0.7)	10 (1.3)	12 (1.2)	9 (1.0)	51 (2.7)	18 (1.3)
Urban fringe	152 (1.2)	20 (1.1)	80 (1.1)	44 (1.6)	3 (0.5)	14 (1.5)	12 (0.9)	11 (0.9)	47 (1.8)	17 (1.2)
Rural	149 (1.3)	20 (1.5)	80 (1.5)	40 (1.7)	2 (0.4)	12 (1.9)	12 (1.3)	13 (1.3)	51 (2.6)	12 (1.2)
Region										
Northeast	153 (2.0)	19 (1.7)	81 (1.7)	46 (2.6)	4 (0.9)	26 (2.6)	7 (1.1)	11 (1.3)	43 (3.2)	13 (1.4)
Midwest	153 (1.5)	17 (1.4)	83 (1.4)	45 (2.0)	3 (0.6)	12 (2.2)	12 (1.6)	15 (1.5)	51 (2.6)	10 (1.0)
South	147 (1.4)	23 (1.4)	77 (1.4)	37 (1.7)	2 (0.5)	6 (1.1)	14 (1.2)	9 (1.3)	49 (2.0)	22 (1.5)
West	† (†)	† (†)	† (†)	† (†)	† (†)	† (†)	† (†)	† (†)	† (†)	† (†)

—Not available.
†Not applicable.
#Rounds to zero.
‡Reporting standards not met.
[1]Scale ranges from 0 to 300.
[2]Basic denotes partial mastery of the knowledge and skills that are fundamental for proficient work at a given grade.
[3]Proficient represents solid academic performance. Students reaching this level have demonstrated competency over challenging subject matter.
[4]Advanced signifies superior performance for a given grade.

[5]Advanced economics includes Advanced Placement, International Baccalaureate, and honors courses.
NOTE: Includes public and private schools. Excludes persons unable to be tested due to limited proficiency in English or due to a disability (if the accommodations provided were not sufficient to enable the test to properly reflect the students' economics proficiency). Detail may not sum to totals due to rounding. Race categories exclude persons of Hispanic ethnicity. Totals include other racial/ethnic groups not shown separately. Standard errors appear in parentheses.
SOURCE: U.S. Department of Education, National Center for Education Statistics, National Assessment of Educational Progress (NAEP), 2006 Economics Assessment, retrieved August 23, 2007, from the NAEP Data Explorer (http://nces.ed.gov/nationsreportcard/nde/). (This table was prepared August 2007.)

Table 130. Percentage of students attaining geography achievement levels, by grade level and selected student characteristics: 2001

Selected student characteristic	Percent of 4th-graders				Percent of 8th-graders				Percent of 12th-graders			
	Below Basic	At or above Basic	At or above Proficient	At Advanced	Below Basic	At or above Basic	At or above Proficient	At Advanced	Below Basic	At or above Basic	At or above Proficient	At Advanced
1	2	3	4	5	6	7	8	9	10	11	12	13
All students	26 (1.2)	74 (1.2)	21 (1.0)	2 (0.3)	26 (0.9)	74 (0.9)	30 (1.2)	4 (0.6)	29 (0.9)	71 (0.9)	25 (1.1)	1 (0.3)
Sex												
Male	25 (1.3)	75 (1.3)	24 (1.4)	3 (0.5)	25 (1.0)	75 (1.0)	33 (1.5)	5 (0.7)	27 (1.1)	73 (1.1)	28 (1.5)	2 (0.4)
Female	28 (1.6)	72 (1.6)	18 (1.1)	1 (0.4)	27 (1.2)	73 (1.2)	26 (1.4)	3 (0.6)	30 (1.0)	70 (1.0)	21 (1.0)	1 (0.3)
Race/ethnicity												
White	13 (1.3)	87 (1.3)	29 (1.5)	3 (0.5)	14 (0.9)	86 (0.9)	39 (1.7)	5 (0.8)	19 (0.9)	81 (0.9)	31 (1.4)	2 (0.4)
Black	56 (2.1)	44 (2.1)	5 (0.9)	# (†)	60 (2.3)	40 (2.3)	6 (0.8)	# (†)	65 (2.3)	35 (2.3)	4 (0.7)	# (†)
Hispanic	51 (3.0)	49 (3.0)	6 (1.0)	# (†)	52 (1.9)	48 (1.9)	10 (1.0)	1 (0.2)	48 (2.6)	52 (2.6)	10 (1.4)	# (†)
Asian/Pacific Islander	23 (3.4)	77 (3.4)	25 (3.0)	1 (0.9)	21 (3.4)	79 (3.4)	32 (3.2)	4 (1.8)	28 (4.3)	72 (4.3)	26 (4.7)	1 (0.7)
Free/reduced-price lunch eligibility												
Eligible	49 (2.2)	51 (2.2)	6 (0.9)	# (†)	50 (1.8)	50 (1.8)	11 (1.2)	1 (0.3)	49 (2.3)	51 (2.3)	11 (1.6)	# (†)
Not eligible	14 (1.1)	86 (1.1)	29 (1.5)	3 (0.6)	17 (0.9)	83 (0.9)	37 (1.7)	5 (0.8)	25 (1.2)	75 (1.2)	26 (1.6)	1 (0.4)
Not available	16 (2.5)	84 (2.5)	27 (3.2)	3 (0.8)	21 (2.1)	79 (2.1)	33 (2.5)	4 (0.9)	24 (2.0)	76 (2.0)	31 (2.1)	2 (0.4)
Region												
Northeast	22 (3.7)	78 (3.7)	24 (2.2)	3 (0.9)	22 (2.5)	78 (2.5)	34 (3.3)	4 (1.3)	29 (2.3)	71 (2.3)	26 (4.1)	2 (1.1)
Southeast	28 (2.5)	72 (2.5)	18 (1.9)	1 (0.6)	27 (2.4)	73 (2.4)	26 (1.6)	3 (0.6)	33 (1.6)	67 (1.6)	21 (1.3)	1 (0.3)
Central	18 (1.7)	82 (1.7)	30 (2.5)	3 (0.7)	18 (2.3)	82 (2.3)	38 (3.7)	6 (1.3)	24 (1.8)	76 (1.8)	28 (1.9)	1 (0.5)
West	34 (2.7)	66 (2.7)	14 (1.7)	1 (0.3)	34 (1.7)	66 (1.7)	23 (1.7)	2 (0.6)	30 (1.9)	70 (1.9)	23 (1.8)	1 (0.4)

†Not applicable.
#Rounds to zero.
NOTE: Includes public and private schools. Excludes students unable to be tested due to limited proficiency in English or due to a disability (if the accommodations provided were not sufficient to enable the test to properly reflect the students' proficiency in geography). Race categories exclude persons of Hispanic ethnicity. Totals include other racial/ethnic groups not shown separately. Detail may not sum to totals because of rounding. Standard errors appear in parentheses.
SOURCE: U.S. Department of Education, National Center for Education Statistics, National Assessment of Educational Progress (NAEP), *The Nation's Report Card: Geography 2001*. (This table was prepared July 2002.)

Table 131. Average mathematics scale score, by age and selected student and school characteristics: Selected years, 1973 through 2004

Selected student and school characteristic	1973		1978		1982		1986		1990		1992		1994		1996		1999		2004	
1	2		3		4		5		6		7		8		9		10		11	
9-year-olds																				
All students	219	(0.8)	219	(0.8)	219	(1.1)	222	(1.0)	230	(0.8)	230	(0.8)	231	(0.8)	231	(0.8)	232	(0.8)	241	(0.9)
Sex																				
Male	218	(0.7)	217	(0.7)	217	(1.2)	222	(1.1)	229	(0.9)	231	(1.0)	232	(1.0)	233	(1.2)	233	(1.0)	243	(1.1)
Female	220	(1.1)	220	(1.0)	221	(1.2)	222	(1.2)	230	(1.1)	228	(1.0)	230	(0.9)	229	(0.7)	231	(0.9)	240	(1.1)
Race/ethnicity																				
White	225	(1.0)	224	(0.9)	224	(1.1)	227	(1.1)	235	(0.8)	235	(0.8)	237	(1.0)	237	(1.0)	239	(0.9)	247	(0.9)
Black	190	(1.8)	192	(1.1)	195	(1.6)	202	(1.6)	208	(2.2)	208	(2.0)	212	(1.6)	212	(1.4)	211	(1.6)	224	(2.1)
Hispanic	202	(2.4)	203	(2.2)	204	(1.3)	205	(2.1)	214	(2.1)	212	(2.3)	210	(2.3)	215	(1.7)	213	(1.9)	230	(2.0)
Region																				
Northeast	227	(1.9)	227	(1.9)	226	(1.8)	226	(2.7)	236	(2.1)	235	(1.9)	238	(2.2)	236	(2.0)	242	(1.7)	245	(2.0)
Southeast	208	(1.3)	209	(1.2)	210	(2.5)	218	(2.5)	224	(2.4)	221	(1.7)	229	(1.4)	227	(2.0)	226	(2.6)	240	(2.2)
Central	224	(1.5)	224	(1.5)	221	(2.7)	226	(2.3)	231	(1.3)	234	(1.6)	233	(1.8)	233	(2.3)	233	(1.4)	240	(1.5)
West	216	(2.2)	213	(1.3)	219	(1.8)	217	(2.4)	228	(1.8)	229	(2.3)	226	(1.6)	229	(1.3)	228	(1.7)	241	(1.8)
13-year-olds																				
All students	266	(1.1)	264	(1.1)	269	(1.1)	269	(1.2)	270	(0.9)	273	(0.9)	274	(1.0)	274	(0.8)	276	(0.8)	281	(1.0)
Sex																				
Male	265	(1.3)	264	(1.3)	269	(1.4)	270	(1.1)	271	(1.2)	274	(1.1)	276	(1.3)	276	(0.9)	277	(0.9)	283	(1.2)
Female	267	(1.1)	265	(1.1)	268	(1.1)	268	(1.5)	270	(0.9)	272	(1.0)	273	(1.0)	272	(1.0)	274	(1.1)	279	(1.0)
Race/ethnicity																				
White	274	(0.9)	272	(0.8)	274	(1.0)	274	(1.3)	276	(1.1)	279	(0.9)	281	(0.9)	281	(0.9)	283	(0.8)	288	(0.9)
Black	228	(1.9)	230	(1.9)	240	(1.6)	249	(2.3)	249	(2.3)	250	(1.9)	252	(3.5)	252	(1.3)	251	(2.6)	262	(1.6)
Hispanic	239	(2.2)	238	(2.0)	252	(1.7)	254	(2.9)	255	(1.8)	259	(1.8)	256	(1.9)	256	(1.6)	259	(1.7)	265	(2.0)
Parents' highest level of education																				
Not high school graduate	—	(†)	245	(1.2)	251	(1.4)	252	(2.3)	253	(1.8)	256	(1.0)	255	(2.1)	254	(2.4)	256	(2.8)	262	(2.2)
Graduated high school	—	(†)	263	(1.0)	263	(0.8)	263	(1.2)	263	(1.2)	263	(1.2)	266	(1.1)	267	(1.1)	264	(1.1)	271	(1.7)
Some education after high school	—	(†)	273	(1.2)	275	(0.9)	274	(0.8)	277	(1.0)	278	(1.0)	277	(1.6)	277	(1.4)	279	(0.9)	283	(1.0)
Graduated college	—	(†)	284	(1.2)	282	(1.5)	280	(1.4)	280	(1.0)	283	(1.0)	285	(1.2)	283	(1.2)	286	(1.0)	292	(0.9)
Region																				
Northeast	275	(2.4)	273	(2.4)	277	(2.0)	277	(2.2)	275	(2.3)	274	(2.2)	284	(1.5)	275	(2.1)	279	(2.7)	284	(2.1)
Southeast	255	(3.2)	253	(3.3)	258	(2.2)	263	(1.4)	266	(1.9)	271	(2.5)	269	(2.0)	270	(1.8)	270	(2.3)	278	(2.1)
Central	271	(1.8)	269	(1.8)	273	(2.1)	266	(4.5)	272	(2.4)	275	(1.5)	275	(3.4)	280	(1.3)	278	(1.8)	283	(2.2)
West	262	(1.9)	260	(1.9)	266	(2.4)	270	(2.1)	269	(1.6)	272	(1.4)	272	(1.7)	273	(1.9)	276	(1.4)	280	(1.4)
17-year-olds																				
All students	304	(1.1)	300	(1.0)	298	(0.9)	302	(0.9)	305	(0.9)	307	(0.9)	306	(1.0)	307	(1.2)	308	(1.0)	307	(0.8)
Sex																				
Male	309	(1.2)	304	(1.0)	301	(1.0)	305	(1.2)	306	(1.1)	309	(1.1)	309	(1.4)	310	(1.3)	310	(1.4)	308	(1.0)
Female	301	(1.1)	297	(1.0)	296	(1.0)	299	(1.0)	303	(1.1)	305	(1.1)	304	(1.1)	305	(1.4)	307	(1.0)	305	(0.9)
Race/ethnicity																				
White	310	(1.1)	306	(0.9)	304	(0.9)	308	(1.0)	309	(1.0)	312	(0.8)	312	(1.1)	313	(1.4)	315	(1.1)	313	(0.7)
Black	270	(1.3)	268	(1.3)	272	(1.2)	279	(2.1)	289	(2.8)	286	(2.2)	286	(1.8)	286	(1.7)	283	(1.5)	285	(1.6)
Hispanic	277	(2.2)	276	(2.3)	277	(1.8)	283	(2.9)	284	(2.9)	292	(2.6)	291	(3.7)	292	(2.1)	293	(2.5)	289	(1.8)
Parents' highest level of education																				
Not high school graduate	—	(†)	280	(1.2)	279	(1.0)	279	(2.3)	285	(2.2)	285	(2.3)	284	(2.4)	281	(2.4)	289	(1.8)	287	(2.4)
Graduated high school	—	(†)	294	(0.8)	293	(0.8)	293	(1.0)	294	(0.9)	298	(1.7)	295	(1.1)	297	(2.4)	299	(1.6)	295	(1.1)
Some education after high school	—	(†)	305	(0.9)	304	(0.9)	305	(1.2)	308	(1.0)	308	(1.1)	305	(1.3)	307	(1.5)	308	(1.6)	306	(1.1)
Graduated college	—	(†)	317	(1.0)	312	(1.0)	314	(1.4)	316	(1.3)	316	(1.0)	318	(1.4)	317	(1.3)	317	(1.2)	317	(0.9)
Region																				
Northeast	312	(1.8)	307	(1.8)	304	(2.0)	307	(1.9)	304	(2.1)	311	(2.0)	313	(2.9)	309	(3.0)	313	(2.4)	310	(1.4)
Southeast	296	(1.8)	292	(1.7)	292	(2.1)	297	(1.4)	301	(2.3)	301	(1.9)	301	(1.6)	303	(2.1)	300	(1.4)	302	(1.3)
Central	306	(1.8)	305	(1.9)	302	(1.4)	304	(1.9)	311	(2.1)	312	(2.0)	307	(2.2)	314	(2.0)	310	(2.0)	313	(1.0)
West	303	(2.0)	295	(1.8)	294	(1.9)	299	(2.7)	302	(1.5)	303	(2.3)	305	(2.4)	304	(2.3)	310	(2.0)	303	(1.9)

—Not available.
†Not applicable.
NOTE: Excludes persons not enrolled in school and those who were unable to be tested due to limited proficiency in English or due to a disability. Includes public and private schools. Scale ranges from 0 to 500. A score of 150 implies the knowledge of some basic addition and subtraction facts, and most students at this level can add two-digit numbers without regrouping. They recognize simple situations in which addition and subtraction apply. A score of 200 implies considerable understanding of two-digit numbers and knowledge of some basic multiplication and division facts. A score of 250 implies an initial understanding of the four basic operations. Students at this level can also compare information from graphs and charts and are developing an ability to analyze simple logical relations. A score of 300 implies an ability to compute decimals, simple fractions, and percents. Stu-

dents at this level can identify geometric figures, measure lengths and angles, and calculate areas of rectangles. They are developing the skills to operate with signed numbers, exponents, and square roots. A score of 350 implies an ability to apply a range of reasoning skills to solve multistep problems. Students at this level can solve routine problems involving fractions and percents, recognize properties of basic geometric figures, and work with exponents and square roots. Race categories exclude persons of Hispanic ethnicity. Totals include other racial/ethnic groups not shown separately. Some data have been revised from previously published figures. Standard errors appear in parentheses.
SOURCE: U.S. Department of Education, National Center for Education Statistics, National Assessment of Educational Progress (NAEP), *NAEP 2004 Trends in Academic Progress*; and unpublished tabulations, NAEP Data Explorer (http://nces.ed.gov/nationsreportcard/nde/), retrieved July 2005. (This table was prepared July 2005.)

Table 132. Percentage of students at or above selected mathematics proficiency levels, by age, sex, and race/ethnicity: Selected years, 1978 through 2004

Selected characteristic	9-year-olds[1]				13-year-olds[2]				17-year-olds[2]			
	Simple arithmetic facts[3]	Beginning skills and understanding[4]	Numerical operations and beginning problem solving[5]	Moderately complex procedures and reasoning[6]	Beginning skills and understanding[4]	Numerical operations and beginning problem solving[5]	Moderately complex procedures and reasoning[6]	Multistep problem solving and algebra[7]	Beginning skills and understanding[4]	Numerical operations and beginning problem solving[5]	Moderately complex procedures and reasoning[6]	Multistep problem solving and algebra[7]
1	2	3	4	5	6	7	8	9	10	11	12	13
Total												
1978	96.7 (0.3)	70.4 (0.9)	19.6 (0.7)	0.8 (0.1)	94.6 (0.5)	64.9 (1.2)	18.0 (0.7)	1.0 (0.2)	99.8 (0.1)	92.0 (0.5)	51.5 (1.1)	7.3 (0.4)
1982	97.1 (0.3)	71.4 (1.2)	18.8 (1.0)	0.6 (0.1)	97.7 (0.4)	71.4 (1.2)	17.4 (0.9)	0.5 (0.1)	99.9 (‡)	93.0 (0.5)	48.5 (1.3)	5.5 (0.4)
1986	97.9 (0.3)	74.1 (1.2)	20.7 (0.9)	0.6 (0.2)	98.6 (0.2)	73.3 (1.6)	15.8 (1.0)	0.4 (0.1)	99.9 (‡)	95.6 (0.5)	51.7 (1.4)	6.5 (0.5)
1990	99.1 (0.2)	81.5 (1.0)	27.7 (0.9)	1.2 (0.3)	98.5 (0.2)	74.7 (1.0)	17.3 (1.0)	0.4 (0.1)	100.0 (‡)	96.0 (0.5)	56.1 (1.4)	7.2 (0.6)
1992	99.0 (0.2)	81.4 (0.8)	27.8 (0.9)	1.2 (0.3)	98.7 (0.3)	77.9 (1.1)	18.9 (1.0)	0.4 (0.2)	100.0 (‡)	96.6 (0.5)	59.1 (1.3)	7.2 (0.6)
1994	99.0 (0.2)	82.0 (0.7)	29.9 (1.1)	1.3 (0.4)	98.5 (0.3)	78.1 (1.1)	21.3 (1.4)	0.6 (0.2)	100.0 (‡)	96.5 (0.5)	58.6 (1.4)	7.4 (0.8)
1996	99.1 (0.2)	81.5 (0.8)	29.7 (1.0)	1.6 (0.3)	98.8 (0.2)	78.6 (0.9)	20.6 (1.2)	0.6 (0.1)	100.0 (‡)	96.8 (0.4)	60.1 (1.7)	7.4 (0.8)
1999	98.9 (0.2)	82.5 (0.8)	30.9 (1.1)	1.7 (0.3)	98.7 (0.2)	78.8 (1.0)	23.2 (1.0)	0.9 (0.2)	100.0 (‡)	96.8 (0.5)	60.7 (1.6)	8.4 (0.8)
2004	99.3 (0.1)	88.6 (0.8)	41.9 (1.2)	— (†)	98.6 (0.2)	83.5 (1.0)	29.0 (1.1)	— (†)	— (†)	96.7 (0.4)	58.6 (1.3)	6.9 (0.6)
Male												
1978	96.2 (0.5)	68.9 (1.0)	19.2 (0.6)	0.7 (0.2)	93.9 (0.5)	63.9 (1.3)	18.4 (0.9)	1.1 (0.2)	99.9 (0.1)	93.0 (0.5)	55.1 (1.2)	9.5 (0.6)
1982	96.5 (0.5)	68.8 (1.3)	18.1 (1.1)	0.6 (0.1)	97.5 (0.6)	71.3 (1.4)	18.9 (1.2)	0.7 (0.2)	100.0 (‡)	93.9 (0.6)	51.9 (1.5)	6.9 (0.7)
1986	98.0 (0.5)	74.0 (1.4)	20.9 (1.1)	0.7 (0.3)	98.5 (0.3)	73.8 (1.8)	17.6 (1.1)	0.5 (0.2)	99.9 (‡)	96.1 (0.6)	54.6 (1.8)	8.4 (0.9)
1990	99.0 (0.3)	80.6 (1.0)	27.5 (1.0)	1.3 (0.4)	98.2 (0.3)	75.1 (1.8)	19.0 (1.2)	0.5 (0.2)	99.9 (‡)	95.8 (0.8)	57.6 (1.4)	8.8 (0.8)
1992	99.0 (0.3)	81.9 (1.0)	29.4 (1.2)	1.4 (0.3)	98.8 (0.4)	78.1 (1.6)	20.7 (1.1)	0.8 (0.3)	100.0 (‡)	96.9 (0.6)	60.5 (1.8)	9.1 (0.7)
1994	99.1 (0.3)	82.3 (0.9)	31.5 (1.6)	1.4 (0.4)	98.3 (0.4)	78.9 (1.5)	23.9 (1.6)	0.8 (0.2)	100.0 (‡)	97.3 (0.6)	60.2 (2.1)	9.3 (1.0)
1996	99.1 (0.2)	82.5 (1.1)	32.7 (1.7)	2.0 (0.5)	98.7 (0.3)	79.8 (1.4)	23.0 (1.6)	1.2 (0.3)	100.0 (‡)	97.0 (0.7)	62.7 (1.8)	9.5 (1.3)
1999	98.8 (0.3)	82.6 (0.9)	32.4 (1.3)	1.9 (0.4)	98.5 (0.3)	79.3 (1.1)	25.4 (1.2)	1.2 (0.2)	100.0 (‡)	96.5 (0.8)	63.1 (2.1)	9.8 (1.1)
2004	99.3 (0.2)	89.3 (0.9)	43.5 (1.2)	— (†)	98.3 (0.3)	82.8 (1.2)	32.6 (1.6)	— (†)	— (†)	96.6 (0.6)	60.6 (1.6)	8.8 (1.0)
Female												
1978	97.2 (0.3)	72.0 (1.1)	19.9 (1.0)	0.8 (0.2)	95.2 (0.5)	65.9 (1.2)	17.5 (0.7)	0.9 (0.2)	99.7 (0.1)	91.0 (0.6)	48.2 (1.3)	5.2 (0.7)
1982	97.6 (0.3)	74.0 (1.3)	19.6 (1.1)	0.5 (0.1)	98.0 (0.3)	71.4 (1.3)	15.9 (1.0)	0.4 (0.2)	99.9 (‡)	92.1 (0.6)	45.3 (1.4)	4.1 (0.4)
1986	97.8 (0.4)	74.3 (1.3)	20.6 (1.3)	0.6 (0.3)	98.6 (0.3)	72.7 (1.9)	14.1 (1.3)	0.3 (0.1)	100.0 (‡)	95.1 (0.7)	48.9 (1.7)	4.7 (0.6)
1990	99.1 (0.3)	82.3 (1.3)	27.9 (1.3)	1.0 (0.3)	98.9 (0.2)	74.4 (1.3)	15.7 (1.0)	0.2 (0.1)	100.0 (‡)	96.2 (0.8)	54.7 (1.8)	5.6 (0.8)
1992	99.0 (0.3)	80.9 (1.1)	26.3 (1.5)	1.0 (0.4)	98.6 (0.2)	77.7 (1.1)	17.2 (1.4)	0.3 (‡)	100.0 (‡)	96.3 (0.8)	57.7 (1.6)	5.2 (0.8)
1994	98.9 (0.4)	81.7 (0.9)	28.3 (1.3)	1.1 (0.4)	98.7 (0.3)	77.3 (1.0)	18.7 (1.4)	0.5 (0.3)	100.0 (‡)	96.0 (0.6)	57.2 (1.4)	5.5 (0.9)
1996	99.1 (0.4)	80.7 (0.9)	26.7 (1.1)	1.2 (0.4)	98.8 (0.3)	77.4 (1.1)	18.4 (1.5)	0.5 (0.2)	100.0 (‡)	96.7 (0.6)	57.6 (2.2)	5.3 (0.8)
1999	99.0 (0.2)	82.5 (1.2)	29.4 (1.4)	1.6 (0.4)	99.0 (0.4)	78.4 (1.2)	21.0 (1.3)	0.6 (0.3)	100.0 (‡)	97.2 (0.4)	58.5 (1.9)	7.1 (1.1)
2004	99.3 (0.2)	87.9 (1.0)	40.3 (1.5)	— (†)	98.8 (0.3)	84.1 (1.1)	25.6 (1.1)	— (†)	— (†)	96.8 (0.5)	56.7 (1.6)	5.1 (0.6)
White												
1978	98.3 (0.2)	76.3 (1.0)	22.9 (0.9)	0.9 (0.2)	97.6 (0.3)	72.9 (0.9)	21.4 (0.7)	1.2 (0.2)	100.0 (‡)	95.6 (0.3)	57.6 (1.1)	8.5 (0.5)
1982	98.5 (0.3)	76.8 (1.2)	21.8 (1.1)	0.6 (0.1)	99.1 (0.1)	78.3 (0.9)	20.5 (1.0)	0.6 (0.1)	100.0 (‡)	96.2 (0.3)	54.7 (1.4)	6.4 (0.5)
1986	98.8 (0.2)	79.6 (0.9)	24.6 (1.0)	0.8 (0.3)	99.3 (0.3)	78.9 (1.7)	18.6 (1.2)	0.4 (0.1)	100.0 (‡)	98.0 (0.4)	59.1 (1.7)	7.9 (0.7)
1990	99.6 (0.2)	86.9 (0.9)	32.7 (1.0)	1.5 (0.3)	99.4 (0.1)	82.0 (1.0)	21.0 (1.2)	0.4 (0.2)	100.0 (‡)	97.6 (0.3)	63.2 (1.6)	8.3 (0.7)
1992	99.6 (0.1)	86.9 (0.7)	32.4 (1.0)	1.4 (0.3)	99.6 (0.2)	84.9 (1.1)	22.8 (1.3)	0.4 (0.2)	100.0 (‡)	98.3 (0.4)	66.4 (1.4)	8.7 (0.9)
1994	99.6 (0.2)	87.0 (0.8)	35.3 (1.3)	1.5 (0.4)	99.3 (0.2)	85.5 (0.9)	25.6 (1.6)	0.7 (0.3)	100.0 (‡)	98.4 (0.4)	67.0 (1.4)	9.4 (1.1)
1996	99.6 (0.1)	86.6 (0.8)	35.7 (1.4)	2.0 (0.4)	99.6 (0.2)	86.4 (1.0)	25.4 (1.5)	0.8 (0.2)	100.0 (‡)	98.7 (0.4)	68.7 (2.2)	9.2 (1.0)
1999	99.6 (0.1)	88.6 (0.8)	37.1 (1.4)	2.2 (0.4)	99.4 (0.3)	86.7 (0.9)	29.0 (1.3)	1.2 (0.3)	100.0 (‡)	98.7 (0.4)	69.9 (2.0)	10.4 (1.1)
2004	99.7 (0.1)	92.6 (0.6)	49.0 (1.4)	— (†)	99.1 (0.2)	90.5 (0.8)	36.0 (1.3)	— (†)	— (†)	98.4 (0.5)	69.0 (1.3)	8.5 (0.8)
Black												
1978	88.4 (1.0)	42.0 (1.4)	4.1 (0.6)	# (†)	79.7 (1.5)	28.7 (2.1)	2.3 (0.5)	# (†)	98.8 (0.3)	70.7 (1.7)	16.8 (1.6)	# (†)
1982	90.2 (1.0)	46.1 (2.4)	4.4 (0.8)	# (†)	90.2 (1.6)	37.9 (2.5)	2.9 (1.0)	# (†)	99.7 (0.2)	76.4 (1.5)	17.1 (1.5)	# (†)
1986	93.9 (1.4)	53.4 (2.5)	5.6 (0.9)	# (†)	95.4 (0.9)	49.0 (3.7)	4.0 (1.4)	# (†)	100.0 (‡)	85.6 (2.5)	20.8 (2.8)	# (†)
1990	96.9 (0.9)	60.0 (2.8)	9.4 (1.7)	# (†)	95.4 (1.1)	48.7 (3.6)	3.9 (1.6)	# (†)	99.9 (‡)	92.4 (2.2)	32.8 (4.5)	2.0 (1.0)
1992	96.6 (1.1)	59.8 (2.6)	9.6 (1.4)	# (†)	95.0 (1.4)	51.0 (2.7)	4.0 (0.7)	# (†)	100.0 (‡)	89.6 (2.5)	29.8 (3.9)	0.9 (‡)
1994	97.4 (1.0)	65.9 (2.4)	11.1 (1.7)	# (†)	95.6 (1.6)	51.0 (3.9)	6.4 (2.4)	# (†)	100.0 (‡)	90.6 (1.8)	29.8 (3.4)	# (†)
1996	97.3 (0.8)	65.3 (2.4)	10.0 (1.2)	# (†)	96.2 (1.3)	53.7 (2.6)	4.8 (1.1)	# (†)	100.0 (‡)	90.6 (1.3)	31.2 (2.5)	0.9 (‡)
1999	96.4 (0.6)	63.3 (2.1)	12.3 (1.5)	# (†)	96.5 (1.1)	50.8 (4.0)	4.4 (1.4)	# (†)	99.9 (‡)	88.6 (2.0)	26.6 (2.7)	1.0 (‡)
2004	97.6 (0.7)	77.0 (2.4)	23.6 (2.0)	— (†)	97.2 (0.6)	67.2 (2.2)	9.0 (1.1)	— (†)	— (†)	91.7 (1.9)	26.0 (2.6)	0.9 (0.5)

See notes at end of table.

Table 132. Percentage of students at or above selected mathematics proficiency levels, by age, sex, and race/ethnicity: Selected years, 1978 through 2004—Continued

Selected characteristic	9-year-olds[1]				13-year-olds[2]				17-year-olds[2]			
	Simple arithmetic facts[3]	Beginning skills and understanding[4]	Numerical operations and beginning problem solving[5]	Moderately complex procedures and reasoning[6]	Beginning skills and understanding[4]	Numerical operations and beginning problem solving[5]	Moderately complex procedures and reasoning[6]	Multistep problem solving and algebra[6]	Beginning skills and understanding[4]	Numerical operations and beginning problem solving[5]	Moderately complex procedures and reasoning[6]	Multistep problem solving and algebra[7]
1	2	3	4	5	6	7	8	9	10	11	12	13
Hispanic												
1978	93.0 (1.2)	54.2 (2.8)	9.2 (2.5)	# (†)	86.4 (0.9)	36.0 (2.9)	4.0 (1.0)	# (†)	99.3 (0.4)	78.3 (2.3)	23.4 (2.7)	1.4 (0.6)
1982	94.3 (1.2)	55.7 (2.3)	7.8 (1.7)	# (†)	95.9 (0.9)	52.2 (2.5)	6.3 (1.0)	# (†)	99.8 (†)	81.4 (1.9)	21.6 (2.2)	0.7 (0.4)
1986	96.4 (1.3)	57.6 (2.9)	7.3 (2.8)	# (†)	96.9 (1.4)	56.0 (5.0)	5.5 (1.1)	# (†)	99.4 (†)	89.3 (2.5)	26.5 (4.5)	1.1 (†)
1990	98.0 (0.8)	68.4 (3.0)	11.3 (3.5)	# (†)	96.8 (1.1)	56.7 (3.3)	6.4 (1.7)	# (†)	99.6 (†)	85.8 (4.2)	30.1 (3.1)	1.9 (0.8)
1992	97.2 (1.3)	65.0 (2.9)	11.7 (2.5)	# (†)	98.1 (0.7)	63.3 (2.7)	7.0 (1.2)	# (†)	100.0 (†)	94.1 (2.2)	39.2 (4.9)	1.2 (†)
1994	97.2 (1.2)	63.5 (3.1)	9.7 (1.8)	# (†)	97.1 (1.3)	59.2 (2.2)	6.4 (1.8)	# (†)	100.0 (†)	91.8 (3.6)	38.3 (5.5)	1.4 (†)
1996	98.1 (0.7)	67.1 (2.1)	13.8 (2.3)	# (†)	96.2 (0.8)	58.3 (2.3)	6.7 (1.2)	# (†)	99.9 (†)	92.2 (2.2)	40.1 (3.5)	1.8 (†)
1999	98.1 (0.7)	67.5 (2.5)	10.5 (1.6)	# (†)	97.2 (0.6)	62.9 (2.5)	8.2 (1.4)	# (†)	99.9 (†)	93.6 (2.2)	37.7 (4.1)	3.1 (1.1)
2004	99.6 (0.2)	82.6 (2.4)	26.9 (2.7)	— (†)	97.3 (0.8)	68.4 (3.3)	14.3 (1.8)	— (†)	— (†)	92.1 (2.1)	32.3 (2.1)	1.3 (0.5)

—Not available.
†Not applicable.
#Rounds to zero.
‡Reporting standards not met.
[1]Virtually no students were able to perform multistep problems and algebra.
[2]Virtually all students knew simple arithmetic facts.
[3]Scale score of 150 or above.
[4]Scale score of 200 or above.
[5]Scale score of 250 or above.
[6]Scale score of 300 or above.
[7]Scale score of 350 or above.
NOTE: Excludes persons not enrolled in school and those who were unable to be tested due to limited proficiency in English or due to a disability. Includes public and private schools. Race categories exclude persons of Hispanic ethnicity. Totals include other racial/ethnic groups not shown separately. Standard errors appear in parentheses.
SOURCE: U.S. Department of Education, National Assessment of Educational Progress (NAEP), 1999 *NAEP Trends in Academic Progress* and NAEP Data Explorer (http://nces.ed.gov/nationsreportcard/nde/), retrieved July 2005. (This table was prepared February 2006.)

Table 133. Mathematics performance of 17-year-olds, by highest mathematics course taken, sex, and race/ethnicity: Selected years, 1978 through 2004

Selected characteristic	Percent of students	Average scale score by highest mathematics course taken						Percent of students at or above score levels			
		All areas	Prealgebra or general mathematics	Algebra I	Geometry	Algebra II	Precalculus or calculus	200	250	300	350
1	2	3	4	5	6	7	8	9	10	11	12
1978											
All students	100 (†)	300 (1.0)	267 (0.8)	286 (0.7)	307 (0.7)	321 (0.7)	334 (1.4)	100 (†)	92 (0.5)	52 (1.1)	7 (0.4)
Sex											
Male	49 (0.5)	304 (1.0)	269 (1.0)	289 (0.9)	310 (1.0)	325 (0.8)	337 (2.0)	100 (†)	93 (0.5)	55 (1.2)	10 (0.6)
Female	51 (0.5)	297 (1.0)	264 (0.9)	284 (1.0)	304 (0.8)	318 (0.9)	329 (1.8)	100 (†)	91 (0.6)	48 (1.3)	5 (0.7)
Race/ethnicity											
White	83 (1.3)	306 (0.9)	272 (0.6)	291 (0.6)	310 (0.6)	325 (0.6)	338 (1.1)	100 (†)	96 (0.3)	58 (1.1)	8 (0.5)
Black	12 (1.1)	268 (1.3)	247 (1.6)	264 (1.5)	281 (1.9)	292 (1.4)	297 (6.5)	99 (0.3)	71 (1.7)	17 (1.6)	# (†)
Hispanic	4 (0.5)	276 (2.3)	256 (2.3)	273 (2.8)	294 (4.4)	303 (2.9)	‡ (†)	99 (0.4)	78 (2.3)	23 (2.7)	1 (0.6)
Other[1]	1 (0.1)	313 (3.3)	— (†)	— (†)	— (†)	— (†)	— (†)	100 (†)	94 (2.6)	65 (4.9)	15 (3.2)
1990											
All students	100 (†)	305 (0.9)	273 (1.1)	288 (1.2)	299 (1.5)	319 (1.0)	344 (2.7)	100 (†)	96 (0.5)	56 (1.4)	7 (0.6)
Sex											
Male	49 (0.9)	306 (1.1)	274 (1.7)	291 (1.6)	302 (1.6)	323 (1.2)	347 (2.4)	100 (†)	96 (0.8)	58 (1.4)	9 (0.8)
Female	51 (0.9)	303 (1.1)	271 (1.8)	285 (1.8)	296 (1.8)	316 (1.1)	340 (4.0)	100 (†)	96 (0.8)	55 (1.8)	6 (0.8)
Race/ethnicity											
White	73 (0.5)	309 (1.0)	277 (1.1)	292 (1.6)	304 (1.3)	323 (0.9)	347 (2.8)	100 (†)	98 (0.3)	63 (1.6)	8 (0.7)
Black	16 (0.3)	289 (2.8)	264 (2.2)	278 (4.0)	285 (3.5)	302 (3.2)	— (†)	100 (†)	92 (2.2)	33 (4.5)	2 (1.0)
Hispanic	7 (0.4)	284 (2.9)	— (†)	— (†)	— (†)	306 (3.3)	— (†)	100 (†)	86 (4.2)	30 (3.1)	2 (0.8)
Other[1]	4 (0.5)	312 (5.2)	— (†)	— (†)	— (†)	— (†)	— (†)	100 (†)	98 (‡)	62 (7.0)	16 (4.3)
1994											
All students	100 (†)	306 (1.0)	272 (1.2)	288 (1.4)	297 (1.7)	316 (1.0)	340 (2.2)	100 (†)	97 (0.5)	59 (1.4)	7 (0.8)
Sex											
Male	49 (1.3)	309 (1.4)	274 (1.8)	289 (1.6)	301 (2.1)	320 (1.5)	343 (2.6)	100 (†)	97 (0.6)	60 (2.1)	9 (1.0)
Female	51 (1.3)	304 (1.1)	268 (1.9)	286 (1.9)	293 (1.8)	313 (1.1)	337 (2.8)	100 (†)	96 (0.6)	57 (1.4)	6 (0.9)
Race/ethnicity											
White	73 (0.5)	312 (1.1)	275 (1.4)	292 (1.7)	301 (1.5)	320 (1.0)	344 (2.0)	100 (†)	98 (0.4)	67 (1.4)	9 (1.1)
Black	15 (0.3)	286 (1.8)	— (†)	275 (3.3)	283 (3.8)	297 (2.5)	— (†)	100 (†)	91 (1.8)	30 (3.4)	# (†)
Hispanic	9 (0.3)	291 (3.7)	— (†)	— (†)	— (†)	304 (4.1)	— (†)	100 (†)	92 (3.6)	38 (5.5)	1 (‡)
Other[1]	3 (0.3)	313 (4.5)	— (†)	— (†)	— (†)	— (†)	— (†)	100 (†)	97 (‡)	66 (6.6)	12 (3.6)
1996											
All students	100 (†)	307 (1.2)	269 (1.9)	283 (1.3)	298 (1.3)	316 (1.3)	339 (1.7)	100 (†)	97 (0.4)	60 (1.7)	7 (0.8)
Sex											
Male	50 (1.2)	310 (1.3)	272 (2.5)	286 (1.5)	302 (1.7)	320 (1.7)	342 (2.3)	100 (†)	97 (0.7)	63 (1.8)	9 (1.3)
Female	50 (1.2)	305 (1.4)	265 (2.2)	278 (2.2)	294 (1.5)	313 (1.4)	335 (2.2)	100 (†)	97 (0.6)	58 (2.2)	5 (0.8)
Race/ethnicity											
White	71 (0.6)	313 (1.4)	273 (2.3)	287 (2.0)	304 (1.6)	320 (1.4)	342 (1.9)	100 (†)	99 (0.4)	69 (2.2)	9 (1.0)
Black	15 (0.3)	286 (1.7)	— (†)	272 (2.4)	280 (3.0)	299 (2.2)	— (†)	100 (†)	91 (1.3)	31 (2.5)	1 (‡)
Hispanic	9 (0.7)	292 (2.1)	— (†)	— (†)	— (†)	306 (2.8)	— (†)	100 (†)	92 (2.2)	40 (3.5)	2 (‡)
Other[1]	4 (0.7)	312 (5.7)	— (†)	— (†)	— (†)	— (†)	— (†)	100 (†)	97 (1.2)	64 (7.2)	14 (5.0)
1999											
All students	100 (†)	308 (1.0)	278 (2.8)	285 (1.7)	298 (1.2)	315 (0.8)	341 (1.4)	100 (†)	97 (0.5)	61 (1.6)	8 (0.8)
Sex											
Male	48 (1.0)	310 (1.4)	281 (3.2)	288 (2.6)	301 (1.8)	317 (1.3)	343 (1.9)	100 (†)	96 (0.8)	63 (2.1)	10 (1.1)
Female	52 (1.0)	307 (1.0)	274 (3.2)	282 (2.5)	295 (1.3)	314 (1.1)	340 (2.0)	100 (†)	97 (0.4)	58 (1.9)	7 (1.1)
Race/ethnicity											
White	72 (0.5)	315 (1.1)	282 (3.4)	290 (2.2)	303 (1.5)	320 (0.9)	343 (1.5)	100 (†)	99 (0.4)	70 (2.0)	10 (1.1)
Black	15 (0.4)	283 (1.5)	— (†)	267 (2.9)	281 (2.5)	293 (1.4)	— (†)	100 (†)	89 (2.0)	27 (2.7)	1 (‡)
Hispanic	10 (0.5)	293 (2.5)	— (†)	— (†)	— (†)	308 (3.0)	— (†)	100 (†)	94 (2.2)	38 (4.1)	3 (1.1)
Other[1]	4 (0.2)	320 (4.0)	— (†)	— (†)	— (†)	— (†)	— (†)	100 (†)	100 (†)	76 (6.3)	14 (4.1)
2004											
All students	100 (†)	307 (0.8)	270 (2.6)	282 (1.4)	296 (1.1)	310 (0.7)	336 (1.6)	100 (†)	97 (0.4)	59 (1.3)	7 (0.6)
Sex											
Male	48 (1.1)	308 (1.0)	273 (3.3)	286 (1.8)	298 (1.6)	313 (1.0)	339 (2.3)	100 (†)	97 (0.6)	61 (1.6)	9 (1.0)
Female	52 (1.1)	305 (0.9)	267 (3.6)	278 (1.8)	293 (1.5)	308 (0.9)	332 (1.3)	100 (†)	97 (0.5)	57 (1.6)	5 (0.6)
Race/ethnicity											
White	69 (1.5)	313 (0.7)	276 (2.9)	287 (1.3)	302 (1.0)	316 (0.8)	338 (1.4)	100 (†)	98 (0.4)	69 (1.3)	9 (0.8)
Black	13 (1.1)	285 (1.6)	— (†)	— (†)	279 (2.0)	292 (1.5)	— (†)	100 (†)	92 (1.9)	26 (2.6)	1 (0.5)
Hispanic	14 (1.2)	289 (1.8)	— (†)	— (†)	285 (3.5)	293 (2.5)	321 (2.6)	100 (†)	92 (2.1)	32 (2.1)	1 (0.5)
Other[1]	5 (0.5)	320 (2.8)	— (†)	— (†)	— (†)	— (†)	— (†)	100 (†)	99 (‡)	73 (4.2)	16 (3.8)

—Not available.
†Not applicable.
#Rounds to zero.
‡Reporting standards not met.
[1]Includes Asians/Pacific Islanders and American Indians/Alaska Natives.
NOTE: Score level 200 indicates ability to perform simple additive reasoning and problem solving. Score level 250 indicates ability to perform simple multiplicative reasoning and two-step problem solving. Score level 300 indicates ability to perform reasoning and problem solving involving fractions, decimals, percents, elementary geometry, and simple algebra. Score level 350 indicates ability to perform reasoning and problem solving involving geom-

etry, algebra, and beginning statistics and probability. Scale ranges from 0 to 500. Excludes persons not enrolled in school and those who were unable to be tested due to limited proficiency in English or due to a disability. Includes public and private schools. Race categories exclude persons of Hispanic ethnicity. Detail may not sum to totals because of rounding. Standard errors appear in parentheses.
SOURCE: U.S. Department of Education, National Center for Education Statistics, National Assessment of Educational Progress (NAEP), *NAEP Trends in Academic Progress*, 1996 and 1999; and NAEP Data Explorer (http://nces.ed.gov/nationsreportcard/nde/), retrieved August 2005. (This table was prepared February 2006.)

Table 134. Average mathematics scale score, percentage attaining mathematics achievement levels, and selected statistics on mathematics education of 4th-graders in public schools, by state or jurisdiction: Selected years, 1992 through 2007

State or jurisdiction	Average scale score[1]										Percent of students, 2007								Having 5 or more hours of math instruction each week		Percent of students spending 30 minutes or more on math homework each day,[5] 2003	
	1992		2000		2003		2005		2007		Attaining mathematics achievement levels											
											Below Basic		At or above Basic[2]		At or above Proficient[3]		At Advanced[4]					
1	2		3		4		5		6		7		8		9		10		11		12	
United States	**219**	**(0.8)**	**224**	**(1.0)**	**234**	**(0.2)**	**237**	**(0.2)**	**239**	**(0.2)**	**19**	**(0.2)**	**81**	**(0.2)**	**39**	**(0.3)**	**5**	**(0.1)**	**88**	**(0.4)**	**49**	**(0.2)**
Alabama	208	(1.6)	217	(1.2)	223	(1.2)	225	(0.9)	229	(1.3)	30	(1.7)	70	(1.7)	26	(1.7)	3	(0.5)	91	(1.6)	47	(1.0)
Alaska	—	(†)	—	(†)	233	(0.8)	236	(1.0)	237	(1.0)	21	(1.2)	79	(1.2)	38	(1.5)	6	(0.6)	88	(2.0)	‡	(†)
Arizona	215	(1.1)	219	(1.3)	229	(1.1)	230	(1.1)	232	(1.0)	26	(1.4)	74	(1.4)	31	(1.2)	4	(0.4)	85	(2.2)	51	(1.0)
Arkansas	210	(0.9)	216	(1.1)	229	(0.9)	236	(0.9)	238	(1.1)	19	(1.5)	81	(1.5)	37	(1.6)	4	(0.5)	94	(1.0)	52	(1.3)
California[6]	208	(1.6)	213	(1.6)	227	(0.9)	230	(0.6)	230	(0.7)	30	(0.8)	70	(0.8)	30	(0.9)	4	(0.4)	90	(1.2)	56	(1.3)
Colorado	221	(1.0)	—	(†)	235	(1.0)	239	(1.1)	240	(1.0)	18	(1.3)	82	(1.3)	41	(1.6)	6	(0.6)	90	(2.0)	50	(1.2)
Connecticut	227	(1.1)	234	(1.1)	241	(0.8)	242	(0.8)	243	(1.1)	16	(1.3)	84	(1.3)	45	(1.6)	7	(0.8)	91	(1.9)	42	(1.1)
Delaware	218	(0.8)	—	(†)	236	(0.5)	240	(0.5)	242	(0.4)	13	(0.9)	87	(0.9)	40	(0.9)	4	(0.5)	91	(0.4)	48	(0.9)
District of Columbia	193	(0.5)	192	(1.1)	205	(0.7)	211	(0.8)	214	(0.8)	51	(1.4)	49	(1.4)	14	(0.7)	3	(0.4)	93	(0.5)	52	(0.9)
Florida	214	(1.5)	—	(†)	234	(1.1)	239	(0.7)	242	(0.8)	14	(0.8)	86	(0.8)	37	(0.9)	3	(0.3)	93	(1.1)	50	(1.3)
Georgia	216	(1.2)	219	(1.1)	230	(1.0)	234	(1.0)	235	(0.8)	21	(1.0)	79	(1.0)	32	(1.3)	4	(0.6)	90	(1.9)	48	(1.2)
Hawaii	214	(1.3)	216	(1.0)	227	(1.0)	230	(0.8)	234	(0.8)	23	(1.0)	77	(1.0)	33	(1.2)	4	(0.5)	90	(1.8)	58	(1.1)
Idaho[6]	222	(1.0)	224	(1.4)	235	(0.7)	242	(0.7)	241	(0.7)	15	(0.9)	85	(0.9)	40	(1.3)	5	(0.6)	85	(2.2)	49	(1.2)
Illinois[6]	—	(†)	223	(1.9)	233	(1.1)	233	(1.0)	237	(1.1)	21	(1.2)	79	(1.2)	36	(1.6)	6	(0.8)	80	(2.1)	51	(1.2)
Indiana[6]	221	(1.0)	233	(1.1)	238	(0.9)	240	(0.9)	245	(0.8)	11	(0.9)	89	(0.9)	46	(1.5)	6	(0.8)	77	(3.3)	50	(1.3)
Iowa[6]	230	(1.0)	231	(1.2)	238	(0.7)	240	(0.7)	243	(0.8)	13	(1.0)	87	(1.0)	43	(1.3)	5	(0.7)	79	(3.2)	46	(1.3)
Kansas[6]	—	(†)	232	(1.6)	242	(1.0)	246	(1.0)	248	(0.9)	11	(0.8)	89	(0.8)	51	(1.7)	9	(0.7)	93	(1.5)	48	(1.4)
Kentucky	215	(1.0)	219	(1.4)	229	(1.1)	232	(0.9)	235	(1.0)	21	(1.0)	79	(1.0)	31	(1.4)	3	(0.6)	78	(2.9)	49	(1.2)
Louisiana	204	(1.5)	218	(1.4)	226	(1.0)	230	(0.9)	230	(1.0)	27	(1.4)	73	(1.4)	24	(1.3)	2	(0.3)	94	(1.8)	43	(1.2)
Maine[6]	232	(1.0)	230	(1.0)	238	(0.7)	241	(0.8)	242	(0.8)	15	(1.0)	85	(1.0)	42	(1.3)	6	(0.7)	86	(2.0)	46	(1.1)
Maryland	217	(1.3)	222	(1.2)	233	(1.3)	238	(1.0)	240	(0.8)	20	(1.3)	80	(1.3)	40	(1.3)	8	(0.7)	94	(1.5)	42	(1.2)
Massachusetts	227	(1.2)	233	(1.2)	242	(0.8)	247	(0.8)	252	(0.8)	7	(0.7)	93	(0.7)	58	(1.5)	11	(0.9)	92	(2.1)	46	(1.0)
Michigan[6]	220	(1.7)	229	(1.6)	236	(0.9)	238	(1.2)	238	(1.3)	20	(1.5)	80	(1.5)	37	(1.6)	5	(0.6)	85	(2.8)	46	(1.2)
Minnesota[6]	228	(0.9)	234	(1.3)	242	(0.9)	246	(1.0)	247	(1.0)	13	(1.1)	87	(1.1)	51	(1.6)	9	(0.9)	85	(2.4)	48	(1.3)
Mississippi	202	(1.1)	211	(1.1)	223	(1.0)	227	(0.9)	228	(1.0)	30	(1.8)	70	(1.8)	21	(1.3)	1	(0.2)	92	(1.8)	51	(1.4)
Missouri	222	(1.2)	228	(1.2)	235	(0.9)	235	(0.9)	239	(0.9)	18	(1.0)	82	(1.0)	38	(1.5)	5	(0.7)	87	(2.7)	49	(1.2)
Montana[6]	—	(†)	228	(1.7)	236	(0.8)	241	(0.8)	244	(0.8)	12	(0.8)	88	(0.8)	44	(1.4)	5	(0.7)	85	(2.1)	48	(1.1)
Nebraska	225	(1.2)	225	(1.8)	236	(0.8)	238	(0.9)	238	(1.1)	20	(1.4)	80	(1.4)	38	(1.6)	5	(0.5)	79	(2.9)	50	(1.2)
Nevada	—	(†)	220	(1.0)	228	(0.8)	230	(0.8)	232	(0.9)	26	(1.3)	74	(1.3)	30	(1.4)	3	(0.4)	94	(1.2)	47	(1.5)
New Hampshire	230	(1.2)	—	(†)	243	(0.9)	246	(0.9)	249	(0.8)	9	(0.7)	91	(0.7)	52	(1.5)	7	(0.7)	85	(2.4)	45	(1.1)
New Jersey	227	(1.5)	—	(†)	239	(1.1)	244	(1.1)	249	(1.1)	10	(0.9)	90	(0.9)	52	(2.0)	9	(1.0)	89	(2.7)	45	(1.2)
New Mexico	213	(1.4)	213	(1.5)	223	(1.1)	224	(0.8)	228	(0.9)	30	(1.4)	70	(1.4)	24	(1.3)	2	(0.4)	88	(2.2)	55	(1.2)
New York[6]	218	(1.2)	225	(1.4)	236	(0.9)	238	(0.9)	243	(0.8)	15	(0.9)	85	(0.9)	43	(1.5)	6	(0.6)	87	(2.0)	47	(1.3)
North Carolina	213	(1.1)	230	(1.1)	242	(0.8)	241	(0.9)	242	(0.8)	15	(1.0)	85	(1.0)	41	(1.4)	6	(0.5)	90	(1.4)	50	(1.3)
North Dakota	229	(0.8)	230	(1.2)	238	(0.7)	243	(0.5)	245	(0.5)	9	(0.7)	91	(0.7)	46	(1.2)	5	(0.5)	77	(2.0)	48	(1.2)
Ohio[6]	219	(1.2)	230	(1.5)	238	(1.0)	242	(1.0)	245	(1.0)	13	(1.1)	87	(1.1)	46	(1.6)	7	(0.8)	83	(3.4)	45	(1.2)
Oklahoma	220	(1.0)	224	(1.0)	229	(1.0)	234	(1.0)	237	(0.8)	18	(1.0)	82	(1.0)	33	(1.4)	3	(0.4)	84	(2.9)	49	(1.0)
Oregon[6]	—	(†)	224	(1.8)	236	(0.9)	238	(0.8)	236	(1.0)	21	(1.1)	79	(1.1)	35	(1.5)	4	(0.5)	76	(2.7)	49	(1.2)
Pennsylvania	224	(1.3)	—	(†)	236	(1.1)	241	(1.2)	244	(0.8)	15	(0.9)	85	(0.9)	47	(1.3)	7	(0.7)	87	(2.5)	42	(1.4)
Rhode Island	215	(1.5)	224	(1.1)	230	(1.0)	233	(0.9)	236	(0.9)	20	(1.1)	80	(1.1)	34	(1.2)	3	(0.4)	91	(1.8)	44	(1.3)
South Carolina	212	(1.1)	220	(1.4)	236	(0.9)	238	(0.9)	237	(0.8)	20	(1.0)	80	(1.0)	36	(1.2)	5	(0.5)	89	(1.8)	48	(1.2)
South Dakota	—	(†)	—	(†)	237	(0.7)	242	(0.5)	241	(0.7)	14	(1.0)	86	(1.0)	41	(1.1)	4	(0.5)	81	(2.5)	55	(1.0)
Tennessee	211	(1.4)	220	(1.4)	228	(1.0)	232	(1.2)	233	(0.9)	24	(1.3)	76	(1.3)	29	(1.2)	3	(0.4)	82	(2.6)	50	(1.2)
Texas	218	(1.2)	231	(1.1)	237	(0.9)	242	(0.6)	242	(0.7)	13	(0.8)	87	(0.8)	40	(1.2)	5	(0.4)	92	(1.4)	52	(1.4)
Utah	224	(1.0)	227	(1.3)	235	(0.8)	239	(0.8)	239	(0.9)	17	(1.0)	83	(1.0)	39	(1.6)	4	(0.5)	83	(2.4)	47	(1.3)
Vermont[6]	—	(†)	232	(1.6)	242	(0.8)	244	(0.5)	246	(0.5)	11	(0.7)	89	(0.7)	49	(1.3)	7	(0.6)	88	(0.9)	47	(1.1)
Virginia	221	(1.3)	230	(1.0)	239	(1.1)	241	(0.9)	244	(0.9)	13	(0.8)	87	(0.8)	42	(1.5)	7	(0.8)	85	(2.7)	46	(1.3)
Washington	—	(†)	—	(†)	238	(1.0)	242	(0.9)	243	(1.0)	16	(1.2)	84	(1.2)	44	(1.4)	7	(0.9)	94	(1.4)	50	(1.1)
West Virginia	215	(1.1)	223	(1.3)	231	(0.8)	231	(0.7)	236	(0.9)	19	(1.1)	81	(1.1)	33	(1.4)	3	(0.4)	96	(1.3)	47	(1.2)
Wisconsin[6]	229	(1.1)	—	(†)	237	(0.9)	241	(0.9)	244	(0.9)	15	(1.0)	85	(1.0)	47	(1.5)	7	(0.7)	87	(2.1)	49	(1.2)
Wyoming	225	(0.9)	229	(1.1)	241	(0.6)	243	(0.6)	244	(0.5)	12	(0.7)	88	(0.7)	44	(1.0)	5	(0.5)	91	(0.3)	57	(1.1)
Department of Defense dependents schools[7]	—	(†)	227	(0.6)	237	(0.4)	239	(0.5)	240	(0.4)	14	(0.8)	86	(0.8)	37	(0.9)	3	(0.3)	84	(0.3)	52	(0.7)
Other jurisdictions																						
American Samoa	—	(†)	152	(2.5)	—	(†)	—	(†)	—	(†)	—	(†)	—	(†)	—	(†)	—	(†)	—	(†)	—	(†)
Guam	193	(0.8)	184	(1.7)	—	(†)	—	(†)	—	(†)	—	(†)	—	(†)	—	(†)	—	(†)	—	(†)	—	(†)
Puerto Rico[8]	—	(†)	—	(†)	179	(1.0)	183	(0.9)	—	(†)	—	(†)	—	(†)	—	(†)	—	(†)	—	(†)	61	(1.0)
U.S. Virgin Islands	—	(†)	181	(1.8)	—	(†)	—	(†)	—	(†)	—	(†)	—	(†)	—	(†)	—	(†)	—	(†)	—	(†)

—Not available.
†Not applicable.
‡Reporting standards not met.
[1]Scale ranges from 0 to 500.
[2]*Basic* denotes partial mastery of prerequisite knowledge and skills that are fundamental for proficient work at the 4th-grade level.
[3]*Proficient* represents solid academic performance for 4th-graders. Students reaching this level have demonstrated competency over challenging subject matter.
[4]*Advanced* signifies superior performance.
[5]Percentage of students who report spending 30 minutes, 45 minutes, 1 hour, and over 1 hour on mathematics homework each day.
[6]Did not meet one or more of the guidelines for school participation in 2000. Data are subject to appreciable nonresponse bias.
[7]Prior to 2005, NAEP divided the Department of Defense (DoD) schools into two jurisdictions, domestic and overseas. In 2005, NAEP began combining the DoD domestic and overseas schools into a single jurisdiction. Data shown in this table for years prior to 2005 were recalculated for comparability.
[8]Because of modifications to the 2005 Puerto Rico administration, results from 2003 should not be compared to results from 2005. Although parallel changes were not made in the nation in 2005, within-year comparisons between Puerto Rico and the nation are valid.
NOTE: With the exception of 1992, includes students for whom accommodations were permitted. Excludes students unable to be tested (even with accommodations) due to limited proficiency in English or due to a disability. Some data have been revised from previously published figures. Detail may not sum to totals because of rounding. Standard errors appear in parentheses.
SOURCE: U.S. Department of Education, National Center for Education Statistics, National Assessment of Educational Progress (NAEP), 1992, 2000, 2003, 2005, and 2007 Mathematics Assessments, retrieved May 19, 2008, from the NAEP Data Explorer (http://nces.ed.gov/nationsreportcard/nde/). (This table was prepared May 2008.)

Table 135. Average mathematics scale score and percentage attaining mathematics achievement levels of 8th-graders in public schools, by level of parental education and state or jurisdiction: Selected years, 1990 through 2007

State or jurisdiction	Average scale score[1]							Percent attaining mathematics achievement levels, 2007				Average scale score, by highest level of education attained by parents, 2007[2]			
	1990	1992	1996	2000	2003	2005	2007	Below Basic	At or above Basic[3]	At or above Proficient[4]	At Advanced[5]	Did not finish high school	Graduated high school	Some education after high school	Graduated college
1	2	3	4	5	6	7	8	9	10	11	12	13	14	15	16
United States	262 (1.4)	267 (1.0)	271 (1.2)	272 (0.9)	276 (0.3)	278 (0.2)	280 (0.3)	30 (0.3)	70 (0.3)	31 (0.3)	7 (0.2)	263 (0.5)	270 (0.4)	283 (0.4)	291 (0.3)
Alabama	253 (1.1)	252 (1.7)	257 (2.1)	264 (1.8)	262 (1.5)	262 (1.5)	266 (1.5)	45 (1.7)	55 (1.7)	18 (1.5)	2 (0.4)	256 (1.9)	254 (2.2)	271 (1.6)	275 (2.0)
Alaska	— (†)	— (†)	278 (1.8)	— (†)	279 (0.9)	279 (0.8)	283 (1.1)	27 (1.3)	73 (1.3)	32 (1.4)	7 (0.6)	‡ (†)	‡ (†)	‡ ‡	‡ ‡
Arizona[6]	260 (1.3)	265 (1.3)	268 (1.6)	269 (1.8)	271 (1.2)	274 (1.1)	276 (1.2)	34 (1.5)	66 (1.5)	26 (1.2)	5 (0.7)	261 (2.5)	267 (2.3)	282 (1.9)	287 (1.5)
Arkansas	256 (0.9)	256 (1.2)	262 (1.5)	257 (1.5)	266 (1.2)	272 (1.2)	274 (1.1)	35 (1.3)	65 (1.3)	24 (1.1)	4 (0.5)	260 (3.0)	268 (1.7)	280 (1.9)	282 (1.5)
California[6]	256 (1.3)	261 (1.7)	263 (1.9)	260 (2.1)	267 (1.2)	269 (0.7)	270 (0.8)	41 (1.0)	59 (1.0)	24 (0.8)	5 (0.4)	255 (1.1)	262 (1.2)	277 (1.4)	286 (1.2)
Colorado	267 (0.9)	272 (1.0)	276 (1.1)	— (†)	283 (1.1)	281 (1.2)	286 (0.9)	25 (1.0)	75 (1.0)	37 (1.2)	10 (0.7)	262 (2.4)	273 (2.1)	290 (2.0)	298 (1.2)
Connecticut	270 (1.0)	274 (1.1)	280 (1.1)	281 (1.3)	284 (1.2)	281 (1.4)	282 (1.5)	27 (1.6)	73 (1.6)	35 (1.6)	8 (0.7)	254 (3.6)	265 (2.2)	280 (2.5)	295 (1.3)
Delaware	261 (0.9)	263 (1.0)	267 (0.9)	— (†)	277 (0.7)	281 (0.6)	283 (0.6)	26 (1.1)	74 (1.1)	31 (1.1)	7 (0.7)	271 (2.2)	274 (1.6)	284 (1.5)	292 (1.0)
District of Columbia	231 (0.9)	235 (0.9)	233 (1.3)	235 (1.1)	243 (0.8)	245 (0.9)	248 (0.9)	66 (1.2)	34 (1.2)	8 (0.6)	1 (0.3)	244 (3.1)	239 (1.7)	261 (2.1)	255 (1.4)
Florida	255 (1.2)	260 (1.5)	264 (1.8)	— (†)	271 (1.5)	274 (1.1)	277 (1.3)	32 (1.4)	68 (1.4)	27 (1.4)	5 (0.7)	264 (2.0)	268 (1.5)	284 (1.8)	286 (1.6)
Georgia	259 (1.3)	259 (1.2)	262 (1.6)	265 (1.2)	270 (1.2)	272 (1.1)	275 (1.0)	36 (1.5)	64 (1.5)	25 (1.0)	4 (0.6)	262 (2.6)	263 (1.7)	279 (1.5)	284 (1.3)
Hawaii	251 (0.8)	257 (0.9)	262 (1.0)	262 (1.4)	266 (0.8)	266 (0.7)	269 (0.8)	41 (1.0)	59 (1.0)	21 (0.7)	3 (0.3)	257 (4.5)	258 (1.5)	274 (1.6)	279 (1.2)
Idaho[6]	271 (0.8)	275 (0.7)	— (†)	277 (1.0)	280 (0.9)	281 (0.9)	284 (0.9)	25 (1.1)	75 (1.1)	34 (1.3)	6 (0.6)	262 (2.8)	271 (1.5)	290 (1.3)	294 (1.1)
Illinois[6]	261 (1.7)	— (†)	— (†)	275 (1.7)	277 (1.2)	278 (1.1)	280 (1.1)	30 (1.6)	70 (1.6)	31 (1.5)	7 (0.8)	262 (1.9)	267 (1.9)	282 (1.4)	293 (1.6)
Indiana[6]	267 (1.2)	270 (1.1)	276 (1.4)	281 (1.4)	281 (1.1)	282 (1.0)	285 (1.1)	24 (1.4)	76 (1.4)	35 (1.4)	7 (0.7)	271 (2.3)	276 (1.5)	284 (2.1)	296 (1.4)
Iowa	278 (1.1)	283 (1.0)	284 (1.3)	— (†)	284 (0.8)	284 (0.9)	285 (0.9)	23 (1.1)	77 (1.1)	35 (1.4)	7 (0.6)	262 (2.5)	274 (1.4)	287 (1.6)	295 (1.0)
Kansas[6]	— (†)	— (†)	— (†)	283 (1.7)	284 (1.3)	284 (1.0)	290 (1.1)	19 (1.1)	81 (1.1)	40 (1.5)	9 (0.7)	271 (3.1)	278 (1.9)	291 (1.9)	299 (1.1)
Kentucky	257 (1.2)	262 (1.1)	267 (1.1)	270 (1.3)	274 (1.2)	274 (1.2)	279 (1.1)	31 (1.5)	69 (1.5)	27 (1.2)	5 (0.6)	265 (2.4)	272 (1.7)	283 (1.7)	288 (1.6)
Louisiana	246 (1.2)	250 (1.7)	252 (1.6)	259 (1.5)	266 (1.5)	268 (1.4)	272 (1.4)	36 (1.8)	64 (1.8)	19 (1.2)	2 (0.4)	265 (2.7)	266 (1.6)	275 (1.5)	279 (1.6)
Maine[6]	— (†)	279 (1.0)	284 (1.4)	281 (1.1)	282 (0.9)	281 (0.8)	286 (0.8)	22 (1.1)	78 (1.1)	34 (1.2)	7 (0.7)	267 (4.0)	277 (1.5)	284 (1.7)	295 (1.0)
Maryland	261 (1.4)	265 (1.3)	270 (2.1)	272 (1.7)	278 (1.0)	278 (1.1)	286 (1.2)	26 (1.2)	74 (1.2)	37 (1.4)	10 (1.0)	288 (3.6)	273 (1.9)	283 (1.8)	289 (1.3)
Massachusetts	— (†)	273 (1.0)	278 (1.7)	279 (1.5)	287 (1.1)	292 (0.9)	298 (1.3)	15 (1.0)	85 (1.0)	51 (1.7)	15 (1.0)	277 (3.0)	284 (2.4)	294 (2.2)	307 (0.9)
Michigan[6]	264 (1.2)	267 (1.4)	277 (1.8)	277 (1.9)	276 (2.0)	277 (1.5)	277 (1.4)	34 (1.7)	66 (1.7)	29 (1.4)	6 (0.7)	258 (4.0)	265 (2.1)	279 (1.8)	287 (1.7)
Minnesota	275 (0.9)	282 (1.0)	284 (1.3)	287 (1.4)	291 (1.1)	290 (1.2)	292 (1.0)	19 (0.8)	81 (0.8)	43 (1.6)	11 (0.8)	264 (3.8)	278 (2.3)	290 (2.0)	301 (1.1)
Mississippi	— (†)	246 (1.2)	250 (1.2)	254 (1.1)	261 (1.1)	263 (1.2)	265 (0.8)	46 (1.3)	54 (1.3)	14 (1.0)	2 (0.3)	256 (2.3)	255 (1.4)	272 (1.4)	271 (1.2)
Missouri	270 (1.1)	271 (1.2)	273 (1.4)	271 (1.5)	279 (1.1)	276 (1.3)	281 (1.0)	28 (1.5)	72 (1.5)	30 (1.3)	5 (0.7)	263 (3.0)	270 (1.6)	285 (1.7)	289 (1.3)
Montana[6]	280 (0.9)	— (†)	283 (1.3)	285 (1.5)	286 (0.8)	286 (0.7)	287 (0.7)	21 (1.0)	79 (1.0)	38 (1.1)	7 (0.5)	265 (3.3)	278 (2.1)	286 (1.6)	296 (0.9)
Nebraska	276 (1.0)	278 (1.1)	283 (1.0)	280 (1.2)	282 (0.9)	284 (1.0)	284 (1.0)	26 (1.2)	74 (1.2)	35 (1.4)	8 (0.7)	260 (3.1)	272 (2.2)	288 (1.8)	292 (1.3)
Nevada	— (†)	— (†)	— (†)	265 (0.8)	268 (0.8)	270 (0.8)	271 (1.0)	40 (1.2)	60 (1.2)	23 (1.0)	4 (0.6)	254 (1.7)	267 (1.9)	281 (2.0)	283 (1.3)
New Hampshire	273 (0.9)	278 (1.0)	— (†)	— (†)	286 (0.8)	285 (0.8)	288 (0.7)	22 (1.1)	78 (1.1)	38 (1.1)	8 (0.6)	269 (2.7)	276 (1.6)	285 (1.9)	295 (0.9)
New Jersey	270 (1.1)	272 (1.6)	— (†)	— (†)	281 (1.1)	284 (1.4)	289 (1.2)	23 (1.4)	77 (1.4)	40 (1.6)	10 (0.7)	270 (3.2)	276 (2.3)	288 (1.8)	298 (1.2)
New Mexico	256 (0.7)	260 (0.9)	262 (1.2)	259 (1.3)	263 (1.0)	263 (0.9)	268 (0.9)	43 (1.6)	57 (1.6)	17 (1.1)	3 (0.5)	254 (1.8)	260 (1.6)	272 (1.5)	280 (1.5)
New York[6]	261 (1.4)	266 (2.1)	270 (1.7)	271 (2.2)	280 (1.1)	280 (0.9)	280 (1.2)	30 (1.4)	70 (1.4)	30 (1.2)	7 (0.8)	265 (2.2)	270 (1.9)	283 (1.7)	290 (1.6)
North Carolina	250 (1.1)	258 (1.2)	268 (1.4)	276 (1.3)	281 (1.0)	282 (0.9)	284 (1.1)	27 (1.4)	73 (1.4)	34 (1.3)	8 (0.9)	268 (2.1)	271 (1.8)	287 (1.7)	295 (1.3)
North Dakota	281 (1.2)	283 (1.1)	284 (0.9)	282 (1.1)	287 (0.8)	287 (0.6)	292 (0.7)	14 (0.9)	86 (0.9)	41 (1.2)	7 (0.7)	‡ (†)	277 (1.6)	292 (1.8)	297 (0.8)

See notes at end of table.

Table 135. Average mathematics scale score and percentage attaining mathematics achievement levels of 8th-graders in public schools, by level of parental education and state or jurisdiction: Selected years, 1990 through 2007—Continued

State or jurisdiction	Average scale score[1]							Percent attaining mathematics achievement levels, 2007				Average scale score, by highest level of education attained by parents, 2007[2]			
	1990	1992	1996	2000	2003	2005	2007	Below Basic	At or above Basic[3]	At or above Proficient[4]	At Advanced[5]	Did not finish high school	Graduated high school	Some education after high school	Graduated college
1	2	3	4	5	6	7	8	9	10	11	12	13	14	15	16
Ohio	264 (1.0)	(†)	(†)	281 (1.6)	282 (1.3)	283 (1.1)	285 (1.2)	24 (1.4)	76 (1.4)	35 (1.5)	7 (0.7)	266 (2.6)	274 (1.8)	285 (1.8)	295 (1.5)
Oklahoma	263 (1.3)	268 (1.1)	(†)	270 (1.3)	272 (1.1)	271 (1.0)	275 (0.9)	34 (1.5)	66 (1.5)	21 (1.2)	3 (0.4)	258 (2.6)	268 (1.6)	276 (1.4)	284 (1.2)
Oregon[6]	271 (1.0)	(†)	276 (1.5)	280 (1.5)	281 (1.3)	282 (1.0)	284 (1.1)	27 (1.1)	73 (1.1)	35 (1.3)	9 (0.7)	267 (2.7)	275 (1.8)	285 (1.5)	295 (1.5)
Pennsylvania	266 (1.6)	271 (1.5)	(†)	(†)	279 (1.1)	281 (1.5)	286 (1.1)	23 (1.3)	77 (1.3)	38 (1.3)	8 (0.6)	271 (3.4)	273 (1.9)	288 (1.7)	296 (1.3)
Rhode Island	260 (0.6)	266 (0.7)	269 (0.9)	269 (1.3)	272 (0.7)	272 (0.8)	275 (0.7)	35 (1.1)	65 (1.1)	28 (1.0)	5 (0.5)	255 (3.2)	259 (1.9)	276 (1.6)	288 (1.1)
South Carolina	—	261 (1.0)	261 (1.5)	265 (1.5)	277 (1.3)	281 (0.9)	282 (1.0)	29 (1.1)	71 (1.1)	32 (1.4)	8 (0.8)	270 (2.7)	270 (1.6)	282 (2.0)	291 (1.4)
South Dakota	—	(†)	(†)	(†)	285 (0.8)	287 (0.6)	288 (0.8)	19 (1.0)	81 (1.0)	39 (1.5)	7 (0.6)	267 (2.0)	278 (1.9)	291 (1.5)	295 (0.9)
Tennessee	—	259 (1.4)	263 (1.4)	262 (1.5)	268 (1.8)	271 (1.1)	274 (1.1)	36 (1.4)	64 (1.4)	23 (1.4)	7 (0.6)	260 (3.0)	265 (1.6)	278 (1.7)	283 (1.5)
Texas	258 (1.4)	265 (1.3)	270 (1.4)	273 (1.6)	277 (1.1)	281 (0.6)	286 (1.0)	22 (1.1)	78 (1.1)	35 (1.3)	3 (0.7)	272 (1.5)	279 (1.6)	289 (1.4)	297 (1.3)
Utah	—	274 (0.7)	277 (1.0)	274 (1.2)	281 (1.0)	279 (0.7)	281 (0.9)	28 (1.1)	72 (1.1)	32 (1.2)	9 (0.6)	253 (3.5)	266 (1.7)	282 (1.8)	291 (1.0)
Vermont[6]	—	(†)	279 (1.0)	281 (1.5)	286 (0.8)	287 (0.8)	291 (0.7)	19 (1.0)	81 (1.0)	41 (1.3)	10 (0.8)	267 (3.8)	275 (1.9)	289 (1.6)	301 (1.0)
Virginia	264 (1.5)	268 (1.2)	270 (1.6)	275 (1.3)	282 (1.3)	284 (1.1)	288 (1.1)	23 (1.3)	77 (1.3)	37 (1.4)	9 (0.8)	264 (2.8)	274 (1.7)	288 (1.7)	298 (1.3)
Washington	—	(†)	276 (1.3)	(†)	281 (0.9)	285 (1.0)	285 (1.0)	25 (1.3)	75 (1.3)	36 (1.2)	9 (0.8)	265 (2.3)	275 (2.0)	290 (1.8)	296 (1.2)
West Virginia	256 (1.0)	259 (1.0)	265 (1.0)	266 (1.2)	271 (1.2)	269 (1.0)	270 (1.0)	39 (1.4)	61 (1.4)	19 (0.9)	2 (0.3)	258 (2.3)	263 (1.4)	274 (1.3)	280 (1.2)
Wisconsin	274 (1.3)	278 (1.5)	283 (1.5)	(†)	284 (1.3)	285 (1.2)	286 (1.1)	24 (1.4)	76 (1.4)	37 (1.3)	8 (0.7)	260 (3.3)	275 (1.8)	285 (2.0)	295 (1.2)
Wyoming	272 (0.7)	275 (0.9)	275 (0.9)	276 (1.0)	284 (0.7)	282 (0.8)	287 (0.7)	20 (1.1)	80 (1.1)	36 (1.6)	7 (0.7)	266 (3.8)	279 (1.5)	288 (1.6)	295 (1.2)
Department of Defense dependents schools[7]	—	—	274 (0.9)	277 (1.1)	285 (0.7)	284 (0.7)	285 (0.8)	22 (1.2)	78 (1.2)	33 (1.2)	5 (0.7)	‡	274 (2.5)	286 (1.2)	290 (1.2)
Other jurisdictions															
American Samoa	(†)	(†)	(†)	192 (5.5)	—	—	(†)	—	—	—	—	(†)	(†)	(†)	(†)
Guam	232 (0.7)	235 (1.0)	239 (1.7)	234 (2.6)	(†)	(†)	(†)	—	—	—	—	(†)	(†)	(†)	(†)
Puerto Rico[8]	(†)	(†)	(†)	(†)	212 (1.0)	218 (1.0)	(†)	—	—	—	—	(†)	(†)	(†)	(†)
U.S. Virgin Islands	219 (0.9)	223 (1.1)	(†)	(†)	—	(†)	(†)	—	—	—	—	(†)	(†)	(†)	(†)

—Not available.
†Not applicable.
‡Reporting standards not met.
[1]Scale ranges from 0 to 500.
[2]Excludes students who responded "I don't know" to the question about educational level of parents.
[3]Basic denotes partial mastery of prerequisite knowledge and skills that are fundamental for proficient work at the 8th-grade level.
[4]Proficient represents solid academic performance for 8th-graders. Students reaching this level have demonstrated competency over challenging subject matter.
[5]Advanced signifies superior performance.
[6]Did not meet one or more of the guidelines for school participation in 2000. Data are subject to appreciable nonresponse bias.

[7]Prior to 2005, NAEP divided the Department of Defense (DoD) schools into two jurisdictions, domestic and overseas. In 2005, NAEP began combining the DoD domestic and overseas schools into a single jurisdiction. Data shown in this table for years prior to 2005 were recalculated for comparability.
[8]Because of modifications to the 2005 Puerto Rico administration, results from 2003 should not be compared to results from 2005. Although parallel changes were not made in the nation in 2005, within-year comparisons between Puerto Rico and the nation are valid.
NOTE: Excludes persons not enrolled in school and those who were unable to be tested due to limited proficiency in English or due to a disability. Data for 2000, 2003, 2005, and 2007 include students for whom accommodations were permitted. Detail may not sum to totals because of rounding. Standard errors appear in parentheses.
SOURCE: U.S. Department of Education, National Center for Education Statistics, National Assessment of Educational Progress (NAEP), 1990, 1992, 1996, 2000, 2003, 2005, and 2007 Mathematics Assessments, retrieved May 19, 2008, from the NAEP Data Explorer (http://nces.ed.gov/nationsreportcard/nde/). (This table was prepared May 2008.)

Table 136.   Average mathematics scale scores of 4th-, 8th-, and 12th-graders, by selected student and school characteristics: Selected years, 1990 through 2007

Selected student or school characteristic	1990[1]		1992[1]		1996		2000		2003		2005		2007	
1	2		3		4		5		6		7		8	
4th-graders, all students	**213**	**(0.9)**	**220**	**(0.7)**	**224**	**(1.0)**	**226**	**(0.9)**	**235**	**(0.2)**	**238**	**(0.1)**	**240**	**(0.2)**
Sex														
Male	214	(1.2)	221	(0.8)	224	(1.1)	227	(1.0)	236	(0.3)	239	(0.2)	241	(0.2)
Female	213	(1.1)	219	(1.0)	223	(1.1)	224	(0.9)	233	(0.2)	237	(0.2)	239	(0.2)
Race/ethnicity														
White	220	(1.0)	227	(0.8)	232	(1.0)	234	(0.8)	243	(0.2)	246	(0.1)	248	(0.2)
Black	188	(1.8)	193	(1.4)	198	(1.6)	203	(1.2)	216	(0.4)	220	(0.3)	222	(0.3)
Hispanic	200	(2.2)	202	(1.5)	207	(1.9)	208	(1.5)	222	(0.4)	226	(0.3)	227	(0.3)
Asian/Pacific Islander	225	(4.1)	231	(2.1)	229	(4.2)	‡	(†)	246	(1.1)	251	(0.7)	253	(0.8)
American Indian/Alaska Native	‡	(†)	‡	(†)	217	(5.6)	208	(3.5)	223	(1.0)	226	(0.9)	228	(0.7)
Control of school														
Public	212	(1.1)	219	(0.8)	222	(1.1)	224	(1.0)	234	(0.2)	237	(0.2)	239	(0.2)
Private, total	224	(2.6)	228	(1.1)	235	(1.9)	238	(0.8)	244	(0.7)	246	(0.8)	‡	(†)
Catholic	219	(3.0)	228	(1.2)	232	(2.5)	237	(1.2)	244	(0.8)	244	(0.7)	246	(1.1)
Lutheran	—	(†)	—	(†)	—	(†)	—	(†)	245	(1.5)	245	(1.3)	—	(†)
Conservative Christian	—	(†)	—	(†)	—	(†)	—	(†)	‡	(†)	‡	(†)	—	(†)
8th-graders, all students	**263**	**(1.3)**	**268**	**(0.9)**	**270**	**(0.9)**	**273**	**(0.8)**	**278**	**(0.3)**	**279**	**(0.2)**	**281**	**(0.3)**
Sex														
Male	263	(1.6)	268	(1.1)	271	(1.1)	274	(0.9)	278	(0.3)	280	(0.2)	282	(0.3)
Female	262	(1.3)	269	(1.0)	269	(1.1)	272	(0.9)	277	(0.3)	278	(0.2)	280	(0.3)
Race/ethnicity														
White	270	(1.3)	277	(1.0)	281	(1.1)	284	(0.8)	288	(0.3)	289	(0.2)	291	(0.3)
Black	237	(2.7)	237	(1.3)	240	(1.9)	244	(1.2)	252	(0.5)	255	(0.4)	260	(0.4)
Hispanic	246	(4.3)	249	(1.2)	251	(1.7)	253	(1.3)	259	(0.6)	262	(0.4)	265	(0.4)
Asian/Pacific Islander	275	(5.0)	290	(5.9)	‡	(†)	288	(3.5)	291	(1.3)	295	(0.9)	297	(0.9)
American Indian/Alaska Native	‡	(†)	‡	(†)	‡	(†)	259	(7.5)	263	(1.8)	264	(0.9)	264	(1.2)
Parents' highest level of education														
Did not finish high school	242	(2.0)	249	(1.7)	250	(2.0)	253	(1.4)	257	(0.6)	259	(0.5)	263	(0.5)
Graduated high school	255	(1.6)	257	(1.2)	260	(1.3)	261	(1.0)	267	(0.4)	267	(0.3)	270	(0.4)
Some education after high school	267	(1.6)	271	(1.1)	277	(1.2)	277	(1.1)	280	(0.4)	280	(0.3)	283	(0.4)
Graduated college	274	(1.5)	281	(1.2)	281	(1.2)	286	(1.0)	288	(0.3)	290	(0.2)	292	(0.3)
Control of school														
Public	262	(1.4)	267	(1.0)	269	(1.0)	272	(0.9)	276	(0.3)	278	(0.2)	280	(0.3)
Private, total	271	(2.5)	281	(2.2)	285	(1.8)	286	(1.2)	292	(1.2)	‡	(†)	293	(1.3)
Catholic	271	(3.5)	278	(2.1)	285	(2.3)	284	(1.5)	289	(1.4)	290	(1.2)	292	(1.6)
Lutheran	—	(†)	—	(†)	—	(†)	—	(†)	296	(1.6)	293	(2.3)	—	(†)
Conservative Christian	—	(†)	—	(†)	—	(†)	—	(†)	286	(2.6)	‡	(†)	—	(†)
12th-graders, all students	**294**	**(1.1)**	**299**	**(0.9)**	**302**	**(1.0)**	**300**	**(1.0)**	**—**	**(†)**	**—**	**(†)**	**—**	**(†)**
Sex														
Male	297	(1.4)	301	(1.1)	303	(1.2)	302	(1.2)	—	(†)	—	(†)	—	(†)
Female	291	(1.3)	298	(1.0)	300	(1.2)	299	(1.0)	—	(†)	—	(†)	—	(†)
Race/ethnicity														
White	300	(1.2)	305	(0.9)	309	(1.2)	307	(1.1)	—	(†)	—	(†)	—	(†)
Black	268	(2.0)	275	(1.8)	275	(1.6)	273	(2.0)	—	(†)	—	(†)	—	(†)
Hispanic	276	(3.8)	286	(1.6)	284	(2.2)	282	(2.0)	—	(†)	—	(†)	—	(†)
Asian/Pacific Islander	311	(5.2)	312	(4.2)	305	(2.7)	315	(4.2)	—	(†)	—	(†)	—	(†)
American Indian/Alaska Native	‡	(†)	‡	(†)	‡	(†)	294	(5.0)	—	(†)	—	(†)	—	(†)
Parents' highest level of education														
Did not finish high school	272	(2.1)	278	(1.7)	280	(2.0)	278	(1.6)	—	(†)	—	(†)	—	(†)
Graduated high school	283	(2.0)	288	(1.4)	290	(1.0)	287	(1.3)	—	(†)	—	(†)	—	(†)
Some education after high school	297	(1.2)	299	(1.0)	302	(0.9)	299	(1.2)	—	(†)	—	(†)	—	(†)
Graduated college	306	(1.6)	311	(1.2)	313	(1.3)	312	(1.3)	—	(†)	—	(†)	—	(†)
Control of school														
Public	294	(1.2)	297	(1.0)	301	(1.1)	299	(1.1)	—	(†)	—	(†)	—	(†)
Private, total	300	(3.6)	314	(2.3)	310	(2.6)	315	(1.1)	—	(†)	—	(†)	—	(†)
Catholic	301	(4.6)	311	(2.5)	309	(2.5)	314	(1.4)	—	(†)	—	(†)	—	(†)
Lutheran	—	(†)	—	(†)	—	(†)	—	(†)	—	(†)	—	(†)	—	(†)
Conservative Christian	—	(†)	—	(†)	—	(†)	—	(†)	—	(†)	—	(†)	—	(†)

—Not available.
†Not applicable.
‡Reporting standards not met.
[1]Accommodations were not permitted for this assessment.
NOTE: Scale ranges from 0 to 500. Includes public and private schools. Excludes persons not enrolled in school and those who were unable to be tested due to limited proficiency in English or due to a disability. Race categories exclude persons of Hispanic ethnicity. Some data have been revised from previously published figures. Standard errors appear in parentheses.
SOURCE: U.S. Department of Education, National Center for Education Statistics, National Assessment of Educational Progress (NAEP), 1990, 1992, 1996, 2000, 2003, 2005, and 2007 Mathematics Assessments, retrieved June 16, 2008, from the NAEP Data Explorer (http://nces.ed.gov/nationsreportcard/nde/). (This table was prepared June 2008.)

Table 137. Average mathematics scale score of 8th-graders and percentage reporting various attitudes toward mathematics work, by frequency of attitude and selected student and school characteristics: 2007

Average scale score[1]

Student or school characteristic	Math work is boring — Never or hardly ever	1–2 times a month	1–2 times a week	Almost every day	Math work is engaging and interesting — Never or hardly ever	1–2 times a month	1–2 times a week	Almost every day	Math work is challenging — Never or hardly ever	1–2 times a month	1–2 times a week	Almost every day	Math work is too easy — Never or hardly ever	1–2 times a month	1–2 times a week	Almost every day
(col)	2	3	4	5	6	7	8	9	10	11	12	13	14	15	16	17
All students	278 (0.5)	286 (0.4)	286 (0.3)	279 (0.3)	278 (0.3)	285 (0.3)	285 (0.4)	280 (0.5)	284 (0.4)	286 (0.4)	283 (0.3)	277 (0.4)	276 (0.4)	284 (0.4)	283 (0.3)	283 (0.4)
Sex																
Male	278 (0.6)	287 (0.4)	288 (0.4)	281 (0.4)	279 (0.4)	287 (0.5)	286 (0.5)	282 (0.5)	286 (0.5)	288 (0.5)	285 (0.4)	277 (0.5)	274 (0.5)	285 (0.4)	285 (0.4)	286 (0.6)
Female	278 (0.6)	286 (0.5)	284 (0.4)	277 (0.4)	276 (0.4)	284 (0.5)	284 (0.5)	279 (0.6)	282 (0.5)	285 (0.5)	282 (0.4)	276 (0.5)	277 (0.6)	284 (0.4)	281 (0.4)	280 (0.5)
Race/ethnicity																
White	291 (0.5)	297 (0.4)	295 (0.4)	287 (0.4)	285 (0.3)	294 (0.4)	294 (0.4)	294 (0.6)	293 (0.4)	295 (0.4)	293 (0.3)	288 (0.5)	285 (0.4)	293 (0.4)	293 (0.3)	294 (0.4)
Black	259 (0.8)	263 (0.8)	263 (0.6)	258 (0.6)	259 (0.7)	263 (0.5)	262 (0.5)	259 (0.7)	264 (0.9)	265 (0.8)	262 (0.7)	255 (0.6)	254 (0.8)	261 (0.8)	262 (0.6)	263 (0.7)
Hispanic	262 (0.8)	268 (0.8)	269 (0.7)	264 (0.6)	264 (0.7)	267 (0.7)	267 (0.7)	265 (0.7)	265 (1.2)	270 (0.7)	267 (0.6)	262 (0.6)	258 (1.0)	266 (0.8)	268 (0.6)	267 (1.0)
Asian/Pacific Islander	295 (2.0)	297 (1.7)	303 (1.7)	295 (1.3)	293 (1.5)	298 (1.7)	300 (1.2)	297 (1.5)	306 (2.4)	302 (1.7)	297 (1.2)	290 (1.4)	288 (2.8)	295 (1.7)	299 (1.0)	301 (1.4)
American Indian/Alaska Native	262 (2.8)	266 (4.2)	267 (2.5)	262 (1.7)	262 (2.4)	270 (2.1)	263 (2.5)	264 (2.2)	271 (2.9)	269 (2.5)	267 (1.7)	255 (2.4)	256 (2.8)	263 (3.0)	266 (1.5)	269 (2.8)
Eligibility for free or reduced-price lunch																
Eligible	263 (0.6)	269 (0.5)	269 (0.5)	264 (0.5)	264 (0.5)	268 (0.4)	268 (0.4)	264 (0.6)	269 (0.6)	271 (0.5)	267 (0.4)	260 (0.5)	258 (0.6)	266 (0.5)	268 (0.4)	269 (0.6)
Not eligible	290 (0.6)	296 (0.5)	295 (0.5)	288 (0.4)	286 (0.4)	294 (0.3)	295 (0.5)	293 (0.5)	293 (0.5)	295 (0.4)	293 (0.3)	287 (0.4)	286 (0.4)	293 (0.4)	292 (0.4)	294 (0.4)
Unknown	289 (2.9)	297 (2.0)	297 (2.0)	287 (1.7)	283 (1.5)	293 (2.0)	298 (1.9)	295 (2.9)	292 (2.7)	298 (2.1)	291 (1.6)	288 (2.4)	283 (2.8)	293 (1.8)	294 (1.8)	298 (2.9)
Control of school																
Public	277 (0.4)	285 (0.4)	285 (0.4)	278 (0.3)	277 (0.3)	284 (0.3)	284 (0.3)	279 (0.4)	283 (0.4)	285 (0.4)	282 (0.3)	275 (0.3)	274 (0.4)	283 (0.3)	282 (0.3)	282 (0.4)
Private	291 (2.4)	298 (1.8)	297 (1.5)	289 (1.5)	286 (1.4)	294 (1.6)	298 (1.7)	297 (2.4)	296 (2.5)	298 (1.9)	294 (1.4)	289 (1.8)	288 (2.2)	294 (1.6)	294 (1.4)	299 (2.9)

Percent of students

Student or school characteristic	Math work is boring — Never or hardly ever	1–2 times a month	1–2 times a week	Almost every day	Math work is engaging and interesting — Never or hardly ever	1–2 times a month	1–2 times a week	Almost every day	Math work is challenging — Never or hardly ever	1–2 times a month	1–2 times a week	Almost every day	Math work is too easy — Never or hardly ever	1–2 times a month	1–2 times a week	Almost every day
(col)	2	3	4	5	6	7	8	9	10	11	12	13	14	15	16	17
All students	17 (0.2)	20 (0.2)	27 (0.2)	35 (0.2)	27 (0.2)	24 (0.2)	29 (0.2)	20 (0.2)	12 (0.1)	21 (0.1)	37 (0.2)	30 (0.2)	17 (0.1)	27 (0.2)	40 (0.2)	16 (0.2)
Sex																
Male	16 (0.2)	19 (0.2)	27 (0.3)	38 (0.3)	28 (0.3)	23 (0.2)	30 (0.2)	20 (0.2)	13 (0.2)	21 (0.2)	37 (0.3)	29 (0.3)	16 (0.2)	26 (0.2)	41 (0.3)	18 (0.2)
Female	19 (0.2)	21 (0.2)	28 (0.2)	32 (0.3)	27 (0.3)	25 (0.2)	29 (0.2)	20 (0.2)	11 (0.2)	21 (0.2)	37 (0.3)	30 (0.2)	18 (0.2)	28 (0.3)	39 (0.3)	14 (0.2)
Race/ethnicity																
White	15 (0.2)	20 (0.2)	28 (0.2)	37 (0.3)	30 (0.3)	26 (0.2)	28 (0.2)	17 (0.2)	12 (0.2)	21 (0.2)	37 (0.2)	29 (0.2)	18 (0.2)	29 (0.2)	38 (0.2)	14 (0.2)
Black	24 (0.4)	18 (0.4)	25 (0.4)	32 (0.5)	24 (0.4)	20 (0.4)	29 (0.4)	28 (0.4)	12 (0.3)	19 (0.4)	34 (0.4)	35 (0.6)	17 (0.3)	23 (0.4)	41 (0.6)	19 (0.4)
Hispanic	19 (0.4)	21 (0.4)	27 (0.5)	33 (0.4)	23 (0.4)	23 (0.4)	31 (0.4)	22 (0.4)	12 (0.3)	20 (0.4)	38 (0.4)	30 (0.4)	14 (0.3)	22 (0.4)	44 (0.5)	18 (0.4)
Asian/Pacific Islander	18 (0.6)	23 (0.6)	30 (0.9)	30 (1.0)	19 (0.9)	24 (0.8)	33 (0.8)	23 (0.8)	13 (0.5)	26 (0.7)	37 (0.9)	24 (0.8)	9 (0.6)	22 (0.9)	46 (1.0)	22 (0.7)
American Indian/Alaska Native	18 (1.4)	19 (1.1)	26 (1.1)	38 (1.4)	28 (1.1)	21 (1.1)	30 (1.3)	22 (1.1)	12 (0.8)	19 (1.1)	37 (1.4)	33 (1.9)	17 (1.2)	27 (1.3)	41 (1.3)	15 (1.0)
Eligibility for free or reduced-price lunch																
Eligible	21 (0.2)	19 (0.2)	26 (0.2)	34 (0.2)	25 (0.3)	22 (0.2)	30 (0.2)	24 (0.3)	13 (0.2)	20 (0.3)	36 (0.3)	31 (0.3)	16 (0.2)	24 (0.2)	41 (0.3)	18 (0.3)
Not eligible	15 (0.2)	20 (0.2)	29 (0.2)	36 (0.3)	28 (0.3)	26 (0.2)	29 (0.2)	17 (0.2)	12 (0.2)	22 (0.2)	37 (0.2)	29 (0.3)	17 (0.2)	28 (0.2)	40 (0.2)	15 (0.2)
Unknown	17 (1.0)	22 (0.8)	28 (1.1)	32 (1.3)	27 (1.1)	24 (1.0)	30 (0.9)	19 (0.9)	10 (0.5)	21 (0.8)	38 (0.9)	30 (0.8)	18 (0.8)	33 (0.9)	36 (1.2)	13 (0.7)
Control of school																
Public	17 (0.2)	20 (0.1)	27 (0.2)	36 (0.2)	27 (0.2)	24 (0.2)	29 (0.1)	20 (0.2)	12 (0.1)	21 (0.1)	37 (0.2)	30 (0.2)	17 (0.1)	26 (0.2)	40 (0.2)	16 (0.2)
Private	19 (0.9)	22 (0.8)	28 (1.0)	31 (1.3)	26 (1.1)	25 (1.0)	30 (1.0)	19 (0.8)	10 (0.7)	21 (0.9)	39 (0.9)	31 (0.9)	18 (0.7)	33 (1.0)	37 (1.0)	12 (0.7)

[1]Scale ranges from 0 to 500.

NOTE: Includes public and private schools. Includes students for whom accommodations were permitted. Excludes students unable to be tested (even with accommodations) due to limited proficiency in English or due to a disability. Race categories exclude persons of Hispanic ethnicity. Detail may not sum to totals because of rounding. Standard errors appear in parentheses.

SOURCE: U.S. Department of Education, National Center for Education Statistics, National Assessment of Educational Progress (NAEP), 2007 Mathematics Assessment, retrieved August 13, 2008, from the NAEP Data Explorer (http://nces.ed.gov/nations reportcard/nde/). (This table was prepared August 2008.)

Table 138. Average science scale scores and percentage of 4th-, 8th-, and 12th-graders attaining science achievement levels, by selected student characteristics and percentile: 1996, 2000, and 2005

Selected characteristic, percentile, and achievement level	4th-graders			8th-graders			12th-graders		
	1996[1]	2000	2005	1996[1]	2000	2005	1996[1]	2000	2005
1	2	3	4	5	6	7	8	9	10
All students	147 (1.1)	147 (0.9)	151 (0.3)	149 (0.8)	149 (1.0)	149 (0.3)	150 (0.7)	146 (0.9)	147 (0.6)
Sex									
Male	148 (1.3)	149 (1.1)	153 (0.3)	150 (0.9)	153 (1.1)	150 (0.4)	154 (1.0)	148 (1.1)	149 (0.7)
Female	146 (1.1)	145 (1.0)	149 (0.3)	148 (0.9)	146 (1.1)	147 (0.3)	147 (0.8)	145 (1.0)	145 (0.6)
Race/ethnicity									
White	158 (0.9)	159 (0.7)	162 (0.3)	159 (0.8)	161 (0.8)	160 (0.2)	159 (0.9)	153 (1.2)	156 (0.6)
Black	120 (1.3)	122 (1.0)	129 (0.6)	121 (0.9)	121 (1.4)	124 (0.4)	123 (1.1)	122 (1.7)	120 (0.9)
Hispanic	124 (3.0)	122 (2.3)	133 (0.5)	128 (2.7)	127 (1.4)	129 (0.5)	131 (2.2)	128 (1.7)	128 (1.3)
Asian/Pacific Islander	144 (3.7)	‡ (†)	158 (1.0)	151 (4.2)	153 (2.9)	156 (0.9)	147 (3.3)	149 (3.6)	153 (1.7)
American Indian	129 (11.9)	135 (6.9)	138 (1.9)	148 (3.5)	147 (6.7)	128 (4.0)	144 (7.5)	151 (3.6)	139 (5.3)
Parents' education									
Less than high school	—	—	—	(†)	(†)	128 (0.5)	(†)	(†)	125 (1.4)
High school diploma or equivalent	—	—	—	(†)	(†)	138 (0.5)	(†)	(†)	136 (0.9)
Some college	—	—	—	(†)	(†)	151 (0.4)	(†)	(†)	148 (0.7)
Bachelor's degree or higher	—	—	—	(†)	(†)	159 (0.3)	(†)	(†)	157 (0.6)
Eligible for free or reduced-price lunch									
Eligible	129 (1.7)	127 (1.3)	135 (0.3)	129 (1.6)	127 (1.1)	130 (0.3)	—	—	—
Not eligible	159 (0.9)	158 (1.1)	162 (0.3)	156 (0.9)	159 (1.0)	159 (0.3)	—	—	—
Information not available	151 (3.9)	160 (1.5)	160 (0.9)	157 (2.3)	155 (1.7)	160 (1.5)	—	—	—
Percentile[2]									
10th	99 (2.1)	99 (1.7)	109 (0.5)	103 (1.5)	101 (1.2)	101 (0.6)	105 (1.4)	101 (1.4)	101 (1.2)
25th	125 (1.6)	125 (1.4)	130 (0.4)	127 (1.2)	126 (1.3)	126 (0.4)	128 (1.1)	124 (1.0)	125 (0.8)
50th	150 (1.2)	150 (0.9)	153 (0.4)	152 (0.7)	152 (0.9)	151 (0.3)	152 (1.2)	148 (1.0)	149 (0.8)
75th	172 (1.0)	172 (0.7)	173 (0.3)	174 (0.8)	175 (0.8)	174 (0.3)	174 (0.8)	170 (1.2)	171 (0.8)
90th	190 (0.8)	190 (1.0)	189 (0.3)	192 (0.8)	194 (1.0)	192 (0.3)	192 (0.9)	189 (1.2)	189 (1.2)
Percent attaining science achievement levels									
Achievement level									
Below Basic	37 (1.4)	37 (1.2)	32 (0.4)	40 (1.0)	41 (1.2)	41 (0.4)	43 (1.0)	48 (1.2)	46 (0.8)
At or above Basic[3]	63 (1.4)	63 (1.2)	68 (0.4)	60 (1.0)	59 (1.2)	59 (0.4)	57 (1.0)	52 (1.2)	54 (0.8)
At or above Proficient[4]	28 (1.0)	27 (0.9)	29 (0.4)	29 (0.9)	30 (1.0)	29 (0.3)	21 (0.8)	18 (0.9)	18 (0.6)
At Advanced[5]	3 (0.3)	3 (0.4)	3 (0.1)	3 (0.3)	4 (0.3)	3 (0.1)	3 (0.3)	2 (0.3)	2 (0.2)

—Not available.

†Not applicable.

‡Reporting standards not met.

[1]Testing accommodations (e.g., extended time, small group testing) for children with disabilities and limited-English-proficient students were not permitted on the 1996 science assessment.

[2]The percentile represents a specific point on the percentage distribution of all students ranked by their science score from low to high. For example, 10 percent of students scored at or below the 10th percentile score, while 90 percent of students scored above it.

[3]Basic denotes partial mastery of the knowledge and skills that are fundamental for proficient work.

[4]Proficient represents solid academic performance. Students reaching this level have demonstrated competency over challenging subject matter.

[5]Advanced signifies superior performance.

NOTE: The NAEP science scale ranges from 0 to 300. Race categories exclude persons of Hispanic ethnicity. Standard errors appear in parentheses.

SOURCE: U.S. Department of Education, National Center for Education Statistics, National Assessment of Educational Progress (NAEP), NAEP Data Explorer (http://nces.ed.gov/nationsreportcard/nde/), retrieved November 2006. (This table was prepared November 2006.)

Table 139. Average science scale score for 8th-graders in public schools, by selected student characteristics and state or jurisdiction: 1996, 2000, and 2005

| State or jurisdiction | Average scale score | | | Sex, 2005 | | Race/ethnicity, 2005 | | | | | National School Lunch Program eligibility, 2005 | |
| | 1996[1] | 2000 | 2005 | Male | Female | White | Black | Hispanic | Asian/ Pacific Islander | American Indian/ Alaska Native | Eligible | Not eligible |
1	2	3	4	5	6	7	8	9	10	11	12	13
United States	**148** (0.9)	**148** (1.1)	**147** (0.3)	**149** (0.4)	**145** (0.4)	**159** (0.3)	**123** (0.4)	**127** (0.5)	**155** (0.9)	**134** (1.5)	**130** (0.3)	**158** (0.3)
Alabama	139 (1.6)	143[3] (1.7)	138 (1.3)	138 (1.6)	137 (1.4)	152 (1.3)	114 (1.5)	‡ (†)	‡ (†)	‡ (†)	123 (1.5)	152 (1.4)
Alaska	153[2] (1.3)	— (†)	— (†)	— (†)	— (†)	— (†)	— (†)	— (†)	— (†)	— (†)	— (†)	— (†)
Arizona	145[3] (1.6)	145[3,4] (1.3)	140 (0.9)	141 (1.1)	139 (1.2)	156 (1.0)	125 (3.5)	123 (1.2)	‡ (†)	121 (3.0)	124 (1.2)	152 (1.4)
Arkansas	144[2] (1.3)	142 (1.2)	144 (1.0)	146 (1.3)	142 (1.1)	155 (0.9)	113 (1.3)	136 (4.0)	‡ (†)	‡ (†)	131 (1.3)	157 (0.9)
California	138 (1.7)	129[3,4] (1.8)	136 (0.7)	138 (0.8)	135 (0.8)	154 (0.9)	120 (1.5)	122 (0.8)	152 (1.8)	132 (5.2)	121 (0.9)	150 (0.7)
Colorado	155 (0.9)	— (†)	155 (1.3)	158 (1.4)	152 (1.6)	166 (1.1)	133 (3.7)	134 (2.0)	158 (4.4)	‡ (†)	135 (1.9)	164 (1.2)
Connecticut	155 (1.3)	153 (1.6)	152 (1.0)	153 (1.6)	151 (1.1)	163 (0.9)	124 (2.2)	123 (2.7)	163 (3.6)	‡ (†)	127 (1.7)	161 (1.0)
Delaware	142[3] (0.8)	— (†)	152 (0.6)	154 (0.7)	150 (1.0)	162 (0.6)	134 (1.1)	136 (2.4)	165 (3.4)	‡ (†)	136 (1.0)	158 (0.7)
District of Columbia	113 (0.7)	— (†)	— (†)	— (†)	— (†)	— (†)	— (†)	— (†)	— (†)	— (†)	— (†)	— (†)
Florida	142 (1.6)	— (†)	141 (1.2)	142 (1.2)	140 (1.4)	155 (1.1)	118 (1.5)	131 (2.0)	149 (4.2)	‡ (†)	128 (1.2)	152 (1.2)
Georgia	142 (1.4)	142 (1.6)	144 (1.1)	145 (1.4)	142 (1.2)	159 (1.4)	125 (1.3)	127 (3.6)	163 (5.9)	‡ (†)	127 (1.0)	158 (1.3)
Hawaii	135 (0.7)	130[3] (1.4)	136 (0.8)	138 (1.4)	135 (0.9)	152 (1.7)	‡ (†)	131 (3.9)	133 (1.0)	‡ (†)	124 (1.2)	146 (0.9)
Idaho	— (†)	158[4] (1.0)	158 (1.0)	161 (1.4)	154 (1.0)	161 (0.9)	‡ (†)	131 (2.2)	‡ (†)	‡ (†)	147 (1.2)	164 (1.1)
Illinois	— (†)	148[4] (1.7)	148 (1.1)	150 (1.4)	146 (1.2)	161 (1.2)	120 (1.5)	130 (1.7)	164 (3.7)	‡ (†)	128 (1.2)	161 (1.2)
Indiana	153 (1.4)	154[3,4] (1.4)	150 (1.3)	154 (1.4)	147 (1.7)	156 (1.3)	119 (2.1)	131 (3.1)	‡ (†)	‡ (†)	135 (2.0)	159 (1.4)
Iowa	158[2] (1.2)	— (†)	— (†)	— (†)	— (†)	— (†)	— (†)	— (†)	— (†)	— (†)	— (†)	— (†)
Kansas	— (†)	— (†)	— (†)	— (†)	— (†)	— (†)	— (†)	— (†)	— (†)	— (†)	— (†)	— (†)
Kentucky	147[3] (1.2)	150[3] (1.2)	153 (0.9)	154 (1.3)	151 (1.0)	155 (0.9)	130 (2.4)	‡ (†)	‡ (†)	‡ (†)	145 (1.4)	159 (1.2)
Louisiana	132[3] (1.6)	134[3] (1.5)	138 (1.5)	141 (1.7)	136 (1.6)	153 (1.3)	120 (1.5)	‡ (†)	‡ (†)	‡ (†)	127 (1.4)	153 (1.4)
Maine	163[3] (1.0)	158[4] (0.9)	158 (0.7)	159 (1.0)	156 (1.1)	158 (0.8)	‡ (†)	‡ (†)	‡ (†)	‡ (†)	150 (1.2)	161 (0.8)
Maryland	145[2] (1.5)	146 (1.4)	145 (1.4)	145 (1.7)	144 (1.6)	160 (1.3)	123 (1.8)	132 (6.1)	165 (3.5)	‡ (†)	122 (2.4)	155 (1.3)
Massachusetts	157[3] (1.4)	158[3] (1.1)	161 (1.0)	162 (1.2)	160 (1.2)	168 (1.0)	133 (2.2)	133 (2.2)	166 (3.4)	‡ (†)	142 (2.1)	168 (1.2)
Michigan	153[2] (1.4)	155[4] (1.8)	155 (1.2)	156 (1.6)	154 (1.4)	163 (1.2)	128 (2.3)	132 (3.8)	‡ (†)	‡ (†)	140 (1.9)	161 (1.3)
Minnesota	159 (1.3)	159[4] (1.2)	158 (1.1)	161 (1.5)	155 (1.3)	166 (0.9)	120 (2.6)	133 (4.3)	137 (2.7)	‡ (†)	139 (1.5)	166 (1.1)
Mississippi	133 (1.4)	134 (1.2)	132 (1.2)	135 (1.5)	130 (1.3)	150 (1.0)	114 (1.5)	‡ (†)	‡ (†)	‡ (†)	121 (1.3)	151 (1.1)
Missouri	151 (1.2)	154 (1.2)	154 (1.2)	157 (1.3)	151 (1.4)	161 (0.9)	124 (2.8)	150 (4.9)	‡ (†)	‡ (†)	140 (2.1)	162 (1.3)
Montana	162[2] (1.2)	164[4] (1.4)	162 (0.8)	162 (1.2)	161 (1.0)	165 (0.7)	‡ (†)	‡ (†)	‡ (†)	135 (2.6)	149 (1.4)	168 (0.7)
Nebraska	157 (1.0)	158 (1.4)	— (†)	— (†)	— (†)	— (†)	— (†)	— (†)	— (†)	— (†)	— (†)	— (†)
Nevada	‡ (†)	141[3] (1.0)	138 (0.9)	139 (1.1)	138 (1.3)	150 (1.0)	115 (2.4)	122 (1.3)	150 (3.4)	‡ (†)	124 (1.3)	146 (1.0)
New Hampshire	‡ (†)	— (†)	162 (0.9)	163 (1.0)	161 (1.1)	163 (0.8)	‡ 0.8	‡ (†)	‡ (†)	‡ (†)	149 (1.7)	165 (0.9)
New Jersey	‡ (†)	— (†)	153 (1.2)	157 (1.6)	150 (1.3)	165 (1.1)	131 (2.6)	133 (1.9)	172 (2.4)	‡ (†)	131 (1.9)	162 (1.2)
New Mexico	141[3] (1.0)	139 (1.5)	138 (0.9)	141 (1.2)	135 (1.3)	157 (1.3)	129 (4.5)	129 (1.1)	‡ (†)	124 (1.5)	129 (1.0)	153 (1.4)
New York	146[2] (1.6)	145[4] (2.1)	— (†)	— (†)	— (†)	— (†)	— (†)	— (†)	— (†)	— (†)	— (†)	— (†)
North Carolina	147 (1.2)	145 (1.4)	144 (1.0)	145 (1.3)	143 (1.1)	155 (0.8)	122 (1.6)	132 (3.2)	157 (9.9)	‡ (†)	129 (1.3)	154 (1.0)
North Dakota	162 (0.8)	159[3] (1.1)	163 (0.6)	165 (0.9)	161 (0.9)	166 (0.6)	‡ (†)	‡ (†)	‡ (†)	137 (3.2)	151 (1.5)	168 (0.6)
Ohio	— (†)	159 (1.5)	155 (1.2)	157 (1.7)	154 (1.3)	162 (1.0)	124 (3.3)	142 (5.6)	‡ (†)	‡ (†)	134 (1.8)	165 (1.0)
Oklahoma	— (†)	149 (1.1)	147 (1.3)	149 (1.4)	144 (1.5)	155 (1.1)	120 (2.7)	132 (3.1)	‡ (†)	139 (2.2)	137 (1.5)	156 (1.2)
Oregon	155 (1.6)	154[4] (1.3)	153 (1.0)	155 (1.4)	152 (1.3)	159 (0.9)	127 (5.5)	129 (3.1)	154 (4.6)	‡ (†)	141 (1.8)	160 (1.2)
Pennsylvania	— (†)	— (†)	— (†)	— (†)	— (†)	— (†)	— (†)	— (†)	— (†)	— (†)	— (†)	— (†)
Rhode Island	149[3] (0.8)	148 (0.9)	146 (0.7)	149 (0.9)	144 (0.9)	156 (0.7)	122 (2.2)	115 (1.8)	141 (4.7)	‡ (†)	127 (1.3)	155 (0.8)

See notes at end of table.

Table 139. Average science scale score for 8th-graders in public schools, by selected student characteristics and state or jurisdiction: 1996, 2000, and 2005—Continued

State or jurisdiction	Average scale score			Sex, 2005		Race/ethnicity, 2005					National School Lunch Program eligibility, 2005	
	1996[1]	2000	2005	Male	Female	White	Black	Hispanic	Asian/ Pacific Islander	American Indian/ Alaska Native	Eligible	Not eligible
1	2	3	4	5	6	7	8	9	10	11	12	13
South Carolina	139 [2,3] (1.5)	140 [3] (1.4)	145 (1.1)	146 (1.5)	144 (1.2)	159 (1.3)	127 (1.4)	130 (5.9)	‡ (†)	‡ (†)	131 (1.2)	158 (1.2)
South Dakota	— (†)	— (†)	161 (0.7)	164 (1.0)	158 (0.9)	165 (0.7)	‡ (†)	‡ (†)	‡ (†)	133 (2.7)	149 (1.3)	168 (0.8)
Tennessee	143 (1.8)	145 (1.5)	145 (1.2)	146 (1.5)	144 (1.4)	153 (1.0)	119 (2.2)	‡ (†)	‡ (†)	‡ (†)	131 (1.5)	156 (1.3)
Texas	145 (1.8)	143 (1.7)	143 (0.8)	145 (1.1)	141 (0.9)	160 (0.9)	125 (1.5)	131 (1.1)	161 (3.8)	‡ (†)	129 (1.0)	156 (1.0)
Utah	156 [3] (0.8)	154 (1.0)	154 (0.7)	155 (1.1)	152 (0.9)	158 (0.7)	‡ (†)	130 (2.4)	139 (3.9)	‡ (†)	142 (1.2)	160 (0.9)
Vermont	157 [2,3] (1.0)	159 [3,4] (1.0)	162 (0.6)	163 (0.9)	161 (0.8)	162 (0.6)	‡ (†)	‡ (†)	‡ (†)	‡ (†)	150 (1.3)	166 (0.6)
Virginia	149 [3] (1.6)	151 [3] (1.0)	155 (1.1)	157 (1.3)	153 (1.2)	165 (1.1)	133 (1.6)	141 (2.7)	161 (3.0)	‡ (†)	136 (1.4)	163 (1.1)
Washington	150 [3] (1.3)	— (†)	154 (0.8)	155 (1.2)	153 (1.0)	160 (0.8)	137 (3.1)	128 (3.2)	149 (2.6)	135 (5.8)	140 (1.4)	161 (0.9)
West Virginia	147 (0.9)	146 (1.1)	147 (0.8)	150 (1.0)	144 (0.9)	148 (0.7)	128 (3.3)	‡ (†)	‡ (†)	‡ (†)	137 (0.9)	156 (0.9)
Wisconsin	160 [2] (1.7)	‡ (†)	158 (1.0)	160 (1.3)	156 (1.2)	165 (0.8)	120 (3.1)	133 (3.1)	153 (4.1)	‡ (†)	137 (2.1)	165 (0.9)
Wyoming	158 (0.6)	156 [3] (1.0)	159 (0.6)	161 (1.0)	157 (0.9)	161 (0.6)	‡ (†)	145 (2.3)	‡ (†)	145 (4.5)	148 (1.2)	164 (0.7)
Department of Defense dependents schools[5]	155 [3] (0.6)	158 [3] (0.7)	160 (0.7)	162 (1.1)	158 (1.0)	168 (0.9)	143 (0.7)	160 (1.9)	161 (2.6)	‡ (†)	‡ (†)	‡ (†)
Other jurisdictions												
American Samoa	— (†)	74 (4.2)	— (†)	— (†)	— (†)	— (†)	— (†)	— (†)	— (†)	— (†)	— (†)	— (†)
Guam	120 (1.1)	114 (1.8)	— (†)	— (†)	— (†)	— (†)	— (†)	— (†)	— (†)	— (†)	— (†)	— (†)

—Not available.
†Not applicable.
‡Reporting standards not met.
[1]Accommodations were not permitted for this assessment.
[2]Did not satisfy one or more of the guidelines for school participation in 1996. Data are subject to appreciable nonresponse bias.
[3]Significantly different from 2005 when only one jurisdiction or the nation is being examined.
[4]Did not satisfy one or more of the guidelines for school participation in 2000. Data are subject to appreciable nonresponse bias.
[5]Before 2005, Department of Defense domestic and overseas schools were separate jurisdictions in NAEP. Data for 1996 and 2000 were recalculated for comparability.

NOTE: Excludes persons not enrolled in school and those who were unable to be tested due to limited proficiency in English or due to a disability (if sample not tested with accommodations or if the accommodations provided in 2000 and 2005 were not sufficient to enable the test to properly reflect the students' science proficiency). Scale ranges from 0 to 300. Race categories exclude persons of Hispanic ethnicity. Standard errors appear in parentheses. Some data have been revised from previously published figures.
SOURCE: U.S. Department of Education, National Center for Education Statistics, National Assessment of Educational Progress (NAEP), *NAEP 1996 Science Report Card for the Nation and the States, The Nation's Report Card: Science 2005,* and the NAEP Data Explorer (http://nces.ed.gov/nationsreportcard/nde/, retrieved on December 4, 2006). (This table was prepared December 2006.)

Table 140. Average science scale score of 12th-graders and percentage reporting various attitudes toward science, by selected student and school characteristics: 2005

Student or school characteristic	Like science			Science is boring			Science is useful for problem solving			Good at science		
	Disagree	Not sure	Agree	Disagree	Not sure	Agree	Disagree	Not sure	Agree	Disagree	Not sure	Agree
1	2	3	4	5	6	7	8	9	10	11	12	13
						Average scale score[1]						
All students	137 (0.8)	139 (0.9)	158 (0.7)	156 (0.6)	146 (0.9)	137 (0.8)	137 (1.2)	143 (0.8)	155 (0.7)	134 (0.8)	143 (0.6)	161 (0.8)
Sex												
Male..........................	136 (1.1)	140 (1.1)	160 (0.9)	158 (0.9)	149 (1.3)	138 (1.0)	137 (1.2)	144 (1.1)	158 (0.8)	133 (1.2)	143 (0.9)	163 (1.0)
Female......................	137 (0.9)	138 (1.2)	155 (0.8)	153 (0.7)	145 (1.1)	136 (0.9)	137 (1.5)	143 (0.9)	152 (0.8)	134 (1.0)	143 (0.7)	159 (0.9)
Race/ethnicity												
White........................	145 (0.9)	149 (0.9)	166 (0.6)	165 (0.6)	155 (0.9)	145 (0.9)	145 (1.2)	152 (0.8)	164 (0.6)	142 (0.9)	152 (0.7)	168 (0.7)
Black........................	113 (1.5)	114 (1.7)	129 (1.3)	127 (1.1)	119 (1.5)	113 (1.6)	115 (1.9)	118 (1.6)	125 (1.3)	111 (1.6)	118 (1.3)	130 (1.4)
Hispanic....................	121 (1.7)	119 (1.9)	138 (1.8)	136 (1.9)	125 (1.9)	121 (1.6)	122 (2.0)	127 (2.1)	135 (1.9)	121 (1.8)	126 (1.5)	145 (2.0)
Asian/Pacific Islander....	137 (3.4)	146 (2.7)	163 (2.0)	160 (2.0)	152 (2.9)	141 (3.5)	141 (4.2)	145 (2.9)	161 (2.1)	137 (2.7)	147 (2.2)	169 (2.5)
American Indian/Alaska Native......	‡ (†)	‡ (†)	‡ (†)	‡ (†)	‡ (†)	‡ (†)	‡ (†)	‡ (†)	‡ (†)	‡ (†)	‡ (†)	‡ (†)
Eligibility for free or reduced-price lunch												
Eligible.....................	121 (1.2)	121 (1.3)	139 (1.3)	136 (1.3)	128 (1.6)	120 (1.1)	121 (1.6)	126 (1.4)	136 (1.2)	120 (1.4)	126 (1.0)	142 (1.7)
Not eligible................	141 (0.8)	144 (1.0)	162 (0.6)	161 (0.6)	152 (0.8)	141 (0.9)	142 (1.4)	148 (0.8)	161 (0.7)	138 (0.9)	148 (0.7)	165 (0.7)
Unknown...................	145 (2.0)	153 (2.3)	167 (2.0)	165 (1.8)	156 (2.9)	147 (2.0)	146 (2.8)	153 (2.4)	165 (1.7)	144 (2.0)	155 (2.2)	170 (2.0)
Control of school												
Public.......................	135 (0.8)	138 (0.9)	156 (0.7)	154 (0.7)	145 (0.9)	136 (0.9)	136 (1.2)	142 (0.8)	154 (0.7)	133 (0.8)	142 (0.7)	160 (0.8)
Private......................	‡ (†)	‡ (†)	‡ (†)	‡ (†)	‡ (†)	‡ (†)	‡ (†)	‡ (†)	‡ (†)	‡ (†)	‡ (†)	‡ (†)
						Percent of students						
All students	31 (0.4)	19 (0.4)	50 (0.5)	46 (0.5)	23 (0.5)	31 (0.4)	20 (0.4)	32 (0.5)	48 (0.6)	26 (0.5)	35 (0.5)	39 (0.6)
Sex												
Male..........................	26 (0.6)	19 (0.5)	55 (0.8)	47 (0.8)	23 (0.7)	30 (0.6)	19 (0.5)	31 (0.8)	51 (0.8)	21 (0.6)	35 (0.8)	45 (0.8)
Female......................	35 (0.6)	19 (0.5)	46 (0.6)	45 (0.7)	23 (0.7)	32 (0.7)	20 (0.6)	34 (0.7)	46 (0.8)	31 (0.6)	35 (0.7)	34 (0.6)
Race/ethnicity												
White........................	30 (0.6)	18 (0.5)	52 (0.6)	46 (0.6)	23 (0.6)	31 (0.5)	19 (0.5)	32 (0.6)	49 (0.7)	24 (0.6)	34 (0.6)	42 (0.7)
Black........................	36 (1.0)	19 (0.8)	45 (1.0)	45 (1.0)	18 (0.9)	37 (1.2)	22 (1.1)	30 (0.9)	48 (1.5)	31 (1.3)	30 (1.2)	39 (1.3)
Hispanic....................	28 (1.1)	23 (1.1)	49 (1.2)	47 (1.3)	27 (1.1)	26 (1.1)	22 (1.0)	35 (1.3)	43 (1.2)	28 (1.0)	45 (1.5)	27 (1.3)
Asian/Pacific Islander....	23 (2.0)	24 (2.0)	53 (2.6)	48 (2.6)	28 (2.1)	24 (2.1)	13 (1.6)	31 (2.1)	56 (2.4)	23 (1.6)	40 (2.4)	37 (2.2)
American Indian/Alaska Native......	36 (5.5)	16 (5.1)	47 (7.1)	40 (5.4)	21 (4.2)	39 (4.8)	15 (4.2)	41 (5.3)	44 (6.1)	31 (5.1)	34 (4.2)	35 (4.3)
Eligibility for free or reduced-price lunch												
Eligible.....................	31 (0.8)	21 (0.9)	48 (1.0)	46 (1.0)	24 (0.7)	30 (1.1)	21 (0.9)	32 (1.0)	47 (1.0)	29 (0.7)	39 (1.0)	32 (1.1)
Not eligible................	31 (0.6)	19 (0.6)	51 (0.7)	45 (0.7)	23 (0.6)	32 (0.6)	20 (0.5)	32 (0.6)	48 (0.7)	25 (0.6)	33 (0.6)	42 (0.6)
Unknown...................	29 (1.4)	17 (0.9)	54 (1.5)	48 (1.4)	24 (1.1)	28 (1.2)	16 (0.8)	30 (1.3)	53 (1.7)	24 (1.1)	36 (1.5)	40 (1.8)
Control of school												
Public.......................	31 (0.5)	19 (0.4)	50 (0.6)	46 (0.6)	23 (0.5)	31 (0.5)	20 (0.4)	33 (0.5)	48 (0.6)	26 (0.5)	35 (0.6)	39 (0.6)
Private......................	‡ (†)	‡ (†)	‡ (†)	‡ (†)	‡ (†)	‡ (†)	‡ (†)	‡ (†)	‡ (†)	‡ (†)	‡ (†)	‡ (†)

†Not applicable.
‡Reporting standards not met.
[1]Scale ranges from 0 to 300.
NOTE: Includes public and private schools. Includes students for whom accommodations were permitted. Excludes students unable to be tested (even with accommodations) due to limited proficiency in English or due to a disability. Race categories exclude persons of Hispanic ethnicity. Detail may not sum to totals because of rounding. Standard errors appear in parentheses.

SOURCE: U.S. Department of Education, National Center for Education Statistics, National Assessment of Educational Progress (NAEP), 2005 Science Assessment, retrieved August 15, 2008, from the NAEP Data Explorer (http://nces.ed.gov/nationsreportcard/nde/). (This table was prepared August 2008.)

Table 141. SAT mean scores of college-bound seniors, by race/ethnicity: Selected years, 1986–87 through 2007–08

Race/ethnicity	1986–87	1990–91	1996–97	1999–2000	2000–01	2001–02	2002–03	2003–04	2004–05	2005–06	2006–07	2007–08	1986–87 to 1996–97	1996–97 to 2006–07	2000–01 to 2001–02	2001–02 to 2002–03	2002–03 to 2003–04	2003–04 to 2004–05	2004–05 to 2005–06	2005–06 to 2006–07	2006–07 to 2007–08
1	2	3	4	5	6	7	8	9	10	11	12	13	14	15	16	17	18	19	20	21	22
SAT—Critical reading																					
All students	507	499	505	505	506	504	507	508	508	503	502	502	-2	-3	-2	3	1	0	-5	-1	0
White	524	518	526	528	529	527	529	528	532	527	527	528	2	1	-2	2	-1	4	-5	0	1
Black	428	427	434	434	433	430	431	430	433	434	433	430	6	-1	-3	1	-1	3	1	-1	-3
Mexican American	457	454	451	453	451	446	448	451	453	454	455	454	-6	4	-5	2	3	2	1	1	-1
Puerto Rican	436	436	454	456	457	455	456	457	460	459	459	456	18	5	-2	1	1	3	-1	0	-3
Other Hispanic	464	458	466	461	460	458	457	461	463	458	459	455	2	-7	-2	-1	4	2	-5	1	-4
Asian/Pacific Islander	479	485	496	499	501	501	508	507	511	510	514	513	17	18	0	7	-1	4	-1	4	-1
American Indian/Alaska Native	471	470	475	482	481	479	480	483	489	487	487	485	4	12	-2	1	3	6	-2	0	-2
Other	480	486	512	508	503	502	501	494	495	494	497	496	32	-15	-1	-1	-7	1	-1	3	-1
SAT—Mathematics																					
All students	501	500	511	514	514	516	519	518	520	518	515	515	10	4	2	3	-1	2	-2	-3	0
White	514	513	526	530	531	533	534	531	536	536	534	537	12	8	2	1	-3	5	0	-2	3
Black	411	419	423	426	426	427	426	427	431	429	429	426	12	6	1	-1	1	4	-2	0	-3
Mexican American	455	459	458	460	458	457	457	458	463	465	466	463	3	8	-1	0	1	5	2	1	-3
Puerto Rican	432	439	447	451	451	451	453	452	457	456	454	453	15	7	0	2	-1	5	-1	-2	-1
Other Hispanic	462	462	468	467	465	464	464	465	469	463	463	461	6	-5	-1	0	1	4	-6	0	-2
Asian/Pacific Islander	541	548	560	565	566	569	575	577	580	578	578	581	19	18	3	6	2	3	-2	0	3
American Indian/Alaska Native	463	468	475	481	479	483	482	488	493	494	494	491	12	19	4	-1	6	5	1	0	-3
Other	482	492	514	515	512	514	513	508	513	513	512	512	32	-2	2	-1	-5	5	0	-1	0
SAT—Writing																					
All students	†	†	†	†	†	†	†	†	†	497	494	494	†	†	†	†	†	†	†	-3	0
White	†	†	†	†	†	†	†	†	†	519	518	518	†	†	†	†	†	†	†	-1	0
Black	†	†	†	†	†	†	†	†	†	428	425	424	†	†	†	†	†	†	†	-3	-1
Mexican American	†	†	†	†	†	†	†	†	†	452	450	447	†	†	†	†	†	†	†	-2	-3
Puerto Rican	†	†	†	†	†	†	†	†	†	448	447	445	†	†	†	†	†	†	†	-1	-2
Other Hispanic	†	†	†	†	†	†	†	†	†	450	450	448	†	†	†	†	†	†	†	0	-2
Asian/Pacific Islander	†	†	†	†	†	†	†	†	†	512	513	516	†	†	†	†	†	†	†	1	3
American Indian/Alaska Native	†	†	†	†	†	†	†	†	†	474	473	470	†	†	†	†	†	†	†	-1	-3
Other	†	†	†	†	†	†	†	†	†	493	493	494	†	†	†	†	†	†	†	0	1

†Not applicable.

NOTE: Data are for seniors who took the SAT any time during their high school years through March of their senior year. If a student took a test more than once, the most recent score was used. The SAT was formerly known as the Scholastic Assessment Test and the Scholastic Aptitude Test. Possible scores on each part of the SAT range from 200 to 800. The critical reading section was formerly known as the verbal section. The writing section was introduced in March 2005.

SOURCE: College Entrance Examination Board, College-Bound Seniors: Total Group Profile [National] Report, selected years, 1986–87 through 2007–08, retrieved August 26, 2008, from http://professionals.collegeboard.com/data-reports-research/sat/cb-seniors-2008. (This table was prepared August 2008.)

Table 142. SAT mean scores of college-bound seniors, by sex: 1966–67 through 2007–08

	SAT[1]									Scholastic Aptitude Test (old scale)					
	Critical reading score			Mathematics score			Writing score[2]			Verbal score			Mathematics score		
School year	Total	Male	Female	Total	Male	Female	Total	Male	Female	Total	Male	Female	Total	Male	Female
1	2	3	4	5	6	7	8	9	10	11	12	13	14	15	16
1966–67	543	540	545	516	535	495	†	†	†	466	463	468	492	514	467
1967–68	543	541	543	516	533	497	†	†	†	466	464	466	492	512	470
1968–69	540	536	543	517	534	498	†	†	†	463	459	466	493	513	470
1969–70	537	536	538	512	531	493	†	†	†	460	459	461	488	509	465
1970–71	532	531	534	513	529	494	†	†	†	455	454	457	488	507	466
1971–72	530	531	529	509	527	489	†	†	†	453	454	452	484	505	461
1972–73	523	523	521	506	525	489	†	†	†	445	446	443	481	502	460
1973–74	521	524	520	505	524	488	†	†	†	444	447	442	480	501	459
1974–75	512	515	509	498	518	479	†	†	†	434	437	431	472	495	449
1975–76	509	511	508	497	520	475	†	†	†	431	433	430	472	497	446
1976–77	507	509	505	496	520	474	†	†	†	429	431	427	470	497	445
1977–78	507	511	503	494	517	474	†	†	†	429	433	425	468	494	444
1978–79	505	509	501	493	516	473	†	†	†	427	431	423	467	493	443
1979–80	502	506	498	492	515	473	†	†	†	424	428	420	466	491	443
1980–81	502	508	496	492	516	473	†	†	†	424	430	418	466	492	443
1981–82	504	509	499	493	516	473	†	†	†	426	431	421	467	493	443
1982–83	503	508	498	494	516	474	†	†	†	425	430	420	468	493	445
1983–84	504	511	498	497	518	478	†	†	†	426	433	420	471	495	449
1984–85	509	514	503	500	522	480	†	†	†	431	437	425	475	499	452
1985–86	509	515	504	500	523	479	†	†	†	431	437	426	475	501	451
1986–87	507	512	502	501	523	481	†	†	†	430	435	425	476	500	453
1987–88	505	512	499	501	521	483	†	†	†	428	435	422	476	498	455
1988–89	504	510	498	502	523	482	†	†	†	427	434	421	476	500	454
1989–90	500	505	496	501	521	483	†	†	†	424	429	419	476	499	455
1990–91	499	503	495	500	520	482	†	†	†	422	426	418	474	497	453
1991–92	500	504	496	501	521	484	†	†	†	423	428	419	476	499	456
1992–93	500	504	497	503	524	484	†	†	†	424	428	420	478	502	457
1993–94	499	501	497	504	523	487	†	†	†	423	425	421	479	501	460
1994–95	504	505	502	506	525	490	†	†	†	428	429	426	482	503	463
1995–96	505	507	503	508	527	492	†	†	†	—	—	—	—	—	—
1996–97	505	507	503	511	530	494	†	†	†	—	—	—	—	—	—
1997–98	505	509	502	512	531	496	†	†	†	—	—	—	—	—	—
1998–99	505	509	502	511	531	495	†	†	†	—	—	—	—	—	—
1999–2000	505	507	504	514	533	498	†	†	†	†	†	†	†	†	†
2000–01	506	509	502	514	533	498	†	†	†	†	†	†	†	†	†
2001–02	504	507	502	516	534	500	†	†	†	†	†	†	†	†	†
2002–03	507	512	503	519	537	503	†	†	†	†	†	†	†	†	†
2003–04	508	512	504	518	537	501	†	†	†	†	†	†	†	†	†
2004–05	508	513	505	520	538	504	†	†	†	†	†	†	†	†	†
2005–06	503	505	502	518	536	502	497	491	502	†	†	†	†	†	†
2006–07	502	504	502	515	533	499	494	489	500	†	†	†	†	†	†
2007–08	502	504	500	515	533	500	494	488	501	†	†	†	†	†	†

—Not available.

†Not applicable.

[1]Data for 1966–67 to 1985–86 were converted to the recentered scale by using a formula applied to the original mean and standard deviation. For 1986–87 to 1994–95, individual student scores were converted to the recentered scale and then the mean was recomputed. For 1995–96 to 1998–99, nearly all students received scores on the recentered scale; any score on the original scale was converted to the recentered scale prior to recomputing the mean. From 1999–2000 on, all scores have been reported on the recentered scale.

[2]Writing data are based on students who took the SAT writing section, which was introduced in March 2005.

NOTE: Data for 1966–67 through 1970–71 are estimates derived from the test scores of all participants. Data for 1971–72 and later are for seniors who took the SAT any time during their high school years through March of their senior year. If a student took a test more than once, the most recent score was used. The SAT was formerly known as the Scholastic Assessment Test and the Scholastic Aptitude Test. Possible scores on each part of the SAT range from 200 to 800. The critical reading section was formerly known as the verbal section. SOURCE: College Entrance Examination Board, *College-Bound Seniors: Total Group Profile [National] Report*, 1966–67 through 2007–08, retrieved August 26, 2008, from http://professionals .collegeboard.com/data-reports-research/sat/cb-seniors-2008. (This table was prepared August 2008.)

Table 143. SAT mean scores of college-bound seniors, by selected student characteristics: Selected years, 1995–96 through 2007–08

Selected student characteristic	1995–96			1999–2000			2005–06				2006–07				2007–08			
	Critical reading score[1]	Mathematics score	Percentage distribution	Critical reading score[1]	Mathematics score	Percentage distribution	Critical reading score[1]	Mathematics score	Writing score[2]	Percentage distribution	Critical reading score[1]	Mathematics score	Writing score[2]	Percentage distribution	Critical reading score[1]	Mathematics score	Writing score[2]	Percentage distribution
1	2	3	4	5	6	7	8	9	10	11	12	13	14	15	16	17	18	19
All students	**505**	**508**	**100**	**505**	**514**	**100**	**503**	**518**	**497**	**100**	**502**	**515**	**494**	**100**	**502**	**515**	**494**	**100**
High school rank																		
Top decile	591	606	22	589	608	†	580	604	577	31	580	602	575	32	573	598	569	31
Second decile	530	539	22	528	543	‡	516	537	511	25	516	534	508	26	511	531	505	27
Second quintile	494	496	28	493	500	‡	484	498	476	20	484	497	474	20	481	495	472	20
Third quintile	455	448	24	455	453	‡	—	—	—	—	—	—	—	—	—	—	—	—
Fourth quintile	429	418	4	425	419	‡	—	—	—	—	—	—	—	—	—	—	—	—
Fifth quintile	411	401	1	408	401	‡	—	—	—	—	—	—	—	—	—	—	—	—
Bottom three quintiles[3]	—	—	—	—	—	—	443	449	435	23	444	450	434	22	441	447	431	22
High school grade point average																		
A+ (97–100)	617	632	6	610	628	7	602	621	599	7	604	620	599	7	595	615	592	6
A (93–96)	573	583	14	567	582	16	563	582	559	18	565	581	559	18	559	578	555	18
A- (90–92)	545	554	15	540	553	17	534	552	529	18	534	550	528	18	529	547	523	19
B (80–89)	486	485	49	482	486	47	479	489	471	46	478	486	469	45	474	484	465	47
C (70–79)	432	426	15	428	426	12	426	428	414	11	424	427	411	11	421	423	408	11
D, E, or F (below 70)	414	408	#	405	406	#	406	413	389	#	403	412	388	#	402	411	390	#
High school type																		
Public	502	506	83	501	510	83	500	514	492	83	498	509	488	84	497	510	488	84
Religiously affiliated	525	510	12	529	523	12	531	529	528	11	531	526	527	11	532	531	529	11
Independent	547	556	5	547	566	5	544	573	550	5	546	569	548	5	550	574	553	5
Intended college major[4]																		
Agriculture/natural resources	491	484	2	490	486	1	481	485	469	1	476	480	463	1	478	481	465	1
Architecture/environmental design	492	519	3	494	524	2	488	528	485	3	492	535	486	3	488	532	483	2
Area, ethnic, cultural and gender studies	†	†	†	†	†	†	†	†	†	†	547	514	533	#	554	521	541	#
Arts: visual/performing	520	497	6	518	502	8	516	502	507	9	517	503	507	9	516	502	506	8
Biological sciences	546	545	6	544	548	5	540	554	532	6	540	552	531	6	537	551	528	5
Business and commerce	483	500	13	487	510	14	486	511	481	15	485	510	479	15	481	509	477	15
Communications	527	497	4	526	505	4	522	504	520	4	523	501	519	4	522	502	519	4
Computer or information sciences	497	522	3	499	533	6	503	534	482	4	505	533	481	3	502	529	477	3
Construction trades	†	†	†	†	†	†	†	†	†	†	415	447	402	#	424	460	409	#
Education	487	477	8	483	481	9	480	484	478	8	480	483	476	8	478	482	475	7
Engineering	525	569	8	523	573	8	519	577	506	8	524	579	510	8	522	579	508	8
Engineering technologies/techniques	†	†	†	†	†	†	†	†	†	†	451	491	435	1	462	508	447	1
Foreign/classical languages	556	534	#	558	539	1	572	549	563	1	581	549	569	1	576	545	564	1
General/interdisciplinary	576	553	19	562	545	#	542	532	532	#	†	†	†	†	†	†	†	†
Health and allied services	500	505	19	497	505	16	485	498	483	18	487	498	484	19	486	498	483	19
History	†	†	†	†	†	†	†	†	†	†	556	518	528	1	548	515	518	1
Home economics[5]	458	452	#	462	462	#	462	466	461	#	463	464	458	#	466	467	462	#
Language and literature	605	545	1	608	552	1	597	541	584	2	596	536	581	2	592	533	577	2
Legal professions and studies	†	†	†	†	†	†	†	†	†	†	516	505	504	2	509	505	500	3
Liberal arts and sciences, general studies, and humanities	†	†	†	†	†	†	†	†	†	†	531	509	516	1	554	532	544	1
Library and archival sciences	554	512	†	556	511	†	579	509	542	†	592	517	544	#	587	517	537	#
Mathematics	552	628	1	551	630	1	539	624	537	1	533	614	529	1	525	609	532	1
Mechanic and repair technologies/technician...	†	†	†	†	†	†	†	†	†	†	423	449	405	#	420	449	403	#
Military sciences	503	505	#	505	512	#	510	521	487	1	517	524	492	1	516	518	486	#
Multi/interdisciplinary studies	†	†	†	†	†	†	†	†	†	†	582	584	570	#	598	586	586	#
Natural resources and conservation	†	†	†	†	†	†	†	†	†	†	499	502	481	#	522	519	503	#

See notes at end of table.

Table 143. SAT mean scores of college-bound seniors, by selected student characteristics: Selected years, 1995–96 through 2007–08—Continued

Selected student characteristic	1995–96 Critical reading score[1]	1995–96 Mathematics score	1995–96 Percentage distribution	1999–2000 Critical reading score[1]	1999–2000 Mathematics score	1999–2000 Percentage distribution	2005–06 Critical reading score[1]	2005–06 Mathematics score	2005–06 Writing score[2]	2005–06 Percentage distribution	2006–07 Critical reading score[1]	2006–07 Mathematics score	2006–07 Writing score[2]	2006–07 Percentage distribution	2007–08 Critical reading score[1]	2007–08 Mathematics score	2007–08 Writing score[2]	2007–08 Percentage distribution
	2	3	4	5	6	7	8	9	10	11	12	13	14	15	16	17	18	19
Parks, recreation, leisure, and fitness studies	†	†	†	†	†	†	†	†	†	†	449	462	437	#	455	478	448	1
Personal and culinary services	†	†	†	†	†	†	†	†	†	†	444	440	432	#	459	459	446	#
Philosophy/religion/theology	560	536	#	560	539	1	557	537	535	1	563	538	541	1	569	548	546	#
Physical sciences	575	595	1	569	592	1	557	589	542	2	560	589	545	2	556	586	539	1
Precision production	†	†	†	†	†	†	†	†	†	†	442	462	409	#	436	462	412	#
Psychology	†	†	†	†	†	†	†	†	†	†	506	488	496	4	503	488	496	5
Public affairs and services	458	448	3	459	454	3	462	461	454	3	497	480	488	2	467	452	461	2
Security and protective services	†	†	†	†	†	†	†	†	†	†	455	457	444	2	451	458	440	2
Social sciences and history	532	509	11	532	513	11	539	519	525	9	†	†	†	†	†	†	†	†
Social sciences	†	†	†	†	†	†	†	†	†	†	569	544	551	3	567	546	551	3
Technical and vocational	435	441	1	442	452	1	437	454	421	1	†	†	†	†	†	†	†	†
Theology and religious vocations	†	†	†	†	†	†	†	†	†	†	541	524	521	#	544	525	522	#
Transportation and materials moving	†	†	†	†	†	†	†	†	†	†	476	495	461	#	461	490	445	#
Other	†	†	†	†	†	†	†	†	†	†	443	445	430	1	466	472	456	1
Undecided	500	507	7	512	521	7	512	530	502	3	519	535	508	3	525	540	516	3
Degree-level goal																		
Certificate program	434	439	1	439	453	1	443	462	435	1	442	461	434	1	438	455	430	1
Associate's degree	422	415	2	420	419	2	416	420	409	2	415	419	407	1	416	419	407	1
Bachelor's degree	476	476	23	478	483	25	477	487	469	25	476	485	467	26	475	485	466	27
Master's degree	514	518	29	515	526	31	512	525	505	30	510	522	502	30	505	519	498	31
Doctor's or related degree	548	552	24	547	554	22	539	553	532	20	540	550	531	20	531	542	524	19
Other	430	438	1	442	454	1	439	456	436	1	436	452	432	1	433	449	430	#
Undecided	502	503	20	508	514	19	515	528	508	22	517	527	508	22	512	523	504	21
Family income																		
Less than $20,000	—	—	—	—	—	—	—	—	—	—	—	—	—	—	—	—	—	—
$20,000, but less than $40,000	—	—	—	—	—	—	—	—	—	—	—	—	—	—	—	—	—	—
$40,000, but less than $60,000	—	—	—	—	—	—	—	—	—	—	—	—	—	—	—	—	—	—
$60,000, but less than $80,000	—	—	—	—	—	—	—	—	—	—	—	—	—	—	—	—	—	—
$80,000, but less than $100,000	—	—	—	—	—	—	—	—	—	—	—	—	—	—	—	—	—	—
$100,000, but less than $120,000	—	—	—	—	—	—	—	—	—	—	—	—	—	—	—	—	—	—
$120,000, but less than $140,000	—	—	—	—	—	—	—	—	—	—	—	—	—	—	—	—	—	—
$140,000, but less than $160,000	—	—	—	—	—	—	—	—	—	—	—	—	—	—	—	—	—	—
$160,000, but less than $200,000	—	—	—	—	—	—	—	—	—	—	—	—	—	—	—	—	—	—
More than $200,000	—	—	—	—	—	—	—	—	—	—	—	—	—	—	—	—	—	—
Highest level of parental education																		
No high school diploma	414	439	4	413	442	4	418	445	418	4	421	445	418	4	419	441	417	5
High school diploma	475	474	35	472	477	33	467	478	460	31	466	476	457	31	464	474	455	32
Associate's degree	489	487	8	488	491	9	484	493	474	8	484	492	473	9	482	490	471	9
Bachelor's degree	525	529	28	525	533	29	522	536	514	28	522	533	513	30	518	531	510	30
Graduate degree	556	558	25	558	566	25	558	571	552	25	560	569	552	26	553	565	546	25

—Not available.

†Not applicable.

#Rounds to zero.

‡Reporting standards not met.

[1] Prior to 2006, the critical reading section was known as the verbal section.

[2] Writing data are based on students who took the SAT writing section, which was introduced in March 2005.

[3] Beginning in 2005–06, the College Board has reported third, fourth, and fifth quintiles as the bottom three quintiles instead of reporting them separately as in previous years.

[4] Data may not be comparable over time because of additions to the list of majors and changes in subspecialties within majors.

[5] Home economics was changed to Family and consumer sciences/human sciences as of 2006–07.

NOTE: Data are for seniors who took the SAT any time during their high school years through March of their senior year. If a student took a test more than once, the most recent score was used. The SAT was formerly known as the Scholastic Assessment Test and the Scholastic Aptitude Test. Possible scores on each part of the SAT range from 200 to 800. Detail may not sum to totals because of rounding and survey item nonresponse.

SOURCE: College Entrance Examination Board, College–Bound Seniors: Total Group Profile [National] Report, selected years, 1995–96 through 2007–08, retrieved August 26, 2008, from http://professionals.collegeboard.com/data-reports-research/sat/cb-seniors-2008. (This table was prepared August 2008.)

Table 144. SAT mean scores of college-bound seniors and percentage of graduates taking SAT, by state or jurisdiction: Selected years, 1987–88 through 2007–08

State or jurisdiction	1987–88		1995–96		2000–01		2005–06			2006–07			2007–08			Percent of graduates taking SAT, 2006–07	Percent of graduates taking SAT, 2007–08[1]
	Critical reading	Mathematics	Critical reading	Mathematics	Critical reading	Mathematics	Critical reading	Mathematics	Writing[2]	Critical reading	Mathematics	Writing[2]	Critical reading	Mathematics	Writing[2]		
1	2	3	4	5	6	7	8	9	10	11	12	13	14	15	16	17	18
United States	**505**	**501**	**505**	**508**	**506**	**514**	**503**	**518**	**497**	**502**	**515**	**494**	**502**	**515**	**494**	**48**	**45**
Alabama	554	540	565	558	559	554	565	561	565	563	556	554	565	557	554	9	8
Alaska	518	501	521	513	514	510	517	517	493	519	517	491	520	520	493	48	45
Arizona	531	523	525	521	523	525	521	528	507	519	525	502	516	522	500	32	26
Arkansas	554	536	566	550	562	550	574	568	567	578	566	565	575	567	559	5	5
California	500	508	495	511	498	517	501	518	501	499	516	498	499	515	498	49	48
Colorado	537	532	536	538	539	542	558	564	548	560	565	549	564	570	553	24	21
Connecticut	513	498	507	504	509	510	512	516	511	510	512	511	509	513	513	84	83
Delaware	510	493	508	495	501	499	495	500	484	497	496	486	499	498	490	72	70
District of Columbia	479	461	489	473	482	474	487	472	482	478	462	471	470	455	465	78 [3]	84
Florida	499	495	498	496	498	499	496	497	480	497	496	479	496	497	481	65	54
Georgia	480	473	484	477	491	489	494	496	487	494	495	483	491	493	482	69	70
Hawaii	484	505	485	510	486	515	482	509	472	484	506	473	481	502	470	61	58
Idaho	543	523	543	536	543	542	543	545	525	541	539	519	540	540	517	19	18
Illinois	540	540	564	575	576	589	591	609	586	594	611	588	583	601	578	8	7
Indiana	490	486	494	494	499	501	498	509	486	497	507	483	496	508	481	62	62
Iowa	587	588	590	600	593	603	602	613	591	608	613	586	603	612	582	4	3
Kansas	568	557	579	571	577	580	582	590	566	583	590	569	580	589	564	8	7
Kentucky	551	535	549	544	550	550	562	562	555	567	565	553	568	570	554	10	8
Louisiana	551	533	559	550	564	562	570	571	571	569	567	563	566	664	558	7	7
Maine[4]	508	493	504	498	506	500	501	501	491	466	465	457	469	466	461	100	87
Maryland	509	501	507	504	508	510	503	509	499	500	502	496	499	502	497	70	69
Massachusetts	508	499	507	504	511	515	513	524	510	513	522	511	514	525	513	85	83
Michigan	532	533	557	565	561	572	568	583	555	568	579	553	581	598	572	9	6
Minnesota	546	549	582	593	580	589	591	600	574	596	603	577	596	609	579	9	8
Mississippi	557	539	569	557	566	551	556	541	562	568	549	560	574	556	566	4	3
Missouri	547	539	570	569	577	577	587	591	582	594	594	587	594	597	584	6	5
Montana	547	547	546	547	539	539	538	545	524	538	543	522	541	548	523	28	24
Nebraska	562	561	567	568	562	568	576	583	566	579	585	562	581	585	567	6	5
Nevada	517	510	508	507	509	515	498	508	481	500	506	480	498	506	478	41	40
New Hampshire	523	511	520	514	520	516	520	524	509	521	521	512	521	523	511	83	74
New Jersey	500	495	498	505	499	513	496	515	496	495	510	494	495	513	496	82	76
New Mexico	553	543	554	548	551	542	557	549	543	555	546	540	557	548	540	12	12
New York	497	495	497	499	495	505	493	510	483	491	505	482	488	504	481	89	84
North Carolina	478	470	490	486	493	499	495	513	485	495	509	482	496	511	482	71	63
North Dakota	572	569	596	599	592	599	610	617	588	584	596	562	594	604	568	4	3
Ohio	529	521	530	535	534	539	535	544	521	536	542	522	534	544	521	27	24
Oklahoma	558	542	566	557	567	561	576	574	563	578	571	559	572	572	557	6	6
Oregon	517	507	523	521	526	526	523	529	503	522	526	502	523	527	502	54	53
Pennsylvania	502	489	498	492	500	499	493	500	483	493	499	482	494	501	483	75	71
Rhode Island	508	496	501	491	501	499	495	502	490	496	498	492	495	498	493	68	66
South Carolina	477	468	480	474	486	488	487	498	480	488	496	475	488	497	476	62	61
South Dakota	585	573	574	566	577	582	590	604	578	589	602	567	595	596	575	3	3
Tennessee	560	543	563	552	562	553	573	569	572	574	569	568	571	570	566	13	11
Texas	494	490	495	500	493	499	491	506	487	492	507	482	488	505	480	52	50
Utah	572	553	583	575	575	570	560	557	550	558	556	544	561	557	543	6	6
Vermont	514	499	506	500	511	506	513	519	502	516	518	508	519	523	507	67	64
Virginia	507	498	507	496	510	501	512	513	500	511	511	498	511	512	499	73	68
Washington	525	517	519	519	527	527	527	532	511	526	531	510	526	533	509	53	52
West Virginia	528	519	526	506	527	512	519	510	515	516	507	505	512	501	498	20	19
Wisconsin	549	551	577	586	584	596	588	600	577	587	598	575	587	604	577	6	5
Wyoming	550	545	544	544	547	545	548	555	537	565	571	544	562	574	541	8	6

[1]Participation rate is based on the projection of high school graduates by the Western Interstate Commission for Higher Education (WICHE), and the number of seniors who took the SAT in each state.

[2]Writing data are based on students who took the SAT writing section, which was introduced in March 2005.

[3]Participation rate is based on self-reported 12th-grade enrollment from D.C's public and nonpublic schools because WICHE estimated fewer graduating seniors than actual SAT test takers.

[4]Beginning with the spring SAT administration in 2006, all Maine high school juniors, including all students in their third year of high school, are required to take SAT tests in critical reading, writing, and mathematics.

NOTE: Data are for seniors who took the SAT any time during their high school years through March of their senior year. If a student took a test more than once, the most recent score was used. The SAT was formerly known as the Scholastic Assessment Test and the Scholastic Aptitude Test. Possible scores on each part of the SAT range from 200 to 800. The critical reading section was formerly known as the verbal section.

SOURCE: College Entrance Examination Board, College-Bound Seniors Tables and Related Items, selected years, 1987–88 through 2007–08, retrieved August 26, 2008, from http://professionals.collegeboard.com/data-reports-research/sat/cb-seniors-2008. (This table was prepared August 2008.)

Table 145. ACT score averages and standard deviations, by sex and race/ethnicity, and percentage of ACT test takers, by selected composite score ranges and planned fields of study: Selected years, 1995 through 2008

Score type and test-taker characteristic	Number												Standard deviation[1]										
	1995	1998	1999	2000	2001	2002	2003	2004	2005	2006	2007	2008	1998	1999	2000	2001	2002	2003	2004	2005	2006	2007	2008
1	2	3	4	5	6	7	8	9	10	11	12	13	14	15	16	17	18	19	20	21	22	23	24
Total test takers																							
Number (in thousands) ...	945	995	1,019	1,065	1,070	1,116	1,175	1,171	1,186	1,206	1,301	1,422	†	†	†	†	†	†	†	†	†	†	†
Percentage of graduates	37.5	36.8	36.9	37.6	37.6	38.4	39.0	38.4	38.2	37.8	40.1	43.1	†	†	†	†	†	†	†	†	†	†	†
	Average test score[2]																						
Composite, total	20.8	21.0	21.0	21.0	21.0	20.8	20.8	20.9	20.9	21.1	21.2	21.1	4.7	4.7	4.7	4.7	4.8	4.8	4.8	—	4.8	5.0	5.0
Sex																							
Male	21.0	21.2	21.1	21.2	21.1	20.9	21.0	21.0	21.1	21.2	21.2	21.2	4.9	4.9	4.9	4.9	5.0	5.0	5.0	5.0	—	—	—
Female	20.7	20.9	20.9	20.9	20.9	20.7	20.8	20.9	20.9	21.0	21.0	21.0	4.6	4.6	4.6	4.6	4.7	4.7	4.7	4.7	—	—	—
Race/ethnicity																							
White	—	22.7	22.7	22.7	21.8	21.7	21.7	21.8	21.9	22.0	22.1	22.1	—	—	—	—	—	—	—	—	—	—	—
Black	—	17.9	17.9	17.8	16.9	16.8	16.9	17.1	17.0	17.1	17.0	16.9	—	—	—	—	—	—	—	—	—	—	—
Mexican American	—	19.6	19.6	19.5	18.5	18.2	18.3	18.4	18.4	—	—	—	—	—	—	—	—	—	—	—	†	†	†
Other Hispanic	—	20.7	20.7	20.5	19.4	18.8	19.0	18.8	18.9	—	—	—	—	—	—	—	—	—	—	—	†	†	†
Hispanic	—	—	—	—	—	18.4	18.5	18.5	18.6	18.6	18.7	18.7	†	†	†	†	—	—	—	—	—	—	—
Asian American or Pacific Islander	—	22.6	22.3	22.4	21.7	21.6	21.8	21.9	22.1	22.3	22.6	22.9	—	—	—	—	—	—	—	—	—	—	—
American Indian/Alaska Native	—	20.4	20.4	20.4	18.8	18.6	18.7	18.8	18.7	18.8	18.9	19.0	—	—	—	—	—	—	—	—	—	—	—
Subject area																							
English	20.2	20.4	20.5	20.5	20.5	20.2	20.3	20.4	20.4	20.6	20.7	20.6	5.4	5.5	5.5	5.6	5.8	5.8	5.9	—	5.9	6.0	6.1
Male	19.8	19.9	20.0	20.0	20.0	19.7	19.8	19.9	20.0	20.1	20.2	20.1	5.4	5.5	5.6	5.6	5.8	5.8	5.9	6.0	—	—	—
Female	20.6	20.8	20.9	20.9	20.8	20.6	20.7	20.8	20.8	21.0	21.0	21.0	5.4	5.5	5.5	5.6	5.7	5.8	5.8	5.9	—	—	—
Mathematics	20.2	20.8	20.7	20.7	20.7	20.6	20.6	20.7	20.7	20.8	21.0	21.0	5.1	5.0	5.0	5.0	5.0	5.1	5.0	—	5.0	5.1	5.2
Male	20.9	21.5	21.4	21.4	21.4	21.2	21.2	21.3	21.3	21.5	21.6	21.6	5.3	5.2	5.2	5.2	5.3	4.8	5.3	5.3	—	—	—
Female	19.7	20.2	20.2	20.2	20.2	20.1	20.1	20.2	20.2	20.3	20.4	20.4	4.8	4.7	4.8	4.7	4.8	5.3	4.8	4.8	—	—	—
Reading	21.3	21.4	21.4	21.4	21.3	21.1	21.2	21.3	21.3	21.4	21.5	21.4	6.0	6.0	6.1	6.0	6.1	6.1	6.0	—	6.0	6.1	6.1
Male	21.1	21.1	21.1	21.2	21.1	20.9	21.0	21.1	21.0	21.1	21.2	21.2	6.2	6.1	6.1	6.1	6.3	5.3	6.1	6.1	—	—	—
Female	21.4	21.6	21.6	21.5	21.5	21.3	21.4	21.5	21.5	21.6	21.6	21.5	5.9	5.9	6.0	6.0	6.1	4.8	5.9	6.0	—	—	—
Science reasoning	21.0	21.1	21.0	21.0	21.0	20.8	20.8	20.9	20.9	20.9	21.0	20.8	4.6	4.5	4.5	4.6	4.6	4.6	4.6	—	4.6	4.9	4.9
Male	21.6	21.8	21.5	21.6	21.6	21.3	21.3	21.3	21.4	21.4	21.4	21.3	4.9	4.8	4.8	4.9	4.9	4.9	4.9	4.9	—	—	—
Female	20.5	20.6	20.6	20.6	20.6	20.4	20.4	20.5	20.5	20.5	20.5	20.4	4.3	4.2	4.3	4.3	4.3	4.3	4.3	4.3	—	—	—
	Percent																						
Obtaining composite scores of—																							
28 or above	—	10	10	10	10	10	10	10	10	11	11	12	—	—	—	—	—	—	—	—	—	—	—
17 or below	—	25	25	25	25	27	27	26	26	25	25	26	—	—	—	—	—	—	—	—	—	—	—
Planned major field of study																							
Business[3]	13	12	12	11	11	10	10	9	9	9	8	11	—	—	—	—	—	—	—	—	—	—	—
Engineering[4]	8	8	8	8	7	7	7	6	6	6	5	7	—	—	—	—	—	—	—	—	—	—	—
Social science[5]	9	9	9	9	9	8	8	7	7	6	5	6	—	—	—	—	—	—	—	—	—	—	—
Education[6]	8	9	9	9	8	8	7	7	6	6	5	6	—	—	—	—	—	—	—	—	—	—	—

—Not available.
†Not applicable.
[1]Standard deviations not available for 1995.
[2]Minimum score is 1 and maximum score is 36.
[3]Includes business and management, business and office, and marketing and distribution.
[4]Includes engineering and engineering-related technologies.
[5]Includes social science and philosophy, religion, and theology.
[6]Includes education and teacher education.
NOTE: Race categories exclude persons of Hispanic ethnicity.
SOURCE: ACT, *High School Profile Report*, selected years, 1995 through 2008. (This table was prepared August 2008.)

Table 146. Percentage distribution of elementary and secondary school children, by average grades and selected child and school characteristics: 1996, 1999, and 2003

Distribution of children, by parental reports of average grades in all subjects

Selected characteristic of children and schools	1996				1999				2003			
	Mostly A's	Mostly B's	Mostly C's	Mostly D's or F's	Mostly A's	Mostly B's	Mostly C's	Mostly D's or F's	Mostly A's	Mostly B's	Mostly C's	Mostly D's or F's
1	2	3	4	5	6	7	8	9	10	11	12	13
All students	**39.5** (0.53)	**37.7** (0.56)	**18.5** (0.41)	**4.2** (0.22)	**40.3** (0.52)	**37.7** (0.53)	**17.8** (0.42)	**4.3** (0.23)	**43.6** (0.62)	**37.0** (0.58)	**15.9** (0.52)	**3.6** (0.24)
Sex of child												
Male	32.5 (0.68)	38.3 (0.82)	23.5 (0.63)	5.7 (0.36)	33.7 (0.70)	38.3 (0.73)	21.9 (0.63)	6.2 (0.39)	36.4 (0.72)	38.6 (0.86)	19.8 (0.74)	5.2 (0.40)
Female	46.9 (0.78)	37.2 (0.77)	13.2 (0.60)	2.7 (0.27)	47.0 (0.77)	37.1 (0.76)	13.5 (0.54)	2.4 (0.25)	51.0 (0.84)	35.3 (0.76)	11.9 (0.61)	1.9 (0.24)
Race/ethnicity of child												
White	43.7 (0.66)	36.1 (0.61)	16.5 (0.49)	3.7 (0.27)	44.6 (0.67)	36.1 (0.65)	15.8 (0.50)	3.4 (0.25)	47.8 (0.86)	35.2 (0.75)	14.0 (0.63)	3.1 (0.25)
Black	27.0 (1.40)	41.0 (1.48)	26.2 (1.51)	5.8 (0.67)	27.5 (1.20)	40.3 (1.42)	26.4 (1.22)	5.8 (0.72)	34.5 (1.75)	39.5 (1.65)	20.9 (1.33)	5.0 (0.82)
Hispanic	31.9 (1.40)	43.6 (1.47)	19.6 (1.18)	4.9 (0.70)	33.3 (1.17)	42.7 (1.26)	17.4 (0.98)	6.5 (0.73)	34.9 (1.14)	42.3 (1.24)	18.6 (1.03)	4.2 (0.49)
Other	44.7 (1.80)	33.7 (2.10)	17.1 (1.61)	4.5 (1.12)	45.8 (2.38)	35.8 (2.36)	14.2 (2.03)	4.2 (1.18)	49.3 (2.63)	33.7 (2.32)	14.3 (1.99)	2.7 (0.78)
Highest education level of parents												
Less than high school	29.0 (1.86)	39.0 (1.89)	23.9 (1.66)	8.1 (1.04)	26.3 (1.58)	40.8 (1.82)	22.3 (1.62)	10.5 (1.30)	27.8 (2.17)	41.6 (2.05)	22.7 (2.28)	7.8 (1.46)
High school/GED	30.5 (0.90)	40.5 (1.09)	23.1 (0.91)	5.9 (0.52)	31.6 (0.99)	39.5 (1.06)	23.3 (0.90)	5.6 (0.49)	32.1 (1.20)	41.4 (1.23)	21.7 (1.12)	4.8 (0.57)
Vocational/technical or some college	36.9 (0.99)	40.1 (1.01)	19.1 (0.64)	3.9 (0.43)	38.9 (0.93)	39.0 (0.94)	18.3 (0.75)	3.8 (0.38)	42.0 (1.13)	37.1 (1.19)	16.9 (0.76)	4.0 (0.42)
Bachelor's degree	52.5 (1.40)	32.9 (1.29)	12.7 (1.03)	1.9 (0.34)	51.1 (1.28)	34.9 (1.22)	12.1 (0.35)	1.8 (0.34)	53.2 (1.30)	34.2 (1.29)	10.9 (0.90)	1.7 (0.31)
Graduate/professional degree	58.2 (1.30)	30.9 (1.21)	9.8 (0.86)	1.1 (0.26)	54.8 (1.30)	33.0 (1.23)	10.3 (0.82)	1.9 (0.39)	60.6 (1.67)	30.9 (1.70)	7.5 (0.73)	1.0 (0.24)
Family income												
$5,000 or less	28.9 (2.50)	38.8 (2.39)	23.3 (2.35)	8.9 (1.67)	25.0 (2.59)	42.9 (3.46)	24.4 (2.77)	7.7 (1.77)	31.8 (4.43)	38.9 (4.27)	21.0 (3.53)	8.3 (3.25)
$5,001 to $10,000	26.6 (1.97)	41.9 (2.30)	24.6 (2.33)	6.9 (1.15)	32.1 (2.37)	36.5 (2.35)	24.0 (2.4)	7.4 (1.32)	31.6 (2.90)	40.1 (3.70)	24.9 (2.70)	3.4 (0.98)
$10,001 to $15,000	28.0 (1.98)	39.8 (2.27)	26.0 (1.97)	6.2 (1.10)	30.3 (2.00)	38.9 (2.16)	23.7 (1.92)	7.1 (1.21)	33.5 (3.49)	35.1 (2.85)	23.9 (2.67)	7.5 (1.44)
$15,001 to $20,000	32.7 (2.34)	38.4 (1.99)	21.6 (1.81)	7.3 (1.35)	32.0 (2.03)	40.0 (2.10)	22.3 (1.69)	5.7 (0.94)	34.6 (2.28)	41.1 (2.41)	18.8 (2.00)	5.4 (1.26)
$20,001 to $25,000	34.4 (1.92)	40.8 (2.19)	20.6 (1.77)	4.2 (0.88)	32.8 (1.83)	38.9 (1.88)	21.6 (1.60)	6.7 (1.09)	33.5 (2.51)	42.1 (2.93)	19.8 (1.99)	4.7 (0.96)
$25,001 to $30,000	33.0 (1.88)	42.0 (2.05)	19.8 (1.41)	5.2 (0.76)	37.4 (1.91)	37.4 (1.90)	19.7 (1.54)	5.4 (0.86)	34.5 (2.67)	42.6 (3.13)	17.9 (1.92)	5.0 (1.21)
$30,001 to $35,000	40.0 (1.88)	38.0 (1.66)	18.1 (1.44)	3.9 (0.69)	38.2 (1.88)	38.8 (1.95)	19.2 (1.53)	3.8 (0.75)	35.1 (2.76)	43.1 (2.57)	16.9 (1.84)	5.0 (1.09)
$35,001 to $40,000	40.4 (1.70)	37.3 (1.69)	19.4 (1.22)	2.8 (0.65)	37.5 (1.83)	42.1 (1.89)	17.4 (1.40)	3.0 (0.62)	39.6 (3.20)	37.8 (2.79)	19.1 (1.78)	3.6 (0.93)
$40,001 to $50,000	43.2 (1.49)	36.0 (1.51)	16.8 (1.09)	4.0 (0.57)	45.0 (1.52)	35.1 (1.44)	16.6 (1.14)	3.3 (0.55)	43.9 (2.06)	35.8 (1.95)	15.8 (1.51)	4.4 (0.75)
$50,001 to $75,000	50.2 (1.05)	32.7 (1.04)	14.9 (0.86)	2.2 (0.34)	45.8 (1.20)	36.8 (1.17)	14.5 (0.84)	2.9 (0.41)	48.0 (1.29)	35.0 (1.22)	14.0 (0.81)	3.0 (0.45)
Over $75,000	51.0 (1.58)	36.8 (1.55)	10.9 (0.9)	1.3 (0.31)	51.9 (1.15)	35.4 (1.11)	10.9 (0.72)	1.8 (0.32)	54.0 (1.19)	33.8 (1.18)	11.0 (0.78)	1.2 (0.19)
Child attending public school	38.2 (0.54)	37.9 (0.56)	19.3 (0.44)	4.6 (0.23)	39.0 (0.55)	37.8 (0.56)	18.5 (0.45)	4.7 (0.26)	41.8 (0.64)	37.5 (0.62)	16.8 (0.57)	3.8 (0.26)
Elementary (kindergarten to grade 8)	43.2 (0.75)	36.6 (0.69)	16.3 (0.55)	3.9 (0.26)	43.5 (0.71)	36.6 (0.71)	15.9 (0.54)	4.1 (0.29)	46.1 (0.80)	35.9 (0.84)	14.6 (0.74)	3.4 (0.32)
Secondary (grades 9 to 12)	29.6 (0.89)	40.2 (1.00)	24.5 (0.89)	5.7 (0.46)	31.8 (0.87)	39.9 (0.92)	22.7 (0.79)	5.6 (0.48)	34.6 (0.96)	40.2 (0.97)	20.6 (0.94)	4.6 (0.46)
Child attending private school	50.8 (1.64)	36.1 (1.58)	11.8 (0.96)	1.3 (0.40)	51.9 (1.61)	36.1 (1.55)	11.0 (1.09)	1.0 (0.27)	57.6 (1.72)	33.0 (1.68)	8.1 (0.91)	1.3 (0.45)
Elementary (kindergarten to grade 8)	55.7 (2.02)	35.3 (1.90)	7.5 (0.86)	1.4 (0.57)	56.2 (1.88)	34.4 (1.80)	9.0 (1.21)	0.5 (0.21)	61.6 (2.39)	30.3 (2.28)	7.3 (1.03)	0.8 (0.28)
Secondary (grades 9 to 12)	41.5 (2.97)	37.7 (2.40)	20.4 (2.30)	1.0 (0.44)	41.2 (3.09)	40.6 (3.03)	15.9 (2.31)	2.2 (0.79)	48.8 (3.22)	38.9 (2.94)	10.0 (1.77)	2.3 (1.30)

NOTE: Includes children enrolled in kindergarten through grade 12. Excludes children whose programs have no classes with lettered grades. Race categories exclude persons of Hispanic ethnicity. Detail may not sum to totals because of rounding. Standard errors appear in parentheses.

SOURCE: U.S. Department of Education, National Center for Education Statistics, Parent and Family Involvement in Education/Civic Involvement Survey, Parent Survey, and Parent and Family Involvement in Education Survey of The National Household Education Surveys Program (PFI/CI-NHES:1996, Parent-NHES:1999, and PFI-NHES:2003). (This table was prepared July 2005.)

Table 147. Average number of Carnegie units earned by public high school graduates in various subject fields, by selected student characteristics: Selected years, 1982 through 2005

Graduation year and selected student characteristic	Total	English	History/ social studies	Mathematics Total	Mathematics Less than algebra	Mathematics Algebra or higher	Total	Science General science	Science Biology	Science Chemistry	Science Physics	Foreign languages	Arts	Career/ technical education[1]	Personal use[2]	Computer related[3]
1	2	3	4	5	6	7	8	9	10	11	12	13	14	15	16	17
1982 graduates	**21.58 (0.090)**	**3.93 (0.022)**	**3.16 (0.028)**	**2.63 (0.022)**	**0.90 (0.021)**	**1.74 (0.028)**	**2.20 (0.025)**	**0.73 (0.016)**	**0.94 (0.014)**	**0.34 (0.010)**	**0.17 (0.008)**	**0.99 (0.029)**	**1.47 (0.035)**	**4.62 (0.061)**	**2.58 (0.048)**	**0.12 (0.007)**
Sex																
Male	21.40 (0.108)	3.88 (0.026)	3.16 (0.034)	2.71 (0.030)	0.94 (0.026)	1.77 (0.039)	2.27 (0.031)	0.76 (0.018)	0.91 (0.016)	0.36 (0.014)	0.23 (0.012)	0.80 (0.030)	1.29 (0.044)	4.60 (0.076)	2.69 (0.056)	0.14 (0.012)
Female	21.75 (0.101)	3.98 (0.026)	3.15 (0.029)	2.57 (0.024)	0.86 (0.025)	1.71 (0.032)	2.13 (0.029)	0.71 (0.017)	0.97 (0.017)	0.33 (0.013)	0.12 (0.008)	1.17 (0.036)	1.63 (0.044)	4.64 (0.072)	2.48 (0.049)	0.11 (0.007)
Race/ethnicity																
White	21.69 (0.107)	3.90 (0.025)	3.19 (0.032)	2.68 (0.026)	0.77 (0.023)	1.91 (0.032)	2.27 (0.029)	0.73 (0.017)	0.97 (0.015)	0.38 (0.013)	0.20 (0.010)	1.06 (0.033)	1.53 (0.042)	4.53 (0.071)	2.52 (0.052)	0.13 (0.009)
Black	21.15 (0.169)	4.08 (0.050)	3.08 (0.064)	2.61 (0.043)	1.36 (0.053)	1.25 (0.066)	2.06 (0.049)	0.81 (0.033)	0.90 (0.033)	0.16 (0.023)	0.09 (0.011)	0.72 (0.067)	1.29 (0.063)	4.75 (0.136)	2.60 (0.094)	0.12 (0.016)
Hispanic	21.23 (0.122)	3.94 (0.037)	3.00 (0.037)	2.33 (0.040)	1.21 (0.037)	1.12 (0.047)	1.80 (0.038)	0.75 (0.026)	0.81 (0.025)	0.16 (0.012)	0.07 (0.007)	0.77 (0.042)	1.29 (0.054)	5.22 (0.111)	2.87 (0.081)	0.08 (0.010)
Asian/Pacific Islander	22.46 (0.216)	4.01 (0.091)	3.16 (0.094)	3.15 (0.095)	0.71 (0.063)	2.44 (0.132)	2.64 (0.125)	0.51 (0.061)	1.11 (0.048)	0.61 (0.046)	0.42 (0.048)	1.79 (0.105)	1.31 (0.124)	3.34 (0.226)	3.05 (0.146)	0.22 (0.057)
American Indian/Alaska Native	21.45 (0.330)	3.98 (0.114)	3.25 (0.207)	2.35 (0.129)	1.23 (0.148)	1.12 (0.213)	2.04 (0.090)	0.67 (0.087)	0.84 (0.124)	0.42 (0.087)	0.12 (0.039)	0.48 (0.117)	1.72 (0.338)	4.77 (0.233)	2.84 (0.129)	0.06 (0.024)
Academic track																
Academic[4]	21.75 (0.092)	4.11 (0.026)	3.32 (0.032)	3.04 (0.024)	0.73 (0.027)	2.30 (0.037)	2.65 (0.032)	0.73 (0.018)	1.13 (0.017)	0.53 (0.016)	0.26 (0.012)	1.54 (0.042)	1.91 (0.050)	2.55 (0.042)	2.62 (0.058)	0.10 (0.006)
Career/technical[5]	20.21 (0.090)	3.44 (0.035)	2.63 (0.032)	1.80 (0.032)	1.09 (0.036)	0.71 (0.030)	1.32 (0.026)	0.69 (0.023)	0.57 (0.021)	0.04 (0.006)	0.02 (0.006)	0.18 (0.015)	0.59 (0.029)	7.74 (0.082)	2.51 (0.065)	0.12 (0.016)
Both[6]	20.89 (0.196)	4.04 (0.037)	3.33 (0.046)	2.69 (0.041)	1.02 (0.036)	1.67 (0.054)	2.17 (0.037)	0.79 (0.023)	0.94 (0.019)	0.29 (0.018)	0.14 (0.015)	0.75 (0.036)	1.41 (0.055)	6.03 (0.091)	2.47 (0.064)	0.18 (0.020)
Neither[7]	18.73 (0.141)	3.58 (0.054)	2.70 (0.054)	1.73 (0.045)	1.08 (0.055)	0.65 (0.060)	1.33 (0.051)	0.69 (0.037)	0.59 (0.035)	0.03 (0.008)	0.02 (0.007)	0.22 (0.027)	0.85 (0.063)	5.23 (0.137)	3.06 (0.115)	0.05 (0.011)
1987 graduates	**23.00 (0.157)**	**4.12 (0.022)**	**3.32 (0.037)**	**3.01 (0.029)**	**0.86 (0.030)**	**2.14 (0.042)**	**2.55 (0.046)**	**0.76 (0.033)**	**1.10 (0.020)**	**0.47 (0.015)**	**0.21 (0.011)**	**1.35 (0.049)**	**1.44 (0.044)**	**4.55 (0.084)**	**2.67 (0.073)**	**0.47 (0.022)**
Sex																
Male	22.88 (0.162)	4.08 (0.021)	3.29 (0.037)	3.05 (0.029)	0.91 (0.032)	2.14 (0.045)	2.59 (0.049)	0.79 (0.032)	1.05 (0.021)	0.47 (0.016)	0.26 (0.013)	1.16 (0.051)	1.24 (0.046)	4.64 (0.089)	2.83 (0.081)	0.47 (0.023)
Female	23.12 (0.156)	4.15 (0.026)	3.35 (0.041)	2.96 (0.030)	0.82 (0.032)	2.15 (0.045)	2.52 (0.048)	0.74 (0.035)	1.14 (0.022)	0.47 (0.017)	0.17 (0.012)	1.53 (0.051)	1.63 (0.050)	4.47 (0.094)	2.51 (0.069)	0.47 (0.023)
Race/ethnicity																
White	23.11 (0.189)	4.08 (0.028)	3.29 (0.045)	3.01 (0.034)	0.74 (0.031)	2.27 (0.050)	2.61 (0.058)	0.75 (0.040)	1.12 (0.025)	0.50 (0.020)	0.23 (0.012)	1.38 (0.055)	1.50 (0.055)	4.65 (0.107)	2.60 (0.082)	0.49 (0.027)
Black	22.40 (0.251)	4.22 (0.038)	3.34 (0.073)	2.99 (0.060)	1.40 (0.074)	1.59 (0.054)	2.33 (0.060)	0.90 (0.051)	1.01 (0.036)	0.31 (0.021)	0.10 (0.012)	1.08 (0.094)	1.20 (0.064)	4.52 (0.130)	2.73 (0.120)	0.39 (0.032)
Hispanic	22.84 (0.162)	4.30 (0.055)	3.22 (0.061)	2.81 (0.056)	1.30 (0.049)	1.50 (0.039)	2.24 (0.045)	0.78 (0.028)	1.07 (0.028)	0.29 (0.015)	0.10 (0.013)	1.25 (0.071)	1.34 (0.056)	4.49 (0.169)	3.19 (0.096)	0.42 (0.031)
Asian/Pacific Islander	24.47 (0.332)	4.37 (0.076)	3.65 (0.163)	3.71 (0.094)	0.53 (0.072)	3.18 (0.143)	3.14 (0.116)	0.59 (0.048)	1.17 (0.027)	0.87 (0.069)	0.50 (0.045)	2.07 (0.105)	1.18 (0.077)	3.11 (0.221)	3.23 (0.185)	0.58 (0.033)
American Indian/Alaska Native	23.23 (0.153)	4.22 (0.033)	3.18 (0.044)	2.98 (0.113)	1.35 (0.145)	1.63 (0.097)	2.44 (0.104)	0.81 (0.041)	1.22 (0.073)	0.32 (0.035)	0.09 (0.027)	0.75 (0.138)	1.68 (0.112)	4.92 (0.125)	3.06 (0.050)	0.39 (0.058)
Academic track																
Academic[4]	23.20 (0.153)	4.26 (0.029)	3.55 (0.045)	3.33 (0.031)	0.65 (0.034)	2.68 (0.051)	2.97 (0.053)	0.73 (0.031)	1.23 (0.024)	0.68 (0.022)	0.32 (0.014)	1.92 (0.066)	1.87 (0.059)	2.57 (0.071)	2.73 (0.081)	0.38 (0.017)
Career/technical[5]	21.07 (0.161)	3.62 (0.032)	2.59 (0.040)	2.03 (0.029)	1.29 (0.051)	0.71 (0.041)	1.48 (0.047)	0.74 (0.053)	0.70 (0.037)	0.03 (0.006)	0.01 (0.003)	0.18 (0.024)	0.47 (0.031)	8.07 (0.155)	2.67 (0.112)	0.39 (0.038)
Both[6]	22.53 (0.179)	4.11 (0.025)	3.29 (0.031)	2.93 (0.026)	0.97 (0.045)	1.96 (0.056)	2.37 (0.051)	0.81 (0.038)	1.07 (0.028)	0.35 (0.016)	0.14 (0.011)	1.01 (0.043)	1.20 (0.054)	6.09 (0.085)	2.53 (0.064)	0.64 (0.034)
Neither[7]	19.56 (0.199)	3.55 (0.050)	2.45 (0.071)	2.11 (0.082)	1.62 (0.100)	0.49 (0.094)	1.47 (0.046)	0.84 (0.075)	0.59 (0.051)	0.03 (0.011)	0.00 (0.004)	0.18 (0.040)	0.76 (0.067)	5.10 (0.233)	3.33 (0.249)	0.17 (0.031)
1990 graduates	**23.53 (0.127)**	**4.19 (0.034)**	**3.47 (0.040)**	**3.15 (0.028)**	**0.90 (0.032)**	**2.25 (0.040)**	**2.75 (0.028)**	**0.85 (0.026)**	**1.14 (0.019)**	**0.53 (0.014)**	**0.23 (0.010)**	**1.54 (0.041)**	**1.55 (0.045)**	**4.19 (0.079)**	**2.68 (0.073)**	**0.54 (0.021)**
Sex																
Male	23.35 (0.130)	4.13 (0.035)	3.45 (0.041)	3.16 (0.028)	0.96 (0.038)	2.20 (0.048)	2.78 (0.033)	0.88 (0.027)	1.11 (0.021)	0.52 (0.017)	0.28 (0.012)	1.33 (0.040)	1.31 (0.047)	4.32 (0.084)	2.87 (0.077)	0.50 (0.020)
Female	23.69 (0.132)	4.25 (0.036)	3.50 (0.041)	3.14 (0.033)	0.85 (0.032)	2.29 (0.039)	2.73 (0.027)	0.83 (0.027)	1.17 (0.019)	0.53 (0.014)	0.19 (0.010)	1.72 (0.045)	1.76 (0.050)	4.08 (0.087)	2.51 (0.072)	0.57 (0.026)
Race/ethnicity																
White	23.54 (0.133)	4.12 (0.036)	3.46 (0.045)	3.13 (0.032)	0.80 (0.033)	2.33 (0.041)	2.80 (0.033)	0.84 (0.022)	1.15 (0.020)	0.55 (0.016)	0.25 (0.011)	1.58 (0.049)	1.61 (0.056)	4.22 (0.085)	2.61 (0.076)	0.52 (0.023)
Black	23.40 (0.255)	4.34 (0.044)	3.49 (0.058)	3.20 (0.064)	1.25 (0.059)	1.95 (0.071)	2.68 (0.061)	0.98 (0.068)	1.11 (0.042)	0.42 (0.024)	0.16 (0.020)	1.20 (0.075)	1.34 (0.064)	4.41 (0.166)	2.74 (0.124)	0.60 (0.055)
Hispanic	23.83 (0.210)	4.51 (0.139)	3.42 (0.071)	3.13 (0.058)	1.30 (0.076)	1.83 (0.090)	2.50 (0.046)	0.83 (0.041)	1.10 (0.034)	0.42 (0.034)	0.14 (0.016)	1.57 (0.060)	1.48 (0.072)	4.12 (0.150)	3.10 (0.103)	0.58 (0.048)
Asian/Pacific Islander	24.07 (0.236)	4.50 (0.117)	3.70 (0.126)	3.52 (0.060)	0.70 (0.121)	2.82 (0.159)	2.97 (0.114)	0.68 (0.080)	1.12 (0.085)	0.74 (0.057)	0.42 (0.047)	2.06 (0.150)	1.29 (0.084)	3.07 (0.337)	2.96 (0.221)	0.54 (0.043)
American Indian/Alaska Native	22.64 (0.267)	4.08 (0.092)	3.34 (0.083)	3.04 (0.152)	1.03 (0.084)	2.01 (0.143)	2.48 (0.175)	0.83 (0.090)	1.09 (0.090)	0.42 (0.072)	0.15 (0.039)	1.15 (0.188)	1.11 (0.126)	4.62 (0.190)	2.81 (0.148)	0.60 (0.130)
Academic track																
Academic[4]	23.53 (0.137)	4.30 (0.044)	3.65 (0.047)	3.37 (0.025)	0.68 (0.031)	2.70 (0.038)	3.06 (0.033)	0.81 (0.033)	1.23 (0.021)	0.70 (0.018)	0.32 (0.012)	2.02 (0.046)	1.93 (0.054)	2.41 (0.048)	2.78 (0.096)	0.42 (0.019)
Career/technical[5]	21.73 (0.244)	3.60 (0.063)	2.58 (0.063)	2.07 (0.054)	1.54 (0.060)	0.53 (0.045)	1.82 (0.047)	0.87 (0.031)	0.71 (0.040)	0.03 (0.008)	0.01 (0.004)	0.17 (0.029)	0.42 (0.042)	8.68 (0.179)	2.59 (0.092)	0.46 (0.067)
Both[6]	23.92 (0.128)	4.14 (0.026)	3.38 (0.038)	3.02 (0.031)	1.12 (0.037)	1.90 (0.044)	2.51 (0.031)	0.92 (0.024)	1.09 (0.024)	0.36 (0.015)	0.14 (0.010)	1.07 (0.040)	1.17 (0.049)	6.10 (0.065)	2.53 (0.073)	0.73 (0.034)
Neither[7]	19.81 (0.564)	3.63 (0.153)	2.59 (0.076)	2.01 (0.139)	1.57 (0.176)	0.44 (0.072)	1.47 (0.085)	0.79 (0.080)	0.60 (0.090)	0.04 (0.020)	0.03 (0.018)	0.21 (0.060)	0.79 (0.249)	5.81 (0.529)	3.29 (0.336)	0.36 (0.063)

See notes at end of table.

Table 147. Average number of Carnegie units earned by public high school graduates in various subject fields, by selected student characteristics: Selected years, 1982 through 2005—Continued

Graduation year and selected student characteristic	Total	English	History/ social studies	Mathematics			Science					Foreign languages	Arts	Career/ technical education[1]	Personal use[2]	Computer related[3]
				Total	Less than algebra	Algebra or higher	Total	General science	Biology	Chemistry	Physics					
1	2	3	4	5	6	7	8	9	10	11	12	13	14	15	16	17
1994 graduates	24.17 (0.144)	4.29 (0.026)	3.55 (0.041)	3.33 (0.021)	0.76 (0.029)	2.57 (0.036)	3.04 (0.026)	0.88 (0.024)	1.26 (0.018)	0.62 (0.013)	0.28 (0.011)	1.71 (0.033)	1.66 (0.041)	3.96 (0.069)	2.63 (0.077)	0.64 (0.025)
Sex																
Male	23.79 (0.146)	4.26 (0.028)	3.51 (0.041)	3.32 (0.022)	0.85 (0.032)	2.48 (0.038)	3.03 (0.030)	0.91 (0.026)	1.20 (0.020)	0.59 (0.015)	0.32 (0.014)	1.49 (0.034)	1.43 (0.038)	4.13 (0.074)	2.83 (0.081)	0.63 (0.027)
Female	24.11 (0.147)	4.32 (0.030)	3.59 (0.041)	3.34 (0.023)	0.68 (0.029)	2.66 (0.037)	3.06 (0.028)	0.86 (0.024)	1.31 (0.018)	0.64 (0.014)	0.24 (0.010)	1.93 (0.034)	1.87 (0.051)	3.80 (0.074)	2.44 (0.078)	0.65 (0.027)
Race/ethnicity																
White	24.08 (0.183)	4.23 (0.035)	3.56 (0.049)	3.36 (0.023)	0.70 (0.034)	2.66 (0.041)	3.13 (0.032)	0.89 (0.030)	1.29 (0.022)	0.65 (0.014)	0.30 (0.014)	1.76 (0.039)	1.74 (0.049)	3.96 (0.080)	2.61 (0.096)	0.63 (0.028)
Black	23.28 (0.132)	4.36 (0.034)	3.51 (0.039)	3.23 (0.030)	1.09 (0.067)	2.14 (0.079)	2.80 (0.042)	0.92 (0.051)	1.21 (0.036)	0.49 (0.028)	0.17 (0.013)	1.35 (0.052)	1.36 (0.066)	4.29 (0.121)	2.69 (0.101)	0.64 (0.039)
Hispanic	23.71 (0.131)	4.61 (0.075)	3.45 (0.046)	3.28 (0.041)	0.96 (0.030)	2.32 (0.057)	2.69 (0.046)	0.83 (0.058)	1.19 (0.027)	0.49 (0.047)	0.17 (0.021)	1.73 (0.062)	1.51 (0.046)	3.87 (0.124)	2.93 (0.086)	0.76 (0.044)
Asian/Pacific Islander	23.84 (0.256)	4.60 (0.091)	3.66 (0.097)	3.66 (0.082)	0.67 (0.113)	2.98 (0.189)	3.35 (0.131)	0.30 (0.034)	1.22 (0.042)	0.81 (0.062)	0.48 (0.058)	2.09 (0.085)	1.32 (0.121)	3.01 (0.236)	2.78 (0.123)	0.71 (0.034)
American Indian/Alaska Native	23.40 (0.541)	4.27 (0.113)	3.57 (0.201)	3.11 (0.038)	0.94 (0.108)	2.17 (0.125)	2.82 (0.073)	0.91 (0.057)	1.28 (0.069)	0.50 (0.065)	0.13 (0.039)	1.30 (0.150)	2.01 (0.351)	4.27 (0.256)	3.12 (0.355)	0.53 (0.217)
Academic track																
Academic[4]	23.86 (0.133)	4.37 (0.034)	3.69 (0.042)	3.52 (0.022)	0.58 (0.030)	2.94 (0.039)	3.32 (0.031)	0.83 (0.027)	1.34 (0.021)	0.77 (0.017)	0.37 (0.014)	2.14 (0.040)	2.05 (0.054)	2.28 (0.045)	2.71 (0.071)	0.50 (0.022)
Career/technical[5]	21.20 (0.252)	3.70 (0.055)	2.49 (0.071)	2.20 (0.052)	1.56 (0.066)	0.64 (0.048)	1.69 (0.064)	0.80 (0.049)	0.83 (0.046)	0.03 (0.006)	0.02 (0.007)	0.14 (0.029)	0.34 (0.036)	8.64 (0.214)	2.41 (0.141)	0.55 (0.055)
Both[6]	24.41 (0.149)	4.23 (0.029)	3.45 (0.039)	3.17 (0.023)	0.96 (0.039)	2.21 (0.045)	2.78 (0.031)	0.96 (0.026)	1.19 (0.021)	0.45 (0.016)	0.17 (0.010)	1.24 (0.037)	1.21 (0.036)	6.01 (0.069)	2.52 (0.095)	0.85 (0.039)
Neither[7]	20.56 (0.476)	3.54 (0.130)	2.24 (0.075)	2.25 (0.073)	1.71 (0.121)	0.54 (0.100)	1.53 (0.078)	0.82 (0.076)	0.63 (0.075)	0.05 (0.024)	0.02 (0.011)	0.19 (0.063)	0.56 (0.105)	6.51 (0.347)	4.47 (0.497)	0.33 (0.063)
1998 graduates	25.14 (0.162)	4.25 (0.037)	3.74 (0.038)	3.40 (0.024)	0.67 (0.022)	2.73 (0.034)	3.12 (0.026)	0.89 (0.024)	1.26 (0.021)	0.66 (0.015)	0.31 (0.015)	1.85 (0.039)	1.90 (0.079)	3.99 (0.098)	2.89 (0.076)	0.74 (0.033)
Sex																
Male	24.64 (0.162)	4.19 (0.038)	3.68 (0.040)	3.37 (0.024)	0.74 (0.023)	2.64 (0.034)	3.09 (0.028)	0.93 (0.026)	1.20 (0.021)	0.62 (0.014)	0.33 (0.018)	1.62 (0.040)	1.61 (0.072)	4.25 (0.099)	3.12 (0.079)	0.78 (0.032)
Female	25.04 (0.166)	4.31 (0.039)	3.80 (0.036)	3.42 (0.025)	0.62 (0.023)	2.80 (0.035)	3.17 (0.029)	0.87 (0.023)	1.32 (0.023)	0.70 (0.018)	0.28 (0.015)	2.06 (0.041)	2.15 (0.094)	3.77 (0.114)	2.67 (0.080)	0.71 (0.036)
Race/ethnicity																
White	24.87 (0.178)	4.19 (0.049)	3.77 (0.046)	3.40 (0.028)	0.57 (0.022)	2.84 (0.035)	3.18 (0.028)	0.87 (0.027)	1.28 (0.025)	0.69 (0.017)	0.33 (0.019)	1.90 (0.049)	2.00 (0.078)	3.97 (0.114)	2.80 (0.088)	0.73 (0.037)
Black	24.37 (0.250)	4.28 (0.045)	3.69 (0.050)	3.42 (0.042)	0.90 (0.053)	2.53 (0.072)	3.03 (0.064)	0.97 (0.045)	1.24 (0.038)	0.58 (0.025)	0.22 (0.022)	1.58 (0.062)	1.57 (0.152)	4.33 (0.149)	2.94 (0.080)	0.84 (0.064)
Hispanic	24.69 (0.218)	4.51 (0.055)	3.60 (0.051)	3.28 (0.041)	1.05 (0.055)	2.23 (0.061)	2.81 (0.054)	0.97 (0.042)	1.13 (0.026)	0.50 (0.036)	0.20 (0.020)	1.78 (0.055)	1.78 (0.113)	3.97 (0.121)	3.36 (0.121)	0.71 (0.046)
Asian/Pacific Islander	24.67 (0.195)	4.37 (0.068)	3.92 (0.086)	3.62 (0.029)	0.65 (0.134)	2.97 (0.136)	3.43 (0.079)	0.81 (0.041)	1.26 (0.027)	0.83 (0.037)	0.51 (0.036)	2.29 (0.129)	1.52 (0.056)	3.15 (0.222)	2.95 (0.206)	0.67 (0.050)
American Indian/Alaska Native	23.81 (0.350)	4.18 (0.082)	3.67 (0.093)	3.10 (0.081)	0.90 (0.067)	2.20 (0.100)	2.68 (0.081)	0.98 (0.070)	1.07 (0.056)	0.49 (0.038)	0.15 (0.024)	1.45 (0.132)	1.94 (0.146)	4.02 (0.164)	3.40 (0.212)	0.67 (0.058)
Academic track																
Academic[4]	24.61 (0.160)	4.33 (0.034)	3.87 (0.038)	3.54 (0.023)	0.53 (0.024)	3.00 (0.036)	3.34 (0.030)	0.84 (0.028)	1.33 (0.027)	0.78 (0.016)	0.38 (0.020)	2.24 (0.041)	2.41 (0.122)	2.22 (0.061)	2.97 (0.088)	0.52 (0.024)
Career/technical[5]	22.10 (0.299)	3.46 (0.092)	2.55 (0.079)	2.17 (0.076)	1.30 (0.073)	0.87 (0.065)	1.69 (0.087)	1.05 (0.088)	0.59 (0.068)	0.03 (0.007)	0.01 (0.005)	0.14 (0.025)	0.47 (0.068)	9.12 (0.239)	3.01 (0.227)	0.81 (0.085)
Both[6]	25.38 (0.190)	4.20 (0.046)	3.66 (0.034)	3.30 (0.030)	0.81 (0.027)	2.49 (0.045)	2.94 (0.038)	0.96 (0.030)	1.20 (0.033)	0.54 (0.022)	0.23 (0.016)	1.45 (0.042)	1.31 (0.048)	6.06 (0.083)	2.73 (0.078)	1.03 (0.048)
Neither[7]	20.39 (0.371)	3.21 (0.146)	2.32 (0.235)	2.19 (0.063)	1.59 (0.137)	0.60 (0.087)	1.58 (0.095)	0.88 (0.089)	0.58 (0.052)	0.04 (0.017)	0.08 (0.031)	0.20 (0.047)	0.55 (0.083)	5.64 (0.598)	5.82 (0.379)	0.51 (0.069)
2000 graduates	26.05 (0.201)	4.39 (0.035)	3.83 (0.033)	3.56 (0.028)	0.61 (0.028)	2.95 (0.038)	3.20 (0.038)	0.85 (0.028)	1.29 (0.028)	0.69 (0.018)	0.36 (0.017)	1.95 (0.044)	2.03 (0.054)	4.21 (0.123)	2.88 (0.065)	0.83 (0.032)
Sex																
Male	26.23 (0.206)	4.31 (0.034)	3.76 (0.032)	3.53 (0.031)	0.68 (0.032)	2.86 (0.046)	3.16 (0.039)	0.88 (0.028)	1.20 (0.029)	0.65 (0.017)	0.40 (0.018)	1.71 (0.044)	1.75 (0.051)	4.60 (0.154)	3.09 (0.070)	0.93 (0.036)
Female	26.46 (0.203)	4.46 (0.038)	3.89 (0.035)	3.58 (0.028)	0.55 (0.026)	3.03 (0.036)	3.25 (0.040)	0.82 (0.030)	1.36 (0.029)	0.73 (0.020)	0.33 (0.017)	2.18 (0.049)	2.30 (0.065)	3.82 (0.104)	2.69 (0.063)	0.74 (0.034)
Race/ethnicity																
White	26.57 (0.252)	4.32 (0.037)	3.86 (0.037)	3.56 (0.031)	0.58 (0.032)	2.98 (0.043)	3.24 (0.038)	0.84 (0.031)	1.30 (0.034)	0.70 (0.020)	0.38 (0.020)	1.98 (0.053)	2.12 (0.068)	4.34 (0.164)	2.79 (0.075)	0.81 (0.036)
Black	26.28 (0.242)	4.43 (0.078)	3.75 (0.067)	3.54 (0.042)	0.72 (0.062)	2.82 (0.059)	3.13 (0.058)	0.91 (0.043)	1.26 (0.040)	0.65 (0.027)	0.27 (0.020)	1.70 (0.071)	1.95 (0.134)	4.29 (0.173)	2.98 (0.093)	0.85 (0.055)
Hispanic	25.91 (0.323)	4.69 (0.106)	3.77 (0.075)	3.42 (0.074)	0.74 (0.051)	2.68 (0.107)	2.87 (0.112)	0.85 (0.046)	1.19 (0.067)	0.58 (0.055)	0.24 (0.025)	1.90 (0.070)	1.77 (0.063)	3.83 (0.124)	3.21 (0.147)	0.89 (0.056)
Asian/Pacific Islander	26.66 (0.327)	4.57 (0.069)	3.77 (0.051)	3.96 (0.095)	0.35 (0.035)	3.61 (0.106)	3.71 (0.153)	0.71 (0.082)	1.36 (0.060)	0.96 (0.048)	0.65 (0.037)	2.51 (0.083)	1.79 (0.084)	2.82 (0.160)	3.09 (0.184)	0.92 (0.111)
American Indian/Alaska Native	26.03 (0.315)	4.12 (0.064)	3.75 (0.100)	3.29 (0.083)	0.91 (0.164)	2.38 (0.178)	2.88 (0.112)	0.98 (0.037)	1.25 (0.080)	0.45 (0.044)	0.19 (0.042)	1.40 (0.105)	1.99 (0.220)	4.79 (0.429)	2.89 (0.230)	0.96 (0.074)
Academic track																
Academic[4]	25.82 (0.186)	4.47 (0.040)	3.93 (0.043)	3.70 (0.034)	0.49 (0.024)	3.21 (0.042)	3.39 (0.042)	0.81 (0.033)	1.35 (0.033)	0.80 (0.023)	0.42 (0.019)	2.32 (0.050)	2.52 (0.072)	2.28 (0.049)	2.96 (0.075)	0.54 (0.024)
Career/technical[5]	24.13 (0.369)	3.33 (0.131)	2.62 (0.121)	2.11 (0.086)	1.28 (0.120)	0.82 (0.100)	1.61 (0.116)	0.84 (0.069)	0.65 (0.091)	0.06 (0.018)	0.05 (0.029)	0.15 (0.042)	0.57 (0.062)	9.56 (0.337)	3.50 (0.249)	1.17 (0.220)
Both[6]	27.16 (0.248)	4.33 (0.035)	3.76 (0.034)	3.45 (0.032)	0.74 (0.040)	2.71 (0.054)	3.04 (0.047)	0.89 (0.031)	1.24 (0.033)	0.59 (0.024)	0.30 (0.024)	1.56 (0.057)	1.47 (0.057)	6.46 (0.170)	2.74 (0.074)	1.20 (0.046)
Neither[7]	22.41 (0.500)	3.50 (0.098)	1.86 (0.142)	2.27 (0.088)	1.76 (0.141)	0.51 (0.101)	1.59 (0.099)	1.04 (0.097)	0.48 (0.082)	0.04 (0.018)	0.02 (0.011)	0.20 (0.056)	0.93 (0.096)	5.52 (0.443)	5.72 (0.506)	0.29 (0.051)

See notes at end of table.

Table 147. Average number of Carnegie units earned by public high school graduates in various subject fields, by selected student characteristics: Selected years, 1982 through 2005—Continued

Graduation year and selected student characteristic	Total	English	History/ social studies	Mathematics			Science					Foreign languages	Arts	Career/ technical education[1]	Personal use[2]	Computer related[3]
				Total	Less than algebra	Algebra or higher	Total	General science	Biology	Chemistry	Physics					
1	2	3	4	5	6	7	8	9	10	11	12	13	14	15	16	17
2005 graduates.........	26.68 (0.100)	4.42 (0.022)	3.98 (0.025)	3.57 (0.016)	0.49 (0.015)	3.19 (0.020)	3.34 (0.019)	0.95 (0.019)	1.28 (0.016)	0.74 (0.010)	0.35 (0.011)	1.97 (0.024)	2.05 (0.035)	4.01 (0.058)	3.23 (0.040)	0.93 (0.021)
Sex																
Male..................	26.50 (0.104)	4.36 (0.025)	3.91 (0.028)	3.65 (0.020)	0.54 (0.016)	3.10 (0.024)	3.29 (0.023)	0.97 (0.019)	1.19 (0.016)	0.70 (0.011)	0.39 (0.013)	1.76 (0.026)	1.71 (0.035)	4.35 (0.059)	3.47 (0.043)	1.09 (0.023)
Female...............	26.84 (0.103)	4.48 (0.021)	4.05 (0.025)	3.70 (0.016)	0.44 (0.016)	3.26 (0.021)	3.40 (0.020)	0.92 (0.020)	1.37 (0.017)	0.78 (0.011)	0.32 (0.012)	2.16 (0.025)	2.38 (0.045)	3.68 (0.068)	3.00 (0.044)	0.79 (0.024)
Race/ethnicity																
White.................	26.87 (0.125)	4.32 (0.029)	4.02 (0.030)	3.69 (0.021)	0.44 (0.017)	3.24 (0.026)	3.43 (0.021)	0.96 (0.022)	1.31 (0.018)	0.76 (0.013)	0.38 (0.012)	2.01 (0.027)	2.17 (0.043)	4.12 (0.075)	3.10 (0.049)	0.90 (0.026)
Black..................	26.57 (0.150)	4.54 (0.028)	3.98 (0.045)	3.71 (0.032)	0.63 (0.034)	3.08 (0.047)	3.21 (0.036)	0.99 (0.037)	1.27 (0.025)	0.68 (0.017)	0.27 (0.025)	1.71 (0.040)	1.77 (0.056)	4.11 (0.111)	3.53 (0.076)	1.07 (0.033)
Hispanic.............	25.91 (0.142)	4.80 (0.037)	3.75 (0.039)	3.49 (0.032)	0.65 (0.034)	2.83 (0.034)	2.92 (0.035)	0.92 (0.031)	1.11 (0.020)	0.63 (0.022)	0.24 (0.017)	1.88 (0.035)	1.78 (0.054)	3.69 (0.098)	3.62 (0.058)	1.00 (0.040)
Asian/Pacific Islander......	26.32 (0.189)	4.51 (0.057)	3.94 (0.042)	3.90 (0.004)	0.27 (0.025)	3.62 (0.041)	3.63 (0.057)	0.74 (0.060)	1.31 (0.035)	0.97 (0.027)	0.56 (0.032)	2.43 (0.068)	1.80 (0.076)	2.91 (0.144)	3.21 (0.086)	0.94 (0.054)
American Indian/Alaska Native......	26.48 (0.443)	4.44 (0.098)	4.06 (0.129)	3.53 (0.141)	0.69 (0.087)	2.84 (0.182)	3.02 (0.072)	1.04 (0.060)	1.28 (0.063)	0.52 (0.052)	0.17 (0.036)	1.44 (0.105)	2.44 (0.179)	4.20 (0.258)	3.36 (0.291)	0.82 (0.102)
Other..................	26.09 (0.374)	4.39 (0.095)	3.87 (0.066)	3.72 (0.087)	0.26 (0.043)	3.46 (0.099)	3.50 (0.083)	0.93 (0.057)	1.35 (0.060)	0.81 (0.049)	0.37 (0.047)	2.31 (0.088)	2.12 (0.232)	2.93 (0.263)	3.26 (0.207)	0.72 (0.119)
Academic track																
Academic[4].........	26.53 (0.092)	4.48 (0.024)	4.09 (0.026)	3.78 (0.017)	0.42 (0.014)	3.36 (0.021)	3.50 (0.021)	0.92 (0.017)	1.35 (0.018)	0.82 (0.010)	0.40 (0.012)	2.20 (0.024)	2.29 (0.043)	2.92 (0.039)	3.27 (0.044)	0.80 (0.018)
Career/technical[5]...	24.01 (0.288)	3.56 (0.064)	2.78 (0.051)	2.42 (0.041)	0.96 (0.062)	1.45 (0.074)	1.87 (0.045)	0.90 (0.057)	0.75 (0.037)	0.16 (0.037)	0.05 (0.021)	0.50 (0.052)	1.32 (0.135)	8.16 (0.215)	3.40 (0.148)	0.77 (0.079)
Both[6]...............	27.93 (0.132)	4.36 (0.024)	3.90 (0.032)	3.63 (0.021)	0.61 (0.026)	3.02 (0.029)	3.17 (0.027)	1.06 (0.030)	1.19 (0.018)	0.62 (0.015)	0.29 (0.016)	1.51 (0.030)	1.34 (0.032)	7.01 (0.091)	3.00 (0.045)	1.42 (0.046)
Neither[7]............	22.73 (0.213)	4.08 (0.096)	2.92 (0.044)	2.44 (0.045)	0.87 (0.057)	1.57 (0.056)	2.01 (0.033)	0.84 (0.045)	0.85 (0.033)	0.21 (0.037)	0.09 (0.021)	1.02 (0.051)	2.35 (0.125)	3.86 (0.128)	4.05 (0.177)	0.64 (0.033)

[1]Includes general labor market preparation, consumer and homemaking education, and occupational education in agriculture, business, marketing, health, occupational home economics, trade and industry, and technical courses.

[2]Includes general skills, personal health and physical education, religion, military sciences, special education, and other courses not included in other subject fields.

[3]Though shown separately here, computer-related courses are also included in the mathematics and career/technical categories.

[4]Includes students who complete at least 12 Carnegie units in academic courses, but less than 3 Carnegie units in any occupational education field.

[5]Includes students who complete at least 3 Carnegie units in an occupational education field, but less than 12 Carnegie units in academic courses.

[6]Includes students who complete at least 12 Carnegie units in academic courses and at least 3 Carnegie units in an occupational education field.

[7]Includes students who complete less than 12 Carnegie units in academic courses and less than 3 Carnegie units in an occupational education field.

NOTE: The Carnegie unit is a standard of measurement that represents one credit for the completion of a 1-year course. Data differ slightly from figures appearing in other NCES reports because of differences in taxonomies and case exclusion criteria. Race categories exclude persons of Hispanic ethnicity. Detail may not sum to totals because of rounding. Standard errors appear in parentheses.

SOURCE: U.S. Department of Education, National Center for Education Statistics, High School and Beyond Longitudinal Study of 1980 Sophomores (HS&B-So:80/82), "High School Transcript Study"; and 1987, 1990, 1994, 1998, 2000, and 2005 High School Transcript Study (HSTS). (This table was prepared January 2007.)

Table 148. Average number of Carnegie units earned by public high school graduates in career/technical education courses, by selected student characteristics: Selected years, 1982 through 2005

Graduation year and selected student characteristic	Total	General labor market preparation	Consumer and homemaking education	Occupational education field								
				Total[1]	Agriculture	Business	Marketing	Health	Occupational home economics	Trade and industrial	Technical/ communications	Other
1	2	3	4	5	6	7	8	9	10	11	12	13
1982 graduates	4.62 (0.061)	0.94 (0.018)	0.68 (0.020)	3.00 (0.052)	0.22 (0.018)	1.03 (0.027)	0.16 (0.011)	0.05 (0.005)	0.11 (0.007)	1.04 (0.035)	0.21 (0.009)	0.10 (0.012)
Sex												
Male	4.60 (0.076)	0.93 (0.026)	0.30 (0.014)	3.36 (0.071)	0.36 (0.033)	0.47 (0.020)	0.14 (0.013)	0.02 (0.004)	0.06 (0.006)	1.96 (0.064)	0.24 (0.014)	0.01 (#)
Female	4.64 (0.072)	0.95 (0.020)	1.03 (0.031)	2.67 (0.056)	0.08 (0.010)	1.55 (0.043)	0.18 (0.015)	0.08 (0.009)	0.15 (0.012)	0.20 (0.016)	0.18 (0.009)	0.18 (0.023)
Race/ethnicity												
White	4.53 (0.071)	0.92 (0.021)	0.63 (0.023)	2.97 (0.059)	0.24 (0.021)	1.06 (0.032)	0.15 (0.012)	0.04 (0.005)	0.10 (0.008)	0.99 (0.038)	0.22 (0.011)	0.09 (0.015)
Black	4.75 (0.136)	0.97 (0.046)	0.90 (0.053)	2.88 (0.130)	0.09 (0.019)	1.00 (0.071)	0.22 (0.031)	0.11 (0.024)	0.14 (0.024)	0.95 (0.091)	0.15 (0.021)	0.12 (0.040)
Hispanic	5.22 (0.111)	1.01 (0.036)	0.85 (0.045)	3.36 (0.106)	0.23 (0.034)	1.00 (0.054)	0.17 (0.020)	0.07 (0.021)	0.13 (0.017)	1.38 (0.094)	0.15 (0.014)	0.12 (0.028)
Asian/Pacific Islander	3.34 (0.226)	1.01 (0.129)	0.30 (0.035)	2.03 (0.157)	0.03 (0.015)	0.58 (0.105)	0.04 (0.023)	0.03 (0.013)	0.06 (0.020)	0.88 (0.095)	0.30 (0.061)	0.02 (0.017)
American Indian/Alaska Native	4.77 (0.233)	0.90 (0.093)	0.47 (0.076)	3.40 (0.257)	0.25 (0.086)	0.74 (0.145)	0.14 (0.045)	0.08 (0.041)	0.06 (0.031)	1.88 (0.441)	0.13 (0.038)	0.03 (0.013)
Academic track												
Academic[2]	2.55 (0.042)	0.84 (0.022)	0.60 (0.025)	1.12 (0.020)	0.04 (0.005)	0.46 (0.017)	0.03 (0.003)	0.02 (0.003)	0.06 (0.006)	0.28 (0.013)	0.17 (0.009)	0.02 (#)
Career/technical[3]	7.74 (0.082)	1.02 (0.034)	0.78 (0.036)	5.94 (0.084)	0.58 (0.056)	1.66 (0.075)	0.33 (0.032)	0.08 (0.016)	0.17 (0.018)	2.43 (0.107)	0.21 (0.019)	0.24 (0.048)
Both[4]	6.03 (0.091)	0.86 (0.025)	0.57 (0.033)	4.60 (0.066)	0.29 (0.040)	1.66 (0.059)	0.29 (0.027)	0.09 (0.012)	0.15 (0.016)	1.57 (0.066)	0.29 (0.021)	0.14 (0.028)
Neither[5]	5.23 (0.137)	1.92 (0.130)	1.62 (0.089)	1.68 (0.042)	0.11 (0.030)	0.74 (0.050)	0.09 (0.018)	0.05 (0.024)	0.13 (0.027)	0.37 (0.039)	0.10 (0.016)	0.07 (0.019)
1987 graduates	4.55 (0.084)	0.83 (0.026)	0.61 (0.032)	3.11 (0.060)	0.19 (0.028)	0.96 (0.037)	0.16 (0.014)	0.08 (0.005)	0.11 (0.008)	0.96 (0.036)	0.43 (0.021)	0.11 (0.013)
Sex												
Male	4.64 (0.089)	0.83 (0.035)	0.33 (0.025)	3.47 (0.065)	0.33 (0.047)	0.56 (0.024)	0.13 (0.014)	0.02 (0.003)	0.08 (0.008)	1.73 (0.072)	0.47 (0.023)	0.03 (0.011)
Female	4.47 (0.094)	0.83 (0.023)	0.86 (0.046)	2.77 (0.067)	0.07 (0.012)	1.34 (0.052)	0.19 (0.019)	0.12 (0.010)	0.14 (0.012)	0.23 (0.021)	0.39 (0.022)	0.18 (0.020)
Race/ethnicity												
White	4.65 (0.107)	0.84 (0.030)	0.60 (0.041)	3.20 (0.074)	0.24 (0.039)	0.97 (0.046)	0.16 (0.017)	0.07 (0.005)	0.11 (0.010)	1.00 (0.047)	0.47 (0.026)	0.10 (0.013)
Black	4.52 (0.130)	0.86 (0.026)	0.73 (0.040)	2.92 (0.113)	0.10 (0.016)	1.00 (0.068)	0.17 (0.021)	0.14 (0.027)	0.14 (0.016)	0.76 (0.053)	0.28 (0.032)	0.14 (0.017)
Hispanic	4.49 (0.169)	0.93 (0.069)	0.62 (0.062)	2.95 (0.101)	0.06 (0.020)	0.97 (0.090)	0.16 (0.037)	0.08 (0.020)	0.11 (0.017)	1.00 (0.054)	0.32 (0.020)	0.11 (0.024)
Asian/Pacific Islander	3.11 (0.221)	0.63 (0.064)	0.35 (0.062)	2.13 (0.141)	0.01 (0.006)	0.63 (0.088)	0.13 (0.076)	0.09 (0.020)	0.08 (0.017)	0.47 (0.047)	0.56 (0.065)	0.04 (0.013)
American Indian/Alaska Native	4.92 (0.125)	0.82 (0.048)	0.65 (0.045)	3.45 (0.112)	0.20 (0.036)	1.04 (0.094)	0.08 (0.041)	0.09 (0.021)	0.11 (0.032)	1.32 (0.079)	0.44 (0.062)	0.03 (0.007)
Academic track												
Academic[2]	2.57 (0.071)	0.76 (0.028)	0.57 (0.034)	1.23 (0.027)	0.02 (0.003)	0.45 (0.015)	0.04 (0.005)	0.02 (0.004)	0.04 (0.004)	0.24 (0.011)	0.37 (0.016)	0.02 (0.003)
Career/technical[3]	8.07 (0.155)	0.90 (0.038)	0.77 (0.040)	6.39 (0.121)	0.59 (0.087)	1.40 (0.087)	0.38 (0.053)	0.18 (0.037)	0.25 (0.034)	2.60 (0.077)	0.35 (0.047)	0.34 (0.049)
Both[4]	6.09 (0.085)	0.86 (0.039)	0.55 (0.040)	4.69 (0.051)	0.30 (0.057)	1.54 (0.061)	0.27 (0.024)	0.11 (0.011)	0.17 (0.015)	1.43 (0.080)	0.56 (0.029)	0.15 (0.024)
Neither[5]	5.10 (0.233)	1.77 (0.155)	1.72 (0.280)	1.62 (0.052)	0.07 (0.022)	0.60 (0.089)	0.09 (0.036)	0.05 (0.018)	0.11 (0.029)	0.37 (0.064)	0.13 (0.026)	0.10 (0.046)
1990 graduates	4.19 (0.079)	0.73 (0.023)	0.57 (0.026)	2.89 (0.065)	0.20 (0.022)	0.88 (0.035)	0.16 (0.012)	0.04 (0.005)	0.10 (0.009)	0.87 (0.040)	0.41 (0.013)	0.10 (0.010)
Sex												
Male	4.32 (0.084)	0.70 (0.025)	0.33 (0.020)	3.28 (0.074)	0.31 (0.039)	0.57 (0.030)	0.14 (0.014)	0.02 (0.004)	0.07 (0.009)	1.59 (0.064)	0.43 (0.016)	0.02 (0.006)
Female	4.08 (0.087)	0.76 (0.025)	0.79 (0.038)	2.53 (0.073)	0.09 (0.015)	1.16 (0.049)	0.18 (0.014)	0.06 (0.009)	0.13 (0.012)	0.22 (0.026)	0.39 (0.014)	0.17 (0.016)
Race/ethnicity												
White	4.22 (0.085)	0.71 (0.029)	0.55 (0.030)	2.97 (0.075)	0.24 (0.027)	0.85 (0.033)	0.16 (0.014)	0.04 (0.006)	0.09 (0.009)	0.95 (0.047)	0.40 (0.015)	0.09 (0.011)
Black	4.41 (0.166)	0.82 (0.035)	0.80 (0.066)	2.79 (0.135)	0.06 (0.010)	1.05 (0.080)	0.17 (0.023)	0.04 (0.014)	0.15 (0.023)	0.64 (0.059)	0.40 (0.036)	0.16 (0.029)
Hispanic	4.12 (0.150)	0.75 (0.048)	0.53 (0.058)	2.85 (0.126)	0.15 (0.034)	0.93 (0.105)	0.19 (0.026)	0.02 (0.007)	0.11 (0.023)	0.75 (0.061)	0.41 (0.048)	0.18 (0.042)
Asian/Pacific Islander	3.07 (0.337)	0.69 (0.124)	0.31 (0.030)	2.07 (0.211)	0.04 (0.017)	0.55 (0.057)	0.05 (0.013)	0.01 (0.005)	0.03 (0.010)	0.72 (0.178)	0.48 (0.032)	0.03 (0.010)
American Indian/Alaska Native	4.62 (0.190)	0.74 (0.141)	0.72 (0.123)	3.16 (0.157)	0.36 (0.113)	0.35 (0.091)	0.15 (0.256)	0.02 (0.021)	0.07 (0.041)	0.95 (0.193)	0.44 (0.098)	0.02 (0.008)
Academic track												
Academic[2]	2.41 (0.048)	0.67 (0.022)	0.55 (0.030)	1.19 (0.022)	0.03 (0.004)	0.46 (0.019)	0.04 (0.004)	0.01 (0.003)	0.04 (0.005)	0.22 (0.011)	0.34 (0.013)	0.02 (0.003)
Career/technical[3]	8.68 (0.179)	1.00 (0.071)	0.74 (0.051)	6.95 (0.171)	0.86 (0.111)	1.22 (0.089)	0.28 (0.056)	0.10 (0.030)	0.26 (0.052)	3.10 (0.231)	0.28 (0.026)	0.30 (0.061)
Both[4]	6.10 (0.056)	0.72 (0.026)	0.57 (0.030)	4.81 (0.048)	0.35 (0.044)	1.47 (0.062)	0.33 (0.027)	0.08 (0.010)	0.16 (0.014)	1.50 (0.060)	0.53 (0.024)	0.19 (0.021)
Neither[5]	5.81 (0.529)	2.81 (0.570)	1.26 (0.232)	1.74 (0.075)	0.10 (0.040)	0.46 (0.054)	0.04 (0.017)	0.04 (0.023)	0.08 (0.032)	0.54 (0.092)	0.32 (0.092)	0.04 (0.020)

See notes at end of table.

Table 148. Average number of Carnegie units earned by public high school graduates in career/technical education courses, by selected student characteristics: Selected years, 1982 through 2005—Continued

Graduation year and selected student characteristic	Total	General labor market preparation	Consumer and homemaking education	Occupational education field								
				Total[1]	Agriculture	Business	Marketing	Health	Occupational home economics	Trade and industrial	Technical/ communications	Other
1	2	3	4	5	6	7	8	9	10	11	12	13
1994 graduates	**3.96** (0.068)	**0.64** (0.021)	**0.52** (0.028)	**2.79** (0.057)	**0.24** (0.023)	**0.88** (0.028)	**0.18** (0.015)	**0.08** (0.007)	**0.13** (0.012)	**0.70** (0.027)	**0.35** (0.017)	**0.09** (0.009)
Sex												
Male	4.13 (0.074)	0.70 (0.026)	0.35 (0.026)	3.08 (0.063)	0.37 (0.036)	0.66 (0.023)	0.14 (0.012)	0.03 (0.004)	0.08 (0.008)	1.25 (0.051)	0.36 (0.020)	0.33 (0.005)
Female	3.80 (0.074)	0.58 (0.021)	0.70 (0.035)	2.52 (0.061)	0.11 (0.013)	1.09 (0.039)	0.22 (0.018)	0.12 (0.012)	0.18 (0.017)	0.17 (0.010)	0.34 (0.017)	0.15 (0.015)
Race/ethnicity												
White	3.96 (0.080)	0.63 (0.026)	0.51 (0.028)	2.81 (0.067)	0.27 (0.031)	0.87 (0.031)	0.19 (0.018)	0.08 (0.009)	0.11 (0.012)	0.72 (0.032)	0.35 (0.021)	0.07 (0.010)
Black	4.29 (0.121)	0.72 (0.050)	0.62 (0.036)	2.94 (0.097)	0.13 (0.028)	1.01 (0.050)	0.20 (0.029)	0.11 (0.020)	0.23 (0.023)	0.60 (0.053)	0.29 (0.025)	0.18 (0.023)
Hispanic	3.87 (0.124)	0.64 (0.037)	0.48 (0.027)	2.75 (0.123)	0.13 (0.022)	0.93 (0.064)	0.15 (0.018)	0.07 (0.011)	0.14 (0.026)	0.65 (0.071)	0.36 (0.028)	0.17 (0.024)
Asian/Pacific Islander	3.01 (0.236)	0.51 (0.043)	0.36 (0.057)	2.13 (0.151)	0.14 (0.053)	0.70 (0.046)	0.11 (0.017)	0.06 (0.009)	0.10 (0.028)	0.50 (0.057)	0.46 (0.029)	0.03 (0.009)
American Indian/Alaska Native	4.26 (0.256)	0.80 (0.104)	0.62 (0.091)	2.84 (0.183)	0.36 (0.147)	0.89 (0.197)	0.05 (0.024)	0.15 (0.071)	0.14 (0.044)	0.57 (0.120)	0.44 (0.076)	0.05 (0.043)
Academic track												
Academic[2]	2.28 (0.045)	0.58 (0.022)	0.49 (0.033)	1.21 (0.020)	0.04 (0.003)	0.51 (0.018)	0.05 (0.005)	0.03 (0.004)	0.05 (0.006)	0.20 (0.008)	0.28 (0.015)	0.02 (0.002)
Career/technical[3]	8.64 (0.214)	1.00 (0.077)	0.78 (0.083)	6.86 (0.237)	0.90 (0.119)	1.17 (0.124)	0.34 (0.068)	0.08 (0.023)	0.26 (0.053)	2.89 (0.203)	0.26 (0.048)	0.29 (0.077)
Both[4]	6.01 (0.059)	0.66 (0.027)	0.54 (0.031)	4.81 (0.042)	0.48 (0.047)	1.41 (0.042)	0.37 (0.031)	0.16 (0.015)	0.23 (0.022)	1.25 (0.056)	0.46 (0.020)	0.18 (0.018)
Neither[5]	6.51 (0.347)	3.91 (0.432)	1.08 (0.157)	1.52 (0.097)	0.05 (0.015)	0.48 (0.092)	0.08 (0.030)	0.02 (0.015)	0.07 (0.026)	0.46 (0.057)	0.16 (0.047)	0.06 (0.033)
1998 graduates	**3.99** (0.098)	**0.61** (0.028)	**0.51** (0.034)	**2.87** (0.074)	**0.20** (0.031)	**0.70** (0.032)	**0.16** (0.014)	**0.14** (0.030)	**0.16** (0.013)	**0.78** (0.042)	**0.51** (0.035)	**0.07** (0.009)
Sex												
Male	4.25 (0.099)	0.67 (0.028)	0.35 (0.029)	3.23 (0.085)	0.27 (0.039)	0.59 (0.029)	0.15 (0.012)	0.06 (0.019)	0.10 (0.011)	1.37 (0.077)	0.53 (0.039)	0.02 (0.003)
Female	3.77 (0.114)	0.57 (0.032)	0.66 (0.041)	2.54 (0.080)	0.14 (0.026)	0.80 (0.038)	0.18 (0.018)	0.22 (0.041)	0.21 (0.019)	0.23 (0.013)	0.49 (0.035)	0.12 (0.017)
Race/ethnicity												
White	3.97 (0.114)	0.58 (0.031)	0.49 (0.039)	2.90 (0.087)	0.24 (0.039)	0.69 (0.035)	0.15 (0.015)	0.11 (0.016)	0.14 (0.011)	0.83 (0.053)	0.51 (0.042)	0.06 (0.010)
Black	4.33 (0.149)	0.70 (0.037)	0.68 (0.062)	2.95 (0.115)	0.09 (0.015)	0.83 (0.072)	0.24 (0.029)	0.29 (0.098)	0.23 (0.048)	0.56 (0.040)	0.47 (0.040)	0.11 (0.021)
Hispanic	3.97 (0.121)	0.66 (0.048)	0.49 (0.060)	2.82 (0.104)	0.16 (0.043)	0.64 (0.052)	0.18 (0.021)	0.16 (0.070)	0.17 (0.025)	0.75 (0.047)	0.51 (0.058)	0.10 (0.026)
Asian/Pacific Islander	3.15 (0.222)	0.58 (0.107)	0.27 (0.033)	2.30 (0.119)	0.09 (0.033)	0.64 (0.040)	0.13 (0.017)	0.15 (0.082)	0.14 (0.021)	0.57 (0.094)	0.49 (0.047)	0.02 (0.005)
American Indian/Alaska Native	4.02 (0.164)	0.54 (0.063)	0.55 (0.083)	2.92 (0.162)	0.19 (0.041)	0.70 (0.084)	0.14 (0.035)	0.06 (0.035)	0.14 (0.044)	0.98 (0.167)	0.51 (0.081)	0.03 (0.014)
Academic track												
Academic[2]	2.22 (0.061)	0.54 (0.028)	0.49 (0.032)	1.19 (0.027)	0.03 (0.004)	0.41 (0.023)	0.05 (0.006)	0.03 (0.004)	0.07 (0.007)	0.22 (0.010)	0.33 (0.024)	0.02 (0.003)
Career/technical[3]	9.12 (0.239)	1.40 (0.180)	0.75 (0.117)	6.97 (0.166)	0.62 (0.123)	0.64 (0.061)	0.29 (0.058)	0.11 (0.032)	0.36 (0.079)	3.36 (0.407)	0.66 (0.091)	0.29 (0.167)
Both[4]	6.06 (0.083)	0.62 (0.032)	0.52 (0.041)	4.92 (0.060)	0.41 (0.067)	1.10 (0.049)	0.31 (0.028)	0.29 (0.067)	0.27 (0.027)	1.39 (0.075)	0.74 (0.050)	0.14 (0.016)
Neither[5]	5.64 (0.598)	2.91 (0.592)	1.20 (0.119)	1.53 (0.144)	0.10 (0.031)	0.43 (0.063)	0.06 (0.024)	0.02 (0.014)	0.07 (0.025)	0.31 (0.080)	0.19 (0.055)	0.06 (0.024)
2000 graduates	**4.21** (0.123)	**0.69** (0.035)	**0.49** (0.023)	**3.03** (0.106)	**0.25** (0.029)	**0.74** (0.040)	**0.16** (0.013)	**0.13** (0.018)	**0.17** (0.016)	**0.80** (0.057)	**0.61** (0.027)	**0.08** (0.009)
Sex												
Male	4.85 (0.154)	0.76 (0.042)	0.33 (0.018)	3.76 (0.135)	0.34 (0.041)	0.65 (0.040)	0.14 (0.013)	0.06 (0.012)	0.12 (0.012)	1.38 (0.098)	0.72 (0.032)	0.02 (0.005)
Female	3.99 (0.104)	0.61 (0.032)	0.64 (0.032)	2.74 (0.086)	0.16 (0.022)	0.83 (0.043)	0.17 (0.015)	0.20 (0.025)	0.23 (0.021)	0.25 (0.020)	0.52 (0.026)	0.13 (0.016)
Race/ethnicity												
White	4.59 (0.164)	0.69 (0.045)	0.49 (0.026)	3.41 (0.137)	0.31 (0.039)	0.73 (0.048)	0.14 (0.015)	0.12 (0.016)	0.18 (0.018)	0.90 (0.077)	0.63 (0.034)	0.07 (0.001)
Black	4.54 (0.173)	0.77 (0.049)	0.67 (0.052)	3.10 (0.125)	0.12 (0.027)	0.88 (0.063)	0.22 (0.034)	0.15 (0.022)	0.16 (0.024)	0.51 (0.043)	0.53 (0.041)	0.16 (0.030)
Hispanic	4.16 (0.124)	0.67 (0.054)	0.37 (0.038)	3.12 (0.148)	0.14 (0.021)	0.75 (0.067)	0.18 (0.032)	0.23 (0.101)	0.19 (0.030)	0.65 (0.051)	0.54 (0.028)	0.07 (0.020)
Asian/Pacific Islander	3.13 (0.160)	0.45 (0.055)	0.25 (0.033)	2.42 (0.146)	0.06 (0.014)	0.50 (0.051)	0.10 (0.031)	0.14 (0.038)	0.09 (0.018)	0.43 (0.054)	0.74 (0.103)	0.02 (0.008)
American Indian/Alaska Native	5.51 (0.429)	0.75 (0.117)	0.68 (0.081)	4.08 (0.394)	0.37 (0.131)	0.72 (0.086)	0.14 (0.037)	0.07 (0.025)	0.23 (0.115)	0.99 (0.235)	0.68 (0.087)	0.07 (0.035)
Academic track												
Academic[2]	2.35 (0.049)	0.61 (0.031)	0.47 (0.021)	1.28 (0.024)	0.03 (0.004)	0.39 (0.021)	0.03 (0.004)	0.03 (0.005)	0.08 (0.009)	0.21 (0.010)	0.38 (0.020)	0.02 (0.003)
Career/technical[3]	10.56 (0.337)	1.24 (0.272)	0.59 (0.070)	8.73 (0.365)	0.79 (0.149)	0.63 (0.117)	0.27 (0.064)	0.12 (0.050)	0.35 (0.086)	4.06 (0.438)	0.87 (0.095)	0.14 (0.057)
Both[4]	6.84 (0.170)	0.75 (0.053)	0.50 (0.031)	5.59 (0.132)	0.51 (0.058)	1.20 (0.066)	0.31 (0.025)	0.27 (0.041)	0.29 (0.029)	1.43 (0.115)	0.90 (0.047)	0.15 (0.018)
Neither[5]	5.82 (0.443)	2.83 (0.297)	1.36 (0.331)	1.62 (0.100)	0.05 (0.023)	0.13 (0.032)	0.05 (0.034)	0.04 (0.030)	0.19 (0.053)	0.40 (0.077)	0.32 (0.049)	0.06 (0.023)

See notes at end of table.

Table 148. Average number of Carnegie units earned by public high school graduates in career/technical education courses, by selected student characteristics: Selected years, 1982 through 2005—Continued

Graduation year and selected student characteristic	Total	General labor market preparation	Consumer and homemaking education	Occupational education field								
				Total[1]	Agriculture	Business	Marketing	Health	Occupational home economics	Trade and industrial	Technical/ communications	Other
1	2	3	4	5	6	7	8	9	10	11	12	13
2005 graduates	**4.01** (0.058)	**0.46** (0.021)	**0.51** (0.015)	**3.03** (0.047)	**0.23** (0.014)	**0.60** (0.016)	**0.15** (0.010)	**0.15** (0.010)	**0.23** (0.012)	**0.69** (0.022)	**0.79** (0.020)	**0.07** (0.004)
Sex												
Male	4.35 (0.059)	0.52 (0.025)	0.34 (0.015)	3.49 (0.051)	0.32 (0.020)	0.58 (0.017)	0.15 (0.011)	0.06 (0.006)	0.16 (0.009)	1.19 (0.036)	0.90 (0.022)	0.02 (0.003)
Female	3.68 (0.068)	0.41 (0.020)	0.68 (0.020)	2.59 (0.053)	0.15 (0.012)	0.62 (0.018)	0.15 (0.010)	0.23 (0.016)	0.30 (0.017)	0.22 (0.011)	0.68 (0.021)	0.13 (0.007)
Race/ethnicity												
White	4.12 (0.075)	0.46 (0.024)	0.53 (0.019)	3.13 (0.061)	0.29 (0.017)	0.58 (0.018)	0.15 (0.012)	0.13 (0.011)	0.22 (0.014)	0.78 (0.029)	0.80 (0.024)	0.07 (0.005)
Black	4.11 (0.111)	0.50 (0.036)	0.60 (0.033)	3.01 (0.079)	0.10 (0.018)	0.76 (0.036)	0.18 (0.015)	0.24 (0.022)	0.27 (0.029)	0.44 (0.026)	0.81 (0.047)	0.10 (0.012)
Hispanic	3.69 (0.098)	0.45 (0.029)	0.43 (0.026)	2.81 (0.089)	0.14 (0.018)	0.62 (0.033)	0.14 (0.015)	0.15 (0.020)	0.26 (0.029)	0.63 (0.042)	0.69 (0.027)	0.09 (0.010)
Asian/Pacific Islander	2.91 (0.144)	0.33 (0.046)	0.31 (0.029)	2.27 (0.119)	0.06 (0.019)	0.43 (0.038)	0.13 (0.023)	0.10 (0.022)	0.16 (0.019)	0.47 (0.075)	0.83 (0.047)	0.05 (0.010)
American Indian/Alaska Native	4.20 (0.258)	0.67 (0.170)	0.62 (0.081)	2.91 (0.178)	0.45 (0.129)	0.47 (0.074)	0.08 (0.033)	0.10 (0.029)	0.23 (0.045)	0.57 (0.094)	0.78 (0.110)	0.11 (0.048)
Other	2.93 (0.263)	0.32 (0.047)	0.33 (0.044)	2.28 (0.233)	0.13 (0.086)	0.45 (0.098)	0.20 (0.058)	0.05 (0.023)	0.24 (0.070)	0.29 (0.058)	0.83 (0.109)	0.03 (0.016)
Academic track												
Academic[2]	2.92 (0.039)	0.40 (0.021)	0.53 (0.017)	1.99 (0.026)	0.09 (0.005)	0.48 (0.011)	0.09 (0.006)	0.07 (0.005)	0.19 (0.012)	0.31 (0.011)	0.67 (0.016)	0.04 (0.002)
Career/technical[3]	8.16 (0.215)	1.07 (0.155)	0.45 (0.044)	6.63 (0.168)	0.93 (0.167)	0.56 (0.066)	0.22 (0.066)	0.20 (0.054)	0.47 (0.081)	3.19 (0.215)	0.56 (0.062)	0.19 (0.073)
Both[4]	7.01 (0.091)	0.56 (0.033)	0.44 (0.019)	6.01 (0.081)	0.61 (0.044)	0.99 (0.038)	0.32 (0.024)	0.40 (0.032)	0.34 (0.029)	1.67 (0.053)	1.20 (0.046)	0.16 (0.013)
Neither[5]	3.86 (0.128)	0.85 (0.084)	0.76 (0.044)	2.24 (0.080)	0.25 (0.044)	0.38 (0.025)	0.14 (0.023)	0.07 (0.013)	0.23 (0.025)	0.49 (0.031)	0.52 (0.032)	0.08 (0.016)

#Rounds to zero.
[1]Includes unclassified courses not shown separately.
[2]Includes students who complete at least 12 Carnegie units in academic courses, but less than 3 Carnegie units in any occupational education field.
[3]Includes students who complete at least 3 Carnegie units in an occupational education field, but less than 12 Carnegie units in academic courses.
[4]Includes students who complete at least 12 Carnegie units in academic courses and at least 3 Carnegie units in an occupational education field.
[5]Includes students who complete less than 12 Carnegie units in academic courses and less than 3 Carnegie units in an occupational education field.

NOTE: The Carnegie unit is a standard of measurement that represents one credit for the completion of a 1-year course. Data differ slightly from figures appearing in other NCES reports because of differences in taxonomies and case exclusion criteria. Race categories exclude persons of Hispanic ethnicity. Detail may not sum to totals because of rounding. Standard errors appear in parentheses.
SOURCE: U.S. Department of Education, National Center for Education Statistics, High School and Beyond Longitudinal Study of 1980 Sophomores (HS&B-So:80/82), "High School Transcript Study"; and 1987, 1990, 1994, 1998, 2000, and 2005 High School Transcript Study (HSTS). (This table was prepared January 2007.)

Table 149. Percentage of public and private high school graduates taking selected mathematics and science courses in high school, by sex and race/ethnicity: Selected years, 1982 through 2005

Course (Carnegie units)	1982	1987	1990	1994	1998	2000	2005									
									Sex		Race/ethnicity					
							Total	Male	Female	White	Black	Hispanic	Asian/Pacific Islander	American Indian/ Alaska Native	Other
1	2	3	4	5	6	7	8	9	10	11	12	13	14	15	16
Mathematics¹															
Any mathematics (1.0)	98.5 (0.21)	98.9 (0.24)	99.9 (0.05)	99.8 (0.05)	99.8 (0.06)	99.8 (0.04)	99.9 (0.02)	99.9 (0.03)	100.0 (†)	99.9 (0.02)	100.0 (†)	99.9 (0.05)	100.0 (†)	100.0 (†)	100.0 (†)
Algebra I (1.0)²	55.2 (1.01)	58.8 (1.19)	63.7 (1.54)	65.8 (1.31)	62.8 (1.42)	61.7 (1.66)	62.8 (1.04)	61.5 (1.05)	64.1 (1.13)	60.9 (1.19)	71.8 (1.67)	65.6 (1.73)	58.0 (2.61)	67.9 (4.89)	69.3 (3.49)
Geometry (1.0)	47.1 (0.99)	58.6 (0.97)	63.2 (1.38)	70.0 (1.26)	75.1 (1.06)	78.3 (1.09)	83.3 (0.65)	81.4 (0.71)	85.2 (0.68)	83.4 (0.80)	84.7 (1.03)	80.5 (1.18)	86.1 (1.31)	74.2 (3.20)	89.2 (2.04)
Algebra II (0.5)³	39.9 (0.93)	49.0 (1.69)	52.9 (1.32)	61.1 (1.39)	61.7 (1.77)	67.8 (1.43)	70.3 (1.00)	67.1 (1.11)	73.3 (1.02)	71.2 (1.21)	69.2 (1.64)	62.7 (1.54)	78.3 (3.40)	67.5 (3.58)	81.8 (3.43)
Trigonometry (0.5)	8.1 (0.54)	11.5 (1.54)	9.6 (1.07)	11.7 (1.16)	8.9 (1.07)	7.5 (1.31)	8.3 (0.88)	8.1 (0.91)	8.6 (0.91)	9.6 (1.18)	3.9 (0.59)	4.8 (0.83)	9.4 (1.59)	10.4 (4.80)	13.9 (3.18)
Analysis/pre-calculus (0.5)	6.2 (0.46)	12.8 (0.92)	13.3 (0.95)	17.3 (0.86)	23.1 (1.44)	26.7 (1.40)	29.5 (0.98)	28.0 (1.02)	30.8 (1.05)	32.0 (1.18)	17.9 (1.61)	20.5 (1.42)	48.8 (2.85)	15.9 (3.04)	31.6 (5.16)
Statistics/probability (0.5)	1.0 (0.16)	1.1 (0.31)	1.0 (0.21)	2.0 (0.33)	3.7 (0.54)	5.7 (0.86)	7.7 (0.53)	7.7 (0.57)	7.8 (0.55)	8.5 (0.65)	5.8 (0.84)	3.4 (0.48)	13.0 (1.21)	2.8 (0.99)	12.0 (3.04)
Calculus (1.0)	5.0 (0.43)	6.1 (0.49)	6.5 (0.46)	9.3 (0.56)	11.0 (0.85)	11.6 (0.73)	13.6 (0.53)	14.0 (0.63)	13.2 (0.59)	15.3 (0.62)	5.5 (0.53)	6.3 (0.65)	29.8 (1.65)	7.9 (2.59)	16.6 (2.49)
AP calculus (1.0)	1.6 (0.26)	3.4 (0.47)	4.1 (0.44)	7.0 (0.53)	6.7 (0.49)	7.9 (0.58)	9.2 (0.44)	9.8 (0.54)	8.7 (0.44)	10.1 (0.52)	2.9 (0.35)	5.0 (0.51)	24.6 (1.75)	2.8 (1.42)	10.9 (1.78)
Science¹															
Any science (1.0)	96.4 (0.39)	97.8 (0.32)	99.3 (0.14)	99.5 (0.07)	99.5 (0.09)	99.5 (0.11)	99.6 (0.09)	99.5 (0.11)	99.6 (0.10)	99.7 (0.07)	99.7 (0.12)	99.1 (0.30)	99.3 (0.34)	98.3 (0.73)	100.0 (†)
Biology (1.0)	77.4 (0.87)	86.1 (1.01)	90.9 (0.97)	93.2 (0.97)	92.7 (0.67)	91.2 (1.00)	92.3 (0.63)	90.8 (0.71)	93.7 (0.61)	92.6 (0.72)	93.6 (0.59)	89.1 (1.24)	92.1 (1.83)	92.1 (1.80)	93.9 (2.41)
AP/honors biology (1.0)	10.0 (0.64)	9.4 (0.72)	10.1 (1.02)	11.9 (0.93)	16.2 (1.31)	16.3 (1.46)	16.0 (0.83)	13.9 (0.81)	18.0 (0.94)	17.0 (0.99)	12.0 (1.37)	11.8 (1.38)	24.0 (2.14)	8.3 (1.87)	21.6 (3.61)
Chemistry (1.0)	32.1 (0.84)	44.2 (1.29)	48.9 (1.23)	55.8 (1.04)	60.4 (1.29)	62.0 (1.47)	66.2 (0.92)	62.5 (1.04)	69.7 (0.99)	67.1 (1.04)	63.6 (1.61)	59.2 (2.13)	79.4 (1.60)	49.3 (4.75)	77.8 (3.11)
AP/honors chemistry (1.0)	3.0 (0.33)	3.5 (0.42)	3.5 (0.47)	3.9 (0.53)	4.7 (0.50)	5.8 (0.85)	7.6 (0.53)	7.6 (0.59)	7.6 (0.55)	8.0 (0.58)	4.0 (0.98)	5.7 (0.82)	17.2 (1.41)	4.8 (1.67)	10.5 (2.57)
Physics (1.0)	15.0 (0.62)	20.0 (0.88)	21.5 (0.81)	24.5 (0.87)	28.8 (1.49)	31.4 (1.16)	32.7 (0.92)	34.8 (0.91)	30.8 (1.11)	34.6 (0.88)	25.8 (2.31)	23.3 (1.68)	49.9 (2.42)	18.2 (3.91)	42.7 (4.08)
AP/honors physics (1.0)	1.2 (0.17)	1.8 (0.30)	2.0 (0.38)	2.7 (0.34)	3.0 (0.37)	3.9 (0.61)	5.3 (0.33)	6.6 (0.42)	4.1 (0.34)	5.6 (0.41)	2.5 (0.37)	3.4 (0.50)	14.2 (1.64)	1.5 (0.89)	8.3 (2.24)
Engineering (1.0)	1.2 (0.21)	2.6 (0.63)	4.2 (1.01)	4.5 (0.78)	6.7 (1.75)	3.9 (0.91)	4.3 (0.51)	4.6 (0.59)	4.0 (0.47)	4.4 (0.62)	4.8 (0.87)	3.3 (0.58)	3.7 (1.11)	3.8 (2.15)	4.2 (1.58)
Astronomy (0.5)	1.2 (0.24)	1.0 (0.17)	1.2 (0.31)	1.7 (0.50)	1.9 (0.46)	2.8 (0.59)	2.8 (0.37)	2.9 (0.42)	2.7 (0.34)	3.3 (0.47)	1.4 (0.24)	1.2 (0.25)	3.1 (0.68)	3.5 (1.61)	1.2 (1.19)
Geology/earth science (0.5)	13.6 (1.04)	13.4 (1.66)	24.7 (2.42)	22.9 (2.41)	20.7 (2.34)	17.4 (1.86)	23.1 (1.48)	23.9 (1.51)	22.4 (1.54)	24.0 (1.86)	24.3 (1.88)	19.6 (1.67)	16.2 (2.39)	22.7 (4.39)	23.2 (4.80)
Biology and chemistry (2.0)	29.3 (0.83)	41.4 (1.22)	47.5 (1.23)	53.7 (1.20)	59.0 (1.22)	59.4 (1.49)	64.3 (0.97)	60.3 (1.08)	68.0 (1.03)	65.3 (1.10)	62.0 (1.60)	57.2 (2.29)	75.5 (2.16)	48.0 (4.74)	73.9 (3.97)
Biology, chemistry, and physics (3.0)	11.2 (0.51)	16.5 (0.77)	18.8 (0.70)	21.4 (0.84)	25.4 (1.32)	25.1 (1.09)	27.3 (0.88)	28.2 (0.85)	26.5 (1.10)	29.0 (0.85)	21.3 (2.25)	18.9 (1.63)	42.8 (2.49)	14.1 (3.33)	33.2 (4.02)

†Not applicable.

¹These data only report the percentage of students who earned the indicated credit (0.5 = one semester; 1.0 = one academic year) in each course while in high school and do not count those students who took these courses prior to entering high school.

²Excludes pre-algebra.

³Includes algebra/trigonometry and algebra/geometry.

NOTE: The Carnegie unit is a standard of measurement that represents one credit for the completion of a 1-year course. Data differ slightly from figures appearing in other NCES reports because of differences in taxonomies and case exclusion criteria.

Some data have been revised from previously published figures. Race categories exclude persons of Hispanic ethnicity. Standard errors appear in parentheses.

SOURCE: U.S. Department of Education, National Center for Education Statistics, High School and Beyond Longitudinal Study of 1980 Sophomores (HS&B-So:80/82), "High School Transcript Study"; and 1987, 1990, 1994, 1998, 2000, and 2005 High School Transcript Study (HSTS). (This table was prepared January 2007.)

Table 150. Percentage distribution of public and private high school graduates, by highest level of mathematics and science course completed and selected student characteristics: 2003–04

Student characteristic	Highest level mathematics course taken since 9th grade[1]					Highest level science course taken since 9th grade[2]							
	Level 1	Level 2	Level 3	Level 4	Level 5	Level 1	Level 2	Level 3	Level 4	Level 5	Level 6	Level 7	Level 8
	2	3	4	5	6	7	8	9	10	11	12	13	14
Total	0.6 (0.10)	4.8 (0.33)	44.6 (0.91)	36.1 (0.82)	13.9 (0.53)	0.6 (0.09)	2.2 (0.28)	3.4 (0.36)	25.4 (0.87)	33.3 (0.89)	17.1 (0.82)	9.6 (0.54)	8.5 (0.51)
Sex													
Male	0.7 (0.15)	5.9 (0.45)	45.2 (1.07)	33.6 (0.94)	14.5 (0.71)	0.8 (0.15)	2.8 (0.42)	3.9 (0.42)	27.0 (0.99)	29.8 (0.96)	17.9 (0.88)	8.1 (0.63)	9.7 (0.63)
Female	0.4 (0.10)	3.8 (0.38)	44.0 (1.09)	38.5 (1.03)	13.2 (0.64)	0.3 (0.08)	1.6 (0.23)	2.9 (0.40)	23.8 (1.02)	36.6 (1.09)	16.3 (0.96)	11.1 (0.65)	7.3 (0.57)
Race/ethnicity[3]													
White	0.5 (0.11)	4.2 (0.36)	41.0 (1.09)	38.3 (0.97)	16.0 (0.67)	0.5 (0.09)	1.9 (0.33)	3.1 (0.39)	23.9 (1.06)	32.1 (1.05)	18.2 (0.97)	11.0 (0.70)	9.4 (0.64)
Black	1.3 (0.42)	5.6 (0.96)	51.3 (2.15)	37.0 (2.15)	4.7 (0.67)	0.9 (0.31)	2.3 (0.71)	2.6 (0.64)	31.2 (1.83)	39.8 (2.16)	12.4 (1.66)	6.5 (1.06)	4.3 (0.80)
Hispanic	0.3 (0.16)	6.7 (1.05)	58.6 (1.87)	27.5 (1.73)	6.8 (0.84)	0.7 (0.25)	3.5 (0.73)	4.7 (0.99)	30.9 (1.87)	35.9 (1.87)	15.5 (1.77)	5.5 (0.77)	3.3 (0.54)
Asian/Pacific Islander	0.4 (0.25)	1.8 (0.43)	28.7 (2.37)	35.6 (2.21)	33.4 (2.45)	0.5 (0.27)	1.7 (0.46)	1.3 (0.41)	12.8 (1.46)	25.9 (1.83)	19.0 (1.76)	13.4 (1.34)	25.4 (2.26)
American Indian/Alaska Native	2.4 (2.42)	12.9 (4.68)	62.9 (6.17)	16.1 (5.19)	5.6 (2.65)	† (†)	5.7 (2.96)	4.6 (3.01)	41.9 (8.84)	28.2 (6.50)	12.3 (5.40)	5.3 (2.73)	2.0 (1.12)
Socioeconomic status													
Lowest quarter	1.4 (0.31)	9.2 (0.81)	57.6 (1.39)	25.6 (1.23)	6.2 (0.67)	1.2 (0.27)	3.9 (0.57)	5.1 (0.77)	35.9 (1.53)	33.1 (1.43)	9.2 (0.90)	8.0 (0.80)	3.6 (0.52)
Middle two quarters	0.5 (0.12)	4.7 (0.43)	49.1 (1.05)	35.6 (0.96)	10.0 (0.51)	0.5 (0.11)	2.2 (0.34)	3.8 (0.44)	27.7 (1.12)	34.4 (1.10)	15.9 (0.87)	9.9 (0.65)	5.7 (0.51)
Highest quarter	0.2 (0.09)	1.6 (0.36)	26.9 (1.14)	44.9 (1.26)	26.4 (1.07)	0.2 (0.11)	1.1 (0.30)	1.4 (0.33)	13.4 (0.87)	31.4 (1.30)	25.0 (1.31)	10.3 (0.83)	17.1 (1.04)
Native language[4]													
English	0.6 (0.10)	4.5 (0.33)	43.7 (0.96)	37.4 (0.87)	13.8 (0.56)	0.5 (0.09)	2.1 (0.30)	3.4 (0.36)	24.9 (0.90)	33.7 (0.92)	17.3 (0.85)	9.8 (0.57)	8.3 (0.51)
Non-English	0.5 (0.19)	6.5 (0.92)	50.6 (2.00)	27.9 (1.50)	14.5 (1.23)	0.7 (0.22)	3.0 (0.65)	3.5 (0.77)	28.8 (1.81)	30.2 (1.72)	15.2 (1.51)	8.5 (0.96)	10.2 (1.11)
Parents' education													
High school or less	1.2 (0.26)	8.2 (0.71)	56.0 (1.20)	27.3 (1.06)	7.3 (0.66)	1.0 (0.22)	4.1 (0.56)	4.9 (0.67)	34.5 (1.42)	33.3 (1.32)	9.7 (0.88)	8.8 (0.77)	3.7 (0.50)
Some college	0.6 (0.15)	5.2 (0.52)	51.0 (1.23)	34.7 (1.13)	8.6 (0.57)	0.5 (0.12)	1.8 (0.37)	3.9 (0.55)	28.9 (1.19)	34.8 (1.17)	15.4 (0.91)	9.2 (0.74)	5.5 (0.54)
4-year college degree or more	0.2 (0.08)	2.5 (0.36)	32.8 (1.11)	42.5 (1.10)	22.0 (0.89)	0.4 (0.12)	1.4 (0.29)	2.1 (0.35)	17.2 (0.87)	32.0 (1.12)	22.7 (1.13)	10.4 (0.68)	13.7 (0.83)
Family composition													
Mother and father	0.3 (0.07)	3.9 (0.37)	40.3 (1.05)	38.2 (0.95)	17.3 (0.68)	0.4 (0.09)	1.8 (0.27)	3.1 (0.39)	21.6 (0.97)	32.7 (1.03)	19.9 (0.95)	10.2 (0.65)	10.3 (0.65)
Mother or father and guardian	1.0 (0.34)	4.9 (0.66)	52.1 (1.68)	34.6 (1.56)	7.4 (0.73)	0.7 (0.22)	2.7 (0.52)	4.0 (0.63)	31.7 (1.57)	34.9 (1.54)	11.4 (1.08)	9.4 (0.87)	5.4 (0.82)
Single parent (mother or father)	0.9 (0.23)	6.8 (0.69)	50.4 (1.38)	32.7 (1.34)	9.3 (0.76)	0.9 (0.22)	2.9 (0.53)	3.7 (0.58)	30.3 (1.28)	34.3 (1.38)	13.3 (1.09)	8.4 (0.80)	6.3 (0.62)
Other	1.7 (0.98)	10.4 (2.26)	57.8 (3.23)	24.8 (2.68)	5.4 (1.44)	2.0 (1.01)	4.5 (1.44)	4.4 (1.23)	38.4 (3.02)	30.2 (2.95)	11.5 (1.86)	6.3 (1.61)	2.6 (0.91)
Extracurricular participation													
No participation	1.2 (0.26)	8.9 (0.75)	55.7 (1.38)	29.1 (1.37)	5.0 (0.54)	0.9 (0.21)	3.6 (0.56)	6.2 (0.77)	35.6 (1.30)	31.5 (1.26)	11.1 (0.86)	7.6 (0.85)	3.6 (0.55)
Less than 1 hour a week	0.6 (0.24)	4.9 (0.87)	47.9 (1.84)	35.5 (1.72)	11.1 (0.99)	0.5 (0.28)	2.8 (0.55)	2.3 (0.57)	28.2 (1.87)	33.7 (1.79)	14.8 (1.46)	9.7 (1.05)	8.1 (1.08)
1 to 4 hours a week	0.3 (0.17)	3.5 (0.46)	42.6 (1.47)	38.7 (1.51)	14.9 (0.90)	0.2 (0.10)	2.1 (0.44)	2.8 (0.44)	21.8 (1.20)	34.6 (1.41)	19.7 (1.36)	9.9 (0.82)	8.9 (0.80)
More than 4 hours a week	0.1 (0.08)	1.9 (0.29)	36.4 (1.15)	40.9 (1.13)	20.7 (0.89)	0.2 (0.08)	1.1 (0.23)	2.0 (0.35)	18.2 (1.02)	34.0 (1.14)	21.3 (1.08)	11.0 (0.73)	12.2 (0.71)
Employment													
No employment	0.3 (0.13)	5.4 (0.65)	41.7 (1.50)	34.6 (1.29)	18.0 (1.03)	0.4 (0.15)	2.2 (0.42)	3.2 (0.52)	22.4 (1.21)	32.1 (1.28)	18.8 (1.18)	9.7 (0.79)	11.1 (0.85)
1 to 15 hours a week	0.5 (0.17)	3.3 (0.40)	36.9 (1.26)	40.5 (1.20)	18.7 (0.89)	0.4 (0.12)	1.9 (0.33)	2.7 (0.42)	19.3 (1.33)	32.8 (1.30)	20.5 (1.13)	11.1 (0.83)	10.8 (0.82)
More than 15 hours a week	0.5 (0.15)	4.4 (0.43)	50.6 (1.05)	35.3 (1.01)	9.1 (0.58)	0.3 (0.10)	2.2 (0.40)	3.9 (0.48)	29.4 (1.08)	34.7 (1.10)	14.5 (0.87)	8.9 (0.71)	6.0 (0.55)
School control													
Public	0.6 (0.11)	5.2 (0.36)	46.4 (0.98)	34.9 (0.88)	12.8 (0.55)	0.6 (0.09)	2.4 (0.31)	3.6 (0.39)	26.5 (0.94)	33.3 (0.95)	16.0 (0.86)	9.6 (0.57)	8.0 (0.54)
Catholic	0.1 (0.10)	0.3 (0.12)	24.8 (2.68)	52.4 (2.57)	22.4 (1.84)	0.2 (0.19)	0.4 (0.35)	1.5 (0.74)	15.2 (2.37)	31.5 (2.70)	30.1 (3.00)	9.3 (1.62)	11.7 (1.15)
Other private	0.3 (0.23)	0.1 (0.07)	23.8 (3.01)	45.4 (3.01)	30.4 (3.98)	† (†)	† (†)	0.6 (0.25)	10.3 (2.12)	33.1 (3.72)	28.9 (4.74)	9.5 (2.09)	17.6 (3.33)
Mixed[5]	† (†)	0.3 (0.26)	46.0 (5.07)	43.3 (5.23)	10.4 (3.79)	† (†)	† (†)	0.5 (0.47)	17.1 (3.13)	46.5 (4.86)	15.0 (3.19)	14.2 (4.43)	6.6 (2.44)
School location													
Urban	0.8 (0.25)	4.0 (0.56)	40.2 (1.78)	41.0 (1.74)	14.0 (1.06)	0.6 (0.18)	2.0 (0.55)	1.9 (0.52)	20.9 (1.50)	36.3 (1.68)	20.0 (1.69)	8.3 (0.93)	10.0 (0.94)
Suburban	0.5 (0.12)	4.6 (0.47)	44.7 (1.27)	35.1 (1.04)	15.2 (0.77)	0.5 (0.12)	2.3 (0.37)	3.9 (0.53)	24.9 (1.17)	31.6 (1.24)	17.1 (1.10)	10.3 (0.80)	9.4 (0.81)
Rural	0.5 (0.16)	6.2 (0.77)	48.3 (2.02)	33.6 (1.98)	11.4 (1.08)	0.6 (0.17)	2.1 (0.68)	4.0 (0.91)	31.1 (2.49)	33.6 (2.09)	13.8 (1.77)	10.0 (1.26)	4.9 (0.71)
Mixed[5]	0.4 (0.38)	7.7 (1.93)	62.1 (3.36)	23.6 (2.59)	6.3 (1.56)	1.4 (0.72)	3.3 (1.15)	4.7 (1.48)	39.3 (3.18)	30.9 (3.11)	9.6 (2.10)	7.9 (1.74)	3.0 (0.81)
School region[6]													
Northeast	0.6 (0.23)	5.0 (0.85)	41.7 (2.32)	35.0 (2.00)	17.7 (1.45)	0.5 (0.15)	2.4 (0.93)	5.3 (1.20)	20.6 (1.89)	30.7 (1.98)	22.3 (2.01)	7.7 (1.04)	10.4 (1.22)
Midwest	0.6 (0.21)	5.0 (0.66)	41.7 (1.65)	39.4 (1.14)	13.3 (0.89)	0.5 (0.16)	1.8 (0.41)	3.5 (0.71)	25.3 (1.93)	30.4 (1.83)	17.5 (1.57)	11.3 (1.23)	9.7 (1.16)
South	0.8 (0.19)	4.2 (0.46)	43.0 (1.35)	38.8 (1.14)	13.3 (0.84)	0.7 (0.15)	1.1 (0.27)	2.3 (0.44)	25.8 (1.25)	37.7 (1.54)	15.6 (1.40)	9.3 (0.85)	7.7 (0.75)
West	0.2 (0.09)	5.4 (0.81)	52.8 (2.24)	29.4 (1.90)	12.2 (1.22)	0.6 (0.22)	4.3 (0.79)	3.3 (0.65)	28.9 (2.06)	32.1 (1.84)	14.3 (1.67)	9.8 (1.22)	6.7 (1.02)
Mixed[5]	† (†)	4.5 (4.40)	50.2 (8.23)	37.3 (8.40)	7.9 (4.09)	† (†)	† (†)	8.6 (5.76)	22.4 (6.14)	27.9 (7.74)	21.2 (6.66)	7.2 (3.25)	12.7 (6.74)

† Not applicable.

[1] Level 1 = no math; Level 2 = basic math/prealgebra; Level 3 = core secondary through algebra II; Level 4 = trigonometry, statistics, precalculus; and Level 5 = calculus.

[2] Level 1 = no science; Level 2 = primary physical science; Level 3 = secondary physical science and basic biology; Level 4 = general biology; Level 5 = chemistry I or physics I; Level 6 = chemistry I and physics I; Level 7 = chemistry II or physics II or advanced biology; Level 8 = both Levels 6 and 7.

[3] Race categories exclude persons of Hispanic ethnicity.

[4] The first language students learned to speak when they were children.

[5] Transfer students were classified as "mixed" if their base-year school and their transfer school were in different categories (e.g., a Catholic school student who transferred to a public school or a student who transferred from an urban to a rural school).

[6] Region is defined by the U.S. Census Bureau based on the state in which the school is located.

NOTE: Highest mathematics and science courses taken are based on a taxonomy of course types for which the student received a nonzero credit while in high school. Detail may not sum to totals because of rounding. The academic year extended from September 1, 2003, to August 31, 2004. Standard errors appear in parentheses.

SOURCE: U.S. Department of Education, National Center for Education Statistics, *Academic Pathways, Preparation, and Performances: A Descriptive Overview of the Transcripts From the High School Graduating Class of 2003–04*, Education Longitudinal Study of 2002 (ELS:2002), "High School Transcript Study." (This table was prepared May 2007.)

Table 151. Percentage of public and private high school graduates earning minimum credits in selected combinations of academic courses, by sex and race/ethnicity: Selected years, 1982 through 2005

Year of graduation and course combination taken[1]	All students		Sex				Race/ethnicity									
			Male		Female		White		Black		Hispanic		Asian/Pacific Islander		American Indian/Alaska Native		Other
1	2		3		4		5		6		7		8		9		10
1982 graduates																
4 Eng, 3 SS, 3 Sci, 3 Math, .5 Comp, and 2 FL[2]	2.0	(0.22)	2.3	(0.31)	1.8	(0.27)	2.4	(0.28)	0.7	(0.28)	0.6	(0.22)	5.8	(1.72)	1.1	(0.77)	— (†)
4 Eng, 3 SS, 3 Sci, 3 Math, and 2 FL	9.5	(0.57)	9.1	(0.70)	9.9	(0.71)	10.9	(0.69)	5.2	(1.02)	3.9	(0.57)	17.0	(2.49)	3.3	(1.68)	— (†)
4 Eng, 3 SS, 3 Sci, 3 Math	14.3	(0.66)	15.2	(0.86)	13.4	(0.79)	15.9	(0.79)	11.0	(1.39)	6.7	(0.79)	21.1	(2.65)	8.1	(3.02)	— (†)
4 Eng, 3 SS, 2 Sci, 2 Math	31.5	(1.07)	31.7	(1.26)	31.3	(1.22)	32.4	(1.21)	30.8	(2.32)	25.6	(1.76)	32.0	(3.40)	23.6	(5.39)	— (†)
1987 graduates																
4 Eng, 3 SS, 3 Sci, 3 Math, .5 Comp, and 2 FL[2]	10.6	(0.73)	11.5	(1.01)	9.8	(0.65)	11.3	(0.97)	6.6	(0.91)	5.5	(1.03)	20.5	(2.57)	2.5	(0.86)	— (†)
4 Eng, 3 SS, 3 Sci, 3 Math, and 2 FL	18.1	(0.91)	18.0	(1.13)	18.3	(1.01)	19.0	(1.10)	12.7	(1.15)	10.8	(1.70)	35.7	(4.49)	4.9	(1.40)	— (†)
4 Eng, 3 SS, 3 Sci, 3 Math	24.8	(1.03)	25.9	(1.27)	23.7	(1.07)	26.1	(1.21)	19.6	(1.99)	14.5	(1.69)	39.8	(4.51)	24.3	(3.69)	— (†)
4 Eng, 3 SS, 2 Sci, 2 Math	48.1	(1.74)	48.0	(2.22)	48.4	(1.56)	48.1	(2.15)	48.3	(2.63)	43.9	(1.92)	57.9	(4.82)	61.8	(5.56)	— (†)
1990 graduates																
4 Eng, 3 SS, 3 Sci, 3 Math, .5 Comp, and 2 FL[2]	18.0	(1.06)	17.8	(1.16)	18.2	(1.09)	18.6	(1.21)	15.1	(1.66)	17.8	(2.42)	23.3	(2.23)	7.8	(3.33)	— (†)
4 Eng, 3 SS, 3 Sci, 3 Math, and 2 FL	29.9	(1.26)	28.8	(1.38)	31.0	(1.36)	31.7	(1.46)	22.9	(2.27)	25.4	(2.41)	42.6	(2.95)	9.9	(3.70)	— (†)
4 Eng, 3 SS, 3 Sci, 3 Math	38.2	(1.50)	38.5	(1.69)	37.9	(1.54)	39.2	(1.63)	39.0	(3.57)	29.8	(2.51)	47.4	(3.04)	19.2	(4.70)	— (†)
4 Eng, 3 SS, 2 Sci, 2 Math	65.5	(1.96)	64.3	(2.09)	66.4	(1.98)	64.9	(2.28)	71.3	(3.00)	63.7	(3.01)	69.1	(3.90)	46.3	(6.39)	— (†)
1994 graduates																
4 Eng, 3 SS, 3 Sci, 3 Math, .5 Comp, and 2 FL[2]	25.1	(1.05)	23.4	(0.93)	26.8	(1.32)	26.4	(1.19)	19.0	(1.45)	27.1	(3.75)	35.5	(2.84)	12.9	(3.09)	— (†)
4 Eng, 3 SS, 3 Sci, 3 Math, and 2 FL	39.0	(1.12)	35.0	(1.11)	42.7	(1.33)	41.6	(1.32)	29.6	(1.52)	35.6	(2.94)	50.1	(2.39)	22.5	(4.31)	— (†)
4 Eng, 3 SS, 3 Sci, 3 Math	49.3	(1.45)	47.0	(1.45)	51.5	(1.58)	52.4	(1.67)	43.7	(2.39)	40.3	(3.25)	54.9	(2.46)	46.0	(3.30)	— (†)
4 Eng, 3 SS, 2 Sci, 2 Math	73.9	(1.50)	71.2	(1.63)	76.4	(1.46)	75.1	(1.69)	74.5	(2.32)	74.7	(2.61)	72.3	(3.62)	76.3	(3.60)	— (†)
1998 graduates																
4 Eng, 3 SS, 3 Sci, 3 Math, .5 Comp, and 2 FL[2]	28.6	(1.72)	27.6	(2.12)	30.1	(1.90)	29.6	(1.99)	27.9	(3.36)	20.4	(2.44)	38.6	(4.61)	16.5	(4.65)	— (†)
4 Eng, 3 SS, 3 Sci, 3 Math, and 2 FL	44.2	(1.92)	40.5	(2.19)	48.2	(2.05)	46.2	(2.16)	40.0	(3.41)	32.0	(2.94)	57.8	(4.51)	28.3	(4.53)	— (†)
4 Eng, 3 SS, 3 Sci, 3 Math	55.0	(2.44)	52.9	(2.64)	57.8	(2.48)	56.8	(2.69)	55.6	(4.39)	40.0	(3.28)	66.1	(5.69)	40.0	(4.73)	— (†)
4 Eng, 3 SS, 2 Sci, 2 Math	74.5	(2.18)	72.8	(2.34)	77.0	(2.14)	74.7	(2.64)	76.0	(3.21)	70.1	(2.57)	79.5	(4.76)	76.4	(5.21)	— (†)
2000 graduates																
4 Eng, 3 SS, 3 Sci, 3 Math, .5 Comp, and 2 FL[2]	31.0	(1.53)	28.6	(1.59)	33.2	(1.73)	31.5	(1.55)	28.9	(1.65)	28.4	(5.50)	37.8	(5.45)	16.2	(2.69)	— (†)
4 Eng, 3 SS, 3 Sci, 3 Math, and 2 FL	46.5	(1.46)	40.3	(1.59)	52.1	(1.60)	47.8	(1.56)	44.2	(2.14)	38.4	(5.05)	56.5	(3.13)	25.6	(3.40)	— (†)
4 Eng, 3 SS, 3 Sci, 3 Math	57.2	(1.58)	52.9	(1.65)	61.1	(1.70)	58.1	(1.70)	62.4	(2.44)	46.4	(5.46)	61.1	(3.11)	40.9	(5.56)	— (†)
4 Eng, 3 SS, 2 Sci, 2 Math	77.6	(1.58)	74.2	(1.86)	80.6	(1.44)	77.9	(1.84)	81.2	(2.23)	74.1	(3.24)	74.5	(3.05)	71.2	(4.44)	— (†)
2005 graduates																
4 Eng, 3 SS, 3 Sci, 3 Math, .5 Comp, and 2 FL[2]	36.2	(1.00)	34.6	(0.97)	37.7	(1.23)	35.8	(1.22)	39.9	(1.72)	33.0	(1.86)	42.9	(2.34)	24.5	(3.48)	36.8 (5.09)
4 Eng, 3 SS, 3 Sci, 3 Math, and 2 FL	52.1	(1.00)	46.8	(1.16)	57.2	(1.01)	53.3	(1.20)	51.4	(1.88)	41.8	(2.07)	63.6	(2.19)	36.2	(3.40)	65.7 (3.12)
4 Eng, 3 SS, 3 Sci, 3 Math	64.7	(1.07)	61.1	(1.26)	68.0	(0.99)	65.9	(1.32)	69.6	(1.83)	49.8	(2.29)	69.1	(2.20)	59.3	(3.30)	72.4 (3.44)
4 Eng, 3 SS, 2 Sci, 2 Math	81.8	(1.02)	79.2	(1.18)	84.3	(0.97)	81.2	(1.33)	88.7	(0.93)	77.2	(1.33)	83.7	(1.72)	81.0	(3.18)	87.2 (2.71)

—Not available.
†Not applicable.
[1]Eng = English; SS = social studies; Sci = science; Comp = computer science; and FL = foreign language.
[2]The National Commission on Excellence in Education recommended that all college-bound high school students take these courses as a minimum.

NOTE: Data differ slightly from figures appearing in other NCES reports because of differences in taxonomies and case exclusion criteria. Race categories exclude persons of Hispanic ethnicity. Standard errors appear in parentheses.
SOURCE: U.S. Department of Education, National Center for Education Statistics, High School and Beyond Longitudinal Study of 1980 Sophomores (HS&B-So:80/82), "High School Transcript Study"; and 1987, 1990, 1994, 1998, 2000, and 2005 High School Transcript Study (HSTS). (This table was prepared January 2007.)

Table 152. Public high schools that offered and students enrolled in dual credit, Advanced Placement, and International Baccalaureate courses, by school characteristics: 2003

School characteristic	Total number of high schools		Percent of public high schools						Total enrollments of public high school students[1]					
			Offered dual credit courses		Offered Advanced Placement courses		Offered International Baccalaureate courses		Dual credit courses		Advanced Placement courses		International Baccalaureate courses	
1	2		3		4		5		6		7		8	
All public high schools	16,500	(120)	71	(1.4)	67	(1.1)	2	(0.4)	1,162,000	(53,420)	1,795,400	(54,930)	165,100	(32,820)
Enrollment size														
Less than 500	7,400	(120)	63	(2.5)	40	(2.3)	‡	(†)	185,300	(15,590)	81,100	(8,510)	‡	(†)
500 to 1,199	5,000	(80)	75	(1.7)	82	(1.6)	2	(0.6)	335,100	(24,020)	481,000	(26,970)	24,800	(11,180)
1,200 or more	4,100	(80)	82	(1.8)	97	(0.8)	7	(1.1)	641,600	(47,500)	1,233,300	(47,700)	140,200	(29,740)
School locale														
City	2,700	(110)	65	(3.4)	77	(2.9)	6	(1.3)	246,300	(33,160)	548,400	(32,020)	58,700	(15,920)
Urban fringe	4,100	(130)	74	(1.9)	87	(2.2)	4	(0.9)	458,800	(36,290)	853,200	(41,300)	97,600	(26,990)
Town	2,400	(130)	79	(3.3)	72	(3.8)	1 !	(0.6)	201,700	(20,440)	143,200	(10,970)	8,300 !	(4,770)
Rural	7,200	(220)	70	(2.3)	50	(2.2)	‡	(†)	255,200	(18,150)	250,600	(14,900)	‡	(†)
Region														
Northeast	2,800	(160)	58	(3.5)	84	(2.3)	1	(0.5)	144,800	(20,600)	390,900	(29,210)	7,300 !	(4,880)
Southeast	3,500	(180)	69	(3.4)	69	(2.6)	5	(1.1)	194,000	(19,300)	386,100	(30,540)	65,800	(18,990)
Central	5,200	(190)	80	(2.6)	54	(2.5)	1	(0.4)	333,900	(29,010)	319,300	(22,060)	25,600 !	(14,170)
West	5,100	(230)	71	(2.2)	69	(2.3)	3	(0.9)	489,400	(47,580)	699,100	(48,150)	66,400	(23,380)
Percent minority enrollment[2]														
Less than 6 percent	5,600	(90)	76	(2.5)	58	(2.1)	#	(†)	317,400	(24,840)	267,100	(18,820)	#	(†)
6 to 20 percent	3,800	(80)	78	(2.4)	70	(2.2)	2	(0.6)	380,900	(35,440)	463,800	(21,630)	16,700	(5,470)
21 to 49 percent	3,200	(120)	72	(3.5)	75	(3.0)	5	(1.3)	228,900	(22,890)	528,500	(29,150)	64,300	(19,280)
50 percent or more	3,600	(100)	58	(3.1)	69	(2.5)	4	(1.0)	231,400	(36,220)	497,700	(35,430)	84,100	(26,560)

†Not applicable.
#Rounds to zero.
!Interpret data with caution.
‡Reporting standards not met.
[1]Enrollments may include duplicated counts of students in each type of course, since schools were instructed to count a student enrolled in multiple courses of a particular type for each course in which he or she was enrolled.
[2]Excludes schools not reporting minority enrollment.

NOTE: Data were collected during the 2002–03 12-month school year. Dual credit courses are those in which high school students can earn both high school and postsecondary credits for the same course. Percentages are based on unrounded numbers. Detail may not sum to totals because of rounding or missing data. Standard errors appear in parentheses.
SOURCE: U.S. Department of Education, National Center for Education Statistics, Fast Response Survey System (FRSS), "Dual Credit and Exam-Based Courses," FRSS 85, 2003. (This table was prepared July 2005.)

Table 153. Percentage of high school seniors who say they engage in various activities, by selected student and school characteristics: 1992 and 2004

Activity	Total	Sex		Race/ethnicity					Socioeconomic status[1]			Control of school attended		
		Male	Female	White	Black	Hispanic	Asian/ Pacific Islander	American Indian/ Alaska Native	Low	Middle	High	Public	Catholic	Other private
1	2	3	4	5	6	7	8	9	10	11	12	13	14	15
1992														
At least once a week														
Use personal computer[2]	23.5 (0.55)	27.5 (0.86)	19.6 (0.67)	23.6 (0.59)	25.0 (2.18)	20.5 (1.49)	26.2 (2.06)	18.3 (3.69)	17.8 (1.14)	23.0 (0.71)	28.3 (1.15)	23.4 (0.58)	24.4 (1.92)	24.1 (2.73)
Work on hobbies	38.1 (0.63)	40.9 (0.95)	35.3 (0.83)	39.3 (0.71)	32.6 (2.19)	36.3 (1.73)	34.9 (2.17)	47.7 (6.11)	35.5 (1.51)	37.5 (0.81)	41.0 (1.24)	37.7 (0.66)	41.0 (2.32)	39.7 (3.49)
Perform community service	10.3 (0.43)	9.5 (0.71)	11.1 (0.49)	10.3 (0.53)	10.1 (1.14)	9.9 (1.04)	13.2 (1.56)	5.3 (2.15)	6.6 (0.57)	8.5 (0.40)	16.1 (1.20)	8.9 (0.41)	16.9 (1.99)	23.9 (3.25)
Driving or riding around	67.7 (0.61)	67.8 (0.92)	67.6 (0.79)	70.0 (0.67)	61.0 (2.30)	61.0 (1.72)	64.9 (2.19)	57.4 (6.03)	66.1 (1.25)	68.8 (0.84)	66.8 (1.21)	67.7 (0.64)	69.7 (2.19)	64.5 (3.43)
Visiting with friends at a local hangout	— (†)	— (†)	— (†)	— (†)	— (†)	— (†)	— (†)	— (†)	— (†)	— (†)	— (†)	— (†)	— (†)	— (†)
Talk on phone with friends	80.3 (0.54)	78.8 (0.83)	81.7 (0.68)	82.6 (0.56)	71.7 (2.30)	75.1 (1.43)	82.3 (1.62)	62.5 (6.24)	75.6 (1.11)	79.4 (0.80)	85.2 (0.93)	79.6 (0.57)	84.5 (2.04)	84.7 (2.50)
Take music, art, or dance class	9.1 (0.33)	6.9 (0.45)	11.4 (0.49)	9.2 (0.38)	8.3 (1.10)	8.7 (1.11)	12.2 (1.27)	9.2 (3.42)	6.2 (0.62)	8.1 (0.42)	13.1 (0.77)	8.9 (0.35)	9.5 (1.19)	12.3 (2.07)
Take sports lessons	6.5 (0.36)	8.4 (0.59)	4.6 (0.41)	6.3 (0.42)	7.0 (0.84)	6.7 (1.14)	8.0 (1.28)	8.2 (2.86)	5.0 (0.58)	6.0 (0.40)	8.5 (0.94)	6.2 (0.35)	8.0 (1.39)	10.2 (2.97)
Play ball or other sports	24.6 (0.56)	35.9 (0.91)	13.2 (0.60)	25.1 (0.64)	22.7 (1.98)	22.7 (1.54)	25.9 (1.99)	25.1 (4.93)	19.1 (0.99)	22.8 (0.68)	31.7 (1.28)	24.0 (0.57)	29.8 (2.33)	27.4 (3.44)
Reading 3 or more hours per week (not for school)	34.8 (0.62)	32.3 (0.91)	37.4 (0.82)	35.4 (0.69)	32.3 (2.31)	34.0 (1.76)	34.7 (2.21)	33.1 (4.74)	30.1 (1.25)	34.8 (0.82)	37.9 (1.26)	34.8 (0.64)	33.9 (2.29)	36.2 (3.54)
Plays video/computer games 3 or more hours per day on weekdays	2.1 (0.16)	3.2 (0.28)	0.9 (0.16)	1.8 (0.16)	3.8 (0.79)	2.0 (0.37)	2.8 (1.03)	1.6 (0.94)	3.0 (0.39)	2.2 (0.26)	1.2 (0.19)	2.2 (0.18)	1.3 (0.39)	0.6 (0.23)
Watches television 3 or more hours per day on weekdays	8.6 (0.35)	8.6 (0.51)	8.7 (0.47)	6.4 (0.34)	22.9 (1.73)	9.0 (1.20)	6.9 (1.16)	8.0 (2.14)	12.9 (0.92)	9.7 (0.51)	4.0 (0.49)	9.0 (0.37)	8.5 (1.42)	3.1 (0.71)
2004														
At least once a week														
Use personal computer at home	85.8 (0.35)	85.6 (0.50)	85.9 (0.48)	90.8 (0.38)	73.9 (1.13)	76.7 (1.06)	94.0 (0.77)	79.0 (3.07)	71.1 (0.90)	87.8 (0.47)	96.3 (0.39)	85.0 (0.37)	96.9 (0.41)	93.9 (0.81)
Work on hobbies	47.2 (0.50)	50.9 (0.71)	43.4 (0.69)	47.8 (0.65)	45.0 (1.29)	45.0 (1.23)	48.5 (1.72)	54.5 (4.93)	44.2 (0.99)	47.3 (0.71)	49.7 (0.97)	47.1 (0.53)	47.3 (1.26)	49.5 (1.61)
Perform community service	18.0 (0.38)	14.9 (0.51)	21.1 (0.57)	17.4 (0.50)	19.5 (1.02)	16.3 (0.92)	25.5 (1.40)	11.8 (2.21)	15.0 (0.71)	16.9 (0.53)	23.1 (0.82)	17.6 (0.41)	23.5 (1.06)	22.4 (1.35)
Driving or riding around	65.5 (0.47)	67.4 (0.66)	63.6 (0.66)	69.9 (0.60)	63.4 (1.21)	52.9 (1.23)	56.3 (1.66)	80.3 (2.73)	58.8 (0.97)	67.2 (0.66)	68.7 (0.90)	65.4 (0.50)	69.2 (1.14)	63.7 (1.56)
Visiting with friends at a local hangout	85.3 (0.35)	88.0 (0.46)	82.4 (0.53)	89.9 (0.40)	79.4 (1.05)	75.7 (1.06)	77.7 (1.40)	83.5 (2.79)	76.5 (0.84)	86.9 (0.48)	90.7 (0.59)	84.8 (0.38)	92.3 (0.64)	89.2 (0.99)
Talk on phone with friends	71.4 (0.35)	65.3 (0.68)	77.7 (0.59)	71.4 (0.60)	78.7 (1.07)	66.1 (1.19)	64.7 (1.62)	75.9 (3.23)	65.3 (0.94)	73.1 (0.64)	74.1 (0.87)	71.1 (0.48)	77.5 (1.04)	72.8 (1.46)
Take music, art, or language class	17.1 (0.37)	13.6 (0.49)	20.6 (0.56)	17.0 (0.49)	18.3 (1.00)	14.9 (0.86)	20.7 (1.28)	18.5 (3.79)	13.2 (0.66)	16.4 (0.52)	22.3 (0.82)	16.8 (0.40)	19.6 (1.00)	22.3 (1.35)
Take sports lessons	12.7 (0.33)	15.5 (0.52)	9.9 (0.41)	12.0 (0.42)	15.1 (0.94)	13.0 (0.82)	13.0 (1.14)	12.4 (1.73)	10.4 (0.62)	12.1 (0.46)	16.2 (0.73)	12.4 (0.36)	18.6 (0.98)	14.6 (1.11)
Play non-school sports	28.3 (0.45)	40.5 (0.70)	15.9 (0.51)	27.2 (0.58)	30.3 (1.19)	29.1 (1.13)	30.8 (1.59)	37.3 (3.84)	26.7 (0.89)	28.3 (0.65)	30.0 (0.90)	28.2 (0.48)	31.5 (1.16)	26.3 (1.43)
Reading 3 or more hours per week (not for school)	33.7 (0.47)	31.5 (0.66)	36.0 (0.67)	33.3 (0.61)	34.6 (1.21)	34.5 (1.18)	32.6 (1.56)	33.6 (4.92)	32.9 (0.94)	32.8 (0.67)	36.3 (0.95)	33.8 (0.50)	29.8 (1.15)	36.2 (1.57)
Plays video/computer games 3 or more hours per day on weekdays	6.3 (0.25)	10.7 (0.44)	1.7 (0.19)	5.6 (0.31)	8.2 (0.75)	6.4 (0.61)	7.0 (1.03)	7.8 (2.73)	7.2 (0.52)	6.7 (0.36)	4.4 (0.41)	6.5 (0.27)	3.9 (0.48)	3.6 (0.63)
Watches television/DVDs 3 or more hours per day on weekdays	30.6 (0.46)	31.9 (0.66)	29.2 (0.64)	24.3 (0.56)	51.9 (1.33)	34.7 (1.18)	26.3 (1.62)	34.4 (3.23)	38.4 (0.96)	31.7 (0.67)	20.7 (0.79)	31.4 (0.49)	24.5 (1.07)	16.8 (1.21)
Hours of homework per week														
Less than 1 hour	13.4 (0.36)	17.4 (0.56)	9.4 (0.43)	14.1 (0.47)	15.4 (0.96)	11.6 (0.83)	6.1 (0.86)	14.3 (3.84)	15.7 (0.77)	14.9 (0.52)	8.7 (0.59)	14.1 (0.39)	5.5 (0.55)	5.3 (0.70)
1 to 3 hours	28.8 (0.47)	30.1 (0.67)	27.5 (0.64)	27.3 (0.59)	33.3 (1.30)	33.9 (1.25)	16.8 (1.28)	30.9 (3.14)	32.6 (0.99)	30.3 (0.68)	22.9 (0.84)	29.7 (0.51)	19.6 (0.99)	16.8 (1.23)
4 to 6 hours	25.1 (0.45)	24.6 (0.64)	25.6 (0.64)	25.9 (0.59)	24.1 (1.19)	22.8 (1.11)	25.5 (1.58)	22.6 (2.96)	24.4 (0.92)	25.1 (0.65)	25.6 (0.87)	25.0 (0.49)	27.4 (1.11)	23.8 (1.38)
7 to 12 hours	21.6 (0.43)	19.8 (0.59)	23.4 (0.61)	22.1 (0.56)	17.6 (1.05)	20.8 (1.06)	28.7 (1.56)	25.3 (4.06)	18.1 (0.83)	20.4 (0.59)	26.7 (0.87)	20.7 (0.46)	29.1 (1.14)	32.6 (1.51)
More than 12 hours	11.1 (0.32)	8.1 (0.39)	14.1 (0.50)	10.6 (0.41)	9.5 (0.84)	10.9 (0.82)	22.9 (1.56)	7.0 (1.67)	9.2 (0.63)	9.3 (0.42)	16.1 (0.71)	10.3 (0.34)	18.5 (0.97)	21.4 (1.29)

—Not available.

†Not applicable.

[1]Socioeconomic status (SES) was measured by a composite score on parental education and occupations, and family income. The "low" SES group is the lowest quartile; the "middle" SES group is the middle two quartiles; and the "high" SES group is the upper quartile.

[2]Question does not specify where computer is used.

NOTE: Race categories exclude persons of Hispanic ethnicity. Standard errors appear in parentheses.

SOURCE: U.S. Department of Education, National Center for Education Statistics, National Education Longitudinal Study of 1988 (NELS:88/92), "Second Follow-up Student Survey, 1992"; and Education Longitudinal Study of 2002 (ELS:2002), "First Follow-up, 2004." (This table was prepared October 2006.)

Table 154. Percentage of high school sophomores who participate in various school-sponsored extracurricular activities, by selected student characteristics: 1990 and 2002

Selected student characteristic	Academic clubs 1990	Academic clubs 2002	Sports: Any sport 1990	Any sport 2002	Interscholastic[1] 2002	Intramural[1] 2002	Cheerleading and drill team 1990	Cheerleading and drill team 2002	Hobby clubs 1990	Hobby clubs 2002	Music (band, orchestra, chorus, or choir) 1990	Music 2002	Vocational clubs 1990	Vocational clubs 2002
	2	3	4	5	6	7	8	9	10	11	12	13	14	15
All sophomores	**30.7 (0.62)**	**8.4 (0.33)**	**52.2 (0.69)**	**54.8 (0.63)**	**43.8 (0.64)**	**33.0 (0.52)**	**9.1 (0.43)**	**13.7 (0.46)**	**7.3 (0.37)**	**9.5 (0.34)**	**21.5 (0.59)**	**21.5 (0.52)**	**11.7 (0.54)**	**8.3 (0.43)**
Sex														
Male	27.4 (0.83)	6.8 (0.38)	63.0 (0.89)	61.0 (0.81)	55.0 (0.80)	38.5 (0.77)	2.1 (0.45)	8.1 (0.52)	7.9 (0.52)	8.1 (0.41)	15.6 (0.63)	16.3 (0.60)	11.0 (0.65)	7.6 (0.53)
Female	34.0 (0.87)	9.9 (0.46)	41.4 (0.89)	48.5 (0.85)	42.5 (0.84)	27.4 (0.64)	15.8 (0.68)	19.2 (0.63)	6.7 (0.50)	10.9 (0.50)	27.3 (0.85)	26.8 (0.71)	12.3 (0.69)	9.1 (0.53)
Race/ethnicity														
White	31.7 (0.72)	8.9 (0.43)	53.5 (0.78)	57.0 (0.79)	52.3 (0.77)	30.9 (0.68)	8.3 (0.38)	13.2 (0.54)	7.5 (0.46)	9.7 (0.47)	22.3 (0.68)	23.9 (0.65)	12.2 (0.64)	9.3 (0.60)
Black	26.2 (1.91)	7.3 (0.67)	51.4 (2.22)	55.0 (1.48)	47.8 (1.51)	39.6 (1.21)	15.7 (2.34)	18.5 (1.16)	5.2 (0.78)	7.8 (0.68)	23.0 (1.77)	21.6 (1.33)	13.7 (1.84)	7.9 (0.81)
Hispanic	27.2 (1.57)	6.1 (0.60)	43.9 (1.82)	48.3 (1.59)	40.0 (1.57)	35.3 (1.41)	8.3 (0.86)	12.3 (0.97)	6.7 (0.67)	8.0 (0.64)	14.8 (1.19)	13.0 (0.91)	7.4 (0.87)	5.4 (0.63)
Asian/Pacific Islander	36.7 (2.24)	14.3 (1.33)	54.9 (2.86)	47.7 (1.87)	38.6 (1.99)	29.5 (1.37)	5.2 (0.98)	9.1 (1.06)	11.8 (1.47)	15.5 (1.41)	20.6 (2.76)	15.5 (1.56)	5.1 (0.81)	5.2 (0.57)
American Indian/Alaska Native	31.9 (4.66)	5.2 (2.15)	44.2 (5.05)	54.6 (5.33)	44.4 (5.45)	40.8 (5.94)	11.3 (3.06)	10.8 (2.90)	8.4 (2.83)	5.3 (2.23)	17.3 (3.66)	12.3 (3.75)	16.9 (3.30)	14.3 (3.61)
Test performance quartile[2]														
Lowest test quartile	22.5 (1.21)	4.4 (0.43)	47.4 (1.42)	47.7 (1.03)	40.5 (1.04)	38.2 (0.93)	9.5 (0.95)	15.0 (0.82)	6.5 (0.59)	6.3 (0.52)	16.0 (0.87)	15.3 (0.78)	17.3 (1.19)	8.9 (0.63)
Second test quartile	29.9 (1.18)	5.1 (0.44)	50.8 (1.22)	52.5 (1.03)	45.1 (1.03)	37.5 (1.00)	8.6 (0.94)	14.4 (0.74)	6.1 (0.58)	7.3 (0.50)	20.5 (1.08)	18.7 (0.78)	13.2 (0.86)	9.5 (0.70)
Third test quartile	30.3 (1.15)	8.1 (0.56)	51.8 (1.22)	56.5 (1.06)	50.6 (1.05)	32.1 (0.97)	9.2 (0.82)	13.7 (0.74)	7.6 (0.65)	10.8 (0.63)	22.1 (1.05)	23.0 (0.88)	11.4 (0.90)	7.6 (0.64)
Highest test quartile	40.0 (1.17)	15.6 (0.80)	59.0 (1.25)	62.3 (1.04)	58.5 (1.05)	24.3 (0.87)	9.0 (0.72)	11.7 (0.73)	8.7 (0.75)	13.4 (0.75)	26.9 (1.05)	28.7 (1.02)	6.7 (0.60)	7.4 (0.67)
Socioeconomic status[3]														
Low	26.3 (1.05)	5.6 (0.46)	42.0 (1.19)	44.9 (1.09)	37.3 (1.12)	32.3 (0.97)	8.2 (0.82)	13.5 (0.73)	5.8 (0.56)	6.7 (0.50)	18.3 (0.93)	15.6 (0.75)	17.1 (1.15)	9.2 (0.76)
Middle	31.5 (0.89)	7.2 (0.38)	52.7 (0.92)	54.9 (0.82)	48.8 (0.82)	34.1 (0.72)	9.6 (0.65)	14.2 (0.60)	7.1 (0.55)	8.8 (0.39)	22.1 (0.77)	21.6 (0.64)	11.4 (0.67)	8.6 (0.50)
High	34.9 (1.16)	13.3 (0.74)	63.2 (1.21)	64.3 (1.05)	59.9 (1.10)	31.3 (0.90)	9.3 (0.65)	12.8 (0.78)	9.4 (0.68)	13.5 (0.79)	24.4 (1.09)	27.1 (1.02)	6.5 (0.54)	7.0 (0.57)
Region														
Northeast	26.9 (1.35)	7.6 (0.85)	55.7 (1.49)	59.3 (1.36)	52.7 (1.42)	34.9 (1.14)	8.0 (0.66)	14.5 (1.26)	11.0 (1.21)	11.2 (0.78)	22.7 (1.33)	20.8 (1.29)	3.5 (0.46)	4.9 (0.63)
Midwest	33.4 (1.27)	6.8 (0.57)	58.3 (1.27)	57.9 (1.36)	52.7 (1.33)	31.2 (1.15)	8.6 (0.63)	13.7 (0.89)	5.4 (0.53)	8.8 (0.77)	26.6 (1.22)	27.5 (1.07)	11.7 (1.17)	8.0 (1.10)
South	32.6 (1.06)	10.8 (0.58)	46.3 (1.16)	52.7 (0.89)	47.3 (0.92)	32.2 (0.77)	11.3 (0.96)	15.4 (0.76)	5.9 (0.53)	9.8 (0.50)	18.8 (0.93)	21.4 (0.85)	18.6 (1.10)	11.5 (0.73)
West	27.5 (1.32)	7.0 (0.66)	51.6 (1.59)	50.9 (1.53)	43.6 (1.53)	34.5 (1.20)	6.8 (0.71)	10.4 (0.88)	8.7 (0.78)	8.5 (0.77)	18.2 (1.30)	15.8 (0.95)	7.2 (0.86)	7.0 (0.80)
Sophomore's school sector														
Public	31.0 (0.65)	8.1 (0.37)	50.8 (0.70)	53.2 (0.67)	47.2 (0.67)	32.7 (0.55)	9.2 (0.46)	13.8 (0.49)	6.7 (0.38)	8.9 (0.35)	22.1 (0.61)	21.2 (0.53)	12.6 (0.60)	8.8 (0.46)
Catholic	28.6 (2.40)	11.3 (0.51)	66.5 (2.76)	73.1 (1.38)	67.7 (1.61)	35.4 (1.50)	7.1 (1.18)	10.7 (1.06)	12.3 (1.53)	17.1 (1.35)	12.6 (1.60)	18.1 (1.82)	2.8 (0.64)	2.2 (0.37)
Other private	29.1 (4.60)	10.5 (0.56)	68.0 (4.46)	73.9 (2.16)	68.3 (2.81)	37.0 (2.64)	9.9 (2.47)	15.5 (1.96)	13.1 (3.50)	14.8 (2.14)	25.7 (5.01)	33.9 (3.61)	5.5 (2.32)	3.8 (1.02)

[1] Interscholastic refers to competition between teams from different schools. Intramural refers to competition between teams or students within the same school. Data on these categories are available only for 2002.
[2] Composite test performance quartile on mathematics, reading, science, and social studies in 1990 and composite test performance quartile on mathematics, reading, and science in 2002.
[3] Socioeconomic status (SES) was measured by a composite score on parental education and occupations, and family income.

NOTE: Race categories exclude persons of Hispanic ethnicity. Standard errors appear in parentheses.
SOURCE: U.S. Department of Education, National Center for Education Statistics, Education Longitudinal Study of 2002 (ELS:2002); and America's High School Sophomores: A Ten Year Comparison, 1980-1990, National Education Longitudinal Study of 1988 (NELS:88/90), "First Follow-up, 1990." (This table was prepared December 2006.)

Table 155. Percentage distribution of 4th-graders, by time spent on homework and television viewing each day and selected student and school characteristics: Selected years, 1992 through 2000

Selected student and school characteristic	Time spent on homework each day					Amount of television watched each day						
	Don't have	Don't do	Half hour or less	One hour	More than one hour	None	One hour or less	Two hours	Three hours	Four hours	Five hours	Six or more hours
1	2	3	4	5	6	7	8	9	10	11	12	13
1992												
All students	16 (1.6)	2 (0.2)	39 (1.2)	28 (0.9)	15 (0.6)	2 (0.2)	17 (0.8)	21 (0.7)	19 (0.6)	13 (0.6)	9 (0.4)	20 (0.7)
Sex												
Male	18 (1.8)	3 (0.4)	39 (1.4)	26 (1.0)	14 (0.8)	2 (0.3)	16 (0.8)	20 (0.9)	18 (0.9)	13 (0.7)	9 (0.7)	21 (0.9)
Female	14 (1.5)	1 (0.3)	39 (1.4)	30 (1.1)	16 (0.8)	2 (0.3)	18 (1.2)	22 (0.9)	19 (0.9)	13 (0.8)	8 (0.6)	18 (0.9)
Race/ethnicity												
White	18 (1.9)	2 (0.3)	38 (1.5)	29 (1.2)	13 (0.6)	2 (0.3)	18 (0.9)	23 (1.0)	21 (0.8)	14 (0.7)	9 (0.6)	13 (0.8)
Black	10 (1.6)	3 (0.6)	45 (2.3)	24 (1.5)	18 (1.4)	2 (0.5)	11 (1.5)	11 (1.0)	12 (1.0)	10 (1.1)	9 (1.2)	44 (1.9)
Hispanic	11 (1.7)	4 (0.5)	39 (2.2)	28 (1.7)	18 (1.9)	2 (0.5)	15 (1.2)	20 (1.6)	14 (1.3)	13 (1.2)	9 (1.0)	27 (1.6)
Asian/Pacific Islander	10 (4.5)	1 (#)	39 (3.4)	28 (4.3)	22 (3.4)	3 (1.3)	26 (3.7)	17 (2.7)	15 (2.8)	11 (1.9)	7 (1.6)	21 (3.2)
American Indian/Alaska Native	17 (5.0)	4 (2.4)	31 (5.7)	18 (4.2)	30 (5.7)	1 (#)	18 (3.8)	13 (3.3)	16 (3.7)	17 (3.3)	11 (3.3)	23 (4.4)
Control of school												
Public	17 (1.7)	2 (0.3)	40 (1.3)	26 (0.9)	14 (0.6)	2 (0.2)	16 (0.8)	21 (0.9)	19 (0.7)	13 (0.7)	9 (0.5)	21 (0.8)
Private	7 (1.8)	1 (0.2)	34 (2.4)	38 (2.2)	21 (1.9)	2 (0.6)	21 (2.3)	24 (1.5)	18 (1.4)	14 (1.1)	9 (1.0)	12 (1.4)
1994												
All students	13 (0.9)	3 (0.3)	39 (1.0)	30 (0.7)	15 (0.6)	2 (0.2)	17 (0.6)	21 (0.6)	17 (0.5)	13 (0.6)	9 (0.4)	21 (0.7)
Sex												
Male	14 (1.0)	5 (0.5)	39 (1.1)	28 (1.0)	15 (0.7)	2 (0.3)	15 (0.8)	19 (0.8)	16 (0.6)	13 (0.7)	10 (0.6)	25 (0.9)
Female	12 (1.1)	2 (0.2)	40 (1.2)	32 (1.0)	15 (0.8)	2 (0.3)	20 (0.9)	23 (0.8)	17 (0.9)	13 (0.8)	8 (0.6)	17 (0.9)
1998												
All students	8 (0.8)	2 (0.2)	43 (1.0)	31 (0.8)	16 (0.6)	3 (0.5)	21 (0.6)	22 (0.7)	19 (0.6)	11 (0.5)	8 (0.4)	16 (0.6)
Sex												
Male	9 (1.0)	3 (0.3)	41 (1.1)	30 (1.0)	16 (0.8)	3 (0.5)	18 (0.9)	22 (0.9)	18 (1.0)	12 (0.7)	8 (0.6)	18 (1.0)
Female	7 (0.7)	1 (0.2)	44 (1.2)	32 (1.0)	16 (0.7)	3 (0.5)	24 (0.8)	22 (0.8)	19 (0.7)	10 (0.6)	7 (0.5)	14 (0.7)
Race/ethnicity												
White	9 (1.0)	2 (0.2)	43 (1.2)	32 (1.1)	15 (0.7)	3 (0.7)	23 (0.9)	24 (0.8)	20 (0.8)	12 (0.7)	7 (0.6)	11 (0.8)
Black	6 (0.9)	3 (0.8)	45 (1.8)	27 (1.5)	19 (1.5)	2 (0.5)	14 (0.9)	14 (1.1)	14 (1.2)	11 (0.8)	12 (0.9)	34 (1.5)
Hispanic	7 (1.0)	3 (0.5)	42 (1.4)	30 (1.3)	18 (1.2)	3 (0.5)	21 (1.2)	19 (1.0)	18 (1.2)	11 (0.8)	8 (0.8)	19 (1.0)
Asian/Pacific Islander	4 (1.7)	1 (#)	39 (3.2)	36 (2.6)	20 (2.3)	4 (1.1)	26 (2.7)	20 (3.0)	16 (2.5)	10 (2.8)	9 (1.9)	14 (2.4)
American Indian/Alaska Native	8 (2.2)	7 (2.0)	40 (4.9)	27 (2.8)	19 (3.6)	1 (#)	19 (3.6)	19 (2.3)	15 (2.6)	8 (2.1)	12 (3.1)	27 (3.4)
2000												
All students	10 (0.9)	2 (0.2)	43 (0.9)	29 (0.6)	16 (0.7)	2 (0.2)	23 (0.7)	23 (0.6)	17 (0.4)	11 (0.5)	6 (0.4)	18 (0.6)
Sex												
Male	11 (1.1)	3 (0.3)	43 (1.2)	27 (0.8)	16 (0.9)	2 (0.3)	20 (1.1)	21 (0.8)	18 (0.7)	11 (0.6)	7 (0.5)	22 (0.9)
Female	9 (1.0)	1 (0.2)	43 (1.1)	31 (0.9)	16 (0.7)	2 (0.3)	26 (0.9)	24 (0.8)	17 (0.7)	10 (0.6)	6 (0.4)	15 (0.7)
Race/ethnicity												
White	11 (1.1)	1 (0.2)	43 (1.2)	30 (0.8)	15 (0.9)	2 (0.3)	25 (0.9)	25 (0.9)	19 (0.6)	11 (0.6)	6 (0.5)	13 (0.7)
Black	8 (0.9)	4 (0.8)	45 (1.8)	26 (1.3)	17 (1.0)	2 (0.2)	14 (0.9)	13 (1.0)	13 (0.9)	10 (0.9)	8 (0.8)	42 (1.5)
Hispanic	7 (1.0)	3 (0.5)	43 (1.4)	29 (1.3)	18 (1.3)	2 (0.4)	22 (1.2)	21 (1.2)	16 (1.1)	13 (1.0)	7 (0.6)	22 (1.5)
Asian/Pacific Islander	1 (0.7)	3 (0.7)	42 (3.2)	35 (3.2)	21 (3.4)	6 (1.4)	29 (2.7)	28 (3.1)	15 (2.8)	8 (1.6)	7 (1.7)	8 (1.8)
American Indian/Alaska Native	15 (4.7)	7 (2.2)	42 (5.4)	24 (4.5)	13 (2.6)	1 (#)	20 (3.6)	18 (2.2)	21 (3.8)	11 (3.4)	7 (2.2)	23 (3.4)
Control of school												
Public	10 (1.0)	2 (0.2)	44 (1.0)	29 (0.7)	15 (0.7)	2 (0.2)	22 (0.8)	22 (0.7)	17 (0.5)	11 (0.5)	6 (0.4)	19 (0.7)
Private	8 (1.6)	1 (0.4)	37 (1.6)	34 (1.5)	20 (1.7)	5 (1.0)	25 (1.4)	24 (0.9)	19 (0.8)	10 (0.9)	6 (0.7)	11 (1.3)
Type of location												
Central city	8 (1.0)	3 (0.4)	41 (1.4)	30 (1.1)	18 (1.2)	2 (0.4)	21 (0.9)	21 (1.1)	16 (0.6)	10 (0.8)	7 (0.6)	24 (1.3)
Urban fringe/large town	8 (1.3)	2 (0.3)	44 (1.3)	30 (1.2)	16 (1.1)	3 (0.3)	24 (1.3)	24 (1.0)	18 (0.8)	10 (0.7)	6 (0.6)	15 (1.0)
Rural/small town	15 (2.3)	2 (0.5)	44 (2.0)	27 (1.4)	12 (1.2)	2 (0.4)	22 (1.8)	23 (1.4)	18 (1.0)	13 (1.1)	6 (0.7)	16 (1.5)

#Rounds to zero.
NOTE: Race categories exclude persons of Hispanic ethnicity. Detail may not sum to totals because of rounding. Standard errors appear in parentheses.

SOURCE: U.S. Department of Education, National Center for Education Statistics, National Assessment of Educational Progress (NAEP), 1992 through 2000 Reading Assessments; retrieved October 2001 from the NAEP Data Explorer (http://nces.ed.gov/nationsreportcard/nde/). (This table was prepared November 2001.)

Table 156. Percentage of elementary and secondary school students who do homework outside of school, whose parents check that homework is done, and whose parents help with homework, by frequency and selected student and school characteristics: 2003 and 2007

Year and selected characteristic	Percent of students who do homework outside of school	Average hours per week spent by students who do homework outside of school	Distribution of students who do homework outside of school by how frequently they do homework				Percent of students whose parents check that homework is done	Distribution of students by how frequently their parents' help with homework				
			Less than once a week	1 to 2 days per week	3 to 4 days per week	5 or more days a week		No help given	Less than once a week	1 to 2 days per week	3 to 4 days per week	5 or more days per week
1	2	3	4	5	6	7	8	9	10	11	12	13
2003												
All students...............	95.6 (0.23)	9.1 (0.19)	2.9 (0.16)	15.1 (0.45)	43.9 (0.61)	38.2 (0.57)	85.2 (0.33)	— (†)	— (†)	— (†)	— (†)	— (†)
All elementary school students (Kindergarten through grade 8)	96.2 (0.26)	9.2 (0.24)	2.3 (0.18)	12.9 (0.43)	46.5 (0.75)	38.3 (0.73)	94.6 (0.29)	— (†)	— (†)	— (†)	— (†)	— (†)
Sex												
Male...............	95.8 (0.41)	9.6 (0.36)	2.7 (0.26)	13.5 (0.58)	47.4 (0.95)	36.4 (0.93)	95.6 (0.38)	— (††)	— (††)	— (††)	— (††)	— (††)
Female...............	96.7 (0.32)	8.7 (0.32)	2.0 (0.23)	12.3 (0.61)	45.5 (1.08)	40.3 (1.09)	93.4 (0.52)	— (††)	— (††)	— (††)	— (††)	— (††)
Race/ethnicity												
White...............	95.9 (0.37)	9.4 (0.30)	2.8 (0.27)	14.9 (0.64)	47.5 (0.97)	34.7 (1.05)	93.1 (0.44)	— (††)	— (††)	— (††)	— (††)	— (††)
Black...............	97.8 (0.51)	8.0 (0.44)	1.4 (0.35)	8.1 (1.02)	47.6 (1.66)	42.9 (1.61)	98.0 (0.79)	— (††)	— (††)	— (††)	— (††)	— (††)
Hispanic...............	96.3 (0.50)	8.8 (0.57)	1.5 (0.34)	11.8 (0.87)	41.8 (1.37)	44.9 (1.51)	96.4 (0.45)	— (††)	— (††)	— (††)	— (††)	— (††)
Asian...............	95.1 (1.62)	11.1 (1.44)	‡ (†)	6.9 (1.74)	41.1 (4.96)	51.2 (5.30)	96.6 (1.18)	— (††)	— (††)	— (††)	— (††)	— (††)
School type												
Public...............	96.4 (0.25)	9.1 (0.24)	2.5 (0.20)	13.5 (0.47)	47.1 (0.75)	36.9 (0.73)	95.0 (0.28)	— (††)	— (††)	— (††)	— (††)	— (††)
Private...............	94.6 (0.87)	9.6 (0.58)	1.3 (0.31)	8.0 (0.92)	41.8 (1.90)	49.0 (1.81)	91.4 (1.16)	— (††)	— (††)	— (††)	— (††)	— (††)
Poverty status												
Poor...............	95.7 (0.71)	9.6 (0.63)	1.3 (0.34)	14.3 (1.33)	42.4 (1.87)	42.0 (1.75)	96.9 (0.77)	— (††)	— (††)	— (††)	— (††)	— (††)
Nonpoor...............	96.3 (0.28)	9.1 (0.25)	2.6 (0.21)	12.6 (0.45)	47.4 (0.77)	37.5 (0.78)	94.0 (0.31)	— (††)	— (††)	— (††)	— (††)	— (††)
All secondary school students (grades 9 through 12)	94.2 (0.52)	8.8 (0.25)	4.1 (0.40)	20.3 (0.94)	37.6 (1.01)	38.0 (1.04)	62.8 (0.86)	— (†)	— (†)	— (†)	— (†)	— (†)
Sex												
Male...............	91.3 (0.81)	9.0 (0.42)	6.2 (0.72)	23.6 (1.30)	38.1 (1.45)	32.1 (1.15)	66.6 (1.14)	— (††)	— (††)	— (††)	— (††)	— (††)
Female...............	97.2 (0.56)	8.5 (0.27)	2.1 (0.35)	17.0 (1.23)	37.1 (1.35)	43.8 (1.53)	59.0 (1.47)	— (††)	— (††)	— (††)	— (††)	— (††)
Race/ethnicity												
White...............	94.2 (0.64)	8.8 (0.33)	4.4 (0.49)	20.2 (1.21)	36.3 (1.20)	39.0 (1.32)	55.4 (1.12)	— (††)	— (††)	— (††)	— (††)	— (††)
Black...............	95.3 (1.05)	9.3 (0.78)	3.4 (0.82)	21.2 (2.48)	42.9 (2.56)	32.6 (2.49)	80.0 (2.13)	— (††)	— (††)	— (††)	— (††)	— (††)
Hispanic...............	92.2 (1.20)	8.1 (0.45)	4.2 (1.15)	20.9 (2.20)	40.1 (2.39)	34.8 (2.45)	78.6 (1.68)	— (††)	— (††)	— (††)	— (††)	— (††)
Asian...............	100.0 (†)	10.4 (1.48)	‡ (†)	6.7! (2.65)	32.8 (5.65)	59.0 (5.76)	52.6 (4.94)	— (††)	— (††)	— (††)	— (††)	— (††)
School type												
Public...............	93.9 (0.58)	8.7 (0.27)	4.6 (0.44)	21.7 (1.03)	38.7 (1.06)	35.0 (1.02)	64.3 (0.92)	— (††)	— (††)	— (††)	— (††)	— (††)
Private...............	96.6 (1.06)	9.9 (0.47)	‡ (†)	7.1 (1.90)	26.9 (2.88)	65.9 (2.92)	49.4 (3.51)	— (††)	— (††)	— (††)	— (††)	— (††)
Poverty status												
Poor...............	90.1 (1.53)	8.6 (0.74)	4.3 (0.97)	23.2 (3.33)	42.3 (3.16)	30.2 (2.83)	75.3 (2.94)	— (††)	— (††)	— (††)	— (††)	— (††)
Nonpoor...............	95.0 (0.55)	8.8 (0.28)	4.1 (0.43)	19.8 (0.94)	36.7 (1.11)	39.4 (1.05)	60.5 (0.91)	— (††)	— (††)	— (††)	— (††)	— (††)
Coursework												
Enrolled in AP classes...............	98.0 (0.47)	9.6 (0.38)	2.2 (0.46)	13.4 (1.10)	31.9 (1.44)	52.5 (1.66)	53.4 (1.32)	— (††)	— (††)	— (††)	— (††)	— (††)
Not enrolled in AP classes...............	91.5 (0.80)	8.2 (0.34)	5.6 (0.67)	25.4 (1.35)	41.8 (1.43)	27.3 (1.30)	69.7 (1.10)	— (††)	— (††)	— (††)	— (††)	— (††)
2007												
All students...............	94.4 (0.30)	5.4 (0.06)	3.1 (0.34)	13.1 (0.47)	43.6 (0.62)	40.2 (0.60)	85.4 (0.46)	10.2 (0.41)	20.3 (0.51)	31.7 (0.64)	25.3 (0.59)	12.4 (0.41)
All elementary school students (kindergarten through grade 8)	95.0 (0.37)	4.7 (0.07)	2.1 (0.23)	12.3 (0.56)	46.2 (0.73)	39.4 (0.68)	95.0 (0.34)	4.3 (0.34)	13.1 (0.52)	32.6 (0.77)	32.9 (0.76)	17.0 (0.56)

See notes at end of table.

Table 156. Percentage of elementary and secondary school students who do homework outside of school, whose parents check that homework is done, and whose parents help with homework, by frequency and selected student and school characteristics: 2003 and 2007—Continued

Year and selected characteristic	Percent of students who do homework outside of school	Average hours per week spent by students who do homework outside of school	Distribution of students who do homework outside of school by how frequently they do homework				Percent of students whose parents' check that homework is done	Distribution of students by how frequently their parents' help with homework				
			Less than once a week	1 to 2 days per week	3 to 4 days per week	5 or more days a week		No help given	Less than once a week	1 to 2 days per week	3 to 4 days per week	5 or more days per week
1	2	3	4	5	6	7	8	9	10	11	12	13
Sex												
Male	94.6 (0.51)	4.6 (0.09)	2.1 (0.31)	12.4 (0.71)	47.9 (1.19)	37.6 (1.09)	95.3 (0.47)	4.3 (0.39)	12.9 (0.63)	32.3 (1.02)	32.7 (1.28)	17.8 (0.85)
Female	95.4 (0.53)	4.9 (0.10)	2.1 (0.31)	12.2 (0.96)	44.4 (1.13)	41.3 (1.08)	94.6 (0.48)	4.3 (0.56)	13.4 (0.76)	32.9 (1.17)	33.2 (1.17)	16.1 (0.79)
Race/ethnicity												
White	94.7 (0.48)	4.4 (0.07)	2.7 (0.36)	13.7 (0.74)	48.3 (1.05)	35.3 (0.99)	94.0 (0.42)	3.8 (0.37)	15.7 (0.74)	34.9 (0.94)	31.3 (0.92)	14.3 (0.63)
Black	95.5 (1.07)	5.6 (0.27)	1.3! (0.53)	7.0 (1.19)	44.4 (3.40)	47.2 (3.11)	96.1 (0.63)	3.5 (1.03)	7.4 (1.14)	25.2 (2.22)	38.3 (3.36)	25.5 (2.38)
Hispanic	94.8 (0.85)	4.7 (0.11)	1.3 (0.33)	13.5 (1.39)	40.7 (1.94)	44.4 (1.74)	96.1 (0.70)	7.1 (0.95)	10.3 (0.91)	30.1 (1.79)	34.0 (1.78)	18.6 (1.52)
Asian	97.7 (0.97)	5.7 (0.39)	1.0! (0.59)	5.1! (1.53)	39.1 (4.31)	54.8 (4.48)	88.5 (3.44)	3.1! (1.36)	12.8 (2.84)	37.5 (4.52)	30.7 (4.22)	15.9 (2.56)
School type												
Public	95.1 (0.38)	4.7 (0.08)	2.0 (0.25)	12.4 (0.62)	46.1 (0.76)	39.4 (0.73)	95.4 (0.36)	4.4 (0.38)	13.1 (0.55)	32.4 (0.86)	32.9 (0.81)	17.2 (0.64)
Private	94.0 (1.01)	4.8 (0.19)	2.7 (0.63)	11.4 (1.96)	46.7 (2.64)	39.2 (2.46)	91.5 (1.19)	3.6 (0.85)	13.6 (1.48)	34.3 (2.10)	33.5 (2.36)	15.2 (1.68)
Poverty status												
Poor	94.2 (0.99)	4.7 (0.20)	2.9 (0.72)	16.3 (2.18)	39.0 (2.53)	41.7 (2.21)	97.9 (0.55)	6.1 (1.01)	8.8 (1.29)	28.5 (2.44)	35.2 (2.41)	21.3 (1.90)
Nonpoor	95.2 (0.36)	4.8 (0.08)	1.9 (0.22)	11.3 (0.58)	48.0 (0.80)	38.8 (0.75)	94.2 (0.40)	3.9 (0.33)	14.2 (0.56)	33.7 (0.80)	32.4 (0.72)	15.9 (0.58)
Locale												
City	95.2 (0.65)	5.1 (0.13)	1.5 (0.31)	9.1 (0.91)	43.4 (1.58)	46.0 (1.43)	95.4 (0.54)	4.8 (0.67)	11.3 (1.02)	29.1 (1.39)	36.0 (1.41)	16.7 (1.15)
Suburban	95.4 (0.51)	4.9 (0.11)	1.9 (0.37)	9.3 (0.71)	46.1 (1.24)	42.7 (1.19)	93.5 (0.67)	4.4 (0.55)	14.5 (0.85)	33.1 (1.05)	30.8 (1.14)	17.1 (0.91)
Town	93.0 (1.50)	4.1 (0.14)	2.7 (0.79)	18.8 (1.98)	46.4 (2.29)	32.2 (2.08)	96.0 (1.04)	3.2 (0.80)	14.2 (1.62)	35.7 (2.68)	31.1 (2.31)	15.7 (1.62)
Rural	95.0 (0.85)	4.2 (0.15)	3.2 (0.69)	19.5 (1.79)	50.6 (1.90)	26.8 (1.63)	96.3 (0.72)	4.1 (0.94)	13.1 (1.30)	35.5 (2.29)	32.8 (2.23)	14.6 (1.37)
All secondary school students (grades 9 through 12)	93.0 (0.55)	6.8 (0.11)	5.4 (0.85)	14.8 (0.96)	38.0 (1.15)	41.9 (1.18)	64.6 (1.21)	23.1 (1.08)	35.9 (1.26)	29.7 (1.19)	8.8 (0.81)	2.5 (0.34)
Sex												
Male	91.2 (0.80)	6.0 (0.19)	7.4 (1.53)	18.3 (1.59)	38.2 (1.78)	36.0 (1.64)	67.8 (1.88)	24.1 (1.56)	36.9 (1.97)	29.1 (1.84)	8.2 (1.11)	1.8 (0.41)
Female	94.9 (0.79)	7.5 (0.16)	3.3 (0.72)	11.2 (1.10)	37.7 (1.79)	47.9 (1.85)	61.4 (1.78)	22.0 (1.32)	35.0 (1.44)	30.4 (1.35)	9.3 (1.11)	3.3 (0.60)
Race/ethnicity												
White	94.5 (0.52)	6.8 (0.13)	4.2 (0.58)	12.9 (0.91)	38.6 (1.51)	44.3 (1.42)	57.2 (1.54)	22.5 (1.28)	41.1 (1.36)	27.7 (1.43)	6.3 (0.66)	2.3 (0.42)
Black	91.8 (1.98)	6.3 (0.38)	9.3! (5.06)	20.1 (3.86)	41.0 (4.72)	29.7 (3.43)	83.1 (2.84)	19.5 (2.97)	26.5 (4.77)	34.4 (4.03)	16.7 (4.45)	2.9! (1.13)
Hispanic	90.7 (2.11)	6.4 (0.34)	5.9 (1.29)	17.7 (3.55)	36.6 (2.93)	39.9 (3.03)	75.6 (2.71)	26.2 (2.94)	25.8 (2.38)	33.8 (3.49)	11.0 (1.76)	3.3! (1.00)
Asian	93.6 (5.45)	10.3 (1.37)	‡ (†)	13.8! (5.51)	18.5! (6.12)	67.7 (7.18)	59.0 (7.69)	26.4 (7.58)	36.1 (7.55)	26.8 (7.61)	7.6! (3.11)	3.1! (1.83)
School type												
Public	92.3 (0.60)	6.5 (0.11)	5.9 (0.96)	15.9 (1.06)	39.7 (1.26)	38.5 (1.17)	66.1 (1.24)	22.8 (1.16)	35.4 (1.29)	30.0 (1.26)	9.1 (0.87)	2.7 (0.37)
Private	98.5 (0.54)	9.3 (0.39)	0.8! (0.35)	5.9 (1.34)	24.0 (2.72)	69.4 (2.89)	53.1 (3.98)	25.0 (2.64)	40.1 (3.68)	27.5 (4.07)	6.1 (1.36)	1.4! (0.61)
Poverty status												
Poor	89.5 (2.21)	5.5 (0.32)	8.3! (4.42)	19.2 (3.62)	38.7 (4.32)	33.7 (3.69)	81.0 (3.03)	24.2 (3.80)	24.0 (4.21)	36.1 (3.76)	14.0 (3.21)	1.7! (0.63)
Nonpoor	93.7 (0.58)	7.0 (0.12)	4.8 (0.53)	13.9 (0.91)	37.8 (1.27)	43.6 (1.37)	61.4 (1.30)	22.8 (1.05)	38.3 (1.19)	28.5 (1.24)	7.7 (0.66)	2.7 (0.38)
Coursework												
Enrolled in AP classes	96.9 (0.59)	8.5 (0.22)	2.4 (0.70)	7.5 (0.93)	31.9 (1.81)	58.2 (1.97)	56.3 (2.06)	27.4 (1.90)	36.3 (1.69)	28.3 (1.74)	6.0 (0.99)	1.9 (0.43)
Not enrolled in AP classes	90.6 (0.81)	5.7 (0.13)	7.3 (1.31)	19.5 (1.40)	41.9 (1.56)	31.2 (1.42)	70.1 (1.46)	20.2 (1.14)	35.7 (1.70)	30.7 (1.59)	10.5 (1.23)	2.9 (0.51)
Locale												
City	92.8 (1.01)	6.8 (0.22)	6.3 (2.46)	14.1 (1.90)	35.9 (2.32)	43.7 (2.53)	71.5 (1.89)	22.6 (1.88)	33.4 (2.64)	29.3 (2.00)	12.0 (1.80)	2.7 (0.55)
Suburban	93.6 (0.95)	7.5 (0.17)	4.8 (0.86)	11.4 (1.27)	36.5 (1.71)	47.4 (2.07)	58.9 (2.00)	23.6 (1.74)	39.1 (1.79)	27.8 (1.68)	7.5 (1.01)	2.0 (0.47)
Town	89.7 (2.16)	6.4 (0.27)	5.4 (1.48)	13.2 (1.74)	45.9 (3.46)	35.5 (3.17)	64.8 (3.12)	24.3 (2.81)	34.4 (2.96)	27.9 (3.41)	9.3 (1.80)	4.2 (1.54)
Rural	93.9 (1.23)	5.6 (0.29)	5.1 (1.20)	22.7 (2.76)	39.6 (3.04)	32.6 (2.79)	65.5 (2.94)	22.1 (2.69)	34.4 (2.71)	34.8 (3.43)	6.2 (1.53)	2.5 (0.88)

— Not available.
†Not applicable.
‡Reporting standards not met.
!Interpret data with caution.
[1]Refers to one or more parent or other household adult. Only includes students who had homework outside of school.

NOTE: Includes children enrolled in kindergarten through grade 12 and ungraded students. Data based on responses of the parent most knowledgeable about the student's education. Race categories exclude persons of Hispanic ethnicity. Detail may not sum to totals because of rounding. Standard errors appear in parentheses. Totals include data for other racial/ethnic groups not separately shown.
SOURCE: U.S. Department of Education, National Center for Education Statistics, Parent and Family Involvement in Education Survey of the National Household Education Surveys Program (PFI-NHES:2003 and 2007). (This table was prepared June 2008.)

Table 157. Tenth-graders' attendance patterns, by selected student and school characteristics: 1990 and 2002

Attendance pattern	All students	Sex		Race/ethnicity					Socioeconomic status[1]			Control of school attended		
		Male	Female	White	Black	Hispanic	Asian/Pacific Islander	American Indian/Alaska Native	Low	Middle	High	Public	Catholic	Other private
1	2	3	4	5	6	7	8	9	10	11	12	13	14	15
Percentage of 10th-graders in 1990														
Number of days missed in first half of current school year														
None	13.5 (0.44)	16.1 (0.66)	10.7 (0.53)	12.4 (0.48)	19.5 (1.75)	10.4 (0.90)	22.3 (1.74)	10.2 (2.11)	12.3 (0.95)	14.0 (0.61)	15.0 (0.82)	13.4 (0.47)	18.0 (2.16)	15.5 (2.14)
1 or 2 days	21.6 (0.46)	23.0 (0.72)	20.2 (0.59)	21.5 (0.56)	23.7 (1.41)	19.1 (1.17)	27.4 (1.97)	13.5 (4.21)	16.9 (0.75)	22.2 (0.68)	26.0 (0.98)	21.3 (0.46)	26.0 (2.45)	34.0 (3.92)
3 or 4 days	26.1 (0.52)	25.4 (0.71)	26.8 (0.76)	27.3 (0.60)	23.7 (1.51)	23.3 (1.15)	22.7 (2.07)	26.8 (3.39)	22.6 (0.89)	26.4 (0.73)	29.1 (0.99)	26.5 (0.56)	27.3 (2.23)	26.9 (2.93)
5 or more days	38.8 (0.63)	35.5 (0.87)	42.2 (0.84)	38.8 (0.72)	33.2 (1.98)	47.2 (1.71)	27.7 (2.22)	49.4 (3.32)	48.2 (1.18)	37.4 (0.85)	29.9 (1.20)	38.8 (0.65)	28.6 (2.35)	23.6 (3.14)
Number of times late in first half of current school year														
Never	24.7 (0.60)	24.8 (0.80)	24.6 (0.77)	27.4 (0.70)	18.1 (1.33)	17.3 (1.48)	23.0 (1.94)	16.0 (3.20)	24.4 (1.17)	25.0 (0.78)	25.9 (0.95)	24.9 (0.61)	27.5 (2.70)	18.3 (2.76)
1 or 2 days	38.2 (0.62)	38.0 (0.88)	38.4 (0.83)	38.1 (0.69)	40.4 (2.02)	36.7 (1.54)	38.0 (2.22)	35.4 (3.64)	37.5 (1.10)	38.6 (0.84)	38.4 (1.16)	37.8 (0.63)	40.4 (2.26)	44.6 (3.87)
3 or more days	37.1 (0.72)	37.1 (0.96)	37.0 (0.88)	34.5 (0.77)	41.5 (2.16)	46.0 (2.07)	39.0 (2.35)	48.6 (3.51)	38.1 (1.30)	36.4 (0.88)	35.7 (1.23)	37.3 (0.75)	32.1 (2.68)	37.1 (4.07)
Number of times cut classes in first half of current school year														
Never	62.4 (0.71)	60.6 (0.90)	64.2 (0.91)	64.0 (0.80)	63.5 (2.12)	50.5 (1.69)	66.4 (2.36)	48.8 (3.91)	59.0 (1.30)	62.4 (0.91)	65.9 (1.24)	61.0 (0.77)	78.6 (2.36)	70.3 (3.66)
1 or 2 times	22.0 (0.49)	22.3 (0.71)	21.7 (0.67)	21.3 (0.54)	22.5 (1.82)	24.6 (1.44)	20.3 (2.01)	35.1 (3.97)	23.4 (1.09)	21.5 (0.68)	22.2 (1.05)	22.3 (0.52)	16.6 (1.92)	19.9 (3.44)
3 to 6 times	8.4 (0.33)	9.2 (0.45)	7.7 (0.48)	8.1 (0.40)	7.5 (0.81)	12.6 (1.02)	5.7 (0.87)	8.3 (3.25)	9.6 (0.73)	8.2 (0.44)	7.3 (0.56)	8.8 (0.35)	3.2 (0.87)	6.9 (1.28)
More than 6 days	7.2 (0.35)	8.0 (0.49)	6.5 (0.44)	6.5 (0.38)	5.4 (1.03)	12.2 (1.23)	7.6 (1.21)	7.8 (2.04)	8.1 (0.64)	7.9 (0.50)	4.6 (0.43)	7.9 (0.39)	1.6 (0.55)	2.9 (1.03)
Percentage of 10th-graders in 2002														
Number of days missed in first half of current school year														
None	14.3 (0.38)	16.1 (0.51)	12.5 (0.47)	13.0 (0.48)	16.5 (0.84)	14.2 (0.88)	28.3 (1.59)	12.1 (0.14)	13.5 (0.67)	13.9 (0.48)	16.0 (0.79)	14.0 (0.40)	16.1 (1.23)	19.2 (2.22)
1 or 2 days	35.4 (0.52)	36.1 (0.69)	34.8 (0.68)	35.5 (0.66)	38.4 (1.17)	33.5 (1.46)	35.7 (1.58)	25.0 (0.92)	32.8 (0.97)	35.3 (0.72)	38.2 (0.96)	35.0 (0.56)	41.0 (1.62)	39.8 (1.71)
3 to 6 days	33.0 (0.53)	31.9 (0.69)	34.3 (0.69)	34.4 (0.69)	30.7 (1.08)	32.7 (1.01)	24.3 (1.23)	35.5 (1.38)	33.1 (0.87)	32.7 (0.74)	33.8 (0.97)	33.2 (0.56)	33.1 (1.51)	29.9 (2.04)
More than 6 days	17.2 (0.41)	16.0 (0.56)	18.5 (0.59)	17.1 (0.49)	14.3 (0.95)	19.6 (1.09)	11.7 (1.16)	27.4 (0.32)	20.6 (0.90)	18.1 (0.53)	12.0 (0.65)	17.8 (0.44)	9.8 (0.77)	11.1 (1.21)
Number of times late in first half of current school year														
Never	26.0 (0.54)	26.0 (0.73)	26.0 (0.68)	29.8 (0.67)	17.4 (0.86)	20.4 (1.18)	27.4 (1.41)	19.8 (0.35)	24.6 (0.87)	25.8 (0.66)	28.1 (0.94)	25.7 (0.58)	33.3 (1.79)	25.1 (2.28)
1 or 2 days	37.4 (0.54)	36.5 (0.75)	38.4 (0.71)	38.7 (0.66)	36.5 (1.33)	34.9 (1.17)	36.2 (1.52)	35.8 (2.42)	36.9 (0.98)	36.7 (0.72)	39.4 (0.91)	37.3 (0.57)	40.4 (1.32)	38.3 (1.39)
3 or more days	36.5 (0.62)	37.4 (0.82)	35.6 (0.77)	31.5 (0.71)	46.1 (1.48)	44.8 (1.45)	36.4 (1.58)	44.4 (1.89)	38.5 (1.01)	37.5 (0.79)	32.5 (1.05)	37.0 (0.67)	26.3 (1.54)	36.7 (2.11)
Number of times cut classes in first half of current school year														
Never	68.4 (0.70)	68.1 (0.87)	68.8 (0.83)	72.9 (0.75)	64.6 (1.64)	56.3 (1.48)	68.9 (1.76)	70.3 (3.43)	62.4 (1.10)	67.1 (0.86)	77.0 (1.04)	67.1 (0.75)	86.1 (1.39)	80.7 (1.90)
1 or 2 times	18.7 (0.46)	18.8 (0.65)	18.5 (0.58)	16.7 (0.55)	20.2 (1.15)	23.9 (1.01)	17.5 (1.25)	22.2 (3.43)	21.3 (0.79)	19.6 (0.63)	14.2 (0.81)	19.2 (0.49)	11.0 (1.12)	13.7 (1.38)
3 to 6 times	6.8 (0.32)	6.8 (0.40)	6.9 (0.41)	5.7 (0.34)	9.0 (0.76)	9.0 (0.83)	8.2 (1.08)	4.7 (0.29)	7.9 (0.65)	7.1 (0.40)	5.2 (0.47)	7.2 (0.34)	1.8 (0.40)	3.9 (0.57)
More than 6 times	6.1 (0.30)	6.3 (0.40)	5.9 (0.40)	4.7 (0.31)	6.2 (0.67)	10.9 (0.97)	5.3 (0.65)	2.7 (0.32)	8.4 (0.62)	6.2 (0.39)	3.7 (0.38)	6.5 (0.32)	1.0 (0.26)	1.7 (0.47)

[1]Socioeconomic status (SES) was measured by a composite score on parental education and occupations, and family income. The "low" SES group is the lowest quarter; the "middle" SES group is the middle two quarters; and the "high" SES group is the upper quarter.

NOTE: Race categories exclude persons of Hispanic ethnicity. Data for 2002 for persons reporting more than one race are not shown separately, but are included in totals. Detail may not sum to totals because of rounding. Standard errors appear in parentheses.

SOURCE: U.S. Department of Education, National Center for Education Statistics, National Education Longitudinal Study of 1988 (NELS:88/90), "First Follow-up Student Survey, 1990", and Education Longitudinal Study of 2002, Base Year (ELS:02). (This table was prepared November 2005.)

Table 158. Percentage of public schools reporting crime incidents, and number and rate of incidents, by school characteristics and type of incident: 1999–2000 and 2005–06

Type of crime incident	All public schools, 1999–2000	2005–06							
		All public schools	Instruction level of school			Size of enrollment			
			Primary	Middle	High	Less than 300	300 to 499	500 to 999	1,000 or more
1	2	3	4	5	6	7	8	9	10
Number of public schools (in thousands)									
All schools	82 (#)	83 (0.4)	49 (0.6)	16 (0.1)	12 (0.1)	21 (0.5)	24 (0.4)	29 (0.3)	9 (0.1)
Schools with incident	71 (1.0)	71 (1.0)	38 (0.9)	15 (0.1)	12 (0.1)	15 (0.8)	20 (0.6)	26 (0.4)	9 (0.1)
Percent of schools with incident	**86.3 (1.23)**	**85.7 (1.07)**	**77.8 (1.68)**	**98.0 (0.42)**	**98.5 (0.54)**	**73.9 (3.38)**	**85.8 (1.90)**	**90.3 (1.17)**	**97.8 (0.92)**
Violent incidents[2]	**71.4 (1.37)**	**77.7 (1.11)**	**67.3 (1.75)**	**94.4 (0.85)**	**95.2 (0.92)**	**63.7 (3.29)**	**77.3 (2.08)**	**82.1 (1.38)**	**96.5 (1.03)**
Serious violent incidents[3]	19.7 (0.98)	17.1 (0.91)	11.0 (1.22)	25.2 (1.59)	31.8 (1.77)	11.4 (1.63)	11.7 (1.38)	19.2 (1.41)	37.2 (1.82)
Rape or attempted rape[4]	0.7 (0.10)	0.3 (0.07)	# (†)	0.8 ! (0.29)	1.4 (0.37)	‡ (†)	‡ (†)	0.3 ! (0.11)	1.5 (0.44)
Sexual battery other than rape[5]	2.5 (0.33)	2.8 (0.24)	0.8 ! (0.31)	4.6 (0.89)	8.8 (0.95)	0.8 ! (0.34)	2.1 (0.58)	2.8 (0.46)	9.0 (1.05)
Physical attack or fight with weapon[6][7]	5.2 (0.60)	3.0 (0.38)	1.2 ! (0.38)	4.8 (0.65)	6.5 (0.81)	‡ (†)	1.7 ! (0.66)	3.8 (0.76)	7.8 (0.95)
Threat of attack with weapon[7]	11.1 (0.70)	8.8 (0.66)	6.9 (1.05)	12.5 (1.14)	12.7 (1.09)	6.5 (1.37)	6.7 (1.06)	9.8 (1.11)	16.1 (1.51)
Robbery with a weapon[7]	0.5 ! (0.15)	0.4 (0.12)	‡ (†)	0.4 ! (0.19)	1.1 (0.26)	‡ (†)	# (†)	‡ (†)	2.1 (0.55)
Robbery without a weapon[7]	5.3 (0.56)	6.4 (0.59)	3.6 (0.68)	9.1 (0.88)	13.9 (1.25)	5.4 (1.35)	3.2 (0.78)	6.5 (0.77)	16.7 (1.25)
Physical attack or fight without a weapon	63.7 (1.52)	74.3 (1.20)	63.3 (1.97)	91.9 (0.94)	93.5 (1.08)	57.1 (3.60)	73.7 (2.18)	80.1 (1.42)	95.8 (1.00)
Threat of attack without weapon	52.2 (1.47)	52.2 (1.27)	41.7 (2.04)	70.6 (1.74)	70.9 (1.64)	39.5 (2.82)	49.7 (2.33)	55.0 (2.02)	77.9 (1.87)
Theft/larceny[9]	**45.6 (1.37)**	**46.0 (1.07)**	**27.8 (1.55)**	**68.7 (1.48)**	**85.6 (1.32)**	**29.6 (2.52)**	**37.2 (1.91)**	**52.1 (1.83)**	**85.8 (1.64)**
Other incidents[10]	— (†)	**68.2 (1.07)**	**54.8 (1.67)**	**87.8 (0.94)**	**93.6 (1.08)**	**53.2 (3.02)**	**63.4 (2.47)**	**74.2 (2.07)**	**95.1 (1.15)**
Possess firearm/explosive device[11]	5.5 (0.44)	7.2 (0.60)	4.9 (0.79)	8.2 (0.83)	14.4 (1.23)	2.3 ! (0.78)	4.6 (1.08)	9.4 (1.09)	18.0 (1.73)
Possess knife or sharp object	42.6 (1.28)	42.8 (1.23)	33.0 (1.70)	60.3 (1.26)	65.1 (1.81)	24.8 (2.45)	36.6 (2.42)	50.0 (2.22)	76.0 (1.66)
Distribution, possession, or use of illegal drugs	— (†)	25.9 (0.68)	3.4 (0.64)	48.8 (1.58)	79.7 (1.64)	14.7 (1.82)	12.3 (1.10)	28.6 (1.07)	77.2 (1.14)
Distribution, possession, or use of alcohol	— (†)	16.2 (0.68)	1.1 ! (0.41)	21.2 (1.27)	60.6 (1.67)	10.2 (1.62)	8.3 (1.44)	14.4 (0.72)	55.2 (1.41)
Vandalism[12]	51.5 (1.61)	50.5 (1.17)	40.4 (1.80)	67.3 (1.58)	74.1 (1.62)	37.6 (2.68)	44.1 (2.35)	55.5 (2.04)	79.8 (1.85)
Number of incidents (in thousands)	**2,259 (117.0)**	**2,191 (45.0)**	**703 (42.3)**	**722 (22.6)**	**611 (18.4)**	**220 (20.5)**	**420 (26.4)**	**851 (35.7)**	**700 (21.7)**
Violent incidents[2]	**1,466 (103.7)**	**1,489 (39.0)**	**562 (36.6)**	**522 (20.8)**	**314 (14.7)**	**148 (17.0)**	**325 (25.6)**	**610 (30.7)**	**406 (17.9)**
Serious violent incidents[3]	61 (7.0)	59 (6.8)	19 ! (6.5)	19 (2.3)	17 (1.6)	‡ (†)	7 (1.1)	21 (2.4)	19 (2.2)
Rape or attempted rape[4]	1 (0.1)	# (†)	# (†)	# (†)	# (†)	‡ (†)	‡ (†)	# (†)	# (†)
Sexual battery other than rape[5]	4 (1.1)	4 (0.4)	1 ! (0.3)	1 (0.3)	2 (0.3)	# (†)	1 ! (0.2)	1 (0.3)	2 (0.3)
Physical attack or fight with weapon[6][7]	12 (2.5)	7 (1.6)	1 ! (0.2)	4 ! (1.5)	2 (0.2)	‡ (†)	# (†)	4 ! (1.6)	2 (0.5)
Threat of attack with weapon[7]	21 (1.9)	25 (6.5)	13 ! (6.4)	6 (1.0)	5 (0.7)	‡ (†)	2 (0.4)	9 (1.2)	5 (1.2)
Robbery with a weapon[7]	‡ (†)	1 ! (0.2)	‡ (†)	‡ (†)	# (†)	‡ (†)	# (†)	‡ (†)	# (†)
Robbery without a weapon[7]	20 (3.2)	22 (2.5)	5 ! (1.4)	7 (1.3)	9 (1.1)	3 (0.9)	3 (0.9)	6 (0.9)	9 (1.2)
Physical attack or fight without a weapon[7]	807 (59.6)	898 (25.5)	356 (21.8)	315 (13.5)	172 (8.1)	92 (11.7)	207 (15.7)	361 (19.9)	237 (11.1)
Threat of attack without weapon	599 (52.7)	533 (20.3)	186 (18.6)	189 (12.6)	124 (7.5)	44 (5.0)	111 (13.5)	227 (17.6)	150 (9.6)
Theft/larceny[9]	**218 (9.2)**	**243 (6.2)**	**36 (3.6)**	**79 (3.4)**	**106 (3.3)**	**19 (2.2)**	**32 (2.3)**	**90 (4.5)**	**103 (3.2)**
Other incidents[10]	— (†)	**459 (11.2)**	**106 (7.1)**	**121 (4.0)**	**192 (4.7)**	**53 (5.6)**	**64 (3.8)**	**152 (5.9)**	**191 (6.0)**
Possess firearm/explosive device[11]	9 (2.2)	12 (1.9)	6 ! (1.8)	3 (0.4)	3 (0.4)	‡ (†)	1 (0.3)	6 (1.1)	4 (0.7)
Possess knife or sharp object	86 (4.0)	90 (2.3)	30 (1.9)	27 (1.3)	28 (1.1)	9 (1.1)	16 (1.2)	36 (1.6)	29 (1.0)
Distribution, possession, or use of illegal drugs	— (†)	117 (4.3)	2 (0.4)	27 (1.5)	76 (2.9)	9 (1.9)	8 (0.8)	29 (1.6)	71 (2.8)
Distribution, possession, or use of alcohol	— (†)	47 (2.4)	1 ! (0.4)	7 (0.6)	31 (1.4)	5 (1.2)	5 (1.1)	11 (1.0)	26 (1.5)
Vandalism[12]	211 (13.6)	193 (7.2)	67 (5.4)	58 (2.7)	55 (2.4)	28 (4.1)	34 (2.9)	70 (3.9)	61 (3.4)

See notes at end of table.

Table 158. Percentage of public schools reporting crime incidents, and number and rate of incidents, by school characteristics and type of incident: 1999–2000 and 2005–06—Continued

Type of crime incident	All public schools, 1999–2000	2005–06								
		All public schools	Instruction level of school			Size of enrollment			
			Primary	Middle	High	Less than 300	300 to 499	500 to 999	1,000 or more
1	2	3	4	5	6	7	8	9	10
Number of incidents per 100,000 students	4,849 (252.4)	4,584 (95.9)	3,150 (179.3)	7,135 (204.3)	5,010 (151.5)	5,107 (449.1)	4,400 (264.5)	4,309 (168.3)	4,932 (169.4)
Violent incidents[2]	3,147 (223.8)	3,116 (82.3)	2,516 (155.2)	5,158 (191.2)	2,571 (120.8)	3,449 (376.3)	3,403 (256.5)	3,086 (144.6)	2,863 (137.8)
Serious violent incidents[3]	130 (15.2)	124 (14.2)	86 ! (28.7)	186 (22.3)	143 (13.4)	‡ (†)	72 (11.4)	107 (11.8)	135 (15.4)
Rape or attempted rape[4]	1 (0.2)	1 (0.2)	# (†)	1 ! (0.4)	2 ! (0.5)	‡ (†)	‡ (†)	# (†)	1 ! (0.4)
Sexual battery other than rape[5]	9 (2.4)	9 (0.8)	3 ! (1.2)	12 (3.1)	18 (2.4)	‡ (†)	8 ! (2.4)	7 (1.5)	13 (2.0)
Physical attack or fight[6] with weapon[7]	26 (5.4)	15 (3.4)	3 ! (1.0)	41 ! (15.2)	13 (1.9)	4 ! (1.7)	5 ! (2.0)	21 ! (8.0)	15 (3.3)
Threat of attack with weapon[7]	45 (4.1)	52 (13.7)	59 ! (28.3)	59 (9.6)	38 (6.1)	‡ (†)	25 (4.7)	45 (6.3)	38 (8.4)
Robbery[8] with a weapon[7]	‡ (†)	1 ! (0.5)	‡ (†)	‡ (†)	2 ! (0.6)	‡ (†)	# (†)	‡ (†)	3 ! (1.4)
Robbery[8] without a weapon[7]	43 (6.8)	46 (5.2)	21 ! (6.3)	71 (12.7)	71 (9.2)	75 (20.5)	34 (9.8)	32 (4.8)	65 (8.4)
Physical attack or fight without a weapon[7]	1,732 (128.8)	1,878 (54.5)	1,595 (92.1)	3,107 (123.8)	1,412 (65.2)	2,140 (259.3)	2,171 (154.3)	1,828 (92.2)	1,671 (83.9)
Threat of attack without weapon	1,285 (113.2)	1,114 (42.6)	834 (82.1)	1,865 (122.0)	1,015 (62.4)	1,031 (119.4)	1,160 (139.7)	1,151 (88.2)	1,058 (71.2)
Theft/larceny[9]	468 (20.2)	508 (12.8)	161 (15.7)	783 (35.1)	865 (27.3)	430 (49.9)	331 (23.9)	454 (23.1)	724 (22.9)
Other incidents[10]	— (†)	960 (24.4)	474 (31.4)	1,193 (37.3)	1,574 (38.1)	1,227 (128.2)	666 (42.6)	768 (30.6)	1,344 (41.3)
Possess firearm/explosive device[11]	18 (4.8)	26 (4.0)	27 (4.0)	28 (3.8)	23 (3.0)	‡ (†)	12 (2.7)	29 (5.8)	26 (5.0)
Possess knife or sharp object	184 (8.7)	188 (4.9)	135 (8.4)	268 (11.7)	226 (8.7)	218 (26.8)	165 (12.5)	182 (8.1)	203 (6.6)
Distribution, possession, or use of illegal drugs	— (†)	245 (9.3)	9 (1.8)	264 (13.2)	620 (24.2)	202 (42.6)	81 (8.8)	147 (8.2)	504 (19.9)
Distribution, possession, or use of alcohol	— (†)	98 (5.2)	4 ! (1.6)	66 (5.6)	258 (11.2)	122 (27.6)	52 (11.5)	54 (5.1)	182 (9.7)
Vandalism[12]	453 (28.6)	403 (15.)	299 (24.4)	568 (28.3)	448 (19.4)	644 (96.2)	357 (33.5)	355 (19.7)	429 (24.9)

See notes at end of table.

Table 158. Percentage of public schools reporting crime incidents, and number and rate of incidents, by school characteristics and type of incident: 1999–2000 and 2005–06—Continued

	2005–06										
	Urbanicity				Percent minority enrollment[1]				Percent of students eligible for free/reduced-price lunch		
Type of crime incident	City	Urban fringe	Town	Rural	Less than 5	5 to less than 20	20 to less than 50	50 or more	0 to 20	21 to 50	51 or more
1	11	12	13	14	15	16	17	18	19	20	21
Number of public schools (in thousands)											
All schools	21 (0.2)	28 (0.2)	8 (#)	26 (0.3)	17 (0.7)	21 (0.8)	19 (0.9)	26 (0.7)	19 (0.9)	28 (1.1)	36 (1.0)
Schools with incident	19 (0.3)	24 (0.5)	7 (0.3)	21 (0.7)	13 (0.7)	17 (0.7)	16 (0.9)	23 (0.7)	15 (0.7)	24 (0.9)	32 (0.9)
Percent of schools with incident	89.5 (1.45)	87.9 (1.66)	87.0 (3.12)	80.1 (2.61)	79.4 (3.34)	82.6 (2.24)	87.3 (2.02)	90.7 (1.28)	79.4 (2.67)	87.9 (1.95)	87.4 (1.44)
Violent incidents[2]	82.3 (1.77)	78.2 (1.87)	82.2 (3.50)	72.3 (2.69)	71.6 (3.33)	73.5 (2.62)	79.7 (2.07)	82.9 (1.90)	68.0 (2.53)	79.7 (2.16)	81.4 (1.66)
Serious violent incidents[3]	23.9 (2.00)	15.9 (1.29)	15.2 (2.83)	13.6 (1.36)	13.1 (1.68)	15.7 (1.52)	16.6 (2.10)	21.6 (1.89)	12.5 (1.21)	19.2 (1.67)	18.0 (1.31)
Rape or attempted rape[4]	0.4 ! (0.15)	0.6 (0.17)	‡ (†)	‡ (†)	‡ (†)	0.2 ! (0.11)	0.4 ! (0.14)	0.5 ! (0.16)	‡ (†)	0.4 ! (0.14)	0.3 ! (0.10)
Sexual battery other than rape[5]	4.2 (0.75)	3.2 (0.38)	1.8 ! (0.60)	1.6 (0.34)	1.5 (0.42)	2.6 (0.44)	2.6 (0.45)	3.9 (0.72)	2.4 (0.42)	2.8 (0.37)	3.0 (0.49)
Physical attack or fight[6] with weapon[7]	5.2 (0.86)	2.5 (0.47)	2.6 ! (0.88)	1.8 ! (0.75)	‡ (†)	2.2 ! (0.66)	2.5 (0.71)	4.9 (0.86)	1.3 ! (0.41)	2.8 (0.70)	4.0 (0.67)
Threat of attack with weapon[7]	12.1 (1.63)	8.1 (0.96)	6.6 (1.75)	7.7 (1.08)	6.8 (1.33)	8.8 (1.11)	7.9 (1.50)	11.1 (1.37)	6.1 (0.96)	10.0 (1.23)	9.3 (1.05)
Robbery[8] with a weapon[7]	1.5 ! (0.49)	0.2 ! (0.08)	# (†)	# (†)	# (†)	# (†)	‡ (†)	0.8 (0.25)	‡ (†)	0.3 ! (0.10)	0.7 ! (0.28)
Robbery[8] without a weapon[7]	9.0 (1.34)	5.5 (0.77)	6.0 (1.62)	5.5 (1.04)	4.8 (1.20)	4.7 (1.50)	5.9 (1.50)	9.0 (1.00)	4.0 (0.75)	6.8 (1.22)	7.4 (0.82)
Physical attack or fight without a weapon	79.0 (1.77)	74.8 (1.92)	79.0 (3.73)	68.4 (2.64)	67.6 (3.23)	70.5 (2.85)	74.9 (2.53)	80.6 (1.84)	65.3 (2.41)	75.8 (2.41)	77.8 (1.97)
Threat of attack without weapon	55.3 (2.73)	53.3 (2.05)	55.2 (3.66)	47.6 (2.48)	47.1 (3.56)	47.8 (2.74)	55.7 (2.33)	55.2 (2.34)	45.1 (2.27)	55.5 (2.15)	53.4 (1.93)
Theft/larceny[9]	46.8 (1.98)	46.9 (1.73)	48.4 (3.47)	43.7 (2.40)	42.8 (3.53)	43.4 (2.43)	47.9 (2.43)	48.4 (2.28)	45.9 (1.94)	52.5 (1.95)	41.0 (1.68)
Other incidents[10]	72.7 (2.56)	69.9 (1.72)	70.6 (4.38)	62.1 (2.59)	62.4 (3.66)	63.4 (2.18)	71.5 (2.55)	71.9 (2.24)	61.7 (2.87)	72.3 (1.88)	68.5 (1.67)
Possess firearm/explosive device[11]	10.2 (1.41)	7.7 (0.97)	5.8 (1.51)	4.7 (0.83)	3.2 (0.83)	4.5 (0.78)	5.6 (0.95)	12.7 (1.40)	4.6 (0.93)	6.3 (0.88)	9.2 (1.07)
Possess knife or sharp object	47.3 (2.38)	44.0 (1.71)	47.7 (3.68)	36.4 (2.63)	34.3 (2.98)	38.7 (2.19)	46.8 (2.73)	46.9 (2.03)	35.3 (2.66)	44.7 (2.52)	45.3 (1.97)
Distribution, possession, or use of illegal drugs	25.0 (1.16)	25.6 (0.91)	31.0 (1.72)	25.2 (1.63)	22.9 (2.05)	24.7 (1.64)	28.1 (1.85)	26.1 (1.52)	25.3 (1.57)	29.6 (1.55)	23.4 (1.27)
Distribution, possession, or use of alcohol	13.2 (0.92)	16.3 (0.68)	15.5 (1.29)	18.7 (1.90)	16.2 (2.70)	18.0 (1.60)	18.2 (1.60)	12.6 (0.91)	19.3 (1.39)	21.5 (1.78)	10.5 (0.73)
Vandalism[12]	58.3 (2.65)	54.3 (1.83)	51.0 (3.97)	40.0 (2.05)	41.2 (3.03)	48.7 (2.13)	52.9 (2.42)	54.6 (2.25)	47.4 (2.33)	55.6 (2.07)	48.2 (1.72)
Number of incidents (in thousands)	784 (32.9)	777 (27.3)	191 (12.0)	440 (22.7)	260 (21.1)	440 (24.1)	499 (29.0)	931 (39.7)	374 (14.2)	768 (23.9)	1,049 (41.6)
Violent incidents[2]	547 (27.5)	525 (24.3)	129 (9.3)	288 (18.6)	174 (19.5)	270 (17.5)	326 (24.4)	678 (34.1)	210 (10.1)	502 (21.4)	778 (35.2)
Serious violent incidents[3]	30 (6.4)	17 (1.9)	4 (0.9)	9 (1.2)	6 (0.9)	11 (1.7)	16 ! (6.4)	26 (2.9)	7 (1.0)	16 (1.7)	36 (6.6)
Rape or attempted rape[4]	# (†)	# (†)	‡ (†)	‡ (†)	‡ (†)	# (†)	# (†)	# (†)	‡ (†)	# (†)	# (†)
Sexual battery other than rape[5]	2 (0.3)	2 (0.3)	# (†)	1 (0.1)	# (†)	1 (0.2)	1 (0.2)	2 (0.3)	1 (0.2)	1 (0.3)	2 (0.3)
Physical attack or fight[6] with weapon[7]	3 (0.5)	3 ! (1.5)	# (†)	1 ! (0.3)	‡ (†)	1 ! (0.3)	1 ! (0.3)	5 ! (1.6)	1 ! (0.3)	1 (0.3)	5 ! (1.6)
Threat of attack with weapon[7]	15 ! (6.4)	6 (0.8)	1 (0.3)	3 (0.5)	3 (0.7)	5 (1.0)	‡ (†)	8 (1.6)	3 (0.5)	6 (1.0)	16 ! (6.4)
Robbery[8] with a weapon[7]	1 ! (0.2)	# (†)	# (†)	# (†)	# (†)	# (†)	‡ (†)	‡ (†)	‡ (†)	‡ (†)	# (†)
Robbery[8] without a weapon[7]	10 (1.6)	6 (1.0)	2 ! (0.7)	4 (0.8)	2 (0.5)	4 (1.0)	5 (1.2)	10 (1.2)	3 (0.8)	7 (1.1)	12 (1.7)
Physical attack or fight without a weapon[7]	329 (17.2)	318 (16.0)	78 (6.1)	173 (14.0)	107 (14.6)	163 (15.2)	193 (15.2)	410 (22.3)	129 (7.7)	301 (17.1)	468 (20.7)
Threat of attack without weapon	189 (15.4)	190 (12.2)	48 (4.6)	106 (8.0)	61 (7.2)	96 (7.4)	118 (9.2)	242 (18.1)	74 (5.8)	184 (8.2)	275 (18.4)
Theft/larceny[9]	78 (4.6)	90 (3.9)	23 (2.3)	52 (3.5)	31 (2.2)	61 (3.8)	63 (3.5)	82 (4.7)	63 (3.4)	97 (3.8)	82 (5.2)
Other incidents[10]	159 (7.7)	162 (4.2)	38 (2.6)	100 (5.7)	55 (3.4)	109 (7.4)	110 (5.9)	172 (8.1)	102 (5.5)	169 (5.2)	188 (9.4)
Possess firearm/explosive device[11]	6 (1.8)	4 (0.6)	1 (0.2)	2 (0.3)	1 (0.2)	1 (0.2)	8 (1.8)	8 (1.8)	1 (0.3)	3 (0.4)	8 (1.9)
Possess knife or sharp object	31 (1.7)	31 (1.4)	9 (0.7)	20 (1.2)	11 (1.0)	18 (1.3)	22 (1.4)	36 (1.8)	14 (0.9)	32 (1.4)	43 (2.1)
Distribution, possession, or use of illegal drugs	38 (2.1)	43 (1.6)	10 (1.1)	26 (2.4)	13 (1.2)	29 (2.1)	32 (2.3)	39 (2.6)	28 (1.8)	48 (2.4)	41 (3.0)
Distribution, possession, or use of alcohol	12 (1.3)	18 (1.2)	4 (0.6)	13 (1.8)	8 (1.4)	16 (1.5)	12 (1.1)	11 (0.9)	17 (1.5)	21 (1.9)	9 (0.8)
Vandalism[12]	72 (5.3)	68 (3.1)	15 (1.3)	39 (2.7)	23 (2.2)	45 (5.0)	43 (2.8)	77 (4.8)	41 (4.3)	65 (3.1)	86 (5.5)

See notes at end of table.

Table 158. Percentage of public schools reporting crime incidents, and number and rate of incidents, by school characteristics and type of incident: 1999–2000 and 2005–06—Continued

Type of crime incident	Urbanicity				Percent minority enrollment[1]				Percent of students eligible for free/reduced-price lunch		
	City	Urban fringe	Town	Rural	Less than 5	5 to less than 20	20 to less than 50	50 or more	0 to 20	21 to 50	51 or more
1	11	12	13	14	15	16	17	18	19	20	21
Number of incidents per 100,000 students	5,457 (213.5)	4,017 (136.5)	4,702 (278.7)	4,379 (210.0)	4,033 (264.3)	3,734 (177.8)	4,350 (211.4)	5,478 (211.0)	2,931 (110.4)	4,612 (180.0)	5,707 (200.4)
Violent incidents[2]	3,811 (183.9)	2,714 (121.6)	3,188 (218.1)	2,867 (171.9)	2,695 (253.9)	2,291 (137.9)	2,843 (183.7)	3,986 (186.6)	1,641 (79.1)	3,014 (152.6)	4,233 (174.0)
Serious violent incidents[3]	207 (45.5)	87 (9.6)	90 (20.0)	88 (11.6)	89 (12.5)	95 (13.8)	137 ! (56.7)	151 (15.9)	55 (7.7)	99 (10.3)	194 (36.8)
Rape or attempted rape[4]	1 ! (0.3)	1 ! (0.3)	‡ (†)	‡ (†)	‡ (†)	# (†)	1 ! (0.2)	1 ! (0.3)	‡ (†)	1 ! (0.3)	1 ! (0.2)
Sexual battery other than rape[5]	12 (2.0)	9 (1.4)	‡ (1.6)	7 (1.5)	6 ! (2.2)	8 (1.7)	9 (1.6)	10 (1.9)	7 (1.6)	9 (1.5)	10 (1.8)
Physical attack or fight[6] with weapon[7]	19 (3.6)	16 ! (7.8)	9 ! (3.7)	8 ! (3.0)	‡ (†)	7 (1.8)	7 ! (2.4)	29 ! (9.2)	4 ! (1.2)	8 (1.9)	28 ! (8.7)
Threat of attack with weapon[7]	103 ! (44.7)	31 (4.4)	23 (6.2)	30 (4.6)	40 (10.4)	42 (8.4)	‡ (†)	48 (9.2)	21 (3.8)	38 (6.2)	86 ! (35.5)
Robbery[8] with a weapon[7]	4 ! (1.6)	# (†)	# (†)	# (†)	# (†)	# (†)	‡ (†)	3 ! (1.3)	‡ (†)	‡ (†)	2 ! (0.8)
Robbery[8] without a weapon[7]	69 (11.3)	30 (5.3)	53 ! (16.4)	43 (8.1)	37 (8.1)	35 (8.4)	43 (10.7)	60 (7.2)	23 (6.3)	41 (6.5)	67 (9.3)
Physical attack or fight without a weapon	2,289 (110.1)	1,643 (79.9)	1,923 (148.5)	1,726 (129.1)	1,665 (199.2)	1,385 (104.1)	1,679 (107.7)	2,411 (124.8)	1,009 (62.7)	1,809 (109.5)	2,545 (97.7)
Threat of attack without weapon	1,315 (104.7)	984 (63.3)	1,175 (109.3)	1,053 (79.2)	941 (100.8)	812 (58.7)	1,026 (72.3)	1,424 (103.4)	577 (43.6)	1,107 (63.7)	1,494 (94.6)
Theft/larceny[9]	540 (29.0)	465 (19.9)	567 (55.2)	521 (34.7)	482 (40.0)	517 (28.0)	551 (30.4)	482 (27.0)	494 (23.4)	583 (24.5)	448 (27.7)
Other incidents[10]	1,106 (51.7)	838 (23.3)	947 (63.3)	991 (57.5)	856 (53.2)	926 (55.3)	956 (48.6)	1,010 (43.5)	795 (45.4)	1,015 (33.8)	1,025 (48.0)
Possess firearm/explosive device[11]	44 (12.7)	20 (3.2)	17 (4.9)	15 (3.0)	10 (2.5)	11 (2.1)	14 (2.6)	50 (10.8)	10 (2.0)	18 (2.7)	44 (10.2)
Possess knife or sharp object	214 (10.8)	158 (7.6)	216 (18.1)	198 (12.0)	167 (14.2)	153 (8.9)	189 (10.5)	213 (8.7)	114 (7.4)	193 (8.4)	236 (10.3)
Distribution, possession, or use of illegal drugs	266 (14.0)	220 (8.8)	256 (27.4)	258 (24.4)	197 (19.5)	247 (15.3)	275 (20.8)	232 (14.0)	217 (14.1)	289 (16.8)	224 (15.3)
Distribution, possession, or use of alcohol	84 (8.8)	91 (5.9)	95 (13.1)	133 (18.3)	121 (23.3)	132 (12.6)	105 (10.3)	62 (5.2)	131 (11.1)	124 (10.7)	51 (4.4)
Vandalism[12]	498 (37.2)	350 (16.8)	363 (32.9)	387 (27.6)	362 (32.3)	383 (40.7)	373 (22.1)	453 (27.9)	324 (35.1)	391 (19.0)	470 (29.1)

—Not available.
†Not applicable.
#Rounds to zero.
‡Interpret data with caution.
¹Excludes the 2 percent of schools for which race/ethnicity data were missing. For this reason, the detailed results do not sum to the totals.
²Violent incidents include serious violent incidents (i.e., rape or attempted rape, sexual battery other than rape, physical attack or fight with a weapon, threat of physical attack with a weapon, and robbery with or without a weapon) plus physical attack or fight without a weapon and threat of physical attack without a weapon.
³Serious violent incidents include rape or attempted rape, sexual battery other than rape, physical attack or fight with a weapon, threat of physical attack with a weapon, and robbery with or without a weapon.
⁴Rape was defined for respondents as "forced sexual intercourse (vaginal, anal, or oral penetration). This includes penetration from a foreign object."
⁵Sexual battery was defined for respondents as an "incident that includes threatened rape, fondling, indecent liberties, child molestation, or sodomy."
⁶Physical attack or fight was defined for respondents as an "actual and intentional touching or striking of another person against his or her will, or the intentional causing of bodily harm to an individual."
⁷Weapon was defined for respondents as "any instrument or object used with the intent to threaten, injure, or kill. Includes look-alikes if they are used to threaten others."
⁸Robbery was defined for respondents as "the taking or attempting to take anything of value that is owned by another person or organization, under confrontational circumstances by force or threat of force or violence and/or by putting the victim in fear. A key difference between robbery and theft/larceny is that robbery involves a threat or battery."
⁹Theft/larceny (taking things over $10 without personal confrontation) was defined for respondents as "the unlawful taking of another person's property without personal confrontation, threat, violence, or bodily harm. Included are pocket picking, steal-

ing purse or backpack (if left unattended or no force was used to take it from owner), theft from a building, theft from a motor vehicle or motor vehicle parts or accessories, theft of bicycles, theft from vending machines, and all other types of thefts."
¹⁰Other incidents include possession of a firearm or explosive device; possession of a knife or sharp object; distribution, possession, or use of illegal drugs or alcohol; and vandalism.
¹¹Firearm/explosive device was defined as "any weapon that is designed to (or may readily be converted to) expel a projectile by the action of an explosive. This includes guns, bombs, grenades, mines, rockets, missiles, pipe bombs, or similar devices designed to explode and capable of causing bodily harm or property damage."
¹²Vandalism was defined for respondents as "the willful damage or destruction of school property including bombing, arson, graffiti, and other acts that cause property damage. Includes damage caused by computer hacking."
NOTE: Either the school principal or the person most knowledgeable about discipline issues at school completed the SSOCS questionnaire. If the respondent did not provide a value for the total number of specified incidents at the school, the value was imputed to equal the number of specified incidents reported to police. Values associated with violent incidents, serious violent incidents, total incidents, and other incidents were obtained by adding the post-imputed values that comprise each of the preceding composite variables. All public schools include primary schools, middle schools, high schools, and combined schools. The population counts on SSOCS 2000 and 2006 exclude all schools in outlying U.S. territories; nonregular schools such as special education, vocational, alternative/other, and ungraded schools; and schools with a high grade of kindergarten or lower. "At school/at your school" was defined for respondents as including activities happening in school buildings, on school grounds, on school buses, and at places that are holding school-sponsored events or activities. Respondents were instructed to, unless the survey specified otherwise, only respond for those times that were during normal school hours or when school activities/events were in session. Primary schools are defined as schools in which the lowest grade is not higher than grade 3 and the highest grade is not higher than grade 8. Middle schools are defined as schools in which the lowest grade is not lower than grade 4 and the highest grade is not higher than grade 9. High schools are defined as schools in which the lowest grade is not lower than grade 9 and the highest grade is not higher than grade 12. Combined schools include all other combinations of grades, including K–12 schools. Detail may not sum to totals because of rounding.
SOURCE: U.S. Department of Education, National Center for Education Statistics, School Survey on Crime and Safety (SSOCS), 2000 and 2006. (This table was prepared July 2007.)

Table 159. Percentage of schools with various security measures, by school control and selected characteristics: 2003–04

Selected school control and characteristic	Total schools — Number	Total schools — Percentage distribution	Controlled access to school buildings[1]	Controlled access to school grounds[2]	School uniforms	Strict dress code	Daily metal detector checks[3]	Random metal detector checks	Closed lunch[4]	Random sweeps for contraband	Daily presence of police or security	Video surveillance	Violence prevention program
1	2	3	4	5	6	7	8	9	10	11	12	13	14
Public total	87,600 (310)	100.0 (†)	81.5 (0.60)	39.4 (0.83)	13.5 (0.53)	49.3 (0.70)	2.0 (0.21)	5.7 (0.32)	88.0 (0.50)	12.8 (0.48)	24.8 (0.59)	32.5 (0.68)	66.3 (0.73)
School enrollment													
Under 300	25,400 (680)	29.0 (0.77)	74.9 (1.43)	33.3 (1.60)	11.9 (1.02)	44.6 (1.61)	4.1 (0.69)	7.1 (0.89)	83.2 (1.22)	17.6 (1.44)	12.6 (1.29)	25.7 (1.56)	62.6 (1.62)
300 to 499	24,800 (640)	28.4 (0.71)	84.4 (1.04)	36.0 (1.38)	12.3 (1.02)	45.4 (1.38)	0.5 (0.19)	2.8 (0.41)	88.4 (0.95)	8.1 (0.69)	13.4 (0.91)	30.5 (1.34)	66.9 (1.37)
500 to 999	28,200 (560)	32.2 (0.64)	84.7 (0.94)	43.7 (1.31)	15.6 (0.95)	54.4 (1.35)	1.2 (0.18)	4.7 (0.48)	91.9 (0.76)	10.2 (0.61)	29.0 (1.21)	32.8 (1.23)	67.9 (1.32)
1,000 to 1,499	5,500 (260)	6.3 (0.30)	84.9 (1.63)	50.6 (2.91)	18.8 (2.63)	59.4 (2.52)	2.4 (0.58)	12.2 (1.51)	90.6 (1.21)	20.0 (1.50)	67.7 (2.36)	52.2 (2.59)	68.2 (2.02)
1,500 or more	3,600 (210)	4.1 (0.24)	77.9 (2.09)	55.6 (2.64)	8.6 (1.66)	55.6 (2.40)	3.4 (0.61)	14.5 (1.57)	83.7 (2.01)	21.7 (1.88)	90.4 (1.83)	61.5 (2.77)	73.7 (2.09)
Percent of students approved for free or reduced-price school lunch													
Does not participate	3,500 (290)	4.0 (0.33)	69.3 (3.21)	42.1 (3.57)	14.8 (2.59)	41.7 (3.25)	3.1 (0.84)	10.0 (2.22)	54.2 (3.82)	23.1 (2.70)	28.3 (3.39)	37.0 (3.88)	61.5 (3.36)
Less than 15	15,000 (480)	17.1 (0.54)	85.3 (1.42)	31.4 (1.78)	3.1 (0.63)	37.7 (1.76)	† (†)	1.3 (0.27)	85.9 (1.33)	8.9 (0.99)	21.2 (1.31)	32.8 (1.67)	62.8 (2.24)
15 to 29	14,900 (510)	17.0 (0.58)	84.3 (1.28)	37.5 (1.43)	5.0 (0.80)	45.1 (1.86)	0.7 (0.19)	3.1 (0.54)	86.3 (1.29)	10.5 (0.92)	23.8 (1.34)	33.1 (1.59)	61.8 (1.60)
30 to 49	21,600 (590)	24.6 (0.67)	78.8 (1.22)	34.1 (1.53)	7.1 (0.77)	49.9 (1.57)	1.6 (0.37)	4.3 (0.48)	87.7 (1.12)	12.6 (0.64)	23.6 (1.07)	31.2 (1.35)	66.0 (1.54)
50 to 74	17,700 (510)	20.2 (0.58)	81.6 (1.51)	41.9 (1.97)	16.4 (1.36)	53.0 (1.58)	1.9 (0.30)	7.1 (0.79)	91.5 (0.83)	13.1 (1.06)	24.5 (1.59)	32.9 (1.42)	69.3 (1.77)
75 to 100	15,000 (570)	17.1 (0.64)	81.7 (1.58)	53.5 (2.13)	37.8 (1.93)	61.9 (1.96)	5.7 (1.01)	12.4 (1.27)	93.5 (1.06)	16.8 (1.68)	30.3 (1.88)	31.9 (2.03)	72.5 (1.85)
Location of school													
City	22,700 (420)	25.9 (0.49)	84.9 (1.16)	49.0 (1.64)	29.3 (1.48)	56.2 (1.63)	4.8 (0.68)	11.4 (0.83)	91.0 (0.80)	14.4 (0.85)	36.5 (1.09)	34.0 (1.24)	70.4 (1.35)
Suburban	25,600 (510)	29.2 (0.56)	86.4 (0.91)	40.1 (1.55)	11.0 (1.03)	44.2 (1.36)	1.1 (0.25)	3.6 (0.48)	88.0 (0.92)	6.1 (0.49)	26.2 (1.13)	34.7 (1.43)	67.7 (1.60)
Town	13,700 (420)	15.6 (0.48)	79.2 (1.51)	33.3 (1.94)	7.4 (0.96)	49.7 (1.84)	1.0 (0.30)	4.8 (0.73)	83.7 (1.62)	13.8 (1.25)	20.2 (1.39)	31.5 (1.67)	64.9 (2.03)
Rural	25,600 (490)	29.3 (0.55)	74.9 (1.28)	33.6 (1.43)	5.3 (0.82)	48.2 (1.55)	1.0 (0.20)	3.4 (0.36)	87.5 (0.88)	17.6 (1.08)	15.3 (0.81)	29.5 (1.34)	52.1 (1.36)
Level[5]													
Elementary	61,500 (360)	70.2 (0.32)	84.7 (0.65)	39.0 (1.03)	14.7 (0.67)	45.2 (0.94)	0.8 (0.23)	3.4 (0.33)	91.2 (0.62)	5.6 (0.44)	15.5 (0.62)	26.3 (0.77)	68.4 (1.00)
Secondary	19,700 (270)	22.5 (0.32)	75.0 (1.33)	41.4 (1.38)	8.8 (1.11)	59.7 (1.33)	3.7 (0.38)	10.2 (0.64)	80.4 (1.04)	28.2 (1.33)	53.9 (1.61)	51.1 (1.55)	61.3 (1.20)
Combined	6,400 (260)	7.4 (0.30)	70.9 (1.89)	37.2 (2.37)	16.1 (1.40)	57.2 (2.08)	8.8 (1.22)	14.8 (1.72)	80.7 (1.76)	35.0 (2.10)	24.4 (1.83)	34.7 (2.14)	62.3 (2.01)
Private total	27,700 (680)	100.0 (†)	73.5 (1.02)	40.2 (1.08)	55.5 (1.06)	73.7 (1.00)	0.8 (0.21)	0.7 (0.20)	88.4 (0.82)	7.7 (0.61)	5.9 (0.50)	19.4 (0.79)	39.0 (1.07)
School enrollment													
Under 300	22,500 (650)	81.3 (0.67)	72.2 (1.25)	40.3 (1.22)	52.4 (1.22)	71.2 (1.16)	1.0 (0.25)	0.9 (0.24)	88.2 (0.98)	8.0 (0.70)	4.0 (0.55)	15.6 (0.88)	37.4 (1.32)
300 to 499	3,100 (140)	11.3 (0.60)	81.1 (1.95)	39.8 (2.56)	69.3 (2.34)	84.2 (1.92)	‡ (†)	‡ (†)	90.6 (1.63)	5.7 (1.81)	5.5 (1.11)	32.1 (2.44)	48.0 (2.72)
500 to 999	1,800 (120)	6.3 (0.39)	77.8 (3.09)	37.8 (3.30)	71.5 (3.16)	87.2 (2.23)	‡ (†)	‡ (†)	88.3 (2.30)	5.9 (1.44)	22.1 (2.85)	41.3 (3.08)	42.2 (3.23)
1,000 or more	300 (40)	1.1 (0.15)	64.4 (6.81)	50.2 (8.14)	50.1 (6.61)	76.2 (5.48)	‡ (†)	‡ (†)	89.2 (4.06)	16.9 (5.88)	53.2 (7.00)	48.6 (6.59)	48.0 (5.97)
Percent of students approved for free or reduced-price school lunch													
Does not participate	21,100 (570)	76.3 (0.81)	70.3 (1.33)	39.7 (1.21)	51.9 (1.28)	71.5 (1.15)	0.8 (0.26)	0.4 (0.18)	87.4 (0.98)	7.7 (0.68)	6.4 (0.63)	17.8 (0.95)	36.0 (1.23)
Less than 15	3,500 (180)	12.8 (0.61)	85.1 (2.18)	33.7 (2.92)	68.0 (2.72)	84.1 (2.19)	‡ (†)	‡ (†)	91.4 (2.22)	4.1 (1.03)	2.6 (0.87)	23.8 (2.07)	51.8 (3.29)
15 to 29	1,200 (130)	4.3 (0.46)	76.9 (4.48)	41.7 (5.12)	66.5 (4.84)	76.6 (4.77)	‡ (†)	‡ (†)	96.8 (1.69)	4.7 (2.32)	‡ (†)	19.4 (4.12)	41.8 (4.90)
30 or more	1,800 (180)	6.5 (0.58)	86.1 (2.46)	57.1 (4.09)	65.7 (3.56)	76.5 (3.26)	3.1 (1.84)	5.5 (2.19)	89.7 (2.51)	16.8 (3.77)	9.3 (2.60)	29.1 (3.31)	48.0 (3.91)
Level[5]													
Elementary	16,700 (330)	60.5 (1.07)	79.5 (1.19)	44.9 (1.32)	60.6 (1.27)	74.1 (1.32)	0.3 (0.17)	‡ (†)	90.3 (0.94)	2.4 (0.52)	3.1 (0.50)	19.9 (0.97)	39.2 (1.34)
Secondary	2,500 (360)	9.1 (1.14)	62.9 (3.65)	32.2 (3.80)	44.9 (3.53)	70.0 (3.78)	3.1 (1.87)	2.1 (1.16)	73.4 (3.80)	23.3 (3.75)	16.2 (2.99)	24.4 (3.11)	44.3 (4.00)
Combined	8,400 (280)	30.4 (0.77)	64.8 (2.11)	33.2 (1.96)	48.4 (2.00)	74.0 (1.66)	1.2 (0.49)	1.7 (0.56)	89.3 (1.34)	13.5 (1.33)	8.3 (1.15)	16.9 (1.60)	37.1 (2.05)

†Not applicable.

‡Reporting standards not met.

[1]Access to buildings is controlled during school hours (e.g., by locked or monitored doors).

[2]Access to grounds is controlled during school hours (e.g., by locked or monitored gates).

[3]All students must pass through a metal detector each day.

[4]All or most students are required to stay on school grounds during lunch.

[5]Elementary schools have grade 6 or below, with no grade higher than 7; secondary schools have no grade lower than 7; and combined schools have grades lower than 7 and higher than 8.

NOTE: Detail may not sum to totals because of rounding. Standard errors appear in parentheses.

SOURCE: U.S. Department of Education, National Center for Education Statistics, Schools and Staffing Survey (SASS), "Public School Principal Questionnaire" and "Private School Principal Questionnaire", 2003–04. (This table was prepared July 2006.)

Table 160. Number of students suspended and expelled from public elementary and secondary schools, by sex, race/ethnicity, and state: 2006

State	Students suspended[1]							
		Sex		Race/ethnicity				
	Total	Male	Female	White	Black	Hispanic	Asian/Pacific Islander	American Indian/Alaska Native
1	2	3	4	5	6	7	8	9
United States	3,328,750 (20,038)	2,272,290 (13,667)	1,056,470 (6,842)	1,302,410 (9,493)	1,244,820 (11,267)	670,700 (6,889)	63,220 (836)	47,610 (2,861)
Alabama	75,090 (727)	50,580 (485)	24,510 (256)	25,730 (380)	47,810 (690)	960 (11)	260 (#)	330 (26)
Alaska	8,060 (427)	5,660 (306)	2,390 (124)	3,470 (72)	620 (5)	380 (10)	460 (33)	3,120 (402)
Arizona	56,000 (1,117)	40,900 (800)	15,110 (347)	19,130 (291)	5,960 (118)	25,010 (387)	660 (9)	5,250 (973)
Arkansas	34,920 (1,191)	24,870 (910)	10,050 (318)	16,340 (757)	16,310 (819)	1,870 (121)	260 (23)	150 (19)
California	474,590 (11,349)	340,090 (8,199)	134,500 (3,481)	115,320 (3,178)	84,860 (4,117)	242,110 (6,179)	24,690 (770)	7,600 (1,531)
Colorado	47,650 (463)	33,580 (353)	14,070 (142)	22,380 (339)	6,030 (12)	17,600 (185)	850 (7)	790 (72)
Connecticut	36,370 (2,749)	24,240 (1,770)	12,130 (999)	14,430 (1,304)	12,700 (1,536)	8,620 (890)	510 (43)	100 (17)
Delaware[2]	12,150 (†)	7,890 (†)	4,260 (†)	3,890 (†)	7,110 (†)	1,020 (†)	110 (†)	20 (†)
District of Columbia[2]	210 (†)	120 (†)	80 (†)	10 (†)	190 (†)	10 (†)	# (†)	# (†)
Florida	291,820 (3,692)	192,470 (2,270)	99,350 (1,454)	105,550 (1,744)	129,630 (2,599)	54,170 (534)	1,890 (18)	580 (49)
Georgia	143,560 (2,598)	95,080 (1,757)	48,470 (877)	37,670 (1,334)	96,980 (1,684)	7,800 (297)	1,010 (22)	90 (4)
Hawaii[2]	9,770 (†)	6,640 (†)	3,120 (†)	1,290 (†)	290 (†)	310 (†)	7,810 (†)	70 (†)
Idaho	9,100 (434)	6,980 (326)	2,120 (115)	6,850 (385)	90 (5)	1,750 (85)	70 (3)	350 (109)
Illinois	130,650 (2,807)	86,950 (1,987)	43,700 (892)	41,270 (1,742)	63,590 (1,940)	24,340 (637)	1,330 (40)	130 (10)
Indiana	77,460 (2,737)	53,300 (1,860)	24,170 (945)	49,720 (2,094)	22,420 (1,266)	4,850 (557)	310 (30)	160 (17)
Iowa	14,190 (440)	9,860 (294)	4,330 (167)	10,000 (397)	2,950 (64)	930 (37)	160 (16)	140 (6)
Kansas	24,300 (701)	17,160 (531)	7,140 (197)	13,680 (621)	5,920 (67)	3,950 (71)	350 (8)	400 (32)
Kentucky	43,420 (2,319)	29,840 (1,636)	13,580 (734)	32,800 (1,780)	9,870 (1,002)	620 (46)	90 (11)	40 (9)
Louisiana	67,780 (2,535)	44,370 (1,636)	23,410 (911)	23,370 (1,721)	43,040 (1,536)	730 (21)	230 (12)	410 (107)
Maine	8,540 (440)	6,340 (345)	2,200 (114)	7,880 (421)	420 (16)	110 (22)	80 (4)	50 (8)
Maryland[2]	60,550 (†)	38,780 (†)	21,770 (†)	23,600 (†)	26,450 (†)	9,220 (†)	1,000 (†)	290 (†)
Massachusetts	49,930 (2,490)	32,960 (1,580)	16,970 (944)	28,040 (1,627)	7,650 (311)	12,780 (1,231)	1,230 (100)	230 (27)
Michigan	131,750 (5,404)	89,450 (3,547)	42,310 (2,039)	71,480 (2,916)	52,580 (4,227)	5,650 (528)	980 (136)	1,060 (133)
Minnesota	30,780 (674)	21,360 (476)	9,420 (234)	15,760 (541)	9,910 (189)	2,440 (110)	1,130 (17)	1,540 (194)
Mississippi	51,940 (1,756)	34,420 (1,154)	17,520 (623)	13,050 (565)	38,250 (1,495)	380 (34)	120 (18)	130 (35)
Missouri	67,820 (2,020)	47,010 (1,408)	20,810 (643)	32,790 (1,174)	32,560 (1,551)	1,780 (63)	450 (13)	240 (15)
Montana	6,500 (232)	4,600 (163)	1,900 (78)	4,490 (177)	70 (3)	120 (6)	40 (2)	1,780 (157)
Nebraska	10,600 (185)	7,240 (142)	3,360 (49)	5,620 (121)	2,820 (5)	1,770 (71)	100 (2)	280 (25)
Nevada[2]	31,620 (†)	20,690 (†)	10,950 (†)	9,700 (†)	7,360 (†)	12,850 (†)	1,270 (†)	440 (†)
New Hampshire	10,170 (498)	6,770 (399)	3,400 (111)	9,080 (489)	310 (8)	670 (7)	80 (6)	30 (2)
New Jersey	79,030 (3,559)	53,730 (2,347)	25,300 (1,260)	28,260 (2,252)	30,520 (1,609)	18,700 (1,170)	1,490 (104)	70 (12)
New Mexico	17,140 (572)	11,560 (387)	5,570 (196)	3,970 (171)	590 (15)	9,510 (497)	110 (3)	2,960 (79)
New York	106,670 (3,845)	72,970 (2,437)	33,700 (1,456)	49,950 (1,918)	38,640 (2,377)	16,040 (857)	1,360 (88)	680 (124)
North Carolina	149,780 (6,774)	101,920 (4,535)	47,860 (2,350)	50,630 (2,234)	85,000 (4,561)	9,250 (392)	790 (43)	4,100 (1,947)
North Dakota	2,140 (153)	1,460 (100)	670 (59)	1,260 (71)	100 (2)	50 (3)	20 (1)	720 (135)
Ohio	109,370 (4,049)	73,860 (2,696)	35,500 (1,442)	62,880 (2,712)	43,030 (2,880)	2,810 (357)	570 (56)	90 (10)
Oklahoma	31,160 (966)	21,830 (706)	9,330 (286)	14,940 (627)	8,210 (403)	3,150 (78)	200 (7)	4,660 (233)
Oregon	27,470 (1,028)	20,140 (732)	7,330 (322)	19,520 (773)	1,620 (44)	4,870 (339)	590 (21)	880 (73)
Pennsylvania	114,040 (6,402)	74,950 (4,013)	39,090 (2,435)	53,090 (2,856)	52,730 (4,090)	6,950 (568)	1,190 (202)	90 (16)
Rhode Island	12,250 (1,071)	8,040 (776)	4,210 (309)	6,920 (847)	1,930 (200)	2,950 (143)	340 (30)	120 (24)
South Carolina	83,830 (2,289)	54,320 (1,547)	29,520 (828)	25,750 (1,067)	55,540 (1,753)	2,120 (302)	240 (21)	180 (77)
South Dakota	3,100 (161)	2,180 (112)	910 (52)	1,850 (87)	170 (3)	110 (1)	40 (2)	930 (138)
Tennessee	73,380 (2,200)	49,860 (1,562)	23,520 (666)	39,350 (1,655)	31,280 (924)	2,290 (64)	400 (6)	70 (7)
Texas	253,530 (2,298)	173,460 (1,671)	80,070 (693)	46,910 (824)	82,270 (1,276)	121,480 (1,411)	2,410 (16)	460 (12)
Utah	16,350 (119)	11,740 (97)	4,610 (50)	10,020 (98)	540 (8)	4,640 (110)	660 (5)	490 (4)
Vermont	3,430 (136)	2,420 (99)	1,010 (44)	3,260 (129)	100 (8)	30 (4)	30 (3)	20 (2)
Virginia	91,810 (2,805)	61,580 (1,867)	30,230 (991)	35,200 (1,080)	49,590 (2,284)	5,490 (165)	1,370 (38)	170 (13)
Washington	59,920 (1,326)	44,470 (1,011)	15,450 (335)	36,360 (1,082)	7,060 (37)	10,280 (390)	3,180 (33)	3,040 (370)
West Virginia	30,750 (2,986)	21,430 (2,033)	9,330 (962)	27,270 (2,482)	3,090 (548)	310 (73)	50 (11)	30 (8)
Wisconsin	43,680 (1,126)	28,210 (721)	15,460 (449)	18,480 (724)	18,010 (399)	4,650 (65)	660 (16)	1,880 (751)
Wyoming	2,680 (400)	1,970 (288)	710 (119)	2,200 (346)	40 (5)	250 (43)	20 (3)	160 (46)

See notes at end of table.

Table 160. Number of students suspended and expelled from public elementary and secondary schools, by sex, race/ethnicity, and state: 2006—Continued

Students expelled — Standard errors appear in parentheses.

State	Total	Sex: Male	Sex: Female	Race/ethnicity: White	Black	Hispanic	Asian/Pacific Islander	American Indian/Alaska Native
1	10	11	12	13	14	15	16	17
United States	102,080 (1,329)	76,360 (976)	25,720 (398)	38,030 (612)	38,640 (935)	22,140 (388)	1,720 (44)	1,550 (69)
Alabama	1,300 (21)	900 (21)	400 (5)	390 (8)	870 (19)	40 (#)	# (#)	# (†)
Alaska	180 (4)	140 (2)	50 (4)	100 (3)	30 (#)	10 (#)	10 (†)	40 (2)
Arizona	660 (41)	530 (36)	130 (6)	260 (32)	60 (3)	300 (16)	10 (#)	40 (5)
Arkansas	500 (43)	360 (29)	130 (19)	310 (32)	150 (15)	30 (9)	10 (2)	# (†)
California	19,460 (608)	15,600 (477)	3,870 (152)	5,350 (230)	3,010 (128)	9,960 (360)	860 (40)	280 (37)
Colorado	2,210 (62)	1,760 (43)	450 (25)	1,000 (32)	260 (2)	860 (47)	30 (4)	60 (12)
Connecticut	1,330 (135)	970 (87)	360 (56)	470 (54)	490 (80)	340 (53)	20 (1)	# (†)
Delaware	230 (†)	170 (†)	50 (†)	100 (†)	110 (†)	10 (†)	# (†)	# (†)
District of Columbia[2]	130 (†)	70 (†)	60 (†)	# (†)	120 (†)	10 (†)	# (†)	# (†)
Florida	1,120 (71)	860 (60)	270 (12)	530 (39)	420 (33)	160 (9)	# (1)	10 (1)
Georgia	3,660 (170)	2,740 (131)	930 (46)	1,390 (93)	2,100 (92)	150 (15)	20 (2)	# (†)
Hawaii[2]	230 (†)	190 (†)	40 (†)	# (†)	# (†)	70 (†)	# (†)	# (†)
Idaho	190 (11)	140 (9)	40 (5)	140 (†)	# (†)	40 (6)	# (6)	# (†)
Illinois	2,760 (132)	2,040 (80)	730 (60)	890 (116)	1,390 (31)	460 (14)	20 (4)	# (†)
Indiana	6,620 (395)	4,560 (272)	2,060 (137)	4,510 (309)	1,610 (119)	460 (45)	30 (6)	20 (4)
Iowa	200 (39)	160 (31)	40 (8)	160 (34)	20 (3)	20 (6)	# (2)	# (†)
Kansas	850 (63)	630 (35)	220 (30)	430 (58)	280 (7)	110 (6)	20 (1)	10 (6)
Kentucky	540 (110)	370 (72)	170 ! (45)	400 (67)	130 ! (68)	# (†)	# (†)	# (†)
Louisiana	5,800 (212)	4,120 (159)	1,680 (56)	1,500 (113)	4,180 (157)	70 (3)	20 (1)	20 (4)
Maine	160 (21)	130 (14)	40 ! (10)	160 (21)	# (†)	# (#)	# (#)	# (†)
Maryland[2]	1,560 (†)	1,190 (†)	360 (†)	340 (†)	1,010 (†)	140 (†)	20 (†)	# (†)
Massachusetts	530 (35)	410 (27)	120 (12)	200 (31)	180 (8)	110 (7)	10 (2)	20 (6)
Michigan	2,140 (149)	1,610 (113)	530 (46)	1,030 (77)	950 (108)	110 (15)	30 (5)	20 (7)
Minnesota	250 (16)	200 (15)	50 (5)	150 (12)	50 (1)	20 (3)	10 (1)	20 (†)
Mississippi	1,490 (73)	1,090 (64)	400 (15)	290 (47)	1,190 (45)	10 (#)	# (#)	# (†)
Missouri	280 (36)	220 (26)	60 (15)	210 (35)	60 (4)	10 (#)	# (†)	# (†)
Montana	100 (10)	90 (9)	20 (3)	60 (8)	# (†)	# (†)	# (†)	40 (7)
Nebraska	650 (11)	480 (9)	170 (2)	290 (7)	210 (1)	110 (4)	10 (#)	30 (4)
Nevada[2]	1,520 (†)	1,190 (†)	340 (†)	490 (†)	410 (†)	530 (†)	70 (†)	20 (†)
New Hampshire	120 ! (38)	80 ! (22)	40 ! (17)	100 (36)	10 (2)	10 (†)	# (†)	# (†)
New Jersey	270 ! (118)	250 ! (118)	20 ! (5)	100 (49)	70 ! (23)	80 (39)	10 (8)	# (†)
New Mexico	240 (16)	200 (14)	40 (3)	40 (3)	10 (#)	110 (10)	10 (#)	80 (10)
New York	890 (180)	700 (143)	190 (41)	580 (144)	240 ! (75)	60 (11)	30 (3)	10 (7)
North Carolina	1,970 ! (830)	1,480 ! (572)	500 ! (260)	300 (52)	1,580 ! (821)	60 (9)	10 (1)	30 (8)
North Dakota	20 (6)	20 (4)	# (†)	10 (2)	# (†)	# (†)	# (#)	10 (5)
Ohio	8,150 (319)	5,450 (223)	2,700 (115)	2,810 (214)	4,970 (194)	340 (27)	30 (4)	10 (3)
Oklahoma	2,200 (73)	1,550 (55)	650 (23)	1,070 (47)	640 (22)	130 (7)	20 (8)	330 (22)
Oregon	1,890 (140)	1,490 (124)	400 (24)	1,320 (105)	110 (17)	360 (12)	50 (6)	60 (9)
Pennsylvania	2,750 (122)	1,890 (93)	860 (40)	1,110 (88)	1,440 (61)	160 (11)	30 (#)	# (†)
Rhode Island	# (†)	# (†)	# (†)	# (†)	# (†)	# (†)	# (†)	# (†)
South Carolina	5,130 (271)	3,730 (201)	1,400 (81)	1,390 (97)	3,650 (224)	70 (10)	20 (4)	10 (3)
South Dakota	120 ! (52)	90 ! (39)	30 ! (13)	40 (24)	10 (9)	10 (3)	# (†)	80 (29)
Tennessee	3,200 (77)	2,440 (60)	760 (21)	1,350 (70)	1,700 (9)	120 (2)	30 (#)	10 (9)
Texas	11,990 (232)	9,010 (190)	2,980 (50)	2,630 (115)	3,760 (90)	5,450 (91)	120 (#)	30 (#)
Utah	250 (5)	190 (5)	60 (#)	160 (5)	20 (†)	40 (1)	10 (1)	10 (1)
Vermont	40 ! (16)	30 (14)	10 ! (2)	40 (16)	# (†)	# (5)	# (†)	# (†)
Virginia	1,150 (174)	980 (163)	170 (18)	580 (162)	440 (45)	90 (5)	40 (5)	# (†)
Washington	3,470 (130)	2,770 (104)	700 (35)	2,140 (101)	280 (6)	720 (40)	140 (2)	190 (34)
West Virginia	210 (34)	140 (22)	60 (14)	190 (30)	10 ! (5)	# (†)	# (2)	# (†)
Wisconsin	1,470 (65)	1,030 (50)	440 (26)	830 (60)	430 (10)	140 (12)	20 (2)	40 (13)
Wyoming	100 (16)	90 (12)	10 ! (4)	90 (16)	# (†)	10 (#)	# (†)	# (†)

†Not applicable.
#Rounds to zero.
!Interpret data with caution.

[1]A student is counted only once, even if suspended more than once during the same school year.
[2]Data are based on universe counts of schools and school districts; therefore, these figures do not have standard errors.

NOTE: Race categories exclude persons of Hispanic ethnicity. Detail may not sum to totals because of rounding. Standard errors appear in parentheses.
SOURCE: U.S. Department of Education, Office for Civil Rights, Civil Rights Data Collection: 2006. (This table was prepared July 2008.)

Table 161. Percentage of students suspended and expelled from public elementary and secondary schools, by sex, race/ethnicity, and state: 2006

State	Percent suspended								Percent expelled							
	Total	Sex		Race/ethnicity					Total	Sex		Race/ethnicity				
		Male	Female	White	Black	Hispanic	Asian/Pacific Islander	American Indian/Alaska Native		Male	Female	White	Black	Hispanic	Asian/Pacific Islander	American Indian/Alaska Native
1	2	3	4	5	6	7	8	9	10	11	12	13	14	15	16	17
United States	**6.9 (0.04)**	**9.1 (0.06)**	**4.5 (0.03)**	**4.8 (0.04)**	**15.0 (0.14)**	**6.8 (0.07)**	**2.7 (0.04)**	**7.9 (0.49)**	**0.21 (0.003)**	**0.31 (0.004)**	**0.11 (0.002)**	**0.14 (0.002)**	**0.47 (0.011)**	**0.22 (0.004)**	**0.07 (0.002)**	**0.26 (0.013)**
Alabama	10.1 (0.11)	13.3 (0.15)	6.8 (#)	5.8 (0.10)	18.3 (0.32)	4.3 (0.10)	3.2 (0.14)	4.8 (0.49)	0.18 (0.003)	0.24 (0.006)	0.11 (0.002)	0.09 (0.002)	0.33 (0.009)	0.16 (0.003)	# (†)	0.01 (0.001)
Alaska	5.9 (0.35)	8.0 (0.47)	3.6 (0.21)	4.6 (0.13)	10.0 (0.10)	5.9 (0.29)	4.6 (0.50)	8.2 (1.18)	0.13 (0.005)	0.20 (0.007)	0.07 (0.006)	0.13 (0.004)	0.45 (0.003)	0.16 (0.006)	0.13 (0.011)	0.10 (0.009)
Arizona	5.9 (0.14)	8.4 (0.19)	3.3 (0.09)	4.5 (0.10)	11.8 (0.27)	6.4 (0.14)	2.6 (0.05)	10.0 (2.19)	0.07 (0.004)	0.11 (0.008)	0.03 (0.001)	0.06 (0.008)	0.12 (0.006)	0.08 (0.004)	0.03 (#)	0.08 (0.015)
Arkansas	7.3 (0.30)	10.2 (0.43)	4.3 (0.17)	5.0 (0.28)	15.9 (0.96)	4.9 (0.48)	3.5 (0.35)	4.7 (0.63)	0.10 (0.009)	0.15 (0.012)	0.06 (0.008)	0.10 (0.010)	0.14 (0.016)	0.09 ! (0.025)	0.07 ! (0.031)	0.03 (0.002)
California	7.5 (0.18)	10.5 (0.25)	4.4 (0.12)	6.0 (0.18)	17.1 (0.82)	7.9 (0.22)	3.3 (0.13)	12.2 (2.33)	0.31 (0.010)	0.48 (0.015)	0.13 (0.005)	0.28 (0.013)	0.61 (0.030)	0.32 (0.013)	0.11 (0.006)	0.46 (0.068)
Colorado	6.0 (0.09)	8.3 (0.13)	3.7 (0.06)	4.5 (0.09)	13.2 (0.05)	8.1 (0.14)	3.2 (0.03)	3.7 (0.89)	0.28 (0.008)	0.43 (0.012)	0.12 (0.007)	0.20 (0.007)	0.56 (0.005)	0.40 (0.022)	0.12 (0.003)	0.60 (0.138)
Connecticut	6.8 (0.52)	8.9 (0.65)	4.7 (0.39)	4.0 (0.37)	17.2 (2.39)	11.4 (1.39)	2.4 (0.22)	5.2 (0.95)	0.25 (0.026)	0.36 (0.034)	0.14 (0.022)	0.13 (0.016)	0.66 (0.126)	0.45 (0.079)	0.10 (0.017)	0.15 ! (0.069)
Delaware[1]	10.9 (†)	13.8 (†)	7.9 (†)	6.4 (†)	20.1 (†)	9.2 (†)	3.3 (†)	5.5 (†)	0.20 (†)	0.30 (†)	0.10 (†)	0.17 (†)	0.32 (†)	0.06 (†)	0.06 (†)	0.00 (†)
District of Columbia[1]	0.4 (†)	0.4 (†)	0.3 (†)	0.2 (†)	0.4 (†)	0.2 (†)	0.0 (†)	0.0 (†)	0.22 (†)	0.25 (†)	0.20 (†)	0.03 (†)	0.25 (†)	0.17 (†)	0.10 (†)	0.00 (†)
Florida	10.5 (0.14)	13.4 (0.17)	7.3 (0.11)	7.9 (0.16)	19.3 (0.34)	7.7 (0.08)	2.9 (0.03)	7.2 (0.59)	0.04 (0.003)	0.06 (0.004)	0.02 (0.001)	0.04 (0.003)	0.06 (0.005)	0.02 (0.001)	0.01 (#)	0.06 (0.012)
Georgia	8.8 (0.23)	11.4 (0.29)	6.1 (0.16)	4.8 (0.21)	15.0 (0.36)	5.4 (0.27)	2.1 (0.07)	3.7 (0.21)	0.23 (0.011)	0.33 (0.017)	0.12 (0.006)	0.18 (0.013)	0.32 (0.015)	0.11 (0.011)	0.04 (0.005)	0.08 ! (0.035)
Hawaii[1]	5.5 (†)	7.2 (†)	3.6 (†)	4.9 (†)	7.0 (†)	5.7 (†)	5.5 (†)	6.0 (†)	0.00 (†)	0.00 (†)	0.00 (†)	0.00 (†)	0.00 (†)	0.00 (†)	0.00 (†)	0.00 (†)
Idaho	3.6 (0.18)	5.3 (0.26)	1.7 (0.10)	3.3 (0.19)	3.5 (0.21)	5.1 (0.29)	1.6 (0.07)	8.6 ! (2.90)	0.09 (0.005)	0.14 (0.008)	0.03 (0.004)	0.07 (0.005)	# (†)	0.20 (0.018)	# (†)	0.37 (0.111)
Illinois	6.4 (0.15)	8.4 (0.20)	4.4 (0.10)	3.8 (0.17)	14.5 (0.53)	6.0 (0.19)	1.7 (0.08)	2.9 (0.41)	0.14 (0.007)	0.20 (0.008)	0.07 (0.006)	0.08 (0.011)	0.32 (0.011)	0.11 (0.004)	0.03 (0.005)	0.07 (0.008)
Indiana	7.4 (0.28)	9.9 (0.37)	4.7 (0.20)	6.0 (0.27)	17.3 (1.18)	7.4 (0.87)	1.8 (0.24)	6.1 (0.70)	0.63 (0.039)	0.85 (0.053)	0.40 (0.028)	0.54 (0.039)	1.24 (0.111)	0.70 (0.077)	0.19 (0.038)	0.60 ! (0.168)
Iowa	3.0 (0.11)	4.0 (0.14)	1.9 (0.08)	2.4 (0.11)	11.4 (0.31)	3.2 (0.27)	1.6 (0.18)	5.2 (0.25)	0.04 (0.008)	0.07 (0.013)	0.01 (0.004)	0.04 (0.008)	0.07 (0.012)	0.06 ! (0.022)	0.01 (0.001)	0.11 ! (0.074)
Kansas	5.1 (0.18)	6.9 (0.26)	3.1 (0.11)	3.8 (0.20)	14.6 (0.27)	6.6 (0.22)	2.9 (0.10)	5.8 (0.59)	0.18 (0.014)	0.25 (0.015)	0.10 (0.013)	0.12 (0.017)	0.68 (0.019)	0.19 (0.011)	0.12 (0.013)	0.20 ! (0.090)
Kentucky	6.6 (0.36)	8.7 (0.48)	4.3 (0.24)	5.8 (0.33)	13.3 (1.27)	4.0 (0.33)	1.5 (0.19)	3.8 (0.89)	0.08 (0.017)	0.11 (0.021)	0.05 ! (0.014)	0.07 (0.012)	0.18 ! (0.091)	0.01 ! (0.004)	0.03 ! (0.013)	# (†)
Louisiana	10.3 (0.41)	13.2 (0.51)	7.3 (0.31)	7.1 (0.56)	14.6 (0.48)	4.7 (0.16)	2.6 (0.14)	6.8 ! (2.24)	0.89 (0.037)	1.23 (0.054)	0.52 (0.021)	0.45 (0.039)	1.42 (0.056)	0.47 (0.020)	0.17 (0.011)	0.39 (0.109)
Maine	4.6 (0.28)	6.6 (0.41)	2.4 (0.15)	4.5 (0.28)	9.0 (0.38)	5.7 (1.11)	2.9 (0.18)	6.4 (1.13)	0.09 (0.012)	0.13 (0.015)	0.04 ! (0.011)	0.09 (0.012)	0.09 ! (0.022)	0.05 (0.002)	0.07 ! (0.038)	# (†)
Maryland[1]	7.1 (†)	8.9 (†)	5.2 (†)	5.8 (†)	8.2 (†)	12.9 (†)	2.2 (†)	8.5 (†)	0.18 (†)	0.27 (†)	0.09 (†)	0.08 (†)	0.31 (†)	0.27 (†)	0.03 (†)	0.09 (†)
Massachusetts	5.6 (0.28)	7.1 (0.35)	3.9 (0.22)	4.2 (0.25)	10.3 (0.50)	12.0 (1.18)	2.5 (0.25)	5.0 (0.63)	0.06 (0.004)	0.09 (0.006)	0.03 (0.003)	0.03 (0.005)	0.24 (0.013)	0.13 (0.009)	0.02 (0.003)	0.04 (0.003)
Michigan	8.2 (0.34)	10.8 (0.43)	5.4 (0.27)	6.1 (0.27)	17.8 (1.48)	7.4 (0.83)	2.2 (0.34)	6.8 (1.08)	0.13 (0.010)	0.19 (0.014)	0.07 (0.006)	0.09 (0.007)	0.32 (0.040)	0.15 (0.023)	0.06 (0.012)	0.12 ! (0.041)
Minnesota	3.7 (0.10)	5.0 (0.14)	2.4 (0.07)	2.4 (0.09)	14.4 (0.33)	5.4 (0.28)	2.5 (0.05)	10.0 (1.43)	0.03 (0.002)	0.05 (0.004)	0.01 (0.001)	0.02 (0.002)	0.08 (0.002)	0.04 (0.007)	0.01 (0.002)	0.14 ! (0.048)
Mississippi	10.2 (0.33)	13.3 (0.41)	7.0 (0.24)	5.5 (0.26)	14.8 (0.55)	4.3 (0.44)	3.0 (0.47)	12.7 ! (3.08)	0.29 (0.015)	0.42 (0.025)	0.16 (0.006)	0.12 (0.020)	0.46 (0.019)	0.07 (0.007)	0.08 (0.013)	0.09 (0.009)
Missouri	7.3 (0.24)	9.8 (0.32)	4.6 (0.16)	4.6 (0.19)	20.2 (1.07)	5.4 (0.32)	2.9 (0.10)	7.0 (0.51)	0.03 (0.004)	0.05 (0.005)	0.01 (0.003)	0.03 (0.005)	0.04 (0.003)	0.02 (0.001)	0.01 (#)	# (†)
Montana	4.5 (0.18)	6.1 (0.24)	2.7 (0.12)	3.7 (0.17)	4.9 (0.27)	3.5 (0.19)	2.3 (0.16)	9.6 (1.05)	0.07 (0.007)	0.12 (0.013)	0.02 (0.005)	0.05 (0.007)	# (†)	# (†)	# (†)	0.24 (0.040)
Nebraska	3.7 (0.08)	4.9 (0.11)	2.4 (0.05)	2.6 (0.06)	12.6 (0.05)	5.0 (0.30)	1.9 (0.04)	6.7 (0.89)	0.23 (0.005)	0.32 (0.008)	0.12 (0.002)	0.13 (0.004)	0.92 (0.004)	0.32 (0.018)	0.13 (0.001)	0.76 (0.121)
Nevada[1]	7.4 (†)	9.5 (†)	5.2 (†)	5.1 (†)	15.5 (†)	8.5 (†)	3.9 (†)	6.6 (†)	0.36 (†)	0.55 (†)	0.16 (†)	0.26 (†)	0.86 (†)	0.35 (†)	0.22 (†)	0.36 (†)
New Hampshire	5.6 (0.32)	7.2 (0.46)	3.9 (0.18)	5.4 (0.33)	8.7 (0.32)	12.1 (0.23)	2.2 (0.19)	4.8 (0.45)	0.06 ! (0.021)	0.08 ! (0.024)	0.04 ! (0.020)	0.06 ! (0.021)	0.28 (0.065)	0.07 (0.001)	0.03 (0.001)	0.17 (0.011)
New Jersey	5.7 (0.26)	7.5 (0.33)	3.7 (0.19)	3.7 (0.30)	12.4 (0.79)	6.9 (0.51)	1.4 (0.13)	3.7 (0.70)	0.02 ! (0.008)	0.03 ! (0.016)	# (†)	0.01 ! (0.006)	0.03 ! (0.009)	0.03 ! (0.015)	0.01 ! (0.008)	# (†)
New Mexico	5.3 (0.20)	6.9 (0.26)	3.5 (0.14)	4.0 (0.19)	7.0 (0.21)	5.4 (0.31)	2.5 (0.12)	8.3 (0.47)	0.07 (0.005)	0.12 (0.009)	0.03 (0.002)	0.03 (0.003)	0.13 (0.002)	0.06 (0.006)	0.17 (0.006)	0.22 (0.030)
New York	3.8 (0.14)	5.1 (0.17)	2.5 (0.11)	3.4 (0.14)	7.3 (0.45)	2.8 (0.15)	0.7 (0.05)	4.5 (0.97)	0.03 (0.006)	0.05 (0.010)	0.01 (0.003)	0.04 (0.010)	0.04 ! (0.014)	0.01 (0.002)	# (†)	0.07 ! (0.044)
North Carolina	10.8 (0.52)	14.3 (0.66)	7.0 (0.37)	6.5 (0.33)	20.0 (1.06)	7.2 (0.40)	2.7 (0.19)	14.9 ! (8.53)	0.14 ! (0.060)	0.21 ! (0.081)	0.07 ! (0.038)	0.04 (0.007)	0.37 ! (0.193)	0.05 (0.007)	0.03 (0.004)	0.09 ! (0.050)
North Dakota	2.2 (0.17)	2.9 (0.21)	1.4 (0.13)	1.5 (0.10)	5.0 (0.16)	3.1 (0.35)	2.0 (0.12)	8.0 (1.80)	0.02 (0.006)	0.05 (0.008)	# (†)	0.01 (0.002)	0.05 (0.001)	# (†)	# (†)	0.12 ! (0.061)
Ohio	6.2 (0.24)	8.2 (0.30)	4.2 (0.17)	4.6 (0.21)	14.6 (0.99)	6.0 (0.83)	2.1 (0.24)	3.7 (0.45)	0.47 (0.020)	0.61 (0.026)	0.32 (0.014)	0.20 (0.016)	1.69 (0.091)	0.72 (0.078)	0.09 (0.014)	0.21 ! (0.038)
Oklahoma	4.9 (0.17)	6.7 (0.24)	3.0 (0.11)	3.9 (0.18)	12.1 (0.60)	5.3 (0.18)	1.8 (0.07)	4.0 (0.24)	0.34 (0.013)	0.47 (0.019)	0.21 (0.008)	0.28 (0.014)	0.94 (0.039)	0.23 (0.014)	0.16 (0.039)	0.29 (0.021)
Oregon	4.9 (0.18)	7.1 (0.26)	2.7 (0.15)	4.8 (0.19)	8.8 (0.24)	5.5 (0.37)	2.1 (0.08)	7.2 (0.57)	0.34 (0.025)	0.52 (0.044)	0.15 (0.010)	0.32 (0.026)	0.58 (0.093)	0.41 (0.015)	0.18 (0.028)	0.47 (0.070)
Pennsylvania	6.8 (0.37)	8.7 (0.45)	4.8 (0.29)	4.2 (0.23)	18.9 (1.41)	8.7 (0.79)	2.7 (0.46)	3.4 (0.64)	0.16 (0.008)	0.22 (0.011)	0.10 (0.005)	0.09 (0.007)	0.52 (0.031)	0.21 (0.017)	0.06 (0.013)	0.04 (0.002)
Rhode Island	8.4 (0.74)	10.7 (1.00)	5.9 (0.47)	6.7 (0.83)	14.6 (2.07)	12.6 (0.65)	7.2 (0.73)	11.3 (2.92)	# (†)	# (†)	# (†)	# (†)	# (†)	# (†)	# (†)	# (†)
South Carolina	11.9 (0.44)	15.1 (0.56)	8.6 (0.33)	6.9 (0.36)	19.2 (0.89)	6.5 (1.05)	2.9 (0.31)	9.6 ! (4.26)	0.73 (0.043)	1.03 (0.063)	0.40 (0.026)	0.37 (0.029)	1.26 (0.091)	0.20 (0.035)	0.19 (0.047)	0.42 ! (0.169)
South Dakota	2.7 (0.16)	3.7 (0.22)	1.6 (0.11)	1.9 (0.12)	7.1 (0.24)	4.3 (0.16)	3.0 (0.19)	6.3 (1.19)	0.11 ! (0.045)	0.16 ! (0.066)	0.05 ! (0.024)	0.04 ! (0.025)	0.08 ! (0.038)	0.20 ! (0.107)	# (†)	0.55 ! (0.221)
Tennessee	7.2 (0.26)	9.6 (0.35)	4.8 (0.17)	5.5 (0.27)	12.8 (0.38)	5.4 (0.22)	2.7 (0.15)	3.4 (0.36)	0.32 (0.010)	0.47 (0.016)	0.15 (0.006)	0.19 (0.011)	0.70 (0.011)	0.29 (0.011)	0.17 (0.009)	0.29 (0.014)
Texas	5.6 (0.06)	7.4 (0.08)	3.6 (0.04)	2.9 (0.06)	12.7 (0.24)	5.7 (0.08)	1.6 (0.01)	3.1 (0.10)	0.26 (0.005)	0.39 (0.008)	0.13 (0.002)	0.16 (0.007)	0.58 (0.016)	0.26 (0.005)	0.08 (#)	0.20 (0.004)
Utah	3.2 (0.04)	4.5 (0.05)	1.9 (0.03)	2.4 (0.03)	7.8 (0.04)	6.7 (0.07)	4.2 (0.04)	6.9 (0.09)	0.05 (0.001)	0.07 (0.002)	0.02 (#)	0.04 (0.001)	0.22 (0.001)	0.06 (0.002)	0.09 (#)	0.19 (0.020)
Vermont	4.0 (0.18)	5.5 (0.25)	2.4 (0.12)	4.0 (0.18)	5.8 (0.50)	4.1 (0.55)	1.8 (0.23)	5.7 (0.77)	0.05 ! (0.019)	0.08 ! (0.031)	0.02 ! (0.006)	0.05 ! (0.020)	0.06 ! (0.033)	0.12 ! (0.069)	# (†)	# (†)
Virginia	7.2 (0.24)	9.4 (0.31)	4.9 (0.18)	4.7 (0.17)	13.9 (0.73)	5.6 (0.21)	2.1 (0.06)	4.0 (0.34)	0.09 (0.014)	0.15 (0.025)	0.03 (0.003)	0.08 ! (0.022)	0.12 (0.013)	0.09 (0.005)	0.06 (0.003)	0.10 ! (0.045)
Washington	5.9 (0.15)	8.6 (0.21)	3.2 (0.08)	5.3 (0.17)	12.0 (0.09)	7.2 (0.39)	3.7 (0.05)	11.3 (1.36)	0.34 (0.014)	0.53 (0.021)	0.14 (0.007)	0.31 (0.016)	0.48 (0.010)	0.50 (0.035)	0.16 (0.002)	0.69 (0.130)
West Virginia	10.2 (1.02)	13.8 (1.31)	6.4 (0.70)	9.7 (0.91)	21.5 (4.03)	11.2 (3.07)	2.4 (0.54)	8.2 (1.98)	0.07 (0.012)	0.09 (0.015)	0.04 (0.010)	0.07 (0.011)	0.09 ! (0.034)	0.07 ! (0.053)	# (†)	# (†)
Wisconsin	5.0 (0.16)	6.3 (0.20)	3.6 (0.13)	2.7 (0.12)	19.7 (0.60)	7.5 (0.18)	2.1 (0.07)	13.5 ! (5.23)	0.17 (0.008)	0.23 (0.012)	0.10 (0.006)	0.12 (0.009)	0.47 (0.016)	0.22 (0.020)	0.06 (0.008)	0.30 ! (0.105)
Wyoming	2.8 (0.34)	4.0 (0.33)	1.6 (0.88)	2.7 (0.34)	3.2 (0.26)	3.1 (0.43)	1.7 (0.26)	6.4 ! (1.37)	0.11 (0.018)	0.18 (0.027)	0.03 ! (0.010)	0.11 (0.021)	0.23 (0.006)	0.09 (0.005)	0.10 (0.007)	# (†)

†Not applicable.
#Rounds to zero.
!Interpret data with caution.
[1]Data are based on universe counts of schools and school districts; therefore, these figures do not have standard errors.

NOTE: Race categories exclude persons of Hispanic ethnicity. Detail may not sum to totals because of rounding. Standard errors appear in parentheses.
SOURCE: U.S. Department of Education, Office for Civil Rights, Civil Rights Data Collection: 2006. (This table was prepared May 2008.)

Table 162. Percentage of students in grades 9 through 12 who reported experience with drugs and violence on school property, by race/ethnicity, grade, and sex: Selected years, 1997 through 2007

Type of violence or drug-related behavior	1997 total	1999 total	2003 total	2005 total	2007 Total	Race/ethnicity White	Black	Hispanic	Grade 9th	10th	11th	12th
1	2	3	4	5	6	7	8	9	10	11	12	13
Felt too unsafe to go to school[1]	4.0 (0.6)	5.2 (1.3)	5.4 (0.41)	6.0 (0.61)	5.5 (0.39)	4.0 (0.43)	6.5 (0.64)	9.6 (1.00)	6.5 (0.64)	5.4 (0.42)	4.7 (0.61)	4.8 (0.58)
Male	4.1 (0.8)	4.8 (1.6)	5.5 (0.51)	5.7 (0.56)	5.4 (0.44)	3.7 (0.44)	6.8 (1.07)	9.6 (1.09)	5.8 (0.66)	4.8 (0.58)	5.5 (0.93)	5.3 (0.72)
Female	3.9 (0.7)	5.7 (1.5)	5.3 (0.51)	6.3 (0.77)	5.6 (0.53)	4.2 (0.66)	6.3 (0.82)	9.7 (1.24)	7.4 (0.96)	6.0 (0.68)	3.9 (0.61)	4.3 (0.71)
Carried a weapon on school property[1,2]	8.5 (1.5)	6.9 (1.2)	6.1 (0.56)	6.5 (0.46)	5.9 (0.37)	5.3 (0.56)	6.0 (0.46)	7.3 (0.82)	6.0 (0.59)	5.8 (0.61)	5.5 (0.68)	6.0 (0.58)
Male	12.5 (2.9)	11.0 (2.1)	8.9 (0.77)	10.2 (0.82)	9.0 (0.65)	8.5 (0.97)	8.4 (0.64)	10.4 (1.18)	8.7 (0.95)	8.8 (1.04)	8.6 (1.25)	9.8 (1.14)
Female	3.7 (0.7)	2.8 (0.7)	3.1 (0.51)	2.6 (0.31)	2.7 (0.33)	2.1 (0.37)	3.5 (0.55)	4.1 (0.72)	3.1 (0.61)	2.6 (0.71)	2.4 (0.36)	2.3 (0.50)
Threatened or injured with a weapon on school property[3]	7.4 (0.9)	7.7 (0.8)	9.2 (0.77)	7.9 (0.36)	7.8 (0.44)	6.9 (0.52)	9.7 (0.87)	8.7 (0.60)	9.2 (0.69)	8.4 (0.51)	6.8 (0.57)	6.3 (0.64)
Male	10.2 (1.4)	9.5 (1.6)	11.6 (0.97)	9.7 (0.41)	10.2 (0.59)	9.2 (0.72)	11.2 (1.34)	12.0 (0.89)	11.4 (0.88)	10.4 (0.73)	10.5 (1.06)	8.1 (1.01)
Female	4.0 (0.6)	5.8 (1.2)	6.5 (0.61)	6.1 (0.41)	5.4 (0.41)	4.6 (0.52)	8.1 (0.86)	5.4 (0.69)	6.8 (0.80)	6.3 (0.71)	3.2 (0.45)	4.5 (0.75)
Engaged in a physical fight on school property[3]	14.8 (1.3)	14.2 (1.3)	12.8 (0.77)	13.6 (0.56)	12.4 (0.48)	10.2 (0.57)	17.6 (1.10)	15.5 (0.81)	17.0 (0.67)	11.7 (0.86)	11.0 (0.73)	8.6 (0.62)
Male	20.0 (2.0)	18.5 (1.4)	17.1 (0.92)	18.2 (0.92)	16.3 (0.60)	14.5 (0.76)	20.0 (1.66)	18.5 (1.22)	22.3 (1.25)	15.0 (1.06)	14.8 (1.13)	11.1 (0.77)
Female	8.6 (1.5)	9.8 (1.9)	8.0 (0.71)	8.8 (0.51)	8.5 (0.62)	5.9 (0.64)	15.2 (1.10)	12.4 (1.29)	11.4 (1.02)	8.3 (1.08)	7.3 (0.96)	6.2 (0.76)
Property stolen or deliberately damaged on school property[3]	32.9 (2.6)	— (†)	29.8 (0.71)	29.8 (0.77)	27.1 (0.69)	25.9 (0.81)	29.2 (1.25)	29.0 (1.34)	30.6 (1.36)	27.6 (1.19)	25.9 (0.97)	22.9 (1.29)
Male	36.1 (2.6)	— (†)	33.1 (0.87)	31.4 (0.82)	30.4 (0.99)	29.3 (1.08)	32.8 (1.74)	32.0 (1.79)	32.2 (1.70)	29.3 (1.70)	32.1 (1.37)	27.2 (1.86)
Female	29.0 (3.7)	— (†)	26.2 (0.82)	28.0 (1.07)	23.7 (0.73)	22.6 (0.94)	25.6 (1.75)	26.0 (1.70)	28.8 (1.63)	25.8 (1.30)	19.7 (1.14)	18.8 (1.19)
Cigarette use on school property[1]	14.6 (1.5)	14.0 (1.9)	8.0 (0.71)	6.8 (0.41)	5.7 (0.50)	6.4 (0.70)	3.4 (0.52)	4.9 (0.52)	4.2 (0.60)	5.4 (0.57)	5.9 (0.83)	7.4 (0.89)
Male	15.9 (1.7)	14.8 (2.0)	8.2 (0.66)	7.4 (0.41)	6.5 (0.53)	7.1 (0.72)	5.1 (0.92)	5.6 (0.66)	4.7 (0.88)	5.8 (0.85)	7.2 (0.99)	8.9 (0.97)
Female	13.0 (2.2)	13.2 (2.0)	7.6 (0.92)	6.2 (0.61)	4.8 (0.56)	5.6 (0.77)	1.7 (0.39)	4.2 (0.88)	3.7 (0.71)	5.0 (0.90)	4.7 (0.92)	5.9 (1.09)
Smokeless tobacco use on school property[4]	5.1 (1.4)	4.2 (1.8)	5.9 (1.53)	5.0 (0.61)	4.9 (0.71)	6.2 (0.94)	0.9 (0.22)	3.2 (0.56)	4.0 (0.90)	5.9 (0.86)	4.2 (0.74)	5.5 (0.93)
Male	9.0 (2.5)	8.1 (3.5)	8.5 (1.48)	9.2 (1.12)	8.9 (1.31)	11.3 (1.70)	1.5 (0.41)	4.9 (1.02)	6.9 (1.68)	10.4 (1.55)	7.9 (1.40)	10.2 (1.60)
Female	0.4 (0.2)	0.3 (0.2)	3.3 (1.68)	0.8 (0.15)	1.0 (0.20)	1.0 (0.26)	0.2 (0.16)	1.5 (0.40)	0.9 (0.31)	1.3 (0.44)	0.6 (0.21)	1.0 (0.54)
Alcohol use on school property[1]	5.6 (0.7)	4.9 (0.7)	5.2 (0.46)	4.3 (0.31)	4.1 (0.32)	3.2 (0.35)	3.4 (0.63)	7.5 (0.86)	3.4 (0.43)	4.1 (0.50)	4.2 (0.54)	4.9 (0.55)
Male	7.2 (1.3)	6.1 (1.1)	6.0 (0.61)	5.3 (0.41)	4.6 (0.35)	3.8 (0.47)	3.7 (0.70)	7.8 (0.93)	3.4 (0.45)	4.6 (0.68)	4.5 (0.64)	6.3 (0.73)
Female	3.6 (0.7)	3.6 (0.7)	4.2 (0.41)	3.3 (0.31)	3.6 (0.37)	2.6 (0.33)	3.2 (0.78)	7.1 (1.16)	3.4 (0.64)	3.6 (0.62)	3.9 (0.64)	3.4 (0.59)
Marijuana use on school property[1]	7.0 (1.0)	7.2 (1.4)	5.8 (0.66)	4.5 (0.31)	4.5 (0.46)	4.0 (0.61)	5.0 (0.73)	5.4 (0.80)	4.0 (0.52)	4.8 (0.60)	4.0 (0.68)	5.1 (0.73)
Male	9.0 (1.3)	10.1 (2.6)	7.6 (0.87)	6.0 (0.46)	5.9 (0.61)	5.2 (0.87)	7.4 (1.07)	6.9 (1.22)	5.2 (0.74)	6.5 (0.87)	5.3 (1.02)	6.6 (1.04)
Female	4.6 (1.1)	4.4 (0.8)	3.7 (0.46)	3.0 (0.31)	3.0 (0.39)	2.7 (0.43)	2.6 (0.66)	3.9 (0.71)	2.7 (0.65)	3.1 (0.62)	2.7 (0.54)	3.7 (0.72)
Offered, sold, or given an illegal drug on school property[3]	31.7 (1.8)	30.2 (2.4)	28.7 (1.94)	25.4 (1.07)	22.3 (1.04)	20.7 (1.23)	19.3 (1.36)	29.1 (1.94)	21.2 (1.24)	25.3 (1.29)	22.7 (1.41)	19.6 (1.26)
Male	37.4 (2.3)	34.7 (3.3)	31.9 (2.09)	28.8 (1.22)	25.7 (1.15)	24.0 (1.48)	25.1 (1.86)	30.9 (2.08)	25.0 (1.67)	29.5 (1.51)	25.7 (1.42)	22.4 (2.03)
Female	24.7 (2.4)	25.7 (2.4)	25.0 (1.94)	21.8 (1.02)	18.7 (1.16)	17.4 (1.37)	13.4 (1.52)	27.2 (2.32)	17.2 (1.52)	21.0 (1.73)	19.8 (2.12)	16.8 (1.24)

—Not available.
†Not applicable.
[1] One or more times during the 30 days preceding the survey.
[2] Such as a gun, knife, or club.
[3] One or more times during the 12 months preceding the survey.
[4] Used chewing tobacco or snuff one or more times during the 30 days preceding the survey.

NOTE: Totals include other racial/ethnic groups not shown separately. Race categories exclude persons of Hispanic ethnicity. Standard errors appear in parentheses.
SOURCE: U.S. Department of Health and Human Services, Centers for Disease Control and Prevention, Youth Risk Behavior Survey (YRBS), 2007 National YRBS Data Files, retrieved July 15, 2008, from http://www.cdc.gov/HealthyYouth/YRBS/data/index.htm. (This table was prepared July 2008.)

Table 163. Percentage of 12- to 17-year-olds reporting substance abuse during the past 30 days and the past year, by drug used, sex, and race/ethnicity: Selected years, 1982 through 2006

Year, sex, and race/ethnicity	Past 30 days — Any[1]	Past 30 days — Marijuana	Past 30 days — Cocaine	Past 30 days — Alcohol	Past 30 days — Cigarettes	Past year — Any[1]	Past year — Marijuana	Past year — Cocaine	Past year — Alcohol	Past year — Cigarettes
	2	3	4	5	6	7	8	9	10	11
1982	— (†)	9.9 (—)	1.9 (—)	34.9 (—)	— (†)	— (†)	17.7 (—)	3.7 (—)	46.1 (—)	— (†)
1985	13.2 (—)	10.2 (—)	1.5 (—)	41.2 (—)	29.4 (—)	20.7 (—)	16.7 (—)	3.4 (—)	52.7 (—)	29.9 (—)
1988	8.1 (—)	5.4 (—)	1.2 (—)	33.4 (—)	22.7 (—)	14.9 (—)	10.7 (—)	2.5 (—)	45.5 (—)	26.8 (—)
1990	7.1 (—)	4.4 (—)	0.6 (—)	32.5 (—)	22.4 (—)	14.1 (—)	9.6 (—)	1.9 (—)	41.8 (—)	26.2 (—)
1993	5.7 (—)	4.0 (—)	0.4 (—)	23.9 (—)	18.5 (—)	11.9 (—)	8.5 (—)	0.7 (—)	35.9 (—)	22.5 (—)
1994	8.2 (—)	6.0 (—)	0.3 (—)	21.6 (—)	19.9 (—)	15.5 (—)	11.4 (—)	1.1 (—)	36.2 (—)	24.5 (—)
1995	10.9 (—)	8.2 (—)	0.8 (—)	21.1 (—)	20.2 (—)	18.0 (—)	14.2 (—)	1.7 (—)	35.1 (—)	26.6 (—)
1996	9.0 (—)	7.1 (—)	0.6 (—)	18.8 (—)	18.3 (—)	16.7 (—)	13.0 (—)	1.4 (—)	32.7 (—)	24.2 (—)
1997	11.4 (—)	9.4 (—)	1.0 (—)	20.5 (—)	19.9 (—)	18.8 (—)	15.8 (—)	2.2 (—)	34.0 (—)	26.4 (—)
1998	9.9 (—)	8.3 (—)	0.8 (—)	19.1 (—)	18.2 (—)	16.4 (—)	14.1 (—)	1.7 (—)	31.8 (—)	23.8 (—)
1999	9.8 (0.23)	7.2 (0.20)	0.5 (0.06)	16.5 (0.30)	14.9 (0.31)	19.8 (0.32)	14.2 (0.29)	1.6 (0.10)	34.1 (0.41)	23.4 (0.37)
2000	9.7 (0.24)	7.2 (0.21)	0.6 (0.07)	16.4 (0.29)	13.4 (0.28)	18.6 (0.31)	13.4 (0.27)	1.7 (0.12)	33.0 (0.39)	20.8 (0.34)
2001	10.8 (0.26)	8.0 (0.24)	0.4 (0.06)	17.3 (0.33)	13.0 (0.28)	20.8 (0.36)	15.2 (0.32)	1.5 (0.10)	33.9 (0.39)	20.0 (0.35)
2002	11.6 (0.29)	8.2 (0.24)	0.6 (0.07)	17.6 (0.32)	13.0 (0.30)	22.2 (0.38)	15.8 (0.32)	2.1 (0.13)	34.6 (0.42)	20.3 (0.35)
2003	11.2 (0.27)	7.9 (0.24)	0.6 (0.06)	17.7 (0.33)	12.2 (0.29)	21.8 (0.36)	15.0 (0.31)	1.8 (0.11)	34.3 (0.42)	19.0 (0.36)
2004	10.6 (0.27)	7.6 (0.23)	0.5 (0.06)	17.6 (0.32)	11.9 (0.30)	21.0 (0.34)	14.5 (0.31)	1.6 (0.11)	33.9 (0.41)	18.4 (0.35)
2005	9.9 (0.25)	6.8 (0.22)	0.6 (0.06)	16.5 (0.32)	10.8 (0.28)	19.9 (0.35)	13.3 (0.30)	1.7 (0.11)	33.3 (0.41)	17.3 (0.36)
Sex										
Male	10.1 (0.38)	7.5 (0.33)	0.6 (0.10)	15.9 (0.44)	10.7 (0.41)	19.7 (0.51)	13.9 (0.43)	1.6 (0.15)	32.0 (0.58)	16.9 (0.51)
Female	9.7 (0.35)	6.2 (0.29)	0.5 (0.08)	17.2 (0.47)	10.8 (0.39)	20.0 (0.48)	12.8 (0.40)	1.7 (0.15)	34.7 (0.61)	17.8 (0.49)
Race/ethnicity										
White	10.1 (0.31)	7.2 (0.27)	0.7 (0.09)	18.5 (0.42)	12.8 (0.36)	20.5 (0.43)	14.3 (0.36)	2.0 (0.15)	36.0 (0.50)	19.8 (0.44)
Black	11.0 (0.75)	7.2 (0.61)	# (0.01)	11.6 (0.73)	6.5 (0.62)	20.4 (0.99)	13.0 (0.78)	# (0.02)	25.2 (1.01)	10.6 (0.74)
Hispanic	9.4 (0.74)	6.3 (0.64)	0.6 (0.19)	16.7 (0.94)	9.1 (0.76)	19.6 (1.01)	12.3 (0.84)	2.0 (0.32)	34.5 (1.18)	16.8 (0.94)
Asian	3.3 (0.81)	1.5 (0.51)	0.2 (0.16)	7.0 (1.23)	3.0 (0.76)	7.6 (1.28)	3.5 (0.79)	0.4 (0.25)	18.1 (1.87)	6.4 (1.35)
Native Hawaiian/Pacific Islander	‡ (†)	‡ (†)	‡ (†)	‡ (†)	‡ (†)	‡ (†)	‡ (†)	‡ (†)	‡ (†)	‡ (†)
American Indian/Alaska Native	19.2 (3.64)	14.9 (3.45)	‡ (†)	12.2 (2.53)	18.0 (3.26)	29.6 (3.48)	22.2 (3.32)	5.1 (2.37)	32.1 (3.49)	25.0 (3.77)
More than one race	9.7 (1.42)	6.8 (1.19)	1.1 (0.57)	13.0 (1.55)	11.0 (1.53)	21.7 (2.23)	13.6 (1.71)	2.0 (0.69)	34.0 (2.82)	16.7 (2.00)
2006	9.8 (0.27)	6.7 (0.21)	0.4 (0.05)	16.6 (0.32)	10.4 (0.26)	19.6 (0.37)	13.2 (0.31)	1.6 (0.11)	32.9 (0.42)	17.0 (0.35)
Sex										
Male	9.8 (0.36)	6.8 (0.30)	0.4 (0.07)	16.3 (0.44)	10.0 (0.36)	19.5 (0.50)	13.4 (0.42)	1.4 (0.14)	32.2 (0.57)	16.7 (0.46)
Female	9.7 (0.36)	6.4 (0.29)	0.5 (0.08)	17.0 (0.47)	10.7 (0.37)	19.7 (0.49)	12.9 (0.41)	1.9 (0.16)	33.7 (0.58)	17.4 (0.48)
Race/ethnicity										
White	10.0 (0.31)	7.1 (0.26)	0.5 (0.07)	19.2 (0.42)	12.4 (0.35)	20.2 (0.42)	13.9 (0.35)	2.0 (0.15)	36.7 (0.50)	19.5 (0.42)
Black	10.2 (0.66)	6.5 (0.51)	0.2 (0.11)	10.5 (0.71)	6.0 (0.50)	18.6 (0.91)	12.2 (0.71)	0.4 (0.15)	24.1 (0.95)	10.8 (0.69)
Hispanic	8.9 (0.66)	5.8 (0.53)	0.5 (0.14)	15.3 (0.84)	8.2 (0.59)	18.8 (0.98)	12.3 (0.80)	1.7 (0.29)	31.3 (1.10)	15.1 (0.84)
Asian	6.7 (1.52)	3.2 (0.92)	0.1 (0.11)	7.6 (1.86)	5.2 (1.16)	13.7 (2.02)	7.3 (1.33)	0.6 (0.52)	20.2 (2.45)	11.0 (2.06)
Native Hawaiian/Pacific Islander	‡ (†)	‡ (†)	‡ (†)	‡ (†)	‡ (†)	‡ (†)	‡ (†)	‡ (†)	‡ (†)	‡ (†)
American Indian/Alaska Native	18.7 (4.38)	11.3 (2.47)	0.1 (0.10)	20.5 (3.96)	21.2 (3.63)	24.3 (3.09)	17.7 (2.91)	2.2 (1.00)	33.2 (3.97)	25.0 (3.77)
More than one race	11.8 (1.96)	8.4 (1.74)	1.2 (0.73)	16.2 (2.36)	12.7 (1.90)	24.3 (3.09)	13.6 (1.71)	3.0 (1.25)	31.2 (2.74)	19.2 (2.32)

—Not available.
†Not applicable.
#Rounds to zero.
‡Reporting standards not met.
[1]Includes other illegal drug use not shown separately.
NOTE: Marijuana includes hashish usage for 1996 and later years. Due to changes in the survey instrument and administration and to improve comparability with new data, estimates for 1982 through 1993 have been adjusted and may differ from those reported in previous years. Data for 1999 and later years have been revised from previously published figures. Data for 1999 and later years were gathered using Computer Assisted Interviewing (CAI) and may not be directly comparable to previous years. Race categories exclude persons of Hispanic ethnicity. Standard errors appear in parentheses.

SOURCE: U.S. Department of Health and Human Services, Substance Abuse and Mental Health Services Administration, *National Household Survey on Drug Abuse: Main Findings*, selected years, 1982 through 2001, and National Survey on Drug Use and Health, 2002 through 2006. Retrieved July 2, 2008, from www.oas.samhsa.gov/NSDUH/2k6NSDUH/tabs/TOC.htm. (This table was prepared July 2008.)

Table 164. Percentage of high school seniors reporting drug use, by type of drug and reporting period: Selected years, 1975 through 2007

Type of drug	Class of 1975	Class of 1980	Class of 1985	Class of 1990	Class of 1995	Class of 1998	Class of 1999	Class of 2000	Class of 2001	Class of 2002	Class of 2003	Class of 2004	Class of 2005	Class of 2006	Class of 2007
1	2	3	4	5	6	7	8	9	10	11	12	13	14	15	16
Percent reporting having ever used drugs															
Alcohol[1]	90.4 (0.69)	93.2 (0.46)	92.2 (0.48)	89.5 (0.57)	80.7 (0.73)	81.4 (0.72)	80.0 (0.78)	80.3 (0.80)	79.7 (0.81)	78.4 (0.83)	76.6 (0.80)	76.8 (0.80)	75.1 (0.81)	72.7 (0.85)	72.2 (0.83)
Any illicit drug	55.2 (1.68)	65.4 (1.23)	60.6 (1.26)	47.9 (1.33)	48.4 (1.32)	54.1 (1.32)	54.7 (1.40)	54.0 (1.44)	53.9 (1.44)	53.0 (1.44)	51.1 (1.35)	51.1 (1.35)	50.4 (1.35)	48.2 (1.37)	46.8 (1.33)
Marijuana only	19.0 (1.32)	26.7 (1.15)	20.9 (1.05)	18.5 (1.03)	20.3 (1.06)	24.7 (1.14)	25.3 (1.22)	25.0 (1.25)	23.2 (1.22)	23.5 (1.22)	23.4 (1.15)	22.4 (1.13)	23.0 (1.14)	21.3 (1.12)	21.3 (1.09)
Any illicit drug other than marijuana[2]	36.2 (1.33)	38.7 (1.04)	39.7 (1.04)	29.4 (0.99)	28.1 (0.97)	29.4 (0.99)	29.4 (1.05)	29.0 (1.08)	30.7 (1.09)	29.5 (1.08)	27.7 (0.99)	28.7 (1.00)	27.4 (0.99)	26.9 (1.00)	25.5 (0.95)
Use of selected drugs															
Cocaine	9.0 (0.73)	15.7 (0.72)	17.3 (0.74)	9.4 (0.59)	6.0 (0.48)	9.3 (0.59)	9.8 (0.63)	8.6 (0.62)	8.2 (0.60)	7.8 (0.59)	7.7 (0.55)	8.1 (0.56)	8.0 (0.56)	8.5 (0.58)	7.8 (0.54)
Heroin	2.2 (0.21)	1.1 (0.12)	1.2 (0.12)	1.3 (0.13)	1.6 (0.14)	2.0 (0.16)	2.0 (0.17)	2.4 (0.19)	1.8 (0.17)	1.7 (0.16)	1.5 (0.14)	1.5 (0.14)	1.5 (0.14)	1.4 (0.14)	1.5 (0.14)
LSD	11.3 (0.81)	9.3 (0.57)	7.5 (0.52)	8.7 (0.57)	11.7 (0.64)	12.6 (0.67)	12.2 (0.70)	11.1 (0.69)	10.9 (0.69)	8.4 (0.61)	5.9 (0.49)	4.6 (0.43)	3.5 (0.38)	3.3 (0.37)	3.4 (0.37)
Marijuana/hashish	47.3 (1.68)	60.3 (1.27)	54.2 (1.29)	40.7 (1.30)	41.7 (1.30)	49.1 (1.33)	49.7 (1.40)	48.8 (1.45)	49.0 (1.45)	47.8 (1.35)	46.1 (1.35)	45.7 (1.35)	44.8 (1.36)	42.3 (1.36)	41.8 (1.31)
PCP	— (†)	9.6 (0.33)	4.9 (0.24)	2.8 (0.19)	2.7 (0.18)	3.9 (0.22)	3.4 (0.22)	3.4 (0.23)	3.5 (0.23)	3.1 (0.22)	2.5 (0.18)	1.6 (0.15)	2.4 (0.18)	2.2 (0.17)	2.1 (0.17)
Percent reporting use of drugs in the past 12 months															
Alcohol[1]	84.8 (0.84)	87.9 (0.59)	85.6 (0.63)	80.6 (0.73)	73.7 (0.81)	74.3 (0.81)	73.8 (0.86)	73.2 (0.89)	73.3 (0.89)	71.5 (0.91)	70.1 (0.86)	70.6 (0.86)	68.6 (0.87)	66.5 (0.90)	66.4 (0.88)
Any illicit drug	45.0 (1.64)	53.1 (1.26)	46.3 (1.26)	32.5 (1.21)	39.0 (1.26)	41.4 (1.28)	42.1 (1.35)	40.9 (1.39)	41.4 (1.39)	41.0 (1.38)	39.3 (1.29)	38.8 (1.29)	38.4 (1.28)	36.5 (1.29)	35.9 (1.25)
Marijuana only	18.8 (1.29)	22.7 (1.06)	18.9 (0.99)	14.6 (0.91)	19.6 (1.02)	21.2 (1.06)	21.4 (1.12)	20.5 (1.14)	19.8 (1.12)	20.1 (1.13)	19.5 (1.05)	18.3 (1.02)	18.8 (1.03)	17.3 (1.01)	17.4 (0.99)
Any illicit drug other than marijuana[2]	26.2 (1.15)	30.4 (0.92)	27.4 (0.89)	17.9 (0.79)	19.4 (0.81)	20.2 (0.82)	20.7 (0.88)	20.4 (0.90)	21.6 (0.92)	20.9 (0.91)	19.8 (0.83)	20.5 (0.85)	19.7 (0.83)	19.2 (0.84)	18.5 (0.80)
Use of selected drugs															
Cocaine	5.6 (0.52)	12.3 (0.58)	13.1 (0.59)	5.3 (0.40)	4.0 (0.35)	5.7 (0.42)	6.2 (0.46)	5.0 (0.43)	4.8 (0.42)	5.0 (0.42)	4.8 (0.39)	5.3 (0.41)	5.1 (0.40)	5.7 (0.43)	5.2 (0.40)
Heroin	1.0 (0.13)	0.5 (0.07)	0.6 (0.07)	0.5 (0.07)	1.1 (0.10)	1.0 (0.10)	1.1 (0.11)	1.5 (0.13)	0.9 (0.13)	1.0 (0.11)	0.8 (0.09)	0.9 (0.09)	0.8 (0.09)	0.8 (0.09)	0.9 (0.09)
LSD	7.2 (0.59)	6.5 (0.43)	4.4 (0.36)	5.4 (0.41)	8.4 (0.49)	7.6 (0.48)	8.1 (0.52)	6.6 (0.49)	6.6 (0.49)	3.5 (0.36)	1.9 (0.25)	2.2 (0.27)	1.8 (0.24)	1.7 (0.24)	2.1 (0.26)
Marijuana/hashish	40.0 (1.61)	48.8 (1.27)	40.6 (1.24)	27.0 (1.15)	34.7 (1.23)	37.5 (1.25)	37.8 (1.33)	36.5 (1.36)	37.0 (1.36)	36.2 (1.35)	34.9 (1.26)	34.3 (1.25)	33.6 (1.24)	31.5 (1.24)	31.7 (1.21)
PCP	— (†)	4.4 (0.20)	2.9 (0.16)	1.2 (0.11)	1.8 (0.13)	2.1 (0.14)	1.8 (0.14)	2.3 (0.16)	1.8 (0.14)	1.1 (0.11)	1.3 (0.11)	0.7 (0.08)	1.3 (0.11)	0.7 (0.09)	0.9 (0.09)
Percent reporting use of drugs in the past 30 days															
Alcohol[1]	68.2 (1.10)	72.0 (0.81)	65.9 (0.85)	57.1 (0.92)	51.3 (0.92)	52.0 (0.92)	51.0 (0.98)	50.0 (1.01)	49.8 (1.01)	48.6 (1.00)	47.5 (0.94)	48.0 (0.94)	47.0 (0.94)	45.3 (0.95)	44.4 (0.92)
Any illicit drug	30.7 (1.35)	37.2 (1.09)	29.7 (1.03)	17.2 (0.87)	23.8 (0.98)	25.6 (1.01)	25.9 (1.07)	24.9 (1.09)	25.7 (1.10)	25.4 (1.09)	24.1 (1.01)	23.4 (1.00)	23.1 (0.99)	21.5 (0.98)	21.9 (0.96)
Marijuana only	15.3 (1.06)	18.8 (0.88)	14.8 (0.80)	9.2 (0.67)	13.8 (0.79)	14.9 (0.82)	15.5 (0.88)	14.5 (0.89)	14.7 (0.89)	14.1 (0.87)	19.5 (0.93)	18.3 (0.91)	12.8 (0.78)	11.7 (0.77)	12.4 (0.76)
Any illicit drug other than marijuana[2]	15.4 (0.80)	18.4 (0.66)	14.9 (0.60)	8.0 (0.47)	10.0 (0.52)	10.7 (0.54)	10.4 (0.56)	10.4 (0.58)	11.0 (0.59)	11.3 (0.60)	10.4 (0.54)	10.8 (0.55)	10.3 (0.54)	9.8 (0.54)	9.5 (0.51)
Use of selected drugs															
Cocaine	1.9 (0.25)	5.2 (0.31)	6.7 (0.35)	1.9 (0.20)	1.8 (0.19)	2.4 (0.22)	2.6 (0.23)	2.1 (0.23)	2.1 (0.23)	2.3 (0.24)	2.1 (0.21)	2.3 (0.22)	2.3 (0.22)	2.5 (0.23)	2.0 (0.20)
Heroin	0.4 (0.08)	0.2 (0.04)	0.3 (0.05)	0.2 (0.04)	0.6 (0.08)	0.5 (0.07)	0.5 (0.07)	0.7 (0.09)	0.4 (0.07)	0.5 (0.08)	0.4 (0.06)	0.5 (0.07)	0.5 (0.07)	0.4 (0.06)	0.4 (0.06)
LSD	2.3 (0.28)	2.3 (0.21)	1.6 (0.18)	1.9 (0.20)	4.0 (0.28)	3.2 (0.26)	2.7 (0.25)	1.6 (0.20)	2.3 (0.24)	0.7 (0.13)	0.6 (0.11)	0.7 (0.12)	0.7 (0.12)	0.6 (0.12)	0.6 (0.11)
Marijuana/hashish	27.1 (1.30)	33.7 (1.07)	25.7 (0.98)	14.0 (0.80)	21.2 (0.94)	22.8 (0.97)	23.1 (1.03)	21.6 (1.04)	22.4 (1.05)	21.5 (0.96)	21.2 (0.94)	19.9 (0.94)	19.8 (0.94)	18.3 (0.92)	18.8 (0.90)
PCP	— (†)	1.4 (0.11)	1.6 (0.12)	0.4 (0.06)	0.6 (0.08)	1.0 (0.10)	0.8 (0.09)	0.9 (0.10)	0.5 (0.10)	0.4 (0.07)	0.6 (0.08)	0.4 (0.06)	0.7 (0.08)	0.4 (0.06)	0.5 (0.07)

—Not available.
†Not applicable.
[1] Survey question changed in 1993; later data are not comparable to figures for earlier years.
[2] Other illicit drugs include any use of LSD or other hallucinogens, crack or other cocaine, or heroin, or any use of other narcotics, amphetamines, barbiturates, or tranquilizers not under a doctor's orders.

NOTE: Standard errors appear in parentheses. Standard errors were calculated from formulas to perform trend analysis over an interval greater than 1 year (for example, a comparison between 1975 and 1990). A revised questionnaire was used in 1982 and later years to reduce the inappropriate reporting of nonprescription stimulants. This slightly reduced the positive responses for some types of drug abuse.
SOURCE: University of Michigan, Institute for Social Research, Monitoring the Future, selected years, 1975 through 2007, retrieved January 3, 2008, from http://www.monitoringthefuture.org/data/07data.html. (This table was prepared January 2008.)

Table 165. Age range for compulsory school attendance and special education services, and policies on year-round schools and kindergarten programs, by state: Selected years, 1997 through 2008

State	Compulsory attendance					Compulsory special education services, 1997[1]	Year-round schools, 2006		Kindergarten education, 2008		
							Has policy on year-round schools	Has districts with year-round schools	School districts required to offer		Attendance required
	2000	2002	2004	2006	2007				Program	Full-day program	
1	2	3	4	5	6	7	8	9	10	11	12
Alabama	7 to 16	7 to 16	7 to 16 [2]	7 to 16	7 to 16	6 to 21		Yes		X	
Alaska	7 to 16	7 to 16	7 to 16 [2]	7 to 16	7 to 16	3 to 22		Yes			
Arizona	6 to 16 [2]	6 to 16 [2]	6 to 16 [2]	6 to 16 [2]	6 to 16 [2]	3 to 22		—	X [3,4]		
Arkansas	5 to 17 [2]	5 to 17 [2]	5 to 17	5 to 17	5 to 17	5 to 21	X	Yes		X	X
California	6 to 18 [2]	6 to 18	6 to 18	6 to 18	6 to 18	Birth to 21	X	Yes	X		
Colorado	—	—	7 to 16	7 to 16	6 to 17	3 to 21		—	X		
Connecticut	7 to 16	7 to 18 [2]	7 to 18 [2]	5 to 18 [5]	5 to 18 [5]	Under 21 [6]		—	X		X
Delaware	5 to 16	5 to 16	5 to 16 [2]	5 to 16	5 to 16	3 to 20		Yes	X	X [7]	X
District of Columbia	—	5 to 18	5 to 18	5 to 18	5 to 18	—	[8]	[8]	X		X
Florida	6 to 16 [9]	6 to 16 [9]	6 to 16 [9]	6 to 16 [9]	6 to 16 [9]	—	X	Yes	X		X
Georgia	6 to 16	6 to 16	6 to 16	6 to 16	6 to 16	Under 21 [6]		Yes		X	
Hawaii	6 to 18	6 to 18	6 to 18	6 to 18	6 to 18	Under 20	X	Yes	X		
Idaho	7 to 16	7 to 16	7 to 16	7 to 16	7 to 16	3 to 21		Yes			
Illinois	7 to 16	7 to 16	7 to 17	7 to 17	7 to 17	3 to 21	X	Yes	X [3]		
Indiana	7 to 16	7 to 16	7 to 16	7 to 18 [2]	7 to 18 [2]	3 to 22		Yes	X		
Iowa	6 to 16 [2]	6 to 16 [2]	6 to 16	6 to 16	6 to 16	Under 21	X	Yes	X		
Kansas	7 to 18 [2]	7 to 18 [2]	7 to 18 [2]	7 to 18 [2]	7 to 18 [2]	Under 21 [10]		—	X		
Kentucky	6 to 16	6 to 16	6 to 16 [2]	6 to 16	6 to 16	Under 21		Yes	X		
Louisiana	7 to 17	7 to 17	7 to 17 [2]	7 to 18 [2]	7 to 18 [2]	3 to 21		Yes		X	X
Maine	7 to 17	7 to 17	7 to 17 [2]	7 to 17 [2]	7 to 17 [2]	5 to 19 [11]		—	X		
Maryland	5 to 16	5 to 16	5 to 16	5 to 16	5 to 16	Under 21	X	—		X	X
Massachusetts	6 to 16	6 to 16	6 to 16	6 to 16 [2]	6 to 16 [2]	3 to 21		—	X		
Michigan	6 to 16	6 to 16	6 to 16	6 to 16	6 to 16	Under 26	X	Yes	X [3,12]		
Minnesota	7 to 18 [2]	7 to 16	7 to 16	7 to 16 [2]	7 to 16 [2]	Under 22		—	X		
Mississippi	6 to 17	6 to 17	6 to 16	6 to 16	6 to 17	Birth to 20		—		X	
Missouri	7 to 16	7 to 16	7 to 16	7 to 16	7 to 16	Under 21		Yes	X		
Montana	7 to 16 [2]	7 to 16 [2]	7 to 16 [2]	7 to 16 [2]	7 to 16 [2]	3 to 18		—	X		
Nebraska	7 to 16	7 to 16	7 to 16	6 to 18	6 to 18	Birth to 21		Yes	X		
Nevada	7 to 17	7 to 17	7 to 17	7 to 17	7 to 18 [2,5]	Under 22		Yes	X		X
New Hampshire	6 to 16	6 to 16	6 to 16	6 to 16	6 to 16 [13]	3 to 21		—			
New Jersey	6 to 16	6 to 16	6 to 16	6 to 16	6 to 16	5 to 21		—		X [14]	
New Mexico	5 to 18	5 to 18	5 to 18 [2]	5 to 18 [2]	5 to 18 [2]	[15]	X	Yes	X		X
New York	6 to 16 [2]	6 to 16	6 to 16	6 to 16 [16]	6 to 16 [16]	Under 21		—	X		
North Carolina	7 to 16	7 to 16	7 to 16	7 to 16	7 to 16	5 to 20	X	Yes		X	
North Dakota	7 to 16	7 to 16	7 to 16	7 to 16	7 to 16	3 to 20 [17]		—			
Ohio	6 to 18	6 to 18	6 to 18	6 to 18	6 to 18	Under 22	X	—	X [3]		X
Oklahoma	5 to 18	5 to 18	5 to 18	5 to 18	5 to 18	3 and up [18]		Yes	X	[19]	X
Oregon	7 to 18	7 to 18	7 to 18 [2]	7 to 18	7 to 18	3 to 21		Yes	X		
Pennsylvania	8 to 17	8 to 17	8 to 17 [2]	8 to 17 [2]	8 to 17 [2]	6 to 21	X	—			
Rhode Island	6 to 16	6 to 16	6 to 16	6 to 16	6 to 16	3 to 21		—	X		X
South Carolina	5 to 16	5 to 16	5 to 16	5 to 17 [5]	5 to 17 [5]	3 to 21		—		X [3,4]	X
South Dakota	6 to 16	6 to 16	6 to 16	6 to 16	6 to 18 [5,20]	Under 21	X	—	X		X
Tennessee	6 to 17	6 to 17	6 to 17	6 to 17 [5]	6 to 17 [5]	3 to 21	X	Yes	X		X
Texas	6 to 18	6 to 18	6 to 18	6 to 18	6 to 18	3 to 21	X	Yes	X		
Utah	6 to 18	6 to 18	6 to 18	6 to 18	6 to 18	3 to 22		Yes	X		
Vermont	7 to 16	6 to 16	6 to 16	6 to 16 [2]	6 to 16 [2]	3 to 21		—	X		
Virginia	5 to 18	5 to 18	5 to 18	5 to 18 [2]	5 to 18 [2]	2 to 21		Yes	X		X
Washington	8 to 17 [2]	8 to 17 [2]	8 to 16 [2]	8 to 18	8 to 18	3 to 21 [21]		Yes	X		
West Virginia	6 to 16	6 to 16	6 to 16	6 to 16	6 to 16	5 to 21	X	Yes		X	X
Wisconsin	6 to 18	6 to 18	6 to 18	6 to 18	6 to 18	Under 21		Yes	X	X [22]	
Wyoming	6 to 16 [2]	6 to 16 [2]	7 to 16 [2]	7 to 16 [2]	7 to 16 [2]	3 to 21		Yes	X		

X State has policy.
—Not available.

[1] Most states have a provision whereby education is provided up to a certain age or completion of secondary school, whichever comes first.

[2] Child may be exempted from compulsory attendance if he/she meets state requirements for early withdrawal with or without meeting conditions for a diploma or equivalency.

[3] State requires districts with full-day programs to offer half-day programs.

[4] Districts may apply for exemptions from the requirement.

[5] Parent/guardian may request a waiver to delay entry to a later age per state law/regulation.

[6] Under 21 or until child graduates from high school.

[7] Full-day requirement becomes effective upon each district's confirming vote and upon specific funding appropriation by the General Assembly.

[8] State did not participate in the 2006 online survey.

[9] Attendance is compulsory until age 18 for Manatee County students, unless they earn a high school diploma prior to reaching their 18th birthday.

[10] To be determined by rules and regulations adopted by the state board.

[11] Must be 5 before October 1, and not 20 before start of school year.

[12] State requires a "program," not necessarily a traditional kindergarten program.

[13] Compulsory attendance age becomes 18 effective July 1, 2009.

[14] Abbott districts only (31). These are districts covered by New Jersey Supreme Court rulings requiring the state to implement comprehensive programs and reforms to improve the education of students in the poorest schools.

[15] School-age unless otherwise provided by law.

[16] New York City and Buffalo require school attendance until age 17 unless employed.

[17] Must not be 21 by September 1.

[18] Children from birth through age 2 are eligible for additional services. Eligibility for special education services ceases upon completion of a secondary education program; no age limit.

[19] Beginning in 2011–12, with the option for districts to transfer intradistrict, interdistrict, or to a licensed child care provider.

[20] Compulsory leaving age becomes 18 effective July 1, 2009; compulsory entry age becomes 5 effective July 1, 2010.

[21] Student may complete school year if 21st birthday occurs while attending school.

[22] Districts are required to provide full-day kindergarten for low-income students.

NOTE: The Education of the Handicapped Act (EHA) Amendments of 1986 make it mandatory for all states receiving EHA funds to serve all 3- to 18-year-old disabled children.

SOURCE: Council of Chief State School Officers, *Key State Education Policies on PK–12 Education*, 2000, 2002, 2004, and 2006; California Department of Education, Safe Schools and Violence Prevention Office, *School Attendance Review Boards*, Feb. 2001; School District of Manatee County Policy and Procedures, retrieved September 18, 2008, from http://www.manatee.k12.fl.us/policy_procedure/pdfs/chapters/Chapter_5.pdf; Education Commission of the States, ECS StateNotes, *Attendance: Compulsory School Age Requirements*, retrieved September 18, 2008, from http://ecs.org/ecsmain.asp?page=/html/issues.asp, and *Kindergarten: State Statutes Regarding Kindergarten* (prepublication copy of 2008 update); and supplemental information from several state education websites. (This table was prepared September 2008.)

Table 166. Minimum length of school year and policy on textbook selection, by state: 2000, 2004, and 2006

State	Minimum length of school year				State policy on textbook selection, 2006					State
	In days			In hours	State recommends or selects textbooks				State standards used in recommendation or selection	
	2000	2004	2006	2006	Recommends	Selects	Either recommends or selects	Local decision		
1	2	3	4	5	6	7	8	9	10	11
Alabama	175	175	175	†			X		X	Alabama
Alaska	180	180	180	†				X		Alaska
Arizona	175 [1]	175	180	†						Arizona
Arkansas	178	178	178	†		X			X	Arkansas
California	175	180	180	†	X				X	California
Colorado	[2]	170	160	450/900 (K⁵); 990 (1–8); 1,080 (9–12)				X		Colorado
Connecticut	180	180	180	900				X		Connecticut
Delaware	[2]	[2]	†	440 (K); 1,060 (1–11); 1,032 (12)						Delaware
District of Columbia	180 [3]	180	180	†	—	—	—	—	—	District of Columbia
Florida	180	180	180	†	X				X	Florida
Georgia	180 [3]	180	180	810 (K–3); 900 (4–5); 990 (6–12)	X				X	Georgia
Hawaii	184	183	179	†	X				X	Hawaii
Idaho	180	170	†	450 (K); 810 (1–3); 900 (4–8); 990 (9–12)	X				X	Idaho
Illinois	180 [4]	185	176	880				X		Illinois
Indiana	180	180	180	900 (1–6); 1,080 (7–12)	X				X	Indiana
Iowa	180	180	180	990 (1–11); 962 (12)				X		Iowa
Kansas	186	186	186 (K–11); 181 (12)	465 (K); 1,116 (1–11); 1,086 (12)						Kansas
Kentucky	175	[2]	175	1,050	X				X	Kentucky
Louisiana	175	177	177	1,062		X			X	Louisiana
Maine	175	180	175	†				X		Maine
Maryland	180	180	180	1,080						Maryland
Massachusetts	180	180	180	425 (K); 900 (1–8); 990 (9–12)				X		Massachusetts
Michigan	180	185	†	549 (K); 1098 (1–12)				X		Michigan
Minnesota	[2]	[2]	[2]	†				X		Minnesota
Mississippi	180	180	180	990	X				X	Mississippi
Missouri	174	174	174	522 (K); 1044 (1–12)						Missouri
Montana	180	180	90 (K); 180 (K–12)	360 (K); 720 (1–3); 1,080 (4–12)						Montana
Nebraska	[2]	[2]	†	400 (K); 1,032 (1–8); 1,080 (9–12)				X		Nebraska
Nevada	180	180	180	†						Nevada
New Hampshire	180	180	180	945 (1–4); 990 (5–12)				X		New Hampshire
New Jersey	180	180	180	†				X	X [5]	New Jersey
New Mexico	180	180	180	450/990 (K⁵); 990 (1–6); 1,080 (7–12)		X			X	New Mexico
New York	180 [3]	180	180	†						New York
North Carolina	180	180	180	1,000		X			X	North Carolina
North Dakota	173	173	173	†				X		North Dakota
Ohio	182	182	182	910						Ohio
Oklahoma	180	180	180	1,080		X			X	Oklahoma
Oregon	[2]	[2]	†	405 (K); 810 (1–3); 900 (4–8); 990 (9–12)		X			X	Oregon
Pennsylvania	180	180	180	450/900 (K⁵); 900 (1–6); 990 (7–12)						Pennsylvania
Rhode Island	180	180	180	†						Rhode Island
South Carolina	180	180	180	†		X			X	South Carolina
South Dakota	—	170	†	875 (1–3); 962.5 (4–12)						South Dakota
Tennessee	180	180	180	†		X			X	Tennessee
Texas	187	180	180	†		X			X	Texas
Utah	180	180	180	990			X		X	Utah
Vermont	175	175	175	350 (K); 700 (1–2); 962.5 (3–12)						Vermont
Virginia	180	180	180	540 (K); 990 (1–12)	X				X	Virginia
Washington	180 [4]	180	180	450 (K); 1,000 (1–12)				X		Washington
West Virginia	180	180	180	†			X		X	West Virginia
Wisconsin	180	180	180	437 (K); 1,050 (1–6); 1,137 (7–12)				X		Wisconsin
Wyoming	175	175	175	450 (K); 900 (1–5); 1,050 (6–8); 1,100 (9–12)						Wyoming

—Not available.
†Not applicable.
X Denotes that the state has a policy. A blank denotes that the state does not have a policy.
[1]1994 data.
[2]No statewide policy; varies by district.
[3]1996 data.
[4]1998 data.

[5]Has state standards, but no policy of state recommendation or selection.
NOTE: Some states allow for different types of school calendars by setting instruction time in both days and hours, while others use only days or only hours. For states in which the number of days or hours varies by grade, the relevant grade(s) appear in parentheses.
SOURCE: Council of Chief State School Officers, *Key State Education Policies on PK–12 Education: 2000, 2004, and 2006*, supplemented by information from several state education agencies. (This table was prepared September 2008.)

Table 167. State requirements for a standard high school diploma: 2006

State	Total required credits for standard diploma, all courses	Required credits in subject areas (in Carnegie units)					High school exit exam required for standard diploma	Characteristics of required exit exams				High school completion credentials	
		English/ language arts	Social studies	Science	Mathe-matics	Other credits		Subjects tested[1]	Exam type[2]	Exam based on stand-ards for 10th grade or higher	Appeals or alter-native route to standard diploma if exam failed	Advanced recog-nition for ex-ceeding standard require-ments	Alternative credential for not meeting all standard require-ments
1	2	3	4	5	6	7	8	9	10	11	12	13	14
Alabama	24	4	4	4	4	8	Yes	EMSH	SB	Yes	No	Yes	Yes
Alaska	21	4	3	2	2	10	Yes	EM	MC	Yes	Yes	No	Yes
Arizona	20	4	2.5	2	2	9.5	Yes	EM	SB	Yes	Yes	Yes	No
Arkansas	21 [3]	4	3	3	3 [3]	8	No	†	†	†	†	No	No
California	13	3	3	2	2	3	Yes	EM	SB	Yes	Yes	Yes	Yes
Colorado	† [4]	† [4]	† [3,4]	† [3]	† [4]	† [4]	No	†	†	†	†	No	No
Connecticut	20	4	3	2	3	8	No	†	†	†	†	No	No
Delaware	22 [3]	4	3	3 [3]	3 [3]	9	No	†	†	†	†	Yes	Yes
District of Columbia	23.5	4	3.5 [3]	3	3 [3]	10	No	†	†	†	†	No	Yes
Florida	24	4	3	3	3 [3]	11	Yes	EM	SB	Yes	Yes	Yes	Yes
Georgia	22	4	3	3	4	8	Yes	EMSH	SB	Yes	Yes	Yes	Yes
Hawaii	22 [3]	4	4	3	3	8	No	†	†	†	†	Yes	Yes
Idaho	21 [3]	4.5	2.5	2 [3]	2 [3]	10	Yes	EM	SB	Yes	Yes	No	No
Illinois	16	3 [3]	2	1 [3]	2 [3]	8	No	†	†	†	†	No	No
Indiana	20	4	2 [3]	2 [3]	2 [3]	10 [3]	Yes	EM	SB	No	Yes	Yes	No
Iowa	† [3]	† [3]	1.5	† [3]	† [3]	1	No	†	†	†	†	No	No
Kansas	21	4	3	2 [3]	2 [3]	10	No	†	†	†	†	No	No
Kentucky	22	4	3	3	3	9	No	†	†	†	†	Yes	Yes
Louisiana	23	4	3	3	3	10	Yes	EMSH	SB	Yes	Yes	Yes	Yes
Maine	16	4	2	2	2	6	No	†	†	†	†	No	No
Maryland	21	4	3	3	3	8	Yes [5]	—	—	—	No	Yes	Yes
Massachusetts	† [4]	† [4]	† [4]	† [4]	† [4]	† [4]	Yes	EM	SB	Yes	Yes	No	Yes
Michigan	† [3,4]	† [3,4]	0.5 [3]	† [3,4]	† [3,4]	† [4]	No	†	†	†	†	No	Yes
Minnesota	† [3,4]	† [3,4]	† [3,4]	† [3,4]	† [3,4]	† [4]	Yes	EM	MC	No	No	No	No
Mississippi	20 [3]	4	3	3 [3]	3 [3]	7	Yes	EMSH	EOC	Yes	Yes	No	Yes
Missouri	22 [3]	3 [3]	2 [3]	2 [3]	2 [3]	13 [3]	No	†	†	†	†	Yes	No
Montana	20	4	2	2	2	10	No	†	†	†	†	No	No
Nebraska	200 hrs [6]	† [4]	† [4]	† [4]	† [4]	† [4]	No	†	†	†	†	No	No
Nevada	22.5	4	2	2	3	11.5	Yes	EM	SB	Yes	No	Yes	Yes
New Hampshire	19.75 [3]	4	2.5 [3]	2 [3]	2 [3]	9.25	No	†	†	†	†	Yes	Yes
New Jersey	22	4	3	3	3	9	Yes	EM	SB	Yes	Yes	No	No
New Mexico	23	4	3 [3]	2 [3]	3	11 [3]	Yes	EMSH	MC	No	Yes	No	Yes
New York	22	4	4	3	3	8	Yes	EMSH	EOC	Yes	Yes	Yes	Yes
North Carolina	20	4	3	3	4	6	Yes	EMT	SB	No	Yes	Yes	Yes
North Dakota	21 [3]	† [4]	† [4]	† [4]	† [4]	† [4]	No	†	†	†	†	No	No
Ohio	20	4	3	3	3 [3]	7	Yes	EMSH	SB	Yes	Yes	Yes	No
Oklahoma	23	4	3	3	3	10	Yes [5]	—	—	—	No	Yes	No
Oregon	22 [3]	3 [3]	3	2 [3]	2 [3]	12	No	†	†	†	†	Yes	Yes
Pennsylvania	† [4]	† [4]	† [4]	† [4]	† [4]	† [4]	No	†	†	†	†	Yes	No
Rhode Island	18 [3]	4	2	2 [3]	3 [3]	7	No	†	†	†	†	No	Yes
South Carolina	24	4	3	3	4	10	Yes	EM	SB	Yes	No	No	Yes
South Dakota	22	4	3	2.5	2.5	10	No	†	†	†	†	Yes	No
Tennessee	20	4	3	3	3	7	Yes	EMS	EOC	Yes	No	No	Yes
Texas	22 [3]	4	3	2	3	10	Yes	EMSH	SB	Yes	No	Yes	Yes
Utah	15 [3]	3 [3]	2.5	2 [3]	2 [3]	5.5	No	†	†	†	†	No	Yes
Vermont	20	4	3	3	3	7	No	†	†	†	†	No	No
Virginia	22	4	3	3	3	9	Yes	EMSH	EOC	Yes	Yes	Yes	Yes
Washington	19	3	2.5	2	2	9.5	Yes [5]	—	—	—	No	No	No
West Virginia	24	4	3 [3]	3	3 [3]	11	No	†	†	†	†	No	Yes
Wisconsin	13	4	3	2	2	2	No	†	†	†	†	No	No
Wyoming	13	4	3	3	3	0	No	†	†	†	†	Yes	Yes

—Not available.

†Not applicable.

[1]Exit exam subjects tested: E = English (including writing), M = Mathematics, S = Science, H = History/social studies, and T = Technology.

[2]Exit exam types: EOC = End-Of-Course, MC = Minimum Competency, and SB = Standards Based.

[3]Number of required credits scheduled to change for classes graduating in 2007 or later.

[4]Graduation requirements are determined locally.

[5]Takes effect for classes graduating in 2007 or later.

[6]Credit hours for graduating classes for Nebraska are not expressed in Carnegie units.

NOTE: Local school districts frequently have other graduation requirements in addition to state requirements. The Carnegie unit is a standard of measurement that represents one credit for the completion of a 1-year course.

SOURCE: Editorial Projects in Education Research Center, Education Week, "What It Takes to Graduate for the Class of 2007," retrieved June 19, 2007, from www.edweek.org/media/ew/dc/2007/40policy-1.pdf; Education Commission of the States, StateNotes, retrieved September 24, 2007, from http://mb2.ecs.org/reports/Report.aspx?id=735; and supplemental information from several state education agencies. (This table was prepared September 2007.)

Table 168. States that use criterion-referenced tests (CRTs) aligned to state standards, by subject area and level: 2006–07

State	Aligned to state standards		Off-the-shelf/ norm-referenced test (NRT)[1]	Criterion-referenced tests,[2] by subject area and level			
	Custom-developed test (CRT)[2]	Augmented or hybrid test[3]		English/ language arts	Mathematics	Science	Social studies/ history
1	2	3	4	5	6	7	8
Alabama	X		X	ES, MS, HS	ES, MS, HS	HS	HS
Alaska	X		X	ES, MS, HS	ES, MS, HS		
Arizona	X	X	X	ES, MS, HS	ES, MS, HS		
Arkansas	X		X	ES, MS, HS	ES, MS, HS	ES, MS	
California	X		X	ES, MS, HS	ES, MS, HS	ES, MS, HS	MS, HS
Colorado	X		X	ES, MS, HS	ES, MS, HS	ES, MS, HS	
Connecticut	X			ES, MS, HS	ES, MS, HS	HS	
Delaware		X		ES, MS, HS	ES, MS, HS	ES, MS, HS	ES, MS, HS
District of Columbia	X			ES, MS, HS	ES, MS, HS		
Florida	X		X	ES, MS, HS	ES, MS, HS	ES, MS, HS	
Georgia	X		X	ES, MS, HS	ES, MS, HS	ES, MS, HS	ES, MS, HS
Hawaii		X		ES, MS, HS	ES, MS, HS		
Idaho	X			ES, MS, HS	ES, MS, HS		
Illinois	X	X		ES, MS, HS	ES, MS, HS	HS	
Indiana	X			ES, MS, HS	ES, MS, HS	ES, MS	
Iowa			X	ES, MS, HS	ES, MS, HS	ES, MS, HS	
Kansas	X			ES, MS, HS	ES, MS, HS		
Kentucky	X		X	ES, MS, HS	ES, MS, HS	ES, MS, HS	ES, MS, HS
Louisiana	X	X		ES, MS, HS	ES, MS, HS	ES, MS, HS	ES, MS, HS
Maine	X		X	ES, MS, HS	ES, MS, HS	ES, MS	
Maryland	X	X		ES, MS, HS	ES, MS, HS	HS	HS
Massachusetts	X			ES, MS, HS	ES, MS, HS	ES, MS, HS	
Michigan	X		X	ES, MS, HS	ES, MS, HS	ES, MS, HS	MS, HS
Minnesota	X			ES, MS, HS	ES, MS, HS		
Mississippi	X		X	ES, MS, HS	ES, MS, HS	ES, MS, HS	HS
Missouri		X		ES, MS, HS	ES, MS, HS		
Montana	X		X	ES, MS, HS	ES, MS, HS		
Nebraska	X			ES, MS, HS			
Nevada	X		X	ES, MS, HS	ES, MS, HS		
New Hampshire	X			ES, MS	ES, MS		
New Jersey	X			ES, MS, HS	ES, MS, HS	ES, MS	
New Mexico	X		X	ES, MS, HS	ES, MS, HS	ES, MS, HS	
New York	X			ES, MS, HS	ES, MS, HS	ES, MS, HS	ES, MS, HS
North Carolina	X			ES, MS, HS	ES, MS, HS	HS	HS
North Dakota	X			ES, MS, HS	ES, MS, HS	ES, MS, HS	
Ohio	X			ES, MS, HS	ES, MS, HS	ES, MS, HS	ES, MS, HS
Oklahoma	X			ES, MS, HS	ES, MS, HS	ES, MS, HS	ES, MS, HS
Oregon	X			ES, MS, HS	ES, MS, HS	MS, HS	
Pennsylvania	X			ES, MS, HS	ES, MS, HS		
Rhode Island	X	X		ES, MS, HS	ES, MS, HS		
South Carolina	X			ES, MS, HS	ES, MS, HS	ES, MS, HS	ES, MS, HS
South Dakota		X	X	ES, MS, HS	ES, MS, HS	ES, MS, HS	
Tennessee	X			ES, MS, HS	ES, MS, HS	ES, MS, HS	ES, MS, HS
Texas	X			ES, MS, HS	ES, MS, HS	ES, MS, HS	MS, HS
Utah	X		X	ES, MS, HS	ES, MS, HS	ES, MS, HS	
Vermont	X			ES, MS	ES, MS		
Virginia	X			ES, MS, HS	ES, MS, HS	ES, MS, HS	ES, MS, HS
Washington	X			ES, MS, HS	ES, MS, HS	ES, MS, HS	
West Virginia	X		X	ES, MS, HS	ES, MS, HS	ES, MS, HS	ES, MS
Wisconsin		X		ES, MS, HS	ES, MS, HS	ES, MS, HS	ES, MS, HS
Wyoming	X			ES, MS, HS	ES, MS, HS		

X State has a test.
[1]Off-the-shelf/norm-referenced tests (NRTs) are commercially developed tests that have not been modified to reflect state content standards.
[2]Custom-developed criterion-referenced tests (CRTs) are explicitly designed to measure state content standards.

[3]Augmented or hybrid tests incorporate elements of both NRTs and CRTs. These tests include NRTs that have been augmented or modified to reflect state standards.
NOTE: ES = elementary school, MS = middle school, and HS = high school.
SOURCE: Quality Counts 2007, Cradle to Career, *Education Week*, 2007. (This table was prepared September 2008.)

Table 169. States using minimum-competency testing, by grade levels assessed, expected uses of standards, and state or jurisdiction: 2001–02

State or jurisdiction	Grade levels in which students are tested on at least one component	Expected uses								
		Student diagnosis or placement[1]	Improvement of instruction[1]	Program evaluation[1]	Student promotion[2]	High school exit requirement	School awards or recognition[3]	Public school performance reporting[3]	Accreditation[3]	Other
1	2	3	4	5	6	7	8	9	10	11
Alabama	3–8,10–12	X	X	X		X	X	X		
Alaska	3,4,6–10	X	X	X				X		
Arizona	2–10		X	X				X		
Arkansas	4–12	X	X	X				X		
California	2–12[4]		X	X	X	X	X	X		(5,6)
Colorado	3–10		X	X				X		
Connecticut	4,6,8,10	X	X	X		X	X	X		
Delaware	2–11	X	X		X		X	X		(6)
Florida	3–11		X	X		X	X	X		
Georgia	K–8,11,12	X	X	X		X	X	X		
Hawaii	3,5,8,10		X	X						
Idaho	K–11		X	X				X		
Illinois	3–5,7–11[4,7]		X	X	X			X		(5)
Indiana	3,6,8,10		X	X				X		
Iowa	4,8,11						X	X	X	
Kansas	4–8,10,11	X	X	X				X	X	
Kentucky	3–12		X	X			X	X		
Louisiana	3–11	X	X	X	X	X		X		
Maine	4,8,11[7]		X	X				X		
Maryland	3,5–12	X	X	X		X	X	X		
Massachusetts	3–8,10[7]	X	X	X		X	X	X		(5)
Michigan	4,5,7,8,11	X	X	X				X	X	
Minnesota	3–12	X	X	X		X				
Mississippi	2–12	X	X	X		X				
Missouri	3–5,7–11	X	X	X			X	X	X	
Montana	4,8,11		X	X						
Nebraska	4,8,11	X	X	X						
Nevada	3–5,8,10–12	X	X	X		X	X	X		
New Hampshire	3,6,10		X	X				X		
New Jersey	4,8,11	X	X	X		X		X	X	(5,8)
New Mexico	K,3–10	X	X	X		X	X	X	X	
New York	4,5,8–12	X	X	X	X	X		X		(5,6)
North Carolina	3–12[4]	X	X	X	X	X		X		
North Dakota	4,8,12	X	X	X	X			X		(6)
Ohio	4,6,9		X	X	X	X	X	X		
Oklahoma	3,5,8,10,11	X	X	X				X	X	
Oregon	3,5,8,10		X	X				X		
Pennsylvania	5,6,8,9,11	X		X			X	X		
Rhode Island	3–5,7–11		X	X				X		
South Carolina	1,3–12[7]	X	X	X		X		X		
South Dakota	2–6,8–11	X	X	X						
Tennessee	3–12	X	X	X		X	X	X		(5,6)
Texas	3–12	X	X	X		X	X	X	X	
Utah	1–12[4]	X	X	X	X		X	X		
Vermont	2,4,5,8,10,11		X	X				X		
Virginia	3–6,8–12	X	X	X	X	X		X	X	
Washington	2–11[4,7]	X	X	X				X		
West Virginia	1–12[7]	X	X	X				X	X	(5,8)
Wisconsin	3,4,8,10	X	X	X				X		
Wyoming	4,8,10–12[7]		X	X				X	X	
Other jurisdictions										
American Samoa	4,6,8,10,12	X	X	X						
Puerto Rico	—	—	—	—	—	—	—	—	—	—
U.S. Virgin Islands	—	—	—	—	—	—	—	—	—	—

—Not available.
X State has program.
[1]Testing program is for instructional purposes.
[2]Testing program is for the purpose of student accountability.
[3]Testing program is for school accountability.
[4]Inclusion is voluntary for students, schools, or school districts for one or more grades.

[5]Endorsed diploma.
[6]Honors diploma.
[7]A sample of students is tested for one or more grades.
[8]High school skills guarantee.
SOURCE: Council of Chief State School Officers, *Annual Survey of State Student Assessment Programs, Fall 2003.* (This table was prepared April 2005.)

Table 170. States requiring testing for initial certification of elementary and secondary teachers, by skills or knowledge assessment and state: 2007 and 2008

State	Assessment for certification, 2007				Assessment for certification, 2008			
	Basic skills exam	Subject-matter exam	Knowledge of teaching exam	Assessment of teaching performance	Basic skills exam	Subject-matter exam	Knowledge of teaching exam	Assessment of teaching performance
1	2	3	4	5	6	7	8	9
Alabama	X	X	X	X	X	X	X	X
Alaska	X				X			
Arizona		X	X			X	X	
Arkansas	X	X	X	X	X	X	X	X
California	X	—		X	X	—		X
Colorado		X				X		
Connecticut	X	X	X	X	X	X	X	X
Delaware	X	X			X	X		
District of Columbia	X	X	—	—	X	X	—	—
Florida	X	X	X		X			X
Georgia	X	X			X	X		
Hawaii	X	X	X	—	X	X	X	—
Idaho		X	X	X		X	X	X
Illinois	X	X	X		X	X	X	
Indiana	X	X		X	X	X		X
Iowa	—		—	—	—		—	—
Kansas		X	X			X	X	
Kentucky		X	X	X	X	X	X	X
Louisiana	X	X	X	X	X	X	X	X
Maine	—	—	—	—	—	—	—	—
Maryland	X	X	X	X	X	X	X	X
Massachusetts	X	X		X	X	X		X
Michigan	X	X		X	X	X		X
Minnesota	X	X	X		X	X	X	
Mississippi	—	—	—	—	—	—	—	—
Missouri	X	X		X	X	X		X
Montana								
Nebraska	X				X			
Nevada	—	X	—	—	—	X	—	—
New Hampshire	X	X			X	X		
New Jersey	—	—	—	—	—	—	—	—
New Mexico	X	X	X	X	X	X	X	X
New York		X	X			X	X	
North Carolina	—	—	—	—	—	—	—	—
North Dakota	—	—	—	—	—	X	—	—
Ohio		X	X	X		X	X	X
Oklahoma	—	—	—	—	—	—	—	—
Oregon	X	X	—	—	X	X	—	—
Pennsylvania	X	X	X	X	X	X	X	X
Rhode Island		X	X	X			X	X
South Carolina		X	X			X	X	
South Dakota	X	X	X	X	X	X	X	X
Tennessee	X	X	X		X	X	X	
Texas	—	—	—	—	—	—	—	—
Utah		X		X		X		X
Vermont	X	X			X	X		
Virginia	X	X	X		X	X	X	
Washington	X	X		X	X	X		X
West Virginia	X	X	X	X	X	X	X	X
Wisconsin	X	X			X	X		
Wyoming	—		—	—	—		—	—

X State requires testing.
—Not available.

SOURCE: National Association of State Directors of Teacher Education and Certification, NASDTEC Knowledgebase, retrieved July 7, 2008, from https://www.nasdtec.info/. (This table was prepared July 2008.)

Table 171. Revenues for public elementary and secondary schools, by source of funds: Selected years, 1919–20 through 2005–06

School year	Total (in thousands)	Federal (in thousands)	Federal revenue per student		State (in thousands)	Local (including intermediate)[1] (in thousands)	Percentage distribution			
			Current dollars	Constant 2006–07 dollars			Total	Federal	State	Local (including intermediate)[1]
1	2	3	4	5	6	7	8	9	10	11
1919–20	$970,121	$2,475	#	$1	$160,085	$807,561	100.0	0.3	16.5	83.2
1929–30	2,088,557	7,334	#	3	353,670	1,727,553	100.0	0.4	16.9	82.7
1939–40	2,260,527	39,810	$2	23	684,354	1,536,363	100.0	1.8	30.3	68.0
1941–42	2,416,580	34,305	1	18	759,993	1,622,281	100.0	1.4	31.4	67.1
1943–44	2,604,322	35,886	2	18	859,183	1,709,253	100.0	1.4	33.0	65.6
1945–46	3,059,845	41,378	2	20	1,062,057	1,956,409	100.0	1.4	34.7	63.9
1947–48	4,311,534	120,270	5	44	1,676,362	2,514,902	100.0	2.8	38.9	58.3
1949–50	5,437,044	155,848	6	53	2,165,689	3,115,507	100.0	2.9	39.8	57.3
1951–52	6,423,816	227,711	9	67	2,478,596	3,717,507	100.0	3.5	38.6	57.9
1953–54	7,866,852	355,237	12	94	2,944,103	4,567,512	100.0	4.5	37.4	58.1
1955–56	9,686,677	441,442	14	109	3,828,886	5,416,350	100.0	4.6	39.5	55.9
1957–58	12,181,513	486,484	15	106	4,800,368	6,894,661	100.0	4.0	39.4	56.6
1959–60	14,746,618	651,639	19	129	5,768,047	8,326,932	100.0	4.4	39.1	56.5
1961–62	17,527,707	760,975	20	138	6,789,190	9,977,542	100.0	4.3	38.7	56.9
1963–64	20,544,182	896,956	22	148	8,078,014	11,569,213	100.0	4.4	39.3	56.3
1965–66	25,356,858	1,996,954	47	303	9,920,219	13,439,686	100.0	7.9	39.1	53.0
1967–68	31,903,064	2,806,469	64	384	12,275,536	16,821,063	100.0	8.8	38.5	52.7
1969–70	40,266,923	3,219,557	71	382	16,062,776	20,984,589	100.0	8.0	39.9	52.1
1970–71	44,511,292	3,753,461	82	420	17,409,086	23,348,745	100.0	8.4	39.1	52.5
1971–72	50,003,645	4,467,969	97	481	19,133,256	26,402,420	100.0	8.9	38.3	52.8
1972–73	52,117,930	4,525,000	99	472	20,699,752	26,893,180	100.0	8.7	39.7	51.6
1973–74	58,230,892	4,930,351	108	475	24,113,409	29,187,132	100.0	8.5	41.4	50.1
1974–75	64,445,239	5,811,595	129	508	27,060,563	31,573,079	100.0	9.0	42.0	49.0
1975–76	71,206,073	6,318,345	141	519	31,602,885	33,284,840	100.0	8.9	44.4	46.7
1976–77	75,332,532	6,629,498	150	520	32,526,018	36,177,019	100.0	8.8	43.2	48.0
1977–78	81,443,160	7,694,194	177	575	35,013,266	38,735,700	100.0	9.4	43.0	47.6
1978–79	87,994,143	8,600,116	202	602	40,132,136	39,261,891	100.0	9.8	45.6	44.6
1979–80	96,881,165	9,503,537	228	600	45,348,814	42,028,813	100.0	9.8	46.8	43.4
1980–81	105,949,087	9,768,262	239	563	50,182,659	45,998,166	100.0	9.2	47.4	43.4
1981–82	110,191,257	8,186,466	204	443	52,436,435	49,568,356	100.0	7.4	47.6	45.0
1982–83	117,497,502	8,339,990	211	438	56,282,157	52,875,354	100.0	7.1	47.9	45.0
1983–84	126,055,419	8,576,547	218	438	60,232,981	57,245,892	100.0	6.8	47.8	45.4
1984–85	137,294,678	9,105,569	232	448	67,168,684	61,020,425	100.0	6.6	48.9	44.4
1985–86	149,127,779	9,975,622	253	475	73,619,575	65,532,582	100.0	6.7	49.4	43.9
1986–87	158,523,693	10,146,013	255	468	78,830,437	69,547,243	100.0	6.4	49.7	43.9
1987–88	169,561,974	10,716,687	268	472	84,004,415	74,840,873	100.0	6.3	49.5	44.1
1988–89	192,016,374	11,902,001	296	499	91,768,911	88,345,462	100.0	6.2	47.8	46.0
1989–90	208,547,573	12,700,784	313	504	98,238,633	97,608,157	100.0	6.1	47.1	46.8
1990–91	223,340,537	13,776,066	334	509	105,324,533	104,239,939	100.0	6.2	47.2	46.7
1991–92	234,581,384	15,493,330	368	544	108,783,449	110,304,605	100.0	6.6	46.4	47.0
1992–93	247,626,168	17,261,252	403	577	113,403,436	116,961,481	100.0	7.0	45.8	47.2
1993–94	260,159,468	18,341,483	422	589	117,474,209	124,343,776	100.0	7.1	45.2	47.8
1994–95	273,149,449	18,582,157	421	572	127,729,576	126,837,717	100.0	6.8	46.8	46.4
1995–96	287,702,844	19,104,019	426	563	136,670,754	131,928,071	100.0	6.6	47.5	45.9
1996–97	305,065,192	20,081,287	440	566	146,435,584	138,548,321	100.0	6.6	48.0	45.4
1997–98	325,925,708	22,201,965	481	607	157,645,372	146,078,370	100.0	6.8	48.4	44.8
1998–99	347,377,993	24,521,817	527	654	169,298,232	153,557,944	100.0	7.1	48.7	44.2
1999–2000	372,943,802	27,097,866	578	697	184,613,352	161,232,584	100.0	7.3	49.5	43.2
2000–01	401,356,120	29,100,183	616	719	199,583,097	172,672,840	100.0	7.3	49.7	43.0
2001–02	419,501,976	33,144,633	695	797	206,541,793	179,815,551	100.0	7.9	49.2	42.9
2002–03	440,111,653	37,515,909	779	873	214,277,407	188,318,337	100.0	8.5	48.7	42.8
2003–04	462,026,099	41,923,435	864	947	217,384,191	202,718,474	100.0	9.1	47.1	43.9
2004–05[2]	487,753,525	44,809,532	918	978	228,553,579	214,390,414	100.0	9.2	46.9	44.0
2005–06	520,643,954	47,553,827	968	993	242,151,076	230,939,051	100.0	9.1	46.5	44.4

#Rounds to zero.
[1]Includes a relatively small amount from nongovernmental private sources (gifts and tuition and transportation fees from patrons). These sources accounted for 2.2 percent of total revenues in 2005–06.
[2]Revised from previously published figures.
NOTE: Beginning in 1980–81, revenues for state education agencies are excluded. Beginning in 1988–89, data reflect new survey collection procedures and may not be entirely comparable with figures for earlier years. With the exception of federal revenue per student,

data are not adjusted for changes in the purchasing power of the dollar due to inflation. Detail may not sum to totals because of rounding.
SOURCE: U.S. Department of Education, National Center for Education Statistics, *Biennial Survey of Education in the United States*, 1919–20 through 1955–56; *Statistics of State School Systems*, 1957–58 through 1969–70; *Revenues and Expenditures for Public Elementary and Secondary Education*, 1970–71 through 1986–87; and Common Core of Data (CCD), "National Public Education Financial Survey," 1987–88 through 2005–06. (This table was prepared April 2008.)

Table 172. Revenues for public elementary and secondary schools, by source and state or jurisdiction: 2005–06

State or jurisdiction	Total (in thousands)	Federal			State		Local and intermediate		Private[1]	
		Amount (in thousands)	Per student	Percent of total	Amount (in thousands)	Percent of total	Amount (in thousands)	Percent of total	Amount (in thousands)	Percent of total
1	2	3	4	5	6	7	8	9	10	11
United States	$520,643,954	$47,553,827	$968	9.1	$242,151,076	46.5	$219,411,054	42.1	$11,527,997	2.2
Alabama	6,346,033	758,840	1,023	12.0	3,547,078	55.9	1,742,902	27.5	297,213	4.7
Alaska	1,712,601	291,193	2,185	17.0	1,005,181	58.7	397,097	23.2	19,130	1.1
Arizona	8,833,520	1,040,249	950	11.8	4,272,320	48.4	3,295,908	37.3	225,043	2.5
Arkansas	4,282,506	485,100	1,023	11.3	2,432,920	56.8	1,221,672	28.5	142,814	3.3
California	63,785,872	6,889,913	1,070	10.8	37,847,078	59.3	18,451,803	28.9	597,078	0.9
Colorado	7,269,475	530,970	681	7.3	3,089,571	42.5	3,353,235	46.1	295,698	4.1
Connecticut	8,711,814	417,629	726	4.8	3,351,644	38.5	4,812,373	55.2	130,167	1.5
Delaware	1,533,399	126,940	1,050	8.3	969,854	63.2	419,118	27.3	17,486	1.1
District of Columbia	1,201,091	146,698	1,908	12.2	†	†	1,043,987	86.9	10,406	0.9
Florida	24,816,807	2,502,270	935	10.1	9,795,679	39.5	11,677,319	47.1	841,539	3.4
Georgia	16,117,459	1,487,715	931	9.2	7,155,591	44.4	6,986,870	43.3	487,284	3.0
Hawaii	2,703,718	223,580	1,223	8.3	2,431,735	89.9	24,489	0.9	23,914	0.9
Idaho	1,909,489	206,418	788	10.8	1,073,734	56.2	595,806	31.2	33,532	1.8
Illinois	22,344,947	1,866,900	884	8.4	6,619,663	29.6	13,379,203	59.9	479,182	2.1
Indiana	11,211,313	771,230	745	6.9	5,504,585	49.1	4,641,800	41.4	293,699	2.6
Iowa	4,734,934	407,201	842	8.6	2,158,230	45.6	2,035,011	43.0	134,492	2.8
Kansas	4,934,817	444,335	951	9.0	2,692,219	54.6	1,678,185	34.0	120,078	2.4
Kentucky	5,909,930	691,004	1,016	11.7	3,383,793	57.3	1,723,256	29.2	111,877	1.9
Louisiana	6,760,714	1,250,505	1,911	18.5	2,933,287	43.4	2,521,778	37.3	55,144	0.8
Maine	2,372,152	233,741	1,196	9.9	1,004,899	42.4	1,090,113	46.0	43,399	1.8
Maryland	10,680,716	663,204	771	6.2	4,189,323	39.2	5,521,778	51.7	306,411	2.9
Massachusetts	13,850,962	772,305	795	5.6	6,507,612	47.0	6,362,253	45.9	208,792	1.5
Michigan	18,978,793	1,560,410	896	8.2	11,259,666	59.3	5,817,633	30.7	341,084	1.8
Minnesota	9,191,384	595,175	709	6.5	6,543,838	71.2	1,756,010	19.1	296,361	3.2
Mississippi	4,132,345	856,727	1,731	20.7	2,108,727	51.0	1,062,454	25.7	104,436	2.5
Missouri	8,908,447	794,318	866	8.9	2,982,806	33.5	4,793,582	53.8	337,741	3.8
Montana	1,372,561	192,565	1,324	14.0	633,923	46.2	491,871	35.8	54,202	3.9
Nebraska	2,972,026	297,318	1,037	10.0	946,683	31.9	1,588,082	53.4	139,943	4.7
Nevada	3,696,968	263,761	640	7.1	958,743	25.9	2,351,149	63.6	123,315	3.3
New Hampshire	2,363,964	130,585	635	5.5	926,256	39.2	1,257,929	53.2	49,194	2.1
New Jersey	22,799,624	1,001,813	718	4.4	9,642,530	42.3	11,666,137	51.2	489,144	2.1
New Mexico	3,148,752	456,396	1,397	14.5	2,241,203	71.2	399,076	12.7	52,077	1.7
New York	46,776,452	3,383,866	1,202	7.2	19,859,481	42.5	23,184,410	49.6	348,695	0.7
North Carolina	11,137,110	1,199,692	847	10.8	6,966,133	62.5	2,711,280	24.3	260,005	2.3
North Dakota	958,109	151,235	1,539	15.8	347,093	36.2	415,223	43.3	44,557	4.7
Ohio	21,106,426	1,603,474	872	7.6	9,217,115	43.7	9,601,190	45.5	684,646	3.2
Oklahoma	4,859,546	649,719	1,024	13.4	2,591,377	53.3	1,386,928	28.5	231,521	4.8
Oregon	5,427,586	529,706	959	9.8	2,737,046	50.4	2,017,639	37.2	143,195	2.6
Pennsylvania	22,683,987	1,839,508	1,005	8.1	8,028,829	35.4	12,397,030	54.7	418,619	1.8
Rhode Island	2,047,019	156,794	1,022	7.7	840,435	41.1	1,026,534	50.1	23,256	1.1
South Carolina	6,706,259	682,419	973	10.2	3,033,281	45.2	2,756,180	41.1	234,379	3.5
South Dakota	1,094,021	180,528	1,480	16.5	361,531	33.0	519,381	47.5	32,581	3.0
Tennessee	7,307,380	816,764	856	11.2	3,105,334	42.5	2,946,470	40.3	438,812	6.0
Texas	39,691,436	4,772,813	1,055	12.0	13,421,855	33.8	20,633,862	52.0	862,905	2.2
Utah	3,441,688	330,297	650	9.6	1,897,355	55.1	1,139,144	33.1	74,892	2.2
Vermont	1,348,836	101,868	1,054	7.6	1,154,694	85.6	70,845	5.3	21,430	1.6
Virginia	12,922,017	866,993	714	6.7	5,112,423	39.6	6,677,050	51.7	265,550	2.1
Washington	9,759,939	877,922	851	9.0	5,933,610	60.8	2,641,095	27.1	307,311	3.1
West Virginia	2,910,905	350,462	1,248	12.0	1,739,376	59.8	792,670	27.2	28,397	1.0
Wisconsin	9,726,952	586,486	670	6.0	5,086,692	52.3	3,824,235	39.3	229,538	2.4
Wyoming	1,149,155	116,274	1,378	10.1	507,043	44.1	510,007	44.4	15,830	1.4
Other jurisdictions										
American Samoa	86,082	70,136	4,277	81.5	15,856	18.4	0	0.0	89	0.1
Guam	207,709	53,030	1,711	25.5	0	0.0	153,756	74.0	923	0.4
Northern Marianas	66,905	29,372	2,507	43.9	37,210	55.6	302	0.5	21	#
Puerto Rico	2,917,236	932,924	1,656	32.0	1,984,178	68.0	12	#	122	#
U.S. Virgin Islands	193,291	40,294	2,406	20.8	0	0.0	152,852	79.1	145	0.1

†Not applicable.
#Rounds to zero.
[1]Includes revenues from gifts, and tuition and fees from patrons.
NOTE: Excludes revenues for state education agencies. Detail may not sum to totals because of rounding.

SOURCE: U.S. Department of Education, National Center for Education Statistics, Common Core of Data (CCD), "National Public Education Financial Survey," 2005–06. (This table was prepared April 2008.)

Table 173. Revenues for public elementary and secondary schools, by source and state or jurisdiction: 2004–05

State or jurisdiction	Total (in thousands)	Federal				State		Local and intermediate		Private[1]	
		Amount (in thousands)	Per student	Percent of total	Amount (in thousands)	Percent of total	Amount (in thousands)	Percent of total	Amount (in thousands)	Percent of total	
1	2	3	4	5	6	7	8	9	10	11	
United States	$487,753,525	$44,809,532	$918	9.2	$228,553,579	46.9	$203,343,370	41.7	$11,047,044	2.3	
Alabama	5,861,380	701,287	960	12.0	3,253,486	55.5	1,619,362	27.6	287,246	4.9	
Alaska	1,679,646	303,626	2,283	18.1	957,820	57.0	379,757	22.6	38,442	2.3	
Arizona	8,152,664	952,009	912	11.7	3,898,118	47.8	3,094,253	38.0	208,285	2.6	
Arkansas	4,034,796	449,442	970	11.1	2,349,685	58.2	1,086,930	26.9	148,739	3.7	
California	59,481,350	6,657,894	1,034	11.2	35,234,574	59.2	17,007,135	28.6	581,747	1.0	
Colorado	6,911,807	481,395	628	7.0	2,954,905	42.8	3,192,500	46.2	283,008	4.1	
Connecticut	8,015,309	425,653	737	5.3	3,062,150	38.2	4,404,119	54.9	123,387	1.5	
Delaware	1,376,724	130,091	1,092	9.4	851,355	61.8	377,357	27.4	17,921	1.3	
District of Columbia	1,285,489	159,467	2,079	12.4	†	†	1,116,821	86.9	9,201	0.7	
Florida	22,633,476	2,379,726	902	10.5	9,533,209	42.1	9,943,670	43.9	776,872	3.4	
Georgia	14,726,455	1,412,133	909	9.6	6,466,311	43.9	6,384,779	43.4	463,232	3.1	
Hawaii	2,274,165	236,974	1,294	10.4	1,986,614	87.4	23,455	1.0	27,122	1.2	
Idaho	1,816,509	195,816	765	10.8	1,043,927	57.5	545,954	30.1	30,813	1.7	
Illinois	21,281,907	1,839,581	877	8.6	6,758,417	31.8	12,236,951	57.5	446,958	2.1	
Indiana	11,278,665	738,593	723	6.5	5,326,048	47.2	4,927,437	43.7	286,587	2.5	
Iowa	4,481,531	374,422	783	8.4	2,051,947	45.8	1,931,836	43.1	123,326	2.8	
Kansas	4,468,190	454,091	968	10.2	2,431,195	54.4	1,471,766	32.9	111,138	2.5	
Kentucky	5,379,257	658,612	976	12.2	3,049,129	56.7	1,562,117	29.0	109,399	2.0	
Louisiana	6,057,201	841,364	1,162	13.9	2,878,017	47.5	2,277,234	37.6	60,587	1.0	
Maine	2,308,518	227,117	1,142	9.8	946,282	41.0	1,093,729	47.4	41,390	1.8	
Maryland	9,886,032	660,276	763	6.7	3,729,271	37.7	5,214,729	52.7	281,756	2.9	
Massachusetts	12,735,802	768,309	788	6.0	5,442,172	42.7	6,353,090	49.9	172,232	1.4	
Michigan	18,365,247	1,545,106	882	8.4	11,043,486	60.1	5,441,696	29.6	334,959	1.8	
Minnesota	8,687,246	567,845	677	6.5	6,050,153	69.6	1,785,980	20.6	283,268	3.3	
Mississippi	3,642,050	577,162	1,165	15.8	1,965,158	54.0	994,460	27.3	105,270	2.9	
Missouri	8,373,954	745,815	824	8.9	2,859,179	34.1	4,447,068	53.1	321,891	3.8	
Montana	1,293,161	194,794	1,328	15.1	584,289	45.2	462,144	35.7	51,933	4.0	
Nebraska	2,800,202	289,540	1,013	10.3	877,246	31.3	1,495,402	53.4	138,013	4.9	
Nevada	3,393,152	256,921	642	7.6	920,244	27.1	2,102,903	62.0	113,086	3.3	
New Hampshire	2,242,384	126,743	613	5.7	879,428	39.2	1,188,299	53.0	47,915	2.1	
New Jersey	21,738,449	956,048	686	4.4	9,450,496	43.5	10,859,897	50.0	472,008	2.2	
New Mexico	3,049,760	502,763	1,542	16.5	2,133,707	70.0	361,283	11.8	52,006	1.7	
New York	43,649,605	3,198,727	1,128	7.3	18,768,008	43.0	21,341,592	48.9	341,277	0.8	
North Carolina	10,438,325	1,133,112	818	10.9	6,544,270	62.7	2,508,292	24.0	252,651	2.4	
North Dakota	920,566	148,495	1,477	16.1	340,259	37.0	388,285	42.2	43,528	4.7	
Ohio	19,912,038	1,526,501	830	7.7	8,752,118	44.0	8,962,880	45.0	670,539	3.4	
Oklahoma	4,621,537	634,278	1,008	13.7	2,466,399	53.4	1,302,954	28.2	217,906	4.7	
Oregon	4,999,669	507,585	919	10.2	2,439,989	48.8	1,913,721	38.3	138,374	2.8	
Pennsylvania	21,439,695	1,784,412	976	8.3	7,717,500	36.0	11,550,684	53.9	387,099	1.8	
Rhode Island	1,878,044	149,862	958	8.0	725,609	38.6	977,939	52.1	24,634	1.3	
South Carolina	6,267,520	661,614	940	10.6	2,837,312	45.3	2,544,947	40.6	223,648	3.6	
South Dakota	1,061,844	179,863	1,465	16.9	355,969	33.5	494,426	46.6	31,586	3.0	
Tennessee	6,942,997	791,171	841	11.4	2,998,090	43.2	2,710,586	39.0	443,150	6.4	
Texas	36,798,422	4,117,534	935	11.2	13,214,827	35.9	18,646,457	50.7	819,604	2.2	
Utah	3,227,340	325,946	647	10.1	1,775,126	55.0	1,056,361	32.7	69,907	2.2	
Vermont	1,283,411	95,050	966	7.4	1,090,538	85.0	77,898	6.1	19,925	1.6	
Virginia	11,990,159	826,809	686	6.9	4,871,156	40.6	6,044,600	50.4	247,593	2.1	
Washington	9,266,940	875,999	859	9.5	5,629,205	60.7	2,464,831	26.6	296,904	3.2	
West Virginia	2,779,795	329,154	1,175	11.8	1,684,324	60.6	738,290	26.6	28,028	1.0	
Wisconsin	9,432,162	606,013	701	6.4	4,789,269	50.8	3,811,303	40.4	225,577	2.4	
Wyoming	1,130,977	106,791	1,260	9.4	585,593	51.8	423,215	37.4	15,378	1.4	
Other jurisdictions											
American Samoa	86,909	68,421	4,243	78.7	16,589	19.1	1,807	2.1	93	0.1	
Guam	—	—	—	—	—	—	—	—	—	—	
Northern Marianas	63,700	25,691	2,215	40.3	37,210	58.4	773	1.2	25	#	
Puerto Rico	3,017,121	891,609	1,549	29.6	2,125,381	70.4	8	#	122	#	
U.S. Virgin Islands	191,280	38,738	2,358	20.3	0	0.0	152,402	79.7	140	0.1	

—Not available.
†Not applicable.
#Rounds to zero.
[1]Includes revenues from gifts, and tuition and fees from patrons.

NOTE: Excludes revenues for state education agencies. Some data have been revised from previously published figures. Detail may not sum to totals because of rounding.
SOURCE: U.S. Department of Education, National Center for Education Statistics, Common Core of Data (CCD), "National Public Education Financial Survey," 2004–05. (This table was prepared April 2008.)

Table 174. Summary of expenditures for public elementary and secondary education, by purpose: Selected years, 1919–20 through 2005–06

School year	Total expenditures	Current expenditures for public elementary and secondary education							Other current expenditures[2]	Capital outlay[3]	Interest on school debt
		Total	Administration	Instruction	Plant operation	Plant maintenance	Fixed charges	Other school services[1]			
1	2	3	4	5	6	7	8	9	10	11	12
Amounts in thousands of current dollars											
1919–20	$1,036,151	$861,120	$36,752	$632,556	$115,707	$30,432	$9,286	$36,387	$3,277	$153,543	$18,212
1929–30	2,316,790	1,843,552	78,680	1,317,727	216,072	78,810	50,270	101,993	9,825	370,878	92,536
1939–40	2,344,049	1,941,799	91,571	1,403,285	194,365	73,321	50,116	129,141	13,367	257,974	130,909
1949–50	5,837,643	4,687,274	220,050	3,112,340	427,587	214,164	261,469	451,663	35,614	1,014,176	100,578
1959–60	15,613,254	12,329,388	528,408	8,350,738	1,085,036	422,586	909,323	1,033,297	132,566	2,661,786	489,514
1969–70	40,683,429	34,217,773	1,606,646	23,270,158	2,537,257	974,941	3,266,920	2,561,856	635,803	4,659,072	1,170,782
1979–80	95,961,561	86,984,142	4,263,757	53,257,937	9,744,785	(4)	11,793,934	7,923,729	597,585	6,506,167	1,873,666
1989–90	212,769,564	188,229,359	16,346,991 [5]	113,550,405 [5]	20,261,415 [5]	(4)	—	38,070,548 [5]	2,982,543	17,781,342	3,776,321
1994–95	279,000,318	243,877,582	19,877,848 [5]	150,556,118 [5]	24,542,922 [5]	(4)	—	48,900,694 [5]	5,148,505	24,456,100	5,518,131
1995–96	293,646,490	255,106,683	20,709,652 [5]	157,473,978 [5]	25,724,062 [5]	(4)	—	51,198,992 [5]	4,724,659	27,555,667	6,259,480
1996–97	313,151,046	270,174,298	21,603,056 [5]	167,148,760 [5]	26,837,270 [5]	(4)	—	54,585,210 [5]	4,649,138	31,429,074	6,898,536
1997–98	334,315,020	285,485,370	22,043,101 [5]	176,521,719 [5]	27,952,899 [5]	(4)	—	58,967,649 [5]	4,884,115	36,168,090	7,777,445
1998–99	355,837,818	302,876,294	23,396,918 [5]	186,776,182 [5]	29,396,471 [5]	(4)	—	63,306,722 [5]	5,242,618	39,522,710	8,196,196
1999–2000	381,838,155	323,888,508	25,079,298 [5]	199,968,138 [5]	31,190,295 [5]	(4)	—	67,650,776 [5]	5,457,015	43,357,186	9,135,445
2000–01	410,811,185	348,360,841	26,689,181 [5]	214,333,003 [5]	34,034,158 [5]	(4)	—	73,304,498 [5]	6,063,700	46,220,704	10,165,940
2001–02	435,364,404	368,378,006	28,309,047 [5]	226,668,386 [5]	34,829,109 [5]	(4)	—	78,571,464 [5]	6,530,554	49,960,542	10,495,301
2002–03	454,906,912	387,593,617	29,751,958 [5]	237,731,734 [5]	36,830,517 [5]	(4)	—	83,279,408 [5]	6,873,762	48,940,374	11,499,160
2003–04	474,241,531	403,390,369	30,864,875 [5]	247,444,620 [5]	38,720,429 [5]	(4)	—	86,360,444 [5]	6,927,551	50,842,973	13,080,638
2004–05[6]	499,568,736	425,047,565	32,666,223 [5]	260,046,266 [5]	40,926,881 [5]	(4)	—	91,408,195 [5]	7,691,468	53,528,382	13,301,322
2005–06	528,734,539	449,594,924	34,197,083 [5]	274,179,857 [5]	44,320,217 [5]	(4)	—	96,897,767 [5]	7,417,761	57,375,299	14,346,556
Amounts in thousands of constant 2006–07 dollars											
1919–20	$11,098,635	$9,223,807	$393,666	$6,775,565	$1,239,385	$325,970	$99,466	$389,756	$35,101	$1,644,662	$195,076
1929–30	27,630,127	21,986,272	938,341	15,715,263	2,576,883	939,891	599,522	1,216,372	117,173	4,423,105	1,103,588
1939–40	34,240,392	28,364,577	1,337,612	20,498,304	2,839,162	1,071,027	732,063	1,886,410	195,257	3,768,322	1,912,236
1949–50	50,318,151	40,402,421	1,896,743	26,827,128	3,685,629	1,846,008	2,253,758	3,893,155	306,978	8,741,792	866,942
1959–60	108,472,874	85,658,258	3,671,108	58,016,641	7,538,273	2,935,911	6,317,509	7,178,817	921,001	18,492,723	3,400,892
1969–70	219,855,297	184,914,593	8,682,396	125,753,104	13,711,464	5,268,630	17,654,600	13,844,399	3,435,911	25,177,859	6,326,965
1979–80	252,333,430	228,727,072	11,211,660	140,043,136	25,624,167	(4)	31,012,457	20,835,652	1,571,365	17,108,136	4,926,854
1989–90	342,070,118	302,616,774	26,281,095 [5]	182,555,248 [5]	32,574,324 [5]	(4)	—	61,206,108 [5]	4,795,041	28,587,104	6,071,200
1994–95	378,667,139	330,997,566	26,978,779 [5]	204,339,030 [5]	33,310,350 [5]	(4)	—	66,369,408 [5]	6,987,696	33,192,512	7,489,364
1995–96	387,989,691	337,067,755	27,363,281 [5]	208,067,462 [5]	33,988,728 [5]	(4)	—	67,648,284 [5]	6,242,605	36,408,795	8,270,536
1996–97	402,283,260	347,074,035	27,751,936 [5]	214,724,328 [5]	34,475,965 [5]	(4)	—	70,121,804 [5]	5,972,423	40,374,735	8,862,067
1997–98	421,946,059	360,317,124	27,821,064 [5]	222,791,796 [5]	35,279,946 [5]	(4)	—	74,424,317 [5]	6,164,345	45,648,511	9,816,078
1998–99	441,467,956	375,761,573	29,027,240 [5]	231,722,699 [5]	36,470,548 [5]	(4)	—	78,541,087 [5]	6,504,221	49,033,603	10,168,560
1999–2000	460,433,318	390,555,681	30,241,463 [5]	241,128,321 [5]	37,610,309 [5]	(4)	—	81,575,586 [5]	6,580,253	52,281,557	11,015,828
2000–01	478,960,625	406,150,397	31,116,647 [5]	249,888,691 [5]	39,680,083 [5]	(4)	—	85,464,976 [5]	7,069,607	53,888,254	11,852,367
2001–02	498,756,503	422,016.417	32,431,042 [5]	259,672,886 [5]	39,900,470 [5]	(4)	—	90,012,018 [5]	7,481,449	57,235,146	12,023,491
2002–03	509,937,988	434,481,658	33,351,117 [5]	266,490,658 [5]	41,285,984 [5]	(4)	—	93,353,898 [5]	7,705,295	54,860,797	12,890,238
2003–04	520,230,411	442,508,561	33,857,952 [5]	271,440,201 [5]	42,475,286 [5]	(4)	—	94,735,122 [5]	7,599,340	55,773,396	14,349,114
2004–05[6]	532,004,271	452,644,658	34,787,145 [5]	276,930,308 [5]	43,584,143 [5]	(4)	—	97,343,062 [5]	8,190,852	57,003,823	14,164,937
2005–06	542,407,792	461,221,600	35,081,431 [5]	281,270,240 [5]	45,466,353 [5]	(4)	—	99,403,576 [5]	7,609,587	58,859,043	14,717,563
Percentage distribution											
1919–20	100.0	83.1	3.5	61.0	11.2	2.9	0.9	3.5	0.3	14.8	1.8
1929–30	100.0	79.6	3.4	56.9	9.3	3.4	2.2	4.4	0.4	16.0	4.0
1939–40	100.0	82.8	3.9	59.9	8.3	3.1	2.1	5.5	0.6	11.0	5.6
1949–50	100.0	80.3	3.8	53.3	7.3	3.7	4.5	7.7	0.6	17.4	1.7
1959–60	100.0	79.0	3.4	53.5	6.9	2.7	5.8	6.6	0.8	17.0	3.1
1969–70	100.0	84.1	3.9	57.2	6.2	2.4	8.0	6.3	1.6	11.5	2.9
1979–80	100.0	90.6	4.4	55.5	10.2	(4)	12.3	8.3	0.6	6.8	2.0
1989–90	100.0	88.5	7.7 [5]	53.4 [5]	9.5	(4)	—	17.9 [5]	1.4	8.4	1.8
1994–95	100.0	87.4	7.1 [5]	54.0 [5]	8.8	(4)	—	17.5 [5]	1.8	8.8	2.0
1995–96	100.0	86.9	7.1 [5]	53.6 [5]	8.8	(4)	—	17.4 [5]	1.6	9.4	2.1
1996–97	100.0	86.3	6.9 [5]	53.4 [5]	8.6	(4)	—	17.4 [5]	1.5	10.0	2.2
1997–98	100.0	85.4	6.6 [5]	52.8 [5]	8.4	(4)	—	17.6 [5]	1.5	10.8	2.3
1998–99	100.0	85.1	6.6 [5]	52.5 [5]	8.3	(4)	—	17.8 [5]	1.5	11.1	2.3
1999–2000	100.0	84.8	6.6 [5]	52.4 [5]	8.2	(4)	—	17.7 [5]	1.4	11.4	2.4
2000–01	100.0	84.8	6.5 [5]	52.2 [5]	8.3	(4)	—	17.8 [5]	1.5	11.3	2.5
2001–02	100.0	84.6	6.5 [5]	52.1 [5]	8.0	(4)	—	18.0 [5]	1.5	11.5	2.4
2002–03	100.0	85.2	6.5 [5]	52.3 [5]	8.1	(4)	—	18.3 [5]	1.5	10.8	2.5
2003–04	100.0	85.1	6.5 [5]	52.2 [5]	8.2	(4)	—	18.2 [5]	1.5	10.7	2.8
2004–05[6]	100.0	85.1	6.5 [5]	52.1 [5]	8.2	(4)	—	18.3 [5]	1.5	10.7	2.7
2005–06	100.0	85.0	6.5 [5]	51.9 [5]	8.4	(4)	—	18.3 [5]	1.4	10.9	2.7

—Not available.

[1]Prior to 1959–60, items included under "other school services" were listed under "auxiliary services," a more comprehensive classification that also included community services.

[2]Includes expenditures for summer schools, adult education, community colleges, and community services.

[3]Prior to 1969–70, excludes capital outlay by state and local school housing authorities.

[4]Plant operation also includes plant maintenance.

[5]Data not comparable to figures prior to 1989–90.

[6]Data have been revised from previously published figures.

NOTE: Beginning in 1959–60, includes Alaska and Hawaii. Beginning in 1989–90, state administration expenditures were excluded from both "total" and "current" expenditures. Beginning in 1989–90, extensive changes were made in the data collection procedures. Detail may not sum to totals because of rounding.

SOURCE: U.S. Department of Education, National Center for Education Statistics, *Biennial Survey of Education in the United States*, 1919–20 through 1949–50; *Statistics of State School Systems*, 1959–60 and 1969–70; *Revenues and Expenditures for Public Elementary and Secondary Education, 1979–80*; and Common Core of Data (CCD), "National Public Education Financial Survey," 1989–90 through 2005–06. (This table was prepared April 2008.)

Table 175. Students transported at public expense and current expenditures for transportation: Selected years, 1929–30 through 2005–06

School year	Average daily attendance, all students	Students transported at public expense		Expenditures for transportation (in unadjusted dollars)		Expenditures for transportation (in constant 2006–07 dollars)[1]	
		Number	Percent of total	Total[2] (in thousands)	Average per student transported	Total[2] (in thousands)	Average per student transported
1	2	3	4	5	6	7	8
1929–30	21,265,000	1,902,826	8.9	$54,823	$29	$653,821	$344
1931–32	22,245,000	2,419,173	10.9	58,078	24	822,357	340
1933–34	22,458,000	2,794,724	12.4	53,908	19	831,043	297
1935–36	22,299,000	3,250,658	14.6	62,653	19	930,713	286
1937–38	22,298,000	3,769,242	16.9	75,637	20	1,077,863	286
1939–40	22,042,000	4,144,161	18.8	83,283	20	1,216,546	294
1941–42	21,031,000	4,503,081	21.4	92,922	21	1,216,580	270
1943–44	19,603,000	4,512,412	23.0	107,754	24	1,262,364	280
1945–46	19,849,000	5,056,966	25.5	129,756	26	1,452,041	287
1947–48	20,910,000	5,854,041	28.0	176,265	30	1,544,308	264
1949–50	22,284,000	6,947,384	31.2	214,504	31	1,848,939	266
1951–52	23,257,000	7,697,130	33.1	268,827	35	2,087,958	271
1953–54	25,643,871	8,411,719	32.8	307,437	37	2,333,764	277
1955–56	27,740,149	9,695,819	35.0	353,972	37	2,687,912	277
1957–58	29,722,275	10,861,689	36.5	416,491	38	2,977,157	274
1959–60	32,477,440	12,225,142	37.6	486,338	40	3,378,827	276
1961–62	34,682,340	13,222,667	38.1	576,361	44	3,914,338	296
1963–64	37,405,058	14,475,778	38.7	673,845	47	4,460,066	308
1965–66	39,154,497	15,536,567	39.7	787,358	51	5,037,285	324
1967–68	40,827,965	17,130,873	42.0	981,006	57	5,888,632	344
1969–70	41,934,376	18,198,577	43.4	1,218,557	67	6,585,143	362
1971–72	42,254,272	19,474,355	46.1	1,507,830	77	7,480,083	384
1973–74	41,438,054	21,347,039	51.5	1,858,141	87	8,135,489	381
1975–76	41,269,720	21,772,483	52.8	2,377,313	109	8,750,765	402
1977–78	40,079,590	21,800,000 [3]	54.4	2,731,041	125 [3]	8,901,206	408 [3]
1979–80	38,288,911	21,713,515	56.7	3,833,145	177	10,079,355	464
1980–81	37,703,744	22,272,000 [3]	59.1	4,408,000 [3]	198 [3]	10,387,767 [3]	466 [3]
1981–82	37,094,652	22,246,000 [3]	60.0	4,793,000 [3]	215 [3]	10,396,921 [3]	467 [3]
1982–83	36,635,868	22,199,000 [3]	60.6	5,000,000 [3]	225 [3]	10,399,287 [3]	468 [3]
1983–84	36,362,978	22,031,000 [3]	60.6	5,284,000 [3]	240 [3]	10,597,695 [3]	481 [3]
1984–85	36,404,261	22,320,000 [3]	61.3	5,722,000 [3]	256 [3]	11,043,876 [3]	495 [3]
1985–86	36,523,103	22,041,000 [3]	60.3	6,123,000 [3]	278 [3]	11,486,597 [3]	521 [3]
1986–87	36,863,867	22,397,000 [3]	60.8	6,551,000 [3]	292 [3]	12,022,584 [3]	537 [3]
1987–88	37,050,707	22,158,000 [3]	59.8	6,888,000 [3]	311 [3]	12,138,107 [3]	548 [3]
1988–89	37,268,072	22,635,000 [3]	60.7	7,550,000 [3]	334 [3]	12,717,357 [3]	562 [3]
1989–90	37,799,296	22,459,000 [3]	59.4	8,030,990 [3]	358 [3]	12,911,441 [3]	575 [3]
1990–91	38,426,543	22,000,000 [3]	57.3	8,678,954 [3]	394 [3]	13,229,869 [3]	601 [3]
1991–92	38,960,783	23,165,000 [3]	59.5	8,769,754 [3]	379 [3]	12,953,230 [3]	559 [3]
1992–93	39,570,462	23,439,000 [3]	59.2	9,252,300 [3]	395 [3]	13,252,033 [3]	565 [3]
1993–94	40,146,393	23,858,000 [3]	59.4	9,627,155 [3]	404 [3]	13,440,764 [3]	563 [3]
1994–95	40,720,763	23,693,000 [3]	58.2	9,889,034 [3]	417 [3]	13,421,677 [3]	566 [3]
1995–96	41,501,596	24,155,000 [3]	58.2	10,396,426 [3]	430 [3]	13,736,605 [3]	569 [3]
1996–97	42,262,004	24,090,000 [3]	57.0	10,989,809 [3]	456 [3]	14,117,839 [3]	586 [3]
1997–98	42,765,774	24,342,000 [3]	56.9	11,465,658 [3]	471 [3]	14,471,050 [3]	594 [3]
1998–99	43,186,715	24,898,000 [3]	57.7	12,224,454 [3]	491 [3]	15,166,193 [3]	609 [3]
1999–2000	43,806,726	24,951,000 [3]	57.0	13,007,625 [3]	521 [3]	15,685,033 [3]	629 [3]
2000–01	44,075,930	24,471,000 [3]	55.5	14,052,654 [3]	574 [3]	16,383,848 [3]	670 [3]
2001–02	44,604,592	24,529,000 [4]	55.0	14,799,365 [4]	603 [4]	16,954,256 [4]	691 [4]
2002–03	45,017,360	24,621,000 [4]	54.7	15,648,821 [4]	636 [4]	17,541,892 [4]	712 [4]
2003–04	45,325,731	25,059,000 [4]	55.3	16,348,784 [4]	652 [4]	17,934,183 [4]	716 [4]
2004–05	45,625,458	25,223,000 [4]	55.3	17,459,659 [4]	692 [4]	18,593,263 [4]	737 [4]
2005–06	45,931,617	25,286,000 [4]	55.1	18,864,069 [4]	746 [4]	19,351,900 [4]	765 [4]

[1]Constant dollars based on the Consumer Price Index, prepared by the Bureau of Labor Statistics, U.S. Department of Labor, adjusted to a school-year basis.
[2]Excludes capital outlay for years through 1979–80, and 1989–90 to the latest year. From 1980–81 to 1988–89 total transportation figures include capital outlay.
[3]Estimate based on data appearing in January issues of *School Bus Fleet.*
[4]Estimate based on data reported by *School Transportation News.*
NOTE: Some data have been revised from previously published figures.

SOURCE: U.S. Department of Education, National Center for Education Statistics, *Statistics of State School Systems,* 1929–30 through 1975–76; *Revenues and Expenditures for Public Elementary and Secondary Education,* 1977–78 and 1979–80; Common Core of Data (CCD), "National Public Education Financial Survey," 1987–88 through 2005–06; Bobit Publishing Co., *School Bus Fleet,* "School Transportation: 2000–2001 School Year"; *School Transportation News,* "K–12 Enrollment/Transportation Data," 2001–02 through 2006–07; and unpublished data. (This table was prepared August 2008.)

Table 176. Current expenditures for public elementary and secondary education, by state or jurisdiction: Selected years, 1969–70 through 2005–06

[In thousands of current dollars]

State or jurisdiction	1969–70	1979–80	1980–81	1989–90	1990–91	1995–96	1996–97	1997–98	1998–99	1999–2000	2000–01	2001–02	2002–03	2003–04	2004–05[1]	2005–06
1	2	3	4	5	6	7	8	9	10	11	12	13	14	15	16	17
United States	$34,217,773	$86,984,142	$94,321,093	$188,229,359	$202,037,752	$255,106,683	$270,174,298	$285,485,370	$302,876,294	$323,888,508	$348,360,841	$368,378,006	$387,593,617	$403,390,369	$425,047,565	$449,594,924
Alabama	422,730	1,146,713	1,393,137	2,275,233	2,475,216	3,240,364	3,436,406	3,633,159	3,880,188	4,176,082	4,354,794	4,444,390	4,657,643	4,812,479	5,164,406	5,699,076
Alaska	81,374	377,947	476,368	828,051	854,499	1,045,022	1,069,379	1,092,750	1,137,610	1,183,499	1,229,036	1,284,854	1,326,226	1,354,846	1,442,269	1,529,645
Arizona	281,941	949,753	1,075,362	2,258,660	2,469,543	3,327,969	3,527,473	3,740,889	3,963,455	4,288,739	4,846,105	5,395,814	5,892,227	6,071,785	6,579,957	7,130,341
Arkansas	235,083	666,949	709,394	1,404,545	1,510,092	1,994,748	2,074,113	2,149,237	2,241,244	2,380,331	2,505,179	2,822,877	2,923,401	3,109,644	3,546,999	3,808,011
California	3,831,595	9,172,158	9,936,642	21,485,782	22,748,218	27,334,639	29,909,168	32,759,492	34,379,878	38,129,479	42,908,787	46,265,544	47,983,402	49,215,866	50,918,654	53,436,103
Colorado	369,218	1,243,049	1,369,883	2,451,833	2,642,850	3,360,529	3,577,211	3,886,872	4,140,699	4,401,010	4,758,173	5,151,003	5,551,506	5,666,191	5,994,440	6,368,289
Connecticut	588,710	1,227,892	1,440,881	3,444,520	3,540,411	4,366,123	4,522,718	4,763,653	5,075,580	5,402,836	5,693,207	6,031,062	6,302,988	6,600,767	7,080,396	7,517,025
Delaware	108,747	269,108	270,439	520,953	543,933	726,241	788,715	830,731	872,786	937,630	1,027,224	1,072,875	1,127,745	1,201,631	1,299,349	1,405,465
District of Columbia	141,138	298,448	295,155	639,983	647,901	679,106	632,952	647,202	693,712	780,192	830,299	912,432	902,318	1,011,536	1,067,500	1,057,166
Florida	961,273	2,766,468	3,336,657	8,228,531	9,045,710	11,480,359	12,018,676	12,737,325	13,534,374	13,885,988	15,023,514	15,535,864	16,355,123	17,578,884	19,042,877	20,897,327
Georgia	599,371	1,608,028	1,688,714	4,505,962	4,804,225	6,629,646	7,230,405	7,770,241	8,537,177	9,158,624	10,011,343	10,853,496	11,630,576	11,788,616	12,528,856	13,739,263
Hawaii	141,324	351,889	395,038	700,012	827,579	1,040,682	1,057,069	1,112,351	1,143,713	1,213,695	1,215,968	1,348,381	1,489,092	1,566,792	1,648,086	1,805,521
Idaho	103,107	313,927	352,912	627,794	708,045	1,019,594	1,090,597	1,153,778	1,239,755	1,302,817	1,403,190	1,481,803	1,511,862	1,555,006	1,618,215	1,694,827
Illinois	1,896,067	4,579,355	4,773,179	8,125,493	8,932,538	10,727,091	11,720,249	12,473,064	13,602,965	14,462,773	15,634,490	16,480,787	17,271,301	18,081,827	18,658,428	19,244,908
Indiana	809,105	1,851,292	1,898,194	4,074,578	4,379,142	5,493,653	6,055,055	6,234,563	6,697,468	7,110,930	7,548,487	7,704,547	8,088,684	8,524,980	9,108,931	9,241,986
Iowa	527,086	1,186,659	1,337,504	2,004,742	2,136,561	2,753,425	2,885,943	3,005,421	3,110,585	3,264,336	3,430,885	3,565,796	3,652,022	3,669,797	3,808,200	4,039,389
Kansas	362,593	830,133	958,281	1,848,302	1,938,012	2,488,077	2,568,525	2,684,244	2,841,147	2,971,814	3,264,698	3,450,923	3,510,675	3,658,421	3,718,153	4,039,417
Kentucky	353,265	1,054,459	1,096,472	2,134,011	2,480,363	3,171,495	3,382,062	3,489,205	3,696,331	3,837,794	4,047,392	4,268,608	4,401,627	4,553,382	4,812,591	5,213,620
Louisiana	503,217	1,303,902	1,767,662	2,838,283	3,023,690	3,545,832	3,747,508	4,029,139	4,264,981	4,391,189	4,485,878	4,802,565	5,056,583	5,290,964	5,554,766	5,554,278
Maine	155,907	385,492	401,355	1,048,195	1,070,965	1,313,759	1,372,571	1,433,175	1,510,024	1,604,438	1,704,422	1,812,798	1,909,268	1,969,497	2,056,266	2,119,408
Maryland	721,794	1,783,056	1,937,159	3,894,644	4,240,862	5,311,207	5,529,309	5,843,685	6,165,934	6,545,135	7,044,881	7,480,723	7,933,055	8,198,454	8,682,586	9,381,613
Massachusetts	907,341	2,638,734	2,794,762	4,760,390	4,906,828	6,435,458	6,846,610	7,381,784	7,948,502	8,564,039	9,272,387	9,957,292	10,281,820	10,799,765	11,357,857	12,210,581
Michigan	1,799,945	4,642,847	5,196,249	8,025,621	8,545,805	11,137,877	11,686,124	12,003,818	12,785,480	13,994,294	14,243,597	14,975,150	15,674,698	15,983,044	16,353,921	16,681,981
Minnesota	781,243	1,786,768	1,900,322	3,474,398	3,740,820	4,844,879	5,087,353	5,452,571	5,836,186	6,140,442	6,531,198	6,586,559	6,867,403	7,084,005	7,310,284	7,686,638
Mississippi	262,760	756,018	716,878	1,472,710	1,510,552	2,000,321	2,035,675	2,164,592	2,293,188	2,510,376	2,576,457	2,642,116	2,853,531	3,059,569	3,243,888	3,550,261
Missouri	642,030	1,504,988	1,643,258	3,288,738	3,487,786	4,531,192	4,775,931	5,067,720	5,348,366	5,655,531	6,076,169	6,491,885	6,793,957	6,832,454	7,115,207	7,592,485
Montana	127,176	358,118	380,092	641,345	719,963	868,892	902,252	929,197	955,695	994,770	1,041,760	1,073,005	1,124,291	1,160,838	1,193,182	1,254,360
Nebraska	231,612	581,615	629,017	1,233,431	1,297,643	1,648,104	1,707,455	1,743,775	1,821,310	1,926,500	2,067,290	2,206,946	2,304,223	2,413,404	2,512,914	2,672,629
Nevada	87,273	281,901	287,752	712,898	864,379	1,296,629	1,434,395	1,570,576	1,738,009	1,875,467	1,978,480	2,169,000	2,251,044	2,470,581	2,722,264	2,959,728
New Hampshire	101,370	295,400	340,518	821,671	890,116	1,114,540	1,173,958	1,241,255	1,316,946	1,418,503	1,518,792	1,641,378	1,781,594	1,900,240	2,021,144	2,139,113
New Jersey	1,343,564	3,638,533	3,648,914	8,119,336	8,897,612	11,208,558	11,771,941	12,056,560	12,874,579	13,327,645	14,773,650	15,822,609	17,185,966	18,416,695	19,669,576	20,869,993
New Mexico	183,736	515,451	560,213	1,020,148	1,134,156	1,517,517	1,557,376	1,659,891	1,788,382	1,890,274	2,022,093	2,204,165	2,281,608	2,446,115	2,554,638	2,729,707
New York	4,111,839	8,760,500	9,259,948	18,090,978	19,514,583	23,522,461	24,237,291	25,332,735	26,885,444	28,433,240	30,884,292	32,218,975	34,546,965	36,205,111	38,866,853	41,149,457
North Carolina	676,193	1,880,862	2,112,417	4,342,826	4,605,384	5,582,994	5,964,939	6,497,648	7,097,882	7,713,293	8,201,901	8,543,290	8,766,968	8,994,620	9,835,550	10,476,056
North Dakota	97,895	228,483	254,197	459,391	460,581	557,043	577,498	599,443	625,428	638,946	668,814	711,437	716,007	749,697	832,157	857,774
Ohio	1,639,805	3,836,576	4,149,858	7,994,379	8,407,428	10,408,022	10,948,074	11,448,722	12,138,937	12,974,575	13,893,495	14,774,065	15,888,494	16,662,985	17,167,886	17,829,599
Oklahoma	339,105	1,055,844	1,193,373	1,905,332	2,107,513	2,804,088	2,990,044	3,138,690	3,332,697	3,382,581	3,750,542	3,875,547	3,804,570	3,853,308	4,161,024	4,406,002
Oregon	403,844	1,126,812	1,292,624	2,297,944	2,453,934	3,056,801	3,184,100	3,474,714	3,706,044	3,896,287	4,112,069	4,214,512	4,150,747	4,199,485	4,458,028	4,773,751
Pennsylvania	1,912,644	4,584,320	4,985,115	9,496,788	10,087,322	12,374,073	12,820,704	13,084,859	13,532,211	14,120,112	14,895,316	15,550,975	16,344,439	17,680,332	18,711,100	19,631,006
Rhode Island	145,443	362,046	395,389	801,908	823,655	1,094,185	1,151,888	1,215,595	1,283,859	1,393,143	1,465,703	1,533,455	1,647,587	1,765,585	1,825,900	1,934,429

See notes at end of table.

Table 176. Current expenditures for public elementary and secondary education, by state or jurisdiction: Selected years, 1969–70 through 2005–06—Continued

[In thousands of current dollars]

State or jurisdiction	1969–70	1979–80	1980–81	1989–90	1990–91	1995–96	1996–97	1997–98	1998–99	1999–2000	2000–01	2001–02	2002–03	2003–04	2004–05[1]	2005–06
1	2	3	4	5	6	7	8	9	10	11	12	13	14	15	16	17
South Carolina	367,689	997,984	1,006,088	2,322,618	2,494,254	3,085,495	3,296,661	3,507,017	3,759,042	4,087,355	4,492,161	4,744,809	4,888,250	5,017,833	5,312,739	5,696,629
South Dakota	109,375	238,332	242,215	447,074	481,304	610,640	628,753	665,082	696,785	737,998	796,133	819,296	851,429	887,328	916,563	948,671
Tennessee	473,226	1,319,303	1,429,938	2,790,808	2,903,209	3,726,486	4,145,380	4,409,338	4,638,924	4,931,734	5,170,379	5,501,029	5,674,773	6,056,657	6,446,691	6,681,456
Texas	1,518,181	4,997,689	5,310,181	12,763,954	13,695,327	18,801,462	20,167,238	21,188,676	22,430,153	25,098,703	26,546,557	28,191,128	30,399,603	30,974,890	31,919,107	33,851,773
Utah	179,981	518,251	587,648	1,130,135	1,235,916	1,719,782	1,822,725	1,916,688	2,025,714	2,102,655	2,250,339	2,374,702	2,366,897	2,475,550	2,627,022	2,778,236
Vermont	78,921	189,811	224,901	546,901	599,018	684,864	718,092	749,786	792,664	870,198	934,031	992,149	1,045,213	1,111,029	1,177,478	1,237,442
Virginia	704,677	1,881,519	2,045,412	4,621,071	4,958,213	5,969,608	6,343,768	6,736,863	7,137,419	7,757,596	8,335,805	8,718,554	9,208,329	9,798,239	10,705,162	11,470,735
Washington	699,984	1,825,782	1,791,477	3,550,819	3,906,471	5,394,507	5,587,803	5,987,060	6,098,008	6,399,885	6,782,136	7,103,817	7,359,566	7,549,235	7,870,979	8,239,716
West Virginia	249,404	678,386	754,889	1,316,637	1,473,640	1,806,004	1,847,560	1,905,940	1,986,562	2,086,937	2,157,563	2,219,013	2,349,833	2,415,043	2,527,767	2,651,491
Wisconsin	777,288	1,908,523	2,035,879	3,929,920	4,292,434	5,670,826	5,975,122	6,280,686	6,620,653	6,852,178	7,249,081	7,592,176	7,934,755	8,131,276	8,435,359	8,745,195
Wyoming	69,584	226,067	271,153	509,084	521,549	581,817	591,488	603,901	651,622	683,918	704,695	761,830	791,732	814,092	863,423	965,350
Other jurisdictions																
American Samoa	16,652	—	—	21,838	24,946	30,382	33,780	33,088	35,092	42,335	40,642	46,192	47,566	55,519	58,163	58,539
Guam		—	—	101,130	116,406	158,303	156,561	168,716						182,506		210,119
Northern Marianas		—	—	20,476	26,822	44,337	53,140	56,514	50,450	49,832	49,151	46,508	50,843	47,681	58,400	57,694
Puerto Rico		—	713,000	1,045,407	1,142,863	1,667,540	1,740,074	1,981,603	2,024,499	2,086,414	2,257,837	2,152,724	2,541,385	2,425,372	2,865,945	3,082,295
U.S. Virgin Islands		—	—	128,065	119,950	122,286	122,188	131,315	146,474	135,174	125,252	107,343	125,405	128,250	137,793	146,872

—Not available.

[1]Data have been revised from previously published figures.

NOTE: Beginning in 1980–81, expenditures for state administration are excluded. Data are not adjusted for changes in the purchasing power of the dollar due to inflation. Detail may not sum to totals because of rounding.

SOURCE: U.S. Department of Education, National Center for Education Statistics, *Statistics of State School Systems*, 1969–70; *Revenues and Expenditures for Public Elementary and Secondary Education*, 1979–80 and 1980–81; and Common Core of Data (CCD), "National Public Education Financial Survey," 1989–90 through 2005–06. (This table was prepared April 2008.)

Table 177. Total expenditures for public elementary and secondary education, by function and state or jurisdiction: 2005–06

[In thousands of current dollars]

State or jurisdiction	Total	Elementary/ secondary current expenditures, total	Instruction	Support services								Food services	Enterprise operations[3]	Other current expenditures[1]	Capital outlay[2]	Interest on school debt
				Total	Student support[4]	Instructional staff[5]	General administration	School administration[5]	Operation and maintenance	Student transportation	Other support services					
1	2	3	4	5	6	7	8	9	10	11	12	13	14	15	16	17
United States	$528,734,539	$449,594,924	$274,179,857	$157,128,936	$23,356,971	$21,924,660	$8,920,041	$25,277,042	$44,320,217	$18,864,069	$14,465,937	$17,263,582	$1,022,549	$7,417,761	$57,375,299	$14,346,556
Alabama	6,607,382	5,699,076	3,333,081	1,987,501	293,235	280,361	154,428	351,994	530,584	263,268	113,631	378,494	0	112,922	668,741	126,642
Alaska	1,812,119	1,529,645	874,604	604,600	96,524	83,140	23,169	90,313	201,223	53,350	56,881	44,006	6,435	7,673	236,959	37,842
Arizona	8,529,997	7,130,341	4,418,230	2,379,469	400,463	168,189	114,087	345,801	786,240	271,157	293,533	332,643	0	49,015	1,130,384	220,257
Arkansas	4,424,593	3,808,011	2,292,086	1,318,461	174,344	242,388	111,195	202,831	354,421	137,201	96,081	194,512	2,952	24,995	495,866	95,721
California	65,854,208	53,436,103	32,244,567	19,154,428	2,458,675	3,605,649	483,643	3,615,844	5,380,825	1,305,488	2,304,305	1,926,940	110,168	1,043,342	9,977,703	1,397,060
Colorado	7,781,436	6,368,289	3,576,989	2,577,875	279,312	330,306	98,005	414,402	658,678	182,196	614,975	197,059	16,366	63,862	1,028,764	320,522
Connecticut	8,892,083	7,517,025	4,762,341	2,488,355	452,267	241,434	147,896	423,560	700,823	354,587	167,788	203,003	63,326	140,272	1,088,437	146,349
Delaware	1,684,465	1,405,465	848,259	491,293	67,087	18,332	16,533	78,218	137,357	83,264	90,502	65,913	0	16,160	232,877	30,113
District of Columbia	1,214,589	1,057,166	550,749	480,300	66,358	75,155	26,842	56,040	133,045	74,817	48,044	26,117	0	13,318	144,105	0
Florida	26,827,338	20,897,327	12,352,747	7,578,653	984,592	1,412,223	210,568	1,187,364	2,351,991	886,111	545,803	965,928	0	468,287	4,854,446	607,278
Georgia	15,875,012	13,739,263	8,598,901	4,437,449	654,685	749,691	179,815	846,153	1,022,021	562,896	422,187	660,245	42,668	36,210	1,929,995	169,544
Hawaii	2,026,154	1,805,521	1,077,351	643,718	216,531	65,864	13,835	121,151	141,315	34,786	50,236	84,453	0	59,457	75,965	85,211
Idaho	1,928,348	1,694,827	1,044,784	570,815	94,777	72,729	37,925	95,882	156,760	80,371	32,371	78,884	344	4,519	191,699	37,303
Illinois	21,954,250	19,244,908	11,329,436	7,284,957	1,218,203	894,521	654,225	978,499	1,923,401	953,690	662,418	630,514	0	152,670	2,013,087	543,585
Indiana	10,713,543	9,241,986	5,550,922	3,312,841	407,131	292,916	171,385	524,807	1,010,222	525,698	380,682	378,222	0	63,064	972,015	436,478
Iowa	4,735,943	4,039,389	2,413,984	1,437,035	239,001	191,853	112,641	239,951	377,380	147,484	128,726	183,441	4,929	31,684	596,833	68,036
Kansas	4,506,242	4,039,417	2,419,648	1,432,728	227,655	185,465	131,969	236,330	390,837	161,494	98,978	187,042	0	4,485	326,958	135,381
Kentucky	6,095,728	5,213,620	3,102,318	1,808,047	214,671	289,715	116,717	283,987	486,639	297,615	118,703	292,861	10,394	80,655	674,547	126,907
Louisiana	6,188,015	5,554,278	3,238,598	2,001,244	228,554	278,273	132,918	290,579	626,709	301,977	142,234	314,325	110	68,602	460,156	104,980
Maine	2,299,359	2,119,408	1,393,238	654,871	78,432	73,897	44,569	112,534	213,603	94,935	36,901	71,299	0	24,121	109,867	45,963
Maryland	10,518,434	9,381,613	5,749,590	3,208,571	391,342	500,802	93,522	637,111	851,749	479,639	254,405	262,804	160,648	24,322	993,616	118,882
Massachusetts	13,757,817	12,210,581	7,957,018	3,877,140	670,672	573,530	202,615	506,057	1,081,632	501,087	341,546	376,423	0	59,408	1,200,362	287,467
Michigan	19,878,934	16,681,981	9,442,946	6,714,691	1,210,229	826,690	341,862	1,000,196	1,814,383	738,429	782,902	524,344	0	351,300	1,993,224	852,428
Minnesota	9,531,590	7,686,638	4,949,826	2,390,423	205,659	354,400	237,143	327,650	601,529	422,669	241,374	324,460	21,929	359,612	1,085,449	399,891
Mississippi	3,893,753	3,550,261	2,098,153	1,247,157	160,537	168,934	102,737	195,396	392,180	156,812	70,561	204,667	284	32,942	241,492	69,059
Missouri	8,783,995	7,592,485	4,607,368	2,646,126	357,737	340,038	225,236	426,080	765,953	385,063	146,019	338,991	0	168,899	759,184	263,426
Montana	1,376,246	1,254,360	757,786	444,426	67,429	49,775	37,852	68,833	131,342	57,911	31,284	50,450	1,698	7,208	101,494	13,185
Nebraska	2,974,472	2,672,629	1,697,132	794,824	111,972	86,721	96,612	134,933	232,156	74,008	58,422	104,325	76,347	5,152	241,417	55,274
Nevada	3,940,869	2,959,728	1,809,449	1,048,676	111,762	81,372	52,022	205,662	296,844	110,770	190,246	101,603	0	17,141	753,521	210,478
New Hampshire	2,396,313	2,139,113	1,380,638	696,149	146,729	65,679	71,717	116,102	185,315	90,652	19,955	62,325	0	6,343	201,594	49,263
New Jersey	23,353,204	20,869,993	12,326,559	7,888,876	1,882,174	689,926	512,940	1,396,596	2,157,953	1,131,243	118,045	468,162	186,396	205,034	1,932,542	345,636
New Mexico	3,171,892	2,729,707	1,535,203	1,074,265	263,342	127,030	83,207	169,243	270,780	112,207	48,456	118,814	1,424	28,615	375,544	38,026
New York	46,269,766	41,149,457	28,462,577	11,769,422	1,317,736	1,159,830	793,293	1,666,969	3,675,699	2,162,388	993,507	917,457	0	1,678,175	2,193,877	1,248,257
North Carolina	12,133,667	10,476,056	6,480,355	3,412,034	568,446	419,385	204,289	681,181	846,327	411,307	281,101	583,667	0	49,326	1,240,430	367,854
North Dakota	968,112	857,774	521,320	267,051	34,285	25,234	38,677	40,041	73,710	36,190	18,914	43,067	26,336	6,262	92,968	11,108
Ohio	20,902,539	17,829,599	10,208,622	7,032,294	1,066,791	1,152,174	523,604	1,042,768	1,661,678	823,276	762,003	586,646	2,037	429,510	2,165,875	477,556
Oklahoma	4,832,418	4,406,002	2,497,439	1,617,347	285,058	176,414	126,736	238,377	515,107	145,385	130,270	247,731	43,486	13,487	389,926	43,003
Oregon	5,337,287	4,773,751	2,801,665	1,801,283	337,295	190,418	65,320	301,821	401,853	212,492	292,084	168,874	1,929	18,486	319,232	225,819
Pennsylvania	23,026,118	19,631,006	12,056,932	6,820,355	952,558	746,123	608,593	859,325	2,032,022	938,668	683,066	673,989	79,730	531,743	2,036,129	827,241
Rhode Island	2,046,113	1,934,429	1,164,366	720,537	230,464	92,729	23,532	98,568	160,745	72,967	41,531	49,526	0	49,253	30,490	31,941
South Carolina	6,990,040	5,696,629	3,316,986	2,077,059	391,163	382,203	69,437	327,178	532,598	204,325	170,154	283,923	18,661	70,282	981,123	242,006
South Dakota	1,058,470	948,671	549,811	345,882	52,232	40,846	34,273	47,251	103,297	33,278	34,705	49,025	3,954	3,138	86,270	20,390
Tennessee	7,439,050	6,681,456	4,295,030	2,062,919	227,033	373,152	137,995	368,086	610,957	243,708	101,988	323,507	0	53,328	552,270	151,996
Texas	42,152,918	33,851,773	20,130,884	11,940,056	1,643,051	1,868,113	527,667	1,879,154	3,880,932	951,930	1,189,211	1,780,833	0	303,929	6,170,451	1,826,766
Utah	3,457,129	2,778,236	1,755,649	856,175	102,818	130,275	32,678	168,829	271,289	90,911	59,374	148,977	17,435	86,803	511,816	80,274

See notes at end of table.

Table 177. Total expenditures for public elementary and secondary education, by function and state or jurisdiction: 2005–06—Continued

[In thousands of current dollars]

State or jurisdiction	Total	Elementary/ secondary current expenditures, total	Total expenditures — Current expenditures for elementary and secondary programs												Other current expenditures[3]	Capital outlay[2]	Interest on school debt
			Instruction	Support services									Food services	Enterprise operations[5]			
				Total	Student support[4]	Instructional staff[5]	General administration	School administration	Operation and maintenance	Student transportation	Other support services					
1	2	3	4	5	6	7	8	9	10	11	12	13	14	15	16	17
Vermont	1,314,627	1,237,442	787,788	415,883	91,604	45,601	30,182	82,008	98,612	40,506	27,371	33,253	519	4,145	58,948	14,091
Virginia	13,185,745	11,470,735	7,025,890	3,974,416	548,473	735,159	172,878	665,998	1,116,045	559,362	176,502	468,241	2,187	67,595	1,298,752	348,663
Washington	10,051,241	8,239,716	4,876,294	2,964,303	524,785	385,838	172,355	489,462	764,613	339,971	287,278	279,948	119,171	47,349	1,428,053	336,123
West Virginia	2,749,151	2,651,491	1,589,476	913,026	94,580	101,342	67,395	141,934	273,115	191,666	42,993	148,989	0	36,574	50,086	11,000
Wisconsin	10,131,019	8,745,195	5,352,462	3,100,114	399,759	430,288	229,927	444,101	833,595	330,728	431,716	292,521	99	233,505	511,548	640,770
Wyoming	1,140,656	965,350	571,810	362,813	56,760	52,537	21,380	53,890	102,135	42,135	33,977	30,139	588	3,583	168,213	3,512
Other jurisdictions																
American Samoa	67,460	58,539	30,551	16,041	2,328	6,232	712	2,352	2,469	751	1,197	11,946	0	4,392	4,529	0
Guam	214,020	210,119	120,010	78,935	22,951	5,836	4,195	11,434	25,940	1,653	6,927	11,175	0	0	3,293	607
Northern Marianas	59,817	57,694	46,755	5,147	1,064	325	2,143	286	152	948	229	484	5,308	507	1,616	0
Puerto Rico	3,282,288	3,082,295	2,163,504	671,346	153,625	26,647	13,495	0	309,267	77,973	90,838	246,945	0	96,459	90,094	13,440
U.S. Virgin Islands	161,374	146,872	94,754	47,938	8,922	4,678	6,979	8,664	9,982	5,735	2,979	3,472	708	1,757	12,745	0

[1]Includes expenditures for adult education, community colleges, private school programs funded by local and state education agencies, and community services.

[2]Includes expenditures for property and for buildings and alterations completed by school district staff or contractors.

[3]Includes expenditures for operations funded by sales of products or services (e.g., school bookstore or computer time). Also includes small amounts for direct program support made by state education agencies for local school districts.

[4]Includes expenditures for health, attendance, and speech pathology services.

[5]Includes expenditures for curriculum development, staff training, libraries, and media and computer centers.

NOTE: Excludes expenditures for state education agencies. Detail may not sum to totals because of rounding.

SOURCE: U.S. Department of Education, National Center for Education Statistics, Common Core of Data (CCD), "National Public Education Financial Survey," 2005–06. (This table was prepared April 2008.)

Table 178. Total expenditures for public elementary and secondary education, by function and state or jurisdiction: 2004–05

[In thousands of current dollars]

State or jurisdiction	Total	Current expenditures for elementary and secondary programs													Other current expenditures[3]	Capital outlay[2]	Interest on school debt
		Elementary/ secondary current expenditures, total	Instruction	Support services								Food services	Enterprise operations[3]				
				Total	Student support[4]	Instructional staff[5]	General administration	School administration	Operation and maintenance	Student transportation	Other support services					
1	2	3	4	5	6	7	8	9	10	11	12	13	14	15	16	17
United States	$499,568,736	$425,047,565	$260,046,266	$147,617,798	$22,118,879	$20,387,692	$8,510,315	$24,155,908	$40,926,881	$17,459,659	$14,058,464	$16,423,973	$959,528	$7,691,468	$53,528,382	$13,301,322
Alabama	5,896,594	5,164,406	3,058,443	1,747,349	257,605	236,196	138,174	312,306	469,833	233,281	99,952	358,613	0	106,665	514,084	111,439
Alaska	1,754,755	1,442,269	832,707	562,600	90,704	73,232	21,214	84,440	186,746	51,582	54,682	41,256	5,706	8,821	268,713	34,952
Arizona	7,705,051	6,579,957	4,030,750	2,241,296	359,509	154,226	108,478	326,762	725,236	237,022	330,063	307,911	0	50,305	843,121	231,669
Arkansas	4,099,536	3,546,999	2,158,004	1,202,569	160,385	204,462	109,624	192,519	316,738	125,326	93,514	183,527	2,899	25,400	436,986	90,151
California	63,194,472	50,918,654	30,908,059	18,069,631	2,343,885	3,294,411	463,454	3,432,721	4,929,142	1,234,146	2,371,872	1,837,874	103,091	1,002,841	10,001,834	1,271,142
Colorado	7,272,972	5,994,440	3,392,114	2,391,777	260,673	304,159	85,215	388,027	613,011	184,450	556,242	187,134	23,415	56,764	923,636	298,132
Connecticut	8,383,755	7,080,396	4,505,734	2,321,507	409,057	233,743	140,021	398,570	644,202	330,402	165,511	194,990	58,164	129,658	1,038,302	135,400
Delaware	1,518,723	1,299,349	771,916	466,878	61,864	16,327	14,578	72,635	131,650	80,633	89,191	60,554	0	15,678	181,156	22,541
District of Columbia	1,231,634	1,067,500	565,473	477,023	55,316	81,013	36,357	56,720	122,374	72,374	52,869	25,004	0	13,202	150,932	0
Florida	23,829,096	19,042,877	11,263,480	6,863,247	914,900	1,158,861	205,989	1,098,174	2,120,893	806,217	558,212	916,150	0	440,006	3,803,390	542,823
Georgia	14,533,211	12,528,856	7,899,852	3,970,311	586,475	668,260	170,171	768,497	916,851	485,336	374,720	621,991	36,702	32,926	1,794,899	176,530
Hawaii	1,805,479	1,648,086	1,007,207	559,177	181,120	70,006	20,908	108,724	116,681	23,717	38,022	81,702	0	56,247	62,655	38,491
Idaho	1,844,208	1,618,215	1,000,526	544,119	90,584	67,992	38,208	91,659	149,351	76,103	30,222	73,570	1	4,252	182,681	39,060
Illinois	21,469,001	18,658,428	11,095,296	6,963,256	1,178,623	855,362	633,206	961,248	1,810,144	894,336	630,335	599,876	0	140,974	2,137,492	532,107
Indiana	10,522,467	9,108,931	5,499,308	3,240,898	404,748	301,446	172,511	515,758	970,504	500,067	375,864	368,725	0	62,965	976,112	374,459
Iowa	4,447,291	3,808,200	2,321,413	1,298,184	221,575	190,698	107,000	211,919	334,070	126,516	106,405	178,708	9,895	35,790	538,313	64,989
Kansas	4,127,279	3,718,153	2,211,723	1,330,311	214,352	164,214	132,381	220,718	362,493	149,150	87,003	176,119	0	4,559	272,366	132,201
Kentucky	5,739,358	4,812,591	2,890,808	1,637,928	190,807	268,176	110,675	262,934	431,249	265,516	108,570	275,669	8,187	76,445	734,589	115,733
Louisiana	6,066,206	5,554,766	3,329,812	1,894,461	242,499	290,079	132,883	298,406	499,808	291,985	138,801	330,366	128	51,921	353,887	105,632
Maine	2,245,242	2,056,266	1,372,765	615,894	71,837	67,454	42,906	110,148	199,634	89,603	34,313	67,607	0	22,436	120,400	46,140
Maryland	9,783,967	8,682,586	5,362,276	2,935,675	372,285	457,670	70,793	581,611	771,223	453,489	228,605	250,683	133,952	22,417	964,314	114,649
Massachusetts	12,502,569	11,357,857	7,228,652	3,801,047	695,371	544,820	198,868	489,260	1,059,404	470,245	343,078	328,158	0	192,131	643,310	309,271
Michigan	19,694,819	16,353,921	9,298,039	6,547,315	1,176,858	799,381	352,940	984,319	1,737,256	710,567	785,994	508,566	0	335,192	2,109,244	896,463
Minnesota	8,939,104	7,310,284	4,752,362	2,219,764	202,668	331,253	187,212	311,077	561,682	399,531	226,342	315,989	22,170	332,149	937,735	358,936
Mississippi	3,538,357	3,243,888	1,938,248	1,105,128	155,281	157,291	99,782	183,485	298,998	144,366	65,926	200,057	454	27,505	201,000	65,964
Missouri	8,241,561	7,115,207	4,322,270	2,475,424	341,734	324,032	215,364	405,955	696,524	353,121	138,693	317,513	0	157,872	709,763	258,719
Montana	1,273,750	1,193,182	728,058	415,335	63,976	45,834	36,248	66,799	119,759	53,765	28,954	48,126	1,663	6,580	63,237	10,752
Nebraska	2,811,778	2,512,914	1,596,345	742,605	105,770	83,036	86,942	128,338	219,947	67,228	51,343	99,586	74,378	3,877	242,950	52,038
Nevada	3,477,243	2,722,264	1,699,144	926,157	102,148	105,459	50,549	186,648	265,001	97,766	118,585	96,964	0	18,202	550,475	186,301
New Hampshire	2,239,798	2,021,144	1,309,782	651,292	136,131	61,831	68,408	110,650	170,967	85,358	17,947	60,070	0	6,087	163,783	48,783
New Jersey	22,415,297	19,669,576	11,647,046	7,400,488	1,765,683	651,540	493,065	1,337,960	1,981,627	1,060,819	109,794	456,351	165,691	214,367	2,206,857	324,497
New Mexico	3,083,276	2,554,638	1,430,765	1,008,462	252,900	118,051	78,733	159,463	245,271	109,698	44,347	113,995	1,416	28,481	461,134	39,023
New York	43,294,263	38,866,853	26,731,925	11,256,925	1,296,215	1,051,501	748,760	1,667,793	3,484,296	1,947,529	1,060,831	878,004	0	1,632,037	2,375,026	420,347
North Carolina	11,211,205	9,835,550	6,123,399	3,174,203	529,580	389,855	191,787	642,162	790,405	365,359	265,054	537,948	0	72,874	955,999	346,783
North Dakota	937,057	832,157	510,617	255,346	32,582	23,209	38,501	38,339	69,383	35,392	17,940	42,210	23,984	5,991	88,318	10,591

See notes at end of table.

Table 178. Total expenditures for public elementary and secondary education, by function and state or jurisdiction: 2004–05—Continued
[In thousands of current dollars]

State or jurisdiction	Total	Elementary/ secondary current expenditures, total	Instruction	Current expenditures for elementary and secondary programs — Support services								Food services	Enterprise operations[3]	Other current expenditures[1]	Capital outlay[2]	Interest on school debt
				Total	Student support[4]	Instructional staff[5]	General administration	School administration	Operation and maintenance	Student transportation	Other support services					
1	2	3	4	5	6	7	8	9	10	11	12	13	14	15	16	17
Ohio	20,059,937	17,167,856	9,816,361	6,786,088	1,027,655	1,095,202	494,119	1,091,703	1,553,657	775,774	747,978	563,654	1,764	438,968	2,055,170	397,933
Oklahoma	4,555,577	4,161,024	2,363,927	1,515,602	272,724	166,336	122,817	223,635	476,077	132,730	121,283	237,968	43,527	13,171	342,973	38,409
Oregon	5,521,697	4,458,028	2,619,853	1,677,267	305,938	171,148	62,498	283,041	373,866	196,816	283,961	158,954	1,953	485,192	363,865	214,612
Pennsylvania	21,870,280	18,711,100	11,540,622	6,451,395	899,572	720,808	575,594	821,821	1,911,951	882,870	638,780	643,708	75,375	439,537	1,949,491	770,153
Rhode Island	1,923,342	1,825,900	1,134,114	646,008	185,055	86,278	22,309	91,245	146,777	68,614	45,730	45,778	0	48,763	20,534	28,145
South Carolina	6,525,760	5,312,739	3,142,227	1,889,111	366,397	355,376	64,514	304,752	486,600	163,674	147,797	263,216	18,187	64,385	928,793	219,842
South Dakota	1,064,354	916,563	532,279	333,056	50,768	41,526	33,461	45,548	95,762	31,211	34,780	47,827	3,400	3,021	124,532	20,237
Tennessee	7,129,884	6,446,691	4,161,966	1,971,361	215,183	358,154	125,960	354,649	580,812	228,921	107,683	313,363	0	51,722	468,542	162,879
Texas	39,466,188	31,919,107	19,049,740	11,188,158	1,558,221	1,784,566	507,580	1,782,675	3,528,285	871,408	1,155,423	1,681,209	0	300,575	5,591,288	1,655,219
Utah	3,253,483	2,627,022	1,662,858	802,388	96,842	127,187	30,200	161,269	243,184	84,714	58,992	140,361	21,415	80,249	471,595	74,617
Vermont	1,259,230	1,177,478	752,170	392,963	85,113	44,066	29,497	79,954	91,984	38,651	23,698	30,842	1,504	3,989	63,343	14,420
Virginia	12,152,662	10,705,162	6,565,103	3,699,642	508,516	681,319	161,403	628,778	1,033,579	518,209	167,837	438,526	1,892	69,118	1,180,303	198,079
Washington	9,556,204	7,870,979	4,680,665	2,801,292	494,930	362,898	167,278	465,775	727,758	319,076	263,576	270,739	118,284	45,297	1,292,122	347,806
West Virginia	2,632,237	2,527,767	1,529,908	858,435	88,866	86,130	66,792	138,025	260,613	178,001	40,009	139,424	0	35,227	52,517	16,727
Wisconsin	10,439,481	8,435,359	5,189,139	2,966,702	386,464	415,654	225,947	426,770	800,987	318,895	389,984	279,427	91	216,635	456,158	1,331,330
Wyoming	1,028,099	863,423	511,018	324,752	50,936	45,962	18,441	47,521	92,636	38,099	31,157	27,409	244	2,004	158,465	4,207
Other jurisdictions																
American Samoa	65,647	58,163	29,135	17,283	2,476	4,695	619	2,282	5,175	678	1,358	11,744	0	3,224	4,260	0
Guam	—	—	—	—	—	—	—	—	—	—	—	—	—	—	—	—
Northern Marianas	60,243	58,400	49,060	5,806	1,053	168	4,175	0	0	158	252	443	3,091	372	1,471	0
Puerto Rico	2,997,288	2,865,945	2,086,373	527,207	59,328	66,551	6,967	0	232,588	55,283	106,489	252,365	0	62,319	69,025	0
U.S. Virgin Islands	150,675	137,793	91,064	42,953	7,989	3,785	6,349	8,140	9,749	4,297	2,645	3,093	683	1,515	11,367	0

—Not available.
[1]Includes expenditures for adult education, community colleges, private school programs funded by local and state education agencies, and community services.
[2]Includes expenditures for property and for buildings and alterations completed by school district staff or contractors.
[3]Includes expenditures for operations funded by sales of products or services (e.g., school bookstore or computer time). Also includes small amounts for direct program support made by state education agencies for local school districts.
[4]Includes expenditures for health, attendance, and speech pathology services.
[5]Includes expenditures for curriculum development, staff training, libraries, and media and computer centers.
NOTE: Excludes expenditures for state education agencies. Some data have been revised from previously published figures. Detail may not sum to totals because of rounding.
SOURCE: U.S. Department of Education, National Center for Education Statistics, Common Core of Data (CCD), National Public Education Financial Survey, 2004-05. (This table was prepared April 2008.)

Table 179. Total expenditures for public elementary and secondary education, by function and subfunction: Selected years, 1990–91 through 2005–06

Function and subfunction	Expenditures (in thousands of current dollars)								Percentage distribution of current expenditures for public schools							
	1990–91	1995–96	1999–2000	2000–01	2002–03	2003–04	2004–05[1]	2005–06	1990–91	1995–96	1999–2000	2000–01	2002–03	2003–04	2004–05[1]	2005–06
Total expenditures	$229,429,715	$293,646,490	$381,838,155	$410,811,185	$454,906,912	$474,241,531	$499,568,736	$528,734,539	†	†	†	†	†	†	†	†
Current expenditures for public schools	202,037,752	255,106,683	323,888,508	348,360,841	387,593,617	403,390,369	425,047,565	449,594,924	100.00	100.00	100.00	100.00	100.00	100.00	100.00	100.00
Salaries	132,730,931[2]	165,806,160	210,158,874	224,305,806	246,349,926	252,179,893	261,572,535	273,150,116	65.70	64.99	64.89	64.39	63.56	62.52	61.54	60.75
Employee benefits	33,954,456[2]	44,786,697	53,333,592	57,976,490	68,137,020	74,483,569	81,930,228	87,887,483	16.81	17.56	16.47	16.64	17.58	18.46	19.28	19.55
Purchased services	16,380,643[2]	21,579,562	29,051,785	31,778,754	35,325,876	37,505,263	39,870,015	43,248,725	8.11	8.46	8.97	9.12	9.11	9.30	9.38	9.62
Tuition	1,192,505[2]	1,590,468	2,231,250	2,458,366	3,298,588	3,327,600	3,605,864	4,168,859	0.59	0.62	0.69	0.71	0.82	0.82	0.85	0.93
Supplies	14,805,956[2]	18,756,157	25,896,917	28,262,078	30,528,970	31,907,726	33,870,267	36,690,234	7.33	7.35	8.00	8.11	7.88	7.91	7.97	8.16
Other	2,973,261[2]	2,587,639	3,216,089	3,579,347	3,953,237	3,986,317	4,198,655	4,449,507	1.47	1.01	0.99	1.03	1.02	0.99	0.99	0.99
Instruction	122,223,362	157,473,978	199,968,138	214,333,003	237,731,734	247,444,620	260,046,266	274,179,857	60.50	61.73	61.74	61.53	61.34	61.34	61.18	60.98
Salaries	90,742,284	114,580,985	145,071,564	154,512,089	168,828,934	172,998,433	179,124,955	186,905,065	44.91	44.91	44.79	44.35	43.56	42.89	42.14	41.57
Employee benefits	22,347,524	30,299,566	36,197,167	39,522,678	45,947,180	50,040,333	55,004,561	59,032,817	11.06	11.88	11.18	11.35	11.85	12.40	12.94	13.13
Purchased services	2,722,639	3,825,111	5,839,673	6,430,708	7,289,623	8,242,306	9,014,911	10,102,038	1.35	1.50	1.80	1.85	1.88	2.04	2.12	2.25
Tuition	1,192,505	1,590,468	2,231,250	2,458,366	3,298,588	3,327,600	3,605,864	4,168,859	0.59	0.62	0.69	0.71	0.85	0.82	0.85	0.93
Supplies	4,584,754	6,513,488	9,751,743	10,377,554	11,294,271	11,722,378	12,163,557	12,784,336	2.27	2.55	3.01	2.98	2.91	2.91	2.86	2.84
Other	633,656	664,360	876,741	1,031,608	1,073,139	1,113,570	1,132,418	1,186,741	0.31	0.26	0.27	0.30	0.28	0.28	0.27	0.26
Student support[3]	8,926,010	12,266,136	16,046,845	17,292,756	19,992,229	20,881,322	22,118,879	23,356,971	4.42	4.81	4.95	4.96	5.16	5.18	5.20	5.20
Salaries	6,565,965	8,885,707	11,496,451	12,354,464	14,030,739	14,485,849	15,173,471	15,833,312	3.25	3.48	3.55	3.55	3.62	3.59	3.57	3.52
Employee benefits	1,660,082	2,307,480	2,841,949	3,036,037	3,678,398	4,040,367	4,475,112	4,859,310	0.82	0.90	0.88	0.87	0.95	1.00	1.05	1.08
Purchased services	455,996	687,300	1,180,701	1,328,600	1,646,297	1,708,119	1,799,403	1,979,681	0.23	0.27	0.36	0.38	0.42	0.42	0.42	0.44
Supplies	191,482	247,262	389,044	421,838	470,505	464,635	483,889	497,201	0.09	0.10	0.12	0.12	0.12	0.12	0.11	0.11
Other	52,485	138,387	138,699	151,817	166,291	182,352	187,005	187,468	0.03	0.05	0.04	0.04	0.04	0.05	0.04	0.04
Instructional staff services[4]	8,467,142	10,070,241	14,640,411	15,926,856	18,568,413	19,091,186	20,387,692	21,924,660	4.19	3.95	4.52	4.57	4.79	4.73	4.80	4.88
Salaries	5,560,129	6,418,530	8,971,366	9,790,767	11,312,220	11,483,486	12,108,423	13,005,332	2.75	2.52	2.77	2.81	2.92	2.85	2.85	2.89
Employee benefits	1,408,217	1,719,377	2,169,051	2,356,440	2,909,834	3,157,356	3,546,696	3,898,171	0.70	0.67	0.67	0.68	0.75	0.78	0.83	0.87
Purchased services	622,487	925,403	1,776,849	2,003,598	2,332,965	2,474,229	2,731,885	2,944,703	0.31	0.36	0.55	0.58	0.60	0.61	0.64	0.65
Supplies	776,863	918,189	1,485,730	1,566,954	1,792,008	1,777,640	1,791,507	1,867,878	0.38	0.36	0.46	0.45	0.46	0.44	0.42	0.42
Other	99,445	88,743	237,415	209,097	221,387	198,476	209,181	208,576	0.05	0.03	0.07	0.06	0.06	0.05	0.05	0.05
General administration	5,791,253	5,878,493	6,698,006	7,108,291	7,960,378	8,266,957	8,510,315	8,920,041	2.87	2.30	2.07	2.04	2.05	2.05	2.00	1.98
Salaries	2,603,562	2,901,172	3,179,759	3,351,554	3,680,522	3,732,878	3,725,275	3,860,883	1.29	1.14	0.98	0.96	0.95	0.93	0.88	0.86
Employee benefits	777,381	828,483	938,113	1,000,698	1,166,775	1,262,864	1,375,298	1,479,556	0.38	0.32	0.29	0.29	0.30	0.31	0.32	0.33
Purchased services	1,482,427	1,626,178	1,941,822	2,099,032	2,384,109	2,505,398	2,635,243	2,735,714	0.73	0.64	0.60	0.60	0.62	0.62	0.62	0.61
Supplies	172,898	185,831	196,205	206,137	223,696	217,151	221,376	225,230	0.09	0.07	0.06	0.06	0.06	0.05	0.05	0.05
Other	754,985	336,828	442,107	450,870	505,276	548,666	553,123	618,657	0.37	0.13	0.14	0.13	0.13	0.14	0.13	0.14
School administration	11,695,344	14,831,159	18,381,292	19,580,890	21,791,580	22,597,918	24,155,908	25,277,042	5.79	5.81	5.68	5.62	5.62	5.60	5.68	5.62
Salaries	8,935,903	11,156,460	13,923,730	14,817,213	16,206,443	16,626,755	17,467,947	18,181,910	4.42	4.37	4.30	4.25	4.18	4.12	4.11	4.04
Employee benefits	2,257,783	2,963,991	3,455,390	3,689,689	4,341,364	4,710,083	5,217,866	5,622,342	1.12	1.16	1.07	1.06	1.12	1.17	1.23	1.25
Purchased services	247,750	384,908	573,003	611,638	718,442	754,181	896,782	862,664	0.12	0.15	0.18	0.18	0.19	0.19	0.21	0.19
Supplies	189,711	256,857	337,651	369,257	416,265	399,456	439,418	474,816	0.09	0.10	0.10	0.11	0.11	0.10	0.10	0.11
Other	64,197	68,943	91,519	93,093	109,066	107,444	133,896	135,311	0.03	0.03	0.03	0.03	0.03	0.03	0.03	0.03
Operation and maintenance	21,290,655	25,724,062	31,190,295	34,034,158	36,830,517	38,720,429	40,926,881	44,320,217	10.54	10.08	9.63	9.77	9.50	9.60	9.63	9.86
Salaries	8,849,559	10,454,854	12,745,457	13,461,242	14,596,762	14,811,588	15,344,880	16,028,083	4.38	4.10	3.94	3.86	3.77	3.67	3.61	3.57
Employee benefits	2,633,075	3,129,632	3,531,423	3,778,520	4,476,354	5,019,477	5,483,344	5,840,665	1.30	1.23	1.09	1.08	1.15	1.24	1.29	1.30
Purchased services	5,721,125	7,698,704	8,866,099	9,642,217	9,866,874	10,463,087	10,921,591	11,913,734	2.83	3.02	2.74	2.77	2.55	2.59	2.57	2.65
Supplies	3,761,738	4,214,201	5,801,242	6,871,845	7,543,937	8,091,029	8,832,550	10,147,971	1.86	1.65	1.79	1.97	1.95	2.01	2.08	2.26
Other	325,157	226,670	246,075	280,334	346,590	335,247	344,516	389,764	0.16	0.09	0.08	0.08	0.09	0.08	0.08	0.09

See notes at end of table.

Table 179. Total expenditures for public elementary and secondary education, by function and subfunction: Selected years, 1990–91 through 2005–06—Continued

Function and subfunction	Expenditures (in thousands of current dollars)								Percentage distribution of current expenditures for public schools							
	1990–91	1995–96	1999–2000	2000–01	2002–03	2003–04	2004–05[1]	2005–06	1990–91	1995–96	1999–2000	2000–01	2002–03	2003–04	2004–05[1]	2005–06
1	2	3	4	5	6	7	8	9	10	11	12	13	14	15	16	17
Student transportation[5]	8,678,954	10,396,426	13,007,625	14,052,654	15,648,821	16,348,784	17,459,659	18,864,069	4.30	4.08	4.02	4.03	4.04	4.05	4.11	4.20
Salaries	3,285,127	3,933,969	5,061,209	5,406,092	5,974,787	6,105,136	6,379,953	6,701,455	1.63	1.54	1.56	1.55	1.54	1.51	1.50	1.49
Employee benefits	892,985	1,207,961	1,464,249	1,592,127	1,905,504	2,119,101	2,333,027	2,535,296	0.44	0.47	0.45	0.46	0.49	0.53	0.55	0.56
Purchased services	3,345,232	4,257,805	5,331,435	5,767,462	6,450,377	6,736,968	7,054,340	7,561,565	1.66	1.67	1.65	1.66	1.66	1.67	1.66	1.68
Supplies	961,447	836,450	1,034,323	1,159,350	1,130,478	1,192,548	1,501,906	1,867,495	0.48	0.33	0.32	0.33	0.29	0.30	0.35	0.42
Other	194,163	160,239	116,410	127,623	187,675	195,031	190,433	198,259	0.10	0.06	0.04	0.04	0.05	0.05	0.04	0.04
Other support services[5]	5,587,837	7,039,408	10,188,917	11,439,134	13,231,082	13,488,270	14,058,464	14,465,937	2.77	2.76	3.15	3.28	3.41	3.34	3.31	3.22
Salaries	2,900,394	3,450,836	4,930,099	5,521,381	6,234,410	6,344,591	6,437,831	6,577,129	1.44	1.35	1.52	1.58	1.61	1.57	1.51	1.46
Employee benefits	980,859	1,182,229	1,433,054	1,594,540	2,019,058	2,265,789	2,486,442	2,483,366	0.49	0.46	0.44	0.46	0.52	0.56	0.58	0.55
Purchased services	798,922	1,362,961	2,462,775	2,783,176	3,283,907	3,185,599	3,277,143	3,455,292	0.40	0.53	0.76	0.80	0.85	0.79	0.77	0.77
Supplies	294,527	398,534	573,670	626,889	717,844	766,110	771,940	793,997	0.15	0.16	0.18	0.18	0.19	0.19	0.18	0.18
Other	613,135	644,849	789,319	913,148	975,863	926,181	1,085,102	1,156,153	0.30	0.25	0.24	0.26	0.25	0.23	0.26	0.26
Food services	8,430,490	10,648,844	12,948,807	13,816,635	14,930,942	15,652,674	16,425,973	17,263,582	4.17	4.17	4.00	3.97	3.85	3.88	3.86	3.84
Salaries	—	3,844,285	4,606,262	4,966,092	5,325,744	5,409,803	5,606,416	5,842,948	†	1.51	1.42	1.43	1.37	1.34	1.32	1.30
Employee benefits	—	1,103,433	1,267,921	1,381,923	1,636,523	1,790,483	1,934,067	2,059,918	†	0.43	0.39	0.40	0.42	0.44	0.46	0.46
Purchased services	—	627,902	897,762	923,091	1,155,396	1,252,027	1,332,761	1,464,511	†	0.25	0.28	0.26	0.30	0.31	0.31	0.33
Supplies	—	4,916,299	6,041,001	6,420,201	6,641,477	7,009,747	7,385,373	7,727,182	†	1.93	1.87	1.84	1.71	1.74	1.74	1.72
Other	—	156,924	135,861	125,327	171,801	190,613	165,355	169,023	†	0.06	0.04	0.04	0.04	0.05	0.04	0.04
Enterprise operations[6]	946,705	777,937	818,172	776,463	907,921	896,209	959,528	1,022,549	0.47	0.30	0.25	0.22	0.23	0.22	0.23	0.23
Salaries	—	179,360	172,977	124,913	159,366	181,374	203,383	213,999	†	0.07	0.05	0.04	0.04	0.04	0.05	0.05
Employee benefits	—	44,545	35,861	23,837	56,031	77,717	73,816	76,042	†	0.02	0.01	0.01	0.01	0.02	0.02	0.02
Purchased services	—	183,288	181,666	189,230	197,885	183,349	205,951	228,823	†	0.07	0.06	0.05	0.05	0.05	0.05	0.05
Supplies	—	269,046	286,309	242,052	298,489	267,031	278,751	304,129	†	0.11	0.09	0.07	0.08	0.07	0.07	0.07
Other	—	101,697	141,943	196,430	196,150	188,738	197,628	199,556	†	0.04	0.04	0.06	0.05	0.05	0.05	0.04
Other current expenditures	3,295,717	4,724,659	5,457,015	6,063,700	6,873,762	6,927,551	7,691,468	7,417,761	†	†	†	†	†	†	†	†
Community services	964,370	1,728,669	2,151,043	2,426,189	2,695,832	2,720,844	2,813,379	3,015,207	†	†	†	†	†	†	†	†
Private school programs	527,609	781,148	961,203	1,026,695	1,161,470	1,146,373	1,236,495	1,389,204	†	†	†	†	†	†	†	†
Adult education	1,365,523	1,500,438	1,715,332	1,838,265	2,005,813	1,968,046	1,964,531	2,003,291	†	†	†	†	†	†	†	†
Community colleges	5,356	7,746	265	351	460	210	435	354	†	†	†	†	†	†	†	†
Other	432,858	706,657	629,172	772,200	1,010,187	1,092,079	1,676,529	1,009,704	†	†	†	†	†	†	†	†
Capital outlay[7]	19,771,478	27,555,667	43,357,186	46,220,704	48,940,374	50,842,973	53,528,382	57,375,299	†	†	†	†	†	†	†	†
Public schools	19,655,496	27,457,489	42,231,206	46,078,494	48,833,138	50,731,632	53,430,719	57,281,425	†	†	†	†	†	†	†	†
Other current expenditures	115,982	98,179	125,980	142,210	107,236	111,341	97,663	93,874	†	†	†	†	†	†	†	†
Interest on school debt	4,324,768	6,259,480	9,135,445	10,165,940	11,499,160	13,080,638	13,301,322	14,346,556	†	†	†	†	†	†	†	†

—Not available.
†Not applicable.
[1]Data have been revised from previously published figures.
[2]Includes estimated data for subfunctions of food services and enterprise operations.
[3]Includes expenditures for guidance, health, attendance, and speech pathology services.
[4]Includes expenditures for curriculum development, staff training, libraries, and media and computer centers.
[5]Includes business support services concerned with paying, transporting, exchanging, and maintaining goods and services for local education agencies; central support services, including planning, research, evaluation, information, staff, and data processing services; and other support services.

[6]Includes expenditures for operations funded by sales of products or services (e.g., school bookstore or computer time). Includes very small amounts for direct program support made by state education agencies for local school districts.
[7]Includes expenditures for property, and for buildings and alterations completed by school district staff or contractors.
NOTE: Excludes expenditures for state education agencies. Data are not adjusted for changes in the purchasing power of the dollar due to inflation. Detail may not sum to totals because of rounding.
SOURCE: U.S. Department of Education, National Center for Education Statistics, Common Core of Data (CCD), "National Public Education Financial Survey," 1990–91 through 2005–06. (This table was prepared April 2008.)

Table 180. Expenditures for instruction in public elementary and secondary schools, by subfunction and state or jurisdiction: 2004–05 and 2005–06

[In thousands of current dollars]

State or jurisdiction	2004–05[1]						2005–06					
	Total	Salaries	Employee benefits	Purchased services[2]	Supplies	Tuition and other	Total	Salaries	Employee benefits	Purchased services[2]	Supplies	Tuition and other
1	2	3	4	5	6	7	8	9	10	11	12	13
United States	$260,046,266	$179,124,955	$55,004,561	$9,014,911	$12,163,557	$4,738,282	$274,179,857	$186,905,065	$59,032,817	$10,102,038	$12,784,336	$5,355,600
Alabama	3,058,443	2,021,674	680,251	84,115	258,856	13,547	3,333,081	2,175,489	785,451	88,963	267,903	15,274
Alaska......................	832,707	531,231	186,133	46,394	42,749	26,200	874,604	551,605	223,009	49,074	42,270	8,645
Arizona	4,030,750	3,179,672	557,576	115,671	151,571	26,260	4,418,230	3,434,477	634,618	156,343	159,898	32,893
Arkansas...................	2,158,004	1,521,530	367,406	63,939	180,532	24,596	2,292,086	1,591,696	409,857	65,222	200,079	25,231
California	30,908,059	20,911,505	6,678,137	1,125,388	1,529,163	663,866	32,244,567	21,714,003	6,906,543	1,244,453	1,682,410	697,158
Colorado	3,392,114	2,456,369	519,120	72,994	243,977	99,654	3,576,989	2,547,089	569,917	83,895	263,931	112,157
Connecticut...............	4,505,734	2,986,243	991,740	130,379	120,982	276,390	4,762,341	3,107,055	1,108,456	140,709	114,910	291,211
Delaware...................	771,916	512,941	205,156	2,987	38,482	12,350	848,259	539,577	231,697	20,143	40,627	16,216
District of Columbia	565,473	360,376	40,550	30,991	6,316	127,241	550,749	347,192	41,200	17,803	4,451	140,103
Florida......................	11,263,480	7,337,810	2,019,401	1,208,723	587,634	109,911	12,352,747	8,030,593	2,222,371	1,401,907	601,228	96,648
Georgia....................	7,899,852	5,664,480	1,576,769	128,147	490,659	39,797	8,598,901	6,115,822	1,789,071	163,431	491,763	38,815
Hawaii	1,007,207	665,681	210,249	53,486	63,830	13,961	1,077,351	691,902	244,469	52,252	60,357	28,371
Idaho.......................	1,000,526	699,197	222,461	29,580	48,311	975	1,044,784	728,450	233,496	34,032	47,898	909
Illinois......................	11,095,296	7,885,666	2,238,038	356,286	395,302	220,004	11,329,436	8,140,977	2,154,575	391,569	406,843	235,471
Indiana.....................	5,499,308	3,455,469	1,797,474	70,927	162,986	12,452	5,550,922	3,526,275	1,744,740	72,571	193,510	13,826
Iowa........................	2,321,413	1,663,162	498,228	58,573	79,852	21,597	2,413,984	1,731,958	524,069	45,511	89,930	22,516
Kansas.....................	2,211,723	1,655,302	363,255	57,368	119,840	15,958	2,419,648	1,790,934	404,458	66,163	140,701	17,392
Kentucky	2,890,808	2,092,737	613,045	49,954	123,460	11,611	3,102,318	2,205,061	709,456	51,924	121,934	13,942
Louisiana	3,329,812	2,307,793	752,636	61,216	197,559	10,609	3,238,598	2,177,515	793,923	49,282	196,927	20,951
Maine.......................	1,372,765	861,726	333,789	57,179	41,693	78,378	1,393,238	887,880	322,399	58,272	42,614	82,073
Maryland...................	5,362,276	3,610,219	1,239,470	100,958	183,430	228,199	5,749,590	3,847,724	1,341,982	122,410	192,332	245,141
Massachusetts...........	7,228,652	4,796,360	1,842,373	37,956	153,633	398,330	7,957,018	4,884,790	2,013,601	58,916	238,400	761,311
Michigan	9,298,039	6,014,909	2,564,549	383,609	310,042	24,929	9,442,946	5,968,872	2,744,179	426,491	280,226	23,179
Minnesota.................	4,752,362	3,370,834	975,173	176,749	166,736	62,871	4,949,826	3,492,568	1,021,262	194,868	177,387	63,742
Mississippi	1,938,248	1,404,793	379,872	41,046	100,371	12,167	2,098,153	1,492,214	421,902	43,734	127,045	13,258
Missouri	4,322,270	3,094,449	722,047	136,931	335,380	33,462	4,607,368	3,274,033	787,574	151,285	359,692	34,785
Montana....................	728,058	506,801	140,560	25,432	51,910	3,355	757,786	503,417	140,880	49,564	60,653	3,272
Nebraska	1,596,345	1,108,501	352,418	54,116	53,182	28,128	1,697,132	1,169,220	384,265	58,405	56,945	28,297
Nevada	1,699,144	1,088,201	377,451	32,948	126,400	74,143	1,809,449	1,161,262	397,973	33,122	136,251	80,840
New Hampshire	1,309,782	848,935	275,666	35,141	37,078	112,962	1,380,638	884,470	304,916	36,414	39,495	115,342
New Jersey	11,647,046	7,628,929	2,597,191	340,368	443,463	637,095	12,326,559	7,989,985	2,880,659	352,826	432,088	671,001
New Mexico	1,430,765	1,013,105	283,272	38,143	96,088	158	1,535,203	1,071,394	312,392	42,223	109,054	141
New York...................	26,731,925	17,887,340	6,662,088	1,164,030	778,726	239,741	28,462,577	18,794,178	7,301,789	1,334,518	776,977	255,115
North Carolina	6,123,399	4,596,115	990,340	131,755	398,993	6,196	6,480,355	4,799,375	1,105,231	140,219	429,171	6,359
North Dakota	510,617	363,548	98,238	17,553	25,836	5,441	521,320	373,358	101,422	17,137	24,276	5,127
Ohio........................	9,816,361	6,695,111	2,113,957	345,245	399,486	262,563	10,208,622	6,862,710	2,206,199	454,417	406,198	279,098
Oklahoma.................	2,363,927	1,703,711	434,415	34,074	185,382	6,344	2,497,439	1,798,103	462,598	33,548	196,181	7,009
Oregon.....................	2,619,853	1,657,493	681,410	99,654	148,505	32,791	2,801,665	1,718,148	777,835	109,829	160,561	35,292
Pennsylvania.............	11,540,622	7,729,507	2,485,888	635,032	468,520	221,674	12,056,932	7,929,952	2,678,663	737,825	469,148	241,343
Rhode Island	1,134,114	753,421	274,903	12,306	25,759	67,726	1,164,366	772,229	286,268	12,563	23,097	70,209
South Carolina...........	3,142,227	2,238,242	610,849	86,524	178,774	27,837	3,316,986	2,362,086	646,438	102,456	177,540	28,466
South Dakota.............	532,279	365,791	99,845	23,600	35,901	7,142	549,811	373,393	102,666	24,665	41,604	7,483
Tennessee	4,161,966	2,886,430	758,587	73,576	428,981	14,392	4,295,030	2,967,408	799,330	78,650	435,700	13,942
Texas	19,049,740	14,707,325	2,284,333	620,065	1,234,824	203,192	20,130,884	15,509,624	2,445,856	639,393	1,303,392	232,618
Utah	1,662,858	1,107,737	436,933	30,526	83,024	4,639	1,755,649	1,156,630	471,405	32,342	91,001	4,271
Vermont	752,170	473,927	152,121	39,163	20,803	66,155	787,788	499,246	166,570	42,162	21,655	58,155
Virginia.....................	6,565,103	4,736,658	1,370,229	135,984	315,255	6,978	7,025,890	5,024,000	1,496,214	158,480	337,416	9,779
Washington................	4,680,665	3,349,597	849,318	234,090	204,997	42,662	4,876,294	3,440,702	947,238	235,816	206,837	45,701
West Virginia..............	1,529,908	942,870	479,606	26,299	79,949	1,183	1,589,476	973,077	500,483	27,241	87,742	933
Wisconsin	5,189,139	3,331,504	1,504,302	75,664	178,629	99,040	5,352,462	3,396,493	1,597,047	74,044	181,995	102,883
Wyoming...................	511,018	342,027	115,741	22,078	29,745	1,428	571,810	378,853	134,204	22,954	34,095	1,704
Other jurisdictions												
American Samoa	29,135	17,685	3,419	2,460	3,926	1,645	30,551	19,253	3,722	3,315	2,726	1,535
Guam....................	—	—	—	—	—	—	120,010	89,200	22,040	1,041	7,382	347
Northern Marianas...	49,060	33,266	8,928	3,717	3,145	5	46,755	32,346	8,731	4,129	1,524	26
Puerto Rico............	2,086,373	1,711,416	265,508	9,414	44,005	56,030	2,163,504	1,763,778	266,163	7,074	68,351	58,138
U.S. Virgin Islands....	91,064	71,326	18,147	161	1,398	32	94,754	73,440	19,609	166	1,507	33

—Not available.
[1]Data have been revised from previously published figures.
[2]Includes purchased professional services of teachers or others who provide instruction for students and travel for instructional staff.

NOTE: Excludes expenditures for state education agencies. Detail may not sum to totals because of rounding.
SOURCE: U.S. Department of Education, National Center for Education Statistics, Common Core of Data (CCD), "National Public Education Financial Survey," 2004–05 and 2005–06. (This table was prepared April 2008.)

Table 181. Total and current expenditures per pupil in public elementary and secondary schools: Selected years, 1919–20 through 2005–06

| School year | Expenditure per pupil in average daily attendance | | | | Expenditure per pupil in fall enrollment[1] | | | | |
| | Unadjusted dollars | | Constant 2006–07 dollars[2] | | Unadjusted dollars | | Constant 2006–07 dollars[2] | | |
	Total expenditure[3]	Current expenditure	Total expenditure[3]	Current expenditure	Total expenditure[3]	Current expenditure	Total expenditure[3]	Current expenditure	Annual percent change in current expenditure
1	2	3	4	5	6	7	8	9	10
1919–20	$64	$53	$685	$571	$48	$40	$513	$427	—
1929–30	108	87	1,294	1,034	90	72	1,071	856	—
1931–32	97	81	1,372	1,148	82	69	1,161	972	—
1933–34	76	67	1,175	1,040	65	57	998	884	—
1935–36	88	74	1,306	1,104	74	63	1,105	933	—
1937–38	100	84	1,421	1,195	86	72	1,220	1,026	—
1939–40	106	88	1,545	1,287	92	76	1,339	1,115	—
1941–42	110	98	1,441	1,287	94	84	1,233	1,102	—
1943–44	125	117	1,461	1,371	105	99	1,231	1,155	—
1945–46	146	136	1,632	1,526	124	116	1,391	1,300	—
1947–48	205	181	1,795	1,590	179	158	1,567	1,388	—
1949–50	260	210	2,244	1,813	231	187	1,992	1,609	—
1951–52	314	246	2,443	1,911	275	215	2,139	1,673	—
1953–54	351	265	2,664	2,010	312	236	2,369	1,788	—
1955–56	387	294	2,939	2,234	354	269	2,687	2,042	—
1957–58	447	341	3,198	2,439	408	311	2,917	2,224	—
1959–60	471	375	3,272	2,606	440	350	3,057	2,435	—
1961–62	517	419	3,512	2,846	485	393	3,296	2,670	—
1963–64	559	460	3,698	3,047	520	428	3,442	2,836	—
1965–66	654	538	4,183	3,440	607	499	3,883	3,194	—
1967–68	786	658	4,721	3,952	732	612	4,392	3,676	—
1969–70	955	816	5,161	4,410	879	751	4,751	4,060	—
1970–71	1,049	911	5,393	4,682	970	842	4,986	4,328	6.6
1971–72	1,128	990	5,595	4,910	1,034	908	5,131	4,503	4.0
1972–73	1,211	1,077	5,773	5,135	1,117	993	5,325	4,737	5.2
1973–74	1,364	1,207	5,972	5,286	1,244	1,101	5,445	4,820	1.7
1974–75	1,545	1,365	6,089	5,378	1,423	1,257	5,609	4,955	2.8
1975–76	1,697	1,504	6,248	5,535	1,563	1,385	5,753	5,096	2.9
1976–77	1,816	1,638	6,317	5,696	1,674	1,509	5,821	5,248	3.0
1977–78	2,002	1,823	6,526	5,941	1,842	1,677	6,003	5,464	4.1
1978–79	2,210	2,020	6,586	6,021	2,029	1,855	6,048	5,529	1.2
1979–80	2,491	2,272	6,549	5,974	2,290	2,088	6,021	5,492	-0.7
1980–81	2,742 [4]	2,502	6,462 [4]	5,895	2,529 [4]	2,307	5,961 [4]	5,438	-1.0
1981–82	2,973 [4]	2,726	6,450 [4]	5,913	2,754 [4]	2,525	5,975 [4]	5,477	0.7
1982–83	3,203 [4]	2,955	6,663 [4]	6,146	2,966 [4]	2,736	6,169 [4]	5,691	3.9
1983–84	3,471 [4]	3,173	6,962 [4]	6,365	3,216 [4]	2,940	6,450 [4]	5,896	3.6
1984–85	3,722 [4]	3,470	7,184 [4]	6,698	3,456 [4]	3,222	6,670 [4]	6,219	5.5
1985–86	4,020 [4]	3,756	7,541 [4]	7,045	3,724 [4]	3,479	6,987 [4]	6,527	5.0
1986–87	4,308 [4]	3,970	7,906 [4]	7,287	3,995 [4]	3,682	7,331 [4]	6,757	3.5
1987–88	4,654 [4]	4,240	8,201 [4]	7,472	4,310 [4]	3,927	7,595 [4]	6,920	2.4
1988–89	5,109	4,645	8,606	7,824	4,738	4,307	7,981	7,255	4.8
1989–90	5,550	4,980	8,923	8,006	5,174	4,643	8,319	7,464	2.9
1990–91	5,885	5,258	8,971	8,015	5,486	4,902	8,363	7,472	0.1
1991–92	6,074	5,421	8,972	8,007	5,629	5,023	8,313	7,419	-0.7
1992–93	6,281	5,584	8,997	7,997	5,804	5,160	8,313	7,390	-0.4
1993–94	6,492	5,767	9,063	8,052	5,996	5,327	8,371	7,437	0.6
1994–95	6,725	5,989	9,128	8,128	6,208	5,529	8,426	7,504	0.9
1995–96	6,962	6,147	9,198	8,122	6,443	5,689	8,513	7,517	0.2
1996–97	7,300	6,393	9,377	8,212	6,764	5,923	8,689	7,609	1.2
1997–98	7,703	6,676	9,722	8,425	7,142	6,189	9,014	7,811	2.7
1998–99	8,118	7,013	10,072	8,701	7,533	6,508	9,346	8,074	3.4
1999–2000	8,592	7,394	10,360	8,915	8,033	6,912	9,686	8,335	3.2
2000–01	9,183	7,904	10,706	9,215	8,575	7,380	9,997	8,604	3.2
2001–02	9,614	8,259	11,014	9,461	8,996	7,727	10,305	8,853	2.9
2002–03	9,952	8,610	11,156	9,651	9,299	8,044	10,423	9,017	1.9
2003–04	10,310	8,900	11,310	9,763	9,627	8,310	10,561	9,116	1.1
2004–05	10,781	9,316	11,481	9,921	10,080	8,711	10,735	9,276	1.8
2005–06	11,350	9,788	11,643	10,041	10,615	9,154	10,889	9,391	1.2

—Not available.
[1]Data for 1919–20 to 1953–54 are based on school-year enrollment.
[2]Constant dollars based on the Consumer Price Index, prepared by the Bureau of Labor Statistics, U.S. Department of Labor, adjusted to a school-year basis.
[3]Excludes "Other current expenditures," such as community services, private school programs, adult education, and other programs not allocable to expenditures per student at public schools.
[4]Estimated.
NOTE: Beginning in 1980–81, state administration expenditures are excluded from both "total" and "current" expenditures. Current expenditures include instruction, student support services, food services, and enterprise operations. Total expenditures include current expenditures, capital outlay, and interest on debt. Beginning in 1988–89, extensive changes were made in the data collection procedures. Some data have been revised from previously published figures.
SOURCE: U.S. Department of Education, National Center for Education Statistics, *Biennial Survey of Education in the United States,* 1919–20 through 1955–56; *Statistics of State School Systems,* 1957–58 through 1969–70; *Revenues and Expenditures for Public Elementary and Secondary Education,* 1970–71 through 1986–87; and Common Core of Data (CCD), "National Public Education Financial Survey," 1987–88 through 2005–06. (This table was prepared April 2008.)

Table 182. Total and current expenditures per pupil in fall enrollment in public elementary and secondary education, by function and state or jurisdiction: 2005–06

State or jurisdiction	Total[1]	Total	Instruction	Total	Student support[4]	Instructional staff[5]	General administration	School administration	Operation and maintenance	Student transportation	Other support services	Food services	Enterprise operations[3]	Capital outlay[2]	Interest on school debt
1	2	3	4	5	6	7	8	9	10	11	12	13	14	15	16
United States	**$10,615**	**$9,154**	**$5,583**	**$3,199**	**$476**	**$446**	**$182**	**$515**	**$902**	**$384**	**$295**	**$352**	**$21**	**$1,168**	**$292**
Alabama	8,755	7,683	4,493	2,679	395	378	208	475	715	355	153	510	0	902	171
Alaska	13,538	11,476	6,562	4,536	724	624	174	678	1,510	400	427	330	48	1,778	284
Arizona	7,749	6,515	4,037	2,174	366	154	104	316	718	248	268	304	0	1,033	201
Arkansas	9,278	8,030	4,834	2,780	368	511	234	428	747	289	203	410	6	1,046	202
California	10,068	8,301	5,009	2,976	382	560	75	562	836	203	358	299	17	1,550	217
Colorado	9,897	8,166	4,587	3,306	358	424	126	531	845	234	789	253	21	1,319	411
Connecticut	15,219	13,072	8,281	4,327	786	420	257	737	1,219	617	292	353	110	1,893	254
Delaware	13,796	11,621	7,014	4,062	555	152	137	647	1,136	688	748	545	0	1,926	249
District of Columbia	15,626	13,752	7,164	6,248	863	978	349	729	1,731	973	625	340	0	1,875	0
Florida	9,854	7,812	4,618	2,833	368	528	79	444	879	331	204	361	0	1,815	227
Georgia	9,909	8,595	5,379	2,776	410	469	112	529	639	352	264	413	27	1,207	106
Hawaii	10,758	9,876	5,893	3,521	1,184	360	76	663	773	190	275	462	0	416	466
Idaho	7,343	6,469	3,988	2,179	362	278	145	366	598	307	124	301	1	732	142
Illinois	10,324	9,113	5,365	3,450	577	424	310	463	911	452	314	299	0	953	257
Indiana	10,290	8,929	5,363	3,201	393	283	166	507	976	508	368	365	0	939	422
Iowa	9,730	8,355	4,993	2,972	494	397	233	496	781	305	266	379	10	1,234	141
Kansas	9,629	8,640	5,175	3,064	487	397	282	505	836	345	212	400	0	699	290
Kentucky	8,847	7,668	4,563	2,659	316	426	172	418	716	438	175	431	15	992	187
Louisiana	9,349	8,486	4,948	3,058	349	425	203	444	958	461	217	480	0	703	160
Maine	11,638	10,841	7,127	3,350	401	378	228	576	1,093	486	189	365	0	562	235
Maryland	12,202	10,909	6,685	3,731	455	582	109	741	990	558	296	306	187	1,155	138
Massachusetts	14,094	12,564	8,187	3,989	690	590	208	521	1,113	516	351	387	0	1,235	296
Michigan	11,208	9,575	5,420	3,854	695	474	196	574	1,041	424	449	301	0	1,144	489
Minnesota	10,929	9,159	5,898	2,848	245	422	283	390	717	504	288	387	26	1,293	476
Mississippi	7,800	7,173	4,239	2,520	324	341	208	395	792	317	143	414	1	488	140
Missouri	9,388	8,273	5,021	2,883	390	371	245	464	835	420	159	369	0	827	287
Montana	9,415	8,626	5,211	3,056	464	342	260	473	903	398	215	347	12	698	91
Nebraska	10,359	9,324	5,921	2,773	391	303	337	471	810	258	204	364	266	842	193
Nevada	9,514	7,177	4,388	2,543	271	197	126	499	720	269	461	246	0	1,827	510
New Hampshire	11,615	10,396	6,710	3,383	713	319	349	564	901	441	97	303	0	980	239
New Jersey	16,587	14,954	8,832	5,653	1,349	494	368	1,001	1,546	811	85	335	134	1,385	248
New Mexico	9,620	8,354	4,698	3,288	806	389	255	518	829	343	148	364	4	1,149	116
New York	15,837	14,615	10,109	4,180	468	412	282	592	1,305	768	353	326	0	779	443
North Carolina	8,532	7,396	4,575	2,409	401	296	144	481	598	290	198	412	0	876	260
North Dakota	9,787	8,728	5,304	2,717	349	257	394	407	750	368	192	438	268	946	113
Ohio	11,129	9,692	5,549	3,823	580	626	285	567	903	448	414	319	1	1,177	260
Oklahoma	7,623	6,941	3,935	2,548	449	278	200	376	812	229	205	390	69	614	68
Oregon	9,632	8,645	5,074	3,262	611	345	118	547	728	385	529	306	3	578	409
Pennsylvania	12,287	10,723	6,586	3,726	520	408	332	469	1,110	513	373	368	44	1,112	452
Rhode Island	13,015	12,609	7,589	4,696	1,502	604	153	642	1,048	476	271	323	0	199	208
South Carolina	9,864	8,120	4,728	2,961	558	545	99	466	759	291	243	405	27	1,399	345
South Dakota	8,649	7,775	4,506	2,835	428	335	281	387	847	273	284	402	32	707	167
Tennessee	7,742	7,004	4,502	2,163	238	391	145	386	640	255	107	339	0	579	159
Texas	9,248	7,480	4,448	2,638	363	413	117	415	858	210	263	394	0	1,364	404
Utah	6,629	5,464	3,453	1,684	202	256	64	332	534	179	117	293	34	1,007	158
Vermont	13,561	12,805	8,152	4,304	948	472	312	849	1,020	419	283	344	5	610	146
Virginia	10,809	9,452	5,789	3,275	452	606	142	549	920	461	145	386	2	1,070	287
Washington	9,694	7,984	4,725	2,872	509	374	167	474	741	329	278	271	115	1,384	326
West Virginia	9,658	9,440	5,659	3,251	337	361	240	505	972	682	153	530	0	178	39
Wisconsin	11,309	9,993	6,116	3,542	457	492	263	507	952	378	493	334	0	585	732
Wyoming	13,471	11,437	6,774	4,298	672	622	253	638	1,210	499	403	357	7	1,993	42
Other jurisdictions															
American Samoa	3,837	3,561	1,859	976	142	379	43	143	150	46	73	727	0	276	0
Guam	6,907	6,781	3,873	2,547	741	188	135	369	837	53	224	361	0	106	20
Northern Marianas	5,061	4,924	3,990	439	91	28	183	24	13	81	20	41	453	138	0
Puerto Rico	5,654	5,470	3,839	1,192	273	47	24	0	549	138	161	438	0	160	24
U.S. Virgin Islands	9,529	8,768	5,657	2,862	533	279	417	517	596	342	178	207	42	761	0

[1]Excludes "Other current expenditures," such as community services, private school programs, adult education, and other programs not allocable to expenditures per pupil in public schools.
[2]Includes expenditures for property and for buildings and alterations completed by school district staff or contractors.
[3]Includes expenditures for operations funded by sales of products or services (e.g., school bookstore or computer time).
[4]Includes expenditures for health, attendance, and speech pathology services.

[5]Includes expenditures for curriculum development, staff training, libraries, and media and computer centers.
NOTE: Excludes expenditures for state education agencies. "0" indicates none or less than $0.50. Detail may not sum to totals because of rounding.
SOURCE: U.S. Department of Education, National Center for Education Statistics, Common Core of Data (CCD), "National Public Education Financial Survey," 2005–06. (This table was prepared April 2008.)

Table 183. Total and current expenditures per pupil in fall enrollment in public elementary and secondary education, by function and state or jurisdiction: 2004–05

State or jurisdiction	Total[1]	Current expenditures, capital expenditures, and interest on school debt													Capital outlay[2]	Interest on school debt
		Current expenditures														
		Total	Instruction	Support services									Food services	Enterprise operations[3]		
				Total	Student support[4]	Instructional staff[5]	General administration	School administration	Operation and maintenance	Student transportation	Other support services				
1	2	3	4	5	6	7	8	9	10	11	12	13	14	15	16
United States	$10,080	$8,711	$5,329	$3,025	$453	$418	$174	$495	$839	$358	$288	$337	$20	$1,097	$273
Alabama	7,930	7,073	4,189	2,393	353	323	189	428	643	320	137	491	0	704	153
Alaska..........................	13,130	10,847	6,262	4,231	682	551	160	635	1,404	388	411	310	43	2,021	263
Arizona	7,337	6,307	3,863	2,148	345	148	104	313	695	227	316	295	0	808	222
Arkansas.....................	8,797	7,659	4,660	2,597	346	441	237	416	684	271	202	396	6	944	195
California	9,655	7,905	4,798	2,805	364	511	72	533	765	192	368	285	16	1,553	197
Colorado	9,421	7,826	4,428	3,123	340	397	111	507	800	241	726	244	31	1,206	389
Connecticut.................	14,296	12,263	7,804	4,021	708	405	243	690	1,116	572	287	338	101	1,798	235
Delaware.....................	12,621	10,911	6,482	3,920	519	137	122	610	1,105	677	749	508	0	1,521	189
District of Columbia	15,883	13,915	7,371	6,218	721	1,056	474	739	1,595	943	689	326	0	1,967	0
Florida.........................	8,862	7,215	4,268	2,600	347	439	78	416	804	305	211	347	0	1,441	206
Georgia........................	9,334	8,065	5,085	2,556	378	430	110	495	590	312	241	400	24	1,155	114
Hawaii..........................	9,549	8,997	5,498	3,053	989	382	114	594	637	129	208	446	0	342	210
Idaho...........................	7,185	6,319	3,907	2,125	354	266	149	358	583	297	118	287	0	713	153
Illinois..........................	10,168	8,896	5,290	3,320	562	408	302	458	863	426	301	286	0	1,019	254
Indiana.........................	10,241	8,919	5,384	3,173	396	295	169	505	950	490	368	361	0	956	367
Iowa.............................	9,223	7,962	4,853	2,714	463	399	224	443	698	265	222	374	21	1,125	136
Kansas.........................	8,788	7,926	4,714	2,836	457	350	282	470	773	318	185	375	0	581	282
Kentucky	8,392	7,132	4,284	2,427	283	397	164	390	639	393	161	409	12	1,089	172
Louisiana	8,304	7,669	4,597	2,616	335	401	183	412	690	403	192	456	0	489	146
Maine...........................	11,180	10,342	6,905	3,098	361	339	216	554	1,004	451	173	340	0	606	232
Maryland......................	11,278	10,031	6,195	3,392	430	529	82	672	891	524	264	290	155	1,114	132
Massachusetts..................	12,619	11,642	7,410	3,896	713	558	204	502	1,086	482	352	336	0	659	317
Michigan	11,054	9,338	5,309	3,739	672	456	202	562	992	406	449	290	0	1,204	512
Minnesota	10,265	8,718	5,668	2,647	242	395	223	371	670	476	270	377	26	1,118	428
Mississippi	7,087	6,548	3,913	2,231	313	318	201	370	604	291	133	404	1	406	133
Missouri.......................	8,928	7,858	4,774	2,734	377	358	238	448	769	390	153	351	0	784	286
Montana.......................	8,638	8,133	4,963	2,831	436	312	247	455	816	366	197	328	11	431	73
Nebraska.....................	9,826	8,794	5,586	2,599	370	291	304	449	770	235	180	348	260	850	182
Nevada.........................	8,646	6,804	4,247	2,315	255	264	126	467	662	244	296	242	0	1,376	466
New Hampshire	10,799	9,771	6,332	3,149	658	299	331	535	827	413	87	290	0	792	236
New Jersey..................	15,934	14,117	8,359	5,311	1,267	468	354	960	1,422	761	79	328	119	1,584	233
New Mexico	9,368	7,834	4,387	3,092	776	362	241	489	752	336	136	350	4	1,414	120
New York......................	14,689	13,703	9,425	3,969	457	371	264	588	1,228	687	374	310	0	837	148
North Carolina	8,038	7,098	4,419	2,291	382	281	138	463	570	264	191	388	0	690	250
North Dakota	9,263	8,279	5,080	2,540	324	231	383	381	690	352	178	420	239	879	105
Ohio.............................	10,663	9,330	5,335	3,688	558	595	269	593	844	422	407	306	1	1,117	216
Oklahoma	7,216	6,610	3,755	2,408	433	264	195	355	756	211	193	378	69	545	61
Oregon.........................	9,116	8,069	4,742	3,036	554	310	113	512	677	356	514	288	4	659	388
Pennsylvania................	11,723	10,235	6,313	3,529	492	394	315	450	1,046	483	349	352	41	1,066	421
Rhode Island	11,978	11,667	7,247	4,128	1,182	551	143	583	938	438	292	293	0	131	180
South Carolina..................	9,182	7,549	4,465	2,684	521	505	92	433	691	233	210	374	26	1,320	312
South Dakota....................	8,643	7,464	4,335	2,712	413	338	272	371	780	254	283	389	28	1,014	165
Tennessee	7,521	6,850	4,422	2,095	229	381	134	377	617	243	114	333	0	498	173
Texas	8,891	7,246	4,324	2,540	354	405	115	405	801	198	262	382	0	1,269	376
Utah	6,301	5,216	3,302	1,593	192	253	60	320	483	168	117	279	43	936	148
Vermont	12,763	11,972	7,648	3,995	865	448	300	813	935	393	241	314	15	644	147
Virginia.........................	10,030	8,886	5,449	3,071	422	566	134	522	858	430	139	364	2	980	164
Washington...................	9,324	7,717	4,589	2,746	485	356	164	457	713	313	258	265	116	1,267	341
West Virginia................	9,271	9,024	5,461	3,064	317	307	238	493	930	635	143	498	0	187	60
Wisconsin	11,822	9,755	6,001	3,431	447	481	261	496	926	369	451	323	0	527	1,540
Wyoming.......................	12,110	10,190	6,031	3,833	601	542	218	561	1,093	450	368	323	3	1,870	50
Other jurisdictions															
American Samoa	3,871	3,607	1,807	1,072	154	291	38	142	321	42	84	728	0	264	0
Guam...........................	—	—	—	—	—	—	—	—	—	—	—	—	—	—	—
Northern Marianas........	5,161	5,034	4,229	500	91	15	360	0	0	14	22	38	266	127	0
Puerto Rico..................	5,099	4,979	3,624	916	103	116	12	0	404	96	185	438	0	120	0
U.S. Virgin Islands.........	9,079	8,387	5,543	2,614	486	230	386	495	593	262	161	188	42	692	0

—Not available.

[1]Excludes "Other current expenditures," such as community services, private school programs, adult education, and other programs not allocable to expenditures per pupil in public schools.

[2]Includes expenditures for property and for buildings and alterations completed by school district staff or contractors.

[3]Includes expenditures for operations funded by sales of products or services (e.g., school bookstore or computer time).

[4]Includes expenditures for health, attendance, and speech pathology services.

[5]Includes expenditures for curriculum development, staff training, libraries, and media and computer centers.

NOTE: Excludes expenditures for state education agencies. "0" indicates none or less than $0.50. Some data have been revised from previously published figures. Detail may not sum to totals because of rounding.

SOURCE: U.S. Department of Education, National Center for Education Statistics, Common Core of Data (CCD), "National Public Education Financial Survey," 2004–05. (This table was prepared April 2008.)

Table 184. Current expenditure per pupil in fall enrollment in public elementary and secondary schools, by state or jurisdiction: Selected years, 1969–70 through 2005–06

State or jurisdiction	Unadjusted dollars													
	1969–70	1979–80	1989–90	1994–95	1995–96	1997–98	1998–99	1999–2000	2000–01	2001–02	2002–03	2003–04	2004–05	2005–06
1	2	3	4	5	6	7	8	9	10	11	12	13	14	15
United States	$751	$2,088	$4,643	$5,529	$5,689	$6,189	$6,508	$6,912	$7,380	$7,727	$8,044	$8,310	$8,711	$9,154
Alabama	512	1,520	3,144	4,109	4,343	4,849	5,188	5,638	5,885	6,029	6,300	6,581	7,073	7,683
Alaska.........................	1,059	4,267	7,577	8,033	8,189	8,271	8,404	8,806	9,216	9,564	9,870	10,116	10,847	11,476
Arizona	674	1,865	3,717	4,264	4,476	4,595	4,672	5,030	5,521	5,851	6,283	5,999	6,307	6,515
Arkansas.....................	511	1,472	3,229	4,186	4,401	4,708	4,956	5,277	5,568	6,276	6,482	6,842	7,659	8,030
California	833	2,227	4,502	4,799	4,937	5,644	5,801	6,314	6,987	7,405	7,552	7,673	7,905	8,301
Colorado......................	686	2,258	4,357	5,047	5,121	5,656	5,923	6,215	6,567	6,941	7,384	7,478	7,826	8,166
Connecticut..................	911	2,167	7,463	8,380	8,430	8,901	9,318	9,753	10,127	10,577	11,057	11,436	12,263	13,072
Delaware......................	833	2,587	5,326	6,502	6,696	7,420	7,706	8,310	8,958	9,285	9,693	10,212	10,911	11,621
District of Columbia	947	2,811	7,872	8,290	8,510	8,393	9,650	10,107	12,046	12,102	11,847	12,959	13,915	13,752
Florida.........................	683	1,834	4,597	5,220	5,275	5,552	5,790	5,831	6,170	6,213	6,439	6,793	7,215	7,812
Georgia	539	1,491	4,000	4,828	5,056	5,647	6,092	6,437	6,929	7,380	7,774	7,742	8,065	8,595
Hawaii.........................	792	2,086	4,130	5,597	5,560	5,858	6,081	6,530	6,596	7,306	8,100	8,533	8,997	9,876
Idaho..........................	573	1,548	2,921	3,957	4,194	4,721	5,066	5,315	5,725	6,011	6,081	6,168	6,319	6,469
Illinois.........................	816	2,241	4,521	5,553	5,519	6,242	6,762	7,133	7,631	7,956	8,287	8,606	8,896	9,113
Indiana........................	661	1,708	4,270	5,411	5,621	6,318	6,772	7,192	7,630	7,734	8,057	8,431	8,919	8,929
Iowa	798	2,164	4,190	5,240	5,481	5,998	6,243	6,564	6,930	7,338	7,574	7,626	7,962	8,355
Kansas........................	699	1,963	4,290	5,222	5,374	5,727	6,015	6,294	6,937	7,339	7,454	7,776	7,926	8,640
Kentucky	502	1,557	3,384	4,545	4,807	5,213	5,637	5,921	6,079	6,523	6,661	6,864	7,132	7,668
Louisiana.....................	589	1,629	3,625	4,356	4,447	5,187	5,548	5,804	6,037	6,567	6,922	7,271	7,669	8,486
Maine	649	1,692	4,903	6,029	6,151	6,742	7,155	7,667	8,232	8,818	9,344	9,746	10,342	10,841
Maryland......................	809	2,293	5,573	6,427	6,593	7,034	7,326	7,731	8,260	8,692	9,153	9,433	10,031	10,909
Massachusetts..............	791	2,548	5,766	6,783	7,033	7,778	8,260	8,816	9,509	10,232	10,460	11,015	11,642	12,564
Michigan	841	2,495	5,090	6,465	6,785	7,050	7,432	8,110	8,278	8,653	8,781	9,094	9,338	9,575
Minnesota	855	2,296	4,698	5,626	5,801	6,388	6,814	7,190	7,645	7,736	8,109	8,405	8,718	9,159
Mississippi	457	1,568	2,934	3,798	3,951	4,288	4,565	5,014	5,175	5,354	5,792	6,199	6,548	7,173
Missouri.......................	596	1,724	4,071	4,866	5,092	5,565	5,855	6,187	6,657	7,136	7,495	7,542	7,858	8,273
Montana.......................	728	2,264	4,240	5,137	5,249	5,724	5,974	6,314	6,726	7,062	7,496	7,825	8,133	8,626
Nebraska	700	2,025	4,553	5,555	5,688	5,958	6,256	6,683	7,223	7,741	8,074	8,452	8,794	9,324
Nevada	706	1,908	3,816	4,730	4,892	5,295	5,587	5,760	5,807	6,079	6,092	6,410	6,804	7,177
New Hampshire	666	1,732	4,786	5,567	5,740	6,156	6,433	6,860	7,286	7,935	8,579	9,161	9,771	10,396
New Jersey...................	924	2,825	7,546	9,178	9,361	9,643	10,145	10,337	11,248	11,793	12,568	13,338	14,117	14,954
New Mexico	665	1,870	3,446	4,404	4,604	5,005	5,440	5,825	6,313	6,882	7,125	7,572	7,834	8,354
New York......................	1,194	2,950	7,051	8,311	8,361	8,852	9,344	9,846	10,716	11,218	11,961	12,638	13,703	14,615
North Carolina	570	1,635	4,018	4,703	4,719	5,257	5,656	6,045	6,340	6,495	6,562	6,613	7,098	7,396
North Dakota	662	1,941	3,899	4,482	4,677	5,056	5,442	5,667	6,125	6,709	6,870	7,333	8,279	8,728
Ohio............................	677	1,894	4,531	5,529	5,669	6,198	6,590	7,065	7,571	8,069	8,632	9,029	9,330	9,692
Oklahoma	554	1,810	3,293	4,533	4,549	5,033	5,303	5,395	6,019	6,229	6,092	6,154	6,610	6,941
Oregon........................	843	2,412	4,864	5,649	5,790	6,419	6,828	7,149	7,528	7,642	7,491	7,618	8,069	8,645
Pennsylvania................	815	2,328	5,737	6,565	6,922	7,209	7,450	7,772	8,210	8,537	8,997	9,708	10,235	10,723
Rhode Island	807	2,340	5,908	7,126	7,304	7,928	8,294	8,904	9,315	9,703	10,349	11,078	11,667	12,609
South Carolina	567	1,597	3,769	4,501	4,779	5,320	5,656	6,130	6,631	7,017	7,040	7,177	7,549	8,120
South Dakota................	656	1,781	3,511	4,271	4,220	4,669	5,259	5,632	6,191	6,424	6,547	7,068	7,464	7,775
Tennessee	531	1,523	3,405	4,017	4,172	4,937	5,123	5,383	5,687	5,948	6,118	6,466	6,850	7,004
Texas..........................	551	1,740	3,835	4,779	5,016	5,444	5,685	6,288	6,539	6,771	7,136	7,151	7,246	7,480
Utah............................	595	1,556	2,577	3,409	3,604	3,969	4,210	4,378	4,674	4,899	4,838	4,991	5,216	5,464
Vermont.......................	790	1,930	5,770	6,367	6,488	7,075	7,541	8,323	9,153	9,806	10,454	11,211	11,972	12,805
Virginia........................	654	1,824	4,690	5,421	5,528	6,065	6,350	6,841	7,281	7,496	7,822	8,219	8,886	9,452
Washington...................	853	2,387	4,382	5,477	5,639	6,040	6,110	6,376	6,750	7,039	7,252	7,391	7,717	7,984
West Virginia.................	621	1,749	4,020	5,663	5,881	6,323	6,677	7,152	7,534	7,844	8,319	8,588	9,024	9,440
Wisconsin	793	2,225	5,020	6,301	6,517	7,123	7,527	7,806	8,243	8,634	9,004	9,240	9,755	9,993
Wyoming......................	805	2,369	5,239	5,753	5,826	6,218	6,842	7,425	7,835	8,645	8,985	9,308	10,190	11,437
Other jurisdictions														
American Samoa	—	—	1,781	1,983	2,084	2,175	2,283	2,739	2,588	2,906	2,976	3,493	3,607	3,561
Guam..........................	766	—	3,817	5,016	4,803	5,200	—	—	—	—	—	5,781	—	6,781
Northern Marianas...........	—	—	3,356	5,340	4,999	6,112	5,312	5,120	4,913	4,438	4,519	4,241	5,034	4,924
Puerto Rico...................	—	—	1,605	2,417	2,657	3,211	3,298	3,404	3,685	3,563	4,260	4,147	4,979	5,470
U.S. Virgin Islands...........	—	—	6,043	5,280	5,378	5,932	6,983	6,478	6,437	5,716	6,840	7,239	8,387	8,768

See notes at end of table.

Table 184. Current expenditure per pupil in fall enrollment in public elementary and secondary schools, by state or jurisdiction: Selected years, 1969–70 through 2005–06—Continued

State or jurisdiction	Constant 2006–07 dollars[1]													
	1969–70	1979–80	1989–90	1994–95	1995–96	1997–98	1998–99	1999–2000	2000–01	2001–02	2002–03	2003–04	2004–05	2005–06
1	16	17	18	19	20	21	22	23	24	25	26	27	28	29
United States	$4,060	$5,492	$7,464	$7,504	$7,517	$7,811	$8,074	$8,335	$8,604	$8,853	$9,017	$9,116	$9,276	$9,391
Alabama	2,765	3,998	5,054	5,577	5,738	6,120	6,436	6,798	6,861	6,907	7,062	7,220	7,532	7,882
Alaska	5,724	11,220	12,182	10,903	10,820	10,439	10,426	10,619	10,745	10,956	11,064	11,097	11,551	11,773
Arizona	3,644	4,904	5,976	5,788	5,914	5,800	5,797	6,065	6,437	6,703	7,043	6,581	6,716	6,683
Arkansas.....................	2,761	3,870	5,191	5,682	5,815	5,942	6,148	6,364	6,491	7,190	7,266	7,505	8,156	8,238
California	4,504	5,855	7,239	6,513	6,524	7,124	7,198	7,614	8,147	8,483	8,466	8,417	8,418	8,516
Colorado	3,707	5,937	7,005	6,850	6,766	7,139	7,348	7,494	7,657	7,951	8,277	8,203	8,334	8,377
Connecticut..................	4,922	5,698	11,998	11,374	11,138	11,235	11,561	11,760	11,807	12,117	12,395	12,545	13,059	13,410
Delaware......................	4,504	6,802	8,563	8,824	8,847	9,365	9,560	10,020	10,444	10,636	10,866	11,202	11,619	11,922
District of Columbia	5,117	7,393	12,655	11,252	11,244	10,593	11,972	12,187	14,045	13,865	13,280	14,216	14,819	14,107
Florida.........................	3,689	4,823	7,391	7,084	6,970	7,008	7,183	7,031	7,194	7,118	7,218	7,452	7,683	8,014
Georgia.......................	2,912	3,921	6,431	6,553	6,681	7,127	7,558	7,762	8,078	8,455	8,715	8,493	8,589	8,818
Hawaii	4,280	5,486	6,640	7,597	7,346	7,393	7,545	7,874	7,690	8,370	9,080	9,361	9,581	10,131
Idaho...........................	3,098	4,071	4,696	5,370	5,542	5,958	6,285	6,409	6,674	6,886	6,817	6,766	6,729	6,637
Illinois.........................	4,408	5,893	7,268	7,537	7,292	7,878	8,390	8,601	8,897	9,115	9,289	9,441	9,473	9,349
Indiana........................	3,573	4,492	6,865	7,344	7,428	7,974	8,402	8,673	8,896	8,861	9,032	9,249	9,498	9,160
Iowa............................	4,313	5,691	6,736	7,112	7,242	7,570	7,746	7,915	8,080	8,407	8,490	8,365	8,479	8,571
Kansas........................	3,776	5,161	6,897	7,088	7,100	7,228	7,462	7,589	8,088	8,408	8,356	8,530	8,440	8,863
Kentucky	2,713	4,095	5,440	6,168	6,351	6,579	6,994	7,140	7,087	7,473	7,467	7,530	7,595	7,867
Louisiana	3,185	4,283	5,828	5,912	5,876	6,546	6,883	6,999	7,038	7,523	7,760	7,976	8,167	8,705
Maine	3,508	4,449	7,883	8,182	8,128	8,509	8,877	9,246	9,598	10,102	10,474	10,691	11,014	11,121
Maryland......................	4,373	6,029	8,960	8,723	8,712	8,878	9,089	9,323	9,630	9,958	10,260	10,348	10,682	11,191
Massachusetts..............	4,273	6,699	9,270	9,206	9,293	9,817	10,247	10,631	11,086	11,722	11,725	12,083	12,398	12,888
Michigan	4,547	6,562	8,183	8,775	8,965	8,898	9,221	9,779	9,651	9,913	9,843	9,975	9,945	9,822
Minnesota	4,620	6,039	7,553	7,636	7,665	8,062	8,454	8,670	8,913	8,863	9,090	9,220	9,284	9,396
Mississippi	2,468	4,124	4,716	5,154	5,220	5,412	5,663	6,046	6,033	6,133	6,493	6,800	6,973	7,358
Missouri.......................	3,221	4,533	6,544	6,605	6,728	7,024	7,264	7,460	7,761	8,175	8,401	8,273	8,368	8,487
Montana.......................	3,932	5,952	6,816	6,972	6,935	7,224	7,411	7,613	7,842	8,090	8,402	8,583	8,661	8,849
Nebraska	3,782	5,323	7,319	7,540	7,516	7,520	7,761	8,059	8,422	8,868	9,050	9,272	9,365	9,565
Nevada	3,814	5,018	6,134	6,420	6,464	6,683	6,932	6,945	6,770	6,964	6,829	7,032	7,246	7,363
New Hampshire	3,600	4,555	7,694	7,556	7,584	7,770	7,981	8,272	8,494	9,091	9,617	10,050	10,405	10,665
New Jersey,...................	4,992	7,429	12,131	12,457	12,368	12,171	12,587	12,465	13,114	13,511	14,088	14,632	15,033	15,341
New Mexico	3,594	4,918	5,540	5,977	6,083	6,316	6,749	7,024	7,360	7,885	7,987	8,306	8,342	8,570
New York	6,454	7,758	11,335	11,280	11,048	11,172	11,593	11,873	12,493	12,851	13,408	13,864	14,593	14,993
North Carolina	3,082	4,300	6,460	6,383	6,235	6,635	7,018	7,290	7,392	7,441	7,356	7,254	7,558	7,587
North Dakota	3,580	5,105	6,269	6,083	6,180	6,381	6,752	6,833	7,141	7,686	7,701	8,044	8,817	8,953
Ohio............................	3,656	4,981	7,284	7,504	7,490	7,823	8,175	8,519	8,827	9,244	9,676	9,905	9,936	9,942
Oklahoma	2,993	4,758	5,294	6,152	6,011	6,352	6,579	6,505	7,018	7,136	6,829	6,751	7,039	7,121
Oregon........................	4,557	6,343	7,821	7,667	7,651	8,101	8,471	8,620	8,777	8,755	8,398	8,357	8,593	8,869
Pennsylvania................	4,406	6,123	9,224	8,910	9,146	9,098	9,243	9,372	9,572	9,780	10,085	10,650	10,900	11,001
Rhode Island	4,360	6,154	9,499	9,671	9,651	10,007	10,290	10,737	10,860	11,115	11,601	12,152	12,425	12,935
South Carolina..............	3,066	4,200	6,060	6,110	6,315	6,714	7,017	7,392	7,731	8,039	7,891	7,872	8,039	8,330
South Dakota................	3,546	4,682	5,645	5,797	5,576	5,893	6,524	6,791	7,218	7,359	7,339	7,754	7,949	7,976
Tennessee	2,869	4,005	5,474	5,452	5,512	6,232	6,356	6,491	6,630	6,814	6,858	7,093	7,295	7,185
Texas	2,978	4,575	6,165	6,486	6,628	6,871	7,053	7,582	7,624	7,757	8,000	7,844	7,716	7,674
Utah	3,216	4,092	4,143	4,626	4,763	5,009	5,223	5,279	5,449	5,613	5,423	5,475	5,555	5,606
Vermont	4,267	5,075	9,277	8,641	8,572	8,929	9,355	10,036	10,671	11,234	11,719	12,298	12,749	13,136
Virginia........................	3,537	4,797	7,540	7,357	7,304	7,655	7,878	8,249	8,489	8,587	8,768	9,016	9,463	9,696
Washington...................	4,610	6,277	7,046	7,433	7,451	7,623	7,580	7,689	7,870	8,064	8,130	8,108	8,218	8,191
West Virginia.................	3,358	4,598	6,463	7,687	7,770	7,981	8,284	8,624	8,784	8,986	9,326	9,421	9,609	9,685
Wisconsin	4,286	5,850	8,070	8,551	8,611	8,990	9,339	9,413	9,610	9,891	10,093	10,136	10,388	10,251
Wyoming......................	4,350	6,230	8,423	7,809	7,698	7,848	8,488	8,954	9,135	9,903	10,072	10,211	10,852	11,732
Other jurisdictions														
American Samoa	—	—	2,864	2,691	2,754	2,745	2,832	3,303	3,018	3,329	3,336	3,832	3,841	3,653
Guam	4,142	—	6,137	6,808	6,346	6,563	—	—	—	—	—	6,341	—	6,956
Northern Marianas...........	—	—	5,396	7,247	6,605	7,714	6,590	6,174	5,728	5,084	5,066	4,652	5,361	5,051
Puerto Rico	—	—	2,581	3,281	3,511	4,052	4,092	4,104	4,296	4,082	4,776	4,549	5,302	5,611
U.S. Virgin Islands.............	—	—	9,715	7,166	7,106	7,487	8,663	7,812	7,504	6,548	7,668	7,941	8,932	8,995

—Not available.
[1]Constant dollars based on the Consumer Price Index (CPI), prepared by the Bureau of Labor Statistics, U.S. Department of Labor, adjusted to a school-year basis. The CPI does not account for differences in inflation rates from state to state.
NOTE: Expenditures for state administration are excluded in all years except 1969–70 and 1979–80. Beginning in 1989–90, survey was expanded and coverage of state expenditures for public school districts was improved. Some data have been revised from previously published figures.
SOURCE: U.S. Department of Education, National Center for Education Statistics, *Statistics of State School Systems*, 1969–70; *Revenues and Expenditures for Public Elementary and Secondary Schools*, 1979–80; and Common Core of Data (CCD), "National Public Education Financial Survey," 1989–90 through 2005–06. (This table was prepared April 2008.)

Table 185. Current expenditure per pupil in average daily attendance in public elementary and secondary schools, by state or jurisdiction: Selected years, 1959–60 through 2005–06

State or jurisdiction	Unadjusted dollars													
	1959–60	1969–70	1979–80	1989–90	1995–96	1997–98	1998–99	1999–2000	2000–01	2001–02	2002–03	2003–04	2004–05	2005–06
1	2	3	4	5	6	7	8	9	10	11	12	13	14	15
United States	$375	$816	$2,272	$4,980	$6,147	$6,676	$7,013	$7,394	$7,904	$8,259	$8,610	$8,900	$9,316	$9,788
Alabama	241	544	1,612	3,327	4,716	5,166	5,512	5,758	6,052	6,327	6,642	6,812	7,309	7,980
Alaska.........................	546	1,123	4,728	8,431	9,012	9,074	9,209	9,668	9,998	10,419	10,770	11,074	11,851	12,537
Arizona	404	720	1,971	4,053	4,860	5,122	5,235	5,478	6,032	6,470	6,784	6,908	7,218	7,637
Arkansas......................	225	568	1,574	3,485	4,710	4,999	5,193	5,628	5,942	6,676	6,981	7,307	8,243	8,748
California	424 [2]	867	2,268	4,391	5,108	5,795	6,045	6,401	7,063	7,439	7,601	7,708	7,989	8,416
Colorado	396	738	2,421	4,720	5,521	6,099	6,386	6,702	7,082	7,284	7,826	8,416	8,558	8,938
Connecticut..................	436	951	2,420	7,837	8,817	9,218	9,620	10,122	10,525	11,022	11,302	11,755	12,655	13,461
Delaware......................	456	900	2,861	5,799	7,267	7,963	8,336	8,809	9,720	9,959	10,257	11,049	11,770	12,330
District of Columbia	431	1,018	3,259	8,955	9,565	9,225	10,611	11,935	13,204	14,557	14,735	15,414	15,074	17,877
Florida.........................	318	732	1,889	4,997	5,894	6,183	6,443	6,383	6,620	6,679	6,922	7,269	7,731	8,376
Georgia........................	253	588	1,625	4,275	5,377	6,059	6,534	6,903	7,431	7,870	8,308	8,278	8,577	9,164
Hawaii.........................	325	841	2,322	4,448	6,051	6,409	6,648	7,090	7,106	7,919	8,770	9,341	9,705	10,747
Idaho..........................	290	603	1,659	3,078	4,465	5,012	5,379	5,644	6,077	6,391	6,454	6,559	6,698	6,861
Illinois.........................	438	909	2,587	5,118	6,128	7,111	7,676	8,084	8,659	8,967	9,309	9,710	10,020	10,282
Indiana........................	369	728	1,882	4,606	6,040	6,786	7,249	7,652	8,128	8,268	8,582	9,033	9,640	9,558
Iowa	368	844	2,326	4,453	5,772	6,295	6,548	6,925	7,340	7,714	7,943	8,017	8,341	8,460
Kansas........................	348	771	2,173	4,752	5,971	6,406	6,708	6,962	7,681	8,342	8,373	8,804	9,037	9,905
Kentucky......................	233	545	1,701	3,745	5,545	6,125	6,501	6,784	7,174	7,536	7,728	7,976	8,379	8,975
Louisiana......................	372	648	1,792	3,903	4,988	5,644	6,019	6,256	6,553	7,061	7,492	7,846	8,288	8,568
Maine..........................	283	692	1,824	5,373	6,546	7,238	7,688	8,247	8,879	9,517	10,114	10,504	11,153	11,760
Maryland......................	393	918	2,598	6,275	7,382	7,812	7,865	8,273	8,833	9,266	9,801	10,140	10,790	11,719
Massachusetts................	409	859	2,819	6,237	7,613	8,299	8,750	9,375	10,073	10,808	11,161	11,583	12,208	13,128
Michigan......................	415	904	2,640	5,546	7,166	7,717	8,142	8,886	9,031	9,428	9,847	10,049	10,328	10,598
Minnesota.....................	425	904	2,387	4,971	6,162	6,795	7,183	7,499	7,960	8,050	8,440	8,934	9,273	9,761
Mississippi	206	501	1,664	3,094	4,250	4,575	4,871	5,356	5,535	5,719	6,186	6,601	6,994	7,699
Missouri.......................	344	709	1,936	4,507	5,626	6,096	6,393	6,764	7,265	7,700	8,002	8,022	8,360	8,834
Montana.......................	411	782	2,476	4,736	5,847	6,448	6,768	6,990	7,484	7,861	8,391	8,771	9,108	9,653
Nebraska	337	736	2,150	4,842	6,083	6,584	6,856	7,360	7,688	8,238	8,550	9,270	9,638	10,170
Nevada	430	769	2,088	4,117	5,320	5,758	5,934	6,148	6,150	6,477	6,496	6,780	7,198	7,720
New Hampshire	347	723	1,916	5,304	5,958	6,487	6,780	7,082	7,656	8,230	8,900	9,391	10,043	10,698
New Jersey	388	1,016	3,191	8,139	9,955	10,233	10,748	10,903	11,752	12,197	13,093	13,776	14,666	15,362
New Mexico	363	707	2,034	3,515	4,587	4,984	5,363	5,835	6,320	6,886	7,126	7,653	7,933	8,426
New York......................	562	1,327	3,462	8,062	9,549	9,970	10,514	10,957	11,887	12,343	13,211	13,926	15,054	16,095
North Carolina	237	612	1,754	4,290	5,090	5,667	6,088	6,505	6,817	6,970	7,057	7,114	7,628	7,940
North Dakota	367	690	1,920	4,189	4,979	5,353	5,820	6,078	6,467	7,112	7,315	7,791	8,776	9,239
Ohio	365	730	2,075	5,045	6,266	6,808	7,254	7,816	8,403	8,928	9,427	9,799	9,984	10,306
Oklahoma	311	604	1,926	3,508	4,881	5,389	5,684	5,770	6,458	6,672	6,540	6,599	7,086	7,449
Oregon........................	448	925	2,692	5,474	6,615	7,348	7,787	8,129	8,545	8,725	8,514	8,640	8,799	9,294
Pennsylvania..................	409	882	2,535	6,228	7,492	7,777	8,026	8,380	8,847	9,196	9,648	10,393	11,014	11,530
Rhode Island	413	891	2,601	6,368	7,936	8,627	9,049	9,646	10,116	10,552	11,377	12,279	12,685	13,917
South Carolina................	220	613	1,752	4,082	5,096	5,643	6,003	6,545	7,210	7,549	7,759	7,893	8,302	8,795
South Dakota.................	347	690	1,908	3,731	4,780	5,281	5,613	6,037	6,581	6,890	7,192	7,607	7,960	8,273
Tennessee	238	566	1,635	3,664	4,548	5,274	5,521	5,837	6,108	6,476	6,674	7,047	7,426	7,580
Texas..........................	332	624	1,916	4,150	5,473	5,910	6,161	6,771	7,039	7,302	7,714	7,711	7,814	8,085
Utah...........................	322	626	1,657	2,764	3,867	4,256	4,478	4,692	5,029	5,294	5,247	5,427	5,654	5,809
Vermont	344	807	1,997	6,227	6,837	7,500	7,984	8,799	9,559	10,229	10,903	11,675	12,579	13,377
Virginia........................	274	708	1,970	4,672	5,433	5,936	6,129	6,491	7,664	7,928	8,300	8,761	9,441	10,046
Washington....................	420	915	2,568	4,702	6,074	6,535	6,595	6,914	7,312	7,626	7,882	8,051	8,362	8,702
West Virginia..................	258	670	1,920	4,360	6,325	6,779	7,189	7,637	8,148	8,451	9,025	9,076	9,321	9,756
Wisconsin	413	883	2,477	5,524	7,094	7,680	8,062	8,299	8,797	9,237	9,538	9,834	10,141	10,484
Wyoming.......................	450	856	2,527	5,577	6,243	6,718	7,393	7,944	8,466	9,321	9,906	10,351	11,087	12,415
Other jurisdictions														
American Samoa	—	—	—	1,908	2,159	2,243	2,354	2,807	2,743	2,983	3,121	3,671	3,801	3,842
Guam..........................	236	820	—	4,234	4,947	5,286	—	—	—	—	—	6,449	—	7,095
Northern Marianas..........	—	—	—	3,007	5,863	7,016	5,973	5,720	5,481	4,934	5,221	4,746	5,669	5,307
Puerto Rico	106	—	—	1,750	3,039	3,648	3,771	3,859	4,191	4,013	4,743	4,534	5,304	5,897
U.S. Virgin Islands..........	271	—	—	6,767	6,155	6,758	7,714	7,238	7,795	6,248	7,747	8,077	8,698	9,637

See notes at end of table.

Table 185. Current expenditure per pupil in average daily attendance in public elementary and secondary schools, by state or jurisdiction: Selected years, 1959–60 through 2005–06—Continued

State or jurisdiction	Constant 2006-07 dollars[1]													
	1959–60	1969–70	1979–80	1989–90	1995–96	1997–98	1998–99	1999–2000	2000–01	2001–02	2002–03	2003–04	2004–05	2005–06
1	16	17	18	19	20	21	22	23	24	25	26	27	28	29
United States	$2,606	$4,410	$5,974	$8,006	$8,122	$8,425	$8,701	$8,915	$9,215	$9,461	$9,651	$9,763	$9,921	$10,041
Alabama	1,675	2,940	4,238	5,349	6,231	6,520	6,838	6,944	7,056	7,249	7,446	7,473	7,783	8,186
Alaska	3,796	6,066	12,431	13,555	11,907	11,453	11,425	11,658	11,656	11,936	12,072	12,148	12,621	12,861
Arizona	2,804	3,892	5,182	6,516	6,422	6,465	6,494	6,606	7,032	7,412	7,605	7,578	7,686	7,834
Arkansas	1,564	3,067	4,140	5,603	6,223	6,309	6,442	6,786	6,927	7,648	7,825	8,016	8,778	8,975
California	2,946 [2]	4,686	5,963	7,059	6,749	7,314	7,500	7,718	8,235	8,522	8,521	8,456	8,507	8,634
Colorado	2,752	3,987	6,366	7,589	7,295	7,698	7,923	8,081	8,256	8,344	8,773	9,232	9,113	9,169
Connecticut	3,030	5,141	6,364	12,599	11,650	11,635	11,935	12,205	12,270	12,627	12,669	12,895	13,477	13,809
Delaware	3,166	4,864	7,523	9,323	9,601	10,050	10,342	10,622	11,333	11,409	11,498	12,121	12,534	12,649
District of Columbia	2,995	5,503	8,570	14,397	12,638	11,643	13,164	14,391	15,395	16,676	16,518	16,909	16,053	18,339
Florida	2,207	3,957	4,967	8,034	7,788	7,804	7,993	7,697	7,718	7,651	7,759	7,974	8,232	8,593
Georgia	1,761	3,177	4,274	6,872	7,105	7,647	8,106	8,324	8,664	9,015	9,312	9,081	9,134	9,401
Hawaii	2,255	4,542	6,105	7,152	7,995	8,089	8,248	8,550	8,285	9,072	9,831	10,246	10,335	11,024
Idaho	2,013	3,260	4,363	4,948	5,899	6,326	6,673	6,806	7,085	7,321	7,235	7,195	7,133	7,039
Illinois	3,046	4,915	6,801	8,228	8,097	8,975	9,523	9,748	10,095	10,273	10,435	10,651	10,671	10,548
Indiana	2,561	3,934	4,950	7,406	7,980	8,565	8,993	9,227	9,476	9,472	9,620	9,909	9,909	9,805
Iowa	2,555	4,562	6,117	7,159	7,626	7,945	8,124	8,350	8,558	8,837	8,904	8,794	8,883	8,678
Kansas	2,416	4,166	5,714	7,639	7,890	8,085	8,322	8,395	8,955	9,557	9,386	9,658	9,623	10,161
Kentucky	1,619	2,946	4,473	6,021	7,327	7,730	8,065	8,181	8,364	8,633	8,663	8,749	8,923	9,207
Louisiana	2,584	3,502	4,712	6,276	6,590	7,123	7,468	7,543	7,640	8,090	8,398	8,607	8,826	8,790
Maine	1,964	3,742	4,795	8,638	8,649	9,135	9,539	9,944	10,352	10,903	11,337	11,523	11,877	12,064
Maryland	2,728	4,963	6,831	10,089	9,754	9,860	9,758	9,976	10,299	10,615	10,987	11,123	11,490	12,022
Massachusetts	2,841	4,642	7,413	10,027	10,060	10,475	10,856	11,305	11,744	12,382	12,512	12,706	13,001	13,467
Michigan	2,884	4,885	8,943	8,917	9,468	9,740	10,102	10,715	10,529	10,801	11,038	11,023	10,998	10,872
Minnesota	2,954	4,883	6,276	7,991	8,142	8,576	8,912	9,043	9,281	9,223	9,461	9,801	9,875	10,013
Mississippi	1,431	2,707	4,375	4,974	5,616	5,774	6,043	6,458	6,453	6,552	6,935	7,242	7,448	7,898
Missouri	2,390	3,829	5,091	7,246	7,434	7,694	7,932	8,156	8,470	8,821	8,970	8,800	8,903	9,063
Montana	2,854	4,225	6,512	7,615	7,725	8,138	8,397	8,429	8,726	9,006	9,406	9,621	9,700	9,902
Nebraska	2,341	3,980	5,653	7,784	8,037	8,310	8,506	8,874	8,963	9,437	9,584	10,169	10,264	10,433
Nevada	2,990	4,158	5,491	6,619	7,029	7,267	7,362	7,413	7,171	7,421	7,282	7,437	7,666	7,919
New Hampshire	2,412	3,907	5,038	8,527	7,872	8,188	8,411	8,540	8,926	9,429	9,976	10,301	10,695	10,975
New Jersey	2,692	5,492	8,392	13,085	13,154	12,915	13,335	13,147	13,701	13,973	14,677	15,112	15,618	15,759
New Mexico	2,520	3,821	5,348	5,651	6,060	6,290	6,664	7,036	7,369	7,889	7,988	8,395	8,448	8,644
New York	3,902	7,170	9,104	12,961	12,617	12,583	13,045	13,212	13,859	14,140	14,809	15,276	16,032	16,511
North Carolina	1,648	3,309	4,613	6,897	6,726	7,153	7,553	7,844	7,948	7,985	7,911	7,804	8,123	8,146
North Dakota	2,548	3,727	5,049	6,735	6,579	6,756	7,221	7,329	7,540	8,148	8,200	8,546	9,346	9,478
Ohio	2,536	3,945	5,455	8,110	8,279	8,592	9,000	9,425	9,797	10,228	10,567	10,749	10,632	10,572
Oklahoma	2,163	3,267	5,066	5,639	6,449	6,801	7,052	6,957	7,529	7,643	7,331	7,239	7,546	7,642
Oregon	3,115	4,997	7,078	8,801	8,740	9,273	9,661	9,802	9,963	9,995	9,543	9,477	9,371	9,534
Pennsylvania	2,845	4,765	6,665	10,013	9,898	9,815	9,957	10,105	10,315	10,535	10,815	11,401	11,729	11,828
Rhode Island	2,872	4,816	6,839	10,237	10,486	10,888	11,226	11,632	11,794	12,088	12,754	13,469	13,509	14,277
South Carolina	1,529	3,310	4,607	6,562	6,733	7,122	7,448	7,893	8,407	8,649	8,698	8,658	8,841	9,023
South Dakota	2,410	3,728	5,016	5,999	6,315	6,665	6,964	7,279	7,673	7,893	8,062	8,344	8,477	8,487
Tennessee	1,654	3,059	4,300	5,890	6,009	6,656	6,850	7,039	7,121	7,419	7,481	7,730	7,908	7,776
Texas	2,309	3,373	5,037	6,673	7,232	7,459	7,644	8,165	8,206	8,365	8,647	8,459	8,321	8,294
Utah	2,240	3,384	4,356	4,443	5,110	5,371	5,555	5,658	5,864	6,065	5,882	5,953	6,021	5,960
Vermont	2,389	4,362	5,251	10,011	9,034	9,466	9,905	10,610	11,144	11,718	12,222	12,808	13,396	13,723
Virginia	1,905	3,825	5,180	7,510	7,178	7,492	7,603	7,827	8,936	9,083	9,304	9,610	10,054	10,306
Washington	2,921	4,946	6,753	7,560	8,025	8,247	8,182	8,337	8,525	8,736	8,836	8,832	8,905	8,928
West Virginia	1,796	3,620	5,050	7,010	8,357	8,556	8,918	9,209	9,500	9,681	10,117	9,957	9,926	10,008
Wisconsin	2,870	4,770	6,513	8,880	9,373	9,693	10,003	10,007	10,257	10,582	10,691	10,787	10,799	10,755
Wyoming	3,129	4,626	6,644	8,967	8,249	8,479	9,172	9,579	9,870	10,678	11,105	11,354	11,807	12,736
Other jurisdictions														
American Samoa	—	—	—	3,067	2,852	2,831	2,921	3,385	3,198	3,417	3,498	4,027	4,048	3,941
Guam	1,642	4,430	—	6,808	6,537	6,672	—	—	—	—	—	7,074	---	7,278
Northern Marianas	—	—	—	4,835	7,747	8,855	7,411	6,897	6,390	5,652	5,852	5,206	6,037	5,444
Puerto Rico	738	—	—	2,813	4,015	4,605	4,678	4,653	4,886	4,597	5,316	4,974	5,648	6,050
U.S. Virgin Islands	1,880	—	—	10,880	8,133	8,530	9,570	8,728	9,088	7,158	8,684	8,861	9,263	9,886

—Not available.
[1]Constant dollars based on the Consumer Price Index (CPI), prepared by the Bureau of Labor Statistics, U.S. Department of Labor, adjusted to a school-year basis. The CPI does not account for differences in inflation rates from state to state.
[2]Estimated by the National Center for Education Statistics.
NOTE: State administration expenditures are excluded in all years except 1959–60, 1969–70, and 1979–80. Beginning in 1989–90, extensive changes were made in the data collection procedures. There are discrepancies in average daily attendance reporting practices from state to state. Some data have been revised from previously published figures.
SOURCE: U.S. Department of Education, National Center for Education Statistics, *Statistics of State School Systems*, 1959–60 and 1969–70; *Revenues and Expenditures for Public Elementary and Secondary Education*, 1979–80; and Common Core of Data (CCD), "National Public Education Financial Survey," 1989–90 through 2005–06. (This table was prepared April 2008.)

CHAPTER 3
Postsecondary Education

Postsecondary education includes an array of diverse educational experiences offered by American colleges and universities, and technical and vocational institutions. For example, a community college may offer vocational training or the first 2 years of training at the college level. A university typically offers a full undergraduate course of study leading to a bachelor's degree, as well as first-professional and graduate programs leading to advanced degrees. Vocational and technical institutions offer training programs that are designed to prepare students for specific careers. Community groups, religious organizations, libraries, and businesses provide other types of educational opportunities for adults.

This chapter provides an overview of the latest statistics on postsecondary education, which includes academic, vocational, and continuing professional education programs after high school. However, to maintain comparability over time, most of the data in the *Digest* are for degree-granting institutions, which are defined as postsecondary institutions that grant an associate's or higher degree and whose students are eligible to participate in the Title IV federal financial aid programs.[1] Degree-granting institutions include almost all 2- and 4-year colleges and universities; they exclude institutions offering only vocational programs of less than 2 years' duration and continuing education programs. The degree-granting institution classification is very similar to the higher education institution classification that the National Center for Education Statistics (NCES) used prior to 1996–97.[2] This chapter highlights historical data that enable the reader to observe long-range trends in college education in America.

Other chapters provide related information on postsecondary education. Data on price indexes and on the number of degrees held by the general population are shown in chapter 1. Chapter 4 contains tabulations on federal funding for postsecondary education. Information on employment outcomes for college graduates is shown in chapter 5. Chapter 7 contains data on college libraries and use of computers by young adults. Further information on survey methodologies is presented in Appendix A: Guide to Sources and in the publications cited in the table source notes.

Enrollment

Enrollment in degree-granting institutions increased by 14 percent between 1987 and 1997 (table 188 and figure 11). Between 1997 and 2007, enrollment increased at a faster rate (26 percent), from 14.5 million to 18.2 million. Much of the growth between 1997 and 2007 was in full-time enrollment; the number of full-time students rose 34 percent, while the number of part-time students rose 15 percent. During the same time period, the number of females rose 29 percent, compared to an increase of 22 percent in the number of males. Enrollment increases can be affected both by population growth and by rising rates of enrollment. Between 1997 and 2007, the number of 18- to 24-year-olds increased from 25.5 million to 29.5 million, an increase of 16 percent (table 15), and the percentage of 18- to 24-year-olds enrolled in college remained relatively stable (37 percent in 1997 and 39 percent in 2007) (table 204). In addition to the enrollment in accredited 2-year colleges, 4-year colleges, and universities, about 447,000 students attended non-degree-granting, Title IV eligible, postsecondary institutions in fall 2006 (table 186).

The number of young students has been growing more rapidly than the number of older students, but this pattern is expected to shift (table 190 and figure 13). Between 1995 and 2006, the enrollment of students under age 25 increased by 33 percent. Enrollment of people 25 and over rose by 13 percent during the same period. From 2006 to 2017, NCES projects a rise of 10 percent in enrollments of people under 25, and a rise of 19 percent in enrollments of people 25 and over.

Enrollment trends have differed at the undergraduate, graduate, and first-professional levels. Undergraduate enrollment generally increased during the 1970s, but dipped from 10.8 million to 10.6 million between 1983 and 1985 (table 205). From 1985 to 1992, undergraduate enrollment increased each year, rising 18 percent before declining 2 percent and stabilizing between 1993 and 1996. Undergraduate enrollment rose 25 percent between 1997 and 2007. Graduate enrollment had been steady at about 1.3 million in the late 1970s and early 1980s, but rose about 67 percent between 1985 and 2007

---

[1] Title IV programs, which are administered by the U.S. Department of Education, provide financial aid to postsecondary students.

[2] Included among degree-granting institutions are some institutions (primarily 2-year colleges) that were not previously designated as higher education institutions. Excluded from degree-granting institutions are a few institutions that were previously designated as higher education institutions even though they did not award an associate's or higher degree. Institutions of higher education were accredited by an agency or association that was recognized by the U.S. Department of Education, or recognized directly by the Secretary of Education. Institutions of higher education offered courses that led to an associate's or higher degree, or were accepted for credit towards a degree.

(table 206). After rising 60 percent between 1970 and 1980, enrollment in first-professional programs stabilized in the 1980s (table 207). First-professional enrollment began rising again in the 1990s and showed an increase of 18 percent between 1997 and 2007.

Since 1984, the number of females in graduate schools has exceeded the number of males (table 206). Between 1997 and 2007, the number of male full-time graduate students increased by 32 percent, compared to a 63 percent increase for female graduate students. Among part-time graduate students, the number of males increased by 10 percent and the number of females increased by 23 percent.

The percentage of American college students who are minorities has been increasing. In 1976, 15 percent were minorities, compared with 32 percent in 2007 (table 226). Much of the change from 1976 to 2007 can be attributed to rising numbers of Hispanic and Asian or Pacific Islander students. During that time period, the percentage of Asian or Pacific Islander students rose from 2 percent to 7 percent and the Hispanic percentage rose from 4 percent to 11 percent. The percentage of Black students was 9 percent at the beginning of the time period and it fluctuated during the early part of the period before rising to 13 percent in 2007. Nonresident aliens for whom race/ethnicity is not reported made up 3 percent of the total enrollment in 2007.

Despite the sizable numbers of small degree-granting colleges, most students attend the larger colleges and universities. In fall 2006, 41 percent of institutions had fewer than 1,000 students; however, these campuses enrolled 4 percent of college students (table 234). While 12 percent of the campuses enrolled 10,000 or more students, they accounted for 55 percent of total college enrollment.

In 2006, the five colleges with the highest enrollment were University of Phoenix Online Campus, with 165,373 students; Ohio State University, with 51,818 students; Miami-Dade College, with 51,329 students; Arizona State University at the Tempe Campus, with 51,234 students; and the University of Florida, with 50,912 students (table 236).

Faculty, Staff, and Salaries

Approximately 3.6 million people were employed in colleges and universities in the fall of 2007, including 2.6 million professional and 0.9 million nonprofessional staff (table 245). In the fall of 2007, there were 1.4 million faculty members in degree-granting institutions, including 0.7 million full-time and 0.7 million part-time faculty. The proportion of executive, administrative, and managerial staff was 6 percent in 2007, compared to 5 percent in 1976 (table 244). The proportion of other non-teaching professional staff rose from 10 percent in 1976 to 20 percent in 2007, while the proportion of nonprofessional staff (including technical and paraprofessional, clerical and secretarial, skilled crafts, and service and maintenance staff) declined from 42 percent to 26 percent. The full-time-equivalent (FTE) student/FTE staff ratio at colleges and universities was lower in 2007 (5.0) than in 1976 (5.4). The FTE student/FTE faculty ratio declined from 16.6 in 1976 to 14.9 in 2007.

Colleges differ in their practices of employing part-time and full-time staff. In fall 2007, 48 percent of the employees at public 2-year colleges were employed full time, compared with 68 percent at public 4-year colleges and universities, 67 percent at private 4-year colleges and universities, and 66 percent at private 2-year colleges (table 245). A higher percentage of the faculty at public 4-year colleges and universities were employed full time (68 percent) than at private 4-year colleges and universities (48 percent), private 2-year colleges (46 percent), or public 2-year colleges (31 percent). In general, the number of full-time staff has been growing at a slower rate than the number of part-time staff (table 243). Between 1997 and 2007, the number of full-time staff increased by 25 percent compared to an increase of 39 percent in the number of part-time staff. Most of the increase in the part-time staff was due to the increase in the number of part-time faculty (59 percent) and instruction and research assistants (48 percent) during this time period.

In fall 2007, minorities made up 17 percent of U.S. faculty (based on a total faculty count excluding persons whose race/ethnicity was unknown) (table 246). Seven percent of the faculty were Black, 6 percent were Asian/Pacific Islander, 4 percent were Hispanic, and 1 percent were American Indian/Alaska Native. About four-fifths of the faculty were White, with 43 percent being White males and 36 percent being White females. Minorities made up about 18 percent of executive, administrative, and managerial staff in 2007 and about 33 percent of nonprofessional staff. The proportions of minority staff at public 4-year colleges (23 percent), private 4-year colleges (22 percent), and public 2-year colleges (22 percent) were similar, with the proportion at private 2-year colleges (27 percent) being slightly higher.

On average, full-time instructional faculty and staff spent 58 percent of their time teaching in 2003 (table 250). Research and scholarship accounted for 20 percent of their time, and 22 percent was spent on other activities (administration, professional growth, etc.).

Faculty salaries generally lost purchasing power from 1972–73 to 1980–81, when average salaries for faculty on 9-month contracts declined 17 percent after adjustment for inflation (table 257). During the 1980s, average salaries rose and recouped most of the losses. Between 1997–98 and 2007–08, there was a further increase in average faculty salaries, resulting in an average of about 4 percent higher than the 1972–73 average, after adjustment for inflation. The average salary in current dollars for males in 2007–08 ($76,935) was higher than the average for females ($63,347). Between 1997–98 and 2007–08, the average salary for males increased by 5 percent and the average salary for females increased by 6 percent, after adjustment for inflation.

The percentage of faculty with tenure has declined in recent years. About 50 percent of full-time instructional faculty had tenure in 2005–06, compared with 56 percent in 1993–94 (table 264). A difference existed between the percentage of males and females with tenure. Fifty-five percent of males compared to 41 percent of females had tenure in 2005–06. About 52 percent of the instructional faculty at public institutions had tenure, compared to 45 percent of faculty at private not-for-profit institutions.

Degrees

During the 2007–08 academic year, 4,352 accredited institutions offered degrees at the associate's degree level or above (table 266). These included 2,675 4-year institutions and 1,677 2-year institutions. Institutions awarding various degrees in 2006–07 numbered 2,725 for associate's degrees, 2,256 for bachelor's degrees, 1,695 for master's degrees, and 648 for doctor's degrees (table 278).

Growing numbers of people are completing college degrees. Between 1996–97 and 2006–07, the number of associate's, bachelor's, master's, first-professional, and doctor's degrees rose (table 268). During this period, associate's degrees increased 27 percent, bachelor's degrees increased 30 percent, master's degrees increased 44 percent, first-professional degrees increased 14 percent, and doctor's degrees increased 32 percent. Since the mid-1980s, more females than males have earned associate's, bachelor's, and master's degrees. In 2006–07, the number of females earning doctor's degrees exceeded the number of males. Also, the number of females receiving all types of degrees has increased at a faster rate than the number for males. Between 1996–97 and 2006–07, the number of bachelor's degrees awarded to males increased by 25 percent, while the number awarded to females increased by 34 percent. The number of males earning doctor's degrees was about 11 percent higher in 2006–07 than in 1996–97, while the number of females earning doctor's degrees rose by 62 percent.

Of the 1,524,000 bachelor's degrees conferred in 2006–07, the largest numbers of degrees were conferred in the fields of business (328,000), social sciences and history (164,000), education (106,000), and health sciences (102,000) (table 271). At the master's degree level, the largest numbers of degrees were in the fields of education (177,000) and business (150,000) (table 272). The fields with the largest number of degrees at the doctor's degree level were health professions and related clinical sciences (8,400), education (8,300), engineering (8,100), biological and biomedical sciences (6,400), psychology (5,200), and physical sciences (4,800) (table 273).

In recent years, the numbers of bachelor's degrees conferred have followed patterns that differed significantly by field of study. While the number of degrees increased 30 percent overall between 1996–97 and 2006–07, there was substantial variation among the different fields of study, as well as shifts in the patterns of change during this time period (table 271). The number of bachelor's degrees conferred in the combined fields of engineering and engineering technologies declined 1 percent between 1996–97 and 2001–02, but then rose 10 percent between 2001–02 and 2006–07 (table 271 and figure 15). The number of engineering and engineering technologies degrees conferred in 2006–07 was about 8 percent higher than the number conferred in 1996–97. The number of degrees in the health professions declined by 17 percent between 1996–97 and 2001–02, but then rose 40 percent between 2001–02 and 2006–07. Similarly, the number of degrees in biological sciences decreased 7 percent between 1996–97 and 2001–02, but then increased 26 percent between

2001–02 and 2006–07; and the number in the physical sciences declined by 9 percent between 1996–97 and 2001–02, but increased 18 percent between 2001–02 and 2006–07. Some technical fields experienced a contrasting pattern. After an increase of 98 percent between 1996–97 and 2001–02, the number of degrees in computer and information sciences decreased 16 percent between 2001–02 and 2006–07. Other fields with sizable numbers of degrees (over 5,000) that showed increases of over 30 percent between 2001–02 and 2006–07 included security and protective services (54 percent); parks, recreation, and leisure studies (45 percent); and transportation and materials moving (41 percent).

Fifty-eight percent of the students who enrolled in a 4-year college or university as first-time freshmen in 1995–96 had completed a bachelor's degree by 2001 (table 329). About 7 percent of students had completed a certificate or associate's degree, 14 percent were still enrolled without having received a degree, and 21 percent were no longer working toward a bachelor's degree.

Finances

For the 2007–08 academic year, annual prices for undergraduate tuition, room, and board were estimated to be $11,164 at public institutions and $28,846 at private institutions (table 331). Between 1997–98 and 2007–08, prices for undergraduate tuition, room, and board at public institutions rose by 30 percent, and prices at private institutions rose by 23 percent, after adjustment for inflation.

In 2005–06, average total expenditures per full-time-equivalent (FTE) student at public degree-granting colleges were $24,126 (table 362). This total reflects an increase of about 2 percent between 2003–04 and 2005–06, after adjustment for inflation. In 2005–06, public 4-year colleges had average total expenditures per FTE student of $32,483, compared to $11,053 at public 2-year colleges. At private not-for-profit colleges, total expenditures per FTE student rose 15 percent between 1996–97 and 2005–06, after adjustment for inflation (table 364). In 2005–06, total expenditures per FTE student at private not-for-profit colleges were $40,156, with an average of $40,394 at 4-year colleges and $18,240 at 2-year colleges. The expenditures per FTE student at for-profit institutions were $11,336 in 2005–06, which was about 3 percent lower than in 1998–99, after adjustment for inflation (table 366). The difference between average expenditures per FTE student at for-profit 4-year colleges ($10,897) and for-profit 2-year colleges ($12,558) was relatively small compared to the differences at 2-year versus 4-year public and private not-for-profit colleges.

As of June 30, 2007, the market value of the endowment funds of the 120 colleges and universities with the largest endowment amounts was $322 billion, reflecting an increase of 18 percent compared to 2006, after adjustment for inflation (tables 31 and 359). The five colleges with the largest endowments in 2007 were Harvard University, Yale University, Stanford University, Princeton University, and University of Texas System.

Figure 11. Enrollment, degrees conferred, and expenditures in degree-granting institutions: 1960–61 through 2006–07

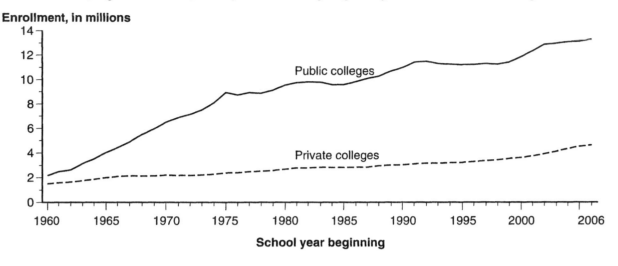

Enrollment, in millions

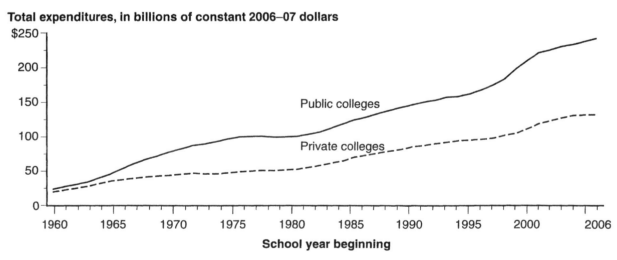

Degrees, in millions

Total expenditures, in billions of constant 2006–07 dollars

SOURCE: U.S. Department of Education, National Center for Education Statistics, *Opening Fall Enrollment in Higher Education*, 1960 through 1965; *Financial Statistics of Higher Education*, 1960–61 through 1964–65; *Earned Degrees Conferred*, 1960–61 through 1964–65; Higher Education General Information Survey (HEGIS), "Fall Enrollment in Institutions of Higher Education," 1966 through 1985, "Degrees and Other Formal Awards Conferred," 1965–66 through 1985–86, and "Financial Statistics of Institutions of Higher Education," 1965–66 through 1985–86; and 1986–87 through 2006–07 Integrated Postsecondary Education Data System, "Fall Enrollment Survey" (IPEDS-EF:86–99), "Completions Survey" (IPEDS-C:87–99), "Finance Survey" (IPEDS-F:FY87–99), Fall 2001 through Fall 2007, and Spring 2001 through Spring 2007.

Figure 12. Percentage change in total enrollment in degree-granting institutions, by state: Fall 2000 through fall 2006

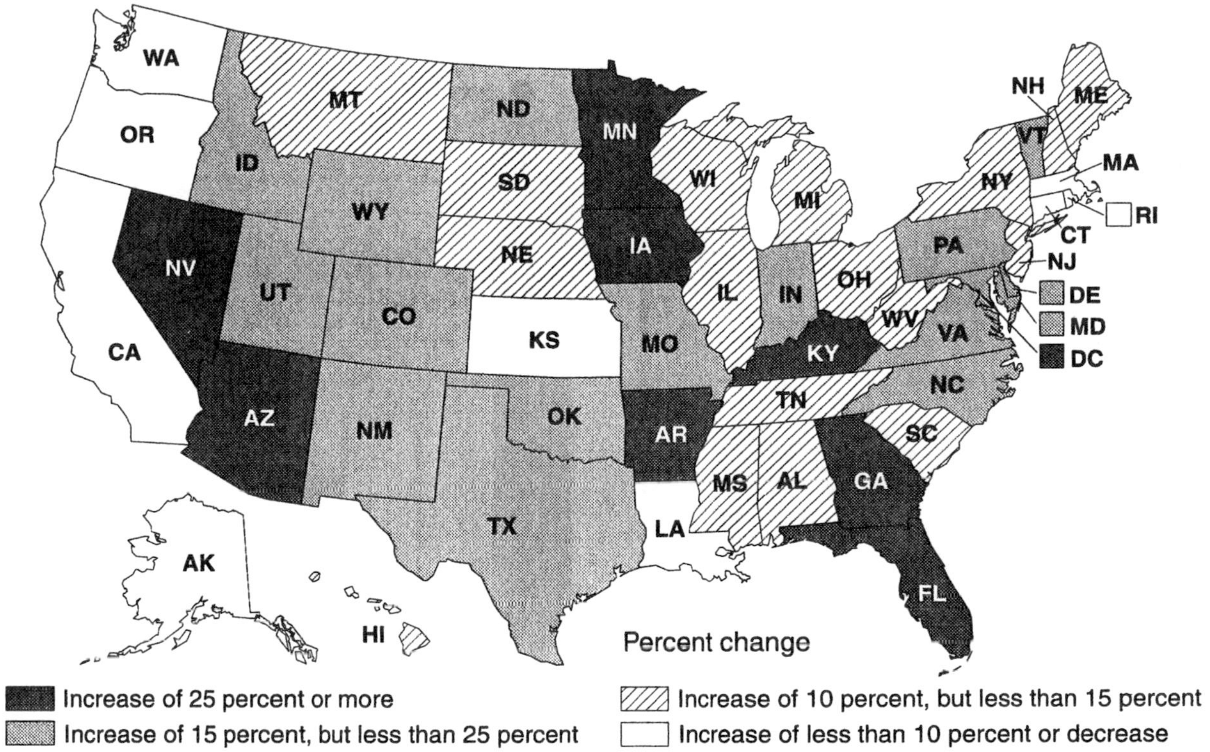

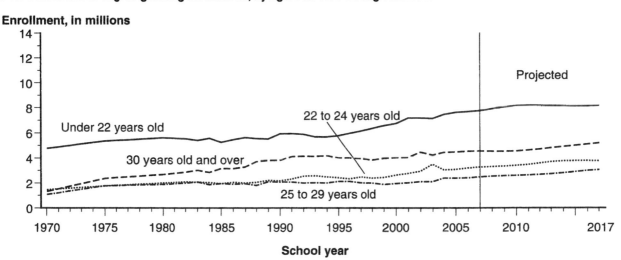

WA
OR
CA
NV
ID
MT
WY
UT
AZ
CO
NM
ND
SD
NE
KS
OK
TX
MN
IA
MO
AR
LA
WI
IL
MI
IN
OH
KY
TN
MS
AL
GA
FL
SC
NC
VA
WV
PA
NY
VT
NH
ME
MA
RI
CT
NJ
DE
MD
DC
AK
HI
Percent change
Increase of 25 percent or more
Increase of 15 percent, but less than 25 percent
Increase of 10 percent, but less than 15 percent
Increase of less than 10 percent or decrease

SOURCE: U.S. Department of Education, National Center for Education Statistics, 2000 and 2006 Integrated Postsecondary Education Data System, Spring 2001 and Spring 2007.

Figure 13. Enrollment in degree-granting institutions, by age: Fall 1970 through fall 2017

Enrollment, in millions
14
12
10
8
6
4
2
0
Projected
22 to 24 years old
Under 22 years old
30 years old and over
25 to 29 years old
1970
1975
1980
1985
1990
1995
2000
2005
2010
2017
School year

SOURCE: U.S. Department of Education, National Center for Education Statistics, Higher Education General Information Survey (HEGIS), "Fall Enrollment in Institutions of Higher Education" surveys, 1970 through 1985; 1986–87 through 2006–07 Integrated Postsecondary Education Data System, "Fall Enrollment Survey" (IPEDS-EF:86–99), and Spring 2001 through Spring 2007; and *Projections of Education Statistics to 2017*.

Figure 14. Full-time-equivalent (FTE) students per staff member in public and private degree-granting institutions, by type of staff: 1976 and 2007

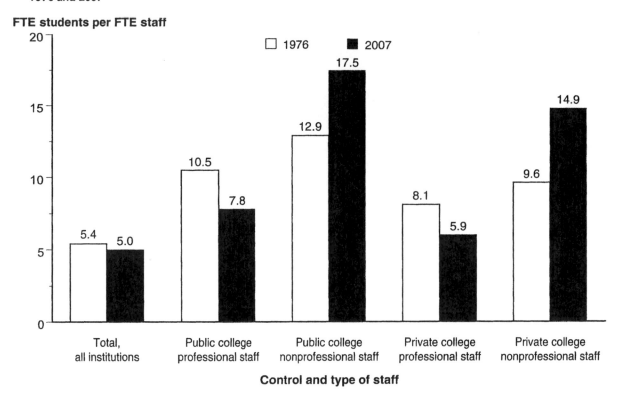

SOURCE: U.S. Department of Education, National Center for Education Statistics, Higher Education General Information Survey (HEGIS), "Staff" survey, 1976, and "Fall Enrollment in Higher Education" survey, 1976; and 2007 Integrated Postsecondary Education Data System, Winter 2007–08 and Spring 2007.

Figure 15. Trends in bachelor's degrees conferred by degree-granting institutions in selected fields of study: 1996–97, 2001–02, and 2006–07

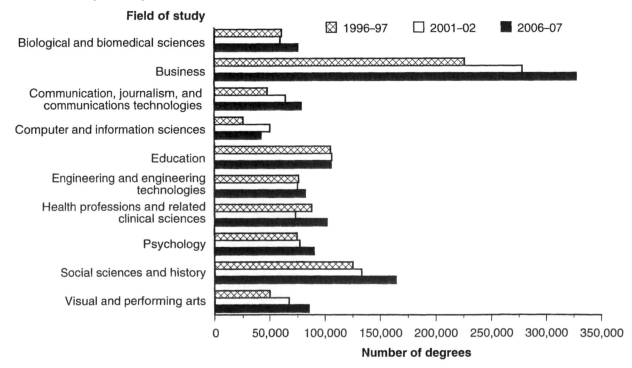

SOURCE: U.S. Department of Education, National Center for Education Statistics, 1996–97, 2001–02, and 2006–07 Integrated Postsecondary Education Data System, "Completions Survey" (IPEDS-C:96–97), and Fall 2001 and Fall 2007.

Figure 16. Percentage distribution of total revenues of public degree-granting institutions, by source of funds: 2005–06

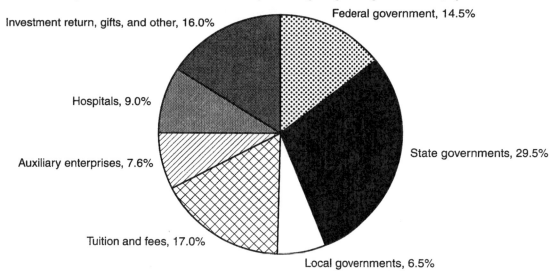

Investment return, gifts, and other, 16.0%

Federal government, 14.5%

Hospitals, 9.0%

State governments, 29.5%

Auxiliary enterprises, 7.6%

Tuition and fees, 17.0%

Local governments, 6.5%

Total revenues = $246.2 billion

NOTE: Detail may not sum to totals because of rounding. Other nonoperating revenues exclude federal, state, and local appropriations.
SOURCE: U.S. Department of Education, National Center for Education Statistics, 2005–06 Integrated Postsecondary Education Data System (IPEDS), Spring 2007.

Figure 17. Percentage distribution of total revenues of private not-for-profit degree-granting institutions, by source of funds: 2005–06

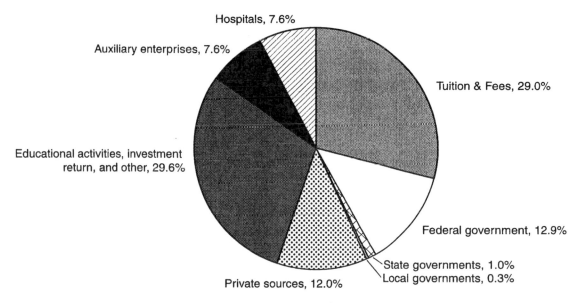

Hospitals, 7.6%

Auxiliary enterprises, 7.6%

Tuition & Fees, 29.0%

Educational activities, investment return, and other, 29.6%

Federal government, 12.9%

State governments, 1.0%
Local governments, 0.3%

Private sources, 12.0%

Total revenues = $152.7 billion

NOTE: Detail may not sum to totals because of rounding.
SOURCE: U.S. Department of Education, National Center for Education Statistics, 2005–06 Integrated Postsecondary Education Data System (IPEDS), Spring 2007.

Table 186. Enrollment, staff, and degrees conferred in postsecondary institutions participating in Title IV programs, by type and control of institution, sex of student, type of staff, and type of degree: Fall 2005, fall 2006, and 2006–07

Selected characteristic	All Title IV participating institutions[1]	Degree-granting institutions[2]					Non-degree-granting institutions[3]				
				Private					Private		
		Total	Public	Total	Not-for-profit	For-profit	Total	Public	Total	Not-for-profit	For-profit
1	2	3	4	5	6	7	8	9	10	11	12
Enrollment, fall 2006											
Total	18,205,474	17,758,870	13,180,133	4,578,737	3,512,866	1,065,871	446,604	101,531	345,073	30,589	314,484
4-year institutions	11,240,834	11,240,330	6,955,013	4,285,317	3,473,710	811,607	504	35	469	469	0
Males	4,870,221	4,870,076	3,078,769	1,791,307	1,476,005	315,302	145	13	132	132	0
Females	6,370,613	6,370,254	3,876,244	2,494,010	1,997,705	496,305	359	22	337	337	0
2-year institutions	6,650,734	6,518,540	6,225,120	293,420	39,156	254,264	132,194	51,065	81,129	16,351	64,778
Males	2,766,327	2,704,739	2,600,635	104,104	13,876	90,228	61,588	26,598	34,990	4,188	30,802
Females	3,884,407	3,813,801	3,624,485	189,316	25,280	164,036	70,606	24,467	46,139	12,163	33,976
Less-than-2-year institutions	313,906	†	†	†	†	†	313,906	50,431	263,475	13,769	249,706
Males	79,253	†	†	†	†	†	79,253	18,691	60,562	4,905	55,657
Females	234,653	†	†	†	†	†	234,653	31,740	202,913	8,864	194,049
Staff, fall 2005											
Total	3,428,811	3,379,087	2,267,687	1,111,400	971,425	139,975	49,724	23,594	26,130	3,618	22,512
Professional staff	2,496,068	2,459,885	1,640,704	819,181	700,202	118,979	36,183	15,841	20,342	2,590	17,752
Administrative	201,571	196,324	101,011	95,313	85,125	10,188	5,247	1,292	3,955	388	3,567
Faculty	1,314,506	1,290,426	841,188	449,238	361,523	87,715	24,080	11,114	12,966	1,768	11,198
Faculty assistants	317,146	317,141	257,952	59,189	59,061	128	5	2	3	0	3
Other professionals	662,845	655,994	440,553	215,441	194,493	20,948	6,851	3,433	3,418	434	2,984
Nonprofessional staff	932,743	919,202	626,983	292,219	271,223	20,996	13,541	7,753	5,788	1,028	4,760
Student/staff ratio	5.2	5.2	5.7	4.0	3.6	7.2	8.7	4.0	13.0	8.1	13.8
Degrees conferred, 2006–07											
Less-than-1-year awards and 1- to 4-year awards	729,037	437,946	331,216	106,730	19,550	87,180	291,091	58,424	232,667	14,645	218,022
4-year institutions	52,796	52,669	21,090	31,579	16,204	15,375	127	0	127	127	0
Males	18,565	18,534	9,459	9,075	5,894	3,181	31	0	31	31	0
Females	34,231	34,135	11,631	22,504	10,310	12,194	96	0	96	96	0
2-year institutions	451,438	385,277	310,126	75,151	3,346	71,805	66,161	26,776	39,385	4,914	34,471
Males	193,664	165,342	142,048	23,294	1,604	21,690	28,322	12,856	15,466	1,339	14,127
Females	257,774	219,935	168,078	51,857	1,742	50,115	37,839	13,920	23,919	3,575	20,344
Less-than-2-year institutions	224,803	†	†	†	†	†	224,803	31,648	193,155	9,604	183,551
Males	57,360	†	†	†	†	†	57,360	12,615	44,745	3,662	41,083
Females	167,443	†	†	†	†	†	167,443	19,033	148,410	5,942	142,468
Associate's degrees	728,118	728,114	566,535	161,579	43,829	117,750	4	4	0	0	0
4-year institutions	164,251	164,251	68,370	95,881	37,503	58,378	0	0	0	0	0
Males	63,860	63,860	26,575	37,285	13,753	23,532	0	0	0	0	0
Females	100,391	100,391	41,795	58,596	23,750	34,846	0	0	0	0	0
2-year institutions	563,864	563,863	498,165	65,698	6,326	59,372	1	1	0	0	0
Males	211,327	211,327	184,451	26,876	1,869	25,007	0	0	0	0	0
Females	352,537	352,536	313,714	38,822	4,457	34,365	1	1	0	0	0
Less-than-2-year institutions	3	†	†	†	†	†	3	3	0	0	0
Males	0	†	†	†	†	†	0	0	0	0	0
Females	3	†	†	†	†	†	3	3	0	0	0
Bachelor's degrees	1,524,092	1,524,092	975,513	548,579	477,805	70,774	0	0	0	0	0
Males	649,570	649,570	420,594	228,976	195,996	32,980	0	0	0	0	0
Females	874,522	874,522	554,919	319,603	281,809	37,794	0	0	0	0	0
Master's degrees	604,607	604,607	291,971	312,636	261,700	50,936	0	0	0	0	0
Males	238,189	238,189	114,983	123,206	105,315	17,891	0	0	0	0	0
Females	366,418	366,418	176,988	189,430	156,385	33,045	0	0	0	0	0
First-professional degrees	90,064	90,064	36,855	53,209	52,746	463	0	0	0	0	0
Males	45,057	45,057	17,471	27,586	27,344	242	0	0	0	0	0
Females	45,007	45,007	19,384	25,623	25,402	221	0	0	0	0	0
Doctor's degrees	60,616	60,616	36,230	24,386	22,483	1,903	0	0	0	0	0
Males	30,251	30,251	18,985	11,266	10,616	650	0	0	0	0	0
Females	30,365	30,365	17,245	13,120	11,867	1,253	0	0	0	0	0

†Not applicable.
[1]Includes degree-granting and non-degree-granting institutions.
[2]Data are for degree-granting institutions, which grant associate's or higher degrees and participate in Title IV federal financial aid programs.

[3]Data are for institutions that did not offer accredited 4-year or 2-year degree programs, but were participating in Title IV federal financial aid programs. Includes some schools with nonaccredited degree programs.
SOURCE: U.S. Department of Education, National Center for Education Statistics, fall 2005, fall 2006, and 2006–07 Integrated Postsecondary Education Data System (IPEDS), Winter 2005–06, Spring 2007, and Fall 2007. (This table was prepared July 2008.)

Table 187. Historical summary of faculty, students, degrees, and finances in degree-granting institutions: Selected years, 1869–70 through 2006–07

Selected characteristic	1869–70	1879–80	1889–90	1899–1900	1909–10	1919–20	1929–30	1939–40	1949–50	1959–60	1969–70	1979–80	1989–90	1999–2000	2005–06	2006–07
1	2	3	4	5	6	7	8	9	10	11	12	13	14	15	16	17
Total institutions[1]	563	811	998	977	951	1,041	1,409	1,708	1,851	2,004	2,525	3,152	3,535	4,084	4,276	4,314
Total faculty[2]	5,553[3]	11,522[3]	15,809[3]	23,868	36,480	48,615	82,386	146,929	246,722	380,554	450,000[4]	675,000[4]	824,220[5]	1,027,830[5]	1,290,426[5]	—
Males	4,887[3]	7,328[3]	12,704[3]	19,151	29,132	35,807	60,017	106,328	186,189	296,773	346,000[4]	479,000[4]	534,254[5]	602,469[5]	714,453[5]	—
Females	666[3]	4,194[3]	3,105[3]	4,717	7,348	12,808	22,369	40,601	60,533	83,781	104,000[4]	196,000[4]	289,966[5]	425,361[5]	575,973[5]	—
Total fall enrollment[6]	52,286[3]	115,817[3]	156,756[3]	237,592	355,213[3]	597,880	1,100,737	1,494,203	2,659,021	3,639,847	8,004,660	11,569,899	13,538,560	14,791,224	17,487,475	17,758,870
Males	41,160[3]	77,972[3]	100,453[3]	152,254	214,648[3]	314,938	619,935	893,250	1,853,068	2,332,617	4,746,201	5,682,877	6,190,015	6,490,646	7,455,925	7,574,815
Females	11,126[3]	37,845[3]	56,303[3]	85,338	140,565[3]	282,942	480,802	600,953	805,953	1,307,230	3,258,459	5,887,022	7,348,545	8,300,578	10,031,550	10,184,055
Earned degrees conferred																
Associate's, total	—	—	—	—	—	—	—	—	—	—	206,023	400,910	455,102	564,933	713,066	728,114
Males	—	—	—	—	—	—	—	—	—	—	117,432	183,737	191,195	224,721	270,095	275,187
Females	—	—	—	—	—	—	—	—	—	—	88,591	217,173	263,907	340,212	442,971	452,927
Bachelor's, total[7]	9,371	12,896	15,539	27,410	37,199	48,622	122,484	186,500	432,058	392,440	792,316	929,417	1,051,344	1,237,875	1,485,242	1,524,092
Males	7,993	10,411	12,857	22,173	28,762	31,980	73,615	109,546	328,841	254,063	451,097	473,611	491,696	530,367	630,600	649,570
Females	1,378	2,485	2,682	5,237	8,437	16,642	48,869	76,954	103,217	138,377	341,219	455,806	559,648	707,508	854,642	874,522
Master's, total[8]	0	879	1,015	1,583	2,113	4,279	14,969	26,731	58,183	74,435	208,291	298,081	324,301	457,056	594,065	604,607
Males	0	868	821	1,280	1,555	2,985	8,925	16,508	41,220	50,898	125,624	150,749	153,653	191,792	237,896	238,189
Females	0	11	194	303	558	1,294	6,044	10,223	16,963	23,537	82,667	147,332	170,648	265,264	356,169	366,418
First-professional, total[7]	—	—	—	—	—	—	—	—	—	—	34,918	70,131	70,988	80,057	87,655	90,064
Males	—	—	—	—	—	—	—	—	—	—	33,077	52,716	43,961	44,239	44,038	45,057
Females	—	—	—	—	—	—	—	—	—	—	1,841	17,415	27,027	35,818	43,617	45,007
Doctor's, total	1	54	149	382	443	615	2,299	3,290	6,420	9,829	29,866	32,615	38,371	44,808	56,067	60,616
Males	1	51	147	359	399	522	1,946	2,861	5,804	8,801	25,890	22,943	24,401	25,028	28,634	30,251
Females	0	3	2	23	44	93	353	429	616	1,028	3,976	9,672	13,970	19,780	27,433	30,365
Finances							_In thousands of current dollars_									
Current-fund revenue	—	—	—	$35,084	$76,883	$199,922	$554,511	$715,211	$2,374,645	$5,785,537	$21,515,242	$58,519,982	$139,635,477	—	—	—
Educational and general income	—	—	$21,464	—	67,917	172,929	483,065	571,283	1,833,845	4,688,352	16,486,177	—	134,655,571	—	—	—
Current-fund expenditures	—	—	—	—	—	—	507,142	674,688	2,245,661	5,601,376	21,043,113	56,913,588	—	—	—	—
Educational and general expenditures	—	—	—	—	—	—	377,903	521,990	1,706,444	4,685,258	16,845,212	44,542,843	105,585,076	—	—	—
Value of physical property	—	—	95,426	253,599	457,594	747,333	2,065,049	2,753,780[9]	4,799,964	13,548,548	42,093,580	83,733,387	164,635,000	—	—	—
Market value of endowment funds	—	—	78,788[10]	194,998[10]	323,661[10]	569,071[10]	1,372,068[10]	1,686,283[10]	2,601,223[10]	5,322,080[10]	11,206,632	20,743,045	67,978,726	—	—	—

—Not available.

[1]Prior to 1979–80, excludes branch campuses.
[2]Total number of different individuals (not reduced to full-time equivalent). Beginning in 1959–60, data are for the first term of the academic year.
[3]Estimated.
[4]Estimated number of senior instructional staff. Excludes graduate assistants.
[5]Because of revised survey procedures, data may not be directly comparable with figures prior to 1989–90.
[6]Data for 1869–70 to 1949–50 are for resident degree-credit students who enrolled at any time during the academic year.
[7]From 1869–70 to 1959–60, first-professional degrees are included under bachelor's degrees.
[8]Figures for years prior to 1969–70 are not precisely comparable with later data.
[9]Includes unexpended plant funds.
[10]Book value. Includes other nonexpendable funds.

NOTE: Data through 1989–90 are for institutions of higher education, while later data are for degree-granting institutions. Degree-granting institutions grant associate's or higher degrees and participate in Title IV federal financial aid programs. The degree-granting classification is very similar to the earlier higher education classification, but it includes more 2-year colleges and excludes a few higher education institutions that did not grant degrees. (See Guide to Sources for details.) Detail may not sum to totals because of rounding.
SOURCE: U.S. Department of Education, National Center for Education Statistics, _Biennial Survey of Education in the United States; Education Directory, Colleges and Universities; Faculty and Other Professional Staff in Institutions of Higher Education; Fall Enrollment in Colleges and Universities; Earned Degrees Conferred; Financial Statistics of Institutions of Higher Education;_ Higher Education General Information Survey (HEGIS), "Fall Enrollment in Institutions of Higher Education," "Degrees and Other Formal Awards Conferred," and "Financial Statistics of Institutions of Higher Education" surveys; and 1989 through 2007 Integrated Postsecondary Education Data System, "Fall Enrollment Survey" (IPEDS-EF:89–99), "Fall Staff Survey" (IPEDS-S:89–99), "Finance Survey" (IPEDS-F:FY90–00), "Completions Survey" (IPEDS-C:90–00), "Institutional Characteristics Survey" (IPEDS-IC:89–99), Winter 2005–06, Spring 2007, and Fall 2007. (This table was prepared July 2008.)

Table 188. Total fall enrollment in degree-granting institutions, by attendance status, sex of student, and control of institution: Selected years, 1947 through 2007

Year	Total enrollment	Attendance status			Sex of student			Control of institution			
		Full-time	Part-time	Percent part-time	Male	Female	Percent female	Public	Private		
									Total	Not-for-profit	For-profit
1	2	3	4	5	6	7	8	9	10	11	12
1947[1]	2,338,226	—	—	—	1,659,249	678,977	29.0	1,152,377	1,185,849	—	—
1948[1]	2,403,396	—	—	—	1,709,367	694,029	28.9	1,185,588	1,217,808	—	—
1949[1]	2,444,900	—	—	—	1,721,572	723,328	29.6	1,207,151	1,237,749	—	—
1950[1]	2,281,298	—	—	—	1,560,392	720,906	31.6	1,139,699	1,141,599	—	—
1951[1]	2,101,962	—	—	—	1,390,740	711,222	33.8	1,037,938	1,064,024	—	—
1952[1]	2,134,242	—	—	—	1,380,357	753,885	35.3	1,101,240	1,033,002	—	—
1953[1]	2,231,054	—	—	—	1,422,598	808,456	36.2	1,185,876	1,045,178	—	—
1954[1]	2,446,693	—	—	—	1,563,382	883,311	36.1	1,353,531	1,093,162	—	—
1955[1]	2,653,034	—	—	—	1,733,184	919,850	34.7	1,476,282	1,176,752	—	—
1956[1]	2,918,212	—	—	—	1,911,458	1,006,754	34.5	1,656,402	1,261,810	—	—
1957	3,323,783	—	—	—	2,170,765	1,153,018	34.7	1,972,673	1,351,110	—	—
1959	3,639,847	2,421,016	1,218,831 [2]	33.5	2,332,617	1,307,230	35.9	2,180,982	1,458,865	—	—
1961	4,145,065	2,785,133	1,359,932 [2]	32.8	2,585,821	1,559,244	37.6	2,561,447	1,583,618	—	—
1963	4,779,609	3,183,833	1,595,776 [2]	33.4	2,961,540	1,818,069	38.0	3,081,279	1,698,330	—	—
1964	5,280,020	3,573,238	1,706,782 [2]	32.3	3,248,713	2,031,307	38.5	3,467,708	1,812,312	—	—
1965	5,920,864	4,095,728	1,825,136 [2]	30.8	3,630,020	2,290,844	38.7	3,969,596	1,951,268	—	—
1966	6,389,872	4,438,606	1,951,266 [2]	30.5	3,856,216	2,533,656	39.7	4,348,917	2,040,955	—	—
1967	6,911,748	4,793,128	2,118,620 [2]	30.7	4,132,800	2,778,948	40.2	4,816,028	2,095,720	2,074,041	21,679
1968	7,513,091	5,210,155	2,302,936	30.7	4,477,649	3,035,442	40.4	5,430,652	2,082,439	2,061,211	21,228
1969	8,004,660	5,498,883	2,505,777	31.3	4,746,201	3,258,459	40.7	5,896,868	2,107,792	2,087,653	20,139
1970	8,580,887	5,816,290	2,764,597	32.2	5,043,642	3,537,245	41.2	6,428,134	2,152,753	2,134,420	18,333
1971	8,948,644	6,077,232	2,871,412	32.1	5,207,004	3,741,640	41.8	6,804,309	2,144,335	2,121,913	22,422
1972	9,214,860	6,072,389	3,142,471	34.1	5,238,757	3,976,103	43.1	7,070,635	2,144,225	2,123,245	20,980
1973	9,602,123	6,189,493	3,412,630	35.5	5,371,052	4,231,071	44.1	7,419,516	2,182,607	2,148,784	33,823
1974	10,223,729	6,370,273	3,853,456	37.7	5,622,429	4,601,300	45.0	7,988,500	2,235,229	2,200,963	34,266
1975	11,184,859	6,841,334	4,343,525	38.8	6,148,997	5,035,862	45.0	8,834,508	2,350,351	2,311,448	38,903
1976	11,012,137	6,717,058	4,295,079	39.0	5,810,828	5,201,309	47.2	8,653,477	2,358,660	2,314,298	44,362
1977	11,285,787	6,792,925	4,492,862	39.8	5,789,016	5,496,771	48.7	8,846,993	2,438,794	2,386,652	52,142
1978	11,260,092	6,667,657	4,592,435	40.8	5,640,998	5,619,094	49.9	8,785,893	2,474,199	2,408,331	65,868
1979	11,569,899	6,794,039	4,775,860	41.3	5,682,877	5,887,022	50.9	9,036,822	2,533,077	2,461,773	71,304
1980	12,096,895	7,097,958	4,998,937	41.3	5,874,374	6,222,521	51.4	9,457,394	2,639,501	2,527,787	111,714 [3]
1981	12,371,672	7,181,250	5,190,422	42.0	5,975,056	6,396,616	51.7	9,647,032	2,724,640	2,572,405	152,235 [3]
1982	12,425,780	7,220,618	5,205,162	41.9	6,031,384	6,394,396	51.5	9,696,087	2,729,693	2,552,739	176,954 [3]
1983	12,464,661	7,261,050	5,203,611	41.7	6,023,725	6,440,936	51.7	9,682,734	2,781,927	2,589,187	192,740
1984	12,241,940	7,098,388	5,143,552	42.0	5,863,574	6,378,366	52.1	9,477,370	2,764,570	2,574,419	190,151
1985	12,247,055	7,075,221	5,171,834	42.2	5,818,450	6,428,605	52.5	9,479,273	2,767,782	2,571,791	195,991
1986	12,503,511	7,119,550	5,383,961	43.1	5,884,515	6,618,996	52.9	9,713,893	2,789,618	2,572,479	217,139 [4]
1987	12,766,642	7,231,085	5,535,557	43.4	5,932,056	6,834,586	53.5	9,973,254	2,793,388	2,602,350	191,038 [4]
1988	13,055,337	7,436,768	5,618,569	43.0	6,001,896	7,053,441	54.0	10,161,388	2,893,949	2,673,567	220,382
1989	13,538,560	7,660,950	5,877,610	43.4	6,190,015	7,348,545	54.3	10,577,963	2,960,597	2,731,174	229,423
1990	13,818,637	7,820,985	5,997,652	43.4	6,283,909	7,534,728	54.5	10,844,717	2,973,920	2,760,227	213,693
1991	14,358,953	8,115,329	6,243,624	43.5	6,501,844	7,857,109	54.7	11,309,563	3,049,390	2,819,041	230,349
1992	14,487,359	8,162,118	6,325,241	43.7	6,523,989	7,963,370	55.0	11,384,567	3,102,792	2,872,523	230,269
1993	14,304,803	8,127,618	6,177,185	43.2	6,427,450	7,877,353	55.1	11,189,088	3,115,715	2,888,897	226,818
1994	14,278,790	8,137,776	6,141,014	43.0	6,371,898	7,906,892	55.4	11,133,680	3,145,110	2,910,107	235,003
1995	14,261,781	8,128,802	6,132,979	43.0	6,342,539	7,919,242	55.5	11,092,374	3,169,407	2,929,044	240,363
1996	14,367,520	8,302,953	6,064,567	42.2	6,352,825	8,014,695	55.8	11,120,499	3,247,021	2,942,556	304,465
1997	14,502,334	8,438,062	6,064,272	41.8	6,396,028	8,106,306	55.9	11,196,119	3,306,215	2,977,614	328,601
1998	14,506,967	8,563,338	5,943,629	41.0	6,369,265	8,137,702	56.1	11,137,769	3,369,198	3,004,925	364,273
1999	14,791,224	8,786,494	6,004,730	40.6	6,490,646	8,300,578	56.1	11,309,399	3,481,825	3,051,626	430,199
2000	15,312,289	9,009,600	6,302,689	41.2	6,721,769	8,590,520	56.1	11,752,786	3,559,503	3,109,419	450,084
2001	15,927,987	9,447,502	6,480,485	40.7	6,960,815	8,967,172	56.3	12,233,156	3,694,831	3,167,330	527,501
2002	16,611,711	9,946,359	6,665,352	40.1	7,202,116	9,409,595	56.6	12,751,993	3,859,718	3,265,476	594,242
2003	16,911,481	10,326,133	6,585,348	38.9	7,260,264	9,651,217	57.1	12,858,698	4,052,783	3,341,048	711,735
2004	17,272,044	10,610,177	6,661,867	38.6	7,387,262	9,884,782	57.2	12,980,112	4,291,932	3,411,685	880,247
2005	17,487,475	10,797,011	6,690,464	38.3	7,455,925	10,031,550	57.4	13,021,834	4,465,641	3,454,692	1,010,949
2006	17,758,870	10,957,305	6,801,565	38.3	7,574,815	10,184,055	57.3	13,180,133	4,578,737	3,512,866	1,065,871
2007	18,248,128	11,269,892	6,978,236	38.2	7,815,914	10,432,214	57.2	13,490,780	4,757,348	3,571,150	1,186,198

—Not available.

[1]Degree-credit enrollment only.

[2]Includes part-time resident students and all extension students.

[3]Large increases are due to the addition of schools accredited by the Accrediting Commission of Career Schools and Colleges of Technology.

[4]Because of imputation techniques, data are not consistent with figures for other years.

NOTE: Data through 1995 are for institutions of higher education, while later data are for degree-granting institutions. Degree-granting institutions grant associate's or higher degrees and participate in Title IV federal financial aid programs. The degree-granting classification is very similar to the earlier higher education classification, but it includes more 2-year colleges and excludes a few higher education institutions that did not grant degrees. (See Guide to Sources for details.)

SOURCE: U.S. Department of Education, National Center for Education Statistics, *Biennial Survey of Education in the United States*; *Opening Fall Enrollment in Higher Education*, 1963 through 1965; Higher Education General Information Survey (HEGIS), "Fall Enrollment in Colleges and Universities" surveys, 1966 through 1985; and 1986 through 2007 Integrated Postsecondary Education Data System, "Fall Enrollment Survey" (IPEDS-EF:86–99), and Spring 2001 through Spring 2008. (This table was prepared October 2008.)

Table 189. Total fall enrollment in degree-granting institutions, by control and type of institution: 1963 through 2007

	All institutions					Public institutions					Private institutions				
		4-year					4-year					4-year			
Year	Total	Total	University	Other 4-year	2-year	Total	Total	University	Other 4-year	2-year	Total	Total	University	Other 4-year	2-year
1	2	3	4	5	6	7	8	9	10	11	12	13	14	15	16
1963[1]	4,779,609	3,929,248	—	—	850,361	3,081,279	2,341,468	—	—	739,811	1,698,330	1,587,780	—	—	110,550
1964[1]	5,280,020	4,291,094	—	—	988,926	3,467,708	2,592,929	—	—	874,779	1,812,312	1,698,165	—	—	114,147
1965[1]	5,920,864	4,747,912	—	—	1,172,952	3,969,596	2,928,332	—	—	1,041,264	1,951,268	1,819,580	—	—	131,688
1966[1]	6,389,872	5,063,902	—	—	1,325,970	4,348,917	3,159,748	—	—	1,189,169	2,040,955	1,904,154	—	—	136,801
1967	6,911,748	5,398,986	2,186,235	3,212,751	1,512,762	4,816,028	3,443,975	1,510,333	1,933,642	1,372,053	2,095,720	1,955,011	675,902	1,279,109	140,709
1968	7,513,091	5,720,269	2,266,120	3,454,149	1,792,822	5,430,652	3,783,652	1,592,707	2,190,945	1,647,000	2,082,439	1,936,617	673,413	1,263,204	145,822
1969	8,004,660	5,937,127	2,420,429	3,516,698	2,067,533	5,896,868	3,962,522	1,738,493	2,224,029	1,934,346	2,107,792	1,974,605	681,936	1,292,669	133,187
1970	8,580,887	6,261,502	2,534,336	3,727,166	2,319,385	6,428,134	4,232,722	1,832,694	2,400,028	2,195,412	2,152,753	2,028,780	701,642	1,327,138	123,973
1971	8,948,644	6,369,355	2,594,470	3,774,885	2,579,289	6,804,309	4,346,990	1,913,626	2,433,364	2,457,319	2,144,335	2,022,365	680,844	1,341,521	121,970
1972	9,214,860	6,458,674	2,620,749	3,837,925	2,756,186	7,070,635	4,429,696	1,941,040	2,488,656	2,640,939	2,144,225	2,028,978	679,709	1,349,269	115,247
1973	9,602,123	6,590,023	2,629,796	3,960,227	3,012,100	7,419,516	4,529,895	1,950,653	2,579,242	2,889,621	2,182,607	2,060,128	679,143	1,380,985	122,479
1974	10,223,729	6,819,735	2,702,306	4,117,429	3,403,994	7,988,500	4,703,018	2,006,723	2,696,295	3,285,482	2,235,229	2,116,717	695,583	1,421,134	118,512
1975	11,184,859	7,214,740	2,838,266	4,376,474	3,970,119	8,834,508	4,998,142	2,124,221	2,873,921	3,836,366	2,350,351	2,216,598	714,045	1,502,553	133,753
1976	11,012,137	7,128,816	2,780,289	4,348,527	3,883,321	8,653,477	4,901,691	2,079,929	2,821,762	3,751,786	2,358,660	2,227,125	700,360	1,526,765	131,535
1977	11,285,787	7,242,845	2,793,418	4,449,427	4,042,942	8,846,993	4,945,224	2,070,032	2,875,192	3,901,769	2,438,794	2,297,621	723,386	1,574,235	141,173
1978	11,260,092	7,231,625	2,780,729	4,451,222	4,028,467	8,785,893	4,912,203	2,062,295	2,849,908	3,873,690	2,474,199	2,319,422	718,434	1,601,314	154,777
1979	11,569,899	7,353,233	2,839,582	4,513,651	4,216,666	9,036,822	4,980,012	2,099,525	2,880,487	4,056,810	2,533,077	2,373,221	740,057	1,633,164	159,856
1980	12,096,895	7,570,608	2,902,014	4,668,594	4,526,287	9,457,394	5,128,612	2,154,283	2,974,329	4,328,782	2,639,501	2,441,996	747,731	1,694,265	197,505 [2]
1981	12,371,672	7,655,461	2,901,344	4,754,117	4,716,211	9,647,032	5,166,324	2,152,474	3,013,850	4,480,708	2,724,640	2,489,137	748,870	1,740,267	235,503 [2]
1982	12,425,780	7,654,074	2,883,735	4,770,339	4,771,706	9,696,087	5,176,434	2,152,547	3,023,887	4,519,653	2,729,693	2,477,640	731,188	1,746,452	252,053 [2]
1983	12,464,661	7,741,195	2,888,813	4,852,382	4,723,466	9,682,734	5,223,404	2,154,790	3,068,614	4,459,330	2,781,927	2,517,791	734,023	1,783,768	264,136
1984	12,241,940	7,711,167	2,870,329	4,840,838	4,530,773	9,477,370	5,198,273	2,138,621	3,059,652	4,279,097	2,764,570	2,512,894	731,708	1,781,186	251,676
1985	12,247,055	7,715,978	2,870,692	4,845,286	4,531,077	9,479,273	5,209,540	2,141,112	3,068,428	4,269,733	2,767,782	2,506,438	729,580	1,776,858	261,344
1986	12,503,511	7,823,963	2,897,207	4,926,756	4,679,548	9,713,893	5,300,202	2,160,646	3,139,556	4,413,691	2,789,618	2,523,761	736,561	1,787,200	265,857 [3]
1987	12,766,642	7,990,420	2,929,327	5,061,093	4,776,222	9,973,254	5,432,200	2,188,008	3,244,192	4,541,054	2,793,388	2,558,220	741,319	1,816,901	235,168 [3]
1988	13,055,337	8,180,182	2,978,593	5,201,589	4,875,155	10,161,388	5,545,901	2,229,868	3,316,033	4,615,487	2,893,949	2,634,281	748,725	1,885,556	259,668
1989	13,538,560	8,387,671	3,019,115	5,368,556	5,150,889	10,577,963	5,694,303	2,266,056	3,428,247	4,883,660	2,960,597	2,693,368	753,059	1,940,309	267,229
1990	13,818,637	8,578,554	3,044,670	5,533,884	5,240,083	10,844,717	5,848,242	2,290,464	3,557,778	4,996,475	2,973,920	2,730,312	754,206	1,976,106	243,608
1991	14,358,953	8,707,053	3,065,429	5,641,624	5,651,900	11,309,563	5,904,748	2,301,222	3,603,526	5,404,815	3,049,390	2,802,305	764,207	2,038,098	247,085
1992	14,487,359	8,764,969	3,050,345	5,714,624	5,722,390	11,384,567	5,900,012	2,283,834	3,616,178	5,484,555	3,102,792	2,864,957	766,511	2,098,446	237,835
1993	14,304,803	8,738,936	3,022,728	5,716,208	5,565,867	11,189,088	5,851,760	2,259,692	3,592,068	5,337,328	3,115,715	2,887,176	763,036	2,124,140	228,539
1994	14,278,790	8,749,080	3,009,072	5,740,008	5,529,710	11,133,680	5,825,213	2,244,636	3,580,577	5,308,467	3,145,110	2,923,867	764,436	2,159,431	221,243
1995	14,261,781	8,769,252	2,999,641	5,769,611	5,492,529	11,092,374	5,814,545	2,235,939	3,578,606	5,277,829	3,169,407	2,954,707	763,702	2,191,005	214,700
1996	14,367,520	8,804,193	2,984,965	5,819,228	5,563,327	11,120,499	5,806,036	2,226,529	3,579,507	5,314,463	3,247,021	2,998,157	758,436	2,239,721	248,864
1997	14,502,334	8,896,765	2,995,886	5,900,879	5,605,569	11,196,119	5,835,433	2,231,273	3,604,160	5,360,686	3,306,215	3,061,332	764,613	2,296,719	244,883
1998	14,506,967	9,017,653	3,021,136	5,996,517	5,489,314	11,137,769	5,891,806	2,249,825	3,641,981	5,245,963	3,369,198	3,125,847	771,311	2,354,536	243,351
1999	14,791,224	9,198,525	3,044,369	6,154,156	5,592,699	11,309,399	5,969,950	2,266,494	3,703,456	5,339,449	3,481,825	3,228,575	777,875	2,450,700	253,250
2000	15,312,289	9,363,858	3,061,812	6,302,046	5,948,431	11,752,786	6,055,398	2,280,122	3,775,276	5,697,388	3,559,503	3,308,460	781,690	2,526,770	251,043
2001	15,927,987	9,677,408	3,126,907	6,550,501	6,250,579	12,233,156	6,236,455	2,336,922	3,899,533	5,996,701	3,694,831	3,440,953	789,985	2,650,968	253,878
2002	16,611,711	10,082,332	3,210,271	6,872,061	6,529,379	12,751,993	6,481,613	2,403,149	4,078,464	6,270,380	3,859,718	3,600,719	807,122	2,793,597	258,999
2003	16,911,481	10,417,247	3,242,639	7,174,608	6,494,234	12,858,698	6,649,441	2,419,631	4,229,810	6,209,257	4,052,783	3,767,806	823,008	2,944,798	284,977
2004	17,272,044	10,726,181	3,258,982	7,467,199	6,545,863	12,980,112	6,736,536	2,426,495	4,310,041	6,243,576	4,291,932	3,989,645	832,487	3,157,158	302,287
2005	17,487,475	10,999,420	3,271,620	7,727,800	6,488,055	13,021,834	6,837,605	2,443,682	4,393,923	6,184,229	4,465,641	4,161,815	827,938	3,333,877	303,826
2006	17,758,870	11,240,330	3,306,973	7,933,357	6,518,540	13,180,133	6,955,013	2,459,874	4,495,139	6,225,120	4,578,737	4,285,317	847,099	3,438,218	293,420
2007	18,248,128	11,630,198	3,349,214	8,280,984	6,617,930	13,490,780	7,166,661	2,490,615	4,676,046	6,324,119	4,757,348	4,463,537	858,599	3,604,938	293,811

—Not available.

[1]Data for 2-year branch campuses of 4-year institutions are included with the 4-year institutions.

[2]Large increases are due to the addition of schools accredited by the Accrediting Commission of Career Schools and Colleges of Technology.

[3]Because of imputation techniques, data are not consistent with figures for other years.

NOTE: Data through 1995 are for institutions of higher education, while later data are for degree-granting institutions. Degree-granting institutions grant associate's or higher degrees and participate in Title IV federal financial aid programs. The degree-granting classification is very similar to the earlier higher education classification, but it includes more 2-year colleges and excludes a few higher education institutions that did not grant degrees. (See Guide to Sources for details.) Some data have been revised from previously published figures.

SOURCE: U.S. Department of Education, National Center for Education Statistics, *Opening Fall Enrollment in Higher Education*, 1965; Higher Education General Information Survey (HEGIS), "Fall Enrollment in Institutions of Higher Education" surveys, 1966 through 1985; and 1986 through 2007 Integrated Postsecondary Education Data System, "Fall Enrollment Survey" (IPEDS-EF:86–99), and Spring 2001 through Spring 2008. (This table was prepared October 2008.)

Table 190. Total fall enrollment in degree-granting institutions, by sex, age, and attendance status: Selected years, 1970 through 2017

[In thousands]

Sex, age, and attendance status	1970	1980	1990	1995	2000	2001	2002	2003	2004	2005	2006	Projected 2008	Projected 2012	Projected 2017
1	2	3	4	5	6	7	8	9	10	11	12	13	14	15
Males and females	8,581	12,097	13,819	14,262	15,312	15,928	16,612	16,911	17,272	17,487	17,759	18,200	19,048	20,080
14 to 17 years old	259	247	177	148	145	133	202	151	200	199	231	191	190	211
18 and 19 years old	2,600	2,901	2,950	2,894	3,531	3,595	3,571	3,479	3,578	3,610	3,769	3,953	3,940	3,960
20 and 21 years old	1,880	2,424	2,761	2,705	3,045	3,408	3,366	3,473	3,651	3,778	3,648	3,723	3,993	3,958
22 to 24 years old	1,457	1,989	2,144	2,411	2,617	2,760	2,932	3,482	3,036	3,072	3,193	3,289	3,584	3,753
25 to 29 years old	1,074	1,871	1,982	2,120	1,960	2,014	2,102	2,106	2,386	2,384	2,401	2,531	2,658	3,035
30 to 34 years old	487	1,243	1,322	1,236	1,265	1,290	1,300	1,368	1,329	1,354	1,409	1,434	1,616	1,813
35 years old and over	823	1,421	2,484	2,747	2,749	2,727	3,139	2,852	3,092	3,090	3,107	3,080	3,066	3,350
Males	5,044	5,874	6,284	6,343	6,722	6,961	7,202	7,260	7,387	7,456	7,575	7,822	8,213	8,568
14 to 17 years old	130	99	87	61	63	54	82	60	78	78	82	82	79	85
18 and 19 years old	1,349	1,375	1,421	1,338	1,583	1,629	1,616	1,558	1,551	1,592	1,705	1,799	1,793	1,787
20 and 21 years old	1,095	1,259	1,368	1,282	1,382	1,591	1,562	1,492	1,743	1,778	1,673	1,705	1,827	1,790
22 to 24 years old	964	1,064	1,107	1,153	1,293	1,312	1,342	1,605	1,380	1,355	1,470	1,512	1,641	1,692
25 to 29 years old	783	993	940	962	862	905	890	930	1,045	978	1,051	1,117	1,183	1,342
30 to 34 years old	308	576	537	561	527	510	547	592	518	545	557	572	649	729
35 years old and over	415	507	824	986	1,012	961	1,164	1,025	1,073	1,130	1,037	1,035	1,040	1,144
Females	3,537	6,223	7,535	7,919	8,591	8,967	9,410	9,651	9,885	10,032	10,184	10,378	10,835	11,512
14 to 17 years old	129	148	90	87	82	79	121	91	122	121	149	109	110	127
18 and 19 years old	1,250	1,526	1,529	1,557	1,948	1,966	1,955	1,922	2,027	2,018	2,064	2,154	2,148	2,174
20 and 21 years old	786	1,165	1,392	1,424	1,663	1,817	1,804	1,981	1,908	2,000	1,975	2,018	2,167	2,169
22 to 24 years old	493	925	1,037	1,258	1,324	1,448	1,590	1,877	1,657	1,717	1,724	1,777	1,943	2,061
25 to 29 years old	291	878	1,043	1,159	1,099	1,110	1,212	1,177	1,341	1,406	1,350	1,413	1,475	1,692
30 to 34 years old	179	667	784	675	738	780	753	776	812	809	852	862	967	1,084
35 years old and over	409	914	1,659	1,760	1,736	1,767	1,976	1,827	2,018	1,960	2,070	2,044	2,026	2,206
Full-time	5,816	7,098	7,821	8,129	9,010	9,448	9,946	10,326	10,610	10,797	10,957	11,263	11,817	12,430
14 to 17 years old	242	223	144	123	125	122	161	121	165	131	166	131	132	150
18 and 19 years old	2,406	2,669	2,548	2,387	2,932	2,929	2,942	2,953	3,028	3,037	3,155	3,304	3,297	3,339
20 and 21 years old	1,647	2,075	2,151	2,109	2,401	2,662	2,759	2,767	2,911	3,030	2,944	3,006	3,231	3,234
22 to 24 years old	881	1,121	1,350	1,517	1,653	1,757	1,922	2,144	2,074	2,097	2,093	2,162	2,369	2,515
25 to 29 years old	407	577	770	908	878	883	1,013	1,072	1,131	1,136	1,217	1,280	1,340	1,554
30 to 34 years old	100	251	387	430	422	494	465	512	490	549	605	613	687	786
35 years old and over	134	182	471	653	599	602	684	758	812	818	778	767	759	852
Males	3,505	3,689	3,808	3,807	4,111	4,300	4,501	4,638	4,739	4,803	4,879	5,055	5,305	5,457
14 to 17 years old	124	87	71	54	51	43	65	50	63	36	66	64	62	66
18 and 19 years old	1,265	1,270	1,230	1,091	1,250	1,329	1,327	1,307	1,313	1,357	1,409	1,486	1,482	1,478
20 and 21 years old	990	1,109	1,055	999	1,106	1,249	1,275	1,218	1,385	1,460	1,331	1,358	1,454	1,426
22 to 24 years old	650	665	742	789	839	854	936	1,041	960	951	1,003	1,034	1,125	1,155
25 to 29 years old	327	360	401	454	415	397	467	503	509	439	562	599	635	722
30 to 34 years old	72	124	156	183	195	216	183	242	201	238	232	239	271	305
35 years old and over	75	74	152	238	256	212	247	277	310	321	275	275	276	305
Females	2,311	3,409	4,013	4,321	4,899	5,148	5,445	5,688	5,871	5,994	6,078	6,208	6,511	6,973
14 to 17 years old	117	136	73	69	74	78	96	71	103	94	100	67	70	84
18 and 19 years old	1,140	1,399	1,318	1,296	1,682	1,600	1,615	1,646	1,716	1,680	1,746	1,818	1,816	1,861
20 and 21 years old	657	966	1,096	1,111	1,296	1,413	1,484	1,549	1,526	1,569	1,612	1,649	1,777	1,808
22 to 24 years old	231	456	608	729	814	903	985	1,103	1,113	1,146	1,090	1,128	1,244	1,360
25 to 29 years old	80	217	369	455	463	486	546	569	622	697	654	681	706	832
30 to 34 years old	28	127	231	247	227	277	282	270	289	311	372	374	416	481
35 years old and over	59	108	319	415	343	390	437	481	502	497	503	492	483	547
Part-time	2,765	4,999	5,998	6,133	6,303	6,480	6,665	6,585	6,662	6,690	6,802	6,937	7,231	7,650
14 to 17 years old	17	38	32	25	20	11	41	30	35	68	65	60	58	61
18 and 19 years old	194	418	402	507	599	666	628	526	549	573	614	648	643	621
20 and 21 years old	233	441	610	596	644	746	607	706	741	748	704	716	762	724
22 to 24 years old	576	844	794	894	964	1,003	1,010	1,338	963	976	1,100	1,127	1,215	1,238
25 to 29 years old	668	1,209	1,213	1,212	1,083	1,132	1,088	1,034	1,255	1,248	1,184	1,251	1,317	1,481
30 to 34 years old	388	905	935	805	843	796	835	856	839	805	805	821	928	1,027
35 years old and over	689	1,145	2,012	2,093	2,150	2,126	2,456	2,094	2,280	2,272	2,329	2,313	2,307	2,498
Males	1,540	2,185	2,476	2,535	2,611	2,661	2,701	2,622	2,648	2,653	2,696	2,767	2,907	3,111
14 to 17 years old	5	17	16	7	11	11	17	10	15	41	16	18	17	18
18 and 19 years old	84	202	191	246	333	300	288	250	239	235	297	313	311	309
20 and 21 years old	105	201	313	283	276	342	287	274	358	318	341	347	372	364
22 to 24 years old	314	392	365	365	454	458	405	564	419	405	466	478	517	537
25 to 29 years old	456	594	539	508	447	508	423	427	536	539	488	518	548	621
30 to 34 years old	236	397	381	378	332	294	364	350	317	306	325	333	378	423
35 years old and over	340	382	672	748	757	749	917	748	764	809	762	761	764	839
Females	1,225	2,814	3,521	3,598	3,692	3,820	3,964	3,963	4,014	4,038	4,106	4,170	4,324	4,539
14 to 17 years old	12	20	17	18	9	1	24	20	19	27	48	42	41	43
18 and 19 years old	110	215	211	261	266	366	340	276	311	338	318	336	332	312
20 and 21 years old	128	240	297	313	368	404	320	433	382	430	363	369	390	360
22 to 24 years old	262	452	429	529	510	545	605	774	543	571	634	649	699	701
25 to 29 years old	212	616	674	704	636	624	666	608	720	709	696	733	769	861
30 to 34 years old	151	507	554	427	511	502	471	507	523	499	480	488	551	604
35 years old and over	349	762	1,340	1,345	1,393	1,377	1,539	1,346	1,516	1,464	1,567	1,552	1,543	1,659

NOTE: Distributions by age are estimates based on samples of the civilian noninstitutional population from the U.S. Census Bureau's Current Population Survey. Data through 1995 are for institutions of higher education, while later data are for degree-granting institutions. Degree-granting institutions grant associate's or higher degrees and participate in Title IV federal financial aid programs. The degree-granting classification is very similar to the earlier higher education classification, but it includes more 2-year colleges and excludes a few higher education institutions that did not grant degrees. (See Guide to Sources for details.) Detail may not sum to totals because of rounding.

SOURCE: U.S. Department of Education, National Center for Education Statistics, Higher Education General Information Survey (HEGIS), "Fall Enrollment in Colleges and Universities" surveys, 1970 and 1980; 1990 through 2006 Integrated Postsecondary Education Data System, "Fall Enrollment Survey" (IPEDS-EF:90–99), and Spring 2001 through Spring 2007; and Projections of Education Statistics to 2017. U.S. Department of Commerce, Census Bureau, Current Population Survey (CPS), October, selected years, 1970 through 2007. (This table was prepared August 2008.)

Table 191. Total fall enrollment in degree-granting institutions, by level of enrollment, sex, age, and attendance status of student: 2007

Age of student and attendance status	All levels			Undergraduate			First-professional			Graduate		
	Total	Males	Females	Total	Males	Females	Total	Males	Females	Total	Males	Females
1	2	3	4	5	6	7	8	9	10	11	12	13
All students	18,248,128	7,815,914	10,432,214	15,603,771	6,727,600	8,876,171	350,764	177,988	172,776	2,293,593	910,326	1,383,267
Under 18	668,426	277,582	390,844	668,193	277,489	390,704	18	5	13	215	88	127
18 and 19	3,963,371	1,794,001	2,169,370	3,961,149	1,793,284	2,167,865	1,291	464	827	931	253	678
20 and 21	3,642,872	1,647,492	1,995,380	3,612,195	1,635,396	1,976,799	11,926	4,454	7,472	18,751	7,642	11,109
22 to 24	3,009,713	1,381,504	1,628,209	2,474,561	1,168,612	1,305,949	133,563	61,463	72,100	401,589	151,429	250,160
25 to 29	2,550,482	1,091,510	1,458,972	1,710,195	728,331	981,864	138,825	74,285	64,540	701,462	288,894	412,568
30 to 34	1,365,912	551,208	814,704	944,123	357,944	586,179	31,764	19,067	12,697	390,025	174,197	215,828
35 to 39	980,818	368,814	612,004	709,012	251,299	457,713	13,326	7,895	5,431	258,480	109,620	148,860
40 to 49	1,266,171	423,603	842,568	935,783	304,967	630,816	12,314	6,613	5,701	318,074	112,023	206,051
50 to 64	627,603	208,067	419,536	445,568	150,103	295,465	6,197	2,902	3,295	175,838	55,062	120,776
65 and over	77,379	31,040	46,339	70,608	27,847	42,761	288	132	156	6,483	3,061	3,422
Age unknown	95,381	41,093	54,288	72,384	32,328	40,056	1,252	708	544	21,745	8,057	13,688
Full-time	11,269,892	5,029,444	6,240,448	9,840,978	4,396,868	5,444,110	316,549	159,328	157,221	1,112,365	473,248	639,117
Under 18	171,784	69,033	102,751	171,705	69,000	102,705	15	4	11	64	29	35
18 and 19	3,383,318	1,522,297	1,861,021	3,381,502	1,521,669	1,859,833	1,286	461	825	530	167	363
20 and 21	2,964,697	1,346,897	1,617,800	2,937,292	1,335,936	1,601,356	11,695	4,354	7,341	15,710	6,607	9,103
22 to 24	1,986,776	949,700	1,037,076	1,572,230	778,160	794,070	128,394	58,966	69,428	286,152	112,574	173,578
25 to 29	1,284,698	584,798	699,900	776,416	346,671	429,745	127,726	68,108	59,618	380,556	170,019	210,537
30 to 34	565,710	235,321	330,389	365,008	135,611	229,397	26,135	15,665	10,470	174,567	84,045	90,522
35 to 39	347,864	130,397	217,467	241,500	81,381	160,119	9,555	5,666	3,889	96,809	43,350	53,459
40 to 49	380,043	125,982	254,061	270,137	84,186	185,951	7,527	4,056	3,471	102,379	37,740	64,639
50 to 64	145,757	47,812	97,945	93,913	30,478	63,435	3,153	1,449	1,704	48,691	15,885	32,806
65 and over	4,868	2,260	2,608	3,185	1,471	1,714	149	68	81	1,534	721	813
Age unknown	34,377	14,947	19,430	28,090	12,305	15,785	914	531	383	5,373	2,111	3,262
Part-time	6,978,236	2,786,470	4,191,766	5,762,793	2,330,732	3,432,061	34,215	18,660	15,555	1,181,228	437,078	744,150
Under 18	496,642	208,549	288,093	496,488	208,489	287,999	3	1	2	151	59	92
18 and 19	580,053	271,704	308,349	579,647	271,615	308,032	5	3	2	401	86	315
20 and 21	678,175	300,595	377,580	674,903	299,460	375,443	231	100	131	3,041	1,035	2,006
22 to 24	1,022,937	431,804	591,133	902,331	390,452	511,879	5,169	2,497	2,672	115,437	38,855	76,582
25 to 29	1,265,784	506,712	759,072	933,779	381,660	552,119	11,099	6,177	4,922	320,906	118,875	202,031
30 to 34	800,202	315,887	484,315	579,115	222,333	356,782	5,629	3,402	2,227	215,458	90,152	125,306
35 to 39	632,954	238,417	394,537	467,512	169,918	297,594	3,771	2,229	1,542	161,671	66,270	95,401
40 to 49	886,128	297,621	588,507	665,646	220,781	444,865	4,787	2,557	2,230	215,695	74,283	141,412
50 to 64	481,846	160,255	321,591	351,655	119,625	232,030	3,044	1,453	1,591	127,147	39,177	87,970
65 and over	72,511	28,780	43,731	67,423	26,376	41,047	139	64	75	4,949	2,340	2,609
Age unknown	61,004	26,146	34,858	44,294	20,023	24,271	338	177	161	16,372	5,946	10,426
Percentage distribution												
All students	100.0	100.0	100.0	100.0	100.0	100.0	100.0	100.0	100.0	100.0	100.0	100.0
Under 18	3.7	3.6	3.7	4.3	4.1	4.4	#	#	#	#	#	#
18 and 19	21.7	23.0	20.8	25.4	26.7	24.4	0.4	0.3	0.5	#	#	#
20 and 21	20.0	21.1	19.1	23.1	24.3	22.3	3.4	2.5	4.3	0.8	0.8	0.8
22 to 24	16.5	17.7	15.6	15.9	17.4	14.7	38.1	34.5	41.7	17.5	16.6	18.1
25 to 29	14.0	14.0	14.0	11.0	10.8	11.1	39.6	41.7	37.4	30.6	31.7	29.8
30 to 34	7.5	7.1	7.8	6.1	5.3	6.6	9.1	10.7	7.3	17.0	19.1	15.6
35 to 39	5.4	4.7	5.9	4.5	3.7	5.2	3.8	4.4	3.1	11.3	12.0	10.8
40 to 49	6.9	5.4	8.1	6.0	4.5	7.1	3.5	3.7	3.3	13.9	12.3	14.9
50 to 64	3.4	2.7	4.0	2.9	2.2	3.3	1.8	1.6	1.9	7.7	6.0	8.7
65 and over	0.4	0.4	0.4	0.5	0.4	0.5	0.1	0.1	0.1	0.3	0.3	0.2
Age unknown	0.5	0.5	0.5	0.5	0.5	0.5	0.4	0.4	0.3	0.9	0.9	1.0
Full-time	100.0	100.0	100.0	100.0	100.0	100.0	100.0	100.0	100.0	100.0	100.0	100.0
Under 18	1.5	1.4	1.6	1.7	1.6	1.9	#	#	#	#	#	#
18 and 19	30.0	30.3	29.8	34.4	34.6	34.2	0.4	0.3	0.5	#	#	#
20 and 21	26.3	26.8	25.9	29.8	30.4	29.4	3.7	2.7	4.7	1.4	1.4	1.4
22 to 24	17.6	18.9	16.6	16.0	17.7	14.6	40.6	37.0	44.2	25.7	23.8	27.2
25 to 29	11.4	11.6	11.2	7.9	7.9	7.9	40.3	42.7	37.9	34.2	35.9	32.9
30 to 34	5.0	4.7	5.3	3.7	3.1	4.2	8.3	9.8	6.7	15.7	17.8	14.2
35 to 39	3.1	2.6	3.5	2.5	1.9	2.9	3.0	3.6	2.5	8.7	9.2	8.4
40 to 49	3.4	2.5	4.1	2.7	1.9	3.4	2.4	2.5	2.2	9.2	8.0	10.1
50 to 64	1.3	1.0	1.6	1.0	0.7	1.2	1.0	0.9	1.1	4.4	3.4	5.1
65 and over	#	#	#	#	#	#	#	#	0.1	0.1	0.2	0.1
Age unknown	0.3	0.3	0.3	0.3	0.3	0.3	0.3	0.3	0.2	0.5	0.4	0.5
Part-time	100.0	100.0	100.0	100.0	100.0	100.0	100.0	100.0	100.0	100.0	100.0	100.0
Under 18	7.1	7.5	6.9	8.6	8.9	8.4	#	#	#	#	#	#
18 and 19	8.3	9.8	7.4	10.1	11.7	9.0	#	#	#	#	#	#
20 and 21	9.7	10.8	9.0	11.7	12.8	10.9	0.7	0.5	0.8	0.3	0.2	0.3
22 to 24	14.7	15.5	14.1	15.7	16.8	14.9	15.1	13.4	17.2	9.8	8.9	10.3
25 to 29	18.1	18.2	18.1	16.2	16.4	16.1	32.4	33.1	31.6	27.2	27.2	27.1
30 to 34	11.5	11.3	11.6	10.0	9.5	10.4	16.5	18.2	14.3	18.2	20.6	16.8
35 to 39	9.1	8.6	9.4	8.1	7.3	8.7	11.0	11.9	9.9	13.7	15.2	12.8
40 to 49	12.7	10.7	14.0	11.6	9.5	13.0	14.0	13.7	14.3	18.3	17.0	19.0
50 to 64	6.9	5.8	7.7	6.1	5.1	6.8	8.9	7.8	10.2	10.8	9.0	11.8
65 and over	1.0	1.0	1.0	1.2	1.1	1.2	0.4	0.3	0.5	0.4	0.5	0.4
Age unknown	0.9	0.9	0.8	0.8	0.9	0.7	1.0	0.9	1.0	1.4	1.4	1.4

#Rounds to zero.
NOTE: Degree-granting institutions grant associate's or higher degrees and participate in Title IV federal financial aid programs. Detail may not sum to totals because of rounding.

SOURCE: U.S. Department of Education, National Center for Education Statistics, 2007 Integrated Postsecondary Education Data System (IPEDS), Spring 2007. (This table was prepared October 2008.)

Table 192. Total fall enrollment in degree-granting institutions, by control and type of institution, age, and attendance status of student: 2007

Age of student and attendance status	All institutions			Public institutions			Private (not-for-profit and for-profit) institutions			Private not-for-profit institutions only		
	Total	4-year	2-year	Total	4-year	2-year	Total	4-year	2-year	Total	4-year	2-year
1	2	3	4	5	6	7	8	9	10	11	12	13
All students	18,248,128	11,630,198	6,617,930	13,490,780	7,166,661	6,324,119	4,757,348	4,463,537	293,811	3,571,150	3,537,664	33,486
Under 18	668,426	226,437	441,989	603,430	164,703	438,727	64,996	61,734	3,262	60,050	58,797	1,253
18 and 19	3,963,371	2,496,501	1,466,870	3,087,771	1,667,313	1,420,458	875,600	829,188	46,412	784,185	776,105	8,080
20 and 21	3,642,872	2,540,470	1,102,402	2,749,406	1,698,286	1,051,120	893,466	842,184	51,282	768,560	763,235	5,325
22 to 24	3,009,713	2,108,489	901,224	2,286,919	1,437,269	849,650	722,794	671,220	51,574	557,120	552,583	4,537
25 to 29	2,550,482	1,690,509	859,973	1,765,751	962,096	803,655	784,731	728,413	56,318	529,744	525,022	4,722
30 to 34	1,365,912	855,514	510,398	919,828	440,675	479,153	446,084	414,839	31,245	269,966	267,016	2,950
35 to 39	980,818	584,732	396,086	654,855	279,752	375,103	325,963	304,980	20,983	192,261	189,966	2,295
40 to 49	1,266,171	718,209	547,962	858,630	332,290	526,340	407,541	385,919	21,622	249,823	246,893	2,930
50 to 64	627,603	332,951	294,652	447,534	160,410	287,124	180,069	172,541	7,528	118,491	117,375	1,116
65 and over	77,379	17,459	59,920	70,649	10,981	59,668	6,730	6,478	252	5,268	5,206	62
Age unknown	95,381	58,927	36,454	46,007	12,886	33,121	49,374	46,041	3,333	35,682	35,466	216
Full-time	11,269,892	8,577,299	2,692,593	7,686,981	5,244,841	2,442,140	3,582,911	3,332,458	250,453	2,664,502	2,643,207	21,295
Under 18	171,784	100,932	70,852	137,294	68,699	68,595	34,490	32,233	2,257	30,484	30,135	349
18 and 19	3,383,318	2,379,998	1,003,320	2,534,326	1,574,654	959,672	848,992	805,344	43,648	767,454	760,108	7,346
20 and 21	2,964,697	2,355,947	608,750	2,116,672	1,553,773	562,899	848,025	802,174	45,851	741,936	737,467	4,225
22 to 24	1,986,776	1,642,119	344,657	1,404,007	1,103,749	300,258	582,769	538,370	44,399	449,656	446,735	2,921
25 to 29	1,284,698	1,011,469	273,229	763,452	537,312	226,140	521,246	474,157	47,089	325,658	323,127	2,531
30 to 34	565,710	425,187	140,523	303,239	188,066	115,173	262,471	237,121	25,350	130,701	129,371	1,330
35 to 39	347,864	254,514	93,350	170,684	94,094	76,590	177,180	160,420	16,760	79,146	78,154	992
40 to 49	380,043	275,167	104,876	176,521	88,159	88,362	203,522	187,008	16,514	89,721	88,639	1,082
50 to 64	145,757	105,578	40,179	66,065	31,490	34,575	79,692	74,088	5,604	36,587	36,195	392
65 and over	4,868	2,990	1,878	2,608	894	1,714	2,260	2,096	164	1,364	1,347	17
Age unknown	34,377	23,398	10,979	12,113	3,951	8,162	22,264	19,447	2,817	12,039	11,929	110
Part-time	6,978,236	3,052,899	3,925,337	5,803,799	1,921,820	3,881,979	1,174,437	1,131,079	43,358	906,648	894,457	12,191
Under 18	496,642	125,505	371,137	466,136	96,004	370,132	30,506	29,501	1,005	29,566	28,662	904
18 and 19	580,053	116,503	463,550	553,445	92,659	460,786	26,608	23,844	2,764	16,731	15,997	734
20 and 21	678,175	184,523	493,652	632,734	144,513	488,221	45,441	40,010	5,431	26,868	25,768	1,100
22 to 24	1,022,937	466,370	556,567	882,912	333,520	549,392	140,025	132,850	7,175	107,464	105,848	1,616
25 to 29	1,265,784	679,040	586,744	1,002,299	424,784	577,515	263,485	254,256	9,229	204,086	201,895	2,191
30 to 34	800,202	430,327	369,875	616,589	252,609	363,980	183,613	177,718	5,895	139,265	137,645	1,620
35 to 39	632,954	330,218	302,736	484,171	185,658	298,513	148,783	144,560	4,223	113,115	111,812	1,303
40 to 49	886,128	443,042	443,086	682,109	244,131	437,978	204,019	198,911	5,108	160,102	158,254	1,848
50 to 64	481,846	227,373	254,473	381,469	128,920	252,549	100,377	98,453	1,924	81,904	81,180	724
65 and over	72,511	14,469	58,042	68,041	10,087	57,954	4,470	4,382	88	3,904	3,859	45
Age unknown	61,004	35,529	25,475	33,894	8,935	24,959	27,110	26,594	516	23,643	23,537	106
	Percentage distribution											
All students	100.0	100.0	100.0	100.0	100.0	100.0	100.0	100.0	100.0	100.0	100.0	100.0
Under 18	3.7	1.9	6.7	4.5	2.3	6.9	1.4	1.4	1.1	1.7	1.7	3.7
18 and 19	21.7	21.5	22.2	22.9	23.3	22.5	18.4	18.6	15.8	22.0	21.9	24.1
20 and 21	20.0	21.8	16.7	20.4	23.7	16.6	18.8	18.9	17.5	21.5	21.6	15.9
22 to 24	16.5	18.1	13.6	17.0	20.1	13.4	15.2	15.0	17.6	15.6	15.6	13.5
25 to 29	14.0	14.5	13.0	13.1	13.4	12.7	16.5	16.3	19.2	14.8	14.8	14.1
30 to 34	7.5	7.4	7.7	6.8	6.1	7.6	9.4	9.3	10.6	7.6	7.5	8.8
35 to 39	5.4	5.0	6.0	4.9	3.9	5.9	6.9	6.8	7.1	5.4	5.4	6.9
40 to 49	6.9	6.2	8.3	6.4	4.6	8.3	8.6	8.6	7.4	7.0	7.0	8.7
50 to 64	3.4	2.9	4.5	3.3	2.2	4.5	3.8	3.9	2.6	3.3	3.3	3.3
65 and over	0.4	0.2	0.9	0.5	0.2	0.9	0.1	0.1	0.1	0.1	0.1	0.2
Age unknown	0.5	0.5	0.6	0.3	0.2	0.5	1.0	1.0	1.1	1.0	1.0	0.6
Full-time	100.0	100.0	100.0	100.0	100.0	100.0	100.0	100.0	100.0	100.0	100.0	100.0
Under 18	1.5	1.2	2.6	1.8	1.3	2.8	1.0	1.0	0.9	1.1	1.1	1.6
18 and 19	30.0	27.7	37.3	33.0	30.0	39.3	23.7	24.2	17.4	28.8	28.8	34.5
20 and 21	26.3	27.5	22.6	27.5	29.6	23.0	23.7	24.1	18.3	27.8	27.9	19.8
22 to 24	17.6	19.1	12.8	18.3	21.0	12.3	16.3	16.2	17.7	16.9	16.9	13.7
25 to 29	11.4	11.8	10.1	9.9	10.2	9.3	14.5	14.2	18.8	12.2	12.2	11.9
30 to 34	5.0	5.0	5.2	3.9	3.6	4.7	7.3	7.1	10.1	4.9	4.9	6.2
35 to 39	3.1	3.0	3.5	2.2	1.8	3.1	4.9	4.8	6.7	3.0	3.0	4.7
40 to 49	3.4	3.2	3.9	2.3	1.7	3.6	5.7	5.6	6.6	3.4	3.4	5.1
50 to 64	1.3	1.2	1.5	0.9	0.6	1.4	2.2	2.2	2.2	1.4	1.4	1.8
65 and over	#	#	0.1	#	#	0.1	0.1	0.1	0.2	0.1	0.1	0.2
Age unknown	0.3	0.3	0.4	0.2	0.1	0.3	0.6	0.6	1.1	0.5	0.5	0.5
Part-time	100.0	100.0	100.0	100.0	100.0	100.0	100.0	100.0	100.0	100.0	100.0	100.0
Under 18	7.1	4.1	9.5	8.0	5.0	9.5	2.6	2.6	2.3	3.3	3.2	7.4
18 and 19	8.3	3.8	11.8	9.5	4.8	11.9	2.3	2.1	6.4	1.8	1.8	6.0
20 and 21	9.7	6.0	12.6	10.9	7.5	12.6	3.9	3.5	12.5	3.0	2.9	9.0
22 to 24	14.7	15.3	14.2	15.2	17.4	14.2	11.9	11.7	16.5	11.9	11.8	13.3
25 to 29	18.1	22.2	14.9	17.3	22.1	14.9	22.4	22.5	21.3	22.5	22.6	18.0
30 to 34	11.5	14.1	9.4	10.6	13.1	9.4	15.6	15.7	13.6	15.4	15.4	13.3
35 to 39	9.1	10.8	7.7	8.3	9.7	7.7	12.7	12.8	9.7	12.5	12.5	10.7
40 to 49	12.7	14.5	11.3	11.8	12.7	11.3	17.4	17.6	11.8	17.7	17.7	15.2
50 to 64	6.9	7.4	6.5	6.6	6.7	6.5	8.5	8.7	4.4	9.0	9.1	5.9
65 and over	1.0	0.5	1.5	1.2	0.5	1.5	0.4	0.4	0.2	0.4	0.4	0.4
Age unknown	0.9	1.2	0.6	0.6	0.5	0.6	2.3	2.4	1.2	2.6	2.6	0.9

#Rounds to zero.
NOTE: Degree-granting institutions grant associate's or higher degrees and participate in Title IV federal financial aid programs. Detail may not sum to totals because of rounding.

SOURCE: U.S. Department of Education, National Center for Education Statistics, 2007 Integrated Postsecondary Education Data System (IPEDS), Spring 2008. (This table was prepared October 2008.)

Table 193. Total fall enrollment in degree-granting institutions, by level of enrollment, sex, attendance status, and type and control of institution: 2007

Attendance status, and type and control of institution	Total			Undergraduate			First-professional			Graduate		
	Total	Males	Females	Total	Males	Females	Total	Males	Females	Total	Males	Females
1	2	3	4	5	6	7	8	9	10	11	12	13
Total	**18,248,128**	**7,815,914**	**10,432,214**	**15,603,771**	**6,727,600**	**8,876,171**	**350,764**	**177,988**	**172,776**	**2,293,593**	**910,326**	**1,383,267**
Full-time	11,269,892	5,029,444	6,240,448	9,840,978	4,396,868	5,444,110	316,549	159,328	157,221	1,112,365	473,248	639,117
Part-time	6,978,236	2,786,470	4,191,766	5,762,793	2,330,732	3,432,061	34,215	18,660	15,555	1,181,228	437,078	744,150
4-year	**11,630,198**	**5,045,343**	**6,584,855**	**8,986,150**	**3,957,143**	**5,029,007**	**350,764**	**177,988**	**172,776**	**2,293,284**	**910,212**	**1,383,072**
Full-time	8,577,299	3,839,336	4,737,963	7,148,487	3,206,801	3,941,686	316,549	159,328	157,221	1,112,263	473,207	639,056
Part-time	3,052,899	1,206,007	1,846,892	1,837,663	750,342	1,087,321	34,215	18,660	15,555	1,181,021	437,005	744,016
2-year	**6,617,930**	**2,770,571**	**3,847,359**	**6,617,621**	**2,770,457**	**3,847,164**	†	†	†	**309**	**114**	**195**
Full-time	2,692,593	1,190,108	1,502,485	2,692,491	1,190,067	1,502,424	†	†	†	102	41	61
Part-time	3,925,337	1,580,463	2,344,874	3,925,130	1,580,390	2,344,740	†	†	†	207	73	134
Public	**13,490,780**	**5,857,299**	**7,633,481**	**12,137,583**	**5,300,572**	**6,837,011**	**142,646**	**68,399**	**74,247**	**1,210,551**	**488,328**	**722,223**
Full-time	7,686,981	3,516,489	4,170,492	6,995,302	3,202,891	3,792,411	136,267	65,294	70,973	555,412	248,304	307,108
Part-time	5,803,799	2,340,810	3,462,989	5,142,281	2,097,681	3,044,600	6,379	3,105	3,274	655,139	240,024	415,115
Public 4-year	7,166,661	3,190,280	3,976,381	5,813,773	2,633,667	3,180,106	142,646	68,399	74,247	1,210,242	488,214	722,028
Full-time	5,244,841	2,417,717	2,827,124	4,553,264	2,104,160	2,449,104	136,267	65,294	70,973	555,310	248,263	307,047
Part-time	1,921,820	772,563	1,149,257	1,260,509	529,507	731,002	6,379	3,105	3,274	654,932	239,951	414,981
Public 2-year	6,324,119	2,667,019	3,657,100	6,323,810	2,666,905	3,656,905	†	†	†	309	114	195
Full-time	2,442,140	1,098,772	1,343,368	2,442,038	1,098,731	1,343,307	†	†	†	102	41	61
Part-time	3,881,979	1,568,247	2,313,732	3,881,772	1,568,174	2,313,598	†	†	†	207	73	134
Private	**4,757,348**	**1,958,615**	**2,798,733**	**3,466,188**	**1,427,028**	**2,039,160**	**208,118**	**109,589**	**98,529**	**1,083,042**	**421,998**	**661,044**
Full-time	3,582,911	1,512,955	2,069,956	2,845,676	1,193,977	1,651,699	180,282	94,034	86,248	556,953	224,944	332,009
Part-time	1,174,437	445,660	728,777	620,512	233,051	387,461	27,836	15,555	12,281	526,089	197,054	329,035
Private 4-year	4,463,537	1,855,063	2,608,474	3,172,377	1,323,476	1,848,901	208,118	109,589	98,529	1,083,042	421,998	661,044
Full-time	3,332,458	1,421,619	1,910,839	2,595,223	1,102,641	1,492,582	180,282	94,034	86,248	556,953	224,944	332,009
Part-time	1,131,079	433,444	697,635	577,154	220,835	356,319	27,836	15,555	12,281	526,089	197,054	329,035
Private 2-year	293,811	103,552	190,259	293,811	103,552	190,259	†	†	†	†	†	†
Full-time	250,453	91,336	159,117	250,453	91,336	159,117	†	†	†	†	†	†
Part-time	43,358	12,216	31,142	43,358	12,216	31,142	†	†	†	†	†	†
Not-for-profit	3,571,150	1,515,794	2,055,356	2,470,327	1,046,794	1,423,533	205,860	108,427	97,433	894,963	360,573	534,390
Full-time	2,664,502	1,168,466	1,496,036	2,054,958	890,766	1,164,192	178,490	93,108	85,382	431,054	184,592	246,462
Part-time	906,648	347,328	559,320	415,369	156,028	259,341	27,370	15,319	12,051	463,909	175,981	287,928
Not-for-profit 4-year	3,537,664	1,504,100	2,033,564	2,436,841	1,035,100	1,401,741	205,860	108,427	97,433	894,963	360,573	534,390
Full-time	2,643,207	1,159,775	1,483,432	2,033,663	882,075	1,151,588	178,490	93,108	85,382	431,054	184,592	246,462
Part-time	894,457	344,325	550,132	403,178	153,025	250,153	27,370	15,319	12,051	463,909	175,981	287,928
Not-for-profit 2-year	33,486	11,694	21,792	33,486	11,694	21,792	†	†	†	†	†	†
Full-time	21,295	8,691	12,604	21,295	8,691	12,604	†	†	†	†	†	†
Part-time	12,191	3,003	9,188	12,191	3,003	9,188	†	†	†	†	†	†
For-profit	1,186,198	442,821	743,377	995,861	380,234	615,627	2,258	1,162	1,096	188,079	61,425	126,654
Full-time	918,409	344,489	573,920	790,718	303,211	487,507	1,792	926	866	125,899	40,352	85,547
Part-time	267,789	98,332	169,457	205,143	77,023	128,120	466	236	230	62,180	21,073	41,107
For-profit 4-year	925,873	350,963	574,910	735,536	288,376	447,160	2,258	1,162	1,096	188,079	61,425	126,654
Full-time	689,251	261,844	427,407	561,560	220,566	340,994	1,792	926	866	125,899	40,352	85,547
Part-time	236,622	89,119	147,503	173,976	67,810	106,166	466	236	230	62,180	21,073	41,107
For-profit 2-year	260,325	91,858	168,467	260,325	91,858	168,467	†	†	†	†	†	†
Full-time	229,158	82,645	146,513	229,158	82,645	146,513	†	†	†	†	†	†
Part-time	31,167	9,213	21,954	31,167	9,213	21,954	†	†	†	†	†	†

†Not applicable.
NOTE: Degree-granting institutions grant associate's or higher degrees and participate in Title IV federal financial aid programs.

SOURCE: U.S. Department of Education, National Center for Education Statistics, 2007 Integrated Postsecondary Education Data System (IPEDS), Spring 2008. (This table was prepared October 2008.)

Table 194. Total fall enrollment in degree-granting institutions, by level of enrollment, sex, attendance status, and type and control of institution: 2006

Attendance status, and type and control of institution	Total			Undergraduate			First-professional			Graduate		
	Total	Males	Females	Total	Males	Females	Total	Males	Females	Total	Males	Females
1	2	3	4	5	6	7	8	9	10	11	12	13
Total	**17,758,870**	**7,574,815**	**10,184,055**	**15,184,302**	**6,513,756**	**8,670,546**	**343,446**	**173,808**	**169,638**	**2,231,122**	**887,251**	**1,343,871**
Full-time	10,957,305	4,879,315	6,077,990	9,571,079	4,264,606	5,306,473	309,158	155,211	153,947	1,077,068	459,498	617,570
Part-time	6,801,565	2,695,500	4,106,065	5,613,223	2,249,150	3,364,073	34,288	18,597	15,691	1,154,054	427,753	726,301
4-year	**11,240,330**	**4,870,076**	**6,370,254**	**8,666,011**	**3,809,102**	**4,856,909**	**343,446**	**173,808**	**169,638**	**2,230,873**	**887,166**	**1,343,707**
Full-time	8,313,999	3,719,478	4,594,521	6,927,857	3,104,806	3,823,051	309,158	155,211	153,947	1,076,984	459,461	617,523
Part-time	2,926,331	1,150,598	1,775,733	1,738,154	704,296	1,033,858	34,288	18,597	15,691	1,153,889	427,705	726,184
2-year	**6,518,540**	**2,704,739**	**3,813,801**	**6,518,291**	**2,704,654**	**3,813,637**	†	†	†	**249**	**85**	**164**
Full-time	2,643,306	1,159,837	1,483,469	2,643,222	1,159,800	1,483,422	†	†	†	84	37	47
Part-time	3,875,234	1,544,902	2,330,332	3,875,069	1,544,854	2,330,215	†	†	†	165	48	117
Public	**13,180,133**	**5,679,404**	**7,500,729**	**11,847,426**	**5,133,850**	**6,713,576**	**139,736**	**66,728**	**73,008**	**1,192,971**	**478,826**	**714,145**
Full-time	7,495,563	3,406,146	4,089,417	6,823,841	3,103,019	3,720,822	133,058	63,392	69,666	538,664	239,735	298,929
Part-time	5,684,570	2,273,258	3,411,312	5,023,585	2,030,831	2,992,754	6,678	3,336	3,342	654,307	239,091	415,216
Public 4-year	6,955,013	3,078,769	3,876,244	5,622,555	2,533,300	3,089,255	139,736	66,728	73,008	1,192,722	478,741	713,981
Full-time	5,103,764	2,338,923	2,764,841	4,432,126	2,035,833	2,396,293	133,058	63,392	69,666	538,580	239,698	298,882
Part-time	1,851,249	739,846	1,111,403	1,190,429	497,467	692,962	6,678	3,336	3,342	654,142	239,043	415,099
Public 2-year	6,225,120	2,600,635	3,624,485	6,224,871	2,600,550	3,624,321	†	†	†	249	85	164
Full-time	2,391,799	1,067,223	1,324,576	2,391,715	1,067,186	1,324,529	†	†	†	84	37	47
Part-time	3,833,321	1,533,412	2,299,909	3,833,156	1,533,364	2,299,792	†	†	†	165	48	117
Private	**4,578,737**	**1,895,411**	**2,683,326**	**3,336,876**	**1,379,906**	**1,956,970**	**203,710**	**107,080**	**96,630**	**1,038,151**	**408,425**	**629,726**
Full-time	3,461,742	1,473,169	1,988,573	2,747,238	1,161,587	1,585,651	176,100	91,819	84,281	538,404	219,763	318,641
Part-time	1,116,995	422,242	694,753	589,638	218,319	371,319	27,610	15,261	12,349	499,747	188,662	311,085
Private 4-year	4,285,317	1,791,307	2,494,010	3,043,456	1,275,802	1,767,654	203,710	107,080	96,630	1,038,151	408,425	629,726
Full-time	3,210,235	1,380,555	1,829,680	2,495,731	1,068,973	1,426,758	176,100	91,819	84,281	538,404	219,763	318,641
Part-time	1,075,082	410,752	664,330	547,725	206,829	340,896	27,610	15,261	12,349	499,747	188,662	311,085
Private 2-year	293,420	104,104	189,316	293,420	104,104	189,316	†	†	†	†	†	†
Full-time	251,507	92,614	158,893	251,507	92,614	158,893	†	†	†	†	†	†
Part-time	41,913	11,490	30,423	41,913	11,490	30,423	†	†	†	†	†	†
Not-for-profit	3,512,866	1,489,881	2,022,985	2,448,240	1,033,031	1,415,209	201,623	105,992	95,631	863,003	350,858	512,145
Full-time	2,615,559	1,145,995	1,469,564	2,029,845	877,003	1,152,842	174,485	90,964	83,521	411,229	178,028	233,201
Part-time	897,307	343,886	553,421	418,395	156,028	262,367	27,138	15,028	12,110	451,774	172,830	278,944
Not-for-profit 4-year	3,473,710	1,476,005	1,997,705	2,409,084	1,019,155	1,389,929	201,623	105,992	95,631	863,003	350,858	512,145
Full-time	2,589,590	1,135,163	1,454,427	2,003,876	866,171	1,137,705	174,485	90,964	83,521	411,229	178,028	233,201
Part-time	884,120	340,842	543,278	405,208	152,984	252,224	27,138	15,028	12,110	451,774	172,830	278,944
Not-for-profit 2-year	39,156	13,876	25,280	39,156	13,876	25,280	†	†	†	†	†	†
Full-time	25,969	10,832	15,137	25,969	10,832	15,137	†	†	†	†	†	†
Part-time	13,187	3,044	10,143	13,187	3,044	10,143	†	†	†	†	†	†
For-profit	1,065,871	405,530	660,341	888,636	346,875	541,761	2,087	1,088	999	175,148	57,567	117,581
Full-time	846,183	327,174	519,009	717,393	284,584	432,809	1,615	855	760	127,175	41,735	85,440
Part-time	219,688	78,356	141,332	171,243	62,291	108,952	472	233	239	47,973	15,832	32,141
For-profit 4-year	811,607	315,302	496,305	634,372	256,647	377,725	2,087	1,088	999	175,148	57,567	117,581
Full-time	620,645	245,392	375,253	491,855	202,802	289,053	1,615	855	760	127,175	41,735	85,440
Part-time	190,962	69,910	121,052	142,517	53,845	88,672	472	233	239	47,973	15,832	32,141
For-profit 2-year	254,264	90,228	164,036	254,264	90,228	164,036	†	†	†	†	†	†
Full-time	225,538	81,782	143,756	225,538	81,782	143,756	†	†	†	†	†	†
Part-time	28,726	8,446	20,280	28,726	8,446	20,280	†	†	†	†	†	†

†Not applicable.
NOTE: Degree-granting institutions grant associate's or higher degrees and participate in Title IV federal financial aid programs.

SOURCE: U.S. Department of Education, National Center for Education Statistics, 2006 Integrated Postsecondary Education Data System (IPEDS), Spring 2007. (This table was prepared September 2007.)

Table 195. Total fall enrollment in degree-granting institutions, by level of enrollment, sex, attendance status, and type and control of institution: 2005

Attendance status, and type and control of institution	Total			Undergraduate			First-professional			Graduate		
	Total	Males	Females	Total	Males	Females	Total	Males	Females	Total	Males	Females
1	2	3	4	5	6	7	8	9	10	11	12	13
Total	17,487,475	7,455,925	10,031,550	14,963,964	6,408,871	8,555,093	337,024	169,831	167,193	2,186,487	877,223	1,309,264
Full-time	10,797,011	4,803,388	5,993,623	9,446,430	4,200,863	5,245,567	303,468	151,859	151,609	1,047,113	450,666	596,447
Part-time	6,690,464	2,652,537	4,037,927	5,517,534	2,208,008	3,309,526	33,556	17,972	15,584	1,139,374	426,557	712,817
4-year	10,999,420	4,775,557	6,223,863	8,476,138	3,728,572	4,747,566	337,024	169,831	167,193	2,186,258	877,154	1,309,104
Full-time	8,150,209	3,649,622	4,500,587	6,799,667	3,047,104	3,752,563	303,468	151,859	151,609	1,047,074	450,659	596,415
Part-time	2,849,211	1,125,935	1,723,276	1,676,471	681,468	995,003	33,556	17,972	15,584	1,139,184	426,495	712,689
2-year	6,488,055	2,680,368	3,807,687	6,487,826	2,680,299	3,807,527	†	†	†	229	69	160
Full-time	2,646,802	1,153,766	1,493,036	2,646,763	1,153,759	1,493,004	†	†	†	39	7	32
Part-time	3,841,253	1,526,602	2,314,651	3,841,063	1,526,540	2,314,523	†	†	†	190	62	128
Public	13,021,834	5,589,223	7,432,611	11,697,730	5,046,002	6,651,728	138,207	65,602	72,605	1,185,897	477,619	708,278
Full-time	7,408,761	3,350,485	4,058,276	6,747,911	3,051,732	3,696,179	131,727	62,492	69,235	529,123	236,261	292,862
Part-time	5,613,073	2,238,738	3,374,335	4,949,819	1,994,270	2,955,549	6,480	3,110	3,370	656,774	241,358	415,416
Public 4-year	6,837,605	3,019,831	3,817,774	5,513,730	2,476,679	3,037,051	138,207	65,602	72,605	1,185,668	477,550	708,118
Full-time	5,021,745	2,295,456	2,726,289	4,360,934	1,996,710	2,364,224	131,727	62,492	69,235	529,084	236,254	292,830
Part-time	1,815,860	724,375	1,091,485	1,152,796	479,969	672,827	6,480	3,110	3,370	656,584	241,296	415,288
Public 2-year	6,184,229	2,569,392	3,614,837	6,184,000	2,569,323	3,614,677	†	†	†	229	69	160
Full-time	2,387,016	1,055,029	1,331,987	2,386,977	1,055,022	1,331,955	†	†	†	39	7	32
Part-time	3,797,213	1,514,363	2,282,850	3,797,023	1,514,301	2,282,722	†	†	†	190	62	128
Private	4,465,641	1,866,702	2,598,939	3,266,234	1,362,869	1,903,365	198,817	104,229	94,588	1,000,590	399,604	600,986
Full-time	3,388,250	1,452,903	1,935,347	2,698,519	1,149,131	1,549,388	171,741	89,367	82,374	517,990	214,405	303,585
Part-time	1,077,391	413,799	663,592	567,715	213,738	353,977	27,076	14,862	12,214	482,600	185,199	297,401
Private 4-year	4,161,815	1,755,726	2,406,089	2,962,408	1,251,893	1,710,515	198,817	104,229	94,588	1,000,590	399,604	600,986
Full-time	3,128,464	1,354,166	1,774,298	2,438,733	1,050,394	1,388,339	171,741	89,367	82,374	517,990	214,405	303,585
Part-time	1,033,351	401,560	631,791	523,675	201,499	322,176	27,076	14,862	12,214	482,600	185,199	297,401
Private 2-year	303,826	110,976	192,850	303,826	110,976	192,850	†	†	†	†	†	†
Full-time	259,786	98,737	161,049	259,786	98,737	161,049	†	†	†	†	†	†
Part-time	44,040	12,239	31,801	44,040	12,239	31,801	†	†	†	†	†	†
Not-for-profit	3,454,692	1,464,299	1,990,393	2,418,368	1,017,578	1,400,790	197,289	103,439	93,850	839,035	343,282	495,753
Full-time	2,563,732	1,121,161	1,442,571	1,996,647	860,065	1,136,582	170,560	88,744	81,816	396,525	172,352	224,173
Part-time	890,960	343,138	547,822	421,721	157,513	264,208	26,729	14,695	12,034	442,510	170,930	271,580
Not-for-profit 4-year	3,411,170	1,448,647	1,962,523	2,374,846	1,001,926	1,372,920	197,289	103,439	93,850	839,035	343,282	495,753
Full-time	2,534,793	1,109,075	1,425,718	1,967,708	847,979	1,119,729	170,560	88,744	81,816	396,525	172,352	224,173
Part-time	876,377	339,572	536,805	407,138	153,947	253,191	26,729	14,695	12,034	442,510	170,930	271,580
Not-for-profit 2-year	43,522	15,652	27,870	43,522	15,652	27,870	†	†	†	†	†	†
Full-time	28,939	12,086	16,853	28,939	12,086	16,853	†	†	†	†	†	†
Part-time	14,583	3,566	11,017	14,583	3,566	11,017	†	†	†	†	†	†
For-profit	1,010,949	402,403	608,546	847,866	345,291	502,575	1,528	790	738	161,555	56,322	105,233
Full-time	824,518	331,742	492,776	701,872	289,066	412,806	1,181	623	558	121,465	42,053	79,412
Part-time	186,431	70,661	115,770	145,994	56,225	89,769	347	167	180	40,090	14,269	25,821
For-profit 4-year	750,645	307,079	443,566	587,562	249,967	337,595	1,528	790	738	161,555	56,322	105,233
Full-time	593,671	245,091	348,580	471,025	202,415	268,610	1,181	623	558	121,465	42,053	79,412
Part-time	156,974	61,988	94,986	116,537	47,552	68,985	347	167	180	40,090	14,269	25,821
For-profit 2-year	260,304	95,324	164,980	260,304	95,324	164,980	†	†	†	†	†	†
Full-time	230,847	86,651	144,196	230,847	86,651	144,196	†	†	†	†	†	†
Part-time	29,457	8,673	20,784	29,457	8,673	20,784	†	†	†	†	†	†

†Not applicable.
NOTE: Degree-granting institutions grant associate's or higher degrees and participate in Title IV federal financial aid programs.

SOURCE: U.S. Department of Education, National Center for Education Statistics, 2005 Integrated Postsecondary Education Data System (IPEDS), Spring 2006. (This table was prepared August 2006.)

Table 196. Total fall enrollment in degree-granting institutions, by attendance status, sex of student, and type and control of institution: Selected years, 1970 through 2006

Attendance status and sex of student, type and control of institution	1970	1975	1980[1]	1985	1990	1995	2000	2001	2002	2003	2004	2005	2006
1	2	3	4	5	6	7	8	9	10	11	12	13	14
Total	8,580,887	11,184,859	12,096,895	12,247,055	13,818,637	14,261,781	15,312,289	15,927,987	16,611,711	16,911,481	17,272,044	17,487,475	17,758,870
Full-time	5,816,290	6,841,334	7,097,958	7,075,221	7,820,985	8,128,802	9,009,600	9,447,502	9,946,359	10,326,133	10,610,177	10,797,011	10,957,305
Males	3,504,095	3,926,753	3,689,244	3,607,720	3,807,752	3,807,392	4,111,093	4,299,890	4,501,098	4,637,872	4,739,355	4,803,388	4,879,315
Females	2,312,195	2,914,581	3,408,714	3,467,501	4,013,233	4,321,410	4,898,507	5,147,612	5,445,261	5,688,261	5,870,822	5,993,623	6,077,990
Part-time	2,764,597	4,343,525	4,998,937	5,171,834	5,997,652	6,132,979	6,302,689	6,480,485	6,665,352	6,585,348	6,661,867	6,690,464	6,801,565
Males	1,539,547	2,222,244	2,185,130	2,210,730	2,476,157	2,535,147	2,610,676	2,660,925	2,701,018	2,622,392	2,647,907	2,652,537	2,695,500
Females	1,225,050	2,121,281	2,813,807	2,961,104	3,521,495	3,597,832	3,692,013	3,819,560	3,964,334	3,962,956	4,013,960	4,037,927	4,106,065
4-year	6,261,502	7,214,740	7,570,608	7,715,978	8,578,554	8,769,252	9,363,858	9,677,408	10,082,332	10,417,247	10,726,181	10,999,420	11,240,330
Full-time	4,587,379	5,080,256	5,344,163	5,384,614	5,937,023	6,151,755	6,792,551	7,073,011	7,390,323	7,675,740	7,926,639	8,150,209	8,313,999
Males	2,732,796	2,891,192	2,809,528	2,781,412	2,926,360	2,929,177	3,115,252	3,233,608	3,365,427	3,475,294	3,572,783	3,649,622	3,719,478
Females	1,854,583	2,189,064	2,534,635	2,603,202	3,010,663	3,222,578	3,677,299	3,839,403	4,024,896	4,200,446	4,353,856	4,500,587	4,594,521
Part-time	1,674,123	2,134,484	2,226,445	2,331,364	2,641,531	2,617,497	2,571,307	2,604,397	2,692,009	2,741,507	2,799,542	2,849,211	2,926,331
Males	936,189	1,092,461	1,017,813	1,034,804	1,124,780	1,084,753	1,047,917	1,052,007	1,083,223	1,094,929	1,116,883	1,125,935	1,150,598
Females	737,934	1,042,023	1,208,632	1,296,560	1,516,751	1,532,744	1,523,390	1,552,390	1,608,786	1,646,578	1,682,659	1,723,276	1,775,733
Public 4-year	4,232,722	4,998,142	5,128,612	5,209,540	5,848,242	5,814,545	6,055,398	6,236,455	6,481,613	6,649,441	6,736,536	6,837,605	6,955,013
Full-time	3,086,491	3,469,821	3,592,193	3,623,341	4,033,654	4,084,711	4,371,218	4,532,209	4,724,056	4,864,164	4,943,811	5,021,745	5,103,764
Males	1,813,584	1,947,823	1,873,397	1,863,689	1,982,369	1,951,140	2,008,618	2,082,146	2,166,759	2,224,876	2,259,946	2,295,456	2,338,923
Females	1,272,907	1,521,998	1,718,796	1,759,652	2,051,285	2,133,571	2,362,600	2,450,063	2,557,297	2,639,288	2,683,865	2,726,289	2,764,841
Part-time	1,146,231	1,528,321	1,536,419	1,586,199	1,814,588	1,729,834	1,684,180	1,704,246	1,757,557	1,785,277	1,792,725	1,815,860	1,851,249
Males	609,422	760,469	685,051	693,115	764,248	720,402	683,100	687,436	706,041	712,865	716,569	724,375	739,846
Females	536,809	767,852	851,368	893,084	1,050,340	1,009,432	1,001,080	1,016,810	1,051,516	1,072,412	1,076,156	1,091,485	1,111,403
Private 4-year	2,028,780	2,216,598	2,441,996	2,506,438	2,730,312	2,954,707	3,308,460	3,440,953	3,600,719	3,767,806	3,989,645	4,161,815	4,285,317
Full-time	1,500,888	1,610,435	1,751,970	1,761,273	1,903,369	2,067,044	2,421,333	2,540,802	2,666,267	2,811,576	2,982,828	3,128,464	3,210,235
Males	919,212	943,369	936,131	917,723	943,991	978,037	1,106,634	1,151,462	1,198,668	1,250,418	1,312,837	1,354,166	1,380,555
Females	581,676	667,066	815,839	843,550	959,378	1,089,007	1,314,699	1,389,340	1,467,599	1,561,158	1,669,991	1,774,298	1,829,680
Part-time	527,892	606,163	690,026	745,165	826,943	887,663	887,127	900,151	934,452	956,230	1,006,817	1,033,351	1,075,082
Males	326,767	331,992	332,762	341,689	360,532	364,351	364,817	364,571	377,182	382,064	400,314	401,560	410,752
Females	201,125	274,171	357,264	403,476	466,411	523,312	522,310	535,580	557,270	574,166	606,503	631,791	664,330
Not-for-profit 4-year	2,021,121	2,198,451	2,413,693	2,463,000	2,671,069	2,853,890	3,050,575	3,119,781	3,218,389	3,297,180	3,369,435	3,411,170	3,473,710
Full-time	1,494,625	1,596,074	1,733,014	1,727,707	1,859,124	1,989,457	2,226,028	2,285,510	2,364,851	2,441,119	2,494,090	2,534,793	2,589,590
Males	914,020	930,842	921,253	894,080	915,100	931,956	996,113	1,015,634	1,045,439	1,073,652	1,092,100	1,109,075	1,135,163
Females	580,605	665,232	811,761	833,627	944,024	1,057,501	1,229,915	1,269,876	1,319,412	1,367,467	1,401,990	1,425,718	1,454,427
Part-time	526,496	602,377	680,679	735,293	811,945	864,433	824,547	834,271	853,538	856,061	875,345	876,377	884,120
Males	325,693	329,662	327,986	336,168	352,106	351,874	332,814	331,645	337,765	335,954	341,391	339,572	340,842
Females	2,021,121	2,198,451	352,693	399,125	459,839	512,559	491,733	502,626	515,773	520,107	533,954	536,805	543,278
2-year	2,319,385	3,970,119	4,526,287	4,531,077	5,240,083	5,492,529	5,948,431	6,250,579	6,529,379	6,494,234	6,545,863	6,488,055	6,518,540
Full-time	1,228,911	1,761,078	1,753,795	1,690,607	1,883,962	1,977,047	2,217,049	2,374,491	2,556,036	2,650,393	2,683,538	2,646,802	2,643,306
Males	771,299	1,035,561	879,716	826,308	881,392	878,215	995,841	1,066,282	1,135,671	1,162,578	1,166,572	1,153,766	1,159,837
Females	457,612	725,517	874,079	864,299	1,002,570	1,098,832	1,221,208	1,308,209	1,420,365	1,487,815	1,516,966	1,493,036	1,483,469
Part-time	1,090,474	2,209,041	2,772,492	2,840,470	3,356,121	3,515,482	3,731,382	3,876,088	3,973,343	3,843,841	3,862,325	3,841,253	3,875,234
Males	603,358	1,129,783	1,167,317	1,175,926	1,351,377	1,450,394	1,562,759	1,608,918	1,617,795	1,527,463	1,531,024	1,526,602	1,544,902
Females	487,116	1,079,258	1,605,175	1,664,544	2,004,744	2,065,088	2,168,623	2,267,170	2,355,548	2,316,378	2,331,301	2,314,651	2,330,332
Public 2-year	2,195,412	3,836,366	4,328,782	4,269,733	4,996,475	5,277,829	5,697,388	5,996,701	6,270,380	6,209,257	6,243,576	6,184,229	6,225,120
Full-time	1,129,165	1,662,621	1,595,493	1,496,905	1,716,843	1,840,590	2,000,008	2,155,496	2,333,312	2,406,233	2,425,621	2,387,016	2,391,799
Males	720,440	988,701	811,871	742,673	810,664	818,605	891,282	961,588	1,034,547	1,060,015	1,065,127	1,055,029	1,067,223
Females	408,725	673,920	783,622	754,232	906,179	1,021,985	1,108,726	1,193,908	1,298,765	1,346,218	1,360,494	1,331,987	1,324,576
Part-time	1,066,247	2,173,745	2,733,289	2,772,828	3,279,632	3,437,239	3,697,380	3,841,205	3,937,068	3,803,024	3,817,955	3,797,213	3,833,321
Males	589,439	1,107,680	1,152,268	1,138,011	1,317,730	1,417,488	1,549,407	1,596,441	1,604,673	1,514,539	1,517,834	1,514,363	1,533,412
Females	476,808	1,066,065	1,581,021	1,634,817	1,961,902	2,019,751	2,147,973	2,244,764	2,332,395	2,288,485	2,300,121	2,282,850	2,299,909
Private 2-year	123,973	133,753	197,505	261,344	243,608	214,700	251,043	253,878	258,999	284,977	302,287	303,826	293,420
Full-time	99,746	98,457	158,302	193,702	167,119	136,457	217,041	218,995	222,724	244,160	257,917	259,786	251,507
Males	50,859	46,860	67,845	83,635	70,728	59,610	104,559	104,694	101,124	102,563	101,445	98,737	92,614
Females	48,887	51,597	90,457	110,067	96,391	76,847	112,482	114,301	121,600	141,597	156,472	161,049	158,893
Part-time	24,227	35,296	39,203	67,642	76,489	78,243	34,002	34,883	36,275	40,817	44,370	44,040	41,913
Males	13,919	22,103	15,049	37,915	33,647	32,906	13,352	12,477	13,122	12,924	13,190	12,239	11,490
Females	10,308	13,193	24,154	29,727	42,842	45,337	20,650	22,406	23,153	27,893	31,180	31,801	30,423
Not-for-profit 2-year	113,299	112,997	114,094	108,791	89,158	75,154	58,844	47,549	47,087	43,868	42,250	43,522	39,156
Full-time	91,514	82,158	83,009	76,547	62,003	54,033	46,670	36,750	35,511	32,172	28,903	28,939	25,969
Males	46,030	40,548	34,968	30,878	25,946	23,265	21,950	17,965	16,677	14,371	12,347	12,086	10,832
Females	45,484	41,610	48,041	45,669	36,057	30,768	24,720	18,785	18,834	17,801	16,556	16,853	15,137
Part-time	21,785	30,839	31,085	32,244	27,155	21,121	12,174	10,799	11,576	11,696	13,347	14,583	13,187
Males	12,097	18,929	11,445	10,786	7,970	6,080	4,499	3,540	3,547	3,238	3,385	3,566	3,044
Females	9,688	11,910	19,640	21,458	19,185	15,041	7,675	7,259	8,029	8,458	9,962	11,017	10,143

[1]Large increase in private 2-year institutions in 1980 is due to the addition of schools accredited by the Accrediting Commission of Career Schools and Colleges of Technology.
NOTE: Data through 1995 are for institutions of higher education, while later data are for degree-granting institutions. Degree-granting institutions grant associate's or higher degrees and participate in Title IV federal financial aid programs. The degree-granting classification is very similar to the earlier higher education classification, but it includes more 2-year colleges and excludes a few higher education institutions that did not grant degrees. (See Guide to Sources for details.)
SOURCE: U.S. Department of Education, National Center for Education Statistics, Higher Education General Information Survey (HEGIS), "Fall Enrollment in Colleges and Universities" surveys, 1970 through 1985; and 1990 through 2006 Integrated Postsecondary Education Data System, "Fall Enrollment Survey" (IPEDS-EF:90–99), and Spring 2001 through Spring 2007. (This table was prepared June 2008.)

Table 197. Fall enrollment and number of degree-granting institutions, by control and affiliation of institution: Selected years, 1980 through 2006

Control and affiliation	Total enrollment						Enrollment, fall 2006					Number of institutions[1]				
								Full-time		Part-time						
	Fall 1980	Fall 1990	Fall 2000	Fall 2003[2]	Fall 2004	Fall 2005	Total	Males	Females	Males	Females	Fall 1980	Fall 1990	Fall 2000	Fall 2005	Fall 2006
1	2	3	4	5	6	7	8	9	10	11	12	13	14	15	16	17
All institutions	12,096,895	13,818,637	15,312,289	16,911,481	17,272,044	17,487,475	17,758,870	4,879,315	6,077,990	2,695,500	4,106,065	3,226	3,501	4,056	4,253	4,301
Public institutions	9,457,394	10,844,717	11,752,786	12,858,698	12,980,112	13,021,834	13,180,133	3,406,146	4,089,417	2,273,258	3,411,312	1,493	1,548	1,676	1,675	1,686
Federal	50,989	50,669	16,917	20,636	20,090	20,197	17,344	11,239	4,266	506	1,333	12	17	12	13	14
State	(²)	7,181,380	9,548,090	10,488,733	10,643,035	10,691,230	10,849,760	2,977,569	3,585,118	1,711,263	2,575,810	(²)	978	1,355	1,352	1,363
Local	(²)	3,508,941	2,078,090	2,176,997	2,128,924	2,123,212	2,127,983	370,276	443,173	530,387	784,147	(²)	523	277	265	264
Other public	9,406,405	103,727	109,689	172,332	188,063	187,195	185,046	47,062	56,860	31,102	50,022	1,481	30	32	45	45
Private institutions	2,639,501	2,973,920	3,559,503	4,052,783	4,291,932	4,465,641	4,578,737	1,473,169	1,988,573	422,242	694,753	1,733	1,953	2,380	2,578	2,615
Independent not-for-profit	1,521,614	1,474,818	1,577,242	1,708,561	1,758,209	1,783,462	1,814,579	612,224	729,086	189,612	283,657	795	709	729	753	745
For-profit	111,714	213,693	450,084	711,735	880,247	1,010,949	1,055,871	327,174	519,009	78,356	141,332	164	322	724	933	979
Religiously affiliated[3]	1,006,173	1,285,409	1,532,177	1,632,487	1,653,476	1,671,230	1,638,287	533,771	740,478	154,274	269,764	774	922	927	892	891
Advent Christian Church	143	—	—	—	—	—	—	—	—	—	—	1	—	—	—	—
African Methodist Episcopal Zion Church	1,091	88	34	1,312	1,343	1,269	1,300	706	514	50	30	3	1	1	3	3
African Methodist Episcopal	4,541	3,220	5,980	4,026	3,788	3,475	3,116	1,472	1,459	99	86	6	5	6	5	5
American Baptist	6,131	10,800	15,410	16,073	14,545	14,358	14,381	3,894	5,408	1,594	3,485	11	15	17	16	16
American Evangelical Lutheran Church	—	—	743	1,413	1,414	1,435	1,429	630	704	39	56	—	—	1	1	1
American Lutheran and Lutheran Church in America	3,092	—	—	—	—	—	—	—	—	—	—	3	—	—	—	—
American Lutheran	21,608	—	—	—	—	—	—	—	—	—	—	13	—	—	—	—
Assemblies of God Church	7,814	8,307	14,272	13,321	13,826	14,095	14,560	5,282	6,782	1,206	1,290	10	11	14	14	15
Baptist	38,231	99,510	107,610	120,140	120,898	126,649	130,113	42,871	57,030	12,802	17,410	33	69	68	73	74
Brethren Church	3,925	958	2,088	8,762	8,437	8,003	8,035	2,416	2,908	1,012	1,699	3	3	3	3	3
Brethren in Christ Church	1,301	2,239	2,797	5,866	5,974	6,320	6,391	1,910	2,629	777	1,075	1	1	1	4	4
Christian and Missionary Alliance Church	1,705	2,519	5,278	5,866	5,974	6,320	6,391	1,910	2,629	777	1,075	3	1	1	4	4
Christian Church (Disciples of Christ)	14,913	30,397	35,984	41,436	43,139	44,923	45,537	12,540	19,991	5,043	7,963	12	18	16	17	17
Christian Churches and Churches of Christ	1,342	2,263	7,277	9,078	9,529	9,686	9,405	3,805	3,867	958	775	7	8	18	19	19
Christian Methodist Episcopal	2,486	2,174	1,502	3,647	3,517	3,778	3,863	1,796	1,861	69	137	4	4	1	3	3
Christian Reformed Church	5,408	4,488	5,999	5,963	5,774	5,757	5,748	2,591	2,782	178	197	3	2	3	3	3
Church of Christ (Scientist)	2,773	2,557	—	—	—	—	—	—	—	—	—	6	8	—	—	—
Church of God of Prophecy	—	249	—	—	—	—	—	—	—	—	—	1	1	—	—	—
Church of God	6,082	5,627	12,540	13,743	13,669	14,030	14,753	4,652	6,451	1,663	1,987	9	9	7	7	7
Church of New Jerusalem	170	—	—	—	—	—	—	—	—	—	—	1	—	—	—	—
Church of the Brethren	8,482	4,463	4,187	4,660	5,293	5,382	5,494	2,144	2,852	203	295	6	5	4	5	5
Church of the Nazarene	11,716	10,779	16,661	19,657	19,957	20,418	20,868	6,629	9,296	1,808	3,135	10	9	12	10	10
Churches of Christ	9,343	14,611	30,140	32,226	32,766	33,072	33,028	11,132	13,614	3,297	4,985	9	19	19	20	19
Cumberland Presbyterian	594	746	1,112	1,610	1,625	1,710	2,381	711	858	309	503	2	2	2	2	2
Evangelical Congregational Church	80	88	148	153	156	170	177	17	6	92	62	1	1	1	1	1
Evangelical Covenant Church of America	1,401	1,035	2,387	2,531	2,563	2,684	3,023	735	1,251	315	722	1	2	3	1	1
Evangelical Free Church of America	833	2,355	4,022	2,846	2,972	3,063	3,028	830	728	955	515	1	2	3	2	2
Evangelical Lutheran Church	743	49,210	49,085	53,310	54,138	54,726	54,970	20,955	27,949	2,316	3,750	3	33	34	35	35
Free Methodist	5,543	5,902	7,323	8,921	8,929	9,250	9,345	2,587	4,746	607	1,405	5	3	4	4	4
Free Will Baptist Church	1,132	1,177	2,378	2,955	3,244	3,519	3,842	1,101	1,782	440	519	4	3	4	4	4
Friends United Meeting	1,109	—	—	—	—	—	—	—	—	—	—	6	—	—	—	—
Friends	5,157	5,844	10,898	12,009	12,681	13,387	13,568	4,464	6,213	1,083	1,803	5	6	8	7	7
General Conference Mennonite Church	820	1,243	1,059	252	255	184	196	139	48	9	0	2	2	1	—	—
Greek Orthodox	204	148	132	—	—	—	—	—	—	—	—	1	1	1	1	1
Interdenominational	1,254	11,103	9,788	21,461	22,120	22,493	23,066	7,510	8,788	2,991	3,777	4	17	14	23	24

See notes at end of table.

Table 197. Fall enrollment and number of degree-granting institutions, by control and affiliation of institution: Selected years, 1980 through 2006—Continued

Control and affiliation	Total enrollment						Enrollment, fall 2006					Number of institutions[1]				
							Total	Full-time		Part-time						
	Fall 1980	Fall 1990	Fall 2000	Fall 2003[2]	Fall 2004	Fall 2005		Males	Females	Males	Females	Fall 1980	Fall 1990	Fall 2000	Fall 2005	Fall 2006
1	2	3	4	5	6	7	8	9	10	11	12	13	14	15	16	17
Jewish	5,738	12,217	14,182	7,608	7,777	7,847	8,412	6,201	1,040	466	705	24	63	62	33	33
Latter-Day Saints	39,172	42,274	44,680	48,105	49,636	50,840	52,091	22,150	23,007	3,561	3,373	4	4	4	4	4
Lutheran Church—Missouri Synod	11,727	13,827	18,866	21,189	22,748	19,686	21,107	5,907	7,885	2,201	5,114	15	14	13	12	12
Lutheran Church in America	23,877	5,796	4,322	4,500	4,441	8,243	8,238	3,331	4,190	217	500	20	5	2	3	3
Mennonite Brethren Church	1,344	1,864	2,390	2,889	2,813	2,751	3,124	673	1,106	452	893	3	3	3	3	3
Mennonite Church	4,008	2,859	3,553	3,922	4,112	4,186	4,150	1,527	2,089	189	345	6	5	5	6	6
Missionary Church Inc.	487	699	1,647	1,848	1,988	1,959	2,081	535	891	217	438	1	1	1	1	1
Moravian Church	2,434	2,511	2,939	3,193	3,363	3,116	3,059	665	1,613	149	632	2	2	2	2	2
Multiple Protestant denominations	5,526	211	4,690	4,686	5,092	5,159	5,156	1,315	1,326	1,504	1,011	8	1	7	7	7
North American Baptist	155	—	124	136	105	107	100	45	21	15	19	1	—	1	1	1
Pentecostal Holiness Church	767	566	976	977	1,013	1,105	1,097	421	432	127	117	3	3	2	3	3
Presbyterian U.S.A. and United Presbyterian	47,144	77,700	78,950	82,350	81,207	82,141	81,921	29,528	41,403	3,519	7,471	57	70	64	60	59
Presbyterian Church in America	—	1,877	4,499	4,371	4,370	2,953	2,893	1,044	858	691	300	—	1	5	3	3
Protestant Episcopal	5,396	4,559	5,479	4,953	5,360	4,970	5,015	2,211	2,393	200	211	12	9	12	11	11
Protestant, other	4,072	38,136	30,116	19,107	11,244	11,589	11,026	3,865	4,494	1,278	1,389	11	44	34	20	20
Reformed Church in America	2,713	5,525	6,002	6,321	6,424	6,311	6,460	2,549	3,451	203	257	4	4	5	5	5
Reformed Episcopal Church	67	—	—	—	—	—	—	—	—	—	—	1	—	—	—	—
Reformed Presbyterian Church	2,014	1,556	2,355	3,143	3,180	3,090	2,946	1,108	1,334	259	245	4	2	2	3	3
Reorganized Latter-Day Saints Church	4,274	4,793	3,390	—	—	—	—	—	—	—	—	2	1	2	—	—
Roman Catholic	422,842	530,585	636,336	684,418	695,069	694,517	706,245	194,672	298,878	70,698	141,997	229	239	239	241	240
Russian Orthodox	47	38	106	89	103	104	106	67	16	15	8	1	1	1	1	1
Seventh-Day Adventists	19,168	15,771	19,223	21,551	22,498	22,848	23,232	7,476	10,053	2,008	3,695	11	11	13	13	13
Southern Baptist	85,281	49,493	54,275	38,313	41,762	38,710	40,747	11,321	15,869	5,409	8,148	54	29	32	21	22
Nondenominational	—	6,758	23,573	32,257	25,465	26,340	27,164	7,436	9,009	5,063	5,656	—	14	16	16	17
Unitarian Universalist	87	82	132	188	197	200	218	47	82	25	64	2	2	2	2	2
United Brethren Church	545	601	938	969	959	1,005	1,071	397	480	103	91	1	1	1	1	1
United Church of Christ	14,169	20,175	23,709	23,661	28,499	28,651	26,993	8,577	11,995	2,044	4,377	16	18	18	20	19
United Methodist	127,099	148,851	171,109	180,177	185,853	191,468	192,958	67,945	89,897	12,471	22,645	91	96	100	99	97
Wesleyan Church	3,583	5,311	11,128	15,059	16,778	18,043	19,288	6,186	11,437	601	1,064	5	4	4	6	6
Wisconsin Evangelical Lutheran Synod	808	931	1,660	1,726	1,641	1,571	1,561	627	779	88	67	1	3	2	2	2
Other religiously affiliated	462	5,743	2,534	7,410	7,227	7,884	8,211	2,426	3,933	581	1,271	1	9	4	10	10

—Not available.
[1]Counts of institutions in this table may be lower than reported in other tables, because counts in this table include only institutions reporting separate enrollment data.
[2]Included under "Other public."
[3]Religious affiliation as reported by institution.
NOTE: Data through 1995 are for institutions of higher education, while later data are for degree-granting institutions. Degree-granting institutions grant associate's or higher degrees and participate in Title IV federal financial aid programs. The degree-granting classification is very similar to the earlier higher education classification, but it includes more 2-year colleges and excludes a few higher education institutions that did not grant degrees. (See Guide to Sources for details.) Some data have been revised from previously published figures.
SOURCE: U.S. Department of Education, National Center for Education Statistics, Higher Education General Information Survey (HEGIS), "Fall Enrollment in Institutions of Higher Education" and "Institutional Characteristics" surveys, 1980; and 1990 through 2006 Integrated Postsecondary Education Data System, "Fall Enrollment Survey" (IPEDS-EF-90–95), "Institutional Characteristics Survey" (IPEDS-IC-90–95), and Spring 2003 through Spring 2007. (This table was prepared June 2008.)

Table 198. Total first-time freshmen fall enrollment in degree-granting institutions, by attendance status, sex of student, and type and control of institution: 1955 through 2007

Year	Total, all freshmen	Full-time	Part-time	Males			Females			4-year		2-year	
				Total	Full-time	Part-time	Total	Full-time	Part-time	Public	Private	Public	Private
1	2	3	4	5	6	7	8	9	10	11	12	13	14
1955[1]	670,013	—	—	415,604	—	—	254,409	—	—	283,084 [2]	246,960 [2]	117,288 [2]	22,681 [2]
1956[1]	717,504	—	—	442,903	—	—	274,601	—	—	292,743 [2]	261,951 [2]	137,406 [2]	25,404 [2]
1957[1]	723,879	—	—	441,969	—	—	281,910	—	—	293,544 [2]	262,695 [2]	140,522 [2]	27,118 [2]
1958[1]	775,308	—	—	465,422	—	—	309,886	—	—	328,242 [2]	272,117 [2]	146,379 [2]	28,570 [2]
1959[1]	821,520	—	—	487,890	—	—	333,630	—	—	348,150 [2]	291,691 [2]	153,393 [2]	28,286 [2]
1960[1]	923,069	—	—	539,512	—	—	383,557	—	—	395,884 [2]	313,209 [2]	181,860 [2]	32,116 [2]
1961[1]	1,018,361	—	—	591,913	—	—	426,448	—	—	438,135 [2]	336,449 [2]	210,101 [2]	33,676 [2]
1962[1]	1,030,554	—	—	598,099	—	—	432,455	—	—	445,191 [2]	324,923 [2]	224,537 [2]	35,903 [2]
1963[1]	1,046,424	—	—	604,282	—	—	442,142	—	—	—	—	—	—
1964[1]	1,224,840	—	—	701,524	—	—	523,316	—	—	539,251 [2]	363,348 [2]	275,413 [2]	46,828 [2]
1965[1]	1,441,822	—	—	829,215	—	—	612,607	—	—	642,233 [2]	398,792 [2]	347,788 [2]	53,009 [2]
1966	1,554,337	—	—	889,516	—	—	664,821	—	—	626,472 [2]	382,889 [2]	478,459 [2]	66,517 [2]
1967	1,640,936	1,335,512	305,424	931,127	761,299	169,828	709,809	574,213	135,596	644,525	368,300	561,488	66,623
1968	1,892,849	1,470,653	422,196	1,082,367	847,005	235,362	810,482	623,648	186,834	724,377	378,052	718,562	71,858
1969	1,967,104	1,525,290	441,814	1,118,269	876,280	241,989	848,835	649,010	199,825	699,167	391,508	814,132	62,297
1970	2,063,397	1,587,072	476,325	1,151,960	896,281	255,679	911,437	690,791	220,646	717,449	395,886	890,703	59,359
1971	2,119,018	1,606,036	512,982	1,170,518	895,715	274,803	948,500	710,321	238,179	704,052	384,695	971,295	58,976
1972	2,152,778	1,574,197	578,581	1,157,501	858,254	299,247	995,277	715,943	279,334	680,337	380,982	1,036,616	54,843
1973	2,226,041	1,607,269	618,772	1,182,173	867,314	314,859	1,043,868	739,955	303,913	698,777	378,994	1,089,182	59,088
1974	2,365,761	1,673,333	692,428	1,243,790	896,077	347,713	1,121,971	777,256	344,715	745,637	386,391	1,175,759	57,974
1975	2,515,155	1,763,296	751,859	1,327,935	942,198	385,737	1,187,220	821,098	366,122	771,725	395,440	1,283,523	64,467
1976	2,347,014	1,662,333	684,681	1,170,326	854,597	315,729	1,176,688	807,736	368,952	717,373	413,961	1,152,944	62,736
1977	2,394,426	1,680,916	713,510	1,155,856	839,848	316,008	1,238,570	841,068	397,502	737,497	404,631	1,185,648	66,650
1978	2,389,627	1,650,848	738,779	1,141,777	817,294	324,483	1,247,850	833,554	414,296	736,703	406,669	1,173,544	72,711
1979	2,502,896	1,706,732	796,164	1,179,846	840,315	339,531	1,323,050	866,417	456,633	760,119	415,126	1,253,854	73,797
1980	2,587,644	1,749,928	837,716	1,218,961	862,458	356,503	1,368,683	887,470	481,213	765,395	417,937	1,313,591	90,721
1981	2,595,421	1,737,714	857,707	1,217,680	851,833	365,847	1,377,741	885,881	491,860	754,007	419,257	1,318,436	103,721
1982	2,505,466	1,688,620	816,846	1,199,237	837,223	362,014	1,306,229	851,397	454,832	730,775	404,252	1,254,193	116,246
1983	2,443,703	1,678,071	765,632	1,159,049	824,609	334,440	1,284,654	853,462	431,192	728,244	403,882	1,189,869	121,708
1984	2,356,898	1,613,185	743,713	1,112,303	786,099	326,204	1,244,595	827,086	417,509	713,790	402,959	1,130,311	109,838
1985	2,292,222	1,602,038	690,184	1,075,736	774,858	300,878	1,216,486	827,180	389,306	717,199	398,556	1,060,275	116,192
1986	2,219,208	1,589,451	629,757	1,046,527	768,856	277,671	1,172,681	820,595	352,086	719,974	391,673	990,973	116,588 [3]
1987	2,246,359	1,626,719	619,640	1,046,615	779,226	267,389	1,199,744	847,493	352,251	757,833	405,113	979,820	103,593
1988	2,378,803	1,698,927	679,876	1,100,026	807,319	292,707	1,278,777	891,608	387,169	783,358	425,907	1,048,914	120,624
1989	2,341,035	1,656,594	684,441	1,094,750	791,295	303,455	1,246,285	865,299	380,986	762,217	413,836	1,048,529	116,453 [3]
1990	2,256,624	1,617,118	639,506	1,045,191	771,372	273,819	1,211,433	845,746	365,687	727,264	400,120	1,041,097	88,143
1991	2,277,920	1,652,983	624,937	1,068,433	798,043	270,390	1,209,487	854,940	354,547	717,697	392,904	1,070,048	97,271
1992	2,184,113	1,603,737	580,376	1,013,058	760,290	252,768	1,171,055	843,447	327,608	697,393	408,306	993,074	85,340
1993	2,160,710	1,608,274	552,436	1,007,647	762,240	245,407	1,153,063	846,034	307,029	702,273	410,688	973,545	74,204
1994	2,133,205	1,603,106	530,099	984,558	751,081	233,477	1,148,647	852,025	296,622	709,042	405,917	952,468	65,778
1995	2,168,831	1,646,812	522,019	1,001,052	767,185	233,867	1,167,779	879,627	288,152	731,836	419,025	954,595	63,375
1996	2,274,319	1,739,852	534,467	1,046,662	805,982	240,680	1,227,657	933,870	293,787	741,164	427,442	989,536	116,177
1997	2,219,255	1,733,512	485,743	1,026,058	806,054	220,004	1,193,197	927,458	265,739	755,362	442,397	923,954	97,542
1998	2,212,593	1,775,412	437,181	1,022,656	825,577	197,079	1,189,937	949,835	240,102	792,772	460,948	858,417	100,456
1999	2,351,932	1,845,407	506,525	1,091,802	863,377	228,425	1,260,130	982,030	278,100	818,957	473,562	952,319	107,094
2000	2,427,551	1,918,093	509,458	1,123,948	894,432	229,516	1,303,603	1,023,661	279,942	842,228	498,532	952,175	134,616
2001	2,497,078	1,989,179	507,899	1,152,837	926,393	226,444	1,344,241	1,062,786	281,455	866,619	508,030	988,726	133,703
2002	2,570,611	2,053,065	517,546	1,170,609	945,938	224,671	1,400,002	1,107,127	292,875	886,297	517,621	1,037,267	129,426
2003	2,591,754	2,102,394	489,360	1,175,856	965,075	210,781	1,415,898	1,137,319	278,579	918,602	537,726	1,004,428	130,998
2004	2,630,243	2,147,546	482,697	1,190,268	981,591	208,677	1,439,975	1,165,955	274,020	925,249	562,485	1,009,082	133,427
2005	2,657,338	2,189,884	467,454	1,200,055	995,610	204,445	1,457,283	1,194,274	263,009	953,903	606,712	977,224	119,499
2006	2,707,213	2,219,853	487,360	1,228,665	1,015,585	213,080	1,478,548	1,204,268	274,280	990,262	598,412	1,013,080	105,459
2007	2,776,168	2,293,855	482,313	1,267,030	1,052,600	214,430	1,509,138	1,241,255	267,833	1,023,543	633,296	1,016,262	103,067

—Not available.

[1] Excludes first-time freshmen in occupational programs not creditable towards a bachelor's degree.

[2] Data for 2-year branches of 4-year college systems are aggregated with the 4-year institutions.

[3] Because of imputation techniques, data are not consistent with figures for other years.

NOTE: Data through 1995 are for institutions of higher education, while later data are for degree-granting institutions. Degree-granting institutions grant associate's or higher degrees and participate in Title IV federal financial aid programs. The degree-granting classification is very similar to the earlier higher education classification, but it includes more 2-year colleges and excludes a few higher education institutions that did not grant degrees. (See Guide to Sources for details.) Beginning in fall 2000, data are for first-time degree/certificate-seeking undergraduates. Alaska and Hawaii are included in all years.

SOURCE: U.S. Department of Education, National Center for Education Statistics, *Biennial Survey of Education in the United States; Opening Fall Enrollment in Higher Education*, 1963 through 1965; Higher Education General Information Survey (HEGIS), "Fall Enrollment in Colleges and Universities" surveys, 1966 through 1985; and 1986 through 2007 Integrated Postsecondary Education Data System, "Fall Enrollment Survey" (IPEDS-EF:86–99), and Spring 2001 through Spring 2008. (This table was prepared November 2008.)

Table 199. Total first-time freshmen fall enrollment in degree-granting institutions, by attendance status, sex, control of institution, and state or jurisdiction: Selected years, 2000 through 2006

State or jurisdiction	Total, fall 2000	Total, fall 2002	Total, fall 2003	Total, fall 2004	Total, fall 2005	Fall 2006 Total	Full-time Total	Full-time Males	Full-time Females	Part-time Total	Part-time Males	Part-time Females	Public institutions	Private institutions
1	2	3	4	5	6	7	8	9	10	11	12	13	14	15
United States	2,427,551	2,570,611	2,591,754	2,630,243	2,657,338	2,707,213	2,219,853	1,015,585	1,204,268	487,360	213,080	274,280	2,003,342	703,871
Alabama	43,411	43,065	42,813	42,737	42,461	42,821	37,841	17,084	20,757	4,980	2,285	2,695	37,549	5,272
Alaska	2,432	2,661	2,753	2,760	2,899	2,984	2,360	1,109	1,251	624	233	391	2,856	128
Arizona	46,646	46,879	44,687	50,521	76,987	63,830	51,310	19,817	31,493	12,520	5,914	6,606	36,353	27,477
Arkansas	22,695	23,021	24,536	24,110	24,480	23,545	21,021	9,577	11,444	2,524	1,065	1,459	20,529	3,016
California	246,128	274,436	246,913	259,869	266,989	294,343	207,707	93,666	114,041	86,636	41,268	45,368	243,069	51,274
Colorado	43,201	44,525	46,088	45,341	47,330	52,309	40,083	18,266	21,817	12,226	5,147	7,079	37,767	14,542
Connecticut	24,212	26,408	26,531	27,295	27,520	27,913	24,387	11,261	13,126	3,526	1,358	2,168	17,517	10,396
Delaware	7,636	9,299	8,766	8,253	8,763	8,259	7,381	3,171	4,210	878	309	569	7,206	1,053
District of Columbia	9,150	10,462	10,231	11,350	11,334	9,996	9,260	3,857	5,403	736	251	485	1,425	8,571
Florida	109,931	125,322	130,724	138,561	136,694	143,052	109,298	48,855	60,443	33,754	13,910	19,844	102,910	40,142
Georgia	67,616	75,130	82,588	83,314	74,267	76,298	62,899	27,390	35,509	13,399	5,471	7,928	61,510	14,788
Hawaii	8,931	9,211	9,073	8,492	8,466	8,316	6,385	2,779	3,606	1,931	890	1,041	6,521	1,795
Idaho	10,669	12,950	11,370	11,801	12,549	11,555	10,104	4,424	5,680	1,451	625	826	8,470	3,085
Illinois	107,592	110,013	115,453	103,212	111,724	109,524	91,752	41,759	49,993	17,772	8,166	9,606	68,609	40,915
Indiana	59,320	62,691	62,478	61,520	61,915	64,138	56,169	26,468	29,701	7,969	3,688	4,281	45,629	18,509
Iowa	39,564	43,860	41,835	43,352	41,242	38,985	31,277	15,447	15,830	7,708	2,848	4,860	26,037	12,948
Kansas	31,424	29,271	29,681	28,393	29,173	29,057	24,253	12,205	12,048	4,804	2,286	2,518	25,865	3,192
Kentucky	34,140	37,998	38,390	39,485	37,766	38,697	33,237	14,129	19,108	5,460	2,056	3,404	28,765	9,932
Louisiana	45,383	43,149	46,406	43,572	32,018	35,643	32,269	13,678	18,591	3,374	1,445	1,929	30,507	5,136
Maine	9,231	10,287	10,710	10,760	11,181	11,465	10,186	4,869	5,317	1,279	476	803	7,759	3,706
Maryland	35,552	40,346	42,258	45,815	44,288	47,166	35,956	16,119	19,837	11,210	4,647	6,563	39,701	7,465
Massachusetts	66,044	67,654	68,490	70,869	70,873	71,764	64,038	29,145	34,893	7,726	2,841	4,885	33,693	38,071
Michigan	84,998	88,325	88,497	88,078	93,221	96,812	73,513	33,877	39,636	23,299	9,818	13,481	79,550	17,262
Minnesota	63,893	64,246	62,436	61,042	57,822	54,004	46,796	22,833	23,963	7,208	3,062	4,146	39,206	14,798
Mississippi	30,356	37,841	34,337	33,646	33,665	32,480	27,952	11,856	16,096	4,528	1,743	2,785	30,205	2,275
Missouri	48,639	49,730	51,066	51,431	52,678	52,569	46,242	20,509	25,733	6,327	2,673	3,654	35,992	16,577
Montana	7,771	7,868	8,538	8,484	8,654	8,554	7,497	3,875	3,622	1,057	433	624	7,781	773
Nebraska	19,027	19,928	20,670	18,855	19,015	18,519	16,394	7,867	8,527	2,125	923	1,202	14,354	4,165
Nevada	10,490	10,236	9,575	13,995	15,117	15,052	9,453	4,038	5,415	5,599	2,717	2,882	13,219	1,833
New Hampshire	13,143	12,408	12,832	12,420	12,692	12,985	11,737	5,366	6,371	1,248	497	751	7,861	5,124
New Jersey	52,233	55,624	56,108	57,564	58,396	61,540	52,624	25,116	27,508	8,916	3,789	5,127	51,379	10,161
New Mexico	15,261	15,834	16,604	16,827	16,653	16,961	13,257	6,182	7,075	3,704	1,737	1,967	15,741	1,220
New York	168,181	171,246	178,097	180,253	181,328	182,929	172,388	80,299	92,089	10,541	4,469	6,072	105,368	77,561
North Carolina	69,343	78,576	76,673	81,444	79,628	84,968	66,392	29,496	36,896	18,576	7,596	10,980	67,540	17,428
North Dakota	8,929	9,149	10,154	9,477	8,296	8,365	7,889	4,272	3,617	476	193	283	7,281	1,084
Ohio	98,823	100,076	104,007	104,334	102,800	103,531	90,995	42,343	48,652	12,536	5,508	7,028	72,319	31,212
Oklahoma	35,094	34,659	37,491	34,948	35,318	34,751	28,237	13,069	15,168	6,514	2,775	3,739	28,965	5,786
Oregon	26,946	27,112	27,239	28,402	28,944	29,704	22,262	10,090	12,172	7,442	3,441	4,001	23,882	5,822
Pennsylvania	125,578	131,518	131,515	132,339	132,758	137,903	121,112	57,663	63,449	16,791	6,462	10,329	78,302	59,601
Rhode Island	13,789	14,819	15,070	15,388	15,277	16,103	14,644	6,916	7,728	1,459	573	886	7,359	8,744
South Carolina	32,353	37,589	37,649	37,868	38,469	39,557	34,108	14,676	19,432	5,449	2,195	3,254	32,478	7,079
South Dakota	8,597	9,124	9,577	9,076	8,780	9,280	8,283	4,042	4,241	997	379	618	7,410	1,870
Tennessee	43,327	44,876	45,880	47,991	49,076	50,120	45,803	19,910	25,893	4,317	1,743	2,574	33,589	16,531
Texas	181,813	188,647	197,110	205,221	202,388	198,219	138,804	64,484	74,320	59,415	27,552	31,863	173,707	24,512
Utah	24,953	28,866	27,763	26,787	28,501	29,402	21,507	9,719	11,788	7,895	3,960	3,935	21,970	7,432
Vermont	6,810	6,583	6,341	6,343	7,684	7,191	6,658	3,407	3,251	533	212	321	4,078	3,113
Virginia	52,661	56,031	60,269	66,621	68,005	73,708	60,889	26,664	34,225	12,819	5,418	7,401	54,802	18,906
Washington	36,287	36,549	38,919	37,393	38,367	37,269	33,188	15,455	17,733	4,081	1,843	2,238	29,870	7,399
West Virginia	15,659	16,826	17,858	16,602	16,675	16,926	15,807	7,476	8,331	1,119	405	714	14,295	2,631
Wisconsin	53,662	57,559	56,167	55,331	55,326	55,816	46,640	22,188	24,452	9,176	3,469	5,707	45,860	9,956
Wyoming	4,209	6,230	6,326	6,519	6,661	6,104	5,378	3,390	1,988	726	316	410	4,501	1,603
U.S. Service Academies	3,818	3,898	4,212	4,182	4,225	4,231	4,231	3,432	799	0	0	0	4,231	†
Other jurisdictions	39,609	40,931	43,361	43,506	41,800	42,847	39,413	17,296	22,117	3,434	1,533	1,901	16,003	26,844
American Samoa	297	477	536	575	597	531	295	121	174	236	96	140	531	0
Federated States of Micronesia	786	952	1,102	1,389	761	1,112	909	440	469	203	103	100	1,112	0
Guam	770	756	749	724	1,117	1,149	673	265	408	476	231	245	1,110	39
Marshall Islands	199	224	133	179	12	6	6	3	3	0	0	0	6	0
Northern Marianas	333	241	307	255	199	192	176	69	107	16	6	10	192	0
Palau	147	103	110	115	105	134	124	69	55	10	2	8	134	0
Puerto Rico	36,773	37,547	39,944	39,471	38,648	39,343	36,895	16,236	20,659	2,448	1,082	1,366	12,538	26,805
U.S. Virgin Islands	304	631	480	798	361	380	335	93	242	45	13	32	380	0

†Not applicable.
NOTE: Degree-granting institutions grant associate's or higher degrees and participate in Title IV federal financial aid programs. Data are for first-time degree/certificate-seeking undergraduates.

SOURCE: U.S. Department of Education, National Center for Education Statistics, 2000 through 2006 Integrated Postsecondary Education Data System, Spring 2001 through Spring 2007. (This table was prepared June 2008.)

Table 200. Recent high school completers and their enrollment in college, by sex: 1960 through 2007

[Numbers in thousands]

Year	Number of high school completers[1] Total	Males	Females	Enrolled in college[2] Total Number	Total Percent	Males Number	Males Percent	Females Number	Females Percent
1	2	3	4	5	6	7	8	9	10
1960	1,679 (43.8)	756 (31.8)	923 (29.6)	758 (40.9)	45.1 (2.13)	408 (29.5)	54.0 (3.18)	350 (28.2)	37.9 (2.80)
1961	1,763 (46.0)	790 (33.2)	973 (31.3)	847 (42.9)	48.0 (2.09)	445 (30.8)	56.3 (3.10)	402 (29.9)	41.3 (2.77)
1962	1,838 (43.6)	872 (31.5)	966 (30.0)	900 (43.2)	49.0 (2.05)	480 (31.1)	55.0 (2.96)	420 (30.0)	43.5 (2.80)
1963	1,741 (44.2)	794 (32.1)	947 (30.0)	784 (41.5)	45.0 (2.09)	415 (29.8)	52.3 (3.11)	369 (28.8)	39.0 (2.78)
1964	2,145 (43.0)	997 (31.9)	1,148 (28.5)	1,037 (45.6)	48.3 (1.89)	570 (32.9)	57.2 (2.75)	467 (31.4)	40.7 (2.54)
1965	2,659 (47.7)	1,254 (35.1)	1,405 (32.0)	1,354 (51.4)	50.9 (1.70)	718 (36.7)	57.3 (2.45)	636 (35.8)	45.3 (2.33)
1966	2,612 (45.0)	1,207 (33.8)	1,405 (29.0)	1,309 (50.2)	50.1 (1.72)	709 (36.0)	58.7 (2.49)	600 (34.8)	42.7 (2.32)
1967	2,525 (37.9)	1,142 (28.4)	1,383 (24.3)	1,311 (40.9)	51.9 (1.42)	658 (28.9)	57.6 (2.09)	653 (28.9)	47.2 (1.92)
1968	2,606 (37.3)	1,184 (28.2)	1,422 (23.8)	1,444 (41.7)	55.4 (1.39)	748 (29.6)	63.2 (2.00)	696 (29.3)	48.9 (1.89)
1969	2,842 (36.0)	1,352 (26.8)	1,490 (23.7)	1,516 (42.5)	53.3 (1.34)	812 (30.3)	60.1 (1.90)	704 (29.7)	47.2 (1.85)
1970	2,758 (37.4)	1,343 (26.1)	1,415 (26.8)	1,427 (42.2)	51.7 (1.36)	741 (29.7)	55.2 (1.94)	686 (29.8)	48.5 (1.90)
1971	2,875 (38.0)	1,371 (26.6)	1,504 (27.1)	1,538 (43.2)	53.5 (1.33)	790 (30.3)	57.6 (1.90)	749 (30.8)	49.8 (1.84)
1972	2,964 (37.8)	1,423 (27.0)	1,542 (26.4)	1,459 (43.1)	49.2 (1.31)	750 (30.4)	52.7 (1.89)	709 (30.5)	46.0 (1.81)
1973	3,058 (37.1)	1,460 (27.6)	1,599 (24.6)	1,424 (43.0)	46.6 (1.29)	730 (30.6)	50.0 (1.87)	694 (30.2)	43.4 (1.77)
1974	3,101 (38.6)	1,491 (27.8)	1,611 (26.8)	1,475 (43.7)	47.6 (1.28)	736 (30.8)	49.4 (1.85)	740 (31.1)	45.9 (1.77)
1975	3,185 (38.6)	1,513 (27.3)	1,672 (27.2)	1,615 (44.8)	50.7 (1.26)	796 (31.2)	52.6 (1.83)	818 (32.1)	49.0 (1.75)
1976	2,986 (39.8)	1,451 (28.9)	1,535 (27.3)	1,458 (43.6)	48.8 (1.31)	685 (30.4)	47.2 (1.87)	773 (31.2)	50.3 (1.82)
1977	3,141 (40.7)	1,483 (29.7)	1,659 (27.7)	1,590 (45.4)	50.6 (1.29)	773 (31.8)	52.1 (1.87)	817 (32.4)	49.3 (1.77)
1978	3,163 (39.7)	1,485 (29.3)	1,677 (26.7)	1,585 (45.2)	50.1 (1.28)	759 (31.6)	51.1 (1.87)	827 (32.4)	49.3 (1.76)
1979	3,160 (40.0)	1,475 (29.2)	1,685 (27.2)	1,559 (45.1)	49.3 (1.28)	744 (31.4)	50.4 (1.88)	815 (32.4)	48.4 (1.76)
1980	3,088 (39.4)	1,498 (28.4)	1,589 (27.3)	1,523 (44.6)	49.3 (1.30)	700 (30.9)	46.7 (1.86)	823 (32.0)	51.8 (1.81)
1981	3,056 (42.2)	1,491 (30.4)	1,565 (29.1)	1,648 (45.8)	53.9 (1.30)	817 (32.4)	54.8 (1.86)	831 (32.4)	53.1 (1.82)
1982	3,100 (40.4)	1,509 (29.0)	1,592 (28.2)	1,569 (46.9)	50.6 (1.36)	741 (32.7)	49.1 (1.95)	828 (33.6)	52.0 (1.90)
1983	2,963 (41.6)	1,389 (30.4)	1,573 (28.2)	1,562 (46.7)	52.7 (1.39)	721 (32.3)	51.9 (2.03)	841 (33.6)	53.4 (1.91)
1984	3,012 (36.5)	1,429 (28.7)	1,584 (21.9)	1,663 (46.0)	55.2 (1.37)	801 (32.7)	56.0 (1.99)	862 (32.3)	54.5 (1.90)
1985	2,668 (40.1)	1,287 (28.7)	1,381 (27.9)	1,540 (45.1)	57.7 (1.45)	755 (31.6)	58.6 (2.08)	785 (32.1)	56.8 (2.02)
1986	2,786 (38.6)	1,332 (28.5)	1,454 (26.0)	1,498 (45.0)	53.8 (1.43)	743 (31.7)	55.8 (2.06)	755 (31.9)	51.9 (1.99)
1987	2,647 (40.9)	1,278 (29.8)	1,369 (28.0)	1,503 (45.1)	56.8 (1.46)	746 (31.9)	58.3 (2.09)	757 (31.9)	55.3 (2.04)
1988	2,673 (47.0)	1,334 (34.1)	1,339 (32.3)	1,575 (50.3)	58.9 (1.57)	761 (35.6)	57.1 (2.24)	814 (35.4)	60.7 (2.20)
1989	2,450 (46.5)	1,204 (32.9)	1,246 (32.8)	1,460 (48.7)	59.6 (1.64)	693 (34.0)	57.6 (2.35)	767 (34.8)	61.6 (2.27)
1990	2,362 (43.0)	1,173 (30.6)	1,189 (30.2)	1,420 (45.9)	60.1 (1.60)	680 (32.2)	58.0 (2.29)	740 (32.6)	62.2 (2.24)
1991	2,276 (41.0)	1,140 (29.0)	1,136 (29.0)	1,423 (44.8)	62.5 (1.62)	660 (31.4)	57.9 (2.33)	763 (31.9)	67.1 (2.22)
1992	2,397 (40.4)	1,216 (29.1)	1,180 (28.1)	1,483 (45.4)	61.9 (1.58)	729 (32.3)	60.0 (2.24)	754 (31.8)	63.8 (2.23)
1993	2,342 (41.4)	1,120 (30.6)	1,223 (27.7)	1,467 (45.4)	62.6 (1.59)	670 (31.9)	59.9 (2.33)	797 (32.1)	65.2 (2.17)
1994	2,517 (38.1)	1,244 (27.9)	1,273 (25.9)	1,559 (43.0)	61.9 (1.43)	754 (30.6)	60.6 (2.05)	805 (30.2)	63.2 (1.99)
1995	2,599 (40.9)	1,238 (29.9)	1,361 (27.7)	1,610 (44.5)	61.9 (1.41)	775 (31.3)	62.6 (2.03)	835 (31.5)	61.3 (1.95)
1996	2,660 (40.5)	1,297 (29.5)	1,363 (27.7)	1,729 (46.1)	65.0 (1.42)	779 (32.4)	60.1 (2.09)	950 (32.5)	69.7 (1.92)
1997	2,769 (41.8)	1,354 (31.0)	1,415 (27.9)	1,856 (47.3)	67.0 (1.38)	860 (33.6)	63.6 (2.01)	995 (32.9)	70.3 (1.87)
1998	2,810 (43.9)	1,452 (31.0)	1,358 (31.0)	1,844 (48.3)	65.6 (1.38)	906 (34.4)	62.4 (1.96)	938 (33.9)	69.1 (1.93)
1999	2,897 (41.5)	1,474 (29.9)	1,423 (28.8)	1,822 (47.8)	62.9 (1.38)	905 (34.1)	61.4 (1.95)	917 (33.4)	64.4 (1.95)
2000	2,756 (45.3)	1,251 (33.6)	1,505 (29.7)	1,745 (48.4)	63.3 (1.41)	749 (33.4)	59.9 (2.13)	996 (34.4)	66.2 (1.88)
2001	2,549 (46.5)	1,277 (33.7)	1,273 (32.0)	1,574 (47.5)	61.8 (1.48)	767 (33.7)	60.1 (2.11)	808 (33.3)	63.5 (2.08)
2002	2,796 (42.7)	1,412 (31.3)	1,384 (29.0)	1,824 (46.1)	65.2 (1.31)	877 (33.0)	62.1 (1.88)	947 (32.1)	68.4 (1.82)
2003	2,677 (42.2)	1,306 (29.9)	1,372 (29.7)	1,711 (45.2)	63.9 (1.35)	799 (31.5)	61.2 (1.97)	913 (32.3)	66.5 (1.86)
2004	2,752 (40.0)	1,327 (29.1)	1,425 (27.3)	1,835 (44.9)	66.7 (1.31)	815 (31.5)	61.4 (1.95)	1,020 (31.6)	71.5 (1.74)
2005	2,675 (40.8)	1,262 (31.5)	1,414 (24.9)	1,834 (44.8)	68.6 (1.31)	839 (32.2)	66.5 (1.94)	995 (30.6)	70.4 (1.77)
2006	2,692 (44.6)	1,328 (32.7)	1,363 (30.1)	1,776 (46.4)	66.0 (1.33)	875 (33.2)	65.8 (1.90)	901 (32.4)	66.1 (1.87)
2007	2,955 (42.6)	1,511 (30.0)	1,444 (30.3)	1,986 (47.0)	67.2 (1.26)	999 (33.4)	66.1 (1.78)	986 (33.1)	68.3 (1.79)

[1]Individuals ages 16 to 24 who graduated from high school or completed a GED during the preceding 12 months.
[2]Enrollment in college as of October of each year for individuals ages 16 to 24 who completed high school during the preceding 12 months.
NOTE: Data are based on sample surveys of the civilian population. High school completion data in this table differ from figures appearing in other tables because of varying survey procedures and coverage. High school completers include GED recipients. Standard errors appear in parentheses. Detail may not sum to totals because of rounding.
SOURCE: American College Testing Program, unpublished tabulations, derived from statistics collected by the Census Bureau, 1960 through 1969. U.S. Department of Commerce, Census Bureau, Current Population Survey (CPS), October, 1970 through 2007. (This table was prepared July 2008.)

Table 201. Recent high school completers and their enrollment in college, by race/ethnicity: 1960 through 2007
[Numbers in thousands]

Year	Number of high school completers[1]				Enrolled in college[2]									
	Total	White	Black[3]	Hispanic[3]	Total		White		Black[3]		Hispanic[3]			
					Number	Percent	Number	Percent	Number	Percent	Number	Annual Percent		3-year moving average
1	2	3	4	5	6	7	8	9	10	11	12	13		14
1960	1,679 (43.8)	1,565 (44.7)	(†)	(†)	758 (40.9)	45.1 (2.13)	717 (40.2)	45.8 (2.21)	(†)	(†)	(†)	(†)	—	(†)
1961	1,763 (46.0)	1,612 (46.9)	(†)	(†)	847 (42.9)	48.0 (2.09)	798 (42.2)	49.5 (2.19)	(†)	(†)	(†)	(†)	—	(†)
1962	1,838 (43.6)	1,660 (45.2)	(†)	(†)	900 (43.2)	49.0 (2.05)	840 (42.4)	50.6 (2.15)	(†)	(†)	(†)	(†)	—	(†)
1963	1,741 (44.2)	1,615 (45.2)	(†)	(†)	784 (41.5)	45.0 (2.09)	736 (40.7)	45.6 (2.17)	(†)	(†)	(†)	(†)	—	(†)
1964	2,145 (43.0)	1,964 (45.4)	(†)	(†)	1,037 (45.6)	48.3 (1.89)	967 (44.8)	49.2 (1.98)	(†)	(†)	(†)	(†)	—	(†)
1965	2,659 (47.7)	2,417 (50.6)	(†)	(†)	1,354 (51.4)	50.9 (1.70)	1,249 (50.4)	51.7 (1.78)	(†)	(†)	(†)	(†)	—	(†)
1966	2,612 (45.0)	2,403 (48.0)	(†)	(†)	1,309 (50.2)	50.1 (1.72)	1,243 (49.6)	51.7 (1.79)	(†)	(†)	(†)	(†)	—	(†)
1967	2,525 (37.9)	2,267 (40.3)	(†)	(†)	1,311 (40.9)	51.9 (1.42)	1,202 (40.1)	53.0 (1.50)	(†)	(†)	(†)	(†)	—	(†)
1968	2,606 (37.3)	2,303 (40.4)	(†)	(†)	1,444 (41.7)	55.4 (1.39)	1,304 (40.9)	56.6 (1.47)	(†)	(†)	(†)	(†)	—	(†)
1969	2,842 (36.0)	2,538 (39.8)	(†)	(†)	1,516 (42.5)	53.3 (1.34)	1,402 (42.0)	55.2 (1.41)	(†)	(†)	(†)	(†)	—	(†)
1970	2,758 (37.4)	2,461 (40.7)	(†)	(†)	1,427 (42.2)	51.7 (1.36)	1,280 (41.2)	52.0 (1.44)	(†)	(†)	(†)	(†)	—	(†)
1971	2,875 (38.0)	2,596 (41.1)	(†)	(†)	1,538 (43.2)	53.5 (1.33)	1,402 (42.5)	54.0 (1.40)	(†)	(†)	(†)	(†)	—	(†)
1972	2,964 (37.8)	2,520 (31.2)	316 (18.3)	101 (14.2)	1,459 (43.1)	49.2 (1.31)	1,252 (39.0)	49.7 (1.42)	141 (16.7)	44.6 (4.62)	46 (11.7)	45.0 (9.74)	—	(†)
1973	3,058 (37.1)	2,590 (30.8)	324 (18.5)	119 (13.7)	1,424 (43.0)	46.6 (1.29)	1,238 (39.2)	47.8 (1.40)	105 (15.2)	32.5 (4.30)	64 (13.0)	54.1 (9.01)	48.7	(5.33)
1974	3,101 (38.6)	2,620 (31.4)	325 (19.0)	121 (15.2)	1,475 (43.7)	47.6 (1.28)	1,236 (39.4)	47.2 (1.39)	154 (17.4)	47.2 (4.58)	57 (12.9)	46.9 (8.94)	53.0	(5.09)
1975	3,185 (38.6)	2,701 (31.9)	302 (15.4)	132 (15.8)	1,615 (44.8)	50.7 (1.26)	1,381 (40.5)	51.1 (1.37)	126 (13.6)	41.7 (3.97)	77 (14.5)	58.0 (8.44)	52.5	(4.88)
1976	2,986 (39.8)	2,492 (33.1)	290 (15.8)	152 (16.2)	1,458 (43.6)	48.8 (1.31)	1,217 (39.1)	48.8 (1.43)	129 (13.8)	44.4 (4.08)	80 (14.8)	52.7 (7.97)	53.8	(4.68)
1977	3,141 (40.7)	2,618 (34.0)	325 (19.3)	155 (16.0)	1,590 (45.4)	50.6 (1.29)	1,331 (40.8)	50.8 (1.41)	161 (17.9)	49.5 (4.65)	79 (14.8)	50.8 (7.96)	48.5	(4.72)
1978	3,163 (39.7)	2,615 (33.7)	345 (18.4)	135 (15.3)	1,585 (45.2)	50.1 (1.28)	1,321 (40.6)	50.5 (1.41)	160 (17.7)	46.4 (4.51)	56 (13.0)	42.0 (8.44)	45.9	(4.69)
1979	3,160 (40.0)	2,629 (32.7)	319 (19.7)	155 (16.1)	1,559 (45.1)	49.3 (1.28)	1,313 (40.5)	49.9 (1.41)	149 (17.5)	46.7 (4.69)	70 (14.3)	45.0 (7.92)	46.4	(4.83)
1980	3,088 (39.4)	2,554 (30.9)	350 (19.7)	130 (17.1)	1,523 (44.6)	49.3 (1.30)	1,273 (39.6)	49.8 (1.43)	149 (17.7)	42.7 (4.44)	68 (14.4)	52.3 (8.70)	49.8	(4.78)
1981	3,056 (42.2)	2,490 (34.1)	349 (20.5)	146 (17.6)	1,648 (45.8)	53.9 (1.30)	1,367 (40.5)	54.9 (1.44)	149 (17.8)	42.7 (4.44)	76 (15.1)	52.1 (8.19)	49.2	(4.68)
1982	3,100 (40.4)	2,474 (32.9)	382 (19.6)	173 (18.2)	1,569 (46.9)	50.6 (1.36)	1,303 (41.5)	52.7 (1.52)	137 (17.9)	35.8 (4.33)	75 (15.8)	43.2 (7.96)	49.8	(4.94)
1983	2,963 (41.6)	2,363 (33.1)	390 (21.1)	138 (17.8)	1,562 (46.7)	52.7 (1.39)	1,301 (40.9)	55.0 (1.55)	149 (18.7)	38.2 (4.34)	75 (15.7)	54.2 (8.96)	47.3	(4.73)
1984	3,012 (36.5)	2,331 (29.1)	433 (18.5)	187 (17.0)	1,663 (46.0)	55.2 (1.37)	1,375 (39.9)	59.0 (1.54)	172 (19.4)	39.8 (4.15)	83 (16.2)	44.3 (7.67)	49.9	(4.89)
1985	2,668 (40.1)	2,104 (32.3)	332 (19.3)	141 (19.7)	1,540 (45.1)	57.7 (1.45)	1,264 (39.2)	60.1 (1.62)	140 (17.8)	42.2 (4.78)	72 (17.0)	51.0 (9.76)	46.5	(5.19)
1986	2,786 (38.6)	2,146 (30.3)	378 (18.4)	169 (21.7)	1,498 (45.0)	53.8 (1.43)	1,219 (38.8)	56.8 (1.62)	140 (17.9)	36.9 (4.38)	74 (17.7)	44.0 (8.85)	42.9	(5.21)
1987	2,647 (40.9)	2,040 (32.4)	333 (20.6)	176 (20.9)	1,503 (45.1)	56.8 (1.46)	1,195 (38.7)	58.6 (1.65)	174 (19.3)	52.2 (4.82)	59 (16.1)	33.5 (8.25)	44.9	(5.04)
1988	2,673 (47.0)	2,013 (37.9)	378 (22.3)	179 (26.6)	1,575 (50.3)	58.9 (1.57)	1,230 (42.9)	61.1 (1.79)	168 (21.1)	44.4 (4.91)	102 (23.6)	57.1 (10.14)	48.6	(5.99)
1989	2,450 (46.5)	1,889 (37.3)	332 (21.3)	168 (26.5)	1,460 (48.7)	59.6 (1.64)	1,147 (41.7)	60.7 (1.85)	177 (20.9)	53.4 (5.27)	93 (22.9)	55.1 (10.51)	51.6	(6.33)
1990	2,362 (43.0)	1,819 (32.2)	331 (21.9)	121 (21.8)	1,420 (45.9)	60.1 (1.60)	1,147 (38.5)	63.0 (1.80)	155 (19.7)	46.8 (5.08)	52 (16.0)	42.7 (10.82)	51.7	(5.70)
1991	2,276 (41.0)	1,727 (30.3)	310 (20.2)	154 (23.5)	1,423 (44.8)	62.5 (1.62)	1,129 (37.2)	65.4 (1.82)	144 (18.8)	46.4 (5.25)	88 (19.9)	57.2 (9.58)	51.6	(5.52)
1992	2,397 (40.4)	1,724 (30.9)	354 (21.4)	198 (23.0)	1,483 (45.4)	61.9 (1.58)	1,109 (37.4)	64.3 (1.84)	171 (20.2)	48.2 (4.92)	109 (21.0)	55.0 (8.50)	58.1	(5.04)
1993	2,342 (41.4)	1,719 (32.6)	304 (20.4)	201 (23.1)	1,467 (45.4)	62.6 (1.59)	1,082 (37.9)	62.9 (1.85)	169 (19.6)	55.6 (5.28)	125 (21.9)	62.2 (8.22)	55.4	(4.97)
1994	2,517 (38.1)	1,915 (27.0)	316 (17.9)	178 (17.3)	1,559 (43.0)	61.9 (1.43)	1,236 (35.5)	64.5 (1.61)	161 (16.7)	50.8 (4.42)	87 (14.0)	49.1 (6.28)	55.0	(3.23)

See notes at end of table.

Table 201. Recent high school completers and their enrollment in college, by race/ethnicity: 1960 through 2007—Continued

[Numbers in thousands]

CHAPTER 3: Postsecondary Education 293
Enrollment

Year	Number of high school completers[1]				Enrolled in college[2]									
					Total		White		Black[3]		Hispanic[3]			
												Percent		3-year moving average
	Total	White	Black[3]	Hispanic[3]	Number	Percent	Number	Percent	Number	Percent	Number	Annual		
	2	3	4	5	6	7	8	9	10	11	12	13		14
1995	2,599 (40.9)	1,861 (30.1)	349 (19.2)	288 (19.4)	1,610 (44.5)	61.9 (1.41)	1,197 (36.1)	64.3 (1.64)	179 (17.6)	51.2 (4.20)	155 (17.6)	53.7 (4.92)		51.2 (3.18)
1996	2,660 (40.5)	1,875 (30.8)	406 (17.3)	227 (18.9)	1,729 (46.1)	65.0 (1.42)	1,264 (37.5)	67.4 (1.67)	227 (19.0)	56.0 (4.03)	115 (16.3)	50.8 (5.79)		56.7 (2.97)
1997	2,769 (41.8)	1,909 (31.8)	384 (19.2)	336 (19.0)	1,856 (47.3)	67.0 (1.38)	1,301 (38.1)	68.2 (1.64)	225 (19.4)	58.5 (4.12)	220 (19.7)	65.6 (4.53)		54.6 (2.94)
1998	2,810 (43.9)	1,980 (33.0)	386 (20.2)	314 (20.8)	1,844 (48.3)	65.6 (1.38)	1,357 (39.0)	68.5 (1.61)	239 (20.0)	61.9 (4.05)	149 (18.3)	47.4 (4.92)		51.8 (2.79)
1999	2,897 (41.5)	1,978 (31.8)	436 (15.2)	329 (20.9)	1,822 (47.8)	62.9 (1.38)	1,311 (38.6)	66.3 (1.64)	257 (19.1)	58.9 (3.86)	139 (18.0)	42.3 (4.76)		47.5 (2.84)
2000	2,756 (45.3)	1,938 (32.9)	393 (20.0)	300 (22.4)	1,745 (48.4)	63.3 (1.41)	1,272 (38.8)	65.7 (1.66)	216 (19.5)	54.9 (4.11)	159 (19.2)	52.9 (5.03)		49.0 (2.96)
2001	2,549 (46.5)	1,834 (34.8)	381 (20.3)	241 (21.1)	1,574 (47.5)	61.8 (1.48)	1,178 (38.7)	64.3 (1.72)	210 (19.4)	55.0 (4.17)	124 (17.4)	51.7 (5.63)		52.7 (2.93)
2002	2,796 (42.7)	1,903 (31.3)	382 (19.1)	344 (21.6)	1,824 (46.1)	65.2 (1.31)	1,314 (36.5)	69.1 (1.55)	227 (18.7)	59.4 (3.90)	184 (19.2)	53.6 (4.46)		54.6 (2.75)
2003[4]	2,677 (42.2)	1,832 (30.8)	327 (18.4)	314 (20.9)	1,711 (45.2)	63.9 (1.35)	1,213 (35.9)	66.2 (1.61)	188 (17.4)	57.5 (4.25)	184 (18.9)	58.6 (4.61)		58.0 (2.66)
2004[4]	2,752 (40.0)	1,854 (30.9)	398 (15.5)	286 (19.9)	1,835 (44.9)	66.7 (1.31)	1,276 (36.1)	68.8 (1.57)	249 (17.9)	62.5 (3.77)	177 (18.4)	61.8 (4.76)		58.1 (2.60)
2005[4]	2,675 (40.8)	1,799 (30.5)	345 (16.6)	390 (20.6)	1,834 (44.8)	68.6 (1.31)	1,317 (35.4)	73.2 (1.52)	192 (17.1)	55.7 (4.15)	211 (19.7)	54.0 (4.18)		57.9 (2.51)
2006[4]	2,692 (44.6)	1,805 (33.2)	318 (20.6)	382 (22.1)	1,776 (46.4)	66.0 (1.33)	1,237 (36.7)	68.5 (1.60)	177 (17.9)	55.5 (4.33)	222 (20.5)	57.9 (4.18)		58.6 (2.43)
2007[4]	2,955 (42.6)	2,043 (29.9)	416 (20.6)	355 (22.3)	1,986 (47.0)	67.2 (1.26)	1,421 (36.8)	69.5 (1.49)	232 (19.5)	55.7 (3.78)	227 (20.7)	64.0 (4.22)		— †

—Not available.
†Not applicable.
[1]Individuals ages 16 to 24 who graduated from high school or completed a GED during the preceding 12 months.
[2]Enrollment in college as of October of each year for individuals ages 16 to 24 who completed high school during the preceding 12 months.
[3]Due to the small sample size, data are subject to relatively large sampling errors. A 3-year moving average is an arithmetic average of the year immediately indicated, the year immediately preceding, and the year immediately following. Moving averages are used to produce more stable estimates.

[4]White and Black data exclude persons identifying themselves as more than one race.
NOTE: High school completion data in this table differ from figures appearing in other tables because of varying survey procedures and coverage. High school completers include GED recipients. Race categories exclude persons of Hispanic ethnicity. Total includes persons of other racial/ethnic groups not separately shown. Standard errors appear in parentheses.
SOURCE: American College Testing Program, unpublished tabulations, derived from statistics collected by the Census Bureau, 1960 through 1969. U.S. Department of Commerce, Census Bureau, Current Population Survey (CPS), October, 1970 through 2007. (This table was prepared July 2008.)

Table 202. Graduation rates of previous year's 12th-graders and college attendance rates of those who graduated, by selected high school characteristics: 1999–2000 and 2003–04

Selected high school characteristic	For 1998–99 school year		College attendance rate of 1998–99 graduates in 1999–2000			For 2002–03 school year		College attendance rate of 2002–03 graduates in 2003–04		
	Number of high schools with 12th-graders	Graduation rate of 12th-graders[1]	Total	4-year institutions	2-year institutions	Number of high schools with 12th-graders	Graduation rate of 12th-graders[1]	Total	4-year institutions	2-year institutions
1	2	3	4	5	6	7	8	9	10	11
Public high schools	**20,000** (230)	**91.4** (0.32)	**66.8** (0.41)	**42.9** (0.47)	**24.0** (0.30)	**22,500** (400)	**89.8** (0.50)	**72.3** (0.39)	**44.1** (0.62)	**28.2** (0.59)
Percent minority students										
Less than 5 percent	6,400 (170)	94.9 (0.28)	65.5 (0.75)	45.8 (0.74)	19.7 (0.43)	6,100 (220)	92.7 (1.41)	70.4 (0.84)	45.6 (0.89)	24.8 (0.60)
5 to 19 percent	4,800 (180)	93.6 (0.34)	68.4 (0.80)	45.9 (0.89)	22.5 (0.53)	5,200 (270)	92.0 (1.12)	75.4 (0.71)	50.1 (1.05)	25.4 (0.74)
20 to 49 percent	4,000 (170)	91.3 (0.45)	67.0 (0.93)	41.8 (0.88)	25.2 (0.70)	4,700 (180)	90.8 (0.68)	72.1 (0.80)	43.7 (1.09)	28.4 (1.07)
50 percent or more	4,800 (150)	86.7 (1.00)	66.1 (0.82)	38.2 (1.01)	27.9 (0.79)	6,500 (280)	85.5 (1.01)	71.0 (1.09)	38.3 (1.35)	32.7 (1.21)
Community type										
Central city	3,600 (150)	87.9 (0.80)	69.3 (0.86)	43.8 (1.00)	25.5 (0.80)	4,400 (260)	85.9 (1.08)	73.3 (1.00)	45.6 (1.41)	27.7 (1.14)
Urban fringe/large town	7,900 (170)	92.6 (0.36)	68.8 (0.70)	44.3 (0.66)	24.5 (0.43)	9,400 (300)	90.9 (0.78)	74.5 (0.46)	45.5 (0.89)	29.0 (0.84)
Rural/small town	8,500 (180)	93.0 (0.44)	59.3 (0.54)	38.3 (0.52)	21.0 (0.40)	8,700 (290)	92.7 (0.43)	65.0 (0.59)	38.1 (0.68)	26.9 (0.54)
Private high schools	**7,600** (240)	**99.1** (0.11)	**89.5** (0.62)	**76.5** (0.87)	**13.0** (0.48)	**8,200** (260)	**98.2** (0.27)	**92.8** (0.63)	**79.5** (1.12)	**13.3** (0.73)
Percent minority students										
Less than 5 percent	2,700 (150)	98.5 (0.41)	86.4 (0.99)	71.5 (1.52)	14.9 (1.08)	2,500 (180)	97.2 (0.87)	89.0 (1.77)	73.8 (2.86)	15.3 (1.60)
5 to 19 percent	2,500 (130)	99.4 (0.08)	91.5 (0.91)	81.3 (1.13)	10.2 (0.58)	2,900 (170)	99.0 (0.18)	94.1 (0.70)	82.6 (1.58)	11.5 (1.18)
20 to 49 percent	1,400 (100)	99.0 (0.15)	92.7 (0.89)	79.0 (1.55)	13.6 (1.47)	1,700 (140)	97.6 (0.43)	94.7 (1.06)	83.4 (1.94)	11.3 (1.45)
50 percent or more	1,000 (110)	99.0 (0.29)	84.0 (3.08)	66.6 (4.69)	17.4 (2.10)	1,100 (140)	97.9 (0.48)	92.4 (1.67)	73.2 (2.91)	19.2 (2.34)
Community type										
Central city	2,900 (150)	99.0 (0.20)	90.7 (0.79)	78.0 (1.30)	12.6 (0.76)	2,500 (180)	97.9 (0.53)	94.0 (1.01)	81.9 (1.70)	12.1 (1.05)
Urban fringe/large town	2,900 (150)	99.3 (0.09)	90.1 (0.86)	76.9 (1.31)	13.1 (0.82)	4,000 (220)	98.3 (0.26)	92.5 (0.72)	79.2 (1.27)	13.3 (1.03)
Rural/small town	1,800 (140)	98.5 (0.33)	80.5 (2.40)	66.3 (2.63)	14.2 (1.48)	1,700 (150)	98.5 (0.34)	89.5 (1.87)	71.3 (3.82)	18.2 (2.81)

[1]Includes only students who were enrolled in 12th grade in fall of the school year and graduated with a diploma by the end of the following summer.
NOTE: Data are based on a sample survey and may not be strictly comparable with data reported elsewhere. Includes all schools, including combined schools, with students enrolled in the 12th grade. Some data have been revised from previously published figures. Detail may not sum to totals because of rounding. Standard errors appear in parentheses.

SOURCE: U.S. Department of Education, National Center for Education Statistics, Schools and Staffing Survey (SASS), "Public School Questionnaire," 1999–2000 and 2003–04, "Private School Questionnaire," 1999–2000 and 2003–04, and "Charter School Questionnaire," 1999–2000. (This table was prepared August 2006.)

Table 203. Estimated rate of 2005–06 high school graduates attending degree-granting institutions, by state: 2006

State	Number of high school graduates			Attending public or private degree-granting institutions				
				Freshmen graduating from high school in the previous 12 months, fall 2006			Estimated rate of high school graduates going to college	Estimated rate of high school graduates going to college in home state
					State residents enrolled in institutions			
	Total[1]	Public, 2005–06	Private, 2004–05	Attending colleges located in the state[2]	In any state[3]	In their home state[4]		
1	2	3	4	5	6	7	8	9
United States[5]	3,111,324	2,815,544	295,790	1,955,510	1,929,453	1,559,301	62.0	50.1
Alabama	43,898	37,918	5,980	32,225	27,019	24,334	61.5	55.4
Alaska	7,641	7,361	280	2,197	3,503	1,964	45.8	25.7
Arizona	56,501	54,091	2,410	31,177	25,423	22,104	45.0	39.1
Arkansas	30,090	28,790	1,300	18,800	17,063	15,093	56.7	50.2
California	375,515	343,515	32,000	208,107	210,481	190,199	56.1	50.7
Colorado	46,784	44,424	2,360	29,351	29,748	23,020	63.6	49.2
Connecticut	46,782	36,222	10,560	24,017	29,429	15,554	62.9	33.2
Delaware	8,635	7,275	1,360	7,047	5,727	3,758	66.3	43.5
District of Columbia	4,350	3,150 [6]	1,200	8,786	2,448	633	56.3	14.6
Florida	151,506	134,686	16,820	97,162	91,149	80,682	60.2	53.3
Georgia	80,348	73,498	6,850	54,763	55,094	45,503	68.6	56.6
Hawaii	13,662	10,922	2,740	5,916	7,534	4,772	55.1	34.9
Idaho	16,606	16,096	510	8,495	7,608	5,549	45.8	33.4
Illinois	141,907	126,817	15,090	74,362	85,730	63,453	60.4	44.7
Indiana	62,740	57,920	4,820	47,986	40,088	34,811	63.9	55.5
Iowa	36,313	33,693	2,620	27,137	22,131	18,087	60.9	52.3
Kansas	31,978	29,818	2,160	22,338	20,985	17,854	65.6	55.8
Kentucky	42,109	38,449	3,660	28,574	25,883	23,043	61.5	54.7
Louisiana	42,285	33,275	9,010	27,476	27,009	24,046	63.9	56.9
Maine	16,190	12,950	3,240	9,347	9,887	6,399	61.1	39.5
Maryland	63,346	55,536	7,810	34,244	42,002	26,681	66.3	42.1
Massachusetts	71,322	61,272	10,050	59,053	51,800	34,476	72.6	48.3
Michigan	111,902	102,582	9,320	71,513	72,171	64,796	64.5	57.9
Minnesota	63,648	58,898	4,750	40,372	43,181	31,876	67.8	50.1
Mississippi	27,218	23,848	3,370	22,445	20,532	18,870	75.4	69.3
Missouri	66,087	58,417	7,670	40,254	38,136	31,686	57.7	47.9
Montana	11,113	10,283	830	6,458	6,271	4,680	56.4	42.1
Nebraska	22,124	19,764	2,360	14,424	14,219	11,599	64.3	52.4
Nevada	17,125	16,455	670	7,949	8,936	6,832	52.2	39.9
New Hampshire	16,228	13,988	2,240	11,247	10,483	5,470	64.6	33.7
New Jersey	101,979	90,049	11,930	44,444	71,620	40,390	70.2	39.6
New Mexico	19,062	17,822	1,240	12,349	13,549	10,652	71.1	55.9
New York	188,687	161,817	26,870	143,264	141,574	113,145	75.0	60.0
North Carolina	81,840	76,710	5,130	61,718	53,787	48,693	65.7	59.5
North Dakota	7,652	7,192	460	6,875	5,504	4,014	71.9	52.5
Ohio	131,446	117,356	14,090	77,478	78,210	65,391	59.5	49.7
Oklahoma	38,047	36,497	1,550	25,193	22,659	20,185	59.6	53.1
Oregon	35,004	32,394	2,610	17,767	16,680	12,716	47.7	36.3
Pennsylvania	146,100	127,830 [6]	18,270	104,005	89,940	74,112	61.6	50.7
Rhode Island	11,908	10,108	1,800	12,501	6,513	3,876	54.7	32.5
South Carolina	37,800	34,970	2,830	30,349	26,275	23,556	69.5	62.3
South Dakota	9,069	8,589 [6]	480	7,029	6,539	5,026	72.1	55.4
Tennessee	56,160	50,880	5,280	38,440	36,039	30,654	64.2	54.6
Texas	251,085	240,485	10,600	131,102	139,043	122,878	55.4	48.9
Utah	30,080	29,050	1,030	18,280	13,921	12,697	46.3	42.2
Vermont	8,039	6,779	1,260	6,306	4,380	1,898	54.5	23.6
Virginia	75,437	69,597	5,840	53,544	51,499	41,342	68.3	54.8
Washington	63,963	60,213	3,750	28,892	31,129	23,988	48.7	37.5
West Virginia	17,523	16,763	760	13,562	10,147	8,841	57.9	50.5
Wisconsin	68,923	63,003	5,920	42,596	42,040	33,999	61.0	49.3
Wyoming	5,567	5,527	40	4,299	3,231	2,367	58.0	42.5

[1]Total includes public high school graduates for 2005–06 and private high school graduates for 2004–05.

[2]All of the new students reported by the institutions in that state; i.e., all in-migrants and "remaining" students. Also, includes students who are not residents of the United States..

[3]All U.S. resident students living in a particular state when admitted to an institution in any state. Students may be enrolled in any state.

[4]Students who attend institutions in their home state.

[5]U.S. total enrollment includes some students not identified by state.

[6]Projected data from NCES 2008-078, *Projections of Education Statistics to 2017.*

NOTE: Detail may not sum to totals because of rounding.

SOURCE: U.S. Department of Education, National Center for Education Statistics, Common Core of Data (CCD), "State Nonfiscal Survey of Public Elementary/Secondary Education," 2006–07; "Private School Survey (PSS)," 2005–06; and 2006 Integrated Postsecondary Education Data System (IPEDS), Spring 2007. (This table was prepared October 2008.)

Table 204. Enrollment rates of 18- to 24-year-olds in degree-granting institutions, by type of institution and sex and race/ethnicity of student: 1967 through 2007

	Enrollment as a percent of all 18- to 24-year-olds[1]								Enrollment as a percent of all 18- to 24-year-old high school completers[1]							
	All students			Sex		Race/ethnicity			All students			Sex		Race/ethnicity		
Year	Total	2-year	4-year	Male	Female	White	Black	Hispanic	Total	2-year	4-year	Male	Female	White	Black	Hispanic
1	2	3	4	5	6	7	8	9	10	11	12	13	14	15	16	17
1967[2]	25.5 (0.44)	— (†)	— (†)	33.1 (0.71)	19.2 (0.54)	26.9 (0.48)	13.0 (1.16)	— (†)	33.7 (0.55)	— (†)	— (†)	44.7 (0.87)	25.1 (0.67)	34.5 (0.58)	23.3 (1.96)	— (†)
1968[2]	26.1 (0.44)	— (†)	— (†)	34.1 (0.70)	19.5 (0.53)	27.5 (0.48)	14.5 (1.18)	— (†)	34.2 (0.54)	— (†)	— (†)	45.9 (0.86)	25.0 (0.66)	34.9 (0.57)	25.2 (1.92)	— (†)
1969[2]	27.3 (0.44)	— (†)	— (†)	35.2 (0.69)	20.9 (0.54)	28.7 (0.47)	16.0 (1.20)	— (†)	35.0 (0.53)	— (†)	— (†)	45.6 (0.82)	26.4 (0.65)	35.6 (0.56)	27.2 (1.90)	— (†)
1970[2]	25.7 (0.42)	— (†)	— (†)	32.1 (0.65)	20.3 (0.52)	27.1 (0.45)	15.5 (1.15)	— (†)	32.6 (0.50)	— (†)	— (†)	41.0 (0.78)	25.5 (0.63)	33.2 (0.53)	26.0 (1.81)	— (†)
1971[2]	26.2 (0.41)	— (†)	— (†)	32.5 (0.63)	20.8 (0.52)	27.2 (0.44)	18.2 (1.19)	— (†)	33.2 (0.49)	— (†)	— (†)	41.5 (0.76)	26.0 (0.63)	33.5 (0.52)	29.2 (1.78)	— (†)
1972	25.5 (0.37)	— (†)	17.1 (0.31)	30.2 (0.56)	21.2 (0.47)	27.2 (0.41)	18.3 (1.18)	13.4 (1.83)	31.9 (0.44)	— (†)	21.2 (0.38)	38.2 (0.66)	26.3 (0.57)	32.6 (0.48)	27.2 (1.65)	25.8 (3.27)
1973	24.0 (0.35)	6.9 (0.21)	17.0 (0.31)	27.7 (0.54)	20.5 (0.46)	25.5 (0.40)	15.9 (1.09)	16.1 (2.02)	29.7 (0.42)	8.5 (0.26)	21.1 (0.37)	34.6 (0.63)	25.3 (0.55)	30.2 (0.46)	23.8 (1.55)	29.1 (3.36)
1974	24.6 (0.35)	7.6 (0.22)	17.0 (0.31)	27.7 (0.53)	21.7 (0.47)	25.8 (0.40)	17.6 (1.14)	18.0 (1.95)	30.5 (0.42)	9.4 (0.27)	21.1 (0.37)	34.7 (0.63)	26.7 (0.56)	30.5 (0.46)	26.2 (1.60)	32.3 (3.17)
1975	26.3 (0.36)	9.0 (0.23)	17.3 (0.31)	29.0 (0.53)	23.7 (0.48)	27.4 (0.40)	20.4 (1.18)	20.4 (2.09)	32.5 (0.42)	11.1 (0.28)	21.4 (0.37)	36.2 (0.63)	29.2 (0.57)	32.3 (0.46)	31.5 (1.69)	35.5 (3.27)
1976	26.7 (0.35)	6.4 (0.20)	20.2 (0.32)	28.2 (0.52)	25.2 (0.48)	27.6 (0.40)	22.5 (1.20)	20.0 (2.00)	33.1 (0.42)	8.0 (0.24)	25.1 (0.39)	35.6 (0.62)	30.9 (0.57)	32.8 (0.46)	33.4 (1.66)	35.9 (3.22)
1977	26.1 (0.38)	6.8 (0.22)	19.4 (0.35)	28.1 (0.56)	24.3 (0.52)	27.2 (0.43)	21.1 (1.18)	17.2 (1.87)	32.5 (0.46)	8.4 (0.27)	24.1 (0.42)	35.6 (0.68)	29.7 (0.61)	32.3 (0.50)	31.3 (1.63)	31.5 (3.11)
1978	25.3 (0.38)	6.6 (0.22)	18.7 (0.34)	27.1 (0.55)	23.6 (0.51)	26.5 (0.43)	20.1 (1.15)	15.2 (1.74)	31.4 (0.45)	8.2 (0.26)	23.2 (0.41)	34.1 (0.66)	28.8 (0.60)	31.3 (0.49)	29.6 (1.58)	27.2 (2.89)
1979	25.0 (0.37)	6.3 (0.21)	18.7 (0.34)	25.9 (0.54)	24.2 (0.52)	26.3 (0.43)	19.8 (1.13)	16.7 (1.77)	31.2 (0.45)	7.8 (0.26)	23.4 (0.41)	32.9 (0.66)	29.6 (0.61)	31.3 (0.49)	29.4 (1.58)	30.2 (2.93)
1980	25.7 (0.38)	7.1 (0.22)	18.6 (0.33)	26.4 (0.54)	25.0 (0.52)	27.3 (0.43)	19.4 (1.12)	16.1 (1.64)	31.8 (0.45)	8.8 (0.27)	23.0 (0.40)	33.5 (0.66)	30.3 (0.61)	32.1 (0.49)	27.6 (1.51)	29.9 (2.80)
1981	26.1 (0.37)	7.5 (0.22)	18.6 (0.33)	27.1 (0.54)	25.2 (0.51)	27.7 (0.43)	19.9 (1.09)	16.6 (1.63)	32.4 (0.44)	9.3 (0.27)	23.1 (0.40)	34.7 (0.65)	30.4 (0.60)	32.7 (0.49)	28.0 (1.46)	29.9 (2.69)
1982	26.6 (0.39)	7.7 (0.24)	18.9 (0.35)	27.2 (0.57)	26.0 (0.55)	28.1 (0.46)	19.9 (1.14)	16.8 (1.77)	33.0 (0.47)	9.6 (0.29)	23.4 (0.42)	34.5 (0.68)	31.6 (0.64)	33.3 (0.52)	28.1 (1.52)	29.2 (2.83)
1983	26.2 (0.39)	7.4 (0.23)	18.8 (0.35)	27.3 (0.57)	25.1 (0.54)	27.9 (0.46)	19.2 (1.12)	17.3 (1.77)	32.5 (0.47)	9.2 (0.29)	23.3 (0.42)	35.0 (0.69)	30.3 (0.63)	33.0 (0.52)	27.0 (1.50)	31.5 (2.94)
1984	27.1 (0.40)	7.3 (0.24)	19.8 (0.36)	28.6 (0.58)	25.6 (0.55)	28.9 (0.47)	20.3 (1.15)	17.9 (1.80)	33.2 (0.47)	9.0 (0.29)	24.2 (0.43)	36.0 (0.70)	30.6 (0.64)	33.9 (0.53)	27.2 (1.47)	29.9 (2.77)
1985	27.8 (0.41)	7.4 (0.24)	20.4 (0.37)	28.4 (0.60)	27.2 (0.57)	30.0 (0.48)	19.6 (1.16)	16.9 (1.84)	33.7 (0.48)	8.9 (0.29)	24.8 (0.44)	36.3 (0.70)	32.3 (0.65)	34.9 (0.55)	26.0 (1.47)	26.8 (2.75)
1986	27.9 (0.42)	7.6 (0.25)	20.3 (0.37)	28.2 (0.60)	27.6 (0.58)	29.7 (0.50)	21.9 (1.21)	17.6 (1.76)	34.0 (0.49)	9.3 (0.30)	24.8 (0.44)	35.3 (0.71)	32.8 (0.67)	34.5 (0.56)	28.6 (1.52)	29.4 (2.72)
1987	29.6 (0.43)	8.1 (0.26)	21.5 (0.39)	30.6 (0.62)	28.7 (0.59)	31.9 (0.51)	22.8 (1.25)	17.5 (1.73)	36.2 (0.50)	10.0 (0.31)	26.3 (0.46)	38.3 (0.73)	34.4 (0.68)	37.3 (0.58)	29.5 (1.54)	28.4 (2.61)
1988	30.3 (0.47)	8.8 (0.29)	21.5 (0.42)	30.2 (0.68)	30.4 (0.66)	33.2 (0.57)	21.2 (1.33)	17.0 (2.00)	37.2 (0.55)	10.8 (0.35)	26.5 (0.50)	38.3 (0.81)	36.3 (0.75)	38.6 (0.63)	28.1 (1.69)	30.8 (3.31)
1989	30.9 (0.48)	8.0 (0.28)	22.9 (0.44)	30.2 (0.68)	31.6 (0.67)	34.2 (0.58)	23.4 (1.38)	16.1 (1.90)	38.1 (0.56)	9.9 (0.34)	28.2 (0.52)	38.3 (0.81)	37.9 (0.77)	39.8 (0.65)	30.7 (1.72)	28.7 (3.12)
1990	32.0 (0.47)	8.7 (0.28)	23.3 (0.43)	32.3 (0.68)	31.8 (0.66)	35.1 (0.57)	25.4 (1.37)	15.8 (1.67)	39.1 (0.54)	10.6 (0.34)	28.5 (0.50)	40.0 (0.79)	38.3 (0.75)	40.4 (0.63)	32.7 (1.68)	28.7 (2.79)
1991	33.3 (0.48)	9.7 (0.30)	23.6 (0.43)	32.8 (0.68)	33.6 (0.67)	36.8 (0.58)	23.5 (1.34)	17.9 (1.72)	41.0 (0.55)	11.9 (0.37)	29.1 (0.51)	41.5 (0.80)	40.5 (0.77)	42.4 (0.64)	31.2 (1.68)	34.3 (2.94)
1992	34.4 (0.49)	9.9 (0.31)	24.4 (0.44)	32.7 (0.68)	36.0 (0.69)	37.3 (0.59)	25.2 (1.37)	21.3 (1.87)	41.7 (0.56)	12.1 (0.37)	29.7 (0.51)	40.7 (0.80)	42.7 (0.77)	42.6 (0.64)	33.5 (1.71)	36.8 (2.90)
1993	34.0 (0.49)	9.8 (0.30)	24.2 (0.44)	33.6 (0.69)	34.4 (0.68)	36.8 (0.59)	24.5 (1.35)	21.7 (1.88)	41.3 (0.56)	11.9 (0.37)	29.4 (0.51)	41.7 (0.80)	40.9 (0.77)	42.3 (0.65)	32.4 (1.69)	35.5 (2.79)
1994	34.6 (0.42)	9.1 (0.26)	25.5 (0.39)	33.1 (0.59)	36.0 (0.60)	38.1 (0.58)	27.7 (1.17)	18.8 (1.10)	42.3 (0.52)	11.2 (0.31)	31.2 (0.46)	41.6 (0.70)	43.0 (0.68)	43.7 (0.57)	35.6 (1.42)	33.1 (1.76)
1995	34.3 (0.44)	8.9 (0.27)	25.4 (0.41)	33.1 (0.63)	35.5 (0.63)	37.9 (0.55)	27.5 (1.18)	20.7 (1.13)	42.3 (0.51)	11.0 (0.33)	31.3 (0.48)	41.7 (0.73)	43.0 (0.72)	44.0 (0.61)	35.4 (1.43)	35.2 (1.74)
1996	35.5 (0.47)	9.5 (0.29)	26.1 (0.43)	34.1 (0.66)	37.0 (0.67)	39.5 (0.59)	27.4 (1.23)	20.1 (1.18)	43.4 (0.54)	11.5 (0.35)	31.9 (0.50)	42.5 (0.77)	44.3 (0.75)	45.1 (0.64)	35.9 (1.51)	34.5 (1.83)
1997	36.8 (0.47)	9.9 (0.29)	27.0 (0.43)	35.0 (0.66)	38.7 (0.67)	40.6 (0.59)	29.8 (1.25)	22.4 (1.21)	45.2 (0.54)	12.1 (0.35)	33.1 (0.51)	44.0 (0.77)	46.3 (0.75)	46.6 (0.64)	39.5 (1.54)	36.0 (1.77)
1998	36.5 (0.46)	10.2 (0.29)	26.3 (0.42)	34.5 (0.65)	38.6 (0.66)	40.6 (0.59)	29.8 (1.24)	20.4 (1.11)	45.2 (0.53)	12.6 (0.36)	32.6 (0.50)	44.3 (0.77)	46.1 (0.74)	46.9 (0.64)	40.0 (1.54)	33.9 (1.68)
1999	35.6 (0.46)	9.1 (0.27)	26.5 (0.42)	34.1 (0.64)	37.0 (0.65)	39.4 (0.58)	30.4 (1.24)	18.7 (1.08)	43.7 (0.52)	11.2 (0.33)	32.5 (0.49)	42.9 (0.75)	44.4 (0.73)	45.3 (0.63)	39.2 (1.50)	31.6 (1.68)
2000	35.5 (0.45)	9.4 (0.28)	26.0 (0.41)	32.6 (0.62)	38.4 (0.65)	38.7 (0.57)	30.5 (1.21)	21.7 (1.12)	43.2 (0.52)	11.5 (0.33)	31.8 (0.48)	40.8 (0.73)	45.6 (0.72)	44.1 (0.62)	39.3 (1.46)	36.2 (1.69)
2001	36.3 (0.45)	9.8 (0.28)	26.6 (0.41)	33.6 (0.63)	39.0 (0.64)	39.5 (0.57)	31.4 (1.22)	21.7 (1.10)	44.3 (0.51)	11.9 (0.33)	32.4 (0.48)	42.4 (0.73)	46.1 (0.72)	45.4 (0.62)	40.2 (1.45)	34.8 (1.61)
2002	36.7 (0.43)	9.7 (0.26)	27.0 (0.39)	33.7 (0.59)	39.7 (0.61)	40.9 (0.55)	31.9 (1.18)	19.9 (0.94)	44.7 (0.48)	11.8 (0.31)	32.9 (0.46)	42.5 (0.69)	46.7 (0.68)	46.7 (0.59)	40.2 (1.39)	31.6 (1.38)
2003[3]	37.8 (0.43)	10.2 (0.27)	27.7 (0.39)	34.3 (0.59)	41.3 (0.61)	41.6 (0.55)	32.3 (1.20)	23.5 (1.02)	45.7 (0.48)	12.3 (0.32)	33.4 (0.46)	42.8 (0.69)	47.2 (0.67)	47.2 (0.59)	41.4 (1.43)	35.8 (1.42)
2004[3]	38.0 (0.42)	9.4 (0.25)	28.6 (0.39)	34.7 (0.59)	41.2 (0.61)	41.7 (0.55)	31.8 (1.18)	24.7 (1.02)	45.8 (0.48)	11.3 (0.30)	34.5 (0.46)	43.0 (0.68)	48.4 (0.67)	47.4 (0.59)	40.8 (1.41)	37.3 (1.40)
2005[3]	38.9 (0.43)	9.6 (0.26)	29.2 (0.40)	35.3 (0.59)	42.5 (0.61)	42.8 (0.55)	33.1 (1.18)	24.8 (1.02)	46.8 (0.48)	11.6 (0.31)	35.2 (0.46)	44.3 (0.68)	49.1 (0.67)	48.6 (0.59)	41.4 (1.39)	37.4 (1.41)
2006[3]	37.3 (0.42)	9.6 (0.25)	27.8 (0.39)	34.1 (0.58)	40.6 (0.60)	41.0 (0.54)	32.6 (1.16)	23.6 (0.99)	45.0 (0.47)	11.5 (0.30)	33.5 (0.45)	42.2 (0.67)	47.7 (0.67)	46.5 (0.58)	42.0 (1.38)	35.5 (1.37)
2007[3]	38.8 (0.42)	10.9 (0.27)	27.9 (0.39)	35.5 (0.58)	42.1 (0.60)	42.6 (0.54)	33.1 (1.15)	26.6 (1.02)	46.1 (0.47)	13.0 (0.32)	33.1 (0.44)	43.4 (0.66)	48.6 (0.66)	47.8 (0.58)	40.1 (1.32)	39.2 (1.37)

—Not available.
†Not applicable.
[1]Includes students who were enrolled in college, but did not report high school completion.
[2]White and Black data include persons of Hispanic ethnicity.
[3]White and Black data exclude persons identifying themselves as multiracial.
NOTE: Data are based on sample surveys of the civilian noninstitutional population. Percents based on 18- to 24-year-old high school completers for 1992 and later years use a slightly different definiton of completion and may not be precisely comparable with figures for other years. All college students are counted as high school completers. Totals include other racial/ethnic groups not separately shown. Race categories exclude persons of Hispanic ethnicity except where otherwise noted. Standard errors appear in parentheses.
SOURCE: U.S. Department of Commerce, Census Bureau, Current Population Survey (CPS), October, 1967 through 2007. (This table was prepared August 2008.)

Table 205. Total undergraduate fall enrollment in degree-granting institutions, by attendance status, sex of student, and control of institution: 1967 through 2007

[In thousands]

Year	Total	Full-time	Part-time	Males	Females	Males Full-time	Males Part-time	Females Full-time	Females Part-time	Males Public	Males Private	Females Public	Females Private
1	2	3	4	5	6	7	8	9	10	11	12	13	14
1967	6,016	4,345	1,671	3,502	2,514	2,569	933	1,775	738	2,492	1,010	1,802	712
1968	6,476	4,740	1,735	3,781	2,695	2,810	971	1,930	764	2,787	994	1,995	700
1969	6,884	4,992	1,892	4,008	2,877	2,952	1,055	2,040	837	2,996	1,012	2,162	715
1970	7,369	5,280	2,089	4,250	3,119	3,096	1,153	2,184	935	3,236	1,014	2,384	735
1971	7,744	5,513	2,231	4,418	3,326	3,201	1,217	2,312	1,015	3,427	991	2,581	746
1972	7,942	5,489	2,453	4,429	3,514	3,121	1,308	2,368	1,146	3,466	963	2,757	757
1973	8,260	5,579	2,681	4,538	3,722	3,134	1,403	2,444	1,278	3,580	958	2,943	779
1974	8,799	5,726	3,072	4,766	4,033	3,192	1,574	2,535	1,499	3,800	966	3,232	801
1975	9,679	6,168	3,511	5,257	4,422	3,459	1,798	2,709	1,713	4,245	1,012	3,581	841
1976	9,435	6,033	3,401	4,906	4,528	3,244	1,662	2,789	1,739	3,951	955	3,669	859
1977	9,717	6,094	3,623	4,897	4,820	3,188	1,709	2,906	1,914	3,937	960	3,906	914
1978	9,684	5,963	3,722	4,761	4,923	3,069	1,692	2,894	2,029	3,812	949	3,975	948
1979	9,998	6,079	3,919	4,820	5,178	3,087	1,733	2,993	2,185	3,865	955	4,182	996
1980	10,475	6,362	4,113	5,000	5,475	3,227	1,773	3,135	2,340	4,015	985	4,427	1,048
1981	10,755	6,449	4,305	5,108	5,646	3,260	1,848	3,189	2,458	4,090	1,018	4,558	1,088
1982	10,825	6,484	4,341	5,170	5,655	3,299	1,871	3,184	2,470	4,140	1,031	4,573	1,081
1983	10,846	6,514	4,332	5,158	5,688	3,304	1,854	3,210	2,478	4,117	1,042	4,580	1,107
1984	10,618	6,348	4,270	5,007	5,611	3,195	1,812	3,153	2,459	3,990	1,017	4,504	1,107
1985	10,597	6,320	4,277	4,962	5,635	3,156	1,806	3,163	2,471	3,953	1,010	4,525	1,110
1986	10,798	6,352	4,446	5,018	5,780	3,146	1,871	3,206	2,575	4,002	1,015	4,658	1,122
1987	11,046	6,463	4,584	5,068	5,978	3,164	1,905	3,299	2,679	4,076	992	4,842	1,136
1988	11,317	6,642	4,674	5,138	6,179	3,206	1,931	3,436	2,743	4,113	1,024	4,990	1,189
1989	11,743	6,841	4,902	5,311	6,432	3,279	2,032	3,562	2,869	4,272	1,039	5,216	1,216
1990	11,959	6,976	4,983	5,380	6,579	3,337	2,043	3,639	2,940	4,353	1,027	5,357	1,223
1991	12,439	7,221	5,218	5,571	6,868	3,436	2,135	3,786	3,082	4,531	1,040	5,617	1,251
1992	12,538	7,244	5,293	5,583	6,955	3,425	2,158	3,820	3,135	4,537	1,046	5,679	1,275
1993	12,324	7,179	5,144	5,484	6,840	3,382	2,102	3,797	3,043	4,447	1,036	5,565	1,276
1994	12,263	7,169	5,094	5,422	6,840	3,342	2,081	3,827	3,013	4,394	1,028	5,551	1,290
1995	12,232	7,145	5,086	5,401	6,831	3,297	2,105	3,849	2,982	4,380	1,021	5,524	1,307
1996	12,327	7,299	5,028	5,421	6,906	3,339	2,082	3,960	2,947	4,383	1,038	5,553	1,354
1997	12,451	7,419	5,032	5,469	6,982	3,380	2,089	4,039	2,943	4,408	1,060	5,599	1,383
1998	12,437	7,539	4,898	5,446	6,991	3,428	2,018	4,111	2,880	4,361	1,085	5,589	1,402
1999	12,681	7,735	4,946	5,559	7,122	3,516	2,044	4,219	2,903	4,431	1,128	5,679	1,443
2000	13,155	7,923	5,232	5,778	7,377	3,588	2,190	4,335	3,042	4,622	1,156	5,917	1,460
2001	13,716	8,328	5,388	6,004	7,711	3,769	2,236	4,559	3,152	4,804	1,200	6,182	1,529
2002	14,257	8,734	5,523	6,192	8,065	3,934	2,258	4,800	3,265	4,960	1,232	6,473	1,592
2003	14,480	9,045	5,435	6,227	8,253	4,049	2,179	4,997	3,256	4,956	1,271	6,567	1,686
2004	14,781	9,284	5,496	6,340	8,441	4,141	2,199	5,144	3,297	5,009	1,331	6,641	1,799
2005	14,964	9,446	5,518	6,409	8,555	4,201	2,208	5,246	3,310	5,046	1,363	6,652	1,903
2006	15,184	9,571	5,613	6,514	8,671	4,265	2,249	5,306	3,364	5,134	1,380	6,714	1,957
2007	15,604	9,841	5,763	6,728	8,876	4,397	2,331	5,444	3,432	5,301	1,427	6,837	2,039

NOTE: Data include unclassified undergraduate students. Data through 1995 are for institutions of higher education, while later data are for degree-granting institutions. Degree-granting institutions grant associate's or higher degrees and participate in Title IV federal financial aid programs. The degree-granting classification is very similar to the earlier higher education classification, but it includes more 2-year colleges and excludes a few higher education institutions that did not grant degrees. (See Guide to Sources for details.) Detail may not sum to totals because of rounding. Some data have been revised from previously published figures.
SOURCE: U.S. Department of Education, National Center for Education Statistics, Higher Education General Information Survey (HEGIS), "Fall Enrollment in Colleges and Universities" surveys, 1967 through 1985; and 1986 through 2007 Integrated Postsecondary Education Data System, "Fall Enrollment Survey" (IPEDS-EF:86–99), and Spring 2001 through Spring 2008. (This table was prepared October 2008.)

Table 206. Total graduate fall enrollment in degree-granting institutions, by attendance status, sex of student, and control of institution: 1969 through 2007

Year	Total	Full-time	Part-time	Males	Females	Males Full-time	Males Part-time	Females Full-time	Females Part-time	Males Public	Males Private	Females Public	Females Private
1	2	3	4	5	6	7	8	9	10	11	12	13	14
1969	955,438	363,752	591,686	589,747	365,691	252,262	337,485	111,490	254,201	392,885	196,862	273,071	92,620
1970	1,038,832	378,842	659,990	635,291	403,541	263,454	371,837	115,388	288,153	427,801	207,490	304,621	98,920
1971	1,011,722	388,012	623,710	615,073	396,649	268,781	346,292	119,231	277,418	415,337	199,736	296,174	100,475
1972	1,065,762	393,260	672,502	626,721	439,041	267,543	359,178	125,717	313,324	427,227	199,494	330,239	108,802
1973	1,123,462	409,272	714,190	647,156	476,306	272,488	374,668	136,784	339,522	441,463	205,693	357,692	118,614
1974	1,189,549	427,598	761,951	662,768	526,781	275,780	386,988	151,818	374,963	454,302	208,466	398,112	128,669
1975	1,263,137	453,052	810,085	699,892	563,245	290,308	409,584	162,744	400,501	480,801	219,091	424,878	138,367
1976	1,333,254	463,701	869,553	714,741	618,513	287,319	427,422	176,382	442,131	478,039	236,702	453,735	164,778
1977	1,317,727	472,584	845,143	700,368	617,359	288,873	411,495	183,711	433,648	457,559	242,809	443,364	173,995
1978	1,318,789	472,291	846,498	687,710	631,079	283,959	403,751	188,332	442,747	441,402	246,308	452,619	178,460
1979	1,308,518	475,675	832,843	669,391	639,127	279,803	389,588	195,872	443,255	426,827	242,564	457,016	182,111
1980	1,344,073	484,855	859,218	674,853	669,220	280,939	393,914	203,916	465,304	426,565	248,288	474,437	194,783
1981	1,342,555	483,854	858,701	673,849	668,706	276,950	396,899	206,904	461,802	419,263	254,586	467,667	201,039
1982	1,322,293	484,705	837,588	669,690	652,603	279,578	390,112	205,127	447,476	416,849	252,841	452,709	199,894
1983	1,340,137	497,380	842,757	677,329	662,808	286,469	390,860	210,911	451,897	418,418	258,911	453,776	209,032
1984	1,345,271	501,027	844,244	671,812	673,459	286,293	385,519	214,734	458,725	411,241	260,571	458,730	214,729
1985	1,376,181	509,010	867,171	676,578	699,603	288,906	387,672	220,104	479,499	413,567	263,011	476,773	222,830
1986	1,435,135	521,830	913,305	693,159	741,976	294,160	398,999	227,670	514,306	432,781	260,378	508,371	233,605
1987	1,452,075	526,729	925,346	693,470	758,605	293,544	399,926	233,185	525,420	429,028	264,442	515,601	243,004
1988	1,471,680	553,112	918,568	697,340	774,340	304,292	393,048	248,820	525,520	429,265	268,075	520,038	254,302
1989	1,521,578	572,442	949,136	710,252	811,326	309,085	401,167	263,357	547,969	436,980	273,272	540,603	270,723
1990	1,586,165	599,101	987,064	737,352	848,813	321,412	415,940	277,689	571,124	456,065	281,287	567,311	281,502
1991	1,639,135	641,905	997,230	760,966	878,169	341,493	419,473	300,412	577,757	470,601	290,365	579,523	298,646
1992	1,668,737	665,538	1,003,199	772,433	896,304	351,141	421,292	314,397	581,907	473,960	298,473	583,621	312,683
1993	1,688,413	688,372	1,000,041	770,980	917,433	354,701	416,279	333,671	583,762	473,272	297,708	590,375	327,058
1994	1,721,469	705,759	1,015,710	775,829	945,640	358,574	417,255	347,185	598,455	471,915	303,914	602,640	343,000
1995	1,732,470	717,120	1,015,350	767,512	964,958	355,726	411,786	361,394	603,564	464,011	303,501	609,665	355,293
1996	1,742,260	736,905	1,005,355	759,411	982,849	357,993	401,418	378,912	603,937	455,960	303,451	612,591	370,258
1997	1,753,489	752,246	1,001,243	757,869	995,620	359,520	398,349	392,726	602,894	452,156	305,713	618,235	377,385
1998	1,767,557	753,578	1,013,979	754,286	1,013,271	355,131	399,155	398,447	614,824	443,963	310,323	622,896	390,375
1999	1,806,803	780,838	1,025,965	766,055	1,040,748	363,239	402,816	417,599	623,149	446,363	319,692	630,142	410,606
2000	1,850,271	813,103	1,037,168	779,616	1,070,655	377,450	402,166	435,653	635,002	447,172	332,444	642,178	428,477
2001	1,903,730	843,070	1,060,660	795,718	1,108,012	387,724	407,994	455,346	652,666	460,031	335,687	659,448	448,564
2002	2,035,652	926,191	1,109,461	846,845	1,188,807	421,448	425,397	504,743	684,064	487,064	359,781	699,780	489,027
2003	2,101,875	984,719	1,117,156	866,531	1,235,344	440,403	426,128	544,316	691,028	491,406	375,125	709,828	525,516
2004	2,156,885	1,024,298	1,132,587	878,776	1,278,109	447,867	430,909	576,431	701,678	485,600	393,176	708,176	569,933
2005	2,186,487	1,047,113	1,139,374	877,223	1,309,264	450,666	426,557	596,447	712,817	477,619	399,604	708,278	600,986
2006	2,231,122	1,077,068	1,154,054	887,251	1,343,871	459,498	427,753	617,570	726,301	478,826	408,425	714,145	629,726
2007	2,293,593	1,112,365	1,181,228	910,326	1,383,267	473,248	437,078	639,117	744,150	488,328	421,998	722,223	661,044

NOTE: Data include unclassified graduate students. Data through 1995 are for institutions of higher education, while later data are for degree-granting institutions. Degree-granting institutions grant associate's or higher degrees and participate in Title IV federal financial aid programs. The degree-granting classification is very similar to the earlier higher education classification, but it includes more 2-year colleges and excludes a few higher education institutions that did not grant degrees. (See Guide to Sources for details.)

SOURCE: U.S. Department of Education, National Center for Education Statistics, Higher Education General Information Survey (HEGIS), "Fall Enrollment in Colleges and Universities" surveys, 1969 through 1985; and 1986 through 2007 Integrated Postsecondary Education Data System, "Fall Enrollment Survey" (IPEDS-EF:86–99), and Spring 2001 through Spring 2008. (This table was prepared October 2008.)

Table 207. Total first-professional fall enrollment in degree-granting institutions, by attendance status, sex of student, and control of institution: 1969 through 2007

Year	Total	Full-time	Part-time	Males	Females	Males Full-time	Males Part-time	Females Full-time	Females Part-time	Males Public	Males Private	Females Public	Females Private
1	2	3	4	5	6	7	8	9	10	11	12	13	14
1969	164,737	143,081	21,656	148,926	15,811	131,368	17,558	11,713	4,098	64,241	84,685	8,354	7,457
1970	173,411	157,384	16,027	158,649	14,762	144,270	14,379	13,114	1,648	68,956	89,693	6,501	8,261
1971	192,668	176,224	16,444	174,058	18,610	159,386	14,672	16,838	1,772	98,233	75,825	9,430	9,180
1972	206,659	190,039	16,620	183,443	23,216	168,990	14,453	21,049	2,167	79,723	103,720	10,842	12,374
1973	218,990	201,663	17,327	186,297	32,693	171,731	14,566	29,932	2,761	81,811	104,486	16,138	16,555
1974	235,452	216,329	19,123	194,079	41,373	178,926	15,153	37,403	3,970	84,271	109,808	20,085	21,288
1975	242,267	219,886	22,381	192,100	50,167	177,117	14,983	42,769	7,398	79,240	112,860	23,557	26,610
1976	244,292	220,124	24,168	189,810	54,482	171,967	17,843	48,157	6,325	77,873	111,937	23,468	31,014
1977	251,357	226,318	25,039	191,451	59,906	173,165	18,286	53,153	6,753	78,189	113,262	24,901	35,005
1978	256,904	232,540	24,364	192,221	64,683	174,906	17,315	57,634	7,049	77,748	114,473	26,839	37,844
1979	263,404	238,949	24,455	193,363	70,041	176,394	16,969	62,555	7,486	77,122	116,241	29,026	41,015
1980	277,767	251,359	26,408	199,344	78,423	181,448	17,896	69,911	8,512	81,022	118,322	33,415	45,008
1981	274,595	248,328	26,267	192,936	81,659	175,414	17,522	72,914	8,745	77,562	115,374	34,177	47,482
1982	278,425	252,108	26,317	191,200	87,225	173,941	17,259	78,167	9,058	76,273	114,927	37,183	50,042
1983	278,529	249,636	28,893	188,096	90,433	169,071	19,025	80,565	9,868	74,938	113,158	38,484	51,949
1984	278,598	249,708	28,890	184,949	93,649	166,286	18,663	83,422	10,227	73,722	111,227	40,186	53,463
1985	274,200	246,619	27,581	179,792	94,408	162,368	17,424	84,251	10,157	71,373	108,419	40,435	53,973
1986	270,401	245,647	24,754	173,851	96,550	158,557	15,294	87,090	9,460	70,326	103,525	41,699	54,851
1987	268,332	241,807	26,525	170,129	98,203	153,668	16,461	88,139	10,064	68,089	102,040	41,947	56,256
1988	267,109	241,228	25,881	166,912	100,197	151,045	15,867	90,183	10,014	66,196	100,716	42,743	57,454
1989	274,451	247,812	26,639	168,773	105,678	152,511	16,262	95,301	10,377	67,548	101,225	45,090	60,588
1990	273,366	245,854	27,512	166,798	106,568	149,805	16,993	96,049	10,519	66,071	100,727	45,674	60,894
1991	280,531	252,012	28,519	169,875	110,656	152,356	17,519	99,656	11,000	64,821	105,054	46,661	63,995
1992	280,922	252,138	28,784	168,620	112,302	151,025	17,595	101,113	11,189	63,511	105,109	47,178	65,124
1993	292,431	259,764	32,667	172,788	119,643	153,873	18,915	105,891	13,752	63,973	108,815	49,681	69,962
1994	294,713	263,311	31,402	173,956	120,757	155,018	18,938	108,293	12,464	63,844	110,112	50,153	70,604
1995	297,592	266,414	31,178	173,897	123,695	155,056	18,841	111,358	12,337	63,594	110,303	51,478	72,217
1996	298,312	267,209	31,103	172,742	125,570	154,107	18,635	113,102	12,468	63,742	109,000	52,923	72,647
1997	298,258	267,218	31,040	169,627	128,631	151,325	18,302	115,893	12,738	63,667	105,960	54,582	74,049
1998	302,473	271,049	31,424	168,846	133,627	150,361	18,485	120,688	12,939	63,800	105,046	56,898	76,729
1999	303,190	270,581	32,609	165,134	138,056	146,613	18,521	123,968	14,088	63,762	101,372	59,123	78,933
2000	306,625	273,571	33,054	163,885	142,740	145,397	18,488	128,174	14,566	63,137	100,748	60,977	81,763
2001	308,647	276,792	31,855	160,666	147,981	143,536	17,130	133,256	14,725	63,566	97,100	64,240	83,741
2002	318,982	285,916	33,066	162,881	156,101	145,482	17,399	140,434	15,667	64,665	98,216	67,629	88,472
2003	329,242	296,161	33,081	166,361	162,881	148,787	17,574	147,374	15,507	64,497	101,864	69,864	93,017
2004	334,529	301,543	32,986	168,438	166,091	150,860	17,578	150,683	15,408	64,636	103,802	71,120	94,971
2005	337,024	303,468	33,556	169,831	167,193	151,859	17,972	151,609	15,584	65,602	104,229	72,605	94,588
2006	343,446	309,158	34,288	173,808	169,638	155,211	18,597	153,947	15,691	66,728	107,080	73,008	96,630
2007	350,764	316,549	34,215	177,988	172,776	159,328	18,660	157,221	15,555	68,399	109,589	74,247	98,529

NOTE: Data through 1995 are for institutions of higher education, while later data are for degree-granting institutions. Degree-granting institutions grant associate's or higher degrees and participate in Title IV federal financial aid programs. The degree-granting classification is very similar to the earlier higher education classification, but it includes more 2-year colleges and excludes a few higher education institutions that did not grant degrees. (See Guide to Sources for details.)

SOURCE: U.S. Department of Education, National Center for Education Statistics, Higher Education General Information Survey (HEGIS), "Fall Enrollment in Colleges and Universities" surveys, 1969 through 1985; and 1986 through 2007 Integrated Postsecondary Education Data System, "Fall Enrollment Survey" (IPEDS-EF:86–99), and Spring 2001 through Spring 2008. (This table was prepared October 2008.)

Table 208. Total fall enrollment in degree-granting institutions, by state or jurisdiction: Selected years, 1970 through 2006

State or jurisdiction	Fall 1970	Fall 1980	Fall 1990	Fall 2000	Fall 2001	Fall 2002	Fall 2003	Fall 2004	Fall 2005	Fall 2006	Percent change, 2000 to 2006
1	2	3	4	5	6	7	8	9	10	11	12
United States	8,580,887	12,096,895	13,818,637	15,312,289	15,927,987	16,611,711	16,911,481	17,272,044	17,487,475	17,758,870	16.0
Alabama	103,936	164,306	218,589	233,962	236,146	246,414	253,846	255,826	256,389	258,408	10.4
Alaska	9,471	21,296	29,833	27,953	27,756	29,546	31,035	30,869	30,231	29,853	6.8
Arizona	109,619	202,716	264,148	342,490	366,485	401,605	435,767	490,925	545,597	567,192	65.6
Arkansas	52,039	77,607	90,425	115,172	122,282	127,372	133,950	138,399	143,272	147,391	28.0
California	1,257,245	1,790,993	1,808,740	2,256,708	2,380,090	2,474,024	2,340,698	2,374,045	2,399,833	2,434,774	7.9
Colorado	123,395	162,916	227,131	263,872	269,292	282,343	289,424	300,914	302,672	308,383	16.9
Connecticut	124,700	159,632	168,604	161,243	165,027	170,606	170,976	172,775	174,675	176,716	9.6
Delaware	25,260	32,939	42,004	43,897	47,104	49,228	49,595	49,804	51,612	51,238	16.7
District of Columbia	77,158	86,675	79,551	72,689	87,252	91,014	95,297	99,988	104,897	109,505	50.6
Florida	235,525	411,891	588,086	707,684	753,554	792,079	840,108	866,665	872,662	885,651	25.1
Georgia	126,511	184,159	251,786	346,204	376,098	397,604	411,102	434,283	426,650	435,403	25.8
Hawaii	36,562	47,181	56,436	60,182	62,079	65,368	67,481	67,225	67,083	66,893	11.2
Idaho	34,567	43,018	51,881	65,594	69,674	72,072	75,390	76,311	77,708	77,872	18.7
Illinois	452,146	644,245	729,246	743,918	748,444	776,622	796,815	801,401	832,967	830,676	11.7
Indiana	192,668	247,253	284,832	314,334	338,715	342,064	350,102	356,801	361,253	368,013	17.1
Iowa	108,902	140,449	170,515	186,974	194,822	202,546	213,958	217,646	227,722	238,634	26.3
Kansas	102,485	136,605	163,733	179,968	184,943	188,049	190,306	191,590	191,752	193,146	7.3
Kentucky	98,591	143,066	177,852	188,341	214,839	225,489	235,743	240,097	244,969	248,914	32.2
Louisiana	120,728	160,058	186,840	223,800	228,871	232,140	244,537	246,301	197,713	224,147	0.2
Maine	34,134	43,264	57,186	58,473	61,127	63,308	64,222	65,415	65,551	66,149	13.1
Maryland	149,607	225,526	259,700	273,745	288,224	300,269	307,613	312,493	314,151	319,460	16.7
Massachusetts	303,809	418,415	417,833	421,142	425,071	431,224	436,102	439,245	443,316	451,526	7.2
Michigan	392,726	520,131	569,803	567,631	585,998	605,835	616,012	620,980	626,751	634,489	11.8
Minnesota	160,788	206,691	253,789	293,445	308,233	323,791	339,597	349,021	361,701	375,899	28.1
Mississippi	73,967	102,364	122,883	137,389	137,882	147,077	148,584	152,115	150,457	151,137	10.0
Missouri	183,930	234,421	289,899	321,348	331,580	348,146	359,749	365,204	374,775	377,098	17.3
Montana	30,062	35,177	35,876	42,240	44,932	45,111	47,240	47,173	47,850	47,501	12.5
Nebraska	66,915	89,488	112,831	112,117	113,817	116,737	119,511	121,053	121,236	124,500	11.0
Nevada	13,669	40,455	61,728	87,893	93,368	95,671	100,849	105,961	110,705	112,270	27.7
New Hampshire	29,400	46,794	59,510	61,718	65,031	68,523	69,608	70,163	69,893	70,669	14.5
New Jersey	216,121	321,610	324,286	335,945	346,507	361,733	372,632	380,374	379,758	385,656	14.8
New Mexico	44,461	58,283	85,500	110,739	112,861	120,997	127,040	131,577	131,337	131,828	19.0
New York	806,479	992,237	1,048,286	1,043,395	1,057,794	1,107,270	1,126,085	1,141,525	1,152,081	1,160,364	11.2
North Carolina	171,925	287,537	352,138	404,652	427,784	447,335	464,437	472,709	484,392	495,633	22.5
North Dakota	31,495	34,069	37,878	40,248	42,843	45,800	48,402	49,533	49,389	49,519	23.0
Ohio	376,267	489,145	557,690	549,553	569,223	587,996	603,399	614,234	616,350	619,942	12.8
Oklahoma	110,155	160,295	173,221	178,016	189,785	198,423	207,791	207,625	208,053	206,236	15.9
Oregon	122,177	157,458	165,741	183,065	191,378	204,565	198,786	199,985	200,033	197,594	7.9
Pennsylvania	411,044	507,716	604,060	609,521	630,299	654,826	676,121	688,780	692,340	707,132	16.0
Rhode Island	45,898	66,869	78,273	75,450	77,235	77,417	79,085	80,377	81,382	81,734	8.3
South Carolina	69,518	132,476	159,302	185,931	191,590	202,007	207,601	208,910	210,444	212,422	14.2
South Dakota	30,639	32,761	34,208	43,221	45,534	47,751	55,816	48,708	48,768	48,931	13.2
Tennessee	135,103	204,581	226,238	263,910	258,534	261,899	276,999	278,055	283,070	290,530	10.1
Texas	442,225	701,391	901,437	1,033,973	1,076,678	1,152,369	1,175,336	1,229,197	1,240,707	1,252,709	21.2
Utah	81,687	93,987	121,303	163,776	177,045	178,932	183,462	194,324	200,691	202,151	23.4
Vermont	22,209	30,628	36,398	35,489	36,351	36,537	37,695	38,639	39,915	41,095	15.8
Virginia	151,915	280,504	353,442	381,893	389,853	404,966	414,945	425,181	439,166	456,172	19.5
Washington	183,544	303,603	263,384	320,840	325,132	338,820	345,566	343,524	348,482	348,154	8.5
West Virginia	63,153	81,973	84,790	87,888	91,319	93,723	97,005	97,884	99,547	100,519	14.4
Wisconsin	202,058	269,086	299,774	307,179	315,850	329,443	329,738	331,506	335,258	340,158	10.7
Wyoming	15,220	21,147	31,326	30,004	31,095	32,605	33,695	33,955	35,334	34,693	15.6
U.S. Service Academies[1]	17,079	49,808	48,692	13,475	14,561	14,420	14,628	14,754	15,265	12,191	-9.5
Other jurisdictions	67,237	137,749	164,618	194,633	201,642	211,204	218,058	220,920	223,165	226,175	16.2
American Samoa	0	976	1,219	297	1,178	1,367	1,537	1,550	1,579	1,607	441.1
Federated States of Micronesia	0	224	975	1,576	2,243	2,173	2,558	2,608	2,283	2,539	61.1
Guam	2,719	3,217	4,741	5,215	4,869	5,157	4,710	4,642	6,064	5,789	11.0
Marshall Islands	0	0	0	328	220	224	601	623	604	647	97.3
Northern Marianas	0	0	661	1,078	982	1,299	1,237	1,101	967	968	-10.2
Palau	0	0	491	581	579	668	727	651	651	679	16.9
Puerto Rico	63,073	131,184	154,065	183,290	188,430	197,781	203,951	207,180	208,625	211,458	15.4
U.S. Virgin Islands	1,445	2,148	2,466	2,268	3,141	2,535	2,737	2,565	2,392	2,488	9.7

[1]Data for 2000 and later years reflect substantial changes in survey coverage.
NOTE: Data through 1990 are for institutions of higher education, while later data are for degree-granting institutions. Degree-granting institutions grant associate's or higher degrees and participate in Title IV federal financial aid programs. The degree-granting classification is very similar to the earlier higher education classification, but it includes more 2-year colleges and excludes a few higher education institutions that did not grant degrees. (See Guide to Sources for details.)

SOURCE: U.S. Department of Education, National Center for Education Statistics, Higher Education General Information Survey (HEGIS), "Fall Enrollment in Colleges and Universities" surveys, 1970 and 1980; and 1990 through 2006 Integrated Postsecondary Education Data System, "Fall Enrollment Survey" (IPEDS-EF:90), and Spring 2001 through Spring 2007. (This table was prepared May 2008.)

Table 209. Total fall enrollment in public degree-granting institutions, by state or jurisdiction: Selected years, 1970 through 2006

State or jurisdiction	Fall 1970	Fall 1980	Fall 1990	Fall 2000	Fall 2001	Fall 2002	Fall 2003	Fall 2004	Fall 2005	Fall 2006	Percent change, 2000 to 2006
1	2	3	4	5	6	7	8	9	10	11	12
United States	6,428,134	9,457,394	10,844,717	11,752,786	12,233,156	12,751,993	12,858,698	12,980,112	13,021,834	13,180,133	12.1
Alabama	87,884	143,674	195,939	207,435	208,385	217,883	225,347	226,989	228,153	230,668	11.2
Alaska	8,563	20,561	27,792	26,559	26,550	28,314	29,821	29,515	28,866	28,595	7.7
Arizona	107,315	194,034	248,213	284,522	294,174	307,496	310,679	317,974	320,865	331,441	16.5
Arkansas	43,599	66,068	78,645	101,775	108,950	113,509	119,920	123,973	128,117	131,407	29.1
California	1,123,529	1,599,838	1,594,710	1,927,771	2,043,182	2,121,106	1,978,831	1,987,283	2,008,155	2,047,565	6.2
Colorado	108,562	145,598	200,653	217,897	222,815	233,740	236,883	239,308	234,509	231,901	6.4
Connecticut	73,391	97,788	109,556	101,027	104,066	108,522	108,815	110,354	111,705	112,476	11.3
Delaware	21,151	28,325	34,252	34,194	36,510	37,344	37,621	38,243	38,682	38,118	11.5
District of Columbia	12,194	13,900	11,990	5,499	5,589	5,603	5,424	5,388	5,595	5,769	4.9
Florida	189,450	334,349	489,081	556,912	588,921	617,754	643,784	649,857	648,999	651,908	17.1
Georgia	101,900	140,158	196,413	271,755	298,215	317,180	330,052	335,979	342,012	346,138	27.4
Hawaii	32,963	43,269	45,728	44,579	45,994	48,163	50,316	50,569	50,157	49,990	12.1
Idaho	27,072	34,491	41,315	53,751	56,673	57,996	60,481	60,695	60,303	59,211	10.2
Illinois	315,634	491,274	551,333	534,155	534,280	554,093	566,137	563,593	555,149	552,777	3.5
Indiana	136,739	189,224	223,953	240,023	259,258	258,627	262,957	266,916	267,298	271,704	13.2
Iowa	68,390	97,454	117,834	135,008	140,227	145,798	149,195	149,776	148,907	151,052	11.9
Kansas	88,215	121,987	149,117	159,976	164,173	167,741	169,384	170,149	170,319	170,531	6.6
Kentucky	77,240	114,884	147,095	151,973	178,349	188,518	196,474	197,991	201,579	204,198	34.4
Louisiana	101,127	136,703	158,290	189,213	194,790	197,547	207,923	208,218	181,043	192,554	1.8
Maine	25,405	31,878	41,500	40,662	42,425	44,850	46,714	47,284	47,519	47,770	17.5
Maryland	118,988	195,051	220,783	223,797	236,795	246,792	251,984	256,582	256,073	260,921	16.6
Massachusetts	116,127	183,765	186,035	183,248	186,891	187,874	189,334	187,873	188,295	192,164	4.9
Michigan	339,625	454,147	487,359	467,861	482,154	495,676	501,821	500,873	505,586	511,776	9.4
Minnesota	130,567	162,379	199,211	218,617	225,941	235,513	242,531	241,245	240,853	244,106	11.7
Mississippi	64,968	90,661	109,038	125,355	125,656	134,130	134,318	137,543	135,896	136,626	9.0
Missouri	132,540	165,179	200,093	201,509	206,721	214,022	216,777	214,561	217,722	218,475	8.4
Montana	27,287	31,178	31,865	37,387	39,368	40,615	42,444	42,289	42,997	42,995	15.0
Nebraska	51,454	73,509	94,614	88,531	89,639	92,111	93,432	93,195	93,181	94,486	6.7
Nevada	13,576	40,280	61,242	83,120	86,790	89,547	94,205	96,773	100,043	101,856	22.5
New Hampshire	15,979	24,119	32,163	35,870	37,224	40,958	41,324	40,642	41,007	41,530	15.8
New Jersey	145,373	247,028	261,601	266,921	275,655	289,275	298,906	305,034	304,315	308,374	15.5
New Mexico	40,795	55,077	83,403	101,450	103,758	111,667	117,245	121,339	120,976	121,668	19.9
New York	449,437	563,251	616,884	583,417	584,607	610,756	613,895	623,192	626,222	635,785	9.0
North Carolina	123,761	228,154	285,405	329,422	350,684	367,861	383,720	389,143	396,755	406,068	23.3
North Dakota	30,192	31,709	34,690	36,014	38,560	41,134	43,383	43,275	42,808	42,949	19.3
Ohio	281,099	381,765	427,613	411,161	425,265	441,738	450,369	454,377	453,001	452,962	10.2
Oklahoma	91,438	137,188	151,073	153,699	163,336	171,369	178,012	179,281	179,225	178,015	15.8
Oregon	108,483	140,102	144,427	154,756	162,645	173,698	166,129	165,375	163,752	160,059	3.4
Pennsylvania	232,982	292,499	343,478	339,229	353,950	370,386	381,254	384,525	380,271	388,251	14.5
Rhode Island	25,527	35,052	42,350	38,458	39,149	38,867	39,937	39,920	40,008	40,374	5.0
South Carolina	47,101	107,683	131,134	155,519	158,661	167,563	171,893	172,386	174,686	176,415	13.4
South Dakota	23,936	24,328	26,596	34,857	37,310	37,760	38,179	37,598	37,548	38,028	9.1
Tennessee	98,897	156,835	175,049	202,530	194,696	194,202	196,088	199,904	200,394	205,056	1.2
Texas	365,522	613,552	802,314	896,534	935,826	1,006,549	1,035,872	1,071,926	1,081,335	1,094,139	22.0
Utah	49,588	59,598	86,108	123,046	133,790	135,778	140,282	145,182	148,960	148,228	20.5
Vermont	12,536	17,984	20,910	20,021	20,480	21,238	22,607	22,980	24,090	24,385	21.8
Virginia	123,279	246,500	291,286	313,780	326,758	337,286	341,948	343,391	349,195	357,823	14.0
Washington	162,718	276,028	227,632	273,928	277,023	293,007	298,079	293,145	296,756	297,048	8.4
West Virginia	51,363	71,228	74,108	76,136	78,304	79,741	82,273	83,274	85,148	86,501	13.6
Wisconsin	170,374	235,179	253,529	249,737	257,888	268,010	266,805	266,884	268,928	272,246	9.0
Wyoming	15,220	21,121	30,623	28,715	29,545	30,666	31,666	31,597	32,611	32,860	14.4
U.S. Service Academies[1]	17,079	49,808	48,692	13,475	14,561	14,420	14,628	14,754	15,265	12,191	-9.5
Other jurisdictions	46,680	60,692	66,244	84,464	85,535	86,484	85,665	83,831	82,341	80,685	-4.5
American Samoa	0	976	1,219	297	1,178	1,367	1,537	1,550	1,579	1,607	441.1
Federated States of Micronesia	0	224	975	1,576	2,243	2,173	2,558	2,608	2,283	2,539	61.1
Guam	2,719	3,217	4,741	5,215	4,869	5,038	4,546	4,470	5,875	5,603	7.4
Marshall Islands	0	0	0	328	220	224	601	623	604	647	97.3
Northern Marianas	0	0	661	1,078	982	1,299	1,237	1,101	967	968	-10.2
Palau	0	0	491	581	579	668	727	651	651	679	16.9
Puerto Rico	42,516	54,127	55,691	73,121	73,173	73,180	71,722	70,263	67,990	66,154	-9.5
U.S. Virgin Islands	1,445	2,148	2,466	2,268	2,291	2,535	2,737	2,565	2,392	2,488	9.7

[1]Data for 2000 and later years reflect substantial changes in survey coverage.
NOTE: Data through 1990 are for institutions of higher education, while later data are for degree-granting institutions. Degree-granting institutions grant associate's or higher degrees and participate in Title IV federal financial aid programs. The degree-granting classification is very similar to the earlier higher education classification, but it includes more 2-year colleges and excludes a few higher education institutions that did not grant degrees. (See Guide to Sources for details.)

SOURCE: U.S. Department of Education, National Center for Education Statistics, Higher Education General Information Survey (HEGIS), "Fall Enrollment in Colleges and Universities" surveys, 1970 and 1980; and 1990 through 2006 Integrated Postsecondary Education Data System, "Fall Enrollment Survey" (IPEDS-EF:90), and Spring 2001 through Spring 2007. (This table was prepared May 2008.)

Table 210. Total fall enrollment in private degree-granting institutions, by state or jurisdiction: Selected years, 1970 through 2006

State or jurisdiction	Fall 1970	Fall 1980	Fall 1990	Fall 2000	Fall 2001	Fall 2002	Fall 2003	Fall 2004	Fall 2005	Fall 2006	Percent change, 2000 to 2006
1	2	3	4	5	6	7	8	9	10	11	12
United States	2,152,753	2,639,501	2,973,920	3,559,503	3,694,831	3,859,718	4,052,783	4,291,932	4,465,641	4,578,737	28.6
Alabama	16,052	20,632	22,650	26,527	27,761	28,531	28,499	28,837	28,236	27,740	4.6
Alaska	908	735	2,041	1,394	1,206	1,232	1,214	1,354	1,365	1,258	-9.8
Arizona	2,304	8,682	15,935	57,968	72,311	94,109	125,088	172,951	224,732	235,751	306.7
Arkansas	8,440	11,539	11,780	13,397	13,332	13,863	14,030	14,426	15,155	15,984	19.3
California	133,716	191,155	214,030	328,937	336,908	352,918	361,867	386,762	391,678	387,209	17.7
Colorado	14,833	17,318	26,478	45,975	46,477	48,603	52,541	61,606	68,163	76,482	66.4
Connecticut	51,309	61,844	59,048	60,216	60,961	62,084	62,161	62,421	62,970	64,240	6.7
Delaware	4,109	4,614	7,752	9,703	10,594	11,884	11,974	11,561	12,930	13,120	35.2
District of Columbia	64,964	72,775	67,561	67,190	81,663	85,411	89,873	94,600	99,302	103,736	54.4
Florida	46,075	77,542	99,005	150,772	164,633	174,325	196,324	216,808	223,663	233,743	55.0
Georgia	24,611	44,001	55,373	74,449	77,883	80,424	81,050	98,304	84,638	89,265	19.9
Hawaii	3,599	3,912	10,708	15,603	16,085	17,205	17,165	16,656	16,926	16,903	8.3
Idaho	7,495	8,527	10,566	11,843	13,001	14,076	14,909	15,616	17,405	18,661	57.6
Illinois	136,512	152,971	177,913	209,763	214,164	222,529	230,678	237,808	277,818	277,899	32.5
Indiana	55,929	58,029	60,879	74,311	79,457	83,437	87,145	89,885	93,955	96,309	29.6
Iowa	40,512	42,995	52,681	53,966	54,595	56,748	64,763	67,870	78,815	87,582	62.3
Kansas	14,270	14,618	14,616	19,992	20,770	20,308	20,922	21,441	21,433	22,615	13.1
Kentucky	21,351	28,182	30,757	36,368	36,490	36,971	39,269	42,106	43,390	44,716	23.0
Louisiana	19,601	23,355	28,550	34,587	34,081	34,593	36,614	38,083	16,670	31,593	-8.7
Maine	8,729	11,386	15,686	17,811	18,702	18,458	17,508	18,131	18,032	18,379	3.2
Maryland	30,619	30,475	38,917	49,948	51,429	53,477	55,629	55,911	58,078	58,539	17.2
Massachusetts	187,682	234,650	231,798	237,894	238,180	243,350	246,768	251,372	255,021	259,362	9.0
Michigan	53,101	65,984	82,444	99,770	103,844	110,159	114,191	120,107	121,165	122,713	23.0
Minnesota	30,221	44,312	54,578	74,828	82,292	88,278	97,066	107,776	120,848	131,793	76.1
Mississippi	8,999	11,703	13,845	12,034	12,226	12,947	14,266	14,572	14,561	14,511	20.6
Missouri	51,390	69,242	89,806	119,839	124,859	134,124	142,972	150,643	156,723	158,623	32.4
Montana	2,775	3,999	4,011	4,853	5,564	4,496	4,796	4,884	4,853	4,506	-7.2
Nebraska	15,461	15,979	18,217	23,586	24,178	24,626	26,079	27,858	28,055	30,014	27.3
Nevada	93	175	486	4,773	6,578	6,124	6,644	9,188	10,662	10,414	118.2
New Hampshire	13,421	22,675	27,347	25,848	27,807	27,565	28,284	29,521	28,886	29,139	12.7
New Jersey	70,748	74,582	62,685	69,024	70,852	72,458	73,726	75,340	75,443	77,282	12.0
New Mexico	3,666	3,206	2,097	9,289	9,103	9,330	9,795	10,238	10,361	10,160	9.4
New York	357,042	428,986	431,402	459,978	473,187	496,514	512,190	518,333	525,859	524,579	14.0
North Carolina	48,164	59,383	66,733	75,230	77,100	79,474	80,717	83,566	87,637	89,565	19.1
North Dakota	1,303	2,360	3,188	4,234	4,283	4,666	5,019	6,258	6,581	6,570	55.2
Ohio	95,168	107,380	130,077	138,392	143,958	146,258	153,030	159,857	163,349	166,980	20.7
Oklahoma	18,717	23,107	22,148	24,317	26,449	27,054	29,179	28,344	28,828	28,221	16.1
Oregon	13,694	17,356	21,314	28,309	28,733	30,867	32,657	34,610	36,281	37,535	32.6
Pennsylvania	178,062	215,217	260,582	270,292	276,349	284,440	294,867	304,255	312,069	318,881	18.0
Rhode Island	20,371	31,817	35,923	36,992	38,086	38,550	39,148	40,457	41,374	41,360	11.8
South Carolina	22,417	24,793	28,168	30,412	32,929	34,444	35,708	36,524	35,758	36,007	18.4
South Dakota	6,703	8,433	7,612	8,364	8,224	9,991	17,637	11,110	11,220	10,903	30.4
Tennessee	36,206	47,746	51,189	61,380	63,838	67,697	80,911	78,151	82,676	85,474	39.3
Texas	76,703	87,839	99,123	137,439	140,852	145,820	139,464	157,271	159,372	158,570	15.4
Utah	32,099	34,389	35,195	40,730	43,255	43,154	43,180	49,142	51,731	53,923	32.4
Vermont	9,673	12,644	15,488	15,468	15,871	15,299	15,088	15,659	15,825	16,710	8.0
Virginia	28,636	34,004	62,156	68,113	63,095	67,680	72,997	81,790	89,971	98,349	44.4
Washington	20,826	27,575	35,752	46,912	48,109	45,813	47,487	50,379	51,726	51,106	8.9
West Virginia	11,790	10,745	10,682	11,752	13,015	13,982	14,732	14,610	14,399	14,018	19.3
Wisconsin	31,684	33,907	46,245	57,442	57,962	61,433	62,933	64,622	66,330	67,912	18.2
Wyoming	0	26	703	1,289	1,550	1,939	2,029	2,358	2,723	1,833	42.2
Other jurisdictions	20,557	77,057	98,374	110,169	116,107	124,720	132,393	137,089	140,824	145,490	32.1
American Samoa	0	0	0	0	0	0	0	0	0	0	†
Federated States of Micronesia	0	0	0	0	0	0	0	0	0	0	†
Guam	0	0	0	0	0	119	164	172	189	186	†
Marshall Islands	0	0	0	0	0	0	0	0	0	0	†
Northern Marianas	0	0	0	0	0	0	0	0	0	0	†
Palau	0	0	0	0	0	0	0	0	0	0	†
Puerto Rico	20,557	77,057	98,374	110,169	115,257	124,601	132,229	136,917	140,635	145,304	31.9
U.S. Virgin Islands	0	0	0	0	850	0	0	0	0	0	†

†Not applicable.
NOTE: Data through 1990 are for institutions of higher education, while later data are for degree-granting institutions. Degree-granting institutions grant associate's or higher degrees and participate in Title IV federal financial aid programs. The degree-granting classification is very similar to the earlier higher education classification, but it includes more 2-year colleges and excludes a few higher education institutions that did not grant degrees. (See Guide to Sources for details.)

SOURCE: U.S. Department of Education, National Center for Education Statistics, Higher Education General Information Survey (HEGIS), "Fall Enrollment in Colleges and Universities" surveys, 1970 and 1980; and 1990 through 2006 Integrated Postsecondary Education Data System, "Fall Enrollment Survey" (IPEDS-EF:90), and Spring 2001 through Spring 2007. (This table was prepared May 2008.)

Table 211. Total fall enrollment in all degree-granting institutions, by attendance status, sex, and state or jurisdiction: 2005 and 2006

State or jurisdiction	Total	Fall 2005 Full-time Males	Full-time Females	Part-time Males	Part-time Females	Total	Fall 2006 Full-time Males	Full-time Females	Part-time Males	Part-time Females
1	2	3	4	5	6	7	8	9	10	11
United States	17,487,475	4,803,388	5,993,623	2,652,537	4,037,927	17,758,870	4,879,315	6,077,990	2,695,500	4,106,065
Alabama	256,389	73,011	97,047	33,448	52,883	258,408	73,405	97,737	33,387	53,879
Alaska	30,231	5,783	7,261	6,094	11,093	29,853	5,744	7,168	6,078	10,863
Arizona	545,597	145,697	207,474	77,511	114,915	567,192	146,018	217,651	81,709	121,814
Arkansas	143,272	39,654	54,229	18,343	31,046	147,391	39,919	54,902	19,248	33,322
California	2,399,833	542,176	679,567	515,013	663,077	2,434,774	552,589	687,488	523,741	670,956
Colorado	302,672	83,152	96,823	49,096	73,601	308,383	86,463	102,272	48,210	71,438
Connecticut	174,675	49,549	61,624	22,764	40,738	176,716	50,945	62,361	22,744	40,666
Delaware	51,612	13,913	19,126	6,476	12,097	51,238	13,973	19,272	6,166	11,827
District of Columbia	104,897	25,805	36,227	16,655	26,210	109,505	26,975	37,433	16,799	28,298
Florida	872,662	212,355	282,656	146,656	230,995	885,651	217,238	288,201	148,347	231,865
Georgia	426,650	119,710	162,697	52,204	92,039	435,403	123,259	166,642	52,654	92,848
Hawaii	67,083	16,667	23,225	10,919	16,272	66,893	16,814	23,136	10,823	16,120
Idaho	77,708	24,793	28,364	9,848	14,703	77,872	24,598	28,508	9,844	14,922
Illinois	832,967	219,365	267,014	137,446	209,142	830,676	220,542	265,781	136,671	207,682
Indiana	361,253	116,230	134,604	45,364	65,055	368,013	117,783	138,279	45,710	66,241
Iowa	227,722	68,344	80,951	29,436	48,991	238,634	69,222	82,594	32,242	54,576
Kansas	191,752	53,832	59,415	31,372	47,133	193,146	54,728	60,238	31,049	47,131
Kentucky	244,969	64,284	88,379	40,874	51,432	248,914	64,118	88,535	42,322	53,939
Louisiana	197,713	60,519	86,134	18,422	32,638	224,147	68,410	94,260	21,948	39,529
Maine	65,551	18,322	22,367	8,107	16,755	66,149	18,543	22,773	8,084	16,749
Maryland	314,151	73,877	95,040	53,669	91,565	319,460	75,699	96,974	54,867	91,920
Massachusetts	443,316	137,526	167,817	50,202	87,771	451,526	140,366	170,534	51,063	89,563
Michigan	626,751	164,820	199,653	102,314	159,964	634,489	167,380	201,133	103,652	162,324
Minnesota	361,701	100,227	128,471	51,918	81,085	375,899	102,651	131,797	54,036	87,415
Mississippi	150,457	46,358	69,104	11,232	23,763	151,137	46,453	69,470	11,440	23,774
Missouri	374,445	99,431	126,375	58,664	89,975	377,098	101,287	127,839	57,834	90,138
Montana	47,850	16,875	18,785	4,643	7,547	47,501	16,978	18,380	4,626	7,517
Nebraska	121,236	37,187	42,701	17,132	24,216	124,500	38,160	44,017	17,654	24,669
Nevada	110,705	23,214	30,164	25,117	32,210	112,270	22,421	29,708	26,870	33,271
New Hampshire	69,893	21,540	26,106	7,740	14,507	70,669	21,679	26,664	7,767	14,559
New Jersey	379,758	105,101	123,299	57,986	93,372	385,656	108,827	125,028	59,165	92,636
New Mexico	131,337	29,352	39,563	23,988	38,434	131,828	29,590	39,247	25,188	37,803
New York	1,152,081	357,281	453,230	124,854	216,716	1,160,364	364,706	456,940	124,379	214,339
North Carolina	484,392	131,161	177,862	62,405	112,964	495,633	133,179	179,337	65,135	117,982
North Dakota	49,389	18,562	18,832	5,009	6,986	49,519	18,578	18,347	5,089	7,505
Ohio	616,350	187,336	230,097	77,315	121,602	619,942	191,086	232,916	75,639	120,301
Oklahoma	208,053	61,510	73,696	28,378	44,469	206,236	60,289	72,543	28,657	44,747
Oregon	200,033	55,268	65,691	33,383	45,691	197,594	54,973	66,399	31,729	44,493
Pennsylvania	692,340	232,614	269,765	67,850	122,111	707,132	236,656	273,731	69,801	126,944
Rhode Island	81,382	27,002	31,904	8,037	14,439	81,734	27,804	32,023	8,005	13,902
South Carolina	210,444	60,370	81,955	21,575	46,544	212,422	60,844	83,344	22,014	46,220
South Dakota	48,768	15,560	17,177	5,512	10,519	48,931	15,333	17,031	5,779	10,788
Tennessee	283,070	88,230	116,131	29,094	49,615	290,530	89,996	119,283	29,351	51,900
Texas	1,240,707	313,684	381,292	222,342	323,389	1,252,709	314,819	380,919	225,125	331,846
Utah	200,691	62,751	59,320	39,134	39,486	202,151	62,227	59,198	39,837	40,889
Vermont	39,915	14,161	14,772	3,468	7,514	41,095	15,003	15,293	3,584	7,215
Virginia	439,166	118,351	150,181	67,327	103,307	456,172	121,835	156,255	71,188	106,894
Washington	348,482	97,592	118,426	54,445	78,019	348,154	97,051	117,838	54,077	79,188
West Virginia	99,547	33,780	40,272	9,489	16,006	100,519	34,233	40,404	9,574	16,308
Wisconsin	335,258	96,589	118,639	46,404	73,626	340,158	98,424	118,577	48,409	74,748
Wyoming	35,334	10,396	9,375	5,863	9,700	34,693	9,608	9,293	6,190	9,602
U.S. Service Academies	15,265	12,521	2,744	0	0	12,191	9,894	2,297	0	0
Other jurisdictions	223,165	66,463	102,684	20,737	33,281	226,175	67,256	105,052	20,634	33,233
American Samoa	1,579	290	475	310	504	1,607	340	475	294	498
Federated States of Micronesia	2,283	791	762	375	355	2,539	823	884	409	423
Guam	6,064	1,085	1,644	1,184	2,151	5,789	1,045	1,686	1,197	1,861
Marshall Islands	604	254	219	67	64	647	284	243	62	58
Northern Marianas	967	260	482	88	137	968	253	468	86	161
Palau	651	212	219	67	153	679	212	240	61	166
Puerto Rico	208,625	63,240	97,951	18,428	29,006	211,458	63,967	100,095	18,269	29,127
U.S. Virgin Islands	2,392	331	932	218	911	2,488	332	961	256	939

NOTE: Degree-granting institutions grant associate's or higher degrees and participate in Title IV federal financial aid programs.

SOURCE: U.S. Department of Education, National Center for Education Statistics, 2005 and 2006 Integrated Postsecondary Education Data System (IPEDS), Spring 2006 and Spring 2007. (This table was prepared May 2007.)

Table 212. Total fall enrollment in public degree-granting institutions, by attendance status, sex, and state or jurisdiction: 2005 and 2006

		Fall 2005					Fall 2006			
		Full-time		Part-time			Full-time		Part-time	
State or jurisdiction	Total	Males	Females	Males	Females	Total	Males	Females	Males	Females
1	2	3	4	5	6	7	8	9	10	11
United States	13,021,834	3,350,485	4,058,276	2,238,738	3,374,335	13,180,133	3,406,146	4,089,417	2,273,258	3,411,312
Alabama.....................................	228,153	62,860	83,551	31,665	50,077	230,668	63,873	84,283	31,543	50,969
Alaska.......................................	28,866	5,531	6,829	5,872	10,634	28,595	5,528	6,806	5,834	10,427
Arizona......................................	320,865	64,483	76,722	73,119	106,541	331,441	65,287	76,219	77,293	112,642
Arkansas....................................	128,117	34,002	47,396	17,506	29,213	131,407	34,031	47,843	18,238	31,295
California	2,008,155	411,841	510,396	475,100	610,818	2,047,565	425,282	516,744	485,506	620,033
Colorado....................................	234,509	61,238	69,071	40,588	63,612	231,901	61,417	68,628	40,184	61,672
Connecticut................................	111,705	28,158	34,549	17,571	31,427	112,476	29,121	35,050	17,513	30,792
Delaware....................................	38,682	11,155	15,117	4,358	8,052	38,118	11,168	15,252	4,073	7,625
District of Columbia	5,595	905	1,377	1,069	2,244	5,769	1,294	1,492	992	1,991
Florida.......................................	648,999	143,833	191,635	118,594	194,937	651,908	147,182	194,674	118,784	191,268
Georgia......................................	342,012	91,393	120,265	47,018	83,336	346,138	94,138	123,448	46,550	82,002
Hawaii..	50,157	12,392	15,638	8,645	13,482	49,990	12,448	15,284	8,807	13,451
Idaho...	60,303	17,933	19,850	8,963	13,557	59,211	17,470	19,114	8,871	13,756
Illinois.......................................	555,149	132,315	150,582	108,988	163,264	552,777	134,055	150,458	107,476	160,788
Indiana.......................................	267,298	82,048	91,174	39,547	54,529	271,704	82,951	93,122	40,033	55,598
Iowa..	148,907	46,620	49,458	22,002	30,827	151,052	46,792	49,105	23,190	31,965
Kansas.......................................	170,319	46,988	51,209	28,992	43,130	170,531	47,664	51,520	28,512	42,835
Kentucky....................................	201,579	51,892	68,773	36,850	44,064	204,198	51,758	68,343	38,120	45,977
Louisiana...................................	181,043	56,570	76,081	17,649	30,743	192,554	58,408	78,426	20,094	35,626
Maine...	47,519	12,712	14,734	6,748	13,325	47,770	12,811	14,812	6,774	13,373
Maryland....................................	256,073	58,801	73,872	45,175	78,225	260,921	60,534	75,309	46,542	78,536
Massachusetts............................	188,295	48,702	58,062	28,910	52,621	192,164	49,987	58,688	29,412	54,077
Michigan....................................	505,586	134,903	156,891	84,999	128,793	511,776	137,103	158,950	85,526	130,197
Minnesota..................................	240,853	69,756	77,948	38,053	55,096	244,106	71,128	78,089	38,658	56,231
Mississippi................................	135,896	41,987	61,441	10,548	21,920	136,626	42,152	61,732	10,780	21,962
Missouri.....................................	217,722	59,306	72,933	31,956	53,527	218,475	60,205	73,495	31,545	53,230
Montana.....................................	42,997	15,290	16,570	4,283	6,854	42,995	15,513	16,273	4,304	6,905
Nebraska....................................	93,181	27,738	29,873	15,116	20,454	94,486	28,061	30,081	15,531	20,813
Nevada.......................................	100,043	19,112	24,258	24,841	31,832	101,856	18,704	23,825	26,544	32,783
New Hampshire	41,007	11,649	13,940	5,569	9,849	41,530	11,910	14,468	5,349	9,803
New Jersey.................................	304,315	79,713	96,592	48,385	79,625	308,374	82,726	97,734	49,289	78,625
New Mexico................................	120,976	26,023	34,258	23,323	37,372	121,668	26,441	34,111	24,542	36,574
New York....................................	626,222	181,802	223,026	81,916	139,478	635,785	187,340	227,520	82,402	138,523
North Carolina	396,755	99,205	135,553	57,674	104,323	406,068	100,115	135,303	61,084	109,566
North Dakota	42,808	16,545	15,470	4,686	6,107	42,949	16,536	15,212	4,735	6,466
Ohio..	453,001	133,533	158,752	63,639	97,077	452,962	136,472	159,535	61,701	95,254
Oklahoma..................................	179,225	50,140	60,979	26,236	41,870	178,015	48,811	59,732	26,961	42,511
Oregon......................................	163,752	43,121	48,893	30,418	41,320	160,059	42,616	48,639	28,709	40,095
Pennsylvania..............................	380,271	125,517	139,428	41,224	74,102	388,251	129,510	142,160	41,473	75,108
Rhode Island	40,008	9,271	13,444	5,603	11,690	40,374	9,777	13,679	5,653	11,265
South Carolina............................	174,686	48,413	64,478	19,609	42,186	176,415	48,873	65,577	19,980	41,985
South Dakota.............................	37,548	12,996	12,894	3,953	7,705	38,028	12,980	12,941	4,193	7,914
Tennessee	200,394	58,276	76,438	24,165	41,515	205,056	59,874	77,883	24,292	43,007
Texas	1,081,335	259,954	315,314	204,267	301,800	1,094,139	261,490	314,088	208,132	310,429
Utah..	148,960	40,934	36,636	35,703	35,687	148,228	39,287	35,249	36,401	37,291
Vermont.....................................	24,090	7,218	8,363	2,497	6,012	24,385	7,473	8,557	2,619	5,736
Virginia......................................	349,195	88,693	107,294	60,538	92,670	357,823	91,224	110,560	62,196	93,843
Washington................................	296,756	79,941	94,634	50,152	72,029	297,048	80,176	94,838	49,346	72,688
West Virginia..............................	85,148	29,101	32,819	8,719	14,509	86,501	29,749	33,181	8,794	14,777
Wisconsin..................................	268,928	77,667	90,812	39,874	60,575	272,246	78,958	89,869	41,988	61,431
Wyoming....................................	32,611	7,788	9,260	5,863	9,700	32,860	7,849	9,219	6,190	9,602
U.S. Service Academies..............	15,265	12,521	2,744	0	0	12,191	9,894	2,297	0	0
Other jurisdictions	82,341	24,984	39,115	6,735	11,507	80,685	24,645	38,843	6,493	10,704
American Samoa.........................	1,579	290	475	310	504	1,607	340	475	294	498
Federated States of Micronesia..............	2,283	791	762	375	355	2,539	823	884	409	423
Guam...	5,875	1,029	1,567	1,158	2,121	5,603	985	1,600	1,185	1,833
Marshall Islands..........................	604	254	219	67	64	647	284	243	62	58
Northern Marianas	967	260	482	88	137	968	253	468	86	161
Palau...	651	212	219	67	153	679	212	240	61	166
Puerto Rico.................................	67,990	21,817	34,459	4,452	7,262	66,154	21,416	33,972	4,140	6,626
U.S. Virgin Islands	2,392	331	932	218	911	2,488	332	961	256	939

NOTE: Degree-granting institutions grant associate's or higher degrees and participate in Title IV federal financial aid programs.

SOURCE: U.S. Department of Education, National Center for Education Statistics, 2005 and 2006 Integrated Postsecondary Education Data System (IPEDS), Spring 2006 and Spring 2007. (This table was prepared June 2008.)

Table 213. Total fall enrollment in private degree-granting institutions, by attendance status, sex, and state or jurisdiction: 2005 and 2006

State or jurisdiction	Total	Fall 2005				Total	Fall 2006			
		Full-time		Part-time			Full-time		Part-time	
		Males	Females	Males	Females		Males	Females	Males	Females
1	2	3	4	5	6	7	8	9	10	11
United States	4,465,641	1,452,903	1,935,347	413,799	663,592	4,578,737	1,473,169	1,988,573	422,242	694,753
Alabama	28,236	10,151	13,496	1,783	2,806	27,740	9,532	13,454	1,844	2,910
Alaska	1,365	252	432	222	459	1,258	216	362	244	436
Arizona	224,732	81,214	130,752	4,392	8,374	235,751	80,731	141,432	4,416	9,172
Arkansas	15,155	5,652	6,833	837	1,833	15,984	5,888	7,059	1,010	2,027
California	391,678	130,335	169,171	39,913	52,259	387,209	127,307	170,744	38,235	50,923
Colorado	68,163	21,914	27,752	8,508	9,989	76,482	25,046	33,644	8,026	9,766
Connecticut	62,970	21,391	27,075	5,193	9,311	64,240	21,824	27,311	5,231	9,874
Delaware	12,930	2,758	4,009	2,118	4,045	13,120	2,805	4,020	2,093	4,202
District of Columbia	99,302	24,900	34,850	15,586	23,966	103,736	25,681	35,941	15,807	26,307
Florida	223,663	68,522	91,021	28,062	36,058	233,743	70,056	93,527	29,563	40,597
Georgia	84,638	28,317	42,432	5,186	8,703	89,265	29,121	43,194	6,104	10,846
Hawaii	16,926	4,275	7,587	2,274	2,790	16,903	4,366	7,852	2,016	2,669
Idaho	17,405	6,860	8,514	885	1,146	18,661	7,128	9,394	973	1,166
Illinois	277,818	87,050	116,432	28,458	45,878	277,899	86,487	115,323	29,195	46,894
Indiana	93,955	34,182	43,430	5,817	10,526	96,309	34,832	45,157	5,677	10,643
Iowa	78,815	21,724	31,493	7,434	18,164	87,582	22,430	33,489	9,052	22,611
Kansas	21,433	6,844	8,206	2,380	4,003	22,615	7,064	8,718	2,537	4,296
Kentucky	43,390	12,392	19,606	4,024	7,368	44,716	12,360	20,192	4,202	7,062
Louisiana	16,670	3,949	10,053	773	1,895	31,593	10,002	15,834	1,854	3,903
Maine	18,032	5,610	7,633	1,359	3,430	18,379	5,732	7,961	1,310	3,376
Maryland	58,078	15,076	21,168	8,494	13,340	58,539	15,165	21,665	8,325	13,384
Massachusetts	255,021	88,824	109,755	21,292	35,150	259,362	90,379	111,846	21,651	35,486
Michigan	121,165	29,917	42,762	17,315	31,171	122,713	30,277	42,183	18,126	32,127
Minnesota	120,848	30,471	50,523	13,865	25,989	131,793	31,523	53,708	15,378	31,184
Mississippi	14,561	4,371	7,663	684	1,843	14,511	4,301	7,738	660	1,812
Missouri	156,723	40,125	53,442	26,708	36,448	158,623	41,082	54,344	26,289	36,908
Montana	4,853	1,585	2,215	360	693	4,506	1,465	2,107	322	612
Nebraska	28,055	9,449	12,828	2,016	3,762	30,014	10,099	13,936	2,123	3,856
Nevada	10,662	4,102	5,906	276	378	10,414	3,717	5,883	326	488
New Hampshire	28,886	9,891	12,166	2,171	4,658	29,139	9,769	12,196	2,418	4,756
New Jersey	75,443	25,388	26,707	9,601	13,747	77,282	26,101	27,294	9,876	14,011
New Mexico	10,361	3,329	5,305	665	1,062	10,160	3,149	5,136	646	1,229
New York	525,859	175,479	230,204	42,938	77,238	524,579	177,366	229,420	41,977	75,816
North Carolina	87,637	31,956	42,309	4,731	8,641	89,565	33,064	44,034	4,051	8,416
North Dakota	6,581	2,017	3,362	323	879	6,570	2,042	3,135	354	1,039
Ohio	163,349	53,803	71,345	13,676	24,525	166,980	54,614	73,381	13,938	25,047
Oklahoma	28,828	11,370	12,717	2,142	2,599	28,221	11,478	12,811	1,696	2,236
Oregon	36,281	12,147	16,798	2,965	4,371	37,535	12,357	17,760	3,020	4,398
Pennsylvania	312,069	107,097	130,337	26,626	48,009	318,881	107,146	131,571	28,328	51,836
Rhode Island	41,374	17,731	18,460	2,434	2,749	41,360	18,027	18,344	2,352	2,637
South Carolina	35,758	11,957	17,477	1,966	4,358	36,007	11,971	17,767	2,034	4,235
South Dakota	11,220	2,564	4,283	1,559	2,814	10,903	2,353	4,090	1,586	2,874
Tennessee	82,676	29,954	39,693	4,929	8,100	85,474	30,122	41,400	5,059	8,893
Texas	159,372	53,730	65,978	18,075	21,589	158,570	53,329	66,831	16,993	21,417
Utah	51,731	21,817	22,684	3,431	3,799	53,923	22,940	23,949	3,436	3,598
Vermont	15,825	6,943	6,409	971	1,502	16,710	7,530	6,736	965	1,479
Virginia	89,971	29,658	42,887	6,789	10,637	98,349	30,611	45,695	8,992	13,051
Washington	51,726	17,651	23,792	4,293	5,990	51,106	16,875	23,000	4,731	6,500
West Virginia	14,399	4,679	7,453	770	1,497	14,018	4,484	7,223	780	1,531
Wisconsin	66,330	18,922	27,827	6,530	13,051	67,912	19,466	28,708	6,421	13,317
Wyoming	2,723	2,608	115	0	0	1,833	1,759	74	0	0
Other jurisdictions	140,824	41,479	63,569	14,002	21,774	145,490	42,611	66,209	14,141	22,529
American Samoa	0	0	0	0	0	0	0	0	0	0
Federated States of Micronesia	0	0	0	0	0	0	0	0	0	0
Guam	189	56	77	26	30	186	60	86	12	28
Marshall Islands	0	0	0	0	0	0	0	0	0	0
Northern Marianas	0	0	0	0	0	0	0	0	0	0
Palau	0	0	0	0	0	0	0	0	0	0
Puerto Rico	140,635	41,423	63,492	13,976	21,744	145,304	42,551	66,123	14,129	22,501
U.S. Virgin Islands	0	0	0	0	0	0	0	0	0	0

NOTE: Degree-granting institutions grant associate's or higher degrees and participate in Title IV federal financial aid programs.

SOURCE: U.S. Department of Education, National Center for Education Statistics, 2005 and 2006 Integrated Postsecondary Education Data System (IPEDS), Spring 2006 and Spring 2007. (This table was prepared June 2008.)

Table 214. Total fall enrollment in private not-for-profit degree-granting institutions, by attendance status, sex, and state or jurisdiction: 2005 and 2006

State or jurisdiction	Total	Fall 2005 Full-time Males	Fall 2005 Full-time Females	Fall 2005 Part-time Males	Fall 2005 Part-time Females	Total	Fall 2006 Full-time Males	Fall 2006 Full-time Females	Fall 2006 Part-time Males	Fall 2006 Part-time Females
1	2	3	4	5	6	7	8	9	10	11
United States	3,454,692	1,121,161	1,442,571	343,138	547,822	3,512,866	1,145,995	1,469,564	343,886	553,421
Alabama	23,076	8,382	11,047	1,462	2,185	22,588	8,008	10,945	1,465	2,170
Alaska	941	188	345	112	296	855	180	303	137	235
Arizona	9,684	3,303	3,872	1,101	1,408	8,592	3,099	3,320	990	1,183
Arkansas	13,781	5,121	6,055	787	1,818	14,349	5,279	6,098	961	2,011
California	277,096	85,794	113,418	33,139	44,745	274,931	86,206	114,407	30,990	43,328
Colorado	31,096	8,722	11,459	4,546	6,369	31,667	8,627	11,642	4,782	6,616
Connecticut	59,995	20,621	26,077	4,789	8,508	60,956	21,107	26,185	4,858	8,806
Delaware	12,930	2,758	4,009	2,118	4,045	13,120	2,805	4,020	2,093	4,202
District of Columbia	71,695	22,348	31,171	7,763	10,413	72,783	22,687	31,229	7,800	11,067
Florida	146,782	44,242	54,785	22,423	25,332	149,448	45,345	56,101	22,759	25,243
Georgia	62,149	21,389	31,467	3,394	5,899	63,562	21,923	31,983	3,514	6,142
Hawaii	14,294	3,522	5,838	2,244	2,690	14,278	3,609	6,091	1,991	2,587
Idaho	15,661	6,159	7,575	806	1,121	16,871	6,451	8,369	900	1,151
Illinois	209,775	64,804	84,179	22,730	38,062	214,533	66,854	87,006	22,602	38,071
Indiana	78,761	29,372	35,997	4,661	8,731	80,263	30,112	37,208	4,552	8,391
Iowa	54,591	19,133	24,954	3,583	6,921	55,430	19,367	24,962	3,783	7,318
Kansas	20,152	6,468	7,403	2,352	3,929	21,191	6,674	7,828	2,509	4,180
Kentucky	29,360	9,419	13,172	2,533	4,236	30,097	9,638	13,630	2,523	4,306
Louisiana	9,829	2,334	5,295	515	1,685	24,630	8,100	11,121	1,685	3,724
Maine	17,069	5,460	7,016	1,324	3,269	16,958	5,590	7,265	1,213	2,890
Maryland	52,156	13,189	17,864	8,132	12,971	52,590	13,338	18,484	7,833	12,935
Massachusetts	250,752	86,736	108,097	20,977	34,942	254,962	88,270	110,398	21,214	35,080
Michigan	112,951	26,590	38,487	16,962	30,912	114,353	26,864	37,872	17,654	31,963
Minnesota	68,859	21,875	30,038	6,174	10,772	70,249	21,998	30,032	6,554	11,665
Mississippi	12,732	3,998	6,389	649	1,696	12,781	3,930	6,493	635	1,723
Missouri	138,762	34,237	43,485	25,630	35,410	140,695	35,402	44,823	25,120	35,350
Montana	4,853	1,585	2,215	360	693	4,506	1,465	2,107	322	612
Nebraska	25,920	8,697	11,707	1,910	3,606	27,039	9,244	12,182	1,999	3,614
Nevada	644	202	267	58	117	761	241	396	47	77
New Hampshire	24,352	8,816	10,187	1,802	3,547	24,419	8,829	10,233	1,876	3,481
New Jersey	70,032	23,654	24,003	9,096	13,279	71,714	24,170	24,644	9,383	13,517
New Mexico	3,489	869	1,458	389	773	3,450	886	1,305	371	888
New York	477,333	159,748	204,239	40,353	72,993	477,439	162,253	204,486	39,294	71,406
North Carolina	83,473	30,722	40,053	4,556	8,142	83,596	31,488	40,846	3,767	7,495
North Dakota	5,682	1,924	2,974	250	534	5,555	1,931	2,800	258	566
Ohio	137,437	46,442	57,217	11,981	21,797	138,359	47,182	57,359	12,091	21,727
Oklahoma	22,142	8,254	9,187	2,136	2,565	21,430	8,443	9,120	1,658	2,209
Oregon	28,097	9,013	12,837	2,513	3,734	29,390	9,453	13,578	2,563	3,796
Pennsylvania	268,039	89,782	112,143	23,349	42,765	273,765	90,709	114,147	24,166	44,743
Rhode Island	40,828	17,598	18,047	2,434	2,749	40,747	17,856	17,902	2,352	2,637
South Carolina	33,701	11,184	16,627	1,836	4,054	33,441	11,060	16,611	1,930	3,840
South Dakota	7,891	2,019	3,346	761	1,765	7,788	1,896	3,257	862	1,773
Tennessee	65,177	23,272	30,948	4,105	6,852	67,197	23,766	31,838	4,245	7,348
Texas	125,111	41,437	49,492	15,456	18,726	125,017	41,646	50,141	14,528	18,702
Utah	42,472	17,958	18,972	2,883	2,659	44,443	19,017	20,025	2,950	2,451
Vermont	15,302	6,599	6,230	971	1,502	16,177	7,185	6,548	965	1,479
Virginia	63,818	21,048	29,459	5,247	8,064	69,273	21,924	30,632	7,078	9,639
Washington	41,623	13,355	19,976	3,315	4,977	41,520	12,829	19,403	3,702	5,586
West Virginia	11,365	3,903	5,662	541	1,259	11,271	3,798	5,635	569	1,269
Wisconsin	60,982	16,916	25,831	5,930	12,305	61,837	17,261	26,554	5,793	12,229
Wyoming	0	0	0	0	0	0	0	0	0	0
Other jurisdictions	121,568	34,118	54,734	12,780	19,936	124,539	34,476	56,708	12,866	20,489
American Samoa	0	0	0	0	0	0	0	0	0	0
Federated States of Micronesia	0	0	0	0	0	0	0	0	0	0
Guam	189	56	77	26	30	186	60	86	12	28
Marshall Islands	0	0	0	0	0	0	0	0	0	0
Northern Marianas	0	0	0	0	0	0	0	0	0	0
Palau	0	0	0	0	0	0	0	0	0	0
Puerto Rico	121,379	34,062	54,657	12,754	19,906	124,353	34,416	56,622	12,854	20,461
U.S. Virgin Islands	0	0	0	0	0	0	0	0	0	0

NOTE: Degree-granting institutions grant associate's or higher degrees and participate in Title IV federal financial aid programs.

SOURCE: U.S. Department of Education, National Center for Education Statistics, 2005 and 2006 Integrated Postsecondary Education Data System (IPEDS), Spring 2006 and Spring 2007. (This table was prepared June 2008.)

Table 215. Total fall enrollment in degree-granting institutions, by control and type of institution and state or jurisdiction: 2005 and 2006

State or jurisdiction	2005 Public 4-year	2005 Public 2-year	2005 Private 4-year Total	2005 Private 4-year Not-for-profit	2005 Private 2-year Total	2005 Private 2-year Not-for-profit	2006 Public 4-year	2006 Public 2-year	2006 Private 4-year Total	2006 Private 4-year Not-for-profit	2006 Private 2-year Total	2006 Private 2-year Not-for-profit
1	2	3	4	5	6	7	8	9	10	11	12	13
United States	6,837,605	6,184,229	4,161,815	3,411,170	303,826	43,522	6,955,013	6,225,120	4,285,317	3,473,710	293,420	39,156
Alabama	149,752	78,401	27,526	22,820	710	256	153,857	76,811	27,417	22,588	323	0
Alaska	27,765	1,101	1,365	941	0	0	27,514	1,081	1,258	855	0	0
Arizona	120,020	200,845	211,287	9,414	13,445	270	129,579	201,862	223,708	8,592	12,043	0
Arkansas	80,346	47,771	14,528	13,610	627	171	82,435	48,972	15,281	14,180	703	169
California	609,397	1,398,758	353,786	270,300	37,892	6,796	626,283	1,421,282	350,484	268,172	36,725	6,759
Colorado	154,706	79,803	58,930	30,876	9,233	220	153,945	77,956	67,886	31,495	8,596	172
Connecticut	65,478	46,227	60,387	58,362	2,583	1,633	65,987	46,489	61,635	59,116	2,605	1,840
Delaware	24,704	13,978	12,751	12,751	179	179	24,070	14,048	12,948	12,948	172	172
District of Columbia	5,595	0	99,302	71,695	0	0	5,769	0	103,736	72,783	0	0
Florida	371,553	277,446	203,001	144,774	20,662	2,008	398,451	253,457	216,586	149,349	17,157	99
Georgia	197,418	144,594	79,669	61,108	4,969	1,041	208,784	137,354	84,336	62,485	4,929	1,077
Hawaii	27,827	22,330	15,749	13,459	1,177	835	27,571	22,419	15,758	13,437	1,145	841
Idaho	48,289	12,014	16,893	15,661	512	0	46,641	12,570	17,982	16,871	679	0
Illinois	202,325	352,824	272,200	208,830	5,618	945	202,853	349,924	270,111	213,624	7,788	909
Indiana	207,329	59,969	83,019	78,110	10,936	651	207,109	64,595	86,610	79,760	9,699	503
Iowa	66,789	82,118	77,321	53,547	1,494	1,044	66,605	84,447	87,200	55,259	382	171
Kansas	96,057	74,262	19,757	19,201	1,676	951	96,524	74,007	21,340	20,729	1,275	462
Kentucky	116,910	84,669	38,597	29,360	4,793	0	117,961	86,237	39,389	30,097	5,327	0
Louisiana	147,529	33,514	12,733	9,829	3,937	0	143,497	49,057	27,431	24,528	4,162	102
Maine	35,084	12,435	16,945	16,945	1,087	124	35,068	12,702	16,839	16,839	1,540	119
Maryland	136,827	119,246	54,417	52,156	3,661	0	143,981	116,940	54,863	52,590	3,676	0
Massachusetts	104,086	84,209	251,730	248,679	3,291	2,073	106,607	85,557	256,207	253,126	3,155	1,836
Michigan	290,001	215,585	118,378	112,647	2,787	304	289,257	222,519	120,576	114,286	2,137	67
Minnesota	130,529	110,324	115,510	67,395	5,338	1,464	129,285	114,821	128,212	68,786	3,581	1,463
Mississippi	69,598	66,298	12,732	12,732	1,829	0	69,448	67,178	12,781	12,781	1,730	0
Missouri	130,980	86,742	148,291	137,509	8,432	1,253	132,145	86,330	150,911	139,529	7,712	1,166
Montana	33,863	9,134	4,368	4,368	485	485	34,149	8,846	4,039	4,039	467	467
Nebraska	52,961	40,220	27,447	25,811	608	109	53,655	40,831	29,217	26,944	797	95
Nevada	83,672	16,371	7,734	644	2,928	0	85,297	16,559	7,393	761	3,021	0
New Hampshire	27,257	13,750	27,470	24,030	1,416	322	28,251	13,279	27,873	24,099	1,266	320
New Jersey	152,430	151,885	74,200	69,891	1,243	141	154,289	154,085	76,291	71,714	991	0
New Mexico	56,839	64,137	9,840	3,489	521	0	56,866	64,802	9,633	3,450	527	0
New York	354,914	271,308	493,245	471,407	32,614	5,926	362,835	272,950	493,696	471,295	30,883	6,144
North Carolina	196,248	200,507	86,091	82,740	1,546	733	202,381	203,687	87,166	82,900	2,399	696
North Dakota	33,603	9,205	4,797	4,797	1,784	885	33,530	9,419	5,964	4,949	606	606
Ohio	279,039	173,962	142,155	135,827	21,194	1,610	279,275	173,687	144,098	137,187	22,882	1,172
Oklahoma	113,608	65,617	26,181	22,142	2,647	0	112,414	65,601	25,493	21,430	2,728	0
Oregon	83,239	80,513	33,436	27,891	2,845	206	83,321	76,738	34,562	29,350	2,973	40
Pennsylvania	256,194	124,077	277,146	262,396	34,923	5,643	262,108	126,143	283,933	267,519	34,948	6,246
Rhode Island	23,966	16,042	40,828	40,828	546	0	24,001	16,373	40,747	40,747	613	0
South Carolina	95,803	78,883	33,819	32,833	1,939	868	96,577	79,838	33,999	32,554	2,008	887
South Dakota	32,063	5,485	10,682	7,353	538	538	32,610	5,418	10,426	7,311	477	477
Tennessee	125,565	74,829	71,549	64,612	11,127	565	128,505	76,551	73,894	66,534	11,580	663
Texas	537,844	543,491	139,782	124,022	19,590	1,089	546,949	547,190	139,300	123,967	19,270	1,050
Utah	113,164	35,796	47,712	41,237	4,019	1,235	109,405	38,823	50,195	43,126	3,728	1,317
Vermont	18,575	5,515	15,147	14,885	678	417	18,792	5,593	16,028	15,717	682	460
Virginia	194,228	154,967	82,535	63,818	7,436	0	197,247	160,576	90,189	69,273	8,160	0
Washington	106,333	190,423	50,874	41,623	852	0	111,397	185,651	50,480	41,520	626	0
West Virginia	67,341	17,807	12,193	11,365	2,206	0	67,472	19,029	12,057	11,271	1,961	0
Wisconsin	153,571	115,357	65,665	60,450	665	532	157,067	115,179	67,081	61,248	831	589
Wyoming	13,126	19,485	115	0	2,608	0	13,203	19,657	78	0	1,755	0
U.S. Service Academies	15,265	0	†	†	†	†	12,191	0	†	†	†	†
Other jurisdictions	72,126	10,215	126,693	117,615	14,131	3,953	70,683	10,002	132,169	121,395	13,321	3,144
American Samoa	0	1,579	0	0	0	0	0	1,607	0	0	0	0
Federated States of Micronesia	0	2,283	0	0	0	0	0	2,539	0	0	0	0
Guam	3,034	2,841	189	189	0	0	3,176	2,427	186	186	0	0
Marshall Islands	0	604	0	0	0	0	0	647	0	0	0	0
Northern Marianas	967	0	0	0	0	0	968	0	0	0	0	0
Palau	0	651	0	0	0	0	0	679	0	0	0	0
Puerto Rico	65,733	2,257	126,504	117,426	14,131	3,953	64,051	2,103	131,983	121,209	13,321	3,144
U.S. Virgin Islands	2,392	0	0	0	0	0	2,488	0	0	0	0	0

†Not applicable.
NOTE: Degree-granting institutions grant associate's or higher degrees and participate in Title IV federal financial aid programs.

SOURCE: U.S. Department of Education, National Center for Education Statistics, 2005 and 2006 Integrated Postsecondary Education Data System (IPEDS), Spring 2006 and Spring 2007. (This table was prepared June 2008.)

Table 216. Total fall enrollment in degree-granting institutions, by level of enrollment and state or jurisdiction: 2004, 2005, and 2006

State or jurisdiction	Fall 2004			Fall 2005			Fall 2006		
	Undergraduate	First-professional	Graduate	Undergraduate	First-professional	Graduate	Undergraduate	First-professional	Graduate
1	2	3	4	5	6	7	8	9	10
United States	14,780,630	334,529	2,156,885	14,963,964	337,024	2,186,487	15,184,302	343,446	2,231,122
Alabama	218,372	4,436	33,018	219,253	4,403	32,733	220,520	4,493	33,395
Alaska	28,563	0	2,306	27,903	0	2,328	27,463	0	2,390
Arizona	410,416	3,178	77,331	456,881	3,330	85,386	476,547	3,259	87,386
Arkansas	125,636	1,836	10,927	129,484	1,879	11,909	132,112	1,966	13,313
California	2,107,426	33,845	232,774	2,135,461	33,817	230,555	2,172,354	33,243	229,177
Colorado	248,396	4,169	48,349	249,616	4,246	48,810	255,412	4,261	48,710
Connecticut	139,071	3,524	30,180	141,332	3,409	29,934	142,926	3,294	30,496
Delaware	41,907	1,167	6,730	43,382	1,072	7,158	42,488	985	7,765
District of Columbia	59,930	9,790	30,268	62,888	9,992	32,017	65,318	9,965	34,222
Florida	761,390	14,804	90,471	764,577	15,733	92,352	775,171	16,503	93,977
Georgia	377,266	7,998	49,019	372,269	8,381	46,000	378,947	9,015	47,441
Hawaii	58,025	604	8,596	57,843	645	8,595	57,527	646	8,720
Idaho	68,613	582	7,116	70,335	563	6,810	70,754	575	6,543
Illinois	667,249	17,859	116,293	692,401	18,021	122,545	688,043	18,116	124,517
Indiana	308,358	6,469	41,974	312,058	6,590	42,605	317,963	6,687	43,363
Iowa	193,908	7,124	16,614	203,453	7,067	17,202	212,715	7,051	18,868
Kansas	168,160	2,501	20,929	168,065	2,479	21,208	168,244	2,447	22,455
Kentucky	210,589	4,647	24,861	215,536	4,546	24,887	219,194	4,758	24,962
Louisiana	211,901	6,399	28,001	172,908	4,413	20,392	194,567	6,086	23,494
Maine	57,394	825	7,196	57,622	820	7,109	58,512	832	6,805
Maryland	252,340	4,322	55,831	252,964	4,383	56,804	255,933	4,431	59,096
Massachusetts	328,335	16,091	94,819	331,242	15,657	96,417	335,511	16,635	99,380
Michigan	529,083	12,583	79,314	536,745	13,244	76,762	545,001	13,817	75,671
Minnesota	280,739	7,819	60,463	283,616	7,852	70,233	289,018	8,115	78,766
Mississippi	135,449	2,525	14,141	133,642	2,588	14,227	134,699	2,090	14,348
Missouri	296,969	11,559	56,676	304,992	11,908	57,545	306,201	11,581	59,316
Montana	42,743	472	3,958	43,403	527	3,920	42,990	595	3,916
Nebraska	103,765	3,618	13,670	103,581	3,646	14,009	105,611	3,672	15,217
Nevada	95,563	923	9,475	99,548	988	10,169	100,760	995	10,515
New Hampshire	59,199	726	10,238	59,081	736	10,076	59,405	742	10,522
New Jersey	321,494	6,184	52,696	321,118	6,069	52,571	326,358	6,109	53,189
New Mexico	114,794	981	15,802	115,048	1,018	15,271	115,875	1,009	14,944
New York	914,620	30,479	196,426	921,458	30,741	199,882	928,563	31,201	200,600
North Carolina	417,786	7,610	47,313	426,106	7,926	50,360	436,662	8,051	50,920
North Dakota	44,774	432	4,327	44,153	803	4,433	44,042	837	4,640
Ohio	526,569	13,231	74,434	529,891	13,252	73,207	533,652	13,286	73,004
Oklahoma	182,767	4,519	20,339	183,568	4,570	19,915	182,340	4,431	19,465
Oregon	174,619	4,777	20,589	174,100	4,559	21,374	170,742	4,678	22,174
Pennsylvania	571,322	19,053	98,405	574,319	19,299	98,722	585,006	19,983	102,143
Rhode Island	69,674	1,515	9,188	70,518	1,512	9,352	71,175	1,508	9,051
South Carolina	184,413	3,392	21,105	185,252	3,384	21,808	187,254	3,361	21,807
South Dakota	43,202	626	4,880	43,206	626	4,936	42,985	678	5,268
Tennessee	239,918	5,913	32,224	243,912	5,921	33,237	250,974	6,018	33,538
Texas	1,082,667	20,367	126,163	1,093,491	20,420	126,796	1,104,529	20,745	127,435
Utah	176,909	1,443	15,972	182,892	1,439	16,360	183,518	1,419	17,214
Vermont	33,313	957	4,369	34,161	969	4,785	34,923	958	5,214
Virginia	360,484	9,039	55,658	373,041	9,821	56,304	387,593	10,276	58,303
Washington	310,944	4,867	27,713	315,154	4,870	28,458	314,862	4,925	28,367
West Virginia	85,388	1,928	10,568	86,803	1,997	10,747	87,292	2,143	11,084
Wisconsin	293,127	4,389	33,990	296,743	4,456	34,059	300,932	4,524	34,702
Wyoming	30,337	432	3,186	31,684	437	3,213	30,928	451	3,314
U.S. Service Academies	14,754	0	0	15,265	0	0	12,191	0	0
Other jurisdictions	193,506	3,775	23,639	193,766	3,871	25,528	195,038	4,051	27,086
American Samoa	1,550	0	0	1,579	0	0	1,607	0	0
Federated States of Micronesia	2,608	0	0	2,283	0	0	2,539	0	0
Guam	4,417	0	225	5,850	0	214	5,536	0	253
Marshall Islands	623	0	0	604	0	0	647	0	0
Northern Marianas	1,101	0	0	967	0	0	968	0	0
Palau	651	0	0	651	0	0	679	0	0
Puerto Rico	180,204	3,775	23,201	179,647	3,871	25,107	180,790	4,051	26,617
U.S. Virgin Islands	2,352	0	213	2,185	0	207	2,272	0	216

NOTE: Degree-granting institutions grant associate's or higher degrees and participate in Title IV federal financial aid programs.

SOURCE: U.S. Department of Education, National Center for Education Statistics, 2004, 2005, and 2006 Integrated Postsecondary Education Data System (IPEDS), Spring 2005, Spring 2006, and Spring 2007. (This table was prepared June 2008.)

Table 217. Total fall enrollment in degree-granting institutions, by control, level of enrollment, type of institution, and state or jurisdiction: 2006

State or jurisdiction	Public Undergraduate Total	Public Undergraduate 4-year	Public Undergraduate 2-year	Public First-professional	Public Graduate	Private Undergraduate Total	Private Undergraduate 4-year	Private Undergraduate 2-year	Private First-professional	Private Graduate
1	2	3	4	5	6	7	8	9	10	11
United States	11,847,426	5,622,555	6,224,871	139,736	1,192,971	3,336,876	3,043,456	293,420	203,710	1,038,151
Alabama	196,633	119,822	76,811	2,772	31,263	23,887	23,564	323	1,721	2,132
Alaska	26,428	25,347	1,081	0	2,167	1,035	1,035	0	0	223
Arizona	304,253	102,391	201,862	1,864	25,324	172,294	160,251	12,043	1,395	62,062
Arkansas	118,766	69,794	48,972	1,882	10,759	13,346	12,643	703	84	2,554
California	1,931,686	510,404	1,421,282	8,306	107,573	240,668	203,943	36,725	24,937	121,604
Colorado	198,481	120,525	77,956	2,689	30,731	56,931	48,335	8,596	1,572	17,979
Connecticut	97,487	50,998	46,489	1,356	13,633	45,439	42,834	2,605	1,938	16,863
Delaware	34,285	20,237	14,048	0	3,833	8,203	8,031	172	985	3,932
District of Columbia	5,300	5,300	0	235	234	60,018	60,018	0	9,730	33,988
Florida	594,432	340,975	253,457	6,886	50,590	180,739	163,582	17,157	9,617	43,387
Georgia	311,068	173,714	137,354	3,253	31,817	67,879	62,950	4,929	5,762	15,624
Hawaii	43,439	21,020	22,419	641	5,910	14,088	12,943	1,145	5	2,810
Idaho	52,771	40,201	12,570	575	5,865	17,983	17,304	679	0	678
Illinois	502,019	152,095	349,924	4,693	46,065	186,024	178,236	7,788	13,423	78,452
Indiana	236,645	172,050	64,595	4,472	30,587	81,318	71,619	9,699	2,215	12,776
Iowa	136,352	51,905	84,447	2,466	12,234	76,363	75,981	382	4,585	6,634
Kansas	150,303	76,296	74,007	2,369	17,859	17,941	16,666	1,275	78	4,596
Kentucky	181,245	95,008	86,237	3,360	19,593	37,949	32,622	5,327	1,398	5,369
Louisiana	169,997	120,940	49,057	3,242	19,315	24,570	20,408	4,162	2,844	4,179
Maine	43,268	30,566	12,702	264	4,238	15,244	13,704	1,540	568	2,567
Maryland	222,725	105,785	116,940	3,629	34,567	33,208	29,532	3,676	802	24,529
Massachusetts	168,110	82,553	85,557	423	23,631	167,401	164,246	3,155	16,212	75,749
Michigan	445,314	222,795	222,519	6,865	59,597	99,687	97,550	2,137	6,952	16,074
Minnesota	219,017	104,196	114,821	3,998	21,091	70,001	66,420	3,581	4,117	57,675
Mississippi	123,034	55,856	67,178	1,461	12,131	11,665	9,935	1,730	629	2,217
Missouri	194,766	108,436	86,330	2,784	20,925	111,435	103,723	7,712	8,797	38,391
Montana	38,617	29,771	8,846	595	3,783	4,373	3,906	467	0	133
Nebraska	82,157	41,326	40,831	1,321	11,008	23,454	22,657	797	2,351	4,209
Nevada	92,291	75,732	16,559	995	8,570	8,469	5,448	3,021	0	1,945
New Hampshire	36,709	23,430	13,279	0	4,821	22,696	21,430	1,266	742	5,701
New Jersey	273,745	119,660	154,085	4,097	30,532	52,613	51,622	991	2,012	22,657
New Mexico	107,801	42,999	64,802	1,009	12,858	8,074	7,547	527	0	2,086
New York	568,083	295,133	272,950	4,710	62,992	360,480	329,597	30,883	26,491	137,608
North Carolina	363,879	160,192	203,687	3,465	38,724	72,783	70,384	2,399	4,586	12,196
North Dakota	38,131	28,712	9,419	837	3,981	5,911	5,305	606	0	659
Ohio	397,957	224,519	173,438	8,230	46,775	135,605	112,813	22,882	5,056	26,229
Oklahoma	158,805	93,204	65,601	2,968	16,242	23,535	20,807	2,728	1,463	3,223
Oregon	142,920	66,182	76,738	1,833	15,306	27,822	24,849	2,973	2,845	6,868
Pennsylvania	343,734	217,591	126,143	6,128	38,389	241,272	206,324	34,948	13,855	63,754
Rhode Island	35,830	19,457	16,373	556	3,988	35,345	34,732	613	952	5,063
South Carolina	155,970	76,132	79,838	2,591	17,854	31,284	29,276	2,008	770	3,953
South Dakota	33,124	27,706	5,418	624	4,280	9,861	9,384	477	54	988
Tennessee	181,008	104,457	76,551	2,903	21,145	69,966	58,386	11,580	3,115	12,393
Texas	980,844	433,654	547,190	12,288	101,007	123,685	104,415	19,270	8,457	26,428
Utah	136,933	98,110	38,823	973	10,322	46,585	42,857	3,728	446	6,892
Vermont	22,027	16,434	5,593	406	1,952	12,896	12,214	682	552	3,262
Virginia	307,646	147,070	160,576	4,999	45,178	79,947	71,787	8,160	5,277	13,125
Washington	277,233	91,582	185,651	2,583	17,232	37,629	37,003	626	2,342	11,135
West Virginia	74,644	55,615	19,029	2,143	9,714	12,648	10,687	1,961	0	1,370
Wisconsin	248,198	133,019	115,179	2,546	21,502	52,734	51,903	831	1,978	13,200
Wyoming	29,125	9,468	19,657	451	3,284	1,803	48	1,755	0	30
U.S. Service Academies	12,191	12,191	†	0	0	†	†	†	†	†
Other jurisdictions	73,321	63,319	10,002	1,524	5,840	121,717	108,396	13,321	2,527	21,246
American Samoa	1,607	0	1,607	0	0	0	0	0	0	0
Federated States of Micronesia	2,539	0	2,539	0	0	0	0	0	0	0
Guam	5,350	2,923	2,427	0	253	186	186	0	0	0
Marshall Islands	647	0	647	0	0	0	0	0	0	0
Northern Marianas	968	968	0	0	0	0	0	0	0	0
Palau	679	0	679	0	0	0	0	0	0	0
Puerto Rico	59,259	57,156	2,103	1,524	5,371	121,531	108,210	13,321	2,527	21,246
U.S. Virgin Islands	2,272	2,272	0	0	216	0	0	0	0	0

†Not applicable.
NOTE: Degree-granting institutions grant associate's or higher degrees and participate in Title IV federal financial aid programs.

SOURCE: U.S. Department of Education, National Center for Education Statistics, 2006 Integrated Postsecondary Education Data System (IPEDS), Spring 2007. (This table was prepared June 2008.)

Table 218. Total fall enrollment in degree-granting institutions, by control, level of enrollment, type of institution, and state or jurisdiction: 2005

State or jurisdiction	Public					Private				
	Undergraduate			First-professional	Graduate	Undergraduate			First-professional	Graduate
	Total	4-year	2-year			Total	4-year	2-year		
1	2	3	4	5	6	7	8	9	10	11
United States	11,697,730	5,513,730	6,184,000	138,207	1,185,897	3,266,234	2,962,408	303,826	198,817	1,000,590
Alabama	194,753	116,352	78,401	2,696	30,704	24,500	23,790	710	1,707	2,029
Alaska	26,759	25,658	1,101	0	2,107	1,144	1,144	0	0	221
Arizona	294,515	93,670	200,845	1,972	24,378	162,366	148,921	13,445	1,358	61,008
Arkansas	116,375	68,604	47,771	1,879	9,863	13,109	12,482	627	0	2,046
California	1,891,784	493,026	1,398,758	8,134	108,237	243,677	205,785	37,892	25,683	122,318
Colorado	199,952	120,149	79,803	2,613	31,944	49,664	40,431	9,233	1,633	16,866
Connecticut	96,581	50,354	46,227	1,378	13,746	44,751	42,168	2,583	2,031	16,188
Delaware	34,966	20,988	13,978	0	3,716	8,416	8,237	179	1,072	3,442
District of Columbia	5,169	5,169	0	232	194	57,719	57,719	0	9,760	31,823
Florida	593,134	315,688	277,446	6,452	49,413	171,443	150,781	20,662	9,281	42,939
Georgia	307,511	162,917	144,594	3,251	31,250	64,758	59,789	4,969	5,130	14,750
Hawaii	43,657	21,327	22,330	640	5,860	14,186	13,009	1,177	5	2,735
Idaho	53,520	41,506	12,014	563	6,220	16,815	16,303	512	0	590
Illinois	504,353	151,529	352,824	4,576	46,220	188,048	182,430	5,618	13,445	76,325
Indiana	232,315	172,346	59,969	4,439	30,544	79,743	68,807	10,936	2,151	12,061
Iowa	134,144	52,026	82,118	2,472	12,291	69,309	67,815	1,494	4,595	4,911
Kansas	150,341	76,079	74,262	2,389	17,589	17,724	16,048	1,676	90	3,619
Kentucky	178,596	93,927	84,669	3,389	19,594	36,940	32,147	4,793	1,157	5,293
Louisiana	158,291	124,777	33,514	3,452	19,300	14,617	10,680	3,937	961	1,092
Maine	42,875	30,440	12,435	259	4,385	14,747	13,660	1,087	561	2,724
Maryland	219,934	100,688	119,246	3,585	32,554	33,030	29,369	3,661	798	24,250
Massachusetts	165,005	80,796	84,209	412	22,878	166,237	162,946	3,291	15,245	73,539
Michigan	438,567	222,982	215,585	6,747	60,272	98,178	95,391	2,787	6,497	16,490
Minnesota	215,971	105,647	110,324	3,769	21,113	67,645	62,307	5,338	4,083	49,120
Mississippi	121,884	55,586	66,298	1,998	12,014	11,758	9,929	1,829	590	2,213
Missouri	194,674	107,932	86,742	2,770	20,278	110,318	101,886	8,432	9,138	37,267
Montana	38,700	29,566	9,134	527	3,770	4,703	4,218	485	0	150
Nebraska	81,386	41,166	40,220	1,316	10,479	22,195	21,587	608	2,330	3,530
Nevada	90,622	74,251	16,371	988	8,433	8,926	5,998	2,928	0	1,736
New Hampshire	36,552	22,802	13,750	0	4,455	22,529	21,113	1,416	736	5,621
New Jersey	269,626	117,741	151,885	3,989	30,700	51,492	50,249	1,243	2,080	21,871
New Mexico	106,582	42,445	64,137	1,018	13,376	8,466	7,945	521	0	1,895
New York	557,715	286,407	271,308	4,704	63,803	363,743	331,129	32,614	26,037	136,079
North Carolina	355,536	155,029	200,507	3,401	37,818	70,570	69,024	1,546	4,525	12,542
North Dakota	38,133	28,928	9,205	803	3,872	6,020	4,236	1,784	0	561
Ohio	397,856	224,123	173,733	8,280	46,865	132,035	110,841	21,194	4,972	26,342
Oklahoma	159,797	94,180	65,617	2,945	16,483	23,771	21,124	2,647	1,625	3,432
Oregon	146,894	66,381	80,513	1,775	15,083	27,206	24,361	2,845	2,784	6,291
Pennsylvania	335,932	211,855	124,077	6,058	38,281	238,387	203,464	34,923	13,241	60,441
Rhode Island	35,065	19,023	16,042	553	4,390	35,453	34,907	546	959	4,962
South Carolina	154,204	75,321	78,883	2,573	17,909	31,048	29,109	1,939	811	3,899
South Dakota	32,969	27,484	5,485	569	4,010	10,237	9,699	538	57	926
Tennessee	176,759	101,930	74,829	2,840	20,795	67,153	56,026	11,127	3,081	12,442
Texas	968,697	425,206	543,491	11,951	100,687	124,794	105,204	19,590	8,469	26,109
Utah	137,825	102,029	35,796	978	10,157	45,067	41,048	4,019	461	6,203
Vermont	21,505	15,990	5,515	406	2,179	12,656	11,978	678	563	2,606
Virginia	299,557	144,590	154,967	4,957	44,681	73,484	66,048	7,436	4,864	11,623
Washington	276,873	86,450	190,423	2,577	17,306	38,281	37,429	852	2,293	11,152
West Virginia	73,609	55,802	17,807	1,997	9,542	13,194	10,988	2,206	0	1,205
Wisconsin	245,450	130,093	115,357	2,498	20,980	51,293	50,628	665	1,958	13,079
Wyoming	28,995	9,510	19,485	437	3,179	2,689	81	2,608	0	34
U.S. Service Academies	15,265	15,265	0	0	0	†	†	†	†	†
Other jurisdictions	74,874	64,659	10,215	1,514	5,953	118,892	104,761	14,131	2,357	19,575
American Samoa	1,579	0	1,579	0	0	0	0	0	0	0
Federated States of Micronesia	2,283	0	2,283	0	0	0	0	0	0	0
Guam	5,661	2,820	2,841	0	214	189	189	0	0	0
Marshall Islands	604	0	604	0	0	0	0	0	0	0
Northern Marianas	967	967	0	0	0	0	0	0	0	0
Palau	651	0	651	0	0	0	0	0	0	0
Puerto Rico	60,944	58,687	2,257	1,514	5,532	118,703	104,572	14,131	2,357	19,575
U.S. Virgin Islands	2,185	2,185	0	0	207	0	0	0	0	0

†Not applicable.
NOTE: Degree-granting institutions grant associate's or higher degrees and participate in Title IV federal financial aid programs.

SOURCE: U.S. Department of Education, National Center for Education Statistics, 2005 Integrated Postsecondary Education Data System (IPEDS), Spring 2006. (This table was prepared August 2006.)

Table 219. Full-time-equivalent fall enrollment in degree-granting institutions, by control and type of institution: 1967 through 2007

Year	All institutions			Public institutions			Private institutions		
	Total	4-year	2-year	Total	4-year	2-year	Total	4-year	2-year
1	2	3	4	5	6	7	8	9	10
1967	5,499,360	4,448,302	1,051,058	3,777,701	2,850,432	927,269	1,721,659	1,597,870	123,789
1968	5,977,768	4,729,522	1,248,246	4,248,639	3,128,057	1,120,582	1,729,129	1,601,465	127,664
1969	6,333,357	4,899,034	1,434,323	4,577,353	3,259,323	1,318,030	1,756,004	1,639,711	116,293
1970	6,737,819	5,145,422	1,592,397	4,953,144	3,468,569	1,484,575	1,784,675	1,676,853	107,822
1971	7,148,558	5,357,647	1,790,911	5,344,402	3,660,626	1,683,776	1,804,156	1,697,021	107,135
1972	7,253,757	5,406,833	1,846,924	5,452,854	3,706,238	1,746,616	1,800,903	1,700,595	100,308
1973	7,453,463	5,439,230	2,014,233	5,629,563	3,721,037	1,908,526	1,823,900	1,718,193	105,707
1974	7,805,452	5,606,247	2,199,205	5,944,799	3,847,543	2,097,256	1,860,653	1,758,704	101,949
1975	8,479,698	5,900,408	2,579,290	6,522,319	4,056,502	2,465,817	1,957,379	1,843,906	113,473
1976	8,312,502	5,848,001	2,464,501	6,349,903	3,998,450	2,351,453	1,962,599	1,849,551	113,048
1977	8,415,339	5,935,076	2,480,263	6,396,476	4,039,071	2,357,405	2,018,863	1,896,005	122,858
1978	8,348,482	5,932,357	2,416,125	6,279,199	3,996,126	2,283,073	2,069,283	1,936,231	133,052
1979	8,487,317	6,016,072	2,471,245	6,392,617	4,059,304	2,333,313	2,094,700	1,956,768	137,932
1980	8,819,013	6,161,372	2,657,641	6,642,294	4,158,267	2,484,027	2,176,719	2,003,105	173,614 [1]
1981	9,014,521	6,249,847	2,764,674	6,781,300	4,208,506	2,572,794	2,233,221	2,041,341	191,880 [1]
1982	9,091,648	6,248,923	2,842,725	6,850,589	4,220,648	2,629,941	2,241,059	2,028,275	212,784
1983	9,166,398	6,325,222	2,841,176	6,881,479	4,265,807	2,615,672	2,284,919	2,059,415	225,504
1984	8,951,695	6,292,711	2,658,984	6,684,664	4,237,895	2,446,769	2,267,031	2,054,816	212,215
1985	8,943,433	6,294,339	2,649,094	6,667,781	4,239,622	2,428,159	2,275,652	2,054,717	220,935
1986	9,064,165	6,360,325	2,703,842	6,778,045	4,295,494	2,482,551	2,286,122	2,064,831	221,291 [2]
1987	9,229,736	6,486,504	2,743,230	6,937,690	4,395,728	2,541,961	2,292,045	2,090,776	201,269 [2]
1988	9,464,271	6,664,146	2,800,125	7,096,905	4,505,774	2,591,131	2,367,366	2,158,372	208,994
1989	9,780,881	6,813,602	2,967,279	7,371,590	4,619,828	2,751,762	2,409,291	2,193,774	215,517
1990	9,983,436	6,968,008	3,015,428	7,557,982	4,740,049	2,817,933	2,425,454	2,227,959	197,495
1991	10,360,606	7,081,454	3,279,152	7,862,845	4,795,704	3,067,141	2,497,761	2,285,750	212,011
1992	10,436,776	7,129,379	3,307,397	7,911,701	4,797,884	3,113,817	2,525,075	2,331,495	193,580
1993	10,351,415	7,120,921	3,230,494	7,812,394	4,765,983	3,046,411	2,539,021	2,354,938	184,083
1994	10,348,072	7,137,341	3,210,731	7,784,396	4,749,524	3,034,872	2,563,676	2,387,817	175,859
1995	10,334,956	7,172,844	3,162,112	7,751,815	4,757,223	2,994,592	2,583,141	2,415,621	167,520
1996	10,481,886	7,234,541	3,247,345	7,794,895	4,767,117	3,027,778	2,686,991	2,467,424	219,567
1997	10,615,028	7,338,794	3,276.234	7,869,764	4,813,849	3,055,915	2,745,264	2,524,945	220,319
1998	10,698,775	7,467,828	3,230,947	7,880,135	4,868,857	3,011,278	2,818,640	2,598,971	219,669
1999	10,943,609	7,638,976	3,304,633	8,020,074	4,944,554	3,075,520	2,923,535	2,694,422	229,113
2000	11,267,025	7,795,139	3,471,886	8,266,932	5,025,588	3,241,344	3,000,093	2,769,551	230,542
2001	11,765,945	8,087,980	3,677,965	8,639,154	5,194,035	3,445,119	3,126,791	2,893,945	232,846
2002	12,331,319	8,439,064	3,892,255	9,061,411	5,406,283	3,655,128	3,269,908	3,032,781	237,127
2003	12,687,597	8,744,188	3,943,409	9,240,724	5,557,680	3,683,044	3,446,873	3,186,508	260,365
2004	13,000,994	9,018,024	3,982,970	9,348,081	5,640,650	3,707,431	3,652,913	3,377,374	275,539
2005	13,200,790	9,261,634	3,939,156	9,390,216	5,728,327	3,661,889	3,810,574	3,533,307	277,267
2006	13,403,097	9,456,166	3,946,931	9,503,558	5,824,768	3,678,790	3,899,539	3,631,398	268,141
2007	13,782,702	9,769,560	4,013,142	9,739,709	5,994,230	3,745,479	4,042,993	3,775,330	267,663

[1]Large increases are due to the addition of schools accredited by the Accrediting Commission of Career Schools and Colleges of Technology in 1980 and 1981.
[2]Because of imputation techniques, data are not consistent with figures for other years.
NOTE: Data through 1995 are for institutions of higher education, while later data are for degree-granting institutions. Degree-granting institutions grant associate's or higher degrees and participate in Title IV federal financial aid programs. The degree-granting classification is very similar to the earlier higher education classification, but it includes more 2-year colleges and excludes a few higher education institutions that did not grant degrees. (See Guide to Sources for details.) Some data have been revised from previously published figures.
SOURCE: U.S. Department of Education, National Center for Education Statistics, Higher Education General Information Survey (HEGIS), "Fall Enrollment in Colleges and Universities" surveys, 1967 through 1985; and 1986 through 2007 Integrated Postsecondary Education Data System, "Fall Enrollment Survey" (IPEDS-EF:86–99), and Spring 2001 through Spring 2008. (This table was prepared October 2008.)

Table 220. Full-time-equivalent fall enrollment in degree-granting institutions, by control and type of institution and state or jurisdiction: 2000, 2005, and 2006

| | Public | | | | | | Private | | | | | |
| | 4-year | | | 2-year | | | 4-year | | | 2-year | | |
State or jurisdiction	2000	2005	2006	2000	2005	2006	2000	2005	2006	2000	2005	2006
1	2	3	4	5	6	7	8	9	10	11	12	13
United States	5,025,588	5,728,327	5,824,768	3,241,344	3,661,889	3,678,790	2,769,551	3,533,307	3,631,398	230,542	277,267	268,141
Alabama	111,322	122,089	125,339	48,545	54,149	52,975	23,518	24,777	24,555	646	682	438
Alaska	16,335	18,444	18,322	473	464	460	672	950	844	307	0	0
Arizona	87,301	101,763	105,540	85,778	101,330	101,929	43,188	204,596	215,950	9,129	12,315	11,465
Arkansas	57,897	67,440	68,850	21,519	30,820	30,876	10,995	12,931	13,463	1,475	587	534
California	476,027	537,136	553,957	707,558	756,014	765,677	250,026	299,701	298,048	34,875	36,155	35,156
Colorado	109,844	123,746	123,595	41,322	44,001	43,076	30,615	48,212	57,475	6,336	8,679	8,167
Connecticut	46,826	53,737	54,555	20,934	26,403	26,785	48,714	52,654	53,488	1,480	1,468	1,532
Delaware	20,427	22,467	21,986	6,939	8,175	8,547	6,549	9,059	9,166	142	165	161
District of Columbia	3,364	3,615	3,984	0	0	0	56,196	75,302	78,175	0	0	0
Florida	190,472	288,146	308,188	173,433	161,069	147,029	107,473	164,325	174,208	15,440	20,271	16,806
Georgia	136,069	165,257	175,496	66,571	93,177	88,384	62,132	71,354	74,287	3,935	4,885	4,742
Hawaii	17,015	22,587	22,201	14,996	13,324	13,464	11,649	12,833	13,032	1,669	1,011	1,020
Idaho	34,125	38,426	37,365	6,807	7,863	7,709	2,500	15,658	16,683	8,921	512	679
Illinois	164,592	174,262	175,008	186,533	202,067	201,600	164,273	228,174	224,994	4,689	4,302	6,476
Indiana	155,982	173,220	173,576	28,131	34,737	37,705	61,851	74,106	77,531	5,034	9,931	8,876
Iowa	61,763	60,039	59,739	44,717	54,279	55,192	43,869	61,945	67,996	2,156	1,325	354
Kansas	74,307	79,530	79,918	39,457	44,234	44,575	15,014	16,028	17,212	1,061	1,519	1,238
Kentucky	86,080	98,519	99,194	32,239	50,916	50,779	25,793	32,508	32,819	5,283	4,006	4,544
Louisiana	126,372	127,570	124,388	27,130	23,174	32,849	27,203	11,324	24,093	2,956	3,738	4,018
Maine	24,678	26,946	26,997	4,797	8,062	8,209	12,954	14,205	14,394	955	906	1,129
Maryland	94,929	107,870	111,939	57,367	68,582	68,512	35,969	41,391	41,970	622	3,271	3,224
Massachusetts	78,452	83,859	85,855	47,972	51,788	52,394	198,476	218,514	222,513	3,084	2,229	2,144
Michigan	223,981	244,054	244,145	101,794	123,231	128,009	75,020	89,727	90,806	1,224	2,412	1,853
Minnesota	95,345	107,648	107,428	65,167	73,317	75,517	54,476	91,830	99,896	8,244	4,665	3,424
Mississippi	56,107	61,350	61,153	47,245	53,618	54,372	9,677	11,300	11,346	775	1,719	1,661
Missouri	99,187	107,799	108,768	46,793	55,186	55,449	84,889	110,262	112,792	6,292	8,009	7,352
Montana	28,278	29,744	29,884	3,900	6,228	6,053	3,336	3,771	3,520	491	443	419
Nebraska	44,374	45,346	45,973	20,812	24,784	24,946	18,750	23,983	25,615	2,057	570	767
Nevada	27,631	57,119	57,293	20,468	8,065	8,104	2,519	7,425	7,014	1,959	2,839	2,903
New Hampshire	21,064	23,682	24,422	5,442	7,348	7,321	20,646	23,540	23,752	1,078	1,178	1,005
New Jersey	111,449	121,784	122,967	79,367	100,103	103,141	51,557	60,042	61,731	3,074	1,174	991
New Mexico	39,779	45,356	45,904	29,541	36,232	36,058	6,799	8,787	8,491	1,296	521	527
New York	269,664	291,025	299,723	168,911	193,460	194,670	366,833	423,483	425,665	20,670	29,085	27,082
North Carolina	140,203	170,110	175,132	96,999	120,991	119,636	67,622	77,971	79,838	981	1,539	2,145
North Dakota	24,728	29,236	29,087	6,515	6,785	6,807	3,697	4,472	5,164	290	1,381	559
Ohio	215,993	242,020	243,382	92,749	107,524	108,568	107,773	120,727	122,479	9,565	19,365	20,771
Oklahoma	79,786	94,992	93,433	34,997	40,640	40,133	21,723	23,339	23,125	327	2,628	2,728
Oregon	59,588	69,555	69,399	46,099	47,788	46,205	23,928	29,290	30,289	1,090	2,565	2,760
Pennsylvania	211,132	229,883	235,617	58,759	75,863	77,293	202,341	234,653	238,457	27,497	31,891	31,518
Rhode Island	17,967	19,653	19,908	8,650	9,215	9,567	33,022	37,676	37,708	0	546	613
South Carolina	74,309	84,069	85,011	41,804	50,418	51,079	25,929	30,142	30,403	1,301	1,784	1,804
South Dakota	23,881	25,541	25,773	4,193	4,873	4,842	6,688	8,284	7,946	114	279	245
Tennessee	99,636	108,494	110,924	53,146	49,705	50,880	52,015	64,564	66,524	4,303	10,198	10,481
Texas	358,523	439,659	446,934	268,057	314,319	311,875	101,852	117,380	117,606	12,580	17,974	17,711
Utah	71,982	84,056	80,985	16,454	20,574	21,285	35,110	44,420	46,663	2,076	2,913	2,973
Vermont	13,581	16,156	16,496	1,845	2,490	2,543	13,313	13,718	14,625	360	595	591
Virginia	147,370	164,960	168,557	72,913	84,570	87,673	51,517	72,292	77,264	5,470	7,127	7,752
Washington	83,899	95,677	98,950	114,754	120,908	118,215	34,489	44,776	43,724	3,467	694	548
West Virginia	58,171	58,546	58,606	3,969	11,934	13,004	8,891	10,895	10,769	1,931	2,123	1,841
Wisconsin	130,661	138,334	140,124	56,195	65,178	64,872	45,510	53,896	55,212	546	485	659
Wyoming	9,665	10,546	10,607	10,588	11,914	11,947	0	115	78	1,289	2,608	1,755
U.S. Service Academies	13,475	15,265	12,191	0	0	0	†	†	†	†	†	†
Other jurisdictions	66,376	63,840	62,945	7,200	7,250	7,109	83,619	105,927	110,810	8,844	13,127	12,399
American Samoa	0	0	0	214	1,038	1,081	0	0	0	0	0	0
Federated States of Micronesia	0	0	0	1,308	1,798	1,986	0	0	0	0	0	0
Guam	2,802	2,465	2,576	777	1,289	1,083	0	155	162	0	0	0
Marshall Islands	0	0	0	166	517	567	0	0	0	0	0	0
Northern Marianas	0	833	821	707	0	0	0	0	0	0	0	0
Palau	0	0	0	450	505	528	0	0	0	0	0	0
Puerto Rico	61,987	58,830	57,781	3,578	2,103	1,864	83,619	105,772	110,648	8,844	13,127	12,399
U.S. Virgin Islands	1,587	1,712	1,767	0	0	0	0	0	0	0	0	0

†Not applicable.
NOTE: Degree-granting institutions grant associate's or higher degrees and participate in Title IV federal financial aid programs.

SOURCE: U.S. Department of Education, National Center for Education Statistics, 2000 through 2006 Integrated Postsecondary Education Data System (IPEDS), Spring 2001 through Spring 2007. (This table was prepared June 2008.)

Table 221. Full-time-equivalent fall enrollment in degree-granting institutions, by control and state or jurisdiction: Selected years,1980 through 2006

State or jurisdiction	Total						Public			Private		
	1980	1990	2000	2004	2005	2006	1990	2000	2006	1990	2000	2006
1	2	3	4	5	6	7	8	9	10	11	12	13
United States	8,819,013	9,983,436	11,267,025	13,000,994	13,200,790	13,403,097	7,557,982	8,266,932	9,503,558	2,425,454	3,000,093	3,899,539
Alabama	138,910	174,610	184,031	203,150	201,697	203,307	154,343	159,867	178,314	20,267	24,164	24,993
Alaska	10,073	18,496	17,787	20,160	19,858	19,626	17,087	16,808	18,782	1,409	979	844
Arizona	127,114	167,617	225,396	368,620	420,004	434,884	153,500	173,079	207,469	14,117	52,317	227,415
Arkansas	64,307	74,449	91,886	108,671	111,778	113,723	63,472	79,416	99,726	10,977	12,470	13,997
California	1,099,559	1,156,288	1,468,486	1,608,720	1,629,006	1,652,838	979,663	1,183,585	1,319,634	176,625	284,901	333,204
Colorado	123,589	159,032	188,117	221,261	224,638	232,313	138,350	151,166	166,671	20,682	36,951	65,642
Connecticut	112,612	115,791	117,954	131,992	134,262	136,360	70,870	67,760	81,340	44,921	50,194	55,020
Delaware	26,284	31,612	34,057	38,514	39,866	39,860	26,059	27,366	30,533	5,553	6,691	9,327
District of Columbia	62,126	61,549	59,560	76,440	78,917	82,159	7,294	3,364	3,984	54,255	56,196	78,175
Florida	290,647	383,385	486,818	624,502	633,811	646,231	302,579	363,905	455,217	80,806	122,913	191,014
Georgia	152,369	198,549	268,707	343,524	334,673	342,909	149,115	202,640	263,880	49,434	66,067	79,029
Hawaii	35,859	41,097	45,329	49,959	49,755	49,717	32,496	32,011	35,665	8,601	13,318	14,052
Idaho	33,938	41,275	52,353	61,683	62,459	62,436	31,408	40,932	45,074	9,867	11,421	17,362
Illinois	432,365	493,364	520,087	573,703	608,805	608,078	353,247	351,125	376,608	140,117	168,962	231,470
Indiana	193,445	222,835	250,998	287,320	291,994	297,688	168,984	184,113	211,281	53,851	66,885	86,407
Iowa	120,083	138,565	152,505	171,328	177,588	183,281	95,772	106,480	114,931	42,793	46,025	68,350
Kansas	101,147	118,969	129,839	141,263	141,311	142,943	106,570	113,764	124,493	12,399	16,075	18,450
Kentucky	113,709	137,651	149,395	184,413	185,949	187,336	111,858	118,319	149,973	25,793	31,076	37,363
Louisiana	132,780	154,132	183,661	204,063	165,806	185,348	129,357	153,502	157,237	24,775	30,159	28,111
Maine	34,471	42,021	43,384	49,695	50,119	50,729	29,876	29,475	35,206	12,145	13,909	15,523
Maryland	149,202	169,972	188,887	218,455	221,114	225,645	141,950	152,296	180,451	28,022	36,591	45,194
Massachusetts	315,937	320,299	327,984	351,157	356,390	362,906	130,962	126,424	138,249	189,337	201,560	224,657
Michigan	366,058	389,814	402,019	454,224	459,424	464,813	326,952	325,775	372,154	62,862	76,244	92,659
Minnesota	162,559	190,608	223,232	270,329	277,460	286,265	143,424	160,512	182,945	47,184	62,720	103,320
Mississippi	85,621	103,957	113,804	129,192	127,987	128,532	92,269	103,352	115,525	11,688	10,452	13,007
Missouri	180,156	210,104	237,161	274,323	281,256	284,361	142,953	145,980	164,217	67,151	91,181	120,144
Montana	29,428	29,905	36,005	40,147	40,186	39,876	26,835	32,178	35,937	3,070	3,827	3,939
Nebraska	68,505	80,989	85,993	94,395	94,683	97,301	65,739	65,186	70,919	15,250	20,807	26,382
Nevada	22,467	33,814	52,577	71,681	75,448	75,314	33,392	48,099	65,397	422	4,478	9,917
New Hampshire	39,456	45,762	48,230	55,392	55,748	56,500	24,948	26,508	31,743	20,814	21,724	24,757
New Jersey	218,838	221,468	245,447	281,732	283,103	288,830	174,324	190,816	226,108	47,144	54,631	62,722
New Mexico	43,722	59,517	77,415	90,885	90,896	90,980	57,870	69,320	81,962	1,647	8,095	9,018
New York	760,305	798,696	826,078	926,102	937,053	947,140	446,379	438,575	494,393	352,317	387,503	452,747
North Carolina	235,266	269,025	305,805	360,438	370,611	376,751	208,321	237,202	294,768	60,704	68,603	81,983
North Dakota	30,188	33,118	35,230	42,226	41,874	41,617	30,276	31,243	35,894	2,842	3,987	5,723
Ohio	369,342	420,499	426,080	484,846	489,636	495,200	317,837	308,742	351,950	102,662	117,338	143,250
Oklahoma	115,701	128,203	136,833	162,024	161,599	159,419	108,933	114,783	133,566	19,270	22,050	25,853
Oregon	110,649	120,176	130,705	149,906	149,198	148,653	101,424	105,687	115,604	18,752	25,018	33,049
Pennsylvania	404,192	464,179	499,729	566,077	572,290	582,885	261,305	269,891	312,910	202,874	229,838	269,975
Rhode Island	50,628	60,168	59,639	65,794	67,090	67,796	28,804	26,617	29,475	31,364	33,022	38,321
South Carolina	109,346	127,225	143,343	164,813	166,413	168,297	101,918	116,113	136,090	25,307	27,230	32,207
South Dakota	27,873	28,256	34,876	39,056	38,977	38,806	22,128	28,074	30,615	6,128	6,802	8,191
Tennessee	161,058	175,961	209,100	229,125	232,961	238,809	130,184	152,782	161,804	45,777	56,318	77,005
Texas	527,724	637,742	741,012	878,489	889,332	894,126	553,436	626,580	758,809	84,306	114,432	135,317
Utah	78,199	94,012	125,622	147,506	151,963	151,906	63,495	88,436	102,270	30,517	37,186	49,636
Vermont	25,572	29,072	29,099	31,775	32,959	34,255	16,048	15,426	19,039	13,024	13,673	15,216
Virginia	199,549	251,708	277,270	316,516	328,949	341,246	202,285	220,283	256,230	49,423	56,987	85,016
Washington	194,440	189,521	236,609	259,263	262,055	261,437	160,889	198,653	217,165	28,632	37,956	44,272
West Virginia	60,394	68,235	72,962	82,375	83,498	84,220	59,229	62,140	71,610	9,006	10,822	12,610
Wisconsin	206,790	229,975	232,912	254,467	257,893	260,867	192,107	186,856	204,996	37,868	46,056	55,871
Wyoming	14,725	21,888	21,542	24,549	25,183	24,387	21,185	20,253	22,554	703	1,289	1,833
U.S. Service Academies[1]	49,736	48,281	13,475	14,754	15,265	12,191	48,281	13,475	12,191	†	†	†
Other jurisdictions	117,637	140,954	166,039	166,039	193,263	193,263	55,908	73,576	70,054	85,046	92,463	123,209
American Samoa	824	952	214	1,018	1,038	1,081	952	214	1,081	0	0	0
Federated States of Micronesia	195	549	1,308	2,169	1,798	1,986	549	1,308	1,986	0	0	0
Guam	2,115	2,956	3,579	3,271	3,909	3,821	2,956	3,579	3,659	0	0	162
Marshall Islands	0	0	166	540	517	567	0	166	567	0	0	0
Northern Marianas	0	376	707	931	833	821	376	707	821	0	0	0
Palau	0	423	450	504	505	528	423	450	528	0	0	0
Puerto Rico	113,285	134,193	158,028	178,767	179,832	182,692	49,147	65,565	59,645	85,046	92,463	123,047
U.S. Virgin Islands	1,218	1,505	1,587	1,778	1,712	1,767	1,505	1,587	1,767	0	0	0

†Not applicable.
[1]Data for 2000 and later years reflect substantial change in survey coverage.
NOTE: Data through 1990 are for institutions of higher education, while later data are for degree-granting institutions. Degree-granting institutions grant associate's or higher degrees and participate in Title IV federal financial aid programs. The degree-granting classification is very similar to the earlier higher education classification, but it includes more 2-year colleges and excludes a few higher education institutions that did not grant degrees. (See Guide to Sources for details.)
SOURCE: U.S. Department of Education, National Center for Education Statistics, Higher Education General Information Survey (HEGIS), "Fall Enrollment in Colleges and Universities" 1980 survey; and 1990 through 2006 Integrated Postsecondary Education Data System, "Fall Enrollment Survey" (IPEDS-EF:90), and Spring 2001 through Spring 2007. (This table was prepared June 2008.)

Table 222. Total full-year enrollment in degree-granting institutions, by control and type of institution and state or jurisdiction: 2005–06 and 2006–07

| | 2005–06 | | | | | | | 2006–07 | | | | | | |
| | | | | Private 4-year | | Private 2-year | | | | | Private 4-year | | Private 2-year | |
State or jurisdiction	Total	Public 4-year	Public 2-year	Not-for-profit	For-profit	Not-for-profit	For-profit	Total	Public 4-year	Public 2-year	Not-for-profit	For-profit	Not-for-profit	For-profit
1	2	3	4	5	6	7	8	9	10	11	12	13	14	15
United States	23,991,421	8,374,606	9,699,901	4,225,516	1,220,011	55,998	415,389	24,331,235	8,576,216	9,678,362	4,289,856	1,301,627	45,488	439,686
Alabama	337,913	185,398	115,899	28,048	7,868	0	700	341,917	188,571	116,503	27,114	8,527	0	1,202
Alaska	54,086	47,904	3,937	1,366	879	0	0	51,961	46,307	3,808	964	882	0	0
Arizona	875,017	148,392	368,467	11,925	326,492	0	19,741	873,090	154,409	366,980	10,952	323,205	0	17,544
Arkansas	188,861	96,816	73,379	15,595	1,774	184	1,113	192,844	98,856	74,570	16,395	1,847	178	998
California	3,360,414	689,971	2,171,227	316,527	122,410	11,537	48,742	3,437,034	709,701	2,230,713	320,765	112,201	1,758	61,896
Colorado	439,650	199,601	128,622	39,923	58,812	232	12,460	434,324	197,220	126,205	40,881	57,603	278	12,137
Connecticut	222,138	80,150	65,801	69,270	2,753	2,576	1,588	224,049	77,745	66,967	71,823	3,476	2,716	1,322
Delaware	64,383	28,038	19,583	16,558	0	204	0	64,243	27,358	19,565	17,115	0	205	0
District of Columbia	136,844	11,563	0	82,425	42,856	0	0	143,765	12,623	0	83,549	47,593	0	0
Florida	1,238,787	512,161	390,618	197,916	108,012	250	29,830	1,261,318	562,750	353,069	200,361	115,208	214	29,716
Georgia	584,967	249,389	226,831	69,998	31,059	1,218	6,472	588,151	260,310	212,839	71,902	35,272	1,295	6,533
Hawaii	90,849	34,771	31,797	18,951	3,404	1,337	589	88,430	33,807	31,897	18,449	2,822	0	1,455
Idaho	110,352	66,909	18,347	22,005	1,998	0	1,093	109,735	65,508	19,274	22,195	1,652	0	1,106
Illinois	1,289,105	233,859	680,622	260,907	101,035	1,322	11,360	1,293,628	234,744	682,793	267,710	93,835	2,132	12,414
Indiana	490,131	251,599	104,708	107,102	12,200	752	13,770	506,629	254,753	110,860	109,326	20,728	614	10,348
Iowa	312,461	78,305	123,782	74,941	35,026	158	249	351,162	78,793	124,710	74,938	72,160	174	387
Kansas	277,228	116,631	124,831	32,820	985	525	1,436	275,034	116,211	124,638	30,812	826	516	2,031
Kentucky	308,438	137,534	116,065	34,398	12,446	0	7,995	313,707	138,080	118,677	35,283	13,338	0	8,329
Louisiana	283,719	180,642	74,108	17,171	4,637	119	7,042	291,867	173,409	78,740	28,109	3,922	0	7,687
Maine	86,496	45,705	17,334	21,206	0	155	2,096	90,094	45,742	18,582	23,055	0	136	2,579
Maryland	413,945	167,268	173,104	65,367	3,610	0	4,596	415,387	173,774	168,252	64,429	4,755	0	4,177
Massachusetts	574,076	145,037	123,122	297,220	3,847	2,508	2,342	582,147	145,092	125,748	302,589	3,851	2,496	2,371
Michigan	845,015	338,329	347,457	146,365	9,396	324	3,144	865,137	337,398	365,912	149,958	7,451	0	4,418
Minnesota	478,427	155,819	161,597	79,476	76,776	1,959	2,800	500,191	158,137	164,655	82,883	91,495	108	2,913
Mississippi	203,975	82,486	102,966	16,724	0	0	1,799	195,342	82,734	93,747	16,373	0	0	2,488
Missouri	521,503	163,753	133,523	191,580	18,694	1,595	12,358	514,628	157,741	132,526	191,379	17,182	1,924	13,876
Montana	62,326	40,914	15,227	5,517	0	668	0	61,343	40,765	14,779	5,086	0	713	0
Nebraska	186,761	64,001	82,164	35,776	3,535	218	1,067	190,113	63,668	83,248	38,120	3,564	208	1,305
Nevada	154,468	112,985	24,950	966	9,967	0	5,600	158,764	124,934	17,884	1,689	9,113	0	5,144
New Hampshire	92,588	34,034	18,501	31,907	5,463	916	1,767	91,884	33,966	19,101	31,485	5,389	644	1,299
New Jersey	488,160	180,222	217,625	83,043	6,167	0	1,103	499,913	182,846	223,475	85,661	6,463	0	1,468
New Mexico	190,312	69,896	105,868	4,714	9,099	0	735	185,119	69,189	103,155	4,005	8,043	0	727
New York	1,472,978	437,933	393,672	560,762	31,345	8,061	41,205	1,483,322	445,348	395,586	562,700	30,596	8,297	40,795
North Carolina	619,842	230,505	283,724	97,166	5,856	809	1,782	615,714	228,697	280,936	97,081	6,142	842	2,016
North Dakota	59,111	38,728	12,258	5,721	1,448	956	0	60,294	38,501	12,666	6,357	1,914	856	0
Ohio	822,933	343,411	263,887	168,287	10,655	1,644	35,049	824,398	343,812	259,411	166,998	10,634	1,960	41,583
Oklahoma	275,080	137,993	96,034	30,448	6,270	0	4,335	269,127	144,049	88,954	24,771	5,721	0	5,632
Oregon	304,542	113,188	144,542	32,965	8,576	266	5,005	307,268	112,779	146,467	34,475	8,174	0	5,373
Pennsylvania	890,731	314,059	188,612	310,058	23,416	8,627	45,959	908,166	315,675	193,062	313,441	29,126	10,060	46,802
Rhode Island	98,841	29,536	22,407	46,180	0	0	718	99,911	29,618	22,929	46,367	0	0	997
South Carolina	270,771	113,683	111,048	40,933	2,200	942	1,965	274,234	113,061	113,060	42,092	2,986	1,043	1,992
South Dakota	63,857	41,675	6,353	9,302	5,728	799	0	63,348	42,237	6,454	8,996	4,951	710	0
Tennessee	360,880	150,101	104,903	76,291	12,740	702	16,143	367,202	151,572	107,498	77,675	12,844	769	16,844
Texas	1,692,783	640,396	845,615	148,557	24,367	1,425	32,423	1,714,192	647,759	862,260	147,913	21,985	1,403	32,872
Utah	280,658	148,656	64,551	50,776	10,431	1,604	4,640	291,779	155,773	66,843	54,007	9,695	1,728	3,733
Vermont	53,243	23,072	9,310	19,622	421	490	328	54,109	23,349	9,410	20,001	816	533	0
Virginia	594,628	233,003	235,398	80,925	31,312	0	13,990	614,638	235,193	242,186	89,852	33,449	0	13,958
Washington	525,296	135,271	324,035	51,001	13,771	0	1,218	517,283	182,567	270,116	51,434	12,034	0	1,132
West Virginia	125,424	79,799	25,088	14,787	1,566	0	4,184	153,782	80,458	26,034	14,742	29,028	0	3,520
Wisconsin	449,444	179,842	175,878	84,028	8,565	916	215	452,113	205,298	149,120	85,599	9,055	978	2,063
Wyoming	50,593	17,282	30,524	0	144	0	2,643	50,700	16,624	31,498	0	74	0	2,504
U.S. Service Academies	16,391	16,391	†	†	†	†	†	16,705	16,705	†	†	†	†	†
Other jurisdictions	261,095	78,711	13,566	136,374	13,994	4,452	13,998	260,216	79,046	10,808	136,695	14,452	4,529	14,686
American Samoa	2,345	0	2,345	0	0	0	0	2,259	2,259	0	0	0	0	0
Federated States of Micronesia	3,202	0	3,202	0	0	0	0	3,324	0	3,324	0	0	0	0
Guam	7,712	3,586	3,933	193	0	0	0	7,456	4,046	3,206	204	0	0	0
Marshall Islands	887	0	887	0	0	0	0	1,033	0	1,033	0	0	0	0
Northern Marianas	1,250	1,250	0	0	0	0	0	1,286	1,286	0	0	0	0	0
Palau	910	0	910	0	0	0	0	892	0	892	0	0	0	0
Puerto Rico	241,419	70,505	2,289	136,181	13,994	4,452	13,998	240,906	68,395	2,353	136,491	14,452	4,529	14,686
U.S. Virgin Islands	3,370	3,370	0	0	0	0	0	3,060	3,060	0	0	0	0	0

†Not applicable.
NOTE: Includes students who enrolled at any point during a 12-month period ending during the summer of the academic year indicated. Degree-granting institutions grant associate's or higher degrees and participate in Title IV federal financial aid programs.

SOURCE: U.S. Department of Education, National Center for Education Statistics, 2005–06 and 2006–07 Integrated Postsecondary Education Data System (IPEDS), Fall 2006 and Fall 2007. (This table was prepared August 2008.)

Table 223. Residence and migration of all freshmen students in degree-granting institutions, by state or jurisdiction: Fall 2006

State or jurisdiction	Total freshman enrollment in institutions located in the state	State residents enrolled in institutions		Ratio of in-state students		Migration of students		
		In any state[1]	In their home state	To freshman enrollment (col. 4/col. 2)	To residents enrolled in any state (col. 4/col. 3)	Out of state (col. 3 - col. 4)	Into state[2] (col. 2 - col. 4)	Net (col. 8 - col. 7)
1	2	3	4	5	6	7	8	9
United States	2,707,213	2,652,859	2,178,745	0.80	0.82	474,114	528,468	54,354
Alabama	42,821	36,076	32,131	0.75	0.89	3,945	10,690	6,745
Alaska..........................	2,984	4,865	2,673	0.90	0.55	2,192	311	-1,881
Arizona	63,830	40,143	35,781	0.56	0.89	4,362	28,049	23,687
Arkansas......................	23,545	22,458	19,495	0.83	0.87	2,963	4,050	1,087
California	294,343	288,532	262,691	0.89	0.91	25,841	31,652	5,811
Colorado	52,309	48,488	39,842	0.76	0.82	8,646	12,467	3,821
Connecticut..................	27,913	34,171	19,029	0.68	0.56	15,142	8,884	-6,258
Delaware	8,259	7,159	4,791	0.58	0.67	2,368	3,468	1,100
District of Columbia	9,996	3,372	873	0.09	0.26	2,499	9,123	6,624
Florida..........................	143,052	133,339	119,012	0.83	0.89	14,327	24,040	9,713
Georgia........................	76,298	77,954	64,734	0.85	0.83	13,220	11,564	-1,656
Hawaii..........................	8,316	9,905	6,613	0.80	0.67	3,292	1,703	-1,589
Idaho............................	11,555	10,894	8,032	0.70	0.74	2,862	3,523	661
Illinois..........................	109,524	114,437	88,819	0.81	0.78	25,618	20,705	-4,913
Indiana.........................	64,138	56,055	48,691	0.76	0.87	7,364	15,447	8,083
Iowa	38,985	30,353	26,567	0.68	0.88	3,786	12,418	8,632
Kansas.........................	29,057	27,945	23,437	0.81	0.84	4,508	5,620	1,112
Kentucky......................	38,697	36,113	31,878	0.82	0.88	4,235	6,819	2,584
Louisiana	35,643	36,171	31,603	0.89	0.87	4,568	4,040	-528
Maine...........................	11,465	12,323	8,281	0.72	0.67	4,042	3,184	-858
Maryland	47,166	55,605	37,580	0.80	0.68	18,025	9,586	-8,439
Massachusetts..............	71,764	64,399	45,306	0.63	0.70	19,093	26,458	7,365
Michigan	96,812	98,597	88,775	0.92	0.90	9,822	8,037	-1,785
Minnesota	54,004	56,226	43,528	0.81	0.77	12,698	10,476	-2,222
Mississippi	32,480	29,941	27,251	0.84	0.91	2,690	5,229	2,539
Missouri	52,569	50,072	41,849	0.80	0.84	8,223	10,720	2,497
Montana.......................	8,554	8,573	6,540	0.76	0.76	2,033	2,014	-19
Nebraska	18,519	18,328	15,218	0.82	0.83	3,110	3,301	191
Nevada	15,052	16,087	13,285	0.88	0.83	2,802	1,767	-1,035
New Hampshire	12,985	12,435	6,709	0.52	0.54	5,726	6,276	550
New Jersey...................	61,540	91,099	56,605	0.92	0.62	34,494	4,935	-29,559
New Mexico	16,961	18,138	14,218	0.84	0.78	3,920	2,743	-1,177
New York.......................	182,929	179,150	146,632	0.80	0.82	32,518	36,297	3,779
North Carolina	84,968	77,524	69,953	0.82	0.90	7,571	15,015	7,444
North Dakota	8,365	7,000	5,009	0.60	0.72	1,991	3,356	1,365
Ohio.............................	103,531	105,677	89,300	0.86	0.85	16,377	14,231	-2,146
Oklahoma	34,751	31,642	28,236	0.81	0.89	3,406	6,515	3,109
Oregon.........................	29,704	28,072	23,147	0.78	0.82	4,925	6,557	1,632
Pennsylvania................	137,903	122,574	103,521	0.75	0.84	19,053	34,382	15,329
Rhode Island	16,103	9,669	6,770	0.42	0.70	2,899	9,333	6,434
South Carolina..............	39,557	35,635	31,555	0.80	0.89	4,080	8,002	3,922
South Dakota	9,280	8,674	6,797	0.73	0.78	1,877	2,483	606
Tennessee	50,120	48,579	41,047	0.82	0.84	7,532	9,073	1,541
Texas	198,219	205,143	183,466	0.93	0.89	21,677	14,753	-6,924
Utah.............................	29,402	22,276	20,441	0.70	0.92	1,835	8,961	7,126
Vermont	7,191	5,175	2,399	0.33	0.46	2,776	4,792	2,016
Virginia.........................	73,708	68,372	55,756	0.76	0.82	12,616	17,952	5,336
Washington...................	37,269	40,743	31,427	0.84	0.77	9,316	5,842	-3,474
West Virginia.................	16,926	13,744	11,637	0.69	0.85	2,107	5,289	3,182
Wisconsin	55,816	55,898	46,121	0.83	0.83	9,777	9,695	-82
Wyoming	6,104	4,368	3,255	0.53	0.75	1,113	2,849	1,736
U.S. Service Academies.....	4,231	†	439[3]	†	†	-439	3,792	4,231
State unknown[4]..............	†	32,691	†	†	†	32,691	†	-32,691
Other jurisdictions	42,847	44,166	42,413	0.99	0.96	1,753	434	-1,319
American Samoa............	531	644	531	1.00	0.82	113	0	-113
Federated States of Micronesia	1,112	1,269	1,112	1.00	0.88	157	0	-157
Guam............................	1,149	1,175	1,012	0.88	0.86	163	137	-26
Marshall Islands.............	6	30	6	1.00	0.20	24	0	-24
Northern Marianas	192	206	158	0.82	0.77	48	34	-14
Palau............................	134	121	86	0.64	0.71	35	48	13
Puerto Rico...................	39,343	39,898	39,144	0.99	0.98	754	199	-555
U.S. Virgin Islands	380	823	364	0.96	0.44	459	16	-443
Foreign countries.............	†	38,652	†	†	†	38,652	†	-38,652
Residence unknown	†	14,383	†	†	†	14,383	†	-14,383

†Not applicable.
[1]Students residing in a particular state when admitted to an institution anywhere—either in their home state or another state.
[2]Includes students coming to U.S. colleges from foreign countries and other jurisdictions.
[3]Students whose residence is in the same state as the service academy.
[4]Institution unable to determine student's home state.

NOTE: Includes all first-time postsecondary students enrolled at reporting institutions. Degree-granting institutions grant associate's or higher degrees and participate in Title IV federal financial aid programs.
SOURCE: U.S. Department of Education, National Center for Education Statistics, 2006 Integrated Postsecondary Education Data System (IPEDS), Spring 2007. (This table was prepared June 2008.)

Table 224. Residence and migration of all freshmen students in degree-granting institutions who graduated from high school in the previous 12 months, by state or jurisdiction: Fall 2006

| State or jurisdiction | Total freshman enrollment in institutions located in the state | State residents enrolled in institutions | | Ratio of in-state students | | Migration of students | | |
| | | In any state[1] | In their home state | To freshman enrollment (col. 4/col. 2) | To residents enrolled in any state (col. 4/col. 3) | Out of state (col. 3 - col. 4) | Into state[2] (col. 2 - col. 4) | Net (col. 8 - col. 7) |
1	2	3	4	5	6	7	8	9
United States	1,955,510	1,929,453	1,559,301	0.80	0.81	370,152	396,209	26,057
Alabama	32,225	27,019	24,334	0.76	0.90	2,685	7,891	5,206
Alaska	2,197	3,503	1,964	0.89	0.56	1,539	233	-1,306
Arizona	31,177	25,423	22,104	0.71	0.87	3,319	9,073	5,754
Arkansas	18,800	17,063	15,093	0.80	0.88	1,970	3,707	1,737
California	208,107	210,481	190,199	0.91	0.90	20,282	17,908	-2,374
Colorado	29,351	29,748	23,020	0.78	0.77	6,728	6,331	-397
Connecticut	24,017	29,429	15,554	0.65	0.53	13,875	8,463	-5,412
Delaware	7,047	5,727	3,758	0.53	0.66	1,969	3,289	1,320
District of Columbia	8,786	2,448	633	0.07	0.26	1,815	8,153	6,338
Florida	97,162	91,149	80,682	0.83	0.89	10,467	16,480	6,013
Georgia	54,763	55,094	45,503	0.83	0.83	9,591	9,260	-331
Hawaii	5,916	7,534	4,772	0.81	0.63	2,762	1,144	-1,618
Idaho	8,495	7,608	5,549	0.65	0.73	2,059	2,946	887
Illinois	74,362	85,730	63,453	0.85	0.74	22,277	10,909	-11,368
Indiana	47,986	40,088	34,811	0.73	0.87	5,277	13,175	7,898
Iowa	27,137	22,131	18,987	0.70	0.86	3,144	8,150	5,006
Kansas	22,338	20,985	17,854	0.80	0.85	3,131	4,484	1,353
Kentucky	28,574	25,883	23,043	0.81	0.89	2,840	5,531	2,691
Louisiana	27,476	27,009	24,046	0.88	0.89	2,963	3,430	467
Maine	9,347	9,887	6,399	0.68	0.65	3,488	2,948	-540
Maryland	34,244	42,002	26,681	0.78	0.64	15,321	7,563	-7,758
Massachusetts	59,053	51,800	34,476	0.58	0.67	17,324	24,577	7,253
Michigan	71,513	72,171	64,796	0.91	0.90	7,375	6,717	-658
Minnesota	40,372	43,181	31,876	0.79	0.74	11,305	8,496	-2,809
Mississippi	22,445	20,532	18,870	0.84	0.92	1,662	3,575	1,913
Missouri	40,254	38,136	31,686	0.79	0.83	6,450	8,568	2,118
Montana	6,458	6,271	4,680	0.72	0.75	1,591	1,778	187
Nebraska	14,424	14,219	11,599	0.80	0.82	2,620	2,825	205
Nevada	7,949	8,936	6,832	0.86	0.76	2,104	1,117	-987
New Hampshire	11,247	10,483	5,470	0.49	0.52	5,013	5,777	764
New Jersey	44,444	71,620	40,390	0.91	0.56	31,230	4,054	-27,176
New Mexico	12,349	13,549	10,652	0.86	0.79	2,897	1,697	-1,200
New York	143,264	141,574	113,145	0.79	0.80	28,429	30,119	1,690
North Carolina	61,718	53,787	48,693	0.79	0.91	5,094	13,025	7,931
North Dakota	6,875	5,504	4,014	0.58	0.73	1,490	2,861	1,371
Ohio	77,478	78,210	65,391	0.84	0.84	12,819	12,087	-732
Oklahoma	25,193	22,659	20,185	0.80	0.89	2,474	5,008	2,534
Oregon	17,767	16,680	12,716	0.72	0.76	3,964	5,051	1,087
Pennsylvania	104,005	89,940	74,112	0.71	0.82	15,828	29,893	14,065
Rhode Island	12,501	6,513	3,876	0.31	0.60	2,637	8,625	5,988
South Carolina	30,349	26,275	23,556	0.78	0.90	2,719	6,793	4,074
South Dakota	7,029	6,539	5,026	0.72	0.77	1,513	2,003	490
Tennessee	38,440	36,039	30,654	0.80	0.85	5,385	7,786	2,401
Texas	131,102	139,043	122,878	0.94	0.88	16,165	8,224	-7,941
Utah	18,280	13,921	12,697	0.69	0.91	1,224	5,583	4,359
Vermont	6,306	4,380	1,898	0.30	0.43	2,482	4,408	1,926
Virginia	53,544	51,499	41,342	0.77	0.80	10,157	12,202	2,045
Washington	28,892	31,129	23,988	0.83	0.77	7,141	4,904	-2,237
West Virginia	13,562	10,147	8,841	0.65	0.87	1,306	4,721	3,415
Wisconsin	42,596	42,040	33,999	0.80	0.81	8,041	8,597	556
Wyoming	4,299	3,231	2,367	0.55	0.73	864	1,932	1,068
U.S. Service Academies	2,295	†	157 [3]	†	†	-157	2,138	2,295
State unknown[4]	†	13,504	†	†	†	13,504	†	-13,504
Other jurisdictions	34,623	35,757	34,418	0.99	0.96	1,339	205	-1,134
American Samoa	425	530	425	1.00	0.80	105	0	-105
Federated States of Micronesia	867	971	867	1.00	0.89	104	0	-104
Guam	637	693	554	0.87	0.80	139	83	-56
Marshall Islands	6	24	6	1.00	0.25	18	0	-18
Northern Marianas	117	146	103	0.88	0.71	43	14	-29
Palau	91	76	52	0.57	0.68	24	39	15
Puerto Rico	32,239	32,776	32,173	1.00	0.98	603	66	-537
U.S. Virgin Islands	241	541	238	0.99	0.44	303	3	-300
Foreign countries	†	24,473	†	†	†	24,473	†	-24,473
Residence unknown	†	450	†	†	†	450	†	-450

†Not applicable.
[1]Students residing in a particular state when admitted to an institution anywhere—either in their home state or another state.
[2]Includes students coming to U.S. colleges from foreign countries and other jurisdictions.
[3]Students whose residence is in the same state as the service academy.
[4]Institution unable to determine student's home state.

NOTE: Includes all first-time postsecondary students who graduated from high school in the previous 12 months and were enrolled at reporting institutions. Degree-granting institutions grant associate's or higher degrees and participate in Title IV federal financial aid programs.
SOURCE: U.S. Department of Education, National Center for Education Statistics, 2006 Integrated Postsecondary Data System (IPEDS), Spring 2007. (This table was prepared June 2008.)

Table 225. Residence and migration of all freshmen students in 4-year degree-granting institutions who graduated from high school in the previous 12 months, by state or jurisdiction: Fall 2006

State or jurisdiction	Total freshman enrollment in institutions located in the state	State residents enrolled in institutions		Ratio of in-state students		Migration of students		
		In any state[1]	In their home state	To freshman enrollment (col. 4/col. 2)	To residents enrolled in any state (col. 4/col. 3)	Out of state (col. 3 - col. 4)	Into state[2] (col. 2 - col. 4)	Net (col. 8 - col. 7)
1	2	3	4	5	6	7	8	9
United States	1,359,444	1,336,048	995,126	0.73	0.74	340,922	364,318	23,396
Alabama	21,967	17,434	15,068	0.69	0.86	2,366	6,899	4,533
Alaska..........................	2,183	3,363	1,951	0.89	0.58	1,412	232	-1,180
Arizona........................	20,407	15,479	12,435	0.61	0.80	3,044	7,972	4,928
Arkansas......................	14,098	12,078	10,517	0.75	0.87	1,561	3,581	2,020
California	111,313	118,446	99,031	0.89	0.84	19,415	12,282	-7,133
Colorado......................	23,135	23,105	17,076	0.74	0.74	6,029	6,059	30
Connecticut..................	18,145	23,453	9,749	0.54	0.42	13,704	8,396	-5,308
Delaware......................	5,100	3,786	1,925	0.38	0.51	1,861	3,175	1,314
District of Columbia	8,786	2,279	633	0.07	0.28	1,646	8,153	6,507
Florida.........................	66,465	61,953	52,139	0.78	0.84	9,814	14,326	4,512
Georgia........................	38,659	39,478	30,465	0.79	0.77	9,013	8,194	-819
Hawaii.........................	3,250	4,791	2,141	0.66	0.45	2,650	1,109	-1,541
Idaho..........................	7,188	6,093	4,443	0.62	0.73	1,650	2,745	1,095
Illinois.........................	50,569	61,661	40,070	0.79	0.65	21,591	10,499	-11,092
Indiana........................	43,495	35,409	30,608	0.70	0.86	4,801	12,887	8,086
Iowa............................	18,484	13,940	11,083	0.60	0.80	2,857	7,401	4,544
Kansas........................	13,695	13,258	10,409	0.76	0.79	2,849	3,286	437
Kentucky......................	21,302	18,694	16,124	0.76	0.86	2,570	5,178	2,608
Louisiana.....................	22,556	21,615	19,222	0.85	0.89	2,393	3,334	941
Maine..........................	7,371	7,880	4,506	0.61	0.57	3,374	2,865	-509
Maryland......................	19,201	27,242	12,407	0.65	0.46	14,835	6,794	-8,041
Massachusetts..............	48,975	41,718	24,755	0.51	0.59	16,963	24,220	7,257
Michigan......................	48,644	49,113	42,178	0.87	0.86	6,935	6,466	-469
Minnesota....................	26,301	29,727	18,884	0.72	0.64	10,843	7,417	-3,426
Mississippi	8,808	7,364	5,866	0.67	0.80	1,498	2,942	1,444
Missouri.......................	27,347	25,246	19,471	0.71	0.77	5,775	7,876	2,101
Montana.......................	5,276	4,828	3,555	0.67	0.74	1,273	1,721	448
Nebraska......................	10,741	10,315	8,146	0.76	0.79	2,169	2,595	426
Nevada........................	6,687	7,553	5,667	0.85	0.75	1,886	1,020	-866
New Hampshire.............	9,139	8,290	3,557	0.39	0.43	4,733	5,582	849
New Jersey...................	24,407	51,429	20,777	0.85	0.40	30,652	3,630	-27,022
New Mexico	6,797	8,249	5,700	0.84	0.69	2,549	1,097	-1,452
New York......................	103,926	102,974	75,141	0.72	0.73	27,833	28,785	952
North Carolina	44,551	36,863	32,094	0.72	0.87	4,769	12,457	7,688
North Dakota	5,539	3,912	2,847	0.51	0.73	1,065	2,692	1,627
Ohio............................	61,708	62,411	50,328	0.82	0.81	12,083	11,380	-703
Oklahoma.....................	17,523	15,219	13,171	0.75	0.87	2,048	4,352	2,304
Oregon........................	12,968	12,191	8,474	0.65	0.70	3,717	4,494	777
Pennsylvania.................	83,335	69,620	54,557	0.65	0.78	15,063	28,778	13,715
Rhode Island	11,510	5,526	2,973	0.26	0.54	2,553	8,537	5,984
South Carolina..............	20,491	16,585	14,089	0.69	0.85	2,496	6,402	3,906
South Dakota................	5,547	4,993	3,714	0.67	0.74	1,279	1,833	554
Tennessee	27,204	25,038	20,035	0.74	0.80	5,003	7,169	2,166
Texas..........................	79,928	88,738	73,378	0.92	0.83	15,360	6,550	-8,810
Utah............................	14,110	10,097	9,045	0.64	0.90	1,052	5,065	4,013
Vermont.......................	5,946	4,005	1,661	0.28	0.41	2,344	4,285	1,941
Virginia........................	37,671	35,816	26,187	0.70	0.73	9,629	11,484	1,855
Washington...................	19,773	21,750	15,088	0.76	0.69	6,662	4,685	-1,977
West Virginia.................	11,118	7,821	6,792	0.61	0.87	1,029	4,326	3,297
Wisconsin.....................	32,315	31,272	23,939	0.74	0.77	7,333	8,376	1,043
Wyoming......................	1,495	1,672	898	0.60	0.54	774	597	-177
U.S. Service Academies....	2,295	†	157 [3]	†	†	-157	2,138	2,295
State unknown[4].............	†	4,276	†	†	†	4,276	†	-4,276
Other jurisdictions	29,036	30,086	28,870	0.99	0.96	1,216	166	-1,050
American Samoa.............	†	84	†	†	†	84	0	-84
Federated States of Micronesia	†	68	†	†	†	68	0	-68
Guam...........................	532	583	449	0.84	0.77	134	83	-51
Marshall Islands.............	†	9	†	†	†	9	0	-9
Northern Marianas	117	143	103	0.88	0.72	40	14	-26
Palau...........................	†	24	†	†	†	24	0	-24
Puerto Rico...................	28,146	28,645	28,080	1.00	0.98	565	66	-499
U.S. Virgin Islands	241	530	238	0.99	0.45	292	3	-289
Foreign countries...........	†	21,929	†	†	†	21,929	†	-21,929
Residence unknown	†	417	†	†	†	417	†	-417

†Not applicable.
[1]Students residing in a particular state when admitted to an institution anywhere—either in their home state or another state.
[2]Includes students coming to U.S. colleges from foreign countries and other jurisdictions.
[3]Students whose residence is in the same state as the service academy.
[4]Institution unable to determine student's home state.

NOTE: Includes all first-time postsecondary students who graduated from high school in the previous 12 months and were enrolled at reporting institutions. Degree-granting institutions grant associate's or higher degrees and participate in Title IV federal financial aid programs.
SOURCE: U.S. Department of Education, National Center for Education Statistics, 2006 Integrated Postsecondary Education Data System (IPEDS), Spring 2007. (This table was prepared June 2008.)

Table 226. Total fall enrollment in degree-granting institutions, by race/ethnicity, sex, attendance status, and level of student: Selected years, 1976 through 2007

Race/ethnicity, sex, attendance status, and level of student	Fall enrollment (in thousands)										Percentage distribution of students									
	1976	1980	1990	2000	2002	2003	2004	2005	2006	2007	1976	1980	1990	2000	2002	2003	2004	2005	2006	2007
1	2	3	4	5	6	7	8	9	10	11	12	13	14	15	16	17	18	19	20	21
All students, total	**10,985.6**	**12,086.8**	**13,818.6**	**15,312.3**	**16,611.7**	**16,911.5**	**17,272.0**	**17,487.5**	**17,758.9**	**18,248.1**	**100.0**	**100.0**	**100.0**	**100.0**	**100.0**	**100.0**	**100.0**	**100.0**	**100.0**	**100.0**
White	9,076.1	9,833.0	10,722.5	10,462.1	11,140.2	11,280.9	11,422.8	11,495.4	11,572.4	11,756.2	82.6	81.4	77.6	68.3	67.1	66.7	66.1	65.7	65.2	64.4
Total minority	1,690.8	1,948.8	2,704.7	4,321.5	4,880.5	5,032.9	5,259.1	5,407.2	5,590.6	5,867.4	15.4	16.1	19.6	28.2	29.4	29.8	30.4	30.9	31.5	32.2
Black	1,033.0	1,106.8	1,247.0	1,730.3	1,978.7	2,068.4	2,164.7	2,214.6	2,279.6	2,383.4	9.4	9.2	9.0	11.3	11.9	12.2	12.5	12.7	12.8	13.1
Hispanic	383.8	471.7	782.4	1,461.8	1,661.7	1,716.3	1,809.6	1,882.0	1,964.3	2,076.2	3.5	3.9	5.7	9.5	10.0	10.1	10.5	10.8	11.1	11.4
Asian/Pacific Islander	197.9	286.4	572.4	978.2	1,074.2	1,075.6	1,108.7	1,134.4	1,165.5	1,217.9	1.8	2.4	4.1	6.4	6.5	6.4	6.4	6.5	6.6	6.7
American Indian/Alaska Native	76.1	83.9	102.8	151.2	165.9	172.6	176.1	176.3	181.1	190.0	0.7	0.7	0.7	1.0	1.0	1.0	1.0	1.0	1.0	1.0
Nonresident alien	218.7	305.0	391.5	528.7	590.9	597.7	590.2	584.8	595.9	624.5	2.0	2.5	2.8	3.5	3.6	3.5	3.4	3.3	3.4	3.4
Male	**5,794.4**	**5,868.1**	**6,283.9**	**6,721.8**	**7,202.1**	**7,260.3**	**7,387.3**	**7,455.9**	**7,574.8**	**7,815.9**	**100.0**	**100.0**	**100.0**	**100.0**	**100.0**	**100.0**	**100.0**	**100.0**	**100.0**	**100.0**
White	4,813.7	4,772.9	4,861.0	4,634.6	4,897.9	4,929.8	4,988.0	5,007.2	5,046.2	5,146.1	83.1	81.3	77.4	68.9	68.0	67.9	67.5	67.2	66.6	65.8
Total minority	826.6	884.4	1,176.6	1,789.8	1,977.2	2,005.3	2,083.7	2,139.2	2,212.6	2,336.6	14.3	15.1	18.7	26.6	27.5	27.6	28.2	28.7	29.2	29.9
Black	469.9	463.7	484.7	635.3	708.6	730.7	758.4	774.1	795.4	838.1	8.1	7.9	7.7	9.5	9.8	10.1	10.3	10.4	10.5	10.7
Hispanic	209.7	231.6	353.9	627.1	699.0	709.3	745.1	774.6	810.0	861.6	3.6	3.9	5.6	9.3	9.7	9.8	10.1	10.4	10.7	11.0
Asian/Pacific Islander	108.4	151.3	294.9	465.9	503.9	498.2	511.6	522.0	536.0	562.5	1.9	2.6	4.7	6.9	7.0	6.9	6.9	7.0	7.1	7.2
American Indian/Alaska Native	38.5	37.8	43.1	61.4	65.7	67.1	68.6	68.4	71.2	74.4	0.7	0.6	0.7	0.9	0.9	0.9	0.9	0.9	0.9	1.0
Nonresident alien	154.1	210.8	246.3	297.3	327.0	325.2	315.6	309.5	316.1	333.2	2.7	3.6	3.9	4.4	4.5	4.5	4.3	4.2	4.2	4.3
Female	**5,191.2**	**6,218.7**	**7,534.7**	**8,590.5**	**9,409.6**	**9,651.2**	**9,884.8**	**10,031.6**	**10,184.1**	**10,432.2**	**100.0**	**100.0**	**100.0**	**100.0**	**100.0**	**100.0**	**100.0**	**100.0**	**100.0**	**100.0**
White	4,262.4	5,060.1	5,861.5	5,827.5	6,242.3	6,351.2	6,434.8	6,488.2	6,526.2	6,610.1	82.1	81.4	77.8	67.8	66.3	65.8	65.1	64.7	64.1	63.4
Total minority	864.2	1,064.4	1,528.1	2,531.7	2,903.3	3,027.5	3,175.4	3,268.0	3,378.0	3,530.9	16.6	17.1	20.3	29.5	30.9	31.4	32.1	32.6	33.2	33.8
Black	563.1	643.0	762.3	1,095.0	1,270.2	1,337.7	1,406.3	1,440.4	1,484.2	1,545.3	10.8	10.3	10.1	12.7	13.5	13.9	14.2	14.4	14.6	14.8
Hispanic	174.1	240.1	428.5	834.7	962.7	1,006.9	1,064.5	1,107.3	1,154.3	1,214.5	3.4	3.9	5.7	9.7	10.2	10.4	10.8	11.0	11.3	11.6
Asian/Pacific Islander	89.4	135.2	277.5	512.3	570.2	577.4	597.1	612.4	629.5	655.4	1.7	2.2	3.7	6.0	6.1	6.0	6.0	6.1	6.2	6.3
American Indian/Alaska Native	37.6	46.1	59.7	89.7	100.2	105.5	107.5	107.9	110.0	115.6	0.7	0.7	0.8	1.0	1.1	1.1	1.1	1.1	1.1	1.1
Nonresident alien	64.6	94.2	145.2	231.4	263.3	272.5	274.6	275.3	279.8	291.2	1.2	1.5	1.9	2.7	2.8	2.8	2.8	2.7	2.7	2.8
Full-time	**6,703.6**	**7,088.9**	**7,821.0**	**9,009.6**	**9,946.4**	**10,326.1**	**10,610.2**	**10,797.0**	**10,957.0**	**11,269.9**	**100.0**	**100.0**	**100.0**	**100.0**	**100.0**	**100.0**	**100.0**	**100.0**	**100.0**	**100.0**
White	5,512.6	5,717.0	6,016.5	6,231.1	6,784.2	6,982.0	7,129.1	7,220.5	7,267.3	7,394.2	82.2	80.6	76.9	69.2	68.0	67.6	67.2	66.9	66.3	65.6
Total minority	1,030.9	1,137.5	1,514.9	2,368.5	2,721.8	2,872.6	3,015.4	3,117.1	3,221.9	3,382.0	15.4	16.0	19.4	26.3	27.4	27.8	28.4	28.9	29.4	30.0
Black	659.2	685.6	718.3	982.6	1,144.2	1,218.4	1,282.8	1,321.7	1,354.6	1,416.1	9.8	9.7	9.2	10.9	11.5	11.8	12.1	12.2	12.4	12.6
Hispanic	211.1	247.0	394.7	710.3	825.1	882.2	936.6	979.7	1,023.8	1,082.9	3.1	3.5	5.0	7.9	8.3	8.5	8.8	9.1	9.3	9.6
Asian/Pacific Islander	117.7	162.0	347.4	591.2	657.4	670.5	691.4	710.1	735.4	770.0	1.8	2.3	4.4	6.6	6.6	6.5	6.5	6.6	6.7	6.8
American Indian/Alaska Native	43.0	43.0	54.4	84.4	95.1	101.4	104.6	105.6	107.9	113.0	0.6	0.6	0.7	0.9	1.0	1.0	1.0	1.0	1.0	1.0
Nonresident alien	160.0	234.4	289.6	410.0	460.4	471.6	465.6	459.4	468.0	493.7	2.4	3.3	3.7	4.6	4.6	4.6	4.4	4.3	4.3	4.4
Part-time	**4,282.1**	**4,997.9**	**5,997.7**	**6,302.7**	**6,665.4**	**6,585.3**	**6,661.9**	**6,690.5**	**6,801.6**	**6,978.2**	**100.0**	**100.0**	**100.0**	**100.0**	**100.0**	**100.0**	**100.0**	**100.0**	**100.0**	**100.0**
White	3,563.5	4,116.0	4,706.0	4,231.0	4,376.0	4,298.9	4,293.6	4,274.9	4,305.1	4,362.1	83.2	82.4	78.5	67.1	65.7	65.3	64.5	63.9	63.3	62.5
Total minority	659.9	811.3	1,189.8	1,953.0	2,158.7	2,160.3	2,243.7	2,290.1	2,368.6	2,485.4	15.4	16.2	19.8	31.0	32.4	32.8	33.7	34.2	34.8	35.6
Black	373.8	421.2	528.7	747.7	834.6	849.9	881.8	892.9	924.8	967.2	8.7	8.4	8.8	11.9	12.5	12.9	13.2	13.3	13.6	13.9
Hispanic	172.7	224.8	387.7	751.5	836.6	834.0	873.0	902.2	940.5	993.2	4.0	4.5	6.5	11.9	12.6	12.7	13.1	13.5	13.8	14.2
Asian/Pacific Islander	80.2	124.4	225.1	387.1	416.8	405.1	417.3	424.3	430.1	447.9	1.9	2.5	3.8	6.1	6.3	6.2	6.3	6.3	6.3	6.4
American Indian/Alaska Native	33.1	40.9	48.4	66.8	70.8	71.3	71.6	70.7	73.2	77.0	0.8	0.8	0.8	1.1	1.1	1.1	1.1	1.1	1.1	1.1
Nonresident alien	58.7	70.6	101.8	118.7	130.6	126.1	124.6	125.5	127.8	130.8	1.4	1.4	1.7	1.9	2.0	1.9	1.9	1.9	1.9	1.9

See notes at end of table.

Table 226. Total fall enrollment in degree-granting institutions, by race/ethnicity, sex, attendance status, and level of student: Selected years, 1976 through 2007—Continued

Race/ethnicity, sex, attendance status, and level of student	Fall enrollment (in thousands)										Percentage distribution of students									
	1976	1980	1990	2000	2002	2003	2004	2005	2006	2007	1976	1980	1990	2000	2002	2003	2004	2005	2006	2007
1	2	3	4	5	6	7	8	9	10	11	12	13	14	15	16	17	18	19	20	21
Undergraduate, total	**9,419.0**	**10,469.1**	**11,959.1**	**13,155.4**	**14,257.1**	**14,480.4**	**14,780.6**	**14,964.0**	**15,184.3**	**15,603.8**	**100.0**	**100.0**	**100.0**	**100.0**	**100.0**	**100.0**	**100.0**	**100.0**	**100.0**	**100.0**
White	7,740.5	8,480.7	9,272.6	8,983.5	9,564.9	9,664.6	9,771.3	9,828.6	9,885.4	10,046.6	82.2	81.0	77.5	68.3	67.1	66.7	66.1	65.7	65.1	64.4
Total minority	1,535.3	1,778.5	2,467.7	3,884.0	4,376.2	4,498.4	4,695.5	4,820.7	4,977.9	5,221.9	16.3	17.0	20.6	29.5	30.7	31.1	31.8	32.2	32.8	33.5
Black	943.4	1,018.8	1,147.2	1,548.9	1,763.8	1,838.0	1,918.5	1,955.4	2,005.7	2,092.6	10.0	9.7	9.6	11.8	12.4	12.7	13.0	13.1	13.2	13.4
Hispanic	352.9	433.1	724.6	1,351.0	1,533.3	1,579.8	1,666.9	1,733.6	1,810.1	1,915.9	3.7	4.1	6.1	10.3	10.8	10.9	11.3	11.6	11.9	12.3
Asian/Pacific Islander	169.3	248.7	500.5	845.5	927.4	922.7	949.9	971.4	997.9	1,042.1	1.8	2.4	4.2	6.4	6.5	6.4	6.4	6.5	6.6	6.7
American Indian/Alaska Native	69.7	77.9	95.5	138.5	151.7	157.8	160.3	160.4	164.2	171.3	0.7	0.7	0.8	1.1	1.1	1.1	1.1	1.1	1.1	1.1
Nonresident alien	143.2	209.9	218.7	288.0	316.0	317.3	313.8	314.7	321.0	335.3	1.5	2.0	1.8	2.2	2.2	2.2	2.1	2.1	2.1	2.1
Male	**4,896.8**	**4,997.4**	**5,379.8**	**5,778.3**	**6,192.4**	**6,227.4**	**6,340.0**	**6,408.9**	**6,513.8**	**6,727.6**	**100.0**	**100.0**	**100.0**	**100.0**	**100.0**	**100.0**	**100.0**	**100.0**	**100.0**	**100.0**
White	4,052.2	4,054.9	4,184.4	4,010.1	4,245.6	4,263.1	4,309.9	4,330.4	4,364.6	4,455.9	82.8	81.1	77.8	69.4	68.6	68.5	68.0	67.6	67.0	66.2
Total minority	748.2	802.7	1,069.3	1,618.0	1,787.1	1,806.5	1,877.0	1,926.6	1,993.3	2,107.5	15.3	16.1	19.9	28.0	28.9	29.0	29.6	30.1	30.6	31.3
Black	430.7	428.2	448.0	577.0	642.2	660.4	684.7	697.5	715.7	754.1	8.8	8.6	8.3	10.0	10.4	10.6	10.8	10.9	11.0	11.2
Hispanic	191.7	211.2	326.9	582.6	649.2	656.8	690.5	718.5	752.0	802.0	3.9	4.2	6.1	10.1	10.5	10.5	10.9	11.2	11.5	11.9
Asian/Pacific Islander	91.1	128.5	254.5	401.9	435.4	427.9	439.1	448.1	460.6	483.6	1.9	2.6	4.7	7.0	7.0	6.9	6.9	7.0	7.1	7.2
American Indian/Alaska Native	34.8	34.8	39.9	56.4	60.3	61.5	62.7	62.5	65.0	67.8	0.7	0.7	0.7	1.0	1.0	1.0	1.0	1.0	1.0	1.0
Nonresident alien	96.4	139.8	126.1	150.2	159.7	157.7	153.1	151.8	155.9	164.2	2.0	2.8	2.3	2.6	2.6	2.5	2.4	2.4	2.4	2.4
Female	**4,522.1**	**5,471.7**	**6,579.3**	**7,377.1**	**8,064.7**	**8,253.0**	**8,440.6**	**8,555.1**	**8,670.5**	**8,876.2**	**100.0**	**100.0**	**100.0**	**100.0**	**100.0**	**100.0**	**100.0**	**100.0**	**100.0**	**100.0**
White	3,688.3	4,425.8	5,088.2	4,973.3	5,319.3	5,401.5	5,461.4	5,498.2	5,520.9	5,590.6	81.6	80.9	77.3	67.4	66.0	65.4	64.7	64.3	63.7	63.0
Total minority	787.0	975.8	1,398.5	2,266.0	2,589.1	2,691.8	2,818.5	2,894.0	2,984.5	3,114.4	17.4	17.8	21.3	30.7	32.1	32.6	33.4	33.8	34.4	35.1
Black	512.7	590.6	699.2	971.9	1,121.6	1,177.7	1,233.8	1,257.8	1,290.0	1,338.5	11.3	10.8	10.6	13.2	13.9	14.3	14.6	14.7	14.9	15.1
Hispanic	161.2	221.8	397.6	768.4	884.1	923.0	976.3	1,015.0	1,058.1	1,113.9	3.6	4.1	6.0	10.4	11.0	11.2	11.6	11.9	12.2	12.5
Asian/Pacific Islander	78.2	120.2	246.0	443.6	492.0	494.8	510.8	523.2	537.3	558.5	1.7	2.2	3.7	6.0	6.1	6.0	6.1	6.1	6.2	6.3
American Indian/Alaska Native	34.9	43.1	55.5	82.1	91.4	96.3	97.6	98.0	99.2	103.6	0.8	0.8	0.8	1.1	1.1	1.2	1.2	1.1	1.1	1.2
Nonresident alien	46.8	70.1	92.6	137.8	156.3	159.6	160.7	162.9	165.2	171.2	1.0	1.3	1.4	1.9	1.9	1.9	1.9	1.9	1.9	1.9
Graduate, total	**1,322.5**	**1,340.9**	**1,586.2**	**1,850.3**	**2,035.7**	**2,101.9**	**2,156.9**	**2,186.5**	**2,231.1**	**2,293.6**	**100.0**	**100.0**	**100.0**	**100.0**	**100.0**	**100.0**	**100.0**	**100.0**	**100.0**	**100.0**
White	1,115.6	1,104.7	1,228.4	1,258.5	1,348.0	1,381.9	1,413.3	1,428.7	1,445.3	1,465.0	84.4	82.4	77.4	68.0	66.2	65.7	65.5	65.3	64.8	63.9
Total minority	134.5	144.0	190.5	359.4	421.0	448.1	475.4	495.7	519.4	548.3	10.2	10.7	12.0	19.4	20.7	21.3	22.0	22.7	23.3	23.9
Black	78.5	75.1	83.9	157.9	189.6	204.5	220.4	233.2	247.2	263.5	5.9	5.6	5.3	8.5	9.3	9.7	10.2	10.7	11.1	11.5
Hispanic	26.4	32.1	47.2	95.4	112.3	119.6	125.8	130.7	135.8	140.9	2.0	2.4	3.0	5.2	5.5	5.7	5.8	6.0	6.1	6.1
Asian/Pacific Islander	24.5	31.6	53.2	95.8	107.1	111.5	115.9	118.4	121.9	127.8	1.9	2.4	3.4	5.2	5.3	5.3	5.4	5.4	5.5	5.6
American Indian/Alaska Native	5.1	5.2	6.2	10.3	11.9	12.5	13.4	13.4	14.5	16.1	0.4	0.4	0.4	0.6	0.6	0.6	0.6	0.6	0.6	0.7
Nonresident alien	72.4	92.2	167.3	232.3	266.6	272.0	268.1	262.1	266.4	280.3	5.5	6.9	10.5	12.6	13.1	12.9	12.4	12.0	11.9	12.2
Male	**707.9**	**672.2**	**737.4**	**779.6**	**846.8**	**866.5**	**878.8**	**877.2**	**887.3**	**910.3**	**100.0**	**100.0**	**100.0**	**100.0**	**100.0**	**100.0**	**100.0**	**100.0**	**100.0**	**100.0**
White	589.1	538.5	538.8	502.6	531.6	543.0	552.9	551.2	553.3	559.7	83.2	80.1	73.1	64.5	62.8	62.7	62.9	62.8	62.4	61.5
Total minority	63.7	65.0	82.1	135.1	152.7	160.8	168.0	172.7	178.3	186.2	9.0	9.7	11.1	17.3	18.0	18.6	19.1	19.7	20.1	20.5
Black	32.0	28.2	29.3	48.9	56.7	60.5	63.9	66.7	69.4	73.5	4.5	4.2	4.0	6.3	6.7	7.0	7.3	7.6	7.8	8.1
Hispanic	14.6	15.7	20.6	36.5	41.7	44.3	46.2	47.5	49.0	50.2	2.1	2.3	2.8	4.7	4.9	5.1	5.3	5.4	5.5	5.5
Asian/Pacific Islander	14.4	18.6	29.7	45.8	50.0	51.4	53.1	53.8	54.9	57.2	2.0	2.8	4.0	5.9	5.9	5.9	6.0	6.1	6.2	6.3
American Indian/Alaska Native	2.7	2.5	2.6	3.8	4.3	4.5	4.7	4.7	4.9	5.3	0.4	0.4	0.3	0.5	0.5	0.5	0.5	0.5	0.6	0.6
Nonresident alien	55.1	68.7	116.4	142.0	162.5	162.7	157.9	153.3	155.7	164.5	7.8	10.2	15.8	18.2	19.2	18.8	18.0	17.5	17.5	18.1
Female	**614.6**	**668.7**	**848.8**	**1,070.7**	**1,188.8**	**1,235.3**	**1,278.1**	**1,309.3**	**1,343.9**	**1,383.3**	**100.0**	**100.0**	**100.0**	**100.0**	**100.0**	**100.0**	**100.0**	**100.0**	**100.0**	**100.0**
White	526.5	566.2	689.5	756.0	816.4	838.8	860.4	877.5	892.0	905.3	85.7	84.7	81.2	70.6	68.7	67.9	67.3	67.0	66.4	65.4
Total minority	70.8	79.0	108.3	224.4	268.3	287.3	307.5	323.0	341.1	362.1	11.5	11.8	12.8	21.0	22.6	23.3	24.1	24.7	25.4	26.2
Black	46.5	46.9	54.6	109.0	132.9	143.9	156.4	166.4	177.7	190.0	7.6	7.0	6.4	10.2	11.2	11.7	12.2	12.7	13.2	13.7
Hispanic	11.8	16.4	26.6	58.8	70.6	75.2	79.5	83.2	86.8	90.7	1.9	2.4	3.1	5.5	5.9	6.1	6.2	6.4	6.5	6.6
Asian/Pacific Islander	10.1	13.0	23.6	50.0	57.1	60.1	62.8	64.6	67.0	70.6	1.6	1.9	2.8	4.7	4.8	4.9	4.9	5.0	5.0	5.1
American Indian/Alaska Native	2.4	2.7	3.6	6.5	7.7	8.1	8.7	8.7	9.5	10.8	0.4	0.4	0.4	0.6	0.6	0.7	0.7	0.7	0.7	0.8
Nonresident alien	17.3	23.5	50.9	90.3	104.1	109.2	110.2	108.8	110.8	115.9	2.8	3.5	6.0	8.4	8.8	8.8	8.6	8.3	8.2	8.4

See notes at end of table.

Table 226. Total fall enrollment in degree-granting institutions, by race/ethnicity, sex, attendance status, and level of student: Selected years, 1976 through 2007—Continued

Race/ethnicity, sex, attendance status, and level of student	Fall enrollment (in thousands)										Percentage distribution of students									
	1976	1980	1990	2000	2002	2003	2004	2005	2006	2007	1976	1980	1990	2000	2002	2003	2004	2005	2006	2007
1	2	3	4	5	6	7	8	9	10	11	12	13	14	15	16	17	18	19	20	21
First-professional, total	**244.1**	**276.8**	**273.4**	**306.6**	**319.0**	**329.2**	**334.5**	**337.0**	**343.4**	**350.8**	**100.0**	**100.0**	**100.0**	**100.0**	**100.0**	**100.0**	**100.0**	**100.0**	**100.0**	**100.0**
White	220.0	247.7	221.5	220.1	227.4	234.4	238.2	238.1	241.7	244.7	90.1	89.5	81.0	71.8	71.3	71.2	71.2	70.7	70.4	69.8
Total minority	21.1	26.3	46.5	78.1	83.3	86.4	88.1	90.8	93.4	97.3	8.6	9.5	17.0	25.5	26.1	26.3	26.3	27.0	27.2	27.7
Black	11.2	12.8	15.9	23.5	25.3	25.9	25.9	26.0	26.8	27.3	4.6	4.6	5.8	7.7	7.9	7.9	7.7	7.7	7.8	7.8
Hispanic	4.5	6.5	10.7	15.4	16.1	16.9	17.0	17.7	18.4	19.3	1.9	2.4	3.9	5.0	5.1	5.1	5.1	5.3	5.4	5.5
Asian/Pacific Islander	4.1	6.1	18.7	36.8	39.6	41.3	42.9	44.6	45.7	48.0	1.7	2.2	6.8	12.0	12.4	12.6	12.8	13.2	13.3	13.7
American Indian/Alaska Native	1.3	0.8	1.1	2.3	2.2	2.3	2.4	2.5	2.5	2.6	0.5	0.3	0.4	0.8	0.7	0.7	0.7	0.7	0.7	0.7
Nonresident alien	3.1	2.9	5.4	8.4	8.3	8.4	8.2	8.1	8.4	8.8	1.3	1.0	2.0	2.7	2.6	2.5	2.5	2.4	2.5	2.5
Male	**189.6**	**198.5**	**166.8**	**163.9**	**162.9**	**166.4**	**168.4**	**169.8**	**173.8**	**178.0**	**100.0**	**100.0**	**100.0**	**100.0**	**100.0**	**100.0**	**100.0**	**100.0**	**100.0**	**100.0**
White	172.4	179.5	137.8	122.0	120.7	123.6	125.2	125.6	128.3	130.5	90.9	90.5	82.6	74.4	74.1	74.3	74.3	74.0	73.8	73.3
Total minority	14.7	16.7	25.3	36.8	37.4	38.0	38.7	39.8	40.9	42.9	7.7	8.4	15.1	22.4	22.9	22.9	23.0	23.4	23.6	24.1
Black	7.2	7.4	7.4	9.5	9.7	9.8	9.8	9.9	10.3	10.5	3.8	3.7	4.4	5.8	6.0	5.9	5.8	5.8	5.9	5.9
Hispanic	3.5	4.6	6.4	8.0	8.1	8.2	8.3	8.6	8.9	9.4	1.8	2.3	3.8	4.9	5.0	5.0	4.9	5.1	5.1	5.3
Asian/Pacific Islander	2.9	4.1	10.8	18.1	18.5	18.8	19.4	20.1	20.5	21.7	1.5	2.1	6.5	11.1	11.3	11.3	11.5	11.9	11.8	12.2
American Indian/Alaska Native	1.0	0.5	0.6	1.2	1.1	1.1	1.2	1.2	1.2	1.3	0.5	0.3	0.4	0.7	0.7	0.7	0.7	0.7	0.7	0.7
Nonresident alien	2.5	2.3	3.8	5.1	4.8	4.7	4.5	4.4	4.5	4.6	1.3	1.1	2.3	3.1	2.9	2.8	2.7	2.6	2.6	2.6
Female	**54.5**	**78.4**	**106.6**	**142.7**	**156.1**	**162.9**	**166.1**	**167.2**	**169.6**	**172.8**	**100.0**	**100.0**	**100.0**	**100.0**	**100.0**	**100.0**	**100.0**	**100.0**	**100.0**	**100.0**
White	47.6	68.1	83.7	98.1	106.6	110.8	113.0	112.5	113.3	114.2	87.3	86.9	78.5	68.7	68.3	68.0	68.0	67.3	66.8	66.1
Total minority	6.4	9.6	21.3	41.3	46.0	48.4	49.4	51.0	52.4	54.4	11.7	12.3	20.0	28.9	29.4	29.7	29.8	30.5	30.9	31.5
Black	3.9	5.5	8.5	14.0	15.6	16.1	16.1	16.2	16.5	16.8	7.2	7.0	8.0	9.8	10.0	9.9	9.7	9.7	9.7	9.7
Hispanic	1.0	1.9	4.3	7.4	8.0	8.7	8.6	9.1	9.5	10.0	1.9	2.4	4.0	5.2	5.2	5.3	5.2	5.5	5.6	5.8
Asian/Pacific Islander	1.1	2.0	7.9	18.7	21.2	22.5	23.5	24.5	25.2	26.4	2.1	2.6	7.4	13.1	13.5	13.8	14.1	14.6	14.8	15.3
American Indian/Alaska Native	0.2	0.3	0.5	1.1	1.2	1.2	1.2	1.3	1.3	1.3	0.4	0.3	0.5	0.8	0.7	0.7	0.7	0.8	0.8	0.8
Nonresident alien	0.5	0.6	1.6	3.3	3.5	3.7	3.7	3.7	3.9	4.2	1.0	0.8	1.5	2.3	2.3	2.2	2.2	2.2	2.3	2.4

NOTE: Race categories exclude persons of Hispanic ethnicity. Because of underreporting and nonreporting of racial/ethnic data, some figures are slightly lower than corresponding data in other tables. Data through 1990 are for institutions of higher education, while later data are for degree-granting institutions. Degree-granting institutions grant associate's or higher degrees and participate in Title IV federal financial aid programs. The degree-granting classification is very similar to the earlier higher education classification, but it includes more 2-year colleges and excludes a few higher education institutions that did not grant degrees. (See Guide to Sources for details.) Detail may not sum to totals because of rounding.

SOURCE: U.S. Department of Education, National Center for Education Statistics, Higher Education General Information Survey (HEGIS), "Fall Enrollment in Colleges and Universities" surveys, 1976 and 1980; and 1990 through 2007 Integrated Postsecondary Education Data System (IPEDS), "Fall Enrollment Survey" (IPEDS-EF:90), and Spring 2001 through Spring 2008. (This table was prepared October 2008.)

Table 227. Total fall enrollment in degree-granting institutions, by race/ethnicity of student and type and control of institution: Selected years, 1976 through 2007

Race/ethnicity of student and type and control of institution	Fall enrollment (in thousands)										Percentage distribution of students									
	1976	1980	1990	2000	2002	2003	2004	2005	2006	2007	1976	1980	1990	2000	2002	2003	2004	2005	2006	2007
1	2	3	4	5	6	7	8	9	10	11	12	13	14	15	16	17	18	19	20	21
All students, total	**10,985.6**	**12,086.8**	**13,818.6**	**15,312.3**	**16,611.7**	**16,911.5**	**17,272.0**	**17,487.5**	**17,758.9**	**18,248.1**	**100.0**	**100.0**	**100.0**	**100.0**	**100.0**	**100.0**	**100.0**	**100.0**	**100.0**	**100.0**
White	9,076.1	9,833.0	10,722.5	10,462.1	11,140.2	11,280.9	11,422.8	11,495.4	11,572.4	11,756.2	82.6	81.4	77.6	68.3	67.1	66.7	66.1	65.7	65.2	64.4
Total minority	1,690.8	1,948.8	2,704.7	4,321.5	4,880.5	5,032.9	5,259.1	5,407.2	5,590.6	5,867.4	15.4	16.1	19.6	28.2	29.4	29.8	30.4	30.9	31.5	32.2
Black	1,033.0	1,106.8	1,247.0	1,730.3	1,978.7	2,068.4	2,164.7	2,214.6	2,279.6	2,383.4	9.4	9.2	9.0	11.3	11.9	12.2	12.5	12.7	12.8	13.1
Hispanic	383.8	471.7	782.4	1,461.8	1,661.7	1,716.3	1,809.6	1,882.0	1,964.3	2,076.2	3.5	3.9	5.7	9.5	10.0	10.1	10.5	10.8	11.1	11.4
Asian/Pacific Islander	197.9	286.4	572.4	978.2	1,074.2	1,075.6	1,108.7	1,134.4	1,165.5	1,217.9	1.8	2.4	4.1	6.4	6.5	6.4	6.4	6.5	6.6	6.7
American Indian/Alaska Native	76.1	83.9	102.8	151.2	165.9	172.6	176.1	176.3	181.1	190.0	0.7	0.7	0.7	1.0	1.0	1.0	1.0	1.0	1.0	1.0
Nonresident alien	218.7	305.0	391.5	528.7	590.9	597.7	590.2	584.8	595.9	624.5	2.0	2.5	2.8	3.5	3.6	3.5	3.4	3.3	3.4	3.4
Public	8,641.0	9,456.4	10,844.7	11,752.8	12,752.0	12,858.7	12,980.1	13,021.8	13,180.1	13,490.8	100.0	100.0	100.0	100.0	100.0	100.0	100.0	100.0	100.0	100.0
White	7,094.5	7,656.1	8,385.4	7,963.4	8,490.5	8,534.0	8,546.3	8,518.2	8,540.5	8,640.3	82.1	81.0	77.3	67.8	66.6	66.4	65.8	65.4	64.8	64.0
Total minority	1,401.2	1,596.2	2,199.2	3,446.3	3,867.4	3,936.7	4,062.4	4,130.8	4,256.6	4,448.8	16.2	16.9	20.3	29.3	30.3	30.6	31.3	31.7	32.3	33.0
Black	831.2	876.1	976.4	1,319.2	1,487.0	1,532.7	1,574.6	1,580.4	1,612.6	1,667.6	9.6	9.3	9.0	11.2	11.7	11.9	12.1	12.1	12.2	12.4
Hispanic	336.8	406.2	671.4	1,229.3	1,388.7	1,414.8	1,477.4	1,525.6	1,594.3	1,685.4	3.9	4.3	6.2	10.5	10.9	11.0	11.4	11.7	12.1	12.5
Asian/Pacific Islander	165.7	239.7	461.0	770.5	851.6	845.0	866.1	881.9	903.8	942.5	1.9	2.5	4.3	6.6	6.7	6.6	6.7	6.8	6.9	7.0
American Indian/Alaska Native	67.5	74.2	90.4	127.3	140.0	144.3	144.4	143.0	145.9	153.3	0.8	0.8	0.8	1.1	1.1	1.1	1.1	1.1	1.1	1.1
Nonresident alien	145.3	204.2	260.0	343.1	394.1	387.9	371.4	372.8	383.1	401.7	1.7	2.2	2.4	2.9	3.1	3.0	2.9	2.9	2.9	3.0
Private	2,344.6	2,630.4	2,973.9	3,559.5	3,859.7	4,052.8	4,291.9	4,465.6	4,578.7	4,757.3	100.0	100.0	100.0	100.0	100.0	100.0	100.0	100.0	100.0	100.0
White	1,981.6	2,176.9	2,337.0	2,498.7	2,649.8	2,746.9	2,876.5	2,977.3	3,032.0	3,116.0	84.5	82.8	78.6	70.2	68.7	67.8	67.0	66.7	66.2	65.5
Total minority	289.6	352.7	505.5	875.2	1,013.2	1,096.2	1,196.7	1,276.4	1,333.9	1,418.6	12.4	13.4	17.0	24.6	26.3	27.0	27.9	28.6	29.1	29.8
Black	201.8	230.7	270.6	411.1	491.6	535.7	590.1	634.2	667.0	715.7	8.6	8.8	9.1	11.5	12.7	13.2	13.7	14.2	14.6	15.0
Hispanic	47.0	65.6	111.0	232.5	273.1	301.5	332.2	356.4	370.1	390.7	2.0	2.5	3.7	6.5	7.1	7.4	7.7	8.0	8.1	8.2
Asian/Pacific Islander	32.2	46.7	111.5	207.7	222.6	230.6	242.6	252.4	261.7	275.4	1.4	1.8	3.7	5.8	5.8	5.7	5.7	5.7	5.7	5.8
American Indian/Alaska Native	8.6	9.7	12.4	23.9	25.9	28.4	31.8	33.3	35.2	36.7	0.4	0.4	0.4	0.7	0.7	0.7	0.7	0.7	0.8	0.8
Nonresident alien	73.4	100.8	131.4	185.6	196.8	209.7	218.8	212.0	212.8	222.8	3.1	3.8	4.4	5.2	5.1	5.2	5.1	4.7	4.6	4.7
4-year, total	**7,106.5**	**7,565.4**	**8,578.6**	**9,363.9**	**10,082.3**	**10,417.2**	**10,726.2**	**10,999.4**	**11,240.3**	**11,630.2**	**100.0**	**100.0**	**100.0**	**100.0**	**100.0**	**100.0**	**100.0**	**100.0**	**100.0**	**100.0**
White	5,999.0	6,274.5	6,768.1	6,658.0	7,053.8	7,202.8	7,359.0	7,496.9	7,603.4	7,781.0	84.4	82.9	78.9	71.1	70.0	69.1	68.6	68.2	67.6	66.9
Total minority	931.0	1,049.9	1,486.1	2,266.1	2,540.3	2,710.0	2,868.0	3,009.5	3,134.4	3,320.5	13.1	13.9	17.3	24.2	25.2	26.0	26.7	27.4	27.9	28.6
Black	603.7	634.3	722.8	995.4	1,119.7	1,188.5	1,258.9	1,313.4	1,361.7	1,441.7	8.5	8.4	8.4	10.6	11.1	11.4	11.7	11.9	12.1	12.4
Hispanic	173.6	216.6	358.2	617.9	702.9	783.7	837.2	900.5	950.0	1,008.7	2.4	2.9	4.2	6.6	7.0	7.5	7.8	8.2	8.5	8.7
Asian/Pacific Islander	118.7	162.1	357.2	576.3	633.1	650.3	678.0	700.0	722.7	768.1	1.7	2.1	4.2	6.2	6.3	6.2	6.3	6.4	6.4	6.5
American Indian/Alaska Native	35.0	36.9	47.9	76.5	84.6	90.4	93.9	95.6	100.0	108.6	0.5	0.5	0.6	0.8	0.8	0.9	0.9	0.9	0.9	0.9
Nonresident alien	176.5	240.9	324.3	439.7	488.3	501.5	499.2	493.1	502.5	528.7	2.5	3.2	3.8	4.7	4.8	4.8	4.7	4.5	4.5	4.5
Public	4,892.9	5,127.6	5,848.2	6,055.4	6,481.6	6,649.4	6,736.5	6,837.6	6,955.0	7,166.7	100.0	100.0	100.0	100.0	100.0	100.0	100.0	100.0	100.0	100.0
White	4,120.2	4,243.0	4,605.6	4,311.2	4,551.7	4,611.0	4,642.9	4,678.1	4,720.8	4,813.6	84.2	82.7	78.8	71.2	70.2	69.3	68.9	68.4	67.9	67.2
Total minority	666.7	740.8	1,046.2	1,486.4	1,636.2	1,744.7	1,811.5	1,876.9	1,942.8	2,045.3	13.6	14.4	17.9	24.5	25.2	26.2	26.9	27.5	27.9	28.5
Black	421.8	438.2	495.1	627.8	682.5	717.9	741.2	754.0	771.0	801.7	8.6	8.5	8.5	10.4	10.5	10.8	11.0	11.0	11.1	11.2
Hispanic	129.3	156.4	262.5	420.0	468.1	528.4	555.8	595.6	629.8	668.6	2.6	3.1	4.5	6.9	7.2	7.9	8.3	8.7	9.1	9.3
Asian/Pacific Islander	87.5	117.2	250.6	381.3	422.8	432.0	447.4	460.1	473.2	498.5	1.8	2.3	4.3	6.3	6.5	6.5	6.6	6.7	6.8	7.0
American Indian/Alaska Native	28.2	29.0	38.0	57.2	62.7	66.4	67.0	67.2	69.7	76.5	0.6	0.6	0.7	0.9	1.0	1.0	1.0	1.0	1.0	1.1
Nonresident alien	106.0	143.8	196.4	257.8	293.7	293.8	282.2	282.6	291.4	307.8	2.2	2.8	3.4	4.3	4.5	4.4	4.2	4.1	4.2	4.3
Private	2,213.6	2,437.8	2,730.3	3,308.5	3,600.7	3,767.8	3,989.6	4,161.8	4,285.3	4,463.5	100.0	100.0	100.0	100.0	100.0	100.0	100.0	100.0	100.0	100.0
White	1,878.8	2,031.5	2,162.5	2,346.9	2,502.1	2,591.8	2,716.1	2,818.8	2,882.6	2,967.5	84.9	83.3	79.2	70.9	69.5	68.8	68.1	67.7	67.3	66.5
Total minority	264.3	309.2	439.8	779.7	904.1	968.3	1,056.5	1,132.5	1,191.6	1,275.3	11.9	12.7	16.1	23.6	25.1	25.7	26.5	27.2	27.8	28.6
Black	182.0	196.1	227.7	367.6	437.2	470.7	517.7	559.4	591.6	640.0	8.2	8.0	8.3	11.1	12.1	12.5	13.0	13.4	13.8	14.3
Hispanic	44.3	60.2	95.7	197.9	234.7	255.3	281.3	304.9	320.2	340.1	2.0	2.5	3.5	6.0	6.5	6.8	7.1	7.3	7.6	7.6
Asian/Pacific Islander	31.2	44.9	106.6	195.0	210.3	218.3	230.5	239.8	249.5	263.1	1.4	1.8	3.9	5.9	5.8	5.8	5.8	5.8	5.8	5.9
American Indian/Alaska Native	6.8	7.9	9.9	19.3	21.9	23.9	26.9	28.4	30.3	32.1	0.3	0.3	0.4	0.6	0.6	0.6	0.7	0.7	0.7	0.7
Nonresident alien	70.5	97.1	127.9	181.9	194.5	207.7	217.0	210.4	211.1	220.8	3.2	4.0	4.7	5.5	5.4	5.5	5.4	5.1	4.9	4.9

See notes at end of table.

Table 227. Total fall enrollment in degree-granting institutions, by race/ethnicity of student and type and control of institution: Selected years, 1976 through 2007—Continued

Race/ethnicity of student and type and control of institution	Fall enrollment (in thousands)										Percentage distribution of students									
	1976	1980	1990	2000	2002	2003	2004	2005	2006	2007	1976	1980	1990	2000	2002	2003	2004	2005	2006	2007
1	2	3	4	5	6	7	8	9	10	11	12	13	14	15	16	17	18	19	20	21
2-year, total	3,879.1	4,521.4	5,240.1	5,948.4	6,529.4	6,494.2	6,545.9	6,488.1	6,518.5	6,617.9	100.0	100.0	100.0	100.0	100.0	100.0	100.0	100.0	100.0	100.0
White	3,077.1	3,558.5	3,954.3	3,804.1	4,086.5	4,078.1	4,063.8	3,998.6	3,969.1	3,975.2	79.3	78.7	75.5	64.0	62.6	62.8	62.1	61.6	60.9	60.1
Total minority	759.8	898.9	1,218.6	2,055.4	2,340.3	2,319.9	2,391.2	2,397.7	2,456.1	2,546.9	19.6	19.9	23.3	34.6	35.8	35.7	36.5	37.0	37.7	38.5
Black	429.3	472.5	524.3	734.9	859.1	879.8	905.8	901.1	917.9	941.7	11.1	10.4	10.0	12.4	13.2	13.5	13.8	13.9	14.1	14.2
Hispanic	210.2	255.1	424.2	843.9	958.9	932.5	972.4	981.5	1,014.3	1,067.4	5.4	5.6	8.1	14.2	14.7	14.4	14.9	15.1	15.6	16.1
Asian/Pacific Islander	79.2	124.3	215.2	401.9	441.0	425.3	430.7	434.4	442.8	456.4	2.0	2.8	4.1	6.8	6.8	6.5	6.6	6.7	6.8	6.9
American Indian/Alaska Native	41.2	47.0	54.9	74.7	81.3	82.3	82.2	80.7	81.1	81.4	1.1	1.0	1.0	1.3	1.2	1.3	1.3	1.2	1.2	1.2
Nonresident alien	42.2	64.1	67.1	89.0	102.6	96.2	90.9	91.8	93.4	95.8	1.1	1.4	1.3	1.5	1.6	1.5	1.4	1.4	1.4	1.4
Public	3,748.1	4,328.8	4,996.5	5,697.4	6,270.4	6,209.3	6,243.6	6,184.2	6,225.1	6,324.1	100.0	100.0	100.0	100.0	100.0	100.0	100.0	100.0	100.0	100.0
White	2,974.3	3,413.1	3,779.8	3,652.2	3,938.8	3,923.1	3,903.4	3,840.1	3,819.7	3,826.7	79.4	78.8	75.7	64.1	62.8	63.2	62.5	62.1	61.4	60.5
Total minority	734.5	855.4	1,153.0	1,959.9	2,231.2	2,192.0	2,251.0	2,253.9	2,313.8	2,403.6	19.6	19.8	23.1	34.4	35.6	35.3	36.1	36.4	37.2	38.0
Black	409.5	437.9	481.4	691.4	804.7	814.8	833.4	826.3	842.5	865.9	10.9	10.1	9.6	12.1	12.8	13.1	13.3	13.4	13.5	13.7
Hispanic	207.5	249.8	408.9	809.2	920.5	886.4	921.6	930.0	964.4	1,016.8	5.5	5.8	8.2	14.2	14.7	14.3	14.8	15.0	15.5	16.1
Asian/Pacific Islander	78.2	122.5	210.3	389.2	428.7	413.0	418.6	421.8	430.6	444.1	2.1	2.8	4.2	6.8	6.8	6.7	6.7	6.8	6.9	7.0
American Indian/Alaska Native	39.3	45.2	52.4	70.1	77.2	77.8	77.4	75.7	76.2	76.8	1.0	1.0	1.0	1.2	1.2	1.3	1.2	1.2	1.2	1.2
Nonresident alien	39.2	60.3	63.6	85.2	100.4	94.1	89.2	90.2	91.6	93.9	1.0	1.4	1.3	1.5	1.6	1.5	1.4	1.5	1.5	1.5
Private	131.0	192.6	243.6	251.0	259.0	285.0	302.3	303.8	293.4	293.8	100.0	100.0	100.0	100.0	100.0	100.0	100.0	100.0	100.0	100.0
White	102.8	145.4	174.5	151.8	147.7	155.1	160.4	158.4	149.4	148.5	78.5	75.5	71.6	60.5	57.0	54.4	53.1	52.1	50.9	50.6
Total minority	25.3	43.5	65.6	95.5	109.1	127.9	140.2	143.8	142.3	143.3	19.3	22.6	26.9	38.0	42.1	44.9	46.4	47.3	48.5	48.8
Black	19.8	34.6	42.9	43.5	54.4	65.0	72.5	74.8	75.4	75.7	15.1	17.9	17.6	17.3	21.0	22.8	24.0	24.6	25.7	25.8
Hispanic	2.6	5.3	15.3	34.7	38.3	46.2	50.8	51.4	49.8	50.6	2.0	2.8	6.3	13.8	14.8	16.2	16.8	16.9	17.0	17.2
Asian/Pacific Islander	0.9	1.8	4.9	12.7	12.3	12.3	12.1	12.6	12.2	12.3	0.7	0.9	2.0	5.1	4.7	4.3	4.0	4.2	4.2	4.2
American Indian/Alaska Native	1.8	1.8	2.5	4.5	4.1	4.4	4.9	5.0	4.9	4.6	1.4	0.9	1.0	1.8	1.6	1.6	1.6	1.6	1.7	1.6
Nonresident alien	3.0	3.7	3.5	3.8	2.2	2.0	1.7	1.6	1.7	2.0	2.3	1.9	1.4	1.5	0.9	0.7	0.6	0.5	0.6	0.7

SOURCE: U.S. Department of Education, National Center for Education Statistics, Higher Education General Information Survey (HEGIS), "Fall Enrollment in Colleges and Universities" surveys, 1976 and 1980; and 1990 through 2007 Integrated Postsecondary Education Data System (IPEDS), "Fall Enrollment Survey" (IPEDS-EF:90), and Spring 2001 through Spring 2008. (This table was prepared October 2008.)

NOTE: Race categories exclude persons of Hispanic ethnicity. Because of underreporting and nonreporting of racial/ethnic data, some figures are slightly lower than corresponding data in other tables. Data through 1990 are for institutions of higher education, while later data are for degree-granting institutions. Degree-granting institutions grant associate's or higher degrees and participate in Title IV federal financial aid programs. The degree-granting classification is very similar to the earlier higher education classification, but it includes more 2-year colleges and excludes a few higher education institutions that did not grant degrees. (See Guide to Sources for details.) Detail may not sum to totals because of rounding.

Table 228. Fall enrollment in degree-granting institutions, by race/ethnicity of student and by state or jurisdiction: 2007

State or jurisdiction	Total	Minority							Percentage distribution							
		White	Total	Black	Hispanic	Asian/ Pacific Islander	American Indian/ Alaska Native	Non-resident alien	Total	White	Minority					
											Total	Black	Hispanic	Asian/ Pacific Islander	American Indian/ Alaska Native	Non-resident alien
1	2	3	4	5	6	7	8	9	10	11	12	13	14	15	16	17
United States	**18,248,128**	**11,756,236**	**5,867,418**	**2,383,351**	**2,076,156**	**1,217,910**	**190,001**	**624,474**	**100.0**	**64.4**	**32.2**	**13.1**	**11.4**	**6.7**	**1.0**	**3.4**
Alabama	268,183	173,823	88,060	77,410	4,575	3,980	2,095	6,300	100.0	64.8	32.8	28.9	1.7	1.5	0.8	2.3
Alaska	30,616	21,439	8,377	1,006	1,251	1,708	4,412	800	100.0	70.0	27.4	3.3	4.1	5.6	14.4	2.6
Arizona	624,147	390,606	211,842	73,707	95,162	23,807	19,156	21,699	100.0	62.6	33.9	11.8	15.2	3.8	3.1	3.5
Arkansas	152,168	112,516	36,453	28,620	3,743	2,366	1,724	3,199	100.0	73.9	24.0	18.8	2.5	1.6	1.1	2.1
California	2,529,522	1,054,586	1,394,667	195,687	698,027	477,765	23,188	80,269	100.0	41.7	55.1	7.7	27.6	18.9	0.9	3.2
Colorado	310,637	232,152	73,540	19,861	36,446	12,656	4,577	4,945	100.0	74.7	23.7	6.4	11.7	4.1	1.5	1.6
Connecticut	179,005	127,084	44,175	19,385	15,388	8,238	664	7,746	100.0	71.0	24.7	10.8	8.9	4.6	0.4	4.3
Delaware	52,343	36,411	14,422	10,362	2,112	1,768	130	1,510	100.0	69.6	27.6	19.8	4.0	3.4	0.3	2.9
District of Columbia	115,153	53,357	54,878	41,641	5,626	7,089	522	6,918	100.0	46.3	47.7	36.2	4.9	6.2	0.5	6.0
Florida	913,793	507,172	377,467	162,670	177,632	33,295	3,870	29,154	100.0	55.5	41.3	17.8	19.4	3.6	0.4	3.2
Georgia	453,711	262,953	177,299	143,329	13,864	18,712	1,394	13,459	100.0	58.0	39.1	31.6	3.1	4.1	0.3	3.0
Hawaii	66,601	16,593	44,415	1,305	2,029	40,718	363	5,593	100.0	24.9	66.7	2.0	3.0	61.1	0.5	8.4
Idaho	78,846	69,287	7,487	731	4,107	1,637	1,012	2,072	100.0	87.9	9.5	0.9	5.2	2.1	1.3	2.6
Illinois	837,018	537,737	272,306	121,450	99,164	48,795	2,897	26,975	100.0	64.2	32.5	14.5	11.8	5.8	0.3	3.2
Indiana	380,477	310,273	55,908	34,120	12,026	8,314	1,448	14,296	100.0	81.5	14.7	9.0	3.2	2.2	0.4	3.8
Iowa	256,259	215,715	33,141	17,123	8,925	5,550	1,543	7,403	100.0	84.2	12.9	6.7	3.5	2.2	0.6	2.9
Kansas	194,102	154,967	29,968	12,176	9,529	5,098	3,165	9,167	100.0	79.8	15.4	6.3	4.9	2.6	1.6	4.7
Kentucky	258,213	222,845	31,026	23,712	3,369	3,118	827	4,342	100.0	86.3	12.0	9.2	1.3	1.2	0.3	1.7
Louisiana	224,754	139,707	79,064	66,282	5,959	5,193	1,630	5,983	100.0	62.2	35.2	29.5	2.7	2.3	0.7	2.7
Maine	67,173	61,547	4,215	1,215	874	1,235	891	1,411	100.0	91.6	6.3	1.8	1.3	1.8	1.3	2.1
Maryland	327,597	184,070	129,734	91,521	14,022	22,752	1,439	13,793	100.0	56.2	39.6	27.9	4.3	6.9	0.4	4.2
Massachusetts	463,366	329,669	105,357	37,817	31,383	34,210	1,947	28,340	100.0	71.1	22.7	8.2	6.8	7.4	0.4	6.1
Michigan	643,279	484,157	134,699	89,090	18,759	21,259	5,591	24,423	100.0	75.3	20.9	13.8	2.9	3.3	0.9	3.8
Minnesota	392,393	314,775	66,719	35,069	9,063	17,666	4,921	10,899	100.0	80.2	17.0	8.9	2.3	4.5	1.3	2.8
Mississippi	155,232	88,413	64,743	61,261	1,489	1,389	604	2,076	100.0	57.0	41.7	39.5	1.0	0.9	0.4	1.3
Missouri	384,366	300,035	73,675	48,815	11,743	10,653	2,464	10,656	100.0	78.1	19.2	12.7	3.1	2.8	0.6	2.8
Montana	47,371	40,035	6,266	320	909	611	4,426	1,070	100.0	84.5	13.2	0.7	1.9	1.3	9.3	2.3
Nebraska	127,378	108,753	15,262	6,082	5,051	3,108	1,021	3,363	100.0	85.4	12.0	4.8	4.0	2.4	0.8	2.6
Nevada	116,276	69,514	43,802	9,834	18,856	13,414	1,698	2,960	100.0	59.8	37.7	8.5	16.2	11.5	1.5	2.5
New Hampshire	70,724	63,112	5,736	1,477	1,843	1,938	478	1,876	100.0	89.2	8.1	2.1	2.6	2.7	0.7	2.7
New Jersey	398,136	232,585	149,061	56,496	56,710	34,588	1,267	16,490	100.0	58.4	37.4	14.2	14.2	8.7	0.3	4.1
New Mexico	134,375	56,621	73,886	4,008	55,138	2,706	12,034	3,868	100.0	42.1	55.0	3.0	41.0	2.0	9.0	2.9
New York	1,172,811	696,109	402,275	161,612	138,407	97,756	4,500	74,427	100.0	59.4	34.3	13.8	11.8	8.3	0.4	6.3
North Carolina	502,330	334,541	156,082	121,482	15,120	13,701	5,779	11,707	100.0	66.6	31.1	24.2	3.0	2.7	1.2	2.3
North Dakota	49,945	42,386	5,477	846	601	587	3,443	2,082	100.0	84.9	11.0	1.7	1.2	1.2	6.9	4.2
Ohio	630,497	503,776	108,554	78,169	13,784	14,073	2,528	18,167	100.0	79.9	17.2	12.4	2.2	2.2	0.4	2.9
Oklahoma	206,382	144,178	52,956	18,869	8,031	5,133	20,923	9,248	100.0	69.9	25.7	9.1	3.9	2.5	10.1	4.5
Oregon	202,928	162,464	34,396	5,135	12,088	13,792	3,381	6,068	100.0	80.1	16.9	2.5	6.0	6.8	1.7	3.0
Pennsylvania	725,397	563,113	136,669	77,618	25,163	31,806	2,082	25,615	100.0	77.6	18.8	10.7	3.5	4.4	0.3	3.5
Rhode Island	82,900	64,806	15,061	4,979	5,991	3,697	394	3,033	100.0	78.2	18.2	6.0	7.2	4.5	0.5	3.7

See notes at end of table.

Table 228. Fall enrollment in degree-granting institutions, by race/ethnicity of student and by state or jurisdiction: 2007—Continued

State or jurisdiction	Total	White	Minority					Nonresident alien	Percentage distribution							
			Total	Black	Hispanic	Asian/ Pacific Islander	American Indian/ Alaska Native		Total	White	Minority					Nonresident alien
											Total	Black	Hispanic	Asian/ Pacific Islander	American Indian/ Alaska Native	
1	2	3	4	5	6	7	8	9	10	11	12	13	14	15	16	17
South Carolina	217,755	145,723	68,855	60,347	4,053	3,570	885	3,177	100.0	66.9	31.6	27.7	1.9	1.6	0.4	1.5
South Dakota	49,747	43,424	5,397	763	580	498	3,556	926	100.0	87.3	10.8	1.5	1.2	1.0	7.1	1.9
Tennessee	297,785	220,327	70,828	58,227	5,748	5,718	1,135	6,630	100.0	74.0	23.8	19.6	1.9	1.9	0.4	2.2
Texas	1,269,098	630,579	589,604	159,492	350,776	68,139	11,197	48,915	100.0	49.7	46.5	12.6	27.6	5.4	0.9	3.9
Utah	203,679	173,975	23,254	3,079	11,179	6,608	2,388	6,450	100.0	85.4	11.4	1.5	5.5	3.2	1.2	3.2
Vermont	42,191	38,251	3,094	858	990	999	247	846	100.0	90.7	7.3	2.0	2.3	2.4	0.6	2.0
Virginia	478,268	319,728	145,703	95,054	20,250	28,045	2,354	12,837	100.0	66.9	30.5	19.9	4.2	5.9	0.5	2.7
Washington	352,075	263,229	77,897	15,326	21,743	34,471	6,357	10,949	100.0	74.8	22.1	4.4	6.2	9.8	1.8	3.1
West Virginia	116,848	101,738	12,822	7,807	2,673	1,799	543	2,288	100.0	87.1	11.0	6.7	2.3	1.5	0.5	2.0
Wisconsin	343,747	291,905	44,620	18,976	10,812	10,846	3,986	7,222	100.0	84.9	13.0	5.5	3.1	3.2	1.2	2.1
Wyoming	35,246	31,440	3,154	387	1,674	412	681	652	100.0	89.2	8.9	1.1	4.7	1.2	1.9	1.8
U.S. Service Academies	15,285	12,035	3,070	743	1,219	924	184	180	100.0	78.7	20.1	4.9	8.0	6.0	1.2	1.2
Other jurisdictions	**226,849**	**727**	**225,147**	**2,031**	**212,361**	**10,728**	**27**	**975**	**100.0**	**0.3**	**99.2**	**0.9**	**93.6**	**4.7**	**#**	**0.4**
American Samoa	1,767	5	1,568	1	1	1,566	0	194	100.0	0.3	88.7	0.1	0.1	88.6	0.0	11.0
Federated States of Micronesia	2,379	1	2,378	0	0	2,378	0	0	100.0	#	100.0	0.0	0.0	100.0	0.0	0.0
Guam	5,244	253	4,926	44	39	4,834	9	65	100.0	4.8	93.9	0.8	0.7	92.2	0.2	1.2
Marshall Islands	557	0	553	0	0	553	0	4	100.0	0.0	99.3	0.0	0.0	99.3	0.0	0.7
Northern Marianas	901	18	683	1	0	682	0	200	100.0	2.0	75.8	0.1	0.0	75.7	0.0	22.2
Palau	668	0	668	0	0	668	0	0	100.0	0.0	100.0	0.0	0.0	100.0	0.0	0.0
Puerto Rico	212,949	315	212,271	54	212,175	30	12	363	100.0	0.1	99.7	#	99.6	#	#	0.2
U.S. Virgin Islands	2,384	135	2,100	1,931	146	17	6	149	100.0	5.7	88.1	81.0	6.1	0.7	0.3	6.3

#Rounds to zero.

NOTE: Race categories exclude persons of Hispanic ethnicity. Degree-granting institutions grant associate's or higher degrees and participate in Title IV federal financial aid programs. Detail may not sum to totals because of rounding.

SOURCE: U.S. Department of Education, National Center for Education Statistics, 2007 Integrated Postsecondary Education Data System (IPEDS), Spring 2008. (This table was prepared October 2008.)

Table 229. Fall enrollment in degree-granting institutions, by race/ethnicity of student and by state or jurisdiction: 2006

State or jurisdiction	Total	Minority							Percentage distribution							
		White	Total	Black	Hispanic	Asian/Pacific Islander	American Indian/Alaska Native	Non-resident alien	Total	White	Minority					
											Total	Black	Hispanic	Asian/Pacific Islander	American Indian/Alaska Native	Non-resident alien
1	2	3	4	5	6	7	8	9	10	11	12	13	14	15	16	17
United States	17,758,870	11,572,441	5,590,555	2,279,605	1,964,319	1,165,482	181,149	595,874	100.0	65.2	31.5	12.8	11.1	6.6	1.0	3.4
Alabama	258,408	167,920	84,454	74,706	4,050	3,800	1,898	6,034	100.0	65.0	32.7	28.9	1.6	1.5	0.7	2.3
Alaska	29,853	21,141	7,813	1,034	1,117	1,581	4,081	899	100.0	70.8	26.2	3.5	3.7	5.3	13.7	3.0
Arizona	567,192	360,355	185,717	55,215	90,784	21,477	18,241	21,120	100.0	63.5	32.7	9.7	16.0	3.8	3.2	3.7
Arkansas	147,391	109,804	34,703	27,615	3,270	2,172	1,646	2,884	100.0	74.5	23.5	18.7	2.2	1.5	1.1	2.0
California	2,434,774	1,034,747	1,324,996	187,898	654,999	459,765	22,334	75,031	100.0	42.5	54.4	7.7	26.9	18.9	0.9	3.1
Colorado	308,383	232,271	70,639	17,782	36,023	12,389	4,445	5,473	100.0	75.3	22.9	5.8	11.7	4.0	1.4	1.8
Connecticut	176,716	127,253	42,550	18,867	14,902	8,081	680	6,933	100.0	72.0	24.1	10.7	8.4	4.6	0.4	3.9
Delaware	51,238	35,948	13,869	10,173	1,918	1,588	190	1,421	100.0	70.2	27.1	19.9	3.7	3.1	0.4	2.8
District of Columbia	109,505	51,407	51,256	38,900	5,202	6,710	444	6,842	100.0	46.9	46.8	35.5	4.8	6.1	0.4	6.2
Florida	885,651	496,599	360,699	158,812	166,973	31,185	3,729	28,353	100.0	56.1	40.7	17.9	18.9	3.5	0.4	3.2
Georgia	435,403	259,541	163,159	133,082	11,804	16,917	1,356	12,703	100.0	59.6	37.5	30.6	2.7	3.9	0.3	2.9
Hawaii	66,893	17,181	43,665	1,372	2,022	39,892	379	6,047	100.0	25.7	65.3	2.1	3.0	59.6	0.6	9.0
Idaho	77,872	68,678	6,956	662	3,812	1,514	968	2,238	100.0	88.2	8.9	0.9	4.9	1.9	1.2	2.9
Illinois	830,676	538,571	266,857	118,401	97,790	47,705	2,961	25,248	100.0	64.8	32.1	14.3	11.8	5.7	0.4	3.0
Indiana	368,013	302,625	52,138	31,669	11,059	7,989	1,421	13,250	100.0	82.2	14.2	8.6	3.0	2.2	0.4	3.6
Iowa	238,634	204,409	27,153	13,280	7,605	5,134	1,134	7,072	100.0	85.7	11.4	5.6	3.2	2.2	0.5	3.0
Kansas	193,146	155,644	29,008	11,733	9,153	4,983	3,139	8,494	100.0	80.6	15.0	6.1	4.7	2.6	1.6	4.4
Kentucky	248,914	215,226	29,187	22,312	3,041	3,072	752	4,501	100.0	86.5	11.7	9.0	1.2	1.2	0.3	1.8
Louisiana	224,147	140,645	77,604	65,386	5,786	5,029	1,403	5,898	100.0	62.7	34.6	29.2	2.6	2.2	0.6	2.6
Maine	66,149	60,517	4,221	1,322	842	1,161	896	1,411	100.0	91.5	6.4	2.0	1.3	1.8	1.4	2.1
Maryland	319,460	181,719	124,237	88,870	13,296	20,951	1,320	13,504	100.0	56.9	38.9	27.8	4.1	6.6	0.4	4.2
Massachusetts	451,526	324,618	99,702	36,392	28,745	32,639	1,926	27,206	100.0	71.9	22.1	8.1	6.4	7.2	0.4	6.0
Michigan	634,489	479,689	131,638	87,311	17,371	20,985	5,371	23,162	100.0	75.6	20.7	13.8	2.8	3.3	0.8	3.7
Minnesota	375,899	307,300	58,443	29,338	8,161	16,405	4,539	10,156	100.0	81.8	15.5	7.8	2.2	4.4	1.2	2.7
Mississippi	151,137	86,658	62,502	59,252	1,310	1,332	608	1,977	100.0	57.3	41.4	39.2	0.9	0.9	0.4	1.3
Missouri	377,098	296,135	71,091	47,311	11,080	10,274	2,426	9,872	100.0	78.5	18.9	12.5	2.9	2.7	0.6	2.6
Montana	47,501	40,308	6,191	290	826	549	4,526	1,002	100.0	84.9	13.0	0.6	1.7	1.2	9.5	2.1
Nebraska	124,500	107,174	14,160	5,635	4,539	2,938	1,048	3,166	100.0	86.1	11.4	4.5	3.6	2.4	0.8	2.5
Nevada	112,270	69,523	40,355	8,884	17,025	12,802	1,644	2,392	100.0	61.9	35.9	7.9	15.2	11.4	1.5	2.1
New Hampshire	70,669	63,365	5,572	1,459	1,781	1,840	492	1,732	100.0	89.7	7.9	2.1	2.5	2.6	0.7	2.5
New Jersey	385,656	227,923	142,228	54,650	53,089	33,272	1,217	15,505	100.0	59.1	36.9	14.2	13.8	8.6	0.3	4.0
New Mexico	131,828	56,265	72,869	3,861	54,690	2,641	11,677	2,694	100.0	42.7	55.3	2.9	41.5	2.0	8.9	2.0
New York	1,160,364	694,500	391,841	160,707	133,361	92,922	4,851	74,023	100.0	59.9	33.8	13.8	11.5	8.0	0.4	6.4
North Carolina	495,633	330,869	154,177	121,528	13,675	12,945	6,029	10,587	100.0	66.8	31.1	24.5	2.8	2.6	1.2	2.1
North Dakota	49,519	42,584	5,117	798	522	568	3,229	1,818	100.0	86.0	10.3	1.6	1.1	1.1	6.5	3.7
Ohio	619,942	498,179	104,447	75,639	12,845	13,468	2,495	17,316	100.0	80.4	16.8	12.2	2.1	2.2	0.4	2.8
Oklahoma	206,236	144,925	52,474	18,542	7,526	5,023	21,383	8,837	100.0	70.3	25.4	9.0	3.6	2.4	10.4	4.3
Oregon	197,594	159,740	32,018	4,832	10,860	12,966	3,360	5,836	100.0	80.8	16.2	2.4	5.5	6.6	1.7	3.0
Pennsylvania	707,132	553,601	129,281	74,113	22,835	30,366	1,967	24,250	100.0	78.3	18.3	10.5	3.2	4.3	0.3	3.4
Rhode Island	81,734	64,379	14,422	5,041	5,573	3,467	341	2,933	100.0	78.8	17.6	6.2	6.8	4.2	0.4	3.6

See notes at end of table.

Table 229. Fall enrollment in degree-granting institutions, by race/ethnicity of student and by state or jurisdiction: 2006—Continued

State or jurisdiction	Total	White	Minority					Non-resident alien	Percentage distribution							
			Total	Black	Hispanic	Asian/ Pacific Islander	American Indian/ Alaska Native		Total	White	Minority					Non-resident alien
											Total	Black	Hispanic	Asian/ Pacific Islander	American Indian/ Alaska Native	
1	2	3	4	5	6	7	8	9	10	11	12	13	14	15	16	17
South Carolina	212,422	142,731	66,418	58,560	3,651	3,349	858	3,273	100.0	67.2	31.3	27.6	1.7	1.6	0.4	1.5
South Dakota	48,931	42,777	5,254	728	487	476	3,563	900	100.0	87.4	10.7	1.5	1.0	1.0	7.3	1.8
Tennessee	290,530	215,369	69,287	57,065	5,464	5,464	1,294	5,874	100.0	74.1	23.8	19.6	1.9	1.9	0.4	2.0
Texas	1,252,709	637,680	566,964	156,044	339,190	65,059	6,671	48,065	100.0	50.9	45.3	12.5	27.1	5.2	0.5	3.8
Utah	202,151	174,907	21,780	2,747	10,185	6,603	2,245	5,464	100.0	86.5	10.8	1.4	5.0	3.3	1.1	2.7
Vermont	41,095	37,345	2,929	793	921	968	247	821	100.0	90.9	7.1	1.9	2.2	2.4	0.6	2.0
Virginia	456,172	308,033	136,556	89,979	18,298	26,040	2,239	11,583	100.0	67.5	29.9	19.7	4.0	5.7	0.5	2.5
Washington	348,154	261,736	76,245	15,015	20,748	34,150	6,332	10,173	100.0	75.2	21.9	4.3	6.0	9.8	1.8	2.9
West Virginia	100,519	89,905	8,332	5,430	1,252	1,284	366	2,282	100.0	89.4	8.3	5.4	1.2	1.3	0.4	2.3
Wisconsin	340,158	291,230	42,082	17,597	10,087	10,467	3,931	6,846	100.0	85.6	12.4	5.2	3.0	3.1	1.2	2.0
Wyoming	34,693	31,174	2,895	391	1,487	379	638	624	100.0	89.9	8.3	1.1	4.3	1.1	1.8	1.8
U.S. Service Academies	12,191	9,618	2,424	582	887	746	209	149	100.0	78.9	19.9	4.8	7.3	6.1	1.7	1.2
Other jurisdictions	226,175	661	224,728	2,100	211,213	11,389	26	786	100.0	0.3	99.4	0.9	93.4	5.0	#	0.3
American Samoa	1,607	5	1,436	0	4	1,432	0	166	100.0	0.3	89.4	0.0	0.2	89.1	0.0	10.3
Federated States of Micronesia	2,539	3	2,536	0	0	2,536	0	0	100.0	0.1	99.9	0.0	0.0	99.9	0.0	0.0
Guam	5,789	317	5,413	58	40	5,309	6	59	100.0	5.5	93.5	1.0	0.7	91.7	0.1	1.0
Marshall Islands	647	0	647	0	0	647	0	0	100.0	0.0	100.0	0.0	0.0	100.0	0.0	0.0
Northern Marianas	968	32	727	0	0	727	0	209	100.0	3.3	75.1	0.0	0.0	75.1	0.0	21.6
Palau	679	0	679	0	0	679	0	0	100.0	0.0	100.0	0.0	0.0	100.0	0.0	0.0
Puerto Rico	211,458	158	211,108	44	211,015	35	14	192	100.0	0.1	99.8	#	99.8	#	#	0.1
U.S. Virgin Islands	2,488	146	2,182	1,998	154	24	6	160	100.0	5.9	87.7	80.3	6.2	1.0	0.2	6.4

#Rounds to zero.
NOTE: Race categories exclude persons of Hispanic ethnicity. Degree-granting institutions grant associate's or higher degrees and participate in Title IV federal financial aid programs. Detail may not sum to totals because of rounding.

SOURCE: U.S. Department of Education, National Center for Education Statistics, 2006 Integrated Postsecondary Education Data System (IPEDS), Spring 2007. (This table was prepared June 2008.)

Table 230. Total number of degree-granting institutions and fall enrollment in these institutions, by type and control of institution and percentage of minority enrollment: 2007

Minority percentage of total enrollment	Total, all institution types	Public institutions								Not-for-profit institutions								For-profit institutions		
		Total	Research university, very high[1]	Research university, high[2]	Doctoral/research[3]	Master's[4]	Baccalaureate[5]	Special focus[6]	2-year	Total	Research university, very high[1]	Research university, high[2]	Doctoral/research[3]	Master's[4]	Baccalaureate[5]	Special focus[6]	2-year	Total	4-year	2-year
1	2	3	4	5	6	7	8	9	10	11	12	13	14	15	16	17	18	19	20	21
All institutions																				
Number of institutions	4,339	1,682	63	75	27	264	177	47	1,029	1,521	33	27	45	343	533	549	91	1,036	488	548
Total enrollment	18,248,128	13,490,780	1,958,392	1,421,682	381,309	2,531,979	795,513	77,786	6,324,119	3,571,150	483,670	303,612	324,909	1,307,936	791,958	325,579	33,486	1,186,198	925,873	260,325
U.S. residents	17,623,654	13,089,102	1,825,874	1,351,651	369,862	2,457,329	780,268	73,851	6,230,267	3,377,402	413,459	280,942	307,034	1,264,965	770,642	307,831	32,529	1,157,150	897,834	259,316
White	11,756,236	8,640,255	1,340,593	973,988	266,107	1,666,129	516,859	49,892	3,826,667	2,481,920	277,293	209,570	207,038	946,217	591,364	229,887	20,551	634,061	506,083	127,978
Minority	5,867,418	4,448,847	485,281	377,663	103,755	791,200	263,409	23,959	2,403,560	895,482	136,166	71,372	99,996	313,748	179,278	77,944	11,978	523,089	391,751	131,338
Black	2,383,351	1,667,616	121,028	159,229	67,420	342,853	104,670	6,480	865,936	410,014	31,575	31,572	38,046	158,959	113,761	29,798	6,303	305,721	236,278	69,443
Hispanic	2,076,156	1,685,439	134,569	124,159	16,770	275,031	113,519	4,565	1,016,826	235,267	32,571	16,326	33,871	99,996	36,503	16,486	2,514	155,450	107,350	48,100
Asian/Pacific Islander	1,217,910	942,520	215,432	78,559	12,621	147,509	35,375	8,966	444,058	226,500	69,569	21,895	26,450	55,244	24,415	27,560	1,367	48,890	37,950	10,940
American Indian/ Alaska Native	190,001	153,272	14,252	15,716	6,944	25,807	9,845	3,948	76,760	23,701	2,451	1,579	1,629	7,549	4,599	4,100	1,794	13,028	10,173	2,855
Nonresident alien	624,474	401,678	132,518	70,031	11,447	74,650	15,245	3,935	93,852	193,748	70,211	22,670	17,875	42,971	21,316	17,748	957	29,048	28,039	1,009
90.0 percent or more minority enrollment																				
Number of institutions	179	63	0	2	3	21	6	4	27	68	0	0	0	3	45	13	7	48	17	31
Total enrollment	396,335	292,302	0	19,196	23,703	115,346	33,366	2,871	97,820	68,979	0	0	0	9,735	51,405	4,863	2,976	35,054	16,720	18,334
U.S. residents	390,237	287,456	0	19,103	23,162	112,934	32,746	2,871	96,640	67,851	0	0	0	9,567	50,521	4,787	2,976	34,930	16,673	18,257
Minority	373,191	273,682	0	17,873	22,230	107,727	31,671	2,723	91,458	66,316	0	0	0	9,040	49,857	4,587	2,832	33,193	15,815	17,378
75.0 to 89.9 percent minority enrollment																				
Number of institutions	217	71	0	2	1	9	8	1	50	31	0	2	0	5	10	8	6	115	45	70
Total enrollment	804,932	683,098	0	58,336	9,065	89,568	89,254	584	436,291	43,364	0	14,396	0	13,617	8,458	4,860	2,033	78,470	39,197	39,273
U.S. residents	780,436	661,200	0	53,774	8,939	85,839	86,089	584	425,975	42,140	0	13,726	0	13,446	8,104	4,834	2,030	77,096	38,043	39,053
Minority	660,282	559,260	0	45,060	6,976	74,341	76,467	521	355,895	37,415	0	13,616	0	11,296	6,904	3,964	1,635	63,607	31,262	32,345
50.0 to 74.9 percent minority enrollment																				
Number of institutions	524	177	7	3	2	20	7	4	134	82	0	0	3	17	18	31	13	265	128	137
Total enrollment	2,398,143	1,991,883	192,953	61,938	15,380	359,169	32,522	2,743	1,327,178	139,785	0	0	43,621	56,220	21,924	13,157	4,863	266,475	188,480	77,995
U.S. residents	2,316,167	1,921,065	180,228	57,314	14,751	339,367	31,534	2,669	1,295,202	135,201	0	0	42,130	54,393	21,369	12,495	4,814	259,901	182,277	77,624
Minority	1,461,834	1,213,429	112,722	33,193	10,780	212,677	22,020	1,552	820,485	82,948	0	0	23,871	35,227	13,229	7,787	2,834	165,457	117,328	48,129
25.0 to 49.9 percent minority enrollment																				
Number of institutions	1,174	476	15	21	5	63	35	16	321	378	22	8	24	93	82	131	18	320	170	150
Total enrollment	6,037,939	4,111,813	496,200	472,305	69,615	579,817	243,456	34,256	2,216,164	1,275,543	352,269	91,434	175,107	428,477	117,993	102,195	8,068	650,583	586,439	64,144
U.S. residents	5,805,415	3,997,291	465,471	445,906	67,284	564,335	238,883	31,700	2,183,712	1,176,385	295,883	84,150	163,515	415,649	113,368	95,949	7,871	631,739	567,747	63,992
Minority	2,134,424	1,480,765	169,443	163,022	22,441	213,697	83,857	13,194	815,111	417,210	107,876	25,899	58,843	148,978	39,320	33,564	2,730	236,449	211,519	24,930
10.0 to 24.9 percent minority enrollment																				
Number of institutions	1,339	540	35	32	12	95	64	19	283	608	11	14	15	157	200	186	25	191	98	93
Total enrollment	6,225,552	4,662,315	1,129,869	606,775	208,127	905,516	230,742	32,091	1,549,195	1,442,723	131,401	150,264	90,538	602,824	314,619	143,794	9,283	120,514	78,676	41,838
U.S. residents	6,001,320	4,509,551	1,048,823	580,866	201,361	885,394	227,983	31,036	1,534,088	1,372,735	117,576	137,691	86,144	581,772	305,660	135,056	8,886	118,984	77,291	41,693
Minority	1,072,593	799,701	190,588	104,867	36,558	148,802	38,480	5,576	274,830	250,904	28,290	28,030	16,097	99,554	52,105	25,345	1,483	21,988	14,616	7,372

See notes at end of table.

Table 230. Total number of degree-granting institutions and fall enrollment in these institutions, by type and control of institution and percentage of minority enrollment: 2007—Continued

Minority percentage of total enrollment	Total, all institution types	Public institutions								Not-for-profit institutions								For-profit institutions		
		Total	Research university, very high[1]	Research university, high[2]	Doctoral/ research[3]	Master's[4]	Baccalau-reate[5]	Special focus[6]	2-year	Total	Research university, very high[1]	Research university, high[2]	Doctoral/ research[3]	Master's[4]	Baccalau-reate[5]	Special focus[6]	2-year	Total	4-year	2-year
1	2	3	4	5	6	7	8	9	10	11	12	13	14	15	16	17	18	19	20	21
Less than 10.0 percent minority enrollment																				
Number of institutions.	906	355	6	15	4	56	57	3	214	454	0	3	3	68	178	180	22	97	30	67
Total enrollment...........	2,385,227	1,749,369	139,370	203,132	55,419	482,563	166,173	5,241	697,471	600,756	0	47,518	15,643	197,063	277,559	56,710	6,263	35,102	16,361	18,741
U.S. residents............	2,330,079	1,712,539	131,352	194,688	54,365	469,460	163,033	4,991	694,650	583,040	0	45,375	15,245	190,138	271,620	54,710	5,952	34,500	15,803	18,697
Minority	165,094	122,010	12,528	13,648	4,770	33,956	10,914	393	45,801	40,689	0	3,827	1,185	14,653	17,863	2,697	464	2,395	1,211	1,184

[1]Research universities with a very high level of research activity.
[2]Research universities with a high level of research activity.
[3]Institutions that award at least 20 doctor's degrees per year, but did not have high levels of research activity.
[4]Institutions that award at least 50 master's degrees per year.
[5]Institutions that primarily emphasize undergraduate education.
[6]Four-year institutions that award degrees primarily in single fields of study, such as medicine, business, fine arts, theology, and engineering. Includes some institutions that have 4-year programs, but have not reported sufficient data to identify program category. Also includes institutions classified as 4-year under the IPEDS system, which had been classified as 2-year in the Carnegie classification system because they primarily award associate's degrees.

NOTE: Relative levels of research activity for research universities were determined by an analysis of research and development expenditures, science and engineering research staffing, and doctoral degrees conferred, by field. Further information on the research index ranking may be obtained from http://www.carnegiefoundation.org/classifications/index.asp?key=798#related. Degree-granting institutions grant associate's or higher degrees and participate in Title IV federal financial aid programs. Some institutions do not report separate enrollment data for each branch campus. For this reason, counts of institutions in this table are somewhat lower than the figures appearing in some other tables. Race categories exclude persons of Hispanic ethnicity.
SOURCE: U.S. Department of Education, National Center for Education Statistics, 2007 Integrated Postsecondary Education Data System (IPEDS), Spring 2008. (This table was prepared October 2008.)

Table 231. Number and percentage of students enrolled in postsecondary institutions, by level, disability status, and selected student characteristics: 2003–04

Selected student characteristic	Undergraduate						Graduate and first-professional[1]					
	All students		Students with disabilities[2]		Nondisabled students		All students		Students with disabilities[2]		Nondisabled students	
1	2		3		4		5		6		7	
Number of students (in thousands)	19,054	(0.0)	2,156	(36.7)	16,897	(36.7)	2,826	(19.9)	189	(14.0)	2,637	(21.1)
Sex (percent)	100.0	(†)	100.0	(†)	100.0	(†)	100.0	(†)	100.0	(†)	100.0	(†)
Male	42.4	(0.39)	42.1	(0.84)	42.4	(0.39)	41.9	(1.23)	38.0	(3.50)	42.2	(1.29)
Female	57.6	(0.39)	57.9	(0.84)	57.6	(0.39)	58.1	(1.23)	62.0	(3.50)	57.8	(1.29)
Race/ethnicity of student (percent)	100.0	(†)	100.0	(†)	100.0	(†)	100.0	(†)	100.0	(†)	100.0	(†)
White	63.1	(0.76)	65.1	(0.99)	62.9	(0.76)	68.3	(1.05)	67.0	(3.39)	68.4	(1.09)
Black	14.0	(0.62)	13.2	(0.78)	14.1	(0.62)	9.6	(0.68)	12.5	(2.99)	9.3	(0.69)
Hispanic	12.7	(0.43)	12.3	(0.62)	12.8	(0.44)	7.7	(0.73)	7.9	(1.85)	7.6	(0.74)
Asian/Pacific Islander	5.9	(0.22)	3.8	(0.37)	6.2	(0.23)	11.0	(0.53)	5.9	(1.36)	11.3	(0.56)
American Indian/Alaska Native	0.9	(0.11)	1.2	(0.22)	0.9	(0.10)	0.6	(0.11)	0.4	(0.24)	0.6	(0.11)
Other	3.3	(0.11)	4.4	(0.31)	3.2	(0.11)	2.9	(0.30)	6.3	(1.59)	2.7	(0.31)
Age (percent)	100.0	(†)	100.0	(†)	100.0	(†)	100.0	(†)	100.0	(†)	100.0	(†)
15 to 23	56.8	(0.52)	45.8	(1.07)	58.2	(0.49)	11.2	(0.44)	8.5	(1.46)	11.4	(0.46)
24 to 29	17.3	(0.28)	15.5	(0.59)	17.5	(0.28)	39.6	(0.93)	33.9	(2.69)	40.0	(1.00)
30 or older	25.9	(0.42)	38.7	(1.06)	24.3	(0.39)	49.2	(1.03)	57.6	(2.72)	48.6	(1.08)
Attendance status (percent)	100.0	(†)	100.0	(†)	100.0	(†)	100.0	(†)	100.0	(†)	100.0	(†)
Full-time, full-year	38.6	(0.45)	33.5	(0.72)	39.2	(0.45)	32.7	(1.01)	28.9	(2.76)	32.9	(1.03)
Part-time or part-year	61.4	(0.45)	66.5	(0.72)	60.8	(0.45)	67.3	(1.01)	71.1	(2.76)	67.1	(1.03)
Student housing status (percent)	100.0	(†)	100.0	(†)	100.0	(†)	—	(†)	—	(†)	—	(†)
On-campus	13.8	(0.36)	10.7	(0.46)	14.2	(0.38)	—	(†)	—	(†)	—	(†)
Off-campus	55.2	(0.47)	61.5	(0.81)	54.4	(0.47)	—	(†)	—	(†)	—	(†)
With parents or relatives	31.0	(0.41)	27.7	(0.73)	31.4	(0.40)	—	(†)	—	(†)	—	(†)
Dependency status (percent)	100.0	(†)	100.0	(†)	100.0	(†)	100.0	(†)	100.0	(†)	100.0	(†)
Dependent	49.7	(0.56)	39.4	(0.95)	51.0	(0.55)	‡	(†)	‡	(†)	‡	(†)
Independent, unmarried	15.2	(0.25)	19.5	(0.72)	14.7	(0.25)	47.5	(1.01)	48.1	(3.03)	47.5	(1.03)
Independent, married	7.9	(0.18)	9.1	(0.50)	7.8	(0.17)	18.8	(0.81)	15.7	(2.45)	19.0	(0.82)
Independent with dependents	27.1	(0.42)	32.0	(0.78)	26.5	(0.42)	33.7	(1.11)	36.2	(3.64)	33.6	(1.11)
Veteran status (percent)	100.0	(†)	100.0	(†)	100.0	(†)	100.0	(†)	100.0	(†)	100.0	(†)
Veteran	3.4	(0.16)	6.2	(0.52)	3.0	(0.14)	3.8	(0.46)	2.7	(0.66)	3.9	(0.48)
Not veteran	96.6	(0.16)	93.8	(0.52)	97.0	(0.14)	96.2	(0.46)	97.3	(0.66)	96.1	(0.48)
Field of study (percent)	100.0	(†)	100.0	(†)	100.0	(†)	100.0	(†)	100.0	(†)	100.0	(†)
Business/management	15.6	(0.33)	14.6	(0.66)	15.7	(0.33)	16.1	(1.02)	12.7	(3.46)	16.4	(1.05)
Education	6.7	(0.23)	6.3	(0.42)	6.8	(0.23)	23.7	(1.53)	29.7	(3.09)	23.3	(1.64)
Engineering/computer science	4.7	(0.25)	3.8	(0.35)	4.8	(0.26)	8.1	(0.59)	4.3	(1.02)	8.4	(0.62)
Health	12.9	(0.37)	12.2	(0.59)	13.0	(0.37)	13.2	(0.87)	9.9	(1.76)	13.4	(0.90)
Humanities	10.3	(0.26)	10.8	(0.52)	10.3	(0.25)	7.3	(0.72)	6.3	(1.04)	7.4	(0.75)
Law	‡	(†)	‡	(†)	‡	(†)	5.5	(0.35)	5.6	(1.13)	5.5	(0.36)
Life/physical sciences	4.5	(0.12)	4.2	(0.29)	4.5	(0.12)	3.5	(0.23)	3.6	(0.92)	3.5	(0.23)
Social/behavioral sciences	7.0	(0.17)	7.3	(0.34)	7.0	(0.18)	5.5	(0.35)	7.8	(1.84)	5.3	(0.33)
Vocational/technical	2.4	(0.14)	2.9	(0.24)	2.3	(0.15)	‡	(†)	‡	(†)	‡	(†)
Undeclared	21.3	(0.51)	22.0	(0.79)	21.2	(0.52)	9.5	(1.02)	9.4	(1.71)	9.5	(1.06)
Other	14.6	(0.34)	15.9	(0.68)	14.4	(0.34)	7.6	(0.58)	10.6	(2.21)	7.4	(0.56)

—Not available.
†Not applicable.
‡Reporting standards not met.
[1]First-professional includes chiropractic medicine, medicine, dentistry, optometry, osteopathic medicine, pharmacy, podiatry, veterinary medicine, law, and theology.
[2]Students with disabilities are those who reported that they had one or more of the following conditions: a specific learning disability, a visual handicap, hard of hearing, deafness, a speech disability, an orthopedic handicap, or a health impairment.

NOTE: Data include Puerto Rico. Detail may not sum to totals because of survey item non-response and rounding. Race categories exclude persons of Hispanic ethnicity. Standard errors appear in parentheses.
SOURCE: U.S. Department of Education, National Center for Education Statistics, 2003–04 National Postsecondary Student Aid Study (NPSAS:04). (This table was prepared August 2005.)

Table 232. Enrollment in postsecondary education, by student level, type of institution, age, and major field of study: 2003–04

Field of study	All students				Undergraduate								Graduate and first-professional
	Total (in thousands)	Percentage distribution, by age			2-year institutions[1]				4-year institutions				Total (in thousands)
		Under 25	25 to 35	Over 35	Total (in thousands)	Percentage distribution, by age			Total (in thousands)	Percentage distribution, by age			
						Under 25	25 to 35	Over 35		Under 25	25 to 35	Over 35	
1	2	3	4	5	6	7	8	9	10	11	12	13	14
Total	21,880 (19.9)	55.7 (0.47)	25.8 (0.36)	18.4 (0.32)	9,588 (23.7)	51.7 (0.70)	26.1 (0.49)	22.3 (0.49)	9,466 (23.7)	70.7 (0.76)	18.2 (0.44)	11.1 (0.44)	2,826 (19.9)
Agriculture and related sciences	95 (8.5)	72.0 (3.40)	19.2 (3.08)	8.8 (2.59)	36 (5.4)	62.0 (6.50)	23.2 (5.90)	14.8 (5.69)	52 (4.7)	82.7 (3.35)	13.4 (2.93)	3.9 (2.14)	8 (2.5)
Architecture and related services	126 (10.6)	68.0 (2.59)	24.8 (2.32)	7.2 (1.37)	46 (5.1)	57.2 (5.52)	28.7 (4.85)	14.0 (3.41)	68 (8.9)	80.4 (3.03)	16.8 (3.04)	2.8 (1.22)	12 (1.6)
Area, ethnic, and gender studies	44 (4.3)	63.2 (4.41)	21.2 (3.81)	15.6 (3.58)	‡ (†)	‡ (†)	‡ (†)	‡ (†)	30 (3.5)	80.7 (4.26)	12.3 (3.98)	7.0 (2.88)	8 (1.4)
Biological and biomedical sciences	500 (16.0)	77.6 (1.22)	18.2 (1.14)	4.2 (0.52)	94 (7.8)	70.8 (3.89)	21.1 (3.25)	8.1 (1.92)	350 (13.0)	87.4 (1.11)	10.4 (0.95)	2.1 (0.40)	56 (3.8)
Business, management, and marketing	3,431 (72.1)	51.1 (1.14)	28.3 (0.87)	20.5 (0.81)	1,170 (30.0)	51.7 (1.11)	25.7 (0.97)	22.7 (0.96)	1,805 (53.6)	60.7 (1.88)	23.2 (1.16)	16.1 (1.23)	456 (29.6)
Communication and journalism	433 (18.8)	82.3 (1.14)	12.8 (1.07)	4.9 (0.89)	72 (7.0)	81.1 (3.43)	13.2 (2.70)	5.6 (1.73)	334 (15.8)	86.9 (1.33)	10.3 (1.16)	2.8 (0.88)	27 (5.9)
Communications technologies/technicians	112 (9.9)	65.4 (3.54)	19.5 (2.76)	15.1 (2.88)	45 (5.9)	64.3 (6.32)	16.0 (3.85)	19.7 (5.14)	63 (7.6)	69.8 (4.82)	19.2 (3.86)	10.9 (3.37)	‡ (†)
Computer and information sciences	998 (36.7)	49.3 (1.33)	29.2 (1.15)	21.5 (1.18)	436 (21.6)	45.6 (2.00)	28.7 (1.95)	25.7 (1.68)	494 (23.6)	56 (2.15)	27 (1.50)	17 (1.59)	69 (9.2)
Construction trades	95 (12.9)	46.4 (5.16)	29.9 (3.67)	23.7 (3.82)	75 (12.4)	38.4 (5.63)	34.5 (4.17)	27.0 (4.78)	20 (2.7)	77.7 (5.53)	12.0 (5.22)	10.3 (4.73)	‡ (†)
Criminal justice	452 (21.0)	59.5 (1.96)	28.5 (1.73)	12.0 (1.18)	210 (14.2)	56.4 (2.96)	31.0 (2.50)	12.5 (1.72)	231 (16.9)	64.1 (2.73)	24.0 (2.06)	11.9 (1.88)	11 (3.1)
Economics	89 (7.0)	82.2 (2.53)	15.9 (2.26)	1.9 (0.80)	8 (2.0)	90.4 (6.26)	7.7 (6.28)	1.9 (0.98)	70 (6.7)	90.3 (2.29)	8.2 (1.93)	1.5 (0.94)	11 (1.4)
Education	1,951 (65.3)	48.0 (1.45)	30.2 (2.00)	21.8 (1.24)	491 (19.1)	55.9 (2.61)	22.6 (1.91)	21.5 (1.87)	790 (37.5)	73.5 (1.53)	16.3 (1.27)	10.2 (0.89)	670 (42.9)
Engineering	683 (51.6)	68.7 (1.87)	22.2 (1.18)	9.1 (1.56)	140 (9.6)	64.4 (3.62)	21.0 (2.46)	14.7 (2.41)	416 (42.3)	82.9 (1.80)	13.3 (1.68)	3.8 (0.62)	127 (13.8)
Engineering technologies/technicians	252 (15.1)	51.8 (2.80)	26.7 (2.45)	21.4 (2.45)	131 (10.5)	43.9 (3.81)	29.8 (3.76)	26.2 (3.64)	109 (9.6)	64.3 (3.77)	21.9 (3.28)	13.8 (2.42)	12 (2.8)
English language and literature/letters	273 (12.4)	72.4 (1.65)	19.3 (1.44)	8.4 (0.99)	48 (5.6)	74.7 (3.84)	17.8 (2.94)	7.4 (2.86)	192 (9.4)	79.9 (1.70)	13.1 (1.48)	7.0 (1.14)	33 (4.0)
Family and consumer/human sciences	104 (8.4)	54.7 (3.41)	22.8 (3.11)	22.5 (2.82)	44 (6.1)	37.2 (5.07)	32.5 (4.51)	30.3 (4.71)	52 (5.6)	73.8 (4.07)	12.8 (2.86)	13.4 (4.42)	‡ (†)
Foreign languages and literatures	104 (7.0)	55.0 (2.93)	24.3 (2.42)	20.7 (2.71)	28 (4.6)	38.7 (5.75)	22.8 (4.36)	38.5 (6.46)	59 (4.3)	73.6 (3.36)	16.9 (3.06)	9.5 (2.51)	16 (2.4)
Geography	37 (6.0)	59.4 (7.32)	21.8 (4.30)	18.8 (8.13)	‡ (†)	‡ (†)	‡ (†)	‡ (†)	25 (4.3)	72.9 (6.19)	16.0 (5.06)	11.1 (3.86)	5 (1.0)
Health professions and related sciences	2,672 (72.4)	45.6 (0.78)	32.9 (0.70)	21.5 (0.77)	1,646 (48.9)	41.8 (1.01)	34.1 (0.92)	24.1 (0.82)	692 (36.8)	60.8 (1.77)	23.2 (1.32)	16.0 (1.17)	334 (24.9)
History	220 (11.2)	70.8 (2.29)	18.9 (2.01)	10.3 (1.77)	36 (4.5)	60.2 (7.09)	18.7 (5.12)	21.1 (7.11)	159 (9.6)	81.6 (1.82)	13.2 (1.63)	5.2 (1.40)	26 (3.9)
International relations and affairs	41 (4.1)	76.3 (4.19)	17.1 (3.78)	6.6 (2.81)	‡ (†)	‡ (†)	‡ (†)	‡ (†)	29 (3.0)	88.6 (2.52)	10.6 (2.64)	0.8 (0.73)	‡ (†)
Legal professions and studies	273 (13.9)	39.7 (2.13)	43.2 (1.93)	17.1 (2.12)	78 (9.9)	41.3 (3.67)	32.4 (3.62)	26.3 (4.31)	41 (5.3)	53.9 (5.25)	27.0 (4.56)	19.1 (4.57)	153 (9.9)
Liberal arts, sciences and humanities	900 (40.5)	62.0 (1.71)	21.0 (1.16)	17.0 (1.36)	616 (38.1)	61.3 (2.36)	21.1 (1.66)	17.5 (1.74)	260 (15.8)	67.5 (1.62)	18.8 (1.26)	13.8 (1.35)	24 (3.6)
Library science	22 (5.5)	13.3 (4.65)	50.4 (8.62)	36.4 (8.32)	‡ (†)	‡ (†)	‡ (†)	‡ (†)	‡ (†)	‡ (†)	‡ (†)	‡ (†)	17 (4.7)
Mathematics and statistics	114 (7.1)	65.3 (3.28)	25.2 (2.49)	9.6 (1.79)	28 (4.1)	57.7 (7.71)	33.0 (6.20)	9.4 (4.13)	63 (5.0)	81.1 (3.39)	12.3 (2.57)	6.7 (2.10)	23 (2.8)
Mechanic and repair technologies	195 (14.8)	51.2 (2.56)	29.5 (1.89)	19.3 (1.97)	173 (14.0)	49.9 (2.71)	28.9 (1.86)	21.1 (2.19)	22 (4.4)	61.1 (7.36)	33.9 (6.80)	5.1 (3.51)	‡ (†)
Military technologies	‡ (†)	‡ (†)	‡ (†)	‡ (†)	‡ (†)	‡ (†)	‡ (†)	‡ (†)	‡ (†)	‡ (†)	‡ (†)	‡ (†)	‡ (†)
Multi/interdisciplinary studies	71 (7.0)	55.7 (4.17)	30.3 (3.26)	14.1 (2.51)	26 (3.0)	50.8 (6.76)	33.8 (6.25)	15.4 (3.13)	38 (6.2)	67.6 (6.16)	22.8 (4.74)	9.7 (3.79)	11 (2.6)
Natural resources and conservation	58 (6.8)	69.4 (5.72)	24.1 (5.61)	6.5 (2.20)	12 (2.2)	73.5 (7.90)	13.6 (5.97)	12.9 (6.91)	35 (5.7)	87.7 (4.13)	12.1 (4.05)	0.2 (0.23)	11 (2.6)
Natural sciences, other	59 (6.3)	66.5 (4.74)	26.3 (4.86)	7.2 (2.01)	12 (2.3)	72.0 (8.58)	16.1 (6.59)	11.9 (6.15)	34 (5.0)	76.8 (5.59)	20.3 (5.48)	2.9 (1.44)	13 (3.3)
Parks, recreation, and fitness studies	109 (8.4)	79.7 (2.56)	17.2 (2.24)	3.1 (1.23)	23 (4.0)	78.6 (5.92)	14.2 (4.45)	7.2 (4.33)	80 (7.2)	82.5 (3.18)	15.7 (2.89)	1.9 (1.25)	‡ (†)
Personal and culinary services	283 (39.4)	60.2 (2.83)	26.0 (1.62)	13.8 (1.97)	224 (29.7)	58.2 (2.32)	26.7 (1.49)	15.1 (1.73)	59 (30.4)	68.3 (8.13)	22.9 (5.22)	8.8 (5.46)	‡ (†)
Philosophy and religious studies	75 (6.7)	62.7 (3.76)	21.3 (2.42)	16.0 (3.18)	7 (1.7)	44.9 (12.50)	17.5 (9.13)	37.6 (13.01)	53 (5.6)	78.1 (3.39)	15.5 (2.78)	6.3 (1.87)	15 (3.0)
Physical sciences	153 (8.1)	66.0 (2.64)	27.2 (2.40)	6.8 (1.19)	24 (4.1)	75.8 (6.10)	15.9 (5.97)	8.3 (4.48)	95 (5.7)	78.9 (3.43)	15.8 (2.94)	5.3 (1.67)	34 (2.7)
Political science and government	209 (9.3)	80.3 (1.87)	14.7 (1.58)	5.1 (1.09)	27 (3.9)	66.4 (6.79)	25.6 (5.67)	8.0 (4.26)	167 (8.2)	87.6 (1.67)	9.7 (1.44)	2.7 (0.83)	15 (2.3)

See notes at end of table.

Table 232. Enrollment in postsecondary education, by student level, type of institution, age, and major field of study: 2003–04—Continued

	All students				Undergraduate								Graduate and first-professional
	Total (in thousands)	Percentage distribution, by age			Total (in thousands)	2-year institutions[1]			Total (in thousands)	4-year institutions			Total (in thousands)
		Under 25	25 to 35	Over 35		Percentage distribution, by age				Percentage distribution, by age			
Field of study						Under 25	25 to 35	Over 35		Under 25	25 to 35	Over 35	
1	2	3	4	5	6	7	8	9	10	11	12	13	14
Precision production	10 (2.1)	47.1 (10.35)	15.9 (5.84)	37.0 (11.06)	8 (2.0)	45.6 (11.79)	14.1 (6.18)	40.3 (12.10)	‡ (†)	‡ (†)	‡ (†)	‡ (†)	‡ (†)
Psychology	617 (20.8)	67.7 (1.57)	22.2 (1.14)	10.2 (0.98)	147 (11.4)	65.3 (3.61)	22.4 (2.92)	12.3 (2.46)	400 (15.2)	76.4 (1.49)	16.3 (1.21)	7.3 (0.80)	69 (7.0)
Public administration and social services	278 (27.0)	34.6 (3.09)	34.1 (2.77)	31.3 (3.04)	62 (7.6)	42.0 (4.76)	26.6 (4.41)	31.4 (4.61)	126 (19.5)	44.6 (6.29)	25.3 (3.69)	30.1 (4.59)	90 (10.7)
Residency programs	153 (9.0)	60.7 (2.63)	32.3 (2.45)	7.1 (1.20)	73 (7.2)	61.7 (4.25)	28.2 (3.56)	10.2 (2.11)	42 (4.1)	76.6 (4.99)	18.8 (3.82)	4.6 (2.46)	39 (3.1)
Science technologies/technicians	38 (5.9)	47.1 (5.77)	32.2 (5.21)	20.7 (4.29)	14 (2.8)	33.7 (9.00)	41.6 (9.19)	24.7 (8.35)	22 (5.0)	58.2 (8.99)	22.3 (7.96)	19.5 (5.89)	‡ (†)
Security and criminal justice	78 (7.9)	62.3 (5.22)	24.2 (3.60)	13.5 (3.25)	55 (7.6)	63.4 (6.25)	28.4 (4.96)	8.2 (2.62)	19 (3.3)	62.1 (9.36)	9.4 (3.27)	28.5 (9.27)	‡ (†)
Social sciences, other	116 (8.2)	55.3 (3.70)	26.0 (3.03)	18.7 (2.58)	32 (4.8)	57.4 (5.99)	23.8 (5.50)	18.9 (4.12)	66 (5.7)	64.8 (4.67)	20.7 (3.68)	14.5 (3.45)	18 (2.6)
Sociology	198 (12.0)	62.5 (2.96)	25.1 (2.43)	12.4 (2.31)	48 (6.9)	46.8 (6.33)	29.5 (6.14)	23.8 (7.41)	139 (8.8)	72.2 (3.12)	20.5 (2.62)	7.3 (1.68)	11 (1.6)
Theology and religious vocations	118 (20.2)	31.8 (4.58)	29.0 (4.99)	39.2 (4.02)	‡ (†)	‡ (†)	‡ (†)	‡ (†)	46 (10.7)	57.8 (4.51)	16.4 (3.81)	25.8 (5.18)	65 (14.9)
Transportation and materials moving	49 (7.3)	64.3 (7.30)	19.0 (3.95)	16.7 (5.23)	26 (4.2)	48.7 (7.74)	28.2 (6.05)	23.1 (4.62)	22 (5.6)	85.2 (13.25)	5.3 (3.46)	9.5 (10.49)	‡ (†)
Visual and performing arts	664 (27.0)	73.9 (1.27)	17.2 (1.27)	8.9 (0.80)	197 (11.6)	69.2 (2.90)	18.7 (2.39)	12.0 (2.02)	422 (23.6)	81.4 (1.81)	13.3 (1.64)	5.3 (0.71)	45 (6.3)
Undeclared or not in a degree program	4,328 (103.0)	53.7 (0.81)	22.2 (0.51)	24.1 (0.76)	2,890 (87.5)	50.3 (1.04)	23.5 (0.69)	26.1 (1.02)	1,169 (35.1)	71.8 (1.07)	15.6 (0.86)	12.5 (0.73)	268 (29.2)

†Not applicable.
‡Reporting standards not met.
[1]Includes less-than-2-year schools and schools not identified by level.

NOTE: Because of different survey editing and processing procedures, enrollment data in this table may differ from those appearing in other tables. Includes students who enrolled at any time during the 2003–04 academic year. Data include Puerto Rico. Detail may not sum to totals because of rounding. Standard errors appear in parentheses.
SOURCE: U.S. Department of Education, National Center for Education Statistics, 2003–04 National Postsecondary Student Aid Study (NPSAS:04), unpublished tabulations. (This table was prepared September 2005.)

Table 233. Graduate enrollment in science and engineering programs in degree-granting institutions, by discipline division: Fall 1994 through fall 2006

Discipline of engineering or science	1994	1995	1996	1997	1998	1999	2000	2001	2002	2003	2004	2005	2006	Percent change, 1994 to 2006
1	2	3	4	5	6	7	8	9	10	11	12	13	14	15
Total, all sciences and engineering	**504,399**	**499,640**	**494,079**	**487,208**	**485,627**	**493,256**	**493,311**	**509,607**	**540,404**	**567,121**	**574,463**	**582,226**	**597,643**	**18.5**
Engineering	113,024	107,201	103,224	101,148	100,038	101,691	104,112	109,493	119,668	127,377	123,566	120,565	123,041	8.9
Aerospace	3,715	3,343	3,208	3,083	3,137	3,349	3,407	3,451	3,685	4,048	4,089	4,170	4,482	20.6
Agricultural	1,061	1,037	1,012	941	975	986	943	947	952	1,058	1,041	1,059	1,073	1.1
Biomedical	2,750	2,732	2,732	2,847	2,855	3,069	3,197	3,599	4,338	5,301	5,807	6,067	6,482	135.7
Chemical	7,639	7,452	7,408	7,288	7,093	6,883	7,056	6,913	7,414	7,516	7,452	7,173	7,261	-4.9
Civil	19,925	19,218	18,528	17,193	16,517	16,226	16,451	16,665	17,713	18,890	18,561	18,114	17,802	-10.7
Electrical	33,020	30,861	29,941	30,787	31,384	31,822	33,611	36,100	39,948	41,763	38,995	37,450	38,265	15.9
Engineering science	2,089	1,955	1,751	1,647	1,701	1,627	1,632	1,798	2,121	2,240	2,198	1,951	2,046	-2.1
Industrial/manufacturing	13,992	13,475	12,675	11,957	11,221	11,803	12,119	12,940	14,033	14,313	13,852	13,650	13,829	-1.2
Mechanical	17,761	16,363	15,509	15,045	14,696	14,956	15,235	15,852	17,139	18,393	17,852	17,373	17,919	0.9
Metallurgical/materials	5,228	4,956	4,747	4,688	4,680	4,481	4,377	4,721	4,992	5,131	5,059	5,160	5,268	0.8
Mining	424	373	371	348	304	328	287	240	267	278	308	279	244	-42.5
Nuclear	1,246	1,154	980	868	821	830	792	801	795	885	971	1,013	1,099	-11.8
Petroleum	624	610	562	561	571	642	627	656	766	849	845	808	813	30.3
Other engineering	3,550	3,672	3,800	3,895	4,083	4,689	4,378	4,810	5,505	6,712	6,536	6,298	6,458	81.9
All sciences	391,375	392,439	390,855	386,060	385,589	391,565	389,199	400,114	420,736	439,744	450,897	461,661	474,602	21.3
Physical sciences	34,466	33,399	32,333	31,105	30,575	30,691	30,385	31,038	32,341	34,298	35,761	36,375	36,901	7.1
Astronomy	973	912	874	778	820	832	888	916	990	1,080	1,119	1,191	1,211	24.5
Chemistry	19,803	19,570	19,334	18,774	18,482	18,416	18,105	18,366	19,045	20,049	20,776	21,101	21,351	7.8
Physics	13,162	12,425	11,728	11,147	10,809	10,869	10,841	11,248	11,701	12,555	13,298	13,472	13,722	4.3
Other physical sciences	528	492	397	406	464	574	551	508	605	614	568	611	617	16.9
Earth, atmospheric, and ocean sciences	15,957	15,716	15,183	14,548	14,258	14,083	13,941	13,841	14,240	14,620	15,131	14,836	14,920	-6.5
Atmospheric sciences	1,109	1,072	1,086	1,092	965	913	963	924	1,036	1,150	1,086	1,146	1,079	-2.7
Geosciences	7,713	7,582	7,304	6,959	6,687	6,637	6,596	6,544	6,712	6,889	7,358	7,212	7,177	-6.9
Oceanography	2,870	2,723	2,615	2,479	2,562	2,624	2,668	2,585	2,618	2,695	2,801	2,760	2,770	-3.5
Other environmental sciences	4,265	4,339	4,178	4,018	4,044	3,909	3,714	3,788	3,874	3,886	3,886	3,718	3,894	-8.7
Mathematical sciences	19,573	18,504	18,008	16,719	16,485	16,257	15,650	16,651	18,163	19,465	19,931	20,210	20,815	6.3
Mathematics and applied mathematics	16,457	15,386	14,948	14,027	13,827	13,521	12,823	13,569	14,702	15,569	15,964	16,106	16,649	1.2
Statistics	3,116	3,118	3,060	2,692	2,658	2,736	2,827	3,082	3,461	3,896	3,967	4,104	4,166	33.7
Computer sciences	34,158	33,458	34,626	35,991	38,027	42,478	47,350	52,196	55,269	53,696	50,016	47,978	47,653	39.5
Life sciences	143,560	148,286	148,948	148,486	149,634	151,345	148,080	150,252	159,356	170,374	178,600	185,553	194,313	35.4
Agricultural sciences	12,242	12,768	12,301	12,203	12,168	12,312	12,023	12,235	12,698	13,197	13,445	13,123	13,016	6.3
Biological sciences	58,033	58,344	57,749	56,705	56,695	56,959	56,282	57,639	61,088	64,701	66,565	68,479	69,941	20.5
Anatomy	1,018	850	878	856	785	749	795	735	906	908	897	938	961	-5.6
Biochemistry	5,615	5,562	5,275	5,102	5,148	5,101	4,966	4,917	5,190	5,552	5,612	5,814	5,824	3.7
Biology	14,208	14,280	14,611	14,646	14,277	13,989	13,407	13,352	13,822	14,770	15,458	15,681	16,463	15.9
Biometry/epidemiology	2,710	2,810	3,005	2,896	3,514	3,704	3,615	3,817	4,071	4,439	4,674	4,805	4,789	76.7
Biophysics	794	845	833	748	737	710	751	877	953	1,032	1,180	1,183	1,203	51.5
Botany	2,748	2,295	2,213	2,082	2,042	1,974	1,904	1,921	1,973	1,901	1,831	1,860	1,850	-32.7
Cell biology	3,829	4,174	4,207	4,300	4,379	4,637	4,820	4,911	5,375	5,689	5,830	6,177	6,553	71.1
Ecology	1,566	1,702	1,632	1,640	1,670	1,704	1,762	1,888	1,967	2,230	2,185	2,165	2,162	38.1
Entomology/parasitology	1,263	1,241	1,234	1,161	1,168	1,145	1,104	1,170	1,191	1,206	1,241	1,126	1,114	-11.8
Genetics	1,699	1,712	1,741	1,776	1,727	1,783	1,712	1,841	1,909	2,073	2,129	2,155	2,154	26.8
Microbiology, immunology, and virology	5,094	5,026	4,912	4,805	4,773	4,815	4,814	4,798	5,208	5,256	5,375	5,401	5,324	4.5
Nutrition	4,791	5,071	4,918	4,604	4,486	4,508	4,413	4,429	4,539	4,695	4,771	4,817	5,042	5.2
Pathology	1,707	1,670	1,656	1,674	1,580	1,580	1,531	1,637	1,613	1,541	1,557	1,593	1,612	-5.6
Pharmacology	2,839	2,710	2,663	2,597	2,730	2,757	2,963	3,140	3,234	3,357	3,122	3,114	2,985	5.1
Physiology	2,378	2,540	2,377	2,298	2,151	2,083	2,015	1,967	2,076	2,328	2,409	2,399	2,416	1.6
Zoology	2,028	1,958	1,808	1,627	1,586	1,523	1,445	1,411	1,349	1,301	1,236	1,264	1,145	-43.5
Other biosciences	3,746	3,898	3,786	3,893	3,942	4,197	4,265	4,828	5,712	6,423	7,058	7,987	8,344	122.7
Health fields	73,285	77,174	78,898	79,578	80,771	82,074	79,775	80,378	85,570	92,476	98,590	103,951	111,356	51.9
Medical fields	15,065	15,538	15,363	15,470	16,643	17,276	16,407	17,363	19,166	20,574	20,866	21,414	23,441	55.6
Other health fields	58,220	61,636	63,535	64,108	64,128	64,798	63,368	63,015	66,404	71,902	77,724	82,537	87,915	51.0
Dentistry	1,298	1,338	1,388	1,491	1,518	1,467	1,430	1,494	1,446	1,654	1,946	1,748	1,614	24.3
Nursing	26,997	28,405	27,388	26,861	25,591	25,074	23,457	23,609	24,715	26,649	29,781	31,670	35,846	32.8
Pharmaceutical sciences	2,887	2,808	2,846	2,710	2,882	3,422	3,611	3,679	4,538	5,493	5,218	6,091	6,315	118.7
Speech pathology/audiology	11,356	11,982	12,857	13,212	13,198	13,600	13,636	13,193	13,368	13,694	14,045	14,821	14,847	30.7
Veterinary sciences	922	975	997	1,224	1,288	1,314	1,367	1,476	1,691	1,719	1,732	1,970	2,067	124.2
Other health related	14,760	16,128	18,059	18,610	19,651	19,921	19,867	19,564	20,646	22,693	25,002	26,237	27,226	84.5
Psychology	54,554	53,641	53,122	53,126	52,557	51,727	50,466	50,454	51,152	52,162	54,126	57,282	57,653	5.7
Psychology, general	18,356	12,519	12,787	13,098	12,733	12,798	12,488	12,488	12,609	13,118	13,771	14,283	13,947	-24.0
Clinical psychology	12,684	17,647	16,833	17,249	17,098	16,238	15,429	15,638	14,969	15,364	16,089	16,620	16,622	31.0
Other psychology	23,514	23,475	23,502	22,779	22,726	22,691	22,549	22,328	23,574	23,680	24,266	26,379	27,084	15.2
Social sciences	89,107	89,435	88,635	86,085	84,053	84,984	83,327	85,682	90,215	95,129	97,332	99,427	102,347	14.9
Agricultural economics	2,289	2,338	2,117	2,043	1,995	2,014	2,079	2,161	2,187	2,318	2,195	2,127	2,158	-5.7
Anthropology	7,665	7,693	7,773	7,560	7,577	7,633	7,626	7,491	7,481	7,789	7,826	7,750	8,150	6.3
Economics (except agricultural)	12,913	12,673	12,080	11,097	10,701	10,562	10,748	11,408	12,009	12,316	12,318	11,805	12,132	-6.0
Geography	4,502	4,371	4,331	4,287	4,326	4,250	4,036	4,304	4,383	4,721	4,809	4,800	4,750	5.5
History and philosophy of science	387	401	409	443	508	557	532	571	663	737	994	965	968	150.1
Linguistics	3,279	3,194	3,156	3,068	2,935	2,799	2,674	2,744	2,875	3,028	2,941	3,187	3,074	-6.3
Political science	34,317	34,298	33,252	32,083	30,828	31,372	31,131	31,805	34,934	36,880	39,023	40,780	41,784	21.8
Sociology	9,498	9,564	9,425	9,413	9,058	8,966	8,652	8,812	8,946	9,127	8,874	9,108	9,035	-4.9
Sociology/anthropology	987	941	923	948	857	741	745	808	719	773	839	848	837	-15.2
Other social sciences	13,270	13,962	15,169	15,143	15,268	16,090	15,104	15,578	16,018	17,440	17,513	18,147	19,459	46.6

NOTE: The survey on which this table is based includes institutions in other jurisdictions, including Guam, Puerto Rico, and the U.S. Virgin Islands. Some data have been revised from previously published figures. Detail may not sum to totals because of rounding.

SOURCE: National Science Foundation, Division of Science Resources Studies, Survey of Graduate Students and Postdoctorates in Science and Engineering, 1994 through 2006. (This table was prepared Septermber 2008.)

Table 234. Number of degree-granting institutions and enrollment in these institutions, by size, type, and control of institution: Fall 2006

Type and control of institution	Total	Under 200	200 to 499	500 to 999	1,000 to 2,499	2,500 to 4,999	5,000 to 9,999	10,000 to 19,999	20,000 to 29,999	30,000 or more
1	2	3	4	5	6	7	8	9	10	11
Number of institutions										
Total	4,301	499	603	645	909	651	495	317	126	56
Doctoral, extensive[1]	151	0	0	0	2	2	12	48	52	35
Doctoral, intensive[2]	107	0	1	1	4	15	29	38	17	2
Master's[3]	637	1	4	26	138	188	172	86	16	6
Baccalaureate[4]	629	19	38	139	302	104	20	5	2	0
Specialized institutions[5]	1,101	283	301	232	180	70	21	10	2	2
2-year	1,676	196	259	247	283	272	241	130	37	11
Public	1,686	16	50	92	334	376	390	265	113	50
Doctoral, extensive[1]	102	0	0	0	0	1	0	23	47	31
Doctoral, intensive[2]	63	0	0	0	2	2	13	31	13	2
Master's[3]	274	0	0	1	20	51	112	73	13	4
Baccalaureate[4]	105	0	1	11	40	32	15	4	2	0
Specialized institutions[5]	99	3	10	11	35	24	9	4	1	2
Art, music, or design	2	0	0	1	1	0	0	0	0	0
Engineering or technology	8	0	1	0	3	3	1	0	0	0
Medical or other health	30	2	4	3	16	4	1	0	0	0
Other specialized	59	1	5	7	15	17	7	4	1	2
2-year	1,043	13	39	69	237	266	241	130	37	11
Private	2,615	483	553	553	575	275	105	52	13	6
Doctoral, extensive[1]	49	0	0	0	2	1	12	25	5	4
Doctoral, intensive[2]	44	0	1	1	2	13	16	7	4	0
Master's[3]	363	1	4	25	118	137	60	13	3	2
Baccalaureate[4]	524	19	37	128	262	72	5	1	0	0
Specialized institutions[5]	1,002	280	291	221	145	46	12	6	1	0
Art, music, or design	91	16	25	12	27	8	3	0	0	0
Business and management	147	28	51	35	18	10	4	1	0	0
Engineering or technology	65	6	10	29	11	6	0	3	0	0
Medical or other health	134	36	43	28	23	4	0	0	0	0
Theological	297	163	85	36	10	3	0	0	0	0
Other specialized	268	31	77	81	56	15	5	2	1	0
2-year	633	183	220	178	46	6	0	0	0	0
Enrollment of institutions										
Total	17,758,870	56,399	204,525	468,124	1,512,881	2,318,556	3,474,957	4,397,472	3,072,096	2,253,860
Doctoral, extensive[1]	3,462,707	0	0	0	4,125	9,758	89,519	704,346	1,295,348	1,359,611
Doctoral, intensive[2]	1,291,243	0	237	890	7,754	57,425	217,098	516,944	410,808	80,087
Master's[3]	4,066,656	80	1,363	19,921	256,691	674,762	1,211,821	1,169,873	396,967	335,178
Baccalaureate[4]	1,177,044	2,289	14,239	108,044	489,431	341,135	120,231	57,216	44,459	0
Specialized institutions[5]	1,242,680	30,878	101,964	166,751	276,749	237,850	144,443	147,576	49,726	86,743
2-year	6,518,540	23,152	86,722	172,518	478,131	997,626	1,691,845	1,801,517	874,788	392,241
Public	13,180,133	2,354	18,052	71,669	588,182	1,382,016	2,762,775	3,680,280	2,756,990	1,917,815
Doctoral, extensive[1]	2,756,539	0	0	0	0	4,869	0	356,509	1,175,568	1,219,593
Doctoral, intensive[2]	927,944	0	0	0	3,902	7,327	96,704	425,706	314,218	80,087
Master's[3]	2,517,192	0	0	671	39,808	195,643	822,551	995,969	323,399	139,151
Baccalaureate[4]	366,901	0	495	9,032	65,306	110,983	91,690	44,936	44,459	0
Specialized institutions[5]	386,437	339	4,022	8,863	62,355	83,929	59,985	55,643	24,558	86,743
Art, music, or design	3,131	0	0	845	2,286	0	0	0	0	0
Engineering or technology	24,198	0	438	0	5,506	11,709	6,545	0	0	0
Medical or other health	53,245	147	1,662	2,061	30,316	13,382	5,677	0	0	0
Other specialized	305,863	192	1,922	5,957	24,247	58,838	47,763	55,643	24,558	86,743
2-year	6,225,120	2,015	13,535	53,103	416,811	979,265	1,691,845	1,801,517	874,788	392,241
Private	4,578,737	54,045	186,473	396,455	924,699	936,540	712,182	717,192	315,106	336,045
Doctoral, extensive[1]	706,168	0	0	0	4,125	4,889	89,519	347,837	119,780	140,018
Doctoral, intensive[2]	363,299	0	237	890	3,852	50,098	120,394	91,238	96,590	0
Master's[3]	1,549,464	80	1,363	19,250	216,883	479,119	389,270	173,904	73,568	196,027
Baccalaureate[4]	810,143	2,289	13,744	99,012	424,125	230,152	28,541	12,280	0	0
Specialized institutions[5]	856,243	30,539	97,942	157,888	214,394	153,921	84,458	91,933	25,168	0
Art, music, or design	106,952	1,787	8,919	8,294	41,129	24,096	22,727	0	0	0
Business and management	147,440	3,046	17,499	25,318	28,063	34,312	26,585	12,617	0	0
Engineering or technology	108,670	490	3,162	20,711	15,559	20,751	0	47,997	0	0
Medical or other health	85,825	3,929	13,842	20,261	35,765	12,028	0	0	0	0
Theological	95,339	17,904	25,893	25,966	14,813	10,763	0	0	0	0
Other specialized	312,017	3,383	28,627	57,338	79,065	51,971	35,146	31,319	25,168	0
2-year	293,420	21,137	73,187	119,415	61,320	18,361	0	0	0	0

[1]Doctoral, extensive institutions are committed to graduate education through the doctorate, and award 50 or more doctor's degrees per year across at least 15 disciplines.

[2]Doctoral, intensive institutions are committed to education through the doctorate, and award at least 10 doctor's degrees per year across 3 or more disciplines or at least 20 doctor's degrees overall.

[3]Master's institutions offer a full range of baccalaureate programs and are committed to education through the master's degree. They award at least 20 master's degrees per year.

[4]Baccalaureate institutions primarily emphasize undergraduate education.

[5]Specialized 4-year institutions award degrees primarily in single fields of study, such as medicine, business, fine arts, theology, or engineering. Includes some institutions that have 4-year programs, but have not reported sufficient data to identify program category. Also includes institutions classified as 4-year under the IPEDS system, which had been classified as 2-year in the Carnegie system because they primarily award associate's degrees.

SOURCE: U.S. Department of Education, National Center for Education Statistics, 2006 Integrated Postsecondary Education Data System (IPEDS), Spring 2007. (This table was prepared June 2008.)

Table 235. Selected statistics for degree-granting institutions enrolling more than 15,000 students in 2006: Selected years, 1990 through 2007

Line number	Institution	State	Con-trol[1]	Type[2]	Total fall enrollment					Fall enrollment, 2006		
										Total	Sex	
					Fall 1990	Fall 2000	Fall 2003	Fall 2004	Fall 2005		Male	Female
1	2	3	4	5	6	7	8	9	10	11	12	13
i	**United States, all institutions[5]**	†	†	†	**13,818,637**	**15,312,289**	**16,911,481**	**17,272,044**	**17,487,475**	**17,758,870**	**7,574,815**	**10,184,055**
ii	Colleges with enrollment over 15,000	†	†	†	5,591,224	6,004,345	6,687,366	6,836,875	6,962,684	7,127,189	3,196,878	3,930,311
1	Auburn University, Main Campus	AL	1	1	21,537	21,860	23,152	22,928	23,333	23,547	11,896	11,651
2	Troy University	AL	1	1	5,024	12,541	17,613	20,855	26,880	27,938	11,646	16,292
3	University of Alabama	AL	1	1	19,794	19,277	20,290	20,929	21,793	23,838	11,021	12,817
4	University of Alabama at Birmingham	AL	1	1	15,356	14,951	16,357	16,693	16,572	16,561	6,571	9,990
5	University of Alaska, Anchorage	AK	1	1	17,490	14,794	16,607	16,261	16,412	16,163	6,389	9,774
6	Arizona State University at the Tempe Campus	AZ	1	1	42,936	44,126	48,901	49,171	51,612	51,234	25,560	25,674
7	Glendale Community College	AZ	1	2	18,512	20,091	20,692	20,649	20,070	19,133	8,310	10,823
8	Mesa Community College	AZ	1	2	19,818	22,821	26,138	27,332	26,528	25,881	11,946	13,935
9	Northern Arizona University	AZ	1	1	16,992	19,964	18,820	19,137	18,773	20,555	7,561	12,994
10	Pima Community College	AZ	1	2	28,766	28,078	31,216	31,545	30,884	32,532	14,286	18,246
11	Rio Salado College	AZ	1	2	10,480	11,275	14,527	16,092	17,415	17,952	6,611	11,341
12	University of Arizona	AZ	1	1	35,729	34,488	37,083	36,932	37,036	36,805	17,455	19,350
13	University of Phoenix, Online Campus	AZ	3	1		14,783	75,588	115,794	117,309	165,373	57,341	108,032
14	University of Arkansas, Main Campus	AR	1	1	14,732	15,346	16,405	17,269	17,821	17,926	9,046	8,880
15	American River College	CA	1	2	18,716	28,420	26,513	30,055	30,527	31,908	15,635	16,273
16	Bakersfield College	CA	1	2	10,776	14,466	14,177	15,482	14,725	15,850	6,534	9,316
17	California Polytechnic State U. San Luis Obispo	CA	1	1	17,751	16,877	18,303	17,582	18,475	18,722	10,543	8,179
18	California State Polytechnic University, Pomona	CA	1	1	19,468	18,424	19,804	19,003	19,885	20,510	11,435	9,075
19	California State University, Chico	CA	1	1	16,633	15,912	15,516	15,734	15,919	16,250	7,521	8,729
20	California State University, Fresno	CA	1	1	19,960	19,056	22,342	19,781	20,371	22,098	9,023	13,075
21	California State University, Fullerton	CA	1	1	25,592	28,381	32,592	32,744	35,040	35,921	14,695	21,226
22	California State University, Long Beach	CA	1	1	33,987	30,918	34,715	33,479	34,547	35,574	13,807	21,767
23	California State University, Los Angeles	CA	1	1	21,597	19,593	20,637	20,307	20,034	20,565	7,658	12,907
24	California State University, Northridge	CA	1	1	31,167	29,066	33,426	31,341	33,243	34,560	13,829	20,731
25	California State University, Sacramento	CA	1	1	26,336	25,714	28,375	27,972	27,932	28,529	11,619	16,910
26	California State University, San Bernardino	CA	1	1	11,923	14,909	16,927	16,194	16,431	16,479	5,729	10,750
27	Cerritos College	CA	1	2	15,886	24,536	23,129	22,155	22,349	22,434	10,124	12,310
28	Chaffey College	CA	1	2	10,985	15,220	17,435	17,963	17,188	17,916	6,943	10,973
29	City College of San Francisco	CA	1	2	24,408	39,386	42,043	42,438	43,255	44,392	18,751	25,641
30	College of the Canyons	CA	1	2	4,815	10,528	14,553	13,953	15,947	17,067	10,038	7,029
31	De Anza College	CA	1	2	21,948	22,770	25,081	22,792	22,694	22,938	11,247	11,691
32	Diablo Valley College	CA	1	2	20,255	21,581	21,116	20,287	19,851	19,302	9,136	10,166
33	East Los Angeles College	CA	1	2	12,447	27,199	22,284	23,969	23,632	27,481	13,192	14,289
34	El Camino Community College District	CA	1	2	25,789	24,067	25,563	24,732	23,895	23,488	10,647	12,841
35	Foothill College	CA	1	2	12,811	14,193	18,006	16,609	17,123	16,936	8,010	8,926
36	Fresno City College	CA	1	2	14,710	19,351	21,755	21,540	21,917	22,040	10,418	11,622
37	Fullerton College	CA	1	2	17,548	19,993	18,720	19,774	19,611	19,995	9,483	10,512
38	Glendale Community College	CA	1	2	12,072	15,596	14,377	15,872	15,480	15,727	6,345	9,382
39	Grossmont College	CA	1	2	15,357	16,309	17,827	17,288	16,381	16,530	6,954	9,576
40	Long Beach City College	CA	1	2	18,378	20,926	23,877	23,177	22,641	23,509	10,539	12,970
41	Los Angeles City College	CA	1	2	14,479	15,174	15,877	15,958	16,283	15,654	6,555	9,099
42	Los Angeles Pierce College	CA	1	2	16,970	16,111	17,720	17,381	17,859	18,690	8,040	10,650
43	Los Angeles Valley College	CA	1	2	16,457	17,393	17,027	16,688	16,130	16,767	6,707	10,060
44	Modesto Junior College	CA	1	2	11,300	15,158	17,291	17,177	17,810	18,034	7,327	10,707
45	Mount San Antonio College	CA	1	2	20,563	28,329	26,440	27,927	27,195	29,079	13,333	15,746
46	National University	CA	2	1	8,836	16,848	17,064	25,684	26,035	25,844	9,744	16,100
47	Orange Coast College	CA	1	2	22,365	23,315	22,520	23,194	22,412	22,680	11,313	11,367
48	Palomar College	CA	1	2	16,707	21,062	23,691	25,040	25,146	26,118	13,357	12,761
49	Pasadena City College	CA	1	2	19,581	22,948	27,876	27,584	27,199	25,873	11,543	14,330
50	Rio Hondo College	CA	1	2	12,048	19,506	16,795	16,748	19,012	20,121	11,236	8,885
51	Riverside Community College	CA	1	2	15,683	22,107	29,664	30,101	29,160	29,486	13,078	16,408
52	Sacramento City College	CA	1	2	14,474	20,878	19,232	21,409	21,784	22,615	9,301	13,314
53	Saddleback College	CA	1	2	14,527	18,563	13,735	18,621	18,351	18,243	8,105	10,138
54	San Diego City College	CA	1	2	13,737	27,165	15,120	15,036	15,204	16,203	7,340	8,863
55	San Diego Mesa College	CA	1	2	23,410	21,233	22,548	22,467	21,066	21,131	9,857	11,274
56	San Diego State University	CA	1	1	35,493	31,609	32,803	32,043	31,802	33,441	13,975	19,466
57	San Francisco State University	CA	1	1	29,343	26,826	29,686	28,804	28,804	29,628	11,674	17,954
58	San Joaquin Delta College	CA	1	2	14,792	16,973	17,131	17,011	16,949	17,121	6,991	10,130
59	San Jose State University	CA	1	1	30,334	26,698	28,932	29,044	29,975	29,604	13,568	16,036
60	Santa Ana College	CA	1	2	20,532	27,571	23,329	26,496	32,096	33,203	20,200	13,003
61	Santa Barbara City College	CA	1	2	11,031	13,834	15,206	15,735	15,811	21,016	9,082	11,934
62	Santa Monica College	CA	1	2	18,108	27,868	23,401	27,459	28,908	28,337	12,174	16,163
63	Santa Rosa Junior College	CA	1	2	20,475	27,020	25,137	24,176	24,293	24,806	10,625	14,181
64	Sierra College	CA	1	2	11,637	17,517	18,105	18,248	18,444	18,339	8,047	10,292
65	Southwestern College	CA	1	2	13,010	17,994	18,716	18,342	19,324	19,446	8,425	11,021
66	Stanford University	CA	2	1	14,724	18,549	17,824	18,836	19,042	17,747	10,436	7,311
67	University of California, Berkeley	CA	1	1	30,634	31,277	33,065	32,803	33,547	33,920	16,447	17,473

See notes at end of table.

Table 235. Selected statistics for degree-granting institutions enrolling more than 15,000 students in 2006: Selected years, 1990 through 2007—Continued

Fall enrollment, 2006					Earned degrees conferred, 2006–07					Total expenses and deductions, 2005–06 (in thousands)[3]	Full-time-equivalent enrollment		
Attendance status			Student level										Line number
Full-time	Part-time	Percent minority[4]	Under-graduate	Postbacca-laureate	Associate's	Bachelor's	Master's	First professional	Doctor's		Fall 2005	Fall 2006	
14	15	16	17	18	19	20	21	22	23	24	25	26	27
10,957,305	6,801,565	31.5	15,184,302	2,574,568	728,114	1,524,092	604,607	90,064	60,616	$353,576,647	13,200,790	13,403,097	i
4,504,781	2,622,408	34.5	5,861,234	1,265,955	175,900	715,588	292,354	36,031	40,052	161,380,994	5,294,341	5,453,417	ii
20,120	3,427	12.4	19,367	4,180	†	3,799	816	207	204	580,567	21,318	21,457	1
11,784	16,154	46.6	20,069	7,869	441	2,215	2,906	†	†	181,050	17,510	18,088	2
20,252	3,586	14.5	19,471	4,367	†	3,131	1,183	152	160	496,556	19,789	21,631	3
11,349	5,212	31.5	11,284	5,277	†	1,814	960	249	192	1,707,178	13,366	13,370	4
7,351	8,812	24.7	15,322	841	660	847	356	†	†	213,193	10,864	10,883	5
37,297	13,937	24.4	41,815	9,419	†	7,282	2,146	198	376	1,032,345	44,279	42,792	6
5,727	13,406	37.1	19,133	†	1,049	†	†	†	†	76,608	10,796	10,228	7
7,816	18,065	30.6	25,881	†	1,697	†	†	†	†	104,098	14,337	13,881	8
13,844	6,711	24.2	14,523	6,032	†	2,877	1,757	†	88	321,199	15,275	16,387	9
9,280	23,252	42.0	32,532	†	2,081	†	†	†	†	155,235	16,471	17,087	10
1,752	16,200	26.2	17,952	†	357	†	†	†	†	66,328	6,924	7,191	11
30,504	6,301	26.9	28,442	8,363	†	5,564	1,382	354	460	1,262,364	33,197	32,946	12
165,373	0	32.7	118,453	46,920	2,918	13,257	15,458	†	121	489,553	117,309	165,373	13
13,604	4,322	12.4	14,350	3,576	†	2,382	939	139	115	522,232	15,088	15,263	14
8,278	23,630	41.1	31,908	†	1,715	†	†	†	†	120,071	15,821	16,211	15
5,553	10,297	61.3	15,850	†	991	†	†	†	†	95,729	8,566	9,010	16
17,440	1,282	25.8	17,794	928	†	3,613	417	†	†	272,326	17,716	17,944	17
16,260	4,250	66.4	18,650	1,860	†	3,768	467	†	†	250,601	17,257	17,924	18
14,326	1,924	22.9	14,927	1,323	†	2,900	346	†	†	182,506	14,762	15,083	19
17,008	5,090	54.2	19,127	2,971	†	3,384	670	†	7	259,431	17,980	19,011	20
23,913	12,008	58.6	30,703	5,218	†	6,295	1,430	†	†	302,358	28,018	28,631	21
26,139	9,435	58.5	29,795	5,779	†	6,110	1,531	†	†	353,263	28,845	29,816	22
13,473	7,092	78.5	15,375	5,190	†	3,097	1,128	†	†	219,348	15,730	16,208	23
23,536	11,024	56.9	28,491	6,069	†	5,682	1,623	†	†	335,578	26,883	27,823	24
20,727	7,802	46.9	23,928	4,601	†	4,953	824	†	†	288,806	23,370	23,786	25
12,224	4,255	59.4	13,156	3,323	†	2,595	775	†	†	179,807	13,658	13,857	26
6,076	16,358	81.1	22,434	†	1,161	†	†	†	†	110,707	11,728	11,568	27
5,827	12,089	68.1	17,916	†	1,368	†	†	†	†	90,724	9,563	9,886	28
8,440	35,952	72.8	44,392	†	1,230	†	†	†	†	250,797	20,151	20,510	29
6,509	10,558	45.3	17,067	†	871	†	†	†	†	75,180	8,334	10,054	30
8,984	13,954	66.0	22,938	†	1,010	†	†	†	†	(6)	13,582	13,669	31
6,730	12,572	41.1	19,302	†	597	†	†	†	†	86,558	11,566	10,951	32
6,478	21,003	87.4	27,481	†	1,213	†	†	†	†	95,032	11,976	13,529	33
7,438	16,050	73.8	23,488	†	1,103	†	†	†	†	132,549	12,997	12,827	34
4,095	12,841	50.8	16,936	†	513	†	†	†	†	91,678	8,472	8,406	35
7,593	14,447	67.4	22,040	†	1,205	†	†	†	†	115,511	12,569	12,443	36
8,245	11,750	58.8	19,995	†	960	†	†	†	†	134,164	11,965	12,190	37
4,811	10,916	43.0	15,727	†	640	†	†	†	†	112,416	8,406	8,476	38
6,617	9,913	40.5	16,530	†	1,116	†	†	†	†	68,011	9,983	9,945	39
7,257	16,252	68.9	23,509	†	874	†	†	†	†	152,470	12,385	12,713	40
5,233	10,421	73.7	15,654	†	681	†	†	†	†	86,911	9,183	8,732	41
5,362	13,328	58.1	18,690	†	870	†	†	†	†	73,242	9,480	9,837	42
4,471	12,296	62.9	16,767	†	778	†	†	†	†	72,673	8,342	8,599	43
6,490	11,544	48.0	18,034	†	1,189	†	†	†	†	114,639	10,360	10,366	44
9,147	19,932	77.6	29,079	†	2,202	†	†	†	†	150,127	14,821	15,839	45
8,845	16,999	39.4	7,002	18,842	86	963	3,425	†	†	129,028	15,100	15,391	46
9,448	13,232	49.5	22,680	†	1,414	†	†	†	†	116,634	13,700	13,890	47
8,249	17,869	40.2	26,118	†	1,369	†	†	†	†	112,039	13,743	14,248	48
8,331	17,542	76.7	25,873	†	1,670	†	†	†	†	146,893	14,460	14,220	49
4,639	15,482	82.6	20,121	†	767	†	†	†	†	89,367	9,537	9,837	50
8,808	20,678	61.4	29,486	†	2,283	†	†	†	†	158,624	15,542	15,750	51
6,909	15,706	63.6	22,615	†	1,063	†	†	†	†	96,124	11,892	12,182	52
6,374	11,869	30.4	18,243	†	937	†	†	†	†	83,524	10,371	10,359	53
2,943	13,260	63.6	16,203	†	674	†	†	†	†	93,625	7,088	7,395	54
5,581	15,550	52.4	21,131	†	1,055	†	†	†	†	134,451	10,896	10,802	55
25,817	7,624	44.2	27,911	5,530	†	6,433	1,773	†	46	409,636	27,317	28,788	56
21,709	7,919	57.1	24,529	5,099	†	5,230	1,498	†	15	372,459	24,114	24,810	57
6,817	10,304	64.4	17,121	†	3,783	†	†	†	†	116,017	10,158	10,276	58
20,744	8,860	59.8	22,482	7,122	†	4,043	2,312	†	†	317,745	23,897	24,170	59
4,278	28,925	62.8	33,203	†	1,292	†	†	†	†	115,254	13,724	13,989	60
6,640	14,376	35.0	21,016	†	1,167	†	†	†	†	106,785	9,467	11,467	61
9,861	18,476	56.7	28,337	†	1,465	†	†	†	†	162,533	16,115	16,064	62
7,786	17,020	26.1	24,806	†	1,139	†	†	†	†	138,047	13,329	13,500	63
6,651	11,688	19.8	18,339	†	2,382	†	†	†	†	93,257	10,649	10,575	64
6,646	12,800	85.2	19,446	†	1,081	†	†	†	†	98,732	10,954	10,943	65
14,136	3,611	32.5	6,422	11,325	†	1,709	2,137	249	720	2,734,986	15,325	15,530	66
32,056	1,864	53.0	23,863	10,057	†	6,629	1,966	377	903	1,592,030	31,893	32,764	67

See notes at end of table.

Table 235. Selected statistics for degree-granting institutions enrolling more than 15,000 students in 2006: Selected years, 1990 through 2007—Continued

Line number	Institution	State	Control[1]	Type[2]	Total fall enrollment					Fall enrollment, 2006		
										Total	Sex	
					Fall 1990	Fall 2000	Fall 2003	Fall 2004	Fall 2005		Male	Female
1	2	3	4	5	6	7	8	9	10	11	12	13
68	University of California, Davis	CA	1	1	23,890	26,094	29,402	29,210	28,815	29,628	13,405	16,223
69	University of California, Irvine	CA	1	1	16,808	20,211	24,273	24,344	24,400	25,230	12,803	12,427
70	University of California, Los Angeles	CA	1	1	36,420	36,890	37,055	35,966	35,625	36,611	16,901	19,710
71	University of California, Riverside	CA	1	1	8,708	13,015	17,296	17,104	16,622	16,875	8,173	8,702
72	University of California, San Diego	CA	1	1	17,790	20,197	24,105	24,663	25,320	26,247	13,076	13,171
73	University of California, Santa Barbara	CA	1	1	18,385	19,962	20,847	21,026	21,016	21,082	9,847	11,235
74	University of California, Santa Cruz	CA	1	1	10,054	12,144	14,997	15,036	15,012	15,364	7,241	8,123
75	University of Southern California	CA	2	1	28,374	29,194	31,606	32,160	32,836	33,389	17,165	16,224
76	Colorado State University	CO	1	1	26,828	26,807	28,186	27,973	27,780	27,636	13,127	14,509
77	Colorado Technical University Online	CO	3	1	†	†	†	3,969	6,734	16,314	7,195	9,119
78	Metropolitan State College of Denver	CO	1	1	17,400	17,688	20,261	20,761	21,010	21,154	9,494	11,660
79	University of Colorado at Boulder	CO	1	1	28,600	29,352	32,423	32,362	31,589	31,665	16,887	14,778
80	U of Colorado at Denver and Health Sciences Center	CO	1	1	11,512	13,737	15,746	16,610	19,766	20,162	8,150	12,012
81	University of Connecticut	CT	1	1	25,497	19,393	22,053	22,694	23,185	23,557	11,413	12,144
82	University of Delaware	DE	1	1	20,818	19,072	21,121	21,238	20,982	20,380	8,827	11,553
83	George Washington University	DC	2	1	19,103	20,527	23,417	24,092	24,099	24,531	11,059	13,472
84	Strayer University	DC	3	1	2,916	1,425	20,138	23,667	27,309	30,654	10,902	19,752
85	Broward Community College	FL	1	2	24,365	27,389	32,030	32,948	31,835	30,607	12,054	18,553
86	Embry Riddle Aeronautical University, Worldwide	FL	2	1	†	†	9,568	13,292	14,691	15,570	13,637	1,933
87	Florida Atlantic University	FL	1	1	12,767	21,046	24,932	25,319	25,645	25,325	9,879	15,446
88	Florida Community College at Jacksonville	FL	1	2	20,974	20,838	25,692	24,769	23,627	22,732	8,788	13,944
89	Florida International University	FL	1	1	22,466	31,945	33,228	34,865	36,904	37,997	16,412	21,585
90	Florida State University	FL	1	1	28,170	33,971	36,884	38,431	39,146	39,973	17,422	22,551
91	Hillsborough Community College	FL	1	2	19,134	18,497	22,006	22,123	21,377	21,293	8,437	12,856
92	Miami-Dade College	FL	1	1	50,078	46,834	58,490	57,026	54,169	51,329	19,814	31,515
93	Nova Southeastern University	FL	2	1	9,562	18,587	23,522	25,430	26,335	25,960	7,503	18,457
94	Palm Beach Community College	FL	1	2	18,392	17,326	22,660	22,554	21,686	21,563	8,262	13,301
95	Saint Petersburg College	FL	1	1	20,012	19,900	23,859	24,102	24,382	24,558	9,020	15,538
96	University of Central Florida	FL	1	1	21,541	33,713	41,535	42,465	44,856	46,646	20,868	25,778
97	University of Florida	FL	1	1	35,477	45,114	47,858	47,993	49,693	50,912	23,986	26,926
98	University of Miami	FL	2	1	13,841	13,963	15,235	15,250	15,674	15,670	7,323	8,347
99	University of North Florida	FL	1	1	8,021	12,550	13,966	14,533	15,234	15,954	6,608	9,346
100	University of South Florida	FL	1	1	32,326	35,561	40,945	42,238	42,660	43,636	17,462	26,174
101	Valencia Community College	FL	1	2	18,438	27,565	29,269	29,556	29,544	30,245	12,854	17,391
102	Georgia Institute of Technology, Main Campus	GA	1	1	12,241	14,805	16,643	16,841	17,135	17,936	12,966	4,970
103	Georgia Perimeter College	GA	1	2	13,944	13,708	18,986	20,316	20,461	19,955	7,642	12,313
104	Georgia Southern University	GA	1	1	12,249	14,184	15,704	16,100	16,646	16,425	7,901	8,524
105	Georgia State University	GA	1	1	23,336	23,625	28,042	27,261	25,967	26,135	10,343	15,792
106	Kennesaw State University	GA	1	1	10,018	13,360	17,477	17,955	18,551	19,844	7,685	12,159
107	University of Georgia	GA	1	1	28,395	31,288	33,878	33,405	33,660	33,959	14,358	19,601
108	University of Hawaii at Manoa	HI	1	1	18,799	17,263	19,862	20,549	20,644	20,357	9,010	11,347
109	Boise State University	ID	1	1	13,367	16,287	18,332	18,332	18,385	18,829	8,594	10,235
110	American Intercontinental University Online	IL	3	1	†	†	†	†	32,880	24,073	8,573	15,500
111	College of DuPage	IL	1	2	29,185	28,862	30,378	29,854	27,117	26,032	11,814	14,218
112	College of Lake County	IL	1	2	13,526	14,441	15,822	15,868	15,745	15,558	6,644	8,914
113	DePaul University	IL	2	1	15,711	20,548	23,610	23,570	23,145	23,149	10,643	12,506
114	DeVry University, Illinois	IL	3	1	3,303	4,095	12,800	14,407	13,990	16,113	8,467	7,646
115	Illinois State University	IL	1	1	22,662	20,755	20,860	20,757	20,653	20,521	8,606	11,915
116	Loyola University Chicago	IL	2	1	14,780	12,605	13,362	13,909	14,764	15,194	5,440	9,754
117	Moraine Valley Community College	IL	1	2	13,601	12,972	15,780	16,077	15,929	15,693	6,625	9,068
118	Northern Illinois University	IL	1	1	24,509	23,248	25,260	24,820	25,208	25,313	11,688	13,625
119	Northwestern University	IL	2	1	17,041	16,952	17,625	17,747	18,065	18,486	9,459	9,027
120	Southern Illinois University, Carbondale	IL	1	1	24,078	22,552	21,387	21,589	21,441	21,003	11,610	9,393
121	Triton College	IL	1	2	16,759	16,927	15,023	15,597	15,845	15,738	6,945	8,793
122	University of Illinois at Chicago	IL	1	1	24,959	24,942	25,764	24,865	24,812	24,644	10,979	13,665
123	University of Illinois at Urbana, Champaign	IL	1	1	38,163	38,465	40,458	40,687	41,938	42,738	22,648	20,090
124	William Rainey Harper College	IL	1	2	16,509	15,021	14,991	15,265	15,026	15,053	6,625	8,428
125	Ball State University	IN	1	1	20,343	19,004	20,490	20,507	20,351	20,030	9,342	10,688
126	Indiana University, Bloomington	IN	1	1	35,451	37,076	38,589	37,821	37,958	38,247	18,426	19,821
127	Indiana University-Purdue University, Indianapolis	IN	1	1	27,517	27,525	29,860	29,953	29,933	29,764	12,445	17,319
128	Purdue University, Main Campus	IN	1	1	37,588	39,667	40,376	40,108	40,151	40,609	24,065	16,544

See notes at end of table.

Table 235. Selected statistics for degree-granting institutions enrolling more than 15,000 students in 2006: Selected years, 1990 through 2007—Continued

Fall enrollment, 2006					Earned degrees conferred, 2006–07					Total expenses and deductions, 2005–06 (in thousands)[3]	Full-time-equivalent enrollment		Line number
Attendance status			Student level										
Full-time	Part-time	Percent minority[4]	Under-graduate	Postbacca-laureate	Associate's	Bachelor's	Master's	First professional	Doctor's		Fall 2005	Fall 2006	
14	15	16	17	18	19	20	21	22	23	24	25	26	27
26,955	2,673	52.8	23,417	6,211	†	6,015	882	402	474	2,286,896	27,260	28,011	68
24,153	1,077	63.3	20,719	4,511	†	5,230	923	97	298	1,426,493	23,724	24,569	69
35,420	1,191	53.4	25,432	11,179	†	6,991	2,296	573	734	3,412,404	34,909	35,894	70
16,305	570	72.1	14,792	2,083	†	3,337	378	†	177	460,075	16,090	16,533	71
25,043	1,204	57.3	21,369	4,878	†	5,061	901	148	387	2,091,279	24,553	25,522	72
20,431	651	39.0	18,212	2,870	†	4,859	576	†	310	625,023	20,570	20,688	73
14,802	562	40.7	13,961	1,403	†	3,411	274	†	132	451,778	14,669	15,025	74
29,206	4,183	40.4	16,729	16,660	†	4,676	4,002	687	691	1,744,634	30,365	30,812	75
21,494	6,142	12.8	21,437	6,199	†	4,169	965	129	211	622,828	24,031	23,815	76
16,314	†	38.5	14,098	2,216	22	2,940	1,143	†	†	105,826	6,734	16,314	77
12,405	8,749	26.0	21,154	†	†	2,510	†	†	†	107,918	15,998	15,936	78
25,886	5,779	15.3	26,363	5,302	†	5,728	962	162	319	790,616	27,919	28,079	79
9,288	10,874	22.1	11,036	9,126	†	1,652	1,696	353	163	906,798	13,164	13,495	80
19,759	3,798	18.5	16,347	7,210	22	4,354	1,444	270	339	835,629	20,834	21,216	81
17,546	2,834	14.0	16,934	3,446	161	3,417	773	†	224	603,647	19,138	18,652	82
15,897	8,634	25.5	10,813	13,718	189	2,209	3,108	685	264	776,728	18,899	19,259	83
7,659	22,995	63.5	21,940	8,714	714	2,262	1,795	†	†	145,506	6,172	16,645	84
9,997	20,610	59.5	30,607	†	2,679	†	†	†	†	177,757	17,384	16,917	85
3,991	11,579	25.0	11,681	3,889	694	2,524	978	†	‡	(6)	8,019	8,518	86
13,497	11,828	38.3	21,082	4,243	192	4,345	1,098	†	74	358,392	18,220	18,157	87
6,907	15,825	34.2	22,732	†	3,027	†	†	†	†	151,942	12,685	12,220	88
22,921	15,076	76.9	31,712	6,285	62	5,324	1,921	86	100	506,645	27,800	28,887	89
33,108	6,865	24.9	31,347	8,626	151	7,189	1,989	281	350	780,045	35,043	35,748	90
6,842	14,451	44.5	21,293	†	2,098	†	†	†	†	107,836	11,717	11,694	91
18,291	33,038	87.7	51,329	†	6,519	44	†	†	†	362,378	33,094	31,623	92
13,579	12,381	51.8	5,413	20,547	8	1,497	4,198	1,002	911	396,244	17,842	18,347	93
6,777	14,786	43.3	21,563	†	2,341	†	†	†	†	108,415	11,747	11,741	94
7,800	16,758	20.9	24,558	†	2,696	463	†	†	†	161,841	14,564	14,563	95
32,845	13,801	26.7	39,678	6,968	205	8,478	1,833	†	212	574,740	36,757	38,246	96
44,374	6,538	27.1	35,110	15,802	479	8,568	3,062	1,163	794	1,745,853	45,946	47,009	97
14,324	1,346	37.9	10,509	5,161	†	2,460	1,101	520	187	1,360,000	14,766	14,856	98
10,678	5,276	21.8	14,124	1,830	409	2,561	598	†	13	162,982	12,154	12,757	99
28,489	15,147	29.1	34,438	9,198	338	6,726	2,093	105	229	877,359	33,575	34,387	100
12,522	17,723	47.6	30,245	†	4,116	†	†	†	†	155,361	17,795	18,472	101
16,115	1,821	23.2	12,361	5,575	†	2,542	1,300	†	459	859,741	16,051	16,808	102
8,881	11,074	51.9	19,955	†	1,514	†	†	†	‡	112,231	12,948	12,599	103
13,529	2,896	24.7	14,483	1,942	†	2,300	447	†	63	185,086	14,852	14,642	104
17,712	8,423	40.6	19,109	7,026	†	3,793	1,660	208	170	432,928	20,860	21,024	105
13,106	6,738	16.2	17,698	2,146	†	2,505	791	†	†	159,820	14,569	15,762	106
29,353	4,606	13.9	25,437	8,522	†	6,203	1,528	470	388	1,017,933	30,596	31,119	107
14,590	5,767	61.3	14,037	6,320	†	2,836	1,094	171	149	728,328	17,175	16,789	108
11,375	7,454	12.1	17,040	1,789	323	1,829	440	†	5	225,970	14,038	14,331	109
24,073	0	43.1	20,911	3,162	5,126	5,736	2,646	†	†	263,780	32,880	24,073	110
8,909	17,123	32.4	26,032	†	1,528	†	†	†	†	151,800	14,939	14,658	111
4,608	10,950	37.6	15,558	†	877	†	†	†	†	86,515	8,285	8,284	112
16,251	6,898	30.3	14,893	8,256	†	2,842	2,323	360	29	352,610	18,786	18,954	113
6,240	9,873	46.9	11,327	4,786	265	1,963	1,208	†	†	146,096	5,787	10,078	114
17,828	2,693	11.7	17,885	2,636	†	4,306	671	†	49	332,586	18,877	18,852	115
12,783	2,411	26.7	9,725	5,469	†	1,877	1,256	418	165	354,412	13,254	13,717	116
6,660	9,033	24.7	15,693	†	1,226	†	†	†	†	71,017	9,768	9,693	117
19,321	5,992	23.7	18,816	6,497	†	3,756	1,553	87	107	420,798	21,328	21,569	118
15,305	3,181	25.6	9,179	9,307	†	2,089	2,665	416	462	1,245,029	16,191	16,533	119
16,803	4,200	21.6	16,294	4,709	68	4,328	897	195	145	555,637	18,870	18,401	120
3,716	12,022	48.4	15,738	†	825	†	†	†	†	57,160	7,865	7,752	121
20,230	4,414	43.4	15,006	9,638	†	3,286	1,737	545	317	1,744,272	21,946	21,896	122
39,249	3,489	23.6	31,472	11,266	†	7,035	2,582	320	698	1,719,622	39,876	40,565	123
6,267	8,786	35.1	15,053	†	1,476	†	†	†	†	112,285	9,146	9,217	124
16,963	3,067	9.2	17,082	2,948	392	3,576	884	†	72	342,150	18,334	18,125	125
33,707	4,540	10.6	29,828	8,419	59	6,181	1,838	281	370	979,720	35,170	35,423	126
17,754	12,010	15.3	21,193	8,571	444	2,828	1,760	651	68	994,085	22,369	22,468	127
35,979	4,630	11.5	32,668	7,941	588	5,927	1,377	224	613	1,210,225	37,283	37,766	128

See notes at end of table.

Table 235. Selected statistics for degree-granting institutions enrolling more than 15,000 students in 2006: Selected years, 1990 through 2007—Continued

Line number	Institution	State	Control[1]	Type[2]	Total fall enrollment					Fall enrollment, 2006		
											Sex	
					Fall 1990	Fall 2000	Fall 2003	Fall 2004	Fall 2005	Total	Male	Female
1	2	3	4	5	6	7	8	9	10	11	12	13
129	Des Moines Area Community College	IA	1	2	10,553	10,998	13,719	15,256	16,046	16,853	7,493	9,360
130	Iowa State University	IA	1	1	25,737	26,845	27,380	26,380	25,741	25,462	14,310	11,152
131	Kaplan University	IA	3	1	641	376	9,195	10,881	20,042	25,168	6,503	18,665
132	Kirkwood Community College	IA	1	2	8,623	11,645	15,030	15,432	15,110	15,064	6,983	8,081
133	University of Iowa	IA	1	1	28,785	28,311	29,745	28,442	28,426	28,816	13,589	15,227
134	Johnson County Community College	KS	1	2	13,740	16,383	18,432	18,612	18,673	19,088	8,703	10,385
135	Kansas State University	KS	1	1	21,137	21,929	23,050	23,151	23,182	23,141	11,425	11,716
136	University of Kansas, Main Campus	KS	1	1	26,434	25,920	26,814	26,980	26,934	26,773	13,286	13,487
137	Eastern Kentucky University	KY	1	1	15,290	13,285	15,951	16,183	16,219	15,763	6,118	9,645
138	University of Kentucky	KY	1	1	22,538	23,114	25,397	25,686	25,672	26,382	12,487	13,895
139	University of Louisville	KY	1	1	22,979	19,771	20,605	20,729	20,726	20,785	9,622	11,163
140	Western Kentucky University	KY	1	1	15,170	15,481	18,380	18,485	18,634	18,660	7,534	11,126
141	Louisiana State University and A & M College	LA	1	1	26,112	31,527	31,934	32,241	34,128	29,925	14,281	15,644
142	Southeastern Louisiana University	LA	1	1	10,262	14,525	15,656	15,465	16,054	15,106	5,518	9,588
143	University of Louisiana at Lafayette	LA	1	1	15,764	15,742	16,208	16,561	17,075	16,302	6,907	9,395
144	Community College of Baltimore County	MD	1	2	—	18,168	20,025	19,968	19,622	19,446	7,212	12,234
145	Johns Hopkins University	MD	2	1	13,363	17,774	18,820	18,626	19,225	19,708	9,502	10,206
146	Montgomery College	MD	1	2	14,361	20,923	21,671	22,256	22,263	22,893	10,336	12,557
147	Towson University	MD	1	1	15,035	16,729	17,188	17,667	18,011	18,921	6,997	11,924
148	University of Maryland, College Park	MD	1	1	34,829	33,189	35,329	34,933	35,369	35,102	18,012	17,090
149	University of Maryland, University College	MD	1	1	14,476	18,276	25,857	28,374	27,429	33,096	14,093	19,003
150	Boston University	MA	2	1	27,996	28,318	29,049	29,596	30,957	31,574	13,527	18,047
151	Harvard University	MA	2	1	22,851	24,279	24,851	24,648	25,017	25,778	13,074	12,704
152	Northeastern University	MA	2	1	30,510	23,897	22,944	22,932	22,604	23,411	11,324	12,087
153	University of Massachusetts, Amherst	MA	1	1	26,025	24,416	24,310	24,646	25,093	25,593	12,810	12,783
154	Central Michigan University	MI	1	1	18,286	26,845	27,758	27,683	27,221	26,710	11,049	15,661
155	Eastern Michigan University	MI	1	1	25,011	23,561	24,419	23,862	23,486	22,950	9,113	13,837
156	Grand Rapids Community College	MI	1	2	12,054	13,400	14,039	14,144	14,798	15,224	7,361	7,863
157	Grand Valley State University	MI	1	1	11,725	18,569	21,429	22,063	22,565	23,295	8,949	14,346
158	Lansing Community College	MI	1	2	22,343	16,011	18,575	19,471	20,057	20,394	9,321	11,073
159	Macomb Community College	MI	1	2	31,538	22,001	22,245	20,471	20,596	21,131	10,039	11,092
160	Michigan State University	MI	1	1	44,307	43,366	44,542	44,836	45,166	45,520	20,695	24,825
161	Oakland Community College	MI	1	2	28,069	23,188	24,145	24,296	24,287	24,123	10,174	13,949
162	Oakland University	MI	1	1	12,400	15,235	16,575	16,902	17,339	17,737	6,580	11,157
163	University of Michigan, Ann Arbor	MI	1	1	36,391	38,103	39,031	39,533	39,993	40,025	20,655	19,370
164	Wayne County Community College District	MI	1	2	11,986	9,008	11,684	11,858	14,764	19,265	5,713	13,552
165	Wayne State University	MI	1	1	33,872	30,408	32,208	32,386	32,160	32,061	13,259	18,802
166	Western Michigan University	MI	1	1	26,989	28,657	29,178	27,829	26,239	24,841	11,765	13,076
167	Capella University	MN	3	1	†	36	9,574	12,599	13,907	17,203	5,798	11,405
168	Saint Cloud State University	MN	1	1	17,075	15,181	16,133	16,077	15,954	16,334	7,340	8,994
169	University of Minnesota, Twin Cities	MN	1	1	57,168	45,481	49,474	50,954	51,175	50,402	23,662	26,740
170	Walden University	MN	3	1	422	1,544	8,227	13,553	22,168	27,412	6,566	20,846
171	Mississippi State University	MS	1	1	14,391	16,561	16,173	15,934	16,101	16,206	8,401	7,805
172	University of Mississippi, Main Campus	MS	1	1	11,288	12,118	13,780	14,497	14,901	15,220	7,129	8,091
173	Missouri State University	MO	1	1	19,480	17,703	18,930	19,114	18,928	19,218	8,246	10,972
174	University of Missouri, Columbia	MO	1	1	25,058	23,309	26,805	27,003	27,930	28,184	13,279	14,905
175	University of Missouri, St. Louis	MO	1	1	15,393	15,397	15,599	15,498	15,548	15,528	6,074	9,454
176	Webster University	MO	2	1	8,745	13,783	18,740	19,038	18,407	18,963	7,775	11,188
177	University of Nebraska at Lincoln	NE	1	1	24,453	22,268	22,559	21,792	21,675	22,106	11,592	10,514
178	Community College of Southern Nevada	NV	1	1	14,161	29,905	34,204	33,627	34,551	35,414	16,591	18,823
179	University of Nevada, Las Vegas	NV	1	1	17,937	22,041	26,161	27,339	28,134	27,912	12,155	15,757
180	University of Nevada, Reno	NV	1	1	11,487	13,149	15,534	15,950	16,336	16,663	7,538	9,125
181	Montclair State University	NJ	1	1	13,067	13,502	15,204	15,637	16,063	16,076	5,897	10,179
182	Rutgers University, New Brunswick/Piscataway	NJ	1	1	33,016	35,236	35,318	34,696	34,449	34,392	16,148	18,244
183	Central New Mexico Community College	NM	1	2	9,739	17,265	22,077	22,927	23,107	22,615	9,227	13,388
184	New Mexico State University, Main Campus	NM	1	1	14,812	14,958	16,174	16,428	16,072	16,415	7,215	9,200
185	University of New Mexico, Main Campus	NM	1	1	23,950	23,670	25,686	26,242	26,172	25,721	10,956	14,765
186	Columbia University in the City of New York	NY	2	1	18,242	19,639	21,322	21,648	21,983	22,317	11,171	11,146
187	Cornell University	NY	2	1	11,533	12,043	19,620	19,518	19,642	19,639	10,452	9,187

See notes at end of table.

Table 235. Selected statistics for degree-granting institutions enrolling more than 15,000 students in 2006: Selected years, 1990 through 2007—Continued

Fall enrollment, 2006					Earned degrees conferred, 2006–07					Total expenses and deductions, 2005–06 (in thousands)[3]	Full-time-equivalent enrollment		Line number
Attendance status			Student level										
Full-time	Part-time	Percent minority[4]	Under-graduate	Postbacca-laureate	Associate's	Bachelor's	Master's	First professional	Doctor's		Fall 2005	Fall 2006	
14	15	16	17	18	19	20	21	22	23	24	25	26	27
6,609	10,244	12.1	16,853	†	1,459	†	†	†	†	101,500	9,625	10,048	129
22,180	3,282	9.0	20,440	5,022	†	4,269	752	97	296	806,836	23,705	23,422	130
5,075	20,093	24.5	24,199	969	2,189	1,561	225	†	†	177,277	5,306	12,961	131
8,590	6,474	9.1	15,064	†	1,949	†	†	†	†	103,379	10,714	10,764	132
23,125	5,691	9.6	20,738	8,078	†	4,219	1,296	550	376	1,838,408	25,081	25,308	133
6,997	12,091	15.8	19,088	†	1,091	†	†	†	†	133,273	10,784	11,056	134
18,261	4,880	8.4	18,761	4,380	78	3,550	679	106	152	493,011	20,080	20,122	135
21,308	5,465	12.4	20,822	5,951	†	3,927	1,351	462	327	663,501	23,595	23,398	136
11,438	4,325	5.9	13,623	2,140	210	1,979	678	†	†	215,178	13,337	13,120	137
21,745	4,637	9.0	19,292	7,090	†	3,613	1,371	361	292	1,646,220	23,073	23,500	138
14,901	5,884	16.4	14,995	5,790	22	2,328	1,276	346	135	633,497	17,065	17,197	139
13,903	4,757	11.1	16,063	2,597	258	2,383	811	†	†	224,213	15,714	15,747	140
26,805	3,120	15.3	24,583	5,342	†	4,617	998	261	274	818,646	31,711	28,015	141
11,807	3,299	20.1	13,544	1,562	77	1,740	382	†	0	143,075	13,637	13,090	142
13,391	2,911	22.1	14,923	1,379	†	2,047	382	†	42	173,091	15,083	14,539	143
6,846	12,600	39.1	19,446	†	1,410	†	†	†	†	145,451	11,270	11,076	144
11,196	8,512	22.3	5,738	13,970	†	1,464	3,758	122	397	3,082,842	14,021	14,453	145
8,792	14,101	53.3	22,893	†	1,692	†	†	†	†	210,328	13,047	13,526	146
14,425	4,496	19.5	15,374	3,547	†	3,120	995	†	12	238,502	15,286	16,128	147
29,832	5,270	31.5	25,154	9,948	†	6,107	1,968	26	653	1,234,445	31,972	31,823	148
3,632	29,464	49.9	22,898	10,198	169	2,809	2,123		11	218,411	12,500	15,107	149
25,492	6,082	23.9	18,521	13,053	0	3,883	3,313	695	540	1,295,646	27,540	27,836	150
19,584	6,194	27.4	9,968	15,810	9	1,802	3,352	840	683	2,999,503	21,492	21,983	151
18,493	4,918	21.0	18,001	5,410	63	3,083	1,248	302	167	546,034	19,551	20,402	152
20,576	5,017	16.2	19,823	5,770	83	4,235	1,155	†	293	730,497	22,024	22,449	153
19,743	6,967	17.6	20,129	6,581	†	3,535	2,246	†	105	315,306	22,431	22,358	154
13,445	9,505	23.1	18,245	4,705	†	2,945	1,150	†	18	284,535	17,694	17,122	155
6,630	8,594	19.9	15,224	†	1,427	†	†	†	†	109,316	9,275	9,515	156
17,963	5,332	11.3	19,578	3,717	†	3,440	913	†	†	264,230	19,247	19,994	157
6,712	13,682	19.1	20,394	†	1,342	†	†	†	†	137,013	10,822	11,306	158
7,986	13,145	10.9	21,131	†	2,190	†	†	†	†	114,065	11,910	12,399	159
39,825	5,695	16.9	35,821	9,699	†	7,930	1,910	362	493	1,498,644	41,470	42,027	160
7,931	16,192	20.8	24,123	†	1,816	†	†	†	†	159,953	13,272	13,367	161
11,258	6,479	14.3	13,701	4,036	†	2,112	951	†	61	181,195	13,458	13,761	162
37,320	2,705	24.6	25,555	14,470	†	5,941	3,347	707	789	4,119,405	38,169	38,337	163
3,822	15,443	81.2	19,265	†	1,014	†	†	†	†	103,970	7,106	9,007	164
17,975	14,086	37.7	20,892	11,169	†	2,379	2,236	475	213	730,871	23,436	23,483	165
18,677	6,164	10.4	20,081	4,760	†	4,527	1,281	†	95	437,342	22,193	21,008	166
1,843	15,360	36.9	2,478	14,725	†	323	1,550	†	667	134,367	1,683	7,730	167
12,308	4,026	6.8	14,707	1,627	120	2,408	376	†	†	158,770	13,558	13,889	168
36,049	14,353	15.8	32,113	18,289	†	6,618	3,019	848	819	2,182,281	41,726	41,474	169
19,329	8,083	27.8	1,434	25,978	†	136	6,004	†	185	129,798	16,031	22,432	170
13,002	3,204	22.3	12,630	3,576	†	2,588	778	54	107	483,178	14,072	14,220	171
13,466	1,754	16.3	12,661	2,559	†	2,376	492	234	103	303,010	13,728	14,145	172
13,981	5,237	6.5	16,234	2,984	†	2,807	777	†	8	207,807	15,775	16,019	173
24,110	4,074	11.0	21,484	6,700	†	4,736	1,350	289	293	1,437,990	25,285	25,641	174
6,667	8,861	19.6	12,459	3,069	†	2,039	718	44	52	183,634	10,188	10,151	175
6,403	12,560	42.3	3,888	15,075	†	1,233	5,427	†	12	147,329	11,095	11,215	176
18,809	3,297	8.8	17,371	4,735	8	3,217	802	124	274	696,872	19,660	20,056	177
7,989	27,425	48.7	35,414	†	1,611	16	†	†	†	148,890	18,920	19,056	178
17,562	10,350	37.7	21,876	6,036	†	3,463	1,011	223	82	442,719	21,988	21,624	179
11,467	5,196	18.9	13,134	3,529	†	1,964	490	53	75	470,572	13,407	13,469	180
10,987	5,089	33.3	12,365	3,711	†	2,482	804	†	9	232,445	12,758	12,919	181
28,432	5,960	38.6	26,691	7,701	†	5,569	1,441	199	406	1,485,056	30,577	30,680	182
6,677	15,938	58.0	22,615	†	1,296	†	†	†	†	114,797	12,358	12,028	183
12,874	3,541	54.9	13,210	3,205	26	2,191	770	†	85	424,763	13,526	14,241	184
17,858	7,863	45.2	18,554	7,167	10	2,999	1,110	293	185	1,234,778	21,190	20,874	185
19,067	3,250	29.2	7,318	14,999	†	1,950	5,134	635	568	2,540,033	20,090	20,320	186
19,601	38	27.3	13,562	6,077	†	3,467	1,701	267	485	1,520,875	19,616	19,615	187

See notes at end of table.

Table 235. Selected statistics for degree-granting institutions enrolling more than 15,000 students in 2006: Selected years, 1990 through 2007—Continued

Line number	Institution	State	Control[1]	Type[2]	Total fall enrollment					Fall enrollment, 2006		
											Sex	
					Fall 1990	Fall 2000	Fall 2003	Fall 2004	Fall 2005	Total	Male	Female
1	2	3	4	5	6	7	8	9	10	11	12	13
188	CUNY, Bernard M. Baruch College	NY	1	1	15,849	15,698	15,126	15,537	15,756	15,730	7,452	8,278
189	CUNY, Borough of Manhattan Community College	NY	1	2	14,819	15,875	18,465	18,854	18,776	18,457	7,117	11,340
190	CUNY, Brooklyn College	NY	1	1	16,605	15,039	15,513	15,384	15,281	15,947	5,956	9,991
191	CUNY, Hunter College	NY	1	1	19,639	20,011	20,797	20,243	20,843	20,899	6,220	14,679
192	CUNY, Queens College	NY	1	1	18,072	15,061	16,993	17,395	17,638	18,107	6,561	11,546
193	Monroe Community College	NY	1	2	13,545	15,315	16,596	17,502	17,294	17,110	7,825	9,285
194	Nassau Community College	NY	1	2	21,537	19,621	20,984	21,446	20,979	21,229	10,109	11,120
195	New York University	NY	2	1	32,813	37,150	38,188	39,408	40,004	40,870	16,645	24,225
196	Saint John's University, New York	NY	2	1	19,105	18,621	19,777	19,813	20,346	20,069	8,273	11,796
197	Stony Brook University	NY	1	1	17,624	19,924	22,344	21,685	22,011	22,522	10,650	11,872
198	Suffolk County Community College	NY	1	2	†	†	20,980	21,117	21,180	21,859	9,417	12,442
199	SUNY at Albany	NY	1	1	17,400	16,751	16,998	16,293	17,040	17,434	8,188	9,246
200	SUNY at Buffalo	NY	1	1	27,638	24,830	27,255	27,276	27,220	27,823	14,429	13,394
201	Syracuse University	NY	2	1	21,900	18,186	18,639	18,247	18,734	19,082	8,586	10,496
202	Touro College	NY	2	1	4,456	8,092	18,174	19,618	22,540	23,651	9,429	14,222
203	Appalachian State University	NC	1	1	11,931	13,227	14,343	14,653	14,653	15,117	7,221	7,896
204	Central Piedmont Community College	NC	1	2	16,311	14,908	16,245	16,400	16,636	17,942	7,297	10,645
205	East Carolina University	NC	1	1	17,564	18,750	21,756	22,767	23,164	24,351	9,280	15,071
206	North Carolina State University at Raleigh	NC	1	1	27,199	28,619	29,854	29,957	30,148	31,130	17,411	13,719
207	University of North Carolina at Chapel Hill	NC	1	1	23,878	24,892	26,359	26,878	27,276	27,717	11,563	16,154
208	University of North Carolina at Charlotte	NC	1	1	14,699	17,241	19,605	19,846	20,772	21,519	9,734	11,785
209	University of North Carolina at Greensboro	NC	1	1	12,882	13,125	14,870	15,329	16,147	16,872	5,345	11,527
210	Bowling Green State University, Main Campus	OH	1	1	18,657	18,096	18,534	18,989	19,016	19,108	8,440	10,668
211	Columbus State Community College	OH	1	2	13,290	18,094	23,297	21,941	22,014	22,745	9,615	13,130
212	Cuyahoga Community College District	OH	1	2	23,157	19,518	23,231	24,664	24,788	24,289	9,163	15,126
213	Kent State University, Kent Campus	OH	1	1	24,434	21,924	24,242	24,347	23,622	22,697	8,888	13,809
214	Miami University, Oxford	OH	1	1	15,835	16,757	16,863	17,161	16,722	16,329	7,334	8,995
215	Ohio State University, Main Campus	OH	1	1	54,087	47,952	50,731	50,995	50,504	51,818	26,383	25,435
216	Ohio University, Main Campus	OH	1	1	18,505	19,920	20,452	20,143	20,461	20,610	9,963	10,647
217	Owens Community College	OH	1	2	6,857	15,845	19,341	19,671	20,595	18,739	10,221	8,518
218	Sinclair Community College	OH	1	2	16,367	19,026	19,860	19,622	18,937	19,103	8,257	10,846
219	University of Akron, Main Campus	OH	1	1	28,801	21,363	21,452	21,598	21,049	21,882	10,331	11,551
220	University of Cincinnati, Main Campus	OH	1	1	31,013	27,327	26,817	27,178	27,932	28,327	13,528	14,799
221	University of Toledo, Main Campus	OH	1	1	24,691	19,491	20,594	19,480	19,201	19,374	9,701	9,673
222	Wright State University, Main Campus	OH	1	1	16,393	13,964	14,648	15,985	16,207	16,088	6,980	9,108
223	Oklahoma State University, Main Campus	OK	1	1	19,827	18,676	23,844	23,819	23,692	23,499	11,896	11,603
224	Tulsa Community College	OK	1	2	17,955	16,270	16,931	17,143	16,770	16,632	6,352	10,280
225	University of Central Oklahoma	OK	1	1	14,232	14,099	15,044	14,598	15,859	15,588	6,368	9,220
226	University of Oklahoma, Norman Campus	OK	1	1	20,774	24,205	27,146	27,483	26,506	25,923	13,141	12,782
227	Oregon State University	OR	1	1	16,361	16,758	18,958	19,153	19,224	19,352	10,167	9,185
228	Portland Community College	OR	1	2	21,888	24,209	24,135	24,505	23,955	23,618	10,221	13,397
229	Portland State University	OR	1	1	16,921	18,889	23,081	23,444	23,929	24,254	10,836	13,418
230	University of Oregon	OR	1	1	18,840	17,801	19,992	20,296	20,347	20,348	9,586	10,762
231	Community College of Allegheny County	PA	1	2	20,553	15,556	19,103	19,292	18,404	18,110	7,682	10,428
232	Community College of Philadelphia	PA	1	2	15,151	15,953	20,615	20,606	17,102	16,870	5,519	11,351
233	Drexel University	PA	2	1	11,926	13,128	17,000	17,656	18,466	19,860	10,366	9,494
234	Pennsylvania State U. Penn State Main Campus	PA	1	1	38,864	40,571	41,795	41,289	40,709	42,914	23,531	19,383
235	Temple University	PA	1	1	29,714	28,355	32,877	33,551	33,695	33,865	15,072	18,793
236	University of Pennsylvania	PA	2	1	21,868	21,853	23,243	23,305	23,704	23,743	11,424	12,319
237	University of Pittsburgh, Main Campus	PA	1	1	28,120	26,329	26,795	26,731	26,559	26,860	12,556	14,304
238	Community College of Rhode Island	RI	1	2	16,620	15,583	16,223	16,293	16,042	16,373	6,286	10,087
239	University of Rhode Island	RI	1	1	16,047	14,362	14,791	14,749	15,095	15,062	6,347	8,715
240	Clemson University	SC	1	1	15,714	17,465	17,016	17,110	17,165	17,309	9,307	8,002
241	University of South Carolina, Columbia	SC	1	1	25,613	23,728	25,288	25,596	27,065	27,390	11,505	15,885
242	Middle Tennessee State University	TN	1	1	14,865	19,121	21,744	22,322	22,554	22,863	10,625	12,238
243	University of Memphis	TN	1	1	20,681	19,986	19,911	20,668	20,465	20,562	7,985	12,577
244	University of Tennessee	TN	1	1	26,055	25,890	27,281	27,792	28,512	28,901	13,878	15,023
245	Austin Community College District	TX	1	2	24,251	25,735	30,638	35,622	31,908	33,039	14,498	18,541
246	Central Texas College	TX	1	2	4,815	14,636	17,255	18,351	17,792	17,726	9,160	8,566
247	Collin County Community College District	TX	1	2	9,059	12,996	16,574	17,702	18,457	19,332	8,453	10,879
248	El Paso Community College	TX	1	2	17,081	18,001	24,569	24,569	26,078	26,667	26,105	10,292	15,813
249	Houston Community College System	TX	1	2	36,437	40,929	37,846	39,715	39,516	42,526	17,326	25,200
250	North Harris Montgomery Community College District	TX	1	2	15,653	24,554	34,471	35,788	39,949	40,846	16,217	24,629
251	Sam Houston State University	TX	1	1	12,753	12,358	13,460	14,371	15,357	15,959	6,585	9,374

See notes at end of table.

Table 235. Selected statistics for degree-granting institutions enrolling more than 15,000 students in 2006: Selected years, 1990 through 2007—Continued

Fall enrollment, 2006					Earned degrees conferred, 2006–07					Total expenses and deductions, 2005–06 (in thousands)[3]	Full-time-equivalent enrollment		
Attendance status			Student level										Line number
Full-time	Part-time	Percent minority[4]	Undergraduate	Postbaccalaureate	Associate's	Bachelor's	Master's	First professional	Doctor's		Fall 2005	Fall 2006	
14	15	16	17	18	19	20	21	22	23	24	25	26	27
10,465	5,265	53.0	12,796	2,934	†	2,550	1,129	†	†	163,872	12,582	12,501	188
10,859	7,598	75.9	18,457	†	2,213	†	†	†	†	144,396	13,484	13,410	189
8,984	6,963	48.8	12,111	3,836	†	1,994	1,160	†	†	171,503	11,099	11,649	190
11,438	9,461	46.2	15,805	5,094	†	2,116	1,307	†	†	239,300	15,046	15,084	191
9,813	8,294	41.3	13,662	4,445	†	2,142	1,332	†	†	188,581	12,419	12,990	192
10,032	7,078	25.5	17,110	†	2,419	†	†	†	†	118,656	12,590	12,408	193
13,868	7,361	40.9	21,229	†	2,713	†	†	†	†	179,377	16,030	16,339	194
31,081	9,789	32.0	20,965	19,905	750	4,734	5,765	967	364	2,402,387	33,938	34,839	195
13,847	6,222	44.3	14,983	5,086	62	2,228	1,022	521	84	345,782	16,391	16,297	196
18,257	4,265	40.0	14,847	7,675	†	2,981	1,610	147	364	1,390,628	18,622	19,846	197
12,281	9,578	25.1	21,859	†	2,659	†	†	†	†	165,110	14,927	15,497	198
14,014	3,420	22.6	12,457	4,977	†	2,770	1,341	†	163	465,853	14,786	15,286	199
23,336	4,487	18.8	18,506	9,317	1	3,939	1,971	576	394	792,802	24,338	25,011	200
16,071	3,011	19.4	13,156	5,926	2	2,819	1,535	207	142	610,027	17,080	17,233	201
12,952	10,699	39.2	12,107	11,544	856	2,189	3,642	351	156	169,556	16,459	17,107	202
13,185	1,932	6.7	13,447	1,670	†	2,425	603	†	3	254,828	13,471	13,923	203
7,261	10,681	41.0	17,942	†	971	†	†	†	†	105,782	9,647	10,847	204
18,607	5,744	20.7	18,587	5,764	†	3,401	1,359	60	59	575,312	19,983	20,775	205
24,026	7,104	16.7	23,730	7,400	130	4,601	1,457	75	411	965,076	25,811	26,750	206
22,911	4,806	21.1	17,124	10,593	†	3,787	1,871	601	512	1,842,583	24,250	24,704	207
15,520	5,999	21.7	17,032	4,487	†	3,111	976	†	48	298,111	17,079	17,807	208
12,400	4,472	25.2	13,024	3,848	†	2,195	906	†	74	273,885	13,512	14,097	209
16,595	2,513	13.4	16,085	3,023	†	3,012	981	†	91	345,581	17,521	17,549	210
9,589	13,156	27.3	22,745	†	1,428	†	†	†	†	136,971	13,434	14,006	211
10,114	14,175	35.7	24,289	†	1,558	†	†	†	†	233,891	15,179	14,873	212
18,186	4,511	11.0	18,136	4,561	†	3,748	1,287	†	136	392,976	20,287	19,912	213
15,322	1,007	8.6	14,551	1,778	308	3,758	417	†	45	451,403	16,083	15,699	214
45,187	6,631	15.3	38,479	13,339	†	8,643	2,635	834	667	3,285,885	46,417	47,746	215
18,841	1,769	6.9	17,026	3,584	58	3,970	894	104	162	430,618	19,406	19,525	216
6,493	12,246	16.4	18,739	†	1,090	†	†	†	†	91,518	11,064	10,604	217
7,374	11,729	20.3	19,103	†	1,399	†	†	†	†	137,146	11,273	11,312	218
15,486	6,396	16.7	18,015	3,867	367	2,292	829	132	94	357,355	17,265	18,044	219
21,434	6,893	17.2	19,977	8,350	160	3,113	1,698	331	261	918,631	23,749	24,082	220
14,959	4,415	17.8	16,067	3,307	152	2,707	634	250	77	342,024	16,637	16,693	221
12,722	3,366	17.1	12,215	3,873	†	2,150	1,069	88	52	313,427	14,050	14,016	222
18,288	5,211	16.3	18,895	4,604	†	3,712	802	67	195	554,403	20,522	20,275	223
5,947	10,685	21.0	16,632	†	1,955	†	†	†	†	105,293	9,668	9,534	224
10,486	5,102	21.6	14,309	1,279	†	2,290	427	†	†	118,481	12,685	12,511	225
19,434	6,489	21.4	19,573	6,350	†	3,888	1,467	174	174	596,519	22,467	21,889	226
16,171	3,181	15.8	15,828	3,524	†	3,294	621	128	179	609,300	17,381	17,417	227
8,576	15,042	22.9	23,618	†	1,757	†	†	†	†	187,113	13,580	13,626	228
13,635	10,619	19.6	17,998	6,256	†	3,143	1,640	†	36	294,805	17,423	17,762	229
17,900	2,448	13.3	16,529	3,819	†	3,721	940	168	170	489,163	18,902	18,851	230
7,374	10,736	19.5	18,110	†	1,889	†	†	†	†	116,139	11,214	10,978	231
5,365	11,505	64.5	16,870	†	1,527	†	†	†	†	120,772	9,188	9,228	232
13,417	6,443	24.3	12,909	6,951	27	2,382	1,379	253	134	584,131	15,500	15,905	233
40,502	2,412	12.5	36,612	6,302	71	9,604	1,131	18	646	2,969,259	39,207	41,432	234
26,110	7,755	31.8	24,674	9,191	7	4,808	1,349	802	392	1,805,842	28,746	29,106	235
19,492	4,251	27.6	11,922	11,821	2	2,823	2,996	653	483	4,197,595	21,293	21,137	236
22,123	4,737	14.6	17,246	9,614	†	3,630	2,045	586	410	1,322,710	23,587	23,914	237
6,127	10,246	24.8	16,373	†	1,145	†	†	†	†	93,879	9,215	9,567	238
11,774	3,288	13.7	11,875	3,187	†	2,008	556	85	85	362,502	12,771	13,033	239
15,154	2,155	10.3	14,172	3,137	†	2,946	803	†	138	536,595	16,022	15,976	240
21,664	5,726	19.5	18,648	8,742	11	3,725	1,612	397	244	665,256	23,422	23,816	241
18,255	4,608	17.5	20,643	2,220	†	3,635	556	†	17	271,240	19,765	20,053	242
13,856	6,706	40.0	15,984	4,578	†	2,442	850	113	112	336,899	16,319	16,457	243
25,264	3,637	13.2	20,619	8,282	†	3,670	1,643	548	347	1,250,824	26,132	26,641	244
9,218	23,821	38.3	33,039	†	1,021	†	†	†	†	164,629	16,577	17,216	245
3,158	14,568	55.2	17,726	†	2,241	†	†	†	†	100,638	7,899	8,049	246
7,598	11,734	29.5	19,332	†	1,116	†	†	†	†	88,463	10,997	11,538	247
10,027	16,078	88.5	26,105	†	1,839	†	†	†	†	134,394	16,099	15,425	248
13,263	29,263	68.5	42,526	†	2,190	†	†	†	†	257,126	21,370	23,088	249
7,732	33,114	40.4	40,846	†	2,191	†	†	†	†	211,190	18,198	18,850	250
12,300	3,659	26.9	13,778	2,181	†	2,543	602	†	43	169,574	13,245	13,708	251

See notes at end of table.

Table 235. Selected statistics for degree-granting institutions enrolling more than 15,000 students in 2006: Selected years, 1990 through 2007—Continued

Line number	Institution	State	Con-trol[1]	Type[2]	Total fall enrollment					Fall enrollment, 2006		
											Sex	
					Fall 1990	Fall 2000	Fall 2003	Fall 2004	Fall 2005	Total	Male	Female
1	2	3	4	5	6	7	8	9	10	11	12	13
252	San Antonio College	TX	1	2	20,083	19,253	20,831	20,563	19,933	20,202	8,157	12,045
253	San Jacinto College, Central Campus	TX	1	2	9,424	10,507	22,747	24,519	24,322	23,753	10,072	13,681
254	South Texas College	TX	1	1	†	11,319	15,334	17,130	16,233	18,460	7,540	10,920
255	Tarrant County College District	TX	1	2	28,161	26,868	32,667	34,136	34,892	34,777	14,312	20,465
256	Texas A & M University	TX	1	1	41,171	44,026	44,813	44,435	44,910	45,380	23,924	21,456
257	Texas State University, San Marcos	TX	1	1	20,940	22,423	26,306	26,783	27,129	27,485	12,020	15,465
258	Texas Tech University	TX	1	1	25,363	24,558	28,549	28,325	28,001	27,996	15,294	12,702
259	University of Houston	TX	1	1	33,115	32,123	35,066	35,180	35,344	34,334	16,539	17,795
260	University of North Texas	TX	1	1	27,160	27,054	31,065	31,155	31,958	33,395	14,312	19,083
261	University of Texas at Arlington	TX	1	1	24,782	20,424	24,979	25,297	25,432	24,825	11,611	13,214
262	University of Texas at Austin	TX	1	1	49,617	49,996	51,426	50,377	49,696	49,697	24,282	25,415
263	University of Texas at Brownsville	TX	1	1	1,448	9,072	10,604	11,560	13,316	15,688	6,426	9,262
264	University of Texas at El Paso	TX	1	1	16,524	15,224	18,542	18,918	19,268	19,842	8,811	11,031
265	University of Texas at San Antonio	TX	1	1	15,489	18,830	24,665	26,175	27,337	28,379	13,223	15,156
266	University of Texas, Pan American	TX	1	1	12,337	12,759	15,914	17,030	17,048	17,337	7,114	10,223
267	Brigham Young University	UT	2	1	31,662	32,554	33,008	34,347	34,067	34,185	17,856	16,329
268	Salt Lake Community College	UT	1	2	13,344	21,596	24,056	24,725	24,111	24,241	12,293	11,948
269	University of Utah	UT	1	1	24,922	24,948	28,436	28,933	30,558	30,511	16,494	14,017
270	Utah Valley State College	UT	1	1	7,879	20,946	23,803	24,149	24,180	23,305	13,295	10,010
271	Weber State University	UT	1	1	13,449	16,050	18,821	18,498	18,142	18,303	9,066	9,237
272	George Mason University	VA	1	1	20,308	23,408	28,246	28,874	29,728	29,889	13,333	16,556
273	James Madison University	VA	1	1	11,251	15,326	16,203	16,108	16,938	17,393	6,744	10,649
274	Liberty University	VA	2	1	18,533	6,192	9,050	10,475	12,458	17,798	9,019	8,779
275	Northern Virginia Community College	VA	1	2	35,194	37,073	38,097	37,392	37,740	38,166	17,444	20,722
276	Old Dominion University	VA	1	1	16,729	18,969	20,802	20,595	21,274	21,625	8,845	12,780
277	Tidewater Community College	VA	1	2	17,726	20,184	23,088	22,691	23,718	24,938	9,815	15,123
278	University of Virginia, Main Campus	VA	1	1	21,110	22,411	23,077	23,341	23,765	24,068	10,717	13,351
279	Virginia Commonwealth University	VA	1	1	21,764	24,066	26,631	28,303	29,168	30,189	12,198	17,991
280	Virginia Polytechnic Institute and State University	VA	1	1	25,568	27,869	27,755	27,619	27,979	28,470	16,445	12,025
281	University of Washington, Seattle Campus	WA	1	1	33,854	36,139	39,135	39,199	39,251	39,524	18,794	20,730
282	Washington State University	WA	1	1	18,412	20,492	22,712	23,241	23,544	23,655	11,228	12,427
283	West Virginia University	WV	1	1	20,854	21,987	24,260	25,255	26,051	27,115	14,078	13,037
284	Milwaukee Area Technical College	WI	1	2	21,600	14,296	17,767	18,524	18,545	17,774	7,411	10,363
285	University of Wisconsin, Madison	WI	1	1	43,209	40,658	40,879	40,455	40,793	41,028	19,490	21,538
286	University of Wisconsin, Milwaukee	WI	1	1	26,020	23,578	25,440	26,832	27,502	28,309	12,941	15,368

—Not available.
†Not applicable.
[1]Publicly controlled institutions are identified by a "1"; private, not-for-profit, by a "2"; and private, for-profit, by a "3."
[2]The types of institutions are identified as follows: "1" for 4-year institutions; and "2" for 2-year institutions.

[3]Includes private and some public institutions reporting total expenses and deductions under Financial Accounting Standards Board (FASB) reporting standards and public institutions reporting total expenses and deductions under Governmental Accounting Standards Board (GASB) 34/35 reporting standards.
[4]Minority students who are U.S. citizens or resident aliens as a percentage of total enrollment, including nonresident aliens.

Table 235. Selected statistics for degree-granting institutions enrolling more than 15,000 students in 2006: Selected years, 1990 through 2007—Continued

Fall enrollment, 2006					Earned degrees conferred, 2006–07					Total expenses and deductions, 2005–06 (in thousands)[3]	Full-time-equivalent enrollment		Line number
Attendance status		Percent minority[4]	Student level										
Full-time	Part-time		Under-graduate	Postbacca-laureate	Associate's	Bachelor's	Master's	First professional	Doctor's		Fall 2005	Fall 2006	
14	15	16	17	18	19	20	21	22	23	24	25	26	27
8,039	12,163	53.0	20,202	†	1,227	†	†	†	†	96,149	11,768	12,123	252
8,931	14,822	50.4	23,753	†	1,631	†	†	†	†	143,533	14,840	13,907	253
6,741	11,719	96.2	18,460	†	1,367	9	†	†	†	105,802	10,249	11,470	254
12,336	22,441	38.4	34,777	†	2,178	†	†	†	†	189,212	19,858	19,870	255
40,654	4,726	18.2	36,580	8,800	†	8,132	1,768	129	598	1,557,884	41,663	42,489	256
20,737	6,748	28.7	23,568	3,917	†	4,673	1,073	†	24	308,573	22,840	23,364	257
24,415	3,581	18.4	22,851	5,145	†	4,673	1,053	231	192	520,996	25,742	25,796	258
24,088	10,246	53.3	27,400	6,934	†	4,810	1,373	539	239	662,617	28,828	28,178	259
23,103	10,292	28.2	26,637	6,758	†	4,791	1,549	†	196	380,302	25,923	27,077	260
15,787	9,038	38.1	19,205	5,620	†	3,833	1,714	†	124	303,739	20,003	19,298	261
45,232	4,465	34.0	37,037	12,660	†	8,521	2,684	579	779	1,738,108	46,946	47,087	262
5,943	9,745	90.9	14,867	821	†	919	183	†	†	137,452	8,703	9,845	263
12,211	7,631	77.8	16,561	3,281	†	2,463	729	†	39	272,802	14,812	15,193	264
19,645	8,734	57.3	24,398	3,981	†	3,656	889	†	46	311,410	22,151	23,059	265
11,639	5,698	89.3	15,076	2,261	†	2,404	631	†	13	203,294	13,467	13,869	266
29,616	4,569	9.1	30,480	3,705	†	6,966	1,075	149	80	807,767	31,223	31,394	267
7,915	16,326	15.7	24,241	†	2,692	†	†	†	†	138,226	13,519	13,396	268
20,018	10,493	11.3	23,983	6,528	†	4,829	1,441	277	345	1,966,266	24,396	24,185	269
11,568	11,737	8.4	23,305	†	1,781	1,479	†	†	†	164,534	16,650	16,304	270
8,606	9,697	10.3	17,849	454	1,630	1,940	171	†	†	148,514	13,481	12,505	271
16,267	13,622	31.6	18,221	11,668	†	3,726	2,544	206	181	434,969	21,120	21,443	272
16,033	1,360	11.2	16,013	1,380	†	3,475	521	†	17	283,317	16,098	16,556	273
11,435	6,363	18.4	13,707	4,091	129	1,774	655	62	21	141,781	10,508	13,952	274
13,238	24,928	43.1	38,166	†	2,815	†	†	†	†	157,845	21,133	21,607	275
12,528	9,097	29.4	15,464	6,161	†	2,765	1,290	†	101	250,407	15,616	16,002	276
8,482	16,456	41.3	24,938	†	2,011	†	†	†	†	100,077	13,177	14,007	277
19,998	4,070	20.1	14,676	9,392	†	3,367	1,634	504	348	1,806,884	21,002	21,503	278
21,211	8,978	29.2	21,068	9,121	†	3,306	1,478	357	191	656,134	23,594	24,663	279
25,678	2,792	15.1	21,997	6,473	48	4,884	1,367	89	356	826,337	26,214	26,710	280
33,029	6,495	32.8	27,836	11,688	†	7,020	2,628	499	631	2,889,527	35,407	35,570	281
19,402	4,253	14.7	19,554	4,101	†	4,797	702	219	175	714,504	21,061	21,064	282
23,777	3,338	7.3	20,590	6,525	†	3,620	1,459	396	148	652,897	24,003	25,035	283
5,484	12,290	38.0	17,774	†	1,537	†	†	†	†	220,894	10,080	9,610	284
36,347	4,681	11.6	29,639	11,389	†	6,194	1,944	650	775	1,931,143	38,129	38,169	285
21,344	6,965	15.3	23,595	4,714	†	3,478	1,178	†	101	389,710	23,464	24,046	286

[5]Data for total enrollment in 1990 are for institutions of higher education, rather than degree-granting institutions.
[6]Data included with parent institution or central office.
NOTE: Degree-granting institutions grant associate's or higher degrees and participate in Title IV federal financial aid programs.

SOURCE: U.S. Department of Education, National Center for Education Statistics, 1990 through 2007 Integrated Postsecondary Education Data System, "Fall Enrollment Survey" (IPEDS-EF:90), Spring 2001 through Spring 2007, and Fall 2007. (This table was prepared July 2008.)

Table 236. Enrollment of the 120 largest degree-granting college and university campuses, by selected characteristics and institution: Fall 2006

Institution	State	Rank[1]	Control[2]	Type[3]	Total enrollment	Institution	State	Rank[1]	Control[2]	Type[3]	Total enrollment
1	2	3	4	5	6	1	2	3	4	5	6
University of Phoenix, Online Campus	AZ	1	3	1	165,373	University of California, Davis	CA	61	1	1	29,628
Ohio State University, Main Campus	OH	2	1	1	51,818	San Jose State University	CA	62	1	1	29,604
Miami-Dade College	FL	3	1	1	51,329	Riverside Community College	CA	63	1	2	29,486
Arizona State University at the Tempe Campus	AZ	4	1	1	51,234	Mount San Antonio College	CA	64	1	2	29,079
University of Florida	FL	5	1	1	50,912	University of Tennessee	TN	65	1	1	28,901
Universit of Minnesota, Twin Cities	MN	6	1	1	50,402	University of Iowa	IA	66	1	1	28,816
University of Texas at Austin	TX	7	1	1	49,697	California State University, Sacramento	CA	67	1	1	28,529
University of Central Florida	FL	8	1	1	46,646	Virginia Polytechnic Institute and State University	VA	68	1	1	28,470
Michigan State University	MI	9	1	1	45,520	University of Texas at San Antonio	TX	69	1	1	28,379
Texas A & M University	TX	10	1	1	45,380	Santa Monica College	CA	70	1	2	28,337
City College of San Francisco	CA	11	1	2	44,392	University of Cincinnati, Main Campus	OH	71	1	1	28,327
University of South Florida	FL	12	1	1	43,636	University of Wisconsin, Milwaukee	WI	72	1	1	28,309
Pennsylvania State U, Penn State Main Campus	PA	13	1	1	42,914	University of Missouri, Columbia	MO	73	1	1	28,184
University of Illinois at Urbana, Champaign	IL	14	1	1	42,738	Texas Tech University	TX	74	1	1	27,996
Houston Community College System	TX	15	1	2	42,526	Troy University	AL	75	1	1	27,938
University of Wisconsin, Madison	WI	16	1	1	41,028	University of Nevada, Las Vegas	NV	76	1	1	27,912
New York University	NY	17	2	1	40,870	SUNY at Buffalo	NY	77	1	1	27,823
North Harris Montgomery Community College District	TX	18	1	2	40,846	University of North Carolina at Chapel Hill	NC	78	1	1	27,717
Purdue University, Main Campus	IN	19	1	1	40,609	Colorado State University	CO	79	1	1	27,636
University of Michigan, Ann Arbor	MI	20	1	1	40,025	Texas State University, San Marcos	TX	80	1	1	27,485
Florida State University	FL	21	1	1	39,973	East Los Angeles College	CA	81	1	2	27,481
University of Washington, Seattle Campus	WA	22	1	1	39,524	Walden University	MN	82	3	1	27,412
Indiana University, Bloomington	IN	23	1	1	38,247	University of South Carolina, Columbia	SC	83	1	1	27,390
Northern Virginia Community College	VA	24	1	2	38,166	West Virginia University	WV	84	1	1	27,115
Florida International University	FL	25	1	1	37,997	University of Pittsburgh, Main Campus	PA	85	1	1	26,860
University of Arizona	AZ	26	1	1	36,805	University of Kansas, Main Campus	KS	86	1	1	26,773
University of California, Los Angeles	CA	27	1	1	36,611	Central Michigan University	MI	87	1	1	26,710
California State University, Fullerton	CA	28	1	1	35,921	University of Kentucky	KY	88	1	1	26,382
California State University, Long Beach	CA	29	1	1	35,574	University of California, San Diego	CA	89	1	1	26,247
Community College of Southern Nevada	NV	30	1	1	35,414	Georgia State University	GA	90	1	1	26,135
University of Maryland, College Park	MD	31	1	1	35,102	Palomar College	CA	91	1	2	26,118
Tarrant County College District	TX	32	1	2	34,777	El Paso Community College	TX	92	1	2	26,105
California State University, Northridge	CA	33	1	1	34,560	College of DuPage	IL	93	1	2	26,032
Rutgers University, New Brunswick/Piscataway	NJ	34	1	1	34,392	Nova Southeastern University	FL	94	2	1	25,960
University of Houston	TX	35	1	1	34,334	University of Oklahoma, Norman Campus	OK	95	1	1	25,923
Brigham Young University	UT	36	2	1	34,185	Mesa Community College	AZ	96	1	2	25,881
University of Georgia	GA	37	1	1	33,959	Pasadena City College	CA	97	1	2	25,873
University of California, Berkeley	CA	38	1	1	33,920	National University	CA	98	2	1	25,844
Temple University	PA	39	1	1	33,865	Harvard University	MA	99	2	1	25,778
San Diego State University	CA	40	1	1	33,441	University of New Mexico, Main Campus	NM	100	1	1	25,721
University of North Texas	TX	41	1	1	33,395	University of Massachusetts, Amherst	MA	101	1	1	25,593
University of Southern California	CA	42	2	1	33,389	Iowa State University	IA	102	1	1	25,462
Santa Ana College	CA	43	1	2	33,203	Florida Atlantic University	FL	103	1	1	25,325
University of Maryland, University College	MD	44	1	1	33,096	Northern Illinois University	IL	104	1	1	25,313
Austin Community College District	TX	45	1	2	33,039	University of California, Irvine	CA	105	1	1	25,230
Pima Community College	AZ	46	1	2	32,532	Kaplan University	IA	106	3	1	25,168
Wayne State University	MI	47	1	1	32,061	Tidewater Community College	VA	107	1	2	24,938
American River College	CA	48	1	2	31,908	Western Michigan University	MI	108	1	1	24,841
University of Colorado at Boulder	CO	49	1	1	31,665	University of Texas at Arlington	TX	109	1	1	24,825
Boston University	MA	50	2	1	31,574	Santa Rosa Junior College	CA	110	1	2	24,806
North Carolina State University at Raleigh	NC	51	1	1	31,130	University of Illinois at Chicago	IL	111	1	1	24,644
Strayer University	DC	52	3	1	30,654	Saint Petersburg College	FL	112	1	1	24,558
Broward Community College	FL	53	1	2	30,607	George Washington University	DC	113	2	1	24,531
University of Utah	UT	54	1	1	30,511	East Carolina University	NC	114	1	1	24,351
Valencia Community College	FL	55	1	2	30,245	Cuyahoga Community College District	OH	115	1	2	24,289
Virginia Commonwealth University	VA	56	1	1	30,189	Portland State University	OR	116	1	1	24,254
Louisiana State University and A & M College	LA	57	1	1	29,925	Salt Lake Community College	UT	117	1	2	24,241
George Mason University	VA	58	1	1	29,889	Oakland Community College	MI	118	1	2	24,123
Indiana U-Purdue U, Indianapolis	IN	59	1	1	29,764	American Intercontinental University Online	IL	119	3	1	24,073
San Francisco State University	CA	60	1	1	29,628	University of Virginia, Main Campus	VA	120	1	1	24,068

[1]College and university campuses ranked by fall 2006 enrollment data.
[2]Publicly controlled institutions are identified by a "1"; private, not-for-profit, by a "2"; and private, for-profit, by a "3."
[3]The types of institutions are identified as follows: "1" for 4-year institutions; and "2" for 2-year institutions.

NOTE: Degree-granting institutions grant associate's or higher degrees and participate in Title IV federal financial aid programs.
SOURCE: U.S. Department of Education, National Center for Education Statistics, 2006 Integrated Postsecondary Education Data System (IPEDS), Spring 2007. (This table was prepared July 2007.)

Table 237. Enrollment and degrees conferred in degree-granting women's colleges, by selected characteristics and institution: Fall 2006 and 2006–07

Institution[1]	State	Type and control[2]	Enrollment, fall 2006							Degrees awarded to females, 2006–07			
			Total	Females	Percent female	Males, full-time	Females, full-time	Males, part-time	Females, part-time	Associate's	Bachelor's	Master's	Doctor's
1	2	3	4	5	6	7	8	9	10	11	12	13	14
Total..........................	†	†	102,202	95,677	93.6	2,516	66,761	4,009	28,916	734	14,435	5,809	282
Judson College.....................	AL	3	305	290	95.1	2	230	13	60	0	41	†	†
Mills College	CA	3	1,393	1,300	93.3	87	1259	6	41	0	199	127	13
Mount Saint Mary's College...	CA	3	2,384	2,166	90.9	109	1585	109	581	137	339	58	15
Scripps College	CA	3	890	880	98.9	6	875	4	5	0	216	†	†
Saint Joseph College.............	CT	3	1,803	1,687	93.6	18	899	98	788	0	218	159	†
Trinity Washington University....	DC	3	1,597	1,434	89.8	43	745	120	689	0	124	215	†
Agnes Scott College	GA	3	914	907	99.2	5	861	2	46	0	161	25	†
Brenau University	GA	3	2,407	2,110	87.7	115	1291	182	819	0	309	163	†
Spelman College	GA	3	2,290	2,290	100.0	0	2191	0	99	0	437	†	†
Wesleyan College	GA	3	632	618	97.8	6	395	8	223	0	77	31	†
Lexington College..................	IL	3	57	57	100.0	0	48	0	9	1	1	†	†
Saint Mary-of-the-Woods College	IN	3	1,668	1,611	96.6	0	478	57	1133	1	131	20	†
Saint Mary's College..............	IN	3	1,527	1,519	99.5	6	1495	2	24	0	349	†	†
Midway College	KY	3	1,321	1,167	88.3	91	849	63	318	46	195	†	†
College of Notre Dame of Maryland.....................	MD	3	3,259	2,855	87.6	16	669	388	2186	0	338	301	0
Bay Path College..................	MA	3	1,479	1,448	97.9	23	1135	8	313	68	293	61	†
Mount Holyoke College..........	MA	3	2,153	2,149	99.8	1	2100	3	49	0	525	1	†
Pine Manor College	MA	3	501	497	99.2	4	490	0	7	3	71	0	†
Regis College	MA	3	1,315	1,262	96.0	15	812	38	450	108	196	83	†
Simmons College	MA	3	4,650	4,188	90.1	86	2354	376	1834	0	462	761	93
Smith College	MA	3	3,092	3,040	98.3	50	2978	2	62	0	670	136	4
Wellesley College	MA	3	2,370	2,318	97.8	0	2200	52	118	0	585	†	†
College of Saint Benedict	MN	3	2,059	2,059	100.0	0	2029	0	30	0	440	†	†
College of St. Catherine	MN	3	5,246	4,934	94.1	129	3087	183	1847	172	511	273	48
Cottey College	MO	4	318	318	100.0	0	316	0	2	119	†	†	†
Stephens College	MO	3	964	918	95.2	31	731	15	187	1	134	35	†
College of Saint Mary............	NF	3	960	960	100.0	0	712	0	248	67	140	23	†
College of Saint Elizabeth	NJ	3	1,982	1,766	89.1	29	770	187	996	0	268	130	†
Georgian Court College........	NJ	3	3,047	2,678	87.9	93	1467	276	1211	0	353	225	†
Barnard College....................	NY	3	2,350	2,350	100.0	0	2300	0	50	0	597	†	†
College of New Rochelle..........	NY	3	6,600	5,939	90.0	390	4282	271	1657	0	844	392	†
Marymount College of Fordham U.[3]..................	NY	3	521	477	91.6	27	397	17	80	0	201	†	†
Wells College.......................	NY	3	478	402	84.1	74	395	2	7	0	80	†	†
Bennett College for Women...	NC	3	607	607	100.0	0	591	0	16	0	81	†	†
Meredith College	NC	3	2,138	2,115	98.9	2	1720	21	395	0	345	30	†
Peace College	NC	3	653	653	100.0	0	622	0	31	0	124	†	†
Salem College	NC	3	1,094	1,050	96.0	15	666	29	384	0	168	62	†
Ursuline College	OH	3	1,639	1,505	91.8	49	805	85	700	0	203	89	†
Bryn Mawr College	PA	3	1,799	1,698	94.4	75	1524	26	174	0	300	113	20
Carlow College	PA	3	2,154	2,005	93.1	79	1235	70	770	0	277	107	†
Cedar Crest College.............	PA	3	1,932	1,835	95.0	17	983	80	852	0	326	35	†
Chatham College..................	PA	3	1,590	1,389	87.4	93	932	108	457	0	108	200	†
Moore College of Art and Design	PA	3	546	542	99.3	0	469	4	73	0	107	†	†
Rosemont College...............	PA	3	995	915	92.0	10	488	70	427	0	104	109	†
Wilson College.....................	PA	3	770	697	90.5	14	350	59	347	5	75	†	†
Columbia College..................	SC	3	1,446	1,401	96.9	19	1102	26	299	0	162	260	†
Converse College	SC	3	1,981	1,735	87.6	20	789	226	946	0	167	196	†
Texas Woman's University	TX	1	11,832	10,783	91.1	553	6160	496	4623	0	1233	1126	69
Hollins University	VA	3	1,061	1,001	94.3	14	814	46	187	0	182	84	†
Mary Baldwin College...........	VA	3	1,755	1,609	91.7	45	1087	101	522	0	236	57	†
Randolph College..................	VA	3	715	712	99.6	1	669	2	43	0	138	8	†
Sweet Briar College..............	VA	3	751	725	96.5	18	689	8	36	0	102	6	†
Alverno College	WI	3	2,480	2,437	98.3	19	1652	24	785	6	296	40	†
Mount Mary College	WI	3	1,732	1,669	96.4	17	989	46	680	0	196	68	†

†Not applicable.
[1]Data are for colleges and universities identified by the Women's College Coalition as women's colleges in 2008. Excludes women's colleges whose IPEDS data are reported together with a coed institution or coordinate men's college. The following institutions were excluded for this reason: The Women's College of the University of Denver; Newcomb College Institute of Tulane University; Douglass College of Rutgers University; and Russell Sage College of the Sage Colleges.

[2]1 = public, 4-year; 3 = private not-for-profit, 4-year; and 4 = private not-for-profit, 2-year.
[3]Institution closed in 2007.
NOTE: Degree-granting institutions grant associate's or higher degrees and participate in Title IV federal financial aid programs.
SOURCE: U.S. Department of Education, National Center for Education Statistics, 2006 and 2006–07 Integrated Postsecondary Education Data System (IPEDS), Spring 2007 and Fall 2007. (This table was prepared July 2008.)

Table 238. Enrollment and degrees conferred in degree-granting institutions that serve large proportions of undergraduate Hispanic students, by selected characteristics and institution: Fall 2006 and 2006–07

Institution	Type and control[1]	Enrollment, fall 2006					Degrees awarded to Hispanics, 2006–07				
		Total	Hispanic	Percent Hispanic[2]	Hispanic undergraduate	Hispanic postbacca-laureate	Associate's	Bachelor's	Master's	First-professional	Doctor's
1	2	3	4	5	6	7	8	9	10	11	12
Total, 50 states and District of Columbia............	†	2,284,868	965,365	42.3	923,553	41,812	46,309	35,403	8,909	561	220
Total, 50 states, District of Columbia, and Puerto Rico................................	†	2,494,287	1,174,380	47.1	1,104,081	70,299	50,576	52,470	14,400	1,135	453
Arizona											
Apollo College/Phoenix Inc..........................	6	2,684	1,018	37.9	1,018	†	42	†	†	†	†
Arizona College of Allied Health..................	6	134	44	32.8	44	†	6	†	†	†	†
Arizona Western College.............................	2	6,579	3,415	51.9	3,415	†	248	†	†	†	†
Art Center Design College, Tucson	5	379	113	29.8	113	†	1	14	†	†	†
Art Institute of Phoenix................................	5	1,055	280	26.5	280	†	8	43	†	†	†
Art Institute of Tucson.................................	5	115	36	31.3	36	†	19	1	†	†	†
Brown Mackie College, Tucson....................	5	360	136	37.8	135	1	47	21	†	†	†
Bryman School	6	1,195	486	40.7	486	†	155	†	†	†	†
Bryman School, East...................................	6	215	54	25.1	54	†	11	†	†	†	†
Central Arizona College...............................	2	6,471	2,193	33.9	2,193	†	80	†	†	†	†
Cochise College	2	4,127	1,408	34.1	1,408	†	164	†	†	†	†
Estrella Mountain Community College	2	5,894	2,274	38.6	2,274	†	94	†	†	†	†
Everest College, Mesa................................	5	361	102	28.3	102	†	0	0	†	†	†
GateWay Community College.......................	2	7,671	2,193	28.6	2,193	†	75	†	†	†	†
International Institute of the Americas, Mesa	5	217	77	35.5	77	†	5	2	†	†	†
International Institute of the Americas, Phoenix	5	482	190	39.4	190	†	14	5	†	†	†
International Institute of the Americas, Tucson..............	5	443	212	47.9	212	†	13	3	†	†	†
ITT Technical Institute, Tucson....................	5	464	172	37.1	172	†	22	2	†	†	†
Lamson College..	6	422	134	31.8	134	†	4	†	†	†	†
Phoenix College	2	12,213	5,013	41.0	5,013	†	252	†	†	†	†
Pima Community College	2	32,532	10,307	31.7	10,307	†	566	†	†	†	†
Pima Medical Institute	6	602	289	48.0	289	†	21	†	†	†	†
Refrigeration School Inc..............................	6	355	111	31.3	111	†	6	†	†	†	†
Remington College, Tempe Campus	5	273	94	34.4	94	†	8	5	†	†	†
South Mountain Community College	2	4,268	1,901	44.5	1,901	†	124	†	†	†	†
Universal Technical Institute of Arizona Inc	6	2,978	753	25.3	753	†	313	†	†	†	†
University of Phoenix, Southern Arizona Campus..........	5	2,831	902	31.9	746	156	†	81	50	†	†
Arkansas											
Ecclesia College	3	251	103	41.0	103	†	0	1	†	†	†
California											
Allan Hancock College.................................	2	12,321	4,675	37.9	4,675	†	415	†	†	†	†
American Intercontinental University	5	1,100	475	43.2	468	7	0	14	1	†	†
Antelope Valley College...............................	2	12,156	3,659	30.1	3,659	†	210	†	†	†	†
Argosy University, Orange County...............	5	1,108	232	20.9	120	112	3	13	15	†	8
Art Institute of California, Inland Empire	5	299	137	45.8	137	†	0	0	†	†	†
Art Institute of California, Los Angeles	5	2,073	779	37.6	779	†	21	47	†	†	†
Art Institute of California, Orange County	5	1,637	461	28.2	461	†	6	14	†	†	†
Art Institute of California, San Diego	5	2,035	602	29.6	602	†	24	70	†	†	†
Bakersfield College......................................	2	15,850	7,371	46.5	7,371	†	357	†	†	†	†
Barstow Community College	2	2,858	782	27.4	782	†	101	†	†	†	†
Brooks College, Long Beach	6	591	242	40.9	242	†	48	†	†	†	†
Brooks College, Sunnyvale..........................	6	373	129	34.6	129	†	17	†	†	†	†
Bryan College	6	856	295	34.5	295	†	0	†	†	†	†
Cabrillo College..	2	14,217	3,826	26.9	3,826	†	182	†	†	†	†
California College, San Diego.......................	5	443	149	33.6	149	†	39	2	†	†	†
California Design College	5	699	189	27.0	189	†	6	4	†	†	†
California School of Culinary Arts.................	6	1,504	595	39.6	595	†	123	†	†	†	†
California State Polytechnic University, Pomona	1	20,510	6,136	29.9	5,611	525	†	888	86	†	†
California State University, Bakersfield........	1	7,711	2,984	38.7	2,527	457	†	438	83	†	†
California State University, Channel Islands	1	3,123	853	27.3	799	54	†	103	5	†	†
California State University, Dominguez Hills........	1	12,068	4,741	39.3	3,874	867	†	647	195	†	†
California State University, Fresno...............	1	22,098	7,274	32.9	6,392	882	†	794	143	†	1
California State University, Fullerton............	1	35,921	10,693	29.8	9,620	1,073	†	1,505	206	†	†
California State University, Long Beach........	1	35,574	9,809	27.6	8,431	1,378	†	1,392	276	†	†
California State University, Los Angeles.......	1	20,565	9,741	47.4	7,740	2,001	†	1,308	370	†	†
California State University, Monterey Bay.....	1	3,818	1,199	31.4	1,112	87	†	191	6	†	†
California State University, Northridge..........	1	34,560	11,324	32.8	9,687	1,637	†	1,360	357	†	†
California State University, San Bernardino..........	1	16,479	6,067	36.8	5,132	935	†	818	163	†	†
California State University, Stanislaus	1	8,374	2,612	31.2	2,216	396	†	339	32	†	†
Canada College...	2	5,579	2,242	40.2	2,242	†	54	†	†	†	†
Cerritos College...	2	22,434	12,802	57.1	12,802	†	559	†	†	†	†
Chaffey College	2	17,916	8,149	45.5	8,149	†	505	†	†	†	†
Charles Drew University of Medicine and Science	3	175	44	25.1	35	9	4	11	3	†	†
Citrus College...	2	11,467	5,308	46.3	5,308	†	269	†	†	†	†
College of the Canyons................................	2	17,067	4,808	28.2	4,808	†	156	†	†	†	†
College of the Desert...................................	2	8,447	4,265	50.5	4,265	†	217	†	†	†	†
College of the Sequoias...............................	2	9,959	4,733	47.5	4,733	†	311	†	†	†	†
Concorde Career College, Garden Grove......	6	477	149	31.2	149	†	15	†	†	†	†
Concorde Career College, San Bernardino.......	6	682	334	49.0	334	†	27	†	†	†	†
Concorde Career College, San Diego	6	405	154	38.0	154	†	0	†	†	†	†
Contra Costa College...................................	2	6,870	1,796	26.1	1,796	†	96	†	†	†	†
Cypress College	2	12,898	3,840	29.8	3,840	†	183	†	†	†	†
DeVry University, California..........................	5	6,005	1,835	30.6	1,705	130	36	286	27	†	†
East Los Angeles College	2	27,481	18,288	66.5	18,288	†	840	†	†	†	†

See notes at end of table.

Table 238. Enrollment and degrees conferred in degree-granting institutions that serve large proportions of undergraduate Hispanic students, by selected characteristics and institution: Fall 2006 and 2006–07—Continued

Institution	Type and control[1]	Enrollment, fall 2006					Degrees awarded to Hispanics, 2006–07				
		Total	Hispanic	Percent Hispanic[2]	Hispanic under-graduate	Hispanic postbacca-laureate	Associate's	Bachelor's	Master's	First-professional	Doctor's
1	2	3	4	5	6	7	8	9	10	11	12
East San Gabriel Valley Regional Occupational Program	2	700	269	38.4	269	†	7	†	†	†	†
El Camino College, Compton Center	2	2,750	1,049	38.1	1,049	†	10	†	†	†	†
El Camino Community College District	2	23,488	8,206	34.9	8,206	†	298	†	†	†	†
Everest College, City of Industry	6	907	812	89.5	812	†	†	†	†	†	†
Everest College, Ontario Metro	5	838	495	59.1	495	†	6	†	†	†	†
Everest College, West Los Angeles	6	550	329	59.8	329	†	0	†	†	†	†
Evergreen Valley College	2	8,654	2,867	33.1	2,867	†	121	†	†	†	†
Fashion Careers College	6	132	46	34.8	46	†	14	†	†	†	†
Fashion Institute of Design & Merchandising, Orange	6	552	153	27.7	153	†	†	†	†	†	†
Fremont College	6	108	48	44.4	48	†	15	†	†	†	†
Fresno City College	2	22,040	10,078	45.7	10,078	†	414	†	†	†	†
Fresno Pacific University	3	2,321	633	27.3	441	192	0	102	20	†	†
Fullerton College	2	19,995	7,190	36.0	7,190	†	301	†	†	†	†
Gavilan College	2	5,185	2,288	44.1	2,288	†	104	†	†	†	†
Hartnell College	2	9,766	5,731	58.7	5,731	†	282	†	†	†	†
Heald College, Fresno	6	807	446	55.3	446	†	15	†	†	†	†
Heald College, Hayward	6	880	312	35.5	312	†	75	†	†	†	†
Heald College, Salinas	6	424	299	70.5	299	†	88	†	†	†	†
Heald College, San Francisco	6	311	77	24.8	77	†	14	†	†	†	†
Heald College, San Jose	6	686	328	47.8	328	†	91	†	†	†	†
Heald College, Stockton	6	586	240	41.0	240	†	37	†	†	†	†
Humphreys College, Stockton	3	630	203	32.2	193	10	79	20	†	3	†
Imperial Valley College	2	8,137	7,241	89.0	7,241	†	333	†	†	†	†
Interamerican College	3	57	52	91.2	35	17	†	5	†	†	†
ITT Technical Institute, Anaheim	5	778	436	56.0	436	†	66	6	†	†	†
ITT Technical Institute, Clovis	5	156	77	49.4	77	†	0	0	†	†	†
ITT Technical Institute, Lathrop	5	651	260	39.9	260	†	46	10	†	†	†
ITT Technical Institute, Oxnard	5	472	247	52.3	247	†	32	21	†	†	†
ITT Technical Institute, San Bernardino	5	1,226	652	53.2	652	†	108	23	†	†	†
ITT Technical Institute, San Diego	5	970	416	42.9	416	†	58	13	†	†	†
ITT Technical Institute, San Dimas	5	832	576	69.2	576	†	57	5	†	†	†
ITT Technical Institute, Sylmar	5	902	550	61.0	550	†	85	11	†	†	†
ITT Technical Institute, Torrance	5	666	384	57.7	384	†	68	5	†	†	†
LA College International	5	137	73	53.3	73	†	9	1	†	†	†
La Sierra University	3	1,896	514	27.1	455	59	†	61	11	†	1
Long Beach City College	2	23,509	8,160	34.7	8,160	†	248	†	†	†	†
Los Angeles City College	2	15,654	6,637	42.4	6,637	†	230	†	†	†	†
Los Angeles County College of Nursing and Allied Health	2	287	76	26.5	76	†	30	†	†	†	†
Los Angeles Harbor College	2	8,868	4,009	45.2	4,009	†	220	†	†	†	†
Los Angeles Mission College	2	7,251	5,394	74.4	5,394	†	264	†	†	†	†
Los Angeles Pierce College	2	18,690	5,946	31.8	5,946	†	192	†	†	†	†
Los Angeles Trade Technical College	2	13,393	7,063	52.7	7,063	†	238	†	†	†	†
Los Angeles Valley College	2	16,767	7,208	43.0	7,208	†	267	†	†	†	†
Los Medanos College	2	7,809	2,063	26.4	2,063	†	39	†	†	†	†
Maric College, Bakersfield	6	235	146	62.1	146	†	1	†	†	†	†
Maric College, Fresno	6	484	285	58.9	285	†	9	†	†	†	†
Maric College, Modesto Campus	6	305	168	55.1	168	†	48	†	†	†	†
Maric College, Palm Springs	6	475	242	50.9	242	†	8	†	†	†	†
Maric College, Panorama City	6	267	179	67.0	179	†	21	†	†	†	†
Maric College, Sacramento Campus	6	656	173	26.4	173	†	16	†	†	†	†
Maric College, San Diego	6	1,293	342	26.5	342	†	35	†	†	†	†
Maric College, Vista	6	329	125	38.0	125	†	33	†	†	†	†
Merced College	2	10,116	4,198	41.5	4,198	†	153	†	†	†	†
Modesto Junior College	2	18,034	5,927	32.9	5,927	†	272	†	†	†	†
Mount Saint Mary's College	3	2,384	1,091	45.8	930	161	62	131	25	†	0
Mount San Antonio College	2	29,079	13,137	45.2	13,137	†	825	†	†	†	†
Mount San Jacinto CC District	2	12,493	3,582	28.7	3,582	†	252	†	†	†	†
Mount Sierra College	5	604	263	43.5	263	†	†	32	†	†	†
National Hispanic University	3	553	479	86.6	421	58	2	14	†	†	†
Newschool of Architecture and Design	5	437	102	23.3	79	23	†	1	1	†	†
Oxnard College	2	6,379	4,186	65.6	4,186	†	298	†	†	†	†
Pacific Oaks College	3	1,028	327	31.8	99	228	†	25	39	†	†
Palo Verde College	2	4,116	1,112	27.0	1,112	†	44	†	†	†	†
Pasadena City College	2	25,873	9,114	35.2	9,114	†	434	†	†	†	†
Pima Medical Institute	6	606	275	45.4	275	†	17	†	†	†	†
Platt College, Los Angeles	5	102	68	66.7	68	†	13	1	†	†	†
Platt College, Newport Beach	5	116	32	27.6	32	†	10	10	†	†	†
Platt College, Ontario	5	287	142	49.5	142	†	26	13	†	†	†
Platt College, San Diego	5	267	70	26.2	70	†	15	13	†	†	†
Porterville College	2	3,665	1,926	52.6	1,926	†	133	†	†	†	†
Quality College of Culinary Careers	6	35	14	40.0	14	†	†	†	†	†	†
Reedley College	2	11,782	5,990	50.8	5,990	†	344	†	†	†	†
Remington College, San Diego Campus	5	428	214	50.0	214	†	52	9	†	†	†
Rio Hondo College	2	20,121	13,451	66.9	13,451	†	492	†	†	†	†
Riverside Community College	2	29,486	11,627	39.4	11,627	†	752	†	†	†	†
Sage College	6	415	137	33.0	137	†	3	†	†	†	†
San Bernardino Valley College	2	12,090	5,400	44.7	5,400	†	293	†	†	†	†
San Diego City College	2	16,203	5,563	34.3	5,563	†	181	†	†	†	†
San Diego State University, Imperial Valley Campus	1	873	785	89.9	589	196	†	160	8	†	†
San Joaquin Delta College	2	17,121	5,048	29.5	5,048	†	765	†	†	†	†

See notes at end of table.

Table 238. Enrollment and degrees conferred in degree-granting institutions that serve large proportions of undergraduate Hispanic students, by selected characteristics and institution: Fall 2006 and 2006–07—Continued

Institution	Type and control[1]	Enrollment, fall 2006					Degrees awarded to Hispanics, 2006–07				
		Total	Hispanic	Percent Hispanic[2]	Hispanic undergraduate	Hispanic postbacca-laureate	Associate's	Bachelor's	Master's	First-professional	Doctor's
1	2	3	4	5	6	7	8	9	10	11	12
San Joaquin Valley College, Bakersfield	6	816	454	55.6	454	†	117	†	†	†	†
San Joaquin Valley College, Fresno	6	680	379	55.7	379	†	187	†	†	†	†
San Joaquin Valley College, Fresno Aviation Campus	6	64	21	32.8	21	†	12	†	†	†	†
San Joaquin Valley College, Modesto Campus	6	380	166	43.7	166	†	12	†	†	†	†
San Joaquin Valley College, Rancho Cucamonga	6	696	440	63.2	440	†	88	†	†	†	†
San Joaquin Valley College, Visalia	6	1,040	530	51.0	530	†	193	†	†	†	†
San Jose City College	2	9,510	3,332	35.0	3,332	†	86	†	†	†	†
Santa Ana College	2	33,203	15,403	46.4	15,403	†	652	†	†	†	†
Santa Barbara Business College, Bakersfield	6	450	250	55.6	250	†	35	†	†	†	†
Santa Barbara Business College, Santa Maria	6	196	119	60.7	119	†	17	†	†	†	†
Santa Barbara Business College, Ventura	6	313	203	64.9	203	†	39	†	†	†	†
Santa Monica College	2	28,337	8,135	28.7	8,135	†	327	†	†	†	†
Santiago Canyon College	2	12,462	5,143	41.3	5,143	†	140	†	†	†	†
South Coast College	6	252	86	34.1	86	†	9	†	†	†	†
Southern California Institute of Technology	5	228	113	49.6	113	†	2	15	†	†	†
Southwestern College	2	19,446	12,052	62.0	12,052	†	593	†	†	†	†
Taft College	2	9,527	4,424	46.4	4,424	†	44	†	†	†	†
University of California, Merced	1	1,286	350	27.2	332	18	†	14	0	†	†
University of California, Riverside	1	16,875	4,149	24.6	3,899	250	†	744	52	†	7
University of La Verne	3	7,482	2,659	35.5	1,707	952	0	389	194	6	9
University of Phoenix, Central Valley Campus	5	2,137	803	37.6	724	79	†	81	22	†	†
University of Phoenix, San Diego Campus	5	3,771	929	24.6	722	207	1	87	47	†	†
University of Phoenix, Southern California Campus	5	14,739	4,693	31.8	3,848	845	1	425	165	†	†
Ventura College	2	11,757	4,651	39.6	4,651	†	311	†	†	†	†
Victor Valley College	2	9,916	3,020	30.5	3,020	†	268	†	†	†	†
West Hills College, Coalinga	2	2,469	1,434	58.1	1,434	†	106	†	†	†	†
West Hills College, Lemoore	2	3,619	1,543	42.6	1,543	†	136	†	†	†	†
West Los Angeles College	2	8,680	2,480	28.6	2,480	†	78	†	†	†	†
Western Career College, Antioch/Walnut Creek	6	319	83	26.0	83	†	†	†	†	†	†
Western Career College, San Jose	6	357	124	34.7	124	†	†	†	†	†	†
Westwood College, Anaheim	5	1,065	604	56.7	604	†	11	95	†	†	†
Westwood College, Inland Empire	5	1,281	819	63.9	819	†	11	72	†	†	†
Westwood College, Los Angeles	5	1,015	744	73.3	744	†	1	114	0	†	†
Westwood College, South Bay	5	628	377	60.0	377	†	13	20	†	†	†
Whittier College	3	2,054	523	25.5	384	139	†	59	17	27	†
Woodbury University	3	1,485	483	32.5	456	27	†	74	8	†	†
Wyotech, Fremont	6	1,554	565	36.4	565	†	40	†	†	†	†
Wyotech, Long Beach	6	1,073	807	75.2	807	†	0	†	†	†	†
Wyotech, West Sacramento	6	570	152	26.7	152	†	20	†	†	†	†
Yuba College	2	9,060	2,428	26.8	2,428	†	147	†	†	†	†
Colorado											
Adams State College	1	8,442	1,210	14.3	758	452	7	75	45	†	†
College America, Denver	5	476	135	28.4	135	†	35	21	†	†	†
Colorado State University, Pueblo	1	6,205	1,495	24.1	1,303	192	†	173	7	†	†
Community College of Denver	2	8,782	3,104	35.3	3,104	†	98	†	†	†	†
Everest College, Thornton	6	936	324	34.6	324	†	33	†	†	†	†
Heritage College	6	582	151	25.9	151	†	59	†	†	†	†
Intellitec College, Grand Junction	6	684	241	35.2	241	†	10	†	†	†	†
Kaplan College, Denver	6	339	164	48.4	164	†	16	†	†	†	†
Lincoln College of Technology	6	788	202	25.6	202	†	47	†	†	†	†
Otero Junior College	2	1,631	491	30.1	491	†	23	†	†	†	†
Pima Medical Institute	6	659	193	29.3	193	†	9	†	†	†	†
Pueblo Community College	2	5,056	1,791	35.4	1,791	†	130	†	†	†	†
Trinidad State Junior College	2	1,732	675	39.0	675	†	72	†	†	†	†
Connecticut											
Capital Community College	2	3,550	1,051	29.6	1,051	†	47	†	†	†	†
Florida											
Acupuncture and Massage College	5	206	96	46.6	89	7	†	†	†	†	†
Al Miami International U of Art and Design	5	2,550	865	33.9	860	5	27	95	1	†	†
American Intercontinental University	5	1,871	718	38.4	693	25	0	52	16	†	†
Argosy University, Tampa	5	660	63	9.5	10	53	†	3	10	†	3
Art Institute of Fort Lauderdale Inc	5	3,058	1,089	35.6	1,089	†	62	131	†	†	†
Barry University	3	8,882	2,768	31.2	1,937	831	†	453	157	25	10
Broward Community College	2	30,607	8,295	27.1	8,295	†	583	†	†	†	†
Carlos Albizu University, Miami Campus	3	1,079	857	79.4	345	512	†	81	130	†	4
City College, Casselberry	4	99	36	36.4	36	†	20	†	†	†	†
City College, Miami	3	269	176	65.4	176	†	35	7	†	†	†
College of Business and Technology	6	93	75	80.6	75	†	21	†	†	†	†
College of Business and Technology, Flagler Campus	6	158	157	99.4	157	†	0	†	†	†	†
College of Business and Technology, Hialeah Campus	6	71	71	100.0	71	†	0	†	†	†	†
DeVry University, Florida	5	2,940	834	28.4	703	131	18	113	33	†	†
Everest Institute	6	606	495	81.7	495	†	111	†	†	†	†
Everest University, Tampa	5	1,242	450	36.2	444	6	27	21	2	†	†
Florida Career College	5	3,666	1,506	41.1	1,506	†	109	†	†	†	†
Florida College of Natural Health	5	204	146	71.6	146	†	36	†	†	†	†
Florida International University	1	37,997	22,586	59.4	19,893	2,693	35	3,169	814	40	22
Florida Metropolitan University, South Orlando	5	3,772	968	25.7	945	23	80	19	4	†	†
Florida National College	6	1,796	1,720	95.8	1,720	†	281	†	†	†	†
Florida Technical College	6	831	259	31.2	259	†	87	†	†	†	†

See notes at end of table.

Table 238. Enrollment and degrees conferred in degree-granting institutions that serve large proportions of undergraduate Hispanic students, by selected characteristics and institution: Fall 2006 and 2006–07—Continued

Institution	Type and control[1]	Enrollment, fall 2006					Degrees awarded to Hispanics, 2006–07				
		Total	Hispanic	Percent Hispanic[2]	Hispanic under-graduate	Hispanic postbacca-laureate	Associate's	Bachelor's	Master's	First-professional	Doctor's
1	2	3	4	5	6	7	8	9	10	11	12
Herzing College	5	182	53	29.1	53	†	8	0	†	†	†
High-Tech Institute, Orlando	6	1,084	372	34.3	372	†	110	†	†	†	†
International Academy of Design and Technology	5	1,158	334	28.8	334	†	12	32	†	†	†
ITT Technical Institute, Fort Lauderdale	5	575	188	32.7	188	†	39	1	†	†	†
ITT Technical Institute, Lake Mary	5	510	129	25.3	129	†	18	1	†	†	†
ITT Technical Institute, Miami	5	557	441	79.2	441	†	86	11	†	†	†
Jones College, Miami Campus	3	94	45	47.9	45	†	†	†	†	†	†
Keiser Career College, Greenacres	6	716	207	28.9	207	†	32	†	†	†	†
Le Cordon Bleu College of Culinary Arts, Miami	6	669	358	53.5	358	†	184	†	†	†	†
Medvance Institute, Miami	6	164	94	57.3	94	†	†	†	†	†	†
Miami Dade College	1	51,329	33,871	66.0	33,871	†	4,010	31	†	†	†
National School of Technology Inc	6	466	366	78.5	366	†	39	†	†	†	†
Nova Southeastern University	3	25,960	4,692	18.1	1,489	3,203	0	348	719	256	50
Saint John Vianney College Seminary	3	56	11	19.6	11	0	†	1	†	†	†
Saint Thomas University	3	2,517	969	38.5	546	423	†	130	87	47	†
Trinity International University	3	280	110	39.3	86	24	†	42	5	†	†
Valencia Community College	2	30,245	7,667	25.3	7,667	†	778	†	†	†	†
Illinois											
Argosy University, Chicago	5	1,077	52	4.8	14	38	†	2	8	†	3
City Colleges of Chicago, Harry S Truman College	2	12,229	6,006	49.1	6,006	†	55	†	†	†	†
City Colleges of Chicago, Malcolm X College	2	6,442	2,029	31.5	2,029	†	36	†	†	†	†
City Colleges of Chicago, Richard J Daley College	2	10,105	6,903	68.3	6,903	†	159	†	†	†	†
City Colleges of Chicago, Wilbur Wright College	2	11,061	5,503	49.8	5,503	†	151	†	†	†	†
Coyne American Institute Inc	6	610	224	36.7	224	†	6	†	†	†	†
Fox College Inc	6	192	89	46.4	89	†	37	†	†	†	†
ITT Technical Institute, Burr Ridge	5	280	101	36.1	101	†	33	3	†	†	†
ITT Technical Institute, Mount Prospect	5	533	141	26.5	141	†	30	4	†	†	†
Lexington College	3	57	16	28.1	16	†	0	1	†	†	†
Lincoln College of Technology	6	1,367	499	36.5	499	†	5	†	†	†	†
Morton College	2	5,049	3,872	76.7	3,872	†	213	†	†	†	†
Northeastern Illinois University	1	12,056	3,179	26.4	2,828	351	†	278	63	†	†
Northwestern Business College	6	1,093	361	33.0	361	†	33	†	†	†	†
Northwestern Business College, Southwestern Campus	6	1,122	379	33.8	379	†	53	†	†	†	†
Saint Augustine College	3	1,299	1,085	83.5	1,085	†	164	11	†	†	†
Triton College	2	15,738	4,377	27.8	4,377	‖	123	†	†	†	†
Waubonsee Community College	2	8,843	2,677	30.3	2,677	†	61	†	†	†	†
Westwood College, Chicago Loop	5	824	263	31.9	263	†	7	29	†	†	†
Westwood College, O'Hare Airport	5	520	220	42.3	220	†	3	25	†	†	†
Kansas											
Dodge City Community College	2	1,766	425	24.1	425	†	27	†	†	†	†
Donnelly College	3	528	160	30.3	160	†	22	†	†	†	†
Seward County Community College	2	1,627	401	24.6	401	†	46	†	†	†	†
Massachusetts											
Gibbs College, Boston	6	520	139	26.7	139	†	9	†	†	†	†
Urban College of Boston	4	670	353	52.7	353	†	40	†	†	†	. †
Nevada											
ITT Technical Institute, Henderson	5	681	186	27.3	186	†	27	5	†	†	†
New Jersey											
Berkeley College	5	2,729	997	36.5	997	†	68	98	†	†	†
Gibbs College	6	991	301	30.4	301	†	12	†	†	†	†
Hudson County Community College	2	6,703	3,163	47.2	3,163	†	223	†	†	†	†
New Jersey City University	1	8,522	2,784	32.7	2,310	474	†	287	67	†	†
Passaic County Community College	2	7,301	3,560	48.8	3,560	†	131	†	†	†	†
Saint Peters College	3	3,117	776	24.9	646	130	3	84	40	†	†
Union County College	2	11,166	3,224	28.9	3,224	†	138	†	†	†	†
New Mexico											
Art Center Design College, Albuquerque	5	262	92	35.1	92	†	3	7	†	†	†
Central New Mexico Community College	2	22,615	10,038	44.4	10,038	†	522	†	†	†	†
Clovis Community College	2	3,657	1,061	29.0	1,061	†	53	†	†	†	†
College of Santa Fe at Albuquerque	3	1,239	506	40.8	298	208	2	76	†	†	†
College of the Southwest	3	526	196	37.3	169	27	†	30	3	†	†
Eastern New Mexico University, Main Campus	1	4,122	1,189	28.8	1,008	181	1	137	31	†	†
Eastern New Mexico University, Roswell	2	3,890	1,598	41.1	1,598	†	107	†	†	†	†
Eastern New Mexico University, Ruidoso	2	805	202	25.1	202	†	3	†	†	†	†
International Institute of the Americas	5	351	230	65.5	230	†	19	0	†	†	†
ITT Technical Institute, Albuquerque	5	657	311	47.3	311	†	60	16	†	†	†
Luna Community College	2	2,007	1,696	84.5	1,696	†	80	†	†	†	†
Mesalands Community College	2	545	216	39.6	216	†	13	†	†	†	†
National American University, Albuquerque	5	329	137	41.6	137	†	7	14	†	†	†
National American University, Rio Rancho	5	190	80	42.1	80	†	9	12	†	†	†
New Mexico Highlands University	1	3,747	1,998	53.3	1,350	648	2	199	136	†	†
New Mexico Junior College	2	2,656	1,198	45.1	1,198	†	85	†	†	†	†
New Mexico State University, Alamogordo	2	1,897	624	32.9	624	†	48	†	†	†	†
New Mexico State University, Carlsbad	2	1,223	590	48.2	590	†	36	†	†	†	†
New Mexico State University, Dona Ana	2	6,921	4,855	70.1	4,855	†	327	†	†	†	†
New Mexico State University, Grants	2	695	263	37.8	263	†	28	†	†	†	†
New Mexico State University, Main Campus	1	16,415	7,712	47.0	6,552	1,160	13	874	217	†	20
Northern New Mexico College	1	2,252	1,595	70.8	1,595	†	88	1	†	†	†
Pima Medical Institute	6	527	256	48.6	256	†	7	†	†	†	†

See notes at end of table.

Table 238. Enrollment and degrees conferred in degree-granting institutions that serve large proportions of undergraduate Hispanic students, by selected characteristics and institution: Fall 2006 and 2006–07—Continued

Institution	Type and control[1]	Enrollment, fall 2006					Degrees awarded to Hispanics, 2006–07				
		Total	Hispanic	Percent Hispanic[2]	Hispanic under-graduate	Hispanic postbacca-laureate	Associate's	Bachelor's	Master's	First-professional	Doctor's
1	2	3	4	5	6	7	8	9	10	11	12
Santa Fe Community College	2	3,873	1,786	46.1	1,786	†	114	†	†	†	†
University of New Mexico, Los Alamos Campus	2	758	315	41.6	315	†	26	†	†	†	†
University of New Mexico, Main Campus	1	25,721	8,300	32.3	6,758	1,542	5	968	230	74	20
University of New Mexico, Taos Branch	2	1,233	668	54.2	668	†	22	†	†	†	†
University of New Mexico, Valencia County Branch	2	1,559	924	59.3	924	†	43	†	†	†	†
University of Phoenix, New Mexico Campus	5	4,572	3,056	66.8	2,446	610	†	400	148	†	†
Western New Mexico University	1	2,584	1,189	46.0	1,043	146	51	52	21	†	†
New York											
Art Institute of New York City	6	1,512	499	33.0	499	†	66	†	†	†	†
ASA Institute of Business and Computer Technology	6	3,079	1,257	40.8	1,257	†	329	†	†	†	†
Berkeley College	5	3,052	867	28.4	867	†	38	104	†	†	†
Boricua College	3	1,020	862	84.5	833	29	151	161	22	†	†
College of Mount Saint Vincent	3	1,812	526	29.0	461	65	2	69	17	†	†
College of Westchester	6	980	318	32.4	318	†	80	†	†	†	†
CUNY Borough of Manhattan Community College	2	18,457	5,491	29.8	5,491	†	586	†	†	†	†
CUNY Bronx Community College	2	8,717	4,219	48.4	4,219	†	361	†	†	†	†
CUNY City College	1	13,155	3,813	29.0	3,194	619	†	354	137	†	†
CUNY Hostos Community College	2	4,697	2,597	55.3	2,597	†	232	†	†	†	†
CUNY John Jay College Criminal Justice	1	14,645	5,289	36.1	4,965	324	67	535	68	†	†
CUNY LaGuardia Community College	2	14,185	4,569	32.2	4,569	†	499	†	†	†	†
CUNY Lehman College	1	10,814	4,776	44.2	4,186	590	†	548	141	†	†
CUNY New York City College of Technology	1	13,368	3,304	24.7	3,304	†	163	127	†	†	†
DeVry Institute of Technology & Keller Graduate School	5	1,432	375	26.2	326	49	18	39	15	†	†
Interboro Institute	6	2,827	1,351	47.8	1,351	†	310	†	†	†	†
Katharine Gibbs School, New York City	6	2,243	798	35.6	798	†	50	†	†	†	†
Long Island University, Brentwood	3	904	69	7.6	20	49	†	0	17	†	†
Mandl, The College of Allied Health	6	582	264	45.4	264	†	79	†	†	†	†
Mercy College, Main Campus	3	9,120	2,532	27.8	1,734	798	46	296	266	†	†
Monroe College, Main Campus	5	4,361	2,396	54.9	2,364	32	579	283	3	†	†
Plaza College	5	701	225	32.1	225	†	65	†	†	†	†
Professional Business College	4	568	171	30.1	171	†	53	†	†	†	†
Technical Career Institutes	6	3,127	1,356	43.4	1,356	†	385	†	†	†	†
Vaughn College of Aeronautics and Technology	3	1,097	421	38.4	421	†	33	†	†	†	†
Wood Tobe-Coburn School	6	291	159	54.6	159	†	128	†	†	†	†
Oregon											
Mount Angel Seminary	3	196	23	11.7	17	6	†	5	0	3	†
Pennsylvania											
Pace Institute	6	207	75	36.2	75	†	10	†	†	†	†
Pennsylvania School of Business	6	190	115	60.5	115	†	0	†	†	†	†
Texas											
Academy of Health Care Professions	6	270	132	48.9	132	†	3	†	†	†	†
American Intercontinental University	5	376	155	41.2	152	3	2	25	3	†	†
Art Institute of Houston	5	1,601	433	27.0	433	†	60	21	†	†	†
ATI Career Training Center	6	792	247	31.2	247	†	11	†	†	†	†
Austin Business College	6	177	92	52.0	92	†	46	†	†	†	†
Baptist University of the Americas	3	114	71	62.3	71	†	2	15	†	†	†
Bradford School of Business	6	100	68	68.0	68	†	10	†	†	†	†
Brazosport College	1	3,809	986	25.9	986	†	56	1	†	†	†
Brookhaven College	2	10,269	2,721	26.5	2,721	†	91	†	†	†	†
Center for Advanced Legal Studies	5	77	22	28.6	20	2	21	†	†	†	†
Coastal Bend College	2	3,267	2,127	65.1	2,127	†	135	†	†	†	†
Computer Career Center	6	294	255	86.7	255	†	15	†	†	†	†
Del Mar College	2	11,352	6,674	58.8	6,674	†	496	†	†	†	†
El Centro College	2	6,157	1,891	30.7	1,891	†	92	†	†	†	†
El Paso Community College	2	26,105	22,246	85.2	22,246	†	1,560	†	†	†	†
Everest College, Arlington	6	730	212	29.0	212	†	30	†	†	†	†
Galveston College	2	2,119	533	25.2	533	†	47	†	†	†	†
Hallmark College of Technology/Aeronautics	6	752	449	59.7	449	†	226	†	†	†	†
Houston Community College System	2	42,526	12,460	29.3	12,460	†	550	†	†	†	†
Howard College	2	3,006	1,050	34.9	1,050	†	63	†	†	†	†
ITT Technical Institute, Arlington	6	691	211	30.5	211	†	54	†	†	†	†
ITT Technical Institute, Austin	6	709	255	36.0	255	†	71	†	†	†	†
ITT Technical Institute, Houston North	6	385	143	37.1	143	†	56	†	†	†	†
ITT Technical Institute, Houston West	6	412	161	39.1	161	†	56	†	†	†	†
ITT Technical Institute, Richardson	6	659	191	29.0	191	†	65	†	†	†	†
ITT Technical Institute, San Antonio	6	699	410	58.7	410	†	130	†	†	†	†
ITT Technical Institute, Webster	6	306	113	36.9	113	†	30	†	†	†	†
Laredo Community College	2	8,152	7,714	94.6	7,714	†	612	†	†	†	†
Midland College	1	5,819	1,791	30.8	1,791	†	190	†	†	†	†
Mountain View College	2	7,022	3,245	46.2	3,245	†	154	†	†	†	†
Northwest Vista College	2	9,568	4,234	44.3	4,234	†	249	†	†	†	†
Odessa College	2	4,647	2,205	47.4	2,205	†	109	†	†	†	†
Our Lady of the Lake University, San Antonio	3	2,783	1,871	67.2	1,322	549	†	252	165	†	4
Palo Alto College	2	7,591	4,687	61.7	4,687	†	370	†	†	†	†
Remington College, Dallas Campus	6	1,424	413	29.0	413	†	51	†	†	†	†
Remington College, Fort Worth Campus	6	730	198	27.1	198	†	26	†	†	†	†
Remington College, Houston Campus	6	912	295	32.3	295	†	38	†	†	†	†
Remington College, North Houston Campus	6	564	192	34.0	192	†	19	†	†	†	†
Saint Edward's University	3	5,224	1,510	28.9	1,342	168	†	225	45	†	†

See notes at end of table.

Table 238. Enrollment and degrees conferred in degree-granting institutions that serve large proportions of undergraduate Hispanic students, by selected characteristics and institution: Fall 2006 and 2006–07—Continued

Institution	Type and control[1]	Enrollment, fall 2006					Degrees awarded to Hispanics, 2006–07				
		Total	Hispanic	Percent Hispanic[2]	Hispanic under-graduate	Hispanic postbacca-laureate	Associate's	Bachelor's	Master's	First-professional	Doctor's
1	2	3	4	5	6	7	8	9	10	11	12
Saint Mary's University	3	3,904	2,190	56.1	1,669	521	†	320	91	40	1
Saint Philip's College	2	9,264	4,271	46.1	4,271	†	315	†	†	†	†
San Antonio College	2	20,202	9,116	45.1	9,116	†	494	†	†	†	†
San Jacinto Community College	2	23,753	8,131	34.2	8,131	†	453	†	†	†	†
South Plains College	2	9,045	2,563	28.3	2,563	†	138	†	†	†	†
South Texas College	1	18,460	17,493	94.8	17,493	†	1,292	9	†	†	†
Southwest Collegiate Institute for the Deaf	2	113	32	28.3	32	†	1	†	†	†	†
Southwest Institute of Technology	6	38	19	50.0	19	†	11	†	†	†	†
Southwest Texas Junior College	2	5,022	4,121	82.1	4,121	†	405	†	†	†	†
Southwestern Adventist University	3	867	221	25.5	199	22	4	28	5	†	†
Sul Ross State University	1	2,773	1,606	57.9	1,225	381	1	203	88	†	†
Texas A & M International University	1	4,917	4,394	89.4	3,577	817	†	641	189	†	0
Texas A & M University, Corpus Christi	1	8,585	3,290	38.3	2,669	621	†	427	138	†	7
Texas A & M University, Kingsville	1	6,728	4,073	60.5	3,458	615	†	691	114	†	18
Texas Culinary Academy	6	801	257	32.1	257	†	39	†	†	†	†
Texas State Technical College, Harlingen	2	4,281	3,797	88.7	3,797	†	233	†	†	†	†
University of Houston, Downtown	1	11,449	4,105	35.9	4,085	20	†	644	5	†	†
University of Phoenix, San Antonio Campus	5	742	410	55.3	348	62	†	10	21	†	0
University of Saint Thomas	3	3,524	934	26.5	563	371	†	84	77	1	0
University of Texas at Brownsville	1	15,688	14,127	90.0	13,551	576	†	831	133	†	†
University of Texas at El Paso	1	19,842	14,618	73.7	12,763	1,855	†	1,839	417	†	10
University of Texas at San Antonio	1	28,379	12,465	43.9	10,993	1,472	†	1,786	351	†	9
University of Texas Health Science Center at San Antonio	1	2,874	719	25.0	276	443	†	121	53	39	4
University of Texas of the Permian Basin	1	3,462	1,221	35.3	1,021	200	†	183	36	†	†
University of Texas, Pan American	1	17,337	15,190	87.6	13,415	1,775	†	2,148	500	†	7
University of the Incarnate Word	3	5,388	3,109	57.7	2,697	412	2	378	101	0	2
Victoria College	2	4,051	1,309	32.3	1,309	†	83	†	†	†	†
Virginia College, Austin	6	603	183	30.3	183	†	39	†	†	†	†
Western Technical College, El Paso, Diana Drive	6	413	304	73.6	304	†	65	†	†	†	†
Western Technical College, El Paso, Plaza Circle	6	570	548	96.1	548	†	163	†	†	†	†
Westwood College, Dallas	6	527	171	32.4	171	†	27	†	†	†	†
Westwood College, Fort Worth	6	409	138	33.7	138	†	21	†	†	†	†
Westwood College, Houston South	6	395	157	39.7	157	†	26	†	†	†	†
Wharton County Junior College	2	6,089	1,550	25.5	1,550	†	97	†	†	†	†
Utah											
Eagle Gate College	6	172	72	41.9	72	†	1	†	†	†	†
Washington											
Heritage University	3	1,336	568	42.5	465	103	8	48	34	†	†
Yakima Valley Community College	2	4,308	1,312	30.5	1,312	†	153	†	†	†	†
Puerto Rico											
American University of Puerto Rico, Bayamon	3	1,550	1,545	99.7	1,506	39	27	221	4	†	†
American University of Puerto Rico, Manati	3	1,473	1,473	100.0	1,473	†	8	164	0	†	†
Atlantic College	3	952	952	100.0	880	72	24	141	29	†	†
Bayamon Central University	3	3,036	3,036	100.0	2,439	597	18	271	129	†	†
Caguas Institute of Mechanical Technology	6	2,976	2,976	100.0	2,976	†	29	†	†	†	†
Caribbean University, Bayamon	3	2,404	2,404	100.0	1,900	504	18	104	124	†	†
Caribbean University, Carolina	3	902	902	100.0	522	380	13	31	115	†	†
Caribbean University, Ponce	3	1,501	1,501	100.0	996	505	13	49	147	†	†
Caribbean University, Vega Baja	3	1,355	1,355	100.0	785	570	24	64	206	†	†
Carlos Albizu University	3	906	906	100.0	204	702	†	63	72	†	85
Centro de Estudios Multidisciplinarios, Humacao	4	488	488	100.0	488	†	115	†	†	†	†
Centro de Estudios Multidisciplinarios, San Juan	4	837	837	100.0	837	†	150	†	†	†	†
Colegio Biblico Pentecostal de Puerto Rico	3	236	233	98.7	233	†	†	23	†	†	†
Colegio de Cinematografia Artes y Television	6	364	364	100.0	364	†	10	†	†	†	†
Colegio Pentecostal Mizpa	3	224	224	100.0	224	†	18	16	†	†	†
Colegio Universitario de San Juan	1	853	853	100.0	853	†	147	54	†	†	†
Columbia Centro Universitario, Caguas	5	950	950	100.0	876	74	91	91	30	†	†
Columbia Centro Universitario, Yauco	5	477	477	100.0	477	†	54	14	†	†	†
EDIC College	6	536	536	100.0	536	†	44	†	†	†	†
EDP College of Puerto Rico Inc	5	904	904	100.0	839	65	61	60	9	†	†
EDP College of Puerto Rico Inc, San Sebastian	5	815	815	100.0	815	†	37	39	†	†	†
Escuela de Artes Plasticas de Puerto Rico	1	484	484	100.0	484	†	†	41	†	†	†
Huertas Junior College	6	1,562	1,562	100.0	1,562	†	272	†	†	†	†
Humacao Community College	4	501	501	100.0	501	†	95	†	†	†	†
ICPR Junior College, Arecibo	6	446	446	100.0	446	†	136	†	†	†	†
ICPR Junior College, General Institutional	6	401	401	100.0	401	†	101	†	†	†	†
ICPR Junior College, Mayaguez	6	514	514	100.0	514	†	73	†	†	†	†
Instituto Tecnologico de Puerto Rico, Recinto de Guayama	2	671	671	100.0	671	†	†	†	†	†	†
Instituto Tecnologico de Puerto Rico, Recinto de Ponce	2	731	731	100.0	731	†	213	†	†	†	†
Instituto Tecnologico de Puerto Rico, Recinto de San Juan	2	701	701	100.0	701	†	†	†	†	†	†
Inter American U of Puerto Rico, Aguadilla	3	4,323	4,323	100.0	4,131	192	46	362	31	†	†
Inter American U of Puerto Rico, Arecibo	3	4,695	4,695	100.0	4,426	269	29	413	101	†	†
Inter American U of Puerto Rico, Barranquitas	3	2,399	2,399	100.0	2,331	68	32	244	21	†	†
Inter American U of Puerto Rico, Bayamon	3	5,150	5,150	100.0	5,089	61	38	438	9	†	†
Inter American U of Puerto Rico, Fajardo	3	2,256	2,256	100.0	2,234	22	11	189	†	†	†
Inter American U of Puerto Rico, Guayama	3	2,347	2,347	100.0	2,297	50	50	225	28	†	†
Inter American U of Puerto Rico, Metro	3	10,598	10,598	100.0	6,865	3,733	44	793	787	†	32
Inter American U of Puerto Rico, Ponce	3	5,367	5,367	100.0	5,111	256	80	420	50	†	†
Inter American U of Puerto Rico, San German	3	5,967	5,967	100.0	4,894	1,073	33	531	231	†	6

See notes at end of table.

Table 238. Enrollment and degrees conferred in degree-granting institutions that serve large proportions of undergraduate Hispanic students, by selected characteristics and institution: Fall 2006 and 2006–07—Continued

Institution	Type and control[1]	Enrollment, fall 2006					Degrees awarded to Hispanics, 2006–07				
		Total	Hispanic	Percent Hispanic[2]	Hispanic under-graduate	Hispanic postbacca-laureate	Associate's	Bachelor's	Master's	First-professional	Doctor's
1	2	3	4	5	6	7	8	9	10	11	12
John Dewey College, University Division.........................	3	1,272	1,272	100.0	1,272	†	106	79	†	†	†
National College of Business and Technology, Arecibo...	5	1,514	1,514	100.0	1,514	†	142	69	†	†	†
National College of Business and Technology, Bayamo..	5	2,171	2,171	100.0	2,171	†	294	50	†	†	†
National College of Business and Technology, Rio Grande	5	1,060	1,060	100.0	1,060	†	164	2	†	†	†
Ponce Paramedical College Inc..................................	6	2,879	2,879	100.0	2,879	†	87	†	†	†	†
Pontifical Catholic U of Puerto Rico, Arecibo.................	3	684	684	100.0	435	249	1	53	73	†	†
Pontifical Catholic U of Puerto Rico, Mayaguez	3	1,651	1,651	100.0	1,422	229	2	180	62	†	†
Pontifical Catholic U of Puerto Rico, Ponce..................	3	7,380	7,346	99.5	5,241	2,105	8	640	209	149	32
Puerto Rico Conservatory of Music............................	1	367	367	100.0	331	36	†	34	11	†	†
Ramirez College of Business and Technology................	6	429	429	100.0	429	†	55	†	†	†	†
Universal Technology College of Puerto Rico................	4	1,318	1,318	100.0	1,318	†	71	†	†	†	†
Universidad Adventista de las Antillas........................	3	889	808	90.9	738	70	24	84	4	†	†
Universidad Central Del Caribe	3	402	386	96.0	115	271	13	12	8	53	†
Universidad Del Este..	3	10,503	10,503	100.0	10,138	365	117	872	61	†	†
Universidad Del Turabo...	3	15,339	15,339	100.0	12,143	3,196	79	975	982	†	†
Universidad Metropolitana......................................	3	12,112	12,112	100.0	9,525	2,587	79	708	729	†	†
Universidad Politecnica de Puerto Rico.......................	3	5,844	5,844	100.0	5,136	708	†	470	129	†	†
University of Phoenix, Puerto Rico Campus..................	5	2,883	2,691	93.3	1,047	1,644	†	82	332	†	†
University of Puerto Rico in Ponce	1	3,265	3,265	100.0	3,265	†	74	372	†	†	†
University of Puerto Rico, Aguadilla..........................	1	3,218	3,218	100.0	3,218	†	45	322	†	†	†
University of Puerto Rico, Arecibo............................	1	4,041	4,041	100.0	4,041	†	44	501	†	†	†
University of Puerto Rico, Bayamon..........................	1	4,565	4,565	100.0	4,565	†	58	479	†	†	†
University of Puerto Rico, Carolina...........................	1	3,937	3,937	100.0	3,937	†	123	464	†	†	†
University of Puerto Rico, Cayey University College	1	3,626	3,626	100.0	3,626	†	1	524	†	†	†
University of Puerto Rico, Humacao..........................	1	4,306	4,289	99.6	4,289	†	121	449	†	†	†
University of Puerto Rico, Mayaguez..........................	1	12,380	12,380	100.0	11,305	1,075	†	1,438	108	†	3
University of Puerto Rico, Medical Sciences Campus.....	1	2,420	2,391	98.8	431	1,960	39	133	225	194	3
University of Puerto Rico, Rio Piedras Campus	1	19,075	19,048	99.9	15,275	3,773	†	2,375	364	178	72
University of Puerto Rico, Utuado.............................	1	1,514	1,514	100.0	1,514	†	46	97	†	†	†
University of Sacred Heart.....................................	3	5,523	5,523	100.0	4,536	987	3	542	71	†	†

†Not applicable.

[1] 1 = public, 4-year; 2 = public, 2-year; 3 = private not-for-profit, 4-year; 4 = private not-for-profit, 2-year; 5 = private for-profit, 4-year; and 6 = private for-profit, 2-year.

[2] Hispanic headcount enrollment (U.S. citizens and permanent residents only) as a percentage of total headcount enrollment, including both resident and nonresident students. Hispanic and total headcount enrollment include graduate as well as undergraduate students.

NOTE: Degree-granting institutions grant associate's or higher degrees and participate in Title IV federal financial aid programs. This table includes institutions that serve large proportions of Hispanic undergraduate students, defined as institutions with a full-time-equivalent undergraduate enrollment of Hispanic students at 25 percent or more of full-time-equivalent undergraduate enrollment of U.S. citizens. Data for Hispanics include only persons who were U.S. citizens or permanent residents.

SOURCE: U.S. Department of Education, National Center for Education Statistics, 2006 and 2006–07 Integrated Postsecondary Education Data System (IPEDS), Spring 2007 and Fall 2007. (This table was prepared July 2008.)

Table 239. Enrollment and degrees conferred in degree-granting tribally controlled institutions, by institution: Fall 2000 through fall 2006, and 2005–06 and 2006–07

Institution	Type and control[1]	Total enrollment										Degrees to American Indians/Alaska Natives			
									2006			Associate's		Bachelor's	
		2000	2001	2002	2003	2004	2005	Total	Total American Indian/ Alaska Native	Percent American Indian/ Alaska Native	Undergraduate American Indian/ Alaska Native	2005–06	2006–07	2005–06	2006–07
1	2	3	4	5	6	7	8	9	10	11	12	13	14	15	16
Tribally controlled institutions[2]	†	13,680	14,075	15,468	17,776	17,605	17,167	17,255	13,635	79.0	13,526	1,322	1,245	186	144
Alaska															
Ilisagvik College	2	322	279	316	417	214	278	203	138	68.0	138	3	5	†	†
Arizona															
Diné College	2	1,712	1,685	1,822	1,878	1,935	1,825	1,669	1,635	98.0	1635	231	215	†	†
Tohono O'odham Community College	2	—	—	—	181	169	270	198	195	98.5	195	5	20	†	†
Kansas															
Haskell Indian Nations University	1	918	967	887	918	928	918	889	889	100.0	889	99	106	70	50
Michigan															
Bay Mills Community College	2	360	368	430	386	401	406	550	325	59.1	325	6	8	†	†
Saginaw Chippewa Tribal College	2	—	—	41	66	109	123	125	108	86.4	108	6	10	†	†
Minnesota															
Fond du Lac Tribal and Community College	2	999	1,023	1,315	1,735	1,775	1,981	2,181	310	14.2	310	25	39	†	†
Leech Lake Tribal College	2	240	174	244	162	195	189	198	172	86.9	172	12	15	†	†
White Earth Tribal and Community College	4	—	79	99	81	67	61	106	67	63.2	67	0	3	†	†
Montana															
Blackfeet Community College	4	299	341	418	546	561	485	467	442	94.6	442	65	55	†	†
Chief Dull Knife College	2	461	442	268	442	356	554	359	285	79.4	285	22	18	†	†
Fort Belknap College	2	295	170	158	215	257	175	161	148	91.9	148	20	13	†	†
Fort Peck Community College	2	400	419	443	419	504	408	441	369	83.7	369	20	14	†	†
Little Big Horn College	2	320	203	275	394	291	259	312	290	92.9	290	43	36	†	†
Salish Kootenai College	3	1,042	976	1,109	1,100	1,130	1,142	1,092	866	79.3	866	79	60	25	17
Stone Child College	2	38	242	83	434	347	344	397	370	93.2	370	21	22	†	†
Nebraska															
Little Priest Tribal College	4	141	88	146	130	154	109	95	82	86.3	82	13	8	†	†
Nebraska Indian Community College	2	170	191	118	190	190	107	115	105	91.3	105	12	3	†	†
New Mexico															
Institute of American Indian and Alaska Native Culture	1	139	44	155	154	176	113	192	174	90.6	174	8	13	28	22
Navajo Technical College	2	841	299	283	300	306	333	392	388	99.0	388	41	32	†	†
Southwestern Indian Polytechnic Institute	2	304	723	777	936	772	614	561	561	100.0	561	65	56	†	†
North Dakota															
Candeska Cikana Community College	2	9	169	160	190	197	198	233	219	94.0	219	20	29	†	†
Fort Berthold Community College	2	50	50	249	274	285	241	196	190	96.9	190	37	14	†	†
Sitting Bull College	1	22	194	214	317	289	287	286	254	88.8	254	32	33	†	3
Turtle Mountain Community College	3	686	684	897	959	787	615	788	739	93.8	739	65	44	11	0
United Tribes Technical College	4	204	302	463	466	536	885	606	543	89.6	543	83	98	†	†
South Dakota															
Oglala Lakota College[2]	1	1,174	1,270	1,279	1,441	1,501	1,302	1,485	1,355	91.2	1295	78	69	39	39
Sinte Gleska University[2]	3	900	895	787	1,055	1,400	1,123	969	778	80.3	729	73	54	13	13
Sisseton-Wahpeton College	2	250	275	285	287	287	290	279	251	90.0	251	25	22	†	†
Washington															
Northwest Indian College	1	524	600	667	643	519	495	623	506	81.2	506	27	37	†	0
Wisconsin															
College of the Menominee Nation	4	371	407	530	499	507	532	513	427	83.2	427	33	37	†	†
Lac Courte Oreilles Ojibwa Community College	2	489	516	550	561	460	505	574	454	79.1	454	53	57	†	†

—Not available.
†Not applicable.
[1]1 = public, 4-year; 2 = public, 2-year; 3 = private not-for-profit, 4-year; and 4 = private not-for-profit, 2-year.
[2]"Total American Indian/Alaska Native" enrollment (column 10) includes graduate students and therefore does not equal "Undergraduate American Indian/Alaska Native" enrollment (column 12).

NOTE: These colleges are, with few exceptions, tribally controlled and located on reservations. They are all members of the American Indian Higher Education Consortium. Degree-granting institutions grant associate's or higher degrees and participate in Title IV federal financial aid programs. Totals include persons of other racial/ethnic groups not separately identified.
SOURCE: U.S. Department of Education, National Center for Education Statistics, 2000 through 2006, 2005–06, and 2006–07 Integrated Postsecondary Education Data System (IPEDS), Spring 2001 through Spring 2007, Fall 2006, and Fall 2007. (This table was prepared July 2008.)

Table 240. Fall enrollment, degrees conferred, and expenditures in degree-granting historically Black colleges and universities, by institution: 2005, 2005–06, 2006, and 2006–07

Institution	State	Type and control[1]	Total enrollment, fall 2005	Enrollment, fall 2006		Degrees conferred, 2006–07					Total expenditures, 2005–06 (in thousands)
				Total	Black enrollment	Associate's	Bachelor's	Master's	First-professional	Doctor's	
1	2	3	4	5	6	7	8	9	10	11	12
Total.........	†	†	311,768	308,774	255,150	3,800	30,778	7,028	1,671	581	$6,402,943
Alabama A&M University[2].............	AL	1	6,182	6,076	5,439	†	559	279	†	11	123,860
Alabama State University	AL	1	5,469	5,565	5,315	†	508	188	†	39	99,977
Bishop State Community College........	AL	2	4,883	4,070	2,528	333	†	†	†	†	33,898
Concordia College............	AL	3	850	827	787	21	54	†	†	†	6,147
Gadsden State Community College........	AL	2	5,421	5,206	1,022	476	†	†	†	†	41,901
H. Councill Trenholm State Technical College, Trenholm.......	AL	2	1,439	1,318	804	123	†	†	†	†	18,004
J. F. Drake Technical College...........	AL	2	729	690	401	63	†	†	†	†	7,514
Lawson State Community College...........	AL	2	3,371	3,141	2,594	192	†	†	†	†	34,172
Miles College	AL	3	1,758	1,738	1,730	†	177	†	†	†	19,562
Oakwood College	AL	3	1,751	1,771	1,622	5	265	†	†	†	35,621
Shelton State Community College, C. A. Fredd campus.......	AL	2	5,754	5,413	1,579	261	†	†	†	†	41,516
Stillman College...........	AL	3	804	815	777	†	116	†	†	†	19,868
Talladega College	AL	3	368	425	419	†	44	†	†	†	9,309
Tuskegee University[2]	AL	3	2,880	2,842	2,679	†	323	43	63	1	102,157
Arkansas Baptist College	AR	3	287	408	406	8	38	†	†	†	4,518
Philander Smith College	AR	3	785	580	571	†	108	†	†	†	12,099
University of Arkansas, Pine Bluff[2]	AR	1	3,231	3,128	2,956	0	376	31	†	†	69,434
Delaware State University[2]	DE	1	3,722	3,690	3,025	†	404	138	†	2	80,082
Howard University............	DC	3	10,930	10,771	9,629	†	1,344	429	410	117	737,797
University of the District of Columbia[2]	DC	1	5,363	5,534	4,632	147	306	55	†	†	110,702
University of the District of Columbia, David A. Clark, School of Law	DC	1	232	†	†	†	†	†	†	†	—
Bethune-Cookman College	FL	3	3,090	3,111	2,892	†	341	†	†	†	50,060
Edward Waters College	FL	3	839	842	812	†	140	†	†	†	17,743
Florida A&M University[2]...........	FL	1	12,154	11,907	10,897	63	1,318	288	195	29	270,401
Florida Memorial College...........	FL	3	2,004	1,867	1,611	†	246	44	†	†	36,944
Albany State College	GA	1	3,649	3,927	3,584	1	396	130	†	†	54,586
Clark Atlanta University	GA	3	4,469	4,514	4,474	†	702	186	†	42	91,248
Fort Valley State University[2]	GA	1	2,174	2,176	2,072	17	293	32	†	†	50,191
Interdenominational Theological Center...........	GA	3	447	466	432	†	†	0	91	7	9,038
Morehouse College	GA	3	3,029	2,933	2,849	†	563	†	†	†	77,828
Morehouse School of Medicine	GA	3	272	286	212	†	†	19	46	0	120,142
Paine College	GA	3	828	913	904	†	83	†	†	†	18,943
Savannah State College	GA	1	3,091	3,241	3,065	†	370	44	†	†	45,561
Spelman College...........	GA	3	2,318	2,290	2,281	†	437	†	†	†	72,496
Kentucky State University[2]...........	KY	1	2,386	2,498	1,626	48	193	47	†	†	56,375
Dillard University...........	LA	3	1,993	1,124	1,099	†	179	†	†	†	114,775
Grambling State University	LA	1	5,164	5,065	4,570	36	517	170	†	3	77,307
Southern University and A&M College, Baton Rouge[2].........	LA	1	10,364	8,624	8,154	4	822	307	†	8	153,187
Southern University at New Orleans	LA	1	—	2,197	2,132	10	287	157	†	†	32,509
Southern University at Shreveport...........	LA	2	2,536	2,387	1,993	284	†	†	†	†	22,679
Xavier University of Louisiana	LA	3	3,091	3,012	2,419	†	348	28	122	†	95,493
Bowie State University...........	MD	1	5,319	5,291	4,751	†	621	369	†	13	69,351
Coppin State College...........	MD	1	4,306	4,104	3,817	†	376	108	†	†	54,766
Morgan State University	MD	1	6,438	6,705	6,133	†	821	92	†	36	150,775
University of Maryland, Eastern Shore[2]...........	MD	1	3,870	4,130	3,357	†	436	58	†	13	88,223
Lewis College of Business...........	MI	4	304	67	67	†	†	†	†	†	2,854
Alcorn State University[2]...........	MS	1	3,544	3,584	3,221	33	397	127	†	†	64,747
Coahoma Community College...........	MS	2	1,946	1,838	1,777	205	†	†	†	†	20,776
Hinds Community College, Utica Campus...........	MS	2	1,396	1,125	1,046	69	0	0	0	0	—
Jackson State University...........	MS	1	8,416	8,256	7,717	†	834	360	†	66	172,240
Mississippi Valley State University...........	MS	1	3,165	3,162	2,992	†	424	87	†	†	69,202
Rust College...........	MS	3	970	920	842	8	130	†	†	†	14,495
Tougaloo College...........	MS	3	933	913	908	3	128	†	†	†	30,716

See notes at end of table.

Table 240. Fall enrollment, degrees conferred, and expenditures in degree-granting historically Black colleges and universities, by institution: 2005, 2005–06, 2006, and 2006–07—Continued

Institution	State	Type and control[1]	Total enrollment, fall 2005	Enrollment, fall 2006		Degrees conferred, 2006–07					Total expenditures, 2005–06 (in thousands)
				Total	Black enrollment	Associate's	Bachelor's	Master's	First-profes-sional	Doctor's	
1	2	3	4	5	6	7	8	9	10	11	12
Harris-Stowe State College	MO	1	1,662	1,868	1,684	†	123	†	†	†	19,676
Lincoln University[2]	MO	1	3,180	3,224	1,155	87	297	67	†	†	41,397
Bennett College for Women	NC	3	572	607	581	†	81	†	†	†	17,994
Elizabeth City State University	NC	1	2,664	2,681	2,137	†	350	18	†	†	59,045
Fayetteville State University	NC	1	6,072	6,301	4,697	†	685	162	†	2	86,259
Johnson C. Smith University	NC	3	1,404	1,470	1,459	†	228	†	†	†	33,427
Livingstone College	NC	3	895	907	883	†	122	†	†	†	18,017
North Carolina Agricultural and Technical State University[2]	NC	1	11,103	11,098	9,916	†	1,321	324	†	6	205,945
North Carolina Central University	NC	1	8,219	8,675	7,218	†	774	348	123	†	146,845
Saint Augustine's College	NC	3	1,163	1,247	1,157	†	187	†	†	†	26,047
Shaw University	NC	3	2,762	2,882	2,791	12	368	11	24	†	41,677
Winston-Salem State University	NC	1	5,566	5,650	4,684	†	747	77	†	†	98,483
Central State University	OH	1	1,623	1,766	1,698	†	166	1	†	†	51,392
Wilberforce University	OH	3	1,170	863	808	†	209	2	†	†	19,103
Langston University[2]	OK	1	3,151	2,788	2,238	1	160	27	†	2	51,488
Cheyney University of Pennsylvania	PA	1	1,560	1,667	1,611	†	149	50	†	†	42,214
Lincoln University of Pennsylvania	PA	1	2,278	2,423	2,259	†	229	191	†	†	48,293
Allen University	SC	3	624	530	527	†	61	†	†	†	13,377
Benedict College	SC	3	2,552	2,531	2,510	†	303	†	†	†	52,756
Claflin College	SC	3	1,728	1,758	1,654	†	273	30	†	†	34,943
Clinton Junior College	SC	4	123	108	108	18	†	†	†	†	2,323
Denmark Technical College	SC	2	1,408	1,377	1,322	106	†	†	†	†	11,413
Morris College	SC	3	863	824	824	†	140	†	†	†	16,834
South Carolina State University[2]	SC	1	4,446	4,384	4,214	†	474	125	†	39	100,952
Voorhees College	SC	3	709	710	698	†	170	†	†	†	16,126
Fisk University	TN	3	920	953	857	†	148	13	†	†	27,533
Lane College	TN	3	1,213	1,370	1,356	†	156	†	†	†	17,442
Le Moyne-Owen College	TN	3	809	714	711	†	127	†	†	†	16,046
Meharry Medical College	TN	3	707	730	580	†	†	10	113	6	112,606
Tennessee State University[2]	TN	1	8,880	9,038	6,737	114	982	328	†	46	157,505
Huston-Tillotson College	TX	3	706	742	589	†	94	†	†	†	15,108
Jarvis Christian College	TX	3	572	675	638	†	86	†	†	†	11,806
Paul Quinn College	TX	3	790	784	699	†	105	†	†	†	12,352
Prairie View A&M University[2]	TX	1	7,912	8,006	7,147	†	838	737	†	10	151,770
Saint Philip's College	TX	2	9,792	9,264	1,463	773	†	†	†	†	54,758
Southwestern Christian College	TX	3	251	202	186	33	2	†	†	†	5,443
Texas College	TX	3	807	755	685	1	76	†	†	†	11,564
Texas Southern University	TX	1	11,903	11,224	9,544	†	780	151	311	41	170,703
Wiley College	TX	3	827	862	756	†	161	†	†	†	18,402
Hampton University	VA	3	6,309	6,152	5,402	4	917	114	51	20	148,330
Norfolk State University	VA	1	6,096	6,238	5,535	52	709	234	†	7	122,637
Saint Paul's College	VA	3	717	681	668	†	139	†	†	†	15,942
Virginia State University[2]	VA	1	5,055	4,872	4,595	4	716	137	†	5	95,827
Virginia Union University	VA	3	1,700	1,599	1,533	†	197	†	120	5	23,391
Virginia University of Lynchburg	VA	3	—	178	174	8	14	†	2	5	1,305
Bluefield State College	WV	1	1,708	1,923	231	96	233	†	†	†	20,930
West Virginia State College	WV	1	3,491	3,502	612	†	464	7	†	†	54,948
University of the U.S. Virgin Islands, St. Thomas Campus[2]	VI	1	2,392	2,488	1,998	81	193	48	†	†	66,782

—Not available.

†Not applicable.

[1] 1 = public, 4-year; 2 = public, 2-year; 3 = private not-for-profit, 4-year; and 4 = private not-for-profit, 2-year.

[2] Land-grant institution.

NOTE: Excludes historically Black colleges and universities that are not participating in Title IV programs. Historically Black colleges and universities are degree-granting institutions established prior to 1964 with the principal mission of educating Black Americans. Federal regulations, 20 U.S. Code, Section 1061 (2), allow for certain exceptions to the founding date. Totals include persons of other racial/ethnic groups not separately identified. Detail may not sum to totals because of rounding.

SOURCE: U.S. Department of Education, National Center for Education Statistics, 2005 through 2007 Integrated Postsecondary Education Data System (IPEDS), Fall 2006, Fall 2007, Spring 2006, and Spring 2007. (This table was prepared September 2008.)

Table 241. Selected statistics on degree-granting historically Black colleges and universities, by control and type of institution: Selected years, 1990 through 2007

Enrollment, degrees, type of revenues, and type of expenditures	Total	Public			Private		
		Total	4-year	2-year	Total	4-year	2-year
1	2	3	4	5	6	7	8
Number of institutions, fall 2007	100	51	40	11	49	47	2
Fall enrollment							
Total enrollment, fall 1990	257,152	187,046	171,969	15,077	70,106	68,528	1,578
Males	105,157	76,541	70,220	6,321	28,616	28,054	562
Males, Black	82,897	57,255	54,041	3,214	25,642	25,198	444
Females	151,995	110,505	101,749	8,756	41,490	40,474	1,016
Females, Black	125,785	86,949	80,883	6,066	38,836	38,115	721
Total enrollment, fall 2000	275,680	199,725	175,404	24,321	75,955	75,306	649
Males	108,164	78,186	68,322	9,864	29,978	29,771	207
Males, Black	87,319	60,029	56,017	4,012	27,290	27,085	205
Females	167,516	121,539	107,082	14,457	45,977	45,535	442
Females, Black	139,920	96,677	89,260	7,417	43,243	42,810	433
Total enrollment, fall 2006	308,774	234,505	198,676	35,829	74,269	74,094	175
Males	118,865	89,194	75,234	13,960	29,671	29,576	95
Males, Black	96,508	69,205	63,846	5,359	27,303	27,208	95
Females	189,909	145,311	123,442	21,869	44,598	44,518	80
Females, Black	158,642	116,689	105,519	11,170	41,953	41,873	80
Full-time enrollment, fall 2006	243,078	174,865	155,327	19,538	68,213	68,054	159
Males	96,790	69,483	61,633	7,850	27,307	27,219	88
Females	146,288	105,382	93,694	11,688	40,906	40,835	71
Part-time enrollment, fall 2006	65,696	59,640	43,349	16,291	6,056	6,040	16
Males	22,075	19,711	13,601	6,110	2,364	2,357	7
Females	43,621	39,929	29,748	10,181	3,692	3,683	9
Earned degrees conferred, 2006–07							
Associate's	3,800	3,679	794	2,885	121	103	18
Males	1,137	1,099	156	943	38	28	10
Males, Black	479	446	89	357	33	23	10
Females	2,663	2,580	638	1,942	83	75	8
Females, Black	1,450	1,377	372	1,005	73	65	8
Bachelor's	30,778	20,648	20,648	†	10,130	10,130	†
Males	10,618	7,148	7,148	†	3,470	3,470	†
Males, Black	9,070	5,967	5,967	†	3,103	3,103	†
Females	20,160	13,500	13,500	†	6,660	6,660	†
Females, Black	17,580	11,439	11,439	†	6,141	6,141	†
Master's	7,028	6,099	6,099	†	929	929	†
Males	1,885	1,639	1,639	†	246	246	†
Males, Black	1,318	1,121	1,121	†	197	197	†
Females	5,143	4,460	4,460	†	683	683	†
Females, Black	3,987	3,400	3,400	†	587	587	†
First-professional	1,671	629	629	†	1,042	1,042	†
Males	651	252	252	†	399	399	†
Males, Black	424	123	123	†	301	301	†
Females	1,020	377	377	†	643	643	†
Females, Black	719	248	248	†	471	471	†
Doctor's	581	378	378	†	203	203	†
Males	215	131	131	†	84	84	†
Males, Black	138	72	72	†	66	66	†
Females	366	247	247	†	119	119	†
Females, Black	284	181	181	†	103	103	†
Financial statistics, 2005–06[1]	In thousands of current dollars						
Total revenue	$6,882,901	$4,251,501	$3,944,904	$306,597	$2,631,400	$2,626,155	$5,245
Student tuition and fees	1,399,176	737,021	690,686	46,335	662,155	659,521	2,635
Federal government[2]	1,812,650	958,846	860,053	98,794	853,804	852,872	931
State governments	1,809,745	1,727,134	1,592,286	134,848	82,611	82,611	0
Local governments	162,811	140,644	131,164	9,480	22,167	22,167	0
Private gifts and grants[3]	402,373	92,257	90,869	1,389	310,115	309,032	1,084
Investment return (gain or loss)	219,739	43,484	40,487	2,998	176,255	176,214	40
Educational activities	8,306	—	—	—	8,306	8,306	0
Auxiliary (essentially self-supporting) enterprises	627,754	368,161	360,827	7,334	259,593	259,477	116
Hospitals and other sources	440,347	183,953	178,534	5,419	256,394	255,955	439
Total expenditures	6,402,943	3,973,199	3,686,569	286,630	2,429,744	2,424,566	5,177
Instruction	1,757,292	1,132,350	1,023,107	109,243	624,942	623,014	1,928
Research	398,057	246,841	246,685	156	151,216	151,167	49
Academic support	502,397	346,497	324,950	21,547	155,901	155,897	4
Institutional support	1,101,505	542,885	505,843	37,043	558,620	556,654	1,966
Auxiliary (essentially self-supporting) enterprises	637,159	391,497	378,948	12,549	245,663	245,520	143
Other expenditures	2,006,532	1,313,129	1,207,036	106,093	693,403	692,315	1,088

—Not available.

†Not applicable.

[1]Totals (column 2) of public and private institutions together are approximate because public and private not-for-profit institutions fill out different survey forms with different accounting concepts.

[2]Includes independent operations.

[3]Includes contributions from affiliated entities.

NOTE: Historically Black colleges and universities are degree-granting institutions established prior to 1964 with the principal mission of educating Black Americans. Federal regulations, 20

U.S. Code, Section 1061 (2), allow for certain exceptions to the founding date. Federal, state, and local governments revenue includes appropriations, grants, contracts, and independent operations. Totals include persons of other racial/ethnic groups not separately identified. Detail may not sum to totals because of rounding.

SOURCE: U.S. Department of Education, National Center for Education Statistics, 1990 through 2007 Integrated Postsecondary Education Data System, "Fall Enrollment Survey" (IPEDS-EF:90), Spring 2001, Spring 2007, and Fall 2007. (This table was prepared October 2008.)

Table 242. Fall enrollment in degree-granting historically Black colleges and universities, by type and control of institution: 1976 through 2006

Year	Total enrollment	Males	Females	4-year	2-year	Public Total	Public 4-year	Public 2-year	Private Total	Private 4-year	Private 2-year
1	2	3	4	5	6	7	8	9	10	11	12
All students											
1976	222,613	104,669	117,944	206,676	15,937	156,836	143,528	13,308	65,777	63,148	2,629
1977	226,062	104,178	121,884	209,898	16,164	158,823	145,450	13,373	67,239	64,448	2,791
1978	227,797	104,216	123,581	211,651	16,146	163,237	150,168	13,069	64,560	61,483	3,077
1979	230,124	105,494	124,630	214,147	15,977	166,315	153,139	13,176	63,809	61,008	2,801
1980	233,557	106,387	127,170	218,009	15,548	168,217	155,085	13,132	65,340	62,924	2,416
1981	232,460	106,033	126,427	217,152	15,308	166,991	154,269	12,722	65,469	62,883	2,586
1982	228,371	104,897	123,474	212,017	16,354	165,871	151,472	14,399	62,500	60,545	1,955
1983	234,446	106,884	127,562	217,909	16,537	170,051	155,665	14,386	64,395	62,244	2,151
1984	227,519	102,823	124,696	212,844	14,675	164,116	151,289	12,827	63,403	61,555	1,848
1985	225,801	100,698	125,103	210,648	15,153	163,677	150,002	13,675	62,124	60,646	1,478
1986	223,275	97,523	125,752	207,231	16,044	162,048	147,631	14,417	61,227	59,600	1,627
1987	227,994	97,085	130,909	211,654	16,340	165,486	150,560	14,926	62,508	61,094	1,414
1988	239,755	100,561	139,194	223,250	16,505	173,672	158,606	15,066	66,083	64,644	1,439
1989	249,096	102,484	146,612	232,890	16,206	181,151	166,481	14,670	67,945	66,409	1,536
1990	257,152	105,157	151,995	240,497	16,655	187,046	171,969	15,077	70,106	68,528	1,578
1991	269,335	110,442	158,893	252,093	17,242	197,847	182,204	15,643	71,488	69,889	1,599
1992	279,541	114,622	164,919	261,089	18,452	204,966	188,143	16,823	74,575	72,946	1,629
1993	282,856	116,397	166,459	262,430	20,426	208,197	189,032	19,165	74,659	73,398	1,261
1994	280,071	114,006	166,065	259,997	20,074	206,520	187,735	18,785	73,551	72,262	1,289
1995	278,725	112,637	166,088	259,409	19,316	204,726	186,278	18,448	73,999	73,131	868
1996	273,018	109,498	163,520	253,654	19,364	200,569	182,063	18,506	72,449	71,591	858
1997	269,167	106,865	162,302	248,860	20,307	194,674	175,297	19,377	74,493	73,563	930
1998	273,472	108,752	164,720	248,931	24,541	198,603	174,776	23,827	74,869	74,155	714
1999	274,212	108,398	165,814	249,169	25,043	199,704	175,364	24,340	74,508	73,805	703
2000	275,680	108,164	167,516	250,710	24,970	199,725	175,404	24,321	75,955	75,306	649
2001	289,985	112,874	177,111	260,547	29,438	210,083	181,346	28,737	79,902	79,201	701
2002	299,041	115,466	183,575	269,020	30,021	218,433	189,183	29,250	80,608	79,837	771
2003	306,727	117,795	188,932	274,326	32,401	228,096	196,077	32,019	78,631	78,249	382
2004	308,939	118,129	190,810	276,136	32,803	231,179	198,810	32,369	77,760	77,326	434
2005	311,768	120,023	191,745	272,666	39,102	235,875	197,200	38,675	75,893	75,466	427
2006	308,774	118,865	189,909	272,770	36,004	234,505	198,676	35,829	74,269	74,094	175
Black students											
1976	190,305	84,492	105,813	179,848	10,457	129,770	121,851	7,919	60,535	57,997	2,538
1978	192,243	82,452	109,791	181,862	10,381	132,987	125,391	7,596	59,256	56,471	2,785
1980	190,989	81,818	109,171	181,237	9,752	131,661	124,236	7,425	59,328	57,001	2,327
1982	182,639	78,874	103,765	171,942	10,697	126,368	117,562	8,806	56,271	54,380	1,891
1984	180,803	76,819	103,984	171,401	9,402	124,445	116,845	7,600	56,358	54,556	1,802
1986	178,628	74,276	104,352	167,971	10,657	123,555	114,502	9,053	55,073	53,469	1,604
1988	194,151	78,268	115,883	183,402	10,749	133,786	124,438	9,348	60,365	58,964	1,401
1990	208,682	82,897	125,785	198,237	10,445	144,204	134,924	9,280	64,478	63,313	1,165
1991	218,366	87,380	130,986	207,449	10,917	152,864	143,411	9,453	65,502	64,038	1,464
1992	228,963	91,949	137,014	217,614	11,349	159,585	149,754	9,831	69,378	67,860	1,518
1993	231,198	93,110	138,088	219,431	11,767	161,444	150,867	10,577	69,754	68,564	1,190
1994	230,162	91,908	138,254	218,565	11,597	161,098	150,682	10,416	69,064	67,883	1,181
1995	229,418	91,132	138,286	218,379	11,039	159,925	149,661	10,264	69,493	68,718	775
1996	224,201	88,306	135,895	213,309	10,892	156,851	146,753	10,098	67,350	66,556	794
1997	222,331	86,641	135,690	210,741	11,590	153,039	142,326	10,713	69,292	68,415	877
1998	223,745	87,163	136,582	211,822	11,923	154,244	142,985	11,259	69,501	68,837	664
1999	226,407	88,057	138,350	213,729	12,678	156,115	144,124	11,991	70,292	69,605	687
2000	227,239	87,319	139,920	215,172	12,067	156,706	145,277	11,429	70,533	69,895	638
2001	238,638	90,718	147,920	224,417	14,221	164,354	150,831	13,523	74,284	73,586	698
2002	247,292	93,538	153,754	231,834	15,458	172,203	157,507	14,696	75,089	74,327	762
2003	253,257	95,703	157,554	236,753	16,504	180,104	163,977	16,127	73,153	72,776	377
2004	257,545	96,750	160,795	241,030	16,515	184,708	168,619	16,089	72,837	72,411	426
2005	256,584	96,891	159,693	238,030	18,554	186,047	167,916	18,131	70,537	70,114	423
2006	255,150	96,508	158,642	238,446	16,704	185,894	169,365	16,529	69,256	69,081	175

NOTE: Data through 1995 are for institutions of higher education, while later data are for degree-granting institutions. Degree-granting institutions grant associate's or higher degrees and participate in Title IV federal financial aid programs. The degree-granting classification is very similar to the earlier higher education classification, but it includes more 2-year colleges and excludes a few higher education institutions that did not grant degrees. (See Guide to Sources for details.)

SOURCE: U.S. Department of Education, National Center for Education Statistics, Higher Education General Information Survey (HEGIS), "Fall Enrollment in Colleges and Universities," 1976 through 1985 surveys; and 1986 through 2006 Integrated Postsecondary Education Data System, "Fall Enrollment Survey" (IPEDS-EF:86–99), and Spring 2001 through Spring 2007. (This table was prepared October 2008.)

Table 243. Employees in degree-granting institutions, by sex, employment status, control and type of institution, and primary occupation: Selected years, fall 1987 through fall 2007

Sex, employment status, control and type of institution, and primary occupation	1987	1989	1991	1993	1995	1997	1999	2001	2003	2005	2007	Percent change, 1997 to 2007
1	2	3	4	5	6	7	8	9	10	11	12	13
All institutions	**2,337,534**	**2,473,116**	**2,545,235**	**2,602,612**	**2,662,075**	**2,752,504**	**2,883,175**	**3,083,353**	**3,187,907**	**3,379,087**	**3,561,428**	**29.4**
Professional staff	1,437,975	1,531,071	1,595,460	1,687,287	1,744,867	1,835,916	1,950,861	2,132,150	2,268,268	2,459,885	2,629,401	43.2
Executive/administrative/managerial	133,719	144,670	144,755	143,675	147,445	151,363	159,888	152,038	184,913	196,324	217,518	43.7
Faculty (instruction/research/public service)	793,070	824,220	826,252	915,474	931,706	989,813	1,027,830	1,113,183	1,173,593	1,290,426	1,371,390	38.6
Graduate assistants	161,464	163,298	197,751	202,819	215,909	222,724	239,738	261,136	292,061	317,141	328,979	47.7
Other professional	349,722	398,883	426,702	425,319	449,807	472,016	523,405	605,793	617,701	655,994	711,514	50.7
Nonprofessional staff	899,559	942,045	949,775	915,325	917,208	916,588	932,314	951,203	919,639	919,202	932,027	1.7
Males	**1,164,067**	**1,212,924**	**1,227,591**	**1,256,037**	**1,274,676**	**1,315,311**	**1,365,812**	**1,451,773**	**1,496,867**	**1,581,498**	**1,650,350**	**25.5**
Professional staff	850,451	880,766	895,591	930,933	946,134	982,870	1,026,882	1,105,053	1,160,417	1,240,030	1,302,131	32.5
Executive/administrative/managerial	82,882	87,951	85,423	82,748	82,127	81,931	83,883	79,348	91,604	95,223	102,258	24.8
Faculty (instruction/research/public service)	529,413	534,254	525,599	561,123	562,893	587,420	602,469	644,514	663,723	714,453	743,812	26.6
Graduate assistants	98,608	98,887	119,125	120,384	123,962	125,873	132,607	142,120	156,881	167,529	173,121	37.5
Other professional	139,548	159,674	165,444	166,678	177,152	187,646	207,923	239,071	248,209	262,825	282,940	50.8
Nonprofessional staff	313,616	332,158	332,000	325,104	328,542	332,441	338,930	346,720	336,450	341,468	348,219	4.7
Females	**1,173,467**	**1,260,192**	**1,317,644**	**1,346,575**	**1,387,399**	**1,437,193**	**1,517,363**	**1,631,580**	**1,691,040**	**1,797,589**	**1,911,078**	**33.0**
Professional staff	587,524	650,305	699,869	756,354	798,733	853,046	923,979	1,027,097	1,107,851	1,219,855	1,327,270	55.6
Executive/administrative/managerial	50,837	56,719	59,332	60,927	65,318	69,432	76,005	72,690	93,309	101,101	115,260	66.0
Faculty (instruction/research/public service)	263,657	289,966	300,653	354,351	368,813	402,393	425,361	468,669	509,870	575,973	627,578	56.0
Graduate assistants	62,856	64,411	78,626	82,435	91,947	96,851	107,131	119,016	135,180	149,612	155,858	60.9
Other professional	210,174	239,209	261,258	258,641	272,655	284,370	315,482	366,722	369,492	393,169	428,574	50.7
Nonprofessional staff	585,943	609,887	617,775	590,221	588,666	584,147	593,384	604,483	583,189	577,734	583,808	-0.1
Full-time	**1,689,069**	**1,779,044**	**1,812,912**	**1,783,510**	**1,801,371**	**1,828,507**	**1,918,676**	**2,043,208**	**2,083,142**	**2,179,864**	**2,281,223**	**24.8**
Professional staff	947,733	1,000,396	1,031,797	1,039,094	1,066,510	1,104,834	1,180,173	1,283,684	1,337,568	1,432,107	1,526,823	38.2
Executive/administrative/managerial	128,809	138,454	139,116	137,834	140,990	144,529	153,722	146,523	178,691	190,078	210,257	45.5
Faculty (instruction/research/public service)	523,420	524,426	535,623	545,706	550,822	568,719	590,937	617,868	630,092	675,624	703,463	23.7
Other professional	295,504	337,516	357,058	355,554	374,698	391,586	435,514	519,293	528,785	566,405	613,103	56.6
Nonprofessional staff	741,336	778,648	781,115	744,416	734,861	723,673	738,503	759,524	745,574	747,757	754,400	4.2
Part-time	**648,465**	**694,072**	**732,323**	**819,102**	**860,704**	**923,997**	**964,499**	**1,040,145**	**1,104,765**	**1,199,223**	**1,280,205**	**38.6**
Professional staff	490,242	530,675	563,663	648,193	678,357	731,082	770,688	848,466	930,700	1,027,778	1,102,578	50.8
Executive/administrative/managerial	4,910	6,216	5,639	5,841	6,455	6,834	6,166	5,515	6,222	6,246	7,261	6.2
Faculty (instruction/research/public service)	269,650	299,794	290,629	369,768	380,884	421,094	436,893	495,315	543,501	614,802	667,927	58.6
Graduate assistants	161,464	163,298	197,751	202,819	215,909	222,724	239,738	261,136	292,061	317,141	328,979	47.7
Other professional	54,218	61,367	69,644	69,765	75,109	80,430	87,891	86,500	88,916	89,589	98,411	22.4
Nonprofessional staff	158,223	163,397	168,660	170,909	182,347	192,915	193,811	191,679	174,065	171,445	177,627	-7.9
Public 4-year	**1,184,934**	**1,307,524**	**1,341,914**	**1,333,533**	**1,383,476**	**1,418,661**	**1,470,842**	**1,558,576**	**1,569,870**	**1,656,709**	**1,741,699**	**22.8**
Professional staff	711,714	791,319	826,633	855,913	893,345	932,972	987,622	1,069,161	1,115,312	1,200,168	1,278,894	37.1
Executive/administrative/managerial	55,967	64,343	63,674	59,678	60,590	61,984	64,336	60,245	70,397	74,241	81,364	31.3
Faculty (instruction/research/public service)	322,635	350,720	358,376	374,021	384,399	404,109	417,086	438,459	450,123	486,691	518,221	28.2
Graduate assistants	125,603	131,970	144,344	170,916	178,342	182,481	196,393	218,260	239,600	257,578	266,429	46.0
Other professional	207,509	244,286	260,239	251,298	270,014	284,398	309,807	352,197	355,192	381,658	412,880	45.2
Nonprofessional staff	473,220	516,205	515,281	477,620	490,131	485,689	483,220	489,415	454,558	456,541	462,805	-4.7
Private 4-year	**720,474**	**722,841**	**734,509**	**762,034**	**770,004**	**786,634**	**857,820**	**912,924**	**988,895**	**1,073,764**	**1,157,226**	**47.1**
Professional staff	418,340	431,403	442,524	473,372	495,383	517,485	569,579	627,364	701,244	789,179	867,234	67.6
Executive/administrative/managerial	56,307	57,861	57,148	59,230	62,314	62,580	69,626	65,739	84,306	90,415	103,183	64.9
Faculty (instruction/research/public service)	224,870	232,980	232,893	251,948	262,660	278,541	296,737	325,713	364,166	430,305	472,628	69.7
Graduate assistants	24,896	22,231	23,989	28,880	33,853	36,064	38,597	41,611	52,101	59,147	62,550	73.4
Other professional	112,267	118,331	128,494	133,314	136,556	140,300	164,619	194,301	200,671	209,312	228,873	63.1
Nonprofessional staff	302,134	291,438	291,985	288,662	274,621	269,149	288,241	285,560	287,651	284,585	289,992	7.7
Public 2-year	**401,327**	**413,245**	**441,414**	**478,980**	**482,454**	**512,086**	**517,967**	**578,394**	**593,466**	**610,978**	**620,784**	**21.2**
Professional staff	285,512	287,418	306,631	337,371	336,661	358,367	364,703	408,792	422,756	440,536	449,372	25.4
Executive/administrative/managerial	18,203	19,289	20,772	21,531	21,806	22,822	21,459	22,566	25,872	26,770	27,363	19.9
Faculty (instruction/research/public service)	230,114	226,578	222,532	276,413	272,434	290,451	296,239	332,665	341,643	354,497	358,925	23.6
Graduate assistants	10,767	8,928	29,216	2,762	3,401	3,561	4,170	1,215	323	374	0	-100.0
Other professional	26,428	32,623	34,111	36,665	39,020	41,533	42,835	52,346	54,918	58,895	63,084	51.9
Nonprofessional staff	115,815	125,827	134,783	141,609	145,793	153,719	153,264	169,602	170,710	170,442	171,412	11.5
Private 2-year	**30,799**	**29,506**	**27,398**	**28,065**	**26,141**	**35,123**	**36,546**	**33,459**	**35,676**	**37,636**	**41,719**	**18.8**
Professional staff	22,409	20,931	19,672	20,631	19,478	27,092	28,957	26,833	28,956	30,002	33,901	25.1
Executive/administrative/managerial	3,242	3,177	3,161	3,236	2,735	3,977	4,467	3,488	4,338	4,898	5,608	41.0
Faculty (instruction/research/public service)	15,451	13,942	12,451	13,092	12,213	16,712	17,768	16,346	17,661	18,933	21,616	29.3
Graduate assistants	198	169	202	261	313	618	578	50	37	42	0	-100.0
Other professional	3,518	3,643	3,858	4,042	4,217	5,785	6,144	6,949	6,920	6,129	6,677	15.4
Nonprofessional staff	8,390	8,575	7,726	7,434	6,663	8,031	7,589	6,626	6,720	7,634	7,818	-2.7

NOTE: Degree-granting institutions grant associate's or higher degrees and participate in Title IV federal financial aid programs. Beginning in 2007, includes institutions with fewer than 15 full-time employees; these institutions did not report staff data prior to 2007. By definition, all graduate assistants are part-time.

SOURCE: U.S. Department of Education, National Center for Education Statistics, 1987 through 2007 Integrated Postsecondary Education Data System (IPEDS), "Fall Staff Survey" (IPEDS-S:87–99), and Winter 2001–02 through Winter 2007–08. (This table was prepared October 2008.)

Table 244. Total and full-time-equivalent staff in degree-granting institutions, by employment status, control of institution, and occupation: Fall 1976, fall 1997, and fall 2007

Control of institution and primary occupation	Fall 1976					Fall 1997				Fall 2007			
	Total		Full-time equivalent (FTE)			Total		Full-time equivalent (FTE)		Total		Full-time equivalent (FTE)	
	Number	Percent	Full-time	Total	FTE students per FTE staff	Number	Percent	Total	FTE students per FTE staff	Number	Percent	Total	FTE students per FTE staff
1	2	3	4	5	6	7	8	9	10	11	12	13	14
All institutions	**1,863,790**	**100.0**	**1,339,911**	**1,541,339**	**5.4**	**2,752,504**	**100.0**	**2,179,536**	**4.9**	**3,561,428**	**100.0**	**2,762,069**	**5.0**
Professional staff	1,073,119	57.6	709,400	845,456	9.8	1,835,916	66.7	1,377,136	7.7	2,629,401	73.8	1,935,211	7.1
Executive/administrative/ managerial	101,263	5.4	97,003	98,972	84.0	151,363	5.5	147,673	71.9	217,518	6.1	213,610	64.5
Faculty (instruction/research/public service)	633,210	34.0	434,071	500,533	16.6	989,813	36.0	709,048	15.0	1,371,390	38.5	927,178	14.9
Graduate assistants	160,086	8.6	28,007	82,684	100.5	222,724	8.1	92,108	115.2	328,979	9.2	136,364	101.1
Other professionals	178,560	9.6	150,319	163,267	50.9	472,016	17.1	428,307	24.8	711,514	20.0	658,059	20.9
Nonprofessional staff	790,671	42.4	630,511	695,883	11.9	916,588	33.3	802,400	13.2	932,027	26.2	826,858	16.7
Public	**1,329,122**	**100.0**	**946,354**	**1,092,558**	**5.8**	**1,930,747**	**100.0**	**1,504,764**	**5.2**	**2,362,483**	**100.0**	**1,811,840**	**5.4**
Professional staff	769,836	57.9	502,325	601,942	10.5	1,291,339	66.9	948,674	8.3	1,728,266	73.2	1,255,632	7.8
Executive/administrative/ managerial	60,733	4.6	58,649	59,579	106.6	84,806	4.4	82,696	95.2	108,727	4.6	106,710	91.3
Faculty (instruction/research/public service)	448,733	33.8	313,367	357,761	17.7	694,560	36.0	494,390	15.9	877,146	37.1	601,617	16.2
Graduate assistants	127,925	9.6	19,076	63,420	100.1	186,042	9.6	75,792	103.8	266,429	11.3	108,541	89.7
Other professionals	132,445	10.0	111,233	121,182	52.4	325,931	16.9	295,796	26.6	475,964	20.1	438,765	22.2
Nonprofessional staff	559,286	42.1	444,029	490,616	12.9	639,408	33.1	556,090	14.2	634,217	26.8	556,207	17.5
Private	**534,668**	**100.0**	**393,557**	**448,781**	**4.4**	**821,757**	**100.0**	**674,772**	**4.1**	**1,198,945**	**100.0**	**950,229**	**4.3**
Professional staff	303,283	56.7	207,075	243,514	8.1	544,577	66.3	428,462	6.4	901,135	75.2	679,579	5.9
Executive/administrative/ managerial	40,530	7.6	38,354	39,393	49.8	66,557	8.1	64,977	42.2	108,791	9.1	106,900	37.8
Faculty (instruction/research/public service)	184,477	34.5	120,704	142,772	13.7	295,253	35.9	214,658	12.8	494,244	41.2	325,561	12.4
Graduate assistants	32,161	6.0	8,931	19,264	101.9	36,682	4.5	16,317	168.2	62,550	5.2	27,823	145.3
Other professionals	46,115	8.6	39,086	42,085	46.6	146,085	17.8	132,511	20.7	235,550	19.6	219,295	18.4
Nonprofessional staff	231,385	43.3	186,482	205,267	9.6	277,180	33.7	246,310	11.1	297,810	24.8	270,650	14.9

NOTE: Data for 1976 are for institutions of higher education, while later data are for degree-granting institutions. Degree-granting institutions grant associate's or higher degrees and participate in Title IV federal financial aid programs. The degree-granting classification is very similar to the earlier higher education classification, but it includes more 2-year colleges and excludes a few higher education institutions that did not grant degrees. (See Guide to Sources for details.) Beginning in 2007, includes institutions with fewer than 15 full-time employees; these institutions did not report staff data prior to 2007. By definition, all graduate assistants are part-time in 1997 and 2007. Detail may not sum to totals because of rounding.
SOURCE: U.S. Department of Education, National Center for Education Statistics, Higher Education General Information Survey (HEGIS), "Staff Survey," 1976; and 1997 and 2007 Integrated Postsecondary Education Data System, "Fall Staff Survey" (IPEDS-S:97), and Winter 2007–08. (This table was prepared October 2008.)

Table 245. Employees in degree-granting institutions, by employment status, sex, control and type of institution, and primary occupation: Fall 2007

Control and type of institution and primary occupation	Full-time and part-time					Full-time				Part-time		
	Total			Females		Total						
	Number	Percentage distribution	Males	Number	Percent of all employees	Number	Percent of all employees	Males	Females	Total	Males	Females
1	2	3	4	5	6	7	8	9	10	11	12	13
All institutions	3,561,428	100.0	1,650,350	1,911,078	53.7	2,281,223	64.1	1,042,024	1,239,199	1,280,205	608,326	671,879
Professional staff	2,629,401	73.8	1,302,131	1,327,270	50.5	1,526,823	58.1	757,208	769,615	1,102,578	544,923	557,655
Executive/administrative/managerial	217,518	6.1	102,258	115,260	53.0	210,257	96.7	99,587	110,670	7,261	2,671	4,590
Faculty (instruction/research/public service)	1,371,390	38.5	743,812	627,578	45.8	703,463	51.3	409,115	294,348	667,927	334,697	333,230
Graduate assistants	328,979	9.2	173,121	155,858	47.4	†	†	†	†	328,979	173,121	155,858
Other professional	711,514	20.0	282,940	428,574	60.2	613,103	86.2	248,506	364,597	98,411	34,434	63,977
Nonprofessional staff	932,027	26.2	348,219	583,808	62.6	754,400	80.9	284,816	469,584	177,627	63,403	114,224
Technical and paraprofessionals	192,974	5.4	79,271	113,703	58.9	152,654	79.1	64,086	88,568	40,320	15,185	25,135
Clerical and secretarial	445,109	12.5	65,870	379,239	85.2	349,275	78.5	41,249	308,026	95,834	24,621	71,213
Skilled crafts	61,973	1.7	58,057	3,916	6.3	59,345	95.8	56,311	3,034	2,628	1,746	882
Service and maintenance	231,971	6.5	145,021	86,950	37.5	193,126	83.3	123,170	69,956	38,845	21,851	16,994
Public 4-year	1,741,699	100.0	822,840	918,859	52.8	1,180,486	67.8	556,846	623,640	561,213	265,994	295,219
Professional staff	1,278,894	73.4	643,974	634,920	49.6	791,021	61.9	404,110	386,911	487,873	239,864	248,009
Executive/administrative/managerial	81,364	4.7	40,651	40,713	50.0	78,488	96.5	39,535	38,953	2,876	1,116	1,760
Faculty (instruction/research/public service)	518,221	29.8	295,966	222,255	42.9	354,290	68.4	214,736	139,554	163,931	81,230	82,701
Graduate assistants	266,429	15.3	139,488	126,941	47.6	†	†	†	†	266,429	139,488	126,941
Other professional	412,880	23.7	167,869	245,011	59.3	358,243	86.8	149,839	208,404	54,637	18,030	36,607
Nonprofessional staff	462,805	26.6	178,866	283,939	61.4	389,465	84.2	152,736	236,729	73,340	26,130	47,210
Technical and paraprofessionals	100,769	5.8	41,960	58,809	58.4	82,967	82.3	35,120	47,847	17,802	6,840	10,962
Clerical and secretarial	202,153	11.6	27,812	174,341	86.2	163,223	80.7	17,289	145,934	38,930	10,523	28,407
Skilled crafts	40,866	2.3	38,674	2,192	5.4	39,786	97.4	37,861	1,925	1,080	813	267
Service and maintenance	119,017	6.8	70,420	48,597	40.8	103,489	87.0	62,466	41,023	15,528	7,954	7,574
Public 2-year	620,784	100.0	266,145	354,639	57.1	300,948	48.5	121,980	178,968	319,836	144,165	175,671
Professional staff	449,372	72.4	204,580	244,792	54.5	187,129	41.6	81,653	105,476	262,243	122,927	139,316
Executive/administrative/managerial	27,363	4.4	12,622	14,741	53.9	26,597	97.2	12,303	14,294	766	319	447
Faculty (instruction/research/public service)	358,925	57.8	169,225	189,700	52.9	112,870	31.4	52,642	60,228	246,055	116,583	129,472
Graduate assistants	0	0.0	0	0	†	†	†	†	†	0	0	0
Other professional	63,084	10.2	22,733	40,351	64.0	47,662	75.6	16,708	30,954	15,422	6,025	9,397
Nonprofessional staff	171,412	27.6	61,565	109,847	64.1	113,819	66.4	40,327	73,492	57,593	21,238	36,355
Technical and paraprofessionals	43,047	6.9	16,781	26,266	61.0	28,249	65.6	11,155	17,094	14,798	5,626	9,172
Clerical and secretarial	86,243	13.9	13,729	72,514	84.1	53,922	62.5	4,746	49,176	32,321	8,983	23,338
Skilled crafts	5,900	1.0	5,186	714	12.1	5,072	86.0	4,677	395	828	509	319
Service and maintenance	36,222	5.8	25,869	10,353	28.6	26,576	73.4	19,749	6,827	9,646	6,120	3,526
Private 4-year[1]	1,157,226	100.0	544,896	612,330	52.9	772,224	66.7	352,645	419,579	385,002	192,251	192,751
Professional staff	867,234	74.9	439,443	427,791	49.3	527,273	60.8	262,675	264,598	339,961	176,768	163,193
Executive/administrative/managerial	103,183	8.9	46,744	56,439	54.7	99,674	96.6	45,548	54,126	3,509	1,196	2,313
Faculty (instruction/research/public service)	472,628	40.8	268,790	203,838	43.1	226,375	47.9	137,016	89,359	246,253	131,774	114,479
Graduate assistants	62,550	5.4	33,633	28,917	46.2	†	†	†	†	62,550	33,633	28,917
Other professional	228,873	19.8	90,276	138,597	60.6	201,224	87.9	80,111	121,113	27,649	10,165	17,484
Nonprofessional staff	289,992	25.1	105,453	184,539	63.6	244,951	84.5	89,970	154,981	45,041	15,483	29,558
Technical and paraprofessionals	48,175	4.2	20,118	28,057	58.2	40,709	84.5	17,481	23,228	7,466	2,637	4,829
Clerical and secretarial	151,354	13.1	23,423	127,931	84.5	127,691	84.4	18,479	109,212	23,663	4,944	18,719
Skilled crafts	15,088	1.3	14,119	969	6.4	14,396	95.4	13,706	690	692	413	279
Service and maintenance	75,375	6.5	47,793	27,582	36.6	62,155	82.5	40,304	21,851	13,220	7,489	5,731
Private not-for-profit 4-year	1,016,690	100.0	473,463	543,227	53.4	714,515	70.3	327,160	387,355	302,175	146,303	155,872
Professional staff	743,614	73.1	374,251	369,363	49.7	484,123	65.1	242,524	241,599	259,491	131,727	127,764
Executive/administrative/managerial	94,129	9.3	42,399	51,730	55.0	90,760	96.4	41,256	49,504	3,369	1,143	2,226
Faculty (instruction/research/public service)	382,390	37.6	217,794	164,596	43.0	215,509	56.4	130,660	84,849	166,881	87,134	79,747
Graduate assistants	62,440	6.1	33,600	28,840	46.2	†	†	†	†	62,440	33,600	28,840
Other professional	204,655	20.1	80,458	124,197	60.7	177,854	86.9	70,608	107,246	26,801	9,850	16,951
Nonprofessional staff	273,076	26.9	99,212	173,864	63.7	230,392	84.4	84,636	145,756	42,684	14,576	28,108
Technical and paraprofessionals	46,395	4.6	18,974	27,421	59.1	39,361	84.8	16,526	22,835	7,034	2,448	4,586
Clerical and secretarial	137,800	13.6	19,472	118,328	85.9	115,560	83.9	14,913	100,647	22,240	4,559	17,681
Skilled crafts	14,979	1.5	14,056	923	6.2	14,303	95.5	13,653	650	676	403	273
Service and maintenance	73,902	7.3	46,710	27,192	36.8	61,168	82.8	39,544	21,624	12,734	7,166	5,568

See notes at end of table.

Table 245. Employees in degree-granting institutions, by employment status, sex, control and type of institution, and primary occupation: Fall 2007—Continued

Control and type of institution and primary occupation	Full-time and part-time					Full-time				Part-time		
	Total		Males	Females		Total		Males	Females	Total	Males	Females
	Number	Percentage distribution		Number	Percent of all employees	Number	Percent of all employees					
1	2	3	4	5	6	7	8	9	10	11	12	13
Private for-profit 4-year	**140,536**	**100.0**	**71,433**	**69,103**	**49.2**	**57,709**	**41.1**	**25,485**	**32,224**	**82,827**	**45,948**	**36,879**
Professional staff	123,620	88.0	65,192	58,428	47.3	43,150	34.9	20,151	22,999	80,470	45,041	35,429
Executive/administrative/managerial	9,054	6.4	4,345	4,709	52.0	8,914	98.5	4,292	4,622	140	53	87
Faculty (instruction/research/public service)	90,238	64.2	50,996	39,242	43.5	10,866	12.0	6,356	4,510	79,372	44,640	34,732
Graduate assistants	110	0.1	33	77	70.0	†	†	†	†	110	33	77
Other professional	24,218	17.2	9,818	14,400	59.5	23,370	96.5	9,503	13,867	848	315	533
Nonprofessional staff	16,916	12.0	6,241	10,675	63.1	14,559	86.1	5,334	9,225	2,357	907	1,450
Technical and paraprofessionals	1,780	1.3	1,144	636	35.7	1,348	75.7	955	393	432	189	243
Clerical and secretarial	13,554	9.6	3,951	9,603	70.8	12,131	89.5	3,566	8,565	1,423	385	1,038
Skilled crafts	109	0.1	63	46	42.2	93	85.3	53	40	16	10	6
Service and maintenance	1,473	1.0	1,083	390	26.5	987	67.0	760	227	486	323	163
Private 2-year[1]	**41,719**	**100.0**	**16,469**	**25,250**	**60.5**	**27,565**	**66.1**	**10,553**	**17,012**	**14,154**	**5,916**	**8,238**
Professional staff	33,901	81.3	14,134	19,767	58.3	21,400	63.1	8,770	12,630	12,501	5,364	7,137
Executive/administrative/managerial	5,608	13.4	2,241	3,367	60.0	5,498	98.0	2,201	3,297	110	40	70
Faculty (instruction/research/public service)	21,616	51.8	9,831	11,785	54.5	9,928	45.9	4,721	5,207	11,688	5,110	6,578
Graduate assistants	0	0.0	0	0	†	†	†	†	†	0	0	0
Other professional	6,677	16.0	2,062	4,615	69.1	5,974	89.5	1,848	4,126	703	214	489
Nonprofessional staff	7,818	18.7	2,335	5,483	70.1	6,165	78.9	1,783	4,382	1,653	552	1,101
Technical and paraprofessionals	983	2.4	412	571	58.1	729	74.2	330	399	254	82	172
Clerical and secretarial	5,359	12.8	906	4,453	83.1	4,439	82.8	735	3,704	920	171	749
Skilled crafts	119	0.3	78	41	34.5	91	76.5	67	24	28	11	17
Service and maintenance	1,357	3.3	939	418	30.8	906	66.8	651	255	451	288	163
Private not-for-profit 2-year	**6,707**	**100.0**	**2,490**	**4,217**	**62.9**	**4,161**	**62.0**	**1,558**	**2,603**	**2,546**	**932**	**1,614**
Professional staff	5,314	79.2	2,049	3,265	61.4	3,136	59.0	1,226	1,910	2,178	823	1,355
Executive/administrative/managerial	749	11.2	330	419	55.9	724	96.7	320	404	25	10	15
Faculty (instruction/research/public service)	3,485	52.0	1,329	2,156	61.9	1,545	44.3	597	948	1,940	732	1,208
Graduate assistants	0	0.0	0	0	†	†	†	†	†	0	0	0
Other professional	1,080	16.1	390	690	63.9	867	80.3	309	558	213	81	132
Nonprofessional staff	1,393	20.8	441	952	68.3	1,025	73.6	332	693	368	109	259
Technical and paraprofessionals	210	3.1	89	121	57.6	161	76.7	68	93	49	21	28
Clerical and secretarial	655	9.8	42	613	93.6	477	72.8	20	457	178	22	156
Skilled crafts	44	0.7	36	8	18.2	39	88.6	34	5	5	2	3
Service and maintenance	484	7.2	274	210	43.4	348	71.9	210	138	136	64	72
Private for-profit 2-year	**35,012**	**100.0**	**13,979**	**21,033**	**60.1**	**23,404**	**66.8**	**8,995**	**14,409**	**11,608**	**4,984**	**6,624**
Professional staff	28,587	81.6	12,085	16,502	57.7	18,264	63.9	7,544	10,720	10,323	4,541	5,782
Executive/administrative/managerial	4,859	13.9	1,911	2,948	60.7	4,774	98.3	1,881	2,893	85	30	55
Faculty (instruction/research/public service)	18,131	51.8	8,502	9,629	53.1	8,383	46.2	4,124	4,259	9,748	4,378	5,370
Graduate assistants	0	0.0	0	0	†	†	†	†	†	0	0	0
Other professional	5,597	16.0	1,672	3,925	70.1	5,107	91.2	1,539	3,568	490	133	357
Nonprofessional staff	6,425	18.4	1,894	4,531	70.5	5,140	80.0	1,451	3,689	1,285	443	842
Technical and paraprofessionals	773	2.2	323	450	58.2	568	73.5	262	306	205	61	144
Clerical and secretarial	4,704	13.4	864	3,840	81.6	3,962	84.2	715	3,247	742	149	593
Skilled crafts	75	0.2	42	33	44.0	52	69.3	33	19	23	9	14
Service and maintenance	873	2.5	665	208	23.8	558	63.9	441	117	315	224	91

†Not applicable.

[1]Includes not-for-profit and for-profit private institutions.

NOTE: Degree-granting institutions grant associate's or higher degrees and participate in Title IV federal financial aid programs. Beginning in 2007, includes institutions with fewer than 15 full-time employees; these institutions did not report staff data prior to 2007. By definition, all graduate assistants are part-time. Detail may not sum to totals because of rounding.

SOURCE: U.S. Department of Education, National Center for Education Statistics, 2007 Integrated Postsecondary Education Data System (IPEDS), Winter 2007–08. (This table was prepared October 2008.)

Table 246. Employees in degree-granting institutions, by race/ethnicity, sex, employment status, control and type of institution, and primary occupation: Fall 2007

Sex, employment status, control and type of institution, and primary occupation	Total	White	Minority						Race/ ethnicity unknown	Nonresident alien[2]
			Number	Percent[1]	Black	Hispanic	Asian/Pacific Islander	American Indian/ Alaska Native		
1	2	3	4	5	6	7	8	9	10	11
All institutions	3,561,428	2,496,754	771,235	22.5	353,146	202,098	194,934	21,057	132,455	160,984
Professional staff	2,629,401	1,894,641	471,726	18.7	191,204	110,052	156,969	13,501	110,362	152,672
Executive/administrative/managerial	217,518	173,948	38,859	18.2	21,047	10,074	6,517	1,221	3,751	960
Faculty (instruction/research/public service)	1,371,390	1,038,982	224,294	17.2	87,107	51,660	78,593	6,934	67,208	40,906
Graduate assistants	328,979	169,028	50,193	16.3	12,634	11,548	24,712	1,299	20,812	88,946
Other professional	711,514	512,683	158,380	22.9	70,416	36,770	47,147	4,047	18,591	21,860
Nonprofessional staff	932,027	602,113	299,509	32.9	161,942	92,046	37,965	7,556	22,093	8,312
Males	1,650,350	1,162,198	325,342	20.5	132,776	86,906	96,635	9,025	65,065	97,745
Professional staff	1,302,131	940,145	212,229	17.0	73,877	50,476	81,787	6,089	55,725	94,032
Executive/administrative/managerial	102,258	83,941	16,027	15.9	8,275	4,230	3,017	505	1,723	567
Faculty (instruction/research/public service)	743,812	566,918	115,731	16.3	38,030	27,201	46,965	3,535	34,907	26,256
Graduate assistants	173,121	84,204	23,606	14.5	4,781	5,384	12,864	577	10,751	54,560
Other professional	282,940	205,082	56,865	20.7	22,791	13,661	18,941	1,472	8,344	12,649
Nonprofessional staff	348,219	222,053	113,113	33.4	58,899	36,430	14,848	2,936	9,340	3,713
Females	1,911,078	1,334,556	445,893	24.2	220,370	115,192	98,299	12,032	67,390	63,239
Professional staff	1,327,270	954,496	259,497	20.4	117,327	59,576	75,182	7,412	54,637	58,640
Executive/administrative/managerial	115,260	90,007	22,832	20.2	12,772	5,844	3,500	716	2,028	393
Faculty (instruction/research/public service)	627,578	472,064	108,563	18.2	49,077	24,459	31,628	3,399	32,301	14,650
Graduate assistants	155,858	84,824	26,587	18.2	7,853	6,164	11,848	722	10,061	34,386
Other professional	428,574	307,601	101,515	24.3	47,625	23,109	28,206	2,575	10,247	9,211
Nonprofessional staff	583,808	380,060	186,396	32.6	103,043	55,616	23,117	4,620	12,753	4,599
Full-time	2,281,223	1,637,653	546,549	24.4	258,723	142,177	131,394	14,255	40,312	56,709
Professional staff	1,526,823	1,148,334	298,966	19.9	121,801	67,185	101,874	8,106	27,812	51,711
Executive/administrative/managerial	210,257	167,877	37,897	18.3	20,578	9,841	6,301	1,177	3,563	920
Faculty (instruction/research/public service)	703,463	540,460	119,906	17.3	37,930	24,975	53,661	3,340	11,875	31,222
Other professional	613,103	439,997	141,163	23.5	63,293	32,369	41,912	3,589	12,374	19,569
Nonprofessional staff	754,400	489,319	247,583	33.4	136,922	74,992	29,520	6,149	12,500	4,998
Part-time	1,280,205	859,101	224,686	18.9	94,423	59,921	63,540	6,802	92,143	104,275
Professional staff	1,102,578	746,307	172,760	16.9	69,403	42,867	55,095	5,395	82,550	100,961
Executive/administrative/managerial	7,261	6,071	962	13.6	469	233	216	44	188	40
Faculty (instruction/research/public service)	667,927	498,522	104,388	17.0	49,177	26,685	24,932	3,594	55,333	9,684
Graduate assistants	328,979	169,028	50,193	16.3	12,634	11,548	24,712	1,299	20,812	88,946
Other professional	98,411	72,686	17,217	18.7	7,123	4,401	5,235	458	6,217	2,291
Nonprofessional staff	177,627	112,794	51,926	30.9	25,020	17,054	8,445	1,407	9,593	3,314
Public 4-year	1,741,699	1,192,314	389,312	23.0	165,686	99,448	112,930	11,248	45,870	114,203
Professional staff	1,278,894	891,372	239,157	19.3	83,612	54,468	93,951	7,126	38,241	110,124
Executive/administrative/managerial	81,364	65,133	15,006	18.6	8,463	3,505	2,496	542	850	375
Faculty (instruction/research/public service)	518,221	391,312	89,288	17.7	27,159	19,683	39,560	2,886	14,423	23,198
Graduate assistants	266,429	140,632	41,288	16.3	10,390	9,651	20,117	1,130	13,030	71,479
Other professional	412,880	294,295	93,575	23.2	37,600	21,629	31,778	2,568	9,938	15,072
Nonprofessional staff	462,805	300,942	150,155	33.0	82,074	44,980	18,979	4,122	7,629	4,079
Private 4-year	1,157,226	817,613	238,471	21.7	118,255	57,150	59,060	4,006	58,771	42,371
Professional staff	867,234	630,656	146,358	17.9	64,991	31,201	47,434	2,732	50,465	39,755
Executive/administrative/managerial	103,183	83,035	17,152	17.0	9,049	4,590	3,224	289	2,510	486
Faculty (instruction/research/public service)	472,628	352,157	72,313	16.4	30,175	14,204	26,385	1,549	32,888	15,270
Graduate assistants	62,550	28,396	8,905	16.3	2,244	1,897	4,595	169	7,782	17,467
Other professional	228,873	167,068	47,988	21.7	23,523	10,510	13,230	725	7,285	6,532
Nonprofessional staff	289,992	186,957	92,113	32.7	53,264	25,949	11,626	1,274	8,306	2,616
Public 2-year	620,784	457,580	132,444	22.3	63,580	42,014	21,567	5,283	26,387	4,373
Professional staff	449,372	348,022	78,136	18.2	38,180	22,127	14,488	3,341	20,448	2,766
Executive/administrative/managerial	27,363	21,619	5,375	19.8	2,854	1,545	654	322	281	88
Faculty (instruction/research/public service)	358,925	279,492	57,942	17.0	27,140	16,551	11,899	2,352	19,065	2,426
Graduate assistants	0	0	0	†	0	0	0	0	0	0
Other professional	63,084	46,911	14,819	23.9	8,186	4,031	1,935	667	1,102	252
Nonprofessional staff	171,412	109,558	54,308	32.8	25,400	19,887	7,079	1,942	5,939	1,607
Private 2-year	41,719	29,247	11,008	27.3	5,625	3,486	1,377	520	1,427	37
Professional staff	33,901	24,591	8,075	24.7	4,421	2,256	1,096	302	1,208	27
Executive/administrative/managerial	5,608	4,161	1,326	24.1	681	434	143	68	110	11
Faculty (instruction/research/public service)	21,616	16,021	4,751	22.9	2,633	1,222	749	147	832	12
Graduate assistants	0	0	0	†	0	0	0	0	0	0
Other professional	6,677	4,409	1,998	31.2	1,107	600	204	87	266	4
Nonprofessional staff	7,818	4,656	2,933	38.6	1,204	1,230	281	218	219	10

†Not applicable.
[1]Minority staff as a percentage of total staff, excluding race/ethnicity unknown.
[2]Race/ethnicity not collected.
NOTE: Degree-granting institutions grant associate's or higher degrees and participate in Title IV federal financial aid programs. Race categories exclude persons of Hispanic ethnicity. Beginning in 2007, includes institutions with fewer than 15 full-time employees; these

institutions did not report staff data prior to 2007. By definition, all graduate assistants are part-time.
SOURCE: U.S. Department of Education, National Center for Education Statistics, 2007 Integrated Postsecondary Education Data System (IPEDS), Winter 2007–08. (This table was prepared October 2008.)

Table 247. Number of full-time-equivalent (FTE) staff and faculty, and FTE staff and faculty/FTE student ratios in degree-granting institutions, by control and type of institution and state or jurisdiction: Fall 2005

State or jurisdiction	Full-time-equivalent (FTE) staff				FTE faculty				FTE faculty as a percent of FTE staff				FTE students per FTE staff				FTE students per FTE faculty			
	Public		Private		Public		Private		Public		Private		Public		Private		Public		Private	
	4-year	2-year	4-year	2-year	4-year	2-year	4-year	2-year	4-year	2-year	4-year	2-year	4-year	2-year	4-year	2-year	4-year	2-year	4-year	2-year
1	2	3	4	5	6	7	8	9	10	11	12	13	14	15	16	17	18	19	20	21
United States	**1,337,858**	**405,524**	**857,095**	**30,159**	**387,475**	**191,218**	**289,756**	**12,858**	**29.0**	**47.2**	**33.8**	**42.6**	**4.3**	**9.0**	**4.1**	**9.2**	**14.8**	**19.2**	**12.2**	**21.6**
Alabama	29,738	5,857	4,597	208	7,948	2,761	1,704	53	26.7	47.1	37.1	25.4	4.1	9.2	5.4	3.3	15.4	19.6	14.5	12.9
Alaska	4,972	140	278	†	1,588	31	97	†	31.9	22.4	34.8	†	3.7	3.3	3.3	†	11.6	14.8	9.8	†
Arizona	23,427	10,702	14,699	1,035	5,593	4,958	6,132	476	23.9	46.3	41.7	46.0	4.3	9.5	13.9	11.9	18.2	20.4	33.4	25.9
Arkansas	15,459	3,957	2,549	72	4,270	1,788	837	26	27.6	45.2	32.8	36.5	4.4	7.8	5.1	8.1	15.8	17.2	15.4	22.2
California	126,789	58,480	73,072	3,793	35,941	31,196	27,098	1,632	28.3	53.3	37.1	43.0	4.2	12.9	4.1	9.5	14.9	24.2	11.1	22.1
Colorado	24,434	5,538	8,186	670	10,358	2,554	3,109	310	42.4	46.1	38.0	46.3	5.1	7.9	5.9	13.0	11.9	17.2	15.5	28.0
Connecticut	13,005	2,976	20,025	239	3,522	1,518	6,634	104	27.1	51.0	33.1	43.3	4.1	8.9	2.6	6.2	15.3	17.4	7.9	14.1
Delaware	5,133	1,302	994	27	1,270	545	435	13	24.7	41.9	43.7	47.2	4.4	6.3	9.1	6.0	17.7	15.0	20.8	12.8
District of Columbia	1,038	†	20,201	†	398	†	6,120	†	38.3	†	30.3	†	3.5	†	3.7	†	9.1	†	12.3	†
Florida	52,063	19,482	30,603	1,851	18,289	7,837	11,443	715	35.1	40.2	37.4	38.6	5.5	8.3	5.4	11.0	15.8	20.6	14.4	28.3
Georgia	38,197	12,163	19,087	553	10,160	5,792	7,020	206	26.6	47.6	36.8	37.2	4.3	7.7	3.7	8.8	16.3	16.1	10.2	23.8
Hawaii	6,044	1,519	1,987	84	2,169	775	1,039	41	35.9	51.0	52.3	48.7	3.7	8.8	6.5	12.1	10.4	17.2	12.4	24.8
Idaho	6,853	1,095	1,773	67	2,326	438	851	34	33.9	40.0	48.0	50.1	5.6	7.2	8.8	7.6	16.5	17.9	18.4	15.2
Illinois	49,092	19,804	53,627	655	11,369	8,683	17,699	250	23.2	43.8	33.0	38.2	3.5	10.2	4.3	6.6	15.3	23.3	12.9	17.2
Indiana	40,415	3,747	16,541	832	10,691	2,060	5,427	360	26.5	55.0	32.8	43.2	4.3	9.3	4.5	11.9	16.2	16.9	13.7	27.6
Iowa	18,769	6,026	11,491	170	5,115	2,452	4,003	67	27.3	40.7	34.8	39.7	3.2	9.0	5.4	7.8	11.7	22.1	15.5	19.7
Kansas	17,834	6,174	2,948	254	5,642	2,584	1,087	104	31.6	41.8	36.9	40.7	4.5	7.2	5.4	6.0	14.1	17.1	14.7	14.7
Kentucky	25,927	5,546	5,802	391	7,096	2,741	2,146	177	27.4	49.4	37.0	45.1	3.8	9.2	5.6	10.2	13.9	18.6	15.1	22.7
Louisiana	23,344	3,282	6,161	344	7,215	1,760	2,051	155	30.9	53.6	33.3	45.2	5.5	7.1	1.8	10.9	17.7	13.2	5.5	24.0
Maine	6,201	991	3,631	109	1,848	558	1,040	55	29.8	56.3	28.6	50.6	4.3	8.1	3.9	8.3	14.6	14.5	13.7	16.4
Maryland	27,142	10,508	21,736	262	9,498	4,642	5,626	137	35.0	44.2	25.9	52.4	4.0	6.5	1.9	12.5	11.4	14.8	7.4	23.8
Massachusetts	20,604	6,892	72,655	284	6,024	2,912	24,273	140	29.2	42.3	33.4	49.6	4.1	7.5	3.0	7.9	13.9	17.8	9.0	15.9
Michigan	53,963	12,496	12,251	191	16,186	6,058	4,972	73	30.0	48.5	40.6	38.0	4.5	9.9	7.3	12.6	15.1	20.3	18.0	33.2
Minnesota	24,612	7,338	14,046	606	5,957	3,610	5,363	244	24.2	49.2	38.2	40.3	4.4	10.0	6.5	7.7	18.1	20.3	17.1	19.1
Mississippi	21,257	6,171	1,887	179	4,404	2,914	680	92	20.7	47.2	36.0	51.3	2.9	8.7	6.0	9.6	13.9	18.4	16.6	18.7
Missouri	29,048	7,037	27,764	1,025	8,625	3,024	10,118	443	29.7	43.0	36.4	43.2	3.7	7.8	4.0	7.8	12.5	18.2	10.9	18.1
Montana	6,376	889	814	101	1,974	345	325	36	31.0	38.8	39.9	35.4	4.7	7.0	4.6	4.4	15.1	18.0	11.6	12.5
Nebraska	12,677	2,851	5,362	88	3,635	1,355	1,888	38	28.7	47.5	35.2	43.3	3.6	8.7	4.5	6.4	12.5	18.3	12.7	14.9
Nevada	8,862	1,083	819	282	2,987	506	548	112	33.7	46.8	66.9	39.8	6.4	7.5	9.1	10.1	19.1	15.9	13.6	25.3
New Hampshire	5,249	1,243	7,310	161	1,437	723	1,898	56	27.4	58.2	26.0	35.0	4.5	5.9	3.2	7.3	16.5	10.2	12.4	20.9
New Jersey	35,075	9,844	14,195	148	9,849	4,244	4,867	49	28.1	43.1	34.3	32.9	3.5	10.2	4.2	7.9	12.4	23.6	12.3	24.1
New Mexico	14,685	5,274	1,129	35	3,383	2,013	637	19	23.0	38.2	56.4	54.7	3.1	6.9	7.8	14.7	13.4	18.0	13.8	26.9
New York	48,911	21,034	124,176	3,359	18,066	9,613	39,831	1,367	36.9	45.7	32.1	40.7	6.0	9.2	3.4	8.7	16.1	20.1	10.6	21.3
North Carolina	42,161	20,486	31,229	214	10,972	11,245	8,338	75	26.0	54.9	26.7	34.9	4.0	5.9	2.5	7.2	15.5	10.8	9.4	20.6
North Dakota	6,255	1,094	694	346	2,020	439	317	68	32.3	40.2	45.7	19.7	4.7	6.2	6.4	4.0	14.5	15.4	14.1	20.3
Ohio	53,405	11,845	26,934	1,774	15,381	5,749	9,558	778	28.8	48.5	35.5	43.8	4.5	9.1	4.2	10.9	15.7	18.7	12.6	24.9
Oklahoma	21,386	4,628	4,621	211	5,910	1,810	1,706	106	27.6	39.1	36.9	50.1	4.4	8.8	5.1	12.4	16.1	22.5	13.7	24.8
Oregon	20,873	7,896	5,786	288	6,149	3,276	2,441	105	29.5	41.5	42.2	36.4	3.3	6.1	5.1	8.9	11.3	14.6	12.0	24.4
Pennsylvania	52,782	8,413	64,639	4,174	17,965	4,143	21,319	1,917	34.0	49.2	33.0	45.9	4.4	9.0	3.6	7.6	12.8	18.3	11.0	16.6
Rhode Island	3,410	859	9,203	65	1,029	436	2,687	26	30.2	50.7	29.2	39.4	5.8	10.7	4.1	8.4	19.1	21.1	14.0	21.3

See notes at end of table.

Table 247. Number of full-time-equivalent (FTE) staff and faculty, and FTE staff and faculty/FTE student ratios in degree-granting institutions, by control and type of institution and state or jurisdiction: Fall 2005—Continued

State or jurisdiction	Full-time-equivalent (FTE) staff				FTE faculty				FTE faculty as a percent of FTE staff				FTE students per FTE staff				FTE students per FTE faculty			
	Public		Private		Public		Private		Public		Private		Public		Private		Public		Private	
	4-year	2-year	4-year	2-year	4-year	2-year	4-year	2-year	4-year	2-year	4-year	2-year	4-year	2-year	4-year	2-year	4-year	2-year	4-year	2-year
1	2	3	4	5	6	7	8	9	10	11	12	13	14	15	16	17	18	19	20	21
South Carolina	19,621	6,219	5,323	163	5,649	2,899	1,840	54	28.8	46.6	34.6	32.9	4.3	8.1	5.7	11.0	14.9	17.4	16.4	33.3
South Dakota	4,848	622	1,504	52	1,565	313	560	27	32.3	50.3	37.2	51.9	5.3	7.8	5.5	5.4	16.3	15.6	14.8	10.3
Tennessee	25,766	5,481	27,866	922	7,322	2,556	6,584	405	28.4	46.6	23.6	43.9	4.2	9.1	2.3	11.1	14.8	19.4	9.8	25.2
Texas	119,326	38,131	28,734	1,843	27,622	16,795	9,744	767	23.1	44.0	33.9	41.6	3.7	8.2	4.1	9.8	15.9	18.7	12.0	23.4
Utah	16,335	2,765	6,340	340	5,398	1,171	2,265	151	33.0	42.3	35.7	44.5	5.1	7.4	7.0	8.6	15.6	17.6	19.6	19.2
Vermont	4,685	363	3,800	366	1,549	193	1,185	136	33.1	53.1	31.2	37.1	3.4	6.9	3.6	1.6	10.4	12.9	11.6	4.4
Virginia	38,492	7,654	15,192	705	12,097	4,240	5,130	345	31.4	55.4	33.8	49.0	4.3	11.0	4.8	10.1	13.6	19.9	14.1	20.6
Washington	53	8,140	5,899	3,514	20			50	29.5	43.9	44.5	37.5	3.5	9.0	5.7	13.1	11.8	20.5	12.7	35.0
West Virginia	10,414	992	1,967	112	3,740	609	679	50	35.9	61.4	34.5	44.8	5.6	12.0	5.5	19.0	15.7	19.6	16.0	42.3
Wisconsin	28,711	11,263	12,963	101	8,373	5,644	4,892	28	29.2	50.1	37.7	28.3	4.8	5.8	4.2	4.8	16.5	11.5	11.0	17.0
Wyoming	2,981	1,935	†	358	994	811	†	216	33.3	41.9	†	60.4	3.5	6.2	†	7.3	10.6	14.7	†	12.1
U.S. Service Academies	1,647	†	†	†	767	†	†	†	46.6	†	†	†	9.3	†	†	†	19.9	†	†	†
Other jurisdictions	15,794	1,276	10,322	1,004	4,941	506	4,178	479	31.3	39.7	40.5	47.7	4.0	5.7	10.3	13.1	12.9	14.3	25.4	27.4
American Samoa	†	210	†	†	†	86	†	†	†	41.0	†	†	†	4.9	†	†	†	12.0	†	†
Federated States of Micronesia	†	340	†	†	†	105	†	†	†	30.9	†	†	†	5.3	†	†	†	17.1	†	†
Guam	610	227	21	†	187	89	5	†	30.6	39.2	23.8	†	4.0	5.7	7.4	†	13.2	14.5	31.0	†
Marshall Islands	†	130	†	†	†	51	†	†	†	39.2	†	†	†	4.0	†	†	†	10.1	†	†
Northern Marianas	190	†	†	†	78	†	†	†	41.1	†	†	†	4.4	†	†	†	10.7	†	†	†
Palau	†	140	†	†	†	42	†	†	†	29.7	†	†	†	3.6	†	†	†	12.2	†	†
Puerto Rico	14,329	228	10,301	1,004	4,511	133	4,173	479	31.5	58.4	40.5	47.7	4.1	9.2	10.3	13.1	13.0	15.8	25.3	27.4
U.S. Virgin Islands	665	†	†	†	165	†	†	†	24.8	†	†	†	2.6	†	†	†	10.4	†	†	†

†Not applicable.

NOTE: Degree-granting institutions grant associate's or higher degrees and participate in Title IV federal financial aid programs. Data are for degree-granting institutions with 15 or more full-time employees; institutions with fewer than 15 employees did not report staff data prior to 2007.

SOURCE: U.S. Department of Education, National Center for Education Statistics, 2005 Integrated Postsecondary Education Data System (IPEDS), Winter 2005–06 and Spring 2006. (This table was prepared August 2006.)

Table 248. Number of instructional faculty in degree-granting institutions, by employment status and control and type of institution: Selected years, fall 1970 through fall 2005

[In thousands]

Year	Total	Employment status			Control				Type	
		Full-time	Part-time	Percent full-time	Public	Private			4-year	2-year
						Total	Not-for-profit	For-profit		
1	2	3	4	5	6	7	8	9	10	11
1970	474	369	104	77.9	314	160	—	—	382	92
1971[1]	492	379	113	77.0	333	159	—	—	387	105
1972	500	380	120	76.0	343	157	—	—	384	116
1973[1]	527	389	138	73.8	365	162	—	—	401	126
1974[1]	567	406	161	71.6	397	170	—	—	427	140
1975[1]	628	440	188	70.1	443	185	—	—	467	161
1976	633	434	199	68.6	449	184	—	—	467	166
1977	678	448	230	66.1	492	186	—	—	485	193
1979[1]	675	445	230	65.9	488	187	—	—	494	182
1980[1]	686	450	236	65.6	495	191	—	—	494	192
1981	705	461	244	65.4	509	196	—	—	493	212
1982[1]	710	462	248	65.1	506	204	—	—	493	217
1983	724	471	254	65.0	512	212	—	—	504	220
1984[1]	717	462	255	64.4	505	212	—	—	504	213
1985[1]	715	459	256	64.2	503	212	—	—	504	211
1986[1]	722	459	263	63.6	510	212	—	—	506	216
1987[2]	793	523	270	66.0	553	240	—	—	548	246
1989[2]	824	524	300	63.6	577	247	—	—	584	241
1991[2]	826	536	291	64.8	581	245	—	—	591	235
1993[2]	915	546	370	59.6	650	265	254	11	626	290
1995[2]	932	551	381	59.1	657	275	261	14	647	285
1997[2]	990	569	421	57.5	695	295	271	24	683	307
1999[c]	1,028	591	437	57.5	713	315	285	30	714	314
2001[2]	1,113	618	495	55.5	771	342	306	36	764	349
2003[2,3]	1,174	630	544	53.7	792	382	330	52	814	359
2005[2]	1,290	676	615	52.4	841	449	362	88	917	373

—Not available.

[1]Estimated on the basis of enrollment. For methodological details on estimates, see National Center for Education Statistics, *Projections of Education Statistics to 2000*.

[2]Because of revised survey methods, data are not directly comparable with figures for years prior to 1987.

[3]Data revised from previously published figures.

NOTE: Includes faculty members with the title of professor, associate professor, assistant professor, instructor, lecturer, assisting professor, adjunct professor, or interim professor (or the equivalent). Excluded are graduate students with titles such as graduate or teaching fellow who assist senior faculty. Data through 1995 are for institutions of higher education, while later data are for degree-granting institutions. Degree-granting institutions grant associate's or higher degrees and participate in Title IV federal financial aid programs. The degree-granting classification is very similar to the earlier higher education classification, but it includes more 2-year colleges and excludes a few higher education institutions that did not grant degrees. (See Guide to Sources for details.) Data are for degree-granting institutions with 15 or more full-time employees; institutions with fewer than 15 employees did not report staff data prior to 2007. Detail may not sum to totals because of rounding.

SOURCE: U.S. Department of Education, National Center for Education Statistics, Higher Education General Information Survey (HEGIS), *Employees in Institutions of Higher Education*, 1970 and 1972, and "Staff Survey" 1976; *Projections of Education Statistics to 2000*; 1987 through 2005 Integrated Postsecondary Education Data System (IPEDS), "Fall Staff Survey" (IPEDS-S:87–99), and Winter 2001–02 through Winter 2005–06; and U.S. Equal Employment Opportunity Commission, Higher Education Staff Information Survey (EEO-6), 1977, 1981, and 1983. (This table was prepared August 2007.)

Table 249. Full-time instructional faculty in degree-granting institutions, by race/ethnicity, sex, and academic rank: Fall 2003, fall 2005, and fall 2007

| Sex and academic rank | Total | White | Minority | | | | Asian/Pacific Islander | American Indian/Alaska Native | Race/ ethnicity unknown | Nonresident alien[2] |
			Number	Percent[1]	Black	Hispanic				
1	2	3	4	5	6	7	8	9	10	11
2003										
Total	630,092	505,186	97,164	15.6	33,106	20,046	41,043	2,969	6,589	21,153
Professors	165,521	144,116	19,402	11.8	5,323	3,415	10,161	503	821	1,182
Associate professors	132,729	109,106	20,763	15.8	7,199	3,860	9,178	526	902	1,958
Assistant professors	152,688	112,657	28,579	19.0	9,449	5,301	13,172	657	2,008	9,444
Instructors	93,087	73,292	16,688	18.2	6,757	4,786	4,314	831	1,349	1,758
Lecturers	23,307	18,338	3,578	15.6	1,202	1,078	1,198	100	315	1,076
Other faculty	62,760	47,677	8,154	13.2	3,176	1,606	3,020	352	1,194	5,735
2005										
Total	675,624	527,900	109,964	16.5	35,458	22,818	48,457	3,231	9,703	28,057
Professors	169,192	145,936	20,856	12.4	5,484	3,793	11,060	519	1,014	1,386
Associate professors	138,444	112,507	22,429	16.4	7,402	4,319	10,144	564	1,296	2,212
Assistant professors	159,689	114,470	31,253	19.9	9,897	5,728	14,922	706	2,809	11,157
Instructors	98,555	76,359	18,368	19.0	7,462	5,261	4,740	905	1,853	1,975
Lecturers	27,215	20,982	4,342	16.2	1,286	1,233	1,714	109	480	1,411
Other faculty	82,529	57,646	12,716	15.8	3,927	2,484	5,877	428	2,251	9,916
Males	401,507	313,685	62,923	15.9	17,029	12,486	31,711	1,697	5,668	19,231
Professors	126,788	109,128	15,706	12.5	3,498	2,680	9,180	348	764	1,190
Associate professors	84,783	68,383	13,893	16.5	3,947	2,551	7,099	296	835	1,672
Assistant professors	86,182	60,244	16,671	19.7	4,459	3,003	8,903	306	1,601	7,666
Instructors	46,481	36,034	8,360	18.4	2,987	2,581	2,320	472	978	1,109
Lecturers	12,976	9,898	1,980	15.6	595	495	839	51	264	834
Other faculty	44,297	29,998	6,313	14.7	1,543	1,176	3,370	224	1,226	6,760
Females	274,117	214,215	47,041	17.4	18,429	10,332	16,746	1,534	4,035	8,826
Professors	42,404	36,808	5,150	12.2	1,986	1,113	1,880	171	250	196
Associate professors	53,661	44,124	8,536	16.0	3,455	1,768	3,045	268	461	540
Assistant professors	73,507	54,226	14,582	20.2	5,438	2,725	6,019	400	1,208	3,491
Instructors	52,074	40,325	10,008	19.5	4,475	2,680	2,420	433	875	866
Lecturers	14,239	11,084	2,362	16.8	691	738	875	58	216	577
Other faculty	38,232	27,648	6,403	17.2	2,384	1,308	2,507	204	1,025	3,156
2007										
Total	703,463	540,460	119,906	17.3	37,930	24,975	53,661	3,340	11,875	31,222
Professors	173,395	147,867	22,734	13.2	5,839	4,128	12,239	528	1,309	1,485
Associate professors	143,692	115,274	24,255	17.1	7,855	4,714	11,082	604	1,628	2,535
Assistant professors	168,508	117,618	34,940	21.2	10,642	6,329	17,290	679	3,593	12,357
Instructors	101,429	77,609	19,470	19.7	7,480	5,800	5,225	965	2,350	2,000
Lecturers	31,264	23,470	5,326	17.4	1,602	1,492	2,081	151	661	1,807
Other faculty	85,175	58,622	13,181	15.9	4,512	2,512	5,744	413	2,334	11,038
Males	409,115	314,375	67,147	16.7	17,782	13,468	34,178	1,719	6,660	20,933
Professors	127,488	108,404	16,882	13.3	3,646	2,874	10,018	344	973	1,229
Associate professors	86,660	68,982	14,760	17.2	4,110	2,768	7,570	312	1,038	1,880
Assistant professors	88,741	60,407	18,207	21.0	4,607	3,265	10,037	298	1,945	8,182
Instructors	46,599	35,795	8,665	19.0	2,928	2,782	2,463	492	1,066	1,073
Lecturers	14,784	11,045	2,367	16.4	721	613	956	77	347	1,025
Other faculty	44,843	29,742	6,266	14.4	1,770	1,166	3,134	196	1,291	7,544
Females	294,348	226,085	52,759	18.2	20,148	11,507	19,483	1,621	5,215	10,289
Professors	45,907	39,463	5,852	12.8	2,193	1,254	2,221	184	336	256
Associate professors	57,032	46,292	9,495	16.8	3,745	1,946	3,512	292	590	655
Assistant professors	79,767	57,211	16,733	21.4	6,035	3,064	7,253	381	1,648	4,175
Instructors	54,830	41,814	10,805	20.2	4,552	3,018	2,762	473	1,284	927
Lecturers	16,480	12,425	2,959	18.3	881	879	1,125	74	314	782
Other faculty	40,332	28,880	6,915	17.6	2,742	1,346	2,610	217	1,043	3,494

[1]Minority faculty as a percentage of total faculty, excluding race/ethnicity unknown.
[2]Race/ethnicity not collected.
NOTE: Degree-granting institutions grant associate's or higher degrees and participate in Title IV federal financial aid programs. Beginning in 2007, includes institutions with fewer than 15 full-time employees; these institutions did not report staff data prior to 2007. By definition, all graduate assistants are part-time. Race categories exclude persons of Hispanic

ethnicity. Totals may differ from figures reported in other tables because of varying survey methodologies.
SOURCE: U.S. Department of Education, National Center for Education Statistics, 2003, 2005 and 2007 Integrated Postsecondary Education Data System (IPEDS), Winter 2003–04, Winter 2005–06, and Winter 2007–08. (This table was prepared October 2008.)

Table 250. Percentage distribution of full-time faculty and instructional staff in degree-granting institutions, by type and control of institution, selected instruction activities, and number of classes taught for credit: Fall 2003

Instruction activity and number of classes	All institutions	Research Public	Research Private	Doctoral Public	Doctoral Private	Comprehensive Public	Comprehensive Private	Private liberal arts	Public 2-year	Other
1	2	3	4	5	6	7	8	9	10	11
Number of full-time faculty and instructional staff										
(in thousands)	681.8 (0.05)	162.1 (0.85)	63.5 (1.58)	51.3 (0.76)	21.7 (0.79)	107.3 (2.98)	41.4 (1.59)	49.6 (1.80)	114.6 (1.09)	70.2 (3.36)
Percentage distribution	100.0 (†)	23.8 (0.12)	9.3 (0.23)	7.5 (0.11)	3.2 (0.12)	15.7 (0.44)	6.1 (0.23)	7.3 (0.26)	16.8 (0.16)	10.3 (0.49)
Average hours worked per week	53.3 (0.13)	55.6 (0.21)	55.8 (0.42)	54.0 (0.38)	52.4 (0.59)	53.2 (0.31)	51.8 (0.53)	54.0 (0.39)	49.2 (0.34)	53.1 (0.49)
Paid activities within institution	45.4 (0.12)	48.8 (0.19)	47.8 (0.36)	45.9 (0.31)	44.7 (0.47)	44.4 (0.27)	42.9 (0.55)	45.6 (0.39)	40.9 (0.27)	45.1 (0.59)
Unpaid activities within institution	3.8 (0.04)	3.1 (0.08)	3.3 (0.15)	3.9 (0.14)	3.8 (0.20)	4.4 (0.13)	4.4 (0.15)	4.4 (0.11)	4.2 (0.12)	3.6 (0.22)
Paid activities outside institution	2.2 (0.05)	1.8 (0.08)	2.7 (0.21)	2.1 (0.13)	2.3 (0.25)	2.3 (0.12)	2.2 (0.17)	2.0 (0.13)	2.3 (0.12)	2.8 (0.24)
Unpaid activities outside institution	1.9 (0.03)	1.9 (0.05)	2.0 (0.09)	2.1 (0.11)	1.7 (0.11)	2.1 (0.09)	2.3 (0.12)	2.0 (0.14)	1.7 (0.08)	1.6 (0.10)
Work time distribution (percent)	100.0 (†)	100.0 (†)	100.0 (†)	100.0 (2.08)	100.0 (†)	100.0 (†)	100.0 (†)	100.0 (†)	100.0 (†)	100.0 (†)
Teaching	58.2 (0.27)	43.5 (0.43)	43.1 (0.76)	55.5 (0.72)	55.0 (1.15)	64.7 (0.70)	67.5 (0.78)	65.9 (0.80)	78.4 (0.65)	55.0 (1.61)
Research/scholarship	20.0 (0.44)	33.2 (0.42)	34.0 (0.84)	22.3 (0.72)	24.6 (0.84)	15.0 (0.49)	11.2 (0.57)	12.7 (0.67)	3.7 (0.26)	18.7 (0.97)
Other	21.7 (0.17)	23.2 (0.45)	22.8 (0.67)	22.2 (0.64)	20.4 (1.21)	20.4 (0.66)	21.3 (0.75)	21.3 (0.73)	17.9 (0.54)	26.3 (1.27)
Faculty/staff distribution by instruction activity (percent)										
Distribution by hours taught per week	100.0 (†)	100.0 (†)	100.0 (†)	100.0 (†)	100.0 (†)	100.0 (†)	100.0 (†)	100.0 (†)	100.0 (†)	100.0 (†)
Less than 4.0	30.3 (0.44)	48.9 (0.83)	52.2 (1.31)	30.0 (1.70)	26.5 (1.74)	16.3 (1.08)	14.9 (1.06)	15.5 (1.15)	14.5 (0.86)	36.0 (2.35)
4.0 to 5.9	5.8 (0.21)	8.4 (0.50)	8.8 (0.77)	6.0 (0.58)	8.4 (1.37)	4.1 (0.53)	4.1 (0.57)	4.1 (0.57)	2.5 (0.33)	6.7 (0.99)
6.0 to 7.9	13.8 (0.37)	20.0 (0.80)	15.2 (1.20)	22.2 (1.14)	22.0 (1.77)	12.0 (0.78)	11.0 (1.43)	13.3 (1.48)	4.4 (0.60)	9.0 (0.88)
8.0 to 9.9	12.5 (0.30)	9.0 (0.49)	9.3 (0.87)	16.9 (1.20)	19.3 (1.76)	21.5 (0.93)	18.7 (1.78)	19.5 (1.83)	5.7 (0.61)	7.2 (0.98)
10.0 to 14.9	18.2 (0.39)	7.9 (0.55)	8.8 (0.88)	15.1 (1.13)	15.0 (1.53)	31.5 (1.24)	32.7 (2.15)	33.5 (1.93)	14.7 (0.90)	19.6 (1.95)
15.0 or more	19.4 (0.40)	5.8 (0.43)	5.7 (0.67)	9.7 (0.92)	8.7 (1.34)	14.6 (0.93)	18.5 (1.92)	14.1 (1.39)	58.2 (1.47)	21.5 (1.73)
Distribution by number of students taught	100.0 (†)	100.0 (†)	100.0 (†)	100.0 (†)	100.0 (†)	100.0 (†)	100.0 (†)	100.0 (†)	100.0 (†)	100.0 (†)
Less than 25	30.6 (0.46)	46.0 (0.84)	51.5 (1.56)	29.7 (1.53)	31.9 (1.88)	16.8 (1.25)	16.5 (1.23)	20.8 (1.44)	15.9 (0.94)	36.8 (1.96)
25 to 49	17.0 (0.34)	17.0 (0.83)	16.9 (1.06)	17.1 (0.99)	18.8 (1.74)	17.9 (0.96)	22.7 (1.57)	25.4 (1.62)	12.0 (0.77)	13.4 (1.41)
50 to 74	16.2 (0.33)	11.9 (0.69)	10.0 (0.99)	16.3 (1.29)	20.9 (1.64)	18.7 (0.77)	26.5 (1.32)	24.4 (1.40)	16.2 (0.86)	14.4 (1.07)
75 to 99	13.0 (0.30)	7.6 (0.51)	6.2 (0.57)	13.9 (0.91)	11.2 (0.95)	17.5 (0.86)	17.6 (1.15)	15.8 (1.09)	18.1 (0.78)	11.5 (1.03)
100 to 149	14.2 (0.39)	7.6 (0.54)	7.0 (0.78)	13.2 (0.87)	9.9 (1.21)	19.4 (1.22)	13.1 (1.61)	10.6 (0.96)	25.7 (0.98)	14.9 (1.58)
150 or more	9.0 (0.27)	9.8 (0.59)	8.4 (0.73)	9.8 (0.87)	7.4 (1.04)	9.7 (0.85)	3.6 (0.72)	3.0 (0.62)	12.1 (0.86)	8.9 (0.63)
Distribution by student classroom contact hours per week[1]	100.0 (†)	100.0 (†)	100.0 (†)	100.0 (†)	100.0 (†)	100.0 (†)	100.0 (†)	100.0 (†)	100.0 (†)	100.0 (†)
Less than 50	24.2 (0.40)	38.3 (0.83)	42.7 (1.33)	23.2 (1.52)	22.0 (1.53)	11.9 (1.04)	12.6 (1.02)	12.2 (1.05)	11.9 (0.77)	30.8 (1.87)
50 to 99	5.3 (0.23)	7.7 (0.56)	7.0 (0.82)	6.4 (0.68)	7.0 (1.20)	4.3 (0.52)	2.7 (0.55)	4.9 (0.48)	2.5 (0.39)	5.2 (0.88)
100 to 199	7.1 (0.20)	9.4 (0.54)	10.7 (0.87)	8.0 (0.88)	8.6 (1.38)	6.2 (0.62)	4.5 (0.66)	7.2 (1.02)	3.4 (0.43)	6.1 (0.99)
200 to 349	9.0 (0.28)	10.9 (0.52)	10.4 (0.83)	10.4 (0.88)	12.8 (1.74)	8.6 (0.71)	10.9 (1.38)	11.9 (1.27)	3.6 (0.54)	6.8 (0.79)
350 to 499	7.7 (0.24)	8.0 (0.44)	8.1 (0.83)	10.6 (1.03)	11.5 (1.03)	7.9 (0.91)	10.2 (0.79)	12.4 (0.93)	3.5 (0.40)	4.6 (0.70)
500 or more	46.8 (0.44)	25.6 (0.74)	21.2 (1.21)	41.4 (1.36)	38.0 (1.81)	61.1 (1.46)	59.1 (1.75)	51.4 (2.13)	75.0 (1.16)	46.6 (2.30)
Distribution by total classroom credit hours	100.0 (†)	100.0 (†)	100.0 (†)	100.0 (†)	100.0 (†)	100.0 (†)	100.0 (†)	100.0 (†)	100.0 (†)	100.0 (†)
Less than 4.0	31.8 (0.54)	48.9 (0.82)	52.1 (1.55)	30.1 (1.46)	29.0 (1.75)	18.0 (1.03)	17.5 (1.44)	23.7 (2.18)	15.4 (0.84)	38.1 (2.23)
4.0 to 5.9	6.6 (0.22)	9.4 (0.54)	10.2 (0.63)	6.8 (0.67)	10.5 (1.53)	3.5 (0.35)	4.5 (0.61)	5.6 (0.67)	3.7 (0.44)	7.0 (0.83)
6.0 to 7.9	15.0 (0.37)	21.6 (0.66)	14.0 (1.04)	25.1 (1.29)	21.3 (1.71)	14.2 (0.94)	12.2 (1.04)	11.4 (1.15)	6.6 (0.72)	10.1 (1.07)
8.0 to 9.9	14.8 (0.33)	10.4 (0.60)	10.7 (0.84)	19.9 (1.28)	20.8 (1.47)	25.3 (1.15)	23.4 (1.73)	19.1 (1.16)	8.1 (0.60)	10.0 (1.19)
10.0 to 14.9	20.2 (0.38)	7.7 (0.51)	9.7 (0.99)	14.8 (1.17)	13.2 (1.40)	32.0 (1.20)	35.4 (1.94)	32.5 (2.20)	24.3 (1.28)	22.3 (1.38)
15.0 or more	11.6 (0.31)	1.9 (0.24)	3.2 (0.52)	3.3 (0.64)	5.2 (0.99)	7.0 (0.88)	6.9 (0.71)	7.7 (1.28)	41.8 (1.50)	12.5 (1.17)

See notes at end of table.

Table 250. Percentage distribution of full-time faculty and instructional staff in degree-granting institutions, by type and control of institution, selected instruction activities, and number of classes taught for credit: Fall 2003—Continued

Instruction activity and number of classes	All institutions	Research		Doctoral		Comprehensive		Private liberal arts	Public 2-year	Other
		Public	Private	Public	Private	Public	Private			
1	2	3	4	5	6	7	8	9	10	11
Faculty/staff distribution by number of classes taught for credit (percent)										
Faculty/staff with undergraduate classes only, by total for-credit courses	100.0 (†)	100.0 (†)	100.0 (†)	100.0 (†)	100.0 (†)	100.0 (†)	100.0 (†)	100.0 (†)	100.0 (†)	100.0 (†)
1	11.0 (0.43)	24.2 (2.40)	20.2 (2.97)	14.1 (2.91)	10.0 (2.52)	10.5 (1.31)	9.3 (1.13)	9.9 (0.98)	8.7 (0.75)	11.2 (2.17)
2	17.4 (0.62)	38.0 (2.80)	31.2 (3.96)	24.2 (3.05)	38.6 (5.05)	14.6 (1.51)	18.5 (2.14)	22.7 (2.32)	10.7 (0.77)	13.7 (2.29)
3	23.7 (0.65)	22.6 (2.21)	30.8 (3.42)	31.1 (2.98)	37.3 (3.60)	28.6 (1.89)	30.3 (2.48)	34.3 (2.57)	16.0 (0.96)	17.3 (2.77)
4	21.9 (0.73)	10.8 (1.43)	11.7 (2.99)	20.4 (1.92)	10.9 (2.75)	33.3 (1.87)	30.7 (2.77)	21.1 (2.22)	16.9 (1.00)	28.4 (2.48)
5 or more	26.1 (0.70)	4.4 (0.86)	6.1 (1.74)	10.1 (1.97)	3.2 (1.15)	13.0 (1.56)	11.2 (1.53)	12.0 (1.44)	47.6 (1.49)	29.4 (2.14)
Faculty/staff with graduate classes only, by total for-credit courses	100.0 (†)	100.0 (†)	100.0 (†)	100.0 (†)	100.0 (†)	100.0 (†)	100.0 (†)	100.0 (†)	‡	100.0 (†)
1	40.1 (1.21)	50.4 (2.17)	48.0 (3.69)	34.3 (3.04)	25.9 (4.02)	23.6 (3.86)	13.0 (3.72)	15.8 (6.35)	‡	37.8 (3.15)
2	31.0 (1.07)	26.3 (1.81)	27.9 (2.93)	39.1 (3.32)	50.7 (4.02)	33.6 (5.32)	28.7 (4.00)	31.6 (12.42)	‡	32.9 (2.93)
3	16.7 (0.88)	14.3 (1.38)	13.3 (2.60)	16.3 (2.76)	14.1 (3.52)	29.6 (4.35)	36.3 (4.99)	22.7 (9.79)	‡	13.4 (2.48)
4	7.1 (0.80)	4.5 (1.24)	7.4 (2.07)	7.4 (2.04)	3.7 (1.44)	10.1 (3.39)	16.5 (3.92)	16.7 (8.04)	‡	7.2 (2.21)
5 or more	5.1 (0.52)	4.4 (0.69)	3.4 (1.33)	2.9 (1.62)	5.7 (2.80)	3.1 (1.52)	5.5 (2.85)	13.1 (6.95)	‡	8.7 (1.94)
Faculty/staff with both undergraduate and graduate classes, by total for-credit courses	100.0 (†)	100.0 (†)	100.0 (†)	100.0 (†)	100.0 (†)	100.0 (†)	100.0 (†)	100.0 (†)	‡	100.0 (†)
1	23.3 (0.68)	32.5 (1.37)	38.4 (1.89)	21.1 (2.17)	20.2 (2.37)	9.0 (1.04)	10.3 (2.14)	9.4 (2.00)	‡	24.8 (3.18)
2	33.4 (0.83)	44.3 (1.36)	42.8 (2.33)	37.1 (2.15)	37.8 (2.58)	19.6 (1.30)	19.0 (2.78)	18.3 (2.62)	‡	18.7 (3.00)
3	24.3 (0.70)	15.5 (0.99)	12.4 (1.37)	26.5 (1.75)	32.0 (3.01)	38.1 (1.91)	34.8 (2.85)	29.5 (3.77)	‡	21.2 (3.06)
4	12.2 (0.54)	4.5 (0.64)	3.7 (1.06)	10.1 (1.37)	6.6 (2.02)	23.4 (1.69)	24.4 (3.39)	27.5 (3.74)	‡	16.6 (3.55)
5 or more	6.7 (0.43)	3.1 (0.45)	2.8 (0.78)	5.2 (0.75)	3.2 (1.74)	9.9 (1.01)	11.4 (2.07)	15.2 (3.65)	‡	18.6 (2.88)

†Not applicable.
‡Reporting standards not met.
[1]Distribution by student classroom contact hours per week is based on the number of contact hours that faculty and instructional staff spend each week with students during classroom instruction multiplied by the number of students taught.

NOTE: Totals may differ from figures reported in other tables because of varying survey methodologies. Detail may not sum to totals because of rounding. Standard errors appear in parentheses.
SOURCE: U.S. Department of Education, National Center for Education Statistics, 2004 National Study of Postsecondary Faculty (NSOPF:04). (This table was prepared December 2008.)

Table 251. Percentage distribution of part-time faculty and instructional staff in degree-granting institutions, by type and control of institution, selected instruction activities, and number of classes taught for credit: Fall 2003

Instruction activity and number of classes	All institutions	Research		Doctoral		Comprehensive		Private liberal arts	Public 2-year	Other
		Public	Private	Public	Private	Public	Private			
1	2	3	4	5	6	7	8	9	10	11
Number of part-time faculty and instructional staff										
(in thousands)	530.0 (0.02)	39.7 (0.78)	23.2 (0.96)	20.8 (0.82)	15.4 (0.83)	60.3 (2.49)	53.5 (2.17)	28.4 (2.19)	230.1 (2.00)	58.7 (3.38)
Percentage distribution	100.0 (†)	7.5 (0.15)	4.4 (0.18)	3.9 (0.15)	2.9 (0.16)	11.4 (0.47)	10.1 (0.41)	5.4 (0.41)	43.4 (0.38)	11.1 (0.64)
Average hours worked per week	39.9 (0.30)	41.1 (0.85)	42.6 (1.24)	43.5 (1.37)	42.1 (1.29)	38.8 (1.01)	42.7 (1.14)	39.6 (1.23)	38.0 (0.45)	41.8 (1.18)
Paid activities within institution	13.7 (0.13)	19.0 (0.61)	14.0 (0.65)	16.4 (0.76)	13.5 (0.97)	14.9 (0.48)	12.1 (0.56)	13.5 (0.73)	12.5 (0.19)	14.2 (0.46)
Unpaid activities within institution	1.7 (0.06)	1.8 (0.25)	2.5 (0.25)	2.3 (0.28)	2.8 (0.37)	2.3 (0.19)	2.7 (0.12)	2.6 (0.17)	2.1 (0.08)	2.5 (0.17)
Paid activities outside institution	22.1 (0.28)	18.3 (0.98)	23.9 (1.34)	23.3 (1.55)	24.1 (1.40)	19.9 (1.00)	26.6 (1.38)	21.9 (0.98)	21.6 (0.41)	23.3 (1.06)
Unpaid activities outside institution	2.3 (0.06)	2.0 (0.25)	2.2 (0.25)	1.6 (0.28)	1.7 (0.37)	1.8 (0.19)	1.3 (0.12)	1.6 (0.17)	1.7 (0.08)	1.8 (0.17)
Work time distribution (percent)	100.0 (†)	100.0 (†)	100.0 (†)	100.0 (†)	100.0 (†)	100.0 (†)	100.0 (†)	100.0 (†)	100.0 (†)	100.0 (†)
Teaching	88.3 (0.32)	74.1 (1.79)	80.6 (1.89)	84.9 (1.71)	87.2 (1.87)	90.8 (0.83)	90.4 (0.70)	90.2 (1.20)	91.3 (0.43)	85.4 (1.19)
Research/scholarship	3.9 (0.80)	13.3 (1.62)	7.0 (0.97)	7.4 (1.35)	5.2 (1.42)	3.2 (0.46)	2.4 (0.49)	2.6 (0.54)	2.1 (0.21)	4.4 (0.61)
Other	7.8 (0.20)	12.6 (1.04)	12.4 (1.75)	7.6 (1.03)	7.6 (1.22)	6.0 (0.63)	7.2 (0.81)	7.2 (0.92)	6.6 (0.40)	10.3 (0.93)
Faculty/staff distribution by instruction activity (percent)										
Distribution by hours taught per week	100.0 (†)	100.0 (†)	100.0 (†)	100.0 (†)	100.0 (†)	100.0 (†)	100.0 (†)	100.0 (†)	100.0 (†)	100.0 (†)
Less than 4.0	45.3 (0.80)	58.1 (2.25)	62.4 (3.87)	53.3 (2.71)	48.0 (2.67)	45.5 (1.68)	39.8 (2.34)	44.8 (2.96)	41.3 (1.30)	46.5 (2.46)
4.0 to 5.9	12.2 (0.48)	9.3 (1.25)	12.9 (2.46)	12.5 (1.49)	15.0 (1.57)	9.7 (1.25)	17.7 (2.07)	13.2 (1.73)	11.7 (0.71)	12.6 (1.62)
6.0 to 7.9	14.3 (0.57)	12.5 (1.50)	10.1 (1.69)	14.5 (1.76)	14.3 (2.01)	19.4 (1.68)	12.9 (2.14)	13.8 (1.98)	14.5 (1.04)	13.0 (1.72)
8.0 to 9.9	10.4 (0.47)	8.9 (1.22)	5.6 (1.46)	8.3 (1.82)	7.8 (1.58)	10.8 (1.11)	11.7 (1.93)	10.7 (1.54)	11.3 (0.73)	9.5 (1.45)
10.0 to 14.9	9.4 (0.47)	7.5 (1.27)	3.0 (1.16)	5.5 (1.29)	7.3 (2.03)	8.0 (1.27)	7.7 (1.29)	8.3 (1.55)	11.7 (0.99)	9.8 (1.27)
15.0 or more	8.3 (0.43)	3.6 (0.90)	6.0 (1.94)	5.9 (1.50)	7.6 (1.26)	6.5 (1.05)	10.3 (1.61)	9.1 (2.38)	9.5 (0.67)	8.5 (1.19)
Distribution by number of students taught	100.0 (†)	100.0 (†)	100.0 (†)	100.0 (†)	100.0 (†)	100.0 (†)	100.0 (†)	100.0 (†)	100.0 (†)	100.0 (†)
Less than 25	52.0 (0.82)	55.6 (2.16)	68.9 (3.98)	44.6 (2.38)	56.9 (3.29)	41.6 (2.07)	57.9 (2.45)	60.5 (2.34)	49.7 (1.37)	54.0 (3.15)
25 to 49	24.9 (0.58)	17.4 (1.54)	16.9 (2.13)	27.4 (2.51)	20.7 (2.48)	24.5 (2.10)	29.4 (1.90)	24.1 (1.76)	26.7 (0.97)	22.6 (2.74)
50 to 74	12.1 (0.54)	11.6 (1.23)	3.7 (1.15)	12.5 (1.71)	9.8 (2.48)	17.5 (1.52)	8.5 (0.77)	10.0 (1.65)	12.9 (0.95)	11.7 (1.55)
75 to 99	5.8 (0.30)	5.4 (0.89)	4.1 (1.57)	7.6 (1.52)	6.8 (1.62)	6.7 (1.22)	2.0 (0.44)	3.7 (0.97)	6.2 (0.48)	7.5 (1.18)
100 to 149	3.4 (0.23)	4.8 (1.07)	2.0 (0.72)	4.2 (1.46)	2.9 (0.89)	7.2 (1.14)	1.8 (0.55)	1.2 (0.66)	3.2 (0.41)	2.4 (0.76)
150 or more	1.9 (0.19)	5.2 (0.96)	4.5 (1.35)	3.7 (0.94)	2.8 (1.12)	2.6 (0.59)	0.4 (0.30)	0.4 (0.34)	1.2 (0.35)	1.7 (0.44)
Distribution by student classroom contact hours per week[1]	100.0 (†)	100.0 (†)	100.0 (†)	100.0 (†)	100.0 (†)	100.0 (†)	100.0 (†)	100.0 (†)	100.0 (†)	100.0 (†)
Less than 50	33.9 (0.80)	41.6 (2.52)	53.4 (3.98)	27.7 (2.98)	40.2 (2.67)	25.4 (1.88)	36.0 (2.52)	38.2 (2.66)	31.3 (1.34)	36.7 (3.40)
50 to 99	17.0 (0.54)	13.1 (1.46)	17.5 (2.13)	23.0 (3.38)	17.0 (2.30)	18.9 (1.40)	19.5 (1.53)	17.4 (1.97)	16.6 (0.96)	14.5 (1.65)
100 to 199	13.2 (0.49)	13.3 (1.51)	8.5 (1.44)	14.2 (2.34)	7.5 (1.56)	14.8 (1.72)	13.3 (1.65)	14.1 (2.01)	13.4 (0.82)	13.5 (2.19)
200 to 349	11.2 (0.46)	10.8 (1.29)	5.6 (1.42)	10.9 (1.97)	12.3 (1.88)	10.3 (1.80)	13.5 (0.93)	10.1 (1.26)	11.4 (0.66)	12.1 (1.62)
350 to 499	7.2 (0.34)	6.1 (0.98)	3.0 (0.96)	7.7 (1.74)	8.5 (1.74)	10.2 (1.00)	4.5 (0.64)	5.5 (0.95)	8.0 (0.69)	6.0 (0.93)
500 or more	17.5 (0.58)	15.1 (1.89)	12.1 (2.50)	16.5 (2.29)	14.5 (2.58)	20.3 (1.97)	13.3 (1.53)	14.6 (2.85)	19.3 (0.98)	17.2 (1.87)
Distribution by total classroom credit hours	100.0 (†)	100.0 (†)	100.0 (†)	100.0 (†)	100.0 (†)	100.0 (†)	100.0 (†)	100.0 (†)	100.0 (†)	100.0 (†)
Less than 4.0	53.3 (0.89)	59.8 (2.39)	67.5 (3.65)	62.2 (2.96)	55.4 (2.34)	52.0 (2.05)	51.3 (2.05)	58.9 (2.14)	50.2 (1.43)	52.2 (3.00)
4.0 to 5.9	11.7 (0.52)	12.2 (1.52)	11.8 (2.12)	10.8 (1.63)	10.6 (1.81)	9.3 (1.09)	14.1 (1.77)	10.3 (1.68)	12.2 (0.75)	11.5 (1.68)
6.0 to 7.9	16.9 (0.55)	12.8 (1.61)	10.2 (2.20)	14.9 (1.96)	18.7 (2.12)	23.1 (2.10)	18.1 (1.22)	15.4 (1.81)	16.5 (0.98)	17.5 (1.62)
8.0 to 9.9	9.4 (0.42)	8.2 (0.92)	6.2 (1.22)	8.5 (1.64)	8.3 (2.03)	9.5 (0.99)	9.0 (1.08)	8.3 (1.34)	10.8 (0.81)	7.4 (1.33)
10.0 to 14.9	6.6 (0.35)	5.6 (1.48)	1.8 (0.75)	3.6 (0.97)	4.8 (1.22)	3.8 (0.81)	5.2 (0.82)	5.1 (1.57)	8.1 (0.62)	9.2 (1.54)
15.0 or more	2.1 (0.21)	1.4 (0.58)	2.5 (0.91)	‡ (†)	2.2 (0.78)	2.2 (0.57)	2.3 (0.64)	2.0 (0.80)	2.2 (0.31)	2.2 (0.63)

See notes at end of table.

Table 251. Percentage distribution of part-time faculty and instructional staff in degree-granting institutions, by type and control of institution, selected instruction activities, and number of classes taught for credit: Fall 2003—Continued

Instruction activity and number of classes	All institutions	Research		Doctoral		Comprehensive		Private liberal arts	Public 2-year	Other
		Public	Private	Public	Private	Public	Private			
1	2	3	4	5	6	7	8	9	10	11
Faculty/staff distribution by number of classes taught for credit (percent)										
Faculty/staff with undergraduate classes only, by total for-credit courses	100.0 (†)	100.0 (†)	100.0 (†)	100.0 (†)	100.0 (†)	100.0 (†)	100.0 (†)	100.0 (†)	100.0 (†)	100.0 (†)
1	49.2 (0.90)	53.1 (3.85)	62.3 (5.20)	58.8 (4.27)	45.4 (4.58)	48.4 (2.43)	54.1 (2.78)	53.7 (3.42)	47.9 (1.20)	43.2 (3.57)
2	29.7 (0.86)	31.2 (3.04)	28.5 (5.51)	26.9 (3.12)	39.8 (4.33)	33.1 (2.35)	29.2 (2.27)	25.0 (2.20)	29.3 (1.24)	29.7 (2.70)
3	12.5 (0.47)	9.4 (1.83)	6.9 (2.33)	11.5 (2.36)	13.1 (3.15)	10.8 (1.26)	9.4 (1.35)	10.2 (1.62)	13.9 (0.84)	13.7 (1.71)
4	5.3 (0.41)	4.6 (1.41)	‡ (†)	‡ (†)	‡ (†)	4.0 (1.06)	5.4 (1.08)	5.6 (1.95)	5.9 (0.65)	6.9 (1.73)
5 or more	3.3 (0.32)	1.7 (1.03)	‡ (†)	2.6 (1.27)	1.3 (1.11)	3.7 (0.95)	1.8 (0.77)	5.5 (1.69)	3.1 (0.44)	6.5 (1.87)
Faculty/staff with graduate classes only, by total for-credit courses	100.0 (†)	100.0 (†)	100.0 (†)	100.0 (†)	100.0 (†)	100.0 (†)	100.0 (†)	100.0 (†)	100.0 (†)	100.0 (†)
1	72.6 (1.73)	71.7 (5.24)	81.7 (4.89)	81.8 (4.93)	72.2 (5.28)	74.8 (5.62)	62.2 (3.67)	69.9 (6.67)	‡	75.6 (5.21)
2	16.6 (1.30)	20.6 (4.61)	7.4 (3.23)	10.8 (4.07)	16.2 (4.50)	12.9 (4.45)	23.3 (2.37)	18.8 (5.77)	‡	16.4 (3.91)
3	5.3 (0.93)	4.0 (2.25)	5.7 (2.74)	7.4 (4.52)	5.7 (3.51)	3.7 (2.40)	7.6 (2.41)	2.9 (2.09)	‡	3.8 (2.34)
4	3.1 (0.81)	‡ (†)	5.2 (3.18)	‡ (†)	4.0 (1.41)	5.2 (3.55)	3.9 (1.32)	6.6 (4.24)	‡	‡ (†)
5 or more	2.4 (0.53)	3.7 (2.05)	‡ (†)	‡ (†)	‡ (†)	‡ (†)	2.9 (1.38)	‡ (†)	‡	3.0 (1.45)
Faculty/staff with both undergraduate and graduate classes, by total for-credit courses	100.0 (†)	100.0 (†)	100.0 (†)	100.0 (†)	100.0 (†)	100.0 (†)	100.0 (†)	100.0 (†)	100.0 (†)	100.0 (†)
1	46.5 (2.05)	51.3 (5.19)	46.4 (10.59)	59.3 (5.24)	63.7 (8.93)	38.0 (6.03)	38.9 (4.23)	44.1 (8.69)	‡	47.4 (6.18)
2	28.7 (1.96)	29.6 (4.47)	36.3 (8.39)	18.5 (6.24)	18.1 (5.75)	30.7 (3.91)	32.7 (5.11)	35.1 (9.57)	‡	23.9 (5.54)
3	13.5 (1.78)	11.3 (3.25)	11.4 (5.72)	16.9 (6.27)	‡ (†)	17.8 (4.04)	16.6 (3.72)	12.3 (4.69)	‡	9.5 (4.84)
4	5.9 (1.19)	3.3 (1.63)	‡ (†)	‡ (†)	7.8 (5.97)	7.9 (3.54)	5.4 (3.06)	5.8 (2.25)	‡	10.0 (4.03)
5 or more	5.4 (1.18)	4.4 (2.08)	‡ (†)	5.0 (2.36)	‡ (†)	5.7 (2.75)	6.4 (2.36)	2.7 (2.30)	‡	9.2 (4.56)

†Not applicable.
‡Reporting standards not met.
[1]Distribution by student classroom contact hours per week is based on the number of contact hours that faculty and instructional staff spend each week with students during classroom instruction multiplied by the number of students taught.

NOTE: Totals may differ from figures reported in other tables because of varying survey methodologies. Detail may not sum to totals because of rounding. Standard errors appear in parentheses.
SOURCE: U.S. Department of Education. National Center for Education Statistics, 2004 National Study of Postsecondary Faculty (NSOPF:04). (This table was prepared December 2008.)

Table 252. Full-time and part-time faculty and instructional staff in degree-granting institutions, by type and control of institution and selected characteristics: Fall 1992, fall 1998, and fall 2003

Selected characteristic	Number (in thousands) 1992	1998	2003	Fall 2003 Total	Research Public	Research Private	Doctoral Public	Doctoral Private	Comprehensive Public	Comprehensive Private	Private liberal arts	Public 2-year	Other
1	2	3	4	5	6	7	8	9	10	11	12	13	14
Full-time faculty and instructional staff													
Number (in thousands)	528.3	560.4	681.8	681.8 (0.05)	162.1 (0.85)	63.5 (1.58)	51.3 (0.76)	21.7 (0.79)	107.3 (2.98)	41.4 (1.59)	49.6 (1.80)	114.6 (1.09)	70.2 (3.36)
Percentage distribution	†	†	†	100.0 (†)	23.8 (0.12)	9.3 (0.23)	7.5 (0.11)	3.2 (0.12)	15.7 (0.44)	6.1 (0.23)	7.3 (0.26)	16.8 (0.16)	10.3 (0.49)
				Percentage distribution of full-time faculty and instructional staff									
Total	†	†	†	100.0 (†)	100.0 (†)	100.0 (†)	100.0 (†)	100.0 (†)	100.0 (†)	100.0 (†)	100.0 (†)	100.0 (†)	100.0 (†)
Sex													
Male	352.7	356.9	420.4	61.7 (0.35)	69.9 (0.62)	68.8 (0.90)	62.8 (1.29)	66.7 (2.04)	58.8 (0.84)	57.6 (2.03)	59.7 (1.14)	50.5 (1.08)	60.3 (1.41)
Female	175.5	203.5	261.4	38.3 (0.35)	30.1 (0.62)	31.2 (0.90)	37.2 (1.29)	33.3 (2.04)	41.2 (0.84)	42.4 (2.03)	40.3 (1.14)	49.5 (1.08)	39.7 (1.41)
Race/ethnicity													
White	456.7	477.0	547.7	80.3 (0.27)	79.0 (0.50)	77.6 (0.73)	81.3 (1.33)	82.7 (1.55)	78.0 (1.12)	85.6 (1.02)	86.0 (0.81)	80.9 (0.84)	79.8 (1.14)
Black	27.4	28.4	38.1	5.6 (0.17)	3.7 (0.26)	4.9 (0.49)	4.1 (0.50)	5.1 (0.73)	8.7 (0.73)	4.8 (0.65)	6.3 (0.69)	6.9 (0.43)	4.7 (0.81)
Hispanic	13.9	18.5	23.8	3.5 (0.10)	2.9 (0.18)	3.5 (0.36)	2.9 (0.37)	2.2 (0.53)	3.6 (0.23)	2.4 (0.36)	2.3 (0.26)	5.8 (0.44)	3.1 (0.44)
Asian/Pacific Islander	27.7	32.5	62.3	9.1 (0.16)	13.2 (0.45)	12.8 (0.63)	10.1 (1.17)	9.3 (1.40)	7.9 (0.34)	5.9 (0.74)	3.8 (0.33)	4.2 (0.44)	11.3 (0.94)
American Indian/Alaska Native	2.6	4.0	10.0	1.5 (0.11)	1.1 (0.17)	1.2 (0.40)	1.6 (0.35)	0.7 (0.36)	1.8 (0.50)	1.2 (0.38)	1.6 (0.31)	2.2 (0.36)	1.0 (0.32)
Age													
Under 30	7.6	8.8	11.9	1.7 (0.13)	1.7 (0.24)	1.5 (0.23)	1.8 (0.37)	1.3 (0.44)	1.7 (0.29)	2.3 (0.56)	2.1 (0.41)	1.8 (0.36)	1.7 (0.68)
30 to 34	35.4	32.2	47.2	6.9 (0.21)	7.5 (0.44)	8.6 (0.89)	7.2 (0.82)	5.9 (0.73)	6.5 (0.74)	7.0 (0.92)	8.9 (0.73)	5.1 (0.52)	6.4 (0.75)
35 to 39	66.8	60.1	77.1	11.3 (0.29)	12.8 (0.58)	14.3 (1.35)	11.8 (0.95)	8.9 (1.45)	10.1 (0.86)	9.6 (0.88)	12.8 (1.22)	9.0 (0.70)	11.1 (1.05)
40 to 44	90.2	81.9	92.6	13.6 (0.31)	15.3 (0.57)	15.0 (0.75)	11.9 (0.83)	11.8 (1.36)	12.1 (0.78)	14.4 (1.15)	12.3 (0.75)	12.7 (0.88)	14.4 (1.38)
45 to 49	97.7	96.8	105.3	15.4 (0.32)	15.9 (0.53)	14.6 (1.24)	16.5 (1.38)	16.0 (1.89)	15.2 (0.75)	13.0 (1.18)	14.3 (1.10)	14.7 (0.70)	18.0 (1.36)
50 to 54	94.9	104.7	114.4	16.8 (0.34)	16.3 (0.66)	14.6 (0.87)	16.0 (1.09)	14.9 (1.34)	16.6 (0.90)	17.1 (1.26)	16.5 (1.00)	19.3 (0.84)	17.1 (1.35)
55 to 59	67.3	90.2	111.6	16.4 (0.37)	13.9 (0.66)	12.0 (0.61)	15.1 (1.01)	16.5 (1.60)	17.3 (0.99)	16.8 (1.24)	15.6 (0.87)	21.9 (1.05)	16.8 (1.46)
60 to 64	44.6	55.0	78.3	11.5 (0.31)	10.7 (0.58)	10.9 (0.74)	13.8 (0.90)	12.8 (1.54)	13.4 (0.72)	12.9 (1.42)	11.8 (1.10)	10.5 (0.68)	9.4 (0.83)
65 or older	23.8	30.6	43.3	6.3 (0.23)	6.0 (0.40)	8.6 (0.64)	5.9 (0.83)	11.8 (1.53)	7.1 (0.67)	6.8 (0.78)	5.7 (0.80)	4.9 (0.67)	5.2 (0.59)
Highest degree													
Less than bachelor's	6.3	6.7	10.0	1.5 (0.12)	0.2 (0.09)	0.2 (0.14)	0.2 (0.09)	‡ (†)	0.1 (0.07)	‡ (†)	0.8 (0.26)	6.1 (0.58)	2.4 (0.64)
Bachelor's	20.9	22.5	29.4	4.3 (0.24)	2.0 (0.27)	2.0 (0.41)	2.9 (0.51)	1.6 (1.17)	3.1 (0.63)	2.8 (2.10)	2.1 (0.53)	11.1 (0.97)	6.9 (0.82)
Master's	155.8	156.0	179.8	26.4 (0.39)	12.3 (0.49)	9.9 (0.93)	20.3 (1.19)	12.9 (1.19)	22.7 (1.08)	28.7 (2.10)	27.2 (1.71)	63.3 (1.22)	25.5 (1.68)
First-professional	58.3	51.7	56.1	8.2 (0.30)	11.8 (0.53)	18.4 (1.19)	4.7 (0.49)	9.7 (1.47)	2.0 (0.30)	3.5 (0.89)	0.9 (0.18)	1.6 (0.30)	21.3 (1.99)
Doctoral	283.8	323.5	406.6	59.6 (0.48)	73.7 (0.61)	69.4 (1.45)	71.9 (1.30)	75.4 (2.03)	72.1 (1.34)	65.0 (2.47)	69.1 (1.92)	17.9 (1.13)	43.8 (2.47)
Academic rank													
Professor	160.6	172.2	194.4	28.5 (0.54)	33.8 (0.95)	34.0 (1.15)	27.3 (1.34)	30.3 (2.37)	29.8 (1.23)	24.8 (1.61)	28.5 (1.79)	21.7 (1.89)	22.9 (1.39)
Associate professor	123.7	132.0	149.6	21.9 (0.37)	23.3 (0.63)	22.0 (1.12)	25.9 (1.54)	31.6 (1.73)	23.2 (1.30)	27.0 (1.41)	24.6 (1.27)	12.1 (1.22)	22.3 (1.47)
Assistant professor	124.3	125.0	158.1	23.2 (0.41)	22.5 (0.68)	26.6 (1.38)	23.5 (1.36)	21.6 (1.63)	28.3 (1.08)	31.8 (2.00)	30.3 (1.14)	10.3 (1.12)	25.2 (1.37)
Instructor	73.9	74.9	82.7	12.1 (0.42)	4.3 (0.27)	5.0 (0.79)	9.0 (0.94)	4.5 (0.89)	7.6 (0.81)	6.8 (1.02)	6.6 (0.91)	37.5 (2.13)	13.9 (1.30)
Lecturer	11.9	14.1	21.9	3.2 (0.22)	4.6 (0.34)	4.9 (0.59)	5.4 (0.80)	2.5 (0.40)	5.4 (0.99)	1.9 (0.67)	1.0 (0.23)	1.0 (0.09)	0.9 (0.27)
Other	17.1	26.3	56.5	8.3 (0.32)	10.6 (0.64)	7.1 (0.54)	8.5 (0.59)	8.9 (1.25)	5.7 (0.94)	7.3 (1.12)	8.8 (1.11)	8.3 (0.80)	7.9 (0.90)
No rank	16.9	15.8	18.6	2.7 (0.19)	0.8 (0.14)	0.4 (0.20)	0.5 (0.25)	0.6 (0.45)	0.1 (0.05)	0.5 (0.10)	0.2 (0.10)	9.8 (0.88)	7.0 (1.14)
Base salary													
Under $10,000	13.8	9.7	4.4	0.7 (0.07)	0.8 (0.19)	0.7 (0.31)	0.8 (0.26)	‡ (†)	0.5 (0.20)	0.3 (0.18)	0.6 (0.18)	0.6 (0.15)	0.9 (0.35)
$10,000 to 24,999	29.4	19.3	19.0	2.8 (0.15)	2.5 (0.28)	3.0 (0.44)	3.8 (0.55)	1.7 (0.74)	3.1 (0.36)	2.9 (0.45)	2.6 (0.58)	2.9 (0.42)	2.4 (0.59)
$25,000 to 39,999	181.8	123.7	79.7	11.7 (0.42)	8.0 (0.49)	5.6 (0.66)	13.0 (0.65)	6.6 (1.03)	12.2 (1.12)	12.8 (1.85)	15.2 (1.38)	18.0 (1.44)	12.0 (1.28)
$40,000 to 54,999	163.8	171.1	192.4	28.2 (0.45)	19.2 (0.78)	15.5 (1.13)	27.4 (1.10)	21.3 (2.12)	34.0 (1.40)	38.8 (1.63)	39.6 (1.64)	37.1 (1.48)	25.7 (1.55)
$55,000 to 69,999	76.7	106.2	147.7	21.7 (0.52)	18.9 (0.58)	15.4 (0.99)	22.3 (1.05)	26.4 (2.02)	24.1 (1.26)	24.9 (1.78)	23.1 (1.34)	24.3 (1.58)	20.9 (1.43)
$70,000 to 84,999	32.1	57.9	94.8	13.9 (0.32)	15.3 (0.64)	16.0 (1.01)	14.7 (1.03)	15.6 (1.52)	14.7 (1.21)	10.5 (1.18)	11.2 (1.46)	12.9 (1.10)	12.0 (1.38)
$85,000 to 99,999	11.1	28.1	50.7	7.4 (0.29)	11.1 (0.54)	9.8 (0.80)	7.8 (0.79)	10.1 (1.32)	8.1 (0.78)	4.0 (1.15)	3.7 (0.56)	3.6 (0.59)	5.7 (0.58)
$100,000 or more	19.6	44.4	93.1	13.7 (0.34)	24.1 (0.76)	34.0 (1.20)	10.2 (0.82)	18.2 (1.63)	3.3 (0.46)	5.8 (0.90)	4.0 (0.57)	0.8 (0.21)	20.4 (2.00)

See notes at end of table.

Table 252. Full-time and part-time faculty and instructional staff in degree-granting institutions, by type and control of institution and selected characteristics: Fall 1992, fall 1998, and fall 2003—Continued

Selected characteristic	Number (in thousands)			Fall 2003									
					Research		Doctoral		Comprehensive		Private liberal arts	Public 2-year	Other
	1992	1998	2003	Total	Public	Private	Public	Private	Public	Private			
1	2	3	4	5	6	7	8	9	10	11	12	13	14
Part-time faculty and instructional staff													
Number (in thousands)	376.7	416.0	530.0	530.0 (0.02)	39.7 (0.78)	23.2 (0.96)	20.8 (0.82)	15.4 (0.83)	60.3 (2.49)	53.5 (2.17)	28.4 (2.19)	230.1 (2.00)	58.7 (3.38)
Percentage distribution	†	†	†	100.0 (†)	7.5 (0.15)	4.4 (0.18)	3.9 (0.15)	2.9 (0.16)	11.4 (0.47)	10.1 (0.41)	5.4 (0.41)	43.4 (0.38)	11.1 (0.64)
Percentage distribution of part-time faculty and instructional staff													
Total	†	†	†	100.0 (†)	100.0 (†)	100.0 (†)	100.0 (†)	100.0 (†)	100.0 (†)	100.0 (†)	100.0 (†)	100.0 (†)	100.0 (†)
Sex													
Male	208.7	217.0	275.9	52.1 (0.45)	50.4 (1.97)	60.2 (1.92)	50.2 (2.26)	58.4 (3.34)	50.0 (1.59)	53.9 (1.53)	50.3 (1.95)	50.7 (0.57)	55.4 (1.66)
Female	168.0	199.1	254.1	47.9 (0.45)	49.6 (1.97)	39.8 (1.92)	49.8 (2.26)	41.6 (3.34)	50.0 (1.59)	46.1 (1.53)	49.7 (1.95)	49.3 (0.57)	44.6 (1.66)
Race/ethnicity													
White	332.8	364.4	451.6	85.2 (0.38)	82.4 (1.63)	85.8 (1.78)	87.9 (2.19)	88.9 (1.99)	87.2 (1.89)	91.0 (0.85)	86.2 (1.59)	83.7 (0.54)	83.0 (1.84)
Black	18.3	18.9	29.7	5.6 (0.20)	2.7 (0.72)	4.1 (1.14)	2.4 (1.01)	2.8 (0.99)	4.7 (1.20)	2.8 (0.40)	8.1 (1.27)	6.9 (0.25)	7.2 (1.02)
Hispanic	11.2	15.5	18.7	3.5 (0.13)	3.2 (0.56)	2.5 (0.78)	4.1 (0.81)	2.8 (0.66)	3.1 (0.39)	2.4 (0.30)	2.1 (0.48)	4.4 (0.21)	3.0 (0.57)
Asian/Pacific Islander	12.2	13.2	20.3	3.8 (0.22)	9.9 (1.39)	6.4 (1.05)	4.5 (1.14)	4.9 (1.79)	3.3 (0.59)	1.9 (0.61)	2.7 (0.63)	2.9 (0.23)	4.7 (1.02)
American Indian/Alaska Native	2.3	4.0	9.7	1.8 (0.22)	1.8 (0.68)	‡ (†)	1.1 (0.69)	0.6 (0.35)	1.7 (0.61)	1.9 (0.42)	0.9 (0.35)	2.1 (0.38)	2.1 (0.70)
Age													
Under 30	20.5	15.1	22.8	4.3 (0.30)	5.6 (0.94)	3.1 (1.11)	8.9 (1.75)	4.8 (1.58)	5.7 (1.04)	1.8 (0.51)	3.8 (0.72)	4.4 (0.46)	3.1 (0.72)
30 to 34	35.9	37.1	43.4	8.2 (0.38)	10.0 (1.32)	8.8 (1.79)	6.8 (1.20)	6.5 (1.81)	8.1 (1.11)	7.9 (1.16)	8.9 (1.33)	8.2 (0.68)	7.6 (1.11)
35 to 39	58.9	47.2	54.6	10.3 (0.48)	8.7 (1.36)	9.4 (1.48)	8.3 (1.74)	12.5 (2.38)	11.1 (1.55)	9.7 (0.88)	10.8 (1.78)	10.4 (0.74)	10.8 (1.35)
40 to 44	70.0	60.4	61.0	11.5 (0.44)	12.9 (1.78)	11.4 (1.81)	13.2 (2.26)	11.2 (2.26)	11.9 (1.34)	10.1 (1.18)	12.2 (1.37)	11.3 (0.78)	11.3 (1.40)
45 to 49	68.0	72.1	76.5	14.4 (0.48)	15.6 (1.51)	16.0 (1.54)	16.3 (2.42)	7.9 (1.93)	11.3 (1.17)	14.3 (1.27)	14.0 (1.95)	14.6 (0.75)	17.1 (1.84)
50 to 54	45.1	69.8	82.8	15.6 (0.42)	14.5 (1.39)	12.2 (1.49)	16.3 (2.27)	16.5 (2.76)	18.5 (1.50)	18.5 (1.24)	15.0 (1.66)	15.9 (0.72)	15.8 (1.57)
55 to 59	28.8	47.1	77.0	14.5 (0.48)	12.1 (1.53)	14.4 (2.14)	13.5 (1.99)	14.2 (2.99)	14.8 (1.35)	14.2 (1.32)	13.7 (1.69)	15.3 (0.71)	14.1 (1.59)
60 to 64	22.9	28.8	51.6	9.7 (0.50)	8.4 (1.38)	9.6 (1.78)	8.0 (1.86)	12.5 (2.58)	11.2 (1.30)	10.5 (1.38)	9.5 (1.41)	9.7 (0.85)	8.5 (1.25)
65 or older	26.6	38.4	60.3	11.4 (0.46)	12.3 (1.49)	15.1 (1.95)	8.7 (1.61)	13.8 (2.90)	12.2 (1.19)	13.1 (1.85)	12.1 (1.93)	10.1 (0.77)	11.7 (2.06)
Highest degree													
Less than bachelor's	17.2	20.3	41.1	7.8 (0.59)	2.2 (0.59)	2.5 (1.27)	0.5 (0.28)	2.1 (0.76)	2.1 (0.61)	0.7 (0.28)	0.9 (0.38)	14.3 (1.21)	7.6 (1.51)
Bachelor's	62.7	58.8	83.8	15.8 (0.55)	9.9 (1.32)	10.9 (1.94)	13.9 (2.09)	7.6 (2.48)	13.1 (1.84)	7.5 (1.08)	8.6 (1.52)	21.5 (1.17)	15.9 (1.67)
Master's	190.2	225.1	273.1	51.5 (0.80)	35.6 (2.39)	36.6 (3.36)	53.8 (3.16)	41.7 (3.47)	57.8 (2.32)	64.4 (2.33)	61.0 (2.21)	52.1 (1.63)	44.7 (3.32)
First-professional	39.6	36.0	38.5	7.3 (0.39)	16.7 (1.98)	21.3 (2.68)	7.7 (1.52)	13.6 (2.41)	4.2 (0.79)	4.8 (0.90)	7.2 (1.50)	3.3 (0.49)	14.4 (1.83)
Doctor's	58.9	75.8	93.5	17.6 (0.60)	35.6 (2.56)	28.7 (3.88)	24.1 (3.30)	35.0 (2.65)	22.7 (1.83)	22.6 (1.88)	22.2 (2.09)	8.7 (0.66)	17.4 (2.28)
Academic rank													
Professor	32.3	30.2	23.3	4.4 (0.30)	8.1 (1.54)	5.6 (1.18)	4.6 (1.43)	5.7 (1.40)	5.7 (1.01)	2.4 (0.55)	4.4 (0.85)	3.2 (0.52)	6.0 (1.03)
Associate professor	22.5	19.4	14.6	2.8 (0.22)	4.3 (0.94)	6.0 (1.45)	2.6 (1.14)	2.9 (1.03)	2.1 (0.69)	3.1 (0.79)	4.7 (1.11)	1.5 (0.27)	4.8 (1.07)
Assistant professor	24.2	23.1	19.8	3.7 (0.29)	11.0 (1.49)	11.9 (3.02)	3.3 (0.80)	7.0 (1.73)	2.0 (0.49)	3.0 (0.86)	5.1 (1.81)	0.8 (0.20)	8.3 (1.24)
Instructor	215.4	205.4	187.7	35.4 (0.83)	20.8 (1.72)	20.5 (1.67)	28.7 (2.27)	20.1 (3.25)	25.4 (2.41)	21.9 (1.64)	24.5 (2.13)	48.5 (1.54)	35.2 (2.66)
Lecturer	45.3	46.3	40.9	7.7 (0.41)	21.5 (1.67)	18.6 (2.30)	13.2 (2.07)	9.6 (1.72)	15.8 (2.18)	8.6 (2.32)	6.7 (1.72)	2.7 (0.42)	2.7 (0.80)
Other	27.6	75.2	230.9	43.6 (0.85)	33.3 (2.17)	38.2 (2.49)	45.4 (2.50)	53.4 (3.25)	47.7 (3.01)	59.7 (3.84)	52.2 (3.03)	40.5 (1.38)	38.3 (3.23)
No rank	9.3	16.5	12.8	2.4 (0.20)	1.0 (0.30)	1.6 (1.20)	2.3 (0.80)	1.4 (0.81)	1.2 (0.39)	1.2 (0.32)	2.3 (0.70)	2.8 (0.39)	4.6 (1.10)
Base salary													
Under $10,000	280.5	256.2	340.5	64.2 (0.60)	43.7 (2.35)	54.7 (2.80)	65.1 (2.94)	59.3 (3.10)	66.0 (2.44)	71.8 (2.97)	67.5 (2.75)	66.6 (1.02)	63.5 (1.97)
$10,000 to $24,999	68.1	112.4	140.8	26.6 (0.60)	29.3 (2.32)	27.5 (2.55)	24.7 (2.63)	30.3 (3.38)	26.3 (2.05)	21.4 (2.40)	23.4 (2.00)	28.1 (0.97)	24.6 (1.74)
$25,000 to $39,999	15.8	26.3	27.5	5.2 (0.32)	12.2 (1.38)	7.7 (1.76)	5.7 (1.48)	4.8 (1.72)	4.9 (1.09)	4.4 (1.15)	5.3 (1.24)	4.1 (0.46)	4.7 (0.92)
$40,000 to $54,999	5.3	11.8	9.6	1.8 (0.14)	5.8 (1.05)	5.0 (1.18)	1.9 (0.70)	3.0 (1.00)	1.6 (0.44)	0.9 (0.31)	1.1 (0.55)	0.5 (0.15)	4.0 (0.83)
$55,000 to $69,999	2.2	4.2	4.7	0.9 (0.15)	3.0 (0.65)	2.0 (1.00)	1.4 (0.71)	1.0 (0.65)	0.9 (0.59)	0.8 (0.31)	1.6 (0.65)	0.4 (0.14)	0.3 (0.25)
$70,000 to $84,999	1.1	2.4	1.9	0.4 (0.07)	2.2 (0.57)	0.9 (0.55)	‡ (†)	‡ (†)	‡ (†)	‡ (†)	‡ (†)	‡ (†)	0.9 (0.30)
$85,000 to $99,999	0.9	#	1.5	0.3 (0.07)	1.0 (0.46)	1.0 (0.51)	‡ (†)	‡ (†)	‡ (†)	‡ (†)	‡ (†)	0.2 (0.10)	0.2 (0.12)
$100,000 or more	2.7	#	3.5	0.7 (0.10)	2.9 (0.63)	1.3 (0.72)	‡ (†)	1.2 (0.75)	‡ (†)	0.4 (0.27)	‡ (†)	0.1 (0.07)	1.8 (0.56)

†Not applicable.
#Rounds to zero.
‡Reporting standards not met.

NOTE: Totals may differ from figures reported in other tables because of varying survey methodologies. Race categories exclude persons of Hispanic ethnicity. Detail may not sum to totals because of rounding. Standard errors appear in parentheses.
SOURCE: U.S. Department of Education, National Center for Education Statistics, 1993, 1999, and 2004 National Study of Postsecondary Faculty (NSOPF:93;99;04). (This table was prepared January 2009.)

Table 253. Full-time and part-time faculty and instructional staff in degree-granting institutions, by race/ethnicity, sex, and selected characteristics: Fall 2003

Selected characteristic	Number (in thousands)	Percent	White		Black		Hispanic		Asian/Pacific Islander		American Indian/Alaska Native	
			Male	Female	Male	Female	Male	Female	Male	Female	Male	Female
1	2	3	4	5	6	7	8	9	10	11	12	13
Full-time faculty and instructional staff												
Number (in thousands)	681.8 (0.05)	†	338.4 (2.63)	209.3 (2.45)	19.5 (1.03)	18.5 (0.87)	13.4 (0.60)	10.4 (0.56)	43.2 (1.00)	19.0 (1.03)	5.8 (0.57)	4.2 (0.50)
Percentage distribution..........	†	100.0	49.6 (0.39)	30.7 (0.36)	2.9 (0.15)	2.7 (0.13)	2.0 (0.09)	1.5 (0.08)	6.3 (0.15)	2.8 (0.15)	0.8 (0.08)	0.6 (0.07)
Type and control												
Public research..........	162.1 (0.85)	100.0	55.4 (0.67)	23.6 (0.59)	2.1 (0.27)	1.7 (0.19)	1.8 (C.16)	1.1 (0.15)	10.0 (0.47)	3.2 (0.35)	0.6 (0.14)	0.6 (0.11)
Private research..........	63.5 (1.58)	100.0	54.7 (1.00)	22.9 (0.80)	2.2 (0.30)	2.7 (0.37)	2.1 (C.30)	1.4 (0.31)	8.9 (0.66)	3.9 (0.48)	0.8 (0.39)	0.4 (0.23)
Public doctoral..........	51.3 (0.76)	100.0	50.2 (1.48)	31.1 (1.22)	2.1 (0.44)	2.0 (0.30)	1.6 (0.20)	1.3 (0.27)	7.9 (1.27)	2.2 (0.56)	1.0 (0.32)	0.6 (0.22)
Private doctoral..........	21.7 (0.79)	100.0	56.0 (2.39)	26.7 (1.94)	3.0 (0.70)	2.1 (0.42)	1.4 (0.49)	0.8 (0.38)	5.8 (1.06)	3.5 (0.93)	0.6 (0.34)	‡ (†)
Public comprehensive..........	107.3 (2.98)	100.0	45.9 (1.03)	32.1 (0.98)	4.7 (0.64)	4.0 (0.42)	2.1 (1.20)	1.6 (0.19)	5.3 (0.40)	2.6 (0.28)	0.8 (0.23)	1.0 (0.33)
Private comprehensive..........	41.4 (1.59)	100.0	48.9 (2.00)	36.7 (1.93)	2.3 (0.53)	2.4 (0.44)	1.6 (0.31)	0.8 (0.22)	4.1 (0.65)	1.9 (0.53)	0.6 (0.26)	0.6 (0.30)
Private liberal arts..........	49.6 (1.80)	100.0	51.9 (1.20)	34.1 (0.99)	3.5 (0.56)	2.8 (0.36)	1.0 (0.20)	1.3 (0.27)	2.2 (0.28)	1.5 (0.29)	1.0 (0.24)	0.6 (0.18)
Public 2-year..........	114.6 (1.09)	100.0	40.8 (1.19)	40.1 (0.90)	3.1 (0.29)	3.8 (0.34)	3.0 (0.38)	2.7 (0.34)	2.2 (0.27)	2.1 (0.39)	1.3 (0.30)	0.8 (0.19)
Other..........	70.2 (3.36)	100.0	48.3 (1.65)	31.5 (1.20)	2.4 (0.59)	2.3 (0.59)	1.7 (0.36)	1.5 (0.29)	7.2 (0.87)	4.1 (0.78)	0.7 (0.34)	0.3 (0.14)
Academic rank												
Professor..........	194.4 (3.67)	100.0	65.5 (0.74)	20.3 (0.61)	2.6 (0.27)	1.1 (0.21)	1.8 (0.13)	0.8 (0.13)	5.7 (0.42)	1.1 (0.21)	0.8 (0.14)	0.4 (0.12)
Associate professor..........	149.6 (2.56)	100.0	51.6 (0.98)	28.4 (0.78)	3.1 (0.42)	2.4 (0.26)	1.7 (0.19)	1.3 (0.15)	7.0 (0.52)	2.9 (0.36)	1.0 (0.21)	0.5 (0.11)
Assistant professor..........	158.1 (2.81)	100.0	41.0 (0.83)	33.6 (0.81)	3.1 (0.37)	3.3 (0.38)	2.3 (0.22)	1.9 (0.15)	8.7 (0.49)	4.3 (0.35)	0.7 (0.16)	0.6 (0.15)
Instructor..........	82.7 (2.85)	100.0	38.2 (1.23)	41.2 (1.09)	3.2 (0.56)	4.4 (0.57)	2.5 (0.37)	2.3 (0.31)	3.1 (0.44)	3.1 (0.48)	0.9 (0.26)	1.1 (0.31)
Lecturer..........	21.9 (1.48)	100.0	36.7 (2.59)	43.9 (2.21)	2.9 (0.91)	3.0 (0.91)	1.3 (0.38)	3.8 (0.77)	2.4 (0.89)	4.0 (0.99)	1.3 (0.52)	0.7 (0.30)
Other..........	56.5 (2.15)	100.0	38.8 (1.51)	39.8 (1.37)	2.5 (0.54)	3.3 (0.56)	1.7 (0.22)	2.2 (0.35)	7.0 (0.98)	2.8 (0.56)	0.6 (0.39)	0.6 (0.18)
No rank..........	18.6 (1.28)	100.0	40.2 (2.37)	43.0 (2.45)	1.5 (0.52)	2.0 (0.83)	2.3 (0.75)	0.7 (0.24)	4.5 (1.17)	3.8 (1.39)	1.1 (0.74)	0.8 (0.46)
Age												
Under 35..........	59.1 (1.77)	100.0	39.4 (1.31)	33.4 (1.36)	2.9 (0.53)	4.7 (0.62)	2.5 (0.40)	2.8 (0.41)	8.9 (0.85)	4.2 (0.70)	0.6 (0.25)	0.5 (0.17)
35 to 44..........	169.8 (2.78)	100.0	43.7 (0.96)	30.2 (0.82)	2.7 (0.31)	3.4 (0.36)	2.8 (0.25)	1.8 (0.18)	9.3 (0.45)	5.0 (0.44)	0.8 (0.17)	0.5 (0.16)
45 to 54..........	219.7 (3.28)	100.0	47.0 (0.86)	34.4 (0.79)	3.1 (0.28)	2.6 (0.22)	1.8 (0.17)	1.6 (0.18)	5.7 (0.32)	2.2 (0.25)	1.0 (0.16)	0.6 (0.12)
55 to 64..........	190.0 (3.10)	100.0	57.1 (0.74)	28.7 (0.59)	2.8 (0.26)	1.9 (0.17)	1.4 (0.12)	1.1 (0.13)	4.1 (0.36)	1.4 (0.24)	0.9 (0.17)	0.7 (0.12)
65 to 69..........	31.8 (1.43)	100.0	67.6 (2.05)	20.2 (1.82)	1.7 (0.50)	2.0 (0.61)	1.6 (0.44)	0.4 (0.19)	4.5 (0.94)	1.1 (0.42)	0.3 (0.20)	‡ (†)
70 or older..........	11.5 (0.67)	100.0	69.0 (3.16)	15.7 (2.71)	5.4 (1.54)	1.6 (0.93)	0.7 (0.43)	‡ (†)	3.8 (1.40)	‡ (†)	1.3 (0.81)	‡ (†)
Base salary												
Under $10,000..........	4.4 (0.49)	100.0	39.7 (5.71)	34.2 (5.09)	5.8 (0.92)	4.5 (2.39)	0.6 (0.48)	4.4 (1.96)	7.8 (3.27)	2.9 (1.67)	‡ (†)	‡ (†)
$10,000 to 24,999..........	19.0 (1.03)	100.0	43.2 (2.61)	34.8 (2.40)	1.3 (0.37)	3.2 (0.89)	2.1 (0.61)	2.4 (0.60)	6.5 (1.23)	4.6 (0.93)	0.8 (0.51)	1.1 (0.48)
$25,000 to 39,999..........	79.7 (2.90)	100.0	36.0 (1.21)	44.5 (1.25)	2.9 (0.55)	3.7 (0.46)	1.8 (0.29)	2.1 (0.62)	3.8 (0.68)	3.6 (0.48)	0.7 (0.26)	0.8 (0.23)
$40,000 to 54,999..........	192.4 (3.09)	100.0	42.2 (0.95)	38.2 (0.79)	2.7 (0.27)	3.7 (0.37)	1.9 (0.18)	1.8 (0.14)	5.0 (0.43)	2.6 (0.27)	1.0 (0.15)	0.9 (0.14)
$55,000 to 69,999..........	147.7 (3.54)	100.0	48.7 (0.88)	31.9 (0.80)	3.1 (0.35)	2.5 (0.28)	2.0 (0.25)	1.6 (0.21)	6.0 (0.43)	2.6 (0.31)	1.0 (0.23)	0.6 (0.15)
$70,000 to 84,999..........	94.8 (2.19)	100.0	55.8 (1.29)	24.2 (1.14)	2.9 (0.39)	1.7 (0.40)	2.4 (0.34)	1.0 (0.20)	8.1 (0.67)	2.6 (0.41)	0.5 (0.23)	0.5 (0.19)
$85,000 to 99,999..........	50.7 (1.98)	100.0	61.9 (1.58)	18.5 (1.03)	3.8 (0.69)	1.5 (0.38)	1.5 (0.41)	1.0 (0.28)	8.3 (1.06)	2.5 (0.57)	0.2 (0.24)	0.2 (0.12)
$100,000 or more..........	93.1 (2.29)	100.0	66.9 (0.99)	13.7 (0.74)	2.4 (0.38)	1.6 (0.33)	2.1 (0.29)	0.8 (0.17)	9.0 (0.80)	2.8 (0.50)	0.6 (0.20)	0.1 (0.09)
Total household income												
Under $10,000..........	‡ (†)	100.0	‡ (†)	‡ (†)	‡ (†)	‡ (†)	‡ (†)	‡ (†)	‡ (†)	‡ (†)	‡ (†)	‡ (†)
$10,000 to 24,999..........	3.0 (0.33)	100.0	42.0 (6.54)	29.3 (6.12)	1.4 (1.13)	2.5 (1.38)	‡ (†)	2.7 (1.60)	9.8 (3.74)	8.7 (3.59)	‡ (†)	‡ (†)
$25,000 to 39,999..........	20.1 (1.13)	100.0	36.5 (2.68)	39.0 (2.28)	3.3 (1.56)	4.5 (0.97)	1.5 (0.43)	2.5 (0.62)	7.3 (1.56)	3.8 (0.95)	0.6 (0.39)	0.9 (0.29)
$40,000 to 54,999..........	55.0 (1.76)	100.0	39.8 (1.66)	38.4 (1.42)	2.9 (0.59)	4.2 (1.42)	2.5 (0.35)	1.9 (0.29)	6.2 (0.80)	2.5 (0.51)	0.4 (0.18)	1.2 (0.31)
$55,000 to 69,999..........	86.2 (1.56)	100.0	43.1 (1.23)	34.2 (1.21)	4.1 (0.50)	4.4 (0.42)	2.1 (0.29)	1.9 (0.17)	5.6 (0.56)	2.5 (0.37)	1.1 (0.26)	1.0 (0.29)
$70,000 to 84,999..........	75.2 (2.19)	100.0	50.6 (1.20)	31.2 (1.11)	2.4 (0.40)	2.8 (0.45)	1.9 (0.26)	1.3 (0.17)	6.3 (0.59)	2.1 (0.40)	0.9 (0.30)	0.5 (0.17)
$85,000 to 99,999..........	95.0 (2.16)	100.0	46.7 (1.15)	32.5 (0.83)	2.8 (0.39)	3.0 (0.58)	2.7 (0.32)	1.6 (0.24)	7.0 (0.81)	2.5 (0.50)	0.6 (0.18)	0.5 (0.14)
$100,000 or more..........	347.3 (3.57)	100.0	50.9 (0.52)	27.5 (0.52)	2.6 (0.18)	1.9 (0.16)	1.7 (0.4)	1.3 (0.11)	6.3 (0.29)	3.0 (0.24)	0.9 (0.11)	0.4 (0.07)

See notes at end of table.

Table 253. Full-time and part-time faculty and instructional staff in degree-granting institutions, by race/ethnicity, sex, and selected characteristics: Fall 2003—Continued

Selected characteristic	Number (in thousands)	Percent	White Male	White Female	Black Male	Black Female	Hispanic Male	Hispanic Female	Asian/Pacific Islander Male	Asian/Pacific Islander Female	American Indian/Alaska Native Male	American Indian/Alaska Native Female
1	2	3	4	5	6	7	8	9	10	11	12	13
Part-time faculty and instructional staff												
Number (in thousands)	530.0 (0.02)	†	235.5 (2.44)	216.1 (2.87)	13.8 (0.91)	15.9 (0.75)	10.2 (0.61)	8.5 (0.56)	10.9 (0.82)	9.4 (0.97)	5.5 (0.78)	4.2 (0.77)
Percentage distribution	‡ (†)	100.0	44.4 (0.46)	40.8 (0.54)	2.6 (0.17)	3.0 (0.14)	1.9 (0.12)	1.6 (0.10)	2.1 (0.15)	1.8 (0.18)	1.0 (0.15)	0.8 (0.15)
Type and control												
Public research	39.7 (0.78)	100.0	41.7 (1.93)	40.7 (2.12)	1.1 (0.37)	1.6 (0.60)	1.5 (0.40)	1.7 (0.43)	4.5 (1.03)	5.4 (0.90)	1.6 (0.67)	‡ (†)
Private research	23.2 (0.96)	100.0	51.1 (2.51)	34.7 (2.29)	2.7 (1.00)	1.4 (0.57)	1.5 (0.62)	0.9 (0.51)	3.6 (1.07)	2.8 (0.77)	‡ (†)	‡ (†)
Public doctoral	20.8 (0.82)	100.0	44.3 (2.27)	43.6 (2.39)	1.4 (0.85)	1.0 (0.47)	1.9 (0.68)	2.2 (0.61)	2.6 (0.86)	1.9 (0.83)	‡ (†)	1.1 (0.68)
Private doctoral	15.4 (0.83)	100.0	51.7 (3.99)	37.3 (3.60)	1.7 (0.77)	1.1 (0.55)	1.6 (0.64)	1.2 (0.36)	3.4 (1.06)	1.4 (0.90)	‡ (†)	0.6 (0.35)
Public comprehensive	60.3 (2.49)	100.0	43.1 (1.34)	44.1 (2.18)	2.3 (0.74)	2.4 (0.79)	1.6 (0.31)	1.5 (0.32)	2.0 (0.38)	1.3 (0.43)	1.0 (0.43)	0.7 (0.34)
Private comprehensive	53.5 (2.17)	100.0	49.1 (1.43)	41.9 (1.56)	1.7 (0.34)	1.1 (0.21)	1.0 (0.19)	1.4 (0.26)	1.1 (0.54)	0.8 (0.35)	1.0 (0.30)	0.9 (0.32)
Private liberal arts	28.4 (2.19)	100.0	44.2 (1.98)	42.0 (2.14)	2.5 (0.85)	5.6 (1.24)	1.1 (0.42)	1.0 (0.35)	1.7 (0.61)	1.1 (0.49)	0.9 (0.35)	‡ (†)
Public 2-year	230.1 (2.00)	100.0	42.8 (0.70)	41.0 (0.67)	2.9 (0.22)	4.0 (0.18)	2.4 (0.20)	2.0 (0.19)	1.5 (0.18)	1.4 (0.19)	1.1 (0.23)	1.0 (0.25)
Other	58.7 (3.38)	100.0	45.7 (1.83)	37.3 (2.14)	4.2 (0.79)	3.0 (0.74)	2.2 (0.53)	0.8 (0.22)	2.4 (0.75)	2.4 (0.92)	1.0 (0.40)	1.1 (0.50)
Academic rank												
Professor	23.3 (1.58)	100.0	59.3 (2.83)	25.0 (2.60)	4.0 (1.17)	2.6 (0.84)	0.6 (0.35)	1.0 (0.41)	3.6 (0.96)	‡ (†)	2.0 (1.08)	1.2 (0.85)
Associate professor	14.6 (1.18)	100.0	43.7 (4.03)	39.5 (3.88)	2.8 (0.84)	2.0 (1.02)	1.8 (0.92)	1.4 (0.49)	6.3 (2.27)	1.6 (0.85)	‡ (†)	‡ (†)
Assistant professor	19.8 (1.53)	100.0	38.8 (3.39)	42.7 (3.37)	2.8 (1.19)	2.5 (1.23)	1.3 (0.68)	1.0 (0.42)	4.8 (1.65)	6.0 (1.62)	‡ (†)	‡ (†)
Instructor	187.7 (4.42)	100.0	41.5 (1.09)	43.9 (1.11)	2.5 (0.30)	3.4 (0.25)	2.2 (0.24)	1.7 (0.22)	1.6 (0.25)	1.6 (0.28)	1.1 (0.26)	0.6 (0.18)
Lecturer	40.9 (2.15)	100.0	41.4 (2.05)	40.1 (1.96)	2.7 (0.63)	2.1 (0.77)	2.1 (0.45)	1.7 (0.42)	3.7 (0.80)	4.2 (0.93)	1.6 (0.56)	0.4 (0.25)
Other	230.9 (4.51)	100.0	46.5 (1.01)	39.9 (1.04)	2.5 (0.29)	3.1 (0.28)	1.8 (0.23)	1.5 (0.17)	1.3 (0.22)	1.3 (0.31)	0.9 (0.22)	1.0 (0.22)
No rank	12.8 (1.07)	100.0	43.8 (3.52)	39.8 (4.63)	2.4 (1.26)	0.9 (0.43)	2.8 (1.31)	3.5 (1.34)	2.0 (0.94)	1.8 (1.15)	‡ (†)	‡ (†)
Age												
Under 35	66.2 (2.30)	100.0	35.3 (1.73)	43.1 (2.04)	3.2 (0.63)	4.3 (0.53)	3.0 (0.49)	3.0 (0.35)	2.4 (0.52)	3.6 (0.93)	1.6 (0.68)	0.4 (0.23)
35 to 44	115.6 (3.03)	100.0	40.7 (1.42)	41.5 (1.41)	2.6 (0.39)	3.0 (0.33)	2.5 (0.30)	2.4 (0.32)	2.6 (0.37)	2.9 (0.45)	0.7 (0.24)	1.2 (0.30)
45 to 54	159.3 (3.22)	100.0	41.7 (1.13)	44.0 (1.17)	2.9 (0.34)	3.2 (0.33)	1.6 (0.24)	1.5 (0.19)	2.1 (0.35)	1.3 (0.26)	0.9 (0.24)	0.8 (0.27)
55 to 64	128.6 (3.31)	100.0	48.2 (1.09)	40.4 (1.06)	2.1 (0.35)	2.8 (0.35)	1.3 (0.30)	0.6 (0.10)	1.6 (0.32)	0.9 (0.23)	1.1 (0.34)	1.0 (0.26)
65 to 69	33.5 (1.81)	100.0	62.8 (3.10)	27.6 (2.83)	2.3 (0.81)	0.9 (0.32)	1.6 (0.54)	1.3 (0.55)	1.3 (0.52)	‡ (†)	1.5 (0.63)	‡ (†)
70 or older	26.8 (1.83)	100.0	58.3 (2.99)	30.7 (3.32)	2.4 (0.79)	1.6 (0.70)	2.5 (0.87)	‡ (†)	2.1 (0.65)	0.8 (0.42)	‡ (†)	‡ (†)
Base salary												
Under $10,000	340.5 (3.17)	100.0	45.4 (0.68)	39.9 (0.77)	2.6 (0.23)	3.5 (0.23)	1.9 (0.17)	1.6 (0.12)	1.6 (0.17)	1.4 (0.26)	1.1 (0.20)	1.0 (0.20)
$10,000 to 24,999	140.8 (3.17)	100.0	41.3 (1.36)	43.6 (1.50)	2.8 (0.38)	2.3 (0.25)	2.1 (0.26)	1.8 (0.24)	2.3 (0.40)	2.4 (0.40)	0.9 (0.25)	0.5 (0.18)
$25,000 to 39,999	27.5 (1.72)	100.0	47.3 (3.06)	38.8 (2.72)	3.3 (0.83)	1.6 (0.98)	1.2 (0.58)	1.6 (0.55)	3.2 (1.02)	1.9 (0.61)	0.8 (0.51)	‡ (†)
$40,000 to 54,999	9.6 (0.74)	100.0	48.2 (4.55)	34.0 (4.33)	0.7 (0.40)	1.4 (0.68)	3.2 (1.19)	‡ (†)	6.2 (2.60)	3.8 (1.70)	‡ (†)	‡ (†)
$55,000 to 69,999	4.7 (0.78)	100.0	45.5 (6.46)	40.4 (6.35)	1.2 (0.72)	3.8 (2.18)	‡ (†)	2.2 (1.08)	‡ (†)	5.1 (2.57)	‡ (†)	‡ (†)
$70,000 to 84,999	1.9 (0.35)	100.0	39.0 (11.51)	43.0 (10.25)	‡ (†)	‡ (†)	‡ (†)	‡ (†)	‡ (†)	5.6 (4.00)	‡ (†)	‡ (†)
$85,000 to 99,999	1.5 (0.39)	100.0	33.4 (13.01)	51.7 (13.73)	‡ (†)	‡ (†)	‡ (†)	‡ (†)	‡ (†)	‡ (†)	‡ (†)	‡ (†)
$100,000 or more	3.5 (0.53)	100.0	47.4 (7.01)	37.1 (5.35)	‡ (†)	‡ (†)	‡ (†)	‡ (†)	10.8 (5.15)	‡ (†)	‡ (†)	‡ (†)
Total household income												
Under $10,000	1.3 (0.37)	100.0	25.7 (13.36)	46.4 (14.12)	‡ (†)	‡ (†)	6.5 (5.17)	‡ (†)	‡ (†)	‡ (†)	‡ (†)	‡ (†)
$10,000 to 24,999	28.5 (1.93)	100.0	36.5 (3.33)	42.5 (3.42)	2.0 (0.71)	4.0 (0.80)	1.7 (0.53)	2.4 (0.55)	1.6 (0.76)	3.5 (1.71)	3.7 (1.34)	2.2 (1.01)
$25,000 to 39,999	47.7 (1.92)	100.0	35.5 (2.27)	46.5 (2.32)	3.4 (0.71)	3.9 (0.66)	2.2 (0.44)	1.8 (0.47)	1.7 (0.55)	2.9 (0.92)	1.1 (0.46)	1.0 (0.43)
$40,000 to 54,999	55.7 (2.52)	100.0	38.1 (2.05)	46.2 (2.35)	3.2 (0.71)	3.4 (0.52)	3.1 (0.67)	2.5 (0.60)	1.1 (0.40)	1.1 (0.35)	0.8 (0.54)	0.5 (0.21)
$55,000 to 69,999	87.2 (2.95)	100.0	41.1 (1.50)	43.0 (1.48)	1.9 (0.38)	4.1 (0.38)	1.7 (0.37)	2.5 (0.35)	2.1 (0.42)	1.6 (0.45)	0.8 (0.27)	1.0 (0.37)
$70,000 to 84,999	58.1 (2.66)	100.0	44.7 (2.15)	41.2 (2.38)	2.3 (0.44)	2.3 (0.57)	2.3 (0.41)	1.3 (0.34)	1.4 (0.41)	2.0 (0.58)	1.1 (0.41)	1.1 (0.37)
$85,000 to 99,999	66.4 (2.39)	100.0	48.6 (1.85)	38.4 (1.81)	2.4 (0.59)	3.1 (0.52)	1.8 (0.37)	1.2 (0.34)	1.9 (0.49)	1.3 (0.41)	0.6 (0.29)	0.7 (0.25)
$100,000 or more	185.1 (3.59)	100.0	34.9 (0.68)	37.0 (0.91)	2.8 (0.32)	2.1 (0.26)	1.5 (0.21)	1.0 (0.17)	2.8 (0.34)	1.6 (0.25)	0.8 (0.22)	0.4 (0.17)

†Not applicable.
‡Reporting standards not met.
NOTE: Totals may differ from figures reported in other tables because of varying survey methodologies. Race categories exclude persons of Hispanic ethnicity. Detail may not sum to totals because of rounding. Standard errors appear in parentheses.

SOURCE: U.S. Department of Education, National Center for Education Statistics, 2003 National Study of Postsecondary Faculty (NSOPF:04). (This table was prepared January 2009.)

Table 254. Full-time and part-time faculty and instructional staff in degree-granting institutions, by field and faculty characteristics: Fall 1992, fall 1998, and fall 2003

Selected characteristic	Number (in thousands)			Fall 2003										
	1992	1998	2003	All fields	Agriculture and home economics	Business	Education	Engineering	Fine arts	Health	Humanities[1]	Natural sciences[2]	Social sciences[3]	Other[4]
1	2	3	4	5	6	7	8	9	10	11	12	13	14	15
Full-time faculty and instructional staff														
Number (in thousands)	528	560	682	681.8 (0.05)	16.9 (0.80)	43.2 (1.40)	50.9 (1.89)	33.4 (1.32)	43.3 (1.68)	93.9 (2.67)	58.8 (1.82)	127.2 (2.19)	88.7 (2.07)	125.5 (2.36)
Percentage distribution	†	†	†	100.0 (†)	2.5 (0.12)	6.3 (0.21)	7.5 (0.28)	4.9 (0.19)	6.3 (0.25)	13.8 (0.39)	8.6 (0.27)	18.7 (0.32)	13.0 (0.30)	18.4 (0.35)
Total	528	560	682	100.0	100.0	100.0	100.0	100.0	100.0	100.0	100.0	100.0	100.0	100.0
Percentage distribution of full-time faculty and instructional staff														
Sex														
Male	353	357	420	61.7 (0.35)	64.6 (2.88)	68.5 (1.61)	39.3 (1.57)	91.5 (1.06)	61.9 (1.38)	46.7 (1.32)	45.3 (1.47)	74.5 (0.88)	64.3 (1.13)	64.0 (0.94)
Female	176	203	261	38.3 (0.35)	35.4 (2.88)	31.5 (1.61)	60.7 (1.57)	8.5 (1.06)	38.1 (1.38)	53.3 (1.32)	54.7 (1.47)	25.5 (0.88)	35.7 (1.13)	36.0 (0.94)
Race/ethnicity														
White	457	477	548	80.3 (0.27)	87.8 (1.61)	79.5 (1.51)	80.5 (1.26)	70.9 (1.85)	86.4 (1.24)	79.7 (0.84)	80.7 (1.31)	77.8 (0.75)	81.4 (1.09)	82.0 (0.69)
Black	27	28	38	5.6 (0.17)	2.3 (0.76)	4.5 (0.79)	7.8 (1.01)	5.4 (0.99)	6.0 (0.88)	5.0 (0.50)	5.6 (0.58)	4.1 (0.48)	7.3 (0.72)	6.1 (0.44)
Hispanic	14	19	24	3.5 (0.10)	2.5 (0.76)	2.3 (0.51)	4.7 (0.63)	2.6 (0.47)	3.3 (0.75)	3.0 (0.32)	6.7 (0.53)	2.9 (0.30)	4.0 (0.47)	2.9 (0.33)
Asian/Pacific Islander	28	33	62	9.1 (0.16)	6.4 (1.34)	12.2 (1.22)	4.8 (0.70)	20.1 (1.64)	2.9 (0.74)	10.7 (0.79)	5.2 (0.94)	14.3 (0.69)	5.9 (0.71)	7.1 (0.49)
American Indian/Alaska Native	3	4	10	1.5 (0.11)	1.0 (0.49)	1.6 (0.37)	2.2 (0.40)	1.0 (0.57)	1.4 (0.38)	1.6 (0.33)	1.8 (0.35)	0.8 (0.17)	1.4 (0.22)	1.8 (0.32)
Age														
Under 30	8	9	12	1.7 (0.13)	2.0 (0.67)	0.7 (0.31)	2.6 (0.79)	1.6 (0.48)	1.6 (0.45)	1.1 (0.26)	1.8 (0.33)	1.3 (0.21)	1.8 (0.35)	2.7 (0.41)
30 to 34	35	32	47	6.9 (0.21)	5.6 (1.27)	4.0 (0.71)	6.8 (0.83)	7.0 (0.99)	6.2 (0.84)	6.3 (0.60)	8.2 (0.74)	6.8 (0.41)	7.6 (0.47)	7.9 (0.52)
35 to 39	67	60	77	11.3 (0.29)	7.5 (1.19)	11.0 (1.15)	7.6 (0.95)	11.3 (1.18)	10.5 (1.20)	13.1 (0.88)	10.9 (0.88)	12.0 (0.65)	12.7 (0.92)	10.9 (0.74)
40 to 44	90	82	93	13.6 (0.31)	13.3 (1.63)	11.8 (1.43)	9.9 (1.03)	15.0 (1.21)	12.3 (1.75)	15.0 (0.91)	13.6 (1.15)	15.4 (0.79)	13.7 (0.79)	12.8 (0.69)
45 to 49	98	97	105	15.4 (0.32)	15.4 (1.84)	17.9 (1.51)	12.7 (1.04)	17.1 (1.70)	18.0 (1.42)	17.3 (0.95)	14.8 (1.24)	15.5 (0.86)	12.9 (0.79)	15.0 (0.66)
50 to 54	95	105	114	16.8 (0.34)	25.3 (2.31)	19.0 (1.30)	17.6 (1.27)	15.2 (1.61)	18.5 (1.38)	19.9 (1.03)	14.1 (1.04)	14.8 (0.64)	14.2 (0.89)	17.1 (0.93)
55 to 59	67	90	112	16.4 (0.37)	16.8 (1.83)	18.8 (1.32)	21.9 (1.43)	15.1 (2.32)	16.8 (1.58)	15.4 (0.80)	16.6 (1.07)	13.3 (0.75)	16.2 (0.85)	17.3 (0.73)
60 to 64	45	55	78	11.5 (0.31)	10.4 (1.61)	10.9 (1.11)	13.7 (1.27)	10.3 (1.33)	11.4 (1.12)	7.8 (0.62)	12.9 (1.07)	12.5 (0.64)	14.0 (0.76)	10.6 (0.61)
65 or older	24	31	43	6.3 (0.23)	3.7 (1.20)	5.9 (0.74)	7.2 (0.74)	7.5 (1.09)	4.7 (0.32)	4.1 (0.51)	7.0 (0.81)	8.5 (0.54)	6.8 (0.59)	5.6 (0.53)
Highest degree														
Less than bachelor's	6	7	10	1.5 (0.12)	1.0 (0.68)	0.2 (0.12)	1.7 (0.74)	2.6 (0.77)	1.4 (0.46)	1.7 (0.31)	0.2 (0.12)	0.1 (0.09)	‡ (†)	4.4 (0.54)
Bachelor's	21	23	29	4.3 (0.24)	6.4 (1.71)	4.0 (0.80)	4.0 (0.64)	6.5 (1.22)	9.1 (1.10)	5.5 (0.69)	1.1 (0.31)	1.4 (0.23)	1.0 (0.26)	7.9 (0.67)
Master's	156	156	180	26.4 (0.39)	29.2 (2.18)	31.8 (1.69)	35.5 (1.37)	13.2 (1.64)	53.9 (1.82)	22.9 (1.16)	35.1 (1.42)	14.9 (0.72)	12.5 (0.72)	34.4 (1.24)
First-professional	58	52	56	8.2 (0.30)	† (†)	2.1 (0.45)	1.1 (0.35)	0.5 (0.30)	1.1 (0.41)	41.1 (1.32)	0.4 (0.18)	3.0 (0.35)	0.5 (0.19)	8.7 (0.76)
Doctor's	284	324	407	59.6 (0.48)	63.0 (2.74)	61.9 (1.73)	57.7 (1.53)	77.1 (2.08)	34.6 (1.96)	28.9 (1.06)	63.2 (1.43)	80.6 (0.67)	86.0 (0.74)	44.6 (1.23)
Academic rank														
Professor	161	172	194	28.5 (0.54)	33.0 (2.71)	29.1 (1.66)	21.9 (1.41)	37.6 (1.69)	28.4 (1.85)	20.1 (0.93)	26.2 (1.46)	35.5 (0.87)	35.4 (1.20)	23.5 (1.09)
Associate professor	124	132	150	21.9 (0.37)	21.0 (2.55)	22.6 (1.32)	17.6 (1.07)	25.3 (1.77)	23.7 (1.64)	23.5 (0.96)	20.0 (1.27)	23.4 (0.93)	22.8 (0.97)	19.9 (1.08)
Assistant professor	124	125	158	23.2 (0.41)	19.2 (1.79)	23.4 (1.51)	23.8 (1.56)	19.6 (1.67)	23.2 (1.75)	32.2 (1.12)	21.7 (1.30)	21.1 (0.82)	24.8 (1.22)	19.2 (0.73)
Instructor	74	75	83	12.1 (0.42)	9.9 (1.60)	13.4 (1.37)	12.6 (1.18)	9.1 (1.39)	9.7 (1.01)	15.3 (0.90)	14.9 (1.17)	7.7 (0.56)	5.7 (0.53)	18.7 (1.02)
Lecturer	12	14	22	3.2 (0.22)	3.4 (1.50)	3.6 (0.68)	3.0 (0.60)	2.0 (0.52)	4.3 (0.64)	1.9 (0.37)	7.9 (0.78)	2.1 (0.25)	2.3 (0.42)	3.6 (0.57)
Other	17	26	57	8.3 (0.32)	11.8 (2.16)	4.9 (0.64)	18.2 (1.57)	5.4 (0.82)	7.1 (1.03)	5.5 (0.50)	5.7 (0.69)	6.7 (0.48)	6.4 (0.67)	12.4 (0.76)
No rank	17	16	19	2.7 (0.19)	1.8 (1.37)	3.0 (0.68)	2.9 (1.05)	0.9 (0.38)	3.6 (1.24)	1.5 (0.27)	3.6 (0.67)	3.5 (0.48)	2.6 (0.47)	2.7 (0.36)

See notes at end of table.

Table 254. Full-time and part-time faculty and instructional staff in degree-granting institutions, by field and faculty characteristics: Fall 1992, fall 1998, and fall 2003—Continued

Selected characteristic	Number (in thousands) 1992	1998	2003	Fall 2003 All fields	Agriculture and home economics	Business	Education	Engineering	Fine arts	Health	Humanities[1]	Natural sciences[2]	Social sciences[3]	Other[4]
1	2	3	4	5	6	7	8	9	10	11	12	13	14	15
Part-time faculty and instructional staff														
Number (in thousands)	377	416	530	530.0 (0.02)	7.3 (0.97)	44.9 (2.98)	63.5 (2.57)	14.0 (1.49)	47.8 (3.65)	57.8 (3.06)	58.9 (2.05)	63.7 (2.46)	53.0 (2.39)	119.2 (3.48)
Percentage distribution	†	†	†	100.0 (†)	1.4 (0.18)	8.5 (0.56)	12.0 (0.48)	2.7 (0.28)	9.0 (0.69)	10.9 (0.58)	11.1 (0.39)	12.0 (0.46)	10.0 (0.45)	22.5 (0.66)
Total	377	416	530	100.0 (†)	100.0 (†)	100.0 (†)	100.0 (†)	100.0 (†)	100.0 (†)	100.0 (†)	100.0 (†)	100.0 (†)	100.0 (†)	100.0 (†)
Percentage distribution of part-time faculty and instructional staff														
Sex														
Male	209	217	276	52.1 (0.45)	32.0 (6.05)	69.6 (1.89)	29.1 (1.71)	90.8 (2.68)	51.4 (2.26)	34.5 (1.60)	31.6 (1.86)	58.2 (2.22)	60.5 (1.90)	66.2 (1.41)
Female	168	199	254	47.9 (0.45)	68.0 (6.05)	30.4 (1.89)	70.9 (1.71)	9.2 (2.68)	48.6 (2.26)	65.5 (1.60)	68.4 (1.86)	41.8 (2.22)	39.5 (1.90)	33.8 (1.41)
Race/ethnicity														
White	333	364	452	85.2 (0.38)	91.4 (3.66)	86.8 (1.54)	85.1 (1.34)	85.4 (2.89)	88.7 (1.22)	85.0 (1.14)	83.0 (1.14)	83.4 (1.35)	84.2 (1.62)	85.5 (0.80)
Black	18	19	30	5.6 (0.20)	2.7 (1.61)	6.7 (0.96)	6.6 (0.98)	2.0 (1.26)	3.0 (0.70)	5.2 (0.68)	5.0 (0.71)	6.0 (0.66)	5.8 (0.75)	6.5 (0.57)
Hispanic	11	16	19	3.5 (0.13)	‡ (†)	2.2 (0.79)	5.1 (0.71)	2.6 (0.64)	2.7 (0.52)	2.2 (0.47)	6.5 (0.81)	2.2 (0.40)	3.7 (0.61)	3.6 (0.39)
Asian/Pacific Islander	12	13	20	3.8 (0.22)	‡ (†)	3.0 (0.80)	1.6 (0.43)	8.4 (2.11)	2.9 (0.70)	6.5 (1.17)	4.2 (0.71)	7.1 (0.89)	2.7 (1.04)	2.5 (0.34)
American Indian/Alaska Native	2	4	10	1.8 (0.22)	‡ (†)	1.4 (0.54)	1.5 (0.37)	1.6 (1.03)	2.8 (0.84)	1.0 (0.35)	1.3 (0.38)	1.4 (0.60)	3.6 (0.91)	1.9 (0.36)
Age														
Under 30	20	15	23	4.3 (0.30)	6.4 (2.51)	2.3 (0.70)	2.7 (0.64)	2.8 (1.78)	4.4 (0.79)	3.7 (0.72)	5.7 (0.95)	7.2 (1.15)	3.5 (0.66)	4.3 (0.60)
30 to 34	36	37	43	8.2 (0.38)	7.7 (2.78)	6.7 (1.28)	7.0 (1.03)	1.8 (0.99)	9.4 (1.24)	8.9 (1.01)	10.0 (1.01)	7.6 (1.16)	10.6 (1.17)	7.7 (0.62)
35 to 39	59	47	55	10.3 (0.48)	5.5 (1.97)	9.6 (1.49)	8.7 (1.21)	10.7 (3.34)	11.7 (1.38)	9.5 (1.34)	8.7 (1.07)	10.2 (1.16)	9.9 (1.27)	12.6 (1.20)
40 to 44	70	60	61	11.5 (0.44)	6.3 (2.79)	10.5 (1.35)	7.9 (0.88)	15.6 (3.25)	12.0 (1.13)	14.9 (1.54)	9.2 (0.91)	10.1 (1.19)	11.2 (1.26)	13.8 (0.96)
45 to 49	68	72	76	14.4 (0.48)	17.4 (5.26)	13.1 (1.45)	11.7 (1.12)	11.4 (3.50)	16.4 (1.68)	19.7 (1.56)	14.3 (1.65)	9.5 (1.05)	13.1 (1.24)	16.5 (1.13)
50 to 54	45	70	83	15.6 (0.42)	16.4 (4.15)	16.3 (1.42)	17.4 (1.41)	22.3 (3.60)	18.4 (1.76)	15.9 (1.55)	14.1 (1.35)	11.9 (1.34)	11.1 (1.29)	17.1 (1.15)
55 to 59	29	47	77	14.5 (0.48)	17.6 (4.45)	17.9 (2.01)	15.5 (1.58)	11.7 (2.89)	14.6 (1.78)	11.5 (1.27)	13.8 (1.46)	15.6 (1.56)	17.5 (1.88)	12.8 (0.82)
60 to 64	23	29	52	9.7 (0.50)	18.0 (5.10)	11.5 (1.25)	13.1 (1.26)	6.5 (1.96)	5.7 (1.05)	6.7 (1.13)	12.7 (1.42)	12.8 (1.67)	10.9 (1.29)	6.6 (0.76)
65 or older	27	38	60	11.4 (0.46)	4.7 (2.09)	12.2 (1.65)	15.8 (1.26)	17.2 (3.46)	7.4 (1.33)	9.3 (1.22)	11.6 (1.50)	15.0 (1.99)	12.2 (1.48)	8.6 (0.79)
Highest degree														
Less than bachelor's	17	20	41	7.8 (0.59)	5.5 (2.53)	1.8 (0.79)	3.7 (0.96)	17.1 (4.44)	9.1 (1.42)	17.3 (1.86)	1.1 (0.57)	0.9 (0.47)	0.5 (0.25)	16.2 (1.31)
Bachelor's	63	59	84	15.8 (0.55)	26.7 (5.80)	13.9 (1.84)	12.0 (1.25)	17.9 (3.50)	28.2 (2.09)	16.2 (1.61)	12.9 (1.65)	16.1 (1.46)	3.2 (0.82)	19.4 (1.11)
Master's	190	225	273	51.5 (0.80)	50.3 (6.09)	66.5 (2.34)	63.0 (1.84)	32.3 (4.61)	54.7 (2.95)	30.2 (1.86)	70.2 (2.33)	49.0 (1.94)	55.5 (1.83)	41.6 (1.56)
First-professional	40	36	39	7.3 (0.39)	2.0 (1.63)	6.3 (1.10)	1.9 (0.45)	† (†)	0.9 (0.39)	25.2 (2.12)	2.3 (0.55)	4.3 (0.85)	3.1 (0.62)	11.2 (1.00)
Doctor's	59	76	94	17.6 (0.60)	15.5 (4.57)	11.5 (1.48)	19.4 (1.61)	31.2 (4.13)	7.1 (1.39)	11.1 (1.28)	13.4 (1.80)	29.7 (1.72)	37.7 (1.90)	11.7 (0.94)
Academic rank														
Professor	32	30	23	4.4 (0.30)	8.9 (4.03)	4.6 (1.06)	3.4 (0.55)	5.9 (2.27)	3.9 (1.05)	5.4 (0.84)	3.5 (0.75)	4.8 (0.82)	4.7 (1.01)	4.1 (0.63)
Associate professor	23	19	15	2.8 (0.22)	‡ (†)	2.3 (0.74)	1.9 (0.47)	5.7 (2.24)	3.7 (0.92)	5.4 (0.89)	1.6 (0.35)	3.3 (0.63)	2.9 (0.60)	1.6 (0.30)
Assistant professor	24	23	20	3.7 (0.29)	2.8 (1.76)	1.5 (0.55)	2.0 (0.50)	3.3 (1.97)	3.6 (0.86)	15.1 (1.64)	1.7 (0.64)	2.8 (0.66)	3.7 (0.89)	1.7 (0.34)
Instructor	215	205	188	35.4 (0.83)	39.9 (5.70)	29.2 (2.00)	37.0 (2.11)	25.3 (4.10)	33.6 (2.12)	36.5 (2.40)	42.9 (2.29)	32.4 (2.05)	30.4 (1.85)	38.2 (1.54)
Lecturer	45	46	41	7.7 (0.41)	14.8 (4.39)	7.6 (1.52)	6.8 (0.97)	9.3 (2.49)	9.7 (1.16)	4.7 (0.93)	11.2 (1.10)	7.8 (1.02)	9.5 (1.20)	5.8 (0.67)
Other	28	75	231	43.6 (0.85)	30.8 (5.98)	51.8 (2.46)	46.6 (1.78)	49.4 (5.02)	42.4 (3.00)	30.5 (1.88)	37.4 (2.23)	45.8 (2.02)	46.0 (2.22)	46.6 (1.47)
No rank	9	16	13	2.4 (0.20)	‡ (†)	3.0 (0.75)	2.1 (0.59)	†	3.2 (1.10)	2.4 (0.68)	1.7 (0.49)	3.1 (0.79)	2.8 (0.71)	2.1 (0.40)

†Not applicable.
‡Reporting standards not met.
[1]Excludes history and philosophy.
[2]Excludes computer sciences.
[3]Includes history.
[4]Includes philosophy, law, occupationally specific programs, computer sciences, and other.

NOTE: Totals may differ from figures reported in other tables because of varying survey methodologies. Race categories exclude persons of Hispanic ethnicity. Detail may not sum to totals because of survey item nonresponse and rounding. Standard errors appear in parentheses.
SOURCE: U.S. Department of Education, National Center for Education Statistics, 1993, 1999, and 2004 National Study of Postsecondary Faculty (NSOPF:93;99:04). (This table was prepared January 2009.)

Table 255. Full-time and part-time faculty and instructional staff in degree-granting institutions, by race/ethnicity, sex, and program area: Fall 1998 and fall 2003

Program area	Number (in thousands) 1998	Number (in thousands) 2003	Percentage distribution, fall 2003 Total	White Male	White Female	Black Male	Black Female	Hispanic Male	Hispanic Female	Asian/Pacific Islander Male	Asian/Pacific Islander Female	American Indian/Alaska Native Male	American Indian/Alaska Native Female
1	2	3	4	5	6	7	8	9	10	11	12	13	14
Full-time faculty and instructional staff	560 (4.8)	682 (#)	100.0	49.6 (0.39)	30.7 (0.36)	2.9 (0.15)	2.7 (0.13)	2.0 (0.09)	1.5 (0.08)	6.3 (0.15)	2.8 (0.15)	0.8 (0.08)	0.6 (0.07)
Agriculture and home economics	10 (0.4)	17 (0.8)	100.0	58.9 (3.03)	28.9 (2.72)	‡ (†)	1.8 (0.73)	1.2 (0.46)	1.3 (0.52)	3.6 (1.13)	2.8 (0.86)	‡ (†)	0.6 (0.35)
Business	39 (1.1)	43 (1.4)	100.0	53.2 (1.49)	26.2 (1.71)	2.5 (0.73)	2.0 (0.44)	1.8 (0.43)	0.5 (0.16)	9.7 (1.06)	2.5 (0.46)	1.3 (0.35)	0.4 (0.17)
Communications	10 (1.0)	16 (1.4)	100.0	48.1 (3.39)	38.7 (3.30)	2.0 (0.73)	3.3 (0.94)	1.9 (0.53)	1.5 (0.59)	1.9 (0.87)	0.6 (0.39)	1.1 (0.77)	0.9 (0.64)
Education	40 (1.4)	51 (1.9)	100.0	32.5 (1.49)	48.0 (1.64)	3.0 (0.60)	4.9 (0.64)	1.5 (0.34)	3.2 (0.52)	1.3 (0.43)	3.5 (0.59)	0.9 (0.25)	1.3 (0.34)
Teacher education	14 (0.6)	18 (1.0)	100.0	31.1 (2.31)	54.4 (2.54)	2.1 (0.86)	5.2 (1.10)	0.4 (0.24)	3.1 (0.89)	‡ (†)	2.1 (0.87)	0.5 (0.25)	0.9 (0.44)
Other education	26 (1.3)	33 (1.5)	100.0	33.3 (2.09)	44.4 (2.46)	3.4 (0.84)	4.7 (0.75)	2.2 (0.51)	3.2 (0.57)	1.9 (0.64)	4.2 (0.81)	1.1 (0.40)	1.5 (0.45)
Engineering	25 (0.9)	33 (1.3)	100.0	65.6 (1.93)	5.3 (0.90)	4.9 (0.84)	0.5 (0.26)	2.2 (0.42)	0.4 (0.17)	17.9 (1.61)	2.2 (0.63)	0.8 (0.53)	‡ (†)
Fine arts	33 (1.4)	43 (1.7)	100.0	52.8 (1.68)	33.6 (1.36)	4.4 (0.83)	1.6 (0.34)	2.0 (0.59)	1.3 (0.44)	1.5 (0.42)	1.4 (0.59)	1.2 (0.36)	0.3 (0.18)
Health sciences	84 (2.0)	94 (2.7)	100.0	36.2 (1.23)	43.5 (1.15)	1.6 (0.26)	3.4 (0.44)	1.6 (0.25)	1.4 (0.19)	6.6 (0.60)	4.1 (0.57)	0.7 (0.22)	1.0 (0.28)
First-professional	40 (1.6)	45 (1.7)	100.0	53.9 (1.58)	20.1 (1.42)	2.2 (0.49)	2.5 (0.58)	2.2 (0.40)	1.3 (0.30)	10.6 (1.08)	5.3 (0.89)	1.1 (0.37)	0.8 (0.39)
Nursing	20 (0.6)	20 (1.2)	100.0	3.5 (0.86)	84.6 (2.21)	‡ (†)	5.3 (1.29)	‡ (†)	0.7 (0.27)	‡ (†)	3.4 (1.10)	‡ (†)	1.8 (0.85)
Other health sciences	24 (1.0)	29 (1.4)	100.0	31.0 (1.98)	52.0 (2.05)	1.5 (0.50)	3.6 (0.84)	1.6 (0.44)	1.9 (0.48)	4.8 (1.02)	2.6 (0.71)	2.0 (1.20)	0.7 (0.31)
Humanities	81 (1.8)	90 (2.4)	100.0	47.3 (1.40)	35.0 (1.33)	2.4 (0.43)	2.6 (0.39)	2.2 (0.24)	2.9 (0.31)	2.9 (0.48)	2.9 (0.54)	0.9 (0.23)	0.9 (0.25)
English and literature	40 (1.2)	39 (1.5)	100.0	38.8 (1.90)	46.0 (2.10)	2.1 (0.45)	4.5 (0.70)	1.3 (0.27)	1.9 (0.50)	0.8 (0.34)	2.7 (0.87)	0.5 (0.18)	1.4 (0.39)
Foreign languages	15 (0.8)	20 (1.0)	100.0	36.2 (1.86)	36.7 (2.07)	2.7 (0.89)	0.9 (0.46)	5.1 (0.75)	8.3 (1.07)	4.0 (1.11)	4.5 (1.01)	0.7 (0.43)	0.8 (0.44)
History	14 (0.6)	18 (1.0)	100.0	59.4 (2.90)	23.0 (2.12)	2.7 (0.80)	2.4 (0.94)	1.9 (0.71)	1.2 (0.52)	5.0 (1.49)	3.2 (0.91)	1.0 (0.45)	‡ (†)
Philosophy	12 (0.8)	13 (1.0)	100.0	72.3 (3.55)	16.6 (2.33)	2.3 (1.11)	‡ (†)	1.0 (0.35)	‡ (†)	4.0 (1.49)	‡ (†)	2.0 (1.20)	‡ (†)
Law	8 (0.6)	10 (1.0)	100.0	54.5 (3.56)	29.9 (3.63)	3.3 (1.10)	4.0 (2.03)	0.9 (0.68)	2.4 (1.15)	2.8 (1.36)	2.0 (1.12)	‡ (†)	‡ (†)
Natural sciences	111 (2.1)	151 (2.5)	100.0	57.3 (1.12)	20.3 (0.80)	2.5 (0.31)	1.5 (0.22)	2.0 (0.20)	0.9 (0.15)	11.2 (0.65)	3.3 (0.35)	0.6 (0.16)	0.3 (0.09)
Biological sciences	40 (1.3)	59 (1.7)	100.0	55.4 (1.69)	21.6 (1.30)	2.2 (0.48)	1.2 (0.28)	1.9 (0.39)	1.2 (0.31)	11.1 (1.13)	4.8 (0.67)	0.3 (0.17)	0.3 (0.12)
Physical sciences	27 (0.8)	36 (1.3)	100.0	68.9 (2.03)	12.8 (1.50)	2.6 (0.59)	0.7 (0.31)	1.4 (0.29)	0.6 (0.19)	9.4 (1.05)	3.0 (0.64)	0.4 (0.33)	‡ (†)
Mathematics	26 (1.0)	32 (1.3)	100.0	52.2 (2.15)	22.7 (1.84)	3.8 (0.67)	2.6 (0.67)	2.8 (0.67)	0.7 (0.28)	11.7 (1.41)	1.8 (0.67)	1.2 (0.56)	0.3 (0.18)
Computer sciences	17 (0.9)	24 (1.2)	100.0	51.0 (2.74)	25.1 (2.15)	1.5 (0.59)	2.0 (0.58)	2.3 (0.52)	0.9 (0.31)	13.5 (1.69)	2.0 (0.66)	1.1 (0.48)	0.6 (0.36)
Social sciences	58 (1.3)	70 (1.8)	100.0	52.2 (1.46)	29.0 (1.23)	3.7 (0.45)	4.1 (0.81)	2.6 (0.36)	1.7 (0.35)	3.4 (0.58)	1.9 (0.48)	0.9 (0.25)	0.6 (0.15)
Economics	9 (0.6)	12 (0.7)	100.0	62.3 (3.46)	18.0 (3.09)	3.5 (0.92)	‡ (†)	3.1 (1.13)	‡ (†)	8.9 (2.18)	3.2 (2.24)	‡ (†)	‡ (†)
Political science	8 (0.5)	10 (0.7)	100.0	67.1 (3.74)	16.8 (2.59)	2.8 (1.19)	3.2 (1.62)	5.1 (1.57)	‡ (†)	2.9 (1.31)	‡ (†)	‡ (†)	‡ (†)
Psychology	20 (0.7)	25 (1.1)	100.0	46.3 (2.33)	37.8 (2.16)	3.4 (1.01)	3.4 (1.99)	1.6 (0.42)	2.7 (0.70)	1.1 (0.49)	1.2 (0.39)	0.6 (0.34)	‡ (†)
Sociology	9 (0.4)	9 (0.6)	100.0	49.9 (3.72)	30.1 (3.42)	3.9 (1.69)	8.0 (2.43)	3.0 (0.97)	1.4 (0.92)	1.1 (0.89)	1.3 (0.75)	‡ (†)	‡ (†)
Other social sciences	13 (0.6)	14 (0.9)	100.0	45.2 (3.59)	30.5 (3.09)	4.8 (1.33)	3.9 (1.28)	1.9 (0.80)	2.4 (0.71)	4.7 (1.50)	3.7 (1.22)	1.9 (0.75)	1.1 (0.54)
Occupationally specific programs	16 (0.8)	27 (1.1)	100.0	60.7 (2.47)	24.2 (2.16)	4.2 (1.16)	1.9 (0.55)	2.5 (0.63)	0.8 (0.26)	2.0 (0.92)	1.4 (0.46)	1.9 (0.62)	0.5 (0.36)
All other programs	44 (1.2)	29 (1.4)	100.0	42.0 (2.03)	37.4 (2.00)	4.7 (1.01)	6.0 (1.01)	1.7 (0.44)	1.7 (0.53)	3.2 (0.99)	2.0 (0.64)	0.7 (0.31)	0.6 (0.28)

See notes at end of table.

Table 255. Full-time and part-time faculty and instructional staff in degree-granting institutions, by race/ethnicity, sex, and program area: Fall 1998 and fall 2003—Continued

Program area	Number (in thousands) 1998	Number (in thousands) 2003	Percentage distribution, fall 2003 Total	White Male	White Female	Black Male	Black Female	Hispanic Male	Hispanic Female	Asian/Pacific Islander Male	Asian/Pacific Islander Female	American Indian/Alaska Native Male	American Indian/Alaska Native Female
1	2	3	4	5	6	7	8	9	10	11	12	13	14
Part-time faculty and instructional staff	416 (5.9)	530 (#)	100.0	44.4 (0.46)	40.8 (0.54)	2.6 (0.17)	3.0 (0.14)	1.9 (0.12)	1.6 (0.10)	2.1 (0.15)	1.8 (0.18)	1.0 (0.15)	0.8 (0.15)
Agriculture and home economics	3 (0.2)	7 (1.0)	100.0	30.8 (6.24)	60.6 (6.30)	‡ (†)	2.1 (1.46)	‡ (†)	‡ (†)	‡ (†)	‡ (†)	‡ (†)	‡ (†)
Business	32 (1.8)	45 (3.0)	100.0	60.6 (1.96)	26.2 (1.73)	4.3 (0.70)	2.3 (0.54)	1.7 (0.77)	0.5 (0.28)	2.0 (0.69)	1.0 (0.50)	1.0 (0.52)	0.4 (0.23)
Communications	10 (1.0)	14 (1.2)	100.0	47.7 (3.71)	39.3 (3.89)	2.1 (0.97)	2.8 (0.95)	0.5 (0.36)	1.5 (0.99)	‡ (†)	0.8 (0.52)	3.5 (1.82)	1.1 (0.86)
Education	34 (1.6)	64 (2.6)	100.0	25.3 (1.65)	59.8 (2.11)	1.4 (0.41)	5.2 (0.90)	1.7 (0.37)	3.4 (0.49)	0.4 (0.19)	1.3 (0.38)	0.3 (0.15)	1.2 (0.36)
Teacher education	13 (1.0)	29 (1.8)	100.0	22.2 (2.41)	63.9 (2.84)	0.9 (0.35)	6.4 (1.17)	1.3 (0.41)	2.2 (0.52)	‡ (†)	0.9 (0.52)	‡ (†)	1.6 (0.69)
Other education	20 (1.2)	34 (1.8)	100.0	27.9 (2.53)	56.4 (2.98)	1.9 (0.66)	4.1 (1.17)	2.0 (0.57)	4.5 (0.77)	0.5 (0.24)	1.6 (0.60)	‡ (†)	0.8 (0.37)
Engineering	9 (0.8)	14 (1.5)	100.0	78.6 (3.70)	6.8 (2.77)	‡ (1.22)	‡ (†)	1.7 (0.46)	0.9 (0.46)	8.0 (2.13)	‡ (†)	‡ (†)	‡ (†)
Fine arts	38 (1.5)	48 (3.6)	100.0	44.8 (2.06)	43.9 (2.44)	1.7 (0.54)	1.3 (0.34)	1.8 (0.49)	0.9 (0.25)	1.0 (0.36)	1.9 (0.58)	2.1 (0.84)	0.7 (0.30)
Health sciences	49 (2.2)	58 (3.1)	100.0	27.9 (1.65)	57.1 (1.74)	1.2 (0.41)	4.0 (0.52)	0.8 (0.26)	1.4 (0.38)	4.0 (0.87)	2.4 (0.72)	0.5 (0.32)	0.5 (0.23)
First-professional	15 (1.3)	17 (1.2)	100.0	47.2 (3.33)	34.7 (3.64)	2.0 (1.03)	2.1 (0.92)	1.2 (0.72)	0.9 (0.45)	6.4 (2.10)	5.1 (2.41)	‡ (†)	‡ (†)
Nursing	12 (0.8)	13 (1.3)	100.0	‡ (†)	86.3 (2.04)	‡ (†)	8.0 (1.30)	‡ (†)	1.4 (0.56)	‡ (†)	1.3 (1.03)	‡ (†)	0.9 (0.47)
Other health sciences	21 (1.7)	28 (2.0)	100.0	29.4 (2.86)	56.4 (3.07)	1.2 (0.66)	3.2 (0.76)	0.8 (0.32)	1.7 (0.70)	4.3 (1.23)	1.4 (0.56)	‡ (†)	0.7 (0.40)
Humanities	74 (2.1)	80 (2.5)	100.0	35.9 (1.52)	49.2 (1.61)	1.6 (0.35)	2.9 (0.45)	2.3 (0.35)	2.9 (0.44)	0.9 (0.30)	2.7 (0.55)	1.0 (0.33)	0.6 (0.22)
English and literature	43 (1.4)	44 (1.9)	100.0	29.5 (2.31)	58.5 (2.47)	1.2 (0.33)	4.3 (0.78)	1.0 (0.35)	1.3 (0.37)	1.0 (0.41)	1.6 (0.46)	0.8 (0.34)	0.8 (0.29)
Foreign languages	12 (1.2)	15 (1.2)	100.0	16.6 (3.57)	52.0 (3.38)	1.4 (0.83)	2.0 (0.80)	7.2 (1.50)	11.4 (1.97)	‡ (†)	7.9 (2.18)	‡ (†)	‡ (†)
History	11 (0.7)	11 (1.0)	100.0	61.1 (4.58)	28.9 (4.15)	1.5 (0.89)	0.5 (0.38)	2.5 (1.05)	‡ (†)	‡ (†)	1.0 (0.63)	3.7 (1.99)	‡ (†)
Philosophy	9 (0.6)	10 (1.2)	100.0	65.7 (4.20)	26.0 (4.60)	3.5 (1.71)	0.5 (0.28)	0.6 (0.46)	‡ (†)	1.8 (1.18)	‡ (†)	‡ (†)	0.7 (0.40)
Law	11 (0.8)	11 (1.2)	100.0	52.6 (4.43)	32.8 (4.18)	4.4 (1.41)	2.0 (0.82)	2.2 (1.05)	‡ (†)	3.5 (1.89)	‡ (†)	1.0 (0.86)	‡ (†)
Natural sciences	65 (2.2)	90 (2.9)	100.0	50.5 (1.72)	32.4 (1.73)	3.8 (0.44)	2.7 (0.36)	1.9 (0.41)	0.7 (0.16)	4.2 (0.61)	2.3 (0.46)	1.0 (0.34)	0.5 (0.26)
Biological sciences	11 (0.9)	16 (1.0)	100.0	41.7 (3.76)	40.1 (3.78)	2.2 (0.67)	2.1 (0.90)	1.0 (0.39)	1.0 (0.40)	5.6 (2.32)	5.3 (1.63)	‡ (†)	‡ (†)
Physical sciences	11 (0.8)	16 (1.1)	100.0	57.8 (3.30)	28.7 (3.42)	3.9 (1.37)	0.9 (0.52)	1.9 (1.05)	0.9 (0.41)	3.1 (1.06)	2.6 (0.99)	‡ (†)	‡ (†)
Mathematics	24 (1.4)	32 (2.3)	100.0	46.6 (3.20)	36.0 (3.04)	4.4 (0.78)	3.1 (0.83)	1.4 (0.48)	0.5 (0.24)	3.9 (0.85)	1.8 (0.64)	1.3 (0.85)	0.9 (0.59)
Computer sciences	19 (1.2)	26 (1.7)	100.0	56.4 (2.98)	25.3 (2.64)	4.1 (1.03)	3.7 (0.60)	3.0 (0.93)	0.7 (0.39)	4.2 (1.10)	0.9 (0.45)	1.4 (0.63)	‡ (†)
Social sciences	41 (2.4)	42 (2.0)	100.0	49.8 (1.85)	32.9 (2.09)	3.7 (0.68)	3.0 (0.66)	2.5 (0.65)	1.5 (0.31)	0.9 (0.48)	2.3 (1.23)	1.5 (0.65)	2.0 (0.62)
Economics	4 (0.5)	5 (0.8)	100.0	68.6 (7.36)	9.3 (4.08)	7.2 (3.52)	‡ (†)	7.0 (4.24)	‡ (†)	‡ (†)	‡ (†)	‡ (†)	‡ (†)
Political science	4 (0.4)	5 (0.8)	100.0	71.1 (5.32)	11.9 (3.93)	5.7 (2.79)	1.7 (1.32)	3.9 (2.30)	1.0 (0.67)	‡ (†)	‡ (†)	‡ (†)	‡ (†)
Psychology	18 (2.1)	18 (1.2)	100.0	42.2 (3.36)	44.4 (3.12)	2.0 (0.76)	3.0 (0.91)	1.4 (0.64)	1.7 (0.58)	‡ (†)	0.6 (0.52)	1.9 (1.11)	2.2 (0.93)
Sociology	6 (0.5)	7 (0.9)	100.0	44.6 (6.09)	30.7 (6.03)	4.0 (1.61)	4.1 (1.54)	1.7 (0.98)	1.6 (0.76)	‡ (†)	‡ (†)	1.7 (1.52)	5.7 (3.43)
Other social sciences	10 (0.9)	8 (0.8)	100.0	46.2 (4.24)	36.4 (4.19)	3.8 (2.28)	4.5 (1.85)	1.8 (1.04)	1.9 (0.83)	4.2 (1.10)	2.8 (1.29)	‡ (†)	‡ (†)
Occupationally specific programs	17 (1.1)	37 (2.4)	100.0	68.2 (2.51)	18.6 (2.19)	4.5 (1.03)	1.8 (0.63)	4.0 (0.92)	0.6 (0.23)	0.6 (0.32)	0.3 (0.19)	1.1 (0.50)	0.4 (0.25)
All other programs	35 (1.6)	19 (1.2)	100.0	41.8 (3.30)	42.6 (2.95)	2.5 (0.81)	5.5 (1.46)	1.9 (0.58)	2.6 (0.90)	0.9 (0.75)	1.2 (0.63)	‡ (†)	‡ (†)

†Not applicable.
#Rounds to zero.
‡Reporting standards not met.

NOTE: Totals may differ from figures reported in other tables because of varying survey methodologies. Race categories exclude persons of Hispanic ethnicity. Detail may not sum to totals because of rounding and nonresponse to program area question. Standard errors appear in parentheses.
SOURCE: U.S. Department of Education, National Center for Education Statistics, 1999 and 2004 National Study of Postsecondary Faculty (NSOPF:99;04). (This table was prepared December 2008.)

Table 256. Average base salary of full-time faculty and instructional staff in degree-granting institutions, by type and control of institution and field of instruction: Selected years, 1987–88 through 2003–04

[In constant 2006–07 dollars]

Program area	Institutions — All	Institutions — Public	Institutions — Private	Research — Public	Research — Private	Doctoral — Public	Doctoral — Private	Comprehensive — Public	Comprehensive — Private	Private liberal arts	Public 2-year	Other
1	2	3	4	5	6	7	8	9	10	11	12	13
1987–88 salaries	**$69,300** (—)	**$69,930** (—)	**$67,870** (—)	**$91,190** (—)	**$83,240** (—)	**$77,380** (—)	**$81,950** (—)	**$64,940** (—)	**$56,670** (—)	**$50,790** (—)	**$57,070** (—)	**$54,000** (—)
Agriculture and home economics	69,400	69,770	†	—	†	62,310	‡	67,220	—	‡	—	†
Business	64,800	65,580	63,130	—	†	70,410	†	62,180	64,910	42,110	58,305	50,548
Education	58,000	60,900	48,020	—	†	62,040	†	59,820	47,980	‡	58,915	†
Engineering	74,780	73,640	78,910	—	†	76,100	†	72,070	73,740	‡	52,700	†
Fine arts	54,200	56,640	49,230	—	†	54,650	†	56,380	47,510	49,390	57,601	†
Health	92,900	92,310	94,090	110,490	—	101,790	96,360	81,820	68,300	‡	53,020	49,819
Humanities	60,760	63,150	57,100	70,170	—	55,330	66,330	63,880	53,120	54,610	62,249	53,710
Natural sciences	68,480	69,320	66,590	88,420	—	71,500	67,190	66,860	55,520	54,080	56,851	‡
Social sciences	66,220	66,610	65,500	87,430	—	63,660	‡	64,360	55,310	51,170	58,798	63,495
Other	64,040	63,360	65,650	‡	†	65,060	‡	59,950	51,180	‡	54,086	†
1992–93 salaries	**67,080** (—)	**66,980** (—)	**67,310** (—)	**91,620** (—)	**80,840** (—)	**73,760** (—)	**80,220** (—)	**62,290** (—)	**61,950** (—)	**53,890** (—)	**56,360** (—)	**57,950** (—)
Agriculture and home economics	68,480	69,450	‡	—	78,400	63,710	77,870	62,130	77,040	‡	56,990	†
Business	70,500	71,550	67,770	—	93,400	84,230	70,550	68,380	54,370	46,290	60,180	48,110
Education	60,220	61,960	53,880	—	71,360	60,450	‡	59,380	65,680	46,430	59,040	†
Engineering	79,590	80,100	77,620	87,490	95,650	76,740	78,830	69,760	51,290	‡	55,350	80,260
Fine arts	58,110	56,270	60,910	123,490	59,210	56,400	54,250	56,070	65,420	54,090	53,750	48,840
Health	79,670	77,480	85,540	104,670	105,230	91,440	94,700	54,870	58,340	60,680	51,260	60,010
Humanities	58,680	59,580	56,770	64,000	63,050	56,810	61,490	58,790	66,840	53,950	58,990	52,350
Natural sciences	69,020	68,030	71,520	96,210	79,390	74,040	81,160	65,770	57,060	53,760	56,790	60,360
Social sciences	65,830	66,030	65,410	84,930	76,110	69,770	70,910	62,570	59,760	58,000	57,740	63,580
Other	63,870	62,210	67,360	94,080	73,060	62,700	88,590	64,960	52,190	52,190	53,950	56,140
1998–99 salaries	**70,530** (489)	**69,550** (538)	**73,350** (1,078)	**82,380** (1,013)	**101,200** (3,111)	**81,223** (2,297)	**87,140** (2,462)	**62,210** (715)	**61,260** (1,392)	**54,090** (882)	**55,380** (525)	**58,590** (1,964)
Agriculture and home economics	72,500 (2,935)	75,300 (2,190)	‡ (†)	83,540 (2,919)	‡ (†)	68,530 (5,998)	‡ (†)	72,730 (1,945)	‡ (†)	‡ (†)	54,870 (2,590)	‡ (†)
Business	69,270 (1,248)	67,740 (1,424)	72,900 (2,473)	85,900 (4,164)	100,430 (9,821)	57,550 (3,538)	86,040 (7,079)	51,110 (2,227)	73,500 (2,309)	52,510 (3,631)	57,250 (1,536)	52,650 (6,105)
Education	59,290 (1,122)	59,880 (1,290)	57,200 (2,267)	66,270 (2,194)	94,380 (6,181)	79,830 (2,973)	‡ (†)	55,290 (6,193)	54,190 (2,379)	50,690 (2,520)	53,750 (1,615)	51,410 (4,608)
Engineering	78,660 (1,615)	77,250 (1,767)	83,950 (3,707)	86,680 (2,978)	‡ (†)	51,990 (1,583)	‡ (†)	55,550 (1,823)	71,840 (7,248)	‡ (†)	55,980 (2,098)	‡ (†)
Fine arts	56,640 (1,440)	55,960 (1,427)	58,390 (3,477)	61,220 (3,501)	‡ (†)	106,500 (5,457)	‡ (†)	55,980 (3,390)	61,820 (8,590)	53,930 (2,081)	57,020 (2,868)	45,400 (3,973)
Health	93,340 (1,880)	89,020 (1,923)	105,300 (4,597)	106,100 (3,444)	124,150 (9,395)	58,360 (3,162)	115,380 (6,152)	57,790 (1,321)	58,780 (5,050)	55,320 (4,559)	54,110 (1,417)	66,230 (4,200)
Humanities	59,130 (802)	59,380 (951)	57,640 (1,492)	66,910 (2,463)	70,760 (5,274)	79,950 (2,301)	61,210 (3,238)	63,460 (1,647)	57,790 (2,205)	53,590 (1,964)	55,890 (1,490)	53,600 (2,344)
Natural sciences	71,130 (892)	70,630 (964)	72,640 (2,074)	81,820 (1,713)	98,980 (4,939)	86,340 (16,948)	76,580 (3,792)	56,270 (1,390)	59,260 (2,467)	52,900 (1,652)	54,750 (1,089)	68,940 (6,459)
Social sciences	72,840 (2,205)	73,760 (2,797)	70,450 (3,039)	85,700 (3,873)	97,440 (8,284)	70,030 (2,982)	73,100 (3,625)	56,890 (2,200)	57,610 (2,226)	58,700 (2,930)	58,550 (1,969)	61,080 (4,828)
Other	64,700 (1,089)	62,560 (1,138)	71,460 (2,589)	74,310 (2,527)	100,050 (8,098)	—	80,800 (4,448)	—	65,530 (3,733)	53,520 (2,330)	54,170 (1,265)	57,880 (4,793)
2003–04 salaries	**73,940** (415)	**77,640** (977)	**72,320** (389)	**86,410** (706)	**98,550** (1,475)	**69,098** (861)	**90,660** (2,087)	**63,670** (899)	**63,530** (1,696)	**60,220** (1,140)	**65,330** (780)	**72,240** (3,370)
Agriculture and home economics	70,790 (1,710)	72,020 (1,833)	57,700 (5,414)	77,190 (2,188)	‡ (†)	70,590 (5,851)	‡ (†)	62,600 (3,400)	‡ (†)	‡ (†)	58,880 (3,571)	‡ (†)
Business	81,170 (1,360)	78,730 (1,409)	87,170 (2,968)	99,650 (4,061)	121,610 (8,372)	83,970 (4,236)	96,060 (6,388)	78,000 (1,734)	74,950 (2,561)	66,450 (2,960)	61,040 (1,712)	68,480 (6,374)
Education	62,620 (946)	63,390 (1,204)	60,550 (1,867)	71,700 (2,342)	80,220 (9,735)	62,240 (2,613)	60,790 (5,991)	61,870 (2,461)	59,180 (2,319)	59,560 (2,926)	59,820 (2,093)	54,440 (2,993)
Engineering	84,090 (1,591)	79,970 (1,424)	97,860 (4,026)	92,000 (2,647)	107,860 (4,679)	80,320 (3,500)	‡ (†)	69,660 (3,236)	83,420 (15,670)	‡ (†)	58,530 (1,651)	‡ (†)
Fine arts	58,670 (797)	59,330 (820)	57,730 (1,435)	64,270 (1,630)	64,150 (3,988)	58,110 (1,758)	‡ (†)	55,430 (1,857)	53,860 (3,000)	54,020 (1,675)	58,090 (2,367)	60,840 (3,204)
Health	98,480 (1,735)	95,730 (1,664)	104,450 (4,101)	118,230 (2,179)	116,190 (3,698)	84,570 (6,498)	101,250 (15,300)	60,210 (1,530)	67,320 (5,173)	54,990 (4,803)	86,480 (3,416)	103,050 (8,695)
Humanities	59,970 (814)	58,430 (941)	63,150 (1,514)	61,840 (1,876)	69,670 (3,756)	55,240 (2,287)	74,430 (4,072)	60,240 (1,991)	58,170 (2,163)	60,790 (2,140)	56,040 (1,586)	54,090 (3,099)
Natural sciences	77,540 (947)	74,290 (894)	85,320 (2,097)	87,080 (1,359)	99,870 (3,799)	71,740 (1,853)	89,400 (3,737)	63,230 (1,351)	61,150 (5,784)	61,150 (2,039)	65,880 (1,655)	84,710 (7,845)
Social sciences	70,850 (669)	69,280 (681)	74,040 (1,474)	79,320 (1,604)	96,340 (3,078)	66,190 (2,093)	69,640 (2,041)	66,190 (1,483)	60,590 (3,540)	64,770 (2,402)	59,760 (1,592)	65,040 (2,869)
Other	65,740 (726)	64,590 (823)	68,380 (1,401)	75,110 (2,045)	91,070 (2,343)	65,590 (1,403)	72,650 (3,037)	61,130 (1,510)	62,340 (1,850)	56,860 (1,462)	59,970 (1,263)	62,240 (2,795)

—Not available.
†Not applicable.
‡Reporting standards not met.

SOURCE: U.S. Department of Education, National Center for Education Statistics, 1988, 1993, 1999, and 2004 National Study of Postsecondary Faculty (NSOPF:88;93;99;04). (This table was prepared August 2007.)

NOTE: Constant dollars based on the Consumer Price Index, prepared by the Bureau of Labor Statistics, U.S. Department of Labor, adjusted to an academic-year basis. Totals may differ from figures reported in other tables because of varying survey methodologies. Standard errors appear in parentheses.

Table 257. Average salary of full-time instructional faculty on 9-month contracts in degree-granting institutions, by academic rank, control and type of institution, and sex: Selected years, 1970–71 through 2007–08

Sex and academic year	All faculty	Academic rank						Public institutions			Private institutions		
		Professor	Associate professor	Assistant professor	Instructor	Lecturer	No rank	Total	4-year	2-year	Total	4-year	2-year
1	2	3	4	5	6	7	8	9	10	11	12	13	14
							Current dollars						
Total													
1970–71	$12,710	$17,958	$13,563	$11,176	$9,360	$11,196	$12,333	$12,953	$13,121	$12,644	$11,619	$11,824	$8,664
1972–73	13,856	19,191	14,580	12,032	10,737	11,637	12,676	14,016	14,417	12,919	13,452	13,622	9,288
1974–75	15,622	21,277	16,146	13,295	12,691	12,575	13,532	15,879	16,271	14,897	14,912	15,092	10,242
1975–76	16,659	22,649	17,065	13,986	13,672	12,906	15,196	16,942	17,400	15,820	15,921	16,116	10,901
1978–79	19,820	26,470	20,047	16,374	13,193	15,281	18,725	20,179	20,722	18,844	18,807	19,010	12,496
1979–80	21,348	28,388	21,451	17,465	14,023	16,122	20,262	21,798	22,349	20,429	20,105	20,318	13,250
1980–81	23,302	30,753	23,214	18,901	15,178	17,301	22,334	23,745	24,373	22,177	22,093	22,325	15,065
1981–82	25,449	33,437	25,278	20,608	16,450	18,756	24,331	25,886	26,591	24,193	24,255	24,509	15,926
1982–83	27,196	35,540	26,921	22,056	17,601	20,072	25,557	27,488	28,293	25,567	26,393	26,691	16,595
1984–85	30,447	39,743	29,945	24,668	20,230	22,334	27,683	30,646	31,764	27,864	29,910	30,247	18,510
1985–86	32,392	42,268	31,787	26,277	20,918	23,770	29,088	32,750	34,033	29,590	31,402	31,732	19,436
1987–88	35,897	47,040	35,231	29,110	22,728	25,977	31,532	36,231	37,840	32,209	35,049	35,346	21,867
1989–90	40,133	52,810	39,392	32,689	25,030	28,990	34,559	40,416	42,365	35,516	39,464	39,817	24,601
1990–91	42,165	55,540	41,414	34,434	26,332	30,097	36,395	42,317	44,510	37,055	41,788	42,224	24,088
1991–92	43,851	57,433	42,929	35,745	30,916	30,456	37,783	43,641	45,638	38,959	44,376	44,793	25,673
1992–93	44,714	58,788	43,945	36,625	28,499	30,543	37,771	44,197	46,515	38,935	45,985	46,427	26,105
1993–94	46,364	60,649	45,278	37,630	28,828	32,729	40,584	45,920	48,019	41,040	47,465	47,880	28,435
1994–95	47,811	62,709	46,713	38,756	29,665	33,198	41,227	47,432	49,738	42,101	48,741	49,379	25,613
1995–96	49,309	64,540	47,966	39,696	30,344	34,136	42,996	48,837	51,172	43,295	50,466	50,819	31,915
1996–97	50,829	66,659	49,307	40,687	31,193	34,962	44,200	50,303	52,718	44,584	52,112	52,443	32,628
1997–98	52,335	68,731	50,828	41,830	32,449	35,484	45,268	51,638	54,114	45,919	54,039	54,379	33,592
1998–99	54,097	71,322	52,576	43,348	33,819	36,819	46,250	53,319	55,948	47,285	55,981	56,284	34,821
1999–2000	55,888	74,410	54,524	44,978	34,918	38,194	47,389	55,011	57,950	48,240	58,013	58,323	35,925
2001–02	59,742	80,792	58,724	48,796	46,959	41,798	46,569	58,524	62,013	50,837	62,818	63,088	33,139
2002–03	61,330	83,466	60,471	50,552	48,304	42,622	46,338	60,014	63,486	52,330	64,533	64,814	34,826
2003–04	62,579	85,333	61,746	51,798	49,065	43,648	47,725	60,874	64,340	53,076	66,666	66,932	36,322
2004–05	64,234	88,158	63,558	53,308	49,730	44,514	48,942	62,346	66,053	53,932	68,755	68,995	37,329
2005–06	66,172	91,208	65,714	55,106	50,883	45,896	50,425	64,158	67,951	55,405	71,016	71,263	38,549
2006–07	68,585	94,870	68,153	57,143	53,278	47,478	52,161	66,566	70,460	57,466	73,419	73,636	41,138
2007–08	71,085	98,548	70,826	59,294	55,325	49,392	54,405	68,981	72,857	59,646	76,133	76,341	43,402
Males													
1972–73	14,422	19,414	14,723	12,193	11,147	12,106	13,047	14,545	14,944	13,268	14,116	14,253	9,571
1974–75	16,303	21,532	16,282	13,458	13,350	13,232	14,008	16,522	16,918	15,350	15,709	15,852	10,633
1975–76	17,414	22,902	17,209	14,174	14,430	13,579	15,761	17,661	18,121	16,339	16,784	16,946	11,378
1978–79	20,777	26,727	20,221	16,602	13,441	15,927	19,400	21,080	21,628	19,475	19,935	20,086	13,048
1979–80	22,394	28,672	21,651	17,720	14,323	16,932	20,901	22,789	23,350	21,131	21,317	21,472	13,938
1980–81	24,499	31,082	23,451	19,227	15,545	18,281	23,170	24,873	25,509	22,965	23,493	23,669	16,075
1981–82	26,796	33,799	25,553	21,025	16,906	19,721	25,276	27,149	27,864	25,085	25,849	26,037	16,834
1982–83	28,664	35,956	27,262	22,586	18,160	21,225	26,541	28,851	29,661	26,524	28,159	28,380	17,346
1984–85	32,182	40,269	30,392	25,330	21,159	23,557	28,670	32,240	33,344	28,891	32,028	32,278	19,460
1985–86	34,294	42,833	32,273	27,094	21,693	25,238	30,267	34,528	35,786	30,758	33,656	33,900	20,412
1987–88	38,112	47,735	35,823	30,086	23,645	27,652	32,747	38,314	39,898	33,477	37,603	37,817	22,641
1989–90	42,763	53,650	40,131	33,781	25,933	31,162	35,980	42,959	44,834	37,081	42,312	42,595	25,218
1990–91	45,065	56,549	42,239	35,636	27,388	32,398	38,036	45,084	47,168	38,787	45,019	45,319	25,937
1991–92	46,848	58,494	43,814	36,969	33,359	32,843	39,422	46,483	48,401	40,811	47,733	48,042	26,825
1992–93	47,866	59,972	44,855	37,842	29,583	32,512	39,365	47,175	49,392	40,725	49,518	49,837	27,402
1993–94	49,579	61,857	46,229	38,794	29,815	34,796	42,251	48,956	50,989	42,938	51,076	51,397	30,783
1994–95	51,228	64,046	47,705	39,923	30,528	35,082	43,103	50,629	52,874	44,020	52,653	53,036	29,639
1995–96	52,814	65,949	49,037	40,858	30,940	36,135	44,624	52,163	54,448	45,209	54,364	54,649	33,301
1996–97	54,465	68,214	50,457	41,864	31,738	36,932	45,688	53,737	56,162	46,393	56,185	56,453	34,736
1997–98	56,115	70,468	52,041	43,017	33,070	37,481	46,822	55,191	57,744	47,690	58,293	58,576	36,157
1998–99	58,048	73,260	53,830	44,650	34,741	38,976	47,610	57,038	59,805	48,961	60,392	60,641	38,040
1999–2000	60,084	76,478	55,939	46,414	35,854	40,202	48,788	58,984	62,030	50,033	62,631	62,905	38,636
2001–02	64,320	83,356	60,300	50,518	48,844	44,519	48,049	62,835	66,577	52,360	67,871	68,100	33,395
2002–03	66,126	86,191	62,226	52,441	50,272	45,469	47,412	64,564	68,322	53,962	69,726	69,976	34,291
2003–04	67,485	88,262	63,466	53,649	50,985	46,214	48,973	65,476	69,248	54,623	72,021	72,250	35,604
2004–05	69,337	91,290	65,394	55,215	51,380	46,929	50,102	67,130	71,145	55,398	74,318	74,540	34,970
2005–06	71,569	94,733	67,654	57,099	52,519	48,256	51,811	69,191	73,353	56,858	76,941	77,143	38,215
2006–07	74,167	98,563	70,168	59,150	55,061	49,641	53,665	71,797	76,072	58,971	79,491	79,663	41,196
2007–08	76,935	102,555	72,940	61,368	57,116	51,804	56,196	74,389	78,673	61,166	82,681	82,850	42,995

See notes at end of table.

Table 257. Average salary of full-time instructional faculty on 9-month contracts in degree-granting institutions, by academic rank, control and type of institution, and sex: Selected years, 1970–71 through 2007–08—Continued

Sex and academic year	All faculty	Academic rank						Public institutions			Private institutions		
		Professor	Associate professor	Assistant professor	Instructor	Lecturer	No rank	Total	4-year	2-year	Total	4-year	2-year
1	2	3	4	5	6	7	8	9	10	11	12	13	14
Females													
1972–73	11,925	17,123	13,827	11,510	10,098	10,775	11,913	12,250	12,300	12,165	11,044	11,219	8,888
1974–75	13,471	19,012	15,481	12,858	11,740	11,543	12,619	13,892	13,831	13,987	12,233	12,423	9,735
1975–76	14,308	20,308	16,364	13,522	12,572	11,901	14,094	14,762	14,758	14,769	13,030	13,231	10,201
1978–79	17,080	24,143	19,300	15,914	12,966	14,465	17,482	17,646	17,627	17,676	15,388	15,611	11,898
1979–80	18,396	25,910	20,642	16,974	13,750	15,142	19,069	19,042	18,985	19,134	16,539	16,787	12,541
1980–81	19,996	27,959	22,295	18,302	14,854	16,168	20,843	20,673	20,608	20,778	18,073	18,326	13,892
1981–82	21,802	30,438	24,271	19,866	16,054	17,676	22,672	22,524	22,454	22,632	19,743	20,024	14,984
1982–83	23,261	32,221	25,738	21,130	17,102	18,830	23,855	23,892	23,876	23,917	21,451	21,785	15,845
1984–85	25,941	35,824	28,517	23,575	19,362	21,004	26,050	26,566	26,813	26,172	24,186	24,560	17,575
1985–86	27,576	38,252	30,300	24,966	20,237	22,273	27,171	28,299	28,680	27,693	25,523	25,889	18,504
1987–88	30,499	42,371	33,528	27,600	21,962	24,370	29,605	31,215	31,820	30,228	28,621	28,946	21,215
1989–90	34,183	47,663	37,469	31,090	24,320	26,995	32,528	34,796	35,704	33,307	32,650	33,010	24,002
1990–91	35,881	49,728	39,329	32,724	25,534	28,111	34,179	36,459	37,573	34,720	34,359	34,898	22,585
1991–92	37,534	51,621	40,766	34,063	28,873	28,550	35,622	37,800	38,634	36,517	36,828	37,309	24,683
1992–93	38,385	52,755	41,861	35,032	27,700	28,922	35,792	38,356	39,470	36,710	38,460	38,987	25,068
1993–94	40,058	54,746	43,178	36,169	28,136	31,048	38,474	40,118	41,031	38,707	39,902	40,378	26,142
1994–95	41,369	56,555	44,626	37,352	29,072	31,677	38,967	41,548	42,663	39,812	40,908	41,815	22,851
1995–96	42,871	58,318	45,803	38,345	29,940	32,584	41,085	42,871	43,986	41,086	42,871	43,236	30,671
1996–97	44,325	60,160	47,101	39,350	30,819	33,415	42,474	44,306	45,402	42,531	44,374	44,726	30,661
1997–98	45,775	61,965	48,597	40,504	32,011	33,918	43,491	45,648	46,709	43,943	46,106	46,466	30,995
1998–99	47,421	64,236	50,347	41,894	33,152	35,115	44,723	47,247	48,355	45,457	47,874	48,204	31,524
1999–2000	48,997	67,079	52,091	43,367	34,228	36,607	45,865	48,714	50,168	46,340	49,737	50,052	32,951
2001–02	52,662	72,542	56,186	46,824	45,262	39,538	45,003	52,123	53,895	49,290	54,149	54,434	32,921
2002–03	54,105	75,028	57,716	48,380	46,573	40,265	45,251	53,435	55,121	50,717	55,881	56,158	35,296
2003–04	55,378	76,652	59,095	49,689	47,404	41,536	46,519	54,408	56,117	51,591	57,921	58,192	36,896
2004–05	56,926	79,160	60,809	51,154	48,351	42,455	47,860	55,700	57,714	52,568	59,919	60,143	39,291
2005–06	58,665	81,514	62,860	52,901	49,533	43,934	49,172	57,462	59,437	54,082	61,830	62,092	38,786
2006–07	61,016	85,090	65,237	54,974	51,832	45,693	50,812	59,781	61,875	56,127	64,246	64,481	41,099
2007–08	63,347	88,301	67,816	57,111	53,889	47,407	52,837	62,129	64,226	58,318	66,528	66,745	43,670
		Constant 2006–07 dollars[1]											
Total													
1970–71	65,312	92,280	69,699	57,431	48,097	57,534	63,378	66,565	67,428	64,975	59,705	60,762	44,522
1972–73	66,076	91,514	69,528	57,375	51,200	55,491	60,447	66,837	68,749	61,605	64,149	64,958	44,293
1974–75	61,574	83,863	63,640	52,401	50,020	49,566	53,337	62,586	64,134	58,718	58,774	59,485	40,368
1975–76	61,319	83,370	62,816	51,482	50,327	47,506	55,936	62,363	64,049	58,231	58,603	59,324	40,125
1978–79	59,067	78,885	59,744	48,798	39,316	45,538	55,802	60,136	61,754	56,157	56,048	56,651	37,240
1979–80	56,135	74,648	56,405	45,925	36,873	42,392	53,278	57,319	58,766	53,719	52,866	53,426	34,841
1980–81	54,913	72,472	54,705	44,542	35,768	40,771	52,632	55,957	57,437	52,262	52,064	52,610	35,502
1981–82	55,204	72,531	54,833	44,703	35,683	40,685	52,779	56,151	57,681	52,479	52,614	53,166	34,546
1982–83	56,564	73,918	55,992	45,873	36,608	41,747	53,155	57,171	58,845	53,176	54,894	55,513	34,515
1984–85	58,765	76,707	57,796	47,611	39,045	43,106	53,430	59,149	61,307	53,780	57,728	58,379	35,726
1985–86	60,767	79,294	59,632	49,295	39,242	44,592	54,568	61,438	63,845	55,510	58,909	59,528	36,461
1987–88	63,258	82,895	62,085	51,298	40,051	45,776	55,567	63,847	66,682	56,759	61,764	62,287	38,534
1989–90	64,522	84,902	63,331	52,554	40,241	46,608	55,560	64,977	68,110	57,099	63,446	64,015	39,551
1990–91	64,275	84,663	63,129	52,490	40,139	45,879	55,479	64,507	67,849	56,485	63,700	64,365	36,719
1991–92	64,770	84,830	63,407	52,797	45,664	44,984	55,807	64,459	67,408	57,544	65,544	66,160	37,920
1992–93	64,044	84,201	62,942	52,458	40,819	43,746	54,099	63,303	66,623	55,766	65,864	66,498	37,390
1993–94	64,731	84,674	63,213	52,537	40,248	45,693	56,661	64,111	67,041	57,297	66,268	66,846	39,699
1994–95	64,891	85,110	63,401	52,601	40,262	45,057	55,954	64,376	67,505	57,141	66,152	67,018	34,762
1995–96	65,152	85,276	63,376	52,450	40,094	45,103	56,809	64,528	67,613	57,205	66,680	67,146	42,169
1996–97	65,297	85,633	63,342	52,267	40,072	44,913	56,781	64,621	67,723	57,274	66,945	67,370	41,915
1997–98	66,053	86,747	64,151	52,794	40,954	44,785	57,133	65,173	68,299	57,956	68,204	68,633	42,397
1998–99	67,115	88,486	65,227	53,780	41,957	45,679	57,380	66,150	69,411	58,663	69,453	69,828	43,200
1999–2000	67,392	89,726	65,746	54,236	42,105	46,056	57,143	66,335	69,877	58,170	69,954	70,328	43,319
2001–02	68,440	92,556	67,275	55,901	53,796	47,885	53,350	67,045	71,042	58,239	71,964	72,275	37,964
2002–03	68,749	93,563	67,786	56,668	54,147	47,778	51,944	67,274	71,166	58,661	72,340	72,655	39,039
2003–04	68,647	93,608	67,733	56,821	53,823	47,881	52,353	66,777	70,580	58,223	73,131	73,422	39,844
2004–05	68,405	93,882	67,685	56,769	52,959	47,404	52,120	66,393	70,341	57,434	73,219	73,475	39,753
2005–06	67,883	93,567	67,413	56,531	52,199	47,083	51,729	65,817	69,708	56,838	72,853	73,106	39,545
2006–07	68,585	94,870	68,153	57,143	53,278	47,478	52,161	66,566	70,460	57,466	73,419	73,636	41,138
2007–08	68,545	95,027	68,295	57,176	53,349	47,627	52,461	66,517	70,254	57,515	73,412	73,614	41,852

See notes at end of table.

Table 257. Average salary of full-time instructional faculty on 9-month contracts in degree-granting institutions, by academic rank, control and type of institution, and sex: Selected years, 1970–71 through 2007–08—Continued

Sex and academic year	All faculty	Academic rank						Public institutions			Private institutions		
		Professor	Associate professor	Assistant professor	Instructor	Lecturer	No rank	Total	4-year	2-year	Total	4-year	2-year
1	2	3	4	5	6	7	8	9	10	11	12	13	14
Males													
1972–73	68,774	92,580	70,210	58,145	53,157	57,727	62,217	69,362	71,262	63,271	67,314	67,968	45,641
1974–75	64,257	84,868	64,174	53,046	52,618	52,153	55,212	65,121	66,682	60,502	61,918	62,479	41,910
1975–76	64,099	84,301	63,344	52,175	53,116	49,983	58,015	65,010	66,701	60,145	61,782	62,376	41,881
1978–79	61,917	79,651	60,260	49,475	40,055	47,465	57,813	62,822	64,455	58,038	59,408	59,858	38,884
1979–80	58,885	75,394	56,932	46,595	37,663	44,522	54,959	59,925	61,400	55,564	56,055	56,461	36,651
1980–81	57,734	73,247	55,264	45,310	36,633	43,080	54,602	58,615	60,114	54,119	55,363	55,778	37,882
1981–82	58,126	73,316	55,429	45,607	36,672	42,779	54,828	58,890	60,442	54,414	56,071	56,478	36,516
1982–83	59,617	74,783	56,701	46,976	37,770	44,145	55,201	60,006	61,691	55,166	58,567	59,026	36,077
1984–85	62,114	77,722	58,659	48,889	40,838	45,467	55,335	62,226	64,356	55,762	61,816	62,299	37,559
1985–86	64,335	80,354	60,543	50,828	40,696	47,346	56,780	64,774	67,134	57,701	63,138	63,596	38,292
1987–88	67,161	84,118	63,128	53,019	41,667	48,729	57,707	67,517	70,309	58,994	66,264	66,642	39,898
1989–90	68,751	86,253	64,518	54,310	41,692	50,099	57,845	69,065	72,080	59,616	68,026	68,479	40,544
1990–91	68,696	86,201	64,387	54,321	41,750	49,386	57,980	68,725	71,901	59,126	68,626	69,083	39,537
1991–92	69,196	86,397	64,715	54,604	49,272	48,511	58,227	68,657	71,490	60,280	70,503	70,959	39,621
1992–93	68,558	85,898	64,246	54,201	42,372	46,567	56,383	67,568	70,745	58,330	70,925	71,382	39,247
1993–94	69,218	86,360	64,542	54,161	41,626	48,579	58,988	68,349	71,187	59,947	71,309	71,757	42,978
1994–95	69,528	86,925	64,747	54,184	41,434	47,614	58,501	68,715	71,762	59,745	71,462	71,982	40,227
1995–96	69,782	87,138	64,792	53,985	40,881	47,745	58,962	68,922	71,941	59,734	71,830	72,207	44,000
1996–97	69,967	87,630	64,818	53,780	40,772	47,444	58,692	69,032	72,147	59,597	72,177	72,521	44,623
1997–98	70,824	88,939	65,682	54,292	41,739	47,306	59,095	69,658	72,880	60,191	73,573	73,931	45,635
1998–99	72,017	90,890	66,783	55,394	43,101	48,355	59,068	70,764	74,197	60,743	74,925	75,234	47,195
1999–2000	72,451	92,220	67,453	55,967	43,234	48,477	58,830	71,124	74,798	60,332	75,522	75,853	46,589
2001–02	73,686	95,493	69,080	57,874	55,956	51,002	55,046	71,984	76,271	59,984	77,753	78,015	38,257
2002–03	74,126	96,618	69,753	58,785	56,353	50,969	53,148	72,374	76,587	60,490	78,161	78,441	38,439
2003–04	74,029	96,821	69,621	58,851	55,929	50,695	53,722	71,825	75,963	59,920	79,005	79,256	39,057
2004–05	73,839	97,217	69,639	58,800	54,716	49,976	53,355	71,488	75,764	58,995	79,143	79,380	37,240
2005–06	73,420	97,183	69,403	58,575	53,877	49,504	53,151	70,980	75,250	58,328	78,931	79,138	39,204
2006–07	74,167	98,563	70,168	59,150	55,061	49,641	53,665	71,797	76,072	58,971	79,491	79,663	41,196
2007–08	74,187	98,891	70,334	59,176	55,075	49,953	54,188	71,731	75,863	58,980	79,727	79,890	41,459
Females													
1972–73	56,865	81,652	65,935	54,887	48,155	51,381	56,811	58,418	58,656	58,009	52,666	53,499	42,382
1974–75	53,095	74,935	61,020	50,679	46,274	45,496	49,736	54,753	54,515	55,130	48,217	48,965	38,370
1975–76	52,665	74,753	60,234	49,773	46,276	43,805	51,879	54,340	54,325	54,363	47,964	48,702	37,548
1978–79	50,901	71,949	57,517	47,424	38,640	43,106	52,099	52,587	52,531	52,675	45,858	46,524	35,456
1979–80	48,373	68,132	54,278	44,633	36,157	39,817	50,144	50,071	49,921	50,315	43,489	44,142	32,976
1980–81	47,122	65,887	52,540	43,130	35,005	38,101	49,118	48,717	48,564	48,965	42,590	43,187	32,737
1981–82	47,293	66,026	52,648	43,093	34,824	38,343	49,180	48,858	48,707	49,093	42,826	43,435	32,503
1982–83	48,380	67,015	53,531	43,947	35,570	39,164	49,615	49,692	49,659	49,744	44,615	45,310	32,955
1984–85	50,068	69,143	55,040	45,501	37,370	40,539	50,278	51,274	51,751	50,514	46,681	47,403	33,921
1985–86	51,732	71,760	56,842	46,836	37,964	41,784	50,972	53,088	53,803	51,951	47,881	48,567	34,713
1987–88	53,746	74,667	59,083	48,637	38,701	42,945	52,170	55,007	56,074	53,268	50,436	51,009	37,385
1989–90	54,956	76,627	60,239	49,983	39,099	43,401	52,296	55,942	57,402	53,547	52,491	53,070	38,588
1990–91	54,695	75,804	59,952	49,883	38,923	42,852	52,101	55,577	57,275	52,926	52,375	53,197	34,428
1991–92	55,439	76,246	60,212	50,312	42,647	42,169	52,615	55,832	57,064	53,937	54,396	55,106	36,458
1992–93	54,978	75,561	59,957	50,177	39,675	41,425	51,264	54,937	56,532	52,580	55,086	55,840	35,904
1993–94	55,927	76,433	60,282	50,496	39,282	43,347	53,714	56,010	57,284	54,040	55,709	56,372	36,498
1994–95	56,148	76,758	60,568	50,695	39,458	42,992	52,887	56,390	57,903	54,034	55,521	56,752	31,014
1995–96	56,645	77,054	60,519	50,665	39,559	43,053	54,285	56,645	58,118	54,287	56,645	57,127	40,526
1996–97	56,941	77,283	60,508	50,550	39,591	42,926	54,564	56,916	58,325	54,636	57,004	57,457	39,388
1997–98	57,774	78,207	61,336	51,121	40,402	42,809	54,891	57,613	58,952	55,462	58,192	58,646	39,120
1998–99	58,832	79,694	62,463	51,975	41,130	43,565	55,485	58,617	59,991	56,396	59,395	59,804	39,110
1999–2000	59,082	80,886	62,813	52,294	41,273	44,142	55,305	58,741	60,494	55,878	59,975	60,355	39,733
2001–02	60,330	83,104	64,367	53,642	51,852	45,294	51,555	59,712	61,743	56,467	62,034	62,360	37,714
2002–03	60,650	84,104	64,699	54,232	52,207	45,136	50,725	59,899	61,789	56,853	62,641	62,952	39,566
2003–04	60,748	84,085	64,826	54,508	52,001	45,564	51,030	59,684	61,559	56,594	63,538	63,835	40,474
2004–05	60,622	84,299	64,757	54,475	51,490	45,211	50,967	59,402	61,461	55,979	63,809	64,048	41,842
2005–06	60,182	83,622	64,485	54,269	50,814	45,070	50,444	58,948	60,974	55,481	63,429	63,698	39,789
2006–07	61,016	85,090	65,237	54,974	51,832	45,693	50,812	59,781	61,875	56,127	64,246	64,481	41,099
2007–08	61,084	85,146	65,393	55,071	51,963	45,713	50,949	59,909	61,931	56,235	64,151	64,361	42,110

[1]Constant dollars based on the Consumer Price Index, prepared by the Bureau of Labor Statistics, U.S. Department of Labor, adjusted to an academic-year basis.
NOTE: Data through 1995–96 are for institutions of higher education, while later data are for degree-granting institutions. Degree-granting institutions grant associate's or higher degrees and participate in Title IV federal financial aid programs. The degree-granting classification is very similar to the earlier higher education classification, but it includes more 2-year colleges and excludes a few higher education institutions that did not grant degrees.

(See Guide to Sources for details.) Data for 1987–88 and later years include imputations for nonrespondent institutions.
SOURCE: U.S. Department of Education, National Center for Education Statistics, Higher Education General Information Survey (HEGIS), "Faculty Salaries, Tenure, and Fringe Benefits" surveys, 1970–71 through 1985–86; and 1987–88 through 2007–08 Integrated Postsecondary Education Data System, "Salaries, Tenure, and Fringe Benefits of Full-Time Instructional Faculty Survey" (IPEDS-SA:87–99), and Winter 2001–02 through Winter 2007–08. (This table was prepared October 2008.)

Table 258. Average salary of full-time instructional faculty on 9-month contracts in degree-granting institutions, by sex, academic rank, and control and type of institution: Selected years, 1999–2000 through 2007–08

[In current dollars]

Academic year, control and type of institution	All faculty			Academic rank									No academic rank
				Professor			Associate professor			Assistant professor	Instructor	Lecturer	
	Total	Males	Females	Total	Males	Females	Total	Males	Females				
1	2	3	4	5	6	7	8	9	10	11	12	13	14
1999–2000													
All institutions	$55,888	$60,084	$48,997	$74,410	$76,478	$67,079	$54,524	$55,939	$52,091	$44,978	$34,918	$38,194	$47,389
Public	55,011	58,984	48,714	72,475	74,501	65,568	54,641	55,992	52,305	45,285	35,007	37,403	47,990
4-year	57,950	62,030	50,168	75,204	76,530	69,619	55,681	56,776	53,599	45,822	33,528	37,261	40,579
Doctoral[1]	62,686	67,294	52,605	81,651	82,900	75,116	57,938	59,190	55,332	48,438	33,334	39,184	39,068
Master's[2]	52,664	55,505	48,068	66,505	67,062	64,715	53,001	53,665	51,888	43,394	33,223	34,208	42,995
Other 4-year	48,280	50,263	44,957	61,327	61,653	60,236	49,888	50,390	48,987	42,304	35,829	36,007	38,345
2-year	48,240	50,033	46,340	57,806	59,441	55,501	48,056	49,425	46,711	41,984	37,634	40,061	48,233
Not-for-profit	58,172	62,788	49,881	78,512	80,557	70,609	54,300	55,836	51,687	44,423	34,670	40,761	41,415
4-year	58,425	63,028	50,117	78,604	80,622	70,774	54,388	55,898	51,809	44,502	34,813	40,783	41,761
Doctoral[1]	74,347	79,678	61,442	97,751	99,341	89,614	63,780	65,347	60,477	53,946	41,820	43,538	46,135
Master's[2]	51,202	54,326	46,413	65,331	66,591	61,378	51,202	52,474	49,167	41,922	33,913	37,266	44,364
Other 4-year	47,743	49,962	44,218	62,007	62,613	59,974	47,285	47,564	46,876	38,937	31,978	33,531	34,809
2-year	37,583	39,933	34,733	39,454	38,431	40,571	36,349	37,342	35,608	31,818	27,696	25,965	40,373
For-profit	29,543	30,023	28,942	45,505	44,248	49,693	48,469	53,548	43,389	33,043	29,894	—	27,958
2001–02													
All institutions	59,742	64,320	52,662	80,792	83,356	72,542	58,724	60,300	56,186	48,796	46,959	41,798	46,569
Public	58,524	62,835	52,123	78,387	80,921	70,564	58,663	60,182	56,220	48,956	48,279	40,809	46,772
4-year	62,013	66,577	53,895	81,726	83,363	75,471	60,041	61,275	57,864	49,697	36,820	40,361	53,777
Doctoral[1]	67,466	72,667	56,888	89,087	90,612	81,891	62,756	64,209	59,982	52,900	36,830	41,806	59,090
Master's[2]	55,804	58,793	51,309	71,330	71,939	69,575	56,881	57,530	55,856	46,707	36,351	38,632	41,032
Other 4-year	50,137	52,328	46,697	64,117	64,790	62,060	52,374	53,158	51,074	44,982	38,927	35,319	39,308
2-year	50,837	52,360	49,290	60,614	62,426	58,337	50,436	51,647	49,282	44,487	52,505	45,610	45,756
Not-for-profit	62,947	67,997	54,271	85,867	88,323	77,203	58,871	60,545	56,163	48,504	37,637	44,762	46,043
4-year	63,189	68,212	54,515	86,009	88,424	77,447	58,969	60,624	56,284	48,616	37,981	44,794	46,888
Doctoral[1]	80,193	86,125	66,467	106,925	108,606	98,797	69,302	70,937	66,025	59,390	43,262	47,065	51,461
Master's[2]	54,850	58,035	50,268	70,234	71,594	66,435	55,206	56,574	53,177	45,328	38,823	39,649	49,832
Other 4-year	51,357	53,517	48,033	67,474	68,148	65,483	51,029	51,385	50,521	41,938	33,732	40,348	39,106
2-year	33,595	33,785	33,419	40,221	39,661	40,840	38,481	38,860	38,149	31,096	30,617	23,484	33,614
For-profit	33,891	35,773	31,539	54,882	74,425	38,346	43,124	48,298	39,286	33,884	29,957	—	31,987
2005–06													
All institutions	66,172	71,569	58,665	91,208	94,733	81,514	65,714	67,654	62,860	55,106	50,883	45,896	50,425
Public	64,158	69,191	57,462	87,599	91,080	78,412	65,107	67,077	62,231	55,029	52,297	44,628	50,096
4-year	67,951	73,353	59,437	91,600	93,976	83,946	66,745	68,475	64,013	56,181	40,044	44,598	47,107
Doctoral[1]	73,985	80,186	62,865	100,403	102,366	92,511	70,259	72,242	66,876	59,777	39,961	45,422	46,126
Master's[2]	60,338	63,599	55,992	77,776	78,734	75,465	62,045	62,996	60,709	52,352	39,424	43,241	45,777
Other 4-year	56,117	58,617	52,836	72,348	74,162	68,815	59,091	60,179	57,427	49,860	42,287	43,941	51,912
2-year	55,405	56,858	54,082	65,740	67,782	63,544	54,870	55,825	54,004	48,425	57,224	45,427	50,513
Not-for-profit	71,203	77,136	61,985	98,253	101,638	88,144	66,877	68,753	64,074	55,278	41,302	49,777	53,231
4-year	71,419	77,314	62,212	98,378	101,713	88,379	66,981	68,818	64,226	55,367	41,494	49,786	53,907
Doctoral[1]	89,278	96,862	74,490	122,784	125,275	112,800	78,684	81,043	74,518	67,151	46,016	51,647	55,222
Master's[2]	61,186	64,596	56,637	78,400	80,151	74,214	61,777	63,056	60,038	50,948	41,530	45,110	57,098
Other 4-year	58,344	60,800	54,868	76,571	77,504	74,285	57,964	58,039	57,860	47,877	38,394	45,837	45,605
2-year	39,101	38,817	39,307	47,174	48,786	45,945	42,433	43,628	41,753	35,437	36,264	38,908	39,399
For-profit	42,480	42,878	42,027	60,111	59,423	61,417	56,621	55,546	58,393	47,598	35,661	—	41,579
2007–08													
All institutions	71,085	76,935	63,347	98,548	102,555	88,301	70,826	72,940	67,816	59,294	55,325	49,392	54,405
Public	68,981	74,389	62,129	94,723	98,753	84,839	70,289	72,373	67,353	59,433	56,934	47,840	53,552
4-year	72,857	78,673	64,226	99,092	101,952	90,663	72,079	73,894	69,327	60,766	43,927	47,812	51,177
Doctoral[1]	79,165	85,985	67,719	108,727	110,982	100,390	75,823	77,967	72,317	64,545	43,279	47,936	50,108
Master's[2]	64,908	68,220	60,757	84,110	85,157	81,818	67,116	67,977	65,957	56,727	42,201	47,708	50,202
Other 4-year	59,515	61,692	56,768	73,901	76,668	69,301	62,785	63,714	61,455	53,208	50,222	46,591	54,092
2-year	59,646	61,166	58,318	69,905	71,845	67,931	58,354	59,289	57,533	51,607	62,646	48,652	53,965
Not-for-profit	76,289	82,853	66,655	106,056	109,775	95,725	71,867	74,016	68,744	59,042	44,666	54,023	59,772
4-year	76,471	83,008	66,834	106,162	109,843	95,906	71,952	74,082	68,848	59,125	44,785	54,033	60,132
Doctoral[1]	93,742	102,556	78,277	131,417	134,431	120,488	84,164	87,143	79,185	70,023	49,025	56,288	64,028
Master's[2]	64,760	68,274	60,296	82,946	84,728	79,017	65,075	66,371	63,392	53,942	44,814	49,252	60,114
Other 4-year	62,909	65,512	59,359	83,437	84,067	81,980	62,525	62,580	62,447	51,356	40,944	48,342	51,660
2-year	44,318	43,229	45,072	52,077	53,951	50,488	48,563	46,818	49,684	41,308	41,046	34,622	46,027
For-profit	47,246	48,932	45,121	55,400	55,365	55,473	60,719	66,938	55,388	51,813	38,788	—	35,862

—Not available.

[1]Institutions that awarded 20 or more doctor's degrees during the previous academic year.

[2]Institutions that awarded 20 or more master's degrees, but less than 20 doctor's degrees, during the previous academic year.

NOTE: Degree-granting institutions grant associate's or higher degrees and participate in Title IV federal financial aid programs.

SOURCE: U.S. Department of Education, National Center for Education Statistics, 1999–2000 through 2007–08 Integrated Postsecondary Education Data System, "Salaries, Tenure, and Fringe Benefits of Full-Time Instructional Faculty Survey" (IPEDS-SA:99), and Winter 2001–02 through Winter 2007–08. (This table was prepared October 2008.)

Table 259. Average salary of full-time instructional faculty on 9-month contracts in degree-granting institutions, by control and type of institution and state or jurisdiction: 2006–07

[In current dollars]

State or jurisdiction	All institu-tions	Public institutions Total	Public 4-year Total	Public 4-year Doctoral[1]	Public 4-year Master's[2]	Public 4-year Other	Public 2-year	Not-for-profit Total	Not-for-profit 4-year Total	Not-for-profit 4-year Doctoral[1]	Not-for-profit 4-year Master's[2]	Not-for-profit 4-year Other	Not-for-profit 2-year	For-profit institutions
1	2	3	4	5	6	7	8	9	10	11	12	13	14	15
United States	$68,585	$66,566	$70,460	$76,921	$62,298	$59,057	$57,466	$73,581	$73,769	$91,291	$62,518	$60,500	$42,043	$46,053
Alabama	59,770	61,275	66,081	74,593	56,347	62,794	49,532	51,667	51,667	64,460	52,658	40,041	†	†
Alaska	61,861	62,694	62,629	64,251	61,496	†	72,865	47,355	47,355	†	51,310	37,961	†	†
Arizona	71,965	72,220	77,243	78,802	65,007	66,957	63,628	61,562	61,562	†	65,760	56,933	†	†
Arkansas	52,062	52,266	56,690	62,198	50,443	51,835	41,526	50,914	51,165	†	52,723	49,950	26,814	†
California	80,843	79,122	81,796	95,397	70,081	69,953	76,114	87,836	87,950	98,319	73,091	80,755	59,976	78,566
Colorado	63,281	62,285	66,209	72,767	53,113	51,469	44,582	69,531	69,531	72,055	67,820	48,364	†	†
Connecticut	83,336	78,435	82,998	93,230	72,791	†	64,740	89,272	89,272	102,964	78,867	68,564	†	43,854
Delaware	79,208	79,532	83,758	85,856	64,908	†	61,852	76,162	76,162	58,121	92,816	†	†	†
District of Columbia	81,791	71,442	71,442	†	69,938	79,879	†	83,489	83,489	84,048	76,680	†	†	47,660
Florida	65,065	64,937	70,234	74,011	62,297	60,068	50,621	65,243	65,243	76,312	64,047	49,412	†	82,742
Georgia	62,839	61,588	64,564	75,190	54,312	49,951	43,324	66,395	66,582	92,851	59,006	50,812	51,781	†
Hawaii	66,635	67,462	71,589	75,582	†	57,647	57,933	63,275	63,275	†	58,651	78,288	†	†
Idaho	54,070	54,675	55,661	57,434	55,965	42,519	49,217	47,260	47,260	†	46,563	47,810	†	†
Illinois	70,404	66,256	68,723	74,186	57,091	†	61,757	76,943	77,105	94,231	62,692	55,206	37,858	24,234
Indiana	65,052	64,808	67,966	72,867	55,391	52,910	42,901	65,582	65,741	90,663	57,282	55,518	40,023	35,347
Iowa	61,109	64,789	74,060	77,504	62,470	†	46,661	55,009	55,009	55,497	52,328	56,420	†	†
Kansas	58,274	60,739	66,825	71,879	55,738	51,521	46,308	42,954	43,410	†	46,970	37,475	34,936	†
Kentucky	56,845	58,316	62,394	73,170	56,441	†	48,188	50,613	50,613	57,906	45,468	52,679	†	†
Louisiana	56,546	55,663	57,562	63,670	50,053	55,787	44,589	60,963	60,963	64,394	62,336	49,818	†	†
Maine	63,082	58,878	60,937	66,577	64,721	50,886	51,415	69,846	70,070	†	52,967	77,852	51,030	†
Maryland	69,179	67,656	71,421	83,365	60,936	61,073	60,762	74,222	74,222	88,795	59,700	65,201	†	†
Massachusetts	85,179	71,086	76,905	86,304	67,214	71,727	56,351	91,648	91,800	104,004	75,740	75,371	44,816	43,033
Michigan	72,106	74,322	75,205	81,982	61,206	52,714	70,544	59,466	59,466	41,145	58,049	60,699	†	†
Minnesota	65,826	67,608	74,139	95,702	63,189	57,904	57,818	61,709	61,725	62,193	57,713	63,444	46,965	‡
Mississippi	52,277	52,717	57,986	60,180	48,785	†	45,886	48,322	48,322	†	52,084	38,392	†	†
Missouri	61,001	58,962	61,508	70,719	54,570	53,916	50,812	65,178	65,502	88,400	50,788	46,920	45,082	53,542
Montana	52,901	54,499	56,783	59,833	51,084	45,134	39,438	42,731	44,341	†	42,633	45,328	29,845	†
Nebraska	59,691	61,745	66,528	76,404	58,258	†	45,663	54,312	54,376	66,285	50,962	46,711	34,360	†
Nevada	72,581	72,723	74,268	80,293	†	60,163	61,097	59,057	59,057	†	59,057	†	†	†
New Hampshire	70,125	68,214	74,202	79,914	64,824	66,116	46,913	73,975	73,975	88,121	63,019	57,354	†	42,110
New Jersey	82,559	80,743	86,547	94,185	81,386	†	66,371	87,070	87,070	103,753	66,738	63,176	†	38,139
New Mexico	57,946	57,625	63,062	69,279	52,760	40,650	44,999	64,721	64,721	†	68,479	60,512	†	†
New York	76,918	71,056	74,337	86,054	71,454	65,323	64,478	82,704	82,934	94,461	64,596	73,775	44,065	41,570
North Carolina	60,919	58,457	70,680	75,940	63,704	60,194	43,013	68,888	69,071	91,893	52,775	50,741	37,289	†
North Dakota	50,399	51,834	54,564	58,899	46,641	43,397	40,469	41,791	43,661	†	45,556	41,923	32,908	†
Ohio	65,507	67,000	70,691	72,604	64,265	55,838	54,322	62,301	62,357	76,192	56,061	61,994	51,749	29,621
Oklahoma	58,120	58,433	62,085	70,720	54,129	45,015	45,505	56,810	56,810	63,602	56,534	40,925	†	‡
Oregon	59,944	59,130	60,913	64,478	48,877	51,893	56,707	62,441	62,441	56,967	65,046	61,348	†	†
Pennsylvania	73,112	71,254	74,028	82,044	70,075	60,440	56,006	75,323	75,606	96,017	62,897	67,241	42,962	37,257
Rhode Island	77,582	68,594	71,993	78,161	60,921	†	57,407	83,430	83,430	102,503	72,142	79,242	†	†
South Carolina	57,941	59,066	66,001	74,854	57,825	51,851	44,544	52,827	52,997	†	60,439	48,920	42,454	†
South Dakota	52,532	54,228	56,877	58,575	57,363	40,023	41,264	46,125	46,125	†	46,961	45,669	28,380	34,333
Tennessee	59,855	58,674	62,640	65,151	58,169	†	45,774	62,371	62,558	82,564	46,599	50,557	28,380	‡
Texas	63,709	62,671	68,262	74,252	58,165	45,825	50,598	68,661	68,839	80,522	64,056	52,210	32,328	‡
Utah	65,763	60,184	63,204	70,560	54,667	54,399	45,802	81,097	81,419	83,802	60,590	†	52,430	†
Vermont	64,256	62,444	62,444	69,186	50,180	47,037	†	65,948	69,176	†	73,764	52,111	39,644	†
Virginia	66,950	69,492	74,723	81,927	60,899	63,124	51,509	59,399	59,399	57,486	60,953	58,429	†	†
Washington	67,453	68,542	81,927	89,376	65,744	53,453	50,579	63,163	63,163	†	63,299	62,079	†	40,987
West Virginia	53,951	55,810	57,430	66,896	54,921	50,444	43,635	44,730	44,730	49,223	43,917	43,585	†	†
Wisconsin	64,208	65,578	65,241	77,761	55,885	†	66,126	58,652	58,751	73,225	53,427	52,587	45,233	†
Wyoming	58,362	58,362	68,282	68,282	†	†	47,891	†	†	†	†	†	†	†
U.S. Service Academies	108,062	108,062	108,062	†	†	108,062	†	†	†	†	†	†	†	†
Other jurisdictions	52,930	53,257	57,251	†	62,017	51,719	29,600	28,527	28,527	24,472	30,435	†	†	†
American Samoa	28,461	28,461	†	†	†	†	28,461	†	†	†	†	†	†	†
Federated States of Micronesia	21,373	21,373	†	†	†	†	21,373	†	†	†	†	†	†	†
Guam	53,436	53,436	57,538	†	57,538	†	45,579	†	†	†	†	†	†	†
Marshall Islands	27,188	27,188	†	†	†	†	27,188	†	†	†	†	†	†	†
Northern Marianas	41,174	41,174	41,174	†	†	41,174	†	†	†	†	†	†	†	†
Palau	17,079	17,079	†	†	†	†	17,079	†	†	†	†	†	†	†
Puerto Rico	56,942	57,482	57,482	†	63,319	52,338	†	28,527	28,527	24,472	30,435	†	†	†
U.S. Virgin Islands	60,214	60,214	60,214	†	60,214	†	†	†	†	†	†	†	†	†

†Not applicable.
‡Reporting standards not met.
[1]Institutions that awarded 20 or more doctor's degrees during the previous academic year.
[2]Institutions that awarded 20 or more master's degrees, but less than 20 doctor's degrees, during the previous academic year.

NOTE: Degree-granting institutions grant associate's or higher degrees and participate in Title IV federal financial aid programs. Data include imputations for nonrespondent institutions.
SOURCE: U.S. Department of Education, National Center for Education Statistics, 2006–07 Integrated Postsecondary Education Data System (IPEDS), Winter 2006–07. (This table was prepared August 2007.)

Table 260. Average salary of full-time instructional faculty on 9-month contracts in degree-granting institutions, by control and type of institution and state or jurisdiction: 2005–06

[In current dollars]

State or jurisdiction	All institu-tions	Public institutions						Not-for-profit institutions						For-profit institutions
		Total	4-year institutions				2-year	Total	4-year institutions				2-year	
			Total	Doctoral[1]	Master's[2]	Other			Total	Doctoral[1]	Master's[2]	Other		
1	2	3	4	5	6	7	8	9	10	11	12	13	14	15
United States	$66,172	$64,158	$67,951	$73,985	$60,338	$56,117	$55,405	$71,203	$71,419	$89,278	$61,186	$58,344	$39,101	$42,480
Alabama	56,542	57,677	61,908	69,453	53,242	62,285	47,094	50,515	50,708	62,981	49,506	45,149	31,315	†
Alaska	59,309	60,029	59,966	62,188	58,439	†	69,531	47,154	47,154	†	50,851	37,540	†	†
Arizona	69,344	69,893	74,324	75,208	60,540	†	62,495	59,850	59,850	†	62,570	55,753	†	44,418
Arkansas	50,398	50,655	55,027	59,926	49,446	49,170	40,094	48,978	49,216	†	50,434	48,271	26,560	†
California	78,292	76,730	80,576	92,260	70,754	71,119	72,402	84,702	84,811	94,955	71,900	77,788	60,556	63,078
Colorado	61,734	60,715	64,440	71,089	50,881	50,571	44,013	68,710	68,710	70,366	69,261	46,645	†	‡
Connecticut	80,368	75,255	79,452	89,268	69,711	†	62,198	86,463	86,463	99,253	77,018	66,473	†	44,501
Delaware	76,668	77,123	80,529	82,710	62,494	†	61,199	72,557	72,557	56,848	86,453	†	†	†
District of Columbia	79,713	68,037	68,037	†	66,385	76,663	†	81,706	81,706	82,414	74,541	†	†	44,100
Florida	62,485	62,375	67,730	70,501	56,167	58,496	49,933	62,701	62,701	73,491	60,879	47,895	†	75,216
Georgia	61,093	60,111	63,242	73,427	53,103	50,051	42,991	63,821	63,974	88,424	55,659	51,505	51,470	†
Hawaii	64,403	64,869	69,127	72,846	†	55,501	55,318	62,541	62,541	†	57,148	78,254	†	†
Idaho	51,057	51,596	52,633	52,950	54,219	44,184	46,269	45,324	45,324	†	45,138	45,497	†	†
Illinois	68,314	64,623	67,029	72,055	56,408	†	60,270	74,172	74,326	97,883	62,537	53,770	34,491	19,867
Indiana	63,341	63,187	66,223	70,896	54,255	52,907	41,809	63,693	63,854	85,224	56,548	53,966	37,640	34,133
Iowa	58,504	61,896	70,701	73,669	61,382	†	44,943	53,253	53,293	53,736	51,944	53,907	45,057	38,479
Kansas	56,527	58,781	64,701	69,719	53,931	53,664	45,215	41,771	42,344	†	44,782	39,481	33,873	†
Kentucky	55,386	56,760	60,891	71,458	55,038	†	46,462	49,509	49,509	55,902	44,110	51,070	†	†
Louisiana	55,146	53,315	55,259	60,260	48,569	53,010	41,040	66,574	66,574	70,935	67,404	45,267	†	†
Maine	60,601	55,810	57,862	63,119	61,105	48,682	49,412	67,883	68,105	†	51,932	75,141	47,393	†
Maryland	66,871	65,237	68,649	79,984	59,090	58,610	59,168	72,101	72,101	91,401	61,952	48,134	†	†
Massachusetts	81,355	66,515	71,938	82,645	60,944	†	52,737	88,137	88,279	99,692	73,514	72,071	42,881	45,295
Michigan	70,308	72,473	73,103	79,699	59,564	52,066	69,814	58,048	58,132	37,305	55,850	60,201	32,233	†
Minnesota	64,140	66,104	71,604	90,410	62,545	54,562	57,718	59,651	59,684	64,466	56,349	60,388	40,993	37,093
Mississippi	49,182	49,472	54,085	56,082	45,882	†	43,596	46,557	46,557	†	50,351	37,432	†	†
Missouri	58,962	57,029	59,327	68,819	52,393	52,103	49,650	62,859	63,262	81,881	51,454	46,587	40,100	55,711
Montana	51,192	52,588	54,597	57,448	48,156	43,465	39,199	42,117	43,808	†	39,671	44,559	29,128	†
Nebraska	58,204	60,446	65,152	74,419	57,349	†	44,472	52,001	52,052	62,715	50,436	44,939	‡	†
Nevada	69,790	69,868	71,063	76,905	†	57,184	60,872	61,679	61,679	†	†	61,679	†	†
New Hampshire	68,522	66,901	73,406	79,727	63,403	66,867	44,249	71,922	71,922	92,328	62,095	54,319	†	41,261
New Jersey	78,502	76,587	81,181	88,981	75,769	†	65,320	83,323	83,376	96,078	63,889	61,936	45,607	36,304
New Mexico	56,415	56,141	60,957	65,618	51,648	38,167	43,945	62,199	62,199	†	62,199	†	†	†
New York	73,760	67,098	70,043	82,230	66,976	62,581	61,314	80,451	80,664	93,626	63,123	70,804	41,721	36,884
North Carolina	57,638	55,024	66,324	70,925	60,001	57,101	40,989	65,967	66,139	87,638	51,399	48,575	36,808	†
North Dakota	47,422	48,671	51,140	54,446	46,714	41,333	38,853	40,072	41,993	†	43,250	40,839	31,881	†
Ohio	63,592	65,071	68,547	70,169	65,363	54,664	53,139	60,575	60,656	80,304	56,338	59,104	48,541	20,342
Oklahoma	54,515	54,741	58,002	65,507	51,591	41,464	43,243	53,579	53,579	61,265	53,651	36,006	†	†
Oregon	57,589	56,604	58,828	62,509	46,617	51,099	53,636	60,945	60,945	54,728	63,729	60,400	†	†
Pennsylvania	70,936	69,305	71,745	80,175	67,136	59,142	55,508	72,919	73,264	94,752	61,902	64,592	40,319	37,555
Rhode Island	75,146	66,547	70,076	75,570	60,173	†	55,184	80,879	80,879	100,267	69,127	99,874	†	†
South Carolina	56,472	57,702	64,592	71,337	56,914	51,432	43,594	50,850	51,156	†	56,708	47,113	37,313	†
South Dakota	50,822	52,266	54,513	56,790	54,935	38,425	41,164	45,324	45,324	†	47,502	39,532	†	34,885
Tennessee	57,891	56,700	60,053	63,088	54,671	†	45,379	60,433	60,683	79,604	45,764	49,478	26,510	†
Texas	62,273	61,397	67,077	73,133	58,209	43,819	49,278	66,377	66,582	76,726	58,485	52,117	31,923	†
Utah	64,644	58,299	61,790	67,372	52,555	44,909	43,899	79,637	79,938	82,410	57,733	†	50,323	†
Vermont	61,644	59,831	59,831	65,630	49,445	46,183	†	63,249	67,112	†	71,883	45,855	31,948	†
Virginia	64,272	66,439	71,601	78,433	58,536	60,834	48,659	57,682	57,682	61,837	58,406	56,468	†	‡
Washington	64,563	65,403	78,485	85,129	62,559	†	48,739	61,247	61,247	†	61,724	58,224	†	‡
West Virginia	51,456	53,008	54,657	63,444	53,087	48,764	42,004	43,546	43,546	47,767	41,608	43,383	†	34,413
Wisconsin	62,866	64,352	64,198	76,398	55,200	†	64,609	56,888	56,974	67,448	51,662	52,123	44,677	†
Wyoming	56,149	56,149	64,563	64,563	†	†	46,630	†	†	†	†	†	†	†
U.S. Service Academies	104,134	104,134	104,134	†	†	104,134	†	†	†	†	†	†	†	†
Other jurisdictions	50,399	50,711	54,076	†	58,484	49,346	30,024	29,829	29,829	†	29,889	‡	†	†
American Samoa	28,052	28,052	†	†	†	†	28,052	†	†	†	†	†	†	†
Federated States of Micronesia	20,925	20,925	†	†	†	†	20,925	†	†	†	†	†	†	†
Guam	51,463	51,463	54,366	†	54,366	†	46,175	†	†	†	†	†	†	†
Marshall Islands	25,926	25,926	†	†	†	†	25,926	†	†	†	†	†	†	†
Northern Marianas	41,137	41,137	41,137	†	†	41,137	†	†	†	†	†	†	†	†
Palau	†	†	†	†	†	†	†	†	†	†	†	†	†	†
Puerto Rico	54,091	54,614	54,614	†	60,460	49,884	†	29,829	29,829	†	29,889	‡	†	†
U.S. Virgin Islands	52,871	52,871	52,871	†	52,871	†	†	†	†	†	†	†	†	†

†Not applicable.
‡Reporting standards not met.
[1]Institutions that awarded 20 or more doctor's degrees during the previous academic year.
[2]Institutions that awarded 20 or more master's degrees, but less than 20 doctor's degrees, during the previous academic year.

NOTE: Degree-granting institutions grant associate's or higher degrees and participate in Title IV federal financial aid programs. Data include imputations for nonrespondent institutions.
SOURCE: U.S. Department of Education, National Center for Education Statistics, 2005–06 Integrated Postsecondary Education Data System (IPEDS), Winter 2005–06. (This table was prepared August 2007.)

Table 261. Average salary of full-time instructional faculty on 9-month contracts in 4-year degree-granting institutions, by type and control of institution, rank of faculty, and state or jurisdiction: 2006–07

[In current dollars]

State or jurisdiction	Public doctoral[1]			Public master's[2]			Not-for-profit doctoral[1]			Not-for-profit master's[2]		
	Professor	Associate professor	Assistant professor	Professor	Associate professor	Assistant professor	Professor	Associate professor	Assistant professor	Professor	Associate professor	Assistant professor
1	2	3	4	5	6	7	8	9	10	11	12	13
United States	$105,174	$73,137	$62,327	$80,555	$64,279	$54,440	$126,444	$81,281	$68,245	$80,056	$62,837	$52,092
Alabama	101,523	71,091	59,736	75,070	60,651	50,394	81,268	60,601	54,124	64,756	55,474	45,309
Alaska	83,997	65,834	55,360	79,990	66,299	53,861	†	†	†	66,591	54,138	45,288
Arizona	104,652	72,363	64,021	95,973	74,783	63,345	†	†	†	106,278	90,445	80,246
Arkansas	87,468	67,267	55,103	65,335	55,215	47,228	†	†	†	62,598	56,035	46,367
California	120,839	78,614	69,417	85,705	67,447	58,934	127,483	87,486	73,045	93,712	73,332	59,641
Colorado	97,983	72,179	61,670	74,153	56,453	48,749	99,433	73,783	58,351	90,472	59,016	51,934
Connecticut	122,166	84,771	69,882	87,921	68,651	56,928	146,988	75,983	69,034	104,742	76,355	61,481
Delaware	119,511	80,715	66,466	77,650	64,392	59,927	63,900	63,623	55,661	115,379	89,074	54,064
District of Columbia	†	†	†	83,239	66,181	56,573	119,168	80,266	64,626	96,926	71,681	56,386
Florida	101,686	71,505	63,203	85,738	68,584	55,833	108,167	72,237	63,438	83,951	63,070	52,842
Georgia	105,985	72,413	62,875	70,412	56,953	49,768	128,746	78,586	67,558	65,780	58,776	49,339
Hawaii	96,077	71,600	63,136	†	†	†	†	†	†	75,844	66,449	55,378
Idaho	75,986	60,499	51,120	72,810	59,119	51,421	†	†	†	†	†	†
Illinois	104,714	70,735	62,132	78,294	62,887	52,678	137,621	83,854	70,470	77,871	61,830	51,249
Indiana	100,372	70,337	60,099	75,463	58,418	51,183	124,630	80,072	64,055	73,931	58,061	50,008
Iowa	103,972	73,087	63,705	80,690	63,614	53,696	62,404	55,576	45,982	70,406	53,325	43,863
Kansas	96,059	69,251	58,952	75,775	58,569	48,198	†	†	†	54,864	47,507	42,614
Kentucky	96,652	69,406	59,248	77,883	60,763	51,960	70,030	56,508	47,547	52,351	46,263	40,354
Louisiana	89,255	65,127	56,332	67,267	55,482	47,410	99,655	68,290	53,859	82,698	60,145	49,560
Maine	79,681	67,832	54,650	82,843	64,108	49,986	†	†	†	71,187	58,570	47,796
Maryland	115,420	79,528	70,139	79,942	63,266	57,227	117,648	77,240	65,392	73,223	57,940	51,071
Massachusetts	108,860	85,723	66,922	80,517	65,723	56,650	140,285	86,826	75,845	101,896	74,213	60,841
Michigan	109,591	76,546	63,764	78,833	63,618	53,314	‡	‡	‡	71,075	57,552	48,674
Minnesota	118,952	79,928	68,898	77,790	62,512	54,067	79,161	63,978	53,685	69,681	57,782	49,969
Mississippi	84,953	64,394	56,221	59,480	52,676	47,106	†	†	†	65,605	51,898	45,769
Missouri	98,184	68,314	57,690	69,253	55,785	48,442	127,675	77,508	66,816	62,040	52,832	44,824
Montana	75,175	58,438	52,532	62,403	52,855	48,953	†	†	†	50,238	40,257	38,892
Nebraska	102,906	72,001	62,554	73,202	61,841	50,511	94,035	66,652	52,745	63,167	51,658	45,645
Nevada	111,668	82,254	63,070	†	†	†	†	†	†	67,423	‡	49,206
New Hampshire	99,318	73,134	60,925	77,545	61,852	52,236	114,637	78,812	61,118	79,456	60,015	49,686
New Jersey	124,941	88,397	69,645	103,298	80,732	63,543	143,260	83,589	69,980	85,612	71,936	55,974
New Mexico	88,210	66,059	58,032	63,020	54,844	48,837	†	†	†	‡	†	†
New York	112,002	79,373	65,482	92,041	70,939	59,365	130,230	86,601	71,168	84,159	65,320	54,442
North Carolina	108,920	75,179	65,770	83,261	67,485	58,448	130,363	85,029	65,997	62,644	53,818	45,595
North Dakota	76,191	62,369	55,526	62,755	51,636	45,722	†	†	†	58,258	49,066	43,017
Ohio	99,707	69,780	58,258	82,007	63,895	55,365	103,418	70,801	60,690	70,558	56,416	47,546
Oklahoma	97,358	69,875	59,975	69,100	57,945	51,643	90,229	64,128	50,550	66,416	52,848	47,763
Oregon	85,778	64,082	58,258	62,175	50,183	41,678	69,395	55,802	49,046	87,276	64,112	51,877
Pennsylvania	114,201	80,446	65,883	91,446	73,414	58,704	126,931	85,979	74,672	82,383	65,761	54,524
Rhode Island	96,773	70,904	60,724	70,475	61,201	50,946	134,168	82,884	73,571	91,420	71,754	61,112
South Carolina	102,188	72,102	64,984	72,659	61,521	51,410	†	†	†	76,233	60,524	46,651
South Dakota	79,902	60,278	52,353	73,354	60,171	51,527	†	†	†	54,003	48,599	45,706
Tennessee	87,097	65,608	54,832	73,347	59,080	48,233	114,265	72,328	59,842	56,012	48,549	42,322
Texas	104,050	71,006	63,130	77,468	63,012	54,786	109,685	76,332	70,291	81,270	62,774	52,324
Utah	92,485	67,966	60,255	67,832	54,717	48,162	106,727	78,830	68,999	70,391	59,895	55,654
Vermont	94,770	70,628	60,815	57,462	47,254	38,216	†	†	†	101,234	71,151	57,533
Virginia	112,647	78,990	64,462	77,000	63,358	53,583	71,029	58,248	50,546	80,279	63,076	49,899
Washington	118,202	85,719	74,665	79,318	67,050	62,893	†	†	†	79,221	63,397	53,446
West Virginia	85,984	64,669	54,192	67,057	56,364	45,840	61,545	49,892	44,667	52,842	46,532	39,361
Wisconsin	100,053	71,744	61,827	69,262	56,602	50,073	99,659	73,394	61,371	65,455	55,159	47,118
Wyoming	89,853	67,840	60,155	†	†	†	†	†	†	†	†	†
U.S. Service Academies	†	†	†	†	†	†	†	†	†	†	†	†
Other jurisdictions	†	†	†	71,170	58,578	51,328	†	†	†	†	†	†
American Samoa	†	†	†	†	†	†	†	†	†	†	†	†
Federated States of Micronesia	†	†	†	†	†	†	†	†	†	†	†	†
Guam	†	†	†	77,900	59,273	46,303	†	†	†	†	†	†
Marshall Islands	†	†	†	†	†	†	†	†	†	†	†	†
Northern Marianas	†	†	†	†	†	†	†	†	†	†	†	†
Palau	†	†	†	†	†	†	†	†	†	†	†	†
Puerto Rico	†	†	†	70,235	57,669	53,008	†	†	†	†	‡	‡
U.S. Virgin Islands	†	†	†	77,025	61,788	51,088	†	†	†	†	†	†

†Not applicable.
‡Reporting standards not met.
[1]Institutions that awarded 20 or more doctor's degrees during the previous academic year.
[2]Institutions that awarded 20 or more master's degrees, but less than 20 doctor's degrees, during the previous academic year.

NOTE: Degree-granting institutions grant associate's or higher degrees and participate in Title IV federal financial aid programs. Data include imputations for nonrespondent institutions.
SOURCE: U.S. Department of Education, National Center for Education Statistics, 2006–07 Integrated Postsecondary Education Data System (IPEDS), Winter 2006–07. (This table was prepared August 2007.)

Table 262. Average salary of full-time instructional faculty on 9-month contracts in 4-year degree-granting institutions, by type and control of institution, rank of faculty, and state or jurisdiction: 2005–06

[In current dollars]

State or jurisdiction	Public doctoral[1]			Public master's[2]			Not-for-profit doctoral[1]			Not-for-profit master's[2]		
	Professor	Associate professor	Assistant professor	Professor	Associate professor	Assistant professor	Professor	Associate professor	Assistant professor	Professor	Associate professor	Assistant professor
1	2	3	4	5	6	7	8	9	10	11	12	13
United States	$100,403	$70,259	$59,777	$77,776	$62,045	$52,352	$122,784	$78,684	$67,151	$78,400	$61,777	$50,948
Alabama	94,705	68,376	52,006	70,010	57,627	48,095	80,362	59,511	50,932	59,789	52,964	43,407
Alaska	81,356	61,602	54,567	75,950	61,834	52,435	†	†	†	66,344	51,013	46,266
Arizona	99,654	68,580	60,630	88,806	70,080	58,380	†	†	†	61,151	77,634	81,977
Arkansas	83,050	64,206	51,949	63,056	53,676	46,135	†	†	†	60,561	51,907	44,427
California	116,367	75,376	66,805	85,933	68,202	57,853	122,761	81,933	70,711	90,944	71,122	58,495
Colorado	94,499	70,017	59,680	67,664	53,156	46,613	93,979	69,131	57,979	90,528	62,674	52,953
Connecticut	116,731	82,299	65,753	84,582	66,245	54,949	140,473	73,449	66,121	101,789	74,278	59,735
Delaware	112,945	78,661	64,003	77,265	65,066	59,403	62,111	59,374	54,522	112,488	82,031	52,035
District of Columbia	†	†	†	81,026	56,759	53,666	117,905	78,646	63,894	94,433	71,112	53,759
Florida	95,296	68,522	59,883	80,560	61,204	50,310	105,262	68,551	59,651	80,581	61,077	49,795
Georgia	102,658	69,254	61,720	69,750	55,754	48,418	133,220	69,771	77,638	61,505	55,847	47,037
Hawaii	92,243	68,434	60,475	†	†	†	†	†	†	72,414	64,310	54,635
Idaho	69,957	55,967	49,063	67,880	56,106	49,314	†	†	†	†	†	†
Illinois	101,104	69,721	60,845	76,980	62,225	51,538	136,450	84,690	74,239	76,992	64,278	51,385
Indiana	97,365	68,679	58,059	73,814	57,880	50,351	118,548	76,870	64,317	71,265	57,098	48,706
Iowa	98,494	70,898	61,041	79,014	62,688	52,979	61,722	53,060	44,517	69,530	52,045	43,976
Kansas	91,131	66,506	56,843	73,388	56,831	47,276	†	†	†	52,738	45,736	41,206
Kentucky	93,838	67,541	56,867	75,575	58,862	51,398	67,689	55,884	45,940	51,406	45,055	39,945
Louisiana	83,352	61,636	54,007	64,730	53,499	45,863	99,386	69,749	60,607	88,476	64,006	53,629
Maine	74,979	63,521	51,084	78,884	59,142	46,901	†	†	†	66,261	55,707	47,445
Maryland	110,361	76,459	68,170	81,770	64,955	54,862	119,306	84,960	68,919	79,405	62,587	51,871
Massachusetts	102,660	82,956	63,902	71,840	59,557	51,298	134,193	83,785	73,115	99,185	71,916	59,593
Michigan	106,000	74,149	62,043	77,291	61,794	51,889	‡	‡	‡	68,273	56,265	46,773
Minnesota	112,643	74,890	64,839	77,449	61,930	53,125	78,783	64,621	54,476	71,175	56,629	47,789
Mississippi	78,249	59,374	52,091	56,770	50,236	44,123	†	†	†	63,670	51,740	45,024
Missouri	95,211	66,890	55,898	66,912	53,567	46,784	116,146	73,707	62,562	65,211	54,863	45,641
Montana	71,914	56,814	50,200	59,162	49,635	44,489	†	†	†	44,845	39,802	34,738
Nebraska	99,378	70,174	60,092	71,136	60,337	49,891	87,630	64,425	50,355	63,295	50,664	43,915
Nevada	104,841	76,978	59,566	†	†	†	†	†	†	†	†	†
New Hampshire	99,402	73,464	61,705	76,026	61,761	51,431	118,484	80,974	61,862	77,415	57,613	49,252
New Jersey	118,492	84,110	66,643	96,394	76,139	59,227	131,814	77,109	66,516	83,578	69,470	53,958
New Mexico	83,734	62,820	54,350	60,672	52,344	47,914	‡	‡	‡	68,552	57,344	49,028
New York	106,736	75,289	62,950	85,620	66,176	55,147	127,488	84,988	70,910	81,415	64,754	53,080
North Carolina	100,938	69,256	61,112	76,658	62,499	55,037	125,596	81,102	62,807	61,784	52,600	44,422
North Dakota	72,859	60,476	53,725	61,629	51,519	44,721	†	†	†	56,243	47,389	40,865
Ohio	96,124	67,811	55,561	80,134	64,015	53,371	108,148	75,323	58,553	71,992	56,413	48,210
Oklahoma	88,749	64,547	54,778	64,634	55,527	48,199	87,696	61,656	48,293	63,574	51,909	43,354
Oregon	82,602	62,316	55,672	58,664	48,145	39,883	65,773	54,934	48,342	87,002	63,517	48,542
Pennsylvania	110,195	77,383	64,331	88,363	70,907	56,359	125,277	82,786	73,645	81,941	64,434	52,957
Rhode Island	93,008	67,604	59,702	68,717	59,707	49,388	128,378	80,752	69,781	88,270	68,384	58,856
South Carolina	95,441	68,792	60,162	70,924	59,651	49,647	†	†	†	72,507	54,989	45,831
South Dakota	77,356	58,204	50,208	69,809	57,621	49,462	†	†	†	57,395	49,756	44,080
Tennessee	84,387	63,707	53,322	67,708	54,986	45,471	110,437	69,850	60,282	54,962	46,692	41,395
Texas	100,479	69,013	62,239	77,039	62,754	54,729	104,612	73,554	66,092	73,872	58,204	47,577
Utah	87,373	64,348	57,755	65,532	52,520	46,343	105,000	76,626	67,769	67,639	59,287	52,358
Vermont	89,943	66,966	57,152	56,442	46,263	36,795	†	†	†	96,759	68,737	56,444
Virginia	107,396	75,963	62,056	73,731	61,673	51,248	74,474	60,138	50,390	75,534	59,626	48,449
Washington	111,741	80,860	71,838	75,453	63,142	57,609	†	†	†	77,197	61,852	52,153
West Virginia	80,062	61,759	51,126	63,178	53,784	42,446	60,281	50,256	43,455	46,494	45,642	38,240
Wisconsin	97,138	69,793	60,298	67,985	55,956	48,837	88,780	67,119	56,812	63,927	53,453	45,455
Wyoming	84,189	65,326	57,458	†	†	†	†	†	†	†	†	†
U.S. Service Academies	†	†	†	†	†	†	†	†	†	†	†	†
Other jurisdictions	†	†	†	66,876	56,200	47,432	†	†	†	†	†	34,771
American Samoa	†	†	†	†	†	†	†	†	†	†	†	†
Federated States of Micronesia	†	†	†	†	†	†	†	†	†	†	†	†
Guam	†	†	†	70,593	57,448	45,495	†	†	†	†	†	†
Marshall Islands	†	†	†	†	†	†	†	†	†	†	†	†
Northern Marianas	†	†	†	†	†	†	†	†	†	†	†	†
Palau	†	†	†	†	†	†	†	†	†	†	†	†
Puerto Rico	†	†	†	66,529	56,384	49,001	†	†	†	†	†	34,771
U.S. Virgin Islands	†	†	†	67,123	53,781	45,165	†	†	†	†	†	†

†Not applicable.
‡Reporting standards not met.
[1]Institutions that awarded 20 or more doctor's degrees during the previous academic year.
[2]Institutions that awarded 20 or more master's degrees, but less than 20 doctor's degrees, during the previous academic year.

NOTE: Degree-granting institutions grant associate's or higher degrees and participate in Title IV federal financial aid programs. Data include imputations for nonrespondent institutions.
SOURCE: U.S. Department of Education, National Center for Education Statistics, 2005–06 Integrated Postsecondary Education Data System (IPEDS), Winter 2005–06. (This table was prepared August 2007.)

Table 263. Average benefit expenditure for full-time instructional faculty on 9-month contracts in degree-granting institutions, by type of benefit and control of institution: Selected years, 1977–78 through 2006–07

						Average benefit expenditure per full-time faculty member receiving benefit							
	Average total benefit per full-time faculty member	Retirement plans			Medical/ dental plans	Guaranteed disability income protection	Tuition plan for dependents	Housing plan	Social Security taxes	Unemploy- ment compen- sation taxes	Group life insurance	Worker's compen- sation taxes	Other benefits
Control and year		Total	Vested within 5 years	Vested after 5 years									
1	2	3	4	5	6	7	8	9	10	11	12	13	14

						Current dollars							
Total													
1977–78	$3,203	$1,725	$1,739	$1,691	$521	$96	$1,410	$886	$899	$109	$105	$80	$288
1982–83	5,799	2,731	2,741	2,703	1,111	151	1,993	1,639	1,712	146	138	114	915
1987–88	7,227	3,677	3,494	4,028	1,682	132	1,585	2,004	2,379	134	178	190	716
1989–90	8,241	4,048	3,974	4,192	2,339	147	2,070	2,643	2,764	121	182	49	637
1992–93	10,473	4,397	4,391	4,410	3,266	179	2,196	2,574	3,168	143	237	344	874
1997–98	12,263	5,289	5,195	5,498	3,535	218	2,765	4,100	3,562	158	195	340	1,274
1998–99	12,580	5,256	5,268	5,228	3,726	213	3,012	3,698	3,668	152	190	347	1,093
1999–2000	13,227	5,292	5,365	5,125	3,989	237	3,362	4,187	3,793	146	190	343	1,415
2002–03	15,552	5,781	6,039	5,208	5,396	264	3,308	4,329	4,158	170	211	411	1,032
2003–04[1]	16,437	5,895	6,161	5,281	5,919	261	3,506	6,101	4,260	191	215	435	1,188
2004–05	17,269	6,211	6,429	5,682	6,314	272	4,072	4,176	4,354	225	199	481	1,229
2005–06	18,082	6,402	6,571	6,010	6,863	280	4,511	5,599	4,451	228	210	473	1,262
2006–07	18,783	6,710	6,851	6,361	7,217	280	5,029	6,914	4,627	176	217	484	1,390
Public													
1977–78	3,252	1,791	1,833	1,724	560	99	430	846	911	99	105	88	94
1982–83	5,920	2,846	2,880	2,776	1,189	153	576	1,027	1,741	139	140	115	980
1987–88	7,146	3,815	3,602	4,086	1,757	140	404	1,172	2,399	109	180	192	611
1989–90	8,361	4,186	4,128	4,259	2,425	154	605	1,767	2,771	97	182	60	602
1992–93	10,280	4,467	4,469	4,464	3,352	188	693	1,135	3,122	117	250	318	827
1997–98	12,114	5,432	5,302	5,617	3,646	219	830	2,614	3,482	133	187	340	1,442
1998–99	12,192	5,249	5,230	5,276	3,830	202	828	1,826	3,553	127	183	348	1,065
1999–2000	12,756	5,258	5,297	5,200	4,131	237	962	2,283	3,660	121	176	347	1,463
2002–03	15,097	5,703	5,968	5,323	5,565	274	978	2,415	4,005	142	198	402	1,058
2003–04[1]	15,916	5,757	6,044	5,330	6,127	262	1,022	4,589	4,073	173	206	425	1,080
2004–05	16,769	6,104	6,321	5,760	6,498	274	1,280	3,655	4,161	202	189	479	1,227
2005–06	17,594	6,308	6,458	6,078	7,126	279	1,483	4,418	4,237	210	202	446	1,247
2006–07	18,299	6,620	6,743	6,419	7,446	281	1,609	393	4,409	149	202	494	1,400
Private													
1977–78	3,071	1,509	1,542	905	404	89	2,025	890	873	131	103	60	838
1982–83	5,462	2,340	2,404	1,295	886	146	3,403	1,798	1,648	170	134	113	212
1987–88	7,438	3,280	3,306	2,906	1,488	120	3,666	2,303	2,337	197	175	184	977
1989–90	7,954	3,657	3,718	2,478	2,112	134	4,259	3,032	2,750	188	182	25	712
1992–93	10,958	4,206	4,259	2,877	3,039	163	4,523	2,956	3,267	212	207	402	957
1997–98	12,629	4,915	5,023	2,531	3,255	216	5,513	4,228	3,735	222	209	339	1,024
1998–99	13,519	5,274	5,327	3,879	3,468	231	6,722	3,936	3,915	219	205	345	1,151
1999–2000	14,366	5,380	5,471	3,354	3,638	237	6,951	4,349	4,074	213	215	335	1,337
2002–03	16,660	5,981	6,153	2,983	4,964	249	6,943	4,348	4,490	247	236	429	988
2003–04[1]	17,687	6,245	6,346	4,225	5,395	259	7,481	6,104	4,667	239	231	457	1,357
2004–05	18,465	6,483	6,603	4,092	5,849	269	7,600	4,455	4,775	284	217	484	1,231
2005–06	19,258	6,637	6,756	5,037	6,195	281	8,594	6,001	4,914	275	223	528	1,287
2006–07	19,942	6,935	7,027	5,382	6,632	278	9,610	7,750	5,097	248	246	465	1,373

						Constant 2006–07 dollars[2]							
Total													
1977–78	10,440	5,621	5,669	5,512	1,697	312	4,595	2,889	2,931	354	341	260	937
1982–83	12,061	5,680	5,701	5,622	2,311	313	4,145	3,408	3,561	305	288	238	1,902
1987–88	12,735	6,479	6,157	7,098	2,964	233	2,793	3,532	4,192	236	314	334	1,261
1989–90	13,249	6,508	6,389	6,740	3,760	236	3,329	4,250	4,444	195	293	79	1,024
1992–93	15,000	6,298	6,290	6,317	4,678	256	3,146	3,686	4,537	205	339	493	1,252
1997–98	15,478	6,675	6,556	6,939	4,462	275	3,490	5,174	4,496	199	246	429	1,609
1998–99	15,607	6,521	6,536	6,486	4,622	264	3,737	4,588	4,550	189	236	431	1,356
1999–2000	15,949	6,382	6,469	6,180	4,810	286	4,054	5,048	4,574	176	229	414	1,706
2002–03	17,433	6,481	6,770	5,838	6,049	296	3,708	4,852	4,661	190	237	460	1,157
2003–04	18,031	6,466	6,758	5,793	6,493	286	3,846	6,693	4,674	209	236	478	1,303
2004–05	18,390	6,615	6,846	6,051	6,724	290	4,336	4,447	4,637	240	212	512	1,308
2005–06	18,550	6,568	6,741	6,166	7,041	287	4,628	5,744	4,566	234	215	485	1,295
2006–07	18,783	6,710	6,851	6,361	7,217	280	5,029	6,914	4,627	176	217	484	1,390
Public													
1977–78	10,599	5,837	5,974	5,619	1,826	324	1,401	2,758	2,970	323	342	287	305
1982–83	12,313	5,920	5,990	5,774	2,472	318	1,198	2,136	3,621	288	291	239	2,039
1987–88	12,593	6,723	6,348	7,200	3,097	247	713	2,065	4,227	193	317	339	1,078
1989–90	13,442	6,729	6,636	6,847	3,899	248	973	2,840	4,454	155	293	96	967
1992–93	14,725	6,398	6,401	6,394	4,801	269	992	1,626	4,472	167	359	456	1,185
1997–98	15,289	6,856	6,692	7,090	4,602	277	1,047	3,299	4,395	168	236	429	1,819
1998–99	15,126	6,512	6,489	6,545	4,751	250	1,027	2,265	4,407	157	227	432	1,322
1999–2000	15,382	6,340	6,387	6,270	4,982	286	1,160	2,753	4,414	146	212	419	1,765
2002–03	16,923	6,393	6,690	5,967	6,238	308	1,097	2,707	4,490	159	222	450	1,186
2003–04	17,459	6,315	6,630	5,846	6,721	268	1,121	5,033	4,468	190	226	466	1,184
2004–05	17,858	6,500	6,732	6,134	6,920	292	1,363	3,892	4,431	216	201	510	1,307
2005–06	18,049	6,471	6,625	6,235	7,311	286	1,521	4,532	4,347	216	208	458	1,279
2006–07	18,299	6,620	6,743	6,419	7,446	281	1,609	393	4,409	149	202	494	1,400

See notes at end of table.

Table 263. Average benefit expenditure for full-time instructional faculty on 9-month contracts in degree-granting institutions, by type of benefit and control of institution: Selected years, 1977–78 through 2006–07—Continued

	Average total benefit per full-time faculty member	Average benefit expenditure per full-time faculty member receiving benefit												
		Retirement plans			Medical/ dental plans	Guaranteed disability income protection	Tuition plan for dependents	Housing plan	Social Security taxes	Unemployment compensation taxes	Group life insurance	Worker's compensation taxes	Other benefits
Control and year		Total	Vested within 5 years	Vested after 5 years									
1	2	3	4	5	6	7	8	9	10	11	12	13	14
Private													
1977–78...................	10,011	4,917	5,025	2,951	1,318	290	6,601	2,900	2,844	426	337	196	2,731
1982–83...................	11,360	4,867	5,000	2,694	1,844	303	7,077	3,739	3,428	354	279	235	442
1987–88...................	13,107	5,781	5,827	5,121	2,622	211	6,461	4,059	4,119	348	308	324	1,722
1989–90...................	12,788	5,880	5,977	3,984	3,395	215	6,847	4,875	4,422	303	293	40	1,145
1992–93...................	15,695	6,025	6,100	4,121	4,353	234	6,478	4,234	4,680	303	297	575	1,370
1997–98...................	15,939	6,204	6,340	3,194	4,108	273	6,957	5,337	4,715	281	264	428	1,293
1998–99...................	16,772	6,544	6,610	4,812	4,302	286	8,339	4,883	4,857	272	255	428	1,428
1999–2000...............	17,323	6,487	6,597	4,044	4,386	286	8,381	5,244	4,913	257	260	404	1,612
2002–03...................	18,676	6,705	6,897	3,344	5,565	279	7,783	4,874	5,033	276	265	481	1,107
2003–04...................	19,402	6,851	6,961	4,635	5,918	284	8,207	6,696	5,120	262	254	501	1,489
2004–05...................	19,664	6,904	7,032	4,358	6,229	287	8,093	4,745	5,086	303	231	515	1,311
2005–06...................	19,756	6,809	6,931	5,167	6,355	289	8,816	6,156	5,041	282	229	541	1,321
2006–07...................	19,942	6,935	7,027	5,382	6,632	278	9,610	7,750	5,097	248	246	465	1,373

[1]Data revised from previously published figures.
[2]Constant dollars based on the Consumer Price Index, prepared by the Bureau of Labor Statistics, U.S. Department of Labor, adjusted to an academic-year basis.
NOTE: Data through 1992–93 are for institutions of higher education, while later data are for degree-granting institutions. Degree-granting institutions grant associate's or higher degrees and participate in Title IV federal financial aid programs. The degree-granting classification is very similar to the earlier higher education classification, but it includes more 2-year colleges and excludes a few higher education institutions that did not grant degrees. (See Guide to Sources for details.)
SOURCE: U.S. Department of Education, National Center for Education Statistics, Higher Education General Information Survey (HEGIS), "Faculty Salaries, Tenure, and Fringe Benefits" surveys, 1977–78 and 1982–83; and 1987–88 through 2006–07 Integrated Postsecondary Education Data System, "Salaries, Tenure, and Fringe Benefits of Full-Time Instructional Faculty Survey" (IPEDS-SA:87–99), and Winter 2002–03 through Winter 2006–07. (This table was prepared August 2007.)

Table 264. Percentage of full-time instructional staff with tenure for degree-granting institutions with a tenure system, by academic rank, sex, and control and type of institution: Selected years, 1993–94 through 2005–06

Academic year, control and type of institution	Percent with tenure														
	Total			Professor			Associate professor			Assistant professor			Instructor	Lecturer	No academic rank
	Total	Male	Female	Total	Male	Female	Total	Male	Female	Total	Male	Female			
1	2	3	4	5	6	7	8	9	10	11	12	13	14	15	16
1993–94															
All institutions	56.2	62.6	42.7	91.9	92.8	87.7	76.8	77.5	75.1	14.4	13.6	15.5	38.3	10.8	26.0
Public institutions	58.9	65.4	45.6	92.6	93.6	87.5	80.8	81.6	78.9	17.1	16.1	18.5	45.5	7.2	28.6
4-year	56.3	63.5	39.3	94.3	94.7	92.0	80.4	81.2	78.4	13.8	13.0	14.8	4.4	5.4	6.1
Doctoral[1]	54.5	62.1	35.0	94.2	94.7	90.1	81.3	82.1	79.2	7.3	6.7	8.3	2.8	2.1	5.4
Master's[2]	60.5	67.7	46.1	95.4	95.5	95.0	79.3	80.0	77.7	23.0	23.0	22.9	6.4	11.7	11.0
Other	51.1	56.3	40.0	88.4	88.8	86.4	76.5	77.3	74.8	22.7	22.8	22.6	4.6	15.0	6.4
2-year	69.9	75.4	63.0	80.7	83.7	75.5	84.2	86.4	81.5	47.7	51.1	44.6	68.9	39.9	65.7
Not-for-profit institutions	49.5	56.0	35.5	90.3	90.8	88.1	67.6	68.1	66.5	9.0	8.7	9.4	6.1	21.9	18.9
4-year	49.5	56.0	35.4	90.3	90.8	88.0	67.6	68.1	66.5	9.0	8.7	9.4	5.5	21.6	15.7
Doctoral[1]	47.6	53.5	31.9	90.5	90.8	88.5	62.5	63.4	60.0	3.7	3.7	3.7	8.9	29.2	15.4
Master's[2]	51.8	59.2	38.2	90.8	91.1	89.8	71.3	72.2	69.6	13.4	13.6	13.1	2.6	0.7	10.5
Other	50.4	57.4	37.2	89.4	90.4	85.1	70.6	70.9	70.2	11.9	11.9	11.9	3.9	3.4	20.0
2-year	47.9	54.5	38.5	88.0	84.3	94.3	63.8	65.1	62.7	12.0	12.3	11.9	20.0	86.7	68.6
For-profit institutions	33.8	39.0	27.8	95.2	94.1	100.0	—	—	—	‡	‡	‡	32.9	—	—
1999–2000															
All institutions	53.7	59.6	43.2	92.8	93.1	91.2	76.8	76.9	76.7	11.8	11.0	12.9	34.1	3.4	18.3
Public institutions	55.9	62.0	45.6	93.9	94.4	91.9	81.0	81.2	80.7	14.1	13.1	15.4	39.8	4.1	21.2
4-year	53.2	60.3	39.3	94.2	94.6	92.5	80.8	81.0	80.3	10.0	9.5	10.6	3.9	3.0	4.0
Doctoral[1]	50.4	58.0	34.5	92.9	93.6	89.3	79.9	80.2	79.4	4.7	4.4	5.2	2.1	1.5	1.4
Master's[2]	59.1	66.0	48.0	96.9	96.9	96.8	82.7	83.0	82.1	18.1	17.8	18.5	6.4	5.9	25.3
Other	54.7	61.2	43.2	94.9	95.1	94.0	80.7	81.3	79.7	21.8	24.1	18.8	5.8	7.2	49.3
2-year	67.7	70.6	64.5	91.2	92.2	89.7	83.3	83.6	83.1	53.8	56.0	52.0	60.4	21.2	64.4
Not-for-profit institutions	48.2	54.2	36.8	90.3	90.5	89.7	68.0	67.8	68.4	7.5	6.8	8.2	1.8	1.2	7.4
4-year	48.1	54.1	36.7	90.3	90.5	89.7	68.0	67.8	68.5	7.4	6.8	8.1	1.6	1.2	4.1
Doctoral[1]	43.4	49.6	29.6	88.6	88.7	87.6	62.6	62.8	62.2	3.0	2.8	3.2	1.0	1.3	0.5
Master's[2]	52.3	59.4	41.4	91.2	91.6	90.0	72.0	73.0	70.3	12.1	11.9	12.3	0.9	0.8	22.3
Other	53.5	59.3	44.0	93.5	93.8	92.8	73.1	71.2	76.0	9.9	9.4	10.5	3.6	1.6	23.5
2-year	59.7	63.3	53.6	96.0	96.0	96.0	57.1	61.3	54.3	31.6	36.7	28.3	30.2	—	65.8
For-profit institutions	77.4	77.2	77.6	47.4	50.0	33.3	—	—	—	—	—	—	86.1	—	71.9
2003–04															
All institutions	50.4	56.0	41.5	91.8	92.0	91.1	74.6	74.2	75.3	9.0	8.2	9.9	30.7	2.1	22.5
Public institutions	53.0	58.6	44.2	93.6	93.8	92.9	78.9	78.7	79.4	11.1	10.2	12.1	35.7	2.6	28.6
4-year	50.2	56.9	38.5	93.9	94.0	93.7	78.7	78.4	79.2	7.5	7.0	8.2	2.4	1.7	4.4
Doctoral[1]	48.9	56.0	35.2	92.7	92.9	91.9	77.9	77.9	77.9	3.9	3.6	4.3	1.3	1.2	2.3
Master's[2]	52.9	59.2	43.9	96.5	96.6	96.3	79.8	79.0	81.0	12.7	11.9	13.6	3.4	2.5	10.4
Other	51.2	57.0	43.0	95.1	95.1	95.0	81.9	81.7	82.2	18.9	20.3	17.2	5.2	3.7	37.0
2-year	65.2	68.3	62.2	90.5	91.3	89.6	81.3	82.1	80.6	45.9	48.8	43.5	57.2	22.0	69.8
Not-for-profit institutions	44.6	50.2	34.9	88.2	88.5	87.2	66.2	65.5	67.3	5.2	4.6	5.9	4.0	0.7	3.3
4-year	44.6	50.3	34.9	88.2	88.5	87.1	66.2	65.5	67.3	5.2	4.6	5.9	3.7	0.7	2.8
Doctoral[1]	40.1	46.3	27.7	86.8	87.2	84.8	60.8	60.8	60.6	2.1	2.0	2.2	0.4	0.6	0.3
Master's[2]	48.7	54.6	40.5	88.4	88.9	86.8	69.8	69.4	70.4	9.1	8.2	9.9	0.8	1.0	23.0
Other	51.9	57.2	44.0	92.1	91.9	92.6	73.7	72.4	75.6	6.7	6.2	7.2	14.9	1.3	15.5
2-year	47.7	43.0	51.9	92.2	87.5	96.3	65.4	61.9	67.7	15.6	14.3	16.7	38.6	37.5	55.6
For-profit institutions	69.2	78.1	57.6	76.5	70.0	85.7	—	—	—	—	—	—	69.4	‡	81.7
2005–06															
All institutions	49.6	55.2	41.0	91.3	91.6	90.5	73.6	73.0	74.5	8.0	7.4	8.6	28.4	1.8	26.1
Public institutions	51.5	57.1	43.3	92.8	93.1	91.8	77.7	77.3	78.4	9.8	9.1	10.6	33.8	2.3	29.9
4-year	48.7	55.4	37.8	93.1	93.3	92.7	77.7	77.3	78.5	6.1	5.8	6.6	2.1	1.6	3.8
Doctoral[1]	47.2	54.2	34.5	91.6	92.0	90.1	75.9	75.7	76.4	2.7	2.6	2.8	1.2	1.3	2.1
Master's[2]	52.3	58.7	43.6	96.5	96.6	96.5	81.0	80.3	82.0	11.4	10.9	11.9	2.9	2.1	5.1
Other	49.1	54.0	42.2	95.4	95.0	96.2	82.6	83.0	81.9	17.6	18.3	16.8	4.9	2.3	34.3
2-year	64.1	67.2	61.2	89.5	90.7	88.2	77.9	77.8	77.9	44.1	46.8	41.8	56.2	22.4	70.3
Not-for-profit institutions	45.1	51.1	35.5	88.3	88.5	87.6	65.4	64.7	66.6	4.6	4.3	4.9	0.7	0.5	9.8
4-year	45.1	51.1	35.4	88.3	88.5	87.6	65.4	64.7	66.6	4.6	4.3	4.9	0.4	0.5	9.4
Doctoral[1]	40.7	47.2	28.3	86.2	86.7	84.1	57.7	57.5	58.1	1.8	1.8	1.8	0.2	0.3	1.8
Master's[2]	49.1	55.0	41.1	89.7	90.2	88.3	71.6	71.6	71.6	8.5	8.1	8.8	0.7	1.1	20.9
Other	52.5	57.8	44.8	92.7	92.3	93.9	74.5	73.5	75.9	5.5	5.4	5.6	0.7	1.5	45.7
2-year	45.2	50.0	41.2	86.3	91.7	81.5	69.7	92.9	52.6	15.4	8.6	20.9	34.5	‡	50.0
For-profit institutions	69.3	67.1	72.5	70.3	65.6	100.0	—	—	—	—	—	—	78.9	‡	—

—Not available.

‡Reporting standards not met.

[1]Institutions that awarded 20 or more doctor's degrees during the previous academic year.

[2]Institutions that awarded 20 or more master's degrees, but less than 20 doctor's degrees, during the previous academic year.

NOTE: The coverage of this table differs from similar tables published in editions of the *Digest* prior to 2003. Previous tenure tabulations included only instructional staff classified as full-time faculty; this table includes all staff with full-time instructional duties, including faculty and other instructional staff. Data for 1993–94 are for institutions of higher education, while later data are for degree-granting institutions. Degree-granting institutions grant associate's or higher degrees

and participate in Title IV federal financial aid programs. The degree-granting classification is very similar to the earlier higher education classification, but it includes more 2-year colleges and excludes a few higher education institutions that did not grant degrees. (See Guide to Sources for details.) Data are for degree-granting institutions with 15 or more full-time employees; institutions with fewer than 15 employees did not report staff data prior to 2007. Some data have been revised from previously published figures.

SOURCE: U.S. Department of Education, National Center for Education Statistics, 1993–94 through 2005–06 Integrated Postsecondary Education Data System, "Fall Staff Survey" (IPEDS-S:93–99), Winter 2003–04, and Winter 2005–06. (This table was prepared August 2007.)

Table 265. Degree-granting institutions, by control and type of institution: Selected years, 1949–50 through 2007–08

Year	All institutions			Public			Private			Not-for-profit			For-profit		
	Total	4-year	2-year	Total	4-year	2-year	Total	4-year, total	2-year, total	Total	4-year	2-year	Total	4-year	2-year
1	2	3	4	5	6	7	8	9	10	11	12	13	14	15	16
Excluding branch campuses															
1949–50	1,851	1,327	524	641	344	297	1,210	983	227	—	—	—	—	—	—
1959–60	2,004	1,422	582	695	367	328	1,309	1,055	254	—	—	—	—	—	—
1969–70	2,525	1,639	886	1,060	426	634	1,465	1,213	252	—	—	—	—	—	—
1970–71	2,556	1,665	891	1,089	435	654	1,467	1,230	237	—	—	—	—	—	—
1971–72	2,606	1,675	931	1,137	440	697	1,469	1,235	234	—	—	—	—	—	—
1972–73	2,665	1,701	964	1,182	449	733	1,483	1,252	231	—	—	—	—	—	—
1973–74	2,720	1,717	1,003	1,200	440	760	1,520	1,277	243	—	—	—	—	—	—
1974–75	2,747	1,744	1,003	1,214	447	767	1,533	1,297	236	—	—	—	—	—	—
1975–76	2,765	1,767	998	1,219	447	772	1,546	1,320	226	—	—	—	—	—	—
1976–77	2,785	1,783	1,002	1,231	452	779	1,554	1,331	223	—	—	—	—	—	—
1977–78	2,826	1,808	1,018	1,241	454	787	1,585	1,354	231	—	—	—	—	—	—
1978–79	2,954	1,843	1,111	1,308	463	845	1,646	1,380	266	—	—	—	—	—	—
1979–80	2,975	1,863	1,112	1,310	464	846	1,665	1,399	266	—	—	—	—	—	—
1980–81	3,056	1,861	1,195	1,334	465	869	1,722	1,396	326[1]	—	—	—	—	—	—
1981–82	3,083	1,883	1,200	1,340	471	869	1,743	1,412	331[1]	—	—	—	—	—	—
1982–83	3,111	1,887	1,224	1,336	472	864	1,775	1,415	360[1]	—	—	—	—	—	—
1983–84	3,117	1,914	1,203	1,325	474	851	1,792	1,440	352	—	—	—	—	—	—
1984–85	3,146	1,911	1,235	1,329	461	868	1,817	1,450	367	—	—	—	—	—	—
1985–86	3,155	1,915	1,240	1,326	461	865	1,829	1,454	375	—	—	—	—	—	—
Including branch campuses															
1974–75	3,004	1,866	1,138	1,433	537	896	1,571	1,329	242	—	—	—	—	—	—
1975–76	3,026	1,898	1,128	1,442	545	897	1,584	1,353	231	—	—	—	—	—	—
1976–77	3,046	1,913	1,133	1,455	550	905	1,591	1,363	228	1,536	1,348	188	55	15	40
1977–78	3,095	1,938	1,157	1,473	552	921	1,622	1,386	236	—	—	—	—	—	—
1978–79	3,134	1,941	1,193	1,474	550	924	1,660	1,391	269	1,564	1,376	188	96	15	81
1979–80	3,152	1,957	1,195	1,475	549	926	1,677	1,408	269	—	—	—	—	—	—
1980–81	3,231	1,957	1,274	1,497	552	945	1,734	1,405	329[1]	1,569	1,387	182	165	18	147
1981–82	3,253	1,979	1,274	1,498	558	940	1,755	1,421	334[1]	—	—	—	—	—	—
1982–83	3,280	1,984	1,296	1,493	560	933	1,787	1,424	363[1]	—	—	—	—	—	—
1983–84	3,284	2,013	1,271	1,481	565	916	1,803	1,448	355	—	—	—	—	—	—
1984–85	3,331	2,025	1,306	1,501	566	935	1,830	1,459	371	1,616	1,430	186	214	29	185
1985–86	3,340	2,029	1,311	1,498	566	932	1,842	1,463	379	—	—	—	—	—	—
1986–87	3,406	2,070	1,336	1,533	573	960	1,873	1,497	376	1,635	1,462	173	238	35	203
1987–88	3,587	2,135	1,452	1,591	599	992	1,996	1,536	460	1,673	1,487	186	323	49	274
1988–89	3,565	2,129	1,436	1,582	598	984	1,983	1,531	452	1,658	1,478	180	325	53	272
1989–90	3,535	2,127	1,408	1,563	595	968	1,972	1,532	440	1,656	1,479	177	316	53	263
1990–91	3,559	2,141	1,418	1,567	595	972	1,992	1,546	446	1,649	1,482	167	343	64	279
1991–92	3,601	2,157	1,444	1,598	599	999	2,003	1,558	445	1,662	1,486	176	341	72	269
1992–93	3,638	2,169	1,469	1,624	600	1,024	2,014	1,569	445	1,672	1,493	179	342	76	266
1993–94	3,632	2,190	1,442	1,625	604	1,021	2,007	1,586	421	1,687	1,506	181	320	80	240
1994–95	3,688	2,215	1,473	1,641	605	1,036	2,047	1,610	437	1,702	1,510	192	345	100	245
1995–96	3,706	2,244	1,462	1,655	608	1,047	2,051	1,636	415	1,706	1,519	187	345	117	228
1996–97	4,009	2,267	1,742	1,702	614	1,088	2,307	1,653	654	1,693	1,509	184	614	144	470
1997–98	4,064	2,309	1,755	1,707	615	1,092	2,357	1,694	663	1,707	1,528	179	650	166	484
1998–99	4,048	2,335	1,713	1,681	612	1,069	2,367	1,723	644	1,695	1,531	164	672	192	480
1999–2000	4,084	2,363	1,721	1,682	614	1,068	2,402	1,749	653	1,681	1,531	150	721	218	503
2000–01	4,182	2,450	1,732	1,698	622	1,076	2,484	1,828	656	1,695	1,551	144	789	277	512
2001–02	4,197	2,487	1,710	1,713	628	1,085	2,484	1,859	625	1,676	1,541	135	808	318	490
2002–03	4,168	2,466	1,702	1,712	631	1,081	2,456	1,835	621	1,665	1,538	127	791	297	494
2003–04	4,236	2,530	1,706	1,720	634	1,086	2,516	1,896	620	1,664	1,546	118	852	350	502
2004–05	4,216	2,533	1,683	1,700	639	1,061	2,516	1,894	622	1,637	1,525	112	879	369	510
2005–06	4,276	2,582	1,694	1,693	640	1,053	2,583	1,942	641	1,647	1,534	113	936	408	528
2006–07	4,314	2,629	1,685	1,688	643	1,045	2,626	1,986	640	1,640	1,533	107	986	453	533
2007–08	4,352	2,675	1,677	1,685	653	1,032	2,667	2,022	645	1,624	1,532	92	1,043	490	553

—Not available.

[1]Large increases are due to the addition of schools accredited by the Accrediting Commission of Career Schools and Colleges of Technology.

NOTE: Data through 1995–96 are for institutions of higher education, while later data are for degree-granting institutions. Degree-granting institutions grant associate's or higher degrees and participate in Title IV federal financial aid programs. The degree-granting classification is very similar to the earlier higher education classification, but it includes more 2-year colleges and excludes a few higher education institutions that did not grant degrees. (See Guide to Sources for details.) Changes in counts of institutions over time are partly affected by increasing or decreasing numbers of institutions submitting separate data for branch campuses.

SOURCE: U.S. Department of Education, National Center for Education Statistics, *Education Directory, Colleges and Universities*, 1949–50 through 1965–66; Higher Education General Information Survey (HEGIS), "Institutional Characteristics of Colleges and Universities" surveys, 1966–67 through 1985–86; and 1986–87 through 2007–08 Integrated Postsecondary Education Data System, "Institutional Characteristics Survey" (IPEDS-IC:86–99), and Fall 2000 through Fall 2007. (This table was prepared July 2008.)

Table 266. Degree-granting institutions and branches, by type and control of institution and state or jurisdiction: 2007–08

State or jurisdiction	Total	All public institutions	Public 4-year — Total	Research university, very high[1]	Research university, high[2]	Doctoral/research university[3]	Master's[4]	Baccalaureate[5]	Special focus[6]	Public 2-year	All not-for-profit institutions	Not-for-profit 4-year — Total	Research university, very high[1]	Research university, high[2]	Doctoral/research university[3]	Master's[4]	Baccalaureate[5]	Special focus[6]	Not-for-profit 2-year	For-profit — Total	For-profit — 4-year	For-profit — 2-year
1	2	3	4	5	6	7	8	9	10	11	12	13	14	15	16	17	18	19	20	21	22	23
United States	4,352	1,665	653	63	75	27	264	177	47	1,032	1,624	1,532	33	27	45	344	534	549	92	1,043	490	553
Alabama	68	39	14	3	3	0	9	1	0	25	18	18	0	0	1	2	10	5	0	11	8	3
Alaska	7	5	3	0	1	0	2	0	0	2	1	1	0	0	0	1	0	0	0	1	1	0
Arizona	76	27	6	2	1	0	3	0	0	21	10	10	0	0	0	2	2	6	0	39	25	14
Arkansas	49	33	11	1	1	1	5	0	1	22	12	11	0	0	0	1	9	1	1	4	3	1
California	416	147	35	8	1	0	19	5	2	112	142	138	3	1	11	27	22	74	4	127	59	68
Colorado	80	27	12	3	1	1	2	5	0	15	13	12	0	1	0	3	3	5	1	40	22	18
Connecticut	46	22	10	1	0	0	4	4	1	12	18	16	1	1	2	6	5	2	2	6	4	2
Delaware	10	5	2	1	0	0	1	0	0	3	5	4	0	0	1	1	1	1	1	0	0	0
District of Columbia	16	2	2	1	0	0	1	0	1	0	11	11	1	3	1	3	0	3	0	3	3	0
Florida	184	40	19	3	3	2	2	8	1	21	55	54	1	1	2	11	21	18	1	89	52	37
Georgia	135	74	24	2	1	1	13	6	1	50	34	31	1	1	0	4	17	8	3	27	18	9
Hawaii	22	10	4	1	0	0	0	3	0	6	6	6	0	0	0	2	1	3	0	6	4	2
Idaho	14	7	4	0	1	1	1	1	0	3	4	4	0	1	2	1	2	1	0	3	2	1
Illinois	177	60	12	2	2	1	7	0	0	48	85	81	2	2	2	16	24	35	4	32	19	13
Indiana	106	29	15	2	1	2	6	4	0	14	43	42	1	0	0	9	21	11	1	34	18	16
Iowa	65	19	3	2	0	0	0	0	0	16	36	35	0	0	0	5	20	10	1	10	9	1
Kansas	60	32	8	2	1	0	4	0	1	24	22	21	0	0	0	6	12	3	1	6	3	3
Kentucky	71	24	8	1	1	1	5	1	0	16	27	27	1	0	1	3	14	9	0	20	7	13
Louisiana	84	52	17	1	2	1	9	1	3	35	10	10	0	0	0	2	4	3	1	22	4	18
Maine	30	15	8	0	1	0	1	6	0	7	13	12	1	1	0	3	6	3	1	2	0	2
Maryland	57	29	13	1	3	0	8	1	1	16	21	21	1	1	0	4	7	8	0	7	4	3
Massachusetts	122	31	15	1	0	2	7	2	3	16	83	79	5	3	1	14	25	31	4	8	4	4
Michigan	105	45	15	3	2	2	7	1	0	30	52	52	0	1	1	9	23	19	0	8	5	3
Minnesota	112	42	11	1	0	0	8	2	0	31	37	36	0	0	3	6	11	16	1	33	28	5
Mississippi	42	26	9	0	4	0	4	0	1	17	11	11	1	0	0	3	4	4	0	5	0	5
Missouri	128	34	13	1	3	0	6	3	0	21	56	52	1	1	0	12	12	26	4	38	17	21
Montana	23	18	6	0	1	0	1	3	1	12	5	4	0	0	0	2	2	1	1	0	0	0
Nebraska	42	15	7	1	0	0	3	2	1	8	19	17	0	0	0	3	9	5	2	8	5	3
Nevada	23	7	6	0	2	0	0	4	0	1	2	2	0	0	1	0	1	1	0	14	7	7
New Hampshire	28	12	5	0	1	0	2	2	0	7	14	13	1	0	1	2	6	3	1	2	1	1
New Jersey	60	33	14	1	2	0	9	1	1	19	23	23	1	1	1	9	3	8	0	4	3	1
New Mexico	42	28	8	1	0	0	1	1	1	20	5	5	0	0	0	4	1	0	0	9	8	1
New York	307	78	43	3	3	0	20	13	4	35	185	165	6	5	6	39	30	79	20	44	14	30
North Carolina	130	75	16	2	2	2	6	3	1	59	45	44	1	1	0	5	28	9	1	10	7	3
North Dakota	22	14	7	0	2	0	1	3	0	7	6	5	1	0	1	2	1	3	1	2	2	0
Ohio	207	61	30	2	7	1	1	15	4	31	78	71	1	1	1	18	26	24	7	68	7	61
Oklahoma	59	29	17	0	2	0	6	7	2	12	14	14	1	1	1	3	5	4	0	16	8	8
Oregon	60	26	9	2	1	1	3	2	1	17	25	25	1	0	2	3	9	11	0	9	5	4
Pennsylvania	263	65	44	2	1	1	16	22	2	21	116	101	1	1	3	30	36	28	15	82	8	74
Rhode Island	14	3	2	1	1	0	1	0	0	1	10	10	0	0	0	4	1	4	1	1	0	1
South Carolina	66	33	13	1	1	1	4	5	1	20	25	23	0	0	0	4	14	5	2	8	5	3
South Dakota	24	12	7	0	1	1	0	3	2	5	8	7	0	0	1	1	3	3	1	4	4	0
Tennessee	105	22	9	1	2	2	5	0	0	13	49	46	1	1	2	10	17	17	3	34	17	17
Texas	214	109	45	2	6	3	21	5	8	64	57	53	1	1	2	16	17	16	4	48	13	35
Utah	36	14	7	1	1	0	2	3	0	7	4	3	0	1	0	1	1	0	1	18	12	6

See notes at end of table.

Table 266. Degree-granting institutions and branches, by type and control of institution and state or jurisdiction: 2007–08—Continued

State or jurisdiction	Total	All public institutions — Total	Public 4-year institutions — Total	Research university, very high[1]	Research university, high[2]	Doctoral/research university[3]	Master's[4]	Baccalaureate[5]	Special focus[6]	Public 2-year	All not-for-profit institutions	Not-for-profit 4-year institutions — Total	Research university, very high[1]	Research university, high[2]	Doctoral/research university[3]	Master's[4]	Baccalaureate[5]	Special focus[6]	Not-for-profit 2-year	For-profit institutions — Total	4-year	2-year
1	2	3	4	5	6	7	8	9	10	11	12	13	14	15	16	17	18	19	20	21	22	23
Vermont	25	6	5	0	1	0	2	2	0	1	17	16	0	0	0	5	9	2	1	2	2	0
Virginia	112	39	15	2	4	0	6	3	0	24	35	35	0	0	1	7	20	7	0	38	20	18
Washington	76	43	13	2	0	0	6	4	1	30	18	18	0	0	0	10	3	5	0	15	12	3
West Virginia	44	23	12	0	1	0	1	9	1	11	9	9	0	0	0	2	6	1	0	12	2	10
Wisconsin	73	31	14	1	1	0	9	3	0	17	30	28	0	1	0	10	10	7	2	12	8	4
Wyoming	10	8	1	0	1	0	0	0	0	7	0	0	0	0	0	0	0	0	0	2	1	1
U.S. Service Academies	5	5	5	0	0	0	0	5	0	0	†	†	†	†	†	†	†	†	†	†	†	†
Other jurisdictions	83	25	18	0	1	0	2	12	3	7	41	37	0	0	2	5	19	11	4	17	8	9
American Samoa	1	1	1	0	0	0	0	1	0	0	0	0	0	0	0	0	0	0	0	0	0	0
Federated States of Micronesia	1	1	0	0	0	0	0	0	0	1	0	0	0	0	0	0	0	0	0	0	0	0
Guam	3	2	1	0	0	0	1	0	0	1	1	1	0	0	0	0	0	1	0	0	0	0
Marshall Islands	1	1	0	0	0	0	0	0	0	1	0	0	0	0	0	0	0	0	0	0	0	0
Northern Marianas	1	1	1	0	0	0	0	1	0	0	0	0	0	0	0	0	0	0	0	0	0	0
Palau	1	1	0	0	0	0	0	0	0	1	0	0	0	0	0	0	0	0	0	0	0	0
Puerto Rico	74	17	14	0	1	0	1	9	3	3	40	36	0	0	2	5	19	10	4	17	8	9
U.S. Virgin Islands	1	1	1	0	0	0	0	1	0	0	0	0	0	0	0	0	0	0	0	0	0	0

†Not applicable.
[1]Research universities with a very high level of research activity.
[2]Research universities with a high level of research activity.
[3]Institutions that award at least 20 doctor's degrees per year, but did not have a high level of research activity.
[4]Institutions that award at least 50 master's degrees per year.
[5]Institutions that primarily emphasize undergraduate education.
[6]Four-year institutions that award degrees primarily in single fields of study, such as medicine, business, fine arts, theology, and engineering. Includes some institutions that have 4-year programs, but have not reported sufficient data to identify program cate-gory. Also includes institutions classified as 4-year under the IPEDS system, which had been classified as 2-year in the Carnegie classification system because they primarily award associate's degrees.

NOTE: Relative levels of research activity for research universities were determined by an analysis of research and development expenditures, science and engineering research staffing, and doctoral degrees conferred, by field. Further information on the research index ranking may be obtained from http://www.carnegiefoundation.org/classifications/index.asp?key=798#related.

Degree-granting institutions grant associate's or higher degrees and participate in Title IV federal financial aid programs.

SOURCE: U.S. Department of Education, National Center for Education Statistics, 2007-08 Integrated Postsecondary Education Data System (IPEDS), Fall 2007. (This table was prepared July 2008.)

Table 267. Degree-granting institutions that have closed their doors, by control and type of institution: 1969–70 through 2007–08

Year	All institutions			Public			Private								
							Total			Not-for-profit			For-profit		
	Total	4-year	2-year	Total	4-year	2-year	Total	4-year	2-year	Total	4-year	2-year	Total	4-year	2-year
1	2	3	4	5	6	7	8	9	10	11	12	13	14	15	16
Excluding branch campuses															
1969–70	18	8	10	3	0	3	15	8	7	—	—	—	—	—	—
1970–71	32	9	23	9	0	9	23	9	14	—	—	—	—	—	—
1971–72	12	3	9	3	0	3	9	3	6	—	—	—	—	—	—
1972–73	19	12	7	2	0	2	17	12	5	—	—	—	—	—	—
1973–74	18	11	7	0	0	0	18	11	7	—	—	—	—	—	—
1974–75	17	13	4	3	0	3	14	13	1	—	—	—	—	—	—
1975–76	8	6	2	2	1	1	6	5	1	—	—	—	—	—	—
1976–77	8	5	3	0	0	0	8	5	3	—	—	—	—	—	—
1977–78	12	9	3	0	0	0	12	9	3	—	—	—	—	—	—
1978–79	9	4	5	0	0	0	9	4	5	—	—	—	—	—	—
1979–80	6	5	1	0	0	0	6	5	1	—	—	—	—	—	—
1980–81	4	3	1	0	0	0	4	3	1	—	—	—	—	—	—
1981–82	7	6	1	0	0	0	7	6	1	—	—	—	—	—	—
1982–83	7	4	3	0	0	0	7	4	3	—	—	—	—	—	—
1983–84	4	4	0	0	0	0	4	4	0	—	—	—	—	—	—
1984–85	4	4	0	0	0	0	4	4	0	—	—	—	—	—	—
1985–86	10	6	4	1	0	1	9	6	3	—	—	—	—	—	—
1986–87 and 1987–88	25	19	6	1	0	1	24	19	5	—	—	—	—	—	—
1988–89	14	6	8	0	0	0	14	6	8	—	—	—	—	—	—
1989–90	12	6	6	0	0	0	12	6	6	—	—	—	—	—	—
1990–91	10	4	6	0	0	0	10	4	6	—	—	—	—	—	—
1991–92	10	7	3	0	0	0	10	7	3	—	—	—	—	—	—
Including branch campuses															
1969–70	24	10	14	5	1	4	19	9	10	—	—	—	—	—	—
1970–71	35	10	25	11	0	11	24	10	14	—	—	—	—	—	—
1971–72	14	5	9	3	0	3	11	5	6	—	—	—	—	—	—
1972–73	21	12	9	4	0	4	17	12	5	—	—	—	—	—	—
1973–74	20	12	8	1	0	1	19	12	7	—	—	—	—	—	—
1974–75	18	13	5	4	0	4	14	13	1	—	—	—	—	—	—
1975–76	9	7	2	2	1	1	7	6	1	—	—	—	—	—	—
1976–77	9	6	3	0	0	0	9	6	3	—	—	—	—	—	—
1977–78	12	9	3	0	0	0	12	9	3	—	—	—	—	—	—
1978–79	9	4	5	0	0	0	9	4	5	—	—	—	—	—	—
1979–80	6	5	1	0	0	0	6	5	1	—	—	—	—	—	—
1980–81	4	3	1	0	0	0	4	3	1	—	—	—	—	—	—
1981–82	7	6	1	0	0	0	7	6	1	—	—	—	—	—	—
1982–83	7	4	3	0	0	0	7	4	3	—	—	—	—	—	—
1983–84	5	5	0	1	1	0	4	4	0	—	—	—	—	—	—
1984–85	4	4	0	0	0	0	4	4	0	—	—	—	—	—	—
1985–86	12	8	4	1	1	0	11	7	4	—	—	—	—	—	—
1986–87 and 1987–88	26	19	7	1	0	1	25	19	6	—	—	—	—	—	—
1988–89	14	6	8	0	0	0	14	6	8	—	—	—	—	—	—
1989–90	19	8	11	0	0	0	19	8	11	—	—	—	—	—	—
1990–91	18	6	12	0	0	0	18	6	12	—	—	—	—	—	—
1991–92	26	8	18	1	0	1	25	8	17	—	—	—	—	—	—
1992–93	24	6	18	0	0	0	24	6	18	—	—	—	—	—	—
1993–94	38	10	28	1	0	1	37	10	27	—	—	—	—	—	—
1994–95	15	8	7	2	0	2	13	8	5	—	—	—	—	—	—
1995–96	21	8	13	1	1	0	20	7	13	—	—	—	—	—	—
1996–97	36	13	23	2	0	2	34	13	21	—	—	—	—	—	—
1997–98	5	0	5	0	0	0	5	0	5	—	—	—	—	—	—
1998–99	7	1	6	1	0	1	6	1	5	—	—	—	—	—	—
1999–2000	16	3	13	3	0	3	13	3	10	—	—	—	—	—	—
2000–01	14	9	5	0	0	0	14	9	5	—	—	—	—	—	—
2001–02	15	2	13	0	0	0	15	2	13	—	—	—	—	—	—
2002–03	13	7	6	0	0	0	13	7	6	—	—	—	—	—	—
2003–04	13	6	7	0	0	0	13	6	7	—	—	—	—	—	—
2004–05	3	1	2	0	0	0	3	1	2	1	1	0	2	0	2
2005–06	11	6	5	1	1	0	10	5	5	5	4	1	5	1	4
2006–07	13	4	9	0	0	0	13	4	9	6	4	2	7	0	7
2007–08	26	10	16	0	0	0	26	10	16	9	6	3	17	4	13

—Not available

NOTE: This table indicates the year by which the institution no longer operated (generally it closed at the end of or during the prior year). Data through 1995–96 are for institutions of higher education, while later data are for degree-granting institutions. Degree-granting institutions grant associate's or higher degrees and participate in Title IV federal financial aid programs. The degree-granting classification is very similar to the earlier higher education classification, but it includes more 2-year colleges and excludes a few higher education institutions that did not grant degrees. (See Guide to Sources for details.)

SOURCE: U.S. Department of Education, National Center for Education Statistics, *Education Directory, Higher Education*, 1969–70 through 1974–75; *Education Directory, Colleges and Universities*, 1975–76 through 1983–84; *1982–83 Supplement to the Education Directory, Colleges and Universities;* and 1986–87 through 2007–08 Integrated Postsecondary Education Data System, "Institutional Characteristics Survey" (IPEDS-IC:86-99), and Spring 2000 through Spring 2008. (This table was prepared September 2008.)

Table 268. Degrees conferred by degree-granting institutions, by level of degree and sex of student: Selected years, 1869–70 through 2017–18

Year	Associate's degrees			Bachelor's degrees			Master's degrees			First-professional degrees			Doctor's degrees[1]		
	Total	Males	Females	Total	Males	Females	Total	Males	Females	Total	Males	Females	Total	Males	Females
1	2	3	4	5	6	7	8	9	10	11	12	13	14	15	16
1869–70	—	—	—	9,371 [2]	7,993 [2]	1,378 [2]	0	0	0	(3)	(3)	(3)	1	1	0
1879–80	—	—	—	12,896 [2]	10,411 [2]	2,485 [2]	879	868	11	(3)	(3)	(3)	54	51	3
1889–90	—	—	—	15,539 [2]	12,857 [2]	2,682 [2]	1,015	821	194	(3)	(3)	(3)	149	147	2
1899–1900	—	—	—	27,410 [2]	22,173 [2]	5,237 [2]	1,583	1,280	303	(3)	(3)	(3)	382	359	23
1909–10	—	—	—	37,199 [2]	28,762 [2]	8,437 [2]	2,113	1,555	558	(3)	(3)	(3)	443	399	44
1919–20	—	—	—	48,622 [2]	31,980 [2]	16,642 [2]	4,279	2,985	1,294	(3)	(3)	(3)	615	522	93
1929–30	—	—	—	122,484 [2]	73,615 [2]	48,869 [2]	14,969	8,925	6,044	(3)	(3)	(3)	2,299	1,946	353
1939–40	—	—	—	186,500 [2]	109,546 [2]	76,954 [2]	26,731	16,508	10,223	(3)	(3)	(3)	3,290	2,861	429
1949–50	—	—	—	432,058 [2]	328,841 [2]	103,217 [2]	58,183	41,220	16,963	(3)	(3)	(3)	6,420	5,804	616
1959–60	—	—	—	392,440 [2]	254,063 [2]	138,377 [2]	74,435	50,898	23,537	(3)	(3)	(3)	9,829	8,801	1,028
1969–70	206,023	117,432	88,591	792,316	451,097	341,219	208,291	125,624	82,667	34,918	33,077	1,841	29,866	25,890	3,976
1970–71	252,311	144,144	108,167	839,730	475,594	364,136	230,509	138,146	92,363	37,946	35,544	2,402	32,107	27,530	4,577
1971–72	292,014	166,227	125,787	887,273	500,590	386,683	251,633	149,550	102,083	43,411	40,723	2,688	33,363	28,090	5,273
1972–73	316,174	175,413	140,761	922,362	518,191	404,171	263,371	154,468	108,903	50,018	46,489	3,529	34,777	28,571	6,206
1973–74	343,924	188,591	155,333	945,776	527,313	418,463	277,033	157,842	119,191	53,816	48,530	5,286	33,816	27,365	6,451
1974–75	360,171	191,017	169,154	922,933	504,841	418,092	292,450	161,570	130,880	55,916	48,956	6,960	34,083	26,817	7,266
1975–76	391,454	209,996	181,458	925,746	504,925	420,821	311,771	167,248	144,523	62,649	52,892	9,757	34,064	26,267	7,797
1976–77	406,377	210,842	195,535	919,549	495,545	424,004	317,164	167,783	149,381	64,359	52,374	11,985	33,232	25,142	8,090
1977–78	412,246	204,718	207,528	921,204	487,347	433,857	311,620	161,212	150,408	66,581	52,270	14,311	32,131	23,658	8,473
1978–79	402,702	192,091	210,611	921,390	477,344	444,046	301,079	153,370	147,709	68,848	52,652	16,196	32,730	23,541	9,189
1979–80	400,910	183,737	217,173	929,417	473,611	455,806	298,081	150,749	147,332	70,131	52,716	17,415	32,615	22,943	9,672
1980–81	416,377	188,638	227,739	935,140	469,883	465,257	295,739	147,043	148,696	71,956	52,792	19,164	32,958	22,711	10,247
1981–82	434,526	196,944	237,582	952,998	473,364	479,634	295,546	145,532	150,014	72,032	52,223	19,809	32,707	22,224	10,483
1982–83	449,620	203,991	245,629	969,510	479,140	490,370	289,921	144,697	145,224	73,054	51,250	21,804	32,775	21,902	10,873
1983–84	452,240	202,704	249,536	974,309	482,319	491,990	284,263	143,595	140,668	74,468	51,378	23,090	33,209	22,064	11,145
1984–85	454,712	202,932	251,780	979,477	482,528	496,949	286,251	143,390	142,861	75,063	50,455	24,608	32,943	21,700	11,243
1985–86	446,047	196,166	249,881	987,823	485,923	501,900	288,567	143,508	145,059	73,910	49,261	24,649	33,653	21,819	11,834
1986–87	436,304	190,839	245,465	991,264	480,782	510,482	289,349	141,269	148,080	71,617	46,523	25,094	34,041	22,061	11,980
1987–88	435,085	190,047	245,038	994,829	477,203	517,626	299,317	145,163	154,154	70,735	45,484	25,251	34,870	22,615	12,255
1988–89	436,764	186,316	250,448	1,018,755	483,346	535,409	310,621	149,354	161,267	70,856	45,046	25,810	35,720	22,648	13,072
1989–90	455,102	191,195	263,907	1,051,344	491,696	559,648	324,301	153,653	170,648	70,988	43,961	27,027	38,371	24,401	13,970
1990–91	481,720	198,634	283,086	1,094,538	504,045	590,493	337,168	156,482	180,686	71,948	43,846	28,102	39,294	24,756	14,538
1991–92	504,231	207,481	296,750	1,136,553	520,811	615,742	352,838	161,842	190,996	74,146	45,071	29,075	40,659	25,557	15,102
1992–93	514,756	211,964	302,792	1,165,178	532,881	632,297	369,585	169,258	200,327	75,387	45,153	30,234	42,132	26,073	16,059
1993–94	530,632	215,261	315,371	1,169,275	532,422	636,853	387,070	176,085	210,985	75,418	44,707	30,711	43,185	26,552	16,633
1994–95	539,691	218,352	321,339	1,160,134	526,131	634,003	397,629	178,598	219,031	75,800	44,853	30,947	44,446	26,916	17,530
1995–96	555,216	219,514	335,702	1,164,792	522,454	642,338	406,301	179,081	227,220	76,734	44,748	31,986	44,652	26,841	17,811
1996–97	571,226	223,948	347,278	1,172,879	520,515	652,364	419,401	180,947	238,454	78,730	45,564	33,166	45,876	27,146	18,730
1997–98	558,555	217,613	340,942	1,184,406	519,956	664,450	430,164	184,375	245,789	78,598	44,911	33,687	46,010	26,664	19,346
1998–99	559,954	218,417	341,537	1,200,303	518,746	681,557	439,986	186,148	253,838	78,439	44,339	34,100	44,077	25,146	18,931
1999–2000	564,933	224,721	340,212	1,237,875	530,367	707,508	457,056	191,792	265,264	80,057	44,239	35,818	44,808	25,028	19,780
2000–01	578,865	231,645	347,220	1,244,171	531,840	712,331	468,476	194,351	274,125	79,707	42,862	36,845	44,904	24,728	20,176
2001–02	595,133	238,109	357,024	1,291,900	549,816	742,084	482,118	199,120	282,998	80,698	42,507	38,191	44,160	23,708	20,452
2002–03	634,016	253,451	380,565	1,348,811	573,258	775,553	513,339	211,664	301,675	80,897	41,887	39,010	46,042	24,351	21,691
2003–04	665,301	260,033	405,268	1,399,542	595,425	804,117	558,940	229,545	329,395	83,041	42,169	40,872	48,378	25,323	23,055
2004–05	696,660	267,536	429,124	1,439,264	613,000	826,264	574,618	233,590	341,028	87,289	43,849	43,440	52,631	26,973	25,658
2005–06	713,066	270,095	442,971	1,485,242	630,600	854,642	594,065	237,896	356,169	87,655	44,038	43,617	56,067	28,634	27,433
2006–07	728,114	275,187	452,927	1,524,092	649,570	874,522	604,607	238,189	366,418	90,064	45,057	45,007	60,616	30,251	30,365
2007–08[4]	718,000	272,000	446,000	1,563,000	658,000	904,000	631,000	248,000	383,000	91,800	46,000	45,800	61,700	30,000	31,700
2008–09[4]	731,000	277,000	454,000	1,603,000	675,000	928,000	649,000	258,000	391,000	93,300	46,800	46,400	61,700	30,100	31,600
2009–10[4]	741,000	282,000	459,000	1,634,000	689,000	945,000	659,000	265,000	393,000	94,400	47,500	46,900	63,500	31,300	32,300
2010–11[4]	743,000	283,000	459,000	1,653,000	699,000	954,000	663,000	269,000	394,000	95,100	48,000	47,100	63,800	31,700	32,100
2011–12[4]	745,000	285,000	460,000	1,667,000	707,000	961,000	670,000	273,000	398,000	96,100	48,500	47,600	63,500	31,700	31,800
2012–13[4]	747,000	286,000	461,000	1,681,000	713,000	968,000	680,000	277,000	402,000	97,200	49,100	48,100	66,700	33,300	33,400
2013–14[4]	750,000	287,000	463,000	1,692,000	718,000	974,000	694,000	284,000	411,000	98,900	49,800	49,200	68,200	34,000	34,200
2014–15[4]	755,000	288,000	467,000	1,700,000	720,000	980,000	712,000	291,000	422,000	101,000	50,500	50,500	69,900	34,800	35,100
2015–16[4]	757,000	288,000	470,000	1,703,000	718,000	985,000	730,000	297,000	433,000	103,100	51,200	51,900	71,600	35,500	36,100
2016–17[4]	763,000	288,000	475,000	1,711,000	718,000	993,000	745,000	302,000	443,000	105,000	51,800	53,200	73,400	36,300	37,200
2017–18[4]	773,000	290,000	483,000	1,730,000	723,000	1,007,000	759,000	306,000	452,000	106,700	52,300	54,400	75,300	37,000	38,200

—Not available.
[1]Includes Ph.D., Ed.D., and comparable degrees at the doctoral level. Excludes first-professional, such as M.D., D.D.S., and law degrees.
[2]Includes first-professional degrees.
[3]First-professional degrees are included with bachelor's degrees.
[4]Projected.
NOTE: Data through 1994–95 are for institutions of higher education, while later data are for degree-granting institutions. Degree-granting institutions grant associate's or higher degrees and participate in Title IV federal financial aid programs. The degree-granting classification is very similar to the earlier higher education classification, but it includes more 2-year colleges and excludes a few higher education institutions that did not grant degrees. (See Guide to Sources for details.) Some data have been revised from previously published figures. Detail may not sum to totals because of rounding.
SOURCE: U.S. Department of Education, National Center for Education Statistics, *Earned Degrees Conferred*, 1869–70 through 1964–65; *Projections of Education Statistics to 2017*; Higher Education General Information Survey (HEGIS), "Degrees and Other Formal Awards Conferred" surveys, 1965–66 through 1985–86; and 1986–87 through 2006–07 Integrated Postsecondary Education Data System, "Completions Survey" (IPEDS-C:87–99), and Fall 2000 through Fall 2007. (This table was prepared July 2008.)

Table 269. Associate's degrees conferred by degree-granting institutions, by discipline division: 1995–96 through 2006–07

Discipline division	1995–96	1996–97	1997–98	1998–99	1999–2000	2000–01	2001–02	2002–03	2003–04	2004–05	2005–06	2006–07
1	2	3	4	5	6	7	8	9	10	11	12	13
Total	555,216	571,226	558,555	559,954	564,933	578,865	595,133	634,016	665,301	696,660	713,066	728,114
Agriculture and natural resources, total	6,182	6,463	6,673	6,632	6,666	6,649	6,494	6,210	6,283	6,404	6,168	5,838
Agriculture, agriculture operations, and related sciences	4,723	5,021	5,206	5,220	5,292	5,200	5,125	4,892	4,959	5,137	4,958	4,638
Natural resources and conservation	1,459	1,442	1,467	1,412	1,374	1,449	1,369	1,318	1,324	1,267	1,210	1,200
Architecture and related services	256	316	265	405	392	417	443	440	492	583	656	517
Area, ethnic, cultural, and gender studies	110	82	97	85	113	73	94	120	105	115	124	164
Biological and biomedical sciences	2,049	2,133	2,113	2,213	1,448	1,443	1,534	1,496	1,456	1,709	1,827	2,060
Business, management, and marketing	90,945	92,228	87,672	86,964	86,106	87,059	86,713	89,627	92,065	96,067	96,933	99,998
Accounting	15,926	16,017	14,807	14,325	13,562	13,158	12,315	13,229	14,506	13,988	13,620	14,232
Business, general	11,397	11,385	11,311	11,514	12,283	12,621	12,936	13,054	13,387	12,050	13,297	12,725
Business administration and management	28,901	29,804	28,793	28,615	28,486	28,947	30,268	33,112	33,652	42,979	43,868	47,684
Business and management, other	15,910	15,197	14,148	14,027	13,398	13,122	13,269	13,108	14,909	13,042	13,925	14,486
Management information systems	4,539	4,936	4,261	4,526	5,394	6,016	6,417	5,600	4,214	2,812	2,179	2,007
Secretarial and related programs	14,272	14,889	14,352	13,957	12,983	13,195	11,508	11,524	11,397	11,196	10,044	8,864
Communications	2,187	2,030	2,368	2,639	2,754	2,949	2,819	2,589	2,444	2,545	2,629	2,609
Communications technologies	2,807	2,863	2,642	2,528	2,625	3,038	3,006	3,304	3,401	3,516	3,380	3,095
Computer and information sciences	12,500	14,607	18,185	22,445	28,185	34,356	40,127	46,234	41,845	36,173	31,246	27,712
Construction trades	2,141	1,928	2,172	2,137	2,337	2,682	2,639	3,009	3,560	3,512	3,850	3,895
Education	9,809	10,587	9,461	10,165	8,510	9,533	9,611	11,205	12,465	13,329	14,475	13,021
Engineering	2,158	1,921	2,118	2,012	1,722	1,795	1,691	2,177	2,737	2,441	2,162	2,136
Engineering-related technologies	40,447	41,349	40,784	42,362	43,732	42,366	40,217	39,998	36,915	33,548	30,461	29,199
English language and literature/letters	813	892	1,035	1,032	947	877	864	896	828	995	1,105	1,249
Family and consumer sciences	7,651	7,998	7,811	8,063	8,031	8,329	9,208	9,496	9,478	9,707	9,488	9,124
Foreign languages, literatures, and linguistics	1,612	1,768	1,674	1,705	1,059	1,100	1,085	1,050	1,047	1,234	1,161	1,207
Health professions and related sciences	104,775	102,077	94,940	93,218	86,676	84,656	82,361	90,716	106,208	122,520	134,931	145,436
Dental assisting	4,564	4,866	4,904	6,628	5,569	5,193	5,223	5,498	5,652	5,813	6,085	6,313
Emergency medical technician–ambulance and paramedic	889	1,048	975	918	1,152	1,134	1,203	1,410	1,617	1,825	1,980	2,008
Medical lab technician	2,982	2,641	2,370	2,033	1,644	1,502	1,384	1,496	1,678	1,932	2,030	2,160
Medical assisting	4,941	5,019	5,102	5,358	5,414	5,863	4,748	5,859	8,499	10,411	12,367	12,071
Nursing assisting	7	13	23	12	7	2	0	8	4	38	101	158
Practical nursing	605	429	499	447	575	619	814	916	1,049	1,388	1,481	1,509
Nursing, R.N. and other	56,469	52,983	47,329	43,029	40,767	40,278	40,800	45,117	51,552	58,007	62,095	66,516
Health sciences, other	34,318	35,078	33,738	34,793	31,548	30,065	28,189	30,412	36,157	43,106	48,792	54,701
Legal professions and studies	11,916	11,242	9,890	9,133	8,842	8,119	7,815	8,412	9,466	9,885	10,509	10,391
Liberal arts and sciences, general studies, and humanities	174,970	181,341	186,248	181,977	187,454	196,843	207,163	217,361	227,650	240,131	244,689	250,030
Library science	94	126	96	86	98	103	96	87	114	108	136	84
Mathematics	758	792	844	823	675	695	685	732	801	807	753	827
Mechanics and repairers	12,519	12,126	10,576	10,781	11,678	12,689	12,063	12,028	12,553	13,619	14,454	15,432
Military technologies	556	556	22	42	65	120	62	85	293	355	610	781
Multi/interdisciplinary studies	8,619	9,182	9,402	8,661	11,784	10,439	13,205	14,067	14,794	13,888	14,473	15,838
Parks, recreation, leisure, and fitness studies	897	885	840	819	819	790	764	805	923	966	1,128	1,251
Personal and culinary services	7,720	8,172	7,648	8,933	9,203	9,786	9,325	12,607	14,239	16,311	17,162	16,103
Philosophy and religion	84	91	101	297	209	299	359	379	404	422	367	375
Physical sciences and science technologies	2,612	2,526	2,286	2,399	2,460	2,337	2,308	2,190	2,676	2,814	2,902	3,404
Physical sciences	1,749	1,728	1,584	1,679	1,350	1,207	1,346	1,141	1,588	1,626	1,733	2,015
Science technologies	863	798	702	720	1,110	1,130	962	1,049	1,088	1,188	1,169	1,389
Precision production trades	1,727	1,773	1,929	2,201	2,308	2,256	2,260	2,287	1,968	2,039	1,977	1,973
Psychology	1,583	1,612	1,765	1,625	1,455	1,554	1,705	1,785	1,887	1,942	1,944	2,213
Public administration and social services	4,218	4,270	4,156	3,881	3,656	3,333	3,323	3,534	3,728	4,027	4,415	4,338
Security and protective services	19,196	19,889	19,002	17,430	16,298	16,425	16,689	18,614	20,573	23,749	26,425	28,208
Criminal justice and corrections	15,990	16,644	15,915	14,448	13,487	13,589	13,603	15,155	17,040	19,942	22,351	23,917
Fire control and safety	2,523	2,638	2,480	2,395	2,364	2,346	2,619	2,941	3,012	3,366	3,554	3,811
Security and protective services, other	683	607	607	587	447	490	467	518	521	441	520	480
Social sciences and history	4,021	4,056	4,196	4,550	5,136	5,132	5,593	5,720	6,245	6,533	6,730	7,080
Social sciences	3,727	3,741	3,910	4,254	4,812	4,877	5,304	5,404	5,875	6,233	6,308	6,673
History	294	315	286	296	324	255	289	316	370	300	422	407
Theology and religious vocations	608	574	570	476	636	576	414	425	492	581	570	608
Transportation and material moving workers	1,551	1,572	977	1,101	956	1,028	1,122	1,211	1,217	1,435	1,472	1,674
Visual and performing arts	13,534	13,593	14,980	17,640	17,100	18,435	20,911	23,120	23,949	22,650	21,754	20,244
Fine arts, general	1,515	1,516	1,281	3,029	1,314	1,435	1,521	1,763	1,326	1,623	1,651	1,758
Design and music	10,579	10,459	11,591	12,026	12,780	14,410	16,388	18,342	18,836	17,482	16,387	15,467
Visual and performing arts, other	1,440	1,618	2,108	2,585	3,006	2,590	3,002	3,015	3,787	3,545	3,716	3,019
Not classified by field of study	1,591	7,606	3,017	2,494	2,798	584	365	0	0	0	0	0

SOURCE: U.S. Department of Education, National Center for Education Statistics, 1995–96 through 2006–07 Integrated Postsecondary Education Data System, "Completions Survey" (IPEDS-C:94–99), and Fall 2000 through Fall 2007. (This table was prepared September 2008.)

Table 270. Associate's degrees and other subbaccalaureate awards conferred by degree-granting institutions, by length of curriculum, sex of student, and discipline division: 2006–07

Discipline division	Less-than-1-year awards			1- to less-than-4-year awards			Associate's degrees		
	Total	Males	Females	Total	Males	Females	Total	Males	Females
1	2	3	4	5	6	7	8	9	10
Total	248,941	112,007	136,934	189,005	71,869	117,136	728,114	275,187	452,927
Agriculture and natural resources, total	3,376	2,495	881	1,626	1,030	596	5,838	3,626	2,212
Agriculture, agriculture operations and related sciences	2,315	1,554	761	1,554	975	579	4,638	2,710	1,928
Natural resources and conservation	1,061	941	120	72	55	17	1,200	916	284
Architecture and related services	164	95	69	178	67	111	517	231	286
Area, ethnic, cultural, and gender studies	379	101	278	121	36	85	164	53	111
Biological and biomedical sciences	111	32	79	29	11	18	2,060	676	1,384
Business, management, and marketing	32,981	10,608	22,373	15,589	3,836	11,753	99,998	32,996	67,002
Accounting	4,173	809	3,364	3,279	652	2,627	14,232	3,203	11,029
Business, general	1,159	705	454	956	441	515	12,725	5,057	7,668
Business administration and management	6,768	2,600	4,168	3,302	1,239	2,063	47,684	18,105	29,579
Business and management, other	11,845	4,352	7,493	2,196	725	1,471	14,486	4,738	9,748
Management information systems	408	287	121	605	428	177	2,007	1,237	770
Secretarial and related programs	8,628	1,855	6,773	5,251	351	4,900	8,864	656	8,208
Communications	470	252	218	446	273	173	2,609	1,311	1,298
Communications technologies	753	475	278	768	511	257	3,095	1,874	1,221
Computer and information sciences	8,403	5,378	3,025	4,856	3,070	1,786	27,712	20,459	7,253
Construction trades	8,946	8,455	491	7,266	6,975	291	3,895	3,696	199
Education	2,949	307	2,642	1,830	152	1,676	13,021	1,773	11,248
Engineering	192	135	57	58	47	11	2,136	1,835	301
Engineering-related technologies	7,594	6,368	1,226	6,475	5,594	881	29,199	25,155	4,044
English language and literature/letters	995	365	630	266	101	165	1,249	378	871
Family and consumer sciences	10,739	1,686	9,053	3,521	670	2,851	9,124	333	8,791
Foreign languages, literatures, and linguistics	799	220	579	463	47	416	1,207	195	1,012
Health professions and related sciences	92,276	17,911	74,365	86,344	11,071	75,273	145,436	21,214	124,222
Dental assisting	2,784	156	2,628	5,663	268	5,395	6,313	277	6,036
Emergency medical technician–ambulance and paramedic	12,352	8,484	3,868	3,277	2,497	780	2,008	1,358	650
Medical lab technician	264	22	242	397	220	177	2,160	518	1,642
Medical assisting	10,836	654	10,182	13,748	692	13,056	12,071	667	11,404
Nursing assisting	24,438	2,477	21,961	244	25	219	158	10	148
Practical nursing	4,327	431	3,896	29,529	2,917	26,612	1,509	129	1,380
Nursing, R.N. and other	2,047	189	1,858	4,430	481	3,949	66,516	8,222	58,294
Health sciences, other	35,228	5,498	29,730	29,056	3,971	25,085	54,701	10,033	44,668
Legal professions and studies	1,558	208	1,350	2,266	297	1,969	10,391	1,046	9,345
Liberal arts and sciences, general studies, and humanities	318	82	236	4,271	1,771	2,500	250,030	93,711	156,319
Library science	163	10	153	52	9	43	84	8	76
Mathematics	40	23	17	7	4	3	827	548	279
Mechanics and repairers	17,103	15,900	1,203	21,177	20,349	828	15,432	14,720	712
Military technologies	74	65	9	5	5	0	781	641	140
Multi/interdisciplinary studies	525	231	294	873	280	593	15,838	6,578	9,260
Parks, recreation, leisure, and fitness studies	347	174	173	182	72	110	1,251	749	502
Personal and culinary services	6,922	1,662	5,260	9,564	1,637	7,927	16,103	8,417	7,686
Philosophy and religion	11	8	3	74	49	25	375	115	260
Physical sciences and science technologies	291	146	145	303	136	167	3,404	1,948	1,456
Physical sciences	27	14	13	12	5	7	2,015	1,149	866
Science technologies	264	132	132	291	131	160	1,389	799	590
Precision production trades	6,019	5,666	353	4,985	4,752	233	1,973	1,849	124
Psychology	138	16	122	25	1	24	2,213	517	1,696
Public administration and social services	845	161	684	549	108	441	4,338	596	3,742
Security and protective services	20,893	15,689	5,204	5,265	3,927	1,338	28,208	15,481	12,727
Criminal justice and corrections	15,547	10,769	4,778	3,812	2,578	1,234	23,917	11,671	12,246
Fire control and safety	5,185	4,822	363	1,377	1,321	56	3,811	3,531	280
Security and protective services, other	161	98	63	129	81	48	480	279	201
Social sciences and history	352	193	159	200	103	97	7,080	2,494	4,586
Social sciences	344	192	152	191	98	93	6,673	2,252	4,421
History	8	1	7	9	5	4	407	242	165
Theology and religious vocations	139	53	86	445	230	215	608	313	295
Transportation and material moving workers	16,659	14,735	1,924	2,102	2,022	80	1,674	1,442	232
Visual and performing arts	5,417	2,102	3,315	6,824	2,626	4,198	20,244	8,209	12,035
Fine arts, general	3,056	1,137	1,919	4,105	1,523	2,582	1,758	574	1,184
Design and music	1,863	709	1,154	2,310	861	1,449	15,467	6,097	9,370
Visual and performing arts, other	498	256	242	409	242	167	3,019	1,538	1,481

SOURCE: U.S. Department of Education, National Center for Education Statistics, 2006–07 Integrated Postsecondary Education Data System (IPEDS), Fall 2007. (This table was prepared September 2008.)

Table 271. Bachelor's degrees conferred by degree-granting institutions, by field of study: Selected years, 1970–71 through 2006–07

Field of study	1970–71	1975–76	1980–81	1985–86	1990–91	1995–96	1996–97	1997–98	1998–99	1999–2000	2000–01	2001–02	2002–03	2003–04	2004–05	2005–06	2006–07
1	2	3	4	5	6	7	8	9	10	11	12	13	14	15	16	17	18
Total	839,730	925,746	935,140	987,823	1,094,538	1,164,792	1,172,879	1,184,406	1,200,303	1,237,875	1,244,171	1,291,900	1,348,811	1,399,542	1,439,264	1,485,242	1,524,092
Agriculture and natural resources	12,672	19,402	21,886	16,823	13,124	21,425	22,597	23,276	23,916	24,238	23,370	23,331	23,348	22,835	23,002	23,053	23,133
Architecture and related services	5,570	9,146	9,455	9,119	9,781	8,352	7,944	7,652	8,246	8,462	8,480	8,808	9,056	8,838	9,237	9,515	9,717
Area, ethnic, cultural, and gender studies	2,579	3,577	2,887	3,021	4,776	5,633	5,692	5,976	6,009	6,212	6,160	6,390	6,634	7,181	7,569	7,879	8,194
Biological and biomedical sciences	35,683	54,085	43,003	38,320	39,377	60,750	63,679	65,583	64,608	63,005	59,865	59,415	60,104	61,509	64,611	69,178	75,151
Business	115,396	143,171	200,521	236,700	249,165	226,623	225,934	232,079	240,947	256,070	263,515	278,217	293,391	307,149	311,574	318,042	327,531
Communication, journalism, and related programs	10,324	20,045	29,428	41,666	51,650	47,320	47,230	49,385	51,384	55,760	58,013	62,791	67,895	70,968	72,715	73,955	74,783
Communications technologies	478	1,237	1,854	1,479	1,397	853	664	878	1,076	1,298	1,178	1,245	1,933	2,034	2,523	2,981	3,637
Computer and information sciences	2,388	5,652	15,121	42,337	25,159	24,506	25,422	27,829	30,574	37,788	44,142	50,365	57,433	59,488	54,111	47,480	42,170
Education	176,307	154,437	108,074	87,147	110,807	105,384	105,116	105,833	107,086	108,034	105,458	106,295	105,845	106,278	105,451	107,238	105,641
Engineering	45,034	38,733	63,642	77,391	62,448	62,257	61,418	60,252	58,260	58,822	58,315	59,627	62,655	63,558	64,906	67,045	67,092
Engineering technologies	5,148	7,943	11,713	19,731	17,303	15,829	14,339	14,397	14,405	14,597	14,660	15,052	14,664	14,669	14,837	14,565	14,980
English language and literature/letters	63,914	41,452	31,922	34,083	51,064	49,928	48,641	49,016	49,800	50,106	50,569	52,375	53,699	53,984	54,379	55,096	55,122
Family and consumer sciences/human sciences	11,167	17,409	18,370	13,847	13,920	14,353	14,886	15,654	16,059	16,321	16,421	16,938	17,929	19,172	20,074	20,775	21,400
Foreign languages, literatures, and linguistics	20,988	17,068	11,638	11,550	13,937	14,832	14,487	15,279	15,821	15,886	16,128	16,258	16,912	17,754	18,386	19,410	20,275
Health professions and related clinical sciences	25,223	53,885	63,665	65,309	59,875	86,087	87,997	86,843	85,214	80,863	75,933	72,887	71,261	73,934	80,685	91,973	101,810
Legal professions and studies	545	531	776	1,223	1,827	2,123	2,083	2,079	1,960	1,969	1,991	2,003	2,474	2,841	3,161	3,302	3,596
Liberal arts and sciences, general studies, and humanities	7,481	18,855	21,643	21,336	30,526	33,997	34,776	33,202	34,772	36,104	37,962	39,333	40,480	42,106	43,751	44,898	44,255
Library science	1,013	843	375	155	90	58	48	73	78	154	52	74	99	72	76	76	82
Mathematics and statistics	24,801	15,984	11,078	16,122	14,393	12,713	12,401	11,795	11,966	11,418	11,171	11,950	12,505	13,327	14,351	14,770	14,954
Military technologies	357	952	42	255	183	7	4	3	2	7	21	3	6	10	40	33	168
Multi/interdisciplinary studies	6,346	13,778	13,061	13,829	17,879	27,149	26,887	26,960	27,545	28,561	27,189	28,943	28,639	29,162	30,243	32,012	33,792
Parks, recreation, leisure and fitness studies	1,621	5,182	5,729	4,623	4,315	12,974	14,246	15,422	16,532	17,571	17,948	18,885	21,432	22,164	22,888	25,490	27,430
Philosophy and religious studies	8,149	8,447	6,776	6,396	7,423	7,541	7,832	8,384	8,506	8,535	8,717	9,473	10,344	11,152	11,584	11,985	11,969
Physical sciences and science technologies	21,410	21,458	23,936	21,711	16,334	19,627	19,496	19,362	18,285	18,331	17,919	17,799	17,950	17,983	18,905	20,318	21,073
Precision production	0	0	0	2	2	12	19	52	43	33	31	47	42	61	64	55	23
Psychology	38,187	50,278	41,068	40,628	58,655	73,416	74,308	74,107	73,636	74,194	73,645	76,775	78,650	82,098	85,614	88,134	90,039
Public administration and social services	5,466	15,440	16,707	11,887	14,350	19,849	20,649	20,408	20,287	20,185	19,447	19,392	19,900	20,552	21,769	21,986	23,147
Security and protective services	2,045	12,507	13,707	12,704	16,806	24,810	25,165	25,076	24,601	24,877	25,211	25,536	26,200	28,175	30,723	35,319	39,206
Social sciences and history	155,324	126,396	100,513	93,840	125,107	126,479	124,891	125,040	124,658	127,101	128,036	132,874	143,256	150,357	156,892	161,485	164,183
Theology and religious vocations	3,720	5,490	5,808	5,510	4,799	5,292	5,542	5,855	6,235	6,789	6,945	7,762	7,962	8,126	9,284	8,548	8,696
Transportation and materials moving	0	225	263	1,838	2,622	3,561	3,547	3,206	3,383	3,395	3,748	4,020	4,631	4,824	4,904	5,349	5,657
Visual and performing arts	30,394	42,138	40,479	37,241	42,186	49,296	50,083	52,077	54,404	58,791	61,148	66,773	71,482	77,181	80,955	83,297	85,186
Not classified by field of study	0	0	0	0	13,258	1,756	4,856	1,373	5	2,398	783	264	0	0	0	0	0

NOTE: The new Classification of Instructional Programs was initiated in 2002–03. The figures for earlier years have been reclassified when necessary to make them conform to the new taxonomy. To facilitate trend comparisons, certain aggregations have been made of the degree fields as reported in the IPEDS "Completions Survey": "Agriculture and natural resources" includes Agriculture, agriculture operations, and related sciences and Natural resources and conservation; "Business" includes Business, management, marketing, and related support services and Personal and culinary services; and

"Engineering technologies" includes Engineering technologies/technicians, Construction trades, and Mechanic and repair technologies/technicians.
SOURCE: U.S. Department of Education, National Center for Education Statistics, Higher Education General Information Survey (HEGIS), "Degrees and Other Formal Awards Conferred" surveys, 1970–71 through 1985–86; and 1990–91 through 2006–07 Integrated Postsecondary Education Data System, "Completions Survey" (IPEDS-C-91–99), and Fall 2000 through Fall 2007. (This table was prepared September 2008.)

Table 272. Master's degrees conferred by degree-granting institutions, by field of study: Selected years, 1970–71 through 2006–07

Field of study	1970–71	1975–76	1980–81	1985–86	1990–91	1995–95	1997–98	1998–99	1999–2000	2000–01	2001–02	2002–03	2003–04	2004–05	2005–06	2006–07
1	2	3	4	5	6	7	8	9	10	11	12	13	14	15	16	17
Total	230,509	311,771	295,739	288,567	337,168	406,301	430,164	439,986	457,056	468,476	482,118	513,339	558,940	574,618	594,065	604,607
Agriculture and natural resources	2,457	3,340	4,003	3,801	3,295	4,551	4,464	4,404	4,360	4,272	4,503	4,492	4,783	4,746	4,640	4,623
Architecture and related services	1,705	3,215	3,153	3,260	3,490	3,993	4,347	4,172	4,268	4,302	4,566	4,925	5,424	5,674	5,743	5,951
Area, ethnic, cultural, and gender studies	1,032	993	802	915	1,233	1,652	1,528	1,438	1,544	1,555	1,541	1,509	1,683	1,755	2,080	1,699
Biological and biomedical sciences	5,623	6,453	5,759	5,043	4,796	6,544	6,788	6,913	6,781	6,955	6,937	6,990	7,657	8,199	8,681	8,747
Business	26,490	42,592	57,888	66,676	78,255	93,554	101,652	107,477	111,532	115,602	119,725	127,685	139,347	142,617	146,406	150,211
Communication, journalism, and related programs	1,770	2,961	2,896	3,500	4,123	5,080	5,611	5,293	5,169	5,218	5,510	6,053	6,535	6,762	7,244	6,773
Communications technologies	86	165	209	308	204	481	486	263	356	427	470	442	365	433	501	499
Computer and information sciences	1,588	2,603	4,218	8,070	9,324	10,579	11,765	12,858	14,990	16,911	17,173	19,509	20,143	18,416	17,055	16,232
Education	87,666	126,061	96,713	74,816	87,352	104,936	113,374	118,048	123,045	127,829	135,189	147,883	162,345	167,490	174,620	176,572
Engineering	16,813	16,472	16,893	21,529	24,454	26,892	25,146	24,734	24,850	25,259	24,908	28,338	32,698	32,633	30,989	29,472
Engineering technologies	134	328	323	617	996	2,054	2,181	2,004	1,876	2,013	2,149	2,332	2,499	2,500	2,541	2,690
English language and literature/letters	10,441	8,599	5,742	5,335	6,784	7,657	7,587	7,288	7,022	6,763	7,097	7,428	7,956	8,468	8,845	8,742
Family and consumer sciences/human sciences	1,452	2,179	2,570	2,011	1,541	1,712	1,838	1,736	1,882	1,838	1,683	1,607	1,794	1,827	1,983	2,080
Foreign languages, literatures, and linguistics	5,480	4,432	2,934	2,690	3,049	3,443	3,181	3,106	3,037	3,035	3,075	3,049	3,124	3,407	3,539	3,443
Health professions and related clinical sciences	5,330	12,164	16,176	18,603	21,354	33,920	39,567	40,707	42,593	43,623	43,560	42,748	44,939	46,703	51,380	54,531
Legal professions and studies	955	1,442	1,832	1,924	2,057	2,751	3,228	3,308	3,750	3,829	4,053	4,141	4,243	4,170	4,453	4,486
Liberal arts and sciences, general studies, and humanities	885	2,633	2,375	1,586	2,213	2,778	2,801	3,101	3,256	3,193	2,754	3,314	3,697	3,680	3,702	3,634
Library science	7,001	8,037	4,859	3,564	4,763	5,099	4,871	4,752	4,577	4,727	5,113	5,295	6,015	6,213	6,448	6,767
Mathematics and statistics	5,191	3,857	2,567	3,131	3,549	3,651	3,409	3,286	3,208	3,209	3,350	3,620	4,191	4,477	4,730	4,884
Military technologies	2	0	43	83	0	136	0	0	0	0	0	0	0	0	0	202
Multi/interdisciplinary studies	926	1,287	2,363	2,890	2,117	2,762	3,067	3,073	3,487	3,475	3,708	3,781	4,047	4,252	4,491	4,762
Parks, recreation, leisure, and fitness studies	218	571	643	570	483	1,684	1,917	2,011	2,322	2,354	2,580	2,978	3,199	3,740	3,992	4,110
Philosophy and religious studies	1,326	1,358	1,231	1,193	1,471	1,363	1,396	1,357	1,376	1,386	1,371	1,578	1,578	1,647	1,739	1,716
Physical sciences and science technologies	6,336	5,428	5,246	5,860	5,281	5,807	5,328	5,124	4,810	5,049	5,012	5,109	5,570	5,678	5,922	5,839
Precision production	0	0	0	0	0	8	10	7	5	2	2	3	13	6	9	5
Psychology	5,717	10,167	10,223	9,845	11,349	15,152	15,142	15,688	15,740	16,539	16,357	17,161	17,898	18,830	19,770	21,037
Public administration and social services	7,785	15,209	17,803	15,692	17,905	24,229	25,144	24,925	25,594	25,268	25,448	25,903	28,250	29,552	30,510	31,131
Security and protective services	194	1,197	1,538	1,074	1,108	1,812	2,000	2,249	2,609	2,514	2,935	2,956	3,717	3,991	4,277	4,906
Social sciences and history	16,539	15,953	11,945	10,564	12,233	15,012	14,938	14,431	14,066	13,791	14,112	14,630	16,110	16,952	17,369	17,665
Theology and religious vocations	2,692	3,258	4,163	4,543	4,803	5,030	4,649	4,679	5,534	4,850	4,909	5,133	5,486	5,815	6,092	6,446
Transportation and materials moving	0	0	0	454	406	919	736	713	697	756	709	765	728	802	784	985
Visual and performing arts	6,675	8,817	8,629	8,420	8,657	10,280	11,145	10,753	10,918	11,404	11,595	11,982	12,906	13,183	13,530	13,767
Not classified by field of study	0	0	0	0	8,523	780	868	88	1,802	528	24	0	0	0	0	0

NOTE: The new Classification of Instructional Programs was initiated in 2002–03. The figures for earlier years have been reclassified when necessary to make them conform to the new taxonomy. To facilitate trend comparisons, certain aggregations have been made of the degree fields as reported in the IPEDS "Completions Survey". "Agriculture and natural resources" includes Agriculture, agriculture operations, and related sciences and Natural resources and conservation; "Business" includes Business, management, marketing, and related support services and Personal and culinary services; and

"Engineering technologies" includes Engineering technologies/technicians, Construction trades, and Mechanic and repair technologies/technicians.
SOURCE: U.S. Department of Education, National Center for Education Statistics, Higher Education General Information Survey (HEGIS), "Degrees and Other Formal Awards Conferred" surveys, 1970–71 through 1985–86; and 1990–91 through 2005–07 Integrated Postsecondary Education Data System, "Completions Survey" (IPEDS-C:91–99), and Fall 2000 through Fall 2007. (This table was prepared September 2008.)

Table 273. Doctor's degrees conferred by degree-granting institutions, by field of study: Selected years, 1970–71 through 2006–07

Field of study	1970–71	1975–76	1980–81	1985–86	1990–91	1995–96	1997–98	1998–99	1999–2000	2000–01	2001–02	2002–03	2003–04	2004–05	2005–06	2006–07
1	2	3	4	5	6	7	8	9	10	11	12	13	14	15	16	17
Total	32,107	34,064	32,958	33,653	39,294	44,652	46,010	44,077	44,808	44,904	44,160	46,042	48,378	52,631	56,067	60,616
Agriculture and natural resources	1,086	928	1,067	1,158	1,185	1,259	1,290	1,231	1,168	1,127	1,148	1,229	1,185	1,173	1,194	1,272
Architecture and related services	36	82	93	73	135	141	131	123	129	153	183	152	173	179	201	178
Area, ethnic, cultural, and gender studies	143	186	161	156	159	183	176	187	205	216	212	186	209	189	226	233
Biological and biomedical sciences	3,595	3,313	3,591	3,352	4,034	5,035	5,236	5,024	5,180	4,953	4,823	5,003	5,242	5,578	5,775	6,354
Business	774	906	808	923	1,185	1,366	1,290	1,201	1,194	1,180	1,156	1,252	1,481	1,498	1,711	2,029
Communication, journalism, and related programs	145	196	171	212	259	338	354	347	347	368	374	394	418	465	461	479
Communications technologies	0	8	11	6	13	7	5	5	10	2	9	4	8	3	3	1
Computer and information sciences	128	244	252	344	676	869	858	801	779	768	752	816	909	1,119	1,416	1,595
Education	6,041	7,202	7,279	6,610	6,189	6,246	6,261	6,394	6,409	6,284	6,549	6,832	7,088	7,681	7,584	8,261
Engineering	3,687	2,872	2,598	3,444	5,316	6,381	5,996	5,432	5,390	5,542	5,187	5,276	5,923	6,547	7,396	8,062
Engineering technologies	1	2	10	12	14	50	42	29	31	62	58	57	58	54	75	61
English language and literature/letters	1,554	1,514	1,040	895	1,056	1,395	1,489	1,407	1,470	1,330	1,291	1,246	1,207	1,212	1,254	1,178
Family and consumer sciences/human sciences	123	178	247	307	229	375	386	323	327	354	311	376	329	331	340	337
Foreign languages, literatures, and linguistics	1,084	1,245	931	768	889	1,020	1,118	1,049	1,086	1,078	1,003	1,042	1,031	1,027	1,074	1,059
Health professions and related clinical sciences	518	617	868	1,139	1,534	1,651	1,975	1,920	2,053	2,242	2,913	3,329	4,361	5,868	7,128	8,355
Legal professions and studies	20	76	60	54	90	91	66	58	74	286	79	105	119	98	129	143
Liberal arts and sciences, general studies, and humanities	32	162	121	90	70	75	87	78	83	102	113	78	95	109	84	77
Library science	39	71	71	62	56	53	48	55	68	58	45	62	47	42	44	52
Mathematics and statistics	1,199	856	728	742	978	1,158	1,215	1,090	1,075	997	923	1,007	1,060	1,176	1,293	1,351
Multi/interdisciplinary studies	109	190	285	405	424	764	843	754	792	784	765	899	876	983	987	1,093
Parks, recreation, leisure, and fitness studies	2	15	42	39	28	104	129	137	134	177	151	199	222	207	194	218
Philosophy and religious studies	555	556	411	480	464	550	590	584	598	600	610	662	595	586	578	637
Physical sciences and science technologies	4,324	3,388	3,105	3,521	4,248	4,512	4,520	4,142	3,963	3,911	3,760	3,858	3,815	4,114	4,489	4,846
Psychology	2,144	3,157	3,576	3,593	3,932	4,141	4,541	4,695	4,731	5,091	4,759	4,835	4,827	5,106	4,921	5,153
Public administration and social services	174	292	362	382	430	499	499	532	537	574	571	599	649	673	704	726
Security and protective services	1	9	21	21	28	38	39	48	52	44	49	72	54	94	80	85
Social sciences and history	3,660	4,157	3,122	2,955	3,012	3,760	4,127	3,855	4,095	3,930	3,902	3,850	3,811	3,819	3,914	3,844
Theology and religious vocations	312	1,022	1,273	1,185	1,076	1,517	1,451	1,440	1,630	1,461	1,350	1,329	1,304	1,422	1,429	1,573
Transportation and materials moving	0	0	0	3	0	0	0	0	0	0	0	0	0	0	0	0
Visual and performing arts	621	620	654	722	838	1,067	1,163	1,130	1,127	1,167	1,114	1,293	1,282	1,278	1,383	1,364
Not classified by field of study	0	0	0	0	747	7	85	6	71	63	0	0	0	0	0	0

NOTE: Includes Ph.D., Ed., and comparable degrees at the doctoral level. Excludes first-professional degrees such as M.D., D.D.S., and law degrees. The new Classification of Instructional Programs was initiated in 2002–03. The figures for earlier years have been reclassified when necessary to make them conform to the new taxonomy. To facilitate trend comparisons, certain aggregations have been made of the degree fields as reported in the IPEDS "Completions Survey": "Agriculture and natural resources" includes Agriculture, agriculture operations, and related sciences and Natural resources and conservation; "Business" includes Business, management, marketing, and related support services and Personal and culinary services;

and "Engineering technologies" includes Engineering technologies/technicians, Construction trades, and Mechanic and repair technologies/technicians.
SOURCE: U.S. Department of Education, National Center for Education Statistics, Higher Education General Information Survey (HEGIS), "Degrees and Other Formal Awards Conferred" surveys, 1970–71 through 1985–86; and 1990–91 through 2006–07 Integrated Postsecondary Education Data System, "Completions Survey" (IPEDS-C:91–99), and Fall 2000 through Fall 2007. (This table was prepared September 2008.)

Table 274. Bachelor's, master's, and doctor's degrees conferred by degree-granting institutions, by field of study and year: Selected years, 1970–71 through 2006–07

Degree and year	Number of degrees conferred								Percentage distribution of degrees conferred							
	Total degrees	Humanities[1]	Social and behavioral sciences[2]	Natural sciences[3]	Computer sciences and engineering[4]	Education	Business	Other fields[5]	Total degrees	Humanities[1]	Social and behavioral sciences[2]	Natural sciences[3]	Computer sciences and engineering[4]	Education	Business	Other fields[5]
1	2	3	4	5	6	7	8	9	10	11	12	13	14	15	16	17
Bachelor's degrees																
1970–71	839,730	143,571	193,511	81,894	52,570	176,307	115,396	76,481	100.0	17.1	23.0	9.8	6.3	21.0	13.7	9.1
1975–76	925,746	150,805	176,674	91,527	52,328	154,437	143,171	156,804	100.0	16.3	19.1	9.9	5.7	16.7	15.5	16.9
1980–81	935,140	134,214	141,581	78,017	90,476	108,074	200,521	182,257	100.0	14.4	15.1	8.3	9.7	11.6	21.4	19.5
1985–86	987,823	132,966	134,468	76,153	139,459	87,147	236,700	180,930	100.0	13.5	13.6	7.7	14.1	8.8	24.0	18.3
1990–91	1,094,538	172,590	183,762	70,104	104,910	110,807	249,165	203,200	100.0	15.8	16.8	6.4	9.6	10.1	22.8	18.6
1995–96	1,164,792	193,668	199,895	93,090	102,592	105,384	226,623	243,540	100.0	16.6	17.2	8.0	8.8	9.0	19.5	20.9
2000–01	1,244,171	214,818	201,681	88,955	117,117	105,458	263,515	252,627	100.0	17.3	16.2	7.1	9.4	8.5	21.2	20.3
2002–03	1,348,811	236,152	221,906	90,559	134,752	105,845	293,391	266,206	100.0	17.5	16.5	6.7	10.0	7.8	21.8	19.7
2003–04	1,399,542	246,646	232,455	92,819	137,715	106,278	307,149	276,480	100.0	17.6	16.6	6.6	9.8	7.6	21.9	19.8
2004–05	1,439,264	256,151	242,506	97,867	133,854	105,451	311,574	291,861	100.0	17.8	16.8	6.8	9.3	7.3	21.6	20.3
2005–06	1,485,242	263,125	249,619	104,266	129,090	107,238	318,042	313,862	100.0	17.7	16.8	7.0	8.7	7.2	21.4	21.1
2006–07	1,524,092	267,489	254,222	111,178	124,242	105,641	327,531	333,789	100.0	17.6	16.7	7.3	8.2	6.9	21.5	21.9
Master's degrees																
1970–71	230,509	29,457	22,256	17,150	18,535	87,666	26,490	28,955	100.0	12.8	9.7	7.4	8.0	38.0	11.5	12.6
1975–76	311,771	31,377	26,120	15,738	19,403	126,061	42,592	50,480	100.0	10.1	8.4	5.0	6.2	40.4	13.7	16.2
1980–81	295,739	28,239	22,168	13,572	21,434	96,713	57,888	55,725	100.0	9.5	7.5	4.6	7.2	32.7	19.6	18.8
1985–86	288,567	27,572	20,409	14,034	30,216	74,816	66,676	54,844	100.0	9.6	7.1	4.9	10.5	25.9	23.1	19.0
1990–91	337,168	30,327	23,582	13,626	34,774	87,352	78,255	69,252	100.0	9.0	7.0	4.0	10.3	25.9	23.2	20.5
1995–96	406,301	34,965	30,164	16,002	39,525	104,936	93,554	87,155	100.0	8.6	7.4	3.9	9.7	25.8	23.0	21.5
2000–01	468,476	35,661	30,330	15,213	44,183	127,829	115,602	99,658	100.0	7.6	6.5	3.2	9.4	27.3	24.7	21.3
2002–03	513,339	37,774	31,791	15,719	50,179	147,883	127,685	102,308	100.0	7.4	6.2	3.1	9.8	28.8	24.9	19.9
2003–04	558,940	40,477	34,008	17,418	55,340	162,345	139,347	110,005	100.0	7.2	6.1	3.1	9.9	29.0	24.9	19.7
2004–05	574,618	42,207	35,782	18,354	53,549	167,490	142,617	114,619	100.0	7.3	6.2	3.2	9.3	29.1	24.8	19.9
2005–06	594,065	44,018	37,139	19,333	50,585	174,620	145,406	121,964	100.0	7.4	6.3	3.3	8.5	29.4	24.6	20.5
2006–07	604,607	44,209	38,702	19,470	48,394	176,572	150,211	127,049	100.0	7.3	6.4	3.2	8.0	29.2	24.8	21.0
Doctor's degrees																
1970–71	32,107	4,410	5,804	9,118	3,816	6,041	774	2,144	100.0	13.7	18.1	28.4	11.9	18.8	2.4	6.7
1975–76	34,064	5,495	7,314	7,557	3,118	7,202	906	2,472	100.0	16.1	21.5	22.2	9.2	21.1	2.7	7.3
1980–81	32,958	4,876	6,698	7,424	2,860	7,279	808	3,013	100.0	14.8	20.3	22.5	8.7	22.1	2.5	9.1
1985–86	33,653	4,701	6,548	7,615	3,800	6,610	923	3,456	100.0	14.0	19.5	22.6	11.3	19.6	2.7	10.3
1990–91	39,294	4,976	6,944	9,260	6,006	6,189	1,185	4,734	100.0	12.7	17.7	23.6	15.3	15.8	3.0	12.0
1995–96	44,652	6,571	7,901	10,705	7,300	6,246	1,366	4,563	100.0	14.7	17.7	24.0	16.3	14.0	3.1	10.2
2000–01	44,904	6,738	9,021	9,861	6,372	6,284	1,180	5,448	100.0	15.0	20.1	22.0	14.2	14.0	2.6	12.1
2002–03	46,042	6,735	8,685	9,868	6,149	6,832	1,252	6,521	100.0	14.6	18.9	21.4	13.4	14.8	2.7	14.2
2003–04	48,378	6,599	8,638	10,117	6,890	7,088	1,481	7,565	100.0	13.6	17.9	20.9	14.2	14.7	3.1	15.6
2004–05	52,631	6,806	8,925	10,868	7,720	7,681	1,498	9,133	100.0	12.9	17.0	20.6	14.7	14.6	2.8	17.4
2005–06	56,067	7,015	8,835	11,557	8,887	7,584	1,711	10,478	100.0	12.5	15.8	20.6	15.9	13.5	3.1	18.7
2006–07	60,616	7,214	8,997	12,551	9,718	8,261	2,029	11,846	100.0	11.9	14.8	20.7	16.0	13.6	3.3	19.5

[1]Includes degrees in Area, ethnic, cultural, and gender studies; English language and literature/letters; Foreign languages, literatures, and linguistics; Liberal arts and sciences, general studies, and humanities; Multi/interdisciplinary studies; Philosophy and religious studies; Theology and religious vocations; and Visual and performing arts.

[2]Includes Psychology; and Social sciences and history.

[3]Includes Biological and biomedical sciences; Mathematics and statistics; and Physical sciences and science technologies.

[4]Includes Computer and information sciences; Engineering; and Engineering technologies.

[5]Includes Agriculture and natural resources; Architecture and related services; Communication, journalism, and related programs; Communications technologies; Family and consumer sciences/human sciences; Health professions and related clini-

cal sciences; Legal professions and studies; Library science; Military technologies; Parks, recreation, leisure, and fitness studies; Precision production; Public administration and social services; Security and protective services; Transportation and materials moving; and Not classified by field of study.

NOTE: Detail may not sum to totals because of rounding.
SOURCE: U.S. Department of Education, National Center for Education Statistics, Higher Education General Information Survey (HEGIS), "Degrees and Other Formal Awards Conferred" surveys, 1970–71 through 1985–86; and 1990–91 through 2006–07 Integrated Postsecondary Education Data System, "Completions Survey" (IPEDS-C:91–96), and Fall 2001 through Fall 2007. (This table was prepared September 2008.)

Table 275. Bachelor's, master's, and doctor's degrees conferred by degree-granting institutions, by sex of student and discipline division: 2006–07

Discipline division	Bachelor's degrees requiring 4 or 5 years			Master's degrees			Doctor's degrees (Ph.D., Ed.D., etc.)[1]		
	Total	Males	Females	Total	Males	Females	Total	Males	Females
1	2	3	4	5	6	7	8	9	10
All fields, total	1,524,092	649,570	874,522	604,607	238,189	366,418	60,616	30,251	30,365
Agriculture and natural resources	23,133	12,309	10,824	4,623	2,174	2,449	1,272	768	504
Agriculture, agriculture operations, and related sciences	14,473	7,539	6,934	2,089	1,020	1,069	778	465	313
Agriculture, general	1,400	838	562	251	122	129	14	8	6
Agricultural business and management, general	858	572	286	44	27	17	0	0	0
Agribusiness/agricultural business operations	1,651	1,116	535	33	17	16	0	0	0
Agricultural economics	863	611	252	381	229	152	166	110	56
Farm/farm and ranch management	91	66	25	10	8	2	0	0	0
Agricultural/farm supplies retailing and wholesaling	75	46	29	0	0	0	0	0	0
Agricultural business technology	0	0	0	0	0	0	0	0	0
Agricultural business and management, other	421	265	156	8	3	5	0	0	0
Agricultural mechanization, general	272	255	17	2	2	0	0	0	0
Agricultural power machinery operation	0	0	0	0	0	0	0	0	0
Agricultural mechanics and equipment/machine technology	0	0	0	0	0	0	0	0	0
Agricultural mechanization, other	25	25	0	0	0	0	0	0	0
Agricultural production operations, general	67	43	24	18	13	5	0	0	0
Animal/livestock husbandry and production	30	14	16	0	0	0	0	0	0
Aquaculture	36	27	9	24	19	5	7	5	2
Crop production	32	26	6	8	7	1	3	2	1
Horse husbandry/equine science and management	7	0	7	0	0	0	0	0	0
Agricultural and food products processing	36	15	21	3	1	2	7	5	2
Equestrian/equine studies	402	23	379	0	0	0	0	0	0
Agricultural and domestic animal services, other	6	0	6	0	0	0	0	0	0
Applied horticulture/horticultural operations, general	205	128	77	16	8	8	11	7	4
Ornamental horticulture	147	96	51	4	1	3	3	3	0
Landscaping and groundskeeping	191	123	68	10	5	5	0	0	0
Turf and turfgrass management	115	112	3	0	0	0	0	0	0
Floriculture/floristry operations and management	0	0	0	0	0	0	1	1	0
Applied horticulture/horticultural business services, other	17	15	2	0	0	0	0	0	0
International agriculture	13	4	9	11	5	6	0	0	0
Agricultural and extension education services	33	13	20	14	4	10	3	2	1
Agricultural communication/journalism	183	43	140	16	2	14	0	0	0
Agricultural public services, other	61	34	27	0	0	0	0	0	0
Animal sciences, general	3,990	1,134	2,856	346	127	219	132	76	56
Agricultural animal breeding	24	8	16	6	4	2	5	4	1
Animal health	0	0	0	4	0	4	0	0	0
Animal nutrition	0	0	0	0	0	0	3	2	1
Dairy science	125	70	55	10	7	3	2	2	0
Livestock management	6	1	5	0	0	0	0	0	0
Poultry science	120	70	50	15	4	11	13	7	6
Animal sciences, other	107	34	73	7	3	4	2	2	0
Food science	809	257	552	262	87	175	130	53	77
Food technology and processing	5	3	2	2	1	1	0	0	0
Food science and technology, other	21	15	6	13	6	7	7	4	3
Plant sciences, general	270	196	74	99	54	45	46	23	23
Agronomy and crop science	394	315	79	128	78	50	84	59	25
Horticultural science	733	477	256	81	46	35	33	20	13
Agricultural and horticultural plant breeding	0	0	0	9	5	4	10	9	1
Plant protection and integrated pest management	10	3	7	9	3	6	1	1	0
Range science and management	147	102	45	60	34	26	8	4	4
Plant sciences, other	64	47	17	41	19	22	11	9	2
Soil science and agronomy, general	110	79	31	79	39	40	54	36	18
Soil chemistry and physics	0	0	0	1	0	1	0	0	0
Soil sciences, other	11	9	2	14	4	10	7	3	4
Agriculture, agriculture operations, and related sciences, other	290	209	81	50	26	24	15	8	7
Natural resources and conservation	8,660	4,770	3,890	2,534	1,154	1,380	494	303	191
Natural resources/conservation, general	1,035	628	407	318	139	179	72	45	27
Environmental studies	2,781	1,238	1,543	454	177	277	60	28	32
Environmental science	1,989	998	991	582	245	337	96	52	44
Environmental science/studies	0	0	0	0	0	0	0	0	0
Natural resources conservation and research, other	0	0	0	7	5	2	3	2	1
Natural resources management and policy	364	231	133	319	140	179	42	26	16
Natural resource economics	15	9	6	10	3	7	3	2	1
Water, wetlands, and marine resources management	63	26	37	41	16	25	1	0	1
Land use planning and management/development	31	17	14	57	37	20	6	5	1
Natural resources management and policy, other	105	66	39	8	3	5	0	0	0
Fishing and fisheries sciences and management	169	114	55	85	42	43	20	13	7
Forestry, general	581	426	155	269	126	143	80	55	25
Forest sciences and biology	157	124	33	100	67	33	38	27	11
Forest management/forest resources management	92	77	15	33	23	10	7	5	2
Urban forestry	31	22	9	5	4	1	0	0	0
Wood science and wood products/pulp and paper technology	94	86	8	26	19	7	7	6	1
Forest resources production and management	1	1	0	12	8	4	4	4	0
Forest technology/technician	7	6	1	0	0	0	6	5	1
Forestry, other	36	29	7	11	6	5	4	0	4
Wildlife and wildlands science and management	927	562	365	177	88	89	33	23	10
Natural resources and conservation, other	182	110	72	20	6	14	12	5	7

See notes at end of table.

Table 275. Bachelor's, master's, and doctor's degrees conferred by degree-granting institutions, by sex of student and discipline division: 2006–07—Continued

Discipline division	Bachelor's degrees requiring 4 or 5 years			Master's degrees			Doctor's degrees (Ph.D., Ed.D., etc.)[1]		
	Total	Males	Females	Total	Males	Females	Total	Males	Females
1	2	3	4	5	6	7	8	9	10
Architecture and related services	9,717	5,393	4,324	5,951	3,304	2,647	178	104	74
Architecture	5,869	3,452	2,417	3,278	1,984	1,294	87	49	38
City/urban, community and regional planning	757	478	279	2,008	1,066	942	68	42	26
Environmental design/architecture	828	471	357	22	8	14	17	11	6
Interior architecture	817	60	757	34	9	25	0	0	0
Landscape architecture	1,015	659	356	488	186	302	1	1	0
Architectural history and criticism, general	17	11	6	16	4	12	4	0	4
Architectural technology/technician	61	41	20	0	0	0	0	0	0
Architecture and related services, other	353	221	132	105	47	58	1	1	0
Area, ethnic, cultural, and gender studies	8,194	2,572	5,622	1,699	617	1,082	233	95	138
African studies	35	8	27	25	7	18	2	2	0
American/United States studies/civilization	1,666	588	1,078	237	86	151	75	26	49
Asian studies/civilization	647	291	356	93	53	40	1	0	1
East Asian studies	422	204	218	103	45	58	16	7	9
Central/Middle and Eastern European studies	6	3	3	10	7	3	0	0	0
European studies/civilization	159	37	122	19	5	14	0	0	0
Latin American studies	552	154	398	277	94	183	5	2	3
Near and Middle Eastern studies	154	71	83	114	53	61	37	25	12
Pacific Area/Pacific rim studies	13	6	7	6	0	6	0	0	0
Russian studies	87	33	54	67	26	41	0	0	0
Scandinavian studies	21	7	14	5	1	4	1	0	1
South Asian studies	12	7	5	21	7	14	1	1	0
Southeast Asian studies	1	0	1	13	7	6	0	0	0
Western European studies	3	0	3	60	25	35	1	1	0
Canadian studies	1	1	0	0	0	0	0	0	0
Slavic studies	7	2	5	0	0	0	0	0	0
Ural-Altaic and Central Asian studies	0	0	0	9	8	1	3	2	1
Regional studies (US, Canadian, foreign)	29	17	12	2	0	2	6	1	5
Chinese studies	16	6	10	9	4	5	0	0	0
French studies	37	6	31	0	0	0	6	3	3
German studies	57	20	37	4	1	3	3	0	3
Italian studies	44	9	35	6	0	6	1	0	1
Japanese studies	44	22	22	6	4	2	0	0	0
Korean studies	0	0	0	4	3	1	0	0	0
Spanish and Iberian studies	18	6	12	0	0	0	1	0	1
Tibetan studies	1	0	1	0	0	0	0	0	0
Area studies, other	570	224	346	64	25	39	3	0	3
African-American/Black studies	757	259	498	102	34	68	27	13	14
American Indian/Native American studies	186	75	111	20	11	9	8	5	3
Hispanic-American, Puerto Rican, and Mexican-American/Chicano studies	324	103	221	33	9	24	2	0	2
Asian-American studies	159	64	95	20	10	10	0	0	0
Women's studies	1,195	40	1,155	150	7	143	7	0	7
Gay/lesbian studies	4	0	4	0	0	0	0	0	0
Ethnic, cultural minority, and gender studies, other	461	136	325	85	21	64	19	4	15
Area, ethnic, cultural, and gender studies, other	506	173	333	135	64	71	8	3	5
Biological and biomedical sciences	75,151	29,951	45,200	8,747	3,568	5,179	6,354	3,221	3,133
Biology/biological sciences, general	52,527	20,146	32,381	2,679	1,084	1,595	788	403	385
Biomedical sciences, general	1,535	583	952	321	137	184	227	103	124
Biochemistry	5,022	2,445	2,577	231	102	129	526	306	220
Biophysics	87	67	20	40	22	18	134	97	37
Molecular biology	563	253	310	140	57	83	261	141	120
Molecular biochemistry	334	165	169	22	16	6	59	33	26
Molecular biophysics	0	0	0	1	1	0	17	9	8
Structural biology	0	0	0	0	0	0	3	2	1
Radiation biology/radiobiology	5	0	5	20	12	8	8	6	2
Biochemistry/biophysics and molecular biology	452	214	238	78	36	42	119	66	53
Biochemistry, biophysics and molecular biology, other	75	36	39	2	1	1	4	1	3
Botany/plant biology	172	68	104	90	28	62	130	57	73
Plant pathology/phytopathology	11	4	7	49	16	33	65	36	29
Plant physiology	0	0	0	5	3	2	16	8	8
Plant molecular biology	0	0	0	1	1	0	7	4	3
Botany/plant biology, other	7	1	6	13	4	9	9	3	6
Cell/cellular biology and histology	470	217	253	29	13	16	163	81	82
Anatomy	312	130	182	87	47	40	69	34	35
Developmental biology and embryology	0	0	0	25	9	16	33	16	17
Neuroanatomy	0	0	0	4	0	4	4	4	0
Cell/cellular and molecular biology	1,596	713	883	102	37	65	333	171	162
Cell biology and anatomy	6	3	3	11	3	8	28	17	11
Cell/cellular biology and anatomical sciences, other	387	172	215	130	58	72	135	55	80
Microbiology, general	1,498	668	830	182	76	106	217	112	105
Medical microbiology and bacteriology	705	287	418	91	32	59	192	92	100
Virology	0	0	0	2	1	1	17	9	8
Parasitology	0	0	0	0	0	0	2	2	0
Immunology	0	0	0	36	16	20	129	57	72
Microbiological sciences and immunology, other	144	52	92	58	14	44	110	53	57
Zoology/animal biology	1,687	623	1,064	141	53	88	98	61	37

See notes at end of table.

Table 275. Bachelor's, master's, and doctor's degrees conferred by degree-granting institutions, by sex of student and discipline division: 2006–07—Continued

Discipline division	Bachelor's degrees requiring 4 or 5 years			Master's degrees			Doctor's degrees (Ph.D., Ed.D., etc.)[1]		
	Total	Males	Females	Total	Males	Females	Total	Males	Females
1	2	3	4	5	6	7	8	9	10
Entomology	108	45	63	186	82	104	93	61	32
Animal physiology	196	83	113	71	31	40	62	31	31
Animal behavior and ethology	34	9	25	3	1	2	5	3	2
Wildlife biology	198	116	82	14	5	9	5	2	3
Physiology, human and animal	0	0	0	0	0	0	0	0	0
Zoology/animal biology, other	0	0	0	1	1	0	0	0	0
Genetics, general	242	101	141	62	20	42	157	60	97
Molecular genetics	94	41	53	25	10	15	71	34	37
Animal genetics	78	33	45	31	13	18	39	18	21
Plant genetics	0	0	0	8	5	3	5	3	2
Human/medical genetics	6	1	5	66	10	56	60	23	37
Genetics, plant and animal	0	0	0	0	0	0	0	0	0
Genetics, other	0	0	0	4	2	2	6	4	2
Physiology, general	907	365	542	285	167	118	151	82	69
Molecular physiology	0	0	0	6	4	2	26	9	17
Cell physiology	0	0	0	6	1	5	15	7	8
Endocrinology	0	0	0	4	1	3	4	2	2
Reproductive biology	0	0	0	6	1	5	1	1	0
Neurobiology and neurophysiology	307	121	186	17	13	4	92	57	35
Cardiovascular science	0	0	0	3	2	1	4	4	0
Exercise physiology	762	350	412	41	17	24	11	6	5
Vision science/physiological optics	200	59	141	4	0	4	9	3	6
Pathology/experimental pathology	20	4	16	115	37	78	146	70	76
Oncology and cancer biology	0	0	0	17	5	12	53	23	30
Medical physiology	0	0	0	0	0	0	0	0	0
Physiology, pathology, and related sciences, other	21	10	11	2	1	1	22	16	6
Pharmacology	59	29	30	115	58	57	208	103	105
Molecular pharmacology	0	0	0	6	3	3	33	15	18
Neuropharmacology	0	0	0	8	7	1	1	1	0
Toxicology	49	18	31	50	22	28	94	43	51
Molecular toxicology	0	0	0	2	0	2	5	2	3
Environmental toxicology	20	9	11	9	4	5	23	12	11
Pharmacology and toxicology	66	32	34	23	10	13	40	19	21
Biometry/biometrics	21	15	6	12	2	10	16	6	10
Biostatistics	17	9	8	253	92	161	113	51	62
Bioinformatics	118	70	48	149	86	63	56	44	12
Biomathematics and bioinformatics, other	9	6	3	4	2	2	5	3	2
Biotechnology	488	246	242	536	220	316	4	2	2
Ecology	638	282	356	199	74	125	166	90	76
Marine biology and biological oceanography	843	268	575	197	84	113	60	31	29
Evolutionary biology	24	6	18	12	5	7	36	16	20
Aquatic biology/limnology	61	35	26	11	6	5	0	0	0
Environmental biology	196	92	104	45	16	29	7	2	5
Population biology	0	0	0	5	2	3	8	4	4
Conservation biology	120	62	58	38	12	26	2	0	2
Epidemiology	0	0	0	628	187	441	203	55	148
Ecology, evolution, systematics and population biology, other	274	106	168	35	12	23	56	28	28
Biological and biomedical sciences, other	1,380	481	899	843	356	487	278	136	142
Business, management, marketing, and personal and culinary services	327,531	166,350	161,181	150,211	84,115	66,096	2,029	1,188	841
Business, management, marketing, and related support services	326,795	166,000	160,795	150,204	84,114	66,090	2,029	1,188	841
Business/commerce, general	21,826	11,914	9,912	9,704	5,810	3,894	394	235	159
Business administration and management, general	128,365	64,455	63,910	89,010	51,829	37,181	837	491	346
Purchasing, procurement/acquisitions and contracts management	313	169	144	229	121	108	0	0	0
Logistics and materials management	1,036	742	294	288	185	103	2	2	0
Office management and supervision	437	179	258	8	1	7	0	0	0
Operations management and supervision	2,471	1,697	774	1,078	668	410	14	11	3
Nonprofit/public/organizational management	567	242	325	748	222	526	4	0	4
Customer service management	47	23	24	6	2	4	0	0	0
E-commerce/electronic commerce	293	185	108	267	153	114	12	8	4
Transportation/transportation management	61	42	19	39	26	13	0	0	0
Business administration, management and operations, other	7,943	4,090	3,853	3,403	2,040	1,363	39	27	12
Accounting	41,964	18,018	23,946	10,415	4,773	5,642	35	19	16
Accounting technology/technician and bookkeeping	119	59	60	4	1	3	0	0	0
Auditing	0	0	0	45	25	20	0	0	0
Accounting and finance	967	298	669	714	254	460	0	0	0
Accounting and business/management	382	153	229	52	27	25	1	1	0
Accounting and related services, other	380	200	180	303	194	109	2	1	1
Administrative assistant and secretarial science, general	39	8	31	5	0	5	0	0	0
Executive assistant/executive secretary	0	0	0	0	0	0	0	0	0
Business/office automation/technology/data entry	124	62	62	0	0	0	0	0	0
General office occupations and clerical services	0	0	0	0	0	0	0	0	0
Business operations support and secretarial services, other	13	5	8	67	23	44	0	0	0
Business/corporate communications	493	144	349	176	37	139	0	0	0
Business/managerial economics	4,254	2,830	1,424	280	151	129	57	42	15
Entrepreneurship/entrepreneurial studies	1,216	794	422	220	158	62	0	0	0
Franchising and franchise operations	0	0	0	0	0	0	0	0	0
Small business administration/management	167	82	85	62	35	27	0	0	0

See notes at end of table.

Table 275. Bachelor's, master's, and doctor's degrees conferred by degree-granting institutions, by sex of student and discipline division: 2006–07—Continued

Discipline division	Bachelor's degrees requiring 4 or 5 years			Master's degrees			Doctor's degrees (Ph.D., Ed.D., etc.)[1]		
	Total	Males	Females	Total	Males	Females	Total	Males	Females
1	2	3	4	5	6	7	8	9	10
Entrepreneurial and small business operations, other	35	25	10	9	5	4	0	0	0
Finance, general	29,078	19,251	9,827	4,393	2,966	1,427	59	34	25
Banking and financial support services	507	314	193	147	107	40	4	1	3
Financial planning and services	242	180	62	212	143	69	0	0	0
International finance	9	4	5	119	64	55	0	0	0
Investments and securities	654	337	317	255	174	81	0	0	0
Public finance	0	0	0	0	0	0	0	0	0
Finance and financial management services, other	233	134	99	446	286	160	0	0	0
Hospitality administration/management, general	4,633	1,699	2,934	256	98	158	15	7	8
Tourism and travel services management	505	217	288	171	90	81	0	0	0
Hotel/motel administration/management	1,745	770	975	109	47	62	7	5	2
Restaurant/food services management	447	239	208	5	1	4	0	0	0
Resort management	73	32	41	0	0	0	0	0	0
Hotel/motel and restaurant management	0	0	0	0	0	0	0	0	0
Hospitality administration/management, other	563	228	335	20	13	7	3	2	1
Human resources management/personnel administration, general	5,447	1,694	3,753	4,051	988	3,063	44	15	29
Labor and industrial relations	820	417	403	570	202	368	10	6	4
Organizational behavior studies	3,282	1,249	2,033	1,848	696	1,152	272	139	133
Labor studies	31	15	16	0	0	0	1	1	0
Human resources development	283	75	208	640	201	439	6	5	1
Human resources management and services, other	765	359	406	1,590	586	1,004	0	0	0
International business/trade/commerce	5,285	2,507	2,778	3,010	1,792	1,218	23	12	11
Management information systems, general	8,771	6,413	2,358	5,499	3,806	1,693	30	21	9
Information resources management/CIO training	129	101	28	326	247	79	37	29	8
Knowledge management	8	4	4	73	39	34	1	1	0
Management information systems and services, other	320	244	76	42	28	14	0	0	0
Management science, general	4,697	2,639	2,058	1,655	809	846	17	9	8
Business statistics	42	31	11	25	13	12	5	1	4
Actuarial science	516	314	202	94	49	45	0	0	0
Management sciences and quantitative methods, other	269	149	120	352	165	187	11	7	4
Marketing/marketing management, general	32,407	14,477	17,930	2,183	954	1,229	43	26	17
Marketing research	47	16	31	102	45	57	1	1	0
International marketing	112	18	94	60	16	44	0	0	0
Marketing, other	1,049	525	524	107	52	55	5	4	1
Real estate	882	610	272	533	403	130	1	1	0
Taxation	0	0	0	1,138	510	628	0	0	0
Insurance	615	386	229	90	58	32	4	2	2
Sales, distribution, and marketing operations, general	1,378	679	699	266	142	124	3	2	1
Merchandising and buying operations	110	27	83	9	0	9	0	0	0
Retailing and retail operations	209	64	145	14	0	14	0	0	0
Selling skills and sales operations	307	164	143	1	0	1	0	0	0
General merchandising/sales/related marketing operations, other	237	83	154	0	0	0	0	0	0
Fashion merchandising	1,948	61	1,887	2	0	2	0	0	0
Apparel and accessories marketing operations	237	16	221	1	0	1	0	0	0
Tourism and travel services marketing operations	40	14	26	0	0	0	0	0	0
Tourism promotion operations	66	23	43	0	0	0	0	0	0
Vehicle and vehicle parts and accessories marketing operations	132	120	12	0	0	0	0	0	0
Business and personal/financial services marketing operations	17	7	10	0	0	0	0	0	0
Special products marketing operations	144	43	101	14	9	5	0	0	0
Hospitality and recreation marketing operations	72	55	17	24	9	15	0	0	0
Specialized merchandising/sales/related marketing operations, other	68	16	52	49	19	30	0	0	0
Construction management	1,455	1,356	99	139	100	39	0	0	0
Business/management/marketing/related support services, other	2,397	1,208	1,189	2,432	1,447	985	30	20	10
Personal and culinary services	736	350	386	7	1	6	0	0	0
Funeral service and mortuary science, general	160	77	83	0	0	0	0	0	0
Cosmetology/cosmetologist, general	0	0	0	0	0	0	0	0	0
Cooking and related culinary arts, general	20	11	9	0	0	0	0	0	0
Baking and pastry arts/baker/pastry chef	53	15	38	2	0	2	0	0	0
Culinary arts/chef training	321	163	158	0	0	0	0	0	0
Restaurant, culinary, and catering management/manager	148	68	80	0	0	0	0	0	0
Meat cutting/meat cutter	0	0	0	0	0	0	0	0	0
Food service, waiter/waitress, and dining room management/manager	0	0	0	0	0	0	0	0	0
Institutional food workers	1	0	1	0	0	0	0	0	0
Institutional food workers and administrators, general	0	0	0	0	0	0	0	0	0
Culinary arts and related services, other	33	16	17	5	1	4	0	0	0
Communication and communications technologies	78,420	29,009	49,411	7,272	2,485	4,787	480	188	292
Communication, journalism, and related programs	74,783	26,444	48,339	6,773	2,153	4,620	479	188	291
Communication studies/speech communication and rhetoric	32,535	11,120	21,415	2,164	611	1,553	277	102	175
Mass communication/media studies	7,752	2,857	4,895	634	231	403	92	40	52
Communication and media studies, other	1,134	349	785	270	103	167	26	13	13
Journalism	12,045	3,871	8,174	1,432	465	967	8	3	5
Broadcast journalism	935	384	551	64	10	54	11	3	8
Photojournalism	172	71	101	0	0	0	0	0	0
Journalism, other	884	318	566	133	45	88	0	0	0
Radio and television	5,890	3,304	2,586	321	139	182	17	9	8
Digital communication and media/multimedia	961	587	374	149	93	56	11	8	3

See notes at end of table.

Table 275. Bachelor's, master's, and doctor's degrees conferred by degree-granting institutions, by sex of student and discipline division: 2006–07—Continued

Discipline division	Bachelor's degrees requiring 4 or 5 years			Master's degrees			Doctor's degrees (Ph.D., Ed.D., etc.)[1]		
	Total	Males	Females	Total	Males	Females	Total	Males	Females
1	2	3	4	5	6	7	8	9	10
Radio, television, and digital communication, other	383	181	202	11	7	4	0	0	0
Organizational communication, general	989	306	683	167	38	129	3	1	2
Public relations/image management	3,938	751	3,187	193	42	151	0	0	0
Advertising	4,581	1,291	3,290	262	70	192	7	2	5
Political communication	49	16	33	0	0	0	0	0	0
Health communication	18	2	16	17	3	14	1	0	1
Public relations, advertising and applied communication, other	485	141	344	89	14	75	0	0	0
Publishing	0	0	0	72	13	59	0	0	0
Communication, journalism, and related programs, other	2,032	895	1,137	795	269	526	26	7	19
Communications technologies/technicians and support services	3,637	2,565	1,072	499	332	167	1	0	1
Communications technology/technician	65	44	21	77	52	25	0	0	0
Photographic and film/video technology/technician and assistant	32	20	12	0	0	0	0	0	0
Radio and television broadcasting technology/technician	481	271	210	138	73	65	1	0	1
Recording arts technology/technician	393	345	48	1	1	0	0	0	0
Audiovisual communications technologies/technicians, other	205	188	17	0	0	0	0	0	0
Graphic communications, general	200	85	115	15	11	4	0	0	0
Printing management	78	37	41	11	7	4	0	0	0
Prepress/desktop publishing and digital imaging design	50	21	29	0	0	0	0	0	0
Animation/interactive technology/video graphics/special effects	1,796	1,361	435	203	143	60	0	0	0
Graphic and printing equipment operator, general production	67	29	38	0	0	0	0	0	0
Printing press operator	11	4	7	0	0	0	0	0	0
Computer typography and composition equipment operator	0	0	0	0	0	0	0	0	0
Graphic communications, other	24	14	10	0	0	0	0	0	0
Communications technologies/technicians and support services, other	235	146	89	54	45	9	0	0	0
Computer and information sciences and support services	42,170	34,342	7,828	16,232	11,985	4,247	1,595	1,267	328
Computer and information sciences, general	12,570	10,524	2,046	5,761	4,367	1,394	749	619	130
Artificial intelligence and robotics	0	0	0	40	31	9	10	9	1
Information technology	6,777	5,281	1,496	785	557	228	15	11	4
Computer and information sciences, other	106	85	21	13	8	5	1	0	1
Computer programming/programmer, general	554	459	95	94	68	26	0	0	0
Computer programming, specific applications	20	11	9	50	30	20	0	0	0
Computer programming, other	249	206	43	0	0	0	0	0	0
Data processing and data processing technology/technician	186	146	40	21	12	9	0	0	0
Information science/studies	5,119	3,820	1,299	2,519	1,658	861	90	59	31
Computer systems analysis/analyst	1,050	803	247	261	190	71	8	7	1
Computer science	8,496	7,366	1,130	4,415	3,422	993	657	522	135
Web page, digital/multimedia and information resources design	746	529	217	40	26	14	0	0	0
Data modeling/warehousing and database administration	69	36	33	0	0	0	0	0	0
Computer graphics	741	591	150	63	44	19	0	0	0
Computer software and media applications, other	176	142	34	57	40	17	0	0	0
Computer systems networking and telecommunications	2,500	2,056	444	508	376	132	6	5	1
System administration/administrator	83	73	10	2	0	2	0	0	0
System, networking, and LAN/WAN management/manager	216	190	26	0	0	0	0	0	0
Computer and information systems security	946	827	119	287	242	45	0	0	0
Web/multimedia management and webmaster	56	35	21	0	0	0	0	0	0
Computer/information tech. services admin. and management, other	532	386	146	437	291	146	1	1	0
Computer and information sciences and support services, other	978	776	202	879	623	256	58	34	24
Education	105,641	22,516	83,125	176,572	40,164	136,408	8,261	2,681	5,580
Education, general	2,476	483	1,993	26,668	6,162	20,506	1,295	349	946
Bilingual and multilingual	187	7	180	1,198	276	922	17	5	12
Multicultural education	0	0	0	19	2	17	14	1	13
Indian/Native American education	0	0	0	0	0	0	0	0	0
Bilingual, multilingual, and multicultural education, other	0	0	0	0	0	0	0	0	0
Curriculum and instruction	1	1	0	16,616	3,305	13,311	981	243	738
Educational leadership and administration, general	37	16	21	18,477	6,784	11,693	2,789	978	1,811
Administration of special education	0	0	0	28	8	20	6	2	4
Adult and continuing education administration	5	2	3	194	50	144	57	16	41
Educational, instructional, and curriculum supervision	43	4	39	1,186	368	818	68	19	49
Higher education/higher education administration	0	0	0	1,541	501	1,040	362	148	214
Community college education	0	0	0	46	17	29	16	3	13
Elementary and middle school administration/principalship	0	0	0	1,160	420	740	44	17	27
Secondary school administration/principalship	0	0	0	363	160	203	48	18	30
Urban education and leadership	53	13	40	229	71	158	35	11	24
Superintendency and educational system administration	0	0	0	521	168	353	15	4	11
Elementary, middle and secondary education/administration	0	0	0	0	0	0	0	0	0
Educational administration and supervision, other	0	0	0	1,119	413	706	319	126	193
Educational/instructional media design	37	21	16	3,904	1,169	2,735	143	59	84
Educational evaluation and research	0	0	0	43	16	27	39	11	28
Educational statistics and research methods	0	0	0	49	16	33	16	7	9
Educational assessment, testing, and measurement	0	0	0	56	9	47	23	7	16
Educational assessment, evaluation, and research, other	0	0	0	21	2	19	0	0	0
International and comparative education	0	0	0	153	31	122	9	3	6
Social and philosophical foundations of education	3	0	3	489	136	353	142	63	79
Special education and teaching, general	6,549	657	5,892	13,063	2,071	10,992	217	43	174
Education/teaching of individuals with hearing impairments/deafness	168	5	163	164	24	140	4	1	3

See notes at end of table.

Table 275. Bachelor's, master's, and doctor's degrees conferred by degree-granting institutions, by sex of student and discipline division: 2006–07—Continued

Discipline division	Bachelor's degrees requiring 4 or 5 years			Master's degrees			Doctor's degrees (Ph.D., Ed.D., etc.)[1]		
	Total	Males	Females	Total	Males	Females	Total	Males	Females
1	2	3	4	5	6	7	8	9	10
Education/teaching of the gifted and talented	0	0	0	328	34	294	1	0	1
Education/teaching of individuals with emotional disturbances	124	11	113	122	19	103	2	2	0
Education/teaching of individuals with mental retardation	238	22	216	115	14	101	1	1	0
Education/teaching of individuals with multiple disabilities	106	25	81	391	51	340	0	0	0
Educ/teach. of individuals with orthopedic/physical health impair.	9	1	8	23	3	20	3	1	2
Education/teaching of individuals with vision impairments/blindness	30	3	27	83	15	68	0	0	0
Educ/teach. of individuals with specific learning disabilities	293	33	260	1,082	161	921	2	1	1
Education/teaching of individuals with speech/language impairments	270	6	264	176	2	174	0	0	0
Education/teaching of individuals with autism	0	0	0	5	0	5	0	0	0
Education/teaching of individuals who are developmentally delayed	0	0	0	0	0	0	0	0	0
Educ/teach. of individuals in early childhood spec. educ. programs	70	2	68	334	28	306	3	0	3
Special education and teaching, other	389	39	350	671	101	570	8	2	6
Counselor education/school counseling and guidance services	37	10	27	12,237	2,067	10,170	283	89	194
College student counseling and personnel services	0	0	0	812	205	607	13	8	5
Student counseling and personnel services, other	1	0	1	167	27	140	0	0	0
Adult and continuing education and teaching	39	20	19	1,265	369	896	172	53	119
Elementary education and teaching	42,424	4,112	38,312	18,407	2,062	16,345	48	9	39
Junior high/intermediate/middle school education and teaching	2,436	540	1,896	1,165	253	912	2	1	1
Secondary education and teaching	4,174	1,694	2,480	7,998	2,951	5,047	26	7	19
Teacher education, multiple levels	1,243	164	1,079	4,770	1,095	3,675	43	4	39
Montessori teacher education	0	0	0	129	8	121	0	0	0
Waldorf/Steiner teacher education	0	0	0	0	0	0	0	0	0
Kindergarten/preschool education and teaching	2,008	55	1,953	453	16	437	15	2	13
Early childhood education and teaching	8,408	302	8,106	2,188	89	2,099	15	2	13
Pre-elementary/early childhood/kindergarten teacher education	0	0	0	0	0	0	0	0	0
Teacher educ. and prof. dev., specific levels and methods, other	310	70	240	4,527	935	3,592	62	23	39
Agricultural teacher education	479	213	266	484	129	355	54	25	29
Art teacher education	1,621	272	1,349	989	166	823	34	9	25
Business teacher education	519	206	313	317	122	195	4	1	3
Driver and safety teacher education	0	0	0	4	1	3	0	0	0
English/language arts teacher education	2,793	549	2,244	1,249	282	967	17	5	12
Foreign language teacher education	126	16	110	215	35	180	16	7	9
Health teacher education	1,675	490	1,185	623	182	441	52	10	42
Family and consumer sciences/home economics teacher education	420	15	405	89	2	87	6	2	4
Technology teacher education/industrial arts teacher education	799	647	152	539	310	229	14	5	9
Sales and marketing operations/marketing and dist. teacher educ.	38	13	25	18	3	15	0	0	0
Mathematics teacher education	2,133	781	1,352	1,757	586	1,171	49	20	29
Music teacher education	3,483	1,331	2,152	1,145	438	707	65	35	30
Physical education teaching and coaching	8,947	5,112	3,835	2,248	1,194	1,054	113	62	51
Reading teacher education	145	14	131	8,248	393	7,855	53	6	47
Science teacher education/general science teacher education	755	284	471	864	295	569	54	21	33
Social science teacher education	694	352	342	269	127	142	2	2	0
Social studies teacher education	2,291	1,265	1,026	781	423	358	0	0	0
Technical teacher education	262	172	90	179	65	114	66	20	46
Trade and industrial teacher education	1,264	795	469	352	131	221	20	10	10
Computer teacher education	22	14	8	962	300	662	3	1	2
Biology teacher education	378	138	240	226	66	160	0	0	0
Chemistry teacher education	64	21	43	42	17	25	0	0	0
Drama and dance teacher education	130	15	115	56	13	43	0	0	0
French language teacher education	58	11	47	22	4	18	0	0	0
German language teacher education	13	3	10	2	1	1	0	0	0
Health occupations teacher education	11	3	8	34	13	21	1	0	1
History teacher education	838	493	345	96	50	46	0	0	0
Physics teacher education	35	25	10	25	16	9	0	0	0
Spanish language teacher education	414	68	346	157	27	130	0	0	0
Speech teacher education	198	74	124	7	3	4	0	0	0
Geography teacher education	14	9	5	0	0	0	0	0	0
Latin teacher education	6	1	5	2	0	2	0	0	0
School librarian/library media specialist	4	2	2	170	11	159	0	0	0
Psychology teacher education	6	1	5	1	0	1	0	0	0
Teacher educ. and prof. dev., specific subject areas, other	530	143	387	1,556	334	1,222	37	7	30
Teaching Eng. as a second/foreign language/ESL language instructor	124	16	108	2,275	487	1,788	19	5	14
Teaching French as a second or foreign language	0	0	0	1	0	1	0	0	0
Teacher assistant/aide	0	0	0	0	0	0	0	0	0
Adult literacy tutor/instructor	0	0	0	37	1	36	0	0	0
Teaching assistants/aides, other	0	0	0	0	0	0	0	0	0
Education, other	2,184	634	1,550	5,776	1,253	4,523	224	89	135
Engineering and engineering technologies	82,072	68,230	13,842	32,162	24,865	7,297	8,123	6,422	1,701
Engineering	67,092	54,745	12,347	29,472	22,872	6,600	8,062	6,377	1,685
Engineering, general	1,812	1,420	392	1,384	1,064	320	260	218	42
Aerospace, aeronautical and astronautical engineering	2,828	2,376	452	912	742	170	234	204	30
Agricultural/biological engineering and bioengineering	680	460	220	190	109	81	76	57	19
Architectural engineering	664	504	160	132	92	40	4	2	2
Biomedical/medical engineering	3,149	1,948	1,201	1,227	747	480	563	363	200
Ceramic sciences and engineering	76	57	19	10	8	2	22	17	5
Chemical engineering	4,492	2,888	1,604	957	636	321	835	627	208
Civil engineering, general	9,462	7,456	2,006	3,220	2,360	860	762	571	191

See notes at end of table.

Table 275. Bachelor's, master's, and doctor's degrees conferred by degree-granting institutions, by sex of student and discipline division: 2006–07—Continued

Discipline division	Bachelor's degrees requiring 4 or 5 years			Master's degrees			Doctor's degrees (Ph.D., Ed.D., etc.)[1]		
	Total	Males	Females	Total	Males	Females	Total	Males	Females
1	2	3	4	5	6	7	8	9	10
Geotechnical engineering	0	0	0	5	4	1	0	0	0
Structural engineering	145	110	35	57	45	12	10	8	2
Transportation and highway engineering	0	0	0	86	67	19	5	5	0
Water resources engineering	4	4	0	36	21	15	19	16	3
Civil engineering, other	60	42	18	78	64	14	9	9	0
Computer engineering, general	4,620	4,186	434	1,472	1,142	330	302	254	48
Computer hardware engineering	14	12	2	10	9	1	0	0	0
Computer software engineering	231	221	10	598	432	166	3	3	0
Computer engineering, other	187	159	28	197	164	33	30	25	5
Electrical, electronics and communications engineering	13,089	11,534	1,555	7,777	6,306	1,471	2,042	1,719	323
Engineering mechanics	102	81	21	62	53	9	32	25	7
Engineering physics	414	357	57	66	51	15	35	30	5
Engineering science	325	240	85	188	137	51	83	66	17
Environmental/environmental health engineering	428	244	184	534	287	247	121	69	52
Materials engineering	582	437	145	542	401	141	422	325	97
Mechanical engineering	16,601	14,637	1,964	4,294	3,722	572	1,106	966	140
Metallurgical engineering	149	110	39	62	50	12	24	15	9
Mining and mineral engineering	129	116	13	51	46	5	12	10	2
Naval architecture and marine engineering	338	303	35	22	16	6	6	4	2
Nuclear engineering	384	306	78	221	166	55	83	75	8
Ocean engineering	147	126	21	55	41	14	6	5	1
Petroleum engineering	450	375	75	225	186	39	37	26	11
Systems engineering	600	470	130	1,110	881	229	78	65	13
Textile sciences and engineering	140	58	82	39	20	19	30	12	18
Materials science	218	149	69	173	119	54	195	137	58
Polymer/plastics engineering	60	49	11	46	31	15	42	28	14
Construction engineering	280	265	15	13	10	3	0	0	0
Forest engineering	14	14	0	6	4	2	1	1	0
Industrial engineering	2,780	1,898	882	1,615	1,201	414	301	213	88
Industrial/manufacturing engineering	0	0	0	0	0	0	0	0	0
Manufacturing engineering	253	223	30	246	205	41	14	13	1
Operations research	354	253	101	273	204	69	55	39	16
Surveying engineering	34	33	1	5	2	3	3	3	0
Geological/geophysical engineering	119	79	40	41	32	9	13	11	2
Engineering, other	678	545	133	1,235	995	240	187	141	46
Engineering technologies/construction trades/mechanics and repairers	14,980	13,485	1,495	2,690	1,993	697	61	45	16
Engineering technologies/technicians	14,588	13,114	1,474	2,690	1,993	697	61	45	16
Engineering technology, general	842	765	77	138	108	30	0	0	0
Architectural engineering technology/technician	655	565	90	0	0	0	0	0	0
Civil engineering technology/technician	492	420	72	0	0	0	0	0	0
Electrical/electronic/communications eng. technology/technician	2,190	1,998	192	24	19	5	0	0	0
Laser and optical technology/technician	0	0	0	0	0	0	0	0	0
Telecommunications technology/technician	65	58	7	80	66	14	0	0	0
Electrical/electronic eng. technologies/technicians, other	274	259	15	0	0	0	0	0	0
Biomedical technology/technician	67	48	19	13	4	9	3	2	1
Electromechanical technology/electromechanical eng. technology	111	108	3	0	0	0	0	0	0
Instrumentation technology/technician	23	22	1	0	0	0	0	0	0
Robotics technology/technician	27	25	2	0	0	0	0	0	0
Electromechanical/instrumentation and maintenance technol./tech.	3	3	0	0	0	0	0	0	0
Heating, air conditioning and refrigeration technology/technician	13	13	0	0	0	0	0	0	0
Energy management and systems technology/technician	32	32	0	27	22	5	0	0	0
Solar energy technology/technician	2	2	0	0	0	0	0	0	0
Water quality/wastewater treatment manage./recycling technol./tech.	30	13	17	0	0	0	0	0	0
Environmental engineering technology/environmental technology	56	34	22	68	47	21	0	0	0
Hazardous materials management and waste technology/technician	1	1	0	6	2	4	0	0	0
Environmental control technologies/technicians, other	6	3	3	45	27	18	0	0	0
Plastics engineering technology/technician	67	58	9	3	3	0	0	0	0
Metallurgical technology/technician	0	0	0	0	0	0	0	0	0
Industrial technology/technician	1,703	1,554	149	262	189	73	5	5	0
Manufacturing technology/technician	589	540	49	35	26	9	0	0	0
Industrial/manufacturing technology/technician	0	0	0	0	0	0	0	0	0
Industrial production technologies/technicians, other	316	275	41	17	15	2	0	0	0
Occupational safety and health technology/technician	437	351	86	75	45	30	0	0	0
Quality control technology/technician	8	7	1	66	41	25	0	0	0
Industrial safety technology/technician	50	41	9	8	4	4	0	0	0
Quality control and safety technologies/technicians, other	14	10	4	7	6	1	0	0	0
Aeronautical/aerospace engineering technology/technician	64	60	4	0	0	0	0	0	0
Automotive engineering technology/technician	322	301	21	0	0	0	0	0	0
Mechanical engineering/mechanical technology/technician	1,246	1,180	66	0	0	0	0	0	0
Mechanical engineering related technologies/technicians, other	337	312	25	0	0	0	0	0	0
Mining technology/technician	4	3	1	0	0	0	0	0	0
Petroleum technology/technician	14	13	1	0	0	0	0	0	0
Mining and petroleum technologies/technicians, other	2	1	1	1	1	0	0	0	0
Construction engineering technology/technician	1,713	1,595	118	98	75	23	0	0	0
Surveying technology/surveying	191	171	20	7	5	2	4	4	0
Engineering-related technologies, other	1	0	1	0	0	0	0	0	0
Computer engineering technology/technician	778	698	80	4	3	1	0	0	0

See notes at end of table.

Table 275. Bachelor's, master's, and doctor's degrees conferred by degree-granting institutions, by sex of student and discipline division: 2006–07—Continued

Discipline division	Bachelor's degrees requiring 4 or 5 years			Master's degrees			Doctor's degrees (Ph.D., Ed.D., etc.)[1]		
	Total	Males	Females	Total	Males	Females	Total	Males	Females
1	2	3	4	5	6	7	8	9	10
Computer technology/computer systems technology	441	366	75	0	0	0	0	0	0
Computer software technology/technician	68	66	2	0	0	0	0	0	0
Computer engineering technologies/technicians, other	0	0	0	0	0	0	0	0	0
Drafting/design engineering technologies/technicians, general	37	29	8	0	0	0	0	0	0
CAD/CADD drafting and/or design technology/technician	53	46	7	8	7	1	0	0	0
Electrical/electronics drafting and electrical/electronics	0	0	0	0	0	0	0	0	0
Mechanical drafting and mechanical drafting CAD/CADD	121	96	25	0	0	0	0	0	0
Drafting/design engineering technologies/technicians, other	8	7	1	9	7	2	0	0	0
Engineering/industrial management	368	296	72	1,562	1,178	384	49	34	15
Engineering technologies/technicians, other	747	669	78	127	93	34	0	0	0
Construction trades	129	122	7	0	0	0	0	0	0
Mason/masonry	1	1	0	0	0	0	0	0	0
Carpentry/carpenter	0	0	0	0	0	0	0	0	0
Electrician	0	0	0	0	0	0	0	0	0
Building/home/construction inspection/inspector	0	0	0	0	0	0	0	0	0
Building/construction finishing, mgmt., and inspection	13	12	1	0	0	0	0	0	0
Building/construction finishing, mgmt., and inspection, other	51	47	4	0	0	0	0	0	0
Plumber and pipefitter	0	0	0	0	0	0	0	0	0
Construction trades, other	64	62	2	0	0	0	0	0	0
Mechanic and repair technologies/technicians	263	249	14	0	0	0	0	0	0
Mechanics and repairers, general	0	0	0	0	0	0	0	0	0
Business machine repair	0	0	0	0	0	0	0	0	0
Communications systems installation and repair technology	65	61	4	0	0	0	0	0	0
Industrial electronics technology/technician	0	0	0	0	0	0	0	0	0
Heavy equipment maintenance technology/technician	8	7	1	0	0	0	0	0	0
Industrial mechanics and maintenance technology	0	0	0	0	0	0	0	0	0
Autobody/collision and repair technology/technician	2	2	0	0	0	0	0	0	0
Automobile/automotive mechanics technology/technician	36	35	1	0	0	0	0	0	0
Diesel mechanics technology/technician	22	22	0	0	0	0	0	0	0
Airframe mechanics and aircraft maintenance technology/technician	50	45	5	0	0	0	0	0	0
Aircraft powerplant technology/technician	0	0	0	0	0	0	0	0	0
Avionics maintenance technology/technician	80	77	3	0	0	0	0	0	0
English language and literature/letters	55,122	17,475	37,647	8,742	2,867	5,875	1,178	478	700
English language and literature, general	42,313	13,038	29,275	5,120	1,664	3,456	970	397	581
English composition	441	183	258	72	18	54	6	4	2
Creative writing	2,097	815	1,282	2,449	861	1,588	16	7	9
American literature (United States)	85	28	57	14	3	11	1	1	0
English literature (British and Commonwealth)	872	269	603	146	33	113	35	16	19
Speech and rhetorical studies	7,830	2,659	5,171	559	180	379	92	37	55
Technical and business writing	480	162	318	230	62	168	9	2	7
English language and literature/letters, other	1,004	321	683	152	46	106	41	14	27
Family and consumer sciences/human sciences	21,400	2,594	18,806	2,080	292	1,788	337	73	264
Work and family studies	53	31	22	14	8	6	0	0	0
Family and consumer sciences/human sciences, general	4,450	439	4,011	456	69	387	58	17	41
Business family and consumer sciences/human sciences	265	96	169	3	0	3	5	1	4
Family and consumer sciences/human sciences communication	31	2	29	3	1	2	0	0	0
Consumer merchandising/retailing management	115	11	104	4	0	4	3	1	2
Family and consumer sciences/human sciences business serv, other	0	0	0	0	0	0	0	0	0
Family resource management studies, general	522	247	275	36	3	33	11	5	6
Consumer economics	404	155	249	5	0	5	0	0	0
Consumer services and advocacy	7	0	7	0	0	0	0	0	0
Family and consumer economics and related services, other	311	25	286	5	1	4	6	0	6
Foods, nutrition, and wellness studies, general	1,922	294	1,628	433	46	387	24	7	17
Human nutrition	265	33	232	138	20	118	24	10	14
Food service systems administration/management	674	346	328	6	1	5	0	0	0
Foods, nutrition, and related services, other	21	4	17	16	4	12	0	0	0
Housing and human environments, general	311	57	254	6	0	6	3	2	1
Facilities planning and management	32	24	8	9	9	0	0	0	0
Housing and human environments, other	23	0	23	0	0	0	0	0	0
Human development and family studies, general	6,237	502	5,735	520	83	437	73	12	61
Adult development and aging	32	5	27	24	4	20	0	0	0
Family systems	462	37	425	30	10	20	9	2	7
Child development	1,288	44	1,244	118	8	110	72	8	64
Family and community services	753	76	677	83	7	76	11	1	10
Child care and support services management	229	8	221	46	2	44	0	0	0
Child care provider/assistant	10	0	10	0	0	0	0	0	0
Human development, family studies, and related services, other	234	7	227	31	7	24	8	0	8
Apparel and textiles, general	2,435	140	2,295	75	8	67	18	2	16
Apparel and textile manufacture	53	1	52	0	0	0	0	0	0
Textile science	0	0	0	0	0	0	2	2	0
Apparel and textile marketing management	230	5	225	4	1	3	2	0	2
Fashion and fabric consultant	0	0	0	0	0	0	0	0	0
Family and consumer sciences/human sciences, other	31	5	26	15	0	15	8	3	5

See notes at end of table.

Table 275. Bachelor's, master's, and doctor's degrees conferred by degree-granting institutions, by sex of student and discipline division: 2006–07—Continued

Discipline division	Bachelor's degrees requiring 4 or 5 years			Master's degrees			Doctor's degrees (Ph.D., Ed.D., etc.)[1]		
	Total	Males	Females	Total	Males	Females	Total	Males	Females
1	2	3	4	5	6	7	8	9	10
Foreign languages, literatures, and linguistics.................	20,275	6,173	14,102	3,443	1,058	2,385	1,059	437	622
Foreign languages and literatures, general	1,544	459	1,085	242	59	183	28	14	14
Linguistics..	1,290	446	844	570	171	399	213	86	127
Language interpretation and translation	60	20	40	115	25	90	0	0	0
Comparative literature	859	266	593	183	56	127	136	47	89
Linguistic/comparative/related language studies and serv., other	50	15	35	11	2	9	6	3	3
African languages, literatures, and linguistics..................	2	1	1	3	1	2	1	1	0
East Asian languages, literatures, and linguistics, general.....	113	67	46	53	25	28	22	10	12
Chinese language and literature	261	139	122	30	6	24	2	0	2
Japanese language and literature	545	305	240	31	14	17	9	2	7
Korean language and literature	13	10	3	0	0	0	0	0	0
East Asian languages, literatures, and linguistics, other	104	56	48	22	6	16	20	13	7
Slavic languages, literatures, and linguistics, general	59	22	37	51	20	31	27	6	21
Russian language and literature	311	163	148	18	8	10	4	2	2
Czech language and literature	2	1	1	0	0	0	0	0	0
Polish language and literature	4	1	3	0	0	0	0	0	0
Slavic/Baltic/Albanian languages, lit, and linguistics, other	2	0	2	2	0	2	0	0	0
Germanic languages, literatures, and linguistics, general	96	58	38	38	16	22	26	14	12
German language and literature	1,055	444	611	158	57	101	56	23	33
Scandinavian languages, literatures, and linguistics	10	3	7	3	1	2	3	2	1
Danish language and literature..	1	1	0	0	0	0	0	0	0
Norwegian language and literature	3	0	3	0	0	0	0	0	0
Swedish language and literature	2	0	2	0	0	0	0	0	0
Germanic languages, literatures, and linguistics, other	1	0	1	0	0	0	0	0	0
Modern Greek language and literature..............................	2	2	0	0	0	0	0	0	0
South Asian languages, literatures, and linguistics, general.....	4	0	4	5	4	1	5	5	0
Sanskrit and classical Indian languages, lit., and linguistics	0	0	0	0	0	0	1	1	0
Iranian and Persian languages, lit., and linguistics	1	1	0	0	0	0	0	0	0
Romance languages, literatures, and linguistics, general.....	107	21	86	64	23	41	27	6	21
French language and literature	2,462	485	1,977	364	89	275	95	28	67
Italian language and literature	280	74	206	97	30	67	20	6	14
Portuguese language and literature...................................	28	14	14	14	6	8	2	0	2
Spanish language and literature	9,013	2,309	6,704	982	254	728	195	76	119
Romanian language and literature	2	0	2	0	0	0	0	0	0
Romance languages, literatures, and linguistics, other	78	16	62	62	16	46	43	21	22
American Indian/Native American languages, literatures, and linguistics	0	0	0	0	0	0	0	0	0
Semitic languages, literatures, and linguistics, general	7	4	3	4	2	2	5	4	1
Arabic language and literature	68	35	33	2	1	1	0	0	0
Hebrew language and literature..	27	16	11	14	5	9	3	1	2
Ancient Near Eastern and biblical languages, lit., and linguistics.....	37	30	7	18	11	7	6	5	1
Middle/Near Eastern and Semitic languages, lit., and ling., other.....	50	20	30	57	31	26	23	11	12
Classics and classical languages, lit., and linguistics, general......	1,154	522	632	177	91	86	65	43	22
Ancient/classical Greek language and literature	35	21	14	3	2	1	2	2	0
Latin language and literature	104	43	61	13	4	9	0	0	0
Classics and classical languages, lit., and linguistics, other.........	10	7	3	26	16	10	1	1	0
Celtic languages, literatures, and linguistics...................	2	0	2	2	2	0	1	0	1
Filipino/Tagalog language and literature	5	4	1	0	0	0	0	0	0
American sign language (ASL)..	49	8	41	0	0	0	0	0	0
Linguistics of ASL and other sign languages....................	0	0	0	0	0	0	0	0	0
Sign language interpretation and translation....................	202	17	185	2	1	1	0	0	0
American sign language, other..	0	0	0	0	0	0	0	0	0
Foreign languages, literatures, and linguistics, other........	161	47	114	7	3	4	12	4	8
Health professions and related clinical sciences	101,810	14,325	87,485	54,531	10,636	43,895	8,355	2,242	6,113
Health services/allied health/health sciences, general	2,707	552	2,155	176	42	134	7	1	6
Communication disorders, general....................................	2,063	86	1,977	1,250	54	1,196	27	4	23
Audiology/audiologist and hearing sciences....................	151	12	139	134	8	126	1,024	117	907
Speech-language pathology/pathologist...........................	829	29	800	1,831	47	1,784	22	4	18
Audiology/audiologist and speech-language pathology/pathologist	3,611	168	3,443	2,334	76	2,258	136	25	111
Communication disorders sciences and services, other	86	1	85	79	3	76	12	5	7
Dental clinical sciences, general.......................................	0	0	0	265	177	88	8	2	6
Advanced general dentistry	0	0	0	13	7	6	0	0	0
Oral biology and oral pathology	0	0	0	30	13	17	15	8	7
Dental public health and education....................................	0	0	0	9	3	6	0	0	0
Dental materials (MS, PhD)	0	0	0	1	1	0	0	0	0
Endodontics/endodontology	0	0	0	16	12	4	0	0	0
Oral/maxillofacial surgery	0	0	0	3	3	0	1	0	1
Orthodontics/orthodontology	0	0	0	79	48	31	0	0	0
Pediatric dentistry/pedodontics..	0	0	0	22	11	11	0	0	0
Periodontics/periodontology	0	0	0	31	24	7	0	0	0
Prosthodontics/prosthodontology	0	0	0	12	6	6	0	0	0
Advanced/graduate dentistry and oral sciences, other......	0	0	0	38	19	19	13	5	8
Dental assisting/assistant...	0	0	0	0	0	0	0	0	0
Dental hygiene/hygienist...	1,510	35	1,475	13	0	13	0	0	0
Dental laboratory technology/technician...........................	8	4	4	1	0	1	0	0	0
Dental services and allied professions, other...................	5	0	5	1	1	0	0	0	0
Health/health care administration/management	3,839	814	3,025	5,069	1,483	3,586	96	41	55
Hospital and health care facilities administration/management......................	1,110	250	860	671	238	433	1	1	0

See notes at end of table.

Table 275. Bachelor's, master's, and doctor's degrees conferred by degree-granting institutions, by sex of student and discipline division: 2006–07—Continued

Discipline division	Bachelor's degrees requiring 4 or 5 years			Master's degrees			Doctor's degrees (Ph.D., Ed.D., etc.)[1]		
	Total	Males	Females	Total	Males	Females	Total	Males	Females
1	2	3	4	5	6	7	8	9	10
Health unit manager/ward supervisor	0	0	0	10	3	7	0	0	0
Medical office management/administration	2	0	2	0	0	0	0	0	0
Health information/medical records administration/administrator	644	89	555	30	2	28	0	0	0
Health information/medical records technology/technician	6	2	4	3	3	0	4	4	0
Medical office assistant/specialist	5	0	5	0	0	0	0	0	0
Medical/health management and clinical assistant/specialist	40	8	32	0	0	0	0	0	0
Health/medical claims examiner	0	0	0	0	0	0	0	0	0
Medical administrative/executive assistant and medical secretary	0	0	0	0	0	0	0	0	0
Medical staff services technology/technician	0	0	0	0	0	0	0	0	0
Health and medical administrative services, other	539	111	428	295	68	227	11	4	7
Medical/clinical assistant	7	0	7	0	0	0	0	0	0
Clinical/medical laboratory assistant	13	4	9	0	0	0	0	0	0
Occupational therapist assistant	0	0	0	0	0	0	0	0	0
Pharmacy technician/assistant	0	0	0	0	0	0	0	0	0
Physical therapist assistant	33	6	27	0	0	0	0	0	0
Veterinary/animal health technology/technician and vet. assistant	209	14	195	0	0	0	0	0	0
Anesthesiologist assistant	0	0	0	41	14	27	0	0	0
Pathology/pathologist assistant	13	4	9	4	0	4	0	0	0
Respiratory therapy technician/assistant	0	0	0	0	0	0	0	0	0
Allied health and medical assisting services, other	131	24	107	53	19	34	0	0	0
Cardiovascular technology/technologist	53	18	35	0	0	0	0	0	0
Electrocardiograph technology/technician	0	0	0	0	0	0	0	0	0
Electroneurodiagnostic/electroencephalographic tech./technologist	0	0	0	0	0	0	0	0	0
Emergency medical technology/technician (EMT paramedic)	107	71	36	10	6	4	0	0	0
Nuclear medical technology/technologist	325	139	186	0	0	0	0	0	0
Perfusion technology/perfusionist	7	4	3	16	8	8	0	0	0
Medical radiologic technology/science radiation therapist	1,020	251	769	8	5	3	0	0	0
Respiratory care therapy/therapist	605	158	447	6	3	3	0	0	0
Surgical technology/technologist	3	2	1	0	0	0	0	0	0
Diagnostic medical sonography/sonographer and ultrasound technician	383	74	309	0	0	0	0	0	0
Radiologic technology/science radiographer	665	175	490	4	2	2	2	1	1
Physician assistant	960	310	650	3,274	807	2,467	0	0	0
Athletic training/trainer	2,188	816	1,372	196	83	113	0	0	0
Gene/genetic therapy	11	0	11	0	0	0	0	0	0
Radiation protection/health physics technician	12	2	10	17	12	5	0	0	0
Allied health diagnostic/intervention/treatment professions, other	188	67	121	31	10	21	0	0	0
Cytotechnology/cytotechnologist	93	26	67	9	3	6	0	0	0
Hematology technology/technician	0	0	0	9	5	4	0	0	0
Clinical/medical laboratory technician	34	9	25	0	0	0	0	0	0
Clinical laboratory science/medical technology/technologist	2,244	537	1,707	186	65	121	1	1	0
Histologic technology/histotechnologist	1	1	0	0	0	0	0	0	0
Cytogenetics/genetics/clinical genetics technology/technologist	17	4	13	0	0	0	0	0	0
Clinical/medical laboratory science and allied professions, other	88	22	66	106	43	63	4	2	2
Pre-dentistry studies	72	38	34	0	0	0	0	0	0
Pre-medicine/pre-medical studies	533	240	293	0	0	0	0	0	0
Pre-pharmacy studies	118	51	67	0	0	0	0	0	0
Pre-veterinary studies	121	22	99	0	0	0	0	0	0
Pre-nursing studies	4	1	3	0	0	0	0	0	0
Health/medical preparatory programs, other	516	141	375	20	7	13	0	0	0
Medical scientist (M.S., Ph.D.)	0	0	0	229	108	121	26	14	12
Substance abuse/addiction counseling	247	40	207	184	68	116	0	0	0
Psychiatric/mental health services technician	116	23	93	18	2	16	0	0	0
Clinical/medical social work	149	19	130	301	40	261	6	3	3
Community health services/liaison/counseling	974	134	840	219	39	180	4	1	3
Marriage and family therapy/counseling	3	0	3	1,746	305	1,441	62	22	40
Clinical pastoral counseling/patient counseling	2	1	1	150	50	100	4	1	3
Psychoanalysis and psychotherapy	0	0	0	7	3	4	0	0	0
Mental health counseling/counselor	2	0	2	576	93	483	5	2	3
Genetic counseling/counselor	4	0	4	86	7	79	0	0	0
Mental and social health services and allied professions, other	409	43	366	399	55	344	11	4	7
Nursing/registered nurse training (RN, ASN, BSN, MSN)	57,072	5,794	51,278	6,208	543	5,665	222	14	208
Nursing administration	177	11	166	1,063	61	1,002	17	1	16
Adult health nurse/nursing	12	1	11	449	43	406	0	0	0
Nurse anesthetist	0	0	0	1,304	508	796	0	0	0
Family practice nurse/nurse practitioner	0	0	0	1,461	129	1,332	2	0	2
Maternal/child health and neonatal nurse/nursing	0	0	0	182	5	177	0	0	0
Nurse midwife/nursing midwifery	0	0	0	56	1	55	0	0	0
Nursing science	797	96	701	2,584	182	2,402	280	17	263
Pediatric nurse/nursing	0	0	0	167	7	160	0	0	0
Psychiatric/mental health nurse/nursing	0	0	0	116	20	96	0	0	0
Public health/community nurse/nursing	0	0	0	164	10	154	0	0	0
Perioperative/operating room and surgical nurse/nursing	0	0	0	11	1	10	0	0	0
Licensed practical/voc. nurse training (LPN, LVN, AAS)	7	0	7	0	0	0	0	0	0
Clinical nurse specialist	1	0	1	171	15	156	0	0	0
Critical care nursing	16	0	16	99	13	86	0	0	0
Occupational and environmental health nursing	0	0	0	0	0	0	0	0	0
Nursing, other	1,565	131	1,434	1,776	145	1,631	135	7	128
Opthalmic technician/technologist	3	0	3	1	1	0	0	0	0

See notes at end of table.

Table 275. Bachelor's, master's, and doctor's degrees conferred by degree-granting institutions, by sex of student and discipline division: 2006–07—Continued

Discipline division	Bachelor's degrees requiring 4 or 5 years			Master's degrees			Doctor's degrees (Ph.D., Ed.D., etc.)[1]		
	Total	Males	Females	Total	Males	Females	Total	Males	Females
1	2	3	4	5	6	7	8	9	10
Ophthalmic/optometric support services/allied professions, other	26	15	11	7	4	3	3	1	2
Pharmacy (PharmD, BS/BPharm)	239	112	127	0	0	0	0	0	0
Pharmacy admin. and pharmacy policy and regulatory affairs	0	0	0	119	54	65	32	17	15
Pharmaceutics and drug design	161	55	106	98	44	54	186	110	76
Medicinal and pharmaceutical chemistry	1	0	1	31	16	15	81	47	34
Natural products chemistry and pharmacognosy	0	0	0	4	0	4	12	3	9
Clinical and industrial drug development (M.S., Ph.D.)	16	6	10	192	55	137	0	0	0
Pharmacoeconomics/pharmaceutical economics	0	0	0	12	5	7	2	0	2
Clinical, hospital, and managed care pharmacy	0	0	0	1	1	0	0	0	0
Industrial and physical pharmacy and cosmetic sciences	0	0	0	4	1	3	0	0	0
Pharmacy, pharmaceutical sciences, and administration, other	221	90	131	140	59	81	128	52	76
Public health, general	451	105	346	4,620	1,290	3,330	244	69	175
Environmental health	236	123	113	317	137	180	61	33	28
Health/medical physics	22	16	6	51	37	14	1	1	0
Occupational health and industrial hygiene	54	27	27	83	46	37	14	9	5
Public health education and promotion	952	201	751	444	60	384	47	13	34
Community health and preventive medicine	360	76	284	185	40	145	34	7	27
Maternal and child health	0	0	0	68	4	64	4	0	4
International public health/international health	0	0	0	116	25	91	1	1	0
Health services administration	342	38	304	417	140	277	13	7	6
Public health, other	282	81	201	897	263	634	112	37	75
Art therapy/therapist	85	2	83	273	17	256	0	0	0
Dance therapy/therapist	0	0	0	25	2	23	0	0	0
Music therapy/therapist	243	15	228	39	4	35	1	0	1
Occupational therapy/therapist	870	82	788	2,846	226	2,620	117	17	100
Orthotist/prosthetist	38	22	16	13	6	7	0	0	0
Physical therapy/therapist	561	116	445	2,656	740	1,916	4,667	1,311	3,356
Therapeutic recreation/recreational therapy	372	67	305	28	8	20	6	2	4
Vocational rehabilitation counseling/counselor	217	33	184	901	214	687	8	3	5
Kinesiotherapy/kinesiotherapist	27	7	20	4	0	4	0	0	0
Assistive/augmentative technology and rehabilitation engineering	0	0	0	0	0	0	0	0	0
Rehabilitation and therapeutic professions, other	679	131	548	398	70	328	44	17	27
Veterinary sciences/veterinary clinical sciences, general	26	11	15	184	70	114	126	60	66
Veterinary anatomy	0	0	0	0	0	0	1	1	0
Veterinary physiology	0	0	0	5	2	3	1	0	1
Veterinary microbiology and immunobiology	0	0	0	3	0	3	6	4	2
Veterinary pathology and pathobiology	0	0	0	2	2	0	3	3	0
Veterinary toxicology and pharmacology (M.S., Ph.D.)	0	0	0	1	0	1	0	0	0
Large animal/food animal/equine surgery and medicine	0	0	0	1	1	0	1	1	0
Small/companion animal surgery and medicine	0	0	0	0	0	0	0	0	0
Comparative and laboratory animal medicine	0	0	0	20	1	19	0	0	0
Veterinary preventive medicine epidemiology/public health	0	0	0	8	2	6	0	0	0
Veterinary infectious diseases	0	0	0	4	1	3	1	1	0
Veterinary biomedical and clinical sciences, other	0	0	0	2	0	2	4	2	2
Health aide	0	0	0	0	0	0	0	0	0
Medical illustration/medical illustrator	38	8	30	26	10	16	0	0	0
Medical informatics	8	0	8	54	25	29	23	18	5
Dietetics/dietitian (RD)	1,870	137	1,733	214	13	201	2	0	2
Clinical nutrition/nutritionist	33	6	27	66	5	61	4	1	3
Dietetics/human nutritional services	0	0	0	0	0	0	0	0	0
Dietetics and clinical nutrition services, other	57	3	54	7	1	6	0	0	0
Bioethics/medical ethics	5	0	5	129	58	71	8	2	6
Acupuncture	3	2	1	1,156	421	735	4	2	2
Traditional Chinese/Asian medicine and Chinese herbology	15	5	10	565	170	395	12	6	6
Naturopathic medicine/naturopathy (ND)	0	0	0	0	0	0	16	3	13
Ayurvedic medicine/ayurveda	0	0	0	0	0	0	0	0	0
Acupuncture and oriental medicine	0	0	0	0	0	0	0	0	0
Alternative and complementary medicine and medical systems, other	43	9	34	16	0	16	0	0	0
Direct entry midwifery (LM, CPM)	0	0	0	0	0	0	0	0	0
Alternative and complementary medical support services, other	17	4	13	3	0	3	0	0	0
Massage therapy/therapeutic massage	3	0	3	0	0	0	0	0	0
Asian bodywork therapy	1	0	1	0	0	0	0	0	0
Movement therapy and movement education	19	1	18	20	3	17	3	1	2
Movement and mind-body therapies and education, other	11	3	8	0	0	0	0	0	0
Herbalism/herbalist	21	3	18	13	1	12	0	0	0
Health professions and related clinical sciences, other	3,700	1,028	2,672	910	384	526	164	69	95
Legal professions and studies	3,596	1,008	2,588	4,486	2,335	2,151	143	78	65
Legal studies, general	1,331	446	885	102	34	68	0	0	0
Pre-law studies	261	111	150	0	0	0	0	0	0
Advanced legal research/studies, general (M.C.L., M.L.I., M.S.L.)[2]	24	7	17	547	277	270	108	60	48
Programs for foreign lawyers (LL.M., M.C.L.)	0	0	0	699	390	309	0	0	0
American/U.S. law/legal studies/jurisprudence (M.C.J.)[2]	30	12	18	178	81	97	8	3	5
Banking, corporate, finance, and securities law[2]	0	0	0	116	61	55	0	0	0
Comparative law (LL.M., M.C.L., J.S.D./S.J.D.)	0	0	0	124	72	52	1	1	0
Energy, environment, and natural resources law (M.S.)[2]	0	0	0	24	12	12	0	0	0
Health law (LL.M., M.J., J.S.D./S.J.D.)	0	0	0	79	23	56	1	1	0
International law and legal studies[2]	0	0	0	199	99	100	0	0	0

See notes at end of table.

Table 275. Bachelor's, master's, and doctor's degrees conferred by degree-granting institutions, by sex of student and discipline division: 2006-07—Continued

Discipline division	Bachelor's degrees requiring 4 or 5 years			Master's degrees			Doctor's degrees (Ph.D., Ed.D., etc.)[1]		
	Total	Males	Females	Total	Males	Females	Total	Males	Females
1	2	3	4	5	6	7	8	9	10
International business, trade, and tax law[2]	3	1	2	82	51	31	0	0	0
Tax law/taxation[2]	0	0	0	434	242	192	0	0	0
Legal research and advanced professional studies, other	5	1	4	880	512	368	6	5	1
Legal administrative assistant/secretary	1	0	1	0	0	0	0	0	0
Legal assistant/paralegal	1,496	259	1,237	35	6	29	0	0	0
Court reporting/court reporter	4	0	4	0	0	0	0	0	0
Legal professions and studies, other	441	171	270	987	475	512	19	8	11
Liberal arts and sciences, general studies and humanities	44,255	14,123	30,132	3,634	1,352	2,282	77	38	39
Liberal arts and sciences/liberal studies	27,003	7,730	19,273	2,296	857	1,439	9	6	3
General studies	11,690	4,560	7,130	66	27	39	1	1	0
Humanities/humanistic studies	2,813	927	1,886	656	225	431	53	24	29
Liberal arts and sciences, general studies and humanities, other	2,749	906	1,843	616	243	373	14	7	7
Library science	82	10	72	6,767	1,309	5,458	52	18	34
Library science/librarianship	82	10	72	6,586	1,272	5,314	51	17	34
Library assistant/technician	0	0	0	0	0	0	0	0	0
Library science, other	0	0	0	181	37	144	1	1	0
Mathematics and statistics	14,954	8,360	6,594	4,884	2,859	2,025	1,351	949	402
Mathematics, general	13,146	7,236	5,910	2,680	1,581	1,099	866	635	231
Analysis and functional analysis	0	0	0	0	0	0	0	0	0
Mathematics, other	167	86	81	12	6	6	3	3	0
Applied mathematics	894	586	308	524	350	174	164	120	44
Computational mathematics	54	47	7	16	10	6	11	7	4
Applied mathematics, other	126	86	40	93	73	20	3	3	0
Statistics, general	444	244	200	1,397	731	666	292	172	120
Mathematical statistics and probability	7	4	3	7	3	4	1	1	0
Statistics, other	15	13	2	8	4	4	7	4	3
Mathematics and statistics, other	101	58	43	147	101	46	4	4	0
Military technologies	168	152	16	202	178	24	0	0	0
Military technologies	168	152	16	202	178	24	0	0	0
Multi/interdisciplinary studies	33,792	10,439	23,353	4,762	1,703	3,059	1,093	485	608
Biological and physical sciences	1,684	692	992	238	110	128	43	29	14
Peace studies and conflict resolution	254	91	163	350	122	228	22	9	13
Systems science and theory	130	111	19	228	122	106	18	14	4
Mathematics and computer science	181	146	35	42	25	17	7	7	0
Biopsychology	114	25	89	0	0	0	6	2	4
Gerontology	174	17	157	231	39	192	31	1	30
Historic preservation and conservation	117	27	90	185	44	141	0	0	0
Cultural resource management and policy analysis	0	0	0	10	3	7	0	0	0
Historic preservation and conservation, other	0	0	0	0	0	0	0	0	0
Medieval and renaissance studies	41	12	29	15	7	8	4	2	2
Museology/museum studies	12	2	10	226	40	186	0	0	0
Science, technology and society	288	170	118	120	51	69	16	8	8
Accounting and computer science	8	3	5	0	0	0	0	0	0
Behavioral sciences	1,464	278	1,186	89	28	61	21	3	18
Natural sciences	508	244	264	83	41	42	1	0	1
Nutrition sciences	847	117	730	455	63	392	124	29	95
International/global studies	2,366	859	1,507	125	73	52	0	0	0
Holocaust and related studies	0	0	0	9	4	5	0	0	0
Ancient studies/civilization	92	32	60	6	2	4	3	1	2
Classical, ancient Mediterranean/Near Eastern studies/archaeology	88	31	57	3	1	2	8	2	6
Intercultural/multicultural and diversity studies	120	29	91	89	32	57	0	0	0
Neuroscience	1,681	649	1,032	151	71	80	410	219	191
Cognitive science	350	192	158	5	3	2	24	14	10
Multi/interdisciplinary studies, other	23,273	6,712	16,561	2,102	822	1,280	355	145	210
Parks, recreation, leisure, and fitness studies	27,430	14,190	13,240	4,110	2,116	1,994	218	109	109
Parks, recreation and leisure studies	2,686	1,258	1,428	236	112	124	17	8	9
Parks, recreation and leisure facilities management	2,991	1,581	1,410	289	129	160	13	3	10
Health and physical education, general	8,510	4,440	4,070	1,169	565	604	37	20	17
Sport and fitness administration/management	4,461	3,129	1,332	1,349	837	512	11	9	2
Kinesiology and exercise science	7,755	3,293	4,462	934	425	509	113	59	54
Health and physical education/fitness, other	884	409	475	121	41	80	17	4	13
Parks, recreation, leisure, and fitness studies, other	143	80	63	12	7	5	10	6	4
Philosophy and religious studies	11,969	7,430	4,539	1,716	1,087	629	637	453	184
Philosophy	6,850	4,730	2,120	720	561	159	383	286	97
Logic	2	0	2	8	4	4	5	4	1
Ethics	27	11	16	16	6	10	0	0	0
Philosophy, other	84	47	37	0	0	0	0	0	0
Religion/religious studies	4,095	2,131	1,964	598	313	285	210	132	78
Buddhist studies	0	0	0	3	1	2	0	0	0
Christian studies	189	131	58	68	35	33	0	0	0
Islamic studies	8	4	4	6	1	5	0	0	0

See notes at end of table.

Table 275. Bachelor's, master's, and doctor's degrees conferred by degree-granting institutions, by sex of student and discipline division: 2006–07—Continued

Discipline division	Bachelor's degrees requiring 4 or 5 years			Master's degrees			Doctor's degrees (Ph.D., Ed.D., etc.)[1]		
	Total	Males	Females	Total	Males	Females	Total	Males	Females
1	2	3	4	5	6	7	8	9	10
Jewish/Judaic studies	223	70	153	94	45	49	13	8	5
Religion/religious studies, other	21	13	8	15	11	4	0	0	0
Philosophy and religious studies, other	470	293	177	188	110	78	26	23	3
Physical sciences and science technologies	21,073	12,455	8,618	5,839	3,556	2,283	4,846	3,317	1,529
Physical sciences	20,783	12,295	8,488	5,811	3,539	2,272	4,844	3,315	1,529
Physical sciences	247	143	104	37	23	14	8	5	3
Astronomy	191	117	74	107	65	42	95	59	36
Astrophysics	121	76	45	34	20	14	23	18	5
Planetary astronomy and science	0	0	0	4	3	1	1	1	0
Astronomy and astrophysics, other	20	7	13	7	5	2	9	7	2
Atmospheric physics and dynamics	577	381	196	159	101	58	76	46	30
Atmospheric sciences and meteorology, general	8	6	2	0	0	0	0	0	0
Meteorology	155	95	60	34	23	11	11	8	3
Atmospheric sciences and meteorology, other	5	1	4	0	0	0	0	0	0
Chemistry, general	10,489	5,304	5,185	2,026	1,080	946	2,410	1,514	896
Analytical chemistry	15	7	8	29	13	16	10	7	3
Inorganic chemistry	0	0	0	0	0	0	5	4	1
Organic chemistry	0	0	0	0	0	0	12	10	2
Physical and theoretical chemistry	1	0	1	0	0	0	5	4	1
Polymer chemistry	4	3	1	16	11	5	41	27	14
Chemical physics	12	9	3	3	3	0	6	6	0
Chemistry, other	473	218	255	23	12	11	25	17	8
Geology/earth science, general	2,851	1,670	1,181	1,104	598	506	388	241	147
Geochemistry	5	2	3	13	3	10	5	2	3
Geophysics and seismology	53	36	17	76	49	27	72	48	24
Paleontology	1	0	1	1	0	1	0	0	0
Hydrology and water resources science	28	15	13	28	12	16	7	6	1
Oceanography, chemical and physical	139	59	80	127	54	73	127	69	58
Geological and earth sciences/geosciences, other	242	131	111	88	50	38	41	21	20
Physics, general	4,591	3,621	970	1,566	1,194	372	1,304	1,073	231
Atomic/molecular physics	21	15	6	12	8	4	9	8	1
Elementary particle physics	0	0	0	0	0	0	0	0	0
Nuclear physics	0	0	0	2	2	0	5	1	4
Optics/optical sciences	59	47	12	65	51	14	41	34	7
Solid state and low-temperature physics	0	0	0	0	0	0	0	0	0
Acoustics	7	6	1	22	19	3	5	3	2
Theoretical and mathematical physics	20	18	2	0	0	0	0	0	0
Physics, other	145	116	29	110	90	20	78	58	20
Physical sciences, other	303	192	111	118	50	68	25	18	7
Science technologies/technicians	290	160	130	28	17	11	2	2	0
Biology technician/biotechnology laboratory technician	32	13	19	0	0	0	2	2	0
Nuclear/nuclear power technology/technician	10	10	0	7	5	2	0	0	0
Chemical technology/technician	5	2	3	0	0	0	0	0	0
Physical science technologies/technicians, other	2	2	0	0	0	0	0	0	0
Science technologies/technicians, other	241	133	108	21	12	9	0	0	0
Precision production	23	12	11	5	2	3	0	0	0
Machine tool technology/machinist	0	0	0	0	0	0	0	0	0
Tool and die technology/technician	0	0	0	0	0	0	0	0	0
Welding technology/welder	7	7	0	0	0	0	0	0	0
Precision metal working, other	0	0	0	0	0	0	0	0	0
Furniture design and manufacturing	16	5	11	5	2	3	0	0	0
Psychology	90,039	20,343	69,696	21,037	4,265	16,772	5,153	1,382	3,771
Psychology, general	84,932	19,272	65,660	5,399	1,339	4,060	1,461	460	1,001
Clinical psychology	143	35	108	2,611	503	2,108	2,155	516	1,639
Cognitive psychology and psycholinguistics	56	17	39	16	5	11	6	3	3
Community psychology	229	21	208	337	50	287	3	0	3
Comparative psychology	0	0	0	3	1	2	0	0	0
Counseling psychology	414	75	339	7,430	1,356	6,074	360	95	265
Developmental and child psychology	596	50	546	88	8	80	39	8	31
Experimental psychology	288	74	214	60	22	38	66	25	41
Industrial and organizational psychology	248	89	159	723	247	476	116	48	68
Personality psychology	37	8	29	1	0	1	0	0	0
Physiological psychology/psychobiology	524	137	387	7	5	2	18	7	11
Social psychology	1,005	230	775	54	7	47	31	10	21
School psychology	0	0	0	1,491	187	1,304	242	38	204
Educational psychology	193	23	170	1,200	215	985	382	102	280
Psychometrics and quantitative psychology	1	0	1	6	2	4	3	0	3
Clinical child psychology	0	0	0	6	3	3	12	3	9
Environmental psychology	12	9	3	7	0	7	5	1	4
Geropsychology	0	0	0	2	0	2	0	0	0
Health/medical psychology	19	5	14	28	4	24	16	6	10
Psychopharmacology	0	0	0	75	36	39	0	0	0
Family psychology	38	7	31	16	2	14	20	5	15
Forensic psychology	470	84	386	523	80	443	23	3	20
Psychology, other	834	207	627	954	193	761	195	52	143

See notes at end of table.

Table 275. Bachelor's, master's, and doctor's degrees conferred by degree-granting institutions, by sex of student and discipline division: 2006–07—Continued

Discipline division	Bachelor's degrees requiring 4 or 5 years			Master's degrees			Doctor's degrees (Ph.D., Ed.D., etc.)[1]		
	Total	Males	Females	Total	Males	Females	Total	Males	Females
1	2	3	4	5	6	7	8	9	10
Public administration and social service professions	23,147	4,354	18,793	31,131	7,758	23,373	726	253	473
Human services, general	2,261	412	1,849	496	111	385	29	13	16
Community organization and advocacy	2,077	443	1,634	560	171	389	10	2	8
Public administration	2,582	1,375	1,207	9,163	3,976	5,187	183	86	97
Public policy analysis	887	388	499	2,019	874	1,145	163	64	99
Social work	14,307	1,563	12,744	17,858	2,262	15,596	297	66	231
Youth services/administration	14	2	12	1	0	1	0	0	0
Social work, other	19	4	15	63	6	57	0	0	0
Public administration and social service professions, other	1,000	167	833	971	358	613	44	22	22
Security and protective services	39,206	19,505	19,701	4,906	2,315	2,591	85	43	42
Corrections	533	223	310	8	2	6	0	0	0
Criminal justice/law enforcement administration	10,592	5,417	5,175	1,382	678	704	11	5	6
Criminal justice/safety studies	22,684	11,017	11,667	2,061	903	1,158	69	36	33
Forensic science and technology	584	133	451	517	124	393	0	0	0
Criminal justice/police science	1,651	1,018	633	55	24	31	0	0	0
Security and loss prevention services	66	51	15	35	22	13	0	0	0
Juvenile corrections	2	0	2	0	0	0	0	0	0
Criminalistics and criminal science	95	24	71	0	0	0	0	0	0
Securities services administration/management	18	15	3	194	82	112	0	0	0
Corrections administration	50	31	19	12	2	10	0	0	0
Corrections and criminal justice, other	2,285	1,008	1,277	143	81	62	5	2	3
Fire protection and safety technology/technician	179	158	21	8	6	2	0	0	0
Fire services administration	251	232	19	9	8	1	0	0	0
Fire science/firefighting	58	54	4	35	35	0	0	0	0
Fire protection, other	42	34	8	2	1	1	0	0	0
Security and protective services, other	116	90	26	445	347	98	0	0	0
Social sciences and history	164,183	82,417	81,766	17,665	8,577	9,088	3,844	2,110	1,734
Social sciences	129,737	62,200	67,537	14,521	6,879	7,642	3,037	1,627	1,410
Social sciences, general	8,129	3,102	5,027	615	224	391	13	7	6
Anthropology	7,851	2,390	5,461	1,170	358	812	506	193	313
Physical anthropology	0	0	0	7	3	4	0	0	0
Anthropology, other	22	5	17	4	1	3	1	1	0
Archeology	188	55	133	33	13	20	12	5	7
Criminology	5,483	2,610	2,873	470	200	270	24	13	11
Demography and population studies	0	0	0	25	10	15	4	1	3
Economics, general	22,821	15,915	6,906	2,320	1,491	829	905	619	286
Applied economics	126	88	38	142	84	58	10	7	3
Econometrics and quantitative economics	150	120	30	30	23	7	0	0	0
Development economics and international development	208	61	147	286	108	178	10	4	6
International economics	186	99	87	146	79	67	11	8	3
Economics, other	425	277	148	38	24	14	5	1	4
Geography	4,305	2,818	1,487	834	480	354	207	118	89
Cartography	106	88	18	25	16	9	4	3	1
Geography, other	141	66	75	34	24	10	0	0	0
International relations and affairs	7,766	3,058	4,708	3,684	1,723	1,961	60	35	25
Political science and government, general	38,915	21,025	17,890	1,941	1,063	878	614	357	257
American government and politics (United States)	179	109	70	116	57	59	0	0	0
Canadian government and politics	0	0	0	0	0	0	0	0	0
Political science and government, other	805	426	379	45	15	30	0	0	0
Sociology	28,960	8,674	20,286	1,545	474	1,071	569	210	359
Urban studies/affairs	884	398	486	346	119	227	51	31	20
Social sciences, other	2,087	816	1,271	665	290	375	31	14	17
History	34,446	20,217	14,229	3,144	1,698	1,446	807	483	324
History, general	33,680	19,801	13,879	2,964	1,608	1,356	745	450	295
American history (United States)	84	48	36	24	13	11	10	3	7
European history	38	20	18	2	2	0	0	0	0
History and philosophy of science and technology	114	44	70	28	10	18	27	13	14
Public/applied history and archival administration	26	9	17	50	11	39	0	0	0
Asian history	0	0	0	0	0	0	3	1	2
History, other	504	295	209	76	54	22	22	16	6
Theology and religious vocations	8,696	5,761	2,935	6,446	3,909	2,537	1,573	1,227	346
Bible/biblical studies	2,709	1,697	1,012	443	332	111	21	16	5
Missions/missionary studies and missiology	439	164	275	283	157	126	52	41	11
Religious education	859	427	432	555	247	308	21	10	11
Religious/sacred music	201	120	81	71	32	39	0	0	0
Theology/theological studies	1,280	872	408	2,918	1,851	1,067	766	619	147
Pre-theology/pre-ministerial studies	293	212	81	0	0	0	0	0	0
Talmudic studies	1,058	1,058	0	353	353	0	26	26	0
Theological and ministerial studies, other	328	231	97	503	330	173	359	281	78
Pastoral studies/counseling	499	349	150	670	233	437	141	105	36
Youth ministry	515	356	159	74	38	36	0	0	0
Pastoral counseling and specialized ministries, other	126	44	82	122	59	63	13	12	1
Theology and religious vocations, other	389	231	158	454	277	177	174	117	57

See notes at end of table.

Table 275. Bachelor's, master's, and doctor's degrees conferred by degree-granting institutions, by sex of student and discipline division: 2006–07—Continued

Discipline division	Bachelor's degrees requiring 4 or 5 years			Master's degrees			Doctor's degrees (Ph.D., Ed.D., etc.)[1]		
	Total	Males	Females	Total	Males	Females	Total	Males	Females
1	2	3	4	5	6	7	8	9	10
Transportation and materials moving	5,657	5,043	614	985	828	157	0	0	0
Aeronautics/aviation/aerospace science and technology, general	3,159	2,884	275	22	18	4	0	0	0
Airline/commercial/professional pilot and flight crew	1,225	1,102	123	820	705	115	0	0	0
Aviation/airway management and operations	747	628	119	90	68	22	0	0	0
Air traffic controller	206	163	43	0	0	0	0	0	0
Flight instructor	5	5	0	0	0	0	0	0	0
Air transportation, other	5	5	0	38	30	8	0	0	0
Ground transportation, other	0	0	0	0	0	0	0	0	0
Marine science/merchant marine officer	288	245	43	0	0	0	0	0	0
Marine transportation, other	0	0	0	0	0	0	0	0	0
Transportation and materials moving, other	22	11	11	15	7	8	0	0	0
Visual and performing arts	85,186	32,729	52,457	13,767	5,910	7,857	1,364	625	739
Visual and performing arts, general	1,913	712	1,201	131	50	81	4	0	4
Crafts/craft design, folk art and artisanry	184	48	136	11	4	7	0	0	0
Dance, general	1,820	163	1,657	221	29	192	6	1	5
Ballet	31	1	30	2	0	2	0	0	0
Dance, other	24	2	22	0	0	0	4	0	4
Design and visual communications, general	3,216	1,366	1,850	151	54	97	3	2	1
Commercial and advertising art	2,525	1,082	1,443	221	107	114	0	0	0
Industrial design	1,264	855	409	115	59	56	0	0	0
Commercial photography	78	24	54	17	6	11	0	0	0
Fashion/apparel design	1,827	129	1,698	63	7	56	0	0	0
Interior design	4,030	346	3,684	244	34	210	0	0	0
Graphic design	3,909	1,683	2,226	116	51	65	0	0	0
Illustration	958	470	488	54	31	23	0	0	0
Design and applied arts, other	849	493	356	227	91	136	2	1	1
Drama and dramatics/theatre arts, general	8,763	3,122	5,641	1,141	498	643	95	42	53
Technical theatre/theatre design and technology	337	144	193	75	26	49	0	0	0
Playwriting and screenwriting	101	56	45	102	57	45	0	0	0
Theatre literature, history and criticism	33	14	19	2	1	1	3	1	2
Acting	521	223	298	116	53	63	0	0	0
Directing and theatrical production	48	25	23	43	25	18	0	0	0
Theatre/theatre arts management	74	16	58	61	39	22	0	0	0
Acting and directing	0	0	0	0	0	0	0	0	0
Dramatic/theatre arts and stagecraft, other	229	70	159	84	30	54	2	1	1
Film/cinema studies	2,254	1,450	804	335	181	154	18	9	9
Cinematography and film/video production	3,025	2,127	898	528	303	225	9	2	7
Photography	1,818	584	1,234	195	95	100	0	0	0
Film/video and photographic arts, other	936	575	361	43	22	21	0	0	0
Art/art studies, general	13,040	4,208	8,832	777	331	446	18	2	16
Fine/studio arts, general	8,782	3,086	5,696	1,343	586	757	1	1	0
Art history, criticism and conservation	3,496	464	3,032	678	101	577	200	52	148
Arts management	519	143	376	356	59	297	1	0	1
Drawing	281	86	195	29	15	14	0	0	0
Intermedia/multimedia	678	414	264	89	56	33	0	0	0
Painting	793	291	502	217	103	114	0	0	0
Sculpture	289	141	148	63	33	30	0	0	0
Printmaking	173	62	111	48	17	31	0	0	0
Ceramic arts and ceramics	223	67	156	58	19	39	0	0	0
Fiber, textile and weaving arts	155	8	147	26	2	24	1	1	0
Metal and jewelry arts	106	18	88	30	4	26	0	0	0
Fine arts and art studies, other	1,236	438	798	274	93	181	0	0	0
Music, general	7,326	3,613	3,713	1,682	867	815	413	218	195
Music history, literature, and theory	114	55	59	42	20	22	10	5	5
Music performance, general	3,746	1,885	1,861	2,077	990	1,087	335	153	182
Music theory and composition	490	367	123	219	158	61	59	47	12
Musicology and ethnomusicology	39	27	12	61	16	45	38	16	22
Conducting	0	0	0	91	64	27	32	20	12
Piano and organ	115	52	63	125	43	82	37	14	23
Voice and opera	251	69	182	196	57	139	7	3	4
Music management and merchandising	1,056	601	455	6	1	5	0	0	0
Jazz/jazz studies	256	214	42	94	82	12	10	7	3
Violin, viola, guitar and other stringed instruments	145	52	93	139	44	95	18	7	11
Music pedagogy	41	12	29	29	10	19	3	1	2
Music, other	641	381	260	208	124	84	17	12	5
Visual and performing arts, other	428	195	233	512	162	350	18	7	11

[1]Excludes first-professional, such as M.D., D.D.S., and law degrees.
[2]Includes LL.M. and J.S.D./S.J.D.
NOTE: Aggregations by field of study derived from the Classification of Instructional Programs developed by the National Center for Education Statistics.

SOURCE: U.S. Department of Education, National Center for Education Statistics, 2006-07 Integrated Postsecondary Education Data System (IPEDS), Fall 2007. (This table was prepared June 2008.)

Table 276. Degrees conferred by degree-granting institutions, by control of institution and level of degree: 1969–70 through 2006–07

Year	Public institutions					Private institutions				
	Associate's degrees	Bachelor's degrees	Master's degrees	First-professional degrees[1]	Doctor's degrees[2]	Associate's degrees	Bachelor's degrees	Master's degrees	First-professional degrees[1]	Doctor's degrees[2]
1	2	3	4	5	6	7	8	9	10	11
1969–70	170,966	519,550	134,545	14,542	19,183	35,057	272,766	73,746	20,376	10,683
1970–71	215,645	557,996	151,603	16,139	20,788	36,666	281,734	78,906	21,807	11,319
1971–72	255,218	599,615	167,075	18,521	21,776	36,796	287,658	84,558	24,890	11,587
1972–73	278,132	630,899	174,405	21,872	22,357	38,042	291,463	88,966	28,146	12,420
1973–74	303,188	651,544	184,632	23,208	21,810	40,736	294,232	92,401	30,608	12,006
1974–75	318,474	634,785	193,804	23,612	22,176	41,697	288,148	98,646	32,304	11,907
1975–76	345,006	635,161	206,298	25,766	21,751	46,448	290,585	105,473	36,883	12,313
1976–77	355,650	630,463	208,901	26,344	21,229	50,727	289,086	108,263	38,015	12,003
1977–78	358,874	627,903	202,099	27,097	20,456	53,372	293,301	109,521	39,484	11,675
1978–79	346,808	621,666	192,016	27,785	20,817	55,894	299,724	109,063	41,063	11,913
1979–80	344,536	624,084	187,499	27,942	20,608	56,374	305,333	110,582	42,189	12,007
1980–81	352,391	626,452	184,384	29,128	20,895	63,986	308,688	111,355	42,828	12,063
1981–82	366,732	636,475	182,295	29,611	20,889	67,794 [3]	316,523	113,251	42,421	11,818
1982–83	377,817	646,317	176,246	29,757	21,186	71,803	323,193	113,675	43,297	11,589
1983–84	379,249	646,013	170,693	29,586	21,141	72,991 [3]	328,296	113,570	44,882	12,068
1984–85	377,625	652,246	170,000	30,152	21,337	77,087	327,231	116,251	44,911	11,606
1985–86	369,052	658,586	169,903	29,568	21,433	76,995	329,237	118,664	44,342	12,220
1986–87	358,811	659,260	167,797	29,346	21,870	77,493	332,004	121,552	43,271	12,171
1987–88	354,180	658,491	173,778	29,153	22,488	80,905	336,338	125,539	41,582	12,382
1988–89	357,001	675,675	179,109	28,993	22,970	79,763	343,080	131,512	41,863	12,750
1989–90	375,635	700,015	186,104	28,810	24,641	79,467	351,329	138,197	42,178	13,730
1990–91	398,055	724,062	193,057	29,554	25,681	83,665	370,476	144,111	42,394	13,613
1991–92	420,265	759,475	203,398	29,366	26,820	83,966	377,078	149,440	44,780	13,839
1992–93	430,321	785,112	213,843	29,628	27,392	84,435	380,000	155,742	45,759	14,740
1993–94	444,373	789,148	221,428	29,842	28,524	86,259	380,127	165,042	45,576	14,661
1994–95	451,539	776,670	224,152	29,871	28,917	88,152	383,464	173,477	45,929	15,520
1995–96	454,291	774,070	227,179	29,882	29,516	100,925	390,722	179,122	46,852	15,136
1996–97	465,494	776,677	233,237	31,243	29,838	105,732	396,202	186,164	47,487	16,038
1997–98	455,084	784,296	235,922	31,233	29,715	103,471	400,110	194,242	47,365	16,295
1998–99	448,334	790,287	238,501	31,693	28,134	111,620	410,016	201,485	46,746	15,943
1999–2000	448,446	810,855	243,157	32,247	28,408	116,487	427,020	213,899	47,810	16,400
2000–01	456,487	812,438	246,054	32,633	28,187	122,378	431,733	222,422	47,074	16,717
2001–02	471,660	841,512	249,828	33,439	27,622	123,473	450,388	232,290	47,259	16,538
2002–03[3]	498,279	875,596	265,643	33,549	28,062	135,737	473,215	247,696	47,348	17,980
2003–04	524,875	905,718	285,138	34,499	29,706	140,426	493,824	273,802	48,542	18,672
2004–05	547,519	932,443	291,505	35,768	31,743	149,141	506,821	283,113	51,521	20,888
2005–06	557,134	955,369	293,517	36,269	33,767	155,932	529,873	300,548	51,386	22,300
2006–07	566,535	975,513	291,971	36,855	36,230	161,579	548,579	312,636	53,209	24,386

[1]Includes degrees that require at least 6 years of college work for completion (including at least 2 years of preprofessional training).
[2]Doctor's degrees include Ph.D., Ed.D., and comparable degrees at the doctoral level. Excludes first-professional degrees such as M.D., D.D.S., and law degrees.
[3]Data have been revised from previously published figures.

SOURCE: U.S. Department of Education, National Center for Education Statistics, Higher Education General Information Survey (HEGIS), "Degrees and Other Formal Awards Conferred" surveys, 1969–70 through 1985–86; and 1986–87 through 2006–07 Integrated Postsecondary Education Data System, "Completions Survey" (IPEDS-C:87–99), and Fall 2000 through Fall 2007. (This table was prepared June 2008.)

Table 277. Degrees conferred by degree-granting institutions, by control of institution, level of degree, and field of study: 2006–07

Field of study	Public institutions				Private institutions			
	Associate's degrees	Bachelor's degrees	Master's degrees	Doctor's degrees[1]	Associate's degrees	Bachelor's degrees	Master's degrees	Doctor's degrees[1]
1	2	3	4	5	6	7	8	9
All fields, total	566,535	975,513	291,971	36,230	161,579	548,579	312,636	24,386
Agriculture and natural resources	5,619	20,028	3,912	1,189	219	3,105	711	83
Architecture and related services	455	7,325	3,784	120	62	2,392	2,167	58
Area, ethnic, cultural, and gender studies	153	5,076	1,022	139	11	3,118	677	94
Biological and biomedical sciences	1,958	51,460	5,558	4,320	102	23,691	3,189	2,034
Business	67,236	180,825	52,615	953	48,865	146,706	97,596	1,076
Communications, journalism, and related programs	2,052	51,885	3,299	362	557	22,898	3,474	117
Communications technologies	2,388	909	53	0	707	2,728	446	1
Computer and information sciences	13,179	20,070	7,963	1,073	14,533	22,100	8,269	522
Construction trades	3,026	126	0	0	869	3	0	0
Education	11,945	75,125	84,806	4,916	1,076	30,516	91,766	3,345
Engineering	1,750	51,369	20,176	5,936	386	15,723	9,296	2,126
Engineering technologies[2]	19,502	11,401	1,436	10	9,697	3,187	1,254	51
English language and literature/letters	1,237	38,427	5,828	886	12	16,695	2,914	292
Family and consumer sciences	8,392	18,233	1,482	244	732	3,167	598	93
Foreign languages, literatures, and linguistics	1,195	13,847	2,480	658	12	6,428	963	401
Health professions and related clinical sciences	104,337	62,627	26,920	3,657	41,099	39,183	27,611	4,698
Legal professions and studies	5,408	2,004	1,113	27	4,983	1,592	3,373	116
Liberal arts and sciences, general studies, and humanities	239,766	31,574	1,550	27	10,264	12,681	2,084	50
Library science	84	82	5,599	51	0	0	1,168	1
Mathematics and statistics	819	9,861	3,685	973	8	5,093	1,199	378
Mechanics and repair technologies	9,085	152	0	0	6,347	111	0	0
Military technologies	781	55	0	0	0	113	202	0
Multi/interdisciplinary studies	15,580	24,283	2,902	638	258	9,509	1,860	455
Parks, recreation, leisure and fitness studies	976	20,697	3,341	193	275	6,733	769	25
Philosophy and religious studies	74	5,409	563	252	301	6,560	1,153	385
Physical sciences and science technologies	3,321	14,244	4,371	3,441	83	6,829	1,468	1,405
Precision production	1,817	7	0	0	156	16	5	0
Psychology	2,069	60,637	7,987	2,194	144	29,402	13,050	2,959
Public administration and social service professions	3,930	14,878	19,761	428	408	8,269	11,370	298
Security and protective services	20,624	25,242	2,382	82	7,584	13,964	2,524	3
Social sciences and history	6,959	110,162	10,402	2,505	121	54,021	7,263	1,339
Social sciences	6,567	87,403	8,032	1,984	106	42,334	6,489	1,053
History	392	22,759	2,370	521	15	11,687	774	286
Theology and religious vocations	0	4	0	0	608	8,692	6,446	1,573
Transportation and materials moving	967	2,261	66	0	707	3,396	919	0
Visual and performing arts	9,851	45,228	6,915	956	10,393	39,958	6,852	408

[1]Includes Ph.D., Ed.D., and comparable degrees at the doctoral level. Excludes first-professional degrees, such as M.D., D.D.S., and law degrees.
[2]Excludes "Construction trades" and "Mechanics and repair technologies," which are listed separately.
NOTE: To facilitate trend comparisons, certain aggregations have been made of the degree fields as reported in the IPEDS Fall survey: "Agriculture and natural resources" includes Agriculture, agriculture operations, and related sciences and Natural resources and conservation; and "Business" includes Business management, marketing, and related support services and Personal and culinary services.
SOURCE: U.S. Department of Education, National Center for Education Statistics, 2006–07 Integrated Postsecondary Education Data System (IPEDS), Fall 2007. (This table was prepared June 2008.)

Table 278. Number of degree-granting institutions conferring degrees, by control, level of degree, and field of study: 2006–07

Field of study	Total number of institutions				Public institutions				Private institutions			
	Associate's degrees	Bachelor's degrees	Master's degrees	Doctor's degrees[1]	Associate's degrees	Bachelor's degrees	Master's degrees	Doctor's degrees[1]	Associate's degrees	Bachelor's degrees	Master's degrees	Doctor's degrees[1]
1	2	3	4	5	6	7	8	9	10	11	12	13
All fields, total	**2,725**	**2,256**	**1,695**	**648**	**1,299**	**609**	**515**	**256**	**1,426**	**1,647**	**1,180**	**392**
Agriculture and natural resources	456	580	200	88	428	275	157	82	28	305	43	6
Architecture and related services	61	183	142	34	58	113	98	24	3	70	44	10
Area, ethnic, cultural, and gender studies	51	462	122	43	45	221	78	25	6	241	44	18
Biological and biomedical sciences	220	1,310	463	245	202	500	335	169	18	810	128	76
Business	1,871	1,733	1,043	150	1,134	556	388	90	737	1,177	655	60
Communications, journalism, and related programs	262	1,078	286	63	217	427	189	48	45	651	97	15
Communications technologies	272	148	16	1	236	39	3	0	36	109	13	1
Computer and information sciences	1,432	1,447	448	151	905	499	269	102	527	948	179	49
Construction trades	285	8	0	0	259	7	0	0	26	1	0	0
Education	670	1,189	1,062	302	578	436	448	187	92	753	614	115
Engineering	291	457	301	199	255	249	198	142	36	208	103	57
Engineering technologies[2]	1,129	339	136	8	866	209	92	3	263	130	44	5
English language and literature/ letters	152	1,299	455	144	147	500	308	97	5	799	147	47
Family and consumer sciences	611	327	143	43	564	206	107	34	47	121	36	9
Foreign languages, literatures, and linguistics	167	907	215	89	162	404	157	60	5	503	58	20
Health professions and related clinical sciences	1,716	1,141	827	271	1,058	471	357	148	658	670	470	123
Legal professions and studies	712	187	116	22	424	60	45	5	288	127	71	17
Liberal arts and sciences, general studies, and humanities	1,380	882	188	15	1,089	369	94	5	291	513	94	10
Library science	32	8	68	13	32	8	55	12	0	0	13	1
Mathematics and statistics	153	1,154	333	163	150	484	259	114	3	670	74	49
Mechanics and repair technologies	626	27	0	0	567	10	0	0	59	17	0	0
Military technologies	4	5	1	0	4	4	0	0	0	1	1	0
Multi/interdisciplinary studies	290	822	307	138	268	319	191	90	22	503	116	48
Parks, recreation, leisure and fitness studies	190	727	214	40	164	322	169	36	26	405	45	4
Philosophy and religious studies	51	908	217	110	32	305	93	56	19	603	124	54
Physical sciences and science technologies	307	1,076	322	210	292	472	234	143	15	604	88	67
Precision production	317	3	1	0	306	1	0	0	11	2	1	0
Psychology	175	1,354	640	282	153	500	321	143	22	854	319	139
Public administration and social service professions	315	728	422	113	289	313	281	73	26	415	141	40
Security and protective services	1,117	713	207	18	843	299	127	16	274	414	80	2
Social sciences and history	238	1,334	426	185	213	510	301	127	25	824	125	58
Social sciences	228	1,257	360	166	205	495	253	114	23	762	107	52
History	81	1,202	334	133	78	474	257	92	3	728	77	41
Theology and religious vocations	88	396	306	137	0	1	0	0	88	395	306	137
Transportation and materials moving	100	78	13	0	88	45	4	0	12	33	9	0
Visual and performing arts	759	1,369	408	102	549	468	245	67	210	901	163	35

[1]Includes Ph.D., Ed.D., and comparable degrees at the doctoral level. Excludes first-professional degrees, such as M.D., D.D.S., and law degrees.
[2]Excludes "Construction trades" and "Mechanics and repair technologies," which are listed separately.

SOURCE: U.S. Department of Education, National Center for Education Statistics, 2006–07 Integrated Postsecondary Education Data System (IPEDS), Fall 2007. (This table was prepared July 2008.)

Table 279. Number of institutions and first-professional degrees conferred by degree-granting institutions in dentistry, medicine, and law, by sex of student: Selected years, 1949–50 through 2006–07

Year	Dentistry (D.D.S. or D.M.D.)				Medicine (M.D.)				Law (LL.B. or J.D.)			
	Number of institutions conferring degrees	Degrees conferred			Number of institutions conferring degrees	Degrees conferred			Number of institutions conferring degrees	Degrees conferred		
		Total	Males	Females		Total	Males	Females		Total	Males	Females
1	2	3	4	5	6	7	8	9	10	11	12	13
1949–50	40	2,579	2,561	18	72	5,612	5,028	584	—	—	—	—
1951–52	41	2,918	2,895	23	72	6,201	5,871	330	—	—	—	—
1953–54	42	3,102	3,063	39	73	6,712	6,377	335	—	—	—	—
1955–56	42	3,009	2,975	34	73	6,810	6,464	346	131	8,262	7,974	288
1957–58	43	3,065	3,031	34	75	6,816	6,469	347	131	9,394	9,122	272
1959–60	45	3,247	3,221	26	79	7,032	6,645	387	134	9,240	9,010	230
1961–62	46	3,183	3,166	17	81	7,138	6,749	389	134	9,364	9,091	273
1963–64	46	3,180	3,168	12	82	7,303	6,878	425	133	10,679	10,372	307
1964–65	46	3,108	3,086	22	81	7,304	6,832	472	137	11,583	11,216	367
1965–66	47	3,178	3,146	32	84	7,673	7,170	503	136	13,246	12,776	470
1967–68	48	3,422	3,375	47	85	7,944	7,318	626	138	16,454	15,805	649
1968–69	—	3,408	3,376	32	—	8,025	7,415	610	—	17,053	16,373	680
1969–70	48	3,718	3,684	34	86	8,314	7,615	699	145	14,916	14,115	801
1970–71	48	3,745	3,703	42	89	8,919	8,110	809	147	17,421	16,181	1,240
1971–72	48	3,862	3,819	43	92	9,253	8,423	830	147	21,764	20,266	1,498
1972–73	51	4,047	3,992	55	97	10,307	9,388	919	152	27,205	25,037	2,168
1973–74	52	4,440	4,355	85	99	11,356	10,093	1,263	151	29,326	25,986	3,340
1974–75	52	4,773	4,627	146	104	12,447	10,818	1,629	154	29,296	24,881	4,415
1975–76	56	5,425	5,187	238	107	13,426	11,252	2,174	166	32,293	26,085	6,208
1976–77	57	5,138	4,764	374	109	13,461	10,891	2,570	169	34,104	26,447	7,657
1977–78	57	5,189	4,623	566	109	14,279	11,210	3,069	169	34,402	25,457	8,945
1978–79	58	5,434	4,794	640	109	14,786	11,381	3,405	175	35,206	25,180	10,026
1979–80	58	5,258	4,558	700	112	14,902	11,416	3,486	179	35,647	24,893	10,754
1980–81	58	5,460	4,672	788	116	15,505	11,672	3,833	176	36,331	24,563	11,768
1981–82	59	5,282	4,467	815	119	15,814	11,867	3,947	180	35,991	23,965	12,026
1982–83	59	5,585	4,631	954	118	15,484	11,350	4,134	177	36,853	23,550	13,303
1983–84	60	5,353	4,302	1,051	119	15,813	11,359	4,454	179	37,012	23,382	13,630
1984–85	59	5,339	4,233	1,106	120	16,041	11,167	4,874	181	37,491	23,070	14,421
1985–86	59	5,046	3,907	1,139	120	15,938	11,022	4,916	181	35,844	21,874	13,970
1986–87	58	4,741	3,603	1,138	121	15,428	10,431	4,997	179	36,056	21,561	14,495
1987–88	57	4,477	3,300	1,177	122	15,358	10,278	5,080	180	35,397	21,067	14,330
1988–89	58	4,265	3,124	1,141	124	15,460	10,310	5,150	182	35,634	21,069	14,565
1989–90	57	4,100	2,834	1,266	124	15,075	9,923	5,152	182	36,485	21,079	15,406
1990–91	55	3,699	2,510	1,189	121	15,043	9,629	5,414	179	37,945	21,643	16,302
1991–92	52	3,593	2,431	1,162	120	15,243	9,796	5,447	177	38,848	22,260	16,588
1992–93	55	3,605	2,383	1,222	122	15,531	9,679	5,852	184	40,302	23,182	17,120
1993–94	53	3,787	2,330	1,457	121	15,368	9,544	5,824	185	40,044	22,826	17,218
1994–95	53	3,897	2,480	1,417	119	15,537	9,507	6,030	183	39,349	22,592	16,757
1995–96	53	3,697	2,374	1,323	119	15,341	9,061	6,280	183	39,828	22,508	17,320
1996–97	52	3,784	2,387	1,397	118	15,571	9,121	6,450	184	40,079	22,548	17,531
1997–98	53	4,032	2,490	1,542	117	15,424	9,006	6,418	185	39,331	21,876	17,455
1998–99	53	4,144	2,674	1,470	118	15,562	8,954	6,608	188	39,167	21,628	17,539
1999–2000	54	4,250	2,547	1,703	118	15,286	8,761	6,525	190	38,152	20,638	17,514
2000–01	54	4,391	2,696	1,695	118	15,403	8,728	6,675	192	37,904	19,981	17,923
2001–02	53	4,239	2,608	1,631	118	15,237	8,469	6,768	192	38,981	20,254	18,727
2002–03	53	4,345	2,654	1,691	118	15,034	8,221	6,813	194	39,067	19,916	19,151
2003–04	53	4,335	2,532	1,803	118	15,442	8,273	7,169	195	40,209	20,332	19,877
2004–05	53	4,454	2,505	1,949	120	15,461	8,151	7,310	198	43,423	22,297	21,126
2005–06	54	4,389	2,435	1,954	119	15,455	7,900	7,555	197	43,440	22,597	20,843
2006–07	55	4,596	2,548	2,048	120	15,730	7,987	7,743	200	43,486	22,777	20,709

—Not available.
SOURCE: U.S. Department of Education, National Center for Education Statistics, *Earned Degrees Conferred*, 1949–50 through 1964–65; Higher Education General Information Survey (HEGIS), "Degrees and Other Formal Awards Conferred" surveys, 1965–66 through 1985–86; and 1986–87 through 2006–07 Integrated Postsecondary Education Data System, "Completions Survey" (IPEDS-C:87–99), and Fall 2000 through Fall 2007. (This table was prepared June 2008.)

Table 280. First-professional degrees conferred by degree-granting institutions, by sex of student, control of institution, and field of study: Selected years, 1985–86 through 2006–07

Control of institution and field of study	1985–86	1990–91	1995–96	1997–98	1998–99	1999–2000	2000–01	2001–02	2002–03	2003–04	2004–05 Total	2004–05 Males	2004–05 Females	2005–06 Total	2005–06 Males	2005–06 Females	2006–07 Total	2006–07 Males	2006–07 Females
1	2	3	4	5	6	7	8	9	10	11	12	13	14	15	16	17	18	19	20
Total, all institutions	**73,910**	**71,948**	**76,734**	**78,598**	**78,439**	**80,057**	**79,707**	**80,698**	**80,897**	**83,041**	**87,289**	**43,849**	**43,440**	**87,655**	**44,038**	**43,617**	**90,064**	**45,057**	**45,007**
Dentistry (D.D.S. or D.M.D.)	5,046	3,699	3,697	4,032	4,144	4,250	4,391	4,239	4,345	4,335	4,454	2,505	1,949	4,389	2,435	1,954	4,596	2,548	2,048
Medicine (M.D.)	15,938	15,043	15,341	15,424	15,562	15,286	15,403	15,237	15,034	15,442	15,461	8,151	7,310	15,455	7,900	7,555	15,730	7,987	7,743
Optometry (O.D.)	1,029	1,115	1,231	1,274	1,285	1,293	1,289	1,280	1,281	1,275	1,252	482	770	1,198	490	708	1,311	493	818
Osteopathic medicine (D.O.)	1,547	1,459	1,895	2,110	2,135	2,236	2,450	2,416	2,596	2,722	2,762	1,482	1,280	2,718	1,434	1,284	2,992	1,475	1,517
Pharmacy (Pharm.D.)	903	1,244	2,555	3,660	3,992	5,669	6,324	7,076	7,474	8,221	8,885	2,889	5,996	9,292	3,032	6,260	10,439	3,394	7,045
Podiatry (Pod.D. or D.P.) or podiatric medicine (D.P.M.)	612	589	650	594	578	569	528	474	439	382	343	195	148	347	191	156	331	173	158
Veterinary medicine (D.V.M.)	2,270	2,032	2,109	2,193	2,226	2,251	2,248	2,289	2,354	2,228	2,354	574	1,780	2,370	535	1,835	2,443	537	1,906
Chiropractic (D.C. or D.C.M.)	3,395	2,640	3,379	3,735	3,639	3,809	3,796	3,284	2,718	2,730	2,560	1,665	895	2,564	1,615	949	2,525	1,617	908
Law (LL.B. or J.D.)	35,844	37,945	39,828	39,331	39,167	38,152	37,904	38,981	39,067	40,209	43,423	22,297	21,126	43,440	22,597	20,843	43,486	22,777	20,709
Theology (M. Div, M.H.L., B.D., or Ord. and M.H.L./Rav.)	7,283	5,695	5,879	5,873	5,558	6,129	5,026	5,195	5,360	5,332	5,533	3,565	1,968	5,666	3,760	1,906	5,990	4,000	1,990
Other	43	487	170	372	153	413	348	227	229	165	262	44	218	216	49	167	221	56	165
Total, public institutions	**29,568**	**29,554**	**29,882**	**31,233**	**31,693**	**32,247**	**32,633**	**33,439**	**33,549**	**34,499**	**35,768**	**17,175**	**18,593**	**36,269**	**17,268**	**19,001**	**36,855**	**17,471**	**19,384**
Dentistry (D.D.S. or D.M.D.)	2,827	2,308	2,198	2,468	2,479	2,512	2,477	2,525	2,493	2,498	2,577	1,488	1,089	2,669	1,515	1,154	2,769	1,586	1,183
Medicine (M.D.)	9,991	9,364	9,370	9,474	9,515	9,389	9,408	9,390	9,276	9,418	9,536	5,069	4,467	9,650	4,944	4,706	9,733	4,993	4,740
Optometry (O.D.)	441	477	499	537	488	493	497	503	481	476	477	159	318	462	185	277	518	198	320
Osteopathic medicine (D.O.)	486	493	528	568	548	535	562	538	571	586	568	285	283	585	284	301	637	301	336
Pharmacy (Pharm.D.)	473	808	1,557	2,212	2,503	3,485	3,876	4,382	4,558	4,930	5,352	1,768	3,584	5,523	1,861	3,662	5,903	1,966	3,937
Podiatry (Pod.D. or D.P.) or podiatric medicine (D.P.M.)	0	0	0	103	97	84	84	75	81	64	64	40	24	65	31	34	66	32	34
Veterinary medicine (D.V.M.)	1,931	1,814	1,889	1,971	1,989	2,021	2,017	2,052	2,023	1,912	2,033	473	1,560	2,048	482	1,566	2,116	474	1,642
Chiropractic (D.C. or D.C.M.)	0	0	0	0	0	0	0	0	0	0	0	0	0	0	0	0	0	0	0
Law (LL.B. or J.D.)	13,419	14,290	13,841	13,900	14,074	13,728	13,712	13,974	14,066	14,615	15,161	7,893	7,268	15,267	7,966	7,301	15,113	7,921	7,192
Theology (M. Div, M.H.L., B.D., or Ord. and M.H.L./Rav.)	0	0	0	0	0	0	0	0	0	0	0	0	0	0	0	0	0	0	0
Other	0	0	0	0	0	0	0	0	0	0	0	0	0	0	0	0	0	0	0
Total, private institutions	**44,342**	**42,394**	**46,852**	**47,365**	**46,746**	**47,810**	**47,074**	**47,259**	**47,348**	**48,542**	**51,521**	**26,674**	**24,847**	**51,386**	**26,770**	**24,616**	**53,209**	**27,586**	**25,623**
Dentistry (D.D.S. or D.M.D.)	2,219	1,391	1,499	1,564	1,665	1,738	1,914	1,714	1,852	1,837	1,877	1,017	860	1,720	920	800	1,827	962	865
Medicine (M.D.)	5,947	5,679	5,971	5,950	6,047	5,897	5,995	5,847	5,758	6,024	5,925	3,082	2,843	5,805	2,956	2,849	5,997	2,994	3,003
Optometry (O.D.)	588	638	732	737	797	800	792	777	800	799	775	323	452	736	305	431	793	295	498
Osteopathic medicine (D.O.)	1,061	966	1,367	1,542	1,587	1,701	1,888	1,878	2,025	2,136	2,194	1,197	997	2,133	1,150	983	2,355	1,174	1,181
Pharmacy (Pharm.D.)	430	436	998	1,448	1,489	2,184	2,448	2,694	2,916	3,291	3,533	1,121	2,412	3,769	1,171	2,598	4,536	1,428	3,108
Podiatry (Pod.D. or D.P.) or podiatric medicine (D.P.M.)	612	589	650	491	481	485	444	399	358	318	279	155	124	282	160	122	265	141	124
Veterinary medicine (D.V.M.)	339	218	220	222	237	230	231	237	331	316	321	101	220	322	53	269	327	63	264
Chiropractic (D.C. or D.C.M.)	3,395	2,640	3,379	3,735	3,639	3,809	3,796	3,284	2,718	2,730	2,560	1,665	895	2,564	1,615	949	2,525	1,617	908
Law (LL.B. or J.D.)	22,425	23,655	25,987	25,431	25,093	24,424	24,192	25,007	25,001	25,594	28,262	14,404	13,858	28,173	14,631	13,542	28,373	14,856	13,517
Theology (M. Div, M.H.L., B.D., or Ord. and M.H.L./Rav.)	7,283	5,695	5,879	5,873	5,558	6,129	5,026	5,195	5,360	5,332	5,533	3,565	1,968	5,666	3,760	1,906	5,990	4,000	1,990
Other	43	487	170	372	153	413	348	227	229	165	262	44	218	216	49	167	221	56	165

NOTE: Includes degrees that require at least 6 years of college work for completion (including at least 2 years of preprofessional training).
SOURCE: U.S. Department of Education, National Center for Education Statistics, Higher Education General Information Survey (HEGIS), "Degrees and Other Formal Awards Conferred," 1985–86; and 1990–91 through 2006–07 Integrated Postsecondary Education Data System, "Completions Survey" (IPEDS-C:91–99), and Fall 2000 through Fall 2007. (This table was prepared June 2008.)

Table 281. Associate's degrees conferred by degree-granting institutions, by race/ethnicity and sex of student: Selected years, 1976–77 through 2006–07

Year and sex	Number of degrees conferred							Percentage distribution of degrees conferred						
	Total	White	Black	Hispanic	Asian/ Pacific Islander	American Indian/ Alaska Native	Non-resident alien	Total	White	Black	Hispanic	Asian/ Pacific Islander	American Indian/ Alaska Native	Non-resident alien
1	2	3	4	5	6	7	8	9	10	11	12	13	14	15
Total														
1976–77[1]	404,956	342,290	33,159	16,636	7,044	2,498	3,329	100.0	84.5	8.2	4.1	1.7	0.6	0.8
1980–81[2]	410,174	339,167	35,330	17,800	8,650	2,584	6,643	100.0	82.7	8.6	4.3	2.1	0.6	1.6
1989–90	455,102	376,816	34,326	21,504	13,066	3,430	5,960	100.0	82.8	7.5	4.7	2.9	0.8	1.3
1990–91	481,720	391,264	38,835	25,540	15,257	3,871	6,953	100.0	81.2	8.1	5.3	3.2	0.8	1.4
1992–93	514,756	411,435	42,886	30,283	16,763	4,408	8,981	100.0	79.9	8.3	5.9	3.3	0.9	1.7
1993–94	530,632	419,694	45,523	32,118	18,444	4,876	9,977	100.0	79.1	8.6	6.1	3.5	0.9	1.9
1994–95	539,691	420,656	47,067	35,962	20,677	5,482	9,847	100.0	77.9	8.7	6.7	3.8	1.0	1.8
1995–96	555,216	426,106	52,014	38,254	23,138	5,573	10,131	100.0	76.7	9.4	6.9	4.2	1.0	1.8
1996–97	571,226	429,464	56,306	43,549	25,159	5,984	10,764	100.0	75.2	9.9	7.6	4.4	1.0	1.9
1997–98	558,555	413,561	55,314	45,876	25,196	6,246	12,362	100.0	74.0	9.9	8.2	4.5	1.1	2.2
1998–99	559,954	409,086	57,439	48,670	27,586	6,424	10,749	100.0	73.1	10.3	8.7	4.9	1.1	1.9
1999–2000	564,933	408,772	60,221	51,573	27,782	6,497	10,088	100.0	72.4	10.7	9.1	4.9	1.2	1.8
2000–01	578,865	411,075	63,855	57,288	28,463	6,623	11,561	100.0	71.0	11.0	9.9	4.9	1.1	2.0
2001–02	595,133	417,733	67,343	60,003	30,945	6,832	12,277	100.0	70.2	11.3	10.1	5.2	1.1	2.1
2002–03	634,016	438,261	75,609	66,673	32,629	7,461	13,383	100.0	69.1	11.9	10.5	5.1	1.2	2.1
2003–04	665,301	456,047	81,183	72,270	33,149	8,119	14,533	100.0	68.5	12.2	10.9	5.0	1.2	2.2
2004–05	696,660	475,513	86,402	78,557	33,669	8,435	14,084	100.0	68.3	12.4	11.3	4.8	1.2	2.0
2005–06	713,066	485,297	89,784	80,854	35,201	8,552	13,378	100.0	68.1	12.6	11.3	4.9	1.2	1.9
2006–07	728,114	491,572	91,529	85,410	37,266	8,583	13,754	100.0	67.5	12.6	11.7	5.1	1.2	1.9
Males														
1976–77[1]	209,672	178,236	15,330	9,105	3,630	1,216	2,155	100.0	85.0	7.3	4.3	1.7	0.6	1.0
1980–81[2]	183,819	151,242	14,290	8,327	4,557	1,108	4,295	100.0	82.3	7.8	4.5	2.5	0.6	2.3
1989–90	191,195	158,954	12,502	9,370	6,170	1,364	2,835	100.0	83.1	6.5	4.9	3.2	0.7	1.5
1990–91	198,634	161,858	14,143	10,738	7,164	1,439	3,292	100.0	81.5	7.1	5.4	3.6	0.7	1.7
1992–93	211,964	169,841	15,689	13,014	7,937	1,680	3,803	100.0	80.1	7.4	6.1	3.7	0.8	1.8
1993–94	215,261	170,905	16,931	13,214	8,289	1,837	4,085	100.0	79.4	7.9	6.1	3.9	0.9	1.9
1994–95	218,352	170,251	16,727	15,670	9,252	2,098	4,354	100.0	78.0	7.7	7.2	4.2	1.0	2.0
1995–96	219,514	169,230	17,941	15,740	10,229	1,993	4,381	100.0	77.1	8.2	7.2	4.7	0.9	2.0
1996–97	223,948	168,882	19,394	17,990	10,937	2,068	4,677	100.0	75.4	8.7	8.0	4.9	0.9	2.1
1997–98	217,613	161,212	18,686	19,108	10,953	2,252	5,402	100.0	74.1	8.6	8.8	5.0	1.0	2.5
1998–99	218,417	160,794	19,402	19,379	11,671	2,241	4,930	100.0	73.6	8.9	8.9	5.3	1.0	2.3
1999–2000	224,721	164,315	20,967	20,946	12,010	2,225	4,258	100.0	73.1	9.3	9.3	5.3	1.0	1.9
2000–01	231,645	166,322	22,147	23,350	12,339	2,294	5,193	100.0	71.8	9.6	10.1	5.3	1.0	2.2
2001–02	238,109	170,622	22,806	23,963	13,256	2,308	5,154	100.0	71.7	9.6	10.1	5.6	1.0	2.2
2002–03	253,451	179,163	25,591	26,461	14,057	2,618	5,561	100.0	70.7	10.1	10.4	5.5	1.0	2.2
2003–04	260,033	183,819	25,961	27,828	13,907	2,740	5,778	100.0	70.7	10.0	10.7	5.3	1.1	2.2
2004–05	267,536	188,569	27,151	29,658	13,802	2,774	5,582	100.0	70.5	10.1	11.1	5.2	1.0	2.1
2005–06	270,095	190,139	27,619	30,040	14,224	2,774	5,299	100.0	70.4	10.2	11.1	5.3	1.0	2.0
2006–07	275,187	191,565	28,273	31,646	15,510	2,873	5,320	100.0	69.6	10.3	11.5	5.6	1.0	1.9
Females														
1976–77[1]	195,284	164,054	17,829	7,531	3,414	1,282	1,174	100.0	84.0	9.1	3.9	1.7	0.7	0.6
1980–81[2]	226,355	187,925	21,040	9,473	4,093	1,476	2,348	100.0	83.0	9.3	4.2	1.8	0.7	1.0
1989–90	263,907	217,862	21,824	12,134	6,896	2,066	3,125	100.0	82.6	8.3	4.6	2.6	0.8	1.2
1990–91	283,086	229,406	24,692	14,802	8,093	2,432	3,661	100.0	81.0	8.7	5.2	2.9	0.9	1.3
1992–93	302,792	241,594	27,197	17,269	8,826	2,728	5,178	100.0	79.8	9.0	5.7	2.9	0.9	1.7
1993–94	315,371	248,789	28,592	18,904	10,155	3,039	5,892	100.0	78.9	9.1	6.0	3.2	1.0	1.9
1994–95	321,339	250,405	30,340	20,292	11,425	3,384	5,493	100.0	77.9	9.4	6.3	3.6	1.1	1.7
1995–96	335,702	256,876	34,073	22,514	12,909	3,580	5,750	100.0	76.5	10.1	6.7	3.8	1.1	1.7
1996–97	347,278	260,582	36,912	25,559	14,222	3,916	6,087	100.0	75.0	10.6	7.4	4.1	1.1	1.8
1997–98	340,942	252,349	36,628	26,768	14,243	3,994	6,960	100.0	74.0	10.7	7.9	4.2	1.2	2.0
1998–99	341,537	248,292	38,037	29,291	15,915	4,183	5,819	100.0	72.7	11.1	8.6	4.7	1.2	1.7
1999–2000	340,212	244,457	39,254	30,627	15,772	4,272	5,830	100.0	71.9	11.5	9.0	4.6	1.3	1.7
2000–01	347,220	244,753	41,708	33,938	16,124	4,329	6,368	100.0	70.5	12.0	9.8	4.6	1.2	1.8
2001–02	357,024	247,111	44,537	36,040	17,689	4,524	7,123	100.0	69.2	12.5	10.1	5.0	1.3	2.0
2002–03	380,565	259,098	50,018	40,212	18,572	4,843	7,822	100.0	68.1	13.1	10.6	4.9	1.3	2.1
2003–04	405,268	272,228	55,222	44,442	19,242	5,379	8,755	100.0	67.2	13.6	11.0	4.7	1.3	2.2
2004–05	429,124	286,944	59,251	48,899	19,867	5,661	8,502	100.0	66.9	13.8	11.4	4.6	1.3	2.0
2005–06	442,971	295,158	62,165	50,814	20,977	5,778	8,079	100.0	66.6	14.0	11.5	4.7	1.3	1.8
2006–07	452,927	300,007	63,256	53,764	21,756	5,710	8,434	100.0	66.2	14.0	11.9	4.8	1.3	1.9

[1]Excludes 1,170 males and 251 females whose racial/ethnic group was not available.
[2]Excludes 4,819 males and 1,384 females whose racial/ethnic group was not available.
NOTE: Race categories exclude persons of Hispanic ethnicity. For 1989–90 and later years, reported racial/ethnic distributions of students by level of degree, field of degree, and sex were used to estimate race/ethnicity for students whose race/ethnicity was not reported. (See Guide to Sources for details.) Detail may not sum to totals because of rounding.

SOURCE: U.S. Department of Education, National Center for Education Statistics, Higher Education General Information Survey (HEGIS), "Degrees and Other Formal Awards Conferred" surveys, 1976–77 and 1980–81; and 1989–90 through 2006–07 Integrated Postsecondary Education Data System, "Completions Survey" (IPEDS-C:90–99), and Fall 2000 through Fall 2007. (This table was prepared July 2008.)

Table 282. Associate's degrees conferred by degree-granting institutions, by sex, race/ethnicity, and field of study: 2006–07

Field of study	Total							Males							Females						
	Total	White	Black	Hispanic	Asian/ Pacific Islander	American Indian/ Alaska Native	Non-resident alien	Total	White	Black	Hispanic	Asian/ Pacific Islander	American Indian/ Alaska Native	Non-resident alien	Total	White	Black	Hispanic	Asian/ Pacific Islander	American Indian/ Alaska Native	Non-resident alien
1	2	3	4	5	6	7	8	9	10	11	12	13	14	15	16	17	18	19	20	21	22
All fields, total	728,114	491,572	91,529	85,410	37,266	8,583	13,754	275,187	191,565	28,273	31,646	15,510	2,873	5,320	452,927	300,007	63,256	53,764	21,756	5,710	8,434
Agriculture and natural resources	5,838	5,459	72	172	34	83	18	3,626	3,419	49	95	15	38	10	2,212	2,040	23	77	19	45	8
Architecture and related services	517	316	38	115	29	3	16	231	116	31	62	15	2	5	286	200	7	53	14	1	11
Area, ethnic, cultural, and gender studies	164	39	15	33	6	70	1	53	12	8	13	2	18	0	111	27	7	20	4	52	1
Biological and biomedical sciences	2,060	1,144	192	342	270	58	54	676	383	68	96	83	16	30	1,384	761	124	246	187	42	24
Business	116,101	74,402	18,032	12,413	6,405	1,313	3,536	41,413	27,654	5,135	4,410	2,495	387	1,332	74,688	46,748	12,897	8,003	3,910	926	2,204
Communications, journalism, and related programs	2,609	1,889	244	283	80	21	92	1,311	981	105	144	40	8	33	1,298	908	139	139	40	13	59
Communications technologies	3,095	2,289	344	270	121	27	44	1,874	1,397	207	155	75	15	25	1,221	892	137	115	46	12	19
Computer and information sciences	27,712	18,379	4,301	3,008	1,282	315	427	20,459	14,119	2,617	2,282	943	204	294	7,253	4,260	1,684	726	339	111	133
Construction trades	3,895	3,342	262	170	72	45	4	3,696	3,192	243	148	68	41	4	199	150	19	22	4	4	0
Education	13,021	8,479	2,139	1,542	221	509	131	1,773	1,254	218	162	27	95	17	11,248	7,225	1,921	1,380	194	414	114
Engineering	2,136	1,338	201	291	184	31	91	1,835	1,173	166	246	149	25	76	301	165	35	45	35	6	15
Engineering technologies[1]	29,199	21,284	3,190	2,989	1,144	298	294	25,155	18,555	2,637	2,527	962	231	243	4,044	2,729	553	462	182	67	51
English language and literature/letters	1,249	709	102	286	104	15	33	378	213	29	83	45	3	5	871	496	73	203	59	12	28
Family and consumer sciences	9,124	4,864	1,978	1,679	329	140	134	333	189	68	47	18	2	9	8,791	4,675	1,910	1,632	311	138	125
Foreign languages, literatures, and linguistics	1,207	784	76	262	41	13	31	195	111	13	51	10	1	9	1,012	673	63	211	31	12	22
Health professions and related clinical sciences	145,436	104,730	18,861	12,294	6,672	1,501	1,378	21,214	14,227	2,493	2,245	1,745	196	308	124,222	90,503	16,368	10,049	4,927	1,305	1,070
Legal professions and studies	10,391	6,751	1,937	1,324	228	103	48	1,046	635	206	142	37	20	6	9,345	6,116	1,731	1,182	191	83	42
Liberal arts and sciences, general studies, and humanities	250,030	166,142	27,673	33,684	14,239	2,709	5,583	93,711	63,901	8,982	11,851	5,852	929	2,216	156,319	102,241	18,691	21,833	8,407	1,780	3,367
Library science	84	69	4	5	2	4	0	8	8	0	0	0	0	0	76	61	4	5	2	4	0
Mathematics and statistics	827	462	49	187	85	15	29	548	296	36	133	57	8	18	279	166	13	54	28	7	11
Mechanics and repair technologies	15,432	11,364	1,127	1,780	821	246	94	14,720	10,913	1,040	1,678	781	223	85	712	451	87	102	40	23	9
Military technologies	781	539	106	80	49	7	0	641	447	84	66	39	5	0	140	92	22	14	10	2	0
Multi/interdisciplinary studies	15,838	9,248	1,716	2,589	1,814	106	365	6,578	4,047	729	888	733	44	137	9,260	5,201	987	1,701	1,081	62	228
Parks, recreation, leisure and fitness studies	1,251	873	179	116	32	26	25	749	515	116	72	23	17	6	502	358	63	44	9	9	19
Philosophy and religious studies	375	329	17	17	5	1	6	115	86	12	10	4	1	2	260	243	5	7	1	0	4
Physical sciences and science technologies	3,404	2,212	258	378	376	43	137	1,948	1,295	136	232	181	18	86	1,456	917	122	146	195	25	51
Precision production	1,973	1,735	81	97	41	16	3	1,849	1,630	70	93	39	14	3	124	105	11	4	2	2	0
Psychology	2,213	1,335	214	470	96	77	21	517	307	37	117	27	25	4	1,696	1,028	177	353	69	52	17
Public administration and social service professions	4,338	2,275	1,238	616	78	96	35	596	296	164	101	14	16	5	3,742	1,979	1,074	515	64	80	30
Security and protective services	28,208	18,952	4,171	4,095	592	299	99	15,481	11,675	1,342	1,907	380	134	43	12,727	7,277	2,829	2,188	212	165	56
Social sciences and history	7,080	3,953	723	1,446	609	208	141	2,494	1,464	223	460	248	48	51	4,586	2,489	500	986	361	160	90
Social sciences	6,673	3,666	714	1,366	587	200	140	2,252	1,290	218	411	238	44	51	4,421	2,376	496	955	349	156	89
History	407	287	9	80	22	8	1	242	174	5	49	10	4	0	165	113	4	31	12	4	1
Theology and religious vocations	608	469	105	18	5	4	7	313	224	71	10	2	2	4	295	245	34	8	3	2	3
Transportation and materials moving	1,674	1,276	112	163	65	24	34	1,442	1,120	94	137	52	19	20	232	156	18	26	13	5	14
Visual and performing arts	20,244	14,141	1,772	2,196	1,135	157	843	8,209	5,711	844	983	369	68	234	12,035	8,430	928	1,213	766	89	609

[1]Excludes "Construction trades" and "Mechanics and repair technologies," which are listed separately.

NOTE: Race categories exclude persons of Hispanic ethnicity. Reported racial/ethnic distributions of students by level of degree, field of degree, and sex were used to estimate race/ethnicity for students whose race/ethnicity was not reported. To facilitate trend comparisons, certain aggregations have been made of the degree fields as reported in the IPEDS Fall survey: "Agriculture and natural resources" includes Agriculture, agriculture operations, and related sciences and Natural resources and conservation; and "Business" includes Business management, marketing, and related support services and Personal and culinary services.

SOURCE: U.S. Department of Education, National Center for Education Statistics, 2005–06 Integrated Postsecondary Education Data System (IPEDS), Fall 2006. (This table was prepared June 2007.)

Table 283. Associate's degrees conferred by degree-granting institutions, by sex, race/ethnicity, and field of study: 2005–06

Field of study	Total							Males							Females						
	Total	White	Black	Hispanic	Asian/Pacific Islander	American Indian/Alaska Native	Non-resident alien	Total	White	Black	Hispanic	Asian/Pacific Islander	American Indian/Alaska Native	Non-resident alien	Total	White	Black	Hispanic	Asian/Pacific Islander	American Indian/Alaska Native	Non-resident alien
1	2	3	4	5	6	7	8	9	10	11	12	13	14	15	16	17	18	19	20	21	22
All fields, total	713,066	485,297	89,784	80,854	35,201	8,552	13,378	270,095	190,139	27,619	30,040	14,224	2,774	5,299	442,971	295,158	62,165	50,814	20,977	5,778	8,079
Agriculture and natural resources	6,168	5,733	59	143	70	98	65	3,792	3,575	38	93	23	47	16	2,376	2,158	21	50	47	51	49
Architecture and related services	656	416	49	122	47	2	20	247	141	30	55	16	0	5	409	275	19	67	31	2	15
Area, ethnic, cultural, and gender studies	124	22	21	19	3	54	5	37	7	7	7	1	14	1	87	15	14	12	2	40	4
Biological and biomedical sciences	1,827	1,031	162	280	228	69	57	626	361	67	92	75	16	15	1,201	670	95	188	153	53	42
Business	114,095	73,280	17,764	12,288	6,425	1,366	2,972	40,136	27,013	5,020	4,248	2,365	398	1,092	73,959	46,267	12,744	8,040	4,060	968	1,880
Communications, journalism, and related programs	2,629	1,905	253	279	103	27	62	1,316	988	103	144	40	16	25	1,313	917	150	135	63	11	37
Communications technologies	3,380	2,449	395	333	128	27	48	2,036	1,437	253	235	79	12	20	1,344	1,012	142	98	49	15	28
Computer and information sciences	31,246	20,474	5,011	3,279	1,576	358	548	22,464	15,499	2,930	2,371	1,095	197	372	8,782	4,975	2,081	908	481	161	176
Construction trades	3,850	3,262	239	202	61	74	12	3,633	3,096	213	187	58	69	10	217	166	26	15	3	5	2
Education	14,475	8,994	2,532	2,103	222	513	111	2,232	1,505	332	262	34	78	21	12,243	7,489	2,200	1,841	188	435	90
Engineering	2,162	1,378	224	312	140	23	85	1,861	1,197	193	270	108	20	73	301	181	31	42	32	3	12
Engineering technologies[1]	30,461	22,101	3,336	3,222	1,140	348	314	25,982	19,088	2,609	2,780	970	279	256	4,479	3,013	727	442	170	69	58
English language and literature/letters	1,105	694	94	200	63	13	41	370	233	32	67	24	5	9	735	461	62	133	39	8	32
Family and consumer sciences	9,488	5,172	2,032	1,668	346	140	130	418	246	72	56	25	6	13	9,070	4,926	1,960	1,612	321	134	117
Foreign languages, literatures, and linguistics	1,161	771	64	240	43	17	26	216	125	6	58	17	2	8	945	646	58	182	26	15	18
Health professions and related clinical sciences	134,931	98,252	17,615	10,446	5,844	1,436	1,338	19,668	13,551	2,252	1,944	1,426	178	317	115,263	84,701	15,363	8,502	4,418	1,258	1,021
Legal professions and studies	10,509	6,960	1,768	1,404	209	115	53	1,093	642	210	177	38	19	7	9,416	6,318	1,558	1,227	171	96	46
Liberal arts and sciences, general studies, and humanities	244,689	164,099	26,878	31,962	13,256	2,661	5,833	89,955	61,989	8,638	10,943	5,208	833	2,344	154,734	102,110	18,240	21,019	8,048	1,828	3,489
Library science	136	114	3	11	7	0	1	15	10	1	2	2	0	0	121	104	2	9	5	0	1
Mathematics and statistics	753	400	36	163	90	10	54	483	250	22	116	58	6	31	270	150	14	47	32	4	23
Mechanics and repair technologies	14,454	11,152	1,028	1,347	673	156	98	13,713	10,663	936	1,262	616	146	90	741	489	92	85	57	10	8
Military technologies	610	399	113	54	41	3	0	510	335	92	46	34	3	0	100	64	21	8	7	0	0
Multi/interdisciplinary studies	14,473	8,889	1,646	1,944	1,578	98	318	6,224	3,945	693	777	647	38	124	8,249	4,944	953	1,167	931	60	194
Parks, recreation, leisure and fitness studies	1,128	816	141	89	28	20	34	656	473	83	47	19	16	18	472	343	58	42	9	4	16
Philosophy and religious studies	367	332	4	20	4	2	5	97	70	3	17	2	2	3	270	262	1	3	2	0	2
Physical sciences and science technologies	2,902	1,907	259	282	273	33	148	1,702	1,146	121	171	161	17	86	1,200	761	138	111	112	16	62
Precision production	1,977	1,710	73	100	65	25	4	1,800	1,597	55	84	37	23	4	177	113	18	16	28	2	0
Psychology	1,944	1,205	207	384	83	43	22	446	281	44	81	19	13	8	1,498	924	163	303	64	30	14
Public administration and social service professions	4,415	2,312	1,235	652	98	75	43	642	313	191	97	17	16	8	3,773	1,999	1,044	555	81	59	35
Security and protective services	26,425	18,379	3,673	3,404	547	359	63	14,578	11,308	1,113	1,655	327	145	30	11,847	7,071	2,560	1,749	220	214	33
Social sciences and history	6,730	3,893	735	1,277	509	172	144	2,338	1,398	218	404	210	57	51	4,392	2,495	517	873	299	115	93
Social sciences	6,308	3,592	716	1,208	491	163	138	2,095	1,232	210	351	199	56	47	4,213	2,360	506	857	292	107	91
History	422	301	19	69	18	9	6	243	166	8	53	11	1	4	179	135	11	16	7	8	2
Theology and religious vocations	570	376	148	25	8	2	11	248	170	54	13	5	2	4	322	206	94	12	3	0	7
Transportation and materials moving	1,472	1,149	87	137	48	17	34	1,268	1,002	76	112	40	16	22	204	147	11	25	8	1	12
Visual and performing arts	21,754	15,271	1,900	2,463	1,245	196	679	9,293	6,485	912	1,167	428	85	216	12,461	8,786	988	1,296	817	111	463

[1]Excludes "Construction trades" and "Mechanics and repair technologies."

NOTE: Race categories exclude persons of Hispanic ethnicity. Reported racial/ethnic distributions of students by level of degree, field of degree, and sex were used to estimate race/ethnicity for students whose race/ethnicity was not reported. To facilitate trend comparisons, certain aggregations have been made of the degree fields as reported in the IPEDS Fall survey: "Agriculture and natural resources" includes Agriculture, agriculture operations, and related sciences and Natural resources

and conservation; and "Business" includes Business management, marketing, and related support services and Personal and culinary services.

SOURCE: U.S. Department of Education, National Center for Education Statistics, 2005–06 Integrated Postsecondary Education Data System (IPEDS), Fall 2006. (This table was prepared June 2007.)

Table 284. Bachelor's degrees conferred by degree-granting institutions, by race/ethnicity and sex of student: Selected years, 1976–77 through 2006–07

Year and sex	Number of degrees conferred							Percentage distribution of degrees conferred						
	Total	White	Black	Hispanic	Asian/ Pacific Islander	American Indian/ Alaska Native	Non-resident alien	Total	White	Black	Hispanic	Asian/ Pacific Islander	American Indian/ Alaska Native	Non-resident alien
1	2	3	4	5	6	7	8	9	10	11	12	13	14	15
Total														
1976–77[1]	917,900	807,688	58,636	18,743	13,793	3,326	15,714	100.0	88.0	6.4	2.0	1.5	0.4	1.7
1980–81[2]	934,800	807,319	60,673	21,832	18,794	3,593	22,589	100.0	86.4	6.5	2.3	2.0	0.4	2.4
1989–90	1,051,344	887,151	61,046	32,829	39,230	4,390	26,698	100.0	84.4	5.8	3.1	3.7	0.4	2.5
1990–91	1,094,538	914,093	66,375	37,342	42,529	4,583	29,616	100.0	83.5	6.1	3.4	3.9	0.4	2.7
1992–93	1,165,178	952,194	78,099	45,417	51,481	5,683	32,304	100.0	81.7	6.7	3.9	4.4	0.5	2.8
1993–94	1,169,275	939,008	83,909	50,299	55,689	6,192	34,178	100.0	80.3	7.2	4.3	4.8	0.5	2.9
1994–95	1,160,134	914,610	87,236	54,230	60,502	6,610	36,946	100.0	78.8	7.5	4.7	5.2	0.6	3.2
1995–96	1,164,792	905,846	91,496	58,351	64,433	6,976	37,690	100.0	77.8	7.9	5.0	5.5	0.6	3.2
1996–97	1,172,879	900,809	94,349	62,509	68,859	7,425	38,928	100.0	76.8	8.0	5.3	5.9	0.6	3.3
1997–98	1,184,406	901,344	98,251	66,005	71,678	7,903	39,225	100.0	76.1	8.3	5.6	6.1	0.7	3.3
1998–99	1,200,303	907,245	102,214	70,085	74,197	8,423	38,139	100.0	75.6	8.5	5.8	6.2	0.7	3.2
1999–2000	1,237,875	929,106	108,013	75,059	77,912	8,719	39,066	100.0	75.1	8.7	6.1	6.3	0.7	3.2
2000–01	1,244,171	927,357	111,307	77,745	78,902	9,049	39,811	100.0	74.5	8.9	6.2	6.3	0.7	3.2
2001–02	1,291,900	958,597	116,623	82,966	83,093	9,165	41,456	100.0	74.2	9.0	6.4	6.4	0.7	3.2
2002–03	1,348,811	994,616	124,253	89,029	87,964	9,875	43,074	100.0	73.7	9.2	6.6	6.5	0.7	3.2
2003–04	1,399,542	1,026,114	131,241	94,644	92,073	10,638	44,832	100.0	73.3	9.4	6.8	6.6	0.8	3.2
2004–05	1,439,264	1,049,141	136,122	101,124	97,209	10,307	45,361	100.0	72.9	9.5	7.0	6.8	0.7	3.2
2005–06	1,485,242	1,075,561	142,420	107,588	102,376	10,940	46,357	100.0	72.4	9.6	7.2	6.9	0.7	3.1
2006–07	1,524,092	1,099,850	146,653	114,936	105,297	11,455	45,901	100.0	72.2	9.6	7.5	6.9	0.8	3.0
Males														
1976–77[1]	494,424	438,161	25,147	10,318	7,638	1,804	11,356	100.0	88.6	5.1	2.1	1.5	0.4	2.3
1980–81[2]	469,625	406,173	24,511	10,810	10,107	1,700	16,324	100.0	86.5	5.2	2.3	2.2	0.4	3.5
1989–90	491,696	414,982	23,257	14,932	19,711	1,860	16,954	100.0	84.4	4.7	3.0	4.0	0.4	3.4
1990–91	504,045	421,290	24,800	16,598	21,203	1,938	18,216	100.0	83.6	4.9	3.3	4.2	0.4	3.6
1992–93	532,881	437,262	28,962	19,883	25,303	2,450	19,021	100.0	82.1	5.4	3.7	4.7	0.5	3.6
1993–94	532,422	430,526	30,766	21,834	26,952	2,620	19,724	100.0	80.9	5.8	4.1	5.1	0.5	3.7
1994–95	526,131	417,878	31,793	23,626	28,992	2,739	21,103	100.0	79.4	6.0	4.5	5.5	0.5	4.0
1995–96	522,454	409,565	32,974	25,029	30,669	2,885	21,332	100.0	78.4	6.3	4.8	5.9	0.6	4.1
1996–97	520,515	403,366	33,618	26,318	32,521	2,996	21,698	100.0	77.5	6.5	5.1	6.2	0.6	4.2
1997–98	519,956	399,553	34,510	27,677	33,445	3,151	21,620	100.0	76.8	6.6	5.3	6.4	0.6	4.2
1998–99	518,746	396,996	34,876	28,662	34,225	3,323	20,664	100.0	76.5	6.7	5.5	6.6	0.6	4.0
1999–2000	530,367	402,961	37,024	30,301	35,853	3,464	20,764	100.0	76.0	7.0	5.7	6.8	0.7	3.9
2000–01	531,840	401,780	38,103	31,368	35,865	3,700	21,024	100.0	75.5	7.2	5.9	6.7	0.7	4.0
2001–02	549,816	414,892	39,196	32,951	37,660	3,624	21,493	100.0	75.5	7.1	6.0	6.8	0.7	3.9
2002–03	573,258	430,248	41,494	35,101	40,230	3,870	22,315	100.0	75.1	7.2	6.1	7.0	0.7	3.9
2003–04	595,425	445,483	43,851	37,288	41,360	4,244	23,199	100.0	74.8	7.4	6.3	6.9	0.7	3.9
2004–05	613,000	456,592	45,810	39,490	43,711	4,143	23,254	100.0	74.5	7.5	6.4	7.1	0.7	3.8
2005–06	630,600	467,467	48,079	41,814	45,809	4,203	23,228	100.0	74.1	7.6	6.6	7.3	0.7	3.7
2006–07	649,570	480,558	49,685	44,750	47,582	4,505	22,490	100.0	74.0	7.6	6.9	7.3	0.7	3.5
Females														
1976–77[1]	423,476	369,527	33,489	8,425	6,155	1,522	4,358	100.0	87.3	7.9	2.0	1.5	0.4	1.0
1980–81[2]	465,175	401,146	36,162	11,022	8,687	1,893	6,265	100.0	86.2	7.8	2.4	1.9	0.4	1.3
1989–90	559,648	472,169	37,789	17,897	19,519	2,530	9,744	100.0	84.4	6.8	3.2	3.5	0.5	1.7
1990–91	590,493	492,803	41,575	20,744	21,326	2,645	11,400	100.0	83.5	7.0	3.5	3.6	0.4	1.9
1992–93	632,297	514,932	49,137	25,534	26,178	3,233	13,283	100.0	81.4	7.8	4.0	4.1	0.5	2.1
1993–94	636,853	508,482	53,143	28,465	28,737	3,572	14,454	100.0	79.8	8.3	4.5	4.5	0.6	2.3
1994–95	634,003	496,732	55,443	30,604	31,510	3,871	15,843	100.0	78.3	8.7	4.8	5.0	0.6	2.5
1995–96	642,338	496,281	58,522	33,322	33,764	4,091	16,358	100.0	77.3	9.1	5.2	5.3	0.6	2.5
1996–97	652,364	497,443	60,733	36,191	36,338	4,429	17,230	100.0	76.3	9.3	5.5	5.6	0.7	2.6
1997–98	664,450	501,791	63,741	38,328	38,233	4,752	17,605	100.0	75.5	9.6	5.8	5.8	0.7	2.6
1998–99	681,557	510,249	67,338	41,423	39,972	5,100	17,475	100.0	74.9	9.9	6.1	5.9	0.7	2.6
1999–2000	707,508	526,145	70,989	44,758	42,059	5,255	18,302	100.0	74.4	10.0	6.3	5.9	0.7	2.6
2000–01	712,331	525,577	73,204	46,377	43,037	5,349	18,787	100.0	73.8	10.3	6.5	6.0	0.8	2.6
2001–02	742,084	543,705	77,427	50,015	45,433	5,541	19,963	100.0	73.3	10.4	6.7	6.1	0.7	2.7
2002–03	775,553	564,368	82,759	53,928	47,734	6,005	20,759	100.0	72.8	10.7	7.0	6.2	0.8	2.7
2003–04	804,117	580,631	87,390	57,356	50,713	6,394	21,633	100.0	72.2	10.9	7.1	6.3	0.8	2.7
2004–05	826,264	592,549	90,312	61,634	53,498	6,164	22,107	100.0	71.7	10.9	7.5	6.5	0.7	2.7
2005–06	854,642	608,094	94,341	65,774	56,567	6,737	23,129	100.0	71.2	11.0	7.7	6.6	0.8	2.7
2006–07	874,522	619,292	96,968	70,186	57,715	6,950	23,411	100.0	70.8	11.1	8.0	6.6	0.8	2.7

[1]Excludes 1,121 males and 528 females whose racial/ethnic group was not available.
[2]Excludes 258 males and 82 females whose racial/ethnic group was not available.
NOTE: Race categories exclude persons of Hispanic ethnicity. For 1989–90 and later years, reported racial/ethnic distributions of students by level of degree, field of degree, and sex were used to estimate race/ethnicity for students whose race/ethnicity was not reported. (See Guide to Sources for details.) Detail may not sum to totals because of rounding.

SOURCE: U.S. Department of Education, National Center for Education Statistics, Higher Education General Information Survey (HEGIS), "Degrees and Other Formal Awards Conferred" surveys, 1976–77 and 1980–81; and 1989–90 through 2006–07 Integrated Postsecondary Education Data System, "Completions Survey" (IPEDS-C:90–99), and Fall 2000 through Fall 2007. (This table was prepared July 2008.)

Table 285. Bachelor's degrees conferred by degree-granting institutions, by sex, race/ethnicity, and field of study: 2006–07

Field of study	Total							Males							Females						
	Total	White	Black	Hispanic	Asian/ Pacific Islander	American Indian/ Alaska Native	Non-resident alien	Total	White	Black	Hispanic	Asian/ Pacific Islander	American Indian/ Alaska Native	Non-resident alien	Total	White	Black	Hispanic	Asian/ Pacific Islander	American Indian/ Alaska Native	Non-resident alien
1	2	3	4	5	6	7	8	9	10	11	12	13	14	15	16	17	18	19	20	21	22
All fields, total	1,524,092	1,099,850	146,653	114,936	105,297	11,455	45,901	649,570	480,558	49,685	44,750	47,582	4,505	22,490	874,522	619,292	96,968	70,186	57,715	6,950	23,411
Agriculture and natural resources	23,133	20,116	680	859	901	214	363	12,309	10,961	290	399	383	111	165	10,824	9,155	390	460	518	103	198
Architecture and related services	9,717	6,983	455	948	867	51	413	5,393	3,965	264	541	393	33	197	4,324	3,018	191	407	474	18	216
Area, ethnic, cultural, and gender studies	8,194	4,486	1,095	1,175	1,045	194	199	2,572	1,399	352	363	335	69	54	5,622	3,087	743	812	710	125	145
Biological and biomedical sciences	75,151	50,120	5,950	4,651	11,665	539	2,226	29,951	20,797	1,577	1,807	4,727	209	834	45,200	29,323	4,373	2,844	6,938	330	1,392
Business	327,531	223,221	37,054	24,724	24,361	2,174	15,997	166,350	120,356	13,947	11,099	11,789	995	8,164	161,181	102,865	23,107	13,625	12,572	1,179	7,833
Communications, journalism, and related programs	74,783	56,929	7,528	5,031	3,329	452	1,514	26,444	20,491	2,537	1,698	1,049	147	522	48,339	36,438	4,991	3,333	2,280	305	992
Communications technologies	3,637	2,614	346	306	251	19	101	2,565	1,879	212	231	164	12	67	1,072	735	134	75	87	7	34
Computer and information sciences	42,170	27,626	5,066	2,835	3,937	275	2,431	34,342	23,600	3,262	2,257	3,121	205	1,897	7,828	4,026	1,804	578	816	70	534
Construction trades	129	113	4	6	5	0	1	122	108	3	6	4	0	1	7	5	0	0	1	0	0
Education	105,641	89,868	6,739	5,111	2,043	909	971	22,516	18,979	1,661	979	434	185	278	83,125	70,889	5,078	4,132	1,609	724	693
Engineering	67,092	45,994	3,307	4,092	8,980	316	4,403	54,745	38,574	2,299	3,181	6,934	248	3,509	12,347	7,420	1,008	911	2,046	68	894
Engineering technologies[1]	14,588	11,125	1,396	854	700	141	372	13,114	10,194	1,135	738	617	112	318	1,474	931	261	116	83	29	54
English language and literature/letters	55,122	43,722	4,148	3,669	2,648	378	557	17,475	14,248	1,008	1,164	763	136	156	37,647	29,474	3,140	2,505	1,885	242	401
Family and consumer sciences	21,400	16,334	2,312	1,237	1,052	195	270	2,594	1,885	342	158	145	27	37	18,806	14,449	1,970	1,079	907	168	233
Foreign languages, literatures, and linguistics	20,275	14,420	828	3,366	1,133	129	399	6,173	4,522	214	928	358	41	110	14,102	9,898	614	2,438	775	88	289
Health professions and related clinical sciences	101,810	75,579	11,413	6,069	5,993	777	1,979	14,325	10,146	1,483	1,043	1,182	120	351	87,485	65,433	9,930	5,026	4,811	657	1,628
Legal professions and studies	3,596	2,290	661	356	239	22	28	1,008	684	135	101	80	2	6	2,588	1,606	526	255	159	20	22
Liberal arts and sciences, general studies, and humanities	44,255	29,719	6,040	4,722	2,520	499	755	14,123	9,978	1,799	1,092	844	162	248	30,132	19,741	4,241	3,630	1,676	337	507
Library science	82	78	1	1	0	2	0	10	10	0	0	0	0	0	72	68	1	1	0	2	0
Mathematics and statistics	14,954	10,965	858	956	1,469	66	640	8,360	6,160	415	540	812	37	396	6,594	4,805	443	416	657	29	244
Mechanics and repair technologies	263	197	21	21	11	5	8	249	187	19	19	11	5	8	14	10	2	2	0	0	0
Military technologies	168	150	5	6	4	3	0	152	136	5	6	2	3	0	16	14	0	0	2	0	0
Multi/interdisciplinary studies	33,792	23,266	2,883	4,193	2,326	299	825	10,439	7,459	830	914	859	101	276	23,353	15,807	2,053	3,279	1,467	198	549
Parks, recreation, leisure and fitness studies	27,430	21,467	2,557	1,830	852	242	482	14,190	10,888	1,491	1,017	441	114	239	13,240	10,579	1,066	813	411	128	243
Philosophy and religious studies	11,969	9,750	600	662	692	92	173	7,430	6,157	321	387	401	55	109	4,539	3,593	279	275	291	37	64
Physical sciences and science technologies	21,073	15,909	1,208	953	2,031	157	815	12,455	9,826	522	548	1,018	78	463	8,618	6,083	686	405	1,013	79	352
Precision production	23	17	0	2	3	1	0	12	10	0	1	0	1	0	11	7	0	1	3	0	0
Psychology	90,039	63,219	10,361	8,334	5,922	646	1,557	20,343	14,587	1,879	1,802	1,591	142	342	69,696	48,632	8,482	6,532	4,331	504	1,215
Public administration and social service professions	23,147	13,605	5,355	2,753	820	280	334	4,354	2,604	868	561	195	65	61	18,793	11,001	4,487	2,192	625	215	273
Security and protective services	39,206	25,215	7,162	4,795	1,179	362	493	19,505	13,804	2,575	2,101	649	163	213	19,701	11,411	4,587	2,694	530	199	280
Social sciences and history	164,183	117,453	14,689	13,762	12,626	1,295	4,358	82,417	62,263	5,449	6,012	5,947	583	2,163	81,766	55,190	9,240	7,750	6,679	712	2,195
Social sciences	129,737	88,837	12,993	11,472	11,261	1,024	4,150	62,200	45,075	4,674	4,720	5,248	440	2,043	67,537	43,762	8,319	6,752	6,013	584	2,107
History	34,446	28,616	1,696	2,290	1,365	271	208	20,217	17,188	775	1,292	699	143	120	14,229	11,428	921	998	666	128	88
Theology and religious vocations	8,696	7,323	638	308	222	41	164	5,761	4,956	344	186	134	29	112	2,935	2,367	294	122	88	12	52
Transportation and materials moving	5,657	4,592	296	372	210	67	120	5,043	4,101	268	331	181	58	104	614	491	28	41	29	9	16
Visual and performing arts	85,186	65,385	4,997	5,977	5,261	613	2,953	32,729	24,644	2,179	2,540	2,019	257	1,090	52,457	40,741	2,818	3,437	3,242	356	1,863

[1]Excludes "Construction trades" and "Mechanics and repair technologies," which are listed separately.

NOTE: Race categories exclude persons of Hispanic ethnicity. Reported racial/ethnic distributions of students by level of degree, field of degree, and sex were used to estimate race/ethnicity for students whose race/ethnicity was not reported. To facilitate trend comparisons, certain aggregations have been made of the degree fields as reported in the IPEDS Fall survey: "Agriculture and natural resources" includes Agriculture, agriculture operations, and related sciences and Natural resources

and conservation; and "Business" includes Business management, marketing, and related support services and Personal and culinary services.

SOURCE: U.S. Department of Education, National Center for Education Statistics, 2006–07 Integrated Postsecondary Education Data System (IPEDS), Fall 2007. (This table was prepared July 2008.)

Table 286. Bachelor's degrees conferred by degree-granting institutions, by sex, race/ethnicity, and field of study: 2005–06

Field of study	Total							Males							Females						
	Total	White	Black	Hispanic	Asian/ Pacific Islander	American Indian/ Alaska Native	Non-resident alien	Total	White	Black	Hispanic	Asian/ Pacific Islander	American Indian/ Alaska Native	Non-resident alien	Total	White	Black	Hispanic	Asian/ Pacific Islander	American Indian/ Alaska Native	Non-resident alien
1	2	3	4	5	6	7	8	9	10	11	12	13	14	15	16	17	18	19	20	21	22
All fields, total	1,485,242	1,075,561	142,420	107,588	102,376	10,940	46,357	630,600	467,467	48,079	41,814	45,809	4,203	23,228	854,642	608,094	94,341	65,774	56,567	6,737	23,129
Agriculture and natural resources	23,053	20,190	685	764	806	256	352	12,063	10,861	296	338	547	120	161	10,990	9,389	389	426	459	136	191
Architecture and related services	9,515	6,991	455	826	794	46	403	5,414	4,054	267	463	555	18	217	4,101	2,897	188	363	439	28	186
Area, ethnic, cultural, and gender studies	7,879	4,307	1,167	1,081	1,004	146	174	2,420	1,336	371	317	309	38	49	5,459	2,971	796	764	695	108	125
Biological and biomedical sciences	69,178	46,877	5,409	4,203	10,165	489	2,035	26,651	18,801	1,398	1,573	3,557	164	758	42,527	28,076	4,011	2,630	6,208	325	1,277
Business	318,042	216,567	36,195	23,100	24,154	2,087	15,939	159,683	115,773	13,138	10,355	11,234	926	8,257	158,359	100,794	23,057	12,745	12,920	1,161	7,682
Communications, journalism, and related programs	73,955	56,648	7,325	4,758	3,224	423	1,577	26,135	20,365	2,492	1,609	1,036	146	486	47,820	36,282	4,833	3,149	2,188	277	1,091
Communications technologies	2,981	2,191	295	222	181	15	77	2,007	1,509	159	147	131	11	50	974	682	136	75	50	4	27
Computer and information sciences	47,480	29,864	5,875	3,164	5,180	304	3,093	37,705	25,237	3,502	2,455	3,937	215	2,359	9,775	4,627	2,373	709	1,243	89	734
Construction trades	141	123	9	2	4	0	3	134	113	9	2	4	0	3	7	5	2	0	0	0	0
Education	107,238	91,279	6,884	5,196	1,954	902	1,043	22,448	13,950	1,693	934	397	197	277	84,790	72,329	5,171	4,262	1,557	705	766
Engineering	67,045	45,465	3,355	4,051	9,070	364	4,740	54,036	37,681	2,335	3,179	6,849	290	3,702	13,009	7,784	1,020	872	2,221	74	1,038
Engineering technologies[1]	14,178	10,600	1,536	824	699	140	379	12,604	9,670	1,171	700	624	125	314	1,574	930	365	124	75	15	65
English language and literature/letters	55,096	43,872	4,242	3,545	2,600	341	496	17,316	14,224	1,048	1,090	718	109	127	37,780	29,648	3,194	2,455	1,882	232	369
Family and consumer sciences	20,775	16,083	2,227	1,163	898	160	244	2,436	1,810	328	123	116	14	45	18,339	14,273	1,899	1,040	782	146	199
Foreign languages, literatures, and linguistics	19,410	13,319	799	3,231	1,039	82	440	5,842	4,320	200	849	310	28	135	13,568	9,499	599	2,382	729	54	305
Health professions and related clinical sciences	91,973	69,092	10,268	5,230	5,102	673	1,608	12,914	9,248	1,339	920	1,001	100	306	79,059	59,844	8,929	4,310	4,101	573	1,302
Legal professions and studies	3,302	2,081	578	335	247	35	26	982	643	132	108	81	9	9	2,320	1,438	446	227	166	26	17
Liberal arts and sciences, general studies, and humanities	44,898	30,162	5,701	4,938	2,808	501	788	14,144	10,074	1,614	1,140	875	150	291	30,754	20,088	4,087	3,798	1,933	351	497
Library science	76	73	2	1	0	0	0	5	5	0	0	0	0	0	71	68	2	1	0	0	0
Mathematics and statistics	14,770	10,700	871	892	1,491	68	748	8,115	5,905	437	482	790	35	466	6,655	4,795	434	410	701	33	282
Mechanics and repair technologies	246	173	19	26	17	2	9	239	167	19	25	17	2	9	7	6	0	1	0	0	0
Military technologies	33	32	0	1	0	0	0	29	28	0	1	0	0	0	4	4	0	0	0	0	0
Multi/interdisciplinary studies	32,012	22,495	2,746	3,431	2,252	254	834	9,959	7,206	815	732	780	86	340	22,053	15,289	1,931	2,699	1,472	168	494
Parks, recreation, leisure and fitness studies	25,490	20,189	2,271	1,646	767	205	412	13,310	10,312	1,348	949	367	108	226	12,180	9,877	923	697	400	97	186
Philosophy and religious studies	11,985	9,801	689	654	622	66	153	7,428	6,117	395	425	354	39	98	4,557	3,684	294	229	268	27	55
Physical sciences and science technologies	20,318	15,421	1,178	903	1,818	155	843	11,831	9,421	477	494	884	83	472	8,487	6,000	701	409	934	72	371
Precision production	55	46	1	2	5	0	1	35	34	0	1	0	0	0	20	12	1	1	5	0	1
Psychology	88,134	62,645	9,663	8,051	5,568	628	1,579	19,865	14,474	1,764	1,741	1,430	136	320	68,269	48,171	7,899	6,310	4,138	492	1,259
Public administration and social service professions	21,986	13,168	5,187	2,365	716	239	311	4,126	2,543	861	448	162	49	63	17,860	10,625	4,326	1,917	554	190	248
Security and protective services	35,319	23,208	6,412	4,005	1,013	356	325	17,498	12,659	2,212	1,789	563	145	150	17,821	10,549	4,200	2,236	450	211	175
Social sciences and history	161,485	115,808	14,683	12,818	12,416	1,307	4,453	80,799	61,029	5,554	5,598	5,851	561	2,206	80,686	54,779	9,129	7,220	6,565	746	2,247
Social sciences	128,332	88,131	12,995	10,808	11,085	1,072	4,231	61,365	44,460	4,735	4,503	5,155	431	2,081	66,967	43,671	8,260	6,305	5,940	641	2,150
History	33,153	27,677	1,688	2,010	1,321	235	222	19,434	16,569	819	1,095	696	130	125	13,719	11,108	869	915	625	105	97
Theology and religious vocations	8,548	7,275	553	329	176	42	173	5,593	4,846	310	182	114	22	119	2,955	2,429	243	147	62	20	54
Transportation and materials moving	5,349	4,382	305	290	194	42	136	4,717	3,876	272	246	169	38	116	632	506	33	44	25	4	20
Visual and performing arts	83,297	63,934	4,855	5,541	5,392	612	2,963	32,117	24,190	2,125	2,419	2,047	239	1,097	51,180	39,744	2,730	3,122	3,345	373	1,866

[1]Excludes "Construction trades" and "Mechanics and repair technologies," which are listed separately.
NOTE: Race categories exclude persons of Hispanic ethnicity. Reported racial/ethnic distributions of students by level of degree, field of degree, and sex were used to estimate race/ethnicity for students whose race/ethnicity was not reported. To facilitate trend comparisons, certain aggregations have been made of the degree fields as reported in the IPEDS Fall survey: "Agriculture and natural resources" includes Agriculture, agriculture operations, and related sciences and Natural resources and conservation; and "Business" includes Business management, marketing, and related support services and Personal and culinary services.
SOURCE: U.S. Department of Education, National Center for Education Statistics, 2005–06 Integrated Postsecondary Education Data System (IPEDS), Fall 2006. (This table was prepared June 2007.)

Table 287. Master's degrees conferred by degree-granting institutions, by race/ethnicity and sex of student: Selected years, 1976–77 through 2006–07

Year and sex	Number of degrees conferred							Percentage distribution of degrees conferred						
	Total	White	Black	Hispanic	Asian/ Pacific Islander	American Indian/ Alaska Native	Non-resident alien	Total	White	Black	Hispanic	Asian/ Pacific Islander	American Indian/ Alaska Native	Non-resident alien
1	2	3	4	5	6	7	8	9	10	11	12	13	14	15
Total														
1976–77[1]	316,602	266,061	21,037	6,071	5,122	967	17,344	100.0	84.0	6.6	1.9	1.6	0.3	5.5
1980–81[2]	294,183	241,216	17,133	6,461	6,282	1,034	22,057	100.0	82.0	5.8	2.2	2.1	0.4	7.5
1989–90	324,301	254,299	15,336	7,892	10,439	1,090	35,245	100.0	78.4	4.7	2.4	3.2	0.3	10.9
1990–91	337,168	261,232	16,616	8,887	11,650	1,178	37,605	100.0	77.5	4.9	2.6	3.5	0.3	11.2
1992–93	369,585	279,827	19,744	10,638	13,863	1,405	44,108	100.0	75.7	5.3	2.9	3.8	0.4	11.9
1993–94	387,070	289,536	21,986	11,933	15,411	1,699	46,505	100.0	74.8	5.7	3.1	4.0	0.4	12.0
1994–95	397,629	293,345	24,166	12,905	16,847	1,621	48,745	100.0	73.8	6.1	3.2	4.2	0.4	12.3
1995–96	406,301	298,133	25,822	14,442	18,216	1,778	47,910	100.0	73.4	6.4	3.6	4.5	0.4	11.8
1996–97	419,401	305,005	28,403	15,440	19,061	1,940	49,552	100.0	72.7	6.8	3.7	4.5	0.5	11.8
1997–98	430,164	308,196	30,155	16,248	21,133	2,053	52,379	100.0	71.6	7.0	3.8	4.9	0.5	12.2
1998–99	439,986	313,487	32,541	17,838	22,072	2,016	52,032	100.0	71.2	7.4	4.1	5.0	0.5	11.8
1999–2000	457,056	320,485	35,874	19,253	23,218	2,246	55,980	100.0	70.1	7.8	4.2	5.1	0.5	12.2
2000–01	468,476	320,480	38,265	21,543	24,283	2,481	61,424	100.0	68.4	8.2	4.6	5.2	0.5	13.1
2001–02	482,118	327,645	40,370	22,385	25,411	2,624	63,683	100.0	68.0	8.4	4.6	5.3	0.5	13.2
2002–03	513,339	342,131	44,438	25,047	27,264	2,858	71,601	100.0	66.6	8.7	4.9	5.3	0.6	13.9
2003–04	558,940	369,582	50,657	29,666	30,952	3,192	74,891	100.0	66.1	9.1	5.3	5.5	0.6	13.4
2004–05	574,618	379,350	54,482	31,485	32,783	3,295	73,223	100.0	66.0	9.5	5.5	5.7	0.6	12.7
2005–06	594,065	393,357	58,976	32,438	34,029	3,504	71,761	100.0	66.2	9.9	5.5	5.7	0.6	12.1
2006–07	604,607	399,267	62,574	34,822	36,134	3,575	68,235	100.0	66.0	10.3	5.8	6.0	0.6	11.3
Males														
1976–77[1]	167,396	139,210	7,781	3,268	3,123	521	13,493	100.0	83.2	4.6	2.0	1.9	0.3	8.1
1980–81[2]	145,666	115,562	6,158	3,085	3,773	501	16,587	100.0	79.3	4.2	2.1	2.6	0.3	11.4
1989–90	153,653	114,203	5,474	3,548	5,896	455	24,077	100.0	74.3	3.6	2.3	3.8	0.3	15.7
1990–91	156,482	114,419	5,916	3,936	6,575	488	25,148	100.0	73.1	3.8	2.5	4.2	0.3	16.1
1992–93	169,258	120,783	6,803	4,722	7,545	584	28,821	100.0	71.4	4.0	2.8	4.5	0.3	17.0
1993–94	176,085	124,409	7,424	5,122	8,298	692	30,140	100.0	70.7	4.2	2.9	4.7	0.4	17.1
1994–95	178,598	124,277	8,097	5,487	8,923	659	31,155	100.0	69.6	4.5	3.1	5.0	0.4	17.4
1995–96	179,081	124,847	8,445	5,843	9,400	705	29,841	100.0	69.7	4.7	3.3	5.2	0.4	16.7
1996–97	180,947	125,552	8,960	6,246	9,218	734	30,237	100.0	69.4	5.0	3.5	5.1	0.4	16.7
1997–98	184,375	125,605	9,652	6,512	10,262	782	31,562	100.0	68.1	5.2	3.5	5.6	0.4	17.1
1998–99	186,148	126,674	10,058	7,032	10,491	771	31,122	100.0	68.1	5.4	3.8	5.6	0.4	16.7
1999–2000	191,792	128,046	11,212	7,635	11,047	836	33,016	100.0	66.8	5.8	4.0	5.8	0.4	17.2
2000–01	194,351	125,993	11,568	8,271	11,349	917	36,253	100.0	64.8	6.0	4.3	5.8	0.5	18.7
2001–02	199,120	128,776	11,795	8,430	11,746	993	37,380	100.0	64.7	5.9	4.2	5.9	0.5	18.8
2002–03	211,664	133,398	12,869	9,270	12,518	1,027	42,582	100.0	63.0	6.1	4.4	5.9	0.5	20.1
2003–04	229,545	143,827	14,653	10,813	14,347	1,127	44,778	100.0	62.7	6.4	4.7	6.3	0.5	19.5
2004–05	233,590	147,546	15,733	11,385	15,031	1,160	42,735	100.0	63.2	6.7	4.9	6.4	0.5	18.3
2005–06	237,896	150,954	16,959	11,637	15,803	1,244	41,299	100.0	63.5	7.1	4.9	6.6	0.5	17.4
2006–07	238,189	151,358	17,907	12,362	16,451	1,264	38,847	100.0	63.5	7.5	5.2	6.9	0.5	16.3
Females														
1976–77[1]	149,206	126,851	13,256	2,803	1,999	446	3,851	100.0	85.0	8.9	1.9	1.3	0.3	2.6
1980–81[2]	148,517	125,654	10,975	3,376	2,509	533	5,470	100.0	84.6	7.4	2.3	1.7	0.4	3.7
1989–90	170,648	140,096	9,862	4,344	4,543	635	11,168	100.0	82.1	5.8	2.5	2.7	0.4	6.5
1990–91	180,686	146,813	10,700	4,951	5,075	690	12,457	100.0	81.3	5.9	2.7	2.8	0.4	6.9
1992–93	200,327	159,044	12,941	5,916	6,318	821	15,287	100.0	79.4	6.5	3.0	3.2	0.4	7.6
1993–94	210,985	165,127	14,562	6,811	7,113	1,007	16,365	100.0	78.3	6.9	3.2	3.4	0.5	7.8
1994–95	219,031	169,068	16,069	7,418	7,924	962	17,590	100.0	77.2	7.3	3.4	3.6	0.4	8.0
1995–96	227,220	173,286	17,377	8,599	8,816	1,073	18,069	100.0	76.3	7.6	3.8	3.9	0.5	8.0
1996–97	238,454	179,453	19,443	9,194	9,843	1,206	19,315	100.0	75.3	8.2	3.9	4.1	0.5	8.1
1997–98	245,789	182,591	20,503	9,736	10,871	1,271	20,817	100.0	74.3	8.3	4.0	4.4	0.5	8.5
1998–99	253,838	186,813	22,483	10,806	11,581	1,245	20,910	100.0	73.6	8.9	4.3	4.6	0.5	8.2
1999–2000	265,264	192,439	24,662	11,618	12,171	1,410	22,964	100.0	72.5	9.3	4.4	4.6	0.5	8.7
2000–01	274,125	194,487	26,697	13,272	12,934	1,564	25,171	100.0	70.9	9.7	4.8	4.7	0.6	9.2
2001–02	282,998	198,869	28,575	13,955	13,665	1,631	26,303	100.0	70.3	10.1	4.9	4.8	0.6	9.3
2002–03	301,675	208,733	31,569	15,777	14,746	1,831	29,019	100.0	69.2	10.5	5.2	4.9	0.6	9.6
2003–04	329,395	225,755	36,004	18,853	16,605	2,065	30,113	100.0	68.5	10.9	5.7	5.0	0.6	9.1
2004–05	341,028	231,804	38,749	20,100	17,752	2,135	30,488	100.0	68.0	11.4	5.9	5.2	0.6	8.9
2005–06	356,169	242,403	42,017	20,801	18,226	2,260	30,462	100.0	68.1	11.8	5.8	5.1	0.6	8.6
2006–07	366,418	247,909	44,667	22,460	19,683	2,311	29,388	100.0	67.7	12.2	6.1	5.4	0.6	8.0

[1]Excludes 387 men and 175 women whose racial/ethnic group was not available.
[2]Excludes 1,377 men and 179 women whose racial/ethnic group was not available.
NOTE: Race categories exclude persons of Hispanic ethnicity. For 1989–90 and later years, reported racial/ethnic distributions of students by level of degree, field of degree, and sex were used to estimate race/ethnicity for students whose race/ethnicity was not reported. (See Guide to Sources for details.) Detail may not sum to totals because of rounding.

SOURCE: U.S. Department of Education, National Center for Education Statistics, Higher Education General Information Survey (HEGIS), "Degrees and Other Formal Awards Conferred" surveys, 1976–77 and 1980–81; and 1989–90 through 2006–07 Integrated Postsecondary Education Data System, "Completions Survey" (IPEDS-C:90–99), and Fall 2000 through Fall 2007. (This table was prepared July 2008.)

Table 288. Master's degrees conferred by degree-granting institutions, by sex, race/ethnicity, and field of study: 2006–07

Field of study	Total							Males							Females						
	Total	White	Black	Hispanic	Asian/ Pacific Islander	American Indian/ Alaska Native	Non-resident alien	Total	White	Black	Hispanic	Asian/ Pacific Islander	American Indian/ Alaska Native	Non-resident alien	Total	White	Black	Hispanic	Asian/ Pacific Islander	American Indian/ Alaska Native	Non-resident alien
1	2	3	4	5	6	7	8	9	10	11	12	13	14	15	16	17	18	19	20	21	22
All fields, total	604,607	399,267	62,574	34,822	36,134	3,575	68,235	238,189	151,358	17,907	12,362	16,451	1,264	38,847	366,418	247,909	44,667	22,460	19,683	2,311	29,388
Agriculture and natural resources	4,623	3,469	158	139	147	39	671	2,174	1,623	52	62	57	13	357	2,449	1,836	106	77	90	26	314
Architecture and related services	5,951	3,902	301	391	390	24	943	3,334	2,243	156	217	159	10	519	2,647	1,659	145	174	231	14	424
Area, ethnic, cultural, and gender studies	1,699	995	175	163	128	27	211	617	365	49	61	53	16	73	1,082	630	126	102	75	11	138
Biological and biomedical sciences	8,747	5,525	505	392	989	37	1,299	3,568	2,375	134	132	382	20	525	5,179	3,150	371	260	607	17	774
Business	150,211	87,416	19,746	7,966	12,705	806	21,572	84,115	51,925	7,152	4,285	7,204	420	13,129	66,096	35,491	12,594	3,681	5,501	386	8,443
Communications, journalism, and related programs	6,773	4,404	714	332	374	27	922	2,153	1,489	166	93	120	9	276	4,620	2,915	548	239	254	18	646
Communications technologies	499	203	63	17	33	12	171	332	142	41	15	16	8	110	167	61	22	2	17	4	61
Computer and information sciences	16,232	6,342	1,043	479	2,038	46	6,284	11,985	5,012	641	368	1,406	39	4,519	4,247	1,330	402	111	632	7	1,765
Construction trades	0	0	0	0	0	0	0	0	0	0	0	0	0	0	0	0	0	0	0	0	0
Education	176,572	135,539	18,361	11,857	4,731	1,140	4,944	40,164	31,063	3,843	2,695	953	284	1,321	136,408	104,471	14,518	9,162	3,778	856	3,623
Engineering	29,472	12,415	924	1,131	3,502	70	11,430	22,872	10,117	625	851	2,464	51	8,764	6,600	2,298	299	280	1,038	19	2,666
Engineering technologies[1]	2,690	1,395	229	135	270	16	645	1,993	1,059	148	90	197	12	487	697	336	81	45	73	4	158
English language and literature/letters	8,742	7,119	435	395	312	66	415	2,867	2,406	90	135	85	23	128	5,875	4,713	345	260	227	43	287
Family and consumer sciences	2,080	1,489	233	101	88	5	164	292	207	28	12	12	1	32	1,788	1,282	205	89	76	4	132
Foreign languages, literatures, and linguistics	3,443	1,960	86	530	129	12	726	1,058	647	30	138	34	5	204	2,385	1,313	56	392	95	7	522
Health professions and related clinical sciences	54,531	38,847	5,632	2,875	4,005	358	2,814	10,656	7,067	886	619	1,052	69	943	43,895	31,780	4,746	2,256	2,953	289	1,871
Legal professions and studies	4,486	1,397	257	192	232	15	2,393	2,335	784	95	78	110	7	1,261	2,151	613	162	114	122	8	1,132
Liberal arts and sciences, general studies, and humanities	3,634	2,792	311	205	161	20	145	1,352	1,048	96	72	68	7	61	2,282	1,744	215	133	93	13	84
Library science	6,767	5,651	288	351	311	37	129	1,309	1,090	36	72	73	8	30	5,458	4,561	252	279	238	29	99
Mathematics and statistics	4,884	2,342	169	163	483	15	1,712	2,859	1,430	87	103	250	9	980	2,025	912	82	60	233	6	732
Mechanics and repair technologies	0	0	0	0	0	0	0	0	0	0	0	0	0	0	0	0	0	0	0	0	0
Military technologies	202	178	11	4	7	2	0	178	162	8	2	4	2	0	24	16	3	2	3	0	0
Multi/interdisciplinary studies	4,762	3,306	363	260	280	38	515	1,703	1,130	125	96	93	12	247	3,059	2,176	238	164	187	26	268
Parks, recreation, leisure and fitness studies	4,110	3,233	374	134	113	27	229	2,116	1,639	214	64	51	15	133	1,994	1,594	160	70	62	12	96
Philosophy and religious studies	1,716	1,388	66	66	64	5	127	1,087	876	38	43	43	2	85	629	512	28	23	21	3	42
Physical sciences and science technologies	5,839	3,549	157	185	331	22	1,595	3,556	2,171	74	116	173	13	1,009	2,283	1,378	83	69	158	9	586
Precision production	5	3	0	0	1	0	1	2	1	0	0	1	0	0	3	2	0	0	0	0	1
Psychology	21,037	15,002	2,719	1,523	902	139	752	4,265	3,196	470	262	166	35	136	16,772	11,806	2,249	1,261	736	104	616
Public administration and social service professions	31,131	19,579	5,733	2,677	1,334	328	1,480	7,758	4,829	1,211	613	355	59	691	23,373	14,750	4,522	2,064	979	269	789
Security and protective services	4,906	3,339	929	349	139	40	110	2,315	1,674	322	160	85	17	57	2,591	1,665	607	189	54	23	53
Social sciences and history	17,665	11,240	1,287	952	876	110	3,200	8,577	5,651	486	428	336	47	1,629	9,088	5,589	801	524	540	63	1,571
Social sciences	14,521	8,597	1,150	801	797	55	3,091	6,879	4,192	421	354	302	35	1,575	7,642	4,405	729	447	495	50	1,516
History	3,144	2,643	137	151	79	25	109	1,698	1,459	65	74	34	12	54	1,446	1,184	72	77	45	13	55
Theology and religious vocations	6,446	4,794	600	213	275	20	544	3,909	2,945	290	126	148	14	386	2,537	1,849	310	87	127	6	158
Transportation and materials moving	985	767	78	55	32	9	44	828	652	64	45	26	6	35	157	115	14	10	6	3	9
Visual and performing arts	13,767	9,687	627	590	752	63	2,048	5,910	4,325	250	309	275	31	720	7,857	5,362	377	281	477	32	1,328

[1]Excludes "Construction trades" and "Mechanics and repair technologies," which are listed separately.

NOTE: Race categories exclude persons of Hispanic ethnicity. Reported racial/ethnic distributions of students by level of degree, field of degree, and sex were used to estimate race/ethnicity for students whose race/ethnicity was not reported. To facilitate trend comparisons, certain aggregations have been made of the degree fields as reported in the IPEDS Fall survey. "Agriculture and natural resources" includes Agriculture, agriculture operations, and related sciences and Natu-ral resources and conservation; and "Business" includes Business management, marketing, and related support services and Personal and culinary services.

SOURCE: U.S. Department of Education, National Center for Education Statistics, 2006–07 Integrated Postsecondary Education Data System (IPEDS), Fall 2007. (This table was prepared July 2008.)

Table 289. Master's degrees conferred by degree-granting institutions, by sex, race/ethnicity, and field of study: 2005–06

Field of study	Total							Males							Females						
	Total	White	Black	Hispanic	Asian/ Pacific Islander	American Indian/ Alaska Native	Non-resident alien	Total	White	Black	Hispanic	Asian/ Pacific Islander	American Indian/ Alaska Native	Non-resident alien	Total	White	Black	Hispanic	Asian/ Pacific Islander	American Indian/ Alaska Native	Non-resident alien
1	2	3	4	5	6	7	8	9	10	11	12	13	14	15	16	17	18	19	20	21	22
All fields, total	594,065	393,357	58,976	32,438	34,029	3,504	71,761	237,896	150,954	16,959	11,637	15,803	1,244	41,299	356,169	242,403	42,017	20,801	18,226	2,260	30,462
Agriculture and natural resources	4,640	3,480	128	153	97	42	740	2,280	1,694	51	63	38	21	413	2,360	1,786	77	90	59	21	327
Architecture and related services	5,743	3,791	237	315	372	36	992	3,165	2,179	122	169	150	24	521	2,578	1,612	115	146	222	12	471
Area, ethnic, cultural, and gender studies	2,080	1,223	184	204	159	35	275	771	491	56	66	48	10	100	1,309	732	128	138	111	25	175
Biological and biomedical sciences	8,681	5,602	468	344	920	49	1,298	3,654	2,433	147	162	389	18	505	5,027	3,169	321	182	531	31	793
Business	146,406	86,404	17,933	7,191	11,923	731	22,224	83,550	52,133	6,578	3,920	6,872	360	13,687	62,856	34,271	11,355	3,271	5,051	371	8,537
Communications, journalism, and related programs	7,244	4,730	702	381	380	25	1,026	2,282	1,546	158	117	103	8	350	4,962	3,184	544	264	277	17	676
Communications technologies	501	227	62	22	47	1	142	329	165	43	13	28	1	79	172	62	19	9	19	0	63
Computer and information sciences	17,055	6,680	996	494	2,168	68	6,649	12,470	5,261	584	360	1,423	49	4,793	4,585	1,419	412	134	745	19	1,856
Construction trades	0	0	0	0	0	0	0	0	0	0	0	0	0	0	0	0	0	0	0	0	0
Education	174,620	134,221	18,237	11,233	4,446	1,144	5,339	40,700	31,556	3,852	2,578	962	303	1,449	133,920	102,665	14,385	8,655	3,484	841	3,890
Engineering	30,989	12,570	880	980	3,340	89	13,130	23,855	10,048	615	747	2,344	67	10,034	7,134	2,522	265	233	996	22	3,096
Engineering technologies[1]	2,541	1,363	235	106	249	15	573	1,811	989	132	72	179	11	428	730	374	103	34	70	4	145
English language and literature/letters	8,845	7,247	465	377	293	61	402	2,860	2,416	126	114	79	23	102	5,985	4,831	339	263	214	38	300
Family and consumer sciences	1,983	1,417	225	97	62	17	165	259	191	26	9	5	3	25	1,724	1,226	199	88	57	14	140
Foreign languages, literatures, and linguistics	3,539	2,076	77	489	160	10	727	1,049	649	19	111	56	2	212	2,490	1,427	58	378	104	8	515
Health professions and related clinical sciences	51,380	36,452	5,054	2,780	3,717	349	3,028	10,630	6,963	820	642	1,048	81	1,076	40,750	29,489	4,234	2,138	2,669	268	1,952
Legal professions and studies	4,453	1,549	259	171	223	17	2,234	2,374	844	110	83	111	7	1,219	2,079	705	149	88	112	10	1,015
Liberal arts and sciences, general studies, and humanities	3,702	2,946	298	178	114	20	146	1,403	1,100	112	58	52	9	72	2,299	1,846	186	120	62	11	74
Library science	6,448	5,485	306	240	226	42	149	1,211	1,034	42	51	44	6	34	5,237	4,451	264	189	182	36	115
Mathematics and statistics	4,730	2,268	163	146	412	12	1,729	2,712	1,289	80	93	220	8	1,022	2,018	979	83	53	192	4	707
Mechanics and repair technologies	0	0	0	0	0	0	0	0	0	0	0	0	0	0	0	0	0	0	0	0	0
Military technologies	9	6	0	0	0	0	0	6	5	0	0	0	0	0	3	1	0	0	0	0	0
Multi/interdisciplinary studies	4,491	3,134	325	275	209	37	511	1,560	1,045	91	89	69	10	256	2,931	2,089	234	186	140	27	255
Parks, recreation, leisure and fitness studies	3,992	3,197	327	140	108	9	211	2,069	1,655	164	70	58	4	118	1,923	1,542	163	70	50	5	93
Philosophy and religious studies	1,739	1,358	89	68	64	11	149	1,046	804	47	43	44	10	98	693	554	42	25	20	1	51
Physical sciences and science technologies	5,922	3,583	195	193	266	19	1,666	3,568	2,174	98	113	139	12	1,032	2,354	1,409	97	80	127	7	634
Precision production	9	6	0	0	0	0	2	6	5	0	0	0	0	1	3	1	0	0	0	0	1
Psychology	19,770	14,340	2,403	1,354	803	141	729	4,079	3,065	397	278	160	19	160	15,691	11,275	2,006	1,076	643	122	569
Public administration and social service professions	30,510	19,529	5,474	2,425	1,222	279	1,581	7,572	4,703	1,169	555	338	65	742	22,938	14,826	4,305	1,870	884	214	839
Security and protective services	4,277	2,965	754	288	126	22	122	2,096	1,528	272	147	68	9	72	2,181	1,437	482	141	58	13	50
Social sciences and history	17,369	10,932	1,333	945	883	110	3,166	8,415	5,470	497	437	371	44	1,596	8,954	5,462	836	508	512	66	1,570
Social sciences	14,377	8,439	1,198	806	820	83	3,031	6,792	4,094	433	357	340	31	1,537	7,585	4,345	765	449	480	52	1,494
History	2,992	2,493	135	139	63	27	135	1,623	1,376	64	80	31	13	59	1,369	1,117	71	59	32	14	76
Theology and religious vocations	6,092	4,490	501	194	305	25	577	3,658	2,724	225	127	158	16	408	2,434	1,766	276	67	147	9	169
Transportation and materials moving	784	601	68	46	27	13	29	661	511	58	37	26	9	20	123	90	10	9	1	4	9
Visual and performing arts	13,530	9,491	598	609	707	75	2,050	5,801	4,289	268	313	221	35	675	7,729	5,202	330	296	486	40	1,375

[1] Excludes "Construction trades" and "Mechanics and repair technologies," which are listed separately.

NOTE: Race categories exclude persons of Hispanic ethnicity. Reported racial/ethnic distributions of students by level of degree, field of degree, and sex were used to estimate race/ethnicity for students whose race/ethnicity was not reported. To facilitate trend comparisons, certain aggregations have been made of the degree fields as reported in the IPEDS Fall survey: "Agriculture and natural resources" includes Agriculture, agriculture operations, and related sciences and Natural resources and conservation; and "Business" includes Business management, marketing, and related support services and Personal and culinary services.

SOURCE: U.S. Department of Education, National Center for Education Statistics, 2005–06 Integrated Postsecondary Education Data System (IPEDS), Fall 2006. (This table was prepared June 2007.)

Table 290. Doctor's degrees conferred by degree-granting institutions, by race/ethnicity and sex of student: Selected years, 1976–77 through 2006–07

Year and sex	Number of degrees conferred[1]							Percentage distribution of degrees conferred[1]						
	Total	White	Black	Hispanic	Asian/ Pacific Islander	American Indian/ Alaska Native	Non-resident alien	Total	White	Black	Hispanic	Asian/ Pacific Islander	American Indian/ Alaska Native	Non-resident alien
1	2	3	4	5	6	7	8	9	10	11	12	13	14	15
Total														
1976–77[2]	33,126	26,851	1,253	522	658	95	3,747	100.0	81.1	3.8	1.6	2.0	0.3	11.3
1980–81[3]	32,839	25,908	1,265	456	877	130	4,203	100.0	78.9	3.9	1.4	2.7	0.4	12.8
1989–90	38,371	26,221	1,149	780	1,225	98	8,898	100.0	68.3	3.0	2.0	3.2	0.3	23.2
1990–91	39,294	25,855	1,248	757	1,504	106	9,824	100.0	65.8	3.2	1.9	3.8	0.3	25.0
1992–93	42,132	26,816	1,350	824	1,578	107	11,457	100.0	63.6	3.2	2.0	3.7	0.3	27.2
1993–94	43,185	27,212	1,385	900	2,024	134	11,530	100.0	63.0	3.2	2.1	4.7	0.3	26.7
1994–95	44,446	27,846	1,667	984	2,689	130	11,130	100.0	62.7	3.8	2.2	6.1	0.3	25.0
1995–96	44,652	27,773	1,632	997	2,641	159	11,450	100.0	62.2	3.7	2.2	5.9	0.4	25.6
1996–97	45,876	28,596	1,865	1,120	2,667	175	11,453	100.0	62.3	4.1	2.4	5.8	0.4	25.0
1997–98	46,010	28,803	2,067	1,275	2,339	186	11,340	100.0	62.6	4.5	2.8	5.1	0.4	24.6
1998–99	44,077	27,838	2,136	1,302	2,299	194	10,308	100.0	63.2	4.8	3.0	5.2	0.4	23.4
1999–2000	44,808	27,843	2,246	1,305	2,420	160	10,834	100.0	62.1	5.0	2.9	5.4	0.4	24.2
2000–01	44,904	27,454	2,207	1,516	2,587	177	10,963	100.0	61.1	4.9	3.4	5.8	0.4	24.4
2001–02	44,160	26,903	2,395	1,434	2,319	180	10,929	100.0	60.9	5.4	3.2	5.3	0.4	24.7
2002–03	46,042	27,709	2,522	1,562	2,424	196	11,629	100.0	60.2	5.5	3.4	5.3	0.4	25.3
2003–04	48,378	28,214	2,900	1,662	2,632	217	12,753	100.0	58.3	6.0	3.4	5.4	0.4	26.4
2004–05	52,631	30,261	3,056	1,824	2,911	237	14,342	100.0	57.5	5.8	3.5	5.5	0.5	27.3
2005–06	56,067	31,601	3,122	1,882	3,257	230	15,975	100.0	56.4	5.6	3.4	5.8	0.4	28.5
2006–07	60,616	34,071	3,727	2,034	3,541	249	16,994	100.0	56.2	6.1	3.4	5.8	0.4	28.0
Males														
1976–77[2]	25,036	20,032	766	383	540	67	3,248	100.0	80.0	3.1	1.5	2.2	0.3	13.0
1980–81[3]	22,595	17,310	694	277	655	95	3,564	100.0	76.6	3.1	1.2	2.9	0.4	15.8
1989–90	24,401	15,314	531	419	865	49	7,223	100.0	62.8	2.2	1.7	3.5	0.2	29.6
1990–91	24,756	14,853	597	399	1,017	59	7,831	100.0	60.0	2.4	1.6	4.1	0.2	31.6
1992–93	26,073	14,991	617	437	1,040	52	8,936	100.0	57.5	2.4	1.7	4.0	0.2	34.3
1993–94	26,552	15,150	627	463	1,373	66	8,864	100.0	57.1	2.4	1.7	5.2	0.2	33.4
1994–95	26,916	15,375	730	488	1,756	58	8,509	100.0	57.1	2.7	1.8	6.5	0.2	31.6
1995–96	26,841	15,112	727	514	1,692	80	8,716	100.0	56.3	2.7	1.9	6.3	0.3	32.5
1996–97	27,146	15,499	795	585	1,645	87	8,535	100.0	57.1	2.9	2.2	6.1	0.3	31.4
1997–98	26,664	15,399	824	652	1,392	83	8,314	100.0	57.8	3.1	2.4	5.2	0.3	31.2
1998–99	25,146	14,726	873	625	1,337	92	7,493	100.0	58.6	3.5	2.5	5.3	0.4	29.8
1999–2000	25,028	14,472	876	611	1,356	57	7,656	100.0	57.8	3.5	2.4	5.4	0.2	30.6
2000–01	24,728	13,937	855	687	1,453	76	7,720	100.0	56.4	3.5	2.8	5.9	0.3	31.2
2001–02	23,708	13,330	922	650	1,242	67	7,497	100.0	56.2	3.9	2.7	5.2	0.3	31.6
2002–03	24,351	13,478	915	741	1,243	76	7,898	100.0	55.3	3.8	3.0	5.1	0.3	32.4
2003–04	25,323	13,567	1,015	766	1,293	90	8,592	100.0	53.6	4.0	3.0	5.1	0.4	33.9
2004–05	26,973	14,023	1,049	764	1,403	87	9,647	100.0	52.0	3.9	2.8	5.2	0.3	35.8
2005–06	28,634	14,659	1,081	826	1,555	105	10,408	100.0	51.2	3.8	2.9	5.4	0.4	36.3
2006–07	30,251	15,268	1,282	892	1,703	96	11,010	100.0	50.5	4.2	2.9	5.6	0.3	36.4
Females														
1976–77	8,090	6,819	487	139	118	28	499	100.0	84.3	6.0	1.7	1.5	0.3	6.2
1980–81[3]	10,244	8,598	571	179	222	35	639	100.0	83.9	5.6	1.7	2.2	0.3	6.2
1989–90	13,970	10,907	618	361	360	49	1,675	100.0	78.1	4.4	2.6	2.6	0.4	12.0
1990–91	14,538	11,002	651	358	487	47	1,993	100.0	75.7	4.5	2.5	3.3	0.3	13.7
1992–93	16,059	11,825	733	387	538	55	2,521	100.0	73.6	4.6	2.4	3.4	0.3	15.7
1993–94	16,633	12,053	758	437	651	68	2,666	100.0	72.5	4.6	2.6	3.9	0.4	16.0
1994–95	17,530	12,471	937	496	933	72	2,621	100.0	71.1	5.3	2.8	5.3	0.4	15.0
1995–96	17,811	12,661	905	483	949	79	2,734	100.0	71.1	5.1	2.7	5.3	0.4	15.4
1996–97	18,730	13,097	1,070	535	1,022	88	2,918	100.0	69.9	5.7	2.9	5.5	0.5	15.6
1997–98	19,346	13,404	1,243	623	947	103	3,026	100.0	69.3	6.4	3.2	4.9	0.5	15.6
1998–99	18,931	13,112	1,263	677	962	102	2,815	100.0	69.3	6.7	3.6	5.1	0.5	14.9
1999–2000	19,780	13,371	1,370	694	1,064	103	3,178	100.0	67.6	6.9	3.5	5.4	0.5	16.1
2000–01	20,176	13,517	1,352	829	1,134	101	3,243	100.0	67.0	6.7	4.1	5.6	0.5	16.1
2001–02	20,452	13,573	1,473	784	1,077	113	3,432	100.0	66.4	7.2	3.8	5.3	0.6	16.8
2002–03	21,691	14,231	1,607	821	1,181	120	3,731	100.0	65.6	7.4	3.8	5.4	0.6	17.2
2003–04	23,055	14,647	1,885	896	1,339	127	4,161	100.0	63.5	8.2	3.9	5.8	0.6	18.0
2004–05	25,658	16,238	2,007	1,060	1,508	150	4,695	100.0	63.3	7.8	4.1	5.9	0.6	18.3
2005–06	27,433	16,942	2,041	1,056	1,702	125	5,567	100.0	61.8	7.4	3.8	6.2	0.5	20.3
2006–07	30,365	18,803	2,445	1,142	1,838	153	5,984	100.0	61.9	8.1	3.8	6.1	0.5	19.7

[1]Includes Ph.D., Ed.D, and comparable degrees at the doctoral level. Excludes first-professional degrees, such as M.D., D.D.S., and law degrees.
[2]Excludes 106 men whose racial/ethnic group was not available.
[3]Excludes 116 men and 3 women whose racial/ethnic group was not available.
NOTE: Race categories exclude persons of Hispanic ethnicity. For 1989–90 and later years, reported racial/ethnic distributions of students by level of degree, field of degree, and sex were used to estimate race/ethnicity for students whose race/ethnicity was not reported. (See Guide to Sources for details.) Detail may not sum to totals because of rounding.
SOURCE: U.S. Department of Education, National Center for Education Statistics, Higher Education General Information Survey (HEGIS), "Degrees and Other Formal Awards Conferred" surveys, 1976–77 and 1980–81; and 1989–90 through 2006–07 Integrated Postsecondary Education Data System, "Completions Survey" (IPEDS-C:90–99), and Fall 2000 through Fall 2007. (This table was prepared July 2008.)

Table 291. Doctor's degrees conferred by degree-granting institutions, by sex, race/ethnicity, and field of study: 2006–07

Field of study	Total — Total	Total — White	Total — Black	Total — Hispanic	Total — Asian/Pacific Islander	Total — American Indian/Alaska Native	Total — Non-resident alien	Males — Total	Males — White	Males — Black	Males — Hispanic	Males — Asian/Pacific Islander	Males — American Indian/Alaska Native	Males — Non-resident alien	Females — Total	Females — White	Females — Black	Females — Hispanic	Females — Asian/Pacific Islander	Females — American Indian/Alaska Native	Females — Non-resident alien
1	2	3	4	5	6	7	8	9	10	11	12	13	14	15	16	17	18	19	20	21	22
All fields, total	**60,616**	**34,071**	**3,727**	**2,034**	**3,541**	**249**	**16,994**	**30,251**	**15,268**	**1,282**	**892**	**1,703**	**96**	**11,010**	**30,365**	**18,803**	**2,445**	**1,142**	**1,838**	**153**	**5,984**
Agriculture and natural resources	1,272	634	26	18	30	3	561	768	384	7	12	13	1	351	504	250	19	6	17	2	210
Architecture and related services	178	68	4	9	9	0	88	104	37	3	5	4	0	55	74	31	1	4	5	0	33
Area, ethnic, cultural, and gender studies	233	123	45	16	18	6	25	95	52	20	5	8	3	7	138	71	25	11	10	3	18
Biological and biomedical sciences	6,354	3,463	182	203	566	23	1,917	3,221	1,790	75	99	257	8	992	3,133	1,673	107	104	309	15	925
Business	2,029	928	173	66	148	6	708	1,188	552	78	45	87	5	421	841	376	95	21	61	1	287
Communications, journalism, and related programs	479	268	44	5	19	1	142	188	102	7	3	6	0	70	291	166	37	2	13	1	72
Communications technologies	1	1	0	0	0	0	0	0	0	0	0	0	0	0	1	1	0	0	0	0	0
Computer and information sciences	1,595	496	34	19	127	3	916	1,267	401	20	15	96	2	733	328	95	14	4	31	1	183
Construction trades	0	0	0	0	0	0	0	0	0	0	0	0	0	0	0	0	0	0	0	0	0
Education	8,261	5,394	1,464	383	302	60	658	2,681	1,840	383	125	84	16	233	5,580	3,554	1,081	258	218	44	425
Engineering	8,062	2,143	127	147	552	9	5,084	6,377	1,693	85	97	422	7	4,073	1,685	450	42	50	130	2	1,011
Engineering technologies[1]	61	23	3	3	3	0	29	45	18	2	2	1	0	22	16	5	1	1	2	0	7
English language and literature/letters	1,178	890	68	41	46	9	124	478	386	12	19	16	2	43	700	504	56	22	30	7	81
Family and consumer sciences	337	189	40	10	10	2	86	73	43	5	0	4	1	20	264	146	35	10	6	1	66
Foreign languages, literatures, and linguistics	1,059	533	17	86	62	1	360	437	243	6	37	22	0	129	622	290	11	49	40	1	231
Health professions and related clinical sciences	8,355	6,530	363	255	483	26	698	2,242	1,588	105	87	141	6	315	6,113	4,942	258	168	342	20	383
Legal professions and studies	143	19	4	2	3	0	115	78	7	3	1	1	0	66	65	12	1	1	2	0	49
Liberal arts and sciences, general studies, and humanities	77	59	5	4	1	2	6	38	24	3	4	1	1	5	39	35	2	0	0	1	1
Library science	52	25	6	2	2	0	17	18	8	1	1	1	0	7	34	17	5	1	1	0	10
Mathematics and statistics	1,351	508	24	24	86	1	708	949	360	18	19	54	0	498	402	148	6	5	32	1	210
Mechanics and repair technologies	0	0	0	0	0	0	0	0	0	0	0	0	0	0	0	0	0	0	0	0	0
Military technologies	0	0	0	0	0	0	0	0	0	0	0	0	0	0	0	0	0	0	0	0	0
Multi/interdisciplinary studies	1,093	687	60	48	75	6	217	485	270	31	24	43	3	114	608	417	29	24	32	3	103
Parks, recreation, leisure and fitness studies	218	134	12	7	13	0	52	109	70	3	3	8	0	25	109	64	9	4	5	0	27
Philosophy and religious studies	637	444	28	24	31	2	108	453	317	20	19	19	1	77	184	127	8	5	12	1	31
Physical sciences and science technologies	4,846	2,233	100	107	249	10	2,147	3,317	1,530	57	64	146	9	1,511	1,529	703	43	43	103	1	636
Precision production	0	0	0	0	0	0	0	0	0	0	0	0	0	0	0	0	0	0	0	0	0
Psychology	5,153	3,853	347	297	310	46	300	1,382	1,069	78	70	65	15	85	3,771	2,784	269	227	245	31	215
Public administration and social service professions	726	409	112	34	39	4	128	253	130	34	11	11	2	65	473	279	78	23	28	2	63
Security and protective services	85	58	7	6	2	1	11	43	29	4	3	1	0	6	42	29	3	3	1	1	5
Social sciences and history	3,844	2,139	187	147	167	23	1,181	2,110	1,132	70	80	82	12	734	1,734	1,007	117	67	85	11	447
Social sciences	3,037	1,547	138	104	140	17	1,091	1,627	775	43	54	68	9	678	1,410	772	95	50	72	8	413
History	807	592	49	43	27	6	90	483	357	27	26	14	3	56	324	235	22	17	13	3	34
Theology and religious vocations	1,573	946	213	30	108	3	273	1,227	738	138	20	95	2	234	346	208	75	10	13	1	39
Transportation and materials moving	0	0	0	0	0	0	0	0	0	0	0	0	0	0	0	0	0	0	0	0	0
Visual and performing arts	1,364	874	32	41	80	2	335	625	455	14	22	15	0	119	739	419	18	19	65	2	216

[1]Excludes "Construction trades" and "Mechanics and repair technologies," which are listed separately.

NOTE: Race categories exclude persons of Hispanic ethnicity. Reported racial/ethnic distributions of students by level of degree, field of degree, and sex were used to estimate race/ethnicity for students whose race/ethnicity was not reported. To facilitate trend comparisons, certain aggregations have been made of the degree fields as reported in the IPEDS Fall survey: "Agriculture and natural resources" includes Agriculture, agriculture operations, and related sciences and Natural resources and conservation; and "Business" includes Business management, marketing, and related support services and Personal and culinary services. Includes Ph.D., Ed.D., and comparable degrees at the doctoral level. Excludes first-professional, such as M.D., D.D.S., and law degrees.

SOURCE: U.S. Department of Education, National Center for Education Statistics, 2006–07 Integrated Postsecondary Education Data System (IPEDS), Fall 2007. (This table was prepared July 2008.)

Table 292. Doctor's degrees conferred by degree-granting institutions, by sex, race/ethnicity, and field of study: 2005–06

Field of study	Total							Males							Females						
	Total	White	Black	Hispanic	Asian/ Pacific Islander	American Indian/ Alaska Native	Non-resident alien	Total	White	Black	Hispanic	Asian/ Pacific Islander	American Indian/ Alaska Native	Non-resident alien	Total	White	Black	Hispanic	Asian/ Pacific Islander	American Indian/ Alaska Native	Non-resident alien
1	2	3	4	5	6	7	8	9	10	11	12	13	14	15	16	17	18	19	20	21	22
All fields, total	**56,067**	**31,601**	**3,122**	**1,882**	**3,257**	**230**	**15,975**	**28,634**	**14,659**	**1,081**	**826**	**1,555**	**105**	**10,408**	**27,433**	**16,942**	**2,041**	**1,056**	**1,702**	**125**	**5,567**
Agriculture and natural resources	1,194	592	33	43	32	1	493	710	364	17	24	13	0	292	484	228	16	19	19	1	201
Architecture and related services	201	59	3	9	15	0	115	108	30	2	2	12	0	62	93	29	1	7	3	0	53
Area, ethnic, cultural, and gender studies	226	110	44	15	17	6	34	98	51	14	9	6	1	17	128	59	30	6	11	5	17
Biological and biomedical sciences	5,775	3,243	175	178	491	19	1,669	2,933	1,684	72	87	242	12	836	2,842	1,559	103	91	249	7	833
Business	1,711	787	137	39	102	12	634	1,049	489	62	25	59	7	407	662	298	75	14	43	5	227
Communications, journalism, and related programs	461	275	24	16	18	1	127	206	118	4	7	11	0	66	255	157	20	9	7	1	61
Communications technologies	3	1	0	0	0	0	2	1	0	0	0	0	0	1	2	1	0	0	0	0	1
Computer and information sciences	1,416	410	24	6	105	6	865	1,109	323	15	3	77	3	688	307	87	9	3	28	3	177
Construction trades	0	0	0	0	0	0	0	0	0	0	0	0	0	0	0	0	0	0	0	0	0
Education	7,584	5,107	1,093	362	240	53	729	2,664	1,858	319	131	75	19	262	4,920	3,249	774	231	165	34	467
Engineering	7,396	1,960	116	104	510	7	4,699	5,913	1,576	71	72	369	7	3,818	1,483	384	45	32	141	0	881
Engineering technologies[1]	75	30	5	2	3	1	34	50	18	2	2	3	0	25	25	12	3	0	0	1	9
English language and literature/letters	1,254	965	67	42	48	6	126	510	418	16	11	14	0	51	744	547	51	31	34	6	75
Family and consumer sciences	340	193	33	8	12	3	91	71	42	3	1	3	0	22	269	151	30	7	9	3	69
Foreign languages, literatures, and linguistics	1,074	536	18	102	57	1	360	436	227	7	46	13	1	142	638	309	11	56	44	0	218
Health professions and related clinical sciences	7,128	5,340	356	207	517	18	690	1,959	1,337	78	62	166	8	308	5,169	4,003	278	145	351	10	382
Legal professions and studies	129	46	5	0	7	0	71	68	19	0	0	7	0	42	61	27	5	0	0	0	29
Liberal arts and sciences, general studies, and humanities	84	72	2	3	1	0	6	37	32	1	2	0	0	2	47	40	1	1	1	0	4
Library science	44	23	2	1	2	0	16	20	8	1	1	0	0	10	24	15	1	0	2	0	6
Mathematics and statistics	1,293	465	21	29	67	0	711	911	353	16	17	46	0	479	382	112	5	12	21	0	232
Mechanics and repair technologies	0	0	0	0	0	0	0	0	0	0	0	0	0	0	0	0	0	0	0	0	0
Military technologies	0	0	0	0	0	0	0	0	0	0	0	0	0	0	0	0	0	0	0	0	0
Multi/interdisciplinary studies	987	615	43	52	55	5	217	461	268	16	27	21	3	126	526	347	27	25	34	2	91
Parks, recreation, leisure and fitness studies	194	130	10	6	7	0	41	103	69	4	3	3	0	24	91	61	6	3	4	0	17
Philosophy and religious studies	578	410	41	21	24	3	79	420	297	25	17	19	3	59	158	113	16	4	5	0	20
Physical sciences and science technologies	4,489	2,092	63	100	249	9	1,976	3,143	1,483	38	64	140	9	1,409	1,346	609	25	36	109	0	567
Precision production	0	0	0	0	0	0	0	0	0	0	0	0	0	0	0	0	0	0	0	0	0
Psychology	4,921	3,687	315	290	278	39	312	1,347	1,030	56	75	71	11	104	3,574	2,657	259	215	207	28	208
Public administration and social service professions	704	412	106	28	27	6	125	285	156	37	11	10	3	68	419	256	69	17	17	3	57
Security and protective services	80	57	7	7	5	0	4	42	31	2	6	2	0	1	38	26	5	1	3	0	3
Social sciences and history	3,914	2,244	182	153	181	22	1,132	2,218	1,251	82	82	70	11	722	1,696	993	100	71	111	11	410
Social sciences	3,062	1,591	146	124	139	17	1,045	1,712	847	61	69	57	9	669	1,350	744	85	55	82	8	376
History	852	653	36	29	42	5	87	506	404	21	13	13	2	50	346	249	15	16	29	3	34
Theology and religious vocations	1,429	840	171	27	94	6	291	1,123	675	104	21	75	4	244	306	165	67	6	19	2	47
Transportation and materials moving	0	0	0	0	0	0	0	0	0	0	0	0	0	0	0	0	0	0	0	0	0
Visual and performing arts	1,383	900	26	32	93	6	326	639	452	17	18	28	3	121	744	448	9	14	65	3	205

[1] Excludes "Construction trades" and "Mechanics and repair technologies," which are listed separately.

NOTE: Race categories exclude persons of Hispanic ethnicity. Reported racial/ethnic distributions of students by level of degree, field of degree, and sex were used to estimate race/ethnicity for students whose race/ethnicity was not reported. To facilitate trend comparisons, certain aggregations have been made of the degree fields as reported in the IPEDS Fall survey: "Agriculture and natural resources" includes Agriculture, agriculture operations, and related sciences and Natural resources and conservation; and "Business" includes Business management, marketing, and related support services and Personal and culinary services. Includes Ph.D, Ed.D., and comparable degrees at the doctoral level. Excludes first-professional, such as M.D., D.D.S., and law degrees.

SOURCE: U.S. Department of Education, National Center for Education Statistics, 2005–06 Integrated Postsecondary Education Data System (IPEDS), Fall 2006. (This table was prepared June 2007.)

Table 293. First-professional degrees conferred by degree-granting institutions, by race/ethnicity and sex of student: Selected years, 1976–77 through 2006–07

Year and sex	Number of degrees conferred							Percentage distribution of degrees conferred						
	Total	White	Black	Hispanic	Asian/ Pacific Islander	American Indian/ Alaska Native	Non-resident alien	Total	White	Black	Hispanic	Asian/ Pacific Islander	American Indian/ Alaska Native	Non-resident alien
1	2	3	4	5	6	7	8	9	10	11	12	13	14	15
Total														
1976–77[1]	63,953	58,422	2,537	1,076	1,021	196	701	100.0	91.4	4.0	1.7	1.6	0.3	1.1
1980–81[2]	71,340	64,551	2,931	1,541	1,456	192	669	100.0	90.5	4.1	2.2	2.0	0.3	0.9
1989–90	70,988	60,487	3,409	2,425	3,362	257	1,048	100.0	85.2	4.8	3.4	4.7	0.4	1.5
1990–91	71,948	60,631	3,588	2,547	3,835	261	1,086	100.0	84.3	5.0	3.5	5.3	0.4	1.5
1992–93	75,387	61,165	4,132	2,996	5,176	370	1,548	100.0	81.1	5.5	4.0	6.9	0.5	2.1
1993–94	75,418	60,143	4,444	3,131	5,892	371	1,437	100.0	79.7	5.9	4.2	7.8	0.5	1.9
1994–95	75,800	59,402	4,747	3,231	6,396	413	1,611	100.0	78.4	6.3	4.3	8.4	0.5	2.1
1995–96	76,734	59,525	5,022	3,475	6,627	463	1,622	100.0	77.6	6.5	4.5	8.6	0.6	2.1
1996–97	78,730	60,280	5,301	3,615	7,374	514	1,646	100.0	76.6	6.7	4.6	9.4	0.7	2.1
1997–98	78,598	59,443	5,499	3,552	7,757	561	1,786	100.0	75.6	7.0	4.5	9.9	0.7	2.3
1998–99	78,439	58,720	5,333	3,864	8,152	612	1,758	100.0	74.9	6.8	4.9	10.4	0.8	2.2
1999–2000	80,057	59,637	5,555	3,865	8,584	564	1,852	100.0	74.5	6.9	4.8	10.7	0.7	2.3
2000–01	79,707	58,598	5,416	3,806	9,261	543	2,083	100.0	73.5	6.8	4.8	11.6	0.7	2.6
2001–02	80,698	58,874	5,811	3,965	9,584	581	1,883	100.0	73.0	7.2	4.9	11.9	0.7	2.3
2002–03	80,897	58,740	5,719	4,093	9,798	586	1,961	100.0	72.6	7.1	5.1	12.1	0.7	2.4
2003–04	83,041	60,379	5,930	4,273	9,964	565	1,930	100.0	72.7	7.1	5.1	12.0	0.7	2.3
2004–05	87,289	63,429	6,313	4,445	10,501	564	2,037	100.0	72.7	7.2	5.1	12.0	0.6	2.3
2005–06	87,655	63,590	6,223	4,446	10,645	710	2,041	100.0	72.5	7.1	5.1	12.1	0.8	2.3
2006–07	90,064	64,546	6,474	4,700	11,686	681	1,977	100.0	71.7	7.2	5.2	13.0	0.8	2.2
Males														
1976–77[1]	51,980	47,777	1,761	893	776	159	614	100.0	91.9	3.4	1.7	1.5	0.3	1.2
1980–81[2]	52,194	47,629	1,772	1,131	991	134	537	100.0	91.3	3.4	2.2	1.9	0.3	1.0
1989–90	43,961	38,036	1,671	1,449	1,962	135	708	100.0	86.5	3.8	3.3	4.5	0.3	1.6
1990–91	43,846	37,533	1,679	1,517	2,211	144	762	100.0	85.6	3.8	3.5	5.0	0.3	1.7
1992–93	45,153	37,415	1,801	1,771	2,871	192	1,103	100.0	82.9	4.0	3.9	6.4	0.4	2.4
1993–94	44,707	36,574	1,902	1,780	3,214	222	1,015	100.0	81.8	4.3	4.0	7.2	0.5	2.3
1994–95	44,853	36,147	2,077	1,835	3,490	223	1,081	100.0	80.6	4.6	4.1	7.8	0.5	2.4
1995–96	44,748	35,786	2,112	1,947	3,539	256	1,108	100.0	80.0	4.7	4.4	7.9	0.6	2.5
1996–97	45,564	36,008	2,201	1,985	3,959	290	1,121	100.0	79.0	4.8	4.4	8.7	0.6	2.5
1997–98	44,911	35,172	2,310	1,973	4,017	291	1,148	100.0	78.3	5.1	4.4	8.9	0.6	2.6
1998–99	44,339	34,271	2,197	2,064	4,333	333	1,141	100.0	77.3	5.0	4.7	9.8	0.8	2.6
1999–2000	44,239	34,004	2,313	2,095	4,372	285	1,170	100.0	76.9	5.2	4.7	9.9	0.6	2.6
2000–01	42,862	32,717	2,110	1,977	4,518	278	1,262	100.0	76.3	4.9	4.6	10.5	0.6	2.9
2001–02	42,507	32,224	2,223	2,045	4,613	292	1,110	100.0	75.8	5.2	4.8	10.9	0.7	2.6
2002–03	41,887	31,635	2,174	2,050	4,624	296	1,108	100.0	75.5	5.2	4.9	11.0	0.7	2.6
2003–04	42,169	31,994	2,248	2,080	4,528	275	1,044	100.0	75.9	5.3	4.9	10.7	0.7	2.5
2004–05	43,849	33,268	2,257	2,214	4,709	288	1,113	100.0	75.9	5.1	5.0	10.7	0.7	2.5
2005–06	44,038	33,544	2,290	2,123	4,641	332	1,108	100.0	76.2	5.2	4.8	10.5	0.8	2.5
2006–07	45,057	33,866	2,368	2,266	5,152	335	1,070	100.0	75.2	5.3	5.0	11.4	0.7	2.4
Females														
1976–77[1]	11,973	10,645	776	183	245	37	87	100.0	88.9	6.5	1.5	2.0	0.3	0.7
1980–81[2]	19,146	16,922	1,159	410	465	58	132	100.0	88.4	6.1	2.1	2.4	0.3	0.7
1989–90	27,027	22,451	1,738	976	1,400	122	340	100.0	83.1	6.4	3.6	5.2	0.5	1.3
1990–91	28,102	23,098	1,909	1,030	1,624	117	324	100.0	82.2	6.8	3.7	5.8	0.4	1.2
1992–93	30,234	23,750	2,331	1,225	2,305	178	445	100.0	78.6	7.7	4.1	7.6	0.6	1.5
1993–94	30,711	23,569	2,542	1,351	2,678	149	422	100.0	76.7	8.3	4.4	8.7	0.5	1.4
1994–95	30,947	23,255	2,670	1,396	2,906	190	530	100.0	75.1	8.6	4.5	9.4	0.6	1.7
1995–96	31,986	23,739	2,910	1,528	3,088	207	514	100.0	74.2	9.1	4.8	9.7	0.6	1.6
1996–97	33,166	24,272	3,100	1,630	3,415	224	525	100.0	73.2	9.3	4.9	10.3	0.7	1.6
1997–98	33,687	24,271	3,189	1,579	3,740	270	638	100.0	72.0	9.5	4.7	11.1	0.8	1.9
1998–99	34,100	24,449	3,136	1,800	3,819	279	617	100.0	71.7	9.2	5.3	11.2	0.8	1.8
1999–2000	35,818	25,633	3,242	1,770	4,212	279	682	100.0	71.6	9.1	4.9	11.8	0.8	1.9
2000–01	36,845	25,881	3,306	1,829	4,743	265	821	100.0	70.2	9.0	5.0	12.9	0.7	2.2
2001–02	38,191	26,650	3,588	1,920	4,971	289	773	100.0	69.8	9.4	5.0	13.0	0.8	2.0
2002–03	39,010	27,105	3,545	2,043	5,174	290	853	100.0	69.5	9.1	5.2	13.3	0.7	2.2
2003–04	40,872	28,385	3,682	2,193	5,436	290	886	100.0	69.4	9.0	5.4	13.3	0.7	2.2
2004–05	43,440	30,161	4,056	2,231	5,792	276	924	100.0	69.4	9.3	5.1	13.3	0.6	2.1
2005–06	43,617	30,046	3,933	2,323	6,004	378	933	100.0	68.9	9.0	5.3	13.8	0.9	2.1
2006–07	45,007	30,680	4,106	2,434	6,534	346	907	100.0	68.2	9.1	5.4	14.5	0.8	2.0

[1]Excludes 394 men and 12 women whose racial/ethnic group was not available.
[2]Excludes 598 men and 18 women whose racial/ethnic group was not available.
NOTE: Includes degrees that require at least 6 years of college work for completion (including at least 2 years of preprofessional training). Race categories exclude persons of Hispanic ethnicity. For 1989–90 and later years, reported racial/ethnic distributions of students by level of degree, field of degree, and sex were used to estimate race/ethnicity for students whose race/ ethnicity was not reported. (See Guide to Sources for details.) Detail may not sum to totals because of rounding.
SOURCE: U.S. Department of Education, National Center for Education Statistics, Higher Education General Information Survey (HEGIS), "Degrees and Other Formal Awards Conferred" surveys, 1976–77 and 1980–81; and 1989–90 through 2006–07 Integrated Postsecondary Education Data System, "Completions Survey" (IPEDS-C:90–99), and Fall 2000 through Fall 2007. (This table was prepared July 2008.)

Table 294. First-professional degrees conferred by degree-granting institutions, by sex, race/ethnicity, and field of study: 2006–07

Field of study	Total	White	Black	Hispanic	Asian/ Pacific Islander	American Indian/ Alaska Native	Non-resident alien	Males Total	White	Black	Hispanic	Asian/ Pacific Islander	American Indian/ Alaska Native	Non-resident alien	Females Total	White	Black	Hispanic	Asian/ Pacific Islander	American Indian/ Alaska Native	Non-resident alien
1	2	3	4	5	6	7	8	9	10	11	12	13	14	15	16	17	18	19	20	21	22
All fields, total	90,064	64,546	6,474	4,700	11,686	681	1,977	45,057	33,866	2,368	2,266	5,152	335	1,070	45,007	30,680	4,106	2,434	6,534	346	907
Dentistry (D.D.S. or D.M.D.)	4,596	2,915	210	199	922	28	322	2,548	1,773	83	102	420	18	152	2,048	1,142	127	97	502	10	170
Medicine (M.D.)	15,730	10,340	1,128	736	3,218	123	185	7,987	5,489	384	345	1,614	68	87	7,743	4,851	744	391	1,604	55	98
Optometry (O.D.)	1,311	820	42	52	317	12	68	493	354	7	15	79	4	34	818	466	35	37	238	8	34
Osteopathic medicine (D.O.)	2,992	2,277	113	117	455	20	10	1,475	1,142	41	55	225	9	3	1,517	1,135	72	62	230	11	7
Pharmacy (Pharm.D.)	10,439	6,735	730	442	2,251	78	203	3,394	2,312	224	128	648	24	58	7,045	4,423	506	314	1,603	54	145
Podiatry (Pod.D. or D.P.) or podiatric medicine (D.P.M.)	331	198	58	26	41	3	5	173	119	24	9	17	1	3	158	79	34	17	24	2	2
Veterinary medicine (D.V.M.)	2,443	2,228	55	67	70	12	11	537	489	15	16	15	2	0	1,906	1,739	40	51	55	10	11
Chiropractic medicine (D.C. or D.C.M.)	2,525	2,000	109	110	196	18	92	1,617	1,297	45	74	124	15	62	908	703	64	36	72	3	30
Naturopathic medicine	221	179	8	12	12	2	8	56	46	2	2	3	0	3	165	133	6	10	9	2	5
Law (LL.B. or J.D.)	43,486	32,552	3,189	2,793	3,849	371	732	22,777	17,956	1,119	1,410	1,733	183	376	20,709	14,596	2,070	1,383	2,116	188	356
Theology (M.Div., M.H.L., B.D., or Ord.)	5,990	4,302	832	146	355	14	341	4,000	2,889	424	110	274	11	292	1,990	1,413	408	36	81	3	49

NOTE: Includes degrees that require at least 6 years of college work for completion (including at least 2 years of preprofessional training). Race categories exclude persons of Hispanic ethnicity. Reported racial/ethnic distributions of students by level of degree, field of degree, and sex were used to estimate race/ethnicity for students whose race/ethnicity was not reported.

SOURCE: U.S. Department of Education, National Center for Education Statistics, 2006–07 Integrated Postsecondary Education Data System (IPEDS), Fall 2007. (This table was prepared July 2008.)

Table 295. First-professional degrees conferred by degree-granting institutions, by sex, race/ethnicity, and field of study: 2005–06

Field of study	Total	White	Black	Hispanic	Asian/ Pacific Islander	American Indian/ Alaska Native	Non-resident alien	Males Total	White	Black	Hispanic	Asian/ Pacific Islander	American Indian/ Alaska Native	Non-resident alien	Females Total	White	Black	Hispanic	Asian/ Pacific Islander	American Indian/ Alaska Native	Non-resident alien
1	2	3	4	5	6	7	8	9	10	11	12	13	14	15	16	17	18	19	20	21	22
All fields, total	87,655	63,590	6,223	4,446	10,645	710	2,041	44,038	33,544	2,290	2,123	4,641	332	1,108	43,617	30,046	3,933	2,323	6,004	378	933
Dentistry (D.D.S. or D.M.D.)	4,389	2,810	214	222	799	29	315	2,435	1,748	76	105	346	15	145	1,954	1,062	138	117	453	14	170
Medicine (M.D.)	15,455	10,172	1,159	681	3,145	143	155	7,900	5,445	400	355	1,557	70	73	7,555	4,727	759	326	1,588	73	82
Optometry (O.D.)	1,198	790	34	42	260	9	63	490	385	6	20	56	3	20	708	405	28	22	204	6	43
Osteopathic medicine (D.O.)	2,718	2,113	95	102	373	24	11	1,434	1,184	28	44	158	14	6	1,284	929	67	58	215	10	5
Pharmacy (Pharm.D.)	9,292	5,966	744	368	1,918	91	205	3,032	2,001	245	131	558	21	76	6,260	3,965	499	237	1,360	70	129
Podiatry (Pod.D. or D.P.) or podiatric medicine (D.P.M.)	347	209	41	32	43	2	20	191	136	12	13	17	1	12	156	73	29	19	26	1	8
Veterinary medicine (D.V.M.)	2,370	2,148	51	65	72	18	16	535	490	13	12	11	5	4	1,835	1,658	38	53	61	13	12
Chiropractic medicine (D.C. or D.C.M.)	2,564	1,968	114	115	209	15	143	1,615	1,254	54	65	143	7	92	949	714	60	50	66	8	51
Naturopathic medicine	216	177	5	9	10	2	13	49	39	0	3	2	1	4	167	138	5	6	8	1	9
Law (LL.B. or J.D.)	43,440	33,154	2,939	2,678	3,556	363	750	22,597	18,149	1,033	1,272	1,565	187	391	20,843	15,005	1,906	1,406	1,991	176	359
Theology (M.Div., M.H.L., B.D., or Ord.)	5,666	4,083	827	132	260	14	350	3,760	2,713	423	103	228	8	285	1,906	1,370	404	29	32	6	65

NOTE: Includes degrees that require at least 6 years of college work for completion (including at least 2 years of preprofessional training). Race categories exclude persons of Hispanic ethnicity. Reported racial/ethnic distributions of students by level of degree, field of degree, and sex were used to estimate race/ethnicity for students whose race/ethnicity was not reported.

SOURCE: U.S. Department of Education, National Center for Education Statistics, 2005–06 Integrated Postsecondary Education Data System (IPEDS), Fall 2006. (This table was prepared June 2007.)

Table 296. Degrees in agriculture and natural resources conferred by degree-granting institutions, by level of degree and sex of student: 1970–71 through 2006–07

| | Bachelor's degrees | | | | Master's degrees | | | Doctor's degrees | | |
| | Total | | | | | | | | | |
Year	Number	Annual percent change	Males	Females	Total	Males	Females	Total	Males	Females
1	2	3	4	5	6	7	8	9	10	11
1970–71	12,672	†	12,136	536	2,457	2,313	144	1,086	1,055	31
1971–72	13,516	6.7	12,779	737	2,680	2,490	190	971	945	26
1972–73	14,756	9.2	13,661	1,095	2,807	2,588	219	1,059	1,031	28
1973–74	16,253	10.1	14,684	1,569	2,928	2,640	288	930	897	33
1974–75	17,528	7.8	15,061	2,467	3,067	2,703	364	991	958	33
1975–76	19,402	10.7	15,845	3,557	3,340	2,862	478	928	867	61
1976–77	21,467	10.6	16,690	4,777	3,724	3,177	547	893	831	62
1977–78	22,650	5.5	17,069	5,581	4,023	3,268	755	971	909	62
1978–79	23,134	2.1	16,854	6,280	3,994	3,187	807	950	877	73
1979–80	22,802	-1.4	16,045	6,757	3,976	3,082	894	991	879	112
1980–81	21,886	-4.0	15,154	6,732	4,003	3,061	942	1,067	940	127
1981–82	21,029	-3.9	14,443	6,586	4,163	3,114	1,049	1,079	925	154
1982–83	20,909	-0.6	14,085	6,824	4,254	3,129	1,125	1,149	1,004	145
1983–84	19,317	-7.6	13,206	6,111	4,178	2,989	1,189	1,172	1,001	171
1984–85	18,107	-6.3	12,477	5,630	3,928	2,846	1,082	1,213	1,036	177
1985–86	16,823	-7.1	11,544	5,279	3,801	2,701	1,100	1,158	966	192
1986–87	14,991	-10.9	10,314	4,677	3,522	2,460	1,062	1,049	871	178
1987–88	14,222	-5.1	9,744	4,478	3,479	2,427	1,052	1,142	926	216
1988–89	13,492	-5.1	9,298	4,194	3,245	2,231	1,014	1,183	950	233
1989–90	12,900	-4.4	8,822	4,078	3,382	2,239	1,143	1,295	1,038	257
1990–91	13,124	1.7	8,832	4,292	3,295	2,160	1,135	1,185	953	232
1991–92	15,113	15.2	9,867	5,246	3,730	2,409	1,321	1,205	955	250
1992–93	16,769	11.0	11,079	5,690	3,959	2,474	1,485	1,159	869	290
1993–94	18,056	7.7	11,746	6,310	4,110	2,512	1,598	1,262	969	293
1994–95	19,832	9.8	12,686	7,146	4,234	2,541	1,693	1,256	955	301
1995–96	21,425	8.0	13,531	7,894	4,551	2,642	1,909	1,259	926	333
1996–97	22,597	5.5	13,791	8,806	4,505	2,601	1,904	1,202	875	327
1997–98	23,276	3.0	13,806	9,470	4,464	2,545	1,919	1,290	924	366
1998–99	23,916	2.7	13,864	10,052	4,404	2,377	2,027	1,231	855	376
1999–2000	24,238	1.3	13,843	10,395	4,360	2,356	2,004	1,168	803	365
2000–01	23,370	-3.6	12,840	10,530	4,272	2,251	2,021	1,127	741	386
2001–02	23,331	-0.2	12,630	10,701	4,503	2,340	2,163	1,148	760	388
2002–03	23,348	0.1	12,343	11,005	4,492	2,232	2,260	1,229	790	439
2003–04	22,835	-2.2	11,889	10,946	4,783	2,306	2,477	1,185	758	427
2004–05	23,002	0.7	11,987	11,015	4,746	2,288	2,458	1,173	763	410
2005–06	23,053	0.2	12,063	10,990	4,640	2,280	2,360	1,194	710	484
2006–07	23,133	0.3	12,309	10,824	4,623	2,174	2,449	1,272	768	504
Percent change										
1996–97 to 2001–02	3.2	†	-8.4	21.5	#	-10.0	13.6	-4.5	-13.1	18.7
2001–02 to 2006–07	-0.8	†	-2.5	1.1	2.7	-7.1	13.2	10.8	1.1	29.9

†Not applicable.
#Rounds to zero.
NOTE: Includes degrees in agriculture, agriculture operations, and related sciences and in natural resources and conservation.

SOURCE: U.S. Department of Education, National Center for Education Statistics, Higher Education General Information Survey (HEGIS), "Degrees and Other Formal Awards Conferred" surveys, 1970–71 through 1985–86; and 1986–87 through 2006–07 Integrated Postsecondary Education Data System, "Completions Survey" (IPEDS-C:87–99), and Fall 2000 through Fall 2007. (This table was prepared September 2008.)

Table 297. Degrees in architecture and related services conferred by degree-granting institutions, by level of degree and sex of student: Selected years, 1949–50 through 2006–07

Year	Bachelor's degrees				Master's degrees			Doctor's degrees		
	Total									
	Number	Annual percent change	Males	Females	Total	Males	Females	Total	Males	Females
1	2	3	4	5	6	7	8	9	10	11
1949–50	2,563	†	2,441	122	166	159	7	1	1	0
1959–60	1,801	†	1,744	57	319	305	14	17	17	0
1967–68	3,057	†	2,931	126	1,021	953	68	15	15	0
1969–70	4,105	†	3,888	217	1,427	1,260	167	35	33	2
1970–71	5,570	35.7	4,906	664	1,705	1,469	236	36	33	3
1971–72	6,440	15.6	5,667	773	1,899	1,626	273	50	43	7
1972–73	6,962	8.1	6,042	920	2,307	1,943	364	58	54	4
1973–74	7,822	12.4	6,665	1,157	2,702	2,208	494	69	65	4
1974–75	8,226	5.2	6,791	1,435	2,938	2,343	595	69	58	11
1975–76	9,146	11.2	7,396	1,750	3,215	2,545	670	82	69	13
1976–77	9,222	0.8	7,249	1,973	3,213	2,489	724	73	62	11
1977–78	9,250	0.3	7,054	2,196	3,115	2,304	811	73	57	16
1978–79	9,273	0.2	6,876	2,397	3,113	2,226	887	96	74	22
1979–80	9,132	-1.5	6,596	2,536	3,139	2,245	894	79	66	13
1980–81	9,455	3.5	6,800	2,655	3,153	2,234	919	93	73	20
1981–82	9,728	2.9	6,825	2,903	3,327	2,242	1,085	80	58	22
1982–83	9,823	1.0	6,403	3,420	3,357	2,224	1,133	97	74	23
1983–84	9,186	-6.5	5,895	3,291	3,223	2,197	1,026	84	62	22
1984–85	9,325	1.5	6,019	3,306	3,275	2,148	1,127	89	66	23
1985–86	9,119	-2.2	5,824	3,295	3,260	2,129	1,131	73	56	17
1986–87	8,950	-1.9	5,617	3,333	3,163	2,086	1,077	92	66	26
1987–88	8,603	-3.9	5,271	3,332	3,159	2,042	1,117	98	66	32
1988–89	9,150	6.4	5,545	3,605	3,383	2,192	1,191	86	63	23
1989–90	9,364	2.3	5,703	3,661	3,499	2,228	1,271	103	73	30
1990–91	9,781	4.5	5,788	3,993	3,490	2,244	1,246	135	101	34
1991–92	8,753	-10.5	5,805	2,948	3,640	2,271	1,369	132	93	39
1992–93	9,167	4.7	5,940	3,227	3,808	2,376	1,432	148	105	43
1993–94	8,975	-2.1	5,764	3,211	3,943	2,428	1,515	161	111	50
1994–95	8,756	-2.4	5,741	3,015	3,923	2,310	1,613	141	95	46
1995–96	8,352	-4.6	5,340	3,012	3,993	2,361	1,632	141	96	45
1996–97	7,944	-4.9	5,090	2,854	4,034	2,336	1,698	135	93	42
1997–98	7,652	-3.7	4,966	2,686	4,347	2,537	1,810	131	80	51
1998–99	8,246	7.8	5,157	3,089	4,172	2,394	1,778	123	80	43
1999–2000	8,462	2.6	5,193	3,269	4,268	2,508	1,760	129	85	44
2000–01	8,480	0.2	5,086	3,394	4,302	2,515	1,787	153	83	70
2001–02	8,808	3.9	5,224	3,584	4,566	2,606	1,960	183	117	66
2002–03	9,056	2.8	5,331	3,725	4,925	2,832	2,093	152	83	69
2003–04	8,838	-2.4	5,059	3,779	5,424	3,049	2,375	173	94	79
2004–05	9,237	4.5	5,222	4,015	5,674	3,180	2,494	179	110	69
2005–06	9,515	3.0	5,414	4,101	5,743	3,165	2,578	201	108	93
2006–07	9,717	2.1	5,393	4,324	5,951	3,304	2,647	178	104	74
Percent change										
1996–97 to 2001–02	10.9	†	2.6	25.6	13.2	11.6	15.4	35.6	25.8	57.1
2001–02 to 2006–07	10.3	†	3.2	20.6	30.3	26.8	35.1	-2.7	-11.1	12.1

†Not applicable.
SOURCE: U.S. Department of Education, National Center for Education Statistics, *Earned Degrees Conferred*, 1949–50 and 1959–60; Higher Education General Information Survey (HEGIS), "Degrees and Other Formal Awards Conferred" surveys, 1967–68 through 1985–86; and 1986–87 through 2006–07 Integrated Postsecondary Education Data System, "Completions Survey" (IPEDS-C:87–99), and Fall 2000 through Fall 2007. (This table was prepared September 2008.)

Table 298. Degrees in the biological and biomedical sciences conferred by degree-granting institutions, by level of degree and sex of student: Selected years, 1951–52 through 2006–07

Year	Bachelor's degrees				Master's degrees			Doctor's degrees		
	Total		Males	Females	Total	Males	Females	Total	Males	Females
	Number	Annual percent change								
1	2	3	4	5	6	7	8	9	10	11
1951–52	11,094	†	8,212	2,882	2,307	1,908	399	764	680	84
1953–54	9,279	†	6,710	2,569	1,610	1,287	323	1,077	977	100
1955–56	12,423	†	9,515	2,908	1,759	1,379	380	1,025	908	117
1957–58	14,308	†	11,159	3,149	1,852	1,448	404	1,125	987	138
1959–60	15,576	†	11,654	3,922	2,154	1,668	486	1,205	1,086	119
1961–62	16,915	†	12,136	4,779	2,642	1,982	660	1,338	1,179	159
1963–64	22,723	†	16,321	6,402	3,296	2,348	948	1,625	1,432	193
1965–66	26,916	†	19,368	7,548	4,232	3,085	1,147	2,097	1,792	305
1967–68	31,826	†	22,986	8,840	5,506	3,959	1,547	2,784	2,345	439
1969–70	34,034	†	23,919	10,115	5,800	3,975	1,825	3,289	2,820	469
1970–71	35,683	4.8	25,303	10,380	5,623	3,780	1,843	3,595	3,011	584
1971–72	37,269	4.4	26,314	10,955	5,983	4,050	1,933	3,566	2,963	603
1972–73	42,205	13.2	29,624	12,581	6,153	4,314	1,839	3,569	2,880	689
1973–74	48,224	14.3	33,205	15,019	6,405	4,510	1,895	3,342	2,670	672
1974–75	51,576	7.0	34,559	17,017	6,422	4,551	1,871	3,315	2,598	717
1975–76	54,085	4.9	35,449	18,636	6,453	4,463	1,990	3,313	2,606	707
1976–77	53,420	-1.2	34,150	19,270	6,948	4,666	2,282	3,299	2,601	698
1977–78	51,326	-3.9	31,654	19,672	6,644	4,351	2,293	3,218	2,447	771
1978–79	48,668	-5.2	29,146	19,522	6,631	4,194	2,437	3,410	2,560	850
1979–80	46,190	-5.1	26,757	19,433	6,322	4,032	2,290	3,527	2,626	901
1980–81	43,003	-6.9	24,069	18,934	5,759	3,597	2,162	3,591	2,581	1,010
1981–82	41,425	-3.7	22,687	18,738	5,667	3,375	2,292	3,611	2,579	1,032
1982–83	39,767	-4.0	21,483	18,284	5,693	3,284	2,409	3,331	2,268	1,063
1983–84	38,445	-3.3	20,499	17,946	5,468	3,108	2,360	3,435	2,367	1,068
1984–85	38,229	-0.6	20,017	18,212	5,100	2,770	2,330	3,408	2,302	1,106
1985–86	38,320	0.2	19,950	18,370	5,043	2,719	2,324	3,352	2,236	1,116
1986–87	37,977	-0.9	19,626	18,351	4,980	2,637	2,343	3,397	2,216	1,181
1987–88	36,576	-3.7	18,202	18,374	4,857	2,520	2,337	3,606	2,338	1,268
1988–89	35,957	-1.7	17,935	18,022	5,009	2,583	2,426	3,535	2,245	1,290
1989–90	37,204	3.5	18,305	18,899	4,906	2,492	2,414	3,837	2,425	1,412
1990–91	39,377	5.8	19,358	20,019	4,796	2,396	2,400	4,034	2,547	1,487
1991–92	42,781	8.6	20,748	22,033	4,816	2,411	2,405	4,323	2,676	1,647
1992–93	46,868	9.6	22,795	24,073	4,974	2,505	2,469	4,595	2,767	1,828
1993–94	51,157	9.2	25,002	26,155	5,390	2,644	2,746	4,724	2,809	1,915
1994–95	55,790	9.1	26,628	29,162	5,824	2,885	2,939	4,881	2,901	1,980
1995–96	60,750	8.9	28,782	31,968	6,544	3,180	3,364	5,035	2,929	2,106
1996–97	63,679	4.8	29,432	34,247	6,925	3,389	3,536	5,094	2,890	2,204
1997–98	65,583	3.0	29,511	36,072	6,788	3,301	3,487	5,236	2,970	2,266
1998–99	64,608	-1.5	28,175	36,433	6,913	3,247	3,666	5,024	2,875	2,149
1999–2000	63,005	-2.5	26,310	36,695	6,781	3,131	3,650	5,180	2,887	2,293
2000–01	59,865	-5.0	24,293	35,572	6,955	3,043	3,912	4,953	2,757	2,196
2001–02	59,415	-0.8	23,346	36,069	6,937	2,996	3,941	4,823	2,667	2,156
2002–03	60,104	1.2	22,918	37,186	6,990	2,981	4,009	5,003	2,714	2,289
2003–04	61,509	2.3	23,248	38,261	7,657	3,227	4,430	5,242	2,804	2,438
2004–05	64,611	5.0	24,617	39,994	8,199	3,318	4,881	5,578	2,845	2,733
2005–06	69,178	7.1	26,651	42,527	8,681	3,654	5,027	5,775	2,933	2,842
2006–07	75,151	8.6	29,951	45,200	8,747	3,568	5,179	6,354	3,221	3,133
Percent change										
1996–97 to 2001–02	-6.7	†	-20.7	5.3	0.2	-11.6	11.5	-5.3	-7.7	-2.2
2001–02 to 2006–07	26.5	†	28.3	25.3	26.1	19.1	31.4	31.7	20.8	45.3

†Not applicable.
SOURCE: U.S. Department of Education, National Center for Education Statistics, *Earned Degrees Conferred*, 1951–52 through 1963–64; Higher Education General Information Survey (HEGIS), "Degrees and Other Formal Awards Conferred" surveys, 1965–66 through 1985–86; and 1986–87 through 2006–07 Integrated Postsecondary Education Data System, "Completions Survey" (IPEDS-C:87–99), and Fall 2000 through Fall 2007. (This table was prepared September 2008.)

Table 299. Degrees in biology, microbiology, and zoology conferred by degree-granting institutions, by level of degree: 1970–71 through 2006–07

Year	Biology, general			Microbiology[1]			Zoology[2]		
	Bachelor's	Master's	Doctor's	Bachelor's	Master's	Doctor's	Bachelor's	Master's	Doctor's
1	2	3	4	5	6	7	8	9	10
1970–71	26,294	2,665	536	1,475	456	365	5,721	1,027	878
1971–72	27,473	2,943	580	1,548	470	351	5,518	1,040	836
1972–73	31,185	2,959	627	1,940	517	344	5,763	1,042	803
1973–74	36,188	3,186	657	2,311	505	384	6,128	1,091	677
1974–75	38,748	3,109	637	2,767	552	345	6,110	1,039	697
1975–76	40,163	3,177	624	2,927	585	364	6,077	976	645
1976–77	39,530	3,322	608	2,884	659	325	5,574	985	696
1977–78	37,598	3,094	664	2,695	615	353	5,096	958	624
1978–79	35,962	3,093	663	2,670	597	395	4,738	946	669
1979–80	33,523	2,911	718	2,631	596	376	4,301	922	639
1980–81	31,323	2,598	734	2,414	482	370	3,873	881	613
1981–82	29,651	2,579	678	2,377	470	350	3,615	868	625
1982–83	28,022	2,354	521	2,324	499	358	3,407	738	533
1983–84	27,379	2,313	617	2,349	505	388	3,231	700	521
1984–85	27,593	2,130	658	2,207	471	319	3,069	664	508
1985–86	27,618	2,173	574	2,257	392	362	2,894	618	548
1986–87	27,465	2,022	537	2,159	451	380	2,791	623	464
1987–88	26,838	1,981	576	2,061	404	442	2,537	629	492
1988–89	26,229	2,097	527	1,833	449	423	2,549	634	466
1989–90	27,213	1,998	551	1,973	403	441	2,473	548	545
1990–91	29,285	1,956	632	1,788	343	443	2,641	551	516
1991–92	31,909	1,995	657	1,750	372	532	2,811	530	494
1992–93	34,932	2,000	671	1,798	367	621	3,036	559	465
1993–94	38,103	2,178	665	1,872	359	591	3,162	658	503
1994–95	41,658	2,350	729	1,992	326	572	3,149	586	487
1995–96	44,818	2,606	768	2,220	364	606	3,453	677	501
1996–97	46,632	2,742	693	2,530	363	612	3,438	720	474
1997–98	47,054	2,617	809	2,926	401	585	3,653	685	465
1998–99	46,078	2,608	711	2,871	410	547	3,426	604	461
1999–2000	44,982	2,599	727	3,049	383	551	3,226	616	481
2000–01	42,310	2,582	780	2,779	334	553	3,045	560	380
2001–02	42,281	2,424	689	2,622	325	538	2,979	578	413
2002–03	42,699	2,340	680	2,455	297	507	2,488	379	355
2003–04	43,465	2,529	681	2,365	350	599	2,454	367	245
2004–05	45,540	2,564	712	2,318	390	610	2,159	384	268
2005–06	48,855	2,719	776	2,243	372	612	2,140	384	254
2006–07	52,527	2,679	788	2,347	369	667	2,223	416	263
Percent change									
1996–97 to 2001–02	-9.3	-11.6	-0.6	3.6	-10.5	-12.1	-13.4	-19.7	-12.9
2001–02 to 2006–07	24.2	10.5	14.4	-10.5	13.5	24.0	-25.4	-28.0	-36.3

[1]Includes microbiology, general; medical microbiology and bacteriology; virology; parisitology; immunology; and microbiological sciences and immunology, other.
[2]Includes zoology/animal biology; entomology; animal physiology; animal behavior and ethology; wildlife biology; physiology, human and animal; and zoology/animal biology, other.

SOURCE: U.S. Department of Education, National Center for Education Statistics, Higher Education General Information Survey (HEGIS), "Degrees and Other Formal Awards Conferred" surveys, 1970–71 through 1985–86; and 1986–87 through 2006–07 Integrated Postsecondary Education Data System, "Completions Survey" (IPEDS-C:87–99), and Fall 2000 through Fall 2007. (This table was prepared September 2008.)

Table 300. Degrees in business conferred by degree-granting institutions, by level of degree and sex of student: Selected years, 1955–56 through 2006–07

Year	Bachelor's degrees				Master's degrees			Doctor's degrees		
	Total									
	Number	Annual percent change	Males	Females	Total	Males	Females	Total	Males	Females
1	2	3	4	5	6	7	8	9	10	11
1955–56	42,813	†	38,706	4,107	3,280	3,118	162	129	127	2
1957–58	51,991	†	48,063	3,928	4,223	4,072	151	110	105	5
1959–60	51,076	†	47,262	3,814	4,643	4,476	167	135	133	2
1961–62	49,017	†	45,184	3,833	7,691	7,484	207	226	221	5
1963–64	55,474	†	51,056	4,418	9,251	9,008	243	275	268	7
1965–66	62,721	†	57,516	5,205	12,959	12,628	331	387	370	17
1967–68	79,074	†	72,126	6,948	17,795	17,186	609	441	427	14
1969–70	105,580	†	96,346	9,234	21,561	20,792	769	620	610	10
1970–71	115,396	9.3	104,936	10,460	26,490	25,458	1,032	774	753	21
1971–72	121,917	5.7	110,331	11,586	30,509	29,317	1,192	876	857	19
1972–73	126,717	3.9	113,337	13,380	31,208	29,689	1,519	917	864	53
1973–74	132,304	4.4	115,363	16,941	32,691	30,557	2,134	922	873	49
1974–75	133,639	1.0	111,983	21,656	36,315	33,274	3,041	939	900	39
1975–76	143,171	7.1	114,986	28,185	42,592	37,654	4,938	906	856	50
1976–77	152,010	6.2	116,394	35,616	46,505	39,852	6,653	839	785	54
1977–78	160,775	5.8	117,103	43,672	48,347	40,224	8,123	834	760	74
1978–79	172,392	7.2	119,765	52,627	50,397	40,766	9,631	852	752	100
1979–80	186,264	8.0	123,639	62,625	55,008	42,744	12,264	767	650	117
1980–81	200,521	7.7	126,798	73,723	57,888	43,411	14,477	808	686	122
1981–82	215,190	7.3	130,693	84,497	61,251	44,230	17,021	826	676	150
1982–83	226,442	5.2	131,451	94,991	64,741	45,987	18,754	770	638	132
1983–84	229,013	1.1	129,296	99,717	66,129	46,167	19,962	926	727	199
1984–85	232,282	1.4	127,467	104,815	66,981	46,199	20,782	827	685	142
1985–86	236,700	1.9	128,415	108,285	66,676	45,927	20,749	923	720	203
1986–87	240,346	1.5	128,506	111,840	67,093	44,913	22,180	1,062	808	254
1987–88	242,859	1.0	129,467	113,392	69,230	45,980	23,250	1,063	810	253
1988–89	246,262	1.4	131,098	115,164	73,065	48,540	24,525	1,100	800	300
1989–90	248,568	0.9	132,284	116,284	76,676	50,585	26,091	1,093	818	275
1990–91	249,165	0.2	131,557	117,608	78,255	50,883	27,372	1,185	876	309
1991–92	256,298	2.9	135,263	121,035	84,517	54,609	29,908	1,242	953	289
1992–93	256,473	0.1	135,368	121,105	89,425	57,504	31,921	1,346	969	377
1993–94	246,265	-4.0	128,946	117,319	93,285	59,223	34,062	1,364	980	384
1994–95	233,895	-5.0	121,663	112,232	93,540	58,931	34,609	1,391	1,011	380
1995–96	226,623	-3.1	116,545	110,078	93,554	58,400	35,154	1,366	972	394
1996–97	225,934	-0.3	116,023	109,911	97,204	59,333	37,871	1,336	947	389
1997–98	232,079	2.7	119,379	112,700	101,652	62,357	39,295	1,290	885	405
1998–99	240,947	3.8	122,250	118,697	107,477	64,700	42,777	1,201	843	358
1999–2000	256,070	6.3	128,521	127,549	111,532	67,078	44,454	1,194	812	382
2000–01	263,515	2.9	132,275	131,240	115,602	68,471	47,131	1,180	783	397
2001–02	278,217	5.6	138,343	139,874	119,725	70,463	49,262	1,156	746	410
2002–03	293,391	5.5	145,075	148,316	127,685	75,239	52,446	1,252	820	432
2003–04	307,149	4.7	152,513	154,636	139,347	80,858	58,489	1,481	960	521
2004–05	311,574	1.4	155,940	155,634	142,617	82,151	60,466	1,498	901	597
2005–06	318,042	2.1	159,683	158,359	146,406	83,550	62,856	1,711	1,049	662
2006–07	327,531	3.0	166,350	161,181	150,211	84,115	66,096	2,029	1,188	841
Percent change										
1996–97 to 2001–02	23.1	†	19.2	27.3	23.2	18.8	30.1	-13.5	-21.2	5.4
2001–02 to 2006–07	17.7	†	20.2	15.2	25.5	19.4	34.2	75.5	59.2	105.1

†Not applicable.
NOTE: Includes degrees in business, management, marketing, and related support services and in personal and culinary services.
SOURCE: U.S. Department of Education, National Center for Education Statistics, *Earned Degrees Conferred*, 1955–56 through 1963–64; Higher Education General Information Survey (HEGIS), "Degrees and Other Formal Awards Conferred" surveys, 1965–66 through 1985–86; and 1986–87 through 2006–07 Integrated Postsecondary Education Data System, "Completions Survey" (IPEDS-C:87–99), and Fall 2000 through Fall 2007. (This table was prepared September 2008.)

Table 301. Degrees in communication, journalism, and related programs and in communications technologies conferred by degree-granting institutions, by level of degree and sex of student: 1970–71 through 2006–07

Year	Bachelor's degrees				Master's degrees			Doctor's degrees		
	Total									
	Number	Annual percent change	Males	Females	Total	Males	Females	Total	Males	Females
1	2	3	4	5	6	7	8	9	10	11
1970–71	10,802	†	6,989	3,813	1,856	1,214	642	145	126	19
1971–72	12,340	14.2	7,964	4,376	2,200	1,443	757	111	96	15
1972–73	14,317	16.0	9,074	5,243	2,406	1,546	860	139	114	25
1973–74	17,096	19.4	10,536	6,560	2,640	1,668	972	175	146	29
1974–75	19,248	12.6	11,455	7,793	2,794	1,618	1,176	165	119	46
1975–76	21,282	10.6	12,458	8,824	3,126	1,818	1,308	204	154	50
1976–77	23,214	9.1	12,932	10,282	3,091	1,719	1,372	171	130	41
1977–78	25,400	9.4	13,480	11,920	3,296	1,673	1,623	191	138	53
1978–79	26,457	4.2	13,266	13,191	2,882	1,483	1,399	192	138	54
1979–80	28,616	8.2	13,656	14,960	3,082	1,527	1,555	193	121	72
1980–81	31,282	9.3	14,179	17,103	3,105	1,448	1,657	182	107	75
1981–82	34,222	9.4	14,917	19,305	3,327	1,578	1,749	200	136	64
1982–83	38,647	12.9	16,213	22,434	3,600	1,660	1,940	208	123	85
1983–84	40,203	4.0	16,662	23,541	3,620	1,578	2,042	216	129	87
1984–85	42,102	4.7	17,233	24,869	3,657	1,574	2,083	232	141	91
1985–86	43,145	2.5	17,681	25,464	3,808	1,603	2,205	218	116	102
1986–87	45,521	5.5	18,201	27,320	3,881	1,584	2,297	275	158	117
1987–88	46,916	3.1	18,672	28,244	3,916	1,568	2,348	233	133	100
1988–89	48,889	4.2	19,357	29,532	4,249	1,734	2,515	248	137	111
1989–90	51,572	5.5	20,374	31,198	4,353	1,705	2,648	272	145	127
1990–91	53,047	2.9	20,806	32,241	4,327	1,711	2,616	272	150	122
1991–92	55,144	4.0	21,601	33,543	4,463	1,692	2,771	255	132	123
1992–93	54,907	-0.4	22,154	32,753	5,179	1,969	3,210	301	146	155
1993–94	52,033	-5.2	21,484	30,549	5,388	2,088	3,300	345	174	171
1994–95	48,969	-5.9	20,501	28,468	5,559	2,086	3,473	321	162	159
1995–96	48,173	-1.6	19,868	28,305	5,561	2,153	3,408	345	190	155
1996–97	47,894	-0.6	19,771	28,123	5,552	1,989	3,563	300	155	145
1997–98	50,263	4.9	20,103	30,160	6,097	2,369	3,728	359	171	188
1998–99	52,460	4.4	20,950	31,510	5,556	2,001	3,555	352	183	169
1999–2000	57,058	8.8	22,152	34,906	5,525	2,030	3,495	357	168	189
2000–01	59,191	3.7	22,542	36,649	5,645	1,964	3,681	370	190	180
2001–02	64,036	8.2	23,692	40,344	5,980	2,169	3,811	383	168	215
2002–03	69,828	9.0	25,338	44,490	6,495	2,301	4,194	398	179	219
2003–04	73,002	4.5	25,813	47,189	6,900	2,329	4,571	426	186	240
2004–05	75,238	3.1	26,926	48,312	7,195	2,535	4,660	468	195	273
2005–06	76,936	2.3	28,142	48,794	7,745	2,611	5,134	464	207	257
2006–07	78,420	1.9	29,009	49,411	7,272	2,485	4,787	480	188	292
Percent change										
1996–97 to 2001–02	33.7	†	19.8	43.5	7.7	9.0	7.0	27.7	8.4	48.3
2001–02 to 2006–07	22.5	†	22.4	22.5	21.6	14.6	25.6	25.3	11.9	35.8

†Not applicable.

SOURCE: U.S. Department of Education, National Center for Education Statistics, Higher Education General Information Survey (HEGIS), "Degrees and Other Formal Awards Conferred" surveys, 1970–71 through 1985–86; and 1986–87 through 2006–07 Integrated Postsecondary Education Data System, "Completions Survey" (IPEDS-C:87–99), and Fall 2000 through Fall 2007. (This table was prepared September 2008.)

Table 302. Degrees in computer and information sciences conferred by degree-granting institutions, by level of degree and sex of student: 1970–71 through 2006–07

Year	Bachelor's degrees				Master's degrees			Doctor's degrees		
	Total		Males	Females	Total	Males	Females	Total	Males	Females
	Number	Annual percent change								
1	2	3	4	5	6	7	8	9	10	11
1970–71	2,388	†	2,064	324	1,588	1,424	164	128	125	3
1971–72	3,402	42.5	2,941	461	1,977	1,752	225	167	155	12
1972–73	4,304	26.5	3,664	640	2,113	1,888	225	196	181	15
1973–74	4,756	10.5	3,976	780	2,276	1,983	293	198	189	9
1974–75	5,033	5.8	4,080	953	2,299	1,961	338	213	199	14
1975–76	5,652	12.3	4,534	1,118	2,603	2,226	377	244	221	23
1976–77	6,407	13.4	4,876	1,531	2,798	2,332	466	216	197	19
1977–78	7,201	12.4	5,349	1,852	3,038	2,471	567	196	181	15
1978–79	8,719	21.1	6,272	2,447	3,055	2,480	575	236	206	30
1979–80	11,154	27.9	7,782	3,372	3,647	2,883	764	240	213	27
1980–81	15,121	35.6	10,202	4,919	4,218	3,247	971	252	227	25
1981–82	20,267	34.0	13,218	7,049	4,935	3,625	1,310	251	230	21
1982–83	24,565	21.2	15,641	8,924	5,321	3,813	1,508	262	228	34
1983–84	32,439	32.1	20,416	12,023	6,190	4,379	1,811	251	225	26
1984–85	39,121	20.6	24,737	14,384	7,101	5,064	2,037	248	223	25
1985–86	42,337	8.2	27,208	15,129	8,070	5,658	2,412	344	299	45
1986–87	39,767	-6.1	25,962	13,805	8,481	5,985	2,496	374	322	52
1987–88	34,651	-12.9	23,414	11,237	9,197	6,726	2,471	428	380	48
1988–89	30,560	-11.8	21,143	9,417	9,414	6,775	2,639	551	466	85
1989–90	27,347	-10.5	19,159	8,188	9,677	6,960	2,717	627	534	93
1990–91	25,159	-8.0	17,771	7,388	9,324	6,563	2,761	676	584	92
1991–92	24,821	-1.3	17,685	7,136	9,655	6,980	2,675	772	669	103
1992–93	24,519	-1.2	17,606	6,913	10,353	7,557	2,796	805	689	116
1993–94	24,527	#	17,528	6,999	10,568	7,836	2,732	810	685	125
1994–95	24,737	0.9	17,684	7,053	10,595	7,805	2,790	887	726	161
1995–96	24,506	-0.9	17,757	6,749	10,579	7,729	2,850	869	743	126
1996–97	25,422	3.7	18,527	6,895	10,513	7,526	2,987	857	721	136
1997–98	27,829	9.5	20,372	7,457	11,765	8,343	3,422	858	718	140
1998–99	30,574	9.9	22,298	8,276	12,858	8,871	3,987	801	650	151
1999–2000	37,788	23.6	27,185	10,603	14,990	9,978	5,012	779	648	131
2000–01	44,142	16.8	31,923	12,219	16,911	11,195	5,716	768	632	136
2001–02	50,365	14.1	36,462	13,903	17,173	11,447	5,726	752	581	171
2002–03	57,433	14.0	41,950	15,483	19,509	13,267	6,242	816	648	168
2003–04	59,488	3.6	44,585	14,903	20,143	13,868	6,275	909	709	200
2004–05	54,111	-9.0	42,125	11,986	18,416	13,136	5,280	1,119	905	214
2005–06	47,480	-12.3	37,705	9,775	17,055	12,470	4,585	1,416	1,109	307
2006–07	42,170	-11.2	34,342	7,828	16,232	11,985	4,247	1,595	1,267	328
Percent change										
1996–97 to 2001–02	98.1	†	96.8	101.6	63.4	52.1	91.7	-12.3	-19.4	25.7
2001–02 to 2006–07	-16.3	†	-5.8	-43.7	-5.5	4.7	-25.8	112.1	118.1	91.8

†Not applicable.
#Rounds to zero.
SOURCE: U.S. Department of Education, National Center for Education Statistics, Higher Education General Information Survey (HEGIS), "Degrees and Other Formal Awards Con- ferred" surveys, 1970–71 through 1985–86; and 1986–87 through 2006–07 Integrated Postsecondary Education Data System, "Completions Survey" (IPEDS-C:87–99), and Fall 2000 through Fall 2007. (This table was prepared September 2008.)

Table 303. Degrees in education conferred by degree-granting institutions, by level of degree and sex of student: Selected years, 1949–50 through 2006–07

Year	Bachelor's degrees				Master's degrees			Doctor's degrees		
	Total									
	Number	Annual percent change	Males	Females	Total	Males	Females	Total	Males	Females
1	2	3	4	5	6	7	8	9	10	11
1949–50..........................	61,472	†	31,398	30,074	20,069	12,025	8,044	953	797	156
1959–60..........................	89,002	†	25,556	63,446	33,433	18,057	15,376	1,591	1,279	312
1967–68..........................	133,965	†	31,926	102,039	63,399	30,672	32,727	4,078	3,250	828
1969–70..........................	163,964	†	40,420	123,544	78,020	34,832	43,188	5,588	4,479	1,109
1970–71..........................	176,307	7.5	44,896	131,411	87,666	38,365	49,301	6,041	4,771	1,270
1971–72..........................	190,880	8.3	49,344	141,536	96,668	41,141	55,527	6,648	5,104	1,544
1972–73..........................	193,984	1.6	51,300	142,684	103,777	43,298	60,479	6,857	5,191	1,666
1973–74..........................	184,907	-4.7	48,997	135,910	110,402	44,112	66,290	6,757	4,974	1,783
1974–75..........................	166,758	-9.8	44,463	122,295	117,841	44,430	73,411	6,975	4,856	2,119
1975–76..........................	154,437	-7.4	42,004	112,433	126,061	44,831	81,230	7,202	4,826	2,376
1976–77..........................	143,234	-7.3	39,867	103,367	124,267	42,308	81,959	7,338	4,832	2,506
1977–78..........................	135,821	-5.2	37,410	98,411	116,916	37,662	79,254	7,018	4,281	2,737
1978–79..........................	125,873	-7.3	33,743	92,130	109,866	34,410	75,456	7,170	4,174	2,996
1979–80..........................	118,038	-6.2	30,901	87,137	101,819	30,300	71,519	7,314	4,100	3,214
1980–81..........................	108,074	-8.4	27,039	81,035	96,713	27,548	69,165	7,279	3,843	3,436
1981–82..........................	100,932	-6.6	24,380	76,552	91,601	25,339	66,262	6,999	3,612	3,387
1982–83..........................	97,908	-3.0	23,651	74,257	83,254	22,824	60,430	7,063	3,550	3,513
1983–84..........................	92,310	-5.7	22,200	70,110	75,700	21,164	54,536	6,914	3,448	3,466
1984–85..........................	88,078	-4.6	21,254	66,824	74,667	20,539	54,128	6,614	3,174	3,440
1985–86..........................	87,147	-1.1	20,982	66,165	74,816	20,302	54,514	6,610	3,088	3,522
1986–87..........................	86,788	-0.4	20,705	66,083	72,619	18,955	53,664	5,905	2,745	3,160
1987–88..........................	90,928	4.8	20,947	69,981	75,270	18,777	56,493	5,568	2,530	3,038
1988–89..........................	96,740	6.4	21,643	75,097	79,793	19,616	60,177	5,884	2,522	3,362
1989–90..........................	105,112	8.7	23,007	82,105	84,890	20,469	64,421	6,503	2,776	3,727
1990–91..........................	110,807	5.4	23,417	87,390	87,352	20,448	66,904	6,189	2,614	3,575
1991–92..........................	107,836	-2.7	22,655	85,181	91,225	20,897	70,328	6,423	2,652	3,771
1992–93..........................	107,578	-0.2	23,199	84,379	94,497	21,857	72,640	6,581	2,712	3,869
1993–94..........................	107,440	-0.1	24,424	83,016	97,427	22,656	74,771	6,450	2,555	3,895
1994–95..........................	105,929	-1.4	25,619	80,310	99,835	23,511	76,324	6,475	2,490	3,985
1995–96..........................	105,384	-0.5	26,214	79,170	104,936	24,955	79,981	6,246	2,404	3,842
1996–97..........................	105,116	-0.3	26,242	78,874	108,720	25,518	83,202	6,297	2,367	3,930
1997–98..........................	105,833	0.7	26,285	79,548	113,374	26,814	86,560	6,261	2,334	3,927
1998–99..........................	107,086	1.2	26,224	80,862	118,048	27,997	90,051	6,394	2,298	4,096
1999–2000......................	108,034	0.9	26,103	81,931	123,045	29,081	93,964	6,409	2,295	4,114
2000–01..........................	105,458	-2.4	24,580	80,878	127,829	29,997	97,832	6,284	2,237	4,047
2001–02..........................	106,295	0.8	24,049	82,246	135,189	31,907	103,282	6,549	2,211	4,338
2002–03..........................	105,845	-0.4	22,604	83,241	147,883	34,033	113,850	6,832	2,314	4,518
2003–04..........................	106,278	0.4	22,802	83,476	162,345	37,843	124,502	7,088	2,403	4,685
2004–05..........................	105,451	-0.8	22,513	82,938	167,490	38,863	128,627	7,681	2,557	5,124
2005–06..........................	107,238	1.7	22,448	84,790	174,620	40,700	133,920	7,584	2,664	4,920
2006–07..........................	105,641	-1.5	22,516	83,125	176,572	40,164	136,408	8,261	2,681	5,580
Percent change										
1996–97 to 2001–02.......	1.1	†	-8.4	4.3	24.3	25.0	24.1	4.0	-6.6	10.4
2001–02 to 2006–07.......	-0.6	†	-6.4	1.1	30.6	25.9	32.1	26.1	21.3	28.6

†Not applicable.
SOURCE: U.S. Department of Education, National Center for Education Statistics, *Earned Degrees Conferred*, 1949–50 and 1959–60; Higher Education General Information Survey (HEGIS), "Degrees and Other Formal Awards Conferred" surveys, 1967–68 through 1985–86; and 1986–87 through 2006–07 Integrated Postsecondary Education Data System, "Completions Survey" (IPEDS-C:87–99), and Fall 2000 through Fall 2007. (This table was prepared September 2008.)

Table 304. Degrees in engineering and engineering technologies conferred by degree-granting institutions, by level of degree and sex of student: Selected years, 1949–50 through 2006–07

| | Bachelor's degrees | | | | Master's degrees | | | Doctor's degrees | | |
| | Total | | | | | | | | | |
Year	Number	Annual percent change	Males	Females	Total	Males	Females	Total	Males	Females
1	2	3	4	5	6	7	8	9	10	11
1949–50	52,246	†	52,071	175	4,496	4,481	15	417	416	1
1959–60	37,679	†	37,537	142	7,159	7,133	26	786	783	3
1969–70	44,479	†	44,149	330	15,593	15,421	172	3,681	3,657	24
1970–71	50,182	12.8	49,775	407	16,947	16,734	213	3,688	3,663	25
1971–72	51,258	2.1	50,726	532	17,299	17,009	290	3,708	3,685	23
1972–73	51,384	0.2	50,766	618	16,988	16,694	294	3,513	3,459	54
1973–74	50,412	-1.9	49,611	801	15,851	15,470	381	3,374	3,318	56
1974–75	47,131	-6.5	46,105	1,026	15,837	15,426	411	3,181	3,113	68
1975–76	46,676	-1.0	45,184	1,492	16,800	16,174	626	2,874	2,805	69
1976–77	49,482	6.0	47,238	2,244	16,659	15,891	768	2,622	2,547	75
1977–78	56,150	13.5	52,353	3,797	16,887	15,940	947	2,483	2,424	59
1978–79	62,898	12.0	57,603	5,295	16,012	14,971	1,041	2,545	2,459	86
1979–80	69,387	10.3	62,877	6,510	16,765	15,535	1,230	2,546	2,447	99
1980–81	75,355	8.6	67,573	7,782	17,216	15,761	1,455	2,608	2,499	109
1981–82	80,632	7.0	71,305	9,327	18,475	16,747	1,728	2,676	2,532	144
1982–83	89,811	11.4	78,673	11,138	19,949	18,038	1,911	2,871	2,742	129
1983–84	95,295	6.1	82,841	12,454	21,197	18,916	2,281	3,032	2,864	168
1984–85	97,099	1.9	83,991	13,108	22,124	19,688	2,436	3,269	3,055	214
1985–86	97,122	#	84,050	13,072	22,146	19,545	2,601	3,456	3,220	236
1986–87	93,560	-3.7	80,543	13,017	23,101	20,137	2,964	3,854	3,585	269
1987–88	89,406	-4.4	76,886	12,520	23,839	20,815	3,024	4,237	3,941	296
1988–89	85,982	-3.8	74,020	11,962	25,066	21,731	3,335	4,572	4,160	412
1989–90	82,480	-4.1	70,859	11,621	25,294	21,753	3,541	5,030	4,576	454
1990–91	79,751	-3.3	68,482	11,269	25,450	21,780	3,670	5,330	4,834	496
1991–92	78,058	-2.1	67,104	10,954	26,430	22,444	3,986	5,533	4,998	535
1992–93	78,662	0.8	67,248	11,414	29,149	24,758	4,391	5,894	5,322	572
1993–94	78,662	0.0	66,920	11,742	30,172	25,453	4,719	6,011	5,339	672
1994–95	78,569	-0.1	66,223	12,346	30,031	25,090	4,941	6,173	5,435	738
1995–96	78,086	-0.6	65,430	12,656	28,946	23,928	5,018	6,431	5,623	808
1996–97	75,757	-3.0	63,066	12,691	27,106	22,114	4,992	6,250	5,476	774
1997–98	74,649	-1.5	61,955	12,694	27,327	21,867	5,460	6,038	5,294	744
1998–99	72,665	-2.7	59,703	12,962	26,738	21,394	5,344	5,461	4,676	785
1999–2000	73,419	1.0	59,741	13,678	26,726	21,100	5,626	5,421	4,582	839
2000–01	72,975	-0.6	59,564	13,411	27,272	21,405	5,867	5,604	4,669	935
2001–02	74,679	2.3	60,474	14,205	27,057	21,263	5,794	5,245	4,332	913
2002–03	77,319	3.5	62,884	14,435	30,670	24,170	6,500	5,333	4,415	918
2003–04	78,227	1.2	63,502	14,725	35,197	27,667	7,530	5,981	4,923	1,058
2004–05	79,743	1.9	65,164	14,579	35,133	27,161	7,972	6,601	5,368	1,233
2005–06	81,610	2.3	67,013	14,597	33,530	25,666	7,864	7,471	5,963	1,508
2006–07	82,072	0.6	68,230	13,842	32,162	24,865	7,297	8,123	6,422	1,701
Percent change										
1996–97 to 2001–02	-1.4	†	-4.1	11.9	-0.2	-3.8	16.1	-16.1	-20.9	18.0
2001–02 to 2006–07	9.9	†	12.8	-2.6	18.9	16.9	25.9	54.9	48.2	86.3

†Not applicable.
#Rounds to zero.
NOTE: Includes degrees in engineering, engineering-related technologies, mechanic and repair technologies, and construction trades from 1969–70 through 2006–07.
SOURCE: U.S. Department of Education, National Center for Education Statistics, *Earned Degrees Conferred*, 1949–50 and 1959–60; Higher Education General Information Survey (HEGIS), "Degrees and Other Formal Awards Conferred" surveys, 1969–70 through 1985–86; and 1986–87 through 2006–07 Integrated Postsecondary Education Data System, "Completions Survey" (IPEDS-C:87–99), and Fall 2000 through Fall 2007. (This table was prepared September 2008.)

Table 305. Degrees in chemical, civil, electrical, and mechanical engineering conferred by degree-granting institutions, by level of degree: 1970–71 through 2006–07

Year	Chemical engineering			Civil engineering			Electrical, electronics, and communications engineering			Mechanical engineering		
	Bachelor's	Master's	Doctor's	Bachelor's	Master's	Doctor's	Bachelor's	Master's	Doctor's	Bachelor's	Master's	Doctor's
1	2	3	4	5	6	7	8	9	10	11	12	13
1970–71	3,579	1,100	406	6,526	2,425	446	12,198	4,282	879	8,858	2,237	438
1971–72	3,625	1,154	394	6,803	2,487	415	12,101	4,206	824	8,530	2,282	411
1972–73	3,578	1,051	397	7,390	2,627	397	12,313	3,895	791	8,523	2,141	370
1973–74	3,399	1,044	400	8,017	2,652	368	11,316	3,499	705	7,677	1,843	385
1974–75	3,070	990	346	7,651	2,769	356	10,161	3,469	701	6,890	1,858	340
1975–76	3,140	1,031	308	7,923	2,999	370	9,791	3,774	649	6,800	1,907	305
1976–77	3,524	1,086	291	8,228	2,964	309	9,936	3,788	566	7,703	1,952	283
1977–78	4,569	1,235	259	9,135	2,685	277	11,133	3,740	503	8,875	1,942	279
1978–79	5,568	1,149	304	9,809	2,646	253	12,338	3,591	586	10,107	1,877	271
1979–80	6,320	1,270	284	10,326	2,683	270	13,821	3,836	525	11,808	2,060	281
1980–81	6,527	1,267	300	10,678	2,891	325	14,938	3,901	535	13,329	2,291	276
1981–82	6,740	1,285	311	10,524	2,995	329	16,455	4,462	526	13,922	2,399	333
1982–83	7,185	1,368	319	9,989	3,074	340	18,049	4,531	550	15,675	2,511	299
1983–84	7,475	1,514	330	9,693	3,146	369	19,943	5,078	585	16,629	2,797	319
1984–85	7,146	1,544	418	9,162	3,172	377	21,691	5,153	660	16,794	3,053	409
1985–86	5,877	1,361	446	8,679	2,926	395	23,742	5,534	722	16,194	3,075	426
1986–87	4,991	1,184	497	8,147	2,901	451	24,547	6,183	724	15,450	3,198	528
1987–88	3,917	1,088	579	7,488	2,836	481	23,597	6,688	860	14,900	3,329	596
1988–89	3,663	1,093	602	7,312	2,903	505	21,908	7,028	998	14,843	3,498	633
1989–90	3,430	1,035	562	7,252	2,812	516	20,711	7,225	1,162	14,336	3,424	742
1990–91	3,444	903	611	7,314	2,927	536	19,320	7,095	1,220	13,977	3,516	757
1991–92	3,754	956	590	8,034	3,113	540	17,958	7,360	1,282	14,067	3,653	851
1992–93	4,459	990	595	8,868	3,610	577	17,281	7,870	1,413	14,464	3,982	871
1993–94	5,163	1,032	604	9,479	3,873	651	15,823	7,791	1,470	15,030	4,099	887
1994–95	5,901	1,085	571	9,827	4,077	625	14,929	7,693	1,543	14,794	4,213	890
1995–96	6,319	1,176	670	10,607	3,905	616	13,900	7,103	1,591	14,177	3,881	940
1996–97	6,564	1,131	650	10,437	3,833	640	13,336	6,393	1,512	13,493	3,608	913
1997–98	6,319	1,128	652	9,926	3,795	610	12,995	6,737	1,458	13,071	3,441	933
1998–99	6,033	1,130	572	9,121	3,648	543	12,531	6,690	1,303	12,705	3,258	774
1999–2000	5,807	1,078	590	8,136	3,433	543	12,930	6,926	1,392	12,807	3,273	776
2000–01	5,611	1,083	610	7,588	3,310	571	13,091	6,815	1,417	12,817	3,371	849
2001–02	5,462	973	605	7,665	3,295	574	13,056	6,587	1,235	13,058	3,391	772
2002–03	5,109	1,065	542	7,836	3,596	599	13,627	7,621	1,256	13,693	3,695	747
2003–04	4,742	1,165	623	7,827	3,790	636	14,123	9,511	1,440	14,050	4,420	787
2004–05	4,397	1,183	773	8,186	3,834	713	14,171	9,054	1,566	14,609	4,637	915
2005–06	4,326	1,116	819	9,090	3,768	750	13,966	8,123	1,860	15,850	4,443	1,096
2006–07	4,492	957	835	9,671	3,482	805	13,089	7,777	2,042	16,601	4,294	1,106
Percent change												
1996–97 to 2001–02	-16.8	-14.0	-6.9	-26.6	-14.0	-10.3	-2.1	3.0	-18.3	-3.2	-6.0	-15.4
2001–02 to 2006–07	-17.8	-1.6	38.0	26.2	5.7	40.2	0.3	18.1	65.3	27.1	26.6	43.3

NOTE: From 1970–71 through 1981–82, civil engineering includes construction and transportation engineering. From 1991–92, civil engineering includes geotechnical, structural, transportation, and water resources engineering. Degrees in engineering technologies are not included in this table.

SOURCE: U.S. Department of Education, National Center for Education Statistics, Higher Education General Information Survey (HEGIS), "Degrees and Other Formal Awards Conferred" surveys, 1970–71 through 1985–86; and 1986–87 through 2006–07 Integrated Postsecondary Education Data System, "Completions Survey" (IPEDS-C:87–99), and Fall 2000 through Fall 2007. (This table was prepared September 2008.)

Table 306. Degrees in English language and literature/letters conferred by degree-granting institutions, by level of degree and sex of student: Selected years, 1949–50 through 2006–07

Year	Bachelor's degrees				Master's degrees			Doctor's degrees		
	Total		Males	Females	Total	Males	Females	Total	Males	Females
	Number	Annual percent change								
1	2	3	4	5	6	7	8	9	10	11
1949–50...............	17,240	†	8,221	9,019	2,259	1,320	939	230	181	49
1959–60...............	20,128	†	7,580	12,548	2,931	1,458	1,473	397	314	83
1967–68...............	47,977	†	15,700	32,277	7,916	3,434	4,482	977	717	260
1969–70...............	56,410	†	18,650	37,760	8,517	3,326	5,191	1,213	837	376
1970–71...............	63,914	13.3	22,005	41,909	10,441	4,126	6,315	1,554	1,107	447
1971–72...............	63,707	-0.3	22,580	41,127	10,412	4,066	6,346	1,734	1,173	561
1972–73...............	60,607	-4.9	22,022	38,585	10,035	3,988	6,047	1,817	1,189	628
1973–74...............	54,190	-10.6	20,082	34,108	9,573	3,824	5,749	1,755	1,142	613
1974–75...............	47,062	-13.2	17,689	29,373	9,178	3,463	5,715	1,595	974	621
1975–76...............	41,452	-11.9	15,898	25,554	8,599	3,290	5,309	1,514	895	619
1976–77...............	37,343	-9.9	14,135	23,208	7,824	2,907	4,917	1,373	768	605
1977–78...............	34,799	-6.8	12,972	21,827	7,444	2,623	4,821	1,272	698	574
1978–79...............	33,218	-4.5	12,085	21,133	6,503	2,307	4,196	1,186	639	547
1979–80...............	32,187	-3.1	11,237	20,950	6,026	2,181	3,845	1,196	635	561
1980–81...............	31,922	-0.8	11,082	20,840	5,742	2,026	3,716	1,040	497	543
1981–82...............	33,078	3.6	11,300	21,778	5,593	1,916	3,677	986	467	519
1982–83...............	31,327	-5.3	10,699	20,628	4,866	1,653	3,213	877	419	458
1983–84...............	32,296	3.1	11,007	21,289	4,814	1,681	3,133	899	413	486
1984–85...............	32,686	1.2	11,195	21,491	4,987	1,723	3,264	915	414	501
1985–86...............	34,083	4.3	11,657	22,426	5,335	1,811	3,524	895	390	505
1986–87...............	35,667	4.6	12,133	23,534	5,298	1,819	3,479	853	367	486
1987–88...............	38,106	6.8	12,687	25,419	5,366	1,796	3,570	858	380	478
1988–89...............	41,786	9.7	13,729	28,057	5,716	1,930	3,786	929	405	524
1989–90...............	46,803	12.0	15,437	31,366	6,317	2,125	4,192	986	444	542
1990–91...............	51,064	9.1	16,891	34,173	6,784	2,203	4,581	1,056	469	587
1991–92...............	54,250	6.2	18,314	35,936	7,215	2,441	4,774	1,142	484	658
1992–93...............	55,289	1.9	19,007	36,282	7,537	2,570	4,967	1,201	495	706
1993–94...............	53,150	-3.9	18,214	34,936	7,611	2,620	4,991	1,205	512	693
1994–95...............	51,170	-3.7	17,581	33,589	7,612	2,672	4,940	1,393	589	804
1995–96...............	49,928	-2.4	17,007	32,921	7,657	2,727	4,930	1,395	535	860
1996–97...............	48,641	-2.6	16,325	32,316	7,487	2,650	4,837	1,431	610	821
1997–98...............	49,016	0.8	16,280	32,736	7,587	2,568	5,019	1,489	611	878
1998–99...............	49,800	1.6	16,285	33,515	7,288	2,442	4,846	1,407	560	847
1999–2000...............	50,106	0.6	16,124	33,982	7,022	2,315	4,707	1,470	611	859
2000–01...............	50,569	0.9	15,997	34,572	6,763	2,160	4,603	1,330	533	797
2001–02...............	52,375	3.6	16,457	35,918	7,097	2,270	4,827	1,291	532	759
2002–03...............	53,699	2.5	16,738	36,961	7,428	2,433	4,995	1,246	492	754
2003–04...............	53,984	0.5	16,792	37,192	7,956	2,459	5,497	1,207	479	728
2004–05...............	54,379	0.7	17,154	37,225	8,468	2,615	5,853	1,212	494	718
2005–06...............	55,096	1.3	17,316	37,780	8,845	2,860	5,985	1,254	510	744
2006–07...............	55,122	#	17,475	37,647	8,742	2,867	5,875	1,178	478	700
Percent change										
1996–97 to 2001–02.......	7.7	†	0.8	11.1	-5.2	-14.3	-0.2	-9.8	-12.8	-7.6
2001–02 to 2006–07.......	5.2	†	6.2	4.8	23.2	26.3	21.7	-8.8	-10.2	-7.8

†Not applicable.
#Rounds to zero.
SOURCE: U.S. Department of Education, National Center for Education Statistics, *Earned Degrees Conferred*, 1949–50 and 1959–60; Higher Education General Information Survey (HEGIS), "Degrees and Other Formal Awards Conferred" surveys, 1967–68 through 1985–86; and 1986–87 through 2006–07 Integrated Postsecondary Education Data System, "Completions Survey" (IPEDS-C:87–99), and Fall 2000 through Fall 2007. (This table was prepared September 2008.)

Table 307. Degrees in modern foreign languages and literatures conferred by degree-granting institutions, by level of degree and sex of student: Selected years, 1949–50 through 2006–07

Year	Bachelor's degrees Total Number	Total Annual percent change	Males	Females	Master's degrees Total	Males	Females	Doctor's degrees Total	Males	Females
1	2	3	4	5	6	7	8	9	10	11
1949–50	4,477	†	1,746	2,731	919	456	463	168	135	33
1959–60	4,527	†	1,548	2,979	832	392	440	150	100	50
1967–68	17,499	†	4,450	13,049	3,911	1,555	2,356	491	336	155
1969–70	19,457	†	4,921	14,536	4,154	1,476	2,678	590	369	221
1970–71	19,806	1.8	4,994	14,812	4,847	1,668	3,179	854	536	318
1971–72	18,673	-5.7	4,635	14,038	4,692	1,633	3,059	911	575	336
1972–73	18,989	1.7	4,589	14,400	4,422	1,578	2,844	1,092	650	442
1973–74	18,807	-1.0	4,486	14,321	4,105	1,399	2,706	1,035	575	460
1974–75	17,842	-5.1	4,174	13,668	4,004	1,330	2,674	969	504	465
1975–76	15,731	-11.8	3,718	12,013	3,670	1,235	2,435	1,010	514	496
1976–77	14,162	-10.0	3,416	10,746	3,293	1,019	2,274	875	430	445
1977–78	13,037	-7.9	3,127	9,910	2,913	870	2,043	768	351	417
1978–79	11,957	-8.3	2,845	9,112	2,563	771	1,792	765	363	402
1979–80	11,315	-5.4	2,783	8,532	2,376	704	1,672	639	278	361
1980–81	10,464	-7.5	2,542	7,922	2,255	739	1,516	708	328	380
1981–82	10,014	-4.3	2,426	7,588	2,170	671	1,499	646	281	365
1982–83	10,026	0.1	2,560	7,466	1,891	633	1,258	594	254	340
1983–84	9,829	-2.0	2,611	7,218	1,929	602	1,327	565	242	323
1984–85	10,357	5.4	2,719	7,638	1,879	597	1,282	558	236	322
1985–86	10,407	0.5	2,884	7,523	1,870	562	1,308	523	206	317
1986–87	10,740	3.2	2,988	7,752	1,918	586	1,332	545	230	315
1987–88	10,513	-2.1	2,839	7,674	2,028	665	1,363	534	228	306
1988–89	11,376	8.2	3,037	8,339	2,110	654	1,456	512	216	296
1989–90	11,991	5.4	3,185	8,806	2,225	674	1,551	599	239	360
1990–91	12,704	5.9	3,526	9,178	2,282	710	1,572	647	274	373
1991–92	13,300	4.7	3,679	9,621	2,400	738	1,662	706	284	422
1992–93	13,904	4.5	3,848	10,056	2,683	857	1,826	717	287	430
1993–94	13,761	-1.0	3,960	9,801	2,699	830	1,869	747	273	474
1994–95	13,196	-4.1	3,949	9,247	2,578	790	1,788	814	335	479
1995–96	13,337	1.1	3,881	9,456	2,562	792	1,770	746	292	454
1996–97	13,053	-2.1	3,792	9,261	2,470	753	1,717	793	316	477
1997–98	13,618	4.3	3,926	9,692	2,367	715	1,652	819	327	492
1998–99	14,163	4.0	4,084	10,079	2,267	657	1,610	757	294	463
1999–2000	14,186	0.2	3,939	10,247	2,228	669	1,559	804	311	493
2000–01	14,292	0.7	3,966	10,326	2,244	664	1,580	818	294	524
2001–02	14,236	-0.4	3,945	10,291	2,284	648	1,636	780	313	467
2002–03	14,854	4.3	4,202	10,652	2,256	600	1,656	749	282	467
2003–04	15,408	3.7	4,362	11,046	2,307	662	1,645	743	278	465
2004–05	16,008	3.9	4,494	11,514	2,517	736	1,781	762	295	467
2005–06	16,762	4.7	4,814	11,948	2,637	742	1,895	777	296	481
2006–07	17,344	3.5	5,059	12,285	2,577	731	1,846	748	288	460
Percent change										
1996–97 to 2001–02	9.1	†	4.0	11.1	-7.5	-13.9	-4.7	-1.6	-0.9	-2.1
2001–02 to 2006–07	21.8	†	28.2	19.4	12.8	12.8	12.8	-4.1	-8.0	-1.5

†Not applicable.
NOTE: Includes degrees conferred in a single language or a combination of modern foreign languages. Excludes degrees in linguistics, Latin, classics, ancient and Middle/Near Eastern biblical and Semitic languages, ancient/classical Greek, Sanskrit and classical Indian languages, American sign language, linguistics of sign languages, and sign language interpretation and translation.

SOURCE: U.S. Department of Education, National Center for Education Statistics, *Earned Degrees Conferred*, 1949–50 and 1959–60; Higher Education General Information Survey (HEGIS), "Degrees and Other Formal Awards Conferred" surveys, 1967–68 through 1985–86; and 1986–87 through 2006–07 Integrated Postsecondary Education Data System, "Completions Survey" (IPEDS-C:87–99), and Fall 2000 through Fall 2007. (This table was prepared September 2008.)

Table 308. Degrees in French, German, Italian, and Spanish conferred by degree-granting institutions, by level of degree: Selected years, 1949–50 through 2006–07

Year	French			German			Italian			Spanish		
	Bachelor's	Master's	Doctor's	Bachelor's	Master's	Doctor's	Bachelor's	Master's	Doctor's	Bachelor's	Master's	Doctor's
1	2	3	4	5	6	7	8	9	10	11	12	13
1949–50	1,471	299	53	540	121	40	—	—	—	2,122	373	34
1959–60	1,927	316	58	659	126	21	—	—	—	1,610	261	31
1967–68	7,068	1,301	152	2,368	771	117	—	—	—	6,381	1,188	123
1969–70	7,624	1,409	181	2,652	669	118	242	71	14	7,226	1,372	139
1970–71	7,306	1,437	192	2,601	690	144	201	87	10	7,068	1,456	168
1971–72	6,822	1,421	193	2,477	608	167	287	104	19	6,847	1,421	152
1972–73	6,705	1,277	203	2,520	598	176	313	78	27	7,209	1,298	206
1973–74	6,263	1,195	213	2,425	550	149	292	81	19	7,250	1,217	203
1974–75	5,745	1,077	200	2,289	480	147	329	100	13	6,719	1,228	202
1975–76	4,783	914	190	1,983	471	164	342	85	19	5,984	1,080	176
1976–77	4,228	875	177	1,820	394	126	325	89	16	5,359	930	153
1977–78	3,708	692	155	1,647	357	101	301	58	19	4,832	822	113
1978–79	3,558	576	143	1,524	344	106	236	60	14	4,563	720	118
1979–80	3,285	513	128	1,466	309	94	272	49	9	4,331	685	103
1980–81	3,178	460	115	1,286	294	79	205	65	13	3,870	592	131
1981–82	3,054	485	92	1,327	324	76	208	55	14	3,633	568	140
1982–83	2,871	360	106	1,367	281	68	224	45	18	3,349	506	129
1983–84	2,876	418	86	1,292	241	63	206	41	13	3,254	537	102
1984–85	2,991	385	74	1,411	240	58	190	44	9	3,415	505	115
1985–86	3,015	409	86	1,396	249	73	240	42	10	3,385	521	95
1986–87	3,062	421	85	1,366	234	70	219	53	17	3,450	504	104
1987–88	3,082	437	89	1,350	244	71	224	45	7	3,416	553	93
1988–89	3,297	444	83	1,428	263	59	239	45	17	3,748	552	101
1989–90	3,259	478	115	1,437	253	67	247	38	19	4,176	573	108
1990–91	3,355	480	98	1,543	242	58	253	36	21	4,480	609	125
1991–92	3,371	465	112	1,616	273	85	238	55	18	4,768	647	143
1992–93	3,280	513	98	1,572	317	86	274	50	13	5,233	667	145
1993–94	3,094	479	104	1,580	298	61	264	47	24	5,505	691	160
1994–95	2,764	470	118	1,352	278	83	271	69	31	5,602	709	161
1995–96	2,655	446	113	1,290	305	75	232	44	22	5,995	769	151
1996–97	2,468	414	119	1,214	281	80	234	49	18	6,161	677	175
1997–98	2,530	389	104	1,181	209	94	252	60	25	6,595	781	160
1998–99	2,555	357	116	1,246	238	77	260	41	12	6,964	694	152
1999–2000	2,514	343	129	1,125	184	76	237	48	13	7,031	718	175
2000–01	2,371	376	115	1,143	242	73	286	42	11	7,164	716	185
2001–02	2,396	356	89	1,092	208	64	263	46	15	7,243	792	193
2002–03	2,294	348	75	1,097	188	77	307	54	20	7,619	791	190
2003–04	2,362	361	85	1,031	153	30	279	49	31	7,991	833	199
2004–05	2,394	356	80	1,103	180	56	277	70	12	8,304	919	190
2005–06	2,410	395	84	1,106	172	48	321	94	17	8,690	981	192
2006–07	2,462	364	95	1,055	158	56	280	97	20	9,013	982	195
Percent change												
1996–97 to 2001–02	-2.9	-14.0	-25.2	-10.0	-26.0	-20.0	12.4	-6.1	-16.7	17.6	17.0	10.3
2001–02 to 2006–07	2.8	2.2	6.7	-3.4	-24.0	-12.5	6.5	110.9	33.3	24.4	24.0	1.0

—Not available.
SOURCE: U.S. Department of Education, National Center for Education Statistics, *Earned Degrees Conferred*, 1949–50 and 1959–60; Higher Education General Information Survey (HEGIS), "Degrees and Other Formal Awards Conferred" surveys, 1967–68 through 1985–86; and 1986–87 through 2006–07 Integrated Postsecondary Education Data System, "Completions Survey" (IPEDS-C:87–99), and Fall 2000 through Fall 2007. (This table was prepared July 2008.)

Table 309. Degrees in Arabic, Chinese, Korean, and Russian conferred by degree-granting institutions, by level of degree: 1969–70 through 2006–07

Year	Arabic			Chinese			Korean			Russian		
	Bachelor's	Master's	Doctor's	Bachelor's	Master's	Doctor's	Bachelor's	Master's	Doctor's	Bachelor's	Master's	Doctor's
1	2	3	4	5	6	7	8	9	10	11	12	13
1969–70	—	—	—	81	34	0	—	—	—	768	172	24
1970–71	15	6	4	89	22	8	—	—	—	715	110	14
1971–72	10	4	0	103	20	11	—	—	—	658	150	15
1972–73	12	3	1	98	29	13	—	—	—	622	120	27
1973–74	20	5	1	121	37	5	—	—	—	624	100	27
1974–75	13	11	2	141	26	12	—	—	—	598	106	20
1975–76	10	7	2	150	23	6	—	—	—	531	81	13
1976–77	7	15	1	112	32	6	—	—	—	528	66	19
1977–78	8	3	1	116	23	4	—	—	—	442	50	12
1978–79	4	4	5	91	22	12	—	—	—	465	51	9
1979–80	13	2	5	79	33	7	—	—	—	402	60	6
1980–81	6	7	0	73	20	6	—	—	—	409	68	8
1981–82	15	4	4	68	14	10	—	—	—	324	49	7
1982–83	12	4	1	92	15	7	—	—	—	342	33	5
1983–84	6	2	0	115	14	10	—	—	—	340	39	3
1984–85	9	4	0	97	21	3	—	—	—	432	47	6
1985–86	5	4	0	87	23	11	—	—	—	493	33	3
1986–87	8	1	1	110	16	10	—	—	—	502	54	8
1987–88	9	4	0	103	31	9	—	—	—	472	54	8
1988–89	6	2	1	138	27	8	—	—	—	469	55	6
1989–90	4	0	1	144	33	8	—	—	—	549	52	5
1990–91	9	0	1	150	24	9	—	—	—	593	70	6
1991–92	13	0	0	183	36	14	—	—	—	629	68	7
1992–93	8	3	2	129	54	8	—	—	—	612	68	4
1993–94	8	2	0	112	48	18	—	—	—	611	71	3
1994–95	10	1	1	107	63	16	—	—	—	572	66	3
1995–96	8	3	2	136	42	19	—	—	—	494	58	7
1996–97	9	3	0	152	31	15	—	—	—	455	46	9
1997–98	16	2	1	161	21	13	—	—	—	383	49	9
1998–99	13	3	1	178	20	14	—	—	—	394	29	4
1999–2000	6	4	5	183	18	15	—	—	—	040	33	10
2000–01	7	2	3	183	13	7	—	—	—	335	24	7
2001–02	13	2	2	189	16	12	—	—	—	277	34	5
2002–03	13	3	0	190	12	9	5	0	0	271	16	6
2003–04	13	3	1	186	15	5	9	2	1	301	21	3
2004–05	21	5	0	208	21	8	8	0	0	298	18	0
2005–06	26	4	2	241	20	10	17	4	3	279	28	7
2006–07	68	2	0	261	30	2	13	0	0	311	18	4

—Not available.
SOURCE: U.S. Department of Education, National Center for Education Statistics, Higher Education General Information Survey (HEGIS), "Degrees and Other Formal Awards Conferred" surveys, 1969-70 through 1985-86; and 1986-87 through 2006-07 Integrated Postsecondary Education Data System, "Completions Survey" (IPEDS-C:87-99), and Fall 2000 through Fall 2007. (This table was prepared June 2008.)

Table 310. Degrees in the health professions and related sciences conferred by degree-granting institutions, by level of degree and sex of student: 1970–71 through 2006–07

| | Bachelor's degrees | | | | Master's degrees | | | Doctor's degrees | | |
| | Total | | | | | | | | | |
Year	Number	Annual percent change	Males	Females	Total	Males	Females	Total	Males	Females
1	2	3	4	5	6	7	8	9	10	11
1970–71	25,223	†	5,785	19,438	5,330	2,165	3,165	518	437	81
1971–72	28,611	13.4	7,005	21,606	6,811	2,749	4,062	459	376	83
1972–73	33,562	17.3	7,752	25,810	7,978	3,189	4,789	685	519	166
1973–74	41,421	23.4	9,347	32,074	9,232	3,444	5,788	645	507	138
1974–75	49,002	18.3	10,844	38,158	10,277	3,686	6,591	666	481	185
1975–76	53,885	10.0	11,386	42,499	12,164	3,837	8,327	617	444	173
1976–77	57,222	6.2	11,896	45,326	12,627	3,865	8,762	578	402	176
1977–78	59,445	3.9	11,600	47,845	14,027	3,972	10,055	704	454	250
1978–79	62,095	4.5	11,214	50,881	15,110	4,155	10,955	731	463	268
1979–80	63,848	2.8	11,330	52,518	15,374	4,060	11,314	821	467	354
1980–81	63,665	-0.3	10,531	53,134	16,176	4,024	12,152	868	499	369
1981–82	63,660	#	10,110	53,550	16,212	3,743	12,469	956	527	429
1982–83	65,642	3.1	10,247	55,395	16,941	4,138	12,803	1,093	615	478
1983–84	65,305	-0.5	10,068	55,237	17,351	4,124	13,227	1,077	528	549
1984–85	65,331	#	9,741	55,590	17,442	4,046	13,396	1,142	546	596
1985–86	65,309	#	9,629	55,680	18,603	4,355	14,248	1,139	547	592
1986–87	63,963	-2.1	9,137	54,826	18,442	3,818	14,624	1,120	518	602
1987–88	61,614	-3.7	8,955	52,659	18,774	4,004	14,770	1,188	516	672
1988–89	59,850	-2.9	8,878	50,972	19,493	4,197	15,296	1,329	555	774
1989–90	58,983	-1.4	9,075	49,908	20,406	4,486	15,920	1,449	635	814
1990–91	59,875	1.5	9,619	50,256	21,354	4,423	16,931	1,534	649	885
1991–92	62,779	4.9	10,330	52,449	23,671	4,794	18,877	1,432	576	856
1992–93	68,434	9.0	11,605	56,829	26,190	5,249	20,941	1,451	571	880
1993–94	75,890	10.9	13,377	62,513	28,442	5,813	22,629	1,552	593	959
1994–95	81,596	7.5	14,812	66,784	31,770	6,718	25,052	1,653	647	1,006
1995–96	86,087	5.5	15,942	70,145	33,920	7,017	26,903	1,651	655	996
1996–97	87,997	2.2	16,440	71,557	36,162	7,536	28,626	2,179	926	1,253
1997–98	86,843	-1.3	15,700	71,143	39,567	8,644	30,923	1,975	678	1,297
1998–99	85,214	-1.9	15,187	70,027	40,707	9,202	31,505	1,920	721	1,199
1999–2000	80,863	-5.1	13,342	67,521	42,593	9,500	33,093	2,053	720	1,333
2000–01	75,933	-6.1	12,514	63,419	43,623	9,711	33,912	2,242	798	1,444
2001–02	72,887	-4.0	10,869	62,018	43,560	9,588	33,972	2,913	991	1,922
2002–03	71,261	-2.2	10,096	61,165	42,748	9,280	33,468	3,329	1,030	2,299
2003–04	73,934	3.8	10,017	63,917	44,939	9,670	35,269	4,361	1,261	3,100
2004–05	80,685	9.1	10,858	69,827	46,703	9,816	36,887	5,868	1,710	4,158
2005–06	91,973	14.0	12,914	79,059	51,380	10,630	40,750	7,128	1,959	5,169
2006–07	101,810	10.7	14,325	87,485	54,531	10,636	43,895	8,355	2,242	6,113
Percent change										
1996–97 to 2001–02	-17.2	†	-33.9	-13.3	20.5	27.2	18.7	33.7	7.0	53.4
2001–02 to 2006–07	39.7	†	31.8	41.1	25.2	10.9	29.2	186.8	126.2	218.1

†Not applicable.
#Rounds to zero.
NOTE: Excludes degrees awarded in first-professional fields, such as medicine (M.D.) and dentistry (D.D.S. and D.M.D.).

SOURCE: U.S. Department of Education, National Center for Education Statistics, Higher Education General Information Survey (HEGIS), "Degrees and Other Formal Awards Conferred" surveys, 1970–71 through 1985–86; and 1986–87 through 2006–07 Integrated Postsecondary Education Data System, "Completions Survey" (IPEDS-C:87–99), and Fall 2000 through Fall 2007. (This table was prepared September 2008.)

Table 311. Degrees in mathematics and statistics conferred by degree-granting institutions, by level of degree and sex of student: Selected years, 1949–50 through 2006–07

Year	Bachelor's degrees				Master's degrees			Doctor's degrees		
	Total		Males	Females	Total	Males	Females	Total	Males	Females
	Number	Annual percent change								
1	2	3	4	5	6	7	8	9	10	11
1949–50............	6,382	†	4,942	1,440	974	784	190	160	151	9
1959–60............	11,399	†	8,293	3,106	1,757	1,422	335	303	285	18
1967–68............	23,513	†	14,782	8,731	5,527	4,199	1,328	947	895	52
1969–70............	27,442	†	17,177	10,265	5,636	3,966	1,670	1,236	1,140	96
1970–71............	24,801	-9.6	15,369	9,432	5,191	3,673	1,518	1,199	1,106	93
1971–72............	23,713	-4.4	14,454	9,259	5,198	3,655	1,543	1,128	1,039	89
1972–73............	23,067	-2.7	13,796	9,271	5,028	3,525	1,503	1,068	966	102
1973–74............	21,635	-6.2	12,791	8,844	4,834	3,337	1,497	1,031	931	100
1974–75............	18,181	-16.0	10,586	7,595	4,327	2,905	1,422	975	865	110
1975–76............	15,984	-12.1	9,475	6,509	3,857	2,547	1,310	856	762	94
1976–77............	14,196	-11.2	8,303	5,893	3,695	2,396	1,299	823	714	109
1977–78............	12,569	-11.5	7,398	5,171	3,373	2,228	1,145	805	681	124
1978–79............	11,806	-6.1	6,899	4,907	3,036	1,985	1,051	730	608	122
1979–80............	11,378	-3.6	6,562	4,816	2,860	1,828	1,032	724	624	100
1980–81............	11,078	-2.6	6,342	4,736	2,567	1,692	875	728	614	114
1981–82............	11,599	4.7	6,593	5,006	2,727	1,821	906	681	587	94
1982–83............	12,294	6.0	6,888	5,406	2,810	1,838	972	697	581	116
1983–84............	13,087	6.5	7,290	5,797	2,723	1,773	950	695	569	126
1984–85............	15,009	14.7	8,080	6,929	2,859	1,858	1,001	699	590	109
1985–86............	16,122	7.4	8,623	7,499	3,131	2,028	1,103	742	618	124
1986–87............	16,257	0.8	8,673	7,584	3,283	1,995	1,288	723	598	125
1987–88............	15,712	-3.4	8,408	7,304	3,413	2,052	1,361	750	625	125
1988–89............	15,017	-4.4	8,081	6,936	3,405	2,061	1,344	866	700	166
1989–90............	14,276	-4.9	7,674	6,602	3,624	2,172	1,452	917	754	163
1990–91............	14,393	0.8	7,580	6,813	3,549	2,096	1,453	978	790	188
1991–92............	14,468	0.5	7,668	6,800	3,558	2,151	1,407	1,048	825	223
1992–93............	14,384	-0.6	7,566	6,818	3,644	2,151	1,493	1,138	867	271
1993–94............	14,171	1.5	7,594	6,577	3,682	2,237	1,445	1,125	880	245
1994–95............	13,494	-4.8	7,154	6,340	3,820	2,289	1,531	1,181	919	262
1995–96............	12,713	-5.8	6,847	5,866	3,651	2,178	1,473	1,158	919	239
1996–97............	12,401	-2.5	6,649	5,752	3,504	2,055	1,449	1,134	861	273
1997–98............	11,795	-4.9	6,247	5,548	3,409	1,985	1,424	1,215	903	312
1998–99............	11,966	1.4	6,181	5,785	3,286	1,901	1,385	1,090	803	287
1999–2000............	11,418	-4.6	5,955	5,463	3,208	1,749	1,459	1,075	803	272
2000–01............	11,171	-2.2	5,791	5,380	3,209	1,857	1,352	997	715	282
2001–02............	11,950	7.0	6,333	5,617	3,350	1,913	1,437	923	658	265
2002–03............	12,505	4.6	6,784	5,721	3,620	1,996	1,624	1,007	734	273
2003–04............	13,327	6.6	7,203	6,124	4,191	2,302	1,889	1,060	762	298
2004–05............	14,351	7.7	7,937	6,414	4,477	2,525	1,952	1,176	841	335
2005–06............	14,770	2.9	8,115	6,655	4,730	2,712	2,018	1,293	911	382
2006–07............	14,954	1.2	8,360	6,594	4,884	2,859	2,025	1,351	949	402
Percent change										
1996–97 to 2001–02.......	-3.6	†	-4.8	-2.3	-4.4	-6.9	-0.8	-18.6	-23.6	-2.9
2001–02 to 2006–07.......	25.1	†	32.0	17.4	45.8	49.5	40.9	46.4	44.2	51.7

†Not applicable.
SOURCE: U.S. Department of Education, National Center for Education Statistics, *Earned Degrees Conferred*, 1949–50 and 1959–60; Higher Education General Information Survey (HEGIS), "Degrees and Other Formal Awards Conferred" surveys, 1967–68 through 1985–86; and 1986–87 through 2006–07 Integrated Postsecondary Education Data System, "Completions Survey" (IPEDS-C:87–99), and Fall 2000 through Fall 2007. (This table was prepared September 2008.)

Table 312. Degrees in the physical sciences and science technologies conferred by degree-granting institutions, by level of degree and sex of student: Selected years, 1959–60 through 2006–07

| | Bachelor's degrees | | | | Master's degrees | | | Doctor's degrees | | |
| | Total | | | | | | | | | |
Year	Number	Annual percent change	Males	Females	Total	Males	Females	Total	Males	Females
1	2	3	4	5	6	7	8	9	10	11
1959–60	16,007	†	14,013	1,994	3,376	3,049	327	1,838	1,776	62
1967–68	19,380	†	16,739	2,641	5,499	4,869	630	3,593	3,405	188
1969–70	21,439	†	18,522	2,917	5,908	5,069	839	4,271	4,038	233
1970–71	21,410	-0.1	18,457	2,953	6,336	5,495	841	4,324	4,082	242
1971–72	20,743	-3.1	17,661	3,082	6,268	5,390	878	4,075	3,805	270
1972–73	20,692	-0.2	17,622	3,070	6,230	5,388	842	3,961	3,698	263
1973–74	21,170	2.3	17,669	3,501	6,019	5,157	862	3,558	3,312	246
1974–75	20,770	-1.9	16,986	3,784	5,782	4,949	833	3,577	3,284	293
1975–76	21,458	3.3	17,349	4,109	5,428	4,622	806	3,388	3,097	291
1976–77	22,482	4.8	17,985	4,497	5,281	4,411	870	3,295	2,981	314
1977–78	22,975	2.2	18,083	4,892	5,507	4,583	924	3,073	2,763	310
1978–79	23,197	1.0	17,976	5,221	5,418	4,438	980	3,061	2,717	344
1979–80	23,407	0.9	17,861	5,546	5,167	4,210	957	3,044	2,669	375
1980–81	23,936	2.3	18,052	5,884	5,246	4,172	1,074	3,105	2,733	372
1981–82	24,045	0.5	17,861	6,184	5,446	4,274	1,172	3,246	2,804	442
1982–83	23,374	-2.8	16,988	6,386	5,250	4,131	1,119	3,214	2,767	447
1983–84	23,645	1.2	17,112	6,533	5,541	4,249	1,292	3,269	2,789	480
1984–85	23,694	0.2	17,065	6,629	5,752	4,425	1,327	3,349	2,808	541
1985–86	21,711	-8.4	15,750	5,961	5,860	4,443	1,417	3,521	2,946	575
1986–87	20,060	-7.6	14,365	5,695	5,586	4,193	1,393	3,629	3,004	625
1987–88	17,797	-11.3	12,385	5,412	5,696	4,300	1,396	3,758	3,085	673
1988–89	17,179	-3.5	12,071	5,108	5,691	4,180	1,511	3,795	3,046	749
1989–90	16,056	-6.5	11,026	5,030	5,410	3,996	1,414	4,116	3,328	788
1990–91	16,334	1.7	11,170	5,164	5,281	3,823	1,458	4,248	3,417	831
1991–92	16,948	3.8	11,425	5,523	5,340	3,888	1,452	4,344	3,402	942
1992–93	17,534	3.5	11,819	5,715	5,346	3,803	1,543	4,348	3,404	944
1993–94	18,392	4.9	12,218	6,174	5,648	4,010	1,638	4,595	3,606	989
1994–95	19,161	4.2	12,490	6,671	5,716	3,996	1,720	4,421	3,386	1,035
1995–96	19,627	2.4	12,566	7,061	5,807	3,943	1,864	4,512	3,479	1,033
1996–97	19,496	-0.7	12,213	7,283	5,526	3,732	1,794	4,417	3,411	1,006
1997–98	19,362	-0.7	11,924	7,438	5,328	3,417	1,911	4,520	3,387	1,133
1998–99	18,285	-5.6	11,003	7,282	5,124	3,366	1,758	4,142	3,144	998
1999–2000	18,331	0.3	10,946	7,385	4,810	3,114	1,696	3,963	2,959	1,004
2000–01	17,919	-2.2	10,553	7,366	5,049	3,212	1,837	3,911	2,875	1,036
2001–02	17,799	-0.7	10,292	7,507	5,012	3,135	1,877	3,760	2,719	1,041
2002–03	17,950	0.8	10,562	7,388	5,109	3,211	1,898	3,858	2,792	1,066
2003–04	17,983	0.2	10,476	7,507	5,570	3,364	2,206	3,815	2,753	1,062
2004–05	18,905	5.1	10,934	7,971	5,678	3,457	2,221	4,114	2,966	1,148
2005–06	20,318	7.5	11,831	8,487	5,922	3,568	2,354	4,489	3,143	1,346
2006–07	21,073	3.7	12,455	8,618	5,839	3,556	2,283	4,846	3,317	1,529
Percent change										
1996–97 to 2001–02	-8.7	†	-15.7	3.1	-9.3	-16.0	4.6	-14.9	-20.3	3.5
2001–02 to 2006–08	18.4	†	21.0	14.8	16.5	13.4	21.6	28.9	22.0	46.9

†Not applicable.
SOURCE: U.S. Department of Education, National Center for Education Statistics, *Earned Degrees Conferred*, 1959–60; Higher Education General Information Survey (HEGIS), "Degrees and Other Formal Awards Conferred" surveys, 1967–68 through 1985–86; and 1986–87 through 2006–07 Integrated Postsecondary Education Data System, "Completions Survey" (IPEDS-C:87–99), and Fall 2000 through Fall 2007. (This table was prepared June 2008.)

Table 313. Degrees in chemistry, geology and earth science, and physics conferred by degree-granting institutions, by level of degree: 1970–71 through 2006–07

Year	Chemistry			Geology and earth science[1]			Physics[2]		
	Bachelor's	Master's	Doctor's	Bachelor's	Master's	Doctor's	Bachelor's	Master's	Doctor's
1	2	3	4	5	6	7	8	9	10
1970–71	11,061	2,244	2,093	3,312	1,074	408	5,071	2,188	1,482
1971–72	10,588	2,229	1,943	3,766	1,233	433	4,634	2,033	1,344
1972–73	10,124	2,198	1,827	4,117	1,296	430	4,259	1,747	1,328
1973–74	10,430	2,082	1,755	4,526	1,479	416	3,952	1,655	1,115
1974–75	10,541	1,961	1,773	4,566	1,340	433	3,706	1,574	1,080
1975–76	11,015	1,745	1,578	4,677	1,384	445	3,544	1,700	997
1976–77	11,200	1,717	1,522	5,280	1,446	480	3,420	1,319	945
1977–78	11,304	1,832	1,461	5,648	1,633	419	3,330	1,294	873
1978–79	11,499	1,724	1,475	5,753	1,616	414	3,337	1,319	918
1979–80	11,229	1,671	1,500	5,785	1,623	440	3,396	1,192	830
1980–81	12,682	1,862	1,649	6,332	1,702	404	3,441	1,294	866
1981–82	11,058	1,683	1,682	6,650	1,865	452	3,503	1,318	878
1982–83	10,789	1,582	1,691	6,981	1,784	406	3,793	1,369	873
1983–84	10,698	1,632	1,707	7,524	1,747	408	3,907	1,532	953
1984–85	10,472	1,675	1,735	7,194	1,927	401	4,097	1,523	951
1985–86	10,110	1,712	1,878	5,760	2,036	395	4,180	1,501	1,010
1986–87	9,660	1,695	1,932	3,943	1,835	399	4,318	1,543	1,074
1987–88	9,043	1,671	1,944	3,204	1,722	462	4,100	1,675	1,093
1988–89	8,618	1,742	1,974	2,847	1,609	492	4,352	1,736	1,112
1989–90	8,122	1,643	2,135	2,372	1,399	562	4,155	1,831	1,192
1990–91	8,311	1,637	2,196	2,367	1,336	600	4,236	1,725	1,209
1991–92	8,629	1,746	2,233	2,784	1,245	549	4,098	1,834	1,337
1992–93	8,903	1,822	2,216	3,123	1,195	626	4,063	1,777	1,277
1993–94	9,417	1,968	2,298	3,456	1,221	577	4,001	1,945	1,465
1994–95	9,700	2,062	2,211	4,032	1,280	539	3,823	1,817	1,424
1995–96	10,395	2,214	2,228	4,019	1,288	555	3,679	1,678	1,462
1996–97	10,609	2,203	2,202	4,023	1,258	564	3,376	1,496	1,410
1997–98	10,528	2,108	2,291	3,866	1,227	588	3,441	1,371	1,393
1998–99	10,068	2,002	2,143	3,544	1,200	533	3,213	1,309	1,252
1999–2000	9,989	1,857	2,028	3,516	1,186	492	3,342	1,232	1,208
2000–01	9,466	1,952	2,056	3,495	1,220	472	3,418	1,365	1,169
2001–02	9,084	1,823	1,984	3,449	1,174	494	3,627	1,344	1,096
2002–03	9,013	1,777	2,092	3,381	1,323	466	3,900	1,438	1,089
2003–04	9,016	2,009	2,033	3,312	1,389	463	4,118	1,625	1,119
2004–05	9,664	1,879	2,148	3,276	1,420	476	4,182	1,785	1,254
2005–06	10,606	2,044	2,403	3,322	1,476	505	4,541	1,846	1,341
2006–07	10,994	2,097	2,514	3,319	1,437	640	4,843	1,777	1,442
Percent change									
1996–97 to 2001–02	-14.4	-17.2	-9.9	-14.3	-6.7	-12.4	7.4	-10.2	-22.3
2001–02 to 2006–08	21.0	15.0	26.7	-3.8	22.4	29.6	33.5	32.2	31.6

[1]Includes geology/earth science, general; geochemistry; geophysics; paleontology; hydrology; oceanography; and geological and earth sciences, other.
[2]Includes physics, general; atomic/molecular physics; elementary particle physics; nuclear physics; optics; acoustics; theoretical physics; and physics, other.

SOURCE: U.S. Department of Education, National Center for Education Statistics, Higher Education General Information Survey (HEGIS), "Degrees and Other Formal Awards Conferred" surveys, 1970–71 through 1985–86; and 1986–87 through 2006–07 Integrated Postsecondary Education Data System, "Completions Survey" (IPEDS-C:87–99), and Fall 2000 through Fall 2007. (This table was prepared June 2008.)

Table 314. Degrees in psychology conferred by degree-granting institutions, by level of degree and sex of student: Selected years, 1949–50 through 2006–07

Year	Bachelor's degrees Total Number	Bachelor's degrees Total Annual percent change	Males	Females	Master's degrees Total	Master's degrees Males	Master's degrees Females	Doctor's degrees Total	Doctor's degrees Males	Doctor's degrees Females
1	2	3	4	5	6	7	8	9	10	11
1949–50	9,569	†	6,055	3,514	1,316	948	368	283	241	42
1959–60	8,061	†	4,773	3,288	1,406	981	425	641	544	97
1967–68	23,819	†	13,792	10,027	3,479	2,321	1,158	1,268	982	286
1969–70	33,679	†	19,077	14,602	5,158	2,975	2,183	1,962	1,505	457
1970–71	38,187	13.4	21,227	16,960	5,717	3,395	2,322	2,144	1,629	515
1971–72	43,433	13.7	23,352	20,081	6,764	3,934	2,830	2,277	1,694	583
1972–73	47,940	10.4	25,117	22,823	7,619	4,325	3,294	2,550	1,797	753
1973–74	52,139	8.8	25,868	26,271	8,796	4,983	3,813	2,872	1,987	885
1974–75	51,245	-1.7	24,284	26,961	9,394	5,035	4,359	2,913	1,979	934
1975–76	50,278	-1.9	22,898	27,380	10,167	5,136	5,031	3,157	2,115	1,042
1976–77	47,861	-4.8	20,627	27,234	10,859	5,293	5,566	3,386	2,127	1,259
1977–78	44,879	-6.2	18,422	26,457	10,282	4,670	5,612	3,164	1,974	1,190
1978–79	42,697	-4.9	16,540	26,157	10,132	4,405	5,727	3,228	1,895	1,333
1979–80	42,093	-1.4	15,440	26,653	9,938	4,096	5,842	3,395	1,921	1,474
1980–81	41,068	-2.4	14,332	26,736	10,223	4,066	6,157	3,576	2,002	1,574
1981–82	41,212	0.4	13,645	27,567	9,947	3,823	6,124	3,461	1,856	1,605
1982–83	40,460	-1.8	13,131	27,329	9,981	3,647	6,334	3,602	1,838	1,764
1983–84	39,955	-1.2	12,812	27,143	9,525	3,400	6,125	3,535	1,774	1,761
1984–85	39,900	-0.1	12,706	27,194	9,891	3,452	6,439	3,447	1,739	1,708
1985–86	40,628	1.8	12,605	28,023	9,845	3,347	6,498	3,593	1,724	1,869
1986–87	43,152	6.2	13,395	29,757	11,000	3,516	7,484	4,062	1,801	2,261
1987–88	45,371	5.1	13,579	31,792	10,488	3,256	7,232	3,973	1,783	2,190
1988–89	49,083	8.2	14,265	34,818	11,329	3,465	7,864	4,143	1,773	2,370
1989–90	53,952	9.9	15,336	38,616	10,730	3,377	7,353	3,811	1,566	2,245
1990–91	58,655	8.7	16,067	42,588	11,349	3,329	8,020	3,932	1,520	2,412
1991–92	63,683	8.6	17,062	46,621	11,659	3,335	8,324	3,814	1,490	2,324
1992–93	66,931	5.1	17,942	48,989	12,518	3,380	9,138	4,100	1,570	2,530
1993–94	69,419	3.7	18,668	50,751	13,723	3,763	9,960	4,021	1,497	2,524
1994–95	72,233	4.1	19,570	52,663	15,378	4,210	11,168	4,252	1,562	2,690
1995–96	73,416	1.6	19,836	53,580	15,152	4,090	11,062	4,141	1,380	2,761
1996–97	74,308	1.2	19,408	54,900	15,769	4,155	11,614	4,507	1,495	3,012
1997–98	74,107	-0.3	18,976	55,131	15,142	3,978	11,164	4,541	1,470	3,071
1998–99	73,636	-0.6	18,304	55,332	15,688	3,990	11,698	4,695	1,510	3,185
1999–2000	74,194	0.8	17,451	56,743	15,740	3,821	11,919	4,731	1,529	3,202
2000–01	73,645	-0.7	16,585	57,060	16,539	3,892	12,647	5,091	1,598	3,493
2001–02	76,775	4.3	17,284	59,491	16,357	3,814	12,543	4,759	1,503	3,256
2002–03	78,650	2.4	17,514	61,136	17,161	3,839	13,322	4,835	1,483	3,352
2003–04	82,098	4.4	18,193	63,905	17,898	3,789	14,109	4,827	1,496	3,331
2004–05	85,614	4.3	19,000	66,614	18,830	3,900	14,930	5,106	1,466	3,640
2005–06	88,134	2.9	19,865	68,269	19,770	4,079	15,691	4,921	1,347	3,574
2006–07	90,039	2.2	20,343	69,696	21,037	4,265	16,772	5,153	1,382	3,771
Percent change										
1996–97 to 2001–02	3.3	†	-10.9	8.4	3.7	-8.2	8.0	5.6	0.5	8.1
2001–02 to 2006–08	17.3	†	17.7	17.2	28.6	11.8	33.7	8.3	-8.1	15.8

†Not applicable.
SOURCE: U.S. Department of Education, National Center for Education Statistics, *Earned Degrees Conferred*, 1949–50 and 1959–60; Higher Education General Information Survey (HEGIS), "Degrees and Other Formal Awards Conferred" surveys, 1967–68 through 1985–86; and 1986–87 through 2006–07 Integrated Postsecondary Education Data System, "Completions Survey" (IPEDS-C:87–99), and Fall 2000 through Fall 2007. (This table was prepared June 2008.)

Table 315. Degrees in public administration and social services conferred by degree-granting institutions, by level of degree and sex of student: 1970–71 through 2006–07

	Bachelor's degrees				Master's degrees			Doctor's degrees		
	Total									
Year	Number	Annual percent change	Males	Females	Total	Males	Females	Total	Males	Females
1	2	3	4	5	6	7	8	9	10	11
1970–71	5,466	†	1,726	3,740	7,785	3,893	3,892	174	132	42
1971–72	7,508	37.4	2,588	4,920	8,756	4,537	4,219	193	150	43
1972–73	10,690	42.4	3,998	6,692	10,068	5,271	4,797	198	160	38
1973–74	11,966	11.9	4,266	7,700	11,415	6,028	5,387	201	154	47
1974–75	13,661	14.2	4,630	9,031	13,617	7,200	6,417	257	192	65
1975–76	15,440	13.0	5,706	9,734	15,209	7,969	7,240	292	192	100
1976–77	16,136	4.5	5,544	10,592	17,026	8,810	8,216	292	197	95
1977–78	16,607	2.9	5,096	11,511	17,337	8,513	8,824	357	237	120
1978–79	17,328	4.3	4,938	12,390	17,306	8,051	9,255	315	215	100
1979–80	16,644	-3.9	4,451	12,193	17,560	7,866	9,694	342	216	126
1980–81	16,707	0.4	4,248	12,459	17,803	7,460	10,343	362	212	150
1981–82	16,495	-1.3	4,176	12,319	17,416	6,975	10,441	372	205	167
1982–83	14,414	-12.6	3,343	11,071	16,046	5,961	10,085	347	184	163
1983–84	12,570	-12.8	2,998	9,572	15,060	5,634	9,426	420	230	190
1984–85	11,754	-6.5	2,829	8,925	15,575	5,573	10,002	431	213	218
1985–86	11,887	1.1	2,966	8,921	15,692	5,594	10,098	382	171	211
1986–87	12,328	3.7	2,993	9,335	16,432	5,673	10,759	398	216	182
1987–88	12,385	0.5	2,923	9,462	16,424	5,631	10,793	470	238	232
1988–89	13,162	6.3	3,214	9,948	17,020	5,615	11,405	428	210	218
1989–90	13,908	5.7	3,334	10,574	17,399	5,634	11,765	508	235	273
1990–91	14,350	3.2	3,215	11,135	17,905	5,679	12,226	430	190	240
1991–92	15,987	11.4	3,479	12,508	19,243	5,769	13,474	432	204	228
1992–93	16,775	4.9	3,801	12,974	20,634	6,105	14,529	459	215	244
1993–94	17,815	6.2	3,919	13,896	21,833	6,406	15,427	519	238	281
1994–95	18,586	4.3	3,935	14,651	23,501	6,870	16,631	556	274	282
1995–96	19,849	6.8	4,205	15,644	24,229	6,927	17,302	499	220	279
1996–97	20,649	4.0	4,177	16,472	24,781	6,957	17,824	518	243	275
1997–98	20,408	-1.2	3,881	16,527	25,144	7,025	18,119	499	223	276
1998–99	20,287	-0.6	3,791	16,496	24,925	6,556	18,369	532	239	293
1999–2000	20,185	-0.5	3,816	16,369	25,594	6,808	18,786	537	227	310
2000–01	19,447	-3.7	3,670	15,777	25,268	6,544	18,724	574	263	311
2001–02	19,392	-0.3	3,706	15,686	25,448	6,505	18,943	571	250	321
2002–03	19,900	2.6	3,726	16,174	25,903	6,391	19,512	599	265	334
2003–04	20,552	3.3	3,793	16,759	28,250	7,001	21,249	649	275	374
2004–05	21,769	5.9	4,209	17,560	29,552	7,370	22,182	673	272	401
2005–06	21,986	1.0	4,126	17,860	30,510	7,572	22,938	704	285	419
2006–07	23,147	5.3	4,354	18,793	31,131	7,758	23,373	726	253	473
Percent change										
1996–97 to 2001–02	-6.1	†	-11.3	-4.8	2.7	-6.5	6.3	10.2	2.9	16.7
2001–02 to 2006–07	19.4	†	17.5	19.8	22.3	19.3	23.4	27.1	1.2	47.4

†Not applicable.
SOURCE: U.S. Department of Education, National Center for Education Statistics, Higher Education General Information Survey (HEGIS), "Degrees and Other Formal Awards Conferred" surveys, 1970–71 through 1985–86; and 1986–87 through 2006–07 Integrated Postsecondary Education Data System, "Completions Survey" (IPEDS-C:87–99), and Fall 2000 through Fall 2007. (This table was prepared June 2008.)

Table 316. Degrees in the social sciences and history conferred by degree-granting institutions, by level of degree and sex of student: 1970–71 through 2006–07

Year	Bachelor's degrees				Master's degrees			Doctor's degrees		
	Total		Males	Females	Total	Males	Females	Total	Males	Females
	Number	Annual percent change								
1	2	3	4	5	6	7	8	9	10	11
1970–71............	155,324	†	98,173	57,151	16,539	11,833	4,706	3,660	3,153	507
1971–72............	158,060	1.8	100,895	57,165	17,445	12,540	4,905	4,081	3,483	598
1972–73............	155,970	-1.3	99,735	56,235	17,477	12,605	4,872	4,234	3,573	661
1973–74............	150,320	-3.6	95,650	54,670	17,293	12,321	4,972	4,124	3,383	741
1974–75............	135,190	-10.1	84,826	50,364	16,977	11,875	5,102	4,212	3,334	878
1975–76............	126,396	-6.5	78,691	47,705	15,953	10,918	5,035	4,157	3,262	895
1976–77............	117,040	-7.4	71,128	45,912	15,533	10,413	5,120	3,802	2,957	845
1977–78............	112,952	-3.5	67,217	45,735	14,718	9,845	4,873	3,594	2,722	872
1978–79............	108,059	-4.3	62,852	45,207	12,963	8,395	4,568	3,371	2,501	870
1979–80............	103,662	-4.1	58,511	45,151	12,176	7,794	4,382	3,230	2,357	873
1980–81............	100,513	-3.0	56,131	44,382	11,945	7,457	4,488	3,122	2,274	848
1981–82............	99,705	-0.8	55,196	44,509	12,002	7,468	4,534	3,061	2,237	824
1982–83............	95,228	-4.5	52,771	42,457	11,205	6,974	4,231	2,931	2,042	889
1983–84............	93,323	-2.0	52,154	41,169	10,577	6,551	4,026	2,911	2,030	881
1984–85............	91,570	-1.9	51,226	40,344	10,503	6,475	4,028	2,851	1,933	918
1985–86............	93,840	2.5	52,724	41,116	10,564	6,419	4,145	2,955	1,970	985
1986–87............	96,342	2.7	53,949	42,393	10,506	6,373	4,133	2,916	2,026	890
1987–88............	100,460	4.3	56,377	44,083	10,412	6,310	4,102	2,781	1,849	932
1988–89............	108,151	7.7	60,121	48,030	11,023	6,599	4,424	2,885	1,949	936
1989–90............	118,083	9.2	65,887	52,196	11,634	6,898	4,736	3,010	2,019	991
1990–91............	125,107	5.9	68,701	56,406	12,233	7,016	5,217	3,012	1,956	1,056
1991–92............	133,974	7.1	73,001	60,973	12,702	7,237	5,465	3,218	2,126	1,092
1992–93............	135,703	1.3	73,589	62,114	13,471	7,671	5,800	3,460	2,203	1,257
1993–94............	133,680	-1.5	72,006	61,674	14,561	8,152	6,409	3,627	2,317	1,310
1994–95............	128,154	-4.1	68,139	60,015	14,845	8,207	6,638	3,725	2,319	1,406
1995–96............	126,479	-1.3	65,872	60,607	15,012	8,093	6,919	3,760	2,339	1,421
1996–97............	124,891	-1.3	64,115	60,776	14,787	7,830	6,957	3,989	2,479	1,510
1997–98............	125,040	0.1	63,537	61,503	14,938	7,960	6,978	4,127	2,445	1,682
1998–99............	124,658	-0.3	61,736	62,922	14,431	7,456	6,975	3,855	2,270	1,585
1999–2000............	127,101	2.0	62,062	65,039	14,066	7,024	7,042	4,095	2,407	1,688
2000–01............	128,036	0.7	61,749	66,287	13,791	6,816	6,975	3,930	2,302	1,628
2001–02............	132,874	3.8	64,170	68,704	14,112	6,941	7,171	3,902	2,219	1,683
2002–03............	143,256	7.8	69,517	73,739	14,630	7,202	7,428	3,850	2,196	1,654
2003–04............	150,357	5.0	73,834	76,523	16,110	7,810	8,300	3,811	2,188	1,623
2004–05............	156,892	4.3	77,702	79,190	16,952	8,256	8,696	3,819	2,184	1,635
2005–06............	161,485	2.9	80,799	80,686	17,369	8,415	8,954	3,914	2,218	1,696
2006–07............	164,183	1.7	82,417	81,766	17,665	8,577	9,088	3,844	2,110	1,734
Percent change										
1996–97 to 2001–02.......	6.4	†	0.1	13.0	-4.6	-11.4	3.1	-2.2	-10.5	11.5
2001–02 to 2006–07.......	23.6	†	28.4	19.0	25.2	23.6	26.7	-1.5	-4.9	3.0

†Not applicable.
SOURCE: U.S. Department of Education, National Center for Education Statistics, Higher Education General Information Survey (HEGIS), "Degrees and Other Formal Awards Con- ferred" surveys, 1970–71 through 1985–86; and 1986–87 through 2006–07 Integrated Postsecondary Education Data System, "Completions Survey" (IPEDS-C:87–99), and Fall 2000 through Fall 2007. (This table was prepared June 2008.)

Table 317. Degrees in economics, history, political science and government, and sociology conferred by degree-granting institutions, by level of degree: Selected years, 1949–50 through 2006–07

Year	Economics			History			Political science and government			Sociology		
	Bachelor's	Master's	Doctor's	Bachelor's	Master's	Doctor's	Bachelor's	Master's	Doctor's	Bachelor's	Master's	Doctor's
1	2	3	4	5	6	7	8	9	10	11	12	13
1949–50	14,568	921	200	13,542	1,801	275	6,336	710	127	7,870	552	98
1951–52	8,593	695	239	10,187	1,445	317	4,911	525	147	6,648	517	141
1953–54	6,719	609	245	9,363	1,220	355	5,314	534	153	5,692	440	184
1955–56	6,555	581	232	10,510	1,114	259	5,633	509	203	5,878	402	170
1957–58	7,457	669	239	12,840	1,397	297	6,116	665	170	6,568	397	150
1959–60	7,453	708	237	14,737	1,794	342	6,596	722	201	7,147	440	161
1961–62	8,366	853	268	17,340	2,163	343	8,326	839	214	8,120	578	173
1963–64	10,583	1,104	385	23,668	2,705	507	12,126	1,163	263	10,943	646	198
1965–66	11,555	1,522	458	28,612	3,883	599	15,242	1,429	336	15,038	981	244
1967–68	15,193	1,916	600	35,291	4,845	688	20,387	1,937	457	21,710	1,193	367
1969–70	17,197	1,988	794	43,386	5,049	1,038	25,713	2,105	525	30,436	1,813	534
1970–71	15,758	1,995	721	44,663	5,157	991	27,482	2,318	700	33,263	1,808	574
1971–72	15,231	2,224	794	43,695	5,217	1,133	28,135	2,451	758	35,216	1,044	636
1972–73	14,770	2,225	845	40,943	5,030	1,140	30,100	2,398	747	35,436	1,923	583
1973–74	14,285	2,141	788	37,049	4,533	1,114	30,744	2,448	766	35,491	2,196	632
1974–75	14,046	2,127	815	31,470	4,226	1,117	29,126	2,333	680	31,488	2,112	693
1975–76	14,741	2,087	763	28,400	3,658	1,014	28,302	2,191	723	27,634	2,009	729
1976–77	15,296	2,158	758	25,433	3,393	921	26,411	2,222	641	24,713	1,830	714
1977–78	15,661	1,995	706	23,004	3,033	813	26,069	2,069	636	22,750	1,611	599
1978–79	16,409	1,955	712	21,019	2,536	756	25,628	2,037	563	20,285	1,415	612
1979–80	17,863	1,821	677	19,301	2,367	712	25,457	1,938	535	18,881	1,341	583
1980–81	18,753	1,911	727	18,301	2,237	643	24,977	1,875	484	17,272	1,240	610
1981–82	19,876	1,964	677	17,146	2,210	636	25,658	1,954	513	16,042	1,145	558
1982–83	20,517	1,972	734	16,467	2,041	575	25,791	1,829	435	14,105	1,112	522
1983–84	20,719	1,891	729	16,643	1,940	561	25,719	1,769	457	13,145	1,008	520
1984–85	20,711	1,992	749	16,049	1,921	468	25,834	1,500	441	11,968	1,022	480
1985–86	21,602	1,937	789	16,415	1,061	497	26,439	1,704	439	12,271	965	504
1986–87	22,378	1,855	750	16,997	2,021	534	26,817	1,618	435	12,239	950	451
1987–88	22,911	1,847	770	18,207	2,093	517	27,207	1,579	391	13,024	984	452
1988–89	23,454	1,886	827	20,159	2,121	487	30,450	1,598	452	14,435	1,135	451
1989–90	23,923	1,950	806	22,476	2,369	570	33,560	1,580	480	16,035	1,198	432
1990–91	23,488	1,951	802	24,541	2,591	606	35,737	1,772	468	17,550	1,260	465
1991–92	23,423	2,106	866	26,966	2,754	644	37,805	1,908	535	19,568	1,347	501
1992–93	21,321	2,292	879	27,774	2,952	690	37,931	1,943	529	20,896	1,521	536
1993–94	19,496	2,521	869	27,503	3,009	752	36,097	2,147	616	22,368	1,639	530
1994–95	17,673	2,400	910	26,598	3,091	816	33,013	2,019	637	22,886	1,748	546
1995–96	16,674	2,533	916	26,005	2,898	805	30,775	2,024	634	24,071	1,772	527
1996–97	16,539	2,433	968	25,214	2,901	873	28,969	1,909	686	24,672	1,731	591
1997–98	17,074	2,435	928	25,726	2,895	937	28,044	1,957	705	24,806	1,737	596
1998–99	17,611	2,323	810	24,794	2,633	921	27,418	1,681	696	24,933	1,943	515
1999–2000	18,441	2,168	851	25,247	2,573	984	27,635	1,627	693	25,598	1,996	595
2000–01	19,437	2,139	851	25,090	2,365	931	27,792	1,596	688	25,268	1,845	546
2001–02	20,927	2,330	826	26,001	2,420	924	29,354	1,641	625	25,202	1,928	534
2002–03	23,007	2,582	836	27,757	2,521	861	33,205	1,664	671	26,095	1,897	591
2003–04	24,069	2,824	849	29,808	2,522	855	35,581	1,869	618	26,939	2,009	558
2004–05	24,217	3,092	973	31,398	2,893	819	38,107	1,983	636	28,473	1,499	527
2005–06	23,807	2,941	930	33,153	2,992	852	39,409	2,054	649	28,467	1,547	562
2006–07	23,916	2,962	941	34,446	3,144	807	39,899	2,102	614	28,960	1,545	569
Percent change												
1996–97 to 2001–02	26.5	-4.2	-14.7	3.1	-16.6	5.8	1.3	-14.0	-8.9	2.1	11.4	-9.6
2001–02 to 2006–07	14.3	27.1	13.9	32.5	29.9	-12.7	35.9	28.1	-1.8	14.9	-19.9	6.6

SOURCE: U.S. Department of Education, National Center for Education Statistics, *Earned Degrees Conferred*, 1949–50 through 1963–64; Higher Education General Information Survey (HEGIS), "Degrees and Other Formal Awards Conferred" surveys, 1965–66 through 1985–86; and 1986–87 through 2006–07 Integrated Postsecondary Education Data System, "Completions Survey" (IPEDS-C:87–99), and Fall 2000 through Fall 2007. (This table was prepared September 2008.)

Table 318. Degrees in visual and performing arts conferred by degree-granting institutions, by level of degree and sex of student: 1970–71 through 2006–07

Year	Bachelor's degrees				Master's degrees			Doctor's degrees		
	Total		Males	Females	Total	Males	Females	Total	Males	Females
	Number	Annual percent change								
1	2	3	4	5	6	7	8	9	10	11
1970–71	30,394	†	12,256	18,138	6,675	3,510	3,165	621	483	138
1971–72	33,831	11.3	13,580	20,251	7,537	4,049	3,488	572	428	144
1972–73	36,017	6.5	14,267	21,750	7,254	4,005	3,249	616	449	167
1973–74	39,730	10.3	15,821	23,909	8,001	4,325	3,676	585	440	145
1974–75	40,782	2.6	15,532	25,250	8,362	4,448	3,914	649	446	203
1975–76	42,138	3.3	16,491	25,647	8,817	4,507	4,310	620	447	173
1976–77	41,793	-0.8	16,166	25,627	8,636	4,211	4,425	662	447	215
1977–78	40,951	2.0	15,572	25,379	9,036	4,327	4,709	708	448	260
1978–79	40,969	#	15,380	25,589	8,524	3,933	4,591	700	454	246
1979–80	40,892	-0.2	15,065	25,827	8,708	4,067	4,641	655	413	242
1980–81	40,479	-1.0	14,798	25,681	8,629	4,056	4,573	654	396	258
1981–82	40,422	-0.1	14,819	25,603	8,746	3,866	4,880	670	380	290
1982–83	39,804	-1.5	14,695	25,109	8,763	4,013	4,750	692	404	288
1983–84	40,131	0.8	15,089	25,042	8,526	3,897	4,629	730	406	324
1984–85	38,285	-4.6	14,518	23,767	8,720	3,896	4,824	696	407	289
1985–86	37,241	-2.7	14,236	23,005	8,420	3,775	4,645	722	396	326
1986–87	36,873	-1.0	13,980	22,893	8,508	3,756	4,752	793	447	346
1987–88	37,150	0.8	14,225	22,925	7,939	3,442	4,497	727	424	303
1988–89	38,420	3.4	14,698	23,722	8,267	3,611	4,656	753	446	307
1989–90	39,934	3.9	15,189	24,745	8,481	3,706	4,775	849	472	377
1990–91	42,186	5.6	15,761	26,425	8,657	3,830	4,827	838	466	372
1991–92	46,522	10.3	17,616	28,906	9,353	4,078	5,275	906	504	402
1992–93	47,761	2.7	18,610	29,151	9,440	4,099	5,341	882	478	404
1993–94	49,053	2.7	19,538	29,515	9,925	4,229	5,696	1,054	585	469
1994–95	48,690	-0.7	19,781	28,909	10,277	4,374	5,903	1,080	545	535
1995–96	49,296	1.2	20,126	29,170	10,280	4,361	5,919	1,067	524	543
1996–97	50,083	1.6	20,729	29,354	10,627	4,470	6,157	1,060	525	535
1997–98	52,077	4.0	21,483	30,594	11,145	4,596	6,549	1,163	566	597
1998–99	54,404	4.5	22,281	32,123	10,753	4,543	6,210	1,130	574	556
1999–2000	58,791	8.1	24,003	34,788	10,918	4,672	6,246	1,127	537	590
2000–01	61,148	4.0	24,967	36,181	11,404	4,788	6,616	1,167	568	599
2001–02	66,773	9.2	27,130	39,643	11,595	4,912	6,683	1,114	490	624
2002–03	71,482	7.1	27,922	43,560	11,982	4,975	7,007	1,293	613	680
2003–04	77,181	8.0	30,037	47,144	12,906	5,531	7,375	1,282	572	710
2004–05	80,955	4.9	31,355	49,600	13,183	5,646	7,537	1,278	594	684
2005–06	83,297	2.9	32,117	51,180	13,530	5,801	7,729	1,383	639	744
2006–07	85,186	2.3	32,729	52,457	13,767	5,910	7,857	1,364	625	739
Percent change										
1996–97 to 2001–02	33.3	†	30.9	35.1	9.1	9.9	8.5	5.1	-6.7	16.6
2001–02 to 2006–07	27.6	†	20.6	32.3	18.7	20.3	17.6	22.4	27.6	18.4

†Not applicable.
#Rounds to zero.
SOURCE: U.S. Department of Education, National Center for Education Statistics, Higher Education General Information Survey (HEGIS), "Degrees and Other Formal Awards Con-ferred" surveys, 1970–71 through 1985–86; and 1986–87 through 2006–07 Integrated Postsecondary Education Data System, "Completions Survey" (IPEDS-C:87–99), and Fall 2000 through Fall 2007. (This table was prepared September 2008.)

Table 319. Statistical profile of persons receiving doctor's degrees, by field of study and selected characteristics: 2004–05 and 2005–06

Selected characteristic	All fields, 2004–05	All fields	Business and management	Education	Engineering	Humanities	Life sciences	Physical sciences[1] Total	Mathe-matics	Social sciences and psychology	Other fields
1	2	3	4	5	6	7	8	9	10	11	12
Number of doctor's degrees conferred	43,354	45,596	1,312	6,123	7,191	5,576	9,683	7,461	1,327	6,873	1,377
Sex (percent)[2]											
Male	54.8	54.9	61.2	34.8	79.8	49.4	48.4	72.3	70.4	42.6	43.4
Female	45.2	45.1	38.8	65.2	20.2	50.6	51.6	27.7	29.6	57.4	56.6
Racial/ethnicity (percent)[3]											
White	80.4	80.3	82.6	77.4	76.4	84.0	80.7	85.4	84.0	78.5	77.3
Black	6.5	6.3	8.1	12.3	4.2	4.1	4.6	2.2	3.0	6.7	9.8
Hispanic	5.0	5.2	3.6	5.7	4.7	5.3	4.4	3.6	4.3	6.8	6.2
Asian	5.8	5.9	4.1	2.5	12.4	3.9	8.1	7.0	6.5	5.1	4.0
American Indian/Alaska Native	0.5	0.4	0.9	0.7	0.1	0.6	0.3	0.2	#	0.5	0.5
Other[4]	1.8	1.9	0.7	1.3	2.2	2.2	1.9	1.6	2.2	2.4	2.3
Citizenship (percent)											
United States	60.7	59.0	45.2	81.2	30.4	72.9	62.1	44.4	41.4	70.9	55.6
Non-U.S., permanent resident	3.7	4.0	5.3	2.2	4.2	4.8	4.4	4.6	5.0	3.4	4.4
Non-U.S., temporary visa holder	29.6	31.0	40.3	9.9	59.4	15.9	28.0	45.9	50.3	19.8	32.0
Unknown	6.0	6.0	9.1	6.7	6.0	6.4	5.5	5.0	3.3	5.9	8.1
Median age at doctorate (years)	33.0	32.7	35.2	41.7	30.8	35.0	31.4	30.3	30.0	32.9	36.2
Percent with bachelor's degree in same field as doctorate	52.7	53.8	34.9	29.8	75.7	53.9	48.9	65.1	69.9	55.0	33.2
Median time lapse (years) to doctorate											
Since bachelor's degree completion	9.9	9.5	11.8	16.7	8.1	11.5	8.6	7.7	7.3	9.6	12.5
Since starting graduate school	8.2	7.9	9.2	12.7	6.9	9.7	7.0	6.7	6.7	7.9	9.9
Postdoctoral plans (percent)[5]											
Definite postdoctoral study[6]	24.7	23.7	3.8	3.5	19.2	7.4	45.1	37.3	33.4	21.3	4.3
Fellowship	—	13.0	1.8	1.3	6.8	5.3	27.0	17.7	20.4	14.9	2.1
Research associateship	—	8.6	1.2	1.3	11.3	0.0	12.5	10.7	12.3	4.2	1.5
Traineeship	—	0.3	‡	0.2	0.2	‡	0.7	0.3	0.5	0.2	‡
Intern, clinical residency	—	0.7	‡	0.1	0.3	‡	2.1	0.1	‡	1.4	‡
Other	—	1.2	0.4	0.6	0.7	0.9	3.0	0.5	‡	0.7	0.5
Definite postdoctoral employment[7]	44.9	46.3	78.2	69.3	45.8	57.6	24.8	34.5	41.8	51.6	71.3
Educational institution[8]	—	27.7	60.6	58.0	8.1	48.5	12.3	13.4	24.9	32.3	53.6
Industry, business	—	11.2	10.6	2.5	31.6	2.3	6.0	16.9	12.3	7.1	7.7
Government	—	3.0	2.6	2.8	3.0	1.3	3.2	2.0	2.2	5.4	3.5
Nonprofit organization	—	2.0	1.3	2.9	1.1	2.5	1.4	0.6	0.5	3.9	3.1
Other and unknown	—	2.4	3.2	3.1	2.0	3.0	1.8	1.6	1.9	3.0	3.4
Seeking employment or study	27.9	27.0	15.6	23.3	32.7	31.5	27.0	26.0	22.8	24.1	21.0
Other/unknown	2.5	3.0	2.5	3.9	2.3	3.5	3.1	2.1	2.0	2.9	3.4
Primary work activity after doctorate (percent)[9]											
Research and development	34.0	36.7	42.4	9.9	74.9	12.7	41.9	61.5	45.3	35.4	31.5
Teaching	39.0	38.5	42.9	40.4	8.3	74.7	33.3	27.5	46.8	38.0	48.0
Administration	15.1	13.4	10.2	39.8	5.1	5.6	9.2	3.4	‡	7.8	12.2
Professional services	10.2	9.5	3.8	9.1	8.7	4.3	13.0	6.1	5.9	17.2	7.2
Other	1.6	1.9	0.7	0.8	3.0	2.7	2.5	1.4	‡	1.7	1.1
Region of employment after doctorate (percent)[10]											
New England	6.0	5.9	5.9	3.2	6.0	7.2	6.6	7.3	6.1	6.9	5.0
Middle Atlantic	13.8	13.9	12.5	12.7	10.9	15.1	12.4	16.7	19.2	16.0	13.7
East North Central	13.0	12.8	12.8	15.7	11.2	13.8	12.0	10.7	14.2	12.0	12.9
West North Central	6.3	6.8	7.2	10.3	3.4	8.0	7.6	4.6	5.7	5.5	7.2
South Atlantic	17.3	17.3	18.9	19.4	12.5	17.4	18.8	14.8	19.0	19.6	18.4
East South Central	4.3	4.4	4.7	6.0	2.7	4.9	4.5	2.3	3.6	4.3	5.7
West South Central	8.3	8.2	9.1	9.8	8.6	7.4	8.6	6.5	5.4	7.0	9.4
Mountain	5.6	5.7	3.8	6.7	7.4	5.5	5.1	4.8	4.0	4.8	4.4
Pacific and insular	15.1	15.5	11.1	11.3	26.1	12.2	12.9	23.8	14.2	12.0	10.7
Foreign	10.4	9.4	13.7	4.9	11.0	8.5	11.4	8.4	8.6	11.7	12.5
Region unknown	#	#	0.1	#	#	#	#	#	#	0.1	0.1

—Not available.
#Rounds to zero.
‡Reporting standards not met.
[1]Includes mathematics, computer science, physics and astronomy, chemistry, and earth, atmospheric, and marine sciences.
[2]Distribution by sex based on respondents of known sex only.
[3]Distribution by race/ethnicity based on U.S. citizens of known race only.
[4]Includes Native Hawaiians and other Pacific Islanders and those of more than one race.
[5]Percentages are based on only those doctorate recipients who responded to questions about postdoctoral plans.
[6]Percentages are based on only those doctorate recipients who indicated definite postdoctoral plans for study and who indicated the type of study.
[7]Percentages are based on only those doctorate recipients who indicated definite postdoctoral plans for employment and who indicated the sector of employment.
[8]Includes 2-year, 4-year, and foreign colleges and universities, medical schools, and elementary/secondary schools.

[9]Percentages are based on only those doctorate recipients who indicated definite postdoctoral plans for employment and who indicated their primary work activity.
[10]Percentages are based on only those doctorate recipients who indicated definite postdoctoral plans for employment.
NOTE: The above classification of degrees by field differs somewhat from that in most publications of the National Center for Education Statistics (NCES). One major difference is that history is included under humanities rather than social sciences. Includes Ph.D., Ed.D., and comparable degrees at the doctoral level. Excludes first-professional degrees, such as M.D., D.D.S., and D.V.M. The number of degrees also differs slightly from that reported in the NCES Integrated Postsecondary Education Data System (IPEDS). The above tabulation excludes some nonresearch doctoral degrees such as doctor's degrees in theology. Race categories exclude persons of Hispanic ethnicity. Detail may not sum to totals because of rounding.
SOURCE: *Doctorate Recipients From United States Universities, 2006*, Survey of Earned Doctorates, National Science Foundation, National Institutes of Health, U.S. Department of Education, National Endowment for the Humanities, U.S. Department of Agriculture, and the National Aeronautics and Space Administration. (This table was prepared July 2008.)

Table 320. Degrees conferred by degree-granting institutions, by control, level of degree, and state or jurisdiction: 2006–07

State or jurisdiction	Public					Private				
	Associate's degrees	Bachelor's degrees	Master's degrees	First-professional degrees[1]	Doctor's degrees (Ph.D., Ed.D., etc.)[2]	Associate's degrees	Bachelor's degrees	Master's degrees	First-professional degrees[1]	Doctor's degrees (Ph.D., Ed.D., etc.)[2]
1	2	3	4	5	6	7	8	9	10	11
United States	566,535	975,513	291,971	36,855	36,230	161,579	548,579	312,636	53,209	24,386
Alabama	7,443	18,499	9,095	672	685	822	3,482	662	454	43
Alaska	976	1,419	643	0	33	63	93	73	0	0
Arizona	11,994	18,570	6,039	552	942	13,786	18,035	21,792	354	156
Arkansas	5,534	9,188	2,718	503	215	187	2,291	539	9	3
California	81,968	112,661	26,529	2,396	3,628	13,829	40,651	30,268	6,503	3,496
Colorado	5,638	20,448	5,230	644	795	3,361	8,417	6,442	442	236
Connecticut	3,940	9,370	3,098	382	361	1,129	8,920	5,307	574	467
Delaware	1,243	3,821	911	0	226	153	1,292	1,381	291	57
District of Columbia	147	306	55	65	0	936	9,955	9,555	2,790	628
Florida	47,284	47,879	13,558	1,830	1,825	15,796	25,995	12,015	2,701	1,513
Georgia	10,471	26,860	8,281	925	1,119	2,627	10,558	4,056	1,253	506
Hawaii	2,393	3,586	1,116	171	149	861	2,109	806	0	37
Idaho	1,903	5,149	1,382	171	161	1,042	2,847	227	0	0
Illinois	25,759	33,074	11,542	1,197	1,318	9,421	36,872	26,286	3,656	1,710
Indiana	9,787	25,247	7,560	1,156	1,188	4,323	13,286	4,272	651	284
Iowa	10,553	10,747	2,529	647	680	3,815	11,641	2,015	1,133	198
Kansas	7,177	13,624	4,062	705	503	668	3,441	1,768	132	0
Kentucky	7,425	14,741	5,546	848	427	2,551	4,338	1,776	245	151
Louisiana	3,851	17,400	4,655	832	446	1,123	4,271	1,680	790	155
Maine	1,954	4,334	888	87	50	509	2,566	726	114	9
Maryland	9,874	19,740	7,593	960	951	547	5,954	6,576	180	419
Massachusetts	8,494	14,401	4,762	88	478	2,197	33,484	23,040	4,415	2,847
Michigan	20,217	40,478	15,767	1,698	1,869	4,974	12,802	5,323	1,652	91
Minnesota	12,341	18,420	4,680	848	819	3,476	11,198	11,707	1,071	1,149
Mississippi	8,239	10,032	2,959	415	437	384	2,020	990	175	0
Missouri	8,834	18,382	5,016	771	487	5,160	17,373	12,352	2,031	1,086
Montana	1,434	4,634	1,106	136	133	164	583	53	0	0
Nebraska	4,105	7,440	2,133	350	360	813	4,892	1,418	520	90
Nevada	2,593	5,673	1,501	276	157	1,102	717	558	123	0
New Hampshire	1,801	4,379	1,115	0	59	1,545	3,927	1,902	198	139
New Jersey	14,805	23,830	6,941	1,190	666	1,043	8,897	5,795	584	579
New Mexico	4,595	6,462	2,517	293	278	250	1,377	588	0	0
New York	41,151	48,819	17,452	1,242	1,397	16,624	65,262	46,913	7,330	3,264
North Carolina	17,767	28,312	9,207	859	1,129	1,923	12,951	3,714	1,224	363
North Dakota	1,912	4,763	946	208	182	398	780	371	0	0
Ohio	18,076	37,666	12,407	2,183	1,684	6,099	21,359	8,002	1,333	511
Oklahoma	8,478	15,394	4,113	755	399	1,323	3,498	1,273	394	63
Oregon	6,896	12,921	3,957	481	426	1,234	4,985	2,097	710	128
Pennsylvania	14,385	40,467	10,136	1,687	1,557	11,932	40,575	18,740	3,160	1,958
Rhode Island	1,145	3,191	816	85	86	2,677	6,791	1,414	268	193
South Carolina	6,792	14,345	3,796	665	464	999	5,139	1,316	178	19
South Dakota	1,735	3,520	883	175	89	533	1,445	308	8	2
Tennessee	7,151	16,936	5,087	712	625	3,441	10,336	3,944	738	415
Texas	39,498	75,624	25,101	3,239	3,052	5,203	20,123	7,701	2,086	567
Utah	8,460	12,103	2,554	277	430	1,375	8,819	1,911	149	80
Vermont	860	2,702	492	97	57	415	2,399	1,459	185	3
Virginia	11,898	29,312	10,436	1,354	1,260	5,048	10,432	3,397	1,272	383
Washington	20,110	21,442	4,711	718	838	813	7,718	4,067	624	96
West Virginia	2,728	8,508	2,511	542	173	1,014	2,597	791	0	55
Wisconsin	10,634	23,564	5,433	650	876	1,153	9,082	3,253	509	237
Wyoming	2,087	1,687	406	118	61	718	4	17	0	0
U.S. Service Academies	0	3,443	0	0	0	†	†	†	†	†
Other jurisdictions	1,997	7,785	898	373	83	3,040	9,827	4,964	529	188
American Samoa	217	0	0	0	0	0	0	0	0	0
Federated States of Micronesia	187	0	0	0	0	0	0	0	0	0
Guam	64	266	60	0	0	1	12	0	0	0
Marshall Islands	85	0	0	0	0	0	0	0	0	0
Northern Marianas	103	32	0	0	0	0	0	0	0	0
Palau	31	0	0	0	0	0	0	0	0	0
Puerto Rico	1,229	7,294	790	373	83	3,039	9,815	4,964	529	188
U.S. Virgin Islands	81	193	48	0	0	0	0	0	0	0

†Not applicable.
[1]Includes degrees that require at least 6 years of college work for completion (including at least 2 years of preprofessional training). See Definitions for details.
[2]Excludes first-professional, such as M.D., D.D.S., and law degrees.

SOURCE: U.S. Department of Education, National Center for Education Statistics, 2006–07 Integrated Postsecondary Education Data System (IPEDS), Fall 2007. (This table was prepared July 2008.)

Table 321. Bachelor's and master's degrees conferred by degree-granting institutions, by field of study and state or jurisdiction: 2006–07

State or jurisdiction	Total degrees		Humanities[1]		Social and behavioral sciences[2]		Natural sciences[3]		Computer sciences and engineering[4]		Education		Business/management		Other fields[5]	
	Bachelor's degrees	Master's degrees	Bachelor's degrees	Master's degrees	Bachelor's degrees	Master's degrees	Bachelor's degrees	Master's degrees	Bachelor's degrees	Master's degrees	Bachelor's degrees	Master's degrees	Bachelor's degrees	Master's degrees	Bachelor's degrees	Master's degrees
1	2	3	4	5	6	7	8	9	10	11	12	13	14	15	16	17
United States	1,524,092	604,607	267,489	44,209	254,222	38,702	111,178	19,470	124,242	48,394	105,641	176,572	327,531	150,211	333,789	127,049
Alabama	21,981	9,757	2,380	303	2,511	652	1,672	205	1,904	667	2,330	3,348	5,618	2,355	5,566	2,227
Alaska	1,512	716	220	62	263	51	140	43	109	61	97	275	263	84	420	140
Arizona	36,605	27,831	3,977	546	3,011	457	1,584	270	4,139	532	2,670	9,859	12,651	12,074	8,573	4,093
Arkansas	11,479	3,257	1,580	244	1,370	137	801	120	720	142	1,420	1,243	2,437	637	3,151	734
California	153,312	56,797	35,518	5,753	33,324	5,399	13,353	1,854	12,227	6,249	2,753	14,512	29,017	11,821	27,110	11,209
Colorado	28,865	11,672	5,178	588	4,584	954	2,231	370	3,165	1,184	165	2,468	6,692	4,112	6,400	1,996
Connecticut	18,290	8,405	4,214	683	4,466	479	1,265	421	915	629	662	2,422	3,123	1,968	3,645	1,803
Delaware	5,113	2,292	770	126	897	140	291	59	341	149	527	873	1,241	588	1,046	357
District of Columbia	10,261	9,610	1,343	870	2,938	1,272	479	374	970	750	135	947	2,933	2,736	1,463	2,661
Florida	73,874	25,573	9,403	1,108	11,415	1,476	3,795	686	5,841	1,903	5,329	5,911	19,079	7,742	19,012	6,747
Georgia	37,418	12,337	5,833	790	5,896	756	2,770	430	3,325	1,242	3,743	3,333	8,725	3,294	7,126	2,492
Hawaii	5,695	1,922	888	158	1,126	210	370	82	229	95	368	484	1,437	436	1,277	457
Idaho	7,996	1,609	1,104	114	968	48	535	83	597	145	1,087	556	1,491	215	2,214	448
Illinois	69,946	37,828	12,405	2,456	9,622	2,331	4,482	1,023	6,091	3,070	6,403	10,829	16,229	11,230	14,714	6,889
Indiana	38,533	11,832	6,243	993	4,753	557	2,323	497	4,164	744	4,163	2,844	8,055	3,797	8,822	2,400
Iowa	22,388	4,544	3,194	435	3,003	164	1,509	215	1,705	373	1,960	1,365	5,339	968	5,678	1,024
Kansas	17,065	5,830	2,988	432	2,206	291	1,154	161	1,294	448	1,618	1,940	3,568	1,297	4,237	1,261
Kentucky	19,079	7,322	2,779	478	2,754	507	1,271	220	1,127	493	2,143	3,084	3,702	862	5,303	1,678
Louisiana	21,671	6,335	3,888	576	2,950	266	1,777	360	1,710	541	1,739	1,431	4,801	1,317	4,866	1,844
Maine	6,900	1,614	1,257	135	1,347	22	620	64	417	43	834	695	802	147	1,623	508
Maryland	25,694	14,169	4,222	955	5,467	1,175	2,132	720	2,737	1,967	1,370	3,150	4,622	3,725	5,144	2,477
Massachusetts	47,885	27,802	9,779	2,235	10,743	1,884	3,754	930	3,851	2,346	1,470	7,931	8,934	6,151	9,354	6,325
Michigan	53,280	21,090	7,035	951	7,065	800	3,639	698	5,651	2,394	5,286	6,156	12,180	5,940	12,424	4,151
Minnesota	29,618	16,387	5,514	742	4,778	884	2,681	235	1,956	810	2,605	7,993	6,001	2,806	6,083	2,917
Mississippi	12,052	3,949	1,257	140	1,468	148	1,018	296	752	212	1,786	1,638	2,710	729	3,061	786
Missouri	35,755	17,368	4,952	841	4,911	1,145	2,234	378	2,858	859	3,251	4,427	9,615	6,678	7,934	3,040
Montana	5,217	1,159	758	112	848	83	474	96	525	68	649	317	805	102	1,158	381
Nebraska	12,332	3,551	1,228	174	1,425	210	834	159	739	189	1,431	1,243	3,397	857	3,228	719
Nevada	6,390	2,059	953	115	857	73	373	79	412	143	573	859	1,674	526	1,533	264
New Hampshire	8,306	3,017	1,461	154	1,859	159	620	57	520	144	436	833	1,913	1,086	1,594	584
New Jersey	32,727	12,736	6,645	994	7,250	742	2,695	422	2,424	1,518	2,147	3,653	5,774	2,906	5,792	2,501
New Mexico	7,839	3,105	1,370	268	857	221	530	143	786	261	928	1,039	1,712	496	1,656	677
New York	114,081	64,365	23,463	6,431	22,697	4,275	7,652	1,752	8,420	4,277	7,510	22,575	22,634	11,195	21,705	13,860
North Carolina	41,263	12,921	5,550	964	7,515	546	3,581	512	3,237	1,098	3,474	2,989	7,893	3,576	10,013	3,236
North Dakota	5,543	1,317	517	23	440	39	332	45	497	107	631	245	1,052	379	2,074	479
Ohio	59,025	20,409	8,841	1,903	8,551	1,251	3,860	769	4,707	1,375	6,505	6,163	12,369	4,656	14,192	4,292
Oklahoma	18,892	5,386	2,723	439	2,242	312	1,268	179	1,427	457	2,065	1,276	4,416	1,680	4,751	1,043
Oregon	17,906	6,054	4,153	575	3,538	378	1,387	221	1,306	352	755	2,533	3,083	858	3,684	1,137
Pennsylvania	81,042	28,876	13,909	2,052	12,671	1,694	6,063	942	7,375	2,458	6,597	8,123	16,369	6,393	18,058	7,214
Rhode Island	9,982	2,230	1,487	206	1,487	198	595	127	636	118	674	493	2,819	642	2,284	446
South Carolina	19,484	5,112	2,837	250	3,309	226	1,854	203	1,158	288	1,755	1,988	4,727	926	3,864	1,231
South Dakota	4,965	1,191	380	46	646	113	398	46	559	134	495	351	999	267	1,488	234
Tennessee	27,272	9,031	6,086	621	3,952	498	1,712	226	1,658	513	1,581	3,343	5,643	1,840	6,640	1,990
Texas	95,747	32,802	20,691	2,726	13,273	2,140	7,601	1,278	6,514	3,342	2,121	7,057	22,309	9,211	23,238	7,048
Utah	20,922	4,465	3,086	239	3,420	202	1,465	192	2,072	487	2,337	915	3,932	1,423	4,610	1,007

See notes at end of table.

Table 321. Bachelor's and master's degrees conferred by degree-granting institutions, by field of study and state or jurisdiction: 2006-07—Continued

State or jurisdiction	Total degrees		Humanities[1]		Social and behavioral sciences[2]		Natural sciences[3]		Computer sciences and engineering[4]		Education		Business/management		Other fields[5]	
	Bachelor's degrees	Master's degrees	Bachelor's degrees	Master's degrees	Bachelor's degrees	Master's degrees	Bachelor's degrees	Master's degrees	Bachelor's degrees	Master's degrees	Bachelor's degrees	Master's degrees	Bachelor's degrees	Master's degrees	Bachelor's degrees	Master's degrees
1	2	3	4	5	6	7	8	9	10	11	12	13	14	15	16	17
Vermont	5,101	1,951	1,263	468	1,213	355	365	29	261	204	287	458	685	135	1,027	302
Virginia	39,744	13,833	8,505	1,419	8,692	1,415	3,195	453	3,248	1,461	937	4,247	7,540	2,520	7,627	2,318
Washington	29,160	8,778	6,543	617	5,711	625	2,449	291	2,142	519	1,502	2,354	5,146	2,001	5,667	2,371
West Virginia	11,105	3,302	2,047	156	1,227	116	684	88	816	215	1,098	978	2,009	702	3,224	1,047
Wisconsin	32,646	8,686	4,605	497	5,056	585	2,972	333	2,499	576	2,988	2,763	6,845	2,055	7,681	1,877
Wyoming	1,691	423	93	46	236	41	147	34	183	42	251	63	267	70	514	127
U.S. Service Academies	3,443	0	374	0	984	0	294	0	1,296	0	0	0	254	0	241	0
Other jurisdictions	17,612	5,862	948	132	1,287	365	1,232	131	1,787	255	3,727	2,170	4,944	1,821	3,687	988
Guam	278	60	27	3	26	0	7	2	16	0	61	30	49	8	92	17
Northern Marianas	32	0	0	0	0	0	0	0	0	0	32	0	0	0	0	0
Puerto Rico	17,109	5,754	911	129	1,230	365	1,208	129	1,764	255	3,613	2,114	4,805	1,801	3,578	961
U.S. Virgin Islands	193	48	10	0	31	0	17	0	7	0	21	26	90	12	17	10

[1]Includes degrees in area, ethnic, cultural, and gender studies; English language and literature/letters; foreign languages, literatures, and linguistics; liberal arts and sciences, general studies and humanities; multi/interdisciplinary studies; philosophy and religious studies; theology and religious vocations; and visual and performing arts.

[2]Includes psychology; social sciences; and history.

[3]Includes biological and biomedical sciences; physical sciences; science technologies/technicians; and mathematics and statistics.

[4]Includes computer and information sciences and support services; engineering; engineering technologies/technicians; mechanic and repair technologies/technicians; and construction trades.

[5]Includes agriculture, agricultural operations, and related sciences; natural resources and conservation; architecture and related services; communication, journalism, and related programs; communications technologies/technicians and support services; health professions and related clinical sciences; family and consumer sciences/human sciences; legal professions and studies; library science; military technologies; parks, recreation, leisure, and fitness studies; security and protective services; public administration and social service professions; transportation and materials moving; and not classified by field of study.

SOURCE: U.S. Department of Education, National Center for Education Statistics, 2006–07 Integrated Postsecondary Education Data System (IPEDS), Fall 2007. (This table was prepared July 2008.)

Table 322. Degrees conferred by degree-granting institutions, by level of degree and state or jurisdiction: 2005–06 and 2006–07

State or jurisdiction	2005–06					2006–07				
	Associate's degrees	Bachelor's degrees	Master's degrees	First-professional degrees[1]	Doctor's degrees (Ph.D., Ed.D., etc.)[2]	Associate's degrees	Bachelor's degrees	Master's degrees	First-professional degrees[1]	Doctor's degrees (Ph.D., Ed.D., etc.)[2]
1	2	3	4	5	6	7	8	9	10	11
United States	713,066	1,485,242	594,065	87,655	56,067	728,114	1,524,092	604,607	90,064	60,616
Alabama	8,895	21,995	10,295	1,120	599	8,265	21,981	9,757	1,126	728
Alaska	1,045	1,573	582	0	21	1,039	1,512	716	0	33
Arizona	16,732	32,708	24,777	816	967	25,780	36,605	27,831	906	1,098
Arkansas	5,462	11,340	3,097	526	225	5,721	11,479	3,257	512	218
California	92,737	151,021	56,029	8,721	6,675	95,797	153,312	56,797	8,899	7,124
Colorado	9,645	27,671	11,705	1,078	983	8,999	28,865	11,672	1,086	1,031
Connecticut	4,993	17,786	8,599	1,054	735	5,069	18,290	8,405	956	828
Delaware	1,328	5,410	2,114	320	271	1,396	5,113	2,292	291	283
District of Columbia	1,105	10,556	9,267	2,724	635	1,083	10,261	9,610	2,855	628
Florida	63,489	69,899	24,041	3,992	2,930	63,080	73,874	25,573	4,531	3,338
Georgia	12,990	36,332	12,490	2,086	1,436	13,098	37,418	12,337	2,178	1,625
Hawaii	3,204	5,813	1,991	165	178	3,254	5,695	1,922	171	186
Idaho	3,065	7,781	1,660	152	172	2,945	7,996	1,609	171	161
Illinois	36,303	68,016	37,502	4,648	2,853	35,180	69,946	37,828	4,853	3,028
Indiana	14,836	38,093	11,345	1,685	1,421	14,110	38,533	11,832	1,807	1,472
Iowa	13,837	21,435	4,430	1,732	804	14,368	22,388	4,544	1,780	878
Kansas	7,850	16,677	5,852	762	486	7,845	17,065	5,830	837	503
Kentucky	9,578	18,646	6,896	1,089	515	9,976	19,079	7,322	1,093	578
Louisiana	4,429	19,936	6,476	1,646	521	4,974	21,671	6,335	1,622	601
Maine	2,416	6,544	1,655	214	39	2,463	6,900	1,614	201	59
Maryland	10,131	25,693	13,438	1,122	1,364	10,421	25,694	14,169	1,140	1,370
Massachusetts	11,139	47,024	27,874	4,321	3,001	10,691	47,885	27,802	4,503	3,325
Michigan	24,373	51,756	21,986	3,257	1,811	25,191	53,280	21,090	3,350	1,960
Minnesota	15,125	28,911	15,188	1,767	1,590	15,817	29,618	16,387	1,919	1,968
Mississippi	8,480	11,803	3,834	597	374	8,623	12,052	3,949	590	437
Missouri	13,947	35,231	17,083	2,709	1,462	13,994	35,755	17,368	2,802	1,573
Montana	1,776	5,118	1,103	136	112	1,598	5,217	1,150	130	133
Nebraska	4,909	12,150	3,953	878	414	4,918	12,332	3,551	870	450
Nevada	3,702	6,595	2,152	265	157	3,695	6,390	2,059	399	157
New Hampshire	3,237	8,030	3,068	206	175	3,346	8,306	3,017	198	198
New Jersey	15,338	32,251	12,607	1,696	1,203	15,848	32,727	12,736	1,774	1,245
New Mexico	4,911	7,491	3,347	250	279	4,845	7,839	3,105	293	278
New York	57,524	111,766	63,687	8,639	4,522	57,775	114,081	64,365	8,572	4,661
North Carolina	19,420	39,969	12,347	1,904	1,422	19,690	41,263	12,921	2,083	1,492
North Dakota	2,138	5,487	1,167	206	151	2,310	5,543	1,317	208	182
Ohio	24,205	58,522	20,680	3,520	2,090	24,175	59,025	20,409	3,516	2,195
Oklahoma	9,204	18,909	5,389	1,200	428	9,801	18,892	5,386	1,149	462
Oregon	8,322	17,631	5,936	1,196	577	8,130	17,906	6,054	1,191	554
Pennsylvania	26,282	79,791	27,593	4,792	3,342	26,317	81,042	28,876	4,847	3,515
Rhode Island	3,831	9,686	2,146	354	301	3,822	9,982	2,230	353	279
South Carolina	7,885	19,313	5,076	850	441	7,791	19,484	5,112	843	483
South Dakota	2,315	4,850	1,117	210	76	2,268	4,965	1,191	183	91
Tennessee	10,176	26,330	9,047	1,432	922	10,592	27,272	9,031	1,450	1,040
Texas	43,785	92,027	32,606	5,362	3,203	44,701	95,747	32,802	5,325	3,619
Utah	9,805	20,677	4,640	433	436	9,835	20,922	4,465	426	510
Vermont	1,380	4,981	1,782	272	64	1,275	5,101	1,951	282	60
Virginia	15,987	38,775	13,414	2,490	1,571	16,946	39,744	13,833	2,626	1,643
Washington	21,735	28,570	8,931	1,322	891	20,923	29,160	8,778	1,342	934
West Virginia	3,297	10,033	3,030	479	202	3,742	11,105	3,302	542	228
Wisconsin	11,695	31,434	8,604	1,144	961	11,787	32,646	8,686	1,159	1,113
Wyoming	3,073	1,792	437	116	59	2,805	1,691	423	118	61
U.S. Service Academies	0	3,414	0	0	0	0	3,443	0	0	0
Other jurisdictions	5,116	17,680	5,300	872	242	5,037	17,612	5,862	902	271
American Samoa	213	0	0	0	0	217	0	0	0	0
Federated States of Micronesia	147	0	0	0	0	187	0	0	0	0
Guam	75	327	69	0	0	65	278	60	0	0
Marshall Islands	155	0	0	0	0	85	0	0	0	0
Northern Marianas	108	13	0	0	0	103	32	0	0	0
Palau	39	0	0	0	0	31	0	0	0	0
Puerto Rico	4,303	17,129	5,180	872	242	4,268	17,109	5,754	902	271
U.S. Virgin Islands	76	211	51	0	0	81	193	48	0	0

[1]Includes degrees that require at least 6 years of college work for completion (including at least 2 years of preprofessional training). See Definitions for details.
[2]Excludes first-professional, such as M.D., D.D.S., and law degrees.

SOURCE: U.S. Department of Education, National Center for Education Statistics, 2005–06 and 2006–07 Integrated Postsecondary Education Data System (IPEDS), Fall 2006 and Fall 2007. (This table was prepared July 2008.)

Table 323. Doctor's degrees conferred by the 60 institutions conferring the most doctor's degrees: 1997–98 through 2006–07

Institution	Rank order[1]	Total, 1997–98 to 2006–07	1997–98	1998–99	1999–2000	2000–01	2001–02	2002–03	2003–04	2004–05	2005–06	2006–07
1	2	3	4	5	6	7	8	9	10	11	12	13
United States, all institutions	†	487,693	46,010	44,077	44,808	44,904	44,160	46,042	48,378	52,631	56,067	60,616
Total, 60 institutions conferring most doctorates	†	250,849	25,315	23,709	23,907	23,635	22,811	23,519	24,694	25,979	27,849	29,431
University of California, Berkeley	1	7,812	756	720	756	759	805	772	775	803	763	903
University of Texas at Austin	2	7,291	836	754	659	733	639	674	702	719	796	779
University of Wisconsin, Madison	3	6,859	757	687	729	663	650	656	628	666	648	775
University of Michigan, Ann Arbor	4	6,700	690	650	629	568	610	616	660	725	763	789
Nova Southeastern University	5	6,637	540	537	587	519	555	749	705	777	757	911
University of Minnesota, Twin Cities	6	6,583	729	658	604	632	560	560	592	678	751	819
University of Illinois at Urbana-Champaign	7	6,432	706	646	597	667	602	617	574	636	689	698
University of California, Los Angeles	8	6,368	607	589	606	612	593	596	666	657	708	734
Stanford University	9	6,194	606	574	589	573	548	611	625	671	677	720
Ohio State University, Main Campus	10	6,123	636	561	620	633	617	575	560	590	664	667
University of Florida	11	6,097	456	445	516	574	607	591	694	702	718	794
Harvard University	12	6,073	803	615	602	520	543	548	572	560	627	683
University of Southern California	13	5,680	515	536	481	522	496	559	573	657	650	691
Pennsylvania State University, Main Campus	14	5,594	571	560	513	526	519	503	539	571	646	646
University of Washington, Seattle Campus	15	5,190	479	520	486	486	452	493	503	528	612	631
Massachusetts Institute of Technology	16	5,165	520	486	475	492	501	440	467	581	602	601
Texas A & M University	17	5,147	525	501	490	509	504	442	515	528	535	598
University of Maryland, College Park	18	4,967	474	501	461	430	430	418	482	516	602	653
Purdue University, Main Campus	19	4,945	496	496	468	464	409	463	446	524	566	613
Columbia University in the City of New York	20	4,939	469	414	461	465	452	433	495	603	579	568
Cornell University[2]	21	4,441	474	485	441	423	382	411	412	452	476	485
Michigan State University	22	4,394	451	404	444	414	428	442	430	425	463	493
University of North Carolina at Chapel Hill	23	4,281	382	374	425	398	390	412	439	459	490	512
University of Pennsylvania	24	4,238	436	380	427	376	380	384	413	463	496	483
University of Arizona	25	3,973	411	411	405	359	370	378	398	386	395	460
New York University	26	3,951	446	300	402	368	415	411	407	423	415	364
University of Georgia	27	3,834	369	365	352	351	393	414	404	424	374	388
Indiana University, Bloomington	28	3,798	361	363	409	420	347	367	375	397	389	370
Rutgers University, New Brunswick/Piscataway	29	3,774	402	375	371	392	363	358	382	332	393	406
Johns Hopkins University	30	3,752	360	366	351	384	373	364	362	387	408	397
University of California, Davis	31	3,711	337	310	357	337	346	373	375	389	413	474
Northwestern University	32	3,694	377	309	321	350	349	370	367	366	423	462
University of Pittsburgh, Pittsburgh Campus	33	3,676	380	360	316	360	336	348	382	372	412	410
University of Chicago	34	3,592	368	384	391	371	333	332	331	327	398	357
North Carolina State University at Raleigh	35	3,385	322	358	316	306	300	322	338	343	369	411
Boston University	36	3,306	307	287	274	304	246	270	267	320	491	540
Yale University	37	3,300	365	322	334	313	310	317	332	329	318	360
University of Virginia, Main Campus	38	3,295	302	302	343	316	321	337	358	341	327	348
University of Iowa	39	3,238	327	310	317	334	320	249	300	341	364	376
Virginia Polytechnic Institute and State University	40	3,214	349	349	309	268	326	272	290	329	366	356
Arizona State University at the Tempe Campus	41	3,170	287	273	286	277	313	300	355	314	389	376
University of California, San Diego	42	3,124	310	303	294	285	278	279	327	303	358	387
State University of New York at Buffalo	43	3,089	295	271	303	294	231	269	299	380	353	394
Georgia Institute of Technology, Main Campus	44	2,983	263	228	230	255	257	225	311	355	400	459
University of Colorado at Boulder	45	2,922	309	307	266	292	258	303	286	272	310	319
City University of New York, Graduate School and University Center	46	2,912	333	277	280	250	271	272	298	298	330	303
Florida State University	47	2,853	305	273	263	252	248	290	271	276	325	350
Temple University	48	2,852	285	248	263	238	226	161	334	322	383	392
University of Tennessee	49	2,797	254	255	286	239	276	262	280	281	317	347
Princeton University	50	2,719	263	250	279	268	230	260	276	273	288	332
University of Massachusetts, Amherst	51	2,693	299	270	276	261	287	213	274	267	253	293
University of Missouri, Columbia	52	2,662	277	230	256	278	252	274	251	274	277	293
University of California, Santa Barbara	53	2,622	264	229	232	258	199	251	253	287	339	310
Stony Brook University	54	2,618	265	227	244	231	20	298	285	317	367	364
University of Connecticut	55	2,611	253	227	275	234	221	237	257	261	307	339
Duke University	56	2,559	238	249	230	259	246	253	259	277	271	277
Iowa State University	57	2,556	300	257	238	243	239	228	228	246	281	296
University of Kansas	58	2,518	278	267	246	231	204	232	239	223	271	327
University of Nebraska, Lincoln	59	2,475	282	251	251	235	213	254	236	234	245	274
Louisiana State University and Agricultural & Mechanical College	60	2,471	258	253	275	264	222	211	240	222	252	274

†Not applicable.
[1]Institutions are ranked by the total number of doctor's degrees conferred during the 10-year period ending June 30, 2007.
[2]Includes degrees conferred by the Endowed and Statutory Colleges.
NOTE: Includes Ph.D., Ed.D., and comparable degrees at the doctoral level. Excludes first-professional, such as M.D., D.D.S., and law degrees.

SOURCE: U.S. Department of Education, National Center for Education Statistics, 1997–98 through 2006–07 Integrated Postsecondary Education Data System, "Completions Survey" (IPEDS-C:98–99), and Fall 2000 through Fall 2007. (This table was prepared July 2008.)

Table 324. Percentage distribution of 1990 high school sophomores, by highest level of education completed through 2000 and selected student characteristics: 2000

Student characteristic	Total	Less than high school completion	High school completion	Some post-secondary	Certificate	Associate's degree	Bachelor's or higher degree Total	Bachelor's degree	Master's degree	Professional and doctor's degrees
1	2	3	4	5	6	7	8	9	10	11
Total	100.0	(†)	8.8 (0.73)	17.8 (0.73)	30.2 (0.90)	7.9 (0.44)	6.6 (0.37)	28.7 (0.89)	25.5 (0.81)	2.8 (0.23)	0.4 (0.06)
Sex										
Male	100.0	(†)	8.5 (1.02)	19.7 (1.06)	32.6 (1.27)	6.8 (0.60)	6.6 (0.56)	25.8 (1.16)	23.2 (1.08)	2.2 (0.31)	0.4 (0.09)
Female	100.0	(†)	9.1 (1.00)	15.9 (0.99)	27.9 (1.12)	8.9 (0.67)	6.6 (0.46)	31.5 (1.12)	27.8 (1.03)	3.3 (0.31)	0.4 (0.09)
Race/ethnicity										
White	100.0	(†)	6.8 (0.75)	17.8 (0.75)	27.6 (0.85)	7.2 (0.44)	7.2 (0.46)	33.3 (0.98)	29.4 (0.91)	3.5 (0.30)	0.5 (0.08)
Black	100.0	(†)	11.1 (2.14)	17.9 (2.29)	38.5 (3.51)	12.0 (1.91)	4.1 (0.66)	16.4 (1.68)	15.4 (1.64)	0.8 (0.25)	0.2 (0.08)
Hispanic	100.0	(†)	16.3 (3.23)	18.5 (2.63)	37.8 (2.93)	8.5 (1.43)	7.3 (1.12)	11.6 (1.16)	10.7 (1.10)	0.8 (0.20)	0.1 (0.07)
Asian/Pacific Islander	100.0	(†)	6.5 (3.14)	6.2 (1.33)	32.2 (4.09)	5.7 (1.62)	3.5 (1.37)	46.1 (4.63)	41.0 (4.45)	3.6 (0.91)	1.5 (0.41)
American Indian/Alaska Native	100.0	(†)	21.6 (3.81)	40.1 (8.24)	23.0 (7.29)	6.4 (4.00)	3.0 (0.97)	5.9 (2.35)	5.3 (2.25)	‡ (†)	‡ (†)
Socioeconomic status in 1990[1]										
Low quartile	100.0	(†)	19.9 (1.97)	31.7 (1.84)	25.4 (1.71)	10.6 (1.12)	5.4 (0.69)	6.9 (0.60)	6.5 (0.59)	0.3 (0.10)	# (†)
Middle two quartiles	100.0	(†)	6.1 (0.79)	17.0 (0.90)	34.4 (1.16)	8.2 (0.61)	8.5 (0.60)	25.7 (1.02)	23.6 (1.00)	1.9 (0.26)	0.2 (0.06)
High quartile	100.0	(†)	0.3 (0.10)	5.2 (0.81)	25.5 (1.47)	4.5 (0.79)	4.6 (0.56)	59.8 (1.58)	51.2 (1.48)	7.3 (0.68)	1.4 (0.23)
Test score composite in 1990[2]										
Low quartile	100.0	(†)	19.3 (1.99)	31.8 (2.00)	28.1 (1.93)	11.2 (1.27)	4.9 (0.76)	4.7 (0.50)	4.5 (0.50)	0.2 (0.08)	0.1 (0.05)
Middle two quartiles	100.0	(†)	4.9 (1.00)	17.0 (0.98)	34.4 (1.29)	8.9 (0.62)	9.2 (0.61)	25.5 (1.08)	23.6 (1.05)	1.8 (0.20)	0.1 (0.03)
High quartile	100.0	(†)	0.7 (0.09)	5.3 (0.72)	23.4 (1.23)	2.7 (0.59)	4.7 (0.57)	63.2 (1.44)	53.9 (1.43)	7.7 (0.75)	1.5 (0.24)
Locus of control in 1990[3]										
Low quartile	100.0	(†)	13.6 (1.01)	26.2 (1.85)	29.9 (1.82)	7.6 (0.93)	6.4 (0.84)	16.2 (1.29)	14.9 (1.26)	1.2 (0.24)	0.1 (0.05)
Middle two quartiles	100.0	(†)	6.8 (0.97)	15.6 (0.98)	30.6 (1.21)	8.0 (0.59)	7.2 (0.51)	31.8 (1.16)	28.5 (1.08)	2.7 (0.33)	0.5 (0.10)
High quartile	100.0	(†)	2.3 (0.60)	12.4 (1.24)	30.6 (1.73)	7.1 (1.05)	6.7 (0.76)	40.9 (1.74)	35.2 (1.60)	5.0 (0.62)	0.7 (0.17)
Self-concept in 1990[4]										
Low quartile	100.0	(†)	8.7 (1.08)	20.6 (1.26)	31.9 (1.51)	7.1 (0.62)	6.9 (0.72)	24.8 (1.32)	22.2 (1.26)	2.5 (0.44)	0.2 (0.08)
Middle two quartiles	100.0	(†)	7.9 (1.20)	18.3 (1.16)	28.6 (1.12)	7.6 (0.59)	7.7 (0.58)	29.9 (1.19)	26.5 (1.12)	2.9 (0.30)	0.5 (0.10)
High quartile	100.0	(†)	5.3 (1.20)	13.3 (1.39)	32.4 (2.26)	8.3 (1.16)	5.2 (0.66)	35.5 (1.81)	31.4 (1.66)	3.4 (0.54)	0.7 (0.15)
High school completion timing										
Dropout (never completed)	100.0	(†)	100.0 (†)	‡ (†)	‡ (†)	‡ (†)	‡ (†)	‡ (†)	‡ (†)	‡ (†)	‡ (†)
Early (before January 1992)	100.0	(†)	1.3[5] (0.71)	38.2 (5.06)	29.1 (3.87)	11.9 (2.68)	12.1 (4.28)	7.3 (1.78)	6.0 (1.43)	‡ (†)	‡ (†)
Normal (from January 1992 through August 1992)	100.0	(†)	# (†)	16.2 (0.80)	32.7 (0.99)	7.9 (0.47)	7.4 (0.41)	35.7 (1.00)	31.7 (0.92)	3.4 (0.28)	0.5 (0.08)
Late (after August 1992)	100.0	(†)	0.1 (0.08)	42.0 (3.00)	39.2 (3.14)	13.0 (2.35)	4.0 (0.95)	1.9 (0.52)	1.9 (0.52)	‡ (†)	‡ (†)
Control of school attended in 1992										
Public	100.0	(†)	7.9 (0.70)	19.0 (0.78)	31.0 (1.00)	8.0 (0.48)	7.0 (0.40)	27.2 (0.91)	24.2 (0.83)	2.6 (0.24)	0.4 (0.07)
Private	100.0	(†)	3.3 (0.99)	3.2 (0.56)	25.3 (2.37)	4.2 (1.10)	4.1 (0.77)	60.0 (2.69)	52.4 (2.64)	6.5 (0.99)	1.1 (0.28)
Postsecondary expectations in 1992										
None	100.0	(†)	11.7 (5.67)	52.6 (5.00)	23.3 (4.45)	7.4 (1.43)	1.7 (0.60)	3.3 (0.79)	3.3 (0.79)	‡ (†)	‡ (†)
Some postsecondary	100.0	(†)	3.9 (1.14)	31.1 (1.82)	34.2 (1.89)	15.2 (1.26)	10.7 (0.98)	4.9 (0.71)	4.5 (0.69)	0.3 (0.18)	‡ (†)
Bachelor's degree	100.0	(†)	0.6 (0.33)	6.7 (0.71)	36.5 (1.47)	6.5 (0.92)	7.6 (0.62)	42.1 (1.48)	38.9 (1.42)	3.0 (0.44)	0.2 (0.08)
Master's degree	100.0	(†)	0.2 (0.09)	5.9 (0.93)	26.6 (1.64)	3.0 (0.51)	6.1 (1.01)	58.2 (1.87)	50.8 (1.86)	6.7 (0.67)	0.8 (0.23)
First-professional or doctor's degree	100.0	(†)	0.9 (0.42)	2.2 (0.44)	28.2 (2.51)	4.7 (0.91)	5.6 (0.96)	58.4 (2.44)	48.4 (2.29)	7.8 (1.19)	2.2 (0.40)
Type of start in postsecondary education										
Fall 1992 full-time 4-year	100.0	(†)	‡ (†)	0.6 (0.13)	22.7 (1.11)	2.2 (0.30)	3.7 (0.43)	70.7 (1.20)	61.4 (1.22)	8.0 (0.64)	1.3 (0.19)
Fall 1992 full-time public 2-year	100.0	(†)	‡ (†)	2.1 (0.60)	41.7 (2.34)	13.4 (1.61)	19.3 (1.54)	23.4 (1.79)	22.1 (1.75)	1.2 (0.36)	‡ (†)
Fall 1992 part-time 4-year	100.0	(†)	‡ (†)	‡ (†)	57.1 (7.33)	3.7 (1.91)	3.3 (1.70)	31.9 (6.33)	29.5 (6.17)	2.4 (1.80)	‡ (†)
Fall 1992 part-time public 2-year	100.0	(†)	2.7 (2.04)	2.8 (2.24)	57.6 (4.97)	15.1 (3.78)	9.7 (2.47)	12.2 (3.16)	12.0 (3.15)	‡ (†)	‡ (†)
Other enrollment	100.0	(†)	2.2 (1.36)	12.4 (3.60)	35.3 (4.82)	15.3 (4.64)	8.2 (1.67)	26.5 (4.43)	24.6 (4.39)	1.6 (0.62)	‡ (†)
Never enrolled	100.0	(†)	18.0 (1.39)	35.4 (1.34)	28.8 (1.37)	8.8 (0.66)	4.5 (0.48)	4.5 (0.47)	4.3 (0.46)	0.1 (0.06)	‡ (†)
Parents' educational attainment in 1990										
No high school diploma	100.0	(†)	25.9 (3.46)	26.7 (2.51)	26.8 (2.81)	11.0 (1.77)	3.7 (0.64)	5.9 (0.99)	5.5 (0.97)	0.4 (0.17)	‡ (†)
High school graduate	100.0	(†)	12.7 (1.75)	30.6 (2.12)	26.1 (1.60)	8.3 (0.83)	9.0 (1.10)	13.3 (1.01)	12.1 (1.01)	1.0 (0.20)	0.1 (0.06)
Vocational/some college	100.0	(†)	4.6 (0.53)	17.3 (0.94)	35.1 (1.20)	9.1 (0.81)	8.1 (0.60)	25.7 (1.09)	23.7 (1.08)	1.9 (0.24)	0.2 (0.06)
Bachelor's degree	100.0	(†)	2.9 (1.35)	7.4 (1.24)	29.7 (2.15)	5.6 (0.91)	5.1 (0.64)	49.4 (2.10)	43.6 (2.02)	5.0 (0.74)	0.7 (0.22)
Master's degree	100.0	(†)	0.8 (0.46)	2.5 (0.74)	23.3 (2.49)	4.6 (1.18)	3.4 (0.62)	65.4 (2.50)	55.3 (2.46)	8.6 (1.39)	1.5 (0.39)
First-professional or doctor's degree	100.0	(†)	0.6 (0.38)	1.8 (0.70)	18.3 (4.50)	2.0 (1.20)	4.1 (2.00)	73.3 (4.66)	61.1 (4.47)	9.3 (2.24)	2.9 (0.78)

†Not applicable.
#Rounds to zero.
‡Reporting standards not met.
[1]Socioeconomic status (SES) was measured by a composite score on parental education and occupations, and family income.
[2]Standardized quartile of composite of student assessments in mathematics and reading.
[3]Locus of control measures whether students attribute the events that happened to them, such as performing well on a test, to being under their own control (i.e., internal locus of control) or to being under the control of others or the environment (external locus of control). Higher scores (highest quartile) means greater internal control and lower scores (lowest quartile) means greater external control.

[4]Self-concept measures the degree to which students like and feel positively about themselves and perceive themselves as a person of worth. The NELS:88 variable is the general self-concept scale from Herbert Marsh's Self-Description Questionnaire (SDQ) II (Marsh 1990).
[5]These students' responses to the educational attainment question were not consistent with their transcript data.
NOTE: Race categories exclude persons of Hispanic ethnicity. Detail may not sum to totals because of rounding. Standard errors appear in parentheses.
SOURCE: U.S. Department of Education, National Center for Education Statistics, National Education Longitudinal Study of 1988 (NELS:88/2000), "Fourth Follow-up, Student Survey. 2000." (This table was prepared December 2005.)

Table 325. Mean number of semester credits completed by bachelor's degree recipients, by course area and major: 1976, 1984, and 1992–93

Selected college major	Total	Business	Computer science	Education	Engineering	Mathematics	Biological sciences	Physical sciences	Social sciences and psychology	Other
1	2	3	4	5	6	7	8	9	10	11
1972 high school seniors who completed bachelor's degrees by 1976										
Mean, all majors	124.0	7.8	1.0	9.7	2.3	7.4	7.6	9.0	30.3	48.8
Business and management	124.4	41.2	2.3	0.5	0.4	10.2	2.5	4.8	30.4	32.0
Computer science	133.3	6.6	33.5	0.4	5.3	22.4	1.9	7.8	20.6	34.8
Education	126.4	0.9	0.3	40.2	—	5.0	5.5	4.3	23.9	46.4
Engineering	134.8	1.6	2.0	0.1	50.0	18.2	1.3	20.5	14.0	27.1
English	117.8	0.5	0.1	7.8	0.1	3.2	3.4	3.4	24.2	75.2
Fine arts	124.9	0.3	0.1	6.6	—	1.3	2.5	2.1	13.6	98.4
Life sciences	122.2	0.4	0.8	1.7	—	8.4	35.6	26.2	17.8	31.3
Physical sciences	122.7	0.8	1.4	0.9	1.9	16.2	9.6	49.5	13.1	29.2
Psychology	119.1	2.0	0.5	5.9	0.3	5.5	6.2	5.9	56.0	36.9
Social sciences	120.6	3.4	0.4	3.3	0.4	5.3	3.2	4.3	60.3	40.1
1980 high school seniors who completed bachelor's degrees by 1984										
Mean, all majors	123.5	12.8	3.3	6.2	4.6	8.4	5.3	8.1	27.5	47.2
Business and management	122.8	41.2	4.5	0.6	1.1	8.9	2.2	3.9	27.5	32.7
Computer science	129.3	11.8	27.9	0.3	4.7	21.3	1.8	8.5	19.0	33.9
Education	127.4	0.7	0.3	45.5	0.1	4.4	4.4	3.8	20.8	47.3
Engineering	132.3	1.0	2.3	0.8	52.5	16.2	1.1	20.2	12.3	25.9
English	114.8	1.7	1.5	6.9	—	2.2	2.1	4.7	21.4	74.4
Fine arts	120.5	1.7	0.6	5.1	—	1.7	2.7	1.5	14.1	93.1
Life sciences	121.9	0.7	1.5	1.9	0.2	10.1	33.5	22.6	18.1	33.3
Physical sciences	124.3	0.2	4.9	0.1	2.0	14.1	12.9	48.7	11.6	30.0
Psychology	120.7	3.0	2.7	2.1	—	6.5	5.8	4.2	55.2	41.2
Social sciences	119.2	6.0	1.4	1.0	0.5	5.4	4.4	5.1	52.0	43.3
1988–89 high school graduates who completed bachelor's degrees by 1992–93										
Mean, all majors	126.5	12.8	3.0	5.7	3.2	7.3	6.0	7.6	29.5	51.7
Business and management	123.9	44.4	3.9	0.9	0.1	7.6	2.6	3.3	23.1	37.9
Computer science	127.6	15.7	34.3	0.4	2.4	15.7	1.7	6.4	17.6	33.5
Education	126.8	1.6	1.5	32.6	—	5.9	4.7	4.4	24.5	51.6
Engineering	136.9	1.4	7.0	0.6	57.9	16.7	1.4	19.0	12.2	20.8
English	127.5	1.8	1.0	3.0	0.1	4.0	3.5	3.8	22.7	87.5
Fine arts	129.6	1.8	1.3	2.2	0.8	3.1	2.4	2.6	19.8	95.7
Life sciences	128.9	1.1	1.4	2.1	1.0	8.0	33.8	23.3	20.7	37.5
Physical sciences	129.1	1.1	2.7	1.1	2.3	15.0	7.5	49.3	16.9	33.2
Psychology	125.3	3.8	1.2	3.6	0.1	5.0	4.9	4.5	53.6	48.6
Social sciences	125.5	6.2	1.2	1.8	0.1	4.8	2.9	5.1	55.7	47.6
All bachelor's degree recipients of 1992–93										
Mean, all majors	132.2	14.6	3.7	7.2	5.4	8.3	6.0	7.8	27.3	52.0
Business and management	129.5	46.8	4.7	0.9	0.7	8.8	2.8	3.6	23.6	37.6
Computer science	137.0	17.4	37.1	0.4	5.0	16.7	2.5	7.5	17.3	33.0
Education	135.9	2.2	1.5	40.1	0.3	6.3	5.4	5.0	24.7	50.5
Engineering	142.1	2.1	7.1	0.3	61.3	17.8	1.3	18.1	11.4	22.8
English	128.8	2.9	1.4	4.6	0.1	4.3	3.5	4.2	23.2	84.5
Fine arts	133.4	2.7	2.0	3.2	0.9	3.7	2.5	4.2	19.3	94.7
Life sciences	132.5	1.7	1.6	2.9	0.9	8.7	34.8	22.3	21.3	38.2
Physical sciences	137.8	2.6	2.9	1.9	4.0	15.5	8.2	50.6	18.2	33.9
Psychology	129.0	4.0	1.4	4.2	0.3	5.5	5.1	4.2	52.4	52.0
Social sciences	127.9	6.2	1.4	2.3	0.3	5.6	3.3	5.4	54.8	48.6

—Not available.
NOTE: All majors total includes fields not shown separately. Detail may not sum to totals because of rounding.

SOURCE: U.S. Department of Education, National Center for Education Statistics, National Longitudinal Study of 1972, "Third Follow-up" (NLS:72/76); High School and Beyond Longitudinal Study (HS&B-Sr:80/84); and Baccalaureate and Beyond Longitudinal Study (B&B:93). (This table was prepared January 1999.)

Table 326. Number and percentage of degree-granting institutions with first-year undergraduates using various selection criteria for admission, by type and control of institution: Selected years, 2000–01 through 2007–08

Selection criteria	All institutions			Public institutions			Private institutions								
										Not-for-profit			For-profit		
	Total	4-year	2-year	Total	4-year	2-year	Total	4-year	2-year	Total	4-year	2-year	Total	4-year	2-year
1	2	3	4	5	6	7	8	9	10	11	12	13	14	15	16
	Number of institutions with first-year undergraduates														
2000–01	3,717	2,034	1,683	1,647	580	1,067	2,070	1,454	616	1,383	1,247	136	687	207	480
2005–06	3,880	2,198	1,682	1,638	588	1,050	2,242	1,610	632	1,351	1,240	111	891	370	521
2006–07	3,933	2,254	1,679	1,639	595	1,044	2,294	1,659	635	1,348	1,243	105	946	416	530
2007–08	3,983	2,313	1,670	1,639	608	1,031	2,344	1,705	639	1,334	1,244	90	1,010	461	549
	Percent of institutions														
Open admissions															
2000–01	40.2	12.9	73.2	63.8	12.1	91.9	21.4	13.3	40.7	14.0	11.7	34.6	36.5	22.7	42.5
2005–06	44.7	18.3	79.3	66.1	13.6	95.4	29.2	20.1	52.4	15.3	13.1	40.5	50.2	43.5	54.9
2006–07	44.7	19.5	78.6	66.0	14.1	95.5	29.6	21.5	50.9	15.7	13.7	40.0	49.4	44.7	53.0
2007–08	44.5	19.5	79.2	65.7	14.5	95.9	29.7	21.3	52.1	15.3	13.3	42.2	48.7	42.7	53.7
Some admission requirements[1]															
2000–01	58.4	85.8	25.1	35.4	87.4	7.1	76.6	85.2	56.3	84.5	86.8	63.2	60.7	75.4	54.4
2005–06	53.4	80.5	18.0	33.6	86.1	4.3	67.9	78.5	40.8	84.2	86.5	57.7	43.2	51.6	37.2
2006–07	52.6	78.7	17.5	33.9	85.7	4.3	66.0	76.3	39.2	83.5	85.7	57.1	41.1	48.1	35.7
2007–08	52.6	78.8	16.3	34.1	85.4	3.9	65.5	76.4	36.3	83.9	86.1	53.3	41.2	50.3	33.5
Secondary grades															
2000–01	34.6	58.7	5.5	23.9	63.4	2.4	43.0	56.7	10.7	60.1	64.1	23.5	8.7	12.6	7.1
2005–06	34.1	57.1	4.2	25.9	68.4	2.2	40.1	53.0	7.4	62.8	66.2	25.2	5.7	8.6	3.6
2006–07	33.8	56.2	3.8	26.2	68.7	2.0	39.2	51.7	6.6	62.9	66.2	23.8	5.5	8.4	3.2
2007–08	34.2	56.3	3.6	26.7	68.8	1.9	39.4	51.8	6.3	65.1	67.8	27.8	5.5	8.9	2.7
Secondary class rank															
2000–01	13.7	24.3	1.0	10.9	30.3	0.3	16.0	21.9	2.3	23.2	25.1	5.9	1.6	2.4	1.3
2005–06	11.3	19.4	0.7	10.4	28.7	0.2	11.9	16.0	1.6	19.3	20.5	6.3	0.7	0.8	0.6
2006–07	10.8	18.4	0.7	10.2	27.7	0.2	11.2	15.0	1.4	18.8	19.9	5.7	0.5	0.5	0.6
2007–08	10.3	17.4	0.6	10.2	27.1	0.2	10.5	13.9	1.3	18.1	18.9	6.7	0.4	0.4	0.4
Secondary school record															
2000–01	45.8	70.3	16.2	29.4	72.9	5.8	58.7	69.2	34.1	73.2	75.5	52.2	29.5	30.9	29.0
2005–06	48.5	73.3	15.9	30.8	78.2	4.2	61.4	71.6	35.4	77.6	79.7	55.0	36.7	44.3	31.3
2006–07	47.7	71.6	15.7	30.9	78.0	4.1	59.7	69.3	34.8	76.7	78.7	53.3	35.5	41.1	31.1
2007–08	47.5	71.1	14.7	31.3	78.1	3.7	58.7	68.6	32.4	77.2	79.2	50.0	34.4	40.1	29.5
College preparatory program															
2000–01	15.5	27.3	1.2	16.2	44.0	1.1	14.9	20.7	1.3	22.1	24.1	4.4	0.4	0.5	0.4
2005–06	15.2	26.4	0.6	17.4	47.1	0.8	13.6	18.8	0.3	22.4	24.3	1.8	0.2	0.5	0.0
2006–07	15.4	26.5	0.5	17.8	48.1	0.6	13.7	18.8	0.3	23.1	24.9	1.9	0.2	0.5	0.0
2007–08	15.5	26.3	0.5	18.1	47.7	0.7	13.6	18.7	0.2	23.8	25.4	1.1	0.2	0.4	0.0
Recommendations															
2000–01	20.4	34.4	3.5	2.7	7.4	0.2	34.4	45.1	9.3	46.6	49.2	22.8	10.0	20.8	5.4
2005–06	19.2	31.9	2.5	2.9	7.7	0.2	31.1	40.8	6.3	49.1	51.5	23.4	3.7	5.1	2.7
2006–07	18.3	30.5	2.0	2.6	6.7	0.2	29.6	39.1	4.9	49.0	51.2	22.9	1.9	2.6	1.3
2007–08	18.0	29.5	2.1	2.6	6.7	0.2	28.8	37.6	5.2	49.0	50.6	25.6	2.1	2.4	1.8
Demonstration of competencies[2]															
2000–01	8.0	12.1	3.0	2.2	5.0	0.7	12.7	15.0	7.1	12.1	12.7	7.4	13.7	29.0	7.1
2005–06	7.0	9.8	3.3	2.3	6.1	0.2	10.3	11.1	8.4	10.2	10.3	9.0	10.5	13.8	8.3
2006–07	6.3	9.2	2.3	2.0	5.4	0.1	9.3	10.5	6.0	9.5	9.6	8.6	9.0	13.5	5.5
2007–08	6.1	8.7	2.5	1.8	4.8	0.1	9.0	10.1	6.3	9.4	9.3	11.1	8.5	12.1	5.5
Test scores[3]															
2000–01	47.2	72.5	16.7	33.2	83.4	5.8	58.5	68.2	35.6	70.3	73.4	41.9	34.6	36.7	33.8
2005–06	36.5	62.5	2.6	31.1	82.3	2.4	40.5	55.2	3.0	65.7	70.5	12.6	2.2	4.1	1.0
2006–07	35.6	60.6	2.1	31.2	82.2	2.1	38.8	52.9	2.0	65.1	69.6	12.4	1.3	2.9	0.0
2007–08	34.8	58.4	2.1	31.6	81.7	2.0	37.0	50.0	2.2	64.4	67.9	15.6	0.8	1.7	0.0
TOEFL[4]															
2000–01	43.4	71.2	9.9	30.2	77.4	4.6	54.0	68.7	19.2	66.2	70.1	30.9	29.3	60.4	15.8
2005–06	41.5	67.9	7.1	31.0	79.3	3.9	49.3	63.8	12.3	67.0	70.6	27.0	22.4	41.1	9.2
2006–07	41.4	66.8	7.4	31.1	78.8	3.9	48.8	62.4	13.1	67.1	70.4	28.6	22.6	38.7	10.0
2007–08	41.4	66.3	6.8	30.9	77.5	3.5	48.6	62.3	12.1	67.5	70.0	32.2	23.8	41.6	8.7
No admission requirements, only recommendations for admission															
2000–01	1.4	1.2	1.7	0.8	0.5	0.9	1.9	1.5	2.9	1.5	1.4	2.2	2.8	1.9	3.1
2005–06	1.8	1.1	2.7	0.3	0.3	0.3	2.9	1.4	6.8	0.5	0.4	1.8	6.6	4.9	7.9
2006–07	2.6	1.7	3.9	0.2	0.2	0.2	4.4	2.3	9.9	0.8	0.6	2.9	9.5	7.2	11.3
2007–08	2.9	1.7	4.6	0.2	0.2	0.2	4.8	2.3	11.6	0.8	0.6	4.4	10.1	6.9	12.8

[1]Many institutions have more than one admission requirement.
[2]Formal demonstration of competencies (e.g., portfolios, certificates of mastery, assessment instruments).
[3]Includes SAT, ACT, or other admission tests.
[4]Test of English as a Foreign Language.

NOTE: Detail may not sum to totals because of rounding.
SOURCE: U.S. Department of Education, National Center for Education Statistics, 2000–01 through 2007–08 Integrated Postsecondary Education Data System, Fall 2000 through Fall 2007. (This table was prepared July 2008.)

Table 327. Number of applications, admissions, and enrollees; their distribution across institutions accepting various percentages of applications; and SAT and ACT scores of applicants, by type and control of institution: 2007–08

Application, admission, enrollment, and SAT and ACT score	All institutions			Public institutions			Private institutions			Not-for-profit			For-profit		
	Total	4-year	2-year	Total	4-year	2-year	Total	4-year	2-year	Total	4-year	2-year	Total	4-year	2-year
1	2	3	4	5	6	7	8	9	10	11	12	13	14	15	16
Number of undergraduate institutions reporting application data[1]	3,959	2,290	1,669	1,639	608	1,031	2,320	1,682	638	1,331	1,241	90	989	441	548
Percentage distribution of institutions by their acceptance of applications	100.0	100.0	100.0	100.0	100.0	100.0	100.0	100.0	100.0	100.0	100.0	100.0	100.0	100.0	100.0
No application criteria	44.8	19.7	79.2	65.7	14.5	95.9	30.0	21.6	52.2	15.3	13.4	42.2	49.7	44.7	53.8
90 percent or more accepted	8.4	9.3	7.1	4.1	8.1	1.7	11.4	9.8	15.7	9.8	9.8	10.0	13.5	9.8	16.6
75.0 to 89.9 percent accepted	13.4	19.9	4.5	10.4	26.3	1.0	15.6	17.6	10.5	19.5	20.5	4.4	10.3	9.3	11.1
50.0 to 74.9 percent accepted	21.8	33.8	5.3	14.6	38.0	0.8	26.9	32.3	12.5	37.5	38.7	21.1	12.5	14.3	11.1
25.0 to 49.9 percent accepted	10.1	15.1	3.2	4.6	11.5	0.6	13.9	16.3	7.5	14.6	14.7	12.2	13.0	20.9	6.8
10.0 to 24.9 percent accepted	1.3	1.8	0.7	0.4	1.2	0.0	2.0	2.1	1.7	2.9	2.4	8.9	0.8	1.1	0.5
Less than 10 percent accepted	0.2	0.3	0.1	0.2	0.5	0.0	0.3	0.3	0.2	0.5	0.4	1.1	0.0	0.0	0.0
Number of applications (in thousands)	6,952	6,776	176	3,833	3,758	75	3,119	3,018	101	2,889	2,872	17	230	146	84
Percentage distribution of applications by institutions' acceptance of applications	100.0	100.0	100.0	100.0	100.0	100.0	100.0	100.0	100.0	100.0	100.0	100.0	100.0	100.0	100.0
No application criteria	†	†	†	†	†	†	†	†	†	†	†	†	†	†	†
90 percent or more accepted	4.2	3.4	32.1	5.0	4.4	33.9	3.1	2.2	30.7	1.9	1.8	7.1	19.1	9.6	35.6
75.0 to 89.9 percent accepted	17.7	17.7	16.0	21.0	21.2	11.2	13.5	13.3	19.6	13.2	13.2	10.1	17.9	15.8	21.5
50.0 to 74.9 percent accepted	45.5	45.8	33.4	50.8	51.0	42.3	39.0	39.4	26.7	40.0	39.9	56.7	26.0	29.2	20.5
25.0 to 49.9 percent accepted	25.7	25.9	17.5	20.6	20.7	12.6	31.9	32.3	21.2	31.7	31.8	18.5	34.7	42.1	21.7
10.0 to 24.9 percent accepted	5.9	6.0	1.0	2.5	2.5	0.0	10.1	10.4	1.8	10.7	10.7	7.5	2.3	3.3	0.6
Less than 10 percent accepted	1.1	1.2	#	0.1	0.1	0.0	2.4	2.5	#	2.6	2.6	0.1	0.0	0.0	0.0
Number of admissions (in thousands)	4,048	3,919	129	2,412	2,355	56	1,636	1,564	73	1,489	1,479	10	147	84	63
Percentage distribution of admissions by institutions' acceptance of applications	100.0	100.0	100.0	100.0	100.0	100.0	100.0	100.0	100.0	100.0	100.0	100.0	100.0	100.0	100.0
No application criteria	†	†	†	†	†	†	†	†	†	†	†	†	†	†	†
90 percent or more accepted	6.8	5.6	43.0	7.5	6.6	44.6	5.7	4.0	41.8	3.4	3.3	12.2	29.1	16.1	46.4
75.0 to 89.9 percent accepted	24.6	24.8	18.1	27.2	27.6	12.3	20.7	20.6	22.6	20.5	20.5	14.0	23.0	22.3	24.0
50.0 to 74.9 percent accepted	49.4	50.0	28.4	51.1	51.4	35.8	46.8	47.9	22.7	49.0	49.0	60.5	24.4	30.0	16.8
25.0 to 49.9 percent accepted	17.3	17.5	10.2	13.4	13.6	7.4	22.9	23.4	12.4	22.9	23.0	11.3	22.9	30.6	12.6
10.0 to 24.9 percent accepted	1.8	1.9	0.2	0.7	0.8	0.0	3.4	3.6	0.4	3.7	3.7	2.0	0.7	1.0	0.2
Less than 10 percent accepted	0.2	0.2	0.0	#	#	0.0	0.4	0.4	0.0	0.4	0.4	0.0	0.0	0.0	0.0
Number of enrollees (in thousands)	1,537	1,439	98	950	911	39	587	528	59	468	462	6	119	66	53
Percentage distribution of enrollees by institutions' acceptance of applications	100.0	100.0	100.0	100.0	100.0	100.0	100.0	100.0	100.0	100.0	100.0	100.0	100.0	100.0	100.0
No application criteria	†	†	†	†	†	†	†	†	†	†	†	†	†	†	†
90 percent or more accepted	9.5	7.1	44.9	9.4	7.9	44.4	9.6	5.6	45.3	4.8	4.7	18.1	28.4	12.4	48.3
75.0 to 89.9 percent accepted	24.7	25.2	16.9	27.1	27.7	12.5	20.8	21.0	19.8	21.0	21.2	11.4	20.1	19.5	20.7
50.0 to 74.9 percent accepted	46.5	47.8	26.6	50.0	50.6	36.3	40.8	43.1	20.2	44.8	44.7	52.8	25.1	32.0	16.6
25.0 to 49.9 percent accepted	16.6	16.9	11.3	12.3	12.5	6.8	23.5	24.5	14.2	22.8	23.0	14.6	25.9	35.4	14.2
10.0 to 24.9 percent accepted	2.4	2.5	0.3	1.2	1.2	0.0	4.4	4.8	0.5	5.4	5.4	3.0	0.5	0.7	0.2
Less than 10 percent accepted	0.3	0.4	0.0	#	#	0.0	0.9	1.0	0.0	1.1	1.1	0.0	0.0	0.0	0.0
SAT scores of applicants															
Critical reading, 25th percentile[2]	473	475	408	457	458	411	482	483	405	483	484	405	422	422	‡
Critical reading, 75th percentile[2]	584	585	522	566	568	516	593	595	528	594	595	528	542	542	‡
Mathematics, 25th percentile[2]	477	479	411	468	469	419	483	484	405	483	485	405	438	438	‡
Mathematics, 75th percentile[2]	588	590	520	578	579	532	594	595	511	594	596	511	553	553	‡
ACT scores of applicants															
Composite, 25th percentile[2]	19.9	20.0	16.5	19.1	19.3	16.0	20.3	20.3	17.4	20.3	20.4	17.2	18.2	18.0	‡
Composite, 75th percentile[2]	24.9	25.0	21.3	24.0	24.1	21.0	25.5	25.5	21.7	25.5	25.5	21.6	23.3	23.5	‡
English, 25th percentile[2]	18.9	19.0	15.4	18.0	18.1	15.1	19.5	19.5	15.9	19.5	19.6	15.5	17.1	16.7	‡
English, 75th percentile[2]	25.1	25.2	21.2	24.1	24.2	21.2	25.7	25.8	21.2	25.7	25.8	21.1	22.8	22.9	‡
Mathematics, 25th percentile[2]	18.9	18.9	16.3	18.3	18.4	15.9	19.2	19.2	16.9	19.2	19.2	16.5	17.4	16.9	‡
Mathematics, 75th percentile[2]	24.5	24.6	20.5	23.9	24.1	20.0	24.9	25.0	21.4	24.9	25.0	21.2	22.1	22.0	‡

†Not applicable.
#Rounds to zero.
‡Reporting standards not met.
[1]Excludes institutions not enrolling first-time degree/certificate-seeking undergraduates. The total on this table differs slightly from other counts of undergraduate institutions because approximately 0.4 percent of undergraduate institutions did not report application information.

[2]Data are only for institutions that require test scores for admission. Relatively few 2-year institutions require test scores for admission.
NOTE: Excludes information for the 0.4 percent of institutions that did not respond to survey questions. Detail may not sum to totals because of rounding.
SOURCE: U.S. Department of Education, National Center for Education Statistics, 2007–08 Integrated Postsecondary Education Data System, Fall 2007. (This table was prepared July 2008.)

Table 328. Percentage of degree-granting institutions offering remedial services, by type and control of institution: 1989–90 through 2007–08

Type and control of institution	1989–90	1990–91	1991–92	1992–93	1993–94	1994–95	1995–96	1996–97	1997–98	1998–99	1999–2000	2000–01	2001–02	2002–03	2003–04	2004–05	2005–06	2006–07	2007–08	Change in percentage points	
																				1989–90 to 1997–98	1997–98 to 2007–08
1	2	3	4	5	6	7	8	9	10	11	12	13	14	15	16	17	18	19	20	21	21
All institutions	**76.6**	**77.7**	**78.6**	**78.5**	**79.0**	**79.8**	**79.5**	**80.0**	**76.7**	**76.1**	**76.1**	**75.1**	**73.3**	**72.5**	**72.1**	**72.6**	**72.2**	**72.8**	**72.4**	**#**	**-4.2**
All 4-year	69.6	70.6	71.4	71.5	72.2	73.6	73.0	73.1	72.5	72.0	71.6	71.4	69.0	67.6	67.1	67.4	66.9	67.5	67.2	2.8	-5.3
All 2-year	87.2	88.4	89.2	88.8	89.5	89.1	89.4	91.0	82.2	81.5	82.2	80.4	79.5	79.5	79.7	80.3	80.2	80.9	80.9	-5.0	-1.4
Public institutions	92.4	93.0	93.9	93.5	93.5	93.7	93.7	94.0	93.8	93.6	93.5	93.1	92.3	91.7	91.3	90.6	90.2	90.4	89.7	1.5	-4.2
4-year	82.9	83.5	84.5	84.5	84.6	85.3	85.4	85.1	85.2	84.2	83.6	81.7	79.9	78.4	77.3	75.6	75.2	75.6	74.1	2.3	-11.1
2-year	98.2	98.9	99.6	98.8	98.7	98.6	98.6	99.2	98.7	99.0	99.2	99.7	99.4	99.4	99.5	99.6	99.3	99.5	99.5	0.5	0.8
Private institutions	64.1	65.6	66.3	66.4	67.4	68.6	68.0	68.6	64.2	63.6	63.9	62.8	60.2	59.0	59.0	60.4	60.4	61.4	61.6	0.1	-2.7
4-year	64.5	65.6	66.4	66.5	67.5	69.2	68.4	68.6	67.8	67.7	67.4	67.9	65.3	63.9	63.7	64.7	64.2	64.9	64.9	3.4	-2.9
2-year	63.0	65.5	65.8	65.8	67.0	66.6	66.3	68.4	55.1	52.8	54.4	48.8	45.0	44.8	44.8	47.4	48.8	50.6	51.0	-7.9	-4.0
Not-for-profit	65.0	65.6	66.2	66.7	67.7	69.3	68.9	69.2	69.0	68.6	69.2	67.6	66.1	65.4	65.0	63.1	62.2	62.2	61.4	4.0	-7.6
4-year	64.2	64.9	65.8	66.2	67.0	68.7	68.3	68.3	68.3	68.3	68.5	67.0	65.5	64.7	64.0	62.5	61.3	61.3	60.6	4.0	-7.6
2-year	71.8	71.3	69.9	71.5	73.5	74.0	73.3	77.3	75.4	71.6	76.7	73.6	72.6	74.0	77.1	71.4	74.3	74.8	73.9	3.7	-1.5
For-profit	59.5	65.6	66.6	64.6	65.6	65.2	63.5	65.2	51.7	51.1	51.5	52.7	48.0	45.6	47.4	55.4	57.2	60.1	61.8	-7.8	10.1
4-year	71.7	81.3	79.2	73.7	76.3	76.0	69.2	72.7	63.9	63.4	60.1	72.9	64.5	59.6	62.0	73.7	75.0	77.0	78.4	-7.8	14.5
2-year	57.0	62.0	63.2	62.0	62.1	60.8	60.5	60.8	47.5	46.2	47.7	41.8	37.3	37.2	37.3	42.2	43.4	45.8	47.2	-9.5	-0.3

#Rounds to zero.
NOTE: Data through 1995–96 are for institutions of higher education, while later data are for degree-granting institutions. Degree-granting institutions grant associate's or higher degrees and participate in Title IV federal financial aid programs. The degree-granting classification is very similar to the earlier higher education classification, but it includes more 2-year colleges and excludes a few higher education institutions that did not grant degrees. (See Guide to Sources for details.)

SOURCE: U.S. Department of Education, National Center for Education Statistics, 1989–90 through 2007–08 Integrated Postsecondary Education Data System, "Institutional Characteristics Survey" (IPEDS-IC:89–99), and Fall 2000 through Fall 2007. (This table was prepared July 2008.)

Table 329. Percentage distribution of enrollment and completion status of first-time postsecondary students starting during the 1995–96 academic year, by type of institution and other student characteristics: 2001

Student and institution characteristic	Students starting in 2-year institutions						Students starting in 4-year institutions					
	Highest degree attained				No degree, still enrolled	No degree, not enrolled	Highest degree attained				No degree, still enrolled	No degree, not enrolled
	Total, any degree[1]	Certificate	Associate's	Bachelor's[2]			Total, any degree[1]	Certificate	Associate's	Bachelor's[2]		
1	2	3	4	5	6	7	8	9	10	11	12	13
Total	**38.4** (1.7)	**11.5** (1.2)	**17.3** (1.3)	**9.7** (1.1)	**16.4** (1.4)	**45.2** (1.6)	**65.1** (1.0)	**2.7** (0.3)	**4.0** (0.4)	**58.4** (1.2)	**14.4** (0.6)	**20.5** (0.8)
Sex												
Male	39.2 (2.4)	10.8 (1.6)	18.7 (1.9)	9.7 (1.5)	18.0 (2.2)	42.8 (2.4)	60.6 (1.4)	2.5 (0.4)	3.6 (0.6)	54.6 (1.5)	16.2 (0.9)	23.2 (1.1)
Female	37.7 (2.2)	12.0 (1.6)	15.9 (1.7)	9.8 (1.4)	14.9 (1.7)	47.4 (2.2)	68.7 (1.3)	2.9 (0.3)	4.3 (0.5)	61.6 (1.4)	12.9 (0.8)	18.4 (1.0)
Age when first enrolled												
18 years or younger	43.8 (2.3)	7.3 (1.2)	19.4 (2.0)	17.0 (1.9)	17.8 (2.1)	38.4 (2.1)	70.0 (1.0)	1.8 (0.2)	3.4 (0.4)	64.7 (1.1)	13.4 (0.6)	16.6 (0.7)
19 years	38.2 (4.1)	8.2 (2.0)	24.3 (4.0)	5.7 (1.9)	20.9 (3.6)	40.9 (4.0)	57.1 (2.8)	3.3 (0.9)	6.0 (1.3)	47.9 (2.9)	16.4 (2.0)	26.6 (2.3)
20 to 23 years	29.9 (4.2)	13.1 (3.0)	13.0 (3.4)	3.7 (1.6)	20.1 (4.2)	50.0 (4.8)	37.7 (3.8)	8.7 (2.1)	6.7 (2.1)	22.3 (3.0)	20.9 (3.0)	41.4 (3.6)
24 to 29 years	36.5 (4.8)	25.6 (4.6)	8.4 (2.2)	2.5 (1.5)	11.0 (3.5)	52.6 (5.1)	34.4 (5.5)	4.3 (1.8)	7.2 (3.5)	23.0 (4.7)	22.7 (5.8)	42.9 (6.3)
30 years or over	30.6 (5.5)	14.1 (3.8)	14.5 (3.3)	2.0 (1.5)	8.7 (2.4)	60.7 (5.8)	26.1 (4.3)	11.5 (3.5)	4.3 (1.6)	10.3 (2.8)	17.0 (4.2)	56.9 (5.1)
Race/ethnicity												
White	40.5 (2.0)	10.9 (1.3)	18.2 (1.5)	11.4 (1.6)	16.5 (1.7)	43.0 (2.0)	68.1 (1.1)	2.4 (0.3)	3.8 (0.4)	61.9 (1.3)	12.5 (0.7)	19.4 (0.9)
Black	28.4 (4.2)	16.7 (4.0)	8.5 (2.3)	3.2 (1.3)	13.3 (2.9)	58.3 (4.3)	51.3 (2.6)	4.6 (1.0)	3.2 (0.8)	43.4 (2.8)	20.6 (2.3)	28.2 (2.2)
Hispanic	34.3 (4.8)	11.1 (3.2)	17.8 (3.2)	5.5 (2.3)	18.1 (3.3)	47.6 (4.8)	53.9 (2.3)	3.1 (0.7)	6.8 (1.7)	44.0 (2.4)	20.4 (1.8)	25.7 (2.1)
Asian/Pacific Islander	41.9 (9.2)	11.6 (6.4)	23.0 (8.2)	7.4 (3.7)	21.2 (7.7)	36.9 (8.7)	71.3 (3.1)	0.2 (0.2)	2.0 (0.8)	69.1 (3.1)	13.9 (2.3)	14.8 (2.4)
American Indian/Alaska Native	‡ (†)	‡ (†)	‡ (†)	‡ (†)	‡ (†)	‡ (†)	55.4 (10.6)	‡ (†)	3.7 (3.7)	51.7 (10.7)	26.1 (8.4)	18.5 (6.8)
Highest education level of parents												
High school diploma or less	36.5 (2.3)	13.5 (1.8)	17.0 (1.9)	6.0 (1.2)	12.4 (1.6)	51.1 (2.4)	52.0 (1.6)	4.1 (0.6)	4.8 (0.6)	43.1 (1.6)	16.5 (1.3)	31.5 (1.5)
Some postsecondary	32.8 (3.3)	10.1 (2.1)	14.3 (2.6)	8.4 (2.0)	19.0 (2.8)	48.2 (2.9)	59.5 (1.9)	3.1 (0.7)	5.4 (1.1)	50.9 (2.1)	16.4 (1.4)	24.2 (1.6)
Bachelor's degree	47.7 (4.2)	9.1 (2.3)	22.4 (3.7)	16.2 (3.2)	18.8 (3.5)	33.5 (3.9)	72.1 (1.5)	1.8 (0.4)	4.0 (0.6)	66.3 (1.5)	13.4 (1.1)	14.5 (1.1)
Advanced degree	45.4 (6.0)	3.1 (2.0)	17.2 (4.4)	25.2 (5.5)	25.2 (5.4)	29.4 (6.0)	76.5 (1.7)	1.2 (0.3)	1.4 (0.3)	73.9 (1.7)	11.7 (1.2)	11.8 (1.1)
Dependency status when first enrolled												
Dependent	42.1 (2.2)	8.2 (1.2)	20.1 (1.8)	13.8 (1.7)	18.3 (1.9)	39.6 (2.1)	68.0 (1.0)	2.1 (0.2)	3.6 (0.4)	62.1 (1.2)	14.0 (0.6)	18.1 (0.7)
Independent	32.9 (3.1)	17.6 (2.4)	12.3 (1.9)	3.0 (0.9)	13.8 (2.4)	53.4 (3.5)	35.9 (2.9)	8.8 (1.7)	6.4 (1.6)	20.6 (2.3)	19.1 (2.5)	45.0 (3.2)
Dependent student family income in 1994												
Less than $25,000	43.0 (3.8)	10.9 (2.6)	24.5 (3.4)	7.6 (2.1)	14.3 (2.6)	42.7 (3.5)	58.8 (1.8)	3.4 (0.7)	5.1 (1.0)	50.3 (2.1)	18.6 (1.5)	22.6 (1.5)
$25,000 to $44,999	41.2 (4.5)	10.5 (2.3)	16.4 (2.9)	14.3 (2.7)	19.1 (3.0)	39.6 (3.6)	61.7 (1.7)	2.3 (0.4)	4.4 (0.8)	55.0 (1.7)	15.1 (1.3)	23.1 (1.4)
$45,000 to $69,999	40.2 (3.8)	5.3 (1.8)	22.1 (3.2)	12.8 (2.5)	19.3 (3.5)	40.5 (4.0)	69.1 (1.6)	1.7 (0.4)	3.7 (0.7)	63.6 (1.7)	13.2 (1.0)	17.7 (1.3)
$70,000 or more	44.7 (5.5)	4.5 (1.8)	15.8 (3.6)	24.4 (4.5)	22.1 (4.2)	33.2 (4.8)	77.4 (1.3)	1.6 (0.4)	2.0 (0.4)	73.8 (1.5)	10.7 (1.0)	11.9 (0.9)
Timing of postsecondary enrollment												
Did not delay[3]	43.9 (2.3)	7.0 (1.1)	20.9 (2.0)	15.9 (1.8)	18.4 (2.0)	37.7 (2.1)	69.2 (1.0)	1.9 (0.2)	3.3 (0.4)	64.0 (1.1)	13.7 (0.6)	17.1 (0.7)
Delayed entry	32.8 (2.7)	15.6 (2.0)	13.7 (1.8)	3.5 (1.0)	14.9 (2.0)	52.3 (2.8)	45.0 (2.2)	6.6 (1.0)	7.0 (1.3)	31.4 (2.1)	18.0 (1.6)	37.0 (2.2)
Attendance status when first enrolled												
Full-time	47.3 (2.4)	10.2 (1.4)	21.3 (1.9)	15.8 (2.1)	15.9 (2.0)	36.8 (2.3)	69.3 (1.0)	1.9 (0.2)	4.0 (0.4)	63.3 (1.2)	12.7 (0.6)	18.0 (0.8)
Part-time	29.5 (3.2)	13.9 (2.7)	12.2 (2.3)	3.4 (1.0)	15.6 (2.4)	54.9 (3.4)	33.4 (3.2)	7.3 (2.0)	2.1 (0.8)	23.9 (3.3)	27.3 (3.0)	39.3 (3.4)
Intensity of enrollment through 2001												
Always part-time	13.2 (2.9)	11.5 (2.8)	1.7 (0.8)	# (†)	13.3 (3.0)	73.4 (3.8)	10.3 (2.9)	9.7 (2.9)	0.6 (0.6)	# (†)	12.9 (3.8)	76.8 (4.1)
Mixed	42.3 (2.5)	12.6 (1.7)	20.8 (2.0)	8.9 (1.3)	21.7 (2.1)	36.0 (2.2)	51.7 (1.5)	4.4 (0.6)	5.5 (0.6)	41.8 (1.6)	26.6 (1.3)	21.7 (1.1)
Always full-time	49.5 (3.2)	9.3 (1.4)	22.0 (2.8)	18.1 (3.1)	9.1 (1.8)	41.4 (3.1)	74.2 (1.1)	1.5 (0.2)	3.3 (0.5)	69.4 (1.2)	8.1 (0.6)	17.8 (0.9)
Degree goal at first institution												
Certificate	45.2 (5.1)	38.4 (5.3)	6.2 (2.3)	0.7 (0.4)	6.8 (2.5)	48.0 (4.8)	37.7 (7.0)	16.1 (6.2)	14.2 (7.5)	7.5 (3.0)	19.4 (6.5)	42.8 (6.7)
Associate's degree	40.9 (2.3)	8.7 (1.3)	24.7 (2.1)	7.5 (1.4)	15.6 (2.0)	43.5 (2.3)	52.6 (4.2)	7.3 (2.4)	24.7 (3.7)	20.7 (3.3)	8.9 (2.3)	38.5 (4.2)
Bachelor's degree	40.3[4] (3.7)	6.0[4] (1.9)	11.7[4] (2.4)	22.6[4] (3.3)	21.9[4] (3.5)	37.8[4] (3.4)	67.6 (1.0)	2.1 (0.3)	2.7 (0.3)	62.9 (1.1)	14.2 (0.6)	18.2 (0.7)

See notes at end of table.

Table 329. Percentage distribution of enrollment and completion status of first-time postsecondary students starting during the 1995–96 academic year, by type of institution and other student characteristics: 2001—Continued

Student and institution characteristic	Students starting in 2-year institutions						Students starting in 4-year institutions					
	Highest degree attained				No degree, still enrolled	No degree, not enrolled	Highest degree attained				No degree, still enrolled	No degree, not enrolled
	Total, any degree[1]	Certificate	Associate's	Bachelor's[2]			Total, any degree[1]	Certificate	Associate's	Bachelor's[2]		
1	2	3	4	5	6	7	8	9	10	11	12	13
Worked while enrolled, 1995–96												
Did not work	43.0 (3.0)	13.9 (2.3)	21.5 (2.8)	7.6 (1.9)	10.4 (2.5)	46.6 (3.1)	71.1 (1.3)	2.0 (0.4)	3.7 (0.7)	65.3 (1.6)	11.9 (0.8)	17.0 (1.1)
Worked part time	44.7 (2.6)	8.5 (1.5)	20.9 (2.1)	15.2 (2.0)	18.4 (2.4)	36.9 (2.3)	65.0 (1.3)	2.3 (0.4)	4.0 (0.4)	58.6 (1.4)	14.7 (0.8)	20.3 (1.0)
Worked full time	27.2 (2.6)	14.3 (2.2)	9.6 (1.5)	3.4 (0.9)	17.0 (2.5)	55.8 (2.9)	41.7 (2.6)	7.1 (1.3)	4.2 (1.1)	30.5 (2.5)	21.7 (2.2)	36.6 (2.5)
Control of first institution												
Public	36.7 (1.8)	10.1 (1.3)	16.4 (1.4)	10.3 (1.3)	17.4 (1.6)	45.9 (1.7)	60.5 (1.2)	2.8 (0.3)	4.4 (0.6)	53.3 (1.4)	17.4 (0.8)	22.2 (1.0)
Private, not for profit	58.9 (5.4)	19.3 (4.6)	27.8 (3.9)	11.8 (3.3)	8.4 (2.4)	32.7 (4.6)	73.6 (1.7)	1.8 (0.3)	2.8 (0.5)	68.9 (2.0)	9.3 (0.8)	17.1 (1.3)
Private, for profit	55.6 (3.2)	27.8 (3.9)	25.8 (3.9)	2.0 (0.8)	4.3 (1.2)	40.0 (3.4)	52.8 (10.5)	17.9 (7.2)	14.9 (6.0)	20.0 (5.1)	11.1 (3.1)	36.1 (8.6)
Socioeconomic status in 1995–96[5]												
Not disadvantaged	41.7 (2.8)	8.9 (1.8)	18.1 (2.1)	14.6 (2.0)	20.4 (2.7)	38.0 (2.7)	71.4 (1.1)	2.0 (0.3)	3.3 (0.4)	66.1 (1.3)	12.3 (0.7)	16.3 (0.8)
Minimally disadvantaged	33.9 (2.4)	12.8 (1.7)	14.9 (1.8)	6.2 (1.4)	13.1 (1.6)	53.0 (2.7)	59.8 (1.6)	3.7 (0.6)	5.4 (0.7)	50.8 (1.7)	16.4 (1.2)	23.8 (1.3)
Moderately or highly disadvantaged	43.7 (3.6)	14.6 (3.0)	21.6 (3.4)	7.5 (1.9)	14.5 (2.7)	41.8 (3.7)	47.1 (2.0)	3.7 (0.8)	3.8 (0.8)	39.6 (2.1)	19.5 (1.9)	33.4 (2.1)

†Not applicable.
#Rounds to zero.
‡Reporting standards not met.
[1]Includes a small percentage of students who had attained a degree and were still enrolled. Includes recipients of degrees not shown separately.
[2]Includes a small percentage of students who had attained an advanced degree.
[3]Includes students with a standard high school diploma who enrolled in postsecondary education in the same year as their graduation.
[4]Includes students whose goal was to transfer to a 4-year institution.

[5]Determined by a socioeconomic diversity index that includes parental income as a percentage of the 1994 federal poverty level, parental education, and the proportion of the student body at the student's high school that was eligible for free or reduced-price lunch.
NOTE: Data reflect completion and enrollment status by spring 2001 of first-time postsecondary students starting in academic year 1995–96. Race categories exclude persons of Hispanic ethnicity. Detail may not sum to totals because of rounding. Standard errors appear in parentheses.
SOURCE: U.S. Department of Education, National Center for Education Statistics, 1996/01 Beginning Postsecondary Students Longitudinal Study (BPS:96/01). (This table was prepared August 2003.)

Table 330. Average scores on Graduate Record Examination (GRE) general and subject tests: 1965 through 2007

Academic year ending	Number of GRE takers	GRE takers as a percent of bachelor's degrees[1]	General test sections				Subject tests									
			Verbal	Quantitative	Analytical reasoning	Analytical writing	Biochemistry, cell and molecular biology	Biology	Chemistry	Computer science	Education	Engineering	Literature	Mathematics	Physics	Psychology
1	2	3	4	5	6	7	8	9	10	11	12	13	14	15	16	17
1965	93,792	18.7	530 (124)	533 (137)	† (†)	† (†)	†	617 (117)	628 (114)	† (†)	481 (86)	618 (108)	591 (95)	† (†)	— (†)	556 (91)
1966	123,960	23.8	520 (124)	528 (133)	† (†)	† (†)	†	610 (115)	618 (110)	† (†)	474 (87)	609 (106)	588 (94)	† (†)	— (†)	552 (91)
1967	151,134	27.0	519 (125)	528 (134)	† (†)	† (†)	†	613 (114)	615 (104)	† (†)	476 (90)	603 (104)	582 (91)	† (†)	— (†)	553 (93)
1968	182,432	28.8	520 (124)	527 (135)	† (†)	† (†)	†	614 (114)	617 (104)	† (†)	478 (87)	601 (105)	572 (91)	† (†)	— (†)	547 (93)
1969	206,113	28.3	515 (124)	524 (132)	† (†)	† (†)	†	613 (112)	613 (104)	† (†)	477 (88)	591 (103)	569 (89)	† (†)	— (†)	543 (89)
1970	265,359	33.5	503 (123)	516 (132)	† (†)	† (†)	†	603 (111)	613 (113)	† (†)	462 (92)	586 (110)	556 (90)	† (†)	— (†)	532 (91)
1971	293,600	35.0	497 (125)	512 (134)	† (†)	† (†)	†	603 (114)	618 (117)	† (†)	457 (95)	587 (115)	546 (91)	† (†)	— (†)	530 (92)
1972	293,506	33.1	494 (126)	508 (136)	† (†)	† (†)	†	606 (115)	624 (124)	† (†)	446 (93)	594 (119)	544 (96)	† (†)	— (†)	528 (92)
1973	290,104	31.5	497 (125)	512 (135)	† (†)	† (†)	†	619 (110)	630 (114)	† (†)	459 (96)	593 (114)	545 (96)	† (†)	— (†)	529 (92)
1974	301,070	31.8	492 (126)	509 (137)	† (†)	† (†)	†	624 (110)	634 (115)	† (†)	452 (93)	591 (121)	547 (99)	† (†)	— (†)	530 (95)
1975	298,335	32.3	493 (125)	508 (137)	† (†)	† (†)	†	— (†)	— (†)	† (†)	— (†)	— (†)	— (†)	† (†)	— (†)	— (†)
1976	299,292	32.3	492 (127)	510 (138)	† (†)	† (†)	†	627 (112)	627 (107)	—	454 (93)	594 (119)	539 (101)	† (†)	— (†)	531 (93)
1977	287,715	31.3	490 (129)	514 (139)	498 (126)	† (†)	†	625 (113)	630 (109)	—	453 (93)	592 (115)	532 (101)	† (†)	— (†)	532 (95)
1978	286,383	31.1	484 (128)	518 (135)	504 (128)	† (†)	†	622 (115)	624 (104)	—	452 (91)	594 (114)	530 (102)	† (†)	— (†)	529 (97)
1979	282,482	30.7	476 (130)	517 (135)	512 (129)	† (†)	†	621 (117)	623 (104)	—	451 (89)	592 (115)	525 (102)	† (†)	— (†)	530 (97)
1980	272,281	29.3	474 (131)	522 (136)	516 (129)	† (†)	†	619 (115)	618 (105)	—	449 (90)	590 (116)	521 (105)	† (†)	— (†)	534 (98)
1981	262,855	28.1	473 (128)	523 (136)	520 (129)	† (†)	†	617 (115)	615 (103)	—	453 (90)	590 (116)	520 (99)	† (†)	— (†)	532 (97)
1982	256,381	26.9	469 (130)	533 (137)	521 (128)	† (†)	†	616 (114)	616 (105)	—	456 (89)	593 (115)	521 (100)	† (†)	— (†)	532 (97)
1983	263,674	27.2	473 (131)	541 (138)	528 (128)	† (†)	†	623 (115)	620 (105)	—	459 (90)	599 (114)	527 (98)	† (†)	— (†)	542 (95)
1984	265,221	27.2	475 (130)	541 (139)	530 (129)	† (†)	†	622 (115)	619 (102)	—	461 (90)	604 (114)	530 (97)	† (†)	— (†)	543 (96)
1985	271,972	27.8	474 (126)	545 (140)	534 (128)	† (†)	—	619 (114)	621 (101)	—	459 (89)	615 (120)	531 (95)	† (†)	— (†)	541 (95)
1986	279,428	28.3	475 (126)	552 (140)	536 (129)	† (†)	—	612 (114)	628 (106)	—	464 (87)	616 (119)	527 (96)	† (†)	— (†)	542 (97)
1987	293,560	29.6	477 (126)	550 (140)	537 (129)	† (†)	—	616 (116)	629 (104)	—	465 (86)	619 (119)	526 (95)	† (†)	— (†)	536 (95)
1988	303,703	30.5	483 (123)	557 (140)	541 (129)	† (†)	—	615 (114)	631 (108)	—	467 (85)	622 (120)	525 (94)	† (†)	— (†)	537 (94)
1989	326,096	32.0	484 (125)	560 (142)	545 (129)	† (†)	—	612 (114)	642 (117)	—	465 (87)	626 (116)	528 (91)	† (†)	— (†)	538 (95)
1990	344,572	32.8	486 (123)	562 (143)	544 (131)	† (†)	—	612 (114)	662 (123)	—	461 (84)	617 (111)	523 (92)	† (†)	— (†)	537 (95)
1991	379,882	34.7	485 (122)	562 (141)	549 (131)	† (†)	—	609 (113)	660 (123)	—	457 (85)	611 (111)	523 (93)	† (†)	— (†)	535 (95)
1992	411,528	36.2	483 (117)	561 (140)	548 (129)	† (†)	—	605 (113)	654 (128)	—	462 (82)	610 (117)	525 (92)	† (†)	— (†)	536 (95)
1993	400,246	34.4	481 (117)	557 (140)	543 (133)	† (†)	—	606 (114)	662 (133)	—	462 (80)	602 (115)	516 (94)	† (†)	— (†)	536 (97)
1994	399,395 [2]	34.2	479 (116)	553 (139)	542 (133)	† (†)	—	620 (116)	627 (113)	—	493 [3] (104)	601 (115)	517 (95)	† (†)	— (†)	538 (96)
1995	389,539 [2]	33.6	477 (115)	553 (140)		† (†)	—	622 (116)	675 (138)	—	488 [3] (102)	596 (113)	513 (96)	† (†)	— (†)	544 (98)
1996	376,013 [2]	32.3	473 (114)	558 (139)		† (†)	—	614 (114)	678 (135)	—	489 [3] (104)	604 (119)	512 (97)	† (†)	— (†)	547 (99)
1997	376,062 [2]	32.1	472 (113)	562 (139)		† (†)	—	620 (115)	684 (143)	—	487 [3] (103)	602 (114)	525 (100)	† (†)	— (†)	554 (99)
1998	364,554 [2]	30.8	471 (113)	569 (141)		† (†)	—	628 (113)	686 (137)	—	477 [3] (100)	609 (118)	530 (100)	† (†)	— (†)	563 (100)
1999[4]	396,330	33.0	468 (114)	565 (143)		† (†)	—	626 (114)	684 (137)	—	† (†)	604 (115)	527 (100)	† (†)	— (†)	559 (99)

See notes at end of table.

Table 330. Average scores on Graduate Record Examination (GRE) general and subject tests: 1965 through 2007—Continued

Academic year ending	Number of GRE takers	GRE takers as a percent of bachelor's degrees[1]	General test sections				Subject tests									
			Verbal	Quantitative	Analytical reasoning	Analytical writing	Biochemistry, cell and molecular biology	Biology	Chemistry	Computer science	Education	Engineering	Literature	Mathematics	Physics	Psychology
1	2	3	4	5	6	7	8	9	10	11	12	13	14	15	16	17
2000[4]	397,489	32.1	465 (116)	578 (147)	562 (141)	† (†)	— (†)	629 (114)	686 (133)	— (†)	†	— (†)	530 (99)	— (†)	— (†)	563 (98)
2001	432,667	34.8	— (†)	— (†)	— (†)	† (†)	— (†)	— (†)	— (†)	— (†)	†	— (†)	— (†)	— (†)	— (†)	— (†)
2002	520,547	40.3	473 (123)	597 (151)	571 (139)	† (†)	— (†)	— (†)	— (†)	— (†)	†	† (†)	— (†)	— (†)	— (†)	— (†)
2003[5,6]	571,606	42.4	470 (120)	593 (147)	† (†)	4.2 (0.96)	517 (100)	635 (114)	682 (125)	712 (97)	† (†)	† (†)	538 (98)	620 (131)	669 (151)	580 (101)
2004[5,6,7]	418,463	29.9	469 (120)	597 (148)	† (†)	4.2 (1.00)	517 (101)	643 (115)	675 (120)	715 (93)	† (†)	† (†)	537 (97)	621 (130)	665 (148)	586 (101)
2005[5,6,7]	431,783	30.0	467 (118)	591 (148)	† (†)	4.2 (0.90)	518 (100)	647 (117)	675 (117)	715 (91)	† (†)	† (†)	540 (97)	623 (130)	672 (151)	592 (101)
2006[5,7,8]	508,604	34.2	465 (117)	584 (149)	† (†)	4.1 (0.90)	519 (99)	650 (118)	677 (116)	717 (92)	† (†)	† (†)	541 (97)	627 (129)	678 (153)	598 (101)
2007[5,7,8]	561,060	36.8	462 (119)	584 (151)	† (†)	4.0 (0.90)	521 (97)	650 (120)	689 (115)	715 (91)	† (†)	† (†)	542 (98)	636 (130)	686 (155)	600 (101)

—Not available.
†Not applicable.
[1]GRE takers include examinees from inside and outside of the United States, while the bachelor's degree recipients include U.S. institutions only.
[2]Total includes examinees who received no score on one or more general test measures.
[3]Data reported for 1994 through 1998 are from the revised education test.
[4]Subject test score data reflect the three-year average for all examinees who tested between October 1 three years prior to the reported test year and September 30 of the reported test year. These data are not directly comparable with data for most other years.
[5]Subject test score data reflect the three-year average for all examinees who tested between July 1 three years prior to the reported test year and June 30 of the reported test year. These data are not directly comparable with previous years, except for 1999 and 2000.
[6]Analytical writing test score data reflect the average for all examinees who tested between October 1, 2002, and June 30 of the reported test year.
[7]Verbal and quantitative test score data reflect the three-year average for all examinees who tested between July 1 three years prior to the reported test year and June 30 of the reported test year. These data are not directly comparable with previous years.

[8]Analytical writing test score data reflect the three-year average for all examinees who tested between July 1 three years prior to the reported test year and June 30 of the reported test year.
NOTE: GRE data include test takers from both within and outside of the United States. GRE scores for the verbal, quantitative, and analytical reasoning sections range from 200 to 800. Scores for the analytical writing section range from 0 to 6, in half-point increments. The range of scores is different for the various subject tests, from as low as 200 to as high as 990. The analytical reasoning section of the GRE, a multiple-choice test, was discontinued in September 2002, and replaced by the analytical writing section, an essay-based test. The education subject test was administered for the final time in April 1998. The engineering subject test was administered for the final time in April 2001. Some data have been revised from previously published figures. Standard deviations appear in parentheses.
SOURCE: Graduate Record Examination Board, *Examinee and Score Trends for the GRE General Test, 1964–65* through *1985–86; A Summary of Data Collected From Graduate Record Examinations Test-Takers During 1986–87; Guide to the Use of Scores, 1987–88* through *2001–02; Sex, Race, Ethnicity, and Performance on the GRE General Test, 2000–01* through *2001–02; Factors That Can Influence Performance on the GRE General Test, 2003–04; GRE Volumes by Country, 2000–2007;* and *Interpreting Your GRE Scores, 2005–06, 2006–07,* and *2007–08.* U.S. Department of Education, National Center for Education Statistics, Higher Education General Information Survey (HEGIS), "Degrees and Other Formal Awards Conferred" surveys, 1964–65 through 1985–86; and 1986–87 through 2006–07 Integrated Postsecondary Education Data System (IPEDS), "Completions Survey" (IPEDS-C:87–99); and Fall 2000 through Fall 2007. (This table was prepared August 2008.)

Table 331. Average undergraduate tuition and fees and room and board rates charged for full-time students in degree-granting institutions, by type and control of institution: 1964–65 through 2007–08

	Constant 2006–07 dollars			Current dollars																			
	Total tuition, room, and board			Total tuition, room, and board					Tuition and required fees (in-state for public institutions)					Dormitory rooms					Board (7-day basis)[1]				
					4-year institutions					4-year institutions					4-year institutions					4-year institutions		
Year and control of institution	All insti-tutions	All 4-year	2-year	All insti-tutions	All 4-year	Univer-sities	Other 4-year	2-year	All insti-tutions	All 4-year	Univer-sities	Other 4-year	2-year	All insti-tutions	All 4-year	Univer-sities	Other 4-year	2-year	All insti-tutions	All 4-year	Univer-sities	Other 4-year	2-year
1	2	3	4	5	6	7	8	9	10	11	12	13	14	15	16	17	18	19	20	21	22	23	24
All institutions																							
1976–77	$7,914	$8,963	$5,558	$2,275	$2,577	$2,647	$2,527	$1,598	$924	$1,218	$1,210	$1,223	$346	$603	$611	$649	$584	$503	$748	$748	$788	$719	$750
1977–78	7,857	8,881	5,552	2,411	2,725	2,777	2,685	1,703	984	1,291	1,269	1,305	378	645	654	691	628	525	781	780	818	752	801
1978–79	7,708	8,694	5,448	2,587	2,917	2,967	2,879	1,828	1,073	1,397	1,370	1,413	411	688	696	737	667	575	826	825	860	800	842
1979–80	7,386	8,328	5,205	2,809	3,167	3,223	3,124	1,979	1,163	1,513	1,484	1,530	451	751	759	803	729	628	895	895	936	865	900
1980–81	7,308	8,247	5,256	3,101	3,499	3,535	3,469	2,230	1,289	1,679	1,634	1,705	526	836	846	881	821	705	976	975	1,020	943	1,000
1981–82	7,569	8,570	5,370	3,489	3,951	4,005	3,908	2,476	1,457	1,907	1,860	1,935	590	950	961	1,023	919	793	1,083	1,082	1,121	1,055	1,094
1982–83	8,063	9,164	5,644	3,877	4,406	4,466	4,356	2,713	1,626	2,139	2,081	2,173	675	1,064	1,078	1,150	1,028	873	1,187	1,189	1,235	1,155	1,165
1983–84	8,358	9,521	5,725	4,167	4,747	4,793	4,712	2,854	1,783	2,344	2,300	2,368	730	1,145	1,162	1,211	1,130	916	1,239	1,242	1,282	1,214	1,208
1984–85	8,806	9,960	6,136	4,563	5,160	5,236	5,107	3,179	1,985	2,567	2,539	2,583	821	1,267	1,282	1,343	1,242	1,058	1,310	1,311	1,353	1,282	1,301
1985–86[2]	9,164	10,326	6,316	4,885	5,504	5,597	5,441	3,367	2,181	2,784	2,770	2,793	888	1,338	1,355	1,424	1,309	1,107	1,365	1,365	1,403	1,339	1,372
1986–87	9,554	10,945	6,048	5,206	5,964	6,124	5,857	3,295	2,312	3,042	3,042	3,042	897	1,405	1,427	1,501	1,376	1,034	1,489	1,495	1,581	1,439	1,364
1987–88	9,682	11,053	5,750	5,494	6,272	6,339	6,226	3,263	2,458	3,201	3,168	3,220	809	1,488	1,516	1,576	1,478	1,017	1,549	1,555	1,596	1,529	1,437
1988–89	9,885	11,328	6,018	5,869	6,725	6,801	6,673	3,573	2,658	3,472	3,422	3,499	979	1,575	1,609	1,665	1,573	1,085	1,636	1,644	1,715	1,601	1,509
1989–90	9,979	11,594	5,956	6,207	7,212	7,347	7,120	3,705	2,839	3,800	3,765	3,819	978	1,638	1,675	1,732	1,638	1,105	1,730	1,737	1,850	1,663	1,622
1990–91	10,002	11,588	5,991	6,562	7,602	7,709	7,528	3,930	3,016	4,009	3,958	4,036	1,087	1,743	1,782	1,848	1,740	1,182	1,802	1,811	1,903	1,751	1,660
1991–92	10,453	12,167	6,044	7,077	8,238	8,390	8,142	4,092	3,286	4,385	4,368	4,394	1,189	1,874	1,921	1,996	1,875	1,210	1,918	1,931	2,026	1,872	1,692
1992–93	10,674	12,543	6,026	7,452	8,758	8,934	8,648	4,207	3,517	4,752	4,665	4,795	1,276	1,939	1,991	2,104	1,926	1,240	1,996	2,015	2,165	1,927	1,692
1993–94	11,073	12,979	6,211	7,931	9,296	9,495	9,186	4,449	3,827	5,119	5,104	5,127	1,399	2,057	2,111	2,190	2,068	1,332	2,047	2,067	2,201	1,992	1,718
1994–95	11,272	13,203	6,288	8,306	9,728	9,863	9,646	4,633	4,044	5,391	5,287	5,441	1,488	2,145	2,200	2,281	2,155	1,396	2,116	2,138	2,295	2,049	1,750
1995–96	11,628	13,649	6,243	8,800	10,330	10,560	10,195	4,725	4,338	5,786	5,733	5,812	1,522	2,264	2,318	2,423	2,260	1,473	2,199	2,226	2,404	2,123	1,730
1996–97	11,826	13,926	6,288	9,206	10,841	11,033	10,726	4,895	4,564	6,118	6,055	6,150	1,543	2,365	2,422	2,518	2,368	1,522	2,276	2,301	2,460	2,208	1,830
1997–98	12,101	14,233	6,553	9,588	11,277	11,382	11,205	5,192	4,755	6,351	6,232	6,408	1,695	2,444	2,507	2,575	2,469	1,598	2,389	2,419	2,576	2,327	1,900
1998–99	12,500	14,749	6,564	10,076	11,888	12,123	11,752	5,291	5,013	6,723	6,713	6,728	1,725	2,557	2,626	2,710	2,578	1,616	2,506	2,540	2,700	2,446	1,950
1999–2000	12,594	14,894	6,521	10,444	12,352	12,613	12,198	5,408	5,238	7,044	7,026	7,052	1,721	2,682	2,749	2,845	2,695	1,733	2,524	2,559	2,741	2,451	1,954
2000–01	12,613	15,066	6,365	10,818	12,922	13,177	12,775	5,460	5,377	7,372	7,360	7,377	1,698	2,819	2,893	2,999	2,833	1,744	2,622	2,658	2,818	2,565	2,017
2001–02	13,037	15,625	6,550	11,380	13,639	13,942	13,468	5,718	5,646	7,786	7,788	7,785	1,800	2,981	3,060	3,184	2,992	1,848	2,753	2,793	2,970	2,692	2,070
2002–03	13,467	16,186	7,008	12,014	14,439	14,827	14,233	6,252	6,002	8,309	8,406	8,264	1,903	3,179	3,263	3,377	3,201	2,077	2,832	2,867	3,044	2,767	2,272
2003–04	14,209	17,009	7,355	12,953	15,505	16,096	15,205	6,705	6,608	9,029	9,268	8,924	2,174	3,359	3,448	3,599	3,368	2,208	2,986	3,028	3,230	2,914	2,322
2004–05	14,687	17,581	7,547	13,792	16,509	17,219	16,164	7,086	7,122	9,706	9,706	9,559	2,338	3,569	3,661	3,813	3,582	2,336	3,100	3,142	3,355	3,023	2,413
2005–06	15,007	17,898	7,418	14,629	17,447	18,229	17,075	7,231	7,601	10,279	10,666	10,119	2,417	3,804	3,899	4,050	3,821	2,396	3,224	3,269	3,513	3,135	2,418
2006–07	15,483	18,471	7,466	15,483	18,471	19,304	18,085	7,466	8,092	10,931	11,404	10,738	2,496	4,019	4,116	4,261	4,041	2,527	3,372	3,424	3,640	3,306	2,443
2007–08[3]	15,665	18,670	7,372	16,245	19,362	20,320	18,924	7,645	8,505	11,459	12,016	11,235	2,535	4,208	4,311	4,486	4,221	2,627	3,533	3,592	3,818	3,468	2,483
Public institutions																							
1964–65	6,209	—	4,170	950	—	1,051	867	638	243	—	298	224	99	271	—	291	241	178	436	—	462	402	361
1965–66	6,289	—	4,286	983	—	1,105	904	670	257	—	327	241	109	281	—	304	255	194	445	—	474	408	367
1966–67	6,363	—	4,403	1,026	—	1,171	947	710	275	—	360	259	121	294	—	321	271	213	457	—	490	417	376
1967–68	6,387	—	4,736	1,064	—	1,199	997	789	283	—	366	268	144	313	—	337	292	243	468	—	496	437	402
1968–69	6,393	—	5,054	1,117	—	1,245	1,063	883	295	—	377	281	170	337	—	359	318	278	485	—	509	464	435
1969–70	6,501	—	5,139	1,203	—	1,362	1,135	951	323	—	427	306	178	369	—	395	346	308	511	—	540	483	465
1970–71	6,614	—	5,129	1,287	—	1,477	1,206	998	351	—	478	332	187	401	—	431	375	338	535	—	568	499	473
1971–72	6,732	—	5,323	1,357	—	1,579	1,263	1,073	376	—	526	354	192	430	—	463	400	366	551	—	590	509	515
1972–73	6,953	—	5,708	1,458	—	1,668	1,460	1,197	407	—	566	455	233	476	—	500	455	398	575	—	602	550	566
1973–74	6,642	—	5,578	1,517	—	1,707	1,506	1,274	438	—	581	463	274	480	—	505	464	409	599	—	621	579	591

See notes at end of table.

Table 331. Average undergraduate tuition and fees and room and board rates charged for full-time students in degree-granting institutions, by type and control of institution: 1964–65 through 2007–08—Continued

	Constant 2006–07 dollars			Current dollars																			
	Total tuition, room, and board			Total tuition, room, and board					Tuition and required fees (in-state for public institutions)					Dormitory rooms					Board (7-day basis)[1]				
					4-year institutions					4-year institutions					4-year institutions					4-year institutions		
Year and control of institution	All insti-tutions	All 4-year	2-year	All insti-tutions	All 4-year	Univer-sities	Other 4-year	2-year	All insti-tutions	All 4-year	Univer-sities	Other 4-year	2-year	All insti-tutions	All 4-year	Univer-sities	Other 4-year	2-year	All insti-tutions	All 4-year	Univer-sities	Other 4-year	2-year
	2	3	4	5	6	7	8	9	10	11	12	13	14	15	16	17	18	19	20	21	22	23	24
1974–75	6,161	—	5,278	1,563	—	1,760	1,558	1,339	432	—	599	448	277	506	—	527	497	424	625	—	634	613	638
1975–76	6,132	—	5,102	1,666	—	1,935	1,657	1,386	433	—	642	469	245	544	—	573	533	442	689	—	720	655	699
1976–77	6,222	6,731	5,184	1,789	1,935	2,067	1,827	1,491	479	617	689	564	283	582	592	614	572	465	728	727	763	692	742
1977–78	6,152	6,642	5,181	1,888	2,038	2,170	1,931	1,590	512	655	736	596	306	621	631	649	616	486	755	752	785	720	797
1978–79	5,941	6,392	5,039	1,994	2,145	2,289	2,027	1,591	543	688	777	622	327	655	664	689	641	527	796	793	823	764	837
1979–80	5,693	6,120	4,790	2,165	2,327	2,487	2,198	1,822	583	738	840	662	355	715	725	750	703	574	867	865	898	833	893
1980–81	5,593	6,010	4,777	2,373	2,550	2,712	2,421	2,027	635	804	915	722	391	799	811	827	796	642	940	936	969	904	994
1981–82	5,776	6,227	4,824	2,663	2,871	3,079	2,705	2,224	714	909	1,042	813	434	909	925	970	885	703	1,039	1,036	1,067	1,006	1,086
1982–83	6,125	6,647	4,970	2,945	3,196	3,403	3,032	2,390	798	1,031	1,164	936	473	1,010	1,030	1,072	993	755	1,136	1,134	1,167	1,103	1,162
1983–84	6,330	6,885	5,082	3,156	3,433	3,628	3,285	2,534	891	1,148	1,264	1,052	528	1,087	1,110	1,131	1,092	801	1,178	1,175	1,213	1,141	1,205
1984–85	6,578	7,106	5,418	3,408	3,682	3,899	3,518	2,807	971	1,228	1,366	1,117	584	1,196	1,217	1,237	1,200	921	1,241	1,237	1,276	1,201	1,302
1985–86[2]	6,700	7,238	5,592	3,571	3,859	4,146	3,637	2,981	1,045	1,318	1,536	1,157	641	1,242	1,263	1,290	1,240	960	1,285	1,278	1,320	1,240	1,380
1986–87	6,983	7,594	5,485	3,805	4,138	4,469	3,891	2,989	1,106	1,414	1,651	1,248	660	1,301	1,323	1,355	1,295	979	1,398	1,401	1,464	1,348	1,349
1987–88	7,137	7,759	5,402	4,050	4,403	4,619	4,250	3,066	1,218	1,537	1,726	1,407	706	1,378	1,410	1,410	1,409	943	1,454	1,456	1,482	1,434	1,417
1988–89	7,199	7,880	5,361	4,274	4,678	4,905	4,526	3,183	1,285	1,646	1,846	1,515	730	1,457	1,496	1,483	1,506	965	1,533	1,536	1,576	1,504	1,488
1989–90	7,241	7,999	5,304	4,504	4,975	5,324	4,723	3,299	1,356	1,780	2,035	1,608	756	1,513	1,557	1,561	1,554	962	1,635	1,638	1,728	1,561	1,581
1990–91	7,251	7,992	5,286	4,757	5,243	5,585	5,004	3,467	1,454	1,888	2,159	1,707	824	1,612	1,657	1,658	1,655	1,050	1,691	1,698	1,767	1,641	1,594
1991–92	7,590	8,409	5,351	5,138	5,693	6,050	5,458	3,523	1,628	2,117	2,409	1,931	936	1,731	1,785	1,789	1,782	1,074	1,780	1,792	1,852	1,745	1,612
1992–93	7,704	8,622	5,441	5,379	6,020	6,442	5,740	3,799	1,782	2,349	2,604	2,192	1,025	1,756	1,816	1,856	1,787	1,106	1,841	1,854	1,982	1,761	1,668
1993–94	7,950	8,887	5,579	5,694	6,365	6,710	6,146	3,396	1,942	2,537	2,821	2,360	1,125	1,873	1,934	1,897	1,958	1,190	1,880	1,895	1,993	1,828	1,681
1994–95	8,096	9,053	5,614	5,965	6,670	7,077	6,409	4,137	2,057	2,661	2,977	2,499	1,192	1,959	2,023	1,992	2,044	1,232	1,949	1,967	2,108	1,866	1,712
1995–96	8,266	9,267	5,571	6,256	7,014	7,448	6,730	4,217	2,179	2,843	3,151	2,660	1,259	2,057	2,121	2,104	2,133	1,297	2,020	2,045	2,192	1,937	1,681
1996–97	8,388	9,422	5,657	6,530	7,334	7,792	7,035	4,404	2,271	2,987	3,323	2,778	1,276	2,148	2,214	2,187	2,232	1,339	2,111	2,133	2,282	2,025	1,789
1997–98	8,599	9,685	5,691	6,813	7,673	8,210	7,318	4,509	2,360	3,110	3,486	2,877	1,314	2,225	2,301	2,285	2,312	1,401	2,228	2,263	2,438	2,130	1,795
1998–99	8,817	9,959	5,712	7,107	8,027	8,625	7,631	4,604	2,430	3,229	3,640	2,974	1,327	2,330	2,409	2,408	2,410	1,450	2,347	2,389	2,576	2,247	1,828
1999–2000	8,814	9,978	5,691	7,310	8,275	8,912	7,852	4,720	2,506	3,349	3,768	3,091	1,338	2,440	2,519	2,516	2,521	1,549	2,364	2,406	2,628	2,239	1,834
2000–01	8,845	10,089	5,642	7,586	8,653	9,321	8,218	4,839	2,562	3,501	3,979	3,208	1,333	2,569	2,654	2,657	2,652	1,600	2,455	2,499	2,686	2,358	1,906
2001–02	9,190	10,535	5,885	8,022	9,196	9,948	8,715	5,137	2,700	3,735	4,273	3,409	1,380	2,723	2,816	2,838	2,801	1,722	2,598	2,645	2,837	2,504	2,036
2002–03	9,530	10,971	6,279	8,502	9,787	10,604	9,280	5,601	2,903	4,045	4,686	3,668	1,483	2,950	3,029	3,023	3,032	1,954	2,669	2,712	2,895	2,580	2,164
2003–04	10,143	11,709	6,595	9,247	10,674	11,679	10,063	6,012	3,319	4,587	5,363	4,141	1,702	3,106	3,212	3,232	3,199	2,089	2,822	2,875	3,084	2,724	2,221
2004–05	10,505	12,168	6,789	9,864	11,426	12,588	10,734	6,375	3,629	5,027	5,939	4,512	1,849	3,304	3,418	3,427	3,413	2,174	2,931	2,981	3,222	2,809	2,353
2005–06	10,725	12,421	6,660	10,454	12,108	13,424	11,335	6,492	3,874	5,351	6,399	4,765	1,935	3,545	3,664	3,654	3,672	2,251	3,035	3,093	3,372	2,899	2,306
2006–07	11,049	12,797	6,815	11,049	12,797	14,215	11,983	6,615	4,102	5,665	6,842	5,020	2,018	3,757	3,878	3,875	3,881	2,407	3,191	3,253	3,498	3,083	2,390
2007–08[3]	11,164	12,944	6,717	11,578	13,424	14,915	12,577	6,966	4,307	5,950	7,171	5,291	2,063	3,941	4,072	4,076	4,069	2,495	3,329	3,402	3,669	3,217	2,408
Private institutions																							
1964–65	12,464	—	9,510	1,907	—	2,202	1,810	1,455	1,088	—	1,297	1,023	702	331	—	390	308	289	488	—	515	479	464
1965–66	12,827	—	9,961	2,005	—	2,316	1,899	1,557	1,154	—	1,369	1,086	768	356	—	418	330	316	495	—	529	483	473
1966–67	13,172	—	10,412	2,124	—	2,456	2,007	1,679	1,233	—	1,456	1,162	845	385	—	452	355	347	506	—	548	490	487
1967–68	13,236	—	10,577	2,205	—	2,545	2,104	1,752	1,297	—	1,534	1,237	892	392	—	455	366	366	516	—	556	501	504
1968–69	13,284	—	10,737	2,321	—	2,673	2,237	1,876	1,383	—	1,638	1,335	956	404	—	463	382	391	534	—	572	520	529
1969–70	13,672	—	10,770	2,530	—	2,920	2,420	1,933	1,533	—	1,809	1,468	1,034	435	—	503	409	413	561	—	608	543	546
1970–71	14,070	—	10,807	2,738	—	3,163	2,599	2,103	1,684	—	1,980	1,603	1,109	463	—	542	434	434	586	—	641	562	560
1971–72	14,471	—	10,844	2,917	—	3,375	2,748	2,186	1,820	—	2,133	1,721	1,172	494	—	576	454	449	603	—	666	573	565
1972–73	14,487	—	10,839	3,038	—	3,512	2,934	2,273	1,898	—	2,226	1,846	1,221	524	—	622	490	457	616	—	664	598	595
1973–74	13,853	—	10,552	3,164	—	3,717	3,040	2,410	1,989	—	2,375	1,925	1,303	533	—	622	502	483	642	—	720	613	624

See notes at end of table.

Table 331. Average undergraduate tuition and fees and room and board rates charged for full-time students in degree-granting institutions, by type and control of institution: 1964–65 through 2007–08—Continued

Column groups: Columns 2–4 are **Constant 2006–07 dollars — Total tuition, room, and board**. Columns 5–24 are **Current dollars**: cols 5–9 = Total tuition, room, and board; cols 10–14 = Tuition and required fees (in-state for public institutions); cols 15–19 = Dormitory rooms; cols 20–24 = Board (7-day basis)[1]. Within each current-dollar group: "All inst" / "All 4-year" / "Universities" / "Other 4-year" / "2-year".

Year and control of institution	All inst (2)	4-year (3)	2-year (4)	All inst (5)	All 4-year (6)	Universities (7)	Other 4-year (8)	2-year (9)	All inst (10)	All 4-year (11)	Universities (12)	Other 4-year (13)	2-year (14)	All inst (15)	All 4-year (16)	Universities (17)	Other 4-year (18)	2-year (19)	All inst (20)	All 4-year (21)	Universities (22)	Other 4-year (23)	2-year (24)
1974–75	13,413	—	10,212	3,403	—	4,076	3,156	2,591	2,117	—	2,614	1,954	1,367	586	—	691	536	564	700	—	771	666	660
1975–76	13,483	—	9,979	3,663	—	4,467	3,385	2,711	2,272	—	2,881	2,084	1,427	636	—	753	583	572	755	—	833	718	712
1976–77	13,586	13,832	10,333	3,906	3,977	4,715	3,714	2,971	2,467	2,534	3,051	2,351	1,592	649	651	783	604	607	790	791	882	759	772
1977–78	13,553	13,820	10,260	4,158	4,240	5,033	3,967	3,148	2,624	2,700	3,240	2,520	1,706	698	702	850	648	631	836	838	943	800	811
1978–79	13,453	13,737	10,101	4,514	4,609	5,403	4,327	3,389	2,867	2,958	3,487	2,771	1,831	758	761	916	704	700	889	890	1,000	851	858
1979–80	12,917	13,181	9,864	4,912	5,013	5,891	4,700	3,751	3,130	3,225	3,811	3,020	2,062	827	831	1,001	768	766	955	957	1,078	912	923
1980–81	12,890	13,182	10,140	5,470	5,594	6,569	5,249	4,303	3,498	3,617	4,275	3,390	2,413	918	921	1,086	859	871	1,054	1,056	1,209	1,000	1,019
1981–82	13,374	13,731	10,296	6,166	6,330	7,443	5,947	4,746	3,953	4,113	4,887	3,853	2,605	1,038	1,039	1,229	970	1,022	1,175	1,178	1,327	1,124	1,119
1982–83	14,392	14,821	11,157	6,920	7,126	8,536	6,646	5,364	4,439	4,639	5,583	4,329	3,008	1,181	1,181	1,453	1,083	1,177	1,300	1,306	1,501	1,234	1,179
1983–84	15,059	15,562	11,173	7,508	7,759	9,308	7,244	5,571	4,851	5,093	6,217	4,726	3,099	1,278	1,279	1,531	1,191	1,253	1,380	1,387	1,559	1,327	1,219
1984–85	15,831	16,310	11,973	8,202	8,451	10,243	7,849	6,203	5,315	5,556	6,843	5,135	3,485	1,426	1,426	1,753	1,309	1,424	1,462	1,469	1,647	1,405	1,294
1985–86	16,667	17,312	12,216	8,885	9,228	11,034	8,551	6,512	5,789	6,121	7,374	5,641	3,672	1,553	1,557	1,940	1,420	1,500	1,542	1,551	1,720	1,490	1,340
1986–87	17,758	18,425	11,716	9,676	10,039	12,278	9,276	6,384	6,316	6,658	8,118	6,171	3,684	1,658	1,673	2,097	1,518	1,266	1,702	1,708	2,063	1,587	1,434
1987–88	18,524	18,784	12,473	10,512	10,659	13,075	9,854	7,078	6,988	7,116	8,771	6,574	4,161	1,748	1,760	2,244	1,593	1,380	1,775	1,783	2,060	1,687	1,537
1988–89	18,848	19,327	13,420	11,189	11,474	14,073	10,620	7,967	7,461	7,722	9,451	7,172	4,817	1,849	1,863	2,353	1,686	1,540	1,880	1,889	2,269	1,762	1,609
1989–90	19,322	19,749	13,939	12,018	12,284	15,098	11,374	8,670	8,147	8,396	10,348	7,778	5,196	1,923	1,935	2,411	1,774	1,663	1,948	1,953	2,339	1,823	1,811
1990–91	19,679	20,178	14,180	12,910	13,237	16,503	12,220	9,302	8,772	9,083	11,379	8,389	5,570	2,063	2,077	2,654	1,889	1,744	2,074	2,077	2,470	1,943	1,989
1991–92	20,520	21,059	14,228	13,892	14,258	17,572	13,201	9,632	9,419	9,759	12,037	9,060	5,754	2,221	2,241	2,825	2,042	1,788	2,252	2,257	2,709	2,098	2,090
1992–93	20,960	21,498	14,185	14,634	15,009	18,898	13,882	9,903	9,942	10,294	13,055	9,533	6,059	2,348	2,362	3,018	2,151	1,970	2,344	2,354	2,825	2,197	1,875
1993–94	21,634	22,204	14,529	15,496	15,904	20,097	14,640	10,406	10,572	10,952	13,874	10,100	6,370	2,490	2,506	3,277	2,261	2,067	2,434	2,445	2,946	2,278	1,970
1994–95	21,996	22,533	15,161	16,207	16,602	21,041	15,363	11,170	11,111	11,481	14,537	10,653	6,914	2,587	2,601	3,469	2,347	2,233	2,509	2,520	3,035	2,362	2,023
1995–96	22,737	23,270	15,279	17,208	17,612	22,502	16,198	11,563	11,864	12,243	15,605	11,297	7,094	2,738	2,751	3,680	2,473	2,371	2,606	2,617	3,218	2,429	2,098
1996–97	23,173	23,691	15,357	18,039	18,442	23,520	16,994	11,954	12,498	12,881	16,552	11,871	7,236	2,878	2,889	3,826	2,602	2,537	2,663	2,672	3,142	2,520	2,181
1997–98	23,370	24,069	16,308	18,516	19,070	24,116	17,717	12,921	12,801	13,344	17,220	12,338	7,464	2,954	2,964	3,756	2,731	2,672	2,762	2,761	3,132	2,648	2,785
1998–99	24,029	24,725	16,524	19,368	19,929	25,443	18,430	13,319	13,428	13,973	18,340	12,815	7,884	3,075	3,091	3,914	2,850	2,581	2,865	2,865	3,188	2,765	2,854
1999–2000	24,341	24,968	16,839	20,186	20,706	26,534	19,127	13,965	14,081	14,588	19,307	13,361	8,235	3,224	3,237	4,070	2,976	2,808	2,882	2,881	3,157	2,790	2,922
2000–01	24,913	25,481	17,241	21,368	21,856	27,676	20,247	14,788	15,000	15,470	20,106	14,233	9,067	3,374	3,392	4,270	3,121	2,722	2,993	2,993	3,300	2,893	3,000
2001–02	25,677	26,230	18,130	22,413	22,896	29,115	21,220	15,825	15,742	16,211	21,176	14,923	10,076	3,567	3,576	4,478	3,301	3,116	3,104	3,109	3,462	2,996	2,633
2002–03	26,164	26,665	19,901	23,340	23,787	31,043	21,965	17,753	16,383	16,826	22,716	15,416	10,651	3,752	3,764	4,724	3,478	3,232	3,206	3,197	3,602	3,071	3,870
2003–04	27,012	27,501	21,455	24,624	25,069	32,886	23,153	19,558	17,315	17,763	24,128	16,284	11,545	3,945	3,952	4,979	3,647	3,581	3,364	3,354	3,778	3,222	4,432
2004–05	27,486	27,962	21,398	25,810	26,257	34,761	24,274	20,093	18,154	18,604	25,643	17,050	12,122	4,171	4,170	5,263	3,854	4,243	3,485	3,483	3,855	3,370	3,728
2005–06	27,585	28,023	21,717	26,889	27,317	36,510	25,282	21,170	18,862	19,292	26,954	17,702	12,450	4,380	4,386	5,517	4,063	3,994	3,647	3,639	4,039	3,517	4,726
2006–07	28,439	28,919	20,284	28,439	28,919	38,437	26,823	20,284	20,048	20,517	28,580	18,848	12,708	4,606	4,613	5,691	4,302	4,147	3,785	3,788	4,166	3,672	3,429
2007–08[3]	28,846	29,307	20,936	29,915	30,393	40,640	28,142	21,712	21,113	21,588	30,260	19,798	13,172	4,808	4,812	6,007	4,467	4,451	3,994	3,993	4,373	3,877	4,089
Not-for-profit	30,806	30,931	18,067	31,948	32,078	40,640	29,697	18,737	23,225	23,351	30,260	21,467	11,666	4,729	4,733	6,007	4,349	3,788	3,994	3,993	4,373	3,881	3,283
For-profit	24,078	24,511	22,536	24,971	25,419	†	25,419	23,371	14,364	14,601	†	14,601	13,430	6,645	7,139	†	7,139	4,809	3,961	3,680	†	3,680	5,131

—Not available.
†Not applicable.
[1]Data for 1986–87 and later years reflect a basis of 20 meals per week rather than meals 7 days per week. Because of this revision in data collection and tabulation procedures, data are not entirely comparable with figures for previous years. In particular, data on board rates are somewhat higher than in earlier years because they reflect the basis of 20 meals per week rather than meals served 7 days per week. Since many institutions serve fewer than 3 meals each day, the 1986–87 and later data reflect a more accurate accounting of total board costs.
[2]Room and board data are estimated.
[3]Preliminary data based on fall 2006 enrollment weights.
NOTE: Data are for the entire academic year and are average total charges for full-time attendance. Tuition and fees were weighted by the number of full-time-equivalent undergraduates, but were not adjusted to reflect student residency. Room and board were based on full-time students. Data through 1995–96 are for institutions of higher education, while later data are for degree-granting institutions. Degree-granting institutions grant associate's or higher degrees and participate in Title IV federal financial aid programs. The degree-granting classification is very similar to the earlier higher education classification, but it includes more 2-year colleges and excludes a few higher education institutions that did not grant degrees. (See Guide to Sources for details.) Because of their low response rate, data for private 2-year colleges must be interpreted with caution. Some data have been revised from previously published figures. Detail may not sum to totals because of rounding.
SOURCE: U.S. Department of Education, National Center for Education Statistics, Higher Education General Information Survey (HEGIS), "Institutional Characteristics of Colleges and Universities" surveys, 1965–66 through 1985–86; "Fall Enrollment in Institutions of Higher Education" surveys, 1965 through 1985; and 1986–87 through 2007–08 Integrated Postsecondary Education Data System, "Fall Enrollment Survey" (IPEDS-EF-86–99), "Institutional Characteristics Survey" (IPEDS-C:86–99), Spring 2001 through Spring 2006, and Fall 2000 through Fall 2007. (This table was prepared July 2008.)

Table 332. Average undergraduate tuition and fees and room and board rates charged for full-time students in degree-granting institutions, by type and control of institution and state or jurisdiction: 2006–07 and 2007–08

[In current dollars]

State or jurisdiction	Public 4-year						Private 4-year						Public 2-year, tuition and required fees (in-state)	
	2006–07		2007–08[1]				2006–07		2007–08[1]					
	Total	Tuition and required fees (in-state)	Total	Tuition and required fees (in-state)	Room	Board	Total	Tuition and required fees	Total	Tuition and required fees	Room	Board	2006–07	2007–08[1]
1	2	3	4	5	6	7	8	9	10	11	12	13	14	15
United States	$12,797	$5,666	$13,424	$5,950	$4,072	$3,402	$28,919	$20,517	$30,393	$21,588	$4,812	$3,993	$2,018	$2,063
Alabama	10,686	4,716	11,035	4,907	3,107	3,022	19,380	13,061	21,014	14,116	3,319	3,578	2,802	2,814
Alaska	11,395	4,422	11,719	4,747	4,104	2,868	23,618	16,301	26,883	18,904	3,700	4,279	2,883	3,161
Arizona	11,966	4,665	12,289	4,954	4,477	2,858	22,160	14,450	21,809	13,186	4,759	3,864	1,451	1,478
Arkansas	9,799	4,954	10,598	5,427	2,926	2,244	19,213	13,371	20,096	14,178	2,884	3,033	1,901	1,928
California	14,349	4,445	14,893	4,879	5,212	4,802	33,207	23,258	35,006	24,453	5,812	4,741	674	588
Colorado	12,079	4,645	13,314	5,250	3,946	4,118	28,834	18,832	30,409	19,879	5,633	4,897	2,034	2,076
Connecticut	15,454	7,148	16,263	7,465	4,722	4,076	38,010	27,666	40,245	29,360	6,036	4,849	2,672	2,829
Delaware	15,203	7,414	16,165	7,823	4,954	3,388	19,081	11,710	20,170	12,474	4,094	3,601	2,364	2,490
District of Columbia	†	2,670	†	3,140	†	†	34,071	23,755	35,747	25,010	6,926	3,811	†	†
Florida	10,418	3,009	10,709	2,980	4,385	3,345	26,524	18,299	27,534	19,167	4,554	3,813	1,968	1,862
Georgia	10,320	3,773	10,984	4,006	4,139	2,839	27,188	18,889	29,046	20,175	5,119	3,752	1,730	1,876
Hawaii	11,032	3,923	12,202	4,653	3,785	3,763	20,301	10,756	21,452	11,348	4,360	5,743	1,395	1,566
Idaho	9,528	4,154	9,871	4,381	2,507	2,983	11,851	5,656	10,788	5,933	1,765	3,089	2,006	2,111
Illinois	15,386	8,044	16,795	8,982	4,032	3,781	29,275	20,398	30,833	21,508	5,322	4,003	2,250	2,377
Indiana	13,148	6,287	14,096	6,604	3,585	3,907	29,019	21,784	29,953	22,396	3,845	3,711	2,713	2,819
Iowa	12,583	6,020	13,191	6,219	3,426	3,546	24,075	17,865	25,057	18,556	3,041	3,460	3,137	3,264
Kansas	10,686	4,959	11,338	5,406	2,925	3,007	21,621	15,763	22,653	16,619	2,707	3,327	1,941	2,029
Kentucky	11,902	5,824	12,641	6,342	3,403	2,896	20,968	14,735	22,303	15,713	3,360	3,230	2,630	2,772
Louisiana	9,021	3,761	9,479	3,835	3,113	2,530	28,896	21,100	30,363	22,162	4,637	3,564	1,526	1,641
Maine	12,869	6,564	14,791	7,250	3,760	3,781	30,976	22,609	32,753	23,900	4,473	4,380	3,037	3,270
Maryland	15,209	7,068	15,644	7,141	4,815	3,687	34,579	25,683	36,171	26,865	5,609	3,697	2,950	3,010
Massachusetts	15,211	7,635	16,159	7,922	4,764	3,473	39,391	28,890	41,458	30,487	6,044	4,927	2,975	3,071
Michigan	14,515	7,505	16,003	8,471	3,817	3,715	20,725	13,912	21,874	14,827	3,556	3,491	2,091	2,186
Minnesota	13,780	7,447	14,188	7,707	3,392	3,089	28,671	21,407	30,105	22,057	3,925	3,552	4,339	4,535
Mississippi	10,049	4,456	10,776	4,762	3,200	2,815	17,640	12,193	18,395	12,693	2,941	2,762	1,710	1,720
Missouri	12,585	6,317	13,385	6,643	4,218	2,523	23,421	16,472	25,008	17,464	3,818	3,726	2,278	2,385
Montana	11,294	5,382	11,600	5,418	2,861	3,330	19,891	13,777	21,072	14,729	2,872	3,471	2,827	2,983
Nebraska	11,138	5,184	11,852	5,443	3,174	3,235	21,779	15,673	23,022	16,596	3,281	3,146	1,993	2,128
Nevada	11,581	2,827	12,168	3,053	5,243	3,872	23,189	13,706	25,562	14,786	5,568	5,208	1,695	1,763
New Hampshire	16,606	9,023	18,293	9,610	5,120	3,563	32,972	23,946	34,643	25,281	5,460	3,902	5,593	5,972
New Jersey	18,705	9,333	19,548	9,702	6,209	3,637	33,170	23,428	35,182	24,877	5,540	4,765	2,914	3,054
New Mexico	9,947	3,937	10,610	4,143	3,495	2,973	21,786	14,324	24,023	15,666	4,407	3,950	1,239	1,271
New York	13,683	5,015	14,140	5,065	5,381	3,693	34,317	24,410	36,228	25,885	6,112	4,231	3,289	3,423
North Carolina	10,471	4,040	10,889	4,301	3,648	2,939	27,545	20,220	29,141	21,497	3,921	3,723	1,303	1,377
North Dakota	10,634	5,473	11,134	5,765	2,227	3,141	14,195	9,764	15,156	10,465	2,090	2,601	3,454	3,606
Ohio	16,902	8,995	16,354	8,090	4,703	3,561	28,422	21,038	30,093	22,337	3,939	3,816	3,250	3,197
Oklahoma	9,825	4,174	10,600	4,471	3,243	2,886	21,559	15,228	22,780	16,128	3,370	3,281	2,260	2,356
Oregon	13,185	5,584	13,868	5,939	3,954	3,976	29,936	22,378	31,810	23,952	4,016	3,842	2,832	2,887
Pennsylvania	16,311	9,124	17,187	9,593	4,327	3,267	33,927	25,068	36,019	26,645	5,162	4,212	3,093	3,181
Rhode Island	15,034	6,719	15,775	7,120	4,779	3,876	35,808	25,401	36,476	26,701	5,423	4,351	2,686	2,846
South Carolina	14,194	7,905	15,089	8,389	4,159	2,542	23,560	17,195	24,914	18,289	3,261	3,364	3,108	3,223
South Dakota	10,013	5,062	10,522	5,395	2,378	2,750	19,816	14,463	20,605	15,274	2,655	2,676	3,542	3,730
Tennessee	10,534	5,006	11,340	5,366	3,312	2,662	24,377	17,453	25,802	18,509	3,871	3,422	2,474	2,631
Texas	11,810	5,093	12,367	5,538	3,575	3,254	25,295	18,285	27,116	19,626	4,044	3,446	1,370	1,436
Utah	9,052	3,783	9,706	4,046	2,291	3,369	11,647	5,768	12,913	6,240	3,318	3,354	2,287	2,419
Vermont	17,271	9,774	18,245	10,401	5,021	2,824	30,708	22,399	33,879	25,111	4,741	4,027	4,204	4,420
Virginia	13,143	6,450	13,928	6,887	3,862	3,178	24,632	17,821	26,170	18,892	3,740	3,537	2,361	2,484
Washington	13,070	5,552	13,478	5,353	3,882	4,242	29,144	21,557	31,090	23,127	4,268	3,695	2,666	2,773
West Virginia	10,620	4,099	11,426	4,377	3,730	3,319	21,026	14,571	22,022	15,296	3,203	3,523	2,665	2,700
Wisconsin	11,230	6,045	11,747	6,177	3,376	2,195	27,185	20,225	28,422	21,334	3,660	3,429	3,168	3,369
Wyoming	9,627	2,951	10,068	2,990	3,158	3,920	†	10,500	†	10,890	†	†	1,820	1,918

†Not applicable.

[1]Preliminary data based on fall 2006 enrollment weights.

NOTE: Data are for the entire academic year and are average charges. Tuition and fees were weighted by the number of full-time-equivalent undergraduates, but were not adjusted to reflect student residency. Room and board are based on full-time students. (See Guide to Sources for details.) Degree-granting institutions grant associate's or higher degrees and par-ticipate in Title IV federal financial aid programs. Some data have been revised from previously published figures. Detail may not sum to totals because of rounding.

SOURCE: U.S. Department of Education, National Center for Education Statistics, 2006–07 and 2007–08 Integrated Postsecondary Education Data System (IPEDS), Fall 2006, Fall 2007, and Spring 2007. (This table was prepared July 2008.)

Table 333. Undergraduate tuition and fees and room and board rates for full-time students in degree-granting institutions, by percentile of charges and control and type of institution: 2000–01 through 2007–08

[In current dollars]

Control and type of institution, and year	Tuition, room, and board					Tuition and required fees				
	10th percentile	25th percentile	Median (50th percentile)	75th percentile	90th percentile	10th percentile	25th percentile	Median (50th percentile)	75th percentile	90th percentile
1	2	3	4	5	6	7	8	9	10	11
All public institutions[1]										
2000–01	$5,701	$6,878	$8,279	$9,617	$11,384	$612	$1,480	$2,403	$3,444	$4,583
2001–02	6,153	7,342	8,602	10,136	12,207	468	1,539	2,529	3,648	4,815
2002–03	6,385	7,801	9,138	10,885	13,094	479	1,629	2,656	3,950	5,281
2003–04	6,909	8,522	10,029	12,085	14,440	900	1,800	2,913	4,464	6,149
2004–05	7,265	9,081	10,797	12,842	15,401	900	1,920	3,152	4,977	6,752
2005–06	7,700	9,623	11,348	13,543	16,264	990	2,070	3,329	5,322	6,972
2006–07	8,337	10,125	12,042	14,505	16,965	1,080	2,190	3,490	5,652	7,530
2007–08[2]	8,827	10,861	12,690	15,361	17,979	1,170	2,280	3,703	6,010	7,969
Public 4-year[1]										
2000–01	6,503	7,347	8,468	9,816	11,611	2,118	2,516	3,314	4,094	5,085
2001–02	6,998	7,697	8,881	10,525	12,416	2,272	2,648	3,489	4,373	5,536
2002–03	7,325	8,121	9,446	11,250	13,408	2,356	2,929	3,784	4,780	6,259
2003–04	7,924	9,023	10,447	12,292	14,655	2,609	3,251	4,254	5,702	6,882
2004–05	8,380	9,574	11,022	13,031	15,622	2,880	3,582	4,665	6,081	7,542
2005–06	8,863	10,219	11,596	13,830	16,443	3,094	3,822	5,084	6,458	8,097
2006–07	9,461	10,797	12,272	14,748	17,160	3,206	4,074	5,376	6,825	8,667
2007–08[2]	10,010	11,462	13,033	15,819	18,384	3,355	4,264	5,689	7,272	8,907
Public 2-year[1]										
2000–01	3,321	3,804	4,627	5,750	6,871	310	724	1,387	1,799	2,455
2001–02	3,613	4,078	4,921	6,187	7,060	308	768	1,440	1,888	2,534
2002–03	3,730	4,475	5,347	6,510	7,829	308	780	1,544	2,078	2,680
2003–04	3,874	4,725	5,562	6,983	8,360	478	1,024	1,700	2,325	2,844
2004–05	4,097	4,889	6,021	7,420	9,015	710	1,048	1,803	2,459	3,033
2005–06	4,380	4,822	6,234	7,567	8,993	691	1,109	1,920	2,589	3,100
2006–07	4,487	5,199	6,376	8,035	9,719	670	1,184	2,059	2,713	3,316
2007–08[2]	4,637	5,361	6,558	8,108	10,392	590	1,200	2,091	2,819	3,384
All private institutions										
2000–01	13,514	17,530	22,398	27,280	32,659	7,520	10,716	14,880	18,795	24,336
2001–02	14,675	18,673	23,585	28,788	33,993	7,950	11,350	15,560	19,700	25,485
2002–03	15,400	19,657	24,885	30,453	35,753	8,210	11,356	16,078	20,702	26,646
2003–04	16,332	20,833	26,455	32,242	37,710	8,650	12,020	16,930	21,790	28,400
2004–05	17,144	21,746	27,872	34,342	39,565	9,184	12,750	17,590	22,712	29,786
2005–06	18,243	23,044	29,279	35,783	41,707	9,285	12,840	18,120	24,030	31,444
2006–07	19,102	24,350	31,009	38,448	43,770	8,337	10,125	12,042	14,505	16,965
2007–08[2]	20,005	25,867	32,794	40,778	46,203	10,800	13,387	20,496	27,200	34,998
Not-for-profit[2]	20,033	26,040	32,925	41,000	46,242	11,530	17,520	23,760	30,000	35,290
For-profit[2]	17,636	20,510	26,699	27,620	32,724	10,190	11,820	13,200	15,600	19,769
Private 4-year										
2000–01	13,972	17,714	22,493	27,430	32,659	8,305	11,548	15,420	19,200	24,336
2001–02	14,740	18,790	23,645	28,907	34,064	8,700	12,150	16,200	20,200	25,533
2002–03	15,592	19,755	24,981	30,459	35,743	8,570	12,300	16,620	21,175	26,910
2003–04	16,364	20,833	26,536	32,242	37,710	9,082	12,660	17,524	22,420	28,440
2004–05	17,156	21,808	27,925	34,468	39,565	9,570	13,200	18,170	23,386	29,910
2005–06	18,350	23,238	29,294	35,912	41,707	9,675	12,956	18,900	24,366	31,452
2006–07	19,187	24,500	31,099	38,448	43,792	10,560	14,880	19,924	26,120	33,318
2007–08[2]	20,056	25,984	32,827	41,000	46,204	11,130	14,100	21,190	27,966	35,142
Not-for-profit[2]	20,253	26,171	32,925	41,000	46,242	11,754	17,640	23,845	30,158	35,290
For-profit[2]	17,040	20,510	26,699	27,369	31,512	10,890	12,270	13,200	15,600	19,775
Private 2-year										
2000–01	6,650	6,850	13,220	16,400	21,845	5,013	6,887	8,329	11,064	13,995
2001–02	10,314	11,527	16,118	17,391	24,214	6,085	7,575	9,102	11,704	14,500
2002–03	11,293	12,189	16,919	21,374	29,777	6,353	7,995	9,600	12,280	15,260
2003–04	11,955	14,119	17,124	26,560	40,780	6,800	8,325	10,462	12,892	17,500
2004–05	13,807	15,486	19,844	27,276	34,385	7,008	8,813	10,629	13,548	18,025
2005–06	11,560	15,680	18,410	22,809	43,425	7,560	9,285	11,180	14,196	17,995
2006–07	8,685	16,568	19,115	26,677	40,130	7,980	9,688	11,600	14,833	18,710
2007–08[2]	15,529	17,460	20,362	26,727	40,232	8,336	10,165	12,100	15,070	18,850
Not-for-profit[2]	13,210	16,829	18,104	23,478	36,659	3,635	8,420	11,130	13,988	17,930
For-profit[2]	20,272	22,532	26,727	40,232	40,232	8,665	10,225	12,294	15,127	18,850

[1]Average undergraduate tuition and fees are based on in-state students only.
[2]Preliminary data based on fall 2006 enrollment weights.
NOTE: Data are for the entire academic year and are average rates for full-time students. Student charges were weighted by the number of full-time-equivalent undergraduates, but were not adjusted to reflect student residency. The data have not been adjusted for changes in the purchasing power of the dollar. Degree-granting institutions grant associ-

ate's or higher degrees and participate in Title IV federal financial aid programs. Some data have been revised from previously published figures.
SOURCE: U.S. Department of Education, National Center for Education Statistics, 2000–01 through 2007–08 Integrated Postsecondary Education Data System (IPEDS), Fall 2000 through Fall 2006 and Spring 2001 through Spring 2007. (This table was prepared July 2008.)

Table 334. Average graduate and first-professional tuition and required fees in degree-granting institutions, by first-professional field of study and control of institution: 1987–88 through 2007–08

Year and control	Average full-time graduate tuition and required fees		Average full-time first-professional tuition and required fees in current dollars									
	Current dollars	Constant 2006–07 dollars	Chiropractic	Dentistry	Medicine	Optometry	Osteopathic medicine	Pharmacy	Podiatry	Veterinary medicine	Law	Theology
1	2	3	4	5	6	7	8	9	10	11	12	13
All institutions												
1987–88	$3,599	$6,342	$6,996	$9,399	$9,034	$7,926	$10,674	$5,201	$12,736	$4,503	$6,636	$3,572
1988–89	3,728	6,280	7,972	9,324	9,439	8,503	11,462	4,952	13,232	4,856	7,099	3,911
1989–90	4,135	6,648	8,315	10,515	10,597	9,469	11,888	5,890	14,611	5,470	8,059	4,079
1990–91	4,488	6,841	9,108	10,270	10,571	9,512	12,830	5,889	15,143	5,396	8,708	4,569
1991–92	5,116	7,557	10,226	12,049	11,646	9,610	13,004	6,731	16,257	6,367	9,469	4,876
1992–93	5,475	7,842	11,117	12,710	12,265	10,858	14,297	6,635	17,426	6,771	10,463	5,331
1993–94	5,973	8,339	11,503	14,403	13,074	10,385	15,038	7,960	17,621	7,159	11,552	5,253
1994–95	6,247	8,479	12,324	15,164	13,834	11,053	15,913	8,315	18,138	7,741	12,374	5,648
1995–96	6,741	8,907	12,507	15,647	14,860	11,544	16,785	8,602	18,434	8,208	13,278	5,991
1996–97	7,111	9,135	12,721	16,585	15,481	12,250	17,888	9,207	19,056	8,668	14,081	6,558
1997–98	7,246	9,145	13,144	17,695	16,310	12,679	18,668	9,744	19,355	9,013	14,992	6,832
1998–99	7,685	9,534	13,582	19,051	17,107	14,066	20,000	9,735	19,547	9,392	15,601	7,171
1999–2000	8,071	9,732	14,256	19,576	17,818	14,354	20,903	10,740	20,158	9,867	16,491	7,725
2000–01	8,429	9,828	15,093	22,097	19,151	15,448	21,784	11,273	20,455	10,365	17,795	7,868
2001–02	8,857	10,147	15,632	22,597	19,795	16,148	22,970	12,259	20,886	11,070	18,707	8,737
2002–03	9,226	10,342	16,758	24,517	21,206	16,439	24,379	13,597	21,633	12,142	19,810	9,485
2003–04	10,312	11,312	17,264	26,124	22,892	17,439	26,059	14,987	22,645	13,420	21,305	9,850
2004–05	11,004	11,719	18,535	28,455	24,293	18,048	27,900	15,951	23,631	14,535	22,935	10,412
2005–06	11,621	11,922	19,445	29,729	25,699	18,717	29,320	17,224	24,347	15,526	24,474	10,811
2006–07	12,312	12,312	21,473	32,004	27,086	19,886	30,604	18,634	25,594	16,551	26,042	11,628
2007–08[1]	12,979	12,515	22,655	33,967	28,335	20,986	32,106	19,843	26,431	17,609	27,830	12,111
Public[2]												
1987–88	1,827	3,220	†	4,614	5,245	2,789	5,125	2,462	†	3,523	2,810	
1988–89	1,913	3,222	†	5,286	5,669	3,455	6,269	2,218	†	3,889	2,766	†
1989–90	1,999	3,214	†	5,728	6,259	3,569	6,521	2,816	†	4,505	3,196	
1990–91	2,206	3,363	†	5,927	6,437	3,821	7,188	2,697	†	4,840	3,430	
1991–92	2,524	3,728	†	6,595	7,106	4,161	7,699	2,871	†	5,231	3,933	†
1992–93	2,791	3,998	†	7,006	7,867	5,106	8,404	2,987	†	5,553	4,261	†
1993–94	3,050	4,258	†	7,525	8,329	5,325	8,640	3,567	†	6,107	4,835	
1994–95	3,250	4,411	†	8,125	8,812	5,643	8,954	3,793	†	6,571	5,307	
1995–96	3,449	4,557	†	8,806	9,585	6,130	9,448	4,100	†	6,907	5,821	
1996–97	3,607	4,634	†	9,434	10,057	6,561	9,932	4,884	†	7,343	6,565	
1997–98	3,744	4,725	†	9,762	10,555	7,366	10,358	5,046	19,541	7,472	7,125	
1998–99	3,897	4,834	†	10,259	11,141	7,890	10,858	5,476	19,818	7,707	7,510	
1999–2000	4,043	4,876	†	10,795	11,610	7,922	11,377	5,997	19,578	8,271	7,824	
2000–01	4,243	4,947	†	11,946	12,188	8,452	11,866	6,476	20,228	8,720	8,414	
2001–02	4,496	5,150	†	13,092	13,186	9,619	12,708	7,187	21,254	9,375	9,115	†
2002–03	4,842	5,427	†	13,992	14,591	10,187	13,497	8,304	21,992	10,396	10,172	
2003–04	5,544	6,081	†	15,613	16,500	11,537	14,994	9,424	22,638	11,763	11,838	
2004–05	6,080	6,475	†	17,690	18,078	12,387	16,467	10,332	24,788	12,878	13,155	
2005–06	6,493	6,661	†	19,177	19,473	13,229	17,653	11,444	24,808	13,849	14,544	
2006–07	6,894	6,894	†	20,701	20,627	14,392	18,102	12,523	26,242	14,915	15,658	
2007–08[1]	7,414	7,149	†	22,075	21,574	15,618	19,280	13,510	27,322	15,925	16,985	†
Private												
1987–88	6,769	11,928	6,996	16,201	14,945	11,635	13,311	8,834	12,736	12,544	9,048	3,572
1988–89	6,945	11,698	7,972	16,127	15,610	12,050	13,536	9,692	13,232	13,285	9,892	3,911
1989–90	7,881	12,670	8,315	16,800	16,826	13,640	14,117	10,656	14,611	14,184	10,901	4,079
1990–91	8,507	12,968	9,108	18,270	17,899	13,767	15,009	11,546	15,143	14,159	12,247	4,569
1991–92	9,592	14,168	10,226	20,318	19,225	14,366	16,098	12,937	16,257	15,816	12,946	4,876
1992–93	10,008	14,334	11,117	21,309	19,585	14,459	17,098	13,373	17,426	17,103	13,975	5,331
1993–94	10,790	15,064	11,503	23,824	20,769	14,156	17,720	14,838	17,621	17,433	15,193	5,253
1994–95	11,338	15,389	12,324	24,641	21,819	14,497	18,422	14,894	18,138	17,940	16,201	5,648
1995–96	12,083	15,965	12,507	25,678	23,001	15,235	19,619	15,618	18,434	19,380	17,251	5,991
1996–97	12,537	16,105	12,721	26,618	24,242	15,949	20,714	15,934	19,056	19,526	18,276	6,558
1997–98	12,774	16,122	13,144	29,985	25,249	16,550	21,707	16,575	19,316	18,624	19,311	6,832
1998–99	13,299	16,499	13,582	31,917	26,495	17,848	22,867	16,874	19,492	19,617	20,253	7,171
1999–2000	13,782	16,619	14,256	32,268	27,702	18,317	23,791	18,220	20,259	20,128	21,393	7,725
2000–01	14,420	16,812	15,093	35,234	30,077	19,838	24,719	19,002	20,498	20,883	23,063	7,868
2001–02	15,165	17,373	15,632	36,184	30,438	20,374	25,909	20,325	20,825	21,772	24,019	8,737
2002–03	14,983	16,795	16,758	39,085	31,895	20,197	27,552	21,561	21,551	22,813	25,243	9,485
2003–04	16,209	17,781	17,264	40,414	32,913	20,955	29,095	23,022	22,647	23,941	26,746	9,850
2004–05	16,751	17,839	18,535	43,228	34,296	21,532	30,707	24,152	23,365	25,027	28,175	10,412
2005–06	17,244	17,690	19,445	45,633	35,895	22,162	32,349	25,439	24,240	26,191	29,782	10,811
2006–07	18,108	18,108	21,473	49,135	37,569	23,474	33,986	26,681	25,432	27,135	31,561	11,628
2007–08[1]	18,923	18,247	22,655	51,990	39,307	24,493	35,572	28,181	26,209	28,506	33,616	12,111

†Not applicable.

[1]Preliminary graduate tuition average based on fall 2006 enrollment weights and first-professional tuition average based on 2006–07 degrees.

[2]Data are based on in-state tuition only.

NOTE: Average graduate student tuition weighted by fall full-time-equivalent graduate enrollment. Average first-professional tuition weighted by number of degrees conferred during the academic year. Some year-to-year fluctuations in tuition data may reflect nonreporting by individual institutions. Excludes institutions not reporting degrees conferred and institutions not reporting tuition. Data through 1995–96 are for institutions of higher education, while later data are for degree-granting institutions. Degree-granting institutions grant associate's or higher degrees and participate in Title IV federal financial aid programs. The degree-granting classification is very similar to the earlier higher education classification, but it includes more 2-year colleges and excludes a few higher education institutions that did not grant degrees. (See Guide to Sources for details.) Some data have been revised from previously published figures.

SOURCE: U.S. Department of Education, National Center for Education Statistics, 1987–88 through 2007–08 Integrated Postsecondary Education Data System, "Fall Enrollment Survey" (IPEDS-EF:87–99); "Completions Survey," (IPEDS-C:88–99); "Institutional Characteristics Survey" (IPEDS-IC:87–99); Fall 2000 through Fall 2007; and Spring 2001 through Spring 2007. (This table was prepared August 2008.)

Table 335. Percentage of undergraduates receiving aid, by type and source of aid and selected student characteristics: 2003–04

Selected student characteristic	Enrollment of undergraduates[1] (in thousands)	Any aid — Total[2]	Any aid — Federal	Any aid — Nonfederal	Grants — Total	Grants — Federal	Grants — Nonfederal	Loans — Total	Loans — Federal[3]	Loans — Nonfederal	Work study — Total[4]	Other — Total	Other — Federal	Other — Nonfederal
1	2	3	4	5	6	7	8	9	10	11	12	13	14	15
All undergraduates	19,054 (#)	63.2 (0.36)	48.0 (0.28)	40.9 (0.48)	50.7 (0.41)	27.6 (0.17)	36.8 (0.46)	35.2 (0.23)	34.0 (0.22)	5.9 (0.19)	7.5 (0.22)	3.6 (0.16)	2.9 (0.13)	0.8 (0.09)
Sex														
Male	8,073 (73.8)	60.6 (0.54)	44.8 (0.50)	40.1 (0.58)	46.5 (0.55)	22.8 (0.36)	35.6 (0.57)	33.7 (0.45)	32.3 (0.43)	6.3 (0.29)	7.4 (0.24)	5.3 (0.22)	4.7 (0.21)	0.7 (0.09)
Female	10,980 (73.8)	65.2 (0.41)	50.4 (0.36)	41.4 (0.54)	53.7 (0.47)	31.1 (0.28)	37.7 (0.51)	36.4 (0.34)	35.2 (0.34)	5.6 (0.17)	7.6 (0.25)	2.3 (0.17)	1.5 (0.11)	0.8 (0.11)
Race/ethnicity[5]														
White	12,025 (144.6)	61.5 (0.56)	44.4 (0.53)	41.7 (0.54)	47.8 (0.58)	21.3 (0.39)	37.7 (0.54)	35.5 (0.48)	34.2 (0.48)	6.2 (0.22)	7.3 (0.27)	3.5 (0.18)	2.6 (0.14)	0.9 (0.13)
Black	2,666 (117.6)	75.8 (0.88)	64.6 (1.11)	41.6 (1.07)	64.3 (0.98)	47.7 (1.03)	37.2 (1.01)	43.2 (1.63)	42.0 (1.65)	5.1 (0.46)	8.5 (0.45)	5.1 (0.38)	4.4 (0.34)	0.8 (0.15)
Hispanic	2,426 (81.3)	63.2 (0.82)	51.9 (0.87)	37.4 (1.02)	53.4 (0.84)	37.7 (0.80)	33.3 (1.04)	29.9 (0.96)	28.7 (0.95)	5.4 (0.42)	6.8 (0.52)	3.1 (0.19)	2.5 (0.17)	0.5 (0.09)
Asian/Pacific Islander	1,127 (41.7)	51.5 (1.51)	38.1 (1.18)	37.0 (1.35)	41.2 (1.38)	22.7 (0.87)	33.7 (1.26)	25.3 (0.97)	23.6 (0.87)	5.3 (0.57)	9.1 (0.55)	2.1 (0.32)	1.8 (0.32)	0.3 (0.07)
American Indian/Alaska Native	176 (20.5)	67.4 (3.84)	50.4 (3.94)	46.1 (3.35)	59.1 (3.69)	35.8 (3.44)	41.8 (3.41)	32.5 (2.99)	31.4 (2.98)	5.0 (1.08)	5.1 (1.27)	3.3 (0.98)	2.4 (0.77)	1.0 (0.41)
Age														
Younger than 24	10,820 (98.6)	64.2 (0.49)	49.4 (0.42)	44.7 (0.54)	51.4 (0.47)	25.7 (0.24)	40.5 (0.51)	37.9 (0.42)	36.3 (0.42)	7.5 (0.24)	10.6 (0.31)	2.0 (0.10)	1.6 (0.08)	0.4 (0.05)
24 to 29 years old	3,299 (53.0)	66.8 (0.74)	55.0 (0.76)	35.2 (0.72)	52.7 (0.72)	36.9 (0.55)	30.7 (0.64)	39.5 (0.66)	38.3 (0.68)	5.0 (0.34)	4.1 (0.23)	5.7 (0.42)	5.1 (0.41)	0.6 (0.07)
30 years old or over	4,935 (79.6)	58.8 (0.78)	40.3 (0.72)	36.2 (0.75)	47.6 (0.75)	25.4 (0.49)	32.7 (0.79)	26.7 (0.60)	25.8 (0.60)	3.0 (0.19)	3.0 (0.18)	5.7 (0.35)	4.0 (0.28)	1.7 (0.24)
Marital status														
Not married[6]	14,613 (78.1)	64.4 (0.44)	50.2 (0.32)	42.5 (0.51)	52.0 (0.47)	28.6 (0.19)	38.3 (0.50)	37.6 (0.30)	36.3 (0.30)	6.7 (0.21)	8.9 (0.26)	2.8 (0.13)	2.2 (0.11)	0.6 (0.06)
Married	4,056 (76.4)	57.5 (0.78)	38.1 (0.84)	35.2 (0.76)	44.2 (0.76)	21.1 (0.66)	31.6 (0.70)	26.0 (0.64)	25.1 (0.65)	3.1 (0.22)	2.9 (0.18)	6.3 (0.41)	5.1 (0.35)	1.3 (0.22)
Separated	385 (14.3)	78.5 (1.96)	67.7 (2.43)	37.9 (1.98)	69.8 (2.10)	58.1 (2.22)	33.1 (1.94)	41.8 (2.32)	40.4 (2.39)	4.5 (0.75)	4.0 (0.52)	5.4 (0.73)	4.2 (0.66)	1.2 (0.35)
Attendance status														
Full-time, full-year	7,824 (93.5)	76.1 (0.40)	61.7 (0.42)	54.3 (0.52)	62.2 (0.48)	33.2 (0.32)	49.3 (0.51)	49.9 (0.44)	48.5 (0.43)	9.0 (0.31)	13.5 (0.41)	3.2 (0.17)	2.4 (0.12)	0.8 (0.09)
Part-time or part-year	11,230 (93.5)	54.3 (0.56)	38.5 (0.44)	31.5 (0.59)	42.7 (0.57)	23.6 (0.35)	28.1 (0.57)	25.0 (0.30)	23.8 (0.30)	3.7 (0.16)	3.4 (0.14)	3.9 (0.20)	3.2 (0.19)	0.8 (0.10)
Dependency status and family income														
Dependent	9,476 (106.4)	63.8 (0.53)	48.5 (0.44)	45.9 (0.58)	50.4 (0.51)	22.8 (0.25)	41.7 (0.56)	38.6 (0.46)	37.0 (0.46)	7.9 (0.26)	11.2 (0.32)	1.6 (0.10)	1.3 (0.08)	0.3 (0.04)
Less than $20,000	1,241 (29.1)	62.7 (0.49)	47.5 (0.49)	35.9 (0.57)	51.0 (0.50)	32.3 (0.33)	31.9 (0.56)	32.0 (0.43)	31.0 (0.43)	3.9 (0.19)	4.0 (0.15)	5.6 (0.27)	4.4 (0.24)	1.2 (0.15)
$20,000–$39,999	1,827 (27.3)	77.8 (0.87)	67.2 (0.95)	50.9 (1.13)	75.3 (0.96)	63.7 (0.96)	48.0 (1.12)	36.2 (1.01)	34.9 (1.07)	5.6 (0.46)	14.2 (0.77)	1.6 (0.25)	1.3 (0.23)	0.3 (0.06)
$40,000–$59,999	1,710 (27.5)	76.2 (0.78)	65.2 (0.73)	54.0 (0.92)	69.6 (0.83)	53.6 (0.81)	49.9 (0.86)	43.1 (0.70)	41.8 (0.73)	7.7 (0.45)	15.0 (0.61)	1.7 (0.18)	1.4 (0.17)	0.4 (0.06)
$60,000–$79,999	1,596 (32.7)	63.2 (0.83)	48.0 (0.79)	46.8 (0.83)	48.4 (0.77)	18.0 (0.51)	42.6 (0.81)	41.4 (0.82)	39.9 (0.79)	8.8 (0.36)	12.1 (0.54)	1.8 (0.23)	1.4 (0.20)	0.4 (0.11)
$80,000–$99,999	1,124 (27.5)	58.7 (1.09)	40.9 (1.00)	44.3 (0.94)	40.6 (0.90)	3.3 (0.25)	39.7 (0.91)	39.6 (0.98)	37.7 (0.97)	8.9 (0.42)	10.2 (0.47)	1.6 (0.15)	1.1 (0.13)	0.5 (0.10)
$100,000 or more	1,978 (43.6)	60.5 (1.30)	41.6 (1.05)	44.3 (1.24)	39.9 (1.24)	0.9 (0.15)	39.6 (1.25)	41.1 (1.08)	39.0 (1.03)	9.9 (0.48)	9.6 (0.64)	1.5 (0.32)	1.3 (0.31)	0.1 (0.05)
Independent	9,578 (106.4)	62.7 (0.49)	47.5 (0.49)	35.9 (0.57)	51.0 (0.50)	32.3 (0.33)	31.9 (0.56)	32.0 (0.43)	31.0 (0.43)	3.9 (0.19)	4.0 (0.15)	5.6 (0.27)	4.4 (0.24)	1.2 (0.15)
Less than $9,999	2,157 (36.5)	70.5 (0.79)	61.6 (0.85)	38.5 (0.86)	65.7 (0.76)	56.2 (0.77)	34.0 (0.84)	37.8 (0.85)	36.6 (0.86)	4.7 (0.39)	8.0 (0.46)	4.2 (0.36)	3.0 (0.31)	1.3 (0.17)
$10,000–$19,999	1,745 (43.2)	73.3 (0.86)	62.7 (0.84)	38.6 (0.92)	63.4 (1.05)	49.3 (0.84)	33.9 (0.89)	40.7 (0.97)	39.5 (0.99)	4.9 (0.34)	5.2 (0.34)	5.9 (0.39)	4.6 (0.37)	1.3 (0.21)
$20,000–$29,999	1,512 (35.6)	68.4 (1.05)	55.9 (1.18)	35.0 (0.94)	53.8 (0.96)	37.2 (0.89)	30.5 (0.91)	38.1 (1.09)	37.2 (1.09)	3.8 (0.35)	3.2 (0.28)	6.1 (0.47)	4.4 (0.33)	1.7 (0.30)
$30,000–$49,999	1,809 (44.1)	60.6 (0.89)	42.3 (0.95)	36.1 (0.83)	46.3 (0.77)	23.2 (0.82)	32.4 (0.82)	29.6 (0.84)	28.7 (0.83)	3.8 (0.31)	2.6 (0.27)	6.4 (0.47)	5.5 (0.42)	1.0 (0.17)
$50,000 or more	2,356 (50.8)	45.6 (0.97)	22.0 (0.74)	31.9 (0.92)	30.1 (0.97)	1.8 (0.18)	29.2 (0.95)	18.1 (0.64)	17.2 (0.61)	2.5 (0.22)	0.9 (0.14)	5.7 (0.50)	4.9 (0.49)	0.9 (0.16)
Housing status														
School-owned	2,632 (69.3)	79.2 (0.60)	62.3 (0.78)	64.9 (0.77)	66.3 (0.70)	25.7 (0.59)	60.3 (0.79)	57.2 (0.82)	55.5 (0.83)	12.9 (0.66)	22.6 (0.72)	1.8 (0.16)	1.3 (0.14)	0.4 (0.09)
Off-campus, not with parents	10,524 (89.4)	62.9 (0.50)	47.4 (0.47)	37.9 (0.58)	49.9 (0.56)	28.8 (0.36)	33.7 (0.55)	33.7 (0.40)	32.5 (0.39)	4.8 (0.20)	5.1 (0.19)	4.6 (0.22)	3.7 (0.19)	1.0 (0.13)
With parents	5,899 (77.7)	56.7 (0.69)	42.7 (0.54)	35.5 (0.66)	45.1 (0.65)	26.2 (0.41)	31.8 (0.63)	28.2 (0.55)	26.9 (0.53)	4.7 (0.19)	5.2 (0.23)	2.6 (0.16)	2.1 (0.14)	0.5 (0.07)

#Rounds to zero.

[1]Numbers of undergraduates may not equal figures reported in other tables, since these data are based on a sample survey of students who enrolled at any time during the school year. Includes all postsecondary institutions.
[2]Includes students who reported they were awarded aid, but did not specify the source or type of aid.
[3]Includes Parent Loans for Undergraduate Students (PLUS).
[4]Details on federal and nonfederal work study participants are not available.
[5]Excludes persons not reported by race/ethnicity and persons reporting more than one race.
[6]Includes students who were single, divorced, or widowed.

NOTE: Detail may not sum to totals because of rounding and/or the fact that some students receive aid from multiple sources. Data include undergraduates in degree-granting and non-degree-granting institutions. Estimates for loans include PLUS loans and may differ from previously published figures. Race categories exclude persons of Hispanic ethnicity. Standard errors appear in parentheses. Data include Puerto Rico.
SOURCE: U.S. Department of Education, National Center for Education Statistics, 2003–04 National Postsecondary Student Aid Study (NPSAS:04). (This table was prepared September 2005.)

Table 336. Full-time, first-time degree/certificate seeking undergraduate students enrolled in degree-granting institutions, by participation and average amount awarded in financial aid programs, and type and control of institution: 2000–01 through 2005–06

[In current dollars]

Control and type of institution, and year	Number enrolled	Number receiving financial aid	Percent receiving aid	Percent of enrolled students in student aid programs				Average award for students in aid programs[1]			
				Federal grants	State/local grants	Institutional grants	Student loans[2]	Federal grants	State/local grants	Institutional grants	Student loans[2]
1	2	3	4	5	6	7	8	9	10	11	12
All institutions											
2000–01	1,976,600	1,390,527	70.3	31.6	31.2	31.1	40.1	$2,486	$2,039	$4,740	$3,764
2001–02	2,050,016	1,481,592	72.3	33.3	32.5	31.5	40.7	2,739	2,057	4,918	3,970
2002–03	2,135,613	1,553,024	72.7	34.1	30.9	31.5	41.4	2,947	2,189	5,267	4,331
2003–04	2,178,517	1,610,967	73.9	34.6	31.2	31.9	43.1	2,934	2,226	5,648	4,193
2004–05	2,260,590	1,689,910	74.8	35.2	31.3	31.7	44.0	2,939	2,343	5,958	4,463
2005–06	2,309,543	1,731,315	75.0	33.7	30.8	32.7	44.6	2,959	2,441	6,213	4,831
Public											
2000–01	1,333,236	872,109	65.4	30.0	33.5	22.7	30.7	2,408	1,707	2,275	3,050
2003–04	1,477,260	1,021,788	69.2	32.7	33.7	23.3	33.6	2,868	1,997	2,657	3,431
2004–05	1,497,590	1,045,144	69.8	33.0	34.9	23.5	33.7	2,891	2,138	2,976	3,715
2005–06	1,510,268	1,066,041	70.6	31.1	34.8	25.1	34.2	2,926	2,226	3,162	3,866
4-year											
2000–01	804,793	573,430	71.3	26.6	36.5	29.6	40.7	2,569	2,068	2,616	3,212
2003–04	875,507	658,103	75.2	28.4	36.9	32.0	44.6	2,992	2,436	2,990	3,629
2004–05	888,267	670,365	75.5	28.3	38.2	32.0	44.3	3,048	2,622	3,388	3,998
2005–06	906,948	695,017	76.6	26.6	36.8	34.2	44.4	3,071	2,752	3,573	4,166
2-year											
2000–01	528,443	298,679	56.5	35.2	28.8	12.1	15.3	2,222	1,009	1,004	2,396
2003–04	601,753	363,685	60.4	39.0	29.0	10.7	17.5	2,737	1,184	1,204	2,700
2004–05	609,323	374,779	61.5	39.7	30.2	11.1	18.2	2,728	1,246	1,238	2,712
2005–06	603,320	371,024	61.5	38.0	31.9	11.3	19.0	2,774	1,314	1,297	2,812
Private not-for-profit											
2000–01	439,369	363,044	82.6	28.4	31.8	68.1	57.7	2,879	2,998	7,368	4,019
2003–04	461,800	392,260	84.9	29.2	31.6	71.9	60.4	3,395	2,969	8,970	4,735
2004–05	471,015	400,562	85.0	27.9	31.5	72.9	59.6	3,427	3,057	9,284	4,981
2005–06	471,069	401,908	85.3	26.5	31.3	73.8	59.8	3,426	3,117	9,932	5,270
4-year											
2000–01	419,499	347,638	82.9	27.4	32.2	70.1	58.1	2,930	3,001	7,458	4,000
2003–04	450,065	382,262	84.9	28.5	31.6	72.8	60.4	3,406	2,968	9,047	4,726
2004–05	459,435	390,761	85.1	27.2	31.4	73.8	59.8	3,463	3,059	9,360	4,991
2005–06	460,832	393,429	85.4	26.0	31.2	74.6	59.8	3,437	3,121	10,002	5,264
2-year											
2000–01	19,870	15,406	77.5	49.2	23.9	25.7	49.5	2,269	2,892	2,168	4,509
2003–04	11,735	9,998	85.2	53.5	32.1	36.3	58.0	3,160	3,021	3,011	5,097
2004–05	11,580	9,801	84.6	55.3	35.9	36.5	55.2	2,715	2,996	3,133	4,526
2005–06	10,237	8,479	82.8	51.6	36.1	38.5	55.9	3,176	2,974	3,799	5,531
Private for-profit											
2000–01	203,995	155,374	76.2	49.3	15.2	6.2	63.5	2,312	2,494	1,540	5,517
2003–04	239,457	196,919	82.2	57.0	15.3	7.4	68.4	2,709	2,379	1,649	5,580
2004–05	291,985	244,204	83.6	58.6	12.1	7.5	71.3	2,703	2,380	1,639	5,575
2005–06	328,206	263,366	80.2	55.6	11.4	8.8	70.4	2,725	2,796	1,423	6,454
4-year											
2000–01	81,075	51,739	63.8	36.1	11.9	8.3	57.7	2,295	2,889	1,616	5,749
2003–04	84,771	63,441	74.8	47.5	15.9	12.6	66.4	2,776	2,467	1,795	6,682
2004–05	125,041	99,840	79.8	52.2	10.6	11.2	73.6	2,564	2,189	1,845	5,955
2005–06	157,705	116,237	73.7	46.8	8.9	10.9	67.2	2,490	2,945	1,641	7.046
2-year											
2000–01	122,920	103,635	84.3	58.0	17.3	4.8	67.3	2,319	2,314	1,453	5,387
2003–04	154,686	133,478	86.3	62.2	15.0	4.6	69.5	2,681	2,328	1,430	5,004
2004–05	166,944	144,364	86.5	63.5	13.3	4.7	69.6	2,789	2,494	1,275	5,274
2005–06	170,501	147,129	86.3	63.6	13.7	6.8	73.4	2,885	2,706	1,098	5,951

[1]Average amounts for students participating in indicated programs.
[2]Includes only loans made directly to students. Does not include Parent Loans for Undergraduate Students (PLUS) and other loans made directly to parents.
NOTE: Degree-granting institutions grant associate's or higher degrees and participate in Title IV federal financial aid programs.

SOURCE: U.S. Department of Education, National Center for Education Statistics, 2000–01 through 2005–06 Integrated Postsecondary Education Data System (IPEDS), Spring 2002 through Spring 2007. (This table was prepared May 2008.)

Table 337. Average amount of financial aid awarded to full-time, full-year undergraduates, by type and source of aid and selected student characteristics: 2003–04

Selected student characteristic	Any aid Total[1]	Federal	Nonfederal	Grants Total	Federal	Nonfederal	Loans Total	Federal[2]	Nonfederal	Work study Total[3]	Other Total	Federal	Nonfederal
1	2	3	4	5	6	7	8	9	10	11	12	13	14
All full-time, full-year undergraduates	$9,899 (106.7)	$7,304 (50.5)	$5,586 (109.1)	$5,565 (92.6)	$3,247 (24.2)	$4,828 (103.3)	$7,336 (80.9)	$6,426 (53.2)	$6,089 (158.5)	$1,942 (41.6)	$4,777 (170.1)	$5,283 (197.0)	$3,008 (180.3)
Sex													
Male	9,989 (148.0)	7,416 (76.3)	5,669 (129.5)	5,517 (105.2)	3,160 (27.6)	4,840 (117.0)	7,577 (103.1)	6,522 (66.6)	6,442 (194.6)	2,022 (46.6)	5,215 (240.2)	5,560 (265.3)	3,060 (273.4)
Female	9,831 (114.9)	7,223 (57.0)	5,524 (128.9)	5,600 (106.8)	3,303 (31.3)	4,819 (122.6)	7,159 (85.1)	6,356 (62.7)	5,783 (179.5)	1,886 (49.4)	4,087 (220.1)	4,705 (295.9)	2,969 (214.6)
Race/ethnicity[4]													
White	9,917 (131.5)	7,318 (61.2)	5,733 (122.8)	5,479 (105.1)	3,075 (30.3)	4,887 (111.1)	7,443 (90.2)	6,450 (57.3)	6,222 (174.7)	1,917 (42.5)	4,942 (215.1)	5,669 (264.7)	2,868 (196.9)
Black	10,520 (250.9)	7,901 (162.9)	5,256 (202.5)	5,694 (185.5)	3,442 (41.9)	4,754 (210.2)	7,111 (205.3)	6,510 (154.4)	5,401 (298.1)	1,959 (88.6)	4,338 (303.8)	4,485 (327.7)	2,991 (458.5)
Hispanic	9,006 (199.9)	6,670 (134.9)	4,838 (163.3)	5,399 (146.6)	3,431 (57.7)	4,251 (150.0)	6,990 (221.3)	6,193 (161.0)	5,500 (375.6)	1,985 (99.8)	4,808 (648.2)	5,170 (734.5)	3,401 (866.8)
Asian/Pacific Islander	10,039 (228.5)	6,745 (168.8)	6,180 (244.3)	6,700 (219.9)	3,411 (57.3)	5,545 (236.8)	7,079 (280.3)	6,136 (200.6)	6,728 (584.3)	2,027 (91.0)	4,390 (805.2)	4,321 (856.1)	‡
American Indian/Alaska Native	9,513 (689.1)	7,463 (430.5)	4,271 (605.1)	5,366 (558.4)	3,545 (378.7)	3,859 (568.1)	6,922 (441.8)	6,387 (329.5)	‡	‡	‡	(†)	‡
Age													
Younger than 24	9,984 (127.5)	6,881 (61.9)	6,102 (121.1)	5,958 (109.4)	3,174 (26.6)	5,288 (117.5)	7,224 (86.6)	6,166 (62.7)	6,261 (152.2)	1,895 (42.1)	4,630 (281.1)	5,117 (329.8)	2,794 (269.3)
24 to 29 years old	10,184 (136.4)	8,710 (97.5)	3,809 (136.0)	4,605 (90.2)	3,375 (42.5)	3,161 (106.3)	7,616 (125.4)	7,093 (93.7)	5,320 (393.8)	2,148 (93.0)	5,497 (342.4)	5,762 (364.2)	3,395 (544.4)
30 years old or over	9,086 (154.8)	8,100 (125.7)	3,240 (133.9)	4,114 (84.7)	3,381 (57.5)	2,577 (101.7)	7,688 (140.2)	7,187 (88.9)	5,269 (442.6)	2,372 (143.8)	4,350 (245.2)	4,975 (291.2)	3,080 (222.2)
Marital status													
Not married[5]	10,037 (115.2)	7,215 (53.5)	5,813 (112.6)	5,755 (98.6)	3,256 (24.7)	5,022 (110.0)	7,312 (84.3)	6,337 (56.4)	6,185 (160.6)	1,927 (42.8)	4,758 (201.7)	5,269 (228.0)	3,008 (220.1)
Married	8,785 (160.9)	7,845 (121.0)	3,502 (123.2)	4,013 (100.2)	3,078 (54.3)	2,930 (116.7)	7,671 (125.2)	7,213 (97.8)	5,074 (385.3)	2,243 (124.1)	4,808 (311.2)	5,279 (393.6)	3,043 (268.3)
Separated	9,554 (409.7)	8,315 (330.7)	3,122 (262.7)	4,758 (230.7)	3,719 (114.5)	2,801 (261.4)	6,532 (260.9)	6,318 (250.0)	3,895 (837.8)	1,846 (208.2)	4,939 (710.6)	‡	‡
Dependency status and family income													
Dependent	10,053 (136.5)	6,799 (61.5)	6,256 (126.7)	6,048 (117.8)	3,099 (27.2)	5,412 (123.3)	7,266 (89.3)	6,157 (63.8)	6,333 (153.0)	1,897 (44.1)	4,689 (341.1)	5,145 (403.2)	2,981 (254.6)
Less than $20,000	10,350 (237.7)	7,374 (135.3)	5,401 (172.5)	6,936 (169.8)	4,027 (30.8)	4,975 (174.4)	5,808 (150.1)	5,276 (124.8)	4,661 (307.8)	1,904 (72.9)	4,235 (604.8)	4,484 (689.6)	2,902 (641.4)
$20,000–$39,999	10,551 (194.1)	6,816 (105.9)	5,817 (166.8)	6,445 (130.8)	2,937 (31.8)	5,249 (149.9)	6,280 (130.2)	5,498 (93.8)	5,135 (253.9)	1,948 (72.6)	4,550 (679.1)	4,975 (848.8)	2,725 (618.1)
$40,000–$59,999	9,678 (211.8)	6,083 (127.0)	6,179 (176.6)	5,471 (158.8)	1,749 (47.0)	5,306 (166.0)	6,935 (156.4)	5,765 (123.7)	5,722 (254.8)	1,872 (67.9)	4,622 (542.8)	4,852 (659.3)	‡
$60,000–$79,999	9,755 (219.5)	6,503 (107.5)	6,473 (179.6)	5,461 (162.9)	1,477 (90.6)	5,447 (165.4)	7,617 (144.5)	6,371 (107.3)	6,700 (69.0)	1,820 (69.0)	3,755 (608.4)	4,145 (708.9)	‡
$80,000–$99,999	10,093 (263.8)	6,791 (157.7)	6,897 (248.3)	5,722 (215.3)	2,264 (616.9)	5,709 (211.0)	8,067 (199.1)	6,674 (157.1)	6,959 (321.3)	1,745 (60.3)	6,184 (1,623.3)	6,486 (1,771.4)	‡
$100,000 or more	9,850 (201.3)	7,263 (133.1)	6,868 (180.8)	5,854 (171.4)	1,659 (449.7)	5,849 (169.5)	8,719 (162.6)	7,296 (129.7)	7,971 (343.3)	2,059 (86.0)	5,235 (1,142.2)	6,614 (1,607.4)	‡
Independent	9,552 (96.2)	8,283 (77.5)	3,603 (89.6)	4,515 (63.9)	3,419 (36.8)	3,006 (69.4)	7,486 (100.7)	6,992 (65.4)	5,204 (300.0)	2,143 (68.8)	4,820 (190.8)	5,352 (225.9)	3,020 (206.7)
Less than $10,000	10,450 (139.1)	8,723 (123.3)	3,709 (112.1)	5,411 (79.3)	3,875 (36.9)	3,208 (106.2)	7,014 (113.2)	6,610 (102.7)	5,006 (349.9)	1,975 (84.2)	4,654 (376.2)	5,434 (471.0)	2,901 (393.7)
$10,000–$19,999	10,450 (208.8)	8,215 (139.9)	3,578 (195.9)	4,366 (99.7)	3,244 (54.2)	2,852 (130.2)	7,301 (207.8)	6,746 (121.5)	5,826 (764.2)	2,380 (129.1)	5,139 (359.7)	5,735 (406.7)	2,964 (386.8)
$20,000–$29,999	9,674 (172.2)	8,262 (138.3)	3,528 (205.1)	4,342 (106.7)	3,365 (65.2)	2,978 (147.5)	7,697 (181.9)	7,236 (144.7)	5,520 (813.8)	2,044 (236.9)	4,859 (514.5)	5,575 (717.9)	2,901 (296.9)
$30,000–$49,999	9,494 (256.4)	7,554 (194.3)	3,690 (191.8)	3,387 (136.9)	2,229 (79.0)	2,973 (181.2)	7,977 (187.9)	7,292 (151.3)	5,009 (437.7)	2,351 (215.7)	3,976 (431.7)	4,085 (529.6)	3,233 (503.0)
$50,000 or more	8,700 (232.5)	7,910 (228.1)	3,321 (184.9)	2,765 (166.0)	1,339 (171.6)	2,773 (167.1)	8,391 (223.9)	7,992 (149.4)	4,503 (497.5)	‡	5,445 (571.1)	5,857 (650.1)	3,276 (395.8)
Housing status													
School-owned	13,204 (219.3)	7,856 (82.6)	8,258 (210.4)	7,827 (185.3)	3,273 (51.4)	7,092 (191.2)	8,064 (131.0)	6,628 (85.7)	7,104 (231.6)	1,801 (49.9)	5,391 (565.2)	5,971 (664.9)	3,696 (409.9)
Off-campus, not with parents	9,391 (114.3)	7,735 (83.7)	4,392 (99.5)	4,741 (88.8)	3,307 (33.0)	3,713 (99.1)	7,356 (108.9)	6,659 (75.8)	5,661 (248.7)	2,203 (63.1)	4,826 (216.0)	5,407 (255.3)	2,953 (220.0)
With parents	7,420 (117.8)	6,054 (85.8)	4,032 (97.0)	4,461 (88.5)	3,134 (30.7)	3,534 (104.1)	6,338 (98.8)	5,713 (89.8)	5,045 (148.1)	1,888 (70.5)	4,219 (214.6)	4,531 (234.7)	2,592 (324.3)

†Not applicable.
‡Reporting standards not met.
[1]Includes students who reported they were awarded aid, but did not specify the source or type of aid.
[2]Includes Parent Loans for Undergraduate Students (PLUS).
[3]Details on federal and nonfederal work study participants are not available.
[4]Excludes persons not reported by race/ethnicity and persons reporting more than one race.
[5]Includes students who were single, divorced, or widowed.
NOTE: Rows may not sum to totals because of rounding and/or the fact that some students receive aid from multiple sources. Data include undergraduates in degree-granting and non-degree-granting institutions. Race categories exclude persons of Hispanic ethnicity. Standard errors appear in parentheses. Data include Puerto Rico.
SOURCE: U.S. Department of Education, National Center for Education Statistics, 2003–04 National Postsecondary Student Aid Study (NPSAS:04). (This table was prepared September 2005.)

Table 338. Average amount of financial aid awarded to part-time or part-year undergraduates, by type and source of aid and selected student characteristics: 2003–04

Selected student characteristic	Any aid Total¹	Any aid Federal	Any aid Nonfederal	Grants Total	Grants Federal	Grants Nonfederal	Loans Total	Loans Federal²	Loans Nonfederal	Work study Total³	Other Total	Other Federal	Other Nonfederal
1	2	3	4	5	6	7	8	9	10	11	12	13	14
All part-time or part-year undergraduates	$4,860 (67.1)	$4,765 (51.3)	$2,549 (66.7)	$2,449 (35.3)	$1,983 (18.4)	$2,054 (45.7)	$5,642 (89.2)	$5,145 (64.6)	$4,958 (243.0)	$2,012 (62.7)	$2,891 (119.8)	$2,995 (126.6)	$2,373 (155.8)
Sex													
Male	5,042 (117.0)	4,991 (92.3)	2,783 (103.4)	2,504 (51.7)	1,975 (31.9)	2,208 (63.5)	5,989 (146.4)	5,359 (98.0)	5,268 (401.4)	2,046 (78.8)	3,067 (138.5)	3,112 (143.9)	2,572 (227.5)
Female	4,746 (64.6)	4,634 (56.3)	2,396 (65.9)	2,418 (39.3)	1,986 (20.7)	1,954 (56.2)	5,433 (78.6)	5,017 (71.8)	4,714 (185.4)	1,987 (85.7)	2,589 (134.9)	2,723 (172.1)	2,270 (163.0)
Race/ethnicity⁴													
White	4,837 (100.9)	4,901 (83.0)	2,620 (89.9)	2,370 (48.2)	1,872 (23.6)	2,105 (59.9)	5,764 (123.9)	5,214 (88.4)	5,235 (275.4)	1,963 (85.3)	2,940 (144.6)	3,219 (156.1)	1,952 (175.0)
Black	4,908 (149.4)	4,735 (115.6)	2,187 (94.1)	2,476 (73.3)	2,045 (35.7)	1,901 (97.1)	5,214 (113.7)	5,009 (114.4)	3,669 (196.1)	1,978 (132.7)	2,758 (249.5)	2,826 (267.4)	2,138 (249.8)
Hispanic	4,622 (121.6)	4,306 (105.8)	2,355 (109.2)	2,487 (56.0)	2,089 (26.8)	1,843 (94.0)	5,466 (160.6)	4,927 (120.9)	4,562 (327.4)	1,975 (154.2)	2,795 (261.8)	2,505 (294.9)	4,126 (520.9)
Asian/Pacific Islander	5,316 (253.5)	4,833 (169.9)	3,158 (236.5)	3,046 (161.0)	2,284 (90.1)	2,438 (182.2)	6,313 (358.0)	5,609 (235.5)	4,901 (753.2)	2,496 (181.0)	3,294 (741.3)	‡ (†)	‡ (†)
American Indian/Alaska Native	4,246 (422.6)	4,289 (373.3)	2,090 (282.6)	2,384 (236.4)	2,264 (246.5)	1,697 (212.6)	5,130 (577.6)	4,479 (419.3)	‡ (†)	‡	‡ (†)	‡ (†)	‡ (†)
Age													
Younger than 24	5,273 (128.2)	4,439 (83.7)	3,288 (117.0)	2,952 (63.8)	2,055 (22.1)	2,646 (84.6)	5,369 (139.7)	4,652 (97.0)	5,248 (294.7)	1,943 (75.9)	2,644 (167.4)	2,708 (203.7)	2,229 (331.6)
24 to 29 years old	5,059 (80.3)	5,125 (67.9)	2,168 (82.0)	2,195 (44.2)	1,957 (29.9)	1,629 (61.3)	5,855 (97.1)	5,436 (74.5)	4,902 (339.1)	2,076 (156.7)	3,231 (223.1)	3,296 (246.8)	2,629 (283.4)
30 years old or over	4,260 (86.6)	4,913 (84.4)	1,975 (61.2)	2,069 (40.1)	1,907 (29.8)	1,677 (49.0)	5,852 (110.2)	5,590 (98.4)	4,279 (315.3)	2,160 (142.6)	2,824 (165.9)	2,962 (170.1)	2,359 (200.3)
Marital status													
Not married⁵	5,153 (89.2)	4,729 (59.8)	2,813 (87.8)	2,634 (45.0)	2,028 (20.5)	2,225 (61.4)	5,596 (104.2)	5,005 (70.0)	5,188 (272.6)	1,963 (59.5)	2,952 (137.5)	3,094 (158.1)	2,285 (197.1)
Married	4,142 (86.9)	4,868 (86.5)	2,020 (63.9)	1,984 (42.6)	1,764 (29.6)	1,724 (50.9)	5,837 (115.4)	5,588 (103.9)	4,157 (285.0)	2,318 (208.9)	2,784 (175.2)	2,808 (187.6)	2,569 (267.9)
Separated	4,872 (225.6)	4,826 (210.5)	1,918 (167.7)	2,460 (96.4)	2,155 (70.8)	1,591 (143.2)	5,315 (214.0)	5,089 (185.2)	3,711 (459.0)	‡ (†)	3,226 (627.4)	‡ (†)	‡
Dependency status and family income													
Dependent	5,458 (151.5)	4,454 (97.5)	3,549 (131.2)	3,111 (79.0)	2,043 (27.1)	2,846 (95.0)	5,481 (166.2)	4,672 (114.7)	5,485 (318.9)	1,919 (71.4)	2,405 (182.5)	2,405 (235.4)	2,402 (422.6)
Less than $20,000	5,075 (180.1)	4,205 (111.9)	2,821 (201.0)	3,334 (113.9)	2,483 (37.6)	2,432 (195.4)	4,567 (214.3)	3,998 (173.3)	4,430 (479.1)	1,773 (170.6)	2,540 (534.8)	2,469 (396.7)	‡ (†)
$20,000–$39,999	5,224 (152.0)	4,105 (99.0)	3,171 (160.1)	3,050 (97.5)	1,963 (39.0)	2,654 (123.0)	4,912 (180.3)	4,203 (122.4)	4,830 (484.7)	1,849 (88.9)	2,187 (322.4)	2,145 (393.3)	‡ (†)
$40,000–$59,999	5,370 (293.3)	4,392 (190.6)	3,528 (269.8)	2,740 (175.1)	1,249 (58.8)	2,801 (205.0)	5,308 (260.8)	4,590 (184.9)	5,878 (320.3)	1,868 (116.8)	1,970 (322.2)	3,202 (700.0)	‡ (†)
$60,000–$79,999	5,454 (249.0)	4,526 (206.0)	3,772 (221.7)	3,071 (221.6)	1,301 (129.3)	3,039 (224.1)	5,363 (258.8)	4,595 (217.4)	4,805 (371.6)	2,033 (158.1)	3,230 (464.3)	‡ (†)	‡ (†)
$80,000–$99,999	5,716 (305.5)	4,989 (284.1)	4,060 (307.5)	3,014 (264.5)	776 (300.7)	3,032 (268.9)	6,127 (328.9)	5,103 (303.7)	5,994 (473.4)	2,296 (283.2)	‡ (†)	‡ (†)	‡ (†)
$100,000 or more	6,530 (346.1)	5,697 (314.3)	4,639 (345.6)	3,523 (235.9)	922 (303.9)	3,523 (246.0)	7,394 (393.7)	6,186 (319.1)	7,172 (742.2)	2,014 (160.0)	2,220 (476.3)	2,113 (496.3)	‡ (†)
Independent	4,586 (54.5)	4,917 (50.3)	2,055 (54.8)	2,165 (28.0)	1,959 (19.7)	1,669 (37.7)	5,731 (81.8)	5,399 (66.4)	4,486 (280.0)	2,109 (94.6)	2,981 (132.7)	3,105 (138.7)	2,368 (161.1)
Less than $10,000	5,130 (128.2)	4,876 (104.9)	2,171 (125.3)	2,599 (56.5)	2,255 (30.3)	1,626 (82.1)	5,391 (164.2)	4,935 (112.3)	4,654 (503.2)	1,971 (123.8)	3,248 (288.9)	3,662 (384.1)	2,213 (276.3)
$10,000–$19,999	4,816 (109.4)	4,718 (100.9)	1,947 (98.4)	2,142 (52.0)	1,866 (30.8)	1,483 (86.9)	5,529 (118.4)	5,224 (110.1)	4,198 (316.3)	2,339 (158.3)	3,091 (241.3)	3,350 (308.0)	2,082 (251.0)
$20,000–$29,999	4,789 (102.9)	4,961 (78.1)	1,844 (73.9)	2,196 (48.2)	2,065 (33.6)	1,480 (63.3)	5,472 (117.1)	5,234 (111.4)	4,000 (239.9)	1,664 (246.7)	3,104 (265.3)	3,453 (323.8)	2,042 (196.8)
$30,000–$49,999	4,307 (113.1)	4,773 (122.2)	2,051 (88.9)	1,835 (50.0)	1,381 (32.7)	1,689 (69.4)	5,931 (163.8)	5,580 (139.1)	4,798 (593.7)	2,401 (304.3)	2,954 (228.6)	2,988 (244.9)	2,572 (333.6)
$50,000 or more	3,889 (121.8)	5,508 (169.5)	2,171 (83.8)	1,910 (71.0)	1,152 (227.2)	1,906 (73.5)	6,570 (176.4)	6,280 (158.6)	4,752 (479.6)	2,410 (450.7)	2,726 (194.5)	2,658 (213.2)	3,060 (370.5)
Housing status													
School-owned	8,776 (400.3)	5,858 (201.2)	6,066 (350.0)	4,967 (226.5)	2,208 (78.9)	4,867 (238.4)	6,422 (387.3)	5,146 (203.0)	6,962 (795.5)	1,883 (118.2)	3,237 (383.1)	3,394 (489.3)	‡ (†)
Off-campus, not with parents	4,596 (59.6)	4,775 (55.3)	2,222 (53.8)	2,216 (29.9)	1,943 (21.4)	1,775 (36.2)	5,670 (85.6)	5,242 (70.3)	4,856 (225.5)	2,063 (75.7)	2,891 (148.4)	3,000 (161.0)	2,344 (155.5)
With parents	4,554 (85.8)	4,460 (81.8)	2,283 (77.1)	2,406 (47.5)	2,032 (24.1)	1,871 (67.5)	5,283 (109.0)	4,901 (97.0)	4,134 (206.5)	2,000 (135.3)	2,847 (143.6)	2,931 (148.8)	2,450 (338.0)

†Not applicable.

‡Reporting standards not met.

¹Includes students who reported they were awarded aid, but did not specify the source or type of aid.

²Includes Parent Loans for Undergraduate Students (PLUS).

³Details on federal and nonfederal work study participants are not available.

⁴Excludes persons not reported by race/ethnicity and persons reporting more than one race.

⁵Includes students who were single, divorced, or widowed.

NOTE: Rows may not sum to totals because of rounding and/or the fact that some students receive aid from multiple sources. Data include undergraduates in degree-granting and non-degree-granting institutions. Race categories exclude persons of Hispanic ethnicity. Standard errors appear in parentheses. Data include Puerto Rico.

SOURCE: U.S. Department of Education, National Center for Education Statistics, 2003–04 National Postsecondary Student Aid Study (NPSAS:04). (This table was prepared September 2005.)

Table 339. Amount borrowed, aid status, and sources of aid for full-time and part-time undergraduates, by control and type of institution: 2003–04

Control and type of institution	Number of undergraduates[1] (in thousands)		Cumulative amount borrowed for undergraduate education[2]		Aid status (percent of students)									
					Nonaided		Receiving aid, by source								
							Any aid[3]		Federal		State		Institutional		Other[3]	
1		2		3		4		5		6		7		8		9
Full-time, full-year students															
All institutions..................	7,824	(93.5)	$12,750	(130.4)	23.9	(0.40)	76.1	(0.40)	61.7	(0.42)	23.7	(0.47)	31.4	(0.66)	22.6	(0.35)
Public.....................................	5,662	(78.1)	11,260	(125.7)	28.9	(0.49)	71.1	(0.49)	56.1	(0.47)	22.9	(0.50)	23.6	(0.63)	19.0	(0.38)
4-year doctoral.....................	2,411	(33.2)	12,707	(136.8)	24.5	(0.64)	75.5	(0.64)	58.2	(0.71)	23.7	(0.49)	31.7	(0.72)	21.7	(0.46)
Other 4-year.........................	1,198	(42.8)	11,500	(313.3)	23.0	(1.12)	77.0	(1.12)	64.0	(1.20)	28.7	(1.73)	23.6	(1.58)	20.0	(0.86)
2-year.................................	2,026	(59.1)	8,294	(263.5)	37.7	(1.22)	62.3	(1.22)	48.9	(1.15)	18.7	(0.86)	14.2	(0.99)	14.9	(0.73)
Less-than-2-year..................	27	(2.1)	6,870	(362.3)	33.3	(2.51)	66.7	(2.51)	48.7	(2.75)	17.1	(2.26)	6.4	(1.39)	29.8	(2.76)
Private, not-for-profit................	1,635	(38.9)	15,458	(287.8)	11.4	(0.78)	88.6	(0.78)	73.1	(0.81)	29.3	(1.51)	64.9	(1.77)	33.7	(0.96)
4-year doctoral.....................	668	(27.5)	16,033	(568.0)	15.9	(1.16)	84.1	(1.16)	66.2	(1.69)	23.9	(1.93)	63.6	(2.55)	34.3	(1.66)
Other 4-year.........................	921	(36.8)	15,268	(453.4)	8.2	(1.08)	91.8	(1.08)	77.9	(1.25)	33.1	(2.39)	67.2	(3.44)	33.8	(1.88)
Less-than-4-year..................	47	(4.4)	11,436	(1,847.7)	11.2	(2.63)	88.8	(2.63)	76.8	(4.76)	33.1	(5.58)	37.7	(6.84)	23.5	(3.81)
Private, for-profit	527	(21.6)	15,100	(500.8)	7.9	(0.72)	92.1	(0.72)	86.9	(0.92)	14.6	(1.77)	11.1	(1.42)	27.9	(1.66)
2-year and above	393	(21.0)	16,950	(596.3)	5.2	(0.89)	94.8	(0.89)	90.6	(1.14)	17.4	(2.42)	11.0	(1.95)	30.2	(2.12)
Less-than-2-year..................	134	(3.0)	8,044	(368.5)	15.7	(1.13)	84.3	(1.13)	76.0	(1.31)	6.4	(0.65)	11.4	(0.97)	20.9	(1.22)
Part-time or part-year students															
All institutions	11,230	(93.5)	$11,235	(147.1)	45.7	(0.56)	54.3	(0.56)	38.5	(0.44)	10.1	(0.39)	10.1	(0.42)	17.6	(0.35)
Public.....................................	9,015	(74.6)	10,564	(132.9)	52.4	(0.69)	47.6	(0.69)	32.0	(0.52)	10.0	(0.43)	7.8	(0.37)	15.0	(0.39)
4-year doctoral.....................	1,516	(33.3)	14,333	(271.1)	41.0	(1.12)	59.0	(1.12)	42.9	(0.92)	10.7	(0.53)	14.6	(0.80)	17.8	(0.74)
Other 4-year.........................	984	(47.7)	11,918	(383.1)	43.9	(2.33)	56.1	(2.33)	42.0	(2.03)	10.5	(1.31)	8.9	(1.07)	16.7	(0.99)
2-year.................................	6,449	(59.1)	8,270	(172.4)	56.4	(0.92)	43.6	(0.92)	28.0	(0.66)	9.7	(0.54)	6.1	(0.48)	14.0	(0.51)
Less-than-2-year..................	66	(2.1)	7,520	(880.1)	57.6	(4.11)	42.4	(4.11)	19.6	(1.80)	12.2	(3.37)	4.1	(1.23)	24.0	(3.02)
Private, not-for-profit................	1,204	(37.4)	14,643	(488.0)	23.7	(1.07)	76.3	(1.07)	52.4	(1.42)	13.6	(1.11)	29.8	(2.24)	30.9	(1.37)
4-year doctoral.....................	356	(17.6)	16,301	(720.2)	26.9	(1.48)	73.1	(1.48)	45.8	(2.20)	12.0	(1.28)	38.5	(3.12)	30.5	(1.63)
Other 4-year.........................	786	(37.2)	14,223	(764.6)	22.6	(1.45)	77.4	(1.45)	54.2	(2.21)	14.0	(1.59)	26.4	(3.32)	31.8	(2.19)
Less-than-4-year..................	62	(4.4)	10,792	(1,846.3)	19.3	(3.62)	80.7	(3.62)	66.9	(3.72)	17.8	(3.44)	22.7	(4.44)	21.3	(3.10)
Private, for-profit	1,011	(19.5)	10,727	(382.9)	12.4	(0.54)	87.6	(0.54)	79.8	(0.85)	7.1	(0.81)	6.6	(0.80)	24.6	(1.41)
2-year and above	636	(19.2)	12,883	(562.8)	9.3	(0.72)	90.7	(0.72)	83.3	(1.26)	8.1	(1.29)	6.5	(1.23)	27.3	(2.27)
Less-than-2-year..................	375	(3.0)	6,572	(107.5)	17.7	(0.97)	82.3	(0.97)	73.8	(0.91)	5.3	(0.53)	6.7	(0.93)	19.9	(0.73)

[1]Numbers of undergraduates may not equal figures reported in other tables, since these data are based on a sample survey of students who enrolled at any time during the academic year.
[2]Includes only those students who borrowed to finance their undergraduate education. Excludes loans from family sources.
[3]Includes students who reported that they were awarded aid, but did not specify the source of the aid.

NOTE: Excludes students whose attendance status was not reported. Detail may not sum to totals because of rounding and because some students receive multiple types of aid and aid from different sources. Standard errors appear in parentheses. Data include Puerto Rico. Some data have been revised from previously published figures.
SOURCE: U.S. Department of Education, National Center for Education Statistics, 2003–04 National Postsecondary Student Aid Study (NPSAS:04). (This table was prepared November 2008.)

Table 340. Percentage of full-time, full-year undergraduates receiving aid, by type and source of aid and control and type of institution: Selected years, 1992–93 through 2003–04

Control and type of institution	Any aid: Total[2]	Any aid: Federal	Any aid: Nonfederal	Grants: Total	Grants: Federal	Grants: Nonfederal	Loans: Total	Loans: Federal	Loans: Nonfederal	Work study[1]: Total	Work study[1]: Federal	Other: Total	Other: Federal	Other: Nonfederal
1	2	3	4	5	6	7	8	9	10	11	12	13	14	15
1992–93, all institutions	**58.7 (0.81)**	**45.6 (0.80)**	**37.9 (0.76)**	**48.9 (0.75)**	**29.4 (0.76)**	**34.0 (0.71)**	**32.3 (0.78)**	**31.3 (0.77)**	**2.7 (0.20)**	**10.2 (0.48)**	**6.8 (0.39)**	**9.5 (0.40)**	**5.2 (0.28)**	**4.6 (0.32)**
Public	52.6 (1.03)	40.0 (0.98)	33.0 (0.88)	43.1 (0.94)	27.8 (0.83)	29.1 (0.79)	25.5 (0.89)	24.8 (0.88)	2.0 (0.22)	6.8 (0.43)	4.2 (0.30)	7.9 (0.40)	3.7 (0.27)	4.4 (0.33)
4-year doctoral	54.1 (1.18)	39.3 (1.17)	34.8 (0.81)	42.4 (1.02)	23.8 (0.96)	30.8 (0.74)	31.2 (1.05)	30.4 (1.04)	2.4 (0.26)	7.1 (0.55)	4.3 (0.37)	8.6 (0.43)	5.0 (0.37)	3.9 (0.27)
Other 4-year	57.1 (1.56)	46.1 (1.61)	37.4 (1.69)	46.1 (1.65)	32.1 (1.63)	32.4 (1.55)	32.2 (1.38)	31.1 (1.34)	2.8 (0.59)	9.5 (0.76)	5.4 (0.57)	7.9 (0.63)	4.2 (0.42)	3.8 (0.55)
2-year	47.2 (2.35)	36.0 (2.09)	27.0 (1.96)	41.9 (2.19)	29.9 (1.81)	24.3 (1.87)	12.1 (1.40)	11.7 (1.38)	0.7 (0.24)	4.1 (0.75)	3.0 (0.58)	7.0 (0.94)	1.3 (0.47)	5.7 (0.84)
Less-than-2-year	35.4 (7.28)	31.6 (7.27)	15.7 (6.50)	30.3 (5.52)	26.6 (5.70)	12.8 (5.75)	3.0 (1.63)	3.0 (1.63)	0.6 (0.51)	1.5 (0.98)	1.4 (0.95)	5.1 (2.59)	0.8 (0.62)	4.4 (2.49)
Private, not-for-profit	70.2 (1.52)	53.4 (1.43)	58.0 (1.60)	62.9 (1.50)	27.7 (1.78)	54.1 (1.64)	45.4 (1.33)	43.6 (1.31)	5.0 (0.48)	22.2 (1.11)	15.9 (0.99)	12.1 (0.98)	7.7 (0.54)	5.0 (0.90)
4-year doctoral	63.6 (1.80)	44.5 (1.57)	54.8 (1.78)	56.1 (1.79)	17.3 (1.29)	51.8 (1.70)	40.5 (1.37)	38.5 (1.31)	6.1 (0.65)	18.9 (1.24)	13.2 (1.38)	11.6 (0.96)	7.4 (0.70)	4.5 (0.67)
Other 4-year	76.2 (2.07)	60.8 (2.07)	62.7 (2.66)	69.4 (2.07)	35.6 (2.77)	58.1 (2.81)	50.6 (2.17)	49.0 (2.20)	4.1 (0.77)	27.0 (1.61)	19.7 (1.47)	12.2 (1.80)	7.9 (0.85)	5.3 (1.71)
Less-than-4-year	73.9 (4.01)	63.9 (5.69)	42.0 (5.38)	61.3 (4.73)	47.3 (7.16)	35.4 (6.71)	39.7 (5.73)	38.1 (5.51)	2.5 (0.97)	4.6 (1.36)	3.0 (1.01)	17.2 (3.97)	9.4 (4.28)	7.8 (3.07)
Private, for-profit	77.3 (2.53)	72.4 (2.76)	16.4 (2.97)	57.0 (2.67)	50.9 (2.69)	11.4 (2.75)	52.9 (3.87)	52.4 (3.87)	2.1 (0.66)	1.9 (1.18)	0.8 (0.36)	15.6 (2.42)	11.3 (2.29)	4.5 (1.02)
2-year and above	82.7 (3.43)	77.4 (4.27)	22.7 (5.67)	52.5 (4.19)	43.4 (4.13)	16.4 (5.15)	63.3 (4.16)	63.0 (4.18)	3.0 (1.41)	3.5 (2.55)	1.4 (0.78)	24.6 (4.64)	18.8 (4.48)	6.5 (2.11)
Less-than-2-year	73.2 (3.27)	68.6 (3.26)	11.5 (2.43)	60.4 (3.57)	56.7 (3.75)	7.5 (2.47)	45.0 (5.12)	44.3 (5.09)	1.5 (0.40)	0.7 (0.43)	0.2 (0.09)	8.7 (1.48)	5.6 (1.21)	3.1 (0.86)
1995–96, all institutions	**68.4 (0.76)**	**55.6 (0.79)**	**45.7 (0.85)**	**54.1 (0.80)**	**30.6 (0.79)**	**41.0 (0.82)**	**43.7 (0.80)**	**43.2 (0.80)**	**1.7 (0.24)**	**11.0 (0.55)**	**9.0 (0.46)**	**10.9 (0.43)**	**5.0 (0.27)**	**5.9 (0.36)**
Public	62.8 (0.97)	50.8 (0.97)	39.0 (0.97)	47.5 (0.99)	23.6 (0.99)	34.2 (0.89)	37.2 (0.93)	36.9 (0.92)	0.8 (0.19)	7.0 (0.52)	5.4 (0.42)	9.3 (0.52)	3.7 (0.30)	5.5 (0.42)
4-year doctoral	65.4 (1.16)	51.9 (1.12)	42.2 (1.18)	47.6 (1.20)	26.1 (1.13)	37.2 (1.19)	44.5 (1.10)	44.1 (1.10)	1.4 (0.34)	7.4 (0.74)	5.3 (0.46)	11.0 (0.75)	5.6 (0.58)	5.4 (0.54)
Other 4-year	69.3 (1.38)	59.8 (1.34)	44.5 (1.58)	52.3 (1.48)	34.4 (1.53)	40.0 (1.45)	47.4 (1.60)	47.2 (1.60)	0.4 (0.14)	9.2 (0.86)	6.7 (0.63)	8.6 (0.66)	3.7 (0.45)	4.8 (0.48)
2-year	55.9 (2.29)	44.5 (2.33)	31.3 (2.25)	44.6 (2.36)	31.1 (2.43)	26.9 (1.93)	21.8 (1.85)	21.3 (1.83)	0.4 (0.39)	5.1 (1.16)	4.7 (1.07)	7.4 (1.17)	1.3 (0.35)	6.0 (1.04)
Less-than-2-year	39.5 (9.87)	20.6 (6.51)	27.5 (7.17)	30.9 (7.49)	18.5 (5.86)	16.0 (5.29)	4.4 (2.28)	4.4 (2.28)	# (†)	0.1 (0.14)	0.1 (0.14)	12.6 (4.52)	0.1 (0.06)	12.0 (4.36)
Private, not-for-profit	80.3 (1.12)	64.0 (1.43)	67.6 (1.58)	71.3 (1.34)	28.6 (1.37)	64.8 (1.64)	56.9 (1.41)	56.2 (1.42)	3.4 (0.64)	24.7 (1.45)	21.0 (1.26)	14.0 (0.86)	8.2 (0.61)	6.1 (0.74)
4-year doctoral	70.6 (1.56)	55.4 (1.77)	61.2 (1.84)	61.6 (1.69)	19.3 (0.93)	58.7 (1.92)	50.9 (1.80)	49.9 (1.88)	3.9 (0.84)	22.6 (1.66)	20.2 (1.62)	13.3 (0.86)	8.6 (0.77)	4.9 (0.52)
Other 4-year	85.6 (1.43)	68.3 (1.99)	72.5 (2.19)	77.3 (1.83)	32.5 (2.10)	70.1 (2.27)	60.4 (1.94)	60.0 (1.95)	2.6 (0.59)	27.6 (2.10)	23.0 (1.80)	14.6 (1.29)	8.2 (0.90)	6.7 (1.15)
Less-than-4-year	79.2 (5.71)	67.5 (6.37)	52.0 (8.29)	61.9 (4.87)	40.0 (4.69)	42.0 (6.10)	52.9 (7.57)	51.7 (7.28)	9.3 (7.17)	5.3 (2.22)	4.6 (2.00)	11.4 (3.30)	5.0 (1.43)	6.3 (2.16)
Private, for-profit	86.2 (1.73)	79.7 (2.05)	32.8 (3.11)	61.3 (2.40)	53.9 (2.53)	20.2 (2.64)	67.7 (3.40)	65.5 (3.67)	5.1 (1.89)	0.5 (0.16)	0.5 (0.15)	17.2 (1.74)	7.6 (1.09)	8.9 (1.32)
2-year and above	85.8 (1.85)	80.3 (2.58)	33.0 (3.41)	60.0 (3.02)	49.1 (3.23)	26.0 (3.83)	70.9 (3.50)	70.9 (3.51)	1.4 (0.74)	0.7 (0.26)	0.7 (0.26)	15.3 (1.86)	7.8 (1.36)	6.9 (1.19)
Less-than-2-year	86.6 (2.92)	79.1 (3.16)	32.5 (5.18)	62.5 (3.72)	56.6 (3.83)	14.5 (3.61)	64.6 (5.75)	60.3 (6.32)	8.7 (3.61)	0.3 (0.18)	0.2 (0.15)	19.1 (2.92)	7.4 (1.69)	10.9 (2.33)
1999–2000, all institutions	**72.5 (0.51)**	**57.7 (0.56)**	**51.8 (0.64)**	**58.7 (0.59)**	**30.3 (0.59)**	**48.3 (0.65)**	**45.4 (0.62)**	**44.3 (0.63)**	**6.8 (0.25)**	**11.2 (0.38)**	**8.5 (0.31)**	**9.6 (0.31)**	**5.6 (0.22)**	**1.9 (0.17)**
Public	67.5 (0.64)	52.6 (0.68)	46.0 (0.72)	53.0 (0.70)	29.8 (0.69)	42.5 (0.72)	38.9 (0.74)	37.9 (0.75)	4.4 (0.24)	7.2 (0.36)	5.4 (0.30)	8.2 (0.35)	3.9 (0.22)	1.9 (0.19)
4-year doctoral	71.0 (0.65)	54.7 (0.70)	48.7 (0.74)	53.1 (0.70)	25.7 (0.72)	44.6 (0.71)	48.3 (0.76)	47.2 (0.78)	5.5 (0.36)	8.3 (0.46)	5.8 (0.38)	9.6 (0.45)	6.1 (0.37)	1.6 (0.15)
Other 4-year	75.0 (1.24)	62.2 (1.48)	50.0 (1.61)	57.7 (1.74)	34.5 (2.11)	46.2 (1.60)	49.1 (1.75)	48.2 (1.78)	4.5 (0.46)	10.4 (1.05)	7.7 (0.83)	7.8 (0.69)	3.9 (0.58)	1.7 (0.36)
2-year	58.2 (1.34)	43.8 (1.28)	40.0 (1.56)	49.9 (1.42)	32.1 (1.17)	37.7 (1.60)	20.5 (1.26)	19.6 (1.24)	3.1 (0.47)	3.8 (0.53)	3.4 (0.50)	6.5 (0.74)	1.1 (0.19)	2.4 (0.49)
Less-than-2-year	60.7 (5.94)	48.1 (6.42)	33.6 (4.81)	49.2 (6.35)	40.8 (6.85)	25.0 (5.05)	11.0 (4.14)	11.0 (4.14)	0.3 (0.31)	0.8 (0.77)	# (†)	17.2 (2.19)	0.1 (0.10)	11.7 (2.02)
Private, not-for-profit	84.0 (0.77)	67.6 (1.02)	71.6 (1.27)	74.7 (1.12)	27.7 (1.23)	68.9 (1.36)	59.3 (1.14)	57.7 (1.18)	13.4 (0.65)	24.4 (1.07)	18.8 (0.82)	12.8 (0.67)	9.7 (0.56)	1.5 (0.40)
4-year doctoral	78.8 (1.13)	62.3 (1.41)	69.4 (1.29)	69.7 (1.24)	22.4 (0.95)	66.4 (1.36)	57.3 (1.42)	55.5 (1.43)	15.1 (0.86)	24.7 (1.17)	20.9 (1.06)	12.0 (0.74)	9.9 (0.66)	1.1 (0.20)
Other 4-year	88.3 (1.12)	72.2 (1.53)	74.1 (2.12)	78.7 (1.81)	30.9 (2.13)	71.6 (2.27)	62.2 (1.79)	60.6 (1.87)	12.8 (1.01)	24.8 (1.75)	17.7 (1.26)	13.2 (1.09)	9.6 (0.90)	1.8 (0.73)
Less-than-4-year	81.1 (3.64)	62.6 (3.94)	61.5 (4.76)	73.9 (3.59)	40.0 (3.66)	59.4 (5.18)	40.3 (5.18)	40.2 (5.19)	5.0 (0.80)	15.1 (2.91)	10.9 (2.54)	14.6 (1.94)	8.8 (0.95)	2.0 (0.81)
Private, for-profit	89.2 (1.25)	86.0 (1.50)	35.3 (3.45)	61.8 (2.49)	52.0 (2.95)	28.8 (3.14)	75.0 (2.87)	74.1 (2.93)	7.3 (1.69)	2.3 (0.84)	2.0 (0.83)	16.1 (1.55)	10.9 (1.42)	2.3 (0.50)
2-year and above	88.3 (1.60)	85.3 (1.90)	38.3 (4.46)	58.5 (2.99)	46.3 (3.47)	33.1 (4.01)	79.5 (2.77)	78.7 (2.80)	6.8 (2.15)	2.6 (1.03)	2.1 (1.00)	17.1 (1.91)	12.3 (1.80)	1.8 (0.47)
Less-than-2-year	91.7 (1.27)	88.3 (1.92)	26.1 (3.49)	71.9 (3.47)	69.9 (3.52)	15.6 (3.33)	61.0 (7.08)	59.9 (7.28)	8.9 (1.89)	1.6 (1.41)	1.6 (1.41)	12.9 (2.42)	6.7 (1.87)	3.8 (1.40)
2003–04, all institutions	**76.1 (0.40)**	**61.7 (0.42)**	**54.3 (0.52)**	**62.2 (0.48)**	**33.2 (0.32)**	**49.3 (0.51)**	**49.9 (0.44)**	**48.5 (0.43)**	**9.0 (0.31)**	**13.5 (0.41)**	**10.3 (0.36)**	**3.2 (0.17)**	**2.4 (0.12)**	**0.8 (0.09)**
Public	71.1 (0.49)	56.1 (0.47)	48.3 (0.56)	56.0 (0.58)	31.6 (0.33)	43.7 (0.54)	42.6 (0.46)	41.1 (0.47)	6.0 (0.16)	9.9 (0.34)	7.3 (0.31)	3.3 (0.19)	2.5 (0.13)	0.9 (0.11)
4-year doctoral	75.5 (0.64)	58.2 (0.71)	54.4 (0.55)	58.5 (0.61)	27.8 (0.79)	49.7 (0.57)	51.6 (0.74)	50.1 (0.74)	7.3 (0.31)	10.8 (0.41)	9.9 (0.87)	2.5 (0.20)	2.1 (0.16)	0.4 (0.11)
Other 4-year	77.0 (1.12)	64.0 (1.20)	53.4 (1.36)	58.8 (1.78)	34.6 (1.38)	48.1 (1.33)	52.2 (1.34)	50.5 (1.38)	7.3 (0.49)	12.9 (0.96)	5.3 (0.50)	3.5 (0.44)	2.6 (0.31)	1.0 (0.30)
2-year	62.3 (1.22)	48.9 (1.15)	38.1 (1.22)	51.5 (1.20)	34.5 (0.88)	34.2 (1.17)	26.4 (1.03)	25.1 (1.02)	3.7 (0.26)	7.1 (0.54)	1.1 (0.57)	3.9 (0.38)	2.8 (0.26)	1.2 (0.23)
Less-than-2-year	66.7 (2.51)	48.7 (2.75)	36.5 (2.39)	49.7 (2.87)	36.0 (1.79)	23.1 (2.58)	24.8 (2.52)	24.2 (2.54)	4.1 (0.89)	2.0 (0.76)	22.5 (1.53)	15.0 (2.50)	1.9 (1.00)	13.2 (2.30)
Private, not-for-profit	88.6 (0.78)	73.1 (0.81)	78.3 (1.28)	81.0 (0.97)	31.9 (0.72)	74.5 (1.34)	66.0 (1.03)	64.4 (1.05)	17.0 (0.96)	29.2 (1.26)	23.0 (1.17)	2.1 (0.19)	1.7 (0.18)	0.4 (0.10)
4-year doctoral	84.1 (1.16)	66.2 (1.69)	76.0 (1.74)	75.9 (1.34)	24.3 (3.06)	72.1 (1.54)	60.8 (2.07)	59.0 (2.02)	17.7 (1.85)	27.7 (1.50)	24.2 (1.93)	1.6 (0.26)	1.4 (0.23)	0.3 (0.11)
Other 4-year	91.8 (1.08)	77.9 (1.25)	80.7 (2.77)	85.0 (1.36)	36.5 (2.12)	77.2 (2.75)	70.3 (2.35)	68.8 (2.34)	16.9 (1.64)	31.3 (2.29)	8.6 (2.71)	2.2 (0.29)	2.0 (0.28)	0.3 (0.12)
Less-than-4-year	88.8 (2.63)	76.8 (4.76)	63.4 (5.93)	76.3 (3.71)	49.6 (3.98)	57.4 (6.16)	56.4 (5.05)	54.3 (5.04)	10.1 (2.42)	10.1 (3.38)	3.7 (0.82)	5.0 (1.68)	1.6 (1.02)	3.4 (1.39)
Private, for-profit	92.1 (0.72)	86.9 (0.92)	44.3 (1.90)	69.7 (1.68)	54.8 (1.69)	31.3 (1.38)	79.4 (1.18)	78.2 (1.17)	16.6 (1.45)	3.6 (0.70)	3.1 (0.62)	5.2 (0.69)	4.0 (0.57)	1.2 (0.30)
2-year and above	94.8 (0.89)	90.6 (1.14)	48.0 (2.45)	70.1 (2.17)	53.6 (2.21)	35.0 (2.50)	86.8 (1.43)	86.1 (1.44)	18.1 (1.91)	4.2 (0.93)	1.5 (0.22)	5.5 (0.90)	4.7 (0.76)	0.8 (0.39)
Less-than-2-year	84.3 (1.13)	76.0 (1.31)	33.3 (1.59)	68.4 (1.44)	58.2 (1.61)	20.2 (1.87)	57.7 (1.62)	55.2 (1.59)	12.2 (1.18)	1.7 (0.21)	10.8 (0.41)	4.2 (0.45)	1.9 (0.28)	2.4 (0.30)

†Not applicable.
#Rounds to zero.
[1]Details on nonfederal work study participants are not available.
[2]Includes students who reported they were awarded aid, but did not specify the source of aid.
NOTE: Excludes students whose attendance status was not reported. Detail may not sum to totals because of rounding and because some students receive multiple types of aid and aid from different sources. Standard errors appear in parentheses. The 2003–04 loan estimates include Parent Loans for Undergraduate Students (PLUS) and may differ from previously published figures. Data include Puerto Rico.
SOURCE: U.S. Department of Education, National Center for Education Statistics, 1992–93, 1995–96, 1999–2000, and 2003–04 National Postsecondary Student Aid Studies (NPSAS:93, NPSAS:96, NPSAS:2000, and NPSAS:04). (This table was prepared August 2005.)

Table 341. Average amount of financial aid awarded to full-time, full-year undergraduates, by type and source of aid and control and type of institution: Selected years, 1992–93 through 2003–04

[In current dollars]

Control and type of institution	Any aid			Grants			Loans			Work study[1]		Other		
	Total[2]	Federal	Nonfederal	Total[3]	Federal	Nonfederal	Total	Federal[4]	Nonfederal	Total	Federal	Total	Federal	Nonfederal
1	2	3	4	5	6	7	8	9	10	11	12	13	14	15
1992–93, all institutions...	$5,727 (1,344.4)	$4,296 (334.1)	$3,480 (915.1)	$3,545 (643.2)	$1,985 (31.5)	$3,319 (807.3)	$3,884 (293.1)	$3,762 (198.1)	$2,728 (663.8)	$1,376 (103.1)	$1,290 (92.5)	$2,380 (659.5)	$2,917 (1,391.0)	$2,049 (411.8)
Public...	4,067 (314.4)	3,695 (44.6)	1,797 (261.6)	2,398 (60.4)	1,880 (20.8)	1,655 (325.1)	3,333 (40.8)	3,273 (46.3)	2,022 (132.7)	1,366 (83.7)	1,346 (64.8)	1,645 (157.2)	2,058 (182.8)	1,288 (58.7)
4-year doctoral...	4,753 (349.3)	4,358 (54.7)	2,277 (235.5)	2,713 (106.3)	1,971 (24.5)	2,144 (278.3)	3,635 (59.6)	3,563 (67.8)	2,112 (268.6)	1,434 (115.9)	1,355 (101.7)	1,816 (113.6)	2,409 (180.4)	1,452 (86.8)
Other 4-year...	4,241 (301.7)	3,782 (71.2)	1,658 (84.9)	2,419 (49.2)	1,943 (29.4)	1,453 (122.9)	3,198 (64.0)	3,118 (66.1)	2,155 (204.5)	1,242 (60.9)	1,265 (69.2)	1,786 (204.4)	1,720 (411.2)	1,728 (148.7)
2-year...	2,762 (188.8)	2,619 (99.6)	1,090 (461.2)	1,928 (76.1)	1,723 (60.5)	1,028 (524.2)	2,530 (162.9)	2,561 (152.2)	‡ (†)	1,466 (165.3)	1,474 (155.9)	1,379 (430.9)	2,016 (246.7)	706 (136.1)
Less-than-2-year...	2,299 (322.3)	1,947 (216.9)	1,139 (502.6)	1,974 (304.9)	1,761 (44.0)	875 (163.4)	3,139 (801.1)	2,971 (885.5)	‡ (†)	‡ (†)	‡ (†)	1,889 (1,326.1)	‡ (†)	‡ (†)
Private, not-for-profit...	9,217 (3,036.2)	5,248 (949.3)	6,053 (1,869.0)	6,026 (1,564.2)	2,312 (123.9)	5,741 (1,651.5)	4,433 (809.4)	4,189 (600.2)	3,444 (772.2)	1,359 (267.7)	1,252 (194.0)	3,792 (1,482.9)	7,509 (4,754.3)	3,001 (767.0)
4-year doctoral...	10,240 (932.0)	5,632 (341.1)	6,919 (325.9)	6,811 (241.4)	2,257 (59.1)	6,395 (422.1)	4,883 (142.4)	4,543 (120.9)	3,692 (468.5)	1,519 (63.3)	1,366 (79.7)	5,148 (669.7)	9,576 (1,864.7)	3,859 (795.3)
Other 4-year...	8,284 (1,402.7)	4,923 (362.5)	5,159 (314.9)	5,389 (359.2)	2,234 (70.9)	4,794 (316.0)	4,166 (175.0)	4,019 (155.3)	2,906 (318.3)	1,283 (73.6)	1,181 (61.9)	3,133 (459.9)	‡ (†)	2,646 (349.0)
Less-than-4-year...	7,667 (919.9)	4,750 (224.6)	4,582 (433.6)	4,863 (404.7)	1,971 (24.5)	4,622 (388.6)	3,728 (124.4)	3,636 (110.7)	2,671 (404.7)	1,119 (67.8)	1,103 (66.2)	2,244 (542.9)	‡ (†)	2,154 (602.4)
Private, for-profit...	5,212 (294.1)	4,924 (283.6)	2,349 (1,168.4)	2,117 (307.3)	1,903 (71.3)	1,854 (1,392.4)	4,739 (287.1)	4,678 (285.7)	2,359 (605.3)	2,418 (593.4)	‡ (†)	2,953 (469.2)	2,720 (1,187.6)	3,114 (1,392.4)
2-year and above...	6,010 (328.0)	5,526 (285.2)	2,561 (1,306.6)	2,407 (528.1)	1,863 (141.7)	2,210 (1,954.5)	5,194 (416.9)	5,106 (380.7)	‡ (†)	‡ (†)	‡ (†)	2,679 (689.7)	‡ (†)	2,572 (421.0)
Less-than-2-year...	4,507 (434.0)	4,390 (429.9)	1,989 (1,237.6)	1,918 (157.7)	2,406 (702.0)	1,156 (679.5)	4,242 (420.3)	4,208 (384.3)	‡ (†)	‡ (†)	‡ (†)	3,469 (1,555.8)	‡ (†)	3,704 (1,739.7)
1995–96, all institutions...	$6,860 (240.2)	$5,373 (115.1)	$3,797 (252.9)	$3,897 (211.7)	$2,012 (22.4)	$3,615 (253.2)	$5,020 (94.5)	$4,965 (94.5)	$2,750 (363.1)	$1,370 (75.1)	$1,300 (66.1)	$3,545 (348.5)	$3,578 (570.9)	$3,299 (296.9)
Public...	5,228 (148.0)	4,817 (136.2)	2,214 (73.5)	2,702 (75.7)	1,931 (26.3)	2,075 (72.4)	4,621 (137.9)	4,606 (139.1)	2,351 (563.7)	1,345 (99.5)	1,290 (77.4)	2,896 (233.8)	3,295 (185.7)	2,342 (276.2)
4-year doctoral...	6,289 (164.6)	5,669 (247.7)	2,856 (103.6)	3,185 (142.4)	1,955 (24.3)	2,730 (105.8)	5,177 (232.3)	5,128 (232.5)	2,694 (715.0)	1,313 (199.0)	1,279 (146.7)	3,078 (466.5)	3,484 (328.7)	2,470 (547.6)
Other 4-year...	5,425 (229.2)	4,847 (196.8)	1,983 (62.6)	2,702 (68.3)	1,939 (73.2)	1,847 (53.4)	4,308 (135.0)	4,299 (133.4)	‡ (†)	1,444 (101.8)	1,373 (70.4)	3,218 (219.6)	3,548 (181.3)	2,467 (292.7)
2-year...	3,423 (232.4)	3,464 (206.3)	1,270 (112.5)	2,007 (75.5)	1,741 (185.1)	1,091 (90.6)	3,615 (302.9)	3,675 (319.3)	‡ (†)	1,217 (170.9)	1,217 (175.0)	2,553 (315.8)	2,892 (274.6)	2,167 (409.0)
Less-than-2-year...	2,956 (1,682.4)	2,661 (1,040.1)	2,406 (471.0)	2,374 (113.1)	6,373 (328.2)	2,552 (281.8)	3,601 (563.8)	3,601 (563.8)	‡ (†)	‡ (†)	‡ (†)	1,968 (398.6)	‡ (†)	1,892 (462.1)
Private, not-for-profit...	10,536 (660.4)	6,498 (236.3)	6,399 (585.5)	6,357 (575.8)	2,288 (60.0)	5,988 (567.2)	5,700 (137.2)	5,576 (129.5)	3,108 (620.0)	1,392 (109.0)	1,308 (99.6)	5,144 (943.7)	4,875 (2,475.5)	5,076 (565.7)
4-year doctoral...	13,044 (1,634.7)	7,313 (433.0)	8,447 (1,493.7)	8,238 (1,548.5)	2,266 (60.6)	7,868 (1,464.9)	6,452 (276.3)	6,318 (217.4)	3,560 (1,564.3)	1,655 (238.6)	1,539 (204.2)	9,033 (2,353.8)	7,355 (4,557.8)	9,655 (1,907.6)
Other 4-year...	9,807 (240.4)	6,275 (237.2)	5,695 (133.1)	5,790 (120.0)	2,034 (100.8)	5,330 (125.9)	5,422 (160.7)	5,307 (148.2)	3,345 (329.1)	1,281 (69.1)	1,206 (62.5)	3,838 (319.7)	3,903 (389.4)	3,674 (354.2)
Less-than-4-year...	6,191 (296.1)	5,101 (182.9)	2,854 (302.8)	3,195 (621.5)	1,912 (32.5)	2,765 (618.9)	4,996 (349.4)	4,868 (236.5)	1,280 (90.0)	1,195 (55.0)	1,095 (213.5)	3,803 (1,232.5)	‡ (†)	‡ (†)
Private, for-profit...	6,401 (158.4)	5,874 (114.3)	2,698 (272.8)	2,507 (96.6)	1,951 (32.8)	2,365 (253.3)	5,275 (244.9)	5,212 (229.7)	2,351 (255.0)	‡ (†)	‡ (†)	3,681 (639.8)	3,537 (406.4)	3,694 (823.3)
2-year and above...	7,037 (388.7)	6,373 (328.2)	2,952 (196.7)	2,825 (192.7)	1,901 (32.8)	2,692 (149.4)	5,671 (219.7)	5,621 (224.2)	‡ (†)	‡ (†)	‡ (†)	3,813 (362.0)	3,866 (254.1)	3,654 (625.8)
Less-than-2-year...	5,648 (524.9)	5,273 (460.6)	2,370 (527.5)	2,140 (102.0)	2,354 (88.5)	1,623 (407.0)	4,771 (712.7)	4,679 (678.1)	2,070 (404.1)	‡ (†)	‡ (†)	3,558 (1,104.1)	‡ (†)	3,719 (1,186.2)
1999–2000, all institutions...	$8,516 (78.1)	$6,162 (57.0)	$5,027 (96.5)	$4,979 (68.8)	$2,525 (16.6)	$4,455 (89.7)	$6,279 (71.6)	$5,689 (68.6)	$4,936 (128.1)	$1,673 (32.8)	$1,558 (25.8)	$3,859 (281.4)	$4,277 (148.7)	$3,199 (448.1)
Public...	6,340 (73.8)	5,499 (60.1)	2,998 (57.2)	3,490 (38.2)	2,463 (13.0)	2,621 (42.4)	5,451 (65.1)	5,132 (67.9)	3,927 (212.1)	1,733 (37.9)	1,635 (53.1)	3,390 (337.9)	3,793 (258.5)	2,706 (349.4)
4-year doctoral...	7,557 (85.2)	6,423 (67.6)	3,800 (74.2)	4,106 (56.8)	2,414 (37.9)	3,444 (71.7)	5,948 (73.6)	5,625 (59.0)	3,948 (203.9)	1,791 (53.5)	1,690 (31.2)	3,724 (161.7)	4,052 (229.7)	3,079 (322.3)
Other 4-year...	6,306 (193.2)	5,483 (148.8)	2,634 (141.1)	3,237 (104.2)	2,452 (26.0)	2,240 (99.4)	5,123 (196.7)	4,875 (197.2)	3,632 (477.4)	1,662 (103.3)	1,571 (170.9)	3,925 (555.7)	3,824 (253.8)	3,915 (1,169.7)
2-year...	4,403 (108.7)	4,000 (70.0)	1,994 (82.0)	2,809 (72.3)	2,378 (153.9)	1,625 (49.5)	4,430 (100.4)	3,987 (86.3)	4,159 (453.9)	1,686 (135.2)	1,606 (74.4)	2,892 (443.2)	3,560 (454.2)	1,890 (261.2)
Less-than-2-year...	4,479 (946.6)	4,100 (1,163.3)	2,044 (390.8)	2,847 (210.3)	8,523 (308.2)	1,771 (430.5)	5,539 (1,080.7)	5,487 (1,156.9)	‡ (†)	‡ (†)	‡ (†)	1,946 (794.9)	‡ (†)	‡ (†)
Private, not-for-profit...	13,490 (217.9)	7,262 (78.3)	8,921 (258.2)	8,267 (275.9)	2,705 (70.3)	7,867 (232.7)	7,609 (83.4)	6,479 (83.6)	5,791 (160.1)	1,605 (52.3)	1,475 (30.4)	5,747 (514.0)	6,273 (397.8)	5,186 (1,053.5)
4-year doctoral...	15,670 (268.5)	7,558 (168.8)	10,610 (325.1)	9,853 (290.4)	2,612 (65.5)	9,372 (260.6)	8,353 (145.7)	6,866 (178.5)	6,505 (309.7)	1,819 (52.1)	1,702 (58.7)	7,286 (1,232.3)	7,983 (1,297.9)	6,566 (1,535.6)
Other 4-year...	12,285 (259.4)	6,861 (94.2)	7,917 (256.5)	7,378 (289.6)	2,621 (136.4)	6,976 (254.6)	7,143 (95.6)	6,250 (66.8)	5,147 (195.9)	1,467 (63.1)	1,294 (37.1)	4,899 (560.5)	5,197 (419.4)	4,672 (894.8)
Less-than-4-year...	8,524 (980.8)	6,114 (463.5)	4,945 (617.6)	5,039 (636.8)	2,506 (21.5)	4,460 (709.6)	6,095 (325.9)	5,442 (268.0)	5,520 (1,438.6)	961 (118.6)	875 (79.7)	6,942 (2,351.0)	‡ (†)	‡ (†)

See notes at end of table.

Table 341. Average amount of financial aid awarded to full-time, full-year undergraduates, by type and source of aid and control and type of institution: Selected years, 1992–93 through 2003–04—Continued

[In current dollars]

Control and type of institution	Any aid			Grants			Loans			Work study[1]		Other		
	Total[2]	Federal	Nonfederal	Total[3]	Federal	Nonfederal	Total	Federal[4]	Nonfederal	Total	Federal	Total	Federal	Nonfederal
1	2	3	4	5	6	7	8	9	10	11	12	13	14	15
Private, for-profit	9,302 (344.8)	8,032 (233.5)	3,881 (344.2)	3,498 (189.7)	2,570 (87.1)	2,850 (330.7)	7,464 (256.4)	6,932 (231.5)	6,211 (478.1)	‡ (†)	‡ (†)	3,916 (389.3)	4,553 (710.2)	3,020 (641.3)
2-year and above	9,978 (441.5)	8,523 (308.2)	3,981 (376.5)	3,785 (246.7)	2,459 (96.3)	3,014 (350.4)	7,839 (310.8)	7,325 (280.8)	6,822 (659.0)	‡ (†)	‡ (†)	3,892 (435.5)	‡ (†)	‡ (†)
Less-than-2-year	6,928 (390.3)	6,294 (373.8)	3,314 (597.1)	2,607 (71.8)	2,883 (77.7)	1,266 (411.4)	5,937 (356.6)	5,328 (338.8)	4,681 (617.3)	‡ (†)	‡ (†)	3,973 (952.9)	‡ (†)	4,426 (1,349.6)
2003–04, all institutions	$9,899 (106.7)	$7,304 (50.5)	$5,586 (109.1)	$5,565 (92.6)	$3,247 (24.2)	$4,828 (103.3)	$7,336 (80.9)	$6,426 (53.2)	$6,089 (158.5)	$1,942 (41.6)	$1,787 (42.2)	$4,777 (170.1)	$5,283 (197.0)	$3,008 (180.3)
Public	7,595 (63.7)	6,544 (51.3)	3,581 (47.3)	4,192 (44.2)	3,192 (25.0)	3,063 (42.9)	6,347 (70.9)	5,832 (61.4)	5,065 (134.4)	2,016 (50.4)	1,850 (56.9)	4,497 (177.5)	5,115 (210.1)	2,533 (160.7)
4-year doctoral	9,083 (88.7)	7,619 (71.5)	4,458 (83.0)	4,839 (77.9)	3,193 (49.8)	3,892 (71.1)	7,114 (73.6)	6,525 (60.8)	5,525 (162.5)	2,079 (59.8)	1,912 (61.1)	5,298 (316.2)	5,705 (359.6)	3,046 (321.8)
Other 4-year	7,965 (173.9)	6,671 (122.8)	3,482 (101.4)	4,218 (92.8)	3,161 (39.4)	2,889 (92.7)	5,210 (114.9)	5,660 (120.9)	5,208 (274.5)	1,922 (84.9)	1,794 (101.1)	4,699 (445.6)	5,063 (549.6)	3,352 (375.7)
2-year	5,209 (81.4)	4,943 (86.8)	2,178 (79.1)	3,312 (51.9)	2,798 (102.9)	1,804 (73.7)	4,728 (99.4)	4,399 (93.8)	3,826 (202.6)	2,004 (115.3)	1,803 (117.3)	3,844 (285.9)	4,575 (351.8)	1,942 (140.8)
Less-than-2-year	5,356 (322.4)	5,061 (213.9)	3,045 (267.6)	3,180 (170.7)	2,902 (251.9)	2,474 (256.0)	5,928 (425.1)	5,266 (218.5)	4,767 (614.0)	2,381 (1,059.6)	‡ (†)	3,180 (577.2)	‡ (†)	2,362 (311.3)
Private, not-for-profit	15,530 (283.7)	8,608 (107.7)	9,994 (274.4)	9,230 (260.2)	3,425 (46.3)	8,572 (263.9)	9,037 (155.1)	7,300 (106.4)	7,445 (265.2)	1,819 (68.4)	1,667 (62.2)	6,492 (656.6)	6,808 (787.1)	4,716 (645.6)
4-year doctoral	17,412 (625.5)	9,081 (319.5)	11,363 (403.3)	10,356 (453.3)	3,358 (55.7)	9,708 (436.3)	9,942 (323.5)	7,753 (191.9)	8,335 (357.4)	2,120 (98.9)	1,965 (84.1)	9,388 (1,742.8)	9,930 (2,032.2)	‡ (†)
Other 4-year	15,258 (575.7)	8,404 (217.1)	9,254 (400.1)	8,662 (375.0)	3,545 (232.9)	7,956 (331.4)	8,566 (223.1)	7,066 (144.8)	6,859 (404.1)	1,631 (66.2)	1,468 (60.2)	5,057 (504.3)	5,263 (512.0)	‡ (†)
Less-than-4-year	9,627 (745.1)	6,886 (339.3)	5,149 (629.4)	5,701 (531.8)	3,229 (45.9)	4,517 (598.7)	6,665 (527.1)	6,104 (438.6)	4,513 (847.1)	1,536 (443.7)	1,536 (495.4)	5,573 (1,206.9)	‡ (†)	5,632 (1,099.8)
Private, for-profit	10,998 (291.2)	9,171 (196.0)	4,889 (335.0)	4,199 (155.7)	3,267 (69.7)	3,630 (253.9)	8,647 (277.0)	7,553 (172.7)	5,755 (590.5)	2,877 (322.4)	2,961 (352.8)	4,572 (470.0)	4,380 (569.3)	4,954 (560.1)
2-year and above	12,086 (370.7)	9,902 (251.9)	5,177 (400.9)	4,488 (206.0)	3,013 (53.8)	3,834 (288.0)	9,148 (337.0)	7,956 (211.7)	6,019 (708.7)	3,032 (356.1)	3,157 (376.7)	4,335 (585.5)	4,245 (643.5)	‡ (†)
Less-than-2-year	7,415 (232.4)	6,619 (191.8)	3,668 (199.0)	3,330 (59.4)	3,547 (110.3)	2,594 (238.8)	6,435 (223.6)	5,711 (160.5)	4,603 (234.1)	1,733 (133.2)	1,570 (136.2)	5,474 (323.0)	5,364 (474.4)	5,308 (314.1)

†Not applicable.
‡Reporting standards not met.
[1]Details on nonfederal work study participants are not available.
[2]Includes all grants, scholarships, or tuition waivers received from federal, state, institutional, or private sources, including employers.
[3]Includes students who reported that they were awarded aid, but did not specify the source or type of aid.
[4]Includes Parent Loans for Undergraduate Students (PLUS).

NOTE: Aid averages are for those students who received the specified type of aid. Full-time, full-year students were enrolled full time for 9 or more months from July 1 through June 30. Data include Puerto Rico. Standard errors appear in parentheses.
SOURCE: U.S. Department of Education, National Center for Education Statistics, 1992–93, 1995–96, 1999–2000, and 2003–04 National Postsecondary Student Aid Studies (NPSAS:93, NPSAS:96, NPSAS:2000, and NPSAS:04). (This table was prepared August 2007.)

Table 342. Percentage of part-time or part-year undergraduates receiving aid, by type and source of aid and control and type of institution: Selected years, 1992–93 through 2003–04

Control and type of institution	Any aid			Grants			Loans			Work study[1]		Other		
	Total[2]	Federal	Nonfederal	Total	Federal	Nonfederal	Total	Federal	Nonfederal	Total	Federal	Total	Federal	Nonfederal
1	2	3	4	5	6	7	8	9	10	11	12	13	14	15
1992–93, all institutions	**37.6 (0.80)**	**25.0 (0.83)**	**16.5 (0.44)**	**32.4 (0.76)**	**18.8 (0.77)**	**14.5 (0.39)**	**13.5 (0.50)**	**13.1 (0.49)**	**0.8 (0.09)**	**2.1 (0.13)**	**1.2 (0.09)**	**4.0 (0.26)**	**13.5 (0.49)**	**2.7 (0.24)**
Public	31.7 (0.71)	19.8 (0.67)	14.5 (0.46)	27.6 (0.66)	15.3 (0.60)	12.6 (0.40)	9.3 (0.41)	8.9 (0.39)	0.6 (0.09)	1.7 (0.12)	0.9 (0.09)	3.5 (0.30)	9.3 (0.40)	2.6 (0.29)
4-year doctoral	40.5 (1.02)	27.5 (0.95)	19.5 (0.66)	31.3 (0.85)	17.1 (0.68)	16.6 (0.61)	20.9 (0.83)	20.4 (0.82)	1.1 (0.18)	3.6 (0.32)	2.1 (0.24)	6.2 (0.43)	21.4 (0.84)	3.4 (0.33)
Other 4-year	39.5 (1.24)	28.4 (1.25)	19.2 (1.00)	33.8 (1.17)	22.0 (1.17)	16.1 (0.88)	16.2 (0.99)	15.6 (0.93)	1.3 (0.32)	3.1 (0.42)	1.6 (0.26)	4.1 (0.46)	16.3 (0.98)	2.6 (0.41)
2-year	28.6 (0.91)	16.5 (0.83)	12.7 (0.61)	25.9 (0.87)	13.7 (0.76)	11.2 (0.52)	5.6 (0.44)	5.3 (0.43)	0.4 (0.11)	1.1 (0.11)	0.6 (0.10)	2.9 (0.42)	5.5 (0.43)	2.5 (0.41)
Less-than-2-year	21.2 (3.11)	15.1 (3.55)	6.9 (1.47)	19.4 (3.43)	13.8 (3.90)	6.0 (1.41)	0.7 (0.32)	0.7 (0.32)	# (†)	0.6 (0.36)	0.4 (0.34)	1.7 (0.70)	0.7 (0.32)	1.3 (0.57)
Private, not-for-profit	56.4 (1.96)	35.1 (2.65)	33.7 (1.54)	50.2 (2.12)	23.2 (2.96)	31.7 (1.49)	23.7 (1.38)	23.2 (1.34)	1.8 (0.23)	5.9 (0.71)	3.8 (0.42)	5.3 (0.48)	23.6 (1.36)	2.9 (0.49)
4-year doctoral	51.4 (1.91)	28.3 (1.49)	33.0 (1.91)	44.4 (1.90)	12.8 (0.98)	31.7 (1.91)	24.2 (1.42)	23.3 (1.39)	2.7 (0.47)	5.4 (0.88)	3.1 (0.58)	4.2 (0.48)	23.8 (1.45)	1.5 (0.29)
Other 4-year	59.4 (2.83)	38.1 (4.18)	35.6 (2.25)	53.8 (3.14)	26.8 (4.73)	33.6 (2.19)	24.4 (2.08)	23.9 (2.02)	1.5 (0.32)	7.3 (1.14)	4.8 (0.65)	5.7 (0.62)	24.4 (2.04)	3.4 (0.65)
Less-than-4-year	53.9 (5.17)	35.8 (4.98)	28.4 (4.07)	47.3 (4.83)	28.3 (4.56)	24.4 (4.05)	20.7 (3.59)	20.3 (3.58)	1.2 (0.44)	1.2 (0.66)	1.2 (0.66)	5.8 (1.88)	20.6 (3.55)	3.6 (1.85)
Private, for-profit	71.0 (3.08)	64.4 (3.44)	11.8 (1.58)	55.3 (3.30)	48.8 (3.61)	8.6 (1.34)	42.3 (3.54)	41.9 (3.51)	1.5 (0.46)	0.9 (0.29)	0.4 (0.11)	6.8 (0.95)	42.2 (3.54)	2.5 (0.65)
2-year and above	64.4 (5.75)	54.9 (5.93)	14.3 (2.75)	46.2 (4.25)	35.0 (4.19)	12.1 (2.45)	45.7 (5.59)	45.5 (5.58)	0.9 (0.63)	1.4 (0.58)	0.6 (0.24)	8.0 (1.52)	45.9 (5.61)	2.1 (0.57)
Less-than-2-year	75.5 (2.78)	70.8 (3.36)	10.2 (1.74)	61.5 (4.15)	58.1 (4.52)	6.3 (1.27)	40.0 (4.50)	39.4 (4.42)	1.8 (0.63)	0.5 (0.27)	0.3 (0.08)	5.9 (1.22)	39.7 (4.46)	2.7 (1.03)
1995–96, all institutions	**38.3 (0.84)**	**24.8 (0.73)**	**24.0 (0.71)**	**29.9 (0.76)**	**16.6 (0.62)**	**19.7 (0.62)**	**14.4 (0.49)**	**14.1 (0.48)**	**0.7 (0.16)**	**1.4 (0.12)**	**1.1 (0.11)**	**5.4 (0.36)**	**0.8 (0.07)**	**4.3 (0.35)**
Public	33.7 (0.93)	20.8 (0.77)	21.8 (0.80)	26.6 (0.84)	14.4 (0.66)	17.9 (0.69)	10.5 (0.47)	10.3 (0.46)	0.3 (0.15)	1.2 (0.13)	0.9 (0.12)	4.7 (0.40)	0.5 (0.06)	3.9 (0.39)
4-year doctoral	41.8 (1.25)	31.2 (1.14)	23.7 (1.19)	28.9 (1.13)	16.9 (0.95)	19.0 (1.02)	25.9 (1.09)	25.6 (1.09)	0.7 (0.22)	2.4 (0.37)	1.4 (0.23)	5.8 (0.65)	1.7 (0.34)	3.9 (0.56)
Other 4-year	41.9 (1.54)	30.9 (1.53)	22.8 (1.11)	30.2 (1.23)	18.2 (1.13)	19.3 (1.05)	22.3 (1.39)	22.1 (1.39)	0.4 (0.14)	2.3 (0.41)	2.0 (0.37)	4.8 (0.55)	0.8 (0.18)	3.7 (0.51)
2-year	30.7 (1.23)	17.2 (0.99)	21.1 (1.06)	25.4 (1.11)	13.4 (0.87)	17.5 (0.90)	5.7 (0.57)	5.5 (0.54)	0.3 (0.20)	0.8 (0.15)	0.7 (0.14)	4.4 (0.53)	0.2 (0.05)	3.9 (0.52)
Less-than-2-year	34.3 (6.35)	13.9 (3.57)	26.0 (5.95)	27.8 (6.70)	12.3 (2.89)	17.4 (6.64)	2.2 (1.32)	2.2 (1.32)	# (†)	# (†)	# (†)	8.6 (2.67)	# (†)	8.3 (2.65)
Private, not-for-profit	55.6 (1.64)	34.9 (1.73)	41.5 (1.66)	44.1 (1.68)	17.9 (1.41)	36.1 (1.63)	26.4 (1.44)	26.1 (1.43)	1.4 (0.53)	4.0 (0.50)	3.1 (0.39)	8.6 (1.09)	2.0 (0.28)	6.6 (1.07)
4-year doctoral	51.0 (1.80)	27.7 (1.60)	39.7 (2.08)	39.3 (1.89)	12.0 (1.36)	34.3 (1.97)	24.4 (1.33)	23.6 (1.33)	1.4 (0.63)	4.6 (0.71)	3.7 (0.67)	8.4 (0.86)	2.1 (0.36)	5.9 (0.80)
Other 4-year	58.4 (2.25)	37.0 (2.49)	44.6 (2.25)	47.5 (2.41)	19.1 (2.07)	39.7 (2.28)	27.3 (2.04)	27.2 (2.03)	0.8 (0.28)	4.5 (0.75)	3.3 (0.56)	8.9 (1.65)	1.7 (0.36)	7.1 (1.64)
Less-than-4-year	50.8 (6.21)	39.7 (5.91)	28.3 (5.56)	36.8 (4.69)	24.6 (4.01)	20.5 (3.57)	26.2 (5.37)	25.9 (5.26)	4.3 (3.90)	0.4 (0.19)	0.3 (0.18)	7.8 (2.41)	2.9 (0.97)	5.1 (1.93)
Private, for-profit	74.1 (2.94)	66.5 (3.33)	24.3 (2.58)	53.4 (3.08)	46.4 (3.13)	15.3 (2.37)	50.3 (3.58)	49.3 (3.53)	4.6 (1.50)	0.4 (0.14)	0.4 (0.14)	10.4 (1.15)	4.2 (0.76)	5.8 (0.86)
2-year and above	74.5 (2.80)	66.9 (3.16)	25.5 (2.74)	53.4 (3.30)	44.8 (3.42)	17.9 (2.73)	50.2 (3.77)	49.8 (3.72)	1.7 (1.06)	0.8 (0.27)	0.7 (0.27)	12.2 (1.81)	4.9 (1.07)	6.9 (1.29)
Less-than-2-year	73.8 (4.99)	66.1 (5.67)	23.2 (4.24)	53.5 (5.06)	47.9 (5.14)	13.0 (3.82)	50.5 (5.89)	48.8 (5.83)	7.2 (2.68)	0.1 (0.08)	0.1 (0.08)	8.7 (1.45)	3.5 (1.07)	4.7 (1.12)
1999–2000, all institutions	**44.6 (0.81)**	**29.8 (0.64)**	**27.4 (0.75)**	**35.4 (0.70)**	**18.6 (0.52)**	**25.0 (0.73)**	**18.4 (0.56)**	**17.7 (0.55)**	**2.1 (0.12)**	**1.9 (0.11)**	**1.4 (0.10)**	**5.2 (0.36)**	**1.2 (0.07)**	**1.5 (0.29)**
Public	39.7 (0.85)	24.8 (0.57)	25.3 (0.86)	31.7 (0.78)	15.9 (0.48)	23.3 (0.83)	13.5 (0.41)	13.0 (0.39)	1.3 (0.11)	1.5 (0.11)	1.1 (0.10)	4.5 (0.38)	0.7 (0.06)	1.4 (0.33)
4-year doctoral	51.0 (0.93)	36.8 (0.93)	30.0 (0.83)	35.7 (0.79)	17.9 (0.70)	26.7 (0.70)	31.5 (0.96)	30.3 (0.87)	3.3 (0.42)	3.0 (0.28)	1.9 (0.25)	5.2 (0.35)	2.3 (0.22)	0.8 (0.12)
Other 4-year	51.2 (1.33)	37.0 (1.36)	29.9 (1.10)	39.1 (1.24)	21.5 (1.33)	27.9 (1.10)	27.4 (1.04)	26.6 (1.02)	2.4 (0.34)	3.1 (0.48)	2.5 (0.44)	4.7 (0.43)	0.9 (0.20)	1.0 (0.19)
2-year	34.9 (1.14)	19.8 (0.69)	23.5 (1.20)	29.5 (1.08)	14.4 (0.62)	21.9 (1.16)	6.9 (0.42)	6.5 (0.40)	0.6 (0.10)	0.8 (0.12)	0.7 (0.11)	4.1 (0.52)	0.3 (0.05)	1.5 (0.47)
Less-than-2-year	38.6 (3.11)	21.9 (3.93)	22.2 (1.77)	29.6 (3.16)	18.2 (3.53)	14.4 (2.46)	5.0 (3.12)	4.7 (3.10)	0.4 (0.27)	1.6 (0.47)	0.9 (0.33)	11.1 (2.44)	0.4 (0.26)	7.9 (2.10)
Private, not-for-profit	64.8 (1.02)	44.5 (1.56)	47.2 (1.32)	53.9 (1.15)	22.1 (1.33)	44.8 (1.44)	34.8 (1.48)	33.4 (1.39)	6.0 (0.50)	5.9 (0.52)	4.0 (0.41)	8.2 (0.81)	3.4 (0.36)	1.2 (0.28)
4-year doctoral	60.2 (1.59)	40.9 (1.74)	46.8 (1.64)	49.9 (1.54)	17.0 (1.15)	44.2 (1.48)	35.1 (1.76)	34.1 (1.74)	7.6 (1.01)	6.5 (0.93)	4.7 (0.80)	7.5 (1.12)	3.7 (0.61)	1.7 (0.70)
Other 4-year	66.2 (1.33)	44.6 (2.23)	48.5 (1.78)	54.9 (1.58)	22.2 (1.94)	46.3 (2.02)	34.4 (2.11)	32.8 (1.95)	5.7 (0.63)	5.8 (0.68)	3.7 (0.52)	8.5 (1.15)	2.9 (0.46)	0.9 (0.28)
Less-than-4-year	71.2 (4.24)	57.3 (5.11)	37.2 (6.39)	61.0 (4.36)	41.7 (4.22)	34.4 (6.66)	36.4 (5.14)	35.9 (5.04)	2.9 (0.62)	4.6 (1.49)	3.5 (1.12)	8.6 (1.69)	5.6 (1.40)	2.0 (0.91)
Private, for-profit	83.1 (1.78)	78.5 (1.53)	22.3 (1.82)	58.9 (2.03)	53.3 (2.19)	14.6 (1.69)	62.7 (3.06)	61.2 (3.07)	6.1 (0.86)	0.3 (0.16)	0.3 (0.15)	11.4 (1.84)	4.6 (0.49)	3.9 (1.22)
2-year and above	81.8 (2.03)	77.9 (2.24)	25.4 (2.77)	54.0 (2.92)	45.6 (2.94)	19.3 (2.16)	69.5 (3.09)	68.5 (3.12)	6.0 (1.28)	0.3 (0.24)	0.3 (0.24)	11.1 (1.36)	5.9 (0.80)	2.5 (0.76)
Less-than-2-year	84.7 (2.75)	79.1 (1.97)	18.7 (2.41)	64.5 (2.44)	62.2 (2.45)	9.1 (1.83)	54.8 (6.25)	52.9 (6.32)	6.3 (1.11)	0.4 (0.19)	0.3 (0.18)	11.8 (3.55)	3.1 (0.60)	5.5 (2.15)
2003–04, all institutions	**54.3 (0.56)**	**38.5 (0.44)**	**31.5 (0.59)**	**42.7 (0.57)**	**23.6 (0.35)**	**28.1 (0.57)**	**25.0 (0.30)**	**23.8 (0.30)**	**3.7 (0.16)**	**3.4 (0.14)**	**2.2 (0.09)**	**3.9 (0.20)**	**3.2 (0.19)**	**0.8 (0.10)**
Public	47.6 (0.69)	32.0 (0.52)	28.2 (0.67)	37.6 (0.65)	20.3 (0.38)	25.6 (0.63)	17.5 (0.35)	16.5 (0.35)	2.1 (0.11)	2.9 (0.15)	1.9 (0.10)	3.6 (0.19)	2.9 (0.17)	0.7 (0.12)
4-year doctoral	59.0 (1.12)	42.9 (0.92)	34.9 (1.06)	41.7 (1.10)	20.5 (0.71)	30.7 (1.07)	37.4 (0.88)	35.5 (0.83)	4.8 (0.33)	4.2 (0.37)	2.1 (0.41)	2.9 (0.26)	2.4 (0.27)	0.5 (0.18)
Other 4-year	56.1 (2.33)	42.0 (2.03)	30.6 (2.08)	40.2 (2.56)	22.7 (1.78)	27.6 (1.87)	31.1 (1.58)	30.0 (1.48)	3.3 (0.52)	3.2 (0.58)	1.7 (0.12)	3.2 (0.56)	2.8 (0.53)	0.5 (0.20)
2-year	43.6 (0.92)	28.0 (0.66)	26.2 (0.87)	36.3 (0.88)	20.0 (0.51)	24.2 (0.82)	10.8 (0.37)	10.1 (0.37)	1.3 (0.11)	2.6 (0.18)	1.0 (0.56)	3.8 (0.27)	3.1 (0.22)	0.7 (0.16)
Less-than-2-year	42.4 (4.11)	19.6 (1.80)	30.0 (3.95)	32.4 (3.52)	15.4 (1.63)	20.2 (3.13)	7.5 (1.90)	5.8 (1.26)	2.0 (1.02)	3.3 (1.06)	8.4 (1.16)	9.3 (2.12)	1.4 (0.45)	7.9 (2.10)
Private, not-for-profit	76.3 (1.07)	52.4 (1.42)	55.3 (1.97)	62.6 (1.67)	24.6 (1.04)	52.1 (2.16)	43.5 (1.30)	41.2 (1.25)	8.6 (0.78)	8.4 (0.71)	5.9 (0.64)	4.7 (0.87)	4.3 (0.89)	0.4 (0.12)
4-year doctoral	73.1 (1.48)	45.8 (2.20)	60.1 (2.23)	62.2 (1.70)	19.0 (2.07)	56.4 (2.25)	41.7 (2.06)	38.6 (2.16)	11.0 (1.14)	12.7 (1.40)	5.0 (0.78)	1.2 (0.40)	1.1 (0.41)	‡ (†)
Other 4-year	77.4 (1.45)	54.2 (2.21)	53.8 (3.05)	62.4 (2.43)	25.3 (1.85)	51.0 (3.26)	44.2 (2.09)	42.5 (2.06)	7.5 (1.14)	6.8 (0.86)	2.9 (0.83)	6.3 (1.33)	6.0 (1.39)	0.3 (0.17)
Less-than-4-year	80.7 (3.62)	66.9 (3.72)	47.1 (4.44)	67.1 (3.26)	48.4 (3.52)	40.1 (4.20)	44.0 (5.58)	39.8 (4.53)	8.5 (2.78)	3.8 (1.06)	1.0 (0.31)	4.6 (1.52)	1.4 (0.86)	3.3 (1.36)
Private, for-profit	87.6 (0.54)	79.8 (0.85)	32.8 (1.44)	63.7 (1.20)	51.9 (1.36)	21.2 (1.10)	70.3 (1.03)	68.5 (1.01)	12.2 (1.12)	1.6 (0.23)	1.1 (0.21)	5.4 (0.78)	3.9 (0.77)	1.5 (0.19)
2-year and above	90.7 (0.72)	83.3 (1.26)	36.5 (2.28)	64.5 (1.85)	50.5 (2.15)	24.9 (1.77)	77.9 (1.44)	76.4 (1.40)	13.6 (1.75)	1.3 (0.34)	1.2 (0.15)	5.6 (1.26)	5.1 (1.24)	0.5 (0.18)
Less-than-2-year	82.3 (0.97)	73.8 (0.91)	26.5 (1.13)	62.4 (0.96)	54.2 (0.73)	14.9 (0.91)	57.6 (0.76)	55.0 (0.84)	9.8 (0.53)	2.1 (0.19)	4.2 (0.37)	5.0 (0.46)	1.9 (0.20)	3.2 (0.38)

†Not applicable.
#Rounds to zero.
‡Reporting standards not met.
[1]Details on nonfederal work study participants are not available.
[2]Includes students who reported they were awarded aid, but did not specify the source of aid.
NOTE: Excludes students whose attendance status was not reported. Detail may not sum to totals because of rounding and because some students receive multiple types of aid and aid from different sources. The 2003–04 loan estimates include Parent Loans for Undergraduate Students (PLUS) and may differ from previously published figures. Standard errors appear in parentheses. Data include Puerto Rico.
SOURCE: U.S. Department of Education, National Center for Education Statistics, 1992–93, 1995–96, 1999–2000, and 2003–04 National Postsecondary Student Aid Studies (NPSAS:93, NPSAS:96, NPSAS:2000, and NPSAS:04). (This table was prepared August 2005.)

Table 343. Percentage of full-time and part-time undergraduates receiving federal aid, by aid program and control and type of institution: 2003–04

Control and type of institution	Number of undergraduates[1] (in thousands)		Percent receiving federal aid in 2003–04, by type														
			Any federal aid		Selected Title IV programs[2]												
					Any Title IV aid		Pell		SEOG[3]		CWS[4]		Perkins[5]		Stafford[6]		PLUS[7]	
1	2		3		4		5		6		7		8		9		10	
Full-time, full-year students																		
All institutions	7,824	(93.5)	61.7	(0.42)	60.6	(0.44)	32.1	(0.34)	10.0	(0.37)	10.3	(0.36)	7.0	(0.31)	47.1	(0.44)	6.3	(0.22)
Public	5,662	(78.1)	56.1	(0.47)	54.9	(0.49)	30.6	(0.33)	7.9	(0.33)	7.3	(0.31)	5.3	(0.25)	39.9	(0.46)	4.9	(0.23)
4-year doctoral	2,411	(33.2)	58.2	(0.71)	57.1	(0.75)	26.5	(0.77)	8.0	(0.49)	7.9	(0.34)	8.5	(0.34)	48.2	(0.77)	7.7	(0.33)
Other 4-year	1,198	(42.8)	64.0	(1.20)	63.2	(1.22)	34.0	(1.40)	8.1	(0.67)	9.9	(0.87)	6.3	(0.98)	49.6	(1.37)	5.7	(0.82)
2-year	2,026	(59.1)	48.9	(1.15)	47.4	(1.16)	33.5	(0.88)	7.7	(0.51)	5.3	(0.50)	1.1	(0.16)	24.4	(1.03)	1.2	(0.15)
Less-than-2-year	27	(2.1)	48.7	(2.75)	47.8	(2.70)	35.9	(1.73)	2.3	(0.88)	1.1	(0.57)	‡	(†)	24.1	(2.56)	0.3	(0.28)
Private, not-for-profit	1,635	(38.9)	73.1	(0.81)	72.5	(0.82)	30.4	(0.77)	14.6	(0.92)	23.0	(1.17)	14.0	(0.95)	62.2	(1.05)	11.0	(0.51)
4-year doctoral	668	(27.5)	66.2	(1.69)	65.3	(1.72)	22.9	(3.07)	11.7	(1.78)	22.5	(1.53)	18.1	(1.24)	55.6	(2.22)	11.5	(0.87)
Other 4-year	921	(36.8)	77.9	(1.25)	77.5	(1.26)	35.0	(2.30)	16.9	(1.31)	24.2	(1.93)	11.6	(1.57)	67.4	(2.38)	10.8	(0.90)
Less-than-4-year	47	(4.4)	76.8	(4.76)	75.5	(4.30)	48.0	(3.70)	12.2	(3.24)	8.6	(2.71)	1.3	(0.88)	53.5	(5.17)	8.1	(2.92)
Private, for-profit	527	(21.6)	86.9	(0.92)	86.1	(0.98)	53.2	(1.74)	17.5	(2.05)	3.1	(0.62)	2.6	(0.79)	78.0	(1.17)	6.7	(0.88)
2-year and above	393	(21.0)	90.6	(1.14)	89.6	(1.24)	52.7	(2.24)	16.2	(2.63)	3.7	(0.82)	3.3	(1.07)	85.8	(1.46)	6.8	(1.10)
Less-than-2-year	134	(3.0)	76.0	(1.31)	75.8	(1.33)	54.7	(1.59)	21.4	(2.14)	1.5	(0.22)	0.8	(0.63)	55.0	(1.55)	6.5	(0.89)
Part-time or part-year students																		
All institutions	11,230	(93.5)	38.5	(0.44)	36.3	(0.43)	23.0	(0.34)	4.4	(0.20)	2.2	(0.09)	1.2	(0.08)	23.5	(0.31)	1.2	(0.07)
Public	9,015	(74.6)	32.0	(0.52)	29.8	(0.51)	19.9	(0.38)	2.9	(0.19)	1.9	(0.10)	1.0	(0.08)	16.2	(0.36)	0.7	(0.05)
4-year doctoral	1,516	(33.3)	42.9	(0.92)	41.6	(0.91)	19.8	(0.70)	3.4	(0.36)	2.8	(0.27)	3.3	(0.31)	34.7	(0.84)	2.5	(0.22)
Other 4-year	984	(47.7)	42.0	(2.03)	40.2	(2.07)	22.5	(1.77)	3.4	(0.42)	2.1	(0.41)	2.0	(0.41)	29.3	(1.48)	0.7	(0.18)
2-year	6,449	(59.1)	28.0	(0.66)	25.5	(0.63)	19.6	(0.52)	2.8	(0.22)	1.7	(0.12)	0.3	(0.05)	9.9	(0.37)	0.3	(0.04)
Less-than-2-year	66	(2.1)	19.6	(1.80)	18.4	(1.75)	14.9	(1.61)	2.1	(0.70)	1.0	(0.56)	0.2	(0.24)	5.6	(1.21)	#	(†)
Private, not-for-profit	1,204	(37.4)	52.4	(1.42)	49.2	(1.37)	24.0	(0.99)	6.3	(0.44)	5.9	(0.64)	3.4	(0.45)	40.5	(1.28)	3.2	(0.44)
4-year doctoral	356	(17.0)	45.8	(2.20)	44.8	(2.24)	18.3	(2.01)	6.2	(0.84)	8.4	(1.16)	4.9	(0.67)	37.7	(2.30)	3.4	(0.64)
Other 4-year	786	(37.2)	54.2	(2.21)	49.8	(2.18)	24.8	(1.83)	6.0	(0.66)	5.0	(0.78)	3.0	(0.60)	41.9	(2.08)	3.0	(0.64)
Less-than-4-year	62	(4.4)	66.9	(3.72)	66.3	(3.79)	45.9	(3.05)	9.9	(2.31)	2.9	(0.83)	0.6	(0.62)	39.2	(4.40)	3.6	(1.35)
Private, for-profit	1,011	(19.5)	79.8	(0.85)	78.6	(0.96)	49.8	(1.34)	14.7	(1.37)	1.1	(0.21)	0.9	(0.26)	68.2	(1.02)	4.0	(0.35)
2-year and above	636	(19.2)	83.3	(1.26)	81.9	(1.40)	49.3	(2.10)	14.3	(2.17)	1.0	(0.31)	1.3	(0.41)	76.1	(1.43)	2.8	(0.50)
Less-than-2-year	375	(3.0)	73.8	(0.91)	73.0	(0.90)	50.7	(0.58)	15.5	(0.77)	1.2	(0.15)	0.2	(0.03)	54.7	(0.81)	5.9	(0.38)

†Not applicable.
#Rounds to zero.
‡Reporting standards not met.
[1]Numbers of undergraduates may not equal figures reported in other tables, since these data are based on a sample survey of students who enrolled at any point during the year.
[2]Title IV of the Higher Education Act.
[3]Supplemental Educational Opportunity Grants.
[4]College Work Study. Prior to October 17, 1986, private, for-profit institutions were prohibited by law from spending CWS funds for on-campus work. Includes persons who participated in the program, but had no earnings.

[5]Formerly National Direct Student Loans (NDSL).
[6]Formerly Guaranteed Student Loans (GSL).
[7]Parent Loans for Undergraduate Students.
NOTE: Excludes students whose attendance status was not reported. Detail may not sum to totals because of rounding and because some students receive multiple types of aid and aid from different sources. Data include Puerto Rico.
SOURCE: U.S. Department of Education, National Center for Education Statistics, 2003–04 National Postsecondary Student Aid Study (NPSAS:04). (This table was prepared August 2005.)

Table 344. Amount borrowed, aid status, and sources of aid for full-time, full-year postbaccalaureate students, by level of study and control and type of institution: Selected years, 1992–93 through 2003–04

Level of study, control and type of institution	Cumulative amount borrowed for post-baccalaureate education (in current dollars)		Aid status (percent of students)									
			Nonaided		Receiving aid, by source							
					Any aid[1]		Federal		State		Institutional		Employer
1	2		3		4		5		6		7		8
1992–93, all institutions	$18,572	(706.5)	31.9	(1.03)	68.1	(1.03)	44.4	(1.47)	7.0	(0.66)	40.6	(1.73)	5.3	(0.52)
Master's degree	11,109	(467.1)	37.5	(2.13)	62.5	(2.13)	33.8	(2.01)	5.8	(0.79)	42.4	(2.70)	8.3	(0.87)
Public	9,335	(543.5)	34.6	(1.98)	65.4	(1.98)	33.9	(1.93)	7.8	(1.07)	44.0	(2.31)	7.6	(1.02)
4-year doctoral	9,597	(648.5)	34.3	(2.14)	65.7	(2.14)	32.4	(2.02)	6.7	(1.18)	46.3	(2.52)	7.7	(1.09)
Other 4-year	7,970	(401.3)	36.1	(4.12)	63.9	(4.12)	42.5	(4.41)	14.4	(2.90)	30.4	(4.28)	6.8	(2.59)
Private	13,628	(807.2)	41.6	(4.05)	58.4	(4.05)	33.7	(3.69)	3.2	(1.04)	40.2	(5.27)	9.4	(1.56)
4-year doctoral	13,879	(905.0)	39.3	(4.44)	60.7	(4.44)	34.2	(4.37)	2.9	(1.20)	42.9	(5.75)	8.9	(1.84)
Other 4-year	‡	(†)	56.5	(3.79)	43.5	(3.79)	30.5	(3.17)	5.1	(2.58)	22.8	(2.27)	12.1	(2.27)
Doctor's degree	16,895	(1,432.1)	30.4	(2.28)	69.6	(2.28)	28.3	(2.45)	4.4	(0.71)	51.6	(2.32)	3.0	(0.85)
Public	12,758	(1,004.8)	30.3	(2.77)	69.7	(2.77)	22.3	(2.44)	6.5	(1.02)	55.5	(2.70)	3.9	(1.23)
Private	21,742	(2,707.7)	30.4	(4.11)	69.6	(4.11)	37.8	(4.48)	1.1	(0.73)	45.5	(4.00)	1.7	(0.96)
First-professional	30,045	(1,237.1)	23.0	(1.17)	77.0	(1.17)	68.2	(1.82)	10.0	(1.54)	37.0	(1.89)	2.3	(0.47)
Public	24,469	(1,354.3)	20.7	(1.30)	79.3	(1.30)	72.5	(1.78)	13.4	(2.13)	37.7	(2.04)	2.3	(0.70)
Private	35,301	(2,055.6)	25.1	(1.71)	74.9	(1.71)	64.3	(2.29)	6.8	(1.32)	36.4	(3.10)	2.3	(0.62)
Other graduate	13,102	(2,268.0)	39.3	(5.42)	60.7	(5.42)	42.4	(4.39)	6.7	(1.44)	22.9	(3.01)	6.0	(1.91)
1995–96, all institutions	$27,122	(1,029.4)	23.9	(1.39)	76.1	(1.39)	49.3	(1.80)	4.1	(0.84)	43.4	(2.03)	5.0	(0.61)
Master's degree	18,807	(774.6)	27.4	(2.16)	72.6	(2.16)	43.6	(2.14)	2.4	(0.61)	42.8	(2.49)	6.6	(1.02)
Public	15,905	(749.5)	25.3	(2.63)	74.7	(2.63)	40.7	(2.37)	3.0	(0.89)	45.7	(3.12)	7.1	(1.36)
4-year doctoral	16,910	(865.1)	23.5	(2.96)	76.5	(2.96)	40.5	(2.64)	2.6	(0.78)	47.9	(3.68)	7.6	(1.55)
Other 4-year	11,417	(1,296.4)	34.0	(5.20)	66.0	(5.20)	41.4	(5.45)	5.1	(3.44)	35.0	(3.96)	4.5	(2.55)
Private	22,568	(1,326.4)	30.6	(3.73)	69.4	(3.73)	48.2	(3.98)	1.4	(0.70)	38.3	(4.23)	5.9	(1.50)
4-year doctoral	23,816	(1,530.2)	28.8	(4.56)	71.2	(4.56)	44.6	(4.45)	1.5	(0.97)	42.2	(4.98)	7.1	(2.07)
Other 4-year	20,299	(2,777.3)	34.6	(6.60)	65.4	(6.60)	56.1	(6.87)	1.3	(0.65)	29.7	(7.95)	3.2	(1.39)
Doctor's degree	24,380	(2,127.9)	17.1	(2.70)	82.9	(2.70)	27.6	(2.87)	0.6	(0.35)	75.7	(3.08)	5.5	(1.55)
Public	22,687	(2,716.2)	14.1	(3.31)	85.9	(3.31)	27.6	(3.51)	1.0	(0.54)	77.8	(3.90)	5.9	(1.99)
Private	28,083	(3,178.4)	22.5	(4.39)	77.5	(4.39)	27.6	(4.94)	#	(†)	72.0	(4.88)	4.9	(2.44)
First-professional	37,540	(1,429.1)	16.8	(1.46)	83.2	(1.46)	73.9	(2.31)	9.4	(2.34)	31.6	(3.10)	1.3	(0.48)
Public	34,463	(2,685.1)	14.3	(1.88)	85.7	(1.88)	79.5	(2.30)	9.7	(4.20)	33.5	(5.41)	1.5	(0.82)
Private	40,350	(1,564.7)	19.0	(2.04)	81.0	(2.04)	69.3	(3.50)	9.2	(2.46)	30.0	(3.53)	1.2	(0.56)
Other graduate	13,557	(1,609.5)	43.5	(5.11)	56.5	(5.11)	34.0	(4.61)	2.2	(1.13)	31.4	(4.90)	6.1	(2.67)
Public 4-year doctoral	‡	(†)	36.9	(8.67)	63.1	(8.67)	32.2	(7.80)	4.0	(2.86)	35.2	(9.43)	1.8	(1.71)
Public other 4-year	12,057	(1,706.8)	46.8	(6.29)	53.2	(6.29)	35.0	(5.67)	1.2	(0.88)	29.4	(5.58)	8.3	(3.89)
1999–2000, all institutions	$38,428	(1,233.2)	17.8	(0.73)	82.2	(0.73)	54.0	(1.05)	6.2	(0.53)	48.7	(1.17)	5.8	(0.45)
Master's degree	24,751	(721.5)	20.6	(1.09)	79.4	(1.09)	50.4	(1.33)	5.4	(0.72)	46.2	(1.38)	8.4	(0.88)
Public	20,219	(704.1)	21.5	(1.49)	78.5	(1.49)	45.8	(1.62)	7.7	(1.17)	49.6	(1.74)	6.8	(0.88)
4-year doctoral	19,850	(826.4)	19.8	(1.60)	80.2	(1.60)	43.9	(1.74)	7.2	(1.34)	54.3	(1.93)	7.1	(1.03)
Other 4-year	21,815	(1,104.6)	29.8	(3.69)	70.2	(3.69)	54.9	(4.45)	10.4	(2.31)	26.8	(3.17)	5.3	(1.30)
Private	29,290	(1,160.7)	19.4	(1.59)	80.6	(1.59)	56.3	(2.16)	2.5	(0.60)	41.9	(2.22)	10.4	(1.66)
4-year doctoral	31,307	(1,436.9)	17.5	(1.82)	82.5	(1.82)	57.7	(2.32)	3.0	(0.79)	49.4	(2.56)	8.3	(1.06)
Other 4-year	23,032	(1,217.1)	24.8	(3.30)	75.2	(3.30)	52.4	(5.10)	1.1	(0.36)	20.9	(4.74)	16.3	(5.55)
Doctor's degree	37,234	(4,065.7)	11.5	(1.39)	88.6	(1.39)	30.2	(2.85)	2.6	(0.63)	77.5	(1.73)	5.4	(0.65)
Public	29,929	(1,750.0)	10.7	(1.23)	89.4	(1.23)	26.5	(1.60)	3.2	(0.88)	80.6	(1.71)	7.4	(0.97)
Private	47,129	(7,597.7)	12.7	(2.94)	87.3	(2.94)	35.9	(6.36)	1.6	(0.79)	72.9	(3.44)	2.3	(0.54)
First-professional	57,556	(2,062.5)	11.5	(1.06)	88.5	(1.06)	80.1	(1.48)	9.8	(1.43)	40.2	(2.65)	1.6	(0.44)
Public	48,328	(1,993.7)	11.4	(1.57)	88.6	(1.57)	81.7	(1.81)	13.1	(2.18)	39.5	(2.87)	1.6	(0.64)
Private	65,299	(3,141.0)	11.6	(1.45)	88.4	(1.45)	78.8	(2.29)	7.1	(1.84)	40.8	(4.22)	1.5	(0.60)
Other graduate	21,238	(1,419.4)	37.3	(3.60)	62.7	(3.60)	44.4	(3.70)	6.3	(1.44)	23.3	(3.35)	7.3	(1.82)
2003–04, all institutions	$53,381	(1,380.8)	13.0	(0.95)	87.0	(0.95)	62.4	(1.39)	4.0	(0.85)	40.0	(1.19)	9.2	(1.00)
Master's degree	37,791	(1,624.4)	19.0	(1.84)	81.0	(1.84)	55.8	(2.35)	2.8	(0.66)	35.5	(2.28)	10.4	(1.80)
Public	32,951	(1,623.4)	20.8	(2.36)	79.2	(2.36)	47.4	(2.76)	3.0	(0.71)	44.0	(2.61)	6.7	(1.06)
4-year doctoral	33,691	(1,610.1)	18.3	(1.76)	81.7	(1.76)	47.7	(2.80)	3.2	(0.80)	47.0	(2.73)	7.5	(1.26)
Other 4-year	28,632	(4,916.1)	36.7	(11.02)	63.3	(11.02)	45.7	(11.86)	‡	(†)	24.3	(7.15)	1.2	(0.77)
Private	41,906	(2,592.4)	17.1	(3.35)	82.9	(3.35)	64.5	(4.01)	2.6	(1.19)	20.8	(2.36)	14.4	(3.57)
4-year doctoral	46,266	(3,402.8)	13.5	(2.49)	86.5	(2.49)	63.2	(4.04)	2.3	(1.66)	36.3	(3.47)	12.3	(4.73)
Other 4-year	34,205	(3,071.6)	23.3	(6.71)	76.7	(6.71)	66.7	(7.54)	3.2	(2.29)	9.5	(4.03)	18.0	(6.09)
Doctor's degree	51,664	(2,786.4)	7.1	(0.69)	92.9	(0.69)	39.8	(2.52)	3.0	(0.86)	69.0	(2.65)	8.7	(1.59)
Public	42,551	(1,927.8)	6.3	(0.68)	93.7	(0.68)	36.6	(2.18)	2.7	(0.60)	76.7	(1.91)	8.8	(1.46)
Private	62,265	(5,193.1)	8.3	(1.43)	91.7	(1.43)	44.0	(4.54)	3.5	(2.02)	58.8	(5.01)	8.5	(3.07)
First-professional	75,703	(2,288.9)	7.9	(0.79)	92.1	(0.79)	83.3	(1.19)	6.3	(2.04)	32.5	(1.87)	4.5	(0.67)
Public	65,423	(1,547.2)	7.8	(1.06)	92.2	(1.06)	83.0	(1.58)	5.2	(0.87)	36.7	(1.61)	4.5	(0.88)
Private	84,516	(4,135.7)	8.1	(1.12)	91.9	(1.12)	83.6	(1.82)	7.3	(3.51)	28.9	(2.94)	4.5	(1.06)
Other graduate	35,501	(4,732.1)	17.1	(5.58)	82.9	(5.58)	75.9	(6.54)	3.8	(1.91)	16.2	(4.66)	21.3	(9.96)

†Not applicable.
#Rounds to zero.
‡Reporting standards not met.
[1]Includes students who reported they were awarded aid, but did not specify the source of aid.
NOTE: Total includes some students whose level of study was unknown. Detail may not sum to totals because of rounding and because some students receive multiple types of aid and aid from different sources. Standard errors appear in parentheses. Data include Puerto Rico. Some data have been revised from previously published figures.
SOURCE: U.S. Department of Education, National Center for Education Statistics, 1992–93, 1995–96, 1999–2000, and 2003–04 National Postsecondary Student Aid Studies (NPSAS:93, NPSAS:96, NPSAS:2000, and NPSAS:2004). (This table was prepared November 2008.)

Table 345. Amount borrowed, aid status, and sources of aid for part-time or part-year postbaccalaureate students, by level of study and control and type of institution: Selected years, 1992–93 through 2003–04

Level of study, control and type of institution	Cumulative amount borrowed for post-baccalaureate education (in current dollars)		Aid status (percent of students)										
			Nonaided		Receiving aid, by source								
					Any aid[1]		Federal		State		Institutional		Employer	
1	2		3		4		5		6		7		8	
1992–93, all institutions	$9,577	(476.4)	71.3	(0.84)	28.7	(0.84)	10.8	(0.48)	1.9	(0.19)	12.7	(0.65)	16.7	(0.69)
Master's degree	8,003	(477.5)	71.7	(0.93)	28.3	(0.93)	10.5	(0.56)	1.6	(0.21)	11.1	(0.67)	18.7	(0.85)
Public	7,246	(376.4)	73.9	(0.99)	26.1	(0.99)	10.1	(0.64)	2.5	(0.36)	11.7	(0.79)	14.6	(0.90)
4-year doctoral	8,058	(499.3)	69.6	(1.28)	30.4	(1.28)	11.9	(0.80)	2.5	(0.43)	15.3	(1.03)	14.6	(1.06)
Other 4-year	5,396	(512.1)	81.2	(1.59)	18.8	(1.59)	6.9	(0.99)	2.4	(0.56)	5.5	(1.01)	14.4	(1.30)
Private	8,958	(801.9)	68.6	(1.73)	31.4	(1.73)	11.1	(0.95)	0.4	(0.14)	10.3	(1.02)	24.4	(1.25)
4-year doctoral	9,794	(1,208.0)	66.9	(1.96)	33.1	(1.96)	12.1	(1.30)	0.4	(0.16)	12.1	(1.43)	25.1	(1.65)
Other 4-year	7,313	(534.0)	71.7	(2.92)	28.3	(2.92)	9.3	(1.25)	0.6	(0.27)	6.9	(1.13)	23.1	(2.32)
Doctor's degree	12,858	(1,369.8)	56.2	(2.41)	43.8	(2.41)	8.6	(1.07)	3.5	(0.83)	33.1	(2.18)	12.0	(1.53)
Public	9,628	(1,227.0)	56.1	(2.58)	43.9	(2.58)	8.5	(1.19)	4.4	(1.23)	33.3	(2.48)	12.9	(1.63)
Private	17,048	(2,506.1)	56.4	(4.85)	43.6	(4.85)	8.9	(2.03)	1.6	(0.69)	32.6	(4.21)	10.2	(3.19)
First-professional	26,158	(2,269.0)	42.6	(3.20)	57.4	(3.20)	44.9	(3.10)	3.3	(0.70)	25.7	(2.26)	6.1	(1.16)
Public	21,931	(3,100.7)	50.8	(5.23)	49.2	(5.23)	42.9	(4.44)	3.6	(1.19)	22.2	(3.54)	5.1	(1.87)
Private	27,842	(2,711.4)	37.8	(3.98)	62.2	(3.98)	46.1	(4.24)	3.2	(0.88)	27.8	(2.91)	6.7	(1.50)
Other graduate	7,223	(895.5)	79.7	(1.50)	20.3	(1.50)	7.7	(0.83)	1.7	(0.45)	8.4	(0.97)	13.4	(1.17)
1995–96, all institutions	$16,193	(651.8)	59.3	(1.23)	40.7	(1.23)	13.8	(0.63)	1.4	(0.31)	16.7	(1.20)	16.1	(0.89)
Master's degree	14,635	(739.4)	56.3	(1.53)	43.7	(1.53)	15.1	(0.78)	1.2	(0.23)	16.5	(1.35)	18.4	(1.20)
Public	12,971	(915.3)	57.3	(2.04)	42.7	(2.04)	13.6	(0.91)	1.7	(0.38)	18.5	(1.87)	16.0	(1.35)
4-year doctoral	14,443	(1,152.0)	52.8	(2.74)	47.2	(2.74)	14.8	(1.23)	1.2	(0.41)	22.6	(2.69)	16.6	(1.79)
Other 4-year	9,273	(756.3)	66.4	(2.83)	33.6	(2.83)	11.1	(1.21)	2.8	(0.78)	10.3	(1.59)	14.8	(1.93)
Private	16,904	(1,240.0)	54.9	(2.28)	45.1	(2.28)	17.2	(1.36)	0.5	(0.16)	13.7	(1.92)	21.8	(2.11)
4-year doctoral	19,948	(1,966.7)	55.3	(3.03)	44.7	(3.03)	17.1	(1.70)	0.6	(0.28)	17.2	(2.99)	18.3	(2.33)
Other 4-year	13,006	(1,023.9)	54.5	(3.50)	45.5	(3.50)	16.6	(2.17)	0.3	(0.15)	9.6	(2.10)	25.9	(3.49)
Doctor's degree	19,530	(1,758.5)	48.6	(3.55)	51.4	(3.55)	12.1	(1.72)	0.6	(0.30)	39.3	(3.48)	9.0	(2.03)
Public	16,288	(1,357.9)	46.1	(4.67)	53.9	(4.67)	9.5	(1.92)	0.9	(0.46)	42.5	(4.57)	9.2	(2.44)
Private	24,882	(2,957.7)	53.3	(4.88)	46.7	(4.88)	17.2	(2.84)	#	(†)	33.3	(4.77)	8.6	(3.59)
First-professional	32,803	(2,151.7)	32.2	(5.02)	67.8	(5.02)	47.4	(5.87)	4.3	(1.49)	27.0	(8.08)	7.0	(1.78)
Public	31,882	(2,069.9)	29.6	(5.44)	70.4	(5.44)	59.6	(4.96)	4.0	(1.96)	25.7	(4.64)	7.5	(3.25)
Private	33,160	(2,893.6)	33.1	(6.46)	66.9	(6.46)	43.5	(7.17)	4.3	(1.07)	27.4	(10.53)	6.8	(2.13)
Other graduate	13,008	(1,214.6)	74.0	(1.69)	26.0	(1.69)	7.0	(0.81)	1.9	(0.94)	8.4	(1.25)	13.3	(1.25)
Public 4-year doctoral	15,473	(2,279.8)	67.8	(2.61)	32.2	(2.61)	9.8	(1.57)	0.5	(0.26)	12.4	(2.54)	14.9	(2.07)
Public other 4-year	11,166	(1,313.0)	77.3	(2.20)	22.7	(2.20)	5.5	(0.90)	2.6	(1.42)	6.3	(1.32)	12.4	(1.58)
1999–2000, all institutions	$20,929	(554.5)	52.1	(0.77)	47.9	(0.77)	18.1	(0.60)	1.6	(0.19)	15.9	(0.55)	20.3	(0.67)
Master's degree	17,489	(517.1)	50.3	(0.92)	49.7	(0.92)	18.6	(0.73)	1.4	(0.21)	14.2	(0.68)	23.2	(0.84)
Public	14,420	(613.8)	53.7	(1.30)	46.3	(1.30)	15.9	(0.92)	2.0	(0.33)	15.3	(0.95)	20.6	(1.15)
4-year doctoral	15,891	(781.1)	50.3	(1.61)	49.7	(1.61)	17.1	(1.12)	2.0	(0.43)	17.9	(1.22)	21.5	(1.40)
Other 4-year	10,593	(651.1)	61.5	(2.03)	38.5	(2.03)	13.3	(1.54)	2.0	(0.49)	9.5	(1.43)	18.6	(2.04)
Private	20,692	(801.0)	45.9	(1.28)	54.1	(1.28)	22.0	(1.14)	0.6	(0.22)	12.7	(0.95)	26.5	(1.20)
4-year doctoral	23,434	(1,090.2)	43.6	(1.48)	56.4	(1.48)	23.1	(1.40)	0.8	(0.32)	14.7	(1.16)	25.9	(1.33)
Other 4-year	14,910	(1,092.3)	50.6	(2.47)	49.4	(2.47)	19.7	(1.97)	0.3	(0.18)	8.4	(1.53)	27.7	(2.41)
Doctor's degree	28,829	(1,883.3)	45.5	(1.68)	54.5	(1.68)	14.5	(1.30)	1.0	(0.33)	37.8	(1.69)	13.9	(1.30)
Public	25,423	(1,444.3)	46.4	(2.13)	53.6	(2.13)	11.8	(1.16)	1.5	(0.48)	40.8	(2.01)	12.2	(1.30)
Private	34,511	(3,883.0)	43.4	(2.66)	56.6	(2.66)	18.1	(3.18)	#	(†)	31.4	(2.97)	17.5	(2.96)
First-professional	46,159	(2,527.3)	22.2	(2.29)	77.8	(2.29)	58.1	(4.76)	5.2	(1.35)	28.3	(2.81)	10.1	(1.90)
Public	36,078	(3,271.1)	20.6	(4.87)	79.4	(4.87)	60.7	(6.96)	6.6	(3.17)	23.9	(5.65)	6.5	(3.62)
Private	50,469	(3,018.2)	22.8	(2.56)	77.2	(2.56)	57.0	(6.00)	4.6	(1.40)	30.1	(3.19)	11.5	(2.22)
Other graduate	18,175	(1,363.8)	58.9	(2.85)	41.1	(2.85)	16.8	(2.46)	1.5	(0.74)	9.1	(1.52)	18.6	(2.40)
2003–04, all institutions	$30,422	(786.8)	34.5	(1.29)	65.5	(1.29)	31.4	(1.44)	1.9	(0.45)	19.0	(1.13)	26.0	(1.23)
Master's degree	28,800	(909.7)	32.5	(1.61)	67.5	(1.61)	34.5	(1.60)	1.9	(0.51)	17.0	(1.49)	27.6	(1.47)
Public	25,404	(753.9)	36.7	(1.49)	63.3	(1.49)	28.4	(1.36)	2.3	(0.46)	22.1	(1.37)	24.6	(1.38)
4-year doctoral	25,628	(692.9)	36.1	(1.30)	63.9	(1.30)	27.5	(1.21)	2.2	(0.44)	24.2	(1.47)	24.8	(1.37)
Other 4-year	24,862	(1,861.2)	38.2	(4.02)	61.8	(4.02)	30.7	(3.74)	2.6	(1.22)	16.5	(2.64)	24.1	(3.82)
Private	32,142	(1,784.4)	27.8	(2.78)	72.2	(2.78)	41.1	(3.03)	1.4	(0.82)	11.4	(2.12)	30.9	(2.69)
4-year doctoral	33,160	(1,756.8)	31.2	(2.41)	68.8	(2.41)	38.0	(2.86)	1.8	(1.69)	14.8	(2.28)	28.1	(2.93)
Other 4-year	31,153	(3,011.2)	24.6	(5.15)	75.4	(5.15)	44.0	(4.85)	0.9	(0.46)	8.1	(3.12)	33.7	(4.41)
Doctor's degree	43,069	(2,000.4)	27.8	(1.28)	72.2	(1.28)	22.2	(1.38)	1.9	(0.32)	45.8	(1.91)	19.9	(1.64)
Public	34,644	(1,225.1)	25.6	(1.17)	74.4	(1.17)	18.2	(1.28)	2.6	(0.44)	55.8	(1.21)	17.3	(1.02)
Private	54,577	(4,900.5)	31.7	(3.35)	68.3	(3.35)	29.1	(3.39)	0.7	(0.54)	28.2	(2.86)	24.3	(4.13)
First-professional	54,044	(5,919.7)	24.6	(3.94)	75.4	(3.94)	54.2	(5.50)	6.8	(3.18)	23.6	(4.34)	13.2	(2.65)
Public	64,855	(6,078.7)	20.8	(5.05)	79.2	(5.05)	63.4	(6.24)	3.0	(2.16)	31.2	(5.74)	9.4	(3.26)
Private	50,875	(7,264.1)	25.6	(4.81)	74.4	(4.81)	51.9	(6.84)	7.7	(4.04)	21.7	(5.47)	14.1	(3.24)
Other graduate	23,800	(1,233.8)	48.8	(2.31)	51.2	(2.31)	19.5	(2.61)	1.1	(0.41)	10.3	(1.38)	25.7	(2.55)

†Not applicable.
#Rounds to zero.
[1]Includes students who reported they were awarded aid, but did not specify the source of aid.
NOTE: Total includes some students whose level of study was unknown. Detail may not sum to totals because of rounding and because some students receive multiple types of aid and aid from different sources. Standard errors appear in parentheses. Data include Puerto Rico. Some data have been revised from previously published figures.
SOURCE: U.S. Department of Education, National Center for Education Statistics, 1992–93, 1995–96, 1999–2000, and 2003–04 National Postsecondary Student Aid Studies (NPSAS:93, NPSAS:96, NPSAS:2000, and NPSAS:2004). (This table was prepared November 2008.)

Table 346. Percentage of full-time, full-year postbaccalaureate students receiving aid, by type of aid, level of study, and control and type of institution: Selected years, 1992–93 through 2003–04

Level of study, control and type of institution	Number of students[1] (in thousands)	Any aid[2]	Fellowship grants	Tuition waivers	Assistantships[3]	Employer	Any loans	Stafford[4]	Perkins[5]
1	2	3	4	5	6	7	8	9	10
1992–93, all institutions	673 (—)	68.1 (1.03)	[6] (†)	12.4 (1.00)	14.3 (1.21)	3.3 (0.39)	43.5 (1.49)	41.1 (1.50)	9.0 (0.97)
Master's degree	281 (—)	62.5 (2.13)	[6] (†)	15.7 (1.32)	18.1 (1.92)	5.1 (0.66)	32.5 (2.01)	30.5 (1.99)	5.0 (0.80)
Public	163 (—)	65.4 (1.98)	[6] (†)	20.5 (1.80)	22.4 (1.85)	4.8 (0.76)	32.2 (1.96)	30.8 (1.86)	4.0 (0.74)
4-year doctoral	139 (—)	65.7 (2.14)	[6] (†)	23.3 (1.99)	23.5 (2.09)	4.7 (0.78)	30.6 (2.06)	29.6 (1.94)	3.3 (0.69)
Other 4-year	24 (—)	63.9 (4.12)	[6] (†)	4.4 (2.00)	15.8 (3.34)	5.3 (2.44)	41.5 (4.87)	38.4 (4.64)	8.3 (3.11)
Private	118 (—)	58.4 (4.05)	[6] (†)	8.9 (1.67)	12.2 (3.95)	5.6 (1.08)	32.9 (3.56)	30.0 (3.60)	6.4 (1.66)
4-year doctoral	102 (—)	60.7 (4.44)	[6] (†)	9.5 (1.92)	13.6 (4.50)	5.7 (1.26)	33.6 (4.23)	30.8 (4.32)	6.8 (1.92)
Other 4-year	16 (—)	43.5 (3.79)	[6] (†)	5.4 (0.64)	3.0 (1.45)	4.7 (0.37)	28.7 (2.47)	24.6 (2.50)	4.4 (0.35)
Doctor's degree	120 (—)	69.6 (2.28)	[6] (†)	19.5 (1.95)	27.1 (2.06)	2.2 (0.74)	25.8 (2.44)	23.9 (2.40)	3.5 (0.62)
Public	73 (—)	69.7 (2.77)	[6] (†)	23.1 (2.70)	31.6 (2.63)	3.1 (1.12)	20.6 (2.38)	18.9 (2.30)	2.9 (0.73)
Private	46 (—)	69.6 (4.11)	[6] (†)	13.6 (2.80)	19.9 (3.42)	0.9 (0.59)	34.1 (4.62)	31.9 (4.57)	4.3 (1.15)
First-professional	211 (—)	77.0 (1.17)	[6] (†)	5.6 (0.99)	4.4 (0.66)	1.2 (0.40)	67.8 (1.77)	65.6 (1.72)	19.3 (1.95)
Public	101 (—)	79.3 (1.30)	[6] (†)	5.4 (1.41)	4.3 (0.57)	1.3 (0.60)	71.8 (1.82)	69.9 (1.58)	23.2 (2.73)
Private	110 (—)	74.9 (1.71)	[6] (†)	5.8 (1.25)	4.5 (1.17)	1.2 (0.54)	64.1 (2.21)	61.6 (2.26)	15.7 (1.80)
Other graduate	61 (—)	60.7 (5.42)	[6] (†)	7.5 (1.78)	6.2 (1.93)	3.7 (1.05)	44.4 (4.16)	39.6 (4.30)	2.7 (0.75)
1995–96, all institutions	861 (—)	76.1 (1.39)	[6] (†)	11.7 (1.34)	19.5 (1.42)	5.0 (0.61)	48.7 (1.77)	48.0 (1.79)	8.1 (0.87)
Master's degree	387 (—)	72.6 (2.16)	[6] (†)	13.5 (1.94)	20.2 (1.85)	6.6 (1.02)	43.1 (2.14)	42.5 (2.13)	5.1 (0.75)
Public	236 (—)	74.7 (2.63)	[6] (†)	17.8 (2.85)	28.9 (2.69)	7.1 (1.36)	39.5 (2.39)	38.8 (2.34)	3.5 (0.85)
4-year doctoral	195 (—)	76.5 (2.96)	[6] (†)	19.5 (3.31)	31.1 (3.18)	7.6 (1.55)	39.2 (2.67)	38.6 (2.60)	4.0 (1.00)
Other 4-year	41 (—)	66.0 (5.20)	[6] (†)	9.9 (4.21)	18.1 (3.30)	4.5 (2.55)	40.8 (5.40)	39.8 (5.39)	1.5 (1.11)
Private	151 (—)	69.4 (3.73)	[6] (†)	6.7 (1.91)	6.6 (1.60)	5.9 (1.50)	48.6 (3.96)	48.2 (3.98)	7.6 (1.35)
4-year doctoral	104 (—)	71.2 (4.56)	[6] (†)	6.4 (2.13)	8.8 (2.32)	7.1 (2.07)	44.6 (4.45)	44.6 (4.45)	9.6 (1.75)
Other 4-year	47 (—)	65.4 (6.60)	[6] (†)	7.4 (3.93)	1.9 (0.99)	3.2 (1.39)	57.4 (6.62)	56.1 (6.87)	3.3 (1.68)
Doctor's degree	147 (—)	82.9 (2.70)	[6] (†)	24.3 (3.37)	51.8 (4.06)	5.5 (1.55)	25.2 (2.62)	25.2 (2.62)	1.5 (0.61)
Public	94 (—)	85.9 (3.31)	[6] (†)	30.9 (4.55)	59.9 (4.62)	5.9 (1.99)	26.7 (3.32)	26.7 (3.32)	1.4 (0.69)
Private	53 (—)	77.5 (4.39)	[6] (†)	12.4 (4.38)	37.3 (6.51)	4.9 (2.44)	22.6 (4.28)	22.6 (4.28)	1.7 (1.16)
First-professional	253 (—)	83.2 (1.46)	[6] (†)	3.0 (0.66)	4.0 (0.74)	1.3 (0.48)	74.4 (2.30)	73.0 (2.46)	18.4 (1.86)
Public	115 (—)	85.7 (1.88)	[6] (†)	3.8 (1.03)	4.1 (1.08)	1.5 (0.82)	79.0 (2.37)	78.6 (2.39)	20.7 (2.49)
Private	138 (—)	81.0 (2.04)	[6] (†)	2.4 (0.90)	3.8 (1.03)	1.2 (0.56)	70.6 (3.53)	68.3 (3.76)	16.4 (2.55)
Other graduate	54 (—)	56.5 (5.11)	[6] (†)	9.8 (3.84)	6.4 (2.08)	6.1 (2.67)	31.3 (4.19)	30.9 (4.17)	2.6 (1.09)
Public 4-year doctoral	18 (—)	63.1 (8.67)	[6] (†)	9.2 (8.59)	6.2 (3.12)	1.8 (1.71)	30.2 (7.40)	30.2 (7.40)	0.7 (0.71)
Public other 4-year	36 (—)	53.2 (6.29)	[6] (†)	10.1 (3.83)	6.6 (2.70)	8.3 (3.89)	31.8 (5.05)	31.2 (5.02)	3.6 (1.59)
1999–2000, all institutions	918 (—)	82.2 (0.73)	20.0 (1.02)	11.5 (0.54)	23.2 (0.80)	5.8 (0.45)	53.7 (1.08)	52.0 (1.08)	8.7 (0.87)
Master's degree	395 (—)	79.4 (1.09)	17.2 (1.03)	12.0 (0.88)	22.6 (1.17)	8.4 (0.88)	50.2 (1.36)	48.7 (1.34)	5.9 (0.64)
Public	222 (—)	78.5 (1.49)	15.5 (1.43)	18.5 (1.41)	30.5 (1.67)	6.8 (0.88)	44.4 (1.62)	43.6 (1.62)	3.0 (0.64)
4-year doctoral	184 (—)	80.2 (1.60)	16.6 (1.60)	19.4 (1.65)	34.0 (1.95)	7.1 (1.03)	42.2 (1.74)	41.6 (1.74)	3.1 (0.74)
Other 4-year	38 (—)	70.2 (3.69)	10.7 (3.06)	14.0 (1.99)	13.7 (2.05)	5.3 (1.30)	54.7 (4.48)	53.3 (4.41)	2.2 (1.14)
Private	172 (—)	80.6 (1.59)	19.2 (1.49)	3.6 (0.75)	12.3 (1.55)	10.4 (1.66)	57.7 (2.24)	55.3 (2.18)	9.8 (1.19)
4-year doctoral	127 (—)	82.5 (1.82)	23.4 (1.89)	4.2 (0.98)	14.0 (1.54)	8.3 (1.06)	60.1 (2.48)	56.7 (2.35)	11.5 (1.50)
Other 4-year	46 (—)	75.2 (3.31)	7.7 (2.01)	1.9 (0.67)	7.8 (4.20)	16.3 (5.55)	51.2 (5.08)	51.2 (5.08)	4.9 (1.86)
Doctor's degree	184 (—)	88.6 (1.39)	37.8 (2.28)	23.3 (1.50)	55.0 (2.55)	5.4 (0.65)	29.5 (2.90)	27.9 (2.90)	4.7 (2.89)
Public	111 (—)	89.4 (1.23)	30.1 (1.54)	35.5 (1.79)	63.5 (1.88)	7.4 (0.97)	26.2 (1.67)	24.4 (1.51)	1.1 (0.37)
Private	73 (—)	87.3 (2.94)	49.5 (4.61)	4.9 (1.03)	41.9 (4.98)	2.3 (0.54)	34.4 (6.49)	33.1 (6.55)	10.2 (6.83)
First-professional	253 (—)	88.5 (1.06)	16.4 (2.18)	4.1 (0.79)	6.5 (0.99)	1.6 (0.44)	80.8 (1.41)	78.7 (1.60)	18.0 (1.83)
Public	113 (—)	88.6 (1.57)	12.3 (1.98)	7.3 (1.55)	6.5 (1.55)	1.6 (0.64)	81.8 (1.83)	80.6 (1.82)	20.1 (2.46)
Private	140 (—)	88.4 (1.45)	19.8 (3.62)	1.5 (0.55)	6.5 (1.28)	1.5 (0.60)	79.9 (2.11)	77.2 (2.55)	16.3 (2.69)
Other graduate	86 (—)	62.7 (3.60)	5.3 (1.48)	6.0 (1.68)	7.4 (1.86)	7.3 (1.82)	42.2 (4.08)	40.6 (4.08)	3.1 (1.13)
2003–04, all institutions	923 (27.8)	87.0 (0.95)	38.2 (1.22)	12.8 (0.71)	21.6 (0.93)	9.2 (1.00)	63.6 (1.31)	56.6 (1.44)	11.8 (1.34)
Master's degree	373 (23.4)	81.0 (1.84)	32.3 (2.22)	11.7 (1.20)	21.4 (1.66)	10.4 (1.80)	58.4 (2.14)	50.5 (2.27)	5.5 (0.85)
Public	190 (11.3)	79.2 (2.36)	37.5 (2.30)	18.4 (1.75)	32.9 (2.49)	6.7 (1.06)	48.5 (2.75)	41.0 (2.37)	4.1 (0.87)
4-year doctoral	165 (10.4)	81.7 (1.76)	38.8 (2.42)	19.5 (1.84)	36.1 (2.58)	7.5 (1.26)	48.8 (2.97)	40.4 (2.60)	4.8 (0.98)
Other 4-year	25 (5.1)	63.3 (11.02)	28.8 (8.09)	11.4 (6.20)	11.9 (6.94)	1.2 (0.77)	46.1 (11.92)	44.8 (11.78)	‡ (†)
Private	182 (19.9)	82.9 (3.35)	26.9 (3.54)	4.7 (1.13)	9.5 (1.46)	14.4 (3.57)	68.7 (3.54)	60.4 (4.04)	6.8 (1.42)
4-year doctoral	116 (8.3)	86.5 (2.49)	36.2 (4.29)	6.9 (1.62)	12.0 (1.96)	12.3 (4.73)	69.3 (3.56)	59.1 (4.23)	9.9 (2.21)
Other 4-year	66 (17.3)	76.7 (6.71)	10.5 (3.79)	1.0 (1.03)	5.1 (2.71)	18.0 (6.09)	67.8 (7.01)	62.5 (7.61)	1.6 (1.14)
Doctor's degree	195 (11.3)	92.9 (0.69)	59.6 (2.36)	30.2 (1.66)	48.9 (2.39)	8.7 (1.59)	38.4 (2.58)	33.2 (2.14)	8.7 (1.65)
Public	111 (5.4)	93.7 (0.68)	65.3 (1.77)	41.7 (1.76)	56.7 (1.93)	8.8 (1.46)	34.1 (2.18)	29.8 (2.24)	6.7 (1.43)
Private	83 (8.8)	91.7 (1.43)	51.9 (4.88)	14.7 (1.63)	38.6 (4.06)	8.5 (3.07)	44.2 (4.44)	37.6 (3.67)	11.5 (3.50)
First-professional	280 (7.3)	92.1 (0.79)	37.5 (2.55)	4.3 (1.25)	7.0 (0.83)	4.5 (0.67)	84.7 (1.06)	78.3 (1.45)	24.7 (3.20)
Public	128 (7.0)	92.2 (1.06)	40.3 (2.20)	5.2 (0.63)	9.5 (1.57)	4.5 (0.88)	84.1 (1.59)	77.8 (1.68)	24.9 (1.98)
Private	152 (9.2)	91.9 (1.12)	35.1 (3.69)	3.5 (2.16)	4.9 (0.95)	4.5 (1.06)	85.1 (1.59)	78.8 (2.44)	24.6 (5.71)
Other graduate	76 (14.4)	82.9 (5.58)	15.6 (4.38)	5.4 (2.65)	5.8 (2.33)	21.3 (9.96)	76.3 (6.53)	66.5 (7.83)	3.3 (1.54)

—Not available.
†Not applicable.
‡Reporting standards not met.
[1]Numbers of full-time, full-year postbaccalaureate students may not equal figures reported in other tables, since these data are based on a sample survey of all postbaccalaureate students who enrolled at any time during the school year.
[2]Includes students who reported they were awarded aid, but did not specify the source of aid.
[3]Includes students who received teaching or research assistantships and/or participated in work-study programs.
[4]Formerly Guaranteed Student Loans (GSL).
[5]Formerly National Direct Student Loans (NDSL).

[6]Fellowship estimates for 1992–93 and 1995–96 were based primarily on information provided by institutions and are not comparable to data for 1999–2000 or 2003–04, which were based on information provided by both students and institutions.
NOTE: Excludes students whose attendance status was not reported. Total includes some students whose level of study or control of institution was unknown. Detail may not sum to totals because of rounding and because some students receive aid from multiple sources. Standard errors appear in parentheses. Data include Puerto Rico.
SOURCE: U.S. Department of Education, National Center for Education Statistics, 1992–93, 1995–96, 1999–2000, and 2003–04 National Postsecondary Student Aid Studies (NPSAS:93, NPSAS:96, NPSAS:2000, and NPSAS:04). (This table was prepared September 2005.)

Table 347. Percentage of part-time or part-year postbaccalaureate students receiving aid, by type of aid, level of study, and control and type of institution: Selected years, 1992–93 through 2003–04

Level of study, control and type of institution	Number of students[1] (in thousands)		Percent receiving aid, by type												
			Any aid[2]		Fellowship grants		Tuition waivers		Assistantships[3]		Employer		Loans					
													Any loans		Stafford[4]		Perkins[5]	
1	2		3		4		5		6		7		8		9		10	
1992–93, all institutions....	1,950	(—)	28.7	(0.84)	[6]	(†)	5.1	(0.34)	4.3	(0.30)	7.9	(0.43)	10.5	(0.46)	9.4	(0.43)	1.0	(0.10)
Master's degree	1,322	(—)	28.3	(0.93)	[6]	(†)	4.6	(0.35)	3.8	(0.32)	8.8	(0.52)	10.3	(0.54)	9.3	(0.52)	0.9	(0.12)
Public	773	(—)	26.1	(0.99)	[6]	(†)	4.9	(0.47)	5.2	(0.43)	6.7	(0.50)	9.9	(0.62)	9.0	(0.60)	1.2	(0.16)
4-year doctoral	489	(—)	30.4	(1.28)	[6]	(†)	6.5	(0.64)	6.7	(0.60)	6.7	(0.69)	11.8	(0.76)	10.7	(0.74)	1.5	(0.21)
Other 4-year	284	(—)	18.8	(1.59)	[6]	(†)	2.3	(0.53)	2.6	(0.63)	6.5	(0.77)	6.5	(0.92)	6.0	(0.87)	0.6	(0.24)
Private	549	(—)	31.4	(1.73)	[6]	(†)	4.2	(0.51)	1.8	(0.43)	11.8	(0.91)	11.0	(0.95)	9.7	(0.89)	0.5	(0.17)
4-year doctoral	357	(—)	33.1	(1.96)	[6]	(†)	4.4	(0.67)	2.5	(0.65)	12.1	(1.17)	11.9	(1.27)	10.5	(1.19)	0.6	(0.25)
Other 4-year	192	(—)	28.3	(2.92)	[6]	(†)	3.8	(0.87)	0.7	(0.25)	11.2	(1.48)	9.3	(1.15)	8.1	(1.10)	0.3	(0.17)
Doctor's degree	149	(—)	43.8	(2.41)	[6]	(†)	12.7	(1.70)	17.0	(1.87)	5.5	(1.18)	7.3	(0.98)	6.9	(0.97)	0.8	(0.13)
Public	97	(—)	43.9	(2.58)	[6]	(†)	15.0	(2.09)	17.0	(1.90)	6.4	(1.16)	7.1	(1.00)	6.5	(0.95)	0.7	(0.10)
Private	51	(—)	43.6	(4.85)	[6]	(†)	8.3	(2.62)	17.0	(3.97)	3.7	(2.67)	7.7	(2.04)	7.5	(2.06)	1.2	(0.35)
First-professional	64	(—)	57.4	(3.20)	[6]	(†)	5.9	(1.06)	3.1	(0.84)	3.4	(0.92)	45.6	(3.13)	42.0	(2.89)	6.2	(0.98)
Public	24	(—)	49.2	(5.23)	[6]	(†)	6.8	(1.62)	6.1	(2.09)	2.5	(1.21)	42.4	(4.37)	41.4	(4.27)	8.5	(1.99)
Private	40	(—)	62.2	(3.98)	[6]	(†)	5.4	(1.40)	1.4	(0.52)	3.9	(1.32)	47.5	(4.29)	42.3	(3.95)	4.9	(1.07)
Other graduate	415	(—)	20.3	(1.50)	[6]	(†)	3.4	(0.61)	1.6	(0.36)	6.4	(0.91)	7.1	(0.81)	6.0	(0.70)	0.5	(0.27)
1995–96, all institutions...	1,842	(—)	40.7	(1.23)	[6]	(†)	6.1	(0.64)	7.4	(0.85)	16.1	(0.89)	13.4	(0.63)	13.1	(0.62)	0.9	(0.14)
Master's degree	1,118	(—)	43.7	(1.53)	[6]	(†)	5.6	(0.69)	7.4	(1.06)	18.4	(1.20)	14.5	(0.77)	14.3	(0.76)	0.7	(0.15)
Public	649	(—)	42.7	(2.04)	[6]	(†)	6.0	(0.96)	10.7	(1.74)	16.0	(1.35)	13.2	(0.89)	12.9	(0.87)	0.9	(0.22)
4-year doctoral	432	(—)	47.2	(2.74)	[6]	(†)	7.1	(1.36)	13.7	(2.54)	16.6	(1.79)	14.3	(1.19)	14.2	(1.19)	1.0	(0.31)
Other 4-year	217	(—)	33.6	(2.83)	[6]	(†)	3.9	(0.95)	4.9	(1.08)	14.8	(1.93)	11.0	(1.22)	10.5	(1.19)	0.6	(0.25)
Private	470	(—)	45.1	(2.28)	[6]	(†)	5.1	(0.97)	2.7	(0.57)	21.8	(2.11)	16.4	(1.35)	16.1	(1.33)	0.5	(0.20)
4-year doctoral	255	(—)	44.7	(3.03)	[6]	(†)	4.3	(1.11)	4.0	(0.97)	18.3	(2.33)	17.6	(1.78)	17.0	(1.70)	0.8	(0.36)
Other 4-year	215	(—)	45.5	(3.50)	[6]	(†)	5.9	(1.67)	1.2	(0.45)	25.9	(3.49)	15.0	(2.10)	14.9	(2.10)	0.1	(0.08)
Doctor's degree	181	(—)	51.4	(3.55)	[6]	(†)	12.7	(2.80)	26.0	(3.52)	9.0	(2.03)	12.0	(1.73)	12.0	(1.73)	0.4	(0.24)
Public	119	(—)	53.9	(4.67)	[6]	(†)	15.6	(3.57)	31.9	(4.55)	9.2	(2.44)	9.2	(1.93)	9.2	(1.93)	0.3	(0.27)
Private	62	(—)	46.7	(4.88)	[6]	(†)	7.4	(3.82)	14.7	(4.03)	8.6	(3.59)	17.2	(2.84)	17.2	(2.84)	0.7	(0.45)
First-professional	60	(—)	67.8	(5.02)	[6]	(†)	3.8	(1.16)	3.1	(1.03)	7.0	(1.78)	47.8	(5.75)	45.7	(5.90)	9.5	(2.29)
Public	15	(—)	70.4	(5.44)	[6]	(†)	4.8	(2.47)	7.9	(3.23)	7.5	(3.25)	58.1	(4.96)	57.4	(4.99)	12.2	(2.72)
Private	46	(—)	66.9	(6.46)	[6]	(†)	3.5	(1.33)	1.6	(0.75)	6.8	(2.13)	44.5	(7.10)	41.9	(7.23)	8.6	(2.87)
Other graduate	483	(—)	26.0	(1.69)	[6]	(†)	5.5	(1.07)	1.5	(0.50)	13.3	(1.25)	6.7	(0.81)	6.6	(0.80)	0.5	(0.18)
Public 4-year doctoral	166	(—)	32.2	(2.61)	[6]	(†)	8.6	(2.19)	0.4	(0.22)	14.9	(2.07)	9.7	(1.60)	9.6	(1.57)	0.4	(0.31)
Public other 4-year	317	(—)	22.7	(2.20)	[6]	(†)	3.8	(1.16)	2.1	(0.76)	12.4	(1.58)	5.2	(0.89)	5.0	(0.88)	0.6	(0.23)
1999–2000, all institutions	1,740	(—)	47.9	(0.77)	4.8	(0.32)	5.8	(0.32)	5.4	(0.30)	20.3	(0.67)	18.0	(0.61)	16.9	(0.59)	1.0	(0.17)
Master's degree	1,103	(—)	49.7	(0.92)	4.5	(0.40)	5.1	(0.38)	4.8	(0.38)	23.2	(0.84)	18.4	(0.73)	17.2	(0.71)	0.7	(0.14)
Public	625	(—)	46.3	(1.30)	3.9	(0.56)	6.4	(0.57)	6.3	(0.56)	20.6	(1.15)	15.7	(0.88)	14.7	(0.89)	0.7	(0.17)
4-year doctoral	434	(—)	49.7	(1.61)	4.2	(0.63)	7.4	(0.72)	8.0	(0.78)	21.5	(1.40)	16.7	(1.07)	15.6	(1.08)	0.5	(0.17)
Other 4-year	191	(—)	38.5	(2.03)	3.2	(1.15)	4.1	(0.90)	2.3	(0.55)	18.6	(2.04)	13.5	(1.53)	12.7	(1.52)	1.2	(0.39)
Private	478	(—)	54.1	(1.28)	5.3	(0.58)	3.3	(0.43)	2.8	(0.47)	26.5	(1.20)	21.8	(1.20)	20.5	(1.14)	0.7	(0.24)
4-year doctoral	323	(—)	56.4	(1.48)	6.3	(0.77)	3.6	(0.53)	3.3	(0.57)	25.9	(1.33)	22.7	(1.47)	21.4	(1.39)	0.8	(0.29)
Other 4-year	156	(—)	49.4	(2.47)	3.1	(0.77)	2.7	(0.74)	1.7	(0.86)	27.7	(2.41)	20.0	(2.07)	18.6	(1.96)	0.6	(0.43)
Doctor's degree	153	(—)	54.5	(1.68)	11.2	(1.17)	14.9	(1.21)	21.3	(1.46)	13.9	(1.30)	14.1	(1.27)	13.5	(1.29)	1.3	(0.91)
Public	104	(—)	53.6	(2.13)	9.1	(1.02)	19.4	(1.48)	25.9	(1.74)	12.2	(1.30)	12.3	(1.11)	11.7	(1.11)	0.3	(0.17)
Private	49	(—)	56.6	(2.66)	15.6	(2.81)	5.3	(1.56)	11.4	(1.80)	17.5	(2.96)	18.0	(3.13)	17.3	(3.20)	3.3	(2.74)
First-professional	72	(—)	77.8	(2.29)	10.1	(2.35)	5.3	(1.35)	4.0	(1.67)	10.1	(1.90)	60.7	(4.03)	57.4	(4.83)	7.2	(2.53)
Public	21	(—)	79.4	(4.87)	9.5	(3.72)	4.3	(2.24)	6.6	(4.99)	6.5	(3.62)	65.1	(6.77)	60.7	(6.96)	6.0	(2.12)
Private	52	(—)	77.2	(2.56)	10.3	(2.93)	5.7	(1.69)	2.9	(1.08)	11.5	(2.22)	59.0	(4.88)	56.1	(6.10)	7.6	(3.42)
Other graduate	412	(—)	41.1	(2.85)	2.5	(0.42)	4.4	(0.78)	1.5	(0.34)	16.8	(1.47)	11.1	(1.26)	10.3	(1.23)	0.4	(0.18)
2003–04, all institutions...	1,903	(33.7)	65.5	(1.29)	14.3	(1.11)	5.9	(0.62)	11.5	(0.73)	26.0	(1.23)	31.5	(1.39)	27.4	(1.50)	1.7	(0.21)
Master's degree	1,320	(37.8)	67.5	(1.61)	12.9	(1.48)	5.4	(0.87)	10.2	(0.93)	27.6	(1.47)	34.5	(1.56)	30.2	(1.76)	1.6	(0.27)
Public	689	(27.5)	63.3	(1.49)	13.2	(1.08)	7.4	(0.90)	16.0	(1.08)	24.6	(1.38)	29.0	(1.30)	24.6	(1.37)	2.2	(0.41)
4-year doctoral	499	(18.6)	63.9	(1.30)	14.8	(1.23)	8.3	(1.06)	17.9	(1.04)	24.8	(1.37)	28.0	(1.24)	23.4	(1.24)	2.6	(0.43)
Other 4-year	190	(15.0)	61.8	(4.02)	9.0	(2.11)	5.0	(1.38)	11.2	(2.46)	24.1	(3.82)	31.5	(3.63)	27.8	(3.65)	1.2	(0.91)
Private	631	(45.2)	72.2	(2.78)	12.5	(2.63)	3.3	(1.18)	3.8	(0.81)	30.9	(2.69)	40.5	(2.96)	36.2	(3.44)	0.9	(0.35)
4-year doctoral	313	(26.0)	68.8	(2.41)	15.4	(2.80)	2.9	(0.61)	6.0	(1.20)	28.1	(2.93)	37.4	(2.67)	31.5	(3.14)	1.7	(0.72)
Other 4-year	318	(43.1)	75.4	(5.15)	9.6	(4.26)	3.6	(2.25)	1.8	(0.87)	33.7	(4.41)	43.5	(4.90)	40.9	(5.47)	0.1	(0.15)
Doctor's degree	192	(11.1)	72.2	(1.28)	29.0	(1.60)	15.2	(1.11)	33.4	(1.66)	19.9	(1.64)	22.5	(1.46)	18.0	(1.36)	1.5	(0.29)
Public	122	(5.5)	74.4	(1.17)	34.5	(1.49)	21.0	(1.32)	42.2	(1.32)	17.3	(1.02)	18.2	(1.22)	13.5	(1.15)	1.9	(0.40)
Private	70	(8.7)	68.3	(3.35)	19.2	(2.35)	4.9	(1.10)	17.9	(2.37)	24.3	(4.13)	30.0	(3.57)	25.9	(3.33)	0.8	(0.37)
First-professional	69	(12.1)	75.4	(3.94)	34.6	(6.42)	3.5	(1.70)	6.5	(1.67)	13.2	(2.65)	52.8	(6.17)	46.6	(5.74)	6.1	(1.83)
Public	14	(1.8)	79.2	(5.05)	28.9	(6.70)	7.2	(3.25)	8.3	(3.65)	9.4	(3.26)	64.4	(5.91)	49.6	(6.77)	20.5	(3.71)
Private	56	(12.1)	74.4	(4.81)	36.0	(7.90)	2.5	(1.89)	6.1	(1.98)	14.1	(3.24)	49.9	(7.56)	45.8	(7.07)	2.6	(1.42)
Other graduate	321	(28.6)	51.2	(2.31)	7.2	(1.38)	3.0	(0.63)	5.1	(0.87)	25.7	(2.55)	20.0	(2.69)	17.3	(2.59)	1.0	(0.39)

—Not available.
†Not applicable.
[1]Numbers of part-time or part-year postbaccalaureate students may not equal figures reported in other tables, since these data are based on a sample survey of all postbaccalaureate students enrolled at any time during the school year.
[2]Includes students who reported they were awarded aid, but did not specify the source of aid.
[3]Includes students who received teaching or research assistantships and/or participated in work-study programs.
[4]Formerly Guaranteed Student Loans (GSL).
[5]Formerly National Direct Student Loans (NDSL).

[6]Fellowship estimates for 1992–93 and 1995–96 were based primarily on information provided by institutions and are not comparable to data for 1999–2000 or 2003–04, which were based on information provided by both students and institutions.
NOTE: Excludes students whose attendance status was not reported. Totals include some students whose level of study or control of institution was unknown. Data include Puerto Rico. Detail may not sum to totals because of rounding and because some students receive aid from multiple sources. Standard errors appear in parentheses.
SOURCE: U.S. Department of Education, National Center for Education Statistics, 1992–93, 1995–96, 1999–2000, and 2003–04 National Postsecondary Student Aid Studies (NPSAS:93, NPSAS:96, NPSAS:2000, and NPSAS:04). (This table was prepared September 2005.)

Table 348. Current-fund revenue of degree-granting institutions, by source of funds: Selected years, 1919–20 through 1995–96

[In thousands of current dollars]

		Current-fund revenue, by source of funds									
Year	Total	Student tuition and fees[1]	Federal government[2]	State governments[3]	Local governments	Endowment earnings	Private gifts and grants[4]	Sales and services of educational activities	Auxiliary enterprises	Hospitals[5]	Other current income
1	2	3	4	5	6	7	8	9	10	11	12
Institutions of higher education[6]											
1919–20	$199,922	$42,255	$12,783	$61,690	(7)	$26,482	$7,584	—	$26,993	—	$22,135
1929–30	554,511	144,126	20,658	150,847	(7)	68,605	26,172	—	60,419	—	83,684
1939–40	715,211	200,897	38,860	151,222	$24,392	71,304	40,453	$32,777	143,923	—	11,383
1949–50	2,374,645	394,610	524,319	491,636	61,700	96,341	118,627	111,987	511,265	—	64,160
1959–60	5,785,537	1,157,482	1,036,990	1,374,476	151,715	206,619	382,569	102,525	1,004,283	$187,769	181,110
1969–70	21,515,242	4,419,845	4,130,066	5,873,626	778,162	516,038	1,129,438	612,777	2,900,390	619,578	535,323
1975–76	39,703,166	8,171,942	6,477,178	12,260,885	1,616,975	687,470	1,917,036	645,420	4,547,622	2,494,340	884,298
1976–77	43,436,827	9,024,932	7,169,031	13,285,684	1,626,908	764,788	2,105,070	779,058	4,919,602	2,859,376	902,377
1977–78	47,034,032	9,855,270	6,968,501	14,746,166	1,744,230	832,286	2,320,368	882,715	5,327,821	3,268,956	1,087,719
1978–79	51,837,789	10,704,171	7,851,326	16,363,784	1,573,018	985,242	2,489,366	1,037,130	5,741,309	3,763,453	1,328,991
1979–80	58,519,982	11,930,340	8,902,844	18,378,299	1,587,552	1,176,627	2,808,075	1,239,439	6,481,458	4,373,384	1,641,965
1980–81	65,584,789	13,773,259	9,747,586	20,106,222	1,790,740	1,364,443	3,176,670	1,409,730	7,287,290	4,980,346	1,948,503
1981–82	72,190,856	15,774,038	9,591,805	21,848,791	1,937,669	1,596,813	3,563,558	1,582,922	8,121,611	5,838,565	2,335,084
1982–83	77,595,726	17,776,041	9,631,097	23,065,636	2,031,353	1,720,677	4,052,649	1,723,484	8,769,521	6,531,562	2,293,706
1983–84	84,417,287	19,714,884	10,406,166	24,706,990	2,192,275	1,873,945	4,415,275	1,970,747	9,456,369	7,040,662	2,639,973
1984–85	92,472,694	21,283,329	11,509,125	27,583,011	2,387,212	2,096,298	4,896,325	2,126,927	10,100,410	7,474,575	3,015,483
1985–86	100,437,616	23,116,605	12,704,750	29,911,500	2,544,506	2,275,898	5,410,905	2,373,494	10,674,136	8,226,635	3,199,186
1986–87	108,809,827	25,705,827	13,904,049	31,309,303	2,799,321	2,377,958	5,952,682	2,641,906	11,364,188	9,277,834	3,476,760
1987–88	117,340,109	27,836,781	14,771,954	33,517,166	3,006,263	2,586,441	6,359,282	2,918,090	11,947,778	10,626,566	3,769,787
1988–89	128,501,638	30,806,566	15,893,978	36,031,208	3,363,676	2,914,396	7,060,730	3,315,620	12,855,580	11,991,265	4,268,618
1989–90	139,635,477	33,926,060	17,254,874	38,349,239	3,639,902	3,143,696	7,781,422	3,632,100	13,938,469	13,216,664	4,753,051
1990–91	149,766,051	37,434,462	18,236,082	39,480,874	3,931,239	3,268,629	8,361,265	4,054,703	14,903,127	15,149,672	4,945,998
1991–92	161,395,896	41,559,037	19,833,317	40,586,907	4,159,876	3,442,009	8,977,271	4,520,890	15,758,599	17,240,338	5,317,651
1992–93	170,880,503	45,346,071	21,014,564	41,247,955	4,444,875	3,627,773	9,659,977	5,037,901	16,662,850	18,124,015	5,714,523
1993–94	179,226,601	48,646,538	22,076,385	41,910,288	4,998,306	3,669,536	10,203,062	5,294,030	17,537,514	18,959,776	5,931,167
1994–95	189,120,570	51,506,876	23,243,172	44,343,012	5,165,961	3,988,217	10,866,749	5,603,251	18,336,094	19,100,217	6,967,023
1995–96	197,414,848	54,725,982	23,879,098	45,621,627	5,589,988	4,570,933	11,942,987	5,552,907	18,861,585	18,672,680	7,997,061
Degree-granting institutions											
1995–96	197,973,236	55,260,293	23,939,075	45,692,673	5,607,909	4,562,171	11,903,126	5,530,763	18,867,540	18,611,570	7,998,116

—Not available.

[1]Tuition and fees received from veterans under Public Law 550 are reported under student fees and are not under income from the federal government.
[2]Federally supported student aid that is received through students is included under tuition and auxiliary enterprises.
[3]Includes federal aid received through state channels and regional compacts, through 1959–60.
[4]Beginning in 1969–70, the private grants also include nongovernmental revenue for sponsored research, student aid, and other sponsored programs.
[5]Prior to 1959–60, data for hospitals are included under sales and services of educational activities.
[6]Institutions that were accredited by an agency or association that was recognized by the U.S. Department of Education, or recognized directly by the Secretary of Education.
[7]Income from state and local governments tabulated under "State governments."

NOTE: Degree-granting institutions grant associate's or higher degrees and participate in Title IV federal financial aid programs. The degree-granting classification is very similar to the earlier higher education classification, but it includes more 2-year colleges and excludes a few higher education institutions that did not grant degrees. (See Guide to Sources for details.) Data for years prior to 1969–70 are not entirely comparable with data for later years. Also, some details for 1969–70 are not directly comparable with data for later years. Detail may not sum to totals because of rounding.
SOURCE: U.S. Department of Education, National Center for Education Statistics, Annual Report of the Commissioner of Education, 1919–20; Biennial Survey of Education in the United States, 1929–30 through 1959–60; Higher Education General Information Survey (HEGIS), "Financial Statistics of Institutions of Higher Education," 1969–70 through 1985–86; and 1986–87 through 1995–96 Integrated Postsecondary Education Data System, "Finance Survey" (IPEDS-F:FY86–96). (This table was prepared October 1998.)

Table 349. Current-fund revenue of public degree-granting institutions, by source of funds: Selected years, 1980–81 through 2000–01

Source	1980–81	1985–86	1990–91	1995–96	1996–97	1997–98	1998–99[1]	1999–2000	2000–01
1	2	3	4	5	6	7	8	9	10
	In thousands of current dollars								
Total current-fund revenue....	$43,195,617	$65,004,632	$94,904,506	$123,501,152	$129,504,834	$137,570,935	$144,969,708	$157,313,664	$176,645,215
Tuition and fees...................	5,570,404	9,439,177	15,258,024	23,257,454	24,631,120	26,058,092	27,427,984	29,125,603	31,919,611
Federal government................	5,540,101	6,852,370	9,763,427	13,672,467	14,189,358	14,544,027	15,554,372	16,952,116	19,744,966
Appropriations...................	1,128,101	1,401,367	1,604,548	1,826,738	1,830,604	1,570,329	1,679,660	1,583,132	1,719,963
Unrestricted grants and contracts	529,424	816,364	1,319,035	1,996,861	1,912,736	2,049,105	2,254,726	(2)	(2)
Restricted grants and contracts[3]..	3,812,197	4,481,723	6,629,484	9,598,340	10,173,113	10,586,439	11,287,950	14,819,488	17,088,332
Independent operations (FFRDC)[4]...............	70,379	152,916	210,360	250,529	272,906	338,154	332,037	549,496	936,671
State governments	19,675,968	29,220,586	38,239,978	44,242,546	46,113,543	49,114,782	52,132,474	56,369,564	62,895,892
Appropriations..................	19,006,716	28,071,070	35,898,653	40,081,437	42,026,368	44,737,656	47,369,188	50,818,832	56,268,990
Unrestricted grants and contracts	45,390	88,779	250,168	924,837	690,665	498,485	497,396	(2)	(2)
Restricted grants and contracts ...	623,863	1,060,737	2,091,157	3,236,272	3,396,510	3,878,641	4,265,889	5,550,732	6,626,902
Local governments	1,622,938	2,325,844	3,531,714	5,074,511	5,019,600	5,279,349	5,546,546	6,039,978	7,052,431
Appropriations..................	1,478,001	2,150,459	3,159,789	4,397,098	4,348,960	4,594,289	4,792,860	5,217,976	5,582,287
Unrestricted grants and contracts	9,915	27,852	73,281	184,597	193,262	226,024	275,326	(2)	(2)
Restricted grants and contracts ...	135,022	147,533	298,644	492,815	477,377	459,036	478,360	822,003	1,470,144
Private gifts, grants, and contracts...	1,100,084	2,109,782	3,651,107	5,089,344	5,584,198	6,123,038	6,752,392	7,488,781	8,948,322
Unrestricted	110,462	279,381	529,496	784,979	900,449	993,528	1,127,013	—	—
Restricted........................	989,622	1,830,401	3,121,611	4,304,365	4,683,749	5,129,511	5,625,378	—	—
Endowment income	214,561	398,603	431,235	721,079	784,695	887,093	958,363	1,170,163	1,351,989
Unrestricted	102,888	181,624	147,368	304,860	299,237	330,570	331,074	—	—
Restricted........................	111,673	216,979	283,867	416,219	485,458	556,523	627,288	—	—
Sales and services	8,455,449	12,990,670	21,546,202	27,399,796	28,851,838	30,491,654	31,595,145	33,982,146	38,250,128
Educational activities	943,737	1,596,946	2,700,185	3,528,610	3,888,767	4,142,825	4,559,546	4,817,258	4,988,373
Auxiliary enterprises	4,614,561	6,684,794	9,058,745	11,595,408	12,280,517	13,070,055	13,775,599	15,174,301	16,501,834
Hospitals...................	2,897,151	4,708,930	9,787,271	12,275,778	12,682,554	13,278,773	13,260,000	13,990,587	16,759,921
Other sources	1,016,110	1,667,600	2,482,819	4,043,955	4,330,483	5,072,901	5,002,432	6,185,313	6,401,070
	Percentage distribution								
Total current-fund revenue....	100.0	100.0	100.0	100.0	100.0	100.0	100.0	100.0	100.0
Tuition and fees...................	12.9	14.5	16.1	18.8	19.0	18.9	18.9	18.5	18.1
Federal government................	12.8	10.5	10.3	11.1	11.0	10.6	10.7	10.8	11.2
Appropriations...................	2.6	2.2	1.7	1.5	1.4	1.1	1.2	1.0	1.0
Unrestricted grants and contracts	1.2	1.3	1.4	1.6	1.5	1.5	1.6	(2)	(2)
Restricted grants and contracts[3]..	8.8	6.9	7.0	7.8	7.9	7.7	7.8	9.4	9.7
Independent operations (FFRDC)[4]...............	0.2	0.2	0.2	0.2	0.2	0.2	0.2	0.3	0.5
State governments	45.6	45.0	40.3	35.8	35.6	35.7	36.0	35.8	35.6
Appropriations..................	44.0	43.2	37.8	32.5	32.5	32.5	32.7	32.3	31.9
Unrestricted grants and contracts	0.1	0.1	0.3	0.7	0.5	0.4	0.3	(2)	(2)
Restricted grants and contracts ...	1.4	1.6	2.2	2.6	2.6	2.8	2.9	3.5	3.8
Local governments	3.8	3.6	3.7	4.1	3.9	3.8	3.8	3.8	4.0
Appropriations..................	3.4	3.3	3.3	3.6	3.4	3.3	3.3	3.3	3.2
Unrestricted grants and contracts	#	#	0.1	0.1	0.1	0.2	0.2	(2)	(2)
Restricted grants and contracts ...	0.3	0.2	0.3	0.4	0.4	0.3	0.3	0.5	0.8
Private gifts, grants, and contracts...	2.5	3.2	3.8	4.1	4.3	4.5	4.7	4.8	5.1
Unrestricted	0.3	0.4	0.6	0.6	0.7	0.7	0.8	—	—
Restricted........................	2.3	2.8	3.3	3.5	3.6	3.7	3.9	—	—
Endowment income	0.5	0.6	0.5	0.6	0.6	0.6	0.7	0.7	0.8
Unrestricted	0.2	0.3	0.2	0.2	0.2	0.2	0.2	—	—
Restricted........................	0.3	0.3	0.3	0.3	0.4	0.4	0.4	—	—
Sales and services	19.6	20.0	22.7	22.2	22.3	22.2	21.8	21.6	21.7
Educational activities	2.2	2.5	2.8	2.9	3.0	3.0	3.1	3.1	2.8
Auxiliary enterprises	10.7	10.3	9.5	9.4	9.5	9.5	9.5	9.6	9.3
Hospitals...................	6.7	7.2	10.3	9.9	9.8	9.7	9.1	8.9	9.5
Other sources	2.4	2.6	2.6	3.3	3.3	3.7	3.5	3.9	3.7

—Not available.
#Rounds to zero.
[1]Data were imputed using alternative procedures. (See Guide to Sources for details.)
[2]Included under restricted grants and contracts.
[3]Excludes Pell Grants. Federally supported student aid that is received through students is included under tuition and auxiliary enterprises.
[4]Generally includes only those revenues associated with major federally funded research and development centers (FFRDC).
NOTE: Data through 1990–91 are for institutions of higher education, while later data are for degree-granting institutions. Degree-granting institutions grant associate's or higher degrees

and participate in Title IV federal financial aid programs. The degree-granting classification is very similar to the earlier higher education classification, but it includes more 2-year colleges and excludes a few higher education institutions that did not grant degrees. (See Guide to Sources for details.) Detail may not sum to totals because of rounding.
SOURCE: U.S. Department of Education, National Center for Education Statistics, Higher Education General Information Survey (HEGIS), "Financial Statistics of Institutions of Higher Education," 1980–81 and 1985–86 surveys; and 1990–91 through 2000–01 Integrated Postsecondary Education Data System, "Finance Survey" (IPEDS-F:FY91–00), and Spring 2001 and Spring 2002. (This table was prepared October 2003.)

Table 350. Revenues of public degree-granting institutions, by source of revenue and type of institution: 2003–04, 2004–05, and 2005–06

Type of institution and year	Total revenues	Tuition and fees[1]	Grants and contracts — Total	Federal (excludes Federal Direct Student Loans)	State	Local	Sales and services of auxiliary enterprises[2]	Sales and services of hospitals	Independent operations	Other operating revenues
1	2	3	4	5	6	7	8	9	10	11
				In thousands of current dollars						
All institutions										
2003–04	$221,921,288	$35,150,615	$42,553,845	$28,881,888	$6,585,978	$7,085,979	$16,989,172	$19,587,282	$918,775	$13,478,024
2004–05	234,841,504	38,525,657	44,376,325	30,070,996	6,818,048	7,487,280	17,672,780	21,771,547	590,166	13,830,102
2005–06	246,164,836	41,770,600	45,147,837	30,333,948	7,207,813	7,606,076	18,786,806	22,100,555	635,607	14,483,979
4-year										
2003–04	182,008,588	28,739,354	35,501,531	24,154,274	4,838,356	6,508,901	15,196,430	19,587,282	914,221	12,635,272
2004–05	193,796,724	31,669,001	37,319,268	25,330,597	5,098,257	6,890,414	15,884,386	21,771,547	590,166	13,136,414
2005–06	202,511,496	34,506,560	37,991,199	25,583,341	5,383,780	7,024,078	16,945,544	22,100,555	635,607	13,753,422
2-year										
2003–04	39,912,699	6,411,261	7,052,314	4,727,614	1,747,622	577,078	1,792,742	0	4,554	842,752
2004–05	41,044,779	6,856,656	7,057,057	4,740,399	1,719,792	596,866	1,788,394	0	0	693,689
2005–06	43,653,340	7,264,040	7,156,638	4,750,607	1,824,034	581,998	1,841,262	0	0	730,557
				Percentage distribution						
All institutions										
2003–04	100.00	15.84	19.18	13.01	2.97	3.19	7.66	8.83	0.41	6.07
2004–05	100.00	16.40	18.90	12.80	2.90	3.19	7.53	9.27	0.25	5.89
2005–06	100.00	16.97	18.34	12.32	2.93	3.09	7.63	8.98	0.26	5.88
4-year										
2003–04	100.00	15.79	19.51	13.27	2.66	3.58	8.35	10.76	0.50	6.94
2004–05	100.00	16.34	19.26	13.07	2.63	3.56	8.20	11.23	0.30	6.78
2005–06	100.00	17.04	18.76	12.63	2.66	3.47	8.37	10.91	0.31	6.79
2-year										
2003–04	100.00	16.06	17.67	11.84	4.38	1.45	4.49	0.00	0.01	2.11
2004–05	100.00	16.71	17.19	11.55	4.19	1.45	4.36	0.00	0.00	1.69
2005–06	100.00	16.64	16.39	10.88	4.18	1.33	4.22	0.00	0.00	1.67
				Revenue per full-time-equivalent student in current dollars						
All institutions										
2003–04	$24,016	$3,804	$4,605	$3,126	$713	$767	$1,839	$2,120	$99	$1,459
2004–05	25,122	4,121	4,747	3,217	729	801	1,891	2,329	63	1,479
2005–06	26,215	4,448	4,808	3,230	768	810	2,001	2,354	68	1,542
4-year										
2003–04	32,749	5,171	6,388	4,346	871	1,171	2,734	3,524	164	2,273
2004–05	34,357	5,614	6,616	4,491	904	1,222	2,816	3,860	105	2,329
2005–06	35,353	6,024	6,632	4,466	940	1,226	2,958	3,858	111	2,401
2-year										
2003–04	10,837	1,741	1,915	1,284	475	157	487	0	1	229
2004–05	11,071	1,849	1,903	1,279	464	161	482	0	0	187
2005–06	11,921	1,984	1,954	1,297	498	159	503	0	0	200
				Revenue per full-time-equivalent student in constant 2006–07 dollars[3]						
All institutions										
2003–04	$26,344	$4,173	$5,052	$3,429	$782	$841	$2,017	$2,325	$109	$1,600
2004–05	26,753	4,389	5,055	3,426	777	853	2,013	2,480	67	1,576
2005–06	26,893	4,563	4,932	3,314	787	831	2,052	2,414	69	1,582
4-year										
2003–04	35,925	5,673	7,007	4,768	955	1,285	2,999	3,866	180	2,494
2004–05	36,588	5,979	7,046	4,782	963	1,301	2,999	4,110	111	2,480
2005–06	36,267	6,180	6,804	4,582	964	1,258	3,035	3,958	114	2,463
2-year										
2003–04	11,888	1,910	2,100	1,408	521	172	534	0	1	251
2004–05	11,790	1,970	2,027	1,362	494	171	514	0	0	199
2005–06	12,229	2,035	2,005	1,331	511	163	516	0	0	205

See notes at end of table.

Table 350. Revenues of public degree-granting institutions, by source of revenue and type of institution: 2003–04, 2004–05, and 2005–06—Continued

Type of institution and year	Nonoperating revenues									Other revenues and additions			
	Appropriations			Nonoperating grants			Gifts	Investment income	Other	Capital appropriations	Capital grants and gifts	Additions to permanent endowments	Other
	Federal	State	Local	Federal	State	Local							
1	12	13	14	15	16	17	18	19	20	21	22	23	24
	In thousands of current dollars												
All institutions													
2003–04	$1,605,958	$53,888,233	$7,707,966	$2,565,883	$942,960	$94,400	$4,191,696	$7,164,011	$3,050,039	$4,808,048	$3,149,016	$995,144	$3,080,221
2004–05	1,783,826	55,324,918	7,687,161	2,873,484	945,643	100,139	4,605,829	9,522,937	2,673,544	4,693,914	3,169,179	886,885	3,807,469
2005–06	1,858,625	58,720,088	8,249,690	2,811,434	1,177,322	102,497	4,975,616	9,597,624	2,705,351	5,421,660	2,568,688	1,004,691	4,046,166
4-year													
2003–04	1,473,410	42,504,491	230,203	1,245,113	313,215	27,821	3,956,515	6,936,235	2,714,320	3,438,251	2,672,009	987,743	2,935,172
2004–05	1,635,613	43,165,057	298,771	1,548,299	436,316	30,828	4,328,996	9,105,619	2,322,082	3,303,568	2,742,551	866,193	3,642,049
2005–06	1,720,108	45,591,539	336,424	1,546,322	613,928	33,269	4,713,701	8,927,767	2,330,293	3,680,390	2,250,167	986,771	3,847,930
2-year													
2003–04	132,548	11,383,743	7,477,762	1,320,769	629,745	66,579	235,181	227,777	335,719	1,369,797	477,008	7,401	145,049
2004–05	148,213	12,159,862	7,388,390	1,325,185	509,327	69,311	276,832	417,318	351,463	1,390,345	426,627	20,692	165,419
2005–06	138,517	13,128,549	7,913,266	1,265,113	563,394	69,228	261,914	669,858	375,058	1,741,270	318,521	17,920	198,236
	Percentage distribution												
All institutions													
2003–04	0.72	24.28	3.47	1.16	0.42	0.04	1.89	3.23	1.37	2.17	1.42	0.45	1.39
2004–05	0.76	23.56	3.27	1.22	0.40	0.04	1.96	4.06	1.14	2.00	1.35	0.38	1.62
2005–06	0.76	23.85	3.35	1.14	0.48	0.04	2.02	3.90	1.10	2.20	1.04	0.41	1.64
4-year													
2003–04	0.81	23.35	0.13	0.68	0.17	0.02	2.17	3.81	1.49	1.89	1.47	0.54	1.61
2004–05	0.84	22.27	0.15	0.80	0.23	0.02	2.23	4.70	1.20	1.70	1.42	0.45	1.88
2005–06	0.85	22.51	0.17	0.76	0.30	0.02	2.33	4.41	1.15	1.82	1.11	0.49	1.90
2-year													
2003–04	0.33	28.52	18.74	3.31	1.58	0.17	0.59	0.57	0.84	3.43	1.20	0.02	0.36
2004–05	0.36	29.63	18.00	3.23	1.24	0.17	0.67	1.02	0.86	3.39	1.04	0.05	0.40
2005–06	0.32	30.07	18.13	2.90	1.29	0.16	0.60	1.53	0.86	3.99	0.73	0.04	0.45
	Revenue per full-time-equivalent student in current dollars												
All institutions													
2003–04	$174	$5,832	$834	$278	$102	$10	$454	$775	$330	$520	$341	$108	$333
2004–05	191	5,918	822	307	101	11	493	1,019	286	502	339	95	407
2005–06	198	6,253	879	299	125	11	530	1,022	288	577	274	107	431
4-year													
2003–04	265	7,648	41	224	56	5	712	1,248	488	619	481	178	528
2004–05	290	7,652	53	274	77	5	767	1,614	412	586	486	154	646
2005–06	300	7,959	59	270	107	6	823	1,559	407	642	393	172	672
2-year													
2003–04	36	3,091	2,030	359	171	18	64	62	91	372	130	2	39
2004–05	40	3,280	1,993	357	137	19	75	113	95	375	115	6	45
2005–06	38	3,585	2,161	345	154	19	72	183	102	476	87	5	54
	Revenue per full-time-equivalent student in constant 2006–07 dollars[3]												
All institutions													
2003–04	$191	$6,397	$915	$305	$112	$11	$498	$850	$362	$571	$374	$118	$366
2004–05	203	6,303	876	327	108	11	525	1,085	305	535	361	101	434
2005–06	203	6,415	901	307	129	11	544	1,049	296	592	281	110	442
4-year													
2003–04	291	8,390	45	246	62	5	781	1,369	536	679	527	195	579
2004–05	309	8,149	56	292	82	6	817	1,719	438	624	518	164	688
2005–06	308	8,165	60	277	110	6	844	1,599	417	659	403	177	689
2-year													
2003–04	39	3,391	2,227	393	188	20	70	68	100	408	142	2	43
2004–05	43	3,493	2,122	381	146	20	80	120	101	399	123	6	48
2005–06	39	3,678	2,217	354	158	19	73	188	105	488	89	5	56

[1]Net of allowances and discounts.
[2]After deducting discounts and allowances.
[3]Constant dollars based on the Consumer Price Index, prepared by the Bureau of Labor Statistics, U.S. Department of Labor, adjusted to a school-year basis.
NOTE: Degree-granting institutions grant associate's or higher degrees and participate in Title IV federal financial aid programs. Includes data for public institutions reporting data according to the Financial Accounting Standards Board (FASB) questionnaire. Detail may not sum to totals because of rounding.
SOURCE: U.S. Department of Education, National Center for Education Statistics, 2003–04 through 2005–06 Integrated Postsecondary Education Data System, Spring 2004 through Spring 2007. (This table was prepared May 2008.)

Table 351. Revenues of public degree-granting institutions, by source of revenue and state or jurisdiction: 2005–06

[In thousands of current dollars]

State or jurisdiction	Total revenues	Operating revenue							Nonoperating revenue[1]			Other revenues and additions
		Total	Tuition and fees[2]	Federal grants and contracts	State and local grants and contracts	Sales and services of auxiliary enterprises[3]	Sales and services of hospitals	Independent operations and other	Total	State appropriations	Local appropriations	
1	2	3	4	5	6	7	8	9	10	11	12	13
United States	$246,164,836	$142,925,383	$41,770,600	$30,333,948	$14,813,889	$18,786,806	$22,100,555	$15,119,585	$90,198,247	$58,720,088	$8,249,690	$13,041,206
Alabama	5,256,045	3,371,497	844,301	843,104	220,531	279,991	977,421	206,148	1,692,726	1,302,342	733	191,822
Alaska	661,224	345,008	79,586	147,224	64,318	38,086	0	15,793	285,676	252,512	0	30,541
Arizona	3,958,802	2,005,713	809,863	647,512	154,950	298,471	0	94,917	1,894,842	1,015,117	562,474	58,247
Arkansas	2,647,070	1,653,833	301,646	213,367	139,000	158,189	635,435	206,196	913,835	639,745	23,269	79,402
California	36,714,487	21,526,641	3,498,033	4,009,877	2,339,766	2,606,122	4,205,635	4,867,208	12,830,101	8,275,470	2,218,323	2,357,745
Colorado	3,705,780	3,308,243	1,124,660	873,848	449,640	349,832	243,169	267,093	307,494	15,436	54,422	90,044
Connecticut	2,576,921	1,433,426	417,891	204,103	73,359	179,127	226,828	332,118	968,928	814,255	0	174,567
Delaware	990,433	508,503	259,435	112,164	30,231	87,001	0	19,672	465,486	218,634	0	16,445
District of Columbia ...	125,921	49,008	17,087	16,005	10,901	1,832	0	3,182	72,377	6,554	61,266	4,537
Florida	8,369,970	3,510,513	1,220,462	842,093	751,704	536,148	0	160,106	4,130,654	3,186,756	0	728,804
Georgia	5,216,995	2,825,904	905,343	748,003	386,048	464,221	181,146	141,144	2,166,481	1,959,504	0	224,610
Hawaii	1,262,700	564,296	124,074	299,582	50,585	70,330	0	19,725	549,318	430,451	0	149,087
Idaho	941,193	519,745	182,526	148,629	68,086	84,358	0	36,147	394,850	338,143	7,633	26,598
Illinois	8,485,386	4,593,800	1,479,219	796,056	327,307	720,249	408,406	862,563	3,667,287	1,602,641	768,509	224,298
Indiana	5,080,474	3,263,119	1,378,286	629,657	307,671	651,618	0	295,887	1,696,609	1,338,901	7,379	120,745
Iowa	3,739,770	2,632,767	559,891	549,567	128,314	334,590	761,623	298,781	1,069,596	798,961	73,502	37,407
Kansas	2,668,490	1,508,051	529,496	374,430	114,691	242,487	0	246,947	1,126,968	725,777	211,593	33,470
Kentucky	4,052,056	2,587,954	574,560	558,049	321,542	208,285	805,475	120,043	1,309,854	1,014,939	12,035	154,248
Louisiana	3,509,240	2,117,246	554,601	498,726	363,478	252,569	356,279	91,594	1,230,623	1,084,984	0	161,371
Maine	748,611	429,484	158,923	71,926	63,108	89,194	0	46,333	289,485	231,890	0	29,643
Maryland	4,730,625	2,889,255	1,112,550	678,832	355,986	474,943	0	266,945	1,606,359	1,078,966	253,486	235,010
Massachusetts	3,425,348	2,209,946	764,681	416,603	211,063	269,642	0	547,956	1,146,846	1,039,187	0	68,556
Michigan	11,627,260	7,509,605	2,412,101	1,415,120	425,822	851,302	1,990,453	414,806	3,808,565	1,771,921	535,401	309,091
Minnesota	4,078,160	2,373,958	995,875	543,739	293,938	377,374	0	163,033	1,546,106	1,194,106	0	158,095
Mississippi	3,080,043	1,861,148	349,637	600,873	177,700	185,265	435,612	112,061	1,055,408	774,001	57,539	163,486
Missouri	3,771,158	2,380,012	743,569	322,435	125,512	502,961	517,620	167,915	1,305,920	868,899	128,638	85,227
Montana	842,226	567,552	201,648	177,201	33,536	91,411	0	63,757	261,555	154,770	6,283	13,119
Nebraska	1,749,476	907,064	255,916	190,696	157,710	210,547	20,626	71,569	801,881	532,258	78,470	40,531
Nevada	1,439,438	618,445	219,833	175,294	72,528	85,414	0	65,376	636,350	524,701	0	184,643
New Hampshire	764,240	544,616	244,305	100,395	30,958	141,347	0	27,611	166,911	114,557	0	52,714
New Jersey	5,758,609	3,580,380	1,276,662	577,629	453,458	420,790	722,364	129,476	2,052,341	1,644,413	195,502	125,888
New Mexico	2,652,189	1,501,927	181,287	505,014	155,323	111,756	410,664	137,884	1,005,613	679,588	92,644	144,649
New York	11,272,621	6,076,983	1,781,602	990,477	1,056,031	679,297	1,430,623	138,953	4,697,371	3,500,566	622,550	498,267
North Carolina	7,730,710	3,275,838	1,008,521	811,659	282,806	1,067,770	0	105,082	3,825,049	2,815,090	156,171	629,823
North Dakota	786,473	539,791	200,722	165,814	47,945	80,928	0	44,382	234,915	195,040	1,786	11,767
Ohio	9,801,575	6,606,115	2,431,028	892,464	526,082	776,285	1,639,400	340,856	2,843,732	1,848,717	126,530	351,729
Oklahoma	2,982,104	1,765,569	491,829	371,987	229,393	343,273	0	329,087	1,027,693	782,847	38,081	188,842
Oregon	3,977,502	2,731,702	691,349	673,995	225,822	237,295	724,917	178,325	1,167,698	657,011	161,438	78,102
Pennsylvania	9,510,266	6,889,957	2,521,886	1,111,292	367,869	709,855	1,745,447	433,609	2,549,920	1,371,792	111,721	70,389
Rhode Island	580,204	366,358	176,396	72,053	21,160	75,282	0	21,467	183,668	172,703	0	30,178
South Carolina	3,139,056	2,048,465	820,922	485,532	279,364	269,635	0	193,012	918,059	715,967	50,592	172,533
South Dakota	532,418	345,533	130,059	98,541	36,875	45,478	0	34,581	166,550	153,928	0	20,335
Tennessee	3,346,499	1,555,610	662,454	274,470	276,346	216,037	0	126,303	1,612,101	1,081,753	4,326	178,788
Texas	22,135,206	10,064,032	2,878,437	2,667,629	1,332,172	892,479	1,103,220	1,190,094	9,175,373	4,658,611	971,351	2,895,802
Utah	3,396,432	2,434,763	401,457	419,567	135,911	147,244	821,704	508,880	825,302	669,271	0	136,367
Vermont	627,789	485,877	231,033	113,878	46,843	72,242	0	21,881	131,252	63,740	0	10,660
Virginia	6,662,436	4,097,222	1,344,645	832,134	172,912	760,774	836,616	150,141	2,147,415	1,482,002	1,934	417,800
Washington	6,387,160	3,875,686	923,224	1,023,050	455,849	392,272	796,846	284,445	2,024,891	1,315,804	33	486,583
West Virginia	1,371,117	869,993	332,836	197,945	137,510	152,227	0	49,476	390,395	355,870	0	110,729
Wisconsin	4,906,643	2,704,510	911,289	689,770	294,605	370,170	0	438,676	2,014,737	1,019,374	621,514	187,396
Wyoming	541,092	211,826	51,851	58,164	27,774	43,688	0	30,349	305,866	229,620	32,562	23,400
U.S. Service Academies	1,847,193	280,896	1,111	95,773	1,858	79,126	103,027	0	1,499,219	0	0	67,078
Other jurisdictions	1,554,673	413,988	81,440	186,557	44,467	16,744	49,647	35,133	1,120,549	913,597	45,878	20,136
American Samoa	9,716	5,345	1,334	3,757	0	254	0	0	4,370	0	0	0
Federated States of Micronesia	18,010	12,871	512	10,410	121	959	0	870	5,138	0	0	0
Guam	97,455	46,916	10,738	24,760	2,554	2,844	0	6,020	48,695	29,684	13,827	1,844
Marshall Islands	7,718	3,460	172	2,866	79	343	0	0	3,258	0	2,000	1,000
Northern Marianas ...	16,217	8,722	1,108	5,250	0	0	0	2,364	7,495	7,270	0	0
Palau	9,385	6,508	1,704	3,596	391	744	0	74	2,877	2,385	0	0
Puerto Rico	1,330,120	298,420	55,956	120,941	39,508	6,828	49,647	25,540	1,017,600	874,258	2,996	14,099
U.S. Virgin Islands	66,053	31,745	9,916	14,978	1,814	4,773	0	264	31,116	0	27,055	3,192

[1]Includes other categories not separately shown.
[2]Net of allowances and discounts.
[3]After deducting discounts and allowances.
NOTE: Degree-granting institutions grant associate's or higher degrees and participate in Title IV federal financial aid programs. Includes data for public institutions reporting data according to the Financial Accounting Standards Board (FASB) questionnaire. Detail may not sum to totals because of rounding.
SOURCE: U.S. Department of Education, National Center for Education Statistics, 2005–06 Integrated Postsecondary Education Data System, Spring 2007. (This table was prepared May 2008.)

Table 352. Appropriations from state and local governments for public degree-granting institutions, by state or jurisdiction: Selected years, 1990–91 through 2005–06

[In thousands of current dollars]

State or jurisdiction	State appropriations						Local appropriations					
	1990–91	1995–96	2000–01	2003–04	2004–05	2005–06	1990–91	1995–96	2000–01	2003–04	2004–05	2005–06
1	2	3	4	5	6	7	8	9	10	11	12	13
United States	$35,898,653	$40,081,437	$56,268,990	$53,888,233	$55,324,918	$58,720,088	$3,159,789	$4,397,098	$5,582,287	$7,707,966	$7,687,161	$8,249,690
Alabama	708,191	879,680	991,302	1,095,040	1,132,482	1,302,342	6,796	4,736	4,829	712	667	733
Alaska	168,395	171,580	190,650	217,745	232,868	252,512	260	693	10,340	5,800	0	0
Arizona	591,656	691,335	903,196	888,236	953,653	1,015,117	149,337	217,426	310,762	476,381	498,031	562,474
Arkansas	315,372	437,257	583,794	585,078	601,070	639,745	216	2,524	9,496	20,238	21,810	23,269
California	5,313,052	4,811,297	7,891,669	7,405,508	7,583,950	8,275,470	771,160	1,353,630	1,764,717	2,402,519	2,104,325	2,218,323
Colorado	423,710	497,663	655,037	494,764	494,773	15,436	22,400	28,786	36,840	42,052	46,673	54,422
Connecticut	363,427	462,183	664,356	718,291	770,317	814,255	0	0	0	0	0	0
Delaware	115,729	107,968	193,695	193,911	208,568	218,634	0	12,379	0	0	0	0
District of Columbia ...	0	0	3,019	4,139	5,237	6,554	73,495	68,257	46,933	50,861	51,581	61,266
Florida	1,638,218	1,898,618	2,656,376	2,800,829	2,993,973	3,186,756	1,850	116	2	0	0	0
Georgia	915,303	1,254,216	1,826,961	1,751,732	1,795,886	1,959,504	25,705	17,371	21,615	5,541	0	0
Hawaii	304,131	280,503	395,884	459,620	374,297	430,451	0	0	0	0	0	0
Idaho	177,918	223,108	290,746	317,794	327,898	338,143	6,161	10,435	11,148	5,635	6,050	7,633
Illinois	1,296,895	1,161,833	1,760,300	1,822,869	1,601,567	1,602,641	284,635	418,269	520,136	680,732	725,914	768,509
Indiana	886,124	977,517	1,257,919	1,294,406	1,332,693	1,338,901	1,507	2,831	6,190	6,600	6,992	7,379
Iowa	544,945	649,901	813,805	750,111	752,859	798,961	21,624	29,098	36,129	65,217	67,204	73,502
Kansas	437,413	528,243	664,201	662,320	687,572	725,777	87,026	117,684	160,873	192,994	198,916	211,593
Kentucky	617,915	690,328	939,047	984,564	925,266	1,014,939	4,682	6,041	14,930	10,084	11,605	12,035
Louisiana	566,798	603,825	834,643	1,081,957	1,087,287	1,084,984	1,462	8,061	517	0	0	0
Maine	174,737	158,044	212,144	216,910	227,017	231,890	0	27	0	0	0	0
Maryland	724,223	717,377	999,723	993,743	1,011,728	1,078,966	117,913	136,661	185,034	216,456	233,262	253,486
Massachusetts	471,368	669,102	1,038,998	820,888	932,895	1,039,187	0	1,779	0	0	0	0
Michigan	1,326,884	1,572,241	1,991,098	1,731,675	1,807,688	1,771,921	159,202	215,733	288,112	503,319	519,588	535,401
Minnesota	744,381	901,114	1,174,797	1,120,554	1,083,760	1,194,106	2,040	0	0	0	0	0
Mississippi	365,574	570,035	758,242	757,385	770,130	774,001	25,670	31,725	38,167	55,899	57,258	57,539
Missouri	563,430	669,832	945,746	850,139	870,916	868,899	38,097	72,895	101,562	119,597	122,589	128,638
Montana	110,199	121,730	137,341	148,593	140,638	154,770	3,310	3,526	4,069	5,404	5,424	6,283
Nebraska	318,482	382,465	514,235	486,098	496,169	532,258	36,569	53,004	19,892	68,594	75,677	78,470
Nevada	161,581	223,413	333,117	453,144	471,522	524,701	0	0	0	0	0	0
New Hampshire	71,226	79,376	96,157	106,405	110,435	114,557	6	0	0	0	0	0
New Jersey	854,989	1,045,117	1,246,554	1,410,600	1,547,573	1,644,413	145,010	156,011	172,667	185,689	190,575	195,502
New Mexico	307,083	413,344	538,822	606,600	637,859	679,588	34,364	42,363	60,183	75,811	83,527	92,644
New York	2,313,120	2,202,186	4,461,671	2,894,535	2,956,576	3,500,566	372,650	405,160	431,415	518,520	563,110	622,550
North Carolina	1,351,111	1,686,718	2,221,600	2,334,186	2,562,993	2,815,090	62,785	79,490	113,448	130,037	142,294	156,171
North Dakota	129,986	138,785	188,047	173,578	187,962	195,040	9	170	21	0	1,713	1,786
Ohio	1,360,141	1,488,806	1,922,571	1,821,109	1,846,028	1,848,717	63,899	120,161	101,647	121,944	123,567	126,530
Oklahoma	473,898	536,307	754,540	707,140	725,408	782,847	12,822	18,578	28,367	38,114	35,851	38,081
Oregon	377,476	442,603	640,347	628,220	534,487	657,011	118,499	82,282	106,436	138,313	148,824	161,438
Pennsylvania	962,121	1,110,896	1,331,544	1,282,991	1,345,487	1,371,792	62,794	78,912	94,338	107,355	109,131	111,721
Rhode Island	113,614	121,153	157,137	166,289	168,731	172,703	0	0	0	0	0	0
South Carolina	578,794	647,111	853,139	656,585	673,181	715,967	18,670	25,737	36,060	43,568	46,149	50,592
South Dakota	81,859	105,090	129,680	142,532	147,505	153,928	0	957	0	0	0	0
Tennessee	663,536	850,110	969,316	1,002,907	1,059,503	1,081,753	1,779	2,113	3,824	0	0	4,326
Texas	2,627,916	3,302,958	4,236,852	4,248,841	4,351,691	4,658,611	210,934	280,141	439,342	824,392	869,053	971,351
Utah	304,738	414,407	531,975	600,043	624,935	669,271	0	0	0	0	0	0
Vermont	40,997	42,400	53,605	59,606	61,620	63,740	4	62	0	0	0	0
Virginia	886,208	839,587	1,395,308	1,189,861	1,316,343	1,482,002	973	1,282	1,570	1,872	2,062	1,934
Washington	828,700	914,200	1,200,392	1,162,885	1,209,222	1,315,804	2,470	100	0	0	0	33
West Virginia	263,269	320,198	382,269	361,838	349,317	355,870	574	693	503	310	213	0
Wisconsin	841,192	937,513	1,186,415	1,027,362	1,023,024	1,019,374	197,712	275,712	379,648	565,152	590,122	621,514
Wyoming	120,623	130,162	149,009	196,077	210,359	229,620	12,721	13,489	20,525	22,253	27,406	32,562
U.S. Service Academies	0	0	0	0	0	0	0	0	0	0	0	0
Other jurisdictions	337,393	551,957	709,473	786,856	847,180	913,597	12,724	22,579	20,612	42,679	40,356	45,878
American Samoa	0	0	0	0	0	0	0	9,443	0	3,462	0	0
Federated States of Micronesia	0	11	40	112	0	0	0	2,978	3,327	0	0	0
Guam	28,283	29,975	29,122	27,654	28,960	29,684	10,028	10,118	12,826	12,422	12,866	13,827
Marshall Islands	0	324	1,924	0	0	0	0	0	0	2,200	3,000	2,000
Northern Marianas	0	8,164	9,055	9,054	8,029	7,270	0	0	0	0	0	0
Palau	644	2,040	2,345	299	2,385	2,385	0	0	0	0	0	0
Puerto Rico	277,295	493,833	647,623	749,737	807,807	874,258	2,375	40	4,459	0	0	2,996
U.S. Virgin Islands	31,170	17,610	19,365	0	0	0	320	0	0	24,596	24,489	27,055

NOTE: Data for 1990–91 are for institutions of higher education, while later data are for degree-granting institutions. Degree-granting institutions grant associate's or higher degrees and participate in Title IV federal financial aid programs. The degree-granting classification is very similar to the earlier higher education classification, but it includes more 2-year colleges and excludes a few higher education institutions that did not grant degrees. (See Guide to Sources for details.) Includes data for public institutions reporting data according to the Financial Accounting Standards Board (FASB) questionnaire. Detail may not sum to totals because of rounding.
SOURCE: U.S. Department of Education, National Center for Education Statistics, 1990–91 through 2005–06 Integrated Postsecondary Education Data System, "Finance Survey" (IPEDS-F:FY91–96), and Spring 2001 through Spring 2007. (This table was prepared May 2008.)

Table 353. Total revenue of private not-for-profit degree-granting institutions, by source of funds and type of institution: 1997–98 through 2005–06

Type of institution and year	Total	Student tuition and fees (net of allowances)	Federal appropriations, grants, and contracts[1]	State appropriations, grants, and contracts	Local appropriations, grants, and contracts	Private gifts, grants, and contracts[2]	Investment return (gain or loss)	Educational activities	Auxiliary enterprises	Hospitals	Other
1	2	3	4	5	6	7	8	9	10	11	12

					In thousands of current dollars						
All institutions											
1997–98	$95,240,891	$26,499,174	$11,156,948	$953,624	$520,115	$13,245,613	$22,311,899	$2,656,621	$7,655,732	$6,278,828	$3,962,337
1998–99	95,680,731	28,044,077	11,622,152	1,044,815	545,600	14,253,692	18,735,718	2,703,488	8,028,235	6,784,998	3,917,956
1999–2000	120,625,806	29,651,812	12,191,827	1,117,742	580,237	16,488,984	37,763,518	2,865,606	8,317,607	7,208,600	4,439,874
2000–01	82,174,492	31,318,106	13,378,019	1,176,060	508,365	15,859,313	-3,602,326	3,468,680	8,742,610	7,126,343	4,199,323
2001–02	84,346,652	33,499,121	14,790,235	1,303,772	493,158	15,394,353	-6,545,330	3,220,868	9,317,922	8,083,935	4,788,618
2002–03	105,672,753	36,019,267	16,625,072	1,514,087	474,889	14,380,351	9,340,400	3,056,259	9,833,972	8,942,047	5,486,409
2003–04	134,230,762	38,505,631	18,335,784	1,455,556	485,717	15,847,551	30,896,917	3,290,420	10,325,606	9,657,753	5,429,805
2004–05	140,150,716	41,394,424	19,699,204	1,469,912	488,010	16,738,916	30,431,521	3,595,559	10,823,963	10,377,808	5,131,401
2005–06	152,744,665	44,263,227	19,683,291	1,558,741	517,109	18,346,525	35,634,520	3,716,409	11,610,762	11,536,658	5,877,423
4-year											
1997–98	94,529,717	26,158,716	11,109,406	938,004	519,025	13,120,588	22,244,963	2,641,456	7,584,913	6,278,278	3,934,367
1998–99	94,812,541	27,695,568	11,572,739	1,026,270	543,561	14,044,604	18,705,741	2,684,664	7,965,778	6,784,463	3,789,154
1999–2000	119,708,625	29,257,523	12,133,829	1,098,961	574,746	16,346,616	37,698,219	2,837,784	8,261,507	7,208,600	4,290,841
2000–01	81,568,928	30,996,381	13,318,572	1,156,503	503,002	15,788,869	-3,623,323	3,452,731	8,703,316	7,125,648	4,147,227
2001–02	83,764,907	33,165,965	14,708,582	1,280,787	490,596	15,328,974	-6,547,915	3,206,440	9,263,171	8,083,935	4,784,371
2002–03	105,064,157	35,676,736	16,515,854	1,487,604	470,126	14,319,622	9,338,684	3,041,307	9,779,275	8,942,047	5,492,904
2003–04	133,594,668	38,181,648	18,236,313	1,423,269	480,104	15,789,672	30,854,091	3,277,767	10,287,215	9,657,753	5,406,836
2004–05	139,528,763	41,045,608	19,622,002	1,446,643	484,379	16,671,017	30,408,545	3,581,869	10,784,161	10,377,808	5,106,733
2005–06	152,150,193	43,944,766	19,607,858	1,530,038	515,776	18,288,085	35,603,805	3,699,630	11,573,115	11,536,658	5,850,463
2-year											
1997–98	711,175	340,459	47,541	15,620	1,090	125,024	66,937	15,165	70,818	550	27,970
1998–99	868,190	348,508	49,414	18,545	2,039	209,088	29,977	18,824	62,457	535	128,803
1999–2000	917,181	394,289	57,998	18,781	5,491	142,368	65,299	27,822	56,100	0	149,033
2000–01	605,564	321,724	59,446	19,557	5,363	70,444	20,996	15,949	39,294	694	52,096
2001–02	581,745	333,156	81,653	22,985	2,562	65,379	2,585	14,429	54,750	0	4,246
2002–03	608,596	342,531	109,217	26,483	4,764	60,729	1,716	14,953	54,697	0	-6,495
2003–04	636,094	323,983	99,471	32,287	5,613	57,900	42,826	12,653	38,391	0	22,969
2004–05	621,953	348,815	77,202	23,269	3,631	67,899	22,976	13,690	39,802	0	24,668
2005–06	594,473	318,460	75,433	28,703	1,333	58,441	30,716	16,778	37,648	0	26,960

					Percentage distribution						
All institutions											
1997–98	100.00	27.82	11.71	1.00	0.55	13.91	23.43	2.79	8.04	6.59	4.16
1998–99	100.00	29.31	12.15	1.09	0.57	14.90	19.58	2.83	8.39	7.09	4.09
1999–2000	100.00	24.58	10.11	0.93	0.48	13.67	31.31	2.38	6.90	5.98	3.68
2000–01	100.00	38.11	16.28	1.43	0.62	19.30	-4.38	4.22	10.64	8.67	5.11
2001–02	100.00	39.72	17.54	1.55	0.58	18.25	-7.76	3.82	11.05	9.58	5.68
2002–03	100.00	34.09	15.73	1.43	0.45	13.61	8.84	2.89	9.31	8.46	5.19
2003–04	100.00	28.69	13.66	1.08	0.36	11.81	23.02	2.45	7.69	7.19	4.05
2004–05	100.00	29.54	14.06	1.05	0.35	11.94	21.71	2.57	7.72	7.40	3.66
2005–06	100.00	28.98	12.89	1.02	0.34	12.01	23.33	2.43	7.60	7.55	3.85
4-year											
1997–98	100.00	27.67	11.75	0.99	0.55	13.88	23.53	2.79	8.02	6.64	4.16
1998–99	100.00	29.21	12.21	1.08	0.57	14.81	19.73	2.83	8.40	7.16	4.00
1999–2000	100.00	24.44	10.14	0.92	0.48	13.66	31.49	2.37	6.90	6.02	3.58
2000–01	100.00	38.00	16.33	1.42	0.62	19.36	-4.44	4.23	10.67	8.74	5.08
2001–02	100.00	39.59	17.56	1.53	0.59	18.30	-7.82	3.83	11.06	9.65	5.71
2002–03	100.00	33.96	15.72	1.42	0.45	13.63	8.89	2.89	9.31	8.51	5.23
2003–04	100.00	28.58	13.65	1.07	0.36	11.82	23.10	2.45	7.70	7.23	4.05
2004–05	100.00	29.42	14.06	1.04	0.35	11.95	21.79	2.57	7.73	7.44	3.66
2005–06	100.00	28.88	12.89	1.01	0.34	12.02	23.40	2.43	7.61	7.58	3.85
2-year											
1997–98	100.00	47.87	6.68	2.20	0.15	17.58	9.41	2.13	9.96	0.08	3.93
1998–99	100.00	40.14	5.69	2.14	0.23	24.08	3.45	2.17	7.19	0.06	14.84
1999–2000	100.00	42.99	6.32	2.05	0.60	15.52	7.12	3.03	6.12	0.00	16.25
2000–01	100.00	53.13	9.82	3.23	0.89	11.63	3.47	2.63	6.49	0.11	8.60
2001–02	100.00	57.27	14.04	3.95	0.44	11.24	0.44	2.48	9.41	0.00	0.73
2002–03	100.00	56.28	17.95	4.35	0.78	9.98	0.28	2.46	8.99	0.00	-1.07
2003–04	100.00	50.93	15.64	5.08	0.88	9.10	6.73	1.99	6.04	0.00	3.61
2004–05	100.00	56.08	12.41	3.74	0.58	10.92	3.69	2.20	6.40	0.00	3.97
2005–06	100.00	53.57	12.69	4.83	0.22	9.83	5.17	2.82	6.33	0.00	4.54

See notes at end of table.

Table 353. Total revenue of private not-for-profit degree-granting institutions, by source of funds and type of institution: 1997–98 through 2005–06—Continued

Type of institution and year	Total	Student tuition and fees (net of allowances)	Federal appropriations, grants, and contracts[1]	State appropriations, grants, and contracts	Local appropriations, grants, and contracts	Private gifts, grants, and contracts[2]	Investment return (gain or loss)	Educational activities	Auxiliary enterprises	Hospitals	Other
1	2	3	4	5	6	7	8	9	10	11	12
					Revenue per full-time-equivalent student in current dollars						
All institutions											
1997–98	$38,852	$10,810	$4,551	$389	$212	$5,403	$9,102	$1,084	$3,123	$2,561	$1,616
1998–99	38,379	11,249	4,662	419	219	5,717	7,515	1,084	3,220	2,722	1,572
1999–2000	47,511	11,679	4,802	440	229	6,494	14,874	1,129	3,276	2,839	1,749
2000–01	31,737	12,095	5,167	454	196	6,125	-1,391	1,340	3,376	2,752	1,622
2001–02	31,876	12,660	5,589	493	186	5,818	-2,474	1,217	3,521	3,055	1,810
2002–03	38,645	13,173	6,080	554	174	5,259	3,416	1,118	3,596	3,270	2,006
2003–04	47,917	13,746	6,545	520	173	5,657	11,029	1,175	3,686	3,448	1,938
2004–05	48,842	14,426	6,865	512	170	5,833	10,605	1,253	3,772	3,617	1,788
2005–06	52,506	15,215	6,766	536	178	6,307	12,249	1,278	3,991	3,966	2,020
4-year											
1997–98	39,558	10,947	4,649	393	217	5,491	9,309	1,105	3,174	2,627	1,646
1998–99	38,918	11,368	4,750	421	223	5,765	7,678	1,102	3,270	2,785	1,555
1999–2000	48,160	11,771	4,882	442	231	6,576	15,166	1,142	3,324	2,900	1,726
2000–01	31,995	12,158	5,224	454	197	6,193	-1,421	1,354	3,414	2,795	1,627
2001–02	32,129	12,721	5,642	491	188	5,880	-2,512	1,230	3,553	3,101	1,835
2002–03	38,939	13,223	6,121	551	174	5,307	3,461	1,127	3,624	3,314	2,036
2003–04	48,299	13,804	6,593	515	174	5,708	11,155	1,185	3,719	3,492	1,955
2004–05	49,216	14,478	6,921	510	171	5,880	10,726	1,263	3,804	3,661	1,801
2005–06	52,870	15,270	6,813	532	179	6,355	12,372	1,286	4,021	4,009	2,033
2-year											
1997–98	11,515	5,513	770	253	18	2,024	1,084	246	1,147	9	453
1998–99	15,276	6,132	869	326	36	3,679	527	331	1,099	9	2,266
1999–2000	17,220	7,403	1,089	353	103	2,673	1,226	522	1,053	0	2,798
2000–01	15,214	8,083	1,494	491	135	1,770	528	401	987	17	1,309
2001–02	14,936	8,553	2,096	590	66	1,679	66	370	1,406	0	109
2002–03	16,784	9,446	3,012	730	131	1,675	47	412	1,508	0	-179
2003–04	18,013	9,174	2,817	914	159	1,640	1,213	358	1,087	0	650
2004–05	18,062	10,130	2,242	676	105	1,972	667	398	1,156	0	716
2005–06	19,004	10,181	2,411	918	43	1,868	982	536	1,204	0	862
					Revenue per full-time-equivalent student in constant 2006–07 dollars[3]						
All institutions											
1997–98	$49,036	$13,643	$5,744	$491	$268	$6,820	$11,488	$1,368	$3,942	$3,233	$2,040
1998–99	47,615	13,956	5,784	520	272	7,093	9,324	1,345	3,995	3,377	1,950
1999–2000	57,290	14,083	5,790	531	276	7,831	17,935	1,361	3,950	3,424	2,109
2000–01	37,002	14,102	6,024	530	229	7,141	-1,622	1,562	3,937	3,209	1,891
2001–02	36,517	14,503	6,403	564	214	6,665	-2,834	1,394	4,034	3,500	2,073
2002–03	43,320	14,766	6,815	621	195	5,895	3,829	1,253	4,031	3,666	2,249
2003–04	52,564	15,079	7,180	570	190	6,206	12,099	1,289	4,043	3,782	2,126
2004–05	52,013	15,362	7,311	546	181	6,212	11,294	1,334	4,017	3,851	1,904
2005–06	53,863	15,609	6,941	550	182	6,470	12,566	1,311	4,094	4,068	2,073
4-year											
1997–98	49,927	13,816	5,868	495	274	6,930	11,749	1,395	4,006	3,316	2,078
1998–99	48,284	14,104	5,893	523	277	7,152	9,526	1,367	4,057	3,455	1,930
1999–2000	58,073	14,193	5,886	533	279	7,930	18,288	1,377	4,008	3,497	2,082
2000–01	37,302	14,175	6,091	529	230	7,220	-1,657	1,579	3,980	3,259	1,897
2001–02	36,807	14,574	6,463	563	216	6,736	-2,877	1,409	4,070	3,552	2,102
2002–03	43,650	14,822	6,862	618	195	5,949	3,880	1,264	4,063	3,715	2,282
2003–04	52,983	15,143	7,232	564	190	6,262	12,237	1,300	4,080	3,830	2,144
2004–05	52,411	15,418	7,371	543	182	6,262	11,422	1,345	4,051	3,898	1,918
2005–06	54,237	15,665	6,990	545	184	6,519	12,692	1,319	4,125	4,112	2,086
2-year											
1997–98	14,533	6,957	972	319	22	2,555	1,368	310	1,447	11	572
1998–99	18,952	7,608	1,079	405	45	4,564	654	411	1,363	12	2,812
1999–2000	20,764	8,926	1,313	425	124	3,223	1,478	630	1,270	0	3,374
2000–01	17,738	9,424	1,741	573	157	2,063	615	467	1,151	20	1,526
2001–02	17,110	9,799	2,402	676	75	1,923	76	424	1,610	0	125
2002–03	18,814	10,589	3,376	819	147	1,877	53	462	1,691	0	-201
2003–04	19,759	10,064	3,090	1,003	174	1,799	1,330	393	1,193	0	713
2004–05	19,235	10,788	2,388	720	112	2,100	711	423	1,231	0	763
2005–06	19,496	10,444	2,474	941	44	1,917	1,007	550	1,235	0	884

[1]Includes independent operations.
[2]Includes contributions from affiliated entities.
[3]Constant dollars based on the Consumer Price Index, prepared by the Bureau of Labor Statistics, U.S. Department of Labor, adjusted to a school-year basis.
NOTE: Detail may not sum to totals because of rounding.

SOURCE: U.S. Department of Education, National Center for Education Statistics, 1997–98 through 2005–06 Integrated Postsecondary Education Data System, "Fall Enrollment Survey" (IPEDS-EF:97–99) and "Finance Survey" (IPEDS-F:FY98–99), and Spring 2001 through Spring 2007. (This table was prepared May 2008.)

Table 354. Total revenue of private not-for-profit degree-granting institutions, by source of funds and type of institution: 2005–06

Type of institution	Total	Student tuition and fees (net of allowances)	Federal appropriations, grants, and contracts[1]	State appropriations, grants, and contracts	Local appropriations, grants, and contracts	Private gifts, grants, and contracts[2]	Investment return (gain or loss)	Educational activities	Auxiliary enterprises	Hospitals	Other
1	2	3	4	5	6	7	8	9	10	11	12
					In thousands of current dollars						
Total................................	$152,744,665	$44,263,227	$19,683,291	$1,558,741	$517,109	$18,346,525	$35,634,520	$3,716,409	$11,610,762	$11,536,658	$5,877,423
4-year..............................	152,150,193	43,944,766	19,607,858	1,530,038	515,776	18,288,085	35,603,805	3,699,630	11,573,115	11,536,658	5,850,463
Doctoral, extensive[3]............	82,327,996	12,599,328	15,467,909	676,060	295,553	9,293,974	24,784,719	2,489,408	4,081,331	9,731,100	2,908,614
Doctoral, intensive[4].............	10,491,529	4,841,896	760,639	166,178	22,605	1,007,381	1,744,936	599,124	959,165	0	389,605
Master's[5]........................	22,092,017	12,993,241	939,586	282,557	8,439	2,137,584	2,028,793	146,383	2,745,491	136,053	673,891
Baccalaureate[6]..................	22,369,442	8,724,211	729,570	191,274	7,354	3,515,424	5,532,926	139,679	3,032,897	0	496,107
Specialized institutions[7]........	14,869,209	4,786,091	1,710,153	213,970	181,825	2,333,722	1,512,431	325,037	754,230	1,669,505	1,382,246
Art, music, or design	2,032,205	972,336	19,437	11,845	2,331	354,104	232,401	20,502	138,868	0	280,381
Business and management	854,178	619,700	10,187	10,899	844	42,858	51,708	4,324	90,947	0	22,711
Engineering or technology	434,536	177,411	17,634	3,722	0	76,056	112,990	574	44,946	0	1,203
Medical or other health	7,426,850	1,314,810	1,517,524	151,412	171,533	891,762	538,931	254,994	164,491	1,668,995	752,399
Theological...........................	2,078,732	522,358	44,295	11,382	849	724,070	427,510	15,933	187,004	0	145,331
Tribal[8]...............................	48,618	1,167	32,928	1,958	0	2,530	256	170	1,712	0	7,897
Other specialized	1,994,091	1,178,309	68,149	22,752	6,269	242,343	148,635	28,540	126,262	510	172,323
2-year..............................	594,473	318,460	75,433	28,703	1,333	58,441	30,716	16,778	37,648	0	26,960
Associate's of arts......................	545,808	314,363	40,013	28,256	392	57,400	30,442	16,053	36,475	0	22,415
Tribal[8]...............................	48,665	4,098	35,420	446	941	1,041	274	725	1,173	0	4,546
					Percentage distribution						
Total................................	100.00	28.98	12.89	1.02	0.34	12.01	23.33	2.43	7.60	7.55	3.85
4-year..............................	100.00	28.88	12.89	1.01	0.34	12.02	23.40	2.43	7.61	7.58	3.85
Doctoral, extensive[3]............	100.00	15.30	18.79	0.82	0.36	11.29	30.10	3.02	4.96	11.82	3.53
Doctoral, intensive[4].............	100.00	46.15	7.25	1.58	0.22	9.60	16.63	5.71	9.14	0.00	3.71
Master's[5]........................	100.00	58.81	4.25	1.28	0.04	9.68	9.18	0.66	12.43	0.62	3.05
Baccalaureate[6]..................	100.00	39.00	3.26	0.86	0.03	15.72	24.73	0.62	13.56	0.00	2.22
Specialized institutions[7]........	100.00	32.19	11.50	1.44	1.22	15.69	10.17	2.19	5.07	11.23	9.30
Art, music, or design	100.00	47.85	0.96	0.58	0.11	17.42	11.44	1.01	6.83	0.00	13.80
Business and management	100.00	72.55	1.19	1.28	0.10	5.02	6.05	0.51	10.65	0.00	2.66
Engineering or technology	100.00	40.83	4.06	0.86	0.00	17.50	26.00	0.13	10.34	0.00	0.28
Medical or other health	100.00	17.70	20.43	2.04	2.31	12.01	7.26	3.43	2.21	22.47	10.13
Theological...........................	100.00	25.13	2.13	0.55	0.04	34.83	20.57	0.77	9.00	0.00	6.99
Tribal[8]...............................	100.00	2.40	67.73	4.03	0.00	5.20	0.53	0.35	3.52	0.00	16.24
Other specialized	100.00	59.09	3.42	1.14	0.31	12.15	7.45	1.43	6.33	0.03	8.64
2-year..............................	100.00	53.57	12.69	4.83	0.22	9.83	5.17	2.82	6.33	0.00	4.54
Associate's of arts......................	100.00	57.60	7.33	5.18	0.07	10.52	5.58	2.94	6.68	0.00	4.11
Tribal[8]...............................	100.00	8.42	72.78	0.92	1.93	2.14	0.56	1.49	2.41	0.00	9.34
					Revenue per full-time-equivalent student in current dollars						
Total................................	$52,506	$15,215	$6,766	$536	$178	$6,307	$12,249	$1,278	$3,991	$3,966	$2,020
4-year..............................	52,870	15,270	6,813	532	179	6,355	12,372	1,286	4,021	4,009	2,033
Doctoral, extensive[3]............	133,793	20,475	25,137	1,099	480	15,104	40,278	4,046	6,633	15,814	4,727
Doctoral, intensive[4].............	38,185	17,623	2,768	605	82	3,666	6,351	2,181	3,491	0	1,418
Master's[5]........................	23,262	13,681	989	298	9	2,251	2,136	154	2,891	143	710
Baccalaureate[6]..................	32,889	12,827	1,073	281	11	5,169	8,135	205	4,459	0	729
Specialized institutions[7]........	41,549	13,374	4,779	598	508	6,521	4,226	908	2,108	4,665	3,862
Art, music, or design	42,107	20,147	403	245	48	7,337	4,815	425	2,877	0	5,809
Business and management	15,739	11,419	188	201	16	790	953	80	1,676	0	418
Engineering or technology	20,768	8,479	843	178	0	3,635	5,400	27	2,148	0	57
Medical or other health	110,710	19,599	22,621	2,257	2,557	13,293	8,034	3,801	2,452	24,879	11,216
Theological...........................	27,094	6,808	577	148	11	9,437	5,572	208	2,437	0	1,894
Tribal[8]...............................	22,815	548	15,452	919	0	1,187	120	80	803	0	3,706
Other specialized	22,537	13,317	770	257	71	2,739	1,680	323	1,427	6	1,948
2-year..............................	19,004	10,181	2,411	918	43	1,868	982	536	1,204	0	862
Associate's of arts......................	18,413	10,605	1,350	953	13	1,936	1,027	542	1,231	0	756
Tribal[8]...............................	29,692	2,500	21,611	272	574	635	167	443	715	0	2,773

[1]Includes independent operations.
[2]Includes contributions from affiliated entities.
[3]Doctoral, extensive institutions are committed to graduate education through the doctorate, and award 50 or more doctor's degrees per year across at least 15 disciplines.
[4]Doctoral, intensive institutions are committed to education through the doctorate and award at least 10 doctor's degrees per year across 3 or more disciplines or at least 20 doctor's degrees overall.
[5]Master's institutions offer a full range of baccalaureate programs and are committed to education through the master's degree. They award at least 20 master's degrees per year.
[6]Baccalaureate institutions primarily emphasize undergraduate education.

[7]Specialized 4-year institutions award degrees primarily in single fields of study, such as medicine, business, fine arts, theology, and engineering. Includes some institutions that have 4-year programs, but have not reported sufficient data to identify program category. Also includes institutions classified as 4-year under the IPEDS system, which had been classified as 2-year in the Carnegie system because they primarily award associate's degrees.
[8]Tribally controlled colleges are located on reservations and are members of the American Indian Higher Education Consortium.
NOTE: Detail may not sum to totals because of rounding.
SOURCE: U.S. Department of Education, National Center for Education Statistics, 2005–06 Integrated Postsecondary Education Data System (IPEDS), Spring 2006 and Spring 2007. (This table was prepared May 2008.)

Table 355. Total revenue of private for-profit degree-granting institutions, by source of funds and type of institution: 1999–2000 through 2005–06

Type of institution and year	Total	Student tuition and fees (net of allowances)	Federal appropriations, grants, and contracts	State and local appropriations, grants, and contracts	Private gifts, grants, and contracts	Investment return	Educational activities	Auxiliary enterprises	Other
1	2	3	4	5	6	7	8	9	10
In thousands of current dollars									
All institutions									
1999–2000	$4,321,985	$3,721,032	$198,923	$71,904	$2,151	$18,537	$70,672	$156,613	$82,153
2000–01	4,967,700	4,340,478	187,353	87,348	2,848	19,737	63,392	172,987	93,557
2001–02	6,181,906	5,423,949	211,372	47,486	5,690	17,127	73,085	216,284	186,914
2002–03	7,496,714	6,712,019	282,521	50,265	5,545	15,112	92,380	250,712	88,160
2003–04	8,989,815	8,049,205	397,828	59,112	7,079	16,813	139,125	238,735	81,918
2004–05	10,979,154	9,566,692	673,950	63,227	7,138	24,526	231,957	252,199	159,465
2005–06	12,586,553	11,016,780	799,544	67,008	4,108	43,962	195,099	270,433	189,620
4–year									
1999–2000	2,381,042	2,050,136	103,865	39,460	1,109	10,340	33,764	102,103	40,266
2000–01	2,952,254	2,583,644	81,879	59,922	1,659	12,574	40,081	106,327	66,168
2001–02	3,775,017	3,382,888	64,761	13,137	2,809	10,691	46,676	132,401	121,655
2002–03	4,753,546	4,353,233	108,806	9,757	3,064	5,952	58,281	173,027	41,427
2003–04	6,016,415	5,489,245	196,945	15,076	3,696	10,931	104,314	164,260	31,948
2004–05	7,692,472	6,864,048	345,810	21,146	4,035	17,332	173,830	201,512	64,760
2005–06	9,124,105	8,225,732	399,919	31,576	2,851	35,383	160,863	190,409	77,373
2–year									
1999–2000	1,940,943	1,670,896	95,058	32,444	1,042	8,197	36,908	54,510	41,888
2000–01	2,015,446	1,756,833	105,474	27,426	1,189	7,163	23,311	66,660	27,389
2001–02	2,406,889	2,041,061	146,611	34,349	2,881	6,436	26,409	83,883	65,259
2002–03	2,743,168	2,358,786	173,715	40,508	2,482	9,160	34,099	77,685	46,733
2003–04	2,973,400	2,550,960	200,883	44,036	3,383	5,882	34,811	74,475	49,970
2004–05	3,286,682	2,702,644	328,141	42,081	3,103	7,194	58,127	50,687	94,705
2005–06	3,462,448	2,791,047	399,626	35,431	1,257	8,579	34,236	80,025	112,247
Percentage distribution									
All institutions									
1999–2000	100.00	86.10	4.60	1.66	0.05	0.43	1.64	3.62	1.90
2000–01	100.00	87.37	3.77	1.76	0.06	0.40	1.28	3.48	1.88
2001–02	100.00	87.74	3.42	0.77	0.09	0.28	1.18	3.50	3.02
2002–03	100.00	89.53	3.77	0.67	0.07	0.20	1.23	3.34	1.18
2003–04	100.00	89.54	4.43	0.66	0.08	0.19	1.55	2.66	0.91
2004–05	100.00	87.14	6.14	0.58	0.07	0.22	2.11	2.30	1.45
2005–06	100.00	87.53	6.35	0.53	0.03	0.35	1.55	2.15	1.51
4–year									
1999–2000	100.00	86.10	4.36	1.66	0.05	0.43	1.42	4.29	1.69
2000–01	100.00	87.51	2.77	2.03	0.06	0.43	1.36	3.60	2.24
2001–02	100.00	89.61	1.72	0.35	0.07	0.28	1.24	3.51	3.22
2002–03	100.00	91.58	2.29	0.21	0.06	0.13	1.23	3.64	0.87
2003–04	100.00	91.24	3.27	0.25	0.06	0.18	1.73	2.73	0.53
2004–05	100.00	89.23	4.50	0.27	0.05	0.23	2.26	2.62	0.84
2005–06	100.00	90.15	4.38	0.35	0.03	0.39	1.76	2.09	0.85
2–year									
1999–2000	100.00	86.09	4.90	1.67	0.05	0.42	1.90	2.81	2.16
2000–01	100.00	87.17	5.23	1.36	0.06	0.36	1.16	3.31	1.36
2001–02	100.00	84.80	6.09	1.43	0.12	0.27	1.10	3.49	2.71
2002–03	100.00	85.99	6.33	1.48	0.09	0.33	1.24	2.83	1.70
2003–04	100.00	86.10	6.76	1.48	0.11	0.20	1.17	2.50	1.68
2004–05	100.00	82.23	9.98	1.28	0.09	0.22	1.77	1.54	2.88
2005–06	100.00	80.61	11.54	1.02	0.04	0.25	0.99	2.31	3.24
Revenue per full-time-equivalent student in constant 2006–07 dollars[1]									
All institutions									
1999–2000	$13,550	$11,666	$624	$225	$7	$58	$222	$491	$258
2000–01	12,687	11,085	478	223	7	50	162	442	239
2001–02	15,513	13,611	530	119	14	43	183	543	469
2002–03	15,543	13,916	586	104	11	31	192	520	183
2003–04	15,241	13,647	674	100	12	29	236	405	139
2004–05	14,836	12,927	911	85	10	33	313	341	215
2005–06	14,338	12,550	911	76	5	50	222	308	216
4–year									
1999–2000	13,753	11,842	600	228	6	60	195	590	233
2000–01	15,093	13,209	419	306	8	64	205	544	338
2001–02	15,642	14,017	268	54	12	44	193	549	504
2002–03	15,415	14,116	353	32	10	19	189	561	134
2003–04	15,454	14,100	506	39	9	28	268	422	82
2004–05	14,795	13,202	665	41	8	33	334	388	125
2005–06	14,130	12,738	619	49	4	55	249	295	120
2–year									
1999–2000	13,309	11,458	652	222	7	56	253	374	287
2000–01	14,256	12,426	746	194	8	51	165	472	194
2001–02	15,315	12,987	933	219	18	41	168	534	415
2002–03	15,770	13,560	999	233	14	53	196	447	269
2003–04	14,828	12,766	1,002	220	17	29	174	371	249
2004–05	14,932	12,279	1,491	191	14	33	264	230	430
2005–06	14,919	12,026	1,722	153	5	37	148	345	484

[1]Constant dollars based on the Consumer Price Index, prepared by the Bureau of Labor Statistics, U.S. Department of Labor, adjusted to a school-year basis.
NOTE: Detail may not sum to totals because of rounding.

SOURCE: U.S. Department of Education, National Center for Education Statistics, 1999–2000 through 2005–06 Integrated Postsecondary Education Data System, "Fall Enrollment Survey" (IPEDS-EF:99) and Spring 2001 through Spring 2007. (This table was prepared May 2008.)

Table 356. Total revenue of private for-profit degree-granting institutions, by source of funds and type of institution: 2004–05 and 2005–06

Year and type of institution	Total	Student tuition and fees (net of allowances)	Federal appropriations, grants, and contracts	State and local appropriations, grants, and contracts	Private gifts, grants, and contracts	Investment return (gain or loss)	Educational activities	Auxiliary enterprises	Other
1	2	3	4	5	6	7	8	9	10
In thousands of current dollars									
2004–05									
Total	$10,979,154	$9,566,692	$673,950	$63,227	$7,138	$24,526	$231,957	$252,199	$159,465
4-year	7,692,472	6,864,048	345,810	21,146	4,035	17,332	173,830	201,512	64,760
Doctoral, intensive[1]	79,329	78,887	0	0	0	442	0	0	0
Master's[2]	2,551,021	2,396,116	43,374	0	54	-1,389	71,697	27,678	13,491
Baccalaureate[3]	476,780	440,498	3,345	3,782	862	6,665	6,319	15,200	109
Specialized institutions[4]	4,585,342	3,948,546	299,091	17,364	3,119	11,614	95,815	158,634	51,159
Art, music, or design	827,234	706,285	54,086	719	0	1,890	7,109	49,316	7,829
Business and management	520,637	478,300	8,216	616	3	-18	14,067	7,600	11,853
Engineering or technology	824,963	800,527	2,089	276	141	151	7,890	12,759	1,130
Medical or other health	57,884	46,728	901	14	178	55	5,262	1,524	3,223
Other specialized	2,354,624	1,916,707	233,799	15,740	2,797	9,535	61,487	87,435	27,124
2-year	3,286,682	2,702,644	328,141	42,081	3,103	7,194	58,127	50,687	94,705
2005–06									
Total	12,586,553	11,016,780	799,544	67,008	4,108	43,962	195,099	270,433	189,620
4-year	9,124,105	8,225,732	399,919	31,576	2,851	35,383	160,863	190,409	77,373
Doctoral, intensive[1]	158,948	157,225	0	0	0	1,723	0	0	0
Master's[2]	2,911,279	2,803,498	10,994	0	0	867	82,501	8,675	4,745
Baccalaureate[3]	473,347	430,416	3,218	2,890	440	10,527	7,030	17,626	1,201
Specialized institutions[4]	5,580,532	4,834,594	385,707	28,686	2,411	22,267	71,332	164,108	71,427
Art, music, or design	928,414	829,749	27,183	616	0	4,871	2,500	51,273	12,224
Business and management	652,785	602,799	10,812	930	6	2,476	17,147	12,545	6,071
Engineering or technology	1,028,406	998,215	2,087	233	0	128	9,839	16,324	1,580
Medical or other health	65,786	55,498	822	1	173	133	5,568	1,729	1,862
Other specialized	2,905,140	2,348,333	344,803	26,907	2,232	14,659	36,278	82,238	49,690
2-year	3,462,448	2,791,047	399,626	35,431	1,257	8,579	34,236	80,025	112,247
Percentage distribution									
2005–06									
Total	100.00	87.53	6.35	0.53	0.03	0.35	1.55	2.15	1.51
4-year	100.00	90.15	4.38	0.35	0.03	0.39	1.76	2.09	0.85
Doctoral, intensive[1]	100.00	98.92	0.00	0.00	0.00	1.08	0.00	0.00	0.00
Master's[2]	100.00	96.30	0.38	0.00	0.00	0.03	2.83	0.30	0.16
Baccalaureate[3]	100.00	90.93	0.68	0.61	0.09	2.22	1.49	3.72	0.25
Specialized institutions[4]	100.00	86.63	6.91	0.51	0.04	0.40	1.28	2.94	1.28
Art, music, or design	100.00	89.37	2.93	0.07	0.00	0.52	0.27	5.52	1.32
Business and management	100.00	92.34	1.66	0.14	#	0.38	2.63	1.92	0.93
Engineering or technology	100.00	97.06	0.20	0.02	0.00	0.01	0.96	1.59	0.15
Medical or other health	100.00	84.36	1.25	0.00	0.26	0.20	8.46	2.63	2.83
Other specialized	100.00	80.83	11.87	0.93	0.08	0.50	1.25	2.83	1.71
2-year	100.00	80.61	11.54	1.02	0.04	0.25	0.99	2.31	3.24
Revenue per full-time-equivalent student in current dollars									
2005–06									
Total	$13,977	$12,234	$888	$74	$5	$49	$217	$300	$211
4-year	13,773	12,417	604	48	4	53	243	287	117
Doctoral, intensive[1]	7,936	7,850	0	0	0	86	0	0	0
Master's[2]	9,551	9,198	36	0	0	3	271	28	16
Baccalaureate[3]	13,012	11,831	88	79	12	289	193	485	33
Specialized institutions[4]	18,526	16,049	1,280	95	8	74	237	545	237
Art, music, or design	21,433	19,155	628	14	0	112	58	1,184	282
Business and management	11,861	10,953	196	17	#	45	312	228	110
Engineering or technology	19,199	18,635	39	4	0	2	184	305	29
Medical or other health	13,902	11,728	174	0	37	28	1,177	365	394
Other specialized	20,094	16,242	2,385	186	15	101	251	569	344
2-year	14,543	11,723	1,678	149	5	36	144	336	471

#Rounds to zero.

[1]Doctoral, intensive institutions are committed to education through the doctorate and award at least 10 doctor's degrees per year across 3 or more disciplines or at least 20 doctor's degrees overall.

[2]Master's institutions offer a full range of baccalaureate programs and are committed to education through the master's degree. They award at least 20 master's degrees per year.

[3]Baccalaureate institutions primarily emphasize undergraduate education.

[4]Specialized 4-year institutions award degrees primarily in single fields of study, such as medicine, business, fine arts, theology, and engineering. Includes some institutions that have 4-year programs, but have not reported sufficient data to identify program category. Also includes institutions classified as 4-year under the IPEDS system, which had been classified as 2-year in the Carnegie system because they primarily award associate's degrees.

NOTE: Detail may not sum to totals because of rounding.

SOURCE: U.S. Department of Education, National Center for Education Statistics, 2004–05 and 2005–06 Integrated Postsecondary Education Data System (IPEDS), Spring 2006 and Spring 2007. (This table was prepared May 2008.)

Table 357. Current-fund revenue received from the federal government by the 120 degree-granting institutions receiving the largest amounts, by control and rank order: 2005–06

Institution	Control[1]	Rank order	Revenue from the federal govern-ment[2] (in thousands)	Institution	Control[1]	Rank order	Revenue from the federal govern-ment[2] (in thousands)
1	2	3	4	1	2	3	4
United States (all institutions)	†	†	$56,122,450				
120 institutions receiving the largest amounts	†	†	36,589,862				
California Institute of Technology	2	1	1,832,980	University of Maryland, Baltimore	1	61	209,502
Johns Hopkins University (MD)	2	2	1,596,449	U. of Massachusetts Medical School, Worcester	1	62	208,489
Massachusetts Institute of Technology	2	3	1,101,063	University of Utah	1	63	207,097
Columbia University in the City of New York	2	4	973,055	U. of Texas Southwestern Medical Center at Dallas	1	64	202,085
University of Washington, Seattle Campus	1	5	832,936	University of California, Irvine	1	65	201,679
Stanford University (CA)	2	6	821,865	Princeton University (NJ)	2	66	200,898
University of Chicago (IL)	2	7	799,993	University of New Mexico, Main Campus	1	67	198,161
University of Michigan, Ann Arbor	1	8	677,980	Rutgers University, New Brunswick/Piscataway (NJ)	1	68	197,716
University of Pennsylvania	2	9	653,281	Purdue University, Main Campus (IN)	1	69	195,010
University of California, Los Angeles	1	10	601,537	Florida State University	1	70	190,805
United States Air Force Academy (CO)	1	11	532,307	University of Tennessee	1	71	187,984
University of California, San Francisco	1	12	527,983	George Washington University (DC)	2	72	184,655
Weill Cornell Medical College (NY)	2	13	527,764	Georgetown University (DC)	2	73	179,610
University of California, San Diego	1	14	525,099	Colorado State University	1	74	179,020
University of Pittsburgh, Main Campus (PA)	1	15	518,720	University of South Florida	1	75	177,790
University of Wisconsin, Madison	1	16	518,471	Iowa State University	1	76	174,748
Harvard University (MA)	2	17	517,992	Indiana U.-Purdue U., Indianapolis	1	77	173,208
United States Military Academy (NY)	1	18	512,536	Kaplan University (IA)	3	78	167,174
University of Southern California	2	19	492,188	Arizona State University at the Tempe Campus	1	79	166,731
University of North Carolina at Chapel Hill	1	20	482,946	U. of Medicine and Dentistry of New Jersey	1	80	156,700
Washington University in St Louis (MO)	2	21	468,791	Virginia Commonwealth University	1	81	153,451
New York University	2	22	467,013	Oregon State University	1	82	151,030
Duke University (NC)	2	23	459,274	Yeshiva University (NY)	2	83	150,882
University of Miami (FL)	2	24	457,126	Stony Brook University (NY)	1	84	147,916
Yale University (CT)	2	25	429,713	Virginia Polytechnic Institute and State U.	1	85	145,846
University of Alabama at Birmingham	1	26	402,157	Dartmouth College (NH)	2	86	144,790
University of Minnesota, Twin Cities	1	27	400,646	Louisiana State U. & Ag. & Mech. & Hebert Law Ctr.	1	87	144,195
United States Naval Academy (MD)	1	28	391,044	Mississippi State University	1	88	143,348
Pennsylvania State University, Main Campus	1	29	377,930	Wake Forest University (NC)	2	89	141,211
University of Texas at Austin	1	30	371,174	Wayne State University (MI)	1	90	139,150
Vanderbilt University (TN)	2	31	359,702	U. of Texas Health Science Center at Houston	1	91	138,553
University of Arizona	1	32	346,275	University of Missouri, Columbia	1	92	137,157
University of Illinois at Urbana-Champaign	1	33	345,324	New Mexico State University, Main Campus	1	93	133,229
Texas A & M University	1	34	343,671	Utah State University	1	94	132,947
Cornell University (NY)	2	35	338,956	North Carolina State University at Raleigh	1	95	128,833
Case Western Reserve University (OH)	2	36	335,561	University of Georgia	1	96	128,194
University of California, Berkeley	1	37	334,154	Tulane University of Louisiana	2	97	126,878
Baylor College of Medicine (TX)	2	38	321,382	University of California, Santa Barbara	1	98	126,002
Emory University (GA)	2	39	319,475	University of Texas Medical Branch	1	99	123,614
Howard University (DC)	2	40	317,803	Brown University (RI)	2	100	123,525
Ohio State University, Main Campus	1	41	311,620	State University of New York at Buffalo	1	101	120,712
University of Florida	1	42	305,985	Medical University of South Carolina	1	102	120,472
University of California, Davis	1	43	295,022	University of Nebraska at Lincoln	1	103	117,727
University of Oklahoma Health Sciences Center	1	44	287,709	University of South Carolina, Columbia	1	104	116,401
University of Illinois at Chicago	1	45	278,930	Washington State University	1	105	115,147
Carnegie Mellon University (PA)	2	46	277,509	Rockhurst University (MO)	2	106	114,264
Georgia Institute of Technology, Main Campus	1	47	277,282	University of Alaska, Fairbanks	1	107	113,865
University of Rochester (NY)	2	48	274,977	U. of Texas Health Science Center at San Antonio	1	108	111,933
University of Iowa	1	49	271,891	Indiana University, Bloomington	1	109	111,506
U. of Colorado at Denver and Health Science Center	1	50	266,016	Tufts University (MA)	2	110	111,288
University of Virginia, Main Campus	1	51	258,958	University of Louisville (KY)	1	111	109,296
Northwestern University (IL)	2	52	258,703	University of Massachusetts, Amherst	1	112	107,570
University of Colorado at Boulder	1	53	255,178	University of Nevada, Reno	1	113	106,773
University of Maryland, College Park	1	54	252,364	Medical College of Wisconsin	2	114	103,968
Oregon Health & Science University	1	55	251,513	Kansas State University	1	115	99,227
Michigan State University	1	56	247,074	University of Vermont	1	116	98,600
University of Hawaii at Manoa	1	57	238,992	University of Kansas, Main Campus	1	117	96,575
Boston University (MA)	2	58	238,037	West Virginia University	1	118	92,170
University of Kentucky	1	59	225,210	University of New Hampshire, Main Campus	1	119	91,559
University of Cincinnati, Main Campus	1	60	212,330	University of Oklahoma, Norman Campus	1	120	91,327

†Not applicable.

[1]Publicly controlled institutions are identified by a "1"; private not-for-profit, by a "2"; and private for-profit, by a "3."

[2]Includes federal appropriations, unrestricted and restricted federal contracts and grants, and revenue for independent operations. Independent operations generally include only the revenues associated with major federally funded research and development centers. Federally supported student aid that is received through students is excluded. Data for public,

private not-for-profit, and private for-profit institutions are only roughly comparable because they were collected using different survey instruments.

NOTE: Degree-granting institutions grant associate's or higher degrees and participate in Title IV federal financial aid programs.

SOURCE: U.S. Department of Education, National Center for Education Statistics, 2005–06 Integrated Postsecondary Education Data System (IPEDS), Spring 2007. (This table was prepared June 2008.)

Table 358. Voluntary support for degree-granting institutions, by source and purpose of support: Selected years, 1959–60 through 2006–07

[In millions of current dollars]

Year	Total voluntary support[1]	Sources						Purpose		Voluntary support as a percent of total expenditures[2]
		Alumni	Nonalumni individuals	Corporations	Foundations	Religious organizations	Other	Current operations	Capital purposes	
1	2	3	4	5	6	7	8	9	10	11
1959–60	$815	$191	$194	$130	$163	$80	$57	$385	$430	14.6
1965–66	1,440	310	350	230	357	108	85	675	765	11.5
1970–71	1,860	458	495	259	418	104	126	1,050	810	8.0
1975–76	2,410	588	569	379	549	130	195	1,480	930	6.2
1980–81	4,230	1,049	1,007	778	922	140	334	2,590	1,640	6.6
1985–86	7,400	1,825	1,781	1,702	1,363	211	518	4,022	3,378	7.6
1990–91	10,200	2,680	2,310	2,230	2,030	240	710	5,830	4,370	7.0
1994–95	12,750	3,600	2,940	2,560	2,460	250	940	7,230	5,520	7.0
1995–96	14,250	4,040	3,400	2,800	2,815	255	940	7,850	6,400	7.5
1996–97	16,000	4,650	3,850	3,050	3,200	250	1,000	8,500	7,500	8.0
1997–98	18,400	5,500	4,500	3,250	3,800	300	1,050	9,000	9,400	8.8
1998–99	20,400	5,930	4,810	3,610	4,530	330	1,190	9,900	10,500	9.3
1999–2000	23,200	6,800	5,420	4,150	5,080	370	1,380	11,270	11,930	9.8
2000–01	24,200	6,830	5,200	4,350	6,000	370	1,450	12,200	12,000	9.3
2001–02	23,900	5,900	5,400	4,370	6,300	360	1,570	12,400	11,500	8.5
2002–03	23,600	6,570	4,280	4,250	6,600	360	1,540	12,900	10,700	7.8
2003–04	24,400	6,700	5,200	4,400	6,200	350	1,550	13,600	10,800	7.7
2004–05	25,600	7,100	5,000	4,400	7,000	370	1,730	14,200	11,400	7.6
2005–06	28,000	8,400	5,700	4,600	7,100	375	1,825	15,000	13,000	7.9
2006–07	29,750	8,270	5,650	4,800	8,500	380	2,150	16,100	13,650	8.1

[1]Data are based on sample surveys of colleges and universities.
[2]Total expenditures include current-fund expenditures and additions to plant value through 1995–96.
NOTE: Some data have been revised from previously published figures.
SOURCE: Council for Aid to Education, "Voluntary Support of Education," selected years, 1959–60 through 2006–07. U.S. Department of Education, National Center for Education Statistics, Higher Education General Information Survey (HEGIS), 1965–66 through 1985–86; Financial Statistics of Institutions of Higher Education, 1959–60; and 1986–87 through 2005–06 Integrated Postsecondary Education Data System, "Finance Survey" (IPEDS-F:FY87–99), and Spring 2001 through Spring 2007. (This table was prepared July 2008.)

Table 359. Endowment funds of the 120 colleges and universities with the largest endowments, by rank order: 2006 and 2007

Institution	2007 rank order[1]	Market value of endowment, as of June 30 (in thousands) 2006	2007	Percent change, 2006 to 2007[2]	Institution	2007 rank order[1]	Market value of endowment, as of June 30 (in thousands) 2006	2007	Percent change, 2006 to 2007[2]
1	2	3	4	5	1	2	3	4	5
Total	†	$266,783,518	$322,194,627	20.8					
Harvard University (MA)	1	28,915,706	34,634,906	19.8	Texas Christian University	61	1,016,353	1,187,057	16.8
Yale University (CT)	2	18,030,600	22,530,200	25.0	University of Cincinnati (OH)	62	1,101,100	1,185,400	7.7
Stanford University (CA)	3	14,084,676	17,164,836	21.9	George Washington University (DC)	63	963,697	1,147,451	19.1
Princeton University (NJ)	4	13,044,900	15,787,200	21.0	Carnegie Mellon University (PA)	64	941,525	1,115,740	18.5
University of Texas System	5	13,234,848	15,613,672	18.0	University of Oklahoma[3]	65	960,315	1,114,426	16.0
Massachusetts Institute of Technology	6	8,368,066	9,980,410	19.3	Princeton Theological Seminary (NJ)	66	945,355	1,108,515	17.3
Columbia University (NY)	7	5,937,814	7,149,803	20.4	Berea College (KY)	67	948,738	1,102,272	16.2
University of Michigan	8	5,652,262	7,089,830	25.4	Boston University (MA)	68	916,017	1,101,386	20.2
University of Pennsylvania	9	5,313,268	6,635,187	24.9	University of Missouri System	69	944,054	1,097,846	16.3
Texas A&M University System[3]	10	5,642,978	6,590,300	16.8	Syracuse University (NY)	70	908,371	1,086,143	19.6
Northwestern University (IL)	11	5,140,668	6,503,292	26.5	Lehigh University (PA)	71	939,473	1,085,639	15.6
University of California	12	5,541,930	6,439,436	16.2	Georgetown University (DC)	72	834,497	1,059,343	26.9
University of Chicago (IL)	13	4,867,003	6,204,189	27.5	Baylor University (TX)	73	874,364	1,018,012	16.4
University of Notre Dame (IN)	14	4,436,624	5,976,973	34.7	Tulane University (LA)	74	858,323	1,009,129	17.6
Duke University (NC)	15	4,497,718	5,910,280	31.4	University of Alabama System	75	848,848	999,816	17.8
Washington University (MO)	16	4,684,737	5,567,843	18.9	Trinity University (TX)	76	814,672	991,112	21.7
Emory University (GA)	17	4,870,019	5,561,743	14.2	University of Iowa[3]	77	832,869	982,428	18.0
Cornell University (NY)	18	4,321,199	5,424,733	25.5	University of California, Los Angeles[3]	78	804,869	975,295	21.2
Rice University (TX)	19	3,986,664	4,669,544	17.1	Saint Louis University (MO)	79	824,851	959,486	16.3
University of Virginia	20	3,618,172	4,370,209	20.8	University of Kentucky	80	785,196	957,608	22.0
Dartmouth College (NH)	21	3,092,100	3,760,234	21.6	University of Tennessee System	81	811,138	954,376	17.7
University of Southern California	22	3,065,935	3,715,272	21.2	Middlebury College (VT)	82	775,753	936,354	20.7
Vanderbilt University (TN)	23	2,946,392	3,487,500	18.4	University of Tulsa (OK)	83	816,980	915,320	12.0
University of Minnesota[3]	24	2,224,308	2,804,466	26.1	University of Arkansas[3]	84	763,069	876,839	14.9
Johns Hopkins University (MD)	25	2,350,749	2,800,377	19.1	Vassar College (NY)	85	741,655	869,122	17.2
Brown University (RI)	26	2,290,646	2,780,798	21.4	University of California, Berkeley	86	694,763	837,011	20.5
Ohio State University[3]	27	1,996,839	2,338,103	17.1	Bowdoin College (ME)	87	673,346	827,714	22.9
University of Pittsburgh (PA)	28	1,802,859	2,254,379	25.0	Oberlin College (OH)	88	697,851	816,135	16.9
University of Washington	29	1,794,370	2,184,374	21.7	Rensselaer Polytechnic Institute (NY)	89	682,894	812,996	19.1
University of North Carolina, Chapel Hill[3]	30	1,638,601	2,164,444	32.1	University of Maryland System[3]	90	674,600	810,374	20.1
New York University	31	1,774,700	2,161,800	21.8	University of Louisville (KY)[3]	91	680,251	796,812	17.1
Rockefeller University (NY)	32	1,771,954	2,145,203	21.1	University of Miami (FL)	92	620,435	741,382	19.5
Williams College (MA)	33	1,462,131	1,892,055	29.4	Pepperdine University (CA)	93	538,233	734,924	36.5
California Institute of Technology	34	1,580,922	1,860,052	17.7	Lafayette College (PA)	94	648,292	734,421	13.3
Case Western Reserve University (OH)	35	1,598,566	1,841,234	15.2	University of Colorado[3]	95	590,306	716,656	21.4
Purdue University (IN)	36	1,493,554	1,786,592	19.6	Wesleyan University (CT)	96	619,761	710,800	14.7
Pomona College (CA)	37	1,457,213	1,760,902	20.8	Colgate University (NY)	97	557,121	709,047	27.3
University of Rochester (NY)	38	1,491,275	1,726,318	15.8	Hamilton College (NY)	98	587,582	701,670	19.4
Grinnell College (IA)	39	1,471,804	1,718,313	16.7	Santa Clara University (CA)	99	598,657	697,881	16.6
Boston College (MA)	40	1,447,887	1,670,092	15.3	Washington and Lee University (VA)	100	586,968	692,797	18.0
Amherst College (MA)	41	1,337,158	1,662,377	24.3	Brandeis University (MA)	101	579,654	691,370	19.3
Wellesley College (MA)	42	1,412,410	1,656,565	17.3	Berry College (GA)	102	589,279	683,253	15.9
University of Richmond (VA)	43	1,380,439	1,654,988	19.9	Northeastern University (MA)	103	595,859	679,926	14.1
University of Wisconsin[3]	44	1,425,750	1,645,250	15.4	Macalester College (MN)	104	577,060	675,987	17.1
Pennsylvania State University	45	1,326,390	1,590,000	19.9	Bryn Mawr College (PA)	105	579,747	663,626	14.5
Indiana University[3]	46	1,276,160	1,556,853	22.0	Carleton College (MN)	106	571,955	663,500	16.0
University of Illinois[3]	47	1,252,290	1,515,387	21.0	College of the Holy Cross (MA)	107	544,347	658,855	21.0
Tufts University (MA)	48	1,148,868	1,452,058	26.4	Louisiana State University System	108	593,203	656,710	10.7
Swarthmore College (PA)	49	1,245,281	1,441,232	15.7	Rochester Institute of Technology (NY)	109	568,945	656,218	15.3
Yeshiva University (NY)	50	1,273,327	1,409,576	10.7	Rutgers University (NJ)	110	549,858	654,184	19.0
University of Delaware	51	1,223,203	1,397,492	14.2	Washington State University	111	579,861	650,903	12.3
Smith College (MA)	52	1,156,350	1,360,966	17.7	Denison University (OH)	112	528,121	642,791	21.7
Southern Methodist University (TX)	53	1,122,477	1,327,816	18.3	Texas Tech University	113	540,251	641,640	18.8
Georgia Institute of Technology[3]	54	1,047,724	1,281,162	22.3	Drexel University (PA)	114	526,792	628,467	19.3
Baylor College of Medicine (TX)	55	1,059,393	1,278,011	20.6	University of Georgia[3]	115	518,823	618,838	19.3
University of Nebraska[3]	56	1,153,559	1,277,169	10.7	Mount Holyoke College (MA)	116	510,032	615,376	20.7
Wake Forest University (NC)	57	1,042,558	1,248,695	19.8	Thomas Jefferson University (PA)	117	468,635	614,338	31.1
Michigan State University	58	1,047,792	1,247,713	19.1	University of Utah	118	509,095	610,469	19.9
Kansas University Endowment Association	59	1,049,367	1,238,695	18.0	Bucknell University (PA)	119	522,059	599,399	14.8
University of Florida[3]	60	996,245	1,219,026	22.4	Colby College (ME)	120	482,019	598,729	24.2

†Not applicable.

[1]Institutions ranked by size of endowment in 2007.

[2]Change in market value of endowment. Includes growth from gifts and returns on investments, as well as reductions from expenditures and withdrawals.

[3]Includes foundations.

NOTE: Includes U.S. institutions participating in the National Association of College and University Business Officers (NACUBO) Endowment Study (excludes Canadian institutions participating in the study). Some data have been revised from previously published figures.
SOURCE: National Association of College and University Business Officers, *NACUBO Endowment Study, 2007.* (This table was prepared June 2008.)

Table 360. Current-fund expenditures and current-fund expenditures per full-time-equivalent student in degree-granting institutions, by type and control of institution: Selected years, 1970–71 through 2000–01

	All institutions			4-year institutions			2-year institutions		
	Current-fund expenditures (in millions)		Current-fund expenditures per student, in constant 2006–07 dollars[1]	Current-fund expenditures (in millions)		Current-fund expenditures per student, in constant 2006–07 dollars[1]	Current-fund expenditures (in millions)		Current-fund expenditures per student, in constant 2006–07 dollars[1]
Control of institution and year	Unadjusted dollars	Constant 2006–07 dollars[1]		Unadjusted dollars	Constant 2006–07 dollars[1]		Unadjusted dollars	Constant 2006–07 dollars[1]	
1	2	3	4	5	6	7	8	9	10
All institutions[2]									
1970–71	$23,375	$120,120	$17,828	$21,049	$108,164	$21,021	$2,327	$11,956	$7,508
1975–76	38,903	143,201	16,887	33,811	124,457	21,093	5,092	18,743	7,267
1980–81	64,053	150,945	17,116	55,840	131,592	21,358	8,212	19,353	7,282
1985–86	97,536	182,975	20,459	85,560	160,509	25,500	11,976	22,466	8,481
1986–87	105,764	194,100	21,414	92,985	170,648	26,830	12,779	23,452	8,674
1987–88	113,786	200,516	21,725	100,143	176,472	27,206	13,644	24,043	8,765
1988–89	123,867	208,644	22,045	109,141	183,839	27,586	14,726	24,805	8,859
1989–90	134,656	216,486	22,134	118,578	190,639	27,979	16,077	25,847	8,711
1990–91	146,088	222,691	22,306	128,594	196,024	28,132	17,494	26,667	8,843
1991–92	156,189	230,697	22,267	137,375	202,908	28,653	18,814	27,789	8,474
1992–93	165,241	236,674	22,677	145,300	208,112	29,191	19,941	28,562	8,636
1993–94	173,351	242,020	23,380	152,164	212,440	29,833	21,187	29,580	9,156
1994–95	182,969	248,330	23,998	160,891	218,366	30,595	22,078	29,965	9,333
1995–96	190,476	251,673	24,352	166,954	220,593	30,754	23,522	31,079	9,829
Public institutions									
1970–71	14,996	77,061	15,558	12,899	66,285	19,110	2,097	10,777	7,259
1975–76	26,184	96,382	14,777	21,392	78,742	19,411	4,792	17,639	7,154
1980–81	42,280	99,635	15,000	34,677	81,720	19,652	7,602	17,916	7,212
1985–86	63,194	118,550	17,780	52,184	97,896	23,091	11,010	20,654	8,506
1986–87	67,654	124,160	18,318	56,003	102,778	23,927	11,651	21,383	8,613
1987–88	72,641	128,009	18,451	60,137	105,974	24,108	12,505	22,036	8,669
1988–89	78,946	132,977	18,737	65,349	110,075	24,430	13,597	22,902	8,839
1989–90	85,771	137,893	18,706	70,865	113,929	24,661	14,906	23,964	8,709
1990–91	92,961	141,706	18,749	76,722	116,952	24,673	16,239	24,754	8,785
1991–92	98,847	146,001	18,568	81,334	120,133	25,050	17,513	25,867	8,434
1992–93	104,570	149,775	18,931	86,065	123,270	25,693	18,505	26,505	8,512
1993–94	109,310	152,610	19,534	89,697	125,229	26,276	19,612	27,381	8,988
1994–95	115,465	156,712	20,132	94,895	128,794	27,117	20,570	27,918	9,199
1995–96	119,525	157,926	20,373	97,905	129,359	27,192	21,620	28,566	9,539
1996–97	125,429	161,130	20,671	103,069	132,406	27,775	22,360	28,724	9,487
1997–98	132,846	167,668	21,305	109,190	137,811	28,628	23,656	29,857	9,770
1998–99	140,539	174,358	22,126	115,158	142,870	29,344	25,381	31,488	10,457
1999–2000	152,325	183,679	22,902	124,878	150,582	30,454	27,447	33,097	10,761
2000–01	170,345	198,603	24,024	140,578	163,899	32,613	29,766	34,704	10,707
Private institutions[2]									
1970–71	8,379	43,059	24,127	8,150	41,879	24,975	230	1,180	10,940
1975–76	12,719	46,819	23,919	12,419	45,715	24,793	300	1,104	9,727
1980–81	21,773	51,310	23,572	21,163	49,872	24,897	610	1,438	8,281
1985–86	34,342	64,425	28,310	33,376	62,612	30,473	966	1,812	8,202
1986–87	38,110	69,940	30,593	36,982	67,870	32,870	1,128	2,070	9,353
1987–88	41,145	72,506	31,634	40,006	70,499	33,719	1,139	2,008	9,974
1988–89	44,922	75,667	31,962	43,792	73,764	34,176	1,130	1,903	9,104
1989–90	48,885	78,593	32,621	47,713	76,709	34,967	1,172	1,884	8,740
1990–91	53,127	80,984	33,389	51,872	79,072	35,491	1,255	1,912	9,683
1991–92	57,342	84,696	33,909	56,041	82,774	36,213	1,301	1,922	9,064
1992–93	60,671	86,899	34,414	59,235	84,842	36,390	1,436	2,057	10,624
1993–94	64,041	89,410	35,214	62,466	87,211	37,033	1,575	2,198	11,942
1994–95	67,504	91,618	35,737	65,996	89,572	37,512	1,508	2,046	11,635
1995–96	70,952	93,747	36,292	69,050	91,234	37,768	1,902	2,513	15,003

[1]Constant dollars based on the Consumer Price Index, prepared by the Bureau of Labor Statistics, U.S. Department of Labor, adjusted to a school-year basis.
[2]Data are not available for years after 1995–96.
NOTE: Data through 1994–95 are for institutions of higher education, while later data are for degree-granting institutions. Degree-granting institutions grant associate's or higher degrees and participate in Title IV federal financial aid programs. The degree-granting classification is very similar to the earlier higher education classification, but it includes more 2-year colleges and excludes a few higher education institutions that did not grant degrees. (See Guide to Sources for details.) Private college data not collected on a basis consistent with public institutions after 1995–96. Detail may not sum to totals because of rounding.
SOURCE: U.S. Department of Education, National Center for Education Statistics, Higher Education General Information Survey (HEGIS), "Financial Statistics of Institutions of Higher Education," 1970–71 through 1985–86, "Fall Enrollment in Institutions of Higher Education," 1970 through 1985; 1986–87 through 2000–01 Integrated Postsecondary Education Data System, "Finance Survey" (IPEDS-F:FY86–99), "Fall Enrollment Survey" (IPEDS-F:FY86–99), and Spring 2001 and Spring 2002. (This table was prepared July 2007.)

Table 361. Current-fund expenditures and educational and general expenditures of institutions of higher education, by purpose and per student: Selected years, 1929–30 through 1995–96

Year	Current-fund expenditures, by purpose — Total	Educational and general expenditures — Total	Administration and general expense	Instruction and departmental research	Organized research	Libraries	Plant operation and maintenance	Organized activities related to instructional departments[1]	Extension and public service	Scholarships and fellowships	Other general expenditures	Auxiliary enterprises	Independent operations[2]	Hospitals	Other current expenditures	E&G expenditures per student — Current dollars	E&G expenditures per student — Constant 2006–07 dollars[4]
1	2	3	4	5	6	7	8	9	10	11	12	13	14	15	16	17	18
1929–30	$507,142	$377,903	$42,633	$221,598	$18,007[5]	$9,622	$61,061	(6)	$24,982	(6)	—	$3,127	(5)	(7)	$126,112	$343	$4,094
1939–40	674,688	521,990	62,827	280,248	27,266[5]	19,467	69,612	27,225[7]	35,325	(6)	—	124,184	(5)	(7)	28,514	349	5,103
1949–50	2,245,661	1,706,444	213,070	780,994	225,341[5]	56,147	225,110	119,108[7]	86,674	(6)	—	476,401	(5)	(7)	62,816	698	6,016
1959–60	5,601,376	4,685,258	583,224	1,793,320	1,022,353[5]	135,384	469,943	234,255[7]	205,595	$172,050	$9,134	916,117	(5)	(7)	—	1,287	8,943
1969–70	21,043,113	16,845,212	2,627,993	6,883,844	2,144,076	652,596	1,541,698	648,089	1,362,320[8]	984,594	—	2,769,276	$757,388	$671,236	—	2,104	11,372
1974–75	35,057,563	27,547,620	4,495,391	11,797,823	3,132,132	1,001,868	2,786,768	1,253,824	1,097,788	1,449,542	532,485	4,073,590	1,085,590	2,350,763	—	2,694	10,620
1979–80	56,913,588	44,542,843	7,621,143	18,496,717	5,099,151	1,623,811	4,700,070	2,252,577	1,816,521	2,200,468	732,385	5,485,608	1,127,728	4,757,409	—	3,850	10,123
1980–81	64,052,938	50,073,805	8,681,513	20,733,166	5,657,719	1,759,784	5,350,310	2,513,502	2,057,770	2,504,525	815,516	7,288,089	1,257,934	5,433,111	—	4,139	9,755
1981–82	70,339,448	54,848,752	9,648,069	22,962,527	5,929,894	1,922,416	5,979,281	2,734,038	2,203,726	2,684,945	783,854	7,997,632	1,258,777	6,234,287	—	4,433	9,617
1982–83	75,935,749	58,929,218	10,412,233	24,673,293	6,265,280	2,039,671	6,391,596	3,047,220	2,320,478	2,922,897	856,548	8,614,316	1,406,126	6,986,089	—	4,742	9,864
1983–84	81,993,360	63,741,276	11,561,260	26,436,308	6,723,534	2,231,149	6,729,825	3,300,003	2,499,203	3,301,673	958,321	9,250,196	1,622,233	7,379,654	—	5,114	10,256
1984–85	89,951,263	70,061,324	12,765,452	28,777,183	7,551,892	2,361,793	7,345,482	3,712,460	2,861,095	3,670,355	1,015,613	10,012,248	1,867,550	8,010,141	—	5,723	11,046
1985–86	97,535,742	76,127,965	13,913,724	31,032,099	3,437,367	2,551,337	7,605,226	4,116,061	3,119,533	4,160,174	1,192,449	10,528,303	2,187,361	8,692,113	—	6,216	11,661
1986–87	105,763,557	82,955,555	15,060,576	33,711,146	9,352,309	2,441,184	7,819,032	5,134,267	3,448,453	4,776,100	1,212,488	11,037,333	2,597,655	9,173,014	—	6,635	12,176
1987–88	113,786,476	89,157,430	16,171,015	35,833,563	10,350,931	2,836,498	8,230,986	5,385,083	3,786,362	5,325,358	1,317,633	11,399,953	2,822,632	10,406,461	—	6,984	12,307
1988–89	123,867,184	96,803,377	17,309,956	38,812,690	11,432,170	3,009,870	8,739,895	5,894,409	4,227,323	5,918,666	1,458,397	12,280,063	2,958,962	11,824,782	—	7,415	12,490
1989–90	134,655,571	105,585,076	19,062,179	42,145,987	12,505,961	3,254,239	9,458,262	6,183,405	4,689,758	6,655,544	1,629,742	13,203,984	3,187,224	12,679,286	—	7,799	12,538
1990–91	146,087,836	114,139,901	20,751,966	45,496,117	13,444,040	3,343,892	10,062,581	6,706,881	5,076,177	7,551,184	1,707,063	14,272,247	3,349,824	14,325,865	—	8,260	12,591
1991–92	156,189,161	121,567,157	21,984,118	47,997,196	14,261,554	3,595,834	10,346,580	6,961,184	5,489,298	9,060,000	1,851,393	14,966,100	3,551,592	16,104,313	—	8,466	12,505
1992–93	165,241,040	128,977,968	23,414,977	50,340,914	15,291,309	3,684,852	10,783,727	7,368,118	5,935,095	10,148,373	1,990,603	15,561,508	3,651,891	17,049,672	—	8,903	12,751
1993–94	173,350,617	136,024,350	24,489,022	52,775,599	16,117,610	3,908,412	11,368,496	7,769,499	6,242,414	11,238,010	2,115,288	16,429,341	3,387,323	17,509,603	—	9,509	13,276
1994–95	182,968,610	144,158,002	25,904,821	55,719,707	17,109,541	4,165,761	11,745,905	8,112,930	6,691,485	12,285,328	2,422,524	17,204,917	3,534,332	18,071,359	—	10,096	13,703
1995–96[9]	190,476,163	151,445,605	27,886,345	57,810,033	17,517,887	4,293,363	12,330,885	9,003,700	7,007,413	13,195,102	2,400,876	17,599,061	3,490,511	17,940,986	—	10,619	14,031

—Not available.

[1]Academic support excluding expenditures for libraries.
[2]Generally includes only those expenditures associated with federally funded research and development centers (FFRDCs).
[3]Data for 1929–30 and 1939–40 are based on school-year enrollment.
[4]Constant dollars based on the Consumer Price Index, prepared by the Bureau of Labor Statistics, U.S. Department of Labor, adjusted to a school-year basis.
[5]Expenditures for federally funded research and development centers are included under "Organized research."
[6]Included under "Other current expenditures."
[7]Expenditures for hospitals included under "Organized activities related to instructional departments."
[8]Includes other sponsored programs, which are separately budgeted programs, other than research, which are supported by sponsors outside the institution.

[9]Data for 1995–96 are for degree-granting institutions. The degree-granting classification is very similar to the earlier higher education classification, except that it includes some additional institutions, primarily 2-year colleges, and excludes a few higher education institutions that did not award associate's or higher degrees. (See Guide to Sources for details.)
NOTE: Institutions of higher education were accredited by an agency or association that was recognized by the U.S. Department of Education, or recognized directly by the Secretary of Education. The data in this table reflect limitations of data availability and comparability. Major changes in data collection forms in 1965–66 and 1974–75 cause significant data comparability problems among the three mostly consistent time periods, 1929–30 to 1959–60, 1969–70, and 1974–75 to 1995–96. The largest problems affect Hospitals, independent operations, Organized research, Other sponsored programs, Extension and public service, and Scholarships and fellowships. Detail may not sum to totals because of rounding.
SOURCE: U.S. Department of Education, National Center for Education Statistics, Biennial Survey of Education in the United States, 1929–30 through 1959–60; Higher Education General Information Survey (HEGIS), "Financial Statistics of Institutions of Higher Education," 1969–70 through 1965–86; and 1986–87 through 1995–96 Integrated Postsecondary Education Data System, "Finance Survey" (IPEDS-F:FY87–96). (This table was prepared July 2007.)

Table 362. Expenditures of public degree-granting institutions, by purpose of expenditure and type of institution: 2003–04, 2004–05, and 2005–06

Type of institution and year	Total expenditures	Operating expenditures																Nonoperating expenditures		
		Total	Instruction		Research	Public service	Academic support	Student services	Institutional support	Operation and maintenance of plant	Depreciation	Scholarships and fellowships[1]	Auxiliary enterprises	Hospitals	Independent operations	Other	Total	Interest	Other
			Total	Salaries and wages															
1	2	3	4	5	6	7	8	9	10	11	12	13	14	15	16	17	18	19	20
							In thousands of current dollars												
All institutions																			
2003–04	$205,068,500	$198,321,711	$56,767,947	$39,431,881	$21,408,497	$8,981,907	$13,613,774	$9,426,787	$16,849,813	$12,611,040	$8,999,651	$8,172,682	$15,705,951	$18,471,970	$736,799	$6,574,893	$6,746,790	$2,679,502	$4,067,287
2004–05	215,794,343	208,488,447	59,656,806	41,026,819	22,550,836	9,481,391	14,258,857	10,042,243	17,454,934	13,578,182	9,592,800	8,402,515	16,664,085	20,104,812	658,166	6,042,819	7,305,896	2,999,771	4,316,125
2005–06	226,549,889	219,061,195	62,988,407	43,202,237	23,056,406	9,746,753	15,299,823	10,634,906	18,528,338	15,117,844	10,071,291	8,616,689	17,314,237	20,689,224	744,028	6,253,250	7,488,694	3,404,166	4,084,528
4-year																			
2003–04	167,654,408	161,575,599	42,287,792	29,290,396	21,394,125	8,293,533	10,904,235	6,062,776	11,691,429	9,469,470	7,586,394	5,123,190	13,680,554	18,471,970	711,188	5,898,943	6,078,810	2,240,096	3,838,714
2004–05	177,191,847	170,580,039	44,699,891	30,555,416	22,528,940	8,819,093	11,417,218	6,475,649	12,151,581	10,287,442	8,136,660	5,453,252	14,593,314	20,104,812	658,166	5,254,019	6,611,808	2,526,222	4,085,586
2005–06	186,074,213	179,399,853	47,286,043	32,206,726	23,031,885	9,054,397	12,290,114	6,906,675	12,915,660	11,508,008	8,517,539	5,697,202	15,158,273	20,689,224	744,028	5,600,805	6,674,361	2,856,931	3,817,430
2-year																			
2003–04	37,414,092	36,746,112	14,480,155	10,141,485	14,371	688,374	2,709,539	3,364,011	5,158,384	3,141,570	1,413,258	3,049,492	2,025,397	0	25,612	675,949	667,980	439,406	228,574
2004–05	38,602,497	37,908,408	14,956,915	10,471,403	21,896	662,298	2,841,639	3,566,594	5,303,353	3,290,740	1,456,140	2,949,262	2,070,771	0	0	788,800	694,089	463,549	230,539
2005–06	40,475,676	39,661,343	15,702,364	10,995,511	24,520	692,356	3,009,709	3,728,231	5,612,677	3,609,836	1,553,752	2,919,487	2,155,964	0	0	652,445	814,333	547,234	267,099
							Percentage distribution												
All institutions																			
2003–04	100.00	96.71	27.68	19.23	10.44	4.38	6.64	4.60	8.22	6.15	4.39	3.99	7.66	9.01	0.36	3.21	3.29	1.31	1.98
2004–05	100.00	96.61	27.65	19.01	10.45	4.39	6.61	4.65	8.09	6.29	4.45	3.89	7.72	9.32	0.30	2.80	3.39	1.39	2.00
2005–06	100.00	96.69	27.80	19.07	10.18	4.30	6.75	4.69	8.18	6.67	4.45	3.80	7.64	9.13	0.33	2.76	3.31	1.50	1.80
4-year																			
2003–04	100.00	96.37	25.22	17.47	12.76	4.95	6.50	3.62	6.97	5.65	4.53	3.06	8.16	11.02	0.42	3.52	3.63	1.34	2.29
2004–05	100.00	96.27	25.23	17.24	12.71	4.98	6.44	3.65	6.86	5.81	4.59	3.08	8.24	11.35	0.37	2.97	3.73	1.43	2.31
2005–06	100.00	96.41	25.41	17.31	12.38	4.87	6.60	3.71	6.94	6.18	4.58	3.06	8.15	11.12	0.40	3.01	3.59	1.54	2.05
2-year																			
2003–04	100.00	98.21	38.70	27.11	0.04	1.84	7.24	8.99	13.79	8.40	3.78	8.15	5.41	0.00	0.07	1.81	1.79	1.17	0.61
2004–05	100.00	98.20	38.75	27.13	0.06	1.72	7.36	9.24	13.74	8.52	3.77	7.64	5.36	0.00	0.00	2.04	1.80	1.20	0.60
2005–06	100.00	97.99	38.79	27.17	0.06	1.71	7.44	9.21	13.87	8.92	3.84	7.21	5.33	0.00	0.00	1.61	2.01	1.35	0.66
							Expenditures per full-time-equivalent student in current dollars												
All institutions																			
2003–04	$22,192	$21,462	$6,143	$4,267	$2,317	$972	$1,473	$1,020	$1,823	$1,365	$974	$884	$1,700	$1,999	$80	$712	$730	$290	$440
2004–05	23,084	22,303	6,382	4,389	2,412	1,014	1,525	1,074	1,867	1,453	1,026	899	1,783	2,151	70	646	782	320	462
2005–06	24,126	23,329	6,708	4,601	2,455	1,038	1,629	1,133	1,973	1,610	1,073	918	1,844	2,203	79	666	797	363	435
4-year																			
2003–04	30,166	29,072	7,609	5,270	3,849	1,492	1,962	1,091	2,104	1,704	1,365	922	2,462	3,324	128	1,061	1,094	403	691
2004–05	31,413	30,241	7,925	5,417	3,994	1,563	2,024	1,148	2,154	1,824	1,443	967	2,587	3,564	117	931	1,172	448	724
2005–06	32,483	31,318	8,255	5,622	4,021	1,581	2,145	1,206	2,255	2,009	1,487	995	2,646	3,612	130	978	1,165	499	666
2-year																			
2003–04	10,158	9,977	3,932	2,754	4	187	736	913	1,401	853	384	828	550	0	7	184	181	119	62
2004–05	10,412	10,225	4,034	2,824	6	179	766	962	1,430	888	393	796	559	0	0	213	187	125	62
2005–06	11,053	10,831	4,288	3,003	7	189	822	1,018	1,533	986	424	797	589	0	0	178	222	149	73

See notes at end of table.

Table 362. Expenditures of public degree-granting institutions, by purpose of expenditure and type of institution: 2003–04, 2004–05, and 2005–06—Continued

Type of institution and year	Total expenditures	Operating expenditures																Nonoperating expenditures		
		Total	Instruction		Research	Public service	Academic support	Student services	Institutional support	Operation and maintenance of plant	Depreciation	Scholarships and fellowships[1]	Auxiliary enterprises	Hospitals	Independent operations	Other	Total	Interest	Other
			Total	Salaries and wages															
1	2	3	4	5	6	7	8	9	10	11	12	13	14	15	16	17	18	19	20
						Expenditures per full-time-equivalent student in constant 2006–07 dollars[2]													
All institutions																			
2003–04	$24,344	$23,543	$6,739	$4,681	$2,541	$1,066	$1,616	$1,119	$2,000	$1,497	$1,068	$970	$1,864	$2,193	$87	$781	$801	$318	$483
2004–05	24,583	23,751	6,796	4,674	2,569	1,080	1,624	1,144	1,988	1,547	1,093	957	1,898	2,290	75	688	832	341	492
2005–06	24,750	23,932	6,881	4,720	2,519	1,065	1,671	1,162	2,024	1,652	1,100	941	1,892	2,260	81	683	818	372	446
4-year																			
2003–04	33,092	31,892	8,347	5,781	4,223	1,637	2,152	1,197	2,308	1,869	1,497	1,011	2,700	3,646	140	1,164	1,200	442	758
2004–05	33,453	32,205	8,439	5,769	4,253	1,665	2,156	1,223	2,294	1,942	1,536	1,030	2,755	3,796	124	992	1,248	477	771
2005–06	33,323	32,128	8,468	5,768	4,125	1,622	2,201	1,237	2,313	2,061	1,525	1,020	2,715	3,705	133	1,003	1,195	512	684
2-year																			
2003–04	11,144	10,945	4,313	3,021	4	205	807	1,002	1,536	936	421	908	603	0	8	201	199	131	68
2004–05	11,088	10,889	4,296	3,008	6	190	816	1,024	1,523	945	418	847	595	0	0	227	199	133	66
2005–06	11,339	11,111	4,399	3,080	7	194	843	1,044	1,572	1,011	435	818	604	0	0	183	228	153	75

[1]Excludes discounts and allowances.
[2]Constant dollars based on the Consumer Price Index, prepared by the Bureau of Labor Statistics, U.S. Department of Labor, adjusted to a school-year basis.

NOTE: Degree-granting institutions grant associate's or higher degrees and participate in Title IV federal financial aid programs. Includes data for public institutions reporting data according to the Financial Accounting Standards Board (FASB) questionnaire. Detail may not sum to totals because of rounding.
SOURCE: U.S. Department of Education, National Center for Education Statistics, 2003–04 through 2005–06 Integrated Postsecondary Education Data System (IPEDS), Spring 2004 through Spring 2007. (This table was prepared June 2008.)

Table 363. Expenditures of public degree-granting institutions, by type of institution, purpose of expenditure, and state or jurisdiction: 2003–04, 2004–05, and 2005–06

[In thousands of current dollars]

State or jurisdiction	Total expenditures, 2003–04	Total expenditures, 2004–05	2005–06 All institutions Total[1]	2005–06 All institutions Operating	4-year institutions Total	4-year institutions Operating expenditures Total[1]	4-year institutions Operating expenditures Instruction	4-year institutions Nonoperating	2-year institutions Total	2-year institutions Operating expenditures Total[1]	2-year institutions Operating expenditures Instruction	2-year institutions Nonoperating
1	2	3	4	5	6	7	8	9	10	11	12	13
United States	$205,068,500	$215,794,343	$226,549,889	$219,061,195	$186,074,213	$179,399,853	$47,286,043	$6,674,361	$40,475,676	$39,661,343	$15,702,364	$814,333
Alabama	4,237,484	4,440,310	4,732,672	4,640,527	4,150,555	4,073,628	916,041	76,927	582,118	566,900	224,313	15,218
Alaska	565,748	625,319	649,612	631,880	632,868	616,621	161,475	16,247	16,744	15,259	4,608	1,485
Arizona	3,301,923	3,521,306	3,809,011	3,686,632	2,752,986	2,660,630	795,784	92,356	1,056,025	1,026,002	383,791	30,023
Arkansas	2,187,822	2,329,165	2,538,362	2,482,623	2,221,676	2,175,279	484,422	46,397	316,686	307,344	119,626	9,342
California	31,090,738	32,218,384	34,026,467	32,313,041	25,877,522	24,434,350	5,068,800	1,443,172	8,148,946	7,878,691	3,042,535	270,254
Colorado	3,214,378	3,311,032	3,515,871	3,460,034	3,083,785	3,047,279	854,900	36,506	432,087	412,755	166,823	19,332
Connecticut	2,043,781	2,306,275	2,393,182	2,328,729	2,066,439	2,004,618	515,693	61,821	326,743	324,110	124,508	2,632
Delaware	709,220	757,382	798,725	796,704	683,730	681,708	272,881	2,021	114,995	114,995	49,409	0
District of Columbia	96,418	100,155	116,830	116,830	116,830	116,830	42,394	0	0	0	0	0
Florida	6,915,163	7,460,740	7,793,877	7,685,331	6,273,057	6,172,532	1,896,551	100,525	1,520,820	1,512,798	521,408	8,021
Georgia	4,535,035	4,666,410	5,008,710	4,957,862	4,084,004	4,043,577	1,091,504	40,427	924,706	914,284	365,963	10,422
Hawaii	1,092,964	1,055,358	1,148,545	1,065,089	984,372	904,519	254,903	79,853	164,173	160,570	67,462	3,603
Idaho	803,392	865,207	895,666	877,901	770,498	753,577	262,468	16,921	125,168	124,324	36,876	844
Illinois	8,594,168	7,707,684	8,147,811	8,015,825	6,046,219	5,952,131	1,410,177	94,088	2,101,592	2,063,694	691,059	37,898
Indiana	4,175,315	4,579,970	4,732,305	4,589,772	4,371,696	4,237,754	1,457,056	133,942	360,609	352,017	132,323	8,592
Iowa	3,230,982	3,261,661	3,524,403	3,446,811	2,871,947	2,805,514	580,798	66,434	652,456	641,297	260,966	11,159
Kansas	2,241,525	2,395,901	2,533,777	2,498,511	2,017,598	1,990,170	612,873	27,427	516,179	508,341	185,601	7,839
Kentucky	3,175,931	3,351,737	3,649,151	3,604,166	3,177,725	3,145,932	747,472	31,793	471,426	458,233	177,564	13,193
Louisiana	3,145,740	3,311,847	3,303,679	3,263,551	2,958,193	2,923,796	802,615	34,396	345,486	339,755	140,896	5,732
Maine	669,363	685,520	710,855	704,521	617,299	611,106	163,771	6,192	93,557	93,414	40,630	143
Maryland	3,833,195	4,129,836	4,413,784	4,335,926	3,473,219	3,399,448	916,498	73,771	940,566	936,478	359,867	4,087
Massachusetts	2,607,208	3,076,812	3,345,954	3,289,296	2,739,414	2,688,663	695,025	50,751	606,540	600,632	225,020	5,908
Michigan	9,244,800	9,599,856	10,130,974	9,984,841	8,635,369	8,510,222	2,077,785	125,147	1,495,605	1,474,619	499,738	20,986
Minnesota	3,514,009	3,637,085	3,878,041	3,810,051	3,064,469	3,004,244	864,600	60,225	813,572	805,807	361,316	7,764
Mississippi	2,589,114	2,759,232	2,894,694	2,836,372	2,254,013	2,201,250	444,827	52,762	640,682	635,122	235,416	5,560
Missouri	3,101,006	3,351,500	3,522,278	3,466,064	2,952,195	2,907,478	761,084	44,717	570,083	558,585	222,661	11,497
Montana	709,735	748,026	797,297	781,189	708,661	693,965	169,558	14,696	88,637	87,224	23,638	1,412
Nebraska	1,518,343	1,518,562	1,639,823	1,603,488	1,385,529	1,350,280	396,572	35,249	254,294	253,208	104,270	1,086
Nevada	1,024,383	1,117,126	1,212,202	1,176,282	1,127,527	1,092,174	385,213	35,353	84,675	84,108	34,114	567
New Hampshire	622,227	637,403	695,153	677,907	606,526	589,280	168,344	17,246	88,627	88,627	29,287	0
New Jersey	4,989,041	5,271,538	5,569,181	5,440,231	4,601,285	4,475,117	1,173,900	126,168	967,897	965,114	347,434	2,783
New Mexico	2,142,322	2,286,513	2,427,203	2,383,998	1,971,850	1,938,247	334,518	33,604	455,353	445,751	164,112	9,602
New York	9,772,214	10,305,243	11,031,705	10,526,171	8,847,638	8,382,233	2,365,636	465,406	2,184,066	2,143,938	952,299	40,128
North Carolina	6,071,783	6,501,732	7,037,662	6,824,130	5,540,882	5,329,286	1,726,796	211,597	1,496,780	1,494,845	684,675	1,935
North Dakota	671,955	716,180	753,586	744,558	661,098	652,781	204,633	8,316	92,488	91,777	36,088	711
Ohio	7,952,265	8,494,328	9,091,243	8,935,019	7,871,448	7,729,375	2,096,298	142,073	1,219,795	1,205,644	447,332	14,152
Oklahoma	2,468,242	2,521,594	2,746,540	2,700,542	2,356,885	2,319,998	688,997	36,887	389,655	380,545	146,866	9,111
Oregon	3,260,024	3,476,027	3,722,085	3,592,486	2,910,376	2,821,844	573,299	88,532	811,709	770,642	291,554	41,067
Pennsylvania	7,911,543	8,345,982	8,736,935	8,700,269	7,873,630	7,856,801	1,984,052	16,829	863,305	843,468	346,541	19,837
Rhode Island	513,168	538,384	567,607	563,036	473,728	469,410	123,022	4,318	93,879	93,626	41,232	253
South Carolina	2,535,272	2,716,391	2,902,490	2,860,100	2,326,959	2,289,415	727,520	37,544	575,531	570,685	218,728	4,846
South Dakota	452,975	485,499	500,890	493,402	451,188	444,256	145,492	p6,931	49,703	49,146	21,111	557
Tennessee	2,833,299	3,011,156	3,123,980	3,083,587	2,671,132	2,631,540	918,503	39,592	452,847	452,047	193,182	800
Texas	17,900,265	19,467,672	18,401,632	16,108,832	15,198,438	13,012,011	4,080,898	2,186,427	3,203,194	3,096,820	1,228,372	106,374
Utah	2,743,580	2,882,837	3,074,335	3,023,451	2,834,961	2,791,460	510,551	43,500	239,374	231,991	89,742	7,383
Vermont	529,088	556,927	594,285	583,319	570,589	559,623	143,787	10,966	23,696	23,696	6,728	0
Virginia	4,990,023	5,423,809	5,846,089	5,760,187	5,158,705	5,075,472	1,327,408	83,233	687,384	684,715	326,974	2,669
Washington	5,171,402	5,417,079	5,674,037	5,584,750	4,289,166	4,208,065	1,106,206	81,101	1,384,871	1,376,685	616,640	8,187
West Virginia	1,079,890	1,147,417	1,250,615	1,218,700	1,180,906	1,149,724	343,154	31,182	69,709	68,976	23,699	733
Wisconsin	4,392,455	4,564,833	4,706,156	4,578,656	3,517,186	3,417,356	937,240	99,830	1,188,970	1,161,299	625,417	27,671
Wyoming	443,838	467,251	486,855	482,962	315,180	312,226	98,072	2,954	171,675	170,736	61,949	939
U.S. Service Academies	1,452,747	1,669,152	1,745,065	1,745,055	1,745,065	1,745,055	401,972	10	0	0	0	0
Other jurisdictions	1,365,030	1,438,206	1,461,202	1,439,935	1,384,180	1,364,907	438,356	19,273	77,021	75,028	26,432	1,993
American Samoa	8,229	9,599	10,036	10,036	0	0	0	0	10,036	10,036	3,860	0
Federated States of Micronesia	20,244	17,822	18,132	18,132	0	0	0	0	18,132	18,132	5,012	0
Guam	81,611	89,316	92,412	88,614	68,792	66,607	16,834	2,185	23,620	22,007	7,757	1,613
Marshall Islands	5,208	5,878	6,323	6,323	0	0	0	0	6,323	6,323	3,016	0
Northern Marianas	17,975	16,010	16,168	16,168	16,168	16,168	10,917	0	0	0	0	0
Palau	8,890	8,514	8,913	8,913	0	0	0	0	8,913	8,913	2,069	0
Puerto Rico	1,163,640	1,226,385	1,242,436	1,226,993	1,232,438	1,217,375	396,774	15,063	9,998	9,618	4,717	380
U.S. Virgin Islands	59,234	64,682	66,782	64,757	66,782	64,757	13,831	2,025	0	0	0	0

[1]Includes other categories not separately shown.
NOTE: Degree-granting institutions grant associate's or higher degrees and participate in Title IV federal financial aid programs. Includes data for public institutions reporting data according to the Financial Accounting Standards Board (FASB) questionnaire. Detail may not sum to totals because of rounding.

SOURCE: U.S. Department of Education, National Center for Education Statistics, 2003–04 through 2005–06 Integrated Postsecondary Education Data System (IPEDS), Spring 2005 through Spring 2007. (This table was prepared June 2008.)

Table 364. Total expenditures of private not-for-profit degree-granting institutions, by purpose and type of institution: 1996–97 through 2005–06

Type of institution and year	Total	Instruction	Research	Public service	Academic support	Student services	Institutional support	Auxiliary enterprises[1]	Net grant aid to students[2]	Hospitals	Independent operations	Other
1	2	3	4	5	6	7	8	9	10	11	12	13
In thousands of current dollars												
All institutions												
1996–97	$67,399,563	$21,126,357	$6,702,520	$1,621,583	$4,942,411	$4,430,241	$8,226,648	$7,079,116	$1,529,456	—	—	$11,741,232
1997–98	69,300,699	23,404,428	7,267,877	1,672,991	5,738,254	4,903,988	9,138,895	7,698,614	1,297,749	$6,395,808	$1,782,095	—
1998–99	75,516,696	25,181,848	7,779,001	1,521,440	6,349,076	5,295,059	9,901,658	8,027,492	1,222,565	7,258,939	2,979,619	—
1999–2000	80,613,037	26,012,599	8,381,926	1,446,958	6,510,951	5,688,499	10,585,850	8,300,021	1,180,882	7,355,110	2,753,679	2,396,563
2000–01	85,625,016	27,607,324	9,025,739	1,473,292	7,368,263	6,117,195	11,434,074	9,010,853	1,176,160	7,255,376	3,134,609	2,022,132
2001–02	92,192,297	29,689,041	10,035,480	1,665,884	7,802,637	6,573,185	12,068,120	9,515,829	1,188,690	7,633,043	3,397,979	2,622,409
2002–03	99,748,076	32,062,218	11,079,532	1,878,380	8,156,688	7,096,223	13,157,744	9,936,478	1,173,845	7,586,208	3,879,736	3,741,024
2003–04	104,317,870	33,909,179	12,039,531	1,972,351	8,759,743	7,544,021	13,951,408	10,508,719	1,101,738	8,374,128	4,222,980	1,934,070
2004–05	110,394,127	36,258,473	12,812,857	2,000,437	9,342,064	8,191,737	14,690,328	10,944,342	1,069,591	9,180,775	4,223,779	1,679,741
2005–06	116,817,913	38,465,058	13,242,343	1,941,519	10,217,274	8,965,704	15,667,101	11,741,258	708,158	9,645,428	4,203,523	2,020,548
4-year												
1996–97	66,668,808	20,922,069	6,701,053	1,616,019	4,902,188	4,294,812	8,095,791	7,011,791	1,502,866	—	—	11,622,219
1997–98	68,677,274	23,164,693	7,267,228	1,669,650	5,704,216	4,817,585	8,988,203	7,621,887	1,276,848	6,395,610	1,771,355	—
1998–99	74,805,484	24,823,398	7,778,900	1,513,641	6,308,251	5,224,455	9,766,020	7,957,265	1,198,516	7,257,021	2,978,017	—
1999–2000	79,699,659	25,744,199	8,376,568	1,438,544	6,476,338	5,590,978	10,398,914	8,228,409	1,162,570	7,355,110	2,752,019	2,176,011
2000–01	85,048,123	27,413,897	9,019,966	1,467,325	7,333,851	6,036,478	11,292,310	8,957,973	1,160,660	7,253,479	3,133,099	1,979,086
2001–02	91,612,337	29,492,583	10,035,394	1,658,781	7,768,870	6,497,127	11,914,149	9,470,557	1,173,725	7,632,942	3,396,831	2,571,376
2002–03	99,137,236	31,866,310	11,079,332	1,871,274	8,122,181	7,014,149	12,996,836	9,876,937	1,161,441	7,586,208	3,854,471	3,708,098
2003–04	103,733,257	33,712,542	12,039,080	1,964,898	8,726,505	7,466,472	13,774,084	10,464,984	1,084,880	8,374,128	4,221,611	1,904,075
2004–05	109,789,731	36,051,084	12,812,326	1,993,767	9,307,600	8,101,214	14,516,197	10,899,456	1,051,216	9,180,775	4,223,779	1,652,317
2005–06	116,247,359	38,249,125	13,241,769	1,931,804	10,177,381	8,894,330	15,524,004	11,696,510	699,462	9,645,428	4,203,523	1,984,024
2-year												
1996–97	730,755	204,288	1,467	5,564	40,223	135,429	130,857	67,324	26,590	—	—	119,013
1997–98	623,424	239,735	649	3,341	34,038	86,403	150,692	76,726	20,901	198	10,740	—
1998–99	711,212	358,450	101	7,799	40,826	70,603	135,638	70,226	24,049	1,917	1,602	—
1999–2000	913,378	268,400	5,358	8,415	34,612	97,521	186,936	71,612	18,311	0	1,660	220,553
2000–01	576,893	193,428	5,772	5,967	34,412	80,717	141,764	52,880	15,500	1,896	1,510	43,046
2001–02	579,960	196,459	86	7,102	33,767	76,058	153,971	45,271	14,965	100	1,147	51,033
2002–03	610,840	195,909	200	7,106	34,508	82,074	160,908	59,541	12,404	0	25,265	32,926
2003–04	584,612	196,637	451	7,453	33,238	77,549	177,324	43,735	10,859	0	1,369	29,995
2004–05	604,395	207,389	532	6,670	34,464	90,523	174,131	44,886	18,375	0	0	27,425
2005–06	570,554	215,934	574	9,715	39,893	71,374	143,096	44,748	8,696	0	0	36,524
Percentage distribution												
All institutions												
1996–97	100.00	31.34	9.94	2.41	7.33	6.57	12.21	10.50	2.27	—	—	17.42
1997–98	100.00	33.77	10.49	2.41	8.28	7.08	13.19	11.11	1.87	9.23	2.57	—
1998–99	100.00	33.35	10.30	2.01	8.41	7.01	13.11	10.63	1.62	9.61	3.95	—
1999–2000	100.00	32.27	10.40	1.79	8.08	7.06	13.13	10.30	1.46	9.12	3.42	2.97
2000–01	100.00	32.24	10.54	1.72	8.61	7.14	13.35	10.52	1.37	8.47	3.66	2.36
2001–02	100.00	32.20	10.89	1.81	8.46	7.13	13.09	10.32	1.29	8.28	3.69	2.84
2002–03	100.00	32.14	11.11	1.88	8.18	7.11	13.19	9.96	1.18	7.61	3.89	3.75
2003–04	100.00	32.51	11.54	1.89	8.40	7.23	13.37	10.07	1.06	8.03	4.05	1.85
2004–05	100.00	32.84	11.61	1.81	8.46	7.42	13.31	9.91	0.97	8.32	3.83	1.52
2005–06	100.00	32.93	11.34	1.66	8.75	7.67	13.41	10.05	0.61	8.26	3.60	1.73
4-year												
1996–97	100.00	31.38	10.05	2.42	7.35	6.44	12.14	10.52	2.25	—	—	17.43
1997–98	100.00	33.73	10.58	2.43	8.31	7.01	13.09	11.10	1.86	9.31	2.58	—
1998–99	100.00	33.18	10.40	2.02	8.43	6.98	13.06	10.64	1.60	9.70	3.98	—
1999–2000	100.00	32.30	10.51	1.80	8.13	7.02	13.05	10.32	1.46	9.23	3.45	2.73
2000–01	100.00	32.23	10.61	1.73	8.62	7.10	13.28	10.53	1.36	8.53	3.68	2.33
2001–02	100.00	32.19	10.95	1.81	8.48	7.09	13.00	10.34	1.28	8.33	3.71	2.81
2002–03	100.00	32.14	11.18	1.89	8.19	7.08	13.11	9.96	1.17	7.65	3.89	3.74
2003–04	100.00	32.50	11.61	1.89	8.41	7.20	13.28	10.09	1.05	8.07	4.07	1.84
2004–05	100.00	32.84	11.67	1.82	8.48	7.38	13.22	9.93	0.96	8.36	3.85	1.50
2005–06	100.00	32.90	11.39	1.66	8.75	7.65	13.35	10.06	0.60	8.30	3.62	1.71
2-year												
1996–97	100.00	27.96	0.20	0.76	5.50	18.53	17.91	9.21	3.64	—	—	16.29
1997–98	100.00	38.45	0.10	0.54	5.46	13.86	24.17	12.31	3.35	0.03	1.72	—
1998–99	100.00	50.40	0.01	1.10	5.74	9.93	19.07	9.87	3.38	0.27	0.23	—
1999–2000	100.00	29.39	0.59	0.92	3.79	10.68	20.47	7.84	2.00	0.00	0.18	24.15
2000–01	100.00	33.53	1.00	1.03	5.96	13.99	24.57	9.17	2.69	0.33	0.26	7.46
2001–02	100.00	33.87	0.01	1.22	5.82	13.11	26.55	7.81	2.58	0.02	0.20	8.80
2002–03	100.00	32.07	0.03	1.16	5.65	13.44	26.34	9.75	2.03	0.00	4.14	5.39
2003–04	100.00	33.64	0.08	1.27	5.69	13.27	30.33	7.48	2.88	0.00	0.23	5.13
2004–05	100.00	34.31	0.09	1.10	5.70	14.98	28.81	7.43	3.04	0.00	0.00	4.54
2005–06	100.00	37.85	0.10	1.70	6.99	12.51	25.08	7.84	1.52	0.00	0.00	6.40

See notes at end of table.

Table 364. Total expenditures of private not-for-profit degree-granting institutions, by purpose and type of institution: 1996–97 through 2005–06—Continued

Type of institution and year	Total	Instruction	Research	Public service	Academic support	Student services	Institutional support	Auxiliary enterprises[1]	Net grant aid to students[2]	Hospitals	Independent operations	Other
1	2	3	4	5	6	7	8	9	10	11	12	13
				Expenditure per full-time-equivalent student in current dollars								
All institutions												
1996–97	$27,880	$8,739	$2,772	$671	$2,044	$1,833	$3,403	$2,928	$633	—	—	$4,857
1997–98	28,270	9,547	2,965	682	2,341	2,000	3,728	3,141	529	$2,609	$727	—
1998–99	30,291	10,101	3,120	610	2,547	2,124	3,972	3,220	490	2,912	1,195	—
1999–2000	31,751	10,246	3,301	570	2,564	2,241	4,169	3,269	465	2,897	1,085	944
2000–01	33,069	10,662	3,486	569	2,846	2,363	4,416	3,480	454	2,802	1,211	781
2001–02	34,841	11,220	3,793	630	2,949	2,484	4,561	3,596	449	2,885	1,284	991
2002–03	36,479	11,725	4,052	687	2,983	2,595	4,812	3,634	429	2,774	1,419	1,368
2003–04	37,240	12,105	4,298	704	3,127	2,693	4,980	3,751	393	2,989	1,508	690
2004–05	38,472	12,636	4,465	697	3,256	2,855	5,120	3,814	373	3,199	1,472	585
2005–06	40,156	13,222	4,552	667	3,512	3,082	5,386	4,036	243	3,316	1,445	695
4-year												
1996–97	28,327	8,890	2,847	687	2,083	1,825	3,440	2,979	639	—	—	4,938
1997–98	28,740	9,694	3,041	699	2,387	2,016	3,761	3,190	534	2,676	741	—
1998–99	30,706	10,189	3,193	621	2,589	2,145	4,009	3,266	492	2,979	1,222	—
1999–2000	32,064	10,357	3,370	579	2,605	2,249	4,184	3,310	468	2,959	1,107	875
2000–01	33,359	10,753	3,538	576	2,877	2,368	4,429	3,514	455	2,845	1,229	776
2001–02	35,139	11,312	3,849	636	2,980	2,492	4,570	3,633	450	2,928	1,303	986
2002–03	36,742	11,810	4,106	694	3,010	2,600	4,817	3,661	430	2,812	1,429	1,374
2003–04	37,504	12,188	4,353	710	3,155	2,699	4,980	3,784	392	3,028	1,526	688
2004–05	38,726	12,716	4,519	703	3,283	2,858	5,120	3,845	371	3,238	1,490	583
2005–06	40,394	13,291	4,601	671	3,536	3,091	5,394	4,064	243	3,352	1,461	689
2-year												
1996–97	11,426	3,194	23	87	629	2,118	2,046	1,053	416	—	—	1,861
1997–98	10,094	3,882	11	54	551	1,399	2,440	1,242	338	3	174	—
1998–99	12,514	6,307	2	137	718	1,242	2,387	1,236	423	34	28	—
1999–2000	17,148	5,039	101	158	650	1,831	3,510	1,345	344	0	31	4,141
2000–01	14,494	4,860	145	150	865	2,028	3,562	1,329	389	48	38	1,081
2001–02	14,890	5,044	2	182	867	1,953	3,953	1,162	384	3	29	1,310
2002–03	16,846	5,403	6	196	952	2,263	4,438	1,642	342	0	697	908
2003–04	16,561	5,570	13	211	942	2,197	5,023	1,239	478	0	39	850
2004–05	17,552	6,023	15	194	1,001	2,629	5,057	1,304	534	0	0	796
2005–06	18,240	6,903	18	311	1,275	2,282	4,575	1,431	278	0	0	1,168
				Expenditure per full-time-equivalent student in constant 2006–07 dollars[3]								
All institutions												
1996–97	$35,815	$11,226	$3,562	$862	$2,626	$2,354	$4,372	$3,762	$813	—	—	$6,239
1997–98	35,680	12,050	3,742	861	2,954	2,525	4,705	3,964	668	$3,293	$918	—
1998–99	37,581	12,532	3,871	757	3,160	2,635	4,928	3,995	608	3,612	1,483	—
1999–2000	38,286	12,354	3,981	687	3,092	2,702	5,028	3,942	561	3,493	1,308	1,138
2000–01	38,555	12,431	4,064	663	3,318	2,754	5,149	4,057	530	3,267	1,411	911
2001–02	39,914	12,854	4,345	721	3,378	2,846	5,225	4,120	515	3,305	1,471	1,135
2002–03	40,892	13,144	4,542	770	3,344	2,909	5,394	4,073	481	3,110	1,590	1,534
2003–04	40,851	13,279	4,715	772	3,430	2,954	5,463	4,115	431	3,279	1,654	757
2004–05	40,970	13,456	4,755	742	3,467	3,040	5,452	4,062	397	3,407	1,568	623
2005–06	41,194	13,564	4,670	685	3,603	3,162	5,525	4,140	250	3,401	1,482	713
4-year												
1996–97	36,389	11,420	3,658	882	2,676	2,344	4,419	3,827	820	—	—	6,344
1997–98	36,273	12,235	3,838	882	3,013	2,544	4,747	4,026	674	3,378	936	—
1998–99	38,095	12,641	3,961	771	3,213	2,661	4,973	4,052	610	3,696	1,517	—
1999–2000	38,664	12,489	4,064	698	3,142	2,712	5,045	3,992	564	3,568	1,335	1,056
2000–01	38,893	12,537	4,125	671	3,354	2,761	5,164	4,097	531	3,317	1,433	905
2001–02	40,256	12,959	4,410	729	3,414	2,855	5,235	4,161	516	3,354	1,493	1,130
2002–03	41,187	13,239	4,603	777	3,374	2,914	5,400	4,103	483	3,152	1,601	1,541
2003–04	41,141	13,370	4,775	779	3,461	2,961	5,463	4,150	430	3,321	1,674	755
2004–05	41,240	13,542	4,813	749	3,496	3,043	5,453	4,094	395	3,449	1,587	621
2005–06	41,439	13,635	4,720	689	3,628	3,171	5,534	4,169	249	3,438	1,498	707
2-year												
1996–97	14,679	4,103	29	112	808	2,720	2,628	1,352	534	—	—	2,391
1997–98	12,740	4,899	13	68	696	1,766	3,079	1,568	427	4	219	—
1998–99	15,525	7,825	2	170	891	1,541	2,961	1,533	525	42	35	—
1999–2000	20,678	6,076	121	190	784	2,208	4,232	1,621	415	0	38	4,993
2000–01	16,898	5,666	169	175	1,008	2,364	4,152	1,549	454	56	44	1,261
2001–02	17,058	5,778	3	209	993	2,237	4,529	1,332	440	3	34	1,501
2002–03	18,883	6,056	6	220	1,067	2,537	4,974	1,841	383	0	781	1,018
2003–04	18,167	6,110	14	232	1,033	2,410	5,510	1,359	524	0	43	932
2004–05	18,692	6,414	16	206	1,066	2,800	5,385	1,388	568	0	0	848
2005–06	18,711	7,082	19	319	1,308	2,341	4,693	1,468	285	0	0	1,198

—Not available.
[1]Essentially self-supporting operations of institutions that furnish a service to students, faculty, or staff, such as residence halls and food services.
[2]Excludes tuition and fee allowances and agency transactions, such as student awards made from contributed funds or grant funds.
[3]Constant dollars based on the Consumer Price Index, prepared by the Bureau of Labor Statistics, U.S. Department of Labor, adjusted to a school-year basis.

NOTE: Detail may not sum to totals because of rounding.
SOURCE: U.S. Department of Education, National Center for Education Statistics, 1996–97 through 2005–06 Integrated Postsecondary Education Data System, "Fall Enrollment Survey" (IPEDS-EF:96–99) and "Finance Survey" (IPEDS-F:FY97–99), and Spring 2001 through Spring 2007. (This table was prepared May 2008.)

Table 365. Total expenditures of private not-for-profit degree-granting institutions, by purpose and type of institution: 2005–06

Type of institution	Total	Instruction	Research	Public service	Academic support	Student services	Institutional support	Auxiliary enterprises[1]	Net grant aid to students[2]	Hospitals	Independent operations	Other
1	2	3	4	5	6	7	8	9	10	11	12	13
						In thousands of current dollars						
Total	$116,817,913	$38,465,058	$13,242,343	$1,941,519	$10,217,274	$8,965,704	$15,667,101	$11,741,258	$708,158	$9,645,428	$4,203,523	$2,020,548
4-year	116,247,359	38,249,125	13,241,769	1,931,804	10,177,381	8,894,330	15,524,004	11,696,510	699,462	9,645,428	4,203,523	1,984,024
Doctoral, extensive[3]	59,293,690	18,144,858	10,890,895	834,289	4,398,975	2,356,818	5,301,075	4,641,262	314,828	7,886,714	3,781,031	742,946
Doctoral, intensive[4]	8,573,617	3,304,918	729,269	113,651	1,306,298	700,629	1,342,017	971,512	22,151	0	37,488	45,683
Master's[5]	18,908,356	7,352,819	255,935	190,586	1,845,921	2,498,159	3,492,948	2,586,685	130,190	96,980	149,239	308,894
Baccalaureate[6]	16,922,613	5,937,396	159,386	162,649	1,519,386	2,521,099	3,308,600	2,773,372	156,514	0	74,996	309,217
Specialized institutions[7]	12,549,082	3,509,133	1,206,285	630,629	1,106,801	817,625	2,079,364	723,680	75,779	1,661,734	160,768	577,285
Art, music, or design	1,494,861	578,865	978	23,612	149,060	129,450	298,394	144,665	6,351	0	24,750	138,737
Business and management	789,191	251,850	4,948	1,368	111,317	134,213	179,673	86,865	4,030	0	8,084	6,842
Engineering or technology	361,446	144,134	14,772	3,928	31,831	46,143	71,718	43,380	5,357	0	63	118
Medical or other health	6,568,112	1,360,783	1,162,459	558,079	488,191	165,073	640,875	144,306	11,834	1,661,043	109,772	265,697
Theological	1,644,577	504,006	6,857	19,006	152,818	149,030	461,381	182,946	35,160	0	12,609	120,765
Tribal[8]	48,580	13,429	1,906	4,000	2,277	3,917	13,283	1,765	1,145	0	0	6,857
Other specialized	1,642,316	656,066	14,364	20,636	171,306	189,799	414,039	119,754	11,902	692	5,489	38,268
2-year	570,554	215,934	574	9,715	39,893	71,374	143,096	44,748	8,696	0	0	36,524
Associate's of arts	522,350	207,263	86	4,147	36,697	62,677	130,601	42,104	5,572	0	0	33,202
Tribal[8]	48,204	8,671	488	5,568	3,195	8,696	12,496	2,644	3,124	0	0	3,322
						Percentage distribution						
Total	100.00	32.93	11.34	1.66	8.75	7.67	13.41	10.05	0.61	8.26	3.60	1.73
4-year	100.00	32.90	11.39	1.66	8.75	7.65	13.35	10.06	0.60	8.30	3.62	1.71
Doctoral, extensive[3]	100.00	30.60	18.37	1.41	7.42	3.97	8.94	7.83	0.53	13.30	6.38	1.25
Doctoral, intensive[4]	100.00	38.55	8.51	1.33	15.24	8.17	15.65	11.33	0.26	0.00	0.44	0.53
Master's[5]	100.00	38.89	1.35	1.01	9.76	13.21	18.47	13.68	0.69	0.51	0.79	1.63
Baccalaureate[6]	100.00	35.09	0.94	0.96	8.98	14.90	19.55	16.39	0.92	0.00	0.44	1.83
Specialized institutions[7]	100.00	27.96	9.61	5.03	8.82	6.52	16.57	5.77	0.60	13.24	1.28	4.60
Art, music, or design	100.00	38.72	0.07	1.58	9.97	8.66	19.96	9.68	0.42	0.00	1.66	9.28
Business and management	100.00	31.91	0.63	0.17	14.11	17.01	22.77	11.01	0.51	0.00	1.02	0.87
Engineering or technology	100.00	39.88	4.09	1.09	8.81	12.77	19.84	12.00	1.48	0.00	0.02	0.03
Medical or other health	100.00	20.72	17.70	8.50	7.43	2.51	9.76	2.20	0.18	25.29	1.67	4.05
Theological	100.00	30.65	0.42	1.16	9.29	9.06	28.05	11.12	2.14	0.00	0.77	7.34
Tribal[8]	100.00	27.64	3.92	8.23	4.69	8.06	27.34	3.63	2.36	0.00	0.00	14.11
Other specialized	100.00	39.95	0.87	1.26	10.43	11.56	25.21	7.29	0.72	0.04	0.33	2.33
2-year	100.00	37.85	0.10	1.70	6.99	12.51	25.08	7.84	1.52	0.00	0.00	6.40
Associate's of arts	100.00	39.68	0.02	0.79	7.03	12.00	25.00	8.06	1.07	0.00	0.00	6.36
Tribal[8]	100.00	17.99	1.01	11.55	6.63	18.04	25.92	5.49	6.48	0.00	0.00	6.89
					Expenditure per full-time-equivalent student in current dollars							
Total	$40,156	$13,222	$4,552	$667	$3,512	$3,082	$5,386	$4,036	$243	$3,316	$1,445	$695
4-year	40,394	13,291	4,601	671	3,536	3,091	5,394	4,064	243	3,352	1,461	689
Doctoral, extensive[3]	96,359	29,488	17,699	1,356	7,149	3,830	8,615	7,543	512	12,817	6,145	1,207
Doctoral, intensive[4]	31,205	12,029	2,654	414	4,754	2,550	4,884	3,536	81	0	136	166
Master's[5]	19,910	7,742	269	201	1,944	2,630	3,678	2,724	137	102	157	325
Baccalaureate[6]	24,880	8,729	234	239	2,234	3,707	4,864	4,078	230	0	110	455
Specialized institutions[7]	35,066	9,805	3,371	1,762	3,093	2,285	5,810	2,022	212	4,643	449	1,613
Art, music, or design	30,973	11,994	20	489	3,088	2,682	6,183	2,997	132	0	513	2,875
Business and management	14,542	4,641	91	25	2,051	2,473	3,311	1,601	74	0	149	126
Engineering or technology	17,275	6,889	706	188	1,521	2,205	3,428	2,073	256	0	3	6
Medical or other health	97,909	20,285	17,328	8,319	7,277	2,461	9,553	2,151	176	24,761	1,636	3,961
Theological	21,435	6,569	89	248	1,992	1,942	6,014	2,385	458	0	164	1,574
Tribal[8]	22,797	6,302	895	1,877	1,069	1,838	6,233	828	537	0	0	3,218
Other specialized	18,562	7,415	162	233	1,936	2,145	4,680	1,353	135	8	62	433
2-year	18,240	6,903	18	311	1,275	2,282	4,575	1,431	278	0	0	1,168
Associate's of arts	17,622	6,992	3	140	1,238	2,114	4,406	1,420	188	0	0	1,120
Tribal[8]	29,410	5,290	298	3,397	1,950	5,306	7,624	1,613	1,906	0	0	2,027

[1]Essentially self-supporting operations of institutions that furnish a service to students, faculty, or staff, such as residence halls and food services.
[2]Excludes tuition and fee allowances and agency transactions, such as student awards made from contributed funds or grant funds.
[3]Doctoral, extensive institutions are committed to graduate education through the doctorate, and award 50 or more doctor's degrees per year across at least 15 disciplines.
[4]Doctoral, intensive institutions are committed to education through the doctorate and award at least 10 doctor's degrees per year across 3 or more disciplines or at least 20 doctor's degrees overall.
[5]Master's institutions offer a full range of baccalaureate programs and are committed to education through the master's degree. They award at least 20 master's degrees per year.
[6]Baccalaureate institutions primarily emphasize undergraduate education.

[7]Specialized 4-year institutions award degrees primarily in single fields of study, such as medicine, business, fine arts, theology, and engineering. Includes some institutions that have 4-year programs, but have not reported sufficient data to identify program category. Also includes institutions classified as 4-year under the IPEDS system, which had been classified as 2-year in the Carnegie system because they primarily award associate's degrees.
[8]Tribally controlled colleges are located on reservations and are members of the American Indian Higher Education Consortium.
NOTE: Detail may not sum to totals because of rounding.
SOURCE: U.S. Department of Education, National Center for Education Statistics, 2005–06 Integrated Postsecondary Education Data System (IPEDS), Spring 2006 and Spring 2007. (This table was prepared May 2008.)

Table 366. Total expenditures of private for-profit degree-granting institutions, by purpose and type of institution: 1998–99 through 2005–06

Year and type of institution	Total expenditures, by purpose						
	Total	Instruction	Research and public service	Student services, academic and institutional support	Auxiliary enterprises[1]	Net grant aid to students[2]	Other
1	2	3	4	5	6	7	8
	In thousands of current dollars						
All institutions							
1998–99	$3,153,591	$1,132,766	$27,060	$1,823,453	$135,398	$34,913	—
1999–2000	3,846,246	1,171,732	24,738	2,041,594	144,305	26,278	$437,599
2000–01	4,235,781	1,310,054	22,896	2,337,151	181,243	43,788	340,649
2001–02	5,087,292	1,517,389	16,632	2,977,225	213,195	23,283	339,567
2002–03	6,110,378	1,747,725	17,987	3,670,218	240,380	36,031	398,037
2003–04	7,364,012	1,883,733	8,606	4,592,730	249,472	56,467	573,004
2004–05	8,830,792	2,313,895	7,583	5,693,200	269,883	54,819	491,411
2005–06	10,208,845	2,586,870	8,445	6,569,329	276,587	66,569	701,044
4–year							
1998–99	1,484,139	499,337	6,703	876,636	81,411	20,052	—
1999–2000	2,022,622	595,976	4,393	1,104,001	92,071	11,805	214,377
2000–01	2,414,655	726,328	4,878	1,385,095	113,371	18,519	166,465
2001–02	3,046,929	883,899	3,192	1,842,373	134,740	8,229	174,495
2002–03	3,754,727	1,030,470	5,339	2,337,388	153,528	14,813	213,190
2003–04	4,821,864	1,143,050	3,705	3,108,697	168,069	32,603	365,740
2004–05	5,989,792	1,430,196	3,513	4,110,514	180,036	38,639	226,894
2005–06	7,218,830	1,680,603	4,065	4,985,531	179,064	54,291	315,276
2–year							
1998–99	1,669,451	633,429	20,357	946,817	53,987	14,861	—
1999–2000	1,823,624	575,756	20,345	937,593	52,234	14,473	223,223
2000–01	1,821,126	583,727	18,019	952,056	67,872	25,269	174,184
2001–02	2,040,363	633,490	13,440	1,134,853	78,455	15,054	165,071
2002–03	2,355,650	717,255	12,648	1,332,830	86,853	21,218	184,846
2003–04	2,542,148	740,683	4,901	1,484,033	81,403	23,864	207,264
2004–05	2,840,999	883,699	4,070	1,582,687	89,846	16,181	264,517
2005–06	2,990,015	906,267	4,381	1,583,798	97,523	12,278	385,768
	Percentage distribution						
All institutions							
1998–99	100.00	35.92	0.86	57.82	4.29	1.11	—
1999–2000	100.00	30.46	0.64	53.08	3.75	0.68	11.38
2000–01	100.00	30.93	0.54	55.18	4.28	1.03	8.04
2001–02	100.00	29.83	0.33	58.52	4.19	0.46	6.67
2002–03	100.00	28.60	0.29	60.07	3.93	0.59	6.51
2003–04	100.00	25.58	0.12	62.37	3.39	0.77	7.78
2004–05	100.00	26.20	0.09	64.47	3.06	0.62	5.56
2005–06	100.00	25.34	0.08	64.35	2.71	0.65	6.87
4–year							
1998–99	100.00	33.64	0.45	59.07	5.49	1.35	—
1999–2000	100.00	29.47	0.22	54.58	4.55	0.58	10.60
2000–01	100.00	30.08	0.20	57.36	4.70	0.77	6.89
2001–02	100.00	29.01	0.10	60.47	4.42	0.27	5.73
2002–03	100.00	27.44	0.14	62.25	4.09	0.39	5.68
2003–04	100.00	23.71	0.08	64.47	3.49	0.68	7.59
2004–05	100.00	23.88	0.06	68.63	3.01	0.65	3.79
2005–06	100.00	23.28	0.06	69.06	2.48	0.75	4.37
2–year							
1998–99	100.00	37.94	1.22	56.71	3.23	0.89	—
1999–2000	100.00	31.57	1.12	51.41	2.86	0.79	12.24
2000–01	100.00	32.05	0.99	52.28	3.73	1.39	9.56
2001–02	100.00	31.05	0.66	55.62	3.85	0.74	8.09
2002–03	100.00	30.45	0.54	56.58	3.69	0.90	7.85
2003–04	100.00	29.14	0.19	58.38	3.20	0.94	8.15
2004–05	100.00	31.11	0.14	55.71	3.16	0.57	9.31
2005–06	100.00	30.31	0.15	52.97	3.26	0.41	12.90

See notes at end of table.

Table 366. Total expenditures of private for-profit degree-granting institutions, by purpose and type of institution: 1998–99 through 2005–06—Continued

Year and type of institution	Total	Instruction	Research and public service	Student services, academic and institutional support	Auxiliary enterprises[1]	Net grant aid to students[2]	Other
1	2	3	4	5	6	7	8
	Total expenditures per full-time-equivalent student in current dollars						
All institutions							
1998–99	9,685	3,479	83	5,600	416	107	—
1999–2000	10,000	3,046	64	5,308	375	68	1,138
2000–01	10,781	3,334	58	5,949	461	111	867
2001–02	11,144	3,324	36	6,522	467	51	744
2002–03	11,301	3,232	33	6,788	445	67	736
2003–04	11,381	2,911	13	7,098	386	87	886
2004–05	11,205	2,936	10	7,224	342	70	624
2005–06	11,336	2,873	9	7,295	307	74	778
4–year							
1998–99	9,117	3,068	41	5,385	500	123	—
1999–2000	9,688	2,855	21	5,288	441	57	1,027
2000–01	10,588	3,185	21	6,074	497	81	730
2001–02	11,021	3,197	12	6,664	487	30	631
2002–03	10,862	2,981	15	6,762	444	43	617
2003–04	11,291	2,677	9	7,279	394	76	856
2004–05	10,818	2,583	6	7,424	325	70	410
2005–06	10,897	2,537	6	7,526	270	82	476
2–year							
1998–99	10,252	3,890	125	5,815	332	91	—
1999–2000	10,370	3,274	116	5,332	297	82	1,269
2000–01	11,048	3,541	109	5,776	412	153	1,057
2001–02	11,333	3,519	75	6,303	436	84	917
2002–03	12,081	3,678	65	6,835	445	109	948
2003–04	11,557	3,367	22	6,747	370	108	942
2004–05	12,120	3,770	17	6,752	383	69	1,128
2005–06	12,558	3,806	18	6,652	410	52	1,620
	Total expenditures per full-time-equivalent student in constant 2006–07 dollars[3]						
All institutions							
1998–99	12,016	4,316	103	6,948	516	133	—
1999–2000	12,059	3,674	78	6,401	452	82	1,372
2000–01	10,818	3,346	58	5,969	463	112	870
2001–02	12,766	3,808	42	7,471	535	58	852
2002–03	12,669	3,624	37	7,609	498	75	825
2003–04	12,485	3,194	15	7,787	423	96	971
2004–05	11,933	3,127	10	7,693	365	74	664
2005–06	11,630	2,947	10	7,484	315	76	799
4–year							
1998–99	11,311	3,806	51	6,681	620	153	—
1999–2000	11,683	3,442	25	6,377	532	68	1,238
2000–01	12,345	3,713	25	7,081	580	95	851
2001–02	12,625	3,663	13	7,634	558	34	723
2002–03	12,176	3,342	17	7,580	498	48	691
2003–04	12,386	2,936	10	7,985	432	84	939
2004–05	11,520	2,751	7	7,906	346	74	436
2005–06	11,179	2,603	6	7,721	277	84	488
2–year							
1998–99	12,720	4,826	155	7,214	411	113	—
1999–2000	12,505	3,948	140	6,429	358	99	1,531
2000–01	12,881	4,129	127	6,734	480	179	1,232
2001–02	12,983	4,031	86	7,221	499	96	1,050
2002–03	13,542	4,123	73	7,662	499	122	1,063
2003–04	12,678	3,694	24	7,401	406	119	1,034
2004–05	12,907	4,015	18	7,190	408	74	1,202
2005–06	12,883	3,905	19	6,824	420	53	1,662

—Not available.

[1]Essentially self-supporting operations of institutions that furnish a service to students, faculty, or staff, such as residence halls and food services.

[2]Excludes tuition and fee allowances and agency transactions, such as student awards made from contributed funds or grant funds.

[3]Constant dollars based on the Consumer Price Index, prepared by the Bureau of Labor Statistics, U.S. Department of Labor, adjusted to a school-year basis.

NOTE: Detail may not sum to totals because of rounding.

SOURCE: U.S. Department of Education, National Center for Education Statistics, 1998–99 through 2005–06 Integrated Postsecondary Education Data System, "Fall Enrollment Survey" (IPEDS-EF:98–99) and "Finance Survey" (IPEDS-F:FY99), and Spring 2001 through Spring 2007. (This table was prepared May 2008.)

Table 367. Total expenditures of private for-profit degree-granting institutions, by purpose and type of institution: 2004–05 and 2005–06

Year and type of institution	Total	Instruction	Research and public service	Student services, academic and institutional support	Auxiliary enterprises[1]	Net grant aid to students[2]	Other
1	2	3	4	5	6	7	8
			In thousands of current dollars				
2004–05							
Total	$8,830,792	$2,313,895	$7,583	$5,693,200	$269,883	$54,819	$491,411
4–year	5,989,792	1,430,196	3,513	4,110,514	180,036	38,639	226,894
Doctoral, intensive[3]	67,138	23,009	0	44,129	0	0	0
Master's[4]	1,496,513	301,444	0	1,159,657	20,444	0	14,969
Baccalaureate[5]	419,419	92,803	0	310,302	10,397	0	5,917
Specialized institutions[6]	4,006,723	1,012,941	3,513	2,596,426	149,196	38,639	206,009
Art, music, or design	725,410	173,591	346	430,881	49,453	11,745	59,394
Business and management	450,864	95,579	218	327,396	7,326	1,053	19,293
Engineering or technology	773,888	209,759	30	518,833	9,386	89	35,792
Medical or other health	54,642	16,509	533	24,859	1,156	1,118	10,466
Other specialized	2,001,918	517,503	2,387	1,294,456	81,874	24,634	81,064
2–year	2,840,999	883,699	4,070	1,582,687	89,846	16,181	264,517
2005–06							
Total	10,208,845	2,586,870	8,445	6,569,329	276,587	66,569	701,044
4–year	7,218,830	1,680,603	4,065	4,985,531	179,064	54,291	315,276
Doctoral, intensive[3]	144,472	44,596	0	99,876	0	0	0
Master's[4]	1,755,252	346,749	0	1,367,888	12,631	0	27,984
Baccalaureate[5]	455,937	97,366	0	340,228	11,042	0	7,301
Specialized institutions[6]	4,863,169	1,191,892	4,065	3,177,539	155,391	54,291	279,991
Art, music, or design	818,347	186,928	515	496,558	49,294	9,362	75,690
Business and management	597,710	123,176	356	423,392	10,932	6,007	33,846
Engineering or technology	890,966	224,929	301	630,964	6,779	160	27,833
Medical or other health	64,792	17,326	659	32,839	1,780	1,515	10,673
Other specialized	2,491,355	639,533	2,234	1,593,785	86,606	37,248	131,948
2–year	2,990,015	906,267	4,381	1,583,798	97,523	12,278	385,768
			Percentage distribution				
2005–06							
Total	100.00	25.34	0.08	64.35	2.71	0.65	6.87
4–year	100.00	23.28	0.06	69.06	2.48	0.75	4.37
Doctoral, intensive[3]	100.00	30.87	0.00	69.13	0.00	0.00	0.00
Master's[4]	100.00	19.75	0.00	77.93	0.72	0.00	1.59
Baccalaureate[5]	100.00	21.36	0.00	74.62	2.42	0.00	1.60
Specialized institutions[6]	100.00	24.51	0.08	65.34	3.20	1.12	5.76
Art, music, or design	100.00	22.84	0.06	60.68	6.02	1.14	9.25
Business and management	100.00	20.61	0.06	70.84	1.83	1.00	5.66
Engineering or technology	100.00	25.25	0.03	70.82	0.76	0.02	3.12
Medical or other health	100.00	26.74	1.02	50.68	2.75	2.34	16.47
Other specialized	100.00	25.67	0.09	63.97	3.48	1.50	5.30
2–year	100.00	30.31	0.15	52.97	3.26	0.41	12.90
			Expenditure per full-time-equivalent student in current dollars				
2005–06							
Total	$11,336	$2,873	$9	$7,295	$307	$74	$778
4–year	10,897	2,537	6	7,526	270	82	476
Doctoral, intensive[3]	7,213	2,227	0	4,987	0	0	0
Master's[4]	5,759	1,138	0	4,488	41	0	92
Baccalaureate[5]	12,533	2,676	0	9,352	304	0	201
Specialized institutions[6]	16,144	3,957	13	10,549	516	180	929
Art, music, or design	18,892	4,315	12	11,463	1,138	216	1,747
Business and management	10,861	2,238	6	7,693	199	109	615
Engineering or technology	16,633	4,199	6	11,779	127	3	520
Medical or other health	13,692	3,662	139	6,940	376	320	2,255
Other specialized	17,232	4,423	15	11,024	599	258	913
2–year	12,558	3,806	18	6,652	410	52	1,620

[1]Essentially self-supporting operations of institutions that furnish a service to students, faculty, or staff, such as residence halls and food services.
[2]Excludes tuition and fee allowances and agency transactions, such as student awards made from contributed funds or grant funds.
[3]Doctoral, intensive institutions are committed to education through the doctorate and award at least 10 doctor's degrees per year across 3 or more disciplines or at least 20 doctor's degrees overall.
[4]Master's institutions offer a full range of baccalaureate programs and are committed to education through the master's degree. They award at least 20 master's degrees per year.
[5]Baccalaureate institutions primarily emphasize undergraduate education.

[6]Specialized 4-year institutions award degrees primarily in single fields of study, such as medicine, business, fine arts, theology, and engineering. Includes some institutions that have 4-year programs, but have not reported sufficient data to identify program category. Also includes institutions classified as 4-year under the IPEDS system, which had been classified as 2-year in the Carnegie system because they primarily award associate's degrees.
NOTE: Detail may not sum to totals because of rounding.
SOURCE: U.S. Department of Education, National Center for Education Statistics, 2004–05 and 2005–06 Integrated Postsecondary Education Data System (IPEDS), Spring 2006 and Spring 2007. (This table was prepared May 2008.)

Table 368. Total expenditures of private not-for-profit and for-profit degree-granting institutions, by level and state or jurisdiction: 1998–99 through 2005–06

[In thousands of current dollars]

State or jurisdiction	1998–99	1999–2000	2000–01	2001–02	2002–03	2003–04	2004–05	2005–06 Total	2005–06 4–year	2005–06 2–year	For–profit 2004–05	For–profit 2005–06
1	2	3	4	5	6	7	8	9	10	11	12	13
United States ...	$75,516,696	$80,613,037	$85,625,016	$92,192,297	$99,748,076	$104,317,870	$110,394,127	$116,817,913	$116,247,359	$570,554	$8,830,792	$10,208,845
Alabama	366,326	393,465	400,987	419,872	435,190	440,158	459,250	473,626	473,626	†	60,629	66,036
Alaska	16,663	19,042	19,106	19,823	20,561	20,916	21,076	23,276	23,276	†	3,986	667
Arizona	129,980	143,698	160,787	162,471	182,548	141,307	147,825	144,560	144,560	†	1,095,783	1,301,977
Arkansas	164,307	230,860	197,313	213,645	216,809	224,969	239,357	239,460	237,979	1,481	11,574	15,111
California	7,417,634	7,871,651	8,682,192	9,588,524	10,268,563	10,838,473	10,728,872	11,328,736	11,231,659	97,077	1,243,346	1,343,174
Colorado	335,298	376,887	399,613	430,242	450,245	486,523	524,349	562,544	559,659	2,885	320,550	431,326
Connecticut	1,894,898	2,094,981	2,193,752	2,343,067	2,517,664	2,684,855	2,882,963	3,074,362	3,059,826	14,536	41,931	45,242
Delaware	43,320	52,533	56,670	62,625	70,783	80,634	87,617	93,079	89,846	3,233	†	†
District of Columbia ..	2,641,207	2,267,409	2,230,368	2,387,245	2,530,695	2,673,493	2,824,081	2,922,770	2,922,770	†	127,859	149,019
Florida	1,905,829	2,031,623	2,247,374	2,472,362	2,695,985	2,908,264	3,067,443	3,239,855	3,237,757	2,098	781,280	889,222
Georgia	2,508,080	2,635,438	2,795,105	2,946,777	3,188,042	3,266,674	3,442,374	3,694,276	3,671,325	22,950	261,219	305,720
Hawaii	122,340	209,135	138,660	146,050	152,348	173,261	195,152	199,857	190,606	9,250	24,996	26,844
Idaho	110,393	118,150	130,256	139,029	147,022	152,512	164,694	176,300	176,300	†	13,073	14,859
Illinois	5,130,189	5,668,566	5,910,538	6,188,489	6,304,076	6,666,469	7,113,842	7,310,521	7,300,175	10,346	620,678	753,796
Indiana	1,246,522	1,343,315	1,425,665	1,525,312	1,612,609	1,702,487	1,796,767	1,879,185	1,872,878	6,307	211,310	234,536
Iowa	689,698	740,760	767,891	800,428	847,857	875,162	921,320	961,673	959,746	1,927	146,688	227,505
Kansas	196,897	208,729	222,036	232,720	237,781	252,050	265,476	277,289	267,300	9,989	11,213	12,324
Kentucky	375,598	400,513	406,358	437,092	458,584	457,484	470,392	495,803	495,803	†	114,564	128,781
Louisiana	692,914	746,629	773,107	828,300	876,419	909,744	940,075	1,088,847	1,086,569	2,278	70,241	57,319
Maine	290,439	316,114	341,350	373,835	384,085	399,609	422,938	451,904	450,760	1,144	5,648	6,764
Maryland	2,113,725	2,205,880	2,410,284	2,725,616	3,019,626	3,271,571	3,497,182	3,716,510	3,716,510	†	41,717	48,230
Massachusetts	7,218,867	7,591,344	8,187,834	8,831,619	9,506,793	10,037,913	10,799,206	11,622,482	11,606,326	16,156	64,126	65,825
Michigan	936,454	995,384	1,065,100	1,134,361	1,206,723	1,259,243	1,327,051	1,407,082	1,404,228	2,854	55,391	61,321
Minnesota	930,959	1,004,427	1,093,937	1,164,763	1,157,173	1,222,082	1,297,457	1,358,101	1,333,316	24,785	325,758	471,346
Mississippi	136,859	150,123	156,292	158,464	167,822	170,290	178,142	192,778	192,778	†	8,369	9,143
Missouri	2,019,795	2,144,299	2,380,876	2,561,036	3,355,385	2,961,937	3,128,635	3,336,361	3,313,484	22,877	106,447	292,903
Montana	64,772	69,426	74,446	72,297	78,561	86,364	91,446	91,423	82,676	8,746	†	†
Nebraska	355,512	387,509	422,879	445,634	840,326	510,418	557,724	590,420	588,016	2,404	25,524	31,320
Nevada	7,679	7,006	9,130	10,919	9,657	8,677	9,637	11,116	11,116	†	104,949	113,511
New Hampshire	572,609	589,823	654,213	719,549	786,283	837,504	883,914	932,584	931,427	1,157	41,599	47,395
New Jersey	1,252,181	1,362,090	1,479,492	1,588,295	1,641,561	1,765,956	1,873,156	2,038,712	2,038,712	†	85,429	81,044
New Mexico	47,256	54,280	63,824	60,571	59,119	52,502	54,076	60,376	60,376	†	35,073	36,476
New York	11,511,493	12,519,671	13,099,910	14,177,942	15,800,433	16,557,418	17,680,799	18,471,543	18,402,476	69,067	624,764	625,590
North Carolina	3,292,928	3,530,337	3,845,125	3,978,481	4,219,294	4,439,832	4,808,306	5,158,463	5,143,256	15,207	38,078	52,150
North Dakota	51,613	56,000	59,677	63,207	68,513	83,942	88,860	92,921	65,160	27,761	7,885	10,759
Ohio	2,017,835	2,211,035	2,368,824	2,530,980	2,637,737	2,843,939	3,017,764	3,205,370	3,193,392	11,978	232,605	261,728
Oklahoma	319,214	338,276	360,772	363,611	370,604	367,119	392,427	419,638	419,638	†	72,537	78,814
Oregon	424,420	456,683	447,516	473,270	487,996	512,749	550,322	578,958	575,125	3,833	86,156	91,337
Pennsylvania	7,219,858	7,590,629	7,841,530	8,397,080	8,894,900	9,386,083	9,960,675	10,603,066	10,501,689	101,378	530,515	585,001
Rhode Island	737,297	828,715	897,056	978,710	1,062,719	1,141,689	1,237,106	1,287,905	1,287,905	†	10,073	9,585
South Carolina	392,369	408,127	432,035	483,551	507,157	532,950	563,952	570,769	559,681	11,089	18,374	20,998
South Dakota	64,155	69,555	75,488	90,290	91,028	93,352	99,575	107,581	103,807	3,774	23,477	26,652
Tennessee	1,842,893	1,971,564	2,131,732	2,367,380	2,609,840	2,819,415	3,140,336	3,435,062	3,427,209	7,853	142,256	166,173
Texas	2,249,979	2,490,597	2,662,275	2,921,130	3,142,104	3,266,787	3,379,710	3,542,703	3,527,308	15,395	343,221	374,290
Utah	610,830	648,035	694,025	741,519	785,441	824,774	867,956	888,654	880,355	8,299	62,880	75,959
Vermont	333,738	347,293	369,832	382,794	400,154	426,338	510,623	553,310	532,221	21,089	24,914	24,009
Virginia	891,622	944,905	1,000,236	1,057,465	1,109,551	1,224,687	1,311,743	1,400,161	1,400,161	†	258,642	309,961
Washington	544,781	600,315	594,393	639,129	674,622	737,957	778,678	803,657	803,657	†	104,107	118,880
West Virginia	162,994	170,653	185,101	194,652	201,085	197,437	181,181	181,222	181,222	†	28,634	22,726
Wisconsin	913,475	999,502	1,062,053	1,160,074	1,258,006	1,321,899	1,410,625	1,521,060	1,511,709	9,351	36,044	48,284
Wyoming	†	†	†	†	†	†	†	†	†		34,596	37,211
Other jurisdictions..	413,323	431,216	456,532	494,476	680,257	578,021	615,990	648,562	635,392	13,170	70,535	79,139
Guam	†	†	†	1,160	1,161	999	1,535	2,635	2,635	†	†	†
Puerto Rico	413,323	431,216	456,532	493,316	679,096	577,023	614,455	645,927	632,757	13,170	70,535	79,139

†Not applicable.
NOTE: Detail may not sum to totals because of rounding.

SOURCE: U.S. Department of Education, National Center for Education Statistics, 1998–99 through 2005–06 Integrated Postsecondary Education Data System, "Finance Survey" (IPEDS-F:FY98–99), and Spring 2001 through Spring 2007. (This table was prepared May 2008.)

Table 369. Participants in adult basic and secondary education programs, by type of program and state or jurisdiction: Selected fiscal years, 1990 through 2005

State or jurisdiction	1990	2000	2003	2004				2005			
				Total	Adult basic education	English literacy	Adult secondary education	Total	Adult basic education	English literacy	Adult secondary education
1	2	3	4	5	6	7	8	9	10	11	12
United States	3,535,970	3,306,687	2,679,927	2,627,618	1,044,111	1,168,897	414,610	2,543,953	1,009,706	1,139,965	394,282
Alabama	40,177	22,430	22,019	21,555	17,423	1,576	2,556	19,827	15,691	1,626	2,510
Alaska	5,067	5,396	4,723	3,588	2,206	502	880	3,791	2,434	600	757
Arizona	33,805	55,274	32,492	27,699	10,340	16,140	1,219	26,881	11,205	14,544	1,132
Arkansas	29,065	39,102	38,336	35,512	22,425	5,149	7,938	37,102	22,570	5,868	8,664
California	1,021,227	456,125	565,311	591,574	89,320	435,777	66,477	591,893	96,986	429,024	65,883
Colorado	12,183	13,743	15,137	15,097	4,406	9,295	1,396	15,011	4,244	9,427	1,340
Connecticut	46,434	27,698	33,062	32,878	5,576	14,675	12,627	31,958	4,852	13,891	13,215
Delaware	2,662	3,278	5,953	6,119	3,549	1,698	872	6,339	3,221	1,968	1,140
District of Columbia	19,586	2,828	3,226	3,170	1,165	1,502	503	3,646	1,382	1,845	419
Florida	419,429	399,772	387,710	370,985	145,141	125,891	99,953	348,119	130,805	114,310	103,004
Georgia	69,580	107,980	114,008	118,458	64,728	41,598	12,132	95,434	54,240	31,659	9,535
Hawaii	52,012	16,176	10,687	9,089	1,296	3,919	3,874	7,461	1,895	3,061	2,505
Idaho	11,171	10,542	8,780	7,261	3,795	2,400	1,066	7,744	4,250	2,475	1,019
Illinois	87,121	120,752	130,492	124,404	40,592	68,253	15,559	118,296	30,897	72,311	15,088
Indiana	44,166	41,760	41,397	41,148	21,678	8,315	11,155	43,498	24,181	8,197	11,120
Iowa	41,507	31,757	16,338	12,242	6,053	3,844	2,345	11,989	5,482	3,915	2,592
Kansas	10,274	11,410	10,386	9,788	4,906	3,873	1,009	9,475	4,567	3,830	1,078
Kentucky	28,090	37,061	34,700	32,235	23,030	3,113	6,092	30,931	22,488	2,768	5,675
Louisiana	40,039	38,873	31,998	32,502	24,856	1,910	5,736	29,367	22,621	1,917	4,829
Maine	14,964	9,807	10,485	8,814	3,758	1,469	3,587	8,151	3,645	1,765	2,741
Maryland	41,230	27,556	30,082	30,304	12,712	12,020	5,572	27,055	11,414	10,347	5,294
Massachusetts	34,220	24,565	21,337	21,578	7,471	11,888	2,219	21,448	7,317	12,013	2,118
Michigan	194,178	86,218	70,893	48,273	24,281	13,301	10,691	34,768	20,560	10,843	3,365
Minnesota	45,648	517,693	43,864	44,220	12,196	25,729	6,295	47,174	13,081	27,507	6,586
Mississippi	18,957	40,370	36,614	26,467	21,304	834	4,329	25,675	21,437	781	3,457
Missouri	31,815	38,773	41,928	37,729	24,186	8,036	5,507	37,052	23,518	7,955	5,579
Montana	6,071	4,995	4,437	3,864	2,641	198	1,025	3,291	2,266	199	826
Nebraska	6,158	9,095	10,200	10,267	4,842	4,237	1,188	10,226	4,795	4,217	1,214
Nevada	17,262	22,346	7,601	8,732	1,148	7,015	569	9,981	1,400	8,163	418
New Hampshire	7,198	5,519	6,444	5,866	1,833	1,866	2,167	5,804	1,916	1,925	1,963
New Jersey	64,080	44,712	42,465	41,803	12,918	24,497	4,388	40,889	12,235	25,265	3,389
New Mexico	30,236	29,197	21,587	22,842	12,383	8,466	1,993	24,132	13,409	8,299	2,424
New York	156,611	194,028	138,184	165,618	63,755	90,305	11,558	157,486	59,929	86,111	11,446
North Carolina	109,740	154,786	108,431	110,185	60,695	29,646	19,844	109,047	60,673	29,711	18,663
North Dakota	3,587	1,964	2,145	2,154	1,321	263	570	2,063	1,225	273	565
Ohio	95,476	81,010	59,761	56,607	37,335	9,040	10,232	50,869	33,893	8,031	8,945
Oklahoma	24,307	20,534	21,620	21,164	13,699	4,580	2,885	20,447	13,338	4,480	2,629
Oregon	37,075	27,981	24,863	21,701	9,404	11,023	1,274	21,668	9,753	10,436	1,479
Pennsylvania	52,444	46,836	52,823	53,706	26,222	15,912	11,572	54,274	27,652	16,195	10,427
Rhode Island	7,347	7,950	4,567	5,166	1,995	1,950	1,221	6,697	2,442	3,138	1,117
South Carolina	81,200	132,497	69,284	67,408	44,713	7,524	15,171	65,901	45,497	7,534	12,870
South Dakota	3,184	5,431	3,446	3,607	2,356	598	653	3,517	2,218	545	754
Tennessee	41,721	49,386	46,166	47,755	34,564	6,600	6,591	48,924	35,770	6,738	6,416
Texas	218,747	106,516	128,363	122,773	49,283	66,667	6,823	119,867	49,237	64,726	5,904
Utah	24,841	28,987	32,883	31,429	13,213	11,690	6,526	29,320	14,170	10,218	4,932
Vermont	4,808	4,436	1,937	2,283	1,289	254	740	2,015	1,099	273	643
Virginia	31,649	31,211	31,574	28,037	12,462	12,068	3,507	29,222	12,260	13,020	3,942
Washington	31,776	57,999	55,363	40,193	14,157	23,495	2,541	50,386	18,488	28,296	3,602
West Virginia	21,186	22,403	10,717	10,213	8,048	275	1,890	9,444	7,049	287	2,108
Wisconsin	61,081	27,297	30,437	29,132	13,986	7,618	7,528	26,029	12,748	7,034	6,247
Wyoming	3,578	2,632	2,671	2,424	1,456	403	565	2,379	1,261	404	714
Other jurisdictions	31,400	53,799	54,259	49,410	17,661	3,672	28,077	37,328	7,525	2,784	27,019
American Samoa	—	—	824	833	373	380	80	838	343	410	85
Federated States of Micronesia	—	—	—	—	—	—	—	—	—	—	—
Guam	1,311	902	989	900	572	71	257	1062	552	132	378
Marshall Islands	—	2,963	302	311	112	129	70	—	—	—	—
Northern Marianas	—	527	475	436	27	189	220	740	59	274	407
Palau	—	—	89	—	—	—	—	206	66	56	84
Puerto Rico	28,436	47,974	50,301	45,796	16,079	2,674	27,043	33,463	6,186	1,482	25,795
U.S. Virgin Islands	1,653	1,433	1,279	1,134	498	229	407	1,019	319	430	270

—Not available.
NOTE: Adult basic education provides instruction in basic skills for adults 16 and over functioning at literacy levels below the secondary level. Adult secondary education provides instruction at the high school level for adults who are seeking to pass the GED or obtain an adult high school credential. English literacy instruction is for adults who lack proficiency in English and who seek to improve their literacy and competence in English.

SOURCE: U.S. Department of Education, Office of Vocational and Adult Education, Division of Adult Education and Literacy, "Adult Education Program Facts, Program Year 1990–1991," Enrollment and Participation in the State-Administered Adult Education Program, selected years, 2000 through 2005, retrieved on August 11, 2005, from http://www.ed.gov/about/offices/list/ovae/pi/AdultEd/aedatatables.html. (This table was prepared September 2006.)

Table 370. Participation of employed persons, 17 years old and over, in career-related adult education during the previous 12 months, by selected characteristics of participants: Various years, 1995 through 2005

Characteristic of employed person	1995 — Percent participating in career/job-related courses (2)	1995 — Number of courses per employee (3)	1999 — Percent participating in career/job-related courses (4)	1999 — Number per employee (5)	2003 — Percent participating in career/job-related courses[1] (6)	2003 — Number per employee[1] (7)	2005 — Employed persons, in thousands[1] (8)	2005 — Percent: In career or job-related courses (9)	2005 — Percent: In apprentice programs (10)	2005 — Percent: In personal interest courses (11)	2005 — Percent: In informal learning activities for personal interest (12)	2005 — Number of career/job-related courses taken (in thousands) (13)	2005 — Number per employee (14)
Total	31.1	0.8	30.5 (1.14)	0.7 (0.03)	46.0 (0.70)	0.9 (0.02)	133,386 (1,508.1)	38.8 (0.83)	1.4 (0.24)	21.8 (0.94)	73.5 (1.01)	108,443	0.8 (0.03)
Sex													
Male	29.0	0.7	28.3 (1.15)	0.6 (0.03)	42.7 (1.15)	0.8 (0.03)	71,754 (934.7)	31.7 (1.22)	2.0 (0.37)	18.5 (1.30)	73.4 (1.52)	44,512	0.6 (0.03)
Female	33.4	0.9	32.9 (1.14)	0.8 (0.03)	49.4 (0.99)	1.0 (0.03)	61,632 (1,219.3)	47.1 (1.43)	0.8 (0.23)	25.8 (1.23)	73.6 (1.37)	63,931	1.0 (0.05)
Age													
17 through 24 years	18.6	0.4	19.1 (1.91)	0.4 (0.06)	33.9 (2.31)	0.5 (0.06)	15,027 (1,030.4)	26.4 (3.01)	3.0 (1.03)	25.2 (3.37)	71.4 (3.15)	8,024	0.5 (0.09)
25 through 29 years	31.2	0.8	34.3 (2.44)	0.8 (0.08)	49.7 (2.62)	0.9 (0.05)	14,555 (918.4)	36.1 (2.94)	3.1 (1.12)	24.5 (3.66)	70.9 (4.49)	9,493	0.7 (0.06)
30 through 34 years	31.6	0.8	34.4 (2.50)	0.8 (0.08)	48.4 (2.50)	0.9 (0.03)	15,253 (977.2)	41.0 (3.06)	2.7 (1.10)	23.7 (2.63)	74.0 (2.54)	12,681	0.8 (0.07)
35 through 39 years	35.1	0.9	29.2 (2.15)	0.7 (0.07)	48.8 (2.32)	1.0 (0.05)	15,285 (922.4)	41.7 (4.16)	1.0 (0.46)	21.6 (3.15)	77.7 (3.00)	13,807	0.9 (0.14)
40 through 44 years	36.6	0.9	36.4 (2.44)	0.8 (0.07)	46.1 (2.23)	0.9 (0.06)	18,141 (946.3)	39.8 (2.73)	0.9 (0.48)	23.3 (2.60)	71.2 (3.15)	15,586	0.9 (0.07)
45 through 49 years	39.6	1.0	30.4 (2.42)	0.7 (0.06)	50.8 (2.15)	1.1 (0.05)	18,149 (842.5)	45.0 (2.15)	0.7 (0.29)	19.0 (2.09)	73.5 (2.68)	16,809	0.9 (0.06)
50 through 54 years	34.4	0.9	34.7 (2.57)	0.8 (0.07)	52.5 (2.21)	1.2 (0.08)	14,624 (732.1)	42.6 (2.49)	0.7 (0.32)	19.5 (1.92)	76.3 (2.27)	14,881	1.0 (0.10)
55 through 59 years	26.7	0.7	30.3 (2.83)	0.6 (0.08)	46.3 (2.49)	1.0 (0.06)	10,522 (676.0)	44.7 (2.98)	0.2 (0.12)	18.3 (1.93)	73.0 (2.95)	9,901	0.9 (0.09)
60 through 64 years	21.1	0.5	27.2 (3.80)	0.7 (0.15)	37.8 (2.63)	0.8 (0.08)	6,021 (498.8)	38.9 (3.97)	0.6 (0.43)	23.4 (3.52)	73.0 (4.22)	4,919	0.8 (0.10)
65 and over	13.7	0.4	20.3 (4.21)	0.4 (0.08)	— (—)	— (—)	5,812 (493.3)	21.6 (3.48)	#	17.4 (3.13)	74.2 (3.75)	2,343	0.4 (0.07)
65 through 69 years	—	—	— (†)	— (†)	33.5 (3.42)	0.7 (0.08)	3,385 (415.5)	19.1 (4.05)	#	20.9 (4.88)	75.4 (5.18)	1,102	0.3 (0.08)
70 years and over	—	—	— (†)	— (†)	22.3 (3.35)	0.5 (0.09)	2,427 (282.3)	25.1 (5.81)	#	12.6 (2.93)	72.6 (6.11)	1,241	0.5 (0.14)
Race/ethnicity													
White	33.2	0.8	32.8 (0.98)	0.6 (0.03)	48.5 (0.85)	1.0 (0.02)	94,881 (1,536.6)	41.3 (0.93)	1.2 (0.25)	22.2 (1.11)	75.3 (1.17)	82,511	0.9 (0.03)
Black	26.2	0.7	28.1 (2.34)	1.0 (0.07)	43.4 (2.19)	0.9 (0.06)	13,773 (533.2)	39.2 (3.82)	1.7 (0.83)	23.5 (3.04)	66.9 (3.02)	10,311	0.7 (0.11)
Hispanic	18.1	0.4	16.4 (1.83)	0.5 (0.05)	31.8 (2.32)	0.6 (0.06)	15,741 (681.1)	25.0 (2.66)	2.9 (0.85)	16.2 (2.31)	65.8 (3.39)	8,786	0.6 (0.11)
Asian	—	—	— (†)	— (†)	— (†)	— (†)	3,770 (520.7)	36.9 (7.00)	0.9 (0.90)	32.3 (7.26)	81.1 (5.88)	2,207	0.6 (0.12)
Asian/Pacific Islander	25.5	0.6	32.8 (4.84)	0.4 (0.15)	50.4 (4.77)	0.8 (0.05)	‡ (†)	‡ (†)	‡ (†)	‡ (†)	‡ (†)	‡ (†)	‡ (†)
Pacific Islander	—	—	— (†)	— (†)	— (†)	— (†)	‡ (†)	‡ (†)	‡ (†)	‡ (†)	‡ (†)	‡ (†)	† (†)
American Indian/Alaska Native	34.0	0.9	29.5 (11.52)	0.7 (0.52)	40.0 (15.14)	0.7 (0.25)	‡ (†)	‡ (†)	‡ (†)	‡ (†)	‡ (†)	‡ (†)	‡ (†)
More than one race	—	—	— (†)	— (†)	— (†)	— (†)	3,786 (562.7)	39.1 (6.85)	1.4 (0.85)	22.6 (6.34)	77.6 (8.40)	3,083	0.8 (0.15)
Other races	—	—	— (†)	— (†)	— (†)	— (†)	‡ (†)	‡ (†)	‡ (†)	‡ (†)	‡ (†)	‡ (†)	‡ (†)
Highest level of education completed													
Less than high school completion	8.8	0.1	7.9 (2.29)	0.4 (0.05)	— (†)	— (†)	16,627 (838.2)	10.4 (2.11)	2.4 (0.90)	8.8 (1.54)	57.0 (3.76)	2,592	0.2 (0.03)
Eighth grade or less	—	—	— (†)	— (†)	9.9 (3.11)	0.1 (0.05)	5,016 (599.7)	2.7 (1.12)	4.4 (2.43)	3.8 (1.71)	46.7 (7.11)	197	# (†)
9th through 12th grade, no completion	—	—	— (†)	— (†)	16.3 (2.22)	0.2 (0.04)	11,610 (792.8)	13.7 (2.99)	1.5 (0.78)	11.0 (2.06)	61.5 (4.05)	2,396	0.2 (0.04)
High school completion	20.9	0.4	21.4 (1.45)	0.8 (0.03)	33.2 (1.59)	0.6 (0.03)	34,121 (1,147.2)	24.7 (1.76)	1.3 (0.46)	17.1 (1.89)	63.4 (2.55)	16,640	0.5 (0.05)
Some vocational/technical	32.3	0.8	28.7 (5.76)	0.9 (0.17)	41.7 (3.26)	1.0 (0.11)	3,744 (393.1)	48.2 (5.92)	2.0 (1.56)	25.5 (4.61)	74.0 (5.54)	3,802	1.0 (0.17)
Some college	29.9	0.7	29.0 (1.78)	0.7 (0.06)	45.6 (1.83)	0.9 (0.05)	24,479 (1,067.7)	39.9 (2.36)	1.9 (0.69)	25.2 (2.50)	79.8 (2.04)	18,437	0.8 (0.05)
Associate's degree	39.2	1.0	39.7 (3.07)	0.9 (0.09)	54.5 (2.74)	1.1 (0.07)	9,943 (730.7)	50.4 (3.71)	2.3 (0.84)	19.1 (2.86)	78.4 (3.88)	14,224	1.4 (0.21)
Bachelor's degree	44.6	1.2	43.8 (2.01)	1.0 (0.06)	64.2 (1.42)	1.3 (0.05)	26,475 (902.7)	53.1 (1.88)	0.2 (0.12)	29.0 (1.77)	78.7 (1.94)	28,099	1.1 (0.06)
Some graduate work (or study)	50.2	1.4	46.8 (4.17)	1.2 (0.14)	71.5 (1.87)	1.7 (0.07)	17,398 (735.4)	61.1 (2.16)	1.5 (0.80)	28.6 (2.01)	88.8 (1.16)	24,649	1.4 (0.07)
No degree	44.3	1.2	54.2 (4.94)	1.2 (0.14)	68.3 (4.90)	1.6 (0.15)	2,125 (227.9)	53.8 (5.79)	‡ (†)	39.3 (6.05)	75.0 (5.64)	2,412	1.1 (0.16)
Master's	50.5	1.4	45.3 (2.97)	1.1 (0.11)	73.4 (2.44)	1.7 (0.09)	11,330 (614.7)	62.7 (2.98)	‡ (†)	28.2 (2.27)	90.5 (1.40)	15,394	1.1 (0.09)
Doctor's	40.4	1.0	34.4 (4.79)	0.7 (0.12)	58.9 (6.15)	1.4 (0.25)	1,500 (227.2)	49.0 (5.80)	‡ (†)	28.8 (4.76)	87.8 (4.35)	2,204	1.4 (0.36)
Professional	67.6	2.0	67.6 (6.98)	1.9 (0.31)	75.3 (4.63)	1.6 (0.16)	2,943 (382.7)	66.5 (6.39)	‡ (†)	22.1 (5.05)	92.9 (2.21)	4,639	1.6 (0.21)

See notes at end of table.

Table 370. Participation of employed persons, 17 years old and over, in career-related adult education during the previous 12 months, by selected characteristics of participants: Various years, 1995 through 2005—Continued

Characteristic of employed person	1995 Percent of adults participating in career or job-related courses	1995 Number of career or job-related courses taken, per employee	1999 Percent of adults participating in career or job-related courses	1999 Number of career or job-related courses taken, per employee	2003 Percent of adults participating in career or job-related courses[1]	2003 Number of career or job-related courses taken, per employee[1]	Employed persons, in thousands	2005 Percent of adults participating — In career or job-related courses	2005 Percent of adults participating — In apprentice programs	2005 Percent of adults participating — In personal interest courses	2005 Percent of adults participating — In informal learning activities for personal interest[1]	Number of career or job-related courses taken (in thousands)	Number of career or job-related courses taken, per employee
1	2	3	4	5	6	7	8	9	10	11	12	13	14
Urbanicity													
Urban..............	32.4	0.8	31.5 (1.67)	0.7 (0.05)	48.0 (0.75)	1.0 (0.02)	105,542 (1,279.1)	39.8 (1.06)	1.4 (0.27)	22.6 (0.94)	74.0 (1.13)	88,140	0.8 (0.03)
Urban, inside urbanized area....	33.3	0.8	31.2 (0.99)	0.7 (0.03)	47.7 (0.88)	1.0 (0.02)	— (†)	— (†)	— (†)	— (†)	— (†)	—	— (†)
Urban, outside urbanized area....	27.9	0.7	32.9 (2.48)	0.8 (0.08)	49.5 (2.19)	1.0 (0.06)	— (†)	— (†)	— (†)	— (†)	— (†)	—	— (†)
Rural................	26.9	0.7	27.1 (1.74)	0.6 (0.05)	38.2 (2.08)	0.8 (0.05)	27,845 (849.4)	34.9 (2.18)	1.4 (0.58)	19.1 (2.17)	71.7 (2.30)	20,303	0.7 (0.06)
Occupation													
Executive, administrative, or managerial occupations.............	42.9	1.2	40.6 (2.06)	1.0 (0.07)	61.7 (2.13)	1.3 (0.06)	14,596 (707.6)	53.6 (2.79)	0.4 (0.25)	29.5 (2.89)	77.7 (2.87)	16,567	1.1 (0.09)
Engineers, surveyors, and architects..............	44.2	1.1	52.1 (6.96)	1.0 (0.16)	66.8 (4.60)	1.3 (0.13)	1,987 (244.9)	56.3 (5.68)	‡ (†)	30.5 (6.36)	81.0 (4.73)	2,323	1.2 (0.16)
Natural scientists and mathematicians..............	59.7	1.7	46.0 (6.61)	0.8 (0.14)	60.7 (5.89)	1.2 (0.13)	4,130 (445.4)	51.5 (5.64)	2.1 (1.55)	31.2 (4.83)	85.3 (5.44)	3,693	0.9 (0.11)
Social scientists and workers, religious workers, and lawyers ...	59.5	1.8	56.9 (5.66)	1.7 (0.24)	77.7 (3.90)	1.9 (0.15)	4,697 (480.9)	66.8 (4.48)	‡ (†)	28.3 (3.81)	88.6 (2.95)	7,822	1.7 (0.29)
Teachers, elementary/secondary...............	53.9	1.5	52.1 (3.53)	1.2 (0.11)	76.5 (2.43)	1.5 (0.19)	7,085 (568.5)	67.7 (4.16)	0.6 (0.37)	31.5 (3.93)	83.0 (2.79)	12,233	1.7 (0.13)
Teachers, postsecondary and counselors, librarians, and archivists..............	41.6	1.0	35.6 (5.85)	0.7 (0.14)	65.7 (5.63)	1.8 (0.09)	2,393 (420.9)	53.1 (8.63)	‡ (†)	17.7 (4.91)	90.9 (3.97)	2,122	0.9 (0.09)
Health diagnosing and treating practitioners ...	68.6	2.0	65.2 (11.99)	1.5 (0.50)	88.5 (4.11)	2.0 (0.24)	978 (208.8)	78.9 (7.10)	‡ (†)	27.4 (9.60)	86.6 (5.37)	1,951	2.0 (0.25)
Registered nurses, pharmacists, dieticians, therapists, and physician's assistants..............	72.8	2.2	72.2 (5.04)	1.8 (0.21)	84.9 (2.80)	1.9 (0.11)	2,794 (238.8)	79.7 (4.60)	‡ (†)	29.4 (4.17)	84.3 (3.70)	4,984	1.8 (0.15)
Writers, artists, entertainers, and athletes	23.4	0.5	30.6 (6.21)	0.6 (0.18)	35.1 (4.84)	0.6 (0.11)	2,969 (405.2)	29.9 (5.69)	‡ (†)	31.8 (6.15)	88.9 (4.39)	1,865	0.6 (0.15)
Health technologists and technicians..............	50.0	1.4	41.8 (6.00)	1.0 (0.19)	59.4 (6.12)	1.4 (0.21)	3,060 (436.7)	70.6 (7.31)	2.0 (1.50)	27.8 (6.48)	77.5 (6.40)	4,473	1.5 (0.18)
Technologists and technicians, except health..............	43.8	1.1	37.6 (4.87)	1.0 (0.15)	51.9 (3.47)	1.2 (0.14)	1,774 (336.5)	29.4 (8.10)	‡ (†)	5.3 (2.02)	75.2 (8.98)	1,015	0.6 (0.17)
Marketing and sales occupations..............	25.2	0.6	21.1 (2.27)	0.4 (0.06)	38.7 (2.36)	0.6 (0.05)	14,845 (971.9)	32.3 (3.17)	1.3 (0.92)	20.8 (2.64)	70.5 (3.53)	7,724	0.5 (0.05)
Administrative support occupations, including clerical.................	30.8	0.7	27.4 (2.02)	0.6 (0.05)	45.1 (2.20)	0.8 (0.04)	21,167 (1,179.4)	36.1 (2.95)	0.8 (0.40)	28.2 (2.28)	72.9 (2.37)	15,443	0.7 (0.10)
Service occupations........	22.6	0.6	21.0 (2.15)	0.5 (0.07)	37.2 (2.04)	0.8 (0.06)	17,180 (1,033.7)	33.7 (3.13)	1.1 (0.36)	16.2 (2.31)	69.0 (2.74)	13,029	0.8 (0.10)

See notes at end of table.

Table 370. Participation of employed persons, 17 years old and over, in career-related adult education during the previous 12 months, by selected characteristics of participants: Various years, 1995 through 2005—Continued

Characteristic of employed person	1995 Percent of adults participating in career or job-related courses	1995 Number of career or job-related courses taken, per employee	1999 Percent of adults participating in career or job-related courses	1999 Number of career or job-related courses taken, per employee	2003 Percent of adults participating in career or job-related courses[1]	2003 Number of career or job-related courses taken, per employee[1]	2005 Employed persons, in thousands	2005 In career or job-related courses	2005 In apprentice programs	2005 In personal interest courses	2005 In informal learning activities for personal interest	2005 Number of career or job-related courses taken (in thousands)	2005 Number of career or job-related courses taken, per employee
1	2	3	4	5	6	7	8	9	10	11	12	13	14
Agriculture, forestry, and fishing occupations	12.4	0.3	12.2 (4.09)	0.2 (0.07)	33.9 (6.19)	0.5 (0.09)	2,522 (423.8)	22.4 (7.61)	2.4 (1.69)	23.0 (11.03)	62.9 (11.04)	960	0.4 (0.12)
Mechanics and repairers	29.1	0.7	15.0 (3.40)	0.3 (0.09)	32.1 (3.84)	0.7 (0.11)	5,241 (521.6)	28.3 (4.47)	4.0 (1.44)	12.6 (3.24)	69.3 (4.36)	2,669	0.5 (0.09)
Construction and extractive occupations	18.6	0.3	13.2 (3.16)	0.2 (0.06)	22.1 (2.87)	0.4 (0.06)	6,827 (647.1)	12.4 (3.04)	5.3 (2.26)	7.8 (1.88)	69.0 (5.25)	2,323	0.3 (0.13)
Precision production[2]	25.6	0.6	18.3 (6.52)	0.4 (0.12)	22.5 (6.15)	0.5 (0.13)	10,483 (839.3)	23.5 (3.79)	1.6 (0.90)	14.0 (3.34)	64.9 (3.74)	4,904	0.5 (0.07)
Production workers	14.8	0.3	23.0 (3.17)	0.5 (0.08)	27.6 (3.34)	0.5 (0.07)	— (†)	— (†)	— (†)	— (†)	— (†)	—	— (†)
Transportation and material moving	15.8	0.3	18.4 (3.62)	0.3 (0.06)	25.8 (3.39)	0.4 (0.05)	7,858 (742.5)	15.2 (2.81)	3.4 (1.77)	10.5 (3.10)	62.5 (5.32)	1,935	0.2 (0.05)
Handlers, equipment cleaners, helpers, and laborers	11.7	0.2	6.8 (3.45)	0.2 (0.12)	15.9 (4.27)	0.3 (0.11)	— (†)	— (†)	— (†)	— (†)	— (†)	—	— (†)
Miscellaneous occupations	38.8	1.0	14.2 (4.62)	0.3 (0.08)	63.0 (21.53)	1.5 (0.61)	801 (189.4)	17.2 (6.87)	‡ (†)	8.7 (4.31)	48.3 (13.96)	409	0.5 (0.28)
Annual household income													
$10,000 or less	12.6	0.2	9.5 (3.09)	0.2 (0.05)	— (†)	— (†)	4,425 (444.8)	16.7 (4.35)	0.6 (0.48)	26.2 (7.96)	69.7 (5.72)	1,556	0.4 (0.12)
$5,000 or less	—	—	— (†)	— (†)	19.4 (4.50)	0.3 (0.05)	1,635 (252.7)	19.1 (6.52)	‡ (†)	22.9 (7.91)	60.9 (8.84)	850	0.5 (0.26)
$5,001 to $10,000	—	—	— (†)	— (†)	17.5 (2.85)	0.3 (0.04)	2,791 (454.1)	15.3 (5.68)	‡ (†)	28.1 (12.27)	74.8 (6.88)	706	0.3 (0.10)
$10,001 to $15,000	15.1	0.4	8.3 (1.88)	0.1 (0.03)	20.1 (3.00)	0.3 (0.05)	4,814 (633.4)	22.2 (5.77)	‡ (†)	17.3 (5.25)	64.5 (7.57)	2,189	0.5 (0.12)
$15,001 to $20,000	20.1	0.4	16.3 (2.75)	0.3 (0.05)	22.7 (3.44)	0.4 (0.07)	4,515 (398.8)	18.2 (3.09)	5.7 (2.71)	11.5 (1.96)	60.4 (5.11)	1,322	0.3 (0.05)
$20,001 to $25,000	20.4	0.5	18.8 (2.79)	0.4 (0.08)	29.4 (2.73)	0.5 (0.07)	5,593 (490.2)	23.8 (4.02)	1.1 (0.51)	13.3 (3.21)	71.5 (4.11)	2,817	0.5 (0.10)
$25,001 to $30,000	24.7	0.5	22.2 (2.73)	0.5 (0.07)	27.7 (2.60)	0.5 (0.07)	7,444 (680.4)	31.4 (4.88)	0.7 (0.44)	16.7 (3.77)	73.5 (3.91)	4,322	0.6 (0.11)
$30,001 to $40,000	30.2	0.8	26.6 (2.82)	0.6 (0.07)	40.4 (2.43)	0.8 (0.06)	13,123 (928.5)	35.1 (3.45)	1.5 (0.65)	21.7 (3.71)	69.1 (3.55)	8,224	0.6 (0.06)
$40,001 to $50,000	34.7	0.8	32.3 (2.34)	0.7 (0.07)	47.9 (2.50)	1.0 (0.07)	13,647 (1,058.4)	31.5 (3.01)	1.8 (0.72)	20.1 (3.32)	73.5 (2.78)	10,072	0.7 (0.10)
$50,001 to $75,000	40.0	1.0	36.6 (1.86)	0.9 (0.06)	49.3 (1.57)	1.0 (0.04)	33,665 (1,430.4)	42.7 (1.80)	1.2 (0.51)	20.9 (2.10)	71.3 (2.55)	28,991	0.9 (0.06)
More than $75,000	45.2	1.3	42.5 (1.79)	1.0 (0.06)	60.5 (1.36)	1.3 (0.04)	46,160 (1,263.3)	48.1 (1.57)	1.3 (0.39)	26.0 (1.37)	79.2 (1.55)	48,951	1.1 (0.05)

—Not available.
†Not applicable.
#Rounds to zero.
‡Reporting standards not met.
[1]Estimates are not directly comparable to 1995, 1999, or 2005 estimates due to wording in questionnaire.
[2]For 2005, figures include "Production workers" occupations data.

NOTE: Data do not include persons enrolled in high school or below. Race categories exclude persons of Hispanic ethnicity. Detail may not sum to totals because of rounding. Standard errors appear in parentheses.
SOURCE: U.S. Department of Education, National Center for Education Statistics, Adult Education Survey (AE-NHES:1995, AE-NHES:1999, and AE-NHES:2005) and Adult Education for Work-Related Reasons Survey (AEWR-NHES:2003) of the National Household Education Surveys Program. (This table was prepared August 2006.)

Table 371. Participation rate of persons, 17 years old and over, in adult education during the previous 12 months, by selected characteristics of participants: Selected years, 1991 through 2005

Characteristic of participant	Percent participating in any program				Percent participating, 2005							Percent in informal learning activities for personal interest, 2005
	1991	1995	1999	2001	In any program	In basic skills/ General Educational Development (GED) classes	In English as a second language (ESL) classes	In part-time post-secondary education[1]	In career or job-related courses	In apprentice programs	In personal-interest courses	
1	2	3	4	5	6	7	8	9	10	11	12	13
Total	33.0	40.2 (0.48)	44.5 (0.77)	46.4 (0.55)	44.4 (0.74)	1.3 (0.22)	0.9 (0.17)	5.0 (0.29)	27.0 (0.63)	1.2 (0.18)	21.4 (0.71)	70.5 (0.79)
Sex												
Male	32.6	38.2 (0.65)	41.7 (1.15)	43.1 (0.83)	41.0 (1.20)	1.4 (0.41)	0.9 (0.29)	5.0 (0.44)	24.5 (0.99)	1.7 (0.31)	18.3 (1.08)	70.8 (1.10)
Female	33.2	42.1 (0.59)	47.1 (1.02)	49.5 (0.78)	47.5 (1.01)	1.2 (0.19)	0.9 (0.15)	5.1 (0.37)	29.2 (0.95)	0.7 (0.15)	24.2 (0.88)	70.2 (1.03)
Age												
17 to 24 years	37.8	47.0 (1.12)	49.9 (2.34)	52.8 (2.04)	52.8 (2.79)	6.0 (1.48)	1.7 (0.61)	11.5 (1.34)	21.3 (2.22)	2.7 (0.76)	26.3 (2.60)	69.2 (2.54)
25 to 29 years	40.0	49.6 (1.31)	56.5 (2.53)	52.9 (2.60)	51.6 (3.82)	1.8 (0.48)	3.3 (1.48)	9.1 (1.50)	29.5 (2.48)	3.2 (1.06)	20.9 (2.78)	66.8 (3.75)
30 to 34 years	37.6	47.3 (1.41)	56.2 (2.57)	53.7 (2.18)	52.7 (2.52)	1.9 (0.66)	1.6 (0.64)	8.4 (1.28)	33.8 (2.71)	2.5 (0.89)	23.2 (2.23)	73.8 (2.22)
35 to 39 years	42.1	47.7 (1.15)	50.1 (2.43)	54.0 (1.71)	48.6 (3.21)	0.4 (0.16)	0.7 (0.26)	6.1 (0.90)	32.6 (3.29)	0.9 (0.36)	20.7 (2.67)	75.5 (2.69)
40 to 44 years	49.2	50.9 (1.15)	50.5 (2.43)	53.5 (1.88)	48.9 (2.43)	0.8 (0.31)	0.6 (0.23)	4.7 (0.77)	34.8 (2.30)	0.9 (0.42)	23.4 (2.29)	71.5 (2.62)
45 to 49 years	40.0	48.7 (1.66)	49.8 (2.69)	55.4 (2.02)	49.0 (2.09)	0.6 (0.30)	0.6 (0.25)	3.2 (0.48)	37.7 (1.83)	0.5 (0.23)	19.3 (1.88)	71.6 (2.52)
50 to 54 years	42.5	42.5 (1.38)	47.2 (2.51)	51.1 (2.22)	46.6 (2.36)	0.2 (0.11)	0.3 (0.15)	4.5 (0.75)	35.2 (2.25)	0.6 (0.28)	20.3 (1.64)	69.5 (1.89)
55 to 59 years	26.8	32.2 (1.66)	38.0 (2.60)	44.1 (1.98)	42.2 (2.78)	0.4 (0.29)	0.4 (0.26)	1.9 (0.43)	31.9 (2.39)	0.3 (0.17)	18.0 (1.63)	71.4 (2.56)
60 to 64 years	29.0	23.7 (1.89)	31.4 (2.83)	30.8 (2.18)	37.9 (3.00)	‡ (†)	0.4 (0.29)	0.9 (0.36)	20.9 (2.07)	0.3 (0.20)	24.1 (2.40)	67.6 (3.04)
65 to 69 years	17.4	18.1 (1.46)	25.4 (2.54)	20.5 (1.74)	26.2 (2.67)	‡ (†)	‡ (†)	0.5 (0.22)	8.1 (1.36)	‡ (†)	20.9 (2.41)	62.9 (1.82)
70 years and over	8.6	13.8 (1.09)	15.0 (1.38)	21.7 (1.37)	21.5 (1.44)	0.2 (0.10)	‡ (†)	0.3 (0.23)	4.0 (0.78)	‡ (†)	17.9 (1.33)	62.9 (1.82)
Racial/ethnic group												
White	34.1	41.5 (0.54)	44.4 (0.89)	47.4 (0.59)	45.6 (0.84)	0.9 (0.23)	0.2 (0.08)	4.9 (0.35)	29.1 (0.70)	0.9 (0.17)	22.1 (0.87)	73.0 (0.92)
Black	25.9	37.0 (1.45)	46.3 (2.30)	43.3 (1.50)	46.4 (2.81)	1.9 (0.49)	‡ (†)	5.4 (0.97)	27.0 (2.53)	1.5 (0.73)	23.7 (2.11)	65.3 (2.02)
Hispanic	31.4	33.7 (1.18)	41.3 (2.51)	41.7 (2.28)	37.8 (2.43)	2.6 (0.72)	5.6 (1.22)	5.7 (1.55)	16.9 (1.72)	2.2 (0.63)	15.4 (1.75)	57.5 (2.86)
Asian	—	— (—)	— (—)	— (†)	48.3 (5.39)	1.2 (0.65)	2.6 (1.03)	7.6 (2.62)	27.2 (4.70)	‡ (†)	26.5 (5.06)	81.1 (4.10)
Pacific Islander	—	— (—)	— (†)	— (†)	‡ (†)	‡ (†)	‡ (†)	3.5 (3.71)	‡ (†)	‡ (†)	‡ (†)	‡ (†)
Asian/Pacific Islander	35.9	39.7 (2.92)	51.1 (4.63)	49.5 (3.81)	36.3 (10.17)	‡ (†)	‡ (†)	5.9 (3.05)	23.0 (8.51)	‡ (†)	13.0 (6.16)	70.6 (9.18)
American Indian/Alaska Native	29.3	38.8 (4.85)	36.3 (9.16)	50.2 (8.28)	39.4 (4.94)	5.1 (2.17)	‡ (†)	4.4 (1.82)	23.8 (4.06)	1.3 (0.59)	21.0 (4.13)	77.6 (5.28)
More than one race	—	— (—)	— (†)	— (†)	‡ (†)	‡ (†)	‡ (†)	3.2 (1.07)	‡ (†)	‡ (†)	‡ (†)	‡ (†)
Highest level of education completed												
8th grade or less	7.7	10.0 (1.10)	14.7 (2.92)	19.7 (2.84)	15.5 (2.47)	1.9 (0.57)	4.3 (1.70)	0.4 (0.23)	1.7 (0.55)	1.7 (0.91)	7.3 (1.24)	38.1 (3.27)
9th through 12th grade, no completion	15.8	20.2 (1.38)	25.6 (2.55)	25.5 (1.53)	27.2 (2.40)	7.9 (1.69)	1.1 (0.41)	2.1 (0.57)	7.6 (1.44)	1.5 (0.61)	12.5 (1.53)	55.7 (2.52)
High school completion	24.1	30.7 (0.84)	34.8 (1.37)	33.9 (1.07)	33.0 (1.62)	0.5 (0.24)	0.7 (0.24)	2.5 (0.36)	17.2 (1.18)	1.1 (0.35)	16.8 (1.27)	63.6 (1.93)
Some vocational/technical	34.2	41.9 (2.16)	41.1 (3.97)	50.7 (3.51)	43.3 (4.30)	0.5 (0.55)	‡ (†)	4.5 (1.42)	28.3 (3.71)	1.4 (0.47)	23.2 (3.09)	77.6 (3.98)
Some college	41.4	41.9 (0.92)	51.1 (1.76)	57.4 (1.29)	51.1 (1.79)	0.3 (0.18)	0.8 (0.52)	8.6 (1.06)	28.8 (1.54)	1.9 (0.66)	26.8 (1.80)	79.8 (1.52)
Associate's degree	49.2	56.1 (1.85)	56.6 (2.93)	62.5 (2.15)	56.5 (3.64)	0.5 (0.40)	1.1 (0.51)	6.6 (1.42)	40.8 (3.27)	0.4 (0.17)	20.1 (2.48)	75.9 (3.70)
Bachelor's degree	51.1	56.9 (1.20)	60.3 (1.84)	64.5 (1.39)	59.8 (1.56)	‡ (†)	0.4 (0.17)	6.3 (0.82)	44.1 (1.61)	1.2 (0.61)	28.6 (1.55)	79.3 (1.72)
Some graduate work (or study)	55.1	59.9 (1.55)	63.6 (1.96)	68.9 (1.64)	66.3 (1.99)	‡ (†)	0.5 (0.32)	8.7 (0.86)	49.3 (2.15)	0.4 (0.61)	30.7 (1.77)	88.0 (1.06)
No degree	—	62.2 (2.67)	64.7 (4.39)	64.2 (3.54)	65.3 (4.84)	‡ (†)	‡ (†)	14.5 (2.55)	40.5 (4.68)	1.4 (0.97)	38.7 (4.81)	78.2 (4.34)
Master's	—	59.1 (1.88)	65.7 (2.64)	70.7 (2.10)	67.5 (2.59)	‡ (†)	‡ (†)	8.9 (1.31)	51.4 (2.81)	‡ (†)	30.6 (2.04)	88.8 (1.33)
Doctor's	—	54.0 (6.99)	53.1 (4.73)	63.7 (3.98)	58.0 (4.94)	‡ (†)	0.9 (0.52)	10.1 (3.14)	34.0 (4.53)	‡ (†)	31.4 (3.95)	90.3 (3.26)
Professional	—	65.9 (3.91)	72.5 (5.75)	72.8 (3.79)	68.2 (5.77)	‡ (†)	‡ (†)	1.9 (1.01)	59.0 (6.35)	‡ (†)	23.9 (4.35)	91.6 (2.15)
Urbanicity												
Urban	34.5	41.8 (0.59)	46.0 (0.88)	48.0 (0.70)	45.7 (0.87)	1.4 (0.28)	1.1 (0.21)	5.5 (0.34)	27.8 (0.79)	1.2 (0.20)	22.2 (0.72)	71.4 (0.86)
Urban, inside urbanized area	—	42.3 (0.64)	46.5 (0.95)	49.3 (0.78)	— (†)	— (†)	— (†)	— (†)	— (†)	— (†)	— (†)	— (†)
Urban, outside urbanized area	—	39.5 (1.12)	43.4 (2.23)	41.6 (1.70)	— (†)	— (†)	— (†)	— (†)	— (†)	— (†)	— (†)	— (†)
Rural	28.3	35.4 (0.98)	39.9 (1.58)	41.6 (1.17)	39.2 (2.06)	0.8 (0.22)	0.3 (0.15)	3.5 (0.62)	23.7 (1.39)	1.1 (0.40)	18.5 (1.76)	67.2 (1.77)
Labor force status												
In labor force	40.7	49.8 (0.69)	52.1 (0.94)	— (†)	52.3 (0.93)	1.4 (0.32)	0.8 (0.19)	6.4 (0.39)	37.1 (0.83)	1.5 (0.24)	21.9 (0.91)	73.0 (0.94)
Employed	42.0	50.7 (0.53)	52.5 (0.96)	— (†)	53.4 (0.94)	1.1 (0.31)	0.7 (0.20)	6.5 (0.39)	38.8 (0.83)	1.4 (0.24)	21.8 (0.94)	73.5 (1.01)
Unemployed	26.0	36.6 (1.91)	44.9 (4.60)	— (†)	37.8 (4.26)	5.8 (1.60)	1.9 (0.79)	5.2 (1.37)	13.5 (2.16)	2.1 (1.23)	22.1 (3.99)	66.7 (3.80)
Not in labor force	15.7	21.3 (0.69)	24.9 (1.17)	— (†)	27.6 (1.18)	1.1 (0.24)	1.3 (0.36)	2.3 (0.45)	5.7 (0.55)	0.6 (0.22)	20.5 (0.97)	65.2 (1.27)
Occupation												
Executive, administrative, or managerial occupations	49.3	55.8 (1.92)	57.0 (2.11)	66.2 (1.61)	64.1 (2.73)	0.2 (0.24)	‡ (†)	6.0 (1.10)	51.8 (2.82)	0.4 (0.24)	28.8 (2.89)	78.6 (2.71)
Engineers, surveyors, and architects	62.6	65.5 (4.18)	79.8 (6.01)	68.1 (4.46)	71.2 (5.68)	‡ (†)	‡ (†)	9.3 (3.21)	55.6 (5.60)	‡ (†)	31.4 (6.19)	81.1 (4.63)

See notes at end of table.

Table 371. Participation rate of persons, 17 years old and over, in adult education during the previous 12 months, by selected characteristics of participants: Selected years, 1991 through 2005—Continued

Characteristic of participant	Percent participating in any program					Percent participating, 2005						Percent in informal learning activities for personal interest, 2005
	1991	1995	1999	2001	In any program	In basic skills/General Educational Development (GED) classes	In English as a second language (ESL) classes	In part-time post-secondary education[1]	In career or job-related courses	In apprentice programs	In personal-interest courses	
1	2	3	4	5	6	7	8	9	10	11	12	13
Natural scientists and mathematicians	48.2	72.3 (3.52)	60.5 (6.74)	74.0 (4.46)	69.1 (4.63)	‡ (†)	‡ (†)	9.2 (2.49)	49.6 (5.27)	2.0 (1.47)	30.2 (4.53)	85.5 (5.16)
Social scientists and workers, religious workers, and lawyers	55.6	76.6 (2.61)	79.3 (4.35)	83.5 (3.05)	77.7 (4.11)	‡ (†)	‡ (†)	12.8 (3.16)	64.3 (4.42)	‡ (†)	29.2 (3.52)	89.4 (2.78)
Teachers, elementary/secondary	55.0	54.8 (4.64)	66.5 (5.61)	79.9 (2.95)	79.7 (2.59)	‡ (†)	1.6 (1.00)	8.3 (3.16)	65.0 (3.99)	0.6 (0.34)	31.7 (3.78)	83.8 (2.62)
Teachers, postsecondary and counselors, librarians, and archivists	45.5	76.7 (1.98)	78.4 (3.11)	69.4 (4.61)	61.3 (6.96)	‡ (†)	‡ (†)	4.7 (3.22)	49.0 (8.50)	‡ (†)	19.5 (4.98)	91.7 (3.58)
Health diagnosing and treating practitioners	67.1	71.1 (5.78)	79.8 (9.02)	78.5 (6.38)	88.8 (5.59)	0.6 (0.55)	‡ (†)	15.4 (2.47)	79.5 (6.59)	‡ (†)	31.9 (9.15)	84.5 (5.63)
Registered nurses, pharmacists, dieticians, therapists, and physician's assistants	59.6	86.7 (2.47)	85.4 (4.10)	82.7 (3.83)	85.4 (4.05)	‡ (†)	‡ (†)	7.9 (2.17)	78.2 (4.89)	‡ (†)	27.4 (3.73)	83.1 (3.92)
Writers, artists, entertainers, and athletes	42.9	49.9 (4.37)	50.0 (6.93)	46.8 (6.03)	52.5 (6.59)	0.2 (0.23)	‡ (†)	5.4 (2.16)	27.8 (5.02)	2.2 (1.53)	35.3 (6.42)	88.2 (3.89)
Health technologists and technicians	68.6	74.8 (3.64)	66.9 (6.16)	85.6 (3.25)	72.1 (8.37)	0.2 (0.16)	‡ (†)	6.0 (2.11)	63.2 (8.67)	1.7 (1.23)	24.6 (5.91)	75.6 (7.26)
Technologists and technicians, except health	55.4	64.3 (2.84)	59.6 (5.07)	70.2 (3.32)	33.8 (8.53)	‡ (†)	‡ (†)	7.1 (3.19)	29.1 (7.68)	‡ (†)	6.2 (2.14)	76.0 (8.80)
Marketing and sales occupations	34.4	44.2 (1.34)	44.4 (2.73)	51.1 (2.10)	45.7 (3.00)	1.7 (0.59)	0.4 (0.26)	4.5 (0.88)	30.2 (2.77)	1.4 (0.80)	21.5 (2.43)	68.9 (3.37)
Administrative support occupations, including clerical	29.9	51.7 (1.25)	50.1 (2.29)	58.7 (1.72)	54.6 (2.70)	1.1 (0.53)	‡ (†)	6.6 (0.98)	33.5 (2.70)	1.3 (0.63)	27.7 (2.18)	73.8 (2.33)
Service occupations	25.2	46.5 (1.38)	50.9 (2.74)	49.3 (2.24)	44.7 (2.47)	1.6 (0.39)	1.9 (0.88)	6.8 (1.42)	28.5 (2.64)	1.4 (0.57)	17.5 (2.10)	65.4 (2.71)
Agriculture, forestry, and fishing occupations	14.3	26.4 (3.55)	34.3 (7.16)	46.4 (6.80)	44.4 (9.02)	3.9 (3.49)	5.7 (4.02)	1.1 (0.89)	20.3 (6.92)	2.3 (1.53)	21.6 (10.05)	64.0 (10.03)
Mechanics and repairers	32.1	47.6 (2.70)	42.2 (5.44)	35.1 (3.40)	40.1 (5.10)	0.5 (0.40)	‡ (†)	6.0 (1.89)	27.4 (4.26)	3.8 (1.38)	12.7 (3.18)	69.3 (4.27)
Construction and extractive occupations	21.9	38.0 (2.45)	34.5 (4.78)	32.3 (3.19)	27.6 (3.73)	1.2 (0.68)	1.1 (0.49)	3.2 (1.08)	12.3 (2.54)	5.2 (1.89)	11.4 (2.72)	72.3 (4.48)
Precision production[2]	31.1	43.0 (4.32)	38.3 (8.48)	35.1 (6.19)	33.0 (3.98)	0.5 (0.37)	0.4 (0.16)	4.2 (1.42)	22.2 (3.41)	1.5 (0.81)	13.3 (2.99)	63.9 (3.46)
Production workers	21.1	30.7 (1.29)	38.0 (3.47)	39.4 (2.82)	— (†)	‡ (†)	‡ (†)	‡ (†)	— (†)	‡ (†)	‡ (†)	60.8 (4.98)
Transportation, material moving	20.7	28.4 (2.32)	33.3 (4.25)	30.4 (3.29)	34.6 (5.27)	4.7 (3.29)	3.3 (2.35)	1.3 (0.76)	14.7 (2.63)	3.2 (1.57)	11.2 (2.85)	— (†)
Handler, equipment, cleaners, helpers, and laborers	20.8	25.1 (2.70)	19.6 (4.56)	18.2 (3.20)	— (†)	— (†)	— (†)	— (†)	— (†)	— (†)	— (†)	— (†)
Miscellaneous occupations	—	56.6 (3.61)	43.0 (7.98)	64.9 (7.07)	39.2 (11.25)	‡ (†)	‡ (†)	‡ (†)	15.7 (5.81)	‡ (†)	7.8 (3.63)	52.2 (12.32)
Annual household income												
$5,000 or less	13.6	21.3 (1.59)	21.0 (3.22)	25.1 (2.92)	35.9 (4.83)	3.3 (2.17)	1.8 (1.04)	3.6 (1.52)	13.7 (4.00)	2.3 (1.89)	17.2 (3.59)	52.9 (4.97)
$5,001 to $10,000	17.5	23.9 (1.37)	24.5 (3.39)	28.0 (2.74)	29.6 (4.49)	2.4 (0.92)	1.5 (0.71)	1.7 (0.81)	8.4 (2.11)	‡ (†)	21.8 (4.75)	61.0 (3.75)
$10,001 to $15,000	22.8	26.7 (1.61)	22.8 (2.45)	28.6 (2.30)	25.0 (3.41)	2.4 (0.69)	0.8 (0.33)	3.3 (1.17)	11.3 (2.52)	0.9 (0.66)	15.5 (3.14)	58.6 (4.43)
$15,001 to $20,000	21.9	31.8 (1.55)	31.4 (2.75)	30.2 (2.48)	24.3 (2.54)	1.0 (0.38)	0.5 (0.30)	3.3 (1.19)	10.1 (1.37)	2.6 (1.20)	12.9 (2.00)	61.1 (3.17)
$20,001 to $25,000	26.7	35.8 (1.27)	35.2 (2.81)	35.2 (2.27)	28.2 (2.51)	1.7 (0.78)	1.9 (0.52)	4.4 (1.26)	12.8 (2.04)	1.1 (0.50)	13.6 (1.88)	63.2 (3.11)
$25,001 to $30,000	32.1	37.9 (1.47)	36.7 (2.61)	38.3 (2.43)	38.6 (3.63)	1.4 (0.72)	1.3 (0.51)	6.8 (2.09)	20.2 (3.37)	0.7 (0.38)	18.4 (2.52)	71.0 (3.38)
$30,001 to $40,000	35.6	42.7 (0.86)	45.2 (2.05)	44.6 (1.54)	42.7 (2.65)	1.9 (0.65)	1.0 (0.49)	3.7 (0.68)	22.8 (2.27)	1.1 (0.39)	23.0 (2.49)	68.7 (2.36)
$40,001 to $50,000	44.8	46.8 (1.39)	47.9 (2.31)	49.1 (1.93)	41.4 (2.92)	1.6 (0.53)	2.4 (1.25)	2.9 (0.55)	22.4 (2.00)	1.5 (0.56)	20.5 (2.47)	71.9 (2.62)
$50,001 to $75,000	46.6	52.0 (0.94)	55.1 (1.80)	55.7 (1.48)	47.7 (1.74)	0.4 (0.19)	0.3 (0.17)	5.8 (0.69)	33.0 (1.37)	0.9 (0.36)	20.5 (1.67)	70.6 (2.15)
More than $75,000	48.7	58.0 (1.27)	56.9 (1.66)	59.5 (1.29)	57.5 (1.49)	1.1 (0.53)	0.5 (0.23)	6.7 (0.58)	39.1 (1.35)	1.3 (0.38)	26.9 (1.13)	78.5 (1.34)

—Not available.
†Not applicable.
‡Reporting standards not met.
[1]Includes college and university degree programs, post-degree certificate programs, and vocational certificate programs.
[2]For 2005, figures include "Production workers" occupations data.

NOTE: Adult education is defined as all education activities, except full-time enrollment in higher education credential programs. Data do not include persons enrolled in high school or below. Race categories exclude persons of Hispanic ethnicity. Standard errors appear in parentheses.
SOURCE: U.S. Department of Education, National Center for Education Statistics, Adult Education Survey (AE-NHES:1991, AE-NHES:1995, AE-NHES:1999, and AE-NHES:2005) and Adult Education and Lifelong Learning Survey (AELL-NHES:2001) of the National Household Education Surveys Program. (This table was prepared May 2008.)

Table 372. Number of non-degree-granting Title IV institutions offering postsecondary education, by control and state or jurisdiction: Selected years, 2000–01 through 2007–08

State or jurisdiction	2000–01, total	2005-06					2006-07					2007-08				
		Total	Public	Private			Total	Public	Private			Total	Public	Private		
				Total	Not-for-profit	For-profit			Total	Not-for-profit	For-profit			Total	Not-for-profit	For-profit
1	2	3	4	5	6	7	8	9	10	11	12	13	14	15	16	17
United States	2,297	2,187	320	1,867	219	1,648	2,222	321	1,901	208	1,693	2,199	319	1,880	191	1,689
Alabama	10	9	0	9	2	7	9	0	9	2	7	6	0	6	1	5
Alaska	3	2	1	1	0	1	2	1	1	0	1	2	1	1	0	1
Arizona	33	34	3	31	0	31	35	3	32	0	32	35	3	32	0	32
Arkansas	36	32	3	29	3	26	32	3	29	2	27	32	3	29	2	27
California	230	235	8	227	28	199	244	9	235	26	209	233	9	224	24	200
Colorado	21	26	4	22	2	20	27	4	23	2	21	28	4	24	2	22
Connecticut	37	36	0	36	5	31	38	0	38	5	33	40	0	40	5	35
Delaware	4	6	0	6	1	5	6	0	6	1	5	6	0	6	1	5
District of Columbia	5	6	0	6	2	4	6	0	6	2	4	5	0	5	1	4
Florida	124	126	37	89	4	85	129	37	92	4	88	128	37	91	5	86
Georgia	38	44	1	43	2	41	43	1	42	1	41	44	1	43	1	42
Hawaii	6	5	0	5	0	5	5	0	5	0	5	6	0	6	1	5
Idaho	11	13	0	13	0	13	12	0	12	0	12	12	0	12	0	12
Illinois	88	94	2	92	13	79	92	2	90	12	78	90	2	88	10	78
Indiana	34	28	3	25	1	24	28	3	25	1	24	32	3	29	1	28
Iowa	27	26	0	26	2	24	26	0	26	2	24	25	0	25	2	23
Kansas	23	25	4	21	2	19	27	5	22	2	20	27	6	21	2	19
Kentucky	52	32	0	32	2	30	33	0	33	2	31	34	0	34	2	32
Louisiana	57	57	9	48	2	46	55	10	45	2	43	60	13	47	2	45
Maine	11	9	0	9	3	6	10	0	10	3	7	10	0	10	3	7
Maryland	34	27	0	27	0	27	27	0	27	0	27	27	0	27	0	27
Massachusetts	60	61	5	56	3	53	62	5	57	3	54	61	5	56	3	53
Michigan	72	65	2	63	3	60	69	2	67	3	64	68	1	67	2	65
Minnesota	20	21	0	21	4	17	22	0	22	4	18	21	0	21	3	18
Mississippi	16	20	0	20	0	20	19	0	19	0	19	19	0	19	0	19
Missouri	69	61	25	36	4	32	65	25	40	4	36	60	22	38	4	34
Montana	10	8	0	8	1	7	8	0	8	1	7	7	0	7	1	6
Nebraska	12	10	0	10	3	7	9	0	9	3	6	8	0	8	2	6
Nevada	10	9	0	9	2	7	12	0	12	2	10	13	0	13	1	12
New Hampshire	11	14	0	14	3	11	14	0	14	3	11	16	0	16	3	13
New Jersey	89	91	4	87	10	77	92	4	88	10	78	87	4	83	9	74
New Mexico	6	7	0	7	0	7	7	0	7	0	7	7	0	7	0	7
New York	152	133	32	101	33	68	138	32	106	32	74	140	32	108	31	77
North Carolina	36	29	1	28	2	26	27	1	26	2	24	28	1	27	2	25
North Dakota	5	5	0	5	0	5	6	0	6	0	6	6	0	6	0	6
Ohio	130	119	50	69	12	57	114	49	65	9	56	116	48	68	7	61
Oklahoma	84	78	45	33	0	33	81	45	36	0	36	80	45	35	0	35
Oregon	28	27	0	27	0	27	27	0	27	0	27	25	0	25	0	25
Pennsylvania	167	131	29	102	27	75	129	28	101	28	73	126	28	98	25	73
Rhode Island	12	10	0	10	2	8	10	0	10	2	8	10	0	10	2	8
South Carolina	14	21	0	21	0	21	21	0	21	0	21	20	0	20	0	20
South Dakota	5	6	0	6	3	3	6	0	6	3	3	6	0	6	3	3
Tennessee	54	58	26	32	2	30	62	26	36	1	35	61	26	35	1	34
Texas	161	169	0	169	4	165	169	0	169	4	165	166	1	165	4	161
Utah	26	24	2	22	0	22	26	2	24	0	24	27	2	25	0	25
Vermont	3	4	1	3	1	2	3	1	2	0	2	3	1	2	0	2
Virginia	56	42	7	35	7	28	41	7	34	7	27	37	7	30	6	24
Washington	42	37	1	36	4	32	39	1	38	4	34	41	1	40	4	36
West Virginia	36	31	14	17	7	10	32	14	18	7	11	29	12	17	6	11
Wisconsin	24	22	0	22	8	14	24	0	24	7	17	27	0	27	7	20
Wyoming	3	2	1	1	0	1	2	1	1	0	1	2	1	1	0	1
Other jurisdictions	74	74	0	74	9	65	80	0	80	12	68	72	0	72	13	59
American Samoa	0	0	0	0	0	0	0	0	0	0	0	0	0	0	0	0
Guam	0	0	0	0	0	0	0	0	0	0	0	0	0	0	0	0
Northern Marianas	0	0	0	0	0	0	0	0	0	0	0	0	0	0	0	0
Palau	0	0	0	0	0	0	0	0	0	0	0	0	0	0	0	0
Puerto Rico	74	74	0	74	9	65	80	0	80	12	68	72	0	72	13	59
U.S. Virgin Islands	0	0	0	0	0	0	0	0	0	0	0	0	0	0	0	0

NOTE: Includes all Title IV institutions that did not grant degrees at the associate's or higher level.

SOURCE: U.S. Department of Education, National Center for Education Statistics, 2000–01 through 2007–08 Integrated Postsecondary Education Data System (IPEDS), Fall 2000 through Fall 2007. (This table was prepared July 2008.)

CHAPTER 4
Federal Programs for Education and Related Activities

This chapter provides a summary of federal legislation and funds for education to describe the scope and variety of federal education programs. Data in this chapter primarily reflect outlays and appropriations of federal agencies. These tabulations differ from federal receipts reported in other chapters because of numerous variations in the data collection systems. Federal dollars are not necessarily spent by recipient institutions in the same year they are appropriated. In some cases, institutions cannot identify the source of federal revenues because they flow through state agencies. Some types of revenues, such as tuition and fees, are reported as revenues from students even though they may be supported by federal student aid programs. Some institutions that receive federal education funds are not included in regular surveys conducted by the National Center for Education Statistics (NCES). Thus, the federal programs data tabulated in this chapter are not comparable with figures reported in other chapters. Readers should also be careful about comparing the data on obligations shown in table 380 with the data on outlays and appropriations appearing in other tables in this chapter.

Federal on-budget funding for education increased 342 percent from fiscal year (FY) 1965 to FY 2007, after adjustment for inflation (table 373). Between FY 1965 and FY 1975, federal on-budget funding for education increased 149 percent. After a decrease of less than 1 percent from FY 1975 to FY 1980, there was a further decrease of 16 percent from FY 1980 to FY 1985. Thereafter, federal on-budget funding for education generally increased. After adjustment for inflation, federal on-budget funding for education increased by 14 percent from FY 1985 to FY 1990, by 20 percent from FY 1990 to FY 1995, by 9 percent from FY 1995 to FY 2000, and by 42 percent from FY 2000 to FY 2007.

Between FY 1990 and FY 1995, after adjustment for inflation, federal on-budget funding increased for each of the four major categories reported: elementary and secondary education (by 32 percent), postsecondary education (by 12 percent), other education (by 21 percent), and research at educational institutions (by 7 percent) (table 373 and figure 18). During the FY 1995 to FY 2000 period, federal funding increased for three of these categories: elementary and secondary education (by 19 percent), other education (by 6 percent), and research at educational institutions (by 26 percent). During the same period, however, funding for postsecondary education decreased by 22 percent. For the categories for which FY 2008 data are available, funding was higher in FY 2008 than

in FY 2000. Funds for elementary and secondary education were 34 percent higher in FY 2008 than in FY 2000, funds for postsecondary education were 104 percent higher, and funds for other education were 16 percent higher.[1]

Off-budget support (federal support for education not tied to appropriations) and nonfederal funds generated by federal legislation (e.g., private loans, grants, and aid) showed an increase of 47 percent in constant dollars between FY 1980 and FY 1990 (table 373). These same funds showed an increase of 137 percent between FY 1990 and FY 2000 and an increase of 63 percent between FY 2000 and FY 2008.

According to FY 2007 estimates, $71.8 billion (about 49 percent of the $147.5 billion spent by the federal government on education) came from the U.S. Department of Education (figure 19 and table 374). Large amounts of money also came from the U.S. Department of Health and Human Services ($25.7 billion), the U.S. Department of Agriculture ($15.4 billion), the U.S. Department of Defense ($6.1 billion), the U.S. Department of Labor ($5.4 billion), the U.S. Department of Veterans Affairs ($5.3 billion), the U.S. Department of Energy ($4.6 billion), the National Science Foundation ($4.4 billion), and the National Aeronautics and Space Administration ($3.0 billion).

For FY 2008, estimates of federal program funds are $72.8 billion for elementary and secondary education, $38.0 billion for postsecondary education, and $7.9 billion for other education programs (table 375). In FY 2007, $32.2 billion in federal funds were spent for research at universities and related institutions (FY 2008 data were not available at the time this publication was prepared).

In FY 2007, educational institutions (including local education agencies, state education agencies, and degree-granting institutions) received 66 percent of federal program funds for education (table 376). Another 15 percent was used for postsecondary student support. Other education organizations (including Head Start programs at child care centers, vocational education programs, and federal programs at libraries and museums) received 12 percent of federal program funds for education. Federal institutions received 3 percent, as did other recipients (including American Indian tribes, private nonprofit agencies, and banks).

---

[1] Changes in postsecondary expenditures between 2005 and 2007 resulted primarily from changes in accounting procedures. At the time that this publication was prepared, 2008 data on funding for research at educational institutions were not yet available.

Of the $73.8 billion spent by the U.S. Department of Education in FY 2008, about 40 percent ($29.7 billion) went to local education agencies (school districts) and 11 percent ($8.0 billion) to state education agencies (table 377 and figure 20). About 19 percent ($13.9 billion) went to postsecondary institutions and another 19 percent ($14.3 billion) to postsecondary students. Smaller percentages (totaling 11 percent) went to federal institutions, other education organizations, and other recipients.

Chronology of Federal Education Legislation

A capsule view of the history of federal education activities is provided in the following list of selected legislation:

1787 *Northwest Ordinance* authorized land grants for the establishment of educational institutions.

1802 *An Act Fixing the Military Peace Establishment of the United States* established the U.S. Military Academy. (The U.S. Naval Academy was established in 1845 by the Secretary of the Navy.)

1862 *First Morrill Act* authorized public land grants to the states for the establishment and maintenance of agricultural and mechanical colleges.

1867 *Department of Education Act* authorized the establishment of the U.S. Department of Education.[2]

1876 *Appropriation Act*, U.S. Department of the Treasury, established the U.S. Coast Guard Academy.

1890 *Second Morrill Act* provided for money grants for support of instruction in the agricultural and mechanical colleges.

1911 *State Marine School Act* authorized federal funds to be used for the benefit of any nautical school in any of 11 specified state seaport cities.

1917 *Smith-Hughes Act* provided for grants to states for support of vocational education.

1918 *Vocational Rehabilitation Act* provided for grants for rehabilitation through training of World War I veterans.

1920 *Smith-Bankhead Act* authorized grants to states for vocational rehabilitation programs.

1935 *Bankhead-Jones Act* (Public Law 74-182) authorized grants to states for agricultural experiment stations.

Agricultural Adjustment Act (Public Law 74-320) authorized 30 percent of the annual customs receipts to be used to encourage the exportation and domestic consumption of agricultural commodities. Commodities purchased under this authorization began to be used in school lunch programs in 1936. The National

School Lunch Act of 1946 continued and expanded this assistance.

1936 *An Act to Further the Development and Maintenance of an Adequate and Well-Balanced American Merchant Marine* (Public Law 74-415) established the U.S. Merchant Marine Academy.

1937 *National Cancer Institute Act* established the Public Health Service fellowship program.

1941 *Amendment to Lanham Act of 1940* authorized federal aid for construction, maintenance, and operation of schools in federally impacted areas. Such assistance was continued under Public Law 815 and Public Law 874, 81st Congress, in 1950.

1943 *Vocational Rehabilitation Act* (Public Law 78-16) provided assistance to disabled veterans.

School Lunch Indemnity Plan (Public Law 78-129) provided funds for local lunch food purchases.

1944 *Servicemen's Readjustment Act* (Public Law 78-346), known as the GI Bill, provided assistance for the education of veterans.

Surplus Property Act (Public Law 78-457) authorized transfer of surplus property to educational institutions.

1946 *National School Lunch Act* (Public Law 79-396) authorized assistance through grants-in-aid and other means to states to assist in providing adequate foods and facilities for the establishment, maintenance, operation, and expansion of nonprofit school lunch programs.

George-Barden Act (Public Law 80-402) expanded federal support of vocational education.

1948 *United States Information and Educational Exchange Act* (Public Law 80-402) provided for the interchange of persons, knowledge, and skills between the United States and other countries.

1949 *Federal Property and Administrative Services Act* (Public Law 81-152) provided for donation of surplus property to educational institutions and for other public purposes.

1950 *Financial Assistance for Local Educational Agencies Affected by Federal Activities* (Public Law 81-815 and Public Law 81-874) provided assistance for construction (Public Law 815) and operation (Public Law 874) of schools in federally affected areas.

Housing Act (Public Law 81-475) authorized loans for construction of college housing facilities.

1954 *An Act for the Establishment of the United States Air Force Academy and Other Purposes* (Public Law 83-325) established the U.S. Air Force Academy.

Educational Research Act (Public Law 83-531) authorized cooperative arrangements with universities, colleges, and state educational agencies for educational research.

---

[2] The U.S. Department of Education as established in 1867 was later known as the Office of Education. In 1980, under Public Law 96-88, it became a cabinet-level department. Therefore, for purposes of consistency, it is referred to as the "U.S. Department of Education" even in those tables covering years when it was officially the Office of Education.

School Milk Program Act (Public Law 83-597) provided funds for purchase of milk for school lunch programs.

1956 *Library Services Act* (Public Law 84-597) provided grants to states for extension and improvement of rural public library services.

1957 *Practical Nurse Training Act* (Public Law 84-911) provided grants to states for practical nurse training.

1958 *National Defense Education Act* (Public Law 85-864) provided assistance to state and local school systems for strengthening instruction in science, mathematics, modern foreign languages, and other critical subjects; improvement of state statistical services; guidance, counseling, and testing services and training institutes; higher education student loans and fellowships; foreign language study and training provided by colleges and universities; experimentation and dissemination of information on more effective utilization of television, motion pictures, and related media for educational purposes; and vocational education for technical occupations necessary to the national defense.

Education of Mentally Retarded Children Act (Public Law 85-926) authorized federal assistance for training teachers of the disabled.

Captioned Films for the Deaf Act (Public Law 85-905) authorized a loan service of captioned films for the deaf.

1961 *Area Redevelopment Act* (Public Law 87-27) included provisions for training or retraining of persons in redevelopment areas.

1962 *Manpower Development and Training Act* (Public Law 87-415) provided training in new and improved skills for the unemployed and underemployed.

Migration and Refugee Assistance Act of 1962 (Public Law 87-510) authorized loans, advances, and grants for education and training of refugees.

1963 *Health Professions Educational Assistance Act of 1963* (Public Law 88-129) provided funds to expand teaching facilities and for loans to students in the health professions.

Vocational Education Act of 1963 (Part of Public Law 88-210) increased federal support of vocational education schools; vocational work-study programs; and research, training, and demonstrations in vocational education.

Higher Education Facilities Act of 1963 (Public Law 88-204) authorized grants and loans for classrooms, libraries, and laboratories in public community colleges and technical institutes, as well as undergraduate and graduate facilities in other institutions of higher education.

1964 *Civil Rights Act of 1964* (Public Law 88-352) authorized the Commissioner of Education to arrange for support for institutions of higher education and school districts to provide inservice programs for assisting instructional staff in dealing with problems caused by desegregation.

Economic Opportunity Act of 1964 (Public Law 88-452) authorized grants for college work-study programs for students from low-income families; established a Job Corps program and authorized support for work-training programs to provide education and vocational training and work experience opportunities in welfare programs; authorized support of education and training activities and of community action programs, including Head Start, Follow Through, and Upward Bound; and authorized the establishment of Volunteers in Service to America (VISTA).

1965 *Elementary and Secondary Education Act of 1965* (Public Law 89-10) authorized grants for elementary and secondary school programs for children of low-income families; school library resources, textbooks, and other instructional materials for school children; supplementary educational centers and services; strengthening state education agencies; and educational research and research training.

Health Professions Educational Assistance Amendments of 1965 (Public Law 89-290) authorized scholarships to aid needy students in the health professions.

Higher Education Act of 1965 (Public Law 89-329) provided grants for university community service programs, college library assistance, library training and research, strengthening developing institutions, teacher training programs, and undergraduate instructional equipment. Authorized insured student loans, established a National Teacher Corps, and provided for graduate teacher training fellowships.

National Foundation on the Arts and the Humanities Act (Public Law 89-209) authorized grants and loans for projects in the creative and performing arts and for research, training, and scholarly publications in the humanities.

National Technical Institute for the Deaf Act (Public Law 89-36) provided for the establishment, construction, equipping, and operation of a residential school for postsecondary education and technical training of the deaf.

School Assistance in Disaster Areas Act (Public Law 89-313) provided for assistance to local education agencies to help meet exceptional costs resulting from a major disaster.

1966 *International Education Act* (Public Law 89-698) provided grants to institutions of higher education for the establishment, strengthening, and operation of centers for research and training in international studies and the international aspects of other fields of study.

National Sea Grant College and Program Act (Public Law 89-688) authorized the establishment and operation of Sea Grant Colleges and programs by initiating and supporting programs of education and research in the various fields relating to the development of marine resources.

Adult Education Act (Public Law 89-750) authorized grants to states for the encouragement and expansion of educational programs for adults, including training of teachers of adults and demonstrations in adult education (previously part of Economic Opportunity Act of 1964).

Model Secondary School for the Deaf Act (Public Law 89-694) authorized the establishment and operation, by Gallaudet College, of a model secondary school for the deaf.

1967 *Education Professions Development Act* (Public Law 90-35) amended the Higher Education Act of 1965 for the purpose of improving the quality of teaching and to help meet critical shortages of adequately trained educational personnel.

Public Broadcasting Act of 1967 (Public Law 90-129) established a Corporation for Public Broadcasting to assume major responsibility in channeling federal funds to noncommercial radio and television stations, program production groups, and ETV networks; conduct research, demonstration, or training in matters related to noncommercial broadcasting; and award grants for construction of educational radio and television facilities.

1968 *Elementary and Secondary Education Amendments of 1968* (Public Law 90-247) modified existing programs, authorized support of regional centers for education of children with disabilities, model centers and services for deaf-blind children, recruitment of personnel and dissemination of information on education of the disabled; technical assistance in education to rural areas; support of dropout prevention projects; and support of bilingual education programs.

Handicapped Children's Early Education Assistance Act (Public Law 90-538) authorized preschool and early education programs for disabled children.

Vocational Education Amendments of 1968 (Public Law 90-576) modified existing programs and provided for a National Advisory Council on Vocational Education and collection and dissemination of information for programs administered by the Commissioner of Education.

1970 *Elementary and Secondary Education Assistance Programs, Extension* (Public Law 91-230) authorized comprehensive planning and evaluation grants to state and local education agencies; provided for the establishment of a National Commission on School Finance.

National Commission on Libraries and Information Services Act (Public Law 91-345) established a National Commission on Libraries and Information Science to effectively utilize the nation's educational resources.

Office of Education Appropriation Act (Public Law 91-380) provided emergency school assistance to desegregating local education agencies.

Environmental Education Act (Public Law 91-516) established an Office of Environmental Education to develop curriculum and initiate and maintain environmental education programs at the elementary/secondary levels; disseminate information; provide training programs for teachers and other educational, public, community, labor, and industrial leaders and employees; provide community education programs; and distribute material dealing with the environment and ecology.

Drug Abuse Education Act of 1970 (Public Law 91-527) provided for development, demonstration, and evaluation of curricula on the problems of drug abuse.

1971 *Comprehensive Health Manpower Training Act of 1971* (Public Law 92-257) amended Title VII of the Public Health Service Act, increasing and expanding provisions for health manpower training and training facilities.

1972 *Drug Abuse Office and Treatment Act of 1972* (Public Law 92-255) established a Special Action Office for Drug Abuse Prevention to provide overall planning and policy for all federal drug-abuse prevention functions; a National Advisory Council for Drug Abuse Prevention; community assistance grants for community mental health centers for treatment and rehabilitation of persons with drug-abuse problems; and, in December 1974, a National Institute on Drug Abuse.

Education Amendments of 1972 (Public Law 92-318) established the Education Division in the U.S. Department of Health, Education, and Welfare and the National Institute of Education; general aid for institutions of higher education; federal matching grants for state Student Incentive Grants; a National Commission on Financing Postsecondary Education; State Advisory Councils on Community Colleges; a Bureau of Occupational and Adult Education and State Grants for the design, establishment, and conduct of postsecondary occupational education; and a bureau-level Office of Indian Education. Amended current U.S. Department of Education programs to increase their effectiveness and better meet special needs. Prohibited sex bias in admission to vocational, professional, and graduate schools, and public institutions of undergraduate higher education.

1973 *Older Americans Comprehensive Services Amendment of 1973* (Public Law 93-29) made available to older citizens comprehensive programs of health, education, and social services.

Comprehensive Employment and Training Act of 1973 (Public Law 93-203) provided for opportunities for employment and training to unemployed and underemployed persons. Extended and expanded provisions in the Manpower Development and Training Act of 1962, Title I of the Economic Opportunity Act of 1962, Title I of the Economic Opportunity Act of 1964, and the Emergency Employment Act of 1971 as in effect prior to June 30, 1973.

1974 *Education Amendments of 1974* (Public Law 93-380) provided for the consolidation of certain programs; and established a National Center for Education Statistics.

Juvenile Justice and Delinquency Prevention Act of 1974 (Public Law 93-415) provided for technical assistance, staff training, centralized research, and resources to develop and implement programs to keep students in elementary and secondary schools; and established, in the U.S. Department of Justice, a National Institute for Juvenile Justice and Delinquency Prevention.

1975 *Indian Self-Determination and Education Assistance Act* (Public Law 93-638) provided for increased participation of Indians in the establishment and conduct of their education programs and services.

Harry S Truman Memorial Scholarship Act (Public Law 93-642) established the Harry S Truman Scholarship Foundation and created a perpetual education scholarship fund for young Americans to prepare and pursue careers in public service.

Indochina Migration and Refugee Assistance Act of 1975 (Public Law 94-23) authorized funds to be used for education and training of aliens who have fled from Cambodia or Vietnam.

Education for All Handicapped Children Act (Public Law 94-142) provided that all children with disabilities have available to them a free appropriate education designed to meet their unique needs.

1976 *Educational Broadcasting Facilities and Telecommunications Demonstration Act of 1976* (Public Law 94-309) established a telecommunications demonstration program to promote the development of nonbroadcast telecommunications facilities and services for the transmission, distribution, and delivery of health, education, and public or social service information.

1977 *Youth Employment and Demonstration Projects Act of 1977* (Public Law 95-93) established a youth employment training program that includes, among other activities, promoting education-to-work transition, literacy training and bilingual training, and attainment of certificates of high school equivalency.

Career Education Incentive Act (Public Law 95-207) authorized the establishment of a career education program for elementary and secondary schools.

1978 *Tribally Controlled Community College Assistance Act of 1978* (Public Law 95-471) provided federal funds for the operation and improvement of tribally controlled community colleges for Indian students.

Education Amendments of 1978 (Public Law 95-561) established a comprehensive basic skills program aimed at improving pupil achievement (replaced the existing National Reading Improvement program); and established a community schools program to provide for the use of public buildings.

Middle Income Student Assistance Act (Public Law 95-566) modified the provisions for student financial assistance programs to allow middle-income as well as low-income students attending college or other postsecondary institutions to qualify for federal education assistance.

1979 *Department of Education Organization Act* (Public Law 96-88) established a U.S. Department of Education containing functions from the Education Division of the U.S. Department of Health, Education, and Welfare (HEW) along with other selected education programs from HEW, the U.S. Department of Justice, U.S. Department of Labor, and the National Science Foundation.

1980 *Asbestos School Hazard Detection and Control Act of 1980* (Public Law 96-270) established a program for inspection of schools for detection of hazardous asbestos materials and provided loans to assist educational agencies to contain or remove and replace such materials.

1981 *Education Consolidation and Improvement Act of 1981* (Part of Public Law 97-35) consolidated 42 programs into 7 programs to be funded under the elementary and secondary block grant authority.

1983 *Student Loan Consolidation and Technical Amendments Act of 1983* (Public Law 98-79) established an 8 percent interest rate for Guaranteed Student Loans and an extended Family Contribution Schedule.

Challenge Grant Amendments of 1983 (Public Law 98-95) amended Title III, Higher Education Act, and added authorization of the Challenge Grant program. The Challenge Grant program provides funds to eligible institutions on a matching basis as an incentive to seek alternative sources of funding.

Education of the Handicapped Act Amendments of 1983 (Public Law 98-199) added the Architectural Barrier amendment and clarified participation of children with disabilities in private schools.

1984 *Education for Economic Security Act* (Public Law 98-377) added new science and mathematics programs for elementary, secondary, and postsecondary education. The new programs included magnet schools, excellence in education, and equal access.

Carl D. Perkins Vocational Education Act (Public Law 98-524) continued federal assistance for vocational education through FY 1989. The act replaced the Vocational Education Act of 1963. It provided aid to the states to make vocational education programs accessible to all persons, including disabled and disadvantaged, single parents and homemakers, and the incarcerated.

Human Services Reauthorization Act (Public Law 98-558) created a Carl D. Perkins scholarship program, a National Talented Teachers Fellowship program, a Federal Merit Scholarships program, and a Leadership in Educational Administration program.

1985 *Montgomery GI Bill—Active Duty* (Public Law 98-525), brought about a new GI Bill for individuals who initially entered active military duty on or after July 1, 1985.

Montgomery GI Bill—Selected Reserve (Public Law 98-525), established an education program for members of the Selected Reserve (which includes the National Guard) who enlist, reenlist, or extend an enlistment after June 30, 1985, for a 6-year period.

1986 *Handicapped Children's Protection Act of 1986* (Public Law 99-372) allowed parents of children with disabilities to collect attorneys' fees in cases brought under the Education of the Handicapped Act and provided that the Education of the Handicapped Act does not preempt other laws, such as Section 504 of the Rehabilitation Act.

Drug-Free Schools and Communities Act of 1986 (Part of Public Law 99-570), part of the Anti-Drug Abuse Act of 1986, authorized funding for FYs 1987–89. Established programs for drug abuse education and prevention, coordinated with related community efforts and resources, through the use of federal financial assistance.

1988 *Augustus F. Hawkins-Robert T. Stafford Elementary and Secondary School Improvement Amendments of 1988* (Public Law 100-297) reauthorized through 1993 major elementary and secondary education programs including: Chapter 1, Chapter 2, Bilingual Education, Math-Science Education, Magnet Schools, Impact Aid, Indian Education, Adult Education, and other smaller education programs.

Technology-Related Assistance for Individuals with Disabilities Act of 1988 (Public Law 100-407) provided financial assistance to states to develop and implement consumer-responsive statewide programs of technology-related assistance for persons of all ages with disabilities.

Stewart B. McKinney Homeless Assistance Amendments Act of 1988 (Public Law 100-628) extended for 2 additional years programs providing assistance to the homeless, including literacy training for homeless adults and education for homeless youths.

Tax Reform Technical Amendments (Public Law 100-647) authorized an Education Savings Bond for the purpose of postsecondary educational expenses. The bill grants tax exclusion for interest earned on regular series EE savings bonds.

1989 *Children with Disabilities Temporary Care Reauthorization Act of 1989* (Public Law 101-127) revised and extended the programs established in the Temporary Child Care for Handicapped Children and Crises Nurseries Act of 1986.

Childhood Education and Development Act of 1989 (Part of Public Law 101-239) authorized the appropriations to expand Head Start programs and programs carried out under the Elementary and Secondary Education Act of 1965 to include child care services.

1990 *Excellence in Mathematics, Science and Engineering Education Act of 1990* (Public Law 101-589) was established to promote excellence in American mathematics, science, and engineering education by creating a national mathematics and science clearinghouse, and creating several other mathematics, science, and engineering education programs.

Student Right-To-Know and Campus Security Act (Public Law 101-542) required institutions of higher education receiving federal financial assistance to provide certain information with respect to the graduation rates of student-athletes at such institutions.

Americans with Disabilities Act of 1990 (Public Law 101-336) prohibited discrimination against persons with disabilities.

National and Community Service Act of 1990 (Public Law 101-610) increased school and college-based community service opportunities and authorized the President's Points of Light Foundation.

1991 *National Literacy Act of 1991* (Public Law 102-73) established the National Institute for Literacy, the National Institute Board, and the Interagency Task Force on Literacy. Amended various federal laws to establish and extend various literacy programs.

High-Performance Computing Act of 1991 (Public Law 102-194) directed the President to implement a National High-Performance Computing Program. Provided for: (1) establishment of a National Research and Education Network; (2) standards and guidelines for high performance networks; and (3) the responsibility of certain federal departments and agencies with regard to the Network.

Veterans' Educational Assistance Amendments of 1991 (Public Law 102-127) restored certain educational benefits available to reserve and active-duty personnel under the Montgomery GI Bill to students whose course of studies were interrupted by the Persian Gulf War.

Civil Rights Act of 1991 (Public Law 102-166) amended the Civil Rights Act of 1964, the Age Discrimination in Employment Act of 1967, and the Americans with Disabilities Act of 1990, with regard to employment discrimination. Established the Technical Assistance Training Institute.

1992 *Ready-To-Learn Act* (Public Law 102-545) amended the General Education Provisions Act to establish Ready-To-Learn Television programs to support educational programming and support materials for preschool and elementary school children and their parents, child care providers, and educators.

1993 *Student Loan Reform Act* (Public Law 103-66) reformed the student aid process by phasing in a system of direct lending designed to provide savings for taxpayers and students. Allows students to choose among a variety of repayment options, including income contingency.

National Service Trust Act (Public Law 103-82) amended the National and Community Service Act of 1990 to establish a Corporation for National Service and enhance opportunities for national service. In addition, the Act provided education grants up to $4,725 per year for 2 years to people age 17 years or older who perform community service before, during, or after postsecondary education.

NAEP Assessment Authorization (Public Law 103-33) authorized the use of NAEP for state-by-state comparisons.

1994 *Goals 2000: Educate America Act* (Public Law 103-227) established a new federal partnership through a system of grants to states and local communities to reform the nation's education system. The Act formalized the national education goals and established the National Education Goals Panel.

School-To-Work Opportunities Act of 1994 (Public Law 103-239) established a national framework within which states and communities can develop School-To-Work Opportunities systems to prepare young people for first jobs and continuing education. The Act also provided money to states and communities to develop a system of programs that include work-based learning, school-based learning, and connecting activities components.

Safe Schools Act of 1994 (Part of Public Law 103-227) authorized the award of competitive grants to local educational agencies with serious crime to implement violence prevention activities such as conflict resolution and peer mediation.

1996 *Contract With America: Unfunded Mandates* (Public Law 104-4) curbed the practice of imposing unfunded federal mandates on states and local governments; strengthened the partnership between the federal government and state, local, and tribal governments; ended the imposition, in the absence of full consideration by Congress, of federal mandates on state, local, and tribal governments without adequate funding, in a manner that may displace other essential governmental priorities; and ensured that the federal government pays the costs incurred by those governments in complying with certain requirements under federal statutes and regulations.

Human Rights, Refugee, and Other Foreign Relations Provisions Act of 1996 (Public Law 104-319) made certain provisions with respect to internationally recognized human rights, refugees, and foreign relations to revise U.S. human rights policy.

1997 *The Taxpayer Relief Act of 1997* (Public Law 105-34) enacted the Hope Scholarship and Life-Long Learning Tax Credit provisions into law.

Emergency Student Loan Consolidation Act of 1997 (Public Law 105-78) amended the Higher Education Act to provide for improved student loan consolidation services.

1998 *Workforce Investment Act of 1998* (Public Law 105-220) enacted the Adult Education and Family Literacy Act, and substantially revised and extended, through FY 2003, the Rehabilitation Act of 1973.

Omnibus Consolidated and Emergency Supplemental Appropriations Act, 1999 (Public Law 105-277) enacted the Reading Excellence Act, to promote the ability of children to read independently by the third grade; and earmarked funds to help states and school districts reduce class sizes in the early grades.

Charter School Expansion Act (Public Law 105-278) amended the charter school program, enacted in 1994 as Title X, Part C of the Elementary and Secondary Education Act of 1965.

Carl D. Perkins Vocational and Applied Technology Education Amendments of 1998 (Public Law 105-332) revised, in its entirety, the Carl D. Perkins Vocational and Applied Technology Education Act, and reauthorized the Act through FY 2003.

Assistive Technology Act of 1998 (Public Law 105-394) replaced the Technology-Related Assistance for Individuals with Disabilities Act of 1988 with a new Act, authorized through FY 2004, to address the assistive-technology needs of individuals with disabilities.

1999 *Education Flexibility Partnership Act of 1999* (Public Law 106-25) authorized the Secretary of Education to allow all states to participate in the Education Flexibility Partnership program.

District of Columbia College Access Act of 1999 (Public Law 106-98) established a program to afford high school graduates from the District of Columbia the benefits of in-state tuition at state colleges and universities outside the District of Columbia.

2000 *The National Defense Authorization Act for Fiscal Year 2001* (Public Law 106-398) included, as Title XVIII, the Impact Aid Reauthorization Act of 2000, which extended the Impact Aid programs through FY 2003.

College Scholarship Fraud Prevention Act of 2000 (Public Law 106-420) enhanced federal penalties for offenses involving scholarship fraud; required an annual scholarship fraud report by the Attorney

General, the Secretary of Education, and the Federal Trade Commission (FTC); and required the Secretary of Education, in conjunction with the FTC, to maintain a scholarship fraud awareness website.

Consolidated Appropriations Act 2001 (Public Law 106-554) created a new program of assistance for school repair and renovation, and amended the Elementary and Secondary Education Act of 1965 to authorize credit enhancement initiatives to help charter schools obtain, construct, or repair facilities; reauthorized the Even Start program; and enacted the "Children's Internet Protection Act."

2001 *50th Anniversary of Brown v. the Board of Education* (Public Law 107-41) established a commission for the purpose of encouraging and providing for the commemoration of the 50th anniversary of the 1954 Supreme Court decision *Brown* v. *Board of Education*.

2002 *No Child Left Behind Act of 2001* (Public Law 107-110) provided for the comprehensive reauthorization of the Elementary and Secondary Education Act of 1965, incorporating specific proposals in such areas as testing, accountability, parental choice, and early reading.

Reauthorization of the National Center for Education Statistics and the Creating of the Institute of Education Sciences of 2002 (Public Law 107-279) established the Institute of Education Sciences within the U.S. Department of Education to carry out a coordinated, focused agenda of high-quality research, statistics, and evaluation that is relevant to the educational challenges of the nation.

The Higher Education Relief Opportunities for Students Act of 2001 (Public Law 107-122) provided the Secretary of Education with waiver authority under student financial aid programs under Title IV of the Higher Education Act of 1965, to deal with student and family situations resulting from the September 11, 2001, terrorist attacks.

Established fixed interest rates for student and parent borrowers (Public Law 107-139) under Title IV of the Higher Education Act of 1965.

2003 *The Higher Education Relief Opportunities for Students Act of 2003* (Public Law 108-76) provided the Secretary of Education with waiver authority under student financial aid programs under Title IV of the Higher Education Act of 1965, to deal with student and family situations resulting from wars or national emergencies.

2004 *Assistive Technology Act of 2004* (Public Law 108-364) reauthorized the Assistive Technology program, administered by the Department of Education.

Taxpayer-Teacher Protection Act of 2004 (Public Law 108-409) temporarily stopped excessive special allowance payments to certain lenders under the Federal Family Education Loan (FFEL) Program and increases the amount of loans that can be forgiven for certain borrowers who are highly qualified

mathematics, science, and special education teachers who serve in high-poverty schools for 5 years.

Individuals with Disabilities Education Improvement Act of 2004 (Public Law 108-446) provided a comprehensive reauthorization of the Individuals with Disabilities Education Act.

2005 *Student Grant Hurricane and Disaster Relief Act* (Public Law 109-67) authorized the Secretary of Education to waive certain repayment requirements for students receiving campus-based federal grant assistance if they were residing in, employed in, or attending an institution of higher education located in a major disaster area, or their attendance was interrupted because of the disaster.

Natural Disaster Student Aid Fairness Act (Public Law 109-86) authorized the Secretary of Education during FY 2006 to reallocate campus-based student aid funds to institutions of higher learning in Louisiana, Mississippi, Alabama, and Texas, or institutions that have accepted students displaced by Hurricane Katrina or Rita. The law also waived requirements for matching funds that are normally imposed on institutions and students.

Hurricane Education Recovery Act (*HERA*) (Public Law 109-148, provision in the Defense Department Appropriations Act for FY 2006) provided funds for states affected by Hurricane Katrina to restart school operations, provide temporary emergency aid for displaced students, and assist homeless youth. The law also permitted the Secretary of Education to extend deadlines under the Individuals with Disabilities Education Act for those affected by Katrina or Rita.

2006 *Higher Education Reconciliation Act of 2005* (Public Law 109-171) made various amendments to programs of student financial assistance under Title IV of the Higher Education Act of 1965.

Public Law 109-211 reauthorized the "ED-FLEX" program (under the Education Flexibility Partnership Act of 1999), under which the Secretary permits states to waive certain requirements of federal statutes and regulations if they meet certain conditions.

Carl D. Perkins Career and Technical Education Improvement Act of 2006 (Public Law 109-270) reauthorized the vocational and technical education programs under the Perkins Act through 2012.

Third Higher Education Extension Act of 2006 (Public Law 109-292) extended the Higher Education Act through June 30, 2007, to afford Congress additional time to complete work on a comprehensive reauthorization.

Public Law 109-323 extended, for an additional year (through September 30, 2007), the period for which the Secretary of Education may waive certain fiscal requirements for states in which the President declared disaster areas as a result of Hurricanes Katrina and Rita.

2007 Public Law 110-15 designated the Department of Education Headquarters Building as the "Lyndon Baines Johnson Department of Education Building."

The *America COMPETES Act* (or *"America Creating Opportunities to Meaningfully Promote Excellence in Technology, Education, and Science"*) (Public Law 110-69) creates new STEM (science, technology, engineering, and mathematics) education programs in various agencies, including the Department of Education.

The *College Cost Reduction and Access Act of 2007* (Public Law 110-84) reduces interest rates on student loans and makes other amendments to the Higher Education Act of 1965 to make college more accessible and affordable.

Permanent extension of the *Higher Education Relief Opportunities for Students Act of 2003* (HEROES Act) (Public Law 110-93) gives the Secretary authority to waive or modify any statutory or regulatory provision applicable to the student financial assistance programs under title IV of the Higher Education Act of 1965 as deemed necessary in connection with a war or other military operation or national emergency.

2008 *Ensuring Continued Access to Student Loans Act of 2008* (Public Law 110-227) provides various authorities to the Department of Education, among other provisions, to help ensure that college students and their parents continue to have access to loans in the tight credit market.

The *Higher Education Opportunity Act* (Public Law 110-315) provides a comprehensive reauthorization of the Higher Education Act of 1965.

Figure 18. Federal on-budget funds for education, by level or other educational purpose: Selected years, 1965 through 2008

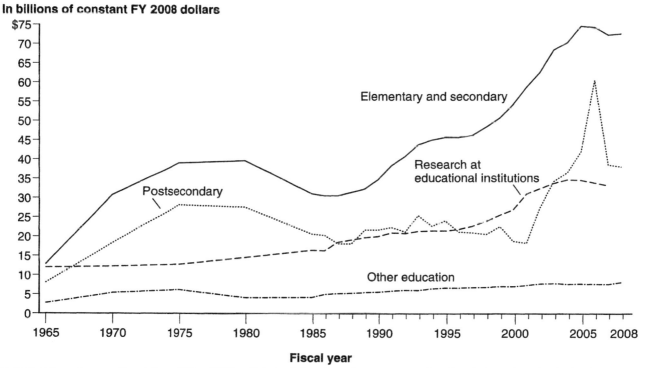

NOTE: Changes in postsecondary expenditures between 2005 and 2007 resulted primarily from changes in accounting procedures. Data for Research at educational institutions not available for 2008.
SOURCE: U.S. Department of Education, Budget Service, unpublished tabulations. U.S. Department of Education, National Center for Education Statistics, unpublished tabulations. U.S. Office of Management and Budget, *Budget of the U.S. Government, Appendix,* fiscal years 1967 through 2009. National Science Foundation, *Federal Funds for Research and Development,* fiscal years 1965 through 2007.

Figure 19. Percentage of federal on-budget funds for education, by agency: Fiscal year 2007

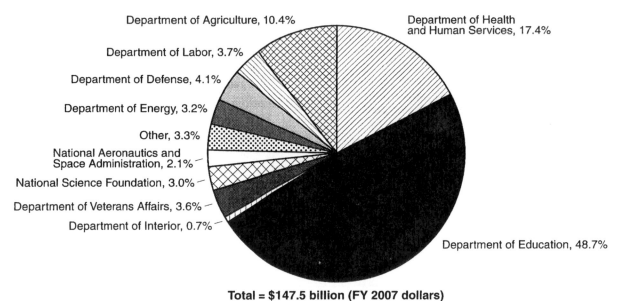

Department of Agriculture, 10.4%

Department of Labor, 3.7%

Department of Defense, 4.1%

Department of Energy, 3.2%

Other, 3.3%

National Aeronautics and Space Administration, 2.1%

National Science Foundation, 3.0%

Department of Veterans Affairs, 3.6%

Department of Interior, 0.7%

Department of Health and Human Services, 17.4%

Department of Education, 48.7%

Total = $147.5 billion (FY 2007 dollars)

NOTE: Detail may not sum to totals because of rounding.
SOURCE: U.S. Department of Education, National Center for Education Statistics, unpublished tabulations. U.S. Office of Management and Budget, *Budget of the U.S. Government, Appendix, Fiscal Year 2009.* National Science Foundation, *Federal Funds for Research and Development, Fiscal Year 2007.*

Figure 20. Department of Education outlays, by type of recipient: Fiscal year 2008

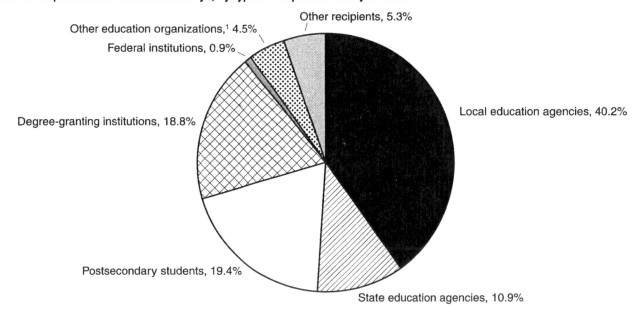

Other education organizations,[1] 4.5%

Federal institutions, 0.9%

Degree-granting institutions, 18.8%

Postsecondary students, 19.4%

Other recipients, 5.3%

Local education agencies, 40.2%

State education agencies, 10.9%

Total outlays = $73.8 billion

[1]Includes funds for vocational education and for federal programs at libraries and museums.
NOTE: Detail may not sum to totals because of rounding.
SOURCE: U.S. Office of Management and Budget, *Budget of the U.S. Government, Fiscal Year 2009.* U.S. Department of Education, Office of the Deputy Secretary, Budget Office, unpublished tabulations.

Table 373. Federal support and estimated federal tax expenditures for education, by category: Selected fiscal years, 1965 through 2008

[In millions of dollars]

Fiscal year	Total on-budget support, off-budget support, and nonfederal funds generated by federal legislation	On-budget support[1] Total	Elementary and secondary	Post-secondary	Other education[3]	Research at educational institutions	Off-budget support and nonfederal funds generated by federal legislation Total	Off-budget support Direct Loan Program[4]	Nonfederal funds Federal Family Education Loan Program[5]	Perkins Loans[6]	Income Contingent Loans[7]	Leveraging Educational Assistance Partnerships[8]	Supplemental Educational Opportunity Grants[9]	Work-Study Aid[10]	Estimated federal tax expenditures for education[2]
	2	3	4	5	6	7	8	9	10	11	12	13	14	15	16
							Current dollars								
1965	$5,354.7	$5,331.0	$1,942.6	$1,197.5	$374.7	$1,816.3	$23.7	†	†	$16.1	†	†	†	$7.6	—
1970	13,359.1	12,526.5	5,830.4	3,447.7	964.7	2,283.6	832.6	†	$770.0	21.0	†	†	†	41.6	—
1975	24,691.5	23,288.1	10,617.2	7,644.0	1,608.5	3,418.4	1,403.4	†	1,233.0	35.7	†	$20.0	†	114.7	$8,605.0
1980	39,349.5	34,493.5	16,027.7	11,115.9	1,548.7	5,801.2	4,856.0	†	4,598.0	31.8	†	76.8	†	149.4	13,320.0
1985	47,753.4	39,027.9	16,901.3	11,174.4	2,107.6	8,844.6	8,725.5	†	8,467.0	21.4	†	76.0	†	161.1	19,105.0
1986	48,357.3	39,962.9	17,049.9	11,283.6	2,620.0	9,009.4	8,394.4	†	8,142.0	20.2	†	72.7	†	159.5	20,425.0
1987	50,724.6	41,194.7	17,535.7	10,300.0	2,820.4	10,538.6	9,529.8	†	9,272.0	20.9	$0.6	76.0	†	160.4	20,830.0
1988	54,078.7	43,454.4	18,564.9	10,657.5	2,981.6	11,250.5	10,624.3	†	10,380.0	20.6	0.5	72.8	†	150.4	17,025.0
1989	59,537.4	48,269.6	19,809.5	13,269.9	3,180.3	12,009.8	11,267.8	†	10,938.0	20.4	0.5	71.9	$22.0	215.0	17,755.0
1990	62,811.5	51,624.3	21,984.4	13,650.9	3,383.0	12,606.0	11,187.2	†	10,826.0	15.0	0.5	59.2	48.8	237.7	19,040.0
1991	70,375.6	57,599.5	25,418.0	14,707.4	3,698.6	13,775.4	12,776.1	†	12,372.0	17.3	0.5	63.5	87.7	235.0	18,995.0
1992	74,481.1	60,483.1	27,926.9	14,387.4	3,992.0	14,176.9	13,998.0	†	13,568.0	17.3	0.5	72.0	97.2	242.9	19,950.0
1993	84,741.5	67,740.6	30,834.3	17,844.0	4,107.2	14,955.1	17,000.8	†	15,524.0	29.3	†	72.4	184.6	190.5	21,010.0
1994	92,781.5	68,254.2	32,304.4	16,177.1	4,483.7	15,289.1	24,527.3	$813.0	23,214.0	52.7	†	72.4	184.6	190.5	22,630.0
1995	95,810.8	71,639.5	33,623.8	17,618.1	4,719.7	15,677.9	24,171.2	5,161.0	18,519.0	52.7	†	63.4	184.6	190.5	24,600.0
1996	96,833.0	71,327.4	34,391.5	15,775.5	4,828.0	16,332.3	25,505.6	8,357.0	16,711.0	31.1	†	31.4	184.6	190.5	26,340.0
1997	103,259.8	73,731.8	35,478.9	15,959.4	5,021.2	17,272.4	29,528.0	9,838.0	19,163.0	52.7	†	50.0	184.6	239.7	28,125.0
1998	107,810.5	76,909.2	37,486.2	15,799.6	5,148.5	18,475.0	30,901.3	10,400.1	20,002.5	45.0	†	25.0	194.3	234.4	29,540.0
1999	113,417.2	82,863.6	39,937.9	17,651.2	5,318.0	19,956.5	30,553.6	9,953.0	20,107.0	33.3	†	25.0	195.9	239.4	37,360.0
2000	119,541.6	85,944.2	43,790.8	15,008.7	5,484.6	21,660.1	33,597.4	10,347.0	22,711.0	33.3	†	50.0	199.7	256.4	39,475.0
2001	130,668.5	94,846.5	48,530.1	14,938.3	5,880.0	25,498.1	35,822.0	10,635.0	24,694.0	25.0	†	80.0	184.0	204.0	41,460.0
2002	150,034.5	109,211.5	52,754.1	22,964.2	6,297.7	27,195.5	40,823.0	11,689.0	28,606.0	25.0	†	104.0	192.0	207.0	—
2003	170,671.5	124,374.5	59,274.2	29,499.7	6,532.5	29,068.1	46,297.0	11,969.0	33,791.0	33.0	†	103.0	202.0	199.0	—
2004	185,176.7	132,420.7	62,653.2	32,433.0	6,576.8	30,757.7	52,756.0	12,840.0	39,266.0	33.0	†	102.0	244.0	271.0	—
2005	203,036.0	146,207.0	68,957.7	38,587.3	6,908.5	31,753.5	56,829.0	12,930.0	43,284.0	0.0	†	101.0	246.0	268.0	—
2006	228,448.6	167,965.6	70,948.2	57,757.7	7,074.5	32,185.1 [11]	60,483.0	12,677.0	47,307.0	0.0	†	100.0	205.0	194.0	—
2007	212,365.7	147,527.7	70,604.2	37,465.3	7,214.9 [11]	32,243.3 [11]	64,838.0	13,022.0	51,320.0	0.0	†	100.0	205.0	191.0	—
2008[11]	—	—	72,839.2	37,968.6	7,877.8	—	67,835.0	14,103.0	53,242.0	0.0	†	98.0	201.0	191.0	—

See notes at end of table.

Table 373. Federal support and estimated federal tax expenditures for education, by category: Selected fiscal years, 1965 through 2008—Continued

[In millions of dollars]

Constant fiscal year 2008 dollars[12]

Fiscal year	Total on-budget support, off-budget support, and nonfederal funds generated by federal legislation	On-budget support[1]					Off-budget support and nonfederal funds generated by federal legislation	Off-budget support			Nonfederal funds				Estimated federal tax expenditures for education[2]
		Total	Elementary and secondary	Post-secondary	Other education[3]	Research at educational institutions	Total	Direct Loan Program[4]	Federal Family Education Loan Program[5]	Perkins Loans[6]	Income Contingent Loans[7]	Leveraging Educational Assistance Partnerships[8]	Supplemental Educational Opportunity Grants[9]	Work-Study Aid[10]	
1	2	3	4	5	6	7	8	9	10	11	12	13	14	15	16
1965	$34,414.1	$34,261.7	$12,484.7	$7,696.2	$2,407.8	$11,673.0	$152.4	†	†	$103.5	†	†	†	$48.8	—
1970	70,051.8	65,685.9	30,573.4	18,078.9	5,058.8	11,974.9	4,365.8	†	$4,037.7	110.0	†	†	†	218.1	—
1975	90,411.4	85,272.8	38,876.4	27,989.7	5,889.7	12,517.0	5,138.6	†	4,514.8	130.6	†	$73.2	†	420.0	$31,508.4
1980	96,953.6	84,988.9	39,490.8	27,388.5	3,815.9	14,293.6	11,964.7	†	11,329.1	78.3	†	189.2	†	368.1	32,819.3
1985	87,260.3	71,316.1	30,884.0	20,419.1	3,851.2	16,161.8	15,944.2	†	15,471.8	39.1	†	138.9	†	294.4	34,910.8
1986	86,252.4	71,279.7	30,411.1	20,125.9	4,673.2	16,069.5	14,972.7	†	14,522.5	36.0	†	129.7	†	284.5	36,431.0
1987	87,992.2	71,460.7	30,419.3	17,867.5	4,892.6	18,281.4	16,531.5	†	16,084.2	36.2	$1.0	131.8	†	278.2	36,133.9
1988	91,057.2	73,168.1	31,259.3	17,945.0	5,020.3	18,943.4	17,889.1	†	17,477.7	34.7	0.8	122.6	†	253.2	28,666.5
1989	96,675.2	78,378.8	32,166.1	21,547.3	5,164.1	19,501.2	18,296.4	†	17,760.8	33.1	0.9	116.7	$35.7	349.1	28,830.1
1990	98,743.7	81,156.7	34,560.8	21,460.1	5,318.3	19,817.5	17,587.0	†	17,019.2	23.6	0.8	93.0	76.7	373.7	29,932.1
1991	106,008.2	86,763.3	38,287.7	22,154.1	5,571.3	20,750.2	19,244.9	†	18,636.2	26.1	0.8	95.7	132.1	354.0	28,612.6
1992	108,473.9	88,087.2	40,672.6	20,953.7	5,813.9	20,647.1	20,386.7	†	19,760.4	25.2	0.8	104.9	141.6	353.8	29,055.1
1993	120,347.5	96,203.3	43,790.0	25,341.6	5,832.9	21,238.8	24,144.1	†	23,466.9	41.5	†	102.9	262.2	270.6	29,837.8
1994	129,145.7	95,005.4	44,965.5	22,517.4	6,241.0	21,281.4	34,140.3	$1,131.6	32,312.4	73.3	†	100.8	257.0	265.2	31,499.5
1995	130,174.5	97,333.9	45,683.4	23,937.1	6,412.4	21,301.0	32,840.5	7,012.1	25,161.1	71.6	†	86.1	250.8	258.9	33,423.1
1996	128,629.6	94,748.9	45,684.5	20,955.7	6,413.4	21,695.3	33,880.8	11,101.2	22,198.3	41.3	†	41.7	245.2	253.1	34,989.2
1997	134,570.1	96,088.7	46,236.8	20,798.6	6,543.7	22,509.6	38,481.4	12,821.1	24,973.6	68.7	†	65.2	240.6	312.4	36,653.0
1998	139,110.7	99,238.0	48,369.4	20,386.6	6,643.2	23,838.8	39,872.7	13,419.5	25,809.7	58.1	†	32.3	250.7	302.5	38,116.2
1999	144,168.3	105,330.6	50,766.4	22,437.0	6,759.9	25,367.3	38,837.7	12,651.6	25,558.7	42.3	†	31.8	249.0	304.3	47,489.5
2000	148,124.0	106,493.5	54,261.2	18,597.3	6,795.9	26,839.1	41,630.5	12,821.0	28,141.2	41.3	†	62.0	247.4	317.7	48,913.5
2001	158,209.2	114,837.1	58,758.6	18,086.8	7,119.3	30,872.3	43,372.1	12,876.5	29,898.7	30.3	†	96.9	222.8	247.0	50,194.4
2002	178,328.8	129,807.1	62,702.8	27,294.9	7,485.3	32,324.2	48,521.6	13,893.4	34,000.7	29.7	†	123.6	228.2	246.0	—
2003	197,588.6	143,989.9	68,622.5	34,152.2	7,562.8	33,652.5	53,598.6	13,856.7	39,120.3	38.2	†	119.2	233.9	230.4	—
2004	208,328.0	148,976.3	70,486.3	36,487.8	7,399.1	34,603.1	59,351.7	14,445.3	44,175.1	37.1	†	114.8	274.5	304.9	—
2005	220,318.7	158,652.3	74,827.5	41,871.9	7,496.6	34,456.4	61,666.4	14,030.6	46,968.4	0.0	†	109.6	266.9	290.8	—
2006	239,768.5	176,288.5	74,463.8	60,619.7	7,425.0	33,779.9 [11]	63,480.0	13,305.2	49,651.1	0.0	†	105.0	215.2	203.6	—
2007	218,122.0	151,526.5	72,518.0	38,480.8	7,410.5	33,117.2 [11]	66,595.5	13,375.0	52,711.1	0.0	†	102.7	210.6	196.2	—
2008[11]	—	—	72,839.2	37,968.6	7,877.8	—	67,835.0	14,103.0	53,242.0	0.0	†	98.0	201.0	191.0	—

—Not available.
†Not applicable.
[1]On-budget support includes federal funds for education programs tied to appropriations.
[2]Losses of tax revenue attributable to provisions of the federal income tax laws that allow a special exclusion, exemption, or deduction from gross income or provide a special credit, preferential rate of tax, or a deferral of tax liability affecting individual or corporate income tax liabilities.
[3]Other education includes libraries, museums, cultural activities, and miscellaneous research.
[4]The William D. Ford Direct Program (commonly referred to as the Direct Loan Program) provides students with the same benefits they are currently eligible to receive under the Federal Family Education Loan (FFEL) program, but provides loans to students through federal capital rather than through private lenders.
[5]Formerly the Guaranteed Student Loan program. Includes new student loans guaranteed by the federal government and disbursed to borrowers.
[6]Student loans created from institutional matching funds (since 1993 one-third of federal capital contributions). Excludes repayments of outstanding loans.
[7]Student loans created from institutional matching funds (one-ninth of the federal contribution). This was a demonstration project that involved only 10 institutions and had unsubsidized interest rates. Program repealed in fiscal year 1992.

[8]Formerly the State Student Incentive Grant program. Starting in fiscal year 2000, amounts under $30.0 million have required dollar-for-dollar state matching contributions, while amounts over $30.0 million have required two-to-one state matching contributions.
[9]Institutions award grants to undergraduate students, and the federal share of such grants may not exceed 75 percent of the total grant.
[10]Employer contributions to student earnings are generally one-third of federal allocation.
[11]Estimated.
[12]Data adjusted by the federal funds composite deflator reported in the U.S. Office of Management and Budget, *Budget of the U.S. Government, Historical Tables, Fiscal Year 2009.*

NOTE: To the extent possible, federal education funds data represent outlays rather than obligations. Some data have been revised from previously published figures. Detail may not sum to totals because of rounding. Changes in postsecondary expenditures between 2005 and 2007 resulted primarily from changes in accounting procedures.

SOURCE: U.S. Department of Education, Budget Service, unpublished tabulations. U.S. Department of Education, National Center for Education Statistics, unpublished tabulations. U.S. Office of Management and Budget, *Budget of the U.S. Government, Appendix,* fiscal years 1967 through 2009. National Science Foundation, *Federal Funds for Research and Development,* fiscal years 1967 through 2007. (This table was prepared October 2008.)

Table 374. Federal on-budget funds for education, by agency: Selected fiscal years, 1970 through 2007

[In thousands of current dollars]

Agency	1970	1975	1980	1985	1990	1995	2000	2005	2006	2007
1	2	3	4	5	6	7	8	9	10	11
Total	$12,526,499	$23,288,120	$34,493,502	$39,027,876	$51,624,342	$71,639,520	$85,944,203	$146,206,999	$167,965,585	$147,527,695
Department of Education	4,625,224	7,350,355	13,137,785	16,701,065	23,198,575	31,403,000	34,106,697	72,893,301	93,571,541	71,808,014
Department of Agriculture	960,910	2,219,352	4,562,467	4,782,274	6,260,843	9,092,089	11,080,031	13,817,553	14,763,772	15,409,677
Department of Commerce	13,990	38,967	135,561	55,114	53,835	88,929	114,575	243,948	214,548	198,461
Department of Defense	821,388	1,009,229	1,560,301	3,119,213	3,605,509	3,879,002	4,525,080	6,320,454	6,461,870	6,066,743
Department of Energy	551,527	764,676	1,605,558	2,247,822	2,561,950	2,692,314	3,577,004	4,339,879	4,197,315	4,649,477
Department of Health and Human Services	1,796,854	3,675,225	5,613,930	5,322,356	7,956,011	12,469,563	17,670,867	26,107,860	25,969,876	25,704,962
Department of Homeland Security	†	†	†	†	†	†	†	624,860	687,394	622,922
Department of Housing and Urban Development	114,709	-52,768	5,314	438	118	1,613	1,400	1,100	900	1,000
Department of the Interior	190,975	300,191	440,547	549,479	630,537	702,796	959,802	1,254,533	1,157,650	962,273
Department of Justice	15,728	61,542	60,721	66,802	99,775	172,350	278,927	608,148	566,934	771,656
Department of Labor	424,494	1,103,935	1,862,738	1,948,685	2,511,380	3,967,914	4,696,100	5,764,500	5,586,500	5,413,500
Department of State	59,742	89,433	25,188	23,820	51,225	54,671	388,349	533,309	555,014	587,120
Department of Transportation	27,534	52,290	54,712	82,035	76,186	135,816	117,054	126,900	142,300	128,700
Department of the Treasury	18	1,118,840	1,247,463	290,276	41,715	49,496	83,000	0	0	0
Department of Veterans Affairs	1,032,918	4,402,212	2,351,233	1,289,849	757,476	1,324,382	1,577,374	4,293,624	4,547,560	5,256,399
Other agencies and programs										
ACTION	†	7,081	2,833	1,761	8,472	†	†	†	†	†
Agency for International Development	88,034	78,896	176,770	198,807	249,786	290,580	332,500	602,100	594,300	656,700
Appalachian Regional Commission	37,838	45,786	19,032	4,745	93	10,623	7,243	8,542	11,027	7,463
Barry Goldwater Scholarship and Excellence in Education Foundation	†	†	†	†	1,033	3,000	3,000	3,000	3,000	3,000
Corporation for National and Community Service	†	†	†	†	†	214,600	386,000	472,000	503,000	395,000
Environmental Protection Agency	19,446	33,875	41,083	60,521	87,481	125,721	98,900	83,400	78,100	72,500
Estimated education share of federal aid to the District of Columbia	33,019	55,487	81,847	107,340	104,940	78,796	127,127	154,962	140,997	168,155
Federal Emergency Management Agency	290	290	1,946	1,828	215	170,400	14,894	†	†	†
General Services Administration	14,775	22,532	34,800	†	†	†	†	†	†	†
Harry S Truman Scholarship fund	†	†	-1,895	1,332	2,883	3,000	3,000	3,000	3,000	3,000
Institute of American Indian and Alaska Native Culture and Arts Development	†	†	†	†	4,305	13,000	2,000	6,000	6,000	6,000
Institute of Museum and Library Services	†	†	†	†	†	†	166,000	250,000	241,000	258,000
James Madison Memorial Fellowship Foundation	†	†	†	†	191	2,000	7,000	2,000	2,000	2,000
Japanese-United States Friendship Commission	†	†	2,294	2,236	2,299	2,000	3,000	3,000	2,000	2,000
Library of Congress	20,478	63,766	151,871	169,310	189,827	241,000	299,000	430,000	435,000	463,000
National Aeronautics and Space Administration	258,366	197,901	255,511	487,624	1,093,303	1,757,900	2,077,830	2,763,120	2,889,157	3,033,534
National Archives and Records Administration	†	†	†	52,118	77,397	105,172	121,879	276,000	276,000	273,000
National Commission on Libraries and Information Science	†	449	2,090	723	3,281	1,000	2,000	1,000	1,000	1,000
National Endowment for the Arts	340	4,754	5,220	5,536	5,577	9,421	10,048	10,976	10,561	11,767
National Endowment for the Humanities	8,459	63,955	142,586	125,671	141,048	151,727	100,014	117,825	120,305	121,086
National Science Foundation	295,628	535,294	808,392	1,147,115	1,588,891	2,086,195	2,955,244	3,993,216	4,060,572	4,368,539
Nuclear Regulatory Commission	†	7,093	32,590	30,261	42,328	22,188	12,200	15,100	12,400	13,200
Office of Economic Opportunity	1,092,410	16,619	†	†	†	†	†	†	†	†
Smithsonian Institution	2,461	5,509	5,153	7,886	5,779	9,961	25,764	45,890	42,092	46,101
United States Arms Control Agency	100	0	661	395	25	†	†	†	†	†
United States Information Agency	8,423	9,405	66,210	143,007	201,547	294,800	†	†	†	†
United States Institute of Peace	†	†	†	†	7,621	12,000	13,000	28,000	101,000	32,000
Other agencies	1,421	5,949	990	432	885	500	300	7,900	9,900	9,745

†Not applicable.
NOTE: To the extent possible, amounts reported represent outlays, rather than obligations. Some data have been revised from previously published figures. Detail may not sum to totals because of rounding. Negative amounts occur when program receipts exceed outlays. Much of the fluctuation in Department of Education funds between 2005 and 2007 was due to changes in postsecondary expenditures that resulted primarily from changes in accounting procedures.

SOURCE: U.S. Department of Education, National Center for Education Statistics, unpublished tabulations. U.S. Office of Management and Budget, *Budget of the U.S. Government, Appendix,* fiscal years 1972 through 2009. National Science Foundation, *Federal Funds for Research and Development,* fiscal years 1970 to 2007. (This table was prepared October 2008.)

Table 375. Federal on-budget funds for education, by level/educational purpose, agency, and program: Selected fiscal years, 1970 through 2008

[In thousands of current dollars]

Level/educational purpose, agency, and program	1970	1980	1985	1990[1]	1995[1]	2000[1]	2005[1]	2006[1,2]	2007[1,2]	2008[1,2]
1	2	3	4	5	6	7	8	9	10	11
Total	$12,526,499	$34,493,502	$39,027,876	$51,624,342	$71,639,520	$85,944,203	$146,206,999	$167,965,585	$147,527,695	—
Elementary/secondary education	5,830,442	16,027,686	16,901,334	21,984,361	33,623,809	43,790,783	68,957,711	70,948,229	70,604,233	$72,839,174
Department of Education[3]	2,719,204	6,629,095	7,296,702	9,681,313	14,029,000	20,039,563	37,477,594	38,863,442	37,562,078	38,900,269
Education for the disadvantaged	1,339,014	3,204,664	4,206,754	4,494,111	6,808,000	8,529,111	14,635,566	14,695,815	14,486,936	15,036,258
Impact aid program[4]	656,372	690,170	647,402	816,366	808,000	877,101	1,262,174	1,141,455	1,162,814	1,388,915
School improvement programs[5]	288,304	788,918	526,401	1,189,158	1,397,000	2,549,971	7,918,091	7,463,468	7,083,651	7,447,908
Indian education	†	93,365	82,328	69,451	71,000	65,285	121,911	120,360	117,992	116,720
English Language Acquisition	21,250	169,540	157,539	188,919	225,000	362,662	667,485	616,075	728,703	797,858
Special education	79,090	821,777	1,017,964	1,616,623	3,177,000	4,948,977	10,940,312	11,836,477	11,777,258	11,771,719
Vocational and adult education	335,174	860,661	658,314	1,306,685	1,482,000	1,462,977	1,967,086	1,987,455	1,955,780	2,125,604
Education Reform—Goals 2000[6]	†	†	†	†	61,000	1,243,479	-35,031	†	†	†
Hurricane Education Recovery								985,797	248,944	215,287
Department of Agriculture	760,477	4,064,497	4,134,906	5,528,950	8,201,294	10,051,278	12,577,265	13,412,550	14,245,994	15,207,897
Child nutrition programs[7]	299,131	3,377,056	3,664,561	4,977,075	7,644,789	9,554,028	11,901,943	12,660,758	13,081,994	14,401,897
McGovern-Dole International Food for Education and Child Nutrition Program[8]	†	†	†	†	†	†	86,000	98,000	98,000	104,000
Agricultural Marketing Service—commodities[9]	341,597	388,000	336,502	350,441	400,000	400,000	399,322	463,792	878,000	542,000
Special milk program	83,800	159,293	15,993	18,707	(7)	(7)	(7)	(7)	(7)	(7)
Estimated education share of Forest Service permanent appropriations	35,949	140,148	117,850	182,727	156,505	97,250	190,000	190,000	188,000	160,000
Department of Commerce	†	54,816	†	†	†	†	†	†	†	†
Local public works program—school facilities[10]	†	54,816	†	†	†	†	†	†	†	†
Department of Defense	143,100	370,846	831,625	1,097,876	1,295,547	1,485,611	1,786,253	1,755,924	1,772,293	1,816,968
Junior Reserve Officers Training Corps (JROTC)	12,100	32,000	55,600	39,300	155,600	210,432	315,122	308,208	324,917	352,821
Overseas dependents schools	131,000	338,846	613,437	864,958	855,772	904,829	1,060,920	1,063,908	1,062,367	1,031,420
Domestic schools[4]	†	†	162,588	193,618	284,175	370,350	410,211	383,808	385,009	432,727
Department of Energy	200	77,633	23,031	15,563	12,646	†	†	†	†	†
Energy conservation for school buildings[11]	†	77,240	22,731	15,213	10,746	†	†	†	†	†
Pre-engineering program	200	393	300	350	1,900	†	†	†	†	†
Department of Health and Human Services	167,333	1,077,000	1,531,059	2,396,793	5,116,559	6,011,036	8,003,348	8,118,935	7,901,700	7,922,700
Head Start[12]	†	735,000	1,075,059	1,447,758	3,534,000	5,267,000	6,842,348	6,851,235	6,888,000	6,878,000
Payments to states for Aid for Families with Dependent Children (AFDC) work programs[13]	†	†	†	459,221	953,000	15,000	—	—	—	—
Social Security student benefits[14]	167,333	342,000	456,000	489,814	629,559	729,036	1,161,000	1,267,700	1,013,700	1,044,700
Department of Homeland Security	†	†	†	†	†	†	500	511	500	618
Tuition assistance for educational accreditation—Coast Guard personnel[15]	†	†	†	†	†	†	500	511	500	618
Department of the Interior	140,705	318,170	389,810	445,267	493,124	725,423	938,506	928,637	728,078	763,733
Mineral Leasing Act and other funds Payments to states— estimated education share	12,294	62,636	127,369	123,811	18,750	24,610	60,290	56,806	52,030	54,000
Payments to counties— estimated education share	16,359	48,953	59,016	102,522	37,490	53,500	79,686	124,000	71,034	74,050
Indian Education Bureau of Indian Education schools	95,850	178,112	177,265	192,841	411,524	466,905	517,647	523,673	518,700	540,734
Johnson-O'Malley assistance[16]	16,080	28,081	25,675	25,556	24,359	17,387	16,510	16,371	12,000	13,782
Education construction	†	†	†	†	†	161,021	263,373	206,787	73,314	80,168
Education expenses for children of employees, Yellowstone National Park	122	388	485	538	1,000	2,000	1,000	1,000	1,000	1,000
Department of Justice	8,237	23,890	36,117	65,997	128,850	224,800	554,500	514,300	719,600	730,000
Vocational training expenses for prisoners in federal prisons	2,720	4,966	8,292	2,066	3,000	1,000	0	1,000	6,000	6,000
Inmate programs[17]	5,517	18,924	27,825	63,931	125,850	223,800	554,500	513,300	713,600	724,000
Department of Labor	420,927	1,849,800	1,945,268	2,505,487	3,957,800	4,683,200	5,654,000	5,355,000	5,226,000	5,018,000
Job Corps	†	469,800	604,748	739,376	1,029,000	1,256,000	1,521,000	1,599,000	1,605,000	1,490,000
Training programs—estimated funds for education programs[18]	420,927	1,380,000	1,340,520	1,766,111	2,928,800	3,427,200	4,133,000	3,756,000	3,621,000	3,528,000

See notes at end of table.

Table 375. Federal on-budget funds for education, by level/educational purpose, agency, and program: Selected fiscal years, 1970 through 2008—Continued

[In thousands of current dollars]

Level/educational purpose, agency, and program	1970	1980	1985	1990[1]	1995[1]	2000[1]	2005[1]	2006[1,2]	2007[1,2]	2008[1,2]
1	2	3	4	5	6	7	8	9	10	11
Department of Transportation .... Tuition assistance for educational accreditation—	45	60	60	46	62	188	†	†	†	†
Coast Guard personnel[15]	45	60	60	46	62	188	†	†	†	†
Department of the Treasury .... Estimated education share of general revenue sharing[19]	†	935,903	273,728	†	†	†	†	†	†	†
State[20]	†	525,019	†	†	†	†	†	†	†	†
Local...............................	†	410,884	273,728	†	†	†	†	†	†	†
Department of Veterans Affairs... Noncollegiate and job training	338,910	545,786	344,758	155,351	311,768	445,052	1,815,000	1,866,000	2,300,564	2,330,000
programs[21] .... Vocational rehabilitation for	281,640	439,993	224,035	12,848	†	†	†	†	†	†
disabled veterans[22]	41,700	87,980	107,480	136,780	298,132	438,635	1,815,000	1,866,000	2,300,564	2,330,000
Dependents' education[23]	15,570	17,813	13,243	5,723	5,961	6,417	—	—	—	—
Service members occupational conversion training act of 1992	†	†	†	†	7,675	†	†	†	†	†
Other agencies Appalachian Regional Commission	33,161	9,157	4,632	93	2,173	2,588	2,962	1,218	1,110	1,200
National Endowment for the Arts	†	4,989	4,399	4,641	7,117	6,002	8,470	8,058	8,825	9,689
Arts in education	†	4,989	4,399	4,641	7,117	6,002	8,470	8,058	8,825	9,689
National Endowment for the Humanities......................	20	330	321	404	997	812	603	0	75	100
Office of Economic Opportunity Head Start[24]	1,072,375 325,700	†	†	†	†	†	†	†	†	†
Other elementary and secondary programs[25]	42,809	†	†	†	†	†	†	†	†	†
Job Corps[25]	144,000	†	†	†	†	†	†	†	†	†
Youth Corps and other training programs[26]	553,368	†	†	†	†	†	†	†	†	†
Volunteers in Service to America (VISTA)[27]	6,498	†	†	†	†		†	†	†	†
Other programs Estimated education share of federal aid to the District of Columbia..........................	25,748	65,714	84,918	86,579	66,871	115,230	138,710	123,653	137,416	138,000
Postsecondary education	**$3,447,697**	**$11,115,882**	**$11,174,379**	**$13,650,915**	**$17,618,137**	**$15,008,715**	**$38,587,287**	**$57,757,738**	**$37,465,287**	**$37,968,605**
Department of Education[3].............	1,187,962	5,682,242	8,202,499	11,175,978	14,234,000	10,727,315	31,420,023	50,624,621	30,052,007	30,267,127
Student financial assistance	†	3,682,789	4,162,695	5,920,328	7,047,000	9,060,317	15,209,515	14,864,129	15,355,736	17,474,372
Federal Direct Student Loan Program	†	†	†	†	840,000	-2,862,240	3,020,992	6,842,092	5,391,146	5,609,564
Federal Family Education Loan Program	2,323	1,407,977	3,534,795	4,372,446	5,190,000	2,707,473	10,777,470	26,336,661	6,033,322	3,941,519
Higher education	1,029,131	399,787	404,511	659,492	871,000	1,530,779	2,053,288	2,058,920	2,399,892	2,694,842
Facilities—loans and insurance	114,199	-19,031	5,307	19,219	-6,000	-2,174	-1,464	-1,304	-1,671	860
College housing loans[28]	†	14,082	-164,061	-57,167	-46,000	-41,886	-33,521	-27,229	-20,722	0
Educational activities overseas	774	3,561	1,838	82	†	†	†	†	†	†
Historically Black Colleges and Universities Capital Financing, Program Account	†	†	†	†	†	150	169	165	318,840	18,235
Gallaudet College and Howard University	38,559	176,829	229,938	230,327	292,000	291,060	339,823	340,664	351,665	329,296
National Technical Institute for the Deaf	2,976	16,248	27,476	31,251	46,000	43,836	53,751	56,670	57,836	54,915
Hurricane Katrina, aid to institutions	†	†	†	†	†	†	†	153,853	165,963	143,524
Department of Agriculture............ Agriculture Extension Service, Second Morrill Act payments to agricultural and mechanical colleges and	†	10,453	17,741	31,273	33,373	30,676	61,957	62,327	64,357	66,709
Tuskegee Institute	†	10,453	17,741	31,273	33,373	30,676	61,957	62,327	64,357	66,709
Department of Commerce	8,277	29,971	2,163	3,312	3,487	3,800	—	—	—	—
Sea Grant Program[29]	†	3,123	2,163	3,312	3,487	3,800	—	—	—	—
Merchant Marine Academy[30].....	6,160	14,809	†	†	†	†	†	†	†	†
State marine schools[30]	2,117	12,039	†	†	†	†	†	†	†	†
Department of Defense................	322,100	545,000	1,041,700	635,769	729,500	1,147,759	1,858,301	1,833,446	1,846,850	1,946,352
Tuition assistance for military personnel	57,500	—	77,100	95,300	127,000	263,303	608,109	563,961	607,515	603,610
Service academies..................	78,700	106,100	196,400	120,613	163,300	212,678	300,760	321,920	354,528	330,156
Senior Reserve Officers Training Corps (SROTC)...............	108,100	—	354,000	193,056	219,400	363,461	537,525	498,165	434,687	549,633
Professional development education[31].........................	77,800	—	414,200	226,800	219,800	308,317	411,907	449,400	450,120	462,953

See notes at end of table.

Table 375. Federal on-budget funds for education, by level/educational purpose, agency, and program: Selected fiscal years, 1970 through 2008—Continued

[In thousands of current dollars]

Level/educational purpose, agency, and program	1970	1980	1985	1990[1]	1995[1]	2000[1]	2005[1]	2006[1,2]	2007[1,2]	2008[1,2]
1	2	3	4	5	6	7	8	9	10	11
Department of Energy............	3,000	57,701	19,475	25,502	28,027	†	†	†	†	†
University laboratory cooperative program	3,000	2,800	6,500	9,402	8,552	‡	‡	‡	‡	‡
Teacher development projects ..	†	1,400	†	†	†					
Energy conservation for buildings—higher education[11].........................	†	53,501	12,705	7,459	7,381	†	†	†	†	†
Minority honors vocational training	‡	‡	150	‡	‡	‡	‡	‡	‡	‡
Honors research program	‡	‡	120	6,472	2,221	‡	‡	‡	‡	‡
Students and teachers	‡	‡	†	2,169	9,873					
Department of Health and Human Services.................................	981,483	2,412,058	516,088	578,542	796,035	954,190	1,433,516	1,264,585	1,159,279	1,176,013
Health professions training programs[32]	353,029	460,736	212,200	230,600	298,302	340,361	581,661	420,115	302,081	318,225
Indian health manpower...........	†	7,187	5,577	9,508	27,000	16,000	27,000	32,000	32,000	36,000
National Health Service Corps scholarships........................	†	70,667	2,268	4,759	78,206	33,300	45,000	40,000	40,000	40,000
National Institutes of Health training grants[33]	†	176,388	217,927	241,356	380,502	550,220	756,014	748,642	761,034	756,024
National Institute of Occupational Safety and Health training grants	8,088	12,899	8,760	10,461	11,660	14,198	23,841	23,828	24,164	25,764
Alcohol, drug abuse, and mental health training programs[34] ...	118,366	122,103	43,617	81,353	†	†	‡	‡	‡	‡
Health teaching facilities[35].........	†	3,078	739	505	365	110				
Social Security postsecondary students' benefits[36]..............	502,000	1,559,000	25,000	†	†	†	†	†	†	†
Department of Homeland Security	‡	‡	‡	‡	‡	‡	36,400	44,000	48,900	52,100
Coast Guard Academy[15]							16,400	22,800	23,400	23,200
Postgraduate training for Coast Guard officers[37]	†	†	†	†	†	†	8,700	11,400	12,800	15,000
Tuition assistance to Coast Guard military personnel[15] ..	†	†	†	†	†	†	11,300	9,800	12,700	13,900
Department of Housing and Urban Development[28]	114,199	‡	‡	‡	‡	‡	‡	‡	‡	‡
College housing loans[28]	114,199									
Department of the Interior............	31,749	80,202	125,247	135,480	159,054	187,179	249,227	165,313	176,695	186,954
Shared revenues, Mineral Leasing Act and other receipts—estimated education share	6,949	35,403	71,991	69,980	82,810	98,740	146,235	59,579	52,400	59,200
Indian programs Continuing education............	9,380	16,909	24,338	34,911	43,907	57,576	76,271	79,610	98,463	101,795
Higher education scholarships.....................	15,420	27,890	28,918	30,589	32,337	30,863	26,721	26,124	25,832	25,959
Department of State	30,850	‡	‡	2,167	3,000	319,000	424,000	443,000	473,000	498,000
Educational exchange[38]	30,850			—	†	319,000	424,000	443,000	473,000	498,000
Mutual educational and cultural exchange activities	30,454	†	†	—	†	303,000	402,000	423,000	453,000	479,000
International educational exchange activities	396	†	†	—	†	16,000	22,000	20,000	20,000	19,000
Russian, Eurasian, and East European Research and Training...............................	†	†	†	2,167	3,000	†	†	†	†	†
Department of Transportation	11,197	12,530	55,569	46,025	59,257	60,300	73,000	71,000	74,000	76,000
Merchant Marine Academy[30].....	†	†	19,898	20,926	30,850	34,000	61,000	63,000	61,000	63,000
State marine schools[30]	†	†	19,777	8,269	8,980	7,000	12,000	8,000	13,000	13,000
Coast Guard Academy[15]	9,342	10,000	11,857	12,074	13,500	15,500	†	†	†	†
Postgraduate training for Coast Guard officers[37]	1,655	2,230	3,499	4,173	5,513	2,500	†	†	†	†
Tuition assistance to Coast Guard military personnel[15] ..	200	300	538	582	414	1,300	†	†	†	†
Department of the Treasury	†	296,750	†	†	†	†	†	†	†	†
General revenue sharing— estimated state share to higher education[19,20]............	†	296,750	†	†	†	†	†	†	†	†

See notes at end of table.

Table 375. Federal on-budget funds for education, by level/educational purpose, agency, and program: Selected fiscal years, 1970 through 2008—Continued

[In thousands of current dollars]

Level/educational purpose, agency, and program	1970	1980	1985	1990[1]	1995[1]	2000[1]	2005[1]	2006[1,2]	2007[1,2]	2008[1,2]
1	2	3	4	5	6	7	8	9	10	11
Department of Veterans Affairs.....	693,490	1,803,847	944,091	599,825	1,010,114	1,132,322	2,478,624	2,681,560	2,955,835	3,061,241
Vietnam-era veterans...............	638,260	1,579,974	694,217	46,998	†	†	†	†	†	†
College student support........	†	1,560,081	679,953	39,458	†	†	†	†	†	†
Work-study	†	19,893	14,264	7,540	†	†	†	†	†	†
Service persons college support	18,900	46,617	35,630	8,911	†	†	†	†	†	†
Post-Vietnam veterans	†	922	82,554	161,475	33,596	3,958	1,136	1,275	914	804
All-volunteer-force educational assistance	†	†	196	269,947	868,394	984,068	2,070,996	2,230,022	2,227,531	2,321,489
Veterans	†	†	†	183,765	760,390	876,434	1,887,239	1,956,747	2,081,097	2,161,585
Reservists	†	†	196	86,182	108,004	107,634	183,757	273,275	146,434	159,904
Veteran dependents' education	36,330	176,334	131,494	100,494	95,124	131,296	388,719	413,136	511,793	555,369
Payments to state education agencies.............................	†	†	†	12,000	13,000	13,000	17,773	17,657	—	—
Reserve Education Assistance Program (REAP)[39]...............	†	†	†	†	†	†	†	19,470	215,597	183,580
Other agencies										
Appalachian Regional Commission	4,105	1,751	—	—	2,741	2,286	4,407	7,876	3,498	3,500
National Endowment for the Humanities	3,349	56,451	49,098	50,938	56,481	28,395	29,253	34,055	40,446	41,000
National Science Foundation	42,000	64,583	60,069	161,884	211,800	389,000	490,000	496,000	527,000	535,000
Science and engineering education programs........	37,000	64,583	60,069	161,884	211,800	389,000	490,000	496,000	527,000	535,000
Sea Grant Program[29].............	5,000	†	†	†	†	†	†	†	†	†
United States Information Agency[40]	8,423	51,095	124,041	181,172	260,800	†	†	†	†	†
Educational and cultural affairs[38]	†	49,546	21,079	35,862	13,600	†	†	†	†	†
Educational and cultural exchange programs[41]	†	†	101,529	145,307	247,200	†	†	†	†	†
Educational exchange activities, international	†	1,549	1,433	3	†	†	†	†	†	†
Information center and library activities................................	8,423	†	†	†	†	†	†	†	†	†
Other programs										
Barry Goldwater Scholarship and Excellence in Education Foundation	†	†	—	1,033	3,000	3,000	3,000	3,000	3,000	4,000
Estimated education share of federal aid to the District of Columbia.................................	5,513	13,143	15,266	14,637	9,468	11,493	14,578	15,954	29,418	42,608
Harry S Truman Scholarship fund	†	-1,895	1,332	2,883	3,000	3,000	3,000	3,000	3,000	3,000
Institute of American Indian and Alaska Native Culture and Arts Development.................	†	†	—	4,305	13,000	2,000	6,000	6,000	6,000	7,000
James Madison Memorial Fellowship Foundation	†	†	—	191	2,000	7,000	2,000	2,000	2,000	2,000
Other education.............	**$964,719**	**$1,548,730**	**$2,107,588**	**$3,383,031**	**$4,719,655**	**$5,484,571**	**$6,908,504**	**$7,074,484**	**$7,214,906**	**$7,877,791**
Department of Education[3]............	630,235	747,706	1,173,055	2,251,801	2,861,000	3,223,355	3,538,862	3,692,930	3,756,445	4,222,866
Administration	47,456	187,317	284,900	328,293	404,000	458,054	548,842	557,837	539,378	565,373
Libraries[42]	108,284	129,127	85,650	137,264	117,000	†	†	†	†	†
Rehabilitative services and disability research	473,091	426,886	798,298	1,780,360	2,333,000	2,755,468	2,973,346	3,115,842	3,177,031	3,603,594
American Printing House for the Blind	1,404	4,349	4,230	5,736	7,000	9,368	16,538	18,901	18,359	23,279
Trust funds and contributions	0	27	-23	148	0	465	136	350	21,677	30,620
Department of Agriculture............	135,637	271,112	336,375	352,511	422,878	444,477	468,631	475,395	515,026	516,316
Extension Service	131,734	263,584	325,986	337,907	405,371	424,174	445,631	451,395	491,026	494,316
National Agricultural Library......	3,903	7,528	10,389	14,604	17,507	20,303	23,000	24,000	24,000	22,000
Department of Commerce	1,226	2,479	†	†	†	†	†	†	†	†
Maritime Administration Training for private sector employees[30].........	1,226	2,479	†	†	†	†	†	†	†	†
Department of Health and Human Services..............................	24,273	37,819	47,195	77,962	138,000	214,000	313,000	312,000	307,000	329,000
National Library of Medicine	24,273	37,819	47,195	77,962	138,000	214,000	313,000	312,000	307,000	329,000
Department of Homeland Security	†	†	†	†	†	†	278,243	194,744	307,076	354,123
Federal Law Enforcement Training Center[43]	†	†	†	†	†	†	159,000	180,000	280,000	340,000
Estimated disaster relief[44]........	†	†	†	†	†	†	119,243	14,744	27,076	14,123
Department of Justice..................	5,546	27,642	25,517	26,920	36,296	34,727	26,148	26,734	28,056	29,457
Federal Bureau of Investigation National Academy..............	2,066	7,234	4,189	6,028	12,831	22,479	15,619	15,931	16,727	17,564
Federal Bureau of Investigation Field Police Academy..........	2,500	7,715	10,220	10,548	11,140	11,962	10,456	10,770	11,308	11,874
Narcotics and dangerous drug training	980	2,416	83	850	325	286	73	33	20	20
National Institute of Corrections	†	10,277	11,025	9,494	12,000	†	†	†	†	†

See notes at end of table.

Table 375. Federal on-budget funds for education, by level/educational purpose, agency, and program: Selected fiscal years, 1970 through 2008—Continued

[In thousands of current dollars]

Level/educational purpose, agency, and program	1970	1980	1985	1990[1]	1995[1]	2000[1]	2005[1]	2006[1,2]	2007[1,2]	2008[1,2]
1	2	3	4	5	6	7	8	9	10	11
Department of State	20,672	25,000	23,791	47,539	51,648	69,349	109,309	112,014	114,120	115,000
Foreign Service Institute	15,857	25,000	23,791	47,539	51,648	69,349	109,309	112,014	114,120	115,000
Center for Cultural and Technical Interchange[38]	4,815	†	†	†	†	†	†	†	†	†
Department of Transportation	3,964	10,212	3,785	1,507	650	700	1,100	700	200	300
Highways training and education grants	2,418	3,412	1,500	—	—	—	—	—	—	—
Maritime Administration Training for private sector employees[30]	†	†	1,135	1,507	650	700	1,100	700	200	300
Urban mass transportation—managerial training grants	1,546	500	1,150	†	†	†	†	†	†	†
Federal Aviation Administration Air traffic controllers second career program	—	6,300	—	—	—	—	—	—	—	—
Department of the Treasury	18	14,584	16,160	41,488	48,000	83,000	†	†	†	†
Federal Law Enforcement Training Center[43]	18	14,584	16,160	41,488	48,000	83,000	†	†	†	†
Other agencies ACTION[45]	†	2,833	1,761	8,472	†	†	†	†	†	†
Estimated education funds	†	2,833	1,761	8,472	†	†	†	†	†	†
Agency for International Development	88,034	99,707	141,847	170,371	260,408	299,000	574,000	566,800	629,200	640,000
Education and human resources	61,570	80,518	115,104	142,801	248,408	299,000	574,000	566,800	629,200	640,000
American schools and hospitals abroad	26,464	19,189	26,743	27,570	12,000	†	†	†	†	†
Appalachian Regional Commission	572	8,124	113	†	5,709	2,369	1,173	1,933	2,855	2,900
Corporation for National and Community Service[45]	‡	‡	‡	‡	214,600	386,000	472,000	503,000	395,000	515,000
Estimated education funds	‡	‡	‡	‡	214,600	386,000	472,000	503,000	395,000	515,000
Federal Emergency Management Agency[46]	290	281	405	215	170,400	14,894	†	†	†	†
Estimated architect/engineer student development program	40	31	155	200	—	—	†	†	†	†
Estimated other training programs[47]	250	250	250	15	—	—	‡	‡	‡	‡
Estimated disaster relief[44]	—	—	—	—	170,400	14,894	‡	‡	‡	‡
General Services Administration Libraries and other archival activities[48]	14,775	34,800	†	†	†	†	†	†	†	†
Institute of Museum and Library Services[42]	†	†	†	†	†	166,000	250,000	241,000	258,000	303,000
Japanese-United States Friendship Commission	†	2,294	2,236	2,299	2,000	3,000	3,000	2,000	2,000	3,000
Library of Congress	29,478	151,871	169,310	189,827	241,000	299,000	430,000	435,000	463,000	360,000
Salaries and expenses	20,700	102,364	130,354	148,985	198,000	247,000	383,000	381,000	413,000	300,000
Books for the blind and the physically handicapped	6,195	31,436	32,954	37,473	39,000	46,000	47,000	54,000	50,000	60,000
Special foreign currency program	2,273	3,492	4,621	10	†	†	†	†	†	†
Furniture and furnishings	310	14,579	1,381	3,359	4,000	6,000	—	—	—	—
National Aeronautics and Space Administration Aerospace education services project[48]	350	882	1,800	3,300	5,923	6,800	—	—	—	—
National Archives and Records Administration Libraries and other archival activities[48]	†	†	52,118	77,397	105,172	121,879	276,000	276,000	273,000	323,000
National Commission on Libraries and Information Science[49]	†	2,090	723	3,281	1,000	2,000	1,000	1,000	1,000	†
National Endowment for the Arts	340	231	1,137	936	2,304	4,046	2,506	2,503	2,942	3,230
National Endowment for the Humanities	5,090	85,805	76,252	89,706	94,249	70,807	87,969	86,250	80,564	81,000

See notes at end of table.

Table 375. Federal on-budget funds for education, by level/educational purpose, agency, and program: Selected fiscal years, 1970 through 2008—Continued

[In thousands of current dollars]

Level/educational purpose, agency, and program	1970	1980	1985	1990[1]	1995[1]	2000[1]	2005[1]	2006[1,2]	2007[1,2]	2008[1,2]
1	2	3	4	5	6	7	8	9	10	11
Smithsonian Institution	2,461	5,153	7,886	5,779	9,961	25,764	45,890	42,092	46,101	53,095
Museum programs and related research	2,261	3,254	4,665	690	3,190	18,000	32,000	33,000	37,000	43,000
National Gallery of Art extension service	200	426	675	474	771	764	890	92	101	95
Woodrow Wilson International Center for Scholars	†	1,473	2,546	4,615	6,000	7,000	13,000	9,000	9,000	10,000
U.S. Information Agency— Center for Cultural and Technical Interchange[38]	†	15,115	18,966	20,375	34,000	†	†	†	†	†
U.S. Institute of Peace	†	†	—	7,621	12,000	13,000	28,000	101,000	32,000	25,000
Other programs Estimated education share of federal aid for the District of Columbia	1,758	2,990	7,156	3,724	2,457	404	1,674	1,389	1,321	1,504
Research programs at universities and related institutions[50]	**$2,283,641**	**$5,801,204**	**$8,844,575**	**$12,606,035**	**$15,677,919**	**$21,660,134**	**$31,753,498**	**$32,185,135**	**$32,243,269**	**—**
Department of Education[51]	87,823	78,742	28,809	89,483	279,000	116,464	456,822	390,548	437,484	428,963
Department of Agriculture	64,796	216,405	293,252	348,109	434,544	553,600	709,700	813,500	584,300	—
Department of Commerce	4,487	48,295	52,951	50,523	85,442	110,775	243,948	214,548	198,461	—
Department of Defense	356,188	644,455	1,245,888	1,871,864	1,853,955	1,891,710	2,675,900	2,872,500	2,447,600	—
Department of Energy	548,327	1,470,224	2,205,316	2,520,885	2,651,641	3,577,004	4,339,879	4,197,315	4,649,477	—
Department of Health and Human Services	623,765	2,087,053	3,228,014	4,902,714	6,418,969	10,491,641	16,357,996	16,274,356	16,336,983	—
Department of Homeland Security	†	†	†	†	†	†	309,717	448,139	266,446	—
Department of Housing and Urban Development	510	5,314	438	118	1,613	1,400	1,100	900	1,000	—
Department of the Interior	18,521	42,175	34,422	49,790	50,618	47,200	66,800	63,700	57,500	—
Department of Justice	1,945	9,189	5,168	6,858	7,204	19,400	27,500	25,900	24,000	—
Department of Labor	3,567	12,938	3,417	5,893	10,114	12,900	110,500	231,500	187,500	—
Department of State	8,220	188	29	1,519	23	†	†	†	†	†
Department of Transportation	12,328	31,910	22,621	28,608	75,847	55,866	52,800	70,600	54,500	—
Department of the Treasury	†	226	388	227	1,498	†	†	†	†	†
Department of Veterans Affairs	518	1,600	1,000	2,300	2,500	†	†	†	†	†
ACTION	†	†	†	†	†	†	†	†	†	†
Agency for International Development	†	77,063	56,960	79,415	30,172	33,500	28,100	27,500	27,500	—
Environmental Protection Agency	19,446	41,083	60,521	87,481	125,721	98,900	83,400	78,100	72,500	—
Federal Emergency Management Agency	†	1,665	1,423	†	†	†	†	†	†	†
National Aeronautics and Space Administration	258,016	254,629	485,824	1,090,003	1,751,977	2,071,030	2,763,120	2,889,157	3,033,534	—
National Science Foundation	253,628	743,809	1,087,046	1,427,007	1,874,395	2,566,244	3,503,216	3,564,572	3,841,539	—
Nuclear Regulatory Commission	†	32,590	30,261	42,328	22,188	12,200	15,100	12,400	13,200	—
Office of Economic Opportunity	20,035	†	†	†	†	†	†	†	†	†
U.S. Arms Control and Disarmament Agency	100	661	395	25	†	†	†	†	†	†
Other agencies	1,421	990	432	885	500	300	7,900	9,900	9,745	—

—Not available.

†Not applicable.

[1]Excludes federal support for medical education benefits under Medicare in the U.S. Department of Health and Human Services. Benefits excluded from total because data before fiscal year (FY) 1990 are not available. This program existed since Medicare began, but was not available as a separate budget item until FY 1990. Excluded amounts are as follows: $4,440,000,000 in FY 1990, $7,510,000,000 in FY 1995, $8,020,000,000 in FY 2000, $8,400,000,000 in FY 2005, $8,400,000,000 in FY 2006, $8,500,000,000 in FY 2007, and an estimated $9,000,000,000 in FY 2008.

[2]Estimated.

[3]The U.S. Department of Education was created in May 1980. It formerly was the Office of Education in the U.S. Department of Health, Education, and Welfare.

[4]Arranges for the education of children who reside on federal property when no suitable local school district can or will provide for the education of these children.

[5]Includes many programs, such as No Child Left Behind, 21st Century Community Learning Centers, Class Size Reduction, Charter Schools, Safe and Drug-Free Schools, and Innovative programs.

[6]Included the School-To-Work Opportunities program, which initiated a national system to be administered jointly by the U.S. Departments of Education and Labor. Programs in the Education Reform program were transferred to the school improvement programs or discontinued in FY 2002. Amounts after FY 2002 reflect balances that are spending out from prior-year appropriations.

[7]Starting in FY 1994, the Special Milk Program has been included in the child nutrition programs.

[8]The Farm Security and Rural Investment Act of 2002 (Public Law 107-171) carries out preschool and school feeding programs in foreign countries to help reduce the incidence of hunger and malnutrition, and improve literacy and primary education.

[9]These commodities are purchased under Section 32 of the Act of August 24, 1935, for use in the child nutrition programs.

[10]Assisted in the construction of public facilities, such as vocational schools, through grants or loans. No funds have been appropriated for this program since FY 1977, and it was completely phased out in FY 1984.

[11]Established in 1979, with funds first appropriated in FY 1980.

[12]Formerly in the Office of Economic Opportunity. In FY 1972, funds were transferred to the U.S. Department of Health, Education, and Welfare, Office of Child Development.

[13]Created by the Family Support Act of 1988 to provide funds for the Job Opportunities and Basic Skills Training program. Replaced by Temporary Assistance for Needy Families program.

[14]After age 18, benefits terminate at the end of the school term or in 3 months, whichever comes first.

[15]Transferred from the U.S. Department of Transportation to the U.S. Department of Homeland Security in March of 2003.

[16]Provides funding for supplemental programs for eligible American Indian students in public schools.

[17]Finances the cost of academic, social, and occupational education courses for inmates in federal prisons.

[18]Some of the work and training programs were in the Office of Economic Opportunity and were transferred to the U.S. Department of Labor in FYs 1971 and 1972. From FY 1994 through FY 2001, included the School-to-Work Opportunities program, which was administered jointly by the U.S. Departments of Education and Labor.

[19]Established in FY 1972 and closed in FY 1986.

[20]The states' share of revenue-sharing funds could not be spent on education in FYs 1981 through 1986.

[21]Provided educational assistance allowances in order to restore lost educational opportunities to those individuals whose careers were interrupted or impeded by reason of active military service between January 31, 1955, and January 1, 1977.

[22]This program is in "Readjustment Benefits" program, Chapter 31, and covers the costs of subsistence, tuition, books, supplies, and equipment for disabled veterans requiring vocational rehabilitation.

[23]This program is in "Readjustment Benefits" program, Chapter 35, and provides benefits to children and spouses of veterans.

[24]Head Start program funds were transferred to the U.S. Department of Health, Education, and Welfare, Office of Child Development, in FY 1972.

[25]Most of these programs were transferred to the U.S. Department of Health, Education, and Welfare, Office of Education, in FY 1972.

[26]Transferred to the U.S. Department of Labor in FYs 1971 and 1972.

[27]Transferred to the ACTION Agency in FY 1972.

[28]Transferred from the U.S. Department of Housing and Urban Development to the U.S. Department of Health, Education, and Welfare, Office of Education, in FY 1979.

[29]Transferred from the National Science Foundation to the U.S. Department of Commerce in October 1970.

[30]Transferred from the U.S. Department of Commerce to the U.S. Department of Transportation in FY 1981.

[31]Includes special education programs (military and civilian); legal education program; flight training; advanced degree program; college degree program (officers); and "Armed Forces Health Professions Scholarship" program.

[32]Does not include higher education assistance loans.

[33]Alcohol, drug abuse, and mental health training programs are included starting in FY 1992.

[34]Beginning in FY 1992, data were included in the National Institutes of Health training grants program.

[35]This program closed in FY 2004.

[36]Postsecondary student benefits were ended by the Omnibus Budget Reconciliation Act of 1981 (Public Law 97-35) and were completely phased out by August 1985.

[37]Includes flight training. Transferred to the U.S. Department of Homeland Security in March of 2003.

[38]Transferred from the U.S. Department of State to the United States Information Agency in 1977, then transferred back to the U.S. Department of State in FY 1998.

[39]Part of the Ronald W. Reagan National Defense Authorization Act for FY 2005 (Public Law 108-375), enacted October 28, 2004. The Reserve Education Assistance Program (REAP) provides educational assistance to members of the National Guard and Reserves who serve on active duty in support of a contingency operation under federal authority on or after September 11, 2001.

[40]Abolished in FY 1998, with functions transferred to the U.S. Department of State and the newly created Broadcasting Board of Governors.

[41]Included in the "Educational and Cultural Affairs" program in FYs 1980 through 1983, and became an independent program in FY 1984.

[42]Transferred from U.S. Department of Education to the Institute of Museum and Library Services in FY 1997.

[43]Transferred to the U.S. Department of Homeland Security in FY 2003.

[44]The disaster relief program repairs and replaces damaged and destroyed school buildings. In FY 1995, funds were for repairs due to the Northridge Earthquake in California. In FY 1995, $74.4 million was spent on school districts, $8.4 million on community colleges, and $87.6 million on colleges and universities. This program was transferred from the Federal Emergency Management Agency to the U.S. Department of Homeland Security in FY 2003.

[45]The National Service Trust Act of 1993 established the Corporation for National and Community Service. In 1993, ACTION became part of this agency.

[46]The Federal Emergency Management Agency was created in 1979, representing a combination of five existing agencies. The funds for the Federal Emergency Management Agency in FY 1970 to FY 1975 were in other agencies. This agency was transferred to the U.S. Department of Homeland Security in March of 2003.

[47]These programs include the Fall-Out Shelter Analysis, Blast Protection Design through FY 1992. Starting in FY 1993, earthquake training and safety for teachers and administrators for grades 1 through 12 are included.

[48]Transferred from the General Services Administration to the National Archives and Records Administration in April 1985.

[49]Public Law 110-161 transferred the National Commission on Libraries and Information Science to the Institute of Museum and Library Services starting in FY 2008.

[50]Includes federal obligations for research and development centers and R & D plant administered by colleges and universities. FY 2006 and FY 2007 data are estimated, except the U.S Department of Education data, which are actual numbers.

[51]FY 1970 includes outlays for the "Research and Training" program. FY 1975 includes the "National Institute of Education" program. FYs 1990 through 2008 include outlays for the Office of Educational Research and Improvement and the Institute for Education Sciences.

NOTE: Some data have been revised from previously published figures. To the extent possible, amounts reported represent outlays rather than obligations. Detail may not sum to totals because of rounding. Negative amounts occur when program receipts exceed outlays. Changes in total postsecondary expenditures between 2005 and 2007 resulted primarily from changes in accounting procedures in the Federal Family Education Loan Program. SOURCE: U.S. Department of Education, Budget Service, unpublished tabulations. U.S. Office of Management and Budget, *Budget of the U.S. Government, Appendix*, fiscal years 1972 through 2009. National Science Foundation, *Federal Funds for Research and Development*, fiscal years 1970 through 2007. (This table was prepared October 2008.)

Table 376. Estimated federal support for education, by type of ultimate recipient and agency: Fiscal year 2007

[In millions of current dollars]

Agency	Total	Local education agencies	State education agencies	Post-secondary students	Degree-granting institutions	Federal institutions	Other education organizations[1]	Other recipients[2]
1	2	3	4	5	6	7	8	9
Total[3]	$212,365.7	$42,859.8	$10,553.2	$47,740.7	$76,294.2	$4,513.5	$18,224.6	$12,179.8
Total program funds—on-budget	147,527.7	42,859.8	8,135.5	21,974.5	47,007.8	4,513.5	18,224.6	4,812.0
Department of Education	71,808.0	29,008.8	7,429.4	14,269.9	13,877.6	613.2	2,931.5	3,677.7
Department of Agriculture	15,409.7	12,615.9	654.1	†	648.7	24.0	976.0	491.0
Department of Commerce	198.5	†	†	†	198.5	†	†	†
Department of Defense	6,066.7	324.9	†	594.1	2,895.6	1,801.9	450.1	†
Department of Energy	4,649.5	†	†	†	4,649.5	†	†	†
Department of Health and Human Services	25,705.0	688.8	†	1,512.9	16,826.2	307.0	6,370.1	†
Department of Homeland Security	622.9	†	†	15.0	277.4	303.4	27.1	†
Department of Housing and Urban Development	1.0	†	†	†	1.0	†	†	†
Department of the Interior	962.3	84.0	52.0	25.8	109.9	518.7	171.8	†
Department of Justice	771.7	†	†	†	24.0	34.1	713.6	†
Department of Labor	5,413.5	†	†	†	187.5	†	5,226.0	†
Department of State	587.1	†	†	†	†	114.1	473.0	†
Department of Transportation	128.7	†	†	†	54.5	61.0	0.2	13.0
Department of Veterans Affairs	5,256.4	†	†	5,256.4	†	†	†	†
Other agencies and programs								
Agency for International Development	656.7	†	†	†	27.5	†	†	629.2
Appalachian Regional Commission	7.5	†	†	†	3.5	†	4.0	†
Barry Goldwater Scholarship and Excellence in Education Foundation	3.0	†	†	†	†	†	3.0	†
Corporation for National and Community Service	395.0	†	†	†	†	†	395.0	†
Environmental Protection Agency	72.5	†	†	†	72.5	†	†	†
Estimated education share of federal aid to the District of Columbia	168.2	137.4	†	†	29.4	†	1.3	†
Harry S Truman scholarship fund	3.0	†	†	†	†	†	3.0	†
Institute of American Indian and Alaska Native Culture and Arts Development	6.0	†	†	†	†	†	6.0	†
Institute of Library and Museum Services	258.0	†	†	†	†	†	258.0	†
James Madison Memorial Fellowship Foundation	2.0	†	†	†	†	†	2.0	†
Japanese-United States Friendship Commission	2.0	†	†	†	†	†	2.0	†
Library of Congress	463.0	†	†	†	†	463.0		†
National Aeronautics and Space Administration	3,033.5	†	†	†	3,033.5	†	†	†
National Archives and Records Administration	273.0	†	†	†	†	273.0	†	†
National Commission on Libraries and Information Science	1.0	†	†	†	†	†	†	1.0
National Endowment for the Arts	11.8	†	†	†	†	†	11.8	†
National Endowment for the Humanities	121.1	†	†	†	†	†	121.1	†
National Science Foundation	4,368.5	†	†	300.4	4,068.1	†	†	†
Nuclear Regulatory Commission	13.2	†	†	†	13.2	†	†	†
Smithsonian Institution	46.1	†	†	†	†	0.1	46.0	†
U.S. Institute of Peace	32.0	†	†	†	†	†	32.0	†
Other agencies	9.7	†	†	†	9.7	†	†	†
Off-budget support and nonfederal funds generated by federal legislation	64,838.0	†	2,417.7	25,766.2	29,286.4	†	†	7,367.8

†Not applicable.

[1]Includes Head Start programs at child care centers, Job Corps and other vocational programs, and federal programs at libraries and museums.

[2]Other recipients include American Indian tribes, private nonprofit agencies, and banks.

[3]Includes on-budget funds, off-budget support, and nonfederal funds generated by federal legislation. Excludes federal tax expenditures.

NOTE: Outlays by type of recipient are estimated based on obligation data. Detail may not sum to totals because of rounding.

SOURCE: U.S. Department of Education, Budget Service, unpublished tabulations. U.S. Department of Education, National Center for Education Statistics, unpublished tabulations. U.S. Office of Management and Budget, *Budget of the U.S. Government, Appendix, Fiscal Year 2009*. National Science Foundation, *Federal Funds for Research and Development, Fiscal Years 2005, 2006, and 2007*. (This table was prepared October 2008.)

Table 377. U.S. Department of Education outlays, by type of recipient and level of education: Selected fiscal years, 1980 through 2008
[In millions of current dollars]

Year and level of education	Total	Local education agencies	State education agencies	Postsecondary students	Postsecondary institutions	Federal institutions	Other education organizations[1]	Other recipients[2]
1	2	3	4	5	6	7	8	9
1980 total	**$13,137.8**	**$5,313.7**	**$1,103.2**	**$2,137.4**	**$2,267.2**	**$249.8**	**$693.8**	**$1,372.7**
Elementary/secondary	6,629.1	5,309.4	662.2	34.2	22.0	62.5	513.4	25.5
Postsecondary	5,682.2	†	99.5	2,103.2	2,166.5	†	†	1,313.0
Other programs	747.7	4.3	341.5	†	†	187.3	180.4	34.2
Education research and statistics	78.7	†	†	†	78.7	†	†	†
1985 total	**16,701.1**	**6,225.0**	**1,502.9**	**2,434.7**	**2,362.3**	**287.3**	**503.9**	**3,385.0**
Elementary/secondary	7,296.7	6,220.8	636.0	58.0	25.2	2.4	322.4	31.9
Postsecondary	8,202.5	†	228.3	2,376.7	2,308.3	†	†	3,289.2
Other programs	1,173.1	4.2	638.6	†	†	284.9	181.5	63.9
Education research and statistics	28.8	†	†	†	28.8	†	†	†
1990 total	**23,198.6**	**8,000.7**	**2,490.3**	**3,859.6**	**3,649.8**	**441.4**	**912.2**	**3,844.4**
Elementary/secondary	9,681.3	7,995.0	700.3	80.5	85.4	113.1	650.7	56.3
Postsecondary	11,176.0	†	261.6	3,779.1	3,475.0	†	†	3,660.4
Other programs	2,251.8	5.7	1,528.5	†	†	328.3	261.5	127.8
Education research and statistics	89.5	†	†	†	89.5	†	†	†
1995 total	**31,403.0**	**11,210.7**	**3,584.0**	**4,964.7**	**5,016.1**	**485.4**	**1,349.2**	**4,792.9**
Elementary/secondary	14,029.0	11,203.3	1,410.0	190.5	170.1	70.3	946.9	37.9
Postsecondary	14,234.0	†	250.8	4,774.2	4,567.0	†	†	4,642.0
Other programs	2,861.0	7.4	1,923.2	†	†	415.1	402.3	113.0
Education research and statistics	279.0	†	†	†	279.0	†	†	†
2000 total	**34,106.7**	**16,016.0**	**4,316.5**	**4,711.7**	**5,005.7**	**506.6**	**1,820.2**	**1,730.1**
Elementary/secondary	20,039.6	16,003.5	1,989.6	260.5	198.9	48.5	1,461.8	76.8
Postsecondary	10,727.3	†	55.2	4,451.2	4,690.3	†	†	1,530.6
Other programs	3,223.4	12.5	2,271.7	†	†	458.1	358.4	122.7
Education research and statistics	116.5	†	†	†	116.5	†	†	†
2001 total	**36,562.0**	**18,027.4**	**4,336.7**	**4,525.6**	**5,793.3**	**600.4**	**2,149.1**	**1,129.7**
Elementary/secondary	22,862.4	18,014.5	1,999.8	392.5	405.9	69.8	1,780.6	199.4
Postsecondary	9,840.7	†	98.5	4,133.1	4,821.9	†	†	787.2
Other programs	3,293.4	12.9	2,238.4	†	†	530.6	368.5	143.1
Education research and statistics	565.5	†	†	†	565.5	†	†	†
2002 total	**46,324.4**	**19,742.1**	**4,967.8**	**8,306.0**	**8,668.2**	**608.9**	**2,200.3**	**1,831.3**
Elementary/secondary	25,246.2	19,729.2	2,429.8	490.0	454.9	77.6	1,829.5	235.3
Postsecondary	17,056.2	†	199.2	7,816.0	7,588.1	†	†	1,452.9
Other programs	3,396.8	12.9	2,338.8	†	†	531.3	370.8	143.1
Education research and statistics	625.2	†	†	†	625.2	†	†	†
2003 total	**57,442.9**	**23,837.7**	**6,164.6**	**11,032.5**	**10,731.8**	**657.8**	**2,478.9**	**2,539.6**
Elementary/secondary	30,749.3	23,882.8	3,141.1	594.3	637.4	109.5	2,105.6	338.6
Postsecondary	22,706.4	†	668.6	10,438.2	9,542.5	†	†	2,057.2
Other programs	3,435.2	14.9	2,354.9	†	†	548.3	373.3	143.8
Education research and statistics	551.9	†	†	†	551.9	†	†	†
2004 total	**62,903.4**	**26,012.4**	**6,334.5**	**12,005.0**	**10,977.0**	**648.9**	**2,730.1**	**4,195.4**
Elementary/secondary	33,689.4	25,990.0	3,611.7	606.2	642.5	126.4	2,300.0	412.6
Postsecondary	25,341.0	†	420.9	11,398.8	9,899.3	†	†	3,621.9
Other programs	3,437.8	22.4	2,301.9	†	†	522.5	430.1	160.9
Education research and statistics	435.2	†	†	†	435.2	†	†	†
2005 total	**72,893.3**	**28,900.2**	**7,126.3**	**14,708.2**	**13,362.4**	**669.8**	**3,023.0**	**5,103.4**
Elementary/secondary	37,477.6	28,878.6	3,971.6	698.1	790.0	145.9	2,578.4	415.0
Postsecondary	31,420.0	†	777.1	14,010.1	12,115.6	†	†	4,517.2
Other programs	3,538.9	21.6	2,377.6	†	†	523.9	444.6	171.2
Education research and statistics	456.8	†	†	†	456.8	†	†	†
2006 total	**93,571.5**	**30,236.6**	**8,331.3**	**22,955.1**	**21,376.1**	**693.2**	**2,902.3**	**7,076.8**
Elementary/secondary	38,863.4	30,214.8	4,098.7	741.5	775.1	168.6	2,455.5	409.2
Postsecondary	50,624.6	†	1,702.4	22,213.6	20,210.5	†	†	6,498.1
Other programs	3,692.9	21.8	2,530.2	†	†	524.6	446.8	169.5
Education research and statistics	390.5	†	†	†	390.5	†	†	†
2007 total	**71,808.0**	**29,008.8**	**7,429.4**	**14,269.9**	**13,877.6**	**613.2**	**2,931.5**	**3,677.7**
Elementary/secondary	37,562.1	28,990.4	4,018.7	824.4	781.5	73.8	2,460.7	412.6
Postsecondary	30,052.0	†	805.5	13,445.5	12,658.6	†	†	3,084.6
Other programs	3,756.4	18.4	2,605.2	†	†	539.4	413.0	180.5
Education research and statistics	437.5	†	†	†	437.5	†	†	†
2008 total	**73,819.2**	**29,657.0**	**8,044.8**	**14,331.0**	**13,899.0**	**629.3**	**3,355.0**	**3,903.3**
Elementary/secondary	38,900.3	29,633.7	4,201.9	835.5	798.6	73.8	2,871.9	484.9
Postsecondary	30,267.1	†	808.9	13,495.5	12,671.4	†	†	3,231.8
Other programs	4,222.9	23.3	3,034.0	†	†	555.5	423.6	186.6
Education research and statistics	429.0	†	†	†	429.0	†	†	†

†Not applicable.

[1]Includes funds for vocational education and for federal programs at libraries and museums.

[2]Other recipients include American Indian tribes, private nonprofit agencies, and banks.

NOTE: Outlays by type of recipient are estimated based on obligation data. Changes in post-secondary expenditures between 2005 and 2007 resulted primarily from changes in account-ing procedures. Some data have been revised from previously published figures. Detail may not sum to totals because of rounding.

SOURCE: U.S. Office of Management and Budget, *Budget of the U.S. Government*, fiscal years 1982 through 2009. U.S. Department of Education, Office of the Deputy Secretary, Budget Office, unpublished tabulations. (This table was prepared October 2008.)

Table 378. U.S. Department of Education appropriations for major programs, by state or jurisdiction: Fiscal year 2007

[In thousands of current dollars]

State or jurisdiction	Total	Grants for the disadvantaged[1]	Block grants to states for school improvement[2]	School assistance in federally affected areas[3]	Career/ technical and adult education[4]	Special education[5]	Language assistance[6]	American Indian education	Degree-granting institutions[7]	Student financial assistance[8]	Rehabilitation services[9]
1	2	3	4	5	6	7	8	9	10	11	12
Total, 50 states and D.C.[10]	$57,790,262	$13,724,471	$5,264,372	$1,044,886	$1,810,201	$11,338,312	$614,091	$95,331	$2,052,517	$18,979,727	$2,866,353
Total, 50 states, D.C., other activities, and other jurisdictions	60,113,877	14,388,314	5,531,867	1,159,153	1,873,051	11,600,112	669,007	95,331	2,095,935	19,721,092	2,980,013
Alabama	977,755	217,034	89,461	3,018	31,409	182,090	3,277	1,662	66,614	323,267	59,924
Alaska	265,989	43,948	27,216	105,490	5,691	36,954	651	9,482	10,290	15,245	11,023
Arizona	1,442,388	297,895	99,926	159,308	37,453	182,922	19,664	10,470	24,266	551,813	58,671
Arkansas	596,507	139,251	57,114	549	19,645	114,413	2,721	289	34,458	189,840	38,228
California	6,765,774	1,924,690	634,027	56,063	223,177	1,242,914	169,058	5,786	197,341	2,022,880	289,837
Colorado	767,845	143,590	61,931	14,245	24,238	153,793	9,812	756	26,590	296,144	36,747
Connecticut	490,455	122,220	50,124	5,263	17,422	133,469	5,460	0	12,264	122,170	22,062
Delaware	151,824	37,687	27,203	81	7,042	34,146	1,354	0	6,958	26,317	11,036
District of Columbia	451,178	49,053	26,956	1,530	6,061	17,848	593	0	262,755	72,235	14,147
Florida	2,879,147	668,524	247,617	9,583	104,807	631,536	40,669	42	54,168	961,095	161,105
Georgia	1,695,252	456,441	159,132	21,237	57,972	318,951	15,123	0	59,382	526,886	80,129
Hawaii	232,820	43,457	27,425	40,898	8,705	40,569	2,578	0	19,494	36,851	12,843
Idaho	275,125	49,925	28,786	7,144	9,815	55,374	1,833	390	9,971	94,600	17,289
Illinois	2,370,221	642,682	223,760	18,813	73,014	510,195	27,485	102	74,998	688,012	111,161
Indiana	1,075,217	255,582	90,547	146	38,806	257,323	6,580	0	23,798	333,666	68,769
Iowa	574,331	78,022	43,481	608	17,842	122,316	2,523	210	26,235	249,004	34,089
Kansas	510,317	106,873	45,480	21,307	16,588	108,411	3,390	1,080	25,435	152,508	29,245
Kentucky	851,317	210,641	85,034	625	28,889	163,752	2,797	0	29,934	276,330	53,313
Louisiana	1,045,667	306,917	118,552	7,842	34,013	190,027	2,176	758	51,787	288,497	45,098
Maine	235,526	48,267	31,299	2,643	8,414	55,952	566	129	1,697	69,666	16,894
Maryland	803,519	203,093	77,275	3,714	27,835	201,765	9,135	73	35,762	202,664	42,202
Massachusetts	1,041,234	230,494	92,334	669	30,657	283,736	11,022	76	32,248	310,846	49,152
Michigan	1,870,275	504,361	193,224	3,855	60,264	400,764	10,373	3,159	39,534	554,459	100,282
Minnesota	839,372	126,747	67,706	14,901	26,906	192,378	6,708	3,354	29,657	325,031	45,985
Mississippi	763,272	194,122	80,748	2,095	21,905	120,037	1,314	341	35,088	263,904	43,717
Missouri	1,202,949	223,942	97,360	21,838	36,183	226,778	3,619	94	29,087	500,509	63,540
Montana	264,385	42,712	32,257	41,974	7,549	37,895	500	2,890	18,085	67,791	12,731
Nebraska	496,446	60,294	32,820	18,969	10,504	74,850	2,382	776	10,175	266,130	19,545
Nevada	289,928	88,399	32,657	3,231	13,509	69,087	6,009	683	13,651	45,592	17,110
New Hampshire	199,351	37,669	29,500	13	8,216	48,188	772	0	3,697	58,924	12,372
New Jersey	1,232,783	275,825	117,159	13,288	44,470	361,315	18,222	58	24,418	319,950	58,076
New Mexico	547,511	114,362	46,343	77,938	13,936	91,486	4,338	7,958	29,322	137,383	24,443
New York	4,293,060	1,303,721	425,784	14,232	107,364	769,889	44,717	1,716	72,628	1,398,661	154,347
North Carolina	1,505,623	339,132	128,298	13,976	54,292	321,813	12,261	3,348	72,493	467,833	92,178
North Dakota	200,484	32,973	27,560	27,969	5,795	27,924	500	1,652	12,913	52,354	10,854
Ohio	2,229,713	490,142	188,868	2,157	69,018	437,599	7,685	0	44,597	866,795	122,851
Oklahoma	780,275	143,228	72,124	39,126	23,863	147,451	3,375	23,553	36,908	248,355	42,291
Oregon	607,152	145,491	55,889	2,096	21,286	129,361	7,633	2,161	15,171	191,210	36,855
Pennsylvania	2,200,840	563,195	203,346	1,259	70,547	428,903	11,343	0	42,082	750,096	130,070
Rhode Island	236,220	54,756	27,526	1,679	8,715	44,808	2,078	0	11,172	73,700	11,787
South Carolina	848,612	207,909	75,625	2,331	29,214	177,038	4,288	5	39,902	259,699	52,601
South Dakota	661,413	41,190	28,051	45,208	6,279	33,348	729	3,508	9,877	482,144	11,080
Tennessee	1,074,534	227,759	93,235	3,405	38,112	233,537	4,781	0	48,195	356,012	68,698
Texas	4,815,579	1,342,768	461,089	89,650	152,483	965,465	87,896	309	154,029	1,341,695	220,195
Utah	485,588	67,111	35,566	9,315	17,164	108,625	3,538	1,202	16,052	198,603	28,412
Vermont	160,302	31,220	26,825	8	5,621	27,080	500	169	9,173	48,691	11,014
Virginia	2,054,911	224,901	94,786	38,289	41,629	283,463	10,295	11	41,710	1,253,181	66,646
Washington	982,569	216,794	88,269	50,023	34,561	223,850	12,795	4,274	42,939	257,624	51,430
West Virginia	412,659	96,781	45,135	34	13,326	76,821	500	0	36,241	116,713	27,108
Wisconsin	881,564	218,921	85,157	12,713	32,548	211,641	5,976	2,246	19,335	235,880	57,147
Wyoming	153,486	31,760	26,785	12,549	5,443	28,455	500	558	7,941	29,471	10,024
Other activities/jurisdictions											
Indian Tribe (Set-Aside)	277,384	98,089	32,163	0	14,769	92,821	5,000	0	0	0	34,543
Other	293,130	68,465	39,552	112,479	13,000	15,000	43,485	0	0	0	1,149
American Samoa	32,042	10,369	6,967	0	567	6,795	1,172	0	1,004	3,849	1,318
Guam	52,227	10,815	10,415	56	1,031	15,202	1,151	0	1,977	9,132	2,446
Marshall Islands	309	0	0	0	0	0	0	0	309	0	0
Federated States of Micronesia	21,450	0	0	0	199	6,579	0	0	1,651	13,022	0
Northern Marianas	18,863	3,938	3,947	0	628	5,168	959	0	1,083	1,657	1,483
Palau	1,323	0	0	0	0	0	0	0	1,323	0	0
Puerto Rico	1,587,011	458,965	165,548	1,573	31,573	110,722	3,086	0	34,441	710,742	70,362
U.S. Virgin Islands	39,875	13,202	8,903	159	1,084	9,514	62	0	1,629	2,963	2,359

[1]Title I includes Grants to Local Education Agencies (Basic, Concentration, Targeted, and Education Finance Incentive Grants); Reading First State Grants; Even Start; Migrant Education Grants; Neglected and Delinquent Children Grants; and Comprehensive School Reform Grants.
[2]Title VI includes Teacher Quality State Grants; 21st Century Community Learning Centers; Educational Technology State Grants; State Grants for Innovative Programs; State Assessments, including No Child Left Behind; Education for the Homeless Children and Youth; Rural and Low-Income Schools Program; Small, Rural School Achievement Program; Safe and Drug Free Schools and Communities State Grants; Mathematics and Science Partnerships; and School Improvement Grants.
[3]Includes Impact Aid—Basic Support Payments; Impact Aid—Payments for Children with Disabilities; and Impact Aid—Construction.
[4]Includes Career and Technical Education State Grants; English Literacy and Civics Education State Grants; Tech-Prep Education; State Grants for Incarcerated Youth Offenders; and Adult Basic and Literacy Education State Grants.
[5]Includes Special Education—Grants to States; Preschool Grants; and Grants for Infants and Families.
[6]Includes Language Acquisition State Grants.

[7]Includes Institutional Aid to Strengthen Higher Education Institutions serving significant numbers of low-income students; Other Special Programs for the Disadvantaged; Cooperative Education; Fund for the Improvement of Postsecondary Education; Fellowships and Scholarships; and annual interest subsidy grants for lenders.
[8]Includes Pell Grants; Leveraging Educational Assistance Partnership; Federal Supplemental Educational Opportunity Grants; Federal Work-Study; Special Allowances; and Federal Family Education Loan Program interest subsidies.
[9]Includes Vocational Rehabilitation State Grants; Supported Employment State Grants; Client Assistance State Grants; Independent Living State Grants; Services for Older Blind Individuals; Protection and Advocacy for Assistive Technology; Assistive Technology State Grant Program; and Protection and Advocacy of Individual Rights.
[10]Total excludes other activities and other jurisdictions.
NOTE: Data reflect revisions to figures in the Budget of the United States Government, Fiscal Year 2009. Detail may not sum to totals because of rounding.
SOURCE: U.S. Department of Education, Budget Service, unpublished tabulations. (This table was prepared September 2008.)

Table 379. Appropriations for Title I, No Child Left Behind Act of 2001, by program and state or jurisdiction: Fiscal years 2007 and 2008

[In thousands of current dollars]

State or jurisdiction	Title I total, 2007	Title I, 2008 Total	Grants to local education agencies[1]	State agency programs Neglected and Delinquent	State agency programs Migrant	Even Start	Reading First State Grants	State Assessments, 2008
1	2	3	4	5	6	7	8	9
Total, 50 states and D.C.[2]	$13,695,783	$14,081,595	$13,245,108	$47,066	$356,326	$58,838	$374,257	$389,628
Total, 50 states, D.C., other activities, and other jurisdictions	14,385,963	14,787,039	13,898,875	48,927	379,771	66,454	393,012	408,732
Alabama	216,895	226,337	215,312	730	2,033	953	7,308	6,628
Alaska	44,237	47,060	38,846	269	6,704	306	936	3,583
Arizona	298,216	292,505	274,874	1,465	6,319	1,139	8,708	8,208
Arkansas	139,313	155,015	144,216	489	5,069	645	4,595	5,232
California	1,909,595	1,883,812	1,698,413	2,561	124,730	7,270	50,838	32,918
Colorado	144,125	147,827	135,347	486	7,073	599	4,321	6,750
Connecticut	122,229	120,892	115,597	1,201	986	472	2,635	5,711
Delaware	37,648	40,431	38,380	518	292	306	936	3,653
District of Columbia	49,127	48,785	47,308	236	0	306	936	3,345
Florida	668,009	703,197	656,163	1,529	22,419	2,950	20,135	15,884
Georgia	456,394	470,040	446,095	1,145	7,926	1,963	12,911	10,984
Hawaii	43,547	46,618	44,323	253	729	306	1,007	3,886
Idaho	49,742	52,499	46,679	270	3,585	306	1,660	4,286
Illinois	643,505	613,591	593,811	970	1,885	2,420	14,505	13,269
Indiana	254,552	261,215	247,042	959	5,093	1,066	7,054	8,113
Iowa	77,798	77,472	72,688	385	1,645	316	2,438	5,294
Kansas	104,529	109,774	95,430	404	11,384	0	2,555	5,225
Kentucky	208,379	223,604	208,484	924	7,059	925	6,214	6,229
Louisiana	305,811	309,163	294,758	1,359	2,373	1,311	9,361	6,477
Maine	48,145	54,329	51,551	206	1,041	306	1,225	3,929
Maryland	202,966	198,786	192,324	937	517	832	4,177	7,370
Massachusetts	230,465	243,726	233,711	1,925	1,595	1,013	5,483	7,699
Michigan	504,440	551,994	527,086	1,058	8,425	2,327	13,099	11,071
Minnesota	127,338	133,032	126,897	203	1,653	557	3,722	7,033
Mississippi	192,788	195,828	187,418	697	585	817	6,309	5,445
Missouri	224,301	236,207	225,118	1,361	1,499	996	7,234	7,591
Montana	42,767	46,039	43,551	115	939	306	1,128	3,714
Nebraska	60,546	67,513	60,224	301	5,043	306	1,640	4,408
Nevada	87,854	84,215	80,812	329	221	363	2,491	5,071
New Hampshire	38,204	40,008	38,198	428	140	306	936	3,993
New Jersey	274,397	299,771	286,906	2,615	2,005	1,240	7,006	9,706
New Mexico	113,983	118,239	113,124	256	853	499	3,507	4,581
New York	1,302,942	1,269,809	1,227,205	2,883	9,319	5,183	25,220	17,314
North Carolina	338,445	379,106	358,529	1,097	5,654	1,608	12,219	10,031
North Dakota	33,001	35,285	33,742	84	218	306	936	3,458
Ohio	489,740	532,497	511,652	2,464	2,431	2,252	13,699	11,968
Oklahoma	142,319	155,535	148,495	235	1,016	661	5,127	5,841
Oregon	145,694	155,357	139,926	1,167	9,420	623	4,221	5,788
Pennsylvania	564,002	590,980	565,478	1,097	8,954	2,487	12,964	12,152
Rhode Island	54,556	55,184	52,998	614	67	306	1,200	3,764
South Carolina	206,815	214,862	205,529	1,488	528	917	6,400	6,398
South Dakota	41,139	43,805	41,539	222	804	306	936	3,625
Tennessee	227,843	249,559	239,240	475	523	1,077	8,244	7,725
Texas	1,340,434	1,406,279	1,299,288	3,015	56,566	5,663	41,747	23,622
Utah	66,935	64,928	60,052	673	1,711	306	2,186	5,497
Vermont	31,228	35,190	32,862	487	600	306	936	3,440
Virginia	224,477	235,732	226,016	1,411	782	1,011	6,512	8,819
Washington	216,459	214,539	191,798	718	15,015	838	6,170	7,954
West Virginia	96,610	103,392	99,573	573	81	439	2,726	4,259
Wisconsin	219,647	206,485	198,986	1,204	605	819	4,870	7,294
Wyoming	31,653	33,545	31,516	574	214	306	936	3,398
Other activities/jurisdictions								
Indian Tribe Set-Aside	98,083	99,607	96,688	0	0	954	1,965	2,000
Other nonstate allocations	57,070	52,468	8,930	1,223	23,445	4,044	14,825	8,732
American Samoa	10,369	10,230	9,525	0	0	81	624	379
Guam	10,815	12,132	11,478	0	0	98	556	815
Northern Marianas	3,938	3,716	3,460	0	0	30	227	256
Puerto Rico	496,703	513,825	510,887	638	0	2,300	0	6,372
U.S. Virgin Islands	13,202	13,467	12,799	0	0	109	559	551

[1]Includes Basic, Concentration, Targeted, and Education Finance Incentive Grants.
[2]Total excludes other activities and other jurisdictions.
NOTE: Detail may not sum to totals because of rounding. These are preliminary estimates for fiscal year 2008. Grants for Innovative Programs has no allocations for fiscal year 2008.

SOURCE: U.S. Department of Education, Budget Service, Elementary, Secondary, and Vocational Education Analysis Division, unpublished tabulations. (This table was prepared May 2008.)

Table 380. Federal obligations for research, development, and R&D plant, by performers, fields of science, and category of obligation: Fiscal years 1999 through 2007

[In millions of current dollars]

Performers, fields of science, and category of obligation	Actual							Estimated		Percent change, 2006 to 2007
	1999	2000	2001	2002	2003	2004	2005	2006	2007	
1	2	3	4	5	6	7	8	9	10	11
Total obligations for research, development, and R&D plant	$77,386.6	$77,356.1	$84,003.0	$90,157.7	$97,927.9	$105,370.7	$112,994.6	$116,872.6	$116,416.5	-0.4
Research and development obligations	75,340.8	72,863.2	79,933.2	85,853.0	93,661.3	101,376.5	109,223.5	113,315.7	112,829.7	-0.4
Performers										
Federal intramural[1]	18,084.7	17,149.8	20,219.8	21,044.8	22,861.6	22,423.2	24,125.4	25,521.5	24,741.5	-3.1
Industrial firms	31,901.6	27,735.5	27,006.2	29,538.2	33,852.7	39,214.6	44,112.5	46,106.2	46,502.1	0.9
FFRDCs[2] administered by industrial firms	1,328.1	1,100.9	1,186.6	1,351.1	1,507.6	1,543.1	1,612.1	1,500.0	1,477.8	-1.5
Universities and colleges	14,959.1	16,815.1	19,587.9	21,290.1	22,693.5	24,169.7	24,841.5	25,332.2	24,968.5	-1.4
FFRDCs[2] administered by universities and colleges	3,896.5	4,053.2	4,617.7	4,641.2	4,754.2	5,400.9	5,686.1	5,888.9	6,136.3	4.2
Other nonprofit institutions	3,608.8	4,216.6	5,138.8	5,739.1	5,706.7	5,623.7	5,910.0	5,956.3	5,751.6	-3.4
FFRDCs[2] administered by nonprofit institutions	913.3	1,231.5	1,269.1	1,404.8	1,352.8	1,443.2	1,649.2	1,724.4	1,949.2	13.0
State and local governments	357.5	224.0	450.6	452.2	400.0	880.1	660.8	657.1	663.8	1.0
Foreign	291.3	336.7	456.5	391.6	532.4	677.9	625.8	629.1	639.1	1.6
Research obligations	33,527.5	38,470.5	44,713.7	48,006.7	51,071.8	53,357.8	53,738.2	54,963.5	55,089.2	0.2
Performers										
Federal intramural[1]	8,685.8	9,449.6	11,130.9	11,857.4	12,419.6	12,085.2	12,349.9	12,634.0	12,674.5	0.3
Industrial firms	4,579.8	4,801.2	5,262.3	5,786.8	6,042.4	6,782.7	6,456.4	6,960.7	6,786.3	-2.5
FFRDCs[2] administered by industrial firms	879.3	700.3	822.3	937.3	1,103.5	1,131.6	1,082.0	1,006.8	977.6	-2.9
Universities and colleges	13,203.8	16,015.9	18,057.1	20,285.4	21,676.5	22,699.1	23,156.0	23,447.0	23,361.4	-0.4
FFRDCs[2] administered by universities and colleges	2,554.1	2,773.2	3,096.3	3,219.4	3,272.6	3,687.3	3,743.4	3,821.2	4,065.8	6.4
Other nonprofit institutions	2,806.7	3,719.8	4,577.9	4,723.0	5,196.3	5,216.4	5,295.8	5,364.6	5,341.2	-0.4
FFRDCs[2] administered by nonprofit institutions	469.5	696.1	739.4	749.6	779.0	795.5	907.8	996.9	1,154.1	15.8
State and local governments	232.4	162.5	308.7	275.5	305.8	532.9	376.8	358.8	356.5	-0.6
Foreign	116.1	152.0	118.9	172.3	276.1	427.0	370.2	373.4	371.8	-0.4
Fields of science										
Life sciences	15,422.5	17,964.7	23,057.3	25,476.8	27,772.2	27,728.5	28,127.8	28,402.0	27,810.6	-2.1
Psychology	632.6	1,626.7	741.9	905.9	1,104.4	1,854.9	1,891.8	1,900.7	1,911.7	0.6
Physical sciences	4,066.2	4,787.9	4,600.8	4,983.2	5,021.6	5,211.1	5,493.7	5,564.3	5,647.6	1.5
Environmental sciences	3,095.3	3,328.8	3,251.7	3,418.3	3,740.9	3,741.6	3,502.6	3,649.1	3,635.7	-0.4
Mathematics and computer sciences	1,980.6	2,205.6	2,610.6	2,630.7	1,104.4	2,949.4	2,983.4	3,064.6	3,181.9	3.8
Engineering	6,263.4	6,346.4	8,100.7	8,274.9	8,405.1	8,866.4	8,552.9	8,975.8	9,487.4	5.7
Social sciences	854.9	1,050.3	1,008.6	1,038.5	1,025.8	1,089.6	1,097.1	1,202.6	1,215.3	1.1
Other sciences	1,212.1	1,160.2	1,245.8	1,278.4	1,329.3	1,916.3	2,088.9	2,204.4	2,198.9	-0.3
Basic research obligations	17,443.7	19,569.8	21,958.1	23,668.3	24,751.4	26,120.7	27,140.3	27,679.8	28,264.4	2.1
Performers										
Federal intramural[1]	3,255.2	3,621.8	4,193.8	4,460.0	4,662.1	4,671.6	4,772.7	4,987.8	4,846.4	-2.8
Industrial firms	1,082.8	1,356.5	917.1	1,231.9	1,279.6	1,969.4	2,051.0	2,161.5	2,211.1	2.3
FFRDCs[2] administered by industrial firms	313.4	171.3	175.1	239.6	312.8	292.2	270.1	269.7	269.1	-0.2
Universities and colleges	9,107.1	10,056.7	11,792.2	12,668.2	13,151.8	13,398.5	13,989.9	14,028.8	14,272.5	1.7
FFRDCs[2] administered by universities and colleges	1,565.5	1,674.0	1,762.1	1,805.2	1,827.8	2,005.8	2,021.2	2,137.8	2,364.3	10.6
Other nonprofit institutions	1,650.0	1,985.3	2,441.7	2,531.7	2,703.9	2,746.1	2,914.2	2,896.3	2,927.9	1.1
FFRDCs[2] administered by nonprofit institutions	354.9	521.6	540.5	563.4	582.1	606.8	670.7	734.5	897.7	22.2
State and local governments	61.4	75.7	71.5	71.5	85.4	197.9	235.9	244.3	253.6	3.8
Foreign	53.4	106.9	64.0	96.8	146.1	232.3	214.6	219.2	221.8	1.2
Fields of science										
Life sciences	9,197.1	10,049.0	12,835.5	14,024.1	14,765.3	14,490.0	15,247.6	15,432.1	15,321.9	-0.7
Psychology	347.3	817.8	292.9	464.6	543.8	979.2	1,040.1	1,046.4	1,055.8	0.9
Physical sciences	3,089.8	3,470.6	3,327.1	3,405.9	3,454.0	3,662.6	3,738.7	3,777.5	4,042.7	7.0
Environmental sciences	1,615.7	1,838.4	1,663.0	1,833.3	1,899.5	2,022.9	1,966.1	2,002.5	2,058.0	2.8
Mathematics and computer sciences	734.9	798.3	957.8	998.7	1,120.2	1,239.1	1,228.4	1,238.9	1,361.2	9.9
Engineering	1,639.7	1,764.2	1,911.5	1,864.9	1,913.1	2,271.7	2,300.5	2,516.4	2,733.5	8.6
Social sciences	246.5	308.0	278.4	361.7	352.8	419.3	391.4	398.7	401.7	0.7
Other sciences	572.5	523.6	691.7	715.2	702.7	1,035.9	1,227.5	1,267.3	1,289.7	1.8
Applied research obligations	16,083.7	18,900.7	22,755.6	24,338.4	26,320.4	27,237.1	26,597.9	27,283.7	26,824.8	-1.7
Performers										
Federal intramural[1]	5,430.6	5,827.8	6,937.2	7,397.4	7,757.5	7,413.6	7,577.2	7,646.2	7,828.1	2.4
Industrial firms	3,497.0	3,444.6	4,345.2	4,554.9	4,762.8	4,813.3	4,405.4	4,799.2	4,575.3	-4.7
FFRDCs[2] administered by industrial firms	565.8	528.9	647.2	697.7	790.7	839.3	811.9	737.2	708.5	-3.9
Universities and colleges	4,096.7	5,959.2	6,864.9	7,617.2	8,524.7	9,300.6	9,166.1	9,418.2	9,088.9	-3.5
FFRDCs[2] administered by universities and colleges	988.6	1,099.2	1,334.2	1,414.1	1,444.8	1,681.6	1,722.2	1,683.4	1,701.5	1.1
Other nonprofit institutions	1,156.7	1,734.5	2,136.2	2,191.3	2,492.5	2,470.3	2,381.6	2,468.4	2,413.3	-2.2
FFRDCs[2] administered by nonprofit institutions	114.6	174.5	198.9	186.2	197.0	188.7	237.1	262.4	256.4	-2.3
State and local governments	171.0	86.9	237.1	204.0	220.4	335.0	140.9	114.5	102.9	-10.2
Foreign	62.8	45.1	54.9	75.6	130.0	194.7	155.6	154.2	150.0	-2.7

See notes at end of table.

Table 380. Federal obligations for research, development, and R&D plant, by performers, fields of science, and category of obligation: Fiscal years 1999 through 2007—Continued

[In millions of current dollars]

Performers, fields of science, and category of obligation	Actual							Estimated		Percent change, 2006 to 2007
	1999	2000	2001	2002	2003	2004	2005	2006	2007	
1	2	3	4	5	6	7	8	9	10	11
Fields of science										
Life sciences	6,225.3	7,915.7	10,221.8	11,452.7	13,007.0	13,238.5	12,880.2	12,970.0	12,488.7	-3.7
Psychology	285.3	808.9	449.0	441.3	560.6	875.6	851.6	854.3	855.9	0.2
Physical sciences	976.4	1,317.3	1,273.6	1,577.4	1,567.6	1,548.6	1,755.0	1,786.8	1,604.9	-10.2
Environmental sciences	1,479.5	1,490.3	1,588.6	1,585.0	1,841.4	1,718.7	1,536.5	1,646.5	1,577.8	-4.2
Mathematics and computer sciences	1,245.7	1,407.3	1,652.8	1,632.0	1,552.2	1,710.3	1,754.9	1,825.7	1,820.7	-0.3
Engineering	4,623.7	4,582.2	6,285.5	6,410.0	6,492.0	6,594.7	6,252.5	6,459.4	6,753.9	4.6
Social sciences	608.3	742.3	730.2	676.9	673.0	670.3	705.8	803.9	813.7	1.2
Other sciences	639.6	636.6	554.1	563.3	626.6	880.5	861.4	937.2	909.2	-3.0
Development obligations	**41,813.1**	**34,392.7**	**35,219.5**	**37,846.3**	**42,589.5**	**48,018.7**	**55,485.3**	**58,352.3**	**57,740.5**	**-1.0**
Performers										
Federal intramural[1]	9,398.9	7,700.2	9,088.9	9,187.4	10,442.0	10,338.0	11,775.5	12,887.5	12,067.0	-6.4
Industrial firms	27,321.8	22,934.4	21,744.0	23,751.4	27,810.3	32,431.8	37,656.1	39,145.5	39,715.7	1.5
FFRDCs[2] administered by industrial firms	448.8	400.6	364.3	413.7	404.1	411.6	530.1	493.2	500.1	1.4
Universities and colleges	1,755.3	799.3	930.8	1,004.7	1,017.0	1,470.6	1,685.6	1,885.2	1,607.1	-14.8
FFRDCs[2] administered by universities and colleges	1,342.3	1,279.9	1,521.4	1,421.8	1,481.6	1,713.5	1,942.8	2,067.7	2,070.5	0.1
Other nonprofit institutions	802.0	496.8	560.8	1,016.1	510.3	407.4	614.1	591.7	410.4	-30.6
FFRDCs[2] administered by nonprofit institutions	443.7	535.4	529.7	655.2	573.7	647.7	741.5	727.5	795.1	9.3
State and local governments	125.1	61.5	141.9	176.7	94.1	347.2	284.1	298.4	307.3	3.0
Foreign	175.2	184.7	337.6	219.2	256.3	250.9	255.6	255.7	267.3	4.5
R&D plant obligations	**2,045.8**	**4,492.8**	**4,069.8**	**4,304.7**	**4,266.5**	**3,994.2**	**3,771.1**	**3,556.9**	**3,586.8**	**0.8**
Performers										
Federal intramural[1]	483.3	573.3	520.4	414.8	609.7	961.3	859.3	817.9	698.3	-14.6
Industrial firms	544.7	2,814.6	2,179.8	2,524.9	1,817.0	1,442.0	1,381.4	1,466.9	1,540.8	5.0
FFRDCs[2] administered by industrial firms	172.8	27.6	41.8	109.1	145.7	188.3	125.7	87.8	21.0	-76.1
Universities and colleges	141.2	213.5	284.7	241.1	686.9	354.3	423.0	294.5	336.7	14.3
FFRDCs[2] administered by universities and colleges	615.5	613.8	615.9	583.3	578.4	603.9	558.3	515.2	595.0	15.5
Other nonprofit institutions	12.2	55.5	27.9	29.1	70.7	164.5	134.6	126.0	138.2	9.6
FFRDCs[2] administered by nonprofit institutions	70.7	193.5	357.5	388.8	333.9	252.4	218.0	197.5	202.8	2.7
State and local governments	5.3	0.9	1.4	2.0	0.8	15.8	55.2	34.7	36.5	5.2
Foreign	—	0.1	40.4	11.7	23.4	11.7	15.6	16.5	17.6	7.0

—Not available.

[1]Includes costs associated with the administration of intramural and extramural programs by federal personnel as well as actual intramural performance.

[2]Federally funded research and development centers.

NOTE: Some data have been revised from previously published figures. Detail may not sum to totals because of rounding. Totals do not include the U.S. Department of Homeland Security.

SOURCE: National Science Foundation, *Federal Funds for Research and Development*, 1997 through 2007. (This table was prepared October 2008.)

CHAPTER 5
Outcomes of Education

This chapter contains tables comparing educational attainment and workforce characteristics. The data show labor force participation and income levels of high school dropouts and high school and college graduates. Population characteristics are provided for many of the measures to help provide comparisons among various demographic groups. Tables 381 to 383 contain data from the U.S. Bureau of Labor Statistics on labor force participation, employment, unemployment, and type of occupation by highest level of educational attainment, sex, age, and race/ethnicity. Tables 384 and 385 provide income comparisons by education level and sex. Table 386 provides literacy scores for adults by education level, employment status, and demographic characteristics. Percentages of high school seniors with various characteristics who work different numbers of hours per week are shown in table 387.

Tables 388 and 389, compiled from U.S. Census Bureau data on high school completers and dropouts, show the labor force participation and college enrollment of high school students within the year after they leave school. The tabulations also provide comparative labor force participation and unemployment rates for high school completers and dropouts. Additional information on college enrollment rates by race/ethnicity and sex has been included to help form a more complete picture of high school outcomes. Table 390 provides data on college enrollment and employment among special education students who have left secondary school. Tables 391 to 394 were prepared from the Recent College Graduates and Baccalaureate and Beyond surveys by the National Center for Education Statistics (NCES). These tables provide data on employment outcomes and salaries for college graduates 1 year after graduation. Tables 395 to 397 deal with drug use and life values of high school seniors and young adults.

Statistics related to outcomes of education appear in other sections of the *Digest*. For example, statistics on educational attainment of the entire population are in chapter 1. More detailed data on the numbers of high school and college graduates are contained in chapters 2 and 3. Chapter 3 contains trend data on the percentage of high school completers going to college. Additional data on the income of people by educational attainment may be obtained from the U.S. Census Bureau in the *Current Population Reports*, Series P-60. The U.S. Bureau of Labor Statistics has a series of publications dealing with the educational characteristics of the labor force. Further information on survey methodologies is in Appendix A: Guide to Sources and in the publications cited in the table source notes.

Labor Force

Adults with higher levels of education generally had higher labor force participation rates than adults with less education (table 381 and figure 21). (People participating in the labor force are those employed or actively seeking employment.) Among people 25 to 64 years old, 86 percent of those with a bachelor's or higher degree participated in the labor force in 2007, compared with 76 percent of those who had completed only high school. In comparison, 64 percent of those ages 25 to 64 who had not completed high school were in the labor force. The 2007 labor force participation rate for those ages 25 to 64 who had completed only high school was higher for Whites (77 percent) and Hispanics (79 percent) than for Asians (74 percent) and Blacks (72 percent) (table 381). Among people ages 25 to 64 with a bachelor's or higher degree, the labor force participation rates for Whites, Blacks, and Hispanics (86 to 88 percent) were higher than the rate for Asians (82 percent).

Unemployment rates were generally higher for people with lower levels of educational attainment than for those with higher levels of educational attainment (table 382). (The unemployment rate is the percentage of people in the labor force who are not employed, but made specific efforts to find employment sometime during the prior 4 weeks.) The 2007 unemployment rate for adults (25 years old and over) who had not completed high school was 7.1 percent, compared with 4.4 percent for those who had completed high school and 2.0 percent for those with a bachelor's or higher degree (figure 22). Younger people tended to have higher unemployment rates than did people 25 years old and over (table 382).

The relative difficulties dropouts have in entering the job market are highlighted by comparing their labor force participation rates to those of other youth. Of the 2006–07 high school completers who were not in college in October 2007, 77 percent were in the labor force (employed or looking for work), and 20 percent of those in the labor force were looking for work (table 388). In comparison, 2006–07 high school dropouts participated in the labor force at a lower rate (56 percent) in October 2007 (table 389).

One year after graduating from college in 1999–2000, 87 percent of individuals receiving bachelor's degrees were employed (77 percent full time and 11 percent part time), 6 percent were unemployed, and 6 percent were not in the labor force (table 392).

Income

Among full-time year-round workers 25 years old and over, the median annual income of males, when adjusted for inflation, increased between 1995 and 1999, but decreased between 1999 and 2007, resulting in a 2007 income that was similar to the 1995 income (table 384). The median annual income for females working full-time year-round rose between 1995 and 2001, and had no consistent trend

between 2001 and 2007, for a net increase of 7 percent for the entire period. Females' incomes remained lower than males' incomes overall, as well as by education level. For example, the median 2007 income for full-time year-round workers with a bachelor's degree was $62,090 for males and $45,770 for females. Among people 25 years old and over who had earnings in 2007, median annual earnings were lower for females than for males ($29,540 vs. $41,540) (table 385 and figure 24).

Figure 21. Labor force participation rate of persons 20 to 64 years old, by age group and highest level of education: 2007

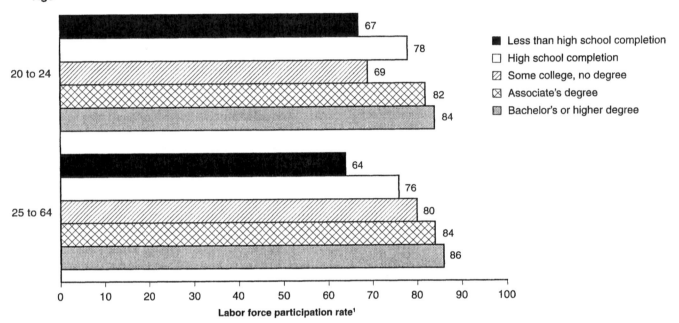

[1]Percentage of the civilian population who are employed or seeking employment.
SOURCE: U.S. Department of Labor, Bureau of Labor Statistics, Office of Employment and Unemployment Statistics, unpublished 2007 annual average data from the Current Population Survey (CPS).

Figure 22. Unemployment rates of persons 25 years old and over, by highest level of education: 2007

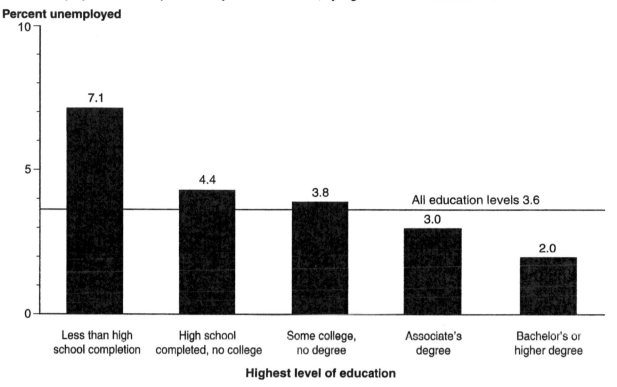

SOURCE: U.S. Department of Labor, Bureau of Labor Statistics, Office of Employment and Unemployment Statistics, unpublished 2007 annual average data from the Current Population Survey (CPS).

Figure 23. Labor force status of 2006–07 high school dropouts and completers not enrolled in college: October 2007

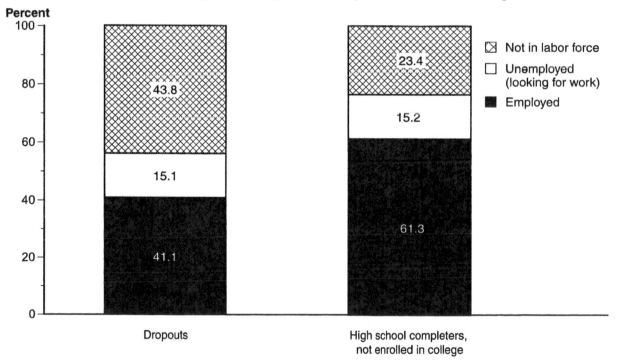

NOTE: Dropouts are persons who have not completed high school, and are not enrolled in school. Detail may not sum to totals because of rounding.
SOURCE: U.S. Department of Commerce, Census Bureau, Current Population Survey (CPS), October 2007.

Figure 24. Median annual earnings of persons 25 years old and over, by highest level of education and sex: 2007

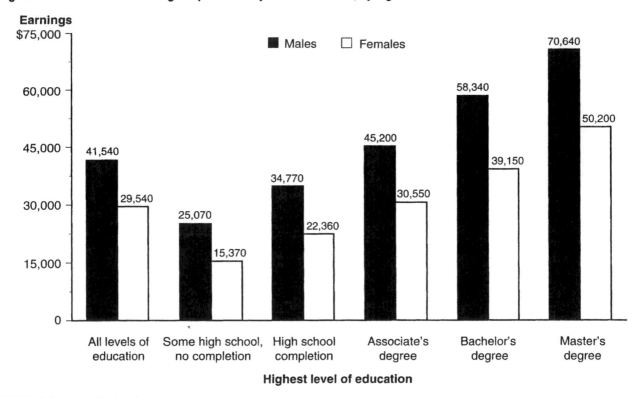

NOTE: Excludes persons without earnings.
SOURCE: U.S. Department of Commerce, Census Bureau, Current Population Survey (CPS), March 2008.

Figure 25. Average salaries of bachelor's degree recipients 1 year after graduation, by field: 1991, 1994, and 2001
(in constant 2006 dollars)

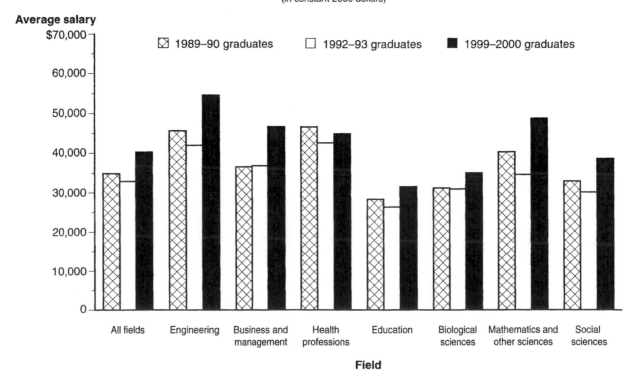

SOURCE: U.S. Department of Education, National Center for Education Statistics, Recent College Graduates Study (RCG), 1991; and 1993/94 and 2000/01 Baccalaureate and Beyond Longitudinal Study (B&B:93/94) and (B&B:2000/01).

Table 381. Labor force participation rates and employment to population ratios of persons 16 to 64 years old, by highest level of education, age, sex, and race/ethnicity: 2007

Age, sex, and race/ethnicity	Labor force participation rate[1]				College			Employment to population ratio[2]				College	
	Total	Less than high school completion[3]	High school completion	Some college, no degree	Associate's degree	Bachelor's or higher degree	Total	Less than high school completion[3]	High school completion	Some college, no degree	Associate's degree	Bachelor's or higher degree	
1	2	3	4	5	6	7	8	9	10	11	12	13
16 to 19 years old[4]	41.3 (0.38)	33.2 (0.44)	60.9 (0.88)	54.3 (1.04)	‡ (†)	‡ (†)	34.8 (0.37)	27.2 (0.42)	51.4 (0.90)	49.7 (1.04)	‡ (†)	‡ (†)
Male	41.1 (0.53)	33.3 (0.61)	63.3 (1.22)	51.5 (1.58)	‡ (†)	‡ (†)	33.9 (0.51)	26.7 (0.57)	52.1 (1.26)	46.6 (1.57)	‡ (†)	‡ (†)
Female	41.5 (0.54)	33.1 (0.64)	58.4 (1.27)	56.5 (1.38)	‡ (—)	‡ (†)	35.8 (0.53)	27.6 (0.60)	50.7 (1.29)	52.2 (1.39)	‡ (†)	‡ (†)
White	46.4 (0.49)	38.6 (0.59)	64.4 (1.09)	58.0 (1.26)	‡ (—)	‡ (†)	40.4 (0.48)	32.7 (0.57)	56.4 (1.13)	53.7 (1.27)	‡ (†)	‡ (†)
Black	29.9 (0.90)	22.1 (0.96)	54.3 (2.29)	41.0 (3.09)	‡ (†)	‡ (†)	21.0 (0.80)	14.9 (0.82)	38.4 (2.23)	33.9 (2.97)	‡ (†)	‡ (†)
Hispanic	37.1 (0.83)	28.6 (0.92)	57.9 (2.00)	57.5 (2.63)	‡ (†)	‡ (†)	30.4 (0.79)	22.6 (0.85)	47.9 (2.02)	52.5 (2.66)	‡ (†)	‡ (†)
Asian	24.3 (1.76)	17.7 (2.01)	36.5 (5.32)	32.5 (3.89)	‡ (†)	‡ (†)	21.4 (1.68)	14.9 (1.88)	32.5 (5.18)	30.2 (3.81)	‡ (†)	‡ (†)
20 to 24 years old[4]	74.4 (0.35)	67.3 (1.08)	77.9 (0.61)	69.4 (0.61)	81.5 (1.19)	83.9 (0.82)	68.4 (0.38)	57.0 (1.14)	70.0 (0.68)	65.2 (0.63)	77.9 (1.27)	79.4 (0.90)
Male	78.7 (0.46)	79.5 (1.21)	85.5 (0.69)	69.6 (0.86)	83.0 (1.69)	84.3 (1.24)	71.7 (0.51)	68.5 (1.39)	76.7 (0.83)	64.8 (0.89)	79.0 (1.83)	78.9 (1.39)
Female	70.1 (0.50)	51.1 (1.67)	68.6 (0.97)	69.1 (0.81)	80.2 (1.57)	83.6 (1.03)	65.0 (0.52)	41.7 (1.64)	61.9 (1.01)	65.4 (0.84)	77.0 (1.66)	79.7 (1.12)
White	76.8 (0.43)	67.3 (1.77)	81.1 (0.77)	70.3 (0.73)	86.3 (1.27)	85.5 (0.91)	71.5 (0.47)	55.9 (1.88)	74.1 (0.86)	66.5 (0.76)	83.1 (1.39)	81.3 (1.00)
Black	68.3 (1.08)	58.1 (3.15)	70.5 (1.71)	67.6 (1.83)	67.8 (4.78)	78.0 (3.44)	57.8 (1.15)	39.9 (3.13)	57.7 (1.85)	60.9 (1.91)	62.7 (4.94)	71.6 (3.75)
Hispanic	74.8 (0.86)	72.1 (1.59)	76.8 (1.41)	72.2 (1.79)	78.2 (3.53)	86.9 (3.06)	69.0 (0.91)	65.3 (1.69)	70.6 (1.52)	67.5 (1.87)	73.8 (3.76)	82.4 (3.45)
Asian	59.5 (1.72)	47.2 (7.32)	65.9 (4.17)	52.0 (2.63)	57.8 (6.08)	71.9 (3.11)	56.2 (1.74)	38.9 (7.15)	63.2 (4.24)	49.4 (2.63)	56.2 (6.11)	67.5 (3.24)
25 to 64 years old	79.1 (0.12)	63.6 (0.41)	76.3 (0.22)	79.7 (0.28)	83.8 (0.35)	85.7 (0.18)	76.2 (0.12)	59.0 (0.42)	72.9 (0.23)	76.7 (0.29)	81.3 (0.37)	84.0 (0.19)
Male	86.6 (0.14)	77.0 (0.48)	84.5 (0.26)	86.4 (0.34)	89.0 (0.44)	92.0 (0.20)	83.5 (0.15)	72.0 (0.52)	80.7 (0.29)	83.3 (0.37)	86.4 (0.48)	90.2 (0.22)
Female	71.8 (0.17)	48.3 (0.60)	67.9 (0.33)	73.7 (0.40)	79.7 (0.48)	79.7 (0.28)	69.2 (0.18)	44.2 (0.59)	65.0 (0.34)	70.7 (0.42)	77.3 (0.50)	78.0 (0.29)
White	80.0 (0.14)	58.5 (0.69)	76.7 (0.27)	79.5 (0.33)	84.2 (0.40)	85.8 (0.21)	77.6 (0.15)	54.0 (0.70)	73.8 (0.28)	76.9 (0.35)	82.1 (0.42)	84.2 (0.22)
Black	75.7 (0.39)	53.4 (1.27)	72.4 (0.67)	79.5 (0.81)	82.7 (1.13)	88.1 (0.64)	71.0 (0.41)	46.4 (1.27)	67.0 (0.71)	74.9 (0.87)	78.7 (1.22)	85.6 (0.70)
Hispanic	77.9 (0.33)	71.3 (0.59)	79.2 (0.59)	82.2 (0.83)	84.2 (1.16)	86.0 (0.75)	74.4 (0.35)	67.0 (0.62)	75.7 (0.63)	78.6 (0.89)	81.3 (1.24)	84.0 (0.79)
Asian	78.2 (0.49)	61.8 (1.97)	73.7 (1.19)	79.2 (1.52)	78.4 (1.86)	82.1 (0.61)	76.0 (0.50)	59.9 (1.98)	71.3 (1.22)	76.3 (1.59)	75.2 (1.95)	80.2 (0.63)

†Not applicable.
‡Reporting standards not met.
[1]Percentage of the civilian population who are employed or seeking employment.
[2]Number of persons employed as a percentage of the civilian population.
[3]Includes persons reporting no school years completed.
[4]Excludes persons enrolled in school.
NOTE: Race categories exclude persons of Hispanic ethnicity. Standard errors appear in parentheses.
SOURCE: U.S. Department of Labor, Bureau of Labor Statistics, Office of Employment and Unemployment Statistics, unpublished 2007 annual average data from the Current Population Survey (CPS). (This table was prepared August 2008.)

Table 382. Unemployment rate of persons 16 years old and over, by age, sex, race/ethnicity, and educational attainment: 2005, 2006, and 2007

Sex, race/ethnicity, and educational attainment	Unemployment rate, 2005 16- to 24-year-olds[1] Total	16 to 19 years	20 to 24 years	25 years old and over	Unemployment rate, 2006 16- to 24-year-olds[1] Total	16 to 19 years	20 to 24 years	25 years old and over	Unemployment rate, 2007 16- to 24-year-olds[1] Total	16 to 19 years	20 to 24 years	25 years old and over
	2	3	4	5	6	7	8	9	10	11	12	13
All persons, all education levels	11.3 (0.16)	16.6 (0.34)	8.8 (0.18)	4.0 (0.04)	10.5 (0.16)	15.4 (0.29)	8.2 (0.17)	3.6 (0.04)	10.5 (0.16)	15.7 (0.30)	8.2 (0.17)	3.6 (0.04)
Less than high school completion	18.5 (0.39)	19.6 (0.49)	16.2 (0.66)	7.6 (0.18)	16.6 (0.38)	17.5 (0.41)	14.3 (0.64)	6.8 (0.17)	17.3 (0.39)	18.3 (0.43)	15.3 (0.67)	7.1 (0.18)
High school completion, no college	12.1 (0.31)	15.6 (0.65)	10.7 (0.34)	4.7 (0.08)	12.0 (0.31)	15.7 (0.57)	10.5 (0.34)	4.3 (0.08)	11.6 (0.30)	15.5 (0.57)	10.1 (0.34)	4.4 (0.08)
Some college, no degree	7.0 (0.24)	9.1 (0.61)	6.5 (0.26)	4.2 (0.10)	6.3 (0.23)	8.1 (0.53)	5.9 (0.25)	3.9 (0.10)	6.5 (0.24)	8.4 (0.54)	6.1 (0.25)	3.8 (0.10)
Associate's degree	6.2 (0.56)	†	6.1 (0.56)	3.3 (0.12)	5.2 (0.50)	†	5.1 (0.50)	3.0 (0.12)	4.5 (0.46)	†	4.4 (0.47)	3.0 (0.12)
Bachelor's or higher degree	5.0 (0.37)	†	5.0 (0.38)	2.3 (0.06)	5.1 (0.37)	†	5.1 (0.37)	2.0 (0.05)	5.5 (0.37)	†	5.4 (0.37)	2.0 (0.05)
Male, all education levels	12.4 (0.23)	18.6 (0.49)	9.6 (0.25)	3.8 (0.06)	11.2 (0.22)	16.9 (0.42)	8.7 (0.24)	3.5 (0.05)	11.6 (0.22)	17.6 (0.44)	8.9 (0.24)	3.6 (0.05)
Less than high school completion	19.0 (0.51)	21.7 (0.69)	14.5 (0.75)	6.4 (0.21)	16.4 (0.48)	18.7 (0.58)	12.3 (0.71)	6.1 (0.20)	17.7 (0.52)	19.9 (0.61)	13.8 (0.77)	6.6 (0.21)
High school completion, no college	12.5 (0.40)	17.1 (0.93)	11.0 (0.44)	4.6 (0.11)	12.3 (0.40)	17.0 (0.81)	10.6 (0.43)	4.3 (0.11)	12.2 (0.40)	17.6 (0.83)	10.3 (0.43)	4.4 (0.11)
Some college, no degree	8.0 (0.37)	10.2 (0.96)	7.5 (0.40)	3.9 (0.14)	6.8 (0.34)	9.5 (0.88)	6.3 (0.36)	3.5 (0.13)	7.3 (0.35)	9.5 (0.88)	6.9 (0.38)	3.6 (0.13)
Associate's degree	6.0 (0.79)	†	6.0 (0.81)	3.3 (0.18)	6.4 (0.79)	†	6.5 (0.81)	3.0 (0.17)	4.9 (0.70)	†	4.8 (0.70)	3.0 (0.17)
Bachelor's or higher degree	5.7 (0.61)	†	5.8 (0.61)	2.3 (0.08)	5.7 (0.60)	†	5.7 (0.60)	1.9 (0.07)	6.4 (0.60)	†	6.4 (0.61)	1.9 (0.07)
Female, all education levels	10.1 (0.21)	14.5 (0.43)	7.9 (0.24)	4.2 (0.06)	9.7 (0.21)	13.8 (0.40)	7.6 (0.23)	3.7 (0.06)	9.4 (0.21)	13.8 (0.40)	7.3 (0.23)	3.6 (0.06)
Less than high school completion	17.9 (0.56)	17.2 (0.64)	19.8 (1.18)	9.7 (0.32)	16.8 (0.55)	16.3 (0.58)	18.7 (1.19)	7.9 (0.29)	16.9 (0.56)	16.5 (0.60)	18.5 (1.21)	8.2 (0.30)
High school completion, no college	11.5 (0.44)	14.2 (0.85)	10.2 (0.50)	4.8 (0.12)	11.5 (0.45)	14.2 (0.80)	10.3 (0.52)	4.3 (0.11)	10.9 (0.43)	13.2 (0.78)	9.8 (0.50)	4.3 (0.11)
Some college, no degree	6.0 (0.30)	8.2 (0.74)	5.5 (0.32)	4.5 (0.15)	5.9 (0.29)	7.1 (0.65)	5.5 (0.32)	4.3 (0.14)	5.9 (0.29)	7.6 (0.67)	5.4 (0.32)	4.1 (0.14)
Associate's degree	6.4 (0.72)	†	6.2 (0.73)	3.3 (0.16)	4.1 (0.58)	†	3.9 (0.58)	3.1 (0.15)	4.0 (0.57)	†	4.0 (0.58)	3.1 (0.15)
Bachelor's or higher degree	4.5 (0.44)	†	4.5 (0.44)	2.4 (0.08)	4.7 (0.44)	†	4.6 (0.44)	2.1 (0.07)	4.8 (0.43)	†	4.6 (0.42)	2.1 (0.07)
White, all education levels	9.2 (0.18)	13.5 (0.37)	7.0 (0.20)	3.3 (0.05)	8.9 (0.18)	12.8 (0.32)	6.8 (0.20)	3.0 (0.04)	8.9 (0.18)	13.1 (0.33)	6.9 (0.20)	3.0 (0.04)
Less than high school completion	16.1 (0.48)	16.0 (0.54)	16.7 (1.10)	7.1 (0.29)	14.9 (0.47)	14.7 (0.46)	15.5 (1.09)	6.5 (0.28)	15.7 (0.49)	15.4 (0.48)	17.0 (1.16)	7.3 (0.30)
High school completion, no college	10.0 (0.36)	12.9 (0.74)	8.7 (0.40)	4.0 (0.09)	10.3 (0.37)	12.9 (0.65)	9.2 (0.42)	3.7 (0.09)	9.8 (0.36)	12.5 (0.64)	8.6 (0.41)	3.8 (0.09)
Some college, no degree	5.7 (0.26)	7.4 (0.65)	5.3 (0.29)	3.5 (0.11)	5.4 (0.26)	6.9 (0.57)	5.0 (0.28)	3.3 (0.11)	5.8 (0.27)	7.4 (0.60)	5.4 (0.29)	3.3 (0.11)
Associate's degree	4.6 (0.57)	†	4.6 (0.58)	3.0 (0.13)	4.0 (0.51)	†	3.9 (0.51)	2.7 (0.13)	3.7 (0.50)	†	3.7 (0.50)	2.6 (0.13)
Bachelor's or higher degree	4.5 (0.40)	†	4.5 (0.40)	2.1 (0.06)	4.9 (0.42)	†	4.8 (0.42)	1.9 (0.06)	5.0 (0.40)	†	5.0 (0.41)	1.9 (0.06)
Black, all education levels	23.0 (0.67)	34.0 (1.40)	18.6 (0.73)	7.6 (0.18)	20.5 (0.63)	29.9 (1.15)	16.4 (0.70)	6.8 (0.17)	19.4 (0.63)	29.7 (1.20)	15.3 (0.67)	6.2 (0.17)
Less than high school completion	38.4 (1.53)	40.4 (1.98)	35.3 (2.40)	14.5 (0.74)	32.2 (1.46)	33.6 (1.61)	29.5 (2.44)	13.0 (0.72)	32.2 (1.54)	32.9 (1.70)	31.4 (2.59)	12.4 (0.73)
High school completion, no college	23.7 (1.13)	30.1 (2.48)	21.6 (1.26)	8.7 (0.32)	22.2 (1.09)	31.5 (2.18)	19.1 (1.19)	8.0 (0.32)	20.8 (1.05)	29.3 (2.09)	18.1 (1.15)	7.4 (0.30)
Some college, no degree	12.7 (0.98)	21.4 (3.10)	11.1 (1.01)	7.7 (0.41)	11.7 (0.94)	14.1 (2.26)	11.2 (1.01)	6.7 (0.38)	10.8 (0.92)	17.3 (2.73)	10.0 (0.95)	5.9 (0.35)
Associate's degree	14.4 (2.82)	†	15.0 (2.92)	5.2 (0.50)	15.3 (2.80)	†	14.2 (2.78)	5.3 (0.49)	8.0 (2.22)	†	7.6 (2.19)	4.9 (0.47)
Bachelor's or higher degree	8.4 (1.83)	†	8.6 (1.87)	3.4 (0.27)	8.7 (1.76)	†	8.4 (1.75)	2.8 (0.23)	8.8 (1.77)	†	8.1 (1.71)	2.9 (0.24)
Hispanic, all education levels	11.3 (0.43)	18.4 (0.98)	8.6 (0.44)	4.8 (0.14)	9.7 (0.40)	15.9 (0.81)	7.2 (0.41)	4.2 (0.13)	10.7 (0.41)	18.1 (0.84)	7.8 (0.42)	4.6 (0.13)
Less than high school completion	14.5 (0.76)	21.7 (1.40)	9.6 (0.82)	6.2 (0.26)	13.1 (0.73)	18.4 (1.14)	9.3 (0.82)	5.5 (0.24)	14.5 (0.77)	21.1 (1.21)	9.5 (0.84)	6.0 (0.25)
High school completion, no college	10.3 (0.71)	16.4 (1.79)	8.4 (0.52)	4.5 (0.25)	9.2 (0.67)	13.9 (1.43)	7.7 (0.71)	4.1 (0.23)	10.2 (0.69)	17.3 (1.57)	8.0 (0.71)	4.4 (0.23)
Some college, no degree	8.6 (0.82)	10.0 (1.94)	8.2 (0.91)	4.1 (0.34)	6.2 (0.70)	10.3 (1.81)	5.2 (0.71)	3.9 (0.32)	6.9 (0.72)	8.8 (1.55)	6.5 (0.79)	4.4 (0.34)
Associate's degree	7.9 (1.86)	†	7.5 (1.87)	4.0 (0.50)	4.5 (1.46)	†	4.5 (1.49)	2.9 (0.41)	5.7 (1.52)	†	5.7 (1.54)	3.5 (0.43)
Bachelor's or higher degree	3.5 (1.42)	†	3.6 (1.46)	2.9 (0.28)	3.7 (1.33)	†	4.1 (1.41)	2.2 (0.24)	6.5 (1.63)	†	5.3 (1.50)	2.3 (0.24)
Asian, all education levels	7.9 (0.81)	12.6 (2.08)	6.5 (0.85)	3.5 (0.19)	7.4 (0.81)	13.7 (2.21)	5.6 (0.81)	2.6 (0.16)	7.0 (0.78)	11.9 (2.08)	5.6 (0.79)	2.8 (0.16)
Less than high school completion	12.9 (2.62)	14.7 (3.15)	5.4 (3.71)	5.5 (0.84)	13.5 (2.85)	‡	‡	3.8 (0.71)	16.9 (3.12)	‡	4.1 (1.63)	3.0 (0.65)
High school completion, no college	7.6 (1.59)	11.7 (4.16)	6.6 (1.68)	4.6 (0.52)	8.8 (1.90)	‡	5.4 (1.81)	3.1 (0.42)	5.7 (1.66)	‡	5.0 (1.20)	3.2 (0.41)
Some college, no degree	6.8 (1.28)	8.3 (3.48)	6.4 (1.37)	3.6 (0.61)	5.9 (1.20)	‡	5.4 (1.26)	3.8 (0.63)	5.6 (1.14)	‡	‡	3.6 (0.58)
Associate's degree	‡	†	6.5 (3.07)	2.7 (0.64)	‡	†	6.7 (3.53)	2.3 (0.56)	‡	†	‡	4.0 (0.74)
Bachelor's or higher degree	‡	†	6.7 (1.74)	3.0 (0.23)	‡	†	5.1 (1.43)	2.1 (0.19)	6.7 (1.54)	†	6.1 (1.49)	2.3 (0.20)

†Not applicable.
‡Reporting standards not met.
[1]Excludes persons enrolled in school.

NOTE: The unemployment rate is the percentage of individuals in the labor force who are not working and who made specific efforts to find employment sometime during the prior 4 weeks. The labor force includes both employed and unemployed persons. Race categories exclude persons of Hispanic ethnicity. Standard errors appear in parentheses.

SOURCE: U.S. Department of Labor, Bureau of Labor Statistics, Office of Employment and Unemployment Statistics, unpublished 2005, 2006, and 2007 annual average data from the Current Population Survey (CPS). (This table was prepared August 2008.)

Table 383. Occupation of employed persons 25 years old and over, by educational attainment and sex: 2007

Occupation and sex	Total employed (in thousands)	Percentage distribution, by highest level of educational attainment							
			High school			College			
		Total	Less than 1 year of high school	1–4 years of high school, no completion	High school completion	Some college, no degree	Associate's degree	Bachelor's degree	Master's or higher degree
1	2	3	4	5	6	7	8	9	10
All persons	**126,172** (229.8)	**100.0**	**3.4** (0.06)	**5.7** (0.08)	**29.2** (0.15)	**17.5** (0.12)	**9.9** (0.10)	**22.2** (0.14)	**12.0** (0.11)
Management, professional, and related	48,666 (218.6)	100.0	0.4 (0.03)	1.1 (0.05)	11.7 (0.17)	12.6 (0.17)	10.3 (0.16)	36.8 (0.25)	27.1 (0.23)
Management, business, and financial operations	20,692 (156.6)	100.0	0.7 (0.07)	1.8 (0.11)	17.1 (0.30)	16.3 (0.30)	8.8 (0.23)	37.6 (0.39)	17.7 (0.31)
Professional and related	27,974 (178.0)	100.0	0.2 (0.03)	0.5 (0.05)	7.7 (0.18)	9.9 (0.21)	11.4 (0.22)	36.1 (0.33)	34.2 (0.33)
Education, training, and library	7,739 (99.5)	100.0	0.2 (0.06)	0.4 (0.08)	7.2 (0.34)	7.4 (0.34)	5.0 (0.29)	36.7 (0.63)	43.1 (0.65)
Preschool and kindergarten teachers	573 (27.6)	100.0	0.2 (0.20)	1.2 (0.53)	14.4 (1.69)	15.4 (1.74)	11.7 (1.55)	41.0 (2.38)	16.1 (1.78)
Elementary and middle school teachers	2,773 (60.4)	100.0	0.1 (0.07)	0.2 (0.09)	2.8 (0.37)	2.3 (0.33)	2.3 (0.33)	47.9 (1.10)	44.3 (1.09)
Secondary school teachers	1,096 (38.2)	100.0	— (†)	— (†)	1.1 (0.36)	1.7 (0.46)	0.9 (0.33)	43.7 (1.73)	52.6 (1.74)
Special education teachers	347 (21.5)	100.0	— (†)	0.3 (0.33)	1.7 (0.81)	2.9 (1.04)	3.2 (1.09)	40.8 (3.05)	51.1 (3.10)
Postsecondary teachers	1,163 (39.3)	100.0	# (†)	0.1 (0.10)	1.1 (0.36)	2.4 (0.52)	2.0 (0.47)	15.0 (1.21)	79.4 (1.37)
Other education, training, and library workers	1,788 (48.6)	100.0	0.6 (0.20)	0.9 (0.26)	20.6 (1.10)	20.2 (1.10)	11.6 (0.88)	27.1 (1.21)	19.0 (1.07)
Service occupations	18,353 (148.6)	100.0	7.6 (0.23)	10.8 (0.26)	39.7 (0.42)	19.1 (0.34)	9.8 (0.25)	11.0 (0.27)	2.0 (0.12)
Sales and office occupations	29,704 (182.4)	100.0	1.2 (0.07)	3.8 (0.13)	34.3 (0.32)	24.9 (0.29)	11.1 (0.21)	20.7 (0.27)	4.0 (0.13)
Natural resources, construction, and maintenance	13,544 (129.5)	100.0	9.3 (0.29)	12.1 (0.32)	43.7 (0.49)	17.5 (0.38)	9.8 (0.30)	6.5 (0.25)	1.1 (0.10)
Production, transportation, and material moving	15,905 (139.3)	100.0	6.9 (0.23)	12.0 (0.30)	48.9 (0.46)	16.8 (0.34)	7.1 (0.23)	7.0 (0.23)	1.2 (0.10)
Male	**67,963** (152.8)	**100.0**	**4.3** (0.09)	**6.6** (0.34)	**30.1** (0.20)	**16.7** (0.16)	**8.6** (0.12)	**21.6** (0.18)	**12.0** (0.14)
Management, professional, and related	24,234 (152.1)	100.0	0.6 (0.06)	1.4 (0.27)	11.7 (0.23)	12.3 (0.24)	7.9 (0.20)	37.1 (0.35)	29.1 (0.33)
Management, business, and financial operations	11,913 (115.9)	100.0	1.0 (0.10)	2.2 (0.48)	17.3 (0.39)	15.2 (0.37)	7.4 (0.27)	38.3 (0.51)	18.6 (0.41)
Professional and related	12,321 (117.6)	100.0	0.2 (0.05)	0.6 (0.24)	6.3 (0.25)	9.5 (0.30)	8.3 (0.28)	35.9 (0.49)	39.2 (0.50)
Education, training, and library	2,080 (51.3)	100.0	0.2 (0.11)	0.4 (0.49)	2.8 (0.41)	4.6 (0.52)	3.0 (0.42)	33.3 (1.18)	55.8 (1.24)
Service occupations	7,786 (96.1)	100.0	8.9 (0.37)	9.8 (1.21)	35.7 (0.62)	20.2 (0.52)	9.6 (0.38)	13.4 (0.44)	2.5 (0.20)
Sales and office occupations	10,788 (111.0)	100.0	1.5 (0.14)	3.8 (0.66)	29.2 (0.50)	22.7 (0.46)	9.7 (0.32)	27.3 (0.49)	5.8 (0.26)
Natural resources, construction, and maintenance	12,986 (120.2)	100.0	9.2 (0.29)	12.2 (1.03)	44.1 (0.50)	17.3 (0.38)	9.8 (0.30)	6.3 (0.24)	1.0 (0.10)
Production, transportation, and material moving	12,168 (116.9)	100.0	6.0 (0.25)	11.8 (1.05)	48.8 (0.52)	17.4 (0.39)	7.4 (0.27)	7.3 (0.27)	1.3 (0.12)
Female	**58,209** (160.3)	**100.0**	**2.4** (0.07)	**4.6** (0.10)	**28.2** (0.21)	**18.4** (0.18)	**11.5** (0.15)	**23.0** (0.19)	**12.0** (0.15)
Management, professional, and related	24,432 (147.3)	100.0	0.3 (0.04)	0.8 (0.06)	11.7 (0.23)	12.9 (0.24)	12.7 (0.23)	36.4 (0.34)	25.2 (0.31)
Management, business, and financial operations	8,779 (98.1)	100.0	0.4 (0.07)	1.3 (0.13)	16.9 (0.44)	17.6 (0.45)	10.7 (0.36)	36.7 (0.57)	16.4 (0.43)
Professional and related	15,653 (125.4)	100.0	0.2 (0.04)	0.5 (0.06)	8.8 (0.25)	10.2 (0.27)	13.7 (0.30)	36.3 (0.42)	30.2 (0.40)
Education, training, and library	5,659 (80.2)	100.0	0.2 (0.06)	0.4 (0.09)	8.9 (0.42)	8.4 (0.41)	5.7 (0.34)	38.0 (0.71)	38.4 (0.71)
Service occupations	10,567 (106.4)	100.0	6.7 (0.27)	11.5 (0.34)	42.6 (0.53)	18.3 (0.41)	10.0 (0.32)	9.2 (0.31)	1.6 (0.14)
Sales and office occupations	18,916 (134.9)	100.0	1.0 (0.08)	3.9 (0.15)	37.1 (0.39)	26.1 (0.35)	11.8 (0.26)	17.0 (0.30)	3.1 (0.14)
Natural resources, construction, and maintenance	558 (25.9)	100.0	10.2 (1.41)	9.3 (1.36)	35.0 (2.22)	22.3 (1.94)	10.2 (1.41)	10.6 (1.43)	2.3 (0.70)
Production, transportation, and material moving	3,736 (65.9)	100.0	9.8 (0.54)	12.8 (0.60)	49.1 (0.90)	15.0 (0.64)	6.1 (0.43)	6.0 (0.43)	1.1 (0.19)

—Not available.
†Not applicable.
#Rounds to zero.

NOTE: Detail may not sum to totals because of rounding. Standard errors appear in parentheses.
SOURCE: U.S. Department of Labor, Bureau of Labor Statistics, Office of Employment and Unemployment Statistics, unpublished 2007 annual average data from the Current Population Survey (CPS). (This table was prepared August 2008.)

Table 384. Median annual income of year-round, full-time workers 25 years old and over, by highest level of educational attainment and sex: 1990 through 2007

(Current dollars; standard errors in parentheses)

Sex and year	Total	Elementary/secondary — Less than 9th grade	Some high school, no completion[1]	High school completion (includes equivalency)[2]	Some college, no degree[3]	Associate's degree[4]	College — Total	Bachelor's degree[6]	Master's degree[4]	Professional degree[4]	Doctor's degree[4]
	2	3	4	5	6	7	8	9	10	11	12
Males											
1990	$30,730 (—)	$17,390 (—)	$20,900 (—)	$26,650 (—)	$31,730 (—)	— (†)	$42,670 (—)	$39,240 (—)	— (†)	— (†)	— (†)
1991	31,610 (—)	17,620 (—)	21,400 (—)	26,780 (175)	31,660 (—)	$33,820 (—)	45,140 (—)	40,910 (—)	$49,730 (—)	$74,000 (—)	$57,190 (—)
1992	32,060 (120)	17,290 (—)	21,270 (—)	27,280 (204)	32,100 (—)	33,430 (—)	45,800 (—)	41,360 (304)	49,970 (304)	76,220 (—)	57,420 (—)
1993	32,360 (124)	16,860 (453)	21,750 (—)	27,370 (322)	32,080 (300)	33,690 (430)	47,740 (707)	42,760 (536)	51,870 (536)	80,550 (—)	63,150 (—)
1994	33,440 (246)	17,530 (545)	22,050 (319)	28,040 (358)	32,280 (517)	35,790 (535)	49,230 (312)	43,660 (633)	53,500 (854)	75,010 (3,040)	61,920 (1,619)
1995	34,550 (275)	18,350 (594)	22,190 (342)	29,510 (184)	33,880 (456)	35,200 (435)	50,480 (303)	45,270 (510)	55,220 (973)	79,670 (2,582)	65,340 (2,188)
1996	35,620 (150)	17,960 (629)	22,720 (414)	30,710 (171)	34,850 (293)	37,130 (774)	51,440 (755)	45,850 (458)	60,510 (945)	85,960 (3,317)	71,230 (3,362)
1997	36,680 (149)	19,290 (600)	24,730 (466)	31,220 (169)	35,950 (291)	38,020 (539)	53,450 (421)	48,620 (851)	61,690 (771)	85,010 (4,253)	76,230 (3,611)
1998	37,910 (291)	19,380 (444)	23,960 (547)	31,480 (388)	36,930 (581)	40,270 (459)	56,520 (439)	51,410 (349)	62,240 (847)	94,740 (12,105)	75,080 (2,507)
1999	40,330 (144)	20,430 (376)	25,040 (535)	33,180 (457)	39,220 (312)	41,640 (460)	60,200 (303)	52,990 (722)	66,240 (690)	100,000 (37,836)	81,690 (3,953)
2000	41,060 (156)	20,790 (235)	25,100 (436)	34,300 (299)	40,340 (214)	41,950 (561)	61,870 (279)	56,330 (573)	68,320 (1,506)	99,410 (20,832)	80,250 (2,446)
2001	41,620 (104)	21,360 (213)	26,210 (251)	34,720 (311)	41,050 (195)	42,780 (673)	62,220 (201)	55,930 (335)	70,900 (687)	100,000 (—)	86,970 (3,013)
2002	41,150 (100)	20,920 (227)	25,900 (207)	33,210 (168)	40,850 (182)	42,860 (719)	61,700 (187)	56,080 (365)	67,280 (1,294)	100,000 (—)	83,310 (2,076)
2003	41,940 (90)	21,220 (191)	26,470 (280)	35,410 (148)	41,350 (175)	42,870 (931)	62,080 (798)	56,500 (393)	70,640 (562)	100,000 (—)	87,130 (2,528)
2004	42,090 (89)	21,660 (220)	26,280 (234)	35,730 (141)	41,900 (323)	44,400 (367)	62,800 (356)	57,220 (653)	71,530 (490)	100,000 (—)	82,400 (2,423)
2005	43,320 (367)	22,330 (398)	27,190 (237)	36,300 (164)	42,420 (812)	47,180 (390)	66,170 (346)	60,020 (235)	75,030 (1,229)	100,000 (—)	85,860 (3,061)
2006	45,760 (134)	22,710 (544)	27,650 (573)	37,030 (406)	43,830 (585)	47,070 (801)	66,930 (241)	60,910 (236)	75,430 (859)	100,000 (—)	100,000 (—)
2007	47,000 (130)	23,380 (461)	29,320 (590)	37,860 (—)	44,900 (585)	49,040 (801)	70,400 (241)	62,090 (236)	76,280 (416)	100,000 (—)	92,090 (1,894)
Females											
1990	21,370 (—)	12,250 (—)	14,430 (—)	18,320 (—)	22,230 (—)	— (†)	30,380 (—)	28,020 (—)	— (†)	— (†)	— (†)
1991	22,040 (—)	12,070 (—)	14,460 (—)	18,840 (—)	22,140 (—)	25,000 (—)	31,310 (—)	29,080 (—)	34,950 (—)	46,740 (—)	43,300 (—)
1992	23,140 (159)	12,960 (—)	14,560 (—)	19,430 (176)	23,160 (—)	25,620 (—)	32,300 (—)	30,330 (294)	36,040 (—)	46,260 (—)	45,790 (—)
1993	23,630 (166)	12,420 (427)	15,390 (—)	19,960 (173)	23,060 (—)	25,880 (295)	34,310 (280)	31,200 (310)	38,610 (606)	50,210 (2,154)	47,250 (—)
1994	24,400 (165)	12,430 (490)	15,130 (328)	20,370 (158)	23,510 (327)	25,940 (428)	35,380 (313)	31,740 (314)	39,460 (556)	50,620 (2,532)	51,120 (2,888)
1995	24,880 (160)	13,580 (559)	15,830 (293)	20,460 (162)	24,000 (274)	27,310 (526)	35,260 (296)	32,050 (273)	40,260 (564)	50,000 (3,635)	48,140 (2,373)
1996	25,810 (131)	14,410 (492)	16,950 (333)	21,180 (143)	25,170 (267)	28,080 (660)	36,460 (481)	33,530 (437)	41,900 (837)	57,620 (4,737)	56,270 (3,300)
1997	26,970 (134)	14,160 (429)	16,700 (335)	22,070 (148)	26,340 (291)	28,810 (513)	38,040 (408)	35,380 (295)	44,950 (760)	61,050 (1,705)	53,040 (3,626)
1998	27,960 (199)	14,470 (492)	16,480 (322)	22,780 (254)	27,420 (271)	29,920 (318)	39,790 (275)	36,560 (305)	45,280 (862)	57,570 (4,479)	57,800 (1,881)
1999	28,840 (216)	15,100 (492)	17,020 (298)	23,060 (279)	27,760 (369)	30,920 (307)	41,750 (439)	37,990 (614)	48,100 (735)	59,900 (3,552)	60,080 (3,130)
2000	30,330 (138)	15,800 (327)	17,920 (434)	24,970 (236)	28,700 (364)	31,070 (231)	42,710 (367)	40,420 (284)	50,140 (328)	58,960 (3,976)	57,080 (2,999)
2001	31,360 (91)	16,690 (255)	19,160 (359)	25,300 (132)	30,420 (186)	32,150 (211)	44,780 (568)	40,990 (231)	50,670 (595)	61,750 (2,421)	62,120 (2,228)
2002	31,010 (83)	16,510 (297)	19,310 (360)	25,180 (121)	29,400 (299)	31,630 (241)	43,250 (291)	40,850 (173)	48,880 (454)	57,020 (3,469)	65,720 (2,268)
2003	31,570 (85)	16,910 (256)	18,940 (327)	26,070 (118)	30,140 (176)	32,250 (489)	45,120 (229)	41,330 (204)	50,160 (263)	66,490 (2,436)	67,210 (2,462)
2004	31,990 (80)	17,020 (241)	19,160 (319)	26,030 (116)	30,820 (135)	33,480 (497)	45,910 (232)	41,680 (172)	51,320 (283)	75,040 (2,436)	66,880 (2,450)
2005	33,080 (242)	16,140 (250)	20,130 (274)	26,290 (134)	31,400 (165)	33,940 (376)	46,950 (441)	42,170 (179)	51,410 (561)	80,460 (2,774)	66,850 (2,490)
2006	35,100 (113)	18,130 (408)	20,130 (270)	26,740 (136)	31,950 (165)	35,160 (283)	49,570 (441)	45,410 (259)	52,440 (561)	76,240 (2,488)	70,520 (1,779)
2007	36,090 (105)	18,260 (461)	20,400 (292)	27,240 (133)	32,840 (415)	36,330 (283)	50,400 (158)	45,770 (262)	55,430 (412)	71,100 (910)	68,990 (2,155)

See notes at end of table.

Table 384. Median annual income of year-round, full-time workers 25 years old and over, by highest level of educational attainment and sex: 1990 through 2007—Continued

[In constant 2007 dollars[7]. Standard errors appear in parentheses]

Sex and year	Total	Elementary/secondary — Less than 9th grade	Elementary/secondary — Some high school, no completion[1]	Elementary/secondary — High school completion (includes equivalency)[2]	College — Some college, no degree[3]	College — Associate's degree[4]	College — Bachelor's or higher degree[5] — Total	College — Bachelor's degree[6]	College — Master's degree[4]	College — Professional degree[4]	College — Doctor's degree[4]
1	2	3	4	5	6	7	8	9	10	11	12
Males											
1990	$48,750 (—)	$27,590 (—)	$33,160 (—)	$42,280 (—)	$50,340 (—)	— (†)	$67,690 (—)	$62,250 (—)	— (†)	— (†)	— (†)
1991	48,130 (—)	26,830 (—)	32,580 (—)	40,770 (259)	46,200 (—)	$51,480 (—)	68,720 (—)	62,270 (449)	$75,710 (—)	$112,650 (—)	$87,060 (—)
1992	47,380 (177)	25,560 (—)	31,440 (—)	40,320 (293)	47,440 (420)	49,410 (—)	67,690 (—)	61,120 (769)	73,850 (—)	112,640 (—)	84,860 (—)
1993	46,430 (178)	24,200 (634)	31,210 (446)	39,270 (451)	46,030 (703)	48,340 (602)	68,500 (989)	61,350 (886)	74,420 (—)	115,580 (—)	90,610 (—)
1994	46,780 (344)	24,530 (741)	30,350 (465)	39,230 (487)	45,160 (603)	50,080 (728)	68,870 (424)	61,090 (694)	74,850 (1,195)	104,940 (4,253)	86,630 (2,265)
1995	47,010 (374)	24,970 (785)	30,180 (547)	40,150 (243)	46,100 (377)	47,890 (575)	68,680 (400)	61,590 (605)	75,120 (1,324)	108,390 (3,513)	88,890 (2,977)
1996	47,070 (198)	23,740 (813)	30,020 (602)	40,580 (221)	46,050 (370)	49,070 (1,000)	67,970 (975)	60,590 (1,099)	79,960 (1,249)	113,600 (4,383)	94,130 (4,443)
1997	47,380 (192)	24,920 (763)	31,940 (696)	40,330 (215)	46,440 (723)	49,120 (686)	69,050 (536)	62,800 (444)	79,690 (996)	109,820 (5,494)	98,480 (4,665)
1998	48,220 (370)	24,650 (553)	30,480 (666)	40,040 (483)	46,980 (376)	51,230 (571)	71,900 (546)	65,390 (899)	79,180 (1,077)	120,510 (15,398)	95,500 (3,189)
1999	50,200 (179)	25,420 (453)	31,160 (525)	41,300 (550)	48,810 (251)	51,820 (554)	74,920 (365)	65,940 (690)	82,440 (859)	124,460 (47,089)	101,660 (4,920)
2000	49,440 (188)	25,030 (275)	30,220 (294)	41,300 (350)	48,570 (225)	50,510 (657)	74,490 (327)	67,830 (392)	82,270 (1,813)	119,700 (25,083)	96,630 (2,945)
2001	48,720 (122)	25,010 (245)	30,680 (239)	40,650 (358)	48,050 (205)	50,080 (776)	72,850 (232)	65,480 (444)	83,010 (804)	117,080 (—)	101,820 (3,528)
2002	47,430 (115)	24,110 (256)	29,850 (316)	38,270 (189)	47,080 (192)	49,390 (810)	71,110 (211)	64,630 (411)	77,540 (1,491)	115,250 (—)	96,010 (2,393)
2003	47,260 (101)	23,910 (210)	29,830 (257)	39,900 (162)	46,590 (343)	48,310 (1,022)	69,950 (876)	63,670 (431)	79,600 (633)	112,690 (—)	98,180 (2,849)
2004	46,190 (98)	23,770 (234)	28,840 (252)	39,210 (150)	45,990 (835)	48,740 (390)	68,930 (—)	62,810 (693)	78,510 (538)	109,760 (—)	90,450 (2,660)
2005	45,990 (390)	23,710 (409)	28,870 (589)	38,540 (169)	45,030 (588)	50,090 (401)	70,250 (378)	63,720 (242)	79,650 (1,305)	106,170 (—)	91,160 (3,250)
2006	47,060 (138)	23,350 (544)	28,440 (590)	38,090 (406)	45,080 (—)	48,410 (801)	68,840 (356)	62,640 (236)	77,580 (883)	102,850 (—)	102,850 (—)
2007	47,000 (130)	23,380 (461)	29,320 (—)	37,860 (—)	44,900 (—)	49,040 (—)	70,400 (241)	62,090 (—)	76,280 (416)	100,000 (—)	92,090 (1,894)
Females											
1990	$33,900 (—)	$19,430 (—)	$22,890 (—)	$29,060 (—)	$35,260 (—)	— (†)	$48,190 (—)	$44,450 (—)	— (†)	— (†)	— (†)
1991	33,560 (—)	18,370 (—)	22,010 (—)	28,670 (—)	33,710 (—)	$38,060 (—)	47,660 (—)	44,270 (434)	$53,200 (—)	$71,160 (—)	$65,920 (—)
1992	34,200 (235)	19,150 (—)	21,520 (—)	28,710 (260)	34,220 (—)	37,870 (—)	47,740 (—)	44,320 (445)	53,260 (—)	68,360 (—)	67,670 (—)
1993	33,910 (238)	17,810 (597)	22,030 (459)	28,640 (248)	33,080 (457)	37,140 (—)	49,230 (392)	44,760 (439)	55,400 (848)	72,050 (3,014)	67,800 (4,041)
1994	34,140 (231)	17,390 (667)	21,170 (399)	28,500 (221)	32,900 (373)	36,290 (413)	49,500 (426)	44,410 (371)	55,200 (756)	70,810 (3,445)	71,520 (3,229)
1995	33,840 (218)	18,470 (739)	21,530 (440)	27,840 (220)	32,650 (353)	37,160 (582)	47,370 (391)	43,610 (577)	54,780 (745)	68,030 (4,804)	65,500 (4,361)
1996	34,110 (173)	19,050 (636)	22,400 (433)	27,980 (189)	33,260 (376)	37,110 (695)	48,180 (621)	44,300 (381)	55,370 (1,081)	76,150 (6,120)	74,360 (4,684)
1997	34,850 (173)	18,290 (546)	21,570 (410)	28,510 (191)	34,020 (345)	37,220 (853)	49,140 (519)	45,700 (388)	58,070 (967)	78,870 (2,169)	68,520 (2,393)
1998	35,560 (253)	18,400 (612)	20,970 (371)	28,980 (323)	34,880 (459)	38,060 (853)	50,610 (519)	46,500 (764)	57,600 (1,073)	73,220 (5,574)	73,520 (3,895)
1999	35,900 (269)	18,790 (394)	21,180 (523)	28,700 (347)	34,550 (438)	38,480 (396)	51,960 (342)	47,280 (342)	59,860 (885)	74,550 (4,277)	74,770 (3,611)
2000	36,520 (166)	19,020 (299)	21,580 (420)	30,070 (284)	34,550 (370)	37,410 (370)	51,420 (529)	48,660 (270)	60,370 (384)	70,990 (4,655)	68,730 (2,608)
2001	36,710 (107)	19,540 (342)	22,430 (415)	29,620 (155)	35,610 (218)	37,640 (270)	52,420 (430)	47,990 (199)	59,320 (686)	72,290 (2,790)	72,730 (2,614)
2002	35,740 (96)	19,030 (288)	22,250 (368)	29,020 (139)	33,880 (345)	36,450 (243)	49,840 (655)	47,080 (230)	56,350 (512)	65,720 (3,909)	75,740 (2,774)
2003	35,570 (96)	19,050 (265)	21,340 (350)	29,380 (133)	33,570 (198)	36,340 (272)	50,840 (328)	46,570 (189)	56,530 (289)	74,930 (2,674)	75,740 (2,689)
2004	35,110 (88)	18,680 (265)	21,030 (291)	28,570 (127)	33,820 (148)	36,750 (537)	50,390 (251)	45,750 (190)	56,330 (300)	82,360 (2,945)	75,600 (2,644)
2005	35,110 (257)	17,140 (291)	21,370 (278)	27,910 (142)	33,340 (175)	36,030 (528)	49,840 (246)	44,770 (266)	54,580 (577)	85,420 (2,559)	70,970 (1,830)
2006	36,090 (116)	18,650 (278)	20,700 (292)	27,500 (142)	32,860 (170)	36,160 (387)	53,980 (454)	46,700 (262)	53,930 (412)	78,410 (910)	72,530 (2,155)
2007	36,090 (105)	18,260 (292)	20,400 (—)	27,240 (133)	32,840 (415)	36,330 (283)	52,400 (158)	45,770 (—)	55,430 (—)	71,100 (—)	68,990 (—)

See notes at end of table.

Table 384. Median annual income of year-round, full-time workers 25 years old and over, by highest level of educational attainment and sex: 1990 through 2007—Continued

Number of persons with income (in thousands)

Sex and year		Elementary/secondary					College					
	Total	Less than 9th grade	Some high school, no completion[1]	High school completion (includes equivalency)[2]	Some college, no degree[3]	Associate's degree[4]	Bachelor's or higher degree[5]					
							Total	Bachelor's degree[6]	Master's degree[4]	Professional degree[4]	Doctor's degree[4]
1	2	3	4	5	6	7	8	9	10	11	12
Males											
1990	44,406 (268.6)	2,250 (73.9)	3,315 (89.3)	16,394 (188.0)	9,113 (144.6)	— (†)	13,334 (171.8)	7,569 (132.6)	— (†)	— (†)	— (†)
1991	44,199 (268.3)	1,807 (66.3)	3,083 (86.2)	15,025 (181.1)	8,034 (136.4)	2,899 (83.6)	13,350 (171.9)	8,456 (139.7)	3,073 (86.1)	1,147 (53.0)	674 (40.7)
1992	44,752 (269.1)	1,815 (66.5)	3,009 (85.2)	14,722 (179.5)	8,067 (136.6)	3,203 (87.8)	13,937 (175.2)	8,719 (141.7)	3,178 (87.5)	1,295 (56.3)	745 (42.8)
1993	45,873 (270.6)	1,790 (66.0)	3,083 (86.2)	14,604 (178.9)	8,493 (140.0)	3,557 (92.4)	14,346 (177.5)	9,178 (145.1)	3,131 (86.8)	1,231 (54.9)	808 (44.5)
1994	47,566 (303.0)	1,895 (69.2)	3,057 (87.6)	15,109 (188.5)	8,783 (146.2)	3,735 (96.6)	14,987 (187.8)	9,636 (152.8)	3,225 (89.9)	1,258 (56.4)	858 (46.9)
1995	48,500 (306.1)	1,946 (72.8)	3,335 (94.9)	15,331 (195.6)	8,908 (152.3)	3,926 (102.8)	15,054 (194.0)	9,597 (157.8)	3,395 (95.7)	1,208 (57.5)	853 (48.4)
1996	49,764 (301.1)	2,041 (69.2)	3,441 (89.6)	15,840 (186.5)	9,173 (144.2)	3,931 (95.6)	15,339 (183.7)	9,898 (149.6)	3,272 (87.4)	1,277 (54.8)	893 (45.9)
1997	50,807 (299.0)	1,914 (67.0)	3,548 (90.9)	16,225 (187.8)	9,170 (143.9)	4,086 (97.4)	15,864 (185.9)	10,349 (152.4)	3,228 (86.7)	1,321 (55.8)	966 (47.7)
1998	52,381 (306.4)	1,870 (66.3)	3,613 (91.7)	16,442 (189.7)	9,375 (145.7)	4,347 (100.4)	16,733 (191.2)	11,058 (157.6)	3,414 (89.2)	1,264 (54.6)	998 (48.5)
1999	53,062 (307.8)	1,993 (68.4)	3,295 (87.7)	16,589 (190.5)	9,684 (148.0)	4,359 (100.6)	17,142 (193.3)	11,142 (158.2)	3,725 (93.1)	1,267 (54.6)	1,008 (48.8)
2000	54,065 (309.7)	1,968 (68.0)	3,354 (88.4)	16,834 (191.7)	9,792 (148.8)	4,729 (104.7)	17,387 (194.6)	11,395 (159.9)	3,680 (92.6)	1,274 (54.8)	1,038 (49.5)
2001	54,013 (224.8)	2,207 (51.4)	3,503 (64.5)	16,314 (135.4)	9,494 (104.9)	4,714 (74.7)	17,780 (140.9)	11,479 (114.8)	3,961 (88.5)	1,298 (39.5)	1,041 (35.4)
2002	54,108 (225.0)	2,154 (50.7)	3,680 (66.1)	16,005 (134.2)	9,603 (105.5)	4,399 (72.2)	18,267 (142.7)	11,829 (116.5)	4,065 (69.4)	1,308 (39.6)	1,065 (35.8)
2003	54,253 (225.2)	2,209 (51.4)	3,369 (63.3)	16,285 (135.3)	9,340 (104.1)	4,696 (74.5)	18,354 (143.0)	11,846 (116.6)	4,124 (69.9)	1,348 (40.2)	1,037 (35.3)
2004	55,469 (227.0)	2,427 (53.8)	3,468 (64.2)	17,067 (138.3)	9,257 (103.6)	4,913 (76.2)	18,338 (142.9)	11,701 (115.9)	4,243 (70.9)	1,305 (39.6)	1,088 (36.1)
2005	56,717 (228.7)	2,425 (53.8)	3,652 (65.9)	17,266 (139.0)	9,532 (105.1)	5,022 (77.0)	18,820 (144.7)	12,032 (117.4)	4,275 (71.2)	1,369 (40.5)	1,144 (37.1)
2006	58,109 (230.6)	2,361 (53.1)	3,872 (67.8)	17,369 (139.4)	9,493 (104.9)	5,110 (77.7)	19,903 (148.4)	12,764 (120.7)	4,542 (73.3)	1,425 (41.3)	1,172 (37.5)
2007	58,147 (230.7)	2,142 (50.6)	3,451 (64.0)	17,224 (138.9)	9,867 (106.8)	5,244 (78.7)	20,218 (149.5)	12,962 (121.6)	4,800 (75.3)	1,332 (40.0)	1,125 (36.7)
Females											
1990	28,636 (234.7)	847 (45.6)	1,861 (67.3)	11,810 (162.8)	6,462 (123.1)	— (†)	7,655 (133.3)	4,704 (105.8)	— (†)	— (†)	— (†)
1991	29,474 (237.1)	733 (42.4)	1,819 (66.5)	10,959 (157.4)	5,633 (115.3)	2,523 (78.1)	7,807 (134.6)	5,263 (111.6)	2,025 (70.1)	312 (27.7)	206 (22.5)
1992	30,346 (239.6)	734 (42.4)	1,659 (63.6)	11,039 (157.9)	5,904 (117.9)	2,655 (80.1)	8,355 (138.9)	5,604 (115.0)	2,192 (72.9)	334 (28.7)	225 (23.5)
1993	30,683 (240.5)	765 (43.3)	1,576 (62.0)	10,513 (154.4)	6,279 (121.4)	3,067 (86.0)	8,483 (139.9)	5,735 (116.3)	2,166 (72.5)	323 (28.2)	260 (25.3)
1994	31,379 (259.2)	696 (42.0)	1,675 (69.3)	10,785 (161.2)	6,256 (124.2)	3,210 (89.7)	8,756 (146.0)	5,901 (120.8)	2,174 (74.0)	398 (31.8)	283 (26.8)
1995	32,673 (268.2)	774 (46.1)	1,763 (69.3)	11,064 (168.6)	6,329 (125.5)	3,336 (94.9)	9,406 (156.3)	6,434 (130.5)	2,268 (78.5)	421 (34.0)	283 (27.9)
1996	33,549 (259.0)	750 (42.1)	1,751 (64.1)	11,363 (159.7)	6,582 (122.9)	3,468 (89.9)	9,636 (147.7)	6,689 (123.9)	2,213 (72.0)	413 (31.2)	322 (27.6)
1997	34,624 (260.1)	791 (43.2)	1,765 (64.4)	11,475 (160.0)	6,628 (123.2)	3,538 (90.7)	10,427 (153.0)	7,173 (128.0)	2,448 (75.7)	488 (34.0)	318 (27.4)
1998	35,628 (265.4)	814 (43.8)	1,878 (66.4)	11,613 (161.3)	7,070 (127.3)	3,527 (90.7)	10,725 (155.4)	7,288 (129.2)	2,639 (78.6)	468 (33.3)	329 (27.9)
1999	37,091 (269.7)	886 (45.7)	1,883 (66.5)	11,824 (162.7)	7,453 (130.6)	3,804 (94.1)	11,242 (158.9)	7,607 (131.9)	2,818 (81.2)	470 (33.3)	346 (28.6)
2000	37,762 (271.6)	930 (46.8)	1,950 (67.7)	11,789 (162.5)	7,391 (130.0)	4,118 (97.8)	11,584 (161.1)	7,899 (134.3)	2,823 (81.2)	509 (34.7)	353 (28.9)
2001	38,228 (197.0)	927 (33.4)	1,869 (47.3)	11,690 (115.8)	7,283 (92.3)	4,190 (70.5)	12,269 (118.5)	8,257 (98.1)	3,089 (60.6)	531 (25.3)	392 (21.7)
2002	38,510 (197.6)	858 (32.1)	1,841 (46.9)	11,687 (115.8)	7,354 (92.7)	4,285 (71.2)	12,484 (119.5)	8,229 (97.9)	3,281 (62.5)	572 (26.2)	402 (22.0)
2003	38,681 (197.9)	882 (32.6)	1,739 (45.6)	11,587 (115.3)	7,341 (92.6)	4,397 (72.2)	12,735 (120.6)	8,330 (98.5)	3,376 (63.4)	567 (26.1)	462 (23.6)
2004	39,072 (198.7)	917 (33.2)	1,797 (46.4)	11,392 (114.4)	7,330 (92.6)	4,505 (73.0)	13,131 (122.4)	8,664 (100.4)	3,451 (64.0)	564 (26.0)	452 (23.3)
2005	40,021 (200.6)	902 (32.9)	1,740 (45.6)	11,419 (114.5)	7,452 (93.3)	4,751 (74.9)	13,758 (125.1)	9,074 (102.6)	3,591 (65.3)	657 (28.1)	437 (22.9)
2006	41,311 (203.2)	934 (33.5)	1,802 (46.4)	11,652 (115.6)	7,613 (94.3)	4,760 (75.0)	14,549 (128.4)	9,645 (105.7)	3,746 (66.7)	662 (28.2)	497 (24.5)
2007	42,196 (204.9)	823 (31.5)	1,649 (44.4)	11,447 (114.7)	7,916 (96.1)	4,891 (76.0)	15,469 (132.1)	9,931 (107.2)	4,389 (72.1)	666 (28.3)	484 (24.1)

—Not available.
†Not applicable.
[1] Includes 1 to 3 years of high school for 1990.
[2] Includes 4 years of high school for 1990.
[3] Includes 1 to 3 years of college and associate's degrees for 1990.
[4] Not reported separately for 1990.
[5] Includes 4 or more years of college for 1990.

[6] Includes 4 years of college for 1990.
[7] Constant dollars based on the Consumer Price Index, prepared by the Bureau of Labor Statistics, U.S. Department of Labor. Standard errors appear in parentheses.
NOTE: Detail may not sum to totals because of rounding.
SOURCE: U.S. Department of Commerce, Census Bureau, Current Population Reports, Series P-60, Money Income of Households, Families, and Persons in the United States and Income, Poverty, and Valuation of Noncash Benefits, 1990 through 1994; Series P-60, Money Income in the United States, 1995 through 2002; and Detailed Income Tabulations from the CPS, 2003 through 2007. Retrieved September 3, 2008, from http://www.census.gov/hhes/www/income/dinctabs.html. (This table was prepared September 2008.)

Table 385. Distribution of earnings and median earnings of persons 25 years old and over, by highest level of educational attainment and sex: 2007

		Elementary/secondary				College		Bachelor's or higher degree				
Sex and earnings	Total	Less than 9th grade	Some high school (no completion)	High school completion (includes equivalency)	Some college, no degree	Associate's degree	Total	Bachelor's degree	Master's degree	Professional degree	Doctor's degree
1	2	3	4	5	6	7	8	9	10	11	12
Total males and females											
(in thousands)...........	196,305 (229.1)	10,824 (113.7)	15,516 (134.8)	61,183 (240.2)	33,812 (191.1)	17,182 (141.4)	57,787 (235.5)	37,559 (199.6)	14,765 (131.7)	2,991 (60.8)	2,472 (55.3)
With earnings.........	135,519 (278.3)	4,462 (74.0)	7,854 (97.5)	39,124 (203.0)	24,280 (165.5)	13,559 (126.6)	46,240 (216.9)	29,752 (180.9)	11,961 (119.3)	2,500 (55.6)	2,027 (50.1)
Distribution of total persons with earnings, by total annual earnings..........	100.0 (†)	100.0 (†)	100.0 (†)	100.0 (†)	100.0 (†)	100.0 (†)	100.0 (†)	100.0 (†)	100.0 (†)	100.0 (†)	100.0 (†)
$1 to $4,999 or loss........	4.9 (0.30)	7.3 (1.61)	8.5 (1.21)	5.8 (0.55)	5.3 (0.70)	4.0 (0.94)	3.5 (0.51)	3.7 (0.64)	3.5 (1.00)	1.9 (2.21)	1.4 (2.46)
$5,000 to $9,999........	5.0 (0.30)	11.1 (1.58)	11.3 (1.19)	5.9 (0.55)	5.2 (0.70)	4.1 (0.94)	2.7 (0.51)	2.9 (0.64)	2.4 (1.01)	1.5 (2.22)	1.6 (2.46)
$10,000 to $14,999........	6.8 (0.29)	18.4 (1.51)	14.2 (1.17)	8.4 (0.54)	6.7 (0.69)	6.0 (0.93)	3.3 (0.51)	3.8 (0.64)	2.4 (1.01)	2.2 (2.21)	2.2 (2.46)
$15,000 to $19,999........	7.4 (0.29)	18.5 (1.51)	13.5 (1.17)	9.8 (0.54)	7.6 (0.69)	6.5 (0.93)	3.5 (0.51)	4.0 (0.63)	2.9 (1.01)	1.7 (2.22)	2.0 (2.46)
$20,000 to $24,999........	8.6 (0.29)	14.4 (1.55)	12.7 (1.18)	11.9 (0.53)	9.1 (0.68)	8.3 (0.92)	4.3 (0.51)	5.1 (0.63)	3.0 (1.01)	2.2 (2.21)	3.1 (2.44)
$25,000 to $29,999........	7.8 (0.29)	9.0 (1.60)	10.2 (1.20)	10.3 (0.54)	9.0 (0.68)	8.4 (0.92)	4.4 (0.51)	5.5 (0.63)	2.8 (1.01)	1.7 (2.22)	1.9 (2.46)
$30,000 to $34,999........	8.5 (0.29)	7.7 (1.61)	7.7 (1.21)	10.1 (0.54)	10.2 (0.68)	9.7 (0.91)	5.9 (0.50)	6.8 (0.63)	4.9 (1.00)	2.7 (2.20)	3.6 (2.44)
$35,000 to $39,999........	7.0 (0.29)	4.1 (1.64)	5.1 (1.23)	7.5 (0.54)	8.4 (0.69)	8.3 (0.92)	5.9 (0.50)	6.9 (0.63)	4.9 (1.00)	2.0 (2.21)	2.2 (2.45)
$40,000 to $49,999........	12.0 (0.28)	4.1 (1.64)	6.9 (1.22)	11.9 (0.53)	12.6 (0.67)	14.2 (0.89)	12.6 (0.49)	13.5 (0.60)	12.7 (0.95)	7.2 (2.15)	6.6 (2.40)
$50,000 to $74,999........	17.6 (0.28)	4.1 (1.64)	7.2 (1.22)	12.9 (0.53)	16.6 (0.66)	20.4 (0.86)	24.3 (0.45)	23.5 (0.57)	27.2 (0.87)	19.4 (2.01)	24.7 (2.15)
$75,000 to $99,999........	6.8 (0.29)	0.5 (1.67)	1.5 (1.25)	3.2 (0.56)	5.0 (0.70)	6.6 (0.93)	12.3 (0.49)	11.0 (0.61)	14.8 (0.94)	12.0 (2.10)	16.8 (2.26)
$100,000 or more........	7.7 (0.29)	0.9 (1.67)	1.1 (1.25)	2.2 (0.56)	4.1 (0.70)	3.6 (0.94)	17.3 (0.47)	13.4 (0.60)	18.5 (0.92)	45.5 (1.65)	34.2 (2.01)
Median earnings[1]........	$35,510 (76)	$18,040 (317)	$20,690 (178)	$28,290 (222)	$32,260 (116)	$36,360 (205)	$51,700 (114)	$47,240 (196)	$56,710 (335)	$89,600 (2,311)	$75,640 (1,441)
Number of males											
(in thousands)........	94,470 (140.8)	5,446 (80.5)	7,853 (95.6)	29,491 (165.1)	15,810 (130.4)	7,436 (93.2)	28,433 (163.2)	18,042 (137.7)	6,886 (89.9)	1,877 (48.0)	1,628 (44.8)
With earnings........	72,216 (181.2)	3,013 (60.5)	4,872 (76.3)	21,701 (148.1)	12,414 (117.5)	5,294 (86.2)	23,921 (153.6)	15,226 (128.3)	5,747 (82.6)	1,602 (44.4)	1,347 (40.8)
Distribution of males with earnings, by total annual earnings........	100.0 (†)	100.0 (†)	100.0 (†)	100.0 (†)	100.0 (†)	100.0 (†)	100.0 (†)	100.0 (†)	100.0 (†)	100.0 (†)	100.0 (†)
$1 to $4,999 or loss........	3.2 (0.41)	4.4 (1.99)	5.7 (1.55)	3.8 (0.74)	3.7 (0.98)	2.5 (1.39)	1.9 (0.72)	2.0 (0.90)	2.3 (1.46)	1.2 (2.78)	1.2 (3.03)
$5,000 to $9,999........	3.4 (0.41)	8.4 (1.95)	8.8 (1.53)	3.9 (0.74)	3.5 (0.99)	2.7 (1.39)	1.5 (0.72)	1.5 (0.90)	1.5 (1.46)	1.4 (2.77)	1.3 (3.02)
$10,000 to $14,999........	5.0 (0.41)	16.7 (1.86)	10.7 (1.51)	5.8 (0.74)	4.4 (0.98)	3.2 (1.39)	2.4 (0.71)	2.6 (0.89)	2.1 (1.46)	2.2 (2.76)	2.2 (3.01)
$15,000 to $19,999........	5.8 (0.40)	17.7 (1.85)	11.2 (1.51)	7.3 (0.73)	5.6 (0.97)	3.8 (1.38)	2.6 (0.71)	2.8 (0.89)	2.5 (1.46)	1.4 (2.77)	1.5 (3.02)
$20,000 to $24,999........	7.3 (0.40)	15.5 (1.87)	13.2 (1.49)	9.7 (0.72)	7.7 (0.95)	5.7 (1.37)	3.1 (0.71)	3.6 (0.89)	2.5 (1.46)	1.9 (2.77)	2.5 (3.01)
$25,000 to $29,999........	6.9 (0.40)	10.0 (1.93)	11.4 (1.51)	9.4 (0.72)	7.0 (0.97)	6.6 (1.36)	3.5 (0.71)	4.2 (0.89)	2.5 (1.46)	1.1 (2.78)	1.9 (3.02)
$30,000 to $34,999........	8.0 (0.40)	9.9 (1.93)	9.1 (1.53)	10.3 (0.72)	9.7 (0.95)	8.3 (1.35)	4.4 (0.71)	5.1 (0.88)	3.5 (1.45)	2.4 (2.76)	3.0 (3.00)
$35,000 to $39,999........	6.8 (0.40)	5.3 (1.98)	6.8 (1.55)	8.4 (0.73)	8.2 (0.96)	8.5 (1.35)	4.5 (0.71)	5.4 (0.88)	3.5 (1.45)	1.2 (2.77)	1.8 (3.02)
$40,000 to $49,999........	12.4 (0.39)	4.9 (1.99)	9.3 (1.52)	14.8 (0.70)	13.7 (0.93)	15.6 (1.29)	10.1 (0.69)	11.7 (0.85)	8.6 (1.41)	4.6 (2.73)	4.6 (2.97)
$50,000 to $74,999........	20.7 (0.37)	5.2 (1.98)	9.9 (1.52)	18.4 (0.69)	22.3 (0.88)	26.4 (1.21)	24.6 (0.63)	25.8 (0.78)	24.4 (1.28)	16.5 (2.55)	21.7 (2.69)
$75,000 to $99,999........	9.0 (0.40)	0.7 (2.03)	2.2 (1.58)	4.9 (0.74)	7.8 (0.96)	10.6 (1.33)	15.4 (0.66)	14.8 (0.84)	17.6 (1.34)	11.0 (2.63)	17.0 (2.77)
$100,000 or more........	11.4 (0.39)	1.3 (2.02)	1.5 (1.59)	3.3 (0.75)	6.5 (0.97)	6.1 (1.37)	26.0 (0.62)	20.4 (0.81)	29.0 (1.24)	54.9 (1.87)	41.5 (2.33)
Median earnings[1]........	$41,540 (92)	$20,660 (232)	$25,070 (337)	$34,770 (350)	$40,090 (280)	$45,200 (473)	$63,270 (955)	$58,340 (935)	$70,640 (533)	$100,000 (—)	$87,160 (2,435)

See notes at end of table.

Table 385. Distribution of earnings and median earnings of persons 25 years old and over, by highest level of educational attainment and sex: 2007—Continued

Sex and earnings	Total	Elementary/secondary			College						
		Less than 9th grade	Some high school (no completion)	High school completion (includes equivalency)	Some college, no degree	Associate's degree	Total	Bachelor's or higher degree			
								Bachelor's degree	Master's degree	Professional degree	Doctor's degree
1	2	3	4	5	6	7	8	9	10	11	12
Number of females											
(in thousands)............	**101,835** (153.3)	**5,379** (80.2)	**7,663** (94.8)	**31,692** (171.9)	**18,002** (138.7)	**9,746** (105.9)	**29,354** (167.5)	**19,517** (143.4)	**7,879** (96.0)	**1,114** (37.1)	**844** (32.4)
With earnings............	63,303 (197.5)	1,449 (42.3)	2,982 (60.3)	17,423 (136.8)	11,866 (115.8)	7,265 (92.4)	22,318 (151.3)	14,526 (126.6)	6,214 (85.9)	899 (33.4)	680 (29.1)
Distribution of females with earnings, by total annual earnings............	100.0 (†)	100.0 (†)	100.0 (†)	100.0 (†)	100.0 (†)	100.0 (†)	100.0 (†)	100.0 (†)	100.0 (†)	100.0 (†)	100.0 (†)
$1 to $4,999 or loss......	6.9 (0.43)	13.2 (2.74)	13.1 (1.91)	8.2 (0.81)	7.0 (0.99)	5.3 (1.28)	5.1 (0.73)	5.5 (0.90)	4.6 (1.38)	3.1 (3.67)	2.2 (4.24)
$5,000 to $9,999......	6.8 (0.43)	16.8 (2.68)	15.4 (1.88)	8.5 (0.81)	7.1 (0.99)	5.3 (1.28)	4.0 (0.73)	4.5 (0.91)	3.2 (1.39)	1.7 (3.70)	2.2 (4.24)
$10,000 to $14,999......	8.8 (0.42)	21.9 (2.59)	19.8 (1.83)	11.7 (0.80)	9.1 (0.98)	8.4 (1.26)	4.1 (0.73)	5.0 (0.90)	2.8 (1.40)	2.1 (3.69)	2.4 (4.24)
$15,000 to $19,999......	9.3 (0.42)	20.2 (2.62)	17.3 (1.86)	13.0 (0.79)	9.7 (0.97)	8.8 (1.25)	4.5 (0.73)	5.2 (0.90)	3.3 (1.39)	2.2 (3.69)	2.9 (4.22)
$20,000 to $24,999......	10.0 (0.42)	11.9 (2.76)	11.8 (1.92)	14.7 (0.78)	10.6 (0.97)	10.5 (1.24)	5.6 (0.73)	6.7 (0.90)	3.5 (1.39)	2.9 (3.67)	4.1 (4.20)
$25,000 to $29,999......	8.8 (0.42)	6.7 (2.84)	8.2 (1.96)	11.4 (0.80)	11.1 (0.97)	10.0 (1.24)	5.5 (0.73)	6.8 (0.90)	3.1 (1.40)	2.6 (3.68)	1.9 (4.24)
$30,000 to $34,999......	9.0 (0.42)	3.2 (2.89)	5.4 (1.99)	9.9 (0.80)	10.8 (0.97)	10.9 (1.24)	7.6 (0.72)	8.7 (0.89)	6.1 (1.37)	3.6 (3.66)	4.6 (4.19)
$35,000 to $39,999......	7.1 (0.43)	1.4 (2.91)	2.3 (2.02)	6.4 (0.82)	8.7 (0.98)	8.1 (1.26)	7.5 (0.72)	8.5 (0.89)	6.2 (1.37)	3.2 (3.67)	2.9 (4.22)
$40,000 to $49,999......	11.5 (0.42)	2.3 (2.90)	3.0 (2.02)	8.2 (0.81)	11.5 (0.97)	12.9 (1.22)	15.3 (0.69)	15.3 (0.85)	16.5 (1.30)	12.0 (3.50)	10.6 (4.05)
$50,000 to $74,999......	14.0 (0.41)	1.9 (2.91)	2.7 (2.02)	6.1 (0.82)	10.6 (0.97)	15.3 (1.21)	23.9 (0.65)	21.0 (0.82)	29.7 (1.19)	24.5 (3.24)	31.0 (3.56)
$75,000 to $99,999......	4.3 (0.43)	# (†)	0.4 (2.04)	1.1 (0.84)	2.2 (1.01)	3.2 (1.29)	9.0 (0.71)	7.0 (0.89)	12.1 (1.33)	13.9 (3.46)	16.3 (3.92)
$100,000 or more......	3.6 (0.44)	0.3 (2.93)	0.5 (2.04)	0.9 (0.84)	1.6 (1.02)	1.5 (1.30)	8.1 (0.72)	6.0 (0.90)	8.7 (1.35)	28.6 (3.15)	19.6 (3.84)
Median earnings[1]......	$29,540 (188)	$14,470 (424)	$15,370 (225)	$22,360 (116)	$27,170 (170)	$30,550 (194)	$42,370 (155)	$39,150 (469)	$50,200 (262)	$66,610 (2,146)	$62,190 (1,847)

—Not available.
†Not applicable.
#Rounds to zero.
[1]Excludes persons without earnings.

NOTE: Detail may not sum to totals because of rounding. Standard errors appear in parentheses.
SOURCE: U.S. Department of Commerce, Census Bureau, Current Population Survey, March 2008. Retrieved September 15, 2008, from http://pubdb3.census.gov/macro/032008/perinc/new03_000.htm. (This table was prepared September 2008.)

Table 386. Literacy skills of adults, by type of literacy, proficiency levels, and selected characteristics: 1992 and 2003

Selected characteristic	Prose literacy[1] Average score 1992	Prose 2003	Prose % Below Basic 2003	Prose % Basic	Prose % Intermediate	Prose % Proficient	Document literacy[2] Average score 1992	Doc 2003	Doc % Below Basic 2003	Doc % Basic	Doc % Intermediate	Doc % Proficient	Quantitative literacy[3] Average score 1992	Quant 2003	Quant % Below Basic 2003	Quant % Basic	Quant % Intermediate	Quant % Proficient
(col)	2	3	4	5	6	7	8	9	10	11	12	13	14	15	16	17	18	19
Total	276 (1.1)	275 (1.3)	14 (0.6)	29 (0.6)	44 (0.7)	13 (0.5)	271 (1.1)	271 (1.2)	12 (0.5)	22 (0.5)	53 (0.7)	13 (0.6)	275 (1.1)	283 (1.2)	22 (0.6)	33 (0.5)	33 (0.5)	13 (0.5)
Sex																		
Male	276 (1.2)	272 (1.5)	15 (0.6)	29 (0.7)	43 (0.7)	13 (0.6)	274 (1.2)	269 (1.5)	14 (0.6)	23 (0.6)	51 (0.8)	13 (0.6)	283 (1.4)	286 (1.3)	21 (0.6)	31 (0.5)	33 (0.5)	16 (0.6)
Female	277 (1.3)	277 (1.4)	12 (0.6)	29 (0.6)	46 (0.8)	14 (0.5)	268 (1.2)	272 (1.2)	11 (0.6)	22 (0.6)	54 (0.8)	13 (0.6)	269 (1.2)	279 (1.3)	22 (0.8)	35 (0.7)	32 (0.7)	11 (0.6)
Age																		
16 to 18 years old	270 (2.3)	267 (2.8)	11 (1.7)	37 (2.5)	48 (2.7)	5 (1.4)	270 (2.2)	270 (2.9)	11 (1.4)	24 (1.8)	56 (2.4)	9 (1.7)	264 (2.5)	267 (3.1)	28 (2.3)	38 (2.1)	28 (2.1)	6 (1.3)
19 to 24 years old	280 (2.0)	276 (2.4)	11 (1.1)	29 (1.3)	48 (1.5)	12 (1.1)	282 (2.2)	282 (2.5)	9 (1.1)	20 (1.2)	58 (1.7)	13 (1.5)	277 (2.0)	279 (2.3)	21 (1.4)	36 (1.3)	33 (1.4)	10 (1.1)
25 to 39 years old	288 (1.3)	283 (1.7)	12 (0.6)	29 (0.7)	45 (0.7)	15 (1.1)	286 (1.2)	286 (1.8)	8 (0.7)	19 (0.7)	56 (1.1)	17 (1.1)	286 (1.3)	292 (1.8)	17 (0.9)	31 (0.8)	35 (0.8)	17 (0.9)
40 to 54 years old	293 (1.2)	282 (2.3)	12 (0.9)	27 (1.1)	47 (1.2)	15 (1.1)	284 (1.2)	284 (1.9)	10 (0.7)	20 (0.8)	54 (0.8)	15 (0.9)	289 (1.8)	289 (1.9)	19 (1.0)	32 (0.9)	34 (0.8)	16 (0.9)
55 to 64 years old	269 (1.4)	278 (1.9)	13 (0.8)	27 (0.9)	44 (1.1)	15 (0.8)	258 (1.4)	270 (2.1)	12 (0.9)	23 (0.9)	54 (1.2)	12 (1.1)	272 (1.8)	289 (1.9)	19 (1.0)	30 (0.8)	34 (0.9)	17 (0.8)
65 years old and older	235 (1.7)	248 (2.0)	23 (1.3)	38 (1.2)	34 (1.4)	4 (0.6)	221 (1.4)	235 (2.0)	27 (1.5)	33 (1.0)	38 (1.4)	3 (0.4)	235 (2.7)	257 (2.2)	34 (1.6)	37 (1.2)	24 (1.2)	5 (0.6)
Race/ethnicity																		
White	287 (1.2)	288 (1.5)	7 (0.5)	25 (0.8)	51 (0.9)	17 (0.9)	281 (1.2)	282 (1.5)	3 (0.5)	19 (0.7)	58 (1.0)	15 (1.0)	288 (1.1)	297 (1.3)	13 (0.7)	32 (0.7)	39 (0.8)	17 (0.8)
Black	237 (1.4)	243 (1.8)	24 (1.4)	43 (1.2)	31 (1.4)	2 (0.4)	230 (1.4)	238 (2.1)	24 (1.7)	35 (1.4)	40 (1.9)	2 (0.5)	222 (1.6)	238 (2.1)	47 (1.8)	36 (1.3)	15 (1.1)	2 (0.4)
Hispanic	234 (2.3)	216 (3.5)	44 (1.8)	30 (1.0)	23 (1.1)	4 (0.8)	238 (1.8)	224 (3.6)	36 (1.6)	26 (0.8)	33 (1.2)	5 (0.5)	233 (2.3)	233 (3.2)	50 (1.7)	29 (0.9)	17 (0.9)	4 (0.5)
Asian/Pacific Islander	255 (6.1)	271 (4.0)	14 (2.0)	32 (2.2)	42 (2.5)	12 (1.8)	259 (6.1)	272 (5.0)	11 (2.2)	22 (2.1)	54 (3.0)	13 (2.3)	268 (7.8)	285 (5.1)	19 (3.0)	34 (2.9)	35 (2.8)	12 (2.5)
Highest level of education																		
Still in high school	268 (2.5)	262 (3.7)	14 (2.5)	37 (2.8)	45 (3.1)	4 (1.5)	270 (2.4)	265 (4.3)	13 (2.3)	24 (2.2)	54 (3.0)	9 (.9)	263 (3.2)	261 (4.2)	31 (2.9)	38 (2.5)	25 (2.3)	5 (1.4)
Less than high school completion	216 (1.4)	207 (2.4)	50 (1.4)	33 (1.0)	16 (0.9)	1 (0.2)	211 (1.5)	208 (2.6)	45 (1.4)	29 (0.7)	25 (1.0)	2 (0.3)	209 (2.1)	211 (2.2)	64 (1.3)	25 (0.8)	10 (0.7)	1 (0.2)
GED/high school equivalency	265 (2.2)	260 (2.1)	10 (1.8)	45 (2.9)	43 (3.0)	3 (1.1)	259 (2.3)	257 (2.5)	13 (1.9)	30 (2.3)	53 (2.8)	4 (1.2)	265 (2.3)	265 (3.1)	26 (3.1)	43 (3.1)	28 (2.9)	3 (1.2)
High school graduate	268 (1.0)	262 (1.3)	13 (1.0)	39 (1.2)	44 (2.4)	6 (1.3)	261 (1.4)	258 (1.5)	13 (1.0)	29 (1.1)	52 (1.4)	5 (0.7)	267 (1.2)	269 (1.6)	24 (1.4)	42 (1.3)	29 (1.3)	5 (0.7)
Vocational/trade/business	268 (2.1)	268 (2.7)	10 (1.8)	36 (2.6)	45 (2.7)	9 (2.1)	273 (2.0)	267 (2.5)	9 (1.5)	26 (2.3)	59 (2.7)	7 (1.7)	280 (2.2)	279 (2.2)	18 (2.1)	41 (2.3)	35 (2.3)	6 (1.4)
Some college	292 (1.0)	287 (1.6)	5 (0.7)	20 (1.5)	59 (1.7)	15 (2.0)	288 (1.6)	294 (1.7)	5 (0.8)	19 (1.5)	65 (.8)	16 (2.2)	295 (1.7)	305 (2.0)	10 (1.1)	36 (1.9)	45 (1.8)	9 (1.1)
Associate's degree	306 (1.9)	298 (2.4)	3 (0.7)	20 (1.5)	56 (2.1)	19 (2.0)	301 (1.9)	291 (2.0)	5 (0.8)	15 (1.3)	66 (2.3)	16 (2.2)	305 (2.0)	305 (2.1)	7 (1.1)	30 (1.9)	45 (2.1)	18 (2.1)
Bachelor's degree	325 (1.9)	314 (2.1)	3 (0.5)	14 (1.0)	53 (1.7)	31 (1.8)	317 (1.9)	303 (2.2)	3 (0.6)	11 (1.2)	62 (2.5)	25 (2.7)	324 (1.8)	323 (1.8)	4 (0.6)	22 (1.2)	43 (1.5)	31 (1.9)
Graduate studies/degree	340 (2.0)	327 (2.8)	1 (0.4)	10 (1.2)	48 (2.3)	41 (2.6)	328 (1.9)	311 (2.8)	1 (0.4)	9 (1.1)	59 (2.6)	31 (2.8)	336 (2.1)	332 (2.1)	3 (0.6)	18 (1.5)	43 (2.1)	36 (2.6)
Employment																		
Full-time	290 (1.3)	285 (1.5)	—	(†)	(†)	(†)	286 (1.2)	281 (1.2)	—	(†)	(†)	(†)	292 (1.3)	296 (1.1)	—	(†)	(†)	(†)
Part-time	285 (1.7)	281 (2.2)	—	(†)	(†)	(†)	279 (1.8)	277 (2.2)	—	(†)	(†)	(†)	281 (1.7)	287 (2.2)	—	(†)	(†)	(†)
Unemployed	263 (2.3)	269 (2.8)	—	(†)	(†)	(†)	261 (2.2)	265 (3.0)	—	(†)	(†)	(†)	261 (3.2)	270 (3.6)	—	(†)	(†)	(†)
Not in labor force	252 (1.4)	255 (1.7)	—	(†)	(†)	(†)	244 (1.5)	250 (1.9)	—	(†)	(†)	(†)	247 (1.9)	261 (1.8)	—	(†)	(†)	(†)
Language spoken before starting school																		
English only	282 (1.2)	283 (1.4)	9 (0.5)	27 (0.7)	49 (0.8)	15 (0.7)	275 (1.2)	276 (1.3)	9 (0.5)	21 (0.6)	56 (0.8)	13 (0.7)	280 (1.2)	289 (1.2)	18 (0.6)	33 (0.6)	35 (0.6)	15 (0.6)
English and Spanish	255 (2.9)	262 (3.1)	14 (2.1)	38 (2.2)	42 (2.4)	6 (1.3)	253 (3.6)	259 (3.4)	12 (2.5)	29 (3.0)	54 (3.8)	5 (1.8)	247 (4.6)	261 (3.8)	31 (3.3)	39 (2.6)	26 (2.8)	4 (1.3)
English and other language	273 (4.0)	278 (3.1)	7 (1.5)	33 (2.8)	51 (3.1)	9 (2.1)	260 (4.5)	268 (3.2)	10 (2.0)	25 (2.3)	57 (2.9)	8 (2.0)	271 (5.6)	289 (4.1)	15 (2.7)	38 (2.7)	34 (3.0)	14 (2.6)
Spanish	205 (2.9)	188 (3.8)	61 (1.8)	25 (1.1)	13 (0.9)	1 (0.3)	216 (2.8)	199 (4.6)	49 (2.0)	25 (1.3)	23 (1.3)	3 (0.4)	212 (3.3)	211 (4.6)	62 (2.3)	25 (1.2)	11 (1.1)	2 (0.5)
Other language	239 (3.4)	249 (4.6)	26 (2.0)	33 (2.0)	34 (2.3)	7 (1.3)	241 (3.7)	257 (4.2)	20 (1.9)	24 (1.0)	46 (2.6)	9 (1.2)	246 (4.3)	270 (4.3)	28 (2.3)	33 (1.7)	43 (2.1)	10 (1.5)

—Not available.

†Not applicable.

[1]Prose literacy refers to the knowledge and skills needed to search, comprehend, and use information from continuous texts. Adults at the Below Basic level, rated 0 to 209, range from being nonliterate in English to being able to locate easily identifiable information in short, commonplace prose texts. At the Basic level, rated 210 to 264, adults are able to read and understand information in short, commonplace prose texts. At the Intermediate level, rated 265 to 339, adults are able to read and understand moderately dense, less commonplace prose texts as well as summarize, make simple inferences, determine cause and effect, and recognize the author's purpose. At the Proficient level, rated 340 to 500, adults are able to read lengthy, complex, abstract prose texts as well as synthesize information and make complex inferences.

[2]Document literacy refers to the knowledge and skills needed to search, comprehend, and use information from noncontinuous texts in various formats. Adults at the Below Basic level, rated 0 to 204, range from being nonliterate in English to being able to locate easily identifiable information and follow instructions in simple documents (e.g., charts or forms). At the Basic level, rated 205 to 249, adults are able to locate and understand information in simple documents. At the Intermediate level, rated 250 to 334, adults are able to locate information in dense, complex documents and make simple inferences about the information. At the Proficient level, rated 335 to 500, adults are able to integrate, synthesize, and analyze multiple pieces of information located in complex documents.

[3]Quantitative literacy refers to the knowledge and skills required to identify and perform computations, either alone or sequentially, using numbers embedded in printed materials. Adults at the Below Basic level, rated 0 to 234, range from being nonliterate in English to being able to locate numbers and use them to perform simple quantitative operations (primarily addition) when the mathematical information is very concrete and familiar. At the Basic level, rated 235 to 289, adults are able to locate easily identifiable quantitative information and use it to solve simple, one-step problems when the arithmetic operation is specified or easily inferred. At the Intermediate level, rated 290 to 349, adults are able to locate less familiar quantitative information and use it to solve problems when the arithmetic operation is not specified or easily inferred. At the Proficient level, rated 350 to 500, adults are able to locate more abstract quantitative information and use it to solve multistep problems when the arithmetic operations are not easily inferred and the problems are more complex.

NOTE: Adults are defined as people age 16 and older living in households or prisons. Adults who could not be interviewed due to language spoken or cognitive or mental disabilities (3 percent in 2003 and 4 percent in 1992) are excluded from this table. Race categories exclude persons of Hispanic ethnicity. Detail may not sum to totals because of rounding. Standard errors appear in parentheses.

SOURCE: U.S. Department of Education, National Center for Education Statistics, 1992 National Adult Literacy Survey (NALS) and 2003 National Assessment of Adult Literacy (NAAL), A First Look at the Literacy of America's Adults in the 21st Century, and supplemental data retrieved July 6, 2006, from http://nces.ed.gov/naal/Excel/2006470_DataTable.xls. (This table was prepared July 2006.)

Table 387. Percentage of 12th-graders working different numbers of hours per week, by selected student characteristics and school locale type: 1992 and 2004

Selected student characteristic and school locale type	Total	Did not work during year	1 to 5	6 to 10	11 to 15	16 to 20	More than 20					
							Total	21 to 25	26 to 30	31 to 35	36 to 40	More than 40
1	2	3	4	5	6	7	8	9	10	11	12	13
1992, total	100.0 (†)	31.8 (—)	6.8 (—)	9.8 (—)	12.7 (—)	16.1 (—)	22.7 (—)	9.8 (—)	5.6 (—)	2.5 (—)	3.3 (—)	1.5 (—)
Sex												
Male	100.0 (†)	33.0 (—)	6.0 (—)	8.9 (—)	11.1 (—)	15.0 (—)	26.0 (—)	10.2 (—)	6.5 (—)	3.1 (—)	4.2 (—)	2.0 (—)
Female	100.0 (†)	30.7 (—)	7.6 (—)	10.7 (—)	14.4 (—)	17.2 (—)	19.5 (—)	9.5 (—)	4.8 (—)	1.9 (—)	2.4 (—)	1.0 (—)
Race/ethnicity												
White	100.0 (—)	27.6 (—)	7.0 (—)	11.2 (—)	14.1 (—)	17.3 (—)	22.8 (—)	10.0 (—)	5.5 (—)	2.6 (—)	3.3 (—)	1.5 (—)
Black	100.0 (—)	47.4 (—)	4.9 (—)	6.5 (—)	7.2 (—)	11.9 (—)	22.1 (—)	8.8 (—)	6.4 (—)	2.4 (—)	2.9 (—)	1.7 (—)
Hispanic	100.0 (—)	38.9 (—)	6.0 (—)	5.3 (—)	11.3 (—)	13.3 (—)	25.2 (—)	10.7 (—)	6.6 (—)	2.4 (—)	4.1 (—)	1.4 (—)
Asian/Pacific Islander	100.0 (—)	43.3 (—)	9.5 (—)	6.7 (—)	9.3 (—)	13.5 (—)	17.7 (—)	8.1 (—)	4.4 (—)	0.8 (—)	3.7 (—)	0.8 (—)
American Indian/Alaska Native	100.0 (—)	45.0 (—)	8.5 (—)	5.6 (—)	6.2 (—)	12.5 (—)	22.3 (—)	12.0 (—)	3.8 (—)	5.0 (—)	0.9 (—)	0.7 (—)
Socioeconomic status quarter[1]												
Low	100.0 (—)	38.2 (—)	5.2 (—)	6.7 (—)	9.5 (—)	13.4 (—)	27.1 (—)	10.2 (—)	6.8 (—)	3.6 (—)	4.3 (—)	2.2 (—)
Middle low	100.0 (—)	29.8 (—)	5.5 (—)	8.3 (—)	11.9 (—)	18.6 (—)	25.9 (—)	10.9 (—)	6.4 (—)	3.2 (—)	4.2 (—)	1.4 (—)
Middle high	100.0 (—)	28.2 (—)	5.8 (—)	10.6 (—)	13.7 (—)	18.4 (—)	23.3 (—)	10.8 (—)	5.9 (—)	2.4 (—)	2.7 (—)	1.6 (—)
High	100.0 (—)	32.5 (—)	10.1 (—)	12.6 (—)	15.0 (—)	14.0 (—)	15.8 (—)	8.0 (—)	3.4 (—)	1.3 (—)	2.1 (—)	1.0 (—)
Locale type of school attended												
Urban	100.0 (—)	35.6 (—)	6.7 (—)	9.4 (—)	12.2 (—)	14.3 (—)	21.7 (—)	9.5 (—)	5.3 (—)	2.3 (—)	3.3 (—)	1.3 (—)
Suburban	100.0 (—)	29.4 (—)	6.6 (—)	9.6 (—)	13.6 (—)	18.3 (—)	22.5 (—)	10.6 (—)	5.7 (—)	2.5 (—)	2.4 (—)	1.4 (—)
Rural	100.0 (—)	31.6 (—)	7.2 (—)	10.6 (—)	12.1 (—)	14.9 (—)	23.7 (—)	9.1 (—)	5.8 (—)	2.7 (—)	4.3 (—)	1.8 (—)
2004, total	100.0 (†)	11.8 (0.38)	8.7 (0.38)	12.2 (0.42)	15.0 (0.39)	18.7 (0.50)	33.5 (0.63)	12.9 (0.40)	8.9 (0.35)	4.4 (0.24)	5.0 (0.26)	2.4 (0.17)
Sex												
Male	100.0 (†)	12.1 (0.55)	8.2 (0.51)	11.2 (0.53)	13.3 (0.54)	18.4 (0.67)	36.9 (0.89)	12.9 (0.56)	9.4 (0.52)	4.9 (0.35)	6.3 (0.44)	3.3 (0.28)
Female	100.0 (†)	11.6 (0.54)	9.3 (0.50)	13.1 (0.58)	16.7 (0.58)	19.0 (0.74)	30.2 (0.80)	13.0 (0.54)	8.3 (0.46)	4.0 (0.33)	3.6 (0.30)	1.4 (0.20)
Race/ethnicity												
White	100.0 (†)	10.9 (0.47)	8.5 (0.48)	13.2 (0.57)	16.3 (0.53)	19.1 (0.60)	31.9 (0.77)	13.1 (0.52)	8.1 (0.40)	4.0 (0.29)	4.5 (0.30)	2.2 (0.21)
Black	100.0 (†)	11.9 (0.94)	8.2 (0.85)	9.1 (0.86)	11.4 (0.94)	18.6 (1.30)	40.7 (1.59)	13.6 (1.11)	11.2 (1.16)	6.5 (0.83)	6.7 (0.86)	2.8 (0.53)
Hispanic	100.0 (†)	13.4 (1.04)	8.4 (0.99)	9.3 (1.00)	12.4 (1.01)	17.6 (1.31)	39.0 (1.59)	12.3 (1.12)	11.6 (1.17)	6.4 (0.75)	6.0 (0.80)	2.7 (0.48)
Asian/Pacific Islander	100.0 (†)	17.1 (1.90)	14.8 (1.87)	12.6 (1.28)	14.9 (1.68)	18.6 (2.06)	21.9 (1.86)	9.2 (1.17)	5.4 (1.01)	2.1 (0.64)	3.9 (0.94)	1.3 (0.45)
American Indian/Alaska Native	100.0 (†)	21.3 (6.29)	14.0 (5.43)	10.8 (4.64)	13.3 (4.01)	18.0 (4.48)	22.6 (5.99)	12.3 (5.22)	3.7 (2.36)	# (†)	3.0 (1.38)	3.5 (1.82)
Socioeconomic status quarter[1]												
Low	100.0 (†)	11.1 (0.78)	7.5 (0.65)	9.5 (0.74)	11.2 (0.78)	18.1 (0.98)	42.6 (1.19)	14.3 (0.88)	11.9 (0.84)	6.3 (0.61)	7.0 (0.59)	3.1 (0.44)
Middle low	100.0 (†)	10.2 (0.72)	7.0 (0.62)	10.8 (0.82)	13.7 (0.80)	19.7 (0.92)	38.5 (1.18)	14.5 (0.90)	9.6 (0.67)	5.2 (0.52)	6.2 (0.59)	3.0 (0.42)
Middle high	100.0 (†)	10.2 (0.69)	8.0 (0.64)	11.7 (0.75)	15.7 (0.78)	19.8 (0.87)	34.5 (1.09)	14.0 (0.85)	9.4 (0.68)	4.5 (0.53)	4.6 (0.48)	2.2 (0.33)
High	100.0 (†)	15.3 (0.80)	11.8 (0.89)	15.7 (0.86)	18.2 (0.91)	17.3 (0.89)	21.7 (0.97)	9.7 (0.60)	5.5 (0.54)	2.3 (0.32)	2.8 (0.34)	1.3 (0.23)
Locale type of school attended												
Urban	100.0 (†)	13.6 (0.69)	10.2 (0.82)	12.7 (0.87)	14.2 (0.89)	16.6 (0.89)	32.8 (1.38)	12.2 (0.80)	9.7 (0.85)	4.7 (0.55)	4.1 (0.50)	2.2 (0.36)
Suburban	100.0 (†)	10.4 (0.55)	8.8 (0.58)	12.5 (0.61)	16.2 (0.57)	19.6 (0.76)	32.5 (0.89)	13.7 (0.62)	8.4 (0.43)	3.9 (0.34)	4.4 (0.35)	2.1 (0.24)
Rural	100.0 (†)	10.9 (0.78)	8.0 (0.73)	12.8 (1.06)	15.4 (0.81)	19.6 (1.10)	33.2 (1.27)	13.2 (0.90)	8.2 (0.71)	4.0 (0.51)	5.3 (0.62)	2.5 (0.39)

—Not available.
†Not applicable.
#Rounds to zero.
[1]Socioeconomic status (SES) was measured by a composite score of parental education and occupations, and family income.

NOTE: Race categories exclude persons of Hispanic ethnicity. Detail may not sum to totals because of rounding.
SOURCE: U.S. Department of Education, National Center for Education Statistics, National Education Longitudinal Study of 1988 (NELS:88/92), "Second Follow-up, Student Survey, 1992"; and Education Longitudinal Study of 2002 (ELS:2002/04), "First Follow-up, Student Survey, 2004." (This table was prepared December 2006.)

Table 388. College enrollment and labor force status of 2005, 2006, and 2007 high school completers, by sex and race/ethnicity: 2005, 2006, and 2007

Selected characteristic	Civilian noninstitutional population			Percentage distribution of population				Civilian labor force[2] Number (in thousands)				Population not in labor force (in thousands)
	Number (in thousands)	Percent	Percent of high school completers	Employed	Unemployed (seeking employment)	Not in labor force	Labor force participation rate of population[1]	Total	Employed	Unemployed (seeking employment)	Unemployment rate	
1	2	3	4	5	6	7	8	9	10	11	12	13
2005 high school completers[3]												
Total	2,675 (107.8)	100.0 (†)	100.0 (†)	49.3 (1.69)	7.8 (0.91)	42.8 (1.30)	57.2 (1.68)	1,529 (68.2)	1,320 (63.4)	209 (25.4)	13.7 (1.55)	1,146 (45.7)
Male	1,262 (74.2)	47.2 (2.09)	47.2 (2.09)	51.7 (2.42)	7.8 (1.30)	40.5 (2.38)	59.5 (2.38)	751 (47.0)	652 (43.9)	99 (17.1)	13.1 (2.12)	511 (38.9)
Female	1,414 (78.2)	52.9 (2.09)	52.9 (2.09)	47.2 (2.21)	7.8 (1.19)	44.9 (2.21)	55.0 (2.21)	778 (46.3)	668 (42.9)	110 (17.5)	14.2 (2.09)	635 (41.9)
White	1,799 (88.9)	67.3 (1.96)	67.3 (1.96)	51.7 (2.06)	6.0 (0.98)	42.3 (1.58)	57.7 (2.04)	1,037 (56.3)	930 (53.3)	107 (18.2)	10.3 (1.66)	762 (37.3)
Black	345 (46.6)	12.9 (1.68)	12.9 (1.68)	40.8 (4.92)	14.5 (3.53)	44.7 (4.98)	55.3 (4.98)	191 (25.6)	141 (22.0)	50 (13.1)	26.2 (5.92)	154 (23.0)
Hispanic	390 (64.4)	14.6 (2.30)	14.6 (2.30)	49.4 (4.71)	11.2 (2.97)	39.4 (4.60)	60.6 (4.60)	237 (28.4)	193 (25.7)	44 (12.3)	18.5 (4.70)	154 (22.9)
Enrolled in college, 2005	1,834 (60.9)	100.0 (†)	68.6 (1.31)	43.4 (2.03)	4.0 (0.80)	52.5 (1.58)	47.4 (2.04)	869 (51.5)	795 (49.3)	73 (15.0)	8.4 (1.66)	965 (42.0)
Male	839 (41.3)	45.7 (1.70)	31.4 (1.31)	43.4 (2.95)	5.0 (1.30)	51.3 (2.97)	48.4 (2.97)	406 (34.7)	364 (32.8)	42 (11.2)	10.3 (2.61)	433 (35.8)
Female	995 (44.8)	54.3 (1.70)	37.2 (1.36)	43.3 (2.62)	3.1 (0.92)	53.5 (2.64)	46.5 (2.64)	463 (35.8)	431 (34.5)	31 (9.3)	6.8 (1.95)	533 (38.4)
2-year	642 (36.7)	35.0 (1.63)	24.0 (1.21)	54.5 (3.44)	6.7 (1.74)	38.3 (2.60)	61.3 (3.37)	393 (34.7)	350 (32.7)	43 (11.5)	11.0 (2.78)	249 (21.4)
4-year	1,192 (49.6)	65.0 (1.63)	44.6 (1.40)	37.4 (2.46)	2.5 (0.80)	60.2 (1.92)	39.9 (2.48)	475 (38.1)	445 (36.9)	30 (9.6)	6.3 (1.96)	717 (36.2)
Full-time students	1,672 (58.3)	92.1 (0.97)	62.5 (0.97)	40.4 (2.10)	3.9 (0.83)	55.7 (1.64)	44.3 (2.13)	741 (47.6)	676 (45.5)	65 (14.2)	8.7 (1.82)	931 (41.2)
Part-time students	162 (18.5)	8.8 (0.97)	6.1 (0.67)	73.8 (6.05)	4.9 (3.00)	21.0 (4.33)	79.0 (5.60)	128 (19.8)	120 (19.2)	8 (5.0)	6.6 (3.85)	34 (7.9)
White	1,317 (51.7)	71.8 (1.53)	49.2 (1.41)	45.3 (2.40)	3.7 (0.91)	51.0 (1.87)	48.9 (2.41)	644 (44.4)	596 (42.7)	48 (12.2)	7.5 (1.82)	672 (35.1)
Black	192 (29.7)	50.3 (2.52)	15.8 (1.03)	33.0 (6.31)	7.2 (3.46)	59.8 (6.58)	40.2 (6.58)	77 (16.3)	63 (14.8)	14 (6.9)	17.8 (8.10)	115 (19.9)
Hispanic	211 (23.6)	49.7 (2.52)	15.6 (1.02)	43.1 (6.34)	2.6 (2.06)	54.3 (6.38)	45.7 (6.38)	96 (18.2)	91 (17.7)	6 (4.4)	5.8 (4.43)	114 (19.8)
Not enrolled in college, 2005	841 (41.8)	100.0 (†)	31.4 (1.31)	62.4 (2.93)	16.2 (2.23)	21.5 (1.92)	78.5 (2.48)	660 (44.9)	525 (40.1)	136 (20.5)	20.6 (2.77)	181 (18.2)
Male	423 (29.7)	50.3 (2.52)	15.8 (1.03)	68.2 (3.90)	13.5 (2.86)	18.4 (3.25)	81.6 (3.25)	345 (32.0)	288 (29.2)	57 (13.0)	16.4 (3.44)	78 (15.2)
Female	418 (29.5)	49.7 (2.52)	15.6 (1.02)	56.5 (4.04)	18.9 (3.19)	24.6 (3.52)	75.4 (3.52)	315 (29.6)	236 (25.6)	79 (14.8)	25.1 (4.07)	103 (16.9)
White	482 (31.8)	57.3 (2.49)	13.0 (1.09)	69.2 (3.68)	12.3 (2.63)	18.5 (2.39)	81.5 (3.10)	393 (34.7)	334 (32.0)	59 (13.5)	15.0 (3.17)	89 (12.8)
Black	153 (18.9)	18.2 (2.06)	5.7 (0.70)	50.6 (7.52)	23.8 (6.4)	25.7 (6.57)	74.3 (6.57)	114 (19.8)	77 (16.3)	36 (11.2)	32.0 (8.14)	39 (11.6)
Hispanic	179 (21.9)	21.3 (2.34)	6.7 (0.80)	56.9 (6.87)	21.3 (5.63)	21.8 (5.73)	78.2 (5.73)	140 (21.9)	102 (18.7)	38 (11.5)	27.3 (6.99)	39 (11.6)
2006 high school completers[3]												
Total	2,692 (108.2)	100.0 (†)	100.0 (†)	46.2 (1.68)	9.0 (0.97)	44.8 (1.30)	55.2 (1.68)	1,484 (67.2)	1,244 (61.6)	241 (27.3)	16.2 (1.68)	1,207 (46.9)
Male	1,328 (76.1)	49.4 (2.09)	49.4 (2.09)	42.8 (2.34)	9.8 (1.41)	47.4 (2.36)	52.6 (2.36)	699 (45.4)	569 (41.0)	130 (19.7)	18.7 (2.54)	629 (43.1)
Female	1,363 (76.9)	50.6 (2.09)	50.6 (2.09)	49.5 (2.26)	8.1 (1.23)	42.4 (2.23)	57.6 (2.23)	785 (46.5)	675 (43.2)	111 (17.5)	14.1 (2.07)	578 (40.0)
White	1,805 (88.3)	67.1 (1.96)	67.1 (1.96)	49.6 (2.06)	8.2 (1.14)	42.2 (1.57)	57.8 (2.04)	1,044 (56.4)	896 (52.3)	149 (21.4)	14.2 (1.90)	761 (37.3)
Black	318 (44.9)	11.8 (1.61)	11.8 (1.61)	29.7 (4.76)	18.2 (4.02)	52.1 (5.21)	47.9 (5.21)	153 (22.9)	95 (18.0)	58 (14.1)	38.0 (7.31)	166 (23.8)
Hispanic	382 (63.9)	14.2 (2.27)	14.2 (2.27)	48.9 (4.75)	7.8 (2.55)	43.3 (4.71)	56.7 (4.71)	217 (27.2)	187 (25.3)	30 (10.1)	13.8 (4.35)	166 (23.8)
Enrolled in college, 2006	1,776 (60.0)	100.0 (†)	66.0 (1.33)	40.5 (2.04)	3.8 (0.80)	55.8 (1.60)	44.2 (2.06)	786 (49.0)	718 (46.9)	67 (14.4)	8.6 (1.76)	990 (42.5)
Male	875 (42.1)	49.2 (1.73)	32.5 (1.32)	35.1 (2.78)	3.8 (1.11)	61.1 (2.84)	38.9 (2.84)	340 (31.7)	307 (30.2)	33 (9.9)	9.7 (2.76)	535 (39.7)
Female	901 (42.7)	50.8 (1.73)	33.5 (1.33)	45.7 (2.77)	3.8 (1.06)	50.5 (2.78)	49.5 (2.78)	446 (35.1)	411 (33.8)	34 (9.8)	7.7 (2.11)	456 (35.5)
2-year	665 (37.3)	37.4 (1.68)	24.7 (1.21)	52.5 (3.39)	6.9 (1.75)	40.6 (2.58)	59.4 (3.34)	395 (34.8)	349 (32.7)	46 (11.9)	11.6 (2.84)	270 (22.2)
4-year	1,111 (47.9)	62.6 (1.68)	41.3 (1.39)	33.2 (2.48)	1.9 (0.73)	64.8 (1.94)	35.2 (2.51)	391 (34.6)	369 (33.6)	21 (8.1)	5.5 (2.03)	720 (36.3)
Full-time students	1,639 (57.8)	92.3 (0.93)	60.9 (1.37)	37.9 (2.10)	3.2 (0.77)	58.8 (1.65)	41.2 (2.13)	675 (45.4)	622 (43.6)	53 (12.8)	7.9 (1.82)	964 (41.9)
Part-time students	137 (17.1)	7.7 (0.93)	5.1 (0.62)	70.4 (6.82)	10.3 (4.57)	19.3 (4.56)	80.7 (5.89)	111 (18.4)	97 (17.2)	14 (6.6)	12.8 (5.58)	26 (7.0)

See notes at end of table.

Table 388. College enrollment and labor force status of 2005, 2006, and 2007 high school completers, by sex and race/ethnicity: 2005, 2006, and 2007—Continued

Selected characteristic	Civilian noninstitutional population		Percentage distribution of population				Labor force participation rate of population[1]	Civilian labor force[2] — Number (in thousands)			Unemployment rate	Population not in labor force (in thousands)
	Number (in thousands)	Percent	Percent of high school completers	Employed	Unemployed (seeking employment)	Not in labor force		Total	Employed	Unemployed (seeking employment)		
1	2	3	4	5	6	7	8	9	10	11	12	13
White	1,237 (49.9)	69.6 (1.59)	46.0 (1.40)	43.4 (2.47)	2.9 (0.84)	53.7 (1.92)	46.3 (2.48)	573 (41.9)	536 (40.5)	36 (10.6)	6.3 (1.79)	664 (34.8)
Black	177 (20.3)	9.9 (1.10)	6.6 (0.74)	27.6 (6.25)	9.9 (4.19)	62.5 (6.77)	37.5 (6.77)	66 (15.1)	49 (13.0)	18 (7.8)	‡ (†)	110 (19.5)
Hispanic	222 (24.2)	12.5 (1.30)	8.2 (0.88)	40.6 (6.13)	4.5 (2.59)	54.9 (6.21)	45.1 (6.21)	100 (18.6)	90 (17.6)	10 (5.9)	10.0 (5.57)	122 (20.4)
Not enrolled in college, 2006	916 (43.6)	100.0 (†)	34.0 (1.33)	57.3 (2.86)	19.0 (2.28)	23.7 (1.90)	76.3 (2.46)	699 (46.2)	525 (40.1)	174 (23.2)	24.9 (2.88)	217 (19.9)
Male	454 (30.7)	49.6 (2.41)	16.9 (1.05)	57.7 (4.00)	21.5 (3.32)	20.9 (3.29)	79.1 (3.29)	359 (32.6)	262 (27.8)	98 (17.0)	27.2 (4.04)	95 (16.8)
Female	462 (31.0)	50.4 (2.41)	17.2 (1.06)	57.0 (3.84)	16.5 (2.88)	26.5 (3.42)	73.5 (3.42)	340 (30.7)	263 (27.0)	76 (14.6)	22.4 (3.78)	122 (18.4)
White	568 (34.4)	62.1 (2.34)	21.1 (1.15)	63.2 (3.54)	19.8 (2.94)	17.0 (2.14)	83.0 (2.76)	472 (38.0)	359 (33.2)	112 (18.6)	23.8 (3.45)	97 (13.3)
Black	142 (18.2)	15.5 (1.86)	5.3 (0.67)	32.4 (7.31)	28.6 (7.06)	39.1 (7.62)	60.9 (7.62)	86 (17.2)	46 (12.6)	40 (11.8)	46.9 (9.99)	55 (13.8)
Hispanic	161 (20.7)	17.6 (2.08)	6.0 (0.76)	60.2 (7.17)	12.4 (4.82)	27.4 (6.54)	72.6 (6.54)	117 (20.0)	97 (18.3)	20 (8.3)	17.0 (6.47)	44 (12.3)
2007 high school completers[3]												
Total	2,955 (113.0)	100.0 (†)	100.0 (†)	44.2 (1.60)	7.6 (0.86)	48.2 (1.24)	51.8 (1.61)	1,531 (68.3)	1,307 (63.1)	224 (26.3)	14.7 (1.59)	1,424 (50.9)
Male	1,511 (80.7)	51.1 (1.99)	51.1 (1.99)	44.5 (2.20)	8.5 (1.23)	47.1 (2.21)	52.9 (2.21)	800 (48.5)	672 (44.5)	128 (19.5)	16.0 (2.23)	711 (45.8)
Female	1,444 (79.0)	48.9 (1.99)	48.9 (1.99)	44.0 (2.18)	6.7 (1.10)	49.4 (2.19)	50.6 (2.19)	731 (44.9)	635 (41.9)	96 (16.4)	13.2 (2.09)	713 (44.4)
White	2,043 (93.4)	69.1 (1.84)	69.1 (1.84)	47.2 (1.93)	5.5 (0.89)	47.3 (1.50)	52.7 (1.93)	1,077 (57.3)	964 (54.2)	113 (18.7)	10.5 (1.64)	967 (42.0)
Black	416 (50.8)	14.1 (1.66)	14.1 (1.66)	36.2 (4.38)	18.4 (3.53)	45.4 (4.54)	54.6 (4.54)	227 (27.9)	151 (22.7)	77 (16.2)	33.7 (5.83)	189 (25.4)
Hispanic	355 (61.8)	12.0 (2.02)	12.0 (2.02)	37.6 (4.78)	6.6 (2.44)	55.8 (4.90)	44.2 (4.90)	157 (23.2)	134 (21.4)	23 (9.0)	14.9 (5.28)	198 (26.0)
Enrolled in college, 2007	1,986 (63.3)	100.0 (†)	67.2 (1.26)	35.9 (1.89)	3.9 (0.76)	60.3 (1.49)	39.7 (1.92)	789 (49.1)	712 (46.7)	77 (15.4)	9.8 (1.86)	1,197 (46.7)
Male	999 (44.9)	50.3 (1.64)	33.8 (1.64)	35.9 (2.62)	2.8 (0.90)	61.2 (2.66)	38.8 (2.66)	387 (33.9)	359 (32.6)	28 (9.2)	7.3 (2.28)	612 (42.5)
Female	986 (44.6)	49.7 (1.64)	33.4 (1.27)	35.8 (2.55)	4.9 (1.15)	59.3 (2.61)	40.7 (2.61)	402 (33.4)	353 (31.3)	49 (11.6)	12.1 (2.72)	585 (40.2)
2-year	711 (38.6)	35.8 (1.57)	24.1 (1.15)	49.0 (3.28)	5.7 (1.53)	45.3 (2.53)	54.7 (3.27)	389 (34.5)	349 (32.7)	41 (11.2)	10.4 (2.73)	322 (24.3)
4-year	1,274 (51.2)	64.2 (1.57)	43.1 (1.33)	28.5 (2.22)	2.9 (0.82)	68.6 (1.76)	31.4 (2.28)	400 (35.0)	363 (33.4)	36 (10.6)	9.1 (2.53)	875 (40.0)
Full-time students	1,851 (61.2)	93.2 (0.82)	62.6 (1.30)	33.5 (1.92)	3.8 (0.78)	62.7 (1.52)	37.3 (1.97)	691 (46.0)	621 (43.6)	70 (14.8)	10.2 (2.02)	1,160 (46.0)
Part-time students	135 (16.9)	6.8 (0.82)	4.6 (0.56)	67.7 (7.05)	4.9 (3.28)	27.3 (5.19)	72.7 (6.72)	98 (17.3)	91 (16.7)	7 (4.5)	6.8 (4.47)	37 (8.2)
White	1,421 (53.3)	71.5 (1.48)	48.1 (1.34)	37.2 (2.25)	3.7 (0.88)	59.2 (1.77)	40.8 (2.28)	580 (42.1)	528 (40.2)	52 (12.7)	9.0 (2.09)	841 (39.2)
Black	232 (23.1)	11.7 (1.12)	7.9 (0.77)	32.0 (5.69)	5.4 (2.76)	62.6 (5.90)	37.4 (5.90)	87 (17.3)	74 (16.0)	13 (6.6)	14.5 (7.02)	145 (22.3)
Hispanic	227 (24.5)	11.4 (1.18)	7.7 (0.81)	34.5 (5.86)	1.4 (1.46)	64.1 (5.92)	35.9 (5.92)	82 (16.8)	78 (16.4)	3 (3.3)	3.9 (4.01)	146 (22.4)
Not enrolled in college, 2007	970 (44.9)	100.0 (†)	32.8 (1.26)	61.3 (2.74)	15.2 (2.03)	23.4 (1.84)	76.6 (2.38)	742 (47.6)	595 (42.7)	147 (21.4)	19.9 (2.58)	227 (20.4)
Male	512 (32.6)	52.8 (2.34)	17.3 (1.02)	61.1 (3.71)	19.5 (3.02)	19.4 (3.01)	80.6 (3.01)	413 (34.9)	313 (30.4)	100 (17.2)	24.1 (3.63)	99 (17.2)
Female	458 (30.8)	47.2 (2.34)	15.5 (0.97)	61.6 (3.79)	10.4 (2.38)	28.0 (3.50)	72.0 (3.50)	330 (30.2)	282 (28.0)	48 (11.5)	14.5 (3.23)	128 (18.9)
White	623 (35.9)	64.2 (2.25)	21.1 (1.10)	70.0 (3.22)	9.7 (2.09)	20.2 (2.18)	79.8 (2.82)	497 (39.0)	436 (36.5)	61 (13.7)	12.2 (2.58)	126 (15.2)
Black	184 (20.7)	19.0 (1.96)	6.2 (0.69)	41.5 (6.75)	34.8 (6.52)	23.7 (5.82)	76.3 (5.82)	141 (22.0)	76 (16.2)	64 (14.9)	45.6 (7.81)	44 (12.3)
Hispanic	128 (18.6)	13.2 (1.80)	4.3 (0.62)	43.2 (8.14)	15.7 (5.98)	41.1 (8.08)	58.9 (8.08)	75 (16.1)	55 (13.8)	20 (8.3)	26.7 (9.47)	53 (13.5)

†Not applicable.

‡Reporting standards not met.

[1]The labor force participation rate is the percentage of persons either employed or seeking employment.

[2]The labor force includes all employed persons plus those seeking employment. The unemployment rate is the percentage of persons in the labor force who are not working and made specific efforts to find employment sometime during the prior 4 weeks.

[3]Includes 16- to 24-year-olds who completed high school between October of the previous year and October of the given year.

NOTE: Enrollment data are for October of given year. Data are based on sample surveys of the civilian noninstitutional population. Percentages are only shown when the base is 75,000 or greater. Even though the standard errors are large, smaller estimates are shown to permit users to combine categories in various ways. Totals include race categories not separately shown. Race categories exclude persons of Hispanic ethnicity. Detail may not sum to totals because of rounding. Standard errors appear in parentheses.
SOURCE: U.S. Department of Commerce, Census Bureau, Current Population Survey (CPS), October 2005, 2006, and 2007. (This table was prepared August 2008.)

Table 389. Labor force status of high school dropouts, by sex and race/ethnicity: Selected years, 1980 through 2007

Year, sex, and race or ethnicity	Number of dropouts (in thousands)	Percent of all dropouts	Percentage distribution of population			Labor force participation rate of dropouts	Dropouts in civilian labor force[1]			Dropouts not in labor force (in thousands)
			Employed	Unemployed (seeking employment)	Not in labor force		Number (in thousands)			
							Total	Unemployed (seeking employment)	Unemployment rate	
1	2	3	4	5	6	7	8	9	10	11
All dropouts[2]										
1980	739 (44.1)	100.0 (†)	43.6 (2.96)	20.2 (2.41)	36.3 (2.87)	63.7 (2.87)	471 (35.2)	149 (19.9)	31.6 (3.50)	268 (26.6)
1985	612 (42.4)	100.0 (†)	43.5 (3.44)	24.0 (2.98)	32.5 (3.25)	67.5 (3.25)	413 (34.8)	147 (20.9)	35.6 (4.06)	199 (24.2)
1990	405 (35.7)	100.0 (†)	46.9 (4.41)	22.2 (3.69)	31.0 (4.08)	69.0 (4.08)	280 (29.7)	90 (16.9)	32.3 (4.99)	125 (19.9)
1995	604 (43.6)	100.0 (†)	47.7 (3.61)	20.0 (2.91)	32.3 (3.38)	67.7 (3.38)	409 (35.9)	121 (19.6)	29.6 (4.03)	195 (24.8)
2000	515 (28.5)	100.0 (†)	48.7 (2.77)	19.2 (3.01)	32.0 (2.59)	68.0 (2.59)	350 (23.5)	99 (17.2)	28.1 (4.16)	165 (16.2)
2003	457 (26.9)	100.0 (†)	40.9 (2.90)	18.4 (3.14)	40.7 (2.89)	59.3 (2.89)	271 (20.7)	84 (15.9)	30.8 (4.86)	186 (17.2)
2004	496 (39.0)	100.0 (†)	32.5 (3.68)	21.4 (3.24)	46.3 (3.03)	53.7 (3.92)	267 (28.6)	106 (18.1)	39.9 (5.27)	229 (20.5)
2005	407 (35.3)	100.0 (†)	38.3 (4.22)	18.9 (3.42)	42.8 (3.32)	57.2 (4.30)	233 (26.7)	77 (15.4)	32.9 (5.42)	174 (17.9)
2006	445 (36.9)	100.0 (†)	40.3 (4.07)	12.5 (2.75)	47.2 (3.20)	52.8 (4.15)	235 (26.8)	55 (13.1)	23.6 (4.87)	210 (19.6)
2007	426 (36.1)	100.0 (†)	41.1 (4.17)	15.1 (3.05)	43.8 (3.25)	56.2 (4.21)	239 (27.1)	64 (14.1)	26.9 (5.04)	187 (18.5)
Male										
1980	422 (32.8)	57.1 (2.91)	50.2 (3.89)	22.0 (3.23)	27.7 (3.48)	72.3 (3.48)	305 (27.9)	93 (15.4)	30.5 (4.21)	117 (17.3)
1985	321 (30.2)	52.5 (3.41)	50.8 (4.71)	30.5 (4.23)	18.7 (3.67)	81.3 (3.67)	261 (27.2)	98 (16.7)	37.5 (5.06)	60 (13.1)
1990	215 (25.6)	53.1 (4.34)	51.2 (5.96)	29.3 (5.43)	19.8 (4.76)	80.2 (4.76)	173 (23.0)	63 (13.9)	36.2 (6.39)	42 (11.3)
1995	339 (32.1)	56.1 (3.53)	52.8 (4.74)	21.2 (3.89)	26.0 (4.17)	74.0 (4.17)	251 (27.7)	72 (14.8)	28.7 (4.99)	88 (16.4)
2000	295 (29.3)	57.3 (3.73)	56.3 (4.94)	18.3 (3.85)	25.6 (4.35)	74.4 (4.35)	220 (25.3)	54 (12.6)	24.5 (4.96)	76 (14.9)
2003	242 (26.6)	53.0 (3.99)	43.8 (5.46)	21.9 (4.55)	34.4 (5.22)	65.6 (5.22)	159 (21.6)	53 (12.5)	33.2 (6.39)	83 (15.6)
2004	278 (28.7)	56.0 (3.84)	35.6 (4.95)	24.1 (4.42)	40.1 (5.07)	59.9 (5.07)	166 (22.2)	67 (14.1)	40.4 (6.56)	112 (18.2)
2005	227 (25.9)	55.8 (4.24)	38.3 (5.56)	21.6 (4.71)	40.3 (5.61)	59.7 (5.61)	136 (20.1)	49 (12.1)	35.9 (7.09)	91 (16.4)
2006	256 (27.6)	57.6 (4.04)	46.3 (5.37)	11.2 (3.39)	42.5 (5.32)	57.5 (5.32)	147 (20.9)	29 (9.2)	19.4 (5.62)	109 (18.0)
2007	233 (26.3)	54.6 (4.16)	41.4 (5.57)	19.0 (4.43)	30.6 (5.53)	60.4 (5.53)	141 (20.4)	44 (11.5)	31.5 (6.75)	92 (16.5)
Female										
1980	317 (27.5)	42.9 (2.82)	34.7 (4.14)	17.7 (3.31)	47.6 (4.34)	52.4 (4.34)	166 (19.9)	56 (11.6)	33.7 (5.68)	151 (19.0)
1985	291 (27.8)	47.5 (3.30)	35.4 (4.58)	16.8 (3.58)	47.8 (4.79)	52.2 (4.79)	152 (20.1)	49 (11.4)	32.2 (6.20)	139 (19.3)
1990	190 (23.3)	46.9 (4.20)	41.6 (6.05)	14.7 (4.35)	43.7 (6.09)	56.3 (6.09)	107 (17.5)	28 (9.0)	26.1 (7.18)	83 (15.4)
1995	265 (27.5)	43.9 (3.42)	40.8 (5.11)	18.5 (4.04)	40.5 (5.10)	59.5 (5.10)	157 (21.2)	49 (11.8)	30.9 (6.24)	107 (17.5)
2000	220 (24.3)	42.7 (3.58)	39.1 (5.40)	20.5 (4.46)	40.6 (5.43)	59.4 (5.43)	131 (18.8)	45 (11.0)	34.2 (6.80)	90 (15.6)
2003	215 (24.0)	47.0 (3.83)	37.7 (5.42)	14.4 (3.93)	47.9 (5.59)	52.1 (5.59)	112 (17.4)	31 (9.1)	27.6 (6.93)	103 (16.6)
2004	218 (24.6)	44.0 (3.72)	28.0 (5.07)	17.9 (4.33)	54.1 (5.63)	45.9 (5.63)	100 (16.7)	39 (10.4)	38.9 (8.13)	118 (18.1)
2005	180 (22.4)	44.2 (4.11)	38.3 (6.04)	15.6 (4.51)	46.0 (6.20)	54.0 (6.20)	97 (16.4)	28 (8.8)	28.8 (7.67)	83 (15.2)
2006	189 (22.9)	42.4 (3.91)	32.3 (5.68)	14.2 (4.24)	53.5 (6.06)	46.5 (6.06)	88 (15.6)	27 (8.6)	30.6 (8.21)	101 (16.8)
2007	193 (23.2)	45.4 (4.02)	40.6 (5.89)	10.4 (3.66)	48.9 (5.99)	51.1 (5.99)	99 (16.6)	20 (7.5)	20.4 (6.76)	95 (16.2)
White[3]										
1980	580 (39.1)	78.5 (2.46)	49.3 (3.37)	18.3 (2.62)	32.4 (3.16)	67.6 (3.16)	392 (32.1)	106 (16.8)	27.0 (3.66)	188 (22.3)
1985	458 (36.7)	74.8 (3.01)	46.7 (4.00)	25.3 (3.50)	27.9 (3.60)	72.1 (3.60)	330 (31.1)	116 (18.6)	35.2 (4.53)	128 (19.4)
1990	303 (30.9)	74.8 (3.83)	51.2 (5.10)	18.5 (3.98)	30.2 (4.69)	69.8 (4.69)	211 (25.8)	56 (13.4)	26.3 (5.42)	92 (17.0)
1995	316 (31.6)	52.3 (3.61)	51.6 (5.00)	18.3 (3.88)	30.1 (4.59)	69.9 (4.59)	221 (26.4)	58 (13.6)	26.2 (5.29)	95 (17.3)
2000	288 (21.4)	55.9 (2.76)	60.2 (3.63)	16.5 (3.79)	23.4 (3.14)	76.6 (3.14)	221 (18.7)	47 (11.9)	21.5 (4.79)	67 (10.3)
2003	226 (18.9)	49.4 (2.95)	48.0 (4.19)	18.2 (4.45)	33.8 (3.97)	66.2 (3.97)	149 (15.4)	41 (11.1)	27.4 (6.33)	76 (11.0)
2004	239 (27.1)	48.2 (3.93)	36.1 (5.44)	14.9 (4.05)	49.0 (4.38)	51.0 (5.66)	122 (19.3)	36 (10.5)	29.2 (7.25)	117 (14.6)
2005	194 (24.4)	47.6 (4.34)	40.3 (6.17)	20.0 (5.05)	39.7 (4.76)	60.3 (6.16)	117 (18.9)	39 (10.9)	33.2 (7.67)	77 (11.9)
2006	214 (25.6)	48.0 (4.15)	48.9 (5.99)	8.2 (3.31)	42.8 (4.58)	57.2 (5.93)	122 (19.4)	18 (7.4)	14.4 (5.59)	92 (13.0)
2007	178 (23.4)	41.8 (4.18)	40.8 (6.45)	11.4 (4.19)	47.7 (5.07)	52.3 (6.56)	93 (16.9)	20 (7.9)	21.8 (7.54)	85 (12.5)
Black[3]										
1980	146 (20.7)	19.8 (2.52)	22.6 (5.97)	27.4 (6.36)	50.0 (7.13)	50.0 (7.13)	73 (14.7)	40 (10.9)	‡ (†)	73 (14.7)
1985	132 (20.9)	21.6 (3.03)	29.5 (7.23)	22.7 (6.64)	47.7 (7.92)	52.3 (7.92)	69 (15.1)	30 (10.0)	‡ (†)	63 (14.4)
1990	86 (17.5)	21.2 (3.83)	30.2 (9.34)	34.9 (9.70)	34.7 (9.68)	65.3 (9.68)	56 (14.1)	30 (10.3)	‡ (†)	30 (10.3)
1995	104 (19.2)	17.2 (2.90)	33.5 (8.73)	25.8 (8.09)	40.8 (9.09)	59.2 (9.09)	62 (14.8)	27 (9.8)	‡ (†)	42 (12.3)
2000	106 (18.7)	20.6 (3.24)	26.7 (7.79)	25.5 (7.68)	47.8 (8.80)	52.2 (8.80)	55 (13.5)	27 (9.4)	‡ (†)	51 (12.9)
2003	81 (16.3)	17.8 (3.25)	29.1 (9.15)	22.9 (8.46)	48.0 (10.06)	52.0 (10.06)	42 (11.8)	19 (7.8)	‡ (†)	39 (11.3)
2004	86 (17.2)	17.3 (3.16)	9.9 (5.99)	44.9 (9.97)	45.2 (9.98)	54.8 (9.98)	47 (12.7)	39 (11.5)	‡ (†)	39 (11.6)
2005	108 (19.3)	26.5 (4.07)	26.5 (7.89)	16.0 (6.56)	57.5 (8.84)	42.5 (8.84)	46 (12.6)	17 (7.7)	‡ (†)	62 (14.6)
2006	69 (15.4)	15.5 (3.19)	‡ (†)	‡ (†)	‡ (†)	‡ (†)	36 (11.2)	17 (7.6)	‡ (†)	33 (10.6)
2007	73 (15.9)	17.2 (3.40)	‡ (†)	‡ (†)	‡ (†)	‡ (†)	43 (12.2)	17 (7.6)	‡ (†)	30 (10.2)
Hispanic										
1980	91 (19.4)	12.3 (2.46)	47.3 (10.66)	18.7 (8.32)	34.1 (10.12)	65.9 (10.12)	60 (15.8)	17 (8.4)	‡ (†)	31 (11.3)
1985	106 (18.7)	17.3 (2.79)	37.7 (8.57)	31.1 (8.19)	31.1 (8.19)	68.9 (8.19)	73 (15.5)	33 (10.5)	‡ (†)	33 (10.5)
1990	67 (15.4)	16.5 (3.48)	‡ (†)	‡ (†)	‡ (†)	‡ (†)	32 (10.7)	10 (6.0)	‡ (†)	35 (11.2)
1995	174 (24.8)	28.8 (3.47)	48.5 (7.15)	20.1 (5.73)	31.4 (6.65)	68.6 (6.65)	119 (20.5)	35 (11.1)	29.3 (7.87)	55 (13.9)
2000	101 (18.2)	19.6 (3.18)	39.0 (8.83)	22.2 (7.52)	38.9 (8.82)	61.1 (8.82)	62 (14.3)	22 (8.6)	‡ (†)	39 (11.3)
2003	124 (20.2)	27.1 (3.77)	40.7 (8.00)	13.8 (5.62)	45.5 (8.11)	54.5 (8.11)	68 (14.9)	17 (7.5)	‡ (†)	57 (13.6)
2004	154 (23.0)	31.0 (3.86)	39.3 (7.32)	17.4 (5.68)	43.2 (7.42)	56.8 (7.42)	87 (17.3)	27 (9.6)	30.7 (9.17)	67 (15.1)
2005	86 (17.2)	21.1 (3.76)	45.1 (9.96)	19.2 (7.89)	35.7 (9.59)	64.3 (9.59)	55 (13.8)	17 (7.6)	‡ (†)	31 (10.3)
2006	136 (21.6)	30.5 (4.06)	35.3 (7.62)	12.6 (5.29)	52.2 (7.97)	47.8 (7.97)	65 (15.0)	17 (7.7)	‡ (†)	71 (15.6)
2007	119 (20.3)	28.0 (4.04)	37.6 (8.24)	23.0 (7.16)	39.5 (8.32)	60.5 (8.32)	72 (15.8)	27 (9.7)	‡ (†)	47 (12.7)

†Not applicable.
‡Reporting standards not met.
[1]The labor force includes all employed persons plus those seeking employment. The labor force participation rate is the percentage of persons either employed or seeking employment. The unemployment rate is the percentage of persons in the labor force who are seeking employment.
[2]Persons 16 to 24 years old who dropped out of school in the 12-month period ending in October of years shown.
[3]Includes persons of Hispanic ethnicity.

NOTE: Data are based on sample surveys of the civilian noninstitutional population. Includes dropouts from any grade, including a small number from elementary and middle schools. Percentages are only shown when the base is 75,000 or greater. Even though the standard errors are large, smaller estimates are shown to permit users to combine categories in various ways. Totals include race categories not separately shown. Race categories exclude persons of Hispanic ethnicity unless otherwise noted. Detail may not sum to totals because of rounding. Standard errors appear in parentheses.
SOURCE: U.S. Department of Commerce, Census Bureau, Current Population Survey (CPS), October, selected years, 1980 through 2007. (This table was prepared August 2008.)

Table 390. Current postsecondary education and employment status, wages earned, and living arrangements of special education students out of secondary school up to 4 years, by type of disability: 2005

Type of disability	Percentage attending postsecondary institutions								Percentage competitively employed[2]		Mean hourly wage at current job[3]		Percentage living independently[4]	
	Any post-secondary[1]		4-year		2-year		Vocational/technical							
1	2		3		4		5		6		7		8	
All disabilities[5]	23.4	(2.62)	7.8	(1.66)	12.9	(2.08)	6.3	(1.51)	69.5	(3.51)	$8.30	(0.32)	28.1	(2.94)
Specific learning disability	25.0	(3.99)	8.8	(2.61)	13.1	(3.12)	6.3 !	(2.24)	77.2	(4.85)	8.30	(0.38)	31.8	(4.53)
Mental retardation	12.0	(3.44)	1.4 !	(1.24)	7.8 !	(2.85)	5.3 !	(2.38)	36.3	(6.04)	7.40	(0.65)	13.7	(3.82)
Emotional disturbance	11.8	(2.95)	2.1 !	(1.31)	8.2 !	(2.54)	4.3 !	(1.86)	64.5	(5.56)	8.90	(0.75)	25.2	(4.21)
Speech or language impairment	36.0	(4.80)	19.6	(3.98)	19.6	(3.98)	6.7 !	(2.51)	71.0	(5.37)	8.00	(0.53)	31.4	(4.85)
Multiple disabilities	25.7	(6.64)	6.7 !	(3.82)	12.5 !	(5.07)	6.7 !	(3.81)	39.8	(8.76)	8.80	(1.17)	6.6 !	(3.91)
Other health impairment	33.3	(4.54)	8.8 !	(2.74)	23.1	(4.09)	11.9	(3.14)	76.2	(4.80)	8.10	(0.38)	20.4	(4.08)
Hearing impairment[6]	50.7	(5.88)	21.2	(4.89)	26.0	(5.22)	12.9 !	(3.99)	56.3	(6.95)	7.70	(0.55)	29.4	(5.66)
Orthopedic impairment	35.8	(5.37)	12.6	(3.72)	22.9	(4.75)	7.5 !	(2.96)	32.0	(6.13)	7.80	(0.97)	25.4	(5.15)
Visual impairment	63.9	(7.60)	34.4	(7.52)	31.7	(7.47)	5.2 !	(3.52)	59.5	(8.79)	9.60	(1.95)	39.9	(8.21)
Autism	35.8	(8.23)	16.1 !	(6.36)	19.0 !	(6.76)	5.1 !	(3.80)	56.0	(9.64)	6.90	(0.69)	17.1 !	(6.51)
Deaf-blindness	24.6 !	(8.26)	12.2 !	(6.42)	8.5 !	(5.47)	8.2 !	(5.26)	37.0	(9.96)	‡	(†)	24.4 !	(8.64)
Traumatic brain injury	17.0 !	(7.57)	4.5 !	(4.20)	11.1 !	(6.33)	5.3 !	(4.54)	50.2	(11.68)	7.80	(0.78)	28.0 !	(9.64)

†Not applicable.
!Interpret data with caution.
‡Reporting standards not met.
[1]Includes 2- and 4-year colleges, and vocational/technical schools.
[2]Competitively employed refers to those receiving more than minimum wage and working in an environment where the majority of workers are not disabled.
[3]Includes wages from noncompetitive jobs.
[4]Living independently includes living alone, with a spouse or roommate, in a college dormitory, in Job Corps housing, or in military housing as a service member.

[5]Includes disability categories with less than 30 youths in the sample, which are not shown separately.
[6]Includes deaf and hard of hearing.
NOTE: Data based on students who had been out of secondary school up to 4 years and had attended special or regular schools in the 1999–2000 or 2000–01 school year. Standard errors appear in parentheses.
SOURCE: U.S. Department of Education, Institute of Education Sciences, National Center for Special Education Research, National Longitudinal Transition Study-2 (NLTS2), Wave 3 parent/youth telephone interview/mail survey, 2005. (This table was prepared August 2006.)

Table 391. Full-time employment status of bachelor's degree recipients 1 year after graduation, by field of study: Selected years, 1976 through 2001

Field of study	Percent employed full time						Percent employed full time in a job closely related to field of study					
	1974–75 graduates in May 1976	1979–80 graduates in May 1981	1983–84 graduates in June 1985	1985–86 graduates in June 1987	1989–90 graduates in June 1991	1999–2000 graduates in July 2001	1974–75 graduates in May 1976	1979–80 graduates in May 1981	1983–84 graduates in June 1985	1985–86 graduates in June 1987	1989–90 graduates in June 1991	1999–2000 graduates in July 2001
1	2	3	4	5	6	7	8	9	10	11	12	13
Total	67	71	73	74	74	84 (0.6)	35	38	38	38	39	52 (0.8)
Professional/technical fields	77	80	82	81	80	88 (0.8)	51	51	47	47	48	63 (1.3)
Arts and sciences fields	56	56	56	62	64	77 (1.1)	18	17	15	25	26	39 (1.3)
Other	65	74	75	74	73	88 (1.2)	36	43	47	36	38	45 (2.2)
Newly qualified to teach	66	75	73	68	74	82 (1.0)	43	56	54	47	58	44 (1.3)
Not newly qualified to teach	67	71	73	74	73	86 (0.7)	33	36	36	37	36	56 (1.1)
Professional/technical fields	80	81	82	82	83	89 (0.9)	52	49	47	47	48	66 (1.5)
Engineering	79	84	84	83	84	87 (2.3)	57	55	53	46	50	71 (3.3)
Business and management	84	83	85	85	83	93 (1.2)	49	44	41	40	42	62 (2.3)
Health	75	77	75	76	86	84 (1.7)	71	66	70	65	83	81 (2.3)
Education[1]	66	67	63	73	67	81 (6.9)	22	29	24	57	39	30 (9.2)
Public affairs and services	—	77	74	72	66	87 (2.8)	—	46	31	37	49	58 (4.6)
Arts and sciences fields	57	56	56	63	64	77 (1.5)	17	16	15	25	23	42 (1.8)
Biological sciences	56	45	43	42	50	66 (3.9)	26	18	17	15	26	47 (5.0)
Physical sciences and mathematics[2]	50	58	51	76	72	89 (2.3)	19	29	20	48	48	66 (3.4)
Psychology	61	56	57	66	59	80 (3.2)	22	17	12	22	22	37 (4.5)
Social sciences	59	61	61	61	68	76 (2.8)	12	10	13	12	16	25 (3.1)
Humanities	56	55	59	59	59	72 (3.5)	12	14	17	19	11	41 (3.9)
Other	68	75	77	75	73	89 (1.5)	36	43	42	36	37	48 (2.8)
Communications	—	71	76	77	75	— (†)	—	31	31	33	29	— (†)
Miscellaneous	66	76	77	74	73	— (†)	35	46	46	38	38	— (†)

—Not available.
†Not applicable.
[1]Includes those who have not finished all requirements for teaching certification or were previously qualified to teach.
[2]Includes computer sciences.
NOTE: Data are from sample surveys of recent college graduates. Notes on methodology are included in the Guide to Sources. Data exclude bachelor's recipients from U.S. Service Academies, deceased graduates, and graduates living at foreign addresses at the time of the survey. Standard errors appear in parentheses. Standard error values are not available for all years.
SOURCE: U.S. Department of Education, National Center for Education Statistics, "Recent College Graduates" surveys, 1976 through 1991; and 2000/01 Baccalaureate and Beyond Longitudinal Study (B&B:2000/01). (This table was prepared September 2003.)

Table 392. Percentage distribution of 1999–2000 bachelor's degree recipients 1 year after graduation, by field of study, time to completion, enrollment status, employment status, occupational area, job characteristics, and annual salaries: 2001

Status	All fields of study	Professional/technical fields					Arts and sciences						
		Business and management	Education	Engineering	Health professions	Public affairs and social services	Biological sciences	Mathematics and physical sciences	Social sciences	History	Humanities	Psychology	Other fields
1	2	3	4	5	6	7	8	9	10	11	12	13	14
Total 1999–2000 graduates	100.0 (†)	100.0 (†)	100.0 (†)	100.0 (†)	100.0 (†)	100.0 (†)	100.0 (†)	100.0 (†)	100.0 (†)	100.0 (†)	100.0 (†)	100.0 (†)	100.0 (†)
Time between high school graduation and degree completion													
4 years or less	32.7 (0.79)	28.2 (1.72)	25.6 (1.80)	23.0 (2.26)	26.2 (2.05)	27.6 (2.58)	44.5 (2.40)	32.5 (2.42)	44.7 (2.37)	42.5 (4.42)	38.1 (2.07)	42.8 (2.37)	31.3 (1.55)
More than 4, up to 5 years	22.9 (0.59)	19.7 (1.40)	25.6 (1.67)	32.4 (2.49)	21.5 (1.75)	23.1 (2.70)	24.6 (2.27)	22.2 (2.00)	22.1 (1.98)	18.3 (2.95)	20.2 (1.50)	18.4 (1.86)	26.3 (1.38)
More than 5, up to 6 years	10.8 (0.48)	10.0 (1.14)	14.2 (1.14)	15.3 (1.14)	11.1 (1.14)	9.1 (-.14)	6.5 (1.14)	11.8 (1.14)	9.5 (1.14)	7.4 (1.14)	11.6 (1.14)	8.5 (1.14)	11.2 (1.14)
More than 6, up to 10 years	14.8 (0.56)	15.3 (1.49)	15.7 (1.66)	15.4 (2.13)	14.9 (1.59)	15.7 (2.93)	16.6 (2.18)	15.0 (2.06)	11.5 (1.43)	12.3 (2.74)	15.4 (1.55)	14.0 (1.78)	14.3 (1.40)
More than 10 years	18.9 (0.62)	26.8 (1.78)	18.6 (1.79)	13.9 (1.81)	26.3 (1.77)	24.6 (2.71)	7.8 (1.44)	18.4 (2.13)	12.2 (1.52)	19.5 (3.47)	14.8 (1.45)	16.4 (1.92)	17.0 (1.45)
Enrollment status													
Enrolled full time	14.2 (0.49)	7.0 (0.91)	6.8 (1.00)	9.7 (1.47)	16.4 (1.35)	11.5 (1.86)	41.5 (2.79)	17.2 (2.00)	23.9 (2.00)	16.7 (2.48)	14.7 (1.24)	23.3 (2.02)	11.1 (0.97)
Enrolled part time	6.5 (0.31)	5.4 (0.80)	11.2 (1.15)	8.9 (1.55)	5.6 (1.00)	7.6 (1.76)	4.0 (0.92)	7.2 (1.40)	4.7 (0.90)	12.2 (3.20)	6.5 (0.94)	7.7 (1.15)	5.0 (0.72)
Not enrolled	79.4 (0.54)	87.6 (1.09)	82.0 (1.45)	81.4 (2.03)	78.1 (1.62)	80.9 (2.34)	54.6 (2.73)	75.6 (2.38)	71.5 (2.14)	71.1 (3.67)	78.9 (1.53)	69.0 (2.13)	83.9 (1.18)
Employment status													
Employed	87.4 (0.44)	91.8 (1.05)	93.9 (0.91)	93.0 (1.39)	88.5 (1.25)	90.9 (1.90)	70.2 (2.49)	88.4 (1.59)	81.2 (1.70)	88.7 (2.27)	85.2 (1.49)	80.8 (1.97)	87.0 (1.02)
Full time	76.5 (0.54)	85.5 (1.29)	84.0 (1.44)	86.0 (1.78)	74.8 (1.67)	85.1 (2.21)	52.6 (2.78)	80.7 (2.02)	56.0 (2.18)	76.8 (2.99)	67.5 (1.83)	64.0 (2.50)	78.6 (1.27)
Part time	10.9 (0.42)	6.2 (0.90)	9.8 (1.15)	6.9 (1.23)	13.7 (1.29)	5.8 (1.23)	17.6 (1.88)	7.7 (1.23)	15.2 (1.71)	11.9 (2.11)	17.7 (1.55)	16.8 (1.92)	8.4 (0.86)
Unemployed[1]	6.2 (0.33)	5.4 (0.90)	2.2 (0.49)	4.4 (1.06)	4.9 (0.90)	4.9 (1.32)	6.7 (1.31)	4.4 (1.06)	7.8 (1.08)	5.5 (1.80)	8.1 (1.07)	9.8 (1.58)	7.8 (0.78)
Not in labor force[2]	6.4 (0.32)	2.9 (0.59)	4.0 (0.74)	2.7 (0.83)	6.6 (0.89)	4.2 (1.04)	23.2 (2.26)	7.3 (1.26)	11.0 (1.40)	5.8 (1.47)	6.7 (0.93)	9.5 (1.38)	5.2 (0.74)
Unemployment rate[3]	4.0 (0.33)	2.9 (0.65)	2.6 (1.38)	2.9 (0.86)	3.1 (0.78)	3.5 (1.01)	8.6 (2.08)	2.8 (1.09)	6.1 (1.25)	7.2 (2.06)	4.9 (1.02)	3.9 (0.92)	3.9 (0.69)
Total employed	100.0 (†)	100.0 (†)	100.0 (†)	100.0 (†)	100.0 (†)	100.0 (†)	100.0 (†)	100.0 (†)	100.0 (†)	100.0 (†)	100.0 (†)	100.0 (†)	100.0 (†)
Occupation													
Business management	25.3 (0.57)	55.4 (1.78)	4.2 (0.83)	11.1 (1.85)	10.8 (1.37)	19.0 (2.68)	15.2 (2.12)	14.6 (2.17)	33.7 (2.07)	22.5 (4.14)	18.1 (1.65)	19.8 (2.24)	22.9 (1.51)
Education	18.1 (0.56)	3.2 (0.65)	81.9 (1.67)	3.0 (1.01)	7.6 (1.09)	11.0 (2.69)	12.6 (1.91)	11.7 (1.90)	13.5 (1.69)	24.0 (3.90)	24.5 (1.72)	21.9 (2.36)	14.2 (1.26)
Engineering	4.8 (0.31)	1.2 (0.33)	# (†)	53.0 (3.11)	# (†)	0.7 (0.47)	1.2 (0.81)	9.2 (1.40)	0.5 (0.24)	# (†)	0.5 (0.37)	# (†)	3.9 (0.76)
Health professions	7.8 (0.38)	1.0 (0.36)	1.6 (0.51)	0.4 (0.30)	61.8 (2.27)	4.3 (1.15)	15.6 (1.96)	2.0 (0.77)	3.4 (0.96)	2.0 (1.97)	1.5 (0.42)	7.9 (1.28)	3.6 (0.67)
Other profession[4]	11.2 (0.42)	2.3 (0.51)	1.5 (0.37)	13.5 (2.08)	5.7 (1.06)	26.7 (2.78)	32.7 (2.82)	16.7 (1.82)	15.2 (1.78)	9.1 (2.34)	10.8 (1.28)	21.2 (2.09)	14.7 (1.19)
Computer science/programming	6.8 (0.37)	9.0 (1.05)	1.2 (0.41)	10.1 (1.93)	0.8 (0.33)	2.3 (1.00)	2.3 (0.70)	35.9 (2.42)	4.9 (1.22)	1.8 (0.97)	5.4 (0.99)	2.1 (0.73)	4.8 (0.94)
Administrative/clerical/support	5.4 (0.33)	5.7 (0.91)	3.5 (0.74)	1.6 (0.60)	2.8 (0.70)	5.1 (1.30)	5.0 (1.40)	3.0 (0.82)	8.8 (1.27)	7.6 (2.15)	8.6 (1.05)	5.9 (1.39)	5.1 (0.73)
Mechanic/operator/laborer	3.3 (0.27)	3.8 (0.78)	1.1 (0.41)	3.6 (1.08)	2.0 (0.74)	2.0 (0.36)	6.1 (1.72)	1.8 (0.68)	1.2 (0.57)	8.3 (2.47)	4.7 (0.85)	2.0 (1.01)	4.8 (0.75)
Sales	6.8 (0.38)	12.2 (1.21)	1.0 (0.45)	1.3 (0.53)	2.9 (0.69)	2.2 (0.79)	3.3 (1.08)	2.0 (0.96)	4.0 (0.91)	11.1 (2.44)	6.8 (1.07)	4.3 (0.93)	12.3 (1.13)
Service	8.1 (0.41)	5.1 (0.83)	3.3 (0.86)	1.7 (0.57)	4.4 (1.05)	5.4 (1.31)	5.0 (1.09)	1.5 (0.54)	11.1 (1.75)	12.2 (2.84)	18.5 (1.60)	11.3 (1.74)	10.7 (1.15)
Military/protective service	2.4 (0.24)	1.2 (0.41)	0.8 (0.47)	0.6 (0.36)	1.2 (0.47)	21.5 (2.39)	1.0 (0.47)	1.7 (0.62)	3.6 (0.81)	1.5 (0.88)	0.6 (0.29)	3.5 (1.02)	2.9 (0.64)
Job characteristics													
Job is start of career	71.4 (0.67)	75.7 (1.60)	86.6 (1.41)	89.1 (1.61)	73.4 (1.88)	75.8 (2.62)	60.0 (3.28)	76.3 (2.37)	62.4 (2.54)	58.9 (4.08)	61.7 (1.98)	56.6 (2.84)	68.1 (1.82)
Job closely related to bachelor's degree	54.0 (0.72)	55.8 (1.66)	82.7 (1.48)	69.3 (2.85)	74.6 (1.95)	59.3 (2.93)	47.1 (3.06)	66.3 (2.62)	29.0 (2.09)	24.8 (3.78)	41.3 (1.95)	35.8 (2.82)	47.0 (2.14)
Annual salaries[5]													
Less than $10,000	1.4 (0.16)	0.4 (0.20)	1.8 (0.57)	0.8 (0.74)	0.6 (0.22)	1.1 (0.58)	1.8 (0.69)	0.8 (0.64)	2.2 (0.70)	3.3 (2.14)	1.8 (0.42)	5.5 (1.48)	1.3 (0.45)
$10,000 to $14,999	2.6 (0.24)	1.0 (0.41)	1.6 (0.42)	0.5 (0.37)	1.3 (0.50)	2.7 (1.44)	4.7 (1.43)	0.7 (0.33)	2.9 (0.79)	2.0 (0.85)	5.4 (0.98)	4.1 (1.24)	3.0 (0.60)
$15,000 to $19,999	5.4 (0.34)	1.8 (0.57)	7.3 (1.14)	1.4 (0.58)	2.8 (0.76)	8.0 (2.16)	9.7 (2.04)	4.2 (1.06)	4.3 (1.03)	8.1 (3.02)	9.1 (1.10)	7.8 (1.85)	7.4 (1.01)
$20,000 to $24,999	11.2 (0.47)	5.7 (0.92)	16.4 (1.76)	1.5 (0.64)	6.4 (1.20)	18.2 (2.74)	13.7 (2.24)	6.6 (1.41)	13.6 (1.79)	11.2 (2.63)	14.7 (1.43)	18.9 (1.99)	15.0 (1.36)
$25,000 to $34,999	36.4 (0.81)	29.3 (1.96)	62.0 (2.18)	5.7 (1.54)	30.2 (2.07)	46.2 (3.38)	37.1 (3.43)	24.7 (2.87)	39.0 (2.77)	47.2 (4.85)	43.3 (2.25)	41.1 (3.12)	37.3 (2.03)
$35,000 to $49,999	28.0 (0.77)	41.1 (2.01)	9.5 (1.24)	44.0 (3.20)	40.3 (2.23)	16.3 (2.39)	25.5 (3.27)	28.3 (2.83)	26.7 (2.41)	26.9 (4.48)	20.2 (1.86)	16.1 (2.38)	24.4 (1.73)
$50,000 to $74,999	12.3 (0.54)	15.9 (1.48)	1.4 (0.59)	43.1 (3.19)	14.7 (1.73)	4.5 (1.58)	5.8 (1.73)	29.5 (2.94)	8.4 (1.58)	1.3 (1.08)	4.9 (1.05)	4.8 (1.22)	9.5 (1.25)
$75,000 or more	2.9 (0.29)	4.9 (0.90)	# (†)	3.0 (0.93)	3.8 (0.99)	2.9 (1.44)	1.7 (1.10)	5.2 (1.13)	2.8 (0.86)	# (†)	0.7 (0.32)	1.8 (1.13)	2.2 (0.60)
Average annual salary[6]	$35,408 (316.0)	$41,008 (941.2)	$27,634 (345.7)	$47,531 (790.0)	$39,441 (1,089.6)	$30,400 (1 054.7)	$30,749 (978.4)	$42,755 (981.0)	$33,892 (916.0)	$29,984 (1,053.2)	$30,102 (846.5)	$28,835 (905.7)	$32,780 (627.5)

†Not applicable.
#Rounds to zero.
[1]Percent of all persons (including those not in the labor force) who are not working, but are looking for work.
[2]Percent not working and not looking for work.
[3]Percent of persons in the labor force (excluding those not in the labor force) who are not working, but are looking for work.
[4]All other professional occupations excluding business, teaching, engineering, and health.
[5]Salaries for those employed full time.
[6]Respondents reporting salaries less than $1,000 or more than $500,000 were excluded.
NOTE: Detail may not sum to totals because of rounding. Standard errors appear in parentheses.
SOURCE: U.S. Department of Education, National Center for Education Statistics, 2000/01 Baccalaureate and Beyond Longitudinal Study (B&B:2000/01). (This table was prepared September 2003.)

Table 393. Enrollment in postbaccalaureate certificate or advanced degree programs and highest degree attained by 1992–93 bachelor's degree recipients, by education characteristics: 2003

Education characteristic	Percent				Distribution by highest degree attained				
		Of those ever enrolled[1]			Bachelor's degree or post-baccalaureate certificate	Advanced degree			
	Ever enrolled	Ever completed[2]	Never completed, no longer enrolled	Currently enrolled		Total	Master's degree	First-professional degree	Doctor's degree
1	2	3	4	5	6	7	8	9	10
Total................................	**42.5**	**63.4**	**23.5**	**17.2**	**74.4**	**25.6**	**19.7**	**4.0**	**1.9**
Undergraduate major									
Professional fields.......	37.4	60.7	24.8	18.3	78.7	21.3	19.0	1.8	0.5
Business and management	27.5	65.0	22.5	15.9	83.3	16.7	14.7	1.8	0.2
Education.................	54.6	56.5	27.1	20.4	71.1	28.9	26.3	1.5	1.1
Health....................	38.0	61.8	24.1	18.4	77.9	22.1	19.4	2.1	0.6
Arts and sciences.........	49.3	64.8	22.4	17.3	69.4	30.7	20.8	6.3	3.6
Arts and humanities.........	46.6	62.7	24.2	18.6	73.0	27.1	21.5	4.3	1.2
Social and behavioral sciences........	49.3	62.2	22.5	19.9	70.8	29.2	21.1	6.1	2.0
Science/math/engineering	51.1	68.4	21.2	14.0	65.7	34.3	20.1	7.7	6.6
Other.......................	36.1	65.7	24.4	13.4	77.6	22.4	18.0	3.4	1.0
Cumulative undergraduate GPA									
Less than 2.75..............	63.5	59.5	25.4	18.5	79.7	20.4	16.8	2.2	1.3
2.75 to 3.74................	51.5	66.1	21.5	17.0	69.4	30.6	21.3	7.1	2.3
3.75 or higher..............	43.7	70.0	22.0	13.1	61.6	38.4	30.1	4.3	4.1
Institution granting bachelor's degree									
Public 4-year...............	40.6	61.2	24.6	18.0	76.6	23.4	18.1	3.5	1.9
Private not-for-profit 4-year.....	47.1	66.3	22.5	16.0	70.0	30.0	22.7	5.3	2.0
Other.......................	33.7	75.3	11.3	14.3	74.6	25.4	22.5	1.6	1.3
Highest degree attained as of 2003									
Bachelor's degree or postbaccalaureate certificate	77.3	7.9	59.1	33.9	100.0	†	†	†	†
Master's degree..............	100.0	100.0	†	7.1	†	100.0	100.0	†	†
Doctor's/first-professional degree	100.0	100.0	†	2.9	†	100.0	†	67.5	32.5
Field of advanced degree[3]									
Business and management	100.0	100.0	†	3.4	†	100.0	98.4	#	1.6
Education...................	100.0	100.0	†	7.4	†	100.0	98.3	0.3	1.4
Health.....................	100.0	100.0	†	4.3	†	100.0	48.7	48.1	3.2
Arts and humanities.........	100.0	100.0	†	7.1	†	100.0	86.6	3.6	9.9
Social and behavioral sciences........	100.0	100.0	†	9.2	†	100.0	89.4	#	10.6
Science/math/engineering	100.0	100.0	†	10.7	†	100.0	76.3	#	23.7
Other.......................	100.0	100.0	†	4.5	†	100.0	43.5	5.1	11.4

†Not applicable.
#Rounds to zero.
[1]Columns are not mutually exclusive; bachelor's degree recipients who are currently enrolled could have completed a prior graduate program.
[2]Includes completion of postbaccalaureate certificates.

[3]Only includes respondents who completed a master's, doctor's, or first-professional degree. These graduates could also have left another graduate program without completing or be currently enrolled in another graduate program.
NOTE: Detail may not sum to totals because of rounding.
SOURCE: U.S. Department of Education, National Center for Education Statistics, 1993/03 Baccalaureate and Beyond Longitudinal Study (B&B:93/03). (This table was prepared August 2006.)

Table 394. Average annual salary of bachelor's degree recipients employed full time 1 year after graduation, by field of study: Selected years, 1976 through 2001

Average salary of degree recipients	Total	Engineering	Business and management	Health professions	Education[1]	Public affairs and social services	Biological sciences	Mathematics and other sciences	Psychology	Social sciences	History	Humanities	Communications	Miscellaneous
1	2	3	4	5	6	7	8	9	10	11	12	13	14	15
Current dollars														
1974–75 recipients—salary in February 1976[2]	$7,600 (†)	$12,200 (†)	$10,200 (†)	$8,600 (†)	$6,300 (†)	— (†)	$6,500 (†)	$7,000 (†)	— (†)	$6,700 (†)	— (†)	$5,800 (†)	— (†)	$6,800 (†)
1979–80 recipients—salary in May 1981[2]	15,200 (†)	22,400 (†)	16,300 (†)	17,300 (†)	11,500 (†)	$13,700 (†)	14,500 (†)	16,300 (†)	$12,500 (†)	14,000 (†)	—	12,600 (†)	—	15,100 (†)
1983–84 recipients—salary in June 1985[2]	17,700 (†)	24,100 (†)	18,700 (†)	20,800 (†)	13,800 (†)	15,100 (†)	15,100 (†)	17,500 (†)	14,600 (†)	15,800 (†)	—	14,000 (†)	$16,200 (†)	18,600 (†)
1985–86 recipients—salary in June 1987	20,400 (†)	26,600 (†)	21,100 (†)	22,600 (†)	15,800 (†)	17,700 (†)	16,400 (†)	22,500 (†)	17,300 (†)	20,300 (†)	—	16,200 (†)	—	17,600 (†)
1989–90 recipients—salary in June 1991	23,600 (†)	30,900 (†)	24,700 (†)	31,500 (†)	19,100 (†)	20,800 (†)	21,100 (†)	27,200 (†)	19,200 (†)	22,200 (†)	—	19,100 (†)	—	20,800 (†)
1992–93 recipients—salary in April 1994[2]	24,200 (†)	30,900 (†)	27,100 (†)	31,300 (†)	19,300 (†)	22,000 (†)	22,600 (†)	25,400 (†)	19,500 (†)	22,100 (†)	$21,000	21,300 (†)	—	21,600 (†)
1999–2000 recipients—salary in 2001[2]	35,400 (320)	47,900 (790)	41,000 (940)	39,400 (1,090)	27,600 (350)	30,400 (1,050)	30,700 (980)	42,800 (940)	28,800 (910)	33,900 (920)	30,000 (1,050)	30,100 (850)	—	32,800 (630)
Constant 2007 dollars														
1974–75 recipients—salary in February 1976[2]	$27,700 (†)	$44,500 (†)	$37,200 (†)	$31,300 (†)	$23,000 (†)	— (†)	$23,700 (†)	$25,500 (†)	— (†)	$24,400 (†)	— (†)	$21,100 (†)	— (†)	$24,800 (†)
1979–80 recipients—salary in May 1981[2]	34,700 (†)	51,100 (†)	37,200 (†)	39,500 (†)	26,200 (†)	31,200 (†)	33,100 (†)	37,200 (†)	28,500 (†)	31,900 (†)	—	28,700 (†)	—	34,400 (†)
1983–84 recipients—salary in June 1985[2]	34,100 (†)	46,500 (†)	36,000 (†)	40,100 (†)	26,600 (†)	29,100 (†)	29,100 (†)	33,700 (†)	28,100 (†)	30,500 (†)	—	27,000 (†)	$31,200 (†)	35,900 (†)
1985–86 recipients—salary in June 1987	37,100 (†)	48,500 (†)	38,500 (†)	41,200 (†)	28,800 (†)	32,300 (†)	29,900 (†)	41,100 (†)	31,600 (†)	37,100 (†)	—	29,600 (†)	—	32,200 (†)
1989–90 recipients—salary in June 1991	35,900 (†)	47,000 (†)	37,600 (†)	47,900 (†)	29,100 (†)	31,700 (†)	32,000 (†)	41,300 (†)	29,200 (†)	33,800 (†)	—	29,000 (†)	—	31,600 (†)
1992–93 recipients—salary in April 1994[2]	33,800 (†)	43,300 (†)	37,900 (†)	43,800 (†)	27,000 (†)	30,800 (†)	31,800 (†)	35,500 (†)	27,200 (†)	30,900 (†)	$29,400	29,800 (†)	—	30,200 (†)
1999–2000 recipients—salary in 2001[2]	41,500 (370)	56,100 (930)	48,000 (1,100)	46,200 (1,280)	32,400 (400)	35,600 (1,240)	36,000 (1,150)	50,100 (1,100)	33,800 (1,060)	39,700 (1,070)	35,100 (1,230)	35,300 (990)	—	38,400 (730)
Percent change, in constant 2007 dollars														
1976 to 2001	49.7 (†)	26.3 (†)	29.2 (†)	47.4 (†)	41.0 (†)	— (†)	52.0 (†)	96.3 (†)	— (†)	62.6 (†)	— (†)	66.8 (†)	—	54.9 (†)
1991 to 2001	15.4 (†)	19.3 (†)	27.6 (†)	-3.6 (†)	11.2 (†)	12.4 (†)	12.4 (†)	21.1 (†)	15.8 (†)	17.4 (†)	— (†)	21.5 (†)	—	21.4 (†)

—Not available.
†Not applicable.
[1]Most educators work 9- to 10-month contracts.
[2]Reported salaries of full-time workers under $2,600 in 1976, $4,200 in 1981, $5,000 in 1985, and $1,000 in 1994 and 2001 were excluded from the tabulations. Also, those with salaries over $500,000 in 1994 and 2001 were excluded.

NOTE: Data exclude bachelor's recipients from U.S. Service Academies, deceased graduates, and graduates living at foreign addresses at the time of the survey. Constant dollars based on the Consumer Price Index, prepared by the Bureau of Labor Statistics, U.S. Department of Labor. Standard errors appear in parentheses.
SOURCE: U.S. Department of Education, National Center for Education Statistics, "Recent College Graduates" surveys, 1976 through 1991; and 1993/94 and 2000/01 Baccalaureate and Beyond Longitudinal Study (B&B:93/94 and B&B:2000/01). (This table was prepared July 2008.)

Table 395. Percentage of 18- to 25-year-olds reporting substance abuse during the past 30 days and the past year, by drug used: Selected years, 1982 through 2006

Year	Percent reporting substance abuse during the past 30 days					Percent reporting substance abuse during past year				
	Illicit drug use			Alcohol	Cigarettes	Illicit drug use			Alcohol	Cigarettes
	Any¹	Marijuana	Cocaine			Any¹	Marijuana	Cocaine		
1	2	3	4	5	6	7	8	9	10	11
1982	— (†)	27.2 (†)	7.0 (†)	66.6 (†)	— (†)	— (†)	37.4 (†)	15.9 (†)	80.6 (†)	— (†)
1985	25.3 (—)	21.7 (—)	8.1 (—)	70.1 (—)	47.4 (—)	37.4 (—)	34.0 (—)	13.6 (—)	84.2 (—)	49.9 (—)
1988	17.9 (—)	15.3 (—)	4.8 (—)	64.7 (—)	45.6 (—)	29.1 (—)	26.1 (—)	10.5 (—)	79.6 (—)	50.9 (—)
1990	15.0 (—)	12.7 (—)	2.3 (—)	62.8 (—)	40.9 (—)	26.1 (—)	23.0 (—)	6.5 (—)	78.1 (—)	45.1 (—)
1991	15.4 (—)	12.9 (—)	2.2 (—)	63.1 (—)	41.7 (—)	26.6 (—)	22.9 (—)	6.7 (—)	80.7 (—)	46.9 (—)
1992	13.1 (—)	10.9 (—)	2.0 (—)	58.6 (—)	41.5 (—)	24.1 (—)	21.2 (—)	5.5 (—)	75.6 (—)	46.8 (—)
1993	13.6 (—)	11.1 (—)	1.6 (—)	58.7 (—)	37.9 (—)	24.2 (—)	21.4 (—)	4.4 (—)	76.9 (—)	43.7 (—)
1994	13.3 (—)	12.1 (—)	1.2 (—)	63.1 (—)	34.6 (—)	24.6 (—)	21.8 (—)	3.6 (—)	78.5 (—)	41.1 (—)
1995	14.2 (—)	12.0 (—)	1.3 (—)	61.3 (—)	35.3 (—)	25.5 (—)	21.8 (—)	4.3 (—)	76.5 (—)	42.5 (—)
1996	15.6 (—)	13.2 (—)	2.0 (—)	60.0 (—)	38.3 (—)	26.8 (—)	23.8 (—)	4.7 (—)	75.3 (—)	44.7 (—)
1997	14.7 (—)	12.8 (—)	1.2 (—)	58.4 (—)	40.6 (—)	25.3 (—)	22.3 (—)	3.9 (—)	75.1 (—)	45.9 (—)
1998	16.1 (—)	13.8 (—)	2.0 (—)	60.0 (—)	41.6 (—)	27.4 (—)	24.1 (—)	4.7 (—)	74.2 (—)	47.1 (—)
1999	16.4 (0.40)	14.2 (0.38)	1.7 (0.12)	57.2 (0.54)	39.7 (0.47)	29.1 (0.48)	24.5 (0.46)	5.2 (0.21)	74.8 (0.48)	47.5 (0.52)
2000	15.9 (0.36)	13.6 (0.34)	1.4 (0.11)	56.8 (0.51)	38.3 (0.48)	27.9 (0.46)	23.7 (0.43)	4.4 (0.18)	74.5 (0.46)	45.8 (0.49)
2001	18.8 (0.41)	16.0 (0.39)	1.9 (0.13)	58.8 (0.50)	39.1 (0.47)	31.9 (0.48)	26.7 (0.48)	5.7 (0.23)	75.4 (0.41)	46.8 (0.48)
2002	20.2 (0.37)	17.3 (0.36)	2.0 (0.12)	60.5 (0.53)	40.8 (0.48)	35.5 (0.46)	29.8 (0.43)	6.7 (0.24)	77.9 (0.41)	49.0 (0.50)
2003	20.3 (0.40)	17.0 (0.37)	2.2 (0.13)	61.4 (0.50)	40.2 (0.47)	34.6 (0.48)	28.5 (0.46)	6.6 (0.23)	78.1 (0.41)	47.6 (0.46)
2004	19.4 (0.40)	16.1 (0.37)	2.1 (0.13)	60.5 (0.51)	39.5 (0.49)	33.9 (0.48)	27.8 (0.47)	6.6 (0.25)	78.0 (0.44)	47.5 (0.52)
2005	20.1 (0.40)	16.6 (0.37)	2.6 (0.15)	60.9 (0.51)	39.0 (0.47)	34.2 (0.47)	28.0 (0.45)	6.9 (0.23)	77.9 (0.43)	47.2 (0.48)
2006	19.8 (0.37)	16.3 (0.35)	2.2 (0.12)	61.9 (0.51)	38.4 (0.47)	34.4 (0.48)	28.0 (0.46)	6.9 (0.24)	78.8 (0.43)	47.0 (0.48)

—Not available.
†Not applicable.
¹Includes other illegal drug use not shown separately.
NOTE: Marijuana includes hashish usage for 1996 and later years. Due to changes in the survey instrument and administration and to improve comparability with new data, estimates for 1982 through 1993 have been adjusted and may differ from those reported in previous years. Data for 1999 have been revised from previously published figures. Data for 1999 and later years were gathered using Computer Assisted Interviewing (CAI) and may not be directly comparable to previous years. Standard errors appear in parentheses.
SOURCE: U.S. Department of Health and Human Services, Substance Abuse and Mental Health Services Administration, *National Household Survey on Drug Abuse: Main Findings*, selected years, 1982 through 2001, and National Survey on Drug Use and Health, 2002 through 2006. Retrieved January 3, 2008, from www.oas.samhsa.gov/NSDUH/2k6NSDUH/tabs/TOC.htm. (This table was prepared January 2008.)

Table 396. Percentage of 18- to 25-year-olds reporting substance abuse during the past 30 days and the past year, by drug used and selected characteristics: 2000 and 2006

Year and selected characteristic	Percent reporting substance abuse during the past 30 days					Percent reporting substance abuse during past year				
	Illicit drug use			Alcohol	Cigarettes	Illicit drug use			Alcohol	Cigarettes
	Any[1]	Marijuana	Cocaine			Any[1]	Marijuana	Cocaine		
1	2	3	4	5	6	7	8	9	10	11
2000										
Total	15.9 (0.36)	13.6 (0.34)	1.4 (0.11)	56.8 (0.51)	38.3 (0.48)	27.9 (0.46)	23.7 (0.43)	4.4 (0.18)	74.5 (0.46)	45.8 (0.49)
Sex										
Male	19.0 (0.52)	16.7 (0.48)	1.7 (0.16)	62.5 (0.67)	41.6 (0.65)	31.9 (0.62)	27.6 (0.58)	5.4 (0.27)	77.2 (0.60)	49.3 (0.66)
Female	12.7 (0.42)	10.6 (0.40)	1.1 (0.13)	51.3 (0.63)	35.0 (0.61)	23.9 (0.57)	19.8 (0.53)	3.4 (0.23)	71.8 (0.59)	42.4 (0.64)
Race/ethnicity										
White	17.6 (0.46)	15.2 (0.43)	1.4 (0.12)	63.3 (0.53)	43.9 (0.59)	30.7 (0.55)	26.4 (0.53)	5.2 (0.23)	80.1 (0.49)	51.9 (0.58)
Black	14.5 (0.79)	13.1 (0.76)	0.4 (0.12)	43.9 (1.11)	25.9 (1.10)	24.7 (1.06)	21.8 (0.93)	1.3 (0.27)	62.5 (1.08)	31.5 (1.09)
Hispanic	10.8 (0.82)	8.3 (0.73)	2.1 (0.44)	44.7 (1.32)	26.5 (1.05)	20.2 (1.02)	15.5 (0.92)	4.1 (0.51)	63.9 (1.26)	34.5 (1.16)
Asian	7.2 (1.22)	5.7 (1.09)	0.5 (0.34)	39.4 (2.15)	22.0 (2.08)	14.0 (1.61)	9.7 (1.40)	1.2 (0.55)	58.4 (2.42)	27.4 (2.01)
Native Hawaiian/Pacific Islander	‡ (†)	6.8 (2.60)	‡ (†)	‡ (—)	‡ (†)	‡ (†)	‡ (†)	1.9 (1.15)	75.9 (4.37)	‡ (†)
American Indian/Alaska Native	17.0 (3.98)	15.1 (3.86)	0.7 (0.35)	‡ (—)	‡ (†)	‡ (†)	‡ (†)	‡ (†)	‡ (†)	‡ (†)
More than one race	27.0 (3.88)	22.8 (3.44)	1.5 (0.82)	59.1 (3.93)	54.9 (3.98)	43.3 (4.20)	36.4 (3.89)	6.4 (1.73)	79.3 (3.61)	61.9 (3.82)
Education										
Less than high school	18.8 (0.77)	16.1 (0.71)	2.2 (0.30)	44.3 (0.97)	45.0 (1.01)	30.3 (0.89)	25.4 (0.84)	5.6 (0.43)	64.1 (0.95)	51.9 (1.00)
High school graduate	15.3 (0.54)	13.1 (0.51)	1.3 (0.17)	52.2 (0.75)	40.9 (0.75)	27.0 (0.69)	22.6 (0.63)	4.4 (0.32)	72.4 (0.67)	47.8 (0.76)
Some college	16.6 (0.68)	14.2 (0.62)	1.1 (0.15)	64.0 (0.84)	35.3 (0.81)	29.2 (0.84)	25.0 (0.79)	4.2 (0.33)	79.6 (0.72)	43.8 (0.82)
College graduate	10.3 (0.78)	9.1 (0.71)	0.9 (0.23)	74.4 (1.26)	26.2 (1.11)	23.0 (1.20)	20.1 (1.11)	2.9 (0.37)	85.7 (1.11)	34.6 (1.23)
Employment status										
Full-time	14.9 (0.46)	12.6 (0.41)	1.4 (0.15)	62.0 (0.65)	41.8 (0.64)	27.2 (0.60)	22.8 (0.56)	4.6 (0.26)	78.8 (0.56)	49.3 (0.63)
Part-time	16.6 (0.77)	14.7 (0.73)	1.4 (0.20)	56.0 (1.02)	33.4 (0.91)	29.0 (0.89)	25.2 (0.85)	4.3 (0.38)	74.7 (0.90)	42.1 (0.91)
Unemployed	25.2 (1.64)	21.8 (1.54)	2.8 (0.65)	53.7 (1.99)	53.0 (2.02)	39.4 (1.89)	33.9 (1.82)	7.4 (1.10)	74.5 (1.69)	59.5 (2.03)
Other[2]	15.3 (0.71)	13.1 (0.67)	1.0 (0.18)	45.1 (1.11)	31.2 (0.95)	25.9 (0.92)	21.7 (0.86)	3.3 (0.31)	62.7 (1.13)	37.9 (1.04)
2006										
Total	19.8 (0.37)	16.3 (0.35)	2.2 (0.12)	61.9 (0.51)	38.4 (0.47)	34.4 (0.48)	28.0 (0.46)	6.9 (0.24)	78.8 (0.43)	47.0 (0.48)
Sex										
Male	23.7 (0.54)	19.9 (0.53)	2.6 (0.20)	65.9 (0.65)	41.9 (0.66)	38.4 (0.64)	31.7 (0.62)	8.4 (0.38)	80.5 (0.58)	50.8 (0.66)
Female	15.8 (0.48)	12.5 (0.44)	1.8 (0.16)	57.3 (0.69)	34.9 (0.60)	30.3 (0.64)	24.2 (0.61)	5.4 (0.28)	77.2 (0.58)	43.1 (0.64)
Race/ethnicity										
White	22.7 (0.49)	18.9 (0.45)	2.6 (0.17)	69.3 (0.54)	44.4 (0.59)	38.9 (0.58)	32.2 (0.56)	8.5 (0.33)	85.1 (0.42)	53.4 (0.59)
Black	17.3 (0.86)	14.5 (0.82)	0.5 (0.14)	46.9 (1.14)	27.5 (1.06)	29.2 (1.13)	24.8 (1.10)	1.6 (0.28)	66.7 (1.16)	33.0 (1.15)
Hispanic	13.9 (0.83)	10.1 (0.71)	2.6 (0.34)	51.5 (1.26)	28.8 (1.11)	25.0 (1.08)	17.9 (0.95)	6.1 (0.56)	69.4 (1.15)	38.3 (1.17)
Asian	9.0 (1.79)	6.7 (1.65)	0.7 (0.41)	49.9 (2.90)	25.0 (2.22)	20.5 (2.22)	15.3 (2.04)	2.6 (0.85)	67.3 (2.74)	33.1 (2.27)
Native Hawaiian/Pacific Islander	‡ (†)	‡ (†)	‡ (†)	‡ (†)	‡ (†)	‡ (†)	‡ (†)	‡ (†)	‡ (†)	‡ (†)
American Indian/Alaska Native	28.5 (4.22)	24.9 (3.72)	3.3 (1.65)	53.1 (4.58)	‡ (†)	45.7 (4.97)	39.6 (4.26)	10.4 (2.68)	73.6 (3.83)	‡ (†)
More than one race	22.4 (3.26)	20.4 (3.22)	2.6 (0.90)	65.6 (3.60)	46.6 (4.12)	40.2 (3.89)	34.0 (3.84)	9.0 (2.40)	87.1 (2.30)	52.5 (4.14)
Education										
Less than high school	22.6 (0.84)	18.5 (0.78)	2.7 (0.31)	47.2 (1.07)	46.4 (1.08)	35.5 (0.98)	27.8 (0.93)	8.4 (0.58)	67.6 (0.99)	53.1 (1.09)
High school graduate	20.3 (0.62)	16.7 (0.57)	2.2 (0.22)	56.5 (0.76)	42.0 (0.74)	34.4 (0.75)	28.1 (0.70)	7.1 (0.39)	75.6 (0.69)	50.0 (0.75)
Some college	19.7 (0.62)	16.3 (0.61)	2.3 (0.22)	69.5 (0.79)	33.8 (0.78)	35.8 (0.78)	29.7 (0.77)	6.6 (0.42)	84.1 (0.64)	43.9 (0.82)
College graduate	14.4 (0.88)	11.7 (0.83)	1.3 (0.27)	79.8 (1.00)	28.5 (1.19)	28.9 (1.15)	23.9 (1.11)	5.0 (0.59)	91.3 (0.73)	37.6 (1.24)
Employment status										
Full-time	19.5 (0.52)	15.5 (0.47)	2.3 (0.19)	67.1 (0.65)	42.0 (0.67)	33.6 (0.64)	26.6 (0.61)	7.5 (0.35)	82.9 (0.56)	50.1 (0.68)
Part-time	20.1 (0.74)	17.1 (0.73)	2.2 (0.25)	63.3 (0.93)	32.7 (0.87)	35.8 (0.93)	30.2 (0.92)	6.2 (0.46)	80.2 (0.74)	42.3 (0.93)
Unemployed	26.1 (1.39)	22.3 (1.34)	2.7 (0.47)	56.7 (1.51)	50.2 (1.58)	40.7 (1.53)	34.5 (1.51)	9.0 (0.88)	75.7 (1.35)	56.1 (1.58)
Other[2]	17.6 (0.83)	14.5 (0.76)	1.9 (0.26)	49.3 (1.21)	32.2 (0.94)	31.9 (1.06)	25.9 (1.05)	5.4 (0.48)	68.0 (1.08)	41.6 (1.04)

†Not applicable.
‡Reporting standards not met.
[1]Includes other illegal drug use not shown separately.
[2]Includes retired persons, disabled persons, homemakers, students, or other persons not in labor force.
NOTE: Marijuana includes hashish usage. Standard errors appear in parentheses.

SOURCE: U.S. Department of Health and Human Services, Substance Abuse and Mental Health Services Administration, National Survey on Drug Use and Health, 2000 and 2006. Retrieved July 10, 2008, from www.oas.samhsa.gov/NSDUH/2k6NSDUH/tabs/TOC.htm. (This table was prepared July 2008.)

Table 397. Percentage of 1972 high school seniors, 1992 high school seniors, and 2004 high school seniors who felt that certain life values were "very important," by sex: Selected years, 1972 through 2004

Life value	Percent of 1972 seniors						Percent of 1992 seniors					Percent of 2004 seniors					
	1972		1974 (2 years after high school)		1976 (4 years after high school)		1992			1994 (2 years after high school)		Total		Male		Female	
	Male	Female	Male	Female	Male	Female	Male	Female	Total	Male	Female	Total		Male		Female	
1	2	3	4	5	6	7	8	9	10	11	12	13		14		15	
Being successful in work	86.5	83.0	81.2	74.9	80.3	69.7	89.0	89.6	90.1	89.9	90.3	91.3	(0.33)	89.7	(0.49)	92.9	(0.40)
Finding steady work	82.3	73.7	74.7	59.9	79.3	62.1	87.1	88.6	89.7	88.7	90.7	87.3	(0.40)	85.6	(0.55)	89.0	(0.49)
Having lots of money	26.0	9.8	17.8	9.1	17.7	9.4	45.3	29.4	35.2	39.5	30.9	35.1	(0.58)	42.7	(0.80)	27.6	(0.69)
Being a leader in the community	14.9	8.0	8.5	4.4	9.2	4.2	—	—	—	—	—	—	(†)	—	(†)	—	(†)
Importance of helping others in the community	—	—	—	—	—	—	—	—	—	—	—	41.7	(0.57)	35.2	(0.77)	48.1	(0.74)
Correcting inequalities	22.5	31.1	16.6	18.2	16.2	17.1	17.0	23.6	—	—	—	19.7	(0.46)	18.1	(0.60)	21.2	(0.67)
Having children	—	—	—	—	—	—	39.0	49.2	—	—	—	49.3	(0.55)	45.4	(0.75)	53.2	(0.78)
Having a happy family life	78.6	85.7	83.1	86.7	84.2	86.4	—	—	—	—	—	81.0	(0.46)	80.1	(0.63)	81.9	(0.64)
Providing better opportunities for my children	66.6	66.2	59.5	61.6	59.8	58.8	74.5	76.5	90.5	90.3	90.8	82.5	(0.45)	82.1	(0.64)	82.9	(0.58)
Living closer to parents or relatives	6.8	8.2	8.3	12.4	7.7	11.9	15.2	18.7	—	—	—	—	(†)	—	(†)	—	(†)
Moving from area	14.3	14.6	8.3	7.4	6.7	6.4	20.7	20.1	—	—	—	—	(†)	—	(†)	—	(†)
Having strong friendships	81.2	78.7	76.5	74.7	76.1	72.1	79.8	80.0	87.6	88.1	87.0	85.5	(0.41)	84.9	(0.56)	86.1	(0.57)
Having leisure time	—	—	60.9	55.1	65.4	60.1	65.3	62.0	—	—	—	69.0	(0.55)	70.2	(0.69)	67.8	(0.74)

—Not available.
†Not applicable.
NOTE: Standard errors appear in parentheses.
SOURCE: U.S. Department of Education, National Center for Education Statistics, National Longitudinal Study of the High School Class of 1972, "Base Year" (NLS:72),

"Second Follow-up" (NLS:72/74), and "Third Follow-up" (NLS:72/76); National Education Longitudinal Study of 1988, "Second Follow-up, Student Survey, 1992" (NELS:88/92) and "Third Follow-up, 1994" (NELS:88/94); and Education Longitudinal Study of 2002, "First Follow-up" (ELS:02/04). (This table was prepared November 2005.)

CHAPTER 6
International Comparisons of Education

This chapter offers a broad perspective on education across the nations of the world. It also provides an international context for examining the condition of education in the United States. Insights into the educational practices and outcomes of the United States are obtained by comparing them with those of other countries. The National Center for Education Statistics (NCES) carries out a variety of activities to provide statistical data for international comparisons of education.

This chapter presents data drawn from materials prepared by the United Nations Educational, Scientific, and Cultural Organization (UNESCO), the Organization for Economic Cooperation and Development (OECD), the International Association for the Evaluation of Educational Achievement (IEA), and the Institute of International Education (IIE). Basic summary data on enrollments, teachers, enrollment ratios, and finances were synthesized from information appearing in *Education at a Glance*, published by OECD. Even though OECD tabulations are very carefully prepared, international data users should be cautioned about the many problems of definition and reporting involved in the collection of data about the educational systems of the world (see the OECD entry in Appendix A: Guide to Sources).

This chapter also presents data from the Trends in International Mathematics and Science Study (TIMSS), carried out under the aegis of the IEA and supported by NCES and the National Science Foundation. This survey was formerly known as the Third International Mathematics and Science Study. TIMSS, conducted every 4 years, is an assessment of fourth- and eighth-graders in mathematics and science. In 1995, TIMSS collected data for both grade 4 and grade 8. In 1999, TIMSS collected data for grade 8 only. With the 2003 data collection, TIMSS offers the first international trend comparisons in mathematics and science at grades 4 and 8. In 2003, the United States and a number of other countries participated in data collection at one or both grade levels: 25 nations collected data on fourth-graders, and 45 nations collected data on eighth-graders. For 15 of these nations, including the United States, TIMSS offers comparisons of fourth-grade student achievement between 1995 and 2003. For 34 of these nations, including the United States, TIMSS also offers comparisons of eighth-grade student achievement between 2003 and at least one prior data collection year, either 1995 or 1999.

This chapter includes additional information on performance scores of 15-year-olds in the areas of reading, mathematics, and science literacy from the Program for International Student Assessment (PISA). PISA also measures general, or cross-curricular, competencies such as learning strategies. While this study focuses on OECD countries, data from some non-OECD countries are also provided.

The role that the United States plays in the world of higher education is illuminated by data on foreign students enrolled in U.S. institutions of higher education. The IIE provides estimates of the number of foreign students and their countries of origin.

Further information on survey methodologies is in Appendix A: Guide to Sources and in the publications cited in the table source notes.

Population

Among the reporting OECD countries in 2005, Mexico had the largest percentage of its population made up of young people ages 5 to 14 (21 percent), followed by Turkey (19 percent) (table 400). Countries with relatively small percentages of people in this age group included Italy, Japan, and Spain (all at 9 percent) and the Czech Republic, Germany, Greece, and Portugal (all at 10 percent). In the United States, the proportion of 5- to 14-year-olds was 14 percent, which was higher than in most of the other OECD countries.

Enrollments

In 2005, about 1.3 billion students were enrolled in schools around the world (table 398). Of these students, 693 million were in elementary-level programs, 511 million were in secondary programs, and 138 million were in postsecondary programs. Between 1990 and 2005, enrollment changes varied from region to region. Changes in elementary enrollment ranged from increases of 68 percent in Africa, 16 percent in Oceania, 15 percent in Asia, and 8 percent in Northern America (defined in UNESCO tabulations as including the United States, Canada, Greenland, Bermuda, St. Pierre, and Miquelon) to a 22 percent decrease in Europe and a 9 percent decrease in Central and South America (figure 26). Over the same period, enrollment increases at the secondary level outpaced increases at the elementary level. At the secondary level, enrollments increased by 164 percent in Central and South America, 97 percent in Africa,

86 percent in Oceania, 70 percent in Asia, 27 percent in Northern America, and 2 percent in Europe.

At the postsecondary level, developing areas of the world also had increases in enrollment between 1990 and 2005 (table 398 and figure 26). Postsecondary enrollment rose by 191 percent in Africa, 169 percent in Asia, 106 percent in Oceania, 114 percent in Central and South America, 68 percent in Europe, and 19 percent in Northern America (figure 26). These increases are due to both growth in the percentages of people attending postsecondary institutions and increases in the total populations in these regions.

In 2005, the reporting OECD countries with the highest proportions of 22- to 25-year-olds enrolled in postsecondary education were Finland (40 percent), followed by Denmark (34 percent), the Republic of Korea and Sweden (both at 32 percent), and Norway and Poland (both at 30 percent) (table 401). The United States' proportion of enrolled 22- to 25-year-olds was 23 percent. Also in 2005, the reporting OECD countries with the highest proportions of 18- to 21-year-olds enrolled in postsecondary education were Greece and the Republic of Korea (both at 65 percent), followed by the United States (45 percent), and Flemish Belgium (43 percent). Postsecondary enrollment varied among countries due partially to differences in how postsecondary education is defined and the age at which postsecondary education begins. For example, programs classified as postsecondary education in some countries may be classified as long-duration secondary education in other countries.

In 2006–07, there were about 583,000 foreign students studying at U.S. colleges and universities (table 420). Fifty-nine percent of these students were from Asian countries. Between 1990 and 2006, the proportion of students at U.S. colleges who were nonresident aliens rose from 2.8 to 3.4 percent (table 226).

Achievement

On the 2003 TIMSS assessment, U.S. fourth-grade students scored 518, on average, in mathematics, exceeding the international average of 495 for the 25 participating educational systems (table 406). (Average scale scores from the TIMSS assessment are based on a range of possible scores from 0 to 1,000. Most participating educational systems represent countries; however, some represent subnational entities with separate educational systems, such as Hong Kong, SAR.[1]) U.S. fourth-graders were outperformed by their peers in 11 educational systems, including 4 Asian educational systems (Chinese Taipei; Hong Kong, SAR; Japan; and Singapore) and 7 European educational systems (Flemish Belgium, England, Hungary, Latvia, Lithuania, the Netherlands, and the Russian Federation). On the other hand, U.S. fourth-graders outscored students in 13 educational systems. In 2003, U.S. eighth-grade students scored 504 in mathematics, on average, exceeding the international aver-

age of 467 for the 45 participating educational systems (table 407). U.S. eighth-graders were outperformed by their peers in 9 educational systems, including 5 Asian educational systems (Chinese Taipei; Hong Kong, SAR; Japan; the Republic of Korea; and Singapore) and 4 European educational systems (Flemish Belgium, Estonia, Hungary, and the Netherlands). On the other hand, U.S. eighth-graders outscored students in 25 educational systems.

On the 2006 PISA, the average score of U.S. 15-year-olds in mathematics literacy was 474, which was lower than the OECD average of 498 (table 403). (Possible scores on PISA assessments range from 0 to 1,000.) The average mathematics literacy score in the United States was lower than the average score in 23 of the other 29 OECD countries for which comparable PISA results were reported, higher than the average score in 4 of the other OECD countries, and not measurably different from the average score in 2 of the OECD countries. Comparable mathematics literacy results were also reported for 27 non-OECD jurisdictions, 8 of which had higher average scores than did the United States. In science literacy, the average score of 15-year-olds in the United States was lower than the average score in 16 of the other 29 OECD countries, higher than the average score in 5 of the other OECD countries, and not measurably different from the average score in 8 of the OECD countries. In 6 of the 27 non-OECD jurisdictions, the science literacy scores of 15-year-olds were higher than the average score in the United States. PISA 2006 reading literacy results were not reported for the United States because of an error in printing the test booklets (for more information, please refer to footnote 3 on table 403 and to the PISA publication cited in the table's source note).

Degrees

In OECD countries, ratios of bachelor's degrees conferred per 100 people at the typical age of graduation in 2005 ranged from 11 in Turkey and 15 in Mexico to 56 in Iceland and 60 in Australia (table 415 and figure 27). The ratio for the United States was 34 degrees per 100 people. In 2005, women had higher bachelor's degree ratios than men in 25 of the 28 OECD countries reporting data.

The percentages of undergraduate degrees awarded in mathematics and science fields—including natural sciences, mathematics and computer science, and engineering—varied across the 28 reporting OECD countries in 2005 (table 416). Three of the reporting OECD countries awarded at least 30 percent of their undergraduate degrees in mathematics and science fields: the Republic of Korea (37 percent), Germany (31 percent), and Finland (30 percent). Four of the countries awarded 15 percent or less of their undergraduate degrees in these fields: Hungary (11 percent), Iceland (14 percent), Norway (14 percent), and the Netherlands (15 percent). In 2005, the United States awarded 17 percent of its undergraduate degrees in mathematics and science fields, a lower percentage than most other reporting countries. The percentages of graduate degrees awarded in mathematics and science fields also ranged widely across countries in

---

[1] Hong Kong, SAR is a Special Administrative Region (SAR) of the People's Republic of China.

2005 (table 417). Nine of the reporting OECD countries awarded at least 30 percent of their graduate degrees in mathematics and science fields: the Republic of Korea (44 percent), Greece (43 percent), Austria (39 percent), Spain (38 percent), the Slovak Republic (37 percent), Portugal (34 percent), Switzerland (32 percent), Germany (31 percent), and Finland (30 percent). Four OECD countries awarded 15 percent or less of their graduate degrees in mathematics and science fields: Hungary (6 percent), Poland (9 percent), the United States (13 percent), and Mexico (15 percent).

Finances

In 2005, per student expenditures at the elementary level of education were at least $7,500 in eight OECD countries (table 418). Specifically, Luxembourg spent $14,100 per student at the elementary level, Iceland $9,300, the United States $9,200, Norway $9,000, Denmark $8,500, Switzerland $8,500, Austria $8,300, and Sweden $7,500. At the secondary level, six countries had expenditures of over $9,000 per student: Luxembourg ($18,800), Switzerland ($12,900),

Norway ($11,000), the United States ($10,400), Austria ($9,800), and Denmark ($9,400). At the higher education level, the following seven countries had expenditures of at least $14,000 per student in 2005: the United States ($24,400), Switzerland ($21,700), Sweden ($15,900), Norway ($15,600), Denmark ($15,000), Austria ($14,800), and Australia ($14,600). These expenditures were adjusted to U.S. dollars using the purchasing-power-parity (PPP) index. This index is considered more stable and comparable than indexes using currency exchange rates.

A comparison of public direct expenditures on education as a percentage of gross domestic product (GDP) in reporting OECD countries shows that national investment in education in 2005 ranged from 3.4 percent in Japan and 3.7 percent in the Slovak Republic to 6.8 percent in Denmark and 7.2 percent in Iceland (table 419 and figure 28). Among reporting OECD countries, the average public investment in education in 2005 was 5.0 percent of GDP. In the United States, the public expenditure on education as a percentage of GDP was 4.8 percent.

Figure 26. Percentage change in enrollment, by selected areas of the world and level of education: 1990 to 2005

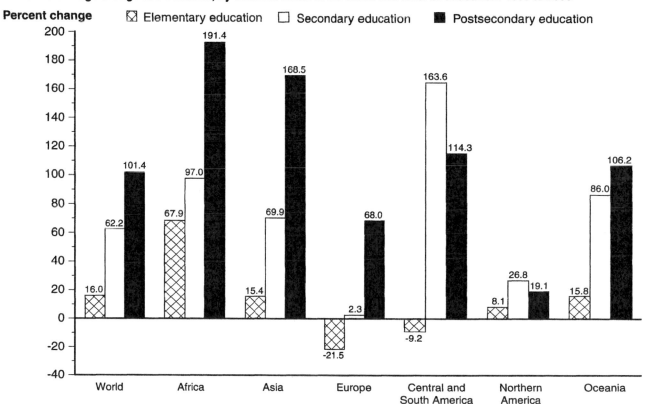

Area of the world

NOTE: Northern America includes Bermuda, Canada, Greenland, St. Pierre and Miquelon, and the United States of America. Hawaii is included in Northern America rather than Oceania. Central and South America includes Latin America and the Caribbean. Oceania includes American Samoa, Australia, Cook Islands, Fiji, French Polynesia, Guam, Kiribati, Marshall Islands, Nauru, New Caledonia, New Zealand, Niue, Norfolk Island, Pacific Islands, Papua New Guinea, Samoa, Solomon Islands, Tokelau, Tonga, Tuvalu, and the Republic of Vanuatu. Data include imputed values for nonrespondent countries.
SOURCE: United Nations Educational, Scientific, and Cultural Organization (UNESCO), *Statistical Yearbook, 1999*, and unpublished tabulations.

Figure 27. Bachelor's degree recipients as a percentage of the population of the typical ages of graduation, by country: 2005

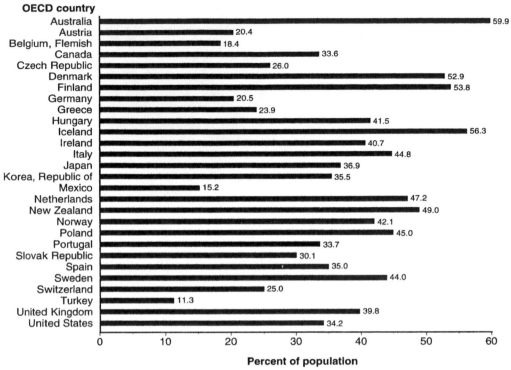

NOTE: Includes graduates of any age. Includes all OECD countries for which comparable data are available.
SOURCE: Organization for Economic Cooperation and Development (OECD), Education Online Database.

Figure 28. Public direct expenditures for education as a percentage of the gross domestic product (GDP), by country: 2005

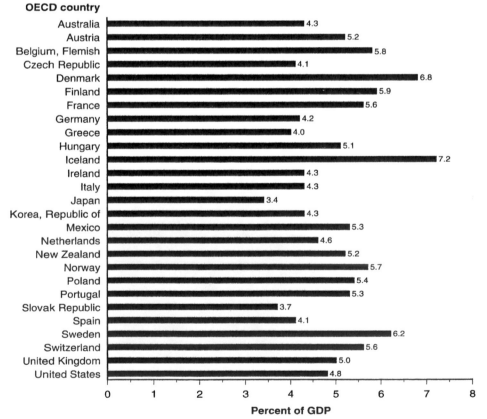

NOTE: Includes all OECD countries for which comparable data are available. Includes all government expenditures for education institutions, plus public subsidies to households for living costs that are not spent at education institutions.
SOURCE: Organization for Economic Cooperation and Development (OECD), *Education at a Glance, 2008.*

Table 398. Selected population and finance statistics, school enrollment, and teachers, by major areas of the world: Selected years, 1980 through 2005

Selected characteristic	World total[1]	Major areas of the world					
		Africa[2]	Asia[3]	Europe[4]	Central and South America[5]	Northern America[5]	Oceania[6]
1	2	3	4	5	6	7	8
1980							
Population, all ages[7] (in thousands)	4,447,090	475,714	2,641,312	693,075	359,307	255,109	22,573
Enrollment, all levels (in thousands)	856,971	78,036	495,155	131,633	87,291	60,041	4,815
First (elementary) level[8]	541,556	62,134	336,174	52,471	65,414	22,611	2,752
Second level[9]	264,379	14,360	144,755	62,734	16,969	23,913	1,647
Third level[10]	51,037	1,542	14,227	16,428	4,908	13,516	416
Teachers, all levels (in thousands)	38,285	2,338	19,641	8,225	3,730	4,079	272
First (elementary) level[8]	19,044	1,661	10,874	2,541	2,260	1,580	129
Second level[9]	15,398	584	7,554	4,387	1,083	1,679	112
Third level[10]	3,843	94	1,213	1,297	387	820	31
Public expenditures on education							
In millions of U.S. dollars	516,400	22,900	93,800	200,600	33,500	155,100	10,400
As a percent of gross national product	4.8	5.3	4.0	5.1[11]	3.8	5.2	5.6
1990							
Population, all ages[7] (in thousands)	5,281,986	629,389	3,184,342	722,109	437,822	282,020	26,304
Enrollment, all levels (in thousands)	980,474	107,871	569,179	131,255	104,968	62,007	5,194
First (elementary) level[8]	596,853	80,640	364,213	48,968	75,505	24,810	2,717
Second level[9]	315,008	24,378	181,652	63,366	22,194	21,569	1,849
Third level[10]	68,613	2,853	23,314	18,922	7,269	15,628	628
Teachers, all levels (in thousands)	47,105	3,791	24,455	9,398	5,131	4,000	330
First (elementary) level[8]	22,626	2,390	12,692	2,812	3,006	1,582	143
Second level[9]	19,380	1,241	9,947	5,076	1,520	1,449	146
Third level[10]	5,100	160	1,816	1,509	605	969	41
Public expenditures on education							
In millions of U.S. dollars	986,500	25,700	199,800	367,500	44,600	330,300	18,600
As a percent of gross national product	4.8	5.6	3.7	5.1[11]	4.1	5.4	5.6
1995							
Population, all ages[7] (in thousands)	5,686,775	719,497	3,437,791	728,034	476,641	296,644	28,168
Enrollment, all levels (in thousands)	1,103,756	130,794	644,609	137,839	116,821	66,510	7,183
First (elementary) level[8]	649,480	95,928	394,304	47,344	82,279	26,501	3,124
Second level[9]	372,724	30,899	219,415	69,448	26,087	23,984	2,891
Third level[10]	81,552	3,966	30,890	21,047	8,455	16,026	1,167
Teachers, all levels (in thousands)	52,047	4,486	26,955	10,113	5,784	4,269	439
First (elementary) level[8]	24,356	2,811	13,499	2,863	3,374	1,649	161
Second level[9]	21,746	1,471	11,273	5,561	1,696	1,528	217
Third level[10]	5,945	205	2,183	1,689	714	1,092	61
2000							
Population, all ages[7] (in thousands)	6,084,908	810,432	3,678,484	731,386	520,405	313,565	30,637
Enrollment, all levels (in thousands)	1,204,015	151,472[12]	704,358[12]	137,084[12]	136,463	67,072	7,567[12]
First (elementary) level[8]	653,681	107,046	404,478[13]	41,652	69,936	27,435	3,134
Second level[9]	452,143	38,044[13]	259,820	70,458	55,213	25,220	3,390
Third level[10]	98,191	6,382[13]	40,061	24,974[13]	11,314	14,417	1,043[13]
Teachers, all levels (in thousands)	57,044[12,14]	5,061[12]	30,025[12]	10,417[12]	6,434	4,662	‡
First (elementary) level[8]	25,701[13]	2,913	15,348[13]	2,755	2,726	1,806	154[13]
Second level[9]	24,703[14]	1,887[13]	12,257	5,777[13]	2,850	1,695	‡
Third level[10]	6,640[14]	262[13]	2,420	1,885	858	1,161	‡
2005							
Population, all ages[7] (in thousands)	6,470,340	909,350	3,912,346	730,314	557,143	328,251	32,937
Enrollment, all levels (in thousands)	1,341,560[12]	191,768[12]	791,490[12]	135,015	142,634	72,771	7,882
First (elementary) level[8]	692,551	135,434	420,181[13]	38,426	68,549	26,813	3,147[12]
Second level[9]	510,825[13]	48,022[13]	308,708[13]	64,802	58,510	27,344	3,440[13]
Third level[10]	138,183[13]	8,312[13]	62,600[13]	31,787	15,575	18,613	1,295[13]
Teachers, all levels (in thousands)	64,438[12,14]	6,003[12]	‡	10,641	7,697[12]	5,023	‡
First (elementary) level[8]	27,179[13]	3,478[13]	16,025[13]	2,678	2,962	1,866	169[13]
Second level[9]	28,452[13,14]	2,206[13]	‡	5,728	3,542	1,806	‡
Third level[10]	8,807[13,14]	319[13]	3,636[13]	2,236	1,194[13]	1,351	‡

‡Reporting standards not met.

[1]Enrollment and teacher data exclude the Democratic People's Republic of Korea.

[2]Excludes Rodrigues and other small islands.

[3]Includes five countries of the former Union of Soviet Socialist Republics (U.S.S.R.), Arab states, and both the Asian and the European portions of Turkey.

[4]Includes all countries of the former U.S.S.R. except Kazakhstan, Uzbekistan, Kyrgyzstan, Tajikistan, and Turkmenistan.

[5]Northern America includes Bermuda, Canada, Greenland, St. Pierre and Miquelon, and the United States of America. Hawaii is included in Northern America rather than in Oceania. Central and South America includes Latin America and the Caribbean.

[6]Includes American Samoa, Australia, Cook Islands, Fiji, French Polynesia, Guam, Kiribati, Marshall Islands, Nauru, New Caledonia, New Zealand, Niue, Norfolk Island, Pacific Islands, Papua New Guinea, Samoa, Solomon Islands, Tokelau, Tonga, Tuvalu, and the Republic of Vanuatu.

[7]Estimate of midyear population.

[8]First-level enrollment generally consists of elementary school, grades 1–6.

[9]Second-level enrollment includes general education, teacher training (at the second level), and technical and vocational education. This level generally corresponds to secondary education in the United States, grades 7–12.

[10]Third-level enrollment includes college and university enrollment, and technical and vocational education beyond the high school level. There is considerable variation in reporting from country to country.

[11]This figure is for Europe, not including the former U.S.S.R.

[12]Estimated.

[13]Estimated by the UNESCO Institute for Statistics.

[14]Includes estimates for major areas of the world not separately shown.

NOTE: Detail may not sum to totals because of rounding. Public expenditure data not available for 1995, 2000, and 2005. Data in this table include imputed values for nonrespondent countries.

SOURCE: United Nations Educational, Scientific, and Cultural Organization (UNESCO), *Statistical Yearbook, 1999*, and unpublished tabulations. (This table was prepared July 2008.)

Table 399. Selected population and enrollment statistics for countries with populations over 10 million, by continent: Selected years, 1990 through 2006

Country[1]	Midyear population (in millions) 1990	2000	2006	Persons per square kilometer, 2006	First level[2] Enrollment (in thousands) 1990–91	2000–01	2005–06	Gross enrollment ratio[5] 1990–91	2000–01	2005–06	Second level[3] Enrollment (in thousands) 1990–91	2000–01	2005–06	Gross enrollment ratio[5] 1990–91	2000–01	2005–06	Third level[4] Enrollment (in thousands) 1990–91	2000–01	2005–06	Gross enrollment ratio[5] 1990–91	2000–01	2005–06
1	2	3	4	5	6	7	8	9	10	11	12	13	14	15	16	17	18	19	20	21	22	23
World total[6]	5,282	6,085	6,549	50	596,853	653,681	692,551[7]	99	101	106[7]	315,008	452,143	510,825[7,8]	52	61	65[7,8]	68,613	98,191	138,183[7,8]	14	19	24[7,8]
Africa																						
Algeria[9]	25	30	33	14	4,189	4,843	4,197	100	108	110	2,176	—	—	61	—	—	286	—	818	11	—	22
Angola	9	13	12	10	990[10]	852	1,391	92	44	60	186	355	—	12	15	15	7	—	—	1	—	—
Burkina Faso	9	11	14	52	504	—	—	33	—	—	99	190	320	7	11	15	5	—	30	1	—	2
Cameroon	11	15	18	38	1,964	2,237[11]	2,998	101	92[11]	107	500	700	698	28	29[8]	24	33	66[8]	120	3	5[3]	7
Cote d'Ivoire	12	16	19	61	1,415	1,944	2,112	67	70	71	361	620[8]	—	22	18[8]	—	30[12]	—	—	—	—	—
Democratic Rep. of the Congo	37	51	62	28	4,562	—	—	70	—	—	1,097[12]	1,253[8]	—	21[12]	—	—	80	—	—	2	—	—
Egypt[9]	56	64	79	79	6,964	7,947[8]	9,795	94	101[8]	103	5,507	8,028[8]	2,993	76	83[8]	27	628[13,14]	—	180	16	—	—
Ethiopia	48	64	77	69	2,466	4,874	10,972	33	63	83	866	2,168	1,454	14	17	46	34	68	110	1	1	2
Ghana[9]	15	19	22	97	1,945	2,561	3,131	75	80	92	—	1,057	2,584	36	37	50	10[15]	55	110	1	3	5
Kenya[9]	23	30	36	63	5,392	5,035	6,101	95	98	106	618[16]	1,909	730	24	39	24	35[15]	89	50	2	3	3
Madagascar	13	16	19	33	1,571	2,208	3,699	103	100	139	323[16]	—	565	18	—	29	36	32	—	3	2	3
Malawi	9	11	13	141	1,401	2,695	2,934	68	139	119	61	487	463	8	32	28	5	20	—	1	—	—
Mali	8	11	12	10	395	1,017	1,610	26	53	80	84	258[8]	—	7	16[8]	52	5[17]	276	—	1	2	12
Morocco[9]	24	29	33	75	2,484	3,670	3,944	67	93	106	1,194	1,541	2,061	35	39	16	256	276	385	11	9	—
Mozambique[9]	14	18	21	26	1,260	2,544	4,173	67	74	105	160	124	367	8	6	11	5[17]	12	11	#	1	1
Niger	8	11	13	10	369	579	1,127	29	30	51	77	106[8]	217	7	6[8]	—	—	—	—	—	—	1
Nigeria[9]	96	127	140	154	13,607	18,802[8]	—	91	96[8]	—	2,908	250	447[8]	25	—	24[8]	208[15,18]	—	—	4[17,18]	—	—
Senegal[9]	8	10	12	64	708	1,108	1,473	59	64	80	—	250	—	16	15	24[8]	19	—	—	3	—	—
South Africa	37	43	48	39	6,952	7,445	3,881	122	107	—	2,742	4,142	—	74	85	34	439[19]	645	741	13	14	15
Sudan	24	34	39	16	2,043	2,567	3,881	53	51	66	732	980	1,447	24	26	34	60[13]	204[8]	325	3	6	—
Tunisia	8	10	10	66	1,406	1,414	1,134	113	114	108	565	1,104[8]	1,247	45	75[8]	85	69	180	—	9	19	31
Uganda	17	22	29	146	2,470[20,21]	6,559	7,364	74	127	117	245[16,21]	547	—	13	16	—	18	56	—	1	3	—
United Republic of Tanzania	25	34	39	44	3,379	4,382	7,960	70	66	110	167	167	—	5	—	—	7[12]	—	—	#	—	—
Zambia	8	10	11	15	1,461	1,590	2,679	99	75	117	190	276	—	24	22	—	15	25[8]	—	2	2[8]	—
Zimbabwe	10	12	12	30	2,116	2,461	2,446	116	98	101	661	844	831	50	42	40	49	49[8]	—	5	4[8]	—
Asia																						
Afghanistan[9]	15	24	31	48	623	749	—	27	19	—	182	—	—	9	19	—	24	—	—	2	—	—
Bangladesh	110	130	147	1,101	11,940	17,668	—	72	109	105	3,593	10,329	—	19	50	38	434	727	781	4	6	—
Cambodia	9	12	14	78	1,330	2,248	2,582	121	106	122	264	351	825	32	17	38	7	22	76	1	2	5
China	1,155	1,261	1,314	141	122,414	113,613	108,925	125	—	111	52,386[18]	81,488	101,195	49	63	76	3,822	7,364	23,361	3	8	22
India	851	1,016	1,112	374	99,118	113,987[24]	139,170	97	99	112	54,180[18]	71,031	—	44	48	—	4,951	9,404	12,853	6	10	12
Indonesia	183	210	232	127	29,754	28,202[8]	28,983	115	111[8]	114	10,965	14,264[8]	16,424	44	55[8]	64	1,773[12]	1,405	3,657	9	—	17
Iran, Islamic Republic of	59	64	70	40	9,370	8,288	7,274	112	94	118	5,085	9,955	—	55	78	—	312[13]	1,405	2,399	10	19	27
Iraq	18	23	27	62	3,328	3,639	—	111	91	100	1,024	1,224	—	47	36	—	170[22]	289	—	12[22]	12	—
Japan	124	127	128	340	9,373	7,529	7,229	100	101	104	11,026	8,782	7,561	97	102	101	2,899[12]	3,982	4,085	30	47	57
Kazakhstan	17	15	15	6	1,197	1,208	973	87	99	104	2,144	2,003	1,982	98	91	95	537	370	781	40	23	53
Korea, North (DPR)	20	22	23	192	—	—	—	105	98	105	—	—	—	90	98	96	—	—	—	39	73	—
Korea, South (Republic of)	43	47	48	490	4,869	3,946	4,031	94	97	—	4,560	4,177	3,786	56	69	—	1,691	2,838	3,210	7	26	—
Malaysia	18	23	24	74	2,456	3,026	4,969	106	89	114	1,456	2,205	2,696	23	38	49	121	549	—	7	26	—
Myanmar	41	46	47	71	5,385	4,858	4,503	108	117[11]	126	1,281	2,268	1,984[8]	23	35	43[8]	196[12]	551[8]	—	4	11[8]	—
Nepal[9]	19	24	28	198	2,789	3,780[11]	4,503	61	71[24]	84	709	1,348	—	33	35	30	94	94	820	5	4	5
Pakistan	119	138	166	213	11,451[23]	13,987[24]	16,688	73	—	110	4,345	—	8,421	23	—	30	—	—	820	3	—	5
Philippines	61	76	92	309	10,427	—	13,007	111	—	—	4,034	—	6,302	73	—	83	1,709	—	2,484	28	—	28
Saudi Arabia[9]	16	21	27	13	1,877	2,775	—	73	105	126	893	—	2,465	44	—	70	154	404	615[8]	12	22	29[8]
Sri Lanka[9]	17	19	21	320	2,112	—	2,280	106	—	—	2,082	1,069	—	74	41	—	55[12,25]	—	—	5	—	—
Syrian Arab Republic	12	16	19	103	2,452	2,775	—	108	105	108	914	1,069	2,465	52	44	70	222	—	—	18	—	—
Taiwan	20	22	23	706	—	—	—	—	—	—	—	—	—	—	—	—	—	—	—	—	—	—
Thailand	56	61	65	126	6,957	6,101	5,844	99	95	105	2,230	—	4,530	30	—	78	1,156[17]	1,900	2,339	19[17]	34	46
Turkey	56	65	70	91	6,862	7,850[8]	7,950[8]	99	96[8]	94[8]	3,808	—	5,388[8]	47	—	79[8]	750	1,588[8]	2,343	13	23	35
Uzbekistan	21	25	27	63	1,778	10,063	2,277	81	107	98	3,295	7,926	4,542	99	65	100	603	732[8]	281	30	9	10
Vietnam	67	79	84	259	8,862	10,063	7,318	103	107[8]	—	3,236	7,926	9,975	32	65	—	130[12]	732[8]	—	2	9	—
Yemen	12	18	21	41	2,679[18]	2,464[8]	—	79[18]	76[8]	—	212[18]	1,151[8]	—	23[18]	43[8]	—	53[12]	173[8]	209[8]	4[12]	10[8]	9[8]

See notes at end of table.

Table 399. Selected population and enrollment statistics for countries with populations over 10 million, by continent: Selected years, 1990 through 2006—Continued

Country[1]	Midyear population (in millions) 1990	2000	2006	Persons per square kilometer, 2006	First level[2] Enrollment (in thousands) 1990–91	2000–01	2005–06	First level Gross enrollment ratio[5] 1990–91	2000–01	2005–06	Second level[3] Enrollment (in thousands) 1990–91	2000–01	2005–06	Second level Gross enrollment ratio[5] 1990–91	2000–01	2005–06	Third level[4] Enrollment (in thousands) 1990–91	2000–01	2005–06	Third level Gross enrollment ratio[5] 1990–91	2000–01	2005–06
1	2	3	4	5	6	7	8	9	10	11	12	13	14	15	16	17	18	19	20	21	22	23
Europe																						
Belgium	10	10	10	343	719	774	733	101	105	102	769	1,058	822	103	145	110	276	356	394	40	57	63
Czech Republic	10	10	10	133	546	645	473	96	104	100	1,268	958	966	91	88	96	118[26]	254	338	16	29	50
France[27]	57	59	63	99	4,149	3,835	4,052	108	106	110	5,522	5,929	5,994	99	110	114	1,699	2,015	2,201	40	53	56
Germany[27]	79	82	82	236	3,431	3,656	3,329	101	105	103	7,398	8,307	8,185	98	98	101	2,049	—	—	34	—	—
Greece	10	11	11	82	813	645	645	98	96	102	851	739	705	93	89	103	283	422	653	36	51	95
Italy[9]	57	58	58	198	3,056	2,836	2,790	103	101	103	5,118	4,404	4,532	83	93	100	1,452	1,770	2,029	32	49	67
Netherlands[9]	15	16	16	487	1,082	1,279	1,277	102	108	107	1,402	1,379	1,423	120	124	118	479	488	580	40	53	60
Poland[9]	38	39	39	127	5,189	3,319	2,602	98	99	98	1,888	3,988	3,317	81	100	100	545	1,580	2,146	22	49	66
Portugal	10	10	11	115	1,020	811	750	123	125	115	670	831	662	67	108	97	186	374	367	23	48	55
Romania[9]	23	22	22	97	1,253	1,189	938	91	102	105	2,858	2,226	2,013	92	81	86	193	453	835	10	24	52
Russian Federation	148	146	142	8	7,596	—	5,165	109	—	96	13,956	—	11,546	93	—	84	5,100	—	9,167	52	—	72
Serbia	9	10	10	115	—	—	312	—	—	99[24]	—	—	623	—	—	87[24]	—	—	—	—	—	—
Spain[9]	39	39	40	81	2,820	2,540	2,501	109	107	105	4,755	3,246	3,091	104	112	119	1,222	1,829	1,789	37	58	67
Ukraine[9]	52	50	47	77	3,991	2,079	1,754	89	105	102	3,408	5,204	3,896	93	97	93	1,652	1,812	2,740	47	50	73
United Kingdom[9]	58	60	61	251	4,533	4,632	4,518	104	102	105	4,336	5,304	5,358	85	101	98	1,258	2,024	2,336	30	58	82
North America																						
Canada	28	31	33	4	2,376	2,456	—	103	99	—	2,292	2,621	—	101	107	—	1,917	1,212	—	95	59	—
Cuba	11	11	11	103	888	1,046	890	98	105	101	1,002	790	928	89	83	94	242	159	682	21	22	88
Guatemala	9	11	12	115	1,165	1,909	2,405	78	104	114	295[12]	504	809	23[12]	38	53	70[17]	—	112[24]	8[17]	—	9[24]
Mexico	83	98	107	56	14,402	14,766	14,595	114	109	113	6,704	9,094	10,883	53	72	87	1,311	1,963	2,447	15	19	26
United States	254	282	298	33	22,429	24,973	24,319	102	101	98	19,277	22,594	24,552	93	94	94	13,819	15,312	17,487	75	80	82
South America																						
Argentina	33	37	40	15	4,985	4,898	—	106	118	—	2,160	3,832	—	71	97	—	1,008[12]	1,767[8]	—	38[12]	53[8]	—
Brazil	148	170	191	23	28,944	20,212	—	106	151	—	3,499	26,097	—	38	104	—	1,540[29]	2,781	—	11	16	—
Chile	13	15	16	22	1,991	1,799	1,695	100	100	104	720	1,391	1,634	73	83	91	262[12]	452	661	21[12]	37	47
Colombia	33	42	44	42	4,247	5,221	5,296	102	112	116	2,378[12,23]	3,569	4,484	50	70	82	487	934	1,315	13	23	31
Ecuador	10	13	14	49	1,846	1,925	2,006	116	115	117	786[18,23]	917	1,103	55	57	68	207	—	—	20	—	—
Peru	22	26	28	22	3,855	4,333	4,026	118	121	116	1,698[8]	2,374	2,760	67	86	94	678	668	952[8]	30	—	35[8]
Venezuela[9]	20	24	26	29	4,053	3,328	3,452	96	102	104	281	1,543	2,105	35	59	77	550	—	1,381[24]	29	28[8]	52[24]
Oceania																						
Australia[9]	17	19	20	3	1,583	1,906	1,939	108	99	105	1,278	2,589	2,537	82	159	150	485[30]	845	1,040	36	65	73

—Not available.
#Rounds to zero.
[1] Selection based on total population for midyear 2006.
[2] First-level enrollment consists of elementary school, typically corresponding to grades 1–6 in the United States.
[3] Second-level enrollment includes general education, teacher training (at the second level), and technical and vocational education.
[4] Third-level enrollment includes college and university enrollment, and technical and vocational education beyond the high school level. There is considerable variation in reporting from country to country.
[5] Data represent the total enrollment of all ages in the school level divided by the population of the specific age groups that correspond to the school level. Adjustments have been made for the varying lengths of first and second level programs. Ratios may exceed 100 because some countries have many students from outside the normal age range.
[6] Enrollment totals and ratios exclude Democratic People's Republic of Korea. Data do not include adult education or special education provided outside regular schools.
[7] World total data for 2004–05.
[8] Estimated by the UNESCO Institute for Statistics.
[9] Classification or data coverage of levels has been revised. Data by level may not be comparable over time.
[10] Data for 1994–95.
[11] Policy change in 2000–01: introduction of free universal primary education.
[12] Data for 1991–92.
[13] Excludes private institutions.
[14] Data refer to universities and exclude Al Azhar.

[15] Excludes nonuniversity institutions (such as teacher training colleges and technical colleges) and excludes distance-learning universities.
[16] General education enrollment only. Excludes teacher training and vocational education enrollments.
[17] Data for 1992–93.
[18] Data for 1993–94.
[19] Not including the former Independent States of Transkei, Bophuthatswana, Venda, and Ciskei.
[20] Estimated.
[21] Data refer to government-aided and maintained schools only.
[22] Data for 1985–86.
[23] Includes preprimary education.
[24] National estimation.
[25] Excludes some nonuniversity institutions.
[26] Includes full-time students only.
[27] Data include both former East and West Germany.
[28] Including vocational education.
[29] Not including former ISCED level 7.
[30] Data do not include Vocational Education and Training Institutes (VETS).

NOTE: Some data have been revised from previously published figures. Detail may not sum to totals because of rounding.

SOURCE: United Nations Educational, Scientific, and Cultural Organization (UNESCO), Statistical Yearbook, 1999; Global Education Digest, 2003 and 2007; unpublished tabulations; and tables 3B, 5, and 14, retrieved July 11, 2008, from http://stats.uis.unesco.org/unesco/ReportFolders/ReportFolders.aspx. World Bank, World Development Indicators, 2000 and World Development Report, 2002. U.S. Department of Commerce, Census Bureau, International Data Base, retrieved July 9, 2008, from http://www.census.gov/ipc/www/idb/index.html. (This table was prepared July 2008.)

Table 400. School-age populations as a percentage of total population, by age group and country: Selected years, 1985 through 2005

Country	5- to 14-year-olds as a percent of total population									15- to 19-year-olds as a percent of total population								
	1985[1]	1990[1]	1995[1]	1998	1999	2002	2003	2004	2005	1985[2]	1990[2]	1995[2]	1998	1999	2002	2003	2004	2005
1	2	3	4	5	6	7	8	9	10	11	12	13	14	15	16	17	18	19
OECD countries																		
Australia	14	13	13	14	14	14	14	14	13	7	6	6	7	7	7	7	7	7
Austria	—	—	—	—	—	12	12	11	11	—	—	—	—	—	6	6	6	6
Belgium	11	11	11	12	12	12	12	12	12	6	5	5	6	6	6	6	6	6
Canada	13	12	12	14	14	—	13	13	13	6	5	5	7	7	—	7	7	7
Czech Republic	(³)	(³)	12	13	12	12	11	11	10	(³)	(³)	6	8	7	7	7	7	6
Denmark	12	10	10	11	12	12	13	13	13	6	6	5	6	5	5	5	5	6
Finland	11	12	11	13	13	12	12	12	12	6	5	5	6	6	6	6	6	6
France	13	12	12	13	13	12	12	12	12	6	6	5	7	7	7	6	6	7
Germany[4]	9	9	10	11	11	11	10	10	10	6	4	4	6	6	6	6	6	6
Greece	—	—	11	11	11	10	10	10	10	—	5	6	7	7	6	6	6	6
Hungary	—	—	—	—	—	12	11	11	11	—	—	—	—	—	6	6	6	6
Iceland	16	15	14	16	16	16	16	15	15	7	7	6	8	8	7	7	7	7
Ireland	18	18	15	16	15	14	14	14	14	8	8	8	9	9	8	8	8	7
Italy	13	10	9	10	10	10	10	10	9	6	6	5	6	5	5	5	5	5
Japan	14	12	10	11	10	10	10	9	9	6	7	5	6	6	6	6	5	5
Korea, Republic of	—	—	14	14	14	14	14	14	14	—	—	7	9	8	7	7	6	7
Luxembourg	10	10	11	12	12	13	13	13	13	5	4	4	6	6	6	6	6	6
Mexico	—	—	—	—	—	22	22	22	21	—	—	—	—	—	10	10	10	10
Netherlands	12	11	11	12	12	12	12	12	12	7	5	5	6	6	6	6	6	6
New Zealand	15	13	13	15	15	15	15	15	15	7	7	6	7	7	7	7	7	7
Norway	13	11	11	13	13	13	14	14	13	6	6	5	6	6	6	6	6	6
Poland	—	—	—	—	—	13	13	12	12	—	—	—	—	—	9	8	8	8
Portugal	—	—	—	—	—	10	11	10	10	—	—	—	—	—	6	6	6	6
Slovak Republic	(³)	(³)	—	—	—	13	13	13	12	(³)	(³)	—	—	—	8	8	8	8
Spain	15	13	10	11	10	10	10	10	9	7	7	6	7	7	6	6	6	5
Sweden	11	10	11	13	13	13	13	13	12	5	5	5	6	6	6	6	6	6
Switzerland	11	10	10	12	12	12	12	11	11	6	5	5	6	6	6	6	6	6
Turkey	21	21	20	21	21	—	19	19	19	9	9	9	11	11	—	9	9	9
United Kingdom	11	11	12	13	13	13	13	13	12	6	5	5	6	6	6	6	7	7
United States	13	13	13	14	15	15	14	14	14	6	5	6	7	7	7	7	7	7
Reporting partner economies																		
Brazil	—	—	—	—	—	20	21	20	19	—	—	—	—	—	11	11	10	10
Chile	—	—	—	—	—	19	18	18	18	—	—	—	—	—	9	9	9	9
Estonia	(³)	(³)	—	—	—	—	—	—	11	(³)	(³)	—	—	—	—	—	—	8
Israel	—	—	—	—	—	18	18	18	18	—	—	—	—	—	9	9	8	8
Russian Federation	(³)	(³)	14	—	14	12	12	11	10	(³)	(³)	—	—	—	8	9	9	9
Slovenia	(³)	(³)	—	—	—	—	—	—	10	(³)	(³)	—	—	—	—	—	—	6

—Not available.
[1] Data are for the 5- to 13-year-old population.
[2] Data are for the 14- to 17-year-old population.
[3] Country did not exist in its current form in the given year.
[4] Data for 1985 are for the former West Germany.

SOURCE: Organization for Economic Cooperation and Development (OECD), *Education at a Glance*, selected years, 1987 through 2001; and Education Online Database, retrieved July 11, 2008, from http://stats.oecd.org/WBOS/Default.aspx. (This table was prepared July 2008.)

Table 401. Percentage of population enrolled in secondary and postsecondary education, by age group and country: Selected years, 1985 through 2005

Country	Secondary, 16 years old, 2005	Secondary, 17 years old, 2005	Postsecondary education (total tertiary education)															
			18 to 21 years old					22 to 25 years old					26 to 29 years old				
			1985	1990	1999	2003	2005	1985	1990	1999	2003	2005	1985	1990	1999	2003	2005
1	2	3	4	5	6	7	8	9	10	11	12	13	14	15	16	17	18
OECD countries																	
Australia	93	80	—	—	31	34	34	—	—	15	20	21	—	—	8	10	10
Austria	92	77	—	—	15	16	16	—	—	20	19	20	—	—	12	9	9
Belgium (Flemish)	101	99	25	—	42	42	43	7	—	15	18	19	2	—	3	5	6
Canada	—	—	—	—	27	—	—	—	—	18	—	—	—	—	7	—	—
Czech Republic	100	97	(¹)	(¹)	17	21	23	(¹)	(¹)	12	16	21	(¹)	(¹)	4	5	6
Denmark	93	85	7	7	8	10	10	16	18	27	30	34	8	9	15	17	20
Finland	96	95	9	14	23	23	24	17	21	35	39	40	8	10	18	19	20
France	97	89	19	25	35	36	36	10	12	20	21	20	4	4	5	5	5
Germany[2]	96	92	9	9	11	13	13	—	16	19	21	23	9	10	11	12	13
Greece	101	75	—	—	54	51	65	—	—	7	25	18	—	—	2	12	8
Hungary	96	92	—	—	20	27	29	—	—	14	19	23	—	—	5	9	9
Iceland	94	83	—	—	7	12	12	—	—	21	26	28	—	—	9	14	16
Ireland	96	76	—	21	33	37	38	—	—	11	12	13	—	—	3	5	5
Italy	88	83	—	—	22	27	29	—	—	21	22	23	—	—	7	8	8
Japan	97	95	—	—	—	—	—	—	—	—	—	—	—	—	—	—	—
Korea, Republic of	95	93	—	—	51	58	65	—	—	26	32	32	—	—	6	7	6
Luxembourg	82	78	—	—	—	—	—	—	—	—	—	—	—	—	—	—	—
Mexico	54	41	—	—	12	15	16	—	—	8	8	9	—	—	1	2	3
Netherlands	95	83	14	18	26	28	29	12	13	20	22	24	6	5	5	6	7
New Zealand	87	70		21	29	28	34	—	15	14	21	23	—	—	8	10	11
Norway	94	92	9	14	19	19	19	14	17	28	29	30	6	8	12	14	14
Poland	97	95	—	—	21	28	31	—	—	21	28	30	—	—	5	7	6
Portugal	80	76	6	—	25	27	27	5	—	17	21	21	2	—	6	8	8
Slovak Republic	95	90	(¹)	(¹)	—	21	22	(¹)	(¹)	—	14	16	(¹)	(¹)	—	4	5
Spain	94	82	15	21	32	34	34	11	14	24	23	22	4	5	8	8	9
Sweden	97	98	8	9	16	17	17	11	11	25	30	32	7	6	12	15	16
Switzerland	90	86	6	6	10	11	12	11	12	17	19	20	5	6	9	9	10
Turkey	55	28	—	7	14	14	20	—	4	9	6	11	—	2	4	2	4
United Kingdom	94	80	15	16	29	30	28	7	11	12	12	13	—	—	6	7	7
United States	96	83	37	41	44	39	45	15	17	18	23	23	8	9	11	11	11
Reporting partner economies																	
Brazil	87	83	—	—	—	9	10	—	—	—	8	9	—	—	—	4	5
Chile	95	89	—	—	—	—	—	—	—	—	—	—	—	—	—	—	—
Estonia	97	92	(¹)	(¹)	—	—	32	(¹)	(¹)	—	—	22	(¹)	(¹)	—	—	12
Israel	95	90	—	—	—	12	12	—	—	—	26	25	—	—	—	16	15
Russian Federation	21	19	(¹)	(¹)	—	—	41	(¹)	(¹)	—	—	26	(¹)	(¹)	—	—	—
Slovenia	98	94	(¹)	(¹)	—	—	37	(¹)	(¹)	—	—	35	(¹)	(¹)	—	—	11

—Not available.
¹Country did not exist in its current form in the given year.
²Data for 1985 are for the former West Germany.
NOTE: Data refer to programs classified by the Organization for Economic Cooperation and Development (OECD) as International Standard Classification of Education (ISCED) level 3, level 5A (first and second award), level 5B, and level 6. ISCED level 3 corresponds to secondary education in the United States. ISCED levels 5A (first and second award), 5B, and 6 together make up total tertiary education, which corresponds to 2-year and 4-year college undergraduate and graduate programs in the United States. Includes both full-time and part-time students. Some increases in enrollment rates may be due to more complete reporting by countries. Enrollment figures may not be directly comparable due to differing definitions of postsecondary (tertiary) education and the age at which it begins. Differences in reference dates between enrollment and population data can result in enrollment rates that exceed 100 percent. Some data have been revised from previously published figures.
SOURCE: Organization for Economic Cooperation and Development (OECD), *Education at a Glance*, selected years, 1987 through 2001; and Education Online Database, retrieved June 30, 2008, from http://stats.oecd.org/WBOS/Default.aspx. (This table was prepared July 2008.)

Table 402. Pupils per teacher in public and private elementary and secondary schools, by level of education and country: Selected years, 1985 through 2006

Country	Elementary								Junior high school (lower secondary)								Senior high school (upper secondary)							
	1985	1990	2000	2002	2003	2004	2005	2006	1985	1990	2000	2002	2003	2004	2005	2006	1985	1990	2000	2002	2003	2004	2005	2006
1	2	3	4	5	6	7	8	9	10	11	12	13	14	15	16	17	18	19	20	21	22	23	24	25
OECD average	—	—	**17.7**	**16.6**	**16.5**	**16.9**	**16.7**	**16.2**	—	—	**15.0**	**14.4**	**14.3**	**13.7**	**13.7**	**13.3**	—	—	**13.9**	**13.1**	**13.0**	**12.7**	**13.0**	**12.4**
Australia	13.8[1]	—	17.3	16.9	16.6	16.4	16.2	16.0	—	—	—	9.8	10.0	10.4	10.6	10.4	3.2	—	—	12.5[2,3]	12.4[2,3]	12.3[2,3]	12.1[2,3]	12.2[2,3]
Austria	11.3	11.6	—	14.4	14.4	15.1	14.1	13.9	9.2	7.7	—	9.8	10.0	10.4	10.6	9.4	15.2	12.4	—	10.3	10.2	11.0	11.3	11.3
Belgium	—	—	15.0[4]	13.1	13.1	12.9	12.8	12.6	—	—	—	—	10.6	10.6	9.4	9.4	—	—	9.7[2,5]	9.3[2,5]	9.6[5]	9.2[5]	9.9[5]	10.2[5]
Canada	18.1	17.1	18.1	—	—	—	—	—	16.0	15.5	18.1	—	—	—	—	—	16.0	15.3	19.5	—	—	—	—	—
Czech Republic	(6)	(6)	19.7	18.9	18.3	17.9	17.5	17.3	(6)	(6)	14.7	14.4	14.3	13.5	13.5	12.3	(6)	—	11.5	12.9[5]	12.6	12.6	12.8	11.9
Denmark	12.7	11.2	10.4	—	—	—	—	—	10.2	9.3	11.4	10.9[7]	10.8[7]	11.3[7]	11.9[7]	11.4[7]	14.8	13.3	14.4	14.2	13.4	—	—	9.7
Finland	—	—	16.9	15.8	16.6	16.3	15.9	15.0	—	—	10.7	10.6	9.8	10.0	10.0	9.7	—	—	17.0[5,8]	16.0[5,8]	15.9[5,8]	16.2[5,8]	18.0[5,8]	15.8[5,8]
France	—	—	19.8	19.4	19.4	19.4	19.4	19.3[9]	—	—	14.7	13.7	13.7	14.1	14.2	14.1[9]	—	—	10.4	10.6	10.6	10.3	10.3	9.7[9]
Germany[10]	20.7	20.3	19.8	18.9	18.7	18.8	18.8	18.7	—	14.6	15.7	15.7	15.6	15.6	15.5	15.5	23.7	21.0	13.9	13.6	13.7	13.9	14.0	14.3
Greece	—	—	13.4	12.5	12.1	11.3	11.1	10.6	16.9	14.6	10.8	9.3	8.7	8.2	7.9	8.0	—	—	10.5	9.3	8.6	8.4	8.8	8.3
Hungary	—	—	10.9	10.8	10.6	10.7	10.6	10.4	—	—	10.9	10.7	10.6	10.2	10.4	10.2	—	—	11.4[5]	13.1	13.2	12.3	12.2	12.3
Iceland	—	—	—	—	—	—	—	—	—	—	12.7[7]	11.4[7]	11.3[7]	11.4[7]	11.3[7]	10.6[7]	—	—	9.7	10.6	10.7[5]	11.1	10.8[5]	10.8[5]
Ireland	12.8	10.7	21.5	19.5	18.7	18.3	17.9	19.4	9.6	8.5	10.4	9.9	10.3	10.3	10.1	10.3	7.2	8.3	15.9[2,5]	14.3[2,5]	13.7[2,5]	14.3[2,5]	15.5[2,5]	14.6[2,5]
Italy	—	10.7	11.0	10.6	10.9	10.7	10.6	10.7	—	8.5	10.4	9.9	10.3	10.3	10.1	10.3	10.8	10.7	10.2	10.3	10.8	11.5	11.0	11.0
Japan	—	20.8[1]	20.9	20.3	19.9	19.6	19.4	19.2	—	18.6	16.8	16.2	15.7	15.3	15.1	14.9	—	16.2	14.0	13.7[5]	13.5[5]	13.2[5]	13.0[5]	12.7[5]
Korea, Republic of	—	—	32.1	31.4	30.2	29.1	28.0	26.7	—	—	21.5	20.7	19.9	20.4	20.8	20.8	—	—	20.9	16.5	16.0	15.9	16.0	15.9
Luxembourg	—	—	15.9[1]	11.6[1]	10.8[1]	—	11.7	11.3[1]	—	—	11.5	14.1	12.6	11.2[1]	12.7	12.6	—	—	9.2[1,2]	9.0[1,2]	9.0[1,2]	9.0[1,2]	9.0[1,2]	9.0[1,2,5]
Mexico	—	—	27.2	26.9	26.7	28.5	28.3	28.0	—	—	34.8	31.5	32.4	33.7	33.7	33.4	—	—	26.5	24.3	24.0	25.2	25.8	25.4
Netherlands	20.2	19.2	16.8[4]	17.0[4]	16.0[4]	15.9[4]	15.9[4]	15.3[4]	12.7	12.4	—	—	—	—	—	—	—	—	17.1[2]	15.9[2]	15.7[2]	15.8[2]	16.2[2]	15.8[2,5]
New Zealand	20.1	19.1	20.6	19.6	19.9	16.7	18.1	17.7	—	—	19.9	19.4	18.8	17.3	16.8	16.6	—	—	13.1	13.8	10.9	12.5	12.9	12.7
Norway	—	—	12.4	10.3[1]	11.7[1]	11.9[1]	—	10.9[1]	—	—	9.9	10.1[1]	10.4[1]	10.5[1]	—	10.2[1]	—	—	9.7	9.2[1,5]	9.2[1,5]	9.6[1,5]	—	9.7[1,5]
Poland	—	—	12.7	12.8	11.9	11.1	11.7	11.5	—	—	11.5	14.1	12.6	—	12.7	12.6	—	—	16.9	13.7	13.5	—	12.9	12.8
Portugal	—	—	12.1	11.0	—	11.1	10.8	10.6	—	—	10.4	9.3	13.9	10.0	8.2	8.3	—	—	7.9	7.5	—	7.3	8.0	7.5[5]
Slovak Republic	(6)	(6)	18.3	20.1	19.4	18.9	18.9	18.6	(6)	(6)	13.5	14.0	13.9	13.9	14.1	13.7	(6)	(6)	12.8	13.3	14.0	14.2	14.3	14.2
Spain	26.8	21.2	14.9	14.6	14.3	14.3	14.3	14.2	21.4	18.8	—	13.7	13.3	12.9	12.5	12.5	15.3	14.8	11.9[2]	8.3	7.9	8.0	8.1	7.8
Sweden	11.6	10.6	12.8	12.5	12.3	12.1	12.2	12.1	10.8	10.2	12.8	12.2	12.1	11.9	12.0	11.4	13.1	11.9	15.2	14.1	14.1	14.0	14.0	13.8
Switzerland	—	—	—	—	—	14.3[1]	14.6[1]	15.1[1]	—	—	—	†	†	11.2[1]	11.7[1]	12.3[1]	—	—	—	13.7	13.5	—	12.9	12.8
Turkey	31.1	30.6	30.5	27.5	25.9	26.5	25.8	26.7	41.3	48.4	17.6[3]	17.6[3]	17.4	17.1	17.0	16.7	11.0	12.1	14.0	17.7	18.0	16.9	16.2	15.8
United Kingdom	19.7	22.0	21.2	19.9	20.0	21.1	20.7	19.8	16.5	18.5	16.3	15.5	15.5	15.2	15.1	14.7	11.1	13.9	12.5[3]	12.5[3]	12.6[3]	12.3[3,5]	11.8[3,5]	11.6[3,5]
United States	17.0	15.6	15.8	15.5	15.5	15.0	14.9	14.6	16.5	15.9	16.3	15.5	15.5	15.2	15.1	14.6	16.2	15.8	14.1	15.6	15.6	16.0	16.0	15.7
Reporting partner economies																								
Brazil	—	—	—	22.4	23.5	23.5	22.9	22.5	—	—	—	17.9	—	18.8	18.1	17.6	—	—	—	16.7	—	18.3	17.6	17.0
Chile	—	—	—	33.1	33.9	27.1	25.9	25.5	—	—	—	32.9	33.5	44.3	25.9	25.5	—	—	—	31.5	32.3	26.8	26.6	26.3
Estonia	(6)	(6)	—	—	—	—	14.1	14.1	(6)	(6)	—	—	—	—	—	12.3	(6)	(6)	—	—	—	—	12.3	13.3
Israel	(6)	(6)	—	20.3	20.9	16.9	17.3	17.2	(6)	(6)	—	13.0	13.4	14.1	13.4	14.1	(6)	(6)	—	14.0	12.9	12.2	13.4	13.2
Russian Federation	(6)	(6)	—	17.1	17.0	17.0	—	—	(6)	(6)	—	—	—	—	11.1	10.2	(6)	(6)	—	11.3[2]	8.5[2]	10.3[2,5]	11.2[5,11]	9.9[2,5,11]
Slovenia	(6)	(6)	—	—	—	—	15.0	14.9	(6)	(6)	—	—	—	—	—	—	(6)	(6)	—	15.6	15.6	16.0	14.6	14.0[5]

—Not available.
†Not applicable.
[1]Public schools only.
[2]Includes junior high school data.
[3]Includes only general programs.
[4]Includes preprimary data.
[5]Includes postsecondary non-higher-education.
[6]Country did not exist in its current form in the given year.
[7]Includes elementary school data.

[8]Includes tertiary type B education (i.e., occupation-specific education corresponding to that offered at the associate's degree level in the United States).
[9]Excludes independent private institutions.
[10]Data for 1985 are for the former West Germany.
[11]Excludes general programs in upper secondary education.
NOTE: In the U.S. data in this table, elementary corresponds to grades 1 through 6, junior high school corresponds to grades 7 through 9, and senior high school corresponds to grades 10 through 12.
SOURCE: Organization for Economic Cooperation and Development (OECD), Education Online Database: Annual National Accounts, Vol. 1, 1997; and Education at a Glance, 2002 through 2008. (This table was prepared July 2008.)

Table 403. Average mathematics literacy, reading literacy, and science literacy scores of 15-year-olds, by sex and country: 2006

Country or other jurisdiction	Mathematics literacy						Reading literacy						Science literacy					
	Total		Male		Female		Total		Male		Female		Total		Male		Female	
1	2		3		4		5		6		7		8		9		10	
OECD total[1]	484	(1.2)	489	(1.3)	478	(1.3)	484	(1.0)	466	(1.2)	502	(1.3)	491	(1.2)	492	(1.4)	490	(1.3)
OECD average[2]	498	(0.5)	503	(0.7)	492	(0.6)	492	(0.6)	473	(0.7)	511	(0.7)	500	(0.5)	501	(0.7)	499	(0.6)
Australia	520	(2.2)	527	(3.2)	513	(2.4)	513	(2.1)	495	(3.0)	532	(2.2)	527	(2.3)	527	(3.2)	527	(2.7)
Austria	505	(3.7)	517	(4.4)	494	(4.1)	490	(4.1)	468	(4.9)	513	(5.5)	511	(3.9)	515	(4.2)	507	(4.9)
Belgium	520	(3.0)	524	(4.1)	517	(3.4)	501	(3.0)	482	(4.1)	522	(3.5)	510	(2.5)	511	(3.3)	510	(3.2)
Canada	527	(2.0)	534	(2.4)	520	(2.0)	527	(2.4)	511	(2.8)	543	(2.5)	534	(2.0)	536	(2.5)	532	(2.1)
Czech Republic	510	(3.6)	514	(4.2)	504	(4.8)	483	(4.2)	463	(5.0)	509	(5.4)	513	(3.5)	515	(4.2)	510	(4.8)
Denmark	513	(2.6)	518	(2.9)	508	(3.0)	494	(3.2)	480	(3.6)	509	(3.5)	496	(3.1)	500	(3.6)	491	(3.4)
Finland	548	(2.3)	554	(2.7)	543	(2.6)	547	(2.1)	521	(2.7)	572	(2.3)	563	(2.0)	562	(2.6)	565	(2.4)
France	496	(3.2)	499	(4.0)	492	(3.3)	488	(4.1)	470	(5.2)	505	(3.9)	495	(3.4)	497	(4.3)	494	(3.6)
Germany	504	(3.9)	513	(4.6)	494	(3.9)	495	(4.4)	475	(5.3)	517	(4.4)	516	(3.8)	519	(4.6)	512	(3.8)
Greece	459	(3.0)	462	(4.3)	457	(3.0)	460	(4.0)	432	(5.7)	488	(3.5)	473	(3.2)	468	(4.5)	479	(3.4)
Hungary	491	(2.9)	496	(3.5)	486	(3.7)	482	(3.3)	463	(3.7)	503	(3.9)	504	(2.7)	507	(3.3)	501	(3.5)
Iceland	506	(1.8)	503	(2.6)	508	(2.2)	484	(1.9)	460	(2.8)	509	(2.3)	491	(1.6)	488	(2.6)	494	(2.1)
Ireland	501	(2.8)	507	(3.7)	496	(3.2)	517	(3.5)	500	(4.5)	534	(3.8)	508	(3.2)	508	(4.3)	509	(3.3)
Italy	462	(2.3)	470	(2.9)	453	(2.7)	469	(2.4)	448	(3.4)	489	(2.8)	475	(2.0)	477	(2.8)	474	(2.5)
Japan	523	(3.3)	533	(4.8)	513	(4.9)	498	(3.6)	483	(5.4)	513	(5.2)	531	(3.4)	533	(4.9)	530	(5.1)
Korea, Republic of	547	(3.8)	552	(5.3)	543	(4.5)	556	(3.8)	539	(4.6)	574	(4.5)	522	(3.4)	521	(4.8)	523	(3.9)
Luxembourg	490	(1.1)	498	(1.7)	482	(1.8)	479	(1.3)	464	(2.0)	495	(2.1)	486	(1.1)	491	(1.8)	482	(1.8)
Mexico	406	(2.9)	410	(3.4)	401	(3.1)	410	(3.1)	393	(3.5)	427	(3.0)	410	(2.7)	413	(3.2)	406	(2.6)
Netherlands	531	(2.6)	537	(3.1)	524	(2.8)	507	(2.9)	495	(3.7)	519	(3.0)	525	(2.7)	528	(3.2)	521	(3.1)
New Zealand	522	(2.4)	527	(3.1)	517	(3.6)	521	(3.0)	502	(3.6)	539	(3.6)	530	(2.7)	528	(3.9)	532	(3.6)
Norway	490	(2.6)	493	(3.3)	487	(2.8)	484	(3.2)	462	(3.8)	508	(3.3)	487	(3.1)	484	(3.8)	489	(3.2)
Poland	495	(2.4)	500	(2.8)	491	(2.7)	508	(2.8)	487	(3.4)	528	(2.8)	498	(2.3)	500	(2.7)	496	(2.6)
Portugal	466	(3.1)	474	(3.7)	459	(3.2)	472	(3.6)	455	(4.4)	488	(3.5)	474	(3.0)	477	(3.7)	472	(3.2)
Slovak Republic	492	(2.8)	499	(3.7)	485	(3.5)	466	(3.1)	446	(4.2)	488	(3.8)	488	(2.6)	491	(3.9)	485	(3.0)
Spain	480	(2.3)	484	(2.6)	476	(2.6)	461	(2.2)	443	(2.6)	479	(2.3)	488	(2.6)	491	(2.9)	486	(2.7)
Sweden	502	(2.4)	505	(2.7)	500	(3.0)	507	(3.4)	488	(4.0)	528	(3.5)	503	(2.4)	504	(2.7)	503	(2.9)
Switzerland	530	(3.2)	536	(3.3)	523	(3.6)	499	(3.1)	484	(3.2)	515	(3.3)	512	(3.2)	514	(3.3)	509	(3.6)
Turkey	424	(4.9)	427	(5.6)	421	(5.1)	447	(4.2)	427	(5.1)	471	(4.3)	424	(3.8)	418	(4.6)	430	(4.1)
United Kingdom	495	(2.1)	504	(2.6)	487	(2.6)	495	(2.3)	480	(3.0)	510	(2.6)	515	(2.3)	520	(3.0)	510	(2.8)
United States[3]	474	(4.0)	479	(4.6)	470	(3.9)	—	(†)	—	(†)	—	(†)	489	(4.2)	489	(5.1)	489	(4.0)
Reporting partner economies																		
Argentina	381	(6.2)	388	(6.5)	375	(7.2)	374	(7.2)	345	(8.3)	399	(7.4)	391	(6.1)	384	(6.5)	397	(6.8)
Azerbaijan	476	(2.3)	475	(2.4)	477	(2.6)	353	(3.1)	343	(3.5)	363	(3.3)	382	(2.8)	379	(3.1)	386	(2.7)
Brazil	370	(2.9)	380	(3.4)	361	(3.0)	393	(3.7)	376	(4.3)	408	(3.7)	390	(2.8)	395	(3.2)	386	(2.9)
Bulgaria	413	(6.1)	412	(6.7)	415	(6.5)	402	(6.9)	374	(7.7)	432	(6.9)	434	(6.1)	426	(6.6)	443	(6.9)
Chile	411	(4.6)	424	(5.5)	396	(4.7)	442	(5.0)	434	(6.0)	451	(5.4)	438	(4.3)	448	(5.4)	426	(4.4)
Colombia	370	(3.8)	382	(4.1)	360	(5.0)	385	(5.1)	375	(5.6)	394	(5.6)	388	(3.4)	393	(4.1)	384	(4.1)
Croatia	467	(2.4)	474	(3.2)	461	(2.8)	477	(2.8)	452	(3.8)	502	(3.3)	493	(2.4)	492	(3.3)	494	(3.1)
Estonia	515	(2.7)	515	(3.3)	514	(3.0)	501	(2.9)	478	(3.2)	524	(3.1)	531	(2.5)	530	(3.1)	533	(2.9)
Hong Kong-China	547	(2.7)	555	(3.9)	540	(3.7)	536	(2.4)	520	(3.5)	551	(3.0)	542	(2.5)	546	(3.5)	539	(3.5)
Indonesia	391	(5.6)	399	(8.3)	382	(4.0)	393	(5.9)	384	(8.7)	402	(4.2)	393	(5.7)	399	(8.2)	387	(3.7)
Israel	442	(4.3)	448	(6.6)	436	(4.3)	439	(4.6)	417	(6.5)	460	(4.6)	454	(3.7)	456	(5.6)	452	(4.2)
Jordan	384	(3.3)	381	(5.3)	388	(3.9)	401	(3.3)	373	(5.6)	428	(3.4)	422	(2.8)	408	(4.5)	436	(3.3)
Kyrgyzstan	311	(3.4)	311	(4.0)	310	(3.4)	285	(3.5)	257	(4.4)	308	(3.3)	322	(2.9)	319	(3.6)	325	(3.0)
Latvia	486	(3.0)	489	(3.5)	484	(3.2)	479	(3.7)	454	(4.3)	504	(3.5)	490	(3.0)	486	(3.5)	493	(3.2)
Liechtenstein	525	(4.2)	525	(7.4)	525	(7.0)	510	(3.9)	486	(7.7)	531	(6.3)	522	(4.1)	516	(7.6)	527	(6.3)
Lithuania	486	(2.9)	487	(3.3)	485	(3.3)	470	(3.0)	445	(3.5)	496	(3.2)	488	(2.8)	483	(3.1)	493	(3.1)
Macao-China	525	(1.3)	530	(2.1)	520	(1.7)	492	(1.1)	479	(1.8)	505	(1.5)	511	(1.1)	513	(1.8)	509	(1.6)
Montenegro	399	(1.4)	405	(2.3)	393	(1.9)	392	(1.2)	370	(2.0)	415	(1.8)	412	(1.1)	411	(1.7)	413	(1.7)
Qatar	318	(1.0)	311	(1.6)	325	(1.3)	312	(1.2)	280	(1.9)	346	(1.6)	349	(0.9)	334	(1.2)	365	(1.3)
Romania	415	(4.2)	418	(4.2)	412	(4.9)	396	(4.7)	374	(4.5)	418	(5.2)	418	(4.2)	417	(4.1)	419	(4.8)
Russian Federation	476	(3.9)	479	(4.6)	473	(3.9)	440	(4.3)	420	(4.8)	458	(4.3)	479	(3.7)	481	(4.1)	478	(3.7)
Serbia	435	(3.5)	438	(4.0)	433	(4.4)	401	(3.5)	381	(3.4)	422	(4.2)	436	(3.0)	433	(3.3)	438	(3.8)
Slovenia	504	(1.0)	507	(1.8)	502	(1.8)	494	(1.0)	467	(1.9)	521	(1.4)	519	(1.1)	515	(2.0)	523	(1.9)
Chinese Taipei	549	(4.1)	556	(4.7)	543	(5.9)	496	(3.4)	486	(4.4)	507	(4.2)	532	(3.6)	536	(4.3)	529	(5.1)
Thailand	417	(2.3)	413	(3.8)	420	(2.6)	417	(2.6)	386	(4.0)	440	(3.0)	421	(2.1)	411	(3.4)	428	(2.5)
Tunisia	365	(4.0)	373	(4.4)	358	(4.4)	380	(4.0)	361	(4.6)	398	(3.9)	386	(3.0)	383	(3.2)	388	(3.5)
Uruguay	427	(2.6)	433	(3.6)	420	(3.1)	413	(3.4)	389	(4.4)	435	(3.8)	428	(2.7)	427	(4.0)	430	(2.7)

—Not available.
†Not applicable.
[1]Illustrates how a country compares with the OECD area as a whole. Computed taking the OECD countries as a single entity, to which each country contributes in proportion to the number of 15-year-olds enrolled in its schools.
[2]Refers to the mean of the data values for all OECD countries, to which each country contributes equally, regardless of the absolute size of the student population of each country.
[3]PISA 2006 reading literacy results are not reported for the United States because of an error in printing the test booklets. In several areas of the reading literacy assessment, students were incorrectly instructed to refer to the passage on the "opposite page" when, in fact, the necessary passage appeared on the previous page. Because of the small number of items used in assessing reading literacy, it was not possible to recalibrate the score to exclude the affected items. Also, as a result of the printing error, the mean performance in mathematics and science may be misestimated by approximately 1 score point. The impact is below one standard error.

NOTE: Possible scores range from 0 to 1,000. Standard errors appear in parentheses.
SOURCE: Organization for Economic Cooperation and Development (OECD), Program for International Student Assessment (PISA), 2006, *PISA 2006 Science Competencies for Tomorrow's World*. (This table was prepared July 2008.)

Table 404. Mean scores and percentage distribution of 15-year-olds scoring at each mathematics literacy proficiency level, by country: 2006

Country or other jurisdiction	Mean score		Below level 1		Level 1		Level 2		Level 3		Level 4		Level 5		Level 6	
1	2		3		4		5		6		7		8		9	
OECD total[2]	484	(1.2)	10.2	(0.35)	16.2	(0.31)	23.2	(0.40)	22.8	(0.40)	16.7	(0.29)	8.3	(0.21)	2.6	(0.10)
OECD average[3]	498	(0.5)	7.7	(0.14)	13.6	(0.15)	21.9	(0.17)	24.3	(0.16)	19.1	(0.16)	10.0	(0.12)	3.3	(0.09)
Australia	520	(2.2)	3.3	(0.28)	9.7	(0.41)	20.5	(0.62)	26.9	(0.57)	23.2	(0.54)	12.1	(0.48)	4.3	(0.47)
Austria	505	(3.7)	7.5	(0.95)	12.5	(1.09)	19.5	(1.06)	23.3	(0.90)	21.3	(1.12)	12.3	(0.79)	3.5	(0.50)
Belgium	520	(3.0)	7.1	(0.85)	10.2	(0.71)	17.0	(0.69)	21.4	(0.67)	21.9	(0.79)	16.0	(0.68)	6.4	(0.40)
Canada	527	(2.0)	2.8	(0.29)	8.0	(0.52)	18.6	(0.65)	27.5	(0.73)	25.1	(0.66)	13.6	(0.58)	4.4	(0.37)
Czech Republic	510	(3.6)	7.2	(0.72)	11.9	(0.84)	20.5	(0.99)	23.0	(0.92)	19.1	(1.06)	12.3	(0.75)	6.0	(0.67)
Denmark	513	(2.6)	3.6	(0.54)	10.0	(0.67)	21.4	(0.78)	28.8	(0.88)	22.5	(0.85)	10.9	(0.58)	2.8	(0.39)
Finland	548	(2.3)	1.1	(0.21)	4.8	(0.53)	14.4	(0.70)	27.2	(0.73)	28.1	(0.83)	18.1	(0.76)	6.3	(0.50)
France	496	(3.2)	8.4	(0.82)	13.9	(1.00)	21.4	(1.16)	24.2	(1.01)	19.6	(0.95)	9.9	(0.67)	2.6	(0.47)
Germany	504	(3.9)	7.3	(1.01)	12.5	(0.80)	21.2	(1.13)	24.0	(1.07)	19.4	(0.90)	11.0	(0.78)	4.5	(0.50)
Greece	459	(3.0)	13.3	(1.10)	19.0	(1.19)	26.8	(0.94)	23.2	(1.12)	12.6	(1.05)	4.2	(0.47)	0.9	(0.17)
Hungary	491	(2.9)	6.7	(0.56)	14.5	(0.80)	25.1	(1.01)	26.5	(0.94)	16.9	(1.07)	7.7	(0.72)	2.6	(0.47)
Iceland	506	(1.8)	5.1	(0.41)	11.7	(0.68)	22.3	(0.88)	26.6	(1.00)	21.7	(0.88)	10.1	(0.65)	2.5	(0.32)
Ireland	501	(2.8)	4.1	(0.50)	12.3	(0.93)	24.1	(1.00)	28.6	(0.90)	20.6	(0.94)	8.6	(0.67)	1.6	(0.25)
Italy	462	(2.3)	13.5	(0.72)	19.3	(0.69)	25.5	(0.75)	22.1	(0.67)	13.3	(0.56)	5.0	(0.36)	1.3	(0.27)
Japan	523	(3.3)	3.9	(0.59)	9.1	(0.71)	18.9	(0.89)	26.1	(1.00)	23.7	(1.03)	13.5	(0.79)	4.8	(0.51)
Korea, Republic of	547	(3.8)	2.3	(0.52)	6.5	(0.71)	15.2	(0.69)	23.5	(1.07)	25.5	(0.99)	18.0	(0.78)	9.1	(1.29)
Luxembourg	490	(1.1)	8.3	(0.55)	14.5	(0.67)	23.2	(0.72)	25.2	(0.83)	18.2	(1.02)	8.2	(0.54)	2.3	(0.28)
Mexico	406	(2.9)	28.4	(1.37)	28.1	(0.88)	25.2	(0.85)	13.1	(0.64)	4.3	(0.40)	0.8	(0.19)	0.1	(0.04)
Netherlands	531	(2.6)	2.4	(0.61)	9.1	(0.82)	18.9	(0.94)	24.3	(0.88)	24.1	(1.06)	15.8	(0.76)	5.4	(0.64)
New Zealand	522	(2.4)	4.0	(0.32)	10.0	(0.79)	19.5	(0.99)	25.5	(1.13)	22.1	(1.02)	13.2	(0.75)	5.7	(0.50)
Norway	490	(2.6)	7.3	(0.73)	14.9	(0.97)	24.3	(0.81)	25.6	(1.01)	17.4	(0.85)	8.3	(0.74)	2.1	(0.25)
Poland	495	(2.4)	5.7	(0.42)	14.2	(0.70)	24.7	(0.80)	26.2	(0.69)	18.6	(0.78)	8.6	(0.67)	2.0	(0.29)
Portugal	466	(3.1)	12.0	(1.05)	18.7	(0.87)	25.1	(0.90)	24.0	(0.92)	14.4	(0.81)	4.9	(0.45)	0.8	(0.20)
Slovak Republic	492	(2.8)	8.1	(0.72)	12.8	(0.86)	24.1	(1.03)	25.3	(0.97)	18.8	(0.87)	8.6	(0.69)	2.4	(0.41)
Spain	480	(2.3)	8.6	(0.52)	16.1	(0.85)	25.2	(0.94)	26.2	(0.61)	16.8	(0.54)	6.1	(0.43)	1.2	(0.18)
Sweden	502	(2.4)	5.4	(0.60)	12.9	(0.83)	23.0	(0.82)	26.0	(0.97)	20.1	(0.89)	9.7	(0.61)	2.9	(0.37)
Switzerland	530	(3.2)	4.6	(0.49)	9.0	(0.60)	17.4	(0.96)	23.2	(0.82)	23.2	(0.91)	15.9	(0.72)	6.8	(0.63)
Turkey	424	(4.9)	24.0	(1.37)	28.1	(1.35)	24.3	(1.25)	12.8	(0.80)	6.7	(0.95)	3.0	(0.77)	1.2	(0.55)
United Kingdom	495	(2.1)	5.9	(0.60)	13.8	(0.70)	24.7	(0.79)	26.3	(0.71)	18.1	(0.60)	8.7	(0.48)	2.5	(0.27)
United States[4]	474	(4.0)	9.9	(1.15)	18.2	(0.91)	26.1	(1.21)	23.1	(1.09)	15.1	(0.99)	6.4	(0.66)	1.3	(0.24)
Reporting partner economies																
Argentina	381	(6.2)	39.4	(2.72)	24.7	(1.46)	20.4	(1.66)	10.6	(1.05)	3.8	(0.56)	0.9	(0.31)	0.1	(0.11)
Azerbaijan	476	(2.3)	0.2	(0.10)	10.4	(0.99)	47.6	(1.64)	34.4	(1.59)	6.6	(0.86)	0.6	(0.26)	0.2	(0.13)
Brazil	370	(2.9)	46.6	(1.40)	25.9	(1.25)	16.6	(0.90)	7.1	(0.58)	2.8	(0.42)	0.8	(0.25)	0.2	(0.10)
Bulgaria	413	(6.1)	29.4	(2.18)	23.9	(1.12)	22.0	(1.04)	14.9	(1.08)	6.7	(0.82)	2.5	(0.57)	0.6	(0.28)
Chile	411	(4.6)	28.2	(1.94)	26.9	(1.20)	23.9	(1.14)	13.9	(1.03)	5.6	(0.71)	1.3	(0.34)	0.1	(0.07)
Colombia	370	(3.8)	44.6	(1.76)	27.3	(1.13)	18.2	(1.27)	7.6	(0.67)	1.9	(0.44)	0.4	(0.18)	#	(†)
Croatia	467	(2.4)	9.3	(0.69)	19.3	(0.92)	28.9	(1.06)	24.3	(0.86)	13.6	(0.67)	4.0	(0.47)	0.8	(0.21)
Estonia	515	(2.7)	2.7	(0.46)	9.4	(0.82)	21.9	(0.91)	30.2	(1.01)	23.3	(1.11)	10.0	(0.63)	2.6	(0.36)
Hong Kong-China	547	(2.7)	2.9	(0.45)	6.6	(0.63)	14.4	(0.84)	22.7	(1.07)	25.6	(0.90)	18.7	(0.78)	9.0	(0.82)
Indonesia	391	(5.6)	35.2	(2.21)	30.5	(1.58)	20.4	(0.99)	10.6	(2.04)	2.8	(0.74)	0.4	(0.16)	#	(†)
Israel	442	(4.3)	22.2	(1.54)	19.8	(1.01)	21.8	(1.03)	18.4	(0.93)	11.8	(0.76)	4.8	(0.54)	1.3	(0.24)
Jordan	384	(3.3)	36.9	(1.44)	29.4	(1.00)	21.9	(0.91)	9.3	(0.79)	2.2	(0.41)	0.2	(0.13)	#	(†)
Kyrgyzstan	311	(3.4)	72.9	(1.54)	16.5	(1.01)	7.1	(0.65)	2.8	(0.46)	0.7	(0.22)	#	(†)	#	(†)
Latvia	486	(3.0)	6.4	(0.62)	14.3	(0.92)	26.3	(0.90)	29.0	(0.96)	17.4	(1.05)	5.5	(0.49)	1.1	(0.28)
Liechtenstein	525	(4.2)	4.0	(1.10)	9.2	(1.98)	18.2	(2.97)	26.4	(3.78)	23.7	(2.92)	12.6	(2.05)	5.8	(1.21)
Lithuania	486	(2.9)	7.8	(0.64)	15.2	(0.77)	25.1	(0.97)	25.1	(1.06)	17.8	(0.83)	7.3	(0.84)	1.8	(0.37)
Macao-China	525	(1.3)	2.6	(0.26)	8.3	(0.63)	20.0	(0.92)	27.3	(0.89)	24.4	(0.76)	13.6	(0.56)	3.8	(0.41)
Montenegro	399	(1.4)	31.6	(0.85)	28.4	(0.80)	23.3	(0.85)	11.8	(0.62)	4.0	(0.38)	0.8	(0.18)	0.1	(0.07)
Qatar	318	(1.0)	71.7	(0.53)	15.5	(0.50)	7.5	(0.59)	3.3	(0.29)	1.4	(0.18)	0.5	(0.10)	0.1	(0.05)
Romania	415	(4.2)	24.7	(2.17)	28.0	(1.88)	26.5	(1.77)	14.1	(1.09)	5.4	(0.83)	1.1	(0.29)	0.1	(0.06)
Russian Federation	476	(3.9)	9.1	(0.94)	17.6	(1.15)	27.0	(1.42)	24.2	(0.93)	14.7	(1.02)	5.7	(0.63)	1.7	(0.30)
Serbia	435	(3.5)	19.6	(1.31)	23.0	(1.06)	26.8	(0.86)	18.7	(0.98)	9.1	(0.66)	2.4	(0.36)	0.4	(0.14)
Slovenia	504	(1.0)	4.6	(0.31)	13.1	(0.75)	23.5	(0.77)	26.0	(0.78)	19.2	(0.79)	10.3	(0.82)	3.4	(0.45)
Chinese Taipei	549	(4.1)	3.6	(0.58)	8.3	(0.73)	14.3	(0.86)	19.4	(0.70)	22.4	(0.84)	20.1	(0.89)	11.8	(0.83)
Thailand	417	(2.3)	23.3	(1.26)	29.7	(1.39)	26.4	(0.92)	14.0	(0.70)	5.3	(0.43)	1.1	(0.22)	0.2	(0.07)
Tunisia	365	(4.0)	48.5	(1.75)	24.0	(1.12)	16.5	(1.06)	8.1	(0.94)	2.4	(0.56)	0.5	(0.23)	#	(†)
Uruguay	427	(2.6)	24.4	(1.05)	21.7	(0.98)	24.3	(0.84)	18.3	(1.08)	8.2	(0.69)	2.6	(0.36)	0.6	(0.16)

†Not applicable.
#Rounds to zero.
[1]Level 1: Able to answer questions involving familiar contexts where all relevant information is present and the questions are clearly defined. Level 2: Able to interpret and recognize situations in contexts that require no more than direct inference, extract relevant information from a single source, and employ direct reasoning for literal interpretations of results. Level 3: Able to execute clearly described procedures, interpret and use representations based on different information sources, and develop short communications reporting their interpretations, results, and reasoning. Level 4: Able to work effectively with explicit models for complex concrete situations that may involve constraints or call for making assumptions, select and integrate different representations, reason with some insight, and construct and communicate explanations and arguments based on their interpretations and actions. Level 5: Able to develop and work with models for complex situations, work strategically using broad, well-developed thinking and reasoning skills, and communicate their interpretations and reasoning. Level 6: Able to conceptualize, generalize, and utilize information, link differ-

ent information sources and representations, and formulate and precisely communicate actions and reflections regarding findings and interpretations.
[2]Illustrates how a country compares with the OECD area as a whole. Computed by taking the OECD countries as a single entity to which each country contributes in proportion to the number of 15-year-olds enrolled in its schools.
[3]Refers to the mean of the data values for all OECD countries, to which each country contributes equally, regardless of the absolute size of the student population of each country.
[4]As a result of a printing error, the mean performance in mathematics may be misestimated by approximately 1 score point. The impact is below one standard error.
NOTE: Possible scores range from 0 to 1,000. Standard errors appear in parentheses. Detail may not sum to totals because of rounding.
SOURCE: Organization for Economic Cooperation and Development (OECD), Program for International Student Assessment (PISA), 2006, *PISA 2006 Science Competencies for Tomorrow's World*. (This table was prepared July 2008.)

Table 405. Mean scores and percentage distribution of 15-year-olds scoring at each scientific literacy proficiency level, by country: 2006

Country or other jurisdiction	Mean score		Percentage distribution at levels of proficiency[1]											
			Below Level 1		Level 1		Level 2		Level 3		Level 4		Level 5		Level 6
1	2		3		4		5		6		7		8		9
OECD total[2]	491	(1.2)	6.9	(0.28)	16.3	(0.30)	24.2	(0.35)	25.1	(0.27)	18.7	(0.30)	7.4	(0.18)	1.4	(0.08)
OECD average[3]	500	(0.5)	5.2	(0.11)	14.1	(0.15)	24.0	(0.17)	27.4	(0.17)	20.3	(0.16)	7.7	(0.10)	1.3	(0.04)
Australia	527	(2.3)	3.0	(0.25)	9.8	(0.46)	20.2	(0.63)	27.7	(0.51)	24.6	(0.53)	11.8	(0.53)	2.8	(0.26)
Austria	511	(3.9)	4.3	(0.88)	12.0	(0.98)	21.8	(1.05)	28.3	(1.05)	23.6	(1.12)	8.8	(0.69)	1.2	(0.20)
Belgium	510	(2.5)	4.8	(0.72)	12.2	(0.62)	20.8	(0.84)	27.6	(0.84)	24.5	(0.77)	9.1	(0.47)	1.0	(0.17)
Canada	534	(2.0)	2.2	(0.27)	7.8	(0.47)	19.1	(0.64)	28.8	(0.58)	27.7	(0.65)	12.0	(0.52)	2.4	(0.25)
Czech Republic	513	(3.5)	3.5	(0.57)	12.1	(0.84)	23.4	(1.17)	27.8	(1.09)	21.7	(0.92)	9.8	(0.86)	1.8	(0.32)
Denmark	496	(3.1)	4.3	(0.64)	14.1	(0.75)	26.0	(1.07)	29.3	(1.04)	19.5	(0.91)	6.1	(0.66)	0.7	(0.18)
Finland	563	(2.0)	0.5	(0.13)	3.6	(0.45)	13.6	(0.68)	29.1	(1.07)	32.2	(0.89)	17.0	(0.72)	3.9	(0.35)
France	495	(3.4)	6.6	(0.71)	14.5	(1.05)	22.8	(1.12)	27.2	(1.09)	20.9	(1.00)	7.2	(0.60)	0.8	(0.17)
Germany	516	(3.8)	4.1	(0.68)	11.3	(0.96)	21.4	(1.06)	27.9	(1.08)	23.6	(0.95)	10.0	(0.62)	1.8	(0.24)
Greece	473	(3.2)	7.2	(0.86)	16.9	(0.88)	28.9	(1.19)	29.4	(1.01)	14.2	(0.83)	3.2	(0.33)	0.2	(0.09)
Hungary	504	(2.7)	2.7	(0.33)	12.3	(0.83)	26.0	(1.15)	31.1	(1.07)	21.0	(0.87)	6.2	(0.57)	0.6	(0.16)
Iceland	491	(1.6)	5.8	(0.50)	14.7	(0.84)	25.9	(0.71)	28.3	(0.92)	19.0	(0.74)	5.6	(0.49)	0.7	(0.18)
Ireland	508	(3.2)	3.5	(0.47)	12.0	(0.82)	24.0	(0.91)	29.7	(0.98)	21.4	(0.87)	8.3	(0.62)	1.1	(0.19)
Italy	475	(2.0)	7.3	(0.46)	18.0	(0.62)	27.6	(0.78)	27.4	(0.61)	15.1	(0.58)	4.2	(0.31)	0.4	(0.09)
Japan	531	(3.4)	3.2	(0.45)	8.9	(0.73)	18.5	(0.86)	27.5	(0.85)	27.0	(1.14)	12.4	(0.63)	2.6	(0.33)
Korea, Republic of	522	(3.4)	2.5	(0.49)	8.7	(0.77)	21.2	(1.05)	31.8	(1.17)	25.5	(0.91)	9.2	(0.83)	1.1	(0.29)
Luxembourg	486	(1.1)	6.5	(0.39)	15.6	(0.65)	25.4	(0.66)	28.6	(0.93)	18.1	(0.71)	5.4	(0.34)	0.5	(0.11)
Mexico	410	(2.7)	18.2	(1.22)	32.8	(0.89)	30.8	(0.95)	14.8	(0.66)	3.2	(0.34)	0.3	(0.09)	#	(†)
Netherlands	525	(2.7)	2.3	(0.38)	10.7	(0.88)	21.1	(0.98)	26.9	(0.87)	25.8	(1.04)	11.5	(0.81)	1.7	(0.24)
New Zealand	530	(2.7)	4.0	(0.43)	9.7	(0.58)	19.7	(0.80)	25.1	(0.71)	23.9	(0.81)	13.6	(0.74)	4.0	(0.37)
Norway	487	(3.1)	5.9	(0.84)	15.2	(0.84)	27.3	(0.79)	28.5	(0.99)	17.1	(0.72)	5.5	(0.44)	0.6	(0.13)
Poland	498	(2.3)	3.2	(0.36)	13.8	(0.63)	27.5	(0.94)	29.4	(1.02)	19.3	(0.80)	6.1	(0.44)	0.7	(0.14)
Portugal	474	(3.0)	5.8	(0.76)	18.7	(1.05)	28.8	(0.92)	28.8	(1.22)	14.7	(0.88)	3.0	(0.35)	0.1	(0.05)
Slovak Republic	488	(2.6)	5.2	(0.60)	15.0	(0.87)	28.0	(0.96)	28.1	(0.99)	17.9	(1.02)	5.2	(0.49)	0.6	(0.14)
Spain	488	(2.6)	4.7	(0.44)	14.9	(0.69)	27.4	(0.77)	30.2	(0.68)	17.9	(0.75)	4.5	(0.38)	0.3	(0.10)
Sweden	503	(2.4)	3.8	(0.44)	12.6	(0.64)	25.2	(0.88)	29.5	(0.90)	21.1	(0.90)	6.8	(0.47)	1.1	(0.21)
Switzerland	512	(3.2)	4.5	(0.52)	11.6	(0.56)	21.8	(0.87)	28.2	(0.81)	23.5	(1.07)	9.1	(0.78)	1.4	(0.27)
Turkey	424	(3.8)	12.9	(0.83)	33.7	(1.31)	31.3	(1.42)	15.1	(1.06)	6.2	(1.15)	0.9	(0.32)	#	(†)
United Kingdom	515	(2.3)	4.8	(0.49)	11.9	(0.61)	21.8	(0.71)	25.9	(0.68)	21.8	(0.62)	10.9	(0.53)	2.9	(0.31)
United States[4]	489	(4.2)	7.6	(0.94)	16.8	(0.88)	24.2	(0.94)	24.0	(0.79)	18.3	(0.97)	7.5	(0.62)	1.5	(0.25)
Reporting partner economies															
Argentina	391	(6.1)	28.3	(2.34)	27.9	(1.39)	25.6	(1.27)	13.6	(1.29)	4.1	(0.63)	0.4	(0.14)	#	(†)
Azerbaijan	382	(2.8)	19.4	(1.50)	53.1	(1.57)	22.4	(1.41)	4.7	(0.86)	0.4	(0.15)	#	(†)	#	(†)
Brazil	390	(2.8)	27.9	(0.99)	33.1	(0.96)	23.8	(0.93)	11.3	(0.88)	3.4	(0.42)	0.5	(0.21)	#	(†)
Bulgaria	434	(6.1)	18.3	(1.72)	24.3	(1.32)	25.2	(1.23)	18.8	(1.14)	10.3	(1.13)	2.6	(0.51)	0.4	(0.18)
Chile	438	(4.3)	13.1	(1.12)	26.7	(1.54)	29.9	(1.18)	20.1	(1.44)	8.4	(1.01)	1.8	(0.32)	0.1	(0.06)
Colombia	388	(3.4)	26.2	(1.71)	34.0	(1.55)	27.2	(1.53)	10.6	(1.04)	1.9	(0.35)	0.2	(0.05)	#	(†)
Croatia	493	(2.4)	3.0	(0.43)	14.0	(0.71)	29.3	(0.91)	31.0	(0.99)	17.7	(0.86)	4.6	(0.44)	0.5	(0.12)
Estonia	531	(2.5)	1.0	(0.23)	6.7	(0.57)	21.0	(0.88)	33.7	(0.96)	26.2	(0.94)	10.1	(0.71)	1.4	(0.27)
Hong Kong-China	542	(2.5)	1.7	(0.36)	7.0	(0.68)	16.9	(0.81)	28.7	(0.95)	29.7	(0.95)	13.9	(0.80)	2.1	(0.30)
Indonesia	393	(5.7)	20.3	(1.71)	41.3	(2.23)	27.5	(1.46)	9.5	(1.99)	1.4	(0.53)	#	(†)	#	(†)
Israel	454	(3.7)	14.9	(1.18)	21.2	(1.01)	24.0	(0.95)	20.8	(0.96)	13.8	(0.80)	4.4	(0.49)	0.8	(0.18)
Jordan	422	(2.8)	16.2	(0.86)	28.2	(0.86)	30.8	(0.83)	18.7	(0.81)	5.6	(0.66)	0.6	(0.20)	#	(†)
Kyrgyzstan	322	(2.9)	58.2	(1.56)	28.2	(1.13)	10.0	(0.81)	2.9	(0.39)	0.7	(0.18)	#	(†)	#	(†)
Latvia	490	(3.0)	3.6	(0.49)	13.8	(0.98)	29.0	(1.19)	32.9	(0.95)	16.6	(0.96)	3.8	(0.39)	0.3	(0.09)
Liechtenstein	522	(4.1)	2.6	(0.99)	10.3	(2.11)	21.0	(2.84)	28.7	(2.58)	25.2	(2.54)	10.0	(1.77)	2.2	(0.84)
Lithuania	488	(2.8)	4.3	(0.44)	16.0	(0.83)	27.4	(0.91)	29.8	(0.85)	17.5	(0.85)	4.5	(0.60)	0.4	(0.15)
Macao-China	511	(1.1)	1.4	(0.24)	8.9	(0.50)	26.0	(0.97)	35.7	(1.14)	22.8	(0.73)	5.0	(0.34)	0.3	(0.09)
Montenegro	412	(1.1)	17.3	(0.79)	33.0	(1.20)	31.0	(0.91)	14.9	(0.65)	3.6	(0.37)	0.3	(0.11)	#	(†)
Qatar	349	(0.9)	47.6	(0.62)	31.5	(0.63)	13.9	(0.49)	5.0	(0.35)	1.6	(0.14)	0.3	(0.09)	#	(†)
Romania	418	(4.2)	16.0	(1.53)	30.9	(1.55)	31.8	(1.62)	16.6	(1.24)	4.2	(0.77)	0.5	(0.14)	#	(†)
Russian Federation	479	(3.7)	5.2	(0.65)	17.0	(1.08)	30.2	(0.93)	28.3	(1.32)	15.1	(1.09)	3.7	(0.46)	0.5	(0.13)
Serbia	436	(3.0)	11.9	(0.91)	26.6	(1.18)	32.3	(1.26)	21.8	(1.18)	6.6	(0.57)	0.8	(0.18)	#	(†)
Slovenia	519	(1.1)	2.8	(0.34)	11.1	(0.72)	23.1	(0.68)	27.6	(1.08)	22.5	(1.13)	10.7	(0.57)	2.2	(0.29)
Chinese Taipei	532	(3.6)	1.9	(0.29)	9.7	(0.82)	18.6	(0.86)	27.3	(0.80)	27.9	(1.03)	12.9	(0.77)	1.7	(0.24)
Thailand	421	(2.1)	12.6	(0.80)	33.5	(1.03)	33.2	(0.88)	16.3	(0.80)	4.0	(0.42)	0.4	(0.12)	#	(†)
Tunisia	386	(3.0)	27.7	(1.12)	35.1	(0.94)	25.0	(0.97)	10.2	(0.98)	1.9	(0.45)	0.1	(0.06)	#	(†)
Uruguay	428	(2.7)	16.7	(1.25)	25.4	(1.09)	29.8	(1.50)	19.7	(1.07)	6.9	(0.54)	1.3	(0.21)	0.1	(0.07)

†Not applicable.
#Rounds to zero.
[1]Level 1: Able to present scientific explanations that are obvious and that follow explicitly from given evidence. Level 2: Able to provide possible explanations in familiar contexts, draw conclusions based on simple investigations, and make literal interpretations of the results of scientific inquiry or technological problem solving. Level 3: Able to select facts to explain phenomena and apply simple models or inquiry strategies, develop short statements using facts, and make decisions based on scientific knowledge. Level 4: Able to select and integrate explanations from different disciplines of science or technology, link those explanations directly to aspects of life situations, and communicate decisions using scientific knowledge and evidence. Level 5: Able to apply scientific concepts and knowledge to many complex life situations, select and evaluate appropriate scientific evidence, bring critical insights to situations, and construct explanations based on evidence and arguments based on critical analysis. Level 6: Able to consistently explain and apply scientific knowledge in a variety of complex life situations, use evidence from different sources to jus-

tify decisions, clearly and consistently demonstrate advanced scientific thinking and reasoning, and develop arguments in support of recommendations and decisions that center on personal, social, or global situations.
[2]Illustrates how a country compares with the OECD area as a whole. Computed by taking the OECD countries as a single entity to which each country contributes in proportion to the number of 15-year-olds enrolled in its schools.
[3]Refers to the mean of the data values for all OECD countries, to which each country contributes equally, regardless of the absolute size of the student population of each country.
[4]As a result of a printing error, the mean performance in science may be misestimated by approximately 1 score point. The impact is below one standard error.
NOTE: Possible scores range from 0 to 1,000. Standard errors appear in parentheses. Detail may not sum to totals because of rounding.
SOURCE: Organization for Economic Cooperation and Development (OECD), Program for International Student Assessment (PISA), 2006, *PISA 2006 Science Competencies for Tomorrow's World*. (This table was prepared July 2008.)

Table 406. Average fourth-grade mathematics scores, by content areas, index of time students spend doing mathematics homework in a normal school week, and country: 2003

Country or other jurisdiction	Mathematics overall	Average score by content area					Index of time students spend doing mathematics homework (TMH)[8] in a normal school week					
		Number[1]	Patterns and relationships[2]	Measurement[3]	Geometry[4]	Data[5]	High TMH[6]		Medium TMH[7]		Low TMH[8]	
							Percent	Mean score	Percent	Mean score	Percent	Mean score
1	2	3	4	5	6	7	8	9	10	11	12	13
International average	495 (0.8)	495 (0.7)	495 (0.7)	495 (0.7)	495 (0.7)	495 (0.6)	18 (0.2)	489 (1.3)	56 (0.3)	500 (0.9)	26 (0.3)	494 (1.6)
Armenia[9]	456 (3.5)	473 (3.0)	461 (4.1)	465 (3.1)	431 (3.8)	417 (3.6)	33 (1.3)	467 (5.1)	65 (1.3)	465 (3.5)	2 (0.3)	‡ (†)
Australia[10]	499 (3.9)	479 (4.3)	495 (3.7)	514 (3.7)	524 (3.7)	525 (3.6)	7 (0.8)	486 (13.0)	43 (2.1)	500 (4.6)	50 (2.1)	505 (4.4)
Belgium (Flemish)	551 (1.8)	549 (1.9)	542 (1.9)	550 (1.4)	533 (1.8)	548 (2.2)	9 (0.7)	538 (3.9)	48 (1.7)	549 (2.7)	43 (2.0)	557 (2.0)
Chinese Taipei	564 (1.8)	568 (1.8)	555 (2.4)	557 (1.6)	553 (2.5)	564 (2.3)	11 (0.6)	546 (3.5)	62 (1.1)	569 (2.0)	27 (1.2)	561 (2.7)
Cyprus	510 (2.4)	514 (2.7)	519 (2.4)	506 (2.3)	505 (2.3)	509 (2.3)	14 (0.6)	494 (4.6)	76 (0.9)	521 (2.4)	10 (0.6)	497 (5.3)
England[10]	531 (3.7)	519 (4.1)	523 (3.9)	535 (3.3)	542 (3.7)	552 (3.4)	4 (0.6)	489 (14.3)	37 (1.8)	531 (4.8)	59 (1.9)	540 (4.2)
Hong Kong, SAR[10,11]	575 (3.2)	574 (3.3)	568 (3.5)	563 (2.7)	557 (2.9)	562 (2.3)	24 (1.0)	575 (3.8)	71 (0.9)	580 (3.2)	5 (0.5)	530 (5.6)
Hungary	529 (3.1)	524 (2.9)	545 (3.7)	532 (2.7)	514 (3.3)	513 (3.2)	17 (0.9)	515 (4.9)	78 (1.1)	538 (3.1)	5 (0.9)	535 (10.6)
Iran, Islamic Republic of	389 (4.2)	410 (3.7)	394 (3.9)	398 (3.2)	416 (3.9)	356 (4.4)	31 (2.3)	404 (5.1)	52 (1.8)	391 (5.0)	17 (2.3)	376 (8.1)
Italy	503 (3.7)	502 (3.6)	496 (4.3)	504 (3.4)	522 (3.5)	497 (3.0)	24 (1.1)	496 (5.2)	52 (1.1)	504 (4.5)	24 (1.6)	512 (3.6)
Japan	565 (1.6)	556 (2.0)	554 (1.4)	568 (1.6)	559 (1.9)	593 (1.6)	8 (0.6)	543 (4.6)	57 (1.8)	568 (2.3)	35 (2.1)	565 (2.7)
Latvia	536 (2.8)	531 (2.6)	532 (3.4)	545 (2.6)	523 (2.2)	526 (2.7)	25 (1.1)	525 (4.1)	71 (1.1)	546 (2.7)	4 (0.6)	517 (9.1)
Lithuania[12]	534 (2.8)	535 (2.9)	531 (3.0)	540 (2.7)	524 (2.2)	517 (2.5)	29 (1.2)	527 (3.8)	66 (1.3)	545 (3.1)	5 (0.6)	510 (10.7)
Moldova, Republic of	504 (4.9)	507 (4.7)	521 (5.1)	505 (4.0)	501 (4.9)	477 (4.3)	31 (2.0)	518 (6.3)	66 (1.9)	504 (5.4)	3 (0.6)	494 (10.9)
Morocco[13]	347 (5.1)	359 (4.7)	360 (4.7)	345 (5.5)	362 (4.9)	355 (5.0)	22 (1.3)	362 (5.9)	58 (1.9)	365 (4.8)	20 (2.1)	353 (12.3)
Netherlands[10]	540 (2.1)	536 (2.2)	527 (2.4)	545 (2.2)	521 (3.2)	553 (2.4)	1 (0.2)	† (†)	10 (0.8)	508 (6.6)	89 (0.9)	546 (1.8)
New Zealand	493 (2.2)	475 (2.3)	495 (2.9)	503 (2.0)	517 (1.8)	522 (2.0)	7 (0.4)	489 (6.7)	41 (1.1)	491 (3.3)	52 (1.3)	504 (3.1)
Norway[14]	451 (2.3)	440 (2.2)	439 (2.7)	475 (2.2)	478 (2.2)	479 (2.3)	12 (1.0)	447 (4.7)	56 (1.8)	462 (3.2)	32 (2.1)	467 (4.0)
Philippines	358 (7.9)	380 (7.4)	382 (7.0)	330 (7.8)	335 (8.8)	384 (7.5)	17 (0.8)	349 (7.0)	52 (1.7)	362 (6.7)	31 (1.9)	372 (15.7)
Russian Federation	532 (4.7)	532 (4.6)	531 (5.0)	538 (3.8)	528 (4.8)	505 (4.1)	38 (1.3)	531 (5.3)	59 (1.2)	537 (4.7)	2 (0.4)	‡ (†)
Scotland[10]	490 (3.3)	475 (3.3)	495 (2.9)	499 (3.1)	511 (2.5)	516 (2.7)	6 (0.8)	477 (6.8)	40 (2.0)	488 (4.2)	54 (2.2)	498 (3.4)
Singapore	594 (5.6)	612 (6.0)	579 (5.4)	566 (4.6)	570 (5.5)	575 (3.9)	40 (1.5)	604 (6.0)	49 (1.3)	595 (5.8)	11 (0.6)	575 (7.2)
Slovenia	479 (2.6)	461 (2.7)	490 (2.7)	497 (2.8)	498 (2.2)	486 (2.7)	14 (0.9)	466 (6.7)	76 (1.2)	490 (2.6)	10 (0.9)	455 (8.6)
Tunisia[13]	339 (4.7)	360 (4.1)	330 (4.7)	308 (5.5)	346 (5.1)	308 (4.7)	22 (2.2)	373 (8.6)	50 (2.8)	365 (6.3)	28 (3.0)	365 (8.0)
United States[10]	518 (2.4)	516 (2.6)	524 (2.7)	500 (2.1)	518 (2.2)	549 (2.0)	12 (0.6)	504 (4.0)	63 (1.3)	524 (2.7)	25 (1.5)	520 (3.5)

†Not applicable.
‡Reporting standards not met.
[1]Topic includes whole numbers; fractions and decimals; integers; and ratio, proportion, and percent.
[2]Topic includes patterns, equations and formulas, and relationships.
[3]Topic includes attributes and units and tools, techniques, and formulas.
[4]Topic includes lines and angles, two- and three-dimensional shapes, congruence and similarity, locations and spatial relationships, and symmetry and transformations.
[5]Topic includes data collection and organization, data representation, and data interpretation.
[6]High level indicates more than 30 minutes of mathematics homework assigned 3–4 times a week.
[7]Medium level indicates more than 30 minutes of mathematics homework assigned no more than twice a week.
[8]Low level indicates no more than 30 minutes of mathematics homework assigned no more than twice a week.

[9]Response rate for the TMH index was at least 70 but less than 85 percent of the students, with missing data having not been explicitly accounted for in the analysis.
[10]Met international guidelines for participation rates only after replacement schools were included.
[11]SAR = Special Administrative Region.
[12]National Desired Population does not cover all of the International Desired Population.
[13]Response rate for the TMH index was at least 50 but less than 70 percent of the students, with missing data having not been explicitly accounted for in the analysis.
[14]Students had received 4 years of formal schooling, but first grade is called "First grade/preschool."
NOTE: TMH index data are provided by students. Data are for fourth-grade students or equivalent in most countries. Possible scores range from 0 to 1,000. Detail may not sum to totals because of rounding. Standard errors appear in parentheses.
SOURCE: International Association for the Evaluation of Educational Achievement (IEA), Trends in International Mathematics and Science Study (TIMSS), 2003, TIMSS 2003 International Mathematics Report, by Ina V.S. Mullis et al. (This table was prepared March 2005.)

Table 407. Average eighth-grade mathematics scores, by content areas, index of time students spend doing mathematics homework in a normal school week, and country: 2003

Country or other jurisdiction	Mathematics overall	Average score by content area					Index of time students spend doing mathematics homework (TMH) in a normal school week					
		Number[1]	Algebra[2]	Measurement[3]	Geometry[4]	Data[5]	High TMH[6]		Medium TMH[7]		Low TMH[8]	
							Percent	Mean score	Percent	Mean score	Percent	Mean score
1	2	3	4	5	6	7	8	9	10	11	12	13
International average[9]	467 (0.5)	467 (0.5)	467 (0.5)	467 (0.5)	467 (0.5)	467 (0.5)	26 (0.2)	468 (0.8)	54 (0.2)	471 (0.6)	19 (0.2)	456 (1.0)
Armenia	478 (3.0)	473 (3.1)	489 (2.6)	488 (3.3)	481 (3.1)	419 (2.7)	35 (1.3)	490 (3.9)	60 (1.2)	478 (3.7)	4 (0.4)	475 (7.5)
Australia	505 (4.6)	498 (4.6)	499 (4.4)	511 (4.3)	491 (4.8)	531 (3.8)	19 (1.6)	520 (6.0)	50 (1.5)	509 (5.4)	31 (2.0)	497 (5.5)
Bahrain	401 (1.7)	380 (1.9)	411 (2.5)	388 (2.1)	438 (2.1)	414 (2.1)	18 (0.8)	387 (3.3)	69 (1.2)	409 (2.0)	13 (1.1)	398 (4.9)
Belgium (Flemish)	537 (2.8)	539 (2.7)	523 (2.8)	535 (2.5)	527 (3.1)	546 (2.9)	13 (1.1)	542 (4.5)	42 (1.4)	546 (3.2)	44 (2.0)	532 (3.7)
Botswana	366 (2.6)	382 (2.2)	377 (2.7)	377 (2.0)	335 (3.9)	375 (2.7)	25 (0.8)	385 (3.9)	53 (0.8)	368 (2.6)	22 (0.9)	355 (3.0)
Bulgaria	476 (4.3)	477 (4.1)	481 (4.0)	473 (4.6)	484 (4.5)	458 (3.9)	33 (1.8)	482 (6.4)	54 (1.5)	478 (4.6)	14 (1.5)	469 (5.4)
Chile	387 (3.3)	390 (3.1)	384 (3.1)	404 (2.9)	378 (3.3)	412 (3.4)	10 (0.7)	387 (6.9)	43 (1.0)	389 (3.8)	47 (1.4)	388 (3.7)
Chinese Taipei	585 (4.6)	585 (4.6)	585 (4.9)	574 (4.4)	588 (5.1)	568 (3.4)	18 (1.5)	611 (6.0)	45 (1.2)	594 (4.4)	37 (2.0)	563 (5.6)
Cyprus	459 (1.7)	464 (1.5)	455 (1.7)	459 (2.2)	457 (2.4)	458 (1.7)	21 (0.3)	459 (2.8)	70 (0.7)	469 (1.8)	9 (0.6)	438 (5.3)
Egypt	406 (3.5)	421 (3.0)	408 (3.9)	401 (3.3)	408 (3.6)	393 (3.2)	26 (0.3)	402 (4.3)	60 (1.0)	418 (3.6)	14 (0.7)	419 (4.7)
England[10]	‡ (†)	‡ (†)	‡ (†)	‡ (†)	‡ (†)	‡ (†)	‡ (†)	‡ (†)	‡ (†)	‡ (†)	‡ (†)	‡ (†)
Estonia	531 (3.0)	523 (3.1)	528 (2.6)	528 (3.0)	540 (2.6)	535 (2.8)	28 (1.3)	519 (4.0)	66 (1.3)	538 (3.2)	7 (1.2)	523 (10.3)
Ghana	276 (4.7)	289 (5.1)	288 (4.8)	262 (3.7)	278 (4.3)	293 (4.1)	24 (0.9)	288 (5.8)	56 (0.9)	280 (4.5)	20 (1.0)	275 (7.5)
Hong Kong, SAR[11,12]	586 (3.3)	586 (3.2)	580 (3.2)	584 (3.3)	588 (3.6)	566 (3.0)	32 (1.9)	600 (3.5)	49 (1.5)	587 (3.6)	19 (1.5)	566 (7.6)
Hungary	529 (3.2)	529 (3.6)	534 (3.1)	525 (3.1)	515 (3.1)	526 (2.9)	20 (1.2)	516 (5.8)	77 (1.2)	537 (3.1)	3 (0.5)	501 (14.1)
Indonesia[13]	411 (4.8)	413 (4.6)	418 (4.5)	394 (4.9)	413 (4.6)	418 (4.0)	37 (1.1)	435 (4.3)	48 (0.8)	406 (5.3)	15 (0.8)	391 (7.3)
Iran, Islamic Republic of	411 (2.4)	416 (2.3)	412 (3.1)	399 (2.6)	437 (3.1)	404 (2.6)	24 (1.2)	420 (3.8)	52 (0.9)	414 (2.8)	25 (1.1)	403 (3.4)
Israel[14]	496 (3.4)	504 (3.3)	498 (3.2)	480 (3.4)	488 (3.7)	492 (3.3)	33 (1.4)	498 (3.9)	55 (1.3)	505 (4.1)	12 (0.9)	479 (6.3)
Italy	484 (3.2)	480 (3.2)	477 (3.4)	500 (3.2)	469 (3.5)	490 (3.0)	54 (1.4)	484 (3.8)	40 (1.1)	487 (3.6)	7 (0.7)	471 (8.0)
Japan	570 (2.1)	557 (2.3)	568 (2.0)	559 (2.0)	587 (2.1)	573 (1.9)	6 (0.7)	565 (10.1)	36 (1.5)	566 (2.8)	58 (1.9)	576 (2.1)
Jordan	424 (4.1)	413 (4.4)	434 (4.4)	418 (4.4)	446 (4.0)	430 (3.5)	25 (0.8)	425 (4.7)	64 (1.1)	437 (4.1)	11 (0.9)	411 (4.9)
Korea, Republic of[15]	589 (2.2)	586 (2.1)	597 (2.2)	577 (2.0)	598 (2.6)	569 (2.0)	11 (1.0)	582 (4.3)	46 (1.6)	592 (2.6)	43 (2.0)	590 (2.8)
Latvia	508 (3.2)	507 (3.2)	508 (3.2)	500 (3.0)	515 (3.3)	506 (3.8)	33 (1.3)	502 (4.7)	61 (1.3)	516 (3.0)	6 (0.7)	508 (9.3)
Lebanon	433 (3.1)	430 (3.3)	448 (3.1)	430 (3.7)	459 (3.0)	394 (4.0)	42 (1.7)	436 (3.5)	52 (1.7)	437 (3.5)	5 (0.6)	412 (7.6)
Lithuania[13]	502 (2.5)	500 (2.7)	501 (2.4)	492 (3.0)	506 (2.5)	502 (2.5)	32 (1.4)	493 (3.1)	63 (1.3)	509 (3.0)	5 (0.8)	490 (8.7)
Macedonia, Republic of[14]	435 (3.5)	438 (3.5)	442 (3.6)	434 (3.6)	442 (3.7)	419 (3.6)	26 (1.1)	440 (4.5)	61 (1.3)	444 (3.9)	13 (1.3)	439 (6.0)
Malaysia	508 (4.1)	524 (4.0)	495 (3.9)	504 (4.5)	495 (4.8)	505 (3.2)	33 (1.3)	515 (4.4)	56 (1.1)	510 (4.5)	11 (0.8)	485 (5.9)
Moldova, Republic of	460 (4.0)	463 (3.8)	464 (4.2)	468 (4.0)	463 (4.7)	428 (3.4)	38 (1.4)	472 (4.3)	57 (1.3)	458 (4.6)	5 (0.5)	437 (8.3)
Morocco[13,16,17]	387 (2.5)	384 (2.7)	400 (2.8)	376 (3.4)	415 (2.3)	374 (2.5)	34 (1.5)	390 (4.5)	52 (1.1)	392 (3.2)	14 (1.0)	380 (4.8)
Netherlands[11]	536 (3.8)	539 (3.6)	514 (4.0)	549 (3.7)	513 (4.1)	560 (3.1)	19 (1.3)	540 (5.2)	62 (1.4)	542 (4.4)	19 (1.7)	518 (6.5)
New Zealand	494 (5.3)	481 (6.0)	490 (5.2)	500 (4.8)	488 (4.6)	526 (5.1)	14 (1.1)	488 (5.1)	49 (1.8)	505 (6.0)	37 (2.1)	492 (7.2)
Norway	461 (2.5)	456 (2.3)	428 (2.7)	481 (2.9)	461 (2.8)	438 (2.5)	25 (1.3)	454 (4.0)	52 (1.3)	466 (2.5)	22 (1.3)	472 (3.5)
Palestinian National Authority	390 (3.1)	385 (3.6)	392 (3.5)	386 (2.8)	423 (3.1)	330 (2.8)	27 (1.1)	393 (3.5)	65 (1.1)	398 (3.5)	8 (0.6)	371 (6.6)
Philippines	378 (5.2)	393 (5.1)	400 (5.2)	372 (4.8)	344 (5.3)	330 (4.5)	24 (0.9)	390 (5.4)	54 (1.0)	382 (5.5)	22 (1.2)	361 (6.6)
Romania	475 (4.8)	474 (4.9)	480 (4.7)	485 (4.7)	476 (4.9)	445 (4.6)	68 (1.6)	492 (4.5)	28 (1.4)	451 (6.4)	3 (0.4)	437 (13.0)

See notes at end of table.

Table 407. Average eighth-grade mathematics scores, by content areas, index of time students spend doing mathematics homework in a normal school week, and country: 2003—Continued

Country or other jurisdiction	Average score by content area						Index of time students spend doing mathematics homework (TMH) in a normal school week					
	Mathematics overall	Number[1]	Algebra[2]	Measurement[3]	Geometry[4]	Data[5]	High TMH[6]		Medium TMH[7]		Low TMH[8]	
							Percent	Mean score	Percent	Mean score	Percent	Mean score
1	2	3	4	5	6	7	8	9	10	11	12	13
Russian Federation..........	508 (3.7)	505 (4.0)	516 (3.2)	507 (3.9)	515 (4.2)	484 (3.2)	53 (1.2)	509 (4.4)	45 (1.2)	511 (3.4)	2 (0.2)	‡ (†)
Saudi Arabia..........	332 (4.6)	307 (5.3)	331 (4.7)	338 (3.4)	382 (4.3)	339 (3.8)	15 (1.0)	315 (8.1)	62 (1.6)	335 (4.6)	23 (1.6)	345 (5.7)
Scotland[11]..........	498 (3.7)	484 (4.2)	488 (3.9)	508 (3.6)	491 (3.3)	531 (3.7)	8 (0.8)	493 (5.8)	46 (2.1)	507 (4.5)	46 (2.5)	496 (4.1)
Serbia[13]..........	477 (2.6)	477 (2.8)	488 (2.5)	475 (2.5)	471 (3.0)	456 (2.6)	25 (1.3)	466 (4.1)	54 (1.2)	481 (3.5)	20 (1.7)	497 (3.5)
Singapore..........	605 (3.6)	618 (3.5)	590 (3.5)	611 (3.6)	580 (3.7)	579 (3.2)	38 (1.1)	621 (3.1)	51 (0.9)	604 (3.8)	11 (0.8)	566 (7.8)
Slovak Republic..........	508 (3.3)	514 (3.3)	505 (3.3)	508 (3.7)	501 (3.6)	495 (2.9)	11 (0.9)	495 (6.4)	81 (1.4)	511 (3.4)	8 (1.3)	500 (7.7)
Slovenia..........	493 (2.2)	498 (2.0)	487 (2.3)	496 (2.3)	483 (2.5)	494 (2.3)	25 (1.1)	482 (2.9)	71 (1.2)	500 (2.5)	4 (0.8)	463 (8.8)
South Africa..........	264 (5.5)	274 (5.4)	275 (5.1)	298 (4.7)	247 (5.4)	296 (5.3)	21 (0.8)	275 (8.1)	58 (0.8)	270 (6.3)	20 (1.0)	260 (5.4)
Sweden..........	499 (2.6)	496 (2.6)	480 (3.0)	512 (2.6)	467 (3.4)	539 (3.0)	4 (0.5)	453 (7.0)	38 (1.4)	494 (3.5)	58 (1.5)	509 (2.7)
Tunisia..........	410 (2.2)	419 (2.3)	405 (2.4)	407 (2.2)	427 (2.0)	387 (2.2)	39 (1.1)	410 (2.7)	50 (1.1)	414 (2.2)	11 (0.9)	414 (4.3)
United States[16]..........	504 (3.3)	508 (3.4)	510 (3.1)	495 (3.2)	472 (3.1)	527 (3.2)	31 (1.0)	518 (4.1)	60 (0.9)	506 (3.2)	9 (0.9)	461 (6.3)

†Not applicable.
‡Reporting standards not met.
[1]Topic includes whole numbers; fractions and decimals; integers; and ratio, proportion, and percent.
[2]Topic includes patterns, algebraic expressions, equations and formulas, and relationships.
[3]Topic includes attributes and units and tools, techniques, and formulas.
[4]Topic includes lines and angles, two- and three-dimensional shapes, congruence and similarity, locations and spatial relationships, and symmetry and transformations.
[5]Topic includes data collection and organization, data representation, data interpretation, and uncertainty and probability.
[6]High level indicates more than 30 minutes of mathematics homework assigned 3–4 times a week.
[7]Medium level includes more than 30 minutes of mathematics homework assigned no more than twice a week.
[8]Low level indicates no more than 30 minutes of mathematics homework assigned no more than twice a week.
[9]The international average of 467 may sometimes appear as 466. In that case, the TIMSS 2003 average for eighth-graders published in the National Center for Education Statistics report reflects the deletion of England from the average.

[10]Did not satisfy guidelines for sample participation rates.
[11]Met guidelines for sample participation rates only after replacement schools were included.
[12]SAR = Special Administrative Region.
[13]National Desired Population does not cover all of International Desired Population.
[14]National Defined Population covers less than 90 percent of National Desired Population.
[15]Korea tested the same cohort of students as other countries, but later in 2003, at the beginning of the next school year.
[16]Nearly satisfied guidelines for sample participation rates only after replacement schools were included.
[17]Response rate for the TMH index was at least 70 but less than 85 percent of the students, with missing data having not been explicitly accounted for in the analysis.
NOTE: TMH index data are provided by students. Data are for eighth grade or equivalent in most countries. Possible scores range from 0 to 1,000. Standard errors appear in parentheses. Detail may not sum to totals because of rounding.
SOURCE: International Association for the Evaluation of Educational Achievement (IEA), Trends in International Mathematics and Science Study (TIMSS), 2003, TIMSS 2003 International Mathematics Report, by Ina V.S. Mullis et al. (This table was prepared April 2005.)

Table 408. Percentage of lesson time spent on various mathematics activities, yearly mathematics instructional time, and mathematics instructional time as a percentage of total instructional time in eighth grade, by country: 2003

Columns 2–9: Percentage of time in mathematics lessons students spend on various activities in a typical week.

Country or other jurisdiction	Reviewing homework	Listening to lecture-style presentations	Working problems with teacher's guidance	Working problems on their own without teacher's guidance	Listening to teachers reteach and clarify content/procedures	Taking tests and quizzes	Participating in classroom management tasks not related to the lesson's content/purpose	Other student activities	Students' average yearly mathematics instructional time, in hours	Mathematics instructional time as a percent of total instructional time
1	2	3	4	5	6	7	8	9	10	12
International average	11 (0.1)	19 (0.1)	22 (0.2)	18 (0.2)	11 (0.1)	10 (0.1)	5 (0.1)	4 (0.1)	123 (0.4)	12 (#)
Armenia	10[1] (0.5)	14[1] (0.8)	26[1] (1.1)	19[1] (0.9)	13[1] (0.6)	11[1] (0.6)	4[1] (0.3)	4[1] (0.3)	‡ (†)	‡ (†)
Australia	8 (0.5)	15 (0.8)	23 (1.2)	28 (1.2)	9 (0.4)	7 (0.4)	7 (0.6)	3 (0.4)	136[1] (2.9)	13[1] (0.3)
Bahrain	13 (0.5)	24 (0.9)	17 (0.5)	12 (0.5)	12 (0.3)	13 (0.5)	6 (0.5)	6 (0.3)	142 (0.8)	16 (0.1)
Belgium (Flemish)	7 (0.4)	14 (1.0)	26 (1.0)	20 (0.9)	16 (0.8)	11 (0.4)	4 (0.3)	2 (0.2)	123[2] (2.2)	13 (0.3)
Botswana	13[1] (0.9)	16[1] (1.1)	19[1] (1.1)	21[1] (1.2)	11[1] (0.8)	10[1] (0.7)	6[1] (0.5)	5[1] (0.4)	‡ (†)	‡ (†)
Bulgaria	10 (0.6)	18 (1.3)	26 (1.0)	16 (0.8)	17 (0.9)	8 (0.5)	3 (0.4)	2 (0.3)	96[1] (1.7)	11[1] (0.2)
Chile	10 (0.4)	18 (0.8)	21 (0.9)	18 (0.8)	14 (0.7)	11 (0.5)	6 (0.4)	3 (0.3)	160[1] (4.1)	14[1] (0.4)
Chinese Taipei	12 (0.5)	42 (1.3)	13 (0.6)	7 (0.5)	9 (0.4)	10 (0.4)	4 (0.3)	3 (0.3)	141 (2.0)	13 (0.2)
Cyprus	22[1] (0.4)	16[1] (0.5)	20[1] (0.5)	14[1] (0.4)	12[1] (0.4)	10[1] (0.5)	5[1] (0.2)	2[1] (0.2)	75[2] (0.4)	8[1] (0.1)
Egypt	11 (0.4)	18 (1.0)	17 (0.8)	15 (0.7)	15 (0.8)	11 (0.4)	6 (0.3)	7 (0.4)	‡ (†)	‡ (†)
England[3]	‡[2] (†)	‡[2] (†)	‡[2] (†)	‡[2] (†)	‡[2] (†)	‡[2] (†)	‡[2] (†)	‡[2] (†)	‡ (†)	‡ (†)
Estonia	10 (0.4)	12 (0.6)	25 (1.0)	25 (0.8)	11 (0.5)	13 (0.6)	3 (0.3)	2 (0.3)	125 (1.2)	12[1] (0.2)
Ghana	11[1] (0.4)	16[1] (0.9)	20[1] (0.8)	18[1] (0.7)	12[1] (0.7)	12[1] (0.4)	7[1] (0.4)	6[1] (0.3)	‡ (†)	‡ (†)
Hong Kong, SAR[4,5]	8 (0.4)	36 (1.5)	18 (0.7)	16 (0.8)	9 (0.7)	6 (0.3)	4 (0.5)	4 (0.4)	145[2] (5.2)	15 (0.5)
Hungary	12 (0.4)	13 (0.7)	25 (0.9)	25 (1.0)	10 (0.4)	10 (0.4)	3 (0.3)	3 (0.3)	112[2] (2.0)	11 (0.2)
Indonesia[6]	12[1] (0.5)	25[1] (1.1)	20[1] (0.9)	14[1] (0.9)	12[1] (0.5)	12[1] (0.7)	3[1] (0.4)	3[1] (0.5)	169[2] (4.4)	13 (0.4)
Iran, Islamic Republic of	12 (0.6)	17 (0.8)	18 (0.7)	14 (0.7)	15 (0.7)	11 (0.5)	6 (0.3)	6 (0.6)	115[2] (3.5)	12[1] (0.4)
Israel[7]	14[1] (0.6)	15[1] (0.8)	22[1] (0.7)	21[1] (0.8)	11[1] (0.4)	10[1] (0.5)	5[1] (0.5)	3[1] (0.3)	‡ (†)	‡[1] (†)
Italy	15 (0.6)	22 (0.8)	19 (0.6)	13 (0.6)	13 (0.4)	11 (0.5)	4 (0.3)	2 (0.3)	132[1] (1.7)	13[1] (0.2)
Japan	7 (0.6)	29 (1.3)	28 (1.1)	11 (1.0)	15 (0.9)	6 (0.4)	2 (0.2)	2 (0.4)	107 (2.6)	10 (0.2)
Jordan	15 (0.7)	23 (1.0)	17 (0.8)	13 (0.8)	11 (0.5)	9 (0.4)	6 (0.4)	6 (0.5)	110 (0.9)	12 (0.2)
Korea, Republic of[8]	6[2] (0.3)	30[2] (1.2)	19[2] (0.6)	20[2] (0.7)	9[2] (0.4)	8[2] (0.4)	5[2] (0.3)	3[2] (0.5)	109[2] (1.2)	9 (0.1)
Latvia	8[1] (0.6)	12[1] (0.7)	25[1] (1.1)	22[1] (0.9)	11[2] (0.6)	15[1] (0.7)	2[1] (0.2)	4[1] (0.4)	122[2] (1.4)	13[1] (0.3)
Lebanon	24[2] (1.6)	17[2] (0.9)	23[2] (1.1)	8[2] (0.8)	10[2] (0.6)	11[2] (0.6)	4[2] (0.4)	2 (0.2)	‡ (†)	‡ (†)
Lithuania[6]	9 (0.5)	7 (0.6)	30 (1.2)	26 (0.9)	11 (0.7)	14 (0.6)	1 (0.2)	2 (0.2)	121[1] (0.9)	11[1] (0.2)
Macedonia, Republic of[7]	7 (0.3)	17 (1.1)	24 (1.1)	23 (1.3)	9 (0.4)	8 (0.4)	3 (0.3)	4 (0.3)	136 (1.7)	14 (0.2)
Malaysia	13 (0.7)	19 (1.0)	26 (1.2)	25 (1.5)	10 (0.4)	6 (0.3)	6 (0.4)	3 (0.4)	114 (2.3)	13 (0.3)
Moldova, Republic of[6,9]	9[2] (0.6)	23[1] (1.0)	18[1] (0.8)	16[1] (0.9)	11[1] (0.5)	9[1] (0.3)	6[1] (0.3)	6[1] (0.4)	127[2] (2.3)	14 (0.3)
Morocco[6,9]	‡ (†)	20[1] (0.9)	16[1] (0.8)	15[1] (1.0)	11[1] (0.5)	16[1] (0.7)	7[1] (0.3)	6[1] (0.4)	193 (3.6)	17 (0.4)
Netherlands[6]	‡[1] (1.1)	13 (0.7)	‡ (2.0)	28 (2.5)	7 (0.5)	8 (0.5)	5 (0.7)	4 (0.4)	94[2] (1.4)	9 (0.4)
New Zealand	7 (0.4)	17 (0.8)	24 (1.1)	23 (1.3)	9 (0.4)	8 (0.4)	7 (0.5)	4 (0.5)	136 (1.7)	14 (0.2)
Norway	8 (0.4)	19 (0.6)	26 (1.2)	25 (1.5)	10 (0.4)	6 (0.3)	4 (0.3)	3 (0.4)	114 (2.3)	13 (0.3)
Palestinian National Authority	13[1] (0.6)	23[1] (1.0)	18[1] (0.8)	16[1] (0.9)	11[1] (0.5)	9[1] (0.3)	6[1] (0.3)	6[1] (0.4)	127[2] (2.3)	14 (0.3)
Philippines	9[1] (0.4)	20[1] (0.9)	16[1] (0.8)	15[1] (1.0)	11[1] (0.5)	16[1] (0.7)	6[1] (0.3)	6[1] (0.4)	193 (3.6)	17 (0.4)
Romania	9 (0.4)	24 (0.8)	29 (1.0)	15 (0.7)	10 (0.4)	9 (0.5)	3 (0.3)	2 (0.2)	120[1] (2.1)	13[1] (0.3)
Russian Federation	11 (0.2)	20 (0.7)	20 (0.7)	18 (0.7)	8 (0.4)	18 (0.5)	1 (0.2)	3 (0.3)	128[1] (2.1)	15[1] (0.3)
Saudi Arabia	15[1] (1.0)	16[1] (1.6)	13[1] (1.0)	8[1] (0.7)	23[1] (2.2)	12[1] (1.0)	6[1] (0.4)	7[1] (0.8)	110[2] (1.0)	11 (0.2)
Scotland[4]	8[1] (0.3)	22[1] (0.7)	26[1] (1.3)	22[1] (1.5)	8[1] (0.5)	4[1] (0.3)	6[1] (0.5)	3[1] (0.5)	142[2] (2.2)	14 (0.5)
Serbia[6]	7 (0.4)	25 (1.4)	23 (1.2)	20 (1.2)	9 (0.3)	7 (0.4)	3 (0.3)	5 (0.5)	107[2] (1.5)	13 (0.2)
Singapore	11 (0.4)	27 (0.7)	19 (0.6)	15 (0.5)	9 (0.3)	8 (0.3)	6 (0.4)	4 (0.4)	114 (1.6)	13 (0.2)

See notes at end of table.

Table 408. Percentage of lesson time spent on various mathematics activities, yearly mathematics instructional time, and mathematics instructional time as a percentage of total instructional time in eighth grade, by country: 2003—Continued

Country or other jurisdiction	Percentage of time in mathematics lessons students spend on various activities in a typical week								Students' average yearly mathematics instructional time, in hours	Mathematics instructional time as a percent of total instructional time
	Reviewing homework	Listening to lecture-style presentations	Working problems with teacher's guidance	Working problems on their own without teacher's guidance	Listening to teachers reteach and clarify content/procedures	Taking tests and quizzes	Participating in classroom management tasks not related to the lesson's content/purpose	Other student activities		
1	2	3	4	5	6	7	8	9	10	11
Slovak Republic	8 (0.3)	17 (0.7)	27 (0.9)	17 (0.7)	13 (0.5)	12 (0.4)	3 (0.3)	3 (0.3)	126 [1] (1.9)	14 [1] (0.3)
Slovenia	11 (0.4)	21 (0.8)	24 (0.7)	22 (0.9)	10 (0.6)	6 (0.3)	2 (0.2)	4 (0.4)	116 (1.3)	11 (0.1)
South Africa	15 [2] (0.9)	13 [2] (0.7)	19 [2] (0.9)	18 [2] (0.9)	11 [2] (0.6)	12 [2] (0.6)	7 [2] (0.4)	5 [2] (0.4)	‡ (†)	‡ (†)
Sweden	4 (0.4)	11 (0.6)	37 (1.8)	28 (1.8)	9 (0.3)	6 (0.3)	3 (0.3)	3 (0.4)	91 [1] (1.6)	10 [1] (0.2)
Tunisia	18 [1] (0.9)	14 [1] (1.0)	17 [1] (0.9)	18 [1] (0.9)	14 [1] (0.8)	13 [1] (0.7)	4 [1] (0.4)	4 [1] (0.5)	‡ (†)	‡ (†)
United States [5]	13 (0.5)	18 (0.7)	21 (0.6)	18 (0.6)	11 (0.3)	11 (0.4)	5 (0.3)	4 (0.4)	135 [2] (2.2)	13 (0.2)

†Not applicable.

#Rounds to zero.

‡Reporting standards not met.

[1] Data available for at least 70 but less than 85 percent of students, with missing data having not been explicitly accounted for in the analysis.

[2] Data available for at least 50 but less than 70 percent of students, with missing data having not been explicitly accounted for in the analysis.

[3] Did not satisfy guidelines for sample participation rates.

[4] Met guidelines for sample participation rates only after replacement schools were included.

[5] SAR = Special Administrative Region.

[6] National Desired Population does not cover all of International Desired Population.

[7] National Defined Population covers less than 90 percent of National Desired Population.

[8] Korea tested the same cohort of students as other countries, but later in 2003, at the beginning of the next school year.

[9] Nearly satisfied guidelines for sample participation rates only after replacement schools were included.

NOTE: Percentage of time in mathematics lessons students spend on various activities in a typical week provided by teachers. Mathematics instructional time provided by teachers and total instructional time provided by schools. Data are for eighth grade or equivalent in most countries. Detail may not sum to totals because of rounding. Standard errors appear in parentheses.

SOURCE: International Association for the Evaluation of Educational Achievement (IEA), Trends in International Mathematics and Science Study (TIMSS), 2003, TIMSS 2003 International Mathematics Report, by Ina V.S. Mullis et al. (This table was prepared April 2005.)

Table 409. Average size and scores of eighth-grade mathematics classes and Index of Teachers' Emphasis on Mathematics Homework (EMH), by country: 2003

Country or other jurisdiction	Overall average class size	Percentage distribution and mean scores of mathematics classes, by average class size								Index of Teachers' Emphasis on Mathematics Homework (EMH)[1]					
		1 to 24 students Percent	1 to 24 students Mean score	25 to 32 students Percent	25 to 32 students Mean score	33 to 40 students Percent	33 to 40 students Mean score	41 or more students Percent	41 or more students Mean score	High EMH[2] Percent	High EMH[2] Mean score	Medium EMH[3] Percent	Medium EMH[3] Mean score	Low EMH[4] Percent	Low EMH[4] Mean score
1	2	3	4	5	6	7	8	9	10	11	12	13	14	15	16
International average	30 (0.1)	29 (0.5)	461 (1.9)	35 (0.5)	473 (1.4)	24 (0.5)	470 (2.1)	13 (0.3)	448 (1.7)	30 (0.5)	473 (1.4)	51 (0.6)	469 (0.9)	19 (0.4)	453 (1.7)
Armenia	27[5] (0.9)	39 (4.4)	474 (5.6)	43 (4.3)	485 (5.0)	7 (1.8)	460 (9.9)	11 (2.8)	462 (8.4)	65[6] (4.5)	481 (4.2)	31 (4.7)	474 (6.6)	4 (2.1)	467 (11.5)
Australia	26 (0.5)	31 (4.2)	482 (9.4)	65 (4.7)	518 (5.9)	4 (2.2)	492 (14.2)	# (†)	‡ (†)	10 (3.0)	544 (19.7)	56 (4.1)	518 (5.9)	34 (3.8)	475 (9.5)
Bahrain	32 (0.1)	6 (0.7)	451 (5.8)	52 (2.7)	402 (2.1)	40 (2.6)	395 (3.5)	3 (†)	412 (3.8)	15 (2.3)	389 (6.1)	72 (3.7)	404 (2.3)	14 (3.1)	396 (8.7)
Belgium (Flemish)	20 (0.3)	90 (2.3)	538 (3.3)	10 (2.3)	553 (10.5)	# (†)	‡ (†)	# (†)	‡ (†)	9 (2.5)	555 (6.5)	30 (3.8)	555 (5.8)	60 (3.9)	529 (5.6)
Botswana	37 (0.4)	1 (0.7)	‡ (†)	14 (2.6)	392 (9.1)	60 (4.3)	380 (3.7)	25 (4.1)	362 (4.1)	44 (4.6)	364 (4.0)	49 (4.5)	368 (4.0)	7 (2.5)	379 (7.0)
Bulgaria	22 (0.5)	64 (4.2)	468 (4.9)	32 (3.9)	503 (8.0)	3 (2.4)	423 (5.0)	1 (#)	‡ (†)	53 (4.2)	483 (6.1)	38 (4.2)	467 (7.7)	9 (2.5)	469 (15.6)
Chile	35 (0.4)	9 (1.5)	385 (17.0)	22 (2.6)	384 (8.1)	47 (3.6)	390 (5.7)	23 (3.0)	389 (6.9)	10 (2.2)	401 (14.9)	49 (3.6)	388 (5.1)	40 (3.3)	383 (5.5)
Chinese Taipei	37 (0.4)	4 (1.5)	598 (28.9)	14 (2.8)	567 (11.5)	65 (4.0)	575 (4.7)	17 (3.2)	636 (8.7)	29 (3.9)	602 (8.6)	39 (3.9)	588 (6.3)	32 (3.9)	570 (7.6)
Cyprus	26 (0.1)	21 (1.9)	463 (3.2)	79 (1.9)	460 (2.0)	# (†)	‡ (†)	# (†)	‡ (†)	35 (3.1)	455 (3.2)	65 (3.1)	462 (2.8)	# (†)	‡ (†)
Egypt	38 (0.6)	3 (1.2)	422 (13.8)	9 (2.1)	428 (11.3)	61 (4.1)	403 (4.3)	27 (3.7)	407 (7.5)	23 (3.3)	401 (8.6)	57 (3.8)	409 (4.8)	20 (3.2)	406 (8.1)
England[7]	‡[8] (†)	† (†)	‡ (†)	† (†)	‡ (†)	† (†)	‡ (†)	† (†)	‡ (†)	†[6] (–)	‡ (†)	† (†)	† (†)	† (†)	† (†)
Estonia	27 (0.5)	32 (3.4)	523 (5.1)	41 (4.2)	530 (4.3)	27 (3.8)	550 (5.4)	# (†)	‡ (†)	12 (2.3)	540 (9.9)	78 (3.2)	532 (3.3)	9 (2.5)	518 (14.1)
Ghana	37[5] (1.0)	16 (2.7)	232 (7.4)	18 (3.1)	249 (8.3)	29 (4.0)	292 (9.0)	37 (4.7)	289 (9.1)	48 (5.0)	271 (7.9)	37 (5.0)	275 (7.1)	15 (3.0)	284 (10.2)
Hong Kong, SAR[9,10]	39 (0.3)	3 (1.1)	504 (28.1)	6 (1.6)	513 (21.3)	49 (4.1)	575 (5.7)	43 (4.1)	612 (4.7)	26 (3.7)	598 (6.0)	50 (4.6)	593 (6.0)	24 (4.0)	566 (10.0)
Hungary	22 (0.4)	64 (3.9)	522 (4.2)	35 (4.0)	540 (6.5)	2 (0.9)	‡ (†)	# (†)	‡ (†)	8 (2.0)	532 (8.9)	90 (2.2)	530 (3.5)	2 (0.9)	‡ (†)
Indonesia[11]	40 (0.5)	3 (1.7)	413 (8.6)	10 (2.8)	366 (20.0)	38 (4.1)	413 (8.3)	48 (4.3)	421 (6.7)	45 (3.9)	421 (7.4)	45 (4.4)	402 (9.4)	10 (2.6)	412 (15.3)
Iran, Islamic Republic of	29 (0.4)	23 (2.9)	397 (5.7)	50 (4.0)	413 (4.5)	25 (3.3)	420 (6.0)	3 (1.4)	431 (13.7)	63 (4.4)	417 (3.2)	26 (4.0)	406 (7.2)	12 (2.8)	399 (9.3)
Israel[12]	34[5] (0.4)	9 (2.2)	512 (18.3)	23 (3.7)	500 (9.2)	64 (4.5)	490 (4.9)	4 (1.7)	531 (4.5)	50 (3.8)	501 (5.4)	44 (4.1)	500 (6.1)	6 (1.7)	438 (17.8)
Italy	22 (0.3)	78 (3.1)	483 (3.4)	22 (3.1)	488 (8.3)	# (†)	‡ (†)	# (†)	‡ (†)	71 (3.5)	482 (3.2)	25 (3.2)	489 (8.4)	4 (1.5)	480 (11.2)
Japan	35 (0.2)	3 (1.2)	561 (6.1)	18 (2.6)	557 (4.5)	78 (2.6)	571 (2.7)	1 (1.0)	‡ (†)	7 (2.2)	583 (23.4)	29 (3.8)	573 (6.9)	64 (3.9)	567 (2.5)
Jordan	35 (0.7)	14 (2.8)	430 (9.4)	26 (3.6)	424 (13.3)	32 (4.4)	417 (5.9)	28 (3.8)	428 (7.4)	30 (3.8)	422 (5.5)	55 (4.4)	430 (6.3)	14 (2.8)	410 (8.6)
Korea, Republic of[13]	37[8] (0.4)	1 (0.9)	‡ (†)	20 (3.0)	569 (4.6)	57 (4.6)	594 (2.9)	22 (3.5)	600 (7.0)	9[14] (2.1)	582 (10.8)	31 (3.6)	589 (4.7)	60 (3.5)	591 (3.5)
Latvia	24 (0.7)	52 (3.5)	497 (4.4)	42 (3.4)	519 (5.5)	3 (1.0)	527 (20.3)	3 (1.7)	506 (12.6)	17 (2.9)	523 (8.8)	75 (3.8)	505 (3.5)	9 (2.6)	500 (11.7)
Lebanon	29 (0.9)	32 (3.9)	429 (6.0)	44 (4.8)	429 (5.1)	16 (3.1)	443 (10.4)	8 (3.1)	464 (8.7)	49 (4.6)	433 (4.6)	45 (4.4)	436 (5.8)	6 (1.9)	401 (13.1)
Lithuania[12]	25 (0.3)	39 (3.2)	486 (4.2)	61 (3.2)	510 (3.0)	# (†)	‡ (†)	# (†)	‡ (†)	13 (2.7)	512 (7.7)	76 (3.6)	501 (3.4)	11 (2.6)	477 (11.3)
Macedonia, Republic of[12]	28 (0.4)	24 (3.5)	439 (9.2)	58 (4.3)	435 (5.9)	17 (3.6)	429 (13.7)	1 (1.0)	‡ (†)	22 (3.3)	450 (8.1)	66 (3.9)	428 (5.2)	12 (2.6)	432 (13.8)
Malaysia	37 (0.4)	1 (0.7)	‡ (†)	18 (3.3)	514 (11.0)	56 (4.4)	563 (5.1)	25 (3.5)	515 (8.8)	60 (4.5)	508 (5.0)	34 (4.2)	515 (8.5)	5 (1.9)	466 (10.1)
Moldova, Republic of	39 (0.6)	56 (4.5)	449 (6.0)	38 (4.6)	460 (7.0)	5 (2.5)	485 (25.2)	1 (0.6)	‡ (†)	43[6] (4.8)	451 (6.1)	52 (5.0)	463 (7.9)	5 (1.9)	468 (10.1)
Morocco[11,15]	54 (0.7)	† (†)	† (†)	† (†)	‡ (†)	† (†)	‡ (†)	# (†)	‡ (†)	54[14] (6.2)	391 (5.9)	37 (6.4)	383 (7.1)	9 (4.1)	389 (11.1)
Netherlands[8]	‡ (†)	33 (3.9)	514 (9.4)	66 (4.1)	546 (5.8)	1 (1.0)	‡ (†)	# (†)	‡ (†)	7 (2.4)	550 (15.3)	82 (3.7)	541 (4.9)	11 (3.1)	495 (14.1)
New Zealand	27 (0.4)	22 (3.0)	469 (8.9)	72 (4.1)	500 (5.7)	6 (3.2)	538 (17.8)	# (†)	‡ (†)	7 (2.1)	479 (15.6)	67 (4.1)	510 (6.6)	25 (4.2)	471 (5.3)
Norway	25 (0.3)	34 (3.8)	467 (4.3)	65 (3.6)	460 (3.5)	1 (0.7)	‡ (†)	1 (0.7)	‡ (†)	25 (3.4)	460 (6.5)	46 (4.3)	465 (3.8)	29 (4.3)	455 (5.0)
Palestinian National Authority	39 (0.6)	6 (2.0)	398 (20.0)	17 (2.8)	393 (7.4)	27 (3.9)	394 (8.9)	50 (3.7)	385 (4.2)	30 (3.7)	389 (6.4)	58 (4.3)	391 (4.6)	12 (2.5)	388 (14.9)
Philippines	54 (0.7)	1 (0.6)	‡ (†)	1 (0.7)	‡ (†)	7 (2.0)	448 (23.4)	91 (2.1)	372 (5.4)	24 (4.0)	358 (10.9)	61 (4.8)	384 (7.1)	15 (3.7)	377 (19.1)
Romania	24 (0.5)	51 (4.5)	469 (6.7)	46 (4.5)	480 (7.4)	3 (1.4)	534 (34.7)	1 (#)	‡ (†)	78 (3.3)	478 (5.5)	21 (3.3)	463 (10.1)	1 (0.7)	‡ (†)
Russian Federation	24 (0.6)	47 (4.2)	500 (5.1)	47 (3.6)	515 (5.0)	6 (3.4)	533 (11.0)	# (†)	‡ (†)	56 (3.5)	514 (4.3)	43 (3.5)	499 (4.7)	1 (0.5)	‡ (†)
Saudi Arabia	28[5] (0.9)	36 (5.3)	333 (7.5)	26 (4.8)	340 (8.1)	29 (5.8)	330 (5.6)	8 (3.0)	325 (4.1)	14 (3.0)	331 (8.9)	69 (3.9)	332 (4.6)	17 (3.0)	346 (15.0)
Scotland[9]	27[5] (0.5)	33 (3.9)	457 (7.2)	56 (4.4)	520 (6.2)	11 (3.4)	548 (10.1)	1 (0.7)	‡ (†)	3 (1.7)	549 (10.6)	45 (4.6)	527 (5.7)	51 (4.5)	477 (6.2)
Serbia[11]	26 (0.4)	38 (3.7)	464 (4.4)	51 (4.0)	483 (3.8)	11 (2.9)	469 (8.2)	# (†)	‡ (†)	34 (4.1)	474 (4.9)	45 (4.3)	481 (4.5)	22 (3.7)	470 (5.6)
Singapore	38 (0.2)	2 (0.6)	‡ (†)	8 (1.6)	613 (18.0)	63 (2.7)	606 (5.0)	26 (2.5)	607 (5.7)	59 (2.4)	620 (4.2)	33 (2.5)	592 (6.6)	8 (1.3)	563 (13.1)

See notes at end of table.

Table 409. Average size and scores of eighth-grade mathematics classes and Index of Teachers' Emphasis on Mathematics Homework (EMH), by country: 2003—Continued

Country or other jurisdiction	Overall average class size	Percentage distribution and mean scores of mathematics classes, by average class size								Index of Teachers' Emphasis on Mathematics Homework (EMH)[1]					
		1 to 24 students		25 to 32 students		33 to 40 students		41 or more students		High EMH[2]		Medium EMH[3]		Low EMH[4]	
		Percent	Mean score	Percent	Mean score	Percent	Mean score	Percent	Mean score	Percent	Mean score	Percent	Mean score	Percent	Mean score
1	2	3	4	5	6	7	8	9	10	11	12	13	14	15	16
Slovak Republic	25 (0.4)	42 (4.6)	498 (4.7)	53 (4.7)	512 (5.4)	5 (1.8)	543 (19.7)	# (†)	‡ (†)	5 (1.5)	510 (12.4)	79 (2.9)	511 (4.0)	16 (2.7)	492 (6.3)
Slovenia	22 (0.3)	70 (4.1)	491 (3.0)	30 (4.1)	500 (4.1)	# (†)	‡ (†)	# (†)	‡ (†)	13 (2.9)	490 (9.2)	85 (3.1)	495 (2.5)	3 (1.0)	473 (9.7)
South Africa	45 [8] (1.3)	4 (1.2)	309 (35.8)	14 (3.0)	290 (23.8)	30 (3.7)	265 (11.7)	52 (4.1)	249 (8.7)	26 [6] (3.4)	266 (9.2)	54 (3.9)	267 (9.6)	20 (3.3)	250 (9.1)
Sweden	21 (0.4)	71 (3.6)	491 (3.3)	27 (3.7)	522 (5.5)	1 (1.0)	‡ (†)	# (†)	‡ (†)	17 (2.8)	503 (7.0)	25 (3.2)	506 (6.0)	59 (3.7)	494 (4.0)
Tunisia	34 [5] (0.3)	1 (1.0)	‡ (†)	26 (3.3)	404 (3.6)	71 (3.5)	412 (3.2)	2 (1.1)	‡ (†)	12 (2.5)	423 (9.1)	84 (3.0)	407 (2.2)	4 (1.6)	442 (11.3)
United States[15]	24 [5] (0.4)	56 (2.9)	504 (3.9)	39 (2.7)	510 (5.1)	4 (1.2)	531 (16.4)	1 (0.7)	‡ (†)	27 (2.5)	531 (8.0)	62 (2.9)	504 (3.8)	11 (2.2)	471 (9.5)

†Not applicable.

#Rounds to zero.

‡Reporting standards not met.

[1]Index based on teachers' responses to two questions about how often they usually assign mathematics homework and how many minutes of mathematics homework they usually assign.

[2]High EMH indicates the assignment of more than 30 minutes of homework in about half of the lessons or more.

[3]Medium level includes all possible combinations of responses not included in the high or low level categories (see below for details on the low level).

[4]Low level indicates no assignment or the assignment of less than 30 minutes of homework in about half the lessons or less.

[5]Class size data available for at least 70 but less than 85 percent of students, with missing data having not been explicitly accounted for in the analysis.

[6]EMH data available for at least 70 but less than 85 percent of students, with missing data having not been explicitly accounted for in the analysis.

[7]Did not satisfy guidelines for sample participation rates.

[8]Class size data available for at least 50 but less than 70 percent of students, with missing data having not been explicitly accounted for in the analysis.

[9]Met guidelines for sample participation rates only after replacement schools were included.

[10]SAR = Special Administrative Region.

[11]National Desired Population does not cover all of International Desired Population.

[12]National Defined Population covers less than 90 percent of National Desired Population.

[13]Korea tested the same cohort of students as other countries, but later in 2003, at the beginning of the next school year.

[14]EMH data available for at least 50 but less than 70 percent of students, with missing data having not been explicitly accounted for in the analysis.

[15]Nearly satisfied guidelines for sample participation rates only after replacement schools were included.

NOTE: Background data provided by teachers. Data are for eighth grade or equivalent in most countries. Possible scores range from 0 to 1,000. Detail may not sum to totals because of rounding. Standard errors appear in parentheses.

SOURCE: International Association for the Evaluation of Educational Achievement (IEA), Trends in International Mathematics and Science Study (TIMSS), 2003, TIMSS 2003 International Mathematics Report, by Ina V.S. Mullis et al. (This table was prepared April 2005.)

Table 410. Eighth-grade students' perceptions about mathematics and hours spent on leisure activities, by country: 2003

Country or other jurisdiction	Index of students' self-confidence in learning mathematics (SCM)[1]						Average hours spent each day[2]							
	High SCM Percent	High SCM Mean score	Medium SCM Percent	Medium SCM Mean score	Low SCM Percent	Low SCM Mean score	Watching TV or videos	Playing computer games	Playing or talking with friends	Doing jobs at home	Playing sports	Reading for enjoyment	Using the Internet	Working at a paid job
1	2	3	4	5	6	7	8	9	10	11	12	13	14	15
Armenia	41 (1.1)	505 (4.0)	40 (1.0)	468 (3.7)	19 (0.9)	462 (4.1)	1.8 (0.03)	0.9 (0.02)	1.7 (0.04)	1.0 (0.02)	1.6 (0.03)	0.7 (0.02)	1.3 (0.04)	0.4 (0.03)
Australia	50 (1.7)	542 (4.5)	31 (1.1)	483 (3.7)	19 (1.2)	451 (6.4)	2.0 (0.03)	1.2 (0.02)	1.6 (0.03)	1.2 (0.02)	1.5 (0.03)	0.9 (0.02)	1.4 (0.03)	0.6 (0.02)
Bahrain	44 (0.9)	437 (2.0)	38 (0.9)	379 (2.4)	18 (0.6)	366 (3.2)	2.0 (0.03)	1.2 (0.03)	1.6 (0.03)	0.9 (0.02)	1.5 (0.03)	0.5 (0.01)	1.3 (0.03)	0.2 (0.02)
Belgium (Flemish)	45 (0.9)	556 (3.2)	30 (0.7)	526 (3.0)	25 (0.8)	518 (3.5)	2.1 (0.03)	1.0 (0.03)	1.9 (0.03)	0.9 (0.03)	1.6 (0.03)	0.5 (0.01)	1.3 (0.02)	0.6 (0.03)
Botswana	38 (0.9)	390 (2.8)	45 (0.8)	361 (2.5)	17 (0.8)	352 (3.4)	1.4 (0.03)	0.5 (0.02)	2.1 (0.04)	2.3 (0.03)	1.5 (0.02)	1.8 (0.03)	0.7 (0.02)	0.6 (0.03)
Bulgaria	33 (1.3)	519 (5.5)	39 (1.4)	467 (4.2)	28 (1.2)	445 (4.8)	2.5 (0.04)	1.1 (0.04)	2.6 (0.05)	1.5 (0.03)	1.2 (0.04)	0.7 (0.03)	1.0 (0.04)	0.3 (0.02)
Chile	35 (1.0)	427 (3.9)	42 (0.7)	369 (3.4)	23 (0.7)	361 (3.9)	2.2 (0.02)	0.7 (0.02)	2.3 (0.02)	1.5 (0.04)	1.8 (0.03)	0.6 (0.01)	0.7 (0.03)	0.3 (0.02)
Chinese Taipei	26 (1.0)	661 (4.1)	30 (0.7)	593 (5.1)	44 (1.1)	534 (4.0)	1.7 (0.03)	1.4 (0.04)	1.4 (0.03)	0.7 (0.01)	1.0 (0.03)	1.0 (0.02)	1.4 (0.04)	0.2 (0.01)
Cyprus	46 (0.8)	503 (2.0)	32 (0.8)	437 (2.2)	22 (0.7)	407 (3.6)	2.1 (0.03)	1.3 (0.02)	2.1 (0.03)	1.0 (0.03)	1.7 (0.03)	0.9 (0.02)	1.2 (0.02)	0.6 (0.02)
Egypt	58 (1.0)	437 (3.3)	35 (0.9)	383 (3.7)	7 (0.4)	374 (5.3)	0.8 (0.02)	0.7 (0.02)	0.8 (0.02)	1.3 (0.03)	1.1 (0.02)	1.0 (0.02)	0.6 (0.02)	0.6 (0.02)
England[3]	‡ (†)	‡ (†)	‡ (†)	‡ (†)	‡ (†)	‡ (†)	2.3 (0.03)	1.1 (0.03)	2.8 (0.03)	1.1 (0.02)	1.4 (0.03)	0.7 (0.02)	1.5 (0.04)	0.4 (0.02)
Estonia	41 (0.9)	569 (3.2)	32 (0.7)	520 (3.1)	28 (0.8)	489 (3.5)	2.3 (0.03)	0.6 (0.02)	1.2 (0.03)	1.5 (0.03)	1.3 (0.02)	1.7 (0.03)	0.8 (0.03)	0.8 (0.02)
Ghana	— (†)	— (†)	— (†)	— (†)	— (†)	— (†)	0.7 (0.02)	2.0 (0.04)	1.6 (0.03)	0.7 (0.01)	1.0 (0.02)	1.1 (0.03)	2.0 (0.03)	0.1 (0.01)
Hong Kong, SAR[4]	30 (0.9)	627 (2.9)	38 (0.7)	581 (4.1)	33 (0.9)	556 (4.0)	2.3 (0.03)	1.1 (0.02)	2.2 (0.03)	1.1 (0.01)	1.5 (0.03)	0.8 (0.02)	0.6 (0.03)	0.2 (0.02)
Hungary	44 (1.0)	574 (3.3)	32 (1.0)	507 (3.9)	24 (0.8)	479 (3.9)	2.1 (0.03)	0.5 (0.02)	2.2 (0.03)	1.1 (0.03)	1.5 (0.03)	0.8 (0.02)	0.6 (0.02)	0.2 (0.02)
Indonesia	27 (1.1)	420 (6.6)	59 (0.8)	408 (4.5)	15 (0.9)	416 (4.7)	1.5 (0.03)	0.5 (0.02)	1.3 (0.03)	2.2 (0.03)	1.1 (0.02)	1.0 (0.02)	0.3 (0.02)	0.8 (0.03)
Iran, Islamic Republic of	35 (0.9)	447 (3.5)	49 (0.8)	399 (2.6)	16 (0.7)	377 (3.4)	1.6 (0.03)	0.4 (0.02)	1.4 (0.03)	1.5 (0.03)	1.4 (0.04)	1.0 (0.02)	0.2 (0.02)	0.7 (0.05)
Israel	59 (1.2)	526 (3.5)	30 (0.9)	461 (3.8)	11 (0.7)	451 (5.7)	2.5 (0.04)	1.9 (0.03)	2.3 (0.03)	1.4 (0.03)	1.6 (0.03)	0.9 (0.04)	1.8 (0.04)	0.6 (0.02)
Italy	46 (0.9)	521 (3.3)	29 (0.9)	466 (3.6)	25 (1.0)	439 (3.4)	1.8 (0.03)	1.0 (0.02)	2.6 (0.03)	1.1 (0.03)	1.8 (0.03)	0.7 (0.02)	0.6 (0.02)	0.9 (0.02)
Japan	17 (0.6)	634 (3.1)	38 (0.7)	580 (2.7)	45 (1.0)	538 (2.3)	2.7 (0.03)	0.9 (0.02)	1.6 (0.04)	0.6 (0.01)	1.3 (0.03)	0.9 (0.02)	0.6 (0.02)	0.1 (0.01)
Jordan	49 (1.2)	463 (4.7)	38 (0.6)	400 (3.7)	13 (0.7)	390 (4.4)	1.5 (0.03)	0.9 (0.03)	1.2 (0.03)	1.3 (0.03)	1.2 (0.03)	0.9 (0.02)	0.6 (0.03)	0.6 (0.03)
Korea, Republic of[5]	30 (0.7)	650 (2.8)	36 (0.6)	592 (2.5)	34 (0.8)	534 (2.3)	1.7 (0.03)	1.5 (0.03)	1.8 (0.03)	0.7 (0.01)	0.7 (0.03)	0.6 (0.01)	1.7 (0.03)	0.1 (0.03)
Latvia	34 (1.0)	555 (3.4)	33 (0.9)	499 (3.2)	33 (1.0)	473 (3.4)	2.4 (0.04)	1.0 (0.03)	2.8 (0.03)	1.6 (0.03)	1.3 (0.03)	0.8 (0.03)	0.8 (0.03)	0.5 (0.02)
Lebanon	43 (1.4)	462 (3.6)	44 (1.1)	416 (3.1)	13 (0.7)	403 (4.4)	1.8 (0.04)	1.3 (0.03)	1.6 (0.04)	1.3 (0.03)	1.6 (0.03)	1.0 (0.02)	1.0 (0.03)	0.8 (0.03)
Lithuania	36 (1.0)	552 (3.1)	37 (0.9)	486 (2.8)	26 (0.9)	456 (2.7)	2.1 (0.03)	1.1 (0.02)	2.6 (0.04)	1.6 (0.04)	1.1 (0.03)	0.6 (0.02)	0.7 (0.03)	0.3 (0.02)
Macedonia, Republic of	33 (1.0)	482 (4.0)	37 (1.0)	418 (4.7)	31 (1.0)	424 (3.9)	2.3 (0.04)	1.3 (0.03)	2.2 (0.03)	1.6 (0.03)	1.8 (0.03)	1.0 (0.02)	0.9 (0.03)	0.7 (0.03)
Malaysia	39 (1.2)	546 (4.2)	45 (1.0)	490 (3.7)	16 (0.7)	471 (4.4)	2.1 (0.04)	0.8 (0.03)	1.5 (0.03)	1.7 (0.02)	1.1 (0.02)	1.2 (0.02)	0.6 (0.02)	0.3 (0.03)
Moldova, Republic of	30 (1.2)	494 (5.0)	50 (0.9)	451 (4.5)	20 (1.1)	441 (5.3)	1.9 (0.04)	0.7 (0.03)	2.0 (0.04)	2.2 (0.06)	1.3 (0.03)	1.1 (0.02)	0.7 (0.03)	0.5 (0.02)
Morocco	‡ (†)	‡ (†)	‡ (†)	‡ (†)	‡ (†)	‡ (†)	1.3 (0.04)	2.3 (0.06)	1.3 (0.03)	1.8 (0.03)	1.5 (0.03)	0.7 (0.02)	1.5 (0.04)	‡ (†)
Netherlands	45 (1.4)	557 (4.4)	33 (1.0)	527 (4.7)	23 (1.0)	511 (4.8)	2.1 (0.05)	1.2 (0.04)	2.0 (0.05)	0.8 (0.02)	1.7 (0.04)	0.5 (0.02)	1.5 (0.04)	0.8 (0.05)
New Zealand	43 (1.4)	534 (6.4)	36 (1.1)	475 (5.4)	21 (0.9)	452 (4.1)	2.1 (0.04)	1.0 (0.04)	1.8 (0.05)	1.0 (0.02)	1.5 (0.03)	0.7 (0.03)	1.3 (0.04)	0.6 (0.03)
Norway	46 (1.1)	502 (2.0)	32 (0.9)	445 (2.9)	21 (0.8)	405 (3.4)	2.2 (0.03)	1.2 (0.03)	2.7 (0.03)	1.0 (0.03)	1.8 (0.03)	0.6 (0.02)	1.2 (0.03)	0.7 (0.02)
Palestinian National Authority	43 (1.0)	428 (3.9)	41 (0.9)	370 (2.9)	16 (0.6)	355 (3.6)	1.2 (0.02)	0.7 (0.02)	1.3 (0.03)	1.5 (0.03)	1.1 (0.02)	1.0 (0.03)	0.5 (0.03)	0.6 (0.03)
Philippines	29 (0.7)	405 (6.1)	59 (0.7)	369 (4.8)	12 (0.5)	366 (6.5)	1.6 (0.04)	0.6 (0.02)	1.7 (0.03)	1.9 (0.03)	1.4 (0.02)	1.2 (0.03)	0.8 (0.04)	0.8 (0.04)
Romania	30 (1.2)	533 (4.6)	45 (1.1)	465 (4.5)	25 (0.9)	442 (5.4)	2.0 (0.04)	0.9 (0.03)	2.1 (0.03)	1.7 (0.05)	1.3 (0.03)	1.0 (0.03)	1.6 (0.04)	0.4 (0.04)
Russian Federation	43 (1.1)	548 (3.0)	30 (1.0)	492 (4.1)	27 (0.8)	466 (4.6)	2.0 (0.03)	1.0 (0.03)	2.5 (0.04)	1.6 (0.03)	1.3 (0.03)	1.1 (0.03)	0.4 (0.02)	0.2 (0.02)
Saudi Arabia	41 (1.4)	361 (4.8)	43 (1.1)	321 (5.4)	16 (0.9)	303 (5.8)	1.6 (0.05)	1.1 (0.03)	1.3 (0.03)	1.5 (0.04)	1.2 (0.04)	0.9 (0.05)	0.8 (0.05)	0.8 (0.03)
Scotland	52 (1.5)	524 (3.9)	32 (1.0)	477 (3.8)	15 (0.9)	456 (5.0)	2.2 (0.03)	1.4 (0.04)	2.7 (0.03)	0.8 (0.02)	1.7 (0.03)	0.6 (0.03)	1.4 (0.03)	0.5 (0.03)
Serbia	44 (1.1)	530 (2.8)	26 (0.9)	458 (3.2)	30 (1.1)	422 (3.4)	2.1 (0.03)	1.0 (0.03)	2.1 (0.03)	1.3 (0.03)	1.3 (0.03)	0.8 (0.02)	0.6 (0.03)	0.3 (0.02)
Singapore	39 (0.8)	639 (3.0)	34 (0.7)	594 (3.9)	27 (0.7)	571 (4.6)	2.3 (0.02)	1.4 (0.03)	1.7 (0.02)	0.7 (0.02)	1.4 (0.03)	0.9 (0.02)	1.6 (0.03)	0.2 (0.02)
Slovak Republic	40 (1.1)	556 (3.7)	35 (1.0)	487 (3.9)	25 (1.0)	462 (4.1)	2.5 (0.03)	1.1 (0.03)	2.8 (0.03)	1.5 (0.04)	1.9 (0.04)	0.9 (0.02)	0.6 (0.02)	0.4 (0.02)
Slovenia	40 (0.9)	533 (3.2)	39 (1.0)	474 (2.5)	20 (0.9)	453 (2.8)	2.2 (0.03)	1.3 (0.03)	2.0 (0.03)	1.2 (0.03)	1.7 (0.03)	0.8 (0.02)	1.1 (0.03)	0.4 (0.02)
South Africa	37 (0.9)	300 (8.3)	48 (0.9)	242 (3.9)	15 (0.8)	255 (9.9)	1.5 (0.03)	0.7 (0.02)	2.0 (0.03)	1.8 (0.02)	1.6 (0.02)	1.6 (0.03)	0.8 (0.02)	0.8 (0.02)
Sweden	49 (1.3)	534 (2.6)	36 (0.9)	477 (3.1)	16 (0.9)	446 (3.4)	2.1 (0.03)	1.1 (0.03)	2.8 (0.03)	1.0 (0.02)	1.5 (0.03)	0.6 (0.02)	1.7 (0.04)	0.4 (0.02)
Tunisia	44 (1.0)	436 (2.7)	36 (0.8)	399 (2.5)	20 (0.9)	384 (2.2)	1.4 (0.02)	0.8 (0.03)	1.5 (0.02)	1.9 (0.03)	1.5 (0.02)	1.3 (0.02)	0.7 (0.02)	0.6 (0.02)
United States	51 (0.8)	534 (3.3)	29 (0.6)	483 (3.5)	20 (0.6)	461 (3.6)	2.2 (0.03)	1.1 (0.02)	2.4 (0.03)	1.2 (0.02)	1.8 (0.02)	0.7 (0.01)	1.8 (0.03)	0.6 (0.02)

—Not available.
†Not applicable.
‡Reporting standards not met.

[1]Index based on students' responses to four statements about mathematics: 1) I usually do well in mathematics; 2) Mathematics is more difficult for me than for many of my classmates (reverse scored); 3) Mathematics is not one of my strengths (reverse scored); 4) I learn things quickly in mathematics. Average is computed across the four items based on a 4-point scale: 1. Agree a lot; 2. Agree a little; 3. Disagree a little; 4. Disagree a lot. Students showing positive attitudes a little or a lot of the time across the four statements were assigned to the high level. Students showing negative attitudes a little or a lot of the time across the four statements were assigned to the low level. Students showing mixed attitudes across the four statements were assigned to the middle level.

[2]Number of hours based on: No time = 0; Less than 1 hour = 0.5; 1–2 hours = 1.5; More than 2, but less than 4 hours = 3; 4 or more hours = 4.5. Activities are not necessarily exclusive; students may have reported engaging in more than one activity at the same time.
[3]Did not satisfy guidelines for sample participation rates.
[4]SAR = Special Administrative Region.
[5]Korea tested the same cohort of students as other countries, but later in 2003, at the beginning of the next school year.
NOTE: Data are for eighth grade or equivalent in most countries. Possible scores range from 0 to 1,000. Detail may not sum to totals because of rounding. Standard errors appear in parentheses.
SOURCE: International Association for the Evaluation of Educational Achievement (IEA), Trends in International Mathematics and Science Study (TIMSS), 2003, TIMSS 2003 International Mathematics Report, by Ina V. S. Mullis et al. (This table was prepared April 2006.)

Table 411. Average mathematics scores at the end of secondary school, by sex, average time spent studying mathematics out of school, and country: 1995

Country	Average score in mathematics			Amount of daily out-of-school study time in mathematics						Average hours[1]
	Total	Males	Females	Less than 1 hour		1 to 2 hours		3 or more hours		
				Percent	Mean score	Percent	Mean score	Percent	Mean score	
1	2	3	4	5	6	7	8	9	10	11
Australia[2]	522 (9.3)	540 (10.3)	510 (9.3)	59 (2.2)	521 (8.3)	36 (2.2)	557 (10.2)	5 (0.8)	534 (13.4)	1.0 (0.04)
Austria[2]	518 (5.3)	545 (7.2)	503 (5.5)	77 (1.7)	526 (5.8)	19 (1.6)	533 (9.4)	4 (0.8)	502 (13.7)	0.6 (0.04)
Canada[2]	519 (2.8)	537 (3.8)	504 (3.5)	56 (2.1)	539 (5.1)	38 (1.9)	547 (5.0)	7 (1.0)	526 (14.6)	1.1 (0.05)
Cyprus[2]	446 (2.5)	454 (4.9)	439 (3.7)	63 (2.1)	435 (4.3)	29 (1.8)	471 (4.8)	8 (1.3)	451 (9.0)	1.0 (0.05)
Czech Republic	466 (12.3)	488 (11.3)	443 (16.8)	92 (1.5)	464 (13.8)	8 (1.4)	482 (17.8)	# (†)	— (†)	0.4 (0.03)
Denmark[2]	547 (3.3)	575 (4.0)	523 (4.0)	68 (2.0)	571 (4.9)	28 (1.6)	563 (4.7)	4 (0.7)	562 (11.9)	0.9 (0.04)
France[2]	523 (5.1)	544 (5.6)	506 (5.3)	59 (2.3)	517 (5.1)	35 (2.3)	539 (6.7)	5 (0.7)	505 (14.7)	1.0 (0.04)
Germany[2]	495 (5.9)	509 (8.7)	480 (8.8)	— (†)	— (†)	— (†)	— (†)	— (†)	— (†)	— (†)
Hungary	483 (3.2)	485 (4.9)	481 (4.8)	74 (0.9)	480 (3.2)	24 (0.8)	496 (5.5)	2 (0.2)	— (†)	0.7 (0.02)
Iceland[2]	534 (2.0)	558 (3.4)	514 (2.2)	79 (1.1)	553 (3.2)	19 (1.1)	542 (7.0)	2 (0.4)	— (†)	0.7 (0.02)
Italy[2]	476 (5.5)	490 (7.4)	464 (6.0)	55 (2.6)	479 (6.3)	40 (2.2)	486 (7.2)	5 (0.9)	477 (11.2)	1.0 (0.05)
Lithuania[2]	469 (6.1)	485 (7.3)	461 (7.7)	67 (1.8)	472 (5.8)	29 (1.7)	480 (5.2)	4 (0.5)	484 (11.5)	0.8 (0.03)
Netherlands[2]	560 (4.7)	585 (5.6)	533 (5.9)	82 (1.7)	606 (6.2)	16 (1.6)	581 (11.1)	1 (0.3)	— (†)	0.7 (0.03)
New Zealand	522 (4.5)	536 (4.9)	507 (6.2)	75 (1.4)	544 (6.1)	23 (1.4)	552 (5.9)	2 (0.3)	— (†)	0.7 (0.03)
Norway[2]	528 (4.1)	555 (5.3)	501 (4.8)	85 (1.4)	541 (5.1)	14 (1.3)	558 (9.5)	1 (0.3)	— (†)	0.5 (0.03)
Russian Federation[2]	471 (6.2)	488 (6.5)	460 (6.6)	56 (2.0)	463 (5.9)	33 (1.4)	484 (7.5)	11 (1.2)	494 (8.1)	1.2 (0.06)
Slovenia[2]	512 (8.3)	535 (12.7)	490 (8.0)	72 (2.7)	521 (9.4)	25 (2.6)	518 (9.5)	2 (0.6)	— (†)	0.7 (0.05)
South Africa[2]	356 (8.3)	365 (9.3)	348 (10.8)	33 (1.8)	394 (17.1)	51 (1.8)	375 (10.9)	17 (1.2)	344 (7.2)	1.7 (0.05)
Sweden	552 (4.3)	573 (5.9)	531 (3.9)	90 (0.9)	579 (5.4)	9 (0.9)	580 (7.8)	1 (0.2)	— (†)	0.4 (0.02)
Switzerland	540 (5.8)	555 (6.4)	522 (7.4)	67 (1.6)	569 (4.9)	28 (1.3)	550 (5.6)	5 (0.9)	522 (10.6)	0.9 (0.04)
United States[2]	461 (3.2)	466 (4.1)	456 (3.6)	76 (1.5)	475 (3.8)	22 (1.5)	486 (5.9)	2 (0.2)	— (†)	0.7 (0.02)

—Not available.
†Not applicable.
#Rounds to zero.
[1]Average hours based on: No time = 0; Less than 1 hour = 0.5; 1–2 hours = 1.5; 3–5 hours = 4; More than 5 hours = 7.
[2]Countries did not meet all International Association for the Evaluation of Educational Achievement sampling specifications.

NOTE: End of secondary school is equivalent to 12th grade in the United States and a few other countries, but ranges from 9th to 14th grades among the survey countries. Possible scores range from 0 to 1,000. Detail may not sum to totals because of rounding. Standard errors appear in parentheses.
SOURCE: International Association for the Evaluation of Educational Achievement (IEA), Trends in International Mathematics and Science Study (TIMSS), 1995, *Mathematics and Science Achievement in the Final Year of Secondary School*, by Ina V. S. Mullis et al. (This table was prepared October 1998.)

Table 412. Average fourth-grade science scores in content areas and average time spent teaching science in school, by country: 2003

Country or other jurisdiction	Average score by content area								Average yearly science instructional time in hours		Science instructional time as a percent of total instructional time[1]	
	Science overall		Life science		Physical science		Earth science					
1	2		3		4		5		6		7	
Armenia	437	(4.3)	435	(4.4)	429	(4.3)	450	(3.6)	‡	(†)	‡	(†)
Australia[2]	521	(4.2)	523	(3.8)	518	(3.9)	518	(4.1)	45 [3]	(2.6)	5	(0.3)
Belgium (Flemish)	518	(1.8)	524	(1.7)	507	(2.3)	522	(1.7)	‡	(†)	‡	(†)
Chinese Taipei	551	(1.7)	540	(1.6)	554	(2.0)	559	(2.6)	84	(1.0)	11	(0.2)
Cyprus	480	(2.4)	482	(2.1)	479	(2.3)	487	(2.5)	46 [3]	(1.4)	5	(0.2)
England[2]	540	(3.6)	532	(3.1)	546	(3.2)	535	(3.5)	‡	(†)	‡	(†)
Hong Kong, SAR[2,4]	542	(3.1)	535	(2.6)	548	(2.7)	536	(2.7)	77 [3]	(5.4)	8	(0.5)
Hungary	530	(3.0)	536	(2.5)	526	(2.7)	526	(3.7)	54 [3]	(1.0)	6	(0.1)
Iran, Islamic Republic of	414	(4.1)	424	(4.6)	419	(4.5)	428	(3.0)	‡	(†)	‡	(†)
Italy	516	(3.8)	521	(3.5)	512	(3.5)	519	(3.7)	73 [5]	(2.3)	8 [5]	(0.3)
Japan	543	(1.5)	530	(1.3)	557	(1.7)	535	(1.9)	81	(1.2)	8	(0.2)
Latvia	532	(2.5)	531	(2.3)	532	(2.6)	534	(2.9)	‡	(†)	‡	(†)
Lithuania[6]	512	(2.6)	516	(2.0)	512	(2.5)	503	(3.2)	53	(1.6)	6	(0.2)
Moldova, Republic of	496	(4.6)	504	(3.9)	489	(3.9)	505	(4.9)	‡	(†)	‡	(†)
Morocco	304	(6.7)	300	(6.1)	308	(7.0)	311	(6.1)	‡	(†)	‡	(†)
Netherlands[2]	525	(2.0)	547	(1.8)	505	(1.9)	503	(2.3)	33 [3]	(1.8)	3	(0.2)
New Zealand	520	(2.5)	520	(2.3)	516	(2.3)	522	(2.3)	65 [3]	(3.5)	7	(0.4)
Norway	466	(2.6)	480	(2.2)	456	(2.3)	473	(2.8)	38 [5]	(1.8)	4 [5]	(0.2)
Philippines	332	(9.4)	330	(9.0)	343	(9.6)	324	(9.2)	176 [5]	(3.2)	16 [5]	(0.4)
Russian Federation	526	(5.2)	526	(4.7)	527	(5.2)	527	(6.0)	33 [3]	(1.2)	5	(0.2)
Scotland[2]	502	(2.9)	506	(3.1)	503	(2.6)	498	(2.6)	‡	(†)	‡	(†)
Singapore	565	(5.5)	506	(3.1)	503	(2.6)	498	(2.6)	64	(0.6)	7	(0.1)
Slovenia	490	(2.5)	489	(2.9)	497	(2.3)	490	(2.7)	75 [5]	(2.2)	9 [5]	(0.3)
Tunisia	314	(5.7)	290	(5.9)	324	(5.3)	336	(4.8)	‡	(†)	‡	(†)
United States[2]	536	(2.5)	537	(2.2)	531	(2.3)	535	(2.5)	83 [5]	(3.0)	8 [5]	(0.3)

†Not applicable.

‡Reporting standards not met.

[1]Computed as the ratio of science instructional time to the total instructional time averaged across students.

[2]Met guidelines for participation rates only after replacement schools were included.

[3]Data are available for at least 50 but less than 70 percent of the students.

[4]SAR = Special Administrative Region.

[5]Data are available for at least 70 but less than 85 percent of the students.

[6]National Desired Population does not cover all of International Desired Population.

NOTE: Data are for fourth grade or equivalent in most countries. Possible scores range from 0 to 1,000. Detail may not sum to totals because of rounding. Standard errors appear in parentheses.

SOURCE: International Association for the Evaluation of Educational Achievement (IEA), Trends in International Mathematics and Science Study (TIMSS), 2003, *TIMSS 2003 International Science Report*, by Michael O. Martin et al. (This table was prepared October 2005.)

Table 413. Average eighth-grade science scores in content areas and average time spent studying out of school, by country: 2003

Country or other jurisdiction	Average score by content area — Science overall	Life science	Chemistry	Physics	Earth science	Environmental science	Index of time students spend doing science homework (TSH) in a normal school week[1] — High TSH Percent	High TSH Mean score	Medium TSH Percent	Medium TSH Mean score	Low TSH Percent	Low TSH Mean score
1	2	3	4	5	6	7	8	9	10	11	12	13
International average	473 (0.5)	474 (0.5)	474 (0.5)	474 (0.5)	474 (0.5)	474 (0.5)	13 (0.2)	458 (1.3)	44 (0.2)	466 (0.9)	43 (0.3)	467 (0.9)
Armenia	461 (3.5)	453[2] (3.3)	466[2] (4.2)	479 (3.2)	460[2] (3.7)	417[2] (4.4)	9 (0.8)	— (†)	35 (1.6)	— (†)	56 (2.0)	— (†)
Australia	527 (3.8)	532[3] (3.8)	506[3] (3.8)	521[3] (3.7)	531[3] (4.2)	536[3] (3.4)	9 (0.8)	520 (6.4)	35 (1.6)	530 (3.3)	56 (2.0)	530 (4.4)
Bahrain	438 (1.8)	445[2] (1.9)	441[2] (2.6)	443[2] (2.0)	440[2] (2.4)	439[2] (3.1)	13 (0.7)	426 (4.1)	56 (1.3)	441 (2.5)	31 (1.4)	445 (2.6)
Belgium (Flemish)	516 (2.5)	526[3] (2.4)	503[3] (2.0)	514[3] (2.5)	508[3] (2.4)	523[3] (2.7)	— (†)	— (†)	— (†)	— (†)	— (†)	— (†)
Botswana	365 (2.8)	370[2] (2.7)	348[3] (3.1)	371[2] (3.2)	361[2] (3.1)	381[2] (3.3)	14 (0.7)	378 (6.1)	45 (1.0)	368 (3.2)	40 (1.2)	366 (3.6)
Bulgaria	479 (5.2)	474 (5.2)	482 (5.7)	485[3] (5.0)	491[3] (4.9)	464[3] (5.0)	— (†)	— (†)	— (†)	— (†)	— (†)	— (†)
Chile	413 (2.9)	427[2] (2.7)	405[2] (3.3)	401 (3.1)	435[2] (3.1)	436[2] (2.9)	— (†)	— (†)	— (†)	— (†)	— (†)	— (†)
Chinese Taipei	571 (3.5)	563[3] (3.1)	584[3] (4.0)	569[3] (3.3)	548[3] (3.1)	560[3] (3.1)	12[4] (1.2)	588[4] (4.6)	37[4] (1.3)	581[4] (4.0)	51[4] (2.1)	561[4] (3.5)
Cyprus	441 (2.0)	437[2] (2.2)	443[2] (2.6)	450[2] (1.7)	447[2] (2.1)	441[2] (2.3)	— (†)	— (†)	— (†)	— (†)	— (†)	— (†)
Egypt	421 (3.9)	425[2] (3.7)	442[2] (3.8)	414[2] (4.1)	403[2] (4.4)	430[2] (4.0)	23 (0.7)	416 (4.4)	64 (0.8)	436 (4.0)	13 (0.6)	430 (6.6)
England[5]	‡ (†)	‡ (†)	‡ (†)	‡ (†)	‡ (†)	‡ (†)	‡ (†)	‡ (†)	‡ (†)	‡ (†)	‡ (†)	‡ (†)
Estonia	552 (2.5)	547[3] (2.4)	552[2] (2.1)	544[3] (2.4)	558[3] (2.9)	540[3] (2.2)	— (†)	— (†)	— (†)	— (†)	— (†)	— (†)
Ghana	255 (5.9)	256[2] (5.6)	276[2] (6.6)	239[2] (5.4)	254[2] (5.6)	267[2] (6.2)	25 (1.2)	267 (8.5)	54 (1.0)	262 (6.0)	22 (1.0)	258 (8.1)
Hong Kong, SAR[6,7]	556 (3.0)	551[3] (2.9)	542[3] (2.6)	555[3] (2.8)	549[3] (2.9)	555[3] (2.6)	6 (0.5)	548 (4.6)	43 (1.4)	563 (2.9)	50 (1.4)	554 (3.9)
Hungary	543 (2.8)	536[3] (2.7)	560[3] (3.1)	536[3] (2.7)	537 (3.1)	528[3] (2.9)	— (†)	— (†)	— (†)	— (†)	— (†)	— (†)
Indonesia[8]	420 (4.1)	424[2] (3.9)	391[2] (3.8)	430[2] (4.0)	431[2] (3.8)	454[2] (3.4)	— (†)	— (†)	— (†)	— (†)	— (†)	— (†)
Iran, Islamic Republic of	453 (2.3)	447[2] (2.6)	445[2] (2.7)	445[2] (3.0)	468[2] (2.9)	487[3] (2.1)	8 (0.7)	451 (5.6)	42 (1.4)	457 (2.9)	49 (1.7)	452 (2.7)
Israel[9]	488 (3.1)	491[3] (3.0)	499[3] (3.4)	484[3] (2.9)	485[3] (3.0)	486[3] (2.9)	13 (0.9)	480 (4.7)	43 (1.6)	485 (4.3)	44 (2.0)	505 (3.4)
Italy	491 (3.1)	498[3] (3.2)	487[3] (3.3)	470 (3.2)	513[3] (4.0)	497[3] (3.0)	14 (1.0)	489 (5.9)	41 (1.1)	487 (3.7)	45 (1.4)	496 (3.7)
Japan	552 (1.7)	549[3] (2.0)	552[3] (2.1)	564[3] (1.9)	530[3] (2.1)	537[3] (2.0)	— (†)	— (†)	— (†)	— (†)	— (†)	— (†)
Jordan	475 (3.8)	448[2] (3.9)	478 (4.4)	465[2] (3.8)	472 (4.0)	492[3] (3.2)	19 (0.9)	466 (4.2)	52 (1.2)	478 (3.9)	29 (1.5)	499 (5.0)
Korea, Republic of[10]	558 (1.6)	558[3] (1.6)	529[3] (2.5)	579[3] (1.6)	540[3] (1.9)	544[3] (1.4)	4 (0.4)	549 (6.3)	26 (1.7)	562 (2.4)	70 (2.0)	559 (1.9)
Latvia	513 (2.9)	511[3] (3.0)	514[3] (3.4)	512[3] (2.9)	514[3] (2.8)	508[3] (3.3)	— (†)	— (†)	— (†)	— (†)	— (†)	— (†)
Lebanon	393 (4.3)	360[2] (5.0)	432[2] (4.9)	419[2] (4.0)	395[2] (4.0)	374[2] (5.1)	— (†)	— (†)	— (†)	— (†)	— (†)	— (†)
Lithuania[8]	519 (2.1)	517 (2.4)	534[3] (2.3)	519[3] (2.7)	512[3] (2.7)	507[3] (2.0)	— (†)	— (†)	— (†)	— (†)	— (†)	— (†)
Macedonia[8]	449 (3.6)	448[2] (3.7)	467[2] (3.9)	458[2] (3.1)	440[2] (4.3)	442[2] (3.7)	20 (1.0)	— (†)	49 (1.4)	— (†)	31 (1.3)	— (†)
Malaysia	510 (3.7)	504[3] (2.5)	514[3] (3.8)	519[3] (3.6)	502[3] (3.8)	513[3] (3.2)	25 (1.0)	513 (4.4)	44 (1.2)	510 (3.6)	31 (1.3)	510 (4.6)
Moldova, Republic of	472 (3.4)	466[2] (3.6)	479 (3.9)	479 (3.7)	475 (4.0)	454[2] (3.8)	— (†)	— (†)	— (†)	— (†)	— (†)	— (†)
Morocco[8,11]	396 (2.5)	390[2] (2.6)	402[2] (2.7)	410[2] (2.7)	397[2] (3.4)	396[2] (3.3)	14[7] (0.7)	391[7] (5.3)	47[7] (1.1)	396[7] (3.4)	39[7] (1.3)	408[7] (3.5)
Netherlands[7]	536 (3.1)	536[3] (3.3)	514[3] (2.6)	538[3] (3.4)	534[3] (3.2)	539[3] (2.8)	— (†)	— (†)	— (†)	— (†)	— (†)	— (†)
New Zealand	520 (5.0)	523[3] (5.1)	501[3] (5.6)	515[3] (4.7)	525[3] (4.8)	525[3] (3.9)	10 (1.3)	519 (6.2)	41 (1.6)	531 (6.9)	48 (2.0)	518 (5.1)
Norway	494 (2.2)	496[3] (2.5)	485[3] (3.0)	488[3] (2.6)	517[3] (2.7)	496[3] (2.2)	13 (0.8)	485 (3.7)	44 (1.2)	493 (3.1)	43 (1.7)	503 (2.3)
Palestinian National Authority	435 (3.2)	435[2] (3.6)	444[2] (3.9)	432[2] (3.6)	439[2] (3.0)	444[2] (3.7)	21 (1.1)	433 (4.4)	56 (1.3)	442 (3.4)	23 (1.3)	441 (4.8)
Philippines[12]	377 (5.8)	387[2] (5.8)	342[2] (6.1)	380[2] (4.7)	377[2] (5.7)	403[2] (5.4)	17 (0.7)	381 (7.5)	50 (0.8)	379 (5.7)	33 (1.2)	381 (7.2)
Romania	470 (4.9)	471 (4.8)	474 (4.9)	473 (4.1)	469 (5.2)	472 (4.7)	— (†)	— (†)	— (†)	— (†)	— (†)	— (†)
Russian Federation	514 (3.7)	514[3] (3.3)	527[3] (4.0)	511[3] (3.4)	518[3] (3.3)	491[3] (3.2)	— (†)	— (†)	— (†)	— (†)	— (†)	— (†)
Saudi Arabia	398 (4.0)	412[2] (3.9)	382[2] (4.8)	394[2] (3.9)	394[2] (4.0)	410[2] (3.8)	8 (0.7)	382 (6.0)	61 (1.5)	402 (4.6)	31 (1.7)	403 (4.6)
Scotland[7]	512 (3.4)	512[3] (3.3)	499[3] (3.2)	515[3] (3.0)	515[3] (3.8)	511[3] (3.5)	3 (0.4)	487 (14.2)	27 (1.4)	508 (5.0)	71 (1.5)	517 (3.4)
Serbia[8]	468 (2.5)	468[2] (2.6)	474 (3.2)	471 (2.6)	471 (3.0)	457[2] (2.4)	— (†)	— (†)	— (†)	— (†)	— (†)	— (†)
Singapore	578 (4.3)	569[3] (4.0)	582[3] (4.2)	579[3] (3.4)	549[3] (3.9)	568[3] (3.8)	18 (0.7)	595 (4.1)	48 (0.7)	585 (4.4)	34 (0.9)	564 (5.5)

See notes at end of table.

Table 413. Average eighth-grade science scores in content areas and average time spent studying out of school, by country: 2003—Continued

Country or other jurisdiction	Average score by content area						Index of time students spend doing science homework (TSH) in a normal school week[1]					
	Science overall	Life science	Chemistry	Physics	Earth science	Environmental science	High TSH		Medium TSH		Low TSH	
							Percent	Mean score	Percent	Mean score	Percent	Mean score
1	2	3	4	5	6	7	8	9	10	11	12	13
Slovak Republic	517 (3.2)	514[3] (2.9)	519[3] (3.6)	519[3] (2.9)	523[3] (3.3)	509[3] (2.8)	— (†)	— (†)	— (†)	— (†)	— (†)	— (†)
Slovenia	520 (1.8)	521[3] (2.2)	532[3] (2.6)	509[3] (1.8)	523[3] (2.2)	515[3] (2.2)	— (†)	— (†)	— (†)	— (†)	— (†)	— (†)
South Africa	244 (6.7)	250[2] (6.0)	285[2] (5.9)	244[2] (6.2)	247[2] (6.3)	251[2] (6.6)	17 (0.7)	234 (9.6)	52 (0.9)	246 (7.9)	32 (0.9)	263 (7.4)
Sweden	524 (2.7)	528[3] (2.7)	526[3] (2.6)	525[3] (2.9)	532[3] (3.3)	499[3] (2.6)	— (†)	— (†)	— (†)	— (†)	— (†)	— (†)
Tunisia	404 (2.1)	417[2] (2.0)	413[2] (2.5)	386[2] (2.5)	408[2] (2.0)	436[2] (2.2)	9 (0.6)	398 (4.0)	35 (0.9)	400 (2.8)	56 (1.2)	411 (2.6)
United States[11]	527 (3.1)	537[3] (3.0)	513[3] (3.2)	515[3] (2.9)	532[3] (2.9)	533[3] (2.9)	13 (0.7)	519 (4.3)	43 (1.4)	530 (3.4)	45 (1.7)	531 (3.7)

—Not available.
†Not applicable.
‡Reporting standards not met.
[1]Index based on students' reports on the frequency and amount of science homework they are given. High level indicates more than 30 minutes of science homework assigned 3–4 times a week. Low level indicates no more than 30 minutes of science homework no more than twice a week. Medium level includes all other possible combinations of responses.
[2]Country average significantly lower than international average.
[3]Country average significantly higher than international average.
[4]Students were asked about natural science; data pertain to grade 8 physics/chemistry course.
[5]Did not satisfy guidelines for sample participation rates.
[6]SAR = Special Administrative Region.

[7]Met guidelines for sample participation rates only after replacement schools were included.
[8]National Desired Population does not cover all of International Desired Population.
[9]National Defined Population covers less than 90 percent of National Desired Population.
[10]Korea tested the same cohort of students as other countries, but later in 2003, at the beginning of the next school year.
[11]Nearly satisfied guidelines for sample participation rates only after replacement schools were included.
[12]Students study only biology at grade 8.
NOTE: Data are for eighth grade or equivalent in most countries. Possible scores range from 0 to 1,000. Detail may not sum to totals because of rounding. Standard errors appear in parentheses.
SOURCE: International Association for the Evaluation of Educational Achievement (IEA), Trends in International Mathematics and Science Study (TIMSS), 2003, TIMSS 2003 International Science Report, by Michael O. Martin et al. (This table was prepared October 2005.)

Table 414. Instructional practices and time spent teaching science in eighth grade, by country: 2003

Country or other jurisdiction	Percent of students who reported doing activity about half the lessons or more												Students' average yearly instructional time in hours									
	Watch the teacher demonstrate an experiment or investigation		Design or plan an experiment or investigation		Conduct an experiment or investigation		Work in small groups on an experiment or investigation		Write explanations about what was observed and why it happened		Relate what is being learned in science to our daily lives		General integrated science		Earth science		Chemistry		Biology		Physics	
1	2		3		4		5		6		7		8		9		10		11		12	
International average	**64**	**(0.2)**	**49**	**(0.2)**	**57**	**(0.3)**	**59**	**(0.3)**	**66**	**(0.2)**	**57**	**(0.2)**	**117**	**(0.7)**	**55**	**(0.6)**	**61**	**(0.8)**	**61**	**(0.8)**	**68**	**(0.6)**
Australia	54	(1.6)	49	(1.7)	60	(2.2)	68	(2.1)	75	(1.5)	42	(1.1)	132[1]	(3.6)	—	(†)	—	(†)	—	(†)	—	(†)
Bahrain	83	(0.8)	63	(0.8)	64	(0.8)	66	(1.1)	68	(0.9)	64	(0.9)	119	(1.1)	—	(†)	—	(†)	—	(†)	—	(†)
Belgium (Flemish)	—	(†)	—	(†)	—	(†)	—	(†)	—	(†)	—	(†)	—	(†)	52[1]	(3.2)	—	(†)	55[1]	(3.3)	58[1]	(2.7)
Botswana	61	(0.9)	45	(0.8)	48	(1.0)	50	(1.1)	61	(0.9)	71	(0.8)	‡	(†)	—	(†)	—	(†)	—	(†)	—	(†)
Bulgaria	—	(†)	—	(†)	—	(†)	—	(†)	—	(†)	—	(†)	—	(†)	53[2]	(2.2)	63[2]	(2.9)	65[1]	(3.2)	64[2]	(3.3)
Chile	57	(1.3)	56	(1.4)	54	(1.5)	61	(1.4)	69	(1.0)	62	(0.7)	118[2]	(2.2)	—	(†)	—	(†)	—	(†)	—	(†)
Chinese Taipei	48[3]	(1.1)	24[3]	(0.9)	36[3]	(1.3)	37[3]	(1.5)	37[3]	(1.1)	40[3]	(1.0)	—	(†)	—	(†)	—[4]	(†)	—	(†)	134[4]	(2.0)
Cyprus	—	(†)	—	(†)	—	(†)	—	(†)	—	(†)	—	(†)	—	(†)	53[1]	(0.7)	34[1]	(1.6)	—	(†)	52[1]	(0.8)
Egypt	80	(0.7)	61	(1.0)	62	(1.0)	60	(0.8)	71	(0.7)	73	(0.7)	‡	(†)	—	(†)	—	(†)	—	(†)	—	(†)
England	‡	(†)	‡	(†)	‡	(†)	‡	(†)	‡	(†)	‡	(†)	‡	(†)	—	(†)	—	(†)	—	(†)	—	(†)
Estonia	—	(†)	—	(†)	—	(†)	—	(†)	—	(†)	—	(†)	‡	(†)	55	(2.9)	65	(3.9)	80	(4.8)	59	(1.8)
Ghana	73	(1.2)	54	(1.3)	55	(1.3)	54	(1.5)	64	(1.5)	75	(1.0)	‡	(†)	—	(†)	—	(†)	—	(†)	—	(†)
Hong Kong, SAR[5]	66	(1.2)	35	(1.0)	71	(1.5)	75	(1.2)	67	(1.2)	61	(0.8)	103[1]	(4.0)	—	(†)	—	(†)	—	(†)	—	(†)
Hungary	—	(†)	—	(†)	—	(†)	—	(†)	—	(†)	—	(†)	—	(†)	58[1]	(2.5)	59[1]	(2.1)	61[1]	(2.8)	57[1]	(2.5)
Indonesia	—	(†)	—	(†)	—	(†)	—	(†)	—	(†)	—	(†)	—	(†)	—	(†)	—	(†)	93[1]	(3.6)	93[1]	(3.3)
Iran, Islamic Republic of	87	(1.0)	66	(1.4)	77	(1.2)	73	(1.5)	78	(1.0)	70	(1.0)	106[1]	(3.7)	—	(†)	—	(†)	—	(†)	—	(†)
Israel	73	(1.6)	56	(1.4)	63	(1.6)	52	(1.8)	76	(1.3)	56	(1.0)	‡	(†)	—	(†)	—	(†)	—	(†)	—	(†)
Italy	26	(1.3)	16	(0.9)	13	(0.8)	12	(0.8)	32	(1.4)	35	(1.1)	69[1]	(1.1)	—	(†)	—	(†)	—	(†)	—	(†)
Japan	66	(1.5)	51	(1.7)	75	(1.7)	79	(1.6)	69	(1.5)	27	(1.1)	99[2]	(1.5)	—	(†)	—	(†)	—	(†)	—	(†)
Jordan	67	(1.5)	56	(1.4)	55	(1.7)	53	(1.6)	66	(1.3)	70	(1.1)	135	(0.8)	—	(†)	—	(†)	—	(†)	—	(†)
Korea, Republic of	31	(1.0)	14	(0.8)	20	(1.1)	39	(1.3)	44	(1.3)	36	(0.9)	103[1]	(2.7)	—	(†)	—	(†)	—	(†)	—	(†)
Latvia	—	(†)	—	(†)	—	(†)	—	(†)	—	(†)	—	(†)	—	(†)	—	(†)	‡	(†)	64[1]	(4.2)	56[1]	(4.1)
Lebanon	—	(†)	—	(†)	—	(†)	—	(†)	—	(†)	—	(†)	‡	(†)	—	(†)	—	(†)	—	(†)	—	(†)
Lithuania	—	(†)	—	(†)	—	(†)	—	(†)	—	(†)	—	(†)	—	(†)	59[2]	(0.4)	65[2]	(1.2)	46[2]	(3.5)	60[2]	(0.8)
Macedonia	—	(†)	—	(†)	—	(†)	—	(†)	—	(†)	—	(†)	—	(†)	53[2]	(1.4)	64[2]	(2.5)	59[2]	(2.0)	79[2]	(1.5)
Malaysia	83	(1.1)	46	(1.3)	71	(1.7)	77	(1.3)	73	(1.0)	72	(1.0)	119	(1.8)	—	(†)	—	(†)	—	(†)	—	(†)
Moldova, Republic of	—	(†)	—	(†)	—	(†)	—	(†)	—	(†)	—	(†)	‡	(†)	—	(†)	—	(†)	—	(†)	—	(†)
Morocco	82	(1.2)	62	(1.3)	61[2]	(1.2)	50	(1.3)	74	(1.0)	65[2]	(1.2)	—	(†)	—[6]	(†)	—[4]	(†)	‡[6]	(†)	‡[4]	(†)
Netherlands	—	(†)	—	(†)	—	(†)	—	(†)	—	(†)	—	(†)	—	(†)	54[1]	(1.7)	—[4]	(†)	58[1]	(1.8)	68[2,4]	(2.4)
New Zealand	60	(2.0)	50	(2.1)	56	(2.5)	66	(2.3)	73	(1.8)	45	(1.3)	132	(2.4)	—	(†)	—	(†)	—	(†)	—	(†)
Norway	40	(1.5)	34	(1.6)	49	(2.2)	49	(2.2)	56	(1.9)	31	(0.9)	92	(2.5)	—	(†)	—	(†)	—	(†)	—	(†)
Palestinian National Authority	70	(1.2)	56	(1.2)	57	(1.0)	54	(1.5)	66	(1.2)	69	(0.9)	101[1]	(1.8)	—	(†)	—	(†)	—	(†)	—	(†)
Philippines[7]	74	(0.9)	58	(1.2)	57	(1.0)	62	(1.1)	72	(1.0)	76	(0.8)	202	(4.2)	—	(†)	—	(†)	—	(†)	—	(†)
Romania	—	(†)	—	(†)	—	(†)	—	(†)	—	(†)	—	(†)	—	(†)	60[2]	(1.1)	67[2]	(2.4)	38[2]	(2.6)	67[2]	(2.4)
Russian Federation	—	(†)	—	(†)	—	(†)	—	(†)	—	(†)	—	(†)	—	(†)	49[2]	(0.7)	59[2]	(1.2)	49[2]	(0.8)	49[2]	(0.9)

See notes at end of table.

Table 414. Instructional practices and time spent teaching science in eighth grade, by country: 2003—Continued

Country or other jurisdiction	Percent of students who reported doing activity about half the lessons or more						Students' average yearly instructional time in hours				
	Watch the teacher demonstrate an experiment or investigation	Design or plan an experiment or investigation	Conduct an experiment or investigation	Work in small groups on an experiment or investigation	Write explanations about what was observed and why it happened	Relate what is being learned in science to our daily lives	General integrated science	Earth science	Chemistry	Biology	Physics
1	2	3	4	5	6	7	8	9	10	11	12
Saudi Arabia.........	68 (1.3)	50 (1.3)	51 (1.4)	43 (1.4)	60 (1.3)	67 (1.0)	106[1] (1.6)	— (†)	— (†)	— (†)	— (†)
Scotland..............	69 (1.4)	54 (1.3)	74 (1.4)	81 (1.2)	83 (1.1)	47 (1.0)	‡ (†)	— (†)	— (†)	— (†)	— (†)
Serbia.................	— (†)	— (†)	— (†)	— (†)	— (†)	— (†)	— (†)	53[2] (2.2)	61[1] (3.7)	53[1] (1.0)	56[1] (2.5)
Singapore............	49 (0.9)	31 (0.6)	55 (1.0)	57 (0.8)	68 (0.8)	58 (0.7)	107 (1.9)	— (†)	— (†)	— (†)	— (†)
Slovak Republic....	— (†)	— (†)	— (†)	— (†)	— (†)	— (†)	— (†)	66[2] (3.9)	76[2] (3.8)	72[2] (5.2)	70[2] (4.5)
Slovenia..............	— (†)	— (†)	— (†)	— (†)	— (†)	— (†)	— (†)	— (†)	59 (1.1)	56 (0.7)	57[2] (0.5)
South Africa.........	72 (1.1)	64 (1.2)	63 (1.1)	70 (1.1)	73 (0.7)	77 (0.7)	‡ (†)	— (†)	— (†)	— (†)	— (†)
Sweden...............	— (†)	— (†)	— (†)	— (†)	— (†)	— (†)	131[2] (7.6)	— (†)	— (†)	— (†)	— (†)
Tunisia................	79 (0.7)	65 (1.0)	69 (1.0)	55 (1.2)	73 (0.8)	54 (0.9)	‡ (†)	— (†)	— (†)	— (†)	— (†)
United States.......	57 (1.3)	48 (1.2)	55 (1.4)	65 (1.5)	65 (1.4)	51 (0.9)	135[1] (2.2)	— (†)	— (†)	— (†)	— (†)

—Not available.
†Not applicable.
‡Reporting standards not met.
[1]Data are available for at least 50 but less than 70 percent of the students.
[2]Data are available for at least 70 but less than 85 percent of the students.
[3]Students in Chinese Taipei were asked about natural science; data pertain to grade 8 physics/chemistry course.
[4]Data reported in physics column are for grade 8 physics/chemistry.
[5]SAR = Special Administrative Region.
[6]Data reported in biology column are for grade 8 biology/earth science.
[7]Students study only biology at grade 8.
NOTE: Data are for eighth grade or equivalent in most countries. Standard errors appear in parentheses. Detail may not sum to totals because of rounding.
SOURCE: International Association for the Evaluation of Educational Achievement (IEA), Trends in International Mathematics and Science Study (TIMSS) 2003, TIMSS 2003 International Science Report, by Michael O. Martin et al. (This table was prepared April 2005.)

Table 415. Number of bachelor's degree recipients per 100 persons of the typical age of graduation, by sex and country: 2002 through 2005

Country	Typical age of graduation	Male and female				Male				Female			
		2002	2003	2004	2005	2002	2003	2004	2005	2002	2003	2004	2005
1	2	3	4	5	6	7	8	9	10	11	12	13	14
OECD countries													
Australia	20–22	50.7	54.8	46.9	59.9	43.0	46.7	37.4	47.9	58.8	63.4	57.0	72.5
Austria	22–23	18.0	19.0	19.6	20.4	17.9	18.7	19.0	19.0	18.1	19.4	20.3	21.8
Belgium (Flemish)	22–24	19.2	—	18.3	18.4	18.7	—	17.5	17.0	19.7	—	19.0	19.8
Canada	22–23	—	—	31.5	33.6	—	—	24.3	25.2	—	—	39.1	42.2
Czech Republic	22–25	15.4	17.3	21.0	26.0	14.3	15.9	18.8	22.6	16.6	18.8	23.4	29.5
Denmark	22–26	34.4	38.6	49.9	52.9	23.4	25.1	35.6	37.2	45.7	52.3	64.4	69.2
Finland	22–28	51.8	55.8	54.7	53.8	37.7	40.4	39.5	38.8	66.4	72.2	70.5	69.7
France	(1)	39.0	41.5	40.0	—	32.9	34.9	33.4	—	45.3	48.4	46.9	—
Germany	25–26	19.2	19.5	20.6	20.5	19.3	19.3	20.3	20.0	19.1	19.7	20.9	21.1
Greece	21–24	—	—	19.1	23.9	—	—	13.3	16.3	—	—	25.4	32.2
Hungary	(1)	31.1	33.6	37.3	41.5	23.2	24.6	26.6	29.0	39.3	43.2	48.4	54.5
Iceland	23–25	40.0	44.2	50.5	56.3	27.2	29.4	31.4	33.6	53.1	59.1	70.3	80.5
Ireland	21–24	30.9	36.8	38.6	40.7	25.6	29.7	31.9	33.3	36.2	44.0	45.3	48.0
Italy	22–25	22.4	27.8	40.1	44.8	19.2	24.0	33.3	37.3	25.6	31.6	47.2	52.7
Japan	22–24	34.1	34.4	36.3	36.9	40.2	40.1	41.4	41.3	27.6	28.5	31.0	32.2
Korea, Republic of	(1)	31.5	31.7	32.3	35.5	31.6	32.1	31.5	34.8	31.3	31.2	33.2	36.2
Mexico	(1)	16.5	14.3	13.8	15.2	15.6	13.3	13.1	14.5	17.4	15.3	14.4	15.9
Netherlands	22–24	38.6	42.5	42.9	47.2	34.4	36.4	37.2	40.2	42.9	48.7	48.6	54.3
New Zealand	21–24	41.6	39.0	47.6	49.0	31.8	29.1	34.9	36.6	51.3	49.1	61.0	62.0
Norway	22–24	41.1	42.0	43.3	42.1	29.7	30.0	31.5	28.8	52.8	54.2	55.3	55.8
Poland	24–25	—	—	44.4	45.0	—	—	32.6	32.8	—	—	56.6	57.6
Portugal	22–23	—	—	32.9	33.7	—	—	20.4	21.7	—	—	45.6	46.0
Slovak Republic	21–24	—	—	28.3	30.1	—	—	24.4	25.6	—	—	32.4	34.8
Spain	20–22	33.1	32.0	35.2	35.0	26.4	25.5	27.5	27.1	40.0	38.9	43.2	43.3
Sweden	23–26	35.2	38.4	39.9	44.0	26.5	28.6	29.7	30.8	44.1	48.5	50.5	57.6
Switzerland	23–26	20.8	20.9	22.4	25.0	23.3	23.5	24.0	26.1	18.3	18.4	20.9	23.9
Turkey	22–28	—	—	14.0	11.3	—	—	15.2	11.8	—	—	12.7	10.7
United Kingdom	21–23	—	—	39.2	39.8	—	—	34.2	34.1	—	—	44.3	45.7
United States	22–24	36.1	33.4	33.2	34.2	29.7	27.6	27.5	28.1	42.9	39.4	39.2	40.7
Reporting partner economies													
Brazil	(1)	—	—	15.6	17.5	—	—	11.8	13.3	—	—	19.4	21.6
Chile	(1)	—	—	25.1	11.5	—	—	22.9	9.7	—	—	27.5	13.4
Estonia	(1)	—	—	—	28.5	—	—	—	17.6	—	—	—	39.5
Israel	22–26	—	—	32.3	32.9	—	—	25.3	25.7	—	—	39.6	40.2
Russian Federation	(1)	—	—	—	45.9	—	—	—	—	—	—	—	—
Slovenia	(1)	—	—	—	21.6	—	—	—	14.3	—	—	—	29.4

—Not available.

[1]Typical age of graduation data not available. Estimates calculated using the age range 22–23.

NOTE: Data in this table refer to degrees classified by the Organization for Economic Cooperation and Development (OECD) as International Standard Classification of Education (ISCED) level 5A, first award. This level corresponds to the bachelor's degree in the United States. The recipients per 100 persons ratio relates the number of people of all ages earning bachelor's degrees in a particular year to the number of people in the population at the typical age of graduation. The typical age is based on full-time attendance and normal progression through the education system (without repeating a year, taking a year off, etc.); this age varies across countries because of differences in their education systems and differences in program duration. Data for Luxembourg are not shown because tertiary students study for only 1 year in Luxembourg. Some data have been revised from previously published figures.

SOURCE: Organization for Economic Cooperation and Development (OECD), *Education at a Glance*, 2004 through 2007; and Education Online Database, retrieved July 1, 2008, from http://stats.oecd.org/WBOS/Default.aspx. (This table was prepared July 2008.)

Table 416. Percentage of bachelor's degrees awarded in mathematics and science, by field and country: Selected years, 1985 through 2005

Country	All mathematics and science degrees[1]						Natural sciences[2]						Mathematics and computer science[3]						Engineering					
	1985	1990	1995	2000	2004	2005	1985	1990	1995	2000	2004	2005	1985	1990	1995	2000	2004	2005	1985	1990	1995	2000	2004	2005
1	2	3	4	5	6	7	8	9	10	11	12	13	14	15	16	17	18	19	20	21	22	23	24	25
OECD countries																								
Australia	—	—	19.3	21.1	24.6	21.1	—	—	9.9	7.6	7.2	5.9	—	—	3.8	5.1	9.7	8.2	—	—	5.6	8.5	7.7	7.0
Austria	16.8	19.6	21.1	25.7	26.0	26.8	5.0	5.3	6.0	5.0	4.8	5.4	4.1	5.2	5.3	3.4	5.6	7.2	7.7	9.0	9.9	17.3	15.6	14.2
Belgium (Flemish)	—	—	—	23.6	25.1	24.7	4.6	—	—	6.4	6.9	5.7	1.7	—	—	2.3	3.1	5.2	—	—	—	14.9	15.1	13.8
Canada	17.1	16.4	16.7	20.0	20.3	20.7	4.9	6.0	6.5	8.1	7.2	6.5	4.5	4.2	3.8	4.3	5.3	5.9	7.7	6.2	6.4	7.6	7.8	8.2
Czech Republic	†	†	—	29.5	29.5	26.7	†	†	—	4.2	4.8	3.9	†	†	—	8.4	4.0	3.8	†	†	—	16.9	20.7	19.0
Denmark	—	—	—	10.5	16.4	16.3	6.3	4.4	2.5	6.8	2.7	2.4	—	—	—	3.1	3.4	3.1	16.2	21.7	17.0	0.6	10.3	10.8
Finland	39.3	33.5	37.2	32.2	30.0	30.0	7.7	4.1	4.0	3.9	3.3	2.7	6.3	5.9	6.9	3.3	5.4	5.6	25.3	23.4	26.3	24.9	21.3	21.7
France	23.8	31.3	31.6	30.1	27.1	26.0	5.0	7.2	6.7	12.2	9.0	6.5	2.3	3.5	5.2	5.5	4.7	6.5	16.5	20.5	19.7	12.5	13.4	14.0
Germany[5]	—	—	—	31.7	30.3	31.3	—	—	—	6.4	6.0	6.3	—	—	—	4.9	7.0	8.1	—	—	—	20.3	17.3	16.9
Greece	—	—	—	—	22.9	25.9	—	—	—	—	11.2	8.3	—	—	—	—	8.2	8.4	—	—	—	—	3.6	9.2
Hungary	—	—	—	12.6	11.9	11.0	—	—	—	1.1	1.4	1.2	—	—	—	1.2	2.4	2.4	—	—	—	10.4	8.1	7.4
Iceland	—	—	—	16.5	17.1	14.1	—	—	—	6.0	4.5	5.0	—	—	—	4.0	6.8	3.5	—	—	—	6.5	5.8	5.5
Ireland	28.8	34.1	32.3	29.3	26.0	17.7	12.8	14.1	16.9	11.5	7.6	3.5	4.0	6.3	4.7	7.2	8.6	4.4	12.0	13.7	10.7	10.6	9.8	9.9
Italy	19.5	19.7	19.5	27.5	24.9	23.9	8.1	7.6	6.8	5.9	5.1	4.8	3.1	3.9	3.8	3.2	2.5	2.2	8.3	8.3	8.9	18.4	17.3	16.9
Japan	—	—	—	23.0	24.4	22.9	2.4	2.1	3.1	0.7	0.8	0.8	1.8	0.6	0.5	3.4	6.1	4.7	19.3	21.0	19.3	18.9	17.5	17.4
Korea, Republic of	—	—	—	36.9	37.6	37.0	—	—	—	6.3	5.9	5.2	—	—	—	4.3	5.3	5.4	—	—	—	26.3	26.4	26.3
Mexico	—	—	15.0	23.0	26.9	27.3	—	—	2.2	2.2	2.6	2.6	—	—	2.8	6.7	8.9	9.3	—	—	9.9	14.1	15.5	15.3
Netherlands	21.8	21.1	—	16.2	15.1	14.9	8.5	7.1	—	3.2	2.5	2.0	1.2	1.6	1.6	1.9	4.5	4.6	12.1	12.4	—	11.1	8.2	7.7
New Zealand	20.5	19.5	16.8	17.8	19.6	19.9	11.7	8.2	—	11.2	6.5	6.7	5.5	5.5	—	1.9	7.8	7.6	3.3	5.8	3.2	4.7	5.3	5.6
Norway	—	12.9	16.8	11.6	16.2	13.7	2.5	2.4	3.1	0.7	0.8	0.8	1.8	0.6	0.5	3.4	6.1	4.7	—	9.9	13.2	7.5	9.3	8.2
Poland	—	—	—	16.7	17.4	17.7	—	—	—	2.7	2.3	2.3	—	—	—	2.0	4.6	5.3	—	—	—	12.0	10.5	10.1
Portugal	—	—	15.0	17.5	—	25.6	6.5	6.7	2.2	1.7	—	6.0	—	—	2.8	3.6	—	6.2	—	10.5	9.9	12.2	—	13.4
Slovak Republic	†	†	—	21.9	23.8	24.6	†	†	—	2.0	3.6	3.7	†	†	—	4.6	4.9	4.4	†	†	—	15.3	15.4	16.5
Spain	13.9	15.0	18.2	22.7	24.5	24.1	5.5	5.7	4.3	5.3	6.5	6.9	1.3	2.6	4.5	4.6	4.9	4.4	7.0	6.7	9.4	13.1	15.2	14.7
Sweden	15.4	24.0	26.4	27.7	31.5	26.9	2.6	4.1	3.9	3.7	4.1	3.6	1.6	4.7	5.5	3.7	4.2	4.0	11.3	15.2	17.0	20.3	23.2	19.2
Switzerland	20.2	23.0	22.3	25.1	24.5	24.2	10.3	11.2	10.4	6.0	6.7	6.9	2.1	3.7	3.7	1.8	5.0	4.7	7.9	8.1	8.3	17.3	12.8	12.7
Turkey	23.0	20.6	20.9	24.1	16.9	22.3	3.6	4.6	5.1	7.4	4.9	6.1	1.6	2.1	2.7	3.6	3.0	4.1	17.8	13.8	13.1	13.1	9.0	12.0
United Kingdom	—	—	—	28.5	27.2	26.0	—	—	—	12.5	9.4	9.2	—	—	—	5.8	8.8	8.3	—	—	—	10.2	9.0	8.4
United States	21.7	16.9	—	17.1	15.8	16.7	6.3	5.1	—	6.6	4.4	4.1	5.5	4.0	3.3	3.9	5.2	5.8	9.8	7.8	6.7	6.6	6.2	6.2
Reporting partner economies																								
Brazil	—	—	—	—	13.4	11.4	—	—	—	—	3.2	3.2	—	—	—	—	4.4	3.5	—	—	—	—	5.8	4.8
Chile	—	—	—	—	22.1	22.9	—	—	—	—	2.9	3.2	—	—	—	—	4.1	2.6	—	—	—	—	15.0	17.2
Estonia	†	†	—	—	—	23.8	†	†	—	—	—	6.3	†	†	—	—	—	6.2	†	†	—	—	—	11.3
Israel	—	—	—	19.0	26.2	26.7	—	—	—	3.1	4.8	5.1	—	—	—	6.8	8.7	7.5	—	—	—	9.1	12.6	14.1
Russian Federation	†	†	—	—	—	—	†	†	—	—	—	—	†	†	—	—	—	—	†	†	—	—	—	—
Slovenia	†	†	—	—	—	17.7	†	†	—	—	—	4.1	†	†	—	—	—	2.0	†	†	—	—	—	11.7

—Not available.

[1]Includes life sciences, physical sciences, mathematics/statistics, computer science, and engineering.
[2]Includes life sciences and physical sciences.
[3]Includes mathematics/statistics and computer science.
[4]Country did not exist in its current form in the given year.
[5]Data for 1985 are for the former West Germany.

NOTE: Data in this table refer to degrees classified by the Organization for Economic Cooperation and Development (OECD) as International Standard Classification of Education (ISCED) level 5A, first award. This level corresponds to the bachelor's degree in the United States. Data for Luxembourg are not shown because tertiary students study for only 1 year in Luxembourg. Some data have been revised from previously published figures.
SOURCE: Organization for Economic Cooperation and Development (OECD), Education Online Database. Retrieved July 9, 2008, from http://stats.oecd.org/WBOS/Default.aspx. (This table was prepared July 2008.)

Table 417. Percentage of graduate degrees awarded in mathematics and science, by field and country: Selected years, 1985 through 2005

Country	All mathematics and science degrees[1]						Natural sciences[2]						Mathematics and computer science[3]						Engineering					
	1985	1990	1996	2000	2004	2005	1985	1990	1996	2000	2004	2005	1985	1990	1996	2000	2004	2005	1985	1990	1996	2000	2004	2005
1	2	3	4	5	6	7	8	9	10	11	12	13	14	15	16	17	18	19	20	21	22	23	24	25
OECD countries																								
Australia	—	—	14.0	15.2	17.9	20.0	—	—	5.4	4.0	2.4	3.1	—	—	3.8	4.9	9.3	8.7	—	—	4.7	6.3	6.1	8.1
Austria	43.3	37.7	38.8	39.2	34.0	38.6	14.2	12.3	17.5	16.7	12.4	15.0	7.3	4.6	4.7	4.7	5.4	6.6	21.7	20.8	16.6	17.7	15.2	16.9
Belgium (Flemish)	—	—	—	19.7	19.1	18.7	—	—	—	12.7	9.6	9.3	—	—	—	4.1	4.8	3.3	—	—	—	7.0	4.6	6.2
Canada	19.7	20.0	22.3	22.4	16.6	18.8	7.5	7.8	7.7	7.4	5.5	5.0	2.8	3.4	3.5	4.1	3.1	4.0	9.4	8.8	11.2	10.9	8.0	9.8
Czech Republic	[4]	[4]	—	21.0	11.8	26.1	[4]	[4]	—	5.3	3.2	8.3	[4]	[4]	—	7.9	2.6	5.6	[4]	[4]	—	7.7	6.0	12.3
Denmark	16.0	22.2	12.3	27.8	24.2	23.4	4.1	5.8	3.1	9.8	7.3	7.5	2.7	4.8	1.5	2.5	9.2	9.2	9.2	11.6	7.8	15.4	7.7	6.7
Finland	47.6	30.6	28.3	28.7	29.6	30.5	24.0	14.7	11.6	11.3	12.1	11.6	6.3	5.4	4.0	2.4	3.0	4.1	17.2	10.5	12.7	14.9	14.5	14.8
France	—	—	—	26.4	34.4	28.4	—	—	—	13.5	17.1	12.5	—	—	—	5.6	8.5	7.0	—	—	—	7.3	8.8	8.9
Germany[5]	27.7	33.2	38.6	38.1	35.1	30.9	18.7	23.5	25.5	24.9	22.1	14.8	1.8	2.3	3.5	3.7	4.0	4.8	7.2	7.4	9.5	9.5	9.1	11.3
Greece	—	—	—	—	49.3	42.8	—	—	—	—	24.8	22.3	—	—	—	—	11.4	5.3	—	—	—	—	13.1	15.2
Hungary	—	—	—	9.9	5.6	6.4	—	—	—	1.7	1.8	1.8	—	—	—	0.7	1.4	1.7	—	—	—	7.5	2.3	2.9
Iceland	—	—	—	35.9	15.9	23.0	—	—	—	19.4	8.8	9.5	—	—	—	#	3.4	3.0	—	—	—	16.5	3.7	10.5
Ireland	31.4	34.5	23.1	28.1	17.5	16.8	18.9	19.5	10.9	6.9	4.8	4.1	2.6	5.8	3.0	15.2	6.5	6.3	9.9	9.3	9.2	6.0	6.2	6.4
Italy	—	—	—	11.7	13.7	15.9	9.5	9.5	10.2	0.3	3.4	3.5	—	—	—	5.8	3.5	3.5	—	—	—	5.7	6.8	8.9
Japan	50.1	54.6	—	—	—	—	—	—	—	—	—	—	—	—	—	—	—	—	40.5	45.1	44.4	41.9	38.0	38.0
Korea, Republic of	—	—	—	48.4	45.4	43.9	—	—	—	8.5	9.7	9.5	—	—	—	5.7	3.3	2.0	—	—	—	34.3	32.4	32.4
Mexico	—	—	—	31.4	16.1	14.7	—	17.7	4.4	18.9	3.4	3.3	—	—	—	4.1	3.6	3.2	—	—	—	8.4	9.2	8.2
Netherlands	45.1	28.9	18.6	20.5	22.5	18.2	20.6	13.8	12.7	11.6	6.7	4.1	5.4	1.5	3.7	1.4	1.3	2.3	7.5	9.7	10.6	1.2	14.4	11.9
New Zealand	40.1	22.6	16.7	22.0	17.2	16.6	24.6	8.0	8.7	14.9	7.4	7.2	3.5	4.7	1.1	4.6	5.6	5.2	15.1	4.0	3.0	7.5	4.1	4.2
Norway	—	33.4	38.3	—	16.5	25.8	17.9	—	—	14.9	7.6	7.8	—	2.1	1.9	—	5.8	11.9	18.7	23.3	27.7	2.5	3.0	6.1
Poland	—	—	—	3.3	4.9	8.7	—	—	—	0.7	1.0	1.5	—	—	—	0.7	1.4	3.7	—	—	—	1.9	2.4	3.5
Portugal	[4]	—	—	39.3	40.7	33.8	[4]	[4]	—	11.7	15.2	12.0	[4]	[4]	—	9.4	10.9	10.0	[4]	[4]	—	18.2	14.6	11.9
Slovak Republic	[4]	[4]	—	38.1	34.5	36.8	[4]	[4]	—	12.6	12.1	10.8	[4]	1.8	—	4.7	4.4	4.2	[4]	5.7	7.1	20.9	18.0	21.8
Spain	35.6	26.9	36.0	36.1	34.9	37.5	28.6	19.7	24.8	23.9	22.7	23.8	1.8	1.4	4.1	5.4	4.8	4.6	5.1	5.7	7.1	6.8	7.4	9.1
Sweden	48.0	48.5	32.3	40.5	32.5	23.7	21.2	19.4	9.2	14.3	10.6	8.0	6.8	9.2	5.9	4.0	4.2	2.8	20.0	19.9	17.1	22.2	17.7	12.9
Switzerland	30.7	30.2	40.1	42.7	26.6	32.0	20.3	22.0	25.8	11.7	10.6	11.7	2.8	1.7	4.1	19.5	2.4	3.4	7.6	6.5	10.1	11.6	13.6	16.9
Turkey	35.8	24.0	—	25.7	19.9	21.4	6.6	7.6	—	7.6	6.1	6.7	2.8	3.3	—	3.0	2.8	3.4	26.3	13.2	—	15.2	10.9	11.2
United Kingdom	—	[4]	—	21.7	19.8	20.3	—	[4]	—	7.4	5.7	5.5	—	[4]	—	5.0	5.9	5.7	—	[4]	—	9.2	8.2	9.0
United States	13.5	14.5	13.8	13.0	12.5	13.5	4.5	4.2	4.0	3.4	1.9	3.3	2.8	3.4	3.2	3.4	3.8	3.5	6.3	6.9	6.7	6.2	6.8	6.7
Reporting partner economies																								
Brazil	—	—	—	—	—	—	—	—	—	—	—	—	—	—	—	—	—	—	—	—	—	—	—	—
Chile	[4]	[4]	—	—	—	8.5	[4]	[4]	—	—	—	2.2	[4]	[4]	—	—	—	1.6	[4]	[4]	—	—	—	4.6
Estonia	[4]	[4]	—	—	—	23.9	[4]	[4]	—	—	—	10.0	[4]	[4]	—	—	—	5.0	[4]	[4]	—	—	—	8.9
Israel	—	—	—	18.1	17.7	17.9	—	—	—	9.2	8.9	8.9	—	—	—	2.8	3.3	3.2	—	—	—	6.1	5.5	5.9
Russian Federation	[4]	[4]	—	—	—	—	[4]	[4]	—	—	—	—	[4]	[4]	—	—	—	—	[4]	[4]	—	—	—	—
Slovenia	[4]	[4]	—	—	—	24.2	[4]	[4]	—	—	—	6.4	[4]	[4]	—	—	—	4.2	[4]	[4]	—	—	—	13.6

—Not available.
#Rounds to zero.
[1]Includes life sciences, physical sciences, mathematics/statistics, computer science, and engineering.
[2]Includes life sciences and physical sciences.
[3]Includes mathematics/statistics and computer science.
[4]Country did not exist in its current form in the given year.
[5]Data for 1985 are for the former West Germany.

NOTE: Data in this table refer to degrees classified by the Organization for Economic Cooperation and Development (OECD) as International Standard Classification of Education (ISCED) level 5A, second award, and as ISCED 6. ISCED 5A, second award, corresponds to master's and first-professional degrees in the United States, and ISCED 6 corresponds to doctor's degrees. Data for Luxembourg are not shown because tertiary students study for only 1 year in Luxembourg. Some data have been revised from previously published figures.

SOURCE: Organization for Economic Cooperation and Development (OECD), Education Online Database. Retrieved July 14, 2008, from http://stats.oecd.org/WBOS/Default.aspx. (This table was prepared July 2008.)

Table 418. Public and private education expenditures per student, by level of education and country: Selected years, 2000 through 2005

Country	Elementary education				Secondary education				Higher education			
	2000	2003	2004	2005	2000	2003	2004	2005	2000	2003	2004	2005
1	2	3	4	5	6	7	8	9	10	11	12	13
	Current dollars											
Australia	$4,967	$5,494	$5,776	$5,992	$6,894	$7,788	$8,160	$8,408	$12,854	$12,406	$14,036	$14,579
Austria	6,560	7,139	7,669	8,259	8,578	8,943	9,446	9,751	10,851	12,344	13,959	14,775
Belgium	4,310	6,180	6,636	6,648	6,889 [1]	7,708 [1]	7,751 [1]	7,731 [1]	10,771	11,824	11,842	11,960
Canada	—	—	—	—	5,947 [2]	—	7,837 [2]	—	14,983	—	—	—
Czech Republic	1,827	2,273	2,791	2,812	3,239	4,088	4,779	4,847	5,431	6,774	6,752	6,649
Denmark	7,074	7,814	8,081	8,513	7,726	8,183	8,849	9,407 [1]	11,981	14,014	15,225	14,959
Finland	4,317	5,321	5,581	5,557	6,094 [1]	7,402 [1]	7,441 [1]	7,324 [1]	8,244	12,047	12,505	12,285
France	4,486	4,939	5,082	5,365	7,636	8,653	8,737	8,927	8,373	10,704	10,668	10,995
Germany	4,198	4,624	4,948	5,014	6,826	7,173	7,576	7,636	10,898	11,594	12,255	12,446
Greece	3,318 [3,4]	4,218 [4]	4,595 [4]	5,146 [4]	3,859 [3]	4,954	5,213	8,423	3,402 [3]	4,924	5,593	6,130
Hungary[3]	2,245	3,286	3,841	4,438	2,446	3,948	3,692	3,806	7,024	8,576	7,095	6,244
Iceland	5,854 [3]	7,752	8,434	9,254	6,518 [3]	6,898	7,721	8,411	7,994 [3]	8,023	8,881	9,474
Ireland	3,385	4,760	5,422	5,732	4,638	6,374	7,110	7,500	11,083	9,341	10,211	10,468
Italy[3]	5,973	7,366	7,390	6,835	7,218	7,938	7,843	7,648	8,065	8,764	7,723	8,026
Japan	5,507	6,350	6,551	6,744	6,266	7,283	7,615	7,908	10,914	11,556	12,193	12,326
Korea, Republic of	3,155	4,098	4,490	4,691	4,069	6,410	6,761	6,645	6,118	7,089	7,068	7,606
Luxembourg	—	11,481 [4]	13,458 [3,4]	14,079 [3,4]	—	17,078	17,876 [3]	18,845 [3]	—	—	—	—
Mexico	1,291	1,656	1,694	1,913	1,615	1,918	1,922	2,180	4,688	5,774	5,778	6,402
Netherlands	4,325	5,836	6,222	6,266	5,912	6,996	7,541	7,741	11,934	13,444	13,846	13,883
New Zealand	—	4,841	5,190	4,780	—	5,693	6,299	6,278	—	8,832	8,866	10,262
Norway	6,550	7,977	8,533	9,001	8,476 [1,3]	10,919 [1]	11,109 [1]	10,995 [1]	13,353 [3]	13,772	14,997	15,552
Poland	2,105 [3]	2,859 [3]	3,130 [3]	3,312 [3]	—	2,951 [3]	2,889 [3]	3,055	3,222 [3]	4,589 [3]	4,412 [3]	5,593 [3]
Portugal	3,672	4,503 [3]	4,681 [3]	4,871 [3]	5,349	6,094 [3]	6,168 [3]	6,473 [3]	4,766	7,200 [3]	7,741 [3]	8,787 [3]
Slovak Republic	1,308	2,020	2,073	2,806	1,927	2,401	2,744	2,716	4,949	4,678	6,535	5,783
Spain	3,941	4,829	4,965	5,502	5,185 [1]	6,418 [1]	6,701	7,211	6,666	8,943	9,378	10,089
Sweden	6,336	7,291	7,469	7,532	6,339	7,662	8,039	8,198	15,097	16,073	16,218	15,946
Switzerland[3]	6,631	8,131	8,570	8,469	9,780	12,209	12,176	12,861	18,450	25,900	21,966	21,734
Turkey[3]	—	869	1,120	—	—	1,428	1,808	—	4,121	—	—	—
United Kingdom	3,877	5,851	5,941	6,361	5,991 [1]	7,290 [1]	7,090 [1]	7,167 [1]	9,657	11,866	11,484	13,506
United States	6,995	8,305	8,805	9,156	8,855	9,590	9,938	10,390	20,358	24,074	22,476	24,370
	Constant 2007 dollars											
Australia	$5,981	$6,192	$6,340	$6,362	$8,301	$8,778	$8,957	$8,927	$15,477	$13,983	$15,408	$15,479
Austria	7,899	8,046	8,418	8,768	10,329	10,080	10,369	10,353	13,065	13,913	15,323	15,687
Belgium	5,190	6,966	7,285	7,058	8,295 [1]	8,688 [1]	8,508 [1]	8,208 [1]	12,969	13,327	12,999	12,698
Canada	—	—	—	—	7,161 [2]	—	8,603 [2]	—	18,041	—	—	—
Czech Republic	2,200	2,562	3,064	2,985	3,900	4,608	5,246	5,146	6,539	7,635	7,412	7,059
Denmark	8,518	8,807	8,871	9,039	9,303	9,223	9,714	9,988 [1]	14,426	15,795	16,713	15,882
Finland	5,198	5,997	6,126	5,900	7,338 [1]	8,343 [1]	8,168 [1]	7,775 [1]	9,926	13,578	13,727	13,043
France	5,401	5,567	5,579	5,696	9,194	9,753	9,591	9,477	10,082	12,065	11,711	11,674
Germany	5,055	5,212	5,432	5,323	8,219	8,085	8,316	8,107	13,122	13,068	13,453	13,214
Greece	3,995 [3,4]	4,754 [4]	5,044 [4]	5,463 [4]	4,647 [3]	5,584	5,722	8,942	4,096 [3]	5,550	6,140	6,509
Hungary[3]	2,703	3,704	4,216	4,712	2,945	4,450	4,053	4,041	8,457	9,666	7,788	6,630
Iceland	7,049 [3]	8,737	9,258	9,825	7,848 [3]	7,775	8,476	8,930	9,625 [3]	9,043	9,749	10,059
Ireland	4,076	5,365	5,952	6,086	5,585	7,184	7,805	7,963	13,345	10,528	11,209	11,114
Italy[3]	7,192	8,302	8,112	7,257	8,691	8,947	8,609	8,120	9,711	9,878	8,478	8,521
Japan	6,631	7,157	7,191	7,160	7,545	8,209	8,359	8,396	13,141	13,025	13,385	13,087
Korea, Republic of	3,799	4,619	4,929	4,980	4,899	7,225	7,422	7,055	7,367	7,990	7,759	8,075
Luxembourg	—	12,940 [4]	14,773 [3,4]	14,948 [3,4]	—	19,249	19,623 [3]	20,008 [3]	—	—	—	—
Mexico	1,554	1,867	1,860	2,031	1,945	2,162	2,110	2,314	5,645	6,508	6,343	6,797
Netherlands	5,208	6,578	6,830	6,653	7,119	7,885	8,278	8,218	14,369	15,153	15,199	14,740
New Zealand	—	5,456	5,697	5,075	—	6,417	6,915	6,666	—	9,955	9,732	10,895
Norway	7,887	8,991	9,367	9,556	10,206 [1,3]	12,307 [1]	12,195 [1]	11,673 [1]	16,078 [3]	15,523	16,463	16,512
Poland	2,535 [3]	3,222 [3]	3,436 [3]	3,516 [3]	—	3,326 [3]	3,171 [3]	3,244	3,880 [3]	5,172 [3]	4,843 [3]	5,938 [3]
Portugal	4,421	5,075 [3]	5,138 [3]	5,172 [3]	6,441	6,869 [3]	6,771 [3]	6,873 [3]	5,739	8,115 [3]	8,497 [3]	9,330 [3]
Slovak Republic	1,575	2,277	2,276	2,979	2,320	2,706	3,012	2,883	5,959	5,273	7,174	6,140
Spain	4,745	5,443	5,450	5,842	6,243 [1]	7,234 [1]	7,356	7,656	8,026	10,080	10,294	10,712
Sweden	7,629	8,218	8,199	7,997	7,633	8,636	8,825	8,704	18,178	18,116	17,803	16,930
Switzerland[3]	7,984	9,165	9,408	8,991	11,776	13,761	13,366	13,654	22,215	29,192	24,113	23,075
Turkey[3]	—	979	1,229	—	—	1,610	1,985	—	4,962	—	—	—
United Kingdom	4,668	6,595	6,522	6,753	7,214 [1]	8,217 [1]	7,783 [1]	7,609 [1]	11,628	13,374	12,606	14,340
United States	8,423	9,361	9,665	9,721	10,662	10,809	10,909	11,031	24,513	27,134	24,672	25,874

—Not available.
[1] Includes postsecondary non-higher-education.
[2] Includes elementary education.
[3] Public institutions only.
[4] Includes preprimary education.

NOTE: Data adjusted to U.S. dollars using the purchasing-power-parity (PPP) index. Constant dollars based on the Consumer Price Index, prepared by the Bureau of Labor Statistics, U.S. Department of Labor.
SOURCE: Organization for Economic Cooperation and Development (OECD), *Education at a Glance*, 2002 through 2008. (This table was prepared July 2008.)

Table 419. Total public direct expenditures on education as a percentage of the gross domestic product, by level and country: Selected years, 1985 through 2005

Country	All institutions							Primary and secondary institutions							Higher education institutions						
	1985	1990	1995	2000[1]	2003[1]	2004[1]	2005[1]	1985	1990	1995	2000[1]	2003[1]	2004[1]	2005[1]	1985	1990	1995	2000[1]	2003[1]	2004[1]	2005[1]
1	2	3	4	5	6	7	8	9	10	11	12	13	14	15	16	17	18	19	20	21	22
Average for OECD countries	**5.3**	**4.9**	**4.9**	**5.2**	**5.3**	**5.0**	**5.0**	**3.7**	**3.5**	**3.5**	**3.5**	**3.7**	**3.5**	**3.5**	**1.1**	**1.0**	**0.9**	**1.2**	**1.1**	**1.1**	**1.0**
Average for all countries listed	**5.3**	**4.9**	**4.9**	**5.1**	**5.3**	**5.0**	**4.9**	**3.7**	**3.5**	**3.5**	**3.5**	**3.7**	**3.5**	**3.5**	**1.1**	**1.0**	**0.9**	**1.2**	**1.1**	**1.0**	**1.0**
OECD countries																					
Australia	5.4	4.3	4.5	5.1	4.3	4.3	4.3	3.5	3.2	3.2	3.9	3.4	3.5	3.4	1.7	1.0	1.2	1.2	0.8	0.8	0.8
Austria	5.6	5.2	5.3	5.8	5.2	5.0	5.2	3.7	3.6	3.8	3.8[2]	3.7	3.6	3.5	1.0	1.0	0.9	1.4[2]	1.1	1.1	1.2
Belgium (Flemish)	6.3	4.8	5.0	5.2	5.9	5.8	5.8	4.0	3.4	3.4	3.4[3]	4.0	4.0	—	1.0	0.8	0.9	1.3[3]	1.2	1.2	1.2
Canada	6.1	5.4	5.8	5.5	—	4.7	4.7	4.1	3.7	4.0	3.3[4]	—	3.2[4]	—	2.0	1.5	1.5	2.0[4]	—	1.4[4]	—
Czech Republic	(5)	(5)	4.8	4.4	4.3	4.2	4.1	(5)	(5)	3.4	3.0[3]	2.9	2.8	2.7	(5)	(5)	0.7	0.8[3]	0.9	0.9	0.8
Denmark	6.2	6.2	6.5	8.4	6.7	6.9	6.8	4.7	4.4	4.2	4.8[2][6]	4.1[6]	4.2[6]	4.4[6]	1.2	1.3	1.3	2.5[2][6]	1.7[6]	1.8[6]	1.6[6]
Finland	5.8	6.4	6.6	6.0	6.0	6.0	5.9	—	4.3	4.2	3.6	3.9	3.9	3.8	—	1.2	1.7	2.0	1.7	1.7	1.7
France	—	5.1	5.8	5.8	5.8	5.7	5.6	—	3.7	4.1	4.1	4.0	3.9	3.8	—	0.8	1.0	1.0	1.1	1.2	1.1
Germany[7]	4.6	—	4.5	4.5	4.4	4.3	4.2	2.8	—	2.9	3.0	2.9	2.8	2.8	1.0	—	1.0	1.1	1.0	1.0	0.9
Greece	—	—	3.7	3.8	4.0	3.3	4.0	—	—	2.8	2.7[2]	2.6[8]	2.1[8]	2.5[8]	—	—	0.8	0.9[2]	1.2	1.1	1.4
Hungary	—	5.0	4.9	4.9	5.5	5.1	5.1	—	3.5	3.3	3.1	3.5	3.3	3.3	—	—	0.8	1.0	1.0	0.9	0.9
Iceland	—	4.3	4.5	6.0	7.5	7.2	7.2	—	3.3	3.4	4.7[2]	5.2[6]	5.2[6]	5.2[6]	—	0.6	0.7	1.1[2]	1.1[6]	1.1[6]	1.1[6]
Ireland	5.6	4.7	4.7	4.4	4.1	4.3	4.3	4.0	3.3	3.3	3.0[3]	3.5	3.3	3.3	0.9	0.9	0.9	1.3[3]	0.7	0.7	1.0
Italy	4.7	5.8	4.5	4.6	4.6	4.4	4.3	3.2	4.1	3.2	3.2	3.5	3.3	3.2	0.6	1.0	0.7	0.8	0.7	0.7	0.6
Japan	—	3.6	3.6	3.6	3.5	3.5	3.4	—	2.9	2.8	2.6[6]	2.7[6]	2.7[6]	2.6[6]	—	0.4	0.4	0.5[6]	0.5[6]	0.5[6]	0.5[6]
Korea, Republic of	—	—	3.6	4.3	4.6	4.4	4.3	—	—	3.0	3.3	3.5	3.5	3.4	—	—	0.3	0.7	0.6	0.5	0.6
Luxembourg	—	—	4.3	—	4.6	4.4	—	—	—	4.2	—	4.0[8]	3.8[8]	3.7[8]	—	—	0.1	—	0.6	—	0.6
Mexico	—	3.2	4.6	4.9	5.6	5.2	5.3	—	2.2	3.0	3.4	4.5	4.4	4.0	—	0.7	0.8	0.9	1.1	1.0	1.0
Netherlands	6.2	5.7	4.6	4.8	4.6	4.6	4.6	4.1	3.6	3.0	3.2	3.2	3.3	3.3	1.5	1.6	1.1	1.3	1.1	1.0	1.0
New Zealand	—	5.5	5.3	7.0	5.7	5.6	5.2	4.1	3.9	3.8	4.9	4.5	4.4	4.0	—	1.2	1.1	1.7	0.9	0.9	0.9
Norway	5.1	6.2	6.8	6.7	6.5	6.2	5.7	4.0	4.1	4.1	3.9	4.6	4.2	3.8	0.7	1.1	1.5	1.7	1.5	1.4	1.3
Poland	—	—	5.2	5.2	5.8	5.4	5.4	—	—	3.3	3.8[2]	4.2	3.7	3.7	—	—	0.8	0.8[2]	1.0	1.1	1.2
Portugal	—	—	5.4	5.7	5.8	5.3	5.3	—	—	4.1	4.2[2]	4.2	3.8	3.7	—	—	1.0	1.0[2]	1.0	0.9	1.3
Slovak Republic	(5)	(5)	4.6	4.2	4.3	4.0	3.7	(5)	(5)	—	2.7[2][3]	2.8[9]	2.6[9]	2.5[9]	(5)	(5)	—	0.7[2][3]	0.8[9]	0.9	0.7[9]
Spain	3.6	4.2	4.8	4.4	4.2	4.2	4.1	2.9	3.2	3.5	3.1	2.8	2.8	2.7	0.4	0.7	0.8	1.0	0.9	0.9	0.9
Sweden	—	5.3	6.6	7.4	6.5	6.5	6.2	—	4.4	4.4	4.9[3]	4.5	4.5	4.2	0.9	1.0	1.6	2.0[3]	1.6	1.6	1.5
Switzerland	4.9	5.0	5.5	5.4	6.0	5.9	5.6	4.0	3.7	4.1	3.9	4.0	3.9	3.9	—	1.0	1.1	1.2	1.6	1.6	1.4
Turkey	—	3.2	2.2	3.5	—	3.8	4.7	—	2.3	1.4	2.4[2]	—	2.9	3.9	—	0.9	0.8	1.1[2]	—	0.9	0.9
United Kingdom	4.9	4.3	4.6	4.8	5.1	5.0	5.0	3.1	3.5	3.8	3.4	4.0	3.8	3.8	1.0	0.7	0.7	1.0	0.8	0.8	0.9
United States	4.7	5.3	5.0	5.0	5.4	5.1	4.8	3.2	3.8	3.5	3.5[4]	3.9	3.7	3.5	1.3	1.4	1.1	1.1[4]	1.2	1.0	1.0
Reporting partner economies																					
Brazil	—	—	—	—	—	—	4.4	—	—	—	—	—	2.9[9]	3.3	—	—	—	—	—	0.7[9]	0.8
Chile	—	—	—	—	—	3.5	3.3	—	—	—	—	—	2.8	2.7	—	—	—	—	—	0.3	0.3
Estonia	(5)	(5)	—	—	—	4.9	4.7	(5)	(5)	—	—	—	3.7	3.5	(5)	(5)	—	—	—	0.9	0.9
Israel	—	—	—	—	7.0	6.6	6.2	—	—	—	—	4.6	4.4	4.2	—	—	—	—	1.3	1.1	1.0
Russian Federation	(5)	(5)	3.4	3.0	3.7	3.6	3.6	(5)	(5)	1.9	1.7	2.1	2.0	1.9	(5)	(5)	0.7	0.5	0.7	0.7	0.8
Slovenia	(5)	(5)	—	—	—	5.4	5.3	(5)	(5)	—	—	3.9	3.9	3.9	(5)	(5)	—	—	1.1	1.1	1.0

—Not available.
[1] Includes public subsidies to households attributable for educational institutions and direct expenditure on educational institutions from international sources, except where noted.
[2] Public subsidies to households not included in public expenditure.
[3] Direct expenditure on education institutions from international sources exceeds 1.5 percent of all public expenditure.
[4] Postsecondary non-higher-education included in higher education.
[5] Country did not exist in its current form in the given year.
[6] Postsecondary non-higher-education included in both secondary and higher education.
[7] Data for 1985 are for the former West Germany.

[8] Preprimary education (for children age 3 and older) is included in primary and secondary education.
[9] Occupation-specific education corresponding to that offered at the associate's degree level in the United States is included in primary and secondary education.

NOTE: Direct public expenditure on educational services includes both amounts spent directly by governments to hire educational personnel and to procure other resources, and amounts provided by governments to public or private institutions, or households. Figures for 1985 also include transfers and payments to private entities, and thus are not strictly comparable with later figures. Some data have been revised from previously published figures.

SOURCE: Organization for Economic Cooperation and Development (OECD), Education Online Database; *Annual National Accounts, Vol. 1, 1997*; and *Education at a Glance*, 2006 through 2008. (This table was prepared August 2008.)

Table 420. Foreign students enrolled in institutions of higher education in the United States and other jurisdictions, by continent, region, and selected countries of origin: Selected years, 1980–81 through 2006–07

Continent, region, and country	1980–81 Number	1980–81 Percent	1985–86 Number	1985–86 Percent	1990–91 Number	1990–91 Percent	1995–96 Number	1995–96 Percent	2000–01 Number	2000–01 Percent	2003–04 Number	2003–04 Percent	2004–05 Number	2004–05 Percent	2005–06 Number	2005–06 Percent	2006–07 Number	2006–07 Percent
1	2	3	4	5	6	7	8	9	10	11	12	13	14	15	16	17	18	19
Total	311,880	100.0	343,780	100.0	407,530	100.0	453,787	100.00	547,867	100.0	572,509	100.0	565,039	100.0	564,766	100.0	582,984	100.0
Africa	38,180	12.2	34,190	9.9	23,800	5.8	20,544	4.6	34,217	6.2	38,150	6.7	36,100	6.4	36,308	6.4	35,802	6.1
East Africa	6,260	2.0	6,730	2.0	7,590	1.9	7,596	1.7	13,516	2.5	14,831	2.6	13,675	2.4	13,635	2.4	13,374	2.3
Kenya	1,930	0.6	1,720	0.5	2,360	0.6	2,534	0.6	6,229	1.1	7,381	1.3	6,728	1.2	6,559	1.2	6,349	1.1
Central Africa	1,130	0.4	1,540	0.4	1,650	0.4	1,346	0.3	1,859	0.3	2,331	0.4	2,505	0.4	2,825	0.5	3,257	0.6
North Africa	7,310	2.3	5,980	1.7	4,540	1.1	3,422	0.8	5,184	0.9	4,487	0.8	3,898	0.7	3,770	0.7	3,700	0.6
Southern Africa	1,480	0.5	2,360	0.7	2,840	0.7	2,657	0.6	3,304	0.6	2,679	0.5	2,240	0.4	2,232	0.4	2,124	0.4
West Africa	22,000	7.1	17,560	5.1	7,180	1.8	5,818	1.3	10,346	1.9	13,821	2.4	13,782	2.4	13,846	2.5	13,344	2.3
Nigeria	17,350	5.6	13,710	4.0	3,710	0.9	2,093	0.5	3,820	0.7	6,140	1.1	6,335	1.1	6,192	1.1	5,943	1.0
Asia	94,640	30.3	156,850	45.6	229,830	56.4	259,893	57.3	302,058	55.1	324,006	56.6	325,112	57.5	327,785	58.0	344,495	59.1
East Asia	51,650	16.6	80,720	23.5	146,020	35.8	166,717	36.7	189,371	34.6	189,874	33.2	192,561	34.1	197,576	35.0	204,023	35.0
China	2,770	0.9	13,960	4.1	39,600	9.7	39,613	8.7	59,939	10.9	61,765	10.8	62,523	11.1	62,582	11.0	67,723	11.6
Hong Kong	9,660	3.1	10,710	3.1	12,630	3.1	12,018	2.6	7,627	1.4	7,353	1.3	7,180	1.3	7,849	1.4	7,722	1.3
Japan	13,500	4.3	13,360	3.9	36,610	9.0	45,531	10.0	46,497	8.5	40,835	7.1	42,215	7.5	38,712	6.9	35,282	6.1
Korea, Republic of	6,150	2.0	18,660	5.4	23,360	5.7	36,231	8.0	45,685	8.3	52,484	9.2	53,358	9.4	59,022	10.5	62,392	10.7
Taiwan	19,460	6.2	23,770	6.9	33,530	8.2	32,702	7.2	28,566	5.2	26,178	4.6	25,914	4.6	27,876	4.9	29,094	5.0
South and Central Asia	14,540	4.7	25,800	7.5	42,370	10.4	45,431	10.0	71,765	13.1	98,138	17.1	97,961	17.3	94,965	16.8	104,457	17.9
India	9,250	3.0	16,070	4.7	28,860	7.1	31,743	7.0	54,664	10.0	79,736	13.9	80,466	14.2	76,503	13.5	83,833	14.4
Nepal	250	0.1	390	0.1	670	0.2	1,219	0.3	2,618	0.5	4,384	0.8	4,861	0.9	6,061	1.1	7,754	1.3
Pakistan	2,990	1.0	5,440	1.6	7,730	1.9	6,427	1.4	6,948	1.3	7,325	1.3	6,296	1.1	5,759	1.0	5,401	0.9
Southeast Asia	28,450	9.1	50,310	14.6	41,440	10.2	47,774	10.5	40,916	7.5	35,994	6.3	34,590	6.1	35,244	6.2	36,015	6.2
Indonesia	3,250	1.0	8,210	2.4	9,520	2.3	12,820	2.8	11,625	2.1	8,880	1.6	7,760	1.4	7,575	1.3	7,338	1.3
Malaysia	6,010	1.9	23,020	6.7	13,610	3.3	14,015	3.1	7,795	1.4	6,483	1.1	6,142	1.1	5,515	1.0	5,281	0.9
Philippines	—	—	3,920	1.1	4,270	1.0	3,127	0.7	3,139	0.6	3,467	0.6	3,531	0.6	3,758	0.7	3,705	0.6
Singapore	—	—	3,930	1.1	4,500	1.1	4,098	0.9	4,166	0.8	3,955	0.7	3,769	0.7	3,909	0.7	3,730	0.6
Thailand	6,550	2.1	6,940	2.0	7,090	1.7	12,165	2.7	11,187	2.0	8,937	1.6	8,637	1.5	8,765	1.6	8,886	1.5
Vietnam	6,490	2.1	3,270	1.0	1,400	0.3	922	0.2	2,022	0.4	3,165	0.6	3,670	0.6	4,597	0.8	6,036	1.0
Europe[1]	25,330	8.1	34,310	10.0	49,640	12.2	67,358	14.8	80,584	14.7	74,134	12.9	85,409	15.1	84,697	15.0	82,731	14.2
France	3,310	1.1	3,680	1.1	5,630	1.4	5,707	1.3	7,273	1.3	6,818	1.2	6,555	1.2	6,640	1.2	6,704	1.1
Germany[2]	3,750	1.2	4,730	1.4	7,000	1.7	9,070	2.0	10,128	1.8	8,745	1.5	8,640	1.5	8,829	1.6	8,656	1.5
Greece	—	—	4,440	1.3	4,360	1.1	3,385	0.7	2,768	0.5	2,126	0.4	2,035	0.4	2,088	0.4	1,986	0.3
Spain	—	—	1,740	0.5	4,300	1.1	4,809	1.1	4,156	0.8	3,631	0.6	3,512	0.6	3,455	0.6	3,575	0.6
Turkey[1]	(¹)	(¹)	(¹)	(¹)	(¹)	(¹)	(¹)	(¹)	(¹)	(¹)	(¹)	(¹)	12,474	2.2	11,622	2.1	11,506	2.0
United Kingdom	4,440	1.4	5,940	1.7	7,300	1.8	7,799	1.7	8,139	1.5	8,439	1.5	8,236	1.5	8,274	1.5	8,438	1.4
Latin America	49,810	16.0	45,480	13.2	47,580	11.7	47,253	10.4	63,634	11.6	69,658	12.2	66,087	11.7	64,769	11.5	64,579	11.1
Caribbean	10,650	3.4	11,100	3.2	12,610	3.1	10,737	2.4	14,423	2.6	15,606	2.7	13,898	2.5	13,855	2.5	13,854	2.4
Central America	12,970	4.2	12,740	3.7	15,950	3.9	14,220	3.1	16,764	3.1	19,264	3.4	19,227	3.4	19,709	3.5	19,743	3.4
Mexico	—	—	5,460	1.6	6,740	1.7	8,667	1.9	10,670	1.9	13,329	2.3	13,063	2.3	13,931	2.5	13,826	2.4
South America	26,190	8.4	21,640	6.3	19,020	4.7	22,296	4.9	32,447	5.9	34,788	6.1	32,962	5.8	31,205	5.5	30,982	5.3
Brazil	—	—	2,840	0.8	3,900	1.0	5,457	1.2	8,846	1.6	7,799	1.4	7,244	1.3	7,009	1.2	7,126	1.2
Colombia	—	—	4,010	1.2	3,180	0.8	3,442	0.8	6,765	1.2	7,533	1.3	7,334	1.3	6,835	1.2	6,750	1.2
Venezuela	11,750	3.8	7,040	2.0	2,890	0.7	4,456	1.0	5,217	1.0	5,575	1.0	5,279	0.9	4,792	0.8	4,523	0.8
Middle East[1]	84,710	27.2	52,720	15.3	33,420	8.2	30,563	6.7	36,858	6.7	31,852	5.6	17,448	3.1	17,806	3.2	22,321	3.8
Iran	47,550	15.2	14,210	4.1	6,260	1.5	2,628	0.6	1,844	0.3	2,321	0.4	2,251	0.4	2,420	0.4	2,795	0.5
Israel	—	—	—	—	—	—	—	—	—	—	3,474	0.6	3,323	0.6	3,419	0.6	3,269	0.6
Jordan	6,140	2.0	6,590	1.9	4,320	1.1	2,222	0.5	2,187	0.4	1,853	0.3	1,754	0.3	1,733	0.3	1,726	0.3
Kuwait	—	—	—	—	—	—	—	—	—	—	1,846	0.3	1,720	0.3	1,703	0.3	1,633	0.3
Lebanon	6,770	2.2	7,090	2.1	3,900	1.0	1,554	0.3	2,005	0.4	2,179	0.4	2,040	0.4	1,950	0.3	1,852	0.3
Saudi Arabia	10,440	3.3	6,900	2.0	3,590	0.9	4,181	0.9	5,273	1.0	3,521	0.6	3,035	0.5	3,448	0.6	7,886	1.4
Turkey[1]	—	—	2,460	0.7	4,080	1.0	7,678	1.7	10,983	2.0	11,398	2.0	(¹)	(¹)	(¹)	(¹)	(¹)	(¹)
North America[3]	14,790	4.7	16,030	4.7	18,950	4.6	23,644	5.2	25,888	4.7	27,650	4.8	28,634	5.1	28,699	5.1	28,756	4.9
Canada	14,320	4.6	15,410	4.5	18,350	4.5	23,005	5.1	25,279	4.6	27,017	4.7	28,140	5.0	28,202	5.0	28,280	4.9
Oceania	4,180	1.3	4,030	1.2	4,230	1.0	4,202	0.9	4,624	0.8	4,534	0.8	4,481	0.8	4,702	0.8	4,300	0.7
Australia	—	—	—	—	—	—	—	—	—	—	2,706	0.5	2,659	0.5	2,806	0.5	2,797	0.5
Unidentified[4]	240	0.1	190	0.1	80	#	30	#	10	#	19	#	37	#	#	#	#	#

—Not available.
#Rounds to zero.
[1]Cyprus (not shown separately) and Turkey were classified as being in the Middle East prior to 2004–05, but in Europe for 2004–05 and later years.
[2]Data for 1980–81 and 1985–86 are for West Germany (Federal Republic of Germany before unification).
[3]Excludes Mexico and Central America, which are included with Latin America.
[4]Home country unknown or undeclared.
NOTE: Totals and subtotals include other countries not shown separately. Data are for "nonimmigrants" (i.e., students who have not migrated to this country). Detail may not sum to totals because of rounding.
SOURCE: Institute of International Education, Open Doors: Report on International Educational Exchange, 1981 through 2007 (selected years). (This table was prepared July 2008.)

CHAPTER 7
Libraries and Educational Technology

This chapter contains statistics on libraries and the use of information technologies. These data show the extent of America's public access to information technologies outside of formal classroom activities. The data also provide a capsule description of the magnitude and availability of library resources.

The first section of the chapter (tables 421 to 426) deals with public libraries, public and private school libraries, and college and university libraries. It contains data on collections, population served, staff, and expenditures. Table 425 provides institutional-level information for the 60 largest college libraries in the country.

The second part of the chapter (tables 427 to 432) provides information on the availability and use of technology at school, home, and work. For example, the percentage of children using computers at school is shown over time. Also included are data on the use of home computers and the Internet by adults and school children, with comparisons among various demographic groups.

Related data may be found in other chapters of the *Digest*. For example, statistics on the number of degrees conferred in computer and information sciences and library sciences are in chapter 3. Further information on survey methodologies is in Appendix A: Guide to Sources and in the publications cited in the table source notes.

Libraries

The average number of library staff per school with a library was 1.8 at public schools in 2003–04 and 1.2 at private schools in 1999–2000 (table 421). On average, public school libraries had smaller numbers of books on a per student basis (1,803 per 100 students) than private school libraries (2,857 per 100 students) in 1999–2000. The number of books on a per student basis in public school libraries in 2003–04 (1,891 per 100 students) was not measurably different from the number in 1999–2000. In 2003–04, public elementary school libraries had larger holdings than public secondary school libraries on a per student basis (2,127 books per 100 students, compared to 1,376 books per 100 students).

Between 1991–92 and 1999–2000, the increase in college library operating expenditures was greater than the increase in enrollment; after adjustment for inflation, library operating expenditures per full-time-equivalent (FTE) student rose 6 percent during this period (table 424). Between 1999–2000 and 2005–06, library operating expenditures per FTE student dropped 12 percent. Overall, there was a net decrease of 7 percent in library operating expenditures per FTE student between 1991–92 and 2005–06. In 2005–06, the average library operating expenditure per FTE student was $472.

In 2005, there were 9,198 public libraries in the United States with a total of 816 million books and serial volumes. The annual number of visits per capita was 4.7, and the annual reference transactions per capita were 1.1 (table 426).

Computers and Technology

In 2005, the average public school contained 154 instructional computers (table 427). One important technological advance that has come to classrooms following the introduction of computers has been connections to the Internet. The percentage of instructional rooms with internet access increased from 51 percent in 1998 to 94 percent in 2005 (figure 29). Nearly all schools had access to the Internet in 2005 (table 427).

The increasing number of computers in schools has coincided with rising percentages of students using computers (table 431). The percentage of elementary and secondary school students using computers at school rose from 70 percent in 1997 to 83 percent in 2003. In 2003, the use of computers at school by elementary and secondary school students varied by age and family income. Among students in elementary and secondary schools, a higher percentage of those age 10 or older than of those younger than 10 used computers at school. In general, a greater percentage of elementary and secondary school students from higher income families than of students from lower income families used computers at school. For example, in 2003, 80 percent of students from families with incomes of $20,000 to $24,999 used computers at school, compared to 86 percent of students from families with incomes of $75,000 or more.

A majority of students in 2003 used computers at home (table 431). In 2003, 68 percent of elementary and secondary school students used computers at home, compared to 43 percent in 1997. Between 1997 and 2003, the percentage of students using computers at home for school work rose from 25 to 47 percent. In 2003, a higher percentage of females than males used computers at home for school work (49 vs. 46 percent). About 54 percent of White elementary and secondary school students used computers at home for school work in 2003, compared to 35 percent of Black students and 34 percent of Hispanic students. A greater percentage of students from higher income families than of students from lower families reported using computers at home for school work. For instance, 63 percent of students from families with incomes of $75,000 or more used a computer at home for school work, compared to 32 percent of students from families with incomes of $20,000 to $24,999.

The percentage of college students using computers at school rose from 63 percent in 1997 to 85 percent in 2003. About 76 percent used computers at home for school work in 2003 (table 431).

Computers are widely used in the workplace. In 2003, 56 percent of all workers used computers at work (table 432). More frequent use of computers at work was associated with higher levels of education and higher incomes. For example, 16 percent of high school dropouts and 40 percent of high school graduates used computers at work, compared to 82 to 87 percent of workers with bachelor's, master's, first-professional, or doctor's degrees. Among the common computer applications used by all employees using computers on the job were Internet and e-mail (75 percent), word processing/desktop publishing (68 percent), spreadsheets/databases (64 percent), and calendar/schedule (57 percent).

Figure 29. Percentage of all public schools and instructional rooms with internet access: Various years, fall 1994 through fall 2005

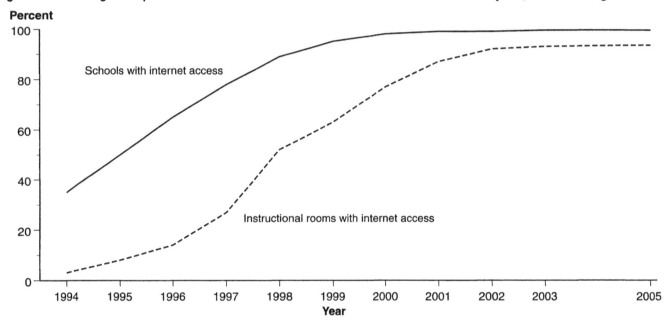

SOURCE: U.S. Department of Education, National Center for Education Statistics, Fast Response Survey System (FRSS), *Internet Access in U.S. Public Schools and Classrooms: 1994–2005.*

Table 421. Selected statistics on school libraries/media centers, by control and level of school: 1999–2000 and 2003–04

Selected statistic	Public, 1999–2000	Public, 2003–04				Private, 1999–2000			
		Total	Elementary	Secondary	Combined elementary/ secondary	Total	Elementary	Secondary	Combined elementary/ secondary
1	2	3	4	5	6	7	8	9	10
Number of schools with libraries	**77,300** (421)	**78,360** (548)	**57,400** (440)	**16,300** (313)	**4,600** (201)	**17,100** (323)	**11,000** (251)	**2,000** (91)	**4,100** (174)
Average number of staff per library	1.89 (0.018)	1.76 (0.014)	1.66 (0.018)	2.09 (0.025)	1.74 (C.116)	1.18 (0.026)	1.01 (0.032)	1.80 (0.083)	1.33 (0.055)
Certified library/media specialists	0.81 (0.007)	0.79 (0.009)	0.73 (0.012)	1.03 (C.018)	0.73 (C.023)	0.23 (0.011)	0.13 (0.009)	0.55 (0.027)	0.35 (0.027)
Full-time	0.65 (0.007)	0.65 (0.009)	0.58 (0.010)	0.92 (0.018)	0.55 (C.027)	0.17 (0.009)	0.07 (0.007)	0.47 (0.025)	0.27 (0.022)
Part-time	0.16 (0.006)	0.14 (0.007)	0.15 (0.009)	0.11 (0.009)	0.18 (0.020)	0.06 (0.005)	0.06 (0.006)	0.07 (0.010)	0.08 (0.013)
Other professional staff	0.17 (0.007)	0.19 (0.008)	0.19 (0.011)	0.14 (0.010)	0.28 (0.036)	0.48 (0.014)	0.47 (0.020)	0.53 (0.039)	0.46 (0.024)
Full-time	0.12 (0.005)	0.13 (0.007)	0.14 (0.009)	0.11 (0.009)	0.16 (0.022)	0.22 (0.009)	0.19 (0.012)	0.33 (0.023)	0.27 (0.020)
Part-time	0.06 (0.004)	0.05 (0.005)	0.05 (0.006)	0.03 (C.004)	0.11 (0.031)	0.25 (0.012)	0.29 (0.017)	0.20 (0.029)	0.19 (0.017)
Other paid employees	0.91 (0.014)	0.78 (0.011)	0.75 (0.013)	0.93 (0.017)	0.73 (0.085)	0.48 (0.014)	0.41 (0.020)	0.72 (0.048)	0.52 (0.030)
Full-time	0.49 (0.008)	0.46 (0.009)	0.41 (0.011)	0.65 (0.017)	0.35 (0.028)	0.14 (0.009)	0.11 (0.011)	0.24 (0.024)	0.18 (0.015)
Part-time	0.41 (0.014)	0.33 (0.012)	0.34 (0.014)	0.28 (0.C14)	0.38 (0.085)	0.34 (0.014)	0.31 (0.018)	0.48 (0.043)	0.34 (0.025)
Percentage of schools' library media centers with certain media equipment									
Telephone	84.8 (0.53)	90.5 (0.55)	89.9 (0.69)	95.3 (0.62)	82.1 (1.94)	53.2 (1.48)	45.3 (2.02)	78.2 (2.67)	62.3 (2.25)
Fax machine	11.5 (0.43)	10.9 (0.50)	6.9 (0.64)	23.1 (1.08)	17.0 (1.94)	6.7 (0.64)	4.8 (0.82)	13.6 (1.38)	8.7 (1.50)
Automated catalog	72.8 (0.69)	82.7 (0.66)	81.9 (0.89)	90.6 (0.76)	63.7 (2.59)	34.2 (1.25)	28.1 (1.54)	55.8 (2.61)	39.9 (2.25)
Automated circulation system	74.4 (0.65)	86.9 (0.61)	86.7 (0.82)	92.8 (0.80)	68.8 (2.45)	29.0 (1.17)	22.9 (1.31)	52.3 (2.48)	33.9 (2.33)
Video laser disc or DVD	43.0 (0.69)	44.1 (0.84)	39.3 (1.02)	61.3 (1.47)	43.2 (2.21)	12.7 (0.67)	10.4 (0.99)	21.2 (1.79)	15.0 (1.40)
Connection to Internet	90.1 (0.57)	95.1 (0.35)	94.1 (0.48)	99.2 (0.22)	92.6 (1.40)	60.6 (1.37)	55.1 (1.77)	81.6 (2.46)	65.2 (2.05)
Video cassette recorders (VCR)	— (†)	86.3 (0.65)	85.4 (0.77)	89.4 (1.21)	86.8 (1.69)	— (†)	— (†)	— (†)	— (†)
Disability assistance technologies, such as TDD	— (†)	11.9 (0.50)	10.2 (0.61)	18.0 (0.79)	11.7 (1.34)	— (†)	— (†)	— (†)	— (†)
Percentage of schools with certain services									
Students permitted to check out computer hardware	2.2 (0.14)	5.2 (0.37)	3.5 (0.45)	10.1 (0.77)	9.6 (1.34)	1.0 (0.17)	0.9 (0.25)	2.2 (0.41)	1.0 (0.29)
Students permitted to check out computer software	6.9 (0.31)	11.7 (0.44)	7.6 (0.56)	23.5 (1.35)	21.7 (2.22)	6.9 (0.57)	3.8 (0.50)	16.6 (1.53)	10.5 (1.59)
Number of library computer stations per 100 students	— (†)	2.3 (0.04)	2.2 (0.05)	2.5 (0.05)	2.7 (0.17)	— (†)	— (†)	— (†)	— (†)
Average holdings per 100 students at the end of the school year[1]									
Books (number of volumes)	1,803 (19.7)	1,891 (45.1)	2,127 (70.2)	1,376 (2C.0)	2,407 (117.7)	2,857 (84.8)	2,801 (86.0)	2,737 (178.3)	3,043 (213.2)
Video materials (tape and disc)	51 (0.8)	68 (3.5)	70 (5.3)	61 (2.1)	87 (13.2)	71 (2.5)	66 (3.3)	72 (6.0)	81 (5.8)
CD-ROM titles	8 (0.3)	12 (0.9)	16 (1.4)	4 (0.3)	10 (1.7)	10 (0.6)	10 (0.8)	10 (1.3)	10 (1.0)
Average additions per 100 students during the school year[1]									
Books (number of volumes)	— (†)	99.3 (2.08)	118.4 (3.13)	61.2 (1.75)	109.2 (6.40)	— (†)	— (†)	— (†)	— (†)
Video materials (tape and disc)	— (†)	4.3 (0.17)	4.4 (0.23)	4.1 (0.9)	5.9 (0.75)	— (†)	— (†)	— (†)	— (†)
CD-ROM titles	— (†)	0.7 (0.09)	0.9 (0.14)	0.3 (0.03)	1.0 (0.23)	— (†)	— (†)	— (†)	— (†)
Total expenditures for library/media materials per pupil[1,2]	$23.37 (0.438)	$16.24 (0.322)	$16.00 (0.469)	$16.11 (0.320)	$21.24 (2.498)	$29.02 (1.050)	$23.60 (1.646)	$38.72 (1.582)	$33.40 (1.831)
Books	9.97 (0.153)	10.99 (0.299)	11.72 (0.452)	9.63 (0.275)	10.19 (0.631)	10.57 (0.625)	9.29 (1.115)	11.18 (0.472)	12.68 (0.834)
Video materials	1.07 (0.022)	0.97 (0.042)	0.91 (0.046)	1.01 (0.0C1)	1.76 (0.617)	1.34 (0.051)	1.04 (0.057)	1.51 (0.106)	1.83 (0.153)
CD-ROM titles	0.59 (0.020)	0.17 (0.016)	0.21 (0.026)	0.10 (0.011)	0.20 (0.040)	0.82 (0.056)	0.72 (0.081)	1.15 (0.109)	0.81 (0.081)
Current serial subscriptions	1.26 (0.016)	1.36 (0.025)	1.06 (0.031)	1.87 (0.049)	2.50 (0.148)	1.34 (0.035)	0.62 (0.030)	2.71 (0.120)	1.86 (0.098)
Electronic subscriptions	0.81 (0.018)	0.88 (0.033)	0.39 (0.042)	1.79 (0.0C1)	1.25 (0.249)	1.35 (0.056)	0.17 (0.036)	3.85 (0.213)	2.08 (0.124)
Value of donated computers, A/V equipment, and other items per student[1,3]	— (†)	$1.56 (0.083)	$1.64 (0.108)	$1.12 (0.074)	$3.88 (0.761)	— (†)	— (†)	— (†)	— (†)

—Not available.
†Not applicable.
[1]Data are for the prior school year.
[2]Includes other expenditures not separately shown.
[3]Includes grants and other contributions.

NOTE: Percentages are based on schools that have library/media centers. Detail may not sum to totals because of rounding. Standard errors appear in parentheses.
SOURCE: U.S. Department of Education, National Center for Education Statistics, Schools and Staffing Survey (SASS), "Public School Library Media Center Questionnaire," 1999–2000 and 2003–04; "Charter School Questionnaire," 1999–2000; and "Private School Library Media Center Questionnaire," 1999–2000, unpublished tabulations. (This table was prepared September 2006.)

Table 422. Selected statistics on public school libraries/media centers, by level and enrollment size of school: 2003–04

Selected statistic	All public school libraries/media centers Total	Elementary school libraries Total	Less than 150	150 to 499	500 to 749	750 or more	Secondary school libraries Total	Less than 500	500 to 749	750 to 1,499	1,500 or more
1	2	3	4	5	6	7	8	9	10	11	12
Number of schools with libraries	78,300 (548)	57,400 (440)	3,200 (273)	29,800 (594)	15,700 (541)	8,600 (343)	16,300 (313)	5,400 (243)	2,900 (149)	4,900 (191)	3,000 (156)
Average number of staff per library	1.76 (0.014)	1.66 (0.018)	1.21 (0.094)	1.62 (0.023)	1.71 (0.029)	1.91 (0.040)	2.09 (0.025)	1.56 (0.040)	1.83 (0.045)	2.25 (0.040)	3.06 (0.088)
Certified library/media specialists	0.79 (0.009)	0.73 (0.012)	0.51 (0.052)	0.70 (0.019)	0.76 (0.019)	0.83 (0.024)	1.03 (0.018)	0.78 (0.032)	0.96 (0.031)	1.12 (0.025)	1.38 (0.050)
Full-time	0.65 (0.007)	0.58 (0.010)	0.16 (0.027)	0.51 (0.016)	0.68 (0.019)	0.76 (0.023)	0.92 (0.018)	0.61 (0.029)	0.88 (0.027)	1.04 (0.025)	1.33 (0.047)
Part-time	0.14 (0.007)	0.15 (0.009)	0.36 (0.044)	0.19 (0.015)	0.08 (0.011)	0.07 (0.014)	0.11 (0.009)	0.17 (0.017)	0.08 (0.017)	0.08 (0.015)	0.06 (0.010)
Other professional staff	0.19 (0.008)	0.19 (0.011)	0.17 (0.048)	0.21 (0.017)	0.18 (0.016)	0.16 (0.018)	0.14 (0.010)	0.15 (0.019)	0.13 (0.020)	0.13 (0.016)	0.15 (0.024)
Full-time	0.13 (0.007)	0.14 (0.009)	0.08 (0.044)	0.15 (0.014)	0.14 (0.015)	0.13 (0.016)	0.11 (0.010)	0.11 (0.019)	0.11 (0.018)	0.11 (0.017)	0.12 (0.023)
Part-time	0.05 (0.005)	0.05 (0.006)	0.09 (0.024)	0.06 (0.008)	0.05 (0.010)	0.04 (0.010)	0.03 (0.004)	0.04 (0.008)	0.02 (0.008)	0.02 (0.004)	0.04 (0.016)
Other paid employees	0.78 (0.011)	0.75 (0.013)	0.53 (0.059)	0.72 (0.018)	0.76 (0.027)	0.91 (0.031)	0.93 (0.017)	0.63 (0.028)	0.74 (0.047)	1.00 (0.033)	1.53 (0.058)
Full-time	0.46 (0.009)	0.41 (0.011)	0.20 (0.036)	0.37 (0.017)	0.43 (0.024)	0.61 (0.028)	0.65 (0.017)	0.39 (0.028)	0.46 (0.031)	0.74 (0.032)	1.16 (0.053)
Part-time	0.33 (0.012)	0.34 (0.014)	0.33 (0.062)	0.35 (0.020)	0.33 (0.024)	0.31 (0.029)	0.28 (0.014)	0.24 (0.025)	0.28 (0.047)	0.26 (0.023)	0.36 (0.032)
Percentage of schools' library media centers with certain media equipment											
Telephone	90.5 (0.55)	89.9 (0.69)	76.4 (4.00)	87.5 (0.99)	93.6 (0.92)	96.2 (0.88)	95.3 (0.62)	88.3 (1.69)	96.6 (1.37)	99.7 (0.10)	99.5 (0.32)
Fax machine	10.9 (0.50)	6.9 (0.64)	12.2 (5.01)	4.9 (0.69)	8.1 (1.24)	9.6 (1.41)	23.1 (1.08)	15.0 (1.71)	17.8 (2.04)	27.4 (1.79)	36.2 (2.31)
Automated catalog	82.7 (0.66)	81.9 (0.89)	54.2 (4.94)	79.6 (1.08)	89.7 (1.08)	85.9 (2.00)	90.6 (0.76)	79.3 (1.89)	92.3 (1.41)	96.7 (0.64)	99.6 (0.20)
Automated circulation system	86.9 (0.61)	86.7 (0.82)	54.6 (4.74)	84.9 (1.18)	93.1 (0.92)	93.4 (1.17)	92.8 (0.80)	83.9 (1.89)	94.3 (1.65)	97.7 (0.48)	99.5 (0.23)
Video laser disc or DVD	44.1 (0.84)	39.3 (1.02)	17.7 (4.56)	38.3 (1.42)	39.6 (1.72)	50.5 (2.51)	61.3 (1.47)	53.4 (3.10)	65.6 (2.86)	63.2 (1.89)	68.7 (2.43)
Connection to Internet	95.1 (0.35)	94.1 (0.48)	81.3 (3.62)	94.4 (0.69)	96.3 (0.69)	94.0 (1.16)	99.2 (0.22)	97.7 (0.66)	99.9 (0.06)	100.0 (#)	99.8 (0.20)
Video cassette recorders (VCR)	86.3 (0.65)	85.4 (0.77)	76.1 (4.11)	84.8 (1.15)	87.7 (1.16)	87.1 (1.40)	89.4 (1.21)	88.4 (2.87)	88.6 (2.36)	91.2 (1.45)	89.0 (1.82)
Disability assistance technologies, such as TDD	11.9 (0.50)	10.2 (0.61)	5.5 (2.03)	8.6 (0.90)	11.5 (1.24)	14.9 (1.95)	18.0 (0.79)	14.1 (1.56)	16.5 (2.17)	18.9 (1.28)	25.0 (2.09)
Percentage of schools with certain services											
Students permitted to check out computer hardware	5.2 (0.37)	3.5 (0.45)	9.4 (4.01)	3.7 (0.69)	1.8 (0.54)	3.7 (1.06)	10.1 (0.77)	13.0 (1.70)	9.2 (1.85)	7.3 (0.86)	10.3 (1.60)
Students permitted to check out computer software	11.7 (0.44)	7.6 (0.56)	15.2 (5.09)	7.5 (0.79)	5.7 (0.85)	8.6 (1.54)	23.5 (1.05)	21.6 (1.86)	22.5 (2.30)	23.9 (1.73)	27.3 (2.33)
Number of library computer stations per 100 students	2.3 (0.04)	2.2 (0.05)	6.2 (0.69)	3.0 (0.11)	1.9 (0.07)	1.4 (0.05)	2.5 (0.05)	4.9 (0.25)	3.0 (0.12)	2.4 (0.06)	1.7 (0.06)
Average holdings per 100 students at the end of the school year[1]											
Books (number of volumes)	1,891 (45.1)	2,127 (70.2)	5,996 (404.4)	2,818 (188.7)	1,937 (46.1)	1,386 (42.3)	1,376 (20.0)	2,886 (97.1)	1,726 (43.4)	1,291 (22.0)	975 (25.5)
Video materials (tape and disc)	68 (3.5)	70 (5.3)	131 (20.0)	88 (13.8)	69 (4.9)	47 (2.8)	61 (2.1)	114 (10.6)	70 (4.8)	62 (3.3)	45 (3.4)
CD-ROM titles	12 (0.9)	16 (1.4)	34 (8.6)	18 (1.9)	19 (3.1)	10 (1.8)	4 (0.3)	13 (2.6)	5 (0.7)	3 (0.4)	2 (0.2)
Average additions per 100 students during the school year[1]											
Books (number of volumes)	99.3 (2.08)	118.4 (3.13)	264.7 (27.02)	144.1 (5.57)	114.5 (5.21)	87.4 (4.91)	61.2 (1.75)	125.7 (7.33)	68.6 (3.18)	60.4 (3.32)	43.8 (2.43)
Video materials (tape and disc)	4.3 (0.17)	4.4 (0.23)	11.7 (2.30)	5.4 (0.46)	4.0 (0.35)	3.3 (0.26)	4.1 (0.19)	7.5 (0.98)	4.8 (0.39)	4.4 (0.39)	2.8 (0.21)
CD-ROM titles	0.7 (0.09)	0.9 (0.14)	4.2 (1.92)	1.3 (0.31)	0.9 (0.20)	0.5 (0.17)	0.3 (0.03)	0.9 (0.16)	0.4 (0.10)	0.3 (0.04)	0.2 (0.03)
Total expenditures for library/media materials per pupil[1,2]	$16.24 (0.322)	$16.00 (0.469)	$37.51 (5.208)	$19.35 (0.825)	$15.45 (0.859)	$11.90 (0.558)	$16.11 (0.320)	$25.80 (1.109)	$18.09 (0.838)	$16.71 (0.675)	$12.64 (0.507)
Books	10.99 (0.299)	11.72 (0.452)	21.69 (3.274)	14.08 (0.745)	11.40 (0.898)	8.94 (0.491)	9.68 (0.275)	14.97 (0.732)	11.25 (0.685)	9.85 (0.523)	7.77 (0.457)
Video materials	0.97 (0.042)	0.91 (0.046)	1.25 (0.208)	0.99 (0.077)	0.91 (0.087)	0.79 (0.065)	1.01 (0.061)	1.58 (0.175)	1.10 (0.093)	1.02 (0.100)	0.84 (0.117)
CD-ROM titles	0.17 (0.016)	0.21 (0.026)	0.37 (0.121)	0.31 (0.061)	0.20 (0.046)	0.08 (0.012)	0.10 (0.011)	0.24 (0.051)	0.10 (0.022)	0.10 (0.011)	0.07 (0.017)
Current serial subscriptions	1.38 (0.025)	1.06 (0.031)	3.02 (0.409)	1.32 (0.064)	0.94 (0.032)	0.82 (0.067)	1.87 (0.049)	3.76 (0.198)	2.28 (0.120)	1.92 (0.076)	1.24 (0.063)
Electronic subscriptions	0.88 (0.033)	0.39 (0.042)	1.02 (0.362)	0.50 (0.096)	0.33 (0.057)	0.31 (0.048)	1.79 (0.061)	2.15 (0.197)	1.85 (0.202)	1.90 (0.108)	1.59 (0.107)
Value of donated computers, A/V equipment, and other items per student[1,3]	$1.56 (0.083)	$1.64 (0.108)	$7.47 (1.785)	$2.24 (0.167)	$1.56 (0.202)	$0.83 (0.118)	$1.12 (0.074)	$3.05 (0.328)	$1.68 (0.201)	$0.98 (0.115)	$0.60 (0.113)

#Rounds to zero.
[1]Data are for the prior school year.
[2]Includes other expenditures not separately shown.
[3]Includes grants and other contributions.

NOTE: Percentages are based on schools that have library/media centers. Detail may not sum to totals because of rounding. Standard errors appear in parentheses.
SOURCE: U.S. Department of Education, National Center for Education Statistics, Schools and Staffing Survey (SASS), "Public School Library Media Center Questionnaire," 2003–04. (This table was prepared September 2006.)

Table 423. Selected statistics on public school libraries/media centers, by state: 2003–04

State	Percent of centers offering selected services/equipment				Average number of staff per library[1]	Books held at end of year per 100 students[2]	Books acquired during year per 100 students[2]	Total expenditure for materials per student[2]	Value of donated computers, A/V equipment, and other items per student[2,3]
	Automated catalog	Automated circulation system	Connection to the Internet	Digital video disk (DVD)					
1	2	3	4	5	6	7	8	9	10
United States	82.7 (0.66)	86.9 (0.61)	95.1 (0.35)	44.1 (0.84)	1.8 (0.01)	1,891 (45.1)	99 (2.1)	$16.2 (0.32)	$1.6 (0.08)
Alabama	87.6 (2.83)	95.9 (1.73)	100.0 (†)	44.0 (4.27)	1.7 (0.07)	1,713 (82.8)	99 (8.0)	15.2 (1.13)	2.6 (0.65)
Alaska	68.5 (4.60)	73.3 (5.55)	86.9 (4.69)	39.5 (5.90)	1.4 (0.03)	3,580 (230.9)	152 (24.2)	19.6 (2.30)	3.0 (1.03)
Arizona	81.5 (2.74)	90.5 (2.74)	93.3 (2.03)	38.8 (4.12)	1.8 (0.03)	2,298 (274.6)	121 (17.1)	15.3 (1.39)	0.9 (0.41)
Arkansas	86.7 (3.02)	93.0 (1.97)	97.0 (1.43)	44.0 (3.98)	1.7 (0.06)	1,931 (101.7)	89 (6.4)	18.1 (1.24)	2.3 (0.51)
California	81.6 (2.42)	87.9 (2.19)	88.7 (2.29)	31.4 (3.10)	1.4 (0.05)	1,488 (62.8)	108 (8.2)	16.5 (0.84)	1.1 (0.26)
Colorado	87.5 (3.96)	87.4 (3.44)	97.4 (1.77)	50.8 (5.03)	1.8 (0.09)	2,289 (423.3)	112 (13.4)	16.1 (1.30)	2.1 (0.64)
Connecticut	66.7 (5.42)	67.7 (5.41)	95.6 (2.46)	55.9 (5.08)	2.0 (0.10)	2,145 (105.2)	113 (17.5)	19.5 (2.16)	1.6 (0.43)
Delaware	97.3 (2.35)	97.8 (1.82)	97.3 (1.99)	29.9 (4.91)	1.6 (0.11)	1,702 (80.8)	75 (6.2)	12.9 (0.83)	1.9 (0.43)
District of Columbia	62.3 (7.68)	77.7 (5.90)	97.5 (2.20)	23.3 (6.71)	1.1 (0.04)	1,715 (307.5)	46 (8.8)	9.3 (2.17)	2.5 (0.74)
Florida	92.4 (2.27)	96.8 (1.72)	96.4 (2.01)	51.9 (4.84)	2.0 (0.08)	1,476 (79.3)	87 (8.6)	13.1 (0.97)	0.9 (0.18)
Georgia	96.4 (2.47)	97.7 (2.05)	98.6 (1.42)	50.8 (5.59)	2.2 (0.06)	1,653 (57.4)	76 (9.1)	14.2 (1.24)	1.4 (0.44)
Hawaii	94.6 (6.01)	95.5 (6.02)	98.1 (0.86)	42.9 (4.78)	1.5 (0.11)	2,029 (147.8)	71 (6.2)	11.5 (2.46)	1.2 (0.23)
Idaho	83.2 (3.01)	89.5 (2.75)	92.7 (2.20)	33.5 (3.84)	1.5 (0.06)	2,340 (102.7)	83 (9.9)	11.9 (1.16)	0.7 (0.18)
Illinois	66.4 (5.04)	70.8 (4.32)	89.2 (3.46)	38.0 (5.47)	2.1 (0.17)	1,703 (82.2)	118 (16.2)	13.7 (1.27)	1.8 (0.44)
Indiana	91.1 (2.83)	93.3 (2.52)	94.6 (2.97)	50.4 (5.76)	1.7 (0.07)	1,977 (95.4)	84 (9.1)	14.9 (0.97)	0.9 (0.30)
Iowa	74.9 (3.43)	78.0 (3.65)	90.6 (3.18)	51.9 (5.11)	2.0 (0.06)	2,605 (121.1)	100 (6.4)	13.9 (0.78)	1.6 (0.52)
Kansas	84.9 (3.50)	86.8 (3.70)	97.2 (1.48)	46.5 (4.24)	1.9 (0.07)	3,059 (142.5)	140 (12.0)	22.2 (2.14)	1.5 (0.35)
Kentucky	89.6 (2.82)	94.1 (2.40)	98.8 (1.02)	56.0 (4.88)	1.7 (0.07)	1,709 (77.6)	91 (8.8)	13.3 (0.65)	0.8 (0.25)
Louisiana	71.1 (4.00)	80.1 (3.26)	96.8 (1.64)	44.5 (4.61)	1.3 (0.05)	1,944 (131.2)	54 (4.6)	15.2 (3.54)	1.9 (0.42)
Maine	62.9 (4.83)	62.7 (4.41)	90.4 (3.73)	30.6 (4.03)	1.6 (0.10)	2,796 (260.5)	102 (8.7)	24.1 (2.68)	2.5 (0.98)
Maryland	82.8 (3.59)	91.0 (3.19)	98.7 (1.50)	46.9 (4.61)	1.6 (0.06)	1,507 (62.8)	125 (24.9)	17.3 (1.74)	1.3 (0.30)
Massachusetts	71.0 (6.43)	70.4 (6.35)	88.0 (5.02)	45.7 (5.69)	1.7 (0.12)	1,841 (126.0)	85 (14.8)	12.5 (1.33)	1.6 (0.44)
Michigan	83.8 (4.23)	82.8 (4.39)	100.0 (†)	48.8 (5.31)	1.8 (0.08)	3,010 (1,266.5)	88 (13.7)	12.8 (1.57)	1.1 (0.47)
Minnesota	92.0 (2.86)	94.6 (2.38)	97.2 (1.41)	59.7 (4.28)	2.1 (0.07)	2,509 (143.1)	111 (9.7)	15.2 (1.08)	2.1 (0.47)
Mississippi	73.2 (4.38)	86.5 (3.43)	95.5 (1.54)	35.6 (4.52)	1.6 (0.06)	1,476 (56.6)	102 (11.2)	14.9 (1.53)	1.4 (0.31)
Missouri	85.8 (3.59)	88.0 (3.33)	96.0 (1.57)	45.0 (4.73)	1.7 (0.06)	2,047 (62.0)	120 (9.0)	22.1 (1.01)	3.3 (0.96)
Montana	62.9 (3.53)	69.2 (3.32)	86.6 (3.36)	37.2 (3.37)	1.5 (0.08)	3,372 (214.8)	147 (17.7)	22.6 (1.40)	3.5 (0.75)
Nebraska	71.8 (4.35)	73.7 (4.27)	82.6 (3.39)	42.4 (5.55)	1.9 (0.09)	3,160 (228.1)	129 (10.4)	21.3 (1.38)	3.5 (0.71)
Nevada	92.2 (4.13)	88.6 (5.05)	93.9 (3.10)	44.2 (4.72)	1.5 (0.06)	1,616 (80.0)	114 (14.3)	13.5 (1.65)	1.4 (0.40)
New Hampshire	65.5 (4.11)	70.6 (4.04)	93.9 (3.02)	45.6 (5.04)	1.8 (0.07)	1,817 (78.5)	96 (11.2)	19.7 (1.28)	1.9 (0.68)
New Jersey	70.0 (6.08)	71.4 (6.08)	97.7 (2.04)	43.1 (6.13)	1.8 (0.08)	2,110 (142.1)	85 (13.6)	21.0 (2.72)	1.1 (0.30)
New Mexico	77.8 (3.58)	85.7 (3.12)	94.0 (1.81)	25.1 (2.74)	1.4 (0.06)	2,153 (105.1)	131 (10.7)	20.7 (1.66)	1.9 (0.43)
New York	76.0 (4.05)	83.9 (3.74)	94.9 (2.59)	47.7 (4.37)	2.2 (0.07)	1,626 (88.6)	95 (7.5)	19.8 (1.93)	2.2 (0.51)
North Carolina	93.3 (2.76)	97.0 (1.95)	96.3 (2.20)	53.0 (5.12)	1.9 (0.08)	1,622 (46.3)	110 (11.9)	18.3 (1.57)	1.1 (0.26)
North Dakota	51.8 (3.25)	53.4 (3.25)	90.1 (2.54)	30.1 (3.17)	1.6 (0.06)	3,710 (168.3)	146 (13.0)	26.1 (1.75)	1.3 (0.42)
Ohio	82.2 (3.47)	82.7 (3.40)	95.9 (2.10)	49.6 (4.89)	1.5 (0.08)	1,669 (78.4)	75 (9.4)	10.9 (0.78)	1.9 (0.46)
Oklahoma	75.5 (2.73)	89.8 (1.87)	95.6 (1.25)	35.0 (2.46)	1.8 (0.04)	2,159 (114.6)	99 (6.2)	15.5 (1.08)	2.5 (0.37)
Oregon	81.1 (4.49)	82.0 (4.69)	100.0 (†)	33.0 (4.61)	1.6 (0.08)	2,631 (221.4)	85 (10.5)	10.7 (0.96)	2.9 (1.11)
Pennsylvania	81.7 (3.59)	87.1 (4.16)	94.8 (3.09)	37.4 (3.87)	1.8 (0.08)	1,961 (83.9)	88 (10.0)	15.1 (0.91)	0.6 (0.16)
Rhode Island	72.3 (4.54)	83.5 (3.79)	98.9 (1.13)	26.4 (5.06)	1.8 (0.08)	1,538 (95.6)	84 (14.5)	16.9 (2.56)	1.5 (0.70)
South Carolina	98.2 (1.69)	99.9 (0.10)	100.0 (†)	46.6 (4.13)	2.1 (0.05)	1,674 (56.6)	94 (11.8)	15.7 (1.16)	2.0 (0.41)
South Dakota	53.6 (4.24)	53.6 (3.92)	89.5 (3.34)	42.6 (4.36)	1.5 (0.08)	3,105 (204.0)	173 (27.6)	22.3 (1.40)	2.1 (0.55)
Tennessee	81.2 (3.63)	89.3 (2.94)	98.6 (0.96)	47.1 (4.72)	1.6 (0.06)	1,652 (56.4)	94 (10.7)	13.0 (1.25)	1.8 (0.33)
Texas	93.7 (1.77)	98.3 (0.71)	99.0 (0.48)	42.4 (4.30)	1.7 (0.06)	1,779 (63.3)	106 (8.6)	18.8 (2.04)	1.6 (0.33)
Utah	87.2 (3.22)	94.8 (2.31)	86.2 (3.96)	51.0 (3.97)	1.4 (0.05)	1,651 (95.2)	84 (7.8)	9.8 (0.56)	1.4 (0.30)
Vermont	74.6 (5.33)	73.5 (5.29)	96.8 (2.06)	38.0 (4.20)	1.7 (0.10)	2,939 (127.9)	138 (10.3)	29.8 (1.27)	1.5 (0.69)
Virginia	95.2 (2.13)	99.5 (0.42)	95.5 (2.14)	52.6 (4.21)	1.9 (0.06)	1,717 (61.9)	88 (6.5)	16.2 (0.70)	1.3 (0.24)
Washington	92.9 (1.78)	96.0 (1.72)	98.9 (1.20)	46.5 (4.30)	2.0 (0.05)	2,060 (93.3)	92 (7.3)	15.7 (2.49)	1.8 (0.47)
West Virginia	42.7 (5.50)	54.6 (5.54)	86.8 (4.34)	33.4 (5.28)	0.9 (0.06)	1,594 (99.8)	74 (10.1)	8.9 (0.65)	1.6 (0.58)
Wisconsin	92.7 (3.07)	91.4 (3.67)	100.0 (†)	55.4 (4.43)	2.1 (0.06)	2,545 (141.8)	121 (8.5)	25.0 (1.26)	1.5 (0.59)
Wyoming	91.2 (3.40)	94.3 (2.92)	96.3 (2.72)	49.7 (5.02)	1.8 (0.07)	3,125 (142.3)	156 (22.4)	21.8 (1.59)	3.1 (0.87)

†Not applicable.
[1]Includes professional and nonprofessional staff.
[2]Data are for the prior school year.
[3]Includes grants and other contributions.

NOTE: Percentages are based on schools that have library/media centers. Standard errors appear in parentheses.
SOURCE: U.S. Department of Education, National Center for Education Statistics, Schools and Staffing Survey (SASS), "Public School Library Media Center Questionnaire," 2003–04. (This table was prepared September 2006.)

Table 424. Collections, staff, and operating expenditures of degree-granting institution libraries: Selected years, 1976–77 through 2005–06

Collections, staff, and operating expenditures	1976–77[1]	1981–82	1984–85	1987–88	1991–92	1994–95	1996–97	1997–98	1999–2000	2001–02	2003–04	2005–06
1	2	3	4	5	6	7	8	9	10	11	12	13
Number of libraries	3,058	3,104	3,322	3,438	3,274	3,303	3,408	3,658	3,527	3,568	3,653	3,617
Number of circulation transactions (in thousands)	—	—	—	—	—	231,503	230,733	216,067	193,948	189,248	200,204	187,236
Enrollment (in thousands)												
Total enrollment[2]	11,121	12,372	12,242	12,767	14,359	14,279	14,300	14,502	14,791	15,928	16,911	17,487
Full-time-equivalent enrollment[2]	8,313	9,015	8,952	9,230	10,361	10,348	10,402	10,615	10,944	11,766	12,688	13,201
Collections (in thousands)												
Number of volumes at end of year	481,442	567,826	631,727	718,504	749,429	776,447	806,717	878,906[3]	913,547	954,030	982,590	1,015,658
Number of volumes added during year	22,367	19,507	20,658	21,907	20,982	21,544	21,346	24,551	24,436	24,574	24,615	22,241
Number of serial subscriptions at end of year	4,670	4,890	6,317	6,416	6,966	6,212	5,709	10,908[4]	7,499	9,855	12,764	16,361
Microform units at end of year	—	—	—	—	—	—	—	1,062,082	1,111,389	1,143,678	1,173,287	1,166,295
Electronic units at end of year[5]	—	—	—	—	—	465	983	3,473	—	—	—	—
Full-time-equivalent (FTE) library staff												
Total staff in regular positions[6]	57,087	58,476	58,476	67,251	67,166	67,433	67,581	68,337	69,123	69,526	69,047	93,590
Librarians and professional staff	23,308	23,816	21,822	25,115	26,341	26,726	27,268	30,041	31,001	32,053	32,280	33,265
Other paid staff	33,779	34,660	38,026	40,733	40,421	40,381	40,022	38,026	37,893	37,473	36,767	36,350
Contributed services	—	—	—	1,403	404	326	291	270	229	—	—	—
Student assistants	—	—	—	33,821	29,075	28,411	27,998	28,373	26,518	25,305	25,038	23,976
FTE student enrollment per FTE staff member	146	154	153	137	154	153	154	155	158	169	184	141
Hours of student and other assistance (in thousands)	39,950	40,068	28,360	—	—	—	—	—	—	—	—	—
Library operating expenditures[7]												
Total operating expenditures (in thousands)	$1,259,637	$1,943,769	$2,404,524	$2,770,075	$3,648,654	$4,013,333	$4,301,815	$4,592,657	$5,023,198	$5,416,716	$5,751,247	$6,234,192
Salaries[8,9,10]	698,090	1,081,894	1,156,138	1,451,551	1,889,368	2,021,233	2,147,842	2,314,380	2,430,541	2,753,404	2,913,221	3,102,561
Hourly wages	68,683	100,847	(10)	(10)	(10)	(10)	(10)	(10)	(10)	(10)	(10)	(10)
Fringe benefits	(9)	(9)	(9)	231,209	—	(9)	(9)	(9)	271,954	(9)	(9)	(9)
Preservation	22,521	30,351	32,939	34,144	43,126	46,554	45,610	42,919	43,832	46,499	42,976	41,102
Furniture/equipment						55,915	56,128	57,013	63,459	—	—	—
Computer hardware/software						128,128	157,949	164,379	160,294	155,791	143,042	153,002
Bibliographic utilities/networks/consortia	—	—	—	—	—	81,106	85,113	89,618	90,264	92,242	101,293	106,268
Information resources	373,699	561,199	750,282	891,281	1,197,293	1,348,933	1,499,249	1,600,995	1,822,277	1,944,490	2,114,555	2,375,485
Books and serial backfiles—paper	—	—	—	—	—	—	—	514,048	552,100	563,007	550,599	572,228
Books and serial backfiles—electronic	—	—	—	—	—	—	—	28,061	33,888	44,792	65,597	93,778
Current serials—paper	—	—	—	—	—	—	—	849,399	945,958	926,105	883,534	830,137
Current serials—electronic	—	—	—	—	—	—	—	125,470	203,371	297,657	480,138	691,585
Audiovisual materials	—	—	—	—	23,879	28,753	28,879	30,623	32,039	37,041	35,216	39,029
Document delivery/interlibrary loan	—	—	—	—	—	12,238	17,645	19,309	20,540	22,913	24,823	26,513
Other collection expenditures	373,699	561,199	750,282	891,281	1,173,414	1,307,942	1,452,725	34,086	34,381	52,976	74,648	81,113
Other library operating expenditures	96,643	169,478	233,957	393,099	518,867	331,463	309,925	323,354	140,579	424,290	436,160	496,877
Operating expenditures per FTE student	152	216	269	300	352	388	414	433	459	460	453	472
Operating expenditures per FTE student in constant 2006–07 dollars[11]	527	468	518	529	520	526	531	546	553	527	497	484
Operating expenditures (percentage distribution)	100.0	100.0	100.0	100.0	100.0	100.0	100.0	100.0	100.0	100.0	100.0	100.0
Salaries[8,9,10]	55.4	55.7	48.1	52.4	51.8	50.4	49.9	50.4	48.4	50.8	50.7	49.8
Hourly wages	5.5	5.2	(10)	(10)	(10)	(10)	(10)	(10)	(10)	(10)	(10)	(10)
Fringe benefits	(9)	(9)	9.6	—	(9)	(9)	(9)	(9)	5.4	(9)	(9)	(9)
Preservation	1.8	1.6	1.4	1.2	1.2	1.2	1.1	0.9	0.9	0.9	0.7	0.7
Information resources	29.7	28.9	31.2	32.2	32.8	33.6	34.9	34.9	36.3	35.9	36.8	38.1
Other[12]	7.7	8.7	9.7	14.2	14.2	14.9	14.2	13.8	9.0	12.4	11.8	12.1
Library operating expenditures as percent of total institutional expenditures for educational and general purposes	3.8	3.5	3.4	3.2	3.0	2.8	—	—	—	—	—	—

—Not available.
[1]Includes data for U.S. territories.
[2]Fall enrollment for the academic year specified.
[3]Includes data for schools newly added to the survey system, so end of year figure for 1997–98 exceeds total of volumes added during the year plus end of year value from 1996–97.
[4]Includes microform and electronic serials.
[5]Electronic files, formerly labeled "Computer files."
[6]Excludes student assistants.
[7]Excludes capital outlay.
[8]Includes salary equivalents of contributed services staff.
[9]Expenditures for fringe benefits included under salaries (except for 1984–85, 1987–88, and 1999–2000).
[10]Hourly wages included under salaries (except for 1976–77 and 1981–82).
[11]Constant dollars based on the Consumer Price Index, prepared by the Bureau of Labor Statistics, U.S. Department of Labor, adjusted to a school-year basis.

[12]Includes furniture/equipment, computer hardware/software, and utilities/networks/consortia as well as expenditures classified as "other library operating expenditures".
NOTE: Data through 1995 are for institutions of higher education, while later data are for degree-granting institutions. Degree-granting institutions grant associate's or higher degrees and participate in Title IV federal financial aid programs. The degree-granting classification is very similar to the earlier higher education classification, but it includes more 2-year colleges and excludes a few higher education institutions that did not grant degrees. (See Guide to Sources for details.) Detail may not sum to totals because of rounding.
SOURCE: U.S. Department of Education, National Center for Education Statistics, *Library Statistics of Colleges and Universities*, selected years, 1976–77 through 1984–85; 1987–88 through 2005–06 Integrated Postsecondary Education Data System, "Academic Libraries Survey" (IPEDS-L:88–98), "Fall Enrollment Survey" (IPEDS-EF:87–99), and Spring 2002 through Spring 2006; Academic Libraries Survey (ALS), 2000 through 2006; and *Academic Libraries: 2006* (NCES 2008-337). (This table was prepared July 2008.)

Table 425. Collections, staff, and operating expenditures of the 60 largest college and university libraries: 2005–06

Institution	Rank order, by number of volumes	Number of volumes at end of year (in thousands)	Number of e-books at end of year	Number of serials at end of year	Full-time-equivalent staff Total	Full-time-equivalent staff Librarians	Operating expenditures (in thousands) Total	Operating expenditures (in thousands) Salaries and wages	Public service hours per week	Gate count per week	Reference transactions per week
1	2	3	4	5	6	7	8	9	10	11	12
Harvard University (MA)	1	15,827	867	98,988	1,265	420	$105,809	$58,047	168	38,945	5,554
Yale University (CT)	2	12,369	167,205	73,953	706	170	74,938	31,304	111	14,599	1,958
University of Illinois at Urbana-Champaign	3	10,371	247,242	63,413	503	99	35,602	19,151	119	84,639	5,264
University of California, Berkeley	4	10,094	—	114,860	531	96	50,253	26,035	98	27,000	3,300
University of Texas at Austin	5	9,022	—	53,125	536	100	41,586	19,810	107	71,992	6,149
Columbia University in the City of NY	6	8,832	342,573	102,901	618	139	51,901	26,064	107	72,484	3,579
Stanford University (CA)	7	8,402	365,000	30,850	697	149	74,233	40,958	105	19,500	2,203
University of Michigan, Ann Arbor	8	8,273	1,028,674	118,654	574	158	49,053	23,204	168	72,696	2,711
University of California, Los Angeles	9	8,157	24,299	77,509	622	125	50,894	26,271	97	69,736	1,975
University of Wisconsin, Madison	10	8,015	502,514	68,560	577	233	40,962	22,381	148	108,354	—
Cornell University (NY)	11	7,521	298,767	77,392	552	116	42,156	21,197	144	101,159	2,047
University of Chicago (IL)	12	7,462	304,016	86,239	318	66	32,301	11,635	144	25,062	802
Indiana University, Bloomington	13	7,242	237,835	71,330	486	97	32,453	14,313	168	87,561	2,346
University of Washington, Seattle Campus	14	6,677	280,140	60,629	463	135	35,218	18,234	142	136,000	2,056
Princeton University (NJ)	15	6,618	222,911	41,775	397	97	41,714	17,639	115	11,777	910
University of Minnesota, Twin Cities	16	6,587	126,892	88,309	408	93	38,322	17,470	100	41,521	3,024
University of North Carolina at Chapel Hill	17	5,817	236	54,591	436	139	34,489	16,203	145	77,538	2,489
Ohio State University, Main Campus	18	5,765	188,722	36,813	435	82	32,966	15,155	168	52,357	6,312
Duke University (NC)	19	5,665	26,000	57,223	359	113	33,532	14,598	137	62,999	2,635
University of Pennsylvania	20	5,571	309,277	47,787	393	120	34,369	15,215	111	36,300	5,000
New York University	21	5,145	769,197	62,537	451	125	41,004	18,186	119	42,795	2,676
University of Virginia, Main Campus	22	5,103	270,603	71,832	373	97	30,273	15,703	149	78,134	3,225
Pennsylvania State U., Penn State Main Campus	23	5,070	18,200	71,230	611	124	48,878	23,496	168	40,417	3,830
University of Arizona	24	5,050	441,889	23,288	237	61	22,547	8,931	168	42,133	659
Rutgers University, New Brunswick/Piscataway	25	5,003	176,995	40,848	321	68	23,161	12,831	105	47,280	1,408
University of Pittsburgh, Main Campus (PA)	26	4,909	224,216	50,232	362	120	30,357	11,869	118	83,242	3,565
University of Kansas, Main Campus	27	4,756	109,272	40,989	258	61	18,300	8,667	140	34,433	1,996
Michigan State University	28	4,736	53,101	35,994	271	69	22,260	10,046	138	41,594	773
Northwestern University (IL)	29	4,688	39,035	45,259	339	94	26,335	12,068	119	26,058	1,638
University of Iowa	30	4,551	324,934	51,374	278	79	25,666	11,335	115	36,630	1,647
University of Oklahoma, Norman Campus	31	4,346	363,116	34,404	153	37	14,444	4,048	117	21,015	640
University of Georgia	32	4,346	84,423	37,226	294	71	23,014	9,487	110	17,735	1,910
University of Florida	33	4,168	273,671	85,169	431	99	27,435	12,339	111	28,421	5,736
University of Southern California	34	3,969	287,712	60,718	375	68	31,894	14,534	159	55,000	1,100
Arizona State University at the Tempe Campus	35	3,896	281,588	30,925	274	72	22,044	9,742	149	73,892	2,317
Johns Hopkins University (MD)	36	3,773	1,488,106	60,858	342	78	31,560	13,369	120	18,982	1,593
Washington University in St. Louis (MO)	37	3,750	197,298	41,339	311	105	37,908	12,923	120	35,000	1,632
University of Tennessee	38	3,735	266,279	35,265	354	123	29,754	11,944	138	39,332	1,743
University of Maryland, College Park	39	3,690	200,000	32,777	304	145	25,284	11,195	162	54,935	4,550
University of Colorado at Boulder	40	3,641	40,677	30,221	212	52	19,210	8,252	104	2,051	2,391
University of Rochester (NY)	41	3,607	13,056	26,760	214	91	18,122	8,231	119	4,196	922
Brigham Young University (UT)	42	3,594	144,910	30,895	380	84	23,943	11,177	105	82,860	3,580
Brown University (RI)	43	3,569	743,698	40,082	208	53	18,945	8,648	154	17,301	466
University of South Carolina, Columbia	44	3,533	691	58,855	277	68	20,422	7,837	152	20,000	3,350
University of Delaware	45	3,471	317,560	12,532	207	52	16,937	7,199	100	19,138	2,052
Louisiana State U. and A&M College	46	3,468	191,428	13,225	212	54	13,454	5,250	100	41,900	896
Wayne State University (MI)	47	3,443	55,429	23,693	267	55	19,054	8,812	168	39,134	1,052
SUNY at Buffalo	48	3,423	103,905	37,288	249	67	19,454	9,965	141	25,000	977
University of Hawaii at Manoa	49	3,413	87,557	156,425	230	66	18,181	8,521	94	27,714	1,732
University of Kentucky	50	3,406	226,680	31,897	263	85	19,569	8,009	140	60,367	1,955
University of California, Santa Barbara	51	3,353	102,925	42,219	238	45	17,131	7,731	103	37,632	1,946
University of New Mexico, Main Campus	52	3,340	195,522	18,143	299	72	21,484	—	103	39,631	1,783
North Carolina State University at Raleigh	53	3,301	278,271	49,480	276	94	22,409	10,033	146	33,325	1,103
Texas A&M University	54	3,300	280,779	45,806	367	91	28,372	11,077	142	47,114	866
University of Missouri, Columbia	55	3,295	25,386	36,244	211	57	14,414	6,051	110	42,000	1,730
University of California, Davis	56	3,258	402,112	41,921	254	54	18,509	8,776	95	33,245	1,289
University of Oregon	57	3,255	230,970	23,186	208	42	13,739	6,921	107	40,581	2,123
University of Notre Dame (IN)	58	3,247	7,443	21,622	261	59	21,694	9,540	126	18,853	574
University of California, San Diego	59	3,236	142,804	24,438	337	58	25,400	13,571	113	65,659	1,477
University of Cincinnati, Main Campus	60	3,209	155,744	42,265	213	51	24,203	10,072	105	29,876	2,241

—Not available.

SOURCE: U.S. Department of Education, National Center for Education Statistics, Academic Libraries Survey (ALS), 2006. (This table was prepared July 2008.)

Table 426. Public libraries, books and serial volumes, library visits, circulation, and reference transactions, by state: Fiscal year 2005

State	Number of public libraries	Number of books and serial volumes (in thousands)	Number of books and serial volumes per capita	Library visits per capita[1]	Circulation per capita	Public library reference transactions per capita[2]
1	2	3	4	5	6	7
United States	9,198 [3]	815,605	2.8	4.7	7.2	1.1
Alabama	207	9,424	2.1	3.2	4.1	0.8
Alaska	89	2,332	3.5	5.2	6.1	0.6
Arizona	86	10,170	1.8	4.0	7.3	0.9
Arkansas	48	5,965	2.3	3.2	4.4	0.7
California	179	79,438	2.2	4.1	5.4	0.9
Colorado	115	11,647	2.6	6.2	11.0	1.3
Connecticut	194	15,005	4.3	6.4	9.0	1.3
Delaware	21	1,696	2.2	5.0	6.9	0.7
District of Columbia	1	2,264	4.1	3.4	2.1	2.1
Florida	78	33,365	1.9	4.1	5.5	1.4
Georgia	58	14,978	1.7	3.7	4.8	1.0
Hawaii	1	3,179	2.5	4.4	5.1	0.7
Idaho	104	3,924	3.2	6.0	8.3	0.6
Illinois	623	41,849	3.7	5.8	8.6	1.5
Indiana	239	24,461	4.3	6.9	12.2	1.0
Iowa	540	12,117	4.1	5.8	9.4	0.6
Kansas	325	10,991	4.8	6.4	10.9	1.2
Kentucky	116	8,483	2.1	4.0	6.0	0.7
Louisiana	67	11,096	2.5	3.1	3.9	0.9
Maine	272	6,365	5.4	5.7	7.5	0.8
Maryland	24	14,521	2.6	5.0	9.4	1.3
Massachusetts	370	31,910	5.0	5.9	7.8	0.8
Michigan	383	33,419	3.4	4.8	6.6	0.9
Minnesota	140	16,152	3.1	5.2	9.9	0.9
Mississippi	50	5,621	1.9	2.9	3.2	0.6
Missouri	149	18,576	3.6	5.0	8.9	1.1
Montana	79	2,760	3.1	4.1	6.2	0.5
Nebraska	270	6,594	4.7	6.5	10.1	0.8
Nevada	22	4,105	1.6	4.1	6.2	0.7
New Hampshire	230	6,052	4.6	4.9	7.7	0.7
New Jersey	306	31,362	3.8	5.4	6.4	0.9
New Mexico	87	4,339	3.0	4.6	6.5	0.9
New York	754	73,757	3.9	5.7	7.5	1.4
North Carolina	75	16,304	1.9	4.0	5.5	1.2
North Dakota	83	2,341	4.2	4.8	7.4	0.7
Ohio	251	47,878	4.2	7.2	15.0	1.6
Oklahoma	113	6,933	2.4	4.6	6.9	0.8
Oregon	125	9,240	2.8	6.2	14.9	0.9
Pennsylvania	458	29,520	2.5	3.6	5.3	0.7
Rhode Island	49	4,357	4.0	5.9	6.8	0.9
South Carolina	42	8,901	2.1	3.6	5.0	1.1
South Dakota	124	3,206	5.3	6.2	9.1	0.9
Tennessee	186	10,955	1.9	3.2	4.1	0.8
Texas	553	44,865	2.1	3.3	4.8	1.1
Utah	71	6,334	2.7	6.9	12.9	1.7
Vermont	184	2,808	4.7	5.7	7.3	0.9
Virginia	91	19,244	2.6	4.6	8.5	1.0
Washington	65	17,769	2.9	7.0	11.1	1.1
West Virginia	97	4,938	2.7	3.3	4.3	0.6
Wisconsin	381	19,696	3.5	6.0	10.3	0.9
Wyoming	23	2,399	4.8	6.2	9.1	1.1

[1]The total number of persons entering the library for any purpose during the year.
[2]A reference transaction is an information contact that involves the knowledge, use, recommendations, interpretation, or instructions in the use of one or more information sources by a member of the library staff.
[3]Consists of 7,433 single-outlet libraries and 1,765 multiple-outlet libraries. Some single-outlet libraries are bookmobiles, and some multiple-outlet libraries consist of or include bookmobiles.

NOTE: Data include imputations for nonresponse. Detail may not sum to totals because of rounding.
SOURCE: U.S. Department of Education, National Center for Education Statistics, Public Libraries Survey (PLS), fiscal year 2005, *Public Libraries in the United States: Fiscal Year 2004*. (This table was prepared May 2008.)

Table 427. Public schools and instructional rooms with internet access, by selected school characteristics: Selected years, 1994 through 2005

Schools, computers, instructional rooms, and access	All public schools	Instructional level[1]		Size of school enrollment			Metropolitan status				Percent of students eligible for free or reduced-price lunch[2]			
		Elementary	Secondary	Less than 300	300 to 999	1,000 or more	City	Urban fringe	Town	Rural	Less than 35 percent	35 to 49 percent	50 to 74 percent	75 percent or more
1	2	3	4	5	6	7	8	9	10	11	12	13	14	15
Estimated total number of schools														
1995	77,850 (—)	57,710 (—)	18,080 (—)	20,670 (—)	50,040 (—)	7,140 (—)	17,910 (—)	18,460 (—)	19,540 (—)	21,940 (—)	37,450 (—)	13,630 (—)	12,810 (—)	13,170 (—)
1998	78,790 (333)	59,170 (293)	19,190 (220)	20,100 (479)	50,560 (467)	8,040 (165)	20,700 (68)	26,270 (98)	11,310 (182)	20,520 (273)	38,160 (1,530)	12,090 (1,185)	13,970 (991)	14,540 (1,263)
1999	78,400 (665)	59,580 (722)	17,110 (521)	20,020 (1,263)	50,390 (681)	7,990 (291)	21,030 (605)	26,250 (514)	11,240 (343)	19,890 (506)	35,650 (1,211)	13,910 (977)	16,100 (1,067)	11,990 (949)
2000	80,130 (650)	59,780 (569)	18,410 (359)	20,070 (697)	51,390 (206)	8,170 (217)	21,120 (1,360)	26,580 (1,746)	11,880 (1,323)	20,550 (1,478)	36,560 (1,215)	12,410 (792)	17,030 (1,071)	13,910 (923)
2001	81,070 (492)	61,640 (527)	17,630 (414)	20,670 (589)	51,970 (274)	8,430 (139)	18,000 (1,416)	26,260 (1,002)	10,180 (746)	26,630 (1,087)	34,930 (1,191)	14,750 (1,203)	16,630 (995)	14,710 (814)
2002	82,040 (780)	62,040 (647)	17,610 (371)	21,430 (761)	51,880 (253)	8,730 (145)	18,550 (963)	26,430 (922)	10,770 (1,080)	26,280 (1,289)	34,990 (1,194)	13,240 (1,050)	19,040 (1,134)	14,770 (862)
2003	82,230 (763)	62,300 (759)	17,890 (396)	21,620 (697)	51,950 (448)	8,660 (154)	18,800 (1,160)	26,490 (1,060)	10,600 (1,098)	26,350 (1,422)	32,500 (1,381)	14,870 (1,111)	18,580 (1,095)	16,290 (999)
2005	82,480 (484)	61,920 (457)	18,910 (332)	20,960 (534)	53,420 (599)	8,100 (398)	19,010 (1,054)	23,820 (1,546)	11,810 (939)	27,850 (1,288)	32,280 (1,158)	14,350 (924)	18,290 (1,268)	17,570 (956)
Percent of schools with internet access[3]														
1994	35 (1.5)	30 (1.9)	49 (2.4)	30 (3.4)	35 (2.0)	58 (3.0)	40 (3.1)	38 (2.9)	29 (2.3)	35 (2.7)	39 (2.3)	35 (4.6)	32 (5.0)	18 (4.6)
1995	50 (1.8)	46 (2.4)	65 (2.7)	39 (3.9)	52 (2.2)	69 (4.1)	47 (4.3)	59 (3.8)	47 (3.7)	48 (3.8)	60 (2.4)	48 (3.9)	41 (4.6)	31 (4.4)
1996	65 (1.8)	61 (2.1)	77 (1.8)	57 (4.4)	66 (2.0)	80 (3.4)	64 (4.5)	75 (3.3)	61 (4.0)	60 (3.3)	74 (2.2)	59 (4.8)	53 (5.1)	53 (5.4)
1998	89 (1.3)	88 (1.6)	94 (2.1)	87 (3.4)	89 (1.4)	95 (2.4)	92 (2.1)	85 (2.8)	90 (3.2)	92 (3.4)	92 (2.0)	93 (2.2)	88 (3.0)	79 (3.7)
1999	95 (0.8)	94 (0.7)	98 (0.8)	96 (1.5)	94 (1.0)	96 (1.7)	93 (1.5)	96 (1.2)	94 (2.5)	96 (1.4)	95 (1.1)	98 (0.9)	96 (1.7)	89 (3.1)
2000	98 (0.5)	97 (0.5)	100[4] (†)	96 (1.7)	98 (0.5)	99 (0.6)	96 (1.1)	98 (1.2)	98 (1.2)	99 (0.9)	99 (0.7)	99 (0.7)	97 (1.3)	94 (1.7)
2001	99 (0.3)	99 (0.4)	100[4] (†)	99 (1.0)	99 (0.4)	100 (†)	97 (1.4)	99 (0.5)	100 (†)	100[4] (†)	99 (0.6)	100 (†)	99 (0.5)	97 (1.1)
2002	99 (0.5)	99 (0.6)	100[4] (†)	96 (1.7)	100[4] (†)	100 (†)	99 (0.7)	100[4] (†)	98 (2.2)	98 (1.0)	98 (1.0)	100 (†)	100 (†)	99 (0.9)
2003	100[4] (†)	99 (0.6)	100 (†)	100 (†)	100[4] (†)	100 (†)	100 (†)	100[4] (†)	100 (†)	100 (†)	100 (†)	100 (†)	100 (†)	99 (0.8)
2005	100[4] (†)	100[4] (†)	100 (†)	100 (†)	99 (0.4)	100 (†)	99 (0.5)	99 (0.6)	100 (†)	100 (†)	99 (0.5)	100 (†)	100 (†)	99 (0.7)
Number of computers for instructional purposes (in thousands)														
1995[5]	5,621 (—)	3,453 (—)	2,021 (—)	850 (—)	3,600 (—)	1,171 (—)	1,497 (—)	1,526 (—)	1,404 (—)	1,195 (—)	2,905 (—)	806 (—)	950 (—)	882 (—)
1998	7,111 (183)	4,519 (145)	2,549 (94)	952 (53)	4,414 (136)	1,744 (106)	2,148 (74)	2,606 (129)	1,047 (58)	1,311 (77)	3,630 (198)	1,105 (114)	1,127 (89)	1,235 (155)
1999	7,806 (147)	4,923 (114)	2,728 (103)	1,021 (76)	4,952 (127)	1,834 (101)	2,320 (113)	2,975 (121)	1,022 (50)	1,489 (75)	3,900 (152)	1,245 (115)	1,429 (116)	1,170 (98)
2000	8,776 (174)	5,296 (149)	3,271 (113)	1,135 (73)	5,524 (121)	2,117 (103)	2,537 (179)	3,396 (213)	1,155 (132)	1,689 (131)	4,394 (147)	1,373 (93)	1,606 (112)	1,384 (107)
2001	10,058 (180)	6,165 (165)	3,654 (98)	1,085 (57)	6,273 (140)	2,700 (85)	2,585 (192)	3,791 (168)	1,134 (78)	2,448 (142)	4,781 (206)	1,707 (120)	1,862 (132)	1,698 (117)
2002	10,711 (237)	6,775 (187)	3,705 (105)	1,347 (101)	6,533 (181)	2,831 (101)	2,862 (158)	4,043 (173)	1,320 (172)	2,686 (164)	4,982 (170)	1,673 (172)	2,265 (137)	1,792 (136)
2003	11,180 (265)	6,879 (234)	4,087 (115)	1,275 (77)	6,709 (179)	3,196 (118)	2,325 (163)	4,188 (177)	1,357 (139)	2,810 (220)	5,049 (252)	1,923 (165)	2,248 (139)	1,960 (110)
2005	12,672 (281)	7,701 (251)	4,783 (148)	1,566 (98)	7,966 (243)	3,139 (163)	3,132 (177)	4,058 (242)	1,819 (193)	3,663 (255)	5,352 (261)	2,193 (185)	2,687 (244)	2,440 (152)
Average number of instructional computers per school														
1995[5]	72 (—)	60 (—)	112 (—)	41 (—)	72 (—)	164 (—)	84 (—)	83 (—)	72 (—)	54 (—)	78 (—)	59 (—)	74 (—)	67 (—)
1998	90 (2.3)	76 (2.4)	133 (4.9)	47 (2.6)	87 (2.5)	217 (13.0)	104 (3.6)	99 (4.9)	93 (5.2)	64 (3.6)	95 (3.7)	91 (6.1)	81 (4.5)	85 (7.7)
1999	100 (2.2)	83 (2.2)	159 (6.4)	51 (2.5)	98 (2.3)	229 (10.7)	110 (4.7)	113 (4.2)	91 (4.2)	75 (3.6)	109 (2.8)	90 (6.8)	89 (5.6)	98 (5.2)
2000	110 (2.0)	89 (2.4)	178 (5.3)	57 (3.1)	106 (2.3)	259 (9.0)	120 (4.9)	128 (4.3)	97 (5.6)	82 (3.6)	120 (3.4)	111 (5.9)	94 (5.7)	99 (5.5)
2001	124 (2.3)	100 (2.7)	207 (6.2)	52 (2.5)	121 (2.6)	320 (10.1)	149 (6.4)	144 (4.7)	111 (6.0)	92 (4.0)	137 (4.9)	116 (5.8)	112 (6.0)	115 (5.0)
2002	131 (2.8)	109 (2.9)	210 (6.4)	63 (4.1)	126 (3.5)	324 (10.8)	144 (6.4)	153 (5.2)	123 (9.3)	102 (4.5)	142 (4.7)	126 (8.5)	119 (5.3)	122 (5.9)
2003	136 (2.6)	110 (3.1)	228 (4.9)	59 (2.9)	129 (3.2)	369 (11.0)	150 (6.1)	158 (5.6)	128 (6.7)	107 (4.9)	155 (5.9)	129 (7.0)	121 (5.6)	120 (5.1)
2005	154 (3.4)	124 (3.8)	253 (6.8)	75 (4.2)	149 (3.9)	388 (13.5)	165 (7.2)	170 (6.3)	154 (13.4)	132 (5.9)	166 (5.5)	153 (9.3)	147 (6.9)	139 (7.4)
Number of instructional computers with internet access (in thousands)														
1995[5]	447 (—)	232 (—)	187 (—)	59 (—)	315 (—)	73 (—)	96 (—)	131 (—)	126 (—)	94 (—)	286 (—)	46 (—)	57 (—)	36 (—)
1998	3,569 (173)	2,100 (148)	1,450 (79)	407 (38)	2,276 (140)	887 (73)	1,026 (87)	1,334 (105)	481 (46)	727 (73)	2,064 (151)	608 (79)	439 (48)	458 (78)
1999	4,809 (145)	2,773 (111)	1,945 (89)	663 (60)	2,988 (132)	1,158 (68)	1,265 (94)	1,887 (93)	691 (59)	966 (70)	2,762 (140)	778 (59)	810 (79)	428 (55)
2000	6,759 (174)	3,813 (136)	2,779 (113)	882 (69)	4,191 (114)	1,686 (97)	1,732 (146)	2,688 (178)	955 (111)	1,335 (91)	3,608 (139)	1,064 (80)	1,215 (93)	858 (87)
2001	8,500 (176)	4,936 (144)	3,357 (92)	874 (61)	5,229 (139)	2,396 (89)	2,175 (164)	3,178 (150)	1,008 (74)	2,139 (137)	4,225 (196)	1,447 (105)	1,529 (114)	1,289 (101)
2002	9,658 (236)	5,912 (183)	3,525 (105)	1,214 (97)	5,827 (183)	2,618 (102)	2,329 (145)	3,677 (160)	1,222 (162)	2,431 (148)	4,586 (167)	1,474 (129)	2,049 (129)	1,549 (122)
2003	10,361 (270)	6,225 (237)	3,935 (117)	1,156 (71)	6,169 (186)	3,036 (122)	2,593 (160)	3,887 (168)	1,284 (128)	2,616 (217)	4,751 (244)	1,724 (158)	2,121 (134)	1,726 (107)
2005	12,245 (274)	7,361 (246)	4,706 (151)	1,515 (98)	7,642 (239)	3,089 (162)	3,009 (173)	3,912 (238)	1,784 (193)	3,541 (239)	5,239 (259)	2,090 (176)	2,583 (228)	2,332 (146)

See notes at end of table.

Table 427. Public schools and instructional rooms with internet access, by selected school characteristics: Selected years, 1994 through 2005—Continued

Schools, computers, instructional rooms, and access	All public schools	Instructional level[1]		Size of school enrollment			Metropolitan status				Percent of students eligible for free or reduced-price lunch[2]			
		Elementary	Secondary	Less than 300	300 to 999	1,000 or more	City	Urban fringe	Town	Rural	Less than 35 percent	35 to 49 percent	50 to 74 percent	75 percent or more
1	2	3	4	5	6	7	8	9	10	11	12	13	14	15
Percent of instructional computers with internet access														
1995	8 (1.7)	7 (2.5)	9 (2.1)	7 (3.4)	9 (2.2)	6 (3.4)	6 (3.0)	9 (2.8)	9 (4.1)	8 (3.4)	10 (2.0)	6 (4.2)	6 (2.9)	4 (4.6)
1998	50 (1.4)	46 (1.6)	57 (2.4)	43 (3.0)	52 (1.7)	51 (3.6)	48 (2.6)	51 (2.4)	46 (3.1)	55 (2.7)	57 (2.2)	55 (3.6)	39 (2.8)	37 (3.6)
1999	62 (1.1)	56 (1.5)	71 (1.2)	65 (2.6)	60 (1.3)	63 (1.8)	55 (2.1)	63 (1.7)	68 (2.5)	65 (2.1)	71 (1.2)	62 (2.9)	57 (2.6)	37 (3.1)
2000	77 (0.8)	72 (1.2)	85 (0.8)	78 (2.8)	76 (1.2)	80 (1.4)	70 (2.1)	79 (1.5)	83 (1.9)	79 (1.3)	82 (1.2)	77 (2.0)	76 (2.5)	62 (2.2)
2001	85 (0.8)	80 (1.1)	92 (0.6)	81 (1.8)	83 (0.8)	89 (1.3)	81 (1.6)	84 (1.2)	89 (1.9)	87 (1.4)	88 (1.1)	85 (2.0)	82 (1.5)	76 (1.6)
2002	90 (0.6)	87 (0.8)	95 (0.8)	90 (1.9)	89 (0.9)	92 (1.0)	87 (1.0)	91 (1.1)	93 (1.6)	90 (1.3)	92 (0.8)	88 (2.3)	90 (1.0)	86 (1.5)
2003	93 (0.4)	90 (0.5)	96 (0.4)	91 (0.7)	92 (0.5)	95 (0.5)	92 (0.7)	93 (1.1)	93 (0.6)	93 (0.7)	95 (0.6)	90 (1.0)	94 (1.0)	88 (0.8)
2005	97	96	98	97	96	98	96	96	98	97	98	95	96	96
Number of public school students per instructional computer with internet access														
1998	12.1 (0.6)	13.6 (0.9)	9.9 (0.4)	9.1 (0.7)	12.3 (0.7)	13.0 (1.0)	14.1 (1.2)	12.4 (0.9)	12.2 (1.2)	8.6 (0.8)	10.6 (0.6)	10.9 (1.2)	15.8 (1.4)	16.8 (2.5)
1999	9.1 (0.3)	10.6 (0.4)	7.0 (0.3)	5.7 (0.4)	9.4 (0.4)	10.0 (0.6)	11.4 (0.8)	9.1 (0.4)	8.2 (0.6)	6.6 (0.4)	7.6 (0.3)	9.0 (0.4)	10.0 (0.8)	16.8 (2.2)
2000	6.6 (0.1)	7.8 (0.2)	5.2 (0.2)	3.9 (0.3)	7.0 (0.1)	7.2 (0.3)	8.9 (0.4)	6.6 (0.2)	6.2 (0.3)	5.0 (0.3)	6.0 (0.2)	6.3 (0.4)	7.2 (0.4)	9.1 (0.7)
2001	5.4 (0.1)	6.1 (0.2)	4.3 (0.1)	4.1 (0.3)	5.6 (0.1)	5.4 (0.2)	5.5 (0.2)	5.7 (0.2)	5.0 (0.3)	4.6 (0.1)	4.9 (0.2)	5.2 (0.2)	5.6 (0.3)	6.8 (0.3)
2002	4.8 (0.1)	5.2 (0.2)	4.1 (0.1)	3.1 (0.2)	5.0 (0.2)	5.1 (0.2)	5.0 (0.2)	4.9 (0.2)	4.4 (0.4)	4.0 (0.2)	4.6 (0.1)	4.5 (0.3)	4.7 (0.2)	5.5 (0.3)
2003	4.4 (0.1)	4.9 (0.2)	3.8 (0.1)	3.2 (0.1)	4.7 (0.1)	4.3 (0.2)	5.0 (0.2)	4.6 (0.2)	4.1 (0.2)	3.8 (0.2)	4.2 (0.1)	4.4 (0.3)	4.4 (0.2)	5.1 (0.2)
2005	3.8 (0.1)	4.1 (0.1)	3.3	2.4 (0.1)	3.9	4.0 (0.1)	4.2 (0.2)	4.1 (0.1)	3.4 (0.2)	3.0 (0.1)	3.8 (0.1)	3.4 (0.2)	3.6 (0.2)	4.0 (0.2)
Number of instructional rooms[6] (in thousands)														
1998	2,709 (41)	1,772 (29)	916 (25)	349 (15)	1,740 (34)	620 (21)	839 (22)	981 (24)	390 (14)	498 (17)	1,372 (60)	413 (39)	451 (29)	471 (42)
1999	2,811 (36)	1,830 (33)	926 (29)	360 (26)	1,805 (39)	645 (30)	857 (29)	1,049 (33)	375 (16)	530 (23)	1,325 (46)	477 (34)	541 (42)	437 (34)
2000	2,905 (35)	1,864 (28)	972 (24)	377 (22)	1,871 (28)	657 (23)	866 (56)	1,086 (61)	413 (47)	541 (39)	1,380 (48)	465 (28)	570 (36)	482 (29)
2001	2,851 (31)	1,854 (30)	929 (18)	332 (17)	1,829 (23)	690 (15)	726 (49)	1,068 (46)	339 (24)	718 (36)	1,299 (48)	486 (34)	551 (35)	510 (29)
2002	2,988 (37)	2,006 (30)	919 (19)	396 (25)	1,896 (20)	696 (16)	748 (36)	1,101 (39)	378 (40)	761 (48)	1,368 (51)	451 (38)	648 (38)	520 (33)
2003	3,004 (47)	1,998 (44)	952 (20)	378 (18)	1,919 (33)	707 (16)	777 (45)	1,104 (51)	375 (38)	748 (54)	1,281 (51)	524 (39)	626 (38)	512 (34)
2005	3,283 (71)	2,152 (70)	1,078 (27)	426 (23)	2,152 (70)	705 (30)	849 (62)	1,050 (61)	439 (41)	945 (67)	1,339 (50)	593 (51)	695 (56)	655 (39)
Percent of instructional rooms[6] with internet access[3]														
1994	3 (0.3)	3 (0.4)	4 (0.6)	3 (0.7)	3 (0.5)	3 (0.6)	4 (0.8)	4 (0.8)	3 (0.6)	3 (0.4)	3 (0.5)	2 (0.4)	4 (1.8)	2 (0.9)
1995	8 (0.7)	8 (1.0)	8 (1.0)	9 (1.6)	8 (1.0)	4 (1.0)	6 (1.3)	8 (1.4)	8 (2.0)	8 (1.5)	10 (1.2)	6 (1.4)	6 (1.9)	3 (1.0)
1996	14 (1.0)	13 (1.5)	16 (1.5)	15 (2.9)	13 (1.2)	16 (2.1)	12 (1.6)	16 (2.2)	14 (1.9)	14 (2.2)	17 (1.6)	12 (2.2)	11 (2.8)	5 (1.8)
1998	51 (1.8)	51 (2.3)	52 (2.1)	54 (3.7)	53 (2.2)	45 (3.9)	47 (3.2)	50 (2.9)	55 (4.0)	57 (3.6)	57 (2.4)	60 (5.1)	41 (3.9)	38 (4.3)
1999	64 (1.6)	62 (1.8)	67 (2.6)	71 (3.2)	64 (1.9)	58 (3.0)	52 (2.6)	67 (2.5)	72 (3.4)	71 (3.0)	73 (2.3)	69 (3.4)	61 (3.1)	38 (4.4)
2000	77 (1.1)	76 (1.5)	79 (1.6)	83 (2.8)	78 (1.5)	70 (2.2)	66 (2.2)	78 (2.0)	87 (2.6)	85 (1.7)	82 (1.5)	81 (2.9)	77 (2.8)	60 (3.3)
2001	87 (0.9)	86 (1.1)	88 (1.2)	87 (2.1)	87 (1.1)	86 (1.7)	82 (2.1)	87 (1.3)	91 (2.2)	89 (1.3)	90 (1.2)	89 (2.2)	87 (2.4)	79 (2.4)
2002	92 (0.6)	92 (0.8)	91 (1.0)	91 (1.9)	93 (0.7)	89 (1.7)	88 (1.6)	92 (0.9)	96 (1.1)	93 (1.0)	95 (0.8)	90 (2.1)	91 (1.4)	89 (1.9)
2003	93 (0.5)	93 (0.7)	94 (0.9)	93 (1.6)	93 (0.7)	94 (1.1)	90 (1.0)	94 (0.9)	97 (0.9)	94 (1.2)	95 (1.0)	93 (1.4)	96 (0.8)	90 (1.5)
2005	94 (1.3)	93 (1.9)	95 (0.9)	92 (1.9)	94 (1.9)	94 (1.5)	88 (3.7)	96 (0.8)	98 (0.7)	95 (1.8)	96 (0.8)	88 (4.3)	96 (0.8)	91 (2.5)

—Not available
†Not applicable.
[1]Data for combined schools are included in the totals and in analyses by other school characteristics, but are not shown separately.
[2]Percent of students eligible for free or reduced-price lunch was not available for some schools. In the 1994 survey, free and reduced-price lunch data came from the Common Core of Data (CCD) only and were missing for 430 schools (percentages presented in this table are based on cases for which data were available). In subsequent years, free and reduced-price lunch information was obtained on the questionnaire, supplemented, if necessary, with CCD data. Missing data ranged from 0 schools (2002, 2003, and 2005) to 10 schools (1999).

[3]Some data differ slightly (e.g., by 1 percent) from previously published figures.
[4]This estimate fell between 99.5 percent and 100.0 percent and therefore was rounded to 100 percent.
[5]Includes computers used for instructional or administrative purposes.
[6]Includes all classrooms, computer labs, and library/media centers.
NOTE: For estimates that are 100 percent, the event defined could have been reported by fewer schools had a different sample been drawn. Standard errors appear in parentheses. Detail may not sum to totals because of rounding.
SOURCE: U.S. Department of Education, National Center for Education Statistics, Fast Response Survey System (FRSS), Internet Access in U.S. Public Schools and Classrooms: 1994–2005; and unpublished tabulations. (This table was prepared July 2007.)

Table 428. Use of the Internet by persons 3 years old and over, by type of use and selected characteristics of students and other users: 2003

Columns 5–14 fall under the heading: *Percent of internet users using the Internet for various activities during the year[1]*

Selected characteristic	Number of persons using the Internet (in thousands)	Percent using the Internet anywhere	Percent using the Internet at school	School assignments	E-mail and messaging	Playing games	Online courses	Product purchases and information	News, weather, and sports	Health information[2]	Government information[3]	Conduct financial transactions[3,4]	Look for jobs[3]
1	2	3	4	5	6	7	8	9	10	11	12	13	14
Total, all persons	**161,636 (309.1)**	**58.7 (0.14)**	**— (†)**	**— (†)**	**82.1 (0.15)**	**42.2 (0.19)**	**5.6 (0.09)**	**71.2 (0.17)**	**60.6 (0.19)**	**39.3 (0.20)**	**44.7 (0.21)**	**30.4 (0.19)**	**18.7 (0.16)**
Sex													
Male	78,070 (343.4)	58.2 (0.21)	— (†)	— (†)	80.4 (0.22)	45.5 (0.27)	5.4 (0.12)	71.8 (0.25)	65.5 (0.26)	34.1 (0.28)	45.5 (0.30)	32.3 (0.28)	19.1 (0.24)
Female	83,567 (348.1)	59.2 (0.20)	— (†)	— (†)	83.7 (0.20)	39.2 (0.26)	5.7 (0.12)	70.6 (0.24)	55.9 (0.26)	44.1 (0.28)	44.0 (0.29)	28.6 (0.26)	18.3 (0.22)
Race/ethnicity													
White	122,243 (353.9)	65.1 (0.17)	— (†)	— (†)	84.8 (0.16)	41.4 (0.22)	5.5 (0.10)	74.4 (0.19)	62.9 (0.21)	41.1 (0.23)	45.9 (0.24)	31.3 (0.22)	17.4 (0.18)
Black	14,898 (131.5)	45.2 (0.45)	— (†)	— (†)	71.1 (0.61)	50.2 (0.67)	5.6 (0.31)	59.7 (0.66)	50.8 (0.67)	33.6 (0.67)	41.1 (0.73)	22.3 (0.62)	25.6 (0.65)
Hispanic	14,038 (132.7)	37.2 (0.43)	— (†)	— (†)	69.6 (0.68)	43.0 (0.73)	5.0 (0.32)	57.2 (0.73)	50.6 (0.74)	30.1 (0.73)	36.4 (0.81)	26.6 (0.74)	21.5 (0.69)
Other	10,457 (133.9)	61.6 (0.65)	— (†)	— (†)	83.3 (0.64)	39.5 (0.84)	7.1 (0.44)	68.4 (0.79)	60.7 (0.83)	37.6 (0.87)	45.4 (0.93)	35.2 (0.89)	21.5 (0.76)
Age													
3 and 4	1,662 (62.5)	19.9 (0.67)	— (†)	— (†)	26.5 (1.67)	64.6 (1.81)	0.6 (0.29)	15.4 (1.36)	11.3 (1.19)	— (†)	— (†)	— (†)	— (†)
5 to 9	8,259 (137.2)	42.0 (0.54)	— (†)	— (†)	33.5 (0.80)	64.8 (0.81)	1.0 (0.17)	17.3 (0.64)	16.6 (0.63)	— (†)	— (†)	— (†)	— (†)
10 to 14	14,570 (179.4)	68.9 (0.49)	— (†)	— (†)	62.4 (0.62)	66.1 (0.60)	1.1 (0.13)	34.4 (0.61)	35.7 (0.61)	6.2 (0.38)	— (†)	— (†)	— (†)
15 to 19	15,768 (186.1)	77.7 (0.45)	— (†)	— (†)	84.0 (0.45)	61.1 (0.60)	5.0 (0.27)	61.3 (0.60)	55.4 (0.61)	13.2 (0.42)	19.3 (0.48)	8.6 (0.34)	10.5 (0.38)
20 to 24	13,800 (174.9)	69.4 (0.50)	— (†)	— (†)	87.1 (0.44)	51.9 (0.65)	8.8 (0.37)	76.4 (0.56)	65.6 (0.62)	28.4 (0.59)	36.2 (0.63)	27.6 (0.59)	30.5 (0.60)
25 to 29	12,492 (167.0)	66.7 (0.53)	— (†)	— (†)	88.7 (0.44)	42.2 (0.68)	8.0 (0.37)	83.1 (0.52)	71.0 (0.62)	44.7 (0.68)	50.2 (0.69)	41.3 (0.68)	31.5 (0.64)
30 to 39	28,580 (242.3)	69.2 (0.35)	— (†)	— (†)	88.6 (0.29)	35.9 (0.44)	7.1 (0.23)	83.6 (0.34)	70.9 (0.41)	45.0 (0.45)	49.9 (0.46)	38.8 (0.44)	23.3 (0.38)
40 to 49	29,978 (247.3)	67.5 (0.34)	— (†)	— (†)	88.3 (0.29)	33.1 (0.42)	6.3 (0.22)	83.4 (0.33)	70.1 (0.41)	48.0 (0.44)	50.9 (0.44)	34.6 (0.42)	19.0 (0.35)
50 to 59	21,911 (215.9)	62.7 (0.40)	— (†)	— (†)	89.3 (0.32)	26.9 (0.46)	5.9 (0.24)	82.1 (0.40)	66.4 (0.49)	50.5 (0.52)	51.2 (0.52)	30.0 (0.48)	12.8 (0.35)
60 to 69	9,677 (148.0)	43.9 (0.51)	— (†)	— (†)	87.5 (0.52)	27.7 (0.70)	3.7 (0.30)	77.8 (0.65)	60.2 (0.77)	49.3 (0.78)	45.6 (0.78)	24.2 (0.67)	6.1 (0.37)
70 or older	4,940 (106.9)	20.1 (0.39)	— (†)	— (†)	86.7 (0.74)	27.9 (0.98)	2.9 (0.37)	67.6 (1.03)	56.8 (1.08)	47.6 (1.09)	37.8 (1.06)	19.0 (0.86)	2.4 (0.34)
Family income[5]													
Less than $10,000	5,290 (112.1)	31.5 (0.63)	— (†)	— (†)	69.3 (1.11)	48.0 (1.20)	6.4 (0.59)	60.6 (1.17)	53.3 (1.20)	33.8 (1.21)	40.4 (1.31)	22.9 (1.12)	34.5 (1.27)
$10,000 to $19,999	8,119 (195.6)	32.5 (0.66)	— (†)	— (†)	70.6 (1.12)	45.0 (1.22)	5.9 (0.58)	60.4 (1.20)	51.3 (1.23)	33.4 (1.23)	39.7 (1.34)	20.7 (1.11)	26.1 (1.20)
$20,000 to $29,999	12,830 (243.1)	43.8 (0.64)	— (†)	— (†)	75.5 (0.84)	46.1 (0.97)	5.4 (0.44)	64.3 (0.34)	54.9 (0.97)	35.8 (0.99)	39.3 (1.04)	24.8 (0.92)	23.6 (0.91)
$30,000 to $39,999	15,730 (267.2)	54.3 (0.65)	— (†)	— (†)	79.4 (0.71)	44.9 (0.88)	5.1 (0.39)	67.0 (0.33)	56.1 (0.88)	36.3 (0.90)	41.9 (0.95)	26.3 (0.85)	21.2 (0.79)
$40,000 to $49,999	13,596 (249.8)	64.8 (0.73)	— (†)	— (†)	80.2 (0.76)	43.7 (0.94)	4.8 (0.40)	70.6 (0.36)	58.0 (0.94)	37.6 (0.97)	41.9 (1.02)	27.3 (0.92)	18.5 (0.80)
$50,000 to $74,999	32,025 (365.2)	71.8 (0.47)	— (†)	— (†)	83.6 (0.46)	42.7 (0.61)	5.1 (0.27)	72.9 (0.55)	61.7 (0.60)	39.7 (0.63)	45.7 (0.67)	31.3 (0.62)	18.2 (0.52)
$75,000 or more	48,795 (429.4)	82.9 (0.34)	— (†)	— (†)	87.3 (0.33)	39.7 (0.49)	6.5 (0.25)	77.7 (0.42)	67.4 (0.47)	44.0 (0.52)	51.5 (0.54)	38.4 (0.53)	15.9 (0.40)
Total, all students	**49,520 (300.6)**	**66.1 (0.27)**	**48.8 (0.28)**	**82.2 (0.26)**	**70.1 (0.32)**	**59.3 (0.34)**	**5.9 (0.16)**	**49.8 (0.35)**	**46.5 (0.35)**	**20.1 (0.33)**	**32.8 (0.45)**	**20.5 (0.39)**	**17.8 (0.37)**
Elementary/secondary[6]	34,636 (262.4)	59.4 (0.31)	43.3 (0.32)	77.9 (0.34)	60.6 (0.40)	64.2 (0.40)	2.0 (0.12)	37.1 (0.40)	36.0 (0.40)	9.3 (0.31)	15.8 (0.53)	5.6 (0.34)	7.0 (0.37)
3 and 4 years old	1,063 (50.1)	23.2 (0.96)	7.6 (0.60)	29.4 (2.15)	25.1 (2.05)	63.5 (2.27)	‡ (†)	12.7 (1.57)	8.5 (1.32)	— (†)	— (†)	— (†)	— (†)
5 to 9 years old	8,116 (136.0)	42.7 (0.55)	26.1 (0.49)	51.6 (0.85)	33.3 (0.81)	64.9 (0.82)	1.0 (0.17)	17.3 (0.65)	16.5 (0.63)	— (†)	— (†)	— (†)	— (†)
10 to 14 years old	14,422 (178.5)	69.4 (0.49)	53.4 (0.53)	85.6 (0.45)	62.4 (0.62)	66.1 (0.61)	1.0 (0.13)	34.2 (0.61)	35.5 (0.61)	5.9 (0.38)	15.8 (0.53)	5.6 (0.34)	7.0 (0.37)
15 years old and over	11,035 (157.5)	79.5 (0.53)	63.6 (0.63)	91.9 (0.40)	81.6 (0.57)	61.3 (0.71)	4.2 (0.29)	57.8 (0.72)	53.6 (0.73)	12.2 (0.48)	15.8 (0.53)	5.6 (0.34)	7.0 (0.37)
College	14,884 (181.2)	89.5 (0.37)	68.1 (0.56)	92.0 (0.34)	92.4 (0.34)	47.8 (0.63)	14.9 (0.45)	79.2 (0.51)	71.1 (0.57)	34.9 (0.60)	45.4 (0.63)	31.5 (0.59)	25.8 (0.55)
Sex													
Male	24,107 (225.2)	64.6 (0.38)	47.7 (0.40)	80.7 (0.39)	66.8 (0.47)	64.1 (0.48)	5.3 (0.22)	50.5 (0.50)	49.9 (0.50)	16.1 (0.44)	31.4 (0.65)	20.2 (0.56)	17.0 (0.52)
Elementary/secondary[6]	17,519 (195.3)	58.4 (0.44)	42.2 (0.44)	76.6 (0.49)	57.2 (0.58)	67.5 (0.54)	2.1 (0.17)	39.4 (0.57)	39.3 (0.57)	7.6 (0.40)	15.4 (0.74)	5.6 (0.47)	6.4 (0.50)
3 and 4 years old	591 (37.4)	24.2 (1.34)	7.2 (0.81)	26.9 (2.81)	23.7 (2.69)	66.4 (2.99)	‡ (†)	11.4 (2.01)	8.7 (1.79)	— (†)	— (†)	— (†)	— (†)
5 to 9 years old	4,051 (97.0)	41.8 (0.77)	25.1 (0.68)	50.4 (1.21)	30.2 (1.11)	66.8 (1.14)	1.2 (0.27)	18.9 (0.95)	17.8 (0.93)	— (†)	— (†)	— (†)	— (†)
10 to 14 years old	7,233 (128.7)	68.1 (0.70)	51.9 (0.75)	84.0 (0.66)	58.0 (0.89)	68.9 (0.84)	1.4 (0.21)	37.6 (0.88)	38.1 (0.88)	4.6 (0.48)	15.4 (0.74)	5.6 (0.47)	6.4 (0.50)
15 years old and over	5,645 (114.1)	77.9 (0.75)	62.8 (0.87)	91.2 (0.58)	79.1 (0.83)	66.3 (0.97)	3.9 (0.40)	59.5 (1.01)	59.6 (1.01)	9.9 (0.61)	15.4 (0.74)	5.6 (0.47)	6.4 (0.50)
College	6,587 (123.0)	90.0 (0.54)	70.2 (0.82)	91.4 (0.53)	92.3 (0.51)	55.1 (0.94)	13.6 (0.65)	79.8 (0.76)	77.9 (0.79)	29.2 (0.86)	45.0 (0.94)	32.7 (0.89)	26.0 (0.83)

See notes at end of table.

Table 428. Use of the Internet by persons 3 years old and over, by type of use and selected characteristics of students and other users: 2003—Continued

Selected characteristic	Number of persons using the Internet (in thousands)	Percent using the Internet anywhere	Percent using the Internet at school	School assignments	E-mail and messaging	Playing games	Online courses	Product purchases and information	News, weather, and sports	Health information[2]	Government information[3]	Conduct financial transactions[3,4]	Look for jobs[3]
1	2	3	4	5	6	7	8	9	10	11	12	13	14
Female	25,413 (230.4)	67.6 (0.37)	49.9 (0.40)	83.6 (0.36)	73.3 (0.43)	54.7 (0.48)	6.5 (0.24)	49.1 (0.48)	43.4 (0.48)	23.8 (0.48)	34.1 (0.62)	20.7 (0.53)	18.6 (0.51)
Elementary/secondary[6]	17,117 (193.2)	60.5 (0.45)	44.4 (0.45)	79.3 (0.48)	64.0 (0.56)	60.8 (0.57)	1.9 (0.16)	34.8 (0.56)	32.6 (0.55)	11.1 (0.48)	16.2 (0.77)	5.7 (0.48)	7.6 (0.56)
3 and 4 years old	472 (33.4)	21.9 (1.37)	8.0 (0.90)	32.5 (3.32)	26.8 (3.14)	60.0 (3.47)	‡ (†)	14.3 (2.48)	8.3 (1.95)	— (†)	— (†)	— (†)	— (†)
5 to 9 years old	4,065 (97.2)	43.7 (0.79)	27.1 (0.71)	52.9 (1.21)	36.3 (1.16)	62.9 (1.17)	0.7 (0.20)	15.7 (0.88)	15.1 (0.86)	— (†)	— (†)	— (†)	— (†)
10 to 14 years old	7,189 (128.3)	70.7 (0.69)	54.9 (0.76)	87.3 (0.60)	66.9 (0.85)	63.3 (0.87)	0.7 (0.15)	30.9 (0.84)	32.9 (0.85)	7.1 (0.57)	— (†)	— (†)	— (†)
15 years old and over	5,390 (111.6)	81.2 (0.74)	64.5 (0.90)	92.6 (0.55)	84.1 (0.77)	56.0 (1.04)	4.4 (0.43)	56.1 (1.04)	47.4 (1.05)	14.6 (0.74)	16.2 (0.77)	5.7 (0.48)	7.6 (0.56)
College	8,297 (137.5)	89.0 (0.50)	66.4 (0.75)	92.4 (0.45)	92.4 (0.45)	42.0 (0.83)	15.9 (0.62)	78.8 (0.69)	65.7 (0.80)	39.4 (0.83)	45.8 (0.84)	30.4 (0.78)	25.7 (0.74)
Race/ethnicity													
White	34,066 (260.6)	73.4 (0.32)	54.0 (0.36)	82.6 (0.32)	74.0 (0.37)	60.1 (0.41)	6.0 (0.20)	52.9 (0.42)	48.8 (0.42)	20.8 (0.40)	34.6 (0.55)	21.9 (0.48)	16.7 (0.43)
Elementary/secondary[6]	23,592 (223.1)	67.1 (0.39)	48.7 (0.41)	78.2 (0.41)	65.1 (0.48)	65.7 (0.48)	1.9 (0.14)	39.9 (0.49)	38.0 (0.49)	9.5 (0.38)	17.3 (0.68)	6.7 (0.45)	5.8 (0.42)
3 and 4 years old	769 (42.6)	26.8 (1.27)	7.2 (0.74)	23.9 (2.37)	24.1 (2.37)	63.5 (2.67)	‡ (†)	9.9 (1.66)	6.5 (1.37)	— (†)	— (†)	— (†)	— (†)
5 to 9 years old	5,557 (113.2)	49.6 (0.73)	30.4 (0.67)	49.7 (1.03)	35.4 (0.99)	65.5 (0.98)	0.9 (0.19)	17.4 (0.78)	17.2 (0.78)	— (†)	— (†)	— (†)	— (†)
10 to 14 years old	9,836 (149.1)	78.2 (0.57)	60.4 (0.67)	87.4 (0.52)	68.5 (0.72)	67.8 (0.72)	0.8 (0.14)	37.0 (0.75)	37.6 (0.75)	5.4 (0.44)	— (†)	— (†)	— (†)
15 years old and over	7,430 (130.4)	87.4 (0.55)	69.6 (0.77)	92.9 (0.46)	87.2 (0.60)	63.4 (0.86)	4.1 (0.36)	63.5 (0.86)	57.4 (0.88)	12.9 (0.60)	17.3 (0.68)	6.7 (0.45)	5.8 (0.42)
College	10,475 (153.6)	92.7 (0.38)	70.3 (0.66)	92.4 (0.40)	94.0 (0.36)	47.5 (0.75)	15.4 (0.54)	82.3 (0.57)	73.1 (0.67)	35.7 (0.72)	46.8 (0.75)	32.7 (0.71)	24.4 (0.65)
Black	5,810 (110.1)	53.0 (0.78)	40.8 (0.77)	82.6 (0.81)	57.4 (1.06)	61.5 (1.05)	5.9 (0.51)	41.9 (1.06)	39.3 (1.05)	18.8 (0.99)	28.2 (1.33)	12.7 (0.99)	22.8 (1.24)
Elementary/secondary[6]	4,137 (96.7)	46.6 (0.87)	36.2 (0.83)	79.1 (1.04)	46.8 (1.27)	64.9 (1.21)	2.0 (0.36)	31.0 (1.18)	31.2 (1.18)	8.7 (0.92)	11.7 (1.42)	1.6 (0.55)	11.5 (1.41)
3 and 4 years old	103 (16.6)	15.0 (2.24)	7.2 (1.62)	51.6 (8.06)	32.5 (7.55)	56.8 (7.99)	‡ (†)	35.3 (7.70)	20.0 (6.45)	— (†)	— (†)	— (†)	— (†)
5 to 9 years old	925 (48.9)	33.1 (1.46)	21.5 (1.27)	58.2 (2.65)	27.1 (2.39)	65.6 (2.56)	0.6 (0.40)	20.0 (2.15)	16.3 (1.99)	— (†)	— (†)	— (†)	— (†)
10 to 14 years old	1,732 (65.8)	53.6 (1.44)	42.7 (1.42)	83.8 (1.45)	45.5 (1.96)	68.6 (1.83)	2.1 (0.57)	29.0 (1.79)	31.6 (1.83)	8.2 (1.33)	— (†)	— (†)	— (†)
15 years old and over	1,377 (59.1)	63.6 (1.69)	54.5 (1.75)	89.2 (1.37)	62.7 (2.13)	60.4 (2.16)	3.1 (0.76)	40.5 (2.17)	41.6 (2.17)	9.2 (1.27)	11.7 (1.42)	1.6 (0.55)	11.5 (1.41)
College	1,673 (64.8)	80.0 (1.43)	60.7 (1.75)	91.4 (1.12)	83.5 (1.48)	53.0 (2.00)	15.4 (1.45)	68.9 (1.85)	59.4 (1.97)	33.9 (1.89)	41.9 (1.97)	21.8 (1.65)	32.2 (1.87)
Hispanic	5,862 (116.2)	49.1 (0.80)	34.9 (0.76)	77.6 (0.95)	58.0 (1.13)	53.3 (1.14)	4.9 (0.49)	38.7 (1.11)	38.1 (1.11)	16.2 (1.02)	27.3 (1.47)	15.9 (1.21)	18.6 (1.29)
Elementary/secondary[6]	4,517 (105.7)	44.2 (0.86)	31.2 (0.80)	74.5 (1.13)	49.1 (1.30)	56.1 (1.29)	2.8 (0.43)	29.1 (1.18)	30.3 (1.19)	8.6 (0.95)	13.9 (1.58)	3.7 (0.87)	9.0 (1.31)
3 and 4 years old	114 (18.6)	15.6 (2.35)	7.2 (1.67)	41.4 (8.08)	16.2 (6.04)	71.0 (7.44)	‡ (†)	7.0 (4.19)	10.6 (5.04)	— (†)	— (†)	— (†)	— (†)
5 to 9 years old	1,095 (56.5)	30.3 (1.33)	17.9 (1.11)	53.6 (2.63)	26.6 (2.33)	59.9 (2.59)	1.8 (0.70)	15.2 (1.89)	15.5 (1.91)	— (†)	— (†)	— (†)	— (†)
10 to 14 years old	1,855 (72.3)	51.9 (1.46)	38.7 (1.42)	78.5 (1.67)	48.2 (2.03)	54.9 (2.02)	1.4 (0.48)	25.5 (1.77)	28.1 (1.82)	6.5 (1.23)	— (†)	— (†)	— (†)
15 years old and over	1,454 (64.5)	63.2 (1.76)	47.9 (1.82)	87.6 (1.51)	69.8 (2.10)	53.7 (2.28)	5.3 (1.02)	45.8 (2.28)	45.8 (2.28)	10.3 (1.39)	13.9 (1.58)	3.7 (0.87)	9.0 (1.31)
College	1,344 (62.2)	78.4 (1.74)	56.9 (2.09)	88.2 (1.54)	88.1 (1.54)	43.9 (2.36)	12.0 (1.55)	71.2 (2.16)	64.2 (2.28)	31.5 (2.21)	41.8 (2.35)	29.0 (2.16)	29.0 (2.16)
Family income[5]													
Less than $10,000	2,642 (84.7)	51.9 (1.22)	41.1 (1.21)	81.4 (1.32)	64.0 (1.63)	56.0 (1.69)	7.9 (0.92)	51.9 (1.70)	50.3 (1.70)	27.1 (1.71)	39.2 (2.07)	25.4 (1.85)	32.9 (1.99)
$10,000 to $19,999	3,477 (95.2)	52.8 (1.07)	41.8 (1.06)	82.2 (1.13)	60.8 (1.45)	52.5 (1.48)	6.9 (0.75)	46.7 (1.48)	42.6 (1.46)	22.6 (1.44)	37.2 (1.90)	19.8 (1.57)	21.4 (1.62)
$20,000 to $29,999	4,226 (103.0)	55.8 (1.00)	42.8 (0.99)	79.7 (1.08)	64.5 (1.29)	56.5 (1.33)	6.8 (0.68)	47.3 (1.34)	43.4 (1.33)	22.8 (1.32)	35.4 (1.75)	19.3 (1.44)	21.7 (1.51)
$30,000 to $39,999	4,860 (108.7)	62.8 (0.96)	45.1 (0.99)	78.5 (1.03)	66.8 (1.18)	60.9 (1.22)	6.6 (0.62)	45.1 (1.25)	41.4 (1.23)	20.5 (1.23)	31.9 (1.68)	20.7 (1.46)	19.1 (1.41)
$40,000 to $49,999	3,812 (98.9)	69.0 (1.09)	49.7 (1.17)	80.2 (1.13)	65.5 (1.35)	60.1 (1.39)	5.5 (0.64)	48.2 (1.41)	41.2 (1.39)	18.7 (1.33)	28.2 (1.82)	17.4 (1.53)	14.8 (1.43)
$50,000 to $74,999	9,038 (130.9)	72.1 (0.70)	51.6 (0.78)	82.0 (0.71)	71.5 (0.83)	60.9 (0.90)	5.0 (0.40)	49.9 (0.92)	46.9 (0.92)	20.2 (0.88)	35.0 (1.23)	20.5 (1.04)	17.2 (0.98)
$75,000 or more	14,314 (132.1)	79.5 (0.53)	57.3 (0.64)	84.3 (0.53)	76.2 (0.62)	61.9 (0.71)	5.9 (0.34)	54.0 (0.73)	51.3 (0.73)	18.6 (0.69)	32.9 (0.97)	22.4 (0.86)	14.6 (0.73)

—Not available.
†Not applicable.
‡Reporting standards not met.
[1]Individuals may be counted in more than one internet activity.
[2]Data are for persons 12 years old and over.
[3]Data are for persons 15 years old and over.
[4]Includes online banking and stock and securities transactions.

[5]Excludes persons whose income data were not available.
[6]Includes prekindergarten through grade 12.
NOTE: Data are based on a sample survey of households and are subject to sampling and nonsampling error. Race categories exclude persons of Hispanic ethnicity. Detail may not sum to totals because of rounding. Standard errors appear in parentheses.
SOURCE: U.S. Department of Commerce, Census Bureau, Current Population Survey (CPS), October 2003, unpublished tabulations. (This table was prepared May 2005.)

Table 429. Number and percentage of home computer users, by type of application and selected characteristics: 1997 and 2003

Selected characteristic	1997		2003										
	Number of home computer users (in thousands)	Percent of persons using computers at home	Number of home computer users (in thousands)	Percent of persons using computers at home	Percent of home computer users using specific applications[1]							
					Word processing	Connect to Internet	E-mail	Spreadsheets/ databases[2]	Graphics/design[2]	School assignments[3]	Household records/ finances[3]	Games
1	2	3	4	5	6	7	8	9	10	11	12	13
Total, age 3 and over	81,013 (600.0)	31.7 (0.16)	156,744 (954.0)	56.9 (0.16)	53.1 (0.22)	82.7 (0.17)	72.7 (0.19)	32.0 (0.23)	37.6 (0.24)	75.9 (0.29)	30.8 (0.22)	58.5 (0.22)
Sex												
Male	41,260 (412.6)	33.1 (0.22)	76,777 (637.8)	57.2 (0.22)	49.5 (0.30)	82.4 (0.23)	70.5 (0.27)	33.7 (0.32)	39.5 (0.33)	73.9 (0.42)	31.6 (0.31)	61.5 (0.29)
Female	39,753 (384.7)	30.3 (0.20)	79,967 (627.8)	56.7 (0.21)	56.7 (0.23)	83.0 (0.21)	74.8 (0.24)	30.3 (0.29)	35.9 (0.30)	77.8 (0.39)	30.1 (0.29)	55.6 (0.28)
Race/ethnicity												
White	68,026 (543.7)	36.9 (0.19)	119,495 (801.4)	63.7 (0.19)	53.9 (0.25)	84.9 (0.18)	75.4 (0.22)	32.6 (0.26)	38.6 (0.27)	75.4 (0.34)	31.8 (0.26)	58.0 (0.25)
Black	4,943 (136.3)	15.6 (0.36)	13,457 (254.7)	40.8 (0.48)	50.5 (0.76)	74.4 (0.67)	62.5 (0.74)	26.8 (0.77)	33.4 (0.82)	79.3 (0.89)	26.9 (0.78)	64.8 (0.73)
Hispanic	4,081 (139.0)	14.5 (0.41)	13,497 (300.2)	35.8 (0.49)	46.6 (0.85)	72.4 (0.76)	59.4 (0.83)	27.8 (0.30)	31.4 (0.93)	74.9 (0.97)	25.1 (0.87)	59.5 (0.83)
Other	3,963 (136.6)	34.8 (0.88)	10,296 (248.9)	60.7 (0.74)	56.3 (0.96)	81.1 (0.76)	71.6 (0.88)	36.4 (1.06)	39.3 (1.07)	76.7 (1.14)	31.4 (1.02)	54.2 (0.97)
Age												
3 to 14	18,774 (249.8)	39.1 (0.39)	30,772 (330.0)	62.6 (0.38)	37.9 (0.48)	57.6 (0.49)	34.5 (0.47)	— (†)	— (†)	61.9 (0.44)	— (†)	86.0 (0.34)
15 and over	62,239 (505.5)	30.0 (0.17)	125,972 (813.4)	55.7 (0.18)	56.8 (0.24)	83.8 (0.15)	82.0 (0.19)	32.0 (0.23)	37.6 (0.24)	92.8 (0.29)	30.8 (0.22)	51.8 (0.24)
15 to 19	8,395 (162.3)	43.1 (0.61)	14,656 (218.2)	72.2 (0.54)	68.9 (0.66)	86.6 (0.49)	77.9 (0.59)	23.2 (0.60)	43.8 (0.71)	93.1 (0.34)	6.2 (0.34)	72.4 (0.64)
20 to 24	4,975 (123.7)	28.5 (0.59)	11,848 (194.7)	59.6 (0.60)	63.7 (0.76)	85.4 (0.54)	80.6 (0.63)	29.9 (0.73)	40.9 (0.78)	94.5 (0.53)	20.5 (0.64)	61.9 (0.77)
25 to 29	5,963 (135.8)	31.7 (0.59)	11,059 (187.7)	59.0 (0.62)	56.0 (0.82)	83.5 (0.52)	83.7 (0.61)	36.2 (0.79)	42.1 (0.81)	94.2 (0.96)	37.1 (0.79)	54.2 (0.82)
30 to 39	15,393 (224.1)	35.8 (0.40)	26,407 (302.3)	64.0 (0.41)	54.3 (0.53)	89.7 (0.32)	83.3 (0.40)	35.5 (0.51)	40.6 (0.52)	89.0 (1.26)	37.6 (0.52)	50.4 (0.53)
40 to 49	15,346 (223.7)	38.3 (0.42)	27,660 (310.4)	62.3 (0.40)	55.4 (0.52)	90.1 (0.31)	82.7 (0.39)	35.3 (0.50)	37.3 (0.50)	88.6 (1.67)	37.5 (0.50)	47.3 (0.52)
50 to 59	7,679 (154.9)	28.5 (0.48)	19,976 (258.5)	57.2 (0.46)	55.4 (0.61)	90.7 (0.35)	83.4 (0.45)	32.5 (0.57)	33.6 (0.58)	90.0 (2.49)	34.4 (0.58)	41.9 (0.60)
60 to 69	3,162 (98.1)	16.2 (0.46)	9,233 (170.6)	41.8 (0.57)	51.8 (0.90)	87.9 (0.59)	81.9 (0.69)	28.5 (0.81)	29.0 (0.82)	69.8 (9.14)	31.8 (0.84)	44.3 (0.89)
70 or older	1,327 (63.2)	5.9 (0.27)	5,134 (125.7)	20.9 (0.45)	43.9 (1.20)	84.5 (0.87)	78.1 (1.00)	20.5 (0.97)	20.6 (0.98)	‡ (†)	25.4 (1.05)	47.0 (1.20)
Family income[4]												
Under $20,000	7,374 (151.6)	11.0 (0.21)	11,951 (195.6)	28.6 (0.38)	48.5 (0.79)	70.1 (0.72)	59.9 (0.77)	23.2 (0.75)	31.5 (0.83)	78.5 (0.85)	22.5 (0.75)	64.4 (0.76)
$20,000 to $29,999	7,819 (156.3)	19.9 (0.35)	12,136 (197.2)	41.4 (0.50)	47.7 (0.78)	74.0 (0.69)	64.5 (0.75)	25.6 (0.77)	32.4 (0.82)	74.8 (1.02)	24.7 (0.76)	63.6 (0.75)
$30,000 to $39,999	10,370 (181.4)	28.5 (0.41)	15,176 (222.4)	52.4 (0.51)	45.6 (0.70)	78.9 (0.57)	68.7 (0.65)	24.9 (0.68)	31.8 (0.73)	72.8 (0.95)	27.1 (0.70)	62.8 (0.68)
$40,000 to $49,999	9,627 (174.4)	36.9 (0.52)	13,300 (207.1)	63.4 (0.57)	50.1 (0.75)	81.9 (0.58)	71.6 (0.68)	28.5 (0.75)	35.6 (0.80)	74.9 (1.03)	28.8 (0.76)	61.5 (0.73)
$50,000 to $74,999	21,685 (270.5)	46.5 (0.40)	31,581 (335.0)	70.8 (0.37)	51.9 (0.49)	85.6 (0.34)	74.8 (0.42)	30.8 (0.50)	37.4 (0.52)	74.9 (0.66)	30.5 (0.50)	59.3 (0.48)
$75,000 or more	24,138 (287.3)	60.3 (0.42)	48,583 (433.0)	82.5 (0.27)	61.3 (0.38)	89.7 (0.24)	79.8 (0.31)	41.2 (0.43)	45.1 (0.43)	77.0 (0.51)	37.8 (0.42)	55.0 (0.39)

—Not available.
†Not applicable.
‡Reporting standards not met.
[1]Individuals may be counted in more than one computer activity.
[2]Data are for persons 15 years old and over.
[3]Data are for students only.
[4]Excludes persons whose income data were not available.
NOTE: Excludes persons under age 3. Race categories exclude persons of Hispanic ethnicity. Detail may not sum to totals because of rounding. Standard errors appear in parentheses.
SOURCE: U.S. Department of Commerce, Census Bureau, Current Population Survey (CPS), October 1997 and October 2003, unpublished tabulations. (This table was prepared August 2004.)

Table 430. Number and percentage of student home computer users, by type of application and selected characteristics: 2003

Selected characteristic of students	Number (in thousands)	Number using computers at home (in thousands)	Percent using computers at home	Percent of home computer users using specific applications[1]							
				Games	Internet	School assignments	E-mail	Word processing	Graphics and design	Spreadsheets and databases	Personal finances
1	2	3	4	5	6	7	8	9	10	11	12
Total, all students	74,911 (312.9)	52,942 (286.3)	70.7 (0.24)	76.2 (0.27)	72.3 (0.28)	75.9 (0.27)	56.5 (0.31)	55.1 (0.32)	— (†)	— (†)	— (†)
Elementary/secondary	58,273 (324.9)	39,364 (282.0)	67.6 (0.30)	82.8 (0.30)	66.0 (0.37)	69.9 (0.36)	46.2 (0.39)	46.8 (0.39)	— (†)	— (†)	— (†)
Under age 5	4,590 (105.0)	2,291 (74.6)	49.9 (1.16)	84.3 (1.19)	29.2 (1.49)	15.1 (1.17)	8.9 (0.93)	9.4 (0.96)	— (†)	— (†)	— (†)
Ages 5 to 9	19,015 (206.6)	11,887 (166.1)	62.5 (0.55)	87.6 (0.47)	45.9 (0.72)	42.0 (0.71)	18.8 (0.56)	22.6 (0.60)	— (†)	— (†)	— (†)
Ages 10 to 14	20,788 (215.0)	14,875 (184.5)	71.6 (0.49)	85.3 (0.45)	74.1 (0.56)	85.1 (0.46)	53.0 (0.64)	56.5 (0.64)	— (†)	— (†)	— (†)
15 years old or over	13,880 (165.7)	10,311 (144.2)	74.3 (0.54)	73.4 (0.64)	85.8 (0.50)	92.4 (0.38)	76.3 (0.61)	69.1 (0.66)	43.1 (0.71)	21.1 (0.59)	4.5 (0.30)
White	8,500 (131.6)	7,186 (121.4)	84.5 (0.57)	75.3 (0.74)	90.2 (0.51)	93.3 (0.43)	81.5 (0.67)	72.1 (0.77)	46.3 (0.86)	22.1 (0.71)	4.7 (0.36)
Black	2,164 (68.8)	1,073 (49.7)	49.6 (1.67)	73.5 (2.09)	73.6 (2.09)	90.3 (1.40)	60.7 (2.31)	59.0 (2.33)	38.9 (2.31)	15.9 (1.73)	3.5 (0.88)
Hispanic	2,298 (75.0)	1,280 (57.5)	55.7 (1.72)	68.2 (2.16)	72.0 (2.08)	87.8 (1.51)	60.8 (2.26)	59.9 (2.27)	30.0 (2.12)	18.2 (1.78)	6.1 (1.11)
Other	918 (45.9)	771 (42.2)	83.9 (1.88)	64.5 (2.68)	83.7 (2.07)	94.3 (1.30)	75.3 (2.41)	69.9 (2.57)	41.4 (2.75)	24.2 (2.40)	2.2 (0.82)
Undergraduate	13,370 (162.9)	10,701 (146.8)	80.0 (0.50)	60.5 (0.69)	89.6 (0.43)	92.8 (0.37)	84.8 (0.51)	77.1 (0.59)	46.5 (0.70)	36.8 (0.68)	21.4 (0.58)
White	8,964 (135.0)	7,551 (124.4)	84.2 (0.56)	60.8 (0.82)	91.1 (0.48)	93.0 (0.43)	86.5 (0.57)	78.7 (0.69)	48.9 (0.84)	37.8 (0.81)	21.1 (0.69)
Black	1,766 (62.8)	1,151 (51.4)	65.2 (1.76)	62.1 (2.22)	83.2 (1.71)	91.1 (1.30)	77.0 (1.93)	72.4 (2.05)	37.7 (2.22)	32.0 (2.13)	23.0 (1.93)
Hispanic	1,544 (62.7)	1,102 (53.6)	71.4 (1.91)	56.8 (2.47)	86.7 (1.69)	92.1 (1.34)	80.5 (1.98)	68.6 (2.32)	38.8 (2.43)	33.4 (2.35)	19.8 (1.99)
Other	1,095 (49.9)	898 (45.4)	82.0 (1.80)	61.5 (2.52)	89.5 (1.59)	94.0 (1.23)	86.3 (1.78)	80.3 (2.06)	47.3 (2.59)	39.4 (2.53)	23.7 (2.20)
Graduate	3,268 (66.0)	2,876 (64.1)	88.0 (0.83)	43.6 (1.35)	93.7 (0.66)	94.6 (0.61)	91.7 (0.75)	86.1 (0.94)	52.2 (1.36)	56.2 (1.35)	45.4 (1.36)
Males	37,323 (253.4)	26,168 (219.6)	70.1 (0.35)	80.1 (0.36)	71.2 (0.41)	73.9 (0.40)	53.0 (0.45)	51.7 (0.45)	— (†)	— (†)	— (†)
Elementary/secondary	30,005 (252.4)	20,050 (211.6)	66.8 (0.43)	84.9 (0.40)	65.3 (0.53)	68.3 (0.51)	43.1 (0.55)	44.2 (0.55)	— (†)	— (†)	— (†)
Under age 5	2,437 (76.9)	1,222 (54.6)	50.2 (1.59)	85.3 (1.59)	30.3 (2.06)	14.9 (1.60)	10.7 (1.38)	9.1 (1.29)	— (†)	— (†)	— (†)
Ages 5 to 9	9,703 (150.9)	6,060 (120.3)	62.5 (0.77)	88.5 (0.64)	44.6 (1.00)	40.7 (0.99)	16.6 (0.75)	20.9 (0.82)	— (†)	— (†)	— (†)
Ages 10 to 14	10,622 (157.5)	7,453 (132.9)	70.2 (0.70)	87.5 (0.60)	73.9 (0.80)	83.3 (0.68)	48.0 (0.91)	53.0 (0.91)	— (†)	— (†)	— (†)
15 years old or over	7,243 (121.9)	5,313 (104.9)	73.4 (0.76)	77.1 (0.84)	84.8 (0.72)	90.9 (0.58)	73.8 (0.88)	66.4 (0.95)	43.3 (0.99)	21.0 (0.82)	4.2 (0.40)
Undergraduate	5,902 (110.4)	4,859 (100.5)	82.3 (0.72)	68.6 (0.97)	89.7 (0.64)	91.7 (0.58)	84.0 (0.77)	75.1 (0.91)	50.2 (1.05)	37.6 (1.01)	22.3 (0.87)
Graduate	1,416 (54.7)	1,259 (51.6)	88.9 (1.22)	48.9 (2.06)	93.8 (0.99)	94.1 (0.97)	91.6 (1.14)	81.2 (1.61)	53.0 (2.05)	58.3 (2.03)	46.9 (2.05)
Females	37,588 (254.1)	26,774 (221.7)	71.2 (0.34)	72.3 (0.40)	73.4 (0.39)	77.8 (0.37)	59.8 (0.44)	58.4 (0.44)	— (†)	— (†)	— (†)
Elementary/secondary	28,269 (246.1)	19,315 (208.0)	68.3 (0.43)	80.7 (0.45)	66.8 (0.53)	71.6 (0.51)	49.4 (0.56)	49.5 (0.56)	— (†)	— (†)	— (†)
Under age 5	2,154 (72.3)	1,069 (51.1)	49.6 (1.69)	83.2 (1.79)	28.0 (2.15)	15.3 (1.72)	6.8 (1.21)	9.8 (1.43)	— (†)	— (†)	— (†)
Ages 5 to 9	9,312 (147.9)	5,827 (118.0)	62.6 (0.79)	86.7 (0.70)	47.1 (1.02)	43.3 (1.02)	21.0 (0.84)	24.4 (0.88)	— (†)	— (†)	— (†)
Ages 10 to 14	10,166 (154.3)	7,422 (132.7)	73.0 (0.69)	83.1 (0.68)	74.4 (0.79)	86.8 (0.62)	57.9 (0.90)	60.0 (0.89)	— (†)	— (†)	— (†)
15 years old or over	6,637 (116.9)	4,997 (101.9)	75.3 (0.77)	69.6 (0.95)	86.7 (0.70)	94.0 (0.49)	78.9 (0.84)	71.8 (0.93)	42.9 (1.02)	21.3 (0.85)	4.9 (0.45)
Undergraduate	7,468 (123.7)	5,842 (109.9)	78.2 (0.70)	53.9 (0.95)	89.6 (0.58)	93.7 (0.47)	85.5 (0.67)	78.8 (0.78)	43.4 (0.95)	36.2 (0.92)	20.6 (0.77)
Graduate	1,852 (62.5)	1,617 (58.5)	87.3 (1.13)	39.5 (1.77)	93.5 (0.89)	95.1 (0.78)	91.8 (0.99)	90.0 (1.09)	51.5 (1.81)	54.5 (1.81)	44.3 (1.80)

—Not available.
†Not applicable.
[1]Individuals may be counted in more than one computer activity.

NOTE: Estimates as of October 1. Race categories exclude persons of Hispanic ethnicity. Detail may not sum to totals because of rounding. Standard errors appear in parentheses.
SOURCE: U.S. Department of Commerce, Census Bureau, Current Population Survey (CPS), October 2003, unpublished tabulations. (This table was prepared May 2005.)

Table 431. Student use of computers, by level of enrollment, age, and student and school characteristics: 1993, 1997, and 2003

Student and school characteristic	1993 Total	1993 Elementary and secondary[1]	1993 College[2]	1997 Total	1997 Elementary and secondary[1]	1997 College[2]	2003 Total	2003 Elementary and secondary[1] Total	2003 Under 5 years old	2003 5 to 9 years old	2003 10 to 14 years old	2003 15 years old or over	2003 College[2]
1	2	3	4	5	6	7	8	9	10	11	12	13	14
Percent of students using computers at school													
Total	59.0 (0.32)	60.1 (0.38)	54.7 (0.71)	68.8 (0.27)	70.4 (0.32)	62.9 (0.60)	83.8 (0.20)	83.5 (0.24)	42.6 (1.14)	80.1 (0.45)	90.3 (0.32)	91.2 (0.35)	84.9 (0.41)
Sex													
Male	59.4 (0.44)	59.9 (0.53)	57.4 (1.04)	70.1 (0.37)	71.0 (0.44)	66.3 (0.88)	83.7 (0.28)	83.4 (0.34)	43.5 (1.57)	79.7 (0.64)	90.1 (0.45)	91.8 (0.47)	85.3 (0.60)
Female	58.7 (0.45)	60.5 (0.54)	52.4 (0.96)	67.6 (0.38)	69.9 (0.46)	60.2 (0.81)	83.8 (0.28)	83.5 (0.35)	41.5 (1.66)	80.7 (0.64)	90.6 (0.45)	90.5 (0.53)	84.6 (0.55)
Race/ethnicity													
White	61.6 (0.37)	63.8 (0.45)	54.0 (0.81)	71.1 (0.32)	73.9 (0.38)	62.1 (0.70)	85.0 (0.24)	84.9 (0.30)	41.1 (1.44)	82.5 (0.56)	92.4 (0.37)	91.9 (0.43)	85.0 (0.49)
Black	51.5 (0.98)	50.6 (0.98)	57.0 (2.54)	66.3 (0.74)	66.1 (0.75)	66.8 (1.78)	82.7 (0.56)	82.5 (0.67)	49.4 (3.18)	78.5 (1.30)	88.0 (0.95)	89.9 (1.01)	83.8 (1.25)
Hispanic	52.3 (1.50)	52.3 (1.16)	52.1 (4.06)	61.5 (0.89)	61.3 (0.69)	62.6 (2.38)	80.3 (0.60)	80.3 (0.71)	39.5 (3.22)	75.6 (1.27)	86.8 (1.01)	88.5 (1.10)	83.0 (1.50)
Other	59.0 (2.24)	57.7 (2.50)	62.7 (4.20)	65.3 (1.32)	65.6 (1.45)	64.6 (2.56)	83.3 (0.77)	81.7 (1.01)	48.9 (4.78)	76.3 (1.89)	86.1 (1.54)	94.1 (1.20)	87.6 (1.30)
Family income[3]													
Less than $5,000	51.2 (1.32)	48.1 (1.50)	62.4 (2.73)	62.1 (1.21)	61.6 (1.41)	63.4 (2.36)	80.9 (1.87)	79.5 (2.31)	42.4 (9.47)	78.3 (3.82)	86.9 (3.39)	86.5 (4.37)	83.8 (3.12)
$5,000 to $9,999	53.3 (1.06)	53.1 (1.17)	54.3 (2.51)	63.5 (1.02)	61.9 (1.14)	70.4 (2.20)	84.4 (1.43)	82.4 (1.74)	49.2 (7.71)	77.8 (3.30)	91.3 (2.18)	88.3 (3.04)	90.1 (2.35)
$10,000 to $14,999	56.4 (1.03)	56.7 (1.13)	55.1 (2.50)	66.2 (0.96)	64.4 (1.06)	65.2 (2.26)	81.7 (1.37)	80.0 (1.61)	50.1 (7.20)	74.1 (3.11)	84.6 (2.41)	90.4 (2.40)	88.0 (2.48)
$15,000 to $19,999	58.1 (1.18)	59.4 (1.30)	52.3 (2.77)	65.9 (1.10)	66.5 (1.21)	63.2 (2.72)	81.3 (1.57)	79.8 (1.84)	26.6 (7.08)	77.0 (3.27)	89.1 (2.38)	89.2 (3.09)	86.7 (2.92)
$20,000 to $24,999	56.4 (1.07)	56.3 (1.18)	56.6 (2.58)	66.9 (0.99)	67.5 (1.10)	64.3 (2.24)	81.3 (1.41)	80.3 (1.61)	43.7 (7.03)	73.0 (3.00)	88.9 (2.16)	92.6 (2.31)	85.3 (2.81)
$25,000 to $29,999	60.0 (1.13)	61.9 (1.25)	52.4 (2.61)	68.5 (1.01)	70.4 (1.11)	61.2 (2.37)	81.9 (1.32)	81.3 (1.48)	35.6 (7.03)	78.0 (2.66)	87.0 (2.21)	90.8 (2.21)	84.4 (2.90)
$30,000 to $34,999	59.1 (1.08)	61.3 (1.20)	50.5 (2.46)	67.6 (0.97)	71.0 (1.05)	53.9 (2.31)	82.2 (1.33)	82.5 (1.46)	40.1 (7.16)	78.5 (2.67)	90.6 (1.86)	88.8 (2.59)	80.9 (3.17)
$35,000 to $39,999	60.7 (1.11)	63.3 (1.21)	49.0 (2.67)	69.0 (0.98)	71.1 (1.08)	60.4 (2.35)	87.1 (1.17)	87.5 (1.30)	54.8 (7.43)	85.2 (2.37)	94.0 (1.53)	90.4 (2.48)	85.7 (2.69)
$40,000 to $49,999	59.3 (0.94)	60.8 (1.04)	53.1 (2.12)	70.5 (0.79)	72.6 (0.85)	60.9 (1.99)	83.5 (1.08)	84.2 (1.18)	47.1 (6.20)	80.0 (2.29)	90.8 (1.56)	90.3 (1.94)	80.4 (2.63)
$50,000 to $74,999	62.6 (0.73)	64.9 (0.82)	55.0 (1.58)	71.7 (0.57)	74.2 (0.63)	63.2 (1.28)	83.8 (0.71)	84.0 (0.80)	35.7 (3.64)	80.5 (1.53)	92.6 (0.94)	92.4 (1.21)	83.1 (1.56)
$75,000 or more	64.6 (0.90)	67.0 (1.04)	58.2 (1.78)	72.1 (0.60)	75.1 (0.68)	63.9 (1.25)	85.6 (0.57)	85.6 (0.65)	39.2 (2.98)	85.3 (1.15)	92.7 (0.81)	93.2 (0.96)	85.8 (1.16)
Control of school													
Public	60.2 (0.34)	61.6 (0.40)	54.0 (0.80)	70.2 (0.28)	72.1 (0.33)	62.3 (0.68)	85.2 (0.21)	85.4 (0.25)	47.7 (1.61)	80.5 (0.48)	90.5 (0.34)	91.2 (0.36)	84.6 (0.46)
Private	52.1 (0.85)	49.8 (1.10)	57.3 (1.52)	60.7 (0.73)	58.6 (0.96)	65.2 (1.27)	75.4 (0.60)	70.5 (0.82)	37.1 (1.61)	77.5 (1.33)	89.1 (1.09)	90.5 (1.36)	86.1 (0.85)
Percent of students using computers at home													
Total	27.0 (0.28)	24.5 (0.33)	36.2 (0.65)	45.1 (0.29)	42.8 (0.34)	53.2 (0.62)	70.7 (0.24)	67.6 (0.30)	49.9 (1.16)	62.5 (0.55)	71.6 (0.49)	74.3 (0.54)	81.6 (0.44)
Sex													
Male	27.4 (0.39)	24.3 (0.45)	40.1 (0.99)	45.2 (0.40)	43.2 (0.48)	53.7 (0.93)	70.1 (0.35)	66.8 (0.43)	50.2 (1.59)	62.5 (0.77)	70.2 (0.70)	73.4 (0.76)	83.6 (0.63)
Female	26.6 (0.39)	24.7 (0.47)	33.0 (0.87)	44.9 (0.40)	42.5 (0.49)	52.8 (0.83)	71.2 (0.34)	68.3 (0.43)	49.6 (1.69)	62.6 (0.79)	73.0 (0.69)	75.3 (0.77)	80.0 (0.60)
Race/ethnicity													
White	32.8 (0.35)	30.8 (0.42)	39.2 (0.76)	54.9 (0.35)	53.9 (0.43)	58.2 (0.72)	80.1 (0.27)	78.3 (0.34)	59.6 (1.43)	74.6 (0.64)	81.8 (0.54)	84.5 (0.57)	85.4 (0.49)
Black	10.9 (0.59)	8.7 (0.54)	22.7 (2.01)	21.1 (0.64)	19.1 (0.62)	31.0 (1.75)	50.2 (0.74)	46.2 (0.88)	31.7 (2.96)	41.6 (1.55)	50.8 (1.46)	49.6 (1.67)	67.5 (1.59)
Hispanic	10.4 (0.90)	7.9 (0.62)	25.0 (3.31)	21.1 (0.74)	18.3 (0.54)	38.8 (2.40)	51.1 (0.76)	47.5 (0.88)	25.8 (2.88)	41.7 (1.46)	52.5 (1.48)	55.7 (1.72)	72.5 (1.79)
Other	28.7 (2.00)	25.8 (2.16)	36.0 (3.99)	49.1 (1.38)	46.5 (1.52)	56.3 (2.66)	74.6 (0.91)	71.3 (1.19)	57.5 (4.73)	61.6 (2.16)	75.7 (1.90)	83.9 (1.88)	83.1 (1.48)

See notes at end of table.

Table 431. Student use of computers, by level of enrollment, age, and student and school characteristics: 1993, 1997, and 2003—Continued

Columns are numbered 1–14. Year groups: 1993 (cols 2–4), 1997 (cols 5–7), 2003 (cols 8–14). Under each of 1993 and 1997: Total, Elementary and secondary, College. Under 2003: Total (col 8); Elementary and secondary — Total (col 9), Under 5 years old (col 10), 5 to 9 years old (col 11), 10 to 14 years old (col 12), 15 years old or over (col 13); College (col 14). Standard errors in parentheses.

Student and school characteristic (1)	1993 Total (2)	1993 Elem. & sec. (3)	1993 College (4)	1997 Total (5)	1997 Elem. & sec. (6)	1997 College (7)	2003 Total (8)	2003 E&S Total (9)	2003 Under 5 (10)	2003 5 to 9 (11)	2003 10 to 14 (12)	2003 15 & over (13)	2003 College (14)
Family income³													
Less than $5,000	9.7 (0.76)	4.3 (0.59)	28.3 (2.43)	22.6 (1.04)	15.2 (1.04)	43.7 (2.43)	44.1 (2.36)	29.8 (2.62)	20.5 (7.74)	29.9 (4.24)	29.5 (4.58)	34.2 (6.07)	75.2 (3.65)
$5,000 to $9,999	8.0 (0.56)	4.2 (0.46)	25.0 (2.08)	15.8 (0.77)	9.3 (0.68)	42.9 (2.39)	47.0 (1.97)	36.6 (2.20)	31.0 (7.14)	30.7 (3.66)	41.3 (3.82)	40.1 (4.65)	77.7 (3.27)
$10,000 to $14,999	11.4 (0.64)	6.7 (0.56)	33.4 (2.26)	18.4 (0.78)	13.6 (0.77)	39.7 (2.32)	47.0 (1.77)	39.3 (1.96)	36.4 (6.93)	32.8 (3.33)	43.2 (3.31)	42.9 (4.03)	75.2 (3.30)
$15,000 to $19,999	15.1 (0.84)	11.2 (0.82)	31.0 (2.44)	20.7 (0.94)	16.5 (0.95)	41.2 (2.77)	48.3 (2.02)	40.8 (2.25)	16.5 (5.95)	33.4 (3.67)	49.1 (3.82)	48.4 (4.97)	74.6 (3.73)
$20,000 to $24,999	16.8 (0.79)	13.6 (0.80)	31.0 (2.27)	30.5 (0.97)	26.2 (1.04)	47.5 (2.34)	53.1 (1.80)	46.6 (2.02)	27.1 (6.29)	41.1 (3.33)	52.5 (3.43)	53.9 (4.39)	77.8 (3.29)
$25,000 to $29,999	21.1 (0.92)	19.1 (0.99)	29.0 (2.28)	34.6 (1.03)	32.0 (1.13)	45.0 (2.42)	59.0 (1.69)	54.7 (1.89)	40.6 (7.21)	47.7 (3.21)	59.5 (3.22)	61.9 (3.72)	78.3 (3.30)
$30,000 to $34,999	24.1 (0.92)	22.6 (1.02)	29.7 (2.15)	38.7 (1.01)	36.1 (1.11)	49.2 (2.32)	64.2 (1.66)	54.7 (1.87)	41.4 (7.19)	54.7 (3.23)	64.9 (3.04)	72.9 (3.66)	76.1 (3.43)
$35,000 to $39,999	27.1 (0.99)	24.9 (1.08)	36.1 (2.44)	44.1 (1.06)	42.6 (1.17)	50.5 (2.40)	67.8 (1.83)	70.0 (1.60)	49.0 (7.46)	63.0 (3.23)	71.9 (2.91)	74.6 (3.66)	78.5 (3.16)
$40,000 to $49,999	32.2 (0.87)	31.6 (0.98)	34.4 (1.92)	50.6 (0.86)	50.4 (0.95)	51.7 (2.04)	73.4 (1.43)	75.9 (1.43)	54.6 (6.18)	68.9 (2.65)	77.5 (2.24)	78.2 (2.70)	86.6 (2.26)
$50,000 to $74,999	43.0 (0.74)	42.9 (0.84)	43.5 (1.52)	61.7 (0.62)	62.2 (0.70)	59.9 (1.30)	79.5 (0.88)	81.3 (0.75)	58.9 (3.74)	74.9 (1.67)	83.8 (1.33)	86.5 (1.56)	87.8 (1.36)
$75,000 or more	56.1 (0.92)	58.1 (1.08)	50.9 (1.74)	74.2 (0.59)	77.2 (0.66)	65.8 (1.23)	87.6 (0.61)	88.6 (0.51)	66.1 (2.89)	85.3 (1.15)	91.0 (0.89)	94.1 (0.90)	91.7 (0.92)
Control of school													
Public	25.3 (0.29)	23.0 (0.34)	34.5 (0.73)	43.2 (0.31)	40.9 (0.37)	52.4 (0.70)	66.3 (0.33)	69.3 (0.77)	41.1 (1.58)	60.4 (0.59)	70.1 (0.52)	73.1 (0.57)	80.9 (0.50)
Private	37.4 (0.80)	35.0 (1.03)	42.5 (1.45)	56.1 (0.75)	56.1 (0.97)	56.1 (1.32)	75.6 (0.77)	78.3 (0.57)	59.3 (1.63)	77.3 (1.34)	84.7 (1.26)	89.3 (1.43)	84.1 (0.90)
Percent of students using computers at home for school work													
Total	**14.8 (0.22)**	**12.0 (0.25)**	**25.0 (0.59)**	**28.6 (0.26)**	**24.8 (0.30)**	**42.5 (0.61)**	**47.2 (0.32)**	**53.6 (0.27)**	**7.5 (0.61)**	**26.2 (0.50)**	**60.9 (0.53)**	**68.6 (0.57)**	**76.0 (0.48)**
Sex													
Male	14.7 (0.31)	11.4 (0.34)	28.2 (0.91)	28.3 (0.37)	24.7 (0.42)	43.3 (0.92)	45.6 (0.45)	51.8 (0.38)	7.5 (0.83)	25.4 (0.69)	58.5 (0.75)	66.7 (0.81)	77.1 (0.72)
Female	14.8 (0.32)	12.5 (0.36)	22.4 (0.77)	28.9 (0.37)	24.9 (0.43)	41.9 (0.82)	48.9 (0.47)	55.4 (0.37)	7.6 (0.89)	27.1 (0.72)	63.4 (0.75)	70.8 (0.82)	75.2 (0.65)
Race													
White	18.0 (0.29)	15.1 (0.33)	27.4 (0.70)	35.0 (0.34)	31.3 (0.40)	47.0 (0.72)	54.1 (0.42)	60.4 (0.33)	7.3 (0.76)	29.1 (0.67)	70.5 (0.64)	78.9 (0.65)	79.8 (0.55)
Black	5.7 (0.44)	4.3 (0.39)	13.4 (1.64)	12.5 (0.51)	10.4 (0.48)	22.8 (1.59)	34.6 (0.84)	39.8 (0.73)	8.2 (1.75)	22.5 (1.32)	43.7 (1.45)	44.8 (1.66)	62.2 (1.65)
Hispanic	5.6 (0.68)	3.6 (0.42)	17.8 (2.92)	12.5 (0.60)	9.8 (0.42)	29.2 (2.24)	33.5 (0.83)	38.3 (0.74)	6.7 (1.65)	20.2 (1.19)	42.6 (1.47)	48.9 (1.73)	66.7 (1.89)
Other	15.8 (1.61)	12.4 (1.63)	24.5 (3.57)	33.6 (1.31)	29.3 (1.39)	45.3 (2.67)	49.4 (1.31)	57.2 (1.03)	10.3 (2.91)	26.8 (1.97)	60.9 (2.16)	79.1 (2.08)	77.8 (1.65)
Family income³													
Less than $5,000	6.6 (0.64)	2.4 (0.45)	21.1 (2.20)	15.1 (0.89)	8.0 (0.79)	35.5 (2.35)	36.5 (2.27)	19.4 (2.27)	4.2 (3.83)	14.4 (3.25)	22.7 (4.21)	30.4 (5.88)	73.8 (3.72)
$5,000 to $9,999	4.7 (0.44)	1.5 (0.28)	18.8 (1.88)	10.4 (0.65)	4.2 (0.47)	36.5 (2.32)	36.5 (1.96)	24.1 (1.96)	4.0 (3.01)	14.0 (2.75)	32.3 (3.62)	34.1 (4.49)	72.8 (3.49)
$10,000 to $14,999	7.2 (0.52)	3.0 (0.38)	27.1 (2.14)	11.4 (0.64)	6.7 (0.56)	32.4 (2.22)	36.9 (1.71)	27.1 (1.78)	14.3 (5.04)	14.4 (2.49)	34.6 (3.18)	36.8 (3.93)	72.2 (3.42)
$15,000 to $19,999	8.5 (0.65)	5.6 (0.60)	20.5 (2.12)	13.2 (0.79)	8.5 (0.72)	36.0 (2.70)	37.2 (1.95)	27.4 (2.04)	0.7 (1.36)	10.8 (2.42)	40.2 (3.75)	42.9 (4.92)	71.5 (3.87)
$20,000 to $24,999	9.7 (0.62)	6.3 (0.57)	24.5 (2.11)	19.4 (0.83)	15.0 (0.84)	37.1 (2.26)	40.5 (1.77)	31.9 (1.89)	8.2 (3.89)	18.9 (2.65)	40.7 (3.38)	48.8 (4.40)	73.4 (3.50)
$25,000 to $29,999	10.3 (0.69)	7.5 (0.66)	21.4 (2.06)	21.9 (0.90)	18.4 (0.94)	35.7 (2.33)	43.4 (1.70)	36.9 (1.84)	8.3 (4.05)	18.0 (2.47)	48.9 (3.28)	55.2 (3.81)	72.2 (3.58)
$30,000 to $34,999	12.9 (0.72)	10.8 (0.75)	20.8 (1.91)	24.4 (0.89)	20.3 (0.93)	40.5 (2.28)	46.8 (1.73)	41.8 (1.89)	8.8 (4.13)	20.4 (2.61)	55.4 (3.17)	64.1 (3.95)	69.0 (3.73)
$35,000 to $39,999	15.2 (0.80)	12.9 (0.83)	24.6 (2.20)	26.5 (0.94)	22.8 (0.99)	41.7 (2.37)	50.9 (1.96)	45.5 (1.96)	7.0 (3.82)	25.9 (2.93)	58.4 (3.19)	66.7 (3.96)	71.8 (3.46)
$40,000 to $49,999	17.1 (0.70)	15.4 (0.76)	23.3 (1.71)	30.1 (0.79)	28.3 (0.86)	38.5 (1.99)	56.9 (1.62)	51.6 (1.62)	12.9 (4.16)	26.3 (2.52)	67.6 (2.51)	71.4 (2.95)	79.0 (2.70)
$50,000 to $74,999	23.1 (0.63)	21.4 (0.70)	28.7 (1.38)	39.3 (0.62)	36.7 (0.70)	48.2 (1.32)	60.9 (1.09)	55.0 (1.09)	4.8 (1.63)	30.2 (1.77)	71.6 (1.62)	81.0 (1.79)	82.4 (1.58)
$75,000 or more	30.2 (0.85)	29.5 (1.00)	32.0 (1.63)	48.3 (0.67)	47.3 (0.78)	51.3 (1.30)	62.8 (0.89)	68.2 (0.75)	6.5 (1.51)	36.2 (1.56)	83.6 (1.15)	90.0 (1.14)	85.7 (1.16)
Control of school													
Public	14.1 (0.24)	11.7 (0.26)	24.1 (0.66)	27.9 (0.28)	24.5 (0.32)	41.9 (0.69)	47.8 (0.35)	53.4 (0.29)	8.0 (0.87)	25.4 (0.53)	59.2 (0.56)	67.5 (0.60)	75.1 (0.55)
Private	18.5 (0.65)	13.8 (0.75)	28.5 (1.33)	32.6 (0.70)	26.9 (0.87)	44.6 (1.32)	43.3 (0.89)	54.7 (0.69)	7.1 (0.85)	32.3 (1.50)	76.5 (1.48)	83.3 (1.73)	79.3 (1.00)

¹Includes students enrolled in prekindergarten through grade 12, ages 3 and above.
²Includes students enrolled at the undergraduate and postbaccalaureate levels.
³Excludes persons whose income data were not available.

NOTE: Data are based on a sample survey of households and are subject to sampling and nonsampling error. Race categories exclude persons of Hispanic ethnicity. Standard errors appear in parentheses.
SOURCE: U.S. Department of Commerce, Census Bureau, Current Population Survey (CPS), October 1993, October 1997, and October 2003, unpublished tabulations. (This table was prepared May 2005.)

Table 432. Percentage of workers, 18 years old and over, using computers on the job, by type of computer application and selected characteristics: 1993, 1997, and 2003

| | | | 2003 | | | | | | | | | |
| | | | | | Percent of on-the-job computer users using specific computer applications[1] | | | | | | | |
Selected characteristic	Percent using computers at work, 1993	Percent using computers at work, 1997	Percent using computers at work	Number using computers at work (in thousands)	Spreadsheets/ databases	Internet/e-mail	Calendar/ schedule	Graphics/design	Programming	Word processing/ desktop publishing	Other uses only	Using 4 or more categories
1	2	3	4	5	6	7	8	9	10	11	12	13
Total	**45.8**	**49.4** (0.24)	**56.1** (0.19)	**76,570**	**64.4** (0.30)	**75.4** (0.27)	**57.0** (0.31)	**29.7** (0.29)	**16.4** (0.23)	**67.8** (0.29)	**8.2** (0.17)	**45.3** (0.31)
Age												
18 to 24	34.4	37.1 (0.66)	38.5 (0.55)	6,575	56.0 (1.06)	62.1 (1.03)	48.9 (1.07)	21.7 (0.88)	12.4 (0.70)	57.9 (1.05)	14.2 (0.74)	33.0 (1.00)
25 to 29	48.3	52.5 (0.70)	56.9 (0.57)	8,203	66.2 (0.90)	75.6 (0.82)	58.3 (0.94)	30.3 (0.88)	18.8 (0.75)	67.8 (0.89)	8.5 (0.53)	47.2 (0.95)
30 to 39	50.7	53.3 (0.46)	59.0 (0.37)	19,225	68.0 (0.58)	78.3 (0.51)	61.8 (0.61)	31.7 (0.58)	18.0 (0.48)	69.8 (0.57)	6.8 (0.31)	49.6 (0.62)
40 to 49	51.3	54.9 (0.47)	60.3 (0.35)	21,772	66.9 (0.55)	77.1 (0.49)	59.0 (0.58)	31.8 (0.55)	17.7 (0.45)	69.7 (0.54)	7.1 (0.30)	48.4 (0.59)
50 to 59	43.9	50.7 (0.61)	60.1 (0.42)	15,423	62.5 (0.67)	76.5 (0.59)	54.6 (0.69)	29.7 (0.64)	15.1 (0.50)	68.1 (0.65)	8.0 (0.38)	43.7 (0.69)
60 or older	27.2	32.6 (0.88)	48.5 (0.67)	5,373	53.8 (1.18)	71.2 (1.07)	46.1 (1.18)	23.5 (1.00)	10.6 (0.72)	63.7 (1.13)	11.1 (0.74)	35.0 (1.12)
Educational attainment and sex												
Not high school completer	10.0	11.9 (0.48)	15.6 (0.50)	2,149	44.1 (1.85)	49.7 (1.86)	40.4 (1.83)	15.3 (1.34)	11.7 (1.20)	43.2 (1.85)	21.6 (1.53)	21.4 (1.53)
High school completer	34.2	36.4 (0.40)	40.4 (0.35)	16,914	53.3 (0.66)	61.4 (0.65)	47.7 (0.66)	18.5 (0.52)	11.8 (0.43)	52.4 (0.66)	14.6 (0.47)	29.3 (0.60)
Some college	50.4	53.6 (0.53)	55.7 (0.42)	15,060	61.5 (0.68)	70.2 (0.64)	53.6 (0.70)	25.3 (0.61)	14.5 (0.50)	62.5 (0.68)	10.0 (0.42)	39.6 (0.69)
Associate's degree	58.2	60.7 (0.81)	62.9 (0.59)	7,813	61.1 (0.95)	71.7 (0.88)	54.4 (0.97)	26.1 (0.86)	15.4 (0.71)	62.6 (0.95)	9.9 (0.58)	39.8 (0.96)
Bachelor's degree	68.8	73.9 (0.50)	82.0 (0.30)	22,540	73.3 (0.51)	85.6 (0.40)	64.2 (0.55)	37.4 (0.56)	20.1 (0.46)	78.0 (0.48)	3.7 (0.22)	57.3 (0.57)
Master's degree	71.2	78.7 (0.81)	87.2 (0.43)	8,292	73.8 (0.83)	90.0 (0.57)	64.9 (0.91)	43.3 (0.94)	20.4 (0.77)	85.6 (0.67)	1.8 (0.25)	62.2 (0.92)
Doctor's or professional degree	66.9	74.6 (1.24)	85.4 (0.67)	3,803	68.8 (1.30)	88.0 (0.91)	66.1 (1.33)	37.5 (1.36)	19.3 (1.11)	81.7 (1.08)	2.9 (0.47)	56.9 (1.39)
Male	40.3	44.1 (0.31)	50.5 (0.25)	36,976	67.2 (0.42)	77.7 (0.37)	58.6 (0.44)	33.8 (0.42)	21.4 (0.37)	65.6 (0.43)	7.8 (0.24)	48.8 (0.45)
Not high school completer	8.5	9.8 (0.53)	12.5 (0.55)	1,095	44.4 (2.59)	48.7 (2.61)	39.4 (2.55)	18.2 (2.01)	13.6 (1.79)	39.7 (2.56)	23.3 (2.21)	20.5 (2.11)
High school completer	24.2	27.1 (0.49)	31.9 (0.45)	7,305	52.1 (1.01)	60.1 (0.99)	45.0 (1.01)	21.6 (0.83)	14.9 (0.72)	45.0 (1.01)	16.1 (0.74)	28.3 (0.91)
Some college	42.8	46.0 (0.71)	49.2 (0.58)	6,718	62.0 (1.02)	71.4 (0.95)	53.0 (1.05)	29.3 (0.96)	18.7 (0.82)	58.2 (1.04)	10.6 (0.65)	40.8 (1.04)
Associate's degree	52.6	55.2 (1.16)	56.9 (0.86)	3,326	64.8 (1.43)	74.1 (1.31)	53.5 (1.49)	33.2 (1.41)	22.1 (1.24)	60.5 (1.46)	9.9 (0.90)	43.7 (1.49)
Bachelor's degree	69.8	74.3 (0.65)	82.5 (0.39)	11,787	77.6 (0.66)	88.4 (0.51)	68.0 (0.74)	40.4 (0.78)	25.6 (0.69)	76.9 (0.67)	2.6 (0.25)	61.7 (0.77)
Master's degree	75.4	79.8 (1.05)	88.0 (0.57)	4,186	78.7 (1.09)	92.1 (0.72)	69.0 (1.23)	44.9 (1.33)	26.8 (1.18)	83.5 (0.99)	1.3 (0.31)	66.2 (1.26)
Doctor's or professional degree	66.5	73.4 (1.43)	85.5 (0.78)	2,559	70.9 (1.55)	88.9 (1.08)	66.5 (1.61)	38.7 (1.66)	21.7 (1.41)	80.1 (1.36)	2.5 (0.53)	58.5 (1.68)
Female	52.4	56.5 (0.32)	62.5 (0.24)	39,594	61.7 (0.42)	73.3 (0.38)	55.5 (0.43)	26.0 (0.38)	11.8 (0.28)	69.8 (0.40)	8.6 (0.24)	42.2 (0.43)
Not high school completer	12.5	15.4 (0.80)	21.0 (0.83)	1,054	43.7 (2.64)	50.7 (2.66)	41.4 (2.62)	12.4 (1.75)	9.7 (1.58)	46.8 (2.66)	19.8 (2.12)	22.3 (2.21)
High school completer	45.2	46.9 (0.56)	50.7 (0.47)	9,609	54.2 (0.88)	62.4 (0.85)	49.7 (0.88)	16.2 (0.65)	9.5 (0.52)	58.0 (0.87)	13.4 (0.60)	30.1 (0.81)
Some college	58.6	61.5 (0.68)	62.4 (0.52)	8,341	61.2 (0.92)	69.3 (0.87)	54.2 (0.94)	22.2 (0.79)	11.1 (0.59)	66.0 (0.90)	9.6 (0.56)	38.5 (0.92)
Associate's degree	63.7	65.4 (0.99)	68.3 (0.70)	4,487	58.4 (1.27)	70.0 (1.18)	55.1 (1.28)	20.7 (1.05)	10.4 (0.79)	64.2 (1.24)	9.9 (0.77)	36.9 (1.24)
Bachelor's degree	67.6	73.5 (0.67)	81.5 (0.40)	10,752	68.7 (0.77)	82.6 (0.63)	60.1 (0.82)	34.1 (0.79)	14.0 (0.58)	79.2 (0.68)	4.9 (0.36)	52.5 (0.83)
Master's degree	66.5	77.5 (1.10)	86.3 (0.58)	4,106	68.9 (1.25)	87.7 (0.88)	60.7 (1.32)	41.7 (1.33)	13.9 (0.93)	87.7 (0.89)	2.3 (0.41)	58.0 (1.33)
Doctor's or professional degree	68.2	†	85.1 (1.09)	1,244	64.5 (2.34)	86.2 (1.69)	65.3 (2.33)	34.9 (2.34)	14.3 (1.72)	85.0 (1.75)	3.9 (0.95)	53.6 (2.44)
Race/ethnicity												
White	48.7	53.8 (0.28)	61.6 (0.21)	59,806	65.5 (0.34)	76.6 (0.30)	56.7 (0.35)	30.7 (0.33)	16.0 (0.26)	68.6 (0.33)	7.8 (0.19)	46.2 (0.35)
Black	36.2	40.0 (0.74)	46.5 (0.61)	6,556	55.4 (1.09)	67.8 (1.02)	56.8 (1.08)	24.2 (0.94)	16.7 (0.82)	61.7 (1.06)	11.6 (0.70)	38.0 (1.06)
Hispanic	29.3	30.2 (0.80)	31.2 (0.61)	5,421	58.9 (1.32)	68.1 (1.25)	56.5 (1.33)	24.8 (1.16)	15.6 (0.97)	63.0 (1.29)	10.4 (0.82)	39.6 (1.31)
Other	—	†	59.4 (0.86)	4,786	68.7 (1.32)	79.2 (1.16)	60.9 (1.39)	31.3 (1.32)	22.9 (1.20)	71.1 (1.29)	6.6 (0.71)	51.0 (1.43)

See notes at end of table.

Table 432. Percentage of workers, 18 years old and over, using computers on the job, by type of computer application and selected characteristics: 1993, 1997, and 2003—Continued

Selected characteristic	Percent using computers at work, 1993	Percent using computers at work, 1997	2003										
			Percent using computers at work	Number using computers at work (in thousands)	Percent of on-the-job computer users using specific computer applications[1]							
					Spreadsheets/ databases	Internet/e-mail	Calendar/ schedule	Graphics/design	Programming	Word processing/ desktop publishing	Other uses only	Using 4 or more categories
1	2	3	4	5	6	7	8	9	10	11	12	13
Occupational group												
Management, business, and financial...	[2]	[2]	80.8 (0.36)	15,840	79.8 (0.55)	88.0 (0.45)	69.1 (0.63)	35.8 (0.66)	18.5 (0.53)	79.9 (0.55)	2.8 (0.23)	61.3 (0.67)
Professional and related occupations ...	[2]	[2]	78.8 (0.31)	22,517	64.4 (0.55)	81.9 (0.44)	58.7 (0.57)	38.9 (0.56)	22.1 (0.48)	74.8 (0.50)	5.2 (0.25)	51.8 (0.58)
Service occupations...	23.2	26.4 (0.51)	28.2 (0.48)	5,898	48.8 (1.12)	58.4 (1.11)	48.9 (1.12)	20.0 (0.90)	12.0 (0.73)	55.3 (1.12)	15.7 (0.82)	29.7 (1.03)
Sales and related occupations...	44.5	51.7 (0.68)	61.1 (0.53)	9,464	61.4 (0.86)	73.0 (0.79)	53.6 (0.89)	26.4 (0.78)	11.7 (0.57)	60.9 (0.87)	11.5 (0.57)	41.0 (0.87)
Office and administrative support...	[2]	[2]	73.9 (0.41)	14,206	63.2 (0.70)	70.4 (0.66)	54.4 (0.72)	19.3 (0.57)	11.5 (0.46)	66.0 (0.69)	8.5 (0.40)	37.5 (0.70)
Farming, fishing, and forestry...	7.9	8.6 (0.80)	10.8 (1.46)	132	55.5 (7.49)	57.7 (7.44)	42.2 (7.44)	20.7 (6.10)	6.5 (3.71)	55.3 (7.49)	9.4 (4.39)	26.1 (6.61)
Construction and extraction...	16.4	18.7 (0.73)	19.0 (0.68)	1,585	56.7 (2.15)	66.0 (2.06)	44.0 (2.15)	25.8 (1.90)	12.7 (1.44)	61.1 (2.12)	9.9 (1.30)	31.8 (2.02)
Installation, maintenance, and repair...	11.7	12.6 (0.79)	42.0 (0.98)	2,229	50.8 (1.83)	61.4 (1.78)	44.5 (1.82)	21.1 (1.49)	18.3 (1.41)	44.4 (1.82)	17.9 (1.40)	29.7 (1.67)
Production occupations...	21.8	23.7 (0.60)	29.6 (0.70)	2,869	52.4 (1.61)	54.9 (1.61)	43.0 (1.60)	26.0 (1.41)	14.9 (1.15)	42.0 (1.59)	17.4 (1.22)	27.5 (1.44)
Transportation and material moving...	11.8	15.1 (0.80)	22.1 (0.71)	1,830	46.4 (2.01)	51.5 (2.02)	43.4 (2.00)	14.5 (1.42)	11.2 (1.27)	40.1 (1.98)	23.1 (1.70)	21.7 (1.66)
Family income[3]												
Less than $20,000...	25.1	26.7 (0.51)	30.1 (0.62)	3,814	51.6 (1.40)	60.1 (1.37)	44.2 (1.39)	22.6 (1.17)	14.0 (0.97)	54.9 (1.39)	16.0 (1.03)	30.6 (1.29)
$20,000 to $29,999...	38.4	38.4 (0.61)	38.8 (0.63)	4,944	56.6 (1.22)	63.2 (1.18)	46.8 (1.23)	21.4 (1.01)	12.9 (0.82)	59.4 (1.21)	12.8 (0.82)	32.0 (1.15)
$30,000 to $39,999...	45.7	45.8 (0.62)	47.0 (0.59)	6,775	57.5 (1.04)	68.0 (0.98)	49.9 (1.05)	23.5 (0.89)	13.4 (0.72)	61.0 (1.02)	12.0 (0.68)	36.5 (1.01)
$40,000 to $49,999...	51.9	52.3 (0.71)	54.3 (0.64)	6,290	61.6 (1.06)	70.9 (0.99)	52.9 (1.09)	26.6 (0.96)	14.4 (0.76)	63.9 (1.05)	9.8 (0.65)	39.3 (1.06)
$50,000 to $74,999...	60.6	59.9 (0.50)	62.2 (0.41)	16,195	63.6 (0.65)	74.8 (0.59)	56.1 (0.67)	28.5 (0.61)	16.5 (0.50)	65.4 (0.65)	8.3 (0.38)	43.6 (0.67)
$75,000 or more...	65.9	69.7 (0.51)	75.0 (0.30)	26,732	72.4 (0.47)	84.3 (0.38)	64.3 (0.51)	36.4 (0.51)	19.2 (0.42)	76.4 (0.45)	4.5 (0.22)	56.3 (0.52)

—Not available.
†Not applicable.
[1]Individuals may be counted in more than one computer activity.
[2]Due to changes in occupational definitions, older data are not comparable to 2003 data.
[3]Excludes persons whose income data were not available.

NOTE: Data are based on a sample survey of households and are subject to sampling and nonsampling error. Race categories exclude persons of Hispanic ethnicity. Detail may not sum to totals because of rounding. Standard errors appear in parentheses. SOURCE: U.S. Department of Commerce, Census Bureau, Current Population Survey (CPS), October 1993, October 1997, and October 2003, unpublished tabulations. (This table was prepared May 2005.)

APPENDIX A
Guide to Sources

Sources and Comparability of Data

The information presented in this report was obtained from many sources, including federal and state agencies, private research organizations, and professional associations. The data were collected using many research methods, including surveys of a universe (such as all colleges) or of a sample, compilations of administrative records, and statistical projections. *Digest* users should take particular care when comparing data from different sources. Differences in sampling, data collection procedures, coverage of target population, timing, phrasing of questions, scope of nonresponse, interviewer training, and data processing and coding mean that results from different sources may not be strictly comparable. Following the general discussion of data accuracy below, descriptions of the information sources and data collection methods are presented, grouped by sponsoring organization. More extensive documentation of a particular survey's procedures does not imply more problems with the data, only that more information is available.

Accuracy of Data

The joint effects of "sampling" and "nonsampling" errors determine the accuracy of any statistic. Estimates based on a sample will differ somewhat from the figures that would have been obtained if a complete census had been taken using the same survey instruments, instructions, and procedures. In addition to such sampling errors, all surveys, both universe and sample, are subject to design, reporting, and processing errors and errors due to nonresponse. To the extent possible, these nonsampling errors are kept to a minimum by methods built into the survey procedures. In general, however, the effects of nonsampling errors are more difficult to gauge than those produced by sampling variability.

Sampling Errors

The samples used in surveys are selected from large numbers of possible samples of the same size that could have been selected using the same sample design. Estimates derived from the different samples would differ from each other. The difference between a sample estimate and the average of all possible samples is called the sampling deviation. The standard, or sampling, error of a survey estimate is a measure of the variation among the estimates from all possible samples and thus is a measure of the precision with which an estimate from a particular sample approximates the average result of all possible samples.

The sample estimate and an estimate of its standard error permit us to construct interval estimates with prescribed confidence that the interval includes the average result of all possible samples. If all possible samples were selected under essentially the same conditions and an estimate and its estimated standard error were calculated from each sample, then (1) approximately 66.7 percent of the intervals from one standard error below the estimate to one standard error above the estimate would include the average value of all possible samples; and (2) approximately 95.0 percent of the intervals from two standard errors below the estimate to two standard errors above the estimate would include the average value of all possible samples. We call an interval from two standard errors below the estimate to two standard errors above the estimate a 95 percent confidence interval.

To illustrate this concept, consider the data and standard errors appearing in table 109. For the 2006 estimate that 9.3 percent of 16- to 24-year-olds were high school dropouts, the table shows that the standard error is 0.22 percent. The sampling error above and below the stated figure is approximately double (1.96) the standard error, or about 0.43 percentage points. Therefore, we can create a 95 percent confidence interval, which is approximately 8.87 to 9.73 (9.3 percent ± 1.96 x 0.22 percent).

Analysis of standard errors can help assess how valid a comparison between two estimates might be. The *standard error of a difference* between two independent sample estimates is equal to the square root of the sum of the squared standard errors of the estimates. The standard error (se) of the difference between independent sample estimates a and b is

$$se_{a\text{-}b} = (se_a^2 + se_b^2)^{1/2}$$

It should be noted that most of the standard error estimates presented in the *Digest* and in the original documents are approximations. That is, to derive estimates of standard errors that would be applicable to a wide variety of items and could be prepared at a moderate cost, a number of approximations were required. As a result, the standard error estimates provide a general order of magnitude rather than the exact standard error for any specific item. The preceding discussion on sampling variability was directed toward a situation concerning one or two estimates. Determining the accuracy of statistical projections is more difficult. In general, the further away the projection date is from the date of the actual data being used for the projection, the greater the probable error in the projections. If, for instance, annual data from 1970 to 2006 are being used to project enrollment in institutions of higher education, the further beyond 2006 one projects, the more variability there is in the projection. One will be less sure of the 2017 enrollment projection than of the 2007 projection. A detailed discussion of the projections methodology is contained in *Projections of Education Statistics to 2017* (National Center for Education Statistics [NCES] 2008-078).

Nonsampling Errors

Universe and sample surveys are subject to nonsampling errors. Nonsampling errors may arise when respondents or interviewers interpret questions differently; when respondents must estimate values, or when coders, keyers, and other processors handle answers differently; when people who should be included in the universe are not; or when people fail to respond (completely or partially). Nonsampling errors usually, but not always, result in an underestimate of total survey error and thus an overestimate of the precision of survey estimates. Since estimating the magnitude of nonsampling errors often would require special experiments or access to independent data, these nonsampling errors are seldom measured.

To compensate for nonresponse, adjustments of the sample estimates are often made. For universe surveys, an adjustment made for either type of nonresponse, total or partial, is often referred to as an imputation, which is often a substitution of the "average" questionnaire response for the nonresponse. For universe surveys, imputations are usually made separately within various groups of sample members that have similar survey characteristics. For sample surveys, missing cases (i.e., total nonresponse) are handled through nonresponse adjustments to the sample weights. For sample surveys, imputation for item nonresponse is usually made by substituting for a missing item the response to that item of a respondent having characteristics that are similar to those of the nonrespondent. For more information, see the *NCES Statistical Standards* (NCES 2003-601).

Although the magnitude of nonsampling error in the data compiled in this *Digest* is frequently unknown, idiosyncrasies that have been identified are noted in the appropriate tables.

National Center for Education Statistics (NCES)

Baccalaureate and Beyond Longitudinal Study

The Baccalaureate and Beyond Longitudinal Study (B&B) is based on the National Postsecondary Student Aid Study (NPSAS) and provides information concerning education and work experience after completing the bachelor's degree. A special emphasis of B&B is on those entering teaching. B&B provides cross-sectional information 1 year after bachelor's degree completion (comparable to the information that was provided in the Recent College Graduates study), while at the same time providing longitudinal data concerning entry into and progress through graduate-level education and the workforce. This information has not been available through follow-ups involving high school cohorts or even college-entry cohorts, both of which are restricted in the number who actually complete a bachelor's degree and continue their education.

B&B followed NPSAS baccalaureate degree completers for a 10-year period after completion, beginning with NPSAS:93. About 11,000 students who completed their degrees in the 1992–93 academic year were included in the first B&B (B&B:93/94). In addition to the student data, B&B collected postsecondary transcripts covering the undergraduate period, which provided complete information on progress and persistence at the undergraduate level. The second B&B follow-up took place in spring 1997 (B&B:93/97) and gathered information on employment history, family formation, and enrollment in graduate programs. The third B&B follow-up occurred in 2003 (B&B:93/03) and provides information concerning graduate study and long-term employment experiences after degree completion.

The most recent B&B cohort, which was associated with NPSAS:2000, included 11,700 students who completed their degrees in the 1999–2000 academic year. The first and only planned follow-up survey of this cohort was conducted in 2001 (B&B:2000/01) and focused on time to degree completion, participation in postbaccalaureate education and employment, and the activities of newly qualified teachers.

Further information on B&B may be obtained from

Kristin Perry
Aurora D'Amico
Postsecondary Studies Division
National Center for Education Statistics
1990 K Street NW
Washington, DC 20006
kristin.perry@ed.gov
aurora.d'amico@ed.gov
http://nces.ed.gov/surveys/b&b

Beginning Postsecondary Students Longitudinal Study

The Beginning Postsecondary Students Longitudinal Study (BPS) provides information on persistence, progress, and attainment from initial time of entry into postsecondary education through entering and leaving the workforce. BPS includes traditional and nontraditional (e.g., older) students and is representative of all beginning students in postsecondary education. BPS follows first-time, beginning students for at least 5 years at approximately 2-year intervals, collecting student data and financial aid reports. By starting with a cohort that has already entered postsecondary education and following it for 5 years, BPS can determine to what extent students who start postsecondary education at various ages differ in their progress, persistence, and attainment. The first BPS was conducted in 1989–90, with follow-ups in 1992 and 1994. The second BPS was conducted in 1995–96, with follow-ups in 1998 and 2001. A third BPS cohort is based on NPSAS:04, with the first BPS follow-up in 2006 and the second in 2009.

Further information on BPS may be obtained from

Aurora D'Amico
Tracy Hunt-White
Postsecondary Studies Division
Postsecondary Cooperative System, Analysis,
    and Dissemination Program
National Center for Education Statistics
1990 K Street NW
Washington, DC 20006
tracy.hunt-white@ed.gov
aurora.d'amico@ed.gov
http://nces.ed.gov/surveys/bps

Common Core of Data

NCES uses the Common Core of Data (CCD) to acquire and maintain statistical data from each of the 50 states, the District of Columbia, the Bureau of Indian Education, Department of Defense dependents schools (overseas and domestic), and the other jurisdictions. Information about staff and students is reported annually at the school, local education agency (LEA) or school district, and state levels. Information about revenues and expenditures is also collected at the state and LEA levels.

Data are collected for a particular school year via an online reporting system open to state education agencies during the school year. Beginning with the 2006–07 school year, nonfiscal CCD data are collected through the Department of Education's Education Data Exchange Network (EDEN). Since the CCD is a universe collection, CCD data are not subject to sampling errors. However, nonsampling errors could come from two sources: nonresponse and inaccurate reporting. Almost all of the states submit the five CCD survey instruments each year, but submissions are sometimes incomplete.

Misreporting can occur when 58 education agencies compile and submit data for approximately 97,000 public schools and over 17,000 local education agencies. Typically, this results from varying interpretations of NCES definitions and differing record-keeping systems. NCES attempts to minimize these errors by working closely with the state education agencies through the National Forum on Education Statistics.

The state education agencies report data to NCES from data collected and edited in their regular reporting cycles. NCES encourages the agencies to incorporate into their own survey systems the NCES items they do not already collect so that these items will also be available for the subsequent CCD survey. Over time, this has meant fewer missing data cells in each state's response, reducing the need to impute data.

NCES subjects data from the state education agencies to a comprehensive edit. Where data are determined to be inconsistent, missing, or out of range, NCES contacts the agencies for verification. NCES-prepared state summary forms are returned to the agencies for verification. Each year, states are also given an opportunity to revise their state-level aggregates from the previous survey cycle.

Further information on the nonfiscal CCD data may be obtained from

John Sietsema
Elementary/Secondary and Library Studies Division
Elementary/Secondary Cooperative System and
    Institutional Studies Program
National Center for Education Statistics
1990 K Street NW
Washington, DC 20006
john.sietsema@ed.gov
http://nces.ed.gov/ccd

Further information on the fiscal CCD data may be obtained from

Frank H. Johnson
Elementary/Secondary and Library Studies Division
Elementary/Secondary Cooperative System and Institutional Studies Program
National Center for Education Statistics
1990 K Street NW
Washington, DC 20006
frank.johnson@ed.gov
http://nces.ed.gov/ccd

Early Childhood Longitudinal Study, Birth Cohort 2001

The Early Childhood Longitudinal Study, Birth Cohort (ECLS-B) is designed to provide decisionmakers, researchers, child care providers, teachers, and parents with nationally representative information about children's early learning experiences and the transition to child care and school. Children's physical and cognitive development, care, and learning experiences at home and school are measured using standardized assessments from birth through kindergarten entry.

Data were collected from a sample of about 10,700 children born in the United States in 2001, representing a population of approximately 4 million. The children participating in the study come from diverse socioeconomic and racial/ethnic backgrounds, with oversamples of Chinese, other Asian and Pacific Islander, American Indian/Alaska Native, twin, and moderately low and very low birth weight children. Children, their parents (including nonresident and resident fathers), their child care providers, and their teachers provide information on children's cognitive, social, emotional, and physical development across multiple settings (e.g., home, child care, and school).

At 9 months (2001–02), 2 years (2003–04), 4 years (2005), 5 years (2006), and 6 years (2007), parents are asked about themselves, their families, and their children; fathers are asked about themselves and the role they play in supporting their child's care and development; and children are observed and assessed. In addition, starting when children are about 2 years old, child care and early education providers are asked to provide information about their own experience and training, their relationship with the child, and the setting's learning environment. When the children are in kindergarten (2006 and 2007), teachers are asked to provide information about the children's early academic skills and the classroom environment. School-level data, merged from two other NCES data sets (the Common Core of Data and the Private School Survey), and residential zip codes collected at each wave, support community descriptions.

Further information on the ECLS-B may be obtained from

Gail Mulligan
Early Childhood, International, and Crosscutting
    Studies Division
Early Childhood and Household Studies Program
National Center for Education Statistics
1990 K Street NW
Washington, DC 20006
gail.mulligan@ed.gov
http://nces.ed.gov/ecls/Birth.asp

Early Childhood Longitudinal Study, Kindergarten Class of 1998–99

The Early Childhood Longitudinal Study, Kindergarten Class of 1998–99 (ECLS-K) was designed to provide detailed information on children's early school experiences. The study began in the fall of 1998. A nationally representative sample of 22,782 children enrolled in 1,277 kindergarten programs during the 1998–99 school year was selected to participate in the ECLS-K. The children attended both public and private kindergartens, and full-day and part-day programs. The sample included children from different racial/ethnic and socioeconomic backgrounds and oversamples of Asian and Pacific Islander children and private school kindergartners. Base-year data were collected in the fall and spring of the kindergarten year. Data were collected again in the fall of first grade (from a 30 percent subsample of schools) and the spring of first grade, and then in the spring of third grade in 2002 and the spring of fifth grade in 2004. The same children were followed through the eighth grade.

The ECLS-K includes a direct child cognitive assessment that is administered one-on-one with each child in the study. The assessment uses a computer-assisted personal interview

(CAPI) approach and a two-stage adaptive testing methodology. In the eighth grade, a two-stage adaptive paper-and-pencil assessment was administered in small groups. The assessment includes three cognitive domains—reading, mathematics, and general knowledge—at kindergarten and first grade. General knowledge was replaced by science at the third, fifth, and eighth grades. Children's height and weight are measured at each data collection point, and a direct measure of children's psychomotor development was administered in the fall of the kindergarten year only. In addition to these measures, the ECLS-K collects information about children's social skills and academic achievement through teacher reports, and through student reports at the third, fifth, and eighth grades.

A computer-assisted telephone interview with the children's parents/guardians is conducted at each data collection point. Parents/guardians are asked to provide key information about their children on subjects such as family demographics (e.g., family members, age, relation to child, race/ethnicity), family structure (e.g., household members and composition), parent involvement, home educational activities (e.g., reading to the child), child health, parental education and employment status, and child's social skills and behaviors.

Data on the schools that children attend and their classrooms are collected by self-administered questionnaires completed by school administrators and classroom teachers. Administrators provide information about the school population, programs, and policies. At the classroom level, data are collected on the composition of the classroom, teaching practices, curriculum, and teacher qualifications and experience. In addition, special education teachers and related services staff provide reports on the services received by children with disabilities.

Further information on the ECLS-K may be obtained from

Chris Chapman
Early Childhood, International, and Crosscutting Studies
    Division
Early Childhood and Household Studies Program
National Center for Education Statistics
1990 K Street NW
Washington, DC 20006
ecls@ed.gov
http://nces.ed.gov/ecls

Education Longitudinal Study of 2002

The Education Longitudinal Study of 2002 (ELS:2002) is a longitudinal survey that is monitoring the transitions of a national probability sample of 10th-graders in public, Catholic, and other private schools. Survey waves follow both students and high school dropouts and monitor the transition of the cohort to postsecondary education, the labor force, and family formation.

In the base year of the study, of 1,221 eligible contacted schools, 752 participated, for an overall weighted school participation rate of approximately 68 percent (62 percent unweighted). Of 17,591 selected eligible students, 15,362 participated, for an overall weighted student response rate of approximately 87 percent. (School and student weighted response rates reflect use of the base weight [design weight] and do not include nonresponse adjustments.) Information for the study is obtained not just from students and their school records, but also from the students' parents, their teachers, their librarians, and the administrators of their schools.

The first follow-up was conducted in 2004, when most sample members were high school seniors. Base-year students who remained in their base schools were resurveyed and tested in mathematics, along with a freshening sample to make the study representative of spring 2004 high school seniors nationwide. Students who were not still at their base schools were administered a questionnaire.

The second follow-up, completed in 2006, continued to follow the sample of students into postsecondary education or work, or both. The next follow-up is scheduled for 2012.

Further information on ELS:2002 may be obtained from

John Wirt
Elementary/Secondary and Libraries Studies Division
Elementary/Secondary Sample Survey Studies Program
National Center for Education Statistics
1990 K Street NW
Washington, DC 20006
john.wirt@ed.gov
http://nces.ed.gov/surveys/els2002

Fast Response Survey System

The Fast Response Survey System (FRSS) was established in 1975 to collect issue-oriented data quickly and with a minimal burden on respondents. The FRSS, whose surveys collect and report data on key education issues at the elementary and secondary levels, was designed to meet the data needs of Department of Education analysts, planners, and decisionmakers when information could not be collected quickly through NCES's large recurring surveys. Findings from FRSS surveys have been included in congressional reports, testimony to congressional subcommittees, NCES reports, and other Department of Education reports. The findings are also often used by state and local education officials.

Data collected through FRSS surveys are representative at the national level, drawing from a universe that is appropriate for each study. The FRSS collects data from state education agencies and national samples of other educational organizations and participants, including local education agencies, public and private elementary and secondary schools, elementary and secondary school teachers and principals, and public libraries and school libraries. To ensure a minimal burden on respondents, the surveys are generally limited to three pages of questions, with a response burden of about 30 minutes per respondent. Sample sizes are rela-

tively small (usually about 1,000 to 1,500 respondents per survey) so that data collection can be completed quickly.

Further information on the FRSS may be obtained from

Peter Tice
Early Childhood, International, and Crosscutting Studies Division
Early Childhood and Household Studies
National Center for Education Statistics
1990 K Street NW
Washington, DC 20006
peter.tice@ed.gov
http://nces.ed.gov/surveys/frss

Condition of America's Public School Facilities: 1999

This report (NCES 2000-032) provides national data about the condition of public schools in 1999 based on a survey conducted by NCES using its Fast Response Survey System (FRSS). Specifically, this report provides information about the condition of school facilities and the costs to bring them into good condition; school plans for repairs, renovations, and replacements; the age of public schools; and overcrowding and practices used to address overcrowding. The results presented in this report are based on questionnaire data for 903 public elementary and secondary schools in the United States. The responses were weighted to produce national estimates that represent all regular public schools in the United States.

Further information about the contents of this report may be obtained from

Peter Tice
Early Childhood, International, and Crosscutting Studies Division
Data Development Program
National Center for Education Statistics
1990 K Street NW
Washington, DC 20006
peter.tice@ed.gov
http://nces.ed.gov/surveys/frss

Internet Access in U.S. Public Schools and Classrooms

The Internet Access in U.S. Public Schools and Classrooms survey is part of the NCES Fast Response Survey System (FRSS). It is designed to assess the federal government's commitment to assist every school and classroom in connecting to the Internet by the year 2000. In 1994, NCES began surveying approximately 1,000 public schools each year about their access to the Internet, access in classrooms, and, since 1996, their type of internet connections. Recent administrations of this survey have been expanded to cover emerging issues. The 2003 survey was designed to update the questions in the 2002 survey and covered the following topics: school connectivity, student access to computers and the Internet, school websites, technologies and procedures to prevent student access to inappropriate websites, and teacher professional development on how to incorporate use of the Internet into the curriculum.

In 2005 respondents were asked about the number of instructional computers with access to the Internet, the types of Internet connections, technologies and procedures used to prevent student access to inappropriate material on the Internet, and the availability of hand-held and laptop computers for students and teachers. Respondents also provided information on teacher professional development in integrating the use of the Internet into the curriculum and using the Internet to provide opportunities and information for teaching and learning.

The 2005 survey on internet access was the last in this series, since internet access in schools has been nearly 100 percent since 2003.

Further information on internet access in public schools and classrooms may be obtained from

Peter Tice
Early Childhood, International, and Crosscutting Studies Division
Data Development Program
National Center for Education Statistics
1990 K Street NW
Washington, DC 20006
peter.tice@ed.gov
http://nces.ed.gov/surveys/frss

Federal Support for Education

NCES prepares an annual compilation of federal funds for education for the *Digest*. Data for U.S. Department of Education programs come from the *Budget of the United States Government*. Budget offices of other federal agencies provide information for all other federal program support except for research funds, which are obligations reported by the National Science Foundation in *Federal Funds for Research and Development*. Some data are estimated, based on reports from the federal agencies contacted and the *Budget of the United States Government*.

Except for money spent on research, outlays are used to report program funds to the extent possible. Some *Digest* tables report program funds as obligations, as noted in the title of the table. Some federal program funds not commonly recognized as education assistance are also included in the totals reported. For example, portions of federal funds paid to some states and counties as shared revenues resulting from the sale of timber and minerals from public lands have been estimated as funds used for education purposes. Parts of the funds received by states (in 1980) and localities (in all years) under the General Revenue Sharing Program are also included, as are portions of federal funds received by the District of Columbia. The share of these funds allocated to education is assumed to be equal to the share of general funds expended for elementary and secondary education by states and localities in the same year as reported by the U.S. Census Bureau in its annual publication, *Government Finances*.

The share of federal funds for the District of Columbia assigned to education is assumed to be equal to the share of the city's general fund expenditures for each level of education.

For the job training programs conducted by the Department of Labor, only estimated sums spent on classroom training have been reported as educational program support.

During the 1970s, the Office of Management and Budget (OMB) prepared an annual analysis of federal education program support. These were published in the *Budget of the United States Government, Special Analyses*. The information presented in this report is not, however, a continuation of the OMB series. A number of differences in the two series should be noted. OMB required all federal agencies to report outlays for education-related programs using a standardized form, thereby assuring agency compliance in reporting. The scope of education programs reported in the *Digest* differs from the scope of programs reported in the OMB reports. Off-budget items such as the annual volume of guaranteed student loans were not included in OMB's reports. Finally, while some mention is made of an annual estimate of federal tax expenditures, OMB did not include them in its annual analysis of federal education support. Estimated federal tax expenditures for education are the difference between current federal tax receipts and what these receipts would be without existing education deductions to income allowed by federal tax provisions.

Recipients' data are estimated based on *Estimating Federal Funds for Education: A New Approach Applied to Fiscal Year 1980* (Miller, V., and Noell, J., 1982, Journal of Education Finance); *Federal Support for Education*, various years; and the *Catalog of Federal Domestic Assistance* (cfda.gov). The recipients' data are estimated and tend to undercount institutions of higher education, students, and local education agencies. This is because some of the federal programs have more than one recipient receiving funds. In these cases, the recipients were put into a "mixed recipients" category, because there was no way to disaggregate the amount each recipient received.

Further information on federal support for education may be obtained from

William Sonnenberg
Early Childhood, International, and Crosscutting Studies Division
Annual Reports Program
National Center for Education Statistics
1990 K Street NW
Washington, DC 20006
william.sonnenberg@ed.gov
http://nces.ed.gov/surveys/AnnualReports/federal.asp

High School and Beyond Longitudinal Study

The High School and Beyond Longitudinal Study (HS&B) is a national longitudinal survey of individuals who were high school sophomores and seniors in 1980. The base-year survey (conducted in 1980) was a probability sample of 1,015 high schools with a target number of 36 sophomores and 36 seniors in each school. A total of 58,270 students participated in the base-year survey. Substitutions were made for nonparticipating schools—but not for students—in those strata where it was possible. Overall, 1,122 schools were selected in the original sample and 811 of these schools participated in the survey. An additional 204 schools were drawn in a replacement sample. Student refusals and absences resulted in an 82 percent completion rate for the survey.

Several small groups in the population were oversampled to allow for special study of certain types of schools and students. Students completed questionnaires and took a battery of cognitive tests. In addition, a sample of parents of sophomores and seniors (about 3,600 for each cohort) was surveyed.

HS&B first follow-up activities took place in the spring of 1982. The sample for the first follow-up survey included approximately 30,000 people who were sophomores in 1980. The completion rate for sample members eligible for on-campus survey administration was about 96 percent. About 89 percent of the students who left school between the base-year and first follow-up surveys (e.g., dropouts, transfer students, and early graduates) completed the first follow-up sophomore questionnaire.

As part of the first follow-up survey of HS&B, transcripts were requested in fall 1982 for an 18,152-member subsample of the sophomore cohort. Of the 15,941 transcripts actually obtained, 1,969 were excluded because the students had dropped out of school before graduation, 799 were excluded because they were incomplete, and 1,057 were excluded because the students graduated before 1982 or the transcripts indicated neither a dropout status nor graduation. Thus, 12,116 transcripts were utilized for the overall curriculum analysis presented in this publication. All courses in each transcript were assigned a 6-digit code based on the Classification of Secondary School Courses (a coding system developed to standardize course descriptions; see http://nces.ed.gov/surveys/hst/courses.asp). Credits earned in each course are expressed in Carnegie units. (The Carnegie unit is a standard of measurement that represents one credit for the completion of a 1-year course. To receive credit for a course, the student must have received a passing grade—"pass," "D," or higher.) Students who transferred from public to private schools or from private to public schools between their sophomore and senior years were eliminated from public/private analyses.

In designing the senior cohort first follow-up survey, one of the goals was to reduce the size of the retained sample while still keeping sufficient numbers of minorities to allow important policy analyses. A total of 11,227 (94 percent) of the 11,995 people subsampled completed the questionnaire. Information was obtained about the respondents' school and employment experiences, family status, and attitudes and plans.

The samples for the second follow-up, which took place in spring 1984, consisted of about 12,000 members of the senior cohort and about 15,000 members of the sophomore cohort. The completion rate for the senior cohort was 91 percent, and the completion rate for the sophomore cohort was 92 percent.

HS&B third follow-up data collection activities were performed in spring 1986. Both the sophomore and senior cohort samples for this round of data collection were the same as those used for the second follow-up survey. The completion rates for the sophomore and senior cohort samples were 91 percent and 88 percent, respectively.

HS&B fourth follow-up data collection activities were performed in 1992, but only surveyed the 1980 sophomore class. They examined aspects of these students' early adult years, such as enrollment in postsecondary education, experience in the labor market, marriage and child rearing, and voting behavior.

Appendix table A-1 contains the maximum number of HS&B cases that are available for tabulations of specific classification variables used throughout this publication.

The standard error (se) of an individual percentage (p) based on HS&B data can be approximated by the formula

$$se_p = \text{DEFT } [p(100 - p)/n]^{1/2}$$

where n is the sample size and DEFT, the square root of the design effect, is a factor used to adjust for the particular sample design used in HS&B. Appendix table A-2 provides the DEFT factors for different HS&B samples and subsamples.

In evaluating a difference between two independent percentages, the standard error of the difference may be conservatively approximated by taking the square root of the sum of the squared standard errors of the two percentages. For example, in the 1986 follow-up of 1980 sophomores, 84.0 percent of the men and 77.2 percent of the women felt that being successful in work was "very important," a difference of 6.8 percentage points. Using the formula and the sample sizes from table A-1 and the DEFT factors from table A-2, the standard errors of the two percentages being compared are calculated to be

$$1.43[(84.0)(16.0)/(5,391)]^{1/2} = .714$$
$$1.43[(77.2)(22.8)/(5,857)]^{1/2} = .784$$

Therefore, the standard error of the difference is

$$(.714^2 + .784^2)^{1/2} = (.510 + .615)^{1/2} = 1.06$$

The sampling error of the difference is approximately double the standard error, or approximately 2.1 percentage points, and the 95 percent confidence interval for the difference is 6.8 ± 2.1, or 4.7 to 8.9 percentage points.

The standard error estimation procedure outlined above does not compensate for survey item nonresponse, which is a source of nonsampling error. (Table A-1 reflects the maximum number of responses that could be tabulated by demographic characteristics.) For example, of the 10,925 respondents in the 1984 follow-up survey of 1980 high school graduates, 372, or 3.4 percent, did not respond to the particular question on whether they had ever used a pocket calculator. Item nonresponse varied considerably. A very low nonresponse rate of 0.1 percent was obtained for a question asking whether the respondent had attended a postsecondary institution. A much higher item nonresponse rate of 12.2 percent was obtained for a question asking if the respondent had used a micro- or minicomputer in high school. Typical item nonresponse rates ranged from 3 to 4 percent.

The Hispanic analyses presented in this publication rely on students' self-identification as members of one of four Hispanic subgroups: Mexican, Mexican-American, Chicano; Cuban; Puerto Rican, Puertorriqueño, Boricuan; or other Hispanic ethnicities.

An NCES series of technical reports and data file user's manuals, available electronically, provides additional information on the survey methodology.

Further information on HS&B may be obtained from

Aurora D'Amico
Postsecondary Studies Division
Postsecondary Cooperative System, Analysis, and Dissemination Program
National Center for Education Statistics
1990 K Street NW
Washington, DC 20006
aurora.d'amico@ed.gov
http://nces.ed.gov/surveys/hsb

High School Transcript Study Tabulations

High school transcript studies have been conducted since 1982 and are associated with a major NCES data collection. The studies collect information that is contained in a student's high school record—courses taken while attending secondary school, information on credits earned, when specific courses were taken, and final grades.

A high school transcript study was conducted in 2004 as part of the Education Longitudinal Study of 2002 (ELS:2002/ 2004). A total of 1,549 schools participated in the request for transcripts, for an unweighted participation rate of approximately 79 percent. Transcript information was received on 14,920 members of the student sample (not just graduates), for an unweighted response rate of 91 percent.

Similar studies were conducted of the coursetaking patterns of 1982, 1987, 1990, 1992, 1994, 1998, and 2000 high school graduates. The 1982 data are based on approximately 12,000 transcripts collected by the High School and Beyond Longitudinal Study (HS&B). The 1987 data are based on approximately 22,799 transcripts from 433 schools obtained as part of the 1987 NAEP High School Transcript Study, a scope comparable to that of the NAEP transcript studies conducted in 1990, 1994, 1998, and 2000. The 1992 data are based on approximately 7,600 transcripts collected by the National Education Longitudinal Study of 1988 (NELS:88/ 92). The 2005 NAEP High School Transcript Study collected a sample of over 26,000 transcripts from 640 public schools and 80 private schools.

Because the 1982 HS&B transcript study used a different method for identifying students with disabilities than was used in NAEP transcript studies after 1982, and in order to make the statistical summaries as comparable as possible, all the counts and percentages in this report are restricted to students whose records indicate that they had not participated in a special education program. This restriction lowers the number of 1990 graduates represented in the tables to 20,866.

Further information on NAEP high school transcript studies may be obtained from

Janis Brown
Assessment Development & Quality Assurance-AD
National Center for Education Statistics
1990 K Street NW
Washington, DC 20006
janis.brown@ed.gov
http://nces.ed.gov/surveys/hst

Further information on all other high school transcript studies may be obtained from

Carl Schmitt
Elementary/Secondary and Library Studies Division
National Center for Education Statistics
1990 K Street NW
Washington, DC 20006
carl.schmitt@ed.gov
http://nces.ed.gov/surveys/hst

Integrated Postsecondary Education Data System

The Integrated Postsecondary Education Data System (IPEDS) surveys approximately 6,800 postsecondary institutions, including universities and colleges, as well as institutions offering technical and vocational education beyond the high school level. IPEDS, which began in 1986, replaced the Higher Education General Information Survey (HEGIS).

IPEDS consists of eight interrelated components that obtain information on who provides postsecondary education (institutions), who participates in it and completes it (students), what programs are offered and what programs are completed, and both the human and financial resources involved in the provision of institutionally based postsecondary education. Until 2000, these components included institutional characteristics, fall enrollment, completions, salaries, finance, and fall staff. Beginning in 2000, data were collected in the fall for institutional characteristics and completions; in the winter for employees by assigned position (EAP), salaries, and fall staff; and in the spring for enrollment, student financial aid, finances, and graduation rates. With the winter 2005–06 survey, the employees by assigned position, fall staff, and salaries components were merged into the human resources component. In 2007–08, the enrollment component was broken into two separate components: 12-month enrollment (collected in the fall) and fall enrollment (collected in the spring).

The degree-granting institutions portion of IPEDS is a census of colleges awarding associate's or higher degrees that are eligible to participate in Title IV financial aid programs. Prior to 1993, data from technical and vocational institutions were collected through a sample survey. Beginning in 1993, all data are gathered in a census of all postsecondary institutions. The tabulations on "institutional characteristics" developed for editions of the *Digest* from 1993 forward are based on lists of all institutions and are not subject to sampling errors.

The definition of institutions generally thought of as offering college and university education changed as of 1996. The old standard for higher education institutions included those institutions that had courses leading to an associate's or higher degree or that had courses accepted for credit toward those degrees. Higher education institutions were accredited by an agency or association that was recognized by the U.S. Department of Education or were recognized directly by the Secretary of Education. Tables, or portions of tables, that use only this standard are noted as "higher education" in the *Digest*. The newer standard includes institutions that award associate's or higher degrees and that are eligible to participate in Title IV federal financial aid programs. Tables that contain any data according to this standard are titled "degree-granting" institutions. Time-series tables may contain data from both series, and they are noted accordingly. The impact of this change on data collected in 1996 was not large. For example, tables on faculty salaries and benefits were only affected to a very small extent. Also, degrees awarded at the bachelor's level or higher were not heavily affected. The largest impact was on private 2-year college enrollment. In contrast, most of the data on public 4-year colleges were affected to a minimal extent. The impact on enrollment in public 2-year colleges was noticeable in certain states, but was relatively small at the national level. Overall, total enrollment for all institutions was about one-half a percent higher in 1996 for degree-granting institutions than for higher education institutions.

Prior to the establishment of IPEDS in 1986, HEGIS acquired and maintained statistical data on the characteristics and operations of institutions of higher education. Implemented in 1966, HEGIS was an annual universe survey of institutions accredited at the college level by an agency recognized by the Secretary of the U.S. Department of Education. These institutions were listed in NCES's *Education Directory, Colleges and Universities*.

HEGIS surveys collected information on institutional characteristics, faculty salaries, finances, enrollment, and degrees. Since these surveys, like IPEDS, were distributed to all higher education institutions, the data presented are not subject to sampling error. However, they are subject to nonsampling error, the sources of which varied with the survey instrument.

The NCES Taskforce for IPEDS Redesign recognized that there were issues related to the consistency of data definitions as well as the accuracy, reliability, and validity of other quality measures within and across surveys. The IPEDS redesign in 2000 provided institution-specific web-based data forms. While the new system shortened data processing time and provided better data consistency, it did not address the accuracy of the data provided by institutions.

Beginning in 2003–04 with the Prior Year Data Revision System, prior-year data have been available to institutions entering current data. This allows institutions to make changes to their prior-year entries either by adjusting the data or by providing missing data. These revisions allow the evaluation of the data's accuracy by looking at the changes made.

NCES conducted a study (NCES 2005-175) of the 2002–03 data that were revised in 2003–04 to determine the accuracy of the imputations, track the institutions that submitted revised data, and analyze the revised data they submitted. When institutions made changes to their data, it was assumed that the revised data were the "true" data. The data were analyzed for the number and type of institutions making changes, the type of changes, the magnitude of the changes, and the impact on published data.

Because NCES imputes missing data, imputation procedures were also addressed by the Redesign Taskforce. For the 2003–04 assessment, differences between revised values and values that were imputed in the original files were compared (i.e., revised value minus imputed value). These differences were then used to provide an assessment of the effectiveness of imputation procedures. The size of the differences also provides an indication of the accuracy of imputation procedures. To assess the overall impact of changes on aggregate IPEDS estimates, published tables for each component were reconstructed using the revised 2002–03 data. These reconstructed tables were then compared to the published tables to determine the magnitude of aggregate bias and the direction of this bias.

Though IPEDS provides the most comprehensive data system for postsecondary education, there are 100 or more entities that collect their own information from postsecondary institutions. This raises the issue of how valid IPEDS data are when compared to education data collected by non-IPEDS sources. In the Data Quality Study, Thomson Peterson data were chosen to assess the validity of IPEDS data because Thomson Peterson is one of the largest and most comprehensive sources of postsecondary data available.

Not all IPEDS components could be compared to Thomson Peterson. Either Thomson Peterson did not collect data related to a particular IPEDS component, or the data items collected by Thomson Peterson were not comparable to the IPEDS items (i.e., the data items were defined differently). Comparisons were made for a selected number of data items in five areas—tuition and price, employees by assigned position, enrollment, student financial aid, and finance. More details on the accuracy and reliability of IPEDS data can be found in the *Integrated Postsecondary Education Data System Data Quality Study* (NCES 2005-175).

Further information on IPEDS may be obtained from

Elise Miller
Postsecondary Studies Division
Postsecondary Institutional Studies Program
National Center for Education Statistics
1990 K Street NW
Washington, DC 20006
elise.miller@ed.gov
http://nces.ed.gov/ipeds

Fall (12-Month Enrollment)

Data on 12-month enrollment are collected for award levels ranging from postsecondary certificates of less than 1 year to doctoral degrees. The 12-month period used is selected by the institution and can be either July 1 through June 30 or September 1 through August 31. Data are collected by race/ethnicity and gender, and include unduplicated headcounts and instructional activity (contact or credit hours). These data are also used to calculate a full-time-equivalent (FTE) enrollment based on instructional activity. FTE enrollment is useful for gauging the size of the educational enterprise at the institution. Prior to the 2007–08 IPEDS data collection, the data collected in the 12-Month Enrollment survey were part of the Fall Enrollment survey. However, to improve the timeliness of the data, a separate survey component was developed in 2007. The data are now collected in the fall for the previous academic year.

Further information on the IPEDS 12-Month Enrollment survey may be obtained from

Jessica Shedd
Postsecondary Studies Division
Postsecondary Institutional Studies Program
National Center for Education Statistics
1990 K Street NW
Washington, DC 20006
jessica.shedd@ed.gov
http://nces.ed.gov/ipeds

Fall (Completions)

This survey was part of the HEGIS series throughout its existence. However, the degree classification taxonomy was revised in 1970–71, 1982–83, 1991–92, and 2002–03. Collection of degree data has been maintained through IPEDS.

Degrees-conferred trend tables arranged by the 2002–03 classification are included in the *Digest* to provide consistent data from 1970–71 to the most recent year. Data in this edition on associate's and other formal awards below the baccalaureate degree, by field of study, cannot be made comparable with figures from prior to 1982–83. The nonresponse rate does not appear to be a significant source of nonsampling error for this survey. The response rate over the years has been high, with both the degree-granting institution response rate and the overall response rate for non-degree-granting institutions at almost 100 percent in fall 2006. Because of the high response rate for degree-granting institutions, nonsampling error caused by imputation is also minimal. Imputation methods and the response bias analysis for the fall 2006 survey are discussed in *Postsecondary Institutions in the United States: Fall 2006 and Degrees and Other Awards Conferred: 2005–06* (NCES 2007-166).

The *Integrated Postsecondary Education Data System Data Quality Study* (NCES 2005-175) indicated that most Title IV institutions supplying revised data on completions in 2003–04 were able to supply missing data for the prior year. The small differences between imputed data for the prior year

and the revised actual data supplied by the institution indicated that the imputed values produced by NCES were acceptable.

Further information on the IPEDS Completions survey may be obtained from

Andrew Mary
Postsecondary Studies Division
Postsecondary Institutional Studies Program
National Center for Education Statistics
1990 K Street NW
Washington, DC 20006
andrew.mary@ed.gov
http://nces.ed.gov/ipeds

Fall (Institutional Characteristics)

This survey collects the basic information necessary to classify institutions, including control, level, and types of programs offered, as well as information on tuition, fees, and room and board charges. Beginning in 2000, the survey collected institutional pricing data from institutions with first-time, full-time, degree/certificate-seeking undergraduate students. Unduplicated full-year enrollment counts and instructional activity are now collected in the Fall Enrollment survey. The overall response rate was at almost 100 percent for Title IV degree-granting institutions for 2007 data.

The *Integrated Postsecondary Education Data System Data Quality Study* (NCES 2005-175) looked at tuition and price in Title IV institutions. Only 8 percent of institutions in 2002–03 and 2003–04 reported the same data to IPEDS and Thomson Peterson consistently across all selected data items. Differences in wordings or survey items may account for some of these inconsistencies.

Further information on the IPEDS Institutional Characteristics survey may be obtained from

Tara Coffey
Postsecondary Studies Division
Postsecondary Institutional Studies Program
National Center for Education Statistics
1990 K Street NW
Washington, DC 20006
tara.coffey@ed.gov
http://nces.ed.gov/ipeds

Winter (Fall Staff)

The fall staff data presented in this publication were collected by NCES through IPEDS, which collects data from postsecondary institutions, including all 2- and 4-year degree-granting education institutions. IPEDS collects staff data biennially, in odd numbered years.

Questionnaires for the 2005–06 Fall Staff survey were completed on the IPEDS data collection website between December 2005 and January 2006; respondents report employment statistics for their institution that cover the payroll period in the fall of the survey year. The 2005–06 survey had an overall response rate of 99.9 percent and a response rate of 99.9 percent for both degree-granting institutions and for non-degree-granting institutions. Imputation methods and the response bias analysis for the 2005–06 Fall Staff survey are discussed in *Employees in Postsecondary Institutions, Fall 2005, and Salaries of Full-Time Instructional Faculty, 2005–06* (NCES 2007-150).

The most recent data quality study, *Integrated Postsecondary Education Data System Data Quality Study* (NCES 2005-175), found that for 2003–04 employee data items, changes were made by 1.2 percent (77) of the institutions that responded. All who made changes made changes that resulted in different employee counts. For both institutional and aggregate differences, the changes had little impact on the original employee count submissions. A large number of institutions reported different staff data to IPEDS and Thomson Peterson; however, the magnitude of the differences was small—usually no more than 17 faculty members for any faculty variable.

Further information on the Fall Staff survey may be obtained from

Sabrina Ratchford
Postsecondary Studies Division
Postsecondary Institutional Studies Program
National Center for Education Statistics
1990 K Street NW
Washington, DC 20006
sabrina.ratchford@ed.gov
http://nces.ed.gov/ipeds

Winter (Salaries, Tenure, and Fringe Benefits of Full-Time Instructional Faculty)

This institutional survey was conducted for most years from 1966–67 to 1987–88; it has been conducted annually since 1989–90, except for 2000–01. Although the survey form has changed a number of times during these years, only comparable data are presented.

Between 1966–67 and 1985–86, this survey differed from other HEGIS surveys in that imputations were not made for nonrespondents. Thus, there is some possibility that the salary averages presented in this report may differ from the results of a complete enumeration of all colleges and universities. Beginning with the surveys for 1987–88, the IPEDS data tabulation procedures included imputations for survey nonrespondents. The response rate for the 2005–06 survey was 99.9 percent for degree-granting institutions. A number of institutions affected by Hurricanes Rita and Katrina did not respond and their data were not imputed. Imputation methods and the response bias analysis for the 2005–06 survey are discussed in *Employees in Postsecondary Institutions, Fall 2005, and Salaries of Full-Time Instructional Faculty, 2005–06* (NCES 2007-150). Although data from this survey are not subject to sampling error, sources of nonsampling error may include computational errors and misclassification in reporting and processing. The electronic reporting system does allow corrections to prior-year reported or missed data, and this should help with these problems. Also, NCES reviews individual institutions' data for internal and longitudinal consistency and contacts institutions to check inconsistent data.

The *Integrated Postsecondary Education Data System Data Quality Study* (NCES 2005-175) found that only 1.3 percent of the responding Title IV institutions in 2003–04 made changes to their salaries data. The differences between the imputed data and the revised data were small and found to have little impact on the published data.

Further information on the Salaries, Tenure, and Fringe Benefits survey may be obtained from

Sabrina Ratchford
Postsecondary Studies Division
Postsecondary Institutional Studies Program
National Center for Education Statistics
1990 K Street NW
Washington, DC 20006
sabrina.ratchford@ed.gov
http://nces.ed.gov/ipeds

Winter/Spring (Fall Enrollment)

This survey has been part of the HEGIS and IPEDS series since 1966. Response rates for this survey have been relatively high, generally exceeding 85 percent. Beginning in 2000, with web-based data collection, higher response rates were attained. In 2005–06, the overall response rates were 100.0 percent for degree-granting 4-year private not-for-profit institutions, 2-year public institutions, and 2-year private not-for-profit institutions; the response rate was 99.8 percent for 4-year public institutions. Imputation methods and the response bias analysis for the 2005–06 survey are discussed in *Enrollment in Postsecondary Institutions, Fall 2005; Graduation Rates, 1999 & 2002 Cohorts; and Financial Statistics, Fiscal Year 2005* (NCES 2007-154).

Beginning with the fall 1986 survey and the introduction of IPEDS (see above), the survey was redesigned. The survey allows (in alternating years) for the collection of age and residence data. Beginning in 2000, the survey collected instructional activity and unduplicated headcount data, which are needed to compute a standardized, full-time-equivalent (FTE) enrollment statistic for the entire academic year.

The *Integrated Postsecondary Education Data System Data Quality Study* (NCES 2005-175) showed that public institutions made the majority of changes to enrollment data during the 2004 revision period. The majority of changes were made to unduplicated headcount data, with the net differences between the original data and the revised data at about 1 percent. Part-time students in general and enrollment in private not-for-profit institutions were often underestimated. The fewest changes by institutions were to Classification of Instructional Programs (CIP) code data. (The CIP is a taxonomic coding scheme that contains titles and descriptions of primarily postsecondary instructional programs.) More institutions provided enrollment data to IPEDS than to Thomson Peterson. A fairly high percentage of institutions that provided data to both provided the same data, and among those that did not, the difference in magnitude was less than 10 percent.

Further information on the IPEDS Fall Enrollment survey may be obtained from

Jessica Shedd
Postsecondary Studies Division
Postsecondary Institutional Studies Program
National Center for Education Statistics
1990 K Street NW
Washington, DC 20006
jessica.shedd@ed.gov
http://nces.ed.gov/ipeds

Spring (Finance)

This survey was part of the HEGIS series and has been continued under IPEDS. Substantial changes were made in the financial survey instruments in fiscal year (FY) 1976, FY 82, FY 87, FY 97, and FY 02. While these changes were significant, considerable effort has been made to present only comparable information on trends in this report and to note inconsistencies. The FY 76 survey instrument contained numerous revisions to earlier survey forms, which made direct comparisons of line items very difficult. Beginning in FY 82, Pell Grant data were collected in the categories of federal restricted grant and contract revenues and restricted scholarship and fellowship expenditures. Finance tables for this publication have been adjusted by subtracting the largely duplicative Pell Grant amounts from the later data to maintain comparability with pre-FY 82 data. The introduction of IPEDS in the FY 87 survey included several important changes to the survey instrument and data processing procedures. Beginning in FY 97, data for private institutions were collected using new financial concepts consistent with Financial Accounting Standards Board (FASB) reporting standards, which provide a more comprehensive view of college finance activities. The data for public institutions continued to be collected using the older survey form. The data for public and private institutions were no longer comparable and, as a result, no longer presented together in analysis tables. In FY 01, public institutions had the option of either continuing to report using Government Accounting Standards Board (GASB) standards or using the new FASB reporting standards. Beginning in FY 02, public institutions had three options: the original GASB standards, the FASB standards, or the new GASB Statement 35 standards (GASB35). Because of the complexity of the multiple forms used by public institutions, finance data for public institutions for some recent years are not presented in the *Digest*.

Possible sources of nonsampling error in the financial statistics include nonresponse, imputation, and misclassification. The response rate has been about 85 to 90 percent for most of the historic years presented in the *Digest*; however, in more recent years, response rates have been much higher because Title IV institutions are required to respond. The 2002 IPEDS data collection was a full-scale web-based col-

lection, which offered features that improved the quality and timeliness of the data. The ability of IPEDS to tailor online data entry forms for each institution based on characteristics such as institutional control, level of institution, and calendar system, and the institutions' ability to submit their data online, were two such features that improved response. The response rate for the FY 06 Finance survey was 100 percent for degree-granting institutions. Imputation methods and the response bias analysis for the FY 06 survey are discussed in *Enrollment in Postsecondary Institutions, Fall 2006*; *Graduation Rates, 2000 & 2003 Cohorts*; *and Financial Statistics, Fiscal Year 2006* (NCES 2008-173).

Two general methods of imputation were used in HEGIS. If prior-year data were available for a nonresponding institution, they were inflated using the Higher Education Price Index and adjusted according to changes in enrollments. If prior-year data were not available, current data were used from peer institutions selected for location (state or region), control, level, and enrollment size of institution. In most cases, estimates for nonreporting institutions in HEGIS were made using data from peer institutions.

Beginning with FY 87, IPEDS included all postsecondary institutions, but maintained comparability with earlier surveys by allowing 2- and 4-year institutions to be tabulated separately. For FY 87 through FY 91, in order to maintain comparability with the historical time series of HEGIS institutions, data were combined from two of the three different survey forms that make up IPEDS. The vast majority of the data were tabulated from form 1, which was used to collect information from public and private not-for-profit 2- and 4-year colleges. Form 2, a condensed form, was used to gather data for 2-year for-profit institutions. Because of the differences in the data requested on the two forms, several assumptions were made about the form 2 reports so that their figures could be included in the degree-granting institution totals.

In IPEDS, the form 2 institutions were not asked to separate appropriations from grants and contracts, nor were they asked to separate state from local sources of funding. For the form 2 institutions, all federal revenues were assumed to be federal grants and contracts, and all state and local revenues were assumed to be restricted state grants and contracts. All other form 2 sources of revenue, except for tuition and fees and sales and services of educational activities, were included under "other." Similar adjustments were made to the expenditure accounts. The form 2 institutions reported instruction and scholarship and fellowship expenditures only. All other educational and general expenditures were allocated to academic support.

The *Integrated Postsecondary Education Data System Data Quality Study* (NCES 2005-175) found that only a small percentage (2.9 percent, or 168) of postsecondary institutions either revised 2002–03 data or submitted data for items they previously left unreported. Though relatively few institutions made changes, the changes made were relatively large—greater than 10 percent of the original data. With a few exceptions, these changes, large as they were, did not greatly affect the aggregate totals.

Again, institutions were more likely to report data to IPEDS than to Thomson Peterson, and there was a higher percentage reporting different values among those reporting to both. The magnitude of the difference was generally greater for research expenditures. It is likely that the large differences are a function of the way institutions report these data to both entities.

Further information on the IPEDS Finance survey may be obtained from

Craig Bowen
Postsecondary Studies Division
Postsecondary Institutional Studies Program
National Center for Education Statistics
1990 K Street NW
Washington, DC 20006
craig.bowen@ed.gov
http://nces.ed.gov/ipeds

Library Statistics

On October 1, 2007, the administration of the Public Libraries Survey (PLS) and the State Library Agencies (StLA) Survey was transferred to the Institute of Museum and Library Services (IMLS). The transfer of these surveys to IMLS is the result of President Bush's fiscal year 2007 budget request.

Public library statistics were collected annually by NCES using the PLS and disseminated annually through the Federal-State Cooperative System (FSCS) for Public Library Data. Descriptive statistics were produced for over 9,200 public libraries. The PLS included information about staffing; operating income and expenditures; type of governance; type of administrative structure; size of collection; and service measures such as reference transactions, public service hours, interlibrary loans, circulation, and library visits. In FSCS, respondents supplied the information electronically, and data were edited and tabulated in machine-readable form.

The respondents were 9,200 public libraries identified in the 50 states and the District of Columbia by state library agencies. At the state level, FSCS was administered by State Data Coordinators, appointed by the Chief Officer of each State Library Agency. The State Data Coordinator collected the requested data from local public libraries and submitted these data to NCES. An annual training conference sponsored by NCES was provided for the State Data Coordinators. All 50 states and the District of Columbia submitted data for individual public libraries, which were also aggregated to state and national levels.

From 1994 through 2006, NCES conducted the StLA Survey for the 50 states and the District of Columbia. A state library agency is the official agency of a state that is charged by state law with the extension and development of public library services throughout the state and that has adequate authority under state law to administer state plans in accor-

dance with the provisions of the Library Services and Technology Act (LSTA) of 2003. The StLA Survey collected data on services, collections, staffing, revenue, and expenditures.

Under the Academic Libraries Survey (ALS), NCES surveyed academic libraries on a 3-year cycle between 1966 and 1988. From 1988 through 1999, ALS was a component of the Integrated Postsecondary Education Data System (IPEDS) and was on a 2-year cycle. Beginning with fiscal year (FY) 2000, ALS was no longer a component of IPEDS, but it remains on a 2-year cycle. ALS provides data on about 3,700 academic libraries. In aggregate, these data provide an overview of the status of academic libraries nationally and statewide. The survey collects data on the libraries in the entire universe of degree-granting institutions. Beginning with the collection of FY 2000 data, the ALS changed to web-based data collection. ALS produces descriptive statistics on academic libraries in postsecondary institutions in the 50 states, the District of Columbia, and the outlying areas.

School library data were collected on the School and Principal Surveys during the 1990–91 Schools and Staffing Survey (SASS). The School Library Media Centers (LMC) Survey became a component of SASS with the 1993–94 administration. Since then, the LMC Survey has been conducted during the 1999–2000, 2003–04, and 2007–08 school years. During the 2003–04 administration, only the public and Bureau of Indian Education (BIE) school library media centers were surveyed. School library questions focus on staff, collections, equipment, services, and expenditures.

Further information on library statistics may be obtained from

Tai Phan
Elementary/Secondary and Library Studies Division
Elementary/Secondary Sample Survey Studies Program
National Center for Education Statistics
1990 K Street NW
Washington, DC 20006
tai.phan@ed.gov
http://nces.ed.gov/surveys/libraries

National Adult Literacy Survey

The National Adult Literacy Survey (NALS), funded by the U.S. Department of Education and 12 states, was created in 1992 as a new measure of literacy. The aim of the survey was to profile the English literacy of adults in the United States based on their performance across a wide array of tasks that reflect the types of materials and demands they encounter in their daily lives.

To gather information on adults' literacy skills, trained staff interviewed a nationally representative sample of nearly 13,600 individuals age 16 and older during the first 8 months of 1992. These participants had been randomly selected to represent the adult population in the country as a whole. Black and Hispanic households were oversampled to ensure reliable estimates of literacy proficiencies and to permit analyses of the performance of these subpopulations. In addition, some 1,100 inmates from 80 federal and state prisons were interviewed to gather information on the proficiencies of the prison population. In total, nearly 26,000 adults were surveyed.

Each survey participant was asked to spend approximately an hour responding to a series of diverse literacy tasks, as well as questions about his or her demographic characteristics, educational background, reading practices, and other areas related to literacy. Based on their responses to the survey tasks, adults received proficiency scores along three scales that reflect varying degrees of skill in prose, document, and quantitative literacy. The results of the 1992 survey were first published in a report, *Adult Literacy in America: A First Look at the Findings of the National Adult Literacy Survey* (NCES 93-275), in September 1993.

Further information on NALS may be obtained from

Sheida White
Assessment Division
Assessment Design and Analysis Program
National Center for Education Statistics
1990 K Street NW
Washington, DC 20006
sheida.white@ed.gov
http://nces.ed.gov/naal/nals_products.asp

National Assessment of Adult Literacy

The 2003 National Assessment of Adult Literacy (NAAL) was conducted to measure both English literacy and health literacy. The assessment was administered to 19,000 adults (including 1,200 prison inmates) age 16 and over in all 50 states and the District of Columbia. Components of the assessment included a background questionnaire, a prison component, the State Assessment of Adult Literacy (SAAL), a health literacy component, the Fluency Addition to NAAL (FAN), and the Adult Literacy Supplemental Assessment (ALSA). The assessment measured literacy directly through the completion of tasks, and results were reported using the following achievement levels: *Below Basic, Basic, Intermediate,* and *Proficient.*

By comparing the 1992 NALS and 2003 NAAL results, NAAL provides an indicator of the progress of adult literacy in the nation.

Further information on NAAL may be obtained from

Sheida White
Assessment Division
Assessment Design and Analysis Program
National Center for Education Statistics
1990 K Street NW
Washington, DC 20006
sheida.white@ed.gov
http://nces.ed.gov/naal

National Assessment of Educational Progress

The National Assessment of Educational Progress (NAEP) is a series of cross-sectional studies initially implemented in 1969 to gather information about selected levels of educational achievement across the country. At the national level, NAEP is divided into two assessments: main NAEP and long-term trend NAEP. NAEP has surveyed students at specific ages (9, 13, and 17) for the long-term trend NAEP and at grades 4, 8, and 11 or 12 for the main NAEP, state NAEP, and long-term writing NAEP. NAEP has also surveyed young adults (ages 25 to 35).

NAEP long-term trend assessments are designed to inform the nation of changes in the basic achievement of America's youth. Nationally representative samples of students have been assessed in science, mathematics, and reading at ages 9, 13, and 17 since the early 1970s. Students were assessed in writing at grades 4, 8, and 11 between 1984 and 1996. To measure trends accurately, assessment items (mostly multiple choice) and procedures have remained unchanged since the first assessment in each subject. Recent trend assessments were conducted in 1994, 1996, 1999, and 2004. Nearly 33,000 students took part in the 2004 trend assessment. Results are reported as average scores for the nation, for regions, and for various subgroups of the population, such as racial and ethnic groups. Data from the trend assessments are available in the most recent report, *NAEP 2004 Trends in Academic Progress* (NCES 2005-464). The most recent long-term trend assessment (of reading and mathematics) was administered in early 2008 with release of data scheduled for 2009.

The 2004 NAEP long-term trend assessments marked the end of tests designed and administered from 1971, marked the beginning of a modified design that provides greater accommodations for students with disabilities and English language learners, and limited the assessments to reading and math. Science and writing are now assessed only in main NAEP.

To ensure that the assessment results can be reported on the same trend line, a "bridge" assessment was administered in addition to the modified assessment. Students were randomly assigned to take either the bridge assessment or the modified assessment. The bridge assessment replicated the instrument given in 1999 and used the same administrative techniques. The 2004 modified assessment provides the basis of comparison for all future assessments, and the bridge links its results to the results from the past 30 years.

In the main national NAEP, a nationally representative sample of students is assessed at grades 4, 8, and 12 in various academic subjects. The assessments change periodically and are based on frameworks developed by the National Assessment Governing Board (NAGB). Items include both multiple-choice and constructed-response (requiring written answers) items. Results are reported in two ways. Average scores are reported for the nation, for participating states and jurisdictions, and for subgroups of the population. In addition, the percentage of students at or above *Basic, Proficient,* and *Advanced* achievement levels is reported for these same groups. The achievement levels are developed by NAGB.

From 1990 until 2001, main NAEP was conducted for states and other jurisdictions that chose to participate (e.g., 47 participated in 1996). Prior to 1992, the national NAEP samples were not designed to support the reporting of accurate and representative state-level results. Separate representative samples of students were selected for each participating jurisdiction. State data are usually available at grades 4 and/or 8, and may not include all subjects assessed in the national-level assessment. In 1994, for example, NAEP assessed reading, geography, and history at the national level at grades 4, 8, and 12; however, only reading at grade 4 was assessed at the state level. In 1996, mathematics and science were assessed nationally at grades 4, 8, and 12; at the state level, mathematics was assessed at grades 4 and 8, and science was assessed at grade 8 only. In 1997, the arts were assessed only at the national level, at grade 8. Reading and writing were assessed in 1998 at the national level for grades 4, 8, and 12 and at the state level for grades 4 and 8; civics was also assessed in 1998 at the national level for grades 4, 8, and 12. These assessments generally involved about 130,000 students at the national and state levels.

In 2002, under the provisions of the No Child Left Behind Act of 2001, all states began to participate in main NAEP and a separate national sample was replaced with the aggregate of all state samples. In 2002, students were assessed in reading and writing at grades 4, 8, and 12 for the national assessment and at grades 4 and 8 for the state assessment. In 2003, reading and mathematics were assessed at grades 4 and 8 for both national and state assessments.

The NAEP national samples in 2003 and 2005 were obtained by aggregating the samples from each state, rather than by obtaining an independently selected national sample. As a consequence, the size of the national sample increased, and smaller differences between scores across years or types of students were found to be statistically significant than would have been detected in previous assessments.

The assessment data presented in this publication were derived from tests designed and conducted by the Education Commission of the States (from 1969 to 1983) and by the Educational Testing Service (ETS) (from 1983 to the present).

Sample sizes and overall participation rates in 2004 for the long-term trend reading assessment for the bridge group were 5,200 9-year-olds (81 percent), 5,700 13-year-olds (77 percent), and 3,800 17-year-olds (55 percent); for those taking the modified assessment, the sizes and rates for the bridge group were 7,300 9-year-olds (80 percent), 7,500 13-year-olds (76 percent), and 7,600 17-year-olds (56 percent). Sample sizes and overall participation rates for the math assessment for the bridge group were 4,600 9-year-olds (80 percent), 4,700 13-year-olds (76 percent), and 4,600 17-year-olds (57 percent); for those taking the modified assessment, the sizes and rates for the bridge group were 7,500 9-year-olds (80 percent), 8,300 13-year-olds (76 percent), and 8,300 17-year-olds (56 percent).

Sample sizes for the reading proficiency portion of the 1999 NAEP long-term trend study were 5,793 for 9-year-olds, 5,933 for 13-year-olds, and 5,288 for 17-year-olds. Overall participation rates were 78 percent, 73 percent, and 59 percent, respectively. Sample sizes for the math and science portions of the 1999 long-term trend study were 6,032 9-year-olds, 5,941 13-year-olds, and 3,795 17-year-olds.

The main NAEP assessments are conducted separately from the long-term assessments. The 2000 mathematics assessment was administered to 13,511 4th-graders, 15,694 8th-graders, and 13,432 12th-graders. The response rates were 96 percent for 4th-graders, 92 percent for 8th-graders, and 77 percent for 12th-graders. The 2003 mathematics assessment was administered to 190,147 4th-graders and 153,189 8th-graders. About 172,000 4th-graders, 162,000 8th-graders, and over 21,000 12th-graders participated in the 2005 assessment.

In 2000, a reading assessment was administered to 77,914 4th-graders. The response rate was 96 percent. In 2002, a reading assessment was administered to 140,487 4th-graders, 115,176 8th-graders, and 14,724 12th-graders. The 2003 reading assessment was administered to 187,581 4th-graders and 155,183 8th-graders. Over 165,000 4th-graders, 159,000 8th-graders, and 21,000 12th-graders participated in the assessment in 2005.

The 1997–98 writing assessment was administered to 19,816 4th-graders, 20,586 8th-graders, and 19,505 12th-graders. The response rates were 95 percent for the 4th-graders, 92 percent for the 8th-graders, and 80 percent for the 12th-graders. The 2002 writing assessment was administered to 139,200 4th-graders, 118,500 8th-graders, and 18,500 12th-graders. The 2007 writing assessment was administered to 139,900 8th-graders and 27,900 12th-graders with response rates of 92 percent and 80 percent respectively.

In 1995–96, a science assessment was administered to 7,305 4th-graders, 7,774 8th-graders, and 7,537 12th-graders. The response rates were 94 percent for the 4th-graders, 94 percent for the 8th-graders, and 93 percent for the 12th-graders. In 2000, a science assessment was administered to 16,749 4th-graders, 16,837 8th-graders, and 15,879 12th-graders. The response rates were 96 percent for the 4th-graders, 92 percent for the 8th-graders, and 76 percent for the 12th-graders. More than 300,000 students in grades 4, 8, and 12 participated in the 2005 science assessment.

The 1993–94 geography assessment was administered to 5,507 4th-graders, 6,878 8th-graders, and 6,234 12th-graders. The response rates for the assessment were 93 percent for the 4th-graders, 93 percent for the 8th-graders, and 90 percent for the 12th-graders. The 2000–01 geography assessment was administered to 7,779 4th-graders, 10,037 8th-graders, and 9,660 12th-graders. The response rates were 95 percent for the 4th-graders, 93 percent for the 8th-graders, and 77 percent for the 12th-graders. The next geography assessment is scheduled for 2009–10.

The 2006 U.S. history assessment, the first since 2001, was administered to over 29,000 students in grades 4, 8, and 12 nationwide. Students in public, private, Department of Defense, and Bureau of Indian Affairs schools were assessed.

The 2006 civics assessment was administered to approximately 25,000 students in grades 4, 8, and 12 nationwide. The response rates for the respective grades were 95 percent, 92 percent, and 72 percent. The previous civics assessment was in 1998.

In 2006, an economics assessment was administered at grade 12 for the first time. Results are based on a nationally representative sample of 11,500 12th-graders from 590 public and private schools. The student participation rate was 72 percent for public school students and 87 percent for private school students.

Information from NAEP is subject to both nonsampling and sampling errors. Two possible sources of nonsampling error are nonparticipation and instrumentation. Certain populations have been oversampled to ensure samples of sufficient size for analysis. Instrumentation nonsampling error could result from failure of the test instruments to measure what is being taught and, in turn, what the students are learning.

Further information on NAEP may be obtained from

Suzanne Triplett
State Support and Constituency Outreach
Assessment Division
National Center for Education Statistics
1990 K Street NW
Washington, DC 20006
suzanne.triplett@ed.gov
http://nces.ed.gov/nationsreportcard

National Education Longitudinal Study of 1988

The National Education Longitudinal Study of 1988 (NELS:88) was the third major secondary school student longitudinal study conducted by NCES. The two studies that preceded NELS:88, the National Longitudinal Study of the High School Class of 1972 (NLS:72) and the High School and Beyond Longitudinal Study (HS&B) in 1980, surveyed high school seniors (and sophomores in HS&B) through high school, postsecondary education, and work and family formation experiences. Unlike its predecessors, NELS:88 began with a cohort of 8th-grade students. In 1988, some 25,000 8th-graders, their parents, their teachers, and their school principals were surveyed. Follow-ups were conducted in 1990 and 1992, when a majority of these students were in the 10th and 12th grades, respectively, and then 2 years after their scheduled high school graduation, in 1994. A fourth follow-up was conducted in 2000.

NELS:88 was designed to provide trend data about critical transitions experienced by young people as they develop, attend school, and embark on their careers. It complements and strengthens state and local efforts by furnishing new information on how school policies, teacher practices, and family involvement affect student educational outcomes (i.e., academic achievement, persistence in school, and par-

ticipation in postsecondary education). For the base year, NELS:88 included a multifaceted student questionnaire, four cognitive tests, a parent questionnaire, a teacher questionnaire, and a school questionnaire.

In 1990, when most of the students were in 10th grade, students, school dropouts, their teachers, and their school principals were surveyed. (Parents were not surveyed in the 1990 follow-up.) In 1992, when most of the students were in 12th grade, the second follow-up conducted surveys of students, dropouts, parents, teachers, and school principals. Also, information from the students' transcripts was collected. The 1994 survey data were collected when most sample members had completed high school. The primary goals of the 1994 survey were (1) to provide data for trend comparisons with NLS:72 and HS&B; (2) to address issues of employment and postsecondary access and choice; and (3) to ascertain how many dropouts had returned to school and by what route. The 2000 follow-up examined the educational and labor market outcomes of the 1988 cohort at a time of transition. Most had been out of high school 8 years; many had completed their postsecondary educations, were embarking on first or even second careers, and were starting families.

Further information on NELS:88 may be obtained from

Jeffrey Owings
Elementary/Secondary and Library Studies Division
National Center for Education Statistics
1990 K Street NW
Washington, DC 20006
jeffrey.owings@ed.gov
http://nces.ed.gov/surveys/nels88

National Household Education Surveys Program

The National Household Education Surveys Program (NHES) is a data collection system that is designed to address a wide range of education-related issues. Surveys have been conducted in 1991, 1993, 1995, 1996, 1999, 2001, 2003, 2005, and 2007. NHES targets specific populations for detailed data collection. It is intended to provide more detailed data on the topics and populations of interest than are collected through supplements to other household surveys.

The topics addressed by NHES:1991 were early childhood education and adult education. About 60,000 households were screened for NHES:1991. In the Early Childhood Education Survey, about 14,000 parents/guardians of 3- to 8-year-olds completed interviews about their children's early educational experiences. Included in this component were participation in nonparental care/education; care arrangements and school; and family, household, and child characteristics. In the NHES:1991 Adult Education Survey, about 9,800 people 16 years of age and older, identified as having participated in an adult education activity in the previous 12 months, were questioned about their activities. Data were collected on programs and up to four courses, including the subject matter, duration, sponsorship, purpose, and cost. Information on the household and the adult's background and current employment was also collected.

In NHES:1993, nearly 64,000 households were screened. Approximately 11,000 parents of 3- to 7-year-olds completed interviews for the School Readiness Survey. Topics included the developmental characteristics of preschoolers; school adjustment and teacher feedback to parents for kindergartners and primary students; center-based program participation; early school experiences; home activities with family members; and health status. In the School Safety and Discipline Survey, about 12,700 parents of children in grades 3 to 12 and about 6,500 youth in grades 6 to 12 were interviewed about their school experiences. Topics included the school learning environment, discipline policy, safety at school, victimization, the availability and use of alcohol/drugs, and alcohol/drug education. Peer norms for behavior in school and substance use were also included in this topical component. Extensive family and household background information was collected, as well as characteristics of the school attended by the child.

In NHES:1995, the Early Childhood Program Participation Survey and the Adult Education Survey were similar to those fielded in 1991. In the Early Childhood component, about 14,000 parents of children from birth to third grade were interviewed out of 16,000 sampled, for a completion rate of 90 percent. In the Adult Education Survey, about 25,000 adults were sampled and 80 percent (20,000) completed the interview.

NHES:1996 covered parent and family involvement in education and civic involvement. Data on homeschooling and school choice also were collected. The 1996 survey screened about 56,000 households. For the Parent and Family Involvement in Education Survey, nearly 21,000 parents of children in grades 3 to 12 were interviewed. For the Civic Involvement Survey, about 8,000 youth in grades 6 to 12, about 9,000 parents, and about 2,000 adults were interviewed. The 1996 survey also addressed public library use. Adults in almost 55,000 households were interviewed to support state-level estimates of household public library use.

NHES:1999 collected end-of-decade estimates of key indicators from the surveys conducted throughout the 1990s. Approximately 60,000 households were screened for a total of about 31,000 interviews with parents of children from birth through 12th grade (including about 6,900 infants, toddlers, and preschoolers) and adults age 16 or older not enrolled in grade 12 or below. Key indicators included participation of children in nonparental care and early childhood programs, school experiences, parent/family involvement in education at home and at school, youth community service activities, plans for future education, and adult participation in educational activities and community service.

NHES:2001 included two surveys that were largely repeats of similar surveys included in earlier NHES collections. The Early Childhood Program Participation Survey was similar in content to the Early Childhood Program Participation Survey fielded as part of NHES:1995, and the Adult Education and Lifelong Learning Survey was similar in content to the Adult Education Survey of NHES:1995. The Before- and After-School Programs and Activities Survey, while containing items fielded in earlier NHES collections, had a number of new items that collected information about what school-age children were doing during the time they spent in child care or in other activities, what parents were looking for in care arrangements and activities, and parent evaluations of care arrangements and activities. Parents of approximately 6,700 children from birth to age 6 who were not yet in kindergarten completed Early Childhood Program Participation Survey interviews. Nearly 10,900 adults completed Adult Education and Lifelong Learning Survey interviews, and parents of nearly 9,600 children in kindergarten through grade 8 completed Before- and After-School Programs and Activities Survey interviews.

NHES:2003 included two surveys: the Parent and Family Involvement in Education Survey and the Adult Education for Work-Related Reasons Survey (the first administration). Whereas previous adult education surveys were more general in scope, this survey had a narrower focus on occupation-related adult education programs. It collected in-depth information about training and education in which adults participated specifically for work-related reasons, either to prepare for work or a career, or to maintain or improve work-related skills and knowledge they already had. The Parent and Family Involvement Survey expanded on the first survey fielded on this topic in 1996. In 2003, screeners were completed with 32,049 households. About 12,700 of the 16,000 sampled adults completed the Adult Education for Work-Related Reasons Survey, for a response rate of 76 percent. For the Parent and Family Involvement in Education Survey, interviews were completed by the parents of about 12,400 of the 14,900 sampled children in kindergarten through grade 12, yielding a unit response rate of 83 percent.

NHES:2005 included surveys that covered adult education, early childhood program participation, and after-school programs and activities. Data were collected from about 8,900 adults for the Adult Education Survey, parents of about 7,200 children for the Early Childhood Program Participation Survey, and parents of nearly 11,700 children for the After-School Programs and Activities Survey. These surveys were substantially similar to the surveys conducted in 2001, with the exceptions that the Adult Education Survey addressed a new topic, informal learning activities for personal interest, and the Early Childhood Program Participation Survey and After-School Programs and Activities Survey did not collect information about before-school care for school-age children.

NHES:2007 fielded the Parent and Family Involvement in Education Survey and the School Readiness Survey. These surveys were similar in design and content to surveys included in the 2003 and 1993 collections, respectively. New features added to the Parent and Family Involvement Survey were questions about supplemental education services provided by schools and school districts (including use of and satisfaction with such services), as well as questions to efficiently identify the school attended by the sampled students. New features added to the School Readiness Survey were questions that collected details about TV programs watched by the sampled children. For the Parent and Family Involvement Survey, interviews were completed with parents of 10,681 sampled children in kindergarten through 12th grade, including 10,370 students enrolled in public or private schools and 311 homeschooled children. For the School Readiness Survey, interviews were completed with parents of 2,633 sampled children ages 3 to 6 and not yet in kindergarten. Parents who were interviewed about children in kindergarten through second grade for the Parent and Family Involvement Survey were also asked some questions about these children's school readiness.

Further information on NHES may be obtained from

Andrew Zukerberg
Early Childhood, International, and Crosscutting Studies Division
Early Childhood and Household Studies Program
National Center for Education Statistics
1990 K Street NW
Washington, DC 20006
andrew.zukerberg@ed.gov
http://nces.ed.gov/nhes

National Longitudinal Study of the High School Class of 1972

The National Longitudinal Study of the High School Class of 1972 (NLS:72) began with the collection of base-year survey data from a sample of about 19,000 high school seniors in the spring of 1972. Five follow-up surveys of these students were conducted in 1973, 1974, 1976, 1979, and 1986. NLS:72 was designed to provide the education community with information on the transitions of young adults from high school through postsecondary education and the workplace.

In addition to the follow-ups, a number of supplemental data collection efforts were undertaken. For example, a Postsecondary Education Transcript Study (PETS) was undertaken in 1984; in 1986, the fifth follow-up included a supplement for those who became teachers.

The sample design for NLS:72 was a stratified, two-stage probability sample of 12th-grade students from all schools, public and private, in the 50 states and the District of Columbia during the 1971–72 school year. During the first stage of sampling, about 1,070 schools were selected for participation in the base-year survey. As many as 18 students were selected at random from each of the sample schools. The sizes of both the school and student samples were increased during the first follow-up survey. Beginning with the first follow-up and continuing through the fourth follow-up,

about 1,300 schools participated in the survey and slightly fewer than 23,500 students were sampled. The response rates for each of the different rounds of data collection were 80 percent or higher.

Sample retention rates across the survey years were quite high. For example, of the individuals responding to the base-year questionnaire, the percentages who responded to the first, second, third, and fourth follow-up questionnaires were about 94, 93, 89, and 83 percent, respectively.

Further information on NLS:72 may be obtained from

Aurora D'Amico
Postsecondary Studies Division
Postsecondary Cooperative System, Analysis, and Dissemination Program
National Center for Education Statistics
1990 K Street NW
Washington, DC 20006
aurora.d'amico@ed.gov
http://nces.ed.gov/surveys/nls72

National Postsecondary Student Aid Study

The National Postsecondary Student Aid Study (NPSAS) is a comprehensive nationwide study of how students and their families pay for postsecondary education. It covers nationally representative samples of undergraduates, graduates, and first-professional students in the 50 states, the District of Columbia, and Puerto Rico, including students attending less-than-2-year institutions, community colleges, 4-year colleges, and major universities. Participants include students who do not receive aid and their parents, as well as students who do receive financial aid and their parents. Study results are used to help guide future federal policy regarding student financial aid. NPSAS was conducted every 3 years. Beginning with the 1999–2000 study, NPSAS is conducted every 4 years.

The first NPSAS was conducted during the 1986–87 school year. Data were gathered from about 1,074 colleges, universities, and other postsecondary institutions; 60,000 students; and 14,000 parents. These data provided information on the cost of postsecondary education, the distribution of financial aid, and the characteristics of both aided and nonaided students and their families.

As a part of NPSAS:93, information on 77,000 undergraduates and graduate students enrolled during the school year was collected at 1,000 postsecondary institutions. The sample included students enrolled at any time between July 1, 1992, and June 30, 1993. About 66,000 students and a subsample of their parents were interviewed by telephone. NPSAS:96 contained information on more than 48,000 undergraduate and graduate students from 973 postsecondary institutions enrolled at any time during the 1995–96 school year. NPSAS:2000 included nearly 62,000 students (49,930 undergraduates, 10,640 graduate students, and 1,200 first-professional students) from 999 postsecondary institutions. NPSAS:04 collected data on 69,100 undergraduates and 31,800 graduate students from 1,360 postsecondary institutions.

Further information on NPSAS may be obtained from

James Griffith
Aurora D'Amico
Postsecondary Studies Division
Postsecondary Longitudinal and Sample Studies Program
National Center for Education Statistics
1990 K Street NW
Washington, DC 20006
james.griffith@ed.gov
aurora.d'amico@ed.gov
http://nces.ed.gov/npsas

National Study of Postsecondary Faculty

The National Study of Postsecondary Faculty (NSOPF) was designed to provide data about faculty to postsecondary researchers, planners, and policymakers. NSOPF is the most comprehensive study of faculty in postsecondary education institutions ever undertaken.

The first cycle of NSOPF (NSOPF:88) was conducted by NCES with support from the National Endowment for the Humanities (NEH) in 1987–88 with a sample of 480 colleges and universities, over 3,000 department chairpeople, and over 11,000 instructional faculty. The second cycle of NSOPF (NSOPF:93) was conducted by NCES with support from NEH and the National Science Foundation in 1992–93. NSOPF:93 was limited to surveys of institutions and faculty, but with a substantially expanded sample of 974 colleges and universities, and 31,354 faculty and instructional staff. The third cycle, NSPOF:99, included 960 degree-granting postsecondary institutions and approximately 18,000 faculty and instructional staff. The fourth cycle of NSOPF was conducted in 2003–04 and included 1,080 degree-granting postsecondary institutions and approximately 26,000 faculty and instructional staff. The fifth cycle is scheduled to take place in 2008–09.

Further information on NSOPF may be obtained from

Linda J. Zimbler
Postsecondary Studies Division
Postsecondary Longitudinal and Sample Studies Program
National Center for Education Statistics
1990 K Street NW
Washington, DC 20006
linda.zimbler@ed.gov
http://nces.ed.gov/surveys/nsopf

Private School Universe Survey

The purposes of the Private School Universe Survey (PSS) data collection activities are (1) to build an accurate and complete list of private schools to serve as a sampling frame for NCES sample surveys of private schools; and (2) to report data on the total number of private schools, teachers, and students in the survey universe. Begun in 1989, the PSS has been conducted every 2 years, and data for the 1989–90, 1991–92, 1993–94, 1995–96, 1997–98, 1999–2000, 2001–02, 2003–04, and 2005–2006 school years have been released.

The PSS produces data similar to that of the CCD for public schools, and can be used for public-private comparisons. The data are useful for a variety of policy and research-relevant issues, such as the growth of religiously affiliated schools, the number of private high school graduates, the length of the school year for various private schools, and the number of private school students and teachers.

The target population for this universe survey is all private schools in the United States that meet the PSS criteria of a private school (i.e., the private school is an institution that provides instruction for any of grades K through 12, has one or more teachers to give instruction, is not administered by a public agency, and is not operated in a private home). The survey universe is composed of schools identified from a variety of sources. The main source is a list frame initially developed for the 1989–90 PSS. The list is updated regularly by matching it with lists provided by nationwide private school associations, state departments of education, and other national guides and sources that list private schools. The other source is an area frame search in approximately 124 geographic areas, conducted by the U.S. Census Bureau.

Further information on the PSS may be obtained from

Steve Broughman
Elementary/Secondary and Libraries Studies Division
Elementary/Secondary Sample Survey Studies Program
National Center for Education Statistics
1990 K Street NW
Washington, DC 20006
stephen.broughman@ed.gov
http://nces.ed.gov/surveys/pss

Projections of Education Statistics

Since 1964, NCES has published projections of key statistics for elementary and secondary schools and institutions of higher education. The latest report is titled *Projections of Education Statistics to 2017* (NCES 2008-078). These projections include statistics for enrollments, instructional staff, graduates, earned degrees, and expenditures. These reports include several alternative projection series and a methodology section describing the techniques and assumptions used to prepare them. Data in this edition of the *Digest* reflect the middle alternative projection series.

Differences between the reported and projected values are, of course, almost inevitable. An evaluation of past projections revealed that, at the elementary and secondary level, projections of enrollments have been quite accurate: mean absolute percentage differences for enrollment ranged from 0.3 to 1.3 percent for projections from 1 to 5 years in the future, while those for teachers were less than 3 percent. At the higher education level, projections of enrollment have been fairly accurate: mean absolute percentage differences were 5 percent or less for projections from 1 to 5 years into the future.

Further information on *Projections of Education Statistics* may be obtained from

William Hussar
Early Childhood, International, and Crosscutting Studies
    Division
Annual Reports Program
National Center for Education Statistics
1990 K Street NW
Washington, DC 20006
william.hussar@ed.gov
http://nces.ed.gov/annuals

Recent College Graduates Study

Between 1976 and 1991, NCES conducted periodic surveys of baccalaureate and master's degree recipients 1 year after graduation with the Recent College Graduates (RCG) Study. The RCG Study—which has been replaced by the Baccalaureate and Beyond Longitudinal Study (B&B) (see listing above)—concentrated on those graduates entering the teaching profession. The study linked respondents' major field of study with outcomes such as whether the respondent entered the labor force or was seeking additional education. Labor force data collected included employment status (unemployed, employed part time, or employed full time), occupation, salary, career potential, relation to major field of study, and need for a college degree. To obtain accurate results on teachers, graduates with a major in education were oversampled. The last two studies oversampled education majors and increased the sampling of graduates with majors in other fields.

For each of the selected institutions, a list of graduates by major field of study was obtained, and a sample of graduates was drawn by major field of study. Graduates in certain major fields of study (e.g., education, mathematics, physical sciences) were sampled at higher rates than were graduates in other fields. Roughly 1 year after graduation, the sample of graduates was located, contacted by mail or telephone, and asked to respond to the questionnaire.

The locating process was more detailed than that in most surveys. Nonresponse rates were directly related to the time, effort, and resources used in locating graduates, rather than to graduates' refusals to participate. Despite the difficulties in locating graduates, RCG response rates are comparable to studies that do not face problems locating their sample membership.

The 1976 study of 1974–75 college graduates was the first, and smallest, of the series. The sample consisted of 211 schools, of which 200 (96 percent) responded. Of the 5,854 graduates in the sample, 4,350 responded, for a response rate of 79 percent.

The 1981 study was somewhat larger, covering 297 institutions and 15,852 graduates. Responses were obtained from 283 institutions, for an institutional response rate of 95 percent, and from 9,312 graduates (716 others were determined to be out of scope), for a response rate of 74 percent.

The 1985 study sampled 404 colleges and 18,738 graduates, of whom 17,853 were found to be in scope. Responses were obtained from 13,200 graduates, for a response rate of 78 percent. The response rate for colleges was 98 percent. The 1987 study sampled 21,957 graduates. Responses were received from 16,878, for a response rate of nearly 80 percent.

The 1991 study sampled 18,135 graduates of 400 bachelor's and master's degree-granting institutions, including 16,172 bachelor's degrees recipients and 1,963 master's degree recipients receiving diplomas between July 1, 1989, and June 30, 1990. Random samples of graduates were selected from lists stratified by field of study. Graduates in education, mathematics, and the physical sciences were sampled at a higher rate, as were minority graduates, to provide a sufficient number of these graduates for analysis purposes. The graduates included in the sample were selected in proportion to the institution's number of graduates. The institutional response rate was 95 percent, and the graduate response rate was 83 percent.

Appendix table A-3 contains sample sizes for number of graduates, by field, for the 1976, 1981, 1985, 1987, and 1991 surveys.

Further information on the RCG Study may be obtained from

Aurora D'Amico
Postsecondary Studies Division
Postsecondary Cooperative System, Analysis, and
    Dissemination Program
National Center for Education Statistics
1990 K Street NW
Washington, DC 20006
aurora.d'amico@ed.gov
http://nces.ed.gov/surveys/b&b

School Survey on Crime and Safety (SSOCS)

The most recent School Survey on Crime and Safety (SSOCS) for which data are available was conducted by NCES in spring/summer of the 2005–06 school year. SSOCS focuses on incidents of specific crimes/offenses and a variety of specific discipline issues in public schools. It also covers characteristics of school policies, school violence prevention programs and policies, and school characteristics that have been associated with school crime. The survey was conducted with a nationally representative sample of regular public elementary, middle, and high schools in the 50 states and the District of Columbia. Special education, alternative, and vocational schools; schools in the other jurisdictions; and schools that taught only prekindergarten, kindergarten, or adult education were not included in the sample.

The sampling frame for the 2006 SSOCS was constructed from the public school universe file created for the 2003–04 Schools and Staffing Survey from the 2003–04 Common Core of Data (CCD) Public Elementary/Secondary School Universe File. The sample was stratified by instructional level, type of locale (urbanicity), and enrollment size. The sample of schools in each instructional level was allocated to each of the 16 cells formed by the cross-classification of the four categories of enrollment size and four types of locale. The sample was allocated to each subgroup in proportion to the sum of the square roots of the total student enrollment in each school in that stratum. The effective sample size within each stratum was then inflated to account for nonresponse. Once the final sample sizes were determined for each of the 64 strata, the subgroups were sorted by region and percent minority enrollment, and an initial sample of 3,565 schools was selected. Of those schools, 2,724 completed the survey. In March 2006, questionnaires were mailed to school principals, who were asked to complete the survey or to have it completed by the person at the school most knowledgeable about discipline issues. The weighted overall response rate was 80.6 percent, and item nonresponse rates ranged from 0 to 33.7 percent. A nonresponse bias analysis was conducted on the 13 items with weighted item nonresponse rates greater than 15 percent, and it was determined that the increased potential for bias in these items was not enough to warrant their exclusion from the data file. Weights were developed to adjust for the variable probabilities of selection and differential nonresponse and can be used to produce national estimates for regular public schools in the 2005–06 school year.

For more information about the SSOCS, contact

Kathryn Chandler
Elementary/Secondary and Libraries Studies Division
Elementary/Secondary Sample Survey Studies Program
National Center for Education Statistics
1990 K Street NW
Washington, DC 20006
kathryn.chandler@ed.gov
http://nces.ed.gov/surveys/ssocs

Schools and Staffing Survey

The Schools and Staffing Survey (SASS) is a set of linked questionnaires used to collect data on the nation's public and private elementary and secondary teaching force, characteristics of schools and school principals, demand for teachers, and school/school district policies. SASS data are collected through a mail questionnaire with telephone follow-up. SASS was first conducted for NCES by the Census Bureau during the 1987–88 school year. SASS subsequently was conducted in 1990–91, 1993–94, 1999–2000, 2003–04, and 2007–08 (2007–08 to be released in June 2009). The 1990–91, 1993–94, 1999–2000, 2003–04, and 2007–08 SASS also obtained data on Bureau of Indian Education

(BIE) schools (schools funded or operated by the BIE). The universe of charter schools in operation in 1998–99 was given the Charter School Questionnaire to complete as part of the 1999–2000 SASS. In the 2003–04 SASS administration, charter schools were not administered a separate questionnaire, but were included in the public school sample. Another change in the 2003–04 administration included a revised data collection methodology using a primary in-person contact with the school with the aim of reducing the field follow-up phase. Also, school library media centers were surveyed only in the public and BIE schools. (See discussion on the School Library Media Centers Survey in "Library Statistics Program," above.)

The 2003–04 SASS estimates are based on a sample consisting of approximately 8,000 public schools, 2,500 private schools, and 145 BIE schools. The public school sample for the 2003–04 SASS was based on an adjusted public school universe file from the 2001–02 school year Common Core of Data (CCD), the compilation of all the nation's public school districts and public schools. The sampling frame includes regular public schools, Department of Defense-operated military base schools in the United States, and other schools, such as special education, vocational, and alternative schools. SASS is designed to provide national estimates for public and private school characteristics and state estimates for school districts, public schools, principals, and teachers. In addition, the teacher survey is designed to allow comparisons between new and experienced teachers and between bilingual/English as a second language (ESL) teachers and other teachers.

The BIE sample consisted of all BIE schools that met the SASS definition of a school.

The private school sample for the 2003–04 SASS was selected from the 2001–02 Private School Universe Survey, supplemented with updates from state lists collected by the Census Bureau and lists by private school associations and religious denominations. Private school estimates are available at the national level and by private school affiliation.

In 2003–04, the weighted response rate for the School District Questionnaire was 82.9 percent. Weighted response rates for the Public School Principal Questionnaire, the Private School Principal Questionnaire, and the BIE-funded School Principal Questionnaire were 82.2 percent, 74.9 percent, and 90.7 percent, respectively.

Weighted response rates in 2003–04 for the Public School Questionnaire, the Private School Questionnaire, and the BIE-funded School Questionnaire were 80.8 percent, 75.9 percent, and 89.5 percent, respectively. The weighted overall response rates were 84.8 percent for public school teachers, 82.4 percent for private school teachers, and 92.0 percent for BIE-funded school teachers.

The Data Analysis System at http://nces.ed.gov/surveys/sass/das.asp may be used to access public school, public teacher, private school, and private teacher public-use data. There is also a methodology report on SASS, the

Quality Profile for SASS, Rounds 1–3: 1987–1995, Aspects of the Quality of Data in the Schools and Staffing Surveys (SASS) (NCES 2000-308).

Further information on SASS may be obtained from

Kerry Gruber
Elementary/Secondary and Libraries Studies Division
Elementary/Secondary Sample Survey Studies Program
National Center for Education Statistics
1990 K Street NW
Washington, DC 20006
kerry.gruber@ed.gov
http://nces.ed.gov/surveys/sass

Teacher Follow–up Survey (TFS)

The Teacher Follow–up Survey is a SASS survey whose purpose is to determine how many teachers remain at the same school, move to another school, or leave the profession in the year following a SASS administration. It is administered to elementary and secondary teachers in the fifty states and the District of Columbia. The TFS uses two questionnaires, one for teachers who left teaching since the previous SASS administration and another for those who are still teaching either in the same school as last year or in a different school. The objective of the TFS is to focus on the characteristics of each group in order to answer questions about teacher mobility and attrition.

Further information on the TFS may be obtained from

Kathryn Chandler
Elementary/Secondary and Libraries Studies Division
Elementary/Secondary Sample Survey Studies Program
National Center for Education Statistics
1990 K Street NW
Washington, DC 20006
kathryn.chandler@ed.gov
http://nces.ed.gov/surveys/sass

Other Department of Education Agencies

Institute of Education Sciences (IES)

SRI International

The National Longitudinal Transition Study-2

The National Longitudinal Transition Study-2 (NLTS-2) is a follow-up of the original National Longitudinal Transition Study conducted from 1985 through 1993. NLTS-2 began in 2001 with a sample of special education students who were ages 13 through 16 and in at least 7th grade on December 1, 2000. The study will continue for 10 years and is designed to provide a national picture of these youths' experiences and achievements as they transition into adulthood. Data will be collected from parents, youth, and schools by survey, telephone interviews, student assessments, and transcripts.

NLTS-2 is designed to align with the original NLTS by including many of the same questions and data items, thus allowing comparisons between the NLTS and NLTS-2 youths' experiences. NLTS-2 also includes items that have been collected in other national databases to permit comparisons between NLTS-2 youth and the general youth population.

Further information on NLTS-2 may be obtained from

Lynn Newman
SRI International
333 Ravenswood Ave.
Menlo Park, CA 94025
lynn.newman@sri.com
http://www.sri.com

Office for Civil Rights

OCR Elementary and Secondary School Survey

The OCR Elementary and Secondary School (E&S) Survey has been used since 1968 by the U.S. Department of Education's Office for Civil Rights (OCR) to obtain trend data from the nation's public elementary and secondary schools. The E&S Survey provides information about the enrollment of students in public schools in every state and about some education services provided to those students. These data are reported by race/ethnicity, sex, and disability.

Data in the E&S Survey are collected pursuant to 34 C.F.R. Section 100.6(b) of the Department of Education regulation implementing Title VI of the Civil Rights Act of 1964. The requirements are also incorporated by reference in Department regulations implementing Title IX of the Education Amendments of 1972, Section 504 of the Rehabilitation Act of 1973, and the Age Discrimination Act of 1975. School, district, state, and national data are currently available. Data from individual public schools and districts are used to generate projected national and state data.

In recent surveys, the sample has been approximately 6,000 districts and 60,000 schools; however, in 2000, data were collected from all public school districts. In sample surveys, the following districts are sampled with certainty: districts having more than 25,000 students; all districts in states having 25 or fewer public school districts; and districts subject to federal court order and monitored by the U.S. Department of Justice. The survey is conducted biennially (with few exceptions). Data currently are available from the 2006 survey.

Data marked with an exclamation point (!) have a nonresponse rate of more than 30 percent. Numbers should be used with caution due to large statistical uncertainty in the estimate. The methodology for flagging "large statistical uncertainties" is based on a standard error for each projected item.

Further information on the E&S Survey can be obtained from

Mary Schifferli
Office for Civil Rights
U.S. Department of Education
555 12th Street SW
Washington, DC 20202
mary.schifferli@ed.gov
http://www.ed.gov/about/offices/list/ocr/data.html?src=rt

Office of Special Education and Rehabilitative Services

Annual Report to Congress on the Implementation of the Individuals With Disabilities Education Act

The Individuals With Disabilities Education Act (IDEA), formerly the Education of the Handicapped Act (EHA), requires the Secretary of Education to transmit to Congress annually a report describing the progress made in serving the nation's children with disabilities. This annual report contains information on children served by public schools under the provisions of Part B of the IDEA and on children served in state-operated programs for the disabled under Chapter I of the Elementary and Secondary Education Act.

Statistics on children receiving special education and related services in various settings and school personnel providing such services are reported in an annual submission of data to the Office of Special Education and Rehabilitative Services (OSERS) by the 50 states, the District of Columbia, and the outlying areas. The child count information is based on the number of children with disabilities receiving special education and related services on December 1 of each year. Count information is available from http://www.ideadata.org.

Since each participant in programs for the disabled is reported to OSERS, the data are not subject to sampling error. However, nonsampling error can arise from a variety of sources. Some states follow a noncategorical approach to the delivery of special education services, but produce counts by disabling condition because Part B of the EHA requires it. In those states that do categorize their disabled students, definitions and labeling practices vary.

Further information on this annual report to Congress may be obtained from

Office of Special Education Programs
Office of Special Education and Rehabilitative Services
U.S. Department of Education
550 12th Street SW
Washington, DC 20065
http://www.ed.gov/about/offices/list/osers/osep/
http://www.ideadata.org

Office of Vocational and Adult Education

Division of Adult Education and Literacy

The Division of Adult Education and Literacy (DAEL) promotes programs that help American adults get the basic skills they need to be productive workers, family members, and citizens. The major areas of support are Adult Basic Education, Adult Secondary Education, and English Language Acquisition. These programs emphasize basic skills such as reading, writing, math, English language competency, and problem solving. Each year, DAEL reports enrollment numbers in state-administered adult education programs for these major areas of support for all 50 states, the District of Columbia, and the eight U.S. jurisdictions (American Samoa, the Federated States of Micronesia, Guam, the Marshall Islands, the Northern Marianas, Palau, Puerto Rico, and the U.S. Virgin Islands).

Further information on DAEL may be obtained from

Office of Vocational and Adult Education
Division of Adult Education and Literacy
U.S. Department of Education
400 Maryland Avenue SW
Washington, DC 20202
http://www.ed.gov/about/offices/list/ovae/pi/AdultEd/

Other Governmental Agencies

Bureau of Labor Statistics

Consumer Price Indexes

The Consumer Price Index (CPI) represents changes in prices of all goods and services purchased for consumption by urban households. Indexes are available for two population groups: a CPI for All Urban Consumers (CPI-U) and a CPI for Urban Wage Earners and Clerical Workers (CPI-W). Unless otherwise specified, data in the *Digest* are adjusted for inflation using the CPI-U. These values are frequently adjusted to a school-year basis by averaging the July through June figures. Price indexes are available for the United States, the four Census regions, size of city, cross-classifications of regions and size classes, and 26 local areas. The major uses of the CPI include as an economic indicator, as a deflator of other economic series, and as a means of adjusting income.

Also available is the Consumer Price Index research series using current methods (CPI-U-RS), which presents an estimate of the CPI-U from 1978 to the present that incorporates most of the improvements that the Bureau of Labor Statistics has made over that time span into the entire series. The historical price index series of the CPI-U does not reflect these changes, though these changes do make the present and future CPI more accurate. The limitations of the CPI-U-RS include considerable uncertainty surrounding the magnitude of the adjustments and the several improvements in the CPI that have not been incorporated into the CPI-U-RS for various reasons. Nonetheless, the CPI-U-RS can serve as a valuable proxy for researchers needing a historical estimate of inflation using current methods.

Further information on consumer price indexes may be obtained from

Consumer Price Indexes
Bureau of Labor Statistics
U.S. Department of Labor
2 Massachusetts Avenue NE
Washington, DC 20212
http://www.bls.gov/cpi

Employment and Unemployment Surveys

Statistics on the employment and unemployment status of the population and related data are compiled by the Bureau of Labor Statistics (BLS) using data from the Current Population Survey (CPS) (see below) and other surveys. The Current Population Survey, a monthly household survey conducted by the U.S. Census Bureau for the Bureau of Labor Statistics, provides a comprehensive body of information on the employment and unemployment experience of the Nation's population, classified by age, sex, race, and various other characteristics.

Further information on unemployment surveys may be obtained from

Bureau of Labor Statistics
U.S. Department of Labor
2 Massachusetts Avenue NE
Washington, DC 20212
cpsinfo@bls.gov
http://www.bls.gov/bls/employment.htm

Census Bureau

Census of Population—Education in the United States

Some tables in this report are based on a part of the decennial census that consists of questions asked of a one-in-six sample of people and housing units in the United States. This sample was asked more detailed questions about income, occupation, and housing costs, in addition to general demographic information.

School Enrollment. People classified as enrolled in school reported attending a "regular" public or private school or college. They were asked whether the institution they attended was public or private and what level of school they were enrolled in.

Educational Attainment. Data for educational attainment were tabulated for people age 15 and older and classified according to the highest grade completed or the highest degree received. Instructions were also given to include the level of the previous grade attended or the highest degree received for people currently enrolled in school.

Poverty Status. To determine poverty status, answers to income questions were used to make comparisons to the appropriate poverty threshold. All people except those who were institutionalized, people in military group quarters and college dormitories, and unrelated people under age 15 were considered. If the total income of each family or unrelated individual in the sample was below the corresponding cutoff, that family or individual was classified as "below the poverty level."

Further information on the 1990 and 2000 Census of Population may be obtained from

Population Division
Census Bureau
U.S. Department of Commerce
Washington, DC 20233
http://www.census.gov/prod/www/abs/decenial.html
http://www.census.gov/main/www/cen2000.html

Current Population Survey

The Current Population Survey (CPS) is a monthly survey of about 60,000 households conducted by the U.S. Census Bureau for the Bureau of Labor Statistics. The CPS is the primary source of information of labor force statistics for the U.S. noninstitutionalized population (e.g., excludes military personnel and their families living on bases and inmates of institutions). In addition, supplemental questionnaires are used to provide further information about the U.S. population. Specifically, in October, detailed questions regarding school enrollment and school characteristics are asked. In March, detailed questions regarding income are asked.

The current sample design, introduced in July 2001, includes about 72,000 households. Each month about 60,000 of the 72,000 households are eligible for interview and of those 7 to 8 percent are not interviewed because of temporary absence or unavailability. Information is obtained each month from those in the household 15 years of age and older and demographic data are collected for children 0–14 years of age. Prior to July 2001, data was collected in the CPS from about 50,000 dwelling units. The samples are initially selected based on the decennial census files and are periodically updated to reflect new housing construction.

The estimation procedure employed for monthly CPS data involves inflating weighted sample results to independent estimates of characteristics of the civilian noninstitutional population in the United States by age, sex, and race. These independent estimates are based on statistics from decennial censuses; statistics on births, deaths, immigration, and emigration; and statistics on the population in the armed services. Generalized standard error tables are provided in the *Current Population* Reports or methods for deriving standard errors can be found within the CPS technical documentation at http://www.census.gov/apsd/tech doc/cps/cps-main.html. The CPS data are subject to both nonsampling and sampling errors.

Caution should also be used when comparing data from 1994 through 2001, which reflect 1990 census-based population controls, with data from 1993 and earlier, which reflect 1980 or earlier census-based population controls, as well as with data from 2002 onward, which reflect 2000 census-based controls. Changes in population controls generally have relatively little impact on summary measures such as means, medians, and percentage distributions. They can have a significant impact on population counts. For example, use of the 1990 census-based population control resulted in about a 1 percent increase in the civilian noninstitutional population and in the number of families and households. Thus, estimates of levels for data collected in 1994 and later years will differ from those for earlier years by more than what could be attributed to actual changes in the population. These differences could be disproportionately greater for certain subpopulation groups than for the total population.

Further information on CPS may be obtained from

Education and Social Stratification Branch
Population Division
Census Bureau
U.S. Department of Commerce
Washington, DC 20233
http://www.census.gov/cps

Dropouts

Each October, the Current Population Survey (CPS) includes supplemental questions on the enrollment status of the population 3 years old and over as part of the monthly basic survey on labor force participation. In addition to gathering the information on school enrollment, with the limitations on accuracy as noted below under "School Enrollment," the survey data permit calculations of dropout rates. Both status and event dropout rates are tabulated from the October CPS. The *Digest* provides information using the status rate calculation. Event rates describe the proportion of students who leave school each year without completing a high school program. Status rates provide cumulative data on dropouts among all young adults within a specified age range. Status rates are higher than event rates because they include all dropouts ages 16 through 24, regardless of when they last attended school.

In addition to other survey limitations, dropout rates may be affected by survey coverage and exclusion of the institutionalized population. The incarcerated population has grown more rapidly and has a higher dropout rate than the general population. Dropout rates for the total population might be higher than those for the noninstitutionalized population if the prison and jail populations were included in the dropout rate calculations. On the other hand, if military personnel, who tend to be high school graduates, were included, it might offset some or all of the impact from the theoretical inclusion of the jail and prison population.

Another area of concern with tabulations involving young people in household surveys is the relatively low coverage ratio compared to older age groups. CPS undercoverage results from missed housing units and missed people within sample households. Overall CPS undercoverage is estimated to be about 8 percent. CPS undercoverage varies with age, sex, and race. Generally, undercoverage is larger for males than for females and larger for Blacks and other races combined than for Whites. For example, in 2007 the undercoverage ratio for Black 20- to 24-year-old males is 31 percent. Ratio estimation to independent age-sex-race-Hispanic population controls partially corrects for the bias due to undercoverage. Further information on CPS methodology may be obtained from http://www.census.gov/cps.

Further information on the calculation of dropouts and dropout rates may be obtained from *Dropout Rates in the United States: 2005* at http://nces.ed.gov/pubs2007/dropout05/ or by contacting

Chris Chapman
Early Childhood, International, and Crosscutting Studies Division
Early Childhood and Household Studies Program
National Center for Education Statistics
1990 K Street NW
Washington, DC 20006
chris.chapman@ed.gov

Educational Attainment

Reports documenting educational attainment are produced by the Census Bureau using March CPS supplement (Annual Social and Economic Supplement (ASEC)) results. The sample size for the 2007 March supplement increased to about 98,000 households, with about 83,000 eligible for interview and about 76,000 interviews completed. The latest release is *Educational Attainment in the United States: 2007*, which may be downloaded at http://www.census.gov/popu lation/www/socdemo/education/cps2007.html.

In addition to the general constraints of CPS, some data indicate that the respondents have a tendency to overestimate the educational level of members of their household. Some inaccuracy is due to a lack of the respondent's knowledge of the exact educational attainment of each household member and the hesitancy to acknowledge anything less than a high school education. Another cause of nonsampling variability is the change in the numbers in the armed services over the years.

The March 2007 basic CPS response rate was 90.6 percent and the ASEC household-level response rate was 91.5 percent for a total supplement response rate of 82.9 percent.

Further information on CPS's educational attainment may be obtained from the CPS website at http://www.cen sus.gov/cps.

Further information on CPS's educational attainment data may be obtained from

Education and Social Stratification Branch
Census Bureau
U.S. Department of Commerce
Washington, DC 20233
http://www.census.gov/population/www/socdemo/
  educ-attn.html

School Enrollment

Each October, the Current Population Survey (CPS) includes supplemental questions on the enrollment status of the population 3 years old and over. Prior to 2001, the October supplement consisted of approximately 47,000 interviewed households. Beginning with the October 2001 supplement, the sample was expanded by 9,000 to a total of approximately 56,000 interviewed households. The main sources of nonsampling variability in the responses to the supplement are those inherent in the survey instrument. The question of current enrollment may not be answered accurately for various reasons. Some respondents may not know current grade information for every student in the household, a problem especially prevalent for households with members in college or in nursery school. Confusion over college credits or hours taken by a student may make it difficult to determine the year in which the student is enrolled. Problems may occur with the definition of nursery school (a group or class organized to provide educational experiences for children), where respondents' interpretations of "educational experiences" vary.

The October 2006 basic CPS household-level response rate was 91.9 percent and the school enrollment supplement person-level response rate was 96.1 percent. Since these rates are determined at different levels they cannot be combined to derive an overall response rate.

Further information on CPS methodology may be obtained from http://www.census.gov/cps.

Further information on the CPS School Enrollment Supplement may be obtained from

Education and Social Stratification Branch
Census Bureau
U.S. Department of Commerce
Washington, DC 20233
http://www.census.gov/population/www/socdemo/
  school.html

Government Finances

The Census Bureau conducts an Annual Survey of Government Finances as authorized by law under Title 13, United States Code, Section 182. This survey covers the entire range of government finance activities: revenue, expenditure, debt, and assets. Revenues and expenditures comprise actual receipts and payments of a government and its agencies, including government-operated enterprises, utilities, and public trust funds. The expenditure-reporting categories comprise all amounts of money paid out by a government and its agencies, with the exception of amounts for debt retirement and for loan, investment, agency, and private trust transactions.

Most of the federal government statistics are based on figures that appear in *The Budget of the United States Government*. Since the classification used by the Census Bureau for reporting state and local government finance statistics differs in a number of important respects from the classification used in the U.S. budget, it was necessary to adjust the federal data. For this report, federal budget expenditures include interest accrued, but not paid, during the fiscal year; Census data on interest are on a disbursement basis.

State government finances are based primarily on the annual Census Bureau Survey of Government Finances. Census analysts compile figures from official records and reports of the state governments for most of the state financial data. States differ in the ways they administer activities; they may fund such activities directly, or they may disburse the money to a lower level government or government agency. Therefore, caution is advised when attempting to make a direct comparison between states on their state fiscal aid data.

The sample of local governments is drawn from the periodic Census of Governments and consists of certain local governments sampled with certainty plus a sample below the certainty level. Finance data for all school districts are collected on an annual basis and released through the NCES Common Core of Data system.

The statistics in *Government Finances* that are based wholly or partly on data from the sample are subject to sampling error. State government finance data are not subject to sampling error. Estimates of major U.S. totals for local governments are subject to a computed sampling variability of less than one-half of 1 percent. The estimates are also subject to the inaccuracies in classification, response, and processing that would occur if a complete census had been conducted under the same conditions as the sample.

Further information on government finances may be obtained from

Governments Division
Census Bureau
U.S. Department of Commerce
Washington, DC 20233
http://www.census.gov/govs/www/

Survey of Income and Program Participation

The main objective of the Survey of Income and Program Participation (SIPP) is to provide accurate and comprehensive information about the income and program participation of individuals and households in the United States, and about the principal determinants of income and program participation. SIPP offers detailed information on cash and noncash income on a subannual basis. The survey also collects data on taxes, assets, liabilities, and participation in government transfer programs. SIPP data allow the government to evaluate the effectiveness of federal, state, and local programs.

The survey design is a continuous series of national panels, with sample size ranging from approximately 14,000 to 36,700 interviewed households. The duration of each panel ranges from 2 1/2 years to 4 years. The SIPP sample is a multistage-stratified sample of the U.S. civilian noninstitutionalized population. For the 1984–93 panels, a panel of households was introduced each year in February. A 4-year panel was introduced in April 1996. A 2000 panel was introduced in February 2000 for two waves. A 3-year 2001 panel was introduced in February 2001. All household members 15 years old and over are interviewed by self-response, if possible. Proxy response is permitted when household members are not available for interviewing.

The SIPP content is built around a "core" of labor force, program participation, and income questions designed to measure the economic situation of people in the United States. These questions expand the data currently available on the distribution of cash and noncash income and are repeated at each interviewing wave. The survey uses a 4-month recall period, with approximately the same number of interviews being conducted in each month of the 4-month period for each wave. Interviews are conducted by personal visit and by decentralized telephone.

The survey has been designed to also provide a broader context for analysis by adding questions on a variety of topics not covered in the core section. These questions are labeled "topical modules" and are assigned to particular interviewing waves of the survey. Topics covered by the modules include personal history, child care, wealth, program eligibility, child support, disability, school enrollment, taxes, and annual income.

Further information on the SIPP may be obtained from

Economics and Statistics Administration
Census Bureau
U.S. Department of Commerce
Washington, DC 20233
http://www.census.gov/sipp/overview.html

National Institute on Drug Abuse

The National Institute on Drug Abuse of the U.S. Department of Health and Human Services is the primary supporter of the long-term study entitled "Monitoring the Future: A Continuing Study of the Lifestyles and Values of Youth," conducted by the University of Michigan Institute for Social Research. One component of the study deals with student drug abuse. Results of the national sample survey have been published annually since 1975. With the exception of 1975, when about 9,400 students participated in the survey, the annual samples comprise roughly 16,000 students in 133 schools. Students complete self-administered questionnaires given to them in their classrooms by University of Michigan personnel. Each year, 8th-, 10th-, and 12th-graders are surveyed (12th-graders since 1975, and 8th- and 10th-graders since 1991). The 8th- and 10th-grade surveys are anonymous,

while the 12th-grade survey is confidential. The 10th-grade samples involve about 17,000 students in 140 schools each year, while the 8th-grade samples have approximately 18,000 students in about 150 schools. In all, approximately 50,000 students from about 420 public and private secondary schools are surveyed annually. Over the years, the response rate has varied from 77 to 86 percent. Beginning with the class of 1976 a randomly selected sample from each senior class has been followed in the years after high school on a continuing basis.

Understandably, there is some reluctance to admit illegal activities. Also, students who are out of school on the day of the survey are nonrespondents, and the survey does not include high school dropouts. The inclusion of absentees and dropouts would tend to increase the proportion of individuals who had used drugs. A 1983 study found that the inclusion of absentees could increase some of the drug usage estimates by as much as 2.7 percentage points. (Details on that study and its methodology were published in *Drug Use Among American High School Students, College Students, and Other Young Adults*, by L.D. Johnston, P.M. O'Malley, and J.G. Bachman, available from the National Clearinghouse on Drug Abuse Information, 5600 Fishers Lane, Rockville, MD 20857.)

Further information on the Monitoring the Future drug abuse survey may be obtained from

National Institute on Drug Abuse
Division of Epidemiology and Statistical Analysis
5600 Fishers Lane
Rockville, MD 20857
http://www.monitoringthefuture.org

National Science Foundation

Federal Funds Survey

The annual Federal Funds Survey is the primary source of information about federal funding for R&D in the United States. It is used by policymakers in the executive and legislative branches of the federal government in determining policies, laws, and regulations affecting science; it is also used by those who follow science trends in every sector of the economy, including university administrators and professors, economic and political analysts, R&D managers inside and outside the government, the science press, and leading members of the science community in the United States and around the world.

The survey is completed by the 15 federal departments and their 70 subagencies and 15 independent agencies that conduct R&D programs. The sample is obtained from information in the president's budget submitted to Congress.

Federal funds data, as collected, span 3 government fiscal years: the fiscal year just completed, the current fiscal year, and the president's budget year. Actual data are collected for the year just completed; estimates are obtained for the current fiscal year and the budget year.

The data is collected and managed online; this system was designed to help improve survey reporting by offering respondents direct online reporting and editing.

The Federal Funds Survey has a response rate of 100 percent with no known item nonresponse, The information included in this survey has been stable since FY 1973, when federal obligations for research to universities and colleges by agency and detailed Science & Engineering fields were added to the survey.

Further information on federal funds for research and development may be obtained from

Research and Development Statistics Program
Division of Science Resources Statistics
National Science Foundation
4201 Wilson Boulevard
Arlington, VA 22230
http://www.nsf.gov/statistics

Survey of Earned Doctorates

The Survey of Earned Doctorates has collected basic statistics from the universe of doctoral recipients in the United States each year since 1958. It has been supported by five federal agencies: the National Science Foundation, in conjunction with the U.S. Department of Education; the National Endowment for the Humanities; the U.S. Department of Agriculture; and the National Institutes of Health.

With the assistance of graduate deans, a survey form is distributed to each person completing the requirements for a doctorate. Of the 45,596 new research doctorates granted in 2006, the response rate was 92 percent. The questionnaire obtains information on sex, race/ethnicity, marital status, citizenship, disabilities, dependents, specialty field of doctorate, educational institutions attended, time spent in completion of doctorate, financial support, education debt, postgraduation plans, and educational attainment of parents.

Further information on the Survey of Earned Doctorates may be obtained from

Human Resources Program
Division of Science Resources Studies
National Science Foundation
4201 Wilson Boulevard
Arlington, VA 22230
http://www.nsf.gov/statistics/srvydoctorates
http://www.norc.org/projects/Survey+of+Earned+
    Doctorates.htm

Survey of Graduate Students and Postdoctorates in Science and Engineering

The Survey of Graduate Students and Postdoctorates in Science and Engineering, also known as the graduate student survey (GSS), is an annual survey at the academic department level of all U.S. institutions offering graduate programs in any science, engineering, or health field. It is an institution-based survey that provides data on the number and characteristics of graduate science and engineering students enrolled in approximately 600 U.S. academic institutions.

Data for the 2006 GSS were collected at the beginning of academic year 2006–07. This survey includes all branch campuses, affiliated research centers, and separately organized components—such as medical or dental schools, nursing schools, and schools of public health—from all academic institutions that offer doctor's and master's degree programs. Only those graduate students enrolled for credit in a master's or doctoral program in science or engineering in the fall of 2006 were included in the survey. M.D., D.O., D.V.M., or D.D.S. candidates, interns, and residents were counted if they were concurrently working on a master's or doctoral degree in science or engineering or were enrolled in a joint M.D./Ph.D. program.

The final 2006 survey universe consisted of 707 reporting units (schools) at 586 graduate institutions: 212 master's-granting institutions and 495 reporting units associated with 374 doctorate-granting institutions.

Further information on the Survey of Graduate Students and Postdoctorates in Science and Engineering may be obtained from

Julia Oliver
GSS Project Officer
Human Resources Statistics Program
National Science Foundation
4201 Wilson Boulevard, Suite 965
Arlington, VA 22230
http://www.nsf.gov/statistics/gradpostdoc

Substance Abuse and Mental Health Services Administration

National Survey on Drug Use and Health

Conducted by the federal government since 1971, the National Survey on Drug Use and Health (NSDUH) is an annual survey of the civilian, noninstitutionalized population of the United States age 12 or older. It is the primary source of information on the prevalence, patterns, and consequences of alcohol, tobacco, and illegal drug abuse. The survey collects data by administering questionnaires to a representative sample of the population (since 1999, the NSDUH interview has been carried out using computer-assisted interviewing). NSDUH collects information from residents of households, noninstitutional group quarters, and civilians living on military bases. The main results of the NSDUH present national estimates of rates of use, numbers of users, and other measures related to illicit drugs, alcohol, and tobacco products.

Prior to 2002, the survey was called the National Household Survey on Drug Abuse (NHSDA). Because of improvements to the survey in 2002, the data from 2002 through 2006 should not be compared with 2001 and earlier NHSDA data to assess changes in substance use over time. The 2006 NSDUH screened 151,288 addresses, and 137,057 completed interviews were obtained. The survey was conducted from January through December 2006. Weighted response rates were 90.6

percent for household screening and 74.2 percent for interviewing. The 2005 NSDUH was the first in a coordinated 5-year sample design providing estimates for all 50 states and the District of Columbia for the years 2005 through 2009. Because the 2005 design enables estimates to be developed by state, states may be viewed as the first level of stratification, as well as a reporting variable.

Further information on the 2006 NSDUH may be obtained from

SAMHSA, Office of Applied Studies
1 Choke Cherry Road, Room 7-1044
Rockville, MD 28057
http://www.oas.samhsa.gov/nsduh.htm

Other Organization Sources

American College Testing Program

The ACT assessment is designed to measure educational development in the areas of English, mathematics, social studies, and natural sciences. The ACT assessment is taken by college-bound high school students and by all graduating seniors in Colorado and Illinois. The test results are used to predict how well students might perform in college.

Prior to the 1984–85 school year, national norms were based on a 10 percent sample of the students taking the test. Since then, national norms are based on the test scores of all students taking the test. Beginning with 1984–85, these norms have been based on the most recent ACT scores available from students scheduled to graduate in the spring of the year. Duplicate test records are no longer used to produce national figures.

Separate ACT standard scores are computed for English, mathematics, science reasoning, and, as of October 1989, reading. ACT standard scores are reported for each subject area on a scale from 1 to 36. The four ACT standard scores have a mean (average) of 21.2 and a standard deviation of 5.0 for test-taking students nationally. A composite score is obtained by taking the simple average of the four standard scores and is an indication of a student's overall academic development across these subject areas.

It should be noted that graduating students who take the ACT assessment are not necessarily representative of graduating students nationally. Students who live in the Midwest, Rocky Mountains, Plains, and South are overrepresented among ACT-tested students as compared to graduating students nationally. These students more often attend public colleges and universities, which require the ACT assessment more often than the SAT test.

Further information on the ACT may be obtained from

The American College Testing Program
500 ACT Drive
P.O. Box 168
Iowa City, IA 52243
http://www.act.org/

American Council on Education

One of the American Council on Education's (ACE) programs and services is the General Educational Development Testing Service (GEDTS), which develops and distributes General Educational Development (GED) tests. A GED credential documents high school-level academic skills. It was first administered in 1942 to returning World War II veterans and first administered to civilians in 1947. ACE publishes the *GED Testing Program Statistical Report*. This report looks at those who take the GED, test performance statistics, and historical information on the GED testing program. Attempting to make comparisons across jurisdictions is problematic since each jurisdiction manages its own GED testing program. As such, each jurisdiction develops its own policies which would be reflected in its testing program outcomes such as pass rates.

Further information on the GED may be obtained from

American Council on Education
One Dupont Circle NW
Washington, DC 20036
http://www.acenet.edu
http://www.gedtest.org

College Entrance Examination Board

The Admissions Testing Program of the College Board comprises a number of college admissions tests, including the Preliminary Scholastic Assessment Test (PSAT) and the Scholastic Assessment Test (SAT). High school students participate in the testing program as sophomores, juniors, or seniors—some more than once during these 3 years. If they have taken the tests more than once, only the most recent scores are tabulated. The PSAT and SAT report subscores in the areas of mathematics and verbal ability.

The SAT results are not representative of high school students or college-bound students nationally since the sample is self-selected, i.e., taken by students who need the results to apply to a particular college or university. Public colleges in many states, particularly in the Midwest, parts of the South, and the West, require ACT scores rather than SAT scores. The proportion of students taking the SAT in these states is very low and is inappropriate for comparison. In recent years, more than 1.4 million high school students have taken the SAT examination annually. The latest version of the SAT, which includes a writing component, was first administered in March 2005.

Further information on the SAT can be obtained from

College Entrance Examination Board
Educational Testing Service
Princeton, NJ 08541
http://www.collegeboard.org/

Commonfund Institute

Commonfund Institute took over management of the Higher Education Price Index (HEPI) in September 2004 from Research Associates of Washington, which originated the index in 1961. HEPI measures average changes in prices of goods and services purchased by colleges and universities through educational and general expenditures. Sponsored research and auxiliary enterprises are not priced by HEPI.

HEPI is based on the prices (or salaries) of faculty and of administrators and other professional service personnel; clerical, technical, service, and other nonprofessional personnel; and contracted services, such as data processing, communication, transportation, supplies and materials, equipment, books and periodicals, and utilities. These represent the items purchased for current operations by colleges and universities. Prices for these items are obtained from salary surveys conducted by various national higher education associations, the American Association of University Professors, the Bureau of Labor Statistics, and the National Center for Education Statistics; and from components of the Consumer Price Index (CPI) and the Producer Price Index (PPI) published by the U.S. Department of Labor, Bureau of Labor Statistics.

The quantities of these goods and services have been kept constant based on the 1971–72 buying pattern of colleges and universities. The weights assigned the various items, which represent their relative importance in the current-fund educational and general budget, are estimated national averages. Variance in spending patterns of individual institutions from these national averages reduces only slightly the applicability of HEPI to any given institutional situation. Modest differences in the weights attached to expenditure categories have little effect on overall index values. This is because HEPI is dominated by the trend in faculty salaries and similar salary trends for other personnel hired by institutions, which minimizes the impact of price changes in other items purchased in relatively small quantities.

Further information on HEPI may be obtained from

Commonfund Institute
15 Old Danbury Road
P.O. Box 812
Wilton, CT 06897-0812
http://www.commonfund.org

Council for Aid to Education

The Council for Aid to Education, Inc. (CAE) is a not-for-profit corporation funded by contributions from businesses. CAE largely provides consulting and research services to corporations and information on voluntary support services to education institutions. Each year, CAE conducts a survey of colleges and universities and private elementary and secondary schools to obtain information on the amounts, sources, and purposes of private gifts, grants, and bequests received during the academic year.

Charitable contributions to colleges and universities in the United States grew by 6.3 percent in 2007 with the average increase in contributions to higher education institutions at 6.5 percent. The $29.75 billion raised in 2007 is the highest total ever reported.

Alumni giving declined by 1.5 percent. However, alumni giving in 2007 is still 16.5 percent higher than it was in 2005. Foundation giving increased by 19.7 percent after increasing 1.4 percent in 2006. Corporate giving increased 4.3 percent over the 2006 amount.

Survey forms are reviewed by CAE for internal consistency before preparing a computerized database. Institutional reports of voluntary support data from the CAE Survey of Voluntary Support of Education are more comprehensive and detailed than the related data in the Integrated Postsecondary Education Data System (IPEDS) Finance survey conducted by NCES. The results from the Survey of Voluntary Support of Education are published in the annual *Voluntary Support of Education*, which may be purchased from CAE.

Further information on voluntary support of education may be obtained from

Ann Kaplan
Council for Aid to Education, Inc.
215 Lexington Avenue
21st Floor
New York, NY 10016
vse@cae.org
http://www.cae.org/content/publications.htm

Council of Chief State School Officers

The Council of Chief State School Officers (CCSSO) is a nonprofit organization of the 57 public officials who head departments of public education in every state, the outlying areas, the District of Columbia, and the U.S. Department of Defense dependents schools. In 1985, the CCSSO founded the State Education Assessment Center to provide a locus of leadership to the states to improve the monitoring and assessment of education. This center has since combined with two other CCSSO centers to form the Division of State Services and Technical Assistance, which supports state education agencies in developing standards-based systems that enable all children to succeed. *Key State Education Policies on PK–12 Education* is one of the publications issued by the State Educators Project. Most of the data are obtained from a member questionnaire, and the remainder of the data are from federal government agencies.

Further information on CCSSO publications may be obtained from

Rolf Blank
State Education Indicators Program
Council of Chief State School Officers
One Massachusetts Avenue NW
7th Floor
Washington, DC 20001
http://www.ccsso.org

Education Commission of the States

Clearinghouse Notes

The Education Commission of the States (ECS) Clearinghouse collects information on laws and standards in the field of education and reports them periodically in *Clearinghouse Notes*. ECS collects information about administrators, principals, and teachers. It also examines policy areas, such as assessment and testing, collective bargaining, early childhood issues, quality education, and school schedules. The information is collected by reading state newsletters, tracking state legislation, and surveying state education agencies. Data are verified by the individual states when necessary. Even though ECS monitors state activity on a continuous basis, it updates the reports only when there is significant change.

StateNotes

ECS regularly issues compilations, comparisons, and summaries of state policies on a number of education issues, including high school graduation requirements and school term information. ECS monitors state education activities for changes in education policies and updates ECS state information accordingly.

Further information on *Clearinghouse Notes* and *StateNotes* is available from

Kathy Christie
Education Commission of the States
700 Broadway, #1200
Denver, CO 80203-3460
kchristie@ecs.org
http://www.ecs.org

Graduate Record Examinations Board

Graduate Record Examinations (GRE) tests are taken by individuals applying to graduate or professional school. GRE offers two types of tests, the General Test and Subject Tests. The General Test, which is mainly offered on computer, measures verbal, quantitative, and analytical writing skills. The writing section consists of two analytical writing tasks and replaced the analytical reasoning section on the general GRE after December 31, 2002. The Subject Tests measure achievement in subject areas that include biochemistry, cell and molecular biology, biology, chemistry, computer science, literature in English, mathematics, physics, and psychology. Each graduate institution or division of the institution determines which GRE tests are required for admission.

Individuals may take GRE tests more than once. Score reports only reflect scores earned within the past 5-year period.

Further information on the GRE may be obtained from

Graduate Record Examinations Board
Educational Testing Service
Princeton, NJ 08541
http://www.gre.org

Institute of International Education

Each year, the Institute of International Education (IIE) conducts a survey of the number of foreign students studying in American colleges and universities and reports these data in the publication *Open Doors*. All of the regionally accredited institutions in NCES's Integrated Postsecondary Education Data System (IPEDS) are surveyed by IIE. The foreign student enrollment data presented in the *Digest* are drawn from IIE surveys that ask institutions for information on enrollment of foreign students, as well as student characteristics, such as country of origin. For the 2006–07 survey, approximately 65.2 percent of the 2,702 institutions surveyed reported data.

Additional information can be obtained from the publication *Open Doors* or by contacting

Sharon Witherell
Institute of International Education–Public Affairs
809 United Nations Plaza
New York, NY 10017-3580
sharonwitherell@iie.org
http://opendoors.iienetwork.org

International Association for the Evaluation of Educational Achievement

The International Association for the Evaluation of Educational Achievement, known as the IEA, is composed of governmental research centers and national research institutions around the world whose aim is to investigate education problems common among countries. Since its inception in 1958, the IEA has conducted more than 23 research studies of cross-national achievement. The regular cycle of studies encompasses learning in basic school subjects. Examples are the Trends in International Mathematics and Science Study (TIMSS) and the Progress in International Reading Literacy Study (PIRLS). IEA projects also include studies of particular interest to IEA members, such as the TIMSS 1999 Video Study of Mathematics and Science Teaching, the Civic Education Study (see below), and studies on information technology in education and preprimary education.

Further information on the International Association for the Evaluation of Educational Achievement may be obtained from

http://www.iea.nl

Civic Education Study

In 1994, the IEA General Assembly, composed of the research institutes participating in IEA projects, decided to undertake a two-phase study of civic knowledge called the Civic Education Study (CivEd). Phase I of CivEd, begun in 1996, was designed to collect extensive documentary evidence and expert opinion describing the circumstances, content, and process of civic education in 24 countries. Phase II, the assessment phase of the study, conducted in 1999, was designed to assess the civic knowledge of 14-year-old students across 28 countries. The assessment items in CivEd were designed to measure knowledge and understanding of key principles that are universal across democracies. Another key component of the Phase II study focuses on measuring the attitudes of students toward civic issues. Although the study was designed as an international comparison, the data collected allow individual countries to conduct in-depth, national-level comparisons and analyses. The next survey is scheduled for 2008–09.

Further information on the IEA Civic Education Study may be obtained from

Daniel McGrath
Early Childhood, International, and Crosscutting Studies Division
International Activities Program
National Center for Education Statistics
1990 K Street NW
Washington, DC 20006
daniel.mcgrath@ed.gov
http://nces.ed.gov/surveys/cived

Trends in International Mathematics and Science Study

The Trends in International Mathematics and Science Study (TIMSS, formerly known as the Third International Mathematics and Science Study) provides reliable and timely data on the mathematics and science achievement of U.S. students compared to that of students in other countries. TIMSS data have been collected in 1995, 1999, 2003, and 2007. TIMSS collects information through mathematics and science achievement tests and questionnaires. The questionnaires request information to help provide a context for the performance scores, focusing on such topics as students' attitudes and beliefs about learning, students' habits and homework, and their lives both in and outside of school; teachers' attitudes and beliefs about teaching and learning, teaching assignments, class size and organization, instructional practices, and participation in professional development activities; and principals' viewpoints on policy and budget responsibilities, curriculum and instruction issues, and student behavior, as well as descriptions of the organization of schools and courses. The assessments and questionnaires are designed to specifications in a guiding framework. The TIMSS framework describes the mathematics and sci-

ence content to be assessed by providing grade-specific objectives, an overview of the assessment design, and guidelines for item development.

Each participating country, like the United States, is required to draw random samples of schools. In the United States, a national probability sample drawn for each study has resulted in over 500 schools and approximately 33,000 students participating in 1995, 221 schools and 9,000 students participating in 1999, and 480 schools and almost 19,000 students participating in 2003. This sample design ensures the appropriate number of schools and students are participating to provide a representative sample of the students in a specific grade in the United States as a whole.

The 2003 U.S. fourth-grade sample achieved an initial school response rate of 70 percent (weighted), with a school response rate of 82 percent after replacement schools were added. From the schools that agreed to participate, students were sampled in intact classes. A total of 10,795 fourth-grade students were sampled for the assessment, and 9,829 participated, for a 95 percent student response rate. The resulting fourth-grade overall response rate, with replacements included, was 78 percent. The U.S. eighth-grade sample achieved an initial school response rate of 71 percent, with a school response rate of 78 percent after replacement schools were added. A total of 9,891 students were sampled for the eighth-grade assessment, and 8,912 completed the assessment, for a 94 percent student response rate. The resulting eighth-grade overall response rate, with replacements included, was 73 percent.

Further information on the study may be obtained from

Patrick Gonzales
Early Childhood, International, and Crosscutting Studies Division
International Activities Program
National Center for Education Statistics
1990 K Street NW
Washington, DC 20006
patrick.gonzales@ed.gov
http://nces.ed.gov/timss/

National Association of College and University Business Officers

The National Association of College and University Business Officers (NACUBO) is a nonprofit professional organization representing chief administrative and financial officers at more than 2,500 colleges and universities across the country. Over two-thirds of all institutions of higher learning in the United States are members of NACUBO. Each year, TIAA-CREF Trust Company, a pension system for educators and a manager of college endowments, conducts an in-depth study of college and university endowments for NACUBO, through its subsidiary, the Trust Company. Endowment assets for 2006 NACUBO Endowment Study participants are for the fiscal year ending June 30, 2006.

Endowments include stocks, bonds, cash, and real estate that colleges and universities receive as gifts. Colleges or universities receiving endowments may not spend the endowment principal, only investment income derived from the principal. Quasi-endowments (year-end surplus assets that institutions choose to treat as permanent capital) may also be included in an investment pool's endowment composition. Also, because donors frequently stipulate that their gifts support specific programs at colleges and universities, the overall size of the endowment can be misleading in terms of available income to support the education of undergraduate students. For example, the income from an endowment gift to a medical school or law school may only be spent on those schools. In such cases, the income would not be available to support undergraduate education. Thus, at some research universities with extensive graduate and professional schools, as little as one-third of the institution's endowment may actually be available to generate income to support undergraduate programs and students.

The 2007 study was administered entirely in a web-based format; there were 785 respondents.

Further information on the 2006 NACUBO Endowment Study may be obtained from

National Association of College and
  University Business Officers
1110 Vermont Ave., N.W., Suite 800
Washington, DC 20005
http://www.nacubo.org

National Association of State Directors of Teacher Education and Certification

The National Association of State Directors of Teacher Education and Certification (NASDTEC) was organized in 1928 to represent professional standards boards and commissions and state departments of education that are responsible for the preparation, licensure, and discipline of educational personnel. Currently, NASDTEC's membership includes all 50 states, the District of Columbia, the U.S. Department of Defense Education Activity, U.S. jurisdictions, and Canadian provinces and territories.

The *NASDTEC Manual on the Preparation & Certification of Educational Personnel (NASDTEC Manual)* was printed between 1984 and 2004, when it was replaced by an online publication, KnowledgeBase. This is an expanded version of the *Manual* and is the most comprehensive source of state-by-state information pertaining to the certification requirements and preparation of teachers and other school personnel in the United States and Canada.

Further information on KnowledgeBase may be obtained from

Roy Einreinhofer, Executive Director
NASDTEC

1225 Providence Rd., PMB #116
Whitinsville, MA 01588
rje@nasdtec.com
http://www.nasdtec.info/

National Catholic Educational Association

The National Catholic Educational Association (NCEA) has been providing leadership and service to Catholic education since 1904. NCEA began to publish *The United States Catholic Elementary and Secondary Schools: Annual Statistical Report on Schools, Enrollment and Staffing* in 1970 because of the lack of educational data on the private sector. The report is based on data gathered by each of the 176 archdiocesan and diocesan offices of education in the United States. These data enable NCEA to present information on school enrollment and staffing patterns for prekindergarten through grade 12. The first part of the report presents data concerning the context of American education, while the following segment focuses on statistical data of Catholic schools. Statistics include enrollment by grade level, ethnicity, and religious affiliation.

Further information on *The United States Catholic Elementary and Secondary Schools: Annual Statistical Report on Schools, Enrollment, and Staffing* may be obtained from

Sister Dale McDonald
National Catholic Educational Association
1077 30th Street NW, Suite 100
Washington, DC 20007-6232
mcdonald@ncea.org
http://www.ncea.org

National Education Association

Estimates of School Statistics

The National Education Association (NEA) produces *Estimates of School Statistics* annually. This report provides projections of public school enrollment, employment and personnel compensation, and finances, as reported by individual state departments of education. The state-level data in *Estimates of School Statistics* allow broad assessments of trends in the above areas. These data should be looked at with the understanding that the state-level data do not necessarily reflect the varying conditions within a state on education issues.

Data in this report are provided by state and District of Columbia departments of education and by other, mostly governmental, sources. Surveys are sent to the departments of education requesting estimated data for the current year and revisions to 4 years of historical data, as necessary. Twice a year, NEA submits current-year estimates on more than 35 education statistics to state departments of education for verification or revision. The estimates are generated using regression analyses and are used in the *Estimates* report only if the states do not provide current data.

Further information on *Estimates of School Statistics* may be obtained from

NEA *Rankings & Estimates* Team—NEA Research
1201 16th Street NW
Washington, DC 20036
http://www.nea.org/aboutnea/contact.html
http://www.nea.org

Status of the American Public School Teacher

The Status of the American Public School Teacher Survey is conducted every 5 years by the National Education Association (NEA). The survey was designed by the NEA Research Division and was initially administered in 1956. The intent of the survey is to solicit information covering various aspects of public school teachers' professional, family, and civic lives.

In the 2000–01 survey, 1,467 public school teachers responded and the response rate was 67.4 percent.

Possible sources of nonsampling errors are nonresponses, misinterpretation, and—when comparing data over years—changes in the sampling method and instrument. Misinterpretation of the survey items should be minimal, as the sample responding is not from the general population, but one knowledgeable about the area of concern. The sampling procedure changed after 1956 and some wording of items has changed over different administrations of the survey.

Since sampling is used, sampling variability is inherent in the data. An approximation to the maximum standard error for estimating the population percentages is 1.4 percent. Approximations for significance for other comparisons appear in appendix table A-6. To estimate the 95 percent confidence interval for population percentages, the maximum standard error of 1.4 percent is multiplied by 2 (1.4 x 2). The resulting percentage (2.8) is added and subtracted from the population estimate to establish upper and lower bounds for the confidence interval.

Further information on the Status of the American Public School Teacher Survey may be obtained from

Steven Liu
National Education Association—Research
1201 16th Street NW
Washington, DC 20036
http://www.nea.org/aboutnea/contact.html
http://www.nea.org

Organization for Economic Cooperation and Development

Education at a Glance (EAG)

The Organization for Economic Cooperation and Development (OECD) publishes analyses of national policies and survey data in education, training, and economics in about 30 countries. The countries surveyed are Australia, Austria, Belgium, Canada, Czech Republic, Denmark, Finland, France, Germany, Greece, Hungary, Iceland, Ireland, Italy, Japan, Korea, Luxembourg, Mexico, Netherlands, New Zealand, Norway, Poland, Portugal, Slovak Republic, Spain, Sweden, Switzerland, Turkey, United Kingdom, and United States. In addition to these OECD countries, several partner countries are surveyed for EAG—Brazil, Chile, Estonia, Israel, Russian Federation, and Slovenia.

To highlight current education issues and create a set of comparative education indicators that represent key features of education systems, OECD initiated the International Education Indicators Project (INES) and charged the Centre for Educational Research and Innovation (CERI) with developing the cross-national indicators for it. The development of these indicators involved representatives of the OECD countries and the OECD Secretariat. Improvements in data quality and comparability among OECD countries have resulted from the country-to-country interaction sponsored through the INES project. The most recent publication in this series is *Education at a Glance, OECD Indicators, 2008*.

The *OECD Handbook for Internationally Comparative Education Statistics: Concepts, Standards, Definitions and Classifications* provides countries with specific guidance on how to prepare information for OECD education surveys; facilitate countries' understanding of OECD indicators and their use in policy analysis; and provides a reference for collecting and assimilating educational data. Chapter 7 of the *OECD Handbook for Internationally Comparative Education Statistics* contains a discussion of data quality issues.

Further information on international education statistics may be obtained from

Andreas Schleicher
Indicators & Analysis Division
OECD Directorate for Education
2, rue André Pascal
F-75775 Paris CEDEX 16
France
andreas.schleicher@oecd.org
http://www.oecd.org

Program for International Student Assessment

The Program for International Student Assessment (PISA) is a system of international assessments that focus on 15-year-olds' capabilities in reading literacy, mathematics literacy, and science literacy. PISA also includes measures of general, or cross-curricular, competencies such as learning strategies. PISA emphasizes functional skills that students have acquired as they near the end of mandatory schooling. PISA is organized by the Organization for Economic Cooperation and Development (OECD), an intergovernmental organization of industrialized countries, and was administered for the first time in 2000, when 43 countries participated. In 2003, 41 countries took part in the assessment, and in 2006, 57 jurisdictions (30 OECD members and 27 nonmembers) participated in the assessment.

PISA is a 2-hour-long paper-and-pencil exam. Assessment items include a combination of multiple-choice and open-ended questions, which require students to come up with their own response. PISA scores are reported on a scale with a mean score of 500 and a standard deviation of 100.

PISA is implemented on a 3-year cycle that began in 2000. Each PISA assessment cycle focuses on one subject in particular, although all three subjects are assessed every 3 years. In the first cycle, PISA 2000, reading literacy was the major focus, occupying roughly two-thirds of assessment time. For 2003, PISA focused on mathematics literacy as well as the ability of students to solve problems in real-life settings. In 2006, PISA focused on science literacy.

The intent of PISA reporting is to provide an overall description of performance in reading literacy, mathematics literacy, and science literacy every 3 years, and to provide a more detailed look at each domain in the years when it is the major focus. These cycles will allow countries to compare changes in trends for each of the three subject areas over time.

To implement PISA, each of the participating countries selects a nationally representative sample of 15-year-olds, regardless of grade level. In the United States, nearly 5,600 students from public and nonpublic schools took the PISA 2006 assessment.

In each country, the assessment is translated into the primary language of instruction; in the United States, all materials are written in English.

Further information on PISA may be obtained from

Holly Xie
Early Childhood, International, and Crosscutting Studies
    Division
International Activities Program

National Center for Education Statistics
1990 K Street NW
Washington, DC 20006
holly.xie@ed.gov
http://nces.ed.gov/surveys/pisa

Phi Delta Kappa/Gallup Poll

Public Attitudes Toward the Public Schools Survey

Each year, the Gallup Poll conducts the Public Attitudes Toward the Public Schools Survey, funded by the Phi Delta Kappa Educational Foundation. The survey includes interviews with adults representing the civilian noninstitutional population, age 18 and older.

Gallup uses an unclustered, directory-assisted, random-digit-dial telephone sample, based on a proportionate stratified sampling design. In 2000, the final sample was weighted so that the distribution corresponded with the U.S. Census Bureau's Current Population Survey (CPS) estimates for the adult population living in households with telephones in the continental United States. The sample used in the 40th (2008) annual survey was made up of a total of 1,002 adults age 18 and older. Field work for the survey was conducted between June 4 and July 3, 2008.

The survey is a sample survey and is subject to sampling error. The size of the error depends largely on the number of respondents providing data. Appendix table A-4 shows the approximate sampling errors associated with different percentages and sample sizes for the survey. Appendix table A-5 provides approximate sampling errors for comparisons of two sample percentages.

For example, an estimated percentage of about 10 percent based on the responses of 1,000 sample members maintains an approximate sampling error of 2 percent at the 95 percent confidence level. The sampling error for the difference in two percentages (50 percent versus 41 percent) based on two samples of 750 members and 400 members, respectively, is about 8 percent at the 95 percent confidence level.

Further information on the Public Attitudes Toward the Public Schools Survey may be obtained from

William Bushaw
Phi Delta Kappa
P.O. Box 789
Bloomington, IN 47402-0789
bbushaw@pdkintl.org
http://www.pdkintl.org

United Nations Educational, Scientific, and Cultural Organization

The United Nations Educational, Scientific, and Cultural Organization (UNESCO) conducts annual surveys of education statistics of its member countries. Data from official surveys are supplemented by information obtained by UNESCO through other publications and sources. Each year, more than 200 countries reply to the UNESCO surveys. In some cases, estimates are made by UNESCO for particular items, such as world and continent totals. While great efforts are made to make them as comparable as possible, the data still reflect the vast differences among the countries of the world in the structure of education. While there is some agreement about the reporting of primary and secondary data, tertiary-level data (i.e., postsecondary education data) present numerous substantive problems. Some countries report only university enrollment, while other countries report all postsecondary enrollment, including enrollment in vocational and technical schools and correspondence programs. A very high proportion of some countries' tertiary-level students attend institutions in other countries. The member countries that provide data to UNESCO are responsible for their validity. Thus, data for particular countries are subject to nonsampling error and perhaps sampling error as well. Users should examine footnotes carefully to recognize some of the data limitations.

Further information on the *Statistical Yearbook* and the *Global Education Digest* may be obtained from

UNESCO Institute for Statistics
Publications
C.P. 6128
Succursale Centre-Ville
Montreal, Quebec, H3C 3J7
Canada
http://www.uis.unesco.org

Table A-1. Respondent counts for selected High School and Beyond surveys: 1982, 1984, and 1986

Classification variable and subgroup	Follow-up survey of 1980 sophomores in 1982	Follow-up survey of 1980 seniors in 1982	Follow-up survey of 1980 sophomores in 1984	Follow-up survey of 1980 seniors in 1984	Follow-up survey of 1980 sophomores in 1986	Follow-up survey of 1980 seniors in 1986
Total respondents (unweighted)	**25,830**	**11,227**	**11,463**	**10,925**	**11,248**	**10,536**
Sex						
Male	12,717	5,213	5,514	5,058	5,391	4,832
Female	13,113	6,014	5,949	5,867	5,857	5,704
Race/ethnicity						
White	17,295	5,180	7,285	5,057	7,194	5,246
Black	3,338	2,724	1,651	2,625	1,585	2,726
Hispanic	4,439	2,749	1,795	2,654	1,745	1,950
Asian or Pacific Islander	413	367	425	355	413	356
American Indian or Alaska Native	248	191	253	185	246	200
Other or unclassified	97	16	54	49	65	58
Socioeconomic status composite (SES)[1]						
Low	6,752	3,940	2,831	3,857	2,751	3,668
Low-middle	6,234	2,390	2,624	2,314	2,559	2,289
High-middle	6,134	2,168	2,849	2,107	2,817	1,995
High	6,341	1,988	3,086	1,936	3,044	1,900
Unclassified	369	741	73	711	77	684
Father's highest level of education						
Less than high school	5,179	—	—	—	—	—
High school completion[2]	11,961	—	—	—	—	—
College graduate[3]	5,169	—	—	—	—	—
Don't know/missing	3,521	—	—	—	—	—
High school program (self-reported)						
Academic	10,152	4,145	6,547	4,007	—	3,899
General	8,789	3,829	3,468	3,764	—	3,602
Vocational	6,664	2,660	3,611	2,581	—	2,481
Unclassified	225	593	56	573	—	554
High school type						
Public	—	9,969	8,647	9,727	—	9,385
Catholic	—	964	2,479	911	—	876
Other private	—	294	337	287	—	275
Postsecondary education status[4]						
Full-time	—	—	4,466	—	—	—
Part-time	—	—	3,275	—	—	—
Never enrolled	—	—	3,678	—	—	—
Missing/unclassified	—	—	44	—	—	—
October 1980 postsecondary education attendance status						
Part-time 2-year public institution	—	—	—	—	—	352
Part-time 4-year public institution	—	—	—	—	—	152
Full-time 2-year public institution	—	—	—	—	—	1,312
Full-time 4-year public institution	—	—	—	—	—	1,986
Full-time 4-year private institution	—	—	—	—	—	1,015
Not a student	—	—	—	—	—	4,523
Other and missing	—	—	—	—	—	1,196
Postsecondary education plans						
No plans	—	—	—	—	—	1,623
Attend vocational/technical school	—	—	—	—	—	1,835
Attend college less than 4 years	—	—	—	—	—	1,528
Earn bachelor's degree	—	—	—	—	—	2,631
Earn advanced degree	—	—	—	—	—	2,265
Missing	—	—	—	—	—	654
Participation in high school extracurricular activities[5]						
Never participated	—	—	—	—	—	1,024
Participated as a member	—	—	—	—	—	4,104
Participated as a leader	—	—	—	—	—	4,457

—Not available.

[1]The SES index is a composite of five equally weighted measures: father's education, mother's education, family income, father's occupation, and presence of certain items in the respondent's household.

[2]Includes attendance at a vocational, trade, or business school; or 2-year college; or attendance at a 4-year college resulting in less than a bachelor's degree.

[3]Includes those with a bachelor's or higher level degree.

[4]Postsecondary education status was determined by students' enrollment in academic or vocational study during the four semesters—fall 1982, spring 1983, fall 1983, and spring 1984—following their scheduled high school graduation. Students who enrolled in full-time study in each of the four semesters were classified as full time. Students who were enrolled in part-time study in any of the four semesters and those who were enrolled in full-time study in fewer than four semesters were classified as part time. Students who had neither enrolled on a full-time nor part-time basis in each of the four semesters were classified as never enrolled.

[5]Responses to questions concerning participation in each of 15 different extracurricular activity areas (i.e., varsity sports, debate, band, subject-matter clubs, etc.) were used to classify students' overall level of participation in extracurricular activities. The difference between the sum of the three category respondent counts and the total sample size is due to missing data.

NOTE: Data from students who dropped out of school between the 10th and 12th grades were not used in analyses of sophomore samples. Race categories exclude persons of Hispanic ethnicity.

SOURCE: U.S. Department of Education, National Center for Education Statistics, High School and Beyond Study of 1980 Sophomores (HS&B-So:80/82, HS&B-So:80/84, and HS&B-So:80/86); and High School and Beyond Study of 1980 Seniors (HS&B-Sr:80/82, HS&B-Sr:80/84, and HS&B-Sr:80/86).

Table A-2. Design effects (DEFF) and root design effects (DEFT) for selected High School and Beyond surveys and subsamples: 1984 and 1986

Subsample characteristic	Follow-up survey of 1980 sophomores in 1984		Follow-up survey of 1980 seniors in1984		Follow-up survey of 1980 sophomores in 1986		Follow-up survey of 1980 seniors in 1986	
	DEFF	DEFT	DEFF	DEFT	DEFF	DEFT	DEFF	DEFT
Total sample	2.40	1.54	2.87	1.69	2.19	1.47	2.28	1.50
Sex								
Male	—	†	—	†	2.07	1.43	2.13	1.45
Female	—	†	—	†	2.06	1.43	2.26	1.50
Race/ethnicity								
White and other	2.06	1.42	2.09	1.44	1.92	1.38	1.70	1.30
Black	2.22	1.47	2.26	1.50	2.19	1.47	2.40	1.54
Hispanic	3.15	1.73	3.72	1.92	3.11	1.76	4.06	2.01
Socioeconomic status composite (SES)[1]								
Low	1.91	1.37	2.28	1.50	1.83	1.35	2.31	1.51
Middle	1.95	1.39	1.81	1.34	2.06	1.42	2.02	1.42
High	2.05	1.42	1.93	1.38	1.92	1.38	1.71	1.30

—Not available.

†Not applicable.

[1]The SES index is a composite of five equally weighted measures: father's education, mother's education, family income, father's occupation, and presence of certain items in the respondent's household.

NOTE: The average design effect for the 1980 sophomore cohort first follow-up (1982) survey is 3.6 (1.89) and the average design effect for the 1980 senior first follow-up (1982) survey is 2.6 (1.62). Race categories exclude persons of Hispanic ethnicity.

SOURCE: U.S. Department of Education, National Center for Education Statistics, High School and Beyond Study of 1980 Sophomores (HS&B-So:80/84 and HS&B-So:80/86); and High School and Beyond Study of 1980 Seniors (HS&B-Sr:80/84 and HS&B-Sr:80/86).

Table A-3. Respondent counts of full-time workers from the Recent College Graduates survey: Selected years, 1976 to 1991

Field of study	Number employed full time				
	1974–75 graduates in May 1976	1979–80 graduates in May 1981	1983–84 graduates in April 1985	1985–86 graduates in April 1987	1989–90 graduates in April 1991
Total respondents (unweighted)	2,464	5,521	6,799	15,024	9,451
Professions	1,840	4,260	3,730	8,987	3,825
Arts and sciences	514	811	2,586	4,869	2,256
Other	110	450	483	1,168	3,370
Newly qualified to teach	1,337	2,469	1,109	2,546	1,966
Not newly qualified to teach	1,127	3,052	5,690	12,478	7,485
Professions	601	1,841	2,809	7,043	2,549
Engineering	80	270	601	915	411
Business and management	290	749	1,532	2,407	1,598
Health	72	252	387	3,106	281
Education[1]	141	464	146	521	188
Public affairs and services	18	106	143	94	71
Arts and sciences	433	770	2,430	4,369	2,006
Biological sciences	83	116	243	380	179
Physical sciences and mathematics	40	103	1,062	1,782	466
Psychology	64	105	189	366	316
Social sciences	107	252	449	780	813
Humanities	139	194	487	1,061	232
Other	93	441	451	1,066	2,930
Communications	7	73	240	392	217
Miscellaneous	86	368	211	674	2,713

[1]Includes those who had not finished all requirements for teaching certification or were previously qualified to teach.

SOURCE: U.S. Department of Education, National Center for Education Statistics, Recent College Graduates (RCG) surveys, 1976, 1981, 1985, 1987, and 1991.

Table A-4. Sampling errors (95 percent confidence level) for percentages estimated from the Gallup Poll: 1992, 1993, and 1996 through 2008

Percent	Size of sample						
	1,500	1,000	750	600	400	200	100
Recommended allowance for sampling error of a percentage							
Percentages near 10 or 90	2	2	3	3	4	5	8
Percentages near 20 or 80	3	3	4	4	5	7	10
Percentages near 30 or 70	3	4	4	5	6	8	12
Percentages near 40 or 60	3	4	5	5	6	9	12
Percentages near 50...................................	3	4	5	5	6	9	13

SOURCE: Phi Delta Kappa, *Phi Delta Kappan*, "The Annual Gallup Poll of the Public's Attitudes Toward the Public Schools," 1992, 1993, and 1996 through 2008.

Table A-5. Sampling errors (95 percent confidence level) for the difference in two percentages estimated from the Gallup Poll: 1992, 1993, and 1996 through 2008

Size of first sample	Size of second sample					
	1,500	1,000	750	600	400	200
Recommended allowance for sampling error of a difference in percentages (percentages near 80 or 20)						
1,500...	4	4	5	5	6	8
1,000...	4	5	5	5	6	8
750...	5	5	5	6	6	8
600...	5	5	6	6	7	8
400...	6	6	6	7	7	9
200...	8	8	8	8	9	10
Recommended allowance for sampling error of a difference in percentages (percentages near 50)						
1,500...	5	5	6	6	7	10
1,000...	5	6	6	7	8	10
750...	6	6	7	7	8	10
600...	6	7	7	7	8	10
400...	7	8	8	8	9	11
200...	10	10	10	10	11	13

SOURCE: Phi Delta Kappa, *Phi Delta Kappan*, "The Annual Gallup Poll of the Public's Attitudes Toward the Public Schools," 1992, 1993, and 1996 through 2008.

Table A-6. Maximum differences required for significance (90 percent confidence level) between sample subgroups from the "Status of the American Public School Teacher" survey: 2000–01

Size of first subgroup	Size of second subgroup						
	100	200	300	400	500	600	700
100...	11.6	10.1	9.5	9.2	9.0	8.9	8.8
200...	10.1	8.2	7.5	7.1	6.9	6.7	6.6
300...	9.5	7.5	6.7	6.3	6.0	5.8	5.7
400...	9.2	7.1	6.3	5.8	5.5	5.3	5.2
500...	9.0	6.9	6.0	5.5	5.2	5.0	4.8
600...	8.9	6.7	5.8	5.3	5.0	4.7	4.6
700...	8.8	6.6	5.7	5.2	4.8	4.6	4.4

SOURCE: National Education Association, *Status of the American Public School Teacher, 2000-01*.

APPENDIX B
Definitions

Academic support This category of college expenditures includes expenditures for support services that are an integral part of the institution's primary missions of instruction, research, or public service. It also includes expenditures for libraries, galleries, audio/visual services, academic computing support, ancillary support, academic administration, personnel development, and course and curriculum development.

Achievement test An examination that measures the extent to which a person has acquired certain information or mastered certain skills, usually as a result of specific instruction.

Achievement levels, NAEP Specific achievement levels for each subject area and grade to provide a context for interesting student performance. At this time they are being used on a trial basis.

> **Basic**—denotes partial mastery of the knowledge and skills that are fundamental for proficient work at a given grade.
>
> **Proficient**—represents solid academic performance. Students reaching this level have demonstrated competency over challenging subject matter.
>
> **Advanced**—signifies superior performance.

Administrative support staff Includes personnel dealing with salary, benefits, supplies, and contractual fees for the office of the principal, full-time department chairpeople, and graduation expenses.

Agriculture Courses designed to improve competencies in agricultural occupations. Included is the study of agricultural production, supplies, mechanization and products, agricultural science, forestry, and related services.

ACT The ACT (formerly the American College Testing Program) assessment program measures educational development and readiness to pursue college-level coursework in English, mathematics, natural science, and social studies. Student performance on the tests does not reflect innate ability and is influenced by a student's educational preparedness.

Alternative schools Alternative schools serve students whose needs cannot be met in a regular, special education, or vocational school. They provide nontraditional education and may serve as an adjunct to a regular school. Although these schools fall outside the categories of regular, special education, and vocational education, they may provide similar services or curriculum. Some examples of alternative schools are schools for potential dropouts; residential treatment centers for substance abuse (if they provide elementary or secondary education); schools for chronic truants; and schools for students with behavioral problems.

Appropriation (federal funds) Budget authority provided through the congressional appropriation process that permits federal agencies to incur obligations and to make payments.

Appropriation (institutional revenues) An amount (other than a grant or contract) received from or made available to an institution through an act of a legislative body.

Associate's degree A degree granted for the successful completion of a sub-baccalaureate program of studies, usually requiring at least 2 years (or equivalent) of full-time college-level study. This includes degrees granted in a cooperative or work-study program.

Auxiliary enterprises This category includes those essentially self-supporting operations which exist to furnish a service to students, faculty, or staff, and which charge a fee that is directly related to, although not necessarily equal to, the cost of the service. Examples are residence halls, food services, college stores, and intercollegiate athletics.

Average daily attendance (ADA) The aggregate attendance of a school during a reporting period (normally a school year) divided by the number of days school is in session during this period. Only days on which the pupils are under the guidance and direction of teachers should be considered days in session.

Average daily membership (ADM) The aggregate membership of a school during a reporting period (normally a school year) divided by the number of days school is in session during this period. Only days on which the pupils are under the guidance and direction of teachers should be considered as days in session. The average daily membership for groups of schools having varying lengths of terms is the average of the average daily memberships obtained for the individual schools.

Bachelor's degree A degree granted for the successful completion of a baccalaureate program of studies, usually requiring at least 4 years (or equivalent) of full-time college-level study. This includes degrees granted in a cooperative or work-study program.

Books Non-periodical printed publications bound in hard or soft covers, or in loose-leaf format, of at least 49 pages, exclusive of the cover pages; juvenile nonperiodical publications of any length found in hard or soft covers.

Budget authority (BA) Authority provided by law to enter into obligations that will result in immediate or future outlays. It may be classified by the period of availability (1-year, multiple-year, no-year), by the timing of congressional action (current or permanent), or by the manner of determining the amount available (definite or indefinite).

Business Program of instruction that prepares individuals for a variety of activities in planning, organizing, directing, and controlling business office systems and procedures.

Capital outlay Funds for the acquisition of land and buildings; building construction, remodeling, and additions; the initial installation or extension of service systems and other built-in equipment; and site improvement. The category also encompasses architectural and engineering services including the development of blueprints.

Carnegie unit The number of credits a student received for a course taken every day, one period per day, for a full year; a factor used to standardize all credits indicated on transcripts across studies.

Catholic school A private school over which a Roman Catholic church group exercises some control or provides some form of subsidy. Catholic schools for the most part include those operated or supported by a parish, a group of parishes, a diocese, or a Catholic religious order.

Central cities The largest cities, with 50,000 or more inhabitants, in a Metropolitan Statistical Area (MSA). Additional cities within the metropolitan area can also be classified as "central cities" if they meet certain employment, population, and employment/residence ratio requirements.

City school See Locale codes.

Class size The membership of a class at a given date.

Classification of Instructional Programs (CIP) The CIP is a taxonomic coding scheme that contains titles and descriptions of primarily postsecondary instructional programs. It was developed to facilitate NCES's collection and reporting of postsecondary degree completions by major field of study using standard classifications that capture the majority of

reportable program activity. It was originally published in 1980 and was revised in 1985, 1990, and 2000.

Classification of Secondary School Courses (CSSC) A modification of the Classification of Instructional Programs used for classifying high school courses. The CSSC contains over 2,200 course codes that help compare the thousands of high school transcripts collected from different schools.

Classroom teacher A staff member assigned the professional activities of instructing pupils in self-contained classes or courses, or in classroom situations; usually expressed in full-time equivalents.

Cohort A group of individuals that have a statistical factor in common, for example, year of birth.

College A postsecondary school which offers general or liberal arts education, usually leading to an associate, bachelor's, master's, doctor's, or first-professional degree. Junior colleges and community colleges are included under this terminology.

Combined Statistical Area (CSA) A combination of areas, each of which contains a core with a substantial population nucleus as well as adjacent communities having a high degree of economic and social integration with that core. A CSA is a region with social and economic ties as measured by commuting, but at lower levels than are found within each component area. CSAs represent larger regions that reflect broader social and economic interactions, such as wholesaling, commodity distribution, and weekend recreation activities.

Combined elementary and secondary school A school which encompasses instruction at both the elementary and the secondary levels; includes schools starting with grade 6 or below and ending with grade 9 or above.

Computer science A group of instructional programs that describes computer and information sciences, including computer programming, data processing, and information systems.

Consolidated Metropolitan Statistical Area (CMSA) An area that meets the requirements of a Metropolitan Statistical Area (MSA—see below) and has a population of 1 million or more, the components of which are large urbanized counties or a cluster of counties (cities and towns in New England) having moderate to substantial commuting and employment interchange.

Constant dollars Dollar amounts that have been adjusted by means of price and cost indexes to eliminate inflationary factors and allow direct comparison across years.

Consumer Price Index (CPI) This price index measures the average change in the cost of a fixed market basket of goods and services purchased by consumers.

Consumption That portion of income which is spent on the purchase of goods and services rather than being saved.

Control of institutions A classification of institutions of elementary/secondary or higher education by whether the institution is operated by publicly elected or appointed officials and derives its primary support from public funds (public control) or by privately elected or appointed officials and derives its major source of funds from private sources (private control).

Credit The unit of value, awarded for the successful completion of certain courses, intended to indicate the quantity of course instruction in relation to the total requirements for a diploma, certificate, or degree. Credits are frequently expressed in terms such as "Carnegie units," "semester credit hours," and "quarter credit hours."

Current dollars Dollar amounts that have not been adjusted to compensate for inflation.

Current expenditures (elementary/secondary) The expenditures for operating local public schools, excluding capital outlay and interest on school debt. These expenditures include such items as salaries for school personnel, fixed charges, student transportation, school books and materials, and energy costs. Beginning in 1980–81, expenditures for state administration are excluded.

Current expenditures per pupil in average daily attendance Current expenditures for the regular school term divided by the average daily attendance of full-time pupils (or full-time equivalency of pupils) during the term. See also Current expenditures and Average daily attendance.

Current-fund expenditures (higher education) Money spent to meet current operating costs, including salaries, wages, utilities, student services, public services, research libraries, scholarships and fellowships, auxiliary enterprises, hospitals, and independent operations; excludes loans, capital expenditures, and investments.

Current-fund revenues (higher education) Money received during the current fiscal year from revenue which can be used to pay obligations currently due, and surpluses reappropriated for the current fiscal year.

Current Population Survey See Appendix A: Guide to Sources.

Degree-granting institutions Postsecondary institutions that are eligible for Title IV federal financial aid programs and grant an associate's or higher degree. For an institution to be eligible to participate in Title IV financial aid programs it must offer a program of at least 300 clock hours in length,

have accreditation recognized by the U.S. Department of Education, have been in business for at least 2 years, and have signed a participation agreement with the Department.

Disabilities, children with Those children evaluated as having any of the following impairments and needing special education and related services because of these impairments. (These definitions apply specifically to data from the U.S. Office of Special Education and Rehabilitative Services presented in this publication.)

Deafness Having a hearing impairment which is so severe that the student is impaired in processing linguistic information through hearing (with or without amplification) and which adversely affects educational performance.

Deaf-blindness Having concomitant hearing and visual impairments which cause such severe communication and other developmental and educational problems that the student cannot be accommodated in special education programs solely for deaf or blind students.

Hearing impairment Having a hearing impairment, whether permanent or fluctuating, which adversely affects the student's educational performance, but which is not included under the definition of "deaf" in this section.

Mental retardation Having significantly subaverage general intellectual functioning, existing concurrently with defects in adaptive behavior and manifested during the developmental period, which adversely affects the child's educational performance.

Multiple disabilities Having concomitant impairments (such as mentally retarded-blind, mentally retarded-orthopedically impaired, etc.), the combination of which causes such severe educational problems that the student cannot be accommodated in special education programs solely for one of the impairments. Term does not include deaf-blind students.

Orthopedic impairment Having a severe orthopedic impairment which adversely affects a student's educational performance. The term includes impairment resulting from congenital anomaly, disease, or other causes.

Other health impairment Having limited strength, vitality, or alertness due to chronic or acute health problems, such as a heart condition, tuberculosis, rheumatic fever, nephritis, asthma, sickle cell anemia, hemophilia, epilepsy, lead poisoning, leukemia, or diabetes which adversely affects the student's educational performance.

Serious emotional disturbance Exhibiting one or more of the following characteristics over a long period of time, to a marked degree, and adversely affecting educational performance: an inability to learn which cannot be explained by intellectual, sensory, or health factors; an inability to build or maintain satisfactory interpersonal relationships with peers and teachers; inappropriate types of behavior or feelings under normal circumstances; a general pervasive mood of unhappiness or depression; or a tendency to develop physical symptoms or fears associated with personal or school problems. This term does not include children who are socially maladjusted, unless they also display one or more of the listed characteristics.

Specific learning disability Having a disorder in one or more of the basic psychological processes involved in understanding or in using spoken or written language, which may manifest itself in an imperfect ability to listen, think, speak, read, write, spell, or do mathematical calculations. The term includes such conditions as perceptual disabilities, brain injury, minimal brain dysfunction, dyslexia, and developmental aphasia. The term does not include children who have learning problems which are primarily the result of visual, hearing, or environmental, cultural, or economic disadvantage.

Speech/language impairment Having a communication disorder, such as stuttering, impaired articulation, language impairment, or voice impairment, which adversely affects the student's educational performance.

Visual impairment Having a visual impairment which, even with correction, adversely affects the student's educational performance. The term includes partially seeing and blind children.

Disposable personal income Current income received by persons less their contributions for social insurance, personal tax, and nontax payments. It is the income available to persons for spending and saving. Nontax payments include passport fees, fines and penalties, donations, and tuitions and fees paid to schools and hospitals operated mainly by the government. See also Personal income.

Doctor's degree An earned degree carrying the title of Doctor. The Doctor of Philosophy degree (Ph.D.) is the highest academic degree and requires mastery within a field of knowledge and demonstrated ability to perform scholarly research. Other doctorates are awarded for fulfilling specialized requirements in professional fields, such as education (Ed.D.), musical arts (D.M.A.), business administration (D.B.A.), and engineering (D.Eng. or D.E.S.). Many doctor's degrees in academic and professional fields require an earned master's degree as a prerequisite. First-professional degrees, such as M.D. and D.D.S., are not included under this heading.

Educational and general expenditures The sum of current funds expenditures on instruction, research, public service, academic support, student services, institutional support, operation and maintenance of plant, and awards from restricted and unrestricted funds.

Educational attainment The highest grade of regular school attended and completed.

Elementary education/programs Learning experiences concerned with the knowledge, skills, appreciations, attitudes, and behavioral characteristics which are considered to be needed by all pupils in terms of their awareness of life within our culture and the world of work, and which normally may be achieved during the elementary school years (usually kindergarten through grade 8 or kindergarten through grade 6), as defined by applicable state laws and regulations.

Elementary school A school classified as elementary by state and local practice and composed of any span of grades not above grade 8. A preschool or kindergarten school is included under this heading only if it is an integral part of an elementary school or a regularly established school system.

Elementary/secondary school As reported in this publication, includes only regular schools (i.e., schools that are part of state and local school systems, and also most not-for-profit private elementary/secondary schools, both religiously affiliated and nonsectarian). Schools not reported include sub-collegiate departments of institutions of higher education, residential schools for exceptional children, federal schools for American Indians, and federal schools on military posts and other federal installations.

Employment Includes civilian, noninstitutional persons who: (1) worked during any part of the survey week as paid employees; worked in their own business, profession, or farm; or worked 15 hours or more as unpaid workers in a family-owned enterprise; or (2) were not working but had jobs or businesses from which they were temporarily absent due to illness, bad weather, vacation, labor-management dispute, or personal reasons whether or not they were seeking another job.

Endowment A trust fund set aside to provide a perpetual source of revenue from the proceeds of the endowment investments. Endowment funds are often created by donations from benefactors of an institution, who may designate the use of the endowment revenue. Normally, institutions or their representatives manage the investments, but they are not permitted to spend the endowment fund itself, only the proceeds from the investments. Typical uses of endowments would be an endowed chair for a particular department or for a scholarship fund. Endowment totals tabulated in this book also include funds functioning as endowments, such as funds left over from the previous year and placed with the endowment investments by the institution. These funds may be withdrawn by the institution and spent as current funds at any time. Endowments are evaluated by two different measures, book value and market value. Book value is the purchase price of the endowment investment. Market value is the current worth of the endowment investment. Thus, the book value of a stock held in an endowment fund would be the purchase price of the stock. The market value of the stock would be its selling price as of a given day.

Engineering Instructional programs that describe the mathematical and natural science knowledge gained by study, experience, and practice and applied with judgment to develop ways to utilize the materials and forces of nature economically. Include programs that prepare individuals to support and assist engineers and similar professionals.

English A group of instructional programs that describes the English language arts, including composition, creative writing, and the study of literature.

Enrollment The total number of students registered in a given school unit at a given time, generally in the fall of a year.

Expenditures Charges incurred, whether paid or unpaid, which are presumed to benefit the current fiscal year. For elementary/secondary schools, these include all charges for current outlays plus capital outlays and interest on school debt. For institutions of higher education, these include current outlays plus capital outlays. For government, these include charges net of recoveries and other correcting transactions other than for retirement of debt, investment in securities, extension of credit, or as agency transactions. Government expenditures include only external transactions, such as the provision of perquisites or other payments in kind. Aggregates for groups of governments exclude intergovernmental transactions among the governments.

Expenditures per pupil Charges incurred for a particular period of time divided by a student unit of measure, such as average daily attendance or fall enrollment.

Extracurricular activities Activities that are not part of the required curriculum and that take place outside of the regular course of study. As used here, they include both school-sponsored (e.g., varsity athletics, drama, and debate clubs) and community-sponsored (e.g., hobby clubs and youth organizations like the Junior Chamber of Commerce or Boy Scouts) activities.

Family A group of two people or more (one of whom is the householder) related by birth, marriage, or adoption and residing together. All such people (including related subfamily members) are considered as members of one family.

Federal funds Amounts collected and used by the federal government for the general purposes of the government. There are four types of federal fund accounts: the general fund, special funds, public enterprise funds, and intragovernmental funds. The major federal fund is the general fund, which is derived from general taxes and borrowing. Federal funds also include certain earmarked collections, such as those generated by and used to finance a continuing cycle of business-type operations.

Federal sources Includes federal appropriations, grants, and contracts, and federally-funded research and development centers (FFRDCs). Federally subsidized student loans are not included.

First-professional degree A degree that signifies both completion of the academic requirements for beginning practice in a given profession and a level of professional skill beyond that normally required for a bachelor's degree. This degree usually is based on a program requiring at least 2 academic years of work prior to entrance and a total of at least 6 academic years of work to complete the degree program, including both prior-required college work and the professional program itself. By NCES definition, first-professional degrees are awarded in the fields of dentistry (D.D.S. or D.M.D.), medicine (M.D.), optometry (O.D.), osteopathic medicine (D.O.), pharmacy (D.Phar.), podiatric medicine (D.P.M.), veterinary medicine (D.V.M.), chiropractic (D.C. or D.C.M.), law (J.D.), and theological professions (M.Div. or M.H.L.).

First-professional enrollment The number of students enrolled in a professional school or program which requires at least 2 years of academic college work for entrance and a total of at least 6 years for a degree. By NCES definition, first-professional enrollment includes only students in certain programs. (See also First-professional degree for a list of programs.)

Fiscal year The yearly accounting period for the federal government, which begins on October 1 and ends on the following September 30. The fiscal year is designated by the calendar year in which it ends; e.g., fiscal year 2006 begins on October 1, 2005, and ends on September 30, 2006. (From fiscal year 1844 to fiscal year 1976, the fiscal year began on July 1 and ended on the following June 30.)

For-profit institution A private institution in which the individual(s) or agency in control receives compensation other than wages, rent, or other expenses for the assumption of risk.

Foreign languages A group of instructional programs that describes the structure and use of language that is common or indigenous to people of the same community or nation, the same geographical area, or the same cultural traditions. Programs cover such features as sound, literature, syntax, phonology, semantics, sentences, prose, and verse, as well as the development of skills and attitudes used in communicating and evaluating thoughts and feelings through oral and written language.

Full-time enrollment The number of students enrolled in higher education courses with total credit load equal to at least 75 percent of the normal full-time course load.

Full-time-equivalent (FTE) enrollment For institutions of higher education, enrollment of full-time students, plus the full-time equivalent of part-time students. The full-time equivalent of the part-time students is estimated using different factors depending on the type and control of institution and level of student.

Full-time-equivalent teacher See Instructional staff.

Full-time instructional faculty Those members of the instruction/research staff who are employed full time as defined by the institution, including faculty with released time for research and faculty on sabbatical leave. Full time counts exclude faculty who are employed to teach less than two semesters, three quarters, two trimesters, or two 4-month sessions; replacements for faculty on sabbatical leave or those on leave without pay; faculty for preclinical and clinical medicine; faculty who are donating their services; faculty who are members of military organizations and paid on a different pay scale from civilian employees; academic officers, whose primary duties are administrative; and graduate students who assist in the instruction of courses.

Full-time worker In educational institutions, an employee whose position requires being on the job on school days throughout the school year at least the number of hours the schools are in session. For higher education, a member of an educational institution's staff who is employed full time.

General administration support services Includes salary, benefits, supplies, and contractual fees for boards of education staff and executive administration. Excludes state administration.

General Educational Development (GED) program Academic instruction to prepare persons to take the high school equivalency examination. See also GED recipient.

GED recipient A person who has obtained certification of high school equivalency by meeting state requirements and passing an approved exam, which is intended to provide an appraisal of the person's achievement or performance in the broad subject matter areas usually required for high school graduation.

General program A program of studies designed to prepare students for the common activities of a citizen, family member, and worker. A general program of studies may include instruction in both academic and vocational areas.

Government appropriation An amount (other than a grant or contract) received from or made available to an institution through an act of a legislative body.

Government grant or contract Revenues from a government agency for a specific research project or other program.

Graduate An individual who has received formal recognition for the successful completion of a prescribed program of studies.

Graduate enrollment The number of students who hold the bachelor's or first-professional degree, or the equivalent, and who are working towards a master's or doctor's degree. First-professional students are counted separately. These enrollment data measure those students who are registered at a particular time during the fall. At some institutions, graduate enrollment also includes students who are in postbaccalaureate classes, but not in degree programs. In most tables, graduate enrollment includes all students in regular graduate programs and all students in postbaccalaureate classes, but not in degree programs (unclassified postbaccalaureate students).

Graduate Record Examination (GRE) Multiple-choice examinations administered by the Educational Testing Service and taken by college students who are intending to attend certain graduate schools. There are two types of testing available: (1) the general exam which measures critical thinking, analytical writing, verbal reasoning, and quantitative reasoning skills, and (2) the subject test which is offered in eight specific subjects and gauges undergraduate achievement in a specific field. The subject tests are intended for those who have majored in or have extensive background in that specific area.

Graduation Formal recognition given an individual for the successful completion of a prescribed program of studies.

Gross domestic product (GDP) The total national output of goods and services valued at market prices. GDP can be viewed in terms of expenditure categories which include purchases of goods and services by consumers and government, gross private domestic investment, and net exports of goods and services. The goods and services included are largely those bought for final use (excluding illegal transactions) in the market economy. A number of inclusions, however, represent imputed values, the most important of which is rental value of owner-occupied housing. GDP, in this broad context, measures the output attributable to the factors of production—labor and property—supplied by U.S. residents.

Handicapped See Disabilities, children with.

Higher education Study beyond secondary school at an institution that offers programs terminating in an associate, baccalaureate, or higher degree.

Higher education institutions (Carnegie classification)

Doctorate-granting Characterized by a significant level and breadth of activity in commitment to doctoral-level education as measured by the number of doctorate recipients and the diversity in doctoral-level program offerings.

Master's Characterized by diverse postbaccalaureate programs (including first-professional), but not engaged in significant doctoral-level education.

Baccalaureate Characterized by primary emphasis on general undergraduate, baccalaureate-level education. Not significantly engaged in postbaccalaureate education.

Special focus Baccalaureate or postbaccalaureate institution emphasizing one area (plus closely related specialties), such as business or engineering. The programmatic emphasis is measured by the percentage of degrees granted in the program area.

Associate's Conferring at least 90 percent of its degrees and awards for work below the bachelor's level.

Tribal Colleges and universities that are members of the American Indian Higher Education Consortium, as identified in IPEDS Institutional Characteristics.

Non-degree-granting Offering undergraduate or graduate study, but not conferring degrees or awards. In this volume, these institutions are included under Specialized.

Higher education institutions (basic classification)

4-year institution An institution legally authorized to offer and offering at least a 4-year program of college-level studies wholly or principally creditable toward a baccalaureate degree. In some tables, a further division between universities and other 4-year institutions is made. A "university" is a postsecondary institution which typically comprises one or more graduate professional schools (see also University). For purposes of trend comparisons in this volume, the selection of universities has been held constant for all tabulations after 1982. "Other 4-year institutions" would include the rest of the nonuniversity 4-year institutions.

2-year institution An institution legally authorized to offer and offering at least a 2-year program of college-level studies which terminates in an associate degree or is principally creditable toward a baccalaureate degree. Also includes some institutions that have a less than 2-year program, but were designated as institutions of higher education in the Higher Education General Information Survey.

Higher Education Price Index A price index which measures average changes in the prices of goods and services purchased by colleges and universities through current-fund education and general expenditures (excluding expenditures for sponsored research and auxiliary enterprises).

High school A secondary school offering the final years of high school work necessary for graduation, usually includes grades 10, 11, 12 (in a 6-3-3 plan) or grades 9, 10, 11, and 12 (in a 6-2-4 plan).

High school program A program of studies designed to prepare students for their postsecondary education and occupation. Three types of programs are usually distinguished—academic, vocational, and general. An academic program is designed to prepare students for continued study at a college or university. A vocational program is designed to prepare students for employment in one or more semiskilled, skilled, or technical occupations. A general program is designed to provide students with the understanding and competence to function effectively in a free society and usually represents a mixture of academic and vocational components.

Hispanic serving institutions pursuant to 302 (d) of Public Law 102-325 (20 U.S.C. 1059c), most recently amended December 20, 1993, in 2(a)(7) of Public Law 103-208, where Hispanic serving institutions are defined as those with full-time-equivalent undergraduate enrollment of Hispanic students at 25 percent or more.

Historically black colleges and universities Accredited institutions of higher education established prior to 1964 with the principal mission of educating black Americans. Federal regulations (20 U.S.C. 1061 (2)) allow for certain exceptions of the founding date.

Household All the people who occupy a housing unit. A house, apartment, mobile home, or other group of rooms, or a single room, is regarded as a housing unit when it is occupied or intended for occupancy as separate living quarters, that is, when the occupants do not live and eat with any other people in the structure, and there is direct access from the outside or through a common hall.

Housing unit A house, an apartment, a mobile home, a group of rooms, or a single room that is occupied as separate living quarters.

Income tax Taxes levied on net income, that is, on gross income less certain deductions permitted by law. These taxes can be levied on individuals or on corporations or unincorporated businesses where the income is taxed distinctly from individual income.

Independent operations A group of self-supporting activities under control of a college or university. For purposes of financial surveys conducted by the National Center for Education Statistics, this category is composed principally of federally funded research and development centers (FFRDC).

Institutional support The category of higher education expenditures that includes day-to-day operational support for colleges, excluding expenditures for physical plant operations. Examples of institutional support include general administrative services, executive direction and planning, legal and fiscal operations, and community relations.

Instruction (colleges and universities) That functional category including expenditures of the colleges, schools, departments, and other instructional divisions of higher education institutions and expenditures for departmental research and public service which are not separately budgeted; includes expenditures for both credit and noncredit activities. Excludes expenditures for academic administration where the primary function is administration (e.g., academic deans).

Instruction (elementary and secondary) Instruction encompasses all activities dealing directly with the interaction between teachers and students. Teaching may be provided for students in a school classroom, in another location such as a home or hospital, and in other learning situations such as those involving co-curricular activities. Instruction may be provided through some other approved medium, such as television, radio, telephone, and correspondence. Instruction expenditures include: salaries, employee benefits, purchased services, supplies, and tuition to private schools.

Instructional staff Full-time-equivalent number of positions, not the number of different individuals occupying the positions during the school year. In local schools, includes all public elementary and secondary (junior and senior high) day-school positions that are in the nature of teaching or in the improvement of the teaching-learning situation; includes consultants or supervisors of instruction, principals, teachers, guidance personnel, librarians, psychological personnel, and other instructional staff, and excludes administrative staff, attendance personnel, clerical personnel, and junior college staff.

Instructional support services Includes salary, benefits, supplies, and contractual fees for staff providing instructional improvement, educational media (library and audiovisual), and other instructional support services.

Junior high school A separately organized and administered secondary school intermediate between the elementary and senior high schools, usually includes grades 7, 8, and 9 (in a 6-3-3 plan) or grades 7 and 8 (in a 6-2-4 plan).

Labor force People employed as civilians, unemployed but looking for work, or in the armed services during the survey week. The "civilian labor force" comprises all civilians classified as employed or unemployed. See also Unemployed.

Land-grant colleges The First Morrill Act of 1862 facilitated the establishment of colleges through grants of land or funds in lieu of land. The Second Morrill Act in 1890 provided for money grants and for the establishment of black land-grant colleges and universities in those states with dual systems of higher education.

Local education agency (LEA) See School district.

Locale codes A classification system to describe a location. The "Metro-Centric" locale codes, developed in the 1980s, classified all schools and school districts based on their county's proximity to metro statistical areas (MSA) and their specific location's population size and density. In 2006, the "Urban-Centric" locale codes were introduced. These locale codes are based on an address's proximity to an urbanized area. For more information see http://nces.ed.gov/ccd/rural_locales.asp.

Pre-2006 Metro-Centric Locale Codes

Large City: A central city of a consolidated metropolitan statistical area (CMSA) or MSA, with the city having a population greater than or equal to 250,000.

Mid-size City: A central city of a CMSA or MSA, with the city having a population less than 250,000.

Urban Fringe of a Large City: Any territory within a CMSA or MSA of a Large City and defined as urban by the Census Bureau.

Urban Fringe of a Mid-size City: Any territory within a CMSA or MSA of a Mid-size City and defined as urban by the Census Bureau.

Large Town: An incorporated place or Census-designated place with a population greater than or equal to 25,000 and located outside a CMSA or MSA.

Small Town: An incorporated place or Census-designated place with a population less than 25,000 and greater than or equal to 2,500 and located outside a CMSA or MSA.

Rural, Outside MSA: Any territory designated as rural by the Census Bureau that is outside a CMSA or MSA of a Large or Mid-size City.

Rural, Inside MSA: Any territory designated as rural by the Census Bureau that is within a CMSA or MSA of a Large or Mid-size City.

2006 Urban-Centric Locale Codes

City, Large: Territory inside an urbanized area and inside a principal city with population of 250,000 or more.

City, Midsize: Territory inside an urbanized area and inside a principal city with population less than 250,000 and greater than or equal to 100,000.

City, Small: Territory inside an urbanized area and inside a principal city with population less than 100,000.

Suburb, Large: Territory outside a principal city and inside an urbanized area with population of 250,000 or more.

Suburb, Midsize: Territory outside a principal city and inside an urbanized area with population less than 250,000 and greater than or equal to 100,000.

Suburb, Small: Territory outside a principal city and inside an urbanized area with population less than 100,000.

Town, Fringe: Territory inside an urban cluster that is less than or equal to 10 miles from an urbanized area.

Town, Distant: Territory inside an urban cluster that is more than 10 miles and less than or equal to 35 miles from an urbanized area.

Town, Remote: Territory inside an urban cluster that is more than 35 miles from an urbanized area.

Rural, Fringe: Census-defined rural territory that is less than or equal to 5 miles from an urbanized area, as well as rural territory that is less than or equal to 2.5 miles from an urban cluster.

Rural, Distant: Census-defined rural territory that is more than 5 miles but less than or equal to 25 miles from an urbanized area, as well as rural territory that is more than 2.5 miles but less than or equal to 10 miles from an urban cluster.

Rural, Remote: Census-defined rural territory that is more than 25 miles from an urbanized area and is also more than 10 miles from an urban cluster.

Mandatory transfer A transfer of current funds that must be made in order to fulfill a binding legal obligation of the institution. Included under mandatory transfers are debt service provisions relating to academic and administrative buildings, including (1) amounts set aside for debt retirement and interest and (2) required provisions for renewal and replacement of buildings to the extent these are not financed from other funds.

Master's degree A degree awarded for successful completion of a program generally requiring 1 or 2 years of full-time college-level study beyond the bachelor's degree. One type of master's degree, including the Master of Arts degree, or M.A., and the Master of Science degree, or M.S., is awarded in the liberal arts and sciences for advanced scholarship in a subject field or discipline and demonstrated ability to perform scholarly research. A second type of master's degree is awarded for the completion of a professionally oriented program, for example, an M.Ed. in education, an M.B.A. in business administration, an M.F.A. in fine arts, an M.M. in music, an M.S.W. in social work, and an M.P.A. in public administration. A third type of master's degree is awarded in professional fields for study beyond the first-professional degree, for example, the Master of Laws (L.L.M.) and Master of Science in various medical specializations.

Mathematics A group of instructional programs that describes the science of numbers and their operations, interrelations, combinations, generalizations, and abstractions and of space configurations and their structure, measurement, transformations, and generalizations.

Mean test score The score obtained by dividing the sum of the scores of all individuals in a group by the number of individuals in that group.

Metropolitan population The population residing in Metropolitan Statistical Areas (MSAs). See Metropolitan Statistical Area.

Metropolitan Statistical Area (MSA) A large population nucleus and the nearby communities which have a high degree of economic and social integration with that nucleus. Each MSA consists of one or more entire counties (or county equivalents) that meet specified standards pertaining to population, commuting ties, and metropolitan character. In New England, towns and cities, rather than counties, are the basic units. MSAs are designated by the Office of Management and Budget. An MSA includes a city and, generally, its entire urban area and the remainder of the county or counties in which the urban area is located. An MSA also includes such additional outlying counties which meet specified criteria relating to metropolitan character and level of commuting of workers into the central city or counties. Specified criteria governing the definition of MSAs recognized before 1980 are published in *Standard Metropolitan Statistical Areas: 1975*, issued by the Office of Management and Budget. New MSAs were designated when 1980 counts showed that they met one or both of the following criteria:

1. Included a city with a population of at least 50,000 within their corporate limits, or

2. Included a Census Bureau-defined urbanized area (which must have a population of at least 50,000) and a total MSA population of at least 100,000 (or, in New England, 75,000).

Migration Geographic mobility involving a change of usual residence between clearly defined geographic units, that is, between counties, states, or regions.

Minimum-competency testing Measuring the acquisition of competence or skills to or beyond a certain specified standard.

National Assessment of Educational Progress (NAEP) See Appendix A: Guide to Sources.

Newly qualified teacher People who: (1) first became eligible for a teaching license during the period of the study referenced or who were teaching at the time of survey, but were not certified or eligible for a teaching license; and (2) had never held full-time, regular teaching positions (as opposed to substitute) prior to completing the requirements for the degree which brought them into the survey.

Nonmetropolitan residence group The population residing outside Metropolitan Statistical Areas. See Metropolitan Statistical Area.

Nonresident alien A person who is not a citizen of the United States and who is in this country on a temporary basis and does not have the right to remain indefinitely.

Nonsupervisory instructional staff People such as curriculum specialists, counselors, librarians, remedial specialists, and others possessing education certification, but not responsible for day-to-day teaching of the same group of pupils.

Not-for-profit institution A private institution in which the individual(s) or agency in control receives no compensation other than wages, rent, or other expenses for the assumption of risk. Not-for-profit institutions may be either independent not-for-profit (i.e., having no religious affiliation) or religiously affiliated.

Obligations Amounts of orders placed, contracts awarded, services received, or similar legally binding commitments made by federal agencies during a given period that will require outlays during the same or some future period.

Occupational home economics Courses of instruction emphasizing the acquisition of competencies needed for getting and holding a job or preparing for advancement in an occupational area using home economics knowledge and skills.

Occupied housing unit Separate living quarters with occupants currently inhabiting the unit. See also Housing unit.

Off-budget federal entities Organizational entities, federally owned in whole or in part, whose transactions belong in the budget under current budget accounting concepts, but that have been excluded from the budget totals under provisions of law.

Operation and maintenance services Includes salary, benefits, supplies, and contractual fees for supervision of operations and maintenance, operating buildings (heating, lighting, ventilating, repair, and replacement), care and upkeep of grounds and equipment, vehicle operations and maintenance (other than student transportation), security, and other operations and maintenance services.

Other foreign languages and literatures Any instructional program in foreign languages and literatures not listed in the table, including language groups and individual languages, such as the non-Semitic African languages, Native American languages, the Celtic languages, Pacific language groups, the Ural-Altaic languages, Basque, and others.

Other support services Includes salary, benefits, supplies, and contractual fees for business support services, central support services, and other support services not otherwise classified.

Other support services staff All staff not reported in other categories. This group includes media personnel, social workers, bus drivers, security, cafeteria workers, and other staff.

Outlays The value of checks issued, interest accrued on the public debt, or other payments made, net of refunds and reimbursements.

Part-time enrollment The number of students enrolled in higher education courses with a total credit load less than 75 percent of the normal full-time credit load.

Personal income Current income received by people from all sources, minus their personal contributions for social insurance. Classified as "people" are individuals (including owners of unincorporated firms), nonprofit institutions serving individuals, private trust funds, and private noninsured welfare funds. Personal income includes transfers (payments not resulting from current production) from government and business such as social security benefits and military pensions, but excludes transfers among people.

Physical plant assets Includes the values of land, buildings, and equipment owned, rented, or utilized by colleges. Does not include those plant values which are a part of endowment or other capital fund investments in real estate; excludes construction in progress.

Postbaccalaureate enrollment The number of graduate and first-professional students working towards advanced degrees and of students enrolled in graduate-level classes, but not enrolled in degree programs. See also Graduate enrollment and First-professional enrollment.

Postsecondary education The provision of formal instructional programs with a curriculum designed primarily for students who have completed the requirements for a high school diploma or equivalent. This includes programs of an academic, vocational, and continuing professional education purpose, and excludes avocational and adult basic education programs.

Private school or institution A school or institution which is controlled by an individual or agency other than a state, a subdivision of a state, or the federal government, which is usually supported primarily by other than public funds, and the operation of whose program rests with other than publicly elected or appointed officials. Private schools and institutions include both not-for-profit and for-profit institutions.

Property tax The sum of money collected from a tax levied against the value of property.

Proprietary (for profit) institution A private institution in which the individual(s) or agency in control receives compensation other than wages, rent, or other expenses for the assumption of risk.

Public school or institution A school or institution controlled and operated by publicly elected or appointed officials and deriving its primary support from public funds.

Pupil/teacher ratio The enrollment of pupils at a given period of time, divided by the full-time-equivalent number of classroom teachers serving these pupils during the same period.

Racial/ethnic group Classification indicating general racial or ethnic heritage based on self-identification, as in data collected by the Census Bureau or on observer identification, as in data collected by the Office for Civil Rights. These categories are in accordance with the Office of Management and Budget standard classification scheme presented below:

White A person having origins in any of the original peoples of Europe, North Africa, or the Middle East. Normally excludes people of Hispanic origin except for tabulations produced by the Census Bureau, which are noted accordingly in this volume.

Black A person having origins in any of the black racial groups in Africa. Normally excludes people of Hispanic origin except for tabulations produced by the Census Bureau, which are noted accordingly in this volume.

Hispanic A person of Mexican, Puerto Rican, Cuban, Central or South American, or other Spanish culture or origin, regardless of race.

Asian A person having origins in any of the original peoples of the Far East, Southeast Asia, or the Indian subcontinent, e.g., China, India, Japan, the Philippines, Vietnam, and Korea.

Native Hawaiian/Other Pacific Islander A person having origins in any of the original peoples of the Pacific Islands, e.g., Hawaii, Guam, and Samoa.

American Indian or Alaska Native A person having origins in any of the original peoples of North America and South America and maintains their cultural identification through tribal affiliation or community recognition.

Related children Related children in a family include own children and all other children in the household who are related to the householder by birth, marriage, or adoption.

Remedial education Instruction for a student lacking those reading, writing, or math skills necessary to perform college-level work at the level required by the attended institution.

Resident population Includes civilian population and armed forces personnel residing within the United States; excludes armed forces personnel residing overseas.

Revenue All funds received from external sources, net of refunds, and correcting transactions. Noncash transactions, such as receipt of services, commodities, or other receipts in kind are excluded, as are funds received from the issuance of debt, liquidation of investments, and nonroutine sale of property.

Rural school See Locale codes.

Salary The total amount regularly paid or stipulated to be paid to an individual, before deductions, for personal services rendered while on the payroll of a business or organization.

Sales and services Revenues derived from the sales of goods or services that are incidental to the conduct of instruction, research, or public service. Examples include film rentals, scientific and literary publications, testing services, university presses, and dairy products.

Sales tax Tax imposed upon the sale and consumption of goods and services. It can be imposed either as a general tax on the retail price of all goods and services sold or as a tax on the sale of selected goods and services.

Scholarships and fellowships This category of college expenditures applies only to money given in the form of outright grants and trainee stipends to individuals enrolled in formal coursework, either for credit or not. Aid to students in the form of tuition or fee remissions is included. College work-study funds are excluded and are reported under the program in which the student is working.

SAT An examination administered by the Educational Testing Service and used to predict the facility with which an individual will progress in learning college-level academic subjects. It was formerly called the Scholastic Assessment Test.

School A division of the school system consisting of students in one or more grades or other identifiable groups and organized to give instruction of a defined type. One school may share a building with another school or one school may be housed in several buildings.

School administration support services Includes salary, benefits, supplies, and contractual fees for the office of the principal, full-time department chairpeople, and graduation expenses.

School climate The social system and culture of the school, including the organizational structure of the school and values and expectations within it.

School district An education agency at the local level that exists primarily to operate public schools or to contract for public school services. Synonyms are "local basic administrative unit" and "local education agency."

Science The body of related courses concerned with knowledge of the physical and biological world and with the processes of discovering and validating this knowledge.

Secondary enrollment The total number of students registered in a school beginning with the next grade following an elementary or middle school (usually 7, 8, or 9) and ending with or below grade 12 at a given time.

Secondary instructional level The general level of instruction provided for pupils in secondary schools (generally covering grades 7 through 12 or 9 through 12) and any instruction of a comparable nature and difficulty provided for adults and youth beyond the age of compulsory school attendance.

Secondary school A school comprising any span of grades beginning with the next grade following an elementary or middle school (usually 7, 8, or 9) and ending with or below grade 12. Both junior high schools and senior high schools are included.

Senior high school A secondary school offering the final years of high school work necessary for graduation.

Serial volumes Publications issued in successive parts, usually at regular intervals, and as a rule, intended to be continued indefinitely. Serials include periodicals, newspapers, annuals, memoirs, proceedings, and transactions of societies.

Social studies A group of instructional programs that describes the substantive portions of behavior, past and present activities, interactions, and organizations of people associated together for religious, benevolent, cultural, scientific, political, patriotic, or other purposes.

Socioeconomic status (SES) For the High School and Beyond study and the National Longitudinal Study of the High School Class of 1972, the SES index is a composite of five equally weighted, standardized components: father's education, mother's education, family income, father's occupation, and household items. The terms high, middle, and low SES refer to the upper, middle two, and lower quartiles of the weighted SES composite index distribution.

Special education Direct instructional activities or special learning experiences designed primarily for students identified as having exceptionalities in one or more aspects of the cognitive process or as being underachievers in relation to general level or model of their overall abilities. Such services usually are directed at students with the following conditions: (1) physically handicapped; (2) emotionally disabled; (3) culturally different, including compensatory education; (4) mentally retarded; and (5) students with learning disabilities. Programs for the mentally gifted and talented are also included in some special education programs. See also Disabilities.

Standardized test A test composed of a systematic sampling of behavior, administered and scored according to specific instructions, capable of being interpreted in terms of adequate norms, and for which there are data on reliability and validity.

Standardized test performance The weighted distributions of composite scores from standardized tests used to group students according to performance.

Standard Metropolitan Statistical Area (SMSA) See Metropolitan Statistical Area (MSA).

Student An individual for whom instruction is provided in an educational program under the jurisdiction of a school, school system, or other education institution. No distinction is made between the terms "student" and "pupil," though "student" may refer to one receiving instruction at any level while "pupil" refers only to one attending school at the elementary or secondary level. A student may receive instruction in a school facility or in another location, such as at home or in a hospital. Instruction may be provided by direct student-teacher interaction or by some other approved medium such as television, radio, telephone, and correspondence.

Student support services Includes salary, benefits, supplies, and contractual fees for staff providing attendance and social work, guidance, health, psychological services, speech pathology, audiology, and other support to students.

Subject-matter club Organizations that are formed around a shared interest in a particular area of study and whose primary activities promote that interest. Examples of such organizations are math, science, business, and history clubs.

Supervisory staff Principals, assistant principals, and supervisors of instruction; does not include superintendents or assistant superintendents.

Tax base The collective value of objects, assets, and income components against which a tax is levied.

Tax expenditures Losses of tax revenue attributable to provisions of the federal income tax laws that allow a special exclusion, exemption, or deduction from gross income or provide a special credit, preferential rate of tax, or a deferral of tax liability affecting individual or corporate income tax liabilities.

Teacher see Instructional staff.

Technical education A program of vocational instruction that ordinarily includes the study of the sciences and mathematics underlying a technology, as well as the methods, skills, and materials commonly used and the services performed in the technology. Technical education prepares individuals for positions—such as draftsman or lab technician—in the occupational area between the skilled craftsman and the professional person.

Title IV Refers to a section of the Higher Education Act of 1965 that covers the administration of the federal student financial aid program.

Title IV eligible institution A postsecondary institution that meets the criteria for participating in the federal student financial aid program. An eligible institution must be any of the following: (1) an institution of higher education (with public or private, non-profit control), (2) a proprietary institution (with private for-profit control), and (3) a postsecondary vocational institution (with public or private, not-for-profit control). In addition, it must have acceptable legal authorization, acceptable accreditation and admission stands, eligible academic program(s), administrative capability, and financial responsibility.

Total expenditure per pupil in average daily attendance Includes all expenditures allocable to per pupil costs divided by average daily attendance. These allocable expenditures include current expenditures for regular school programs, interest on school debt, and capital outlay. Beginning in 1980–81, expenditures for state administration are excluded and expenditures for other programs (summer schools, community colleges, and private schools) are included.

Town school See Locale codes.

Trade and industrial occupations The branch of vocational education which is concerned with preparing people for initial employment or with updating or retraining workers in a wide range of trade and industrial occupations. Such occupations are skilled or semiskilled and are concerned with layout designing, producing, processing, assembling, testing, maintaining, servicing, or repairing any product or commodity.

Transcript An official list of all courses taken by a student at a school or college showing the final grade received for each course, with definitions of the various grades given at the institution.

Trust funds Amounts collected and used by the federal government for carrying out specific purposes and programs according to terms of a trust agreement or statute, such as the social security and unemployment trust funds. Trust fund receipts that are not anticipated to be used in the immediate future are generally invested in interest-bearing government securities and earn interest for the trust fund.

Tuition and fees A payment or charge for instruction or compensation for services, privileges, or the use of equipment, books, or other goods.

Unclassified students Students who are not candidates for a degree or other formal award, although they are taking higher education courses for credit in regular classes with other students.

Unadjusted dollars See Current dollars.

Undergraduate students Students registered at an institution of higher education who are working in a program leading to a baccalaureate degree or other formal award below the baccalaureate, such as an associate degree.

Unemployed Civilians who had no employment but were available for work and: (1) had engaged in any specific job seeking activity within the past 4 weeks; (2) were waiting to be called back to a job from which they had been laid off; or (3) were waiting to report to a new wage or salary job within 30 days.

U.S. Service Academies These institutions of higher education are controlled by the U.S. Department of Defense and the U.S. Department of Transportation. The 5 institutions counted in the NCES surveys of degree granting institutions include: the U.S. Air Force Academy, U.S. Coast Guard Academy, U.S. Merchant Marine Academy, U.S. Military Academy, and the U.S. Naval Academy.

University An institution of higher education consisting of a liberal arts college, a diverse graduate program, and usually two or more professional schools or faculties and empowered to confer degrees in various fields of study. For purposes of maintaining trend data in this publication, the selection of university institutions has not been revised since 1982.

Urban fringe school See Locale codes.

Visual and performing arts A group of instructional programs that generally describes the historic development, aesthetic qualities, and creative processes of the visual and performing arts.

Vocational education Organized educational programs, services, and activities which are directly related to the preparation of individuals for paid or unpaid employment, or for additional preparation for a career, requiring other than a baccalaureate or advanced degree.

APPENDIX C
Index of Table Numbers

Academic rank of faculty in postsecondary institutions, 249, 253
  by field of study, 254, 255
  salaries by, 257, 258, 261, 262
  tenure by, 264
  by type and control of institution, 252
Academic support, expenditures at postsecondary institutions, 364, 365
Achievement of elementary and secondary students. *See also under individual subjects*
  mathematics, 136
  reading, 123
  science, 138
ACT (American College Testing Program) scores, 145, 327
Administration/Administrative staff
  postsecondary institutions, expenditures for, 361, 362
  in public elementary and secondary schools, 80, 81, 82, 83
  public elementary and secondary schools, expenditures for, 174, 176, 177, 178, 179
Admission requirements for postsecondary institutions, 326
Admissions to undergraduate institutions, 327
Adult education, 369, 370, 371
Advanced Placement courses in public secondary schools, 152, 156
Affiliation of postsecondary institutions, 197
Age
  adult education participation, 370, 371
  attendance status at postsecondary institutions, 190
  bachelor's degrees by, 10
  center-based preprimary programs and, 44
  child care arrangements by, 45, 46, 47
  cognitive and motor skills by, 112
  computer usage, 429, 430, 432
  educational attainment by, 8, 9
  enrollment in grades 9 to 12 compared to population, 55
  faculty in postsecondary institutions, 252, 253
  field of study in postsecondary institutions by, 232
  GED (General Educational Development) credentials issued by, 108
  international comparisons of bachelor's degree recipients, 415
  international comparisons of school-age population, 400
  internet usage, 428
  labor force participation by, 381
  language, mathematics and motor skills by, 114
  literacy skills of adults, 386
  mathematics scores by, 131, 132, 133
  mental and physical skills by, 113
  percentage of population enrolled in school by, 6, 7
  population by, 15, 16
  postsecondary enrollment by, 192

  preprimary education and, 43
  range for compulsory school attendance, 165
  reading scores by, 117, 119, 120
  school-age population, by state, 17
  student financial aid by, 335, 337, 338
  students exiting special education, 111
  teachers in public schools, 69
  unemployment rate, 382
Agriculture
  associate's degrees in, 269, 270, 282, 283
  bachelor's degrees in, 10, 271, 285, 286
  degrees conferred in, 275, 277, 296
  doctor's degrees in, 273, 291, 292
  enrollment in postsecondary education, 232
  institutions conferring degrees in, 278
  master's degrees in, 272, 288, 289
Alcohol usage
  by high school seniors, 164
  by teenagers, 163
  violence and drug usage on school property, 162
  by young adults, 395, 396
Algebra course work in high school, 133
Alumni, support for postsecondary institutions, 358
American Indians/Alaska Natives
  ACT (American College Testing Program) scores, 145
  with associate's degrees, 281, 282, 283
  attendance patterns by tenth-graders, 157
  with bachelor's degrees, 10, 284, 285, 286
  course work by high school graduates in mathematics and science, 149, 150
  distribution in public schools, 97
  with doctor's degrees, 290, 291, 292
  educational attainment by state, 12
  employment of high school seniors, 387
  enrollment distribution in public schools by state, 41
  estimates of resident population by age, 16
  with first-professional degrees, 293, 294, 295
  gifted and talented students by state, 53, 54
  high school graduates and dropouts, 107
  with master's degrees, 287, 288, 289
  mathematics scores by grade, 136
  postsecondary institutions
    employment in, 246
    enrollment in, 226, 227
    enrollment in by state, 228, 229
    faculty in, 249, 253, 255
  in public charter and traditional public schools, 101
  reading scores and achievement levels of fourth-graders, 121
  reading scores by grade, 118

SAT scores for college-bound seniors, 141
science scores and achievement levels by grade, 138
science scores of eighth-graders in public schools, 139
suspensions and expulsions from public schools, 160, 161
tribally controlled institutions, 239
Applications to undergraduate institutions, 327
Appropriations for public postsecondary institutions, 352
Arabic, degrees conferred in, 309
Architecture
associate's degrees in, 269, 270, 282, 283
bachelor's degrees in, 10, 271, 285, 286
degrees conferred in, 275, 277, 297
doctor's degrees in, 273, 291, 292
enrollment, postsecondary education, 232
institutions conferring degrees in, 278
master's degrees in, 272, 288, 289
Area studies
associate's degrees in, 269, 270, 282, 283
bachelor's degrees in, 271, 285, 286
degrees conferred in, 275, 277
doctor's degrees in, 273, 291, 292
enrollment, postsecondary education, 232
institutions conferring degrees in, 278
master's degrees in, 272, 288, 289
Arts
associate's degrees in, 269, 270, 282, 283
bachelor's degrees in, 10, 271, 285, 286
Carnegie units earned by high school graduates, 147
degrees conferred in, 275, 277, 318
doctor's degrees in, 273, 291, 292
institutions conferring degrees in, 278
master's degrees in, 272, 288, 289
Asians/Pacific Islanders
ACT (American College Testing Program) scores, 145
with associate's degrees, 281, 282, 283
attendance patterns by tenth-graders, 157
with bachelor's degrees, 10, 284, 285, 286
course work by high school graduates in mathematics and
science, 149, 150
distribution in public schools, 97
with doctor's degrees, 290, 291, 292
educational attainment by state, 12
employment of high school seniors, 387
enrollment distribution in public schools by state, 41
estimates of resident population by age, 16
with first-professional degrees, 293, 294, 295
gifted and talented students by state, 53, 54
high school graduates and dropouts, 107
with master's degrees, 287, 288, 289
mathematics scores by grade, 136
postsecondary institutions
employment in, 246
enrollment in, 226
enrollment in by state, 228, 229
enrollment in by type and control of institution, 227
faculty in, 249, 253, 255
poverty rates, 21
in public charter and traditional public schools, 101
reading scores and achievement levels of fourth-graders, 121
reading scores by grade, 118
SAT scores for college-bound seniors, 141
science scores and achievement levels by grade, 138

science scores of eighth-graders in public schools, 139
suspensions and expulsions from public schools, 160, 161
unemployment rate, 382
Assessment. See Testing
Associate's degrees, 282, 283
by control of institution, 276, 277, 320
by field of study, 269, 270
by gender, 268
number of institutions conferring, 278
by race/ethnicity and gender, 281
by state, 322
Attendance, elementary/secondary education
age range for compulsory, 165
average daily, 40, 175, 185
patterns by tenth-graders, 157
preprimary education status, 43
Attendance status, postsecondary institutions, 188, 190, 196
by control and type of institution, 192
first-professional level, 207
by first-time freshmen, 198, 199
graduate level, 206
institutions with more than 15,000 students, 235
by level, 193, 194, 195
in private postsecondary institutions by state, 213, 214
in public postsecondary institutions by state, 212
by race/ethnicity and gender, 226
by state, 211
student financial aid and
graduate level, 344, 345, 346, 347
undergraduate level, 335, 337, 338, 339, 340, 341, 342, 343
undergraduate level, 205
Attitudes of students
mathematics, 137
science, 140
values of high school seniors, 397
Attrition rate for teachers in public schools, 73
Auxiliary enterprises, postsecondary institutions
current-fund revenues, 348, 349
expenditures for, 361, 362, 364, 365, 366, 367
revenues, 350, 351
revenues to private institutions, 353, 354, 355, 356
Average daily attendance, public elementary and secondary
schools, 40
current expenditures per pupil, 185
transportation expenditures, 175
Averaged freshman graduation rates for public secondary schools,
106

Bachelor's degrees
by control of institution, 276, 277, 320
course work for, 325
employment of recipients of, 391, 392
by field of study, 271, 296–318, 392 (See also Field of study)
by gender, 268
international comparisons of, 415
international comparisons of science and mathematics, 416
number of institutions conferring, 278
number of persons with, 10
by race/ethnicity and gender, 284, 285, 286
salaries of recipients, 394
salaries of teachers by, 76
by state, 321, 322

Behavioral sciences. *See* Social sciences
Benefit expenditures for faculty in postsecondary institutions, 263
Biology
    associate's degrees in, 269, 270, 282, 283
    bachelor's degrees in, 271, 285, 286
    course work for bachelor's degrees, 325
    degrees conferred in, 275, 277, 298, 299
    doctor's degrees in, 273, 291, 292
    enrollment, postsecondary education, 232
    institutions conferring degrees in, 278
    international comparisons of time spent on science, 414
    master's degrees in, 272, 288, 289
Blacks
    ACT (American College Testing Program) scores, 145
    with associate's degrees, 281, 282, 283
    attendance patterns by tenth-graders, 157
    with bachelor's degrees, 10, 284, 285, 286
    child care arrangements by, 45
    college enrollment and labor force status of high school
        graduates, 388
    course work by high school graduates in mathematics and
        science, 149, 150
    distribution in public schools, 97
    with doctor's degrees, 290, 291, 292
    dropouts from high school, 109
    educational attainment, 8, 9, 12
    employment of high school seniors, 387
    enrollment distribution in public schools by state, 41
    estimates of resident population by age, 16
    family characteristics of, 19
    with first-professional degrees, 293, 294, 295
    gifted and talented students by state, 53, 54
    high school graduates and dropouts, 107
    internet usage, 428
    labor force status of high school dropouts, 389
    leisure activities of high school seniors, 153
    with master's degrees, 287, 288, 289
    mathematics scores by age, 132
    mathematics scores by grade, 136
    mathematics scores of 17-year-olds, 133
    percentage of population enrolled in school, 6
    postsecondary institutions
        employment in, 246
        enrollment in, 201, 204, 226
        enrollment in by state, 228, 229
        enrollment in by type and control of institution, 227
        faculty in, 249, 253, 255
        historically black colleges and universities, 240, 241, 242
    poverty rates, 21
    in public charter and traditional public schools, 101
    reading levels by age, 120
    reading scores and achievement levels of fourth-graders, 121
    reading scores by grade, 118
    SAT scores for college-bound seniors, 141
    science scores and achievement levels by grade, 138
    science scores of eighth-graders in public schools, 139
    suspensions and expulsions from public schools, 160, 161
    unemployment rate, 382
    violence and drug usage on school property, 162
Branch campuses, postsecondary institutions, 265, 267

Business and management
    associate's degrees in, 269, 270, 282, 283
    bachelor's and master's degrees in, 321
    bachelor's degrees in, 10, 271, 285, 286
    course work for bachelor's degrees, 325
    degrees conferred in, 274, 275, 277, 300
    doctor's degrees in, 273, 291, 292, 319
    enrollment, postsecondary education, 232
    institutions conferring degrees in, 278
    master's degrees in, 272, 288, 289

Calculus course work in secondary schools, 133
Careers and adult education participation, 370, 371. *See also*
    Occupation
Career/technical education, 148. *See also* Vocational schools/
    education
Carnegie units earned in high school, 147
    state requirements for high school graduation, 167
    in vocational education, 148
Catholic schools. *See also* Private elementary and secondary
    schools
    attendance patterns by tenth-graders, 157
    enrollment and other characteristics, 58
    extracurricular activities of high school sophomores, 154
    leisure activities of high school seniors, 153
    reading scores by grade in, 123
    staff-to-student ratios, 60
    tuition for, 59
Center-based programs, 44, 46, 47. *See also* Preprimary education
Certification of teachers, states requiring test for, 170
Charter schools, 98, 101
Chemical engineering, 305. *See also* Engineering
Chemistry, 313, 414
Child care, 44, 45
    cognitive and motor skills by primary type of, 112
    language, mathematics and motor skills by primary type of, 114
    mental and physical skills by primary type of care, 113
    quality rating of arrangements for, 47
    by type of arrangement, 46
Chinese, degrees conferred in, 309
Cigarettes, teenagers and young adults smoking, 163, 395, 396
Civics, scores and achievement levels by grade, 128
Civil engineering, 305. *See also* Engineering
Classroom teachers. *See* Teachers
Class size
    international comparisons of mathematics, 409
    by teacher characteristics, 67
Closing of postsecondary institutions, 267
Cognitive skills of young children, 112
Collections in college and university libraries, 424, 425
Collections in public libraries, 426
Color knowledge, 114
Communications
    associate's degrees in, 269, 270, 282, 283
    bachelor's degrees in, 10, 271, 285, 286
    degrees conferred in, 275, 277, 301
    doctor's degrees in, 273, 291, 292
    enrollment, postsecondary education, 232
    institutions conferring degrees in, 278
    master's degrees in, 272, 288, 289

Completion status in postsecondary education, 329
Computer and information sciences
    associate's degrees in, 269, 270, 282, 283
    bachelor's and master's degrees in, 321
    bachelor's degrees in, 10, 271, 285, 286
    course work for bachelor's degrees, 325
    degrees conferred in, 274, 275, 277, 302
    doctor's degrees in, 273, 291, 292
    enrollment, postsecondary education, 232
    institutions conferring degrees in, 278
    master's degrees in, 272, 288, 289
Computers
    home use, 429, 430
    number used for instruction in public elementary and secondary
        schools, 427
    usage by educational level, 431
    work use, 432
Construction trades
    associate's degrees in, 269, 270, 282, 283
    bachelor's degrees in, 271, 285, 286
    degrees conferred in, 275, 277
    doctor's degrees in, 273, 291, 292
    enrollment, postsecondary education, 232
    institutions conferring degrees in, 278
    master's degrees in, 272, 288, 289
Consumer Price Index, 31
Control of institutions. *See* Private elementary and secondary
    schools; Private postsecondary institutions; Public elementary
    and secondary schools; Public postsecondary institutions
Course work/Credits
    bachelor's degree recipients, 325
    Carnegie units, average earned by public high school graduates,
        147
    Carnegie units required by state for high school graduation, 167
    dual credit, Advanced Placement and International
        Baccalaureate courses in public secondary schools, 152
    by high school graduates in mathematics and science, 149, 150
    mathematics scores of 17-year-olds and, 133
    minimum earned by high school graduates, 151
    subjects taught in public high schools, 70
Crime at public elementary and secondary schools, 158
Criminal justice enrollment in postsecondary education, 232. *See
    also* Security
Criterion-referenced assessments by state, 168
Current expenditures. *See also* Expenditures
    per pupil in public schools, 181, 183, 185
    in public elementary and secondary schools, 174, 176, 177, 178
Current-fund expenditures. *See also* Expenditures
    postsecondary institutions, 360, 361
Current-fund revenues. *See also* Revenues
    from federal government to postsecondary institutions, 357
    by source for postsecondary institutions, 348, 349

Degree-granting institutions. *See* Postsecondary education
Degrees conferred. *See also individual degrees*
    associate's degrees, 269, 270
    bachelor's degrees, 271
    by control of institution, 276, 277, 278
    doctor's degrees, 273
    first-professional degrees, 279, 280
    at historically black colleges and universities, 240, 241

    at institutions serving large populations of Hispanic students,
        238
    at institutions with more than 15,000 students, 235
    by level and gender, 268
    master's degrees, 272
    number of institutions and enrollment size, 234
    by state, 320, 321, 322
    Title IV postsecondary institutions, 186
    tribally controlled institutions, 239
    at women's colleges, 237
Degrees earned. *See also* Educational attainment; individual
    degrees
    completions by type of institution, 329
    by field of study, 296–318
    by Hispanics, 238
    income by educational attainment, 384, 385
    by teachers in schools, 67, 68, 74
    women's colleges, 237
Dentistry, first-professional degrees in, 279, 280, 294, 295
Department of Education, 377, 378
Dependency status and student financial aid, 335, 337, 338
Disabilities, students with, 51
    exiting special education, 111
    in federally supported programs, 50
    Individuals with Disabilities Education Act, 52
    postsecondary education and employment status of, 390
    postsecondary institution enrollment, 231
Discipline division. *See* Field of study
Disposable personal income, 30. *See also* Income
Distance education, high school participation in, 57
Doctor's degrees
    by control of institution, 276, 277, 320
    by field of study, 273
    by gender, 268
    by institution, 323
    number of institutions conferring, 278
    by race/ethnicity and gender, 290, 291, 292
    by state, 322
    statistical profile of persons receiving, 319
    student financial aid for, 344, 345, 346, 347
Dropouts from high school
    by gender and race/ethnicity, 109
    labor force status, 389
    in school districts of more than 15,000 students, 91
    by state and race/ethnicity, 107
    years of school completed, 110
Drug usage
    by high school seniors, 164
    percentage of students' experiencing, 162
    by teenagers, 163
    by young adults, 395, 396
Dual credits in public secondary schools, 152

Earth sciences, 313, 414. *See also* Science
Economics
    degrees conferred in, 317
    enrollment, postsecondary education, 232
    scores, achievement levels, and course work of high school
        seniors, 129
Education (as field of study)
    associate's degrees in, 269, 270, 282, 283
    bachelor's and master's degrees in, 321

bachelor's degrees in, 10, 271, 285, 286
course work for bachelor's degrees, 325
degrees conferred in, 274, 275, 277, 303
doctor's degrees in, 273, 291, 292, 319
enrollment, postsecondary education, 232
institutions conferring degrees in, 278
master's degrees in, 272, 288, 289, 321
Education, federal support for, 373, 374, 379
by agency, 375, 376
Department of Education appropriations, 378
Department of Education outlays, 377
Education agencies (public), 89
Educational attainment
adult education participation, 370, 371
bachelor's degrees, number of persons with, 10 (*See also*
Bachelor's degrees)
computer usage at work, 432
high school sophomores of 1990, 324
income by, 384, 385
labor force participation by, 381
by largest 25 states, 13
by level of attainment, 8, 9
literacy skills of adults, 386
by metropolitan area, 14
occupations by, 383
parental participation in educational activities with children, 24
parental participation in school activities, 23
parents', children's reading scores by, 117, 123 (*See also*
Parental level of education)
by state, 11
by state and race/ethnicity, 12
of teachers in public schools, 67, 68
unemployment rate, 382
Educational institutions, number of, 5
Eighth grade
international comparisons
of mathematics class size, 409
of mathematics instructional time, 408
of mathematics scores, 407
of science, instructional practices in, 414
of science scores, 413
of students' perceptions of mathematics, 410
mathematics scores, 136
by attitude, 137
in public schools, 135
reading scores, 118, 124
reading scores and achievement levels in public schools, 122
science scores and achievement levels, 138
science scores in public schools, 139
writing scores and achievement levels, 125
Electrical engineering, 305. *See also* Engineering
Elementary and secondary education, 32–185. *See also* Private
elementary and secondary schools; Public elementary and
secondary schools
computer usage by students, 431
enrollment overview, 2
expenditures of educational institutions, 26
expenditures on, 28
expenditures related to gross domestic product, 25
federal support for, 373, 375
number of institutions, 5
participants in, 1

per capita expenditures on, 29
pupil-to-teacher ratios in public and private schools, 64
Elementary schools, 87, 95, 98. *See also* Private elementary and
secondary schools; Public elementary and secondary schools
Emotional attachment to parents, 113
Employees in postsecondary institutions, 243, 245. *See also* Staff
Employment
bachelor's degree recipients and, 391, 392
computer usage on the job, 432
high school dropouts, labor force status, 389
high school graduates, labor force status, 388
high school seniors, 387
ratio to population, 381
special education students' status, 390
of teachers in nonschool environment, 75
Endowment funds, 359
Engineering
associate's degrees in, 269, 270, 282, 283
bachelor's degrees in, 10, 271, 285, 286, 416
course work for bachelor's degrees, 325
degrees conferred in, 275, 277, 304, 305
doctor's degrees in, 273, 291, 292, 319
enrollment, postsecondary education, 232
graduate-level enrollment in, 233
institutions conferring degrees in, 278
international comparisons of bachelor's degree recipients, 416
international comparisons of graduate degrees in, 417
master's degrees in, 272, 288, 289
English and literature
associate's degrees in, 269, 270, 282, 283
bachelor's degrees in, 10, 271, 285, 286
Carnegie units earned by high school graduates, 147
Carnegie units required by state for high school graduation, 167
criterion-referenced assessments by state, 168
degrees conferred in, 275, 277, 306
doctor's degrees in, 273, 291, 292
enrollment, postsecondary education, 232
institutions conferring degrees in, 278
master's degrees in, 272, 288, 289
English as a second language, 369
Enrollment
at all levels of education, 2
in Catholic elementary and secondary schools, 61
in grades 9 to 12 compared to population, 55
international comparisons, 398
international comparisons of secondary and postsecondary
enrollment, 401
in largest 100 school districts, 93
percentage of population enrolled in school, 6, 7
postsecondary institutions
applications and admissions compared to, 327
attendance status, 188, 190, 196, 211
bachelor's degree recipients 1 year after graduation, 392
by control and affiliation, 197
by control and type, 189, 192, 215
degrees conferred at, 234
disabled students in, 231
field of study, 232
first-professional level, 207
first-time freshmen, 198
full-time-equivalent enrollment in, 219, 220
by gender and race/ethnicity, 204

graduate level, 206
historically black colleges and universities, 240, 241, 242
institutions with large populations of Hispanic students, 238
institutions with more than 15,000 students, 235
largest colleges and universities, 236
by level, 191, 193, 194, 195, 216, 217, 218
private institutions by state, 210, 213, 214
public institutions by state, 209, 212
by race/ethnicity, 227, 228, 229
by race/ethnicity and gender, 226
by recent high school completers, 200, 201, 202, 203
by state, 208, 209, 210, 222
Title IV, 186
tribally controlled institutions, 239
undergraduate, 205, 388
women's colleges, 237
preprimary education, 43, 48
in private elementary and secondary schools, 58, 62
public elementary and secondary schools
by capacity level, 103
charter schools, 101
by grade, 37
historical statistics of, 32
by metropolitan status, 90
pupil-to-staff ratios in, 85
pupil-to-teacher ratios in, 63, 64, 66
race/ethnicity distribution in, 41, 97
school size of, 95, 96
by state, 33, 34, 35, 36, 41
in school districts, 88
by school districts of more than 15,000 students, 91
Environment in schools
class size, 67, 409
factors that interfere with instruction, 102
overcrowding in public schools, 103
violence and drug usage, 162
Even Start program, 379
Exit exams for high school diploma, 167
Expenditures
of educational institutions, 25, 26
gross domestic product and income compared to, 30
international comparisons on education, 418, 419
postsecondary institutions
current fund, 360, 361
libraries, 424, 425
private institutions, 364, 365, 366, 367, 368
public institutions, 362, 363
by purpose, 361
by type and control of institution, 360
public elementary and secondary schools
current by state, 176
current per pupil by state, 184, 185
by function and subfunction, 179
historical statistics of, 32
for instruction, 180
by metropolitan status, 90
per pupil, 181
per pupil by state, 182, 183
by purpose, 174, 177, 178, 179
in school districts of more than 15,000 students, 92
for school libraries and media centers, 421, 422, 423
by state and local governments, 27, 28
by state and local governments per capita, 29

Expulsions from school, 160, 161
Extracurricular activities (school sponsored), 154

Faculty, postsecondary
benefit expenditures for, 263
by employment status, 243, 245, 248
by field of study, 254, 255
full-time by race/ethnicity, 249
full-time-equivalent (FTE), 244, 247
historical statistics of degree-granting institutions, 187
instructional activities of, 250, 251
number of, 1, 4
by race/ethnicity and gender, 246, 253
salaries
by field of study, 256
by rank, 257, 258
by state, 259, 260, 261, 262
with tenure, 264
by type and control of institution, 252
Families
care of children in, 44, 45, 46, 47
characteristics of, 19
homeschooled children, 38
median income of, 30 (See also Income, family)
poverty rates by race/ethnicity, 21
preschool literacy activities at home, 49
by status and presence of children, 18
Federal government, 373–380
budget composite deflator, 31
education agencies (public) operated by, 89
expenditures for education, 373, 374
by agency, 375, 376
Department of Education appropriations, 378
Department of Education outlays, 377
research, 380
Title I allocations, 379
funds to largest school districts, 93
grants to undergraduates, 336
programs for students with disabilities, 50
revenues
for postsecondary institutions, 348, 357
private, 353, 354, 355, 356
public, 349, 350, 351
for public elementary and secondary schools, 171, 172, 173
student financial aid, 335, 337, 338, 339, 340, 341, 342, 343, 344, 345
Field of study. See also under individual subjects
associate's degrees by, 269, 270
bachelor's degree recipients, enrollment in postbaccalaureate program, 393
bachelor's degree recipients, salaries by, 394
bachelor's degrees by, 271, 392
bachelor's degrees by course work completed, 325
degrees conferred by, 296–318
doctor's degrees by, 273
faculty in postsecondary institutions, 254, 255
faculty salaries by, 256
first-professional degrees by, 279, 280
full-time employment by, 391
intended major for college-bound seniors, 143
by level and type of institution, 232
master's degrees by, 272

Finances for postsecondary institutions, historical statistics, 187. *See also* Expenditures; Revenues

Financial aid to students
 graduate level, 344, 345, 346, 347
 as part of expenditures for private postsecondary institutions, 364, 365, 366, 367
 public postsecondary institution expenditures, 362
 undergraduates receiving, 335, 336, 337, 338, 339, 340, 341, 342, 343

First-professional degrees
 by control of institution, 276
 by field of study, 279, 280
 by gender, 268
 number of institutions conferring, 279
 by race/ethnicity and gender, 293, 294, 295
 by state, 322

First-professional level
 disabled students enrolled at, 231
 enrollment at, 191, 193, 194, 195
  by attendance status, 207
  by race/ethnicity and gender, 226
  by state, 216, 217, 218
 field of study, 232
 student financial aid for, 344, 345, 346, 347
 tuition and fees for, 334

Foreign languages
 associate's degrees in, 269, 270, 282, 283
 bachelor's degrees in, 10, 271, 285, 286
 Carnegie units earned by high school graduates, 147
 degrees conferred in, 275, 277, 307–309
 doctor's degrees in, 273, 291, 292
 enrollment, postsecondary education, 232
 enrollment in high school, 56
 institutions conferring degrees in, 278
 master's degrees in, 272, 288, 289

Foreign students in United States, 420

Fourth grade
 international comparisons of mathematics, 406
 international comparisons of science, 412
 mathematics scores and achievement levels, 134, 136
 reading scores, 118, 123
 reading scores and achievement levels in public schools, 121
 science scores and achievement levels, 138
 time spent on homework and television, 155
 writing scores and achievement levels, 125

Four-year postsecondary institutions
 admission requirements for, 326
 applications, admissions, and enrollment comparisons, 327
 attendance status at, 196
 with branch campuses, 265
 closing of institutions, 267
 completion status for students, 329
 enrollment in, 189, 192, 193, 194, 195
  by race/ethnicity, 204, 227
  by recent high school completers in, 202
  by state, 215, 217, 218
 expenditures of, 360
  private, 364, 365, 366, 367, 368
  public, 362, 363
 faculty in, 248
  salaries, 258, 259, 260, 261, 262
  tenure, 264
 field of study at, 232

first-time freshmen at, 198
full-time-equivalent enrollment in, 219, 220
full-time-equivalent staff at, 247
historically black colleges and universities, 242
number of institutions, 230
number of institutions by state, 266
remedial coursework offered by, 328
residence and migration of freshmen in postsecondary institutions, 225
revenues of private postsecondary institutions, 354, 355, 356
revenues of public institutions, 350
staff in, 243, 245, 246
student financial aid
 graduate students, 344, 345, 346, 347
 undergraduates, 336, 339, 340, 341, 342, 343
Title IV postsecondary institutions, 186
tuition, fees, and board rates for undergraduates, 331, 332, 333

Free or reduced-price school lunch program
 civics achievement by grade, 128
 crime incidents reported at public schools, 158
 economics achievement of high school seniors, 129
 environmental factors that interfere with instruction, 102
 geography achievement by grade, 130
 history achievement by grade, 126, 127
 mathematics scores of eighth-graders by attitude, 137
 number and percentage of eligible public school students by state, 42
 public elementary and secondary schools with internet access, 427
 public school capacity level and, 103
 schools with security measures, 159
 science achievement by grade, 138
 science achievement of eighth-graders in public schools, 139
 science scores of high school seniors by attitude, 140
 writing achievement, 125

French
 degrees conferred in, 308
 enrollment in high school, 56

Freshmen (postsecondary institutions)
 enrollment by attendance status, 198
 enrollment by state, 199
 residence and migration of, 223, 224, 225

Full-day kindergarten, 165
 mathematics and science skills for 1998 kindergarten cohort, 116
 reading skills for 1998 kindergarten cohort, 115

Full-time attendance at postsecondary institutions, 188, 196
 by age and gender, 190
 by control and affiliation of institution, 197
 by control and type of institution, 192
 first-professional enrollment, 207
 first-time freshmen, 198, 199
 graduate enrollment, 206
 graduate-level student financial aid, 344, 346
 institutions with more than 15,000 students, 235
 by level, 191, 193, 194, 195
 in private institutions by state, 213, 214
 in public institutions by state, 212
 by race/ethnicity and gender, 226
 by state, 211
 student financial aid, 337, 340, 341, 343
 undergraduate, 205

Full-time employment. *See also* Employment
    bachelor's degree recipients and, 391
    in postsecondary institutions, 243, 245, 246, 248, 249, 250
Full-time-equivalent enrollment in postsecondary institutions, 219, 220, 221, 235
Full-time-equivalent staff in postsecondary institutions, 244, 247. *See also* Faculty; Staff
Full-time-equivalent students (postsecondary institutions), expenditures per, 360, 362
Full-time faculty, 249, 250. *See also* Faculty
Full-year enrollment in postsecondary institutions, 222
Funding for public elementary and secondary schools. *See* Revenues

GED (General Educational Development) test, 108
Gender
    ACT (American College Testing Program) scores, 145
    adult education participation, 370, 371
    associate's degrees by, 281, 282, 283
    attendance status at postsecondary institutions, 188, 190, 196
    bachelor's degrees by, 10, 284, 285, 286
    Carnegie units earned by high school graduates, 147, 148
    child care arrangements and, 46, 47
    civics achievement by grade, 128
    cognitive and motor skills by, 112
    college enrollment and labor force status of high school graduates by, 388
    computer usage, 429, 430, 431, 432
    course work and mathematics scores of 17-year-olds, 133
    course work by high school graduates in mathematics and science, 149, 150
    degrees conferred by, 296–298, 300–304, 306, 307, 310–312, 314–316, 318
    degrees conferred by field of study, 275
    doctor's degrees by, 290, 291, 292, 319
    dropouts from high school by, 109
    economics achievement of high school seniors, 129
    educational attainment, 8, 9
        of high school sophomores of 1990, 324
        in largest 25 states, 13
        by metropolitan area, 14
    employment of high school seniors, 387
    enrollment in postsecondary institutions, 200, 226
    enrollment in Title IV postsecondary institutions, 186
    extracurricular activities of high school sophomores, 154
    first-professional degrees by, 279, 280, 293, 294, 295
    geography achievement levels by grade, 130
    gifted and talented students by state, 53, 54
    grades earned by elementary and secondary students, 146
    high school graduates by control of school, 104
    historical statistics of degree-granting institutions, 187
    history achievement by grade, 126, 127
    homework, 156
    income by educational attainment, 384, 385
    international comparisons
        of bachelor's degree recipients, 415
        of mathematics, 411
        of mathematics, reading, and science skills, 403
    internet usage, 428
    labor force participation by, 381

labor force status of high school dropouts, 389
language, mathematics, and motor skills by, 114
leisure activities of high school seniors, 153
life values of high school students, 397
literacy skills of adults, 386
master's degrees by, 287, 288, 289
mathematics and science skills for 1998 kindergarten cohort, 116
mathematics scores
    by age, 131, 132
    of eighth-graders by attitude, 137
    by grade, 136
mental and physical skills by, 113
minimum credits earned by high school graduates, 151
occupations by, 383
percentage of population enrolled in school by, 6
postsecondary institutions
    associate's degrees by field of study, 270
    attendance status and state, 211
    attendance status at public institutions by state, 212
    degrees conferred by, 268
    employment in, 243, 245, 246
    enrollment in, 191, 193, 194, 195, 204
    enrollment in private institutions by state, 213, 214
    faculty in, 249, 252, 253, 254, 255
    faculty salaries by, 257, 258
    faculty with tenure in, 264
    first-professional enrollment at, 207
    first-time freshmen at, 198, 199
    graduate enrollment at, 206
    historically black colleges and universities, 241
    institutions with more than 15,000 students, 235
    undergraduate enrollment at, 205
    women's colleges, 237
reading achievement by age, 117, 120
reading scores by grade, 118, 123
reading skills for 1998 kindergarten cohort, 115
SAT scores for college-bound seniors, 142
science achievement by grade, 138
science scores of high school seniors by attitude, 140
science scores of eighth-graders in public schools, 139
student financial aid, 335, 337, 338
suspensions and expulsions from public schools, 160, 161
teachers' educational attainment in schools by, 68
teachers in public schools, 69
time spent on homework and television by fourth-graders, 155
unemployment rate, 382
violence and drug usage on school property, 162
writing achievement by grade, 125
General Educational Development (GED) test, 108
Geography
    achievement levels by grade, 130
    enrollment, postsecondary education, 232
Geology, 313
Geometry course work in secondary schools, 133
German
    degrees conferred in, 308
    enrollment in high school in, 56
Gifted and talented students, 53, 54
Goals for education for college-bound seniors, 143

Government. *See also* Federal government; Local governments; States
expenditures on education by function, 27
support for education by agency, 374, 375, 376
Grade levels
civics achievement by, 128
enrollment in public elementary and secondary schools by, 34, 35, 36, 37
environmental factors that interfere with instruction, 102
geography achievement levels by, 130
history achievement by, 126, 127
minimum-competency testing by, 169
percentage of children by type of schooling, 39
public elementary and secondary schools by, 94
public elementary schools by, 99
public secondary schools by, 100
reading achievement by, 118, 123
violence and drug usage on school property, 162
writing achievement by, 125
Grades, average
distribution in public schools, 146
SAT scores, 143
Graduate-level studies
disabled students enrolled in, 231
enrollment in, 191, 193, 194, 195
by attendance status, 206
by race/ethnicity and gender, 226
by state, 216, 217, 218
faculty teaching, 250
field of study, 232
at institutions with more than 15,000 students, 235
international comparisons of degrees in science, 417
part-time faculty teaching, 251
in science and engineering postsecondary programs, 233
tuition and fees for, 334
Graduate Record Examination (GRE), 330
Graduation requirements for high school, 167
Grants to students
graduate students receiving, 346, 347
undergraduates receiving, 335, 336, 337, 338, 340, 341, 342, 343
Gross domestic product
expenditures of educational institutions compared to, 25
government expenditures and income compared to, 30
international comparisons of educational expenditures as a percentage of, 419
price index, 31

Half-day kindergarten, 165
mathematics and science skills for 1998 kindergarten cohort, 116
reading skills for 1998 kindergarten cohort, 115
Head Start, 46, 47
Health sciences
associate's degrees in, 269, 270, 282, 283
bachelor's degrees in, 10, 271, 285, 286
degrees conferred in, 275, 277, 310
doctor's degrees in, 273, 291, 292
enrollment, postsecondary education, 232
institutions conferring degrees in, 278
master's degrees in, 272, 288, 289
Higher education. *See* Postsecondary education

High school graduates
Carnegie units earned by, 147
Carnegie units required by state, 167
college enrollment and labor force status, 388
educational attainment of high school sophomores of 1990, 324
enrollment in postsecondary institutions, 200, 201, 202, 203
GED credentialed, 108
by gender and control of school, 104
from private secondary schools, 62
by state, 105, 106
by state and race/ethnicity, 107
students with disabilities, 111
High schools, 95. *See also* Elementary and secondary education; Public elementary and secondary schools
High school seniors
drug usage by, 164
economics achievement, 129
employment of, 387
leisure activities of, 153
life values of, 397
mathematics achievement, 136
reading achievement, 118, 123
science achievement, 138
science achievement by attitude, 140
writing achievement, 125
Hispanics
ACT (American College Testing Program) scores, 145
with associate's degrees, 281, 282, 283
attendance patterns by tenth-graders, 157
with bachelor's degrees, 10, 284, 285, 286
child care arrangements by, 45
college enrollment and labor force status of high school graduates, 388
course work by high school graduates in mathematics and science, 149, 150
distribution in public schools, 97
with doctor's degrees, 290, 291, 292
dropouts from high school, 109
educational attainment, 8, 9, 12
employment of high school seniors, 387
enrollment distribution in public schools by state, 41
estimates of resident population by age, 16
family characteristics of, 19
with first-professional degrees, 293, 294, 295
gifted and talented students by state, 53, 54
high school graduates and dropouts, 107
internet usage, 428
labor force status of high school dropouts, 389
leisure activities of high school seniors, 153
with master's degrees, 287, 288, 289
mathematics scores by age, 132
mathematics scores by grade, 136
mathematics scores of 17-year-olds, 133
percentage of population enrolled in school, 6
postsecondary institutions
employment in, 246
enrollment in, 201, 204, 226
enrollment in by state, 228, 229
enrollment in by type and control of institution, 227
faculty in, 249, 253, 255
serving large proportions of, 238
poverty rates, 21

in public charter and traditional public schools, 101
reading levels by age, 120
reading scores and achievement levels of fourth-graders, 121
reading scores by grade, 118
SAT scores for college-bound seniors, 141
science scores and achievement levels by grade, 138
science scores of eighth-graders in public schools, 139
suspensions and expulsions from public schools, 160, 161
unemployment rate, 382
violence and drug usage on school property, 162
Historically black colleges and universities, 240, 241, 242
Historical summary statistics
  Catholic schools, 61
  degree-granting institutions, 187
  enrollment at all levels, 3
  expenditures of educational institutions, 25, 26
  level of education attained, 8
  number of school districts and public and private schools, 87
  public elementary and secondary schools, 32
History
  achievement by grade, 126, 127
  associate's degrees in, 269, 270, 282, 283
  bachelor's degrees in, 10, 271
  Carnegie units earned by high school graduates, 147
  criterion-referenced assessments by state, 168
  degrees conferred in, 275, 277, 316, 317
  doctor's degrees in, 273
  enrollment, postsecondary education, 232
  institutions conferring degrees in, 278
  master's degrees in, 272
Home activities
  computers, 429, 430
  preschool literacy activities, 49
Homeschooled students, 38, 39
Homework
  international comparisons in mathematics, 406, 407, 411
  international comparisons in science, 413
  mathematics, 134
  parental involvement with, 156
  reading scores by amount of time on, 119
  time fourth-graders spent on, 155
Hospitals
  current-fund revenues for postsecondary institutions, 348, 349
  expenditures at postsecondary institutions for, 361, 362, 364, 365
  revenues for postsecondary institutions, 350
  revenues for private postsecondary institutions, 353, 354
Household income. *See also* Income, family
  adult education participation, 370, 371
  center-based preprimary programs and, 44
  enrollment in preprimary education, 48
  homeschooled children, 38
  by states, 20
Humanities. *See also* Liberal arts and humanities
  bachelor's and master's degrees in, 321
  doctor's degrees in, 319

Illicit drug usage, 395, 396. *See also* Drug usage
Income. *See also* Poverty rates/status; Socioeconomic status
  compared to gross domestic product and government
    expenditures, 30
  by educational attainment, 384, 385

family
  computer usage, 429, 430, 431, 432
  dropouts from high school and, 110
  educational goals for college-bound seniors, 143
  grades earned by elementary and secondary students, 146
  internet usage, 428
  parental participation in educational activities with children, 24
  parental participation in school activities, 23
  student financial aid, 335, 337, 338
high school seniors, 387
household by state, 20 (*See also* Household income)
parental participation in educational activities with children, 24
parental participation in school activities by level of, 23
teacher salaries, 75 (*See also* Salaries)
Index of Teachers' Emphasis on Mathematics Homework (EMH), 409
Individuals with Disabilities Education Act, 51, 52, 111
Instructional levels. *See* Grade levels
Instructional methods in science, 414
Instructional time in mathematics, 134. *See also* Time, use of
Instruction/Instructional staff. *See also* Faculty, postsecondary; Teachers, elementary and secondary
  postsecondary institutions
    expenditures for, 361, 362, 363
    expenditures for at private institutions, 364, 365, 366, 367
    Title IV, 186
  in public elementary and secondary schools, 80, 81, 82, 83
    environmental factors interfering with, 102
    expenditures for, 174, 176, 177, 178, 179, 180
Interest on school debt, 182. *See also* Expenditures
International Baccalaureate programs in public secondary schools, 152
International comparisons, 398–420
  bachelor's degree recipients, 415
  bachelor's degrees in science, 416
  educational expenditures per student, 418
  eighth-graders' perceptions of mathematics, 410
  foreign students enrolled in United States, 420
  graduate degrees in science, 417
  instructional activities in science, 414
  mathematics
    class size for, 409
    instruction time, 408
    scores, 404, 406, 407, 411
  mathematics, reading, and science skills, 403
  population and enrollment, 398, 399
  public direct expenditures on education, 419
  pupils per teacher in elementary and secondary schools, 402
  school-age population, 400
  science scores, 405, 412, 413
  secondary and postsecondary enrollment, 401
International relations, enrollment in postsecondary education, 232
Internet access/usage, 428
  home activities, 429, 430
  public elementary and secondary schools with, 427
Italian
  degrees conferred in, 308
  enrollment in high school in, 56

Japanese, enrollment in high school in, 56
Journalism, 301

Junior high schools, 94. *See also* Public elementary and secondary schools

Kindergarten
    age range for compulsory school attendance, 165
    mathematics and science skills for 1998 cohort, 116
    preschool literacy activities, 49
    reading skills for 1998 cohort, 115
Korean, degrees conferred in, 309

Labor force. *See also* Employment
    dropouts from high school, 110, 389
    high school graduates in, 388
    participation rates, 381
Language initially learned, literacy skills of adults, 386
Language skills, 114
Latin, enrollment in high school in, 56
Legal professions
    associate's degrees in, 269, 270, 282, 283
    bachelor's degrees in, 271, 285, 286
    degrees conferred in, 275, 277
    doctor's degrees in, 273, 291, 292
    enrollment, postsecondary education, 232
    first-professional degrees in law, 279, 280, 294, 295
    institutions conferring degrees in, 278
    master's degrees in, 272, 288, 289
Leisure activities
    of high school seniors, 153
    international comparisons of eighth-graders', 410
    reading scores in school and, 119
Liberal arts and humanities
    associate's degrees in, 269, 270, 282, 283
    bachelor's and master's degrees in, 321
    bachelor's degrees in, 10, 271, 285, 286
    degrees conferred in, 274, 275, 277
    doctor's degrees in, 273, 291, 292, 319
    enrollment, postsecondary education, 232
    institutions conferring degrees in, 278
    master's degrees in, 272, 288, 289
Libraries
    expenditures at postsecondary institutions for, 361
    in postsecondary institutions, 424, 425
    public, 426
    school, 421, 422, 423
Library science
    associate's degrees in, 269, 270, 282, 283
    bachelor's degrees in, 271, 285, 286
    degrees conferred in, 275, 277
    doctor's degrees in, 273, 291, 292
    enrollment, postsecondary education, 232
    institutions conferring degrees in, 278
    master's degrees in, 272, 288, 289
Life sciences. *See also* Biology; Science
    doctor's degrees in, 319
    international comparisons of eighth-graders' scores, 413
    international comparisons of fourth-graders' scores, 412
Life values, 397
Literacy skills, 114, 386
Loans to students
    graduate students receiving, 344, 345, 346, 347

undergraduates receiving, 335, 336, 337, 338, 339, 340, 341, 342, 343
Local communities, public opinion on condition of public schools, 22
Local governments
    expenditures by, 27, 28
    expenditures on education, 29
    grants to undergraduates, 336
    postsecondary institutions
        appropriations for, 352
        revenues for, 348, 349, 350, 351
        revenues for private, 353, 354, 355, 356
    revenues for public elementary and secondary schools, 171, 172, 173

Marital status, 18
Master's degrees
    by control of institution, 276, 277, 320
    by field of study, 272, 296–318
    by gender, 268
    number of institutions conferring, 278
    by race/ethnicity and gender, 287, 288, 289
    salaries of teachers by, 77
    by state, 321, 322
    student financial aid for, 344, 345, 346, 347
Mathematics
    elementary and secondary education
        achievement
            by age, 132
            by grade, 136
            by student and school characteristics, 131
            of eighth-graders by attitude, 137
            of eighth-graders in public schools, 135
            of fourth-graders, 134
            for 1998 kindergarten students by age, 116
        Carnegie units earned by high school graduates, 147
        Carnegie units required by state for high school graduation, 167
        course work and mathematics scores of 17-year-olds, 133
        course work by high school graduates in, 149, 150
        criterion-referenced assessments by state, 168
    international comparisons, 403, 404, 406, 407, 411
        of bachelor's degree recipients, 416
        of class size, 409
        of eighth-graders' perceptions about, 410
        of graduate degrees in, 417
        of time spent in mathematics instruction, 408
    postsecondary education
        associate's degrees in, 269, 270, 282, 283
        bachelor's degrees in, 10, 271, 285, 286
        course work for bachelor's degrees, 325
        degrees conferred in, 275, 277, 311
        doctor's degrees in, 273, 291, 292, 319
        enrollment, postsecondary education, 232
        institutions conferring degrees in, 278
        master's degrees in, 272, 288, 289
    skills in four-year-old children, 114
Mechanical engineering, 305. *See also* Engineering
Media centers in schools, 421, 422, 423
Medicine, first-professional degrees in, 279, 280, 294, 295. *See also* Health sciences
Mental skills, 113

Metropolitan status
  adult education participation, 370, 371
  center-based preprimary programs and, 44
  course work by high school graduates in mathematics and
      science, 150
  crime incidents reported at public schools, 158
  dual credit, Advanced Placement, and International
      Baccalaureate enrollment in public schools, 152
  economics achievement of high school seniors, 129
  educational attainment by, 14
  employment of high school seniors, 387
  high school graduates enrolled in postsecondary institutions by, 202
  homeschooled children, 38
  homework, parental involvement with, 156
  largest school districts, 93
  percentage of children by type of schooling, 39
  public elementary and secondary schools, 90
  public elementary and secondary schools with internet access, 427
  reading achievement of eighth-graders by, 122
  school districts of more than 15,000 students, 91, 92
  schools with security measures, 159
  time spent on homework and television by fourth-graders, 155
Microbiology, degrees in, 299
Middle schools, 94. *See also* Public elementary and secondary schools
Military technologies
  associate's degrees in, 269, 270, 282, 283
  bachelor's degrees in, 271, 285, 286
  degrees conferred in, 275, 277
  enrollment, postsecondary education, 232
  institutions conferring degrees in, 278
  master's degrees in, 272, 288, 289
Minimum-competency testing by state, 169
Minimum length of school year, 166
Minority enrollment in postsecondary institutions, 228, 229, 230.
    See also Race/ethnicity
Mobility
  residence and migration of freshmen in postsecondary
      institutions, 223, 224, 225
  of teachers in public and private schools, 73
Mothers. *See also* Parents
  center-based preprimary programs and, 44
  employment status
    child care arrangements, 46, 47
    language, mathematics and motor skills by, 114
    mental and physical skills developed by children, 113
  level of education and literacy activities, 49 (*See also* Parental
      level of education)
  preprimary education and, 48
Motor skills, 112, 113, 114

Natural sciences. *See also* Science
  enrollment, postsecondary education, 232
  international comparisons of graduate degrees in science, 417
Need-based student financial aid. *See* Financial aid to students
No Child Left Behind Act (2001), 379. *See also* Title I allocations
Non-degree-granting institutions, 186, 372
Nonsectarian private elementary and secondary schools, 58, 59
Not-for-profit private postsecondary institutions, 214. *See also*
    Private postsecondary institutions
    enrollment in, 192
    expenditures of, 364, 365, 368
    revenues to, 353

Occupation
  adult education participation, 370, 371
  bachelor's degree recipients by, 392
  computer usage at work, 432
  by educational attainment, 383
One-parent households, 18, 21
One-teacher schools, 94, 98
Operating expenditures, public postsecondary institutions, 362,
    363
Opinions on education
  public on condition of public schools, 22
  teachers on problems in schools, 71
  teachers on school conditions, 72
Organization of Economic Cooperation and Development (OECD)
  mathematics, reading, and science skills, 403
  mathematics scores, 404
  science scores, 405
Overcrowding in public schools, 103

Parental level of education
  child care arrangements and, 46, 47
  cognitive and motor skills by, 112
  educational achievement of children
    civics, 128
    economics, 129
    history, 126, 127
    mathematics, 131, 135, 136
    reading, 117, 123
    reading of fourth- and eighth-graders, 124
    writing, 125
  educational attainment of high school sophomores of 1990, 324
  educational goals for college-bound seniors, 143
  grades earned by elementary and secondary students, 146
  homeschooled children and, 38
  language, mathematics, and motor skills, 114
  mathematics and science course work by children in school, 150
  mathematics and science skills for 1998 kindergarten cohort,
      116
  mental and physical skills by, 113
  reading skills for 1998 kindergarten cohort, 115
Parents
  emotional attachment of two-year-old children to, 113
  homework, involvement with children's, 156
  involvement in educational activities with children, 24
  preprimary education and characteristics of mothers, 48
  school activities, participation in, 23
Part-time attendance at postsecondary institutions, 188, 196
  by age and gender, 190
  by control and type of institution, 192
  first-professional enrollment, 207
  first-time freshmen, 198, 199
  graduate enrollment, 206, 345
  graduate-level student financial aid, 347
  institutions with more than 15,000 students, 235
  by level, 191, 193, 194, 195
  in private institutions by state, 213, 214
  in public institutions by state, 212
  by race/ethnicity and gender, 226
  by state, 211
  student financial aid, 338, 342, 343
Part-time employment in postsecondary institutions, 243, 245,
    246, 248

Part-time faculty, 251. *See also* Faculty
Performing arts
   associate's degrees in, 269, 270, 282, 283
   bachelor's degrees in, 271, 285, 286
   degrees conferred in, 275, 277, 318
   doctor's degrees in, 273, 291, 292
   enrollment, postsecondary education, 232
   institutions conferring degrees in, 278
   master's degrees in, 272, 288, 289
Pharmacy, first-professional degrees in, 280, 294, 295
Philosophy, religion, and theology
   associate's degrees in, 269, 270, 282, 283
   bachelor's degrees in, 10, 271, 285, 286
   degrees conferred in, 275, 277
   doctor's degrees in, 273, 291, 292
   enrollment, postsecondary education, 232
   institutions conferring degrees in, 278
   master's degrees in, 272, 288, 289
Physical sciences
   associate's degrees in, 269, 270, 282, 283
   bachelor's degrees in, 271, 285, 286
   course work for bachelor's degrees, 325
   degrees conferred in, 274, 275, 277, 312, 313
   doctor's degrees in, 273, 291, 292, 319
   enrollment, postsecondary education, 232
   institutions conferring degrees in, 278
   international comparisons of eighth-graders' scores, 413
   international comparisons of fourth-graders' scores, 412
   master's degrees in, 272, 288, 289
Physical skills, 113
Physics, 313, 414
Podiatry, 280, 294, 295
Political science and government
   degrees conferred in, 317
   enrollment, postsecondary education, 232
Population
   by age and race/ethnicity, 16
   by age group, 15
   gross domestic product and income, 30
   historical statistics of, 32
   international comparisons, 398, 399
   international comparisons of secondary and postsecondary
     enrollment, 401
   percentage enrolled in school, 6, 7
   ratio to employment status, 381
   school-age, by state, 17
Postbaccalaureate education, 393. *See also* Graduate-level studies
Postsecondary education, 186–372
   admission requirements for institutions, 326
   applications, admissions, and enrollment for undergraduates, 327
   closing of institutions, 267
   computer usage by students, 431
   course work in, 325
   Department of Education outlays for, 377
   doctor's degrees by institution, 323
   endowment funds for institutions, 359
   enrollment at all levels, 2
   enrollment status of bachelor's degree recipients, 393
   expenditures on, 25, 26, 28, 361 (*See also under* Expenditures)
   federal support for, 373, 375
   high school graduates enrolling in, 388
   institutions with more than 15,000 students, 235

largest colleges and universities, 236
libraries in institutions, 424, 425
non-degree-granting Title IV institutions, 372
number of institutions, 5, 230, 265
number of institutions by state, 266
participants in, 1
per capita expenditures on, 29
special education students enrolled in, 390
Poverty rates/status
   center-based preprimary programs and, 44
   child care arrangements and, 46, 47
   cognitive and motor skills by, 112
   homework, 156
   language, mathematics, and motor skills by, 114
   in largest 100 school districts, 93
   mental and physical skills by, 113
   by race/ethnicity, 21
   in school districts of more than 15,000 students, 92
   by state, 20
   type of schooling and, 39
Preprimary education
   center-based programs, 44
   child care arrangements, 45, 46
   enrollment and characteristics of children, 48
   enrollment in, 43
   literacy activities at home, 49
   in public elementary schools, 99
   quality of child care arrangements, 47
Preschool programs, 43. *See also* Preprimary education
Price indexes, 31
Primary schools. *See* Private elementary and secondary schools;
   Public elementary and secondary schools
Principals
   in private elementary and secondary schools, 60, 86
   in public elementary and secondary schools, 86
Private elementary and secondary schools
   attendance patterns by tenth-graders, 157
   Catholic schools, 61 (*See also* Catholic schools)
   course work by high school graduates in mathematics and
     science, 149, 150
   enrollment in, 2, 3, 58
   enrollment in grades 9 to 12 compared to population, 55
   expenditures of, 26
   extracurricular activities of high school sophomores, 154
   grades earned by students in, 146
   graduates enrolled in postsecondary institutions, 202, 203
   high school graduates, 62, 104
   historical and projected enrollment statistics, 3
   homework, 156
   leisure activities of high school seniors, 153
   mathematics and science skills for 1998 kindergarten cohort,
     116
   mathematics scores by grade, 136
   mathematics scores of eighth-graders by attitude, 137
   minimum credits earned by high school graduates, 151
   mobility of teachers, 73
   number of, 5, 87
   opinions of teachers on school conditions, 71, 72
   parental participation in educational activities with children, 24
   parental participation in school activities, 23
   participants in, 1
   percentage of children in, 39

preprimary education, 43
principals in, 86
reading scores by grade, 123
reading scores of fourth- and eighth-graders in, 124
reading skills for 1998 kindergarten cohort, 115
school libraries and media centers, 421
science scores by high school seniors by attitude, 140
with security measures, 159
staff-to-student ratios, 60
teachers in, 4, 68
  salaries, 75
  by school affiliation, 58
time spent on homework and television by fourth-graders, 155
tuition for, 59
Private funding for public elementary and secondary schools, 172, 173
Private gifts and grants
postsecondary institutions, 348, 349, 350
revenues to private postsecondary institutions, 353, 354, 355, 356
by source, 358
Private postsecondary institutions
admission requirements for, 326
applications, admissions, and enrollment comparisons, 327
attendance status at, 188, 196, 213
with branch campuses, 265
closing of institutions, 267
by control and affiliation, 197
current-fund revenues, 357
degrees conferred at
  number of degrees, 276, 277, 320
  number of institutions conferring, 234, 278
enrollment, 2, 189, 192, 193, 194, 195
  by race/ethnicity, 227
  by state, 210, 215, 217, 218, 222
expenditures of, 26, 360, 364–368
faculty in, 4, 248, 250, 252, 253
  benefit expenditures for, 263
  part-time, 251
  salaries, 256, 257, 258, 259, 260, 261, 262
  tenure, 264
first-professional level enrollment at, 207
first-time freshmen at, 198, 199
full-time-equivalent enrollment in, 219, 220, 221
full-time-equivalent staff at, 247
graduate enrollment, 206
historically black colleges and universities, 242
non-degree-granting Title IV institutions, 372
not-for-profit institutions, 214
number of, 5, 230, 266
remedial coursework offered by, 328
revenues for by source, 353, 354, 355, 356
staff in, 243, 244, 245, 246
student financial aid
  graduate students receiving, 344, 345, 346, 347
  undergraduate students receiving, 336, 339, 340, 341, 342, 343
Title IV programs, 186
tuition, fees and board rates for undergraduates, 331, 332, 333
tuition and fees for graduate-level studies, 334
undergraduate enrollment at, 205
Problems in schools, opinions of teachers on, 71

Proficiency levels. *See* Achievement of elementary and secondary students; *individual subjects*
Programs with special instructional approaches in public schools, 101
Projections of statistics, enrollment at all levels, 3
Psychology
associate's degrees in, 269, 270, 282, 283
bachelor's degrees in, 10, 271, 285, 286
course work for bachelor's degrees, 325
degrees conferred in, 275, 277, 314
doctor's degrees in, 273, 291, 292, 319
enrollment, postsecondary education, 232
institutions conferring degrees in, 278
master's degrees in, 272, 288, 289
Public administration
associate's degrees in, 269, 270, 282, 283
bachelor's degrees in, 271, 285, 286
degrees conferred in, 275, 277, 315
doctor's degrees in, 273, 291, 292
enrollment, postsecondary education, 232
institutions conferring degrees in, 278
master's degrees in, 272, 288, 289
Public elementary and secondary schools
attendance patterns by tenth-graders, 157
average daily attendance at, 40
charter schools and, 101
course work by high school graduates in mathematics and science, 149, 150
crime incidents reported at, 158
distance education participation, 57
dual credit, Advanced Placement, and International Baccalaureate enrollment, 152
education agencies, 89
elementary schools by state and grade span, 99
enrollment
  at all levels, 2, 3
  by capacity level, 103
  distribution in by state and race/ethnicity, 41
  by grade in, 37
  in grades 9 to 12 compared to population, 55
  by size, 95
  by state, 33, 34, 35, 36
environmental conditions, 102
expenditures, 26
  by function, 177, 178, 179
  for instruction, 180
  per pupil, 181, 182, 183, 184, 185
  by purpose, 174
  by state, 176
  for transportation to school, 175
extracurricular activities of high school sophomores, 154
foreign language enrollment, 56
free or reduced-price lunch program, students eligible for, 42
grades earned by students in, 146
by grade spans included, 94
graduates enrolled in postsecondary institutions, 202, 203
high school graduates, 104, 105, 106
high school graduates and dropouts, 107
historical and projected enrollment statistics, 3
historical statistics for, 32
homework, 156
internet access, 427

leisure activities of high school seniors, 153
mathematics achievement
    of eighth-graders by attitude, 137
    of eighth-graders in, 135
    of fourth-graders in, 134
    by grade, 136
mathematics and science skills for 1998 kindergarten cohort, 116
by metropolitan status, 90
minimum credits earned by high school graduates, 151
mobility of teachers, 73
number of, 5
number of school districts, 87
opinions of teachers on problems in schools, 71
opinions of teachers on school conditions, 72
parental participation in educational activities with children, 24
parental participation in school activities, 23
participants in, 1
percentage of children in, 39
preprimary education, 43
principals in, 86
public opinion on condition of, 22
pupil-to-staff ratios in, 85
pupil-to-teacher ratios, 63, 66
race/ethnicity distribution in, 97
reading achievement (*See also under* Reading)
    of eighth-graders in, 122
    of fourth- and eighth-graders in, 124
    of fourth-graders in, 121
    by grade, 123
reading skills for 1998 kindergarten cohort, 115
revenues by source of funds, 171, 172, 173
school libraries and media centers, 421, 422, 423
school size of public schools, 96
science scores of high school seniors by attitude, 140
science scores of eighth-graders in, 139
secondary schools by state and grade levels, 100
with security measures, 159
staff in, 80, 81, 82, 83
by state and type of school, 98
subjects taught in high school, 70
suspensions and expulsions from, 160, 161
teachers in, 4, 65 (*See also* Teachers)
    characteristics of, 67, 68, 69
    as percentage of staff in, 84
    salaries, 75, 76, 77, 78, 79
time spent on homework and television by fourth-graders, 155
transportation to school, 175
Public libraries, 426
Public opinion. *See* Opinions on education
Public postsecondary institutions
admission requirements for, 326
affiliation of, 197
applications, admissions, and enrollment comparisons, 327
appropriations for by state, 352
attendance status at, 188, 196, 212
with branch campuses, 265
closing of institutions, 267
current-fund revenues, 357
degrees conferred at
    number of degrees, 276, 277, 320
    number of institutions conferring, 234, 278

enrollment, 2, 192, 193, 194, 195
    graduate, 206
    by race/ethnicity, 227
    by state, 209, 215, 217, 218, 222
    undergraduate, 205
enrollment by control and type of institution, 189
expenditures of, 26, 360, 362, 363
faculty in, 4, 248, 250, 252, 253
    benefit expenditures for, 263
    part-time, 251
    salaries, 256, 257, 258, 259, 260, 261, 262
    tenure, 264
first-professional enrollment at, 207
first-time freshmen at, 198, 199
full-time-equivalent enrollment in, 219, 220, 221
full-time-equivalent staff at, 247
historically black colleges and universities, 242
institutions conferring degrees, 278
non-degree-granting Title IV institutions, 372
number of, 5, 230, 266
remedial coursework offered by, 328
revenues, 350
staff in, 243, 244, 245, 246
student financial aid
    graduate students receiving, 344, 345, 346, 347
    undergraduate students receiving, 336, 339, 340, 341, 342, 343
Title IV programs, 186
tuition, fees, and board rates for undergraduates, 331, 332, 333
tuition and fees for graduate-level studies, 334
Pupils
average number in public elementary schools, 99
expenditures per in public schools, 181, 182, 183, 184, 185
to-staff ratios in public elementary and secondary schools, 85
to-teacher ratios, 63, 64
    international comparisons, 402
    by metropolitan status in public schools, 90
    by state in public schools, 66

Race/ethnicity
ACT (American College Testing Program) scores, 145
adult education participation, 370, 371
associate's degrees by, 281, 282, 283
attendance patterns by tenth-graders, 157
bachelor's degrees by, 284, 285, 286
Carnegie units earned by high school graduates, 147
Carnegie units earned by high school graduates in vocational education by, 148
center-based programs and, 44
child care arrangements by, 45, 46, 47
civics achievement by grade, 128
cognitive and motor skills by, 112
college enrollment and labor force status of high school graduates by, 388
computer usage, 429, 430, 431, 432
course work and mathematics scores of 17-year-olds, 133
course work by high school graduates in mathematics and science, 149, 150
distribution in public schools, 97
doctor's degrees by, 290, 291, 292
dropouts from high school by, 109
economics achievement of high school seniors, 129
educational attainment, 8, 9, 12

educational attainment of high school sophomores of 1990, 324
employment of high school seniors, 387
enrollment distribution in public schools by state, 41
enrollment in postsecondary institutions, 201, 226, 227
estimates of resident population by age and, 16
extracurricular activities of high school sophomores, 154
family characteristics by, 19
first-professional degrees by, 293, 294, 295
geography achievement by grade, 130
gifted and talented students by state, 53, 54
grades earned by elementary and secondary students, 146
high school graduates and dropouts by, 107
history achievement by grade, 126, 127
homeschooled children, 38
homework, 155, 156
internet usage, 428
labor force participation by, 381
labor force status of high school dropouts, 389
language, mathematics, and motor skills by, 114
leisure activities of high school seniors, 153
literacy skills of adults, 386
master's degrees by, 287, 288, 289
mathematics and science skills for 1998 kindergarten cohort, 116
mathematics achievement
  by age, 131, 132
  of eighth-graders by attitude, 137
  by grade, 136
mental and physical skills by, 113
minimum credits earned by high school graduates, 151
number of persons with bachelor's degrees, 9, 10
parental participation in educational activities with children, 24
parental participation in school activities, 23
percentage of children by type of schooling, 39
percentage of population enrolled in school by, 6
postsecondary institutions
  employment in, 246
  enrollment in, 204, 226, 227, 228, 229
  faculty in, 249, 252, 253, 254, 255
poverty rates by, 21
preschool literacy activities at home, 49
in public charter and traditional public schools, 101
reading achievement
  by age, 117, 120
  of fourth- and eighth-graders, 124
  of fourth-graders, 121
  by grade, 118, 123
reading skills for 1998 kindergarten cohort, 115
SAT scores for college-bound seniors, 141
school districts of more than 15,000 students, 91
science achievement
  of eighth-graders in public schools, 139
  by grade, 138
  of high school seniors by attitude, 140
student financial aid, 335, 337, 338
suspensions and expulsions from public schools, 160–161
teachers' educational attainment in schools by, 68
time spent on homework and television by fourth-graders, 155
unemployment rate, 382
violence and drug usage on school property, 162
writing achievement by grade, 125

Reading
  achievement
    by age, 119
    by age, gender, and race/ethnicity, 120
    of eighth-graders, 122
    of fourth- and eighth-graders, 124
    of fourth-graders, 121
    by grade, 118, 123
    international comparisons, 403
  preschool literacy activities at home, 49
  skill levels for 1998 kindergarten students by age, 115
Reading First State Grants, 379
Reduced-price lunch program, 42. *See also* Free or reduced-price school lunch program
Regional distribution
  course work by high school graduates in mathematics and science, 150
  doctor's degrees by, 319
  dual credit, Advanced Placement, and International Baccalaureate enrollment in public schools, 152
  economics achievement of high school seniors, 129
  extracurricular activities of high school sophomores, 154
  geography achievement by grade, 130
  history achievement by grade, 126, 127
  homeschooled children, 38
  mathematics achievement by age, 131
  reading achievement by age, 117
  schooling type, percentage of children by, 39
Religious affiliation
  postsecondary institutions, 197
  private elementary and secondary schools, 58, 60
Remedial coursework, postsecondary institutions offering, 328
Research
  expenditures at postsecondary institutions for, 361, 362, 364–367
  federal support for, 373, 375, 380
Residency of freshmen attending in-state postsecondary institutions, 223, 224, 225
Revenues
  postsecondary institutions
    current-fund by source, 348, 349
    from federal government, 357
    private institutions, 353, 354, 355, 356
    for public postsecondary institutions, 351
    by source, 350
    voluntary support, 358
  public elementary and secondary schools
    historical statistics, 32
    by metropolitan status, 90
    source of funds for, 171, 172, 173
  in school districts of more than 15,000 students, 92
Risk factors for students
  mathematics and science skills for 1998 kindergarten cohort, 116
  reading skills for 1998 kindergarten cohort, 115
Room and board for undergraduates at postsecondary institutions, 331, 332, 333
Rural areas, public elementary and secondary schools, 90
Russian
  degrees conferred in, 309
  enrollment in high school in, 56

Salaries
  of bachelor's degree recipients, 392, 394
  faculty in postsecondary institutions, 252, 253
    by academic rank, 257, 258
    by field of instruction, 256
    by state, 259, 260, 261, 262
  of principals in public and private schools, 86
  public postsecondary institutions, expenditures for, 362
  public schools, expenditures for, 179, 180
  of teachers, 74, 75, 76, 77, 78, 79
SAT scores, 143
  applications, admissions, and enrollment for undergraduates, 327
  for college-bound seniors, 141, 142
  by state, 144
Scholarships for college. See Financial aid to students
Scholastic Aptitude Test. See SAT scores
School activities, parental participation in, 23
School-age population
  international comparisons, 400
  by state, 17
School conditions
  crime at public schools, 158
  enrollment under or over capacity, 103
  environmental factors that interfere with instruction, 102
  teachers' opinions on, 72
  violence and drug usage, 162
School districts, 89
  enrollment and poverty in 100 largest, 93
  by enrollment size, 88
  with more than 15,000 students, 91, 92
  number of, 87
School libraries, 421, 422, 423
School lunch program, 42. See also Free or reduced-price school lunch program
School year, length of, 166
Science
  elementary and secondary education
    achievement by grade, 138
    achievement of eighth-graders in public schools, 139
    achievement of high school seniors by attitude, 140
    Carnegie units earned by high school graduates, 147
    Carnegie units required by state for high school graduation, 167
    course work by high school graduates in, 149, 150
    skill levels for 1998 kindergarten students by age, 116
  international comparisons, 403, 405
    of bachelor's degree recipients, 416
    of eighth-graders' scores, 413
    of fourth-graders' scores, 412
    of graduate degrees in, 417
    of instructional practices, 414
  postsecondary education
    associate's degrees in, 269, 270
    bachelor's and master's degrees in, 321
    bachelor's degrees in, 10, 271
    biology degrees, 298, 299
    course work for bachelor's degrees, 325
    degrees conferred in, 274, 275, 277
    doctor's degrees in, 273, 319
    enrollment in, 232
    federal support to institutions for, 380

    graduate-level enrollment in, 233
    institutions conferring degrees in, 278
    master's degrees in, 272
    physical sciences degrees, 312–313
Secondary education for adults, 369
Secondary schools. See Private elementary and secondary schools; Public elementary and secondary schools
Security
  associate's degrees in, 269, 270, 282, 283
  bachelor's degrees in, 271, 285, 286
  degrees conferred in, 275, 277
  doctor's degrees in, 273, 291, 292
  institutions conferring degrees in, 278
  master's degrees in, 272, 288, 289
  schools with measures for, 159
Self-confidence in learning mathematics (SCM), 410. See also Mathematics
Shutdowns of postsecondary institutions, 267
Skills
  in four-year-old children, 114
  literacy skills of adults, 386
  mathematics and science by age, 116
  in mathematics by age, 132
  in nine-month-old children, 112
  reading skills by age, 115
  in two-year-old children, 113
Social sciences
  associate's degrees in, 269, 270, 282, 283
  bachelor's and master's degrees in, 321
  bachelor's degrees in, 10, 271, 285, 286
  course work for bachelor's degrees, 325
  degrees conferred in, 274, 275, 277, 316
  doctor's degrees in, 273, 291, 292, 319
  enrollment, postsecondary education, 232
  institutions conferring degrees in, 278
  master's degrees in, 272, 288, 289
Social services, degrees in, 315
Social studies
  criterion-referenced assessments by state, 168
  high school diploma requirements by state, 167
Socioeconomic status. See also Income
  attendance patterns by tenth-graders, 157
  child care arrangements and, 46, 47
  cognitive and motor skills by, 112
  course work by high school graduates in mathematics and science, 150
  educational attainment of high school sophomores of 1990, 324
  employment of high school seniors, 387
  extracurricular activities of high school sophomores, 154
  language, mathematics, and motor skills by, 114
  leisure activities of high school seniors, 153
  mathematics and science skills for 1998 kindergarten cohort, 116
  mental and physical skills by, 113
  reading skills for 1998 kindergarten cohort, 115
Sociology
  degrees conferred in, 317
  enrollment, postsecondary education, 232
Spanish
  degrees conferred in, 308
  enrollment in high school in, 56
Special education. See also Disabilities, students with
  age range for compulsory attendance, 165

percentage distribution of students in, 51
postsecondary education and employment status of students in, 390
schools by state, 98
students exiting, 111
Staff. *See also* Faculty; Teachers
  in postsecondary institutions, 243–264
    by employment status, 243, 245
    full-time equivalent, 247
    in libraries, 424, 425
    by race/ethnicity and gender, 246
  in private elementary and secondary schools, 60
  in public elementary and secondary schools, 80, 81, 82, 83, 84
  pupil-to-staff ratios in public schools, 85
States
  adult education participation, 369
  age range for compulsory school attendance, 165
  average daily attendance at public schools, 40
  Carnegie units required for high school graduation, 167
  certification test for teachers, 170
  criterion-referenced assessments, 168
  degrees conferred in, 320, 321, 322
  Department of Education appropriations, 378
  education agencies, 89
  educational attainment by, 11, 12, 13
  enrollment in public elementary and secondary schools, 33, 34, 35, 36
  enrollment in public schools by race/ethnicity, 41
  expenditures
    on education per capita, 29
    by governments, 27, 28
    in public elementary and secondary schools, 176, 177, 178, 180, 182, 183, 184, 185
  free or reduced-price lunch program, students eligible for, 42
  gifted and talented students by, 53, 54
  graduates from private schools by state, 62
  high school graduates and dropouts by, 107
  high school graduates by, 105, 106
  high school graduates enrolled in postsecondary institutions by, 203
  household income and poverty rates, 20
  Individuals with Disabilities Education Act, 52
  mathematics scores and achievement levels of eighth-graders in public schools, 135
  mathematics scores and achievement levels of fourth-graders in public schools, 134
  minimum-competency testing by, 169
  policies on textbook selection and length of school year, 166
  postsecondary institutions
    appropriations for, 352
    attendance status and gender, 211, 212
    employment in, 247
    enrollment in, 208, 215, 216, 217, 218, 222, 228, 229
    enrollment in private institutions, 214
    expenditures of private institutions, 368
    expenditures of public institutions, 363
    faculty salaries by, 259, 260, 261, 262
    first-time freshmen at, 199
    full-time-equivalent enrollment in, 220, 221
    institutions with more than 15,000 students, 235
    non-degree-granting Title IV institutions, 372
    number in, 266

    private institutions by, 210, 213
    public institutions by, 209
    residence and migration of freshmen, 223, 224, 225
    revenues of public institutions, 351
    tuition, fees, and board rates for undergraduates, 332
  public elementary and secondary schools by type of school, 98
  public elementary schools by grade span, 99
  public libraries in, 426
  public secondary schools by grade span, 100
  pupil-to-staff ratios in public schools by, 85
  reading scores and achievement levels of eighth-graders by, 122
  reading scores and achievement levels of fourth-graders by, 121
  revenues for public elementary and secondary schools, 171, 172, 173
  SAT scores by, 144
  school-age population, 17
  school districts of more than 15,000 students, 91, 92
  school libraries and media centers by, 423
  science scores of eighth-graders in public schools, 139
  staff in public elementary and secondary schools, 81, 82, 83
  student financial aid from, 339, 344, 345
  suspensions and expulsions from public schools, 160, 161
  teachers
    as percentage of staff in public schools by, 84
    in public elementary and secondary schools, 65, 67
    pupil-to-teacher ratios in public schools by, 66
    salaries of in public schools, 76, 77, 79
  Title I agency programs, 379
Statistics and mathematics. *See also* Mathematics
  bachelor's degrees in, 10
  degrees conferred in, 311
  enrollment, postsecondary education, 232
Status dropouts from high school, 109, 110. *See* also Dropouts from high school
Student financial aid
  graduate level, 344, 345, 346, 347
  undergraduate level, 335, 336, 337, 338, 339, 340, 341, 342, 343
Students. *See* Graduate-level studies; Pupils; Undergraduate-level studies
Student-to-faculty ratios, 247
Subjects taught in public high schools, 70. *See also* Course work/ Credits
Substance abuse. *See* Drug usage
Suburban areas, public elementary and secondary schools, 90
Suspensions from school, 160, 161

Talented students, 53, 54. *See also* Gifted and talented students
Teachers, elementary and secondary
  average class size for in public schools, 67
  in Catholic schools, 61
  characteristics of in public schools, 69
  degrees and teaching experience at the elementary/secondary level, 67, 68
  historical statistics of public schools, 32
  international comparisons, 398, 402
  mobility of, 73
  number of, 1, 4
  opinions on school conditions, 71, 72
  in private elementary and secondary schools, 58, 60, 62
  in public charter and traditional public schools, 101
  in public elementary and secondary schools, 64, 65, 66, 84
  salaries in public and private schools, 75

salaries in public schools, 74, 76, 77, 78, 79
states requiring test for certification, 170
subjects taught in public high schools, 70
Teachers' Emphasis on Mathematics Homework (EMH), 409
Teaching experience
    in public and private schools, 68
    in public schools, 67
    salaries by
        in public and private schools, 75
        in public schools, 74, 76, 77
Technical education, 148. *See also* Vocational schools/education
Teenagers. *See also* High school seniors; Tenth grade
    drug usage by, 162, 163, 164
    international comparisons of mathematics, 404
    international comparisons of mathematics, reading, and science
        skills, 403
    international comparisons of science, 405
Television, 155
Temporary facilities in public schools, 102
Tenth grade
    attendance patterns, 157
    extracurricular activities of high school sophomores, 154
Tenure for faculty, 264
Testing, state
    criterion-referenced assessments, 168
    minimum-competency testing, 169
    teacher certification testing, 170
Textbook selection, 166
Theology, 294, 295. *See also* Philosophy, religion, and theology
Time, use of
    by fourth-graders on homework and television, 155
    on homework, 119
    international comparisons
        on mathematics homework, 406, 407, 411
        in mathematics instruction, 408
        on science homework, 413
        in science instruction, 412, 414
    in mathematics instruction, 134
    minimum length of school year, 166
Time-series studies
    high school sophomores of 1990, 324
    mathematics and science skills for 1998 kindergarten cohort,
        116
Title I allocations
    to largest school districts, 93
    in school districts of more than 15,000 students, 92
    by states, 379
Title IV postsecondary institutions, 186
    non-degree-granting, 372
    number of, 5, 372
Transportation to school, 175
Tribally controlled institutions, 239
Tuition
    for postsecondary institutions, 331–334
    for private elementary and secondary schools, 59
    as revenue to postsecondary institutions, 348, 349, 350, 351
    as revenue to private institutions, 353, 354, 355, 356
    for undergraduates, 331, 332, 333
Two-year postsecondary institutions
    admission requirements for, 326
    applications, admissions, and enrollment comparisons, 327
    attendance status at, 196

with branch campuses, 265
closing of institutions, 267
completion status for students, 329
current-fund revenues for postsecondary institutions, 350
enrollment, 189, 192, 193, 194, 195
    by race/ethnicity, 204, 227
    by recent high school completers in, 202
    by state, 215, 217, 218, 222
expenditures at private institutions, 364–368
expenditures of, 360, 362, 363
faculty in, 248
    salaries, 257, 258, 259, 260
    tenure, 264
field of study at, 232
first-time freshmen at, 198
full-time-equivalent enrollment in, 219, 220
full-time-equivalent staff at, 247
historically black colleges and universities, 242
number of institutions, 230, 266
remedial coursework offered by, 328
revenues to private postsecondary institutions, 354, 355, 356
revenues to public postsecondary institutions, 350
staff in, 243, 245, 246
student financial aid, 336, 339, 340, 341, 342, 343
Title IV postsecondary institutions, 186
tuition, fees, and board rates for undergraduates, 331, 332, 333
undergraduate enrollment at, 205

Underenrollment in public schools, 103
Undergraduate-level studies
    admission requirements for institutions, 326
    applications, admissions, and enrollment comparisons, 327
    disabled students enrolled at, 231
    enrollment, 191, 193, 194, 195
        by attendance status, 205
        by race/ethnicity and gender, 226
        by state, 216, 217, 218
    faculty teaching at, 250
    field of study, 232
    at institutions with more than 15,000 students, 235
    part-time faculty teaching at, 251
    student financial aid, 335, 336, 337, 338, 339, 340, 341, 342,
        343
    tuition, fees, and board rates for, 331, 332, 333
Unemployment rate, 382
    for dropouts from high school, 110, 389
    for high school graduates, 388
United States Department of Education. *See* Department of
    Education
United States history, achievement by grade, 126, 127. *See also*
    History
Universities, 189. *See also* Private postsecondary institutions;
    Public postsecondary institutions
Urbanicity. *See* Metropolitan status

Values of high school seniors, 397
Veterinary medicine, first-professional degrees in, 280, 294, 295
Violent crimes
    percentage of students experiencing, 162
    at public elementary and secondary schools, 158
Visual arts
    associate's degrees in, 269, 270, 282, 283

bachelor's degrees in, 271, 285, 286
degrees conferred in, 275, 277, 318
doctor's degrees in, 273, 291, 292
enrollment, postsecondary education, 232
institutions conferring degrees in, 278
master's degrees in, 272, 288, 289
Vocational schools/education
  Carnegie units earned by high school graduates, 147, 148
  postsecondary institutions, 372
  public secondary schools, 100
Voluntary support for postsecondary institutions, 358

Whites
  ACT (American College Testing Program) scores, 145
  with associate's degrees, 281, 282, 283
  attendance patterns by tenth-graders, 157
  with bachelor's degrees, 10, 284, 285, 286
  child care arrangements by, 45
  college enrollment and labor force status of high school graduates, 388
  course work by high school graduates in mathematics and science, 149, 150
  distribution in public schools, 97
  with doctor's degrees, 290, 291, 292
  dropouts from high school, 109
  educational attainment, 8, 9, 12
  employment of high school seniors, 387
  enrollment distribution in public schools by state, 41
  estimates of resident population by age, 16
  family characteristics of, 19
  with first-professional degrees, 293, 294, 295
  gifted and talented students by state, 53, 54
  high school graduates and dropouts, 107
  internet usage, 428
  labor force status of high school dropouts, 389

leisure activities of high school seniors, 153
  with master's degrees, 287, 288, 289
  mathematics scores by age, 132
  mathematics scores by grade, 136
  mathematics scores of 17-year-olds, 133
  percentage of population enrolled in school, 6
  postsecondary institutions
    employment in, 246
    enrollment in, 201, 204, 226
    enrollment in by state, 228, 229
    enrollment in by type and control of institution, 227
    faculty in, 249, 253, 255
  poverty rates, 21
  in public charter and traditional public schools, 101
  reading levels by age, 120
  reading scores and achievement levels of fourth-graders, 121
  reading scores by grade, 118
  SAT scores for college-bound seniors, 141
  science scores and achievement levels by grade, 138
  science scores of eighth-graders in public schools, 139
  suspensions and expulsions from public schools, 160, 161
  unemployment rate, 382
  violence and drug usage on school property, 162
Women's colleges, 237
Work experience. *See also* Teaching experience
  computer usage, 432
  of principals, 86
Work load of faculty in postsecondary institutions, 250, 251
Writing scores and achievement levels by grade, 125

Year-round schools, 165
Years of school completed, by level of attainment, 8. *See also* Educational attainment

Zoology, degrees in, 299